P9-DCP-319

# C# Professional Projects

# C# Professional Projects

*Geetanjali Arora*
*Balasubramaniam Aiaswamy*
*Nitin Pandey*

*WITH*

NIIT

©2002 by Premier Press, Inc. All rights reserved. No part of this book may be reproduced or transmitted in any form or by any means, electronic or mechanical, including photocopying, recording, or by any information storage or retrieval system without written permission from Premier Press, except for the inclusion of brief quotations in a review.

Premier Press™

The Premier Press logo, top edge printing, and related trade dress are trademarks of Premier Press, Inc. and may not be used without written permission. All other trademarks are the property of their respective owners.

*Important:* Premier Press cannot provide software support. Please contact the appropriate software manufacturer's technical support line or Web site for assistance.

Premier Press and the author have attempted throughout this book to distinguish proprietary trademarks from descriptive terms by following the capitalization style used by the manufacturer.

Information contained in this book has been obtained by Premier Press from sources believed to be reliable. However, because of the possibility of human or mechanical error by our sources, Premier Press, or others, the Publisher does not guarantee the accuracy, adequacy, or completeness of any information and is not responsible for any errors or omissions or the results obtained from use of such information. Readers should be particularly aware of the fact that the Internet is an ever-changing entity. Some facts may have changed since this book went to press.

ISBN: 1-931841-30-6

Library of Congress Catalog Card Number: 2001096998

Printed in the United States of America

02 03 04 05 06 RI 10 9 8 7 6 5 4 3 2 1

**Publisher:**
Stacy L. Hiquet

**Marketing Manager:**
Heather Buzzingham

**Managing Editor:**
Sandy Doell

**Editorial Assistant:**
Margaret Bauer

**Book Production Services:**
Argosy

**Cover Design:**
Mike Tanamachi

# About NIIT

NIIT is a global IT solutions corporation with a presence in 38 countries. With its unique business model and technology-creation capabilities, NIIT delivers software and learning solutions to more than 1,000 clients across the world.

The success of NIIT's training solutions lies in its unique approach to education. NIIT's Knowledge Solutions Business conceives, researches, and develops all of its course material. A rigorous instructional design methodology is followed to create engaging and compelling course content.

NIIT trains over 200,000 executives and learners each year in information technology areas using stand-up training, video-aided instruction, computer-based training (CBT), and Internet-based training (IBT). NIIT has been featured in the *Guinness Book of World Records* for the largest number of learners trained in one year!

NIIT has developed over 10,000 hours of instructor-led training (ILT) and over 3,000 hours of Internet-based training and computer-based training. IDC ranked NIIT among the Top 15 IT training providers globally for the year 2000. Through the innovative use of training methods and its commitment to research and development, NIIT has been in the forefront of computer education and training for the past 20 years.

Quality has been the prime focus at NIIT. Most of the processes are ISO-9001 certified. It was the 12th company in the world to be assessed at Level 5 of SEI-CMM. NIIT's Content (Learning Material) Development facility is the first in the world to be assessed at this highest maturity level. NIIT has strategic partnerships with companies such as Computer Associates, IBM, Microsoft, Oracle, and Sun Microsystems.

# About the Authors

**Geetanjali Arora** is an instructional designer who has worked with the NIIT for almost two years. She has done several projects with the NIIT that include instructor-led training (ILT), computer-based training (CBT), and Web-based training (WBT). She has written on both technical and non-technical subjects. At the NIIT, Geentanjali's responsibilities include scripting, construction, planning, and scheduling. She has also provided training on NexGen and Dreamweaver.

**Balasubramaniam Aiaswamy** is a technical trainer and writer, an instructional designer, a subject matter expert (SME), and an ID reviewer with NIIT's Knowledge Solutions Business division, which develops and reviews instructor-led training (ILT) products for various software and technologies. These technologies include Microsoft Visual InterDev 6.0, Microsoft Site Server 3.0 Commerce Edition, Microsoft Windows CE, Java 2 Micro Edition (J2ME), networking concepts, the installation and administration of a Layer 3 network, and Web security. He is both an MCSD and an MCP in Windows NT. Balasubramaniam has experience in teaching career programs at NIIT's Career Education Group division. He has taught various technical subject areas including networking essentials, SQL Server 7.0, Microsoft Windows NT Server 4.0, Microsoft Visual Basic 6.0, Microsoft Visual C++ 4.0, Windows 32 API programming, HTML, Java, Unix, C, and C++. He has also set up and managed labs for students and administered Novell 3.11 and UNIX (SCO)–based networks.

**Nitin Pandey** works with NIIT as a subject matter expert (SME) for learning content developed on Microsoft technologies. Nitin has been involved in the development of WBTs and seminars for NIIT Online Ltd. and Microsoft. Nitin provides technical support to the development teams, develops sample applications, and provides technical reviews of learning content.

# Contents at a Glance

# Contents

# Introduction

This book provides readers with the knowledge of Visual C# concepts. In addition to the concepts explained in the chapters, the book provides readers with several projects that enable them to create Windows applications, Web services, Web applications, and mobile Web applications. The book aims for providing the readers with extensive knowledge of C# so that they are able to develop live projects using C#. The book is aimed at readers with a basic knowledge of programming.

## Goal of the Book

This book includes overview sections that contain chapters covering the basic concepts of C#. These chapters enable readers to refresh basic programming concepts and understand how these concepts can be applied in C#.

Using the concepts covered in the overview sections, several professional projects have been created in the Professional Projects section. These projects provide readers a hands-on approach to learning Visual C#. The professional projects form a major part of the book, covering both simple and complex concepts of the language. Each professional project focuses on a specific C# concept and includes the case study for the project. The case study of the project gives the readers an idea of the real-life situations where these projects can be applied.

In creating the projects, the simple-to-complex approach has been followed. The book starts with creating simple Windows applications and moves on to creating Web applications, Web services, and finally mobile Web applications.

In addition to the overview and the Professional Projects sections, the book includes the Beyond the Labs and Appendixes section. The Beyond the Labs section includes a chapter on the advanced C# concepts that have not been covered in the earlier sections. This section introduces the concepts of messaging and COM+. Readers can take a step forward towards understanding these concepts in detail and applying them to their applications. The Appendixes section includes appendixes that act as a quick reference for C#.

## How to Use this Book

This book has been organized to facilitate a better grasp of content covered in the book. The various conventions used in the book include the following:

- **Analysis.** The book incorporates an analysis of code, explaining what it does and why, line by line.
- **Tips.** Tips have been used to provide special advice or unusual shortcuts with the software.
- **Notes.** Notes give additional information that may be of interest to the reader, but is not essential to performing the task at hand.
- **Cautions.** Cautions are used to warn users of possible disastrous results if they perform a task incorrectly.
- **New term definitions.** All new terms have been italicized and then defined as a part of the text.

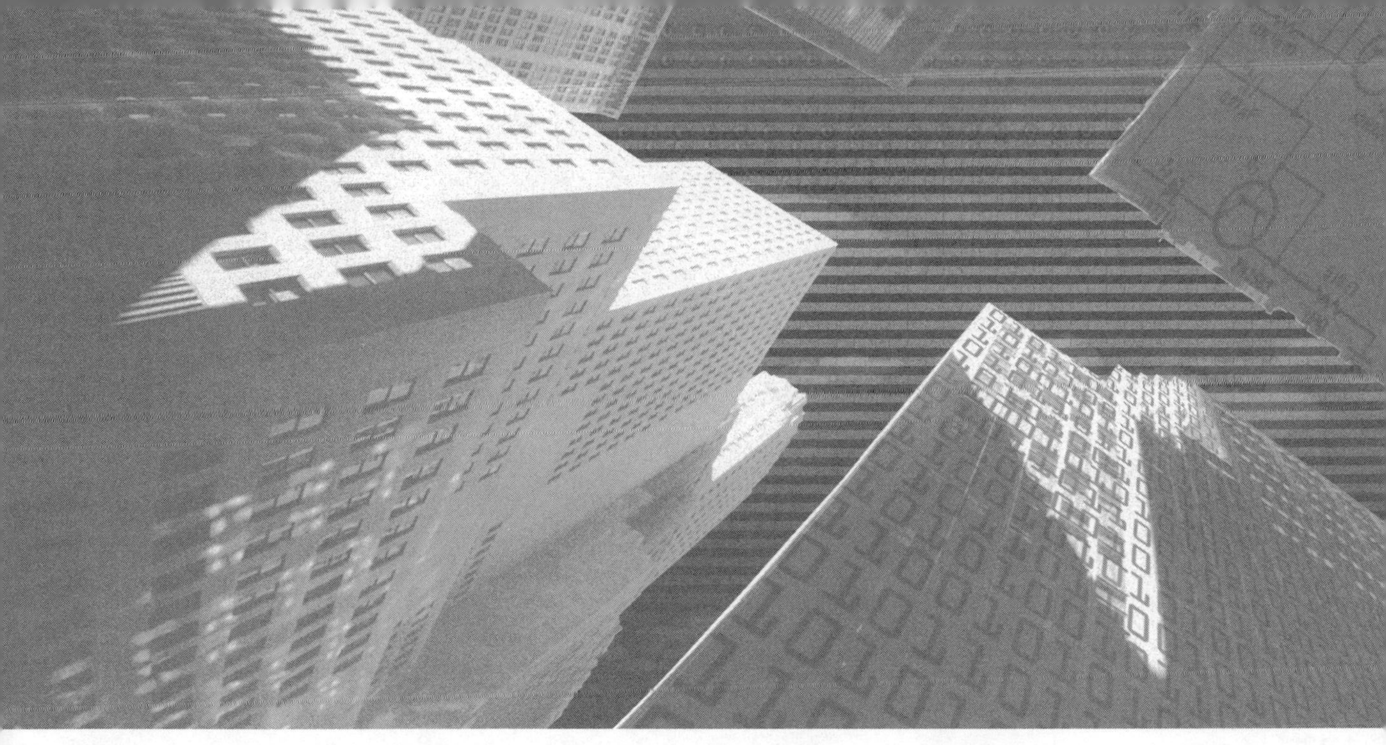

# PART I

## Introduction to C#

# Chapter 1

## Overview of the .NET Framework

Microsoft has released the Visual C# language and its framework—called the .NET Framework—with the aim of providing programmers with complete support for developing applications. This chapter introduces you to the .NET Framework and its components. These components include the CLR (*common language runtime*) and the .NET base class library. In addition, this chapter introduces you to CTS (*common type system*), CLS (*common language specification*), garbage collector, and assembly. Subsequently, the chapter details some of the base classes of C#, such as `Delegate`, `Exception`, and `Thread`, included in the .NET Framework.

## Introduction to the .NET Framework

The *.NET Framework* is a new API (*application programming interface*) that helps programmers to write applications for the Windows platform. In addition, .NET enables you to write programs or applications for a distributed environment. To do so, .NET helps you to create Web services and Web applications. You will learn about Web services and Web applications later in this chapter.

The .NET Framework not only helps you write new programs, but also provides you with the ability to improve the existing programs. The .NET Framework is well designed for communicating with existing COM (*Component Object Model*) components, making the applications written in .NET languages backward-compatible with existing programs.

The .NET Framework provides a complete development framework. The .NET Framework helps you write complex applications by providing you with predefined classes and methods in the .NET base class library and also manages the execution of the applications that you write.

.NET provides you with a library of classes, which contains several base classes called *.NET base classes*. These classes, in turn, define several functions that you can use to write your applications. In addition, .NET provides the .NET Runtime environment called the CLR to execute the code written for the Windows platform. You will learn about the .NET class library and the .NET Runtime environment in detail later in this chapter.

.NET offers an application development environment called *Visual Studio .NET* that consists of several programming languages, such as Visual Basic .NET, Visual C#, Visual FoxPro, and Visual C++ .NET. These programming languages combine the features of the existing languages with several new features to provide a powerful development framework. Following are some of the features of the .NET Framework.

- **Interoperability with other environments.** The need for a new development environment was primarily because the applications developed in existing environments were not platform-independent. For example, applications that you develop for the Windows platform are not compatible with the applications designed for the UNIX environment. With the evolution of the .NET Framework, you can develop applications that can run on the Internet, making them accessible across various platforms. These applications are called *Web applications* and are fully supported by the .NET Framework.

  Interoperability across environments, which is the strongest feature of .NET applications, is a result of .NET's support for MSIL (*Microsoft intermediate language*). At the time of compilation, all the managed code written for the .NET platform is converted to MSIL, which is a set of CPU-independent instructions. When you run the code written for the Windows platform in any other environment, for example UNIX, the compiler compiles the MSIL code to one that UNIX understands, enabling the application to run.
- **Support for developing language-independent applications.** In addition to developing applications that can interoperate with those in a different environment, you can develop applications that are language-independent. Visual Studio .NET provides a common development environment for all languages in the .NET series. This implies that if you develop an application by using any language of the .NET family, the code can be easily translated and used by any other .NET language. For example, a Visual C++ .NET application can be easily converted to a Visual Basic .NET or Visual C# application, and likewise the opposite.
- **Support for OOPs (*object-oriented programming*).** OOPs is not a new concept for C++ programmers. Code in a OOP-based language is written using classes and objects. This not only helps you to write code easily, but also helps reuse your code. As discussed earlier, .NET has a

library of classes that contains methods that you can use to develop your applications. In addition, .NET also supports inheritance, which means that you can derive new classes from existing or base classes, and thus make the base class methods available to the new classes.

- **Support for Web applications.** Creating Web pages using scripting languages such as ASP (*Active Server Pages*) has not been an easy task for programmers worldwide. Therefore, to make coding simpler for the programmers, .NET provides the ASP.NET technology. The applications that use the ASP.NET technology to create Web pages are called Web applications.

  Using ASP.NET, you can create new ASP.NET pages or convert existing ASP pages to ASP.NET pages. ASP.NET also enables you to add high-level functionality to your Web pages by allowing you to create pages in any of the .NET programming languages. For example, using ASP.NET, you can create dynamic Web pages that allow you to access data from an underlying database.
- **Support for Web services.** .NET helps you to create Web services that you can use to create applications for different platforms that access data through the Internet. To do so, the methods of an instance of a class are called across the Internet and can then be used by applications running on various platforms. In addition, Web services help you to access the functionality of a remote server, such as calling a method from a remote server, creating an instance of a class on a remote server, and performing operations on the remote server. Web services use HTTP, which simplifies your task of accessing a remote server. HTTP helps in transferring messages written using XML between client and server.

As you can see, .NET is set to change the style of programming. The components of .NET that make it a user-friendly development environment are discussed in the following sections.

## Common Language Runtime (CLR)

Among the most important components of .NET is the *.NET Runtime*, commonly called the *CLR*. As the name suggests, the CLR is a common run-time environment for the code written in .NET languages. The code in .NET is managed by the CLR and is, therefore, called *managed code*. Managed code contains the information about the code, such as the classes, methods, and variables defined in the code. This information contained in managed code is called *metadata*. The CLR uses metadata to provide safe execution of the program code.

In addition to executing code, the CLR manages memory and threads and helps in the security and interoperability of the code with other languages. Besides providing safe execution of the program, managed code aims at targeting CLR services. These CLR services include locating and loading classes and interoperating with the existing DLL (*Dynamic Link Library*) code and COM objects.

The CLR has also enabled programmers to achieve interoperability across applications written in any of the .NET languages. Because the CLR is the common runtime environment for all .NET applications, all the code in .NET is converted to MSIL and is executed in a similar fashion. As discussed earlier, this code is called managed code. Managed code in .NET is developed using the CTS or CLS classes. The following section discusses CLS and CTS in detail.

## Common Type System (CTS)

As discussed earlier, .NET aims at providing interoperability between applications. To create interoperable applications, you need a set of standard data types that would be used across applications. In addition, you require a set of guidelines to create user-defined classes and objects for the .NET Framework. These standard data types and the set of guidelines are contained in CTS. To ensure interoperability across applications, CTS includes only those data types and features that are compatible across languages.

Consider an example of an application of which a part is created using C++. Subsequently, to provide a visual interface, you need to recreate the entire application in Visual Basic. This means that you need to recreate all the classes that you have used in the C++ application. This is because C++ and Visual Basic are not interoperable. The CTS feature for the .NET Framework simplifies such tedious tasks. If you create a class in any of the languages in the .NET Framework, you can use the same class in another language that is supported by the .NET Framework. Figure 1-1 displays the language interoperability feature of the .NET Framework.

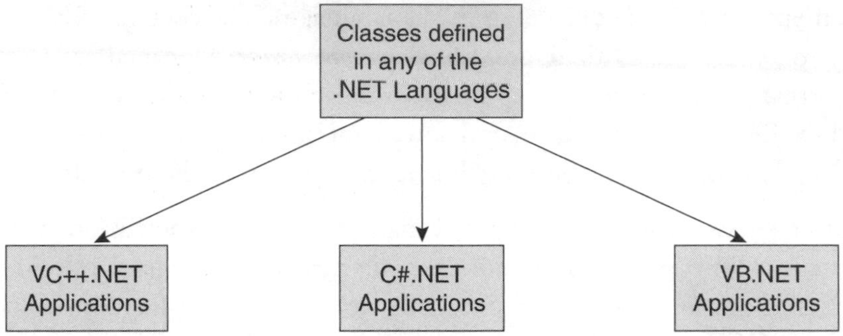


**FIGURE 1-1** *Language interoperability feature of the .NET Framework*

By now, you know that interoperability provided by CTS is a desired feature of all programmers. Following are some of the benefits of the interoperability offered by CTS.

- Inherit a class from a class you created in another language.
- Create an object of a class created in another language. You can also access the methods of the object that you have created.
- Pass an object or a reference of an object as a parameter to the methods of the class that you have written in another language.
- Debug an application that contains the objects of classes written in different languages. The debugger of the .NET Framework also enables you to switch between source code of the applications you have written in different .NET languages.

## Common Language Specification (CLS)

In addition to CTS, another feature that ensures language interoperability in the .NET Framework is CLS. CLS is defined as a set of rules that a .NET language should follow to allow you to create applications that are interoperable with other languages. However, to achieve interoperability across languages, you can only use objects with features listed in the CLS. These features are called *CLS-compliant features.*

For example, C# supports `uint32`, which is a 32-bit unsigned `integer` data type that is not CLS-compliant. The `uint32` data type is not supported by Visual Basic

.NET. If you use the `uint32` data type in a C# class, the class might not be interoperable with Visual Basic .NET applications. Only a CLS-compliant code is fully interoperable across languages. Although you can use the non-CLS feature in a .NET language class, the class might not be available to other .NET languages.

CLS works closely with CTS and MSIL to ensure language interoperability. You can also call CLS as a subset of CTS and MSIL, because CLS does not include all the features of CTS and MSIL. A compiler might not support some of the features of CTS and MSIL and still be CLS-compliant. Following are some of the features of CLS:

- Global methods and variables are not allowed in a CLS-compliant language.
- Some data types, such as unsigned data types, are not allowed in a CLS-compliant language.
- Unique names should be used in a CLS-compliant language. Even if the language is case-sensitive, you must use distinct names for different variables. Languages that are case-insensitive should be able to differentiate between the names.
- Any exception that you want to handle must be derived from the base class `Exception`.
- Pointers are not supported by a CLS-compliant language.

### Garbage Collector

Consider a situation in which you write extensive code for an application, such as that for an airline reservation system. In the application, you define a large number of variables of different data types, but you do not remove the variables from the system memory. In such a case, variables that are not required occupy memory space, resulting in reduced application performance to the extent that the application might even stop running.

The *garbage collection* feature of CLR enables automatic management of system memory. If a variable is not referenced for a long period of time by any application, the garbage collector automatically releases the memory assigned to the variable. This memory clean-up process ensures that there is no unnecessary wastage of system memory and, therefore, prevents memory leakage from the application.

In .NET, the CLR handles the process of garbage collection. To understand the garbage collection system, first look at the mechanism of allocating memory to an application. When you create an application, some memory space is allocated to it. Therefore, all the variables, classes, objects, and other resources that you declare in the application are added to this memory space. This process is called *heap allocation* to an application. When you go on adding data to this heap, there comes a time when the memory allocated to your application becomes full and you cannot add more data to it. This is the time when the garbage collector becomes active.

The garbage collector scans the entire heap and deallocates memory to resources that are no longer in use, thereby creating free spaces in the heap. You can now add more objects to the memory.

## Class Library

As discussed earlier, .NET provides you with several base classes. These base classes are available as a library of classes called the .NET base class library, which is an API similar to MFCs (*Microsoft Foundation Classes*) used with Visual C++ 6.0.

In addition to the base classes, the class library includes interfaces, value types, enumerations, and methods that allow you to perform a wide variety of tasks to make programming easier. Further, the classes contained in the .NET class library have a user-friendly name. This helps you to easily identify the classes that you need to use in your program. For example, if you need to create a thread, you use the `Thread` class. Similarly, to create an exception, you use the `Exception` class. You will learn about these classes later in this chapter.

A class library provides classes that help you create interoperable applications. This implies that the classes defined in the class library can be used to create a Visual C++ .NET, Visual Basic .NET, or C# application. In addition, the methods defined in the classes can also be used by any other .NET programming language.

## Assembly

An *assembly* is a logical structure that contains complied code for the .NET Framework. An assembly can be stored in one file or multiple files and can be .dll or .exe files. You may also include files using COM objects, resource files, or metadata in an assembly. As discussed earlier, metadata stores information about managed code in .NET. Similarly, metadata in an assembly contains information about the assembly. Therefore, assemblies are self-describing.

Before developing applications for the .NET platform, programmers used to create applications by using DLLs. Assemblies offer you several advantages over .dll files. Assemblies contain types, resources, and metadata. Whatever resources you might require for your application, you can simply include them in the assembly. For example, you may include the namespaces containing the classes that you require for your application. This makes developing an application easier for you.

In addition, while working with assemblies, you need not worry about registering your assembly and managing and versioning of your application. Registering your application with the operating system is as simple as copying assembly files to your application directory.

Another important advantage of using assemblies is that they can be either shared or private. The following section will discuss shared and private assemblies in detail.

## Private Assembly

As the name suggests, a *private assembly* is available only to the application for which you create it. When you create a private assembly, you need to provide the assembly along with the executable application. You create a private assembly when you do not need the assembly for another application. For example, if you create an assembly for a skills inventory system of the employees of an organization, you might not require the assembly for another application, such as the hardware inventory system of the organization.

Private assemblies offer you several advantages, such as:

- **Registering the assembly.** You need not register your assembly. To use a private assembly, you only need to copy it to the directory or subdirectory of your application.
- **Securing the application.** A private assembly makes your application safe to use because no other application can access the resources of the private assembly. This implies that no other application can make changes to the private assembly, giving the application full control over the assembly. You do not require security permissions for a private assembly, as these permissions are contained in the application's directory.

- **Applying naming conventions to the resources.** Because the resources in the private assembly are only accessible to your application, you need not worry about the naming convention of these resources. Even if two namespaces in different private assemblies have the same name, it does not affect the performance of any of the application.

### Shared Assembly

Consider a situation in which you need to create an application for different processes of the HR system, such as payroll generation, leave processing, and employee appraisal system. All these processes need to use the `Employee` class. In such a scenario, it is preferable to reuse the same class in all the listed systems instead of creating a class for each application. Therefore, you can create an assembly that you can use in multiple applications. Such an assembly is called a *shared assembly*. You can also use a shared assembly in all .NET languages if the assembly is created according to the CLS standards discussed earlier.

Multiple applications use shared assemblies; therefore, the assemblies cannot be stored with a specific application. Shared assemblies are stored in the assembly cache, which is a special directory in the file system. To store a shared assembly in the assembly cache, you can use .NET utilities, such as `Gacutil.exe` and `Regasm.exe`.

Working with shared assemblies is not as simple as working with private assemblies. Because the resources in the shared assembly can be accessed across applications, you need to be careful with the versioning and naming convention of these resources. Shared assemblies are given a *strong name*, which is a unique name that applications need to specify to access the shared assembly. However, versioning problems can be solved by accessing the resources with the correct version number.

The following features make assembly an important component of .NET applications:

- Self-describing
- Side-by-side
- Version dependency
- Application domain
- Zero-impact installation

These features are discussed in detail in the following subsections.

### Self-Describing

An assembly is self-describing because it consists of metadata that stores information about the assembly, such as the data type of the variables and the methods declared in the assembly. This implies that you need not register an assembly with the registry in the operating system.

### Side-by-Side

The side-by-side feature of an assembly enables you to install multiple versions of the same assembly in an application. Consider a situation in which you need to work with an application for the airline reservation system. The airline company needs to coordinate with different locations of the airline worldwide.

In this case, you need to create and refer to the two versions of the assembly at a time. The side-by-side feature of an assembly enables you to use both versions of the assembly in the same application without resulting in any conflict in the application.

### Version Dependency

An assembly *manifest* is used to maintain versions of the resources in an assembly. The manifest is a part of the assembly that contains metadata. When you refer an assembly from an application, the version of the referenced assembly is stored in the manifest of the application. This enables you to identify the version number of a referenced assembly that you have used during application development, thus taking care of the versioning problems of the assembly.

### Application Domain

The application domain feature of an assembly enables you to execute multiple applications that are independent of each other. These applications are executed as a part of the same process. Because each application is independent of the other, any error in one application does not affect other applications that are a part of the same process.

### Zero-Impact Installation

As discussed earlier, to install an assembly, you do not need to register the assembly with the operating system. You can simply use `copy` or `xcopy` commands to install an assembly. This is called the zero-impact installation feature of assemblies.

## Versioning

A well-known fact about the software industry is the regular change in the requirements of users. In such a dynamic scenario, new and improved versions of applications need to be developed. At numerous instances, when you upgrade an application, it may result in errors in the existing application. This can happen because the component that you upgrade might not be compatible with the earlier versions of the application. Problems in maintaining versions may also lead to problems in maintaining and debugging an application. An assembly includes features such as side-by-side and version dependency, which enable you to install multiple versions of the same assembly simultaneously.

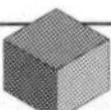

**NOTE**

Every version of an assembly has the following four parts:

```
<Application name> <Major version>.<Minor version>.<Build>.<Revision>
```

Here, `Major version` is the main version number of the application, `Minor version` is a part of the version of the application, and `Build` and `Revision` numbers are generally based on the system date. If you specify "*" in place of `Build` and `Revision`, they are automatically generated based on the system date. `Build` is the number of days since 01/01/00, and `Revision` is the number of seconds since midnight, based on the system time.

For example, if the version name of an application is `ABC 1.2.90.2670`, then `ABC` is the application name. The number `1` refers to the `Major version`, `2` is the `Minor version`, and `90` is the `Build`. The `Build` value of 90 refers to the 90th day after 01/01/00, and `2670` is the number of seconds since the midnight of the 90th day after 01/01/00.

You looked at the components of the .NET Framework, class library being one of them. Now look at some of the .NET base classes contained in the class library.

# An Overview of .NET Framework Base Classes

As discussed earlier, .NET provides you with several predefined base classes in the .NET class library. These classes contain methods that help you to create applications easily. Working with these classes is simple because of their user-friendly names.

The .NET class library consists of numerous base classes. However, in this chapter, you will be introduced to some of the most frequently used classes. You will learn more about these classes in the subsequent chapters.

## Exceptions

Just as in C++, the .NET Framework is designed to handle exceptions. An *exception* is the erroneous execution of an application that results in an unpredicted output. When an exception is generated in a .NET application, an object of the `Exception` class, a .NET base class, is thrown. This object contains information about the error that is generated and the way that the .NET Framework handles the error. For example, the object might contain information about the message to be displayed when the compiler encounters an error or the details of the area within the code where the error was detected.

You can handle exceptions in the .NET Framework by using `try{}`, `catch{}`, and `finally{}` statements. These statements are similar to the statements that you use in C++ for handling exceptions.

## Threads

A *thread* is single executable sequence of code. It is good practice to execute different sections of the application code, which are independent and parallel to each other. You can execute the code in sections by creating threads for each section and executing them simultaneously. For example, until an application prints data on a printer, you can use another thread to read from a file. This process is known as *multithreading*. To use the concept of multithreading in your application, you need to derive your class from the `Thread` class, which is another .NET base class.

## Delegates

`Delegate` is yet another type of special class that consists only of method definitions. Delegates are objects that allow you to pass methods as parameters to another method. Just as with a class, you need to instantiate a delegate. The instance of the delegate is created from the `Delegate` class of the .NET base class library.

In C#, events are special types of delegates that are assigned to trap an event. Any activity performed by a system is known as an *event*. For example, when you press a key or move the mouse pointer, an event is generated. To create an event-driven application, you need to trap the events generated by the system and perform the necessary action. For example, you need to trap the action following a key press or a click of a mouse. To do this, C# provides you with the `Event` delegate.

## Summary

In this chapter, you were introduced to the .NET Framework. The .NET Framework is a new API provided by Microsoft to help programmers develop applications for the distributed environment. In addition, .NET enables you to write applications for the Windows platform. Next, you learned about some of the components of the .NET Framework that make it a user-friendly development environment. These components include the CLR and the .NET class library.

The CLR is the run-time environment for the code written in .NET languages. The CLR includes CLS and CTS, which help you to achieve interoperability of the applications created for the .NET Framework. CTS is a set of guidelines and standard data types that you can use to create user-defined classes and objects for the .NET Framework. CLS is defined as a set of rules that a .NET language should follow to create applications that are interoperable with other languages.

In this chapter, you also learned about a class library. Visual Studio .NET is a development environment that provides you with several base classes containing methods. These base classes are contained in a library of classes called the .NET base class library, which is an API. Finally, you learned about some of the base classes in the class library, such as `Exception`, `Thread`, and `Delegate`.

# Chapter 2

## C# Basics

In this chapter, you will learn about the basics of C#. This chapter will discuss variables and data type casting. You will also learn about arrays and strings used in C#. Finally, you will be introduced to the statements and expressions used in C#.

# Introduction to C#

C# is an advanced version of C and C++ and is designed specially for the .NET environment. C#, pronounced *C sharp*, is a new object-oriented language used by programmers worldwide to develop applications that run on the .NET platform. However, C# is not a part of the .NET environment. C# is a part of Microsoft Visual Studio .NET 7.0. The other languages included in the Visual Studio package are Visual C++ and Visual Basic. Visual Studio 7.0 also includes scripting languages, such as VBScript and JScript. You can use all these languages to create applications that run in the .NET environment. C# is a significant step in the evolution of programming languages, and C# is an ideal solution for high-level business applications. Using C#, you can create a wide range of projects that can be used to build a complete client/server application.

C# builds on the features of C, C++, Visual Basic (VB), and Java to provide a complete environment for developing applications. C# merges the power of C, the object-oriented features of C++, and the graphical interface of VB. In addition, the programs in both C# and Java compile to a byte code.

Now look at the basic components of a C# application.

# Variables

*Variables* are storage locations for values in C#. A variable has a variable name and a data type associated with it. The *data type* represents the type of values that can be stored in the variable. Variables can store characters, character strings, numeric values, or memory addresses.

## Initializing Variables

To use a variable, you first need to declare it. In C#, you can declare a variable by using the following syntax:

```
<modifiers> <data type> <variable1, variable2,..........>;
```

Here, modifiers are the access modifiers that are used to define the accessibility level of a variable. C# supports five types of access modifiers: `public`, `protected internal`, `protected`, `internal`, and `private`. Data type is the type of the variable.

To use a variable in an application, you need to assign a value to it. You can assign a value to a variable by using the assignment operator (=). To assign a value `10` to the `integer` variable `x`, you use the following statement:

```
public int x = 10;
```

In C#, you cannot use a variable without initializing it. You can assign a well-defined initial value to a variable. Such a variable is called an *initially assigned variable*. C# also supports an *initially unassigned variable* that does not have a well-defined initial value assigned to it. However, you need to assign a well-defined value to an initially unassigned variable before using it.

## Variable Modifiers

*Variable modifiers* are used to define the features of a variable. Variable modifiers specify the accessibility levels of a variable. For example, a variable modifier decides whether a variable can be used or modified outside the class in which it is declared. The variable modifiers that are supported by C# are listed in Table 2-1.

**Table 2-1 The Variable Modifiers in C#**

| Variable Modifier | Description |
|---|---|
| `internal` | An `internal` variable is accessed from the current program in which it is declared. |
| `private` | A `private` variable is accessed from the type that contains it. |
| `protected` | A `protected` variable is accessed from the containing class or the types derived from the containing class. |
| `public` | A `public` variable can be accessed from anywhere. |
| `read-only` | A `read-only` variable is assigned a value when the variable is declared initially. If you do not assign a value to a `read-only` variable when it is first declared, the variable takes the default value of that type. As the name indicates, you cannot change the value of a `read-only` variable. |
| `static` | A `static` variable is accessed directly from the class and not from the instance of the class. |

You can specify the variable modifier while declaring a variable.

## Variable Data Types

The data type of a variable defines the type of the variable. Figure 2-1 displays the data types in C#.

## Types of Variables

There are seven types of variables in C#. These are as follows:

- **Static variables.** A static variable has a `static` modifier. You can access a static variable directly from the class to which it belongs. You do not need to create an instance of a class to access a static variable. A static variable becomes active when the program in which it is declared is loaded and becomes inactive when the program terminates.
- **Instance variables.** An instance variable is declared without the `static` modifier.

| Data Type | Description of the Data Type |
|---|---|
| int | An int data type is used to store 32-bit signed integer values. |
| long | A long data type is used to store 64-bit signed integer values. |
| short | A short data type is used to store 16-bit signed integer values. |
| sbyte | A sbyte data type is used to store 8-bit signed integer values. |
| byte | A byte data type is used to store 8-bit unsigned integer values. |
| ushort | An ushort data type is used to store 16-bit unsigned integer values. |
| uint | An uint data type is used to store 32-bit unsigned integer values. |
| ulong | An ulong data type is used to store 64-bit unsigned integer values. |
| float | A float data type is used to store floating point values of single precision. |
| double | A double data type is used to store floating point values of double precision. |
| decimal | A decimal data type is used to store 28-digit decimal numbers. |
| char | A char data type is used to store a Unicode character value. |
| string | A string data type is used to store an array of Unicode characters. |
| object | The object data type is the base type of every type. |
| bool | A bool data type is used to store boolean values, true or false. |

**FIGURE 2-1** *Variable data types*

- **Array elements.** An array element stores the starting address of an array in memory. To access an array element, you need to create an instance of the array.
- **Value parameters.** A value parameter is a variable declared without a `ref` or `out` modifier. When you call a method that contains the value parameter, the parameter becomes active. It takes the value of the argument that you specify in the method. When the method is returned, the value parameter becomes inactive.
- **Reference parameters.** A reference parameter has a `ref` modifier. A reference parameter is initialized with the value of the underlying variable. A reference parameter stores the location of the argument that is specified when the method is declared.
- **Output parameters.** An output parameter is a variable declared with the `out` modifier. The out modifier allows you to pass a variable, which is not initialized, to a method. The variable then takes the value from the method to which it is passed.

- **Local variables.** A local variable is declared within a method. A local variable is not initialized automatically and becomes active when the program that contains the local variable is executed. It becomes inactive when the execution of the immediate code, which contains the local variable, ceases.

## Variable Scope

A *scope* of a variable defines the region of the code from where you can access a variable. To know more about the various scopes of a variable, refer to Table 2-2.

**Table 2-2 Scopes of a Variable**

| Variable Scope | Description |
|---|---|
| Block | You can access the variable only within the code in which it is declared. |
| Procedure | You can access the variable only within the procedure for which it is declared. |
| Namespace | You can access the variable from anywhere within the namespace. |

C# supports several data types, as discussed. There may be instances where you need to convert one data type to another. To do this, C# provides you with data type casting statements.

## Types of Data Type Casting

Data type casting in C# can be of two types:

- Implicit conversion
- Explicit conversion

C# allows you to initialize variables by using the value or reference type. However, a value type can be casted only to another value type. Similarly, a reference type can be casted only to another reference type. When a data type is converted to another data type without any loss of data, this technique is called *implicit conversion.*

For example, you can implicitly convert an `integer` type data type to a `long` data type without any loss of data.

```
int x = 100;
long y;
y = x;
```

Figure 2-2 shows the implicit data type conversions that are permissible.

| Data Type | Permissible Implicit Data Type Conversion |
|---|---|
| int | decimal, long, double, and float |
| long | decimal, double, and float |
| short | int, long, decimal, double, and float |
| sbyte | short, int, long, decimal, double, and float |
| byte | int, uint, long, ulong, short, ushort, decimal, double, and float |
| ushort | int, uint, long, ulong, decimal, double, and float |
| uint | long, ulong, decimal, double, and float |
| ulong | decimal, double, and float |
| float | double |
| char | int, uint, long, ulong, ushort, decimal, double, and float |

**FIGURE 2-2** *Implicit data type conversion*

To convert a `long` data type to an `integer` data type, you use the *explicit data conversion* statements. In addition to all implicit data conversion statements, explicit data conversion statements also include all numeric data type conversions that cannot be implicitly converted. C# provides you with the cast operator to perform explicit data conversion.

```
int x;
long y = 100;
x = (int) y;
```

The `long` data type `y` is converted to `integer` `x` explicitly. An explicit data conversion might lead to some loss of information or may even result in an exception being thrown.

Figure 2-3 shows explicit data type conversions.

| Data Type | Explicit Data Type Conversion |
|---|---|
| int | uint, byte, sbyte, short, ushort, char, and ulong |
| long | int, uint, byte, sbyte, short, ushort, char, and ulong |
| short | uint, ushort, byte, sbyte, char, and ulong |
| sbyte | byte, uint, ulong, char, and ushort |
| byte | char and sbyte |
| ushort | short, byte, sbyte, and char |
| uint | int, short, ushort, byte, sbyte, and char |
| ulong | byte, sbyte, int, uint, short, ushort, long, and char |
| float | int, uint, long, ulong, char, decimal, short, ushort, byte, and sbyte |
| double | int, uint, short, ushort, byte, sbyte, long, ulong, char, float, and double |
| decimal | byte, sbyte, int, uint, short, ushort, long, ulong, char, float, and double |
| char | short, byte, and sbyte |

**FIGURE 2-3** *Explicit data type conversion*

In addition to the data type conversion statements, C# provides you with boxing and unboxing data conversion techniques. You can use *boxing* to convert a value type to an object type. Boxing can be of the type implicit or explicit data conversion.

When you try to convert a value type to an object type, C# creates an instance of the object type. The value stored in the data type is then written to the instance of the object that is created.

Conversely, *unboxing* converts an object type to a value type. Unboxing is an explicit data type conversion technique. To convert an object type to a value type by using unboxing, you first need to create a value type by using boxing. The concept of boxing and unboxing is explained in detail in Chapter 4, "More about Components."

As you have seen earlier, C# uses variables to store values. To store multiple variables as a single data structure, you can use an array.

## Arrays

An *array* is a data structure that acts as a pointer to an address in memory. An array stores a number of variables and has an index attached to it. The *index* of an array is used to access the elements of the array. The *elements* of an array are the variables that are stored in the array. An array can store only the elements of the same data type. For example, an `integer` array can store only the variables of the `integer` type. Unlike C++, an array in C# is an object and, therefore, has methods and properties associated with it.

To access the elements in an array, you use indices. An array can have a single index or multiple indices attached to it. The number of indices on each element of an array defines the *rank* of the array. For example, if an array has one index attached to its elements, the rank of the array is one. Such an array is called a *single-dimensional array*. Similarly, if an array has more than one index, it is called a *multidimensional array*. You will learn more about multidimensional arrays in Chapter 4, in the section "Multidimensional Arrays."

To use an array in a program code, you need to declare and initialize it. In C#, you initialize an array by using the `new` keyword. To initialize an `integer` array with `20` elements, you use the following statement:

```
int [] Integer = new int [20];
```

C# allows you to specify the size of an array dynamically. Therefore, you can declare an array and initialize it at run time. When you declare an array without initializing it, C# creates a null reference to the array. You can then specify the amount of memory required by using the `new` keyword. C# allocates the required memory to the array at run time. For example, you can declare an array `Integer` and then specify the size of the array as `20` by using the `new` keyword.

```
int [] Integer;
Integer = new int [20];
```

When the array is initialized with the value `20`, you can access any elements of the array. The elements of an array are accessed by their indices. The index of an array in C# starts from zero. Therefore, the first element of an array has an index zero. To assign a value `100` to the last element of the array `Integer`, use the following statement:

```
Integer [19] = 100;
```

Similar to integers, you can use arrays to store character values. An array of character values is called a *string*. Strings will now be discussed in detail.

# Strings

C# provides you with a *String* type. In C and C++, an array of characters is called a *string*. String is not a class in C and C++, therefore, working with strings is a problem in C and C++. Simple operations, such as comparing or adding two strings, require a lot of programming. To provide the programmers with a solution to this problem, C# created a `String` class.

## Initializing Strings

You can initialize a string by using the `string` keyword. To initialize a string, `string1`, use the following statement:

```
string string1 = "Hello World";
```

The previous sample code declares a string, `string1`, and initializes it with a value `"Hello World"`.

The assignment of a value to a string takes place by the reference type. When you declare a string, an object of the `String` class is created and placed on the heap. This object of the `String` class has the reference to the memory location where the string is stored.

## Working with Strings

The `String` class in C# is in the `System` namespace. `String` is a class and has several methods associated with it. You can use these methods to perform operations on strings. The commonly used methods in the `String` class are as follows:

- **`Compare()`.** The `Compare()` method is used to compare two strings.
- **`Format()`.** You can use the `Format()` method to format the values in a string. The `Format()` method allows you to specify formatting for each value in a string.
- **`Trim()`.** The `Trim()` method in C# deletes the extra spaces in a string. The `Trim()` method can be used to delete both the leading and trailing spaces.
- **`ToUpper()`.** To change the capitalization of the elements in a string, you can use the `ToLower()` or `ToUpper()` methods. The `ToLower()` method

converts the elements of the string to lowercase. Similarly, you can convert the string to uppercase by using the `ToUpper()` method.

- **`Split()`.** Working with large strings can be a problem. Therefore, the `System.String` class provides the `Split()` method that can be used to break a string into several small strings. You can specify a character from where the string should be split. The `Split()` method breaks the string into substrings at each instance of the given character. The substrings created by the `Split()` method are stored in the form of an array.
- **`IndexOf()`.** The `IndexOf()` method is used to locate a character or substring in the main string. The `IndexOf()` method returns the index of the first instance of the specified character in a string. Similarly, to locate the last occurrence of a character or substring, you can use the `LastIndexOf()` method.
- **`IndexOfAny()`.** If you need to know the index of the first occurrence of any one of a set of characters in a string, you can use the `IndexOfAny()` method. Similarly, the `LastIndexOfAny()` method is used to locate the index of the last occurrence of any one of a set of characters in a string.
- **`Replace()`.** To replace all occurrences of a character or a substring in a string by another character or substring, you use the `Replace()` method.

Simple operations on a string, such as adding or concatenating two strings, can be performed using a (+) operator. You do not require a method for concatenating two strings. For example, to add `string1` and `string2`, you first need to initialize the two strings. You can then use the (+) operator to add the two strings and initialize their value to another string, `string3`. The code sample that follows displays this.

```
string string1 = 'John ';
string string2 = 'Floyd';
string string3 = string1 + string2;
```

The value of `string3` in the previous sample is `John Floyd`.

You have learned about performing simple operations on a string. Now look at the various statements and expressions provided by C#. You can use these statements and expressions to perform specific operations on variables.

# Statements and Expressions

*Statements* in C# are similar to those in C and C++. Statements in C# can be of two types:

- Simple
- Embedded

*Simple statements* include all variable declaration statements and labeled statements. However, all other statements that are embedded and are a part of another statement are called *embedded statements*. All statements in C# are enclosed within curly braces {}.

## Types of Statements

C# supports simple statements and embedded statements, such as *selection*, *iteration*, and *jump* statements. Look at these statements in detail.

### *Simple Statements*

*Simple statements* include all declaration and labeled statements. Simple statements also include statements that are used to call methods.

#### Declaration Statements

A *declaration statement* is used to declare a variable or a constant. You can use a single statement to declare more than one variable or constant. The following is an example of an initializing statement.

```
public int i, y;
i = 45;
y = 37;
```

Similarly, you use declaration statements to declare constants. *Constants* are data types whose value cannot be changed after being declared. The `const` keyword is used to declare a constant. Consider the following code sample:

```
const char x = a;
```

The previous code declares a constant `x` of the type character and assigns a value a to it. The value of the constant `x` cannot be changed throughout the lifetime of `x`.

### Labeled Statements

In addition to declaring variables and constants, you can declare labels in C#. A *labeled statement* is a simple statement that is used to declare a label. The syntax of a labeled statement is as follows:

```
<label1> : <statement1>
```

Here, `label1` is the name of a label and `statement1` specifies the statements to be executed when the control reaches the label. You use a `goto` statement to refer to a label.

### Method Call Statements

A *method call statement* is also a type of a simple statement. A method call statement is used to call a method that is already created. The following code sample is an example of a method call statement:

```
public int x;
x = 100;
MessageBox.Show (x);
```

The previous code calls the `Show` method of the class `MessageBox`.

## *Selection Statements*

C# also provides you with *selection statements*. In cases where the program has to execute one block of statements out of all the available blocks of statements, selection statements are used. In such a case, the program code needs to select the block of statements to be executed, which are therefore called selection statements. The selection of the statements to be executed is based on the value returned by evaluating an expression that follows the selection statement. The selection statements are of two types:

- if-statement
- switch-statement

### if-statement

The *if-statement* is a decision-making statement that selects a specific set of statements to execute. The selection of the set of statements is based on a `Boolean` value that is returned by evaluating a given expression. The syntax of an if-statement is as follows:

```
if (Boolean-expression) statement1
```

The *Boolean expression* returns a value of either `true` or `false`. If the Boolean expression evaluates to `true`, the statement following the Boolean expression is executed. After the execution of statement1, the control passes to the end of the if-statement. If the result of the Boolean expression is `false`, the statements in the `else` block are executed.

Look at the following example of an if-else statement:

```
int x;
if (x >= 0)
{
        MessageBox.Show("x is a positive number.");
}
else
{
        MessageBox.Show("x is a negative number.");
}
```

The previous code tests for the value of `x`, and if the Boolean expression evaluates to `true`, the message `"x is a positive number."` is displayed. However, if the value of the Boolean expression (`x >= 0`) is `false`, the message `"x is a negative number."` is displayed.

If an `else` statement is not provided in the if-statement, the control is transferred to the end of the if-statement when the result of the Boolean expression is `false`.

## switch-statement

Similar to the if-statement, the *switch-statement* is a type of a selection statement. However, a switch-statement is used when there are multiple block statements from which to choose. The syntax of a switch-statement is as follows:

```
-------------
switch (expression)
{
case constant-expression:
       statement
```

```
        jump-statement
[default:
        statement
        jump-statement]
}
-------------
```

The switch statement is written with a `switch` keyword, followed by an expression to be evaluated. The switch statement evaluates an expression, and the set of statements to be executed is selected. The selection is based on the result of the expression. The different sets of statements to be executed are considered as different cases. The `case` keyword is used to define different cases. The result of the statement is matched to the available cases, and the set of statements to be executed is selected. The following is an example of a switch-statement:

```
int x;
switch (x)
{
    case 1:
        MessageBox.Show("x is a positive number.");
        break;
    case 2:
        MessageBox.Show("x is a negative number.");
        break;
    default:
        MessageBox.Show("x is equal to 0.");
        break;
}
```

As shown in the preceding code, you can also include a *`default`* case. The `default` case is executed if the result of the expression does not match any of the available cases. A *`break` statement* is used to pass the control out of the case.

In C and C++, a *fall-through condition* can occur. In a fall-through condition, if you omit any of the `break` statements, the program executes two cases. However, in C#, a fall-through condition is omitted because the compiler throws an error for each case that does not end with a `break` statement. The following code in C# generates an error:

```
int x;
switch (x)
```

```
{
    case 1:
        MessageBox.Show("x is a positive number.");
        break;
    case 2:
        MessageBox.Show("x is a negative number.");
    default:
        MessageBox.Show("x is equal to 0.");
        break;
}
```

If you need to execute two cases, you need to provide an explicit `goto` statement. The syntax for such a code is given as follows:

```
switch (expression)
{
    case 1 :
         statement
         goto case2;
    case 2 :
         statement
         goto default;
    [default:
         statement
         jump-statement]
}
```

In this case, the compiler first executes `case1`, then `case2`, and then the `default` case.

In addition to the selection statements, types of statements also include iteration statements.

## Iteration Statements

The iteration statements are used to execute a set of statements repeatedly until a condition is met. The types of iteration statements are as follows:

- `for` loop
- `foreach` loop

- while loop
- do-while loop

## for Loop

The *for loop* in C# is similar to the for loop in C and C++. The for loop is used to execute a given set of statements until a given expression in the for loop returns true. The syntax of a for loop is as follows:

```
for (initializer; condition; iterator)
{
        ------------------
}
```

Here, initializer is an expression that is evaluated before the control enters the loop. The condition specifies the condition that is evaluated before every iteration is completed. The iterator is the expression that is evaluated after every iteration. The statements in the for loop are continuously executed until the expression returns false.

If you want to transfer the control of execution to the end of the for loop when the control is within the loop, you can use a break statement explicitly. In such a case, the statements within the for loop are not executed even if the condition evaluated is true. Therefore, the iteration stops.

However, if you need to end a particular iteration, you can use a continue statement. The control of execution passes to the end of the statements within the for loop, which ends only the running iteration.

## foreach Loop

The *foreach loop* is introduced in C#. However, it did not exist in C and C++. The foreach loop in C# iterates the statements in the foreach loop for each element in an array or collection. The following example will help you to understand the foreach loop.

```
int [] Integer = {15,89,1000,6}
foreach (int x in Integer)
{
        Console.WriteLine (x)
}
```

Here, `in` is a keyword for the `foreach` loop.

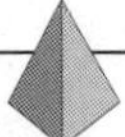

**TIP**

The value of the variable in the `foreach` loop cannot change during the execution of the `foreach` loop.

## while Loop

The *`while` loop* is similar to a `for` loop because it evaluates a condition and executes the statements within the `while` loop until the condition returns `false`. The `while` loop in C# is similar to the `while` loop in C and C++. If the condition that is evaluated results in `false` the first time, the `while` loop is not executed. The syntax of a `while` loop is similar to that of the `for` loop, except that the `while` loop takes only one parameter. The code sample that follows is an example of the `while` loop that is not executed.

```
int x = 20;
while (x < 10)
{
        Console.WriteLine (x);
        x++;
}
```

When the code evaluates the condition for the first time, the result is `false`. Therefore, the control does not enter the loop.

## do-while Loop

The *`do-while` loop* is another form of iteration statements in which the condition is evaluated for the first time after the statements in the `do-while` loop are executed. This implies that the `do-while` loop, in contrast to the `while` loop, is executed at least once. The following code executes the statements in the `do-while` loop once before it checks for the value of `x` and, therefore, displays the value of `x` once.

```
int x = 20;
do {
        Console.WriteLine (x);
} while (x < 10)
```

## Jump Statements

*Jump statements* are also a type of statement in C#. The jump statements are used to pass the control of the execution unconditionally to another line in the program. The line of code to which the control is transferred is called the *target* of the jump statement. The commonly used jump statements in C# are:

- `goto` statement
- `return` statement
- `break` statement
- `continue` statement

The jump statements in C# are similar to those in C and C++.

### `goto` Statement

The *`goto` statement* is used to jump unconditionally to another line in a program. You need to specify the line to which the code jumps using a label. The syntax of the `goto` statement uses the `goto` keyword, such as:

```
goto Label1;
```

where `Label1` specifies the line to which the code passes the control.

**TIP**

The `goto` statement cannot be used in the following cases:

- Jumping into a block of code
- Exiting a `finally` block
- Jumping outside a class

### `return` Statement

A *`return` statement* is another jump statement that is used to end a method of a class. After a method ends, the execution control is transferred to the calling method. If the method that includes the `return` statement has a return type, the method must a return a value of the return type. The syntax of the `return` statement is as follows:

```
return expression;
```

Here, `return` is a keyword that you use to write a `return` statement.

If the method is of the type `void`, the `return` statement does not take an expression. Constructors or destructors also do not require an expression with the `return` statement.

### break Statement

As you have seen, you can use a `return` statement to end a method. Similarly, to end a loop, you use the *`break` statement*. It is used to exit from a loop, such as `for`, `foreach`, `do`, and `do-while` loop. The `break` statement passes the control out of the loop. The `break` statement is written using the `break` keyword.

```
break;
```

For nested loops, the `break` statement passes the control to the end of the innermost loop.

### continue Statement

Similar to a `break` statement, the *`continue` statement* is also used with loops. The `continue` statement is used to end only the current iteration and not the entire loop. The execution again starts for the next iteration. The `continue` keyword is used to specify a `continue` statement.

```
continue;
```

A `continue` statement cannot be used to exit a `finally` block. You will learn about the `finally` block in Chapter 6, "Threads."

Having learned about statements, you need to understand expressions. Expressions are also used to perform operations on variables.

## Expressions

*Expressions* in C# are similar to that of C++. Expressions are defined as a sequence of operands and operators that are used to perform operations. An expression can be of the following types: values, variables, classes, namespaces, indexers, and methods.

## Operators

*Operators* are used to write expressions. Operators specify the kind of operation that is to be performed on the operands. The types of operators supported by C# are displayed in Table 2-3.

**Table 2-3 The Types of Operators in C#**

| Types of Operators | Description |
|---|---|
| Unary operators | Unary operators perform operations on a single operand. For example, the ++ and -- operators are unary operators. Unary operators can either precede or succeed the operand. Unary operators are used with numeric data types. |
| Binary operators | Binary operators perform operations on two operands. For example, +, -, +=, -=, *, and / are binary operators. Binary operators are written between the two operands. Binary operators are also used with numeric operators. |
| Ternary operators | Ternary operators have three operands. C# supports only one ternary operator, ? :. The ? : operator is equivalent to an `if-else` statement. |

Now look at the syntax of the ? : operator.

```
condition ? true value : false value
```

Here, `condition` is the condition of the `if-else` statement. It is a Boolean expression. If the condition evaluates to `true`, the `true` value is returned. Otherwise, the `false` value is returned.

The unary, binary, and ternary operators are further classified according to the operations they perform. Look at the operators supported by C# in detail.

The *arithmetic operators* are used to perform arithmetic operations. C# supports +, -, *, /, and %. These operators are similar to the operators in C++.

The *increment* and *decrement operator* increases or decreases the value of a variable by one. The increment operator is ++, and the decrement operator is --.

The *assignment operator* performs an arithmetic operation and assigns the result to a variable. The commonly used assignment operators are =, +=, -=, *=, /=, %=, &=, |=, <<=, >>=, and ^=.

The *logical operators* supported by C# are &, |, ^, ~, &&, ||, `true`, `false`, and !.

The *relational operators* are also called *comparison operators*. These operators are used to compare two numeric values. An example of relational operators are ==, <, >, <=, >=, and !=.

The *bit shifting operators* are << and >>. These operators are used to shift the bit to the left and right respectively.

The *conditional operator* is the ternary operator ? :, as discussed in the preceding table. The ternary operator ? : is used for the `if-else` construct.

Each type of variable in C# has a specific range. If an operation results in the overflow of the range, C# provides *`checked`* and *`unchecked` operators*. These operators are used to manage the overflow situation. When an operation is performed on the variable marked as `checked`, CLR (*common language runtime*) checks for overflow. If the value overflows, C# throws an exception. If you do not want an overflow check, mark the variable as `unchecked`. No exception is raised in this case even if an overflow occurs and may result in the loss of data.

You can use the *`is` operator* in C# to match the object with the type specified. You use the `is` and `typeof` operators to know the type of objects at run time.

C# provides the *`sizeof` operator* to find the size of the variable in `bytes`. The variable whose size is to be found is passed as a parameter to the `sizeof` operator.

## Operator Overloading

C++ programmers are familiar with the concept of operator overloading. As seen earlier, all operators in C# perform a specified set of operations. However, if you want user-defined implementations, you use *operator overloading*. Many of the available operators in C# can be overloaded. For operator overloading, it is essential that one or both operands in the expression are of the struct type or a user-defined class. To declare an operator overload, use the `operator` keyword. The syntax of an operator overload is:

```
operator operator1
```

## Summary

In this chapter, you learned about the basics of C#. You learned that C# is an object-oriented language that is derived from C and C++. C# is designed to create high-level applications that work on the .NET environment. Next, you learned that variables are storage locations for values in C#. Variables can store characters, character strings, numeric values, or memory addresses. Then you learned that an array is a data structure that acts as a pointer to an address in a memory. An array stores a number of variables and has an index attached to it. C# provides a `String` class to work with strings. `String` is a class in C#. Therefore, it has several methods associated with it.

Finally, you learned about the data conversion statements in C#, along with other statements and expressions. The commonly used statements in C# are of the following types: simple, selection, iteration, and jump. Expressions in C# are a sequence of operators and operands that are used to perform operations.

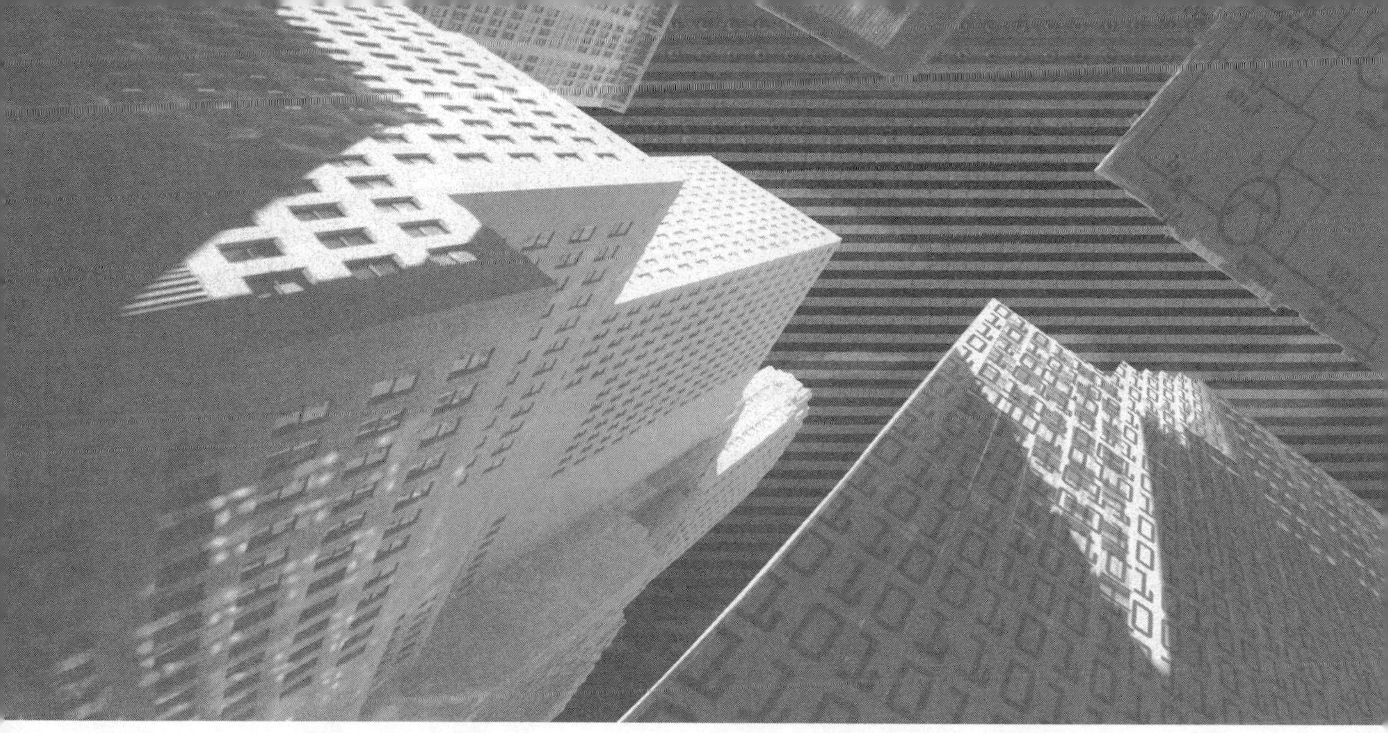

# PART II

## Handling Data

# Chapter 3

## Components of C#

In this chapter, you will learn about the basic components of the C# language, such as classes, namespaces, structs, enumerations, and interfaces. You will also learn about the methods used with classes. Finally, you will learn to write, compile, and execute a simple program in C# by using the `Main()` method.

## Classes

The most important component of C# is a class. A *class* is defined as a data structure used to create *objects*. The instance of a class is called an object. An object contains data and has methods associated with it. The data and methods associated with a class are called the *members* of the class. A class is used to define the data contained in objects. However, classes do not contain data themselves. To use a class in a program, you first need to declare the class.

### Declaring Classes

To declare a class, you use the `class` keyword. A class is declared using the class declaration statement as shown:

```
<modifiers> class <class name>
{
            -----------------
}
```

Here, modifiers specify the accessibility information about the class. A class modifier defines the scope of the class. C# supports several class modifiers, such as `new`, `public`, `private`, `protected`, `internal`, `sealed`, and `abstract`. Take a look at Table 3-1 to learn more about class modifiers.

**Table 3-1 The Class Modifiers in C#**

| Class Modifier | Description |
|---|---|
| `new` | A `new` class modifier is used with nested classes. It is used to hide an inherited class by the same name as the base class. |
| `public` | A `public` class modifier is used to define classes that can be accessed from any program code. |
| `private` | A `private` class modifier is used to define classes that can be accessed from a containing type. A `private` modifier is typically used with a class that contains `static` methods. |
| `protected` | A `protected` class modifier is used to define classes that can be accessed from a containing type or the types derived from the containing types. |
| `internal` | An `internal` class modifier is used to define classes that can be accessed from the current assembly. |
| `sealed` | A `sealed` class modifier is used to prevent a class being derived from a base class. |
| `abstract` | An `abstract` class modifier is used to define a base class of other classes. However, you cannot create instances of an abstract class. An abstract class supports inheritance. However, if you inherit from an abstract class, you need to implement all its abstract methods. An abstract class cannot be a sealed class, as you cannot derive a sealed class. |

After declaring a class, you can use it in a C# project. C# allows you to use the class that you define in other applications. In addition, you can derive a class from an existing class. This concept is called inheritance. Inheritance will now be discussed in detail.

## Inheritance

The concept of inheritance is familiar to C and C++ programmers. *Inheritance* allows a class to be derived from another class known as the *base class*. The class that you derive is called the *derived class*. Inheritance allows you to reuse the data and methods of a class by the derived class. However, the constructors and destructors of the base class are not implicitly inherited. You will learn about the methods, constructors, and destructors used with classes later in this chapter.

In C#, you cannot derive a class from multiple classes. This is known as *single inheritance*. However, you can derive any number of classes from a single class. In addition, a base class of other classes can, in turn, be derived from another class. In C#, the `Object` class is the base class of all classes. The `Object` class lies in the `System` namespace. Here is the syntax of inheriting a derived class from a base class.

```
class <derived class> : <base class>
```

In the previous code, a colon (:) is used to indicate that a class is derived from an existing class. For example,

```
class Class1 : Class2
```

Here, `Class2` is the base class of `Class1`, and therefore, `Class1` inherits all members of `Class2`.

The following example will help you to understand the concept of inheritance.

```
class Employee
{
        public void EmployeeName()
        {
                ------------
        }
}
class Salary : Employee
{
        public void CalculateSalary()
        {
                ----------
        }
}
```

```
class Bonus
{
        static void Main()
        {
                Salary salary1 = new Salary;
                salary1.EmployeeName();
                salary1.CalculateSalary();
        }
}
```

This code declares two classes, `Employee` and `Salary`. The `Salary` class is inherited from the `Employee` class and, therefore, inherits the method declared by the base class. An instance of the derived class is created to access the members of the base class.

As discussed earlier, the derived class implicitly inherits all the members of the base class. However, you can hide any method of the base class so that the derived class cannot access the method. To do so, you declare another method by a signature that is same as that of the base class method. When a compiler finds such a method, it generates a warning. To suppress this warning, you use the `new` keyword. This makes the base class method inaccessible to the derived class.

In the above case, if you need to declare a method with the name `EmployeeName()` in the `Salary` class, you need to include the `new` keyword in the method declaration statement. The next example uses the `new` keyword.

```
class Salary : Employee
{
        new public void EmployeeName()
        {
                ............
        }
}
```

Inheritance allows a derived class to inherit the methods of the base class. However, the constructors and destructors of the base class are not implicitly inherited. The next section looks at the constructors and destructors in detail.

## Constructors

A *constructor* is a default method that is called when an object is initialized from a class. Each class has a constructor with a name that is the same as that of the class. A constructor does not return a value. However, unlike methods, you do not call a constructor. It is automatically called when you create an object of a class.

It is not necessary to declare a constructor for a class. If you do not explicitly declare a constructor, C# automatically creates a default constructor for a class with the same name as that of the class. The following is an example of declaring a constructor:

```
<modifier> <constructor name>
{
            -----------
}
```

Constructor modifiers include `public`, `private`, `protected`, and `internal`. Inside the block of the constructor are the statements that are used to initialize the class that contains the constructor.

To initialize the data members of a class, you can declare a constructor for the class and pass parameters to it. The parameters in this case are the initial values of the data members. To understand the concept of passing parameters to constructors, look at the following example:

```
public class Employee
{
        public Employee()
        {
                string Name = 'John';
        }
        public Employee (string EmployeeName)
        {
                Name = EmployeeName;
        }
}
```

In the previous code, the constructor with the name `Employee()` is declared in the class `Employee`. The constructor takes `EmployeeName` as the parameter and initializes the value of `Name` with `EmployeeName`. Therefore, when you create an instance of the `Employee` class, the object gets initialized. This prevents any other class from accessing the objects of the `Employee` class before initializing the object.

After declaring a constructor, you need to use it to instantiate an object of the class. You use the `new` keyword to instantiate the object of the class.

```
Employee employee1 = new Employee ('Smith');
```

When you pass a value as a parameter, the new value overwrites the initial value. Therefore, the name of the employee is changed to `Smith`. However, if you do not want to change the default value, you can instantiate the constructor without passing a parameter to it, as shown in the following example:

```
Employee employee1 = new Employee();
```

As already discussed, if you do not explicitly declare a constructor, C# creates a default constructor. In this case, C# calls the default constructor of the direct base class. The `base` keyword is used to call the default base class constructor from the derived class. You can also use the `this` keyword if you want to call any other constructor of the base class.

Therefore, if you derive a class `Salary` from the class `Employee`, you can call the constructor of the `Employee` class from the `Salary` class.

```
class Employee
{
        public Employee ()
        {
                 -------------
        }
}
class Salary : Employee
{
         public Salary : base ()
        {
                  -------------
        }
}
```

As you know, it is essential to initialize an instance of a class whenever the instance is created. Similarly, it is also essential to destroy the instance of the class when it goes out of scope. To do this, C# contains destructors that are called when an instance of a class is destroyed.

## Destructors

*Destructors* are not extensively used in C#. To destroy resources from memory, C# uses the garbage collection mechanism. You have learned about this mechanism in Chapter 1, "Overview of the .NET Framework," in the section "Garbage Collector."

Similar to naming a constructor, the destructor takes the same name as that of the class. You can declare a destructor by using the destructor declaration statement. These statements include a tilde (~) sign followed by the name of the class.

```
public class Employee
{
        ~ Employee ()
        {
                -----------------
        }
}
```

In the previous code, `Employee()` is the destructor of the `Employee` class. You can include the statements required to uninitialize variables of the class in the body of the destructor.

You cannot explicitly call a destructor. It is automatically invoked when an instance of a class is not used by any program. In addition, if destructors of the base and derived classes are to be invoked, the derived class destructor is invoked first, followed by the base class constructor.

In addition to the garbage collection system, C# provides you with the `Finalize()`, `Dispose()`, and `Close()` methods. These methods are used to clean up the memory after a resource is destroyed.

### *Finalize()* Method

To destroy data members when they are not needed, you can create the `Finalize()` method. This method is automatically called when the class instance is deleted. The `Finalize()` method cleans the memory before the garbage collection system dereferences the object. You cannot call the `Finalize()` method because it gets automatically invoked when you call the destructor of the class.

Similar to a destructor declaration statement, you can declare the `Finalize()` method by using the tilde (~) sign followed by the name of the containing class.

The `Finalize()` method does not return any value. In addition, you cannot pass parameters to the `Finalize()` method and directly override it.

Before C# calls the `Finalize()` method, it waits for some time after the object instance is no longer used by any program code. This unnecessarily blocks memory and destroys resources in longer time duration. To tackle this problem, C# provides you with the `Dispose()` and `Close()` methods.

### `Dispose()` and `Close()` Methods

In C#, you can explicitly call the `Dispose()` and `Close()` methods to destroy the resources immediately after the class instance is deleted. These methods are not implicitly invoked. Therefore, if you forget to call the `Dispose()` or `Close()` methods, the resources remain in memory until the garbage collection system cleans the memory. To solve this problem, you can use the `Dispose()` and `Close()` methods with the `Finalize()` method. If the `Dispose()` or `Close()` method is not explicitly called, the `Finalize()` method will clean the memory before the garbage collection system is invoked.

Having learned about the `Finalize()`, `Dispose()`, and `Close()` methods, you can take a look at the methods used with classes in detail.

# Methods

A *method* is a logical section of code that can be used to perform a specific operation. An object or a class can call a method to implement the functionality of the method. A method has a return type or can be of the type `void`.

## Declaring a Method

The syntax of method declaration is as shown here:

```
< modifier> <return type> <method name> (parameter1, parameter2, ........)
{
                statements
}
```

Here, `modifier` is the access modifier and `return type` specifies the data type of the value that is returned by the method. The list of parameters that the method takes is specified in the parentheses following the method name.

## Calling a Method

After a method is declared, you can call the method to be used by any class or an object. To call a method, you use the following syntax:

```
object1.method1 (parameter1, parameter2,...);
```

Here, `object1` is the instance of the class that calls the method, `method1` is the name of the method, and the parameter list is specified within parentheses.

## Passing Parameters to Methods

While calling a method, you can pass a list of parameters to the method. The types of parameters that can be passed to a method are:

- Value parameters
- Reference parameters
- Output parameter
- Parameter arrays

The parameters that are passed by value to a method are called *value parameters*. When a variable is passed by value, the method changes the value of the variable in a copy. However, the actual value remains unchanged. Therefore, the value parameters are not affected by the changes that are made to the variables in the method. By default, all variables are passed as value parameters.

The value of variables that are passed by reference, known as *reference parameters*, changes when you modify the variable in a method. When a variable is passed by reference, the variable passes only a reference to the method and not the actual value. Therefore, changes made by the method are made to the original variable and not to its copy. C# overwrites the changes to the original value of the variable. The `ref` keyword is used to pass a variable to a method by reference.

The syntax of a method to which you pass a parameter by reference is:

```
object1.method1 (parameter1, ref parameter2,...);
```

Here, `parameter1` is passed by value. However, `parameter2` is passed by reference. Therefore, the value of `parameter1` will not be affected by the changes made to it during method execution. However, if changes are made to `parameter2` in the method body, the changes will get reflected to its original value.

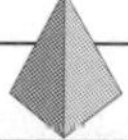

**TIP**

In contrast to variables, strings do not change even when passed by reference. When you make a change to the value of a string, C# creates a new string.

In general, methods return a single value. In C#, you can write methods that return multiple values. To do so, you pass a parameter to the method as an *output parameter*. An output parameter is passed to a method by using the `out` keyword.

```
object1.method1 (out parameter1);
```

Here, `parameter1` is passed to `method1` as an output parameter.

In C#, it is essential that you initialize a variable before using it. Therefore, when you pass an output parameter, it already has some value. C# overwrites this value with the value returned by the method. This is a waste and can be avoided by using the `out` keyword. A variable prefixed with the `out` keyword is an exception, as you can pass it to a method without initializing it. The output parameter is initialized by the value returned by the method. A variable can store an output value only if you pass the variable to the method by reference.

In addition to variables, you can pass arrays as a parameter to a method. However, only a one-dimensional array can be passed to a method. You use the `params` keyword to specify a *parameter array*.

The syntax of passing a parameter array is:

```
object1.method1 (parameter1, params data type[] parameter2);
```

In the previous syntax, `parameter2` is a one-dimensional array, and its type is specified by the data type.

When you declare a parameter array along with other parameters, you must include the parameter array as the last element in the list. In addition, you cannot include a parameter array with a reference or an output parameter. Therefore, the following code will generate an error:

```
object1.method1 (params data type[] parameter1, ref parameter2);
```

## Method Modifiers

Similar to classes, methods in C# also have modifiers. Following are some of the commonly used method modifiers.

- **`static`.** A `static` method cannot be called by any particular instance of a class. To call a `static` method, you need to specify the name of the container class.
- **`new`.** A `new` method in C# is used to suppress the compiler's warning when you try to hide a method of a base class with the same name as the derived class method.
- **`public`.** Similar to the `public` modifier of a class, if you declare a method as `public`, it can be accessed from any location. The method can also be called from outside the class that declares it.
- **`private`.** A method declared as `private` is private to the class that declares it. This implies that a `private` method cannot be called from outside the class that contains the method.
- **`protected`.** A `protected` method modifier is similar to a `protected` class modifier. A method declared as `protected` can be called from the derived classes of the class that contains the method, in addition to the class that declares the method.
- **`internal`.** An `internal` method can be called from anywhere in the assembly.
- **`extern`.** An `extern` method in C# has an unlimited scope. You can use a method declared as `extern` even in a different language.
- **`virtual`.** A derived class of a class that contains a method can override a `virtual` method. You can also implement a `virtual` method dynamically. However, the method that will get invoked will be decided at run time. A `virtual` modifier cannot be used with `static`, `override`, and `abstract` modifiers.
- **`abstract`.** An `abstract` method is a special type of a `virtual` method. An `abstract` method can define a method. However, you cannot implement an `abstract` method. You can only declare an `abstract` method in an `abstract` class.
- **`override`.** The `override` method is used to override an inherited `abstract` or `virtual` method.

- **sealed.** A sealed method is used with an override method to override an inherited virtual method. However, a class inherited from the class containing this method cannot override a sealed method.

## Overloading a Method

*Method overloading* in C# is similar to method overloading in C++. Overloading a method allows you to declare more than one method with the same name in the same class. However, it is required that all methods with the same name take a different number of parameters or have different parameter types. The methods with the same name are called *overloaded methods*.

### Defining Overloaded Methods

Method overloading is useful when you need to perform the same operation on different parameters. For example, you can overload a method Add() to add two integer numbers and two strings. Look at overloading a method with this example:

```
public int Add (int x, int y)
{
            int z = x + y;
            return z;
}
public string Add (string string1, string string2)
{
          string string3 = string1 + string2;
          return string3;
}
```

You will notice that both the methods have the same name, Add(). However, the first Add() method is used to add two integers, x and y, and return an integer z. The second Add() method adds two strings, string1 and string2, and returns a string type string3.

### Calling Overloaded Methods

After declaring a method, you need to call the method. When you call an overloaded method, the C# compiler needs to identify the method that is called. The C# compiler identifies the method based on the type of parameters passed in the method call statement.

```
------------
object1.Add (25, 50)
-------------
```

Because the type of parameters passed to the `Add()` method in the previous statement are `integers`, the C# compiler calls the first `Add()` method.

### Default Parameters

Methods are useful if you want certain parameters of a method not to be explicitly initialized. These parameters then take default values as specified in the body of the method. This feature is provided by the default parameters of C++. C# does not support default parameters. However, to overcome this problem, you can overload methods.

In the previous example, you can create overloads of the method `Add()` to pass default values to it. The code for the `Add()` method in the previous section does not specify any value for either `x` or `y`. However, you can modify the code as shown following to pass a default value to the method.

```
public int Add (int x)
{
            int z = x + 100;
            return z;
}
```

The previous code always adds 100 to the value of `integer x` that is passed as a parameter when the `Add()` method is called by any class.

You have learned about classes and the methods used with classes. However, when you create an instance of a user-defined class, there may be more than one class with the same name. Therefore, to avoid this confusion, C# provides you with namespaces.

## Namespaces

*Namespaces* are containers that are used to logically group similar classes that have related functionality. You can also use namespaces to group similar data types. Therefore, when you refer a data type or a class, their names are automatically prefixed with the name of the namespace. This helps the compiler to understand which class is being referred in your code.

In C#, you need to declare each class in a namespace. However, if you do not explicitly declare a class in a namespace, C# automatically places the class in the default namespace. The default namespace is automatically created with the same name as that of the project. A namespace in C# can have more than one class.

## Declaring Namespaces

C# provides you with several classes that you can use in your program code. Most of these classes are a part of the `System` namespace. You can also declare namespaces in the program code and then add classes to them. A namespace is declared using the `namespace` keyword. While declaring a namespace, you do not need to prefix the namespace declaration with an access modifier. All namespaces in C# are implicitly `public`, as they can be used across all programs.

```
namespace Employee
{
          class Employee
}
```

You can place the `Employee` class in the `Employee` namespace. In addition, you can include other namespaces, classes, structs, enumerations, and interfaces in a namespace. You will learn about structs and enumerations later in this chapter.

C# allows the use of nested namespaces. Therefore, to refer to a namespace within another namespace, you use periods (.) to separate the names of the namespaces. For example,

```
namespace Employee
{
          namespace Salary
          {
                    class Salary
          }
}
```

To refer to the `Salary` class, you need to refer to it as `Employee.Salary.Salary`.

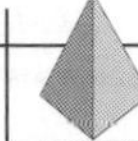

**TIP**

You can have two classes with the same name in different namespaces. However, a namespace cannot contain two classes with the same name.

## Accessing Namespaces

After declaring a namespace, you can access the namespace with the `using` directive. Therefore, to access the namespace `Employee`, use the following statement:

```
using Employee;
```

Additionally, as you have seen earlier, C# allows the use of nested namespaces. It will, however, be tedious to write the complete name of a class repeatedly in the code. To simplify this task, you can declare the class with the `using` keyword in the beginning of the code, such as:

```
using Employee.Salary;
```

In this case, each time you use the class `Salary`, the compiler can discern that the class `Salary` within the `Salary` namespace is being referred.

However, there may be cases when two namespaces contain classes with the same name. To refer to these classes, you need to write the full name in the code. To avoid writing full names in such cases, you can create an alias.

## Aliases

C# allows you to create aliases of a class or a namespace with the `using` keyword. *Aliases* are short names assigned to classes and namespaces. The syntax of an alias is:

```
using <alias> = <class>
```

In the previous example, you can create an alias for the class `Salary`, such as:

```
using aliasSalary = Employee.Salary
```

Now, each time you need to refer to the `Salary` namespace, you can use the alias name, such as:

```
aliasSalary.Salary.CalculateSalary()
```

Here, `CalculateSalary()` is a method in the `Salary` class.

You have learned about classes and namespaces. The next section offers some information about structs. Structs are data structures similar to classes and are important components of C#.

# Structs

Structs are data structures that contain constructors, constants, variables, methods, indexers, properties, operators, and nested types. However, unlike classes, which are reference types, structs are value types. This implies that structs do not require allocation of heap. In addition, a variable declared of the type struct directly contains data, in contrast to a class variable that contains only a reference to the data.

Similar to declaring a class, you can also declare a struct in C#. Structs are declared using the `struct` keyword.

```
<modifier> struct <struct name>
{
            -----------
}
```

Modifiers used with structs are similar to those used with classes. Struct modifiers include `new`, `public`, `private`, `protected`, and `internal`. However, you cannot use the `abstract` and `sealed` modifiers with structs. Structs are implicitly sealed, as they do not support inheritance.

Structs are used to group similar data. This data can then be easily copied from one struct to another. Consider the following example:

```
public struct Employee
{
        public int Empid;
        public string Empname;
        public string Empemail;
        public string Empsalary;
}
```

The previous struct includes variables that are used to store employee information. Once a struct is declared, the variables in the struct are initialized to default values. However, to copy these values from one struct to another, you need first to initialize the struct with the `new` keyword. The `new` keyword is used to call the default constructor of the struct, resulting in initializing the variables declared in the struct.

```
Employee emp1;
Employee emp2;
emp1= new Employee ();
emp1.EmployeeName = 'Steve'
emp1.Employeeemail = 'steve@hotmail.com'
emp1.EmployeeSalary = $1000;
```

Now, to copy these values from `emp1` to `emp2`, you can use the assignment operator (=) as follows:

```
emp2 = emp1;
```

As you can see, a single statement can copy the entire value of one struct to another. However, if you want to use classes to perform this task, you need to create a method. All data is copied from one struct to another; therefore, it is advisable that you create structs to store small amounts of data.

Structs in C# are different from structs in C and C++. Unlike C and C++, all data members of structs in C# are `private` by default. In addition, structs in C# are very similar to classes and can perform most of the things that classes do. However, some differences between structs and classes still exist.

As discussed earlier, structs do not require heap allocation. Instead, structs are stored on stacks of memory. This is how structs differ from classes. Figure 3-1 lists the key differences between structs and classes.

Another important component of C# is enumerations. Similar to classes and structs, enumerations are used to store values. The next section looks at enumerations in detail.

Differences between structs and classes

| Classes | Structs |
| --- | --- |
| Classes are reference types that require allocation of heap. | Structs are value types that do not require allocation of heap. |
| Classes contain a reference to the data. | Structs directly contain the original data. |
| Classes can inherit from other classes and interfaces. | Structs can inherit from interfaces only. |
| Classes are used to store large data (more than 16 bytes). | Structs are used to store less data (16 bytes or less). |
| To instantiate an object of a class, you use the new keyword. | You do not require the new keyword to create a instance of a struct. |

**FIGURE 3-1** *Differences between structs and classes*

# Enumerations

*Enumerations* are data structures that store values with user-friendly names. This set of user-friendly named constants is called an *enumerator list*. The default data type of an enumerator list is an `integer`. Each enumerator has an `integer` base-type called the *underlying-type*. This underlying-type of the enumerator list must contain all the values that might be present in an instance of an enumerator. To use an enumerator in your code, you first need to declare the enumerator. Enumerators are declared using the `enum` keyword.

```
<modifier> enum <enumeration name>
{
        ...............
}
```

The modifiers used with enumerations are `new`, `public`, `private`, `protected`, and `internal`. However, enumerations cannot be of the type `abstract` or `sealed`. Look at the following example to understand enumerations.

```
public enum months
{January, February, March, April, May, June, July, August, September, October,
  November, December};
```

The previous code creates an enumeration with the name `months` and declares all the possible values for `months`. The first element of the enumeration takes a default value of 0 and the successive elements take the previous value plus 1.

You can also specify user-defined values for the elements of an enumeration. For example,

```
public enum months
{January = 1, February, March, April, May, June, July, August, September, October,
   November, December};
```

In this case, the values of `January`, `February`, and `March` are 1, 2, and 3, respectively. In this chapter, you have learned about inheritance in classes. To implement inheritance, C# supports interfaces.

# Interfaces

*Interfaces* are components used to declare a set of methods. However, the data members of an interface are not implemented. As discussed earlier, C# allows you to group related data by using structs. However, to group related methods, properties, indexers, and events, you use interfaces. Interfaces contain only method declarations; therefore, you cannot create an instance of an interface. However, you need to declare an interface by using the `interface` keyword.

```
interface <interface name>
{
        -----------------
}
```

Interface declarations do not include a modifier because all interfaces are `public` by default. Interfaces cannot be `abstract`, `sealed`, `virtual`, or `static`. However, you can use the `new` modifier with nested interfaces. The `new` modifier is used when you need to hide an inherited namespace by the same name as the base namespace.

In situations where you want the members of a class to exhibit certain features, you can group these members in an interface. The class can then implement the interface. The classes in C# can also implement multiple interfaces. Implementing an interface implies that a class is derived from the interface and the class implements all the members of that interface. Consider the following example of the `Employee` class that implements two interfaces:

```
interface Employee
{
        -----------
}
interface Salary
{
        -----------
}
class Employee: Employee, Salary
{
        -----------
}
```

Therefore, the class `Employee` implements all the methods declared in the interfaces `Employee` and `Salary`.

Similar to classes, interfaces can also be inherited. These interfaces are called *explicit base interfaces*. C# does not support multiple inheritance of classes. However, you can achieve multiple inheritance in C# by using interfaces.

In the previous example, if the interface `Salary` was inherited from `Employee`, the interface declaration statement would be:

```
interface Salary: Employee
{
        -----------
}
```

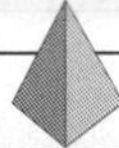

**TIP**

In C#, if a class implements an interface, the class also implicitly implements its base interfaces.

By now, you have learned about the basic components of C# that you can use to write programs in C#. The next sections look at writing a simple program in C# and then compiling and executing it.

# Writing, Compiling, and Executing a C# Program

## Writing a C# Program

Writing a program in C# involves writing the `Main()` method. Before writing a program, you need to select the template from the available templates for C#. C# provides you with a variety of templates, as shown in Figure 3-2.

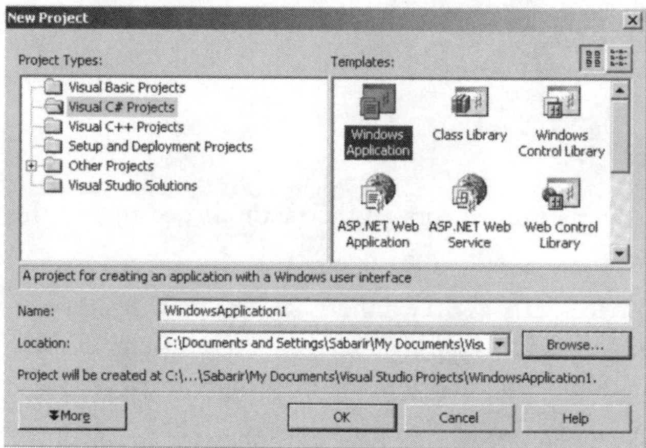


**FIGURE 3-2** *Templates for writing a C# program*

The execution of a C# program starts with the execution of the `Main()` method. Therefore, you need to write the `Main()` method for each program in C#. The `Main()` method is of the type `static` and returns a value of the type `void` or `int`.

If the `Main()` method is of the type `void`, it does not return a value. However, a `Main()` method of the type `integer` returns an `integer` type variable. The following is the syntax of a `Main()` method.

```
<modifier> static <data type> Main ()
```

Here, `modifier` is the access modifier of the `Main()` method and the `data type` is `void` or `integer`.

The modifier of the `Main()` method is explicitly written as `public`. However, it would not make a difference if any other modifier is specified.

The next code is an example of writing a simple program in C#.

```
using System;
class Class1
{
            public static void Main()
             {
                        Console.WriteLine ("This is a sample program in C#");
             }
}
```

The code uses the `using` statement to enable you to use the `System` namespace in the program code. The `class` keyword is then used to declare a class by the name `Class1`. Inside the class declaration is the `static` method `Main()` of the type `void`. The `Console.WriteLine` statement is used to display the text given in double quotes (" ") in the Console window.

## Compiling a C# Program

Once you have written a program, you can compile the program by using the `Build` command in the `Build` menu. The compilation of the program is shown in Figure 3-3.

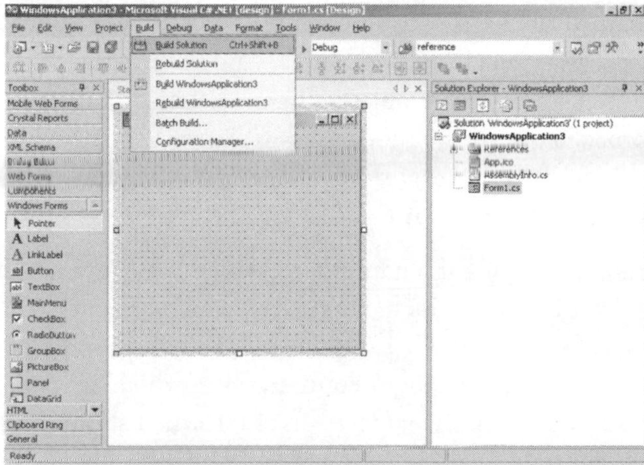

**FIGURE 3-3** *Compiling a C# program*

## Executing a C# Program

After compiling the C# program, you need to execute the program. For executing a program, click the `Start` command in the `Debug` menu.

An example of executing a C# program is shown in Figure 3-4.

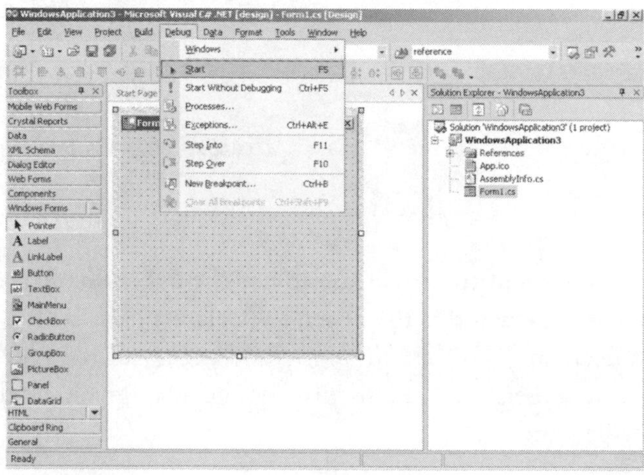


**FIGURE 3-4** *Executing a C# program*

## Summary

In this chapter, you learned about the components of C#. These components include classes, namespaces, structs, enumerations, and interfaces. A class is defined as a data structure used to create objects. The instance of a class is called an object. Next, you learned about the methods used in classes. A method is a logical section of code that can be used to perform a specific operation. A method has a return type or can be of the type `void`.

Another important component of C# is a namespace, which is a container used to logically group similar classes. C# also includes structs, which are data structures containing constructors, constants, variables, methods, indexers, properties, operators, and nested types. You also leaned about enumerations, which are data structures that store values with user-friendly names. You also learned about interfaces, which are components used to declare a set of methods. However, the data members of the interface are not implemented. Finally, you learned to write, execute, and compile a simple program in C#.

# Chapter 4

## More about Components

In Chapter 3, "Components of C#," you learned about some of the components of C#, such as classes, namespaces, and interfaces. In Chapter 4, you will learn about other components provided by C#. These components include arrays, collections, and indexers. This chapter will also cover data conversion by using boxing and unboxing. Finally, you will look at the preprocessor directives in C#.

# Arrays

We introduced the concept of arrays in Chapter 2, "C# Basics," in the section "Arrays." This section will look at arrays in detail. An *array* is a data structure used to store a number of variables and has one or more indices attached to it. Based on the number of indices associated with arrays, arrays are classified as single-dimensional arrays and multidimensional arrays.

## Single-Dimensional Arrays

A *single-dimensional array* has an index attached to its elements. You can initialize a single-dimensional array as follows:

```
<data type> [] <array1> = new <data type> [size];
```

Here, `data type` is the type of data stored in the array, and `size` defines the number of elements in the array.

## Multidimensional Arrays

A *multidimensional array* has more than one index associated with its elements. C# supports two types of multidimensional arrays:

- Rectangular array
- Orthogonal or jagged array

A *rectangular array* has an equal number of columns in each row. An array of rank two is called a two-dimensional array. Therefore, a two-dimensional rectangular array will have two columns in each row. Look at the following statement that declares a two-dimensional rectangular array of three rows.

```
int [,] Integer = { {2,3}, {3,4}, {4,5} };
```

The dimension of an array is not specified while declaring an array. However, the dimension of an array is defined by the number of commas (,) in an array declaration statement. Look at the following example to declare a three-dimensional array with three rows.

```
int [, ,] Integer = { {1,2,3}, {2,3,4}, {3,4,5} };
```

In C#, you can initialize an array by using a `for` loop.

```
int [,] Integer = new int [5,10];
for (int x  = 0; x < 5; x++)
{
     for (int y = 0; y < 10; y++)
     Integer [x,y] = x*y;
}
```

The previous code creates a two-dimensional array with five rows and 10 columns. The variables `x` and `y` denote the number of rows and columns, respectively, in the array `Integer`. The values of `x` and `y` change in a `for` loop. The elements of the array are initialized by the product of the values of the variables `x` and `y`.

As discussed earlier, C# also supports *orthogonal* or *jagged* arrays. An orthogonal array can have a different number of columns in each row. Therefore, while declaring a jagged array, you specify only the number of rows in the array. Just as in a rectangular array, you do not use commas to declare an orthogonal array. Instead, the dimension of a jagged array is specified by the number of square brackets ([]).

```
int [] [] Integer = new int [2] [];
Integer [0] = new int [2];
Integer [1] = new int [5];
```

This code declares a two-dimensional array with two rows. The first row contains two columns and the second row contains five columns.

After declaring an array, you need to perform operations on the array. To do this, C# provides you with several methods. Some of the commonly used methods in arrays are discussed in the next section.

## Methods in Arrays

An array in C# is an object and, therefore, has its own methods. Now look at some of the common methods used with arrays.

The `Length` property is used to determine the size or number of elements in an array. To find out the number of elements in the one-dimensional array `Integer`, you use the following statement:

```
int I = Integer.Length;
```

In this code, the `Length` property derives the size of the array `Integer`, which is then stored in the integer variable `I`.

Similarly, to determine the size of a multidimensional array, you use the `GetLength()` method. The `GetLength()` method returns the number of elements in a specified dimension of a multidimensional array. The dimension of the array is specified as a parameter to the `GetLength()` method.

```
int I = Integer.GetLength (1);
```

Here, the `GetLength()` method is used to find out the size of the second dimension of the multidimensional array `Integer`. The number of elements in the second dimension of the array are then stored in the integer variable `I`.

You can use the `Reverse()` method to reverse the order of the elements of an array. The `Reverse()` method is a static method, so the elements of an array that need to be reversed are sent as a parameter to the `Reverse()` method.

```
Array.Reverse (Integer);
```

This code reverses the order of the elements of the array. The name of the array is passed as a parameter to the method.

The elements of an array can be sorted using the `Sort()` method. Similar to the `Reverse()` method, the name of the array to be sorted is sent as a parameter to the method `Sort()`. The `Sort()` method arranges the elements of an array in ascending order. The elements of the array `Integer` can be sorted as:

```
Array.Sort (Integer);
```

Consider an example of an array that stores the marks of students. This data is sorted to know the maximum and minimum marks obtained by the students.

```
int [] Marks = {70,62,53,44,75,68};
int I = Marks.Length;
Array.Sort (Marks);
for (int x = 0; x < I; x++)
{
     Console.WriteLine (x);
}
```

This code initializes an integer array with the values as specified in the program code. The code then calculates the size of the one-dimensional array `Integer` and stores its value in the variable `I`. The size of the array is determined using the `Length` property. The `Sort()` method is then used to sort the elements of `Integer`. The sorted elements are displayed in the Console window by using the `WriteLine()` method of the `Console` class.

The output of the previous code is:

```
44,53,62,68,70,75
```

In this section, you learned about arrays. An array is a special type of collection in C#. The next section will look at collections in C#.

# Collections

A *collection* is defined as a group of objects that you can access using the `foreach` loop. For example, look at the following code:

```
foreach (string str1 in collection1)
{
     Console.WriteLine (str1):
}
```

In this code, `collection1` is a collection, and the `foreach` loop is used to access objects of `collection1`.

## Creating Collections

All collections in C# are implemented by the `System.Collections.IEnumerable` interface. You have learned about interfaces in Chapter 3 in the section "Interfaces." Interfaces are components used to declare a set of methods that are never implemented. There are several predefined interfaces provided by C#. One of these predefined interfaces is the `IEnumerable` interface that has a `GetEnumerator()` method. This method returns an object of the type `enumerator`. Therefore, every collection has one or more `enumerator` objects associated with it. These objects are used to access data from the associated collection. You can use the `enumerator` object only to read data from a collection, not to modify the collection.

To access the elements of a collection, you create an object that implements the `IEnumerable` interface. To initialize this object, the `MoveNext()` method is called. This method is used to move across the elements of the collection. When the `MoveNext()` method is called for the first time, it moves the `enumerator` object to the first element of the collection.

Once the `enumerator` object is initialized with the first element of the collection, you can then move across the elements of the collection by calling the `MoveNext()` method. The value referred by the `enumerator` object can be read by the `Current` property. This property returns only a reference to the elements of the collection. Therefore, to get the actual value of the element, you can type cast the reference to the type of the element. To find out more about collections, consider the following code sample.

```
public interface IEnumerable
{
        IEnumerator GetEnumerator ();
}
public interface IEnumerator
{
      bool MoveNext();
      object Current
      {
            get;
      }
void Reset();
}
```

This code declares the `GetEnumerator()` method of the `IEnumerable` interface. Next, the `MoveNext()` method of the `IEnumerator` interface, which returns a `Boolean` type variable, is called. The `Current` property of the type `object` is used to read the current element of the collection. You use the `get` property to read the elements of a collection. You can use the `Reset()` method to reset the value of the `enumerator` object.

## Working with Collections

After creating a collection, you can work with it. To do this, you can use the interfaces provided by C#. Figure 4-1 lists some of the interfaces that you can use to work with collections.

| Interface | Description |
|---|---|
| ICollection | The ICollection interface is used to specify the enumerators, size, and methods for synchronizing a collection. |
| IDictionary | The IDictionary interface is used to represent a collection of associated keys and values. |
| IList | The IList interface is used to represent a collection of objects for which you can create individual indices. |
| ICloneable | The ICloneable interface is used to create a new instance of a class. The new instance is created with values that are similar to those of an existing instance. This technique is called cloning. |

**FIGURE 4-1** *Interfaces used with collections*

Each of these interfaces is present in the `System.Collections` namespace. These interfaces have several classes and methods associated with them. The `ArrayList` class will be discussed in detail.

`ArrayList` is an important class present in the `System.Collections` namespace that you can use to create a dynamically increasing array. The `ArrayList` class implements the `IList` interface. When you create an object of the `ArrayList` class, C#

allocates memory to this object. You can specify the initial size of the `ArrayList` object while creating the instance of the `ArrayList` class by using the `new` keyword. You can then add elements to this object. However, if you add more elements to the `ArrayList` than its capacity (the number of elements that an object of `ArrayList` can hold), C# automatically allocates more memory to the `ArrayList` object. Consider the following example to learn about the `ArrayList` class.

```
using System;
using System.Collections;
public class ArrayList1
{
        public static void Main()
        {
                ArrayList list1 = new ArrayList();
                list1.Add("This");
                list1.Add("is");
                list1.Add("a");
                list1.Add("sample");
                list1.Add("ArrayList.");
        }
}
```

This code creates an object of the `ArrayList` class with the name `list1` and then adds elements to this object by using the `Add()` method.

Some of the methods present in the interfaces used with collections are discussed in the following list.

**ICollection Interface:**

- **CopyTo().** The CopyTo() method is used to copy the elements of the ICollection interface to a specified array. You can also specify the starting index from which you want to copy the elements.

**IDictionary Interface:**

- **Add().** The Add() method is used to add an element to the IDictionary interface. You can specify the key and value of the element that is added.

- **Remove().** The Remove() method is used to delete an element from the IDictionary interface. You need to specify the key of the element to be deleted.
- **Clear().** The Clear() method is used to delete all the elements from the IDictionary interface.
- **GetEnumerator().** The GetEnumerator() method is used to return an IDictionaryEnumerator object for the IDictionary interface.
- **Contains().** The Contains() method is used to locate a particular element in the IDictionary interface. You need to specify the key of the element to be located.

**IList Interface:**

- **Add().** The Add() method of the IList interface is used to add elements to the IList interface.
- **Remove().** The Remove() method is used to delete the first occurrence of the object from the IList interface.
- **RemoveAt().** The RemoveAt() method is used to delete the element present at the index value that you specify.
- **Clear().** The Clear() method is used to delete all the elements from the IList interface.
- **Insert().** The Insert() method is used to insert an element at the specified index in the IList interface.
- **IndexOf().** The IndexOf() method is used to find the index value of the specified element.

**ICloneable Interface:**

- **Clone().** The Clone() method is used to create clones of an existing instance of a class.

Having learned about arrays and collections, you need to learn about indexers. Indexers are members that allow you to access objects as if they were the elements of an array.

# Indexers

There may be instances where you need to access the elements of a class as an array. You can do this by using *indexers* provided by C#. To be able to use indexers in classes, you first need to declare an indexer. Indexers are declared as follows:

```
<modifier> <type> this [parameter-list]
```

Here, `modifier` is the indexer modifier and `type` defines the return type of the indexer. The `this` keyword is used as a name of the indexer. Indexers do not have an explicit name. The `parameter-list` in the square brackets defines the data type of the object that has the elements to be accessed.

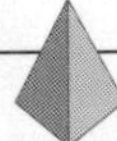

**TIP**

In the indexer declaration statement, you can specify any data type as the index of the elements to be accessed.

For example, consider the following sample code:

```
public int this [int x]
```

This code declares a `public` indexer with the return type as `integer`. Here, the data type of the object is of the `integer` type.

C# allows you to define both read-only and write-only indexers. To read and write data to an indexer, you use the `get` and `set` properties, respectively. The `get` and `set` properties do not take any parameter. However, the `get` property returns the elements of the type as specified in the indexer declaration statement. The `set` property is used to assign values to indexer elements. Consider the following code:

```
class Class1
{
        int variable1, variable2;
       public int this [int x]
       set
       {
              switch (x)
              {
```

```
                    case 0:
                            variable1 = 10;
                    break;
                    case 1:
                            variable2 = 20;
                    break;
            }
}
        get
        {
                switch (x)
                {
                        case 0:
                                return variable1;
                        case 1:
                                return variable2;
                }
        }
}
```

In this code, the switch statements are used to read and write data to the indexer.

In this section, you learned about arrays, collections, and indexers that are used to store and access variables and objects. However, you also need to learn about type casting variables into objects and vice versa. To do this, C# provides you with the techniques of boxing and unboxing.

# Boxing and Unboxing

*Boxing* is a data type conversion technique that is used to implicitly convert a `value` type to either an `object` type or a `reference` type. When you convert a `value` type to an `object` type, C# creates an instance of the `object` type and then copies the `value` type to that instance.

Consider the following example of an implicit data conversion by using boxing.

```
class Class1
{
        public static void Main ()
```

```
            {
                 string string1 = "New String";
                object obj1 = string1;
                Console.WriteLine (obj1);
            }
}
```

This code initializes a `string` type variable with the value "`New String`" and then creates an instance `obj1` of the type `object`. The value of `string1` is now copied to the new instance of object and is displayed in the `Console` window.

In addition to implicit data conversion by using boxing, you can use boxing to explicitly convert data. Look at the following example of an explicit data conversion by using boxing.

```
string string1 = "New String";
object obj1 = (object) string1;
```

This code uses the cast operator to explicitly convert `string1` to an object.

Similar to boxing, *unboxing* is also a data type conversion technique. Unboxing is used to explicitly convert an `object` type to a `value` type. The technique of unboxing is opposite to that of boxing. However, to unbox a `reference` type, it is essential that you first box the `value` type. Unboxing can be only of the explicit conversion type. Consider the following example to understand unboxing.

```
string string1 = "New String";
object obj1 = string1;
string string2 =(string) obj1;
```

While unboxing from one type to another, you need to take care that the resultant variable has enough space to store the initial type. For example, if you try to unbox as `byte` variable type from an `integer` variable type, it may result in an error. In this case, you box a 32-bit `integer` type value to an 8-bit `sbyte` type value. Subsequently, you unbox a smaller value to a larger value. Therefore, the following code generates an error in C#.

```
int x = 100;
object y = (object) x;
sbyte z = (sbyte) y;
```

In addition to data conversion statements, C# provides you with certain commands that influence the compilation of your code. These commands are called preprocessor directives.

# Preprocessor Directives

In C#, *preprocessor directives* are commands that are not executed. However, these commands influence the process of compilation of code. For example, if you do not want the compiler to execute certain part of the code, you can mark the code by using the preprocessor directive. To declare a preprocessor directive, use a # sign, such as:

```
# preprocessor name
```

Some of the commonly used preprocessor directives provided by C# are discussed in the following sections.

## #region and #endregion

C# provides you with the `#region` preprocessor directive that you can use to define a set of statements to be executed as a block. The `#endregion` directive marks the end of such a set of statements. For example:

```
#region Region1
            string EmpName, EmpAddress;
            int Empcode, Empphone;
#endregion
```

Here, `Region1` is the name given to the set of statements marked by the `#region` preprocessor directive.

## #define and #undef

The `#define` and `#undef` preprocessor directives are used to define and remove the definition of a symbol, respectively. These preprocessor directives are similar to a variable declaration statement. However, the symbols created by these directives do not exist. You can use the `#define` and `#undef` directives to declare symbols. However, you cannot create symbols by using these declarations. For example:

```
#define symbol1
```

and

```
#undef symbol1
```

The first line of code defines a symbol with the name `symbol1`, and the second line of code deletes the definition of `symbol1`.

## #if, #endif, #else, and #elif

As discussed earlier, preprocessor directives can be used to prevent a compiler from executing certain sections of code. Similarly, you can also use certain preprocessor directives to conditionally compile certain sections of code. To do this, C# provides you with the `#if`, `#endif`, `#else`, and `#elif` preprocessor directives. These directives are commonly called *conditional preprocessor directives*.

The syntax of an `#if-#endif` command is as follows:

```
#if symbol1
                  -----------------
#endif
```

Here, `symbol1` is a symbol declared by the `#define` preprocessor directive. The statements in the `#if` loop are executed if the symbol following the `#if` keyword has been previously declared using the `#define` command. If `symbol1` has not been previously declared, the compiler reaches the end of `#endif` statement.

You can also direct the compiler to execute a set of statements if the symbol is not defined. This can be done using the `#elif` and `#else` preprocessor directives. Look at the following example.

```
#define Symbol1
class Class1
{
          #if Symbol1
                    Console.WriteLine ("Symbol1 exists")
```

```
        #else
                Console.WriteLine ("Symbol1 does not exist")
        #endif
}
```

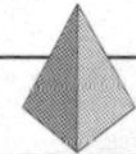

**TIP**

You can also use nested `#if-#elif` loops.

## #error and #warning

The `#error` and `#warning` preprocessor directives are used to raise an error and a warning, respectively. If the compiler encounters the `#warning` preprocessor directive, it issues a warning to the programmer by displaying the text in the `#warning` statement. The compiler then resumes with compilation of the code. However, if the compiler comes across an `#error` preprocessor directive, it generates an error and stops executing the code. The `#error` and `#warning` preprocessor directives are generally used with the conditional preprocessor directives discussed previously.

Look at the following example to have better understanding of the preprocessor directives used in C#.

```
#define Symbol1
using System;
public class Class1
{
        public static void Main()
        {
            #if Symbol1
                Console.WriteLine("Symbol1 is defined");
            #else
                #warning Symbol1 is not defined
            #endif
        }
}
```

The output of the previous code is shown in Figure 4-2.

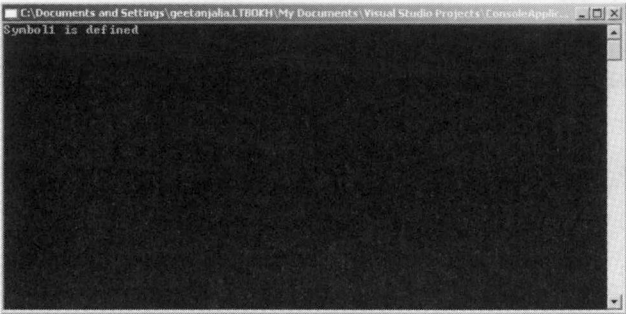

**FIGURE 4-2** *Ouput of the previous code*

## Summary

In this chapter, you learned about arrays and collections. An array is a data structure used to store a number of variables and has one or more indices attached to it. A collection is defined as a group of objects that you can access using the `foreach` loop. An array is a special type of collection in C#. Next, you learned about indexers, which are members that allow you to access objects as if they were the elements of an array.

This chapter also covered techniques to type cast variables into objects and vice versa. To do this, you used the techniques of boxing and unboxing. Boxing is used to convert a `value` type to a `reference` type. Unboxing does the opposite, by converting a `reference` type to a `value` type. Finally, you learned about preprocessor directives in C#. These directives are commands that are not executed by the C# compiler. However, these commands affect the process of code compilation.

# Chapter 5

## Attributes and Properties

In Chapter 3, "Components of C#," you learned about classes and the methods implemented with classes. In this chapter, you will learn about attributes and properties that are used to store extra information about classes.

## Attributes

*Attributes* are used to store additional information about methods and classes. You have extensively used attributes in the previous chapters. For example, the class and method modifiers that store accessibility information about classes and methods, respectively, are attributes placed on these entities. Attributes are elements used with methods, classes, assemblies, and Web services. Attributes can also be used with arguments of a method.

Attributes are similar to preprocessor directives, as the attributes are not compiled during the execution of a program. However, attributes are useful because they provide you with additional information about resources in a program. You can retrieve this information at run time and can then document the information for future use. To retrieve the information stored in attributes, you need to create instances of the `Attribute` class. You will learn about the `Attribute` class later in this chapter.

### Declaring Attributes

Attributes are declared using an attribute declaration statement, such as:

```
[attribute name (attribute parameters)]
```

This statement includes the name of the attribute, followed by the list of parameters in parentheses. You can also define an attribute that does not take any parameter. The attribute declaration statement is immediately followed by the declaration of the entities for which the attribute is defined.

All attributes in C# are derived from the `Attribute` class. The `Attribute` class is global to the .NET Framework. This implies that if you declare an attribute, it can be used by any class defined in the .NET Framework. The next section will discuss the `Attribute` class in detail.

## Attribute Class

You can define an attribute class to store user-defined attributes. The attribute class that you declare also contains information about the entities on which you can place the attributes defined in the class. All attribute classes are derived from the abstract class `Attribute`. The `Attribute` class is contained in the `System` namespace.

Once an attribute is declared in the attribute class, you can place the attribute on any entity. An attribute class can be of the following types:

- **Single-use attribute class.** The attributes declared in a single-use attribute class cannot be placed more than once on the same entity.

```
[color ("Green")]
class Car
{
              --------------
}
```

- **Multiuse attribute class.** The attributes declared in a multiuse attribute class can be placed more than once on the same entity. The following example shows that two values of the attribute `color` can be placed on the class `Car`.

```
[color ("Green"), color ("Blue")]
class Car
{
              --------------
}
```

As discussed earlier, you can create attributes that take parameters. To perform this task, you need to define a parameter list in the default constructor of the attribute class. The attribute class takes two types of parameters. These parameters will now be described in detail.

## Attribute Parameters

The parameters used with attributes include the following:

- **Positional parameters.** Parameters that are declared in the `public` constructor of the attribute class are called *positional parameters*. A positional parameter of an attribute consists of an attribute argument expression and is used with the required parameters.
- **Named parameters.** Parameters that are declared in the `non-static`, `public` read-write field or property of an attribute class are called *named parameters*. They are used to read and write values to an attribute. You use named parameters to define optional parameters of an attribute class.

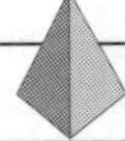

**TIP**

If you need to declare both positional and named parameters for the same attribute class, the positional parameters are followed by the named parameters.

You can also specify the data types of both positional and named parameters. The attribute parameter types supported by C# are `int`, `short`, `long`, `byte`, `char`, `string`, `bool`, `double`, `float`, `object`, `type`, and `enum`. You have learned about these data types in Chapter 2, "C# Basics," in the section "Variable Data Types."

Until now, you have seen that you can define custom attributes and the custom attribute class. However, C# also contains certain default attributes, as discussed in the next section.

## Default Attributes

The C# compiler explicitly recognizes the default parameters provided by C# and compiles the program code accordingly. Following are some of the most commonly used default attributes.

- **`Obsolete` attribute.** As the name suggests, the `Obsolete` attribute is used to mark an element that you should no longer use in any program code. The `Obsolete` attribute is the alias defined for the `ObsoleteAttribute` class in the `System` namespace. To prevent a programmer from using the code marked obsolete, you can generate an error or a warning by passing the error or warning as a parameter to the `Obsolete` attribute. For example:

```
[Obsolete  ("Do not use this method in the code"), true]
```

Here, the first parameter contains the error or warning message to be displayed. The second parameter of the type `bool` specifies whether an error or a warning will be generated. The value of `true` specifies that the compiler will generate an error and stop the execution of the program. However, if the value of this parameter is `false`, the compiler only generates a warning.

- **`Conditional` attribute.** The `Conditional` attribute is used to conditionally compile a set of statements marked with the `Conditional` attribute. You can also mark a method with the `Conditional` attribute. The method or set of statements will then be compiled only if a symbol is defined. Consider the following example:

```
[Conditional ("Symbol1")]
public void Method1()
{
        -----------
}
```

In this code, the call to the function `Method1` will only be made if `Symbol1` is defined. `Symbol1` can be defined using the `#define` preprocessor directive. You have learned about the preprocessor directives available in C# in Chapter 4, "More about Components," in the section "Preprocessor Directives."

- **`AttributeUsage` attribute.** The `AttributeUsage` attribute is used with the attribute class. This attribute takes parameters that store information about the attribute class. To know more about the `AttributeUsage` attribute, consider the following example:

```
[AttributeUsage (AttributeTargets.Class ¦ AttributeTargets.Structs,
  AllowMultiple = true, Inherited = true)]
public class Attribute1 : Attribute
{
        ----------
}
```

The first parameter of the `AttributeUsage` attribute is `AttributeTargets`, which defines the list of entities for which you can declare the attribute. The `AttributeTargets` parameter can take more than one value and is of the type `enum`. You can also use `AttributeTargets.All` to make the attribute applicable to all the entities specified in your program code.

The second parameter of the `AttributeUsage` attribute is the `bool` type parameter named `AllowMultiple`. If this parameter is set to `false`, the attribute class is a single-use attribute class. The `true` value of this parameter indicates that the class is a multi-use attribute class.

The third parameter of the `AttributeUsage` attribute is another `bool` type parameter named `Inherited`. The `Inherited` parameter specifies whether the attribute can be used by the derived classes of the base class for which the attribute is defined. To make the attribute accessible to the derived classes, the value of this parameter is set to `true`. However, the default value of the `Inherited` parameter is `false`, which prevents the use of the attribute by the derived classes.

The next section will discuss properties, which are used to access an attribute of an element.

# Properties

You have seen that you can declare attributes for all the elements in your program code. However, to access an object or a class, you need to declare a *property* member for that object. Just like attributes, properties also store information about objects. In previous discussions, you have been using properties with almost every object that you defined. For example, the name of an object is its property. However, properties cannot be used to define storage locations.

## Declaring Properties

Properties are declared using the property declaration statement, such as:

```
<modifier> <type> <property name>
{
          -----------
}
```

The property modifier includes access modifiers, such as `public`, `private`, `protected`, and `internal`. In addition, the property modifier includes the `new`, `static`, `override`, `abstract`, and `sealed` modifiers. You can use more than one modifier in a property declaration statement. Because a property is not a variable, you cannot pass a property as a `ref` or an `out` parameter.

The property declaration statement also includes the type of the property, followed by its name of the property. Inside the block of the property declaration statement, you include the accessor declaration statements. These statements are executable statements that define the actions to be performed while reading and writing values to an attribute.

Each property that you declare has accessors associated with it. These accessors define statements that enable you to read and write values to a property. The accessors used with properties will now be discussed in detail.

## Accessors

The accessors used with properties are the `get` and `set` accessors. These accessors are followed by a block of statements to be executed when the accessor is invoked.

- **`get` accessor.** The `get` accessor is a method used to read values to a property. The `get` accessor does not take any parameter, but it returns a value of the data type specified in the property declaration statement. In the body of the `get` accessor, you need to include a `return` or a `throw` statement. This prevents the control of execution from going out of the body of the `get` accessor. The expression that follows the `get` accessor in the definition of the property must be of a specific type. You should be able to implicitly convert this type into the data type specified in the property declaration statement.
- **`set` accessor.** The `set` accessor is a method used to write values to a property. The `set` accessor takes a single implicit parameter named `value` but does not return any value. Therefore, the `set` accessor is a `void` method with a parameter that specifies the value to be written. The `return` statement in the `set` accessor is not followed by any expression.

To understand the get and set accessors, look at the following example:

```
public class Car
{
        string color:
        public string Color1
        {
                get
                {
                        return color;
                }
                set
                {
                        color = value;
                }
        }
}
```

This code declares a property Color1 for the class Car. The property declaration statement contains the get and set accessors. When you need to read data from the property, the get accessor is implicitly invoked. The get accessor returns a variable color of the same data type as that of the property. The variable color stores the value read by using the get accessor.

When you need to write a value to a property, the set accessor is invoked. The set accessor takes a parameter named value that specifies the value to be written to the variable color. To write the value Green to the property, you simply need to write the following statement:

```
Car car1 = new Car();
car1.color = "Green";
```

Based on the type of accessors defined in the property declaration statement, properties are classified as follows.

- **read-only property.** The property definition of a read-only property contains only the get accessor.
- **write-only property.** The property definition of a write-only property contains only the set accessor.
- **read-write property.** The property definition of a read-write property contains both the get and set accessors.

In addition to this classification, properties are classified based on the modifier specified in the property declaration statement. As discussed earlier, property modifiers include access modifiers and the `new`, `static`, `override`, `abstract`, and `sealed` modifiers.

## Types of Properties

C# supports the following properties based on the type of modifier used in the property declaration statement.

- **Static property.** A property that is declared with a `static` modifier is a *static property*. A static property cannot be referred by a specific instance of a class. You cannot use the `abstract`, `override`, and `virtual` modifiers with a static property.
- **Instance property.** A property that is not declared with an explicit `static` modifier is an *instance property*. An instance property is referred by a specific instance of a class and is also known as a *non-static property*.

# Summary

In this chapter, you learned about attributes and properties. Attributes are elements used with methods and classes to store additional information about them. Attributes can also be used with the arguments of a method. To retrieve the information stored in attributes, you need to create instances of the `Attribute` class. All attribute classes are derived from the abstract class `Attribute` in the `System` namespace.

Next, you learned about the default attributes provided by C#. These default attributes include the `Obsolete`, `Conditional`, and `AttributeUsage` attributes. The C# compiler explicitly identifies the default parameters provided by C# and compiles the program code accordingly.

Finally, you learned about properties that are used to access an attribute of an element. Each property that you declare has accessors associated with it. These accessors define statements that enable you to read and write values to a property. The accessors used with properties are the `get` and `set` accessors.

# Chapter 6

## Threads

In this chapter, you will be introduced to threads. In addition, you will learn to create and work with threads. This chapter introduces you to the `Thread` class, which is a .NET base class. This class helps you to create and manipulate threads in applications. This chapter also discusses the states and priorities of threads. Finally, the chapter introduces you to the synchronization of variables across threads.

# Introduction to Threads

Threads are a well-known concept to C and C++ programmers. A *thread* is a basic unit of the execution of a program. In other words, a thread is the smallest unit to which the operating system allocates processor time. A thread decides the sequence of execution of a program and is very useful for executing complex applications or even multiple applications simultaneously. In addition, you can have a single application containing multiple threads. When the C# compiler executes a multithreaded application, several threads are executed simultaneously. This makes the execution of a complex application less time-consuming.

In a multithreaded application, you can execute multiple activities simultaneously. For example, consider a situation in which you execute a print command for printing 100 pages. Printing 100 pages takes a substantial amount of time. Therefore, you can have two threads working simultaneously on the system. One thread can be used for printing and the other thread can be used to perform any other activity, such as working in a Word document or a spreadsheet.

All the applications that you create involve one or more threads. However, there are some situations in which threads can be used very effectively. Following are examples of some of these situations.

- As discussed earlier, you use threads to perform operations that can be time-consuming. In such cases, you can create two threads, a *worker thread* and a *user thread*. The worker thread performs time-consuming operations, and the user thread manages user interactions. For example, you can create a worker thread to print 100 pages while the user thread enables you to work in a Word document.

- You can also use threads to transfer data over the network. For example, you need to transfer volumes of data from one branch office to another. In this case, you can create a thread to connect to the server in the other branch.
- You also use threads when you need to execute an application that performs more than one operation. For example, when a data entry operator enters data into a database, this data should be updated automatically in the master database. In this case, you can have a worker thread and a user thread. The user thread accepts the input from the user while the worker thread updates the records in the master database.

You have seen that using threads in your application allows you to perform multiple activities simultaneously. However, extensive use of threads in a single application may even deteriorate the performance of your application. To understand this, let us look at the process of execution of threads. Executing threads requires the use of several operating system resources. These resources execute a thread for a very short period of time, known as the *time slice* of the thread. After executing the thread for this time slice, the Windows operating system chooses another thread to execute. This process of executing multiple threads for a given time slice is called *preemptive multitasking*. If you have multiple threads in a single application, the operating system spends time switching between various threads after a time slice, which may in turn reduce the performance of the application.

By now, you know that your application can have as many threads as required. The next section looks at creating threads for your application.

## Creating Threads

A thread that you create is an instance of the `Thread` class. The `Thread` class is a class in the .NET Framework class library and is located in the `System.Threading` namespace. Therefore, to create an instance of the `Thread` class, you first need to import the `System.Threading` namespace. You can then create the object of the `Thread` class that represents a thread. You can continue to add threads to your application by simply creating multiple instances of the object of the `Thread` class.

To create a thread, you need to declare an instance of the `Thread` class and provide it with the details of the method with which the execution of the thread starts. To do so, you can use the `public void` delegate named `ThreadStart()` of the `System.Threading` namespace. You have learned about delegates in Chapter 1, "Overview of the .NET Framework," in the section "Delegates."

Consider the following example.

```
using System;
using System.Threading;
class Class1
{
  public void Method1()
  {
    Console.WriteLine("Method1 is the starting point of execution of the thread");
  }
  public static void Main()
  {
    Class1 newClass = new Class1();
    Thread Thread1 = new Thread(new ThreadStart(newClass.Method1));
  }
}
```

Here, an instance of the `Thread` class, `Thread1`, is created. The `ThreadStart()` delegate specifies the name of the method, `Method1`, with which the execution of `Thread1` starts. `Method1` is a `public void` function defined in `Class1`. However, creating an instance of the `Thread` class does not make the thread functional. To start the thread, you need to call the `Start()` method. The following code shows the syntax for calling the `Start()` method.

```
Thread1.Start();
```

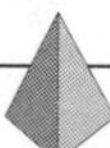

**TIP**

Because the threads that you define can be used across applications, it is advisable that you give a relevant name to your thread. This enables other programmers to reuse the functionality provided by your thread. To give a relevant name to your thread, you can change the value of the `Name` property of the thread.

The following code defines a worker thread for updating the records in the master database. It will give the thread a meaningful name, such as `Update Records Thread`.

```
Thread Thread1 = new Thread(new ThreadStart(newClass.Method1));
Thread1.Name = "Update Records Thread";
```

The previous code snippet creates an instance of the `Thread` class with the name `Thread1` and then assigns a name `Update Records Thread` to the thread.

In addition to the `Name` property that is used to give a meaningful name to a thread, you can use properties to know the status of the executing threads. These properties are defined in the `Thread` class of the `System.Threading` namespace.

- **`IsAlive` property.** The `IsAlive` property is used to specify that the execution of a thread is complete or the thread is still working. The `IsAlive` property returns a `Boolean` value of `true` for the thread that is working and `false` for the thread that is not executing.
- **`ThreadState` property.** The `ThreadState` property indicates the execution status of a thread. In other words, it returns a value specifying whether the execution of the thread has started or not. You will learn about the states of a thread later in this chapter.

## Aborting Threads

You have learned how to create and execute a thread. However, sometimes you may need to stop a running thread. Consider the same old example in which you executed a print command for 100 pages. In this case, a thread is executed to print the required pages. If you need to print some other urgent page, you need to stop the previous print command or, in other words, abort the thread that is printing 100 pages. This section discusses aborting a running thread.

C# provides you with a base class, the `Thread` class, that you can use to perform several operations with threads. The `Thread` class contains several predefined methods that enable you to work with threads. To abort a thread, you use the `Abort()` method of the `Thread` class. The `Abort()` method has the following syntax:

```
Thread1.Abort();
```

Here, `Thread1` is the instance of the `Thread` class. The `Abort()` method does not take any parameters. When you call the `Abort()` method, the C# compiler might not kill the thread instantaneously. To understand why the C# compiler takes time to kill the thread, you first need to understand how the `Abort()` method is executed.

When you call the `Abort()` method of the `Thread` class, the method throws the `ThreadAbortException` exception. In addition to the base class that is used to handle threads, C# provides base classes to generate exceptions. The `Thread-AbortException` is an exception of the `ThreadAbortException` class. C# provides you with no mechanism to handle this exception. In other words, if you try to abort the thread that is being executed inside the `try` block, the C# compiler first executes any associated `finally` blocks before aborting the thread.

As you have seen, .NET provides you with a mechanism for safer killing of threads compared with the earlier environments that killed the targeted thread instantly. Having learned about creating and aborting threads, the next section will continue the discussion about working with threads. It will discuss the `Join()` method that allows you to wait for a thread to finish execution or to be killed by the `Abort()` method.

## Joining Threads

C# allows you to wait for a thread to terminate before the C# compiler proceeds with the execution of the other thread. To do so, the `Thread` class contains a `Join()` method, which takes the following syntax:

```
Thread1.Join();
```

The previous statement calls the `Join()` method of the `Thread` class to wait for `Thread1` to terminate. If you do not know the time the thread takes to terminate, you can also specify the maximum time for which you want the C# compiler to wait before proceeding with the execution of the next thread. If the maximum time limit is not specified, the compiler waits for the thread to terminate on its own.

The `Join()` method is often used with the `Abort()` method. As explained earlier, when you call the `Abort()` method, the thread is not terminated instantly if it is in the middle of the `try` block. This implies that you need to wait for the `finally` statements to be executed before the thread terminates. However, you might not know the time the C# compiler takes to execute the `finally` block, and you are not ready to wait for a long period of time. Therefore, you can call the `Abort()` method followed by the `Join()` method to terminate the thread.

You have learned how to abort and join a thread. In some cases, you might only need to stop or suspend the execution of a thread for a specified time. The following section discusses suspending threads.

## Suspending Threads

You have learned about aborting threads. When a thread is aborted, you cannot resume the execution of the thread. However, when you suspend a thread, you can resume its execution whenever required. To suspend the execution of a thread, you use the `Suspend()` method. The `Suspend()` method is another method of the `Thread` class and does not take any parameters. The syntax of the `Suspend()` method is:

```
Thread1.Suspend();
```

The `Suspend()` method does not kill the thread permanently. It just stops the execution of the thread until it is resumed. Therefore, when you need to restart the execution of a thread, you can call another method of the `Thread` class, the `Resume()` method. The `Resume()` method starts executing the thread from the point at which the execution was suspended. The syntax of the `Resume()` method is shown in the following code.

```
Thread1.Resume();
```

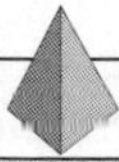

**TIP**

You can only resume the execution of a suspended thread.

Similar to the `Abort()` method, the `Suspend()` method does not instantly stop the execution of the targeted thread. It waits for the thread to reach a safe point before suspending it.

You can also call the `Suspend()` and `Resume()` methods from an executing thread. Therefore, a thread can call the `Suspend()` method to suspend itself or another thread.

For example, if `thread1` suspends itself, another thread needs to call the `Resume()` method to restart its execution. However, if `thread1` suspends another thread, such as thread2, the execution of thread2 is not resumed until thread1 calls the Resume() method on thread2.

In addition to the Suspend() method, you can block the execution of a thread by calling the Sleep() method of the Thread class.

## Making Threads Sleep

The Thread class contains another method, called the Sleep() method, to stop the execution of a thread for a specified time. You can specify the time for which you want to stop the execution of a thread by passing the time as a parameter to the Sleep() method. The time is specified in milliseconds. Consider the following example that puts the thread to sleep for 2 seconds.

```
Thread.Sleep(2000);
```

As you can see in the previous code, the Sleep() method is called by the class itself and not the instance of the class.

You may wonder how the Sleep() method is different from the Suspend() method. Both of these methods are used to stop the execution of a thread for some time. You have seen that the Suspend() method does not instantly stop the execution of the thread. It waits for the thread to reach a safe point before stopping its execution. However, if you need to block the execution of a thread immediately, you can do this by calling the Sleep() method instead of the Suspend() method.

Figure 6-1 shows the difference between the Sleep() and Suspend() methods.

| Suspend() Method | Sleep() Method |
|---|---|
| The Suspend() method is used to block the execution of a thread until you call the Resume() method. | The Sleep() method is used to block the execution of the thread for the time that you specify. |
| The Suspend() method does not suspend the requested thread immediately. | The Sleep() method blocks the execution of the requested thread immediately. |
| You can call the Suspend() method to block the execution of another thread. | The Sleep() method cannot be called to block the execution of another thread. |
| To call the Suspend() method, you use the instance name. | To call the Sleep() method, you use the type name. |

**FIGURE 6-1** *Differences between the* Suspend() *and* Sleep() *methods*

Until now, you have learned about various methods that can be used with threads. To understand more about these operations, here is a simple thread with operations performed on it.

```
using System;
using System.Threading;
class Class1
{
  public void Method1()
  {
    Console.WriteLine("Method1 is the starting point of execution of the thread");
  }
  public static void Main()
  {
      Class1 newClass = new Class1();
      Thread Thread1 = new Thread(new ThreadStart(newClass.Method1));
      Thread1.Name = "Sample Thread";
      Thread1.Start ();
     Console.WriteLine ("The execution of Sample Thread has started.");
    Thread1.Abort();
  }
}
```

The previous code imports the `System` and `System.Threading` namespaces in your program code. The code then creates a class with the name `Class1` and declares a method `Method1` in the class. This method is specified as the starting point of execution of a thread named `Sample Thread`, which is an instance of the `Thread` class. Next, an instance of the `ThreadStart` delegate is created that takes `Method1` as the parameter. The instance of the `Thread` class is used to call the methods of the `Thread` class that perform operations on `Sample Thread`.

The output of the previous code is shown in Figure 6-2.

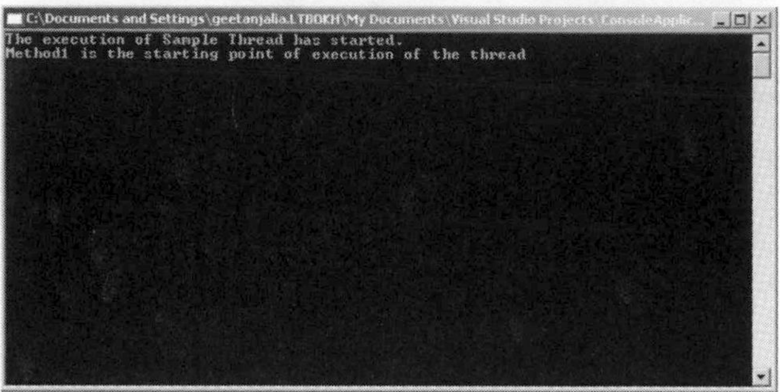


**FIGURE 6-2** *Output of the previous code*

When you call the methods of the `Thread` class, the state of the thread changes. For example, before you start a thread, the thread is not running. After you call the `Start()` method, the state of the thread changes to `Running`. This state changes further when you call the `Suspend()` or `Abort()` methods. In other words, whenever you perform an action on the thread, its state changes. The next section discusses the various states of a thread in detail.

## Thread States

The change in the state of a thread results from the action performed on the thread. In other words, when you call a method of the `Thread` class, it changes the state of the thread. Figure 6-3 shows the effect of various methods of the `Thread` class on the states of a thread.

You have seen that you can suspend, sleep, or abort a running thread. However, if you do not want any other user to change the state of your thread, you can set the priority of your thread to `Highest`. The following section discusses thread priorities in detail.

## Thread Priorities

The thread priorities define the sequence of executing various threads on a system. For example, if you have two threads running on a system, the thread with higher priority is executed first. C# allows you to set different priorities for different threads running simultaneously on your system.

| Methods | States of a Thread |
|---|---|
| Thread.Start() | When you call the Thread.Start() method, the state of a thread changes to *Running*. |
| Thread.Sleep() | When you call the Thread.Sleep() method, the state of a thread changes to *WaitSleepJoin*. This implies that the thread is not running for a specified time. |
| Thread.Suspend() | When the Thread.Suspend() method is called from another thread, the state of a thread changes to *SuspendRequested*. However, when the Thread.Suspend() method is executed, the state of the thread changes to *Suspended*. |
| Thread.Resume() | When you call the Thread.Resume() method, the state of a thread changes to *Running*. |
| Thread.Abort() | When the Thread.Abort() method is called from another thread, the state of a thread changes to *AbortRequested*. However, when the Thread.Abort() method is executed, the state of the thread changes to *Aborted*. |

**FIGURE 6-3** *Effect of methods on the states of a thread*

The priority levels supported by C# are as follows:

- **`Highest`.** A thread with the `Highest` priority is executed first. When the C# compiler finds the thread with the `Highest` priority, it stops executing all other threads until the thread with the `Highest` priority is executed.
- **`AboveNormal`.** A thread with the `AboveNormal` priority is executed before any other threads except the thread with the `Highest` priority.
- **`Normal`.** A thread with the `Normal` priority is third in the priority list. This thread is given a time slice according to the process of preemptive multitasking.
- **`BelowNormal` and `Lowest`.** A thread with the `BelowNormal` or `Lowest` priority is executed only if the operating system does not encounter any other thread with a higher priority. You normally assign these priority levels to threads whose execution is not important to the system.

All of the priority levels mentioned here are a part of an enumeration object known as `ThreadPriorityEnumeration`.

You can see that the priority levels can be set to define the sequence of execution of threads. However, the priority levels that you set are only applicable to the threads of a single process. For example, if you have a multithreaded application with five threads, the sequence in which these threads will be executed is affected by the priority levels. A thread with a higher priority does not affect the execution of threads of another application running on the system.

You can change the priority of a thread by specifying the value in the `ThreadPriority` property of the thread. To understand the syntax of the `ThreadPriority` property, look at the following example:

```
Thread Thread1 = new Thread(new ThreadStart(newClass.Method1));
Thread1.Priority = ThreadPriority.Highest;
```

The previous code sets the priority of `Thread1` as `Highest`. This stops the execution of all the threads with a lower priority level until `Thread1` is executed.

**CAUTION**

You should be very careful while setting priorities because specifying a priority level of `Highest` stops the execution of all the threads running on a system.

You have seen that by specifying the priority level of threads, you can set the sequence of executing multiple threads on your system. In addition to setting the priority levels, you need to synchronize multiple threads. This ensures smooth and bug-free execution of multiple threads simultaneously. The next section will help you understand the concept of synchronization so that the operating system does not encounter any problems while executing multithreaded applications.

## Synchronization

As the name suggests, *synchronization* helps you to synchronize the use of variables and objects accessed by multiple threads running on your system. In simpler words, synchronization ensures that a variable can be accessed by only one thread at a time. Therefore, by preventing multiple threads from accessing a single variable, you can ensure bug-free execution of the threads on your system.

To understand the need for synchronization, consider a scenario in which two threads with the same priority, `thread1` and `thread2`, are running simultaneously on a system. When the first thread is executed in its time slice, it may write some value to a `public` variable, `variable1`. However, in the next time slice, the other thread might try to read or write a value to `variable1`. This situation can result in an error if the process of writing a value to `variable1` is not completed in the first time slice. When another thread reads this variable, it may read the wrong value, resulting in an error. This situation can be avoided by synchronizing the use of `variable1` by only one thread.

C# provides you with the `lock` keyword to synchronize the use of variables and objects. The `lock` statement takes the name of the object or variable to be locked as a parameter by the `lock` keyword. The name of the variable is enclosed in parentheses as shown in the following example:

```
lock (variable1)
{
        -----------
}
```

Here, `variable1` is the name of the variable to be locked by a thread. The statements to be executed after placing a lock on `variable1` are enclosed in curly braces following the `lock` statement. The `lock` statement locks the variable so that no other thread can access it for the time the lock is placed on the variable. To do this, the `lock` statement places an object known as *mutual exclusion lock* or *mutex* on the variable. No other thread is given access to a variable for the time mutex is placed on the variable.

Therefore, if `thread1` places a lock or mutex on `variable1`, the operating system puts `thread2` on sleep for the time mutex is placed on `variable1`.

By now, you know that synchronization is essential to prevent bugs in your multithreaded application. However, excessive synchronization might reduce the performance of your application. Now, look at the problems associated with the use of excessive synchronization.

- When you place a lock on an object, no other thread is allowed to access this object. Therefore, any other thread that needs access to this object waits for the other thread to release the lock. If there are several threads waiting for the thread to release the lock, the overall performance of the application is affected. The performance of the application can be balanced to some extent by placing locks effectively. The lock on the object is placed for the time the compiler executes the statements in the `lock` block. Therefore, if you write minimum code in the lock statement, you can minimize the effect of placing a lock on a variable by an application.

- Placing and releasing a lock on an object is a resource-intensive activity and adds to the overhead cost of the application.
- Another critical problem that occurs while synchronizing objects is *deadlocking*. Consider a situation in which two different objects are locked by two different threads. Now, each thread wants to access the objects locked by the other. If `thread1` wants to access `object1` that is locked by `thread2`, `thread1` enters the sleep mode for the time `thread2` releases the lock on `object1`. However, this never happens, because `thread2` itself enters the sleep mode while trying to access `object2`, which is held by `thread1`. Both the threads go to sleep while waiting for the other to release its lock. This situation results in a deadlock because even the operating system cannot release the lock on the objects. The locks on `object1` and `object2` can only be released by `thread2` and `thread1`, respectively. Therefore, the application hangs.

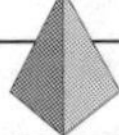

**TIP**

Despite the problems that are discussed here, locks are required on objects in a multithreaded environment. Therefore, you need to be careful while synchronizing the objects in applications.

## Summary

In this chapter, you learned that a thread is a basic unit of execution of a program. In other words, a thread is the smallest unit to which the operating system allocates processor time. Threads allow you to execute multiple applications simultaneously and make the execution of a complex application simple and less time consuming. Therefore, you can create threads for your application. A thread that you create is an instance of the `Thread` class. The `Thread` class is a .NET base class located in the `System.Threading` namespace. You can then create the object of the `Thread` class that represents a thread.

In addition to creating threads, you learned about performing operations on threads that include aborting, sleeping, suspending, and resuming threads. In this chapter, you also learned about various states and priorities of threads. The change in the state of a thread is a result of the action performed on the thread. The thread priorities supported by C# are `Highest`, `AboveNormal`, `Normal`, `BelowNormal`, and `Lowest`. All of these priority levels are a part of an enumeration object known as `ThreadPriorityEnumeration`. Finally, you learned about synchronization, which ensures that a variable can be accessed by only one thread at a time. By preventing multiple threads from accessing a single variable, you can ensure bug-free execution of the threads on your system.

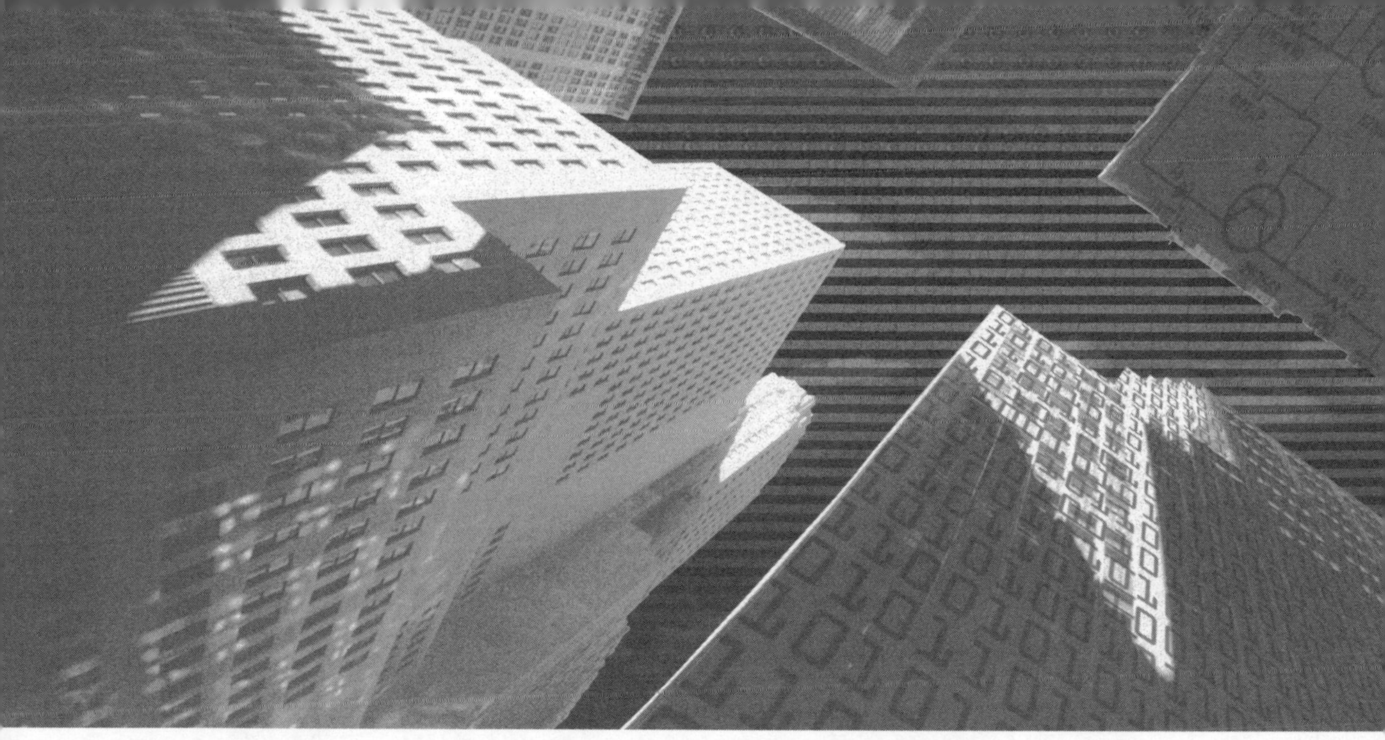

# PART III

## Professional Project 1

# Project 1

## Creating a Customer Maintenance Project

# Project 1 Overview

Now that you have looked at the basics of C#, you can move on to developing projects by using C#. Beginning with this chapter, you will learn more about using C# and its features through projects. These projects will help you to get a better understanding of the features of C#, which will enable you to apply these features in real-life projects.

In this project, you will learn to create a customer maintenance system for CarKare, Inc. This involves creating a Windows application that contains Windows forms. In addition, you will learn to connect these Windows forms to an underlying database such that the Windows forms display data from the SQL database. Finally, you will learn to create crystal reports that provide you with an analysis of the customer data and the data of the job done by a worker in a month.

You will learn to create the Windows application throughout this project. In the next chapter, I will discuss the case study and design of the Windows application.

# Chapter 7

## Project Case Study

You have looked at the basics of C#; you will now move on to developing projects by using C#. Beginning with this chapter, you will learn more about using C# and its features through projects. These projects will help you to get a better understanding of the features of C#, which will enable you to apply these features in real-life projects.

The first project will be to develop a Customer Maintenance project. This chapter covers the case study and design of the project.

## Case Study

CareKar, Inc. is a car maintenance company in Atlanta. The workers of the company get their total compensation as a fixed salary added to allowances that are based on the work they do in a month. In addition, the company gives discounts to their regular customers. Don Burton, the accounts manager of the company, finds it difficult to calculate the gross salary of a worker at the end of a month. Therefore, Don has decided to track the work done by a worker on a daily basis. This would enable him to calculate the allowances given to workers at the end of a month. In addition, he has also decided to track the visits of a customer on a monthly basis. This data would enable him to calculate the discount to be given to a customer.

As a solution to Don's problem, the company has decided to create databases that store information about workers, customers, work done by each worker, and consumable products. Based on the data in the databases, the company will then generate reports to analyze the data. The analysis of the data in the crystal reports will enable Don to find the work done by a worker in a month and, therefore, calculate the worker's gross monthly salary. You will learn to create the Windows forms and crystal reports in the following chapters.

This project covers the creation of a Windows application for CareKar, Inc. However, before proceeding with the actual creation of the project, you must first understand the stages of a project. The following sections discuss the various stages in the development of a project in detail.

# Project Life Cycle

The development life cycle of a project involves three phases:

- Project initiation
- Project execution
- Project deployment

Project development actually starts when the need to develop or significantly change an existing system is identified. In this case, the need is to store, organize, and analyze the data.

After the business need is identified, the different approaches to meet it are reviewed for feasibility and appropriateness. An effective approach would be to create databases to store the data. The data in the databases can then be analyzed by displaying selective data or by grouping the data in a crystal report. I'll now discuss the phases of a project life cycle in detail.

In the *project initiation phase*, a comprehensive list of tasks to be performed is prepared, and responsibilities, depending upon individual skills, are assigned to team members. I will be discussing the tasks that need to be performed when I proceed with the coding of the application.

In the *project execution phase*, the development team develops the application. This phase consists of the following stages:

- Analyzing requirements
- Creating high-level design
- Creating low-level design
- Constructing
- Integration and testing
- User acceptance testing

The final stage in the project life cycle is the *project deployment phase.* In this stage, the application is deployed at the client location, and support is provided to the client for a specified period. In addition, any bugs identified in the application are debugged. This phase consists of the following two stages:

- Implementation
- Operation and maintenance

The following sections discuss each of these stages in detail. To start with, I will discuss the stages of the project execution phase.

## Analyzing Requirements

*Analyzing requirements* is the process of determining and documenting a customer's needs and constraints. Subsequently, based on these requirements, you create a plan for developing the application. The process of analyzing requirements often starts with a problem statement given by a customer or the customer's representative. Analysts organize all the information gathered from the customer and analyze the customer's needs. Finally, they prepare a written description of the customer's problem and define a possible solution.

In this case, the problem statement, as stated by Don Burton, is "CareKar, Inc. needs to analyze data on jobs done by a worker and visits made by a customer." On analyzing the problem statement, the analysts defined the following list of problems faced by CareKar, Inc.

- The company needs to create databases to store and organize data.
- The company needs to analyze the data.
- Based on the analysis of the data, the company needs to find means to serve its customers better and more efficiently.
- Based on the analysis of the data, the company needs to calculate the gross salary of an individual worker.

As a solution to the problems faced by the customer, the analysts proposed that a Windows application with the following features be developed for CareKar, Inc.

- The application communicates with the databases and displays the data in the databases in the Windows forms.
- The application includes a means to create crystal reports that are used for analysis of the data.
- The application is then deployed at the client site.

## High-Level Design

The second stage in the project execution phase is to develop a *high-level design*. In the high-level design phase, the external characteristics of the system, such as interfaces, are designed. In addition, in this phase, the operating environment and various subsystems and their input and output are decided. In this stage, features that require user input or approval from the client are documented, and client approval is obtained for the same. These documents include the functional specifications document of the application, which is presented in a simple language to the client. The functional specifications include the description of the databases, forms, and reports that will be included in the application. This application will be called Customer Maintenance Project.

This project includes Windows forms that display data from an underlying database, CMS (*Customer Maintenance System*). The following section discusses the database design.

### Database Design

The first step in the development of a project is to design a robust database. Before you design a database, it's a good idea to recapitulate the concepts related to a database.

Why do you need a database? A database is a repository of data, a place where you can store data and extract it whenever required. You can store and extract data from a database in various ways. One of the ways is by using SQL (*structured query language*) statements. The following section discusses some of the basic SQL statements used to create and modify the data in a database.

### The SQL Statements

SQL is an ANSI (*American National Standards Institute*) standard for accessing database systems. SQL statements can be used to retrieve and update data in a database. SQL works with databases such as Microsoft Access, DB2 (*Database 2*), Informix, Microsoft SQL Server, Oracle, Sybase, and many others.

Databases contain tables, which contain the data in the form of rows and columns. Table 7-1 shows an example of how data is stored in tables.

**Table 7-1 Displaying Data in a Sales Table**

| City | Sales | Date |
|---|---|---|
| New York | 23600 | Jul-14-2002 |
| Atlanta | 16400 | Jul-12-2002 |
| Seattle | 17300 | Jul-11-2002 |
| Chicago | 19700 | Jul-14-2002 |
| San Francisco | 24200 | Jul-14-2002 |

In this table, `City`, `Sales`, and `Date` are table columns. The rows contain five records each about sales at five cities on a particular date.

You can extract this data from the database by using SQL query statements. The next section will revise basic SQL query statements.

## The `Select` Statement

A database can be queried using SQL `Select` statements. Here is an example of a simple SQL `Select` statement.

```
Select * from Sales
```

This statement extracts all the records from the `Sales` table. The syntax of an SQL `Select` statement is as follows:

```
Select [select-list] from [table name]
```

You can further modify the `Select` statement to extract data from the table based on a condition by using the `where` keyword. For example, consider that you need to only view the sales on July 14, 2002. The following SQL statement provides the required output.

```
select city, sales from Sales where date = 'jul-14-2002'
```

The syntax for the `Select` statement where you extract data based on a condition is as follows:

```
Select [select-list] from [table name] where [search condition]
```

The search operators that you can use with the `where` keyword are described in Table 7-2.

**Table 7-2 Operators Used in a Search Condition**

| Operator | Description |
|---|---|
| = | Equal |
| > | Greater than |
| < | Less than |
| >= | Greater than or equal |
| <= | Less than or equal |
| <> | Not equal |
| Between | Between an inclusive range |
| Like | Search for a pattern in a column |

Table 7-3 shows the `Students` table that contains information about students.

**Table 7-3 The `Students` Table**

| FirstName | LastName | EmailAddress | DOB | City |
|---|---|---|---|---|
| Sandra | Lewis | slewis@aol.com | Jan-04-1971 | Atlanta |
| Elaine | Thorn | ethorn@yahoo.com | Oct-27-1979 | Chicago |
| George | Thomas | gthomas@freemail.com | Aug-25-1976 | Atlanta |
| Simon | Watson | swatson@fastmail.com | Mar-18-1978 | Memphis |
| Larry | Gates | lgates@mymail.com | Jun-12-1981 | Atlanta |
| Michael | Brown | mbrown@aol.com | Feb-02-1972 | Memphis |
| Sarah | Judd | sjudd@zipmail.com | Oct-01-1982 | Chicago |
| Joshua | Johnson | jjohnson@slowmail.com | Apr-24-1977 | Detroit |
| Daniel | Allison | dallison@aol.com | Dec-07-1975 | Chicago |
| Nicholas | Harvey | nharvey@buzz.com | Mar-13-1979 | Detroit |
| Laura | Hansen | lhansen@hotmail.com | Sep-12-1973 | Memphis |

Now, I'll create some SQL statements that will refresh your memory. To select only the students who live in Chicago, modify the `Select` statement, as follows:

```
Select * from Students where city = 'Chicago'
```

Table 7-4 displays the result of the previous query.

**Table 7-4 Students Who Live in Chicago**

| FirstName | LastName | EmailAddress | DOB | City |
|---|---|---|---|---|
| Daniel | Allison | dallison@aol.com | Dec-07-1975 | Chicago |
| Elaine | Thorn | ethorn@yahoo.com | Oct-27-1979 | Chicago |
| Sarah | Judd | sjudd@zipmail.com | Oct-04-1982 | Chicago |

Consider the following SQL statement. The statement returns all rows with last names ending with *n*.

```
Select * from Students where LastName like '%n'
```

Table 7-5 displays the result of the previous query.

**Table 7-5 Students Whose Last Name Ends With *N***

| FirstName | LastName | EmailAddress | DOB | City |
|---|---|---|---|---|
| Daniel | Allison | dallison@aol.com | Dec-07-1975 | Chicago |
| Elaine | Thorn | ethorn@yahoo.com | Oct-27-1979 | Chicago |
| Joshua | Johnson | jjohnson@slowmail.com | Apr-24-1977 | Detroit |
| Laura | Hansen | lhansen@hotmail.com | Sep-12-1973 | Memphis |
| Michael | Brown | mbrown@aol.com | Feb-02-1972 | Memphis |
| Simon | Watson | swatson@fastmail.com | Mar-18-1978 | Memphis |

To alphabetically sort names of all students between Joshua and Michael, use the following SQL statement.

```
Select * from Students where FirstName between 'Joshua' and 'Michael'
```

The result of the previous statement is displayed in Table 7-6.

**Table 7-6 Students Whose First Name Is between Joshua and Michael**

| FirstName | LastName | EmailAddress | DOB | City |
|---|---|---|---|---|
| Joshua | Johnson | jjohnson@slowmail.com | Apr-24-1977 | Detroit |
| Larry | Gates | lgates@mymail.com | Jun-12-1981 | Atlanta |
| Laura | Hansen | lhansen@hotmail.com | Sep-12-1973 | Memphis |
| Michael | Brown | mbrown@aol.com | Feb-02-1972 | Memphis |

Similarly, you can also display only specific columns. For example, to extract only `FirstName`, `LastName`, and `City`, you can use the following `Select` statement.

```
Select FirstName, LastName, City from Students
```

The result of the above SQL statement is shown in Table 7-7.

**Table 7-7 List of First Names, Last Names, and Cities**

| FirstName | LastName | City |
|---|---|---|
| Daniel | Allison | Chicago |
| Elaine | Thorn | Chicago |
| George | Thomas | Atlanta |
| Joshua | Johnson | Detroit |
| Larry | Gates | Atlanta |
| Laura | Hansen | Memphis |
| Michael | Brown | Memphis |
| Nicholas | Harvey | Detroit |
| Sandra | Lewis | Atlanta |
| Sarah | Judd | Chicago |
| Simon | Watson | Memphis |

## The `Insert` Statement

The `Insert` statement inserts a new row in a table. For example, to insert a new record in the `Students` table, you can use the following SQL statement.

```
Insert into Students values ('Sarah', 'Lee', 'slee@yahoo.com', 'Mar-22-1977',
  'Detroit')
```

The preceding SQL statement inserts a new record in the `Students` table with the values mentioned in the SQL statement.

You can also insert data into specific columns. For example, to add only first and last names, you can use the following `Insert` statement.

```
Insert into students (FirstName, LastName)
values ('Jessica', 'Parker')
```

## The `Update` Statement

The `Update` statement modifies the data in a table. For example, consider that Laura Hansen has changed her last name to Brown. The following update statement can help you make the change:

```
Update Students set LastName = 'Brown' where FirstName = 'Laura' and LastName =
  'Hansen'
```

## The `Delete` Statement

The `Delete` statement removes some or all rows from a table. For example, in the `Students` table, to delete the records of all students in Detroit, you use the following SQL statement:

```
Delete from Students where City = 'Detroit'
```

## The `Create` Statement

The `Create` statement can be used to create a database, a table in a database, and indexes in a table. For example, the following `Create` statement can be used to create a database containing customers.

```
Create database Customers
```

The statement to create a table is slightly different from the `Select` statement. Consider a situation where you want to create a table named `Customers` with five columns: `cust_no`, `cust_name`, `cust_addr`, `cust_phone`, and `cust_email`. To create the table `Customers`, you need to use the following SQL statement:

```
Create table Customers
(cust_no char(4),
cust_name char(25),
cust_addr varchar(50),
cust_phone char(12),
cust_email char(20))
```

The first step toward creating a database is to create the design of a database. The following section discusses the fundamentals of a database design.

## Primary and Foreign Keys

To access data stored in a table, you need a way to identify each row stored in the table. For example, consider that George Thomas has changed his e-mail address to georget@aol.com and you need to update the same in the `Students` table. You can execute the following SQL statement to update the information:

```
Update Students set EmailAddress = 'georget@aol.com'
where FirstName = 'George' and LastName = 'Thomas'
```

In this case, the `FirstName` and `LastName` columns identify the rows uniquely in the `Students` table. However, this is not the best way to identify a row because more than one person could have the same combination of the first name and the last name. Therefore, the identifier must uniquely identify all data in the table. In the case of the `Students` table, you can create another column, `StudentID`, that will be unique for every row. Such a unique identifier is called a *primary key*.

Consider the `Customers` table discussed earlier. It has five columns: `cust_no`, `cust_name`, `cust_addr`, `cust_phone`, and `cust_email`. In this table, `cust_no` is the best column to be set as the primary key. This is because this key is unique for each record and can, therefore, identify each row uniquely. You can make a column a primary key when creating the table in the following manner:

```
Create table Customers
(cust_no char(4) primary key,
cust_name char(25),
cust_addr varchar(50),
cust_phone char(12),
cust_email char(20))
```

A *foreign key* is a column or a combination of columns that creates a link between two tables. Adding the primary key column of one table to another table creates a relationship between the tables. This primary key column becomes the foreign key in the other table.

Consider the `Orders` table with the columns `order_no`, `order_price`, `order_quantity`, and `order_date`. To process an order, a customer who ordered the goods must be tracked. To do this, you need to add the `cust_no` column to the `Orders` table. The `cust_no` column, which is the primary key in the `Customers` table, becomes the foreign key in the `Orders` table. You can create a foreign key at the time of creating the table in the following manner:

```
Create table Orders
(order_no char(4)  primary key,
order_price int,
order_quantity int,
order_date datetime,
cust_no char(4) not null
references Customers (cust_no))
```

## Referential Integrity

You learned that foreign keys are used to establish relationships. However, you may be wondering why you need to establish these relationships. To appreciate the need for creating relationships between tables, consider the following scenario. Table 7-8 displays the records in the `Orders` table and Table 7-9 displays the records in the `Customers` table.

**Table 7-8 The `Orders` Table**

| cust_no | cust_name | cust_addr | cust_phone | cust_email |
|---|---|---|---|---|
| C001 | Lee, Lynn & Associates | #106, Crosswood St., Memphis, TN | 901-458-4233 | lee@lla.com |
| C023 | Korex copiers | #286 Central Avenue, Memphis, TN | 901-362-7615 | webmaster@korex.com |
| C035 | Sellmart | #2136 S White Station Memphis, TN | 901-497-5256 | liz@sellmart.com |
| C017 | Plasco & Sons | #1176 South Central Avenue, Memphis, TN | 901-362-2661 | bcroft@aol.com |
| C034 | Plex Cables, Inc. | #1054 Poplar Avenue, Memphis, TN | 901-497-0763 | sales@plexcables.com |

**Table 7-9 The `Customers` Table**

| order_no | order_price | order_quantity | order_date | cust_no |
|---|---|---|---|---|
| O762 | 625 | 2 | 1-12-2002 | C023 |
| O023 | 2175 | 4 | 3-3-2002 | C035 |
| O136 | 175 | 1 | 2-2-2002 | C001 |
| O174 | 550 | 2 | 3-22-2002 | C017 |
| O382 | 1050 | 4 | 1-22-2002 | C023 |

Now, if the record for the customer with `cust_no` C017 is deleted, there will be an order, O174, that will not have a valid `cust_no`. In order to avoid such a condition, you need to establish relationships. When any two tables are related, you cannot delete a record in one table if there is a related record for it in the other table. This is known as *referential integrity*.

Referential integrity provides the following benefits. It prevents users from:

- Adding records to a related table if there is no associated record in the primary table

- Changing values in a primary table when there are related records in the related table
- Deleting records from a primary table if there are related records in the related table

## Normalization

*Normalization* refers to the process of reducing data redundancy. It usually involves splitting data into two or more tables until repeating groups of data are placed in separate tables. The first step in building a database is to examine the data and then break it down into a row and column format. To appreciate the need for normalization, consider the following example.

Consider Table 7-10, which displays the records in the `Product_Orders` table.

**Table 7-10 The `Product_Orders` Table**

| Ord_Id | Ord_Date | Ord_Qty | Ord_Amt | Prod_Id | Prod_Name | Prod_rate |
|---|---|---|---|---|---|---|
| 0014 | 03-13-02 | 3 | $24 | P012 | Soft toys | $8 |
| 0045 | 03-10-01 | 2 | $12 | P003 | Candle stand | $6 |
| 0033 | 02-17-02 | 4 | $32 | P012 | Soft toys | $8 |
| 0021 | 01-25-01 | 1 | $11 | P007 | Pen | $11 |

Consider a situation where you need to reduce the rate of soft toys to $6 because you have a large stock of soft toys. However, in reducing the rate, you had to make changes in two rows. Imagine the effort required to make changes in a table with a large number of records. So, you decided to split this table into two tables, `Orders` and `Products`. Whereas the `Orders` table has the orders that were booked by customers, the `Products` table has the list of products sold by the company.

This type of problem, where the same information needs to be changed in more than one record, is referred to as an *update anomaly*.

The order with `Ord_Id` 0045 was cancelled. So, you decide to delete that record. However, you realized that the details of `Candle stand` would also be lost. The solution to this problem is to split the table into two, `Orders` and `Products`. This type of problem is referred to as a *deletion anomaly*.

Now, consider a situation where you need to change the rate for `Candle stand.` You would need to change the rate for `Ord_Id` 0045 also. This problem is similar to the update anomaly; however, you noticed this only when you added this record. This kind of problem is referred to as an *insertion anomaly*.

Therefore, to design a database without having to encounter these anomalies, you need to normalize the database.

To summarize, the following rules help you design a robust database:

- A table should have a unique identifier.
- A table should not have repeating values or columns.
- A table should store data for only a single type of entity.
- A table should avoid columns with null values.

## Designing a Database

After applying all the concepts discussed so far, you would arrive at the database structure shown in Figure 7-1 for the CMS database.

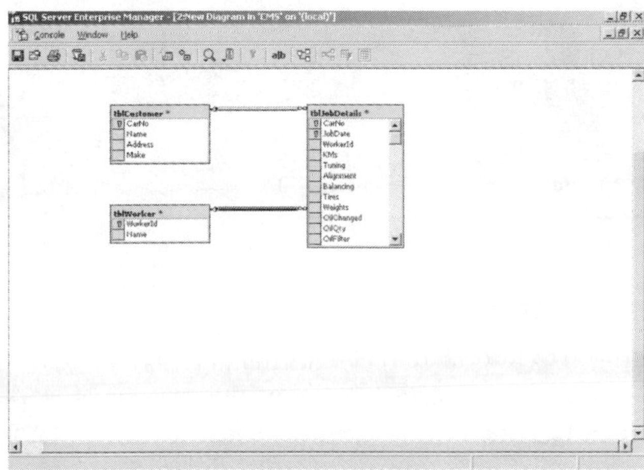


**FIGURE 7-1** *Structure of the CMS database*

The following section discusses the details of each table in the CMS database.

## *The `tblWorker` Table*

The `tblWorker` table is used to store information about a worker. Table 7-11 shows the details of the `tblWorker` table.

**Table 7-11 Details of the `tblWorker` Table**

| Column Name | Data Type | Length | Allow Nulls |
|---|---|---|---|
| WorkerID | int | - | No |
| Name | nvarchar | 50 | Yes |

## *The `tblCustomer` Table*

The `tblCustomer` table stores information about the customers of the organization. Table 7-12 displays the details of the `tblCustomer` table.

**Table 7-12 Details of the `tblCustomer` Table**

| Column Name | Data Type | Length | Allow Nulls |
|---|---|---|---|
| CarNo | nvarchar | 15 | No |
| Name | nvarchar | 255 | Yes |
| Address | nvarchar | 255 | Yes |
| Make | nvarchar | 50 | Yes |

## *The `tblJobDetails` Table*

The `tblJobDetails` table stores information about the job done by a worker in a particular month. It also stores the information about the amount of work done on a car in a particular month. Table 7-13 displays the details of the `tblJobDetails` table.

**Table 7-13 Details of the `tblJobDetails` Table**

| Column Name | Data Type | Length | Allow Nulls |
|---|---|---|---|
| CarNo | nvarchar | 15 | No |
| JobDate | datetime | 15 | No |
| WorkerId | int | - | No |
| KMs | int | - | Yes |
| Tuning | int | - | Yes |
| Alignment | int | - | Yes |
| Balancing | int | - | Yes |
| Tires | int | - | Yes |
| Weights | int | - | Yes |
| OilChanged | int | - | Yes |
| OilQty | int | - | Yes |
| OilFilter | int | - | Yes |
| GearOil | int | - | Yes |
| GearOilQty | int | - | Yes |
| Point | int | - | Yes |
| Condenser | int | - | Yes |
| Plug | int | - | Yes |
| PlugQty | int | - | Yes |
| FuelFilter | int | - | Yes |
| AirFilter | int | - | Yes |
| Remarks | int | - | Yes |

After discussing the database design, the next section will look at the design of the forms that display data from the tables in the databases. The next section discusses the forms used in the Customer Maintenance project.

## Designing the Windows Forms Used in Customer Maintenance Project

The Customer Maintenance project includes the `WorkerForm`, `CustomerForm`, and `JobDetails` forms to access data from the `tblWorker`, `tblCustomer`, and `tblJobDetails` tables, respectively. In addition, the Customer Maintenance project includes the main form, `Form1`, and the `Reports` form.

### *Form1*

`Form1` contains links that a user uses to view different forms created in the Customer Maintenance project. Figure 7-2 shows the layout of `Form1`.

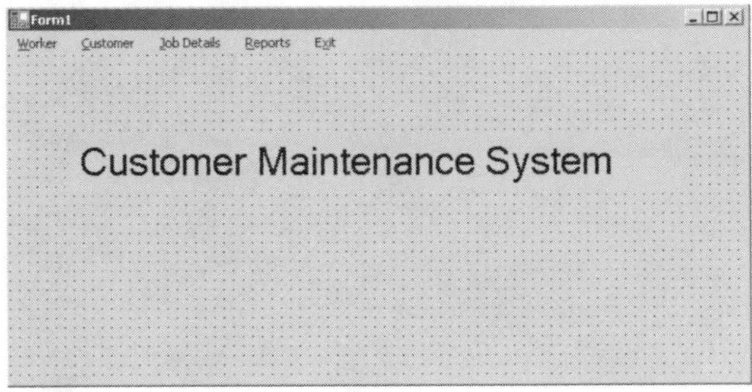


**FIGURE 7-2** *Layout of* `Form1`

### *The* `WorkerForm` *Form*

The layout of the `WorkerForm` form is displayed in Figure 7-3.

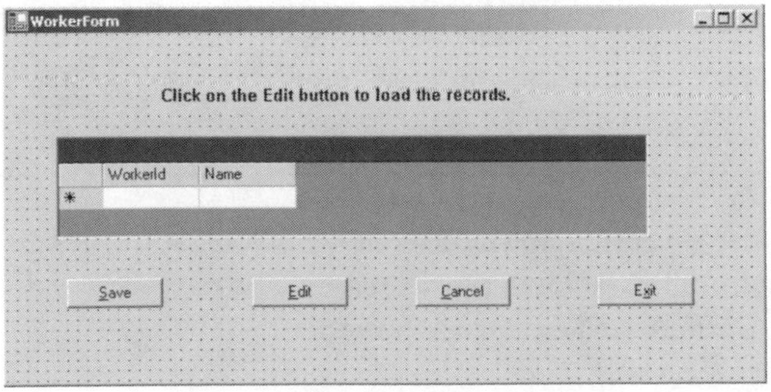

**FIGURE 7-3** *Layout of the* `WorkerForm` *form*

## The CustomerForm Form

The layout of the `CustomerForm` form is displayed in Figure 7-4.

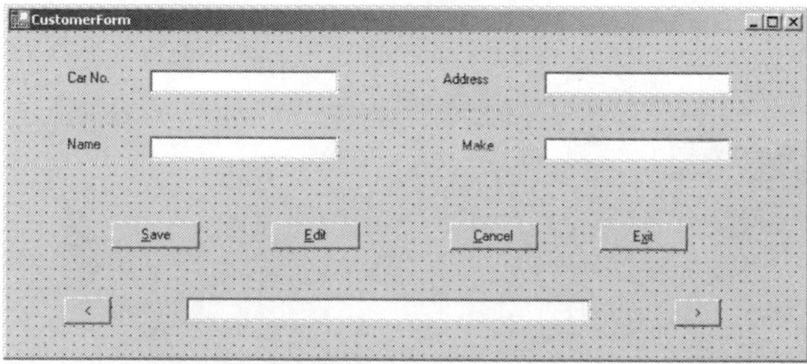


**FIGURE 7-4** *Layout of the* `CustomerForm` *form*

## The JobDetails Form

The layout of the `JobDetails` form is displayed in Figure 7-5.

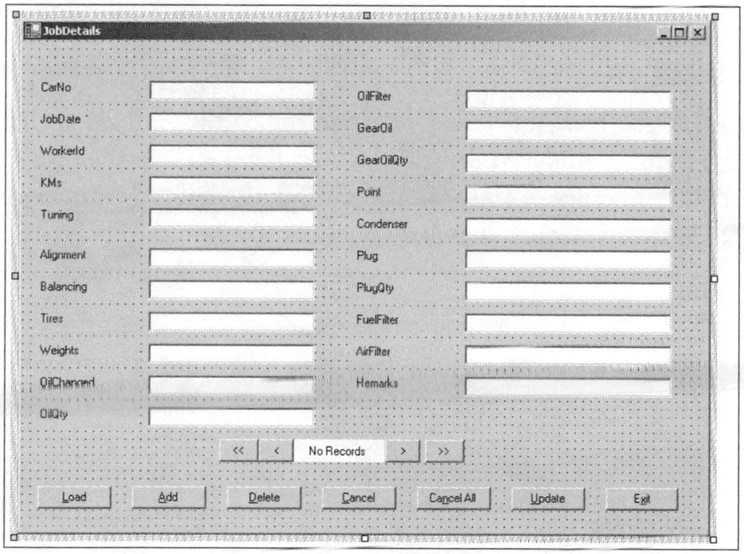

**FIGURE 7-5** *Layout of the* `JobDetails` *form*

### The `Reports` Form

The `Reports` form contains links to various reports created in the Customer Maintenance project. The layout of the `Reports` form is displayed in Figure 7-6.

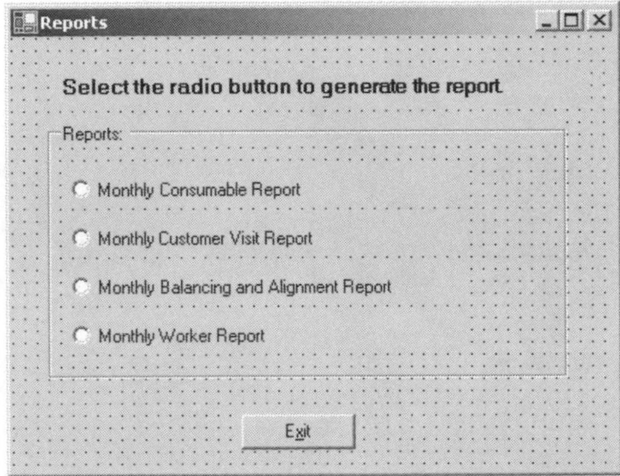


**FIGURE 7-6** *Layout of the* `Reports` *form*

## Low-Level Design

In the *low-level design* phase, a detailed design of the software modules, based on the high-level design, is produced. In addition, the team lays down specifications for various software modules of an application. Modules defined in the high-level design phase are used to create a detailed structure of a system. The system contains subsystems, which are partitioned into one or more design units or modules.

In the low-level design phase, the flow of the different modules in the Customer Maintenance project and the interactions between various interfaces are defined. The flow and the interaction between the interfaces are shown in the following figures.

### The `Form1` Module

The `Form1` module deals with `Form1`. Figure 7-7 shows the flowchart and the interaction of `Form1` with the other modules.

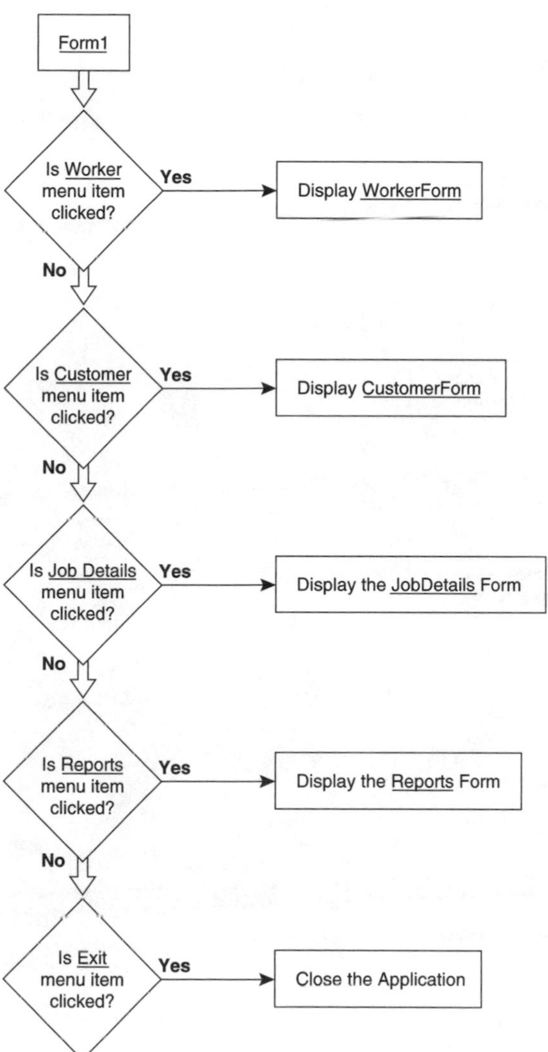


**FIGURE 7-7** *Flowchart of the `Form1` module*

## The `Worker` Module

The `Worker` module consists of `WorkerForm` that contains information about workers. The flowchart of `WorkerForm` is displayed in Figure 7-8.

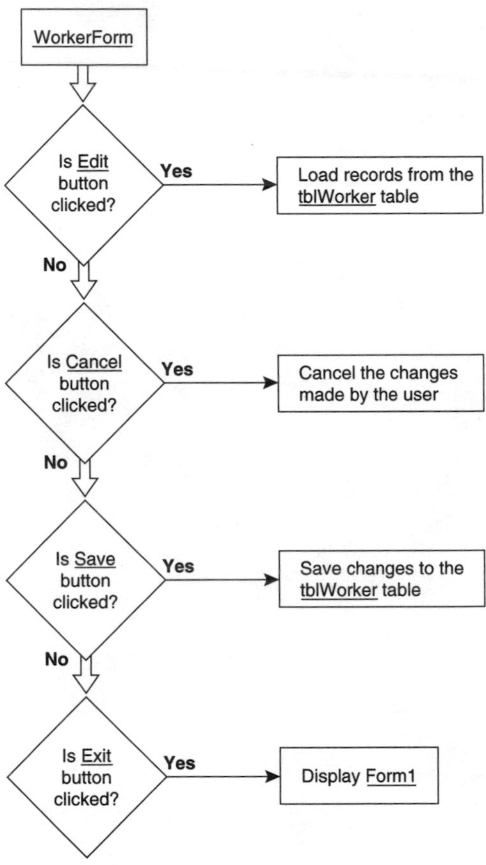


**FIGURE 7-8** *Flowchart of the* `Worker` *module*

## The `Customer` Module

The `Customer` module contains `CustomerForm`. Figure 7-9 displays the flowchart of the `Customer` module.

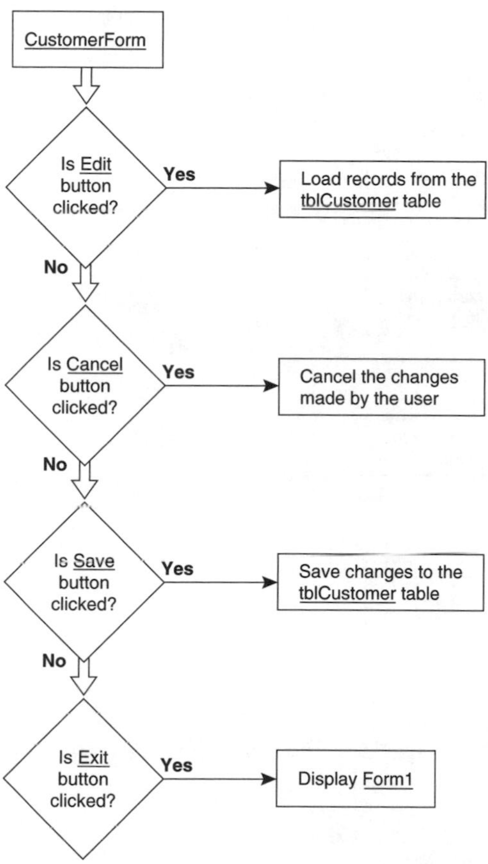


**FIGURE 7-9** *Flowchart of the* `Customer` *module*

## The `Job Details` Module

The `Job Details` module contains the `JobDetails` form. Figure 7-10 displays the flowchart of the `Job Details` module.

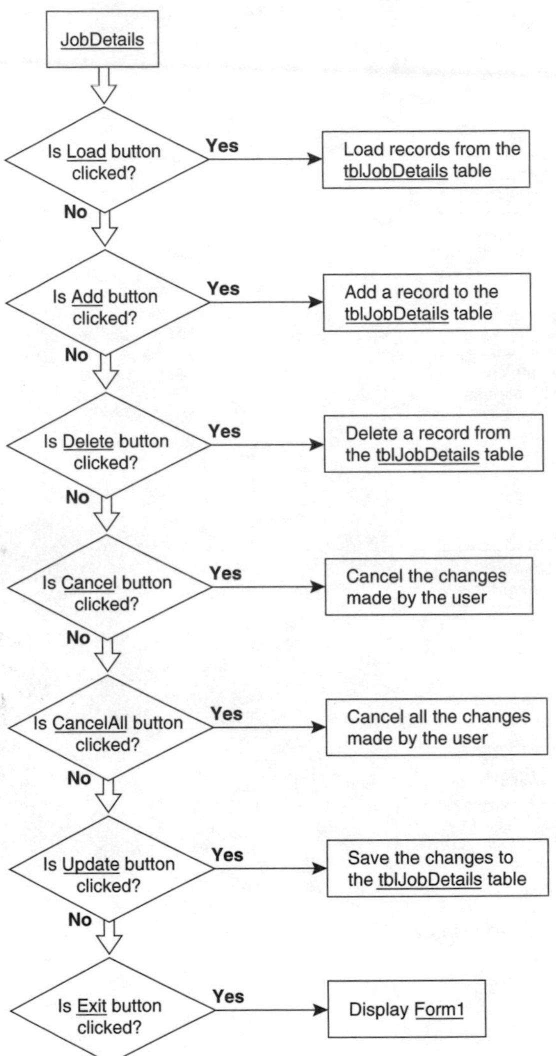


**FIGURE 7-10** *Flowchart of the* `Job Details` *module*

## The `Reports` Module

The `Reports` module contains the `Reports` form. The flowchart of the `Reports` module is displayed in Figure 7-11.

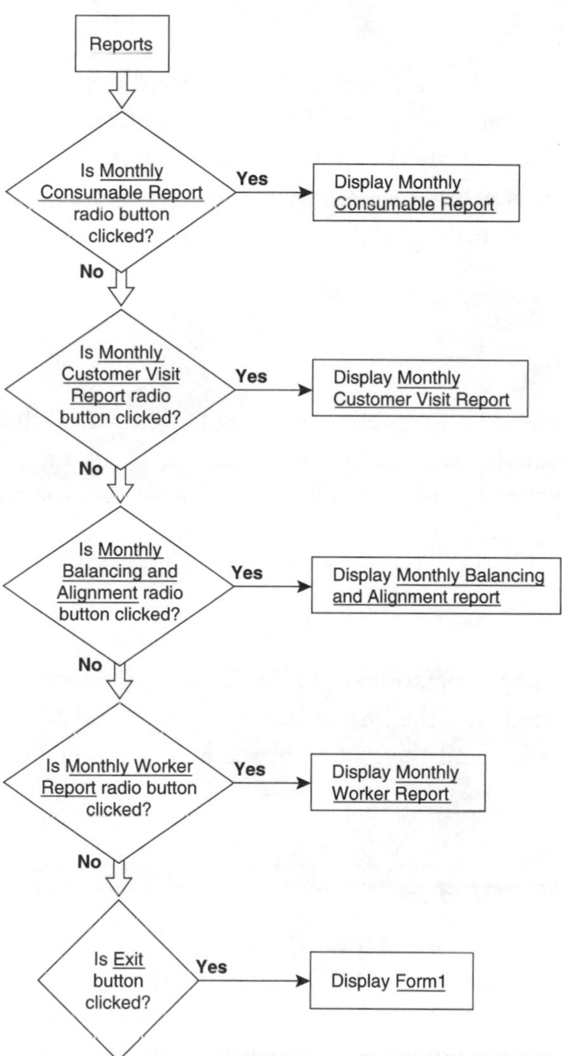


**FIGURE 7-11** *Flowchart of the* `Reports` *module*

## Construction

In the *construction* phase, different software modules are built. This phase uses the output of the low-level design to produce software components. During the construction phase, task responsibilities are assigned to team members. Some team members may need to design and develop an interface, while the others may be required to write the code for database connectivity and business rules.

## Integration and Testing

The integration of different modules and testing are conducted during the *integration and testing* phase. The quality assurance (QA) team validates whether the functional requirements, defined in the requirements document, are met. The development team also submits a test case report to the QA team so that the application that the development team has created can be tested in various possible scenarios.

## User Acceptance Testing

In the *user acceptance* phase, based on the predefined acceptance criteria, the client conducts acceptance testing of the project. In this phase, the acceptance criteria include the fulfillment of all the requirements identified during the requirements analysis phase.

## Implementation

The system is installed and made operational in a production environment. The *implementation* phase is initiated after the system has been tested and accepted by the client. This phase continues until the system operates in a production environment.

## Operations and Maintenance

In the *operations and maintenance* phase, software is monitored for performance in accordance with user requirements. In addition, the modifications that are required are incorporated in the software. Operations continue as long as a system can effectively adapt to an organization's needs. However, when modifications or changes are identified, the system may re-enter the planning phase.

In the next few chapters, you will learn to develop the Windows application, starting with the creation of the Windows forms.

# *Summary*

This chapter introduced you to a project case study. You learned about the different stages in a project life cycle. These stages include project initiation, project execution, and project deployment. Then, you looked at various phases of the project execution stage, such as analyzing requirements, creating high-level design, creating low-level design, constructing, integration and testing, and user acceptance testing.

While learning about the high-level and low-level designs of a project, you learned to create a database design and the layout of the forms used in the Customer Maintenance project. In the forthcoming chapters, I will take you through the process of developing the project.

# Chapter 8

## Windows Forms and Controls

In this chapter, you will be introduced to Visual Studio .NET projects and solutions. In addition, you will learn to create a new project in Visual Studio .NET. This chapter introduces you to console applications and Windows applications. Finally, you will learn to create Windows forms and add controls to the forms used in the Customer Maintenance project.

## Introduction to Visual Studio .NET Projects

*Visual Studio .NET projects* are containers that hold development material for an application. Visual Studio .NET projects contain files, folders, and references to databases, which you require while developing your project. To develop any application in Visual Studio .NET, you need to create a new project by using the New Project dialog box. You will look at creating a new project later in this chapter.

Projects in Visual Studio .NET are contained within *solutions,* which help you create simple or complex applications by using the templates and tools available in Visual Studio .NET. A solution can also contain multiple projects or other solutions. In Visual Studio .NET, after you create a project, it is automatically placed within a solution. Using solutions and projects enables you to manage and organize the files and folders that will be used to create your application. To do this, Visual Studio .NET provides you with a Solution Explorer window in which you can view and manage solutions and projects. Figure 8-1 shows the Solution Explorer window.

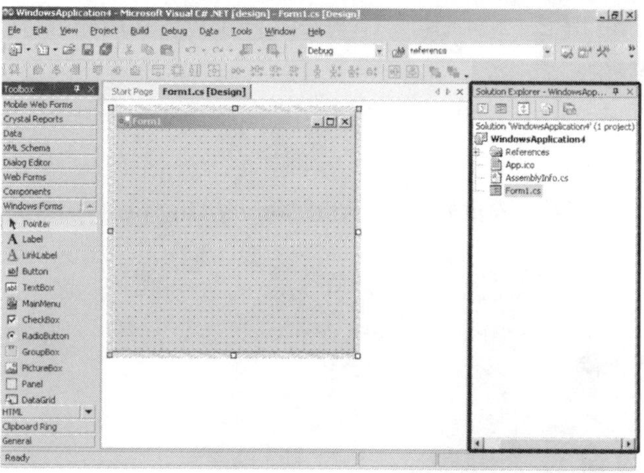

**FIGURE 8-1** *The Solution Explorer window*

A project includes an HTML file, a project file, and source files. In addition, you may include several other files in your project, depending on the complexity of the application you create. For example, you may create an .xsd file to include a dataset in your projcct. You will learn about these files later in this project.

When a project is completed, you usually convert the project into an executable program (.exe), a dynamic-link library (.dll), or a module. The following section discusses how to create a new project.

## Creating a New Project

To create a new project in Visual Studio .NET, perform the following steps:

1. On the Start menu, point to Programs and click on Microsoft Visual Studio .NET.
2. From the list that is displayed, select the Microsoft Visual Studio .NET option.

   The Microsoft Development Environment window is displayed.

3. On the File menu of the Microsoft Development Environment window, point to New.
4. From the list that is displayed, select Project.

   The Add New dialog box is displayed.

Figure 8-2 displays the Project option of the Add New dialog box.

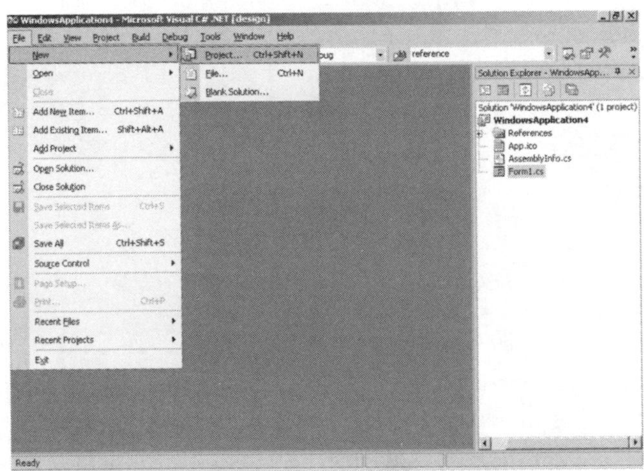


**FIGURE 8-2** *The Project option of the Add New dialog box*

In the Add New dialog box, you need to select the project type and template for creating a new project. In the left panel of the Add New dialog box, select the type of project for your application, for example, a Visual Basic, Visual C++, or Visual C# project. In this book, you will create a project in Visual C#, therefore you should select the Visual C# option.

Having selected the type of project, you need to select the template file. Visual Studio .NET provides you with several template files. To know more about these template files, refer to Figure 8-3.

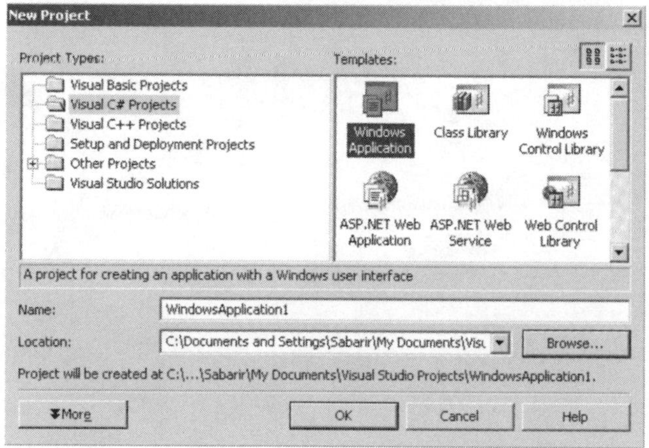


**FIGURE 8-3** *Templates provided by the .NET Framework*

Using the available templates, you can create a variety of applications, such as Windows applications, ASP.NET Web applications, ASP.NET Web services, console applications, and so on. In this chapter, you will learn about console applications and Windows applications. However, ASP.NET Web applications and ASP.NET Web services will be discussed in the next project.

## Console Application

Using Visual Studio .NET templates, you can create applications that display the output in a console window. Such applications are called *console applications*. To create a console application, select the Console Application project template in the right pane of the New Project dialog box. In the Name text box, specify the name SampleConsoleApplication.

When you create a console application, Visual Studio .NET adds the necessary files to the project. These files include References, App.ico, and AssemblyInfo.cs. You will learn about these files later in this chapter.

In addition to the previously mentioned files, a class file with the name `Class1.cs` is created. This file contains empty code for the class module. Figure 8-4 shows the `Class1.cs` file.

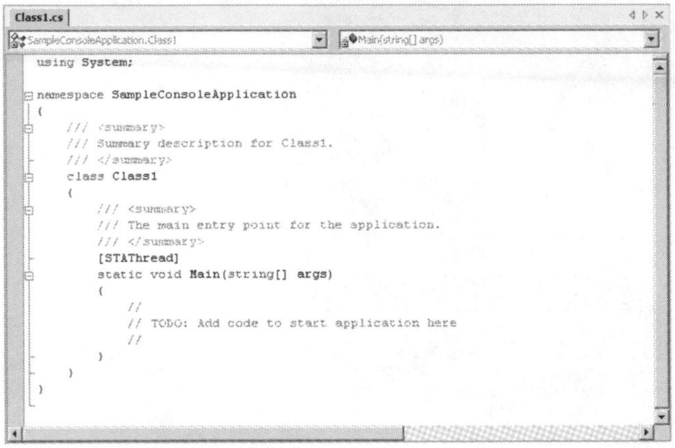

```
using System;

namespace SampleConsoleApplication
{
	/// <summary>
	/// Summary description for Class1.
	/// </summary>
	class Class1
	{
		/// <summary>
		/// The main entry point for the application.
		/// </summary>
		[STAThread]
		static void Main(string[] args)
		{
			//
			// TODO: Add code to start application here
			//
		}
	}
}
```

**FIGURE 8-4** `Class1.cs` *file*

A console application does not have a user interface, and it is run from the command prompt. You can now create a simple console application that displays the message `This is a sample console application.` in the console window.

To display the message, you need to add the following code to the void `Main()` method of the application.

```
static void Main(string[] args)
	{
		Console.WriteLine("This is a sample console application.");
	}
```

The `WriteLine()` method is present in the `Console` class, which lies in the `System` namespace. The `WriteLine()` method is used to write the current line to the Console window. Similarly, to read from the Console window, you can include the `Console.ReadLine()` method in the following manner:

```
static void Main(string[] args)
	{
		Console.WriteLine("This is a sample console application.");
		Console.ReadLine();
	}
```

The output of the previous code is displayed in Figure 8-5.

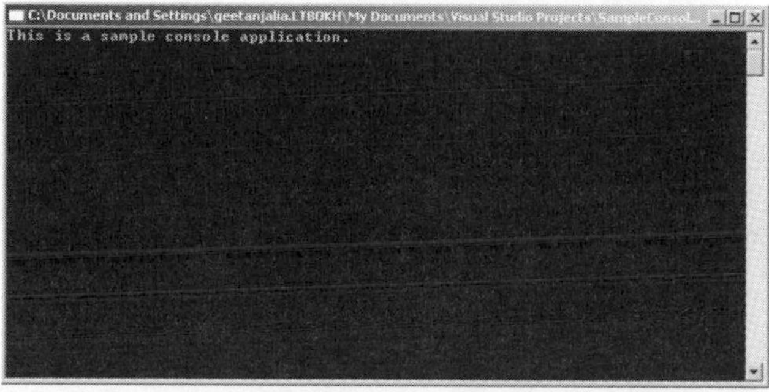


**FIGURE 8-5** *Output of the previous code*

## Windows Applications

Programmers worldwide have been using different programming languages to create Windows applications that can run locally on a computer. However, all of these languages have their own advantages and limitations. For example, C programmers use the Win32 API (*application programming interface*) to create Windows applications. On the other hand, Visual Basic provides programmers with a graphical interface to create forms and applications, and Visual C++ uses MFC (*Microsoft Foundation Classes*) to create Windows applications.

Until now, there was no environment that provided the combined features of these languages. As a result, Microsoft came up with Visual Studio .NET, which provides you with a common framework for developing Windows applications in any of the Visual Studio .NET languages, such as Visual Basic .NET, Visual C++ .NET, and Visual C#. Visual Studio .NET provides a graphical interface for creating applications, and the .NET class library provides you with the classes you can use to write the code for your application. There's no doubt that you can create Windows applications easily and in far less time by using the .NET Framework. The next section will look at creating a Windows application.

To create a Windows application, select the Windows Application project template in the Templates pane of the New Project dialog box. In the Name text box, specify a name for your application, SampleWindowsApplication, and in the Location text box, type the path or browse to the directory in which you want to save your application.

After you create a Windows application with the name SampleWindowsApplication, Visual Studio .NET creates a solution and a project with the same name. The Windows application opens in the Windows Forms Design view. A default form, Form1, is created for you in the design view. Form1 is an instance of the `Form` class of the .NET class library and is an interface for your application.

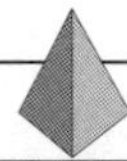

**TIP**

The `Form` class lies in the `System.Windows.Forms` namespace.

In addition to creating a default form, Visual Studio .NET creates the default files and references that you require to create your project. Table 8-1 lists some of these files.

**Table 8-1 The Windows Application Files**

| Files | Description |
|---|---|
| AssemblyInfo.cs | The AssemblyInfo.cs file contains assembly information, such as the versions of the assembly. |
| Form.cs | The Form.cs file contains the code for the default form. |
| References | The References folder includes references to the namespaces that you use for the development of an application. For example, the References folder contains System, System.Data, System.Drawing, System.Windows.Forms, and System.XML files that contain references to the respective namespaces. |

Figure 8-6 displays the default files that are included in the SampleWindowsApplication project.

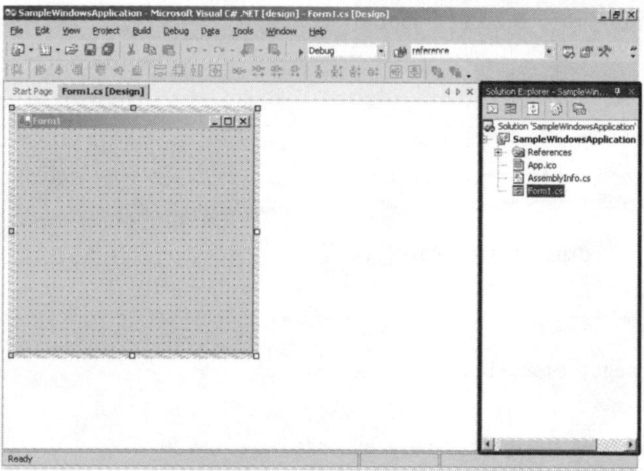

**FIGURE 8-6** *Windows application files*

Visual Studio .NET also creates the code for the default form, Form1, which is created in the Windows application. To view the code behind the form, you can either double-click on the form or select the form and press the F7 key. The following sample shows the code that is automatically generated when you create a Windows application.

```
using System;
using System.Drawing;
using System.Collections;
using System.ComponentModel;
using System.Windows.Forms;
using System.Data;

namespace SampleWindowsApplication
{
     public class Form1 : System.Windows.Forms.Form
     {
         private System.ComponentModel.Container components = null;
         public Form1()
         {
              InitializeComponent();
         }
```

```
        protected override void Dispose( bool disposing )
        {
            if( disposing )
            {
                if (components != null)
                {
                    components.Dispose();
                }
            }
            base.Dispose( disposing );
        }
        #region Windows Form Designer generated code
        private void InitializeComponent()
        {
            this.AutoScaleBaseSize = new System.Drawing.Size(5, 13);
            this.ClientSize = new System.Drawing.Size(292, 273);
            this.Name = "Form1";
            this.Text = "Form1";
            this.Load += new System.EventHandler(this.Form1_Load);
        }
        #endregion

        [STAThread]
        static void Main()
        {
            Application.Run(new Form1());
        }
        private void Form1_Load(object sender, System.EventArgs e)
        {
            --------
        }
    }
}
```

When you create a Windows application in Visual Studio .NET, a default namespace with the same name as that of your application is also created. In this case, a default namespace is created with the name `SampleWindowsApplication`. In addition, Visual Studio .NET includes some of the existing namespaces in the application, such as `System`, `System.Drawing`, `System.Collections`, and so on. Inside the `SampleWindowsApplication` namespace, a `public` class named Form1 is created. When you add controls to the form, the declarations of the controls are added to this class. You will learn to add controls to a form later in this chapter.

The Form1 class contains a default constructor named Form1. The constructor includes the `InitializeComponent()` method. This method contains the statements required to initialize the Windows form used in the application. For example, the `InitializeComponent()` method includes the name of the form. The declaration for the `InitializeComponent()` method is included in the `#region` preprocessor directive.

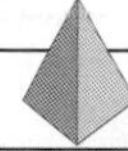

**TIP**

`#region` preprocessor directives are used to demarcate regions.

In addition, the Form1 class contains the `Dispose()` method, which is called to deallocate the memory occupied by the components that are no longer used by the application. The class also includes the `Main()` method, which is the starting point of the execution of the program. Finally, the `public` class includes the declaration of the `Form1_Load` method, which is used in the `InitializeComponent()` method.

This previous code creates a blank form for your application to which you need to add functionality through various controls. The following section discusses how to add controls to your form.

## Adding Controls to a Windows Form

Visual Studio .NET provides you with various Windows form controls that you can add to your application by just dragging the controls to your form. Figure 8-7 displays the Windows form controls available with Visual Studio .NET.

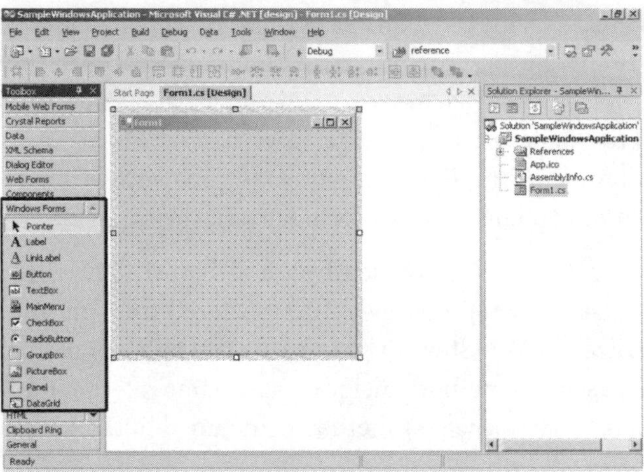


**FIGURE 8-7** *Windows form controls available with Visual Studio .NET*

You will now add a button to `SampleWindowsApplication`. To add a button, drag a Button control to the form. You can place the Button control anywhere in the form. Figure 8-8 shows a Windows form with a Button control.

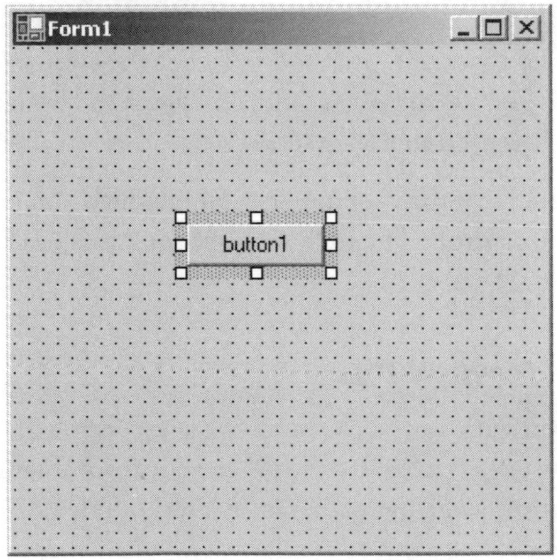


**FIGURE 8-8** *Windows form with a Button control*

As discussed earlier, when you add a control to the form, the declaration of the control is added to the `Form1` class. The following code shows the declaration of the Button control:

```
private System.Windows.Forms.Button button1;
```

As you can see, the button has the text `button1` on it. To change the text displayed on the button, you must change its properties.

## Changing the Properties of a Windows Form Control

You can view the properties of a button in the Properties window. Figure 8-9 displays the Properties window.

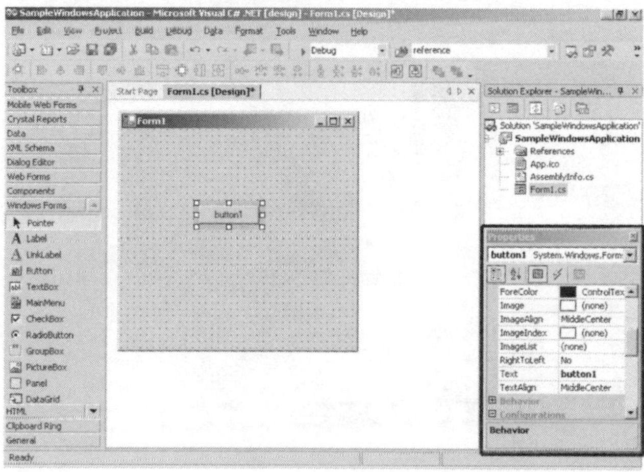

**FIGURE 8-9** *The Properties window*

To change the properties of the button, perform the following steps:

1. Select the button to make it active.
2. In the Properties window, make the following changes to the properties of a button:
   - **Text**: `Welcome`
   - **Name**: `sampleButton`

◆ **Font**:

**Name**: `Arial`

Your button now displays the text `Welcome`. The button that you created, however, does not perform any action. To add some functionality to the button, you need to add code to `button1_Click()` method. You can add code to display a message box when the button is clicked.

```
private void button1_Click(object sender, System.EventArgs e)
      {
            MessageBox.Show("This is a sample Windows Application");
     }
```

The sample Windows application that you created in the preceding code is shown in Figure 8-10.

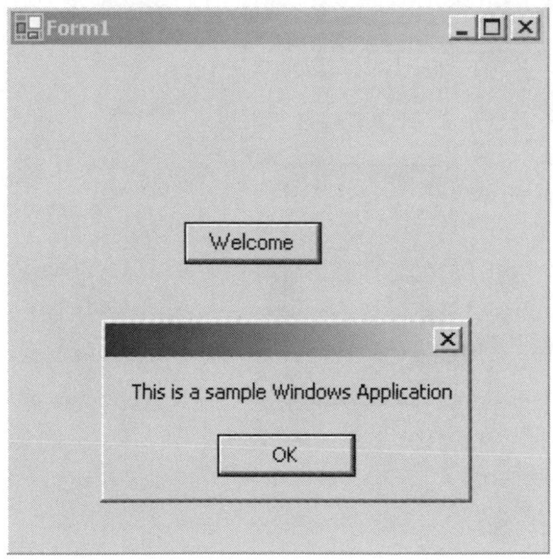


**FIGURE 8-10** *Sample Windows application*

In addition to the Button control, you can create other controls in a Windows application. The following section discusses some of these controls.

## Types of Windows Forms Controls

Windows forms controls are used with Windows forms to accept user input. In addition to using Windows controls that are provided by Visual Studio .NET, you can create custom controls. In this section, you will look at some of the controls provided by Visual Studio .NET.

### Button Control

A Button control is used to allow a user to perform a specified action on the click of a mouse. You can specify the action to be performed in the click event of the button. The following steps will create a Button control in a Windows form, Form1, which displays another form, Form2, when the button is clicked. In addition, Form1 is hidden when the button is pressed. To create the Button control, perform the following steps:

1. Drag a Button control from the Windows Forms toolbox to Form1.
2. Change the following properties of the Button control:
   - **Name:** `btnShow`
   - **Text:** `&Show`
3. Double-click on the Button control to display the code.
4. Add the following code to the `Click` event of the control:

```
private void button1_Click(object sender, System.EventArgs e)
{
                Form2 newForm = new Form2();
                newForm.Show();
               this.Hide();
}
```

**TIP**

If you prefix a letter in the `Text` property of a Button control with an ampersand (&), Visual Studio .NET creates the letter as the access key for the Button control. You can then access the button by using the Alt key in combination with the access key. For example, prefixing an ampersand with the letter *S* in the text property of the Show button allows you to click the Show button by using Alt and S keys.

## Label Control

A Label control is used to display static text or images. You can use a Label control to display the descriptions of controls used in a form. For example, you can create a Label control to specify the description of the Button control that you created in the previous example. To create the Label control, perform the following steps:

1. Drag a Label control from the Windows Forms toolbox to Form1.
2. Change the following properties of the Label control.
   - **Name:** `lblDescription`
   - **Text:** `Click on the Show button to display Form 2`
   - **Font:**

     **Name:** `Arial`

     **Size:** `10`

     **Bold:** `True`

Figure 8-11 shows Form1.

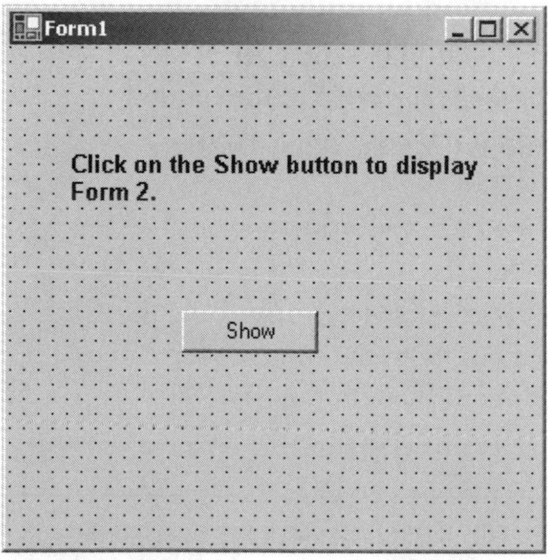


**FIGURE 8-11** *Form1*

## TextBox Control

A TextBox control is used to allow a user to input values to a form. You can also use a TextBox control to display dynamic text. This implies that you can change the value in the text box at run time.

## MainMenu Control

A MainMenu control is used to create menu items in a form. You can drag the MainMenu control to the form to create menu items at run time. You can use the Checked property of the MainMenu control to find whether the control is selected or not. The following steps show you how to create the File menu for Form1.

1. Drag a MainMenu control from the Windows Forms toolbox to the form.

   A menu item is added to the form.
2. Click on the text Type Here and type the name of the first menu item as `&File`.
3. In the text area below the File menu, type `&New` to create the New option.

   Similarly, you can create the Open, Save, Save As, and Exit options.
4. To add a menu item adjacent to the File option, type `&Edit` in the text area to the right of the File menu.

   Similarly, you can create Cut, Copy, and Paste options on the Edit menu.

   However, the menu items that you have created so far do not perform any function. To add functionality to the menu item, you need to add code to the click event of the menu option.
5. Double-click the `New` option to display the code window.
6. Type the following code in the click event of the New option.

```
private void menuItem2_Click_1(object sender, System.EventArgs e)
{
            Form2 newForm = new Form2();
           newForm.Show();
           this.Hide();
}
```

When you click the New option on the File menu, a new form, Form2, is created for you. Similarly, you can write code for other options. Figure 8-12 displays the New option.

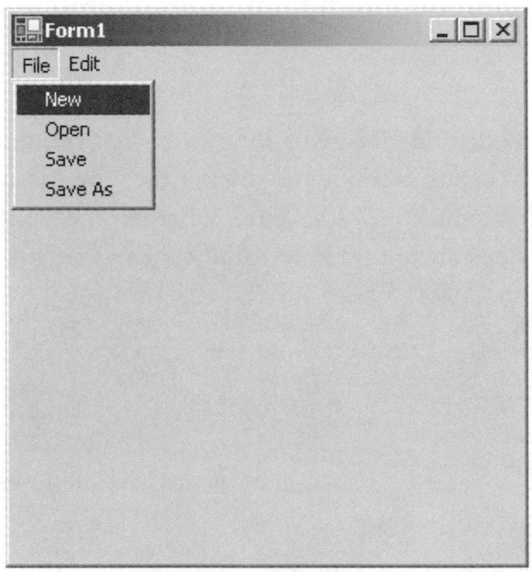


**FIGURE 8-12** *The New option*

## GroupBox Control

A GroupBox control is used to create a group of controls, such as RadioButton, CheckBox, TextBox controls, and so on. You can give a specific name to a GroupBox control that can be used to identify each item in the GroupBox control.

## RadioButton Control

A RadioButton control is used to allow users to select an option from a group of two or more options. You can use a GroupBox control to group RadioButton controls. In the previous example of a Button control, when a user clicks the button, Form2 is displayed. However, in this case, if the user has the option of viewing more than one form, you can create a group of RadioButton controls. To do this, perform the following steps:

1. Drag a GroupBox control to the form.
2. Change the Text property of the GroupBox control to Forms.
3. Drag three RadioButton controls and place them within the GroupBox control.
4. In the Properties window, change the following properties of the RadioButton controls:

   RadioButton1:

   - **Name**: `btnForm1`
   - **Text**: `Form1`

   RadioButton2:

   - **Name**: `btnForm2`
   - **Text**: `Form2`

   RadioButton3:

   - **Name**: `btnForm3`
   - **Text**: `Form3`

To make the radio buttons functional, write the code for the click events of the RadioButton controls.

1. Double-click on `btnForm1` to open the code window.
2. Add the following code to the click event of `btnForm1`.

```
private void btnForm1_CheckedChanged(object sender, System.EventArgs e)
{
                         Form1 newForm = new Form1();
                        newForm.Show();
                        this.Hide();
}
```

The previous code creates an instance of Form1. The instance of Form1 is used to call the `Show()` method to display Form1. The `this.Hide()` statement is used to hide the current form.

Similarly, you can write the code for `btnForm2` and `btnForm3`.

1. Double-click on `btnForm2` to open the code window.

2. Add the following code to the click event of `btnForm2`.

```
private void btnForm2_CheckedChanged(object sender, System.EventArgs e)
{
                    Form2 newForm = new Form2();
                   newForm.Show();
                   this.Hide();
}
```

3. Double-click on `btnForm3` to open the code window.
4. Add the following code to the click event of `btnForm3`:

```
private void btnForm3_CheckedChanged(object sender, System.EventArgs e)
{
                   Form3 newForm = new Form3();
                   newForm.Show();
                   this.Hide();
}
```

5. Save the form by using the Save option on the File menu.

Figure 8-13 shows the GroupBox control with the three radio buttons.

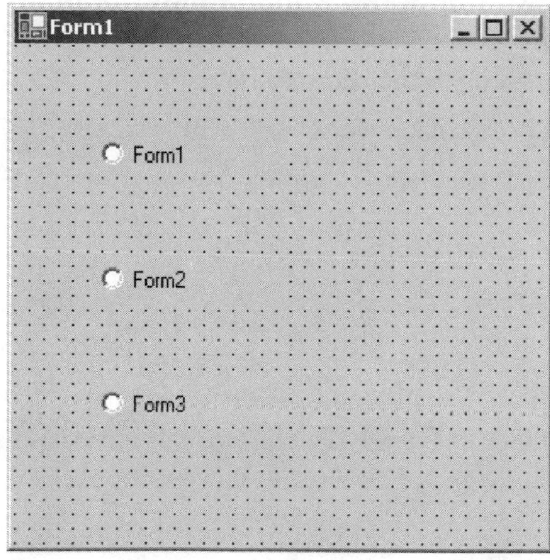


**FIGURE 8-13** *RadioButton controls*

## CheckBox Control

A CheckBox control allows a user to select a state, which can be either True or False. A CheckBox control is similar to a RadioButton control; however, you can create a group of CheckBox controls that allow user to select more than one value. To select an option, a user needs to check the CheckBox control.

To determine whether a CheckBox control is selected or not, you can use the Checked property, which returns a Boolean value, True or False, depending on whether the user has selected the check box or not.

To make a CheckBox control functional, you need to add code to the control. You can use the CheckState property of the CheckBox control to specify the action to be performed, depending on whether the control is checked or not. The CheckState property returns a value of Checked or Unchecked.

## ListBox Control

A ListBox control is used to allow users to select one or more options from a list of items. You can use the SelectionMode property to specify whether a user can select one or multiple options. For example, if you set the SelectionMode property to one, the user can select only one option. However, if the SelectionMode property is set to either MultiSimple or MultiExtended, the user can select multiple options.

To create a ListBox control that allow users to select only one option, perform the following steps:

1. Drag a ListBox control to the form.
2. In the Properties window, set the following properties of the control:
   - **Name**: `listBox1`
   - **SelectionMode**: `One`

   The ListBox control is empty until now. To add values to the control, perform the following steps:
3. In the Properties window, select the Items property by clicking on the ellipsis button.

   The String Collection Editor window is displayed.

4. Add values to the String Collection Editor window by typing each value in a single row.

   You can add values such as `OptionA`, `OptionB`, `OptionC`, `OptionD`, and `OptionE`.

5. Click on the OK button to close the String Collection Editor window.
6. Click on the Save option on the File menu to save the form.

   The values are displayed in the ListBox control. You can now resize the control according to your need. If the options require more space than that provided, a scroll bar appears. Figure 8-14 shows the ListBox control with values added to it.

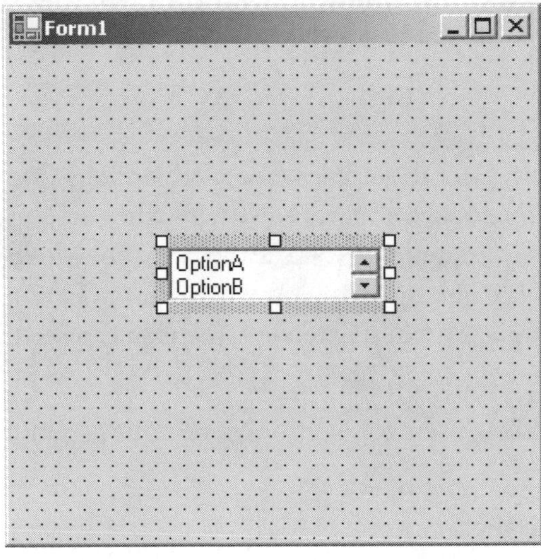


**FIGURE 8-14** *ListBox control*

## ComboBox Control

A ComboBox control allows users to select an option from a list of options. In addition, you can type an option in the ComboBox control if you do not want to select any of the available options.

To determine the option that a user selects, you can use the SelectedIndex property. The SelectedIndex property returns the index value of the item that is selected. However, if you do not select any option, the value returned by the SelectedIndex property is -1.

**NOTE**

Both the ListBox and ComboBox controls are used to allow users to select an option from the items list. However, a ListBox control does not allow a user to enter values. This implies that a user is restricted to selecting an option from the available list. Alternatively, a ComboBox control provides the user with suggested options. The user may or may not select the options that are provided in the ComboBox control.

## MonthCalendar Control

A MonthCalendar control allows users to select a date from a calendar that displays dates and months. By default, the current date is selected. However, a user is allowed to select any other date by clicking on the date value. The user can also change the month by clicking on the arrow buttons that appear at the top of the MonthCalendar control. A MonthCalendar control allows you to select multiple dates. The control also allows you to specify a range of dates that you can select.

## DateTimePicker Control

A DateTimePicker control is used to allow users to select a single date from the calendar of dates that is displayed when a user clicks the Down Arrow button. A user can also type the date in the text box area of the DateTimePicker control. Unlike the MonthCalendar control, you can also specify the time in the DateTimePicker control.

When the user clicks the Down Arrow button, a MonthCalendar control is displayed, which allows you to select a date by clicking on the date in the MonthCalendar control.

Figure 8-15 shows a MonthCalendar control and a DateTimePicker control.

**FIGURE 8-15** *MonthCalendar control and DateTimePicker control*

Having learned about Windows applications in general, you can now apply the concepts to create a Windows application for the Customer Maintenance project.

## Creating a Windows Application for the Customer Maintenance Project

As discussed earlier, you can create a Windows application by using the templates provided by Visual Studio .NET. Name the new project that you create Customer Maintenance Project. When you create the application, Visual Studio .NET creates a default form, Form1, for you. The following section describes adding controls to Form1.

## Creating an Interface for `Form1`

1. Drag a Label control from the Windows Forms toolbox to the form.
2. Click on the Label control to change its properties.

   If the Properties window is not displayed, click on the Properties Window option on the View menu. Alternatively, you can click the F4 key to display the Properties window.
3. Change the following properties of the control:
   - **Text**: `Customer Maintenance System`
   - **Font**:

     **Name**: `Microsoft Sans Serif`

     **Size**: `25`
4. Drag a MainMenu control from the Windows Forms toolbox to the form.

   A menu item is added to the form.
5. Click on the text Type Here and type the name of the first menu item as `&Worker`.

Similarly, you can add more menu items to the form by typing in the area containing the text Type Here. You can add menu items for Customer, Job Details, Reports, and Exit. After adding menu items to the form, you need to change the properties of the menu items.

6. Click on the Worker menu item to change its properties.
7. In the Properties window, change the following properties of the Worker menu item.
   - **Text**: `&Worker`
   - **Shortcut**: `AltW`

Similarly, you can change the properties for the rest of the menu items. Table 8-2 shows the menu items and their corresponding property values.

**Table 8-2 Menu Items and their Corresponding Property Values**

| Menu Item | Property Value |
|---|---|
| Worker | **Text**: `&Worker` |
| | **Shortcut**: `AltW` |
| Customer | **Text**: `&Customer` |
| | **Shortcut**: `AltC` |
| Job Details | **Text**: `&Job Details` |
| | **Shortcut**: `AltJ` |
| Reports | **Text**: `&Reports` |
| | **Shortcut**: `AltR` |
| Exit | **Text**: `E&xit` |
| | **Shortcut**: `AltX` |

Figure 8-16 shows Form1 after the controls are added to it.

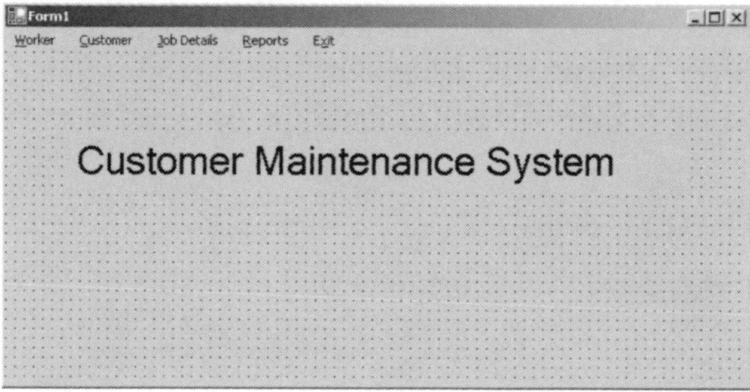


**FIGURE 8-16** *Form1 with the controls*

Similarly, you can create an interface for the rest of the forms.

## Creating an Interface for `WorkerForm`

WorkerForm is used to display the records in the Worker table. You can also add, modify, or delete records from this table by using WorkerForm. However, before creating an interface for WorkerForm, you need to add another form to the project. To add another form, perform the following steps.

1. Right-click on Customer Maintenance Project in the Solution Explorer window and select the Add option.
2. From the list that is displayed, select the Add New Item option.

   The Add New Item dialog box is displayed.
3. In the Templates: pane of the Add New Item dialog box, select the Windows Form icon.
4. In the Name text box, type the name of the form as WorkerForm and click on the Open button.

Visual Studio .NET creates a blank form with the name WorkerForm. You can now add controls to the form. To do so, perform the following steps:

1. Add a Label control, DataGrid control, and four button controls to the form.
2. In the Properties window, change the following properties of the controls:

   Label control:

   - **Name**: `label1`
   - **Text**: `Click on the Edit Button to load the records.`
   - **Font**:

     **Name**: `Arial`

     **Size**: `10`

     **Bold**: `True`

   Button1 control:

   - **Name**: `btnSave`
   - **Text**: `Save`

Button2 control:

- **Name:** `btnEdit`
- **Text:** `Edit`

Button3 control:

- **Name:** `btnCancel`
- **Text:** `Cancel`

Button4 control:

- **Name:** `btnExit`
- **Text:** `Exit`

You will change the properties of a DataGrid control later in this project. Figure 8-17 shows the WorkerForm with the controls added to the form.

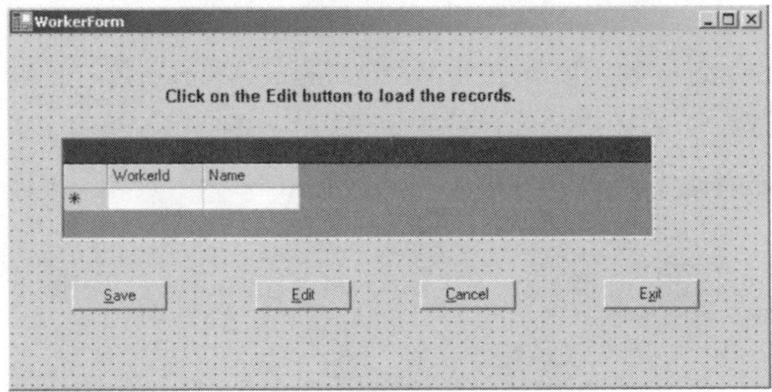


**FIGURE 8-17** *WorkerForm with the controls*

## Creating an Interface for `CustomerForm`

CustomerForm is used to view, add, delete, or modify the records in the Customer table. To create the CustomerForm, perform the following steps:

1. Right-click on Customer Maintenance Project in the Solution Explorer window and select the Add option.
2. From the list that is displayed, select the Add New Item option.

   The Add New Item dialog box is displayed.

3. In the Templates: pane of the Add New Item dialog box, select the Windows Form icon.
4. In the Name text box, type the name of the form as CustomerForm and click on the Open button.

Visual Studio .NET creates a blank form with the name CustomerForm. You can now add controls to the form. To do this, perform the following steps.

1. Add four Label controls to the form.
2. In the Properties window, change the following properties of the controls:

   Label1 control:

   - **Name**: `lblCarNo`
   - **Text**: `Car No.`

   Label2 control:

   - **Name**: `lblName`
   - **Text**: `Name`

   Label3 control:

   - **Name**: `lblAddress`
   - **Text**: `Address`

   Label4 control:

   - **Name**: `lblMake`
   - **Text**: `Make`
3. Add five text boxes to the form.

   You will change the properties of the text boxes after creating DataSet for the form.
4. Add six button controls to the form and change the following properties of the controls:

   Button1 control:

   - **Name**: `btnSave`
   - **Text**: `Save`

   Button2 control:

   - **Name**: `btnEdit`
   - **Text**: `Edit`

Button3 control:

- **Name**: `btnCancel`
- **Text**: `Cancel`

Button4 control:

- **Name**: `btnExit`
- **Text**: `Exit`

Button5 control:

- **Name**: `btnPrevious`
- **Text**: `Previous`

Button6 control:

- **Name**: `btnNext`
- **Text**: `Next`

5. On the File menu, click on the Save option to save the form.

Figure 8-18 shows the layout of CustomerForm.

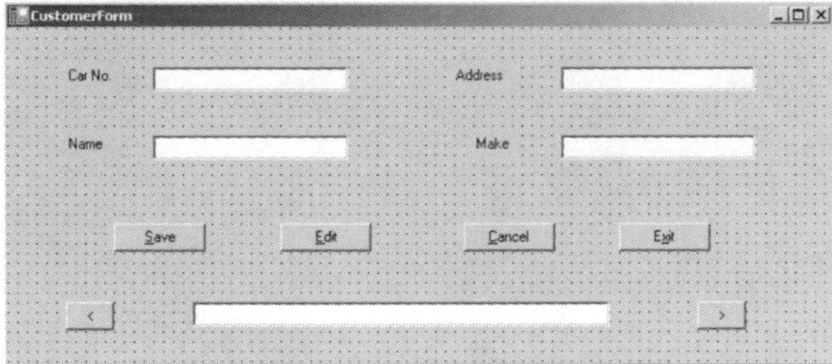


**FIGURE 8-18** *CustomerForm with the controls*

## Creating an Interface for `ReportsForm`

ReportsForm includes a GroupBox control that contains four radio buttons. You can select any radio button to generate a corresponding report. To create ReportsForm, add a new form to the project and name the form ReportsForm. You can now add controls to the form.

1. Add a Label control, a GroupBox, four radio buttons, and a button control to the form.
2. Change the following properties of the control in the Properties window.

   Label control:
   - **Name**: `label1`
   - **Text**: `Select the radio button to generate the report.`
   - **Font**:

     **Name**: `Microsoft Sans Serif`

     **Size**: `10`

     **Bold**: `True`

   GroupBox control:
   - **Name**: `groupBox1`
   - **Text**: `Reports:`

   RadioButton1 control:
   - **Name**: `radioButton1`
   - **Text**: `Monthly Consumable Report`

   RadioButton2 control:
   - **Name**: `radioButton2`
   - **Text**: `Monthly Consumer Visit Report`

   RadioButton3 control:
   - **Name**: `radioButton3`
   - **Text**: `Monthly Balancing and Alignment Report`

   RadioButton4 control:
   - **Name**: `radioButton4`
   - **Text**: `Monthly Worker Report`

   Button control:
   - **Name**: `btnExit`
   - **Text**: `Exit`
3. On the File menu, click on the Save option to save the form.

Figure 8-19 shows the interface of the ReportsForm.

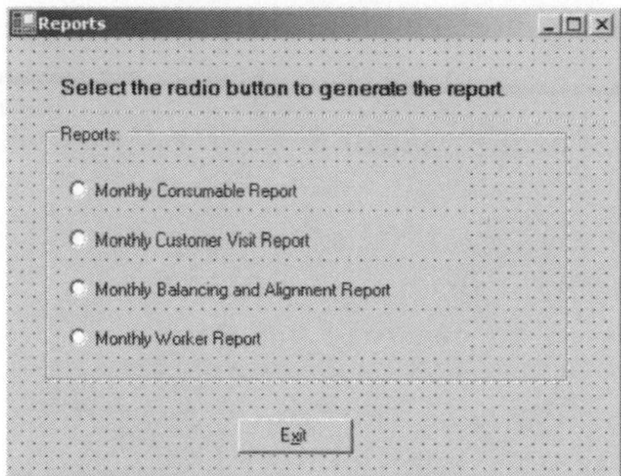


**FIGURE 8-19** *ReportsForm with the controls*

## Creating an Interface for `JobDetailsForm`

JobDetailsForm is used to view and modify the records in the JobDetails table. You can create JobDetailsForm by using Data Form Wizard. Data Form Wizard is used to create forms that interact with an underlying database. You will look at creating JobDetailsForm in the subsequent chapter, which deals with database interactivity in a Windows form.

# Summary

In this chapter, you learned that Visual Studio .NET projects are the containers used to hold the development material for an application. A Visual Studio .NET project contains files, folders, and references to the databases that you may require while developing your project. To develop any application in Visual Studio .NET, you need to create a new project by using the New Project dialog box. You can select the template from the available templates to create a variety of applications, such as Windows applications, ASP.NET Web applications, ASP.NET Web services, console applications, and so on.

Using Visual Studio .NET templates, you can create applications that display the output in a console window. Such applications are called console applications. A console application does not have a user interface and is run from the command prompt. Another type of application that you can create using Visual Studio .NET templates is a Windows application. Visual Studio .NET provides a graphical interface and the classes in the .NET class library for creating Windows applications. Next, you learned to create a sample Windows application and to add controls to the forms in the application. When you create a Windows application by using the templates provided by Visual Studio .NET, a default form, Form1, is created for you in the design view. Form1 is an instance of the `Form` class of the .NET class library and is an interface for your application.

The chapter introduced you to several controls provided in the Windows Forms toolbox. These controls include a Label control, a TextBox control, a Button control, a MainMenu control, a RadioButton control, and so on.

Finally, you used the general concepts explained in the chapter to create the layouts of the forms used in the Customer Maintenance project. These forms include Form1, WorkerForm, CustomerForm, ReportsForm and JobDetailsForm.

# Chapter 9

## Validations and Exception Handling

Validation and exception handling form an integral part of any business application. Your application needs to be robust to withstand any anomalies of application execution.

Anomalies in an application can occur because of unexpected conditions. For example, you may design your application to open a file in the write mode. Although the code will not generate any error if the file is closed, if a user opens the file in another application and then executes your application, your application can generate an unrecoverable error. To avoid such run-time errors, you should implement an exception-handling mechanism in your application.

Exception handling provides many uses in an application. For example, if a user specifies the date in an incorrect format, the user can be allowed to rectify the error and proceed with the registration. Similarly, if the databases pertaining to the application are not responding, the application can display a message to that effect and allow the user to select an alternate location for the database.

This chapter provides an in-depth coverage of the exception-handling capabilities of Visual C#. You will apply exception-handling logic to the Customer Maintenance project. In addition, Visual Studio .NET provides a number of debugging tools that you can use to debug your application. This chapter will also introduce you to the debugging tools and help you use the important ones to debug your application.

## Performing Validations

You should always validate data in a Windows form before updating the data in a database. This method has several benefits, some of which include:

- **Improved response time.** The response time of an application is shorter because the application does not need to attempt to update the data in the database and then retrieve an error message because of incorrect data.
- **Accuracy of data.** The application is less prone to sending incorrect data to the database.

- **Improved database performance.** The load on the database is reduced because it processes optimal transactions only.

In this section, you can learn to validate data for the `JobDetails` form of the Customer Maintenance project.

## Identifying the Validation Mechanism

There are several mechanisms to ensure that only valid values are specified in a user form. Some of these ways are given in the following list:

- Selecting the appropriate Windows control for accepting data
- Trapping incomplete data when users navigate from one control to another
- Validating the form before submitting records to the database

I will now explain each method described here one by one.

### *Selecting Windows Controls*

Often, you can eliminate common errors by using the correct type of controls. For example, instead of using a text box for accepting `date` values from users, you can use the `DateTimePicker` control. Similarly, you can use the `ListBox` control to make the user select an option from a range of options or use the `RadioButton` control to accept one value from a range of values. In this way, the choices available to the user are limited and the user is less likely to make a mistake.

In the `JobDetails` form, the value for the `JobDate` field should be in the `date` format. Therefore, instead of using a `TextBox` control, you should use the `DateTimePicker` control. The steps to add the `DateTimePicker` control to the form are given in the following list:

1. Open the Customer Maintenance project.
2. Double-click on the `JobDetails.cs` form to open the code-behind file.
3. Delete the `TextBox` control from the `JobDate` field.
4. Drag a `DateTimePicker` control from the Toolbox to the form.

The changed form, which is obtained after completing the preceding steps, is shown in Figure 9-1.

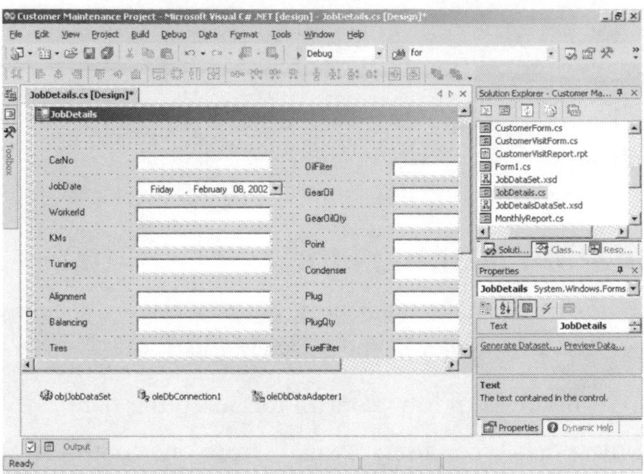


**FIGURE 9-1** *Adding a `DateTimePicker` control to the form*

Run the application and open the `JobDetails` form. You will notice that the current date automatically appears in the form. Similarly, when data is loaded from the database, the `JobDate` field changes to the one that was specified while adding the record, as shown in Figure 9-2.

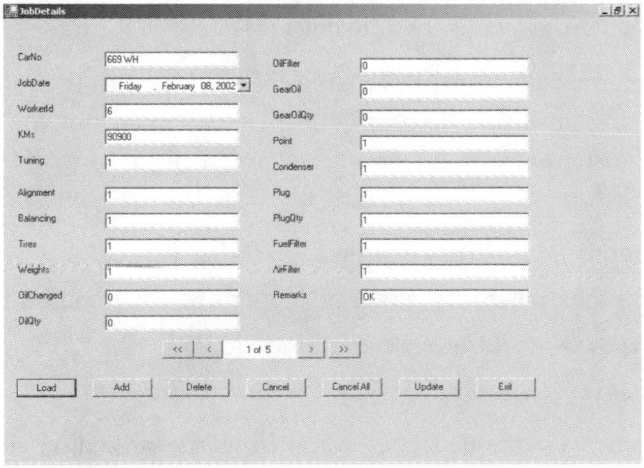

**FIGURE 9-2** *Displaying date and time data from a database*

## Trapping Incomplete Data

There are certain fields in a database that cannot be left blank when you add records to the database. For example, the CMS (*Customer Maintenance System*) database uses the `tblJobDetails` table to store records pertaining to the `JobDetails` form. Follow these steps to check the fields that are mandatory in the `tblJobDetails` table:

1. Open SQL Server Enterprise Manager.
2. In the SQL Server Enterprise Manager window, click on the + (plus) sign next to the name of the SQL server on which the database is installed.
3. In the SQL Server node, expand the CMS database, which stores the `tblJobDetails` table.
4. Click on Tables. The tables in the CMS database will appear.
5. Right-click on tblJobDetails and select Properties. The Table Properties - tblJobDetails dialog box will appear. This dialog box shows the fields of the table in which you can have null values, as displayed in Figure 9-3.

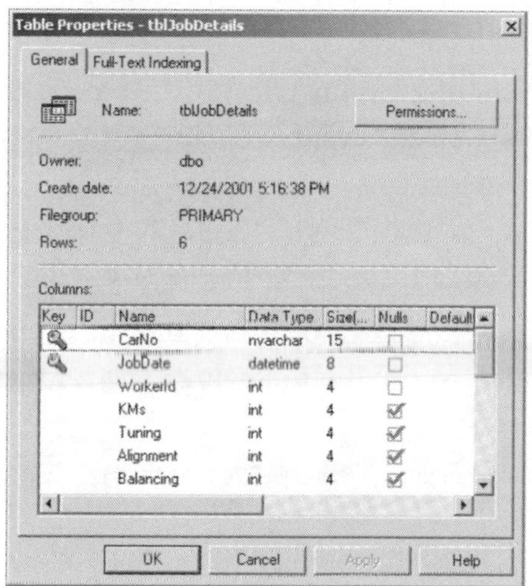


**FIGURE 9-3** *Mandatory fields in a table*

As you can see in Figure 9-3, the CarNo, JobDate, and WorkerId fields are mandatory in the database. The CarNo, JobDate, and WorkerId controls on the JobDetails form represent these fields.

To ensure that a user has specified values for the three fields described above, there are two methods. Either you can validate the required field as soon as a user moves out of it, or you can validate the entire form when the user clicks on the Add or Update button. I examine the procedure to validate an entire form in the next section. In this section, I will describe the ways to validate one field at a time.

When a user selects a control, the Enter event of the control is generated. Similarly, when a user deselects a control, the Leave event of the control is generated. You can use these events to validate controls.

Begin by ensuring that the user has specified a valid car number before the user proceeds to specify the date. When a user tabs out of the CarNo control, the Enter event of the JobDate control and the Leave event of the CarNo control are generated. Therefore, you can check whether the user has specified a valid value for the CarNo either in the Enter event of the JobDate control or in the Leave event of the CarNo control. If the user has not specified a valid value, you can reactivate the CarNo control. To code the functionality, follow these steps:

1. Click on the editCarNo text box in the design view of the JobDetails form.
2. In the Properties window, click on the Events button (the button that has the yellow lightning symbol). All the events available for the TextBox control will appear.
3. From the list of available events, double-click on Leave. The location of this option in the Properties window is shown in Figure 9-4.
4. When you double-click on Leave, Code Editor opens and the event handler for the Leave event is defined. Write the following code for the Leave event of the editCarNo text box:

```
private void editCarNo_Leave(object sender, System.EventArgs e)
{
   if ((editCarNo.Text=="") || (editCarNo.Text==null))
   {
      MessageBox.Show("Please specify a valid value for the car
         number","Error in input");
```

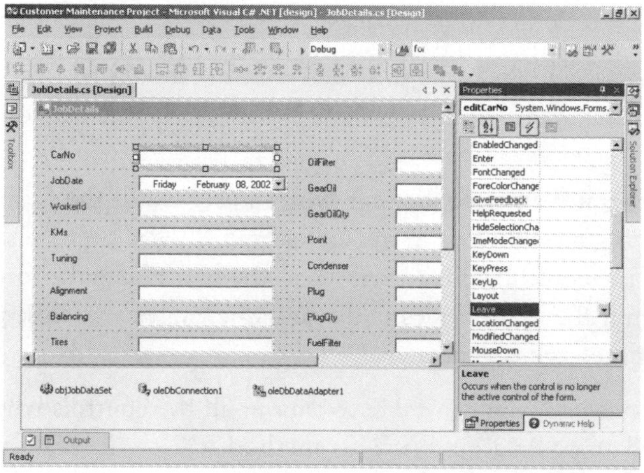

FIGURE 9-4 *Adding event handlers for controls*

```
            editCarNo.Focus();
        }
    }
```

After writing the preceding code, compile and run the application. If you attempt to specify a blank value in the `editCarNo` text box, the application will display an error message and bring the text box into focus, as shown in Figure 9-5.

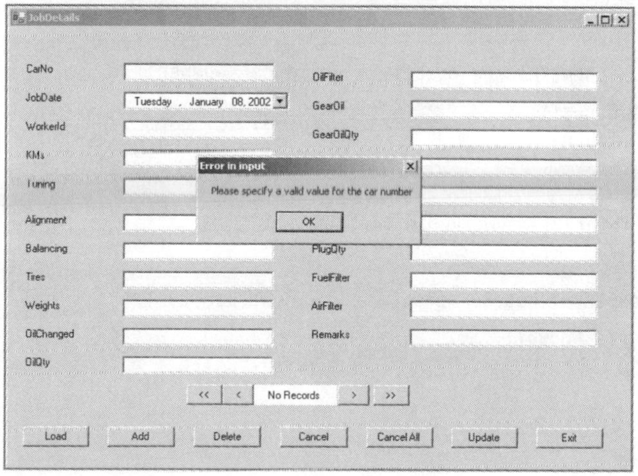

FIGURE 9-5 *Validating data in controls*

The preceding method has two main drawbacks:

- The user cannot decide the order in which controls should be filled. For example, if the user wishes to fill `WorkerId` before `CarNo`, the user cannot do so.
- The control generates an error message when a user closes the form without specifying a valid value in the `CarNo` field. This is because the `Leave` event of the control is fired even when the user closes the form. Therefore, even if the user decides to discard all changes and close the form, the error message is generated.

To overcome these drawbacks, you can validate data in all the controls when the user clicks on the Update or Add button. This method will be discussed in the next section.

## Validating a Form

You can validate data in the `JobDetails` form in the `Click` event of the Update button. Validating all the controls simultaneously saves you the effort of coding events for each `TextBox` control separately. To validate the `JobDetails` form:

1. Open the `JobDetails` form in the Design view.
2. Double-click on the Update button. Code Editor opens.
3. Write the following code for the `Click` event of the `JobDetails` form:

```
if (editCarNo.Text.Length <6)
   {
      MessageBox.Show("Please specify a valid car Number");
      editCarNo.Focus();
      return;
   }
   if (Convert.ToInt32(editWorkerId.Text)<1)
   {
      MessageBox.Show("Please specify a valid worker ID");
      editWorkerId.Focus();
      return;
   }
```

The preceding code displays an error message if the user specifies incorrect values for the `editCarNo` and the `editWorkerId` fields. You will notice that I have not validated the dates and other fields. It is easier to validate these fields by using exception handlers, which will be discussed in the "Handling Exceptions" section of this chapter. Before doing that, the next section will examine the `ErrorProvider` control of Visual Studio .NET.

## Using the ErrorProvider Control

Instead of displaying message boxes each time the user submits an incorrect or incomplete form, you can use the `ErrorProvider` control to show an icon next to the control (which will be referred to as the *error icon* in future references) that has an error. When a user moves the mouse pointer over the error icon, the error message associated with the icon is displayed as a ToolTip.

The `ErrorProvider` control enhances user experience by eliminating the use of message boxes for notifying errors. You have already added the validation code for the `JobDetails` form. Therefore, in this section, you will validate a different form, `CustomerForm`, by using the `ErrorProvider` control. The steps to add the `ErrorProvider` control to the `CustomerForm` form are as follows:

1. Open the `CustomerForm` form in the Design view.
2. Drag the `ErrorProvider` control from the Toolbox to the form. The `ErrorProvider` control will be added to the component tray.
3. Change the `Name` property of `ErrorProvider` to `errCustForm`.
4. Click on the `textBox1` control that represents the Car No. field.
5. In the Properties window, specify a description of the error message in the `Error on errCustForm` property, as shown in Figure 9-6.
6. Repeat Steps 4 and 5 to add error descriptions for all text boxes to the `CustomerForm` form.

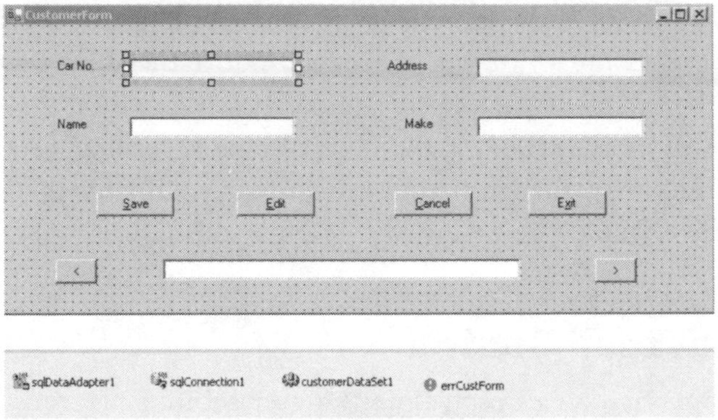

**FIGURE 9-6** *Adding an* `ErrorProvider` *control*

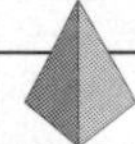

**TIP**

As you add error descriptions to each control in the form, an exclamation point icon appears next to each control.

When you specify an error message with each control during design time, the error icon appears as soon as a user loads the form. To avoid showing an error message even before the user has entered values in the form, you should clear the error message. To clear the error messages associated with controls, use the `SetError` method of the `errCustForm` control. The `SetError` method sets the error message associated with a control. If a blank string is passed to this method, the error message associated with the control is cleared. To clear error messages, add the following code for the `Load` event of the `CustomerForm` form:

```
private void CustomerForm_Load(object sender, System.EventArgs e)
{
    errCustForm.SetError(textBox1,"");
    errCustForm.SetError(textBox2,"");
    errCustForm.SetError(textBox3,"");
    errCustForm.SetError(textBox4,"");
}
```

Next, you need to check for the availability of data in each text box when the user clicks on Save. The code for the `Click` event of the Save button is given as follows:

```
private void btnSave_Click(object sender, System.EventArgs e)
{
   bool flag;
   flag=true;
   if (textBox1.Text=="")
   {
      errCustForm.SetError(textBox1,"Please specify a valid car number.");
      flag=false;
   }
   else
      errCustForm.SetError(textBox1,"");
   if (textBox2.Text=="")
   {
      errCustForm.SetError(textBox2,"Please specify a valid name.");
      flag=false;
   }
   else
      errCustForm.SetError(textBox2,"");
   if (textBox3.Text=="")
   {
      errCustForm.SetError(textBox3,"Please specify a valid address.");
      flag=false;
   }
   else
      errCustForm.SetError(textBox3,"");
   if (textBox4.Text=="")
   {
      errCustForm.SetError(textBox4,"Please specify a valid make.");
      flag=false;
   }
   else
      errCustForm.SetError(textBox4,"");
   if (flag==false)
      return;
```

```
    else
    {
        sqlDataAdapter1.Update(customerDataSet1);
        MessageBox.Show("Database updated!");
    }
}
```

In the preceding code, I have used a variable `flag` of the `bool` data type to determine whether any field has been left blank. When a field is blank, the value of the `flag` variable changes to false and an error message is set on the `ErrorProvider` control. Similarly, after the user specifies a valid value in the field, the error message associated with the field is cleared.

After writing the preceding code, run the form and check the output. To open `CustomerForm`, click on Customer on the main menu of the form. If you click on Save without specifying any value in the `CustomerForm` form, error icons appear for each field in the form, as shown in Figure 9-7.

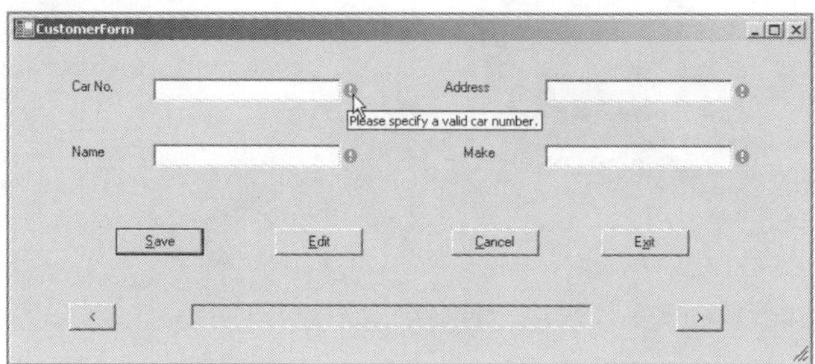


**FIGURE 9-7** *Using an* `ErrorProvider` *control*

# Handling Exceptions

Exceptions are abnormal conditions in an application. For example, if you attempt to update records in a database when one or more of the mandatory fields have been left blank, your application will throw an exception.

If exceptions are not handled by your application, your application will terminate abnormally. In this section, you can learn about ways to handle exceptions in the `JobDetails` form.

## Using the `try` and `catch` Statements

The `try` and `catch` statements form part of structured exception handling. When you know about certain statements of code that may generate an error, you can place those statements in a `try` block. For example, when you specify code to update data in a database or convert data from one format to another, your application can throw an exception. Therefore, you should place these statements in a `try` block.

Whenever statements in a `try` block throw an exception, the `catch` block, which follows the `try` block, catches the exception if the exception is in the same format as that expected by the `catch` block. For example, if you attempt to supply a `string` data type variable instead of an `int` data type, your application will throw an exception of the `FormatException` class. If the `catch` block handles exceptions of the `FormatException` class, the statements of the `catch` block will be executed.

You may wonder if you need to specify `catch` statements for each type of exception that your application generates. It is not mandatory to do so. All exception classes are derived from the `Exception` class of the `System` namespace. Therefore, unless you want to implement different exception handling logic for different types of exceptions, you can use the `Exception` class to handle all exceptions generated by your application.

The syntax for the `try` and `catch` statements is given as follows:

```
try
{
   //The statements that might generate an error
   Statement(s);
}
catch (filter)
```

```
{
   //The statements written here are executed when the statements listed in the Try
   //block fail and the filter specified is true.
   Statement(s);
}
```

The code for the `Click` event of the Update button, after implementing the `try` and `catch` statements, is given as follows:

```
private void btnUpdate_Click(object sender, System.EventArgs e)
{
   if (editCarNo.Text.Length <6)
   {
      MessageBox.Show("Please specify a valid car Number");
      editCarNo.Focus();
      return;
   }
   try
   {
      if (Convert.ToInt32(editWorkerId.Text)<1)
      {
         MessageBox.Show("Please specify a valid worker ID");
         editWorkerId.Focus();
         return;
      }
      if (Convert.ToDateTime(dateTimePicker1.Value) > DateTime.Today)
      {
         MessageBox.Show("Please specify a valid date");
         dateTimePicker1.Focus();
         return;
      }
   }
   catch (Exception exception)
   {
      MessageBox.Show(exception.Message);
   }
}
```

In the preceding code, I used the `try` block for converting the values specified by the user for the `editWorkerId` and `dateTimePicker1` fields to `int` and `date` data types, respectively. If these statements throw any exception, the program control passes to the `catch` block and the description of the error is displayed to the user.

## Using the Debug and Trace Classes

The .NET Framework class library provides the `Debug` and `Trace` classes in the `System.Diagnostics` namespace. The classes can be used to monitor variables in an application. For example, the number of months in a year cannot exceed 12. Therefore, you can use the `Debug` or `Trace` classes to monitor the value of a variable, such as a month. Whenever the value of the variable exceeds 12, the application will throw an assertion failure, which will lead to display of the Debug Assertion Failure dialog box.

**CAUTION**

The `Debug` and `Trace` classes provide the same functionality. However, the `Debug` class is active only in the Debug configuration. Therefore, use the `Debug` class only to debug your application. Do not change application data by using this class because the logic will not work in the Release configuration. Therefore, if you plan to change application data, use the `Trace` class.

You can use the `Debug` and `Trace` classes anywhere in the `JobDetails` form. As an example, I have used the `Assert` method of the `Debug` class to ensure that the date in the `dateTimePicker1` control never exceeds the current date. To do this, complete the following steps:

1. Add a reference to the `System.Diagnostics` namespace by specifying the following line of code in the JobDetails.cs file:

```
using System.Diagnostics;
```

2. Add the following line of code wherever you want to check the value of the `dateTimePicker1` control:

```
Debug.Assert(Convert.ToDateTime(dateTimePicker1.Value) >
                DateTime.Today,"The date has exceeded the current date");
```

When the value in the `dateTimePicker1` control exceeds the current date, a Debug Assertion Failure dialog box is displayed, as shown in Figure 9-8.

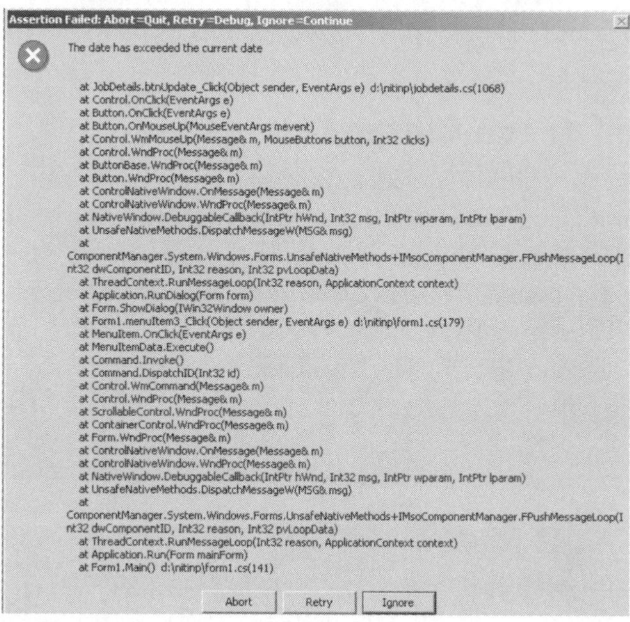


**FIGURE 9-8** *The Debug Assertion Failure dialog box*

# Debugging the Customer Management Application

Visual Studio .NET provides a number of features that simplify the debugging of applications. In this section, you will learn to use the debugging windows and Task List features of Visual Studio .NET. Whereas the debugging windows help you find errors in the program, the Task List helps you maintain a list of pending tasks.

## Using the Debugging Features of Visual Studio .NET

Visual Studio .NET provides 13 debugging windows. Of these, the important ones are listed here.

- **Autos.** The Autos window shows the value of the variable in a code that is currently executing.
- **Watch.** The Watch window can be used to monitor the value of variables. You can add variables to the Watch window and check their values when your application is executing.
- **Call Stack.** The Call Stack window shows the functions and the sequence in which they have been called in an application.
- **Breakpoints.** The Breakpoints window shows all the breakpoints that you have added to your application.
- **Command.** The Command window can be used to check the output of a variable or an expression.
- **Output.** The Output window shows the assemblies and modules that have been loaded by your application.

These windows are available only when you run your application in the Debug mode. When you are in the Debug mode, your application temporarily halts when it encounters a breakpoint. At that time, you can examine the data in each window to determine the state of your application and correct any anomalies.

I will now discuss how to create a breakpoint and then how to use debug windows at the breakpoint.

## Adding Breakpoints to an Application

A breakpoint halts the execution of your application so that you can examine the state of the application, such as the data in variables and the functions that have been invoked in the application. To insert a breakpoint, follow these steps:

1. Click on the line in which you want to insert a breakpoint.
2. Click on the Debug menu and then click on New Breakpoint.
3. The New Breakpoint dialog box opens, which is shown in Figure 9-9. In this dialog box, click on the File tab.
4. The file name and number of the line that you selected in Step 1 are shown in the File tab of the New Breakpoint dialog box. Click on OK to create the new breakpoint.

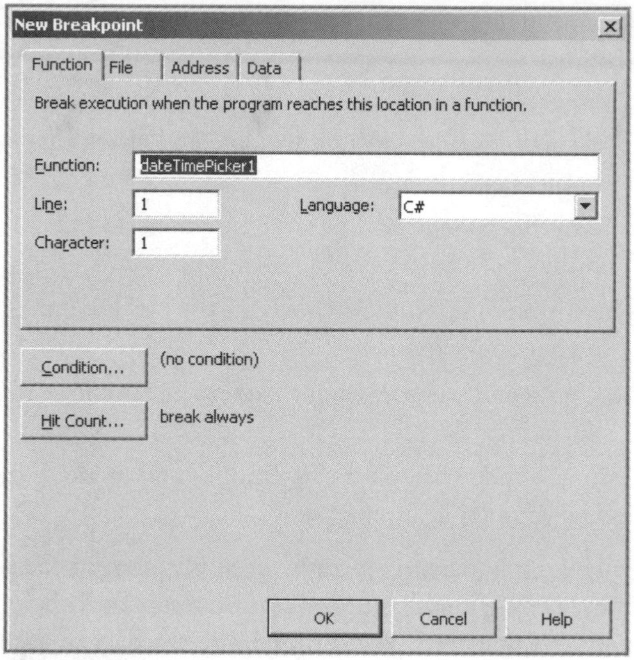

FIGURE 9-9 *Adding a new breakpoint*

## Working with Debugging Windows

To use debugging windows, insert a breakpoint into your application by using the steps given in the preceding section and run your application. When the application encounters a breakpoint, it gets suspended temporarily. In the suspended mode, you can view all the debugging windows. The suspended view of the application is shown in Figure 9-10.

In the suspended view, as you can see in Figure 9-10, the Autos window shows the value stored in the `dateTimePicker1` control and the Breakpoints window shows the breakpoints in the application. Similarly, the Watch and Call Stack windows are shown in Figure 9-11. I have added the `dateTimePicker1` watch expression to the Watch window. The Call Stack window shows the calls to functions that have been already made in the application.

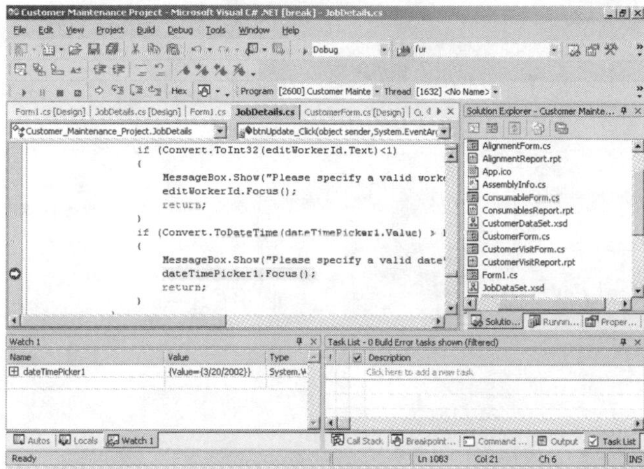


**FIGURE 9-10** *Suspending an application*

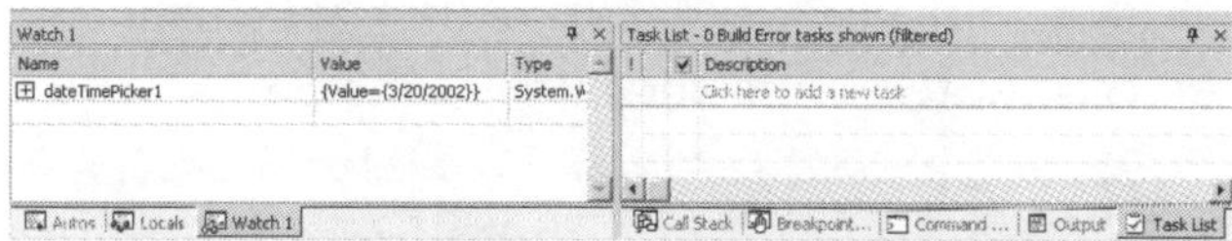


**FIGURE 9-11** *Watch and Call Stack windows*

## Using the Task List

The Task List in Visual Studio .NET is a useful feature that enables you to view a summary of pending tasks in a project. You can use the Task List to view compilation errors, summarize a list of pending tasks, and view the status of pending tasks. To view Task List, follow these steps:

1. Click on the View menu.
2. On the View menu, click on Other Windows and then click on Task List.
3. In the Task List, right-click on the Description field.
4. Click on Show Tasks in the short-cut menu.
5. From the Show Tasks submenu, click on All. All tasks that are currently added to the Task List appear in the Task List, as shown in Figure 9-12.

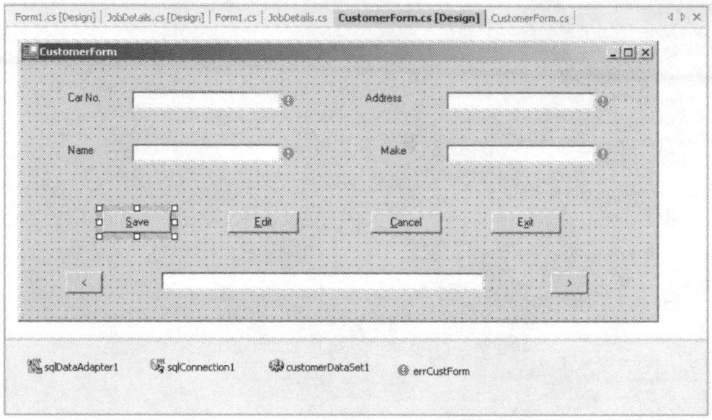

**FIGURE 9-12** *Viewing pending tasks in the Task List*

By default, all compilation errors are added to the Task List. In addition, all comment entries that you create with the keywords `TODO` or `HACK` are also added to the Task List. Therefore, you can create a comment entry such as:

```
//TODO: Add data validation code here
```

This entry will automatically appear in the Task List. Double-clicking on the entry will take to you to the line of code where you made the comment.

You can also add tasks to the Task List directly in the Task List window. Such tasks are referred to as *user-defined tasks*. For user-defined tasks, you can assign a priority of High, Low, or Normal. Figure 9-13 shows a user-defined high-priority task in the Task List.

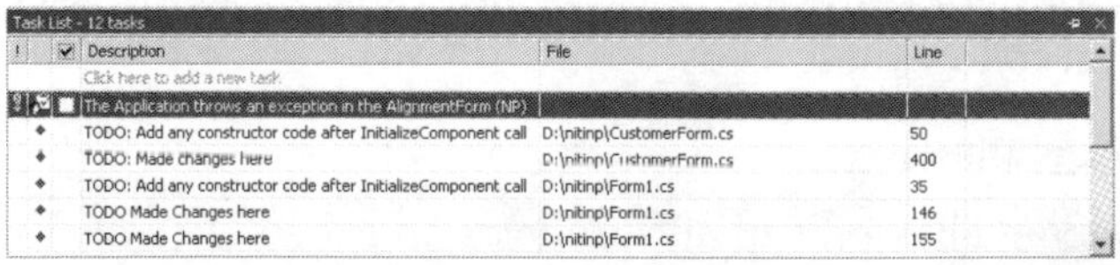

**FIGURE 9-13** *User-defined tasks in the Task List*

# Summary

This chapter explained the concepts for validating code and handling exceptions. There are several ways to ensure that users specify valid data into controls, such as selecting the appropriate Windows control for accepting information, validating data in controls by using the `Leave` event of controls, and validating a form at the `Click` event of a button.

To handle exceptions in applications, you can use the `try` and `catch` statements. You can also use the `Debug` and `Trace` classes of the `System.Diagnostics` namespace to ensure that the values stored in variables remain within expected limits.

Finally, you can use the debugging windows and the Task List feature of Visual Studio .NET to debug your applications.

# Chapter 10

## Database Interaction Using ADO.NET

In most real-life projects, your application needs to interact with a database. To do so, Visual Studio .NET provides you with the *ADO.NET* data access model that helps your application to communicate with data sources, such as a Microsoft SQL Server and Oracle.

ADO.NET is mainly designed to provide data access for distributed applications, such as Web applications. In addition to accessing data from a data source, ADO.NET enables you to modify, add, or delete data from the data source. To provide data access, ADO.NET contains data providers, such as Microsoft Jet OLE DB Provider, Microsoft OLE DB Provider for Oracle, Microsoft OLE DB Provider for SQL Server, and so on. These data providers are used to connect to a corresponding data source, enabling users to access and modify the data in the data source.

In this chapter, you will learn to connect the Windows forms that you have created for the Customer Maintenance project to the corresponding data source. In addition, you will add functionality to the data-bound controls used in these Windows forms. Finally, you will learn to create a form by using the Data Form Wizard.

## Connecting Windows Forms to a Data Source Using ADO.NET

You have seen the design of the database in Chapter 7, "Project Case Study." In addition, you have created forms for the Customer Maintenance project in Chapter 8, "Windows Forms and Controls." You will now learn to connect the forms that you have created to the Customer Maintenance database.

### Creating Form1

Before connecting the WorkerForm, CustomerForm, and JobDetails form to the corresponding data sources, you can add functionality to the menu items that you created in Form1.

Form1 contains menu items used to display the corresponding forms. You have already created these menu items; however, they are not functional. You can add the code to these menu items to make them functional. To do so, perform the following steps:

1. Double-click on `menuItem1` to display the code window.

   When the user clicks the `Worker` menu item, WorkerForm should be displayed. In addition, Form1 should be hidden.

2. To display WorkerForm, add the following code to the `Click` event of `menuItem1`.

```
private void menuItem1_Click (object sender, System.EventArgs e)
{
            WorkerForm newForm = new WorkerForm();
           newForm.ShowDialog(this);
}
```

The previous code creates an instance of WorkerForm named `newForm` and then calls the `ShowDialog()` method to display WorkerForm. The `ShowDialog()` method is used to display WorkerForm as a modal dialog box. As you can see, the `ShowDialog()` method has a parameter `this`. Using the keyword `this` enables you to declare Form1 as the parent form of WorkerForm.

Similarly, you can write the code for the Customer menu item, the Job Details menu item, and the Reports menu item, which are used to display the CustomerForm, the JobDetails form, and the Reports form, respectively.

The Exit menu in Form1 is used to close Form1. Therefore, you need to call the `Close()` method of the `Form` class as follows:

```
private void menuItem5_Click(object sender,
  System.EventArgs e)
{
            this.Close();
}
```

**MODAL AND MODELESS FORMS**

Visual Studio .NET allows you to display a form or a dialog box as modal or modeless in a MDI (*multiple-document interface*) application. A modal dialog box, when active, does not allow you to work with any other form in the application. Therefore, you need to close the form to work with another form in the application. You may even hide the modal form to work with another form.

However, a modeless dialog box allows you to work with another form in the application even if you do not close the modeless form.

## Connecting WorkerForm to the `Workers` Table

In Chapter 8, you created a WorkerForm with a DataGrid control and four Button controls. However, these controls are not functional. You can now add code for these controls to make them functional.

### *Adding Functionality to the DataGrid Control*

Before adding code to make a DataGrid control functional, you first need to understand what a DataGrid control is.

A *DataGrid* control is a type of a data-bound control that is used to display the data from a data source. The data from the data source is displayed in the form of a grid containing rows and columns. You can use a DataGrid control to add, delete, or modify records from an associated data source. In addition, you can use a DataGrid control to display data from one or more tables.

To display the data in a DataGrid control, you first need to bind the control to a data source by using ADO.NET. When a DataGrid control is bound to a data source, Visual Studio .NET automatically creates the rows and columns to display the data. In addition, the data from the data source is loaded to a DataSet object that you create.

A *DataSet* object is a memory cache that provides a relational view of the data from the data source. You can create a dataset to hold data from one or more tables. In addition to displaying the data from a data source, a dataset can be used to store relationships between the tables and the constraints defined for the table.

You will now create a DataSet object that contains data from the `tblWorker` table, which you need to display in the DataGrid control. To create a dataset, you first need to connect to the SQL server that contains the Customer Maintenance database. To do this, Visual Studio .NET provides you with several data adapters, such as OleDbDataAdapter and SqlDataAdapter. These data adapters act as an interface between the dataset and the underlying data source. This implies that a dataset uses a data adapter to communicate with the underlying data source. A data adapter is used to perform the functions of reading and writing data from a dataset to a data source and vice versa.

To create a data adapter, perform the following steps.

1. Drag SqlDataAdapter from the Data toolbox.

   The Data Adapter Configuration Wizard is displayed.

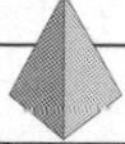

**TIP**

If you need to connect to a database other than a SQL database, you need to use the OleDbDataAdapter.

2. Click on the Next button to start the wizard.
3. In the Choose Your Data Connection page, click on the New Connection button to create a new connection to a SQL database.

   The Data Link Properties window is displayed.
4. In the Provider tab of the Data Link Properties window, select the OLE DB provider to which you want to connect.

   The Microsoft OLE DB Provider for SQL Server option is selected by default. In this case, you will use this option because you need to connect to a SQL database. To connect to some other database, you can select the appropriate option from the OLE DB Provider(s) list.
5. Click on the Next button to proceed with the wizard.

   The Connection page of the Data Link Properties window is displayed.

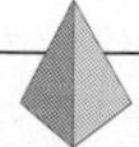

**TIP**

You can also type the name of the server in the combo box.

6. From the Select or enter a server name: combo box, select the server to which you want to connect.
7. In the Enter information to log on to the server: group box, select the authentication mode to connect to a SQL server.

   The Enter information to log on to the server: group box provides you with two radio buttons. To connect to a SQL server by using the Windows authentication mode, you select the Use Windows NT Integrated Security radio button.

However, if you select the Use a specific name and password: radio button, you need to specify the user name and the password in the User name: and Password: text box, respectively. To leave the password blank, check the Blank password check box.

8. Select the Select the database on the server: radio button to select a name of the database to which you want to connect.
9. Select the name of the database from the drop-down list.

   Here, the name of the database is CMS. You may also type the name of the database in the combo box.
10. Click on the Test Connection button to test the connection to the CMS database.

    A message box showing the text `Test connection succeeded.` is displayed if the connection is successful.
11. Click on the OK button to close the message box.
12. Click on the OK button to close the Data Link Properties window.

    The Choose Your Data Connection page is displayed. The name of the database is displayed in the Which data connection should the data adapter use? list box.
13. Click on the Next button to proceed with the wizard.

    The Choose a Query Type page is displayed. The page provides you with several options that the data adapter can use to access the database.
14. Select the Use SQL statements radio button.

    This option allows you to create a SQL statement that enables the data adapter to access the database.
15. Click on the Next button.

    The Generate the SQL statements page is displayed. You can type the query in the What data should the data adapter load into the dataset? text box.
16. Type the following SQL statement in the text box:

```
SELECT WorkerId, Name
FROM tblWorker
```

This SQL statement allows you to select the `WorkerId field` and the `Name` field from the `tblWorker` table. You can also click on the Query Builder button to graphically create the query. The Data Adapter Configuration Wizard uses this SQL statement to create the Insert, Update, and Delete statements to insert, modify, and delete records from the `tblWorker` table.

17. Click on the Next button.

    The View Wizard Results page is displayed. This page displays a list of tasks that the wizard has performed. The Data Adapter Configuration Wizard creates `Select`, `Insert`, `Update`, and `Delete` statements. In addition, the wizard creates table mappings for your database.

18. Click on the Finish button to create the data adapter.

The Data Adapter Configuration Wizard creates a data adapter with the name `sqlDataAdapter1`, which contains information about the table and the fields to which the connection is made. In addition, the Data Adapter Configuration Wizard creates a connection named `sqlConnection1` that contains the information about accessing the CMS database.

After creating a connection by using the Data Adapter Configuration Wizard, you need to generate a dataset. Visual Studio .NET automatically creates a DataSet object when you select the Generate Dataset option in the Data menu. To generate a dataset, perform the following steps:

1. Click anywhere in the form to activate it.
2. In the Data menu, select the Generate Dataset option.

   The Generate Dataset window is displayed.

3. From the Choose a dataset: group box, select the New radio button. In the text box adjacent to the New radio button, type the name of the DataSet object as `workerDataSet`.

   Make sure that the `tblWorker` table is selected in the Choose which table(s) to add to the dataset text box.

4. Check the Add this dataset to the designer. check box.

Selecting the Add this dataset to the designer. check box ensures that the DataSet object is added to the component tray at the bottom of the form in the design view.

5. Click on the OK button to close the Generate Dataset window.

A DataSet object with the name `workerDataSet1` is created. In addition, Visual Studio .NET creates a schema file named `workerDataSet1.xsd` in the Solution Explorer window. This file contains the definition of the dataset. You can double-click on the `workerDataSet1.xsd` file to view the definition of the dataset.

The dataset that you have created contains the data from the `tblWorker` table. However, the data is still not visible to the user. To display the records from the table, you need to bind the DataGrid control to the `workerDataSet1` dataset. Performing the following steps will bind the DataGrid control to the dataset.

1. In the Design view, click on the DataGrid control to display its properties.

   If the Properties window is not displayed, select the Properties Window option from the View menu or press the F4 key.
2. In the Properties window, select the DataSource property.
3. Click on the Down Arrow button to display the list of DataSet objects.
4. From the list that is displayed, select the `workerDataSet1` option.
5. Click on the Down Arrow button of the DataMember property.

   A list of tables in the data source is displayed.
6. Select `tblWorker` from the displayed list.

   A DataGrid control showing the column headings is displayed.
7. Save the form by clicking on the Save option in the File menu.

Figure 10-1 shows the WorkerForm with the DataGrid control.

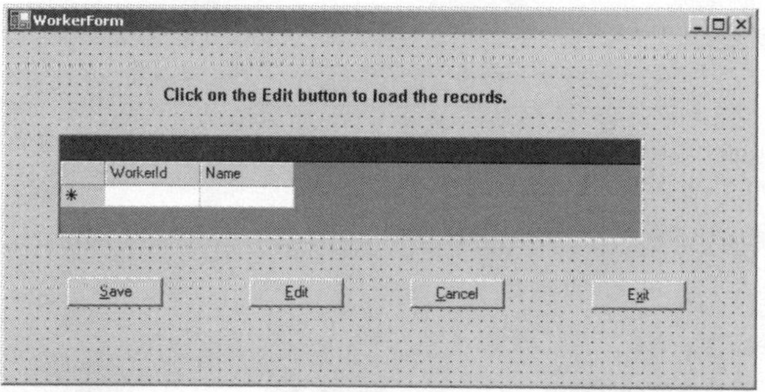


**FIGURE 10-1** *The WorkerForm with the DataGrid control*

As you can see, the DataGrid control contains only the column headings. Visual Studio .NET does not automatically load the records from the table to the DataGrid control. To do so, you need to write the code for the Edit button.

## *Adding Functionality to the Edit Button*

While creating the WorkerForm, you have included four Button controls to the form. However, until now, you have not added code to the buttons. In this section, you will write the code for the `Click` event of the Edit button that loads the records from the data source to the DataGrid control. To do so, perform the following steps:

1. Double-click on the Edit button to open the code window.
2. Add the following code to the `Click` event of the button.

```
private void btnEdit_Click(object sender, System.EventArgs e)
{
        workerDataSet1.Clear();
        sqlDataAdapter1.Fill(workerDataSet1);
}
```

The previous code calls the `Clear()` method of the `System.Data.DataSet` class, which is used to clear records from the tables in the `workerDataSet1` dataset. Then, the `Fill()` method of the data adapter is called to load the records in the dataset. The `Fill()` method accepts the name of the DataSet object as the parameter.

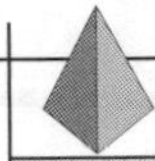

**TIP**

If you are using an `OleDbDataAdapter` to connect to a database, include the following code in the `Click` event of the Edit button.

```
private void btnEdit_Click(object sender, System.EventArgs e)
{
    workerDataSet1.Clear();
    oleDbDataAdapter1.Fill(workerDataSet1);
}
```

When the user clicks on the Edit button, the records from the `tblWorker` table get loaded in the DataGrid control. You can resize the control to display as many records as you want. However, if the records are more than the space provided, a scroll bar is introduced in the DataGrid control. Figure 10-2 shows WorkerForm with the records displayed from the `tblWorker` table.

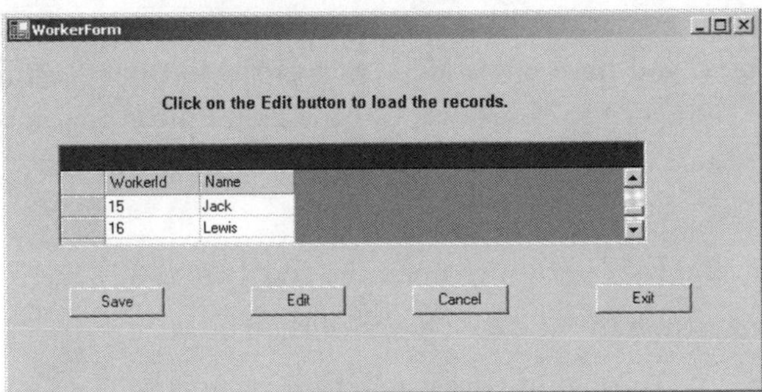


**FIGURE 10-2** *WorkerForm with the records displayed*

## *Adding Functionality to the Save Button*

The Edit button allows you only to view the records. However, when you perform any modifications to the records that are displayed, the updated record is saved only in the dataset. To replicate the changes made by the user to the records in the data source, you need to write the code for the Save button.

Visual Studio .NET provides you with an `Update()` method of the data adapter that you can use to make changes in the underlying data source. Writing the following code in the `Click` event of the Save button will call the `Update()` method.

```
private void btnSave_Click(object sender, System.EventArgs e)
{
                sqlDataAdapter1.Update(workerDataSet1);
                MessageBox.Show("The Worker table is updated.");
}
```

You can make the following changes to the previous code if you are using OleDb-DataAdapter.

```
private void btnSave_Click(object sender, System.EventArgs e)
{
                oleDbDataAdapter1.Update(workerDataSet1);
                MessageBox.Show("The Worker table is updated.");
}
```

The `Update()` method includes the statements for adding, deleting, and modifying records in the database. When a user makes changes to the records and clicks the Save button, the `Update()` method is called. The `Update()` method checks the value of the RowState property to identify the index of the row to which the user has made changes. The `Update()` method then executes the `Insert`, `Delete`, or `Update` command as required.

When the changes are updated to the `tblWorker` table, a message box displaying the text `The Worker table is updated.` is shown. Figure 10-3 shows the message box displaying the message that the changes are updated to the database.

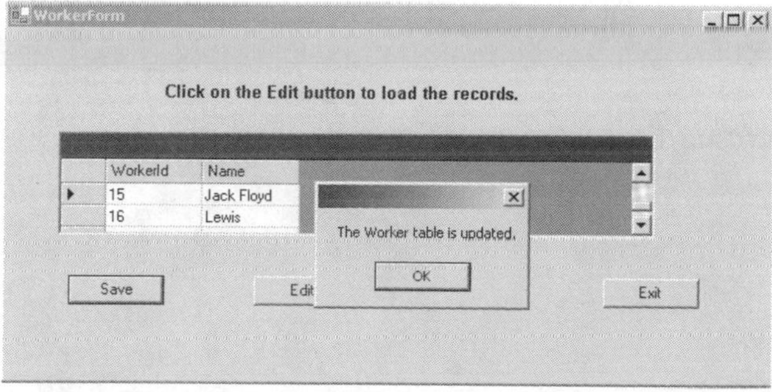


**FIGURE 10-3** *WorkerForm with the message box displayed*

If the user needs to cancel the changes made to the records in the DataSet, the user can click the Cancel button. You can now write the code for the Cancel button.

## Adding Functionality to the Cancel Button

To add functionality to the Cancel button, perform the following steps:

1. Double-click on the Cancel button to display the code window.
2. Add the following code to the `Click` event of the button.

```
private void btnCancel_Click(object sender, System.EventArgs e)
{
            workerDataSet1.Clear();
            sqlDataAdapter1.Fill(workerDataSet1);
}
```

The previous code uses the `Clear()` method of the `DataSet` class to clear all the rows in the dataset.

## Adding Functionality to the Exit Button

After working with the WorkerForm, you need to close the WorkerForm to display the main form, Form1. This can be done by adding the following code to the `Click` event of the Exit button.

```
private void btnExit_Click(object sender, System.EventArgs e)
{
        Form1 newForm = new Form1();
        newForm.Show();
        this.Hide();
}
```

Until now, you have written the code for all the controls in the form. Now consider the entire code for the WorkerForm.

```
using System;
using System.Drawing;
using System.Collections;
using System.ComponentModel;
using System.Windows.Forms;
```

```
namespace Customer_Maintenance_Project
{
    public class WorkerForm : System.Windows.Forms.Form
    {
        private System.Windows.Forms.Button btnSave;
        private System.Windows.Forms.Button btnEdit;
        private System.Windows.Forms.Button btnCancel;
        private System.Windows.Forms.Button btnExit;
        private System.Data.SqlClient.SqlDataAdapter sqlDataAdapter1;
        private System.Data.SqlClient.SqlCommand sqlSelectCommand1;
        private System.Data.SqlClient.SqlCommand sqlInsertCommand1;
        private System.Data.SqlClient.SqlCommand sqlUpdateCommand1;
        private System.Data.SqlClient.SqlCommand sqlDeleteCommand1;
        private System.Data.SqlClient.SqlConnection sqlConnection1;
        private Customer_Maintenance_Project.WorkerDataSet workerDataSet1;
        private System.Windows.Forms.DataGrid dataGrid1;
        private System.Windows.Forms.Label label1;
        private System.ComponentModel.Container components = null;

        public WorkerForm()
        {
            InitializeComponent();
        }

        protected override void Dispose( bool disposing )
        {
            if( disposing )
            {
                if(components != null)
                {
                    components.Dispose();
                }
            }
            base.Dispose( disposing );
        }

        private void WorkerForm_Load(object sender, System.EventArgs e)
        {
```

```
        }

        private void btnSave_Click(object sender, System.EventArgs e)
        {
            sqlDataAdapter1.Update(workerDataSet1);
            MessageBox.Show("The Worker table is updated.");
        }

        private void btnEdit_Click(object sender, System.EventArgs e)
        {
            workerDataSet1.Clear();
            sqlDataAdapter1.Fill(workerDataSet1);
        }

        private void btnExit_Click(object sender, System.EventArgs e)
        {
            Form1 newForm = new Form1();
            newForm.Show();
            this.Hide();
        }
        private void btnCancel_Click(object sender, System.EventArgs e)
        {
            workerDataSet1.Clear();
            sqlDataAdapter1.Fill(workerDataSet1);
        }
    }
}
```

The previous code includes default namespaces, such as `System`, `System.Drawing`, `System.Collections`, `System.ComponentModel`, and `System.Windows.Forms`. Visual Studio .NET creates a default namespace with the same name as that of the project, Customer_Maintenance_Project. Inside the namespace, a class with the same name as that of the form, WorkerForm, is created. The `WorkerForm` class is derived from the `System.Windows.Forms.Form` class.

The `WorkerForm` class includes the declaration of all the controls used in the form. These controls include the Label, Button, DataSet, DataAdapter, and DataGrid controls. In addition, the declaration of the SQL commands, such as `Select`,

`Update`, `Insert`, and `Delete` are included in the `WorkerForm` class. This class also contains a default constructor with the name `WorkerForm`. The constructor is used to call the `InitializeComponent()` method, which is a private void method declared in the `#region` preprocessor directives. The `InitializeComponent()` method contains the statements used to initialize the controls and commands used in the code.

The `WorkerForm` class also includes a protected override of the `Dispose()` method, which is used to deallocate memory to the components that are no longer used by the program code. Finally, the code includes the `Click` event of the button controls that you added in the previous sections.

WorkerForm that you have created is now functional. To test the form, perform the following steps:

1. On the Debug menu, click on the Start option. Alternatively, you can press the F5 key to start debugging.

   You can now click on each button to test the functionality.
2. Click on the Edit button.

   The records in the `tblWorker` table are displayed.
3. Edit a record and click on the Save button.

   A message box showing the text `The Worker table is updated.` is displayed.

Similarly, you can add or delete a record by clicking the Save button. You can also cancel the changes that you made to the records in the dataset by pressing the Cancel button and return to the main form by pressing the Exit button.

As you can see, the main form, Form1, is displayed when you click on the Exit button. Form1 contains the links to the WorkerForm, CustomerForm, JobDetails, and Reports forms. After creating the WorkerForm form, you can now add the functionality to the CustomerForm form.

## Connecting CustomerForm to the `tblCustomer` Table

The CustomerForm is used to display the records from the `tblCustomer` table. To do this, you need to create the DataSet object for the customer records similar to the ones that you created for the worker records. The steps for creating a dataset are the same as discussed earlier, except for the SQL query that you create to select the records from the database.

To create a DataSet object, run the Data Adapter Configuration Wizard. The wizard creates the sqlDataAdapter and sqlConnection objects that you can use to connect to the `tblCustomer` table. However, in the Generate the SQL statements page of the Data Adapter Configuration Wizard, type the following SQL query that selects all the records from the `tblCustomer` table:

```
SELECT CarNo, Name, Address, Make
FROM tblCustomer
```

The previous SQL statement enables the sqlDataAdapter data adapter to connect to the `tblCustomer` table. However, a dataset is still not created. To enable Visual Studio .NET to create a dataset, perform the following steps:

1. Click anywhere in the form to make it active.
2. In the Data menu, select the Generate Dataset option.

   The Generate Dataset window is displayed.
3. From the Choose a dataset: group box, select the New radio button. In the text box adjacent to the New radio button, type the name of the dataset as `customerDataSet`.

   Make sure that the `tblCustomer` table is selected in the Choose which table(s) to add to the dataset text box.
4. Check the Add this dataset to the designer. check box.
5. Click on the OK button to close the Generate Dataset window.

   A DataSet object with the name `customerDataSet1` is added to the component tray at the bottom of the form. Figure 10-4 shows the CustomerForm form with `sqlDataAdapter1`, `sqlConnection1`, and `customerDataSet1` added to the form.

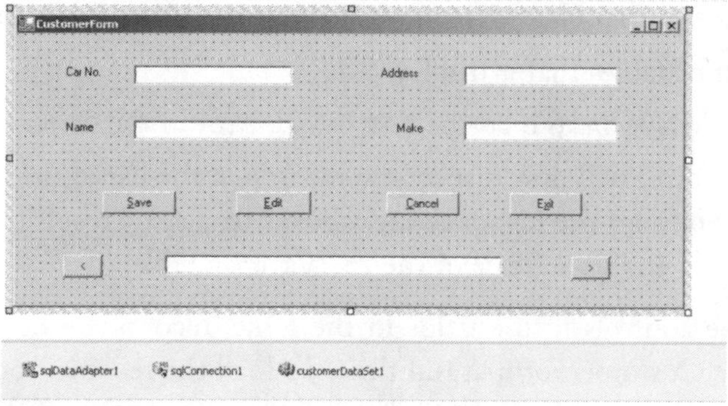

**FIGURE 10-4** *CustomerForm in the design view*

However, generating a DataSet object does not display records in the form. To display records, you can either use a DataGrid control or bind the controls to the fields in the underlying table. In the previous section, you have seen that a DataGrid control displays all the records in the form of a grid. However, you can also display each field in a separate control by binding each control to a field in the table. The following section discusses binding controls to the fields in a table.

## Binding TextBox Controls to Fields in the `tblCustomer` Table

In Chapter 7, you created the interface for the CustomerForm form. CustomerForm includes four text boxes that you can bind to the four column headings in the `tblCustomer` table. You can bind a control to a field in a table by changing the properties of the control. To do so, perform the following steps:

1. Click on a TextBox control to change its properties.

   In the Properties window, change the properties of the TextBox controls.
2. Click on the plus (+) sign to the left of the DataBindings property.

   A list of properties is displayed.
3. Click on the Down Arrow button of the Text property.

   A list of datasets is displayed.

4. Expand the `customerDataSet1` dataset by clicking the plus (+) sign.
5. Expand the list of tables that is displayed.
6. Select the CarNo option to bind the text box control to the `CarNo` field.

   The TextBox control will now display the records in the `CarNo` field. Similarly, you can bind the rest of the text boxes to display records from the `Name`, `Address`, and `Make` fields of the `tblCustomer` table.

Even after binding the controls to the fields in the table, records are not automatically loaded in the CustomerForm at run time. To load the records, you need to call the `Fill()` method of the data adapter in the `Click` event of the Edit button. You can now write the code to load the records in the CustomerForm form at run time.

### *Adding Functionality to the Edit Button*

To write the code for the Edit button, perform the following steps:

1. Double-click on the Edit button to display the code window.
2. Add the following code to the `Click` event of the Edit button.

```
private void btnEdit_Click(object sender, System.EventArgs e)
{
              customerDataSet1.Clear();
             sqlDataAdapter1.Fill(customerDataSet1);
}
```

The previous code calls the `Clear()` method to clear all the records in the dataset. Next, it calls the `Fill()` method to load the records from `customerDataSet1` to CustomerForm. If you are using OleDbDataAdapter, you need to make the following changes to the `Click` event of the Edit button.

```
private void btnEdit_Click(object sender, System.EventArgs e)
{
              customerDataSet1.Clear();
             oleDbDataAdapter1.Fill(customerDataSet1);
}
```

When the user clicks on the Edit button, the records are displayed in the CustomerForm form. Figure 10-5 shows the CustomerForm form with the records displayed.

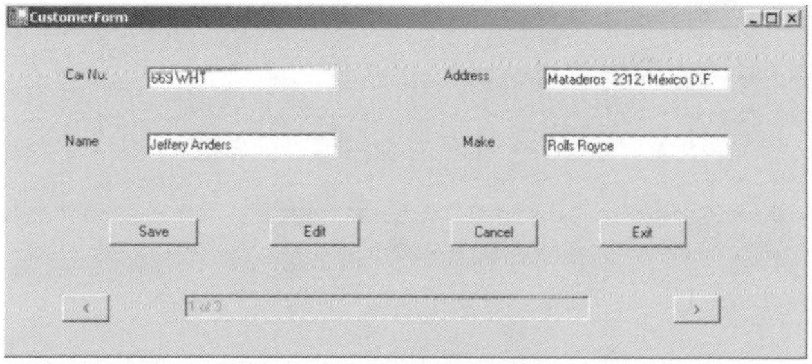

**FIGURE 10-5** *CustomerForm with the records displayed*

When the records are loaded, you can make changes to the records. In addition, you can add or delete a record. To save the changes that you make to the records, you need to write the code for the Save button. The following section discusses how to add code to the Save button.

## Adding Functionality to the Save Button

The Save button is used to save the changes that you make to the records in the `tblCustomer` table. To do so, you need to add the following code to the `Click` event of the Save button.

```
private void btnSave_Click(object sender, System.EventArgs e)
    {
        bool flag;
        flag=true;
        if (textBox1.Text=="")
        {
            errCustForm.SetError(textBox1,"Please specify a valid car number.");
            flag=false;
        }
        else
            errCustForm.SetError(textBox1,"");
            if (textBox2.Text=="")
            {
                errCustForm.SetError(textBox2,"Please specify a valid name.");
                flag=false;
            }
```

```
        else
            errCustForm.SetError(textBox2,"");
            if (textBox3.Text=="")
            {
                errCustForm.SetError(textBox3,"Please specify a valid address.");
                flag=false;
            }
            else
                errCustForm.SetError(textBox3,"");
                if (textBox4.Text=="")
                {
                    errCustForm.SetError(textBox4,"Please specify a valid make.");
                    flag=false;
                }
                else
                    errCustForm.SetError(textBox4,"");
                    if (flag==false)
                    return;
                    else
                    {
                    sqlDataAdapter1.Update(customerDataSet1);
                    MessageBox.Show("Database updated!");
                    }
}
```

Similar to the Cancel and Exit buttons in the WorkerForm, you need to add the functionality to the Cancel and Exit buttons in the CustomerForm form.

As you have seen, a DataGrid control displays all the records in a grid. However, if you are using individual controls to display the fields of a table, as in the case of CustomerForm, a single record is displayed at a time. To view all the records, you need to add Back and Next buttons that allow you to navigate through multiple records.

## Adding Functionality to the Back Button

The Back button allows you to display the previous record of the `tblCustomer` table. To do so, add the following code to the `Click` event of the Back button.

```
private void btnBack_Click_1(object sender, System.EventArgs e)
{
            btnBack.BindingContext[customerDataSet1, "tblCustomer"].Position -=1 ;
            CurrentPosition();
}
```

The previous code uses the `Position` property of the BindingContext object to find the position of the record. To navigate to the previous record, the value of the `Position` property is decremented by one. The code then calls the `CurrentPosition()` method that is used to display the position of the record in the `txtDisplayPosition` text box.

**NOTE**

A BindingContext object is used to manage objects derived from the `Control` class. These controls include all Windows Forms controls, such as TextBox, GroupBox, ListBox, and so on. Each of these controls has an associated BindingContext object. The `BindingContext` class contains several methods that can be used to perform operations on these objects.

The `CurrentPosition()` method is a custom-defined private void method. You can add the code of the `CurrentPosition()` method to the public class CustomerForm.

```
private void CurrentPosition()
{
  int currentPosition, ctr;
  ctr = this.BindingContext[customerDataSet1, "tblCustomer"].Count;
  if(ctr == 0)
  {
    txtDisplayPosition.Text = "(There are no records in the Customer table.)";
  }
```

```
    else
    {
      currentPosition = this.BindingContext[customerDataSet1, "tblCustomer"].Position + 1;
      txtDisplayPosition.Text = currentPosition.ToString() + " of " + ctr.ToString() ;
    }
}
```

The previous code declares two `integer` variables, `currentPosition` and `ctr`. The `Count` property of the BindingContext object is used to find the number of records in `customerDataSet`. The value returned by the `Count` property is stored in the variable `ctr`.

The `if` construct is used to check the value of `ctr`. If the value of `ctr` is equal to zero, it implies that there are no records in the table. However, if the value of `ctr` is not equal to zero, the value of the current record is converted to a `string` by using the `ToString()` method and is then displayed in the `txtDisplayPosition` text box.

Similarly, you can write the code for the Next button. The Next button enables the user to navigate to the next record in the table. To make the Next button functional, add the following code to the `Click` event of the Next button:

```
private void btnNext_Click(object sender, System.EventArgs e)
{
            btnNext.BindingContext[customerDataSet1, "tblCustomer"].Position +=1 ;
            CurrentPosition();
}
```

Figure 10-6 shows CustomerForm.

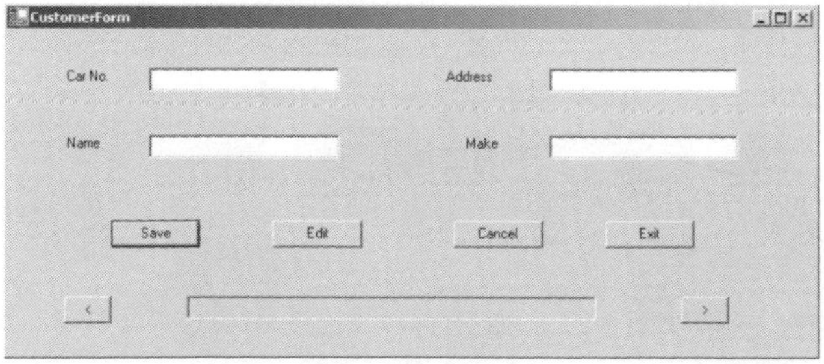

**FIGURE 10-6** *CustomerForm*

After adding the functionality for all the controls, the complete code for the CustomerForm form is as follows:

```
using System;
using System.Drawing;
using System.Collections;
using System.ComponentModel;
using System.Windows.Forms;

namespace Customer_Maintenance_Project
{
   public class CustomerForm : System.Windows.Forms.Form
   {
      private System.Windows.Forms.Button btnSave;
      private System.Windows.Forms.Button btnEdit;
      private System.Windows.Forms.Button btnCancel;
      private System.Windows.Forms.Label lblCarNo;
      private System.Windows.Forms.Label lblName;
      private System.Windows.Forms.Label lblAddress;
      private System.Windows.Forms.Label lblMake;
      private System.Windows.Forms.TextBox textBox1;
      private System.Windows.Forms.TextBox textBox2;
      private System.Windows.Forms.TextBox textBox3;
      private System.Windows.Forms.TextBox textBox4;
      private System.Data.SqlClient.SqlDataAdapter sqlDataAdapter1;
      private System.Data.SqlClient.SqlCommand sqlSelectCommand1;
      private System.Data.SqlClient.SqlCommand sqlInsertCommand1;
      private System.Data.SqlClient.SqlCommand sqlUpdateCommand1;
      private System.Data.SqlClient.SqlCommand sqlDeleteCommand1;
      private System.Data.SqlClient.SqlConnection sqlConnection1;
      private Customer_Maintenance_Project.CustomerDataSet customerDataSet1;
      private System.Windows.Forms.Button btnNext;
      private System.Windows.Forms.Button Exit;
      private System.Windows.Forms.TextBox txtDisplayPosition;
      private System.Windows.Forms.Button btnBack;
      private System.ComponentModel.Container components = null;
      public CustomerForm()
```

```
{
   InitializeComponent();
}
protected override void Dispose( bool disposing )
{
   if( disposing )
   {
      if(components != null)
      {
         components.Dispose();
      }
   }
   base.Dispose( disposing );
}

private void btnEdit_Click(object sender, System.EventArgs e)
{
   customerDataSet1.Clear();
   sqlDataAdapter1.Fill(customerDataSet1);
   CurrentPosition();
}

private void btnSave_Click(object sender, System.EventArgs e)
{
   bool flag;
   flag=true;
   if (textBox1.Text=="")
   {
      errCustForm.SetError(textBox1,"Please specify a valid car number.");
      flag=false;
   }
   else
      errCustForm.SetError(textBox1,"");
   if (textBox2.Text=="")
   {
      errCustForm.SetError(textBox2,"Please specify a valid name.");
      flag=false;
   }
```

```
    else
       errCustForm.SetError(textBox2,"");
    if (textBox3.Text=="")
    {
       errCustForm.SetError(textBox3,"Please specify a valid address.");
       flag=false;
    }
    else
       errCustForm.SetError(textBox3,"");
    if (textBox4.Text=="")
    {
       errCustForm.SetError(textBox4,"Please specify a valid make.");
       flag=false;
    }
    else
       errCustForm.SetError(textBox4,"");
    if (flag==false)
       return;
    else
    {
       sqlDataAdapter1.Update(customerDataSet1);
       MessageBox.Show("Database updated!");
    }
}

private void btnBack_Click(object sender, System.EventArgs e)
{
    btnBack.BindingContext[customerDataSet1, "tblCustomer"].Position -=1 ;
    CurrentPosition();
}

private void btnNext_Click(object sender, System.EventArgs e)
{
    btnNext.BindingContext[customerDataSet1, "tblCustomer"].Position +=1 ;
    CurrentPosition();
}
```

```
private void CustomerForm_Load(object sender, System.EventArgs e)
{
   errCustForm.SetError(textBox1,"");
   errCustForm.SetError(textBox2,"");
   errCustForm.SetError(textBox3,"");
   errCustForm.SetError(textBox4,"");
}

private void CurrentPosition()
{
   int currentPosition, ctr;
   ctr = this.BindingContext[customerDataSet1, "tblCustomer"].Count;
   if(ctr == 0)
   {
      txtDisplayPosition.Text = "(There are no records in the Customer table.)";
   }
   else
   {
      currentPosition = this.BindingContext[customerDataSet1,
         "tblCustomer"].Position + 1;
      txtDisplayPosition.Text = currentPosition.ToString() + " of " +
         ctr.ToString() ;
   }
}

private void btnCancel_Click(object sender, System.EventArgs e)
{

}

private void Exit_Click(object sender, System.EventArgs e)
{
   Form1 newForm1 = new  Form1();
   newForm1.Show();
   this.Hide();
}
```

```
        private void btnBack_Click_1(object sender, System.EventArgs e)
        {
            btnBack.BindingContext[customerDataSet1, "tblCustomer"].Position -=1 ;
                CurrentPosition();
        }
    }
}
```

## Connecting the JobDetails Form to the `tblJobDetails` Table

The JobDetails form is used to display records from the `tblJobDetails` table. Visual Studio .NET provides us with the Data Form Wizard that you can use to generate datasets, add data-bound controls, and add functionality to the controls. Perform the following steps to run the Data Form Wizard.

1. Right-click on Customer Maintenance Project in the Solution Explorer window.
2. From the list that is displayed, point to the Add option and click on the Add New Item option.

   The Add New Item dialog box is displayed.
3. From the Templates: pane, select the Data Form Wizard icon.
4. In the Name text box, type the name as `JobDetails`.
5. Click on the Open button to close the Add New Item dialog box.

   The Data Form Wizard is displayed.
6. Click on the Next button to start the Wizard.

   The Choose the dataset you want to use page is displayed.
7. Select the Create a new dataset named: radio button to create a new dataset.
8. Type the name of the dataset as `JobDataSet` in the text box.

9. Click on the Next button.

   The Choose a data connection page is displayed.
10. From the Which connection should the wizard use? list box, choose the name of the database, CMS.

    You can also create a new connection by using the New Connection button.
11. Click on the Next button.

    The Choose tables or views page is displayed.
12. Add the tables from the list by clicking on the Right Arrow button.

    You can select multiple tables from the available list.
13. Click on the Next button.

    The Choose tables and columns on the form page is displayed.
14. Select the fields that you want to display on the form.

    By default, all the fields are selected. If you do not want to display a field, deselect the field name.
15. Click on the Next button.

    The Choose the display style page is displayed. This page provides you with the option of creating a DataGrid control or individual controls.
16. Select the Single record in individual controls radio button.

    The Add, Delete, Cancel, and Navigation controls check box becomes active. If you do not want a button to appear on the form, you can uncheck the corresponding check box.
17. Click on the Finish button to close the wizard.

Figure 10-7 displays the JobDetails form as created by the wizard.

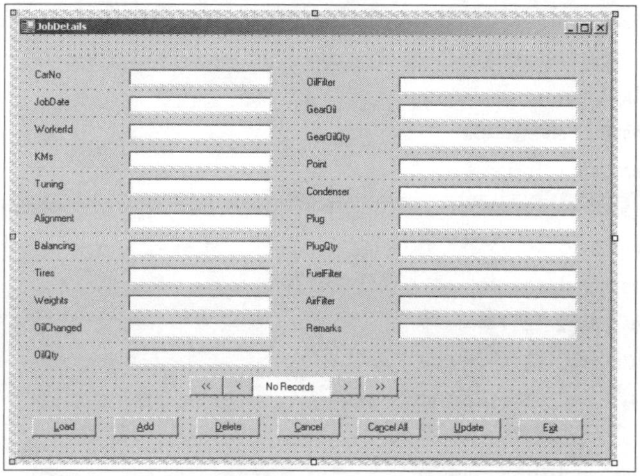

FIGURE 10-7 *The JobDetails form*

As you can see, the Data Form Wizard creates the data-bound controls and buttons for you. You can now change the layout of the form and add an Exit button. When a user clicks the Exit button, Form1 is displayed. In addition, the JobDetails form is hidden. The code for the JobDetails form is as follows:

```
using System;
using System.Drawing;
using System.Collections;
using System.ComponentModel;
using System.Windows.Forms;

namespace Customer_Maintenance_Project
{
  public class JobDetails : System.Windows.Forms.Form
  {
    private System.Data.OleDb.OleDbCommand oleDbSelectCommand1;
    private System.Data.OleDb.OleDbCommand oleDbInsertCommand1;
    private System.Data.OleDb.OleDbCommand oleDbUpdateCommand1;
    private System.Data.OleDb.OleDbCommand oleDbDeleteCommand1;
    private Customer_Maintenance_Project.JobDataSet objJobDataSet;
    private System.Data.OleDb.OleDbConnection oleDbConnection1;
```

```
private System.Data.OleDb.OleDbDataAdapter oleDbDataAdapter1;
private System.Windows.Forms.Button btnLoad;
private System.Windows.Forms.Button btnUpdate;
private System.Windows.Forms.Button btnCancelAll;
private System.Windows.Forms.Label lblCarNo;
private System.Windows.Forms.Label lblJobDate;
private System.Windows.Forms.Label lblWorkerId;
private System.Windows.Forms.Label lblKMs;
private System.Windows.Forms.Label lblTuning;
private System.Windows.Forms.Label lblAlignment;
private System.Windows.Forms.Label lblBalancing;
private System.Windows.Forms.LabellblTires;
private System.Windows.Forms.Label lblWeights;
private System.Windows.Forms.Label lblOilChanged;
private System.Windows.Forms.Label lblOilQty;
private System.Windows.Forms.TextBox editCarNo;
private System.Windows.Forms.TextBox editJobDate;
private System.Windows.Forms.TextBox editWorkerId;
private System.Windows.Forms.TextBox editKMs;
private System.Windows.Forms.TextBox editTuning;
private System.Windows.Forms.TextBox editAlignment;
private System.Windows.Forms.TextBox editBalancing;
private System.Windows.Forms.TextBox editTires;
private System.Windows.Forms.TextBox editWeights;
private System.Windows.Forms.TextBox editOilChanged;
private System.Windows.Forms.TextBox editOilQty;
private System.Windows.Forms.Label lblOilFilter;
private System.Windows.Forms.Label lblGearOil;
private System.Windows.Forms.Label lblGearOilQty;
private System.Windows.Forms.Label lblPoint;
private System.Windows.Forms.Label lblCondenser;
private System.Windows.Forms.Label lblPlug;
private System.Windows.Forms.Label lblPlugQty;
private System.Windows.Forms.Label lblFuelFilter;
private System.Windows.Forms.Label lblAirFilter;
private System.Windows.Forms.Label lblRemarks;
private System.Windows.Forms.TextBox editOilFilter;
```

```
private System.Windows.Forms.TextBox editGearOil;
private System.Windows.Forms.TextBox editGearOilQty;
private System.Windows.Forms.TextBox editPoint;
private System.Windows.Forms.TextBox editCondenser;
private System.Windows.Forms.TextBox editPlug;
private System.Windows.Forms.TextBox editPlugQty;
private System.Windows.Forms.TextBox editFuelFilter;
private System.Windows.Forms.TextBox editAirFilter;
private System.Windows.Forms.TextBox editRemarks;
private System.Windows.Forms.Button btnNavFirst;
private System.Windows.Forms.Button btnNavPrev;
private System.Windows.Forms.Label lblNavLocation;
private System.Windows.Forms.Button btnNavNext;
private System.Windows.Forms.Button btnLast;
private System.Windows.Forms.Button btnAdd;
private System.Windows.Forms.Button btnDelete;
private System.Windows.Forms.Button btnCancel;
private System.Windows.Forms.Button btnExit;
private System.ComponentModel.Container components = null;

public JobDetails()
{
  InitializeComponent();
}

protected override void Dispose( bool disposing )
{
  if( disposing )
  {
    if(components != null)
    {
      components.Dispose();
    }
  }
  base.Dispose( disposing );
}
```

```
public void FillDataSet(Customer_Maintenance_Project.JobDataSet dataSet)
{
    dataSet.EnforceConstraints = false;
    try
    {
        this.oleDbConnection1.Open();
        this.oleDbDataAdapter1.Fill(dataSet);
    }
    catch (System.Exception fillException)
    {
        throw fillException;
    }
    finally
    {
        dataSet.EnforceConstraints = true;
        this.oleDbConnection1.Close();
    }
}

public void UpdateDataSource(Customer_Maintenance_Project.JobDataSet ChangedRows)
{
    try
    {
        if ((ChangedRows != null))
        {
            this.oleDbConnection1.Open();
            oleDbDataAdapter1.Update(ChangedRows);
        }
    }
    catch (System.Exception updateException)
    {
        throw updateException;
    }
    finally
    {
        this.oleDbConnection1.Close();
    }
}
```

```
public void LoadDataSet()
{
    Customer_Maintenance_Project.JobDataSet objDataSetTemp;
    objDataSetTemp = new Customer_Maintenance_Project.JobDataSet();
    try
    {
        this.FillDataSet(objDataSetTemp);
    }
    catch (System.Exception eFillDataSet)
    {
        throw eFillDataSet;
    }
    try
    {
        objJobDataSet.Clear();
        objJobDataSet.Merge(objDataSetTemp);
    }
        catch (System.Exception eLoadMerge)
    {
        throw eLoadMerge;
    }
}

public void UpdateDataSet()
{
    Customer_Maintenance_Project.JobDataSet objDataSetChanges =
      new Customer_Maintenance_Project.JobDataSet();
    this.BindingContext[objJobDataSet,"tblJobDetails"].EndCurrentEdit();
    objDataSetChanges =
       ((Customer_Maintenance_Project.JobDataSet)(objJobDataSet.GetChanges()));
    if ((objDataSetChanges != null))
    {
        try
        {
            this.UpdateDataSource(objDataSetChanges);
            objJobDataSet.Merge(objDataSetChanges);
```

```
                objJobDataSet.AcceptChanges();
                MessageBox.Show("Database Updated!");
            }
            catch (System.Exception eUpdate)
            {
                throw eUpdate;
            }
        }
    }

    private void btnCancelAll_Click(object sender, System.EventArgs e)
    {
        this.objJobDataSet.RejectChanges();
    }

    private void objJobDataSet_PositionChanged()
    {
        this.lblNavLocation.Text = ((((this.BindingContext[objJobDataSet,"tblJobDetails"].
           Position + 1)).ToString() + " of  ")
+ this.BindingContext[objJobDataSet,"tblJobDetails"].Count.ToString());
    }

    private void btnNavNext_Click(object sender, System.EventArgs e)
    {
        this.BindingContext[objJobDataSet,"tblJobDetails"].Position =
           (this.BindingContext[objJobDataSet,"tblJobDetails"].Position + 1);
        this.objJobDataSet_PositionChanged();
    }

    private void btnNavPrev_Click(object sender, System.EventArgs e)
    {
        this.BindingContext[objJobDataSet,"tblJobDetails"].Position =
           (this.BindingContext[objJobDataSet,"tblJobDetails"].Position - 1);
        this.objJobDataSet_PositionChanged();
}
```

```
private void btnLast_Click(object sender, System.EventArgs e)
{
    this.BindingContext[objJobDataSet,"tblJobDetails"].Position =
       (this.objJobDataSet.Tables["tblJobDetails"].Rows.Count - 1);
    this.objJobDataSet_PositionChanged();
}

private void btnNavFirst_Click(object sender, System.EventArgs e)
{
this.BindingContext[objJobDataSet,"tblJobDetails"].Position = 0;
this.objJobDataSet_PositionChanged();
}

private void btnLoad_Click(object sender, System.EventArgs e)
{
    try
    {
        this.LoadDataSet();
    }
    catch (System.Exception eLoad)
    {
        System.Windows.Forms.MessageBox.Show(eLoad.Message);
    }
    this.objJobDataSet_PositionChanged();
}

private void btnUpdate_Click(object sender, System.EventArgs e)
{
       if (editCarNo.Text.Length <6)
       {
    MessageBox.Show("Please specify a valid car Number");
    editCarNo.Focus();
        return;
       }
```

```
        try
        {
    if (Convert.ToInt32(editWorkerId.Text)<1)
    {
         MessageBox.Show("Please specify a valid worker ID");
         editWorkerId.Focus();
         return;
    }
    if (Convert.ToDateTime(dateTimePicker1.Value) > DateTime.Today)
    {
         MessageBox.Show("Please specify a valid date");
         dateTimePicker1.Focus();
         return;
    }
        }
        catch (Exception exception)
        {
    MessageBox.Show(exception.Message);
        }
    try
    {
        this.UpdateDataSet();
    }
    catch (System.Exception eUpdate)
    {
        System.Windows.Forms.MessageBox.Show(eUpdate.Message);
    }
    this.objJobDataSet_PositionChanged();
}

private void btnAdd_Click(object sender, System.EventArgs e)
{
    try
    {
        this.BindingContext[objJobDataSet,"tblJobDetails"].EndCurrentEdit();
        this.BindingContext[objJobDataSet,"tblJobDetails"].AddNew();
    }
```

```
            catch (System.Exception eEndEdit)
        {
            System.Windows.Forms.MessageBox.Show(eEndEdit.Message);
        }
        this.objJobDataSet_PositionChanged();
    }

    private void btnDelete_Click(object sender, System.EventArgs e)
    {
        if ((this.BindingContext[objJobDataSet,"tblJobDetails"].Count > 0))
        {
            this.BindingContext[objJobDataSet,"tblJobDetails"].
               RemoveAt(this.BindingContext[objJobDataSet,"tblJobDetails"].Position);
            this.objJobDataSet_PositionChanged();
        }
    }

    private void btnCancel_Click(object sender, System.EventArgs e)
    {
        this.BindingContext[objJobDataSet,"tblJobDetails"].CancelCurrentEdit();
        this.objJobDataSet_PositionChanged();
    }

    private void btnExit_Click(object sender, System.EventArgs e)
    {
        Form1 newForm1 = new  Form1();
        newForm1.Show();
        this.Hide();
    }

    private void JobDetails_Load(object sender, System.EventArgs e)
    {

    }
  }
}
```

The previous code creates a namespace with the name of the project, `Customer Maintenance Project`. Inside the namespace, the `JobDetails` class is created. This class is derived from the `System.Windows.Forms.Form` class. The `JobDetails` class contains the declaration of all the controls and the SQL statements used in the JobDetails form. In addition, the class contains the declaration of the data adapter, dataset, and the connection objects created by the Data Form Wizard.

The class also contains a default constructor with the name of the class, `JobDetails`. The `JobDetails` constructor includes a method call statement for the `InitializeComponent()` method. The `InitializeComponent()` method is defined in the `#region` preprocessor directives and contains the initialization statements for all the controls and the SQL commands used in the code. The controls are initialized using the `new` keyword.

In addition to the public constructor, the `JobDetails` class defines the `Dispose()` method, which is called to deallocate memory used by the components that are no longer used by the project.

As you can see, the JobDetails form includes the Load, Add, Delete, Cancel, Cancel All, and Update buttons. The following sections discuss each of these buttons in detail.

## *The Load Button*

The Load button is used to display the records in the `JobDetails` table. The `Click` event of the Load button includes the `try` and `catch` statements. In the `try` statement, the `LoadDataSet()` method is called. The `LoadDataSet()` method is used to create a temporary dataset, `objDataSetTemp`, which holds the records returned by the `FillDataSet()` method. This method is called in the `try` statement of the `LoadDataSet()` method. The `try` statement is then followed by the `catch` statement that throws an `eFillDataSet` exception.

After the records are loaded into a temporary dataset, the records from the `tblJobDetails` table are merged in the dataset object, `objJobDataSet`, by using the `Merge()` method. The `Merge()` method takes the name of the temporary dataset as the parameter. Figure 10-8 displays the JobDetails form with records loaded from the `tblJobDetails` table.

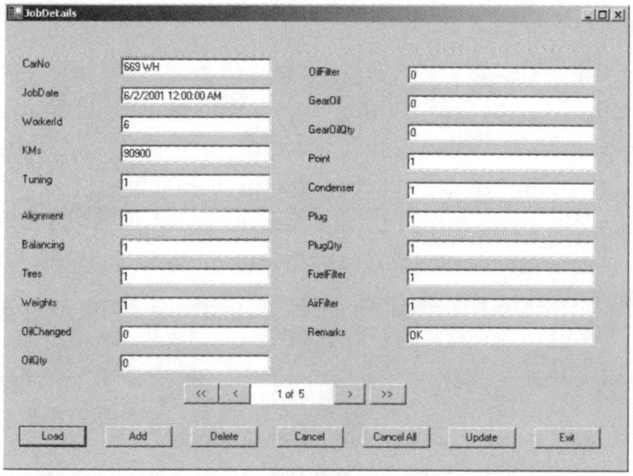

**FIGURE 10-8** *The JobDetails form*

## The Add Button

The Add button is used to add a new record to the `tblJobDetails` table. The `Click` event of the Add button includes `try` and `catch` statements. Inside the `try` statement, a BindingContext object is used to add a new record to the underlying table.

First, the `EndCurrentEdit()` method of the `BindingManagerBase` class is used to stop any edit action that is taking place. Next, the `AddNew()` method of the `BindingManagerBase` class is called that adds a new record to the underlying table. When the record is added, the `objJobDataSet_PositionChanged()` method is used to display the position of the new record in the `lblNavLocation` label.

**NOTE**

The `BindingManagerBase` class is an abstract class in the `System.Windows.Forms` namespace. The methods defined in the `BindingManagerBase` class are used to perform operations on the objects that are bound to same data source.

### The Delete Button

The Delete button is used to delete the displayed record from the tblJobDetails table. In the Click event of the Delete button, an if loop is created that checks whether records are present in the table. The Count property of the BindingContext object is used to find the number of records in the objJobDataSet dataset. If the count is greater than zero, the record at the current position is deleted from the dataset. Next, the objJobDataSet_PositionChanged() method is used to display the position of the next record in the lblNavLocation label.

### The Cancel Button

The Cancel button is used to cancel any changes made to the records in the dataset. To do so, the CancelCurrentEdit() method of the BindingManagerBase class is used. The objJobDataSet_PositionChanged() method is then called to refresh the position of the records in the lblNavLocation label.

### The Cancel All Button

The Cancel All button is used to reject all the changes that are made to the records in the dataset by using the RejectChanges() method. This method rolls back any changes made to the dataset from the time the dataset was created.

### The Update Button

The Update button is used to modify any records in a dataset. The Click event of the Update button includes a call to the UpdateDateSet() method defined in the code. The UpdateDateSet() method creates an instance, objDataSetChanges, of a dataset. The changes made to the objJobDataSet dataset are retrieved by using the GetChanges() method and are stored in the objDataSetChanges dataset.

The UpdateDateSet() method contains an if loop, which is used to check whether changes are made to the objJobDataSet dataset. If the value of objDataSetChanges is not equal to null, the changes made to the objJobDataSet dataset are updated to the underlying data source by using the UpdateDataSource() method. The UpdateDataSource() method is a public void method defined in the JobDetails class. This method calls the Update() method to add, delete, or modify records in the tblJobDetails table.

After creating the `JobDetails` form using the Data Form Wizard, you can test the form by either pressing the F5 key or clicking on the Start command in the Debug menu.

## Summary

In this chapter, you learned about the basics of ADO.NET. ADO.NET is a data access model that helps your application to communicate with data sources, such as the Microsoft SQL Server data source. In addition, by using ADO.NET, your application can interact with other OLE DB data sources, such as Oracle. Next, you learned to create database connections of a Windows form with a data source. Finally, you looked at the code for each of the Windows forms created for the Customer Maintenance project.

# Chapter 11

## Crystal Reports

Crystal reports are a powerful tool used to create and view reports that display selective data. For example, you can create a crystal report to view the sales data of an organization for a particular year.

You have been creating crystal reports in various languages. Visual Studio .NET also provides you with the Crystal Reports Designer tool that helps you create a wide variety of reports easily and efficiently. In addition, you can use the Crystal Reports Designer tool to modify an existing report.

In this chapter, you will be introduced to the Crystal Reports Designer tool. Next, you will learn to create a crystal report by using the Crystal Report Gallery present in the Crystal Reports Designer tool. Finally, you will use the Windows Forms Viewer control to host and view the reports in a Windows form.

## Introduction to the Crystal Reports Designer Tool

Visual Studio .NET provides you with a powerful tool called the *Crystal Reports Designer tool* for creating and modifying crystal reports. It is a common tool for creating reports in the .NET Framework, which can be used by any language supported by the .NET Framework, such as Visual Basic .NET, Visual C#, and Visual C++.

The Crystal Reports Designer tool enables you to create reports that can be hosted in a Windows platform or published as Report Web Services on a Web server. To view a crystal report in a Windows application, Visual Studio .NET provides you with a Windows Forms Viewer control. However, to view a crystal report in a Web application, you use a Web Forms Viewer control. In this chapter, you will be creating crystal reports for a Windows application.

The Crystal Reports Designer tool contains the Crystal Report Gallery, which allows you to select Report Expert. Report Expert is a wizard that helps you create various types of crystal reports. You will learn more about the Crystal Report Gallery and Report Expert in the following sections.

# Creating the Reports Form

The Reports form contains four radio buttons. Clicking on any radio button generates the corresponding report. To add functionality to these radio buttons, perform the following steps:

1. Double-click on the first radio button to open the code window.

   On selecting this radio button, a user should be able to view the ConsumableForm form that contains the report of the consumable products used in a month.
2. To display the ConsumableForm form, add the following code to the `CheckedChanged` event of `radioButton1`.

```
private void radioButton1_CheckedChanged(object sender, System.EventArgs e)
{
        ConsumableForm newForm = new ConsumableForm();
        newForm.Show();
        this.Hide();
}
```

The previous code displays ConsumableForm when the user selects the first radio button. However, you have not yet created the crystal report. The following section discusses how to create crystal reports.

## Creating Crystal Reports

As discussed earlier, Visual Studio .NET provides you with the Crystal Report Gallery that consists of several standard wizards called *Report Experts*. These Report Experts enable you to create crystal reports easily and efficiently. The Crystal Report Gallery also provides you with the option of creating a crystal report by using a blank report or an existing report. In this section, you will learn to create a crystal report by using Report Expert. To open the Crystal Report Gallery, perform the following steps:

1. In the Solution Explorer window, right-click the name of the project, Customer Maintenance Project.
2. From the displayed list, point to the Add option and then select the Add New Item option.

   The Add New Item dialog box is displayed.

3. In the Templates: pane of the Add New Item dialog box, select the Crystal Report icon.
4. In the Name: text box, type `ConsumablesReport.rpt` as the name and click on the Open button.

   The Crystal Report Gallery dialog box is displayed.
5. In the Create a Crystal Report Document group box, select the Using the Report Expert radio button.

You can select the As a Blank Report or the From an Existing Report radio button to create a crystal report by using a blank template or an existing template, respectively.

As discussed earlier, the Crystal Report Gallery provides you with several Report Experts. The following section discusses various Report Experts provided by the Crystal Report Gallery.

## The Report Experts Provided by the Crystal Report Gallery

The Report Experts in Visual Studio .NET allow you to create reports with different formats. Figure 11-1 shows the Crystal Report Gallery dialog box containing various Report Experts.

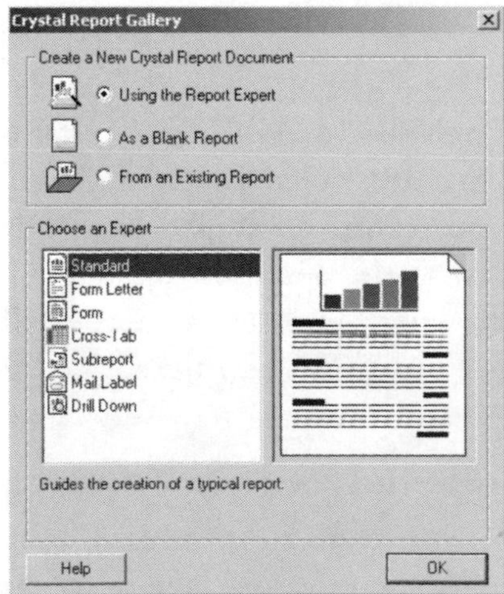


**FIGURE 11-1** *The Crystal Report Gallery dialog box*

Table 11-1 lists various Report Experts in the Crystal Report Gallery dialog box.

**Table 11-1 The Report Experts**

| Report Experts | Description |
|---|---|
| Standard | You can use Standard Report Expert to create a typical report. |
| Form Letter | You can use Form Letter Report Expert to create a report that contains customer information in addition to the standard text. |
| Form | You can use Form Report Expert to create a report in the form of a letterhead that contains the logo of the organization. |
| Cross-Tab | You can use Cross-Tab Report Expert to create a summary of a report in the form of a grid. |
| Subreport | You can use Subreport Report Expert to create another report as a part of the main report. |
| Mail Label | You can use Mail Label Report Expert to create a report that contains multiple columns. |
| Drill Down | You can use Drill Down Report Expert to create a report that contains a summary created by extracting the available information. |

**TIP**

You can see a preview of various Report Experts in the Preview window.

## Creating Crystal Reports Using the Standard Report Expert

In this section, you will be creating a crystal report by using a Standard Report Expert. The next steps continue with the procedure for creating reports.

6. In the Choose an Expert group box of the Crystal Report Gallery dialog box, select the Standard option and click on the OK button.

   The Data tab of Standard Report Expert is displayed.

7. Click on the plus (+) sign adjacent to the OLE DB [ADO] option.

   The OLE DB (ADO) dialog box is displayed. Alternatively, you can double-click on the OLE DB [ADO] option to open the OLE DB (ADO) dialog box.

8. In the OLE DB Provider page, select the Microsoft OLE DB Provider for SQL Server option and click on the Next button.

   The Connection Information page is displayed. You use this page to enter information required to set up a connection with a data source.

9. In the Server: combo box, select the name of the server containing the database from the drop-down list.

   You can also type the name of the server in the combo box. In this page, you can specify the authentication mode to connect to a SQL server.

10. Select the name of the database as CMS from the Database: combo box and click on the Finish button.

    Standard Report Expert creates a connection with the CMS database.

11. Double-click on the CMS database to display a list of tables in the database.

12. Select the table `tblJobDetails` from the available list and click on the Insert Table button.

    The `tblJobDetails` table is now displayed in the Tables in report: list.

13. Click on the Next button.

    The Fields tab is displayed. This page contains a list of all the fields in the `tblJobDetails` table. You can select the fields that you want display in your report.

14. From the list of fields, select the `JobDate`, `Tires`, `Weights`, `OilChanged`, `OilFilter`, `GearOil`, `Point`, `Condenser`, `Plug`, `FuelFilter`, and `AirFilter` fields and click on the Add button.

    The fields that you have selected appear in the Fields to Display: list. You can use the Up Arrow or Down Arrow buttons to increase or decrease the level of display of the fields.

    The name of the field appears in the Column Heading: text box. You can edit the name of a field by selecting the field and changing the text in the Column Heading: text box.

15. Click on the Next button to proceed.

    The Group tab is displayed. This page contains information about the field that you want to use to group data. The records in the `tblJobDetails` table are sorted on the basis of the Group By: field.

16. From the Available Fields: list, select the JobDate field and click on the Add button.

    The JobDate field appears in the Group By: list. You can also specify the sort order of the records in the Sort Order: list box.

17. In the Break: list box, select the for each month option.

    The records in the `tblJobDetails` table will be grouped for each month. This will help the user to view monthly data of the consumable items in the Monthly Consumables report.

18. Click on the Next button.

    The Total tab of Standard Report Expert is displayed. In this page, you can select the fields for which you want to create summarized information. By default, all the fields are selected. You can either add or remove a field by selecting the field and clicking on the Add or Remove button, respectively. The Total tab provides you with a Summary Type: list box, which contains the items that you can select to display the type of summary information. Because you need to know the total number of products consumed within a specified month, choose the summary type Sum.

19. Check the Add Grand Totals check box and click on the Next button.

    The Top N tab is displayed. You can specify the name of the field based on which one you want to sort the groups. This is optional information and you may choose to click on the Next button without specifying any information in this page.

20. Click on the Next button to display the Chart tab.

    The Chart page provides you with several options for including a graph in your report.

21. Click on the Style button if you do not want to include a chart.

    The Style tab is displayed. You can select the formatting style of the report and specify a title in this page. Standard Report Expert provides you with several formatting styles for displaying your report. You can see the preview of a style in the preview window.

22. In the Title: text box, type the name of the report as `Consumable Report`.
23. From the Style: list, select the Standard option and click on the Finish option to create the crystal report.

Figure 11-2 displays the report as created by the Crystal Report Gallery.

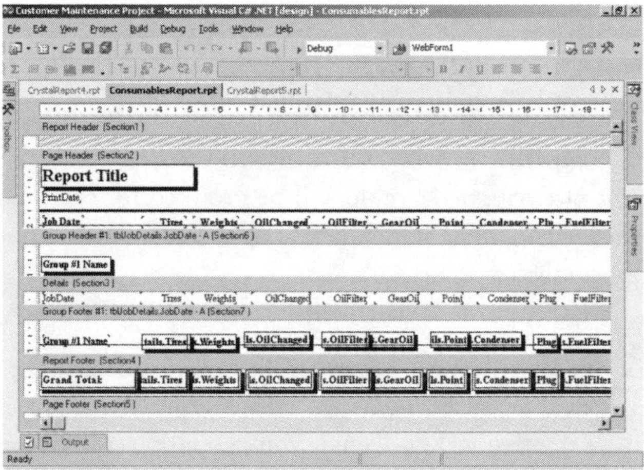

**FIGURE 11-2** *Consumable Report*

If you want, you can make changes to the layout of the report. However, this report does not display the data. To make the data available to users, you need to host the crystal report by using a Windows Forms Viewer control.

## Windows Forms Viewer Control

As discussed earlier, a Windows Forms Viewer control provides you with a means to host and display the data in a report. The Windows Forms Viewer control is available in the Windows Forms toolbox and can be included in a Windows form. Figure 11-3 shows a Windows Forms Viewer control.

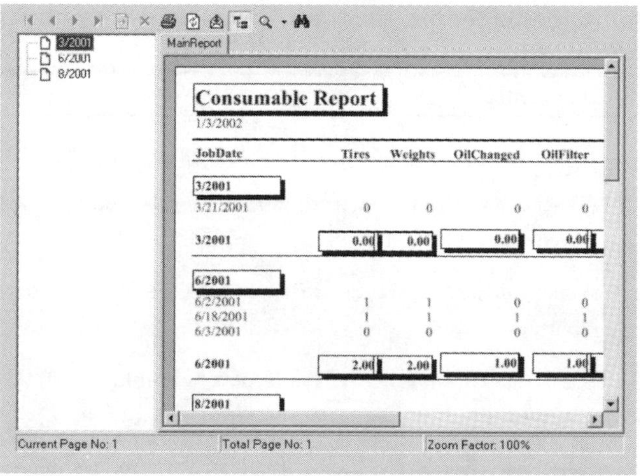

**FIGURE 11-3** *Windows Forms Viewer control*

The left-hand pane of the Windows Forms Viewer control is a Field Explorer window that displays field values, the basis on which the data in the records is grouped. The right-hand pane is used to display the crystal report that you created. On top of the Windows Forms Viewer control is a toolbar containing several buttons that you can use to navigate, refresh, or print the report. Table 11-2 discusses the buttons in the toolbar of the Windows Forms Viewer control.

**Table 11-2 Buttons in the Toolbar of the Windows Forms Viewer Control**

| Buttons | Description |
|---|---|
| Go to First Page | A user can click on the Go to First Page button to view the first page, in case the report contains multiple pages of data. |
| Go to Previous Page | A user can click on the Go to Previous Page button to view the previous page. |
| Go to Next Page | A user can click on the Go to Next Page button to view the next page. |
| Go to Last Page | A user can click on the Go to Last Page button to view the last page. |

*continues*

**Table 11-2 Buttons in the Toolbar of the Windows Forms Viewer Control *(continued)***

| Buttons | Description |
|---|---|
| Go to Page | A user can click on the Go to Page button to view a specified page. |
| Close Current View | A user can click on the Close Current View button to close the current view. This button is active only for Subreport or groups. |
| Print Report | A user can click on the Print Report button to print the data in a report. |
| Refresh Report | A user can click on the Refresh Report button to refresh the data in a report. |
| Export Report | A user can click on the Export Report button to save the report as a Word document (.doc), an Acrobat file (.pdf), an Excel spreadsheet (.xls), or a rich text format (.rtf) file. |
| Toggle Group Tree | A user can click on the Toggle Group Tree button to display or hide the Field Explorer window. |
| Zoom | A user can click on the Zoom button to increase or decrease the zoom percentage of a report. The user can select the zoom percentage from the drop-down list. |
| Search Text | A user can click on the Search Text button to find the specified data in a report. |

The following section discusses creating a Windows Forms Viewer control to display a crystal report.

## Creating the Windows Forms Viewer Control

As discussed earlier, a Windows Forms Viewer control is used to host and display a crystal report. Perform the following steps to create a Windows Forms Viewer control.

1. In the Solution Explorer window, right-click on the project name, Customer Maintenance Project.

2. In the displayed list , point to Add and click on the Add New Item option.

   The Add New Item dialog box is displayed.
3. In the Templates: pane, select the Windows Form option.
4. In the Name: text box, type the name of the form as ConsumableForm and click on the Open button.

   Visual Studio .NET creates a new form for you.

   From the Windows Forms toolbox, drag the CrystalReportViewer and Button controls to the form.

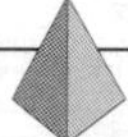

**TIP**

In the Windows Forms toolbox, a Windows Forms Viewer control is called CrystalReportViewer.

Resize the CrystalReportViewer control to occupy maximum area on the form. Figure 11-4 shows ConsumableForm with the CrystalReportViewer control.

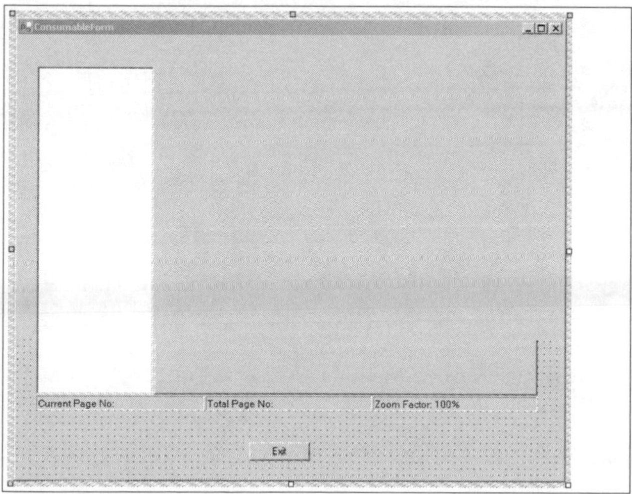


**FIGURE 11-4** *ConsumableForm with the CrystalReportViewer control*

As you can see, the CrystalReportViewer control is empty. To host and display the report in the CrystalReportViewer control, you need to associate the control with ConsumablesReport.rpt. To do so, perform the following steps:

1. Select the CrystalReportViewer control to make it active.
2. In the Properties window, change the value of the ReportSource property of the CrystalReportViewer control.

   The ReportSource property enables you to associate the CrystalReportViewer control with the required crystal report.
3. Click on the down arrow button of the ReportSource property.
4. From the drop-down list, select the Browse option.

   The Browse option enables you to browse for the location of the ConsumablesReport.rpt report.

   After associating the report with the CrystalReportViewer control, you can test the report by clicking on the F5 key or by selecting the Start command on the Debug menu.

   When you run the project and click on the Monthly Consumable Report radio button in the Reports form, the ConsumableForm form is displayed. Figure 11-5 shows the Reports form with the Monthly Consumable Report radio button.

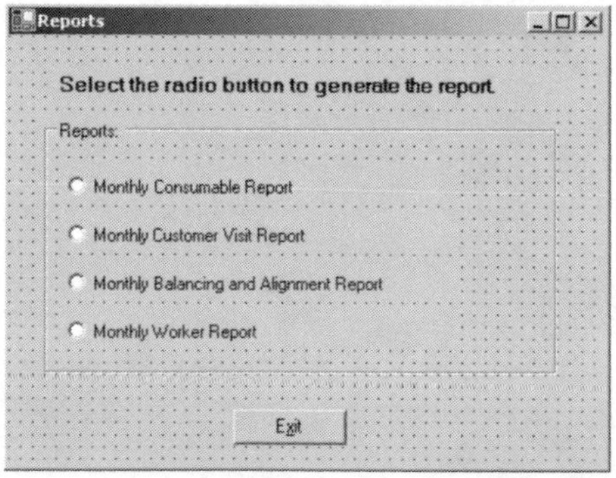

**FIGURE 11-5** *Reports form*

The ConsumableForm form now contains the Consumable Report that you have created. Figure 11-6 shows the Consumable Report as seen at run time.

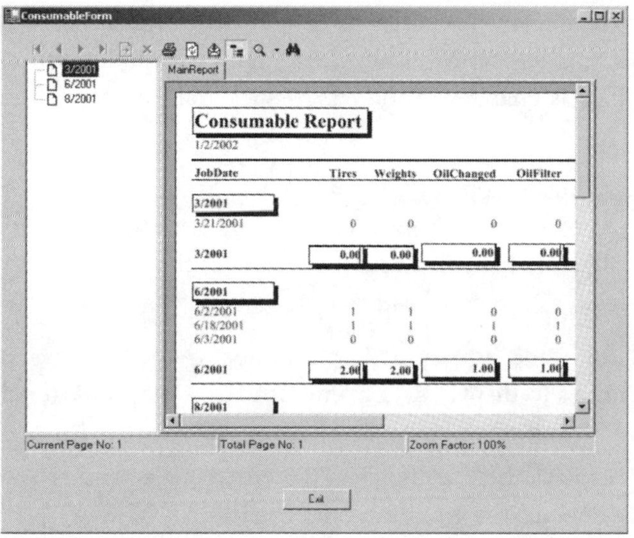


**FIGURE 11-6** *Consumable Report at run time*

To enable a user to return to the Reports form after viewing the report, you can make the Exit button functional. To do so, add the following code to the `Click` event of the Exit button.

```
private void btnExit_Click(object sender, System.EventArgs e)
{
        Reports newForm = new Reports();
        newForm.Show();
        this.Hide();
}
```

After creating the Monthly Consumable report, you can similarly create the Monthly Customer Visit, Monthly Balancing and Alignment, and Monthly Worker reports.

# Creating the Monthly Customer Visit Report

The Monthly Customer Visit report is created to track the number of visits of a customer in a particular month. The procedure for creating the Monthly Customer

Visit report is similar to the one you used to create the Monthly Consumable report. However, while creating the Monthly Customer Visit report, you need to make a few changes, such as changes in the table name, field names, Group By: field, and so on.

Similar to the Monthly Consumable report, you can use Standard Report Expert to create the Monthly Customer Visit report. However, if you want, you can select any other expert. The following list will discuss the changes that you need to make while creating the Monthly Customer Visit report.

1. In the Data tab of Standard Report Expert, select the `tblCustomer` and `tblJobDetails` tables to display data from both these tables. After clicking on the Next button, the Links tab is displayed.

   The Links tab displays the link between the `tblCustomer` and `tblJobDetails` tables. By default, the common field name, CarNo, is selected as the link. However, if required, you can clear the link by clicking on the Clear Links button and then create a new link by dragging the field name from one table to another. Figure 11-7 displays the Links tab of Standard Report Expert.

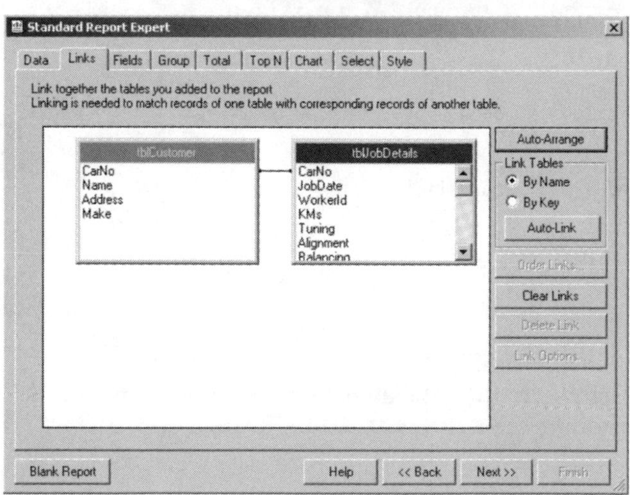


**FIGURE 11-7** *The Links tab of Standard Report Expert*

2. In the Fields tab, select the `CarNo`, `Name`, `Address`, and `Make` fields from the `tblCustomer` table. From the `tblJobDetails` table, select the JobDate option.
3. In the Group By: list, select the `CarNo` and then the `JobDate` fields.
4. In the Title: text box of the Style tab, type the title of the report as Customer Visit Report and select any style from the Style: list.

Figure 11-8 displays the Monthly Customer Visit report as created by the Crystal Report Gallery.

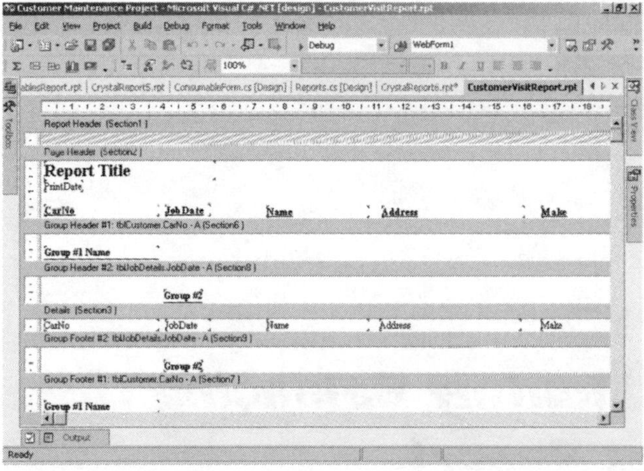


**FIGURE 11-8** *Monthly Customer Visit report in the design view*

After creating the crystal report, you can create a new form, CustomerVisitForm, and include a CrystalReportViewer control to display the report. Figure 11-9 shows the Monthly Customer Visit report as seen at run time.

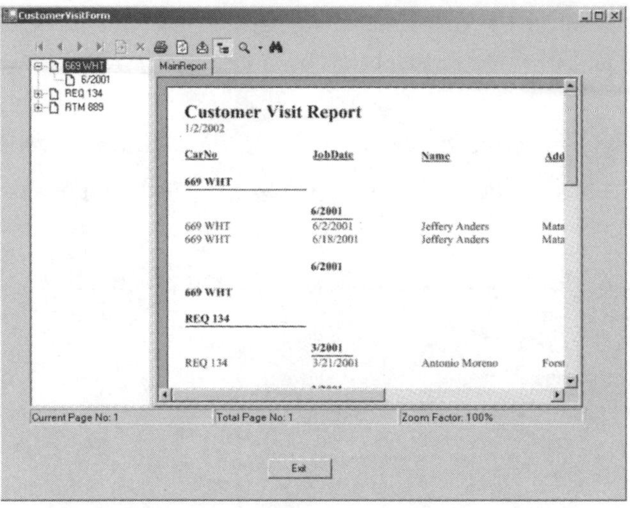


**FIGURE 11-9** *Monthly Customer Visit report at run time*

# Creating the Monthly Balancing and Alignment Report

The Monthly Balancing and Alignment report is created to track the number of balancing and alignment jobs performed by a worker in a month. You can create the Monthly Balancing and Alignment report by using the Crystal Report Gallery as discussed in the previous sections. Figure 11-10 displays the report as created by the Crystal Report Gallery.

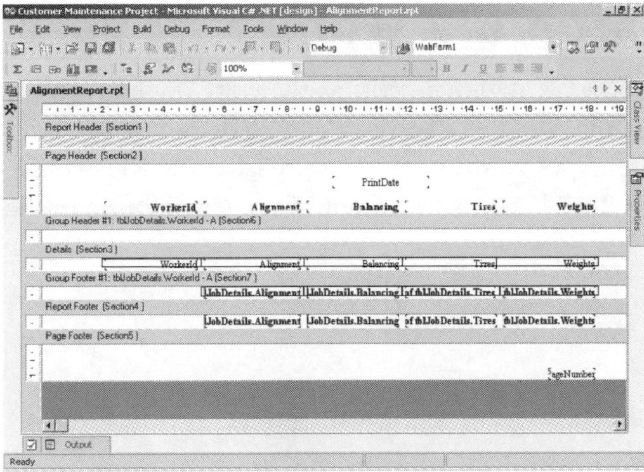

**FIGURE 11-10** *Monthly Balancing and Alignment report in the design view*

You can make changes to the layout of the Monthly Balancing and Alignment report in the design view. However, to display the report at run time, you need to create a new form, AlignmentForm, and then include a CrystalReportViewer control. Figure 11-11 shows the Monthly Balancing and Alignment report at run time.

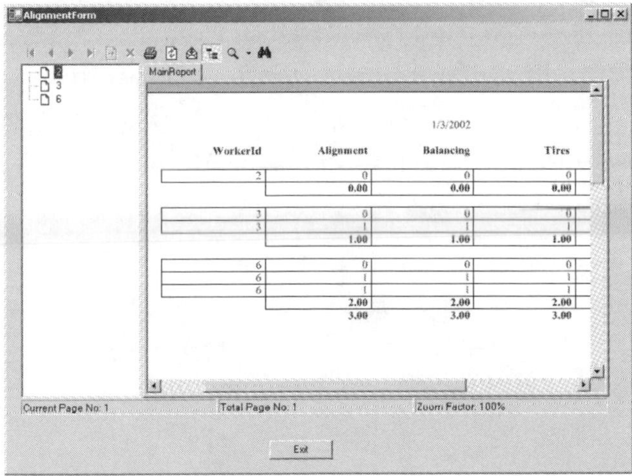

**FIGURE 11-11** *Monthly Balancing and Alignment report at run time*

# Creating the Monthly Worker Report

The Monthly Worker report is used to determine the work done by a worker in a month. You can also use the Monthly Worker report to determine the work done by a worker on a car during a month. You can use the Crystal Report Gallery to create the report. Figure 11-12 shows the output of the Crystal Report Gallery.

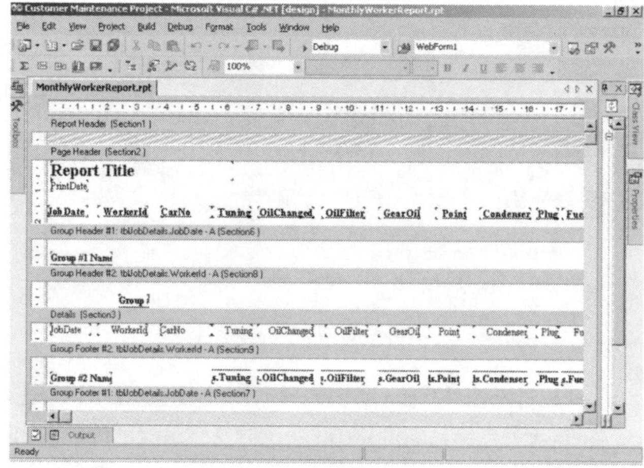


**FIGURE 11-12** *Monthly Worker report in the design view*

To view Monthly Worker report, create a new form, MonthlyReport, and include a CrystalReportViewer control. Figure 11-13 shows the Monthly Worker report with the data displayed.

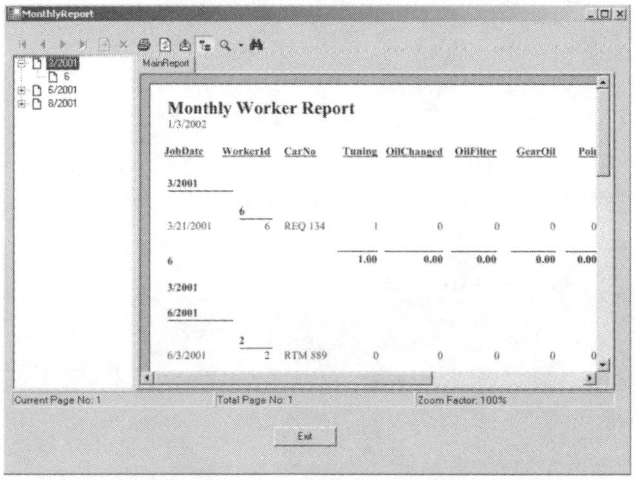


**FIGURE 11-13** *Monthly Worker report at run time*

# Summary

In this chapter, you learned that crystal reports are a powerful tool used to create and view reports that display selective data. Visual Studio .NET provides you with the Crystal Reports Designer tool that helps you create a wide variety of reports easily and efficiently. In addition, you can use the Crystal Reports Designer tool to modify an existing report.

The Crystal Reports Designer tool contains the Crystal Report Gallery, which allows you to select Report Expert. Report Expert is a wizard that enables you to create various kinds of crystal reports. After creating a crystal report by using Report Expert, you can use a Windows Forms Viewer control to view the report. A Windows Forms Viewer control provides you with a means to host and display the data in a report. The Windows Forms Viewer control is available in the Windows Forms toolbox and can be included in a Windows form.

Finally, you learned to create a crystal report by using the Crystal Report Gallery and then host the report by creating a Windows Forms Viewer control.

# Chapter 12

## Deploying a Windows Application

In the preceding chapters, you created the Customer Maintenance project for CareKar, Inc. However, until now, you have not deployed the project at the client site. Visual Studio .NET provides you with the functionality to deploy the application that you have created on any other computer. You can also distribute your application on another computer in the form of a program that can be easily installed on the computer. In this chapter, you will learn to deploy a Windows application.

## Introduction to Deploying a Windows Application

In real-life situations, you often need to execute a Windows application that you have created on a computer other than the computer on which you created the application. This is called *deploying a Windows application*. Deploying a Windows application in Visual Studio .NET can be as simple as compiling the application in the form of an .exe file. You can then execute the application by copying the .exe file of the application on another computer.

However, for huge applications, like the one that you have created for CareKar, Inc., compiling the application as an .exe file may not guarantee the successful deployment of the application. In such cases, you need to create an installation program to deploy your application on another computer. The user can then run the installation program that copies the installation files to the user's computer. In addition, the user is not required to explicitly make changes to the registry of the computer. The installation program modifies the registry, enabling the application to run on the user's computer.

To execute an application in Visual Studio .NET, the application is first converted to managed code that is managed by the CLR (*common language runtime*). To do so, the installation program makes the CLR files, which are required for the execution of the application, available to the application.

The process of deploying an application as an installable program on the user's machine requires you to decide on the location where you need to deploy the application. In addition, you need to identify the method by which the application is to be deployed. To create an installation program for your application, you can use various deployment projects available in Visual Studio .NET, which are discussed in the following section.

## Deployment Projects Available in Visual Studio .NET

A *deployment project* in Visual Studio .NET is a project that enables you to create an installation program to ensure a successful deployment of your application on another computer. Figure 12-1 displays various deployment projects provided by Visual Studio .NET.

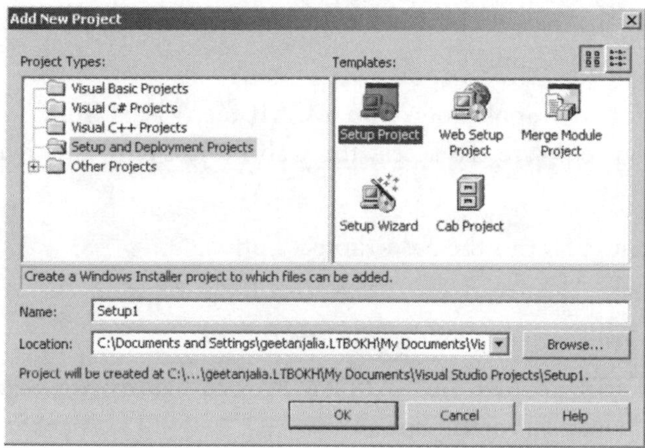


**FIGURE 12-1** *Various deployment projects in Visual Studio .NET*

You can choose the type of deployment project to be used depending on the type of application that you create.

## The CAB Project

The simplest way to deploy a Windows application is to convert the application to a CAB (*cabinet*) file. A *CAB file* is a compressed form of your project. This implies that a CAB file compresses the application into smaller files that occupy less memory on the user's computer. Therefore, converting an application to a CAB project enables the user to store the application in a compressed and organized manner. In addition, the CAB files that you create for your project can be easily transported and deployed on the user's machine.

A CAB file can be used to package the ActiveX controls. Packaging an ActiveX control involves signing the ActiveX control or the application that contains the control. This process is called *Authenticode signing*. This enables the user to identify the source of the application and verify its authenticity. In addition, users can easily download and then install these files on their machines. You will learn about packaging Web applications that can be downloaded from a Web server in Chapter 26, "Deploying the Application."

To enable you to convert your application into a CAB file, Visual Studio .NET provides the Cab Project template. To access the Cab Project template, perform the following steps:

1. On the File menu, point to the Add Project option.
2. From the list that is displayed, select the New Project option.

   The Add New Project dialog box is displayed.
3. In the Project Types: pane of the Add New Project dialog box, select the Setup and Deployment Projects option.

   Various options of deployment projects available in Visual Studio .NET are displayed in the Templates: pane.
4. Select the Cab Project option.

   Figure 12-2 shows the Cab Project option.

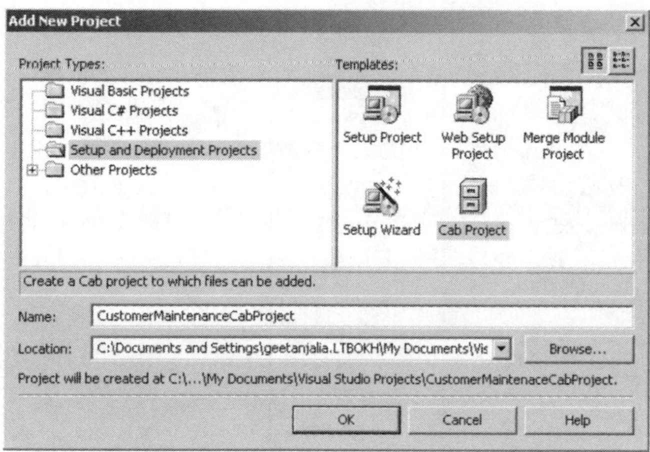


**FIGURE 12-2** *The Cab Project option in the Add New Project dialog box*

5. In the Name: text box, type the name of the Cab Project as `Customer-MaintenanceCabProject`.
6. Browse for the location where you want to save CustomerMaintenance-CabProject by using the Browse button.
7. Click on the OK button to close the Add New Project dialog box.

   CustomerMaintenanceCabProject is added to the Solution Explorer window. Figure 12-3 shows CustomerMaintenanceCabProject added to the Solution Explorer window.

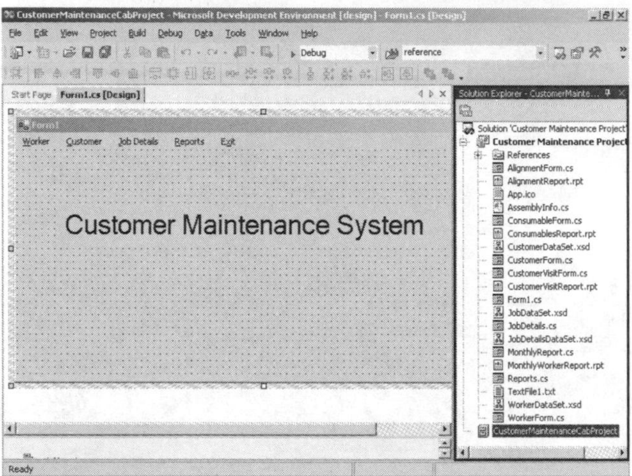


**FIGURE 12-3** *CustomerMaintenanceCabProject in the Solution Explorer window*

The Properties window of the CustomerMaintenanceCabProject project displays information about the project, such as the name, version number, and Web dependencies of the project.

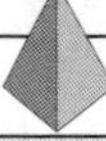

**TIP**

Visual Studio .NET does not specify any Web dependencies of the CAB projects. However, you can create references to any Web dependencies by changing the Web dependencies property of the CAB project. If Web dependencies property is set, all dependencies are automatically downloaded and installed when the CAB file is run.

You can also implement Authenticode signing by checking the Authenticode signing: check box in CustomerMaintenanceCabProject Property Pages. To access CustomerMaintenanceCabProject Property Pages, perform the following step:

1. Click on the View menu and select the Property Pages option. Alternatively, you can press the Shift+F4 keys.

   CustomerMaintenanceCabProject Property Pages is displayed. Figure 12-4 shows CustomerMaintenanceCabProject Property Pages.

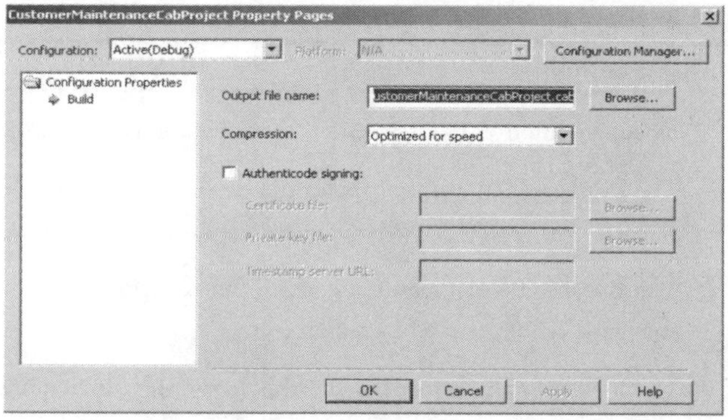

**FIGURE 12-4** *CustomerMaintenanceCabProject Property Pages*

You can also specify the amount by which you want to compress the application in the properties of the CAB project. For example, if you compress an application by a higher amount, the file creation process takes more time compared to compressing a file by lower amounts. However, a file with higher compression level takes less time to download. In addition, the properties of a CAB project allow you to specify the location where you want to store the executable files.

However, the CustomerMaintenanceCabProject project that you have created does not contain the application files. To add the application files to the CAB project, perform the following steps:

1. Right-click on the CustomerMaintenanceCabProject project in the Solution Explorer window.
2. In the displayed list, point to the Add option.

   The displayed list contains the following options.

   - **Project Output.** The Project Output option displays the Add Project Output Group dialog box that provides several options of files that you can add to the CAB project. Table 12-1 displays the file options in the Add Project Output Group dialog box.
   - **File.** The File option enables you to add an arbitrary file other than the files listed in Table 12-1 of the CAB project.

**Table 12-1 File Options in the Add Project Output Group dialog box**

| File Options | Description |
|---|---|
| Documentation Files | Documentation Files contain the documentation of the project. |
| Primary Output | The Primary Output files contain the executable files built by the project. |
| Localized Resources | The Localized Resources files contain the assembly information about the resources used in the project. |
| Debug Symbols | The Debug Symbols files contain the debugging files required for the project. |
| Content Files | Content Files contain all the content files used in the project. |
| Source Files | Source Files contain all the source files used in the project. |

After learning about the types of files that Visual Studio .NET allows you to add to the CAB project, you can continue with the steps to add files to the CustomerMaintenanceCabProject project that you have created.

3. Select the Project Output option.

   The Add Project Output Group dialog box is displayed. The name of the project is displayed in the Project: list box.
4. Select the Primary Output option from the file options in the Add Project Output Group dialog box.

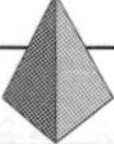

**TIP**

The Primary Output option is a mandatory option. However, you may choose to select any other option to be deployed along with the application.

5. Click on the OK button to close the Add Project Output Group dialog box.

   The Primary Output option is displayed in the Solution Explorer window. You can view the file name and the path of the executable file in the Properties window of the Primary Output option.

6. Select the Primary Output option in the Solution Explorer window to display the Properties window.
7. Click the ellipsis button of the Outputs property.
8. The Outputs dialog box is displayed, which contains information about the executable file for the Customer Maintenance project.

   Figure 12-5 displays the Outputs dialog box.
9. Build the project by clicking on the F5 key.

   Alternatively, you can select the Start option on the Debug menu.

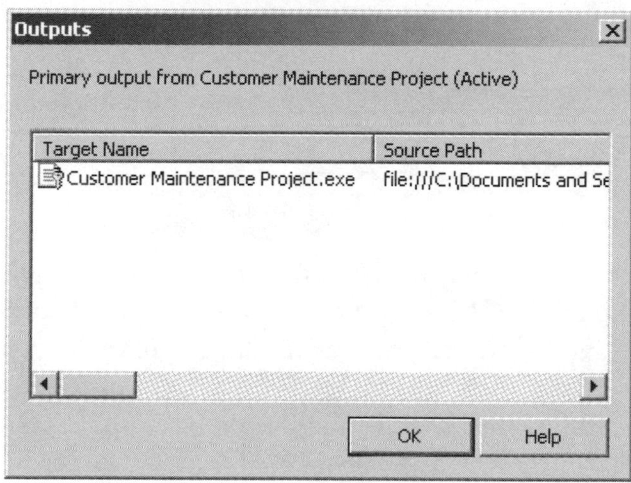


**FIGURE 12-5** *The Outputs dialog box*

To create the executable file, you need to build the CustomerMaintenance-CabProject project, as described in the previous Step 9.

Building the project creates an executable file in the location specified in the Outputs dialog box. The executable file, along with an .osd file, is created in the form of a compressed file. To access these files, you can unzip the CustomerMaintenanceCabProject.CAB file. The .osd file contains the information about the CustomerMaintenanceCabProject.CAB file in the XML format. Figure 12-6 shows the contents of the .osd file.

```
<?XML version="1.0" ENCODING='UTF-8'?>
<!DOCTYPE SOFTPKG SYSTEM "http://www.microsoft.com/standards/osd/osd.dtd">
<?XML::namespace href="http://www.microsoft.com/standards/osd/msicd.dtd" as="MSICD"?>
<SOFTPKG NAME="CustomerMaintenanceCabProject" VERSION="1,0,0,0">
        <TITLE> CustomerMaintenanceCabProject </TITLE>
            <MSICD::NATIVECODE>
                <CODE NAME="Customer&#32;Maintenance&#32;Project">
                    <IMPLEMENTATION>
                        <CODEBASE FILENAME="Customer&#32;Maintenance&#32;Project.exe">
                        </CODEBASE>
                    </IMPLEMENTATION>
                </CODE>
            </MSICD::NATIVECODE>
</SOFTPKG>
```

**FIGURE 12-6** *Contents of the .osd file*

For huge projects, a CAB project may not be sufficient to deploy an application. Therefore, you can combine the CAB project option with the other options provided by Visual Studio .NET. For example, consider the Customer Maintenance project that we have created for CareKar, Inc. This project includes several resource files, such as .xsd files, that contain information about the datasets created to access the tables in the CMS (*Customer Maintenance System*) database. Because these .xsd files are included in the application, they need to be distributed as a part of the application. In such a scenario, it would be appropriate to first convert the application into a CAB file and then create a Setup project. I will discuss the Setup project in the following section.

## The Setup Project

Another deployment project that Visual Studio .NET provides you is the Setup project. The Setup Project template creates the installer files that users can install on their machines to deploy the application. The installer files created by the Setup Project template are called MSI (*Microsoft Windows Installer*) files. These files have an extension of .msi and can be installed on the user's machine by using the Microsoft Installer service.

The Setup Project template creates the MSI files for your application, which include the application files, the resource files, and the information required for the deployment of the application. This information includes the registry information and the steps for the successful installation of the application. In addition, the MSI files include the Visual Studio. NET runtime files that are required for the execution of the Windows application.

> **THE MICROSOFT INSTALLER SERVICE**
>
> The Microsoft Installer service is an installation service provided by Microsoft to optimize the process of deploying an application. For example, the Microsoft Installer service installs the files required for the successful deployment of an application or the component of an application. This service is available as a part of Microsoft Windows 2000 and higher operating systems.

You will now create a Setup project for the Customer Maintenance project by using the Setup templates provided by Visual Studio .NET. Visual Studio .NET provides separate templates for deploying the Windows application and Web applications. The template used to deploy the Windows application, the Setup Project template, creates the MSI files for the application on the user's computer. The template used to deploy Web applications, the Web Setup Project template, creates the MSI files in a virtual directory present on a Web server. In this chapter, I will be discussing the deployment of the Windows application by using the Setup Project template.

To create a Setup project for the Customer Maintenance project, perform the following steps:

1. On the File menu, point to the Add Project option.
2. From the list that is displayed, select the New Project option.

   The Add New Project dialog box is displayed.
3. From the Project Types: pane, select the Setup and Deployment Projects option.
4. In the Templates: pane, select the Setup Project option.
5. In the Name: text box, type the name of the Setup project as CustomerMaintenanceSetupProject.
6. Click on the Browse button to browse to the location where you want to save the Setup project.
7. Click on the OK button to close the Add New Project dialog box.

The Setup Project template creates a file system editor, which is displayed by default. You can also access the file system editor from the View menu. In addition to the file system editor, the View menu provides several other editor options, such as Registry, File Types, User Interface, Custom Actions, and Launch Conditions. To access the editors provided by Visual Studio .NET, perform the following steps:

1. Right-click on CustomerMaintenanceSetupProject in the Solution Explorer window.
2. In the displayed list, point to the View menu.

   The list of file editors is displayed. You can click on any of these options to display the corresponding information. You will learn more about the editors later in this chapter.

Figure 12-7 displays the file system editor as created on the user's machine.

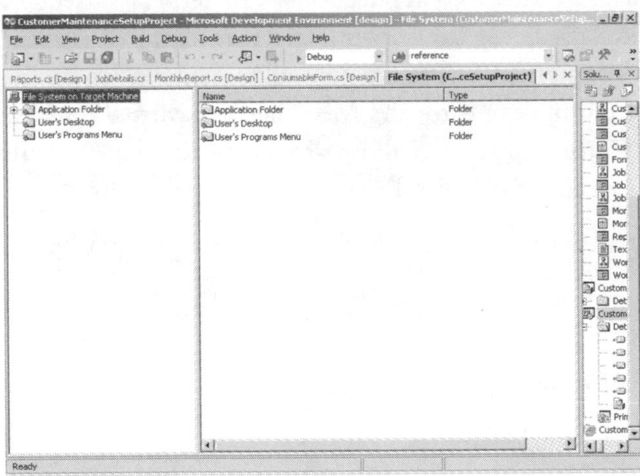

**FIGURE 12-7** *File system editor as created on the user's machine*

As you can see, the folders in the file system editor, such as Application Folder, User's Desktop, and User's Program Menu, are empty. This is because you have not added the output files to the Setup project. You will learn to add the output files later in this chapter.

The Add option of CustomerMaintenanceSetupProject provides you with two options in addition to the Project Output and File options. These additional options are Folder and Assembly.

- **Folder.** The Folder option allows you to add a new folder to the file system editor.
- **Assembly.** The Assembly option allows you to add Visual Studio .NET components from the Component Selector dialog box. The Component Selector dialog box contains a list of components, their versions, and their locations on the hard disk, which you may need to add to the user's machine. Figure 12-8 displays the Component Selector dialog box.

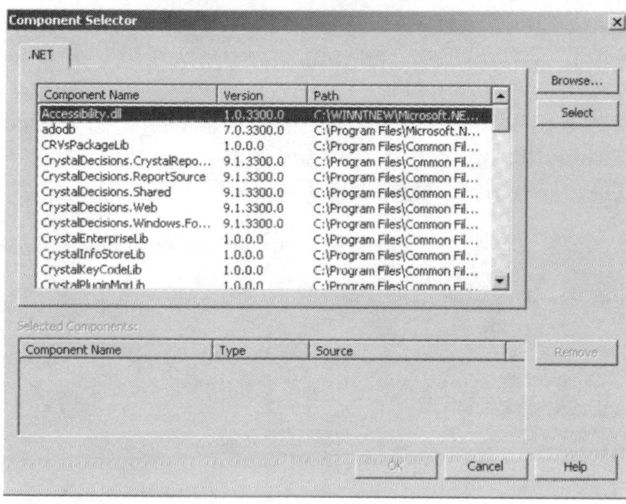


**FIGURE 12-8** *The Component Selector dialog box*

After seeing the options available on the Add menu, you can continue with the process of creating a Setup project. In this project, you will be adding only Project Output. However, you may add the other options to your project, if required.

1. In the user interface for the file system editor, right-click Application Folder.
2. In the displayed list, point to the Add menu and then select the Folder option.

Visual Studio .NET adds a new folder to the file system editor. Alternatively, you can add a new folder by clicking on the Action menu. In the displayed list, point to the Add menu and then select thc Folder option.

3. Name this folder `Output`.

   You may give any name to the folder.

4. On the Action menu, point to the Add option.
5. Select the Project Output option to add the required files to the Setup project.

   The Add Project Output Group dialog box is displayed.

6. In the Add Project Output Group dialog box, select the Primary Output option.

   The Primary Output is created in the Output folder.

You saw the user interface for the file system earlier. The folders did not contain the output files. After adding the Project Output file to the Setup project, the user interface for the file system appears as shown in Figure 12-9.

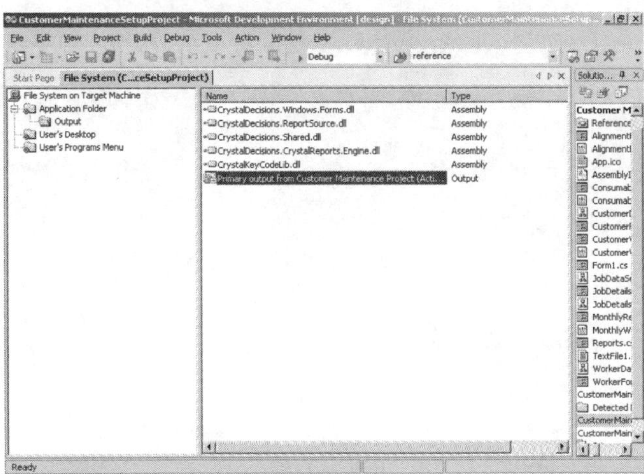


**FIGURE 12-9** *The user interface for the file system editor*

After creating the output file, you need to build the Setup project by performing the following steps:

1. Click on the Build menu.
2. From the drop-down list, select the Build CustomerMaintenanceSetup-Project option.

Building the project creates a MSI file that can be easily deployed on the user's machine. The location and other properties of the MSI file are displayed in the Properties window of the Primary Output file. Figure 12-10 shows the CustomerMaintenanceProject.msi file.

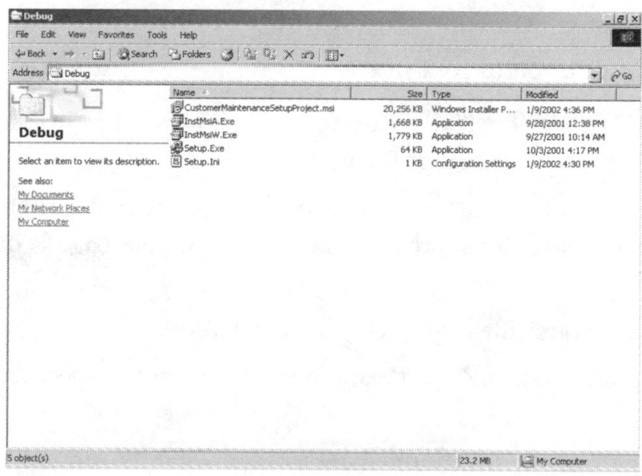

**FIGURE 12-10** *The CustomerMaintenanceProject.msi file*

You can distribute the CustomerMaintenanceProject.msi file that you have created in several ways, such as floppy disks or compact discs. To do this, copy the MSI file that is created to the distribution medium and then run the installation program on the user's machine.

Perform the following steps to install the Windows application on the user's machine.

1. Copy the CustomerMaintenanceProject.msi file to the user's machine.

2. Double-click on the CustomerMaintenanceProject.msi file to start the installation.

   The Windows Installer service prepares the user's machine for the installation. Then, the Welcome page of the Setup wizard is displayed.
3. Click on the Next button to continue.

   The Select Installation Folder page is displayed.
4. Browse for the location where you want to install the application by clicking on the Browse button.
5. Select the Everyone radio button if you want to enable all the users who log on to the machine to access the application.

   By default, the Just me radio button is selected.
6. Click on the Next button to continue.

   The Confirm Installation page is displayed.
7. Click on the Next button to start the installation.

   A progress bar shows the progress of the installation process. When the installation process is complete, the Installation Complete page is displayed.
8. Click on the Close button to complete the installation.

   The CustomerMaintenanceProject.exe file is created in the specified folder.
9. Double-click the CustomerMaintenanceProject.exe file to run the Windows application.

Having tested the application, you can distribute the application to your customer.

## Merge Module

In addition to a CAB or Setup project, you can create a Merge Module project by using the templates provided by Visual Studio .NET. A Merge Module project is used to combine the application files, resource files, registry files, and Setup files in a single package.

You use the Merge Modules for projects that can be shared across applications. This implies that the components used to set up a Merge Modules project can be shared for multiple Merge Module projects. For example, consider a situation in which you need to distribute two applications on a user's computer. In this case, you can have a common set of setup components for both the applications. Therefore, the Merge Module projects are similar to the dynamic link library (.dll) files, which allow applications to share the code.

In addition to the setup components, you can create any component as a Merge Module that needs to be shared across multiple applications. For example, if a resource is used in more than one application, you can deploy the resource as a Merge Module and can then reuse the resource file for multiple applications. However, you cannot install a Merge Module alone. It can be added to the MSI files that you have created in the previous section.

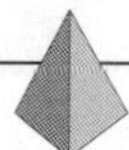

**TIP**

You can add a Merge Module component while creating a MSI file. In addition, the merge module component can be added after the MSI files are created.

Another advantage of creating a Merge Module project is that the project recognizes all the dependencies for a component and tracks the versions of the component. This prevents the user from installing the incorrect version of the component. To further avoid any version problem while installing a component, you must create a Merge Module project that contains the dependencies of the component.

You will now learn how to create a Merge Module project. You can create a Merge Module project similar to the way you created the Setup Project. However, instead of selecting the Setup Project option in the Add New Project dialog box, select the Merge Module option. After performing the required steps, build the Merge Module project to create a .msm file. Figure 12-11 shows the file system editor of the Merge Module project.

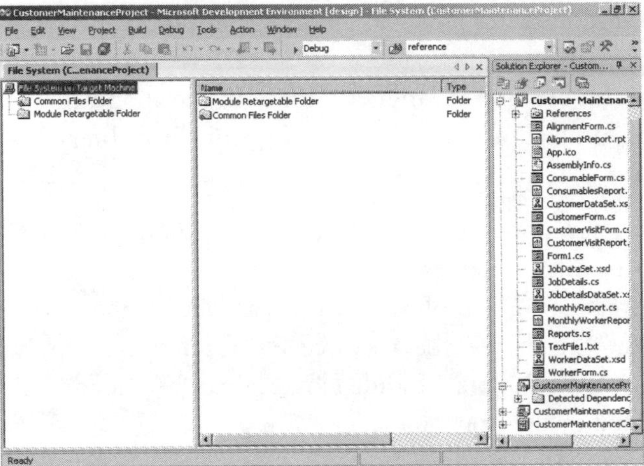

**FIGURE 12-11** *The file system editor of the Merge Module project*

As discussed earlier, to deploy the .msm file, you need to merge the file with a Windows Installer (.msi) file. The MSI file that contains a Merge Module component also stores information about the version of the component. Figure 12-11 displays the .msm file created for the project.

While you install the application, the Windows Installer service adds the version information to a Windows Installer database that enables multiple applications to use a component. If you uninstall any one application, the Windows Installer database ensures that the corresponding component is not uninstalled.

In the preceding sections, you looked at creating various deployment projects by using the templates provided by Visual Studio .NET. However, you can create these deployment projects by using the Setup wizard.

## The Setup Wizard

The Setup wizard is used to create various deployment projects. You can now create a deployment project by using the Setup wizard. To access the Setup wizard, select the Setup Wizard option in the Add New Project dialog box. The Welcome page of the Setup wizard is displayed. To create the deployment project by using the wizard, perform the following steps.

1. On the Welcome page of the wizard, click on the Next button to start the Setup wizard.

   The Choose a project type page is displayed.
2. Click on the radio button to create the type of deployment project.

   The wizard provides you with an option to create a Setup project for a Windows application, a Setup project for a Web application, a Merge Module for a Windows Installer, and a downloadable CAB file.
3. Click on the Next button to display the Choose project outputs to include page.
4. In the Which project output groups do you want to include? text box, check the file options that you want to include in your deployment project, and click on the Next button.

   The Choose files to include page is displayed. This page allows you to add any additional file other than the files that you added in Step 4, such as .txt or .htm files. You can add a file by clicking on the Add button. Because adding additional files is optional, you may choose to proceed further without adding any additional files.
5. Click on the Next button to display the Create Project page.

   The Create Project page displays the summary of the information that you have specified in the Setup wizard. Figure 12-12 displays the summary of the information specified in the Setup wizard.
6. To create the project, click on the Finish button on the Create Project page.

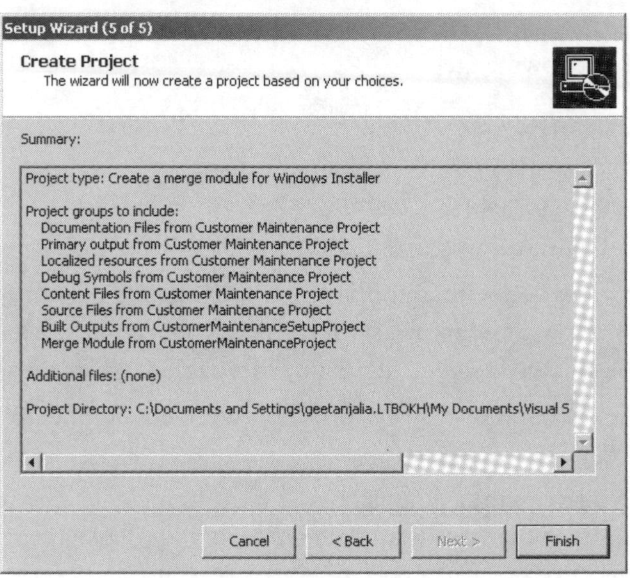


**FIGURE 12-12** *Summary of the information specified in the Setup wizard*

The project created by the wizard is added to the Solution Explorer window. You can now build the deployment project to test it.

When you build the project, Visual Studio .NET creates the output file in the Output folder that you created in the Application Folder. However, Visual Studio .NET enables you to create a shortcut to the output file on the user's machine. The user can then conveniently access the output file by using this shortcut. You can then create a shortcut to the output file.

It is a good practice to create a shortcut for users so that they can easily access your application. To create a shortcut, perform the following steps:

1. Select the Primary output from CustomerMaintenanceProject (Active) file in the Output folder.
2. On the Action menu, select the Create Shortcut to Primary output from CustomerMaintenanceProject (Active) option.

   A shortcut is created in the Output folder. If required, you can rename the shortcut.

Visual Studio .NET allows you to create shortcuts to the user's desktop and the user's program menu. To create a shortcut to the user's desktop, drag the shortcut to the User's Desktop folder. However, to add a shortcut to the user's program menu, drag the shortcut to the User's Program Menu folder in the file system editor. After adding the shortcut, you can build the project.

In this section, you learned about the file system editor. The following section discusses all the default editors in detail.

## Deployment Project Editors

As discussed earlier, while creating a deployment project, you need to specify the information, such as the location where you need to deploy the project, the method of deployment, the registry information, and so on. In addition, you might want to add customized information for the installation of the deployment project. To enable you to specify all this information, Visual Studio .NET provides you with several deployment project editors. By default, there are six deployment project editors. The following sections will look at each of the deployment project editors in detail.

### *The File System Editor*

The file system editor is the default editor that is displayed when you create a deployment project in Visual Studio .NET. You can use the file system editor to add files and folders to your deployment project. By default, the file system editor contains the Application Folder, the User's Desktop folder, and User's Program Menu folder. The folder structure displayed in the file system editor corresponds to the folder structure that will be created on the user's machine. However, Visual Studio .NET allows you modify the default folder structure by adding additional folders to the file system editor.

To add additional folders, perform the following steps:

1. Right-click on the File System on Target Machine option.
2. From the displayed list, select the Add Special Folders option.

A list containing the available folders is displayed. You can select any option to add the corresponding folder to the file system editor. These folders include Fonts Folder, User's Personal Data Folder, Windows Folder, User's Favorites Folder, and so on.

In addition, you can also add several files to the file system editor. For example, you can add output files, such as .exe or .dll files, or additional files, such as .txt or .htm files, to any folder in the file system editor. To add a file to the file system editor, perform the following steps:

1. Select the folder in which you want to add a file.
2. Click on the Action menu and point to the Add option.
3. From the list that is displayed, select the File option.

   The Add Files dialog box is displayed.
4. Browse for the file in the Add Files dialog box and click on the Open button.

The selected files are added to the specified folder.

You can also add shortcuts to the editor as explained in the previous section. Figure 12-13 displays a file system editor with additional files and folders added to it.

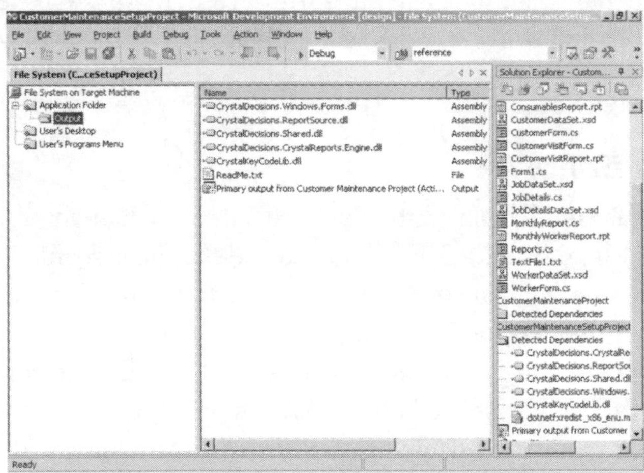


**FIGURE 12-13** *A file system editor with additional files and folders*

As you can see, a file system editor contains the left-hand pane, called the *navigation pane*, and a right-hand pane, called the *details pane*. The navigation pane shows the list of folders, and the details pane contains the files, folders, and shortcuts within the folder that is selected in the navigation pane. When you select a folder, you can view the properties of the folder in the Properties window.

## *The Registry Editor*

When you install an application on the user's computer, you may need to make modifications to the registry of the user's computer. These modifications may include adding registry keys and values to the registry. The registry editor in Visual Studio .NET allows you to write the registry keys and values to the registry. To access the registry editor, perform the following steps:

1. On the View menu, point to the Editor option.
2. In the displayed list, select the Registry option.

   The registry editor as shown in Figure 12-14 is displayed.

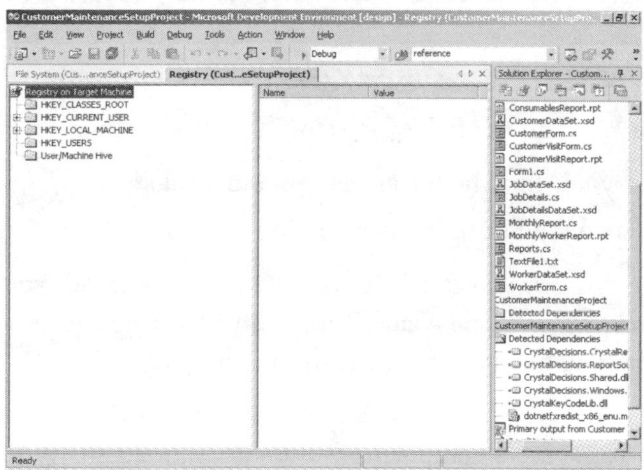


**FIGURE 12-14** *The registry editor*

Similar to the file system editor, the registry editor includes the navigation pane and the details pane. The navigation pane shows a list of existing registry keys on the user's computer. The details pane displays the registry entries for the registry key selected in the navigation pane. The navigation pane contains the name and the values for the corresponding registry entry.

As discussed earlier, you can add registry keys to the registry on the user's computer by using the registry editor. The following section discusses adding registry keys to the registry editor.

### Adding Registry Keys to the Registry Editor

To add a registry key to the registry editor, perform the following steps:

1. Select the registry key in the navigation pane.
2. On the Action menu, select the New Key option.

A new registry key gets added to the selected registry key. You can rename the registry key as required.

Similar to adding registry keys, you can also add values to new or existing keys.

### Adding Registry Values to Registry Keys

To add a registry value, perform the following steps:

1. Select the registry key for which you want to add a value.
2. On the Action menu, point to the New option.

The list that is displayed allows you to add a `string`, `binary`, or `DWORD` type value to the registry keys. Select the String Value, Environment String Value, Binary Value, or DWORD Value options to add the corresponding key value.

When you install the application on the user's machine, the registry values are written to the registry of the user's computer. If values exist for a registry key, the new value is overwritten to the registry key.

Visual Studio .NET also allows you to import an existing registry file to the registry editor, as discussed in the following section.

### Importing Registry Files

A registry file with an extension .reg can be included in the registry editor by performing the following steps:

1. In the registry editor, select the Registry on Target Machine option.

2. On the Action menu, click on the Import option.
3. The Import Registry File dialog box is displayed.
4. Browse for the required registry file, and click on the Open button to import the registry file to your project.

## The File Types Editor

Visual Studio .NET allows you to specify any file type or file association on the user's computer by using the file types editor. To create a file association, you need to associate the file extension with the application that you have created. You can then associate an action to be performed for all file types that you identify. For example, you can associate your application with a Microsoft Word document (.doc file) or a Microsoft Excel worksheet (.xls file). Associating an application with a file type creates an executable file. For example, for a Microsoft Excel worksheet, an executable file, EXCEL.exe, is created. When a file with an extension of .xls is opened, the executable file EXCEL.exe is launched.

Similar to the other editors, you can access the file types editor from the Editor option on the View menu. The file types editor does not contain any file type yet. You will now learn to add a file type to the file type editor.

### Adding File Types to the File Type Editor

To add a file type to the file type editor, perform the following steps:

1. Select the File Types on Target Machine option in the file type editor.
2. On the Action menu, click on the Add File Type option.

Visual Studio .NET creates a new file type for your deployment project. Rename this file MyFileType. This file type does not have a file extension associated with it.

### Associating a File Extension to the File Type

You can now associate a file extension to the MyFileType file type by performing the following steps:

1. Select the MyFileType file type in the file type editor.

   To associate a file extension, change the Extensions property of the file type.

2. In the Properties window, click on the Extensions property.
3. Type the value of the Extensions property as `xls`.

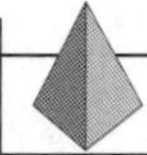

**TIP**

The value for the Extensions property is not preceded with a period.

The file extension that you type is added to the name of the file type, MyFileType. However, you have not yet added an executable file to the file type.

## Adding an Executable File to the File Type

To add an executable file to the file type, perform the following steps:

1. Select the MyFileType file type in the file type editor.

   To add an executable file, change the Command property of the file type.
2. In the Properties window, click on the ellipsis button of the Command property.
3. The Select Item in Project dialog box is displayed.
4. In the Select Item in Project dialog box, select the folder in which you want to add the file from the Look in: list box and click on the Add File button.

   You may also add an output file or an assembly by clicking on the Add Output or Add Assembly button, respectively.
5. The Add Files dialog box is displayed.
6. Browse for the executable file (EXCEL.exe file) and click on the OK button.

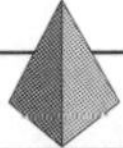

**TIP**

You can add an icon to the executable file by associating the icon file with the icon property of the file type.

As discussed earlier, you can specify the actions to be performed on the file with the .xls extension. The following section describes specifying an action.

## Specifying an Action to be Performed on the File with the .xls Extension

When you create a file type, the Open action is created for you by default. However, you can add more actions to be performed on the file. To specify an action, perform the following steps:

1. Select the MyFileType file type in the file type editor.
2. On the Action menu, click on the Add Action option.

   A new action is added to the MyFileType file type.
3. Rename the action `&Save`.
4. In the Properties window, select the Verb property and type the value of the Verb property as `Save`.

The value in the Verb property is used to identify the action to be performed when the user selects the Save option from the shortcut menu.

In addition to adding actions to the file types, you can specify a default action to be performed when the user double-clicks on a file with the .xls extension. You can create the default action Open. To do this, perform the following steps:

1. Right-click on the Open action.
2. Select the Set As Default option.

Figure 12-15 displays the file type editor.

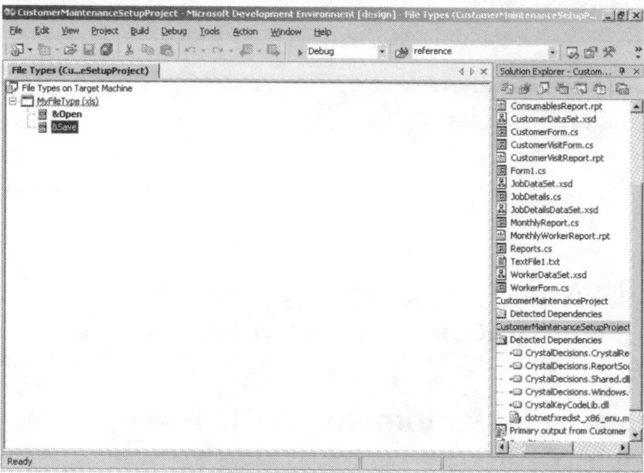


**FIGURE 12-15** *The file type editor*

## User Interface Editor

You have seen the installation process of the Customer Maintenance project. During the installation process, the dialog boxes that are displayed are created by Visual Studio .NET. You can make changes to these dialog boxes or may even add new dialog boxes in Visual Studio .NET. In addition, you can change the properties of the default dialog boxes. To do this, Visual Studio .NET provides you with a user interface editor. Similar to any other editor, you can access a user interface editor from the Editor option on the View menu. Figure 12-16 displays the user interface editor.

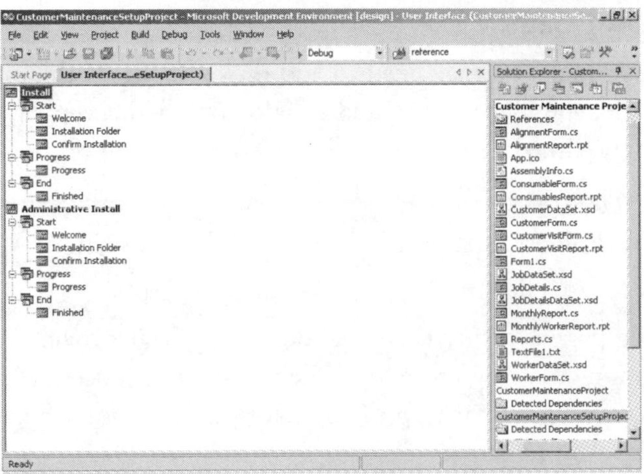

**FIGURE 12-16** *The user interface editor*

As you can see, the user interface editor displays the structure of dialog boxes that will be displayed during the installation process. The user interface editor is a tree view control containing the dialog boxes that are displayed when the user or the system administrator installs the application on the user's machine or the network. The following section discusses customizing the dialog box in the installation process of an application.

## Customizing Dialog Boxes

Visual Studio .NET allows you to customize the interface of a dialog box by performing the following steps:

1. Select the Standard dialog box in the user interface editor.
2. In the Properties window of the dialog box, modify the required property.

In addition to customizing dialog boxes, you may want to add new dialog boxes to the installation process. The next section will discuss adding new dialog boxes.

## Adding New Dialog Boxes

Consider a situation in which you may need to add dialog boxes to the installation process. For example, you may want to add a dialog box that accepts the user and company name at the time of installation. To do this, perform the following steps:

1. Select the Start, Progress, or Finish option in the Install section.
2. On the Action menu, click on the Add Dialog option.

   The Add Dialog page is displayed. The Add Dialog page provides you with several options that you can add to the installation process. You can view a short description of each option by selecting the option. Figure 12-17 shows the Add Dialog page.
3. Select the Register User dialog box on the Add Dialog page.
4. Click on the OK button to add the Register User dialog box.

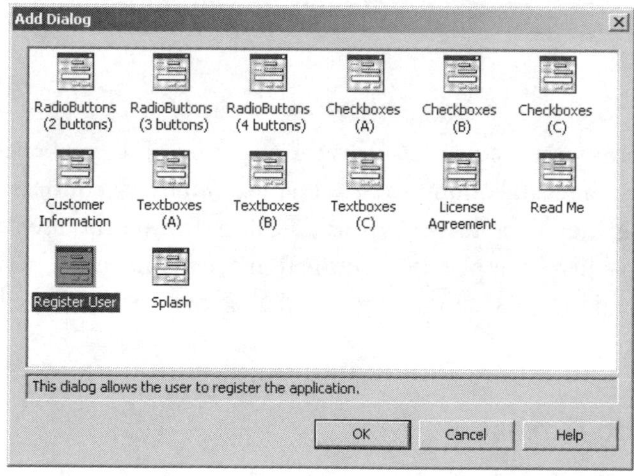


**FIGURE 12-17** *The Add Dialog page*

By default, the Register User dialog box gets added last in the list. You can move the newly added dialog box up or down the list as required. Figure 12-18 displays the Register User dialog box added to the user interface editor.

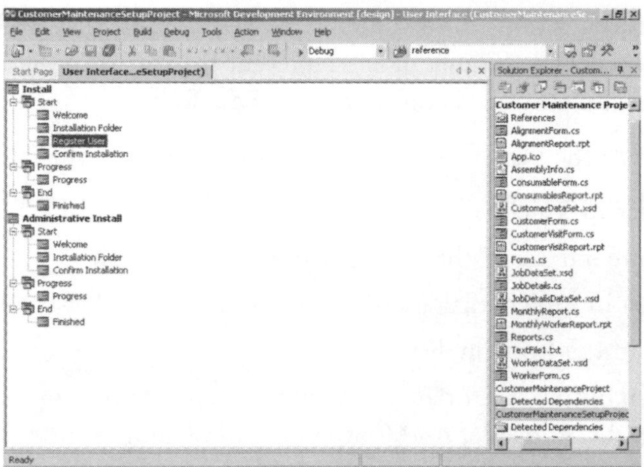


**FIGURE 12-18** *The Register User dialog box added to the user interface editor*

## The Custom Action Editor

Using the custom editor in Visual Studio .NET, you can modify the installation process to perform some additional tasks on the user's computer. This implies that you can add custom actions that the installation process performs while installing the application. You can access the custom action editor in the Editor option of the View menu. Figure 12-19 shows the custom action editor.

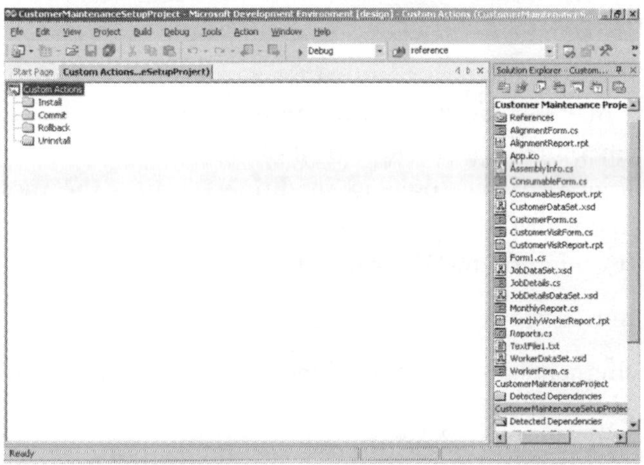


**FIGURE 12-19** *The custom action editor*

As you can see, the custom action editor contains the Install, Commit, Rollback, and Uninstall folders by default. These folders represent the stages of the installation process. You can add custom actions to any of these folders.

To add custom actions to the installation process, perform the following steps:

1. Select any folder to which you want to add a custom action.
2. On the Action menu, select the Add Custom Action option.
3. The Select Item in Project dialog box is displayed.
4. Select a folder in the Look in: list box.
5. To add a file, an output file, or an assembly that contains the custom action, click on the Add File, Add Output, or Add Component button, respectively.

**TIP**

Before adding a custom action to the installation process, you must compile your custom action in the form of executable files, such as .dll or .exe, or scripts, such as VBScript (.vbs file) or JScript (.js file).

6. Click on the OK button to add the custom action.

## The Launch Conditions Editor

When you install an application, the installation process must follow some conditions. These conditions may include the availability of certain files, the required operating system, or the required registry keys. You can apply these conditions by using the launch conditions editor. Applying conditions ensures the successful installation and deployment of the application. To access the launch conditions editor, access the Editor option on the View menu.

To add a launch condition, perform the following steps:

1. Select the Requirements on Target Machine option in the launch condition editor.
2. On the Action menu, select the Add File Launch Condition option.

You may even choose to add a launch condition for a registry, Windows Installer, .NET Framework, or Internet Information Services (IIS).

Visual Studio .NET adds two nodes, Search for File1 and Launch Conditions, to the launch conditions editor. Figure 12-20 displays the launch conditions editor.

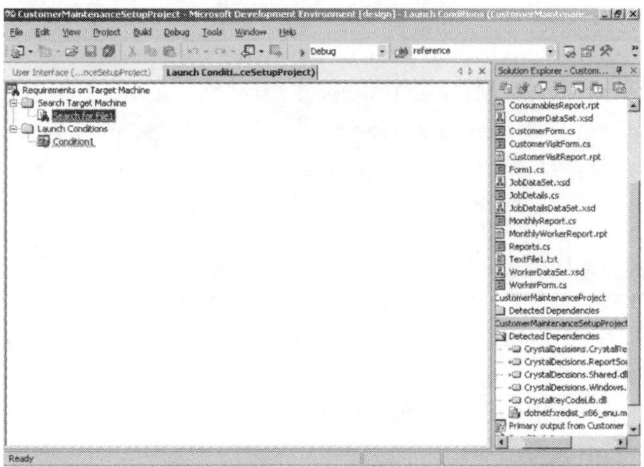


**FIGURE 12-20** *The launch conditions editor*

The properties of the Search for File1 node allow you to specify the properties of the file to be searched during installation. The properties of the Launch Conditions nodes allow you to specify the message to be displayed if the required file is not found.

# Summary

In this chapter, you learned about the basics of deploying a Windows application. Deploying a Windows application allows you to execute a Windows application that you have created on a computer other than the computer on which you created the application. To enable you to deploy an application, Visual Studio .NET provides you with deployment project templates. A deployment project in Visual Studio .NET is a project that enables you to create an installation program to ensure successful deployment of your application on another computer.

Next, you learned about the various deployment project templates available in C#. The simplest way to deploy a Windows application is to convert the application to a CAB file. A CAB file is a zipped form of your project. Another deployment project that Visual Studio .NET provides you is the Setup project. The Setup Project template creates the installer files, called MSI files, that the users can install on their machines to deploy the application. In addition to a CAB or Setup project, you can create a Merge Module project by using the templates provided by Visual Studio .NET. A Merge Module project is used to combine the application files, resource files, registry files, and Setup files in a single package. Visual Studio .NET also provides you with a Setup wizard that you can use to create these deployment projects.

Finally, you learned about the deployment editors, which allow you to specify information, such as the location where you need to deploy the project, the method of deployment, registry information, and so on, while creating a deployment project. By default, Visual Studio .NET contains six types of deployment editors. These editors include the file system, registry, file type, user interface, custom action, and launch conditions editors.

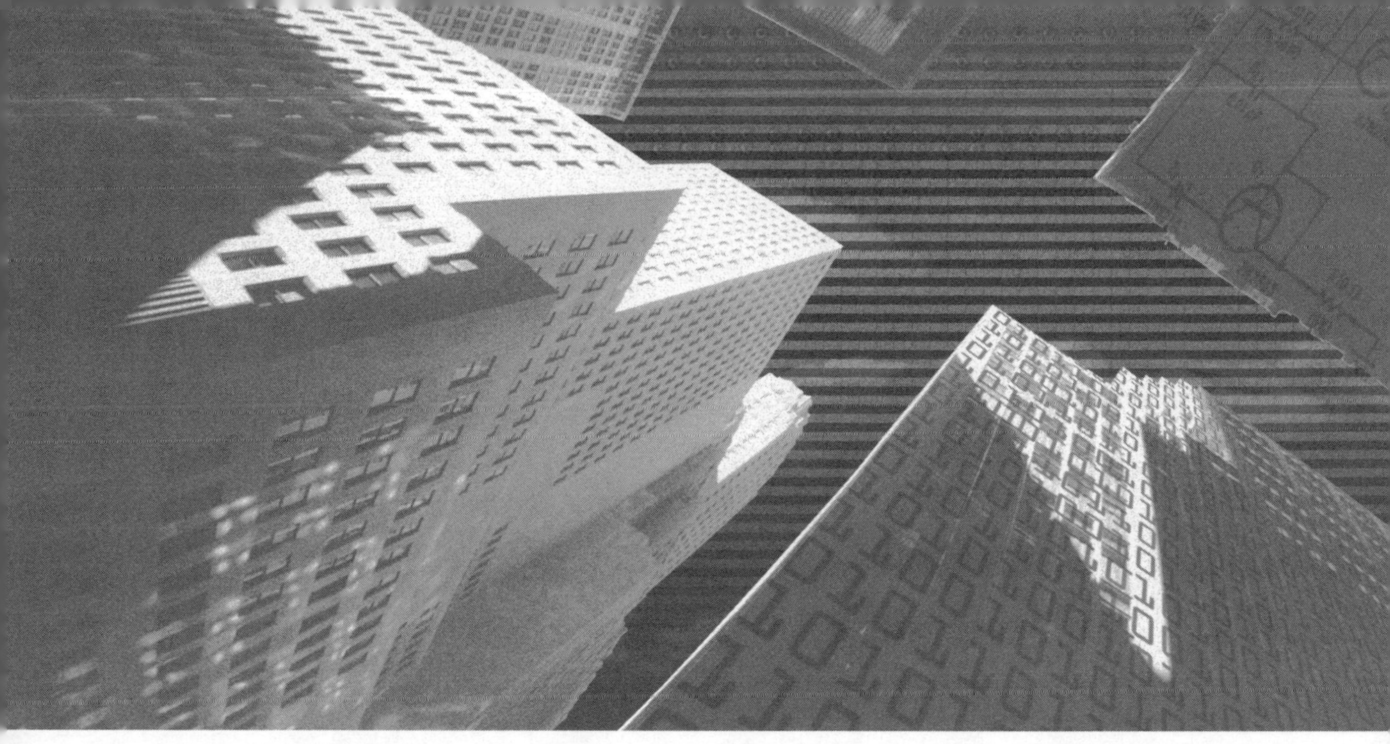

# PART IV

## Professional Project 2

# Project 2

## Creating the Employee Records System (ERS) Project

## Project 2 Overview

The Employee Records System (ERS) is a utility that will be used by the human resources department to view the records of employees in the organization. The basic purpose of such a system is to assist the HR personnel in finding details of the employees.

In this project, I will take you through the process of building the ERS application using the TreeView, ListView, and StatusBar controls and interacting with an XML file.

In the previous project, you learned to develop a Windows application for a car maintenance company. In this project, you will learn to create another Windows application, an Employee Records System (ERS) that displays the details of employees.

# Chapter 13

## Project Case Study and Design

This project describes the procedure to access XML data from a Windows application. It also illustrates the use of important Windows controls, such as the TreeView and ListView controls.

## Case Study

You need to develop an application that enables you to pick up the details of employees from an XML file and display the employee codes in the TreeView control. On clicking an employee code, the details of the employee must be displayed in the ListView control.

This chapter will start developing the ERS project. This project will introduce you to various controls, such as TreeView, ListView, StatusBar, and ListLabel, and their properties and methods. The project will also discuss how to read records from a XML data store. This chapter covers the design of the project.

## Project Life Cycle

You looked at the phases of a DLC (*development life cycle*) of a project in Chapter 7, "Project Case Study," in the section "Case Study." Because we have already discussed the entire life cycle of the project, here I will discuss the design of the application created by the development team for the ERS project. You, as a part of the development team, will analyze the requirements and create a design for the application.

### Analyzing Requirements

To find a solution to a problem faced by a customer, you first need to analyze the customer's requirements in detail. This is done in the analyzing requirements phase of the project life cycle. After analyzing the customer's problems in detail, you create a plan for developing the application. This analysis of the customer's problem is based on the problem statement stated by senior management and the information gathered by the development team.

In this case, the problem statement, as stated by the HR Manager, is, "The details of each employee must be accessible in an easy and simple manner."

Upon analyzing the problem statement, the development team defined the following list of tasks that they need to do:

- The HR department needs to maintain the records of its employee in a data store.
- The HR department needs an application that will enable it to obtain its employee records in a quick and efficient manner.

This application can be extended to add new employee records, modify existing records, and delete records.

## High-Level Design

Based on the plan of the Windows application, the development team created a design of the Windows application in the high-level design phase. The design of the ERS application includes creating the user interface for the Windows form used in the application.

The ERS application consists of a Windows form, as shown in Figure 13-1.

**FIGURE 13-1** *Layout of the ERS form*

To create the layout of the ERS application, as shown in Figure 13-1, you need to include TreeView, ListView, and StatusBar controls. The following section discusses the different controls in detail. The ERS application consists of a main Windows form, called `EmployeeRecordsForm`.

Press F4 to view the properties of the `EmployeeRecordsForm` form. Change the following property values in the Properties window:

```
Name: EmployeeRecordsForm
Auto Scroll: True
MinimizeBox: False
MaximizeBox: False
Size: 728, 408
Text: Employee Records Monitoring System
```

The properties of the `EmployeeRecordsForm` form are as shown in Figure 13-2.

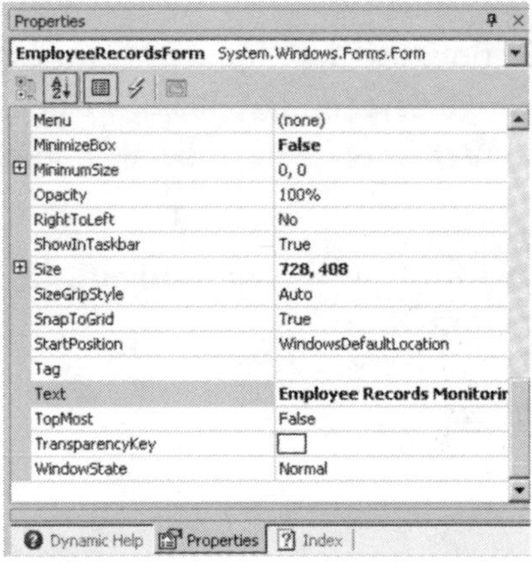


**FIGURE 13-2** *Properties of the* `EmployeeRecordsForm` *form*

Changing the `Name` property changes the name of the form. By setting the `MinimizeBox` and the `MaximizeBox` properties to `False`, you can ensure that the form cannot be maximized or minimized.

## TreeView Control

A TreeView control is a Windows Forms control that you can use to display a hierarchy of nodes. These nodes are called *root* or *parent* nodes. Each root node in the hierarchy can contain one or more nodes, called *child* nodes. The root and parent nodes can be collapsed or expanded.

To add a TreeView control in Visual Studio .NET, you can drag the TreeView control from the Windows Forms toolbox to the `EmployeeRecordsForm` form. Figure 13-3 shows the TreeView control in the Windows Forms toolbox.

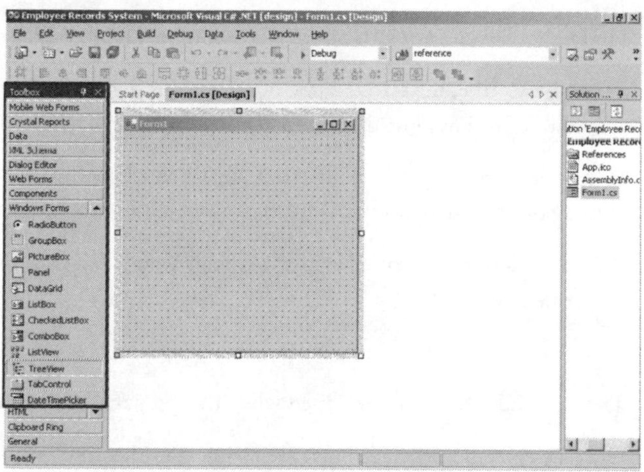


**FIGURE 13-3** *A TreeView control in the Windows Forms toolbox*

You can create a TreeView control by dragging a TreeView control from the Windows Forms toolbox to the form. The appearance of the TreeView control can be changed from the properties window. Table 13-1 lists and explains some of the important TreeView control properties.

**Table 13-1 TreeView Control Properties**

| Property | Description |
|---|---|
| `Name` | Sets the name of the control. |
| `AllowDrop` | Indicates whether the control can accept data that user drags onto it. |
| `BorderStyle` | Sets the border style of the control. The default style is `Fixed3D`, wherein the control has a sunken three-dimensional appearance. |
| `CheckBoxes` | Displays check boxes next to the tree nodes in the control when set to true. |
| `FullRowSelect` | Highlights the entire width of the control when a node is selected. |
| `HideSelection` | When set to true, the selected tree node remains highlighted even after the control has lost the focus. |
| `HotTracking` | When set to true, the tree node labels appear as a hyperlink when the mouse pointer moves over it. |
| `ImageIndex` | Sets the image-list index value of the default image that is displayed by the tree nodes. |
| `ImageList` | Specifies the ImageList that contains the images. |
| `LabelEdit` | The tree node labels can be edited when this property is set to true. |
| `Nodes` | Gets the collection of nodes that are assigned to the TreeView control. |
| `Scrollable` | The TreeView control displays scroll bars when it is set to true. |
| `SelectedImageIndex` | Gets or sets the image list index value of the image that is displayed when a tree node is selected. |
| `ShowLines` | Displays lines connecting the nodes in the control, when set to true. |
| `ShowPlusMinus` | Displays plus sign (+) and minus sign (-) when a node contains child nodes. |
| `ShowRootLines` | Displays lines connecting root nodes in the control when set to true. |
| `Size` | Sets the height and width of the control. |
| `Sorted` | When set to true, the nodes in the control are displayed in a sorted order. |
| `Visible` | When set to true, the control is not displayed. |

You will now create a TreeView control for the application. To create a TreeView control, perform the following steps:

1. Drag a TreeView control from the Windows Forms toolbox to the form. A blank TreeView control is added to the form.
2. Press the F4 key to display the properties of the TreeView control.
3. In the Properties window, change the following properties:

```
Name: treeView1
ShowLines: True
ShowPlusMinus: True
ShowRootLines: True
Size: 240, 352
```

The control does not contain any nodes. You can add both parent and child nodes to the TreeView control by using the `Nodes` property. You can also add nodes programmatically, which will be discussed in the next chapter.

## ListView Control

A ListView control is a Windows Form control that displays a collection of items by using one of the four different possible views. A ListView control enables you to display a list of items with text and images to identify the type of item. You can display the items in a ListView control as large icons, small icons, or a vertical list. The items can also be displayed with column headers identifying the information being displayed in a subitem.

You can create a ListView control by dragging a ListView control from the Windows Forms toolbox to the form. The appearance of the ListView control can be changed from the Properties window. Table 13-2 lists and explains some of the important ListView control properties.

**Table 13-2 ListView Control Properties**

| Property | Description |
|---|---|
| `Name` | Sets the name of the control. |
| `Activation` | Specifies the type of action the user must take to activate an item. |
| `Alignment` | Sets the alignment of items in the control. |
| `AllowDrop` | Indicates whether the control will accept data the user drags onto it or not. |
| `AllowColumnReorder` | Indicates whether the user can drag column headers to reorder columns in the control. |
| `AutoArrange` | Indicates whether items are automatically arranged. |
| `BorderStyle` | Sets the border style of the control. |
| `Columns` | Gets the collection of all column headers that appear in the control. |
| `Dock` | Sets the edge of the parent container to which a control is docked. |
| `FullRowSelect` | Indicates whether clicking an item selects all its subitems. |
| `HeaderStyle` | Sets whether the column header is clickable or not. |
| `Items` | Specifies the collection of items in the control. |
| `LabelWrap` | Indicates whether the item label wraps or not. |
| `LargeImageList` | Specifies the ImageList to use when displaying the items as large icons. |
| `MultiSelect` | Indicates whether multiple items can be selected. |
| `Scrollable` | Indicates whether scroll bars will be displayed. |
| `SmallImageList` | Specifies the ImageList to use when displaying the items. |
| `Sorting` | Sets the sort order for items in the control. |
| `View` | Specifies the manner in which items are displayed in the control. The items can be displayed either as large icons, small icons, in a list manner, or in a details manner. |
| `Visible` | When set to true, the control is not displayed. |

You will now create a ListView control for the application. To create a ListView control, perform the following steps:

1. Drag a ListView control from the Windows Forms toolbox to the form.

   A blank ListView control is added to the form. Similar to the TreeView control, the appearance of the ListView control can be modified by changing its properties.
2. Press the F4 key to display the properties of the ListView control.
3. In the Properties window, change the following properties:

   `Name: listView1`

   `Activation: TwoClick`

   `MultiSelect: False`

   `View: Details`

## *StatusBar Control*

A StatusBar control is a Windows Forms control that typically appears at the bottom of the form and is used to display different types of status information. A StatusBar control can have status bar panels on them that display text or icons to indicate the state. The StatusBar panels can be used to display information about page numbers, spelling and grammar status, and editing modes on the status bar.

Perform the following steps to create a status bar for the application:

1. Drag a StatusBar control from the Windows Forms toolbox to the form.
2. Press F4 and change the following properties:

   `Name: statusBar1`

   `ShowPanels: True`

   Panels can be added to a StatusBar control either at design time through `StatusBarPanel Collection Editor` or at run time through the `StatusBarPanelCollection` class.
3. In the Properties window, click on the Panels property, and then click on the ellipsis (...) button to open StatusBarPanel Collection Editor.
4. Add a panel by clicking the Add button.

5. Change the following values:

   Name: `statusBarPanel1`

   Text: `Click the employee code to view details`

   Width: `240`

The StatusBarPanel Collection Editor is shown in Figure 13-4.

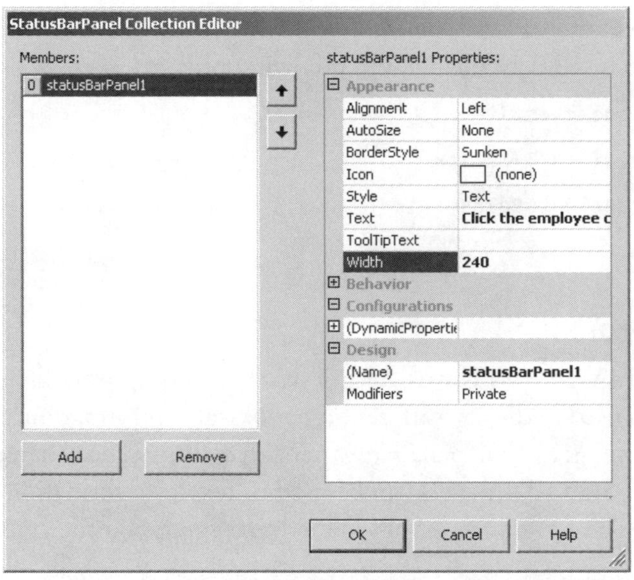


**FIGURE 13-4** *The StatusBarPanel Collection Editor*

## The XML File Schema

The development team decides to store the records of the employees in an XML file. This would facilitate accessing the data store from any system. The schema of this XML file is as follows:

```
<?xml version="1.0"?>
 <EmpRecordsData>
 <Ecode Id="E0001" EmployeeName="Michael Perry">
  <EmpDetails DateofJoin="02-02-1999" Grade="A" salary="1750"/>
  </Ecode>
```

```
<Ecode Id="E0002" EmployeeName="Jenifer Carell">
<EmpDetails DateofJoin="03-22-1999" Grade="B" salary="2500"/>
 </Ecode>
<Ecode Id="E0003" EmployeeName="George Rice">
 <EmpDetails DateofJoin="04-18-1999" Grade="A" salary="1800"/>
 </Ecode>
<Ecode Id="E0004" EmployeeName="Pamela Griffin">
 <EmpDetails DateofJoin="04-27-1999" Grade="E" salary="7000"/>
 </Ecode>
<Ecode Id="E0005" EmployeeName="Simon Watson">
 <EmpDetails DateofJoin="05-03-1999" Grade="A" salary="1650"/>
 </Ecode>
<Ecode Id="E0006" EmployeeName="Daniel Allison">
 <EmpDetails DateofJoin="05-13-1999" Grade="D" salary="5700"/>
 </Ecode>
<Ecode Id="E0007" EmployeeName="Laura Hansen">
 <EmpDetails DateofJoin="06-02-1999" Grade="C" salary="4150"/>
 </Ecode>
<Ecode Id="E0008" EmployeeName="Sarah Judd">
 <EmpDetails DateofJoin="09-11-1999" Grade="B" salary="2600"/>
 </Ecode>
<Ecode Id="E0009" EmployeeName="Joshua Johnson">
 <EmpDetails DateofJoin="09-23-1999" Grade="E" salary="7725"/>
 </Ecode>
<Ecode Id="E0010" EmployeeName="Larry Gates">
 <EmpDetails DateofJoin="10-20-1999" Grade="C" salary="4350"/>
 </Ecode>
<Ecode Id="E0011" EmployeeName="Nicholas Harvey">
 <EmpDetails DateofJoin="10-20-1999" Grade="B" salary="2720"/>
 </Ecode>
<Ecode Id="E0012" EmployeeName="Michael Brown">
 <EmpDetails DateofJoin="11-11-1999" Grade="A" salary="1665"/>
 </Ecode>
<Ecode Id="E0013" EmployeeName="George Lewis">
 <EmpDetails DateofJoin="12-07-1999" Grade="B" salary="3150"/>
 </Ecode>
```

```
<Ecode Id="E0014" EmployeeName="Elaine Thorn">
 <EmpDetails DateofJoin="12-13-1999" Grade="C" salary="4070"/>
 </Ecode>
</EmpRecordsData>
```

This XML data store is saved as EmpRec.xml. The EmpRec.xml file has `Ecode` and `EmpDetails` as its elements. `Id` and `EmployeeName` are attributes of the `Ecode` element. `Date of Join`, `Grade`, and `salary` are attributes that are contained within the `EmpDetails` element.

## Low-Level Design

After completing the analysis and design of the ERS application in the high-level design phase, the development team creates a detailed design of software modules. These software modules are then used to create a detailed structure of the application. In addition to creating software modules, the team decides the flow and interaction of each module.

The flowchart of the project created by the development team is shown in Figure 13-5.

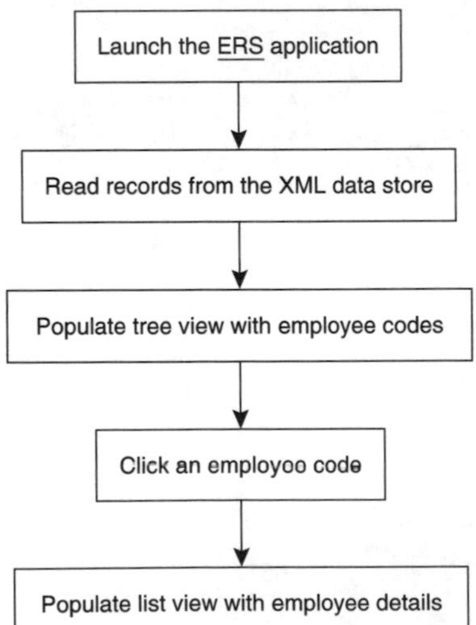


**FIGURE 13-5** *Flowchart of the ERS project*

# Summary

In this chapter, you were introduced to the case study and design of the ERS project. You created the high-level and low-level design of the application. You also learned about different controls and the means of using them. You will learn to develop the application in the next chapter.

# Chapter 14

## Implementing the Business Logic

In this chapter, you will learn to add nodes to the tree view and items to the list view programmatically. You will also learn to read contents of an XML file. You will build the Employee Records System application.

## Populating the TreeView Control

In order to build the application, the first task you need to complete is populating the TreeView control. You have inserted a TreeView control in the form. However, the TreeView control does not contain any nodes. Now you will learn to add nodes to the control programmatically.

In order to add a node, you first need to initialize a new instance of the `TreeNode` class. Calling the constructor of the `TreeNode` class enables you to achieve this. The constructor of the `TreeNode` class is overloaded, as explained in Table 14-1.

**Table 14-1 `TreeNode` Class Constructors**

| Constructor | Description |
|---|---|
| `public TreeNode();` | Initializes a new instance of the `TreeNode` class |
| `public TreeNode(string);` | Initializes a new instance of the `TreeNode` class with the specified label text |
| `public TreeNode(string, TreeNode[]);` | Initializes a new instance of the `TreeNode` class with the specified label text and child tree nodes |
| `public TreeNode(string, int, int);` | Initializes a new instance of the `TreeNode` class with the specified label text and images to be displayed in selected and unselected state |
| `public TreeNode(string, int, int, TreeNode[]);` | Initializes a new instance of the `TreeNode` class with the specified label text, child tree nodes, and images to be displayed in selected and unselected state |

## Displaying Employee Codes in the TreeView Control

You can add a node to the TreeView control using the `Add` method, as follows:

```
treeview1.Nodes.Add(new TreeNode("Root Node")
```

In this code, `treeview1` refers to the TreeView control. The `Nodes` collection contains all child nodes of a particular parent node. The `Add` method of the `TreeNodeCollection` class enables you to add nodes to the collection. For example, the following code explains the manner in which you can add a node with the display text "`My Computer`".

```
tnRootNode = new TreeNode("My Computer");
tvFolderView.Nodes.Add(tnRootNode);
```

The previous code assumes that you have added a TreeView control to the form.

The first task that you need to accomplish is to open the XML data store and read the employee records. You will learn about XML in Chapter 17, "Interacting with a Microsoft Word Document and Event Viewer." You are already aware that the `XmlTextReader` class provides a simple mechanism to access to a stream of XML data in a fast, noncached manner. I will be using the `XmlTextReader` class to read the EmpRec.xml file.

The `XmlTextReader` represents a reader that is advanced using the read methods and properties of the current node. Table 14-2 lists some of the commonly used properties of the `XmlTextReader` class.

**Table 14-2 Properties of the `XmlTextReader` Class**

| Properties | Description |
|---|---|
| EOF | Indicates whether the reader is positioned at the end of the XML stream |
| HasAttributes | Indicates whether current node has any attributes |
| HasValue | Indicates whether current node has any value |
| Item | Obtains the value of the attribute |
| LineNumber | Gets the current line number of the reader |
| LinePosition | Gets the current position of the reader in the line specified |
| Name | Gets the name of the current node |
| ReadState | Gets the state of the reader |
| Value | Gets the text value of the current node |

Table 14-3 lists some of the commonly used properties of the `XmlTextReader` class.

**Table 14-3 Methods of the `XmlTextReader` Class**

| Methods | Description |
|---|---|
| Close | Changes the ReadState to closed |
| GetAttribute | Gets the value of an attribute |
| MoveToAttribute | Moves to the specified attribute |
| MoveToContent | Checks whether the current node is a content node; if not, the reader skips to the next node |
| MoveToElement | Moves to the element that contains the current attribute node |
| MoveToFirstAttribute | Moves to the first attribute |
| MoveToNextAttribute | Moves to the next attribute |
| Read | Reads the next node from the stream |
| ReadAttributeValue | Parses the attribute value into one or more Text, EntityReference, or EndEntity nodes |
| ReadInnerXml | Reads all the content, including markup, as a string |
| ReadOuterXml | Reads the content, including markup, representing the current node and its child nodes |
| ReadString | Reads the contents of an element or a text node as a string |
| Skip | Skips the children of the current node |
| ToString | Returns a string that represents the current object |

Now you need to read the employee codes from the EmpRec.xml file and display them in the tree view control.

You can open the XML file by initializing the `XMLTextReader` class, as follows:

```
XmlTextReader reader= new XmlTextReader ("E:\\BookProj\\EmpRec.xml");
```

where `e:\BookProj\EmpRec.xml` represents the path on your hard disk where the EmpRec.xml file is stored.

I have written the entire code for populating the TreeView control inside a function, `PopulateTreeView`, as given following.

```
protected void PopulateTreeView()
{
  statusBarPanel1.Text="Refreshing Employee Codes. Please wait...";
  this.Cursor = Cursors.WaitCursor;
  treeView1.Nodes.Clear();
  tvRootNode=new TreeNode("Employee Records");
  this.Cursor = Cursors.Default;
  treeView1.Nodes.Add(tvRootNode);

  TreeNodeCollection nodeCollect = tvRootNode.Nodes;
  string strVal="";
  XmlTextReader reader= new XmlTextReader("E:\\BookProj\\EmpRec.xml");

  reader.MoveToElement();
  try
  {
    while(reader.Read())
    {
      if(reader.HasAttributes && reader.NodeType==XmlNodeType.Element)
      {
        reader.MoveToElement();
        reader.MoveToElement();
        reader.MoveToAttribute("Id");
        strVal=reader.Value;
        reader.Read();
        reader.Read();

        if(reader.Name=="Dept")
        {
          reader.Read();
        }
      //create the child nodes
      TreeNode EcodeNode = new TreeNode(strVal);
```

```
        //      Add the Node
        nodeCollect.Add(EcodeNode);
        }
      }
    statusBarPanel1.Text="Click on an employee code to see their record.";
    }
    catch(XmlException e)
    {
      MessageBox.Show("XML Exception :"+e.ToString());
    }
}
```

Figure 14-1 displays the TreeView control populated with the employee codes.

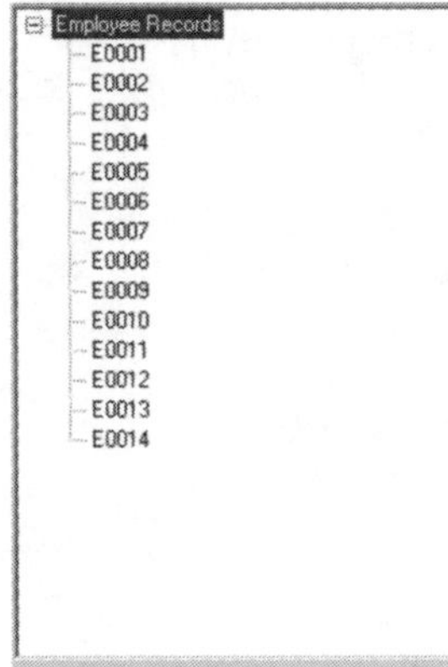


**FIGURE 14-1** *The TreeView control populated with employee codes*

## Event Handling

An event is the result of an action that has occurred. This action could have occurred as a result of user action, such as a mouse click, or could have been the result of a built-in program logic. For example, when a person rings the doorbell, an event takes place. Another person responds to the event by attending the door. The person ringing the bell is called the *event sender* and the person responding is the *event receiver* or *handler*. However, the person triggering the event is not aware of the person who will be handling the event.

To respond to an event, you must provide an event handler method that will handle the events. Suppose you have a simple Windows form that contains a button. When the button is clicked, the event must be handled by an event handler method. The following code shows an event handler.

```
void Button_Clicked(object sender, EventArgs e)
{
    //the program logic
}
```

However, for the event to be handled, you need to tie up your event handler to an instance of the button. You need to create an instance of EventHandler that takes a reference to Button_Clicked as its argument, as shown in the following code:

```
button.Click+=new EventHandler(this.Button_Clicked);
```

This tying up is taken care of by Visual Studio .NET. The following example shows a simple Windows application that handles a button click event.

```
using System;
using System.ComponentModel;
using System.Windows.Forms;
using System.Drawing;
public class EventSampleForm: Form
{
   private Button button;

   public EventSampleForm () : base()
   {
      button = new Button();
      button.Location = new Point(50,100);
      button.Text = "Click Me";
      // To wire the event, create a delegate instance and add it to the Click event.
      button.Click += new EventHandler(this.Button_Clicked);
      Controls.Add(button);
   }
   // The event handler.
   private void Button_Clicked(object sender, EventArgs e)
```

```
    {
        MessageBox.Show("You clicked me!");
    }
    // STAThreadAttribute indicates that Windows Forms uses the
    // single-threaded apartment model.
    [STAThreadAttribute]
    public static void Main(string[] args)
    {
        Application.Run(new EventSampleForm ());
    }
}
```

The essential steps in an event handling application are as follows:

- The source of an event is an instance of `System.Windows.Forms.<control>` control.
- The `<control>` raises an event.
- The delegate for the event is `EventHandler`.
- The form has an event handler called `Control_Event`.
- The `Control_Event` is tied to the event.

## Displaying Employee Details in the ListView Control

In the ERS application, the employee details need to be displayed in the ListView control at the click of an employee code in the TreeView control. Items can be added to ListView control using the `ListView Collection Editor` or programmatically. For this application, you need to add the items programmatically, because the items are dependent on an event, the click of an employee code node in the TreeView control.

However, before the list view control is populated, you need to create column headers for the ListView control. A column header is an item in a ListView control that contains heading text. I have put the code for displaying the column headers in the `initializeListControl` method, as given following.

```
protected void initializeListControl()
{
    listView1.Clear();
    listView1.Columns.Add("Employee Name",225,HorizontalAlignment.Left );
```

```
    listView1.Columns.Add("Date of Join",70,HorizontalAlignment.Right );
    listView1.Columns.Add("Grade",105,HorizontalAlignment.Left );
    listView1.Columns.Add("Salary",105,HorizontalAlignment.Left );
}
```

The `Columns` property of the ListView class contains a collection of all the column headers that appear in the control. The `Columns` property returns a collection containing `ColumnHeader` objects that are displayed in the ListView control. The `ColumnHeader` objects define the text to be displayed for a column and is contained in the `ListView.ColumnHeaderCollection`.

You can add a column header to the collection using the `Add` method. Alternatively, you can create an array of `ColumnHeader` objects and pass it to the `AddRange` method to add a number of column headers.

Table 14-4 explains some of the commonly used methods of the `ListView.ColumnHeaderCollection`.

**Table 14-4 `ListView.ColumnHeaderCollection` Members**

| Method | Description |
|---|---|
| Add | This overloaded method adds a column header to the collection. |
| AddRange | This method adds an array of column headers to the collection. |
| Clear | This method removes all column headers from the collection. |
| Contains | This method determines whether the specified method is contained in the collection. |
| Insert | This method inserts a column header into the collection at the specified index. |
| Remove | This method removes the specified column header from the collection. |
| RemoveAt | This method removes the column header at the specified index from within the collection. |

The final task is to read the EmpRec.xml XML file and display the details of an employee whose employee code has been clicked in the TreeView control.

```
protected void PopulateListView(TreeNode currNode)
{
  initializeListControl();
```

```
    XmlTextReader listRead= new XmlTextReader("E:\\BookProj\\EmpRec.xml");
    listRead.MoveToElement();

    while(listRead.Read())
    {
      string strNodename;
      string strNodePath;
      string name;
      string grade;
      string doj;
      string sal;
      string[] strItemsArr=new String [4];
      listRead.MoveToFirstAttribute();
      strNodename=listRead.Value;
      strNodePath=currNode.FullPath.Remove(0,17);
      if(strNodePath==strNodename)
      {
        ListViewItem lvi;
        listRead.MoveToNextAttribute();
        name=listRead.Value;
        lvi=listView1.Items.Add(name);
        listRead.Read();
        listRead.Read();
        listRead.MoveToFirstAttribute();
        doj=listRead.Value;
        lvi.SubItems.Add(doj);
        listRead.MoveToNextAttribute();
        grade=listRead.Value;
        lvi.SubItems.Add(grade);
        listRead.MoveToNextAttribute();
        sal=listRead.Value;
        lvi.SubItems.Add(sal);
        listRead.MoveToNextAttribute();
        listRead.MoveToElement();
        listRead.ReadString();
      }
    }
  }
```

Figure 14-2 displays the ERS application populated with the employee records.

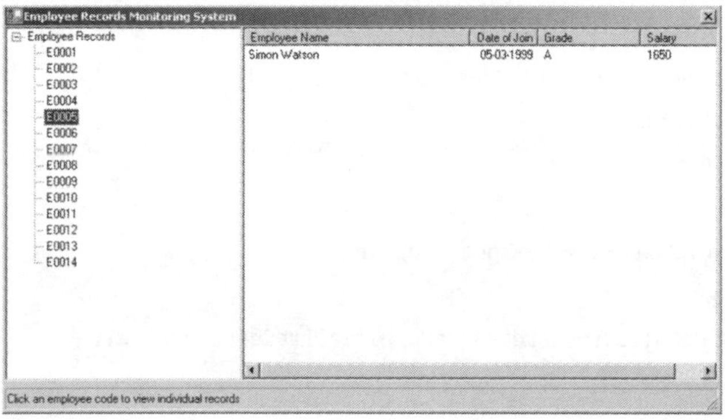

**FIGURE 14-2** *The ERS application*

The code for the entire application is given here.

```
using System;
using System.Drawing;
using System.Collections;
using System.ComponentModel;
using System.Windows.Forms;
using System.Data;
using System.Xml;
using System.Diagnostics;
using System.IO;
namespace EmployeeRecords
{
  /// <summary>
  /// Summary description for Form1.
  /// </summary>
  public class EmployeeRecordsForm : System.Windows.Forms.Form
  {
    private System.Windows.Forms.TreeView treeView1;
    private System.Windows.Forms.ListView listView1;
    private System.Windows.Forms.StatusBar statusBar1;
    private System.Windows.Forms.StatusBarPanel statusBarPanel1;
```

```
/// <summary>
/// Required designer variable.
/// </summary>
private System.ComponentModel.Container components=null;
private TreeNode tvRootNode;
public EmployeeRecordsForm()
{
  // Required for Windows Form Designer support
  InitializeComponent();
  // TODO: Add any constructor code after InitializeComponent call
  PopulateTreeView();
  initializeListControl();
}
/// <summary>
/// Clean up any resources being used.
/// </summary>
protected override void Dispose( bool disposing )
{
  if( disposing )
  {
    if (components != null)
    {
      components.Dispose();
    }
  }
  base.Dispose( disposing );
}
#region Windows Form Designer generated code
/// <summary>
/// Required method for Designer support - do not modify
/// the contents of this method with the code editor.
/// </summary>
private void InitializeComponent()
{
  this.treeView1 = new System.Windows.Forms.TreeView();
  this.listView1 = new System.Windows.Forms.ListView();
  this.statusBar1 = new System.Windows.Forms.StatusBar();
  this.statusBarPanel1 = new System.Windows.Forms.StatusBarPanel();
```

```
 ((System.ComponentModel.ISupportInitialize)(this.statusBarPanel1))
    .BeginInit();
this.SuspendLayout();
this.treeView1.ImageIndex = -1;
this.treeView1.Name = "treeView1";
this.treeView1.SelectedImageIndex = -1;
this.treeView1.Size = new System.Drawing.Size(240, 352);
this.treeView1.TabIndex = 0;
this.treeView1.AfterSelect += new System.Windows.Forms.TreeViewEventHandler
   (this.treeView1_AfterSelect);
//
// listView1
//
this.listView1.Activation = System.Windows.Forms.ItemActivation.TwoClick;
this.listView1.Location = new System.Drawing.Point(240, 0);
this.listView1.Name = "listView1";
this.listView1.Size = new System.Drawing.Size(480, 352);
this.listView1.TabIndex = 1;
this.listView1.View = System.Windows.Forms.View.Details;

//
// statusBar1
//
this.statusBar1.Location = new System.Drawing.Point(0, 357);
this.statusBar1.Name = "statusBar1";
this.statusBar1.Panels.AddRange(new System.Windows.Forms.StatusBarPanel[] {
this.statusBarPanel1});
this.statusBar1.ShowPanels = true;
this.statusBar1.Size = new System.Drawing.Size(720, 24);
this.statusBar1.TabIndex = 2;
//
// statusBarPanel1
//
this.statusBarPanel1.Text = "Click the employee code to view details";
this.statusBarPanel1.Width = 720;
//
// EmployeeRecordsForm
//
```

```
    this.AutoScaleBaseSize = new System.Drawing.Size(5, 13);
    this.AutoScroll = true;
    this.ClientSize = new System.Drawing.Size(720, 381);
    this.Controls.AddRange(new System.Windows.Forms.Control[] {
    this.statusBar1,
    this.listView1,
    this.treeView1});
    this.MaximizeBox = false;
    this.MinimizeBox = false;
    this.Name = "EmployeeRecordsForm";
    this.Text = "Employee Records Monitoring System";
    ((System.ComponentModel.ISupportInitialize)(this.statusBarPanel1))
       .EndInit();
    this.ResumeLayout(false);
  }
  #endregion
  /// <summary>
  /// The main entry point for the application.
  /// </summary>
   [STAThread]
  static void Main()
  {
    Application.Run(new EmployeeRecordsForm());
  }

  protected void PopulateTreeView()
  {
    statusBarPanel1.Text="Refreshing Employee Codes. Please wait...";
    this.Cursor = Cursors.WaitCursor;
    treeView1.Nodes.Clear();
    tvRootNode=new TreeNode("Employee Records");
    this.Cursor = Cursors.Default;
    treeView1.Nodes.Add(tvRootNode);

    TreeNodeCollection nodeCollect = tvRootNode.Nodes;
    string strVal="";
    XmlTextReader reader= new XmlTextReader("E:\\BookProj\\EmpRec.xml");
    reader.MoveToElement();
```

```
  try
  {
    while(reader.Read())
    {
      if(reader.HasAttributes && reader.NodeType==XmlNodeType.Element)
      {
        reader.MoveToElement();
        reader.MoveToElement();
        reader.MoveToAttribute("Id");
        strVal=reader.Value;
        reader.Read();
        reader.Read();
        if(reader.Name=="Dept")
        {
          reader.Read();
        }

        //create the child nodes
        TreeNode EcodeNode = new TreeNode(strVal);
        //    Add the Node
        nodeCollect.Add(EcodeNode);
      }
    }
    statusBarPanel1.Text="Click on an employee code to see their record.";
  }
  catch(XmlException e)
  {
    MessageBox.Show("XML Exception :"+e.ToString());
  }
}

protected void initializeListControl()
{
  listView1.Clear();
  listView1.Columns.Add("Employee Name",225,HorizontalAlignment.Left );
  listView1.Columns.Add("Date of Join",70,HorizontalAlignment.Right );
  listView1.Columns.Add("Grade",105,HorizontalAlignment.Left );
```

```
  listView1.Columns.Add("Salary",105,HorizontalAlignment.Left );
}

protected void PopulateListView(TreeNode currNode)
{
  initializeListControl();
  XmlTextReader listRead= new XmlTextReader("E:\\BookProj\\EmpRec.xml");
  listRead.MoveToElement();

  while(listRead.Read())
  {
    string strNodename;
    string strNodePath;
    string name;
    string grade;
    string doj;
    string sal;
    string[] strItemsArr=new String [4];
    listRead.MoveToFirstAttribute();
    strNodename=listRead.Value;
    strNodePath=currNode.FullPath.Remove(0,17);
    if(strNodePath==strNodename)
    {
      ListViewItem lvi;
      listRead.MoveToNextAttribute();
      name=listRead.Value;
      lvi=listView1.Items.Add(name);
      listRead.Read();
      listRead.Read();
      listRead.MoveToFirstAttribute();
      doj=listRead.Value;
      lvi.SubItems.Add(doj);
      listRead.MoveToNextAttribute();
      grade=listRead.Value;
      lvi.SubItems.Add(grade);
      listRead.MoveToNextAttribute();
      sal=listRead.Value;
      lvi.SubItems.Add(sal);
```

```
            listRead.MoveToNextAttribute();
            listRead.MoveToElement();
            listRead.ReadString();
          }
        }
      }
      private void treeView1_AfterSelect(object sender, System.Windows.Forms
         .TreeViewEventArgs e)
      {
        TreeNode currNode = e.Node;
        if (tvRootNode == currNode )
        {
          initializeListControl();
          statusBarPanel1.Text="Double click the Employee Records";
          return;
        }
        else
        {
          statusBarPanel1.Text="Click an employee code to view individual records";
        }
        PopulateListView(currNode);
      }
    }
  }
```

## Summary

You have learned to develop a Windows application using TreeView, ListView, and StatusBar controls and to interact with a XML file.

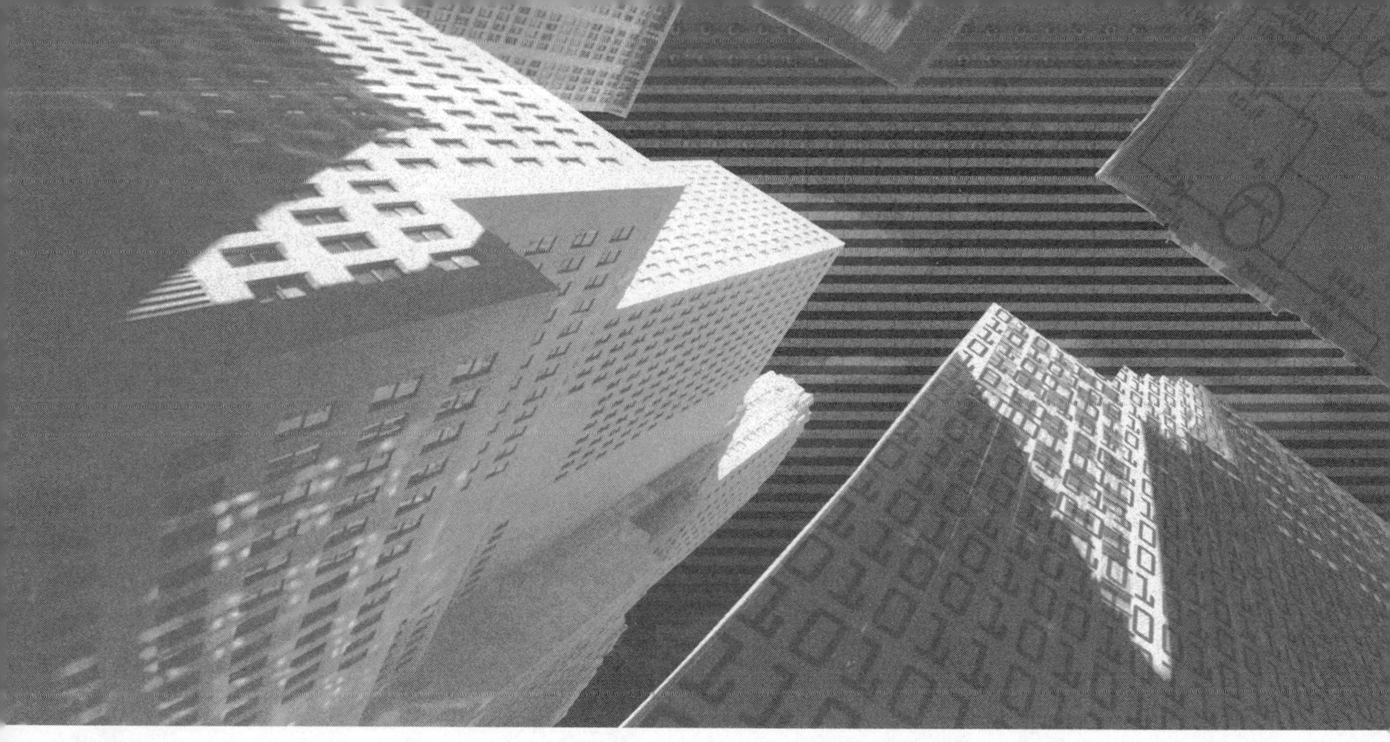

# PART V

## Professional Project 3

# Project 3

## Creating a Creative Learning Project

# Project 3 Overview

In the preceding two projects, you looked at developing Windows applications for a car maintenance company and creating an employee records system application. In this project, you will learn to create another Windows application for a chain of bookstores. This Windows application is called Creative Learning after the name of the chain of bookstores.

The Creative Learning application contains a Windows form that validates the data entered by a user in a Word document. In this project, you will learn to create a Windows form that interacts with a Microsoft Word document. In addition, any errors produced while processing a Word document are logged in Windows Event Viewer. Therefore, you will also learn to access Event Viewer from a Windows form created in Visual Studio .NET.

I will be discussing the creation of the Windows form in the following chapters. The next chapter covers the case study and design of the Creative Learning application.

# Chapter 15

## Project Case Study and Design

In this chapter, I will discuss the case study of the Creative Learning project. In addition, you will be introduced to the project life cycle of the Creative Learning project. The project life cycle includes analyzing the requirements of Creative Learning. Finally, you will create a high-level and low-level design of the Creative Learning application.

## Case Study

Creative Learning is a group of publishers located at New York. Recently, the organization has moved into retailing the books published at the publishing house. To start with, the organization has established bookstores at six locations in New York. However, the organization aims at increasing the number of bookstores in the forthcoming years. In addition, the organization is looking forward to establishing bookstores across all major states in the United States.

To meet the competition in the retail market, the organization has decided to monitor the sales data of all six bookstores for a few months. The management of the organization has decided to develop an application that will track the sales record of each bookstore on a daily basis. The analysis of the tracked data will give the management a fair idea of the performance of each bookstore.

To develop and deploy the application, the senior managers have appointed a development team of three people. The development team comprises the project manager, John Frye, and two application developers, Larry Barrett and Sam Jones. The development team has decided upon a strategy to build the application. To understand the strategy, you first need to understand the sales process at the bookstores.

All of the six bookstores in New York are connected to a main server over a LAN. The main server is located at the head office of Creative Learning in New York. Whenever a book is purchased from any of the bookstores, the salesperson issues a cash memo to the customer. A *cash memo* is a Word document that contains details about the purchase made. The salesperson then sends the copy of the cash memo to the main server over the LAN.

An operator at the head office makes an entry of each cash memo into an XML document. At the end of the day, the data in the XML document is analyzed to determine the sales from each bookstore. This data would then be analyzed at the end of the month to decide the performance of the bookstores.

The development team at Creative Learning has decided to automate the entire process. When a salesperson issues a cash memo to a customer, the salesperson makes a copy of the cash memo in the specified directory on the main server. Then, on the main server, the format of the cash memo is checked for accuracy. Once the format is validated, the entry of the cash memo will be made into the XML document. The data in the document can then be easily analyzed to see the performance of each of the bookstores.

To carry out the entire process, the development team plans to create a Windows application and name it the Creative Learning project. The following section discusses the stages in the life cycle of the Creative Learning project.

# Project Life Cycle

You looked at the phases of a DLC (*development life cycle*) of a project in Chapter 7, "Project Case Study," in the section "Case Study." Therefore, in this chapter, I will not discuss the entire life cycle of the project. However, I will discuss the analysis of the organization's requirements from the development team at Creative Learning. In addition, I will discuss the design of the application created by the development team based on the analysis of the organization's requirements. You, as a part of the development team, will analyze the requirements of Creative Learning and will create a design for the application based on the analysis.

## Analyzing Requirements

To find a solution to a customer's problem, it is essential that you analyze the requirements of the customer in detail. This is done in the *analyzing requirements* phase of the project life cycle. After analyzing the customer's problem in detail, you create a plan for developing the application. This analysis of the customer's problem is based on the problem statement stated by senior managers and the information gathered by the development team.

In the case of Creative Learning, the problem statement, as stated by senior managers, is, "Creative Learning needs to automate the process of analyzing sales data of each bookstore."

Upon analyzing the problem statement, the development team defined the following list of tasks that Creative Learning needs to do:

- The organization needs to analyze the sales data of each bookstore.
- The organization needs to automate the data analysis process.
- Based on the analysis results, the organization will determine the performance of each bookstore.
- Based on the performance of bookstores, the organization plans to move ahead with its growth plans.

To provide a solution to the aforementioned problems of Creative Learning, the development team plans to create a Windows application with the following features:

- The application will receive a copy of the cash memo from a directory on the main server at the head office of Creative Learning.
- The application will validate the format of the cash memo.
- If the format of the cash memo is incorrect, the application will create an event log.
- Alternatively, if the format of the cash memo is correct, an entry for the cash memo will be created in an XML document.

## High-Level Design

Based on the plan of the Windows application, the development team created a design of the Windows application in the high-level design phase. The design of the Creative Learning application includes creating the interface for the Windows form used in the application.

The Creative Learning application consists of a Windows form called Creative Learning. Figure 15-1 shows the layout of the Creative Learning form.

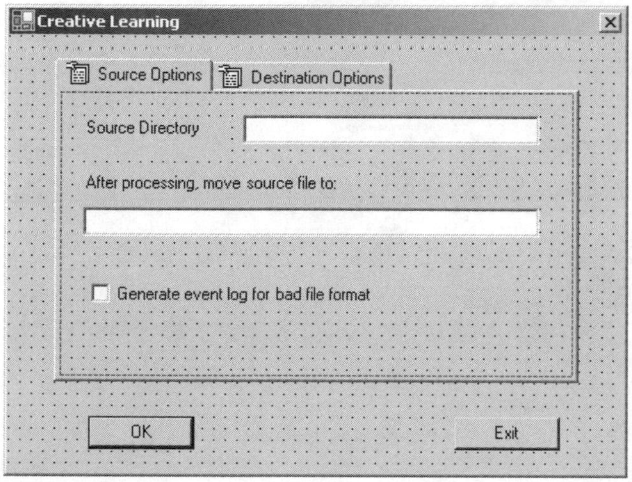

**FIGURE 15-1** *Layout of the Creative Learning form*

To create the layout of the Creative Learning application, as shown in Figure 15-1, you need to include a tab control and two button controls. You have learned about button controls in Chapter 8, "Windows Forms and Controls" in the section "Types of Windows Forms Controls." The following section discusses a TabControl control in detail.

## The TabControl Control

A TabControl control is a Windows forms control that you can use to create multiple tabbed pages in a window or a dialog box. For example, a tab control can be used to display multiple-options pages in a wizard. You can use the arrow keys to shift from one tabbed page to another. A TabControl control has a `TabPages` property that you can modify to add tabbed pages to the tab control. You will learn about adding tabbed pages to a tab control later in this chapter.

To create a tab control in Visual Studio .NET, you can drag the control from the Windows Forms toolbox to the form. Figure 15-2 shows the TabControl control in the Windows Forms toolbox.

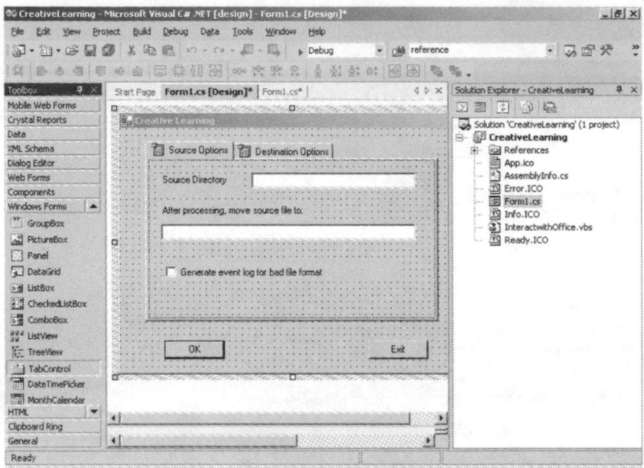

**FIGURE 15-2** *A TabControl control in the Windows Forms toolbox*

You can now create a tab control for your application. To create a tab control, perform the following steps:

1. Drag a TabControl control from the Windows Forms toolbox to the Creative Learning form.

   A blank TabControl control is added to the form. To add pages to the tab control, you need to change the properties of the tab control.
2. Press the F4 key to display the properties of the tab control.
3. In the Properties window, click on the ellipsis button of the TabPages property.

   The TabPage Collection Editor page is displayed. This page allows you to add tabbed pages to the control as a Collection object.
4. To add a tabbed page, click on the Add button.

   A tabbed page with an index `0` is added to the Members: text box. The properties of the tabbed page are displayed in the tabPage1 Properties: window.
5. In the tabPage1 Properties: window, change the following properties of the tabbed page.
   - **`Text:`** `Source Options`
   - **`Name:`** `tabSource`

When you change the name of the tabbed page to `tabSource`, the name of the tabPage1 Properties: window changes to tabSource Properties: window.

6. Repeat Steps 4 and 5 to add another tabbed page to the form.
7. Name the new tabbed page `tabDest`, and change the Text property to Destination Options.

   You can change the order in which the tabbed pages are displayed by clicking on either the Up or Down Arrow buttons.

   Figure 15-3 shows the TabPage Collection Editor page.
8. Click on the OK button to add tabbed pages.

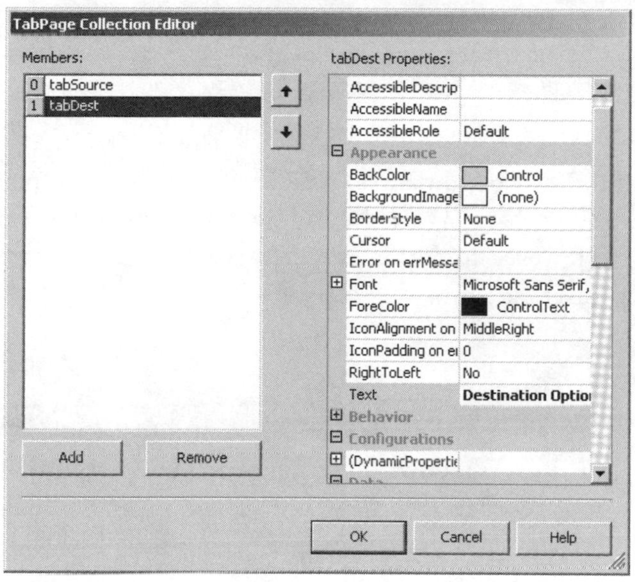


**FIGURE 15-3** *The TabPage Collection Editor page*

The tabbed pages are added, as shown in Figure 15-4. You can resize the tab control to display the tabbed pages.

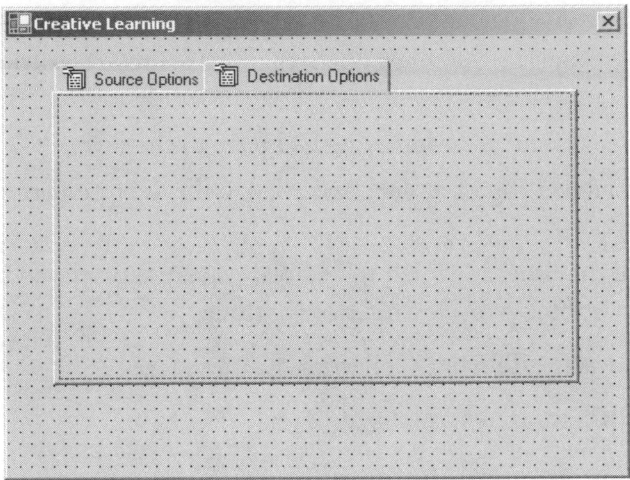


**FIGURE 15-4** *The TabControl control added to the Creative Learning form*

The tabs in the tab control do not contain an image yet. You can add images to the tabs in the tab control by changing the ImageIndex property in the TabPage Collection Editor page. However, to do this, you first need to add an ImageList control to the `Creative Learning` form.

## The ImageList Control

Visual Studio .NET provides you with an ImageList control that you can use to add images to the controls in a Windows form. These include various controls, such as TabControl, Button, ToolBar, TreeView control, and so on. An ImageList control is a collection of images. You can add images to the ImageList control by using the Images property.

However, to associate an ImageList control to a Windows Forms control, you can change the ImageList property of the Windows Forms control. The ImageList control is present in the Windows Forms toolbox, and to add the control to the form, you must drag the control to the form.

To add an ImageList control to the Creative Learning form, perform the following steps:

1. Drag an ImageList control from the Windows Forms toolbox to the form.

An ImageList control with the name ImageList1 is added to the component tray. Figure 15-5 shows the ImageList control added to the component tray of the Creative Learning form.

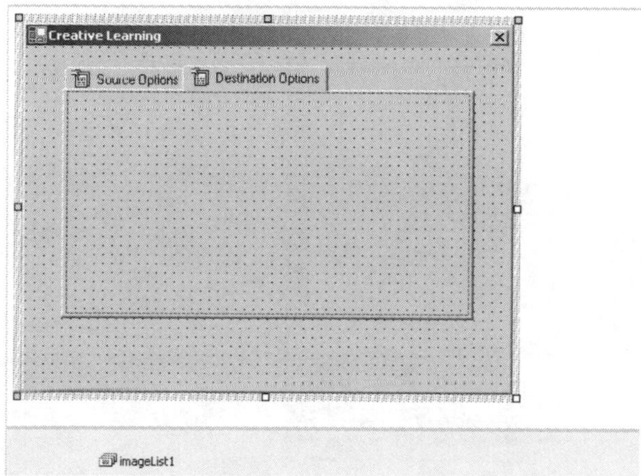


**FIGURE 15-5** *The ImageList control added to the component tray of the Creative Learning form*

Until now, the ImageList control does not contain any image. To add images to the ImageList control, you need to change the Images property of the ImageList control. When you add images to the ImageList control, the images are added to a Collection object of the control. To add images to a ImageList control in Visual Studio .NET, perform the following steps:

2. Click on the ellipsis button of the Images property.

   The Image Collection Editor dialog box is displayed.

3. Click on the Add button to add an image to the Members: textbox.

   You can browse for the image to add it to the ImageList control. The image that you add is included in the `System.Drawing` namespace. The index value of the first image that is added is `0`. As you add more images to the ImageList control, the index value increases. However, in the case of Creative Learning form, you will add only one image.

4. Click on the OK button to close the Image Collection Editor dialog box.

   Figure 15-6 shows the Bitmap image added to the Image Collection Editor dialog box.

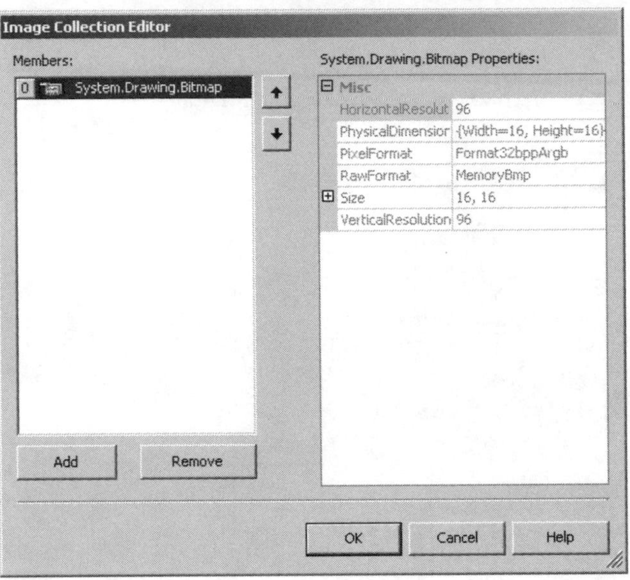


**FIGURE 15-6** *The Bitmap image added to the Image Collection Editor dialog box*

To add the image in the ImageList control to the TabControl control, perform the following steps:

5. Click on the drop-down button of the ImageList property of the TabControl control.
6. From the drop-down list, select the imageList1 option.

   imageList1 is associated with the TabControl control.

   However, the Bitmap image is not presently visible on the tabbed pages. To display the image on the tabbed pages, you need to modify the properties of the tabbed pages on the TabPage Collection Editor page.
7. Click on the ellipsis button of the TabPages property of the tab control to display the properties of the tabbed pages.

   The tabSource tabbed page is selected by default.
8. Click on the drop-down button of the `ImageIndex` property.
9. From the drop-down list, select the `0` option.
10. Repeat Steps 8 and 9 to add an image to the tabDest tabbed page. The images get added to the tabbed pages.

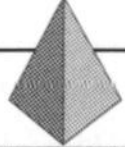

**TIP**

You can add the same image to all tabbed pages or different images to different tabbed pages in a tab control.

Having created the tabbed pages in the tab control, you can add label controls and text boxes to be displayed on the tabbed pages.

## Adding Controls to Tabbed Pages

The tab control that you created contains two tabbed pages, Source Options and Destination Options. You can first add controls to the Source Options page.

The Source Options page consists of a check box control, two label controls, and two text box controls. You can add these controls to the tabSource tabbed page by dragging the controls from the Windows Forms toolbox. Then, change the following properties of the controls.

**Label1**

- Name: `label1`
- Text: `Source Directory`

**Label2**

- Name: `label3`
- Text: `After processing, move source file to:`

**TextBox1**

- Name: `txtSource`

**TextBox2**

- Name: `txtProcessedFile`

#### CheckBox

- Name: `optGenerateLog`
- Text: `Generate event log for bad file format`

After adding controls to the tabSource tabbed page, the page looks as shown in Figure 15-7.

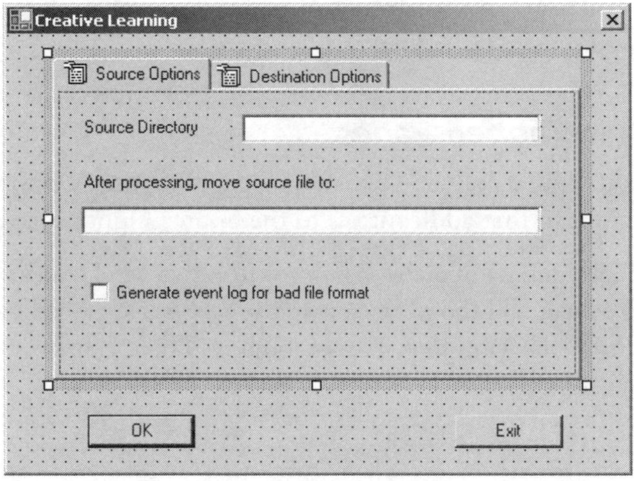


**FIGURE 15-7** *The tabSource page with the controls added*

Similarly, you can add controls to the tabDest page. The tabDest page contains a label, a text box, a list box, a group box, and two button controls. Change the following properties of the controls after adding them to the tabbed page.

#### Label

- Name: `label2`
- Text: `Destination Directory`

#### TextBox

- Name: `txtDest`

#### ListBox

- Name: `lstEvents`

**GroupBox**

- Name: `groupEventLog`
- Text: `Event Log`

**Button1**

- Name: `btnRefresh`
- Text: `Refresh Log`

**Button2**

- Name: `btnViewSummary`
- Text: `View Summary`

Figure 15-8 shows the controls added to the tabDest page.

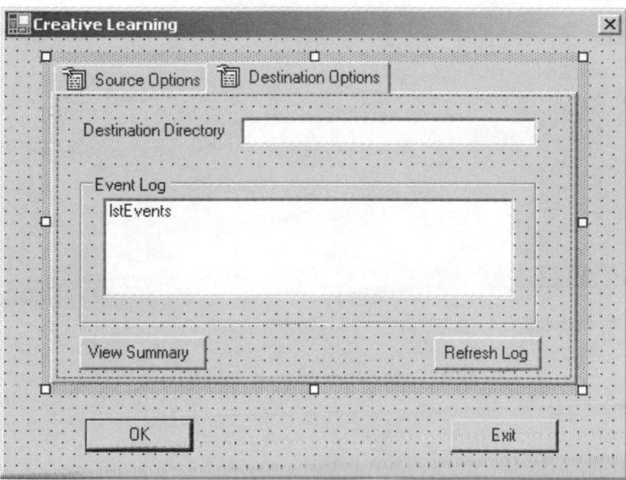


**FIGURE 15-8** *The tabDest page with the controls added*

## Low-Level Design

After creating the design of a form in the high-level design phase, the development team creates a detailed design of software modules. These software modules are then used to create a detailed structure of the application. In addition to creating software modules, the team decides the flow and interaction of each module. This includes creating flowcharts for each module.

Based on the high-level design of the `Creative Learning` form, the development team created the flowchart for the form, as shown in Figure 15-9.

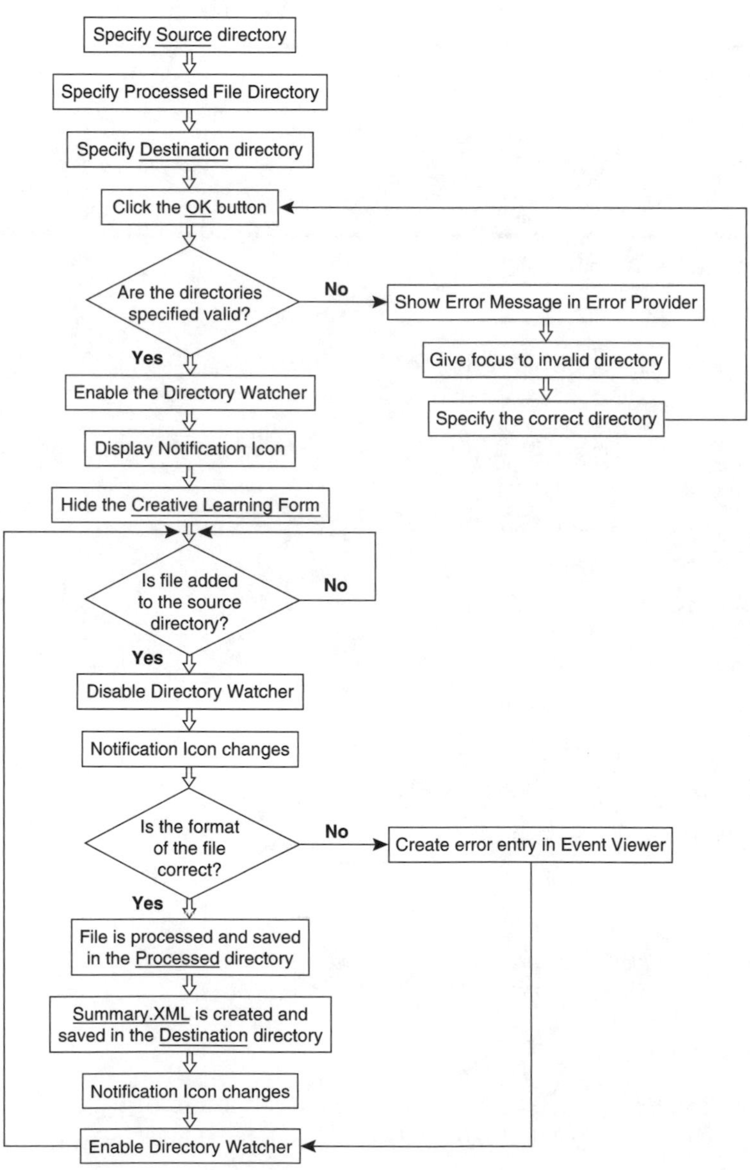


**FIGURE 15-9** *Flowchart of the Creative Learning module*

Having decided the interface and the software module, the development team proceeds with thc construction and testing of the Windows application. After the application is tested and the errors in the application are detected and removed, the application is deployed at the client site. I will discuss writing the code and deploying the Creative Learning application in the next chapter.

# Summary

In this chapter, you were introduced to the project case study. Based on the case study of the project, you analyzed the requirements of Creative Learning and learned to create a detailed high-level and low-level design of the application. You will learn to create and deploy the application in the next chapter.

# Chapter 16

## Implementing the Programming Logic

In the preceding chapter, you looked at the design of the Creative Learning application. This project adds the programming logic to the Creative Learning application.

## Adding the Programming Logic to the Application

Before adding the programming logic to the Creative Learning application, you need to understand how the application works.

1. When the Creative Learning application is run, a user needs to specify the names of the source, destination, and processed file directories.

   The application, by default, specifies the names of the source, destination, and processed file directories as `D:\Creative\Source`, `D:\Creative\Destination`, and `D:\Creative\Processed`. The user may choose to retain the default directory structure or may change the directory structure as required.
2. When the user adds the names of the specified directories and clicks on the OK button, the application checks whether the entered directory structure is valid.
3. If the user enters an invalid directory structure, the application creates an error message in Error Provider and gives focus to the invalid directory.
4. If the user enters a valid directory structure, the application enables the directory watcher.
5. The application then hides the Creative Learning form and displays a notification icon in the status area of the taskbar.
6. While the application is running, it continuously checks whether the user has added a file to the source directory.
7. When the user adds a file to the source directory, the application disables the directory watcher and changes the notification icon in the status area.

8. The application then validates the file format, and if the format of the file is not correct, the application generates an error entry in Event Viewer.
9. Alternatively, if the file format is correct, the application processes the file. Processing of the file includes extracting data, such as `Cash Memo No.` and `Total amount payable` from the cash memo document.
10. Once the file has been processed, the application saves the information from the cash memo document to an XML document, `Summary.XML`. This XML document is then saved in the destination directory as specified by the user.
11. After creating the `Summary.XML` document, the application changes the notification icon again and then enables the directory watcher so that the directory watcher can check the directory for any new file.

You have seen how the application works. You can now code to the application so that the application can be deployed at the client site. To start, add code to the form `Load()` method.

## Adding Code to the Form `Load()` Method

When the form is loaded by using the form `Load()` method, the default values of the source, destination, and processed file directory are displayed in txtSource, txtDest, and txtProcessedFile text boxes, respectively. In addition, the optGenerateLog check box is checked by default. When the optGenerateLog check box is checked, any errors that occur while the application is running are logged in the Event Viewer. However, if desired, the user may choose to uncheck the optGenerateLog check box.

To load the form, specify the following code to the `Load()` method of the Creative Learning form.

```
private void frmCreative_Load(object sender, System.EventArgs e)
{
                    txtSource.Text="D:\\Creative\\Source\\";
                    txtProcessedFile.Text="D:\\Creative\\Processed\\";
                    txtDest.Text="D:\\Creative\\Destination\\";
                    optGenerateLog.Checked=true;
}
```

When the application is run, the Creative Learning form looks as shown in Figure 16-1 and Figure 16-2.

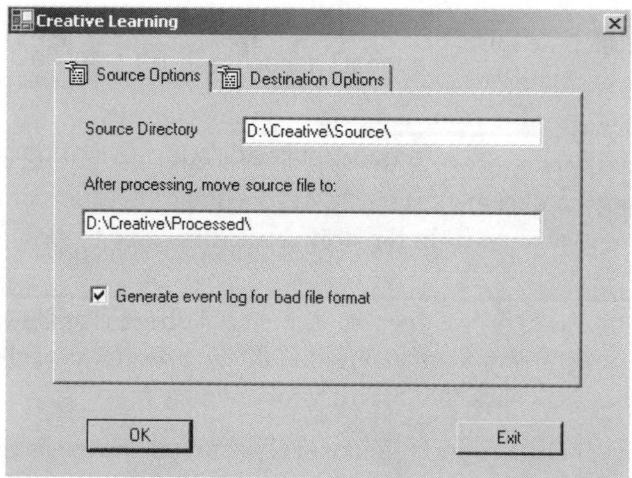


**FIGURE 16-1** *The tabSource page of the Creative Learning form at run time*

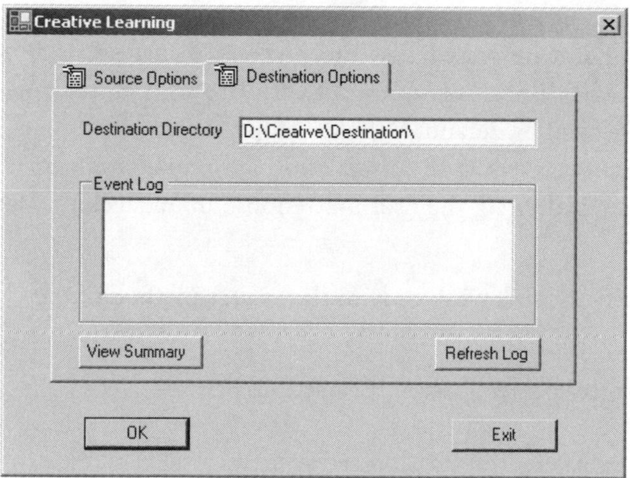


**FIGURE 16-2** *The tabDest page of the Creative Learning form at run time*

## Adding Code to the OK Button

After entering the required information, such as the names of the source, destination, and processed file directory, the user clicks on the OK button. The application then validates the directory structure that is specified by the user. If the directory structure is found to be incorrect, the application creates an error message in Error Provider and then gives the focus to the invalid directory. However, for it to do so, you first need to add an ErrorProvider control from the Windows Forms toolbox.

### *The ErrorProvider Control*

The ErrorProvider control in Windows forms is used to validate data entered by the user in a control. If the data entered by the user is incorrect, the ErrorProvider control displays an icon adjacent to the control in which the user enters the data. You can change the `Icon` property of the ErrorProvider control to specify the icon that is displayed when an error occurs. By default, Visual Studio .NET displays the icon as shown in Figure 16-3.

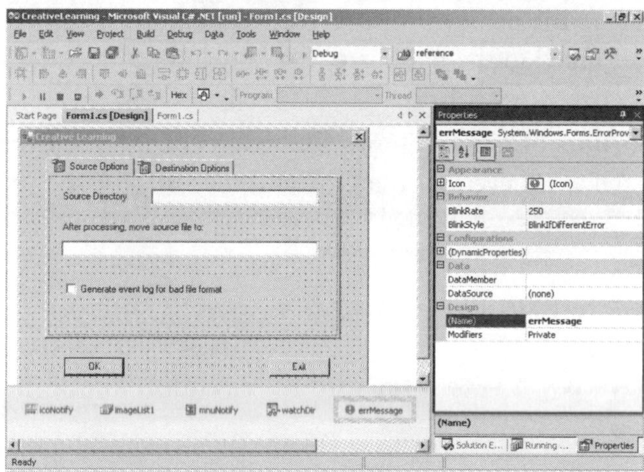


**FIGURE 16-3** *The default icon of the ErrorProvider control*

In addition, the ErrorProvider control displays an error message as a ToolTip when the user points to the icon next to the control. You can specify the error message by using the `SetError()` method of the `ErrorProvider` class. You will learn to specify an error message by using the `SetError()` method later in this chapter.

You can include an ErrorProvider control in the Creative Learning form by performing the following steps:

1. Drag the ErrorProvider control from the Windows Forms toolbox to the form.

   Figure 16-4 shows an ErrorProvider control in the Windows Forms toolbox.

   The ErrorProvider control gets added to the component tray of the form.

2. Change the Name property of the ErrorProvider control to `errMessage`.

   After adding the ErrorProvider control to the form, you need to associate the ErrorProvider control with the control whose value is to be validated. You can do this by passing the name of the control as a parameter to the `SetError()` method of the `ErrorProvider` class. In your project, you need to validate the name of the source, destination, and processed file directories specified in the txtSource, txtDest, and txtProcessedFile text boxes, respectively.

3. To validate the names of the directories entered by the user, add the following code to the `Click` event of the OK button.

```
if (!Directory.Exists(txtSource.Text))
{
   errMessage.SetError(txtSource,"Invalid source directory");
   txtSource.Focus();
   tabControl1.SelectedTab=tabSource;
   return;
}
else
errMessage.SetError(txtSource,"");
```

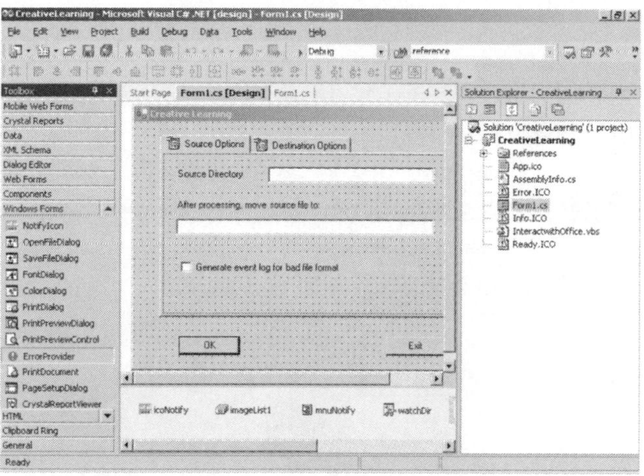

**FIGURE 16-4** *An ErrorProvider control in the Windows Forms toolbox*

The preceding code uses an `if` loop to validate the directory structure. The `if` loop uses the `Exists()` method of the `Directory` class to check whether the path of the directory specified in the txtSource text box exists on the hard disk. If the path of the directory specified in the txtSource text box does not exist, the ErrorProvider control is used to display an error message.

The `SetError()` method is used to display an error message. This method takes the name of the control whose value is to be validated, `txtSource`, and the error message to be displayed as a ToolTip, `Invalid source directory`, as parameters. The `txtSource.Focus();` command is used to set the focus of the application to the txtSource text box. Then, the `SelectedTab` property of the TabControl control is used to set the tabSource tabbed page as the selected page. However, if the directory structure specified by the user is correct, no text is displayed in the ErrorProvider control. Figure 16-5 shows an error message displayed in an Error-Provider control.

Similarly, you can add code to validate the directory structure in the txtDest and txtProcessedFile text boxes.

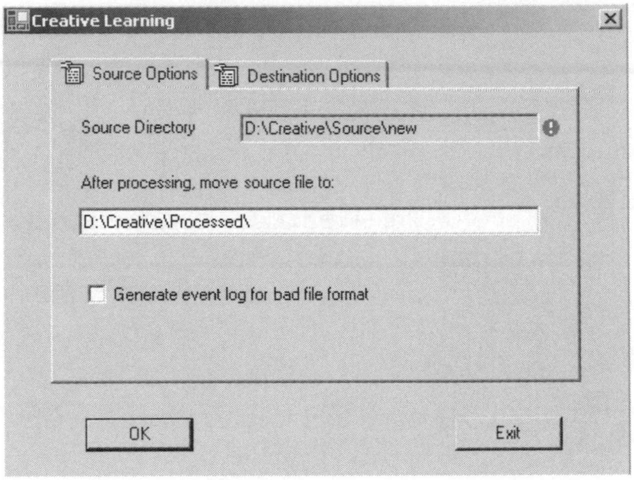

**FIGURE 16-5** *An ErrorProvider control displaying an error message*

Another important aspect of the application is when a user specifies an invalid directory structure, the color of the text box changes to pink. To do this, add the following code to the `KeyUp` event of the txtSource text box.

```
private void txtSource_KeyUp(object sender, System.Windows.Forms.KeyEventArgs e)
{
   if (Directory.Exists(txtSource.Text))
      txtSource.BackColor=Color.White;
   else
      txtSource.BackColor=Color.Pink;
}
```

Similarly, you can add code to the txtDest and txtProcessedFile text boxes.

When the directory structure is validated, you need to enable the directory watcher and display the notification icon in the status area. In addition, you need to hide the Creative Learning form from the taskbar. This will enable your application to appear minimized in the system tray. Before doing that, add a FileSystemWatcher component to the Creative Learning form.

## The FileSystemWatcher Component

The FileSystemWatcher component in Visual Studio .NET is used to monitor the contents of a directory. This implies that you can monitor the contents of a directory by using the FileSystemWatcher component and perform custom actions when the contents of the directory are changed. For example, you can use the FileSystemWatcher component to find any modifications made to the content of the entire directory or one or more files in the specified directory. When a user makes some change to the files in a specified directory, such as adding, deleting, or modifying a file, the FileSystemWatcher component generates an event. For example, when a user adds a file to the specified directory, the `Created` event is generated. You will learn about the `Created` event in Chapter 17, "Interacting with a Microsoft Word Document and Event Viewer."

To add a FileSystemWatcher component to the Creative Learning form, perform the following steps:

1. Drag a FileSystemWatcher component from the Components toolbox.

   The FileSystemWatcher component gets added to the component tray. Figure 16-6 shows the FileSystemWatcher component in the Components toolbox.

2. Change the following properties of the FileSystemWatcher component.

   - `Name: watchDir`
   - `Filter: *.doc`

   Specifying the value of the Filter property to `*.doc` restricts the `watchDir` component to monitoring only Microsoft Word documents.

**TIP**

By default, the `EnableRaisingEvent` property of the FileSystemWatcher component is set to true. Therefore, as soon as the FileSystemWatcher component is enabled, it starts monitoring the specified directory and raises an event when a change occurs.

3. To enable the `watchDir` component, add the following statement to the `Click` event of the OK button.

```
watchDir.EnableRaisingEvents=true;
```

Until now, you have not specified the path of the directory that the `watchDir` component will monitor. In this case, the `watchDir` component needs to monitor the source directory as entered by the user in the txtSource text box.

4. To specify the path of the directory to the `watchDir` component, add the following statement to the `Click` event of the OK button.

```
watchDir.Path=txtSource.Text;
```

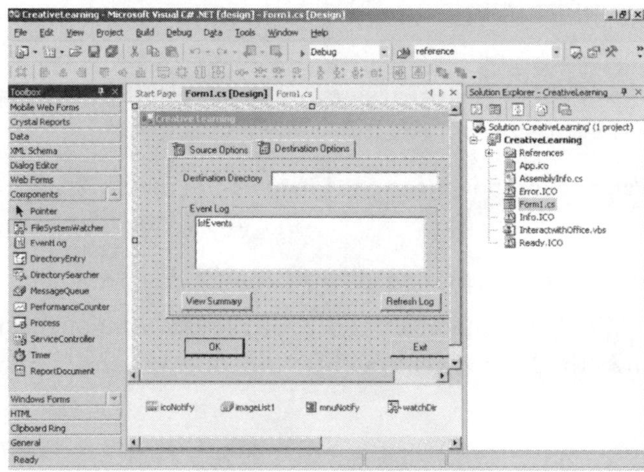


**FIGURE 16-6** *A FileSystemWatcher component in the Components toolbox*

After enabling the `watchDir` component, you need to add a notification icon to the form that is displayed in the status area when the user runs the application. You can do this by adding the NotifyIcon control to your form.

## The NotifyIcon Control

The NotifyIcon control in Visual Studio .NET is used to denote a process running in the background as an icon in the status area. For example, when you print a document, the printer icon is displayed in the status area of the taskbar. To specify the icon to be displayed, you need to change the Icons property of the control.

To add the NotifyIcon control to your form, perform the following steps:

1. Drag the NotifyIcon control from the Windows Forms toolbox to the Creative Learning form.

   A NotifyIcon control with the name `notifyIcon1` gets added to the component tray. Figure 16-7 shows the NotifyIcon control in the Windows Forms toolbox.

2. Change the Name property of the NotifyIcon control to `mnuNotify`.

   To display a notification icon, you need to add the icon file (Ready.ico file) to the bin folder of your application and then create an instance of the icon file.

3. To create an instance of the icon file, add the following statement to the `frmCreative` class in the `CreativeLearning` namespace.

   ```
   private System.Drawing.Icon m_Ready= new System.Drawing.Icon("Ready.ICO");
   ```

4. To display the notification icon, add the following code to the `Click` event of the OK button.

   ```
   icoNotify.Icon=m_Ready;
   icoNotify.Visible=true;
   ```

   After you have specified the notification icon, the user does not need to see the application. Therefore, you can hide the application from the taskbar.

5. To hide the application, add the following code to the `Click` event of the OK button.

   ```
   this.ShowInTaskbar=false;
   this.Hide();
   ```

The entire code for the OK button is as follows:

```
private void btnOK_Click(object sender, System.EventArgs e)
{
   if (!Directory.Exists(txtSource.Text))
   {
      errMessage.SetError(txtSource,"Invalid source directory");
```

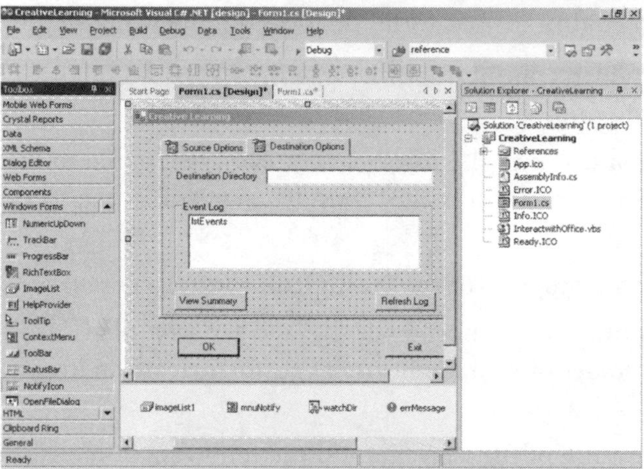

**FIGURE 16-7** *The NotifyIcon control in the Windows Forms toolbox*

```
        txtSource.Focus();
        tabControl1.SelectedTab=tabSource;
        return;
    }
    else
        errMessage.SetError(txtSource,"");
    if (!Directory.Exists(txtDest.Text))
    {
        errMessage.SetError(txtDest,"Invalid destination directory");
        txtDest.Focus();
        tabControl1.SelectedTab=tabDest;
        return;
    }
    else
        errMessage.SetError(txtDest,"");
        if (!Directory.Exists(txtProcessedFile.Text))
    {
        errMessage.SetError(txtProcessedFile,"Invalid processed file directory");
        txtProcessedFile.Focus();
```

```
            tabControl1.SelectedTab=tabSource;
            return;
        }
        else
        errMessage.SetError(txtProcessedFile,"");
        watchDir.Path=txtSource.Text;
        watchDir.EnableRaisingEvents=true;
        icoNotify.Icon=m_Ready;
        icoNotify.Visible=true;
        this.ShowInTaskbar=false;
        this.Hide();
    }
```

Visual Studio .NET also allows you to add a context menu to the NotifyIcon control. The context menu is displayed when the user right-clicks on the notification icon in the status area of the taskbar.

## The ContextMenu Control

The ContextMenu control in Visual Studio .NET allows you to create a menu that consists of frequently used commands. The menu that is created is called a context menu. A context menu is associated with a control in a Windows form. The user can access the context menu by right-clicking on the control in the Windows form.

To add a ContextMenu control to the NotifyIcon control, perform the following steps:

1. Drag a ContextMenu control from the Windows Forms control to the Creative Learning form.

   A ContextMenu control with the name `contextMenu1` is added to the component tray. In addition, a context menu is added to the top of the form.
2. Click on the text Context Menu on the top of the form to add menus to the ContextMenu control.

   A menu item gets added to the ContextMenu control. You can change the text of the menu item by typing the text in the Type Here area.
3. Type the name of the menu item as `Configure Application`.

4. Change the Name property of the menu item to `mnuConfigure`.

   To add another menu item to the ContextMenu control, type the name of the menu item in the Type Here area below the Configure Application menu item.

5. Type the name of the second menu item as `Exit`.

6. Change the Name property of the menu item to `mnuExit`.

   Figure 16-8 displays the ContextMenu control in the design view.

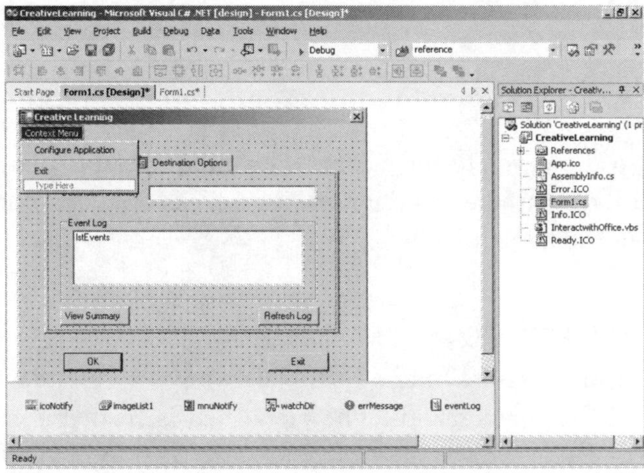

**FIGURE 16-8** *The ContextMenu control in the design view*

However, the menu items that you created do not contain the code so far.

7. To make the mnuConfigure menu item functional, add the following code to the `Click` event of the mnuConfigure menu item.

```
private void mnuConfigure_Click(object sender, System.EventArgs e)
{
                icoNotify.Visible=false;
                this.ShowInTaskbar=true;
                this.Show();
}
```

When the user clicks the mnuConfigure menu item in the context menu, the notify icon disappears and the Creative Learning form is displayed. In addition, the application appears in the taskbar.

8. To make the mnuExit menu item functional, add the following code to the `Click` event of the mnuExit menu item.

```
private void menuItem3_Click(object sender, System.EventArgs e)
{
            Application.Exit();
}
```

When the user clicks the mnuExit menu item, the application terminates. In addition, the user can exit the application by clicking on the Exit button. You will learn to add code to the Exit button later in this chapter.

In addition to adding menu items to the ContextMenu control, you can add code that displays the application when the user double-clicks on the notification icon in the status area of the taskbar.

9. To display the application when the user double-clicks on the notification icon, add the following code to the `DoubleClick` event of the NotifyIcon control.

```
private void icoNotify_DoubleClick(object sender, System.EventArgs e)
{
            icoNotify.Visible=false;
            this.ShowInTaskbar=true;
            this.Show();
}
```

## Adding Code to the Exit Button

Add the following code to the `Click` event of the Exit button. This code will enable the application to terminate when the user clicks on the Exit button.

```
private void btnCancel_Click(object sender, System.EventArgs e)
{
            Application.Exit();
}
```

## Summary

In this chapter, you added functionality to the Creative Learning form. While adding code to the form, you learned about a few new Windows forms controls, such as the ErrorProvider, FileSystemWatcher, NotifyIcon, and ContextMenu controls.

# Chapter 17

## Interacting with a Microsoft Word Document and Event Viewer

In the preceding chapter, you looked at how the Creative Learning application works. However, the way that the Creative Learning application works also involves accessing and processing a Microsoft Word document. In addition, the errors generated during the processing of the Microsoft Word document are trapped in Windows Event Viewer. Therefore, your application needs to interact with both the Microsoft Word document and Windows Event Viewer. This project covers the process of interacting with the Word document and Windows Event Viewer.

# Interacting with a Microsoft Word Document

In the preceding chapter, you learned how to add a FileSystemWatcher component to your application. This component monitors a specified directory for any changes, such as adding or deleting a file. In addition, you changed the Filter property of the FileSystemWatcher component to `*.doc`. Doing this restricts the function of a FileSystemWatcher component to only monitoring the Word document. Therefore, when a user adds a Word file to the source directory, the FileSystemWatcher component generates a `Created` event.

## The `Created` Event

The `Created` event is a public event of the `FileSystemWatcher` class. The `FileSystemWatcher` class generates the `Created` event when a new file is added to a directory specified in the `FullPath` property of the event.

To handle the `Created` event, the `FileSystemWatcher` class contains a delegate `FileSystemEventHandler`. The `FileSystemEventHandler` delegate takes two parameters, the object that causes the event and an argument of the type `FileSystemEventArgs` that contains information about the event. This information includes the name and path of the directory that is monitored by the FileSystemWatcher component.

In this case, each time a new cash memo is added to the source directory, the FileSystemWatcher component raises a `Created` event. Therefore, to access and process the cash memo, you need to add programming logic to the `Created` event of the `FileSystemWatcher` class.

## Adding Code to the `Created` Event

When a file is added to the source directory, your application needs to process the cash memo file. File processing involves extracting data from the cash memo, such as `Cash Memo No.` and `Total amount payable`. This information is then written to an XML document as a chronological summary of the sales recorded at the bookstores of Creative Learning.

### *Displaying a Notification Icon with a ToolTip in the Status Area*

While the application processes one file, you need to disable the FileSystemWatcher component so that the component does not monitor the source directory for that time. In addition, you can change the notification icon in the status area of the taskbar to denote that the application is processing a file. You can also change the text that is displayed when the user points to the notification icon in the status area. You will now add code to the `Created` event to perform the activities mentioned earlier in the chapter.

```
watchDir.EnableRaisingEvents=false;
icoNotify.Icon=m_Info;
icoNotify.Text="Processed: "+ e.Name;
```

The preceding code sets the `EnableRaisingEvents` property of the `FileSystemWatcher` class to `false`. Doing this disables the `watchDir` component for the time the value of the `EnableRaisingEvents` property is set to `true`. Next, the `Icon` property of the NotifyIcon control is changed to display a different icon in the status area. However, before doing this, you need to add the Info.ico file to the bin folder of your application and then create an instance of the Info.ico file by using the following statement:

```
private System.Drawing.Icon m_Info= new System.Drawing.Icon("Info.ICO");
```

Creating an instance of the `Info.ico` file adds the file to the `Icon` class of the `System.Drawing` namespace. When the notification icon is displayed in the status area, you can use the `Text` property of the notification icon to display a ToolTip. The `Text` property appends the word `Processed:` to the name of the file that is being processed. Figure 17-1 displays the notification icon with a ToolTip.

**FIGURE 17-1** *Notification icon with a ToolTip in the status area*

## *Extracting Data from a Word Document*

Your application is now ready to process the Word document. However, to access the Word application, you need to create an instance of the `Word.ApplicationClass` class. After you are able to access the Word application, you can create an instance of the `Word.DocumentClass` class to access the Word document. To do so, add the following statements to the `Created` event of the FileSystemWatcher component.

```
Word.Application wdApp= new Word.ApplicationClass();
Word.Document Doc = new Word.DocumentClass();
```

After creating the instance of the Word document `Doc`, you can use the instance to open the document file that the user adds to the source directory. To do this, you can use the `Open()` method of the `Documents` class. The `Open()` method takes 12 parameters. However, only the first parameter, which is an object containing the file name to be opened, is essential. To pass `FileName` as a parameter to the `Open()` method, you can create an object, `filename`, which stores the name of the file and the full path of the directory where the file is stored. To create the `filename` object, use the following statement:

```
object filename=e.FullPath;
```

**TIP**

The `filename` object is passed as a reference parameter to the `Open()` method.

Except for the first parameter, the rest of the parameters of the `Open()` method are optional. Therefore, you can create an object of the instance of the `Missing` class `optional`.

**NOTE**

The `Missing` class is a public sealed class in the `System.Reflection` namespace. You cannot inherit a `Missing` class.

The `optional` object can now be passed as optional parameters to the `Open()` method. To do this, use the following statements:

```
object optional=System.Reflection.Missing.Value;
Doc=wdApp.Documents.Open(ref filename, ref optional, ref optional,ref optional,ref
   optional,ref optional,ref optional,ref optional,ref optional,ref optional,ref
   optional,ref optional);
```

The preceding code opens the Word document present in the source directory and stores the entire content of the Word document in the instance of the `Word.DocumentClass` class `Doc`. However, in this case, you only require the information in the `Cash Memo No.` and `Total amount payable` fields. Figure 17-2 shows a sample cash memo document.

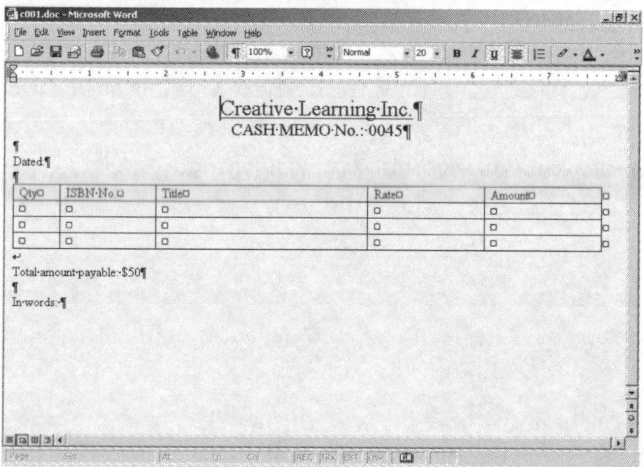


**FIGURE 17-2** *Sample cash memo document*

To retrieve the required data from the cash memo document, add the following code to the `Created` event:

```
Word.Range wdRange;
wdRange=Doc.Paragraphs.Item(2).Range;
string strMemo, strAmount;
int intParacount;
strMemo=wdRange.Text;
strMemo=strMemo.Substring(15,4);
intParacount=Doc.Paragraphs.Count;
intParacount=intParacount-2;
wdRange=Doc.Paragraphs.Item(intParacount).Range;
object count="-1";
object wdCharacter="1";
wdRange.MoveEnd(ref wdCharacter,ref count);
strAmount=wdRange.Text;
strAmount=strAmount.Substring(23);
```

The preceding code creates an object of the type `Range`, `wdRange` that stores the content of the Word document. You then use the `Item` property of the `Paragraphs` collection to retrieve data from a specified paragraph. As shown in Figure 17-2, `Cash Memo No.` is the second paragraph in the cash memo document. Therefore, you need to retrieve the content of the second paragraph of the cash memo document by using the `Range` property. The content that is retrieved is then stored in `wdRange`.

The `Text` property of the `wdRange` object is used to store the text of the paragraph in a `string` type variable, `strMemo`. Until now, the `strMemo` variable stores the entire content of the second paragraph. However, to just retrieve the value of the `Cash Memo No.` field, use the `Substring()` method. The `Substring()` method takes two parameters, the starting position from where the text is retrieved and the number of characters retrieved.

Similarly, you can store the text of the `Total amount payable` field in another `string` type variable, `strAmount`. The `Total amount payable` field is the second last paragraph in the cash memo document. Therefore, you need to declare an integer variable, `intParacount`, that stores the number of paragraphs in a document. You use the `Count` property of the `Paragraphs` collection to count the number of paragraphs in the document.

You can store the data that you have retrieved from the cash memo document in an XML document. However, before storing the data in an XML document, you need to understand the basics of XML.

# Overview of XML

XML (*Extensible Markup Language*) is a standard defined for W3C (*World Wide Web Consortium*) that you can use to store and display data in a structured format. The data in an XML document is displayed as plain text to provide you with a standard interface to display data across multiple platforms. Because of this, XML is extensively used to create applications that run on the Internet. To display data in an XML document, you use tags. You can now write a simple XML code that displays data in the Internet Explorer window. To create an XML document, type the following code in a Notepad file.

```
<?xml version="1.0"?>
<Students>
    <Student>
        < StudentId> St001 </StudentId>
        <LastName> Brown </LastName>
        <FirstName> George </FirstName>
    </Student>
    <Student>
        < StudentId> St002 </StudentId>
        <LastName> Floyd </LastName>
        <FirstName> Nancy </FirstName>
    </Student>
    <Student>
        < StudentId> St003 </StudentId>
        <LastName> Smith </LastName>
        <FirstName> James </FirstName>
    </Student>
</Students>
```

In the preceding code, the first line `<?xml version= "1.0"?>` is an XML declaration statement that is used to indicate to the browser that the document being processed is an XML document. The tag `Student` is used to denote an element that contains `StudentId`, `LastName`, and `FirstName` as nodes.

To view the output of the preceding code, save the Notepad file as `Student.xml` and open the file in Internet Explorer. Figure 17-3 shows the `Student.xml` file in Internet Explorer.

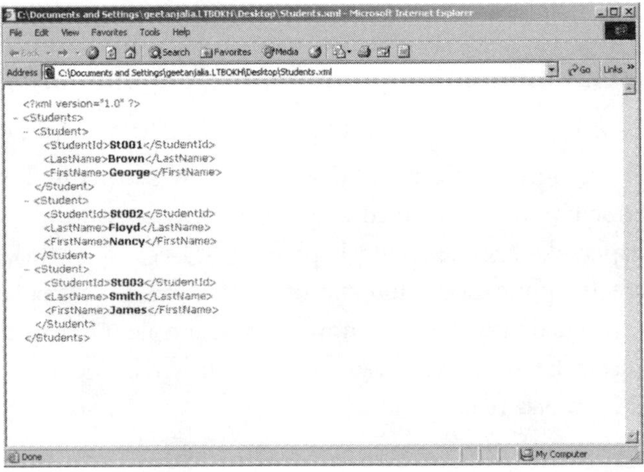


**FIGURE 17-3** *The* `Student.xml` *file in Internet Explorer*

Visual Studio .NET provides you with several classes and APIs (*application programming interfaces*) that you can use to display and process data in an XML document. The following section discusses a few classes that you use to read and write data from an XML document.

## The `XmlReader` Class

The `XmlReader` class is an abstract base class in the Visual Studio .NET base class library that allows you to access XML data. The `XmlReader` class lies in the `System.Xml` namespace and provides you with the ability to create a customized reader. In addition, the `XmlReader` class allows you to implement the functionality of derived classes such as `XmlTextReader`, `XmlValidatingReader`, and `XmlNodeReader`. The `XmlReader` class provides several methods and properties to access data from XML documents.

## The XmlWriter Class

The `XmlWriter` class is another abstract base class in the `System.Xml` namespace that allows you to write data to an XML document. You can use the `XmlWriter` class to create an interface for the XML documents. These XML documents are created using streams generated by the `XmlWriter` class and conform to the W3C and Namespace recommendations. The `XmlWriter` class implements the `XmlTextWriter` class. The `XmlWriter` class contains several methods and classes that you can use to write data to streams.

## Displaying Data in an XML Document

Before writing the code to display data in an XML document, you should first see a sample XML document created by the Creative Learning application. Figure 17-4 shows the sample XML document.

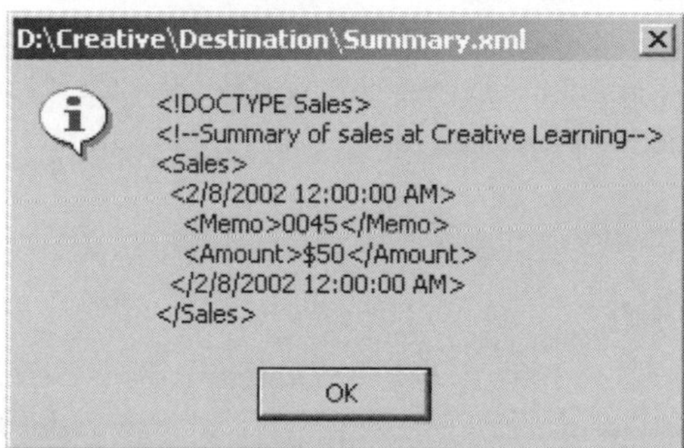


**FIGURE 17-4** *Sample XML document*

To display data in an XML document, you first need to create an object, `xmlWrite`, of the `XmlTextWriter` class in the `System.Xml.XmlWriter` class. After creating the `xmlWrite` object, you can use this object to write data to the XML document. The following section discusses how to add code to the XML document.

## Adding Code to the XML Document

To write data to the XML document, add the following code to the `Created` event.

```
XmlTextWriter xmlWrite;
xmlWrite.Formatting=Formatting.Indented;
xmlWrite.WriteDocType("Sales",null,null,null);
xmlWrite.WriteComment("Summary of sales at Creative Learning");
xmlWrite.WriteStartElement("Sales");
xmlWrite.WriteStartElement(Convert.ToString(DateTime.Today));
xmlWrite.WriteElementString("Memo",strMemo);
xmlWrite.WriteElementString("Amount",strAmount);
xmlWrite.WriteEndElement();
xmlWrite.WriteEndElement();
```

The preceding code creates an object, `xmlWrite`, of the `XmlTextWriter` class. Then, the code uses the `WriteDocType()` method of the `XmlTextWriter` class to write the DOCTYPE declaration of the XML document. The `WriteDocType()` method takes four parameters. The first parameter specifies the name of the DOCTYPE, `Sales`, and is an essential parameter. However, the other three parameters are optional.

## The DOCTYPE Declaration

The DOCTYPE declaration is used to specify DTD (*Document Type Definition*) for an XML document. DTD contains a set of rules that you can use to define the structure and logic of XML documents. You can create a document called a *DTD document* to store the set of rules for a specific XML document. The DTD documents contain rules that conform to W3C standards and are used to define the structure and syntax of the XML documents. In addition, the DTD documents contain the content and values allowed for an XML document as per W3C standards. The DTD document is a file with the extension .dtd.

When you create an XML document, the document is validated against the rules specified in the DTD document. To do this, you need to associate an XML document with a DTD document by using the DOCTYPE declaration. In addition to the name of the document, you can specify the root element of the document.

After discussing the DOCTYPE declaration statement, I will continue with the discussion of the code that is used to write data to the XML document. In addition to specifying a DOCTYPE for your XML document, you can add a comment to the XML document. To add a comment, you can use the `WriteComment()` method of the `XmlTextWriter` class. The `WriteComment()` method takes the text to be displayed in the form of a comment as a parameter.

After specifying the DOCTYPE and a comment to the XML document, you need to add data to the document. The data in an XML document is displayed in the form of elements and nodes. Each element that you specify is enclosed within tags. To specify the starting tag for an element, you use the `WriteStartElement()` method. The `WriteStartElement()` method is a void method in the `XmlTextWriter` class and is used to specify the starting tag for an element and associate the element with the given namespace. The `WriteStartElement()` method takes the name of the element as a parameter.

You can use the `WriteStartElement()` method to start two elements, `Sales` and current date. To specify the current date, use the `DateTime` struct in the `System` namespace. The `Today` property of the `DateTime` struct is used to retrieve the current date. The value returned by the `Today` property of the `DateTime` struct is converted to a `string` type value by using the `ToString()` method of the `Convert` class.

**NOTE**

The `ToString()` method is used to convert a 64-bit signed integer to its equivalent `string` type value represented by the `System.String` class in the specified base. The `ToString()` method is a method in the `Convert` class that lies in the `System` namespace.

Once you have added elements to your XML document, you can add nodes to the elements. To add nodes to the current date element, use the `WriteElementString()` method `XmlWrite` class. When you override the `WriteElementString()` method in a derived class, you can use it to create an element with the parameters that you specify. The `WriteElementString()` method takes the name of the element and its value as the parameter. You can use the `WriteElementString()` method to specify `Memo` and `Amount` as nodes in the current date element.

After adding data to the element, you need to close the element tag. You can do this by using the `WriteEndElement()` method. The `WriteEndElement()` method is a `void` method in the `XmlTextWriter` class.

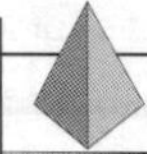

**TIP**

You need to call the `WriteEndElement()` method of the `XmlTextWriter` class as many times as the number of elements in your XML document. This means that calling the `WriteEndElement()` method once will not close all the elements in the XML document.

You have created an object of the `XmlTextWriter` class `xmlWrite`. You have also used it to write the data to an XML document. However, until now, you have not specified the name of the XML document and the directory where the XML document needs to be stored. To do this, add the following statement to the `Created` event. The name of the file is specified as `Summary.xml`, and the destination directory is the directory specified in the `txtDest` text box.

```
xmlWrite= new XmlTextWriter(txtDest.Text + "Summary.xml",null);
```

You can also use the `Intended` enum of the `System.Xml.Formatting` enum to format the data that is displayed in the XML document. The `System.Xml.Formatting` enum is used to specify the format settings for the objects of the `System.Xml.XmlTextWriter` class. Using the `Intended` enum enables you to display the data as per the `System.Xml.XmlTextWriter.Indentation` and `System.Xml.XmlTextWriter.IndentChar` settings. Figure 17-5 shows the XML document before you format the data in the document.

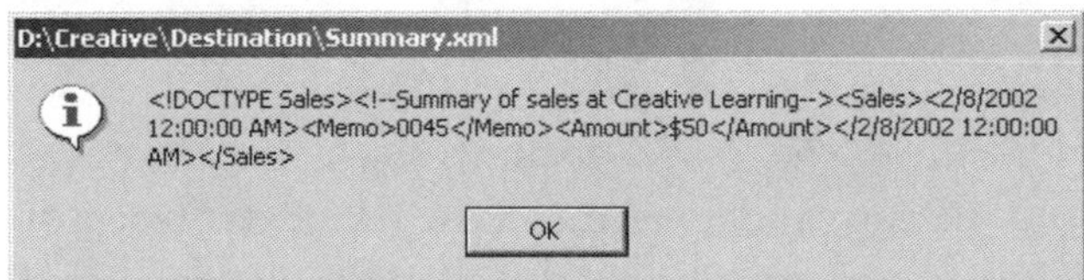


**FIGURE 17-5** *Data in the XML document without formatting*

After the application writes the data to the `Summary.xml` document, the application is ready to process the next document. Therefore, you need to again change the notification icon to Ready.ico. To do this, type the following statement in the `Created` event.

```
icoNotify.Icon=m_Ready;
```

Figure 17-6 shows the Ready.ico notification icon in the status area of the taskbar.

**FIGURE 17-6** *Ready.ico notification icon in the status area of the taskbar*

However, while processing a document, the application might detect an error, such as incorrect or incomplete data in the cash memo document. In such a case, the application generates an error message in Event Log.

## Displaying an Error Message in the Event Log

*Event logging* is a method by which the Microsoft Windows operating system keeps track of all the important software and hardware events running on the system. Tracking the events helps the system administrator to detect the cause of any error that occurs on the system. You can view these software and hardware events in Event Viewer provided by Microsoft Windows. To access Event Viewer, perform the following steps:

1. Point to the Settings option on the Start menu.
2. In the displayed list, click on the Control Panel option.
   The Control Panel window is displayed.
3. In the Control Panel window, click on the Administrative Tools option.
   The Administrative Tools window is displayed.

4. In the Administrative Tools window, click on the Event Viewer option.

   The Event Viewer window is displayed. Figure 17-7 displays the Event Viewer window.

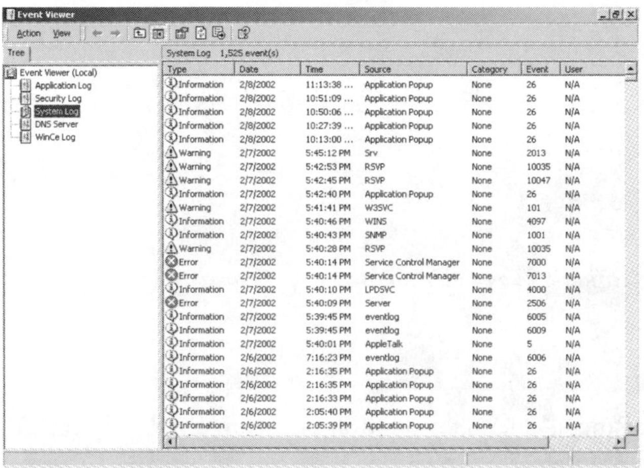

**FIGURE 17-7** *The Event Viewer window*

## The EventLog Component

Visual Studio .NET provides you with the EventLog component to view the events logged in Event Viewer. In addition to reading existing events, you can write event logs to Event Viewer by using the EventLog component. The EventLog component allows you to connect to Microsoft Windows Event Viewer on your local machine or on a remote machine.

You can access the EventLog component from the Components toolbox. Figure 17-8 shows the EventLog component in the Components toolbox.

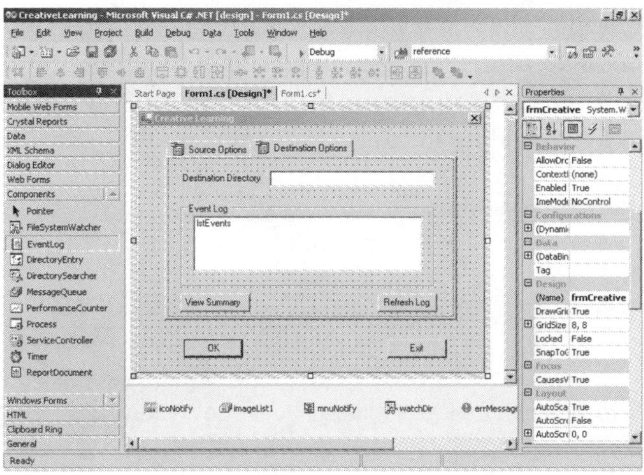

**FIGURE 17-8** *The EventLog component in the Components toolbox*

## Adding the EventLog Component to the Form

To include the EventLog component, drag the EventLog component from the Components toolbox to the Creative Learning form. The EventLog component with a name `eventLog1` is added to the component tray. Change the Name property of the control to eventLog. Figure 17-9 shows the eventLog component added to the component tray.

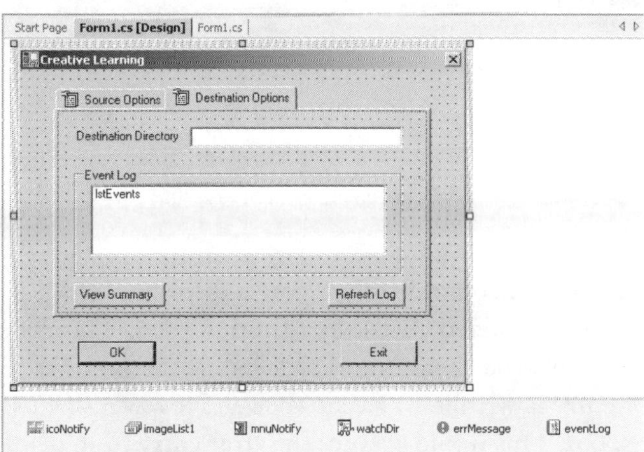


**FIGURE 17-9** *The eventLog component added to the component tray*

In addition to tracking events, Event Viewer can track the errors that are generated by the application while processing the cash memo document. When an error occurs, you can change the notification icon to Error.ico by creating an instance of the Error.ico file by adding the following statement to the `frmCreative` class:

```
private System.Drawing.Icon m_Error= new System.Drawing.Icon("Error.ICO");
```

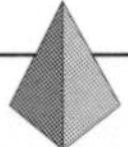

**TIP**

Remember to add the Error.ico file to the bin folder of your application.

To add an error entry to the EventLog component, you need to catch any exception that is generated by the application. The exception can then be written to Event Viewer by using the `WriteEntry()` method.

The `WriteEntry()` method is a `void` method of the `EventLog` class in the `System.Diagnostics` namespace. The `WriteEntry()` method is used to write a message to Event Viewer. The message to be displayed is passed as a parameter to the `WriteEntry()` method. You can now add code to the `Created` event that writes error logs to Event Viewer.

```
catch (Exception catchException)
{
   icoNotify.Icon=m_Error;
   icoNotify.Text="Error in " + e.Name;
   if (optGenerateLog.Checked==true)
      eventLog.WriteEntry(e.Name + ": " + catchException.Message);
}
```

In the preceding code, the Error.ico notification icon is displayed and a ToolTip displaying the error message is added to the notification icon. The code then checks whether the `optGenerateLog` check box is checked. If the user has selected the check box, the error entry is written to Event Viewer. However, the user may choose to clear the check box. This would prevent the error entry from being written to Event Viewer.

Figure 17-10 shows the Error.ico notification icon with an error message displayed in the status area.

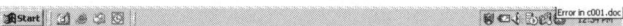

**FIGURE 17-10** *The Error.ico notification icon with an error message*

Figure 17-11 displays the error entry in Event Viewer.

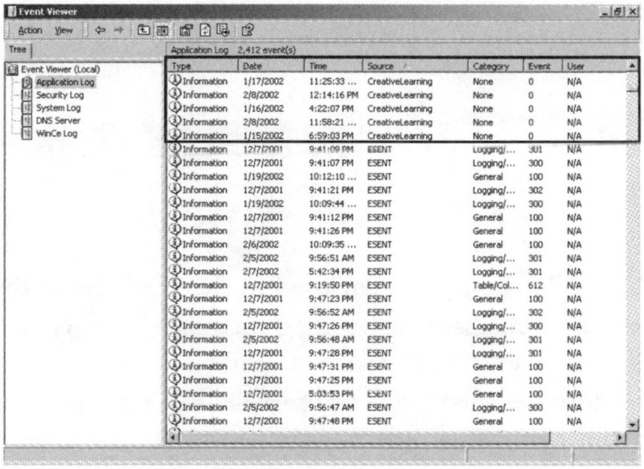

**FIGURE 17-11** *The error entry in Event Viewer*

After writing the data to an XML document, you need to close the object of the `XmlTextWriter` class by using the `Close()` method. In addition, you need to exit the Word application. You can do this by using the `Quit()` method. You can then instantiate the object of the `Word.Application` class to `null` so that the object can refer to another Word document in the source directory. In addition, you need to enable the directory watcher component to monitor the source directory.

```
finally
{
            xmlWrite.Flush();
            xmlWrite.Close();
```

```
            wdApp.Quit(ref optional, ref optional, ref optional);
            wdApp=null;
            watchDir.EnableRaisingEvents=true;
}
```

After the file is processed, you can move it the directory specified in the txtProcessedFile text box. To do this, add the following code to the `Created` event.

```
tryagain:
try
{
        File.Move(e.FullPath,txtProcessedFile.Text+e.Name);
}
catch
{
        goto tryagain;
}
```

The `File.Move()` method call statement is enclosed in the `try` loop so that the application tries to move the processed file to the processed directory until the time the file closes and can be moved. The `Move()` method is used to move the processed file to the directory specified in the txtProcessedFile text box. The path of the source directory and destination directory are passed as parameters to the `Move()` method.

**NOTE**

The `Move()` method is used to move a specified object from the source directory to the destination directory. In addition, you can change the name of the object in the destination directory by passing the new name as a parameter to the `Move()` method.

The events that were generated are visible in Event Viewer. You can also create a list box that displays the event entries that are generated in Event Viewer for your Creative Learning application.

## Displaying Event Entries from Event Viewer

You have created a list box that will display the event entries from Event Viewer. You can now add code to the Refresh Log button. When the user clicks on the Refresh Log button, the event entries from Event Viewer are picked and displayed in the `lstEvents` list box. To do this, add the following code to the `Click` event of the Refresh Log button.

```
private void btnRefresh_Click(object sender, System.EventArgs e)
{
		lstEvents.Items.Clear();
		eventLog.Log="Application";
		eventLog.MachineName=".";
		foreach (EventLogEntry logEntry in eventLog.Entries)
		{
				if (logEntry.Source=="CreativeLearning")
				{
						lstEvents.Items.Add(logEntry.Message);
				}
		}
}
```

The preceding code uses the `Clear()` method to clear the contents of the `lstEvents` list box. The code then sets the `Log` property of the `EventLog` class to the Application Log node of Event Viewer. Specifying the `MachineName` property of the `EventLog` class to `.` (dot) indicates that the event log is created in the Event Viewer of the user's machine.

Next, the `foreach` loop is used to write all the event entries with Source as Creative Learning to the `lstEvents` list box. The `Add()` method of the `ListBox` class adds an entry as an item to the `lstEvents` list box. Figure 17-12 shows the Application Log node of Event Viewer.

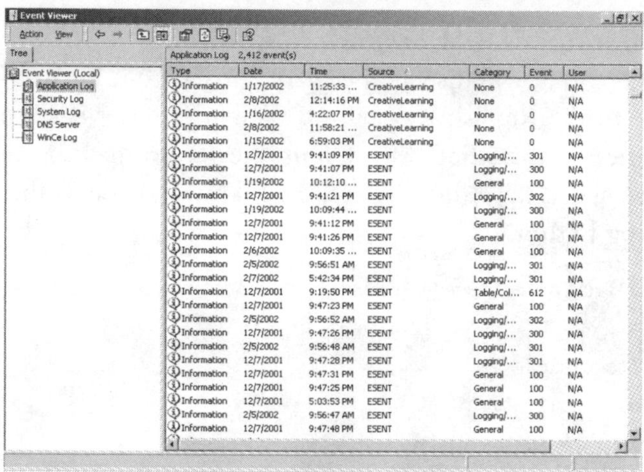


**FIGURE 17-12** *The Application Log node of Event Viewer*

Figure 17-13 displays the error logs in the `lstEvents` list box.

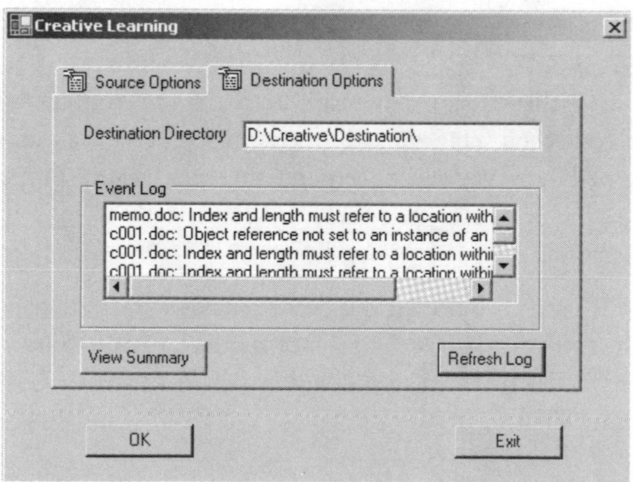


**FIGURE 17-13** *The error logs in the `lstEvents` list box*

In addition to creating a list box to list the event entries for the Creative Learning application, you can display the contents of the `Summary.xml` document in a message box.

## Displaying Data from the `Summary.xml` Document in a Message Box

To display the data from the `Summary.xml` document in a message box, you need to read data from the XML document. To do this, create an instance of the `StreamReader` class `strRead`. The `StreamReader` class is a class in the `System.IO` namespace and implements the `System.IO.TextReader` class. The `TextReader` class represents a reader that is used to read the characters in a byte stream. To create an instance of the `StreamReader` class, use the following statement:

```
StreamReader strRead;
```

After creating the instance, you can use it to read the contents of the `Summary.xml` document in the directory specified in the `txtDest` text box. To read the data from the `Summary.xml` document, use the following statement:

```
strRead= new StreamReader(txtDest.Text+"Summary.xml");
```

The data in the `strRead` object can then be displayed in a message box by using the `Show()` method of the `MessageBox` class. To read the data in the `Summary.xml` document, use the `ReadToEnd()` method of the `StreamReader` class that reads the entire content of the `Summary.xml` document. In addition, you can include the OK button and the Info.ico file in the message box by passing them as parameters to the `Show()` method. To display a message box, type the following statement in the `Click` event of the btnSummary button.

```
try
{
    strRead= new StreamReader(txtDest.Text+"Summary.xml");
    MessageBox.Show(strRead.ReadToEnd(),txtDest.Text+"Summary.xml",MessageBoxButtons
        .OK,MessageBoxIcon.Information);
    strRead.Close();
}
```

After displaying the message box, you need to close the object of the `StreamReader` class. You can close the `strRead` object by using the `Close()` method of the `StreamReader` class. The `Close()` method closes the object and releases any resources associated with the `strRead` object.

Figure 17-14 shows the message box displaying the data from the `Summary.xml` document.

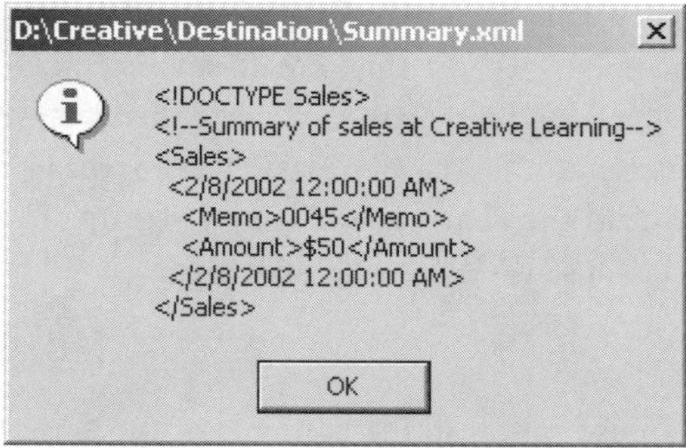


**FIGURE 17-14** *The message box displaying the data from the* `Summary.xml` *document*

If the application generates an exception while reading data from an XML document, you can display the exception that is generated in another message box, as shown in the following statement:

```
catch(Exception exc)
{
   MessageBox.Show("An error was returned: " + exc.Message + "Please check the
      destination folder for summary");
}
```

Figure 17-15 displays the message box with an error.

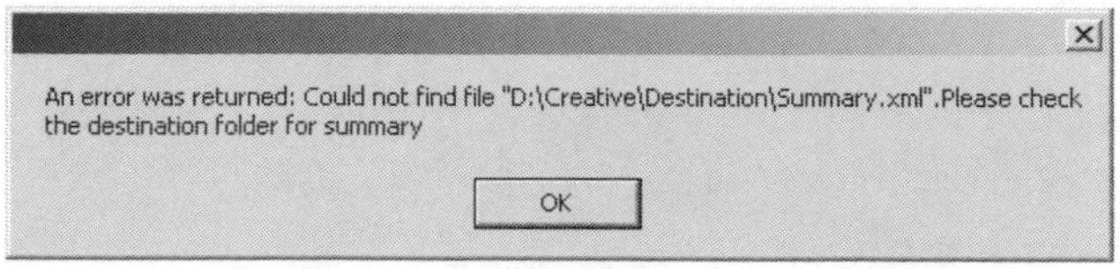

An error was returned: Could not find file "D:\Creative\Destination\Summary.xml".Please check the destination folder for summary

OK

**FIGURE 17-15** *The message box displaying an error message*

You have completed writing code for the application. The following is the complete code for the application.

```
using System;
using System.Drawing;
using System.Collections;
using System.ComponentModel;
using System.Windows.Forms;
using System.Data;
using System.IO;
using System.Diagnostics;
using System.Xml;

namespace CreativeLearning
{
   public class frmCreative : System.Windows.Forms.Form
   {
      private System.Drawing.Icon m_Ready= new System.Drawing.Icon("Ready.ICO");
      private System.Drawing.Icon m_Error= new System.Drawing.Icon("Error.ICO");
      private System.Drawing.Icon m_Info= new System.Drawing.Icon("Info.ICO");
      private System.Windows.Forms.Button btnOK;
      private System.Windows.Forms.Button btnCancel;
      private System.Windows.Forms.NotifyIcon icoNotify;
      private System.Windows.Forms.TabControl tabControl1;
      private System.Windows.Forms.TabPage tabSource;
      private System.Windows.Forms.TabPage tabDest;
      private System.Windows.Forms.ImageList imageList1;
      private System.Windows.Forms.Label label1;
      private System.Windows.Forms.TextBox txtSource;
      private System.Windows.Forms.Label label3;
      private System.Windows.Forms.TextBox txtProcessedFile;
      private System.Windows.Forms.CheckBox optGenerateLog;
      private System.Windows.Forms.ContextMenu mnuNotify;
      private System.Windows.Forms.MenuItem menuItem2;
      private System.Windows.Forms.MenuItem mnuConfigure;
      private System.Windows.Forms.MenuItem mnuExit;
      private System.IO.FileSystemWatcher watchDir;
      private System.Windows.Forms.ErrorProvider errMessage;
```

```
private System.Diagnostics.EventLog eventLog;
private System.Windows.Forms.GroupBox groupEventLog;
private System.Windows.Forms.ListBox lstEvents;
private System.Windows.Forms.Button btnRefresh;
private System.Windows.Forms.TextBox txtDest;
private System.Windows.Forms.Label label2;
private System.Windows.Forms.Button btnSummary;
private System.Diagnostics.EventLog eventLog1;
private System.ComponentModel.IContainer components;

public frmCreative()
{
   InitializeComponent();
}

protected override void Dispose( bool disposing )
{
   if( disposing )
   {
      if (components != null)
      {
         components.Dispose();
      }
   }
   base.Dispose( disposing );
}

static void Main()
{
   Application.Run(new frmCreative());
}
private void frmCreative_Load(object sender, System.EventArgs e)
{
   txtSource.Text="D:\\Creative\\Source\\";
   txtProcessedFile.Text="D:\\Creative\\Processed\\";
   txtDest.Text="D:\\Creative\\Destination\\";
   optGenerateLog.Checked=true;
}
```

```
private void btnOK_Click(object sender, System.EventArgs e)
{
   if (!Directory.Exists(txtSource.Text))
   {
      errMessage.SetError(txtSource,"Invalid source directory");
      txtSource.Focus();
      tabControl1.SelectedTab=tabSource;
      return;
   }
   else
      errMessage.SetError(txtSource,"");
      if (!Directory.Exists(txtDest.Text))
      {
         errMessage.SetError(txtDest,"Invalid destination directory");
         txtDest.Focus();
         tabControl1.SelectedTab=tabDest;
         return;
      }
      else
      errMessage.SetError(txtDest,"");
      if (!Directory.Exists(txtProcessedFile.Text))
      {
         errMessage.SetError(txtProcessedFile,"Invalid processed file
            directory");
         txtProcessedFile.Focus();
         tabControl1.SelectedTab=tabSource;
         return;
      }
      else
         errMessage.SetError(txtProcessedFile,"");
         watchDir.Path=txtSource.Text;
         watchDir.EnableRaisingEvents=true;
         icoNotify.Icon=m_Ready;
         icoNotify.Visible=true;
         this.ShowInTaskbar=false;
         this.Hide();
      }
```

```
private void txtSource_KeyUp(object sender, System.Windows.Forms.KeyEventArgs e)
{
   if (Directory.Exists(txtSource.Text))
      txtSource.BackColor=Color.White;
   else
      txtSource.BackColor=Color.Pink;
}

private void txtProcessedFile_KeyUp(object sender, System.Windows.Forms
   .KeyEventArgs e)
{
   if (Directory.Exists(txtProcessedFile.Text))
      txtProcessedFile.BackColor=Color.White;
   else
   txtProcessedFile.BackColor=Color.Pink;
}

private void menuItem3_Click(object sender, System.EventArgs e)
{
   Application.Exit();
}

private void mnuConfigure_Click(object sender, System.EventArgs e)
{
   icoNotify.Visible=false;
   this.ShowInTaskbar=true;
   this.Show();
}

private void btnCancel_Click(object sender, System.EventArgs e)
{
   Application.Exit();
}

private void icoNotify_DoubleClick(object sender, System.EventArgs e)
{
   icoNotify.Visible=false;
   this.ShowInTaskbar=true;
```

```
    this.Show();
}

private void watchDir_Created(object sender, System.IO.FileSystemEventArgs e)
{
    watchDir.EnableRaisingEvents=false;
    icoNotify.Icon=m_Info;
    icoNotify.Text="Processed: "+ e.Name;
    Word.Application wdApp= new Word.ApplicationClass();
    object optional=System.Reflection.Missing.Value;
    XmlTextWriter xmlWrite;
    xmlWrite= new XmlTextWriter(txtDest.Text + "Summary.xml",null);
    try
    {
        Word.Document Doc = new Word.DocumentClass();
        object filename=e.FullPath;
        Doc=wdApp.Documents.Open(ref filename, ref optional, ref optional,
            ref optional,ref optional,ref optional,ref optional,ref optional,
            ref optional,ref optional,ref optional,ref optional);
        Word.Range wdRange;
        wdRange=Doc.Paragraphs.Item(2).Range;
        string strMemo, strAmount;
        int intParacount;
        strMemo=wdRange.Text;
        strMemo=strMemo.Substring(15,4);
        intParacount=Doc.Paragraphs.Count;
        intParacount=intParacount-2;
        wdRange=Doc.Paragraphs.Item(intParacount).Range;
        object count="-1";
        object wdCharacter="1";
        wdRange.MoveEnd(ref wdCharacter,ref count);
        strAmount=wdRange.Text;
        strAmount=strAmount.Substring(23);
        xmlWrite.Formatting=Formatting.Indented;
        xmlWrite.WriteDocType("Sales",null,null,null);
        xmlWrite.WriteComment("Summary of sales at Creative Learning");
        xmlWrite.WriteStartElement("Sales");
        xmlWrite.WriteStartElement(Convert.ToString(DateTime.Today));
```

```
        xmlWrite.WriteElementString("Memo",strMemo);
        xmlWrite.WriteElementString("Amount",strAmount);
        xmlWrite.WriteEndElement();
        xmlWrite.WriteEndElement();
        iconNotify.Icon=m_Ready;
    }

    catch (Exception catchException)
    {
        icoNotify.Icon=m_Error;
        icoNotify.Text="Error in " + e.Name;
        if (optGenerateLog.Checked==true)
        eventLog.WriteEntry(e.Name + ": " + catchException.Message);
    }

    finally
    {
        xmlWrite.Flush();
        xmlWrite.Close();
        wdApp.Quit(ref optional, ref optional, ref optional);
        wdApp=null;
        watchDir.EnableRaisingEvents=true;
    }

    tryagain:
    try
    {
        File.Move(e.FullPath,txtProcessedFile.Text+e.Name);
    }

    catch
    {
        goto tryagain;
    }
}
```

```
private void btnRefresh_Click(object sender, System.EventArgs e)
{
   lstEvents.Items.Clear();
   eventLog.Log="Application";
   eventLog.MachineName=".";
   foreach (EventLogEntry logEntry in eventLog.Entries)
   {
      if (logEntry.Source=="CreativeLearning")
      {
         lstEvents.Items.Add(logEntry.Message);
      }
   }
}

private void btnSummary_Click(object sender, System.EventArgs e)
{
   StreamReader strRead;
   try
   {
      strRead= new StreamReader(txtDest.Text+"Summary.xml");
      MessageBox.Show(strRead.ReadToEnd(),txtDest.Text+"Summary.xml",
         MessageBoxButtons.OK,MessageBoxIcon.Information);
      strRead.Close();
   }
   catch(Exception exc)
   {
      MessageBox.Show("An error was returned: " + exc.Message + "Please check the
         destination folder for summary");
   }

private void txtDest_KeyUp(object sender, System.Windows.Forms.KeyEventArgs e)
{
   if (Directory.Exists(txtDest.Text))
      txtDest.BackColor=Color.White;
   else
```

```
                txtDest.BackColor=Color.Pink;
            }
        }

    }
```

## Summary

In this chapter, you learned to add code that allows your application to interact with a Word document and Windows Event Viewer.

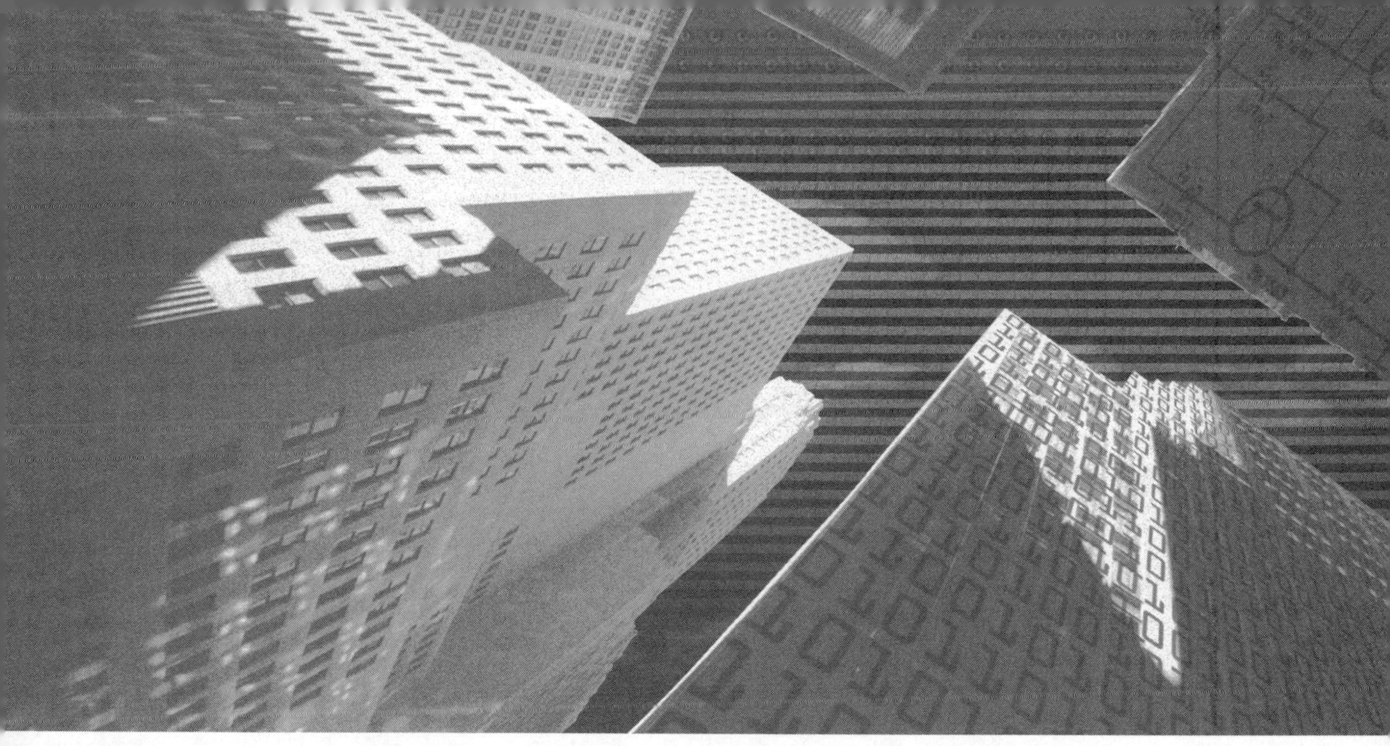

# PART VI

## Professional Project 4

# Project 4

## Creating an Airline Reservation Portal

## Project 4 Overview

An airline portal is an enterprise solution for managing customer and flight information for an airline. The primary function of the portal is to manage flight information and perform reservations and cancellations. However, the duties in an airline also involve performing allied tasks, such as querying the status of flights, managing accounts of executives who perform the reservations, and generating reports to interpret airline performance.

Airline reservation portals were developed as customized applications in which the airline employees primarily managed all customer data and processed customer requests. However, with the advent of the Internet, it is possible to enable customers to access their data through a Web site or a mobile device. These methods of accessing information over the Internet through Web sites and mobile devices has become all the more easier with the advent of ASP.NET.

In this project, I want to show you how to develop an enterprise solution for managing the flight schedules and reservations in an airline. The project uses a blend of the ASP.NET Web applications, ASP.NET Mobile Web Applications, and SQL Server Enterprise Management tools to provide an integrated solution. With the help of the project, you can understand the processes involved in managing business data and also the ability of C# to help you build your application around the business logic.

# Chapter 18

## Project Case Study and Design

In the preceding projects, you developed Windows Forms applications. Windows Forms applications are usually run on desktop computers. For a distributed environment, ASP applications are preferred because a large audience can access them relatively easily.

ASP.NET Web applications are an optimal solution for managing large-scale business applications. You can either deploy these applications on an intranet and make them accessible throughout an organization, or make them securely accessible on the Internet so that Internet users can access and update information on the Web site.

In this project, you will learn to create an ASP.NET Web application for automating the ticketing process of a fictitious airline, SkyShark Airlines. The project, albeit customized for the requirements of SkyShark Airlines, can be easily customized to specific business requirements. This chapter has been written to equip you with the information necessary to begin creating the application.

In this chapter, I present the case study of the application and its design. The design includes the databases and tables, the relationship between database tables, and the structure of the Web forms in the application.

## Airline Profile

Launched in 1999, SkyShark Airlines is a United States-based airline that has rapidly grown in the past three years. High service standards and the exceptional commitment of its employees have resulted in a consistent increase in the customer base of the airline over the past years. Following this positive trend, the airline plans to further its profits in the next financial year with the introduction of new aircrafts and new air routes.

Currently, the airline operates from a corporate office and a number of regional offices. In the current setup, the regional offices interact with users somewhat independently. The only interaction that happens between the regional and the head offices is the daily exchange of customer transactions that have happened during business hours.

The airline plans to add to its existing list of regional offices and enable real-time communication between the regional offices and the corporate office. Each regional office would be connected by an intranet. Subsequently, reservations and cancellations will be performed at each of the regional offices, which will function in an interlinked manner. The data will be collated on a daily basis at the corporate office for the purpose of analysis and reports.

The executives of SkyShark Airlines are categorized into three roles: business management, network administration, and line-of-business operations. Tasks in these roles are well defined and are equally important in the effective functioning of the business transactions. It is important to understand the role of business executives because the design of the application, as you will see later, depends upon these roles. Therefore, in this section, I examine the tasks performed by each business executive.

## Role of a Business Manager

Business managers are responsible for framing policies and ensuring that the business operations perform at the optimal level. In the context of SkyShark Airlines, the duties of business managers are specified in the following list:

- **Introducing new flights.** Business managers are responsible for introducing new flights after analyzing the market opportunities and business trends.
- **Adding new user accounts.** Business managers request for new user accounts for users that need to access custom applications deployed by the airline. When requesting for a new user account, the role of the user is also specified. As a policy, when a new employee joins the airline, business managers send a request for the inclusion of a new user account to the network administrator.
- **Analyzing flight performance.** Business managers analyze the performance of flights to determine whether or not a flight generates the expected revenue. The results of the analysis are also used to determine if the capacity of flights is optimally utilized.
- **Launching frequent flier programs.** Frequent flier programs are used to enable discounts for customers who have either flown the airline more than a predefined number of times or paid more than a predetermined fare. To enable the frequent flier program, business managers use the

flight transaction data and determine which customers should be eligible for the program.

## Role of a Network Administrator

Network administrators are responsible for ensuring around-the-clock connectivity of the corporate office with the regional offices. You should note that network administrators are proficient with database management tools, such as SQL Server Enterprise Manager, because they need to use these tools frequently for accomplishing their tasks. The duties of network administrators are given in the following list:

- **Maintaining Web servers and database servers.** Network administrators ensure that the latest patches and updates available for Web servers and database servers are installed. They examine database logs and Web server logs to ensure that there are no hardware or software-related problems. They also analyze the network usage to determine if the present infrastructure can sustain the demand. If it cannot, ways to scale the hardware infrastructure are determined and implemented.
- **Managing user accounts.** Network administrators create user accounts for users who are authorized to perform flight-related transactions. They also ensure that the user accounts of users who resign from the organization are disabled.
- **Backing up and archiving databases.** Network administrators back up databases daily and also ensure that data that pertains to flights that have departed is periodically archived.

## Role of a Line-of-Business Executive

The line-of-business executives are responsible for performing the reservation and cancellation of tickets for the airline. The responsibilities of these executives are summarized in the following list:

- **Reservation on flights.** Line-of-business executives reserve passengers on flights. While reserving the seats, they generate a ticket that specifies the status and fare to the passenger.
- **Cancellation on flights.** Passengers can approach the line-of-business executives for cancellation of their tickets. When a ticket is cancelled, the fare amount entitled for refund to the passenger is refunded.

- **Reporting flight status.** On demand, line-of-business executives also report the seat availability in the business and executive classes to passengers.
- **Confirmation of reservation.** Line-of-business executives can confirm the ticket of a passenger 72 to 24 hours before the departure of the flight. The confirmation can be carried out over telephone as well as across the reservation counters at regional offices.

Having examined the role of business executives in SkyShark Airlines, you can understand the requirements of the airline portal easily. These requirements are explained in the next section.

# Project Requirements

The airline portal required by the airline should be an integrated solution that allows all business executives and customers to access data that is pertinent to their roles. Notice the inclusion of customers that I made in the preceding sentence. By enabling customers to manage their information, such as their ticket status and the confirmation status of their reservation, the airline wants to reduce the workload of its line-of-business executives and enhance customer experience.

Based on the roles of executives discussed in the previous section, you can infer that the responsibilities of the airline executives are well defined. The airline portal uses the role of these executives as a framework for imparting its functionality. Thus, the portal enables different sets of tasks for business managers, network administrators, and line-of-business executives. In this section, I list all tasks that need to be accomplished in the airline portal and also examine how these tasks will be accomplished.

## Creation and Deletion of User Accounts

The procedure of creating a new user account is given in the following list:

1. A business manager decides when a new user account needs to be created and uses the online portal to send an e-mail message to the network administrator. The username and the role of the user are specified in the e-mail message.

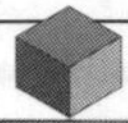

**NOTE**

As a convention, the username selected by the network administrator for a new user account is the same as the Windows 2000 domain account user ID for the user.

2. Network administrators use the online portal to create a new user account. When the new account is created, an e-mail message is triggered to the user. The e-mail message specifies the username, password, and the privacy policy of the airline (as an attachment).
3. When the user logs on for the first time, it is mandatory for the user to change his or her password.

When a user is no longer required to use the airline portal, the network administrator deletes the user account from the airline portal.

## Addition of Flight Details

After you add new user accounts, users can access the airline portal. The next step, after adding user accounts, is to add the details of new flights so that registered users can access the airline portal and perform reservations and cancellations.

To add new flight details, a business manager uses the following information:

- Flight number
- Origin and destination
- Number of seats in the business and executive class
- Fares for the two classes
- Type of aircraft

The business manager adds the information to the airline portal, and the flight is ready to accept reservations and cancellations.

## Reservations

Line-of-business executives perform reservations on flights after flight details are added by business managers. Reservation of passengers on flights is a three-step procedure, as specified following:

1. The passenger supplies the flight number, the class, and the date of journey. The line-of-business executive uses this information to retrieve the flight status. The flight status is intimated to the passenger.
2. If the passenger wishes to continue with the reservation, the line-of-business executive accepts the name and e-mail address of the user to perform the reservation.
3. The e-mail address of the user is optional and is used to check if the customer qualifies for a frequent flier discount. If the customer qualifies for a discount, the discount is deducted from the ticket fare and the ticket is generated.

## Cancellations

If a passenger wishes to cancel a ticket, the passenger approaches the line-of-business with the ticket number. The line-of-business executive cancels the ticket and refunds the fare to the passenger. The refund applicable to a customer is calculated depending upon the departure time of the flight, by using the following scheme:

- If the user has not boarded the flight, as checked by the status in the confirmation of reservations, and the flight has departed, 80 percent of the fare is refunded.
- If the flight has not departed, 10 dollars are subtracted from the fare and the remaining amount is refunded.

## Query of Status

Passengers can query the status of their tickets as well as the status of flights. To query the status, passengers can either contact the line-of-business executives or query the information from the online portal of SkyShark Airlines. The online portal for the airline presents information about flight schedules, flight status, and ticket status. The online portal can also be used to confirm reservations. I will describe the online portal in detail later in this project.

## Confirmation of Tickets

Passengers need to confirm their tickets before the departure of the flight. This practice is established to ensure that seats of passengers who decide not to travel on the scheduled date are offered to the passengers in the waiting list. To confirm their ticket, passengers can use the options given in the following list:

- Use the ticket number to confirm the ticket with the line-of-business executive, either by telephone or in person.
- Use the ticket number and e-mail ID to confirm the reservation on the online portal.

## Creation of Reports

Business managers can generate reports to view the performance of flights. The types of reports supported by the airline portal are specified in the following list:

- **Monthly flight revenue.** The monthly flight revenue report retrieves the total revenue generated from all the flights in a given month. The business manager needs to select the month and year to run the report.
- **Flight revenue report.** The flight revenue report reports the total revenue generated from a flight. To run this report, the business manager needs to specify the flight number.
- **Customer affinity report.** The customer affinity report retrieves the customers who have flown the flight maximum number of times or who have paid the maximum fare. To run this report, the business manager needs to specify how many customer records the application should retrieve. This report is used to launch the frequent fliers program.
- **Total revenue report.** The total revenue report is used to retrieve the total revenue that has been generated by the airline since a given month and year.

## Launch of Frequent Flier Programs

Business managers are responsible for launching frequent flier programs that are used for giving discounts to customers who frequently fly with the airline. Customers are given discounts if they specify either of the parameters specified in the following list:

- **Frequency of flight.** Customers who frequently fly the airline are given a discount of a certain percent on their ticket fare. The business managers determine the frequency of flight and the discount percentage.

- **Total fare collected.** Customers who have paid more than a certain amount as fare are also given discounts. The amount and the discount, in this case as well, are decided by the business manager.

The discount applicable to users is applied when they book a ticket on the airline.

## Summarizing the Tasks

I have explained all the tasks that need to be performed by the airline. I will now sort each task by role, because this information is used for creating the form design.

The tasks of business managers are summarized as follows:

- Add and remove flights
- Request for user IDs
- Generate reports
- Manager frequent flier programs

The tasks of network administrators are summarized as follows:

- Add and delete user accounts
- Back up and archive databases
- Examine Web server and database logs

The tasks of line-of-business executives are summarized as follows:

- Create and cancel reservations
- Query status of flights and tickets
- Confirm tickets

The summarized tasks form the basis of the application. As you will see in the next section, the database structure and the application interface follow closely with the tasks summarized for each business executive.

# Project Design

After having examined the requirements of the application in detail, you can now proceed with designing the application. In the project design stage, you identify the database tables and the relationships between them to finalize the database schema. It is critical to examine all the possible requirements and incorporate them in the database schema because reworking the design later means a lot of wasted effort. After you finalize the database schema, you can finalize interface of your application so that the development team has a framework on which it can work.

In this section, I examine the database schema of the SkyShark Airlines database and the design of the forms. The design of the forms is the interface of the final application.

## Database Design

You arrive at the structure of the database tables after creating the preliminary structure of tables that match the application requirements and then normalizing the structure to eliminate data redundancy. The process is explained in Chapter 7, "Project Case Study," in the section "Normalization."

If you examine the business requirements stated previously, the first task performed in the airline application is the creation of new user accounts. Therefore, I begin with explaining the structure of the `dtUsers` table, which will be used for storing the details of authorized users. Thereafter, I explain each table of the database as it is created.

### *The `dtUsers` Table*

The `dtUsers` table has four columns. Three columns store the username, password, and role of the user, while the fourth one signifies whether or not the user has changed the password after logging on the first time. The structure of the `dtUsers` table is given in Table 18-1.

**Table 18-1 Structure of the `dtUsers` Table**

| Column Name | Data Type | Length | Allow Nulls |
|---|---|---|---|
| `Username` | `char` | 15 | 0 |
| `Password` | `char` | 15 | 0 |
| `Role` | `char` | 10 | 0 |
| `PasswordChanged` | `bit` | 1 | 1 |

**TIP**

In the preceding table structure, the value `0` for Allow Nulls implies that it is mandatory for you to specify a value for the field when you add a new record. Similarly, the value `1` implies that the field is optional when you add a new record. For example, in the `dtUsers` table, the `PasswordChanged` field, which stores a `Boolean` value to specify whether or not the user has changed the password, is optional.

After network administrators create user IDs in the `dtUsers` table, business managers should specify flight details.

## The `dtFltDetails` Table

The `dtFltDetails` table stores details of airline routes flown by the airline. The structure of the `dtFltDetails` table is given in Table 18-2.

**Table 18-2 Structure of the `dtFltDetails` Table**

| Column Name | Data Type | Length | Allow Nulls |
|---|---|---|---|
| `FltNo` | `char` | 10 | 0 |
| `Origin` | `text` | 16 | 0 |
| `Destination` | `text` | 16 | 0 |
| `Deptime` | `datetime` | 8 | 0 |
| `Arrtime` | `datetime` | 8 | 0 |
| `AircraftType` | `char` | 10 | 0 |
| `SeatsExec` | `int` | 4 | 0 |
| `SeatsBn` | `int` | 4 | 0 |
| `FareExec` | `int` | 4 | 0 |
| `FareBn` | `int` | 4 | 0 |
| `LaunchDate` | `datetime` | 8 | 0 |

In the structure of the `dtFltDetails` table given in Table 18-2, I have added a `LaunchDate` field. The `LaunchDate` field is used to store the date on which the flight is launched. This information will be used to display details of newly launched flights on the Web site.

After flight details are added to the `dtFltDetails` table, line-of-business executives can make reservations on the airline. Therefore, I now move on to the table that is used for storing details of reservations, `dtReservations`.

## *The `dtReservations` Table*

The `dtReservations` table is the most frequently used table of the database. The table is used to store details of passengers who have reserved a seat on the flight. The structure of the `dtReservations` table is given in Table 18-3.

**Table 18-3 Structure of the `dtReservations` Table**

| Column Name | Data Type | Length | Allow Nulls |
|---|---|---|---|
| `TicketNo` | `char` | 10 | 0 |
| `FltNo` | `char` | 10 | 0 |
| `DateOfJourney` | `datetime` | 8 | 0 |
| `ClassOfRes` | `char` | 4 | 0 |
| `Name` | `char` | 20 | 0 |
| `EMail` | `char` | 50 | 1 |
| `Fare` | `int` | 4 | 0 |
| `Status` | `int` | 4 | 0 |
| `ReservedBy` | `char` | 15 | 0 |
| `DateOfRes` | `datetime` | 8 | 0 |
| `TicketConfirmed` | `bit` | 1 | 1 |

In the `dtReservations` table, the `TicketConfirmed` and `EMail` fields allow null values. The `TicketConfirmed` field is updated when users confirm their ticket. The e-mail address, when specified by the passenger, is used for enabling the frequent flier program.

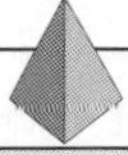

**TIP**

To ensure privacy of data, only customers who specify their e-mail address can query their ticket status on the online portal of SkyShark Airlines.

As a result of a large number of flights flown by the airline, there will be a large amount of data in the `dtReservations` table. However, if you notice, you need to store details of passengers related to those flights that have departed only for the frequent flier programs. Therefore, a network administrator should ideally move the data related to departed flights to another table, which can be used for the frequent fliers program. This type of mechanism will have the following advantages:

- **Archiving database tables easily.** Data that is ready for archiving is automatically moved to another table. Therefore, network administrators can archive database tables easily.
- **Improved performance.** If you use a different database for storing data pertaining to flights that have departed, queries for analyzing data will be directed to the other database and the performance of the `dtReservations` table, which is critical to the online portal, will improve because redundant transactions are eliminated.
- **Easy access to data.** For generating reports, business managers need not access dynamic data in the `dtReservations` table. Instead, they can use the other table to retrieve only the data that is pertinent to analysis.

To implement the logic that I have explained, I have created the `dtDepartedFlights` table, which follows next.

## The `dtDepartedFlights` Table

The `dtDepartedFlights` table has exactly the same structure as the `dtReservations` table. Therefore, I do not replicate it here. You can look the structure up in Table 18-3. After a flight has departed, data pertaining to passengers who have flown the flight is moved to the `dtDepartedFlights` table. This data is used for generating reports and for enabling the frequent flier programs.

Having examined the tables related to flight details and reservations, you can examine the table for cancellations, `dtCancellations`.

## *The dtCancellations Table*

The `dtCancellations` table stores information related to tickets that have been cancelled. This information is required only for accountability of refunded fare and reservations. Therefore, if a passenger whose ticket has been cancelled informs the airline that the ticket should not have been cancelled, the details of the executive who processed the cancellation can be traced and the reasons of the cancellation can be determined. The structure of the `dtCancellations` table is given in Table 18-4.

**Table 18-4 Structure of the `dtCancellations` Table**

| Column Name | Data Type | Length | Allow Nulls |
|---|---|---|---|
| `TicketNo` | `char` | 10 | 0 |
| `Refund` | `int` | 4 | 0 |
| `ProcessedBy` | `char` | 15 | 0 |
| `CancellationDate` | `datetime` | 8 | 0 |

The `dtCancellations` table can be archived on a timely basis to ensure that no redundant data is stored in the database. I will now discuss the next important table, `dtFltStatus`.

## *The dtFltStatus Table*

When a passenger reserves a seat on an airline, the number of seats available for reservation should reduce by one. Similarly, if a flight is overbooked, excess passengers should be placed in queue. The updated status of a flight should be available to passengers when they reserve their seat.

To ensure that an updated status of a flight is always available, I have used the `dtFltStatus` table. As soon as the first ticket is booked on a flight, an entry for the flight is created in the `dtFltStatus` table. This table is updated as reservations and cancellations are made. The structure of the `dtFltStatus` table is given in Table 18-5.

**Table 18-5 Structure of the `dtFltStatus` Table**

| Column Name | Data Type | Length | Allow Nulls |
|---|---|---|---|
| FltNo | char | 10 | 0 |
| StatusDate | datetime | 8 | 0 |
| StatusClass | char | 10 | 0 |
| Status | int | 4 | 0 |

In the structure of the `dtFltStatus` table, the `FltNo`, `StatusDate`, and `StatusClass` fields form a composite key. This implies that the three fields together form a unique combination that can be used to retrieve the status of a specific class of a flight on a specified date.

I will now examine the last two tables that are related to the frequent flier program, `dtPassengerDetails` and `dtFrequentFliers`.

## The `dtPassengerDetails` Table

To enable the frequent fliers program, the `dtPassengerDetails` table retrieves data from the `dtDepartedFlights` table. The `dtPassengerDetails` table uses the e-mail address of passengers to identify the number of times they have flown the airline and the total fare collected from them in these flights. The structure of the `dtPassengerDetails` table is given in Table 18-6.

**Table 18-6 Structure of the `dtPassengerDetails` Table**

| Column Name | Data Type | Length | Allow Nulls |
|---|---|---|---|
| EMail | char | 50 | 0 |
| FareCollected | int | 4 | 0 |
| TotalTimesFlown | int | 4 | 0 |

Whenever a new frequent flier program is launched, data from the `dtPassengerDetails` table is used to determine how many passengers the program will impact. This data is used for enabling discounts to passengers. The discounts are specified in the `dtFrequentFliers` table.

## The `dtFrequentFliers` Table

The `dtFrequentFliers` table is used to specify the discount (expressed in percentage) applicable to customers. Just as in the `dtPassengerDetails` table, the passengers are identified by their e-mail address. The structure of the `dtFrequentFliers` table is given in Table 18-7.

**Table 18-7 Structure of the `dtFrequentFliers` Table**

| Column Name | Data Type | Length | Allow Nulls |
|---|---|---|---|
| `EMail` | `char` | 50 | 0 |
| `Discount` | `int` | 4 | 0 |

When a passenger reserves a ticket, the e-mail address of the passenger is checked in the `dtFrequentFliers` table to query if a discount is applicable to the passenger. If a discount is applicable, the fare is computed after deducting the applicable discount.

## Database Schema

Having examined all the tables of the SkyShark Airlines database, you can infer the database schema by creating relationships between database tables. The schema for the SkyShark Airlines database is shown in Figure 18-1.

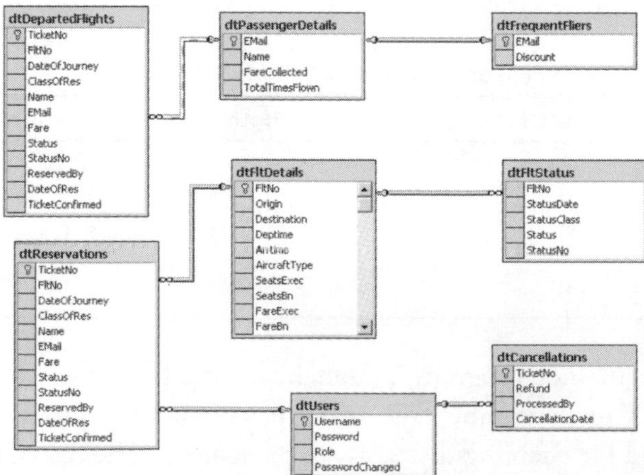


**FIGURE 18-1** *Database schema for SkyShark Airlines*

The relationships between tables in the schema that is shown in Figure 18-1 are explained in Table 18-8.

**Table 18-8 Relationships in the SkyShark Airlines Database**

| Relationship Tables | Relationship | Remarks |
|---|---|---|
| `dtUsers—dtReservations` | One-to-many | One line-of-business executive can perform one or more reservations. |
| `dtUsers—dtCancellations` | One-to-many | One line-of-business executive can perform one or more cancellations. |
| `dtFltDetails—dtReservations` | One-to-many | Tickets on one flight can be booked more than once in the `dtReservations` table. |
| `dtFltDetails—dtFltStatus` | One-to-many | More than one entry for a flight in the `dtFltDetails` table can exist in the `dtFltStatus` table. |
| `dtPassengerDetails—dtDepartedFlights` | One-to-many | A passenger in the `dtPassengerDetails` table could have boarded a number of flights in the `dtDepartedFlights` table. |
| `dtPassengerDetails—dtFrequentFliers` | One-to-one | An entry for the passenger in the `dtFrequentFliers` table should exist in the `dtPassengerDetails` table. |

You have examined each table of the SkyShark Airlines database and the database schema. Next, you will examine the interface of the application—the Web Forms that constitute the application.

## Web Forms Design

As discussed in the previous sections, the Web application for SkyShark Airlines should provide different ASP.NET Web forms for different roles. In this section, I will show you the design of each Web form in the application.

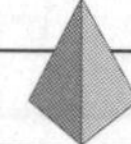

**TIP**

To create Web forms discussed in this section, refer to Chapter 20, "Designing the Application."

### The Login Form

The application has a single login form that allows users to log on by using their logon name and password. The login form, Default.aspx, is shown in Figure 18-2.

**FIGURE 18-2** *The login form for the Web application*

The logon credentials specified by users are validated against the `dtUsers` table. If the logon credentials specified by the user are valid, the role of the user is retrieved from the `dtUsers` database. Next, the user is redirected to the default form for business managers, line-of-business executives, or network administrators, depending upon the user's role.

## Forms for Business Managers

The Web application has four forms for business managers: AddFl.aspx, RequestID.aspx, Reports.aspx, and FreqFl.aspx. The next sections discuss each of these forms.

### The AddFl.aspx Form

The AddFl.aspx form is used to add new flights to the airline. The information specified by business managers in the AddFl.aspx form is stored in the `dtFltDetails` table. The AddFl.aspx form is shown in Figure 18-3. Notice that the prefix *SS* is added to all flight numbers by default, because these initials represent SkyShark Airlines.

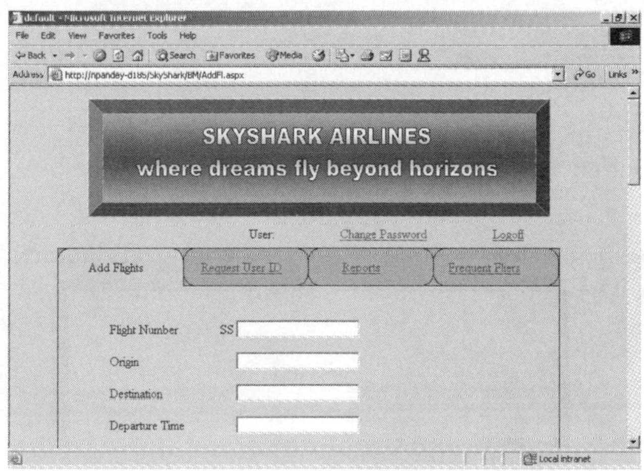


**FIGURE 18-3** *Adding new flights to the airline*

### The RequestID.aspx Form

Business managers use the RequestID.aspx form to request new user IDs. The request is sent to a network administrator by e-mail. The interface of the RequestID.aspx form is shown in Figure 18-4.

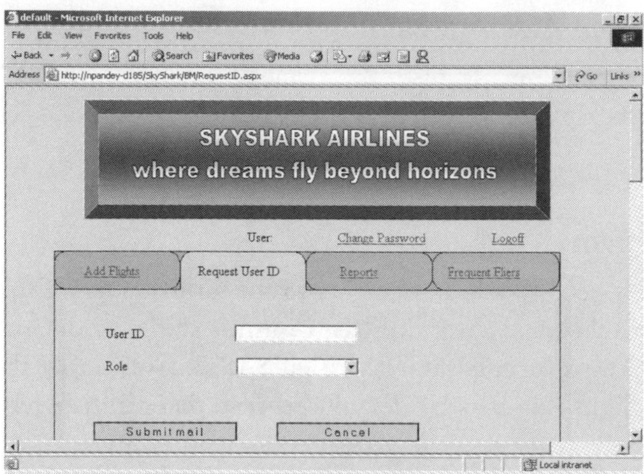


FIGURE 18-4 *Requesting new user accounts*

## The Reports.aspx Form

The Reports.aspx form is used for generating reports. You can view a description of the reports that a business manager can generate in the "Project Requirements" section of this chapter. The Reports.aspx form is shown in Figure 18-5.

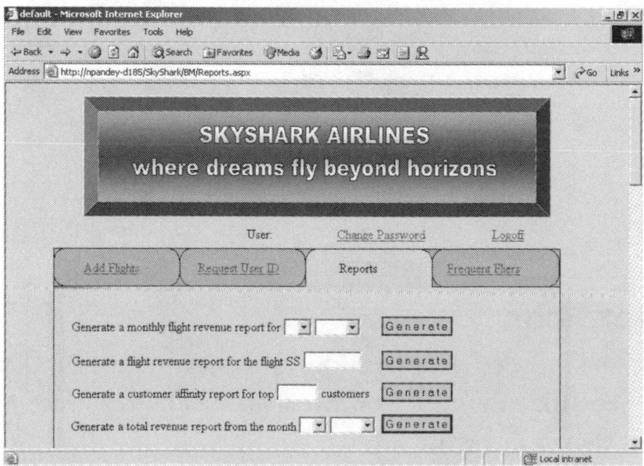


FIGURE 18-5 *Generating reports for analysis*

As you can see in Figure 18-5, you can select parameters for generating reports in the Reports.aspx form. For example, in the monthly flight revenue report, business managers can select the month and year for which the report should be generated. These parameters are internally used by the application to generate the final report.

## The FreqFl.aspx Form

The FreqFl.aspx form is used for managing the frequent fliers program. The form is shown in Figure 18-6.

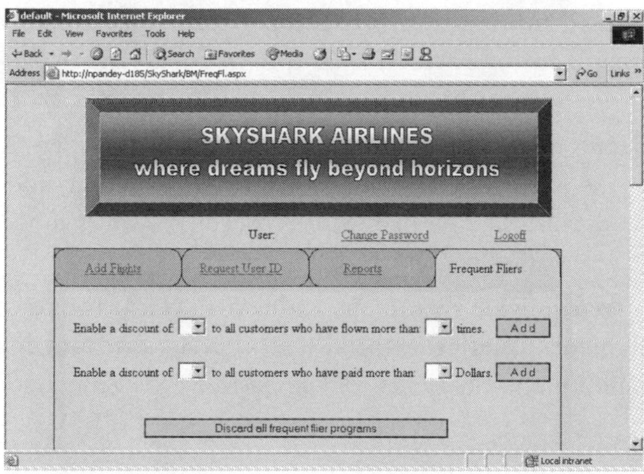


**FIGURE 18-6** *Enabling the frequent fliers program*

The FreqFl.aspx form provides two parameters on which you can enable the frequent fliers program: the number of times that a passenger has flown the flight and the total amount paid by passengers as fare. When a business manager enables the frequent fliers program on these parameters, the eligible passengers are added to the `dtFrequentFliers` table of the SkyShark Airlines database, which is used for enabling discounts to the selected passengers at the time of reservation.

## Forms for Line-of-Business Executives

Line-of-business executives use four Web forms for their daily operations: CreateRes.aspx, CancelRes.aspx, QueryStat.aspx, and ConfirmRes.aspx. A description of these forms is given in this section.

### The CreateRes.aspx Form

The CreateRes.aspx form is used for making reservations to flights. This is the most elaborate of all forms in the Web application. The reservation process is divided into three steps:

1. In Step 1, the line-of-business executive accepts the flight number, class, and date of journey. The information is used to query the status of the flight.
2. In Step 2, the details of the flight and the flight status are displayed to the passenger. If the passenger wants to proceed with the reservation after viewing the details, the line-of-business executive moves to the third step of the reservation process.
3. In Step 3, passengers provide their name and e-mail ID. If the passenger qualifies for the frequent flier program, the appropriate discount is applied to the fare. Finally, the ticket for the passenger is generated.

The CreateRes.aspx form is shown in Figure 18-7.

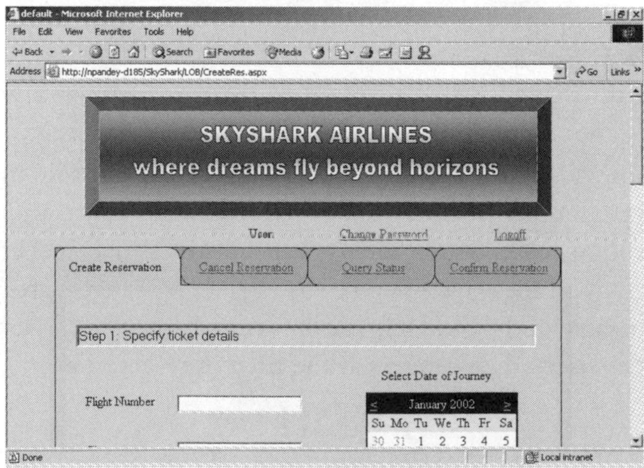


**FIGURE 18-7** *Making reservations to flights*

## The CancelRes.aspx Form

The CancelRes.aspx form is used for canceling reservations. The only parameter required on this form is the ticket number. After the line-of-business executive specifies the ticket number and cancels the reservation, the ticket is marked as canceled and status of the flight is updated in the `dtFltStatus` table. The CancelRes.aspx form is shown in Figure 18-8.

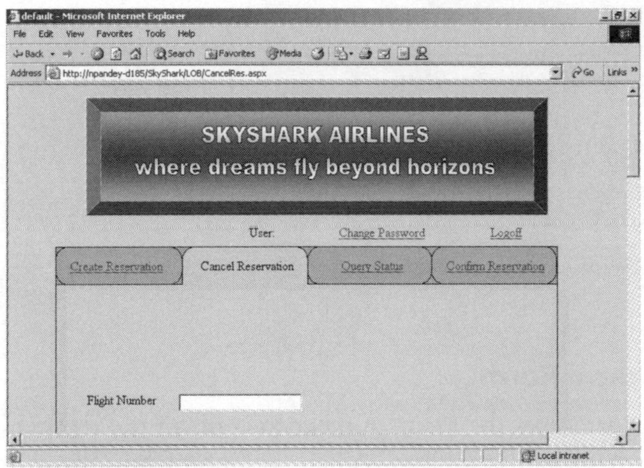


**FIGURE 18-8** *Canceling reservations*

## The QueryStat.aspx Form

The QueryStat.aspx form is used for retrieving the status of flights and tickets. The status of flights is queried from the `dtFltStatus` table by using the date, class, and flight number. Similarly, the status of tickets is retrieved from the `dtReservations` table by using the ticket number. The QueryStat.aspx form is shown in Figure 18-9.

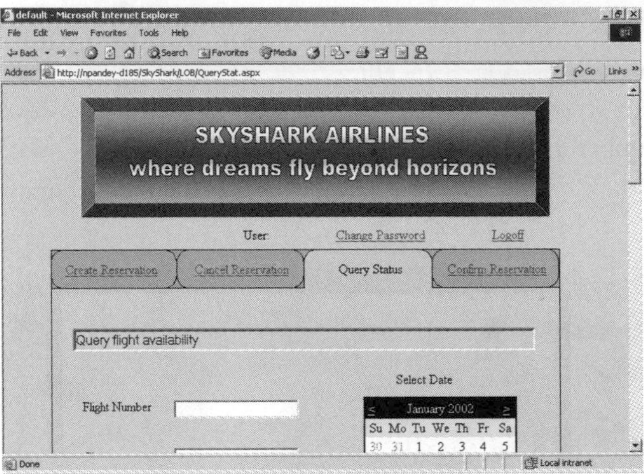


**FIGURE 18-9** *Querying the status of flights and tickets*

## The ConfirmRes.aspx Form

The ConfirmRes.aspx form uses the ticket number to confirm the reservation of a passenger before the departure of a flight. When the line-of-business executive confirms the status of a passenger, the status is updated in the `dtReservations` table. The ConfirmRes.aspx form is shown in Figure 18-10.

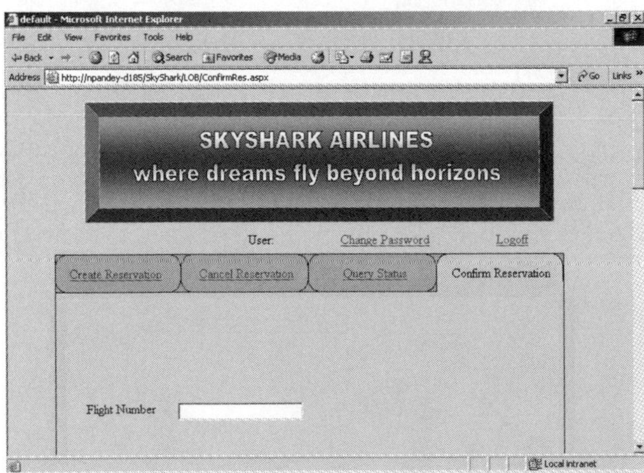


**FIGURE 18-10** *Confirming reservations*

## Forms for Network Administrators

Network administrators can use the SQL Server Enterprise Manager for archiving and backing up databases. However, the SkyShark Airlines application provides two Web forms for simplifying some of the tasks of network administrators. These forms are explained in this section.

### The ManageUsers.aspx Form

The ManageUsers.aspx form is used for adding and deleting user accounts. The details of users added or deleted are updated in the dtUsers database.

I have divided the ManageUsers.aspx form into two sections. The first section is used for adding new users and the second one is used for deleting user accounts. The ManageUsers.aspx form is shown in Figure 18-11.

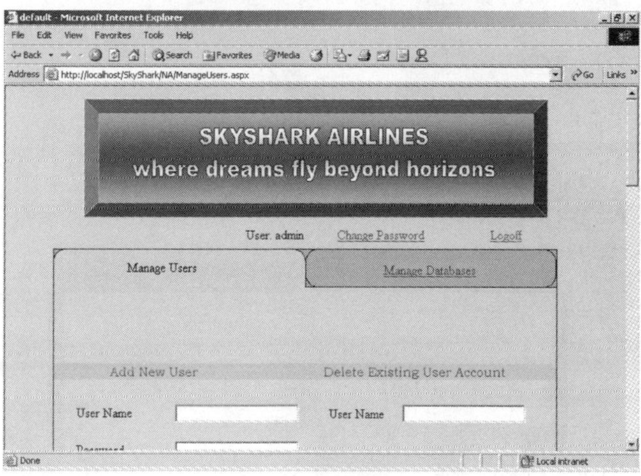


**FIGURE 18-11** *Adding and deleting user accounts*

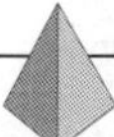

**TIP**

The ManageUsers.aspx form is divided into two sections by using DHTML. You will learn how to implement this functionality in Chapter 20.

## The ManageDatabases.aspx Form

The ManageDatabases.aspx form is used for two tasks:

- **Updating flight information for flights that have departed.** Information for flights that have departed needs to be moved from the `dtReservations` table to the `dtDepartedFlights` table. Network administrators can move this information by the click of a single button on the ManageDatabases.aspx form.
- **Updating customer for the frequent fliers program.** Information pertaining to the frequent fliers program needs to be retrieved from the `dtDepartedFlights` table and updated in the `dtPassengerDetails` table. This information can also be updated from the ManageDatabases.aspx form.

The ManageDatabases.aspx form is shown in Figure 18-12.

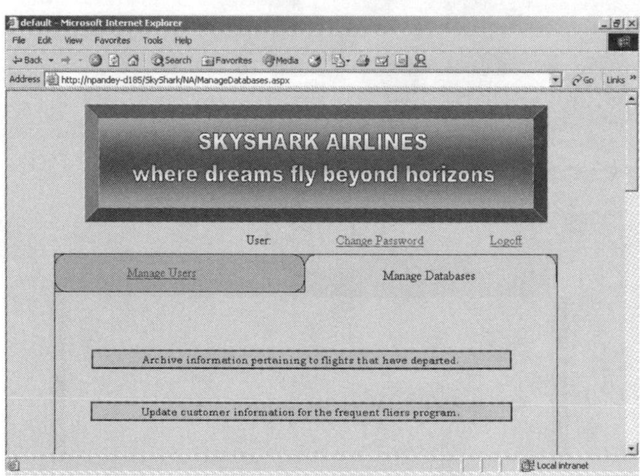


**FIGURE 18-12** *Managing databases*

## *Common Forms of the Application*

Apart from the Default.aspx form, there are some forms that are common across all roles in the organization. These forms are explained in the following list:

- **ChangePassword.aspx.** The ChangePassword.aspx form is used for changing the password of a user. This form has a consistent interface across all roles in the airline.
- **Header.aspx.** The Header.aspx form is used for displaying the header of every form, which contains the banner.
- **Logoff.aspx.** The Logoff.aspx form is used for logging off a user from the Web application. The Logoff.aspx form is shown in Figure 18-13.

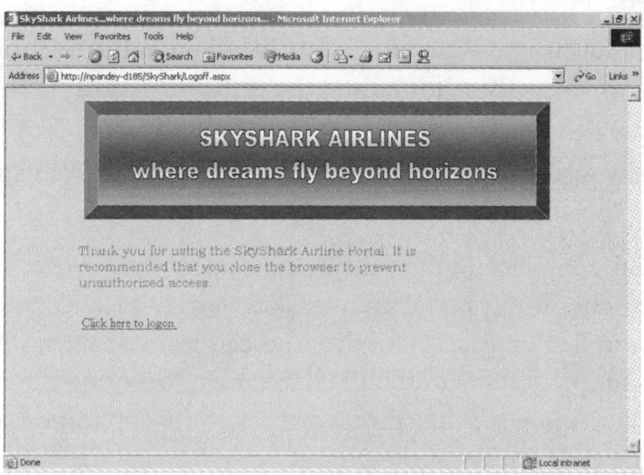


**FIGURE 18-13** *Logging off users from the Web application*

## Enabling Security with the Directory Structure

Whenever you create a new application, you need to secure it. This especially holds true for ASP.NET applications because they need to be protected from unauthorized intruders from the Internet. Security is not an issue that can be dealt with only after applications are complete. Instead, you need to plan for the security of the application from the conception stage.

ASP.NET enables you to implement directory-level security. Thus, you can grant permissions to different uses for accessing forms stored in different directories. This ability of ASP.NET is especially useful for your airline application.

SkyShark Airlines has different roles defined for its executives. Each role has a set of tasks defined for it. These tasks do not overlap. Therefore, your application should not allow a line-of-business executive to add a new flight by using the ASP.NET forms that is to be used by business managers. As a result, you need to authenticate users to access the Web site and restrict users from accessing forms based upon their respective roles.

To enable such a security model on your Web site, you can implement either of the following methods:

- Place ASP.NET forms into different folders based upon the roles of users who need to access these forms and use different security settings for the folders.
- Programmatically manage access to ASP.NET forms of the Web application.

In the airline application, I implement both the methods described above. Different folders are created for forms pertaining to different roles and access to ASP.NET forms is controlled programmatically. You can learn about restricting access to ASP.NET forms programmatically in Chapter 25, "Securing the Application." However, I will examine the directory structure of the application, which is always finalized in the early phases of the project.

In the SkyShark Airlines application, the ASP.NET forms pertaining to the three business roles are given as follows:

- **Business managers.** AddFl.aspx, RequestID.aspx, Reports.aspx, and FreqFl.aspx
- **Line-of-business executives.** CreateRes.aspx, CancelRes.aspx, QueryStat.aspx, and ConfirmRes.aspx
- **Network administrators.** ManageUsers.aspx and ManageDatabases.aspx

The application root directory should therefore have three subdirectories: BM, LOB, and NA. Each of these subdirectories will store files as per the scheme given in the previous list. The final directory structure for the SkyShark Airlines application is given in Figure 18-14.

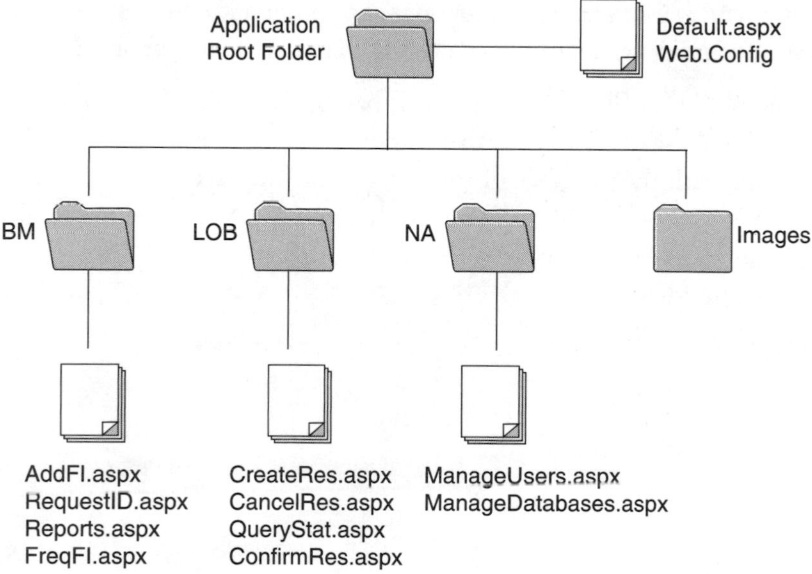


**FIGURE 18-14** *Directory structure for the SkyShark Airlines application*

Note that in the preceding directory structure, I have not shown the Images folder, but in the final application, the Images folder is present in all subdirectories and holds figures that are used on Web pages.

# Summary

The ASP.NET professional project is based upon the business transactions of a fictitious airline, SkyShark Airlines. Executives in SkyShark Airlines can be categorized into three roles: business management, line-of-business operations, and network administrators.

Business managers are responsible for framing policies and analyzing the performance of the airline. Similarly, line-of-business executives are responsible for performing reservations and cancellations, and network administrators perform administrative tasks pertaining to managing databases and user accounts.

The airline portal for SkyShark Airlines is based upon the roles of business executives. The database of SkyShark Airlines comprises eight user-defined tables that are associated with the interface of the portal. The interface of the portal presents different Web forms to business executives based upon their role in the airline.

# Chapter 19

## Basics of ASP.NET Web Applications

In the previous chapter, Chapter 18, "Project Case Study and Design," you studied the case of SkyShark Airlines. You also saw the database schema and Web forms that provide the interface to the application.

All the forms that you viewed in the last chapter are Web forms that are created in ASP.NET. The Web application ASP.NET is the next version of ASP (*Active Server Pages*) 3.0. However, ASP.NET is quite different from ASP because it includes a completely revamped ASP engine and uses the CLR (*common language runtime*) environment for running ASP code.

You will see in this chapter that ASP.NET simplifies Web development by allowing you to separate programming logic from the HTML code that is used to display the page. ASP.NET also provides improved caching and debugging support.

You can write programming logic in ASP.NET by using Visual Basic .NET or Visual C#. In this chapter, I will explore the basic concepts related to ASP.NET, which will help you to start creating the SkyShark Airlines project. The subsequent chapters will build on the concepts covered in this chapter and help you consolidate your learning of ASP.NET.

Visual Studio .NET provides a highly user friendly and powerful interface to simplify development in ASP.NET. For example, the ASP.NET Web application and ASP.NET Web service project templates can be conveniently used to develop Web applications and Web services. These templates provide the Web form and HTML controls that allow you to design a Web form without needing to write a single line of code. Another important aspect that I will explain in this chapter is the use of Visual Studio .NET for creating ASP.NET applications.

## Getting Started with ASP.NET

ASP.NET is a server-side scripting technology that allows you to create dynamic Web sites. ASP.NET is built upon the .NET framework. In this section, I'll explore the new features and the types of applications that you can create in ASP.NET. However, before that, I'll examine the prerequisite software package that is required to create and run ASP.NET applications.

## Prerequisites for ASP.NET Applications

ASP.NET is a component of .NET Framework SDK (*Software Development Kit*). ASP.NET can be downloaded free of cost from the Microsoft site at **http://msdn.microsoft.com**. The software requirements to install the SDK are specified in the following list:

- Windows XP Server or Windows XP Professional
- Windows 2000 Server or Windows 2000 Professional
- Windows NT 4.0 with Service Pack 6a
- IIS (*Internet Information Server*) 5.0 or a later version

In an enterprise environment, you have different development servers and deployment servers. The development servers are used to develop the applications, and the deployment servers are the Web servers on which the application is deployed. You need not install .NET Framework SDK on the deployment servers. Instead, you can install .NET Framework Redistributable, which is also downloadable from the Microsoft Web site.

## New Features in ASP.NET

After having examined the prerequisites to run ASP.NET, I will examine the new features of ASP.NET. The most important features of ASP.NET are specified in the following list:

- **Compiled code.** One of the most prominent differences between ASP and ASP.NET is that the code in ASP.NET is compiled while the code in ASP 3.0 is interpreted. The compilation of code significantly improves the performance of the Web application. It also allows early binding and strong typing of the program code.
- **Support for multiple programming languages.** ASP.NET supports Visual Basic .NET, Visual C#, and JScript. You can use any of these three languages to write your code. You can also use a combination of all three languages to develop your Web application. The development team might code one module for the application in Visual Basic .NET and another in Visual C# and JScript.
- **Support for WYSIWYG (*what you see is what you get*) editors.** Similar to ASP 3.0, ASP.NET applications can be coded in WYSIWYG

HTML editors. In this project, the Visual Studio .NET development platform that you will use to develop the SkyShark Airlines project is a WYSIWYG editor.

- **Improved caching.** ASP.NET optimizes the performance of request processing by providing extensive caching support. ASP.NET exposes a cache API to help programmers cache their own objects. This allows programmers to have greater control over caching of their content. The data in ASP.NET can be cached at two levels, page and fragment. Page-level caching enables you to cache a complete page, and fragment caching enables the caching of only a part of a page.
- **Extensive security.** ASP.NET applications can use Windows, Forms, and Microsoft Passport authentication mechanisms. In ASP 3.0 applications, security is configured at IIS. ASP.NET takes the security model to the next step by allowing you to configure security at the IIS and Web application. You can also enable directory-level security for your Web application. I will explain ASP.NET security in detail later in this chapter and in Chapter 25, "Securing the Application."
- **Debugging and tracing.** An important task in application development is debugging and tracing. When you build your ASP.NET application in Visual Studio .NET, you can use the extensive debugging tools and tracing methods to debug your application.
- **Efficient state management.** State management is the process of maintaining state and page information over multiple requests for the same or different pages. ASP.NET provides easy-to-use application and session-state capabilities. Session and application data can be stored in user-defined objects, which can be updated or queried from time to time.
- **Improved data access.** The ADO.NET architecture provides a reliable and efficient mode of accessing data. Although the topic of ADO.NET is too complicated to cover in a single chapter, I will use the ADO data objects extensively in this project. These objects are explained as they are used.

After having examined the features of ASP.NET, you can now examine the applications that can be created in ASP.NET.

## Types of ASP.NET Applications

In ASP.NET, you can create two types of applications: Web applications and Web services. In this section, I include a brief description of these applications.

### ASP.NET Web Applications

ASP.NET Web applications are applications that interact directly with users through the Internet. The Web sites that you commonly browse on the Internet are Web applications. The Web applications that are built using ASP.NET are ASP.NET Web applications. I will explain ASP.NET Web applications in this project in detail.

### ASP.NET Web Services

Consider a scenario where you need to consolidate the data that is available on three data sources and display it on a Web site. The only way to display output by using Web applications is to create different Web applications and provide links to all applications on a Web site. However, consider that the data that you need to access may be stored on legacy systems and the data may be relevant only when it is consolidated and analyzed.

Implementing such a scenario by using Web applications can be a challenging task. Here, the solution is in ASP.NET Web services. Web services expose the functionality provided by one application to other applications. The functionality exposed by a Web service can be implemented by other Web services or applications in a number of ways, depending upon the business requirements of Web service clients. Therefore, a Web service that exposes a product catalog can be displayed on one Web application as a list and on another Web application with the custom search functionality.

Another advantage offered by Web services is that they are platform-independent. Data is exposed by Web services in an XML format, which is the industry standard. Therefore, any device that can interpret XML can make use of the data that is available from the Web service. I will discuss more of Web services in the next professional project, "Project 5: Creating a Web Portal for a Bookstore."

# Exploring ASP.NET Web Applications

ASP.NET applications include Web pages that are used to interact with a user. These pages are referred to as Web forms. When you browse an ASP.NET Web site, you use its Web forms to retrieve and update information. You can retrieve and update information on an ASP.NET Web site by using Web form server controls. These controls help design the interface of your application and process user data at the server.

In this section, I will explain the concept of Web forms and describe the controls that are provided by ASP.NET.

## Introducing Web Forms

Web forms are ASP.NET components that enable you to create interactive and dynamic Web pages. Web forms also provide you with a rich set of controls that can programmed in any .NET-compatible language, such as Visual Basic .NET and Visual C#.

A Web form comprises two components, programming logic and form interface. By separating the two, ASP.NET makes it easy for you to concentrate on the programming logic of the application without worrying about how the text will be rendered on the Web form. The two components of a Web form are explained as follows:

- **Visual component.** The visual component of a Web form is the .aspx file that contains the code for rendering a Web form.
- **Programming logic.** The programming logic of a Web form is the logic used to generate the output for a Web form. The default option provided by Visual Studio .NET is to create this file as a code-behind file. When you create a code-behind file, the extension of the file is .aspx.cs or .aspx.vb, depending upon whether you are coding your application in Visual C# or Visual Basic .NET. However, you can also create this code in a code-inline model in which the code is written in the .aspx file. This method was used in ASP 3.0.

To create high performance Web forms, you should understand how Web forms are processed. There are two processing methods, client-side and server-side. I will discuss these methods in detail in this section.

## Server-Side Processing

In the server-side processing method, the request from the client is passed to the server for validation. For example, when a user needs to add details about a new flight, the user specifies the required information on a Web form and submits the information to the server for processing. This is an example of server-side processing. In the SkyShark Airlines application, most of the processing needs to be performed at the server side. Therefore, you will see that this method is used most often in the Web forms created in the subsequent chapters of this project.

Each time a Web form is posted to the server for processing, data is processed and the same form or another form is displayed to the user. For example, when you specify flight details and query the database for status of a flight, the information is retrieved and the Web form is reconstructed to display the status of the flight.

Before a Web form is displayed, the `Page_Load` event for the Web form is generated. All server controls are loaded for the Web form in the `Page_Load` event. Similarly, when the user navigates away or closes a Web form, the `Page_Unload` event is generated. In the `Page_Unload` event, the page is removed from the memory and any clean-up code that might be required to free resources is executed.

This procedure has inherent performance overheads. Consider the case where you specify a ticket number and submit the form to retrieve ticket details. All controls will be reinstantiated each time the page is loaded. However, you need to change the values in one or more controls. There should be a way to retain the control state between round trips on the server. ASP.NET offers a solution to this problem. By setting the `IsPostBack` property of controls to true, you can retain the state of a control between round trips. In addition, the initialization code executes only after the `IsPostBack` property is set to true, which helps in averting performance overheads.

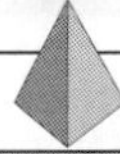

**TIP**

Round trips are generated when a user requests for the Web form that is displayed.

## Client-Side Processing

The client-side processing method is used to perform client-side validation. For example, if a client needs to print a report, it needs to process the document at the client end and not at the server end. If you use client-side validation code, the load on your server can be considerably reduced. The performance of your application improves. In the SkyShark Airlines application, I will use client-side processing to print the reservation ticket that is generated for a passenger.

## Web Form Server Controls

Web form server controls are used for designing the user interface of the application and posting data to the server. Although similar to HTML controls in appearance and operation, server controls run on the server. It is easier to program with these controls because the methods, properties, and events exposed by these controls are consistent and utilize the .NET Framework class library. In this section, I will examine the server controls that are provided by ASP.NET.

### *Summary of Web Form Server Controls*

To access Web form controls, you need to create an ASP.NET Web application. The steps to create an ASP.NET Web application are specified in the following list:

1. Launch Visual Studio .NET.
2. Click on File. The File menu will appear.
3. On the File menu, click on New and then click on Project. The New Project dialog box will appear.
4. In the New Project dialog box, click on Visual C# projects in the Project Types list.
5. Click on ASP.NET Web Application in the Templates list and specify a name and location for the Web application in the Location text box.
6. Click on OK. A new Web application will be created.

In an ASP.NET Web application, Web form controls are available in the Toolbox. Click the View menu and select Toolbox to open Toolbox. The Web form controls are shown in Figure 19-1.

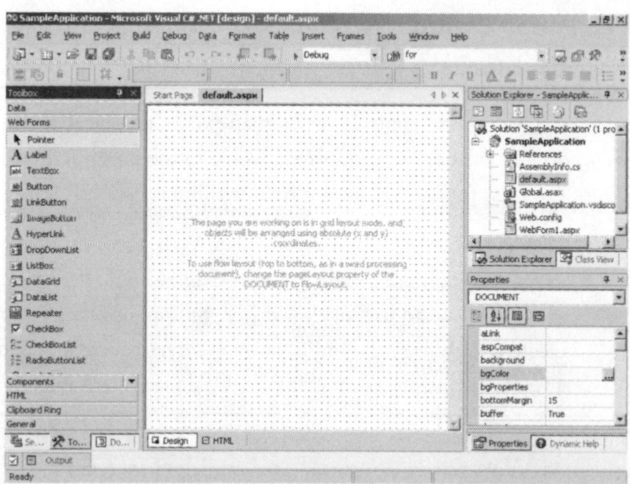

**FIGURE 19-1** *Web form controls in Visual Studio .NET*

As you can see, in the Toolbox, there are different categories of controls available for Web forms. These categories are described in Table 19-1.

**Table 19-1 Types of Web Forms Controls**

| Web Forms Controls | Description |
|---|---|
| User controls | User controls are used to create reusable Web pages. You use user controls to create controls that are reusable across multiple Web pages. For example, you can use a user control to create reusable menus items, tables, toolbars, and so on. |
| Validation controls | Validation controls are used to test the values that the user specifies against the requirements defined by the programmer. A validation control must be associated with another control that accepts user input. For example, you can use a `RequiredFieldValidator` control to check whether the user has specified a value for the control. You can also use `RegularExpressionValidator` to check for a pattern of values that is entered by the user. |

*continues*

**Table 19-1 Types of Web Forms Controls *(continued)***

| Web Forms Controls | Description |
|---|---|
| HTML server controls | HTML server controls are used to expose an object to a server so that the object becomes accessible to the programmers. You can then program these controls within an ASP.NET file. |
| Web form controls | Web form controls are used to create Web pages that have built-in features that are more advanced than HTML Web pages. For example, you can use label, text box, button, or other controls to create a Web page. In addition, Web server controls include advanced controls, such as Image, Calendar, and Table. |

In this section, I will discuss Web form controls and validation controls. These controls will be used frequently in the SkyShark Airlines application. The Web form controls available in ASP.NET with their respective descriptions are given in Table 19-2.

**Table 19-2 Web Form Controls**

| Control | Description |
|---|---|
| `TextBox` | Displays a text box in which users can enter text. |
| `Label` | Displays text that cannot be edited by the user. Commonly used to label other controls on a Web form. |
| `DropDownList` | Allows users to select an option from a list of available options. |
| `ListBox` | Displays a list of options from which users can select multiple options. |
| `Image` | Displays a clickable or nonclickable image. A clickable image can be used to provide a hyperlink to another Web form. |
| `AdRotator` | Displays a list of banners on the Web site. The list of banners can be specified as an XML file. Each time a page is requested, banners are retrieved from the file and displayed sequentially. |
| `CheckBoxList` | Displays a group of check boxes. For example, you can have a `CheckBoxList` control to accept a user's preferences for a party. |

**Table 19-2 Web Form Controls *(continued)***

| Control | Description |
|---|---|
| `RadioButtonList` | Displays a list of radio buttons that allows users to select one option from list of options. For example, you can use a `RadioButtonList` control for gender, which displays two check boxes for Male and Female. |
| `Calendar` | Displays a calendar and allows users to select dates and weeks. You can customize the appearance of the calendar to blend it with your Web application. |
| `LinkButton` | A `LinkButton` control is similar to a `Button` control but it appears like a hyperlink. |
| `ImageButton` | Displays a button on which you can display an image. |
| `HyperLink` | Used to create hyperlinks from one Web form to another. |
| `Table` | Creates a table and provides several useful methods and properties to render a table from the programming logic of the application. |
| `Panel` | Creates a borderless division on the form that serves as a container for other controls. |
| `Repeater Control` | Displays information from a dataset by using a set of HTML elements and controls. The `Repeater` control repeats the HTML elements for each record in the data set. |
| `DataList` | Provides extensive layout and formatting options to display information in a table format. This control is similar to a `Repeater` control but offers greater control over the format of the output. |
| `DataGrid` | The `DataGrid` control can retrieve information from a dataset and display it directly on a form in the table format without requiring a user to specify the structure of data in the dataset. |

ASP.NET provides a number of validation controls that simplify your task of validating user input. Instead of coding validation logic for each control, you can use the validation controls to validate information specified by a user. The validation controls of ASP.NET are summarized in Table 19-3.

**Table 19-3 Validation Controls**

| Control | Description |
|---|---|
| `RequiredFieldValidator` | Ensures that users specify a valid value in the control with which the `RequiredFieldValidator` control is associated. |
| `CompareValidator` | Uses the comparison operators to validate user input with a predefined value of another control or a database field. |
| `RangeValidator` | Validates the user input to determine whether or not it is in a predefined range for numbers, characters, or dates. |
| `RegularExpressionValidator` | Matches user input with a regular expressions. For example, it checks for predictable sequences of characters, such as social security numbers, telephone numbers, and zip codes. |
| `CustomValidator` | Checks the user's entry by using validation logic that you code for your application. |

## *Working with Web Form Server Controls*

Each control has a set of properties that can be used for modifying its state. You can modify the properties of a control at design time or run time.

To modify the properties of a control at design time, follow these steps:

1. Right-click on a control and select Properties. The Properties window for the control will appear. For example, the Properties window of the ListBox control is shown in Figure 19-2.
2. Change the required property of the control. For example, you can change the `ID` of a list box to `lstMonth`.

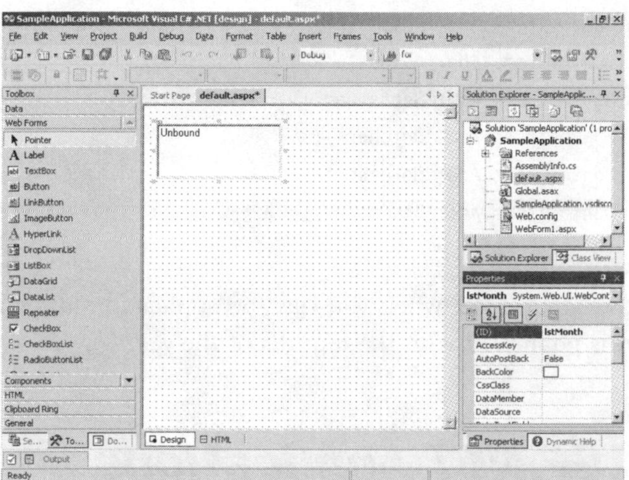


**FIGURE 19-2** *The Properties window of a control*

You can now modify the `Items` property of the list box to add months to the `lstMonth` control programmatically. To change the properties of a control at run time, you use the Code Editor window. Use the following steps to open the Code Editor window and change the properties of a control:

1. Drag a Button control from Toolbox to the form.
2. Double-click the button. The Code Editor window will open.
3. Add the following code to the `Click` event of the button.

```
private void Button1_Click(object sender, System.EventArgs e)
{
            lstMonth.Items.Add("January");
            lstMonth.Items.Add("February");
            lstMonth.Items.Add("March");
            lstMonth.Items.Add("April");
            lstMonth.Items.Add("May");
            lstMonth.Items.Add("June");
```

```
            lstMonth.Items.Add("July");
            lstMonth.Items.Add("August");
            lstMonth.Items.Add("September");
            lstMonth.Items.Add("October");
            lstMonth.Items.Add("November");
            lstMonth.Items.Add("December");
        }
```

After specifying the preceding code, when you run the application and click on the button, the list box is populated with the months of the year.

# Configuring ASP.NET Applications

After you create an ASP.NET application, you need to secure it. You also need to ensure that your application can be ported to Web servers easily. Therefore, two important features of configuring an ASP.NET application are security and deployment. I will include a brief description of these concepts in this section.

## Configuring Security for ASP.NET Applications

ASP.NET applications can be secured at IIS or at the Web application level. The security methods employed at these two levels are described in the following list:

- **IIS.** You can configure application-level security to specify the authentication mode for a Web site or a virtual directory at IIS. You can also configure the file access permissions for the Web site on IIS Server.
- **ASP.NET.** All ASP.NET applications include a Web.Config file that is used for storing the application configuration. You can modify this file for changing the authentication mode of your application, specifying a list of users who are allowed to access your Web site, and specifying the default login page that is displayed when an unauthenticated user requests for a resource that requires authentication. The file-based security mechanism provided by ASP.NET can help implement subdirectory level security for a Web application. For example, you can implement form-based authentication for Web forms in one folder of your application, which is accessible to the registered users on the Web site. You can implement Windows authentication for Web forms in another folder, which is accessible only by corporate employees.

You will learn how to implement different security mechanisms for your Web application in Chapter 25.

## Deploying ASP.NET Applications

You can deploy ASP.NET applications by copying the files in the virtual directory of an application to a virtual directory on the destination server. However, Visual Studio .NET provides a more sophisticated method of deployment. Instead of manually copying all ASP.NET files, you can use the Web Setup deployment project in Visual Studio .NET.

The Web Setup deployment project is a project template that can be configured to accomplish the necessary tasks to deploy a Web application. Some tasks that you can configure using the Web Setup project template are specified in the following list:

- Check for the presence of .NET run-time files and other prerequisite software before installing the application.
- Prompt the user for the name for the virtual directory in which the application should be installed.
- Enforce business rules, such as acceptance of user agreements, before the installation of the software.
- Create databases and add data that might be necessary for the successful execution of your application.

It is advisable to use the Web Setup project template for deploying your ASP.NET applications. However, another easy method to deploy your application is to use the Copy Project feature in Visual Studio .NET. This feature copies the source files of the application to a virtual directory that you specify. You can use this feature only when the computer on which you want to deploy your application is accessible on the network. It is not possible to use it to distribute your application to customers or business partners. I will describe the steps to deploy ASP.NET applications in Chapter 26, "Deploying the Application."

# Creating a Sample ASP.NET Application

After having examined the basic concepts of an ASP.NET application, you can build on your knowledge by attempting a simple ASP.NET application. In this section, I have created a simple application that queries a username and password in a database and displays a welcome message if the user is successfully authenticated.

## Creating a New Project

The first step in creating an ASP.NET application in Visual Studio .NET is to add a new project by using the ASP.NET Web Application template. The steps to add a new ASP.NET Web Application were discussed in the section "Summary of Web Form Server Controls." Create a new project with the name SampleApplication. After creating the new project, proceed to the next section, "Adding Controls to the Project," to add controls to the sample application.

## Adding Controls to the Project

To design the user interface of the application, you need to add controls to the application. The steps to add controls to the Web form are specified in the following list:

1. Click on the View menu and select Toolbox to open Toolbox.
2. Drag a Label control from Toolbox to the default form in the Web application.
3. Change the properties of the label as given here:
   - `ID`=lblCaption
   - `Text`=Please log on
   - `Font`
     - `Bold`=True
     - `Italic`=True
     - `Name`=Georgia
4. Drag two label controls to the form for accepting the username and the password. Change the `Text` property of these label controls to User Name and Password, respectively.
5. Drag two `TextBox` controls to the form and change their `ID` to txtUserName and txtPassword, respectively.
6. Drag a `Button` control to the form and change its `Text` property to Submit. In addition, change the `ID` of the button to btnSubmit.

The basic structure of the form is complete. Next, you need to add validation controls to the form to validate user input before data is processed on the server. To add validation controls to the form, follow these steps:

1. Drag a `RequiredFieldValidator` control to the form for validating the User Name text box. Change the properties of the `RequiredFieldValidator` control as mentioned in the following list:
   - `ErrorMessage`=Invalid user name
   - `ControlToValidate`=txtUserName
2. Drag another `RequiredFieldValidator` control to the form for validating the Password text box. Change the properties of the control as mentioned here:
   - `ErrorMessage`=Invalid password
   - `ControlToValidate`=txtPassword

The interface of the form is complete. However, you can add one more Label control to display a welcome message if the user logs on successfully. Change the `ID` of the label to lblMessage and clear the `Text` property. The complete form is shown in Figure 19-3.

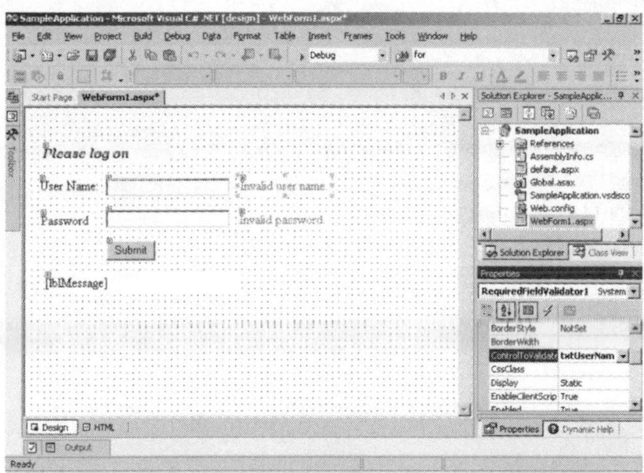


**FIGURE 19-3** *Form to accept username and password*

After having designed the interface of the form, you can code the functionality of the Web application.

## Coding the Application

To code the functionality of the application, you need to create the database structure and use the database to validate users. In this section, I will explain the procedure for creating a database and utilizing it in the application.

### Creating the Database

To validate the username and the password, I have created a database named SampleDatabase and added a Logon table to the database. Next, I added two records to the Logon table. To create a similar structure for your Web application, execute the SQL script given as follows:

```
CREATE DATABASE SampleDatabase
GO
USE SampleDatabase
GO
CREATE TABLE Logon (
            [UserName] [char] (10) COLLATE SQL_Latin1_General_CP1_CI_AS NOT NULL ,
            [Password] [char] (10) COLLATE SQL_Latin1_General_CP1_CI_AS NOT NULL
) ON [PRIMARY]
GO
ALTER TABLE Logon WITH NOCHECK ADD
          CONSTRAINT [PK_Logon] PRIMARY KEY  CLUSTERED
          (
                      [UserName]
           )  ON [PRIMARY]
GO
INSERT INTO LOGON
VALUES ('John', 'password')
GO
INSERT INTO LOGON
VALUES ('Suzan', 'mypassword')
GO
```

### Adding Functionality to the Application

ASP.NET includes data access tools that make it easier for you to interact with databases. The SQL Server .NET data provider is used for accessing SQL Server databases. The data provider provides three primary classes to access databases:

- **`SqlConnection`.** The `SqlConnection` class is used for creating a connection to the database.
- **`SqlDataAdapter`.** The `SqlDataAdapter` class is used for adding, updating, deleting, and selecting records from the database.
- **`DataSet`.** The `DataSet` class is used to cache data that is retrieved from a database. A `DataSet` object comprises a number of `DataTable` objects that contain data retrieved from database tables.

In addition to the three classes described here, ASP.NET provides the `SqlCommand` class that can be used for executing queries on a database.

Visual Studio .NET provides data controls that correspond to the SQL Server data provide classes described in the previous list. These controls are available on the Data tab of the Toolbox. Follow these steps to use the data controls for accessing databases:

1. Drag an `SqlDataAdapter` control from Toolbox to the form. Data Adapter Configuration Wizard will start.
2. On the Welcome screen, click on Next. The Choose Your Data Connection screen of the wizard will appear.
3. On the Choose Your Data Connection screen, click on New Connection. The Data Link Properties dialog box will appear, as shown in Figure 19-4.

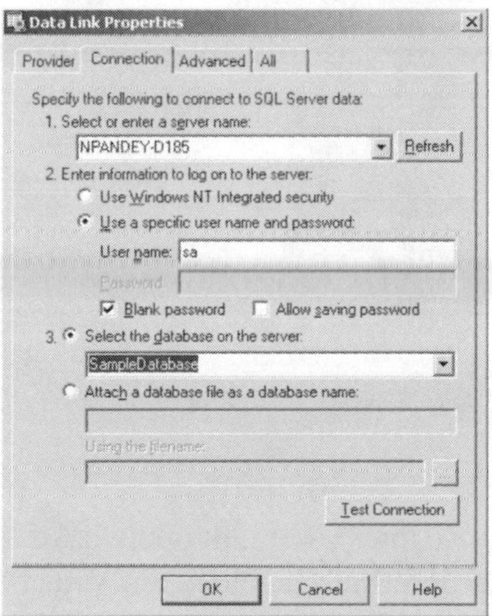


**FIGURE 19-4** *The Data Link Properties dialog box*

4. In the Data Link Properties dialog box, configure the connection to the database that you created in the previous section and click on OK. The data connection that you created will be displayed on the Choose Your Data Connection screen of the Data Adapter Configuration wizard.
5. Click on Next. The Choose Query Type screen will appear.
6. On the Choose Query Type screen, retain the default option and click on Next. The Generate the SQL Statements screen will appear.
7. Specify the SQL Query as specified and click on Next.

```
Select UserName, Password from Logon where (UserName=@username)
```

8. On the View Wizard results screen, click on Finish to complete the wizard.

When you complete the wizard, new SqlDataAdapter and SqlConnection controls are added to your project. These controls appear in Component Designer, as shown in Figure 19-5.

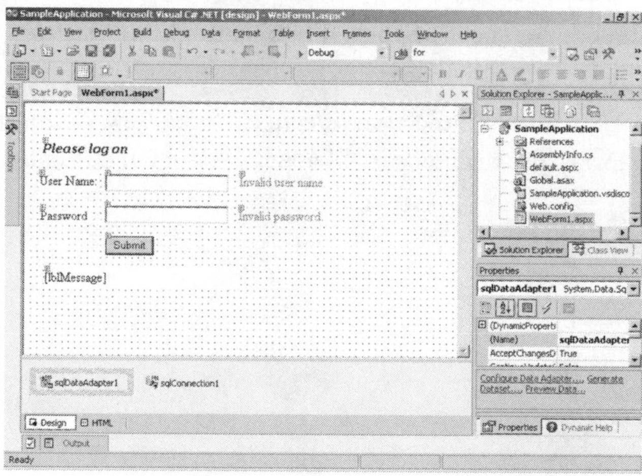

**FIGURE 19-5** *Adding new SqlDataAdapter and SqlConnection controls to the form*

In the preceding steps, you used the Data Adapter Configuration wizard to configure the SqlDataAdapter and SqlConnection controls. However, Visual Studio .NET offers another simple mechanism to configure these controls without traversing the wizard. This method is specified below:

1. Click on the View menu and select Server Explorer to open the Server Explorer window.
2. In the Server Explorer window, navigate to the table for which you want to configure the data adapter. For example, the path to the Logon table is shown in Figure 19-6.
3. Press and hold the mouse button on the name of the table and drag it to the form. Visual Studio .NET will automatically add the SqlData-Adapter and SqlConnection controls to your form.

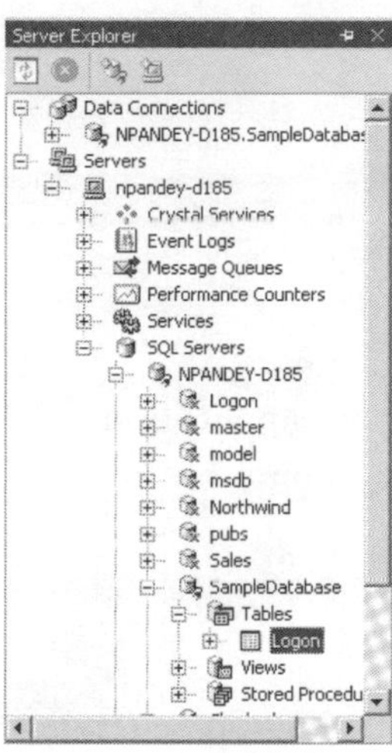


**FIGURE 19-6** *Using the Server Explorer to add data controls*

In the SkyShark Airlines project, I will use Server Explorer to configure the connections to database tables.

After adding data controls to the Web form, you need to add a DataSet control to the form. To add the DataSet control to the form, perform the following steps:

1. Click on the Data menu and then click on Generate Dataset. The Generate Dataset dialog box will appear, as shown in Figure 19-7.
2. Click on OK to configure a new DataSet control and add it to Component Designer.

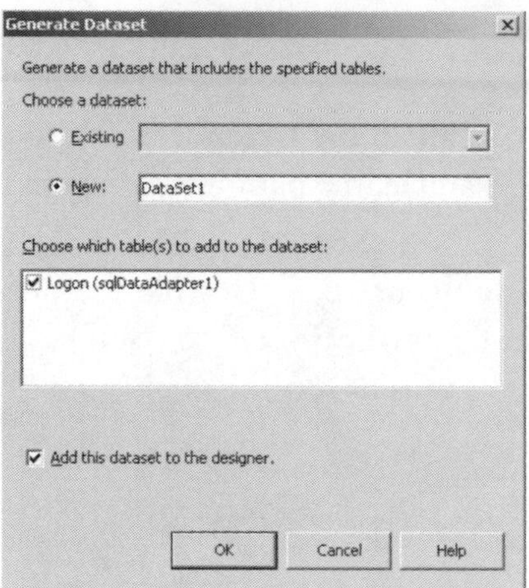


**FIGURE 19-7** *Adding a new DataSet control*

You have added all the required controls to configure your application. In the last step, add the following code for the Click event of the Submit button:

```
private void btnSubmit_Click(object sender, System.EventArgs e)
{
   sqlConnection1.Open();
   sqlDataAdapter1.SelectCommand.Parameters[0].Value=txtUserName.Text.Trim();
   sqlDataAdapter1.Fill(dataSet11, "UserDetails");
   if (dataSet11.Tables["UserDetails"].Rows.Count==0)
   {
      lblMessage.Text="Invalid user name";
   }
   else
   {
      if (dataSet11.Tables["UserDetails"].Rows[0][1].ToString().Trim()==
         txtPassword.Text.Trim())
         lblMessage.Text="Welcome " + txtUserName.Text;
      else
         lblMessage.Text="Invalid password";
   }
   sqlConnection1.Close()
}
```

In the preceding code, the following sequence of tasks is performed:

1. The connection to the database is opened by the `Open` function.
2. The value specified by the user for the username is assigned to the first parameter of the `SELECT` query. The first parameter is `@username`.
3. The `Fill` method of the `SqlDataAdapter` class is used for executing the select query and adding the resultant data to the data set. The `Fill` command accepts two parameters, the name of the data set and the name of the `DataTable` in the data set in which the data should be stored.
4. If the number of rows returned by the select command is 0 as determined by the Count property of the Rows collection of a DataTable, an error message is displayed to the user.
5. If the number of rows returned is greater than 0, the password specified by the user is validated against the password retrieved from the database. The password retrieved from the database is stored in the second column of the first row of a DataSet table and can be accessed at the position Rows[0][1].

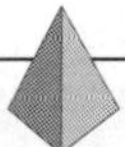

**TIP**

The first member of a collection has the index 0. Therefore, to access the second element, which is the password in this case, the index that needs to be used is 1.

6. If the password specified by the user matches the password retrieved from the database, a welcome message is displayed. If the password does not match, an error message is displayed.

After specifying the preceding code, click on Debug and then Start to run the application. The output of the application, which is generated after you specify a valid username and password, is shown in Figure 19-8.

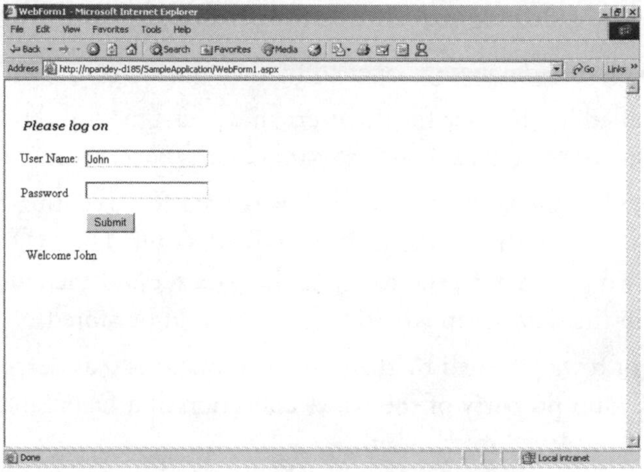

**FIGURE 19-8** *Validating user credentials against a data source*

## Summary

ASP.NET is a server-side scripting language that allows you to create dynamic Web pages. The Web pages that you create in ASP.NET are known as Web forms. Web forms are processed on the server and can be coded in any .NET-compatible scripting language, such as Visual C# or Visual Basic .NET.

ASP.NET provides a number of server controls and validation controls that can be added to Web forms. Some commonly used server controls are Label, TextBox, Button, DropDownList, ListBox, Calendar, and RadioButtonList. Validation controls in ASP.NET help validate user input in a field before data is processed on the server.

To make applications communicate with the database, you can use the SQL Server .NET data provider. The three primary classes provided by this data provider are `SqlConnection`, `SqlDataAdapter`, and `DataSet`. The `SqlConnection` class is used for creating a connection to the database. The `SqlDataAdapter` class is used for updating records in the database, and the `DataSet` class is used to cache the data that is retrieved from the database.

# Chapter 20

## Designing the Application

The last two chapters discussed the project case study and the basics of ASP.NET applications. In this chapter, you will learn how to create the user interface and the database schema of the SkyShark Airlines application. The design of the application is based on the project case study described in Chapter 18, "Project Case Study and Design."

The database schema is usually the first component to be finalized for an application. Any changes in the database schema at a later stage in the development of your application can lead to tremendous developmental overheads. Therefore, I will first finalize the structure of the database and then proceed with the design of forms.

## Creating the Database Schema

I discussed the structure of the database schema in detail in the section "Database Design" of Chapter 18. The schema is displayed in Figure 20-1.

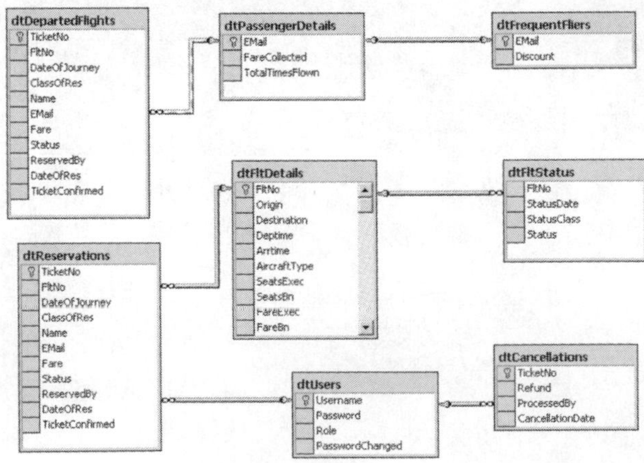


**FIGURE 20-1** *Database schema for SkyShark Airlines*

In this section, you will learn about the steps to create the database schema. You can use either SQL Server Enterprise Manager or Query Analyzer to create the database structure. If you choose SQL Server Enterprise Manager, you can use the MMC (*Microsoft Management Console*) based interface to graphically design your application. However, if you choose Query Analyzer, you need to specify SQL (*structured query language*) statements to design database tables and manage relationships.

In this section, I will examine how to create the database structure by using Query Analyzer.

## Creating Database Tables

To use Query Analyzer for creating databases, you need to open Query Analyzer and connect to the SQL Server on which you want to create the database. The steps to open Query Analyzer and connect to a database are given as follows:

1. Click on Start. The Start menu will appear.
2. From the Programs menu, select Programs and then select Microsoft SQL Server.
3. From the submenu of Microsoft SQL Server, select Query Analyzer. The SQL Query Analyzer window will open.
4. In the SQL Query Analyzer window, the Connect to SQL Server dialog box appears by default. If it does not appear, select the Connect option from the File menu.
5. The Connect to SQL Server dialog box is shown in Figure 20-2. In this dialog box, select the name of the SQL Server from the SQL Server list and specify the username and password to log on to the database.
6. Click on OK to connect to the database.

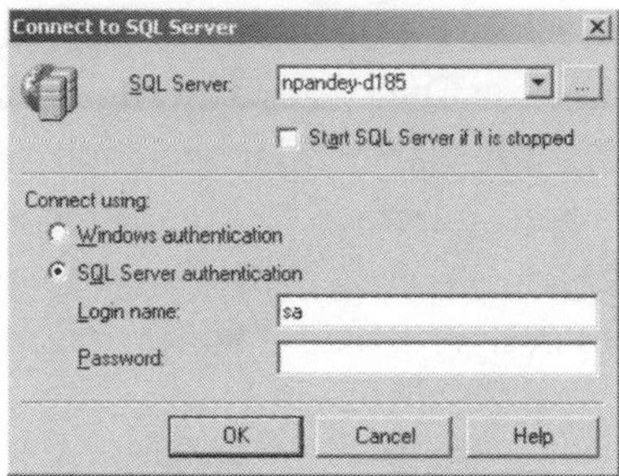


**FIGURE 20-2** *The Connect to SQL Server dialog box*

After connecting to the SQL Server, you need to create the SkyShark Airlines database before you can create the database tables. To create the SkyShark Airlines database, run the following SQL script in Query Analyzer:

```
CREATE DATABASE SkyShark
GO
USE DATABASE SkyShark
GO
```

In the preceding SQL statements, I have created a `SkyShark` database and have changed the database context to `SkyShark`. All tables that I create now will be created in the `SkyShark` database. I now begin creating tables in this database.

**CAUTION**

While executing all SQL statements that follow in this section, ensure that the current database is specified as `SkyShark`. If this is not the case, all database tables will be created in the `Master` database.

### Creating the `dtUsers` Table

The `dtUsers` table is used to store the username, password, and role of all users having access to the SkyShark Airlines application. To create the `dtUsers` table, execute the SQL script given as follows:

```
CREATE TABLE [dbo].[dtUsers] (
	[Username] [char] (15) COLLATE SQL_Latin1_General_CP1_CI_AS NOT NULL ,
	[Password] [char] (15) COLLATE SQL_Latin1_General_CP1_CI_AS NOT NULL ,
	[Role] [char] (10) COLLATE SQL_Latin1_General_CP1_CI_AS NOT NULL ,
	[PasswordChanged] [bit] NULL
) ON [PRIMARY]
GO
```

In the preceding statements, the `dtUsers` table is created and the Username, Password, Role, and Password fields are added to the table.

### Creating the `dtFltDetails` Table

The `dtFltDetails` table is used to store details of all flights by SkyShark Airlines. The script to generate the `dtFltDetails` table is given as follows:

```
CREATE TABLE [dbo].[dtFltDetails] (
	[FltNo] [char] (10) COLLATE SQL_Latin1_General_CP1_CI_AS NOT NULL ,
	[Origin] [text] COLLATE SQL_Latin1_General_CP1_CI_AS NOT NULL ,
	[Destination] [text] COLLATE SQL_Latin1_General_CP1_CI_AS NOT NULL ,
	[Deptime] [datetime] NOT NULL ,
	[Arrtime] [datetime] NOT NULL ,
	[AircraftType] [char] (10) COLLATE SQL_Latin1_General_CP1_CI_AS NOT NULL,
	[SeatsExec] [int] NOT NULL ,
	[SeatsBn] [int] NOT NULL ,
	[FareExec] [int] NOT NULL ,
	[FareBn] [int] NOT NULL ,
	[LaunchDate] [datetime] NOT NULL
) ON [PRIMARY] TEXTIMAGE_ON [PRIMARY]
GO
```

## Creating the `dtReservations` Table

The `dtReservations` table is used to reserve seats for passengers on each flight. The SQL script that generates this table is given as follows:

```
CREATE TABLE [dbo].[dtReservations] (
	[TicketNo] [char] (10) COLLATE SQL_Latin1_General_CP1_CI_AS NOT NULL ,
	[FltNo] [char] (10) COLLATE SQL_Latin1_General_CP1_CI_AS NOT NULL ,
	[DateOfJourney] [datetime] NOT NULL ,
	[ClassOfRes] [char] (10) COLLATE SQL_Latin1_General_CP1_CI_AS NOT NULL ,
	[Name] [char] (20) COLLATE SQL_Latin1_General_CP1_CI_AS NOT NULL ,
	[EMail] [char] (50) COLLATE SQL_Latin1_General_CP1_CI_AS NULL ,
	[Fare] [int] NOT NULL ,
	[Status] [int] NOT NULL ,
	[ReservedBy] [char] (15) COLLATE SQL_Latin1_General_CP1_CI_AS NOT NULL ,
	[DateOfRes] [datetime] NOT NULL ,
	[TicketConfirmed] [bit] NULL
) ON [PRIMARY]
GO
```

## Creating the `dtFltStatus` Table

The `dtFltStatus` table stores the latest ticket availability status. The data in this table is updated in tandem with any new record added to the `dtReservations` or `dtCancellations` table. The script that generates the `dtFltStatus` table is given as follows:

```
CREATE TABLE [dbo].[dtFltStatus] (
	[FltNo] [char] (10) COLLATE SQL_Latin1_General_CP1_CI_AS NOT NULL ,
	[StatusDate] [datetime] NOT NULL ,
	[StatusClass] [char] (10) COLLATE SQL_Latin1_General_CP1_CI_AS NOT NULL ,
	[Status] [int] NOT NULL
) ON [PRIMARY]
GO
```

## Creating the dtCancellations Table

All cancellations made in the dtReservations table are recorded in the dtCancellations table. The query for creating the dtCancellations table is given as follows:

```
CREATE TABLE [dbo].[dtCancellations] (
	[TicketNo] [char] (10) COLLATE SQL_Latin1_General_CP1_CI_AS NOT NULL ,
	[Refund] [int] NOT NULL ,
	[ProcessedBy] [char] (15) COLLATE SQL_Latin1_General_CP1_CI_AS NOT NULL ,
	[CancellationDate] [datetime] NOT NULL
) ON [PRIMARY]
GO
```

## Creating the dtDepartedFlights Table

The dtDepartedFlights table is similar to the dtReservations table. After flight departure, data pertaining to the flight is moved from the dtReservations table to the dtDepartedFlights table. The script that generates the dtDepartedFlights table is given as follows:

```
CREATE TABLE [dbo].[dtDepartedFlights] (
	[TicketNo] [char] (10) COLLATE SQL_Latin1_General_CP1_CI_AS NOT NULL ,
	[FltNo] [char] (10) COLLATE SQL_Latin1_General_CP1_CI_AS NOT NULL ,
	[DateOfJourney] [datetime] NOT NULL ,
	[ClassOfRes] [char] (10) COLLATE SQL_Latin1_General_CP1_CI_AS NOT NULL ,
	[Name] [char] (20) COLLATE SQL_Latin1_General_CP1_CI_AS NOT NULL ,
	[EMail] [char] (50) COLLATE SQL_Latin1_General_CP1_CI_AS NULL ,
	[Fare] [int] NOT NULL ,
	[Status] [int] NOT NULL ,
	[ReservedBy] [char] (10) COLLATE SQL_Latin1_General_CP1_CI_AS NOT NULL ,
	[DateOfRes] [datetime] NOT NULL ,
	[TicketConfirmed] [bit] NULL
) ON [PRIMARY]
GO
```

### Creating the dtPassengerDetails Table

The dtPassengerDetails table is used for storing data pertaining to passengers who have a valid e-mail address. The table is used to make discounts available for the frequent fliers program. To create the dtPassengerDetails table, execute the following script:

```
CREATE TABLE [dbo].[dtPassengerDetails] (
	[EMail] [char] (50) COLLATE SQL_Latin1_General_CP1_CI_AS NOT NULL ,
	[FareCollected] [int] NOT NULL ,
	[TotalTimesFlown] [int] NOT NULL
) ON [PRIMARY]
GO
```

### Creating the dtFrequentFliers Table

The dtFrequentFliers table is used to store a list of passengers eligible for the frequent fliers program. The list is retrieved from the dtPassengerDetails table on the basis of a query specified by business managers. To create the dtFrequentFliers table, run the following script:

```
CREATE TABLE [dbo].[dtFrequentFliers] (
	[EMail] [char] (50) COLLATE SQL_Latin1_General_CP1_CI_AS NOT NULL ,
	[Discount] [int] NOT NULL
) ON [PRIMARY]
GO
```

Now that you have created all the tables, the next step is to set primary keys and specify relationships between tables. You do that in the next section.

## Managing Primary Keys and Relationships

Primary keys are used to ensure that the records in a table are unique. The primary keys for all database tables are listed in Table 20-1.

**Table 20-1 Primary Key Fields in Tables**

| Table Name | Primary Key Field |
|---|---|
| dtUsers | Username |
| dtFltDetails | FltNo |
| dtReservations | TicketNo |
| dtCancellations | TicketNo |
| dtDepartedFlights | TicketNo |
| dtPassengerDetails | EMail |
| dtFrequentFliers | EMail |

To specify primary keys for tables, run the following script:

```
ALTER TABLE [dbo].[dtCancellations] WITH NOCHECK ADD
   CONSTRAINT [PK_dtCancellation] PRIMARY KEY  CLUSTERED
   (
      [TicketNo]
   )  ON [PRIMARY]
GO
ALTER TABLE [dbo].[dtDepartedFlights] WITH NOCHECK ADD
   CONSTRAINT [PK_dtDepartedFlights] PRIMARY KEY  CLUSTERED
   (
      [TicketNo]
   )  ON [PRIMARY]
GO
ALTER TABLE [dbo].[dtFltDetails] WITH NOCHECK ADD
   CONSTRAINT [PK_dtFltDetails] PRIMARY KEY  CLUSTERED
   (
      [FltNo]
   )  ON [PRIMARY]
GO
ALTER TABLE [dbo].[dtFrequentFliers] WITH NOCHECK ADD
   CONSTRAINT [PK_dtFrequentFlier] PRIMARY KEY  CLUSTERED
   (
      [EMail]
   )  ON [PRIMARY]
GO
```

```
ALTER TABLE [dbo].[dtPassengerDetails] WITH NOCHECK ADD
   CONSTRAINT [PK_dtAllCustomers] PRIMARY KEY  CLUSTERED
   (
      [EMail]
   )  ON [PRIMARY]
GO
ALTER TABLE [dbo].[dtReservations] WITH NOCHECK ADD
   CONSTRAINT [PK_dtReservations] PRIMARY KEY  CLUSTERED
   (
      [TicketNo]
   )  ON [PRIMARY]
GO
ALTER TABLE [dbo].[dtUsers] WITH NOCHECK ADD
   CONSTRAINT [PK_dtUsers] PRIMARY KEY  CLUSTERED
   (
      [Username]
   )  ON [PRIMARY]
GO
```

After creating the tables and setting the primary keys, you need to create relationships between tables. Relationships between tables are discussed in Table 18-8 of Chapter 18. To create relationships between tables, run the following code:

```
ALTER TABLE [dbo].[dtCancellations] ADD
   CONSTRAINT [FK_dtCancellation_dtUsers] FOREIGN KEY
   (
      [ProcessedBy]
   ) REFERENCES [dbo].[dtUsers] (
      [Username]
   )
GO
ALTER TABLE [dbo].[dtDepartedFlights] ADD
   CONSTRAINT [FK_dtDepartedFlights_dtPassengerDetails] FOREIGN KEY
   (
      [EMail]
   ) REFERENCES [dbo].[dtPassengerDetails] (
      [EMail]
   ) NOT FOR REPLICATION
```

```
GO
ALTER TABLE [dbo].[dtDepartedFlights] nocheck constraint
[FK_dtDepartedFlights_dtPassengerDetails]
GO
ALTER TABLE [dbo].[dtFltStatus] ADD
   CONSTRAINT [FK_dtFlightStatus_dtFltDetails] FOREIGN KEY
   (
      [FltNo]
   ) REFERENCES [dbo].[dtFltDetails] (
      [FltNo]
   )
GO
ALTER TABLE [dbo].[dtFrequentFliers] ADD
   CONSTRAINT [FK_dtFrequentFlier_dtAllCustomers] FOREIGN KEY
   (
      [EMail]
   ) REFERENCES [dbo].[dtPassengerDetails] (
      [EMail]
   )
GO
ALTER TABLE [dbo].[dtReservations] ADD
   CONSTRAINT [FK_dtReservations_dtFltDetails] FOREIGN KEY
   (
      [FltNo]
   ) REFERENCES [dbo].[dtFltDetails] (
      [FltNo]
   ),
   CONSTRAINT [FK_dtReservations_dtUsers] FOREIGN KEY
   (
      [ReservedBy]
   ) REFERENCES [dbo].[dtUsers] (
      [Username]
   )
GO
```

## Viewing the Database Schema

After you run all the preceding scripts, the database schema is ready. You can view the structure of database tables and their relationships in Enterprise Manager. To view the database schema, follow these steps:

1. Open SQL Server Enterprise Manager.
2. Navigate to the SkyShark database.
3. Right-click on Diagrams in SkyShark and select New Database Diagram. The Create Database Diagram Wizard will appear.
4. In the Welcome screen of the wizard, click on Next. The Select Tables to be Added screen of the wizard will appear. This screen is shown in Figure 20-3.
5. Select all database tables that you created in the previous section and click on Next. The Completing the Create Database Diagram Wizard screen of the wizard will appear.
6. Click Finish to complete the wizard.

After you complete the task by using the wizard, the database schema appears as shown in Figure 20-3.

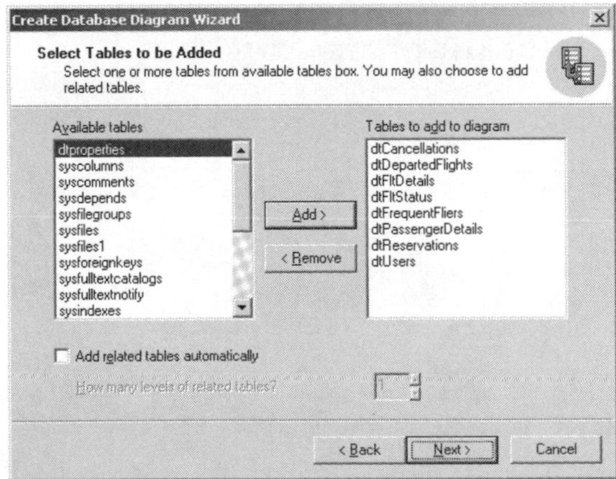


**FIGURE 20-3** *The Select Tables to be Added screen*

# Designing Application Forms

The application provides different forms for users in different roles. For example, business managers are provided with four forms: AddFl.aspx, RequestID.aspx, Reports.aspx, and FreqFl.aspx. All forms pertaining to different roles were discussed in Chapter 18.

In this section, I explain the controls that you need to add to each Web form and the properties of Web forms that you need to configure. After this section, all Web forms for the application will be ready.

## Standardizing the Interface of the Application

All Web forms for the SkyShark Airlines application have a standard interface, which is derived by adding a banner to a header.htm file and including the file on each Web page. Next, I have added a menu bar, which resembles a tab control, on top of each Web form. To do this, I created four similar images with different tabs selected and showing the images at the same position on each Web form. A collage of these images is shown in Figure 20-4.

**FIGURE 20-4** *Creating a menu bar for the application*

Now, when a user selects different screens, distinct images are displayed but give the impression that the same screen contains several tabs.

## Common Forms in the Application

There are a number of common forms used by employees at all positions in SkyShark Airlines. In this section, I will explain the design of these forms.

### Default.aspx

The default.aspx form is the first form displayed when a user visits a Web site. The default.aspx form is the logon form for the Web application. When users visit the Web application, they need to log on by specifying their logon credentials in the default.aspx form. Subsequently, depending upon the position of the user, the user is redirected to other forms of the Web application.

You can change the form WebForm1.aspx, added to the Web application by default, to make the form the default.aspx page. To do so, follow these steps:

1. Right-click on WebForm1.aspx in Solution Explorer and select Rename.
2. Type the name of the form as default.aspx.
3. Double-click on default.aspx to open the code-behind file in the Code Editor window.
4. Change the name of the class to `WebLogonForm`.
5. Return to the design view of the default.aspx form.
6. In the design view of the form, in the `@ Page` directive in the first line, change the name of the class to WebLogonForm. The new `@ Page` directive is given as follows:

```
<%@ Page language="c#" Codebehind="default.aspx.cs" AutoEventWireup="false"
Inherits="SkyShark.WebLogonForm" %>
```

**NOTE**

By performing these steps, you have changed the name and the default class associated with the Web form. These steps need to be carried out for all Web forms that you will add to the project. However, I will not repeat these steps separately for each Web form.

To design the default.aspx form, add controls to it and change their properties as shown in Table 20-2.

**Table 20-2 Controls in the Default.aspx Form**

| Control Type | ID | Properties Changed |
|---|---|---|
| TextBox | txtUserName | None |
| TextBox | txtPassword | TextMode=Password |
| Button | btnSubmit | Text=Submit |
| Label | lblMessage | ForeColor=Red<br>Text=""<br>Font:Bold=True |
| RequiredFieldValidator | RequiredFieldValidator | ControlToValidate=txtUserName<br>ErrorMessage=Please specify a valid user name. |
| RequiredFieldValidator | RequiredFieldValidator2 | ControlToValidate=txtPassword<br>ErrorMessage=Please specify a valid password. |

In the preceding table, I have not included the details of the User Name and Password labels. You need to add these controls to the form as well. The completed default.aspx form is shown in Figure 20-5.

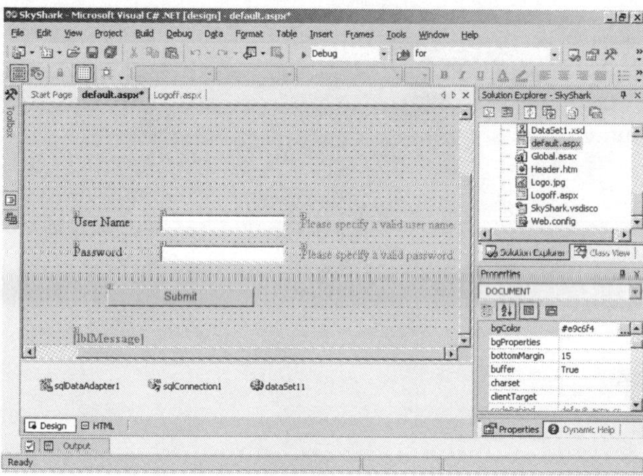


**FIGURE 20-5** *The default.aspx page*

## Logoff.aspx

The Logoff.aspx form is used to display the logoff page when a user logs off from the Web site. The controls I have added to the Logoff.aspx form are summarized in Table 20-3.

**Table 20-3 Controls in the Logoff.aspx Form**

| Control Type | ID | Properties Changed |
|---|---|---|
| TextArea | None | None |
| Hyperlink | HyperLink1 | NavigateUrl=default.aspx |
| | | Text=Click here to logon. |

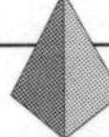

**TIP**

TextArea is an HTML control. Therefore, you need not specify any values for the control.

The Logoff.aspx page is shown in Figure 20-6.

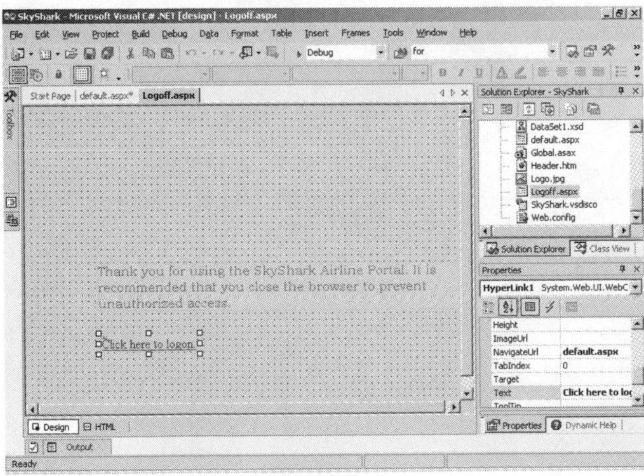

**FIGURE 20-6** *The Logoff.aspx page*

## ChangePassword.aspx

The ChangePassword.aspx form is used by authenticated users to change their passwords. The controls you need to add to the ChangePassword.aspx form are given in Table 20-4.

**Table 20-4 Controls in the ChangePassword.aspx Form**

| Control Type | ID | Properties Changed |
|---|---|---|
| Label | txtUser | Text=Changing Password for: |
| TextBox | txtPassword | TextMode=Password |
| TextBox | txtConfPassword | TextMode=Password |
| Button | btnSubmit | Text=Submit |
| RequiredFieldValidator | RequiredFieldValidator1 | ErrorMessage=Please specify a valid password. |
| | | ControlToValidate=txtPassword |
| RequiredFieldValidator | RequiredFieldValidator2 | ErrorMessage=Please specify a valid password. |
| | | ControlToValidate=txtConfPassword |
| CompareValidator | CompareValidator1 | ErrorMessage=The passwords specified by you do not match. Please try again. |
| | | ControlToValidate=txtConfPassword |
| | | ControlToCompare=txtPassword |

In the ChangePassword.aspx form, the txtUser control is used to display the logon name of the user who is currently logged on. This control is common to all forms in the application. The CompareValidator1 control is used to ensure that the user specifies identical values in the txtPassword and txtConfPassword controls. The completed ChangePassword.aspx form is shown in Figure 20-7.

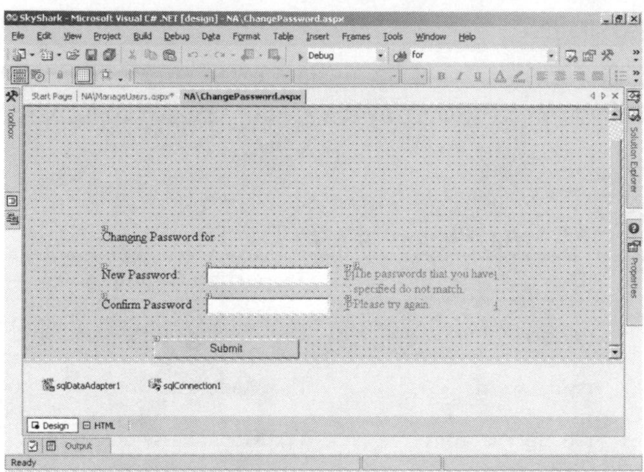


**FIGURE 20-7** *The ChangePassword.aspx form*

## Forms for Network Administrators

The SkyShark Airlines application provides two forms for business managers, ManageUsers.aspx and ManageDatabases.aspx. The ManageUsers.aspx form is used to add and remove user accounts, and the ManageDatabases.aspx form is used to update databases. I will discuss the design of these two forms in this section.

### *ManageUsers.aspx*

The ManageUsers.aspx form is divided into two sections. One section is used to add user accounts and the other is used to remove user accounts. The controls you need to add to the ManageUsers.aspx form are given in Table 20-5.

**Table 20-5 Controls in the ManageUsers.aspx Form**

| Control Type | ID | Properties Changed |
|---|---|---|
| Label | txtUser | Text=Changing Password for: |
| HyperLink | HyperLink1 | NavigateUrl=ChangePassword.aspx |
| | | Text=Change Password |
| HyperLink | HyperLink2 | NavigateUrl=../Logoff.aspx |
| | | Text=Logoff |
| Label | lblMessage | Text="" |
| | | ForeColor=Red |
| | | Font:Bold=True |
| Button (HTML) | AddUser | None (HTML control) |
| Button (HTML) | DeleteUser | None (HTML control) |
| TextBox | txtAddUserName | None |
| TextBox | txtAddPassword | TextMode=Password |
| TextBox | txtAddConfPassword | TextMode=Password |
| ListBox | lstAddRole | Items=BM, NA, LOB |
| Button | btnAddSubmit | Text=Submit |
| TextBox | txtDelUserName | None |
| Button | btnDelDelete | Text=Delete |

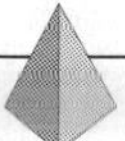

**TIP**

In the ManageUsers.aspx form, items are added to the lstAddRole property by using the ListItem Collection Editor. The ListItem Collection Editor is invoked when you click on the ellipsis button in the Items property.

After you add the controls specified in Table 20-5, the design of the ManageUsers.aspx form is complete and is shown in Figure 20-8.

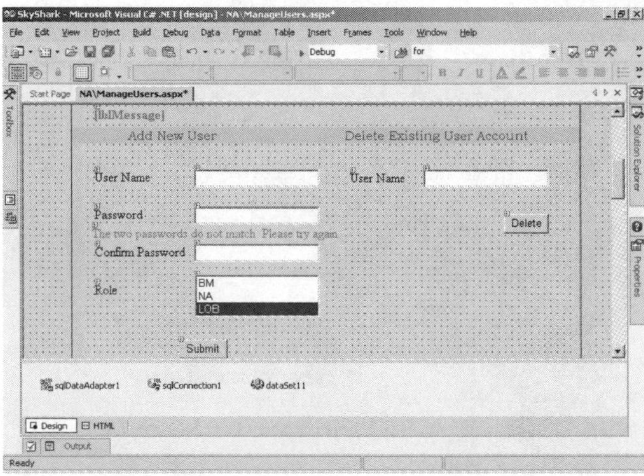


**FIGURE 20-8** *The ManageUsers.aspx form*

## ManageDatabases.aspx

The ManageDatabases.aspx form includes two Button controls used for moving information pertaining to flight departure from the `dtReservations` table to the `dtDepartedFlights` table and from the `dtDepartedFlights` table to the `dtPassengerDetails` table. Apart from the first four controls consistent in all forms and mentioned in Table 20-5, I have added two Button controls to the form. These controls are described in Table 20-6.

**Table 20-6 Controls in the ManageDatabases.aspx Form**

| Control Type | ID | Properties Changed |
|---|---|---|
| Button | btnArchive | Text=Archive information pertaining to flights that have departed.<br>BackColor=Silver<br>BorderColor=Blue<br>Font:Name=Bookman Old Style |
| Button | btnUpdate | Text=Update customer information for the frequent fliers program.<br>BackColor=Silver<br>BorderColor=Blue<br>Font:Name=Bookman Old Style |

## Forms for Business Managers

SkyShark Airlines provides four forms for business managers: AddFl.aspx, RequestID.aspx, Reports.aspx, and FreqFl.aspx. The design of these forms is discussed in this section.

### *AddFl.aspx*

The AddFl.aspx form is used to add details of any new flights introduced by SkyShark Airlines. The design of the AddFl.aspx form is straightforward. Apart from including the first four controls mentioned in Table 20-5, I have added text boxes and validation controls for the flight number, departure time and place, arrival time and destination, aircraft type, number of seats in the executive and business classes, and the fares of the executive and business class fields. I have also added two buttons for submitting and canceling the form. The design of the AddFl.aspx form is shown in Figure 20-9.

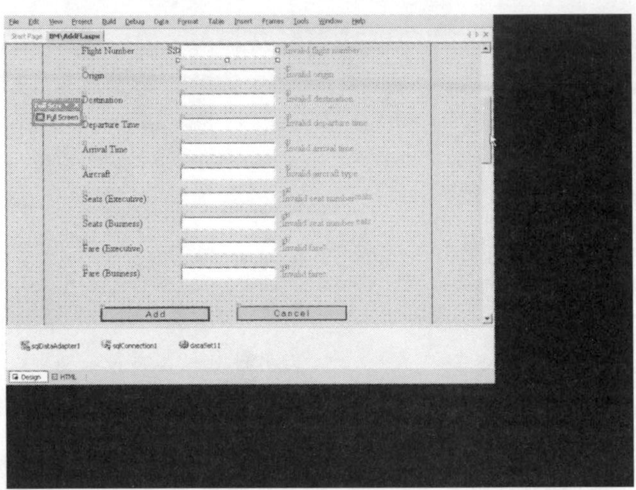

**FIGURE 20-9** *The AddFl.aspx form*

## RequestID.aspx

The RequestID.aspx form is used by business managers to request for new user IDs. The controls in the RequestID.aspx form are listed in Table 20-7.

**Table 20-7 Controls in the RequestID.aspx Form**

| Control Type | ID | Properties Changed |
|---|---|---|
| TextBox | txtUserID | None |
| RequiredFieldValidator | RequiredFieldValidator1 | ErrorMessage=Please specify a valid user name. |
| | | ControlToValidate=txtUserID |
| ListBox | lstRole | Items=Admin, BM, NA |
| Button | btnSubmit | Text=Submit Mail |
| | | BackColor=Silver |
| | | BorderColor=Blue |

The RequestID.aspx form is shown in Figure 20-10.

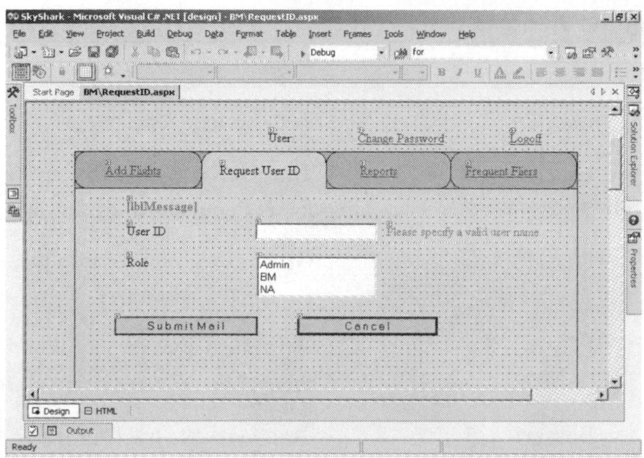


**FIGURE 20-10** *The RequestID.aspx form*

## Reports.aspx

The Reports.aspx form is used to generate reports. The form uses a DataGrid control to display reports corresponding to the type of report selected by the business manager. You can assign a DataView control to the DataGrid control so that data can be formatted and displayed in the form. A DataView control, in turn, retrieves data from a DataSet control. You will learn about using the DataGrid control in Chapter 21, "Implementing the Business Logic."

The controls you need to add to the Reports.aspx page are listed in Table 20-8.

**Table 20-8 Controls in the Reports.aspx Form**

| Control Type | ID | Properties Changed |
|---|---|---|
| Label | Label1 | Text=Select a report: |
| Label | Label2 | Text=Generate a flight usage report for all flights flown by the airline. |
| Label | Label3 | Generate a customer affinity report for top 100 customers |
| Label | Label4 | Generate a total revenue report from the month |
| Buttons (3) | Button1, 2, 3 | Text=Generate<br>BackColor=Silver<br>BorderColor=Blue |
| ListBox | lstMonth | Items=1, 2, 3, 4, 5, 6, 7, 8, 9, 10, 11, 12 |
| ListBox | lstYear | Items=2002, 2003, 2004, 2005 |
| DataGrid | DataGrid1 | BorderColor=#8080FF<br>Font:Name=Bookman Old Style<br>BorderStyle=Inset<br>BorderWidth=2px |

The completed Reports.aspx form is shown in Figure 20-11.

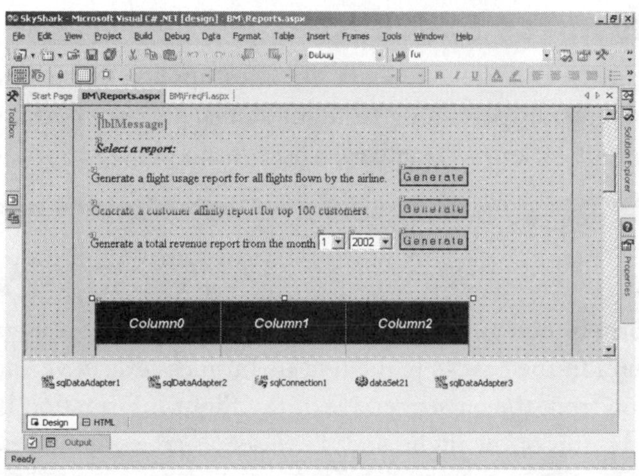


**FIGURE 20-11** *The Reports.aspx form*

## FreqFl.aspx

The FreqFl.aspx form is used to make the frequent fliers program available to passengers. The form is similar to the Reports.aspx form. The FreqFl.aspx form uses the DataGrid control to list users entitled to the frequent fliers program. The design of the FreqFl.aspx form is shown in Figure 20-12.

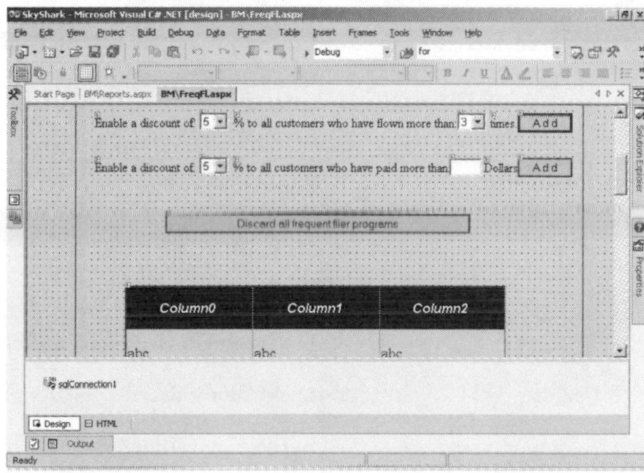


**FIGURE 20-12** *The FreqFl.aspx form*

## Forms for Line-of-Business Executives

Line-of-business executives use the SkyShark Airlines application to manage reservations and answer queries pertaining to flight status. The application provides four forms for line-of-business executives. These forms are described in this section.

### *CreateRes.aspx*

The CreateRes.aspx form is used to make reservations. Making flight reservations is a three-step procedure. In the first step, the line-of-business executive enquires about flight information from the passenger. Next, the flight information is used to find out the fare and status of the flight, and these details are communicated to the passenger. Finally, the name and e-mail address of the passenger are used to make the reservation. The controls added to the CreateRes.aspx form are summarized in Table 20-9.

**Table 20-9 Controls in the CreateRes.aspx Form**

| Control Type | ID | Properties Changed |
|---|---|---|
| Label | Label3 | Text=Step 1: Specify ticket details |
| | | Font:Name=Microsoft Sans Serif |
| | | BorderStyle=Inset |
| TextBox | txtFltNo | None |
| ListBox | lstClass | Items=Executive, Business |
| Calendar | Cal1 | BackColor=White |
| | | BorderColor=Black |
| | | BorderStyle=Double |
| | | Border=2px |
| | | DayNameFormat=FirstTwoLetter |
| Button | btnNext | BackColor=Silver |
| | | BorderColor=Blue |
| | | Font:Name=Microsoft Sans Serif |
| | | Text=Next |

**Table 20-9 Controls in the CreateRes.aspx Form *(continued)***

| Control Type | ID | Properties Changed |
|---|---|---|
| Label | Label4 | Text=Step 2: Confirm flight status and fare with the customer |
| | | Font:Name=Microsoft Sans Serif |
| | | BorderStyle=Inset |
| TextBox(6) | txtTNo, txtFare, txtStatus, txtOrg, txtDest, and txtDepTime | TextBox controls for ticket number, fare, status, origin of flight, destination of flight, and departure time. |
| | | Enabled=False |
| Label | Label5 | Text=Step 3: Confirm booking |
| | | Font:Name=Microsoft Sans Serif |
| | | BorderStyle=Inset |
| TextBox | txtName | None |
| TextBox | txtEMail | None |
| Button | btnCreate | BackColor=Silver |
| | | BorderColor=Blue |
| | | Font:Name=Microsoft Sans Serif |
| | | Text=Create Reservation |
| Button | btnCancel | BackColor=Silver |
| | | BorderColor=Blue |
| | | Font:Name=Microsoft Sans Serif |
| | | Text=Cancel |

The completed CreateRes.aspx form is shown in Figure 20-13.

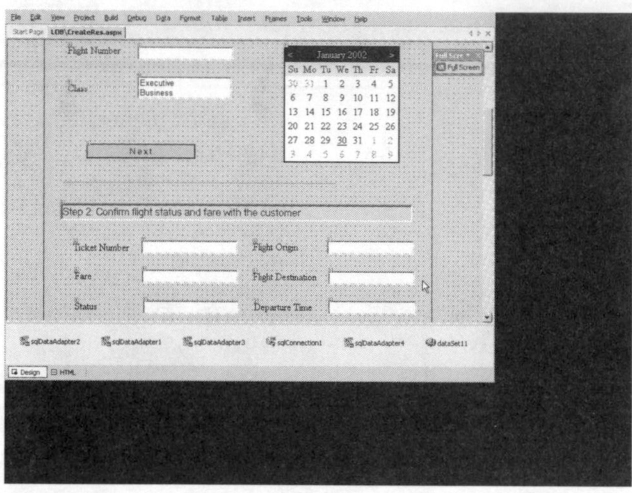


**FIGURE 20-13** *The CreateRes.aspx form*

## CancelRes.aspx

The CancelRes.aspx page is used to cancel reservations. The form uses the ticket number specified by the customer to cancel the reservation. Apart from the standard controls included on every page, I have included three controls in the CancelRes.aspx form. These controls are listed as follows:

- **txtTNo.** The txtTNo control is used to accept the ticket number to be cancelled.
- **RequiredFieldValidator1.** The RequiredFieldValidator1 control is used to ensure that the user specifies a valid value in the txtTNo field.
- **btnCancel.** The btnCancel control is used to cancel reservations.

## QueryStat.aspx

The QueryStat.aspx form is used to enquire about the status of flights and tickets. The first section of the form, which is used to find out the status of flight arrival and departure, uses the same controls that are used in Step1 of the CreateRes.aspx form. The next section, which provides information about the confirmation status of passenger tickets, is similar to the CancelRes.aspx form. The completed QueryStat.aspx form, which will help you design your form, is displayed in Figure 20-14.

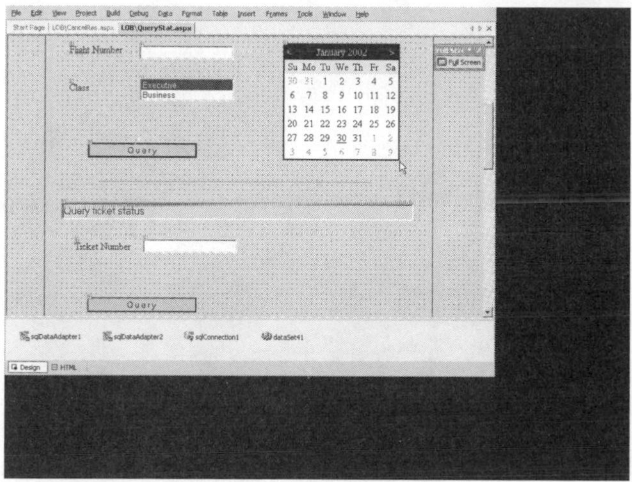


**FIGURE 20-14** *The QueryStat.aspx form*

### ConfirmRes.aspx

The ConfirmRes.aspx form is used to confirm reservations before flight departure. Just as with the CancelRes.aspx form, the ConfirmRes.aspx form uses the ticket number to confirm a reservation.

## Summary

This chapter discussed how to design an application for an airline portal. The first step to design the application is to create the database schema by using either SQL Server Enterprise Manager or Query Analyzer.

The next step is to design the Web forms of the application by using the list of controls specified against each form of the application. Then, you change the default name and classes associated with each Web form. Finally, you update the changed class name in the `@ Page` directive of the Web form so that the application can identify the classes associated with each Web form. The design of your application is now ready.

# Chapter 21

## Implementing the Business Logic

In the last chapter, you designed the forms for the SkyShark Airlines application. In this chapter, you will implement the business logic for running the application and fulfilling the business requirements of SkyShark Airlines that were discussed in Chapter 18, "Project Case Study and Design."

# Coding the Logon and Logoff Functionality

The logon and logoff functionality of the Web application is implemented by the use of Session variables. To log on to the Web site, the user supplies the logon name and password on the default.aspx page. After the user has been successfully authenticated, the username and the role of the user are stored in session variables. These values are used for identifying the user on each page of the Web application. When the user decides to log off, the Session variables for the user are cleared and the user is no longer able to browse the Web site.

**TIP**

You can also authenticate users by using the ASP.NET authentication mechanism. This mechanism is discussed in Chapter 25, "Securing the Application."

The next sections will implement the functionality described previously in the default.aspx and Logoff.aspx forms.

## The Default.aspx Form

The default.aspx form uses the `dtUsers` table to authenticate users. Before you write the code for the default.aspx form, drag the `dtUsers` table from Server Explorer to the design view of the form. Visual Studio .NET automatically configures SqlDataAdapter and SqlConnection controls for the form. You can read a description of these controls in Chapter 19, "Basics of ASP.NET Web Applications," in the section "Coding the Application."

After you add SqlDataAdapter and SqlConnection controls to the form, you can generate a dataset for the form. To generate the dataset, follow these steps:

1. Click anywhere on the form.
2. Click on the Data menu and select Generate Dataset. The Generate Dataset dialog box will appear.
3. In the Generate Dataset dialog box, click on the New option and click on OK.
4. A new DataSet control is added to your project.

All the three data controls are visible in Component Designer in the Design view of the form, as you can see in Figure 21-1.

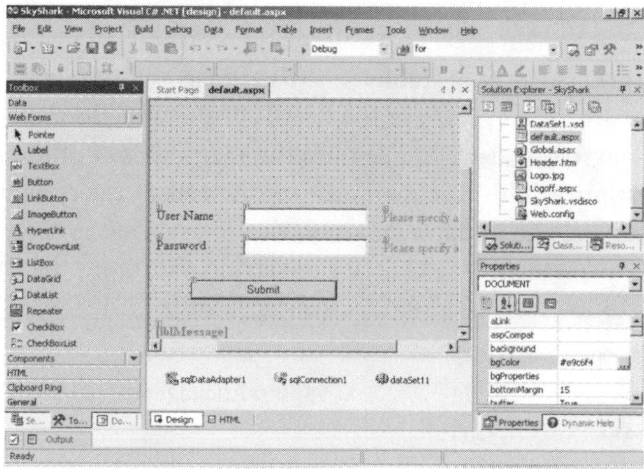


**FIGURE 21-1** *Data controls appear in Component Designer*

A DataAdapter control has a default set of queries associated with it for selecting, inserting, updating, and deleting data from the SQL Server table with which the DataAdapter control is associated. These queries are specified by the SelectCommand, InsertCommand, UpdateCommand, and DeleteCommand properties of the DataAdapter control.

If required, you can change the default queries associated with the DataAdapter control. For example, the default SelectCommand associated with the sqlDataAdapter1 control, which you added to the form for the `dtUsers` table, is `SELECT Username, Password, Role, PasswordChanged FROM dtUsers`. This query returns all the records from the `dtUsers` table.

However, to validate a single user, you need not retrieve all the records from the `dtUsers` table. Therefore, you can modify the SelectCommand property to `SELECT Username, Password, Role, PasswordChanged FROM dtUsers WHERE (UserName=@username)`. The modified query accepts the `@username` parameter at run time and retrieves the record from the table that has the same username as specified by the user.

After you add and configure data controls for the default.aspx form, double-click on Submit to write the code for the `Click` event of the form.

The code for the `Click` event of the Submit button is logically divided into three parts:

1. **Retrieve data from the `dtUsers` table.** The username and password specified by the user are used to retrieve the details of the user from the `dtUsers` table. To retrieve data, you can use the `Fill` method of the sqlDataAdapter1 control. The `Fill` method runs the `SELECT` query associated with the control and updates data into the dataset that is passed to the method as a parameter. The code for retrieving data from the database is given as follows:

   ```
   string username, password;
   int datarows;
   username=txtUserName.Text.Trim();
   password=txtPassword.Text.Trim();
   sqlConnection1.Open();
   sqlDataAdapter1.SelectCommand.Parameters["@UserName"].Value=username;
   datarows=sqlDataAdapter1.Fill(dataSet11,"UserDetails");
   sqlConnection1.Close();
   ```

2. **Check username and password supplied by the user.** If the username specified by the user matches with any record in the database, then the data inserted into the dataset will have at least one row in it. The number of records retrieved from the database can be ascertained by checking the return value of the `Fill` method described previously. If no rows have

been returned by the SELECT query, then the username specified by the user is incorrect. However, if the SELECT query returns data but the password does not match, then the password specified by the user is incorrect. The code that uses the logic described above to check the username and password is given as follows:

```
if (datarows==0)
   lblMessage.Text="Incorrect user name";
else
{
   if (dataSet11.Tables["UserDetails"].Rows[0][1].ToString().
      Trim()==password)
   {
      //The credentials supplied by the user are correct
   }
else
   lblMessage.Text="Incorrect password";
}
```

3. **Store username and role in session variables and redirect the user.** When the user is successfully authenticated, the username and the role of the user are stored in Session variables and the user is redirected to the home page of one of the roles in the organization, depending upon the role of the user retrieved from the database. The code to implement this functionality is given as follows:

```
string Role;
Role=dataSet11.Tables["UserDetails"].Rows[0][2].ToString().Trim();
Session["usrName"]=username;
Session["usrRole"]=Role;
if (Role=="Disabled")
{
   lblMessage.Text="Your account has been disabled. Please contact the
      network administrator.";
   return;
}
FormsAuthentication.GetAuthCookie(username,false);
switch(Role)
```

```
        {
            case "Admin":
                Response.Redirect(".\\NA\\ManageUsers.aspx");
                break;
            case "BM":
                Response.Redirect(".\\BM\\AddFl.aspx");
                break;
            case "LOB":
                Response.Redirect(".\\LOB\\CreateRes.aspx");
                break;
        }
```

The complete code of the `Click` event of Submit button, which incorporates the functionality described previously, is given as follows:

```
private void btnSubmit_Click(object sender, System.EventArgs e)
{
if (Page.IsValid==true)
{
    string username, password;
    int datarows;
    username=txtUserName.Text.Trim();
    password=txtPassword.Text.Trim();
    sqlConnection1.Open();
    sqlDataAdapter1.SelectCommand.Parameters["@UserName"].Value=username;
    datarows=sqlDataAdapter1.Fill(dataSet11,"UserDetails");
    sqlConnection1.Close();
    if (datarows==0)
        lblMessage.Text="Incorrect user name";
    else
    {
        if (dataSet11.Tables["UserDetails"].Rows[0][1].ToString().Trim()==password)
        {
        string Role;
        Role=dataSet11.Tables["UserDetails"].Rows[0][2].ToString().Trim();
        Session["usrName"]=username;
        Session["usrRole"]=Role;
        if (Role=="Disabled")
        {
```

```
            lblMessage.Text="Your account has been disabled. Please
               contact the network administrator.";
            return;
        }
        switch(Role)
        {
            case "Admin":
               Response.Redirect(".\\NA\\ManageUsers.aspx");
               break;
            case "BM":
               Response.Redirect(".\\BM\\AddFl.aspx");
               break;
            case "LOB":
               Response.Redirect(".\\LOB\\CreateRes.aspx");
               break;
        }
    }
    else
        lblMessage.Text="Incorrect password";
}
dataSet11.Clear();
}
}
```

## The Logoff.aspx Form

The Logoff.aspx form is used for logging a user off from the Web site. This form clears the Session variables assigned to the user so that the user is unable to browse any page on the Web application. All code on the Logoff.aspx form is written in the `Load` event of the form. To write the code for the `Load` event, double-click on the form in the Design view. The code for the `Load` event of the Logoff.aspx form is given as follows:

```
private void Page_Load(object sender, System.EventArgs e)
{
    Session.RemoveAll();
}
```

# Coding the Forms for Network Administrators

SkyShark Airlines provides the ManageUsers.aspx and ManageDatabases.aspx forms for network administrators.

By default, when the application is installed, a user account for network administrators is added to the application, with the username and password as Admin and Password, respectively, so that a network administrator can access the ManageUsers.aspx form and create user accounts. You can examine the code for the ManageUsers.aspx form.

## The ManageUsers.aspx Form

The ManageUsers.aspx page is used for adding and deleting user accounts. I will examine the steps to add and delete user accounts separately. However, before examining these tasks, perform the following steps to configure data controls for the ManageUsers.aspx form:

1. Drag the `dtUsers` table from Server Explorer to the Design view of the form.
2. Generate a dataset for the SqlDataAdapter control that is added to the form.
3. Modify the default queries that are associated with the sqlDataAdapter1 control as specified:
   - **SelectCommand.** `SELECT Username FROM dtUsers`
   - **DeleteCommand.** `UPDATE dtUsers SET Role = 'Disabled' WHERE (Username = @Original_Username)`

### Adding User Accounts

To add a user account, you need to perform the following steps:

1. **Check whether the username already exists.** Before adding a record to the `dtUsers` table, you should check whether the user account already exists. You can check usernames by retrieving them from the `dtUsers` table and checking each record. The following code snippet retrieves

records from the `dtUsers` table and compares them with the username specified by the user.

```
string username, password, role;
int selection;
role=lstAddRole.SelectedItem.Text;
username=txtAddUserName.Text.Trim();
password=txtAddPassword.Text.Trim();
selection=lstAddRole.SelectedIndex;
sqlConnection1.Open();
sqlDataAdapter1.Fill(dataSet11, "UserList");
sqlConnection1.Close();
foreach (DataRow myRow in dataSet11.Tables["UserList"].Rows)
{
   if (myRow[0].ToString().Trim().ToLower()==username.ToLower())
   {
      lblMessage.Text="The user name already exists. Please try another
         user name";
      return;
   }
}
```

2. **Add the new user to the database.** If the username specified by the user is unique, the application adds a record to the database by using the SQL query associated with the `InsertCommand` property of the sql-DataAdapter1 control. However, before you execute the query, you need to assign values specified by the user as the parameters to the query. To assign values to parameters, you can use the `Parameters` collection of `InsertCommand`. The code snippet to add a new user to the database is given as follows:

```
sqlDataAdapter1.InsertCommand.Parameters[0].Value=username;
sqlDataAdapter1.InsertCommand.Parameters[1].Value=password;
sqlDataAdapter1.InsertCommand.Parameters[2].Value=role;
sqlConnection1.Open();
sqlDataAdapter1.InsertCommand.ExecuteNonQuery();
sqlConnection1.Close();
```

**NOTE**

Instead of using the code in Step 2, you could also update the DataSet that corresponds to the data in the `dtUsers` table and then invoke the `Update` method of sqlDataAdapter1 to update data in the `dtUsers` table. The ideal scenario to employ that method is when you want to optimize database interaction by caching changes and then sending them to the database at regular intervals.

3. **Send an e-mail message to the registered user.** After adding the new user to the SkyShark Airlines application, use the `SmtpMail` class to send an e-mail message to the registered user. The `Send` method of the `SmtpMail` class uses an object of the `MailMessage` class to send an e-mail message to the user. The code for creating and sending the message is given as follows:

```
MailAttachment attachment= new
MailAttachment("c:\\Inetpub\\wwwroot\\SkyShark\\NA\\PrivacyPolicy.doc");
MailMessage email= new MailMessage();
email.Attachments.Add(attachment);
email.To=username + "@skyshark.com";
email.From="admin@skyshark.com";
email.Subject="Message from SkyShark Airlines";
email.Body="Dear " + username + ",\n\nYour account has been added " +
"to the SkyShark Airlines application. You can log on to the " +
"application at http://npandey-d185/skyshark. \n\nYour logon name" +
" is " + username + " and the password is password. Please change" +
" your password when you log on. \n\n By logging on to the application," +
" you agree to abide by the terms and conditions attached in the mail" +
"\n\n Happy Browsing.\n\n Network Administrator (SkyShark)";
SmtpMail.Send(email);
```

When a new user registers on the Web site, the details of the new user are added to the `dtUsers` table and an e-mail message is sent to the user. The complete code of the `Click` event of the Submit button is obtained by combining the code snippets given earlier. The code is given as follows:

```
private void btnAddSubmit_Click(object sender, System.EventArgs e)
{
   if (txtAddUserName.Text==null || txtAddUserName.Text=="" || txtAddPassword.Text
      ==null || txtAddPassword.Text=="" || txtAddConfPassword.Text
      ==null || txtAddConfPassword.Text=="")
   {
   lblMessage.Text="One or more required values are missing. Try again.";
   }
   if (Page.IsValid)
   {
      string username, password, role;
      int selection;
      role=lstAddRole.SelectedItem.Text;
      username=txtAddUserName.Text.Trim();
      password=txtAddPassword.Text.Trim();
      selection=lstAddRole.SelectedIndex;
      sqlConnection1.Open();
      sqlDataAdapter1.Fill(dataSet11, "UserList");
      sqlConnection1.Close();
      foreach (DataRow myRow in dataSet11.Tables["UserList"].Rows)
      {
      if (myRow[0].ToString().Trim().ToLower()==username.ToLower())
      {
      lblMessage.Text="The user name already exists. Please try another user name";
         return;
      }
   }
   sqlDataAdapter1.InsertCommand.Parameters[0].Value=username;
   sqlDataAdapter1.InsertCommand.Parameters[1].Value=password;
   sqlDataAdapter1.InsertCommand.Parameters[2].Value=role;
   sqlConnection1.Open();
   sqlDataAdapter1.InsertCommand.ExecuteNonQuery();
   sqlConnection1.Close();
   MailAttachment attachment= new MailAttachment("c:\\Inetpub\\wwwroot\\SkyShark\\NA
      \\PrivacyPolicy.doc");
```

```
    MailMessage email= new MailMessage();
    email.Attachments.Add(attachment);
    email.To=username + "@niit.com";
    email.From="nitinp@niit.com";
    email.Subject="Message from SkyShark Airlines";
    email.Body="Dear " + username + ",\n\nYour account has been added " +
    "to the SkyShark Airlines application. You can log on to the " +
    "application at http://npandey-d185/skyshark. \n\nYour logon name" +
    " is " + username + " and the password is password. Please change" +
    " your password when you log on. \n\n By logging on to the application," +
    " you agree to abide by the terms and conditions attached in the mail" +
    "\n\n Happy Browsing.\n\n Network Administrator (SkyShark)";
    SmtpMail.Send(email);
    lblMessage.Text="User added successfully";
    txtAddUserName.Text="";
    dataSet11.Clear();
}
}
```

## Deleting User Accounts

The procedure for deleting user accounts is straightforward. The username specified by the network administrator is checked in the `dtUsers` database to ensure that it exists. Next, the `DeleteCommand` property of the sqlDataAdapter1 control is used to delete the username specified by the network administrator from the database. The code for the `Click` event of the Delete button is given as follows:

```
private void btnDelDelete_Click(object sender, System.EventArgs e)
{
    string username=txtDelUserName.Text.Trim();
    bool userexists=false;
    if (username==null || username=="")
    {
        lblMessage.Text="Please specify a valid user name";
    }
    else
    {
        sqlConnection1.Open();
        sqlDataAdapter1.Fill(dataSet11, "UserList");
```

```
            sqlConnection1.Close();
            foreach (DataRow myRow in dataSet11.Tables["UserList"].Rows)
            {
                if (myRow[0].ToString().Trim().ToLower()==username.ToLower())
                {
                    userexists=true;
                }
            }
            if (userexists==false)
            {
                lblMessage.Text="The user does not exist";
                return;
            }
            sqlDataAdapter1.DeleteCommand.Parameters[0].Value=username;
            sqlConnection1.Open();
            sqlDataAdapter1.DeleteCommand.ExecuteNonQuery();
            sqlConnection1.Close();
            lblMessage.Text="User disabled successfully";
            txtDelUserName.Text="";
        }
    }
```

## The ManageDatabases.aspx Form

The ManageDatabases.aspx form is used for moving data between the `dtReservations` and `dtDepartedFlights` tables. It is also used to update the `dtPassengerDetails` table for the frequent fliers program.

For updating the `dtDepartedFlights` and `dtPassengerDetails` tables, I have created stored procedures in SQL Server. These procedures are called from the SkyShark Airlines application so that the data can be updated directly at the back end. There are several advantages of using a stored procedure in this scenario:

- Since the data is not required in the application, it does not need to be retrieved from the application and then posted back again. This saves a lot of unnecessary network congestion and improves the performance of the application and the database.

- The developer does not need to write unnecessary code for the application. SQL queries that are used in stored procedures can be easily tested by using Query Analyzer.

To move data from the `dtReservations` table to the `dtDepartedFlights` table, you need to write the following stored procedure:

```
CREATE PROCEDURE UpdateReservations
@date datetime
AS
INSERT INTO dtDepartedFlights
SELECT * from dtReservations
WHERE (DateOfJourney < @date) AND (TicketConfirmed=1)
DELETE from dtReservations
WHERE (DateOfJourney < @date)
GO
```

To execute a stored procedure, you need to associate it with an SqlCommand object. Stored procedures can be associated with SqlCommand objects in the same way as you associate SQL Server tables with your application. The stored procedures in the SkyShark Airlines database are shown in Figure 21-2.

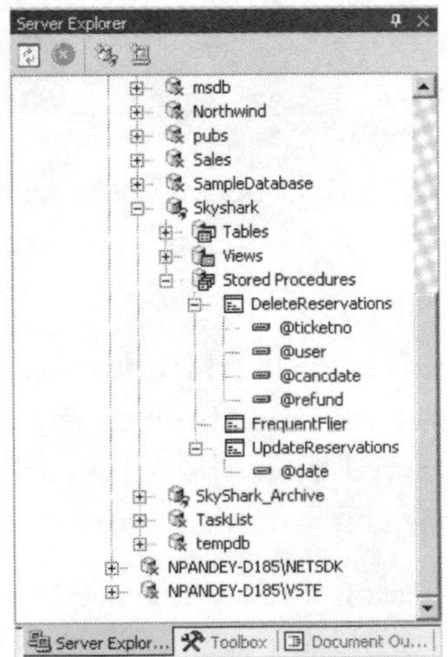


**FIGURE 21-2** *Stored procedures can be accessed from Server Explorer*

To write the code for executing the UpdateReservations stored procedure from the SkyShark Airlines application, drag the Update Reservations stored procedure form Server Explorer to the design view of the form. Visual Studio .NET automatically creates the sqlDataAdapter1 and sqlCommand1 controls. To run the stored procedure when a user clicks on the Archive button, write the following code for the `Click` event of the Archive button:

```
private void BtnArchive_Click(object sender, System.EventArgs e)
{
   lblMessage.Text="";
   sqlConnection1.Open();
   sqlCommand1.Parameters[1].Value=DateTime.Today.Date.ToShortDateString();
   sqlCommand1.ExecuteNonQuery();
   sqlConnection1.Close();
   lblMessage.Text="Done.";
}
```

To move data between the `dtDepartedFlights` and `dtPassengerDetails` tables, I have created the FrequentFlier stored procedure. The definition of this procedure is given as follows:

```
CREATE PROCEDURE FrequentFlier
AS
DELETE dtFrequentFliers
INSERT INTO dtPassengerDetails
SELECT EMail, Sum(Fare), Count(EMail) from dtDepartedFlights
where EMAIL!='NotSpecified' group by EMail
GO
```

To run this procedure, specify the following code in the `Click` event of the Update button:

```
private void btnUpdate_Click(object sender, System.EventArgs e)
{
   lblMessage.Text="";
   sqlConnection1.Open();
   sqlCommand2.ExecuteNonQuery();
   sqlConnection1.Close();
   lblMessage.Text="Done.";
}
```

## The ChangePassword.aspx Form

The ChangePassword.aspx form is included in the folders for network administrators, business managers, and LOB (*line-of-business*) executives. However, I will discuss the coding and functionality of this form in this section only. The functionality remains same across the forms for all the roles.

To add functionality to the ChangePassword.aspx page, drag the `dtUsers` table from Server Explorer to Component Designer. In the resulting sqlDataAdapter1 control that is added to the form, change the UpdateCommand property as mentioned here:

```
UPDATE dtUsers SET Password = @Password, PasswordChanged = '1' WHERE (Username =
   @Original_Username)
```

After specifying the preceding query, double-click on the Submit button to code the functionality for its `Click` event. Write the following code for the `Click` event of the form:

```
private void btnSubmit_Click(object sender, System.EventArgs e)
{
   sqlConnection1.Open();
   sqlDataAdapter1.UpdateCommand.Parameters[0].Value=txtPassword.Text.Trim();
   sqlDataAdapter1.UpdateCommand.Parameters[1].Value=Session["usrName"];
   sqlDataAdapter1.UpdateCommand.ExecuteNonQuery();
   sqlConnection1.Close();
   Response.Redirect("ManageUsers.aspx");
}
```

The preceding code accepts the new password specified by the user as the first parameter and the username, which is retrieved from the Session state variables, as the second parameter to update the password of the user in the `dtUsers` table.

## Restricting Access to Web Forms

One aspect that is common across all Web pages of the application is that the users should be able to access Web forms pertaining to a role only if they are in that role. For example, the ManageUsers.aspx form should be accessible to network administrators only.

The SkyShark Airlines application enforces this constraint by using Session variables. The role of the user is queried from these variables in the `Load` event of all forms. When the role of the user matches with the intended audience of the form, the user is allowed to load the Web form. If the user should not be allowed to access the page, the user is redirected to the default.aspx page. The code that controls access to Web pages in the `Load` event of forms for network administrators is given as follows:

```
private void Page_Load(object sender, System.EventArgs e)
{
    if (Session["usrRole"]==null)
    {
        Response.Redirect("..\\default.aspx");
    }
    if (!(Session["usrRole"].ToString()=="Admin"))
    {
        Response.Redirect("..\\default.aspx");
    }
    else
    {
        txtUser.Text="Changing password for "+ Session["usrName"].ToString();
    }
}
```

**NOTE**

You need to add the code given here in the `Load` event of all forms. The only precaution you need to take is that you should change the value to check in the `if` clause (`(!(Session["usrRole"].ToString()=="Admin"))`) to "BA" for business managers and "LOB" for LOB executives.

# Coding the Forms for Business Managers

Business managers use the AddFl.aspx, RequestID.aspx, Reports.aspx, and FreqFl.aspx forms for their business operations. In this section, you can learn to add functionality to these forms.

## The AddFl.aspx Form

The AddFl.aspx form is used for adding details of new flights. To add data to the AddFl.aspx table, configure SqlConnection and SqlDataAdapter controls by dragging the dtFltDetails table to the form. Next, change the SelectCommand and InsertCommand properties of the sqlDataAdapter1 control as mentioned here:

- SelectCommand= `SELECT FltNo FROM dtFltDetails`
- InsertCommand= `INSERT INTO dtFltDetails (FltNo, Origin, Destination, Deptime, Arrtime, AircraftType, SeatsExec, SeatsBn, FareExec, FareBn, LaunchDate) VALUES (@FltNo, @Origin, @Destination, @Deptime, @Arrtime, @AircraftType, @SeatsExec, @SeatsBn, @FareExec, @FareBn, @LaunchDate)`

The steps to add new flights to the airline are as follows:

1. **Ensure that the flight number is unique.** The flight number specified by the business manager is queried in the `dtFltDetails` table. If the flight number is not unique, an error message is displayed to the user. You need to write the following code to ensure that the flight number is unique:

```
dataSet11.Clear();
sqlConnection1.Open();
sqlDataAdapter1.Fill(dataSet11,"FltNos");
sqlConnection1.Close();
foreach (DataRow myRow in dataSet11.Tables["FltNos"].Rows)
{
   if (myRow[0].ToString().Trim().ToLower()==txtFltNo.Text.ToLower())
```

```
        {
            lblMessage.Text="The flight already exists. Please try another
               flight number.";
            return;
        }
    }
```

2. **Validate the departure and arrival times.** The departure and arrival times for flights need to be specified in the correct format. The departure and arrival times specified by the user are converted into date and time format by using the `ToDateTime` function of the `Convert` class. The resultant values are stored in `TimeSpan` structures. The code to validate departure and arrival times is given as follows:

```
TimeSpan deptime, arrtime;
try
{
   deptime=Convert.ToDateTime(txtDepTime.Text).TimeOfDay;
   arrtime=Convert.ToDateTime(txtDepTime.Text).TimeOfDay;
}
   catch
{
   lblMessage.Text="Invalid departure or arrival time";
   return;
}
```

3. **Update flight details.** The details of the new flight are added as parameters to the `InsertCommand` query. Next, you need to open the connection to the database and execute the query. Then you can close the connection to the database and clear all fields of the AddFl.aspx form. The code snippet to update flight details is given as follows:

```
try
{
sqlDataAdapter1.InsertCommand.Parameters[0].Value=txtFltNo.Text.Trim();
sqlDataAdapter1.InsertCommand.Parameters[1].Value=txtOrigin.Text.Trim();
sqlDataAdapter1.InsertCommand.Parameters[2].Value=txtDestination.
   Text.Trim();
sqlDataAdapter1.InsertCommand.Parameters[3].Value=deptime.ToString();
sqlDataAdapter1.InsertCommand.Parameters[4].Value=arrtime.ToString();
```

```
sqlDataAdapter1.InsertCommand.Parameters[5].Value=txtAircraft.
   Text.Trim();
sqlDataAdapter1.InsertCommand.Parameters[6].Value= Convert.ToInt32
   (txtSeatsExec.Text.Trim());
sqlDataAdapter1.InsertCommand.Parameters[7].Value= Convert.ToInt32
   (txtSeatsBus.Text.Trim());
sqlDataAdapter1.InsertCommand.Parameters[8].Value= Convert.ToInt32
   (txtFareExec.Text.Trim());
sqlDataAdapter1.InsertCommand.Parameters[9].Value= Convert.ToInt32
   (txtFareBn.Text.Trim());
sqlDataAdapter1.InsertCommand.Parameters[10].Value= DateTime.Today.Date.
   ToShortDateString();
sqlConnection1.Open();
sqlDataAdapter1.InsertCommand.ExecuteNonQuery();
}
catch
{
   lblMessage.Text="Unable to add flight details.";
   sqlConnection1.Close();
   return;
}
sqlConnection1.Close();
lblMessage.Text="Flight added successfully.";
txtFareBn.Text="";
txtFareExec.Text="";
txtSeatsBus.Text="";
txtSeatsExec.Text="";
txtArrTime.Text="";
txtDepTime.Text="";
txtDestination.Text="";
txtOrigin.Text="";
txtFltNo.Text="";
txtAircraft.Text="";
}
```

The complete code for the Submit button of the form is obtained by combining the three preceding code snippets.

The form also includes a Cancel button that is used to clear the values of all fields. The code for the `Click` event of the Cancel button is given as follows:

```
private void btnCancel_Click(object sender, System.EventArgs e)
{
    txtFareBn.Text="";
    txtFareExec.Text="";
    txtSeatsBus.Text="";
    txtSeatsExec.Text="";
    txtArrTime.Text="";
    txtDepTime.Text="";
    txtDestination.Text="";
    txtOrigin.Text="";
    txtFltNo.Text="";
    txtAircraft.Text="";
}
```

## The RequestID.aspx Form

The RequestID.aspx form is used for making a request for a new user account. The business manager specifies the username and the role of the new user and submits the request to the network administrator by e-mail. The code for the `Click` event of the Submit button is given as follows:

```
private void btnSubmit_Click(object sender, System.EventArgs e)
{
    string to, from, subject, body;
    to="admin@skyshark.com";
    from=Session["usrName"].ToString() + "@niit.com";
        subject="New User Request";
        body="I would like to request for a new user. The details are given
            below:\n\n"+
        "User Name: " + txtUserID.Text + "\n\nRole: " + lstRole.SelectedItem.Text
            + "\n\nThanks!\n\n" + Session["usrName"].ToString();
    SmtpMail.Send(from, to, subject, body);
    txtUserID.Text="";
    lstRole.SelectedIndex=0;
    lblMessage.Text="Request sent successfully";
}
```

## The Reports.aspx Form

The Reports.aspx form is used for generating reports. The SkyShark Airlines application supports three reports. I have added three SqlDataAdapter controls on the form; one for each report. To add three SqlDataAdapter controls to the form, drag the `dtPassengerDetails` and `dtDepartedFlights` tables to the form. I have added the `dtPassengerDetails` table to the Component Designer twice so that I can configure two sqlDataAdapter controls for the application. The SelectCommand queries associated with each sqlDataAdapter control are given as follows:

- **sqlDataAdapter1.** `SELECT FltNo, SUM(Fare) AS Fare FROM dtDepartedFlights WHERE (DateOfJourney > @date) GROUP BY FltNo`
- **sqlDataAdapter2.** `SELECT FltNo, DateOfJourney, SUM(Fare) AS Revenue FROM dtDepartedFlights GROUP BY DateOfJourney, FltNo`
- **sqlDataAdapter3.** `SELECT TOP 100 EMail, FareCollected, TotalTimesFlown FROM dtPassengerDetails ORDER BY TotalTimesFlown`

In the preceding list, the sqlDataAdapter1 control is used for generating the total revenue report. The total revenue report displays the total revenue generated by each flight after a specified date. The sqlDataAdapter2 control is used for generating the flight usage report for all flights flown by the airline. The flight usage report displays the total daily revenue generated by each flight. Finally, the sqlDataAdapter3 control is used for identifying the top 100 customers who have flown the airline most frequently.

For generating the total revenue report, you need to specify a date from which the report should be generated. After you select the date and click on Generate, the following sequence of steps generates the report:

1. The date is constructed by retrieving the month and year selected by the user and appending 01 to the date. Therefore, if the user has selected the month 07 and the year 2003, the date generated will be 07/01/2003, in the mm/dd/yyyy format.
2. The generated date is passed to the SelectCommand query of sqlDataAdapter1 as a parameter and the result is retrieved in a dataset.
3. The table in the dataset is associated with an object of the `DataView` class, which is bound to the DataGrid1 control to display the output report to the user.

The code to generate the total revenue report is given as follows:

```
private void Button4_Click(object sender, System.EventArgs e)
{
   dataSet21.Clear();
   DataGrid1.DataSource="";
   string month, date, year;
       month=lstMonth.SelectedItem.Text;
   year=lstYear.SelectedItem.Text;
   date=month + "/01/" + year;
   sqlConnection1.Open();
   sqlDataAdapter1.SelectCommand.Parameters[0].Value=date;
   sqlDataAdapter1.Fill(dataSet21,"Revenue");
   sqlConnection1.Close();
   DataView source=new DataView(dataSet21.Tables["Revenue"]);
   DataGrid1.DataSource=source;
   DataGrid1.DataBind();
}
```

The flight usage report does not accept any information from the user because it generates a report for all the flights. The code for this report is straightforward, as given here:

```
private void Button1_Click(object sender, System.EventArgs e)
{
   dataSet21.Clear();
   DataGrid1.DataSource="";
   sqlConnection1.Open();
   sqlDataAdapter2.Fill(dataSet21,"Usage");
   DataView source=new DataView(dataSet21.Tables["Usage"]);
   DataGrid1.DataSource=source;
   DataGrid1.DataBind();
   sqlConnection1.Close();
}
```

Finally, the code of the customer affinity report, which queries the top 100 customers who have flown the airline, is given as follows:

```
private void Button3_Click(object sender, System.EventArgs e)
{
   dataSet21.Clear();
   DataGrid1.DataSource="";
   sqlConnection1.Open();
   sqlDataAdapter3.Fill(dataSet21,"FreqFl");
   DataView source=new DataView(dataSet21.Tables["FreqFl"]);
   DataGrid1.DataSource=source;
   DataGrid1.DataBind();
   sqlConnection1.Close();
}
```

## The FreqFl.aspx Form

The FreqFl.aspx form is used for enabling the frequent flier program. This form is very similar to the Reports.aspx form in its appearance and functionality. The FreqFl.aspx form enables two types of frequent flier programs. In the first program, customers who have flown the airline more than a predetermined number of times are given discounts. In the second program, customers who have paid more than a specified fare are given discounts.

To create the frequent flier programs, I have added an SqlConnection1 control to the form. Next, I have written the following function for enabling discounts to customers based on the number of times that they have flown the airline:

```
private void Button2_Click(object sender, System.EventArgs e)
{
   lblMessage.Text="";
   DataGrid1.DataSource="";
   SqlCommand Command1= new SqlCommand("INSERT INTO dtFrequentFliers Select
      EMail, Discount="+lstDisc1.SelectedItem.Text+ " from dtPassengerDetails where
      TotalTimesFlown > "+ lstTimesFlown.SelectedItem.Text, sqlConnection1);
   sqlConnection1.Open();
   Command1.ExecuteNonQuery();
   lblMessage.Text="Done.";
   SqlDataAdapter DataAdapter = new SqlDataAdapter("SELECT * from
      dtFrequentFliers", sqlConnection1);
```

```
    DataSet ds= new DataSet();
    DataAdapter.Fill(ds);
    DataView source = new DataView(ds.Tables[0]);
    DataGrid1.DataSource=source;
    DataGrid1.DataBind();
    sqlConnection1.Close();
}
```

In the preceding code, I have assigned an SQL query to an object of the SqlDataAdapter class. The query is run and the rows returned are stored in an object of the DataSet class. These rows are displayed on the form by using the DataGrid1 control.

The code for the second frequent fliers program is very similar to the code for the frequent flier program already shown. However, the query that is used for retrieving the records from the database is different. The complete code of the function that retrieves passengers for the frequent fliers program on the basis of the fare that they have paid is given as follows:

```
private void Button1_Click(object sender, System.EventArgs e)
{
    lblMessage.Text="";
    if (txtFare.Text=="" || txtFare.Text==null)
    {
        lblMessage.Text="Invalid parameter for fare collected.";
        return;
    }
    DataGrid1.DataSource="";
    SqlCommand Command1= new SqlCommand("INSERT INTO dtFrequentFliers Select EMail,
        Discount="+lstDisc2.SelectedItem.Text+ " from dtPassengerDetails where
        FareCollected > "+ txtFare.Text, sqlConnection1);
    sqlConnection1.Open();
    Command1.ExecuteNonQuery();
    lblMessage.Text="Done.";
    SqlDataAdapter DataAdapter = new SqlDataAdapter("SELECT * from
        dtFrequentFliers", sqlConnection1);
    DataSet ds= new DataSet();
    DataAdapter.Fill(ds);
```

```
    DataView source = new DataView(ds.Tables[0]);
    DataGrid1.DataSource=source;
    DataGrid1.DataBind();
    sqlConnection1.Close();
}
```

Finally, business managers have the option to discard frequent flier programs. To discard the frequent flier program, you need to delete all the records from the `dtFrequentFliers` table. The code to accomplish this task is given as follows:

```
private void Button3_Click(object sender, System.EventArgs e)
{
    lblMessage.Text="";
    SqlCommand Command1= new SqlCommand("DELETE dtFrequentFliers", sqlConnection1);
    sqlConnection1.Open();
    Command1.ExecuteNonQuery();
    lblMessage.Text="Done.";
    sqlConnection1.Close();
}
```

# Coding the Forms for LOB Executives

LOB executives perform the tasks of reserving and canceling seats for passengers, querying the status of flights and tickets, and confirming the reservation of passengers. In this section, I provide a description of how these tasks are accomplished.

## The CreateRes.aspx Form

The reservation process is a two-stage process. In the first stage, the flight number, class, and date of reservation are used for querying the status of the flight. The code to retrieve the status of the flight by using the flight number is given as follows:

```
private void btnNext_Click(object sender, System.EventArgs e)
{
    dataSet11.Clear();
    sqlConnection1.Open();
```

```
sqlDataAdapter1.Fill(dataSet11, "FltDetails");
sqlConnection1.Close();
bool exists=false;
foreach (DataRow myRow in dataSet11.Tables["FltDetails"].Rows)
{
   if (myRow[0].ToString().Trim().ToLower()==txtFltNo.Text.ToLower())
   {
      exists=true;
      txtOrg.Text=myRow[1].ToString();
      txtDest.Text=myRow[2].ToString();
      txtDepTime.Text=myRow[3].ToString().Substring(myRow[3].ToString().
         Length-11).Trim();
      if(lstClass.SelectedIndex==0)
         txtFare.Text=myRow[8].ToString();
      else
         txtFare.Text=myRow[9].ToString();
   }
}
if (exists==false)
{
   lblMessage.Text="Incorrect flight number. Please try again";
   return;
}
txtTNo.Text="Auto generated";
txtFltNo.Enabled=false;
lstClass.Enabled=false;
Cal1.Enabled=false;
sqlDataAdapter2.SelectCommand.Parameters[0].Value=txtFltNo.Text.Trim();
sqlDataAdapter2.SelectCommand.Parameters[1].Value=Cal1.SelectedDate.
   ToShortDateString();
sqlDataAdapter2.SelectCommand.Parameters[2].Value=lstClass. SelectedItem.Text;
sqlConnection1.Open();
sqlDataAdapter2.Fill(dataSet11, "FltStatus");
if (dataSet11.Tables["FltStatus"].Rows.Count==0)
{
   txtStatus.Text="Available";
}
```

```
    else
    {
        int status=Convert.ToInt32(dataSet11.Tables["FltStatus"].Rows[0][3]);
        if (status<=0)
        {
            txtStatus.Text="Waitlisted (" + Convert.ToString((status-1)) + ")";
        }
        else
        {
            txtStatus.Text="Available";
        }
    }
}
```

After the customer agrees to proceed with the reservation, the details of the flight are retrieved from the `dtFltDetails` and the `dtFltStatus` tables. The status of the flight is retrieved to ensure that the flight status has not changed between the time when the request for reservation was first made to the actual processing of the process. This functionality is achieved by the following code snippet:

```
if (txtName.Text=="" || txtName.Text==null)
{
    lblMessage.Text="Invalid user name";
    return;
}
string TicketNo, DateOfRes, DateOfJourney, FltNo, ClassOfRes, Name, EMail;
int TicketConf, Status, Fare;
try
{
    FltNo=txtFltNo.Text.Trim();
    ClassOfRes=lstClass.SelectedItem.Text;
    Name=txtName.Text;
    DateOfRes=DateTime.Today.Date.ToShortDateString();
    DateOfJourney=Cal1.SelectedDate.ToShortDateString();
    TicketConf=0;
    Fare=Convert.ToInt32(txtFare.Text.Trim());
    dataSet11.Clear();
    sqlConnection1.Open();
```

```
sqlDataAdapter2.SelectCommand.Parameters[0].Value=txtFltNo.Text.Trim();
sqlDataAdapter2.SelectCommand.Parameters[1].Value= Cal1.SelectedDate
   .ToShortDateString();
sqlDataAdapter2.SelectCommand.Parameters[2].Value= lstClass.SelectedItem.Text;
sqlDataAdapter2.Fill(dataSet11, "FltStatus");
if (dataSet11.Tables["FltStatus"].Rows.Count==0)
{
   //fill in the flight details
   sqlDataAdapter1.Fill(dataSet11, "FltDetails");
   string strTotSeats;
   int intTotSeats;
   foreach (DataRow myRow in dataSet11.Tables["FltDetails"].Rows)
   {
      if (myRow[0].ToString().Trim().ToLower()==txtFltNo.Text.ToLower())
      {
         if(lstClass.SelectedIndex==0)
         {
            strTotSeats=myRow[6].ToString();
         }
         else
         {
            strTotSeats=myRow[7].ToString();
         }
         intTotSeats=Convert.ToInt32(strTotSeats);
         sqlDataAdapter2.InsertCommand.Parameters[0].Value= txtFltNo.Text
            .Trim();
         sqlDataAdapter2.InsertCommand.Parameters[1].Value= Cal1.SelectedDate
            .ToShortDateString();
         sqlDataAdapter2.InsertCommand.Parameters[2].Value= lstClass
            .SelectedItem.Text;
         sqlDataAdapter2.InsertCommand.Parameters[3].Value=intTotSeats-1;
         sqlDataAdapter2.InsertCommand.ExecuteNonQuery();
      }
   }
   //set status as available
   Status=1;
}
```

```
    else
    {
       int val=Convert.ToInt32(dataSet11.Tables["FltStatus"].Rows[0][3]);
       if (val<=0)
       {
          Status=val-1;
       }
       else
       {
          Status=1;
       }
       sqlDataAdapter2.UpdateCommand.Parameters[0].Value=txtFltNo.Text.Trim();
       sqlDataAdapter2.UpdateCommand.Parameters[1].Value= Cal1.SelectedDate
          .ToShortDateString();
       sqlDataAdapter2.UpdateCommand.Parameters[2].Value= lstClass.SelectedItem
          .Text;
       sqlDataAdapter2.UpdateCommand.ExecuteNonQuery();
}
```

The information that is retrieved from the database tables is updated into the `dtReservations` table. To update information into the `dtReservations` table, the following code snippet is used:

```
sqlDataAdapter3.Fill(dataSet11, "TicketNos");
int count, maxno, ticketno;
if (dataSet11.Tables["TicketNos"].Rows.Count>0)
{
   maxno=Convert.ToInt32(dataSet11.Tables["TicketNos"].Rows[0][0].ToString());
   for (count=1; count < dataSet11.Tables["TicketNos"].Rows.Count; count++)
   {
      if (maxno < Convert.ToInt32(dataSet11.Tables["TicketNos"].Rows[count][0]
         .ToString()))
   maxno=Convert.ToInt32(dataSet11.Tables["TicketNos"].Rows[count][0].ToString());
   }
}
else
{
   maxno=0;
}
```

```
ticketno=maxno+1;
TicketNo=Convert.ToString(ticketno);
EMail=txtEMail.Text;
if (EMail==null || EMail=="")
{
   EMail="NotSpecified";
}
else
{
   sqlDataAdapter4.SelectCommand.Parameters[0].Value=EMail;
   sqlDataAdapter4.Fill(dataSet11,"FreqFl");
   if (dataSet11.Tables["FreqFl"].Rows.Count==0)
   {
      //do nothing to the fare
   }
   else
   {
      int discount;
   discount=Convert.ToInt32(dataSet11.Tables["FltStatus"].Rows[0][0]);
      discount=(100-discount)/100;
      Fare=Fare-discount;
   }
}
sqlDataAdapter3.InsertCommand.Parameters[0].Value=TicketNo;
sqlDataAdapter3.InsertCommand.Parameters[1].Value=FltNo;
sqlDataAdapter3.InsertCommand.Parameters[2].Value=DateOfJourney;
sqlDataAdapter3.InsertCommand.Parameters[3].Value=ClassOfRes;
sqlDataAdapter3.InsertCommand.Parameters[4].Value=Name;
sqlDataAdapter3.InsertCommand.Parameters[5].Value=EMail;
sqlDataAdapter3.InsertCommand.Parameters[6].Value=Fare;
sqlDataAdapter3.InsertCommand.Parameters[7].Value=Status;
sqlDataAdapter3.InsertCommand.Parameters[8].Value=Session["usrName"].ToString();
sqlDataAdapter3.InsertCommand.Parameters[9].Value=DateOfRes;
sqlDataAdapter3.InsertCommand.Parameters[10].Value=TicketConf;
sqlDataAdapter3.InsertCommand.ExecuteNonQuery();
sqlConnection1.Close();
lblMessage.Text="Reservation complete. Fare is US$ "+ Fare.ToString();
txtFltNo.Text="";
```

```
lstClass.SelectedIndex=0;
Cal1.SelectedDate=DateTime.Today;
txtTNo.Text="";
txtFare.Text="";
txtStatus.Text="";
txtOrg.Text="";
txtDest.Text="";
txtDepTime.Text="";
txtName.Text="";
txtEMail.Text="";
txtFltNo.Enabled=true;
lstClass.Enabled=true;
Cal1.Enabled=true;
Response.Redirect("Ticket.aspx?TNo=" + TicketNo);
}
catch (Exception ex)
{
   lblMessage.Text=ex.Message;
   sqlConnection1.Close();
   txtFltNo.Enabled=true;
   lstClass.Enabled=true;
   Cal1.Enabled=true;
}
}
```

## The CancelRes.aspx Form

The CancelRes.aspx form is used to perform cancellation of reservations. When a ticket is cancelled, the status of the flight needs to be updated in the `dtFltStatus` table. You also need to update the status of the passengers on the flight who are in the waiting list. In addition, you also need to compute the refund amount that is applicable to the passenger.

To perform cancellations, I have used a combination of stored procedures and programming logic. The steps to cancel a reservation are given as follows:

1. Retrieve the fare that the passenger had paid.
2. Compute the refund applicable to the customer, depending upon whether or not the flight has departed.

3. Update status of other passengers who might have been confirmed because of the cancellation of ticket.
4. Create a record in the `dtCancellations` table and delete the reservation of the passenger from the `dtReservations` table.

The first two tasks are performed by programming logic, the code for which is given as follows:

```
lblMessage.Text="";
dataSet51.Clear();
sqlConnection1.Open();
sqlDataAdapter1.SelectCommand.Parameters[0].Value=txtTNo.Text.Trim();
sqlDataAdapter1.Fill(dataSet51, "TicketDetails");
sqlConnection1.Close();
if (dataSet51.Tables["TicketDetails"].Rows.Count==0)
{
   lblMessage.Text="Invalid ticket number";
   return;
}
else
{
   string ticketno, user, cancdate, journeydate;
   int refund, fare;
   ticketno=txtTNo.Text.Trim();
   journeydate=dataSet51.Tables["TicketDetails"].Rows[0][2].ToString();
   fare=Convert.ToInt32(dataSet51.Tables["TicketDetails"]. Rows[0][6].ToString());
   if (Convert.ToDateTime(journeydate)<=DateTime.Today)
   {
      refund=fare-10;
   }
   else
   {
      refund=Convert.ToInt32(fare*0.8);
   }
```

After the refund amount has been calculated, the details of the ticket that needs to be cancelled are passed to a stored procedure that updates the status of other customers booked on the flight and also deletes the customer record from the `dtReservations` database. The code for the DeleteReservations stored procedure, which accomplishes these tasks, is given as follows:

```
CREATE PROCEDURE DeleteReservations
@ticketno char(10), @user char(15), @cancdate datetime, @refund int
AS
Declare @fltno char(10)
Declare @date datetime
Declare @class char(10)
Declare @status int
select @fltno=FltNo, @date=DateOfJourney, @class=ClassOfRes , @status=Status
from dtReservations where TicketNo=@ticketno
Update dtReservations
set Status=Status+1 where FltNo=@fltno and DateOfJourney=@date
and ClassOfRes=@class and Status<@status
Update dtFltStatus
set Status=Status+1 where FltNo=@fltno and StatusDate=@date
and StatusClass=@class
INSERT into dtCancellations
values (@ticketno, @refund, @user, @cancdate)
Delete dtReservations where TicketNo=@ticketno
GO
```

## The QueryStat.aspx Form

The QueryStat.aspx page is used for querying the status of flights and tickets. LOB executives can either use the flight number to query the status of a flight or use the ticket number to query the status of a ticket. In both the cases, an error message is displayed if the number specified is invalid. Otherwise, the status of the flight or ticket is retrieved and displayed to the user.

The following code is used for querying the status of a flight:

```
private void Button2_Click(object sender, System.EventArgs e)
{
   dataSet41.Clear();
   lblMessage.Text="";
   lblStatus.Text="";
   if (txtFltNo.Text=="" || txtFltNo.Text==null)
```

```
    {
        lblMessage.Text="Invalid flight number";
        return;
    }
    else
    {
        sqlConnection1.Open();
        sqlDataAdapter1.SelectCommand.Parameters[0].Value=txtFltNo.Text.Trim();
        sqlDataAdapter1.SelectCommand.Parameters[1].Value=Cal1. SelectedDate
            .ToShortDateString();
        sqlDataAdapter1.SelectCommand.Parameters[2].Value= lstClass.SelectedItem
            .Text;
        sqlDataAdapter1.Fill(dataSet41, "FltStatus");
        sqlConnection1.Close();
        if (dataSet41.Tables["FltStatus"].Rows.Count==0)
        {
            lblStatus.Text="Status: Available";
        }
        else
        {
            string strStatus;
            int status;
            strStatus=dataSet41.Tables["FltStatus"].Rows[0][0].ToString();
            status=Convert.ToInt32(strStatus);
            if (status >= 0)
            {
                lblStatus.Text="Status: Available";
            }
            else
            {
            lblStatus.Text="Status: Overbooked (" + strStatus + ")";
            }
        }
    }
}
```

## The ConfirmRes.aspx Form

The ConfirmRes.aspx form is used for confirming the reservation of customers. The form queries the ticket number specified by the user against the `dtReservations` database. If the ticket number is valid, the data of journey is retrieved from the database to ensure that the flight has not already departed. If both the conditions, validity of ticket number and nondeparture of flight, are fulfilled, the ticket is confirmed and the customer is informed about the same. The code for the `Click` event of the Submit form, which enables you to confirm a reservation, is given as follows:

```
private void btnConfirm_Click(object sender, System.EventArgs e)
{
   lblMessage.Text="";
   lblDetails.Visible=false;
   sqlConnection1.Open();
   dataSet21.Clear();
   sqlDataAdapter1.SelectCommand.Parameters[0].Value=txtTNo.Text.Trim();
   sqlDataAdapter1.Fill(dataSet21, "TicketDetails");
   sqlConnection1.Close();
   if (dataSet21.Tables["TicketDetails"].Rows.Count==0)
   {
      lblMessage.Text="Invalid ticket number.";
      return;
   }
   else
   {
      string DateOfFlight;
         DateOfFlight=dataSet21.Tables["TicketDetails"].Rows[0][2].ToString();
         if (Convert.ToDateTime(DateOfFlight) < Convert.ToDateTime(DateTime.Today
            .ToShortDateString()))
         {
            lblMessage.Text="The flight has already departed";
            return;
         }
         else
         {
            sqlConnection1.Open();
            sqlDataAdapter1.UpdateCommand.Parameters[0].Value= txtTNo.Text.Trim();
```

```
                sqlDataAdapter1.UpdateCommand.ExecuteNonQuery();
                sqlConnection1.Close();
                lblDetails.Text="Ticket confirmed\n(" + dataSet21.Tables
                   ["TicketDetails"].Rows[0][4].ToString() +
                "\n" + dataSet21.Tables["TicketDetails"].Rows[0][2].ToString() + ")";
                lblDetails.Visible=true;
            }
        }
    }
```

## Summary

This chapter provided the necessary code and explanations to implement the functionality for Web forms. The forms of the SkyShark Airlines application have a consistent interface that is created by using a header file and a consistent menu on all Web forms. Most forms of the SkyShark Airlines application include data controls that are used to exchange data with the SkyShark database. Additionally, each Web form includes an authentication mechanism to ensure that the user is authorized to view the Web forms.

# Chapter 22

## Creating the Customer Transaction Portal

In the last chapter, you implemented the business logic for running the application and fulfilling the business requirements of SkyShark Airlines. In this chapter, you will design and create the customer transaction portal for the airline, which will help customers to view details of new flights launched by the company, the status of their tickets, and the status of flights.

## Designing the Form

The customer transaction portal is developed to enhance the experience of customers. This portal provides the following four options to a customer:

- **View New Flights.** This option enables customers to view the five most recently launched flights.
- **View Ticket Status.** This option enables customers to view the status of their tickets.
- **View Flight Status.** This option enables customers to view the booking status of a flight.
- **Confirm Reservation.** This option enables customers to confirm their reservation.

To provide these functionalities, you'll create an ASP.NET Web application. This application will contain only one Web form named wbFrmSkyShark.aspx. This form will display the data corresponding to all four options by using a different set of controls. The design of the wbFrmSkyShark.aspx Web form is displayed in Figure 22-1.

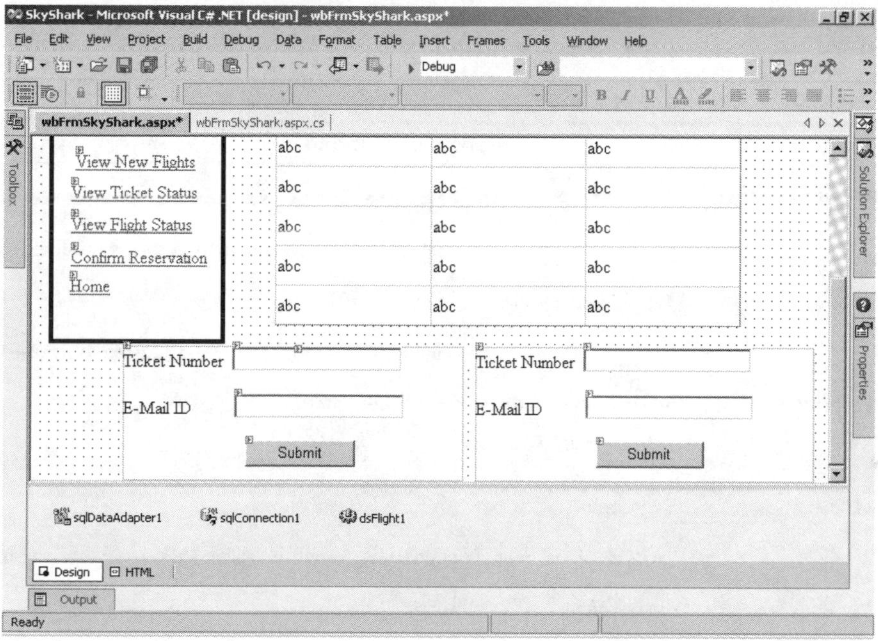


**FIGURE 22-1** *The design of the wbFrmSkyShark.aspx Web form*

The preceding figure does not show all the controls present on the Web form. This is because I've used only a single Web form for all the options. Controls corresponding to each option are organized in various Panels. Table 22-1 lists all these Panels and other controls present on the Web form.

**Table 22-1 Controls in the wbFrmSkyShark.aspx Form**

| Controls | Function |
|---|---|
| Panel1 | Contains controls to display all the options |
| Panel2 | Contains controls used for the View Flight Status option |
| Panel3 | Contains controls used for the View Ticket Status option |
| Panel4 | Contains controls used for the Confirm Reservation option |
| DataGrid1 | Displays the new flights |
| LblStatus | To display various messages to the user |

Of these panels, Table 22-2 lists all the controls present in Panel1.

**Table 22-2 Controls in Panel1**

| Control Type | ID | Properties Changed |
|---|---|---|
| Hyperlink | Hyperlink1 | Text=View New Flights |
| | | NavigateURL = wbFrmSkyShark.aspx?subform=VNF |
| Hyperlink | Hyperlink2 | Text=View Ticket Status |
| | | NavigateURL = wbFrmSkyShark.aspx?subform=VTS |
| Hyperlink | Hyperlink3 | Text=View Flight Status |
| | | NavigateURL = wbFrmSkyShark.aspx?subform=VFS |
| Hyperlink | Hyperlink4 | Text=Confirm Reservation |
| | | NavigateURL = wbFrmSkyShark.aspx?subform=CR |
| Hyperlink | Hyperlink5 | Text=Home |
| | | NavigateURL = wbFrmSkyShark.aspx?subform=H |

If you notice, each panel is placed in different locations on the form. However, at run time, only one panel will appear on the screen, depending on the choice of the user. Therefore, you should align each panel at the same location before loading the form. You can do so by changing the `Left` and `Top` attributes of the panels in the `Load` event of the Web form, as given in the code that follows:

```
private void Page_Load(object sender, System.EventArgs e)
{
   Panel2.Style["left"]="222px";
   Panel2.Style["Top"]="152px";
   Panel3.Style["lcft"]-"222px";
   Panel3.Style["Top"]="152px";
   Panel4.Style["left"]="222px";
   Panel4.Style["Top"]="152px";
}
```

The wbFrmSkyShark.aspx uses the `dtFltDetails` table to retrieve the flight details. Before you write the code for the wbFrmSkyShark.aspx form, drag the `dtFltDetails` table from Server Explorer to the design view of the form. Visual

Studio .NET automatically configures SqlDataAdapter and SqlConnection controls for the form. You can read a description of these controls in Chapter 19, "Basics of ASP.NET Web Applications," in the section "Coding the Application."

After you add SqlDataAdapter and SqlConnection controls to the form, you can generate a dataset for the form. To generate the dataset, follow these steps:

1. Click anywhere on the form.
2. Click on the Data menu and select Generate Dataset. The Generate Dataset dialog box will appear.
3. In the Generate Dataset dialog box, click on the New option and in the corresponding box, enter `dsFlight` and click on OK.
4. A new DataSet control is added to your project.

All three data controls are visible in Component Designer in the Design view of the form, as you can see in Figure 22-1. I will now proceed with the implementation of the functionality that was discussed in the beginning of the chapter.

## The View New Flights Option

This option displays the details of the five most recent flights launched by the SkyShark Airlines in a DataGrid control. To implement this functionality, create a procedure named `Display_NewFlights()`. The code for this procedure is given as follows.

```
public void Display_NewFlights()
{
     string SelStr;
     SelStr = "Select top 5 fltno, origin, destination, deptime, fareexec,
        farebn, launchdate from dtfltdetails order by launchdate";
     SqlCommand SelComm;
     SelComm = new SqlCommand(SelStr, sqlConnection1);
     sqlDataAdapter1.SelectCommand = SelComm;
     sqlDataAdapter1.Fill(dsFlight1,"Details");
     DataView source= new DataView(dsFlight1.Tables["Details"]);
     DataGrid1.DataSource=source;
     DataGrid1.DataBind();
     DataGrid1.Visible = true;
}
```

This procedure will retrieve the data stored in the `fltno`, `origin`, `destination`, `deptime`, `fareexec`, `farebn`, and `launchdate` columns of the `dtFltDetails` table. The retrieved data is displayed in the `DataGrid1` control. This procedure will be called from the `Page_Load` event of the wbFrmSkyShark.aspx page.

## The View Ticket Status Option

This option will enable the customer to view the status of her ticket. To view the status, the customer needs to provide the ticket number and e-mail ID. These values are then validated against the values stored in the `dtReservations` table in the database. If either the ticket number or the e-mail ID provided is incorrect, then a suitable error will be displayed.

You will accept the values from the customer in the `txtTicketNo` and `txtEMail` text boxes contained on Panel3. Table 22-3 lists all the controls contained in Panel3.

**Table 22-3 Controls in Panel3**

| Control Type | ID | Properties Changed |
|---|---|---|
| TextBox | txtTicketNo | None |
| TextBox | txtEMail | None |
| Button | btnSubmit | Text=Submit |

The values entered in the text boxes are validated and the corresponding result is displayed on the click of the Submit button. The code for the `Click` event of the Submit button is given as follows.

```
private void btnSubmit_Click(object sender, System.EventArgs e)
{
     string strSel;
     int status;
     strSel = "Select email, status from dtReservations where TicketNo = @TN";
     SqlCommand SelComm;
     SelComm = new SqlCommand(strSel, sqlConnection1);
     sqlDataAdapter1.SelectCommand = SelComm;
     sqlDataAdapter1.SelectCommand.Parameters.Add("@TN", SqlDbType.Char, 10).Value
        = txtTicketNo.Text ;
```

```
        SqlDataReader rdrTicket;
        sqlConnection1.Open();
        rdrTicket = sqlDataAdapter1.SelectCommand.ExecuteReader();

        if( rdrTicket.Read())
        {
             if( rdrTicket.GetString(0).Trim() == txtEMail.Text )
             {
                  status = rdrTicket.GetInt32(1);
             }
             else
             {
                  lblStatus.ForeColor = Color.Red ;
                  lblStatus.Text = "Incorrect EMail ID!!";
                  return;
             }
        }
        else
        {
             lblStatus.ForeColor = Color.Red ;
             lblStatus.Text = "Incorrect Ticket Number!!";
             return;
        }
         sqlConnection1.Close();
        if(status >= 0)
        {
             lblStatus.ForeColor = Color.Blue ;
             lblStatus.Text = "Your ticket is confirmed";
        }
        else
        {
             lblStatus.ForeColor = Color.Blue ;
             lblStatus.Text = "Your ticket is overbooked by " + Convert.ToString
                (status);
        }
}
```

## The View Flight Status Option

This option will enable the customer to view the booking status of a flight. To view the status, the customer needs to provide the flight number. The code then searches for the booking status of the flight in the `dtFltStatus` table and displays the result. If the flight number is incorrect, then an error message is displayed.

You will accept the values from the customer in the `txtFlightNo` text box contained on Panel2. Table 22-4 lists all the controls contained in Panel2.

**Table 22-4 Controls in Panel2**

| Control Type | ID | Properties Changed |
|---|---|---|
| TextBox | txtFlightNo | None |
| Button | btnSubmit1 | Text=Submit |

The booking status of the flight is displayed on the click of the Submit button. If the value entered is incorrect, an error message is displayed. The code for the `Click` event of the Submit button is given as follows.

```
private void btnSubmit1_Click(object sender, System.EventArgs e)
{
     string strSel;
     int status;
     strSel = "Select status from dtfltstatus where FltNo = @FN";
     SqlCommand SelComm;
     SelComm = new SqlCommand(strSel, sqlConnection1);
     sqlDataAdapter1.SelectCommand = SelComm;
     sqlDataAdapter1.SelectCommand.Parameters.Add("@FN",
   SqlDbType.Char, 10).Value = txtFlightNo.Text ;
     SqlDataReader rdrTicket;
     sqlConnection1.Open();
     rdrTicket = sqlDataAdapter1.SelectCommand.ExecuteReader();
     if( rdrTicket.Read())
     {
          status = rdrTicket.GetInt32(0);
     }
```

```
        else
        {
             lblStatus.ForeColor = Color.Red ;
             lblStatus.Text = "Incorrect Flight Number!!";
             return;
        }
        sqlConnection1.Close();
        if(status >= 0)
        {
        lblStatus.ForeColor = Color.Blue ;
             lblStatus.Text = "Ticket is available";
        }
        else
        {
             lblStatus.ForeColor = Color.Blue ;
             lblStatus.Text = "Flight is overbooked by " +
      Convert.ToString(status);
        }

}
```

## The Confirm Reservation Option

This option will enable the customer to confirm a reservation. To do so, the customer will need to provide the ticket number and the e-mail ID, which are then validated against the values stored in the `dtReservations` table of the database. If either of the two values is incorrect, an appropriate error message is displayed.

You will accept the values from the customer in the `txtTktNo` and `txtEml` text boxes contained on Panel4. Table 22-5 lists various controls present on Panel4.

**Table 22-5 Controls in Panel4**

| Control Type | ID | Properties Changed |
|---|---|---|
| TextBox | txtTktNo | None |
| TextBox | txtEml | None |
| Button | btnSubmit2 | Text=Submit |

These values are validated and the corresponding result is displayed on the click of the Submit button. The code for the `Click` event of the Submit button is given as follows.

```
private void btnSubmit2_Click(object sender, System.EventArgs e)
{
	string strSel;
	bool status;
	strSel = "Select email, ticketconfirmed from dtReservations where
		TicketNo = @TN";
	SqlCommand SelComm;
	SelComm = new SqlCommand(strSel, sqlConnection1);
	sqlDataAdapter1.SelectCommand = SelComm;
	sqlDataAdapter1.SelectCommand.Parameters.Add("@TN",
		SqlDbType.Char, 10).Value = txtTktNo.Text ;
	SqlDataReader rdrTicket;
	sqlConnection1.Open();
	rdrTicket = sqlDataAdapter1.SelectCommand.ExecuteReader();
	if( rdrTicket.Read())
	{
		if( rdrTicket.GetString(0).Trim() == txtEml.Text )
		{
			status = rdrTicket.GetBoolean(1);
		}
	else
		{
			lblStatus.ForeColor = Color.Red ;
			lblStatus.Text = "Incorrect EMail ID!!";
			return;
		}
	}
```

```
        else
        {
            lblStatus.ForeColor = Color.Red ;
            lblStatus.Text = "Incorrect Ticket Number!!";
            return;
        }
        sqlConnection1.Close();
        if(status == true)
        {
            lblStatus.ForeColor = Color.Blue ;
            lblStatus.Text = "Your ticket has already been confirmed!!";
        }
        else
        {
            string UpdStr;
            UpdStr= "Update dtReservations set ticketconfirmed = 1 where
              ticketno = @TN";
            SqlCommand UpdComm;
            UpdComm = new SqlCommand(UpdStr, sqlConnection1);
            sqlDataAdapter1.UpdateCommand = UpdComm;
            sqlDataAdapter1.UpdateCommand.Parameters.Add("@TN",
               SqlDbType.Char, 10).Value = txtTktNo.Text ;
            sqlConnection1.Open();
            sqlDataAdapter1.UpdateCommand.ExecuteNonQuery ();
            sqlConnection1.Close ();
            lblStatus.ForeColor = Color.Blue ;
            lblStatus.Text = "Your ticket has been confirmed!!";
        }
}
```

This finishes the code for various options. These codes are executed after the page is loaded. Therefore, I will now list the code for the `Page_Load` event of the wbFrmSkyShark.aspx page.

```
private void Page_Load(object sender, System.EventArgs e)
{
    // Put user code to initialize the page here
    Panel2.Style["left"]="222px";
```

```
        Panel2.Style["Top"]="152px";
        Panel3.Style["left"]="222px";
        Panel3.Style["Top"]="152px";
        Panel4.Style["left"]="222px";
        Panel4.Style["Top"]="152px";

        if(Request.QueryString.Count == 0)
        {
            return;
        }
        else
        {
        string param;
            param = Request.QueryString.Get(0).ToString();
            switch(param)
            {
                case "VNF":
                Display_NewFlights();
                break;
                case "VTS":
                Panel3.Visible = true;
                break;
                case "VFS":
                Panel2.Visible = true;
                break;
                case "CR":
                Panel4.Visible = true;
                break;
                case "H":
                break;
                default:
                break;
            }
        }
    }
```

This listing completes the coding part. I will now discuss the testing of this application.

# Testing the Application

To test the application, perform the following steps:

1. Execute the application. The wbFrmSkyShark.aspx Web form appears as shown in Figure 22-2.

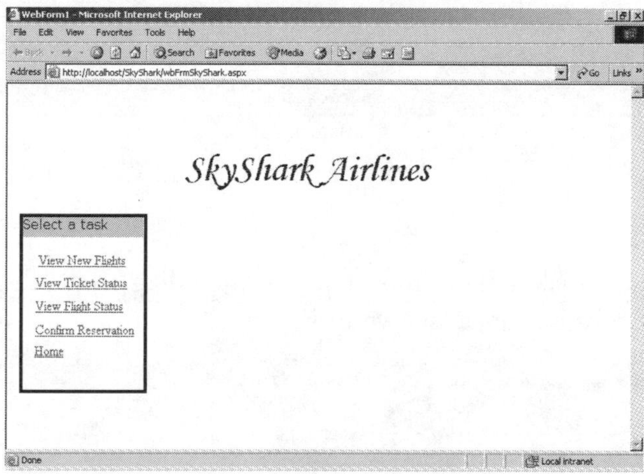


**FIGURE 22-2** *The home page*

2. Click on the View New Flights link. DataGrid1 appears, as shown in Figure 22-3, containing the appropriate records.

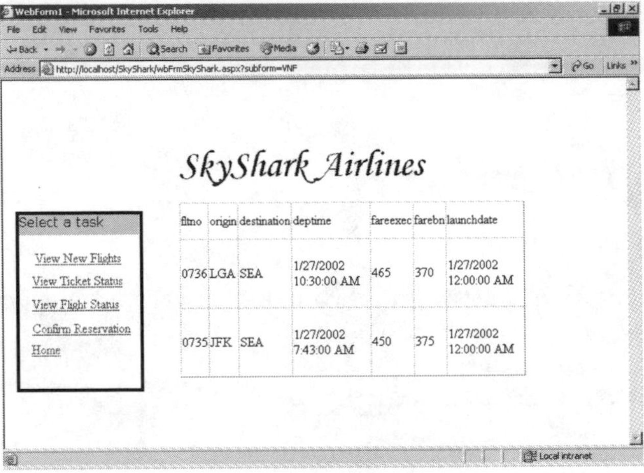


**FIGURE 22-3** *The details of new flights*

3. Click on the View Ticket Status link. The corresponding screen displays two text boxes and a button, as shown in Figure 22-4.

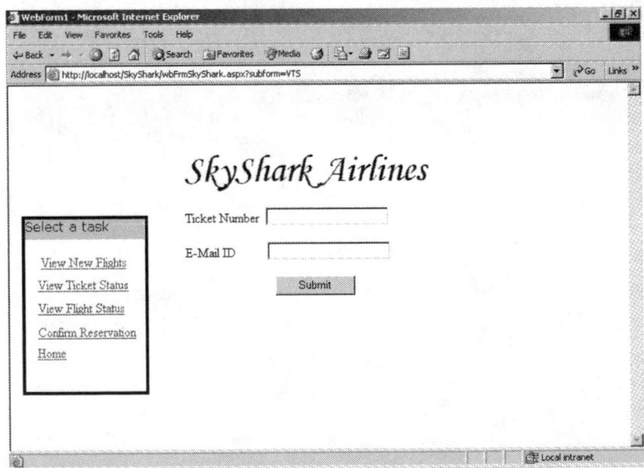


**FIGURE 22-4** *The screen to check the ticket status*

4. Enter test values in both the text boxes and click the Submit button. If both the values are correct, the status is displayed. Otherwise, an error message is displayed.
5. Click on the View Flight Status link. The corresponding screen displays a text box and a button, as shown in Figure 22-5.

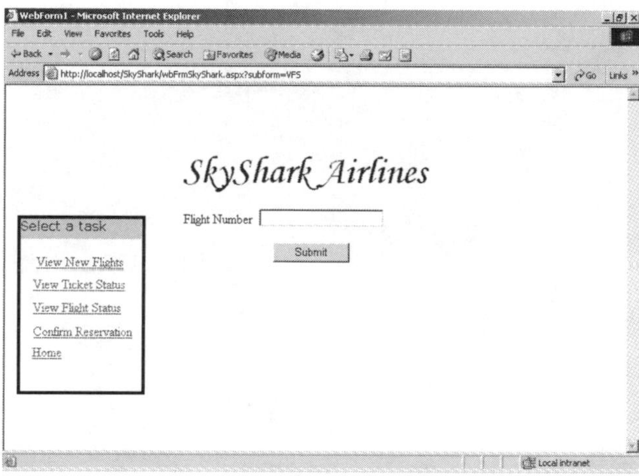


**FIGURE 22-5** *The screen to check the flight status*

6. Enter an appropriate value in the Flight Number text box and click the Submit button. If the provided value is correct, the booking status of the flight is displayed. Otherwise, an error message is displayed.
7. Click on the Confirm Reservation link. The corresponding screen displays two text boxes and a button, as shown in Figure 22-6.

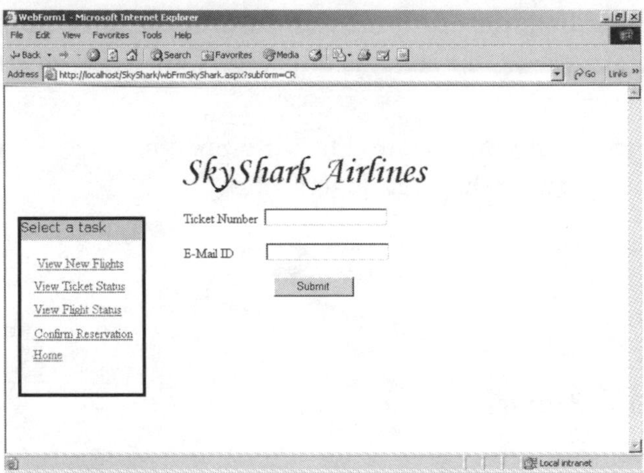


**FIGURE 22-6** *The screen to confirm reservation*

8. Enter some appropriate values in both the text boxes and click the Submit button. If both the values are correct, then the reservation is confirmed. Otherwise, an error message is displayed.
9. Click on the Home link. The home page appears.

This completes the testing of the customer portal of SkyShark Airlines.

# Summary

In this chapter, you learned how to create the customer transaction portal of SkyShark Airlines. Next, you learned about the interface of the form and the programming logic to add functionality to the form. Finally, you examined the steps to test the application and ensure that it operates correctly.

# Chapter 23

## Debugging and Testing the Application

You have developed the SkyShark Airlines application. Suppose you compile the application and run it. The application does run; however, it generates error messages or displays dialog boxes that might not be interpretable by end users. By debugging your application, you can track and eliminate these errors.

Visual Studio .NET provides several options to help you in such situations. In this chapter, I will discuss the various debugging tools provided by Visual Studio .NET to debug these errors. This chapter also discusses the points to be considered while testing the application.

## Locating Errors in Programs

One of the most difficult tasks in developing an application is finding errors. With Visual Studio .NET it is very simple to trace syntax errors. Visual Studio .NET warns you about syntax errors at the time of writing the code itself. In addition, these errors are listed when you compile the program in the Output window.

Visual Studio .NET provides you with a number of debugging tools and options to enable you to write error-free programs. You can see these tools and options while debugging a Visual Studio .NET program in the *break* mode. A program is in break mode when any error halts the execution of your program temporarily. You can also introduce a breakpoint in your application. When your application encounters a breakpoint, it enters the break mode. This mode enables you to examine the status of your application by using other debugging tools provided by Visual Studio .NET.

A program can be forced to enter the break mode by setting a breakpoint. You can set a breakpoint simply by placing the cursor on a line and pressing the F9 key. You can also set a breakpoint as follows: On the Debug menu, click the New Breakpoint option. The New Breakpoint dialog box appears as shown in Figure 23-1.

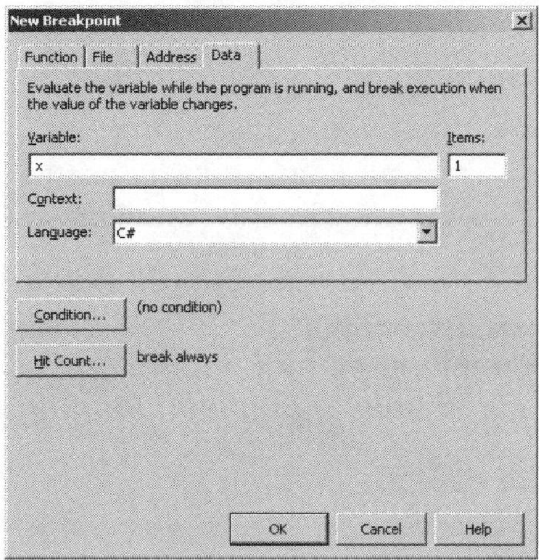


**FIGURE 23-1** *The New Breakpoint dialog box*

You can also enter the break mode from within your code by using the `Stop` statement.

Visual Studio .NET has four types of breakpoints, as follows:

- **Function breakpoint.** Temporarily puts the program execution on hold when the program execution reaches a specific position within a function.
- **File breakpoint.** Causes the program execution to halt when it reaches a specified position within the specified file.
- **Address breakpoint.** Causes the program to break when execution reaches a specific memory location.
- **Data breakpoint.** Causes the program execution to halt when the value of a variable changes.

The advantage of the break mode is that it enables you to modify the values of variables and properties. Now I will discuss other debugging tools available with Visual Studio .NET.

## Watch Window

The Watch window is useful to monitor values of variables and expressions. You can add variables to the Watch window by entering the variable name in the Name column of the window or by selecting QuickWatch option from the Debug window. The Watch window can be invoked only from the break mode. Figure 23-2 displays the Watch window.

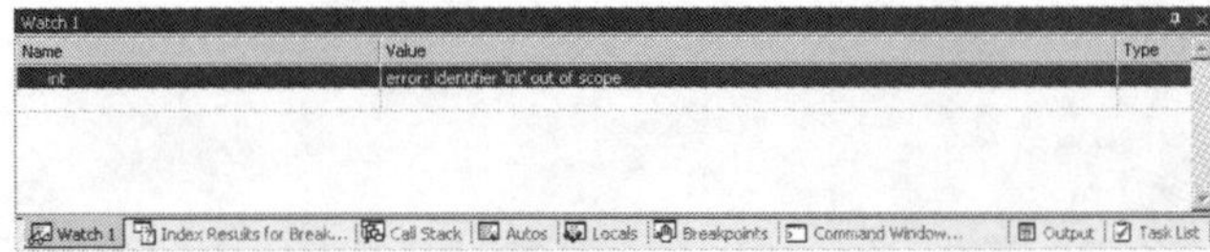


**FIGURE 23-2** *The Watch window*

## Locals Window

The Locals window displays variables that are local to the current execution context, such as the current function or module. In order to open the Locals window, you must be in debugging mode. To open the Locals window, on the Debug menu, point to Windows, and then click Locals. Figure 23-3 shows the Locals window.

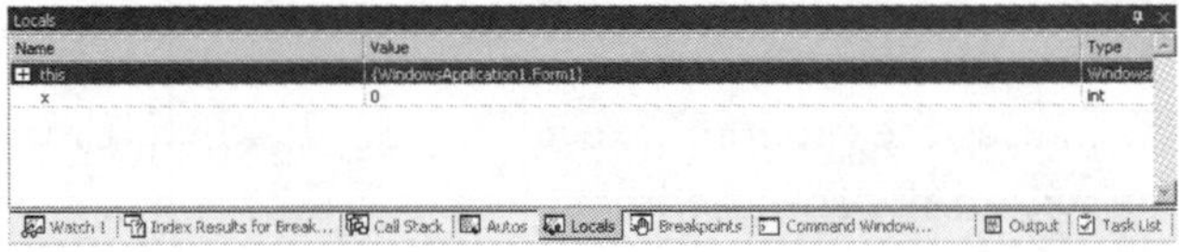


**FIGURE 23-3** *The Locals window*

## Call Stack Window

The Call Stack window lists the functions and procedure calls that are currently loaded in memory in the order in which they were called. You can view this window only in the break mode. The Call Stack window displays the sequence of program execution. The Call Stack window is shown in Figure 23-4.

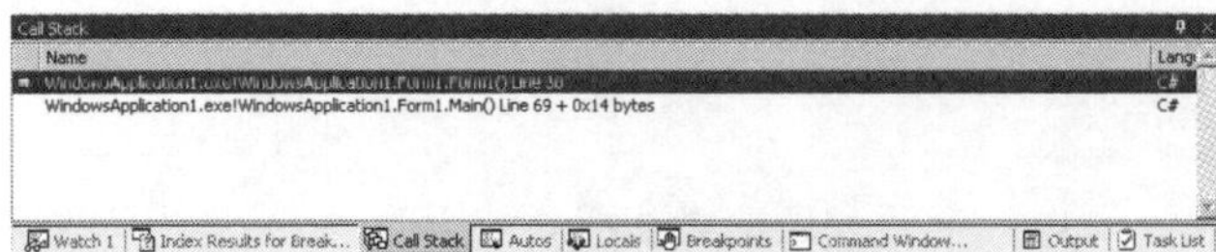

**FIGURE 23-4** *The Call Stack window*

## Autos Window

The Autos window displays the name of all variables in the current and previous statement. You need not specify the name of the variable. The Visual Studio .NET debugger automatically identifies the variables in the current execution location statement and displays them in the window. Figure 23-5 displays the Autos window.

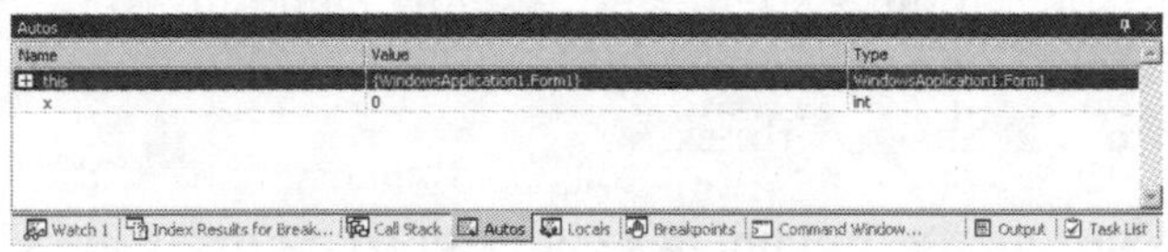

**FIGURE 23-5** *The Autos window*

## Command Window

The Command window is used to evaluate expressions or issue commands when in the debug mode. To open the Command window, perform the following steps:

On the View menu, point to Other Windows.

In the displayed list, click on the Command Window option.

The Command window has two modes, Command and Immediate. Command mode is used to issue Visual Studio .NET commands, while the Immediate mode is used for debugging purposes, evaluating expressions, and printing variable values. For example, `? num`, where `num` represents a variable, will return the value stored in the variable. Figure 23-6 displays the Command window.

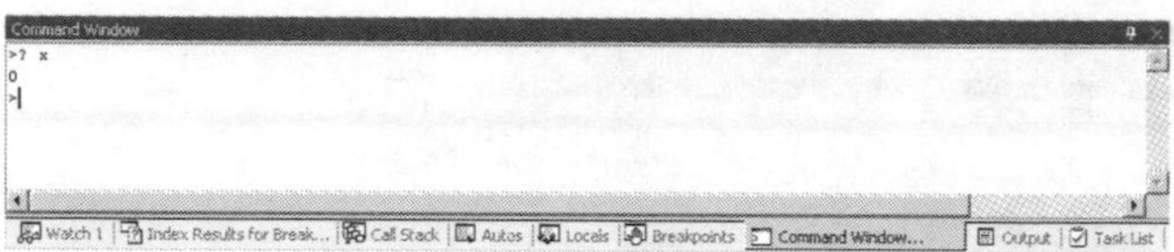


**FIGURE 23-6** *The Command window*

Having learned about the basics of debugging an application, you can test the SkyShark Airlines application. The following section discusses how to test the Web site developed for SkyShark Airlines.

# Testing the Application

After creating the application, you need to test the application. Testing enables you to verify that your application is secure and running smoothly. In addition, testing the Web site ensures that there are no dead links in your Web site. You can now test the Web site for SkyShark Airlines.

While testing the application, you will log in as three different users and test the functionality associated with each of the users. To start with, you will log in as the network administrator. To do this, perform the following steps:

1. Execute the application. The default.aspx page appears as shown in Figure 23-7.

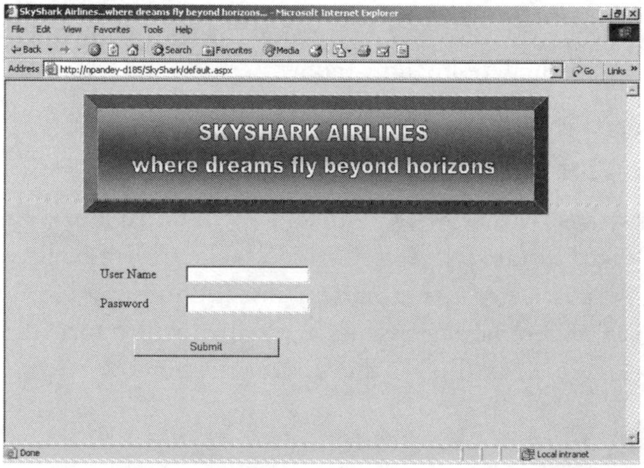

**FIGURE 23-7** *The default.aspx page*

2. In the User Name box, enter the user name as `admin`. The admin account is created by default when you create the application.
3. In the Password box, enter the password as `password`.
4. Click on the Submit button. The ManageUsers.aspx page appears, as shown in Figure 23-8. This page helps the network administrators to add or delete users.

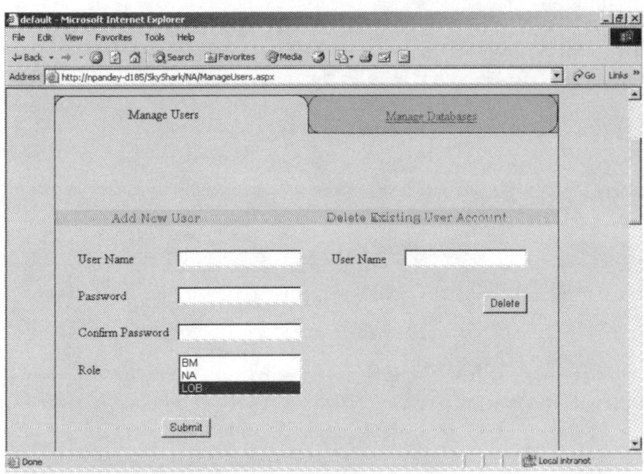


**FIGURE 23-8** *The ManageUsers.aspx page*

5. Next, you will add a new user to the application. This user will be added as a business manager. To do this, enter the following details on the form to add new users:

   User Name: `RobertB`

   Password: `Password`

   Confirm Password: `Password`

   Role: `BM`
6. Click on the Submit button. A message appears, as shown in Figure 23-9, indicating that the user was successfully added. Now you will log on using the credentials of this new user and test the functionality provided to a business manager.

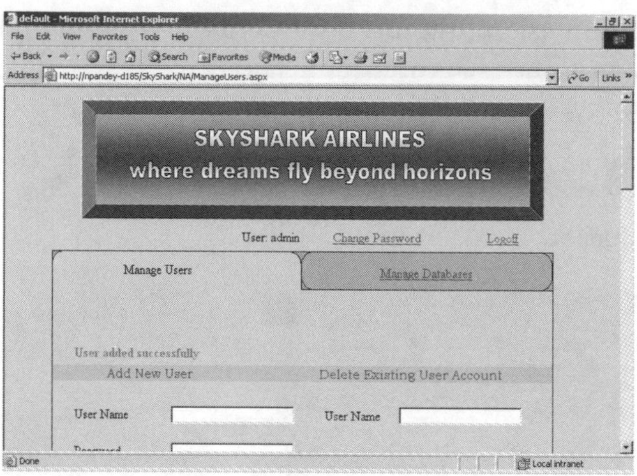


**FIGURE 23-9** *Adding a new user*

7. Click on the Logoff link. The Logoff.aspx page appears as shown in Figure 23-10.

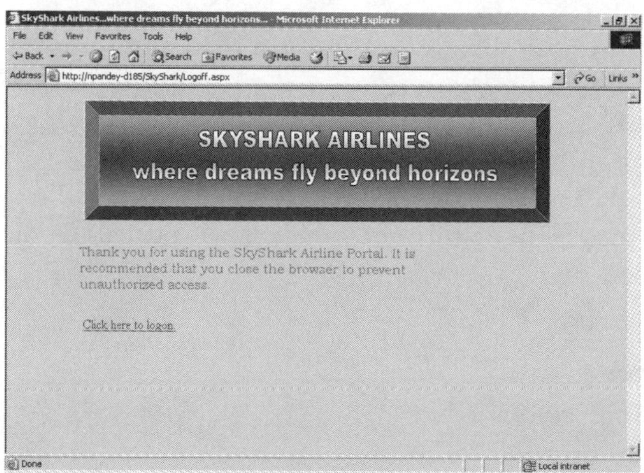


**FIGURE 23-10** *Logging off the application*

8. Click on the Click here to logon link to enter the application as a business manager.
9. Enter the username and password that you entered in Step 5, and click on the Submit button. The Addfl.aspx page appears as shown in Figure 23-11. This page helps a business manager to add new flights. In addition, a business manager can generate various reports.

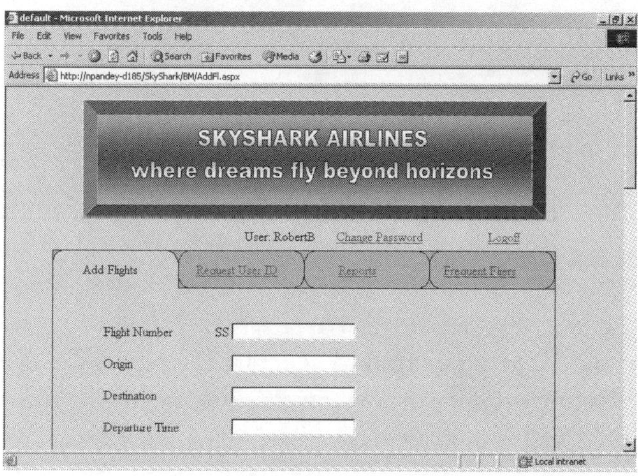


**FIGURE 23-11** *The page to add new flights*

10. Click on the Reports link. The Reports.aspx page appears, as shown in Figure 23-12. A business manager can use this page to view different reports.

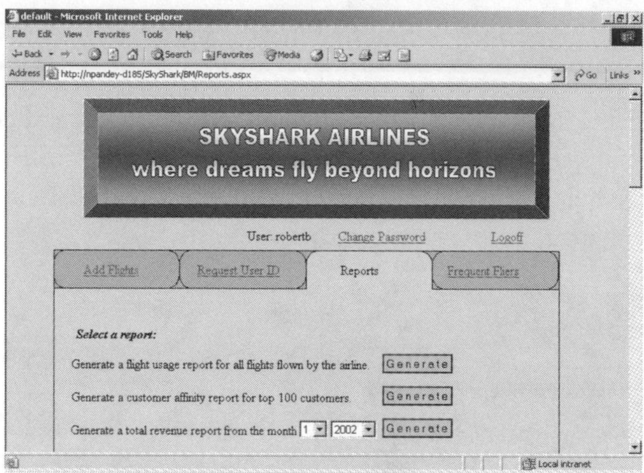


**FIGURE 23-12** *The page to view reports*

11. Click on the second Generate button to generate the report for the top 100 customers. The report appears as shown in Figure 23-13. You will now log in as a line-of-business executive.

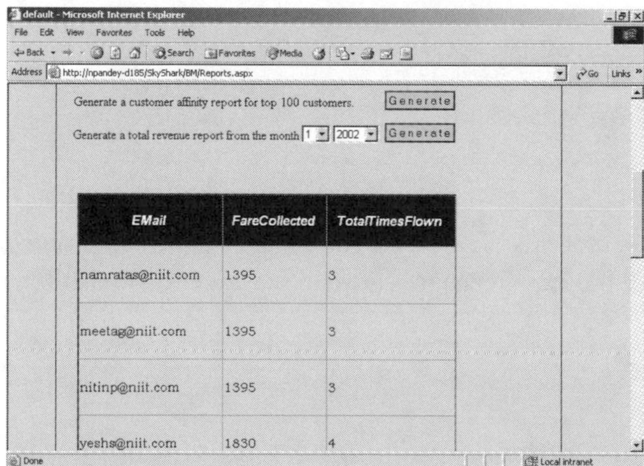


**FIGURE 23-13** *The report generated by the Web site*

12. Click on the Logoff link. The Logoff.aspx page appears.
13. Click on the Click here to logon link to log in to the Web site. The default.aspx page appears.
14. In the User Name box, type the username as `meetag`.
15. In the Password box, type the password as `password`.

    Click on the Submit button. The CreateRes.aspx page appears as shown in Figure 23-14.

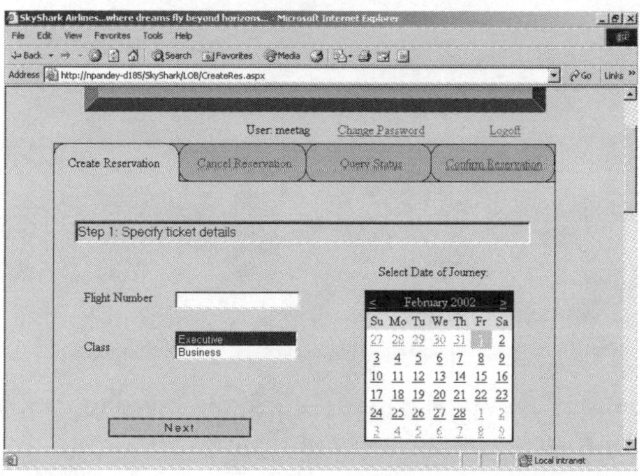


**FIGURE 23-14** *The CreateRes.aspx page*

16. In the Flight Number box, enter `0735`.
17. Click on the Next button. The details of the flight appear, as shown in Figure 23-15. You may need to scroll down.

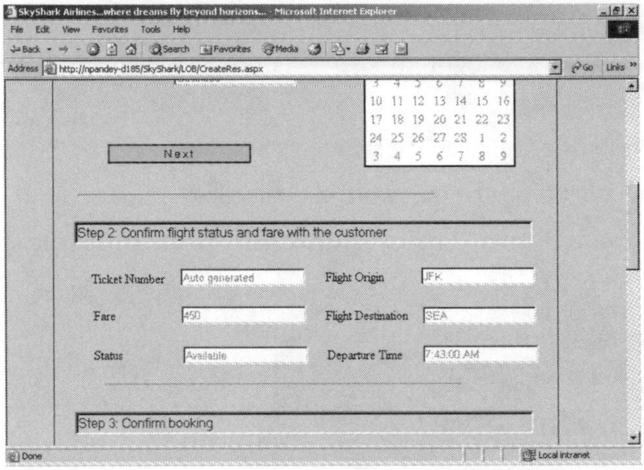

FIGURE 23-15 *The flight details*

18. In the Customer Name box, enter `John Smith`.
19. In the E-Mail ID box, enter `JohnS@xyz.com`.
20. Click on the Create Reservation button. A ticket is issued to the customer in the Ticket.aspx page, as shown in Figure 23-16.

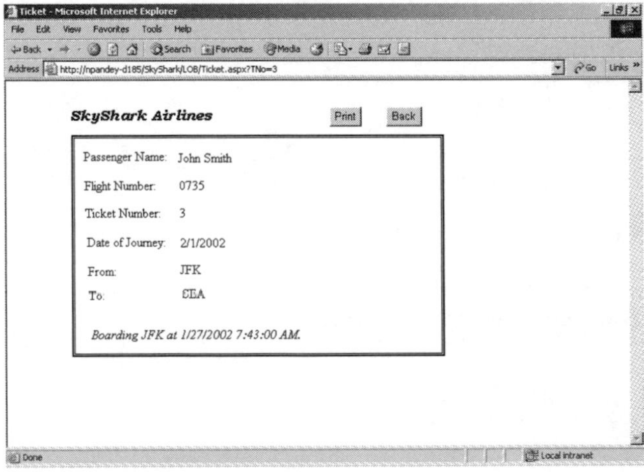


FIGURE 23-16 *The ticket issued to a customer*

21. Click the Back button.
22. Click on the Logoff link.

The user is logged off from the site.

With this, you have tested all the functionalities provided by the system.

# Summary

In this chapter, you learned about the basics of debugging an application. Next, you learned about the tools provided by Visual Studio .NET for debugging an application. Finally, you tested the Web site developed for SkyShark Airlines.

# Chapter 24

## Administering the Application

In the preceding chapters, you learned to create the SkyShark Airlines Web application and test it. After an application is successfully created, a network administrator needs to perform regular maintenance tasks to ensure that the application operates optimally.

Two common tasks that need to be performed by network administrators to ensure that the application operates optimally are database management and Web server management. In this chapter, I explain how these tasks are performed. You need to perform these tasks regularly to ensure that the SkyShark Airlines is operational at all times.

## Managing the Databases

Database management tasks are performed using SQL Server Enterprise Manager. The database management tasks that a network administrator needs to perform for the SkyShark Airlines application are summarized in the following list:

- Manage user accounts
- Move data from the dtReservations and dtPassengerDetails tables
- Back up the SkyShark database
- Export data from the dtDepartedFlights and dtCancellations tables
- Review database logs on a timely basis
- Schedule database maintenance tasks

In the list of preceding tasks, the SkyShark Airlines application can be used to perform the first two tasks. However, SQL Server Enterprise Manager can help you perform the remaining tasks easily. Therefore, in this section, you will learn to use Enterprise Manager to perform database administration tasks.

## Backing Up the SkyShark Airlines Databases

To back up the SkyShark Airlines database, you first need to launch Enterprise Manager. To launch Enterprise Manager in SQL Server 2000, perform the steps given as follows:

1. Click on the Start menu. The Start menu will appear.
2. On the Start menu, point to Programs and then point to Microsoft SQL Server.
3. From the Microsoft SQL Server submenu, select Enterprise Manager. The SQL Server Enterprise Manager window will open.

After you open the SQL Server Enterprise Manager window, navigate to the SkyShark database by performing the following steps:

1. Under Console Root, double-click on Microsoft SQL Servers. The list of SQL Server groups registered on the SQL Server will appear.
2. Click on the + (plus) sign next to the SQL Server groups and then click on the + sign next to the server on which you had created the database.
3. Next, click on the + sign next to the Databases folder. The SkyShark Airlines database will appear in the list of databases, as shown in Figure 24-1.

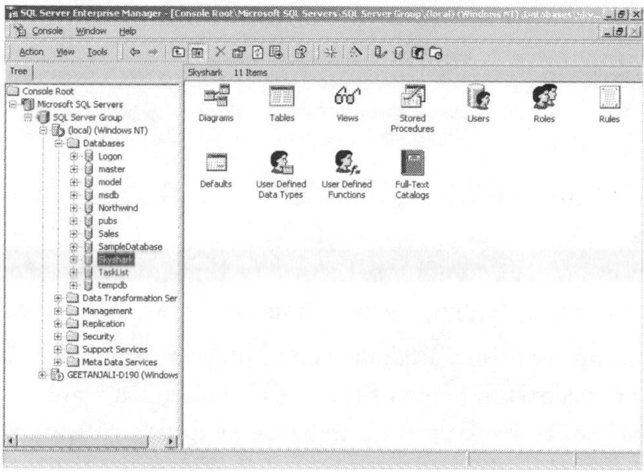


**FIGURE 24-1** *Path to the SkyShark database*

After you navigate to the database, follow these steps to make a backup of the database:

1. Right-click on the name of the database and point to All Tasks.
2. From the All Tasks submenu, select Backup Database. The SQL Server Backup - SkyShark dialog box will appear, which is shown in Figure 24-2.

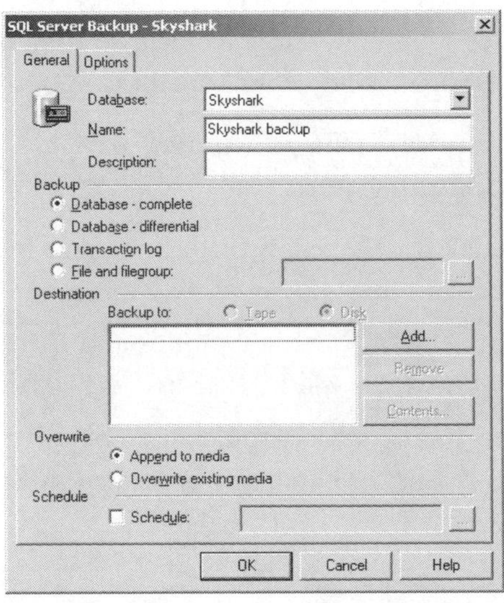


**FIGURE 24-2** *Backing up a database*

3. Before you can back up a database, you need to specify a device to which you want to back up. For example, you can back up a database to a Tape drive or a location on your computer. To specify a new backup device, click on Add. The Select Backup Destination dialog box will appear.
4. In the Select Backup Destination dialog box, you can either specify a backup device or specify the name of the file to which you want to backup the database. To back up the database in a directory, specify the location and name of the file as C:\Program Files\Microsoft SQL Server\MSSQL\BACKUP\SkyShark_Backup in the File name text box.

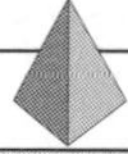

**TIP**

The default location of the backup folder is C:\Program Files\Microsoft SQL Server \MSSQL\BACKUP\.

5. Click on OK to close the Select Backup Destination dialog box. The file name that you specified in Step 5 will appear in the Backup to list.
6. Click on the Options tab of the SQL Server Backup - SkyShark dialog box.
7. On the Options tab, check the Verify backup upon completion option.
8. Click on OK. The SQL Server Backup - SkyShark dialog box will close, and SQL Server will start backing up your database.

SQL Server will display the Backup Progress dialog box when the backup is in progress. Upon successfully completing the backup, it will display a dialog box to indicate that the backup was completed successfully.

Instead of backing up your databases manually each time, you can also create a schedule to back up databases on a regular basis. I will discuss the procedure to periodically back up databases in the "Scheduling Database Maintenance Tasks" section of this chapter.

## Exporting Data from Databases

The dtDepartedFlights and dtPassengerDetails tables are used for storing data pertaining to flights that have departed and the names of passengers on these flights respectively. Data in these tables will tend to become redundant over time. For example, you might not need to maintain a list of passengers who have flown a particular flight that departed a month ago. Therefore, you can archive this data into another data store and delete it from the database.

To move data from one database to another, you can use the SQL Server DTS (*Data Transformation Services*) tasks. To use a DTS task for exporting data from the dtDepartedFlights table, follow these steps:

1. Double-click on SkyShark in SQL Server Enterprise Manager to view a list of objects in the database.

2. Under SkyShark, right-click on Tables and point the mouse over All Tasks. From the All Tasks submenu, select Export Data. The DTS Import/Export Wizard will be launched.
3. On the Welcome screen of the DTS Import/Export Wizard, click on Next. The Choose a Data Source screen of the wizard will appear. Notice that the name of the SkyShark database is already selected in the Database list.
4. Click on Next. The Choose a destination screen of the wizard will appear. This screen is shown in Figure 24-3.

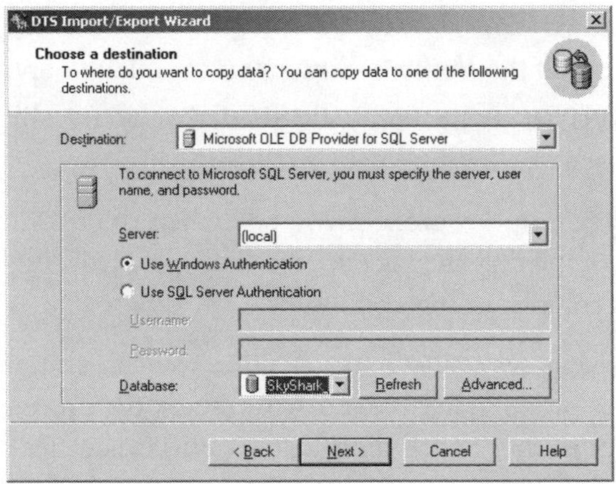


**FIGURE 24-3** *The Choose a destination screen of the DTS Import/Export Wizard*

5. Select the database to which you want to back up data. For example, I have selected the SkyShark_Archive database. Click on Next to continue. The Select Tablc Copy or Query screen will appear.
6. On the Select Table Copy or Query screen, retain the default option to copy a table and click on Next. The Select Source Tables and Views screen will appear as shown in Figure 24-4.

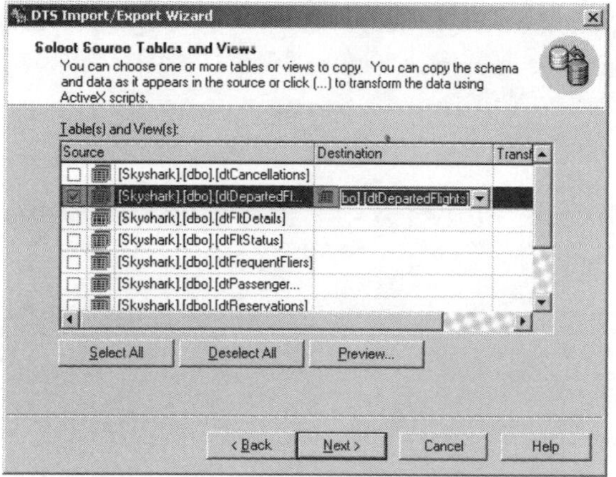


**FIGURE 24-4** *The Select Source Tables and Views screen of the DTS Import/Export Wizard*

7. Check the dtDepartedFlights table and click on Next. The Save, schedule, and replicate package screen will appear.
8. To run the DTS task immediately, click on Next. The Completing the DTS Import/Export screen will appear.
9. Click on Finish to run the DTS task.

While the DTS task executes successfully, the Execute Package dialog box is open. When the task is complete, a dialog box appears signifying the successful execution of the DTS task. Click on OK to close the dialog box and then click on Done to close the Execute Package dialog box.

After you copy data from the dtDepartedFlights table, you can delete the data in this table from the SkyShark database.

## Examining Database Logs

Every activity in SQL Server is logged in a log file. You can examine these log files on a periodic basis to track all activities on the database and identify any errors that SQL Server might encounter. To view the SQL Server log files, follow these steps:

1. In Enterprise Manager, double-click on Management under the entry for the SQL Server for which you want to view log files.

2. Under Management, click on SQL Server Logs. The SQL Server logs appear in the right pane, as shown in Figure 24-5.

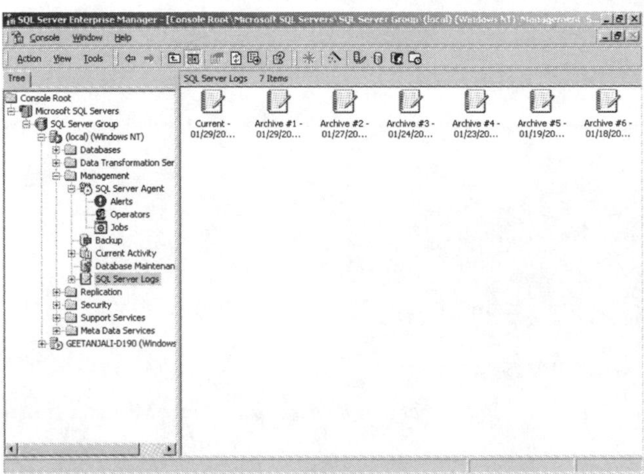

**FIGURE 24-5** *Viewing the SQL Server log files*

3. To view any log file, double-click on the log file. The information logs in the log file that you select will appear. You can view these entries to detect any error in your databases.

## Scheduling Database Maintenance Tasks

Having examined how to back up databases and analyze SQL Server log files, you can examine how to create scheduled database maintenance tasks so that the process of backing up databases is automated. To create a maintenance task for the SkyShark database, follow these steps:

1. Right-click on the name of the database in Enterprise Manager and select the Maintenance Plan menu option from the All Tasks menu. The Database Maintenance Plan Wizard will be launched.
2. On the Welcome screen of the wizard, click on Next. The Select Databases screen of the wizard will appear. Notice that the SkyShark database is already selected.

3. Click on Next until you reach the Specify the Database Backup Plan screen.
4. On the Specify the Database Backup Plan screen, click on Change to specify a schedule for backing up databases. The Edit Recurring Job Schedule screen will appear.
5. On the Edit Recurring Job Schedule screen, specify the schedule to back up databases. For example, I have created a schedule to back up the database daily at 12:00 A.M., as shown in Figure 24-6.

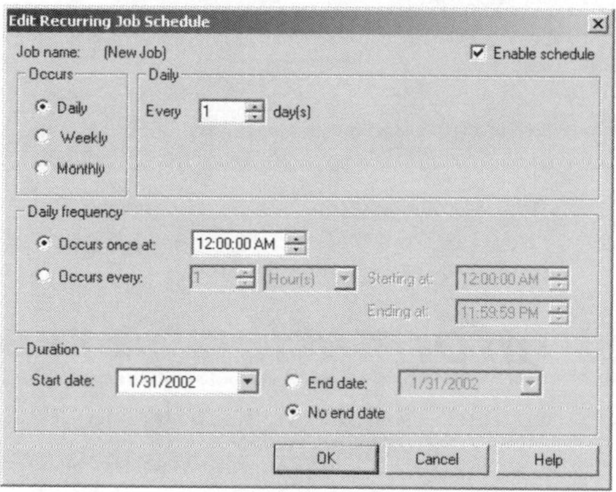


**FIGURE 24-6** *Specifying a schedule to back up databases*

6. Click on OK. The Specify the Database Backup Plan screen will reappear. Click on Next to continue.
7. Click on Next until you reach the Completing the Database Maintenance Plan Wizard screen.
8. On the Completing the Database Maintenance Plan Wizard screen, specify a name for the maintenance plan or retain the default name and click on Finish.

The maintenance tasks that you schedule are listed in the Database Maintenance Plans section of Enterprise Manager as shown in Figure 24-7.

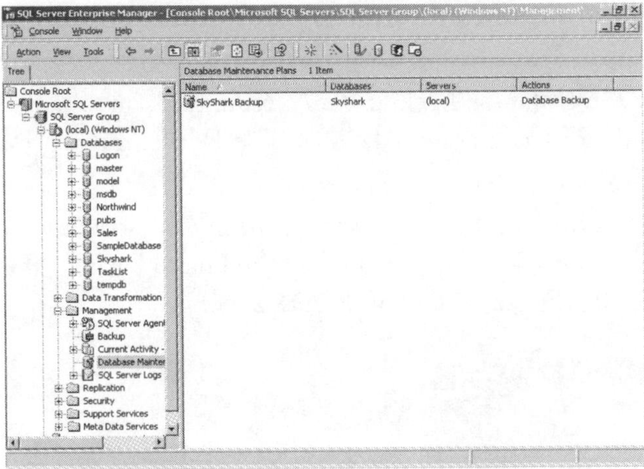

**FIGURE 24-7** *Viewing a list of maintenance tasks*

# Managing Internet Information Server

You can optimize the SkyShark Airlines Web application by modifying the Web.Config file or by using Internet Services Manager, which is the administration tool for IIS (*Internet Information Server*). Internet Services Manager is an MMC (*Microsoft Management Console*) based console that can be used to manage IIS Server. By using Internet Information Services, you can add and remove Web sites, control access to Web sites, and start and stop the IIS server. In this section, you will examine the steps to configure HTTP error pages and Web server log files for the SkyShark Airlines application. To configure the error pages and Web server log files, I will use the Web.Config file and Internet Information Services MMC add-in, respectively.

## Configuring IIS Error Pages

A default set of error pages is associated with IIS. Error pages are HTML pages that are numbered according to the error that they represent. These pages are displayed when HTTP errors occur while browsing the Web site. For example, if IIS encounters an error while processing a request, an internal server error is generated, which is the HTTP error number 500. Similarly, if the user requests a Web page that does not exist, error 404 is generated, which is shown in Figure 24-8.

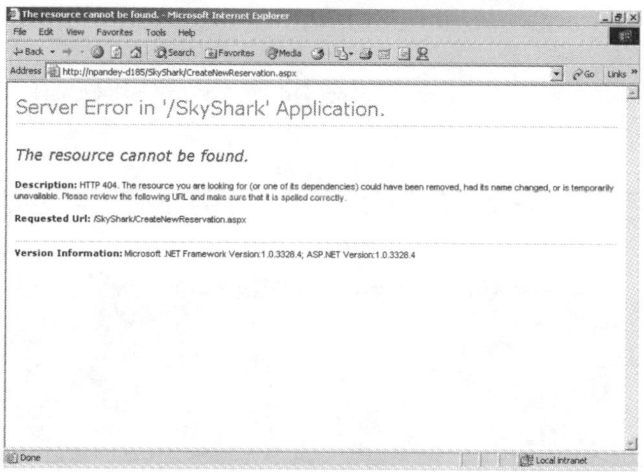


**FIGURE 24-8** *A default error message*

Notice that in the preceding figure, I browsed for the Web form **http://npandey-d185/SkyShark/CreateNewReservation.aspx** that does not exist in the application. You can change the default error pages that are associated with IIS. For example, you can create a new Web page for the 404 error. The Web page might provide links to another page of the Web site or enable the user to send an e-mail message to the network administrator of SkyShark Airlines.

The next section will customize the 404 error page for the Web site. I have created a simple HTML page to which the user should be redirected if a Web page does not exist. The code for the page is given as follows:

```
<html>
<head>
<title>Page Not Found</title>
</head>
<body>
<p align="center"><b><FONT face="MS Sans Serif" size="5">Page Not
   Found.</FONT></b></p>
<HR>
<p>The resource you are looking for (or one of its dependencies) could have been
   removed, had its name changed, or is temporarily unavailable. Please make sure
   that it is spelled correctly or select one of the options given below:</p>
```

```
<p>Report a bug to the <a href="mailto:admin@skyshark.com">System
   administrator</a></p>
<p>Browse to default page of <a href="http://npandey-d185/SkyShark">SkyShark</a>
   Airlines</p>
<HR>
<p><font face="Book Antiqua"><FONT size="2">(C) </FONT><a href="http://npandey-d185
   /skyshark">
<FONT size="2">SkyShark Airlines</FONT></a><FONT size="2"> 2001-
   2002</FONT></font></p>
</body>
</html>
```

Save the file in the root directory of the SkyShark Airlines application with the name Error404.htm. To associate the HTML page with the 404 error, you need to make configuration changes in the Web.Config file. The Web.Config file is an XML-based file that contains information pertaining to the configuration of the application, such as the authentication mode that is supported by the application and the mode of tracking session state of the application.

The Web.Config file includes the `<customError>` element that is used for configuring custom error messages for the application. The `<customError>` element has two attributes that pertain to custom error messages. These attributes are described in the following list:

- **`mode`.** The `mode` attribute is used to enable or disable custom error messages for the Web site. This attribute can have the values `On`, `Off`, or `RemoteOnly`. When the value is `On`, custom error messages are enabled in the application. Similarly, the value `Off` disables custom error messages on the Web site. When the value is `RemoteOnly`, custom error messages are displayed only for remote requests to the Web application.
- **`defaultRedirect`.** Thc `defaultRedirect` attributc is used to identify the location and name default error page that is associated with the Web application.

The `<customError>` element includes a child element `<error>` that is used to configure error pages for specific errors that occur in the Web application. Thus, if you need to specify a specific error page for the 404 error, you need to use the `<error>` element. The `<error>` element includes two attributes: `statusCode` and `redirect`. These attributes are described in the following list:

- **`statusCode`.** The `statusCode` attribute is used for specifying the error number with which you are associating the error page.
- **`redirect`.** The `redirect` element is used to specify the custom page that you want to display when the application encounters the error.

To associate your error page with thc 404 error, open the Web.Config file in Visual Studio .NET. The Web.Config file is located in the root directory of the Web application. In the Web.Config file, locate the `<customError>` element and replace it with the following code:

```
<customErrors mode="On" defaultRedirect="AllErrors.htm">
        <error statusCode="404" redirect="Error404.htm"/>
</customErrors>
```

Save the Web.Config file. After you associate the custom error page with error 404, the error message shown in Figure 24-9 is generated when a user requests a Web page that does not exist.

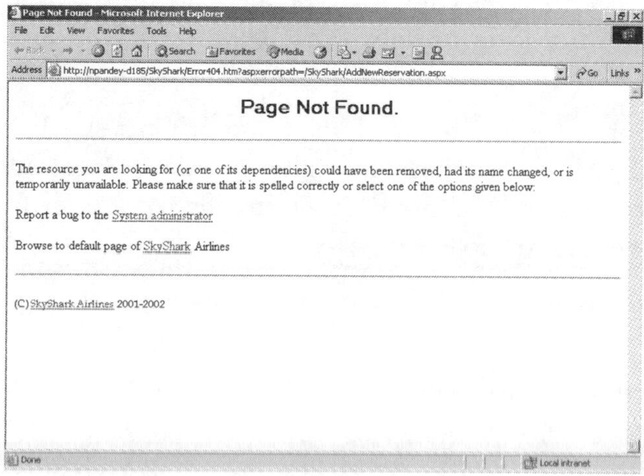


**FIGURE 24-9** *Displaying custom error messages*

## Managing Web Server Log Files

IIS generates log files for all requests that are processed by it. Log files can help you track the users who have visited your Web site or provide useful information about the performance of the IIS server and your application.

You can configure IIS to create log files in a number of formats. Some of the commonly used formats for generating log files are given as follows:

- **W3C Extended Log File.** This format creates ASCII files that contain one entry per request that is processed by IIS. Each entry has a number of fields that provide information about the different parameters of the request. For example, the `#Date` field indicates the date on which the first entry in the log file was made.
- **Microsoft IIS Log.** This format also creates ASCII files that record basic information about each Web request, such as the user's IP address and the number of bytes that were exchanged in processing the request. The Microsoft IIS Log format can be exported to other applications like Microsoft Excel, Microsoft Access, or another RDBMS (*Relational Database Management System*) for proper utilization.
- **ODBC Logging.** This format is used to record log file data in ODBC (*Open Database Connectivity*) compliant databases, such as Microsoft SQL Server. This is a convenient format for analyzing log file data because data from SQL Server databases can be presented in a number of ways.

To configure the location of log files and the format in which logs should be created, you need to use the MMC-based administration console for Internet Information Services. To access the MMC-based administration console for Internet Information Services, perform the following steps:

1. Open the Programs menu by clicking on Start and then selecting Programs.
2. On the Programs menu, point to Administrative Tools and click Internet Services Manager to open the Internet Information Services window.
3. In Internet Information Services, right-click on Default Web Site and select Properties. The Default Web Site Properties dialog box will appear.
4. In the Default Web Site Properties dialog box, select the required logging format from the Active log format list.
5. Click on Properties to configure the location and the frequency with which the log files should be generated. The Extended Logging Properties dialog box will appear.

6. Specify the location of the log files in the Log file directory text box and the frequency for creating new log files in the New Log Time Period section of the Extended Logging Properties dialog box.
7. Click on OK to close the Extended Logging Properties dialog box. The Default Web Site Properties dialog box will reappear.
8. Click on OK to close the Default Web Site Properties dialog box.

After you complete the preceding steps, IIS creates log files at the specified location. You can retrieve log files from time to time and analyze the performance of your Web application.

# Summary

Network administrators can use SQL Server Enterprise Manager to manage databases. You can use the Enterprise Manager to back up databases, review database logs and schedule maintenance tasks.

You can change the default error messages associated with your Web application by designing a new HTML page and associating it with the application by using the Web.Config file. The Web.Config file includes the `<customError>` element, which in turn includes the `<error>` element that is used for mapping the error numbers with the error pages of the application.

IIS creates log files to track all Web requests that are processed by the server. You can select from a number of log file formats to create the log file, depending upon where you want to store the logs and how you want to analyze them.

# Chapter 25

## Securing the Application

Securing a Web site is as important as developing it. You need to ensure that your Web site is safeguarded from hackers and unauthenticated users to prevent any damage to the content or functionality of your Web site. This is essential for the smooth functioning of your Web application. You can implement various security measures to secure your Web site from unintentional access.

In this chapter, you will learn about the authentication mechanisms for Web and database servers. Next, you will use these mechanisms to implement Web server and database security on the SkyShark Airlines application.

# Security in ASP.NET Applications

ASP.NET applications are deployed on IIS (*Internet Information Server*). IIS has security mechanisms that can be implemented to ensure safety of Web applications. In addition to the security mechanisms of IIS, ASP.NET applications have security mechanisms implemented using a Web.Config file that can be used to specify how users are authenticated when accessing the application.

In this section, you will learn about concepts pertaining to securing Web sites by using IIS and ASP.NET. You will also learn about the different authentication mechanisms that can be implemented for securing a Web application.

## Authentication Mechanisms

Authentication is the method of determining whether a user is authorized to view the requested resource. The user is able to access the resources on the server or the Web site only after the authentication process is complete. In this section, I will explain the authentication mechanisms supported by IIS and ASP.NET.

### *IIS Security Mechanisms*

IIS provides built-in support for validating the identity of clients. An ASP.NET application is deployed on IIS, which implies that any security feature made available by IIS is automatically incorporated into your Web application. The authentication methods available with IIS are Anonymous authentication, Basic authentication, Integrated Windows authentication, and Digest authentication. Take a look at Table 25-1 to learn more about each of these methods.

**Table 25-1 IIS Authentication Methods**

| Authentication Method | Description |
|---|---|
| Anonymous | This type of authentication mechanism does not require a user to provide a user ID or password to browse through a Web application. In this mechanism, IIS uses a default logon name and password to request for resources from a Web application. Therefore, this is the least secure authentication medium available for accessing Web site resources. |
| Basic | This type of authentication mechanism does not allow a user to access the resources of a Web application unless the user provides the user ID and password. However, this authentication method has one drawback. The user's password is transmitted over the Internet in an unencrypted form, making it vulnerable to hackers. |
| Integrated Windows | This type of authentication uses the "hashing to track the user" mechanism. In this mechanism, a user need not specify a password to be authenticated. The user is verified over the network by using the user's Windows account logon credentials. This mechanism is generally deployed for internal business processes of organizations, where the users accessing the application are few. |
| Digest | This type of authentication mechanism, just like the Basic authentication mechanism, does not allow a user to access the resources of a Web application unless he or she provides the user ID and password. This mechanism ensures greater security than the Basic authentication method because the user's password is sent over the Internet in an encrypted form. |

### ASP.NET Authentication Mechanisms

To ensure the security of your Web applications, ASP.NET provides three authentication mechanisms: Forms authentication, Passport authentication, and Windows authentication. These three mechanisms are described as follows:

- **Forms authentication.** This authentication mechanism, also called *cookie-based authentication*, is based on a single logon form. Users can access this form anytime they need to log on. A few Web sites allow you to browse through Web forms without the need to log on. However, when you have to log on to a Web site, you are directed to a logon form. After the logon process is successful, you are redirected to the original form. In Forms authentication, a logon form is invoked as soon as an unauthenticated user requests for a Web form. Cookies are vulnerable to attack by hackers and can be easily accessed by other users on the site because cookies are transmitted over the Web in an unencrypted form. However, cookies can be made safer by encryption. In addition, you can embed cookies with the IP address of the original user to restrict unauthenticated users from getting permissions to resources.
- **Passport authentication.** Passport is the default authentication mechanism provided by Microsoft for its Hotmail, MSN, and Passport services. This is a centralized authentication service, which requires fewer resources because you need not implement additional hardware for authentication. Moreover, all users registered for the Passport authentication service are registered users of the Web site. Therefore, Passport authentication caters to a greater number of users as compared to the Forms authentication service. To use the Passport authentication service, you need to download the Passport software development kit.
- **Windows authentication.** Windows authentication is implemented in a Windows 2000 domain. In Windows authentication, users are authenticated against their account in the Windows 2000 domain.

## Securing a Web Site with IIS and ASP.NET

By configuring security settings on IIS and including the Web.Config file, you can create a highly secure environment for your application. Consider the case of the SkyShark Airlines application.

The corporate office and regional offices of SkyShark Airlines are connected on a LAN. Therefore, every user who accesses the Web application has a valid Windows account. Consequently, as the first level of authentication, you can make Windows authentication available on IIS. This ensures that anonymous users do not access the Web site. As the next level of security, you can enable form-based authentication for your ASP.NET application and validate users with their accounts in the `dtUsers` table of SQL Server before they can access the Web site resources.

Therefore, the SkyShark Airlines application has two levels of security. The first level of security is implemented by IIS. Users authenticated by IIS access the Web application and are then authenticated against the `dtUsers` table of the SQL Server database. When users are authenticated, their profile is also retrieved from the `dtUsers` table, which is used to grant access to Web pages. You can view the mechanism of granting permissions to users for accessing Web pages in Chapter 21, "Implementing the Business Logic."

To restrict access to Web pages, the SkyShark Airlines application uses the `Session` variables `usrRole` and `usrName`. The code to initialize these variables is discussed in Chapter 21.

I will now discuss the steps to implement Windows authentication on IIS and Forms authentication on ASP.NET.

# Enabling Authentication in SkyShark Airlines

In the SkyShark Airlines application, you need to enable Windows authentication on the IIS Web server and Forms authentication for the SkyShark Airlines application. In this section, I list the steps to configure these two authentication modes for the SkyShark Airlines application.

## Configuring IIS Authentication

To enable Windows authentication, you can use the IIS console. The steps to open the console and configure the application are given as follows:

1. Click on Start and point to Programs.

2. From the Programs menu, select Administrative Tools and then click on Internet Services Manager. The Internet Information Services window will open.
3. In the Internet Information Services window, double-click on Default Web Site to view a list of Web sites installed on the computer.
4. In Default Web Site, right-click on SkyShark and select Properties. The SkyShark Properties dialog box will appear.
5. Click on the Directory Security tab of the SkyShark Properties dialog box. This tab of the dialog box is shown in Figure 25-1.

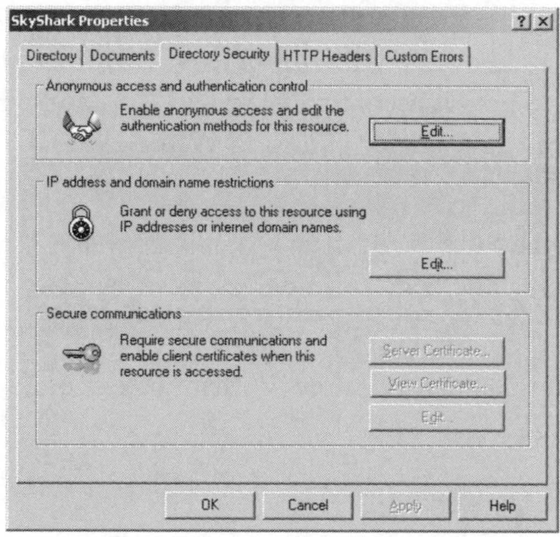


**FIGURE 25-1** *Directory Security tab of the SkyShark Properties dialog box*

6. In the SkyShark Properties dialog box, click on Edit in the Anonymous access and authentication control section.
7. In the Authentication Methods dialog box, clear the Anonymous access option and check the Integrated Windows authentication option, as shown in Figure 25-2.

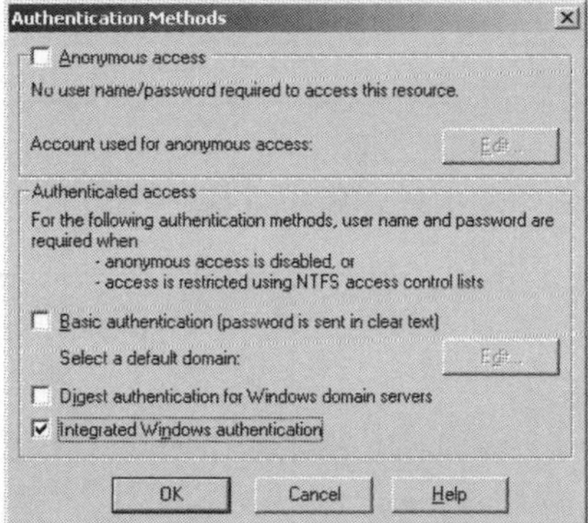


**FIGURE 25-2** *Enabling Integrated Windows authentication*

8. Click on OK to close the Authentication Methods dialog box. The SkyShark Properties dialog box will reappear.
9. Click on OK to close the SkyShark Properties dialog box.

Your Web server is now configured for Windows authentication. Next, you need to configure the Web application to use Form authentication. In the next section, I will discuss Form authentication in ASP.NET.

## Configuring Authentication in ASP.NET

To configure ASP.NET security, you need to specify a default logon page that is displayed to a user if the identity of the user is not validated. The default logon page for SkyShark Airlines is default.aspx. Therefore, if an unauthenticated user tries to navigate directly to a page of the Web application, the user will be directed to the default.aspx page.

ASP.NET provides the `System.Web.Security` namespace that makes the necessary classes available for configuring authentication. To authenticate a user, you need to use the `FormsAuthentication` class of the `System.Web.Security` namespace. Some important functions of this class, which help you to authenticate users on your Web application, are listed in Table 25-2.

**Table 25-2 Methods of the `FormsAuthentication` Class**

| Method | Description |
|---|---|
| `Authenticate` | The `Authenticate` method validates usernames and passwords against those specified in the data store. |
| `GetAuthCookie` | The `GetAuthCookie` method creates an authentication cookie for an authenticated user. The cookie can be used for identifying authenticated users. |
| `RedirectFromLoginPage` | After validating a user, the `RedirectFromLoginPage` method redirects a user to the requested page. |
| `RenewTicketIfOld` | The `RenewTicketIfOld` method renews/revalidates the authentication ticket of a user after it is no longer valid. |
| `SignOut` | The `SignOut` method is used for logging a user off from the Web application. |

To implement Forms authentication, you need to change the `<authentication>` and `<authorization>` elements of the Web.Config file. By default, when you create a new application, authentication is not enabled in your application, as specified by the following line of code in the Web.Config file:

```
<authentication mode="None"/>
```

To enable Forms authentication on your Web site, change the `<authentication>` property as follows:

```
<authentication mode="Forms">
        <forms loginUrl="default.aspx" name=".ASPXFORMSAUTH"/>
</authentication>
<authorization>
        <deny users="?" />
</authorization>
```

In the preceding code snippet, I have changed the authentication mode to `Forms` by changing the mode attribute of the `<authentication>` element.

When the authentication mode is set to `Forms`, the Web application issues a cookie to an authenticated user. You need to specify the suffix of the cookie by using the name attribute of the `<forms>` element. You also need to specify the name of the logon form, where an unauthenticated user is redirected. In the preceding code snippet, I have specified the name of the logon form as default.aspx, which is the logon form for SkyShark Airlines, and the suffix of the cookies is specified as `.ASPXFORMSAUTH`.

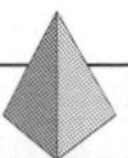

**TIP**

ASP.NET uses the `*` and `?` user types to control access to Web site resources. The `*` user type represents all users and the `?` user type represents anonymous users.

After enabling Forms authentication, you need to prevent Web application access to anonymous users. The `<deny users="?"/>` statement uses the `?` user type to prevent access to anonymous users.

After enabling custom authentication for SkyShark Airlines, you can modify the code of the default.aspx form so that an authentication ticket can be issued to the user after the user's credentials are validated. To issue authentication tickets, the `FormsAuthentication` class provides the `GetAuthCookie` and `RedirectFromLoginPage` methods. The difference in the two methods is that the `GetAuthCookie` method generates an authentication ticket but does not redirect the user to the page requested initially. However, the `RedirectFromLoginPage` method authenticates the user and then redirects the user to the page requested initially.

For the SkyShark Airlines application, you need to use the `GetAuthCookie` method to generate the authentication ticket. You cannot use the `RedirectFromLoginPage` method because you have implemented a custom solution based on Session state variables. These variables redirect the user to Web forms depending upon the role of the users. For example, if you implement the `RedirectFromLoginPage` method, when a line-of-business executive requests the ManageUsers.aspx page, which should be accessible to network administrators only, the `RedirectFromLoginPage` method will authenticate and redirect him to the ManageUsers.aspx page. This should not be the case.

The `GetAuthCookie` method uses two parameters to generate the authentication ticket, the username and the state of the cookie (persistent or not). To generate the authentication ticket for the user by using the `GetAuthCookie` method, add a reference to the `System.Web.Security` namespace in the default.aspx page and call the `GetAuthCookie` method of the `FormsAuthentication` class. The code snippet where you need to make the change is given as follows, and the changes made appear in bold format.

```
if (Role=="Disabled")
{
        lblMessage.Text="Your account has been disabled. Please contact the network
           administrator.";
        return;
}
FormsAuthentication.GetAuthCookie(username,false);
switch(Role)
{
        case "Admin":
```

After you have issued an authentication ticket to the user, you need to remove the ticket when the user logs off from the Web site. To remove the authentication ticket, use the `SignOut` method of the `FormsAuthentication` class in the Logoff.aspx form. The code for the `Load` event of the form, which implements the log off functionality, is given as follows:

```
private void Page_Load(object sender, System.EventArgs e)
{
        Session.RemoveAll();
        FormsAuthentication.SignOut();
}
```

When the user logs off from the Web site, the authentication ticket for the user is removed and the user has restricted access to the Web site.

## Securing SQL Server

Although not directly in the purview of ASP.NET, you need to secure the SkyShark Airlines databases to ensure that the security aspects of the Web application are taken care of. In this section, I briefly describe the authentication process of SQL Server to help you secure SQL Server by using the optimal authentication mode.

To access the resources on SQL Server 2000, you pass through two security stages. The first security stage is the authentication stage. In this stage, you need to enter a valid logon ID and password. After you pass this stage, you are connected to an instance of SQL Server 2000. The next stage is the authorization stage. In this stage, the exact permissions to be granted to a user to access different databases are decided. The user needs to have an account in each of the databases to which the user wants to connect and access resources. This stage also enables you to determine the extent of activities that a user can perform on a specified database. SQL Server 2000 uses two authentication modes:

- **Windows Authentication mode.** The Windows Authentication mode enables you to connect to the SQL Server by using the Windows 2000 domain user account.
- **Mixed Authentication mode.** The Mixed Authentication mode enables you to connect to the SQL Server either by using Windows authentication or by using SQL Server ID-based authentication. If either of the logon credentials is valid, you are able to connect to an instance of SQL Server 2000.

To configure the authentication mode on SQL Server, follow these steps:

1. Open SQL Server Enterprise Manager.
2. Right-click on the name of the SQL Server on which you want to configure authentication and select Properties. The SQL Server Properties (Configure) dialog box will appear.
3. Click on the Security tab. The Security tab of the SQL Server Properties (Configure) dialog box is shown in Figure 25-3.
4. Select the authentication mode that you want to select from the Security section of the SQL Server Properties (Configure) dialog box and click on OK.

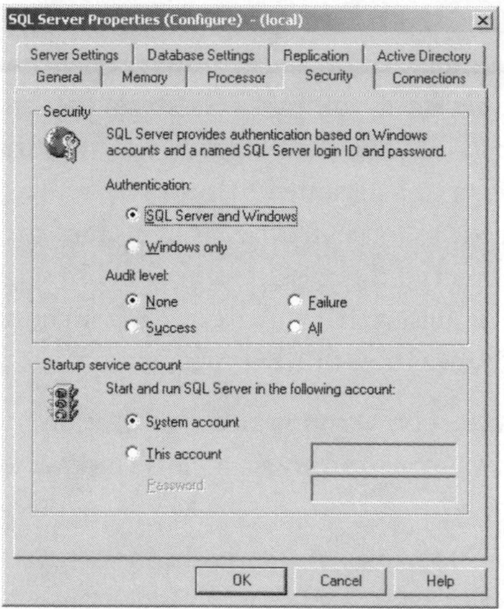


**FIGURE 25-3** *Configuring authentication on SQL Server 2000*

It is recommended that you use the Mixed Authentication mode to secure the SQL Server. In this way, users need not only to have permissions to manage resources on the SQL Server, but also to know SQL Server logon credentials to manage the resource.

# Summary

Authentication for ASP.NET applications can be configured on IIS and in the Web.Config file. IIS supports Basic, Integrated, Windows, and Digest authentication, whereas ASP.NET supports Forms, Passport, and Windows authentication.

To configure the authentication mechanism on IIS, you use SQL Server Enterprise Manager. To configure application security, you need to set the authentication mode to forms in the Web.Config file. You also need to restrict access to anonymous users.

After configuring the Web.Config file, you can use the methods of the `GetAuthCookie` or `RedirectFromLoginPage` methods of the `FormsAuthentication` class to generate an authentication ticket for a user. Finally, you can remove the authentication ticket by using the `SignOut` method when the user logs off from the Web application.

SQL Server offers two authentication modes, Windows and Mixed. For enhanced security, you should implement the Mixed Authentication mode.

# Chapter 26

## Deploying the Application

In this chapter, you will learn to deploy a Web application. Deployment can be described as the process of distributing an entire application or even a component to other computers. You will learn about different deployment scenarios and the situations where you can use a particular method of deployment.

## Deployment Scenarios

The process of deployment has undergone a number of changes compared to the deployment model of applications developed using Visual Studio 6.0. In order to deploy a Visual Studio .NET solution, you need to pass on some information to .NET. This information can be regarding the location, method, and application to be deployed. For deployment purposes, Visual Studio .NET provides templates for four different types of deployment projects, which are as follows:

- **Merge Module project.** This type of project allows you to package all your project files/components into a single module (.msm) file. The Merge Module project enables you to create reusable setup components and share setup code between installers. Merge modules contain components and related files, such as resources and registry entries. Merge modules need to be merged into an installer for each application that uses the component.
- **Setup project.** This type of project is used to create installers for distributing Windows Application projects. The output file is a Windows Installer (.msi) file. The Installer file contains the application files and any dependent files, such as registry entries and setup instructions. The target files are installed in the files system of your local computer.
- **Web Setup project.** This type of project is used to distribute Web Application projects. The files are deployed on a Web server. The Web Setup project automatically takes care of configuration and registration.

- **Cab project.** This type of project is used primarily to package and distribute ActiveX controls so that they can be downloaded from a Web server. This option is employed when you want the code to run on a client computer instead of a server.

The primary aim of deployment is to install the application on a target computer. You can create a new deployment project or even add an existing deployment project to a solution. I will now discuss the process of creating a deployment project.

1. On the File menu, point to Add and click on New Project.
2. In the Add New Project dialog box (refer to Figure 26-1), select the Setup and Deployment option from the Project Types: pane and Setup Project from the Templates: pane.

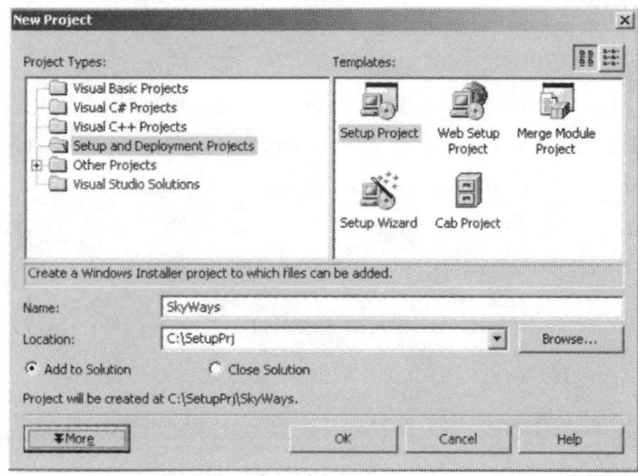


**FIGURE 26-1** *The Add New Project dialog box*

3. Specify the name for the deployment project in the Name: text box and the path in the Location: text box.

The File System editor is opened (refer to Figure 26-2).

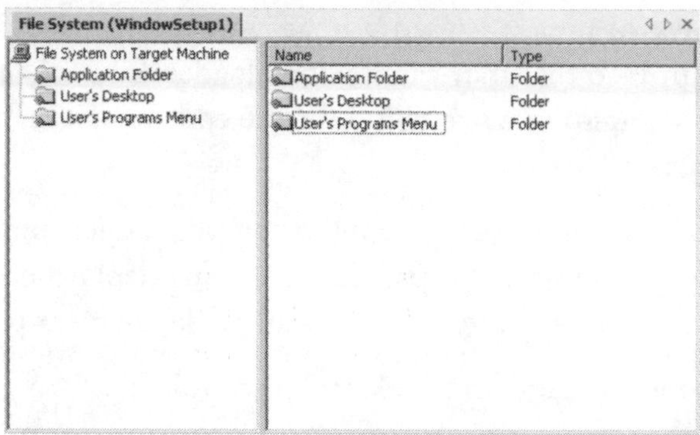


**FIGURE 26-2** *The File System editor*

## Deployment Editors

You might want to specify the location where files should be installed on a target computer and other configuration tasks to be performed during installation. For this purpose, Visual Studio .NET provides you with six deployment editors, which can be used to specify and customize properties and settings for various aspects of deployment. You can open a deployment editor as follows:

1. Select the deployment project in Solution Explorer.
2. On the View menu, point to Editor and then click on the name of the editor that you want to open.

The deployment editors available with Visual Studio .NET are listed as follows:

- File System editor
- Registry editor
- File Types editor
- User Interface editor
- Customs Action editor
- Launch Conditions editor

**NOTE**

The User Interface editor is not available in the case of Merge Module projects, and no editor is available for Cab projects.

I will explain each one of the editors in detail.

### File System Editor

The File System editor presents the file system view of the target computer. The File System editor uses the concept of abstract folders to ensure that files are installed in the location you specify. For example, the Desktop folder compares to the desktop folder on the target computer.

### Registry Editor

The Registry editor enables you to specify the registry keys and values to be added to the registry of the target computer. By default, the Registry editor displays the standard Windows registry keys. You can add your own keys to any registry key or subkey.

### File Types Editor

The File Types editor is used to specify file associations on the target computer. You can associate a file extension with your application and specify the action to be performed for each file type.

### User Interface Editor

The User Interface editor is used to specify and set properties for dialog boxes displayed during installation on the target computer. This editor is a tree control that contains two sections, Install and Administrative Install. The Install section contains dialog boxes to be displayed when the user runs the installer, and the Administrative Install contains dialog boxes to be displayed when the system administrator uploads the installer to a network location. The User Interface editor is shown in Figure 26-3.

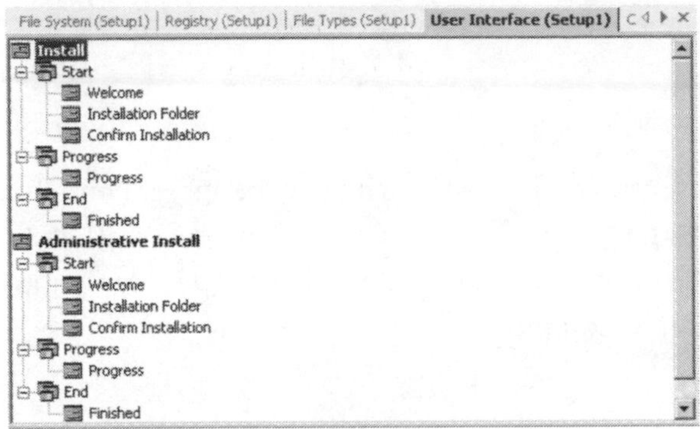


**FIGURE 26-3** *The User Interface editor*

### Customs Action Editor

This editor enables you to specify actions to be performed on the target computer upon the completion of installation. This editor contains four folders, each corresponding to a particular installation phase. The folders are Install, Commit, Rollback, and Uninstall. Custom actions run in the same order in which they are displayed in the editor.

### Launch Conditions Editor

You can specify conditions that need to be fulfilled for installation. For example, you might want to check for a file before installation.

Now that you are aware of the different deployment options and the deployments editors available in Visual Studio .NET, I will guide you through the process of creating the deployment project for the SkyShark Airlines application.

## Deploying the SkyShark Airlines Application

As you know, the SkyShark Airlines application is a Web application. In order to create a deployment project for this application, you will need to create a Web Setup project. Apart from creating Windows Installers for distribution through the traditional medium, such as CDs or DVDs, Visual Studio .NET supports its deployment to a Web server. This is a better option for Web application projects because registration and configuration issues are handled by Visual Studio .NET.

In order to deploy a Web application to a Web server, you create a Web Setup project, build it, copy it to the Web server computer, and run the installer to install the application on the Web server.

## Creating a Deployment Project

Perform the following steps in order to create a deployment project for the SkyShark Airlines application.

1. Open your SkyShark Airlines application.
2. On the File menu, point to Add and click on New Project.
3. In the Add New Project dialog box (refer to Figure 26-4), select the Setup and Deployment option from the Project Types: pane and the Setup Project from the Templates: pane.
4. Enter `SkySharkDeploy` in the Name: text box and the required path in the Location: text box (refer to Figure 26-4).

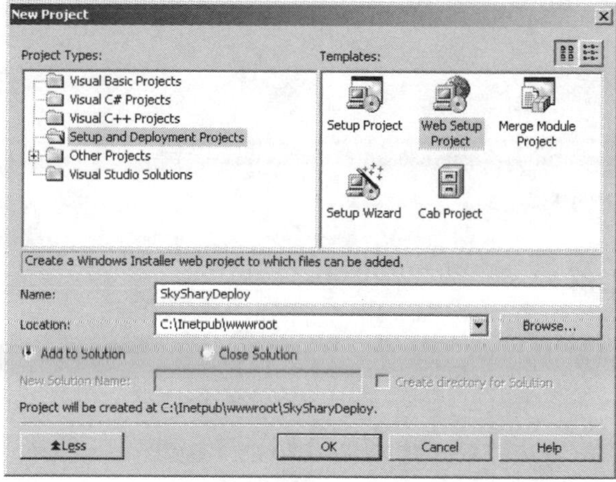


**FIGURE 26-4** *The Add New Project dialog box*

5. Ensure that the Add to Solution radio button is selected.
6. Click on the OK button to create a deployment project.

   The File System editor is displayed.

The window of the File System editor is divided into two parts, a navigation pane on the left and a details pane on the right. The navigation pane contains a hierarchical list of folders representing the file system.

The settings of the File System editor can be modified by changing the properties. However, the actual properties are dependent on the project type and the current selection in the editor. The properties of the File System editor are given in Table 26-1.

**Table 26-1 File System Editor Properties for Web Application Folder**

| Property | Description |
|---|---|
| AllowDirectoryBrowsing | Sets the IIS DirectoryBrowsing property for the selected folder |
| AllowReadAccess | Sets the IIS Read property for the selected folder |
| AllowScriptSourceAccess | Sets the IIS Script source access property for the selected folder |
| AllowWriteAccess | Sets the IIS Write property for the selected folder |
| AlwaysCreate | Specifies whether the selected folder is to be created as part of installation |
| ApplicationProtection | Sets the IIS Application Protection property for the selected folder |
| AppMappings | Sets the IIS Application Mappings property for the selected folder |
| Condition | Sets the Windows Installer condition that must be satisfied |
| DefaultDocument | Specifies the startup file for the selected folder |
| ExecutePermissions | Sets the IIS Execute Permissions property for the selected folder |
| Index | Sets the IIS Index this resource property for the selected folder |

**Table 26-1 File System Editor Properties for Web Application Folder *(continued)***

| Property | Description |
|---|---|
| IsApplication | Specifies whether the IIS application root will be created for the selected folder |
| LogVisits | Sets the IIS Log Visits property for the selected folder |
| Name | Specifies the name for the selected folder |
| Port | Specifies the port where a Web server is located on the target computer |
| Property | Specifies the named property that can be accessed during installation to override the path of a custom folder |
| VirtualDirectory | Specifies the virtual directory on the Web server where a Web application will be installed on the target computer |

## Adding the Output of SkySharkDeploy to the Deployment Project

Perform the following steps to add the project output to the deployment project.

1. Select the Web Application folder.
2. Press F4 to open the Properties window. Set the VirtualDirectory property to SkySharkDeploy.
3. Set the DefaultDocument property to default.aspx.
4. In the File System editor, select the Web Application folder.
5. On the Action menu, point to Add and choose Project Output.
6. In the AddProjectOutputGroup dialog box (refer to Figure 26-5), choose SkyShark from the drop-down list.

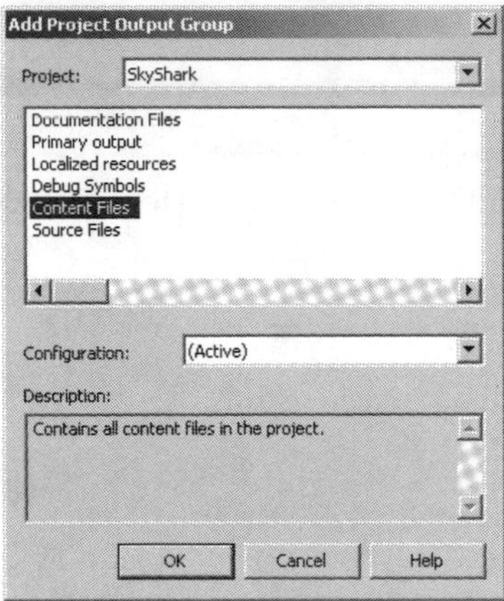


**FIGURE 26-5** *The AddProjectOutputGroup dialog box*

7. Select the Primary output and Content Files from the list and click on OK.

   The File System editor is shown in Figure 26-6.

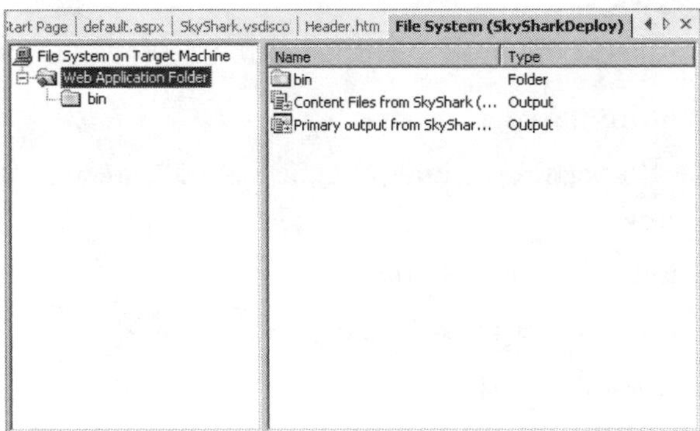


**FIGURE 26-6** *The File System editor*

8. On the Build menu, choose Build SkySharkDeploy.

The SkyShark Airlines application is now ready for deployment. However, the database also needs to be packaged and distributed. For this purpose, you need to create a custom action to create the database and associated tables during installation.

You can create a custom action by performing the steps given as follows.

1. Create an installer class.
2. Create a data connection object.
3. Create a text file that contains the SQL statements to create the database and its associated tables.
4. Add code to the installer class to read the text file.

## Deploying the Project to a Web Server on Another Computer

The steps that follow describe the procedure to deploy the application to a Web server on another computer.

1. In Windows Explorer, navigate to the project and locate the installer. The default path is \documents and setting\yourloginname\My Documents\Visual Studio Projects\WebDeploy\project configuration \SkySharkDeploy.msi. The default project configuration is Debug.
2. Copy the SkySharkDeploy.msi and all other files and subdirectories to the Web server computer.
3. Double-click on the Setup.exe on the Web server to run the installer.

# Summary

Deployment is the process of distributing a ready application or even its component to other computers. Visual Studio .NET provides templates for four different types of deployment projects: Merge Module, Setup, Web Setup, and Cab. Visual Studio .NET provides six deployment editors that enable you to specify the location where files should be installed on a target computer, the registry keys to be added, or any other conditions that need to be fulfilled during installation.

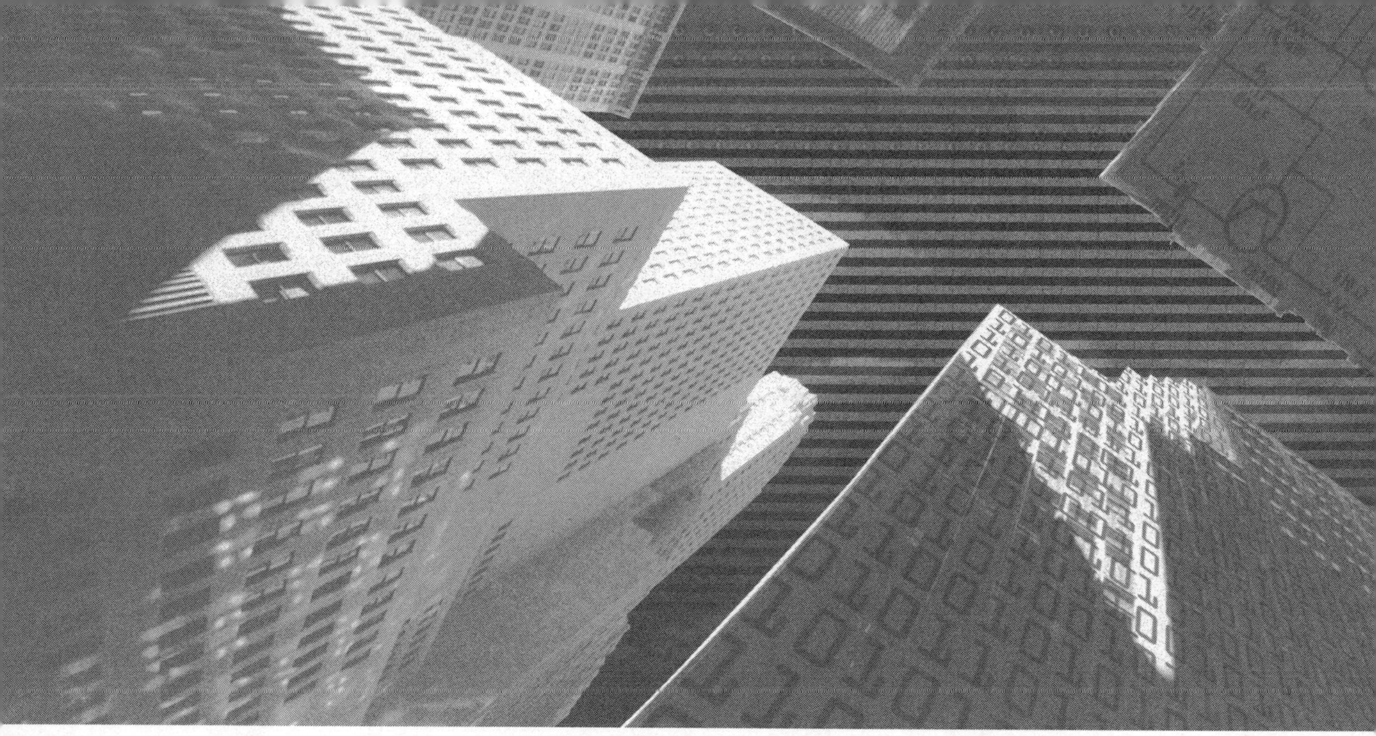

# PART VII

## Professional Project 5

# Project 5

## *Creating a Web Portal for a Bookstore*

# Project 5 Overview

A Web portal for a bookstore is an enterprise solution that allows businesses to interoperate. A portal for a bookstore offers users a variety of books from several publishers. Therefore, implementing Web services with the Web portal enables organizations to share their data with each other. For example, publishers can publish their catalog of books on the Web site of the retailer. Retailers, in turn, can share the data of their customers with the publishers. In addition to sharing data across organizations, these organizations share the business objective of achieving success.

Traditionally, customers used to visit a bookstore to buy a book. However, with the advent and increasing popularity of the Internet, customers can now shop for books on the Internet. In addition, book lovers can keep abreast of virtually all newly published books.

In this context, Bookers Paradise, a chain of retailers of books, has planned to launch its Web site. The Web site will display the catalogs of books from various publishers. To display information about books from the publishers, Bookers Paradise has planned to create Web services for each of the publishers.

In the Web portal project, you will learn to develop a complete solution for Bookers Paradise. You will learn to create a Web portal that accesses data by using Web services. In addition, the data displayed on the portal is stored in the SQL databases that act as the back end. The Web portal and the Web services are created by using the .NET Framework. The language used as the front end will be Visual C# .NET.

In this project, you will learn to create a Web portal for Bookers Paradise. In addition, you will learn to create Web services for two publishers, Deepthoughts Publications and Black and White Publications.

After completing this project, you will be able to appreciate the support that the .NET Framework extends to create Web services. In addition, you will be able to create an integrated business solution in the form of Web portal. This Web portal can then be customized to meet your business requirements.

# Chapter 27

## Project Case Study and Design

In the preceding projects, you learned how to develop Windows applications and an ASP.NET Web application. Windows applications are used to develop applications that can run on a desktop computer. Alternatively, ASP.NET applications are large-scale business applications that can be deployed on an intranet of the organization or on the Internet. However, to find a business solution that integrates applications built on different platforms, you need to create a Web service. In addition to integrating various applications, a Web service can be used to integrate data from various applications developed for different organizations.

In this chapter, I will discuss the case study of the Web portal project. In addition, I will discuss the database and the interface design for the Web portal. You will learn to create the actual application in the forthcoming chapters.

## Organization Profile

Bookers Paradise is chain of retailers, having their retail outlets spread across the United States. Bookers Paradise was established in 1998 as a small bookstore in the city of New York. Since then, the organization has grown to be a chain of more than 50 outlets in the United States. To grow further in the business world and increase its yearly profits, the organization plans to sell the books of two publishers over the Internet. These publishers are Deepthoughts Publications and Black and White Publications.

Deepthoughts Publications is one of the leading book publishers of the United States. Deepthoughts Publications has been publishing books on various subjects ever since it was established in 1991. Deepthoughts Publications publishes high-quality books and, therefore, has a huge clientele. In addition, Deepthoughts Publications has been dealing with a number of retailers, Bookers Paradise being one of them. Therefore, to enable its customers to buy books online, Deepthoughts Publications has decided to create a Web service. This Web service will provide the Web site developed by Bookers Paradise with information about the books published at the publishing house.

Similar to Deepthoughts Publications, Black and White Publications is one of the major book providers of Bookers Paradise. Established in 1994, Black and White Publications has grown to be a leading publishing house in the United States. The organization, with its corporate office located in New York, has its branches spread all over the United States. Black and White Publications shares the corporate goal of increasing its yearly profits with Bookers Paradise. Therefore, Black and White Publications wants to collaborate with Bookers Paradise to sell its books online. To do this, the publishing house plans to create a Web service that provides the site of Bookers Paradise with the information about the books published at its publishing house.

## Project Requirements

Bookers Paradise wants to launch an online bookstore that contains information about books published by Deepthoughts Publications and Black and White Publications. To display the catalog of books on the Web portal, Deepthoughts Publications and Black and White Publications need to host a Web service that is used to expose the information about the books in the form of a catalog. This information includes the ISBN (*International Standard Book Number*) number, the title, the author, and so on. To access the information exposed by the Web services, Bookers Paradise needs to host a Web service client. This Web service client is the Web portal launched by Bookers Paradise. The Web service client displays the book catalogs to the visitors on the site. In addition, the Web service client stores the information about its customers.

The function of the Web service that you create is not limited to providing the Web portal with book catalogs. The customers that visit the site of Bookers Paradise can search for information about the books on the site. For example, the customer can search for books on a particular subject, books written by a particular author, or books published by a particular publisher. To provide customers with the required information, Web services need to expose functions to the Web service client. In addition, the Web service can expose functions that provide information about the availability of the book and the editions of the book released by the publisher.

As stated earlier, a Web service is used to integrate information from various organizations. Therefore, a Web service provides the Web service client with information about books. Similarly, the Web service client shares the data of its customers with the publisher. When customers visit the Web portal for Bookers Paradise, they can view information about the books on the site. In addition, they can query for information on books on the site. When the customer views the information about a book and places an order for the book on the site of Bookers Paradise, the Web service client forwards the purchase request to the publisher of the book. In addition, the information about the customer is sent to the publisher.

The publisher then maintains the customer data along with the information about the book that is released. When the book is delivered to the customer, the publisher updates the status of the book in the database maintained by the publisher. The customer can then query the Web site to know the status of the order placed by the customer. I will discuss the structure of the databases maintained by the retailer and the publisher later in this chapter.

To have a clear understanding of the working of the Web portal, I will first list the tasks that need to be performed by the Web portal. In addition, I will discuss how these will be accomplished.

## Querying for Information about All Books

As discussed earlier, a user can query for the information about the books published by a publisher. The procedure for querying information is as discussed here:

1. A user visits the Web site of Bookers Paradise. On the Main page, the user chooses to view the information about all the books published by the Deepthoughts Publications and the Black and White Publications publishing houses.

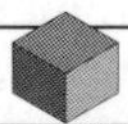

**NOTE**

The user has the option to view the information about all the books or search for information about the books based on criteria. In the next section, you will learn about the procedure for viewing the information about books based on criteria.

2. The Web site sends the request to the Web service hosted by the two publishing houses.
3. The Web service processes the request and sends the result of the query back to the Web site. The user can then view the desired information on the Web site.

**NOTE**

The Web service has certain Web methods that the Web service uses to respond to the queries sent by the Web service client, which is the Web site in this case. You will learn about creating the Web service and the Web methods in the succeeding chapters.

## Querying for Information about Books Based on Criteria

A user who visits the site of Bookers Paradise can view information about the selected books published by Deepthoughts Publications and Black and White Publications. The search for information about books in this case is based on criteria. For example, the user can search for information about books based on category, title, or author. The procedure to search for information based on criteria is given as follows:

1. The user visits the Web site of Bookers Paradise and selects the criteria from the list box in the Main page.
2. The Web site requests the Web service to retrieve the required information.
3. The required information is returned to the Web site in the form of records from the database. This information can then be viewed by the user in the Results form.

After the user has viewed and selected a book to purchase, the user can order the book on the site. The following section covers the procedure for ordering a book on the Web site.

## Ordering a Book on the Web Site

The procedure to order a book on the Web site is as follows:

1. The user selects a book to order in the Orders page.
2. The user then clicks on the Order button to order the book.
3. The user is taken to the Orders page. On the Orders page, the customer details, such as name, address, and credit card information, are specified.
4. After specifying the required details, the user clicks on the Order button.
5. When the `Order` button is clicked, the details submitted by the user is sent to the database maintained by the publishing house.

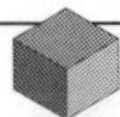

**NOTE**

To send the information submitted by the user to the database of the publishing house, the Web site uses a Web method created in the Web service. You will learn about this method, `AcceptDetails()`, in Chapter 29, "Developing Web Services."

6. The details of the customer and the order placed by the customer are stored in the database at the publishing house.
7. At the site of the publishing house, the request of the user is processed and the book is delivered to the client.

# Project Design

Having examined the project requirements in detail, you need to create a detailed design of the project. You can create a design of the application in the project design stage. The project design stage includes identifying the database design and the database schema. To finalize the database schema, you first need to decide on the tables required in the database. Then, a detailed analysis of the database design is required to identify the relationships between various tables in the database. Based on this, a detailed schema of the database is created. It is critical to examine all possible requirements and incorporate them in the database schema to avoid reworking at a later stage. The following section delineates the database design for the Web portal.

## Database Design

After creating the structure of database tables and normalizing the structure, you arrive at a database schema that is appropriate for your Web portal project. Normalizing the database design helps to remove data redundancy.

In the case of this Web portal, data is not stored in the database of any one organization. Data is spread across the databases of Bookers Paradise and the two publishing houses. It therefore becomes all the more essential for you to carefully plan the database design and normalize the design. This will help you avoid data redundancy across tables in the databases of different organizations. You have learned about the basic concepts of creating an SQL database and normalization in Chapter 7, "Project Case Study," in the section "Normalization."

In addition to creating the database design for the three organizations, you need to establish relationships between the tables in the databases. This will help you program your application to query and update data in the related tables. I will discuss how to create relationships between tables later in this chapter. However, I will first discuss the structure of the tables in the databases of the three organizations.

### *Database Design for Bookers Paradise*

Bookers Paradise plans to launch a Web site that allows visitors to view information about books and to place an order for a book. To do this, Bookers Paradise maintains a database called BookersDB. This database includes two tables, `BookersOrders` and `BookersCustDetails`. The following section discusses these tables in detail.

### The `BookersOrders` Table

The `BookersOrders` table stores information about the order placed by a customer for a book. Therefore, this table includes information such as `OrderNo`, `CustomerID`, and `ISBNNo` of the book. When a customer places an order, a unique identification number, `CustomerID`, is assigned to the customer. In addition, for each order, a unique number, `OrderNo`, is assigned. The `OrderNo` is defined as the primary key for the table. Table 27-1 shows the fields in the `BookersOrders` table in the BookersDB database.

**Table 27-1 Structure of the `BookersOrders` Table**

| Column Name | Data Type | Length | Allow Nulls |
|---|---|---|---|
| OrderNo | char | 10 | 0 |
| CustomerID | char | 6 | 0 |
| ISBNNo | char | 10 | 0 |

**NOTE**

In the preceding structure of the `BookersOrders` table, the value `0` for the `Allow Nulls` column does not allow the user to leave this field blank. However, if you specify the value as `1`, the field is optional when adding a new record. I will be using this convention while discussing the structure of the rest of the tables.

## The `BookersCustDetails` Table

In addition to storing the details of the order, Bookers Paradise wants to store the details of all the customers who place an order for a book. To do this, the `BookersCustDetails` table is created. The `BookersCustDetails` table contains fields such as `CustomerID`, `CustomerName`, `BillingAddress`, and so on. The `CustomerID` field is set as primary key for this table. Table 27-2 shows the details of the `BookersCustDetails` table.

**Table 27-2 Structure of the `BookersCustDetails` Table**

| Column Name | Data Type | Length | Allow Nulls |
|---|---|---|---|
| CustomerID | char | 6 | 0 |
| CustomerName | varchar | 50 | 0 |
| BillingAddress1 | varchar | 50 | 0 |
| BillingAddress2 | varchar | 50 | 0 |
| BillingAddressCity | varchar | 20 | 0 |
| BillingAddressState | varchar | 20 | 0 |

## Database Design for Deepthoughts Publications

If you consider the business requirements for the Web portal project, when a customer places an order for a book, the order, along with the information about the customer, is forwarded to the respective publisher. Deepthoughts Publications then stores this information in a database called DTDB. The DTDB database contains two tables, the `DTCatalog` and the `DTOrders` tables. I will discuss the structure of these tables in the following sections.

### The `DTCatalog` Table

The `DTCatalog` table stores information about the books published by Deepthoughts Publications. This information includes the ISBN number, title, author, date of publishing, price, and category of the book. In addition, the table contains a short description of the book.

Every book published at the publishing house has a unique ISBN number, which is defined as the primary key for the `DTCatalog` table. Table 27-3 shows the structure of the `DTCatalog` table.

**Table 27-3 Structure of the `DTCatalog` Table**

| Column Name | Data Type | Length | Allow Nulls |
|---|---|---|---|
| ISBNNo | char | 10 | 0 |
| BookTitle | varchar | 50 | 0 |
| Author | varchar | 50 | 0 |
| Category | char | 10 | 0 |
| Description | varchar | 50 | 0 |
| DateOfPublication | datetime | 8 | 0 |
| Price | varchar | 8 | 0 |

### The `DTOrders` Table

The `DTOrders` table stores information about an order placed by the customer. In addition, you can store the details of the customer who placed the order. Table 27-4 shows the fields in the `DTOrders` table.

**Table 27-4 Structure of the `DTOrders` Table**

| Column Name | Data Type | Length | Allow Nulls |
|---|---|---|---|
| ISBNNo | char | 10 | 0 |
| OrderNo | char | 5 | 0 |
| DateOfOrder | datetime | 8 | 0 |
| CustomerName | varchar | 50 | 0 |
| CustomerAddress1 | varchar | 50 | 0 |
| CustomerAddress2 | varchar | 50 | 1 |
| CustomerCity | varchar | 20 | 0 |
| CustomerState | varchar | 10 | 0 |
| OrderedBy | varchar | 50 | 0 |
| Status | varchar | 20 | 0 |
| CreditCardType | char | 10 | 0 |
| CreditCardNumber | varchar | 20 | 0 |

The preceding table contains a `Status` column. This column contains information about the status of the delivery of the book to the customer. In addition, Table 27-4 contains a field with the name `OrderedBy`. This field stores the information about the retailer who ordered for the specified book. In our case, the value stored in this field is Bookers Paradise.

The `DTOrders` table also contains information about the credit card of the customer, such as the type of credit card and the credit card number of the customer.

The `DTOrders` table has the combination of `ISBNNo` and `OrderNo` fields as the composite key.

## Database Design for Black and White Publications

Black and White Publications maintains a database called BWDB. Similar to the database of Deepthoughts Publications, the BWDB database stores information about the books published by Black and White Publications and the customers who order the books. To store this information, the BWDB database has two tables, `BWCatalog` and `BWOrders`. The following sections discuss these tables in detail.

## The `BWCatalog` Table

The `BWCatalog` table stores information about the books published by Black and White Publications. Table 27-5 shows the structure of the `BWCatalog` table.

**Table 27-5 Structure of the `BWCatalog` Table**

| Column Name | Data Type | Length | Allow Nulls |
|---|---|---|---|
| ISBNNo | char | 10 | 0 |
| BookName | varchar | 50 | 0 |
| Author | varchar | 50 | 0 |
| Price | decimal | 9 | 0 |
| AboutTheAuthor | varchar | 100 | 1 |
| Category | varchar | 30 | 0 |

As you can see, the `BWCatalog` table stores information such as the ISBN number, name, author, price, and category of the book. In addition, the preceding table contains the `AboutTheAuthor` field. You can store some information about the author of the book in this field. The `ISBNNo` field is set as the primary key for this table.

## The `BWOrders` Table

Similar to the orders table of Deepthoughts Publications, the orders table of Black and White Publications stores information about the orders that are sent by the site of Bookers Paradise. Table 27-6 shows the fields contained in the `BWOrders` table in the BWDB database.

**Table 27-6 Structure of the BWOrders Table**

| Column Name | Data Type | Length | Allow Nulls |
|---|---|---|---|
| ISBNNo | char | 10 | 0 |
| OrderNo | char | 5 | 0 |
| DateOfOrder | datetime | 8 | 0 |
| CustomerName | varchar | 50 | 0 |
| CustomerAddress1 | varchar | 50 | 0 |
| CustomerAddress2 | varchar | 50 | 0 |
| CustomerCity | varchar | 20 | 0 |
| CustomerState | varchar | 20 | 0 |
| RequestedBy | varchar | 20 | 0 |
| Status | varchar | 20 | 0 |
| CreditCardType | char | 10 | 0 |
| CreditCardNumber | varchar | 20 | 0 |

Similar to the `Status` and `OrderedBy` fields of the `DTOrders` table, the `Status` and `RequestedBy` fields of the `BWOrders` table store the status of delivery of the book and the details of the retailer who ordered for the book, respectively.

In addition, the `BWOrders` table contains the credit card information of the customer who orders for a book on the Web site of Bookers Paradise.

## Database Schema

Having created the design of the tables of Bookers Paradise, Deepthoughts Publications and Black and White Publications, you need to establish relationships between the tables of the organizations. Based on these relationships, a detailed database schema is created. I will first discuss the relationships between the tables of Bookers Paradise.

## The Relationships between the Tables of Bookers Paradise

The relationships between the tables of Bookers Paradise are shown in Figure 27-1.

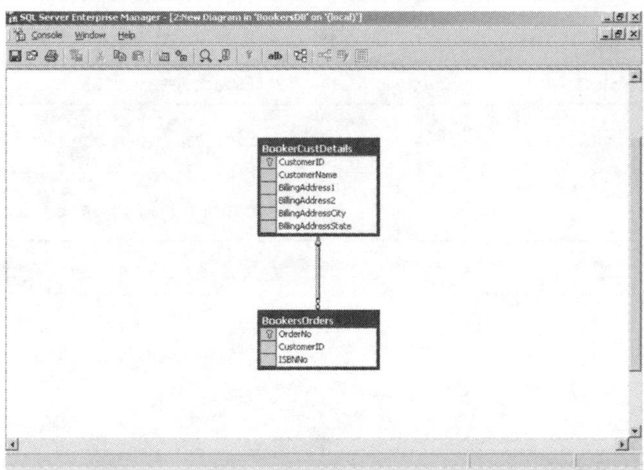


**FIGURE 27-1** *Database schema for Bookers Paradise*

Table 27-7 explains the relationships between the tables of Bookers Paradise shown in Figure 27-1.

**Table 27-7 Relationships in the Tables of Bookers Paradise Database**

| Table1 | Table2 | Type | Description |
|---|---|---|---|
| BookerCustDetails | BookersOrders | One-to-many | One customer can place one or more orders. However, one order can contain orders from only one customer. |

## The Relationships between the Tables of Deepthoughts Publications

The relationships between the tables of Deepthoughts Publications are explained in Table 27-8.

**Table 27-8 Relationships in the Tables of Deepthoughts Publications Database**

| Table1 | Table2 | Type | Description |
|---|---|---|---|
| DTCatalog | DTOrders | Many-to-many | One order can be placed for one book. However, one order can contain one or more books. |

This relationship is shown in Figure 27-2.

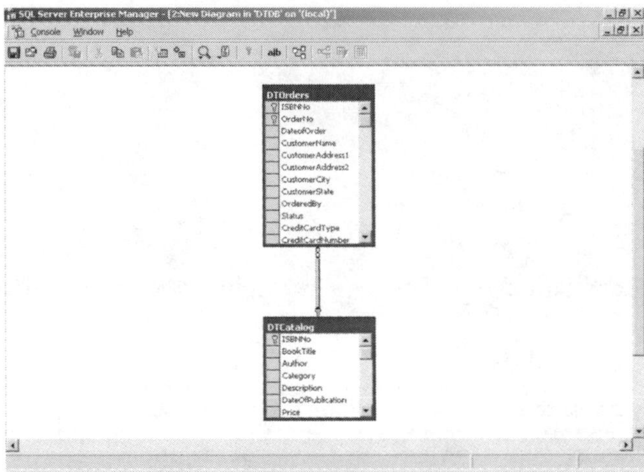


**FIGURE 27-2** *Database schema for Deepthoughts Publications*

## The Relationships between the Tables of Black and White Publications

The relationships between the tables of Black and White Publications are similar to those of Deepthoughts Publications. Figure 27-3 shows the relationships of Black and White Publications.

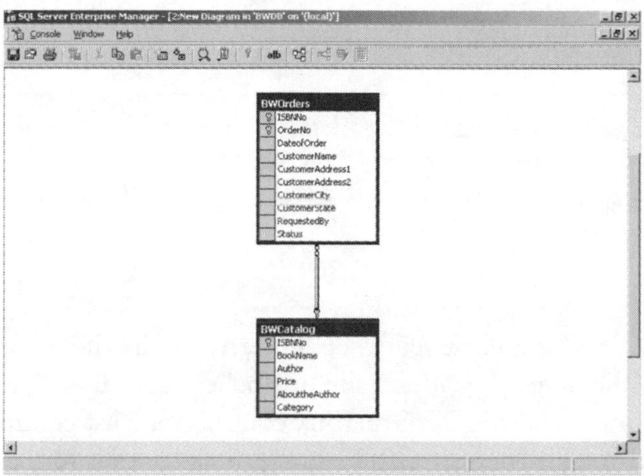


**FIGURE 27-3** *Database schema for Black and White Publications*

The relationships shown in Figure 27-3 are explained in Table 27-9.

**Table 27-9 Relationships in the Tables of Black and White Publications Database**

| Table1 | Table2 | Type | Description |
|---|---|---|---|
| BWCatalog | BWOrders | One-to-many | One order can be placed for one book. However, one order can contain one or more books. |

After you finalize the database schema, you can finalize the interface of your application. Finalizing the interface of the application includes deciding on the Web forms to be included in the application. This will help the development team to have a framework to work on.

## Web Forms Design

The Web site for Bookers Paradise includes five forms, the Main form, the Results form, the Orders form, the Search form, and the Construction form. The following section discusses these forms in detail.

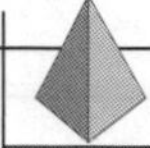

**TIP**

In this chapter, I will only detail the layout of these forms. You will learn to create these forms in Chapter 30, "Developing Web Service Clients."

## The Main Form

The Main form is the first form displayed when a user visits the site of Bookers Paradise. This form is the home page of the site of Booker's Paradise. The Main form consists of one button control, five hyperlink controls, one list control, one text box control, and two table controls. After adding these controls to the form, you need to change the properties of these controls. You will learn to change the properties of the controls in Chapter 30.

Once the controls are added to the form, the Main form looks as shown in Figure 27-4.

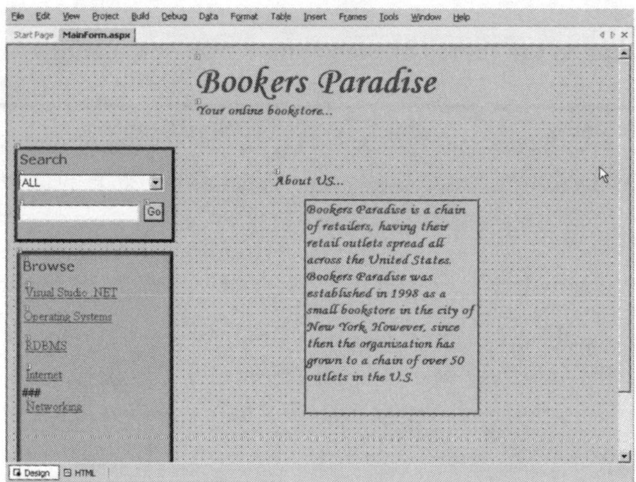


**FIGURE 27-4** *The layout of the Main form*

The Main form allows you to search for information about all the books or only books based on criteria. When the user selects the criteria and clicks on the Go button in the Main form, the Results page is displayed.

## The Results Form

The Results form shows the result of the search performed by the user. In addition, the Results page allows the user to order a book. The Results page includes a data grid, a label, and a hyperlink control.

To add these controls to the form, drag the controls from the Web Forms toolbox. When the controls are added, the Results form looks as shown in Figure 27-5.

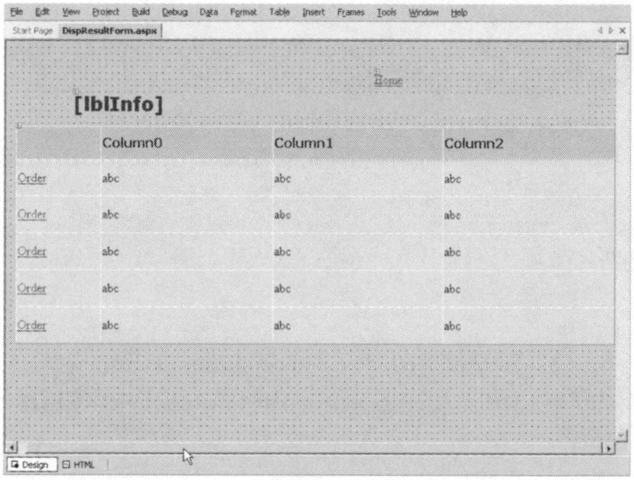

**FIGURE 27-5** *The layout of the Results form*

In the Results page, the user can choose a book to order. To order a book, a user needs to click on the Order button. This takes the user to the Orders page.

## The Orders Form

The Orders form accepts details of the user who wishes to order a book on the Web site of Booker's Paradise. Figure 27-6 shows the layout of the Orders form.

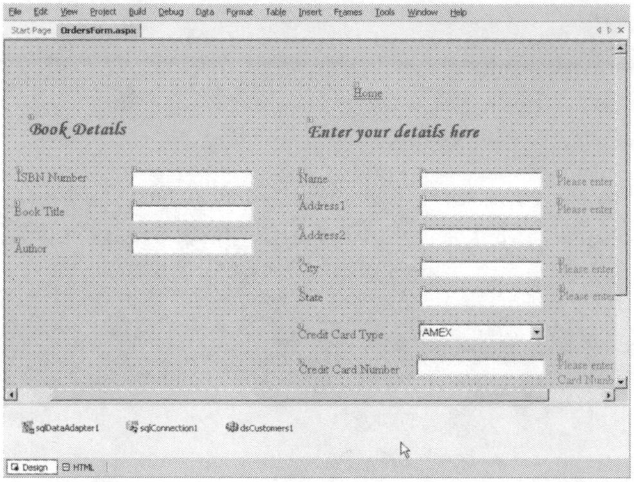

FIGURE 27-6 *The layout of the Orders form*

As you can see in Figure 27-6, the Orders form includes 1 button control, 2 hyperlink controls, 12 label controls, 1 list control, 5 RequiredFieldValidator controls, and 10 text box controls.

## The Search Form

The Main form in the site of Booker's Paradise allows a user to select criteria to search for a book. When a user selects criteria in the list box, the user needs to specify a value for the criteria. In case the user forgets to specify a value, the user is taken to the Search page.

The Search page prompts the user to specify the criteria and a value for the criteria. To do this, the Search page includes a label control, two button controls, four radio buttons, and four text box controls.

Figure 27-7 shows the layout of the Search form.

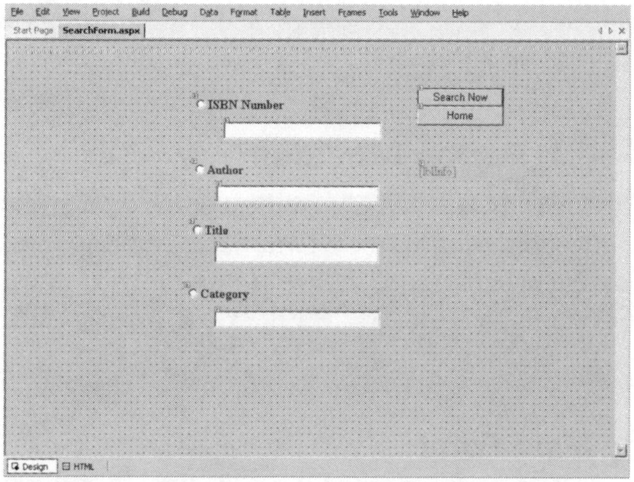

FIGURE 27-7 *The layout of the Search form*

## The Construction Form

The Main form, as you saw in Figure 27-4, includes hyperlink controls. When a user clicks on any of the hyperlink controls, the user is taken to the Construction page. Figure 27-8 shows the Construction page.

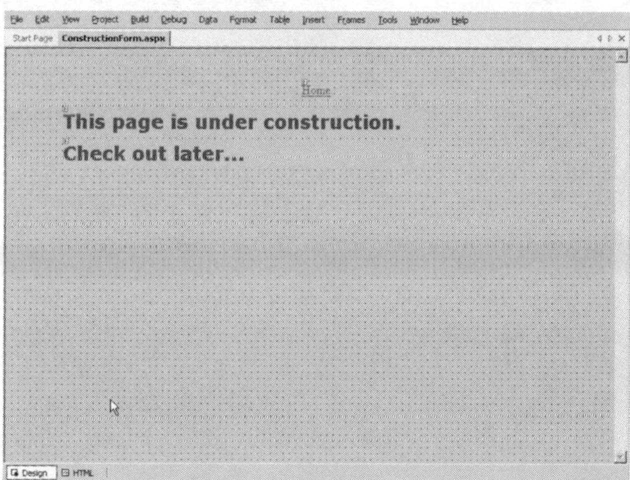


FIGURE 27-8 *The layout of the Construction form*

The Construction form contains a hyperlink control and two label controls. The hyperlink on the Construction page takes you to the Main form.

## Flowcharts for the Web Forms Modules

After seeing the design of all the forms in the Web client application for Booker's Paradise, you can create the flowcharts for these forms. This will help you understand the working of the client application, making it easier for you to write the code for the client application. To begin, create a flowchart for the Main form, which is the home page for the Web site.

### *Flowchart for the Main Form*

In the Main page, the user selects criteria, specifies a value for the criteria, and queries for the information based on the criteria. In addition, the user may choose to click on any of the hyperlinks on the Main form. Based on this functionality, a flowchart for the Main form is created. Figure 27-9 shows the flowchart for the Main form.

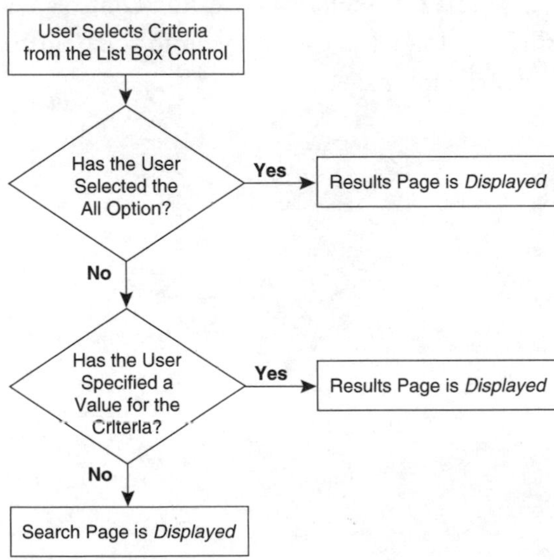


**FIGURE 27-9** *The flowchart for the Main form*

## Flowchart for the Results Form

The Results form allows a user to select a book to order. Based on this, the flowchart for the Results page is shown in Figure 27-10.

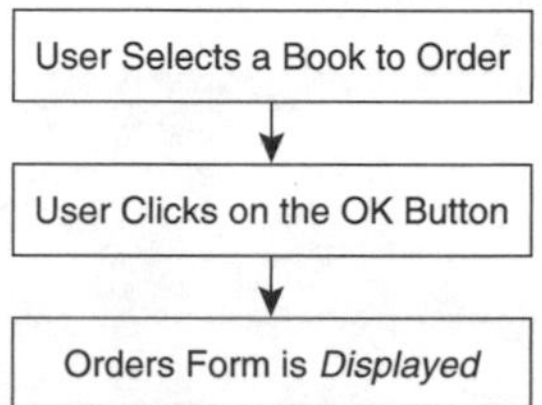


**FIGURE 27-10** *The flowchart for the Results form*

## Flowchart for the Orders Form

The Orders page accepts the information about the customer and passes this information to the database of the publisher. In addition, the information about the book that is ordered is passed to the database of the publisher. To do this, the Orders form works as shown in Figure 27-11.

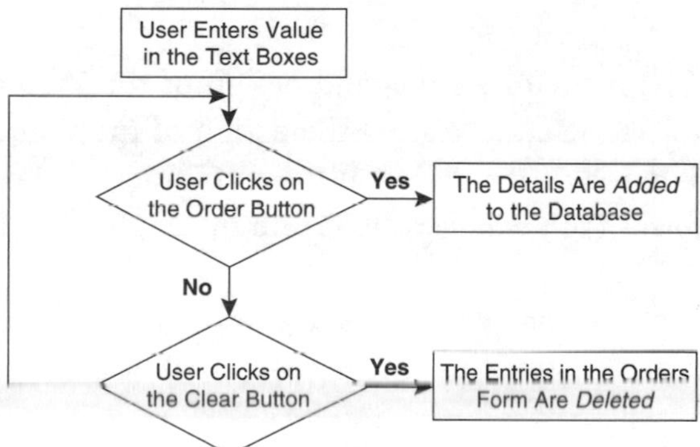


**FIGURE 27-11** *The flowchart for the Orders form*

### Flowchart for the Search Form

In the Search page, the user selects a radio button to choose criteria to search for information about the site. In addition, the user specifies the value for the criteria. Figure 27-12 shows this functionality of the Search page in the form of a flowchart.

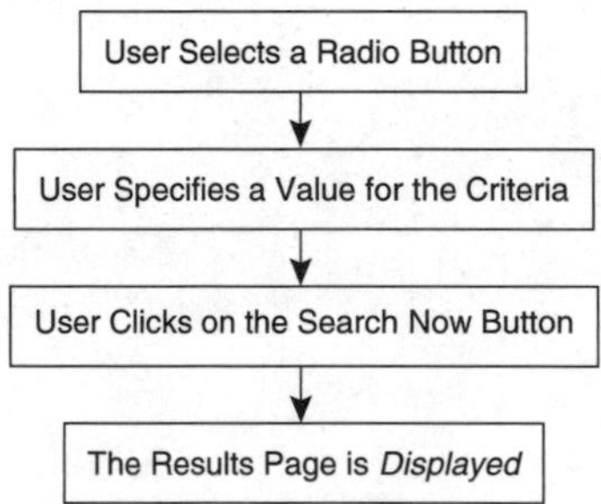


**FIGURE 27-12** *The flowchart for the Search form*

## Summary

In this chapter, you learned about the case study and design of the Web portal project. The design of the project includes creating the design of the application and the supporting databases. Based on the design of the application, you created the flowcharts for the Web forms. You will learn to create the application in the forthcoming chapters.

# Chapter 28

## Exploring ASP.NET Web Services

The ever-changing business scenario has become more and more dependent on the Web for any data transaction or for communication between applications. Because of this dependency, the focus of developers is shifting from creating a desktop application to an application that can access data through the Internet. These applications are mainly distributed applications. *Distributed applications* are scalable applications in which data is shared across applications.

For example, a distributed application consists of a client application that interacts with a middleware application, which contains the business logic for the entire business solution that you create. This intermediate application in turn interacts with the underlying databases that store the data for the application. Therefore, as you can see, a business solution on the whole comprises a number of applications and databases. These applications and databases may be present on a single computer. However, in large-scale business operations, these applications are generally distributed across different computers connected over a network. In such cases, these applications may be created using different programming languages and, in the worst scenario, on different platforms.

To build a complete business solution, it is essential that you integrate these applications. Integration of applications built on various platforms is made simpler with the use of Web services.

In this chapter, you will be introduced to the basics of ASP.NET Web services. In addition, you will learn about the architecture and working of a Web service. Next, you will be introduced to the technologies used in a Web service. These technologies include XML (*Extensible Markup Language*), SOAP (*Simple Object Access Protocol*), WSDL (*Web Services Description Language*), and UDDI (*Universal Description Discovery and Integration*). Finally, you will learn to create a simple Web service in a Visual Studio .NET.

# Introduction to ASP.NET Web Services

You were introduced to Web services in Chapter 1, "Overview of the .NET Framework," in the section "Introduction to the .NET Framework." In this chapter, I will discuss Web services in detail.

As discussed earlier, a Web service is used to integrate different applications that access data through the Internet. To do this, methods in a Web service are called over the Internet, which can then be accessed by applications developed on different platforms. This implies that a Web service is a reusable component, such as a method, that can be used by any Web application running on the Internet. In addition, a Web service can be used by a Windows application. These applications are called *Web service client applications*.

Before developing Web services, DLL (*Dynamic Link Library*) files or components were used to create distributed applications. However, to communicate with a client application, these components use protocols such as RPC (*Remote Procedure Call*), DCOM (*Distributed Component Object Model*), RMI (*Remote Method Invocation*), or IIOP (*Internet Inter-ORB Protocol*). Therefore, communication between a client application and a component depends on various factors, such as hardware platform, programming languages, vendor implementations, and data-encryption schemes. This implies that transferring data between two applications requires a similar infrastructure at the two application sites. However, this scenario cannot be obtained while working with Internet applications. An Internet application can be accessed by various client applications. Therefore, it is essential to build components that can be used to create distributed applications that can be accessed from various platforms. To do this, you can use Web services. Web services allow you to create platform independent distributed applications. The ability to create distributed applications that are independent of the platform is mainly due to the support of a Web service for Internet standards, such as HTTP and XML.

In addition to integrating applications built on different platforms, a Web service allows you to integrate business solutions for one or more organizations. You can create a Web service specific for your organization or customize a Web service created by another organization to your specific requirements. You can also create a Web service that can be used by a single application or be called on the Internet to be used by multiple applications. To call a Web service from the Internet, the

Web service client needs to know the location of the Web service and the input and output information required for accessing the Web service.

A Web service that you create can be a simple one-method service. For example, consider a situation in which you want to know the current time in a particular state. In this case, you can create a method in a Web service that returns the current time in the state that you choose. You can pass the state for which you want to know the current time as a parameter to the method. The method created in a Web service is called a *Web method*. You will learn to about Web methods in detail later in this chapter.

In addition to performing simple tasks by using a Web service method, you can create Web methods that perform complex tasks. In such cases, a Web service may consist of several Web methods performing complex tasks. For example, consider a situation in which you need to validate the username and password entered by a user to log on to a site. This is a very common scenario, as almost all Web sites require a method to validate the username and password. Therefore, in such a case, you can create a Web service that performs data validations. In addition, the Web service that you create can be used to validate data for various Web sites. You can then customize the Web service according the requirements based on your database schema. In this case, the Web site that uses the Web service to perform data validations is called a Web service client application, and the application that hosts the Web service is called a *Web service provider application*.

The data validation scenario that I discussed involves various applications and an underlying database. For example, the Web site that needs to perform data validation is a Web application, which interacts with a database. The database may be created using SQL, Access, Oracle, or any other RDBMS (*Relational Database Management System*). In addition, for the Web application to perform validations based on the data in the database, the Web application uses another application. In this case, another application required to perform validations is a Web service. Therefore, as you can see, multiple applications are involved in a complete business solution. To integrate these applications, a Web service can be used. The next sections will show how a Web service can provide integration of multiple applications.

A Web service uses XML and any other Internet standard, such as HTTP, to create an infrastructure that helps you to integrate applications build on multiple platforms. Because of the support of Web services for XML, these Web services are often referred to as *XML Web services*.

An XML Web service uses SOAP messaging to communicate and transfer data across applications. In addition, SOAP messaging allows a great deal of abstraction between a Web service client and a Web service provider. This implies that using the XML messaging technique allows you to create a client and a service provider independent of each other.

By now, you must have got an idea of the need for a Web service. I will now discuss the architecture of a Web service.

## Web Service Architecture

As discussed earlier, a Web service can be an intermediate application that allows a Web service client application to access data from an underlying database. To do this, the Web service architecture internally consists of four layers. These layers are explained in the following bulleted list.

- **The data layer.** The *data layer* is the first layer in the Web service architecture. This layer contains the data that the Web client application needs to access.
- **The data access layer.** The layer above the data layer is the *data access layer*. The data access layer contains the business logic or the code that allows the Web client application to access the data in the data layer. In addition to storing data, the data access layer is used to secure the data present in the data layer.
- **The business layer.** The third layer in the Web service architecture is the *business layer*. This layer contains the code required for implementing the Web service. The business layer in turn is divided into *business logic* and *business façade* layers. The business logic layer contains all the services provided in a Web service. However, the business façade layer acts as an interface of the Web service.
- **The listener layer.** The layer closest to the Web service client is the *listener layer*. It is the main layer used by the Web service client to communicate with the Web service. When a Web service client wants to access a Web method present in a Web service, the Web service client sends in a request. This request is received by the listener layer. The listener layer then interprets the request sent by the Web service client application. When the client request is processed and the Web service returns the response in the form of an XML message, the listener layer forwards this XML message to the Web service client.

The Web service architecture is explained in Figure 28-1.

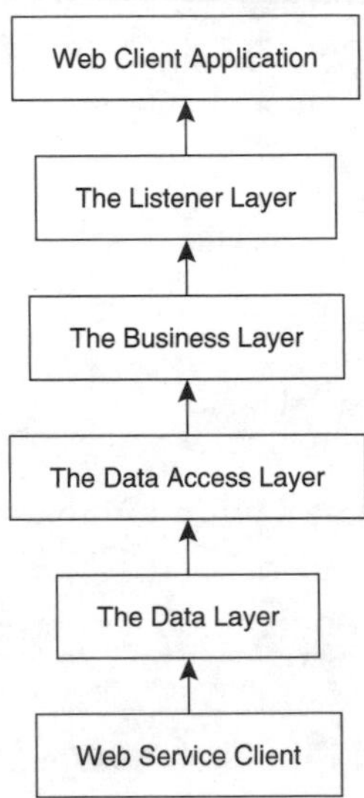


**FIGURE 28-1** *The Web service architecture*

After discussing the four-layered structure of a Web service, I will look at the working of the Web service based on the Web service architecture.

## Working of a Web Service

The working of a Web service involves the client application sending a request for a service. The request made to the Web service is in the form of an XML message using a transfer protocol, such as HTTP. This scenario is somewhat similar to a method call statement that you use to call a particular method. The request for the service is passed to the listener layer, which forwards the request to the Web service provider application. The request is then processed by the Web service provider application. Processing of the request includes the data access layer to retrieve the data requested by the client application. This data is then passed to the listener layer, which in turn forwards the data to the client application. Figure 28-2 shows the working of a Web service.

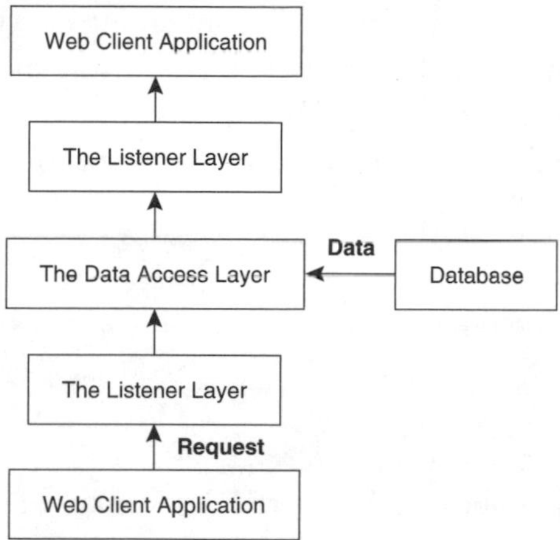


**FIGURE 28-2** *The working of a Web service*

I will now discuss the working of a Web service in detail. When a client application sends a request for a service, you may need to pass arguments. To pass arguments over the network, the arguments are packaged as a SOAP message and passed to the Web method by using a network protocol. You will learn about SOAP in detail later in this chapter.

Then, the Web service decodes the SOAP message to retrieve the arguments passed to the Web method. Once the arguments are passed to the Web method, the method is executed and the return value is passed to the Web client application.

Having learned about the working of a Web service, you can look at the technologies that are used by a Web service.

# Technologies Used in Web Services

You can create Web services by using any language provided by the .NET Framework, such as Visual C# .NET, Visual Basic .NET, and Visual C++ .NET. However, for an application to be able to access a Web service, the client application needs to meet certain requirements. These requirements include a standard format for describing Web services, a standard format for representing data transfer, and a standard for sending methods and the results returned by the methods across the network. In addition, to be able to access a Web service, the Web client application needs to identify a method for locating the Web service and passing inputs to the Web methods.

As a solution to these requirements, technologies such as XML, WSDL, and SOAP were developed. The following sections discuss these technologies in detail.

## XML in a Web Service

XML is a markup language used to describe data in a particular format. This data can be accessed by any application built on any platform. XML allows you to transfer data in a format that is independent of the platform. Therefore, XML is a widely used technology that transfers data across the Internet applications. XML documents store data in the form of text. This makes the XML document easily understood by applications built on different platforms. Moreover, content stored in an XML document is easily transferred over the network.

Having discussed XML in general, you can see how a Web service uses XML. When a Web service client application calls a Web service, the client application passes arguments to the Web method. The Web service processes the Web methods and returns a result to the client application. Because the client application can be built using any platform, the data returned by the Web service is in the form of XML.

## WSDL in a Web Service

WSDL is a markup language that defines a Web service. WSDL is an XML file that contains information about a Web service. This information includes the Web services called by a Web site, the methods included in each of the Web services, and the parameters that you need to pass to the Web methods. In addition, WSDL includes information about the results returned when a request is processed by a Web service. For example, WSDL defines the type of the values returned by a Web method. Therefore, WSDL is a vocabulary defined for the creation of a Web service that the developer may need to use while creating a Web service.

In addition to storing information about the Web methods, WSDL stores information about the format used by a user to access a Web service and specifies the location at which the Web service is available. Therefore, WSDL describes the entire mechanism involved in the transfer of data from a Web service client to the Web service and vice versa.

For example, a Web service client application needs to call a Web method that validates the username and password entered by the user. The Web method is created in a Web service. To call this Web method, the Web service client sends a request to the Web service. The request that is sent to the Web method is specified by WSDL. The request is sent to the Web service in the form of XML messages. In this case, WSDL stores the format in which the request is sent.

In addition, when a Web method is called, you need to pass the username and password as parameters. The information about the type and the format of the parameters is stored in a WSDL file. When the request is processed and the result is returned, WSDL stores the format and other information about the results returned.

## SOAP in a Web Service

To transfer data from a Web service client to a Web service and vice versa, the transfer protocol used is SOAP. SOAP is a protocol based on XML that is used by a client application to access a Web service. In addition to XML, SOAP uses HTTP for the transfer of data. When a client sends a request, the request is in the form of a SOAP message. The SOAP message also includes the parameters and the method call statement. Based on this information in the SOAP message, the appropriate Web method is called.

As discussed earlier, SOAP is a standard protocol used for communication between a Web service client and a Web service. However, SOAP does not define syntax to be followed while transferring data. Instead, SOAP provides a mechanism for packaging data to be transferred across a network. In addition, SOAP is a transfer protocol based on simple Internet standards. The transfer of data using SOAP takes place in the form of a SOAP package. A SOAP package includes an envelope that encapsulates the data to be exchanged.

In addition to these technologies, Web services uses UDDI to identify the Web services provided by various Web service providers. I will now discuss UDDI in detail.

## UDDI in a Web Service

When you develop a Web service, you need to register the Web service in a UDDI directory. UDDI provides a mechanism for the Web service providers to register their Web services. When a Web service is registered with a UDDI directory, an entry for the Web service is created. A UDDI directory maintains an XML file for each Web service registered with the UDDI directory. This XML file contains a pointer to the Web service that is registered in the directory. In addition, the UDDI directory also contains pointers to the WSDL document for a Web service. To do this, the Web service provider needs to first describe the Web service in a WSDL document. Once a WSDL document is created, the Web service can be registered with the UDDI directory. This makes the Web service easily accessible to the Web service clients, as the client applications can discover and identify a Web service from a UDDI directory.

Consider the example of the Web service used to perform user validation. Once you have created the Web service and described it in a WSDL document, you can register the Web service with the UDDI directory. Then, any user who wants to use the Web method can search on the UDDI directory for the required Web method. The UDDI directory returns the list of Web services that are registered with the UDDI directory. The user can then select the required Web method from the list of the available Web services.

A UDDI directory contains white pages, yellow pages, and green pages. The white pages contain information about the organization that provides the Web service. This information includes the name, address, and other contact numbers of the Web service provider company. The yellow pages in a UDDI directory contain information about the companies based on geographical taxonomies. The green pages provide the service interface for the client applications that access the Web service.

After discussing Web services and the technologies used with Web services, I will discuss how Web services fit into the .NET Framework.

# Web Services in the .NET Framework

The .NET Framework provides a complete framework for developing Web services. This implies that in the .NET Framework you can not only create Web services but also deploy, use, and maintain the Web services. The .NET Framework provides you with tools and technologies that you can use to develop a Web service. The following section discusses how to create a Web service in Visual Studio .NET.

Similar to creating a Windows application and a Web application, Visual Studio .NET provides you with a template to create a Web service. The template for creating a Web service is provided in the New Project dialog box. To access the Web service template, perform the following steps:

1. On the File menu, point to the New option.
2. In the displayed list, select the Project option.

   The New Project dialog box is displayed.
3. In the right pane of the New Project dialog box, select the ASP.NET Web Service project template option.
4. In the Location text box, type the address of the Web server on which you will develop the Web service.

In our case, the development server is the local computer. You can also specify the name of the Web service, SampleWebService, in the Location text box. Figure 28-3 shows the New Project dialog box with the ASP.NET Web Service project template selected.

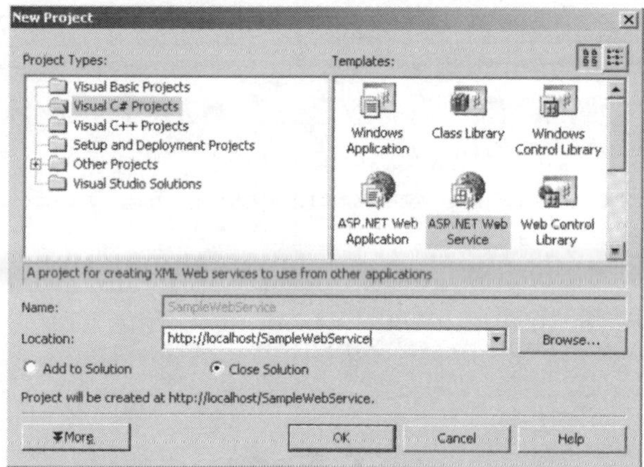


**FIGURE 28-3** *The New Project dialog box*

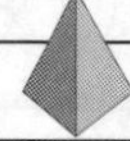

**TIP**

The Web server that you specify as the development server must have the .NET Framework and IIS (*Internet Information Server*) 5.0 or later installed on it. In case you have IIS 5.0 installed on your local computer, you can specify the path in the Location text box of the local computer.

A Web service with the name SampleWebService is created. Figure 28-4 shows the design view for SampleWebService.

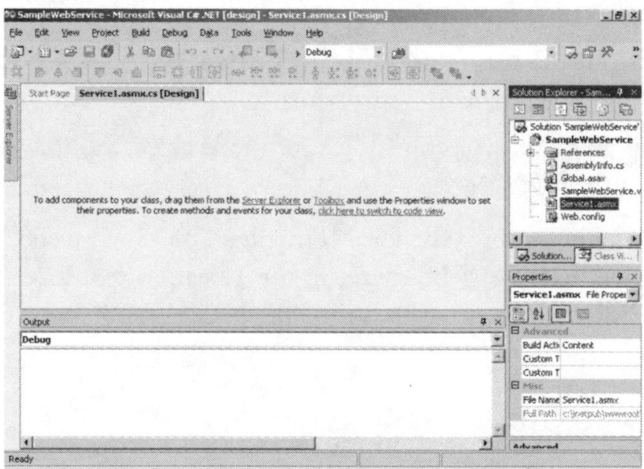


**FIGURE 28-4** *The design view for SampleWebService*

SampleWebService contains the files and references required for the Web service. The description of these files is given in Table 28-1.

**Table 28-1 Files in a Web Service**

| Files | Description |
|---|---|
| `AssemblyInfo.cs` | This file contains the metadata of the assembly for the project. |
| `Service1.asmx.cs` | This file contains the code for the class declared in the Web service. |
| `Service1.asmx` | This file is the entry point of the Web service and contains information about the processing directive of the Web service. The processing directive identifies the class in which the code for the Web service is implemented. |
| `Global.asax.cs` | This file contains the code for handling the events generated in the application. |
| `Global.asax` | This file contains information about handling the events generated in the application. |
| `Web.config` | This file contains information about the configuration settings of ASP.NET resources. |
| `SampleWebService.csproj.webinfo` | This file contains information about the location of the project on the development server. |
| `SampleWebService.vsdisco` | This file contains the description of the Web service that is required by the client application to access the Web service. The file contains the description of the methods and interfaces used in the Web service to enable programmers to communicate with these resources. |
| `SampleWebService.sln` | This solution file contains the metadata of the solution. If your local server is your development server, the `SampleWebService.sln` file exists on the local server. |
| `SampleWebService.csproj` | This project file contains information about the list of files related to a project. |

When you create a Web service, the component designer view for `Service1.asmx` is displayed. The `Service1.asmx.cs` file contains the code for the Web service. You will learn about the default code generated by Visual Studio .NET later in this chapter.

In the .NET Framework, you can create complex Web services that an application can use to access data over the Internet. You will learn about creating complex Web services during the project. However, in this chapter, you will create a simple Web service that will help you to have a better understanding of how to create a Web service.

## Creating a Simple Web Service in the .NET Framework

In this section, I will show how to create a simple Web service in the .NET Framework. Name this Web service SampleWebService. You can create a Web service by using the ASP.NET Web Service template in the New Project dialog box. In the Location: text box of the New Project dialog box, specify the name of the Web service as SampleWebService.

When you click on the OK button in the New Project dialog box, Visual Studio .NET creates a virtual directory with the name of your Web service. In case a Web service with the specified name already exists, Visual Studio .NET prompts you to specify another name for your Web service. Figure 28-5 shows the window displayed when Visual Studio .NET creates a new virtual directory.

**FIGURE 28-5** *The window displayed while creating a new virtual directory*

As you can see, the Web service does not have any user interface or a form. The default file displayed when Visual Studio .NET creates a Web service is `Service1.asmx`. I have already explained the default files generated by Visual Studio .NET in Table 28-1.

After creating the Web service, you need to add Web methods to the Web service. The code behind the Web service is written in the `Service1.asmx.cs` file. To access the `Service1.asmx.cs` file, press the F7 key or double-click the `Service1.asmx` file.

As you can see in the `Service1.asmx.cs` file, Visual Studio .NET generates a default code for your Web service. The following section discusses the default code created by Visual Studio .NET.

## The Default Code Generated for a Web Service

Creating a Web service includes writing the code for Web methods in a Web service. However, before you add Web methods to the Web service, Visual Studio .NET generates a default code as shown:

```
using System;
using System.Collections;
using System.ComponentModel;
using System.Data;
using System.Diagnostics;
using System.Web;
using System.Web.Services;

namespace SampleWebService
{
    public class Service1 : System.Web.Services.WebService
    {
        public Service1()
        {
            InitializeComponent();
        }
    //WEB SERVICE EXAMPLE
        // The HelloWorld() example service returns the string Hello World
        // To build, uncomment the following lines then save and build the project
        // To test this web service, press F5
        //[WebMethod]
        //public string HelloWorld()
```

```
        //{
            //return "Hello World";
        //}
    }
}
```

The preceding code includes the required namespaces in your Web service. In addition, the code creates a namespace with the name of your Web service. Inside the `SampleWebService` namespace, a `public` class with the name `Service1` is declared. This class contains a default constructor, `Service1`. In addition, the code contains a simple Web method with the name `HelloWorld()`. The `HelloWorld()` Web method returns a string `Hello World` when the Web service is run.

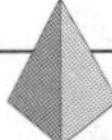

**TIP**

As you can see in the preceding code, the Web method `HelloWorld()` is marked as comment entries. You can remove the front slash (//) signs preceding the Web method declaration statements.

When you remove the comment signs and build the Web service, the Service1.asmx page, as shown in Figure 28-6, is created.

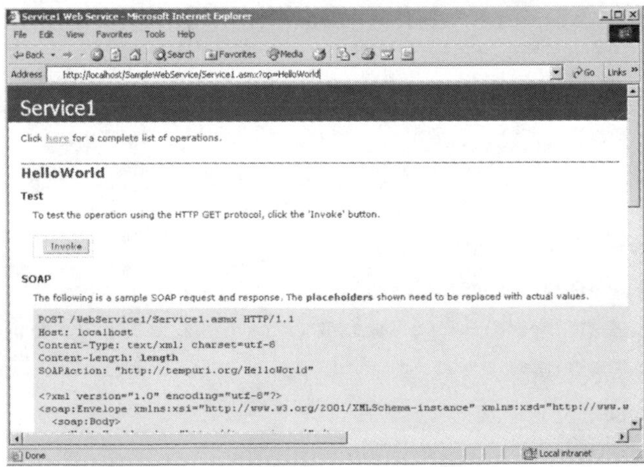


**FIGURE 28-6** *The Service1.asmx page*

As you can see in Figure 28-6, the Service1.asmx page contains the SOAP message used to send a request for a Web service. In addition, the Service1.asmx page contains the response of the request for the Web service. The response for the SampleWebService Web service is in the form of a SOAP message

The Service1.asmx page contains an Invoke button that you can click to test the Web service. When you click on the Invoke button, the Hello World Web service is displayed, as shown in Figure 28-7.

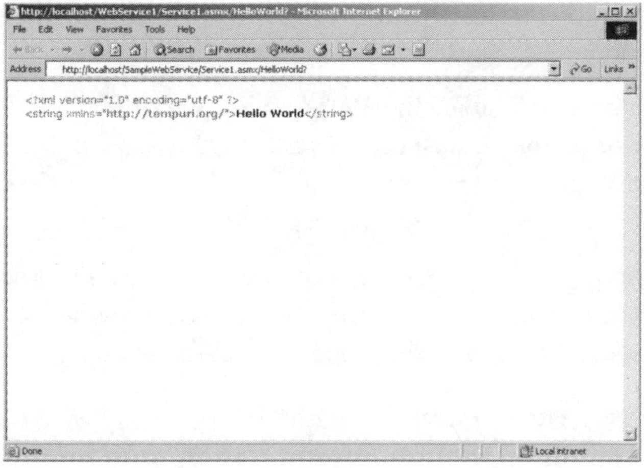


**FIGURE 28-7** *The Hello World Web service*

Having seen a sample Web service, you can now continue with the procedure for creating the SampleWebService Web service.

## Creating a Web Method in the SampleWebService Web Service

Until now, I have not specified the task that the Web method in the SampleWebService Web service would perform. You can create a Web method that returns the day of the week on which a date falls. For example, if January 1, 2002 was Tuesday, the value returned by the Web method will be 2.

When you create a Web service, it is a good practice to specify a summary of the Web service. This will help any user who tries to locate a similar Web service. To add a summary to your Web service, add the following line in the beginning of your Web service.

```
[WebService(Namespace="http://WebServices/SampleWebService", Description="This
   service retrieves the day of the week on which a date falls.")]
```

The preceding statement includes information about the Web service that you create. This information includes the URL that you can use to access the Web service and a short description of the task performed by the Web service.

After providing the information about the Web service, write the code for the Web method required to perform the specified task. In this case, the task performed by the Web method is to return the day of the week on which a specified date falls. Therefore, you need to pass the date as a parameter to the Web method.

Similar to writing a description for the Web service, you can write a short description for the Web method that you declare in the Web service. To write a description for the Web method, add the following code to the Web service.

```
[WebMethod(Description="This method returns the day of the week in integer format.
   It expects a date in mm/dd/yyyy format and returns 8 if the value specified is
   invalid.")]
```

After adding a description of the Web method to the code, write the actual code for the Web method. The code for the Web method is as follows:

```
[WebMethod(Description="This method returns the day of the week in integer format.
   It expects a date in mm/dd/yyyy format and returns 8 if the value specified is
   invalid.")]
public int GetDay(DateTime dt)
{
            System.DayOfWeek dw;
            dw=dt.DayOfWeek;
            switch(dw.ToString())
            {
                        case "Sunday":
                                    return 0;
```

```
                        case "Monday":
                                    return 1;
                        case "Tuesday":
                                    return 2;
                        case "Wednesday":
                                    return 3;
                        case "Thursday":
                                    return 4;
                        case "Friday":
                                    return 5;
                        case "Saturday":
                                    return 6;
                        default:
                                    return 8;
            }
}
```

The preceding code declares a Web method with the name `GetDay()`. The `GetDay()` method takes a parameter `dt` of the struct `DateTime`. The date for which you want to retrieve the day is passed as a parameter `dt` to the `GetDay()` method. In addition, the `GetDay()` method returns an `integer` type value that stores the day on which the specified date falls.

Inside the declaration of the method, the code creates a variable, `dw`, of the enum `DayOfWeek`. This enumeration is present in the `System` namespace and is used to specify a day of the week. Next, the code initializes the `dw` variable to the day for the value passed as a parameter to the `GetDay()` method.

Then, the `switch` case statements are used to return an `integer` value for the day stored in the `dw` variable. To do this, the value stored in the `dw` variable is checked using the `switch` case statements. However, to check for the value stored in the `dw` variable, you first need to convert this value to a `string` type value. To do this, you can use the `ToString()` method.

Once you have written the code for the Web method, your Web service is ready to be tested. The following section discusses the procedure for testing a Web service.

## Testing the SampleWebService Web Service

As already discussed, the Web service does not have an interface. However, to test the Web service, Visual Studio .NET launches the Web service in Internet Explorer. I will now discuss the steps to test SampleWebService.

To test the SampleWebService Web service, click on the Debug menu, and then select the Start option. Alternatively, you can press the F5 key to debug and run the Web service.

Visual Studio .NET launches the Web service in the Internet Explorer window, as shown in Figure 28-8.

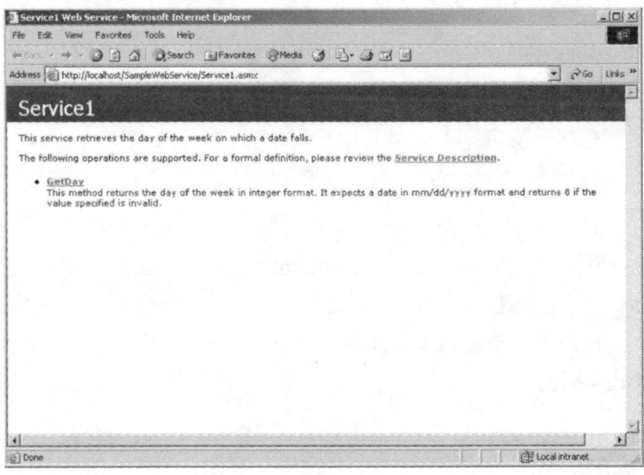


**FIGURE 28-8** *The Service1.asmx page for SampleWebService*

In addition to the description of the Web service and the Web method, the Service1.asmx page contains a link to call the `GetDay()` method. To access the Web method, click on the link.

When you click on the link in the Service1.asmx page, the Service1.asmx page for the `GetDay()` method is displayed. To execute the `GetDay()` method, you need to pass a date as a parameter to the `GetDay()` method and click on the Invoke button. Figure 28-9 shows a parameter passed to the `GetDay()` method.

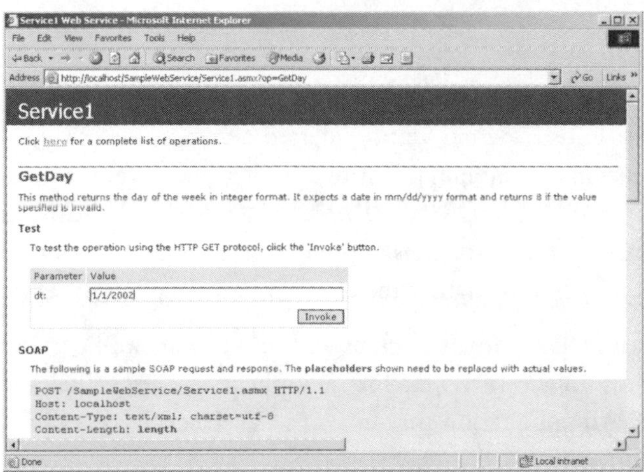


**FIGURE 28-9** *The parameter specified in the* `GetDay()` *method*

The result returned by the SampleWebService Web service is displayed. Figure 28-10 shows the result returned by the Web method.

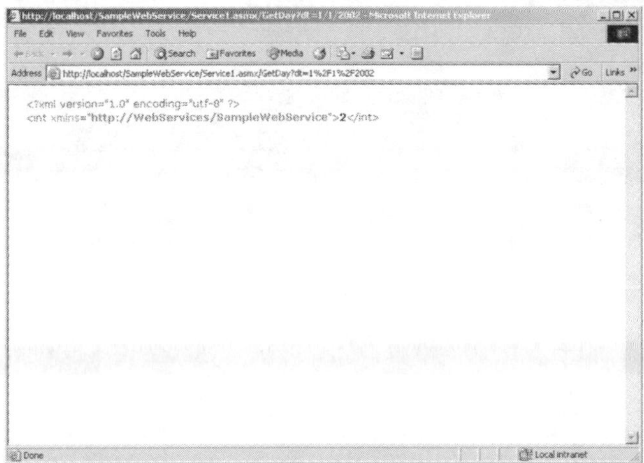


**FIGURE 28-10** *The result returned by the* `GetDay()` *method*

## Summary

In this chapter, you learned about distributed applications. Distributed applications are scalable applications in which data is shared across applications. Therefore, distributed applications include applications built on different platforms or by using different programming languages. To create a large-scale business solution, it is essential that you integrate these applications. Integration of applications built on various platforms is made simpler with the use of Web services.

A Web service is a reusable component, such as a method, that can be used by any Web application running on the Internet. These applications are called Web service client applications. An application that hosts the Web service is called a Web service provider application.

Next, you learned about the architecture of a Web service. The Web service architecture includes a four-layered model. These layers are the data layer, the data access layer, the business layer, and the listener layer. Based on this architecture, you learned about the working of the Web service.

Next, you learned about the role of XML, WSDL, SOAP, and UDDI in a Web service. Based on this knowledge about a Web service, you learned to create a simple Web service using Visual Studio .NET.

# Chapter 29

## Developing Web Services

In the preceding chapters, you looked at the case study and design of the Web site of Bookers Paradise. In addition, you were introduced to the basics of an ASP.NET Web service. Based on the knowledge about Web services, you learned to create a sample Web service by using Visual Studio .NET. This chapter discusses how to create a Web service for Deepthoughts Publications.

## Creating a Web Service for Deepthoughts Publications

A Web service for Deepthoughts Publications provides information about books published at its publishing house. This information is displayed on the Web site of Bookers Paradise. In addition to searching for information about all the books published by Deepthoughts Publications, a user can search for selected books based on criteria.

To start with, you can create a Web service by using the ASP.NET Web Service template provided by Visual Studio .NET. Refer to this Web service as DTWebService. To create the Web service, perform the following steps:

1. On the File menu, point to the New option.
2. In the displayed list, select the Project option.

   The New Project dialog box is displayed.
3. In the Project Types: pane, select the Visual C# Projects option.
4. In the Templates: pane, select the ASP.NET Web Service option.
5. In the Location: text box, type the name of the Web service as `DTWebService`.
6. Click on the OK button to create the DTWebService Web service.

Figure 29-1 shows the New Project dialog box for DTWebService.

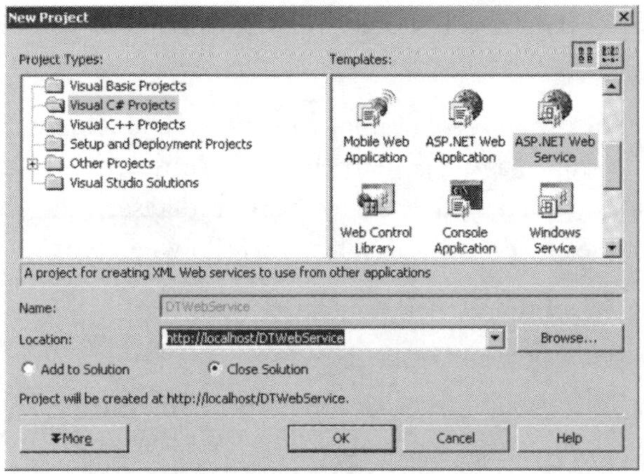


**FIGURE 29-1** *The New Project dialog box for DTWebService*

Visual Studio .NET creates the Web service and the default files in the Web service. I have discussed the default files generated by Visual Studio .NET for a Web service in Chapter 28, "Exploring ASP.NET Web Services," in the section "Web Services in the .NET Framework."

After creating the Web service, add a short description of the Web service. This will help any user looking for a similar Web service. To write a short description, add the following code at the beginning of the Web service.

```
[WebService (Namespace="http://LocalHost/DTWebService/", Description="A service
   displaying catalogs of Deepthoughts publisher")]
```

Because the Web service that you create needs to connect to a database, you need to create a data connection object. To create a data connection object to connect to a database, perform the following steps:

1. In the Server Explorer window, expand the Servers node.

   If the Server Explorer window is not displayed, you can select the Server Explorer option on the View menu.

   When you expand the Servers node, a list of the available SQL servers is displayed.

2. Browse for the DTDB database and drag the `DTCatalog` table to the Service1.asmx page.

Visual Studio .NET automatically adds sqlConnection and sqlDataAdapter components to the Service1.asmx page. When the sqlConnection and sqlDataAdapter components are added, you need to create a dataset that accesses data from the DTDB database. To do this, perform the following steps:

1. On the Data menu, select the Generate Dataset option.

   The Generate Dataset dialog box is displayed.
2. In the Choose a dataset: group box, select the New radio button.
3. Specify the name of the dataset as `dsDetails1`.
4. Check the Add this dataset to the designer window check box.
5. Click on the OK button to close the Generate Dataset dialog box.

The dataset with the name dsDetails1 is added to the Service1.asmx page. Figure 29-2 shows the sqlConnection, sqlDataAdapter, and dataset components added to the Service1.asmx page.

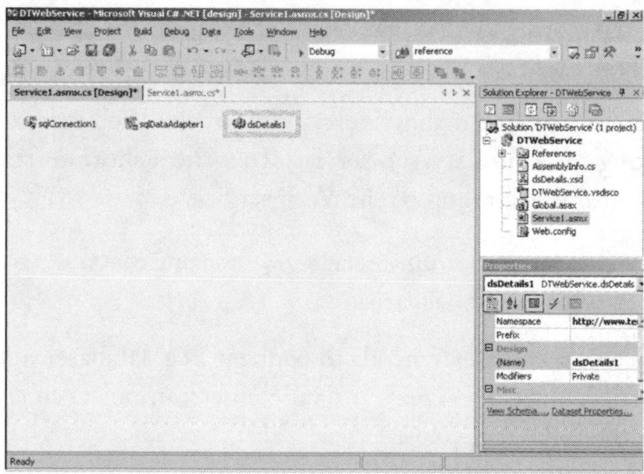

**FIGURE 29-2** *The Service1.asmx page with the components added*

Once a Web service is created and the components are added, you can add Web methods to it. Web methods are required to provide the functionality to the Web site. The following section discusses the Web methods in the Web service of Deepthoughts Publications.

## Creating the `SearchAll()` Web Method

Creating a Web service involves coding for the Web methods in the Web service. In this case, you need to create a Web method that returns information about all the books published at Deepthoughts Publications. Before creating the Web method, add a short description about the Web method.

```
[WebMethod(Description="This method searches for the details of all books published
   by Deepthoughts Publications")]
```

Now add the code for the Web method. The code for the Web method is as displayed:

```
[WebMethod(Description="This method searches for the details of all books published
   by Deepthoughts Publications")]
public DataSet SearchALL()
{
            string SelStr;
            SelStr = "Select * from DTCatalog";
            SqlCommand SelCom;
            SelCom = new SqlCommand(SelStr, sqlConnection1);
            sqlDataAdapter1.SelectCommand = SelCom;
            sqlConnection1.Open();
            sqlDataAdapter1.SelectCommand.ExecuteNonQuery();
            sqlDataAdapter1.Fill(dsDetails1,"Details");
            sqlConnection1.Close();
            return dsDetails1;
}
```

The preceding code declares a `string` variable with the name `SelStr`. Next, the code initializes the `SelStr` variable to a SQL statement that retrieves all the records from the `DTCatalog` table. Next, an instance of the `SqlCommand` class is created with the name `SelCom`. The `SqlCommand` class is present in the `System.Data.SqlClient` namespace. The `SqlCommand` class is used to represent a SQL statement that is executed against a SQL server database. You can derive a class from a `SqlCommand` class.

After declaring the `SelCom` instance, you can initialize it. In the constructor of the `SqlCommand` class, you need to pass two parameters, `SelStr` and `sqlConnection1`. Because the `SqlCommand` class represents all the SQL statements executed against a SQL server database, you need to specify the SQL statement by passing it as a parameter to the constructor. In addition, you need to specify the sqlConnection object for executing the SQL command. This object is passed as a parameter to the constructor of the `SqlCommand` class.

Next, the `SelectCommand` property of the `SqlDataAdapter` class is used to select the records stored in the `SelCom` object. The `SqlDataAdapter` class is present in the `System.Data.SqlClient` namespace and represents the SQL commands used to modify the SQL server database.

Then, the `Open()` method of the SqlConnection class is used to establish a connection with the DTDB database. When a connection with the DTDB database is established, the records in the `DTCatalog` table are retrieved and stored in the dsDetails1 dataset. To do this, the `ExecuteNonQuery()` method of the `SqlCommand` class is executed to return the records that are affected by the SQL command stored in the `SelStr` variable. In this case, all the records in the `DTCatalog` table are returned by the `ExecuteNonQuery()` method. The records returned are then stored in the dataset by using the `Fill()` method of the `DbDataAdapter` class.

Once the records are retrieved, you can close the connection to the DTDB database by using the `Close()` method of the `SqlConnection` class. Finally, the dataset, dsDetails1, is returned when the `SearchAll()` method is called by a Web service client application. To return the dataset, you use the `return` keyword.

After creating the Web method, you can test the Web method by pressing the F5 key. The Service1.asmx page is displayed as shown in Figure 29-3.

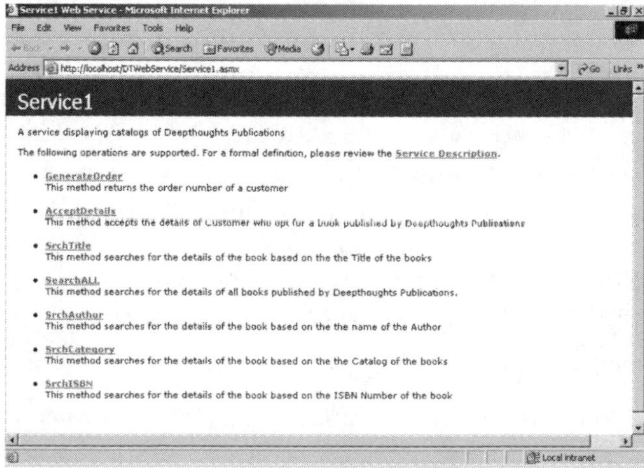


**FIGURE 29-3** *The Service1.asmx page*

The Service1.asmx page contains a link to the `SearchAll()` method. Click on the link to view the Service1.asmx page for the `SearchAll()` method. This page contains an Invoke button. When the user clicks on the Invoke button, the `SearchAll()` method is executed and the results are displayed as shown in Figure 29-4.

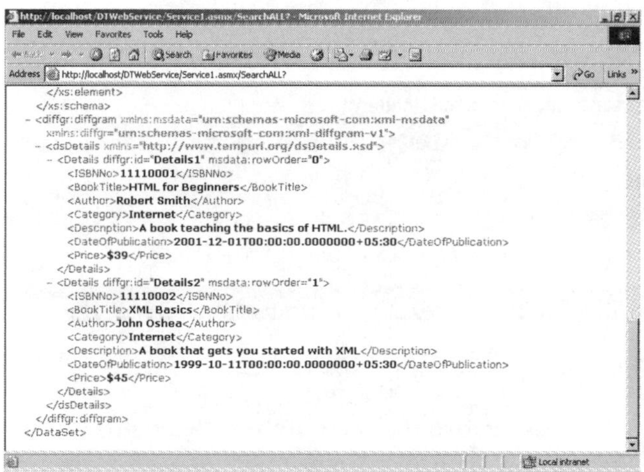


**FIGURE 29-4** *The results returned by the* `SearchAll()` *method*

## Creating the `SrchISBN()` Web Method

You can now create a Web method that returns the records from the `DTCatalog` table with the ISBN number that is passed as a parameter to the Web method. First, write a description for the Web method.

```
[WebMethod(Description="This method searches for the details of the book based on
   the " + " ISBN Number of the book")]
```

After writing the description, you need to write the code for the Web method `SrchISBN()`. The code for the Web method is as follows:

```
[WebMethod(Description="This method searches for the details of the book based on
   the " + " ISBN Number of the book")]
public DataSet SrchISBN(string ISBN)
{
   string SelStr;
```

```
    SelStr = "Select * from DTCatalog where ISBNNo = @ISB";
    SqlCommand SelCom;
    SelCom = new SqlCommand(SelStr, sqlConnection1);
    sqlDataAdapter1.SelectCommand = SelCom;
    sqlDataAdapter1.SelectCommand.Parameters.Add("@ISB",SqlDbType.Char, 10)
       .Value = ISBN;
    sqlConnection1.Open();
    sqlDataAdapter1.SelectCommand.ExecuteNonQuery();
    sqlDataAdapter1.Fill(dsDetails1,"Details");
    sqlConnection1.Close();
    return dsDetails1;
}
```

The preceding code declares a Web method, `SrchISBN()`, which accepts a `string` type parameter named `ISBN`. In the method declaration statement, you also specify the return type of the Web method. Because the `SrchISBN()` Web method returns the records with the specified ISBN number, the return type of the `SrchISBN()` Web method is `Dataset`.

Next, a SQL statement that retrieves the record with the specified ISBN number is created and stored in the `string` type variable `SelStr`. Notice that the parameter specifying the ISBN number is preceded with @ in the SQL statement. This is the syntax for writing SQL queries in Visual Studio .NET.

After the SQL statement is created, the `Add()` method of the `SqlParameterCollection` class is used to add `SqlParameter` to the `SqlParameterCollection` object. The `SqlParameterCollection` object is used to store the parameters associated with the SQL command in the `SqlParameterCollection` object. Next, the `Value` property is used to assign a value to the parameter. In this case, the value assigned to the `@ISB` parameter is the ISBN number, which is passed to the `SrchISBN()` Web method.

After specifying a parameter, you can create a connection to the DTDB database. To do this, you use the `Open()` method. Then, the records affected are retrieved and stored in the dsDetails1 dataset. In this case, the records affected are the ones that match the ISBN number sent as the parameter. After storing the records, close the SQL connection by using the `Close()` method. The dataset is then returned by using the `return` keyword.

After creating the Web method, you can test the Web service. On the Service1.asmx page for the `SrchISBN()` Web method, specify the parameter and click on the Invoke button. Figure 29-5 shows the Service1.asmx page for the `SrchISBN()` Web method.

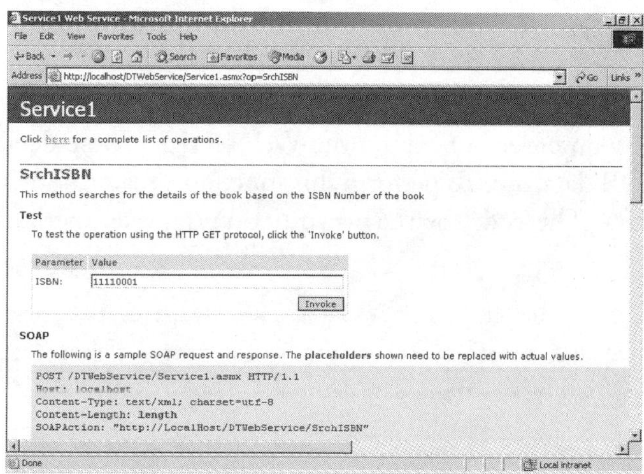


**FIGURE 29-5** *The Service1.asmx page for the* `SrchISBN()` *method*

After clicking on the Invoke button, the Web method is executed and the results are returned as shown in Figure 29-6.

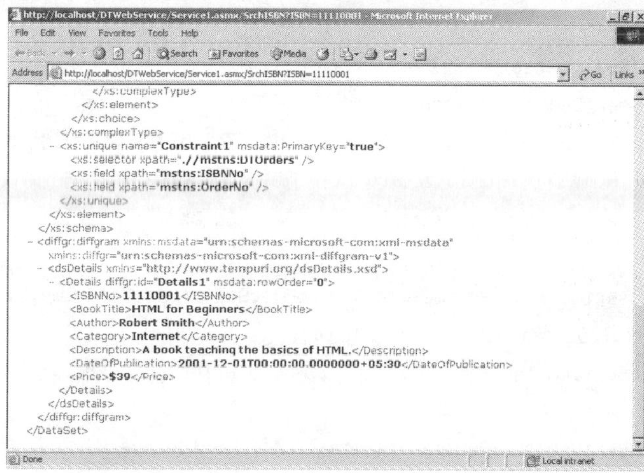


**FIGURE 29-6** *The results returned by the* `SrchISBN()` *method*

Similarly, you can write the code for the Web methods that accept the author, the category, or the title as the parameter.

## Creating the `AcceptDetails()` Web Method

In addition to providing the data to the Web site, DTWebService accepts the details of the customer who orders a book on the Web service. These details are then stored in the DTDB database. To perform this function, create another Web method, `AcceptDetails()`. The code for the `AcceptDetails()` Web method is as shown:

```
public string AcceptDetails(string ISBN, string DateOrder, string CustName, string
   CustAddr1, string CustAddr2, string CustCity, string CustState, string OrdBy,
   string OrdStat, string CardType, string CardNum)
{
   string OrderNo;
   string error;
   error="";
   OrderNo = GenerateOrder();
   string InsStr;
   InsStr = "Insert Into DTOrders Values( @IN, @ON, @DO, @CN, @CA1, @CA2, @CC, @CS,
      @OB, @ST, @CT, @CCN)";
   try
   {
      SqlCommand InsCom;
      InsCom = new SqlCommand(InsStr, sqlConnection1);
      sqlDataAdapter1.InsertCommand = InsCom;
      sqlDataAdapter1.InsertCommand.Parameters.Add("@IN", SqlDbType.Char,10).
         Value = ISBN;
      sqlDataAdapter1.InsertCommand.Parameters.Add("@ON", SqlDbType.Char,5).
         Value = OrderNo;
      sqlDataAdapter1.InsertCommand.Parameters.Add("@DO",SqlDbType.DateTime,8).
         Value = Convert.ToDateTime(DateOrder).Date ;
      sqlDataAdapter1.InsertCommand.Parameters.Add("@CN", SqlDbType.VarChar ,50).
         Value= CustName;
      sqlDataAdapter1.InsertCommand.Parameters.Add("@CA1", SqlDbType.VarChar,50).
         Value= CustAddr1;
      sqlDataAdapter1.InsertCommand.Parameters.Add("@CA2",SqlDbType.VarChar,50).
```

```
            Value=CustAddr2;
         sqlDataAdapter1.InsertCommand.Parameters.Add("@CC",SqlDbType.VarChar,20).
            Value = CustCity;
         sqlDataAdapter1.InsertCommand.Parameters.Add("@CS", SqlDbType.VarChar ,10).
            Value = CustState;
         sqlDataAdapter1.InsertCommand.Parameters.Add("@OB",SqlDbType.VarChar , 50).
            Value=OrdBy;
         sqlDataAdapter1.InsertCommand.Parameters.Add("@ST",SqlDbType.VarChar,20).
            Value=OrdStat;
         sqlDataAdapter1.InsertCommand.Parameters.Add("@CT",SqlDbType.Char,10).
            Value=CardType;
         sqlDataAdapter1.InsertCommand.Parameters.Add("@CCN",SqlDbType.VarChar,20).
            Value=CardNum;
         if(sqlConnection1.State== ConnectionState.Closed )
         {
            sqlConnection1.Open ();
         }
         sqlDataAdapter1.InsertCommand.ExecuteNonQuery();
         sqlConnection1.Close();
      }
      catch(Exception E1)
      {
         error = E1.Message;
      }
      string result;
      if (error.Length != 0)
      {
         result = "Record Not Inserted due to the following reason: \n"+ error;
      }
      else
      {
         result = "Record Inserted!!";
      }
      return result;
   }
```

The preceding code declares a Web method with the name `AcceptDetails()` that returns a `string` type variable. This `string` type variable, `result`, returns a message whether the records are inserted in the DTDB database or not. If an error occurs while attempting to add the records to the DTDB database, the `AcceptDetails()` Web method returns an error.

In addition, the Web method declaration statement accepts 11 parameters, each corresponding to a field in the `DTOrders` table. These parameters include ISBN number, date of ordering, name of the customer, address of the customer, and so on. In addition, the credit card details of the customer are passed as a parameter to the Web method.

Inside the Web method, three `string` variables, `OrderNo`, `error`, and `InsStr`, are declared. The variable `error` is initialized to a null value. However, the `OrderNo` variable is initialized to the `GenerateOrder()` method. The `GenerateOrder()` method is used to autogenerate the order number for any order placed by a customer. You will learn to add code to the `GenerateOrder()` method later in this chapter.

Next, the code creates a SQL statement that inserts a value into the `DTOrders` table. To do this, an `Insert` statement is created. The `Insert` statement accepts 12 parameters, each corresponding to the parameter passed to the `AcceptDetails()` Web method. This `Insert` statement is then stored in the `InsStr` variable.

After creating the SQL statement, a `try` loop is used to enter records to the `DTOrders` table. Inside the `try` loop, an instance, `InsCom`, of the `SqlCommand` class is created and the `Insert` command is passed as a parameter to the constructor of the `SqlCommand` class. Then, the value of the parameter passed to the `AcceptDetails()` Web method is stored in the `SqlParameterCollection` object. This process is repeated for all of the 11 parameters.

Next, an `if` statement is used to check whether the connection to the DTDB database is closed or not. To do this, the `State` property of the `SqlConnection` class is used. If the connection is closed, the code opens the connection by using the `Open()` method. Then, the `ExecuteNonQuery()` method is used to return the records affected by the `Insert` statement and the connection to the SQL database is closed.

While adding records to the DTOrders table, if an exception is generated, the exception is caught in the `catch` loop and stored in the `error` variable. Next, a `string` type variable result is declared that returns the message stating whether the records are added to the database or not. To do this, the `Length` property of the `String` class is used. If the value in the `Length` property is equal to zero, an error message is displayed. However, if the records are added, a message confirming that the records are added is displayed. Figure 29-7 shows the message returned by the `AcceptDetails()` Web method.

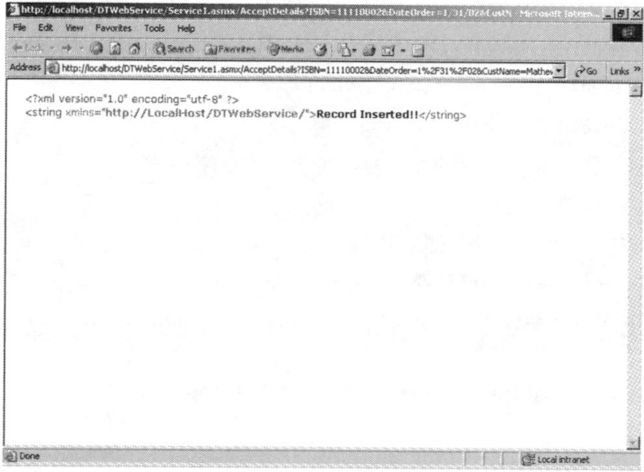


**FIGURE 29-7** *The message returned by the AcceptDetails() Web method*

Until now, I have not added a description for the `AcceptDetails()` Web method. To do this, add the following statement before the Web method:

```
[WebMethod(Description="This method accepts the details of Customer who opt " + "
   for a book published by Deepthoughts Publications")]
```

## Creating the `GenerateOrder()` Web Method

As discussed earlier, when a customer places an order for a book, the details of the book and the customer are returned to the Web service. In addition, an order number for each order is generated automatically. To do this, you need to write code for the `GenerateOrder()` Web method.

However, first add a short description for the Web method.

```
[WebMethod(Description="This method returns the order number of a customer")]
```

Now, add the following code to the Web service:

```
[WebMethod(Description="This method returns the order number of a customer")]
public string GenerateOrder()
{
        string SelStr;
        SelStr = "Select Count(*) From DTOrders";
        SqlCommand SelCom;
        SelCom = new SqlCommand(SelStr, sqlConnection1);
        sqlConnection1.Open();
        sqlDataAdapter1.SelectCommand = SelCom;
        sqlDataAdapter1.Fill(dsDetails1,"Details");
        sqlConnection1.Close();
        string str;
        str = dsDetails1.Tables["Details"].Rows[0][0].ToString ();
        int val;
        val = Convert.ToInt32(str);
        val= val+1;
        if(val>0 & val<=9)
        {
                str = "0000" + Convert.ToString(val);
        }
        else if(val>9 & val<=99)
        {
                str ="000" + Convert.ToString (val);
        }
        else if(val>99 & val <=999)
        {
                str = "00" + Convert.ToString (val);
        }
        else
        {
                str = "0" + Convert.ToString (val);
        }
        return str;
}
```

The preceding code declares a `public` Web method named `GenerateOrder()` that returns a `string` containing the generated order number. Inside the method declaration statement, a `string` type variable named `SelStr` is declared. This variable is then initialized to a SQL statement that selects all the records in the `DTOrders` table. Next, an instance of the `SqlCommand` class is created and initialized to the SQL statement stored in the `SelStr` variable.

Then, the `Open()` method is used to open the SQL connection to the `DTOrders` table. Next, the records in the `DTOrders` table are selected using the `SelectCommand` property. These records are then added to the `dsDetails` dataset by using the `Fill()` method and the connection to the `DTOrders` table is closed.

The code then declares a string type variable named `str` and initializes it to a collection of rows in the `DTOrders` table. To do this, the `Rows` property of the `DataRowCollection` class is used. The value returned by the `Rows` property is converted to a `string` value by using the `ToString()` method and stored in the `str` variable. Next, an `integer` type variable, `val`, is declared and initialized to the 32-bit signed `integer` equivalent of the value stored in the `str` variable. To convert the string type variable to the 32-bit signed integer variable, you use the `ToInt` property of the `System.Convert` class.

The value stored in the variable `val` is the number of records in the `DTOrders` table. Therefore, to generate the next order number, you need to add 1 to the value in the variable `val`. Then, an `if` loop is used to find the range of the value in the variable `val`. If this value lies in the range 0 to 9, the string, O000, is added to this value. However, to do this, you again need to convert the value in the variable `val` to a `string` type value.

Similarly, if the value in the variable `val` lies in the range 9 to 99, the string O00 is added to the value. Therefore, the range of the value is found out and *O* followed by zeros is added to make the order number a four-digit number. This value stored in the variable `str` is returned by the Web method.

After writing the code for the `GenerateOrder()` Web method, you can test the Web method. On testing the Web method, an order number is returned, as shown in Figure 29-8.

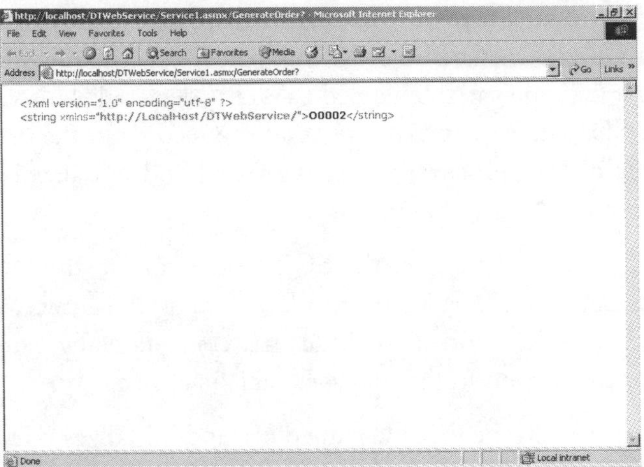


**FIGURE 29-8** *The order number returned by the* `GenerateOrder()` *Web method*

Now look at the entire code for the Web service project that you created. This will help you enhance your understanding of the Web service.

```
using System;
using System.Collections;
using System.ComponentModel;
using System.Data;
using System.Diagnostics;
using System.Web;
using System.Web.Services;
using System.Data.SqlClient ;

namespace DTWebService
{
   [WebService (Namespace="http://LocalHost/DTWebService/", Description="A service
      displaying catalogs of Deepthoughts Publications ")]
   public class Service1 : System.Web.Services.WebService
   {
      public Service1()
```

```
{
   InitializeComponent();
}

private System.Data.SqlClient.SqlCommand sqlSelectCommand1;
private System.Data.SqlClient.SqlCommand sqlInsertCommand1;
private System.Data.SqlClient.SqlCommand sqlUpdateCommand1;
private System.Data.SqlClient.SqlCommand sqlDeleteCommand1;
private System.Data.SqlClient.SqlConnection sqlConnection1;
private System.Data.SqlClient.SqlDataAdapter sqlDataAdapter1;
private DTWebService.dsDetails dsDetails1;

[WebMethod(Description="This method accepts the details of Customer who opt"
   +" for a book published by Deepthoughts Publications")]
public string AcceptDetails(string ISBN, string DateOrder, string CustName,
   string CustAddr1, string CustAddr2, string CustCity, string CustState,
   string OrdBy, string OrdStat, string CardType, string CardNum)
{
   string OrderNo;
   string error;
   error="";
   OrderNo = GenerateOrder();
   string InsStr;
   InsStr = "Insert Into DTOrders Values( @IN, @ON, @DO, @CN, @CA1, @CA2,
      @CC, @CS, @OB, @ST, @CT, @CCN)";
   try
   {
      SqlCommand InsCom;
      InsCom = new SqlCommand(InsStr, sqlConnection1);
      sqlDataAdapter1.InsertCommand = InsCom;
      sqlDataAdapter1.InsertCommand.Parameters.Add("@IN", SqlDbType.Char,10).
         Value = ISBN;
      sqlDataAdapter1.InsertCommand.Parameters.Add("@ON", SqlDbType.Char,5).
         Value = OrderNo;
      sqlDataAdapter1.InsertCommand.Parameters.Add("@DO",
         SqlDbType.DateTime,8).Value = Convert.ToDateTime(DateOrder).Date ;
```

```
        sqlDataAdapter1.InsertCommand.Parameters.Add("@CN", SqlDbType
           .VarChar ,50).Value= CustName;
        sqlDataAdapter1.InsertCommand.Parameters.Add("@CA1", SqlDbType
           .VarChar,50).Value= CustAddr1;
        sqlDataAdapter1.InsertCommand.Parameters.Add("@CA2",SqlDbType
           .VarChar,50).Value=CustAddr2;
        sqlDataAdapter1.InsertCommand.Parameters.Add("@CC",SqlDbType
           .VarChar,20).Value = CustCity;
        sqlDataAdapter1.InsertCommand.Parameters.Add("@CS", SqlDbType
           .VarChar ,10).Value = CustState;
        sqlDataAdapter1.InsertCommand.Parameters.Add("@OB",SqlDbType
           .VarChar , 50).Value=OrdBy;
        sqlDataAdapter1.InsertCommand.Parameters.Add("@ST",SqlDbType
           .VarChar,20).Value=OrdStat;
        sqlDataAdapter1.InsertCommand.Parameters.Add("@CT",SqlDbType
           .Char,10).Value=CardType;
        sqlDataAdapter1.InsertCommand.Parameters.Add("@CCN",SqlDbType
           .VarChar,20).Value=CardNum;

        if(sqlConnection1.State== ConnectionState.Closed )
        {
           sqlConnection1.Open ();
        }

        sqlDataAdapter1.InsertCommand.ExecuteNonQuery();
        sqlConnection1.Close();
     }
     catch(Exception E1)
     {
        error = E1.Message;
                 }
     string result;
     if (error.Length != 0)
     {
        result = "Record Not Inserted due to the following reason: \n"+ error;
     }
```

```
    else
    {
        result = "Record Inserted!!";
    }
    return result;
    }

[WebMethod(Description="This method searches for the details of all books
    published by Deepthoughts Publications ")]
public DataSet SearchALL()
{
    string SelStr;
    SelStr = "Select * from DTCatalog";
    SqlCommand SelCom;
    SelCom = new SqlCommand(SelStr, sqlConnection1);
    sqlDataAdapter1.SelectCommand = SelCom;
    sqlConnection1.Open();
    sqlDataAdapter1.SelectCommand.ExecuteNonQuery();
    sqlDataAdapter1.Fill(dsDetails1,"Details");
    sqlConnection1.Close();
    return dsDetails1;
}

[WebMethod(Description="This method searches for the details of the book
    based on the " +" ISBN Number of the book")]
public DataSet SrchISBN(string ISBN)
{
    string SelStr;
    SelStr = "Select * from DTCatalog where ISBNNo = @ISB";
    SqlCommand SelCom;
    SelCom = new SqlCommand(SelStr, sqlConnection1);
    sqlDataAdapter1.SelectCommand = SelCom;
    sqlDataAdapter1.SelectCommand.Parameters.Add("@ISB",SqlDbType.Char, 10)
        .Value = ISBN;
    sqlConnection1.Open();
    sqlDataAdapter1.SelectCommand.ExecuteNonQuery();
    sqlDataAdapter1.Fill(dsDetails1,"Details");
```

```
        sqlConnection1.Close();
        return dsDetails1;
    }

    [WebMethod(Description="This method searches for the details of the book
        based on the " + " the name of the Author")]
    public DataSet SrchAuthor(string Author)
    {
        string SelStr;
        SelStr = "Select * from DTCatalog where Author = @AU";
        SqlCommand SelCom;
        SelCom = new SqlCommand(SelStr, sqlConnection1);
        sqlDataAdapter1.SelectCommand = SelCom;
        sqlDataAdapter1.SelectCommand.Parameters.Add("@AU",SqlDbType.
            VarChar , 50).Value = Author;
        sqlConnection1.Open();
        sqlDataAdapter1.SelectCommand.ExecuteNonQuery();
        sqlDataAdapter1.Fill(dsDetails1,"Details");
        sqlConnection1.Close();
        return dsDetails1;
    }

    [WebMethod(Description="This method searches for the details of the book
        based on the " +" the Catalog of the books")]
public DataSet SrchCategory(string Catalog)
    {
        string SelStr;
        SelStr = "Select * from DTCatalog where Category = @CA";
        SqlCommand SelCom;
        SelCom = new SqlCommand(SelStr, sqlConnection1);
        sqlDataAdapter1.SelectCommand = SelCom;
        sqlDataAdapter1.SelectCommand.Parameters.Add("@CA",SqlDbType.Char , 10)
            .Value = Catalog;
        sqlConnection1.Open();
        sqlDataAdapter1.SelectCommand.ExecuteNonQuery();
        sqlDataAdapter1.Fill(dsDetails1,"Details");
        sqlConnection1.Close();
```

```
    return dsDetails1;
}

[WebMethod(Description="This method searches for the details of the book
    based on the " + " the Title of the books")]
public DataSet SrchTitle(string BkTitle)
{
    string SelStr;
    SelStr = "Select * from DTCatalog where BookTitle = @BT";
    SqlCommand SelCom;
    SelCom = new SqlCommand(SelStr, sqlConnection1);
    sqlDataAdapter1.SelectCommand = SelCom;
    sqlDataAdapter1.SelectCommand.Parameters.Add("@BT",SqlDbType.VarChar , 50)
       .Value = BkTitle;
    sqlConnection1.Open();
    sqlDataAdapter1.SelectCommand.ExecuteNonQuery();
    sqlDataAdapter1.Fill(dsDetails1,"Details");
    sqlConnection1.Close();
    return dsDetails1;
}

[WebMethod(Description="This method returns the order number of a customer")]
public string GenerateOrder()
    {
    string SelStr;
    SelStr = "Select Count(*) From DTOrders";
    SqlCommand SelCom;
    SelCom = new SqlCommand(SelStr, sqlConnection1);
    sqlConnection1.Open();
    sqlDataAdapter1.SelectCommand = SelCom;
    sqlDataAdapter1.Fill(dsDetails1,"Details");
    sqlConnection1.Close();
    string str;
    str = dsDetails1.Tables["Details"].Rows[0][0].ToString ();
    int val;
    val = Convert.ToInt32(str);
```

```
            val= val+1;
                        if(val>0 & val<=9)
            {
               str = "0000" + Convert.ToString(val);
            }
            else if(val>9 & val<=99)
            {
               str ="000" + Convert.ToString (val);
            }
            else if(val>99 & val <=999)
            {
               str = "00" + Convert.ToString (val);
            }
            else
            {
               str = "0" + Convert.ToString (val);
            }
            return str;
         }
      }
   }
```

After creating the Web service, you can test the Web service.

## Testing the Web Service

To test the Web service, press the F5 key or select the Start option on the Debug menu. Because you have tested most of the Web methods while creating them, you can test the remainder of the Web methods.

### *Testing the `SrchAuthor()` Web Method*

On testing the `SrchAuthor()` Web method, the method returns records for the specified author. Figure 29-9 shows the records returned by the `SrchAuthor()` Web method.

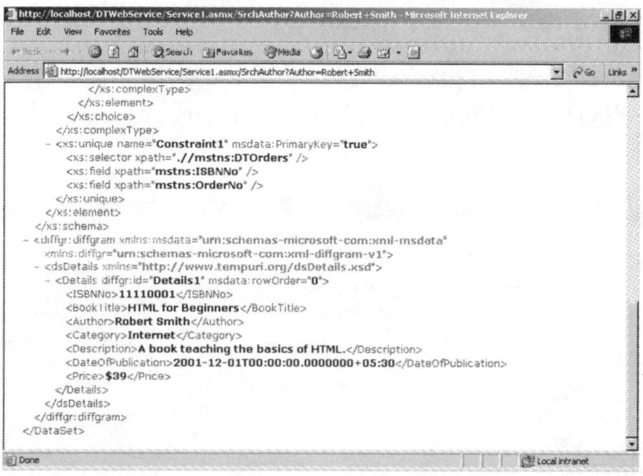


**FIGURE 29-9** *The records returned by the* `SrchAuthor()` *Web method*

## Testing the `SrchCategory()` Web Method

Figure 29-10 shows the records based on the category specified by the user in the `SrchCategory()` Web method.

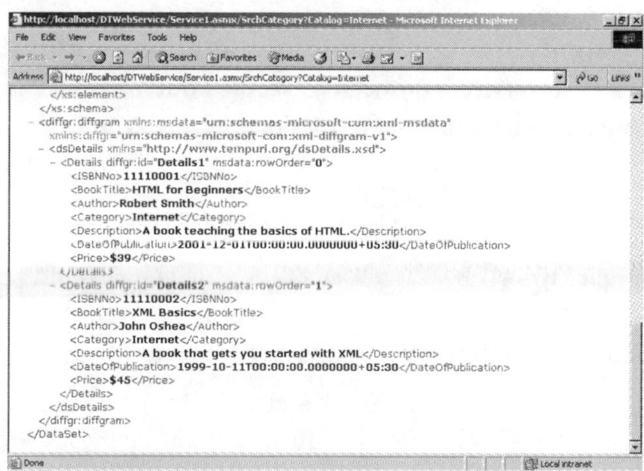


**FIGURE 29-10** *The records returned by the* `SrchCategory()` *Web method*

### Testing the `SrchTitle()` Web Method

When the user wants to search for a particular book, the user can specify the title of the book as the search criteria. Figure 29-11 shows the record returned by the `SrchTitle()` Web method.

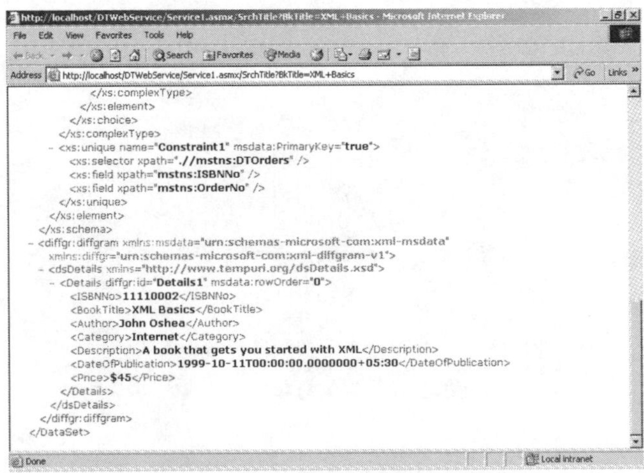


**FIGURE 29-11** *The record returned by the* `SrchTitle()` *Web method*

Once you have created a Web service, you need to secure your Web service. The following section discusses how to secure a Web service.

## Securing a Web Service

It is essential that you secure the Web service that you create. This would prevent anyone else from tampering with your Web service. To secure a Web service, there are several attributes associated with the Web service, as shown:

- Authentication
- Authorization
- Auditing

- Data integrity
- Data privacy
- Data availability

Among all these attributes, authentication is the most important attribute. To provide security to your Web service, you need to have a secure mechanism for authentication. *Authentication* is defined as the process of verifying the details of the user attempting to access the Web service. This verification is done on the basis of the information stored about the user. This information may include a password, an ID, or a thumbprint. These credentials stored for a user are called *principal*. However, to avoid a situation in which an unauthorized user tries to access the Web service by using the password assigned to an authorized user, you need to carefully decide the authentication credentials for your Web service.

## Summary

In this chapter, you learned how to create the DTWebService Web service. While creating the Web service, you added the required Web methods to the Web service. These Web methods include `AcceptDetails()`, `GenerateOrder()`, `SearchALL()`, `SrchISBN()`, `SrchTitle()`, `SrchCategory()`, and `SrchAuthor()`. In this way, you can also create a Web service for Black and White Publications.

After adding the Web methods to the DTWebService Web service, you tested the Web service in the Internet Explorer window. Finally, you learned to secure a Web service.

# Chapter 30

## Developing Web Service Clients

In the preceding chapter, you created a Web service for Deepthoughts Publications. However, to access the Web service, you need to create a Web client application. In this case, the Web client application is the Web site for Bookers Paradise.

In this chapter, you will learn to create the Web service client application. Creating the Web service client application includes creating the Web forms required for the Web site. In addition, you will learn to add code to the Web forms.

# Creating a Web Service Client Application for Bookers Paradise

The Web site for Bookers Paradise displays the information about the books published by Deepthoughts Publications and Black and White Publications. The user can choose to view information about all the books or selected books on the Web site. In addition to viewing information, the user can select a book to order.

When a user orders a book, the details of the book and the customer are added to the database of the publisher. Before writing the code for the client application, you will create the Web forms for the application.

## Creating the Web Forms for the Bookers Paradise Web Site

You have seen the design of the Web forms for the Bookers Paradise Web site in Chapter 27, "Project Case Study and Design," in the section "Web Forms Design." However, in Chapter 27, you did not create the forms. The following sections discuss the creation of the Web forms used in the Bookers Paradise Web site.

## Creating the Main Form

As already discussed in Chapter 27, the Main form consists of four label controls, one button control, five hyperlink controls, one list control, one text box control, and two table controls. To add these controls to the Main form, drag these controls from the Web Forms toolbox and change the properties of the controls. Table 30-1 shows the properties that you need to change for the controls.

**Table 30-1 Properties for the Controls Added to the Main Form**

| Control | Property | Value |
|---|---|---|
| Label1 | ID | Label1 |
| | Text | Browse |
| | Font | Verdana |
| | ForeColor | Purple |
| | BackColor | #FF80FF |
| Label2 | ID | Label2 |
| | Text | Bookers Paradise |
| | Font | Monotype Corsiva, XX-Large |
| | ForeColor | Purple |
| | BackColor | Transparent |
| Label3 | ID | Label3 |
| | Text | Your Online Bookstore… |
| | Font | Monotype Corsiva, Larger |
| | ForeColor | Purple |
| | BackColor | Transparent |
| Label4 | ID | Label4 |
| | Text | About US… |
| | Font | Monotype Corsiva, Larger |
| | ForeColor | Purple |
| | BackColor | Transparent |
| HyperLink1 | ID | HyperLink1 |
| | Text | Visual Studio .NET |
| | NavigateURL | ConstructionForm.aspx |
| | BackColor | #FF80FF |

*continues*

**Table 30-1 Properties for the Controls Added to the Main Form *(continued)***

| Control | Property | Value |
|---|---|---|
| HyperLink2 | ID | HyperLink2 |
| | Text | Operating Systems |
| | NavigateURL | ConstructionForm.aspx |
| | BackColor | #FF80FF |
| HyperLink3 | ID | HyperLink3 |
| | Text | RDBMS |
| | NavigateURL | ConstructionForm.aspx |
| | BackColor | #FF80FF |
| HyperLink4 | ID | HyperLink4 |
| | Text | Networking |
| | NavigateURL | ConstructionForm.aspx |
| | BackColor | #FF80FF |
| HyperLink5 | ID | HyperLink5 |
| | Text | Internet |
| | NavigateURL | ConstructionForm.aspx |
| | BackColor | #FF80FF |
| Button | ID | btnGo |
| | Text | Go |
| List | ID | lstType |
| | Items | All |
| | | Author |
| | | Title |
| | | ISBN Number |
| | | Category |
| Table1 | ID | Table1 |
| | BorderStyle | Outset |
| | ForeColor | Purple |
| | BackColor | #FF80FF |
| | Rows | TableRow0 |
| | | TableRow1 |
| TableRow0 | Cells | TableCell0 |

**Table 30-1 Properties for the Controls Added to the Main Form *(continued)***

| Control | Property | Value |
|---|---|---|
| TableCell0 | Text | Search |
| | Font | Verdana, Small |
| | ForeColor | Purple |
| | VerticalAlign | Top |
| Table2 | ID | Table2 |
| | BorderStyle | Outset |
| | ForeColor | Purple |
| | BackColor | Magenta |
| | Rows | TableRow0 |
| TableRow0 | BorderStyle | Outset |
| | BackColor | #FFC0FF |
| | Cells | TableCell0 |
| TableCell0 | BackColor | #FF80FF |
| TextBox1 | ID | txtSearch |

After creating the form in the design view, the form looks as shown in Figure 30-1.

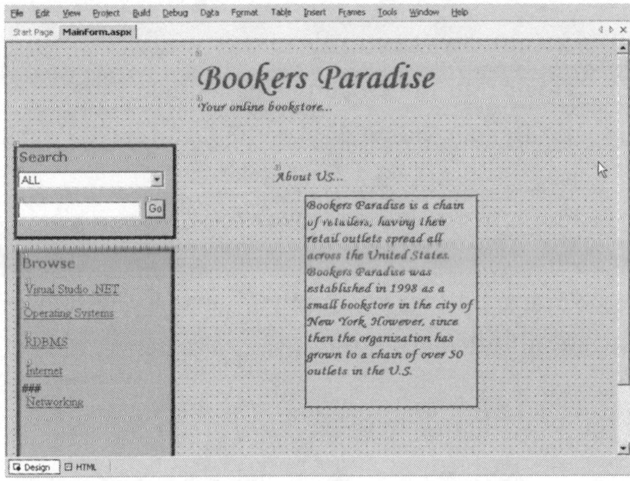


**FIGURE 30-1** *The Main form*

## Creating the Results Form

The Results page is generated to display the results of the user's query. To create the Results form, you need to include a DataGrid, a label, and a hyperlink control. You can name the Results form DispResultForm. After adding the controls, you need to change the properties of the Web form controls as shown in Table 30-2.

**Table 30-2 Properties for the Controls Added to the Results Form**

| Control | Property | Value |
|---|---|---|
| HyperLink1 | ID | HyperLink1 |
| | Text | Home |
| | NavigateURL | MainForm.aspx |
| Lable1 | ID | lblInfo |
| | Font | Verdana, Large |
| | ForeColor | #400040 |
| DataGrid1 | ID | DataGrid1 |
| | BackColor | #E0E0E0 |

After adding the DataGrid control to the form, you need to add button controls to the DataGrid control. To do this, perform the following steps:

1. Select the DataGrid control to view its Properties window.

   Below the Properties window, the Property Builder link is displayed.
2. Click on the Property Builder link to display the DataGrid1 Properties dialog box.
3. In the DataGrid1 Properties dialog box, select the Columns tab in the left hand pane.
4. In the Available columns: list box, expand the Button Column node.
5. Select the Select option and click on the right arrow button to add the Select button.

   When you add the Select button, the text boxes in the ButtonColumn properties area become enabled.

6. In the Text: text box, type the text as `Order`.
7. In the Command name: text box, type the value as `Ord`.
8. In the Button Type: list box, select the value as LinkButton.
9. Click on the OK button to close the DataGrid1 Properties dialog box.

Figure 30-2 shows the DataGrid1 Properties dialog box.

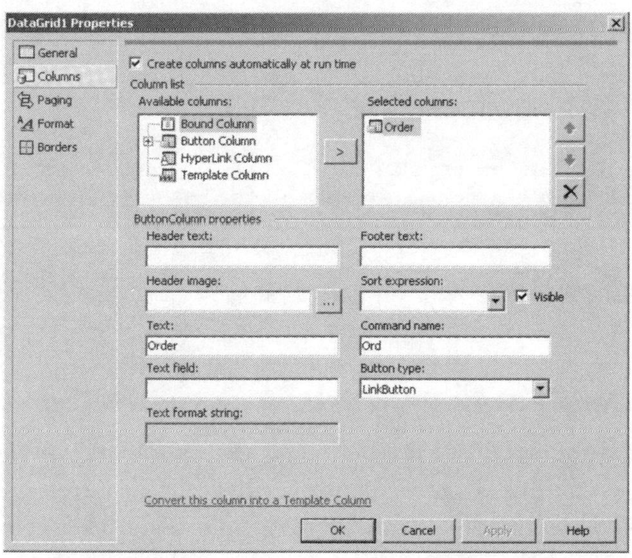


**FIGURE 30-2** *The DataGrid1 Properties dialog box*

When you create the form, the DispResultForm form looks as shown in Figure 30-3.

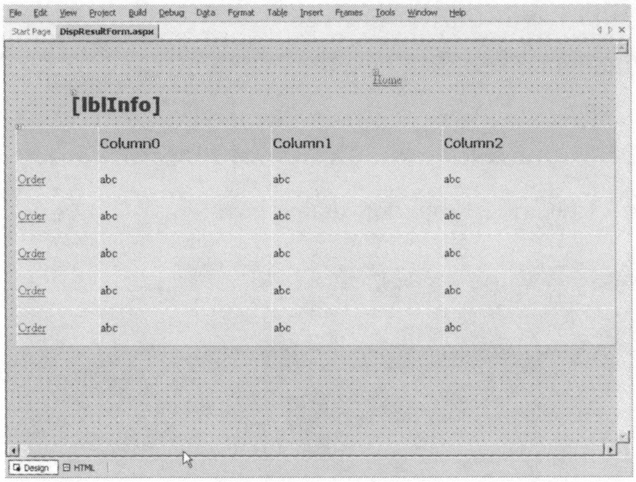

**FIGURE 30-3** *The DispResultForm form*

## Creating the Orders Form

The Orders form stores the details of the book and the customers who order a book at the Web site. To do this, 1 button control, 2 hyperlink controls, 12 label controls, 1 list control, 5 RequiredFieldValidator controls, and 10 text box controls are added to the form. Name this Web form OrdersForm. In the OrdersForm form, change the properties of the controls as shown in Table 30-3.

**Table 30-3 Properties for the Controls Added to the Orders Form**

| Control | Property | Value |
|---|---|---|
| Button1 | ID | btnClear |
| | Text | Clear |
| Button2 | ID | btnOrder |
| | Text | Order |
| HyperLink1 | ID | HyperLink1 |
| | Text | Home |
| | NavigateURL | MainForm.aspx |
| Label1 | ID | Label1 |
| | Text | ISBN Number |
| | ForeColor | Purple |

**Table 30-3 Properties for the Controls Added to the Orders Form *(continued)***

| Control | Property | Value |
|---|---|---|
| Label2 | ID | Label2 |
| | Text | Enter your details here |
| | ForeColor | Purple |
| | Font | Monotype Corsiva, Large |
| Label3 | ID | Label3 |
| | Text | Book Title |
| | ForeColor | Purple |
| Label4 | ID | Label4 |
| | Text | Name |
| | ForeColor | Purple |
| Label5 | ID | Label5 |
| | Text | Address1 |
| | ForeColor | Purple |
| Label6 | ID | Label6 |
| | Text | Address2 |
| | ForeColor | Purple |
| Label7 | ID | Label7 |
| | Text | City |
| | ForeColor | Purple |
| Label8 | ID | Label8 |
| | Text | State |
| | ForeColor | Purple |
| Label9 | ID | Label9 |
| | Text | Author |
| | ForeColor | Purple |
| List | ID | lstCardType |
| | Items | Amex |
| | | Visa |
| | | Master |
| Text Box1 | ID | TextBox1 |
| | TextMode | Multiline |
| | Enabled | False |
| | Font | Verdana |

**Table 30-3 Properties for the Controls Added to the Orders Form *(continued)***

| Control | Property | Value |
|---|---|---|
| Text Box2 | ID | txtAddr1 |
| Text Box3 | ID | txtAddr2 |
| Text Box4 | ID | txtAuthor |
| | Enabled | False |
| Text Box5 | ID | txtCardNumber |
| Text Box6 | ID | txtCity |
| Text Box7 | ID | txtISBN |
| | Enabled | False |
| Text Box8 | ID | txtName |
| Text Box9 | ID | txtState |
| Text Box10 | ID | txtTitle |
| RequiredFieldValidator1 | ID | RequiredFieldValidator1 |
| | ControlToValidate | txtCardNumber |
| | ErrorMessage | Please enter the Credit Card Number |
| RequiredFieldValidator2 | ID | RequiredFieldValidator3 |
| | ControlToValidate | txtName |
| | ErrorMessage | Please enter your Name |
| | Text | Please enter your Name |
| RequiredFieldValidator3 | ID | RequiredFieldValidator4 |
| | ControlToValidate | txtCardNumber |
| | ErrorMessage | Please enter your Name |
| | Text | Please enter your Name |
| RequiredFieldValidator4 | ID | RequiredFieldValidator5 |
| | ControlToValidate | txtAddr1 |
| | ErrorMessage | Please enter the Address |
| RequiredFieldValidator5 | ID | RequiredFieldValidator6 |
| | ControlToValidate | txtCity |
| | ErrorMessage | Please enter the City |

**Table 30-3 Properties for the Controls Added to the Orders Form *(continued)***

| Control | Property | Value |
|---|---|---|
| RequiredFieldValidator6 | ID | RequiredFieldValidator7 |
| | ControlToValidate | txtState |
| | ErrorMessage | Please enter the State |

In addition to the previously mentioned controls, you need to add an sqlDataAdapter, an sqlConnection, and Dataset objects to the OrdersForm form. I have already explained the steps to include these controls to the form in Chapter 29, "Developing Web Services," in the section "Creating a Web Service for Deepthoughts Publications."

Figure 30-4 shows the form after it is created.

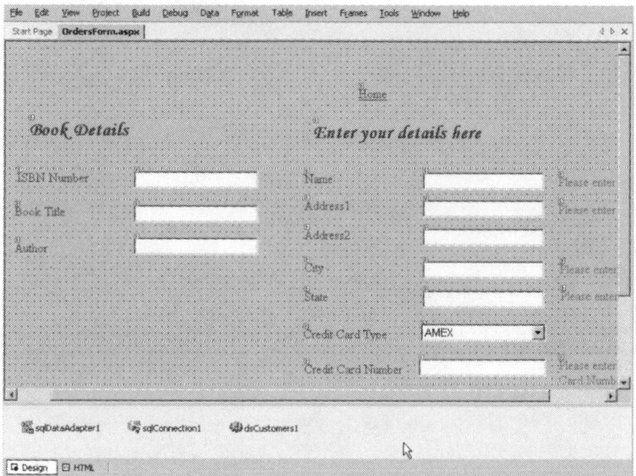


**FIGURE 30-4** *The OrdersForm form*

## Creating the Search Form

The Search form allows a user to search for records based on criteria. Therefore, the user needs to enter the criteria and a value for the criteria. To create the Search form, add a label control, two button controls, four radio buttons, and four text box controls to the form and then change the properties of the controls added to the form. The properties that you need to change in the Search page are specified in Table 30-4.

**Table 30-4 Properties for the Controls Added to the Search Form**

| Control | Property | Value |
|---|---|---|
| Button1 | ID | btnHome |
| | Text | Home |
| Button2 | ID | btnSearch |
| | Text | Search |
| Label1 | ID | lblInfo |
| | ForeColor | Red |
| Radio Button1 | ID | radAuthor |
| | Text | Author |
| | GroupName | Criteria |
| | ForeColor | #400040 |
| Radio Button2 | ID | radCategory |
| | Text | Category |
| | GroupName | Criteria |
| | ForeColor | #400040 |
| Radio Button3 | ID | radISBN |
| | Text | ISBN Number |
| | GroupName | Criteria |
| | ForeColor | #400040 |
| Radio Button4 | ID | radTitle |
| | Text | Title |
| | GroupName | Criteria |
| | ForeColor | #400040 |
| Text Box1 | ID | txtAuthor |
| Text Box2 | ID | txtCategory |
| Text Box3 | ID | txtISBN |
| Text Box4 | ID | txtTitle |

Figure 30-5 shows the Search form when it is created.

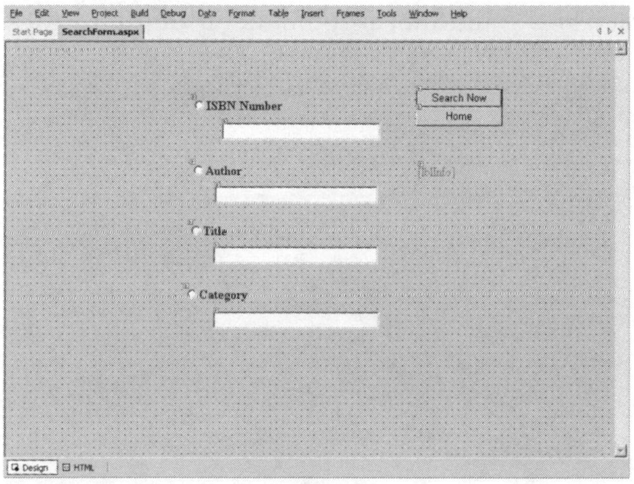


**FIGURE 30-5** *The Search form*

Once the form is created, you can rename the form SearchForm.

## Creating the Construction Form

To create the construction form, add a hyperlink control and two label controls to the form. Rename the form ConstructionForm. Next, you need to change the properties of the controls, as shown in Table 30-5.

**Table 30-5 Properties for the Controls Added to the Construction Form**

| Control | Property | Value |
|---|---|---|
| Label1 | ID | Label1 |
| | Text | This page is under construction. |
| | ForeColor | Purple |
| | Font | Verdana, Large |
| Label2 | ID | Label2 |
| | Text | Check out later... |
| | ForeColor | Purple |
| | Font | Verdana, Large |
| HyperLink1 | ID | HyperLink1 |
| | Text | Home |
| | NavigateURL | MainForm.aspx |

Having created the form, look at the form as shown in Figure 30-6.

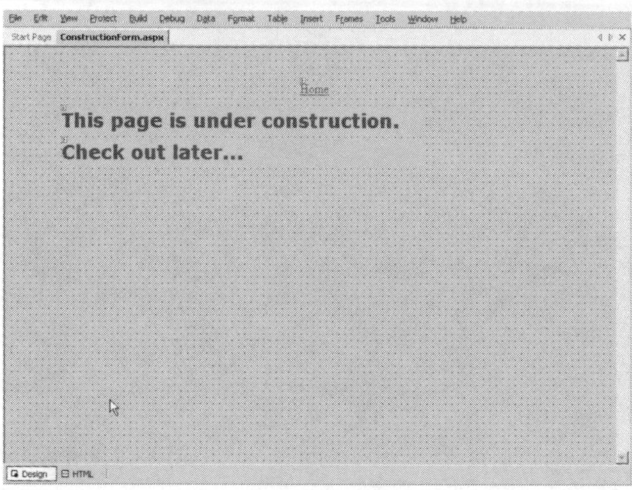


**FIGURE 30-6** *The ConstructionForm form*

## Adding Code to the Web Forms

After creating the forms, add the code to the forms to make them functional. The following section discusses writing code for the Web forms that you have created.

### *Adding Code to the Main Form*

To begin with, write the code for the Main form. Adding functionality to the Main form includes writing code for the button control in the Main form. To add the functionality to the button control, add the following code in the `Click` event of the button control.

```
private void btnGo_Click(object sender, System.EventArgs e)

    string strList;
    string strText;
    strList = lstType.SelectedItem.Text ;
    if(String.Compare(strList, "ALL")==0)
```

```
    {
       strText="Search ALL";
    }
    else
    {
       strText = txtSearch.Text;
    }
       if(strText.Length != 0)
       {
       Response.Redirect ("DispResultForm.aspx?Cat=" + strList + "& str=" + strText);
       }
       else
       {
       Response.Redirect ("SearchForm.aspx");
       }
}
```

The preceding code for the `Click` event of the Go button declares two `string` type variables, `strList` and `strText`. The `strList` variable is used to store the value selected by the user in the list box control. To do this, you use the `Text` property of the `ListItem` class. The `Text` property is used to specify or retrieve values in the list box that is created. To retrieve the selected item, use the `SelectedItem` property of the `ListControl` class.

Next, the `Compare()` method of the `String` class is used to compare the value stored in the `strList` variable to zero. If the value stored in the variable is zero, then the text `Search ALL` is stored in the variable `strText`. However, if the value stored in the variable `strList` is not equal to zero, the value entered by the user in the `txtSearch` text box is assigned to the variable `strText`. Doing this helps you to store the value entered by the user for the selected criteria.

However, there may be cases where the user forgets to specify a value in the `txtSearch` text box. In this case, the user is taken to the `SearchForm` form. Otherwise, the user is taken to the `DispResultForm` where the records matching a given criteria are displayed. To do this, you use an `if` statement that checks whether the length of the value stored in the `strText` variable is zero or not. The length of the variable is found out by using the `Length` property of the `String` class.

To display the form based on the result of the `if` statement, you can use the `Redirect()` method. The `Redirect()` method redirects the user to a new page. The URL of the resultant page is passed as a parameter to the `Redirect()` method.

After writing the code for the `Click` event of the Go button, you can see the code for the MainForm form. The code for the MainForm form is as shown:

```
using System;
using System.Collections;
using System.ComponentModel;
using System.Data;
using System.Drawing;
using System.Web;
using System.Web.SessionState;
using System.Web.UI;
using System.Web.UI.WebControls;
using System.Web.UI.HtmlControls;

namespace BookersClient
{
   public class WebForm1 : System.Web.UI.Page
   {
      protected System.Web.UI.WebControls.TextBox txtSearch;
      protected System.Web.UI.WebControls.Button btnGo;
      protected System.Web.UI.WebControls.DropDownList lstType;
      protected System.Web.UI.WebControls.Table Table2;
      protected System.Web.UI.WebControls.Label Label1;
      protected System.Web.UI.WebControls.HyperLink HyperLink1;
      protected System.Web.UI.WebControls.HyperLink HyperLink2;
      protected System.Web.UI.WebControls.HyperLink HyperLink3;
      protected System.Web.UI.WebControls.HyperLink HyperLink5;
      protected System.Web.UI.WebControls.HyperLink HyperLink4;
      protected System.Web.UI.WebControls.Label Label2;
      protected System.Web.UI.WebControls.Label Label3;
      protected System.Web.UI.WebControls.Label Label4;
      protected System.Web.UI.WebControls.Table Table1;
```

```
        private void Page_Load(object sender, System.EventArgs e)
        {

        }
        private void btnGo_Click(object sender, System.EventArgs e)
        {
            string strList;
            string strText;
            strList = lstType.SelectedItem.Text ;
            if(String.Compare(strList, "ALL")==0)
            {
                strText="Search ALL";
            }
            else
            {
                strText = txtSearch.Text;
            }
            if(strText.Length != 0)
            {
                Response.Redirect ("DispResultForm.aspx?Cat=" + strList + "& str="
                    + strText);
            }
            else
            {
                Response.Redirect ("SearchForm.aspx");
            }
        }
    }
}
```

## Adding Code to the DispResultForm Form

When the user is taken to the DispResultForm form, the records matching the criteria specified in the MainForm page are displayed. Therefore, you need to add code to the `Page_Load()` method as shown:

```
private void Page_Load(object sender, System.EventArgs e)
{
    DTService.Service1 srv1 = new DTService.Service1();
```

```
DataSet ds1;
string strCategory;
string strParam;
strCategory = Request.QueryString.Get(0).ToString();
strParam = Request.QueryString.Get(1).ToString();

switch(strCategory)
{
   case "ALL":
      ds1 = srv1.SearchALL();
   if(ds1.Tables["Details"].Rows.Count != 0)
   {
      DataView source= new DataView(ds1.Tables["Details"]);
      DataGrid1.DataSource=source;
      DataGrid1.DataBind();
      lblInfo.Text = "Your search produced following results";
   }
   else
   {
      DataGrid1.Visible = false;
      lblInfo.Text = "No matching records found!!";
   }
   break;

   case "Title":
        ds1=srv1.SrchTitle (strParam);
      if(ds1.Tables["Details"].Rows.Count !=0)
      {
         DataView source= new DataView(ds1.Tables["Details"]);
         DataGrid1.DataSource=source;
         DataGrid1.DataBind();
         lblInfo.Text = "Your search produced following results...";
      }
      else
      {
         DataGrid1.Visible = false;
         lblInfo.Text = "No matching records found!!";
      }
```

```
break;

case "ISBN Number":
ds1=srv1.SrchISBN (strParam);
if(ds1.Tables["Details"].Rows.Count !=0)
{
   DataView source= new DataView(ds1.Tables["Details"]);
   DataGrid1.DataSource=source;
   DataGrid1.DataBind();
   lblInfo.Text = "Your search produced following results...";
}
else
{
   DataGrid1.Visible = false;
   lblInfo.Text = "No matching records found!!";
}
break;

case "Author":
   ds1=srv1.SrchAuthor (strParam);
   if(ds1.Tables["Details"].Rows.Count !=0)
   {
      DataView source= new DataView(ds1.Tables["Details"]);
      DataGrid1.DataSource=source;
      DataGrid1.DataBind();
      lblInfo.Text = "Your search produced following results";
   }
   else
   {
      DataGrid1.Visible = false;
      lblInfo.Text = "No matching records found!!";
   }
break;
```

```
            case "Category":
            ds1=srv1.SrchCategory(strParam);
               if(ds1.Tables["Details"].Rows.Count !=0)
               {
                  DataView source= new DataView(ds1.Tables["Details"]);
                  DataGrid1.DataSource=source;
                  DataGrid1.DataBind();
                  lblInfo.Text = "Your search produced following results...";
               }
               else
               {
                  DataGrid1.Visible = false;
                  lblInfo.Text = "No matching records found!!";
               }
            break;

         default:
         break;
      }
}
```

The preceding code is used to declare an instance, `srv1`, of the `DTService.Service1` class. In addition, the code declares a dataset object with the name `ds1` and two `string` type variables, `strCategory` and `strParam`. Next, the `strCategory` variable is initialized to the `QueryString` value stored at the index value 0. Similarly, the `strParam` variable is initialized to the `QueryString` value stored at the index value 1.

Then, the `switch` case statements are used to find out the value selected by the user in the list box on the Main page. Based on this value, the records are displayed in the DispResultForm form.

First consider the case in which a user selects the `All` option. In this case, the object, `ds1`, of the dataset is used to call the `SearchALL()` Web method in the Web service that you created in Chapter 29. This will store all the records returned by the `SearchALL()` Web method in the `ds1` dataset object.

However, there may be a case where there are no records to be displayed. In this case, you can display an error message to the user. To do this, you first need to check whether the records in the `Details` data table object are equal to null or not. To find this, you can use the `Count` property of the `InternalDataCollectionBase` class. The `Count` property returns the total number of elements in the data table object. The value that is retuned is then equated to null. If the collection object contains records, then an object, `source`, of the `DataView` class is created and initialized to the records in the `Details` data table object.

Then, the `DataSource` property of the DataGrid object is used to specify a source for the records in the DataGrid control. In this case, the source for the records is the `source` object. Finally, the `DataBind()` method is used to bind the DataGrid control to the source object. Once the records are stored and displayed in the DataGrid control, you can display a message in the `lblInfo` label control. To display the text in the label control, the `Text` property of the control is used. Figure 30-7 shows the records displayed in the DataGrid control.

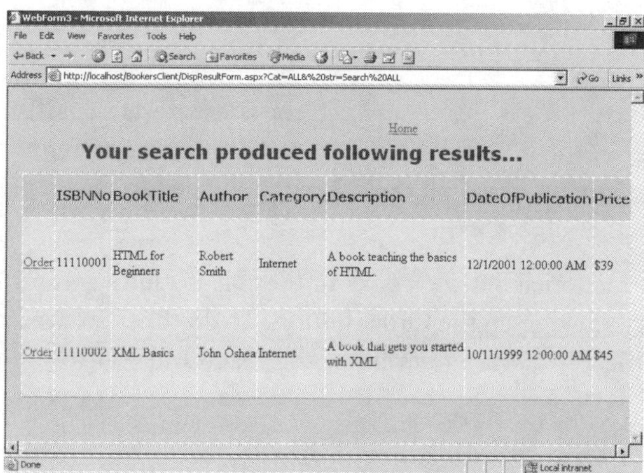


**FIGURE 30-7** *The records displayed in the DataGrid control*

However, in the case where the `Details` data table object does not contain any records, the DataGrid control is made invisible and an error message is displayed in the `lblInfo` label control. Figure 30-8 shows an error message in the `lblInfo` label control.

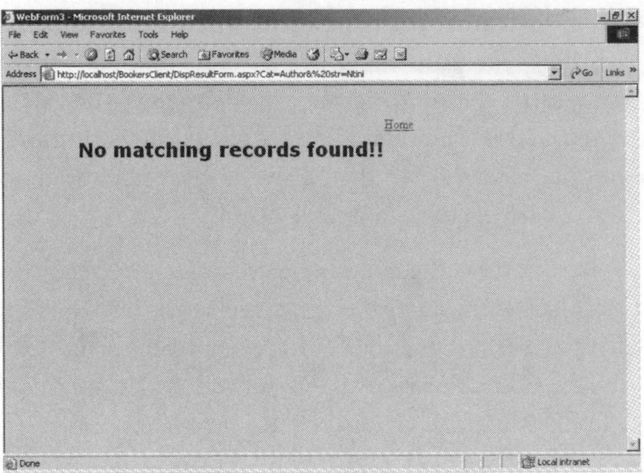


**FIGURE 30-8** *The error message in the* `lblInfo` *label control*

Having understood the code for the case in which the user selects the All option, you can easily add code for the rest of the `switch` cases. The only difference is that in the case of returning records based on the criteria, you need to pass a parameter `strParam` to the DataSet object, `ds1`.

After viewing the information about the books in the DispResultForm form, the user can order a book by clicking on the Order button. To do this, you need to add the following code to the `ItemCommand()` event of the DataGrid control:

```
private void DataGrid1_ItemCommand(object source,
System.Web.UI.WebControls.DataGridCommandEventArgs e)
{
   if(e.CommandName == "Ord")
   {
      string strISBN;
      string strTitle;
      string strAuthor;
      strISBN = e.Item.Cells[1].Text ;
      strTitle = e.Item.Cells[2].Text ;
      strAuthor = e.Item.Cells[3].Text;
```

```
        Response.Redirect ("OrdersForm.aspx?ISBN=" + strISBN + " & Title=" + strTitle
            + " & Author=" + strAuthor);
    }
}
```

The preceding code uses the `CommandName` property in an `if` loop to check whether the `CommandName` specified for the button controls in the DataGrid control is `Ord`. I have discussed the `CommandName` property earlier in this chapter.

Inside the `if` loop, three `string` variables are declared with the names `strISBN`, `strTitle`, and `strAuthor`. These variables store the text in the cells of the DataGrid control. These variables are then passed as parameters to the `Redirect()` method of the `HTTPResponse` class. The page to be displayed using the `Redirect()` method is also passed as a parameter to the `Redirect()` method. In this case, the page to be displayed is the Orders form.

After adding the previously mentioned code to DispResultForm form, have a look at the complete code for the DispResultForm form. The complete code for the DispResultForm form is as shown:

```
using System;
using System.Collections;
using System.ComponentModel;
using System.Data;
using System.Drawing;
using System.Web;
using System.Web.SessionState;
using System.Web.UI;
using System.Web.UI.WebControls;
using System.Web.UI.HtmlControls;

namespace BookersClient
{
public class WebForm3 : System.Web.UI.Page
    {
        protected System.Web.UI.WebControls.Label lblInfo;
        protected System.Web.UI.WebControls.HyperLink HyperLink1;
        protected System.Web.UI.WebControls.DataGrid DataGrid1;
```

```
private void Page_Load(object sender, System.EventArgs e)
{
   DTService.Service1 srv1 = new DTService.Service1();
   DataSet ds1;
   string strCategory;
   string strParam;
   strCategory = Request.QueryString.Get(0).ToString();
   strParam = Request.QueryString.Get(1).ToString();

   switch(strCategory)
   {
      case "ALL":
      ds1 = srv1.SearchALL();
      if(ds1.Tables["Details"].Rows.Count != 0)
      {
         DataView source= new DataView(ds1.Tables["Details"]);
         DataGrid1.DataSource=source;
         DataGrid1.DataBind();
         lblInfo.Text = "Your search produced following results...";
      }
      else
      {
         DataGrid1.Visible = false;
         lblInfo.Text = "No matching records found!!";
      }
      break;

      case "Title":
      ds1=srv1.SrchTitle (strParam);
      if(ds1.Tables["Details"].Rows.Count !=0)
      {
         DataView source= new DataView(ds1.Tables["Details"]);
         DataGrid1.DataSource=source;
         DataGrid1.DataBind();
         lblInfo.Text = "Your search produced following results...";
      }
```

```
else
{
   DataGrid1.Visible = false;
   lblInfo.Text = "No matching records found!!";
}
break;

case "ISBN Number":
   ds1=srv1.SrchISBN (strParam);
   if(ds1.Tables["Details"].Rows.Count !=0)
   {
      DataView source= new DataView(ds1.Tables["Details"]);
      DataGrid1.DataSource=source;
      DataGrid1.DataBind();
      lblInfo.Text = "Your search produced following results...";
   }
   else
   {
      DataGrid1.Visible = false;
      lblInfo.Text = "No matching records found!!";
   }
   break;

   case "Author":
   ds1=srv1.SrchAuthor (strParam);
   if(ds1.Tables["Details"].Rows.Count !=0)
   {
      DataView source= new DataView(ds1.Tables["Details"]);
      DataGrid1.DataSource=source;
      DataGrid1.DataBind();
      lblInfo.Text = "Your search produced following results...";
   }
   else
   {
      DataGrid1.Visible = false;
      lblInfo.Text = "No matching records found!!";
   }
```

```
                break;

                case "Category":
                ds1=srv1.SrchCategory(strParam);
                if(ds1.Tables["Details"].Rows.Count !=0)
                {
                    DataView source= new DataView(ds1.Tables["Details"]);
                    DataGrid1.DataSource=source;
                    DataGrid1.DataBind();
                    lblInfo.Text = "Your search produced following results...";
                }
                else
                {
                    DataGrid1.Visible = false;
                    lblInfo.Text = "No matching records found!!";
                }
                break;
                default:
                break;
            }
        }

private void DataGrid1_ItemCommand(object source, System.Web.UI.WebControls
    .DataGridCommandEventArgs e)
        {
            if(e.CommandName == "Ord")
            {
                string strISBN;
                string strTitle;
                string strAuthor;
                strISBN = e.Item.Cells[1].Text ;
                strTitle = e.Item.Cells[2].Text ;
                strAuthor = e.Item.Cells[3].Text;

                Response.Redirect ("OrdersForm.aspx?ISBN=" + strISBN + " & Title="
                    + strTitle + " & Author=" + strAuthor);
            }
        }
```

```
    }
}
```

## Adding Code to the Search Form

The Search form prompts the user to specify criteria and the value for the criteria. After specifying the criteria and the value, the user needs to click on the Search Now button. Clicking on the Search Now button will display the matching records in the DispResultForm form. In addition, the user can select the Home button to visit the Home page for the Web site of Bookers Paradise.

In order for the Web service to return the required records, you need to track the radio button selected by the user. In addition, you need to track the value specified for the criteria. To do this, you need to add the following code to the `Click` event of the `btnSearch` button:

```
private void btnSearch_Click(object sender, System.EventArgs e)
{
        string strText, strCriteria;
        strText="";
        strCriteria="";
        if(txtISBN.Text.Trim() == "" & txtAuthor.Text.Trim() =="" & txtCategory
          .Text.Trim() =="" & txtTitle.Text.Trim() =="")
        {
                lblInfo.Text ="Please enter a value!!";
                return;
        }

        if(radISBN.Checked == true)
        {
                strText = txtISBN.Text;
                strCriteria = "ISBN Number";
        }
        else if(radAuthor.Checked == true)
        {
                strText = txtAuthor.Text;
                strCriteria = "Author";
        }
        else if(radCategory.Checked == true)
```

```
        {
                strText = txtCategory.Text;
                strCriteria = "Category";
        }
        else if(radTitle.Checked == true)
        {
                strText = txtTitle.Text;
                strCriteria = "Title";
        }

        Response.Redirect ("DispResultForm.aspx?Cat=" + strCriteria + "& str="
          + strText);
}
```

The preceding code declares two `string` variables, `strText` and `strCriteria`, and initializes these variables to a null value. Next, the `Trim()` property of the `String` class is used to check whether the user has entered a value in any of the text box controls in the Search form. To check this, the code uses an `if` loop. If any of the text box controls do not contain a value, the user is prompted to enter a variable. Figure 30-9 shows the message in the `lblInfo` label control.

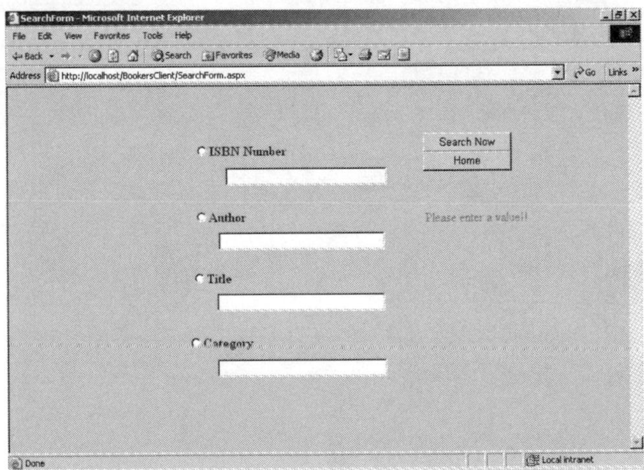


**FIGURE 30-9** *The message in the `lblInfo` label control*

When a user selects any of the radio buttons, you need to track the radio button clicked. To do this, the `Checked` property of the `CheckBox` class is used. The `Checked` property returns a Boolean value. If the radio button is clicked, the value returned by the `Checked` property is `True`. Otherwise, the `Checked` property returns a value `False`.

For the radio button that is selected, the code uses the `strText` variable to store the text in the corresponding text box. In addition, the criteria specified by the user is stored in the `strCriteria` variable. Finally, the `Redirect()` method is used to display the DispResultForm form. The values in the `strText` and `strCriteria` variables are passed to the `Redirect()` method as a parameter.

As already discussed, the Search page contains a Home button. When the Home button is clicked, the Home page of the Web site of Bookers Paradise is displayed. To add this functionality, write the following code for the `Click` event of the Home button:

```
private void btnHome_Click(object sender, System.EventArgs e)
{
        Response.Redirect ("MainForm.aspx");
}
```

The preceding code uses the `Redirect()` method to redirect the user to the MainForm form, which is the Home page in this case.

After adding the preceding code to the SearchForm page, look at the complete code for the SearchForm page.

```
using System;
using System.Collections;
using System.ComponentModel;
using System.Data;
using System.Drawing;
using System.Web;
using System.Web.SessionState;
using System.Web.UI;
using System.Web.UI.WebControls;
using System.Web.UI.HtmlControls;
```

```
namespace BookersClient
{
  public class SearchForm : System.Web.UI.Page
  {
    protected System.Web.UI.WebControls.RadioButton radISBN;
    protected System.Web.UI.WebControls.RadioButton radAuthor;
    protected System.Web.UI.WebControls.RadioButton radTitle;
    protected System.Web.UI.WebControls.RadioButton radCategory;
    protected System.Web.UI.WebControls.TextBox txtISBN;
    protected System.Web.UI.WebControls.TextBox txtAuthor;
    protected System.Web.UI.WebControls.TextBox txtTitle;
    protected System.Web.UI.WebControls.Button btnSearch;
    protected System.Web.UI.WebControls.Label lblInfo;
    protected System.Web.UI.WebControls.Button btnHome;
    protected System.Web.UI.WebControls.TextBox txtCategory;

    private void Page_Load(object sender, System.EventArgs e)
    {

    }

    private void btnSearch_Click(object sender, System.EventArgs e)
    {
      string strText, strCriteria;
      strText="";
      strCriteria="";
      if(txtISBN.Text.Trim() == "" & txtAuthor.Text.Trim() =="" &
          txtCategory.Text.Trim() =="" & txtTitle.Text.Trim() =="")
      {
        lblInfo.Text ="Please enter a value!!";
        return;
      }

      if(radISBN.Checked == true)
      {
        strText = txtISBN.Text;
        strCriteria = "ISBN Number";
      }
```

```
        else if(radAuthor.Checked == true)
        {
          strText = txtAuthor.Text;
          strCriteria = "Author";
        }
        else if(radCategory.Checked == true)
        {
          strText = txtCategory.Text;
          strCriteria = "Category";
        }
        else if(radTitle.Checked == true)
        {
          strText = txtTitle.Text;
          strCriteria = "Title";
        }
        Response.Redirect ("DispResultForm.aspx?Cat="
           + strCriteria + "& str=" + strText);
        }

      private void btnHome_Click(object sender, System.EventArgs e)
      {
        Response.Redirect ("MainForm.aspx");
      }
    }
}
```

## Adding Code to the Orders Form

The Orders form accepts the information about the customer who orders a book on the Web site. This information, along with the information about the book, is added to the database of the publishing house.

When the Orders page is displayed, it contains the information about the book to be ordered. To do this, add the following code to the `Page_Load()` method. The `Page_Load()` method is executed when the page is loaded at run time.

```
private void Page_Load(object sender, System.EventArgs e)
{
        txtISBN.Text = Request.QueryString.Get(0).ToString();
```

```
        txtTitle.Text = Request.QueryString.Get(1).ToString();
        txtAuthor.Text = Request.QueryString.Get(2).ToString();
}
```

The preceding code retrieves the `QueryString` value stored at index 0, 1, and 2 and assigns these values to the `txtISBN`, `txtTitle`, and `txtAuthor` text boxes, respectively.

When the user enters the required details and clicks on the Order button, the information is added to the underlying database. To do this, add the following code to the `Click` event of the `btnOrder` button.

```
private void btnOrder_Click(object sender, System.EventArgs e)
{
        DTService.Service1 srv = new DTService.Service1();
        string strDate, strStatus, strOrderBy;
        strDate = Convert.ToString(DateTime.Today);
        strStatus="Pending";
        strOrderBy="Bookers Paradise";
        string result;

        result = srv.AcceptDetails(txtISBN.Text,
        strDate,
        txtName.Text,
        txtAddr1.Text,
        txtAddr2.Text,
        txtCity.Text,
        txtState.Text,
        strOrderBy,
        strStatus,
        lstCardType.SelectedItem.Text,
        txtCardNumber.Text );

        string orderno;
        orderno = srv.GenerateOrder();

         if (result == "Record Inserted!!")
        {
                string custid;
                custid = InsertBookersDB(orderno);
```

```
            TextBox1.Text = "Dear " + txtName.Text + "!! \n" +
            "Thanks for visiting Bookers Paradise. \n" +
            "Your Customer ID is " + custid + ".\n" +
            "Your order (Number " + orderno + ") will be shipped by "
               + DateTime.Today.AddDays(15).Date + ".";
        }
        else
        {
        TextBox1.Text = "Dear " + txtName.Text + "!! \n" +
        "Thanks for visiting Bookers Paradise \n" +
        "Your request could not be processed due to some internal error. \n"+
        "Please visit later.";
        }
}
```

The preceding code creates an instance of the `DTService.Service1` class. In addition, the code declares three `string` type variables, `strDate`, `strStatus`, and `strOrderBy`. The `strDate` variable is initialized to the current date, which is retrieved by the `Today` property of the `System.DateTime` struct. However, to store the date in a `string` type variable, you first need to convert the date type value to a `string` type value by using the `Convert()` method. Next, the `strStatus` variable is initialized to the value `Pending` and the `strOrderBy` variable to the value `Bookers Paradise`.

Then, a `string` type variable, `result`, is declared and initialized to the value returned by the `AcceptDetails()` Web method. This Web method is used to store the details of the customer and the book, passed as parameters to the Web method, in the `DTDetails` table. You have learned to write the code for the `AcceptDetails()` Web method in Chapter 29 in the section "Creating the `AcceptDetails()` Web Method."

Next, the code declares and initializes another `string` type variable, `orderno`, to the value returned by the `GenerateOrder()` Web method. This method is used to automatically generate an order number for each order that is placed.

Next, a `if` construct is used to check whether records are added to the database. If the records are added, a `string` type variable, `custid`, is declared. This variable is initialized to a value returned by the `InsertBookersDB()` method that is used to automatically create the customer ID for all orders that are placed. You will learn to write a code for the `InsertBookersDB()` method later in this chapter.

Then, a message is displayed in a text box confirming that the order for a book is successfully placed. Figure 30-10 shows a message displayed to the customer.

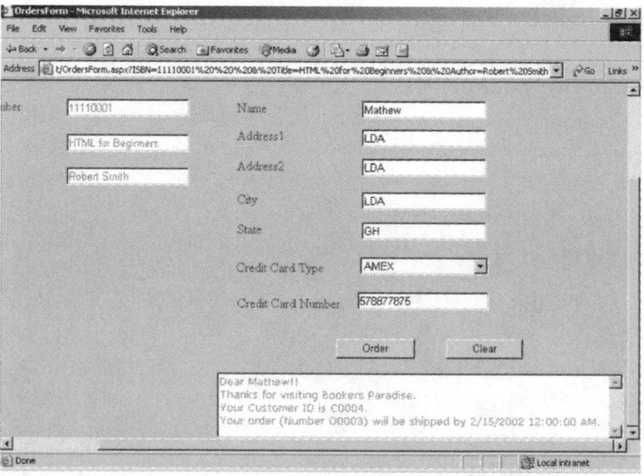


**FIGURE 30-10** *The message displayed to the customer*

However, if the `AcceptDetails()` Web method fails to add the records to the underlying database, an error message is displayed to the customer.

## Adding Code to the `InsertBookersDB()` Method

The `InsertBookersDB()` method is used to automatically generate the customer ID value for all orders that are placed on the Web site. The order number for the order is passed as the parameter to this method. To create the `InsertBookersDB()` method, write the following code:

```
public string InsertBookersDB(string order)
{
	string SelStr;
	 SelStr = "Select Count(*) From BookerCustDetails";
	 SqlCommand SelCom;
	 SelCom = new SqlCommand(SelStr, sqlConnection1);
	 sqlConnection1.Open();
	 sqlDataAdapter1.SelectCommand = SelCom;
	 sqlDataAdapter1.Fill(dsCustomers1,"Customer");
```

```
        sqlConnection1.Close();
        string str;
        str = dsCustomers1.Tables["Customer"].Rows[0][0].ToString ();
        int val;
        val = Convert.ToInt32(str);
        val= val+1;
        if(val>0 & val<=9)
        {
                str = "C000" + Convert.ToString(val);
        }
        else if(val>9 & val<=99)
        {
                str ="C00" + Convert.ToString (val);
        }
        else if(val>99 & val <=999)
        {
                str = "C0" + Convert.ToString (val);
        }
        else
        {
                str = "C" + Convert.ToString (val);
        }
}
```

In the preceding code, a `string` type variable `SelStr` is declared and initialized to a SQL statement that is used to count the records in the `BookersCustDetails` table. Next, an instance, `SelCom`, of the `SqlCommand` class is declared. In the constructor of the `SqlCommand` class, the variable `SelStr` is passed as a parameter. In addition, an object of the sqlConnection component is added as a parameter to the constructor of the `SqlCommand` class.

Once you have assigned the SQL statement to the `SelStr` variable, the connection to the `BookerCustDetails` table is opened by using the `Open()` method. Then, the `Fill()` method is used to fill the sqlDataAdapter component with the data in the dataset. After the records are added to the sqlDataAdapter component, the connection to the `BookerCustDetails` table is closed using the `Close()` method.

The code then declares a `string` type variable `str` and initializes it to a collection of rows in the table. To do this, the `Rows` property of the `DataRowCollection` class is used. The value returned by the `Rows` property is converted to a `string` value by using the `ToString()` method and stored in the `str` variable. Next, an `integer` type variable, `val`, is declared and initialized to the 32-bit signed `integer` equivalent of the value stored in the `str` variable. To convert the `string` type variable to the 32-bit signed integer variable, you use the `ToInt` property of the `System.Convert` class.

Because the value stored in the variable `val` is the number of records in the `BookerCustDetails` table, to generate the next customer ID, you need to add 1 to the value in the variable `val`. Then, an `if` construct is used to find the range of the value in the variable `val`. If this value lies in the range 0 to 9, the string C000 is added to this value. However, to do this, you again need to convert the value in the variable `val` to a `string` type value.

Similarly, if the value in the variable `val` lies in the range 9 to 99, the string C00 is added to the value. Therefore, the range of the value is found out and *C* followed by zeros is added to make the customer ID a four-digit number. This value stored in the variable `str` is returned by the method.

## Adding Code to Store the Customers' Details in the Database

As already discussed, the values entered by the user in the Orders form are stored in the database of Deepthoughts Publications. You can write the code that stores the details about the customers in the underlying database. To do this, add the following code to the Orders page:

```
string InsStr;
InsStr = "Insert Into BookerCustDetails Values(@CID, @CN, @BA1, @BA2, @BC, @BS)";
SqlCommand InsCom;
InsCom = new SqlCommand(InsStr, sqlConnection1);
sqlDataAdapter1.InsertCommand = InsCom;
sqlDataAdapter1.InsertCommand.Parameters.Add("@CID", SqlDbType.Char,6).Value = str;
sqlDataAdapter1.InsertCommand.Parameters.Add("@CN", SqlDbType.VarChar,50)
   .Value = txtName.Text;
sqlDataAdapter1.InsertCommand.Parameters.Add("@BA1", SqlDbType.VarChar ,50)
   .Value= txtAddr1.Text ;
sqlDataAdapter1.InsertCommand.Parameters.Add("@BA2", SqlDbType.VarChar,50)
   .Value= txtAddr2.Text ;
sqlDataAdapter1.InsertCommand.Parameters.Add("@BC",SqlDbType.VarChar,20)
   .Value = txtCity.Text ;
```

```
sqlDataAdapter1.InsertCommand.Parameters.Add("@BS", SqlDbType.VarChar ,10)
   .Value = txtState.Text ;
if(sqlConnection1.State== ConnectionState.Closed )
{
       sqlConnection1.Open ();
}
sqlDataAdapter1.InsertCommand.ExecuteNonQuery();
sqlConnection1.Close();
```

The preceding code declares a `string` type variable `InsStr` and stores an SQL query used to insert values to the `BookerCustDetails` table. The values to be stored are passed to the SQL query. Next, an instance of the `SqlCommand` class is created to connect to the sqlDataAdapter component. Next, the `Add()` method is used to add values in the text box controls to the `SqlParameterCollection` object. To retrieve the value in the text box, the `Text` property is used.

Next, an `if` loop is used to check whether the SQL connection is opened or closed. If the connection is closed, you use the `Open()` method to open the connection. Finally, the `ExecuteNonQuery()` method of the `SqlCommand` class is executed to return the records that are affected by the SQL command stored in the `SelStr` variable. After adding the records, the connection is closed.

Similarly, you can add the code that adds the details of the book for which the user has placed an order in the database of Deepthoughts Publications. You will see the code later in this chapter.

In addition to the Order button, the Orders form contains a Clear button. The following section discusses adding code to the Clear button.

## Adding Code to the Clear Button

The Clear button is used to clear all the values entered by the user in the Orders page. To add this functionality, write the following code in the `Click` event of the `btnClear` button:

```
private void btnClear_Click(object sender, System.EventArgs e)
{
     txtISBN.Text="";
     txtTitle.Text ="";
     txtAuthor.Text ="";
     txtName.Text="";
```

```
        txtAddr1.Text="";
        txtAddr2.Text="";
        txtCity.Text="";
        txtState.Text="";
        TextBox1.Text ="";
        txtCardNumber.Text ="";
        lstCardType.SelectedIndex =0;
}
```

The preceding code writes a null value in all the text box controls.

After adding the previously described code snippets to the Orders page, look at the complete code for the OrdersForm form.

```
using System;
using System.Collections;
using System.ComponentModel;
using System.Data;
using System.Drawing;
using System.Web;
using System.Web.SessionState;
using System.Web.UI;
using System.Web.UI.WebControls;
using System.Web.UI.HtmlControls;
using System.Data.SqlClient ;

namespace BookersClient
{
    public class OrdersForm : System.Web.UI.Page
    {
        protected System.Web.UI.WebControls.Label Label1;
        protected System.Web.UI.WebControls.Label Label4;
        protected System.Web.UI.WebControls.Label Label5;
        protected System.Web.UI.WebControls.Label Label6;
        protected System.Web.UI.WebControls.Label Label7;
        protected System.Web.UI.WebControls.Label Label8;
        protected System.Web.UI.WebControls.TextBox txtISBN;
        protected System.Web.UI.WebControls.TextBox txtName;
```

```
protected System.Web.UI.WebControls.TextBox txtAddr1;
protected System.Web.UI.WebControls.TextBox txtAddr2;
protected System.Web.UI.WebControls.TextBox txtCity;
protected System.Web.UI.WebControls.RequiredFieldValidator
   RequiredFieldValidator3;
protected System.Web.UI.WebControls.RequiredFieldValidator
   RequiredFieldValidator4;
protected System.Web.UI.WebControls.RequiredFieldValidator
   RequiredFieldValidator5;
protected System.Web.UI.WebControls.RequiredFieldValidator
   RequiredFieldValidator6;
protected System.Web.UI.WebControls.Button btnOrder;
protected System.Web.UI.WebControls.Button btnClear;
protected System.Web.UI.WebControls.Label Label2;
protected System.Web.UI.WebControls.Label Label3;
protected System.Web.UI.WebControls.Label Label9;
protected System.Web.UI.WebControls.Label Label10;
protected System.Web.UI.WebControls.Label Label11;
protected System.Web.UI.WebControls.Label Label12;
protected System.Web.UI.WebControls.DropDownList lstCardType;
protected System.Web.UI.WebControls.TextBox txtCardNumber;
protected System.Web.UI.WebControls.TextBox txtTitle;
protected System.Web.UI.WebControls.TextBox txtAuthor;
protected System.Web.UI.WebControls.RequiredFieldValidator
   RequiredFieldValidator1;
protected System.Web.UI.WebControls.TextBox TextBox1;
protected System.Web.UI.WebControls.HyperLink HyperLink1;
protected System.Data.SqlClient.SqlCommand sqlSelectCommand1;
protected System.Data.SqlClient.SqlCommand sqlInsertCommand1;
protected System.Data.SqlClient.SqlCommand sqlUpdateCommand1;
protected System.Data.SqlClient.SqlCommand sqlDeleteCommand1;
protected System.Data.SqlClient.SqlConnection sqlConnection1;
protected System.Data.SqlClient.SqlDataAdapter sqlDataAdapter1;
protected BookersClient.dsCustomers dsCustomers1;
protected System.Web.UI.WebControls.TextBox txtState;
```

```
private void Page_Load(object sender, System.EventArgs e)
{
    // Put user code to initialize the page here
    txtISBN.Text = Request.QueryString.Get(0).ToString();
    txtTitle.Text = Request.QueryString.Get(1).ToString();
    txtAuthor.Text = Request.QueryString.Get(2).ToString();
}

private void btnOrder_Click(object sender, System.EventArgs e)
{
    DTService.Service1 srv = new DTService.Service1();
    string strDate, strStatus, strOrderBy;
    strDate = Convert.ToString(DateTime.Today);
    strStatus="Pending";
    strOrderBy="Bookers Paradise";
    string result;

    result = srv.AcceptDetails(txtISBN.Text,
    strDate,
    txtName.Text,
    txtAddr1.Text,
    txtAddr2.Text,
    txtCity.Text,
    txtState.Text,
    strOrderBy,
    strStatus,
    lstCardType.SelectedItem.Text,
    txtCardNumber.Text );

    string orderno;
    orderno = srv.GenerateOrder();

    if (result == "Record Inserted!!")
    {
        string custid;
        custid = InsertBookersDB(orderno);
```

```
        TextBox1.Text = "Dear " + txtName.Text + "!! \n" +
        "Thanks for visiting Bookers Paradise. \n" +
        "Your Customer ID is " + custid + ".\n" +
        "Your order (Number " + orderno + ") will be shipped by " +
           DateTime.Today.AddDays(15).Date + ".";
    }
    else
    {
        TextBox1.Text = "Dear " + txtName.Text + "!! \n" +
        "Thanks for visiting Bookers Paradise \n" +
        "Your request could not be processed due to some internal error. \n"+
        "Please visit later.";
    }
}

public string InsertBookersDB(string order)
{
    //Code To Generate Customer ID
    string SelStr;
    SelStr = "Select Count(*) From BookerCustDetails";
    SqlCommand SelCom;
    SelCom = new SqlCommand(SelStr, sqlConnection1);
    sqlConnection1.Open();
    sqlDataAdapter1.SelectCommand = SelCom;
    sqlDataAdapter1.Fill(dsCustomers1,"Customer");
    sqlConnection1.Close();
    string str;
    str = dsCustomers1.Tables["Customer"].Rows[0][0].ToString ();
    int val;
    val = Convert.ToInt32(str);
    val= val+1;
    if(val>0 & val<=9)
    {
        str = "C000" + Convert.ToString(val);
    }
```

```
else if(val>9 & val<=99)
{
   str ="C00" + Convert.ToString (val);
}
else if(val>99 & val <=999)
{
   str = "C0" + Convert.ToString (val);
}
else
{
   str = "C" + Convert.ToString (val);
}
//Store customer details
string InsStr;
InsStr = "Insert Into BookerCustDetails Values(@CID, @CN, @BA1, @BA2,
   @BC, @BS)";
SqlCommand InsCom;
InsCom = new SqlCommand(InsStr, sqlConnection1);
sqlDataAdapter1.InsertCommand = InsCom;
sqlDataAdapter1.InsertCommand.Parameters.Add("@CID",
   SqlDbType.Char,6).Value = str;
sqlDataAdapter1.InsertCommand.Parameters.Add("@CN",
   SqlDbType.VarChar,50).Value = txtName.Text;
sqlDataAdapter1.InsertCommand.Parameters.Add("@BA1", SqlDbType
   .VarChar ,50).Value= txtAddr1.Text ;
sqlDataAdapter1.InsertCommand.Parameters.Add("@BA2", SqlDbType.VarChar,50)
   .Value= txtAddr2.Text ;
sqlDataAdapter1.InsertCommand.Parameters.Add("@BC",SqlDbType.VarChar,20)
   .Value = txtCity.Text ;
sqlDataAdapter1.InsertCommand.Parameters.Add("@BS", SqlDbType
   .VarChar ,10).Value = txtState.Text ;
if(sqlConnection1.State== ConnectionState.Closed )
{
   sqlConnection1.Open ();
}
```

```
    sqlDataAdapter1.InsertCommand.ExecuteNonQuery();
    sqlConnection1.Close();
    //Store Order Details
    string InsStr1;
    InsStr1 = "Insert Into BookersOrders Values(@ON, @CID, @ISBN)";
    SqlCommand InsCom1;
    InsCom1 = new SqlCommand(InsStr1, sqlConnection1);
    sqlDataAdapter1.InsertCommand = InsCom1;
    sqlDataAdapter1.InsertCommand.Parameters.Add("@ON", SqlDbType.Char,10)
        .Value = order;
    sqlDataAdapter1.InsertCommand.Parameters.Add("@CID", SqlDbType.Char,6)
        .Value = str;
    sqlDataAdapter1.InsertCommand.Parameters.Add("@ISBN", SqlDbType.Char,10)
        .Value = txtISBN.Text;
    if(sqlConnection1.State== ConnectionState.Closed )
    {
        sqlConnection1.Open ();
    }
    sqlDataAdapter1.InsertCommand.ExecuteNonQuery();
    sqlConnection1.Close();
    return str;
}

private void btnClear_Click(object sender, System.EventArgs e)
{
    txtISBN.Text="";
    txtTitle.Text ="";
    txtAuthor.Text ="";
    txtName.Text="";
    txtAddr1.Text="";
    txtAddr2.Text="";
    txtCity.Text="";
    txtState.Text="";
    TextBox1.Text ="";
    txtCardNumber.Text ="";
    lstCardType.SelectedIndex =0;
}
```

```
        private void btnHome_Click(object sender, System.EventArgs e)
        {
            Response.Redirect ("Mainform.aspx");
        }
    }
}
```

## Adding Code to the Construction Form

The Main form in the Bookers Paradise Web site contains some hyperlinks. On clicking the hyperlinks, the user is taken to the ConstructionForm form. However, the Construction form displays a message that the page to which the user wants to connect is under construction.

The Construction form includes a hyperlink control that takes you to the Home page. The code for the Construction form includes the declarations for the controls added to the form. The code for the Construction form is as shown as follows:

```
using System;
using System.Collections;
using System.ComponentModel;
using System.Data;
using System.Drawing;
using System.Web;
using System.Web.SessionState;
using System.Web.UI;
using System.Web.UI.WebControls;
using System.Web.UI.HtmlControls;

namespace BookersClient
{
        public class ConstructionForm : System.Web.UI.Page
        {
                protected System.Web.UI.WebControls.Label Label2;
                protected System.Web.UI.WebControls.HyperLink HyperLink1;
                protected System.Web.UI.WebControls.Label Label1;
```

```
            private void Page_Load(object sender, System.EventArgs e)
            {

            }
        }
    }
```

## Summary

In this chapter, you learned about how to create the forms required for the Web site of Bookers Paradise. In addition, you learned to add code to the Web forms created for the Web site.

# PART VIII

## Professional Project 6

# Project 6

## Creating a Mobile Application

## Project 6 Overview

In the preceding projects, you have developed Windows applications, Web applications, and Web services. In this project, you will learn to create a mobile Web application for an electronic goods company named Electronix, Inc. The mobile application that you will develop is called MobileCallStatus.

To begin with, I will discuss the case study and design of the MobileCallStatus application. Then, I will discuss the basics of the mobile Web applications that involve the need for developing mobile Web applications. In addition, in this project you will be introduced to the technologies responsible for creating, testing, and deploying mobile Web applications. Finally, based on this knowledge, you will create the MobileCallStatus application.

# Chapter 31

## Project Case Study and Design

In this project, you will learn to create a mobile Web application. I will discuss the case study and design of the mobile Web application in this chapter. In addition, you will learn about the project life cycle of the MobileCallStatus application, which includes creating high-level and low-level designs of the application.

## Case Study

Electronix, Inc. is one of the leading electronic goods companies in the United States. The company has its offices all over the United States, with its head office located in California. The company was established in 1990 and has grown tremendously since then. The company now provides electronic goods services to more than a million customers all over the United States.

Electronix, Inc. has a huge customer support division comprising more than 500 executives across all branches. The customer support executives at Electronix, Inc. provide services to customers over the telephone, the mobile phone, and the Internet. In addition, the engineers of the customer support division visit the customers to solve their problems. Because of this, the engineers need to travel a lot.

The customer support division tracks all the complaints made by the customers in a CRM (*Customer Relations Management*) database. The engineers then access the customer complaint data in the CRM database to discover the pending calls and the new complaints that are logged in the database. The senior managers in the customer support division have realized the need for the engineers to be able to access the customer complaint data while they are traveling. This would enable the engineers to be aware of the pending and new calls without going back to the office. As a result, the engineers can attend to the pending and new calls while they are traveling.

In this context, the senior management has decided to create a mobile application that can be accessed using an engineer's mobile phone. The complaints that are logged in the CRM database are then stored in an XML document. The senior management has decided to create a mobile application that can provide the data from this XML document to the users. The engineers can access the mobile application from their mobile phones to discover the status of the complaints.

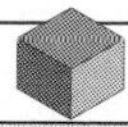

**NOTE**

While creating this application, I am assuming that the customer complaint data is already transformed from the CRM database to an XML document.

To develop the application, the senior managers performed an analysis of the available technologies and decided to create the application by using the mobile technologies available as a part of the .NET platform. This is because the .NET Framework provides an easy and user-friendly framework for developing Web applications for the distributed environment. In addition, the Mobile Internet Toolkit, which is based on the .NET Framework, can be installed on the user's computer. The Mobile Internet Toolkit provides the user with the tools and components that can be used to create a mobile application easily and efficiently.

Therefore, the senior managers have appointed a software developer who has experience in working with the .NET technologies. The software developer has decided to use C# as language to develop this mobile application. The following section discusses the stages in the life cycle of the MobileCallStatus application.

# Project Life Cycle

You are familiar with the phases of a DLC (*development life cycle*) of a project. Therefore, in this chapter, I will only discuss the analysis of the organization's requirements that were done by the software developer at Electronix, Inc. In addition, I will discuss the design of the application created by the software developer based on the analysis of the organization's requirements. You, as a developer, will analyze the requirements of Electronix, Inc., and create a design for the MobileCallStatus application.

## Analyzing Requirements

To develop an application, it is essential that you analyze the requirements of the customer in detail. This analysis is done in the analyzing requirements phase of the project life cycle. Based on the customer's problem, you can create a plan for developing the application. The analysis of the customer's problem is completed on the basis of the problem statement stated by senior managers and the information gathered by the developer.

In the case of Electronix, Inc., the problem statement is as follows: "Electronix, Inc. needs to make the customer complaint data, which contains the status of the calls made by the customers, accessible to the engineers while they are traveling."

After analyzing the problem statement, the developer created a detailed list of tasks to be done while creating the application:

- ◆ The organization needs to make the customer complaint data containing the status of the calls accessible to the engineers while they are traveling.
- ◆ The organization needs to save the time and effort of the engineers.
- ◆ Because the engineers travel a lot, the application should be deployed on a mobile device, such as their mobile phones.

To provide a solution to the problems of Electronix, Inc., the developer plans to create a mobile Web application that can be accessed from the mobile phones of the engineers. The mobile Web application will have the following features:

- ◆ The application will prompt the users to enter their logon name and password.
- ◆ The application will validate the logon name and password of the users.
- ◆ The information about the logon name and password of the users is stored in the Users.xml file.
- ◆ The application will show the pending calls to the users.
- ◆ When a user marks the status of a call as complete, the status is reflected in the Calls.xml file.
- ◆ The application will show the unattended or new calls to the users.
- ◆ When a user accepts a call, the status of the call is changed to pending in the Calls.xml file.

## High-Level Design

Based on the plan that is created by the developer at Electronix, Inc., the developer needs to create a high-level and low-level design of the application in the high-level and low-level design phases, respectively. To create a design of the mobile application, the developer needs to identify the mobile Web forms to be included in the application. In addition, the developer needs to identify the mobile Web form controls to be included in the Web forms. All this is done in the high-level design phase of the DLC of the application.

The MobileCallStatus application consists of four mobile Web forms, frmLogon, frmSelectOption, frmPending, and frmUnattended. You will learn about mobile Web forms in detail in Chapter 32, "Basics of Mobile Applications," in the section, "The Mobile Web Form." However, in this chapter, I will only discuss the designs of the four forms. Figure 31-1 shows the layout of the frmLogon form.

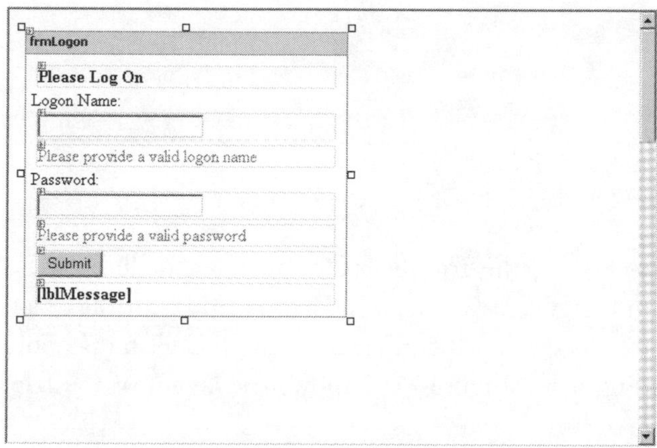


**FIGURE 31-1** *The design of the frmLogon form*

The frmLogon form consists of two Label controls, two TextBox controls, two RequiredFieldValidator controls, and one Command control. You will learn about these controls in detail in Chapter 32 in the section "The Design of the Mobile-TimeRetriever Application."

Figure 31-2 shows the layout of the frmSelectOption form.

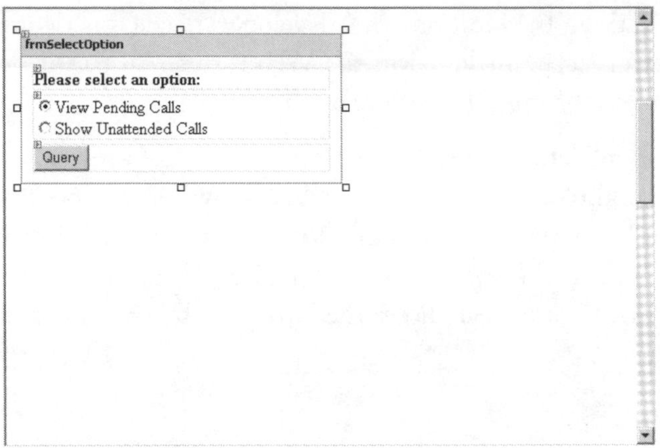


**FIGURE 31-2** *The design of the frmSelectOption form*

As you can see in Figure 31-2, the frmSelectOption form includes a Label, a SelectionList, and a Command control. You will learn to add controls to a mobile Web form in Chapter 32. As discussed earlier, the MobileCallStatus application also includes a frmPending form. Figure 31-3 shows the layout of the frmPending form.

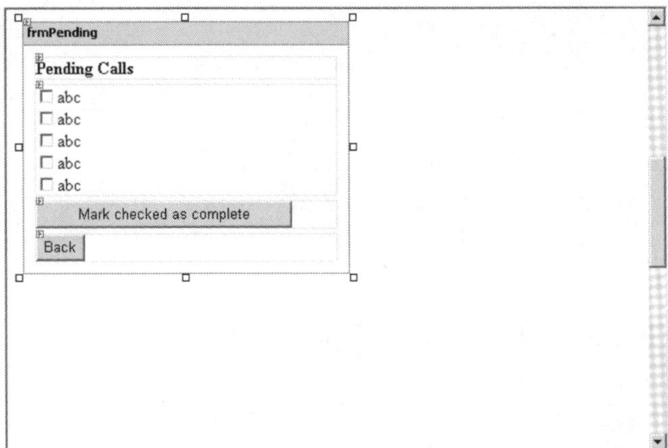


**FIGURE 31-3** *The design of the frmPending form*

The frmPending form includes a Label, a SelectionList, and two Command controls.

In addition to the previously mentioned forms, the MobileCallStatus application contains another form, frmUnattended. Figure 31-4 shows the design of the frmUnattended form.

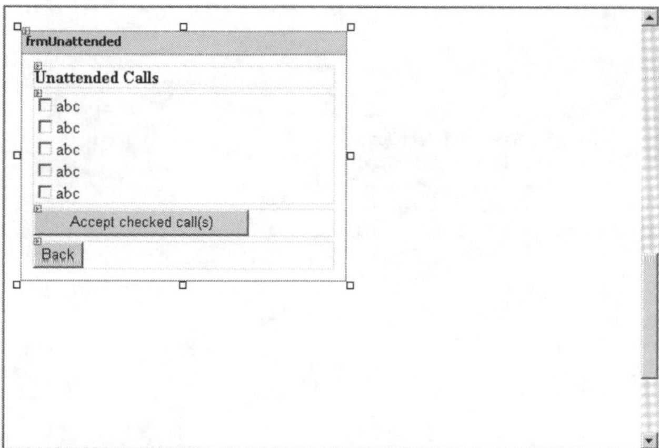


**FIGURE 31-4** *The design of the frmUnattended form*

## Low-Level Design

After creating the design of the forms in the high-level design phase, the developer needs to create a detailed design of the software modules. These software modules are then used to create the applications. In addition to creating software modules, the developer needs to decide the flow and interaction of each module. This includes creating flowcharts for each module. The flowcharts for the software modules are created in the low-level design phase of the DLC of the application. Figure 31-5 shows the flowchart for the frmLogon module.

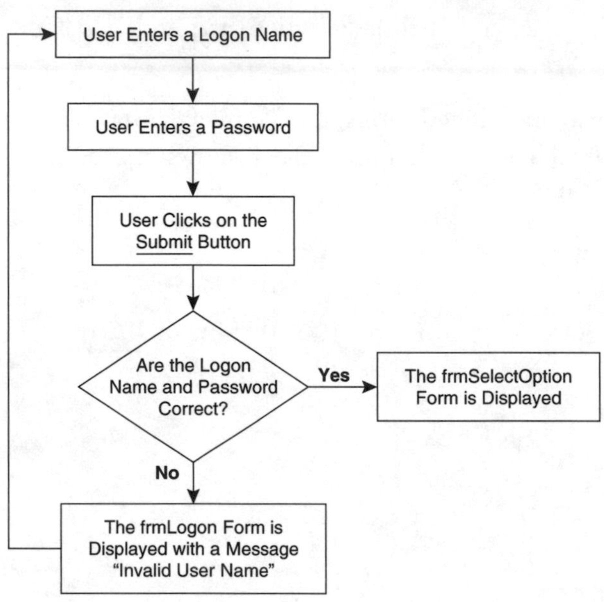


**FIGURE 31-5** *Flowchart of the frmLogon module*

Based on the design of the frmSelectOption form, the developer created the flowchart for the form, as shown in Figure 31-6.

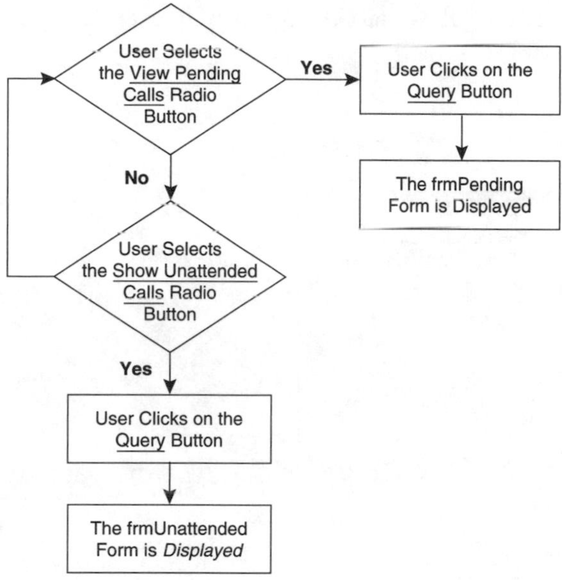


**FIGURE 31-6** *Flowchart of the frmSelectOption module*

Similarly, based on the design of the frmPending form, the developer created the flowchart for the frmPending module. Figure 31-7 shows the flowchart of the frmPending module.

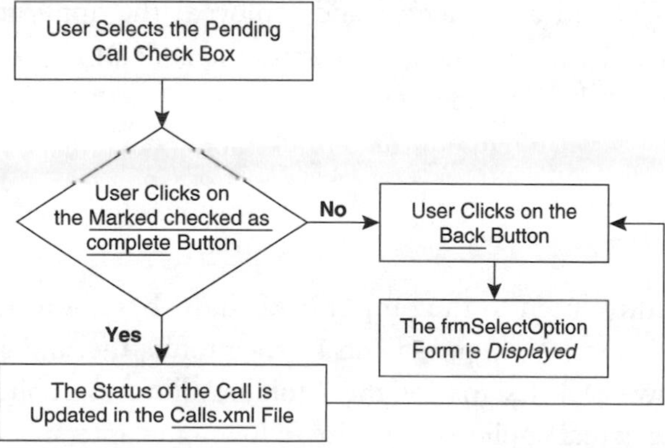


**FIGURE 31-7** *Flowchart of the frmPending module*

In addition, the developed created a flowchart for the frmUnattended module as shown in Figure 31-8.

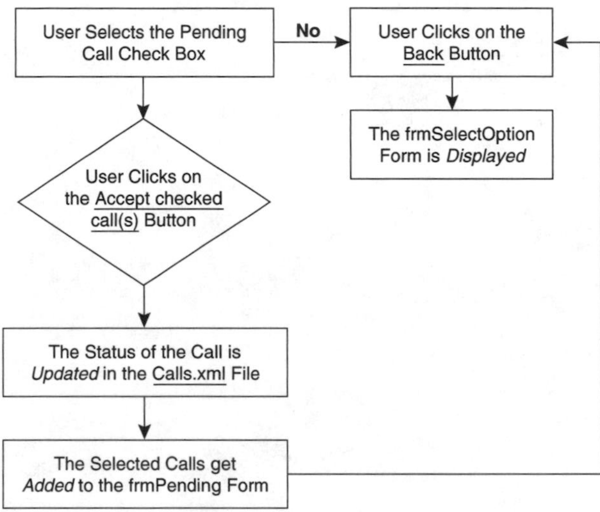


**FIGURE 31-8** *Flowchart of the frmUnattended module*

After the developer has created the interface and the software modules, the developer constructs and tests the mobile application. After the application is tested and the errors in the application are detected and removed, the application is deployed on a mobile device. I will discuss how to write the code of the MobileCallStatus application in the following chapters.

## Summary

In this chapter, you were introduced to the project case study. Based on the case study of the project, you analyzed the requirements of Electronix, Inc. and created detailed high-level and low-level designs for the MobileCallStatus application. You will learn to create the actual application in the following chapters.

# Chapter 32

## Basics of Mobile Applications

Over the years, the Internet has become more of a necessity than a luxury. In today's scenario, the Internet is not restricted only to the business world but has become an essential part of our day-to-day activities. For example, you can search for information on the Internet, shop on the Internet, pay your bills on the Internet, and so on.

Moreover, with the increasing popularity of the Internet, people worldwide want to access the Internet from anywhere and anytime. People no longer want to restrict themselves to accessing the World Wide Web from their personal computers at home or in their offices. Instead, they want to access the Internet from any mobile device, such as Pocket PC handhelds, mobile phones, and so on. To make this possible, software developers around the world are developing applications that can be accessed from mobile devices. Such applications are called *mobile applications*.

In this chapter, I will discuss the basics of mobile applications. In addition, you will learn about the Mobile Internet Toolkit and the basics of the WAP (*Wireless Application Protocol*) and WML (*Wireless Markup Language*) technologies. Finally, you will learn to create a simple mobile Web application that can be accessed from a mobile phone in Visual Studio .NET.

## Overview of Mobile Applications

Mobile applications are the applications that are accessible from various mobile devices. In addition, mobile applications allow you to access a Web site from the mobile devices. Until now, users have not been extensively using the mobile applications, because of the following limitations of the mobile applications:

- Mobile applications running on a mobile device, such as a mobile phone, require higher bandwidths. This adds to the overall cost of running a mobile application.
- Mobile devices have a limited memory and battery life. Therefore, it becomes difficult to run the application for a long time.

- It is difficult for a user to access information from the applications on the Internet, which are designed to be accessed from a personal computer, by using a mobile application. A Web page does not exactly fit the small screen of a mobile device. This makes it difficult for the user to navigate through the Web pages on a small screen.

As a solution to the previously mentioned problems, Visual Studio .NET provides you with the mobile technology that you can use to create applications that can be accessed from mobile devices. These applications contain mobile Web forms that can easily fit to the small screen of the mobile device, making navigation of Web pages possible. In addition, these mobile Web forms can adapt to the memory and bandwidth requirements of various mobile devices from which the Web form is accessed. I will discuss mobile Web forms in detail later in this chapter.

To be able to create mobile applications by using the Visual Studio .NET mobile technology, you need to use the Microsoft Mobile Internet Toolkit. The following section discusses the Mobile Internet Toolkit.

## The Microsoft Mobile Internet Toolkit

The Microsoft Mobile Internet Toolkit provides you with the essential tools for creating, testing, and deploying a mobile application. These tools include the mobile Web forms, components, and controls. These tools provide you with a user-friendly interface for creating mobile applications. Creating a mobile application by using the Mobile Internet Toolkit becomes as simple as creating an ASP.NET Web application in the .NET Framework. You have learned to create an ASP.NET Web application in the .NET Framework in Project 5, "Creating a Web Portal for a Bookstore."

The following list looks at some of the features of the Mobile Internet Toolkit that make it an easy-to-use tool for developing mobile applications.

- The Mobile Internet Toolkit is based on the .NET Framework and, therefore, provides you with all the features of the .NET Framework, such as the toolbox that contains mobile Web controls. You can drag these controls to the form to use them. In addition, the Mobile Internet Toolkit has the Mobile Internet Designer. The Mobile Internet Designer is a visual tool that works as a part of the existing Visual Studio .NET

IDE (*interactive development environment*) and provides you with a visual interface for creating the mobile Web forms. Figure 32-1 shows the Mobile Internet Designer with a blank mobile Web form created by the Mobile Internet Toolkit.

- The Mobile Internet Toolkit creates managed code that can be accessed from various mobile devices.
- The Mobile Internet Toolkit enables you to debug and deploy the mobile Web application on various devices, such as mobile phones, pagers, and PDAs (*personal digital assistants*). In addition, the Mobile Internet Toolkit extends the functionality of the .NET Framework to allow you to create applications that can be accessed from any supporting device.
- In addition to allowing you to test your mobile application on a built-in browser, the Mobile Internet Toolkit allows you to test your application on an emulator by using emulator software. However, to do this, you need to install the emulator and the emulator software. Testing the application on an emulator provides you with a fair idea of how your application will appear on the actual mobile device. An emulator simulates the mobile device environment for you so that you can test your application before deploying it on the actual mobile device.

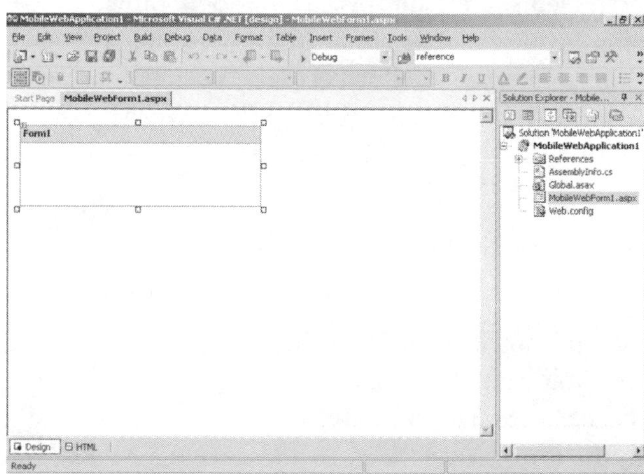


**FIGURE 32-1** *Mobile Internet Designer with a blank mobile Web form*

The Mobile Internet Toolkit is not packaged as a part of Visual Studio .NET. Therefore, to create mobile applications, you need to install the Mobile Internet Toolkit. Microsoft provides a freely downloadable version of the Mobile Internet Toolkit on its site. You can download the Mobile Internet Toolkit from the following link: **http://msdn.microsoft.com/subscriptions/resources/subdwnld.asp**. This link connects you to the MSDN Subscriber Downloads page on the Microsoft Web site. You can then search for the Mobile Internet Toolkit on the page.

**TIP**

You can download the Mobile Internet Toolkit on a computer running Windows NT or higher. In addition, you need to have either the .NET Framework or Visual Studio .NET on your computer before installing the Mobile Internet Toolkit.

After you have downloaded and installed the Mobile Internet Toolkit on your computer, several new project types are added to the New Project dialog box. Figure 32-2 shows the New Project dialog box with the Mobile Web Application project type selected.

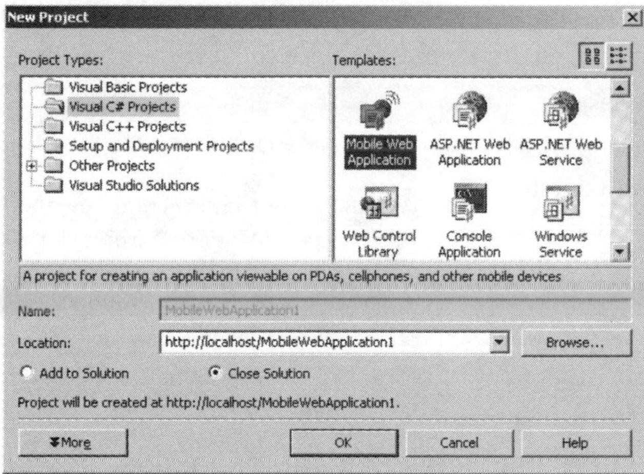


**FIGURE 32-2** *The New Project dialog box with the Mobile Web Application project type selected*

I will discuss how to create a mobile Web application by using the Mobile Web Application project type later in this chapter. I will first discuss the transfer protocol used with the mobile applications that can be accessed from a mobile phone, WAP. However, when you access the mobile application from a PDA, the transfer protocol used will be TCP/IP.

## Overview of WAP

I have already discussed the limitations of the earlier mobile Web applications, such as low memory and CPU capacity and higher bandwidth requirements. As a solution to these problems, a new protocol was developed. This protocol enables a wireless device, such as a mobile phone or a two-way pager, to access a Web site on the Internet. Therefore, this protocol was named WAP. WAP is a communication protocol, or a set of rules, that allows a wireless device to access a mobile application. To enable a user to access a mobile application, the user needs to have a WAP-enabled mobile device, such as a WAP-enabled mobile phone.

WAP is an industry standard developed by the WAP Forum that provides a set of rules for communication between the wireless devices and the world of the Internet. In addition, it provides telephony services for several wireless devices. WAP extends support to several advanced Internet technologies, such as IP (*Internet Protocol*), TCP (*Transmission Control Protocol*), and HTTP (*Hypertext Transfer Protocol*). This makes it possible for a wireless device to utilize the functionality of these Internet technologies.

In addition, the wireless devices have hardware factors suitable for accessing an Internet site from the device. These hardware factors include a small screen, limited RAM, ROM, and a battery. These devices also allow users to navigate through the site by using the one-finger navigation feature, which makes navigation fun for the users. The wireless devices are capable of using the maximum

**THE WAP FORUM**

WAP is a protocol developed by the WAP Forum. The WAP Forum works in coordination with several organizations, such as W3C (*World Wide Web Consortium*), to provide the wireless industry with a global specification for all wireless networks. In this context, the WAP Forum released its first specification, WAP 1.0, in 1998. The WAP Forum has also released its second specification, WAP 2.0. The WAP Forum includes the major wireless technology companies, such as Nokia, Ericsson, Oracle Corporation, and so on.

power of processors, which reduces the overall cost of accessing the application from a wireless device.

To access an Internet site from a mobile device, your mobile device needs to be WAP-enabled. A WAP-enabled mobile device has microbrowser software installed on it. This software is used to send and receive a user's request for accessing a Web site. For example, when a user tries to access a site from the WAP-enabled device, the microbrowser software sends a request to the server to allow the user to access the site. The following section discusses the WAP architecture in detail.

## The WAP Architecture

To understand the concept of the WAP architecture, first have a look at the Web architecture. The Web architecture refers to the architecture involved when a user tries to access a Web site from a Web browser. When a user tries to access a Web site on a Web server, a request for the site is sent from the client to the server. In this case, the client is the Web browser that sends a URL (*Uniform Resource Locator*) request to the server, which is the Web server. Then, at the server site, the request is processed in the form of CGI (*Common Gateway Interface*) scripts, and the content of the site is returned to the client as a response to the user's request. Figure 32-3 shows the Web architecture in detail.

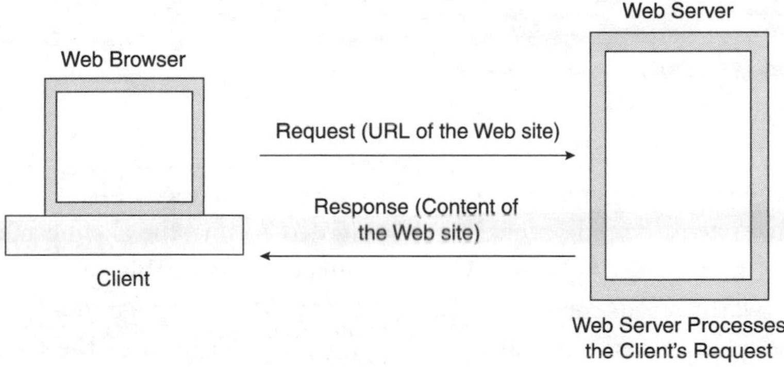


**FIGURE 32-3** *The Web architecture*

After learning about the Web architecture, you can easily understand the WAP architecture. The WAP architecture is similar to the Web architecture, except that the WAP architecture involves a WAP gateway that acts as an interface between the client and the server. A *WAP gateway* is software placed between the client and the server that supports the WAP standards and the Internet protocols, such as HTTP and IP. In addition, the WAP gateway supports XML (*Extensible Markup Language*) and WML. A WAP gateway consists of encoders, decoders, and script compilers that are used for communication between the client and the server.

In the case of a mobile device trying to access an Internet site, the mobile device becomes the client and the Web server is the server from where the site is being accessed. Figure 32-4 shows the WAP architecture in detail.

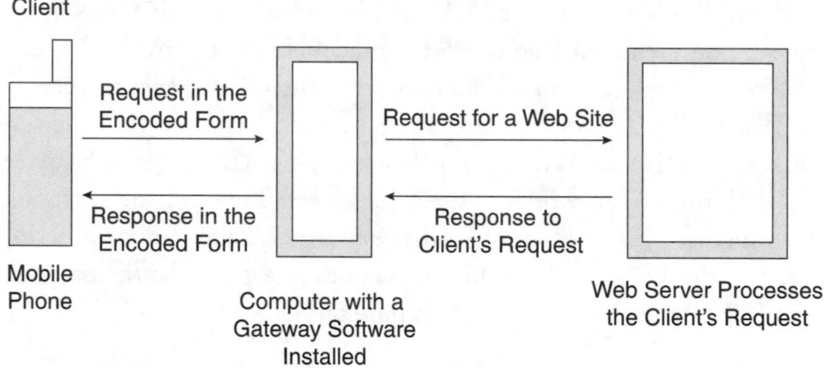


**FIGURE 32-4** *The WAP architecture*

As you can see in the figure, to access a Web site from a client (mobile device), the client first needs to send a request for the site. To do this, the client establishes a connection to the WAP gateway. Once a connection is established, the WAP gateway software uses an encoder to encode or convert the request to a form that is easily understood by the Internet server. This encoded form of the request is then forwarded to the server where the request is further processed.

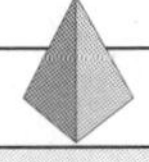

**TIP**

WAP allows users to access only WAP-enabled sites, such as **www.google.com** and **www.yahoo.com**.

Then, as a response to the user's request, the server sends the content of the site to the client. However, a user of a mobile device cannot read this content in the form returned by the server. Therefore, the WAP gateway transfers the content in the Internet language to a form supported by WAP devices, such as WML and WMLScript. WAP uses the WML and WMLScript languages to send and receive data on a wireless device. The data is then displayed to the user by using the microbrowser software on the mobile device.

## Overview of WML

WML is a language based on XML. In addition to releasing specifications on WAP, the WAP Forum releases specifications on WML. Similar to XML, WML provides a standard for describing data. The standards defined for describing data are based on the W3C standards. You have learned about XML in detail in Chapter 17, "Interacting with a Microsoft Word Document and Event Viewer," in the section "Overview of XML."

The standards defined for describing data in WML are stored as rules in a document called DTD (*Document Type Definition*). This implies that the DTD document stores the syntax for describing data in a WML document. In addition, a DTD document can include the definition of the elements to be used in the WML document. The elements in a WML document are enclosed within tags. WML allows the users to define the tags to be used in the WML documents. While describing data in a WML document, you need to associate your WML document to a DTD document.

I have already discussed the use of the microbrowser software. A microbrowser understands and fully supports the syntax of a WML document.

After discussing the technology and the transfer protocol for a mobile Web application, I will discuss a simple mobile Web application. The following section discusses the mobile Web application that includes a mobile Web form.

# Creating a Simple Mobile Web Application by Using the Mobile Internet Toolkit

As discussed earlier, when you install the Mobile Internet Toolkit on your computer, the Mobile Web Application project type is added to the New Project dialog box. You can use this project type option to create a sample mobile Web application. To access the mobile Web application project type, perform the following steps:

1. On the File menu, point to the New option.
2. In the displayed list, click on the Project option.

   The New Project dialog box is displayed.
3. In the Project Types: pane of the New Project dialog box, select the Visual C# option.
4. In the Templates: pane, select the Mobile Web Application option.
5. In the Location: text box, the localhost appears by default. Type the name of the application as `MobileTimeRetriever`.

   Figure 32-5 shows the New Project dialog box.
6. Click on the OK button.

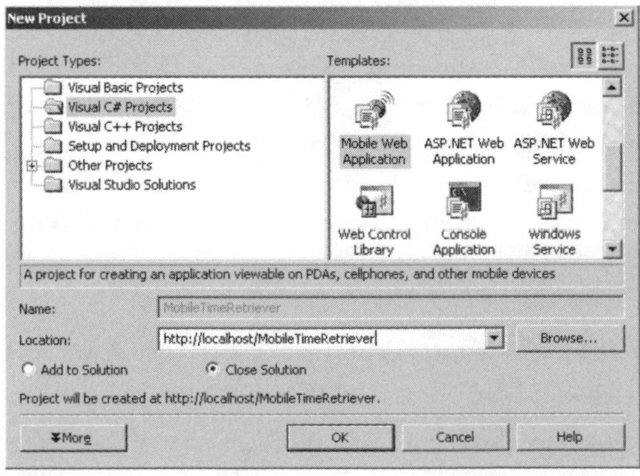


**FIGURE 32-5** *The New Project dialog box for the MobileTimeRetriever application*

The MobileTimeRetriever application opens in the design view. Visual Studio .NET creates a number of default files for the mobile Web application, as displayed in the Solution Explorer window. The MobileWebForm1.aspx file is selected by default. In addition to the default files, Visual Studio .NET creates a blank mobile Web form, Form1, in the design view. Figure 32-6 shows the default files and the mobile Web form.

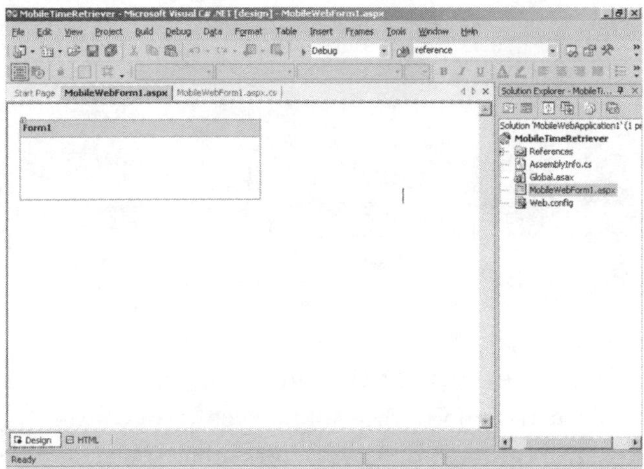


**FIGURE 32-6** *The default files and a blank mobile Web form for the MobileTimeRetriever application*

The following section discusses the mobile Web form in detail.

## The Mobile Web Form

A mobile Web application contains a mobile Web form by default. However, you can add multiple mobile Web forms to the application. All the mobile Web forms that you add to your application appear on a single mobile Web form page in the design view. However, at run time, only one mobile Web form appears to a user at a time. The mobile Web form has an extension .aspx and appears as a control in the mobile Web forms toolbox. When you install the Mobile Internet Toolkit on your computer, the mobile Web forms toolbox is added to the toolbox of Visual Studio .NET. Figure 32-7 shows the mobile Web forms toolbox.

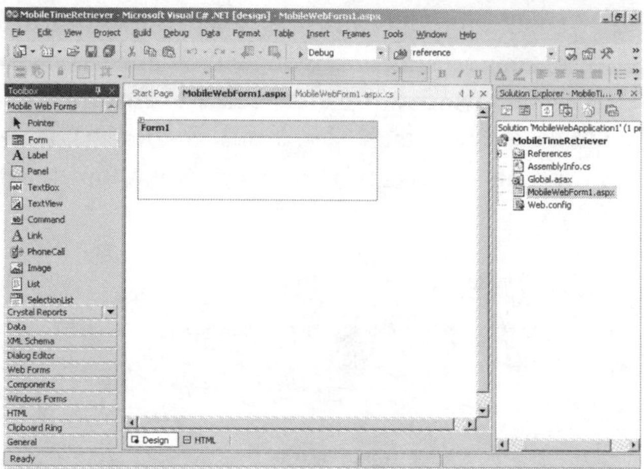


**FIGURE 32-7** *The mobile Web forms toolbox*

As you can see in Figure 32-7, the mobile Web forms toolbox contains several other mobile Web controls in addition to the mobile Web form control. You can add these mobile Web controls to the mobile Web form that you create. You can add the mobile Web controls to either a Form control or a Panel control. However, you cannot directly add the controls to the mobile Web forms page. The Form or Panel control acts as a container to store and display the mobile Web forms controls that need to be displayed in a mobile Web forms page. You will learn more about various mobile Web forms controls later in this chapter.

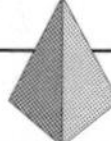

**TIP**

You can add as many mobile Web controls as you want to a Form or Panel control. However, to increase the usability of a mobile Web form, it is advisable that you add the minimum possible controls to a mobile Web form. You can add any number of mobile Web forms to a mobile Web form page.

In addition to the mobile Web forms control, a mobile Web form also contains the content from a Web site. You can display the content of the site in the controls on a mobile Web page. When a user sends a request for a Web page, the content of the Web page is displayed to the user in the format that is supported by the mobile device on a mobile Web form. While displaying data of a site on a mobile device, the mobile Web form page automatically identifies the type of the mobile device and converts the content of the site to the format that can be displayed on the device. Therefore, a mobile Web form acts as an interface that presents the content of a Web page to a user of a mobile device. In addition, a mobile Web page helps hide the code of the Web page from the user by displaying only the content of the Web page to the user.

A mobile Web form is similar to an ASP.NET Web form page. In addition, the process of creating a mobile Web form application is similar to the process of creating an ASP.NET Web form application. In this project, I will discuss how to create a mobile Web form application that can be accessed from a mobile phone.

After discussing mobile Web forms, which are the building blocks of a mobile Web application, in detail, this section will continue with creating a simple mobile Web application, MobileTimeRetriever. The MobileTimeRetriever application is a simple mobile Web application that displays the current time in the city of New York and allows the user to select a city from a list and find the current time in the selected city. The steps to create a mobile Web application are the same as the steps to create a Windows application that you did in the last two projects:

1. Create the interface for the application.
2. Write the code for the application.

However, before creating any mobile Web application, it is essential that you design the mobile Web forms in the application. The following section discusses the design of the MobileTimeRetriever application.

## The Design of the MobileTimeRetriever Application

Designing the application before its actual creation is all the more essential in the case of a mobile Web application. This is because of the smaller screen size of a mobile device. The content of a site in a mobile device is not shown as a single or multiple page Web site. Instead, the entire content of the site is displayed in the form of smaller but logical chunks of data presented in a linear manner. These chunks of data are displayed in the controls on a mobile Web form.

When the data in the controls needs to be displayed, these controls are broken down into smaller units called *screens* by the Mobile Internet Toolkit. The size of the screen is determined by the type of device on which you need to deploy the mobile application. However, while designing a mobile application, you need not worry about the different screen sizes of various mobile devices. The Mobile Internet Toolkit allows you to create applications once for various mobile devices. The code then adapts to the various form factors, such as the screen size, bandwidth, and memory of the accessing client device.

As discussed earlier, the mobile Web forms toolbox contains several tools that you can use to create a mobile application. In addition, the Mobile Internet Toolkit allows you to create custom Web forms tools for your application. In the following sections, I will discuss about the standard controls available. You can then use these standard controls to design a MobileTimeRetriever application.

## The Form Control

I have already discussed Form controls. A Form control is a container used to store and display other mobile Web forms controls. At run time, a single form is displayed at a time. However, you can access multiple forms on a mobile Web page by using the same URL address of the Web page. To add a form to your mobile Web forms page, drag the Form control from the mobile Web forms toolbox to the mobile Web forms page.

## The Panel Control

The Panel control is similar to a Form control in that it can be used to logically group related controls. However, unlike a Form control, you cannot place a Panel control directly on the Web forms page. A Panel control needs to be included in a Form control or another Panel control. Alternatively, you cannot nest a Form control within a Panel control. If you try to include a Form control within a Panel control, an error is generated, as shown in Figure 32-8.

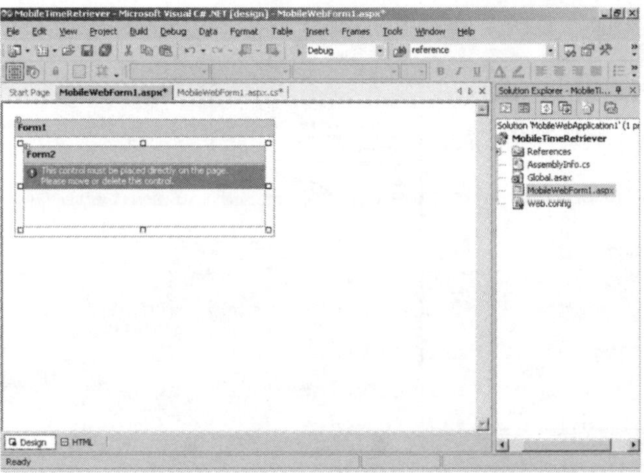


**FIGURE 32-8** *The error displayed on including a Form control within a Panel control*

In addition to organizing controls in a Panel control, you can use a Panel control to set the properties of all the controls within the same Panel control.

## The MobilePage Control

In addition to the Form and Panel controls, Visual Studio .NET provides you with another control called the MobilePage control, which groups related controls. The MobilePage control acts as a container for all other containers in a mobile Web application. This implies that the MobilePage control is the outermost container in a mobile Web application and has an associated URL address. The MobilePage control has a class associated with it called the `MobilePage` class. It is the base class for all the controls in a mobile Web application and stores the information about the style and other properties that are common to the controls in a MobilePage control. Figure 32-9 shows a MobilePage control.

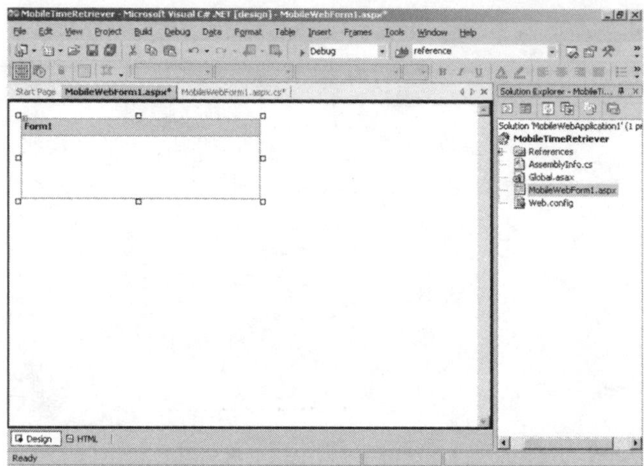

**FIGURE 32-9** *The MobilePage control*

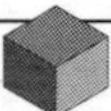

**NOTE**

The MobilePage control is not packaged as a control in the mobile Web forms controls toolbox. Visual Studio .NET automatically creates a MobilePage control for your application. You can add one or more Form controls to the MobilePage control. In addition, the MobilePage control may contain a StyleSheet control.

## The Label Control

A mobile Web form Label control is similar to a Windows forms Label control. A Label control is used to display any text in mobile application. You can add text to a Label control either by setting the `Text` property of the Label control or by programmatically changing the text of the Label control. To add a Label control to your form, drag the Label control from the mobile Web forms toolbox to the Form or Panel control.

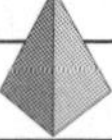

**TIP**

You can have multiple controls in different mobile Web forms. However, you should not give the same name to the controls in different Web forms for the same mobile Web application. You can specify a name for a control by using the `ID` property of the control.

## The TextBox Control

A TextBox control is another control that allows you to display text. You can use a TextBox control to allow users to input text, which is then stored in the `Text` property of the control. Unlike the TextBox control in a Windows application, the TextBox control in a mobile application is used to display single-line text. To display text in multiple lines, you use a TextView control.

## The TextView Control

A TextView control is used to display text in a mobile application, similar to a TextBox control. However, a TextView control is used to display multiple lines of text. You can use the `Text` property of the TextView control to specify the text to be displayed in a TextView control. The `Text` property of the TextView control accepts HTML tags to specify the formatting of the text in the TextView control. Figure 32-10 shows a TextView control in a mobile Web form.

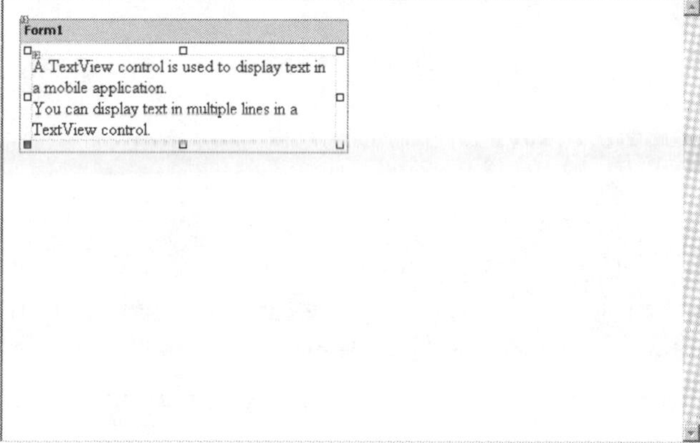


**FIGURE 32-10** *The TextView control in a mobile Web form*

To display the text as it appears in Figure 32-10, add the following text to the Text property of the control.

```
A TextView control is used to display text in a mobile application. <br>
You can display text in multiple lines in a TextView control.
```

### The Link Control

A Link control is a text-based control that creates a text hyperlink. You can use this hyperlink to connect to another form or another mobile Web page. You can specify the name of the form or the URL of the page in the `NavigateURL` property of the control.

### The PhoneCall Control

A PhoneCall control is another text-based control that is used to store a phone number to be called. When a PhoneCall control is accessed from a mobile device, such as a cellular phone, the PhoneCall control dials the number specified in the control.

### The List Control

A List control is used to display a list of items in a mobile device. A user can select any item from the List control. To add items to a List control, use the `Items` property of the control. You can also associate the List control to a data source to display a list of items from a data source. Perform the following steps to display a list of items in a List control.

1. Drag a List control from the mobile Web forms toolbox to a mobile Web form.
2. Select the List control to make it active.
3. In the Properties window of the list control, change the `ID` property of the control to `lstCountry`.

   If the Properties window is not visible, press the F4 key or select the Properties Window option on the View menu.
4. Click on the ellipsis button of the `Items` property to add items to the List control.

The `lstCountry` Properties dialog box is displayed. To associate the List control to a data source, select the General tab. However, you can add items to the List control in the Items tab of the lstCountry Properties dialog box. The Items tab is displayed by default.

5. Click on the Create New Item button to add a new item.

   A new item is added to the list. To change the text of the new item that is added, you can specify the text in the area that shows `Text`.

6. Type the name of the first item as `Australia`.

7. Repeat Steps 5 and 6 to add more items to the List control.

   You can add `Belgium`, `China`, `Germany`, `India`, `Japan`, `France`, `United Kingdom`, and `United States`. You can move an item in the list by using the Up or Down Arrow keys in the lstCountry Properties dialog box. Figure 32-11 shows the lstCountry Properties dialog box.

   Visual Studio .NET allows you to create list items as hyperlinks. To do so, check the Render list items as hyperlinks check box.

8. Click on the OK button to close the lstCountry Properties dialog box.

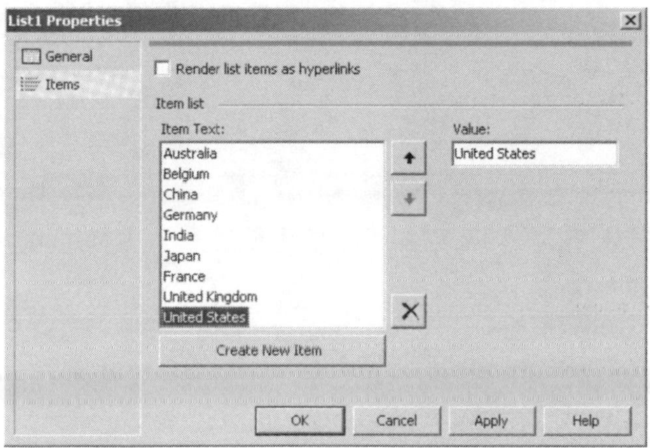


**FIGURE 32-11** *The lstCountry Properties dialog box*

The items are added to the `lstCountry` list control.

## The SelectionList Control

A SelectionList control is similar to a List control because it can be used to display a list of items. However, you can use a SelectionList control to provide users with a choice of options in the form of a drop-down list, radio buttons, check boxes, and combo boxes. A user can select one or more options from a SelectionList control. When a user selects an item from the list, the selected item is not automatically posted to the server. To do this, the user needs to explicitly click on the Command control. You will learn about the Command control later in this chapter.

To display the list of countries as you did in the previous section, you can also use a SelectionList control instead of a List control. To add items to the SelectionList control, use the `Items` property of the control. The procedure for adding items to a SelectionList control is the same as that of adding items to a List control. Figure 32-12 shows the items added to a SelectionList control and a List control.

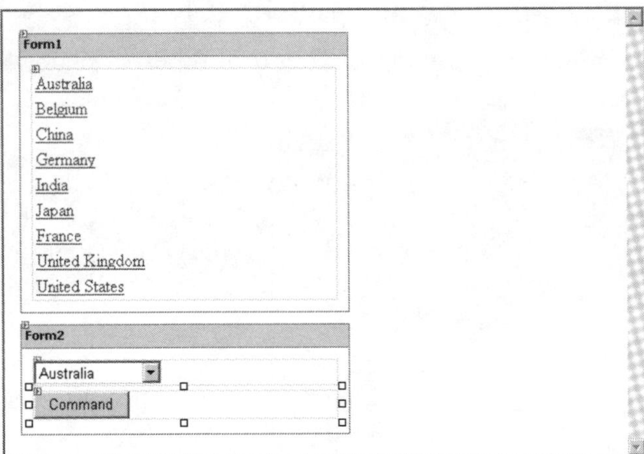


**FIGURE 32-12** *The items added to a SelectionList control and a List control*

## The ObjectList Control

An ObjectList control is also used to display a list of items in a mobile application. However, the list of items in an ObjectList control includes the list of data objects. To display a list of data objects in an ObjectList control, you need to bind the ObjectList control to a data source. You can do this by using the `DataSource` property of the control.

## The Command Control

A Command control is similar to a Button control that is used to post user input to a server. For example, when a user types data in a text box and selects an option from the SelectionList control, the user needs to click the Command button to post this data on the server.

## The Image Control

An Image control is used to display an image in a mobile application. An image control allows you to specify an image in multiple formats, depending on the type of device on which the image needs to be displayed. A file format defined for a type of a device may not be displayed on another type of device.

## The Calendar Control

A Calendar control is used to add a calendar to the mobile Web form page. A user can select a date, month, and year in the Calendar control. You can change the properties of a Calendar control to change the look of the control. Figure 32-13 shows a Calendar control with a date selected.

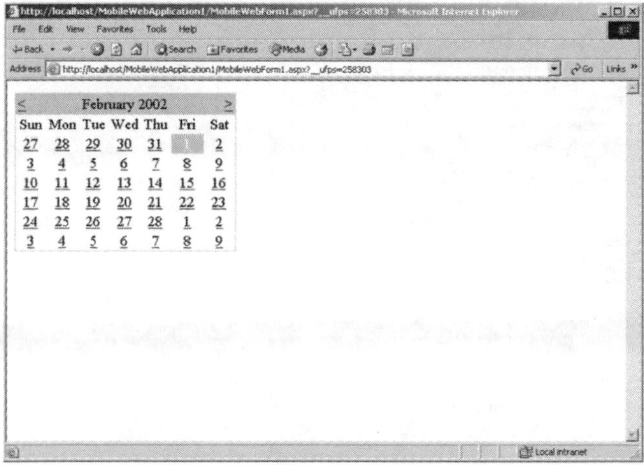


**FIGURE 32-13** *The Calendar control with a date selected*

## The StyleSheet Control

A StyleSheet control is used to store the styles applied to the controls in a mobile Web form page. The StyleSheet control consists of a number of style elements that can be accessed by the name of the element specified in the `Name` property of the style element. A StyleSheet is associated with a mobile Web form page and, therefore, needs to be placed directly on the mobile Web form page. To specify the style elements in a StyleSheet control, perform the following steps:

1. Drag the StyleSheet control to the mobile Web form page.
2. Right-click on the control to add the style elements.

   The StyleSheet1 Styles Editor dialog box is displayed.
3. To add a style to the StyleSheet control, select the style from the Style Types: list box and click on the > button.

The style element is added to the StyleSheet control. Figure 32-14 shows the StyleSheet1 Styles Editor dialog box with the PagerStyle1 style element added to it.

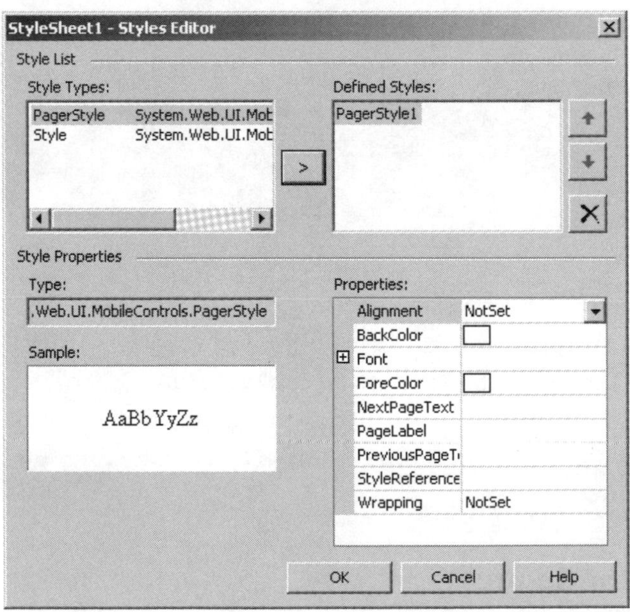


**FIGURE 32-14** *The StyleSheet1 Styles Editor dialog box*

## The Validation Controls

In addition to the previously discussed controls, the mobile Web forms controls also include some validation controls, such as RequiredFieldValidator, RegularExpressionValidator, CompareValidator, RangeValidator, and CustomValidator. The following sections discuss the validation controls in a mobile Web page.

### The RequiredFieldValidator Control

A RequiredFieldValidator control is used to ensure that a user enters a value in the associated control. If the control has a default value, the RequiredFieldValidator control checks whether the value entered by the user is different from its initial value. You can associate a control to the RequiredFieldValidator control by using the `ControlToValidate` property of the RequiredFieldValidator control.

### The RegularExpressionValidator Control

If you need to validate the value of a control entered by a user against an expression, you can associate the control to the RegularExpressionValidator control. To do this, you specify the name of the control in the `ControlToValidate` property of the RegularExpressionValidator control. You can specify the expression to which the value is matched by selecting an expression from the Regular Expression Editor dialog box. You can also create a custom expression in the Regular Expression Editor dialog box. To access the Regular Expression Editor dialog box, click on the ellipsis button of the `ValidationExpression` property.

### The CompareValidator Control

A CompareValidator control is used to compare the values in two controls. You can specify criteria for the values that need to be compared. In addition, you need to specify the control in order to associate it with the CompareValidator control. You can do this by specifying a control in the ControlToCompare property of the CompareValidator control.

### The RangeValidator Control

A RangeValidator control is used to validate that the value of an associated control lies within the range that you specify. You can specify the range by setting the value of the `MaximumValue` and `MinimumValue` properties of the RangeValidator control.

### The CustomValidator Control

A CustomValidator control allows you to write custom code to validate the value specified in a control. You can specify an error message to be displayed when the value entered in the control is incorrect. To display an error message, change the `ErrorMessage` property of the control.

You have seen the validation controls that you can use in a mobile Web application. However, to display the error message when an error occurs, you need to include a ValidationSummary control.

### *The ValidationSummary Control*

A ValidationSummary control is used to display the summary of the errors that occurred when the values entered in the controls are validated by the validation controls. The ValidationSummary control displays the list of error messages as you specify in the `ErrorMessage` property of the validation controls. To display the errors that occur while validating a form, you need to associate the Validation-Summary control with a form. To do this, you specify the name of the form in the `FormToValidate` property of the control. In addition, you can change the font of the error message that is displayed in the ValidationSummary control by changing the `Font` property of the control. Figure 32-15 shows a ValidationSummary control with an error message displayed.

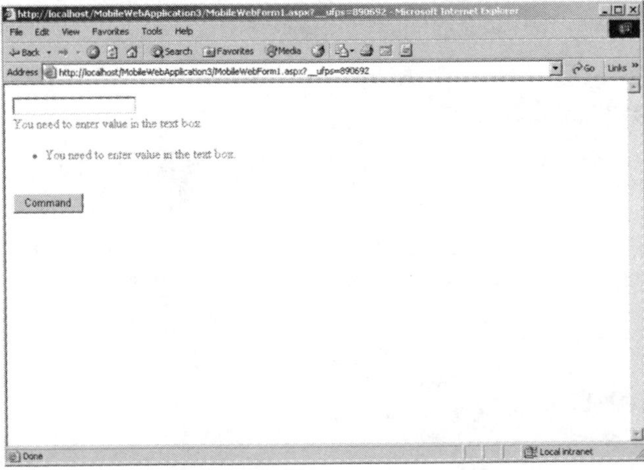


**FIGURE 32-15** *The ValidationSummary control with an error message displayed*

You have learned about various controls that can be used in a mobile Web application. You can now use this knowledge to create the mobile Web forms required for a MobileTimeRetriever application.

## Creating the Interface for the Mobile Web Forms

The MobileTimeRetriever application contains two forms, frmOptions and frmResult. Figure 32-16 shows the interface of the frmOptions form.

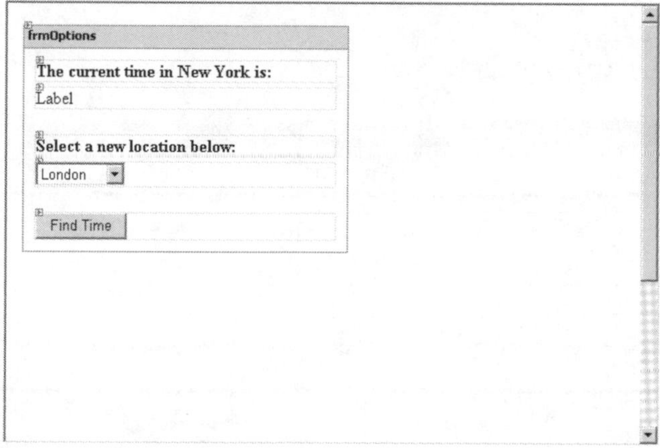


**FIGURE 32-16** *The interface of the frmOptions form*

As you can see, the frmOptions form contains three Label controls, one Command control, and one SelectionList control. To add these controls to the form, drag the controls from the mobile Web forms control toolbox to the form and change the following properties of the controls.

**Label1**

- `ID: lblCurrentTime`
- `Text: The current time in New York is:`
- `Font:`

  `Bold: True`

### Label2

- `ID:` `lblCurTime`
- `Text:` `Label`

### Label3

- `ID:` `lblRegion`
- `Text:` `Select a new location below:`
- `Font:`

  `Bold:` `True`

### Command1

- `ID:` `cmdFindTime`
- `Text:` `Find Time`

### SelectionList

- `ID:` `lstLocations`
- `Items:` The items to be added in the SelectionList control are displayed in Table 32-1.

**Table 32-1 Items to Be Added to the SelectionList Control**

| ItemText | Value | Selected |
| --- | --- | --- |
| London | 1 | Checked |
| Moscow | 2 | Unchecked |
| Bangkok | 3 | Unchecked |
| Singapore | 4 | Unchecked |
| Sydney | 5 | Unchecked |

In the General tab of the lstLocations Properties dialog box, change the following properties:

- **Select Type**: DropDown
- **Rows**: 4

After creating the interface for the frmOptions form, create the interface for the frmResult form. Figure 32-17 shows the interface for the frmResult form.

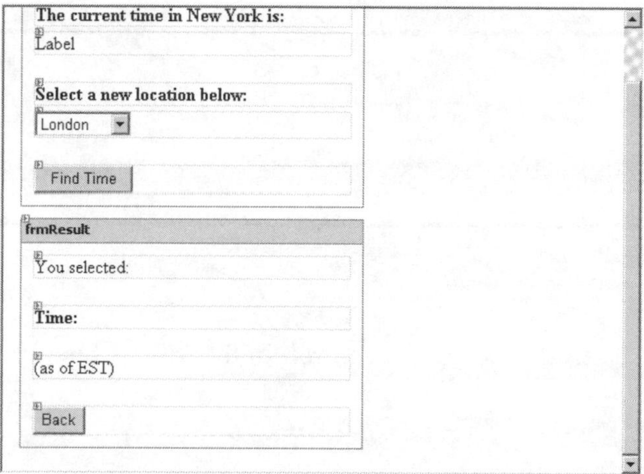


**FIGURE 32-17** *The frmResult form*

The frmResult form contains three Label controls and one Command control. Change the following properties of the controls:

## Label1

- `ID: lblSelLoc`
- `Text: You selected:`

**Label2**

- ID: lblTime
- Text: Time:
- Font:

  Bold: True

**Label3**

- ID: lblOrgLoc
- Text: (as of EST)

**Command1**

- ID: cmdBack
- Text: Back

After creating the interface, add code to the controls in the MobileTimeRetriever application.

## Adding Code to the MobileTimeRetriever Application

Once you have added the controls to the form, Visual Studio .NET automatically creates the declaration statements for the controls. However, to make the controls functional, you need to add code to the `Click` events of the Command controls.

### *Adding Code to the `cmdFindTime` Command Control*

When a user selects the location from a `lstLocations` SelectionList control and clicks on the `cmdFindTime` Command control, the application displays the current time in the selected location. To do this, add the following code to the `Click` event of the `cmdFindTime` Command control.

```
private void cmdFindTime_Click(object sender, System.EventArgs e)
{
   DateTime currentTime= DateTime.Now;
   TimeSpan timeDiff=new TimeSpan(0,0,0);
   switch (lstLocations.Selection.Value)
```

```
        {
            case "1":
                timeDiff=new TimeSpan(5,0,0);
                break;
            case "2":
                timeDiff=new TimeSpan(8,0,0);
                break;
            case "3":
                timeDiff=new TimeSpan(12,0,0);
                break;
            case "4":
                timeDiff=new TimeSpan(13,0,0);
                break;
            case "5":
                timeDiff=new TimeSpan(15,0,0);
                break;
        }
        DateTime newTime=currentTime.Add(timeDiff);
        lblSelLoc.Text="You selected: " + lstLocations.Selection.Text;
        lblTime.Text="Time at the selected location:" + Convert.ToString(newTime);
        lblOrgLoc.Text="(as of " + DateTime.Now + " EST)";
        ActiveForm=frmResult;
    }
```

The previous code creates a variable, `currentTime`, of the struct `DateTime` in the `System` namespace. It then uses the `Now` property of the struct `DateTime` to retrieve the current date and time on the computer. The value returned by the `Now` property is stored in the `currentTime` variable. The code then creates an instance, `timeDiff`, of the `TimeSpan` struct in the `System` namespace. The `TimeSpan` struct is used to represent a time interval. Next, a `switch` case is used to trap the value selected by the user in the SelectionList control. To do this, the `Value` property of the `MobileListItem` class is used.

Then, the instance of the `TimeSpan` struct is used to find the time for different locations. The difference between the time in New York and the selected city is passed as a parameter to `timeDiff`. For example, the difference between the time in New York and London is five hours. Therefore, this time difference in hours is passed as a parameter to the default constructor of `timeDiff`. Similarly, the time difference between other cities is passed to `timeDiff` for different cases of the `switch` statement.

The code then creates another variable of the `DateTime` struct, `newTime`. Then, the `Add()` method of the `DateTime` class is used to add the value stored in `timeDiff` to the value stored in the `currentTime` variable. The result is then stored in the `newTime` variable, which is then converted to a string and displayed in the `lblTime` Label control. The location selected by the user is displayed in the `lblSelLoc` Label control. The time at the original location, New York, is displayed in the `lblOrgLoc` Label control. Finally, the code makes the frmResult form active. Figure 32-18 shows the frmOptions form at run time.

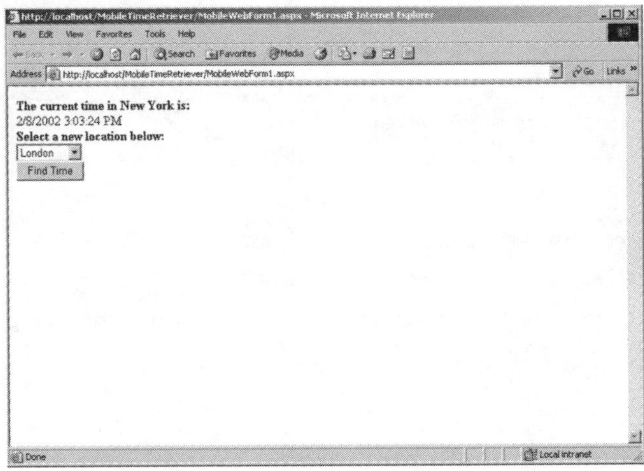


**FIGURE 32-18** *The frmOptions form at run time*

When the user clicks on the Find Time button, the frmResult form becomes active. Figure 32-19 shows the frmResult form at run time.

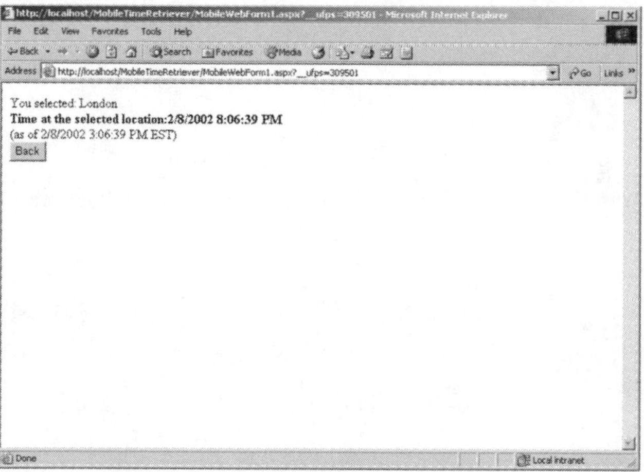


**FIGURE 32-19** *The frmResult form at run time*

To return to the frmOptions form from the frmResult form, the user needs to click on the Back button. The following section discusses how to add code to the Back button.

## Adding Code to the `cmdBack` Command Control

When a user clicks on the Back button, the frmOptions form becomes active. To do this, add the following code to the `Click` event of the `cmdBack` Command control.

```
private void cmdBack_Click(object sender, System.EventArgs e)
{
   ActiveForm=frmOptions;
}
```

The preceding code uses the `ActiveForm` property to set the frmOptions form as active. The entire code of the application is as shown below.

```
using System;
using System.Collections;
using System.ComponentModel;
```

```
using System.Data;
using System.Drawing;
using System.Web;
using System.Web.Mobile;
using System.Web.SessionState;
using System.Web.UI;
using System.Web.UI.MobileControls;
using System.Web.UI.WebControls;
using System.Web.UI.HtmlControls;
using System.Xml;

namespace MobileTimeRetriever
{
   public class MobileWebForm1 : System.Web.UI.MobileControls.MobilePage
   {
      protected System.Web.UI.MobileControls.Label lblCurrentTime;
      protected System.Web.UI.MobileControls.Label lblRegion;
      protected System.Web.UI.MobileControls.SelectionList lstLocations;
      protected System.Web.UI.MobileControls.Command cmdFindTime;
      protected System.Web.UI.MobileControls.Label lblSelLoc;
      protected System.Web.UI.MobileControls.Label lblTime;
      protected System.Web.UI.MobileControls.Command cmdBack;
      protected System.Web.UI.MobileControls.Label lblCurTime;
      protected System.Web.UI.MobileControls.Form frmOptions;
      protected System.Web.UI.MobileControls.Form frmResult;
      protected System.Web.UI.MobileControls.Label lblOrgLoc;

      private void Page_Load(object sender, System.EventArgs e)
      {
         ActiveForm=frmOptions;
         lblCurTime.Text=Convert.ToString(DateTime.Now);
      }

      private void cmdFindTime_Click(object sender, System.EventArgs e)
      {
         DateTime currentTime= DateTime.Now;
         TimeSpan timeDiff=new TimeSpan(0,0,0);
         switch (lstLocations.Selection.Value)
```

```
            {
                case "1":
                    timeDiff=new TimeSpan(5,0,0);
                    break;
                case "2":
                    timeDiff=new TimeSpan(8,0,0);
                    break;
                case "3":
                    timeDiff=new TimeSpan(12,0,0);
                    break;
                case "4":
                    timeDiff=new TimeSpan(13,0,0);
                    break;
                case "5":
                    timeDiff=new TimeSpan(15,0,0);
                    break;
            }
            DateTime newTime=currentTime.Add(timeDiff);
            lblSelLoc.Text="You selected: " + lstLocations.Selection.Text;
            lblTime.Text="Time at the selected location:" + Convert.ToString(newTime);
            lblOrgLoc.Text="(as of " + DateTime.Now + " EST)";
            ActiveForm=frmResult;
        }

        private void cmdBack_Click(object sender, System.EventArgs e)
        {
            ActiveForm=frmOptions;
        }
    }
}
```

In Figures 32-18 and 32-19, you saw the forms in Internet Explorer. To have an idea of the look of the forms in a mobile device, you can view the output of the application in a WAP device emulator. To view the output of the application in an emulator, you need to install the emulator and the WAP gateway. After installing the emulator and the gateway, you need to perform the following steps to view the output in the emulator:

1. On the View menu, point to the Mobile Explorer Browser option.

2. In the displayed list, select the Show Browser option.
3. Type the URL address of the mobile Web page in the Address box of the emulator and then press the Enter key.

The output is shown in the emulator. Figure 32-20 shows the frmOptions form in an emulator.

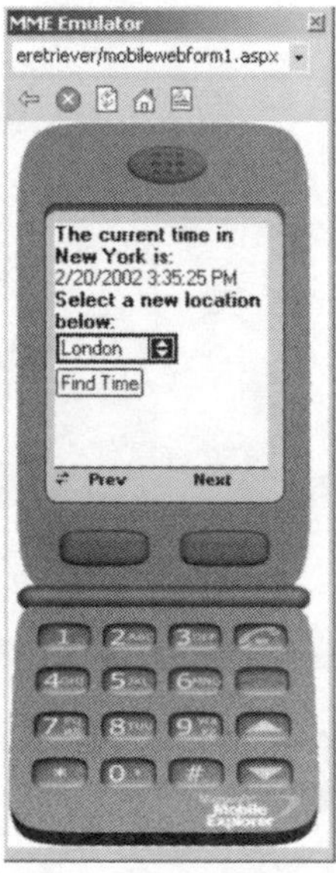


**FIGURE 32-20** *The frmOptions form in an emulator*

Figure 32-21 shows the frmResult form in the emulator.

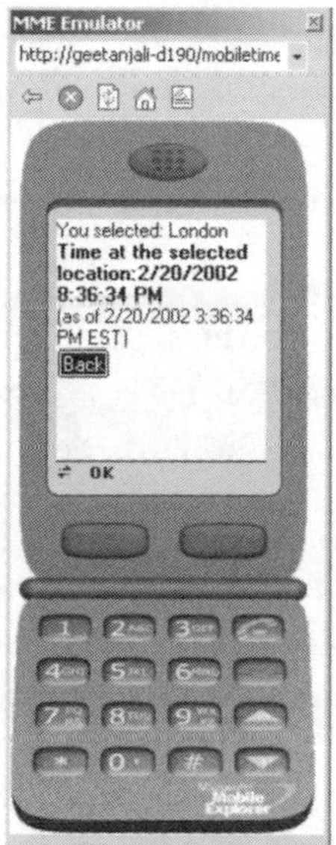


**FIGURE 32-21** *The frmOptions form in an emulator*

**NOTE**

I have used the Microsoft Mobile Explorer 3.0 Emulator and the Ericsson Gateway/Proxy Demo 1.0 gateway to capture the preceding figures.

# Summary

In this chapter, you learned about the basics of a mobile application. Mobile applications are applications that are accessible from various mobile devices. In addition, mobile applications allow you to access a Web site from mobile devices. To create a mobile application, you first need to install the Microsoft Mobile Internet Toolkit. The Mobile Internet Toolkit provides you with the essential tools for creating, testing, and deploying a mobile application. These tools include mobile Web forms, components, and controls.

Next, you learned about the transfer protocol for mobile applications, WAP. WAP is a communication protocol, or a set of rules, that allows a wireless device to access a mobile application. Therefore, to enable a user to access a mobile application, the user needs to have a WAP-enabled mobile device, such as a WAP-enabled mobile phone.

Then you learned about the technology used for rendering the mobile applications on a mobile phone, WML. WML is a language based on XML. Similar to XML, WML provides a standard for describing data. The standards defined for describing data are based on the W3C standards.

Finally, you learned to create a simple mobile Web application, MobileTime-Retriever, that can be accessed from a mobile phone. You can use the same code to create a mobile application that can be accessed from a PDA. However, in that case, the transfer protocol used is TCP/IP.

# Chapter 33

## Implementing the Business Logic

In the preceding chapters, you looked at the case study and design of the MobileCallStatus application. In addition, you were introduced to the basics of a mobile Web application. Based on this learning, you created a simple mobile Web application in the .NET Framework. In this chapter, you will create the forms required for the MobileCallStatus application. You will also add the business logic to the MobileCallStatus application.

## Creating the Forms Required for the MobileCallStatus Application

You have already seen the design of the forms required for the MobileCallStatus application. In this chapter, I will discuss how to create the mobile Web forms for the MobileCallStatus application.

Before creating the mobile Web forms, you need to create a mobile application with the name MobileCallStatus. To create a mobile application with the name MobileCallStatus, perform the following steps:

1. On the File menu, point to the New option.
2. In the displayed list, click on the Project option.

   The New Project dialog box is displayed.
3. In the Project Types: pane of the New Project dialog box, select the Visual C# option.
4. In the Templates: pane, select the Mobile Web Application option.
5. In the Location: text box, the local host appears by default. Type the name of the application as `MobileCallStatus`.
6. Click on the OK button.

Figure 33-1 shows the IDE (*Interactive Development Environment*) for the MobileCallStatus application.

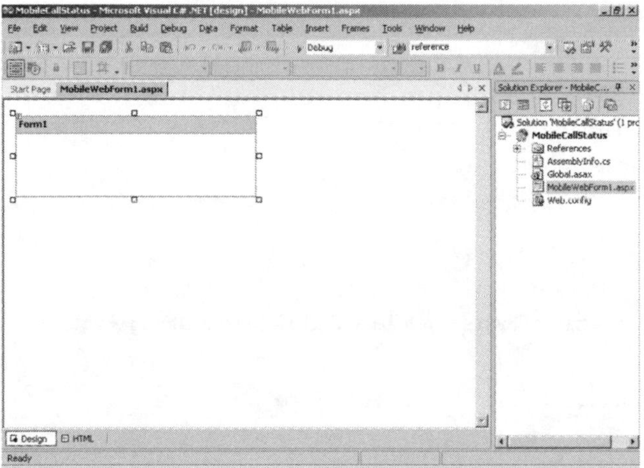

**FIGURE 33-1** *The IDE for the MobileCallStatus application*

As you can see in Figure 33-1, Visual Studio .NET automatically creates the default files. In addition, Visual Studio .NET generates default code. The following section discusses the default code generated by Visual Studio .NET for a mobile application.

## The Default Code Generated by Visual Studio .NET for a Mobile Application

The default code generated by Visual Studio .NET is as follows:

```
using System;
using System.Collections;
using System.ComponentModel;
using System.Data;
using System.Drawing;
using System.Web;
using System.Web.Mobile;
```

```
using System.Web.SessionState;
using System.Web.UI;
using System.Web.UI.MobileControls;
using System.Web.UI.WebControls;
using System.Web.UI.HtmlControls;

namespace MobileCallStatus
{
   public class MobileWebForm1 : System.Web.UI.MobileControls.MobilePage
   {
      protected System.Web.UI.MobileControls.Form Form1;
      private void Page_Load(object sender, System.EventArgs e)
      {

      }
   }
}
```

The preceding code contains the `using` directive statements that allow you to use the namespace and the classes defined in the namespace within the code for your application. In addition, the Visual Studio .NET creates a namespace with the same name as that of the application, `MobileCallStatus`.

Inside the `MobileCallStatus` namespace, a public class with the name `MobileWeb-Form1` is created. The `MobileWebForm1` class is derived from the `MobilePage` class that lies in the `System` namespace. The `MobileWebForm1` class contains the declaration of the instance of the `Form` class, `Form1`. In addition, the `MobileWebForm1` class contains the `Page_Load()` method. You can include the statements required for initializing the mobile page in the `Page_Load()` method.

In addition to the preceding code, Visual Studio .NET creates HTML code for the mobile application. To view the HTML code, switch to the HTML page in the IDE. To do this, select the HTML Source option on the View menu. Figure 33-2 shows the HTML code for the MobileCallStatus application.

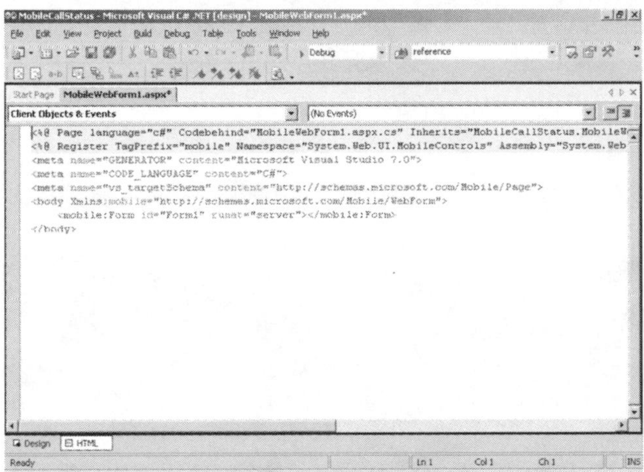

**FIGURE 33-2** *The HTML code for the MobileCallStatus application*

As you can see in Figure 33-2, the first two lines of the HTML code are highlighted. These two lines are called the *prolog* for the MobileCallStatus application. The `@ Page` directive includes the information about the mobile page. This information includes the language used for developing the mobile application, the mobile Web form included in the mobile page, and the base class of the mobile Web page. The `@ Register` directive includes the information about the namespace and the assembly for the mobile Web page.

Next, the HTML code includes the meta information for the HTML code, such as the software and the language used to create the mobile application. In addition, the meta statements include the information about the schema used for creating the mobile Web page. Next, the HTML code contains the `body` tags. Inside the `body` tags, the information about the mobile Web form is included.

After discussing the code generated by Visual Studio .NET, I will continue discussing how to create forms for the MobileCallStatus application.

## Creating the frmLogon Form

You have seen the design of the frmLogon form. You can now create the frmLogon form. To create the frmLogon form, drag two Label controls, two TextBox controls, two RequiredFieldValidator controls, and one Command control to the form. Next, change the following properties of the controls:

### Label1

- ID: `Label1`
- Text: `Please Log On`
- Font:

  Bold: `True`

### Label2

- ID: `lblMessage`
- Visible: `False`
- Font:

  Bold: `True`

### TextBox1

- ID: `TextBox1`

### TextBox2

- ID: `TextBox2`
- Password: `True`

### RequiredFieldValidator1

- ID: `RequiredFieldValidator1`
- ControlToValidate: `TextBox1`
- ErrorMessage: `Please provide a valid logon name`

**RequiredFieldValidator2**

- `ID: RequiredFieldValidator2`
- `ControlToValidate: TextBox2`
- `ErrorMessage: Please provide a valid password`

**Command1**

- `ID: cmdSubmit`
- `Text: Submit`

After you have added the controls and changed the previously mentioned properties, the form appears as shown in Figure 33-3.

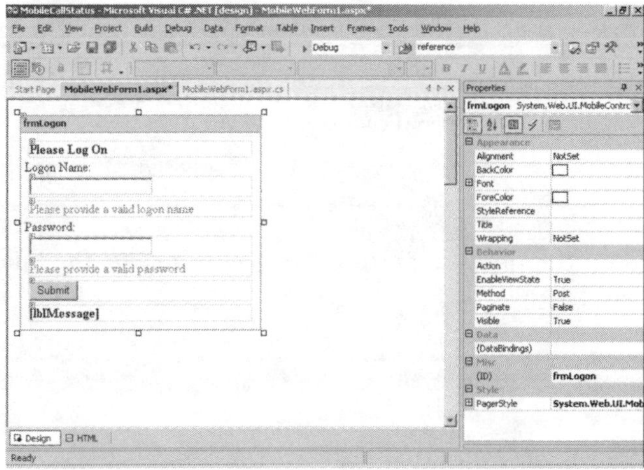

**FIGURE 33-3** *The frmLogon form with the controls added*

## Creating the frmSelectOption Form

The second form required for the MobileCallStatus application is the frmSelectOption form. To create the frmSelectOption form, add a Label, a SelectionList, and a Command control to the form. After adding these controls, change the following properties of the control.

### Label1

- ID: Label2
- Text: Please select an option:
- Font:

  Bold: True

### SelectionList1

- ID: lstOptions
- Items: The items to be added in the SelectionList1 control are displayed in Table 33-1.

**Table 33-1 Items to be Added to the SelectionList Control**

| ItemText | Value | Selected |
|---|---|---|
| View Pending Calls | viewPending | Checked |
| Show Unattended Calls | showUnattended | Unchecked |

In the General tab of the lstOptions Properties dialog box, change the following properties:

- **Select Type:** Radio
- **Rows:** 2

### Command1

- **ID:** cmdLoad
- **Text:** Query

Figure 33-4 shows the frmSelectOption form with the controls added.

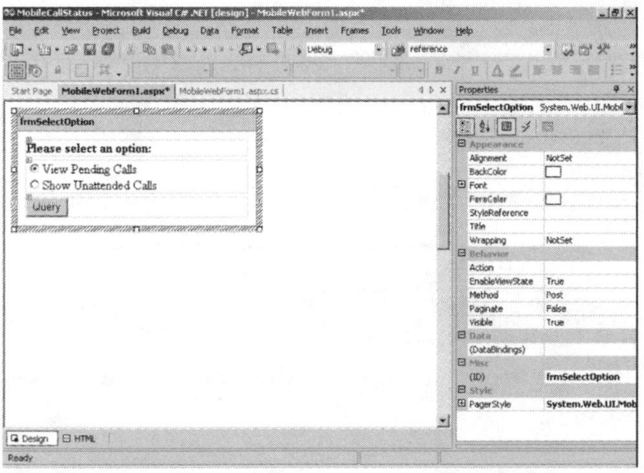

**FIGURE 33-4** *The frmSelectOption form with the controls added*

## Creating the frmPending Form

The frmPending form contains a Label, a SelectionList, and two Command controls. Drag these controls to the form and change the following properties of the controls:

### Label1

- `ID: Label3`
- `Text: Pending Calls`
- `Font:`

  `Bold: True`

### SelectionList1

- `ID: lstPending`
- `Select Type: CheckBox`
- `Rows: 4`

**Command1**

- ID: `cmdUpdate`
- Text: `Mark checked as complete`

**Command2**

- ID: `cmdBack1`
- **Text:** `Back`

When you add controls to the frmPending form, the form appears as shown in Figure 33-5.

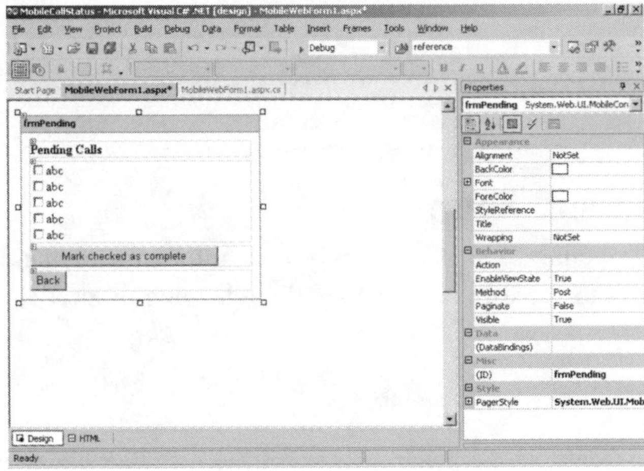

**FIGURE 33-5** *The frmPending form with the controls added*

## Creating the frmUnattended Form

To create the frmUnattended form, drag a Label, a SelectionList, and two Command controls to the form. Then, change the following properties of the controls:

**Label1**

- ID: `Label4`
- Text: `Unattended Calls`

- `Font:`

  `Bold: True`

### SelectionList1

- `ID: lstUnattended`
- `Select Type: CheckBox`
- `Rows: 4`

### Command1

- `ID: cmdAcceptCall`
- `Text: Accept checked call(s)`

### Command2

- `ID: cmdBack2`
- `Text: Back`

Figure 33-6 shows the frmUnattended form with the previously mentioned controls added to the form.

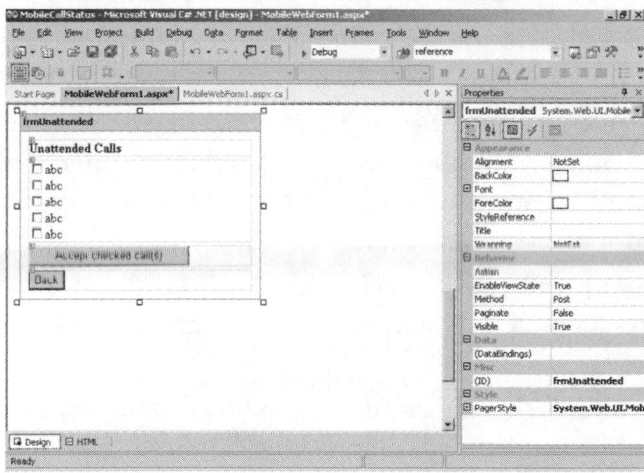


**FIGURE 33-6** *The frmUnattended form with the controls added*

Until now, you have created the interface of the forms required for the MobileCallStatus application. However, the controls that are added to the forms are not functional. To make the controls functional, you need to add code to these controls.

## Adding the Business Logic to the MobileCallStatus Application

You should first understand the working of the MobileCallStatus application. This will help you to write the code for the mobile Web controls in the mobile forms.

1. When a user accesses the MobileCallStatus application, the user needs to enter a logon name and password in the frmLogon form.
2. The user then clicks on the Submit button.
3. The application then validates the logon name and password of the user based on the data in the `Users.xml` file.
4. If the data entered by the user is incorrect, a message is displayed to the user.
5. The user then needs to reenter the logon name and password.
6. The logon name and password are again validated, and the process is repeated until the user enters correct data.
7. When the data entered by the user is validated and found to be correct, the frmSelectOption form is displayed. In the frmSelectOption form, the user can choose to view the incomplete calls or the new calls added to the `Calls.xml` file.
8. To view the pending calls, the user selects the View Pending Calls option and clicks on the Query button. The frmPending form is displayed.
9. However, to view the new calls added to the XML file, the user needs to select the Show Unattended Calls radio button. The user then clicks on the Query button. The frmUnattended form is displayed.

10. In the frmPending form, the user can view the pending calls and click on the Back button to return to the frmSelectOption form. In addition, the user may check the pending calls check boxes and click on the Mark checked as complete button when a call is completed. The status of the call will be changed to `Complete` in the `Calls.xml` file.
11. In the frmUnattended form, the user can view the new calls added to the list in the `Calls.xml` file and click on the Back button to return to the frmSelectOption form. However, if the user wishes to accept any new call, the user needs to check the pending calls check boxes and click on the Accept checked call(s) button. In this case, the status of the accepted calls is changed to `Pending` in the `Calls.xml` file.

To implement the previously listed functionality, you need to add code to the Command controls that are included in the MobileCallStatus application. You can start with the Submit button in the frmLogon form.

## Adding Code to the Submit Button in the frmLogon Form

While writing the code for the Submit button, you first need to set the `Visible` property of the `lblMessage` Label control to `false`. This will make the `lblMessage` control invisible until an error message is generated. To display the error message, you would then need to change the `Visible` property of the control to `true`. However, to make the control invisible, add the following statement to the `Click` event of the `cmdSubmit` button.

```
lblMessage.Visible=false;
```

Next, you need to validate the logon name and password entered by the user. The data entered by the user is validated against the `Users.xml` document. To do this, add the following code to the `Click` event of the `cmdSubmit` button.

```
if (Page.IsValid)
{
   bool found;
   found=false;
   XmlTextReader reader= new XmlTextReader("C:\\ Electronix\\Users.xml");
   reader.MoveToContent();
   while (reader.Read())
```

```
{
    if (reader.HasAttributes)
    {
        reader.MoveToNextAttribute();
        if (reader.Value==TextBox1.Text)
        {
            reader.MoveToNextAttribute();
            if (reader.Value==TextBox2.Text)
            {
                found=true;
                reader.MoveToFirstAttribute();
                ActiveForm=frmSelectOption;
            }
            else
            {
                lblMessage.Text="Invalid Password";
                lblMessage.Visible=true;
            }
        }
    }
}
reader.Close();
if (found==false & lblMessage.Visible==false)
{
    lblMessage.Text="Invalid User Name";
    lblMessage.Visible=true;
}
}
```

The preceding code uses an `if` loop to validate the data entered by the user. To do this, the `IsValid` property of the `Page` is used. The `IsValid` property returns a `Boolean` type value, `true` or `false`. If all the validations applied in the page are successful, the `IsValid` property returns `true`. Alternatively, if any of the validation fails, the `IsValid` property returns `false`. The value returned by the `IsValid` property is stored in the `Boolean` type variable `found`. The variable `found` is initialized to `false`.

Next, an object `reader` of the `XmlTextReader` class is created and initialized to read the `Users.xml` file. The path of the `Users.xml` file is specified in the initialization statement. You have learned about the `XmlTextReader` class in Chapter 17, "Interacting with a Microsoft Word Document and Event Viewer," in the section "The `XmlReader` Class."

The code then uses the `MoveToContent()` method of the `XmlReader` class to check whether the current node in the XML document is a content node. If the current node is not a content node, the reader moves to the next content node. You need to check for the content node to read the values from the content node of the `Users.xml` file.

Then the `Read()` method of the `XmlTextReader` class is used in a `while` loop to read the content of the `Users.xml` file. Inside the `while` loop, the `HasAttributes` property of the `XmlReader` class is used to check whether the current node has any attributes associated with it. The `HasAttributes` property returns a `Boolean` type value. If the current node has an associated attribute, the `HasAttributes` property returns a value, `true`.

Then an `if` loop is used to match the value entered by the user in `TextBox1` to the value in the `reader` object. To do this, the `Value` property of the `XmlTextReader` class is used. If the value in `TextBox1` is the same as the value in the `reader` object, the value of `TextBox2` is matched to the value of the next attribute. The `MoveToNextAttribute()` method is used to move to the next attribute in the `Users.xml` document. If the values of `TextBox1` and `TextBox2` are matched to the values in the attributes of the XML document, the `found` variable is set to `true`. A value of the variable `found`, if set to `true`, indicates that the validations performed in the frmLogon form are successful. In addition, the `reader` object is set to the first attribute in the `Users.xml` file and the frmSelectOption form is displayed to the user. Figure 33-7 shows the `Users.xml` file.

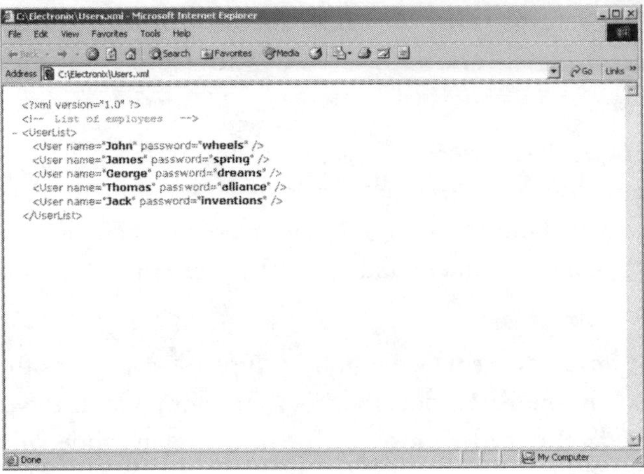


**FIGURE 33-7** *The* `Users.xml` *file*

However, if any of the values, `TextBox1` or `TextBox2`, do not match, an error message is displayed to the user. This would require you to set the `Visible` property of the `lblMessage` Label control to `true`. Figure 33-8 shows the frmLogon form with an error message, Invalid User Name, displayed.

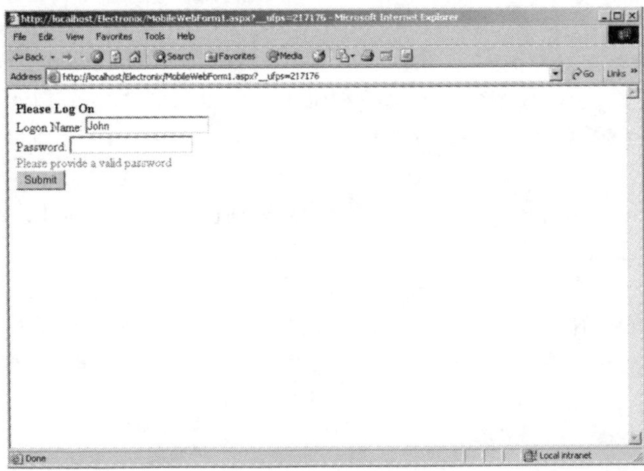


**FIGURE 33-8** *The frmLogon form with an error message displayed*

The preceding code matches the value entered by the user to all the attributes in the `Users.xml` file If the value of the variable `found` is `false`, an error message is displayed. Finally, the `reader` object is closed using the `Close()` method of the `XmlTextReader` class.

## Adding Code to the Query Button in the frmSelectOption Form

When a user selects an option, View Pending Calls or Show Unattended Calls, and clicks on the Query button, the frmPending form or the frmUnattended form is displayed, respectively. Therefore, you first need to track the option selected by the user and display the corresponding form. To do this, add the following code to the `Click` event of the `cmdLoad` button.

```
if (lstOptions.Selection.Value=="viewPending")
{
   ActiveForm=frmPending;
}
else
{
   ActiveForm=frmUnattended;
}
```

The preceding code uses the `Value` property of the `MobileListItem` class to find the option selected by the user and then to display the appropriate form. However, displaying the form requires reading data from the `Calls.xml` file. To display data from the `Calls.xml` file, you need to add the following code to the `Click` event of the `cmdLoad` button.

```
string lstItem;
XmlTextReader reader = new XmlTextReader("C:\\Electronix\\Calls.xml");
reader.MoveToContent();
while (reader.Read())
{
   lstItem="";
   if (reader.HasAttributes)
```

```
    {
        reader.MoveToNextAttribute();
        reader.MoveToNextAttribute();
        if (reader.Value=="Unattended")
        {
            reader.MoveToFirstAttribute();
            lstItem=reader.Value + ": ";
            reader.MoveToElement();
            lstItem=lstItem+ reader.ReadInnerXml();
            lstUnattended.Items.Add(lstItem);
        }
        if (reader.Value=="Pending")
        {
            reader.MoveToFirstAttribute();
            lstItem=reader.Value + ": ";
            reader.MoveToElement();
            lstItem=lstItem+ reader.ReadInnerXml();
            lstPending.Items.Add(lstItem);
        }
    }
}
```

The preceding code creates a variable of the type string, `lstItem`, and initializes it to a null value. In addition, the code creates an instance, `reader`, of the `XmlTextReader` class and initializes it to the `Calls.xml` file. Next, the `MoveToContent()` method of the `XmlReader` class is used to move to the content node in the XML document.

The code uses the `Read()` method to read the data in the `while` loop. Inside the `while` loop, an `if` loop is used to check whether the current node has any attributes associated with it. If the current node has attributes associated with it, the `reader` object is moved to read the second attribute, `status`, in the `Calls.xml` file. Figure 33-9 displays the content of the `Calls.xml` file.

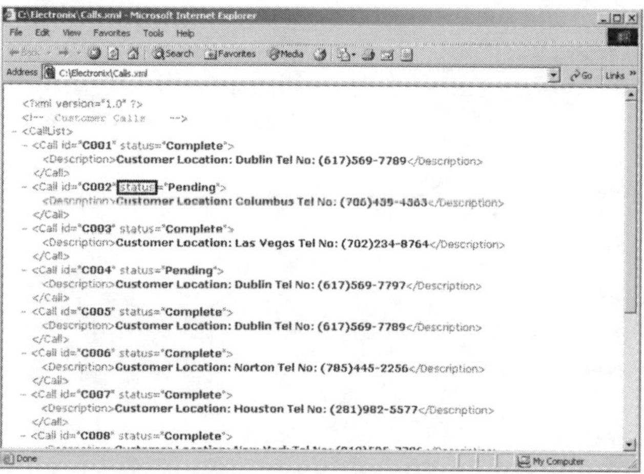

**FIGURE 33-9** *The content of the* `Calls.xml` *file*

If the value of the `status` node is `Unattended`, the `reader` object is moved back to the first attribute of the content node, `id`. To move to the `id` attribute, the `MoveToFirstAttribute()` method of the `XmlTextReader` class is used. Then, the value in the `id` attribute is retrieved using the `Value` property and stored in the `lstItem` variable.

Next, the `reader` object is moved to the `Call` element that contains the `id` attribute. This would enable the `reader` object to read the entire content of the `Call` element with the value of the `status` node as `Unattended`. To read the entire content of the `Call` element as a `string`, you can use the `ReadInnerXml()` method of the `XmlTextReader` class. Then, the content of the `Call` element is stored in the `lstItem` variable and added to the `lstUnattended` SelectionList control by using the `Add()` method of the `MobileListItemCollection()` class.

Similarly, if the user has selected the View Pending Calls option, the content of the `Call` element with the value of the status property as `Pending` is added to the `lstPending` SelectionList control and displayed in the frmPending form. Figure 33-10 shows the frmSelectOption form with the View Pending Calls option selected.

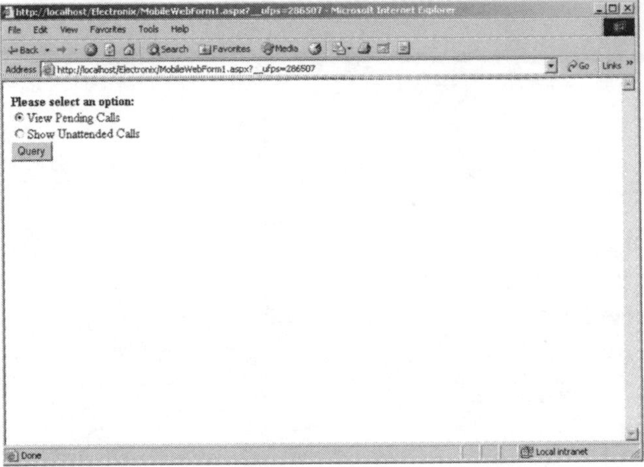


**FIGURE 33-10** *The frmSelectOption form with the View Pending Calls option selected*

## Adding Code to the Mark checked as complete Button in the frmPending Form

When a user checks the pending calls check box and clicks on the Mark checked as complete button, the status of the selected call is changed to `Complete` in the `Calls.xml` file. In addition, the entry of the call is removed from the `lstPending` SelectionList control in the frmPending form. To do this, you need to add the following code to the `Click` event of the `cmdUpdate` button.

```
private void cmdUpdate_Click(object sender, System.EventArgs e)
{
   StreamReader strRead;
   string content, strText;
    int index;
   strRead= new StreamReader("C:\\Electronix\\Calls.xml");
   content=strRead.ReadToEnd();
   strRead.Close();
   for (int i=0; i<lstPending.Items.Count; i++)
   {
      if (lstPending.Items[i].Selected==true)
      {
         strText=lstPending.Items[i].Text;
```

```
            strText=strText.Substring(0,4);
            index=content.IndexOf(strText);
            content=content.Remove(index+14,7);
            content=content.Insert(index+14, "Complete");
        }
    }
    StreamWriter strWrite;
    strWrite = new StreamWriter("C:\\Electronix\\Calls.xml");
    strWrite.Write(content);
    strWrite.Close();
    lstPending.Items.Clear();
    string lstItem;
    XmlTextReader reader;
    reader = new XmlTextReader("C:\\Electronix\\Calls.xml");
    reader.MoveToContent();
    while (reader.Read())
    {
        lstItem="";
        if (reader.HasAttributes)
        {
            reader.MoveToNextAttribute();
            reader.MoveToNextAttribute();
            if (reader.Value=="Pending")
            {
                reader.MoveToFirstAttribute();
                lstItem=reader.Value + ": ";
                reader.MoveToElement();
                lstItem=lstItem+ reader.ReadInnerXml();
                lstPending.Items.Add(lstItem);
            }
        }
    }
    reader.Close();
}
```

The preceding code creates an instance, `strRead`, of thc `StreamReader` class and initializes it to the `Calls.xml` file in the `Electronix` folder. Next, a `string` type variable, `content`, is declared and initialized to the data in the `strRead` object.

However, to do this, you first need to use the `ReadToEnd()` method of the `StreamReader` class to read the entire content stored in the `strRead` object. Once the data in the `strRead` object is stored in the `content` variable, you can close the `strRead` object by using the `Close()` method. Next, a `for` loop is used to add the data in the `content` variable as list items to the `lstPending` SelectionList control. This data is then displayed as a list of calls in the frmPending form. Figure 33-11 shows the list of pending calls at run time.

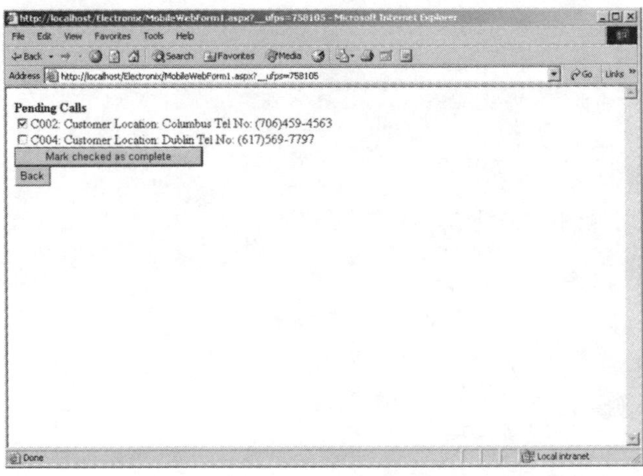


**FIGURE 33-11** *The list of pending calls at run time*

As you can see in Figure 33-11, the user has selected the `C002` pending list check box. After selecting the check box, if the user clicks on the Mark checked as complete button, the status of the `C002` call is changed to `Complete`. You have already added the code to do this in the `Click` event of the `cmdAcceptCall` button. I will now discuss the code.

To write the changes to the `Calls.xml` file, you would need an object of the `StreamWriter` class. Therefore, the code declares and initializes an object, `strWrite`, to the `Calls.xml` file. The `strWrite` object uses the `Write()` method of the `StreamWriter` class to write the changes to the `Calls.xml` file. The data to be written is passed as a parameter to the `Write()` method. After doing this, you can close the `strWrite` object. Figure 33-12 shows the status of the `C002` call changed to `Complete`.

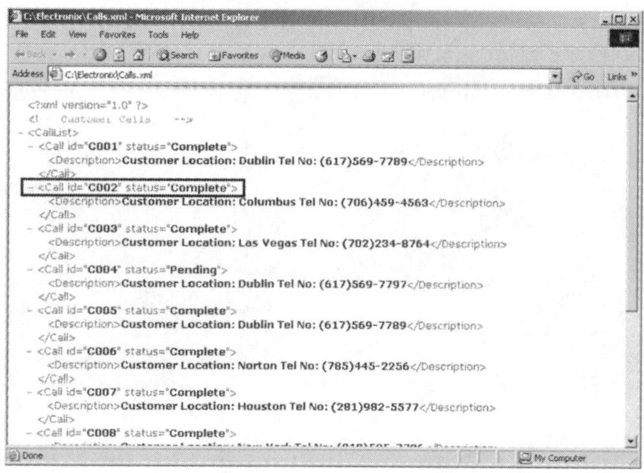


**FIGURE 33-12** *The status of the* `C002` *call changed to* `Complete`

Once the changes are made to the `Calls.xml` file, the changes should be reflected in the frmPending form. To do this, an object reader of the `XmlTextReader` class is created that will read the content of the `Calls.xml` file. This content is then added to the `lstPending` SelectionList control and displayed in the frmPending form.

After the user makes changes to the frmPending form, the user needs to return to the frmSelectOption form. To do this, a Back button is added to the frmPending form.

## Adding Code to the Back Button in the frmPending Form

To display the frmPending form, when the user clicks on the Back button, add the following code to the `cmdBack` button.

```
private void cmdBack1_Click(object sender, System.EventArgs e)
{
   lstPending.Items.Clear();
   ActiveForm=frmSelectOption;
}
```

## Adding Code to the Accept checked call(s) Button in the frmUnattended Form

After writing the code for the `cmdUpdate` button in the frmPending form, you can easily write the code for the `cmdAcceptCall` button. The code for the `Click` event of the `cmdAcceptCall` button is as follows:

```
private void cmdAcceptCall_Click(object sender, System.EventArgs e)
{
    StreamReader strRead;
    string content, strText;
    int index;
    strRead= new StreamReader("C:\\Electronix\\Calls.xml");
    content=strRead.ReadToEnd();
    strRead.Close();
    for (int i=0; i<lstUnattended.Items.Count; i++)
    {
        if (lstUnattended.Items[i].Selected==true)
        {
            strText=lstUnattended.Items[i].Text;
            strText=strText.Substring(0,4);
            index=content.IndexOf(strText);
            content=content.Remove(index+14,10);
            content=content.Insert(index+14, "Pending");
        }
    }
    StreamWriter strWrite;
    strWrite = new StreamWriter("C:\\Electronix\\Calls.xml");
    strWrite.Write(content);
    strWrite.Close();
    lstUnattended.Items.Clear();
    string lstItem;
    XmlTextReader reader;
    reader = new XmlTextReader("C:\\Electronix\\Calls.xml");
    reader.MoveToContent();
    while (reader.Read())
```

```
    {
        lstItem="";
        if (reader.HasAttributes)
        {
            reader.MoveToNextAttribute();
            reader.MoveToNextAttribute();
            if (reader.Value=="Unattended")
            {
                reader.MoveToFirstAttribute();
                lstItem=reader.Value + ": ";
                reader.MoveToElement();
                lstItem=lstItem+ reader.ReadInnerXml();
                lstUnattended.Items.Add(lstItem);
            }
        }
    }
    reader.Close();
}
```

Figure 33-13 shows the frmUnattended form at run time.

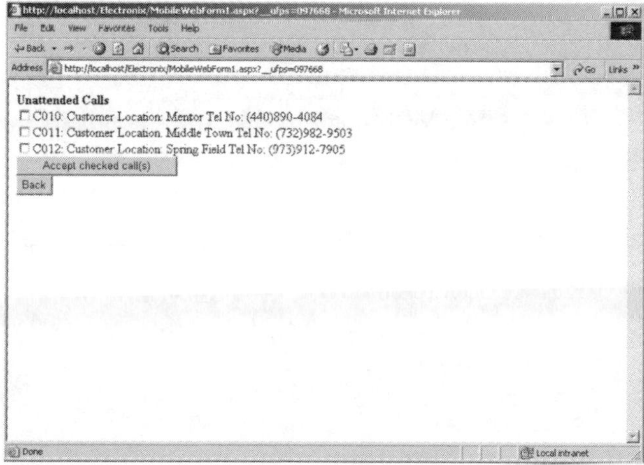


**FIGURE 33-13** *The frmUnattended form at run time*

## Adding Code to the Back Button in the frmUnattended Form

Similar to writing the code for the Back button in the frmPending form, you can add the following code to the Back button of the frmUnattended form.

```
private void cmdBack2_Click(object sender, System.EventArgs e)
{
   stUnattended.Items.Clear();
   ActiveForm=frmSelectOption;
}
```

After creating the MobileCallStatus application, you can test the application in an emulator. The following section discusses how to test a mobile application in an emulator.

# Testing the MobileCallStatus Application in an Emulator

To test your application in an emulator, perform the following steps:

1. On the View menu, point to the Mobile Explorer Browser option.
2. In the displayed list, select the Show Browser option.
3. Type the address of the mobile Web form in the Address box of the emulator and then press Enter.

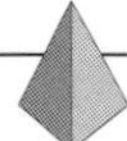

**TIP**

While using an emulator, you can use the keyboard to type the information or navigate through the pages. While working with the actual device, such as a mobile phone, you can use the keys on the mobile phone.

You can type the address of the forms in the Address box to view all the forms in the MobileCallStatus application. Figure 33-14 shows the frmLogon form in an emulator.

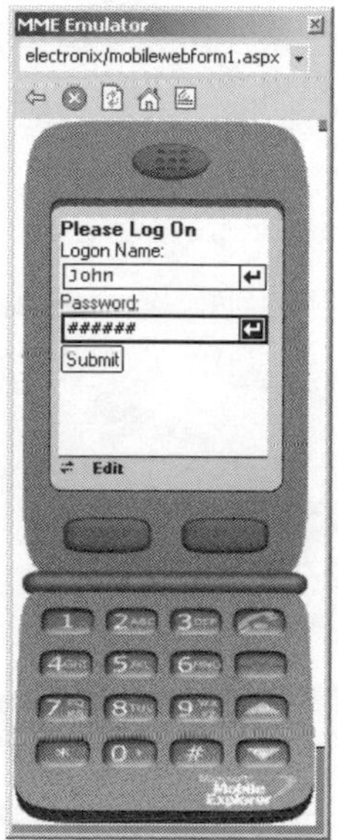


**FIGURE 33-14** *The frmLogon form in an emulator*

Navigating to the next form takes you to the frmSelectOption form, as shown in Figure 33-15.

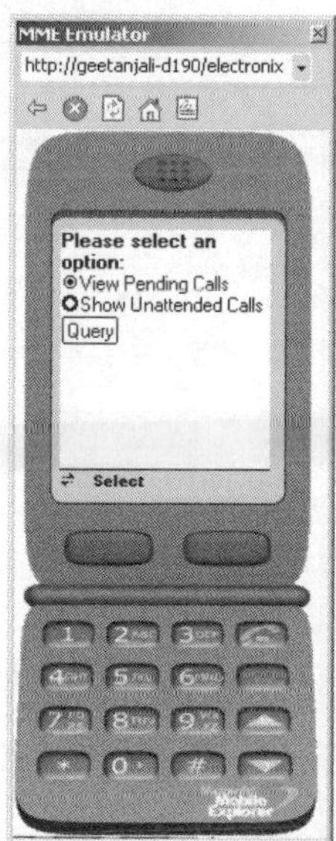


**FIGURE 33-15** *The frmSelectOption form in an emulator*

In the frmSelectOption form, if the user selects the View Pending Calls option, the frmPending form is displayed as shown in Figure 33-16.

**FIGURE 33-16** *The frmPending form in an emulator*

However, if the user selects the Show Unattended Calls option in the frmSelect-Option form, the frmUnattended form is displayed. Figure 33-17 shows the frmUnattended form in an emulator.

**FIGURE 33-17** *The frmUnattended form in an emulator*

# Summary

In this chapter, you created the MobileCallStatus application. While creating the application, you looked at the default code created by Visual Studio .NET for a mobile Web application. Finally, you learned to write the code for the Mobile-CallStatus application.

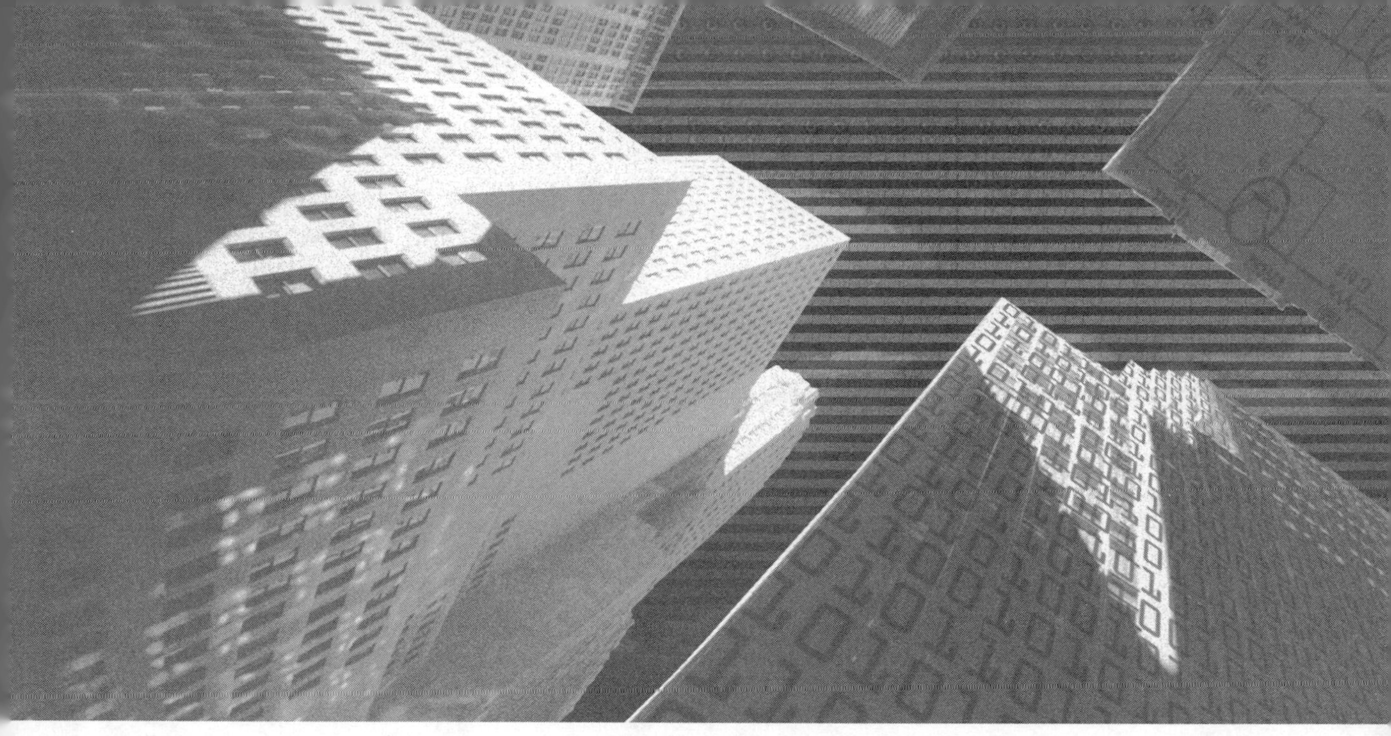

# PART IX

## Beyond the Labs

# Chapter 34

## Advanced C# Concepts

In this chapter, you will learn about COM+, `System.Messaging` namespace, and asynchronous message queuing.

# COM+

Before I introduce you to COM+, you need to understand the concepts of COM, MTS, and Windows DNA.

## What Is COM?

As you might be aware, COM stands for *component object model*, and it is a model for construction of binary-compatible software components introduced by Microsoft. In simple terms, COM is a specification and implementation framework that allows you to create modular, object-oriented, customizable, and upgradeable distributed applications using a number of programming languages. COM enables you to develop components that can communicate with other components irrespective of the programming language or tool you choose to develop it. Therefore, COM allows you to concentrate on developing your application and not bother about the internals of the components.

COM allows clients to invoke services provided by COM-compliant components (COM objects). Services implemented by COM objects are exposed through a set of interfaces that represent the point of contact between clients and the object.

### *Why COM?*

In order to understand the features provided by COM, you first need to understand the rationale for its existence. Binary code has been in use for a long time now. Libraries have been used in C and C++ from the very beginning. Windows programmers have been reusing DLLs (*dynamically linked libraries*). But there were other issues.

Libraries created using C/C++ compilers were often incompatible with executables created using a different C/C++ compiler. Secondly, DLLs were language dependent. Moreover, updating DLLs posed greater problems. Compatibility between versions was not achieved because of memory allocation reasons. Changed DLLs often broke executables designed for an earlier version.

## Benefits of COM

COM was an alternative developed by Microsoft to overcome these problems. The major benefits of COM are:

- COM components can provide functionality in a standard way.
- COM provides for component interoperability.
- COM provides a good versioning mechanism that allows one system component to be updated without requiring updates to other components in the system.
- COM components can be implemented in a number of programming languages.

Before we proceed further, I will take you through some commonly used terms in COM.

### Interfaces

An *interface* is a specification that defines the type of behavior a class must implement. An interface provides a group of related methods that are pure virtual functions. These methods are not implemented in the interface but are implemented in the class that implements the interface. The class that implements the interface methods is referred to as *coclass*. When the coclass is instantiated, the instance that is created is referred to as *component object*.

A class that inherits an interface must implement every member of the interface. An interface enables other programs to access the functionality provided by your component.

Consider the following example, where a COM object behaves like a clock. The clock object supports two interfaces, IClock and IAlarm. The IClock interface provides the methods to set and read current time. The IAlarm interface provides the alarm and methods.

## GUID

COM objects and interfaces are specified using Microsoft IDL (*interface definition language*). In order to avoid problems arising out of two components with same names, every COM component and interface has a GUID (*globally unique identifier*). A GUID is a 128-bit integer that is generated and assigned to every COM component and interface built. It uniquely identifies the component to the operating environment and other software.

## CLSID

Class ID (CLSID) is a unique identifier that is associated with an OLE (*Object Linking and Embedding*) object. If a class is used to create more than one instance of an object, the associated application needs to register its CLSID in the system registry. This enables clients to locate and load the executable code associated with the objects.

## Marshaling

*Marshaling* is the process of packaging and sending interface method calls across thread or process boundaries.

## Type Library

*Type libraries* are binary files (.tlb files) that include information about types and objects exposed by an ActiveX application. A type library can contain any of the following:

- Information about data types
- Description about one or more objects
- Reference to type descriptions from other type libraries

Including the type library with the product ensures that information about objects in the library is made available to users of the application. Type libraries can be shipped as a standalone binary file or a resource in a DLL.

## Stub

*Stub* is an interface-specific object that unpackages the parameters for that interface after they are marshaled across the process boundary and makes the requested method call. The stub runs in the address space of the receiver and communicates with a corresponding proxy in the sender's address space.

## Proxy

A *proxy* is an interface-specific object that packages parameters for that interface in preparation for a remote method call. A proxy runs in the address space of the sender and communicates with a corresponding stub in the receiver's address space.

## Standard Interfaces

Every component must implement at least two interfaces, the *IUnknown* and the *IDispatch* interfaces. The IUnknown interface has three methods, as follows:

- AddRef
- Release
- QueryInterface

COM objects keep track of the number of interface pointers to the object that are in use. When the reference count reaches zero, it can be freed. However, the object is not explicitly freed; instead, all the objects interface pointers and the object frees itself after an appropriate time.

`AddRef` increments the reference count and `Release` documents it. The QueryInterface is the most important method. Because all interfaces inherit from IUnknown, all interfaces must implement QueryInterface. The QueryInterface method provides client access to other interfaces on an object.

IDispatch interface exposes objects, methods, and properties to other programs that support automation. COM components implement the IDispatch interface to enable access by automation clients.

Every COM object runs inside of a server. A single server can support multiple COM objects. A client can access COM objects provided by a server in one the following three ways:

- **In-process server.** Clients can link directly to a library containing the server. The client and server execute in the same process. Communication is accomplished through function calls.
- **RPC (*remote procedure call*).** The client can access a server running in a different process but on the same machine through an interprocess communication mechanism.
- **Remote Object Proxy.** The client can access a remote server running on another machine. The network communication between client and server is accomplished through RPC. The mechanism supporting access to remote servers is called DCOM (*Distributed COM*).

## Functioning of COM Objects

If the client and the server are in the same process, the sharing of data between the two is simple. However, when the server process is separate from the client process, as in a local server or remote server, COM must format and bundle the data in order to share it. This process of preparing the data is called marshaling. Marshaling is accomplished through a proxy object and a stub object that handle the cross-process communication for any particular interface. COM creates the stub in the object's server process and has the stub manage the real interface pointer. COM then creates the proxy in the client's process and connects it to the stub. The proxy then supplies the interface pointer to the client.

The client calls the interfaces of the server through the proxy, which marshals the parameters and passes them to the server stub. The stub unmarshals the parameters and makes the actual call inside the server object. When the call completes, the stub marshals return values and passes them to the proxy, which in turn returns them to the client. The same proxy/stub mechanism is used when the client and server are on different machines.

The internal implementation of marshaling and unmarshaling differs depending on whether the client and server operate on the same machine (COM) or on different machines (DCOM). When a client wishes to create and use a COM object, the client performs the following steps:

1. It invokes the COM API to instantiate a new COM object.
2. COM locates the object implementation and initiates a server process for the object.
3. The server process creates the object and returns an interface pointer at the object.
4. The client can then interact with the newly instantiated COM object through the interface pointer.

## COM Threading Model

Programming multithreading applications is quite a tedious task irrespective of the tool or the language being used. In an application that is single threaded, everything runs synchronously, that is, one after the other, whereas in case of multithreaded applications, the execution sequence is not so straightforward. All requests for a component method are queued up in the message pump, causing all requests to be executed simultaneously. Applications in which multiple threads are active at the same time can be asynchronous.

It is possible that methods in a component execute simultaneously. Data in a component can be changed or accessed by more than one thread, thus losing its concurrency. Therefore, it becomes the responsibility of the component or the application to prevent such simultaneous access by multiple threads or to make the code thread savvy.

Because this is a likely scenario for COM components, the COM architecture provides various threading models, which allows you to create components that are inherently thread savvy but less flexible, or components that can handle threading issues themselves.

You can build COM components that have any of the following threading models:

- Single threaded
- Apartment threaded
- Both single and apartment threaded
- Free threaded

An *apartment* is neither a thread nor a process. It is an execution context in which components exist. Different types of apartments define how a class object can be accessed from different threads in the same process.

An apartment can be an STA (*single threaded apartment*) or an MTA (*multithreaded apartment*). As the name suggests, objects in an STA can be accessed by only one thread at a time. If more than one thread tries to access the object in an STA, the requests are queued in a message pump and access is given serially. The advantage here is that because the access is serialized, you can be sure a component created in this model will never be accessed by more than one thread at a time.

In the case of an MTA, it is possible for multiple threads to enter the apartment, that is, more than one thread can access an object in an MTA. Here, the onus of protecting the data in an object from concurrent access and possible corruption is on the programmer.

A process can have multiple STAs, but only one MTA. The first STA created in the process is called its main STA. When a component is created using the single threaded model, it is forced to run on the same thread that initialized it or on the main STA of the process. This is the least flexible of the COM threading models.

When a component is created as apartment threaded (STA), the object can be loaded into any STA in the process. This ensures that access to the object is synchronized. When a component is created as free threaded, it will be loaded into the process-wise MTA. It is possible for multiple threads to access it simultaneously. The programmer is responsible for creating thread-safe code.

In case a component is created to support both apartment threading and free threading, any client that supports either of these models can access the class object. However, the access to the data must be synchronized by the developer.

## Windows DNA

Now that I have gone though the basics of COM, I will introduce you to COM+. Before that, I will take a quick look at *Windows DNA (Distributed Internet Applications)* architecture. Windows DNA is the application development for the Windows platform. It specifies how to develop robust, scalable, distributed applications using the Windows platform and to extend existing data and external applications to support the Internet.

Windows DNA describes the technologies that provide a complete integrate n-tier development model and the set of services that developers require to build scalable enterprise-level applications on the Windows platform. Figure 34-1 shows the Windows DNA model.

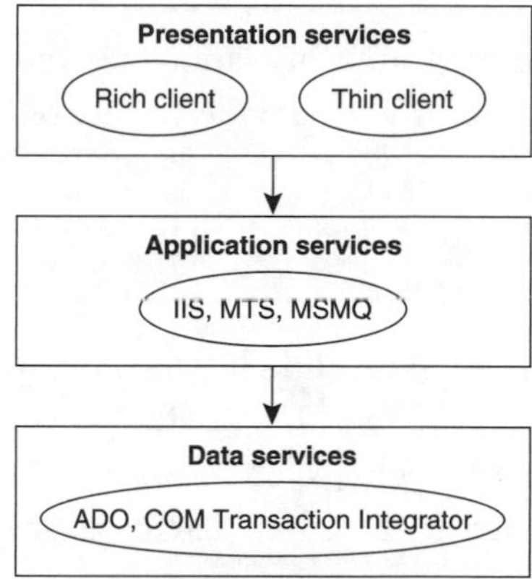


**FIGURE 34-1** *Windows DNA architecture*

Windows DNA addresses the requirements at all tiers of modern distributed applications: presentation, business logic, and data. The presentation services include all applications and technologies that can be used to provide access to the application. They can be HTML, dynamic HTML, and JavaScript viewed through a Web browser (thin client) or a Windows application developed using Win32 API and distributed as executables (rich client).

The application services tier is typically composed of components that bind the presentation and the data layers. The technologies involved in this layer are IIS, COM, ASP, and MTS. This layer handles the business logic and other application services.

The data services layer enables the application to store and retrieve data. The technologies involved in this layer are ADO+ and OLE DB.

Some of the benefits of Windows DNA include:

- Windows DNA provides a very comprehensive, integrated platform for building distributed applications. Commonly needed middle tier services are provided to developers, doing away with the burden of having to build commonly used services.
- Applications can be built faster by using a common services infrastructure of the Windows platform.
- Windows DNA supports a number of programming languages and development tools, providing the developers with a wide variety of choice.
- Windows DNA is designed to provide a high level of interoperability with existing applications and legacy systems.

The core of Windows DNA is the integration of Web and client/server application development models through the COM. Windows DNA defines a common set of services, including components, dynamic HTML, Web browser and server, scripting, transactions, message queuing, security, directory, database and data access, systems management, and user interface. These services are exposed in a unified way through COM.

The application services, infrastructure services, and common interfaces operate in a multitier framework. COM and other protocols and services act as the bond between the application and data layer.

From a technology that was initially designed to promote code reuse, COM has made a very successful transition to design software components that encapsulate business rules and logic. Today, system services are provided through COM.

## Microsoft Transaction Server (MTS)

COM was a component technology designed to enable efficient code reuse. With the release of DCOM in Windows NT 4.0, the technology was expanded to support distributed applications by means of remote component instantiation and method invocations.

This was followed by release of MTS, which allowed developers to build and run their components in MTS as its middle tier. In addition, it provided much needed support for distributed transactions, integrated security, thread pooling, and improved configuration and administration.

## COM+

One of the problems faced by developers building multitier applications is deciding when to use MTS and when to use COM. COM is shipped with Windows NT, whereas MTS needs to be installed as an add-on. MTS is not a part of COM. Moreover, MTS and COM have quite different programming models of their own. MTS is a layer on top of COM, but COM was not modified to accommodate MTS. However, the two are not tightly integrated.

In Windows 2000, COM and MTS have been unified into a single run-time layer and support a common programming model. The new run time has been named COM+. COM+ is a part of Windows 2000.

COM+, just like COM, is based on binary components and interface-based programming. Method calls are remoted across process and computer boundaries using a transparent RPC layer. COM+ components can be upgraded and extended in production without affecting the client applications that use them. They also support distributed transactions and role-based security. Additionally, COM+ provides a built-in thread-pooling scheme and uses attribute programming as its programming model.

In addition to transactional services and integrated security, COM+ exposes services such as synchronization and object pooling. COM+ provides new features, such as queued components and COM+ events that are exposed through configurable attributes and a new threading model called neutral apartment threading. I will now discuss each of these features in brief.

### *Role-Based Security*

COM+ supports role-based as well as process-based security. A role represents the security profile of one or more users in an MTS application. At design time, a developer can set up security checks programmatically through roles. At deployment time, an administrator maps a set of roles to user accounts and group accounts inside a Windows NT domain. Therefore, in role-based security, access to parts of an application are granted or denied on the basis of the logical group or role to which the caller has been assigned. The role-based security model of MTS provides more flexibility than the security model provided by COM.

### Threading

COM+ includes a new threading model, neutral apartment threading. You can use neutral apartments for projects with no user interface. In case of neutral apartments, objects follow the rules for MTAs. However, they can execute on any kind of thread. Each process can have only one neutral apartment.

### Object Pooling

This is a service that enables you to configure a component to have instances of itself kept alive in a pool, ready to be used by clients accessing the component. You can configure and monitor the pool by specifying characteristics such as pool size and creation request timeout values. COM+ manages the pool while the application is running, handling object activation and reuse based on the criteria you have specified. This object reuse leads to significant performance and scaling benefits.

### Queued Components

Queued components are a feature of COM+ that is based on MSMQ (*Microsoft Message Queue Service*). Queued components provide a simple way to invoke and execute components asynchronously. Processing can take place without having to bother about whether the sender is available or not at the other end. With MSMQ, a client application can send request messages even when the server application is offline, and a server can respond to request messages after all client applications have gone offline. In environments where client applications and servers can become disconnected for any number of reasons, this capability allows the distributed application as a whole to stay up and running.

However, this results in extra code for creating, preparing, and sending messages from client applications. It also requires you to write a server-side listener application.

On the other hand, COM+ provides a service, named queued components, that allows you to take advantage of MSMQ without having to explicitly program using the MSMQ API. The queued components service is a layer built on top of MSMQ. The COM+ queued components services enable you to create components that can execute immediately, provided the client and the server are connected or the execution can be deferred until a connection is established.

The benefits of queued processing are:

- Shorter component life span
- Message reliability
- Reduced dependency on component availability
- Efficient server scheduling

## COM+ Events

Events are used to manage a connection between a publisher and one or more subscribers and then manage the delivery of events to those subscribers. In the COM+ event model, applications that send out event notifications are called *publishers*. Applications that receive event notifications are called *subscribers*. The COM+ queued components service is used to make the publisher and subscriber processing time independent by queuing the publisher's message and later replaying it to the subscriber. COM+ events are often called LCEs (*loosely coupled events*) because publishers and subscribers do not have any knowledge of one another. Publishers and subscribers know about event classes, but not about each other. Whether or not you need to use the queued components service depends on the underlying business logic of your application. If you need to have events that are time-independent, you can create them by composing COM+ events with COM+ queued components.

## Working of COM+ Events

Suppose you author an event class that implements one or more interfaces. The methods that are defined in these interfaces represent a set of events. You write subscriber components to implement these interfaces and respond to events when they are triggered. Next, you write a publisher application to create objects from the event class and call various methods when it wants to fire events. The event service takes care of processing the method and delivering the events to every subscriber.

COM+ events store event information from different publishers in an event store in the COM+ catalog. Subscribers query this store and select the events that they want to hear about. Selecting event information from the event store creates a subscription. When an event occurs, the event system looks in this database and finds the interested subscribers, creates a new object of each interested class, and calls a method on that object.

### Automatic Transactions

Automatic transaction processing assumes that COM components are either transaction-aware or transaction-unaware. Transaction-aware components are called transactional components. COM+ looks at the component's transaction requirement before activating an object based on the component.

Once .NET Framework class is marked to participate in a transaction, it will automatically execute within the scope of a transaction. You can control the object's transactional behavior by setting a transaction attribute value in the class. The attribute value, in turn, determines the transactional behavior of the instantiated object. Thus, based on the attribute value, the object will automatically participate or never participate in a transaction.

### Just-in-Time Activation

Just-in-Time (JIT) activation is an automatic service provided by COM+ that can enable you use server resources more efficiently. When a component is configured as JIT activated, COM+ can disable an instance of the component even when a client is holding an active reference to the object. The next time the client calls a method on the object (which the client believes to be still active), COM+ will reactivate the object to the client, just in time.

The primary advantage of JIT activation is that you enable clients to hold references to objects for as long as they need them without tying up server resources.

### Synchronization

Synchronization is a service provided by COM+ for managing concurrency. Synchronization prevents more than one caller from entering the component at a given time. It determines when threads can make calls to an object. Typically, synchronization is needed when you have a multithreaded or a free threaded apartment object. Synchronization prohibits flow across processes or computers and flows from one component to another.

COM+ ensures concurrency by a series of locks for each activity. If a caller tries to enter a COM+ synchronized component that is already being used by another caller, the call is blocked until the lock is released. If the lock is not in use, the lock is acquired and the call is processed. After completing, the lock is released for the next caller. To prevent deadlock, COM+ manages access to all objects across activities by a nested series of calls chained throughout the network.

## .NET Interoperability

.NET provides interoperability features that allow you to work with existing unmanaged code (that is, code running outside the CLR) in COM components as well as Win32 DLLs. .NET CLR enables interoperability by hiding the complexity associated with calls between managed and unmanaged code. The run time automatically generates code to translate calls between the two environments.

When you call a COM object from .NET, the run time generates an RCW (*run-time callable wrapper*). The RCW acts as a surrogate for the unmanaged object (refer to Figure 34-2). The RCW handles all interaction between the .NET client and the COM component. It takes care of creating and binding the COM object, translating and marshaling data between environments, and managing the lifetime of the wrapped COM object.

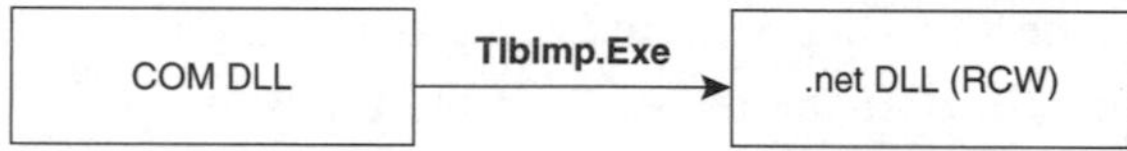


**FIGURE 34-2** *COM DLL-to-RCW conversion*

Even when you call a .NET component from COM, the run time generates a wrapper object called CCW (*COM callable wrapper*). The run time reads the type information for the component from its assembly metadata and generates a CCW. The CCW, like the RCW, acts as a proxy between the unmanaged COM object and the managed .NET component. The CCW takes care of handling all interaction between the COM client and the managed object.

### *COM+ Services*

.NET components can participate in COM+ applications and share context, transactions, synchronization boundaries, and so forth with COM+ components. .NET components that participate in COM+ applications are called *serviced components*. A serviced component is the mechanism that enables context sharing between COM+ and .NET Framework classes.

Serviced components must be registered in the COM+ catalog, typically by using the `regsvcs` tool provided with the .NET Framework SDK. You can specify the exact service requirements for your .NET component by annotating your managed code with service related attributes.

### *Calling Unmanaged APIs from .NET*

.NET also supports calling unmanaged code in Win32 DLLs. This interoperability, referred to as *platform invocation* or simply *P/Invoke*, allows managed code to call into C-language-type API functions. It also handles the marshaling of data types between managed and unmanaged types, finds and invokes the function in the DLL, and facilitates transition from managed to unmanaged code.

## COM Interoperability

COM interoperability provides access to existing COM components without modifying the original component. When you need to incorporate a COM code in to your managed application, import the relevant COM types using the COM Interop (TlbImp.exe) utility.

The TlbImp (*type library importer*) utility is a command-line tool that is shipped along with .NET Framework SDK. It converts a COM type library into .NET Framework metadata. The type library importer also does the following:

- COM coclasses are converted to C# classes with a zero parameter constructor.
- COM structs are converted into C# structs with public fields.

COM interop also allows you to access managed objects. For this purpose, COM interop provides a utility (RegAsm.exe) that exports the managed types into a type library and registers the component as a COM component. At run time, the CLR marshals data between COM objects and managed objects as needed.

### *C# Client Interop*

I will now discuss the steps to be followed to use C# code to interoperate with COM objects.

C# provides support for the following:

- Creating COM objects
- Determining whether a COM interface is implemented by an object

◆ Calling methods on COM interfaces
◆ Implementing objects and interfaces that can be called by COM clients

## Creating a COM Class Wrapper

In order to access COM objects and interfaces from C# code, you need to include a .NET Framework definition for the COM interfaces in your C# code. You can easily accomplish this by using the type library importer utility.

## Declaring a COM Coclass

COM coclasses are represented as classes in C#. These classes must have the `ComImport` attribute associated with them. A coclass is declared as shown in the code snippet that follows:

```
// declare CalcManager as a COM coclass
[ComImport, Guid("E436EBB3-524F-11CE-9F53-0020AF0BA770")]
class CalcManager
{
    //code to do something
}
```

The C# compiler will add a constructor without any parameters that you can call to create an instance of the COM coclass.

## Creating a COM Object

Creating an instance of the COM coclass using the `new` operator is equivalent to using `CoCreateInstance`. The above class can be instantiated as given here:

```
class MainClass
{
    public static void Main()
    {
        CalcManager calc = new CalcManager ();
    }
}
```

### Declaring a COM Interface

COM interfaces are represented in C# as interfaces with `ComImport` and `Guid` attributes. They cannot include any interfaces in their base interface list, and they must declare the interface member functions in the order that the methods appear in the COM interface.

## *Developing COM+ Applications*

When developing COM+ applications, the principal tasks include designing COM components to encapsulate application logic, creating the COM+ application, and administering the application through deployment and maintenance.

### Designing COM Components

The following steps describe a general procedure for good component design:

1. Define the COM classes and implementation classes.
2. Group the classes into components.
3. Integrate the components into a COM+ application.

### Creating the COM+ Application

After designing the COM components, the developer integrates the components into a COM+ application and configures the application. The following steps describe the process:

1. Integrate the components into a COM+ application. You can integrate the components into an existing COM+ application or create a new application for the components. Specify the correct set of attributes for each of the classes. These attributes express the component's dependencies on any services its implementation might rely on, such as transactions, queued components, security, object pooling, and JIT activation.
2. Set up the security framework, that is, define roles and association of roles to classes, interfaces, and methods.
3. Configure environment-specific attributes on classes and applications.
4. Export the application for redistribution and deployment.

### Administering COM+ Applications

Typically, a developer delivers a partially configured COM+ application to the system administrator. The administrator then customizes the application for one or more specific environments. For example, the system administrator adds user accounts in roles and server names in an application. The administrator's tasks include the following:

1. Install the configured COM+ application on an administrative machine.
2. Provide the environment-specific attributes, such as role members and object pool size.
3. Export the fully configured COM+ application.
4. Create an application proxy.

After an application is fully configured for a specific environment, the administrator can then deploy it on test or production machines. This involves installing the fully configured COM+ application on one or more machines.

## *Accessing a COM+ Component from C# Code*

If you want to access an existing COM+ application from C# code, you do not need to modify the existing COM+ application, despite the fact that the execution model of the component is very different.

Following is an example of accessing a DLL from C# code. You can access the DLL in two ways, early binding and late binding. I will first take you through the early binding example.

### Accessing a COM Component Using Early Binding

In order to use an existing COM component, you need to create a RCW using the type library importer (TlbImp.exe) utility, as follows.

Assume you have a COM component with a method `Add` that takes two parameters and returns their sum.

```
'CompAdd.Dll
(class1)
Public Function Add(A As Long, B As Long) As Long
    Add = A + B
End Function
```

Run the TlbImp.exe utility to create a RCW as shown in Figure 34-3.

```
E:\BookProj\AddDll>tlbimp CompAdd.dll /out:CompAddRCW.dll
Microsoft (R) .NET Framework Type Library to Assembly Converter 1.0.3328.4
Copyright (C) Microsoft Corporation 1998-2001.  All rights reserved.

Type library imported to E:\BookProj\AddDll\CompAddRCW.dll

E:\BookProj\AddDll>_
```

**FIGURE 34-3** *Creating an RCW with TlbImp utility*

The preceding command generates a wrapper DLL, called CompAddRcw.dll. You can view this DLL using a utility called `IlDasm.exe`.

Now you need to write code to call the wrapper DLL (`CompAddRcw.dll`) to access the actual DLL (`CompAdd.dll`). The code for calling the DLL is given as follows.

```
//code to access CompAdd.dll
using CompAddRcw;
using System;
namespace AddEarlyBind
{
  class EarlyBinding
  {
    public static void Main()
    {
      CompAddRcw.Class1 objAdd = new CompAddRcw.Class1();
      long lRes;
      int ix=100;
      int iy=200;
      lRes= objAdd.Add( ref ix, ref iy);
      Console.WriteLine(lRes);
    }
  }
}
```

Compile the program with `/r:` switch and execute it to call the COM component.

## Accessing a COM Component Using Late Binding

To implement late binding, you need to use `System.Reflection` namespace, which enables access to the types contained in any assembly. This can be accomplished as follows:

1. Get the interface `IDispatch` using `Type.GetTypeFromProgID("Project1.Class1")`.
2. Create instance using the type ID `Activator.CreateInstance(objAddType)`.
3. Create an array of arguments.
4. Invoke the method using the function `objAddType.InvokeMember`.

The code for implementing the same is as follows.

```
using System.Reflection;
using System;
namespace AddLateBind
{
  class LateBinding
  {
    public static void Main()
    {
      //Get IDispatch Interface
      Type objAddType = Type.GetTypeFromProgID("Project1.Class1");
      //Create Instance
      object objAdd = Activator.CreateInstance(objAddType);
      //Make Array of Arguments
      object[] myArguments = { 100, 200 };
      object obj;
      //Invoke Add Method
      obj = objAddType.InvokeMember("Add", BindingFlags.InvokeMethod,
      null, objAdd, myArguments);
      Console.WriteLine(obj);
    }
  }
}
```

The method `Type.GetTypeFromProgID` is used to load the type information of the COM object. The call to `Activator.CreateInstance` returns an instance of the COM object. Finally, `InvokeMember` function is used to call the method of COM object.

## A Complete Example

The following example describes the process of creating a DLL in C# and accessing it from C# code. I shall first take you through the steps to create a DLL.

### Creating the DLL

1. On the File menu, point to the New option.
2. In the displayed list, click the Project option.

   The New Project dialog box is displayed.
3. In the Project Types: pane of the New Project dialog box, select the Visual C# option.
4. In the Templates: pane, select the Class Library option.
5. Type the name of the application as `Math` in the Name: text box and the desired location in the Location: text box.
6. Click the OK button.
7. Add a method with the following definition.

   ```
   public long Add(long Val1, long Val2)
   {
       return Val1 + Val2;
   }
   ```
8. Add a property, Extra, as shown in the following code.

   ```
   public bool Extra
   {
     get
     {
       return bTest;
     }
     set
     {
       bTest=Extra;
   ```

```
    }
}
```

9. Change the name of Class1 to MathComp. Also change the name of the constructor.
10. Build the component.

## Building the Client

1. On the File menu, point to the New option.
2. In the displayed list, click the Project option.

   The New Project dialog box is displayed.
3. In the Project Types: pane of the New Project dialog box, select the Visual C# option.
4. In the Templates: pane, select the Console Application option.
5. Type the name of the application as `MathClient` in the Name: text box and the desired location in the Location: text box.
6. Click the OK button.
7. On the Project menu, click the Add Reference option.
8. Browse and select the Math.dll you created and add it to the current project (refer to Figure 34-4).

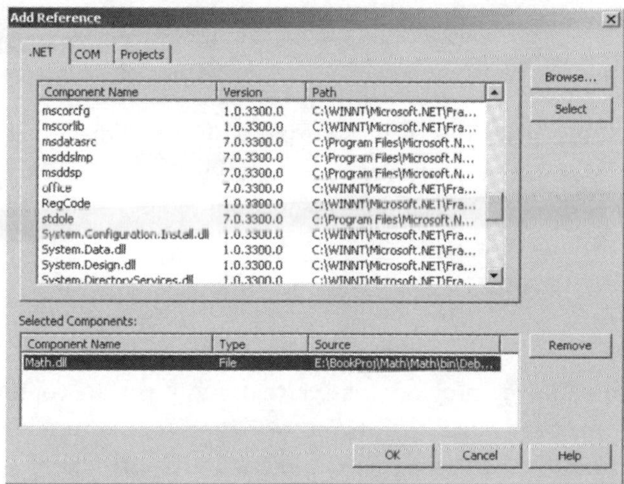


**FIGURE 34-4** *The Add Reference dialog box*

9. Type the following code:

```
using System;
using Math;

namespace MathClient
{
  /// <summary>
  /// Summary description for Class1.
  /// </summary>
  class Class1
  {
     /// <summary>
    /// The main entry point for the application.
    /// </summary>
    [STAThread]
    static void Main(string[] args)
    {
      MathComp obj=new MathComp();
      long lRes=obj.Add(10,20);
      obj.Extra=false;
      Console.Write(lRes);
      return;
    }
  }
}
```

Compile the project and see the output. You can expand on this project further to create a better math application that performs more functions. These steps explain to you the mechanism to create a DLL and access it.

# Messaging

The `System.Messaging` namespace provides classes that allow you to connect to, monitor, and administer message queues on the network and send or receive messages. Before I explain the `System.Messaging` namespace, it is critical to understand message queuing and certain terms related to messaging.

## Benefits of Message Queues

Messaging also provides a powerful and flexible mechanism for interprocess communication between components of a server-based application. The advantages provided by messaging are:

- **Robustness.** Messages are less affected by component failures than direct calls between components, as messages are stored in queues until processed.
- **Message prioritization.** Important messages are received before less important ones. Therefore, you can guarantee adequate response time for critical applications.
- **Offline capabilities.** Messages can be sent to temporary queues and remain there until they are delivered successfully. Moreover, users can continue to perform operations when access to the queue is unavailable. Additional operations can proceed as if the message has already been processed, because the message delivery is guaranteed when the network connection is restored.
- **Transactional messaging.** Several messages can be coupled into a single transaction, ensuring that the messages are delivered in sequence and are successfully retrieved from their destination queue. If any errors occur, the entire transaction is cancelled.
- **Security.** The message queuing technology on which the `MessageQueue` component is based uses Windows security to provide secure access control, provide auditing, and encrypt and authenticate the messages your component sends and receives.

## Limitations

In order to develop `MessageQueue` components your system must meet the following requirements:

- To see queue information in `Server Explorer` or to access queues programmatically, you must install message queuing on your client computer.
- Message queuing can be run in either a domain or a workgroup environment. In the context of message queuing, a domain environment

includes domain controllers that provide a directory service such as *active directory*, and a workgroup environment is any environment that does not provide such a directory service.

## Key Messaging Terms

Before we proceed further, I would like to explain certain key terms.

A *message* is a unit of data sent from one computer to another. A message can be very simple, consisting of just a string of text, or more complex, possibly involving embedded objects or pictures.

Messages are transmitted to queues. A *message queue* is a temporary storage area that holds messages while they are in transit. The message queue manager acts as the intermediary in transmitting a message from its source to its destination. The main purpose of a queue is to provide routing and guarantee the delivery of the message. In case the recipient is not available when a message is sent, the queue holds the message until it can be successfully delivered.

*Message queuing*, Microsoft's messaging technology, provides messaging and message queue facilities for any applications that have Microsoft Windows installed regardless of whether they are on the same network or whether they are online at the same time.

A *message queuing network* is a set of computers that are enabled to send messages back and forth to one another. Different computers in the network play different roles to ensure that messaging proceeds smoothly. Some computers provide information to determine how messages are sent, some hold information about the entire network, while others simply send and receive messages.

During message queuing setup, an administrator makes decisions about which servers can communicate with each other and sets up special roles for specific servers. The computers that make up this message queuing network are called *sites*, and they are connected to one another by site links. Each site link has an associated cost, determined by the administrator, that indicates how quickly messages can be passed across it.

The message queuing administrator also sets up one or more computers in the network that act as *routing servers.* A routing server makes decisions about how a message is delivered by looking at the cost of various site links and determining the quickest and most efficient way to deliver the message across multiple sites.

## Types of Message Queues

There are two main categories of queues, queues created by users and system queues.

### User-Generated Queues

Queues created by users can be any of the following:

*Public queues* are those that are replicated throughout the message network and can potentially be accessed by all of the computers connected by the network.

*Private queues* are queues that are not published across the entire network. They are available only on the local computer that contains them. They can be accessed only by applications that know the full path name of the queue.

*Administration queues* are queues that contain messages acknowledging the delivery of messages sent within a given message queuing network. You specify the administration queue you want your `MessageQueue` components to use.

*Response queues* contain response messages that are returned to the sender application when the message is received by the destination application. You specify the response queue you want your `MessageQueue` components to use.

### System Queues

System queues generally fall in one of the following categories:

*Journal queues* optionally store copies of messages that you send and copies of messages removed from a queue. A single journal queue on each message queuing client stores copies of messages sent from that computer. On the server, a separate journal queue is created for each individual queue. This journal tracks messages removed from that queue.

*Dead-letter queues* store copies of undeliverable or expired messages. If the message that expired or was undeliverable was a transactional message, it is stored in a special kind of dead-letter queue called a *transaction dead-letter queue.* Dead letters are stored on the computer on which the message expired.

*Report queues* contain messages that indicate the route a message took to its destination and can contain test messages. There can be only one report queue per computer.

*Private system queues* are a series of private queues that store administrative and notification messages that the system needs to process messaging actions.

Most of the work you do in your applications will involve accessing public queues and their messages. However, you will most likely use several different kinds of the system queues in your day-to-day operations, depending on your application's need for journal recording, acknowledgement, and other special processing.

### Synchronous and Asynchronous Communication

Messages are sent to and received from a queue as separate processes. Therefore, queue communication is inherently asynchronous. You can also receive messages asynchronously by invoking the `BeginReceive` method and then move on to perform other tasks without waiting for a reply. However, synchronous communication is different from this.

In synchronous communication, the sender of a request waits for a response from the receiver before performing other tasks. The amount of time that the sender must wait depends on the amount of time it takes for the receiver to process the request and send a response.

## `System.Messaging` Namespace

As you know, message queuing is a technology that allows applications running at different times to communicate across heterogeneous networks and systems. Applications send, receive, or read messages from queues. The `MessageQueue` class is a wrapper around message queuing. There are different versions for different operating environments. `System.Messaging` namespace provides classes that allow you to connect to, monitor, and administer message queues on the network and send, receive, or read messages.

Message queuing enables developers to build applications that communicate with other programs quickly in a simple and reliable manner. Messaging ensures guaranteed messages delivery and a fail-proof way to carry out your business processes. For example, suppose you have a retail point-of-sale application that must run 24 hours a day, seven days a week. If the database system behind the application goes down, your sales staff might need to start taking orders manually. Using message queuing, you can set up the system so that the orders that cannot be processed during the downtime are automatically put into a queue and processed as soon as the database comes back up.

You can use an instance of the MessageQueue component to establish connection with existing message queues, examine their contents, and send and receive messages. You can also use Server Explorer of Visual Studio .NET to view message queues on any server to which you have access. You can also add a queue from Server Explorer to your component's designer to automatically create a component that is configured to interact with the queue.

## MessageQueue Class

MessageQueue class provides members for reading and writing message to the queue. The Send method enables your application to write messages to the queue. This method is overloaded and enables you to specify whether to send your message using a message or any other managed object, including application-specific classes.

The Receive, ReceiveById, and ReceiveByCorrelationId methods provide functionality for reading messages from a queue. These methods support transactional queue processing. These methods also provide overloads with timeout parameters that enable processing to continue if the queue is empty. Because these methods are examples of synchronous processing, they interrupt the current thread until a message is available, unless you specify a timeout.

The Peek method is similar to the Receive method, but it does not cause a message to be removed from the queue when it is read. Because the Peek method does not change the queue contents, there are no overloads to support transactional processing.

The BeginPeek, EndPeek, BeginReceive, and EndReceive methods provide ways to asynchronously read messages from the queue. They do not interrupt the current thread while waiting for a message to arrive in the queue.

Other methods of the MessageQueue class provide functionality for retrieving lists of queues by specified criteria and determining if specific queues exist.

In addition, MessageQueue class provides methods for creating and deleting message queues, for setting ACL-based access rights, and for working with the connection cache.

The Message class provides detailed control over the information you send to a queue and is the object used when receiving or peeking messages from a queue.

Besides the message body, the properties of the `Message` class include acknowledgment settings, format selection, identification, authentication and encryption information, timestamps, and transaction data.

Table 34-1 lists the classes in the `System.Messaging` namespace hierarchy.

**Table 34-1 `System.Messaging` Namespace Hierarchy**

| Class | Description |
|---|---|
| AccessControlEntry | Specifies access rights for a user or a computer to perform application-specific implementations of common tasks. |
| AccessControlList | Contains a list of access control entries, specifying access rights for one or more trustees. |
| ActiveXMessageFormatter | Serializes or deserializes primitive data types and other objects to or from the body of a message. |
| BinaryMessageFormatter | Serializes or deserializes an object, or a group of connected objects, to or from the body of a message, using a binary format. |
| DefaultPropertiesToSend | Specifies the default property values that will be used when sending objects other than Message instances to a message queue. |
| Message | Provides access to the properties needed to define a message queuing message. |
| MessageEnumerator | Provides a forward-only cursor to enumerate through messages in a message queue. |
| MessagePropertyFilter | Controls and selects the properties that are retrieved when peeking or receiving messages from a message queue. |
| MessageQueue | Provides access to a queue on a message queuing server. |
| MessageQueueAccessControlEntry | Specifies access rights for a user or a computer to perform message queuing tasks. |
| MessageQueueCriteria | Filters message queues when performing a query. |

**Table 34-1 `System.Messaging` Namespace Hierarchy *(continued)***

| Class | Description |
|---|---|
| MessageQueueEnumerator | Provides a forward-only cursor to enumerate through messages in a message queue. |
| MessageQueueException | The exception that is thrown if a Microsoft message queuing internal error occurs. |
| MessageQueueInstaller | Allows you to install and configure a queue that your application needs in order to run. |
| MessageQueuePermission | Allows control of code access permissions for messaging. |
| MessageQueuePermissionAttribute | Allows declarative `MessageQueue` permission checks. |
| MessageQueuePermissionEntry | Defines the smallest unit of a code access security permission set for messaging. |
| MessageQueuePermissionEntryCollection | Contains a strongly typed collection of `MessageQueuePermissionEntry` objects. |
| MessageQueueTransaction | Provides a message queuing internal transaction. |
| MessagingDescriptionAttribute | Specifies a description for a property or event. |
| PeekCompletedEventArgs | Provides data for the `PeekCompleted` event. When your asynchronous peek operation calls an event handler, an instance of this class is passed to the handler. |
| ReceiveCompletedEventArgs | Provides data for `ReceiveCompleted` event. |
| Trustee | Specifies a user account, group account, or logon session to which an access control entry applies. |
| XmlMessageFormatter | Serializes and deserializes objects to or from the body of a message, using the XML format. |

### *Creating a Queue*

The following steps explain how to create a message queue on your computer using the `MessageQueue` component. Using the `MessageQueue` component, you can send messages and retrieve them from the queue.

1. On the File menu, point to New, and then click Project.
2. In the New Project dialog box, choose Visual C# in the left pane, and Windows Application from the Template: pane.
3. Type the name of the application in the Name: text box and the desired location in the Location: text box.
4. Click the OK button.
5. Open Server Explorer.
6. Expand the Servers node.
7. Expand the node for your local server. The node on your local computer is identified by the computer name.
8. Expand the Message Queues node.
9. Right-click Private Queues and select Create Queue from the shortcut menu.
10. Enter a queue name, such as `Trial`. Do not check Make Transactional.

    A new private queue is created and appears in Server Explorer.
11. Drag the Trial queue from the Server Explorer onto your form. A new MessageQueue component is added to the project.

The MessageQueue component is used to programmatically access the messages contained in the Trial queue created earlier.

## Summary

COM is a specification and implementation framework pioneered by Microsoft that allows you to create binary compatible software components. COM allows you to concentrate on developing your application without bothering about the internals of the components. COM architecture provides various threading models, which enables you to create components that are inherently thread savvy.

MTS is an add-on to Windows NT that allows developers to build and run their components as middle tier. COM+ is the new run time in Windows 2000 that unifies the COM and MTS programming models. COM+ components support attribute programming, distributed transactions, synchronization, thread pooling and other features supported by the COM model. In addition, COM+ provides new features such as neutral apartment threading, queued components, role-based security, JIT activation, automatic transactions, and a new COM+ event model.

C# provides full support for COM+ services. Through COM interoperability, a C# program can call methods of any COM component. The process making this happen involves early and late binding. A .NET component may also be exposed as a COM component. The C# component does not need anything special to be written in the code. However, you can use type library importer utility to register a C# component and create a type library.

Message queuing is a technology that allows applications running at different times to communicate across heterogeneous networks and systems. Applications send, receive, or read messages from queues. The `System.Messaging` namespace provides classes that allow you to connect to, monitor, and administer message queues on the network and send or receive messages. The `MessageQueue` class is a wrapper around message queuing. The `MessageQueue` class provides members for reading and writing messages to the queue.

Messages are sent to and received from a queue as separate processes. Therefore, queue communication is inherently asynchronous. In synchronous communication, the sender of a request waits for a response from the receiver before performing other tasks.

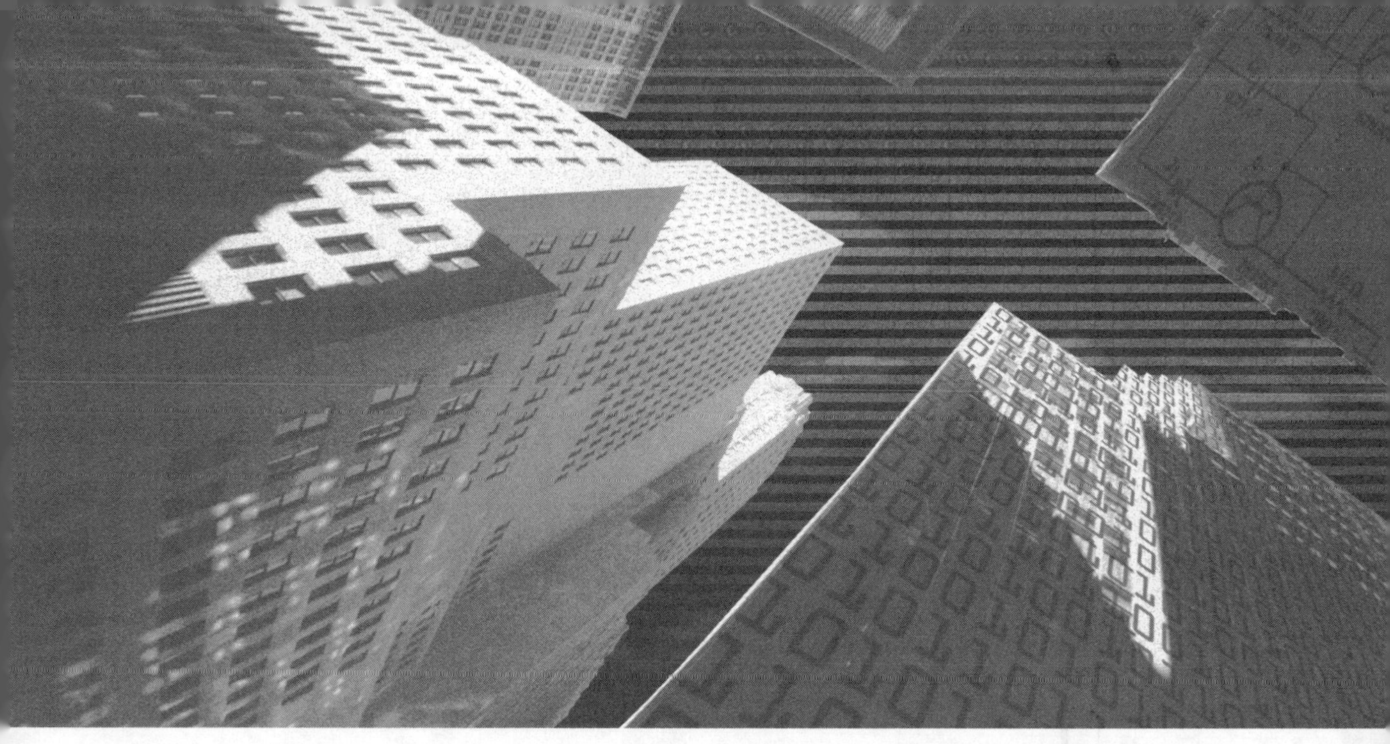

# PART X

## Appendixes

# Appendix A

## Unsafe Code

In this chapter, you will learn about the basics of pointers. You will learn to declare and implement pointers. In addition, you will learn about using pointers with managed code. Finally, you will learn to compile unsafe code.

## Pointers

*Pointers* are not a new concept for C and C++ programmers. A pointer is a variable similar to a reference and points to an address in memory. A pointer stores the actual memory address and makes it available to you.

Pointers are extensively used in C and C++ for dynamic allocation of memory and to directly access the memory. However, if pointers are not used properly, they may lead to memory corruption. To avoid such situations, C# hides most of the memory management operations from the end user. However, there may be cases where you need to have direct access to memory. C# allows you to use pointers in such cases. The following list contains some of the cases where you need to access memory addresses by using pointers.

- You may be required to use pointers when you are working with existing code written in C or C++ that uses pointers.
- You may require pointers to create applications with high performance requirements.
- Pointers allow you to work with the underlying operating system by providing an interface between the program code and the operating system.
- When you are debugging an application, you may be required to have direct access to a particular memory location. In addition to various debugging options provided by Visual Studio .NET, pointers help you in this case by allowing you to access the data stored at the specified memory location.
- Pointers also provide you with an interface to work with advanced COM (*Component Object Model*) applications containing structures that use pointers.

As discussed earlier, if pointers are not used effectively, they can be a problem to programmers. The following list contains some of the problems faced by programmers while using pointers.

- Working with pointers requires extensive and high-level programming. If you are not careful while programming with pointers, you may introduce errors in your code, which may even result in the program crashing.
- When a pointer is no longer used by any program, you need to deallocate its memory. If you forget to deallocate the memory associated with the pointer, it may lead to unpredictable problems in your code. Debugging these problems can be time-consuming and tedious.
- Pointers make the address of a memory location transparent to the users. Therefore, it becomes possible for users to manipulate the memory addresses. This may introduce errors in your code by making it unsafe to use.
- While writing a program that uses pointers, you may make your pointer point to a wrong memory location. Therefore, when your program code accesses an incorrect memory location, it may produce errors or may even result in the program crashing.
- The major problem with using pointers in the program code used to be because of the garbage collection system of CLR (*common language runtime*). The garbage collection system operates in the background to deallocate memory to objects that are no longer used by any program. The garbage collection system also causes the movement of objects within memory. Each time an object is moved, C# updates its reference. However, there is no mechanism by which the programmer is informed about the new memory location of the object. This may cause your pointer to point to a different memory location, thereby introducing errors in the program. As a solution to this problem, the .NET Framework introduced the concept of unsafe code. You will learn about unsafe code later in this appendix.

In spite of these problems, programmers have been extensively using pointers in C and C++. This is mainly because pointers offer several advantages to programmers, thereby helping them to write complex applications. Some of the advantages of using pointers in your code include backward compatibility with code written in C and C++. Pointers also help you to access and manipulate data easily and efficiently, thereby increasing the performance of your application.

Because of the advantages of pointers, C# has retained pointers in some capacity. However, to prevent memory corruption in C#, pointers are used only within blocks of code for which the pointer is required. This restricts the programmer to using pointers only when they are required and marked. You can use the `unsafe` keyword to mark the block of code in which you need to declare a pointer. A class, method, struct, constructor, or block of code within a method can be marked as unsafe. However, you cannot mark a static constructor as unsafe.

When you mark code as unsafe, you inform the compiler that the program is not sure whether the code is safe to execute. Therefore, to execute code marked as unsafe, you need to give full trust to the program code. As discussed earlier, the major problem that you face while working with pointers is because of the garbage collection system of CLR. Therefore, to solve this problem, C# runs the code marked as unsafe outside the garbage collection system. This allows you to perform memory management processes directly. Therefore, you can only declare a pointer in the set of statements marked as unsafe.

## Declaring Pointers

The following syntax shows how to declare a pointer. An asterisk (*) is used to declare a pointer.

```
unsafe class Class1
{
        int *pointer1;
}
```

The preceding code marks the class `Class1` as unsafe. The pointer named `pointer1` is declared in this class. You can also mark a variable as unsafe. However, you can only do this in the block of code that is marked unsafe. After you mark code as unsafe, you need to inform the compiler that your program contains unsafe code. This will allow you to declare pointers in the unsafe code. To inform the compiler about the presence of unsafe code, you use the flag `unsafe` with the compile command. You will learn about the compilation of unsafe code later in this appendix.

C# allows you to declare more than one pointer of the same data type in a single command. In this case, you will use only one asterisk sign, although in C++, you were required to have different asterisk for each pointer declaration. It is an exception in the syntax of a pointer declaration statement.

```
int *pointer1, pointer2;
```

This code will give an error in C++. To declare two pointers in C++, you use the following syntax:

```
int *pointer1, *pointer2;
```

After a pointer is declared, you can use it like any other variable used in the code. However, to use a pointer, you need to initialize the pointer with the address in the memory. Similar to variables, you cannot use a pointer without initializing it. A pointer can also be initialized to a null value.

After initializing a pointer, you can use it with any program code. All programs in C# are classified as managed or unmanaged code. The following section discusses the types of code in detail.

## Types of Code

The code in C# is classified as managed or unmanaged code based on the level of control that CLR has over the code.

### Managed Code

*Managed code* contains some information about the code. This information contained in managed code is called *metadata*. Managed code in the .NET Framework is controlled by CLR, which uses metadata to provide safe execution of the program code. CLR also helps in memory management, security, and interoperability of the code with other languages. In addition to providing safe execution of the program, managed code aims at targeting the CLR services. These CLR services include locating and loading classes and interoperating with the existing DLL (*dynamic link library*) code and COM objects. By default, all code in C# is managed code.

### Unmanaged Code

Code that is marked with the `unsafe` keyword is called *unmanaged code*. The unmanaged code does not provide any information about the code. In other words, unmanaged code does not provide CLR with metadata. CLR is not sure of the safe execution of unmanaged code, and therefore, unmanaged code is considered to be unsafe. You can only run unsafe code in a fully trusted environment. Because of the problems that you face while working with pointers, C# allows you to use pointers in unsafe code.

After declaring a pointer in unsafe code, you need to implement pointers.

## Implementing Pointers

A pointer that you declare must be of the type `pointer`. You can declare a `pointer` type by using the asterisk (*) sign after the `void` keyword or by declaring the pointer as an `unmanaged-type`. For example:

```
void *
```

or

```
unmanaged-type *
```

In the preceding syntax, `void` is the data type of the variable to which the pointer points. This data type is called the *reference type*. However, an `unmanaged-type` can be of any data type other than the reference type. The `unmanaged-type` data types include all `variable` types, `enum`, `pointer`, or `struct`.

While working with pointer types, you need to remember the following guidelines:

- The void type pointer points to any variable type that is not known to the user. Therefore, you cannot use the `indirection operator` with the void type pointer. In addition, you cannot perform any arithmetic operation on the void pointer. However, you can type cast the void pointer to any other pointer type and vice versa. You will learn about the indirection operator and pointer arithmetic later in this appendix.
- Because pointers are of `unmanaged-type`, they are not managed by garbage collector. Therefore, you cannot declare a pointer pointing to a `reference type`.
- C# does not allow a pointer to inherit from an object. In addition, you cannot type cast a pointer type to an object and vice versa. This implies that you can neither box nor unbox a pointer. However, if you convert a pointer to a value type, you can box this value type variable.

As you have seen, pointers are used with unmanaged code. However, in some cases, C# also allows you to use pointers with managed code. The following section discusses the use of pointers with managed code in detail.

## Using Pointers with Managed Code

The main problem of using pointers with managed code is that the garbage collection system of CLR controls the execution of the managed code. The garbage collection system moves the objects internally in the memory. If you use pointers in managed code, the garbage collector does not automatically change the address stored in the pointer. This is because the garbage collector does not have control over pointers. This may cause problems with your code, as the pointer points to incorrect memory locations.

To solve this problem, C# allows you to prevent CLR from moving a specified object in the memory. To do this, you use the `fixed` statement. To understand the `fixed` statement, look at its syntax.

```
fixed (pointer declaration statement)
```

Here, the `fixed` keyword is used to pin the position of the managed object. The pointer declaration statement declares and initializes a pointer with the address of the managed object. Until the C# compiler finishes the compilation of the program code, the garbage collection system is not allowed to move the object that is marked with the `fixed` keyword.

Having seen the use of pointers in managed and unmanaged code, you will learn about the operators that you can use to work with pointers.

## Working with Pointers

In addition to the operators used with variables, C# supports some more operators to be used with pointers.

- **`indirection operator.`** The `indirection operator` is used to retrieve the content stored at the memory address referred by the pointer. In other words, the `indirection operator` converts a pointer to a variable of the `value type`. You can convert a pointer to almost every variable data type or a struct. However, you cannot convert a pointer to a class or an array. This operator is denoted by an asterisk (`*`) sign, and it is also called a `dereference operator`.

- **`address operator`.** The `address operator` is used to retrieve the address of the memory location referred by the pointer. In other words, the `address operator` converts the variable of the `value type` to a pointer. This operator is denoted by the ampersand (`&`) sign.
- **`sizeof operator`.** The `sizeof operator` is used with the `unmanaged-type` pointer to find out the size of the pointer. While allocating memory to the pointer, you may need to know the size of the pointer. The return type of the `sizeof operator` is `integer`, and it can be used to find the size of both default and user-defined unmanaged pointers.
- **`stackalloc operator`.** The `stackalloc operator` is used to allocate memory from the call stack. The `stackalloc operator` has the following syntax:

  ```
  stackalloc <data type>[expression]
  ```

  Here, `data type` is the type of variable that you can store at the new memory location, and `expression` specifies the number of memory locations to be allocated.
- **`->` operator.** The `-> operator` is used to access the struct members by using a pointer. You can use the `-> operator` as follows:

  ```
  <expression> -> <identifier>
  ```

  In the preceding syntax, the `expression` is any unmanaged-type expression, and `identifier` is the struct to which the pointer points.
- **`[]` operator.** The `[] operator` is used to access an element of the pointer. The syntax of the `[] operator` is:

  ```
  <data type>[] <identifier>
  ```

  Here, the `data type` is the type of the pointer, and `identifier` specifies the name of the pointer whose elements are to be accessed.

Working with pointers also involves performing operations on pointers. The following section discusses the pointer arithmetic.

## Pointer Arithmetic

Pointer arithmetic is very similar to the operations performed with variables. However, you cannot perform operations on a `void` type pointer. Similar to variables, you can use the increment (+) and the decrement (-) operators to add and subtract values from a pointer, respectively. For example, to add an integer value to a pointer, you use the following statement:

```
Pointer1 + 20;
```

Because the size of an integer is 4 bytes, the preceding statement adds 80 bytes to the pointer named Pointer1. However, to increment the value of a pointer by 1 byte, you can add a byte or an sbyte to a pointer.

Similarly, you can use the ++, --, and the comparison operators, such as <, >, ==, !=, <=, and >=, to perform operations on pointers.

In addition to performing operations on pointers, you can also type cast pointers.

## *Type Casting Pointers*

As discussed earlier, you can type cast a pointer type to a variable type and vice versa. Pointers are used to store memory addresses, which are integer values. Therefore, it is possible to explicitly convert a pointer to an integer type. You need to convert a pointer to an integer type to display the pointer. The Console.WriteLine method does not take a pointer as a parameter. However, if you convert a pointer to an integer variable, you can pass it as a parameter to the Console.WriteLine method. To know more about pointer type casting, consider the following example:

```
int Integer = 20;
int *Pointer1;
Pointer1 = &Integer;
Console.WriteLine ("The value of Pointer1 is" + (int) Pointer1);
```

Here, a pointer named Pointer1 is declared and initialized with the address of an integer variable named Integer. To display the value of Pointer1, the pointer is type casted to an integer type by using the cast operator.

Because integer data type has a size of 4 bytes, you cannot use it in 64-bit systems. If you type cast a pointer to an integer value, it may result in an overflow condition. Therefore, it is advisable to type cast a pointer to a ulong type value.

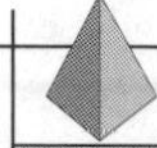

**TIP**

You cannot use the `checked` keyword to track overflow conditions while working with pointers.

C# also allows you to type cast between different `pointer` types. Consider the following example:

```
int Integer = 20;
int *Pointer1;
Pointer1 = &Integer;
sbyte *Pointer2 = (sbyte*) Pointer1;
```

You can only explicitly convert between `pointer` types. C# does not allow an implicit pointer type conversion.

In this chapter, you learned about pointers and the use of pointers in your program code. After writing code that contains a pointer, you need to compile the code. Compilation of code containing pointers is slightly different from the compilation of an ordinary code.

## Compiling Unsafe Code

As discussed earlier, you need to inform the compiler that the code to be executed is marked as unsafe. If you are compiling the program code from the command line, you can add the `unsafe` flag with the compile command, as shown:

```
csc /unsafe file1.cs
```

The preceding statement includes the `unsafe` flag with the `csc` command to inform the compiler that the file named `file1.cs` is marked as unsafe.

You can also compile the unsafe code by setting the Allow unsafe code blocks property to `True` in Visual Studio .NET. To do this, you can do the following steps:

1. Right-click on the project name in the Solution Explorer window.
2. Click on the Properties option in the drop-down list.

   The Property Pages page is displayed.

3. In the right pane, select the Configuration Properties option.
4. Change the value of Allow unsafe code blocks property in the Build option to `True`.

   The default value of this property is `False`.
5. Click on the OK button to close the Property Pages page.

Figure A-1 shows the Allow unsafe code blocks option.

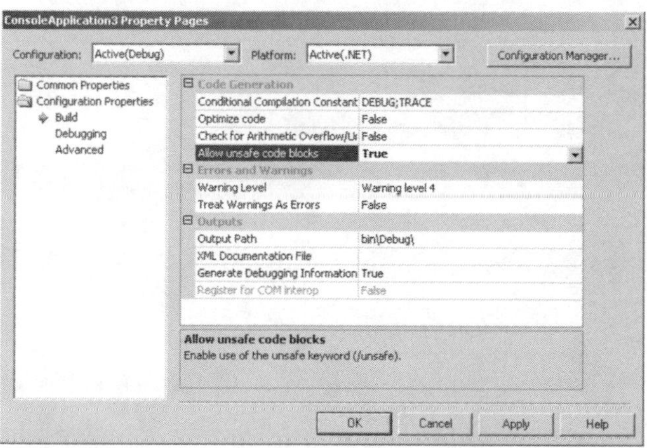


**FIGURE A-1** *Allow unsafe code blocks option*

## Summary

In this chapter, you learned about pointers. A pointer is a variable similar to a reference and points to an address in memory. A pointer stores the actual memory address and makes it available to you. Pointers are extensively used in C and C++ for dynamic allocation of memory and to directly access the memory. Working with pointers requires extensive programming. Therefore, C# allows you to use pointers only within blocks of code for which the pointer is required. You can use the `unsafe` keyword to mark the block of code in which you need to declare a pointer.

Then you learned about the classification of code in C#. All program code in C# is classified as managed or unmanaged code. Managed code contains some information about the code. This information contained in the managed code is called metadata. The code that is marked with the `unsafe` keyword is called unmanaged code. The unmanaged code does not contain metadata.

Next, you learned about the operators used with pointers. These operators include the `indirection operator`, the `address operator`, the `sizeof operator`, the `stackalloc operator`, the `->` `operator`, and the `[]` `operator`. Finally, you learned about the commands used to compile the code that uses pointers.

# Appendix B

## Introduction to Visual Basic .NET

In this appendix, you will learn about the languages of Visual Studio .NET. In addition, you will learn in detail about Visual Basic .NET as an object-oriented programming language. The appendix will also cover the different features of an object-oriented programming language. In addition, you will learn about the components of Visual Basic. NET.

Based on your knowledge of Visual Basic .NET, you will learn to create a simple Visual Basic .NET Windows application and compare a Visual Basic .NET application with a Visual C# .NET application.

## Introduction to the Languages of Visual Studio .NET

The latest version of Visual Studio is Visual Studio .NET, which is based on the .NET Framework. The tools and languages provided by Visual Studio .NET enable you to build applications such as Web-based applications, desktop applications, and mobile applications. In addition, you can create Web services in Visual Studio .NET.

The following programming languages are included in Visual Studio .NET:

- Visual C# .NET
- Visual Basic .NET
- Visual C++ .NET

Visual Studio .NET also supports technologies such as ASP.NET. These technologies enable you to develop and deploy various applications. Visual Studio .NET also includes the MSDN Library, which contains complete documentation on various applications and development tools.

The IDE (*Integrated Development Environment*) of Visual Studio .NET helps you to create applications in various .NET languages. Visual Studio .NET allows the IDE to share tools and create applications in multiple languages.

Visual Studio .NET includes various advanced features compared to the earlier versions of Visual Studio. The following sections discuss the languages included in Visual Studio .NET.

## Visual C# .NET

Visual C# .NET is a new language provided by Visual Studio .NET. Visual C# .NET is an object-oriented language based on languages such as C and C++. You can create applications for the .NET Framework by using Visual C# .NET. Visual C# .NET supports CLR (*common language runtime*). Code written in Visual C# .NET is managed code. Various templates, designers, and wizards, which help you create applications in Visual C# .NET, are provided by IDE. You have learned about Visual C# .NET throughout this book. The next sections will look at the other languages provided by Visual Studio .NET.

## Visual Basic .NET

The latest version of Visual Basic, which is Visual Basic .NET, includes several new features. Unlike the earlier versions of Visual Basic, Visual Basic .NET supports inheritance. Version 4 and Version 6 of Visual Basic supported interfaces but not implementation inheritance. Visual Basic .NET supports both implementation inheritance and interfaces. Overloading is another new feature of Visual Basic .NET, which I will discuss later in this appendix.

Visual Basic .NET also supports multithreading, which allows you to create multithreaded and scalable applications. Visual Basic .NET can also be used with CLS (*common language specification*) and supports structured exception handling.

**COMMON LANGUAGE SPECIFICATION**

A set of rules and constructs supported by the CLR is known as CLS. Visual Basic .NET supports CLS. CLS also shares the objects, classes, or components created in Visual Basic .NET with any other language that supports CLS.

Regardless of the language used in creating the application, CLS ensures that there is interoperability between the different applications. You can derive a class that is based on a class written in Visual C# .NET while you work in Visual Basic .NET, where the data types and variables of the class that is derived matches the base class.

## Visual C++ .NET

The enhanced version of Visual C++ is Visual C++ .NET. Features such as support for managed extensions and attributes are included in Visual C++ .NET.

You can create applications for the .NET Framework by using a set of language extensions of C++ that are included in managed extensions. You can also convert the components that are already present in C++ into components that support the .NET Framework by using managed extensions. Therefore, using managed extensions, the existing code can be reused, saving both time and effort. You can also use managed extensions to merge both unmanaged and managed C++ code in an application.

Attributes that enable you to extend the functionality of a language and simplify the creation of COM components are supported by Visual C++ .NET. You can also apply classes, data members, or member functions to attributes.

## Overview of Visual Basic .NET

The complete framework of Visual Basic .NET is based on the .NET Framework. Visual Basic .NET inherits the various features of the .NET Framework along with features of the earlier versions of Visual Basic. In this section, you will learn about the features of Visual Basic .NET as compared to the features in the earlier versions of Visual Basic.

As discussed earlier, Visual Basic .NET supports implementation inheritance as compared to the earlier versions of Visual Basic that supported interface inheritance. In other words, you can implement only interfaces with the earlier versions of Visual Basic. All the methods of the interface need to be implemented when you implement an interface in Visual Basic 6.0. In addition, the code has to be rewritten each time you implement the interface.

Visual Basic .NET, on the other hand, supports implementation inheritance. This implies that while applications are created in Visual Basic .NET, a class can also be derived from another class, which is known as the *base class*. The methods and properties of the base class are inherited by the derived class. In the derived class, you can either use or override the code that already exists in the base class. Therefore, code can be reused with the help of implementation inheritance. Although multiple interfaces can be implemented in a class in Visual Basic .NET, the class can inherit from only one class.

Visual Basic .NET also provides constructors and procedures, where constructors are used to initialize objects. The `Sub New` procedure replaces the `Class_Initialize` event in Visual Basic .NET. The `Sub New` procedure is executed when an object of the class is created, unlike the `Class_Initialize` event that is available in the earlier versions of Visual Basic. The first procedure to be executed in a class is the `Sub New` procedure. Instead of the `Class_Terminate` event, the `Sub Finalize` procedure is available in Visual Basic .NET. When an object is destroyed, the `Sub`

`Finalize` procedure is automatically called to complete the tasks that remain incomplete. In addition, the `Sub Finalize` procedure can only be called from the class to which it belongs or from the classes from which it is derived.

Visual Basic .NET has another additional feature known as garbage collection. Allocated resources such as objects and variables are monitored by the .NET Framework. In addition, the destroying objects, which are no longer in use, automatically release memory for reusing the objects in the .NET Framework. When an object is set to `Nothing`, in Visual Basic 6.0, it is destroyed automatically, whereas in Visual Basic .NET, it continues to occupy space even when it is set to `Nothing`. In Visual Basic .NET, the garbage collector checks the objects that are not currently used by the applications. The garbage collector releases the memory occupied by the object when any object is found marked for garbage collection.

The `GC` class, the `Sub Finalize` procedure, and the `IDisposable` interface are used to perform garbage selection operations in the .NET Framework. The `System` namespace contains the `GC` class that provides various methods that enable you to control the system garbage collector. In the .NET Framework, a member of the `Object` class, the `Sub Finalize` procedure, acts as a destructor. You can also override this procedure in your applications. However, the `Sub Finalize` procedure is not executed when the application is executed. The `Sub Finalize` procedure is called by the `GC` class to release the memory that is occupied by a destroyed object. However, an explicit way of managing resources in the form of the `IDisposable` interface is provided by the .NET Framework. The `Dispose()` method is included in the `IDisposable` interface. After the `IDisposable` interface is implemented, the `Dispose()` method can be overridden in the applications. You can release resources and database connections in the `Dispose()` method.

Overloading is a feature that enables you to define several procedures with the same name, where each procedure has a different set of arguments. Visual Basic .NET supports this feature of overloading as compared to the earlier versions of Visual Basic. You can use overloading for constructors and properties in a class along with the procedures. The `Overloads` keyword is used for overloading procedures.

Consider a scenario in which a procedure needs to be created to display the address of an employee. The address of the employee should be viewed based on either the employee name or the employee code, which can be done by using the overload feature. You need to create two procedures with the same name but different arguments. The employee name is accepted as the argument by the first procedure, and the employee code is accepted as the argument by the second.

The .NET Framework class library is organized into namespaces. A namespace is referred to as a collection of classes. You can logically group classes within an assembly by using namespaces. In addition to Visual Basic .NET, these namespaces are available in all the .NET languages.

In Visual Basic .NET, you use the `Imports` statement to access the classes in namespaces. Consider an example: To use a button control as defined in the `System.Windows.Forms` namespace, you include the statement mentioned here in the beginning of the program.

```
Imports System.Windows.Forms
```

After the `Imports` statement has been added, a new button can be created using the following code:

```
Dim button1 as Button
```

If you do not include the `Imports` statement in the program, the full reference path of the class to create a button needs to be used. If the `Imports` statement is not used, then the following code can be used for creating a button:

```
Dim button1 as System.Windows.Forms.Button
```

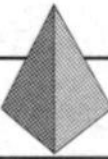

**TIP**

In addition to using the namespaces already available in Visual Basic .NET, you can create your own namespaces. In the next appendix, you will learn how to create a namespace.

As already discussed, Visual Basic .NET also supports multithreading. A multithreaded application can simultaneously handle multiple tasks. Multithreading can also be used to decrease the time taken by an application to respond to user interaction. You need to ensure that a separate thread in the application handles user interaction so that the time taken by an application to respond to user interaction is decreased.

Visual Basic .NET enables you to detect and remove errors at run time by supporting structured exception handling. In Visual Basic .NET, you can use `Try…Catch…Finally` statements to create exception handlers. By using `Try…Catch…Finally` statements, you can create strong and efficient exception handlers to improve the performance of the application.

You have considered the new and added features of Visual Basic .NET. The following sections discuss the features of an object-oriented programming language.

# Features of an Object-Oriented Programming Language

In an object-oriented programming language, objects serve as the building blocks of a programming language, displaying a unique identity and behavior. A chair, a table, and a book are examples of objects that are used every day. An *object* in a programming language is defined as an instance of a class. Applications created in an object-oriented programming language are made up of objects.

An object is qualified as an object-oriented programming language if the following features are supported:

- Abstraction
- Encapsulation
- Inheritance
- Polymorphism

The next sections will consider each of the features mentioned here in detail.

## Abstraction

Before you buy a television set, you consider its size, durability, and features. As a buyer, you may not be interested in knowing about the machinery of the television set. The main features of the television set are more likely to be your primary concern. This is known as *abstraction.* In a programming language, abstraction helps you focus mainly on the essential aspects of an object. The nonessential aspects are normally overlooked.

Visual Basic .NET, like any other programming language, provides abstraction through classes and objects. Attributes and behavior shared by similar objects are defined as *class*. The instance of the class is an *object*. Each object consists of characteristics and attributes that are the properties of the object. In addition, a set of actions can be performed by each object. The actions that are performed are known as *methods*. In Visual Basic .NET, you can specify the various properties and methods that are used for objects while creating classes. Abstraction is mainly used to reduce the complexity of an object by exposing only the essential features and methods of an object. Additionally, abstraction helps you generalize an object as a data type. By declaring classes, you can also generalize objects as data types.

## Encapsulation

Information hiding or *encapsulation* means that the nonessential details of an object are hidden. Consider an example: When you switch your television on, it starts functioning. Needless to say that the internal functioning process remains hidden. In other words, the functioning of the television is hidden or encapsulated.

The method of implementing abstraction is encapsulation. As mentioned earlier, abstraction refers mainly to concentrating on the necessary and essential details of an object while ignoring the unnecessary and nonessential ones. Encapsulation achieves this.

The internal implementation of the classes is hidden from the user by encapsulation. Therefore, encapsulation is displaying only the properties and methods of an object. It helps the developers in hiding the complexity of an object and also uses different implementations of the same object.

## Inheritance

The earlier versions of Visual Basic supported interface inheritance but not implementation inheritance. However, Visual Basic .NET supports both implementation inheritance and interface inheritance.

Implementation inheritance means that a class is derived from an existing class. The derived class is called *subclass*, and the class from which it is derived is called *base class*.

**NOTE**

The classes that are created in Visual Basic .NET are derived from the `Object` class, which is a part of the `System` namespace.

The properties and methods of the base class are inherited by the subclass. In addition, methods and properties can be added to the subclass in order to extend the functionality of the base class. In the derived class, the methods of the base class can also be overridden.

Inheritance also helps you create hierarchies of objects. For example, you can consider a class named `animals`. The `cats` class is derived from the `animals` class, and the `lions` class is derived from the `cats` class.

In the preceding example, the class `lions` inherits the properties and methods of the class `cats`, which in turn inherits all the properties and methods of the class `animals`. Therefore, all the properties and methods of the `lions` class and the `cats` class are inherited by the `animals` class.

All the classes that are created in Visual Basic .NET can be inherited by default. Inheritance helps you create complex objects from simpler ones and reuse the code. After a class is created in Visual Basic .NET, it can also be used as a base class in order to create a derived class.

## Polymorphism

The ability of an object to exist in different forms is known as *polymorphism*. Consider an example to have a proper understanding of the term.

If you decide to buy a television set, you either contact a dealer or call the manufacturing company. If you contact a dealer, the dealer first takes the order and then contacts the company. However, if you contact the company directly, the company contacts the dealers of your region and makes the necessary arrangements to deliver the television set. In this case, the dealer and the company are two different classes. The dealer and the company respond differently to the same order. In object-oriented programming, this is known as polymorphism.

Polymorphism helps you to perform different functions by using the same methods. To elaborate, the implementation of a base class can be changed in the derived classes. Therefore, when two classes are derived from the same class, a method can be created with the same name in both the classes. Based on the task that needs to be performed, you can select the method.

You learned about the features of object-oriented programming language, such as abstraction, encapsulation, inheritance, and polymorphism. Now, have a look at the components of Visual Basic .NET.

# Components of Visual Basic .NET

You have learned about the components of Visual C# .NET throughout this book. This appendix discusses the components of Visual Basic .NET. These components include variables, constants, operators, arrays, collections, procedures, arguments, and functions.

## Variables

Applications deal mostly with different types of data, such as text or numeric. This data needs to be stored by an application for later use and for performing certain operations on the data. It also needs to be stored for performing certain operations, such as calculating totals. A programming language uses variables in order to store data. A temporary memory location is called a *variable* that has a name or a word to refer to and a data type to determine the kind of data it can hold.

Visual Basic .NET provides various data types that help in storing different kinds of data. In the following section, you will learn more about the data types.

### Data Types

The kind of data that a variable can hold is referred to as a data type. `Integer`, `Long`, and `Byte` are some of the data types that are provided by Visual Basic .NET. Table B-1 lists the various data types of Visual Basic .NET.

**Table B-1 Data Types in Visual Basic .NET**

| Data Type | Description |
|---|---|
| `Integer` | The numeric data is stored. This data type stores the `Integer` data as a 32-bit (4 bytes) number. |
| `Long` | The numeric data that can exceed the range supported by the `Integer` data type that is stored. It stores the value of `Long` as a 64-bit (8 bytes) number. |
| `Short` | The smaller range of numeric data (between −32,678 to 32,767) is stored. This data type stores the `Short` data as a 16-bit (2 bytes) number. |
| `Byte` | The binary data is stored. This data type can also store ASCII character values in the numeric form. |
| `Char` | A single character is stored. This data type stores the `Char` data as a 16-bit (2 bytes) unsigned number. |
| `DateTime` | The date and time data is stored. This data type stores the date and time data as IEEE 64-bit (8 bytes) long integers. |
| `String` | The alphanumeric data, which is data containing numbers and text, is stored. |
| `Object` | The data of any type, such as `Integer`, `Boolean`, `String`, or `Long`, is stored. |
| `Double` | The large floating-point numbers are stored. This data type stores the `Double` data as an IEEE 64-bit (8 bytes) floating-point number. |
| `Single` | The single precision floating-point values are stored. This data type stores the `Single` data as an IEEE 32-bit (4 bytes) floating-point number. |
| `Decimal` | The very large floating-point values are stored. This data type stores the `Decimal` data as a 128-bit (16 bytes) signed integer to the power of 10. |
| `Boolean` | The data that can have only two values is stored. This data type stores the `True` and `False` `Boolean` data as a 16-bit (2 bytes) number. |

As compared to the earlier versions of Visual Basic, some changes in data types of Visual Basic .NET are mentioned as follows.

- The `Variant` data type is used to store any type of data in Visual Basic 6.0. This is similar to the `Object` data type in Visual Basic .NET.
- The `Double` data type is used to store a date in Visual Basic 6.0. The `DateTime` data type stores data in the date and time format in Visual Basic .NET.

- The `Currency` data type is not supported by Visual Basic .NET. Instead, the `Decimal` data type is used to store currency values.

After having a look at the various data types, you can now examine how variables are declared in Visual Basic .NET.

### *Variable Declarations*

To provide information about a variable to a program in advance is known as declaring a variable. The `Dim` statement is used to declare a variable. To declare a variable, you can use the following syntax:

```
Dim VariableName As type
```

The `As type` clause in the `Dim` statement is optional, and it defines the object type or the data type of the variable that you are declaring. Now, consider the following statement:

```
Dim int1 as Integer
Dim str1 as String
```

An `Integer` variable known as `int1` is declared by the first statement, and a `String` variable known as `str1` is declared by the second variable.

Variables can also be declared using the identifier type characters. These characters also specify the data type of a variable. You can consider the following statement as an example:

```
Dim str1$
```

In the statement, the identifier type character for a `String` variable is specified by `$`. The various identifier type characters that can be used in Visual Basic .NET are listed in Table B-2.

**Table B-2 Identifier Type Characters in Visual Basic .NET**

| Data Type | Identifier Type Character |
|---|---|
| `Integer` | % |
| `Long` | & |
| `Decimal` | @ |
| `String` | $ |
| `Single` | ! |
| `Double` | # |

You should consider some of the ground rules for naming a variable before discussing the various variable declarations that are possible in Visual Basic .NET. However, it is not necessary for you to follow these naming conventions. Following the naming convention makes the code easy to understand for anyone who wants to understand the code.

Some of the ground rules of naming a variable are:

- A variable must begin with a letter.
- A variable cannot contain a period or identifier type character.
- A variable must not exceed 255 characters.
- A variable must be unique within the same scope, defined as the range from which a variable can be accessed, such as a procedure, a form, or a module.

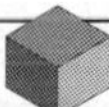

**NOTE**

A *module* is defined as a collection of procedures where a procedure is a set of statements used to perform some specific tasks.

You learned how to declare a variable. You will now learn how to initialize variables.

## Variable Initialization

A variable contains a value when it is declared. Consider the following example: By default, an `Integer` variable contains `0` and a `Boolean` variable stores `False` as the value.

To set a start value, you can initialize a variable. The following code explains the variable:

```
Dim int1 as Integer
int1 = 20
```

An `Integer` variable, `int1`, is declared by the first statement, while the second statement initializes it to the value `20`. In the earlier versions of Visual Basic, the initialization of variables was not allowed in the same line as their declarations. But now, Visual Basic .NET allows it. Therefore, the code can now be written as:

```
Dim int1 As Integer = 20
```

## Variable Scope

The scope of a variable determines the part of the program or application that can use the variable. Consider an example. A variable can be used only within a particular block of code or the entire program. Based on its scope, a variable can be called `local` or module-level. You can also refer to the scope of a variable as its accessibility.

If a variable is declared inside a procedure, it can only be accessed within that procedure. The variable is then referred to as a `local` variable. At times, you need to use a variable across modules within an application or throughout the application. The variable is then referred to as module-level variables. The declaration section of the module declares these variables. Module-level variables can be further classified as `private` or `public`.

The modules that can be used within the module in which they are declared are known as `private` modules. These modules are declared only at the module-level. A `private` variable is declared in the following statements:

```
Private Dim int1 As Integer
```

or

```
Private int1 As Integer
```

The `public` variables can be used across modules and also can be declared at the module-level. A `public` variable is declared in the following statements.

```
Public Dim int1 As Integer
```

or

```
Public int1 As Integer
```

## Constants

Suppose you need to use a particular value in an application. The application needs to calculate and display the percentage of marks obtained by each student in an examination. To calculate the percentage of marks, the application needs to use the maximum score at a number of places. In this case, instead of repeating each value every time, you can use constants. A variable whose value remains the same during the execution of a program is called a *constant*.

To declare a constant, you can use the following statement:

```
Const maxMarks As Integer = 100
```

or

```
Const maxMarks = 100
```

Each of the previously mentioned statements declares a constant by the name `maxMaks` and initializes it with the value `100`. These statements use a `const` keyword to declare a constant.

In case of any change in value, the processing of constants is faster than with variables; only the value at the point of declaring the constant needs to be changed.

You have learned about the variables and related concepts. You will now learn how to perform various operations on these variables.

## Operators

A unit of code that performs an operation on one or more variables or elements is known as an *operator*. An operator can be used to perform various operations, such as arithmetic operations, concatenation operations, comparison operations, and logical operations.

The following operators are supported by Visual Basic .NET:

- **Arithmetic operators.** Used for mathematical calculations.
- **Comparison operators.** Used for comparisons.
- **Assignment operators.** Used for assignment operations.
- **Concatenation operators.** Used for combining strings.
- **Logical/Bitwise operators.** Used for logical operations.

## Arrays

Variables are used to store data. At times, there may be situations where you need to work with multiple variables that store a similar type of information. For example, the names of about 50 employees need to be stored. Declaring these 50 variables is a monotonous and time-consuming task. Therefore, an array can be declared to make the task easy.

A collection of variables of the same data type is called *array*. The variables that form an array have the same name and are known as *array elements*. An *index number* refers to each variable in an array, which is its position in the array. The index number helps in distinguishing one array element from another. As an example, you can declare an array containing 50 variables of the `String` data type in order to store the names of 50 employees. When an array is declared, you need to create and initialize all the variables immediately. When an `Integer` array is declared, all the elements are initialized to 0. As compared to multiple variables, it is easier to manipulate an array and its elements. You can manipulate arrays by using the various loop statements that are provided by Visual Basic .NET.

In Visual Basic .NET, all the arrays that you create are basically derived from the `Array` class of the `System` namespace. You can also use the methods and properties of the `System.Array` type to manipulate these arrays. The next section will discuss how to declare these arrays.

### Declaring Arrays

You need to declare an array before using the array in a program, just like a variable. While declaring an array, you need to specify the array name, the data type of the array, and the number of variables that the array contains. In Visual Basic .NET, you need to declare arrays in a way similar to that in which variables are declared. You can do this by using the `Dim` statement, the `Public` statement, or the `Private` statement. The syntax that is used to declare an array is:

```
Dim ArrayName (NumElements) As DataType
```

In the syntax mentioned, the following list contains specifications:

- **ArrayName.** Specifies the name of the array.
- **NumElements.** Specifies the number of elements that the array can contain.
- **DataType.** Specifies the data type of the elements. This is optional.

While declaring arrays, parentheses need to be included after the array name to differentiate an array from a variable. Consider the following code statement:

```
Dim intArray1(10) As Integer
```

An `Integer` array by the name `intArray1`, which can contain 11 elements, is declared in the code mentioned above. Why are there 11 elements and not 10 as mentioned in the code? It is because arrays are zero-based. The index number, which is between 0 and 10, adds up to 11. The code mentioned previously is part of the statement given here:

```
Dim IntArray () As Integer = New Integer(10) {}
```

## Differences between Visual Basic .NET and Visual Basic 6.0 in Terms of Arrays

I will now discuss some of the basic differences between Visual Basic .NET and the earlier versions of Visual Basic in terms of arrays. By default, the starting index of an array is 0 in Visual Basic 6.0, and you can change the starting index to 1 by using the `Option Base` statement. In addition, the starting index for individual array declarations can be changed. The number of elements in the array is equal to the number specified during an array declaration statement plus one, if the default starting index is set to 0. However, the starting index for every array is 0 and cannot be changed in Visual Basic .NET. The `Option Base` statement is not supported by Visual Basic .NET. Interoperability with arrays of other programming languages is permitted because most programming languages support zero-based arrays.

### Initializing Arrays

Each element of an array is initialized as if it were a separate variable. However, if an array is not initialized, then Visual Basic .NET initializes each array element to the default value of the data type of the array.

Consider the code given here. It explains how to declare and initialize an array.

```
Dim booksArray1(4) As String
booksArray1(0) = "Introducing VB.NET"
booksArray1(1) = "Introducing ADO.NET"
booksArray1(2) = "Introducing VC++.NET"
booksArray1(3) = "Introducing ASP.NET"
booksArray1(4) = "Introducing C#"
```

In the previously mentioned code, an array, `booksArray1`, is declared that can contain five `String` type elements. This array stores `Introducing VB.NET` at index `0`, `Introducing ADO.NET` at index `1`, `Introducing VC++.NET` at index `2`, `Introducing ASP.NET` at index `3`, and `Introducing C#` at index `4`. It may be mentioned that 0 is the starting index or the lower bound that remains fixed for all the arrays. The upper bound or the end index is 4, and it can differ from one array to another.

An array can be declared or initialized in a single line by using the `new` keyword provided by Visual Basic .NET. This example shows how to declare an array by using a single line of code.

```
Dim booksArray1() As String = {"Introducing VB.NET", "Introducing ADO.NET",
"Introducing VC++.NET", "Introducing ASP.NET", "Introducing C#"}
```

To retrieve the values stored in a particular index position, the index number and the name of the array needs to be specified. The following statements illustrate the point:

```
Dim strVar As String
strVar = booksArray1(2)
```

After the execution of the previously mentioned statements, the value of the `String` type variable, `strVar`, which is stored in the index position 2 in `booksArray1`, is retrieved.

## Collections

A collection can be considered as a group of related objects. Generally, a collection is used to work with related objects. However, collections can be made to work with any data type.

### *Standard Collections Provided by Visual Basic .NET*

Visual Basic .NET provides you with several collections that are used to organize and manipulate objects in an efficient way. Consider an example. All the controls in a form are stored in the `Controls` collection. Similarly, all the forms in a Visual Basic .NET project are stored in the `Forms` collection. An efficient way to keep track of the objects that an application needs to create and destroy during run time is provided by a collection.

Consider an example: In an application that you have created, you need to take inputs for five text boxes from the user and then validate the data entered by the user for all of them. One way in which the code can be written is to check for each of the text boxes separately. Another way, which is relatively easy, is to check using the `Controls` collection. Every form has a `Controls` collection that represents all the controls, such as command buttons, labels, text boxes, and so on that are present in the form. You can easily perform the input validation check by using the `Controls` collection.

**NOTE**

`Controls` is the base class for all the controls. It is included in the `System.Windows.Forms` namespace and is provided by Visual Basic .NET.

You have learned about the collections in a brief overview. I will now discuss how you can create your own collections.

### *Creating Collections*

In addition to the various standard collections that are present in Visual Basic .NET, you can create your own collections. For collections, Visual Basic .NET provides the `Collection` class. The syntax for creating a collection is discussed as follows:

```
Dim CollectionName As New Collection()
```

In the preceding syntax, the name of the collection that you want to create is specified by `CollectionName`. An instance of the `Collection` class is created, which is declared by the `New` keyword in the declaration statement

After the creation of the collection, you can manipulate the creation in the same way as you would manipulate the standard collections that are provided by Visual Basic .NET. However, there are some differences between the two. Consider the following example:

```
Dim collection1 as New Collection()
collection1 = Controls
```

The preceding code creates and initializes a `Collection` object, `collection1`, with the `Controls` collection. However, this statement displays an error message. Why is it so? The answer is that the `Controls` collection and the `Collection` class object are not interchangeable and are of different types with different usage. In addition, they do not have the same methods and also do not use the same kinds of index values.

## Procedures

Consider a scenario where you need to perform a particular task repeatedly, for instance, calculating the average of marks obtained by students in a particular subject. In a situation such as this, you can group them in a procedure instead of writing the statements repeatedly. A set of statements grouped together to perform a specific task is called *procedure*. You can organize your applications by using procedures that allow you to chunk and group the program code logically.

After grouping the statements in a procedure, you can call the procedure from anywhere in the application. To call a procedure means to execute a statement that further instructs the compiler to execute the procedure. After executing the code in the procedure, the statement following the statement that called the procedure is executed. The statement that is called by a procedure is called a *calling statement*, and it includes the name of the procedure. The calling statement also includes the data values that are needed by the procedure for performing the tasks that are specified. The data values are also referred to as *arguments* or *parameters*.

Consider the example of calculating average mentioned previously. In this case, you can create a procedure that accepts the maximum and minimum marks obtained by students as data values and calculate the average. To call this procedure, the statement to be called must provide the minimum and maximum marks obtained by students as parameters.

Now consider some of the advantages that are offered by procedures. The first advantage is the reusability of code. In other words, a procedure can be created and used when it is required and if any statement has to be changed, you simply need to make the changes in a single location. This is useful mainly in the case of large and complex applications. The applications that use procedures are easier to debug. Additionally, you can easily trace the errors in a procedure without debugging the entire application code.

Now consider the scope or accessibility of procedures in an application. Similar to classes and variables, procedures have a scope. A procedure is generally declared in a class or a module. Therefore, you can call a procedure from the same class or module in which it is created. The scope of the procedure depends on the access modifiers that you use while the procedures are declared. The access modifiers supported by Visual Basic .NET are listed in Table B-3.

**Table B-3 Access Modifiers for Procedures**

| Access Modifier | Scope |
|---|---|
| `Public` | A procedure with a `Public` access modifier can be called from any class or module in the application. |
| `Private` | A procedure with a `Private` access modifier can be called from the same class or module in which it is declared. |
| `Protected` | A procedure with a `Protected` access modifier can be called from the same class or module in which it is declared. In addition, it can be called from the derived classes of the class in which it is declared. |
| `Friend` | A procedure with a `Friend` access modifier can be called from any class or module that contains its declaration. |

Based on the functionality of procedures, they can be classified as:

- **Sub procedures.** A sub procedure is used to perform a specific task.
- **Function procedures.** A function procedure is used to perform the specific tasks and returns a value to the calling statement.
- **Property procedures.** A property procedure is used to assign or access a value from an object.
- **Event-handling procedures.** An event-handling procedure is used to perform a specific task when a particular event occurs.

## Arguments

As stated earlier, variables, constants, or expressions are accepted as arguments by procedures. As a result, each time a procedure that accepts arguments is called, arguments need to be passed to the procedure. Based on the data values that are passed as arguments, the result can differ for each call to a procedure. Arguments can be passed to procedures by either value or reference.

## Functions

Visual Basic .NET provides various built-in functions that can be used in applications. Some of the built-in functions are `MsgBox`, `InputBox`, `CStr`, `DateDiff`, and `StrComp`. The `Microsoft.VisualBasic` namespace contains a declaration for these built-in functions. These functions can be classified based on the tasks performed by the various built-in functions. The functions can be classified as follows:

- Functions to enhance your programs are performed by the Application enhancement functions. Examples of Application enhancement functions are `MsgBox` and `InputBox`.
- Functions to manipulate strings are performed by String functions. Examples of String functions are `StrComp`, `Len`, and `Trim`.
- Functions to manipulate date and time values are performed by the Date function. Examples of Date functions are `DateDiff`, `Now`, and `Month`.
- Functions to convert one data type to another are performed by the Conversion function. Examples of Conversion functions are `CStr`, `CDate`, and `Val`.

Having discussed the components of Visual Basic .NET, you can use this knowledge to create a simple application in Visual C# .NET.

# Creating a Simple Visual C# .NET Windows Application

In this section, you will create a simple Visual C# .NET Windows application. Then, I will discuss how to create the same application in Visual Basic .NET. Doing this will help you to appreciate how easy it is to convert an application created in one of the languages of the .NET Framework to another. In addition, you will be able to realize how closely the two languages of the .NET Framework, Visual Basic .NET and Visual C# .NET, are related.

Now, I will proceed with creating a simple Windows application in Visual C# .NET. Name this application SampleWindowsApplication. This application accepts a username and password from the user. After specifying the required information, the user clicks on the Submit button. A message box showing the text `The user name and password that you have specified is accepted.` is displayed. In addition, the Windows form consists of an Exit button that is used to exit the Windows application. To create SampleWindowsApplication, include two label controls, two text box controls, and two command controls to the Windows form. Next, change the following properties of the controls:

**Form1**

- Name: `frmAcceptUserInput`
- Text: `Accept User Input`

**Label1**

- Name: `lblUserName`
- Text: `User Name`

**Label2**

- Name: `lblPassword`
- Text: `Password`

### Textbox1

- Name: txtUserName

### Textbox2

- Name: txtPassword
- PasswordChar: [*]

### Button1

- Name: btnSubmit
- Text: submit

### Button2

- Name: btnExit
- Text: Exit

After dragging the controls to the form, your SampleWindowsApplication looks as shown in Figure B-1.

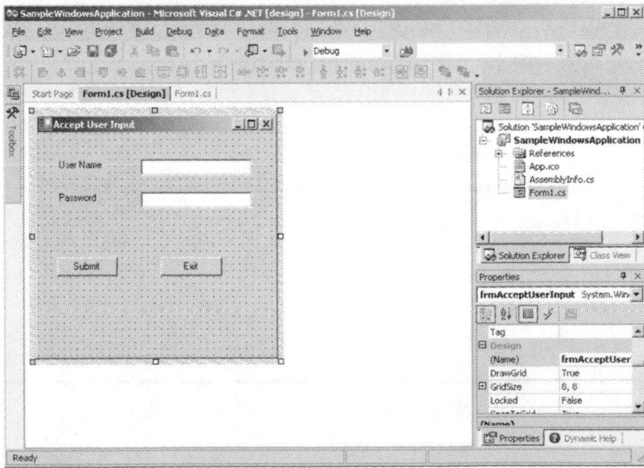

**FIGURE B-1** *SampleWindowsApplication with the controls added*

Now, to add the functionality to the application, you need to write code for the button controls. After adding code to the button controls, the code for the application is as shown:

```
using System.Drawing;
using System.Collections;
using System.ComponentModel;
using System.Windows.Forms;
using System.Data;

namespace SampleWindowsApplication
{
   public class frmAcceptUserInput : System.Windows.Forms.Form
   {
      private System.Windows.Forms.Label lblUserName;
      private System.Windows.Forms.Label lblPassword;
      private System.Windows.Forms.Button btnSubmit;
      private System.Windows.Forms.Button btnExit;
      private System.Windows.Forms.TextBox txtUserName;
      private System.Windows.Forms.TextBox txtPassword;
      private System.ComponentModel.Container components = null;

      public frmAcceptUserInput()
      {
         InitializeComponent();
      }

      protected override void Dispose( bool disposing )
      {
         if( disposing )
         {
            if (components != null)
            {
               components.Dispose();
            }
         }
         base.Dispose( disposing );
      }
```

```
[STAThread]
        static void Main()
        {
           Application.Run(new frmAcceptUserInput());
        }

        private void btnSubmit_Click(object sender, System.EventArgs e)
        {
           MessageBox.Show("The user name and password that you have specified is
              accepted.");
        }

        private void btnExit_Click(object sender, System.EventArgs e)
        {
           Application.Exit();
        }
    }
}
```

After creating an application in Visual C# .NET, you can create this application in Visual Basic .NET.

## Creating a Simple Application in Visual Basic .NET

The steps for creating an application in Visual Basic .NET are similar to the steps for creating an application in Visual C# .NET. Similar to Visual C# .NET, Visual Studio .NET also provides you with a template to create an application in Visual Basic .NET. To create the SampleWindowsApplication by using Visual Basic .NET, perform the following steps:

1. On the File menu, point to the New option.
2. In the displayed list, select the Project option.

   The New Project dialog box is displayed.
3. In the Project Types: pane of the New Project dialog box, select the Visual Basic Projects option.

4. In the Templates: pane, select the Windows Application option.
5. In the Name: text box, type the name of the Windows application as `SampleWindowsApplication1`.
6. Accept the default location as specified in the Location: text box. You may also choose to browse for the location where you want to save the application by clicking on the Browse button.
7. Click on the OK button to close the New Project dialog box.

Figure B-2 shows the New Project dialog box for the SampleWindowsApplication1 project in Visual Basic .NET.

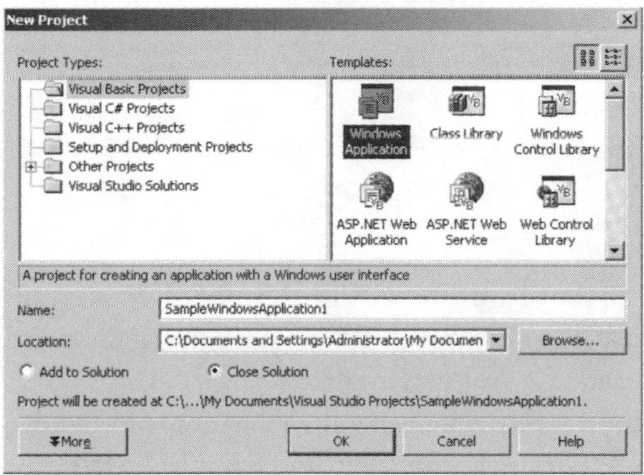


**FIGURE B-2** *The New Project dialog box for SampleWindowsApplication1*

When you click on the OK button, Visual Studio .NET automatically creates the default files and a blank Windows form for you. Click on the Show All Files button in the Solution Explorer window to view a list of all the files created by Visual Studio .NET. Figure B-3 shows the default files and the blank form created by Visual Studio .NET.

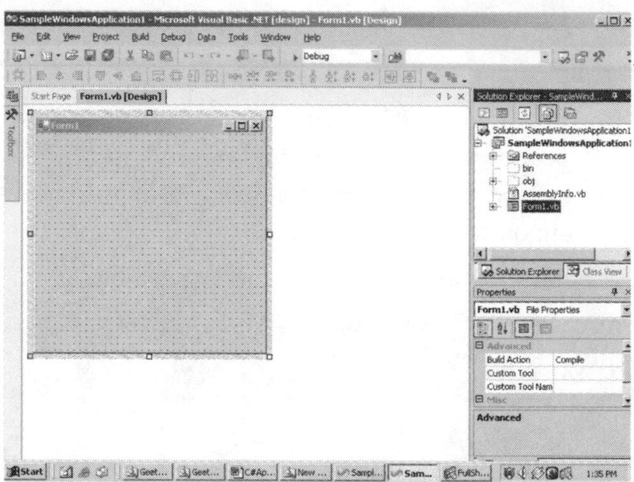

**FIGURE B-3** *The default files and the blank form created by Visual Studio .NET*

As you can see in Figure B-3, the blank form in Visual Basic .NET is created with an extension .vb. In addition, Visual Studio .NET creates some reference files for the SampleWindowsApplication1 project. Similar to Visual C# .NET, Visual Studio .NET creates a solution with the same name as that of the Windows application. Inside the solution, the project with the name SampleWindowsApplication1 is created.

Now, proceed with the creation of the SampleWindowsApplication1 application. To create the application, you need to add controls to the Windows form. Because Visual Basic .NET and Visual C# .NET are languages based on the .NET Framework, the IDE for the Visual Basic .NET applications is the same as that of the Visual C# .NET applications. The IDE for the Visual Basic .NET applications contains a toolbox that contains controls that you can use to create the Windows application. Figure B-4 shows the toolbox that contains standard controls for creating a Windows application in Visual Basic .NET.

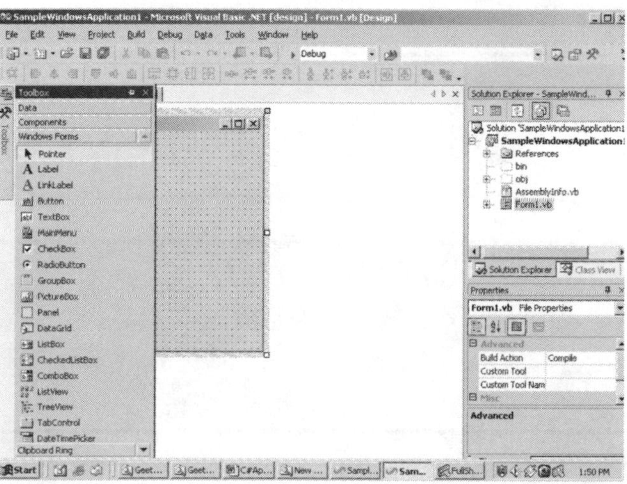


**FIGURE B-4** *The toolbox for creating Windows application*

From the toolbox, drag two label controls, two text box controls, and two button controls and place them on the form. Now in the Properties window of the controls, change the properties of the controls.

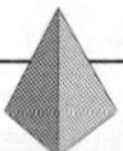

**TIP**

If the Properties window is not displayed, select the control and press the F4 key. Alternatively, you can select the Properties Window option on the View menu.

Change the following properties of the controls:

### Form1

- Name: `Form1`
- Text: `Accept User Input`

### Label1

- Name: `lblUserName`
- Text: `User Name`

### Label2

- Name: `lblPassword`
- Text: `Password`

### Textbox1

- Name: `txtUserName`

### Textbox2

- Name: `txtPassword`
- PasswordChar: [*]

### Button1

- Name: `btnSubmit`
- Text: `submit`

### Button2

- Name: `btnExit`
- Text: `Exit`

After adding the controls, you need to add the code to the button controls to make them functional. The following sections discuss how to write code in Visual Basic .NET.

## Adding Code to the Submit Button

When the user clicks on the Submit button, a message box is displayed. To do this, add the following code to the `Click` event of the Submit button.

```
Private Sub btnSubmit_Click(ByVal sender As System.Object, ByVal e As
    System.EventArgs) Handles btnSubmit.Click
```

```
    MessageBox.Show("The user name and password that you have specified is
       accepted.")
End Sub
```

The preceding code creates a `Sub` procedure with the `private` access modifier for the `Click` event of the Submit button. As you can see in the preceding code, the event handler declaration for the `Click` event includes two parameters, a `sender` object and an `event` argument. In addition, the statement includes a `Handles` keyword. This keyword indicates that whenever a `Click` event occurs for the Submit button, the event is handled by the `Sub` procedure, `btnSubmit_Click`.

Inside the `Sub` procedure, the `Show()` method of the `MessageBox` class is used to display a message. Figure B-5 shows the message box when the user clicks on the Submit button.

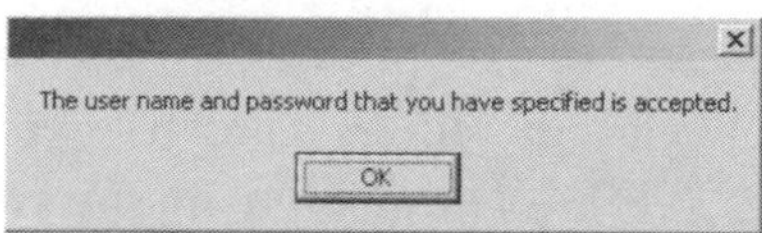


**FIGURE B-5** *The message box displayed when user clicks on the Submit button*

## Adding Code to the Exit Button

On clicking the Exit button, the Windows application should exit. To do this, add the following code to the `Click` event of the Exit button.

```
Private Sub btnExit_Click(ByVal sender As System.Object, ByVal e As
   System.EventArgs) Handles btnExit.Click
   Application.Exit()
End Sub
```

The preceding code creates an event handler `Sub` procedure for the `Click` event of the Exit button. Inside the `Sub` procedure, the `Exit()` sub of the `Application` class is used to exit the application. Figure B-6 shows the Exit button in the Accept User Input form.

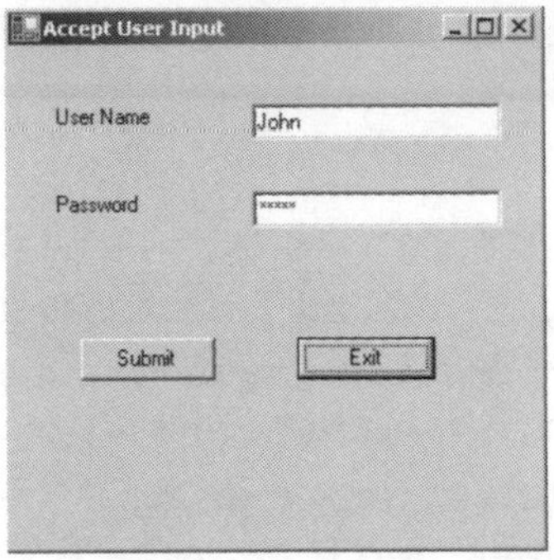

**FIGURE B-6** *The Exit button in the Accept User Input form*

As you can see, writing code for a Visual Basic .NET application is very similar to adding code to the Visual C#. NET application. However, to have a better understanding of the code of Visual Basic .NET as compared to the code of Visual C# .NET, look at the complete code for Visual Basic .NET. The entire code for the SampleWindowsApplication1 application is as follows:

```
Public Class Form1
   Inherits System.Windows.Forms.Form

   Private Sub btnSubmit_Click(ByVal sender As System.Object, ByVal e As
      System.EventArgs) Handles btnSubmit.Click
      MessageBox.Show("The user name and password that you have specified is
         accepted.")
   End Sub

   Private Sub btnExit_Click(ByVal sender As System.Object, ByVal e As
      System.EventArgs) Handles btnExit.Click
      Application.Exit()
   End Sub
End Class
```

The overall code for the Visual Basic .NET application is slightly different from that of the Visual C# .NET. As you can see, the preceding code creates a class `Form1`, which is inherited from the `Form` class. The `Form` class is present in the `System.Windows.Forms` namespace. The `Inherits` keyword is used to inherit a class from a base class. Next, the code contains the declarations for the event handlers for the Submit and Exit buttons.

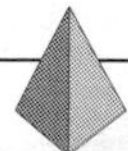

**TIP**

A major difference in the code of Visual Basic .NET and Visual C# .NET is that the statements in Visual Basic .NET are not followed by a semicolon (;) as in Visual C# .NET.

## Summary

In this chapter, you learned about the various languages of Visual Studio .NET. Visual C# .NET, Visual Basic .NET, and Visual C++ .NET are the three main languages of Visual Studio .NET. In addition, you looked at an overview of Visual Basic .NET.

Next, you learned about the different features of an object-oriented programming language. These features include abstraction, encapsulation, inheritance, and polymorphism.

You also learned about the various components of Visual Basic. NET, such as variables, constants, operators, arrays, collections, procedures, arguments, and functions. In addition, you learned to create a simple Visual C# .NET Windows application. Finally, you learned to create the same application by using Visual Basic .NET.

# Appendix C

## Visual Studio .NET Integrated Development Environment

In this appendix, you will learn about the Visual Studio .NET IDE (*integrated development environment*), which enables you to develop applications based on the .NET Framework. You will also learn about the various tools and windows associated with the Framework. In addition, you will learn about the functions of the tools and windows in the Visual Studio .NET Framework.

# Introduction to Visual Studio .NET IDE

The Visual Studio .NET IDE is common to all the .NET languages. You can use the same set of tools and windows across languages to create an application.

When you begin working with Visual Studio .NET, the Start Page is the default screen that is displayed. Alternatively, you can open the Start Page by choosing the Show Start Page command from the Help menu.

The Start Page is the default home page for the Web browser in Visual Studio .NET, and it provides a centralized location to work in Visual Studio .NET. In addition, the Start Page provides various links, such as Get Started, Online Community, and Headlines, to enable a quick and efficient environment for working in Visual Studio. NET. The Start Page in the Visual Studio .NET IDE is shown in Figure C-1.

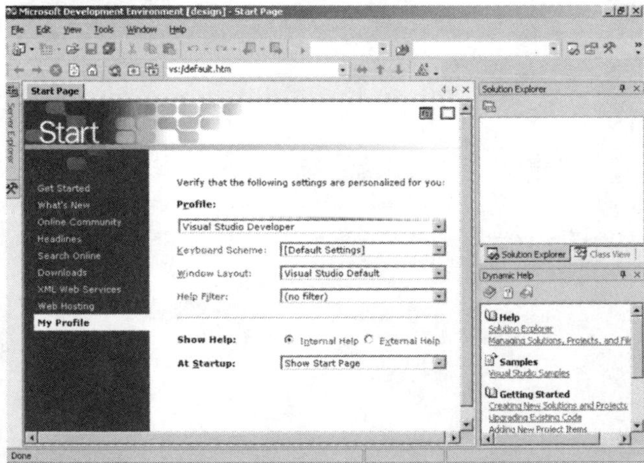


**FIGURE C-1** *The Start Page in the Visual Studio .NET IDE*

I will discuss the windows and tools displayed in IDE in the following sections.

## Menu Bar

The menus that are displayed on the menu bar of the Visual Studio .NET IDE enable you to perform different tasks, such as opening, saving, editing, and formatting files. In addition to these default menus, IDE displays menus that are relevant to the task that is being performed.

The following list takes a look at some commonly used menus in Visual Studio .NET.

- **File.** The File menu provides commands to open and save projects, files, and solutions. In addition, the menu provides commands to add items such as forms, controls, modules, and classes to projects and solutions.
- **Edit.** The Edit menu provides commands such as Cut, Copy, Paste, Delete, Undo, and Redo to perform the tasks associated with them.
- **View.** The View menu provides commands to access the various windows and tools available in Visual Studio .NET.
- **Project.** The Project menu provides commands to add components such as forms, modules, classes, and controls to the projects.
- **Build.** The Build menu provides commands to build projects. This menu also provides the Configuration Manager command to create, modify, and build configurations for solutions and projects.
- **Debug.** The Debug menu provides commands such as Start, Step Into, and Step Over to locate and correct errors in the applications.
- **Format.** The Format menu provides commands such as Align and Center in Form to format controls while working in a designer.
- **Tools.** The Tools menu provides commands such as Debug Processes, Customize Toolbox, Add-in Manager, Customize, and Options to perform the functions associated to them. When these commands are selected, the corresponding dialog box also gets displayed.
- **Window.** The Window menu provides commands such as New Window and Split to work with windows in IDE.
- **Help.** The Help menu provides commands such as Dynamic Help, Contents, Index, Search, and Previous Topic and Next Topic, which takes the content from the MSDN (*Microsoft Developer Network*) library and provides the required information.

**NOTE**

Windows Forms Designer, Web Form Designer, XML Designer, and Component Designer are the designers provided by Visual Studio .NET to design applications quickly and easily.

Figure C-2 shows the menu bar in the Visual Studio .NET IDE.

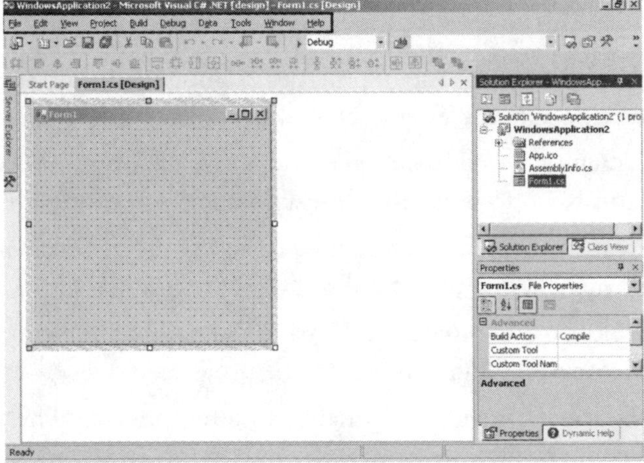

**FIGURE C-2** *The menu bar in the Visual Studio .NET IDE*

## Toolbars

Visual Studio .NET IDE provides the Standard and Web toolbars that are displayed by default. The other toolbars that are provided include the Text Editor, Build, and Debug toolbars.

Depending on the designer, tool, or window that is being used, the toolbars relevant to the performed task will be displayed in IDE. Some of the toolbars available in Visual Studio .NET IDE are described in Table C-1.

**Table C-1 Toolbars Available in Visual Studio .NET**

| Toolbar | Function |
|---|---|
| Build | Used to build applications. |
| Crystal Reports - Insert | Used to open the Insert Summary, Insert Group, Insert Subreport, Insert Chart, and Insert Picture dialog boxes. |
| Crystal Reports - Main | Used to perform basic formatting operations, such as justify text, apply fonts, and access dialog boxes. You can use the Crystal Reports-Main toolbar to access dialog boxes such as Select Expert and Object Properties. |
| Data Design | Used to generate datasets and preview data. |
| Database Diagram | Used to work with database objects. |
| Debug | Used to start and stop debugging of applications. |
| Debug Location | Used to view the program, thread, and stack frame of an error encountered while debugging a program. |
| Design | Used to work with controls in the Web Form Designer. |
| Formatting | Used to format text. |
| Full Screen | Used to work in the full-screen mode. |
| HTML Editor | Used to format, validate, and work with HTML documents. |
| Image Editor | Used to create and manipulate images. |
| Layout | Used to modify the layout of controls in the designer. |
| Source Control | Used to maintain different versions of your applications. |
| Standard | Used to work with solutions, projects, and files. In addition, you can use the Standard toolbar to open windows, such as Solution Explorer and Class View. |
| Style Sheet | Used to format and view style sheets. |
| Table | Used to work with the tables in a database. |
| Text Editor | Used to work in the code editor. |
| Web | Used to browse for Web pages. |
| XML Data | Used to create schemas. |
| XML Schema | Used to preview datasets and edit keys and relations. |

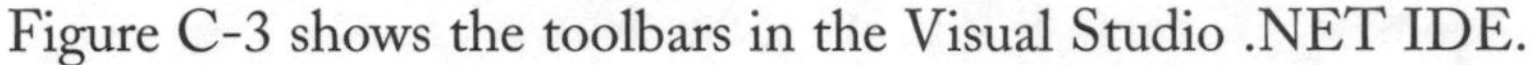

Figure C-3 shows the toolbars in the Visual Studio .NET IDE.

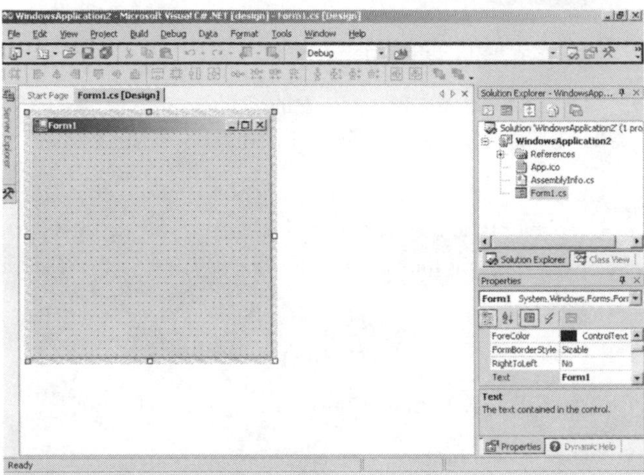


**FIGURE C-3** *The toolbars in the Visual Studio .NET IDE*

Having looked at the toolbars, you can look at the windows in Visual Studio .NET in the next section.

## Visual Studio .NET IDE Windows

As discussed earlier, the Start Page is the first screen that appears when you launch Visual Studio .NET. This page enables you to access existing projects or create new ones. The Start Page is the default home page of Visual Studio .NET IDE, which contains various links providing online help on MSDN. The Start Page also allows you to customize the appearance of IDE by specifying your preferences.

### *The Solution Explorer Window*

A collection of all the projects and files needed for an application is called a *solution*. A project file contains a number of files that need to be executed for working in the project. In Visual Studio .NET IDE, Solution Explorer provides a hierarchical view of all files, solutions, and projects. To open Solution Explorer, you need to select the Solution Explorer command from the View menu. The Solution Explorer window in the Visual Studio .NET IDE is shown in Figure C-4.

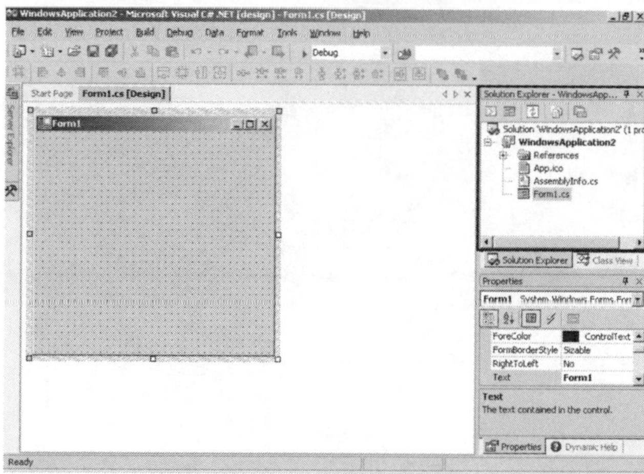


**FIGURE C-4** *The Solution Explorer window in the Visual Studio .NET IDE*

The Solution Explorer window is displayed, which shows a listing of the projects, files, and references present in the solution. You can open a file by double-clicking on the file name in Solution Explorer.

The Solutions Explorer also contains a toolbar that displays the buttons that are specific to the selected file. View Code, Show All Files, and Properties are a few commonly displayed buttons. Figure C-5 shows the toolbar in the Solution Explorer window.

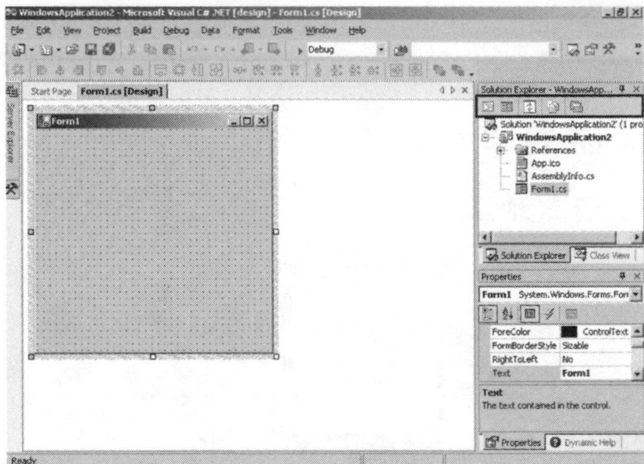

**FIGURE C-5** *The toolbar in the Solution Explorer window*

## The Class View Window

You can view the hierarchical structure of solutions and projects by using the Class View window provided in the Visual Studio .NET IDE. You can open the Class View window by selecting either the Class View tab on the Visual Studio .NET IDE or the Class View command from the View menu. The components are organized in the Class View window based on the project in which they are contained. The Class View window also provides a structured view of the code that helps in understanding the organization of the components within a project. A logical view provided by the Class View window helps in understanding the interrelationships between various components and objects. The Class View window is shown in Figure C-6.

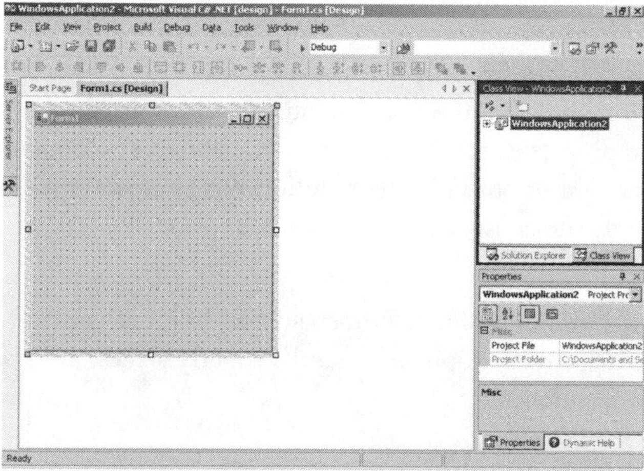


**FIGURE C-6** *The Class View window*

An icon represents each type of component in the Class View window. Each icon represents different types of components, such as namespaces, classes, and interfaces.

You can navigate through the projects in a solution by using the Class View window. You can also view the properties or code for a component by using the Class View window. Consider an example: To view the code associated with a method, right-click the method name in the Class View window and select the Browse Definition command from the context menu. The corresponding code for the selected method is displayed.

A toolbar is also displayed in the Class View window, which displays the Sort By and New Folder buttons. Using the Sort By button, you can sort the files in the order of the alphabet by type. You can use the New Folder button to create virtual folders.

## The Properties Window

The Properties window displays the properties of a component. By selecting the Properties Window command from the View menu, you can open the Properties window. To display the properties associated with the selected components, you need to select the component or object in the Solution Explorer window. You can also view, edit, and modify the components of projects and solutions by using the Properties window.

The Properties window displays different properties for different controls. Various buttons, such as Categorized, Alphabetic, and Property Pages, are also displayed in the Properties window.

To view and modify the properties of a Button control, for example, you open the Solution Explorer window and select the Button control. The properties of the Button control are displayed in the Properties window, as shown in Figure C-7.

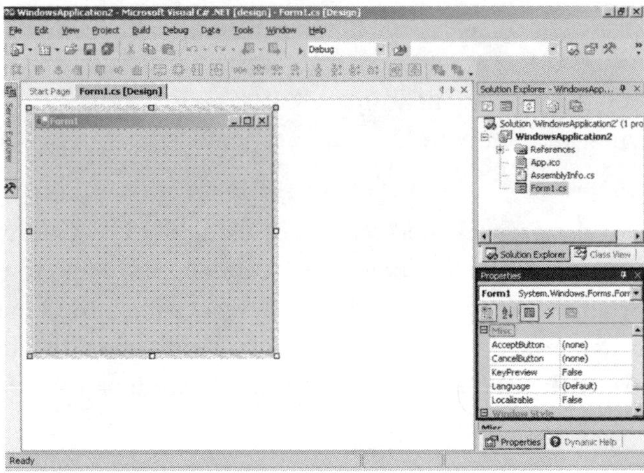


**FIGURE C-7** *The Properties window for a Button control*

## The Dynamic Help Window

The Dynamic Help window in Visual Studio .NET provides access to the information that is relevant to perform a particular task. The Dynamic Help window is displayed when Visual Studio .NET IDE is opened. Alternatively, you can access this command by selecting the Dynamic Help command from the Help menu.

Various links related to the current window or current task are also displayed in the Dynamic Help window. The Dynamic Help window displays information depending on the selection in IDE. The information is organized categorically in the Dynamic Help window. By default, the Dynamic Help window displays the Help, Samples, and Getting Started categories.

Consider an example: When you work in the Class View window, the information related to the Class View window is displayed in the Dynamic Help window. Similarly, if a Button control is selected while working in the designer, the information related to the `Button` class is displayed in the Dynamic Help window, as shown in Figure C-8.

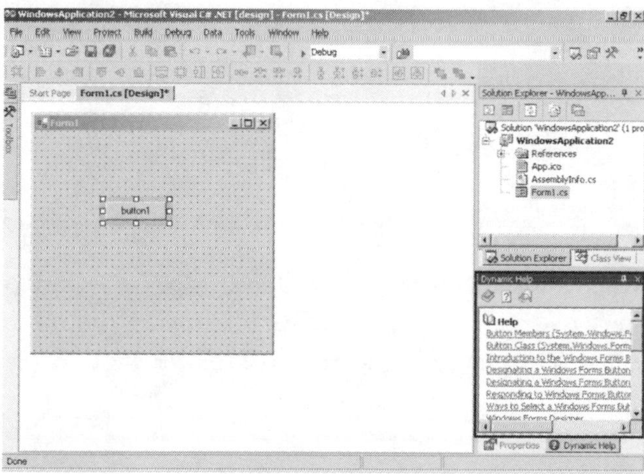


**FIGURE C-8** *The Dynamic Help window for a Button control*

## The Server Explorer Window

In Visual Studio .NET, the Server Explorer window enables server management. You can access the Server Explorer window by selecting the Server Explorer tab displayed on the left margin of the IDE. Alternatively, you can select the Server Explorer command from the View menu to open the Server Explorer window.

The nodes Data Connections and Servers are displayed in the Server Explorer window. The Data Connections node lists the database connections for the databases that are created using the Server Explorer window. The Server node lists the names of the servers that are currently being used. Figure C-9 shows the Server Explorer window.

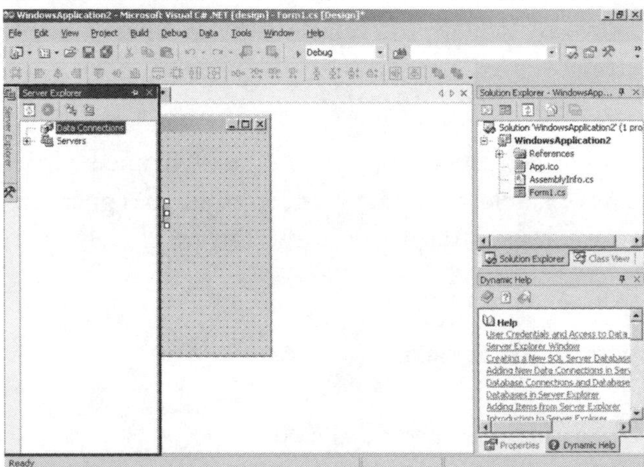


**FIGURE C-9** *The Server Explorer window*

The Server Explorer window also allows you to add event logs, message queues, and performance counters to your project. A toolbar displaying the buttons for commonly used commands is displayed in the Server Explorer window.

## Toolbox

The Toolbox contains various tools available in Visual Studio .NET. The Toolbox can be opened by clicking the Toolbox tab displayed on the left margin of the Visual Studio .NET IDE. You can also open the Toolbox by selecting the Toolbox command from the View menu.

The General and Clipboard Ring tabs are displayed by default. In addition, tools with specific functions are displayed in the toolbox. You can view all the tabs on the Toolbar by selecting the Show All Tabs option from the context menu.

Some of the tabs available in the Toolbox are:

- **General tab.** The General tab, by default, displays only the Pointer control. You can also add controls, such as custom controls, to the General tab. Custom controls refer to user-defined controls. Figure C-10 shows the General tab of the Toolbox.

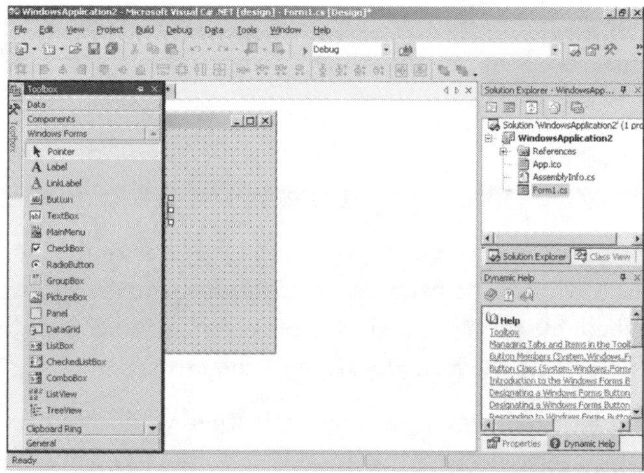


**FIGURE C-10** *The General tab of the Toolbox*

- **Clipboard Ring tab.** The Clipboard Ring tab also displays only the Pointer control by default. The Clipboard Ring tab displays the last 12 items that are added to the clipboard. The clipboard is basically a memory cache maintained by the Microsoft Windows operating system. The Clipboard Ring tab of the Toolbox is shown in Figure C-11.

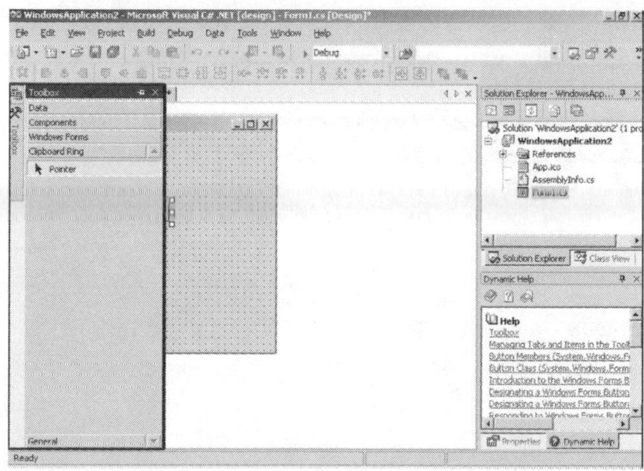


**FIGURE C-11** *The Clipboard Ring tab of the Toolbox*

The Toolbox can also be customized by adding tabs and tools. You can use the Customize Toolbox command from the Tools menu to open the Customize Toolbar dialog box.

## The Task List Window

Visual Studio .NET allows you to mark the code present in your application with comments. The Task List window helps track errors and warnings. These comments are displayed in the table format. To view these errors, you need to double-click the message and determine the exact location of the error.

You can open the Task List window by selecting the Other Windows command from the View menu and then selecting the Task List command from the submenu. The Task List window is shown in Figure C-12.

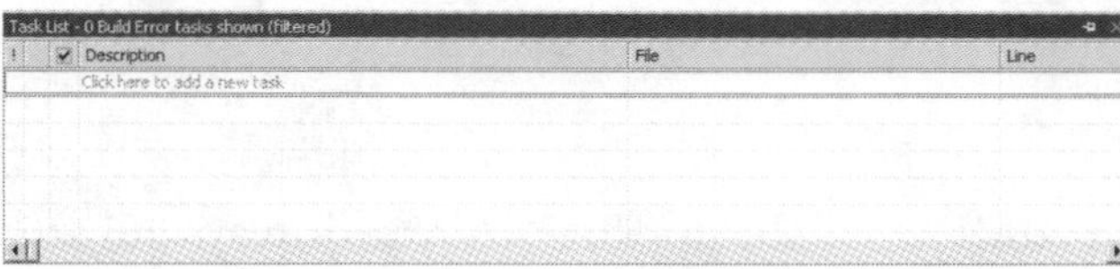


**FIGURE C-12** *The Task List window*

You can also add comments for the errors in the code, which may be useful for later references. Figure C-13 shows a comment for an error in the code.

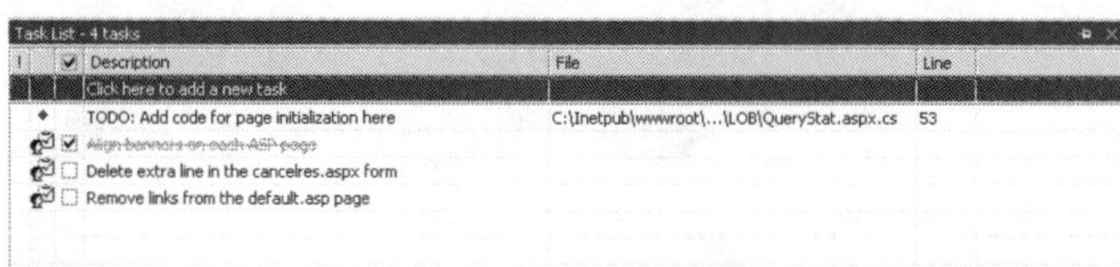


**FIGURE C-13** *A comment for an error in the code*

## Managing Windows

The windows that are displayed in Visual Studio .NET IDE can be managed according to your requirements. The following options are available to perform this function. The next sections will discuss them in detail.

### Hiding Windows

To hide a window, you use the Auto Hide feature of the Visual Studio .NET IDE. The window is then displayed as a tab, which can be clicked to maximize the hidden window. You can apply the Auto Hide feature to various tools of IDE, such as Solution Explorer, Task List, and Toolbox. The Auto Hide feature may be enabled or disabled by toggling the pushpin icon in the upper-right corner of the window. Figure C-14 shows the Auto Hide feature of the Visual Studio .NET IDE.

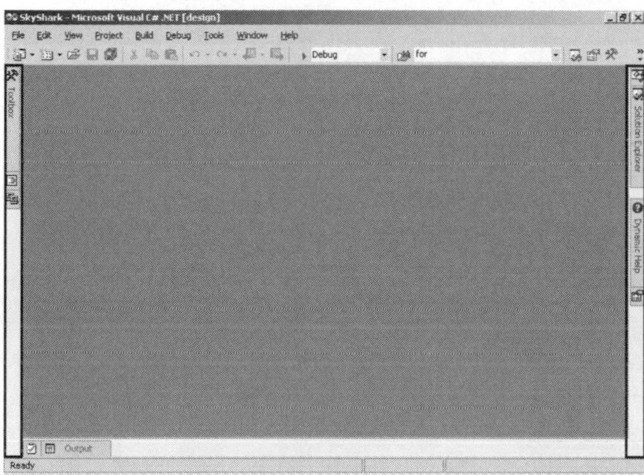


**FIGURE C-14** *The Auto Hide feature of Visual Studio .NET IDE*

### Docking Windows

You can drag the windows present in IDE as per your requirements by using the docking windows feature provided by Visual Studio .NET. The windows can be attached or left free-standing as per your requirements.

# Customizing Visual Studio .NET IDE

The Visual Studio .NET IDE can be customized according to your requirements while creating an application. The following sections will discuss how to customize Visual Studio .NET.

## The Options Dialog Box

The Options dialog box is used for customizing the IDE. This dialog box can be used to specify a default location to save the projects and manipulate the layout of IDE. The Options dialog box can also be used for specifying the user interface elements, such as keyboard mappings, font, and color. The Options dialog box is shown in Figure C-15.

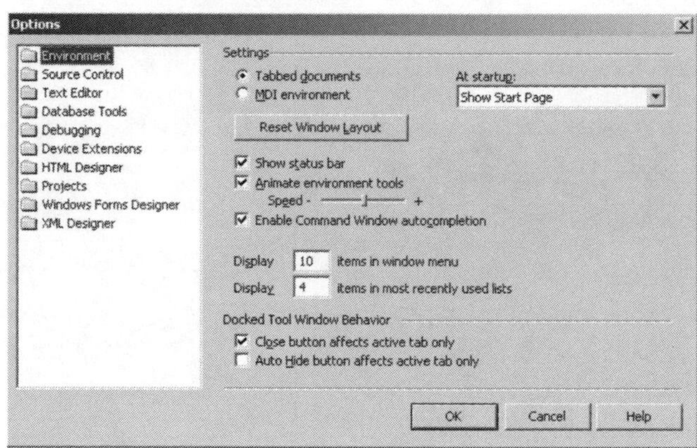


**FIGURE C-15** *The Options dialog box*

You can display the Options dialog box by selecting the Options command from the Tools menu. The dialog box consists of two panes that contain folders such as Environment, Text Editor, and Debugging, and their respective options.

The following sections will discuss some frequently used features of the Environment folder.

### *The General Page*

The General Page is used to change the default settings of IDE. You can use this page to display the Status bar in IDE and specify whether IDE should support the MDI (*Multiple Document Interface*) environment. In addition, you can specify the item to be displayed at the startup. The General Page is shown in Figure C-16.

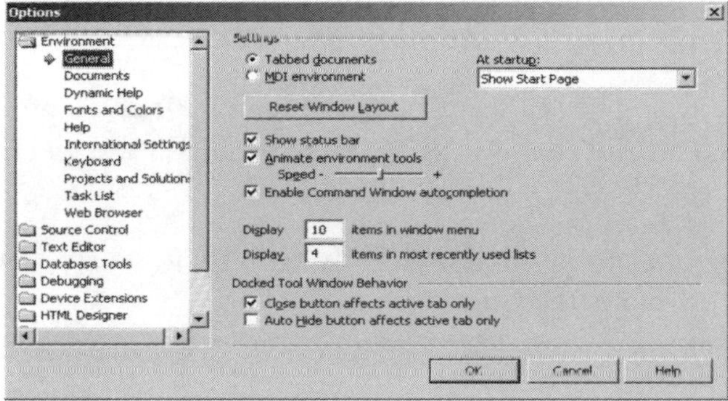


**FIGURE C-16** *The General Page*

## The Fonts and Colors Page

The Fonts and Colors Page is used to customize the font and color settings for the elements having a user interface. Figure C-17 shows the Fonts and Colors Page.

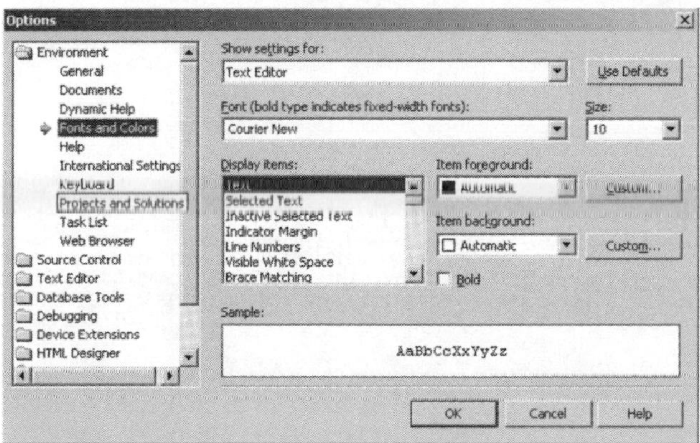


**FIGURE C-17** *The Fonts and Colors Page*

In addition to the pages mentioned previously, the Options dialog box consists of the Documents page, the Dynamic Help page, the Help page, and the Keyboard page.

## The Customize Dialog Box

You use the Customize dialog box to manipulate the toolbars that are present in IDE. You can create and modify your own toolbars. You can also add and remove the existing toolbars.

The Customize dialog box can be displayed by selecting Customize from the Tools menu. Figure C-18 shows the Customize dialog box.

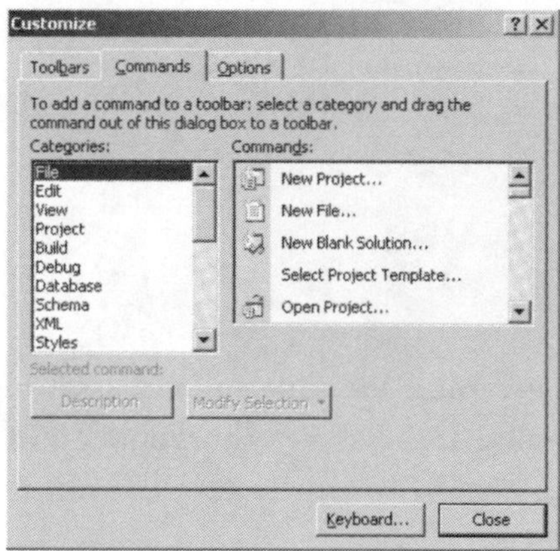


**FIGURE C-18** *The Customize dialog box*

As you can see in Figure C-18, the Customize dialog box contains the Toolbars, Commands, and Options tabs. The following section discusses these tabs in detail.

### *The Toolbars Tab*

The Toolbars tab is used create a toolbar and rename, delete, and reset existing toolbars.

### The Commands Tab

The Commands tab is used to add frequently used commands to toolbars. The Commands tab consists of two lists, Categories and Commands. The Categories list displays commands such as File and Edit, and the Commands list displays the commands for a selected category.

### The Options Tab

The Options tab is used to customize the appearance of toolbars and menu bars.

## Summary

In this chapter, you learned about the Visual Studio .NET IDE that will enable you to develop applications based on the .NET Framework. You also learned about the various windows and tools that are used in the Visual Studio .NET IDE. In addition, you learned about the various functions of windows and tools that enable enhancement of the Visual Studio .NET IDE.

# Index

## B



## C

## E



## F

## J



## K



## L

## N



## O

## Q



## R

## S

# T

## U

## X

## Z

# Professional Topics for the Professional Programmer

The Premier Press *Professional Projects* series offers intermediate to advanced programmers hands-on guides for accomplishing real-world, professional tasks. Each book includes several projects—each one focusing on a specific programming concept and based on a real-world situation. Use the skills developed throughout the book and modify the projects to fit your professional needs!

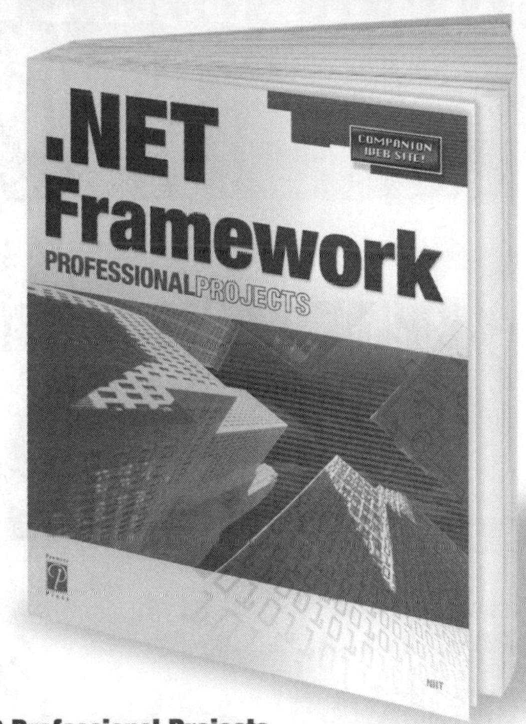


**.NET Framework Professional Projects**
1-931841-24-1
U.S. $49.99 Can. $77.95 U.K. £36.99

**ADO.NET Professional Projects**
1-931841-54-3
U.S. $49.99 Can. $77.95 U.K. £36.99

**ASP.NET Professional Projects**
1-931841-21-7
U.S. $49.99 Can. $77.95 U.K. £36.99

**C# Professional Projects**
1-931841-30-6
U.S. $49.99 Can. $77.95 U.K. £36.99

**Dynamic Web Forms Professional Projects**
1-931841-13-6
U.S. $49.99 Can. $77.95 U.K. £36.99

**J2EE Professional Projects**
1-931841-22-5
U.S. $49.99 Can. $77.95 U.K. £36.99

**PHP Professional Projects**
1-931841-53-5
U.S. $49.99 Can. $77.95 U.K. £36.99

**Streaming Media Professional Projects**
1-931841-14-4
U.S. $49.99 Can. $77.95 U.K. £36.99

**VBA Professional Projects**
1-931841-55-1
U.S. $49.99 Can. $77.95 U.K. £36.99

**Visual Basic.NET Professional Projects**
1-931841-29-2
U.S. $49.99 Can. $77.95 U.K. £36.99

**Visual C++.NET Professional Projects**
1-931841-31-4
U.S. $49.99 Can. $77.95 U.K. £36.99

Premier Press, Inc.
www.premierpressbooks.com

**Call now to order!**
**1.800.428.7267**

# NEED A COMPUTER BOOK? WE'VE GOT YOU COVERED!

## Try a Premier Press Series...

In a Weekend®

Fast & Easy®

Linux®

For The Absolute Beginner

Fast & Easy® Web Development

Administrator's Guide

Game Development

Professional Projects

Premier Press, Inc.
www.premierpressbooks.com

To Order Call
1.800.428.7267

# fast&easy® web development

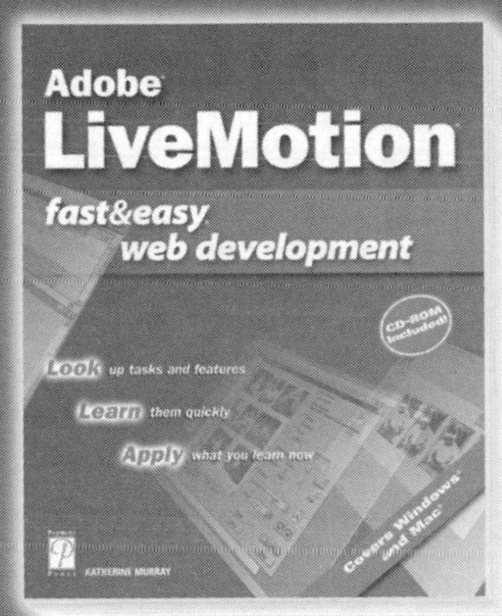


## Less Time. Less Effort. More Development.

Don't spend your time leafing through lengthy manuals looking for the information you need. Spend it doing what you do best—Web development. Premier Press's *fast & easy® web development* series leads the way with step-by-step instructions and real screen shots to help you grasp concepts and master skills quickly and easily.

**Adobe® LiveMotion™ *Fast & Easy® Web Development***
0-7615-3254-4 • CD Included
$29.99 U.S. • $44.95 Can. • £21.99 U.K.

**ASP 3 *Fast & Easy® Web Development***
0-7615-2854-7 • CD Included
$24.99 U.S. • $37.95 Can. • £18.99 U.K.

**CGI *Fast & Easy® Web Development***
0-7615-2938-1 • CD Included
$24.99 U.S. • $37.95 Can. • £18.99 U.K.

**ColdFusion® *Fast & Easy® Web Development***
0-7615-3016-9 • CD Included
$24.99 U.S. • $37.95 Can. • £18.99 U.K.

**Macromedia® Director® 8 and Lingo™ *Fast & Easy® Web Development***
0-7615-3049-5 • CD Included
$24.99 U.S. • $37.95 Can. • £18.99 U.K.

**Macromedia® Dreamweaver® 4 *Fast & Easy® Web Development***
0-7615-3518-7 • CD Included
$29.99 U.S. • $44.95 Can. • £21.99 U.K.

**Macromedia® Dreamweaver® UltraDev™ 4 *Fast & Easy® Web Development***
0-7615-3517-9 • CD Included
$29.99 U.S. • $44.95 Can. • £21.99 U.K.

**Macromedia® Fireworks® 4 *Fast & Easy® Web Development***
0-7615-3519-5 • CD Included
$29.99 U.S. • $44.95 Can. • £21.99 U.K.

**Macromedia® Flash™ 5 *Fast & Easy® Web Development***
0-7615-2930-6 • CD Included
$24.99 U.S. • $37.95 Can. • £18.99 U.K.

**HomeSite™ 4.5 *Fast & Easy® Web Development***
0-7615-3182-3 • CD Included
$29.99 U.S. • $44.95 Can. • £21.99 U.K.

**Java™ 2 *Fast & Easy® Web Development***
0-7615-3056-8 • CD Included
$24.99 U.S. • $37.95 Can. • £18.99 U.K.

**JavaServer Pages™ *Fast & Easy® Web Development***
0-7615-3428-8 • CD Included
$29.99 U.S. • $44.95 Can. • £21.99 U.K.

**PHP *Fast & Easy® Web Development***
0-7615-3055-x • CD Included
$24.99 U.S. • $37.95 Can. • £18.99 U.K.

**XHTML *Fast & Easy® Web Development***
0-7615-2785-0 • CD Included
$24.99 U.S. • $37.95 Can. • £18.99 U.K.

Premier Press, Inc.
www.premierpressbooks.com

**Call now to order!**
**1.800.428.7267**

# GAME DEVELOPMENT.

## IT'S SERIOUS BUSINESS.

"Game programming is without a doubt the most intellectually challenging field of Computer Science in the world. However, we would be fooling ourselves if we said that we are 'serious' people! Writing (and reading) a game programming book should be an exciting adventure for both the author and the reader."

—André LaMothe,
Series Editor

Premier Press, Inc.
www.premierpressbooks.com

PREMIER PRESS

GAME DEVELOPMENT

DISCARD

# THE NORTON ANTHOLOGY OF SHORT FICTION

SIXTH EDITION

DATE DUE

| | |
|---|---|
| June 25, 2012 | |
| OCT 04 2012 | |
| APR 04 2013 | |
| JUL 26 2013 | |
| NOV 11 2013 | |
| NOV 26 2013 | |
| JAN 29 2014 | |
| June 1, 2015 | |
| SEP 20 2016 | |
| Oct. 25, 2017 | |
| APR 09 2018 | |
| NOV 26 2019 | |
| Nov. 15, 2021 | |
| | |
| | |

DEMCO, INC. 38-2931

DISCARD

# THE NORTON ANTHOLOGY OF SHORT FICTION

**SIXTH EDITION**

R. V. CASSILL
BROWN UNIVERSITY

RICHARD BAUSCH
GEORGE MASON UNIVERSITY

W. W. NORTON & COMPANY ▪ NEW YORK ▪ LONDON

AUSTIN COMMUNITY COLLEGE
LIBRARY SERVICES

Copyright © 2000, 1995, 1990, 1986, 1981, 1978 by W. W. Norton & Company, Inc.

All rights reserved.
Printed in the United States of America.

Since this page cannot legibly accommodate all of the copyright notices, pp. 1731–36 constitute an extension of the copyright page.

The text of this book is composed in New Caledonia with the display set in Garamond.
Composition by Binghamton Valley Composition.
Manufacturing by Courier Companies

Library of Congress Cataloging-in-Publication Data

The Norton anthology of short fiction / R. V. Cassill, Richard Bausch.—6th ed.
p. cm.
Includes bibliographical references and index.

**ISBN 0-393-97508-8 (pbk.)**

1. Short stories. I. Cassill, R. V. (Ronald Verlin), date. II. Bausch, Richard, date.
PN6120.2.N59 2000
808.83'1—dc21 99-047447

**W. W. Norton & Company, Inc., 500 Fifth Avenue, New York, N.Y. 10110**
**www.wwnorton.com**

W. W. Norton & Company Ltd., Castle House, 75/76 Wells Street, London W1T 3QT

5 6 7 8 9 0

AUSTIN COMMUNITY COLLEGE
LIBRARY SERVICES

# Contents

# Chronological Table of Contents

The date given for each story is that of first book publication; if, however, the story was published significantly earlier in a journal or magazine, the date of first periodical publication is given instead. (In the anthology itself, when an author is represented by more than one story, his or her stories are ordered chronologically, unless the author's own preferred order is well established—as in the case of Katherine Anne Porter.)

# Preface

The first principle for composing the ideal fiction anthology is self-evident: Fill it with stories that discriminating readers have liked most. "Nothing, of course, will ever take the place of the good old fashion of 'liking' a work of art or not liking it," said Henry James. He called this the "primitive" and the "ultimate" test—stressing at the same time the necessity of other critical tactics and measures to be employed along the way. As usual, James was right.

It can be taken for granted that the anthologist likes the stories he has included, but that is not quite enough. Teaching is a collective enterprise. So, in assembling the contents of this book I leaned very heavily on the advice, opinion, and preferences that my publishers had assembled from correspondence with teachers of fiction at colleges and universities across the country. In a real sense, then, the table of contents represents a collaborative effort. This is a collection that has met James's fundamental test of being liked by many experienced and devoted readers.

An anthology designed as a teaching instrument must also, however, entice and guide those who are just learning to like what has long been delighting others. It must provide the calculated variety that permits the teacher to lead the way with the least encumbrance and the largest resources to draw on. Although this text makes no pretense of displaying "the history of the short story" in a systematic way, the selections were made with a view to supporting those historical interpretations that classroom teachers might elect to develop from it. The chronological table of contents provides the groundwork for such an approach.

Discreet footnoting was designed to make each piece accessible to the contemporary student reader. Many questions are phrased to increase students' awareness of the technical options available to the storyteller, because in assembling the collection I chose works that will demonstrate the spectrum of contemporary techniques and show, in the work of earlier times, that technical variations are in themselves part of the meaning of fiction.

The amplitude of the text has permitted the inclusion of more than one story by several important writers. When this is the case, care was taken to suggest the range as well as the particular voice and manner of the author. Partial lists of each author's books point the way to wider reading.

The Glossary is a handy compilation of critical terms most useful in a disciplined classroom discussion of fiction. And, because talking constructively about stories is so crucial a part of the experience that begins with reading them, I have shaped an introductory part of the book as an initiation to that rewarding practice. The short selections in "Talking about Fiction" are the gleanings of a lifetime in which I sought—and tested in the classroom—examples that would show with maximum brevity, clarity, and force the truly fundamental characteristics of the storyteller's art.

A glance at the table of contents will show you that many things in this book have been frequently anthologized. Some have never appeared before in anthologies. In the old as in the new, the freshness and vitality of the collection as a whole was the governing consideration. The goal was to put together a very large group of stories that would, in detail and overall design, express both the living tradition of short fiction and the culture of which it is a part.

For their generous and invaluable help in the movement toward that goal I want to thank M. H. Abrams, Cornell University; Donald K. Adams, Occidental College; Martha Y. Battle, University of Tennessee at Martin; Steven D. Blume, Marietta College; E. C. Bufkin, University of Georgia; Pat M. Carr, University of Texas at El Paso; Thomas Cooley, Ohio State University; Richard C. Day, Humboldt State University; James E. Evans, University of North Carolina at Greensboro; Suzanne Ferguson, Ohio State University; H. Ramsey Fowler, Memphis State University; John R. Griffin, Southern Colorado State College; Cyril Gulassa, De Anza College; Carolyn Heilbrun, Columbia University; Mary Hesky, Goucher College; Michael Hoffman, University of California at Davis; Irene Honeycutt, Central Piedmont Community College; William L. Howarth, Princeton University; Michael Joyce, Jackson (Michigan) Community College; Sylvan M. Karchmer, University of Houston; Anne Thompson Lee, Bates College; Frank Lentricchia, University of California at Irvine; Michael McKeon, Boston University; Rose Moss, Wellesley College; Raymond M. Olderman, University of Wisconsin; Guy Owen, North Carolina State University at Raleigh; James K. Robinson, University of Cincinnati; Robert Storey, University of Pennsylvania; Walter Waring, Kalamazoo College; Shirley Yarnall, The American University; James L. Yoch, University of Oklahoma.

R. V. CASSILL

# Preface to the Sixth Edition

Continuity and change. For one who has had his hands on the shaping of this anthology for almost a quarter of a century—as I have—the looming imperatives of continuity and change go far beyond any conscious decisions to alter either the contents or the layout of the book.

It is the nebulous spirit of the times that dictates the replacement of some titles with others, as it is the sense that new pieces are, willy-nilly, projections from what is very old and long familiar. Something to be retained in a new form.

As with earlier editions I have drawn on the enthusiasms of other writers and teachers. This time the dependence has been magnified by a quantum leap because Richard Bausch has come to serve as co-editor. His tangents meet with mine in matters of taste and experience. He brings his vitality as a teacher, novelist, short-story writer, and critic with the perspective of his generation to bear on the choices of the old and the new offerings. In collaboration we trace in this edition a pattern of what literature in the form of short fiction may be and should be in the period now dawning. A feature of the new collaboration is the scatter of commentary appended to several stories, comments commissioned with the objective of bringing the contemporary sensibility to bear freshly on old and new fiction.

But although there is continuity in the republic of literature and although this continuity may well be the most important thing you discover in your reading year by year, there is also evolutionary change. Year by year and decade by decade there are shifts in the subject matter preferred by our best writers. There are shifts in the way such subject matter is treated. The substance and tenor of this decade—and of the coming millennium—will not be quite the same as that of any time past. It may be that the linkages themselves will be the surest sign of profound changes in the culture, almost in the species. The tenor and substance will alter as we peer at our books for signs of continuity. The contours of the hills remain, but the winds will change, and part of our devoted reading will be to register the paradox of continuity in all manner of variety.

Throughout, our targets were the eye and heart of the individual student reader. Making the selections of stories, we depended on guesswork as well as the authority of tradition. The guess was ultimately that in some stories or others the student would find a permanent companionship, something that must of necessity be taken along because it has been made alive. When you, reader, have finished this book, it should not be finished with you, still making its claims and offering its justifications—something to outlast the midnight oil and welcome days to come.

It may be tempting to some to consider short fiction as consumer goods laid out on the counter to be consumed as we consume other offerings of consumer society. It is anyone's right to approach it thus, and the delights of consumption may be substantial. I would suggest, however, there are more adventurous metaphors that engage the imagination with more rewards in the quest of each soul for itself. Those we mean to peddle from this stand.

Suppose, for instance, that beyond the crash of colliding millennia and the hissing slide of tectonic plates, the characters in literature cry out to us in diminished voices, "Take us with you. Make us alive." Theirs are the voices of continuity, the continuity that we call human to distinguish it from the brute continuity of passing time and sheer happenstance.

How precious this continuity is cannot be demonstrated by any measure of technological or material ballyhoo about the statistics of national rank among the trading nations. Its value has to be discovered by perceptions accumulated in the privacy of recognitions, accumulated in the conquest of the loneliness each reader brings to his or her task. We overcome the loneliness of the human condition by learning how to read better, by devotion to the grand sum of literary imagination calling to us, summoning it as it summons us.

Others we want to thank for their help of one kind or another are Karen Bausch, Emily Bausch, Patricia Cardente, Kay Cassill, Jesse Cassill, Orin E. Cassill, Kathryn Karlsson, Gloria Oquendo, and Anne Richards. In addition, the fine reference librarians at the Brown University Library, Rochambeau Public Library, Providence, Rhode Island, and the Wellfleet Library, Wellfleet, Massachusetts, came through with timely information when we called upon them.

We would also like to thank the many teachers whose comments on the Fifth Edition have helped us plan the Sixth: Robert C. Adams (Community College of Southern Nevada), Bruce Bashford (SUNY at Stony Brook), Greg Beaumont (Florida State University), Illona Bell (Williams College), Bert Bender (Arizona State University), Barbara Bengels (Hofstra University), Ann Bliss (Western Oregon State College), John C. Bonnell (Malcomb County Community College), Fred Bornhauser (Hunter College-SUNY), Robert Brophy (California State University at Long Beach), Rosellen Brown (University of Houston), Allen Bundy (Long Beach City College), T. P. Caldwell (Mississippi State University), Alan Cheuse (George Mason University), Dennis A. Clarke (SUNY at Stony Brook), Tammy Clewell (The Florida State University), J. L. Cobbs (Kutztown University), Beth Cooley (Gonzaga University), Joanne Craig (Bishop's University), William Doherty (Hofstra University), Edmund Epstein (Queens College), Gary Fincke (Susquehanna University), Mildred Fischer (Glendale College), Elizabeth Flynn (Michigan Technological University), Philip Furia (University of North Carolina at Wilmington), Casey Gilson (Broward Community College), William Goede (Capilano College), Stephen Grecco (Pennsylvania State University), Jill Grindel (University of North Florida), Irving Halpern (San Francisco State University), Howard Hertz (Pasadena City College), Clinton S. Hirst (University of Detroit Mercy), Robert Hughes (University of Hawaii at Manoa), Betty Jo Hypes (West Virginia University), Richard Kocter (Loyola Marymount University), Ann Mairoff (Palomar College), Michael Martone (Syracuse University), G. G. Miller (Florida International University), Linda Miller (Muhlenberg College), Patricia Moran (University of

California at Davis), Jeffrey Moss (California State University), Stephen Murabito (University of Pittsburgh at Greensburg), R. Pearse (Brooklyn College), David Rife (Lycoming College), Fred Willer Robinson (University of San Diego), Martha Ronk (Occidental College), Thomas Russell (University of Memphis), Richard Sheehan (North Hennepin Community College), Richard D. Spiese (California State University at Long Beach), Leslie St. Martin (University of Hawaii), Phyllis Stowell (Saint Mary's College), Elizabeth Tallent (Stanford University), Robert Terrill (Mt. San Antonio College), Burt Thrup (University of North Dakota), Mary Titus (St. Olaf College), John R. Vaccone (Sacramento City College), Margaret M. Walsh (University of Massachusetts-Boston), Mary Webb (University of Nevada at Reno), Linda Wells (Boston University), and Melvin Williams (American International College).

# Talking about Fictio[n]

Discussion and analysis follow naturally from th[e] ... make while we are reading. There need be no deliber[a]... story apart." The illusionistic aspect of fiction begins to ... the instant it is experienced, fading passage by passage be... ing moves from the beginning toward the end. When the sp[...] whole is dissolving in our memory into its component parts, w[...] favorable position to sort them out and ask what each part did t[o] ... imagination along lines imagined by the person who wrote the stor[y].

Readers with some degree of critical experience have the habit o[f] ... aspects of plot, character, tone, theme, imagery, point of view, and num[...] other variations of literary form as they sum up and discuss their reading experience. But before we begin to examine any of these aspects in isolation, we can here consider some truly basic features characteristic of fiction in general. We can do that conveniently with the pieces in this section because they are all brief enough to permit an easy reference from text to commentary. They include a poem, three excerpts from stories printed in full farther along in the book, and four selections that are essentially complete short stories. For all their brevity these four display the unity and completeness you will find in the rest of the stories included in this anthology.

## Character and Setting

*Nothing is more fundamental to creating a story than establishing a spatial, temporal environment and peopling it with actors. Here is an example by a modern master.*

### ERNEST HEMINGWAY

*story from* **In Our Time**[1]

Nick sat against the wall of the church where they had dragged him to be clear of machine-gun fire in the street. Both legs stuck out awkwardly. He had been hit in the spine. His face was sweaty and dirty. The sun shone on his face. The day was very hot. Rinaldi, big backed, his equipment sprawling, lay face downward against the wall. Nick looked straight ahead brilliantly. The pink wall of the house opposite had fallen out from the roof, and an iron bedstead hung twisted toward the street. Two Austrian dead lay in the rubble in the shade of

1. Chapter VI of the pamphlet *in our time*, published in a limited edition in January 1924; each of its chapters was virtually a miniature short story in the mode Hemingway was then perfecting. In the following year these nonconsecutive chapters were printed in alternation with longer stories in an expanded volume called *In Our Time*.

...her dead. Things were getting forward in the
...er bearers would be along any time now. Nick
...ooked at Rinaldi. "Senta[2] Rinaldi. S...ta. You and
...ay still in the ... breathing with
...urned his head careful... away smiling sweatily.
...ting audience.

*...sentence specifies a battle setting (by mention of the machine-... the street) and the particular spot, the foot of a church wall, where ... seated. His name, the bare beginning of characterization, is given, and ... quickly learn that he has been wounded.*

*The ruined house across the street is a consistent and specially meaningful part of the setting. Nick is looking at it "brilliantly"—seeing it, that is, with the sharpened, almost desperate awareness that accompanies his injury. The dead bodies of Austrian soldiers mean (to Nick, who is obliged by his role to see them as enemies) that the battle is "going well." The split between his personal concern and his merely military recognition of things is signaled by his next thought: Because the battle is going well for his side, stretcher bearers will soon come to pick him up. This consoling thought leads directly to one more consoling yet: For him the war is over. With an effort at cheerfulness, Nick puts his realization into words, saying, "we've made a separate peace."*

*His wounded comrade Rinaldi does not answer. Perhaps he can't. His silence suggests that Nick's joy at the prospect of getting out of the war is a limited and probably temporary response to the bad thing that has happened to him. Such a suggestion gives a bleak coloration to the inferences we can make about Nick's future, though the story stops short of any explicit prediction.*

## *Action, Plot, and Complication*

*Much of what we understand and feel about people comes from watching them act in relation to others and to the entanglements they create as the action proceeds. The following story by a medieval writer depends almost exclusively on elements of action in developing the complications that give meaning to its plot.*

### GIRALDIS CAMBRENSIS

#### *from* **Revenge**

. . . The lord of Chateau-roux in France maintained in the castle a man whose eyes he had formerly put out, but who, by long habit, recollected the ways of

2. Listen.

the castle, and the steps leading to the towers revenge, and meditating the destruction of the y doors of the castle, and took the only son and hei to the summit of a high tower, from whence concern by the people beneath. The father of struck with terror, attempted by every possible of his son, but received for answer, that this co same mutilation of those lower parts, which he The father, having in vain entreated mercy, a violent blow to be struck on his body; and th lamentably, as if he had suffered mutilation. Th he felt the greatest pain? When he replied in his and prepared to precipitate the boy. A second blo the castle asserting that the greatest pain was at his ing his disbelief, again carried the boy to the summ time, however, the father, to save his son, really mu he exclaimed that the greatest pain was in his teeth; man who has had experience should be believed, and th my injuries. I shall meet death with more satisfaction, beget any other son, nor receive comfort from this." Then and the boy from the summit of the tower, their limbs w instantly expired. The knight ordered a monastery built on of the boy, which is still extant, and called De Doloribus.[4]

*The revenger's wish to pay back the man who has blin him provides the initial motivation from which the fictional pl The sequence of following events, complicating the plot, repres erating contest of will and cunning between the chief antagonist blows to which the father submits are graduated tests of his affe his son and of his confidence in his ability to outwit his opponent. affection, confidence, and cleverness are attributes of character, we s progress in the action reveals character.*

*The blind man's response to the blows is motivated by his interpre (correct in each case) of what has really happened. Note that in the case o the first two blows a part of what has happened is a further attempt to victimize him, by deceit. At each test the father's confidence diminishes, and he is motivated by this progressive diminishing of confidence, as well as by growing anxiety for his son, to submit to castration. Probably it is his mushrooming panic that prevents his considering what may happen after he has yielded to the demand.*

*The straightforward movement of the plot toward the anticipated end shifts when the revenger declares himself only partially satisfied by the father's castration. The suicide and murder of the boy held hostage carry the action to the point of fully measuring the degree of fury that began it.*

3. Kidneys. 4 Place of Sorrow.

*ıt in this story the characterization—aside from that ɿion itself—is kept to a stark minimum. Nevertheless, nagination to speculate on the variables of sensation usually included in fictional characterization. The ɲent generated by the force of the action carries us into boy may have seen as he looked down from the tower captive. What did he remember as he heard his father ɘ? What did he want his father to do? Perhaps we are even ne answers for such questions; a good story incites the ıtion to go a bit beyond what is actually and literally told.*

## *Point of View*

*ɛed to make judgments about characters by their actions in a ɦat they choose to do and what is done to them. Our response is and given particular coloration by the attitude, personal vision, and ations with which the characters respond as the events of the story This individualized response is called* point of view. *It is an element in told in the third person as well as in the first, though the degree to an author exploits it may vary widely.*

### ALICE WALKER

#### *from* **Everyday Use**

Sometimes I dream a dream in which Dee and I are suddenly brought together on a TV program. . . . Out of a dark and soft-seated limousine I am ushered into a bright room filled with many people. There I meet a smiling, gray, sporty man like Johnny Carson who shakes my hand and tells me what a fine girl I have. Then we are on the stage and Dee is embracing me with tears in her eyes. She pins on my dress a large orchid, even though she has told me once she thinks orchids are tacky flowers.

In real life I am a large, big-boned woman with rough, man-working hands. . . . I can kill and clean a hog as mercilessly as a man. My fat keeps me hot in zero weather. I can work outside all day, breaking ice to get water for washing. I can eat pork liver cooked over an open fire minutes after it comes steaming from the hog. . . .

*This woman is intentionally portraying herself without any attempt to falsify the harsh demands of her life, her daydreams, or her appearance. But her candor and the touch of self-mockery in her dream of appearing on TV are testimony to a certain kind of self-confident pride. She knows who she is, after all, and speaks as someone who knows how to make the best of her strength and her shortcomings.*

*Her narrative voice will remain a stabilizing force throughout the story, guiding the reader's discriminations between th lifestyles as they conflict and compete. Thus the necessary trust to the outcome, in which certain s quished.*

*But it is not only in stories told in the first p objective world through the eyes of a character.*

## FLANNERY O'CON

*from* **Everything That Rises M**

His mother continued to gaze at him but sh momentary discomfort. Her eyes retained thei to be unnaturally red, as if her blood pressu glimmer of sympathy to show on his face. Ha desperately to keep it and carry it through. I a lesson that would last a while, but there seen The Negro refused to come out from behind

*This passage begins with a statement that is e could have been made by a neutral reporter without interest in Julian. But then we are moved briskly to w prejudiced point of view prevails. When we come to the u third sentence, we know that his mother's face seems particula of his intimacy with her and his inverted concern with her blood p We move then beyond his notation of her symptoms into the hostile w is motivating his behavior in the bus. Now we are fully in his point of view, seeing things as he does and beholding the malevolence that shapes his vision. "He would have liked to teach her a lesson that would last a while." This glimpse into his mind underlines his complicity with the deadly forces gathering to finish the woman off.*

*Some stories told in the third person may shift the point of view from that of one character to another's, and in some it is hard to say with certainty that the author has adopted the point of view of* any *of the characters, for some styles and types of diction will indicate that we are reading of matters that could only be known by the writer. There is a great range of possibilities in the distance that can be set between the creator and the imagined creatures populating the printed page. For the reader it is always well to assume that something in the nature of the material has influenced the writer's choice to move in close or keep an Olympian distance. The closer he or she wants to be to the characters in their travails, the more the writer will immerse himself or herself in the point of view of this person or that in the story.*

*In the story from which the following excerpt is taken, Freeman mostly chooses to show what is happening from the point of view of her main female character. But just for a little she lapses, intruding with summary and evaluative comment on certain developments. This "author intrusion" (see Glossary)* dilutes the concreteness and sensuousness of

xxviii ■

nerally shunned because it ... ing rendered.

## E. WILKINS FREEMAN

### *from* A New England Nun

d brother had died, and she was all alone in the world. ...ng of all—a subtle happening which both were too simple ...ouisa's feet had turned into a path, smooth maybe under a ...but so straight and unswerving that it could only meet a check ...d so narrow that there was no room for any one at her side.

*...l find when you read the whole story that such judgmental ...mment is by no means typical of most of the narrative manner. ...s quoted passage we are unmistakably being told things Louisa ...t know about herself, and a projection into the future is made. For ...ment the author is speaking directly to the reader—and perhaps ...essarily lapsing from the disciplined point of view she chose. But if we ...e to call this a fault, we would certainly concede that it is a very minor ...e, which might readily be excused by citing the nature of the material. ...fter all, the narrative covers a period of many years, and compression of some parts is absolutely required. I have cited it here not to criticize it but only to illustrate another of the choices available to the fiction writer.*

## *Indirection*

*The revelations of fiction are not usually made by direct statement. The bottom line is not spelled out in a positive or unambiguous summation. Rather the tactic of the fictional art is to guide, direct, and entice the imagination of the reader to a point where intuition blends with a comprehension of detail to engender a sympathetic understanding still shaded by mysteries of a moral or psychological sort.*

## BARBARA L. GREENBERG

### Important Things

For years the children whimpered and tugged. "Tell us, tell us."

You promised to tell the children some other time, later, when they were old enough.

Now the children stand eye to eye with you and show you their teeth. "Tell us."

"Tell you what?" you ask, ingenuous.

"Tell us The Important Things."

You tell the children there are six continents and five oceans, or vice versa.

You tell your children the little you know about sex. Your children tell you there are better words for what you choose to call The Married Embrace.

You tell your children to be true to themselves. They say they are true to themselves. You tell them they're lying, you always know when they're lying. They tell you you're crazy. You tell them to mind their manners. They think you mean it as a joke; they laugh.

There are tears in your eyes. You tell the children the dawn will follow the dark, the tide will come in, the grass will be renewed, every dog will have its day. You tell them the story of The Littlest Soldier whose right arm, which he sacrificed while fighting for a noble cause, grew back again.

You say that if there were no Evil we wouldn't have the satisfaction of choosing The Good. And if there were no pain, you say, we'd never know our greatest joy, relief from pain.

You offer to bake a cake for the children, a fudge cake with chocolate frosting, their favorite.

"Tell us," say the children.

You say to your children, "I am going to die."

"When?"

"Someday."

"Oh."

You tell your children that they, too, are going to die. They already knew it.

You can't think of anything else to tell the children. You say you're sorry. You *are* sorry. But the children have had enough of your excuses.

"A promise is a promise," say the children.

They'll give you one more chance to tell them of your own accord. If you don't, they'll have to resort to torture.

*This little story is a teaser, crafted not only to keep the children (and the narrator) baffled about what "important things" are but to lure us into our own creative speculation about the great secrets of existence. By a process of elimination, those things we would readily think of as important are dismissed as unsatisfactory. The fundamentals of common knowledge are denied their fundamental status. The challenge to name what is truly important slips by the narrator and is slyly posed to us. Once the attempts at direct answers is used up, the story has put it up to us to scrape our souls for what we have to declare.*

*In some sense most of the stories we will encounter in this book bring us to the same pass, for even in those where the author has come down hard with a positive declaration about what is important, there will be a nimbus or shadowy fringe in which conviction and full comprehension can only be established by our emotional insight and a seizure of implications that are not spelled out in the text. Most stories—much larger than this one in bulk—stir up questions of right and wrong, of what is worth living for and dying for. Truly these are "important things," and authors work with all their skill to guide us to a point where the inexpressible can be sensed. But the best tactic of fiction to move circuitously to the point of revelation. Then those readers who have followed the path of indirections complete the reading transaction by going somewhat farther than they have been led, by drawing from themselves the impassioned judgment that will make the story whole.*

## *The Part and the Whole*

*In our reading of fiction (or any literary form, for that matter) we will often pause to consider the relation between some single word and the overall meaning of the situation and action, between a significant part and the significance of the whole, as in this poem:*

### WILLIAM STAFFORD

**Traveling through the Dark**

Traveling through the dark I found a deer
dead on the edge of the Wilson River road.
It is usually best to roll them into the canyon:
that road is narrow; to swerve might make more dead.

By glow of the tail-light I stumbled back of the car
and stood by the heap, a doe, a recent killing;
she had stiffened already, almost cold.
I dragged her off; she was large in the belly.

My fingers touching her side brought me the reason—
her side was warm; her fawn lay there waiting,
alive, still, never to be born.
Beside that mountain road I hesitated.

The car aimed ahead its lowered parking lights;
under the hood purred the steady engine.
I stood in the glare of the warm exhaust turning red;
around our group I could hear the wilderness listen.

I thought hard for us all—my only swerving—,
then pushed her over the edge into the river.

*Like many other poems, this one tells a story, and our immediate concern with it is to demonstrate how one part—the verb* to swerve*—expands the meaning of the episode, opening dimensions of thought that may be inherent in the action but might elude a casual observer of what is being done.*

*There is probably no way the narrator can save the life of the unborn fawn trapped in the dead body of its mother. Yet the very hopelessness of the fawn's plight calls to him to take sides with it against the threat of extinction. So he faces a dilemma. If he does not kill the fawn by pushing the deer into guiding the reader's discriminations between the claims made by different lifestyles as they conflict and compete. Thus the point of view contributes a necessary trust to the outcome, in which certain strident claims are vanquished.*

*But it is not only in stories told in the first person that we look at the objective world through the eyes of a character.*

## FLANNERY O'CONNOR

### *from* **Everything That Rises Must Converge**

His mother continued to gaze at him but she did not take advantage of his momentary discomfort. Her eyes retained their battered look. Her face seemed to be unnaturally red, as if her blood pressure had risen. Julian allowed no glimmer of sympathy to show on his face. Having got the advantage he wanted desperately to keep it and carry it through. He would have liked to teach her a lesson that would last a while, but there seemed no way to continue the point. The Negro refused to come out from behind his paper.

*This passage begins with a statement that is essentially objective. It could have been made by a neutral reporter without any special insight or interest in Julian. But then we are moved briskly to where Julian's special and prejudiced point of view prevails. When we come to the word* seemed *in the third sentence, we know that his mother's face seems particularly red because of his intimacy with her and his inverted concern with her blood pressure. We move then beyond his notation of her symptoms into the hostile wish that is motivating his behavior in the bus. Now we are fully in his point of view, seeing things as he does and beholding the malevolence that shapes his vision. "He would have liked to teach her a lesson that would last a while." This glimpse into his mind underlines his complicity with the deadly forces gathering to finish the woman off.*

*Some stories told in the third person may shift the point of view from that of one character to another's, and in some it is hard to say with certainty that the author has adopted the point of view of* any *of the characters, for some styles and types of diction will indicate that we are reading of matters that could only be known by the writer. There is a great range of possibilities in the distance that can be set between the creator and the imagined creatures populating the printed page. For the reader it is always well to assume that something in the nature of the material has influenced the writer's choice to move in close or keep an Olympian distance. The closer he or she wants to be to the characters in their travails, the more the writer will immerse himself or herself in the point of view of this person or that in the story.*

*In the story from which the following excerpt is taken, Freeman mostly chooses to show what is happening from the point of view of her main female character. But just for a little she lapses, intruding with summary and evaluative comment on certain developments. This "author intrusion" (see Glossary) is generally shunned because it dilutes the concreteness and sensuousness of the action being rendered.*

## MARY E. WILKINS FREEMAN

### *from* A New England Nun

. . . Louisa's father and brother had died, and she was all alone in the world. But greatest happening of all—a subtle happening which both were too simple to understand—Louisa's feet had turned into a path, smooth maybe under a calm, serene sky, but so straight and unswerving that it could only meet a check at her grave, and so narrow that there was no room for any one at her side.

*You will find when you read the whole story that such judgmental authorial comment is by no means typical of most of the narrative manner. But in this quoted passage we are unmistakably being told things Louisa could not know about herself, and a projection into the future is made. For the moment the author is speaking directly to the reader—and perhaps unnecessarily lapsing from the disciplined point of view she chose. But if we were to call this a fault, we would certainly concede that it is a very minor one, which might readily be excused by citing the nature of the material. After all, the narrative covers a period of many years, and compression of some parts is absolutely required. I have cited it here not to criticize it but only to illustrate another of the choices available to the fiction writer.*

# *Indirection*

*The revelations of fiction are not usually made by direct statement. The bottom line is not spelled out in a positive or unambiguous summation. Rather the tactic of the fictional art is to guide, direct, and entice the imagination of the reader to a point where intuition blends with a comprehension of detail to engender a sympathetic understanding still shaded by mysteries of a moral or psychological sort.*

## BARBARA L. GREENBERG

### Important Things

For years the children whimpered and tugged. "Tell us, tell us."

You promised to tell the children some other time, later, when they were old enough.

Now the children stand eye to eye with you and show you their teeth. "Tell us."

"Tell you what?" you ask, ingenuous.

"Tell us The Important Things."

You tell the children there are six continents and five oceans, or vice versa.

*the river, he will have failed in his duty to other people who will be using the road, and he may be to blame for any accident that might ensue if a car either struck the deer's body or swerved to avoid it.*

*In the ultimate decision to push the entrapped fawn to its doom we see the pattern of all anguishing predicaments in which people who yearn to do good must commit what they believe to be the lesser evil. No wonder the narrator hesitates.*

*Now, consider how the verb* to swerve *(and its other form,* swerving*) intensifies and expands the meaning of that hesitation. In the fourth line* to swerve *is firmly associated with danger of death. That association is recalled to our minds when the narrator, who has paused to think before acting, calls his thought "my only swerving." The dispute in his mind between natural impulse and social duty and the wish for time to seek some gentler alternative is thus equated with a dangerous human weakness. Still, because the double meaning given to* swerving *permits a double vision, we see that the weakness is, simultaneously, a noble and human response, worth the practical risk it entails.*

*Are the processes of thought that expose us to contradictory motivations a weakness, a costly form of nobility, or a mysterious combination of both? That is the multidimensional quandary we are brought to confront by the wordplay in this poem. The story situation applies great pressure on a single word, and just as great pressure applied to carbon produces a diamond, pressure of meaning converging on a single word produces something that will refract special lights back through the whole substance of the story.*

*When you read Herman Melville's* Bartleby, the Scrivener, *you will note how that massive story puts the same sort of presure on the single word* prefer. *Other stories that do not depend so much on wordplay will force a reciprocal action between the whole and some detail of gesture, a bit of unintentionally revealing dialogue or fragmentary glimpse of a passion ordinarily hidden behind a civilized exterior.*

*In some sense, of course, every word and every detail in a story is crucial to the development of meaning in the larger movements of plot or character development. But those special parts that echo, qualify, or expand the larger concept are those to which we direct our closest scrutiny.*

## *Coherence*

*In well-made fiction one thing follows from another, and the connected parts all work together to deliver the effect and meaning. Let's examine the cooperative interconnections of parts in the following.*

## WRIGHT MORRIS

### *story from* **God's Country and My People**[5]

My feet were not big. My knee pants were always below my knees. I preferred to ride a man's bike side-saddle, the sprocket wearing a grease spot on one shin, and my father often wondered what was on my mind. He spoke to Mrs. Healy, in the eighth grade, about it, and she referred him to *Tom Sawyer.* In case I might be too smart for *Tom Sawyer,* she gave him three books by Ralph Henry Barbour.[6] My father read them late at night, in the bathroom, or in the egg-candling[7] room of his produce business, using the light that came through the holes of the candler. If he could believe what he read, all I had on my mind was good clean fun. All I wanted to do was pitch the winning game and win the cross-country run. That seemed a long way to run, but my father believed that I could. Later he hoped to send me to an Eastern school where I would live in a room hung with college pennants, and spend Christmas with my roommate whose younger sister was home from her boarding school. Playing run-sheep-run[8] at night with Lillian Eichler, we stood holding hands in Mrs. Seidel's coal bin, where my breathing was noisy but I had no idea what was on my mind.

*The first two sentences and the first principal clause of the third explain the situation. They define the boy's adolescent foibles, which—as indicated in the second clause of the third sentence—cause the father concern. For the narrator to state here that his father "often wondered" is to expand the time range and the sophistication of the voice recounting the events. The words signal that the narrator is looking back—probably from adulthood—to contemplate a problem that endured through a phase of his youth.*

*Now the fourth sentence adds a particular, concrete action, performed at a specific point in time, which follows coherently from the habitual action recounted in the third sentence. In a story on a larger scale such transition from habitual to specific would ordinarily be accomplished by passing over from narration to a scene. (We might guess that the scene between the father and Mrs. Healy would open with words on the order of:* One day my exasperated father went for help to my eighth grade teacher. "My kid's floundering," he told her. . . .*)*

*Next, characterization of Mrs. Healy is provided by her naive, schoolmarm faith that books will fix whatever is wrong. She is further characterized (and derided in the tone of fond irony that pervades the whole) by her topsy-turvy notion that books by Ralph Henry Barbour are more sophisticated than* Tom Sawyer. *The author thus satirizes not only Mrs. Healy but the quaint provincialism of the milieu in which the action is taking place.*

5. Morris's book consists of photographs by the author with prose vignettes or stories on unnumbered facing pages. 6. American author of juvenile inspirational fiction. 7. A method of checking eggs for edibility by holding them against a lighted hole in a dark-walled box. 8. Variant of hide-and-seek.

*The sixth sentence smoothly continues the line of action and fills in some information about family circumstances that was postponed from the expository opening. That the books are read by night "in the bathroom" must mean that the father and his motherless son live in a single room with adjacent bath. Their poverty and the father's commitment to his son's welfare are indicated by the father's use of light from the egg candler to read by. Frugality and aspiration are seen pathetically blended in the father's nature.*

*As we register this pathos we come to a shift in the direction of the plot action. Intending to come closer to his son by reading the prescribed books, the father is misled into a dream of glory that can only widen the distance between them. Paternal altruism detours into self-indulgent sentimentality. The specific ingredients of the father's reading, given in the eighth and tenth sentences, not only play up the ironic tone of the whole—they retroactively satirize Mrs. Healy and parody the national dream of what we call "upward mobility."*

*Finally, the increasing likelihood that the father's efforts will backfire is confirmed by the eleventh sentence. When the focus of narration shifts to the son, we see he is very far off the track of his father's daydreams.*

*It might appear that in a story so brief no space could be found to individualize Lillian Eichler. A multitude of teenage girls have played run-sheep-run at night in Midwestern towns. Yet the single verb* stood *sets her apart from the nameless multitude. It is not every girl who could be hypnotized (or self-hypnotized) into patience while she waits for the mixed-up boy to discover what truly is on his mind at this opportune moment.*

*From a minimal cast of characters the author has made a maximum statement about human relations by (1) choosing characters whose differences provide meaningful contrast and (2) relying on dramatic progression to show off facets of each character in successive phases of the action. The end of the story was implicit in its beginning. The significant relation between setting and characters is exposed as they interact within a small but dense design. Details that further the plot serve, at the same time, to establish and modulate the tone. The last three words repeat (with ironic variation) something said before—and tie the last knot on an elegantly neat package.*

# *General Questions*

*The following questions are designed to prompt your approaches to your reading and to preparing papers or notes for classroom discussion. It is by no means necessary to prepare systematic answers for all or any of the stories. Obviously not all questions need to be answered in relation to any particular story. But their best use might be in focusing your attention on one or another of those aspects the writer has managed in weaving the whole fabric of the story. Thus they continue the process examined in the previous section and reach onward to the stories that follow.*

## Exposition and Setting

1. How and when has the author introduced the main characters?

2. How much background information or history has the author provided for them? At what point in the story, and by what means, is this background information brought in? What makes such backgrounding necessary or (in cases in which it is scanty or lacking altogether) unnecessary? Are the characters made quickly comprehensible by representing them as familiar types?

3. What means provide us with an understanding of the situation prevailing before the action, properly speaking, begins? To what extent is a prevailing and preexisting conflict used as a jumping-off place for the present action of the story?

4. What is there of special interest or significance in the setting of the story? By what means are we informed about the details of the setting? At what point in the story? How is its relation to the significance of the action expressed?

5. Is the setting vividly represented or merely implied by the way in which events unfold? Has the author assumed that readers would be familiar with the significant qualities to be found in this setting?

6. How is the setting exploited to enhance or control the mood of the story? How does it help to bring out the feelings or emotions experienced by the characters?

7. In stories told in the first person, do we learn essential things about the narrator by the feelings or attention the narrator devotes to the setting?

8. Could the action take place meaningfully in another setting? That is—has the setting been chosen arbitrarily, for its own sake, or because it has an integral connection with the action?

## Plot

1. Do the meaning and emotional impact of this story heavily depend on the working out of the plot? Or is the plot—if it is noticeable at all—subordinate to the other elements?

2. To what extent does the action of the plot emerge from the kinds of characters depicted in the story and their relation to each other?

3. Are there any major breaks or omissions in the chain of causality that links the events or episodes of the plot? Is the outcome of the plot consistent with the actions that initiated it? If there is a surprise ending, does it emerge from some unforeseen but plausible change in direction of the plot line?

4. How is the plot related to the chronology of the story? That is, have some decisive actions, necessary to the plot, taken place before the narration begins? Is the narration halted with an implication of some event still to come that will round out the plot?

5. Test the plot for meaning and credibility by imagining alternative events which, at any point, might have made for a different outcome.

6. What motivations in the characters are necessary to move the plot along?

### Character and Conflict

1. Who is the central character, or who are the central characters? What means has the author used to demonstrate their qualities? To what extent are the characters defined by contrast with minor characters?

2. Do we understand the characters as types or as individuals? By their actions? Their speech? Their thoughts? (It may be useful for you to pick a single instance of action, speech, or thought and ask in what ways it represents the character to whom it is attributed.)

3. Which characters are active and which passive within the pattern of the story?

4. Does the story show growth or change of character? How much of the story's meaning depends on such growth or change?

5. How much of the conflict in the story rises from an opposition between the central character and his or her environment?

6. Is the conflict inherent in the personality of the characters assembled by the author or in the backgrounds they represent?

7. How has the author worked to involve the reader's sympathies for certain characters, and how does this contribute to the reader's assessment of the issues of the conflict?

8. How much are the characters (or their representation) conditioned by their time and place?

### Point of View and Person of Narration

1. Has the author confined the narration to a single point of view? Taking into account the nature of the material in the story, what apparent advantages lie in telling about it from the point of view actually chosen?

2. What potentially interesting aspects of the subject matter have been subordinated or omitted by choice of point of view?

3. In first-person narration, to what extent does the author appear to have identified himself with the narrator? What has the author gained by keeping a distinction between himself and the personality of the narrator?

4. What would be gained or lost by changing the narration from first to

third person, or vice versa? (Class exercises in rewriting parts of stories may be useful in support of this question.)

5. How is the point of view complemented by disciplines of style and diction? How do self-imposed limits of diction reinforce the emotional impact of a story or focus its meaning?

6. Is an illusion of reality enhanced by choice of point of view? A sense of immediacy?

### Theme

1. Does the story make a general statement about life or experience? Can it be stated in the form of a maxim? (The effort to reduce the meaning of any piece of fiction to a short, aphoristic summary can stumble all too readily into simplistic errors. The teacher should point out that summary of any theme is less than a complete understanding of the story from which it comes.)

2. Is the thematic statement accomplished chiefly by the outcome of the action? What qualifications and shadings are given to it by the awareness of the characters of what has happened to them?

3. What values and ideas have been put into the conflict from which the thematic statement comes?

4. Is the theme a traditional one? Has the story given a new twist to traditional wisdom? Where else—in literature, history, or religion—have you encountered a similar theme? Can you recall a poem or another story that makes a comparable thematic statement?

### Description, Representation, and Symbol

1. Pick out some examples of language used by the author to stimulate and control the reader's visualization of the scene. Consider not only individual words and phrases but the accumulations and combinations of nouns, verbs, and their modifiers in paragraph structures.

2. How have the details chosen by the author given the essential appearance of characters or scene? Is the story fully presented to your senses? Comment on the adequacy of the description.

3. Has the author relied on your familiarity with certain scenes, characters, and situations to fill in what has been omitted from the actual text of the story?

4. How has the objectively rendered action of the story helped you to understand the thoughts, emotions, and motivations of the characters? Can you fill in the thought processes of those characters whose thoughts are not described?

5. What objects, acts, or situations have a symbolic meaning? Are the characters aware of these symbolic meanings? Has the author used symbols as a means of communicating to the reader some meanings not implicit in the action and not understood by any character in the story?

**MODE (AS IT APPLIES)**

1. What devices or instances has the author relied on to heighten the comic (pathetic, tragic, satiric, elegiac) effect of the story?

2. What exaggerations or distortions of reality do you find used to shape the material of the story to a particular purpose? Could the same material serve another purpose? (For example, in the case of comedy, could the material have been treated in a way that would produce a tragic effect?)

3. To what extent has the author manipulated the tone of the story to give a special flavor to the material?

4. With what views of life does this story fit best?

5. What satiric or ironic elements can you distinguish in the story? Do these dominate the whole story? Are they consistent with the overall quality of the story, or do they provide tension, variety, and suspense as you wait to learn what the author is really driving at?

6. Does the story appeal chiefly to a romantic or realistic sensibility? Does it tend to stir up pity, contempt, amusement, awe, dismay, admiration, or a desire that life should be different than it is?

# Sherwood Anderson

*Anderson (1876–1941) was born in Camden, Ohio, the son of a roving, likable, improvident, and talkative man, who often appears under one name or another in Anderson's works. After some intermittent schooling, Anderson enlisted in the army for service in Cuba during the Spanish-American War. A few years later—in the spirit of rebellion against industrial and commercial civilization that was to color his writing thereafter—he walked out of his job as manager of an Ohio paint factory. Going to Chicago, then in the ferment of a literary renaissance, he made friends with writers and began to publish his own poetry and fiction. With the appearance in 1919 of* Winesburg, Ohio, *he became famous. As in the collections that followed, the stories of this book show life and desire frustrated by the provincialism of the Midwest. Characteristic of his work is a tone of melancholy reminiscence in which he projects remembered realities on the screen of a philosophic imagination. His autobiography,* A Story-Teller's Story *(1924), is partly fictional, as most of his fiction is partly autobiographical. His novels include* Windy McPherson's Son *(1916),* Poor White *(1920),* Many Marriages *(1923), and* Dark Laughter *(1925). His later collections of stories are* The Triumph of the Egg *(1921),* Horses and Men *(1923), and* "Death in the Woods" and Other Stories *(1933).*

## I Want to Know Why

We got up at four in the morning, that first day in the East. On the evening before, we had climbed off a freight train at the edge of town and with the true instinct of Kentucky boys had found our way across town and to the race track and the stables at once. Then we knew we were all right. Hanley Turner right away found a nigger we knew. It was Bildad Johnson, who in the winter works at Ed Becker's livery barn in our home town, Beckersville. Bildad is a good cook as almost all our niggers are and of course he, like everyone in our part of Kentucky who is anyone at all, likes the horses. In the spring Bildad begins to scratch around. A nigger from our country can flatter and wheedle anyone into letting him do most anything he wants. Bildad wheedles the stable men and the trainers from the horse farms in our country around Lexington. The trainers come into town in the evening to stand around and talk and maybe get into a poker game. Bildad gets in with them. He is always doing little favors and telling about things to eat, chicken browned in a pan, and how is the best way to cook sweet potatoes and corn bread. It makes your mouth water to hear him.

When the racing season comes on and the horses go to the races and there is all the talk on the streets in the evenings about the new colts, and everyone says when they are going over to Lexington or to the spring meeting at Churchill Downs or to Latonia,[1] and the horsemen that have been down to New Orleans or maybe at the winter meeting at Havana in Cuba[2] come home to spend a week before they start out again, at such a time when everything talked about in Beckersville is just horses and nothing else and the outfits start out and horse racing is in every breath of air you breathe, Bildad shows up with a job as cook for some outfit. Often when I think about it, his always going all season to the races and working in the livery barn in the winter where horses are and where men like to come and talk about horses, I wish I was a nigger. It's a foolish thing to say, but that's the way I am about being around horses, just crazy. I can't help it.

Well, I must tell you about what we did and let you in on what I'm talking about. Four of us boys from Beckersville, all whites and sons of men who live in Beckersville regular, made up our minds we were going to the races, not just to Lexington or Louisville, I don't mean, but to the big Eastern track we were always hearing our Beckersville men talk about, to Saratoga.[3] We were all pretty young then. I was just turned fifteen and I was the oldest of the four. It was my scheme. I admit that, and I talked the others into trying it. There was Hanley Turner and Henry Rieback and Tom Tumberton and myself. I had thirty-seven dollars I had earned during the winter working nights and Saturdays in Enoch Myer's grocery. Henry Rieback had eleven dollars and the others, Hanley and Tom, had only a dollar or two each. We fixed it all up and laid low until the Kentucky spring meetings were over and some of our men, the sportiest ones, the ones we envied the most, had cut out. Then we cut out too.

I won't tell you the trouble we had beating our way on freights and all. We went through Cleveland and Buffalo and other cities and saw Niagara Falls. We bought things there, souvenirs and spoons and cards and shells with pictures of the falls on them for our sisters and mothers, but thought we had better not send any of the things home. We didn't want to put the folks on our trail and maybe be nabbed.

We got into Saratoga as I said at night and went to the track. Bildad fed us up. He showed us a place to sleep in hay over a shed and promised to keep still. Niggers are all right about things like that. They won't squeal on you. Often a white man you might meet, when you had run away from home like that, might appear to be all right and give you a quarter or a half dollar or something, and then go right and give you away. White men will do that, but not a nigger. You can trust them. They are squarer with kids. I don't know why.

At the Saratoga meeting that year there were a lot of men from home. Dave Williams and Arthur Mulford and Jerry Myers and others. Then there was a lot from Louisville and Lexington Henry Rieback knew but I didn't. They were professional gamblers and Henry Rieback's father is one too. He is what

1. Racetrack in Covington, Kentucky. Churchill Downs is the famous track in Louisville, Kentucky, where the Kentucky Derby is run every year. 2. I.e., the horse-racing season in Havana. 3. Famous resort town and site of racetrack in upstate New York.

is called a sheet writer and goes away most of the year to tracks. In the when he is home in Beckersville he don't stay there much but goes aw cities and deals faro.[4] He is a nice man and generous, is always sending Henry presents, a bicycle and a gold watch and a boy scout suit of clothes and things like that.

My own father is a lawyer. He's all right, but don't make much money and can't buy me things, and anyway I'm getting so old now I don't expect it. He never said nothing to me against Henry, but Hanley Turner and Tom Tumberton's fathers did. They said to their boys that money so come by is no good and they didn't want their boys brought up to hear gamblers' talk and be thinking about such things and maybe embrace them.

That's all right and I guess the men know what they are talking about, but I don't see what it's got to do with Henry or with horses either. That's what I'm writing this story about. I'm puzzled. I'm getting to be a man and want to think straight and be O. K., and there's something I saw at the race meeting at the Eastern track I can't figure out.

I can't help it, I'm crazy about thoroughbred horses, I've always been that way. When I was ten years old and saw I was growing to be big and couldn't be a rider I was so sorry I nearly died. Harry Hellinfinger in Beckersville, whose father is Postmaster, is grown up and too lazy to work, but likes to stand around in the street and get up jokes on boys like sending them to a hardware store for a gimlet to bore square holes and other jokes like that. He played one on me. He told me that if I would eat a half a cigar I would be stunted and not grow any more and maybe could be a rider. I did it. When father wasn't looking I took a cigar out of his pocket and gagged it down some way. It made me awful sick and the doctor had to be sent for, and then it did no good. I kept right on growing. It was a joke. When I told what I had done and why, most fathers would have whipped me, but mine didn't.

Well, I didn't get stunted and didn't die. It serves Harry Hellinfinger right. Then I made up my mind I would like to be a stableboy, but had to give that up too. Mostly niggers do that work and I knew father wouldn't let me go into it. No use to ask him.

If you've never been crazy about thoroughbreds, it's because you've never been around where they are much and don't know any better. They're beautiful. There isn't anything so lovely and clean and full of spunk and honest and everything as some race horses. On the big horse farms that are all around our town Beckersville there are tracks, and the horses run in the early morning. More than a thousand times I've got out of bed before daylight and walked two or three miles to the tracks. Mother wouldn't of let me go, but father always says "Let him alone." So I got some bread out of the breadbox and some butter and jam, gobbled it and lit out.

At the tracks you sit on the fence with men, whites and niggers, and they chew tobacco and talk, and then the colts are brought out. It's early and the grass is covered with shiny dew and in another field a man is plowing and they are frying things in a shed where the track niggers sleep, and you know how a

4. A card game, favorite of gamblers. "Sheet writer": a bookmaker.

nigger can giggle and laugh and say things that make you laugh. A white man can't do it and some niggers can't, but a track nigger can every time.

And so the colts are brought out and some are just galloped by stableboys, but almost every morning on a big track owned by a rich man who lives maybe in New York, there are always, nearly every morning, a few colts and some of the old race horses and geldings and mares that are cut loose.

It brings a lump up into my throat when a horse runs. I don't mean all horses, but some. I can pick them nearly every time. It's in my blood like in the blood of race track niggers and trainers. Even when they just go slop-jogging along with a little nigger on their backs, I can tell a winner. If my throat hurts and it's hard for me to swallow, that's him. He'll run like Sam Hill[5] when you let him out. If he don't win every time it'll be a wonder and because they've got him in a pocket behind another or he was pulled or got off bad at the post or something. If I wanted to be a gambler like Henry Rieback's father I could get rich. I know I could and Henry says so too. All I would have to do is to wait till that hurt comes when I see a horse and then bet every cent. That's what I would do if I wanted to be a gambler, but I don't.

When you're at the tracks in the morning—not the race tracks but the training tracks around Beckersville—you don't see a horse, the kind I've been talking about, very often, but it's nice anyway. Any thoroughbred, that is sired right and out of a good mare and trained by a man that knows how, can run. If he couldn't, what would he be there for and not pulling a plow?

Well, out of the stables they come and the boys are on their backs and it's lovely to be there. You hunch down on top of the fence and itch inside you. Over in the sheds the niggers giggle and sing. Bacon is being fried and coffee made. Everything smells lovely. Nothing smells better than coffee and manure and horses and niggers and bacon frying and pipes being smoked out of doors on a morning like that. It just gets you, that's what it does.

But about Saratoga. We was there six days and not a soul from home seen us and everything came off just as we wanted it to, fine weather and horses and races and all. We beat our way home and Bildad gave us a basket with fried chicken and bread and other eatables in, and I had eighteen dollars when we got back to Beckersville. Mother jawed and cried, but Pop didn't say much. I told everything we done, except one thing. I did and saw that alone. That's what I'm writing about. It got me upset. I think about it at night. Here it is.

At Saratoga we laid up nights in the hay in the shed Bildad had showed us and ate with the niggers early and at night when the race people had all gone away. The men from home stayed mostly in the grandstand and betting field and didn't come out around the places where the horses are kept except to the paddocks just before a race when the horses are saddled. At Saratoga they don't have paddocks under an open shed as at Lexington and Churchill Downs and other tracks down in our country, but saddle the horses right out in an open place under trees on a lawn as smooth and nice as Banker Bohon's front yard here in Beckersville. It's lovely. The horses are sweaty and nervous and shine and the men come out and smoke cigars and look at them and the trainers are

5. Euphemism for hell.

there and the owners, and your heart thumps so you can hardl

Then the bugle blows for post and the boys that ride com athe. with their silk clothes on and you run to get a place by the fe ning out niggers. th the

I always am wanting to be a trainer or owner, and at the risk of and caught and sent home I went to the paddocks before every race. en boys didn't, but I did.

We got to Saratoga on a Friday, and on Wednesday the next week Mullford Handicap was to be run. Middlestride was in it and Sunstrea weather was fine and the track fast. I couldn't sleep the night before.

What had happened was that both these horses are the kind it make throat hurt to see. Middlestride is long and looks awkward and is a gelding. belongs to Joe Thompson, a little owner from home who only has half a doz horses. The Mullford Handicap is for a mile and Middlestride can't untrac fast. He goes away slow and is always 'way back at the half, then he begins to run and if the race is a mile and a quarter he'll just eat up everything and get there.

Sunstreak is different. He is a stallion and nervous and belongs on the biggest farm we've got in our country, the Van Riddle place that belongs to Mr. Van Riddle of New York. Sunstreak is like a girl you think about sometimes but never see. He is hard all over and lovely too. When you look at his head you want to kiss him. He is trained by Jerry Tillford who knows me and has been good to me lots of times, lets me walk into a horse's stall to look at him close and other things. There isn't anything as sweet as that horse. He stands at the post quiet and not letting on, but he is just burning up inside. Then when the barrier goes up he is off like his name, Sunstreak. It makes you ache to see him. It hurts you. He just lays down and runs like a bird dog. There can't anything I ever see run like him except Middlestride when he gets untracked and stretches himself.

Gee! I ached to see that race and those two horses run, ached and dreaded it too. I didn't want to see either of our horses beaten. We had never sent a pair like that to the races before. Old men in Beckersville said so and the niggers said so. It was a fact.

Before the race, I went over to the paddocks to see. I looked a last look at Middlestride, who isn't such a much standing in a paddock that way, then I went to see Sunstreak.

It was his day. I knew when I see him. I forgot all about being seen myself and walked right up. All the men from Beckersville were there and no one noticed me except Jerry Tillford. He saw me and something happened. I'll tell you about that.

I was standing looking at that horse and aching. In some way, I can't tell how, I knew just how Sunstreak felt inside. He was quiet and letting the niggers rub his legs and Mr. Van Riddle himself put the saddle on, but he was just a raging torrent inside. He was like the water in the river at Niagara Falls just before it goes plunk down. That horse wasn't thinking about running. He don't have to think about that. He was just thinking about holding himself back till the time for the running came. I knew that. I could just in a way see right e was going to do some awful running and I knew it. He wasn't etting on much or prancing or making a fuss, but just waiting. I d Jerry Tillford his trainer knew. I looked up, and then that man and into each other's eyes. Something happened to me. I guess I loved the much as I did the horse because he knew what I knew. Seemed to me wasn't anything in the world but that man and the horse and me. I cried Jerry Tillford had a shine in his eyes. Then I came away to the fence to ait for the race. The horse was better than me, more steadier and, now I now, better than Jerry. He was the quietest and he had to do the running.

Sunstreak ran first of course and he busted the world's record for a mile. I've seen that if I never see anything more. Everything came out just as I expected. Middlestride got left at the post and was 'way back and closed up to be second, just as I knew he would. He'll get a world's record too some day. They can't skin the Beckersville country on horses.

I watched the race calm because I knew what would happen. I was sure. Hanley Turner and Henry Rieback and Tom Tumberton were all more excited than me.

A funny thing that happened to me. I was thinking about Jerry Tillford the trainer and how happy he was all through the race. I liked him that afternoon even more than I ever liked my own father. I almost forgot the horses thinking that way about him. It was because of what I had seen in his eyes as he stood in the paddocks beside Sunstreak before the race started. I knew he had been watching and working with Sunstreak since the horse was a baby colt, had taught him to run and be patient and when to let himself out and not to quit, never. I knew that for him it was like a mother seeing her child do something brave or wonderful. It was the first time I ever felt for a man like that.

After the race that night I cut out from Tom and Hanley and Henry. I wanted to be by myself and I wanted to be near Jerry Tillford if I could work it. Here is what happened.

The track in Saratoga is near the edge of town. It is all polished up and trees around, the evergreen kind, and grass and everything painted and nice. If you go past the track you get to a hard road made of asphalt for automobiles, and if you go along this for a few miles there is a road turns off to a little rummy-looking farmhouse set in a yard.

That night after the race I went along that road because I had seen Jerry and some other men go that way in an automobile. I didn't expect to find them. I walked for a ways and then sat down by a fence to think. It was the direction they went in. I wanted to be as near Jerry as I could. I felt close to him. Pretty soon I went up the side road—I don't know why—and came to the rummy farmhouse. I was just lonesome to see Jerry, like wanting to see your father at night when you are a young kid. Just then an automobile came along and turned in. Jerry was in it and Henry Rieback's father, and Arthur Bedford from home, and Dave Williams and two other men I didn't know. They got out of the car and went into the house, all but Henry Rieback's father who quarreled with them and said he wouldn't go. It was only about nine o'clock, but they were all drunk and the rummy-looking farmhouse was a place for bad women to stay in. That's what it was. I crept up along a fence and looked through a window and saw.

It's what give me the fantods.[6] I can't make it out. The women in the house were all ugly mean-looking women, not nice to look at or be near. They were homely too, except one who was tall and looked a little like the gelding Middlestride, but not clean like him, but with a hard ugly mouth. She had red hair. I saw everything plain. I got up by an old rosebush by an open window and looked. The women had on loose dresses and sat around in chairs. The men came in and some sat on the women's laps. The place smelled rotten and there was rotten talk, the kind a kid hears around a livery stable in a town like Beckersville in the winter but don't ever expect to hear talked when there are women around. It was rotten. A nigger wouldn't go into such a place.

I looked at Jerry Tillford. I've told you how I had been feeling about him on account of his knowing what was going on inside of Sunstreak in the minute before he went to the post for the race in which he made a world's record.

Jerry bragged in that bad woman house as I knew Sunstreak wouldn't never have bragged. He said that he made that horse, that it was him that won the race and made the record. He lied and bragged like a fool. I never heard such silly talk.

And then, what do you suppose he did! He looked at the woman in there, the one that was lean and hard-mouthed and looked a little like the gelding Middlestride but not clean like him, and his eyes began to shine just as they did when he looked at me and at Sunstreak in the paddocks at the track in the afternoon. I stood there by the window—gee!—but I wished I hadn't gone away from the tracks, but had stayed with the boys and the niggers and the horses. The tall rotten-looking woman was between us just as Sunstreak was in the paddocks in the afternoon.

Then, all of a sudden, I began to hate that man. I wanted to scream and rush in the room and kill him. I never had such a feeling before. I was so mad clean through that I cried and my fists were doubled up so my fingernails cut my hands.

And Jerry's eyes kept shining and he waved back and forth, and then he went and kissed that woman and I crept away and went back to the tracks and to bed and didn't sleep hardly any, and then next day I got the other kids to start home with me and never told them anything I seen.

I been thinking about it ever since. I can't make it out. Spring has come again and I'm nearly sixteen and go to the tracks mornings same as always, and I see Sunstreak and Middlestride and a new colt named Strident I'll bet will lay them all out, but no one thinks so but me and two or three niggers.

But things are different. At the tracks the air don't taste as good or smell as good. It's because a man like Jerry Tillford, who knows what he does, could see a horse like Sunstreak run, and kiss a woman like that the same day. I can't make it out. Darn him, what did he want to do like that for? I kept thinking about it and it spoils looking at horses and smelling things and hearing niggers laugh and everything. Sometimes I'm so mad about it I want to fight someone. It gives me the fantods. What did he do it for? I want to know why.

6. Slang for being very shaken and upset.

# MARGARET ATWOOD

*Atwood (1939– ) was born in Ottawa, Ontario. Her father was an entomologist. After her education at the University of Toronto, Radcliffe, and Harvard, she held various jobs as cashier, waitress, market-research writer, and writer of screenplays. She has won numerous prizes for her poetry as well as her fiction. Her novels include* The Edible Woman *(1969),* Surfacing *(1972),* Lady Oracle *(1976),* Life before Man *(1979),* Bodily Harm *(1982),* The Handmaid's Tale *(1985),* Cat's Eye *(1988),* The Robber Bride *(1993), and* Alias Grace *(1996), which has received numerous awards. Many of her stories have been collected in* Dancing Girls and Other Stories *(1978),* Murder in the Dark *(1983),* Bluebeard's Egg *(1983), and* Wilderness Tips *(1989).*

## Death by Landscape

Now that the boys are grown up and Rob is dead, Lois has moved to a condominium apartment in one of the new waterfront developments. She is relieved not to have to worry about the lawn, or about the ivy pushing its muscular little suckers into the brickwork, or the squirrels gnawing their way into the attic and eating the insulation off the wiring, or about strange noises. This building has a security system, and the only plant life is in pots in the solarium.

Lois is glad she's been able to find an apartment big enough for her pictures. They are more crowded together than they were in the house, but this arrangement gives the walls a European look: blocks of pictures, above and beside one another, rather than one over the chesterfield, one over the fireplace, one in the front hall, in the old acceptable manner of sprinkling art around so it does not get too intrusive. This way has more of an impact. You know it's not supposed to be furniture.

None of the pictures is very large, which doesn't mean they aren't valuable. They are paintings, or sketches and drawings, by artists who were not nearly as well known when Lois began to buy them as they are now. Their work later turned up on stamps, or as silk-screen reproductions hung in the principals' offices of high schools, or as jigsaw puzzles, or on beautifully printed calendars sent out by corporations as Christmas gifts, to their less important clients. These artists painted mostly in the twenties and thirties and forties; they painted landscapes. Lois has two Tom Thomsons, three A. Y. Jacksons, a Lawren Harris.

She has an Arthur Lismer, she has a J. E. H. MacDonald. She has a David Milne. They are pictures of convoluted tree trunks on an island of pink wave-smoothed stone, with more islands behind; of a lake with rough, bright, sparsely wooded cliffs; of a vivid river shore with a tangle of bush and two beached canoes, one red, one gray; of a yellow autumn woods with the ice-blue gleam of a pond half-seen through the interlaced branches.

It was Lois who'd chosen them. Rob had no interest in art, although he could see the necessity of having something on the walls. He left all the decorating decisions to her, while providing the money, of course. Because of this collection of hers, Lois's friends—especially the men—have given her the reputation of having a good nose for art investments.

But this is not why she bought the pictures, way back then. She bought them because she wanted them. She wanted something that was in them, although she could not have said at the time what it was. It was not peace: she does not find them peaceful in the least. Looking at them fills her with a wordless unease. Despite the fact that there are no people in them or even animals, it's as if there is something, or someone, looking back out.

When she was thirteen, Lois went on a canoe trip. She'd only been on overnights before. This was to be a long one, into the trackless wilderness, as Cappie put it. It was Lois's first canoe trip, and her last.

Cappie was the head of the summer camp to which Lois had been sent ever since she was nine. Camp Manitou, it was called; it was one of the better ones, for girls, though not the best. Girls of her age whose parents could afford it were routinely packed off to such camps, which bore a generic resemblance to one another. They favored Indian names and had hearty, energetic leaders, who were called Cappie or Skip or Scottie. At these camps you learned to swim well and sail, and paddle a canoe, and perhaps ride a horse or play tennis. When you weren't doing these things you could do Arts and Crafts and turn out dingy, lumpish clay ashtrays for your mother—mothers smoked more, then—or bracelets made of colored braided string.

Cheerfulness was required at all times, even at breakfast. Loud shouting and the banging of spoons on the tables were allowed, and even encouraged, at ritual intervals. Chocolate bars were rationed, to control tooth decay and pimples. At night, after supper, in the dining hall or outside around a mosquito-infested campfire ring for special treats, there were singsongs. Lois can still remember all the words to "My Darling Clementine," and "My Bonnie Lies over the Ocean," with acting-out gestures: a rippling of the hands for "the ocean," two hands together under the cheek for "lies." She will never be able to forget them, which is a sad thought.

Lois thinks she can recognize women who went to these camps, and were good at it. They have a hardness to their handshakes, even now; a way of standing, legs planted firmly and farther apart than usual; a way of sizing you up, to see if you'd be any good in a canoe—the front, not the back. They themselves would be in the back. They would call it the stern.

She knows that such camps still exist, although Camp Manitou does not.

They are one of the few things that haven't changed much. They now offer copper enameling, and functionless pieces of stained glass baked in electric ovens, though judging from the productions of her friends' grandchildren the artistic standards have not improved.

To Lois, encountering it in the first year after the war, Camp Manitou seemed ancient. Its log-sided buildings with the white cement in between the half-logs, its flagpole ringed with whitewashed stones, its weathered gray dock jutting out into Lake Prospect, with its woven rope bumpers and its rusty rings for tying up, its prim round flowerbed of petunias near the office door, must surely have been there always. In truth it dated only from the first decade of the century; it had been founded by Cappie's parents, who'd thought of camping as bracing to the character, like cold showers, and had been passed along to her as an inheritance, and an obligation.

Lois realized, later, that it must have been a struggle for Cappie to keep Camp Manitou going, during the Depression and then the war, when money did not flow freely. If it had been a camp for the very rich, instead of the merely well off, there would have been fewer problems. But there must have been enough Old Girls, ones with daughters, to keep the thing in operation, though not entirely shipshape: furniture was battered, painted trim was peeling, roofs leaked. There were dim photographs of these Old Girls dotted around the dining hall, wearing ample woolen bathing suits and showing their fat, dimpled legs, or standing, arms twined, in odd tennis outfits with baggy skirts.

In the dining hall, over the stone fireplace that was never used, there was a huge molting stuffed moosehead, which looked somehow carnivorous. It was a sort of mascot; its name was Monty Manitou. The older campers spread the story that it was haunted, and came to life in the dark, when the feeble and undependable lights had been turned off or, due to yet another generator failure, had gone out. Lois was afraid of it at first, but not after she got used to it.

Cappie was the same: you had to get used to her. Possibly she was forty, or thirty-five, or fifty. She had fawn-colored hair that looked as if it was cut with a bowl. Her head jutted forward, jigging like a chicken's as she strode around the camp, clutching notebooks and checking things off in them. She was like their minister in church: both of them smiled a lot and were anxious because they wanted things to go well; they both had the same overwashed skins and stringy necks. But all this disappeared when Cappie was leading a singsong, or otherwise leading. Then she was happy, sure of herself, her plain face almost luminous. She wanted to cause joy. At these times she was loved, at others merely trusted.

There were many things Lois didn't like about Camp Manitou, at first. She hated the noisy chaos and spoon-banging of the dining hall, the rowdy singsongs at which you were expected to yell in order to show that you were enjoying yourself. Hers was not a household that encouraged yelling. She hated the necessity of having to write dutiful letters to her parents claiming she was having fun. She could not complain, because camp cost so much money.

She didn't much like having to undress in a roomful of other girls, even in the dim light, although nobody paid any attention, or sleeping in a cabin with seven other girls, some of whom snored because they had adenoids or colds, some of whom had nightmares, or wet their beds and cried about it. Bottom bunks made her feel closed in, and she was afraid of falling out of top ones; she was afraid of heights. She got homesick, and suspected her parents of having a better time when she wasn't there than when she was, although her mother wrote to her every week saying how much they missed her. All this was when she was nine. By the time she was thirteen she liked it. She was an old hand by then.

Lucy was her best friend at camp. Lois had other friends in winter, when there was school and itchy woolen clothing and darkness in the afternoons, but Lucy was her summer friend.

She turned up the second year, when Lois was ten, and a Bluejay. (Chickadees, Bluejays, Ravens, and Kingfishers—these were the names Camp Manitou assigned to the different age groups, a sort of totemic clan system. In those days, thinks Lois, it was birds for girls, animals for boys: wolves, and so forth. Though some animals and birds were suitable and some were not. Never vultures, for instance; never skunks, or rats.)

Lois helped Lucy to unpack her tin trunk and place the folded clothes on the wooden shelves, and to make up her bed. She put her in the top bunk right above her, where she could keep an eye on her. Already she knew that Lucy was an exception to a good many rules; already she felt proprietorial.

Lucy was from the United States, where the comic books came from, and the movies. She wasn't from New York or Hollywood or Buffalo, the only American cities Lois knew the names of, but from Chicago. Her house was on the lake shore and had gates to it, and grounds. They had a maid, all of the time. Lois's family only had a cleaning lady twice a week.

The only reason Lucy was being sent to *this* camp (she cast a look of minor scorn around the cabin, diminishing it and also offending Lois, while at the same time daunting her) was that her mother had been a camper here. Her mother had been a Canadian once, but had married her father, who had a patch over one eye, like a pirate. She showed Lois the picture of him in her wallet. He got the patch in the war. "Shrapnel," said Lucy. Lois, who was unsure about shrapnel, was so impressed she could only grunt. Her own two-eyed, unwounded father was tame by comparison.

"My father plays golf," she ventured at last.

"*Everyone* plays golf," said Lucy. "My *mother* plays golf."

Lois's mother did not. Lois took Lucy to see the outhouses and the swimming dock and the dining hall with Monty Manitou's baleful head, knowing in advance they would not measure up.

This was a bad beginning; but Lucy was good-natured, and accepted Camp Manitou with the same casual shrug with which she seemed to accept everything. She would make the best of it, without letting Lois forget that this was what she was doing.

However, there were things Lois knew that Lucy did not. Lucy scratched the tops off all her mosquito bites and had to be taken to the infirmary to be daubed with Ozonol. She took her T-shirt off while sailing, and although the counselor spotted her after a while and made her put it back on, she burr spectacularly, bright red, with the X of her bathing-suit straps standing out in alarming white; she let Lois peel the sheets of whispery-thin burned skin off her shoulders. When they sang "Alouette" around the campfire, she did not know any of the French words. The difference was that Lucy did not care about the things she didn't know, whereas Lois did.

During the next winter, and subsequent winters, Lucy and Lois wrote to each other. They were both only children, at a time when this was thought to be a disadvantage, so in their letters they pretended to be sisters, or even twins. Lois had to strain a little over this, because Lucy was so blond, with translucent skin and large blue eyes like a doll's, and Lois was nothing out of the ordinary—just a tallish, thinnish, brownish person with freckles. They signed their letters LL, with the L's entwined together like the monograms on a towel. (Lois and Lucy, thinks Lois. How our names date us. Lois Lane, Superman's girlfriend, enterprising female reporter; "I Love Lucy." Now we are obsolete, and it's little Jennifers, little Emilys, little Alexandras and Carolines and Tiffanys.)

They were more effusive in their letters than they ever were in person. They bordered their pages with X's and O's, but when they met again in the summers it was always a shock. They had changed so much, or Lucy had. It was like watching someone grow up in jolts. At first it would be hard to think up things to say.

But Lucy always had a surprise or two, or something to show, some marvel to reveal. The first year she had a picture of herself in a tutu, her hair in a ballerina's knot on the top of her head; she pirouetted around the swimming dock, to show Lois how it was done, and almost fell off. The next year she had given that up and was taking horseback riding. (Camp Manitou did not have horses.) The next year her mother and father had been divorced, and she had a new stepfather, one with both eyes, and a new house, although the maid was the same. The next year when they had graduated from Bluejays and entered Ravens, she got her period, right in the first week of camp. The two of them snitched some matches from their counselor, who smoked illegally, and made a small fire out behind the farthest outhouse, at dusk, using their flashlights. They could set all kinds of fires by now; they had learned how in Campcraft. On this fire they burned one of Lucy's used sanitary napkins. Lois is not sure why they did this, or whose idea it was. But she can remember the feeling of deep satisfaction it gave her as the white fluff singed and the blood sizzled, as if some wordless ritual had been fulfilled.

They did not get caught, but then they rarely got caught at any of their camp transgressions. Lucy had such large eyes, and was such an accomplished liar.

This year Lucy is different again: slower, more languorous. She is no longer interested in sneaking around after dark, purloining cigarettes from the counselor, dealing in black-market candy bars. She is pensive, and hard to wake in the mornings. She doesn't like her stepfather, but she doesn't want to live with her real father either, who has a new wife. She thinks her mother may be having a love affair with a doctor; she doesn't know for sure, but she's seen them smooching in his car, out on the driveway, when her stepfather wasn't there.

It serves him right. She hates her private school. She has a boyfriend, who is sixteen and works as a gardener's assistant. This is how she met him: in the garden. She describes to Lois what it is like when he kisses her—rubbery at first, but then your knees go limp. She has been forbidden to see him, and threatened with boarding school. She wants to run away from home.

Lois has little to offer in return. Her own life is placid and satisfactory, but there is nothing much that can be said about happiness. "You're so lucky," Lucy tells her, a little smugly. She might as well say *boring* because this is how it makes Lois feel.

Lucy is apathetic about the canoe trip, so Lois has to disguise her own excitement. The evening before they are to leave, she slouches into the campfire ring as if coerced, and sits down with a sigh of endurance, just as Lucy does.

Every canoe trip that went out of camp was given a special send-off by Cappie and the section leader and counselors, with the whole section in attendance. Cappie painted three streaks of red across each of her cheeks with a lipstick. They looked like three-fingered claw marks. She put a blue circle on her forehead with fountain-pen ink, and tied a twisted bandanna around her head and stuck a row of frazzle-ended feathers around it, and wrapped herself in a red-and-black Hudson's Bay blanket. The counselors, also in blankets but with only two streaks of red, beat on tom-toms made of round wooden cheese boxes with leather stretched over the top and nailed in place. Cappie was Chief Cappeosota. They all had to say "How!" when she walked into the circle and stood there with one hand raised.

Looking back on this, Lois finds it disquieting. She knows too much about Indians: this is why. She knows, for instance, that they should not even be called Indians, and that they have enough worries without other people taking their names and dressing up as them. It has all been a form of stealing.

But she remembers, too, that she was once ignorant of this. Once she loved the campfire, the flickering of light on the ring of faces, the sound of the fake tom-toms, heavy and fast like a scared heartbeat; she loved Cappie in a red blanket and feathers, solemn, as a chief should be, raising her hand and saying, "Greetings, my Ravens." It was not funny, it was not making fun. She wanted to be an Indian. She wanted to be adventurous and pure, and aboriginal.

"You go on big water," says Cappie. This is her idea—all their ideas—of how Indians talk. "You go where no man has ever trod. You go many moons." This is not true. They are only going for a week, not many moons. The canoe route is clearly marked, they have gone over it on a map, and there are prepared campsites with names which are used year after year. But when Cappie says this—and despite the way Lucy rolls up her eyes—Lois can feel the water stretching out, with the shores twisting away on either side, immense and a little frightening.

"You bring back much wampum," says Cappie. "Do good in war, my braves, and capture many scalps." This is another of her pretenses: that they are boys, and bloodthirsty. But such a game cannot be played by substituting the word "squaw." It would not work at all.

Each of them has to stand up and step forward and have a red line drawn across her cheeks by Cappie. She tells them they must follow the paths of their ancestors (who most certainly, thinks Lois, looking out the window of her apartment and remembering the family stash of daguerreotypes and sepia-colored portraits on her mother's dressing table, the stiff-shirted, black-coated, grim-faced men and the beflounced women with their severe hair and their corseted respectability, would never have considered heading off onto an open lake, in a canoe, just for fun).

At the end of the ceremony they all stood and held hands around the circle, and sang taps. They did not sound very Indian, thinks Lois. It sounded like a bugle call at a military post, in a movie. But Cappie was never one to be much concerned with consistency, or with archeology.

After breakfast the next morning they set out from the main dock, in four canoes, three in each. The lipstick stripes have not come off completely, and still show faintly pink, like healing burns. They wear their white denim sailing hats, because of the sun, and thin-striped T-shirts, and pale baggy shorts with the cuffs rolled up. The middle one kneels, propping her rear end against the rolled sleeping bags. The counselors going with them are Pat and Kip. Kip is no-nonsense; Pat is easier to wheedle, or fool.

There are white puffy clouds and a small breeze. Glints come from the little waves. Lois is in the bow of Kip's canoe. She still can't do a J-stroke very well, and she will have to be in the bow or the middle for the whole trip. Lucy is behind her; her own J-stroke is even worse. She splashes Lois with her paddle, quite a big splash.

"I'll get you back," says Lois.

"There was a stable fly on your shoulder," Lucy says.

Lois turns to look at her, to see if she's grinning. They're in the habit of splashing each other. Back there, the camp has vanished behind the first long point of rock and rough trees. Lois feels as if an invisible rope has broken. They're floating free, on their own, cut loose. Beneath the canoe the lake goes down, deeper and colder than it was a minute before.

"No horsing around in the canoe," says Kip. She's rolled her T-shirt sleeves up to the shoulder; her arms are brown and sinewy, her jaw determined, her stroke perfect. She looks as if she knows exactly what she is doing.

The four canoes keep close together. They sing, raucously and with defiance; they sing "The Quartermaster's Store," and "Clementine," and "Alouette." It is more like bellowing than singing.

After that the wind grows stronger, blowing slantwise against the bows, and they have to put all their energy into shoving themselves through the water.

Was there anything important, anything that would provide some sort of reason or clue to what happened next? Lois can remember everything, every detail; but it does her no good.

They stopped at noon for a swim and lunch, and went on in the afternoon. At last they reached Little Birch, which was the first campsite for overnight. Lois and Lucy made the fire, while the others pitched the heavy canvas tents.

The fireplace was already there, flat stones piled into a U. A burned tin can and a beer bottle had been left in it. Their fire went out, and they had to restart it. "Hustle your bustle," said Kip. "We're starving."

The sun went down, and in the pink sunset light they brushed their teeth and spat the toothpaste froth into the lake. Kip and Pat put all the food that wasn't in cans into a packsack and slung it into a tree, in case of bears.

Lois and Lucy weren't sleeping in a tent. They'd begged to be allowed to sleep out; that way they could talk without others hearing. If it rained, they told Kip, they promised not to crawl dripping into the tent over everyone's legs: they would get under the canoes. So they were out on the point.

Lois tried to get comfortable inside her sleeping bag, which smelled of musty storage and of earlier campers, a stale salty sweetness. She curled herself up, with her sweater rolled up under her head for a pillow and her flashlight inside her sleeping bag so it wouldn't roll away. The muscles of her sore arms were making small pings, like rubber bands breaking.

Beside her Lucy was rustling around. Lois could see the glimmering oval of her white face.

"I've got a rock poking into my back," said Lucy.

"So do I," said Lois. "You want to go into the tent?" She herself didn't, but it was right to ask.

"No," said Lucy. She subsided into her sleeping bag. After a moment she said, "It would be nice not to go back."

"To camp?" said Lois.

"To Chicago," said Lucy. "I hate it there."

"What about your boyfriend?" said Lois. Lucy didn't answer. She was either asleep or pretending to be.

There was a moon, and a movement of the trees. In the sky there were stars, layers of stars that went down and down. Kip said that when the stars were bright like that instead of hazy it meant bad weather later on. Out on the lake there were two loons, calling to each other in their insane, mournful voices. At the time it did not sound like grief. It was just background.

The lake in the morning was flat calm. They skimmed along over the glassy surface, leaving V-shaped trails behind them; it felt like flying. As the sun rose higher it got hot, almost too hot. There were stable flies in the canoes, landing on a bare arm or leg for a quick sting. Lois hoped for wind.

They stopped for lunch at the next of the named campsites, Lookout Point. It was called this because, although the site itself was down near the water on a flat shelf of rock, there was a sheer cliff nearby and a trail that led up to the top. The top was the lookout, although what you were supposed to see from there was not clear. Kip said it was just a view.

Lois and Lucy decided to make the climb anyway. They didn't want to hang around waiting for lunch. It wasn't their turn to cook, though they hadn't avoided much by not doing it, because cooking lunch was no big deal, it was just unwrapping the cheese and getting out the bread and peanut butter, but Pat and Kip always had to do their woodsy act and boil up a billy tin for their own tea.

They told Kip where they were going. You had to tell Kip where you were going, even if it was only a little way into the woods to get dry twigs for kindling. You could never go anywhere without a buddy.

"Sure," said Kip, who was crouching over the fire, feeding driftwood into it. "Fifteen minutes to lunch."

"Where are they off to?" said Pat. She was bringing their billy tin of water from the lake.

"Lookout," said Kip.

"Be careful," said Pat. She said it as an afterthought, because it was what she always said.

"They're old hands," Kip said.

Lois looks at her watch: it's ten to twelve. She is the watchminder; Lucy is careless of time. They walk up the path, which is dry earth and rocks, big rounded pinky-gray boulders or split-open ones with jagged edges. Spindly balsam and spruce trees grow to either side, the lake is blue fragments to the left. The sun is right overhead; there are no shadows anywhere. The heat comes up at them as well as down. The forest is dry and crackly.

It isn't far, but it's a steep climb and they're sweating when they reach the top. They wipe their faces with their bare arms, sit gingerly down on a scorching-hot rock, five feet from the edge but too close for Lois. It's a lookout all right, a sheer drop to the lake and a long view over the water, back the way they've come. It's amazing to Lois that they've traveled so far, over all that water, with nothing to propel them but their own arms. It makes her feel strong. There are all kinds of things she is capable of doing.

"It would be quite a dive off here," says Lucy.

"You'd have to be nuts," says Lois.

"Why?" says Lucy. "It's really deep. It goes straight down." She stands up and takes a step nearer the edge. Lois gets a stab in her midriff, the kind she gets when a car goes too fast over a bump. "Don't," she says.

"Don't what?" says Lucy, glancing around at her mischievously. She knows how Lois feels about heights. But she turns back. "I really have to pee," she says.

"You have toilet paper?" says Lois, who is never without it. She digs in her shorts pocket.

"Thanks," says Lucy.

They are both adept at peeing in the woods: doing it fast so the mosquitoes don't get you, the underwear pulled up between the knees, the squat with the feet apart so you don't wet your legs, facing downhill. The exposed feeling of your bum, as if someone is looking at you from behind. The etiquette when you're with someone else is not to look. Lois stands up and starts to walk back down the path, to be out of sight.

"Wait for me?" says Lucy.

Lois climbed down, over and around the boulders, until she could not see Lucy; she waited. She could hear the voices of the others, talking and laughing, down near the shore. One voice was yelling, "Ants! Ants!" Someone must have sat on an ant hill. Off to the side, in the woods, a raven was croaking, a hoarse single note.

She looked at her watch: it was noon. This is when she heard the shout.

She has gone over and over it in her mind since, so many times that the first, real shout has been obliterated, like a footprint trampled by other footprints. But she is sure (she is almost positive, she is nearly certain) that it was not a shout of fear. Not a scream. More like a cry of surprise, cut off too soon. Short, like a dog's bark.

"Lucy?" Lois said. Then she called "Lucy!" By now she was clambering back up, over the stones of the path. Lucy was not up there. Or she was not in sight.

"Stop fooling around," Lois said. "It's lunchtime." But Lucy did not rise from behind a rock or step out, smiling, from behind a tree. The sunlight was all around; the rocks looked white. "This isn't funny!" Lois said, and it wasn't, panic was rising in her, the panic of a small child who does not know where the bigger ones are hidden. She could hear her own heart. She looked quickly around; she lay down on the ground and looked over the edge of the cliff. It made her feel cold. There was nothing.

She went back down the path, stumbling; she was breathing too quickly; she was too frightened to cry. She felt terrible—guilty and dismayed, as if she had done something very bad, by mistake. Something that could never be repaired. "Lucy's gone," she told Kip.

Kip looked up from the fire, annoyed. The water in the billy can was boiling. "What do you mean, gone?" she said. "Where did she go?"

"I don't know," said Lois. "She's just gone."

No one had heard the shout, but then no one had heard Lois calling, either. They had been talking among themselves, by the water.

Kip and Pat went up to the lookout and searched and called, and blew their whistles. Nothing answered.

Then they came back down, and Lois had to tell exactly what had happened. The other girls all sat in a circle and listened to her. Nobody said anything. They all looked frightened, especially Pat and Kip. They were the leaders. You did not just lose a camper like this, for no reason at all.

"Why did you leave her alone?" said Kip.

"I was just down the path," said Lois. "I told you. She had to go to the bathroom." She did not say *pee* in front of people older than herself.

Kip looked disgusted.

"Maybe she just walked off into the woods and got turned around," said one of the girls.

"Maybe she's doing it on purpose," said another.

Nobody believed either of these theories.

They took the canoes and searched around the base of the cliff, and peered down into the water. But there had been no sound of falling rock; there had been no splash. There was no clue, nothing at all. Lucy had simply vanished.

That was the end of the canoe trip. It took them the same two days to go back that it had taken coming in, even though they were short a paddler. They did not sing.

After that, the police went in a motorboat, with dogs; they were the Mounties and the dogs were German shepherds, trained to follow trails in the woods. But it had rained since, and they could find nothing.

Lois is sitting in Cappie's office. Her face is bloated with crying, she's seen that in the mirror. By now she feels numbed; she feels as if she has drowned. She can't stay here. It has been too much of a shock. Tomorrow her parents are coming to take her away. Several of the other girls who were on the canoe trip are also being collected. The others will have to stay, because their parents are in Europe, or cannot be reached.

Cappie is grim. They've tried to hush it up, but of course everyone in camp knows. Soon the papers will know too. You can't keep it quiet, but what can be said? What can be said that makes any sense? "Girl vanishes in broad daylight, without a trace." It can't be believed. Other things, worse things, will be suspected. Negligence, at the very least. But they have always taken such care. Bad luck will gather around Camp Manitou like a fog; parents will avoid it, in favor of other, luckier places. Lois can see Cappie thinking all this, even through her numbness. It's what anyone would think.

Lois sits on the hard wooden chair in Cappie's office, beside the old wooden desk, over which hangs the thumbtacked bulletin board of normal camp routine, and gazes at Cappie through her puffy eyelids. Cappie is now smiling what is supposed to be a reassuring smile. Her manner is too casual: she's after something. Lois has seen this look on Cappie's face when she's been sniffing out contraband chocolate bars, hunting down those rumored to have snuck out of their cabins at night.

"Tell me again," says Cappie, "from the beginning."

Lois has told her story so many times by now, to Pat and Kip, to Cappie, to the police, that she knows it word for word. She knows it, but she no longer believes it. It has become a story. "I told you," she said. "She wanted to go to the bathroom. I gave her my toilet paper. I went down the path, I waited for her. I heard this kind of shout . . ."

"Yes," says Cappie, smiling confidingly, "but before that. What did you say to one another?"

Lois thinks. Nobody has asked her this before. "She said you could dive off there. She said it went straight down."

"And what did you say?"

"I said you'd have to be nuts."

"Were you mad at Lucy?" says Cappie, in an encouraging voice.

"No," says Lois. "Why would I be mad at Lucy? I wasn't ever mad at Lucy." She feels like crying again. The times when she has in fact been mad at Lucy have been erased already. Lucy was always perfect.

"Sometimes we're angry when we don't know we're angry," says Cappie, as if to herself. "Sometimes we get really mad and we don't even know it. Sometimes we might do a thing without meaning to, or without knowing what will happen. We lose our tempers."

Lois is only thirteen, but it doesn't take her long to figure out that Cappie is not including herself in any of this. By *we* she means Lois. She is accusing

Lois of pushing Lucy off the cliff. The unfairness of this hits her like a slap. "I didn't!" she says.

"Didn't what?" says Cappie softly. "Didn't what, Lois?"

Lois does the worst thing, she begins to cry. Cappie gives her a look like a pounce. She's got what she wanted.

• • •

Later, when she was grown up, Lois was able to understand what this interview had been about. She could see Cappie's desperation, her need for a story, a real story with a reason in it; anything but the senseless vacancy Lucy had left for her to deal with. Cappie wanted Lois to supply the reason, to be the reason. It wasn't even for the newspapers or the parents, because she could never make such an accusation without proof. It was for herself: something to explain the loss of Camp Manitou and of all she had worked for, the years of entertaining spoiled children and buttering up parents and making a fool of herself with feathers stuck in her hair. Camp Manitou was in fact lost. It did not survive.

Lois worked all this out, twenty years later. But it was far too late. It was too late even ten minutes afterwards, when she'd left Cappie's office and was walking slowly back to her cabin to pack. Lucy's clothes were still there, folded on the shelves, as if waiting. She felt the other girls in the cabin watching her with speculation in their eyes. *Could she have done it? She must have done it.* For the rest of her life, she has caught people watching her in this way.

Maybe they weren't thinking this. Maybe they were merely sorry for her. But she felt she had been tried and sentenced, and this is what has stayed with her: the knowledge that she had been singled out, condemned for something that was not her fault.

Lois sits in the living room of her apartment, drinking a cup of tea. Through the knee-to-ceiling window she has a wide view of Lake Ontario, with its skin of wrinkled blue-gray light, and of the willows of Centre Island shaken by a wind, which is silent at this distance, and on this side of the glass. When there isn't too much pollution she can see the far shore, the foreign shore; though today it is obscured.

Possibly she could go out, go downstairs, do some shopping; there isn't much in the refrigerator. The boys say she doesn't get out enough. But she isn't hungry, and moving, stirring from this space, is increasingly an effort.

She can hardly remember, now, having her two boys in the hospital, nursing them as babies; she can hardly remember getting married, or what Rob looked like. Even at the time she never felt she was paying full attention. She was tired a lot, as if she was living not one life but two: her own, and another, shadowy life that hovered around her and would not let itself be realized—the life of what would have happened if Lucy had not stepped sideways, and disappeared from time.

She would never go up north, to Rob's family cottage or to any place with wild lakes and wild trees and the calls of loons. She would never go anywhere near. Still, it was as if she was always listening for another voice, the voice of a person who should have been there but was not. An echo.

While Rob was alive, while the boys were growing up, she could pretend she didn't hear it, this empty space in sound. But now there is nothing much left to distract her.

She turns away from the window and looks at her pictures. There is the pinkish island, in the lake, with the intertwisted trees. It's the same landscape they paddled through, that distant summer. She's seen travelogues of this country, aerial photographs; it looks different from above, bigger, more hopeless: lake after lake, random blue puddles in dark green bush, the trees like bristles.

How could you ever find anything there, once it was lost? Maybe if they cut it all down, drained it all away, they might find Lucy's bones, some time, wherever they are hidden. A few bones, some buttons, the buckle from her shorts.

But a dead person is a body; a body occupies space, it exists somewhere. You can see it; you put it in a box and bury it in the ground, and then it's in a box in the ground. But Lucy is not in a box, or in the ground. Because she is nowhere definite, she could be anywhere.

And these paintings are not landscape paintings. Because there aren't any landscapes up there, not in the old, tidy European sense, with a gentle hill, a curving river, a cottage, a mountain in the background, a golden evening sky. Instead there's a tangle, a receding maze, in which you can become lost almost as soon as you step off the path. There are no backgrounds in any of these paintings, no vistas; only a great deal of foreground that goes back and back, endlessly, involving you in its twists and turns of trees and branch and rock. No matter how far back in you go, there will be more. And the trees themselves are hardly trees; they are currents of energy, charged with violent color.

Who knows how many trees there were on the cliff just before Lucy disappeared? Who counted? Maybe there was one more, afterwards.

Lois sits in her chair and does not move. Her hand with the cup is raised halfway to her mouth. She hears something, almost hears it: a shout of recognition, or of joy.

She looks at the paintings, she looks into them. Every one of them is a picture of Lucy. You can't see her exactly, but she's there, in behind the pink stone island or the one behind that. In the picture of the cliff she is hidden by the clutch of fallen rocks towards the bottom, in the one of the river shore she is crouching beneath the overturned canoe. In the yellow autumn woods she's behind the tree that cannot be seen because of the other trees, over beside the blue sliver of pond; but if you walked into the picture and found the tree, it would be the wrong one, because the right one would be further on.

Everyone has to be somewhere, and this is where Lucy is. She is in Lois's apartment, in the holes that open inwards on the wall, not like windows but like doors. She is here. She is entirely alive.

Bibles and a tambourine. The brother was testifying[7] and while he testified two of the sisters stood together, seeming to say, amen, and the third sister walked around with the tambourine outstretched and a couple of people dropped coins into it. Then the brother's testimony ended and the sister who had been taking up the collection dumped the coins into her palm and transferred them to the pocket of her long black robe. Then she raised both hands, striking the tambourine against the air, and then against one hand, and she started to sing. And the two other sisters and the brother joined in.

It was strange, suddenly, to watch, though I had been seeing these meetings all my life. So, of course, had everybody else down there. Yet, they paused and watched and listened and I stood still at the window. "*'Tis the old ship of Zion,*" they sang, and the sister with the tambourine kept a steady, jangling beat, "*it has rescued many a thousand!*" Not a soul under the sound of their voices was hearing this song for the first time, not one of them had been rescued. Nor had they seen much in the way of rescue work being done around them. Neither did they especially believe in the holiness of the three sisters and the brother, they knew too much about them, knew where they lived, and how. The woman with the tambourine, whose voice dominated the air, whose face was bright with joy, was divided by very little from the woman who stood watching her, a cigarette between her heavy, chapped lips, her hair a cuckoo's nest, her face scarred and swollen from many beatings, and her black eyes glittering like coal. Perhaps they both knew this, which was why, when, as rarely, they addressed each other, they addressed each other as Sister. As the singing filled the air the watching, listening faces underwent a change, the eyes focusing on something within; the music seemed to soothe a poison out of them; and time seemed, nearly, to fall away from the sullen, belligerent, battered faces, as though they were fleeing back to their first condition, while dreaming of their last. The barbecue cook half shook his head and smiled, and dropped his cigarette and disappeared into his joint. A man fumbled in his pockets for change and stood holding it in his hand impatiently, as though he had just remembered a pressing appointment further up the avenue. He looked furious. Then I saw Sonny, standing on the edge of the crowd. He was carrying a wide, flat notebook with a green cover, and it made him look, from where I was standing, almost like a schoolboy. The coppery sun brought out the copper in his skin, he was very faintly smiling, standing very still. Then the singing stopped, the tambourine turned into a collection plate again. The furious man dropped in his coins and vanished, so did a couple of the women, and Sonny dropped some change in the plate, looking directly at the woman with a little smile. He started across the avenue, toward the house. He has a slow, loping walk, something like the way Harlem hipsters walk, only he's imposed on this his own half-beat. I had never really noticed it before.

I stayed at the window, both relieved and apprehensive. As Sonny disappeared from my sight, they began singing again. And they were still singing when his key turned in the lock.

7. Proclaiming his religious belief.

"Hey," he said.

"Hey, yourself. You want some beer?"

"No. Well, maybe." But he came up to the window and stood beside me, looking out. "What a warm voice," he said.

They were singing *If I could only hear my mother pray again!*

"Yes," I said, "and she can sure beat that tambourine."

"But what a terrible song," he said, and laughed. He dropped his notebook on the sofa and disappeared into the kitchen. "Where's Isabel and the kids?"

"I think they want to see their grandparents. You hungry?"

"No." He came back into the living room with his can of beer. "You want to come some place with me tonight?"

I sensed, I don't know how, that I couldn't possibly say no. "Sure. Where?"

He sat down on the sofa and picked up his notebook and started leafing through it. "I'm going to sit in with some fellows in a joint in the Village."

"You mean, you're going to play, tonight?"

"That's right." He took a swallow of his beer and moved back to the window. He gave me a sidelong look. "If you can stand it."

"I'll try," I said.

He smiled to himself and we both watched as the meeting across the way broke up. The three sisters and the brother, heads bowed, were singing *God be with you till we meet again.* The faces around them were very quiet. Then the song ended. The small crowd dispersed. We watched the three women and the lone man walk slowly up the avenue.

"When she was singing before," said Sonny, abruptly, "her voice reminded me for a minute of what heroin feels like sometimes—when it's in your veins. It makes you feel sort of warm and cool at the same time. And distant. And—and sure." He sipped his beer, very deliberately not looking at me. I watched his face. "It makes you feel—in control. Sometimes you've got to have that feeling."

"Do you?" I sat down slowly in the easy chair.

"Sometimes." He went to the sofa and picked up his notebook again. "Some people do."

"In order," I asked, "to play?" And my voice was very ugly, full of contempt and anger.

"Well"—he looked at me with great, troubled eyes, as though, in fact, he hoped his eyes would tell me things he could never otherwise say—"they *think* so. And *if* they think so—!"

"And what do *you* think?" I asked.

He sat on the sofa and put his can of beer on the floor. "I don't know," he said, and I couldn't be sure if he were answering my question or pursuing his thoughts. His face didn't tell me. "It's not so much to *play.* It's to *stand* it, to be able to make it at all. On any level." He frowned and smiled: "In order to keep from shaking to pieces."

"But these friends of yours," I said, "they seem to shake themselves to pieces pretty goddamn fast."

"Maybe." He played with the notebook. And something told me that I should curb my tongue, that Sonny was doing his best to talk, that I should listen. "But of course you only know the ones that've gone to pieces. Some don't—or at least they haven't *yet* and that's just about all *any* of us can say." He paused. "And then there are some who just live, really, in hell, and they know it and they see what's happening and they go right on. I don't know." He sighed, dropped the notebook, folded his arms. "Some guys, you can tell from the way they play, they on something *all* the time. And you can see that, well, it makes something real for them. But of course," he picked up his beer from the floor and sipped it and put the can down again, "they *want* to, too, you've got to see that. Even some of them that say they don't—*some,* not all."

"And what about you?" I asked—I couldn't help it. "What about you? Do *you* want to?"

He stood up and walked to the window and I remained silent for a long time. Then he sighed. "Me," he said. Then: "While I was downstairs before, on my way here, listening to that woman sing, it struck me all of a sudden how much suffering she must have had to go through—to sing like that. It's *repulsive* to think you have to suffer that much."

I said: "But there's no way not to suffer—is there, Sonny?"

"I believe not," he said and smiled, "but that's never stopped anyone from trying." He looked at me. "Has it?" I realized, with this mocking look, that there stood between us, forever, beyond the power of time or forgiveness, the fact that I had held silence—so long!—when he had needed human speech to help him. He turned back to the window. "No, there's no way not to suffer. But you try all kinds of ways to keep from drowning in it, to keep on top of it, and to make it seem—well, like *you.* Like you did something, all right, and now you're suffering for it. You know?" I said nothing. "Well you know," he said, impatiently, "why *do* people suffer? Maybe it's better to do something to give it a reason, *any* reason."

"But we just agreed," I said, "that there's no way not to suffer. Isn't it better, then, just to—take it?"

"But nobody just takes it," Sonny cried, "that's what I'm telling you! *Everybody* tries not to. You're just hung up on the *way* some people try—it's not *your* way!"

The hair on my face began to itch, my face felt wet. "That's not true," I said, "that's not true. I don't give a damn what other people do, I don't even care how they suffer. I just care how *you* suffer." And he looked at me. "Please believe me," I said, "I don't want to see you—die—trying not to suffer."

"I won't," he said flatly, "die trying not to suffer. At least, not any faster than anybody else."

"But there's no need," I said, trying to laugh, "is there? in killing yourself."

I wanted to say more, but I couldn't. I wanted to talk about will power and how life could be—well, beautiful. I wanted to say that it was all within; but was it? or, rather, wasn't that exactly the trouble? And I wanted to promise that I would never fail him again. But it would all have sounded—empty words and lies.

So I made the promise to myself and prayed that I would keep it.

"It's terrible sometimes, inside," he said, "that's what's the trouble. You walk these streets, black and funky and cold, and there's not really a living ass to talk to, and there's nothing shaking, and there's no way of getting it out—that storm inside. You can't talk it and you can't make love with it, and when you finally try to get with it and play it, you realize *nobody's* listening. So *you've* got to listen. You got to find a way to listen."

And then he walked away from the window and sat on the sofa again, as though all the wind had suddenly been knocked out of him. "Sometimes you'll do *anything* to play, even cut your mother's throat." He laughed and looked at me. "Or your brother's." Then he sobered. "Or your own." Then: "Don't worry. I'm all right now and I think I'll *be* all right. But I can't forget—where I've been. I don't mean just the physical place I've been, I mean where I've *been.* And *what* I've been."

"What have you been, Sonny?" I asked.

He smiled—but sat sideways on the sofa, his elbow resting on the back, his fingers playing with his mouth and chin, not looking at me. "I've been something I didn't recognize, didn't know I could be. Didn't know anybody could be." He stopped, looking inward, looking helplessly young, looking old. "I'm not talking about it now because I feel *guilty* or anything like that—maybe it would be better if I did, I don't know. Anyway, I can't really talk about it. Not to you, not to anybody," and now he turned and faced me. "Sometimes, you know, and it was actually when I was most *out* of the world, I felt that I was in it, that I was *with* it, really, and I could play or I didn't really have to *play,* it just came out of me, it was there. And I don't know how I played, thinking about it now, but I know I did awful things, those times, sometimes, to people. Or it wasn't that I *did* anything to them—it was that they weren't real." He picked up the beer can; it was empty; he rolled it between his palms: "And other times—well, I needed a fix, I needed to find a place to lean, I needed to clear a space to *listen*—and I couldn't find it, and I—went crazy, I did terrible things to *me,* I was terrible *for* me." He began pressing the beer can between his hands, I watched the metal begin to give. It glittered, as he played with it like a knife, and I was afraid he would cut himself, but I said nothing. "Oh well. I can never tell you. I was all by myself at the bottom of something, stinking and sweating and crying and shaking, and I smelled it, you know? *my* stink, and I thought I'd die if I couldn't get away from it and yet, all the same, I knew that everything I was doing was just locking me in with it. And I didn't know," he paused, still flattening the beer can, "I didn't know, I still *don't* know, something kept telling me that maybe it was good to smell your own stink, but I didn't think that *that* was what I'd been trying to do—and—who can stand it?" and he abruptly dropped the ruined beer can, looking at me with a small, still smile, and then rose, walking to the window as though it were the lodestone rock. I watched his face, he watched the avenue. "I couldn't tell you when Mama died—but the reason I wanted to leave Harlem so bad was to get away from drugs. And then, when I ran away, that's what I was running from—really. When I came back, nothing had changed, *I* hadn't changed, I was just—older." And he stopped, drumming with his fingers on the windowpane. The sun had vanished, soon darkness would fall. I watched his face. "It can come again," he said, almost as though speaking to himself.

Then he turned to me. "It can come again," he repeated. "I just want you to know that."

"All right," I said, at last. "So it can come again. All right."

He smiled, but the smile was sorrowful. "I had to try to tell you," he said.

"Yes," I said. "I understand that."

"You're my brother," he said, looking straight at me, and not smiling at all.

"Yes," I repeated, "yes. I understand that."

He turned back to the window, looking out. "All that hatred down there," he said, "all that hatred and misery and love. It's a wonder it doesn't blow the avenue apart."

We went to the only nightclub on a short, dark street, downtown. We squeezed through the narrow, chattering, jampacked bar to the entrance of the big room, where the bandstand was. And we stood there for a moment, for the lights were very dim in this room and we couldn't see. Then, "Hello, boy," said the voice and an enormous black man, much older than Sonny or myself, erupted out of all that atmospheric lighting and put an arm around Sonny's shoulder. "I been sitting right here," he said, "waiting for you."

He had a big voice, too, and heads in the darkness turned toward us.

Sonny grinned and pulled a little away, and said, "Creole, this is my brother. I told you about him."

Creole shook my hand. "I'm glad to meet you, son," he said, and it was clear that he was glad to meet me *there,* for Sonny's sake. And he smiled, "You got a real musician in *your* family," and he took his arm from Sonny's shoulder and slapped him, lightly, affectionately, with the back of his hand.

"Well. Now I've heard it all," said a voice behind us. This was another musician, and a friend of Sonny's, a coal-black, cheerful-looking man, built close to the ground. He immediately began confiding to me, at the top of his lungs, the most terrible things about Sonny, his teeth gleaming like a lighthouse and his laugh coming up out of him like the beginning of an earthquake. And it turned out that everyone at the bar knew Sonny, or almost everyone; some were musicians, working there, or nearby, or not working, some were simply hangers-on, and some were there to hear Sonny play. I was introduced to all of them and they were all very polite to me. Yet, it was clear that, for them, I was only Sonny's brother. Here, I was in Sonny's world. Or, rather: his kingdom. Here, it was not even a question that his veins bore royal blood.

They were going to play soon and Creole installed me, by myself, at a table in a dark corner. Then I watched them, Creole, and the little black man, and Sonny, and the others, while they horsed around, standing just below the bandstand. The light from the bandstand spilled just a little short of them and, watching them laughing and gesturing and moving about, I had the feeling that they, nevertheless, were being most careful not to step into that circle of light too suddenly; that if they moved into the light too suddenly, without thinking, they would perish in flame. Then, while I watched, one of them, the small black man, moved into the light and crossed the bandstand and started fooling around with his drums. Then—being funny and being, also, extremely ceremonious—

Creole took Sonny by the arm and led him to the piano. A woman's voice called Sonny's name and a few hands started clapping. And Sonny, also being funny and being ceremonious, and so touched, I think, that he could have cried, but neither hiding it nor showing it, riding it like a man, grinned, and put both hands to his heart and bowed from the waist.

Creole then went to the bass fiddle and a lean, very bright-skinned brown man jumped up on the bandstand and picked up his horn. So there they were, and the atmosphere on the bandstand and in the room began to change and tighten. Someone stepped up to the microphone and announced them. Then there were all kinds of murmurs. Some people at the bar shushed others. The waitress ran around, frantically getting in the last orders, guys and chicks got closer to each other, and the lights on the bandstand, on the quartet, turned to a kind of indigo. Then they all looked different there. Creole looked about him for the last time, as though he were making certain that all his chickens were in the coop, and then he—jumped and struck the fiddle. And there they were.

All I know about music is that not many people ever really hear it. And even then, on the rare occasions when something opens within, and the music enters, what we mainly hear, or hear corroborated, are personal, private, vanishing evocations. But the man who creates the music is hearing something else, is dealing with the roar rising from the void and imposing order on it as it hits the air. What is evoked in him, then, is of another order, more terrible because it has no words, and triumphant, too, for that same reason. And his triumph, when he triumphs, is ours. I just watched Sonny's face. His face was troubled, he was working hard, but he wasn't with it. And I had the feeling that, in a way, everyone on the bandstand was waiting for him, both waiting for him and pushing him along. But as I began to watch Creole, I realized that it was Creole who held them all back. He had them on a short rein. Up there, keeping the beat with his whole body, wailing on the fiddle, with his eyes half closed, he was listening to everything, but he was listening to Sonny. He was having a dialogue with Sonny. He wanted Sonny to leave the shoreline and strike out for the deep water. He was Sonny's witness that deep water and drowning were not the same thing—he had been there, and he knew. And he wanted Sonny to know. He was waiting for Sonny to do the things on the keys which would let Creole know that Sonny was in the water.

And, while Creole listened, Sonny moved, deep within, exactly like someone in torment. I had never before thought of how awful the relationship must be between the musician and his instrument. He has to fill it, this instrument, with the breath of life, his own. He has to make it do what he wants it to do. And a piano is just a piano. It's made out of so much wood and wires and little hammers and big ones, and ivory. While there's only so much you can do with it, the only way to find this out is to try; to try and make it do everything.

And Sonny hadn't been near a piano for over a year. And he wasn't on much better terms with his life, not the life that stretched before him now. He and the piano stammered, started one way, got scared, stopped; started another way, panicked, marked time, started again; then seemed to have found a direction, panicked again, got stuck. And the face I saw on Sonny I'd never seen before. Everything had been burned out of it, and, at the same time, things usually hidden were being burned in, by the fire and fury of the battle which was occurring in him up there.

Yet, watching Creole's face as they neared the end of the first set, I had the feeling that something had happened, something I hadn't heard. Then they finished, there was scattered applause, and then, without an instant's warning, Creole started into something else, it was almost sardonic, it was *Am I Blue?*[8] And, as though he commanded, Sonny began to play. Something began to happen. And Creole let out the reins. The dry, low, black man said something awful on the drums, Creole answered, and the drums talked back. Then the horn insisted, sweet and high, slightly detached perhaps, and Creole listened, commenting now and then, dry, and driving, beautiful and calm and old. Then they all came together again, and Sonny was part of the family again. I could tell this from his face. He seemed to have found, right there beneath his fingers, a damn brand-new piano. It seemed that he couldn't get over it. Then, for a while, just being happy with Sonny, they seemed to be agreeing with him that brand-new pianos certainly were a gas.

Then Creole stepped forward to remind them that what they were playing was the blues. He hit something in all of them, he hit something in me, myself, and the music tightened and deepened, apprehension began to beat the air. Creole began to tell us what the blues were all about. They were not about anything very new. He and his boys up there were keeping it new, at the risk of ruin, destruction, madness, and death, in order to find new ways to make us listen. For, while the tale of how we suffer, and how we are delighted, and how we may triumph is never new, it always must be heard. There isn't any other tale to tell, it's the only light we've got in all this darkness.

And this tale, according to that face, that body, those strong hands on those strings, has another aspect in every country, and a new depth in every generation. Listen, Creole seemed to be saying, listen. Now these are Sonny's blues. He made the little black man on the drums know it, and the bright, brown man on the horn. Creole wasn't trying any longer to get Sonny in the water. He was wishing him Godspeed. Then he stepped back, very slowly, filling the air with the immense suggestion that Sonny speak for himself.

Then they all gathered around Sonny and Sonny played. Every now and again one of them seemed to say, amen. Sonny's fingers filled the air with life, his life. But that life contained so many others. And Sonny went all the way back, he really began with the spare, flat statement of the opening phrase of the song. Then he began to make it his. It was very beautiful because it wasn't hurried and it was no longer a lament. I seemed to hear with what burning he had made it his, and what burning we had yet to make it ours, how we could cease lamenting. Freedom lurked around us and I understood, at last, that he could help us to be free if we would listen, that he would never be free until we did. Yet, there was no battle in his face now, I heard what he had gone through, and would continue to go through until he came to rest in earth. He had made it his: that long line, of which we knew only Mama and Daddy. And

8. A jazz tune by H. Akst and G. Clarke; from *On With the Show*, 1929.

he was giving it back, as everything must be given back, so that, passing through death, it can live forever. I saw my mother's face again, and felt, for the first time, how the stones of the road she had walked on must have bruised her feet. I saw the moonlit road where my father's brother died. And it brought something else back to me, and carried me past it, I saw my little girl again and felt Isabel's tears again, and I felt my own tears begin to rise. And I was yet aware that this was only a moment, that the world waited outside, as hungry as a tiger, and that trouble stretched above us, longer than the sky.

Then it was over. Creole and Sonny let out their breath, both soaking wet, and grinning. There was a lot of applause and some of it was real. In the dark, the girl came by and I asked her to take drinks to the bandstand. There was a long pause, while they talked up there in the indigo light and after awhile I saw the girl put a Scotch and milk on top of the piano for Sonny. He didn't seem to notice it, but just before they started playing again, he sipped from it and looked toward me, and nodded. Then he put it back on top of the piano. For me, then, as they began to play again, it glowed and shook above my brother's head like the very cup of trembling.[9]

9. Isaiah 51.22: "I have taken out of thine hand the cup of trembling . . . thou shalt no more drink it again."

# JAMES BALDWIN

*Baldwin (1924–1987) was born in New York City. Stepson of a revivalist minister and himself active in the ministry for three years, he drew on and refined the passionate eloquence of religious oratory as one ingredient of his style. He began his literary career while living in Paris, during a time when he had to support himself by a variety of odd jobs to supplement his income from writing. Recognition of his talents as a novelist and short-story writer was paralleled by the attention paid to him as an essayist who illumined the American racial dilemma. He directed our conscience to the inequities that blight our country. Much of his work aimed at unraveling the repressive myths of white society and at healing the disastrous estrangement he found in the lives of black people in America. His novels include* Go Tell It on the Mountain *(1953),* Giovanni's Room *(1957),* Another Country *(1962),* Tell Me How Long the Train's Been Gone *(1968),* If Beale Street Could Talk *(1974), and* Just Above My Head *(1979). His books of essays are* Notes of a Native Son *(1955),* Nobody Knows My Name *(1961),* The Fire Next Time *(1963), and* No Name in the Street *(1972). His short stories are collected in* Going to Meet the Man *(1965).*

## Sonny's Blues

I read about it in the paper, in the subway, on my way to work. I read it, and I couldn't believe it, and I read it again. Then perhaps I just stared at it, at the newsprint spelling out his name, spelling out the story. I stared at it in the swinging lights of the subway car, and in the faces and bodies of the people, and in my own face, trapped in the darkness which roared outside.

It was not to be believed and I kept telling myself that, as I walked from the subway station to the high school. And at the same time I couldn't doubt it. I was scared, scared for Sonny. He became real to me again. A great block of ice got settled in my belly and kept melting there slowly all day long, while I taught my classes algebra. It was a special kind of ice. It kept melting, sending trickles of ice water all up and down my veins, but it never got less. Sometimes it hardened and seemed to expand until I felt my guts were going to come spilling out or that I was going to choke or scream. This would always be at a moment when I was remembering some specific thing Sonny had once said or done.

When he was about as old as the boys in my classes his face had been bright and open, there was a lot of copper in it; and he'd had wonderfully direct brown eyes, and great gentleness and privacy. I wondered what he looked like now. He had been picked up, the evening before, in a raid on an apartment downtown, for peddling and using heroin.

I couldn't believe it: but what I mean by that is that I couldn't find any room for it anywhere inside me. I had kept it outside me for a long time. I hadn't wanted to know. I had had suspicions, but I didn't name them, I kept putting them away. I told myself that Sonny was wild, but he wasn't crazy. And he'd always been a good boy, he hadn't ever turned hard or evil or disrespectful, the way kids can, so quick, so quick, especially in Harlem. I didn't want to believe that I'd ever see my brother going down, coming to nothing, all that light in his face gone out, in the condition I'd already seen so many others. Yet it had happened and here I was, talking about algebra to a lot of boys who might, every one of them for all I knew, be popping off needles every time they went to the head.[1] Maybe it did more for them than algebra could.

I was sure that the first time Sonny had ever had horse,[2] he couldn't have been much older than these boys were now. These boys, now, were living as we'd been living then, they were growing up with a rush and their heads bumped abruptly against the low ceiling of their actual possibilities. They were filled with rage. All they really knew were two darknesses, the darkness of their lives, which was now closing in on them, and the darkness of the movies, which had blinded them to that other darkness, and in which they now, vindictively, dreamed, at once more together than they were at any other time, and more alone.

When the last bell rang, the last class ended, I let out my breath. It seemed I'd been holding it for all that time. My clothes were wet—I may have looked as though I'd been sitting in a steam bath, all dressed up, all afternoon. I sat alone in the classroom a long time. I listened to the boys outside, downstairs, shouting and cursing and laughing. Their laughter struck me for perhaps the first time. It was not the joyous laughter which—God knows why—one associates with children. It was mocking and insular, its intent was to denigrate. It was disenchanted, and in this, also, lay the authority of their curses. Perhaps I was listening to them because I was thinking about my brother and in them I heard my brother. And myself.

One boy was whistling a tune, at once very complicated and very simple, it seemed to be pouring out of him as though he were a bird, and it sounded very cool and moving through all that harsh, bright air, only just holding its own through all those other sounds.

I stood up and walked over to the window and looked down into the courtyard. It was the beginning of the spring and the sap was rising in the boys. A teacher passed through them every now and again, quickly, as though he or she couldn't wait to get out of that courtyard, to get those boys out of their sight and off their minds. I started collecting my stuff. I thought I'd better get home and talk to Isabel.

The courtyard was almost deserted by the time I got downstairs. I saw this boy standing in the shadow of a doorway, looking just like Sonny. I almost called

1. Toilet. 2. Heroin.

his name. Then I saw that it wasn't Sonny, but somebody we used to know, a boy from around our block. He'd been Sonny's friend. He'd never been mine, having been too young for me, and, anyway, I'd never liked him. And now, even though he was a grown-up man, he still hung around that block, still spent hours on the street corners, was always high and raggy. I used to run into him from time to time and he'd often work around to asking me for a quarter or fifty cents. He always had some real good excuse, too, and I always gave it to him. I don't know why.

But now, abruptly, I hated him. I couldn't stand the way he looked at me, partly like a dog, partly like a cunning child. I wanted to ask him what the hell he was doing in the school courtyard.

He sort of shuffled over to me, and he said, "I see you got the papers. So you already know about it."

"You mean about Sonny? Yes, I already know about it. How come they didn't get you?"

He grinned. It made him repulsive and it also brought to mind what he'd looked like as a kid. "I wasn't there. I stay away from them people."

"Good for you." I offered him a cigarette and I watched him through the smoke. "You come all the way down here just to tell me about Sonny?"

"That's right." He was sort of shaking his head and his eyes looked strange, as though they were about to cross. The bright sun deadened his damp dark brown skin and it made his eyes look yellow and showed up the dirt in his kinked hair. He smelled funky.[3] I moved a little away from him and I said, "Well, thanks. But I already know about it and I got to get home."

"I'll walk you a little ways," he said. We started walking. There were a couple of kids still loitering in the courtyard and one of them said goodnight to me and looked strangely at the boy beside me.

"What're you going to do?" he asked me. "I mean, about Sonny?"

"Look. I haven't seen Sonny for over a year, I'm not sure I'm going to do anything. Anyway, what the hell *can* I do?"

"That's right," he said quickly, "ain't nothing you can do. Can't much help old Sonny no more, I guess."

It was what I was thinking and so it seemed to me he had no right to say it.

"I'm surprised at Sonny, though," he went on—he had a funny way of talking, he looked straight ahead as though he were talking to himself—"I thought Sonny was a smart boy, I thought he was too smart to get hung."

"I guess he thought so too," I said sharply, "and that's how he got hung. And how about you? You're pretty goddamn smart, I bet."

Then he looked directly at me, just for a minute. "I ain't smart," he said. "If I was smart, I'd have reached for a pistol a long time ago."

"Look. Don't tell *me* your sad story, if it was up to me, I'd give you one." Then I felt guilty—guilty, probably, for never having supposed that the poor bastard *had* a story of his own, much less a sad one, and I asked, quickly, "What's going to happen to him now?"

3. Unwashed.

He didn't answer this. He was off by himself some place.

"Funny thing," he said, and from his tone we might have been discussing the quickest way to get to Brooklyn, "when I saw the papers this morning, the first thing I asked myself was if I had anything to do with it. I felt sort of responsible."

I began to listen more carefully. The subway station was on the corner, just before us, and I stopped. He stopped, too. We were in front of a bar and he ducked slightly, peering in, but whoever he was looking for didn't seem to be there. The juke box was blasting away with something black and bouncy and I half watched the barmaid as she danced her way from the juke box to her place behind the bar. And I watched her face as she laughingly responded to something someone said to her, still keeping time to the music. When she smiled one saw the little girl, one sensed the doomed, still-struggling woman beneath the battered face of the semi-whore.

"I never *give* Sonny nothing," the boy said finally, "but a long time ago I come to school high and Sonny asked me how it felt." He paused, I couldn't bear to watch him, I watched the barmaid, and I listened to the music which seemed to be causing the pavement to shake. "I told him it felt great." The music stopped, the barmaid paused and watched the juke box until the music began again. "It did."

All this was carrying me some place I didn't want to go. I certainly didn't want to know how it felt. It filled everything, the people, the houses, the music, the dark, quicksilver barmaid, with menace; and this menace was their reality.

"What's going to happen to him now?" I asked again.

"They'll send him away some place and they'll try to cure him." He shook his head. "Maybe he'll even think he's kicked the habit. Then they'll let him loose"—he gestured, throwing his cigarette into the gutter. "That's all."

"What do you mean, that's *all?*"

But I knew what he meant.

"I *mean,* that's *all.*" He turned his head and looked at me, pulling down the corners of his mouth. "Don't you know what I mean?" he asked, softly.

"How the hell *would* I know what you mean?" I almost whispered it, I don't know why.

"That's right," he said to the air, "how would *he* know what I mean?" He turned toward me again, patient and calm, and yet I somehow felt him shaking, shaking as though he were going to fall apart. I felt that ice in my guts again, the dread I'd felt all afternoon; and again I watched the barmaid, moving about the bar, washing glasses, and singing. "Listen. They'll let him out and then it'll just start all over again. That's what I mean."

"You mean—they'll let him out. And then he'll just start working his way back in again. You mean he'll never kick the habit. Is that what you mean?"

"That's right," he said, cheerfully. "*You* see what I mean."

"Tell me," I said at last, "why does he want to die? He must want to die, he's killing himself, why does he want to die?"

He looked at me in surprise. He licked his lips. "He don't want to die. He wants to live. Don't nobody want to die, ever."

Then I wanted to ask him—too many things. He could not have answered, or if he had, I could not have borne the answers. I started walking. "Well, I guess it's none of my business."

"It's going to be rough on old Sonny," he said. We reached the subway station. "This is your station?" he asked. I nodded. I took one step down. "Damn!" he said, suddenly. I looked up at him. He grinned again. "Damn it if I didn't leave all my money home. You ain't got a dollar on you, have you? Just for a couple of days, is all."

All at once something inside gave and threatened to come pouring out of me. I didn't hate him any more. I felt that in another moment I'd start crying like a child.

"Sure," I said. "Don't sweat." I looked in my wallet and didn't have a dollar, I only had a five. "Here," I said. "That hold you?"

He didn't look at it—he didn't want to look at it. A terrible, closed look came over his face, as though he were keeping the number on the bill a secret from him and me. "Thanks," he said, and now he was dying to see me go. "Don't worry about Sonny. Maybe I'll write him or something."

"Sure," I said. "You do that. So long."

"Be seeing you," he said. I went on down the steps.

And I didn't write Sonny or send him anything for a long time. When I finally did, it was just after my little girl died, and he wrote me back a letter which made me feel like a bastard.

Here's what he said:

Dear brother,

You don't know how much I needed to hear from you. I wanted to write you many a time but I dug how much I must have hurt you and so I didn't write. But now I feel like a man who's been trying to climb up out of some deep, real deep and funky hole and just saw the sun up there, outside. I got to get outside.

I can't tell you much about how I got here. I mean I don't know how to tell you. I guess I was afraid of something or I was trying to escape from something and you know I have never been very strong in the head (smile). I'm glad Mama and Daddy are dead and can't see what's happened to their son and I swear if I'd known what I was doing I would never have hurt you so, you and a lot of other fine people who were nice to me and who believed in me.

I don't want you to think it had anything to do with me being a musician. It's more than that. Or maybe less than that. I can't get anything straight in my head down here and I try not to think about what's going to happen to me when I get outside again. Sometime I think I'm going to flip and *never* get outside and sometime I think I'll come straight back. I tell you one thing, though, I'd rather blow my brains out than go through this again. But that's what they all say, so they tell me. If I tell you when I'm coming to New York and if you could meet me, I sure would appreciate it. Give my love to Isabel and the kids and I was sure sorry to hear about little Gracie. I wish I could be like Mama and say the Lord's will be done, but I don't know it seems to me that trouble is the one thing that never does get stopped and I don't know what good it does to blame it on the Lord. But maybe it does some good if you believe it.

Your brother,
Sonny

Then I kept in constant touch with him and I sent him whatever I could and I went to meet him when he came back to New York. When I saw him many things I thought I had forgotten came flooding back to me. This was because I had begun, finally, to wonder about Sonny, about the life that Sonny lived inside. This life, whatever it was, had made him older and thinner and it had deepened the distant stillness in which he had always moved. He looked very unlike my baby brother. Yet, when he smiled, when we shook hands, the baby brother I'd never known looked out from the depths of his private life, like an animal waiting to be coaxed into the light.

"How you been keeping?" he asked me.

"All right. And you?"

"Just fine." He was smiling all over his face. "It's good to see you again."

"It's good to see you."

The seven years' difference in our ages lay between us like a chasm: I wondered if these years would ever operate between us as a bridge. I was remembering, and it made it hard to catch my breath, that I had been there when he was born; and I had heard the first words he had ever spoken. When he started to walk, he walked from our mother straight to me. I caught him just before he fell when he took the first steps he ever took in this world.

"How's Isabel?"

"Just fine. She's dying to see you."

"And the boys?"

"They're fine, too. They're anxious to see their uncle."

"Oh, come on. You know they don't remember me."

"Are you kidding? Of course they remember you."

He grinned again. We got into a taxi. We had a lot to say to each other, far too much to know how to begin.

As the taxi began to move, I asked, "You still want to go to India?"

He laughed. "You still remember that. Hell, no. This place is Indian enough for me."

"It used to belong to them," I said.

And he laughed again. "They damn sure knew what they were doing when they got rid of it."

Years ago, when he was around fourteen, he'd been all hipped on the idea of going to India. He read books about people sitting on rocks, naked, in all kinds of weather, but mostly bad, naturally, and walking barefoot through hot coals and arriving at wisdom. I used to say that it sounded to me as though they were getting away from wisdom as fast as they could. I think he sort of looked down on me for that.

"Do you mind," he asked, "if we have the driver drive alongside the park? On the west side—I haven't seen the city in so long."

"Of course not," I said. I was afraid that I might sound as though I were humoring him, but I hoped he wouldn't take it that way.

So we drove along, between the green of the park and the stony, lifeless elegance of hotels and apartment buildings, toward the vivid, killing streets of our childhood. These streets hadn't changed, though housing projects jutted up out of them now like rocks in the middle of a boiling sea. Most of the houses in which we had grown up had vanished, as had the stores from which we had stolen, the basements in which we had first tried sex, the rooftops from which we had hurled tin cans and bricks. But houses exactly like the houses of our past yet dominated the landscape, boys exactly like the boys we once had been found themselves smothering in these houses, came down into the streets for light and air and found themselves encircled by disaster. Some escaped the trap, most didn't. Those who got out always left something of themselves behind, as some animals amputate a leg and leave it in the trap. It might be said, perhaps, that I had escaped, after all, I was a school teacher; or that Sonny had, he hadn't lived in Harlem for years. Yet, as the cab moved uptown through streets which seemed, with a rush, to darken with dark people, and as I covertly studied Sonny's face, it came to me that what we both were seeking through our separate cab windows was that part of ourselves which had been left behind. It's always at the hour of trouble and confrontation that the missing member aches.

We hit 110th Street and started rolling up Lenox Avenue. And I'd known this avenue all my life, but it seemed to me again, as it had seemed on the day I'd first heard about Sonny's trouble, filled with a hidden menace which was its very breath of life.

"We almost there," said Sonny.

"Almost." We were both too nervous to say anything more.

We live in a housing project. It hasn't been up long. A few days after it was up it seemed uninhabitably new, now, of course, it's already rundown. It looks like a parody of the good, clean, faceless life—God knows the people who live in it do their best to make it a parody. The beat-looking grass lying around isn't enough to make their lives green, the hedges will never hold out the streets, and they know it. The big windows fool no one, they aren't big enough to make space out of no space. They don't bother with the windows, they watch the TV screen instead. The playground is most popular with the children who don't play at jacks, or skip rope, or roller skate, or swing, and they can be found in it after dark. We moved in partly because it's not too far from where I teach, and partly for the kids; but it's really just like the houses in which Sonny and I grew up. The same things happen, they'll have the same things to remember. The moment Sonny and I started into the house I had the feeling that I was simply bringing him back into the danger he had almost died trying to escape.

Sonny has never been talkative. So I don't know why I was sure he'd be dying to talk to me when supper was over the first night. Everything went fine, the oldest boy remembered him, and the youngest boy liked him, and Sonny had remembered to bring something for each of them; and Isabel, who is really much nicer than I am, more open and giving, had gone to a lot of trouble about dinner and was genuinely glad to see him. And she's always been able to tease Sonny in a way that I haven't. It was nice to see her face so vivid again and to hear her laugh and watch her make Sonny laugh. She wasn't, or, anyway, she didn't seem to be, at all uneasy or embarrassed. She chatted as though there were no subject which had to be avoided and she got Sonny past his first, faint stiffness. And thank God she was there, for I was filled with that icy dread again. Everything I did seemed awkward to me, and everything I said sounded freighted with hidden meaning. I was trying to remember everything I'd heard about dope addiction and I couldn't help watching Sonny for signs. I wasn't doing it out of malice. I was trying to find out something about my brother. I was dying to hear him tell me he was safe.

"Safe!" my father grunted, whenever Mama suggested trying to move to a neighborhood which might be safer for children. "Safe, hell! Ain't no place safe for kids, nor nobody."

He always went on like this, but he wasn't, ever, really as bad as he sounded, not even on weekends, when he got drunk. As a matter of fact, he was always on the lookout for "something a little better," but he died before he found it. He died suddenly, during a drunken weekend in the middle of the war, when Sonny was fifteen. He and Sonny hadn't ever got on too well. And this was partly because Sonny was the apple of his father's eye. It was because he loved Sonny so much and was frightened for him, that he was always fighting with him. It doesn't do any good to fight with Sonny. Sonny just moves back, inside himself, where he can't be reached. But the principal reason that they never hit it off is that they were so much alike. Daddy was big and rough and loud-talking, just the opposite of Sonny, but they both had—that same privacy.

Mama tried to tell me something about this, just after Daddy died. I was home on leave from the army.

This was the last time I ever saw my mother alive. Just the same, this picture gets all mixed up in my mind with pictures I had of her when she was younger. The way I always see her is the way she used to be on a Sunday afternoon, say, when the old folks were talking after the big Sunday dinner. I always see her wearing pale blue. She'd be sitting on the sofa. And my father would be sitting in the easy chair, not far from her. And the living room would be full of church folks and relatives. There they sit, in chairs all around the living room, and the night is creeping up outside, but nobody knows it yet. You can see the darkness growing against the windowpanes and you hear the street noises every now and again, or maybe the jangling beat of a tambourine from one of the churches close by, but it's real quiet in the room. For a moment nobody's talking, but every face looks darkening, like the sky outside. And my mother rocks a little from the waist, and my father's eyes are closed. Everyone is looking at something a child can't see. For a minute they've forgotten the children. Maybe a kid is lying on the rug, half asleep. Maybe somebody's got a kid in his lap and is absent-mindedly stroking the kid's head. Maybe there's a kid, quiet and big-eyed, curled up in a big chair in the corner. The silence, the darkness coming, and the darkness in the faces frighten the child obscurely. He hopes that the hand which strokes his forehead will never stop—will never die. He hopes that there will never come a time when the old folks won't be sitting around the living room, talking about where they've come from, and what they've seen, and what's happened to them and their kinfolk.

But something deep and watchful in the child knows that this is bound to end, is already ending. In a moment someone will get up and turn on the light. Then the old folks will remember the children and they won't talk any more that day. And when light fills the room, the child is filled with darkness. He knows that every time this happens he's moved just a little closer to that darkness outside. The darkness outside is what the old folks have been talking about. It's what they've come from. It's what they endure. The child knows that they won't talk any more because if he knows too much about what's happened to *them,* he'll know too much too soon, about what's going to happen to *him.*

The last time I talked to my mother, I remember I was restless. I wanted to get out and see Isabel. We weren't married then and we had a lot to straighten out between us.

There Mama sat, in black, by the window. She was humming an old church song, *Lord, you brought me from a long ways off.* Sonny was out somewhere. Mama kept watching the streets.

"I don't know," she said, "if I'll ever see you again, after you go off from here. But I hope you'll remember the things I tried to teach you."

"Don't talk like that," I said, and smiled. "You'll be here a long time yet."

She smiled, too, but she said nothing. She was quiet for a long time. And I said, "Mama, don't you worry about nothing. I'll be writing all the time, and you be getting the checks. . . ."

"I want to talk to you about your brother," she said, suddenly. "If anything happens to me he ain't going to have nobody to look out for him."

"Mama," I said, "ain't nothing going to happen to you *or* Sonny. Sonny's all right. He's a good boy and he's got good sense."

"It ain't a question of his being a good boy," Mama said, "nor of his having good sense. It ain't only the bad ones, nor yet the dumb ones that gets sucked under." She stopped, looking at me. "Your Daddy once had a brother," she said, and she smiled in a way that made me feel she was in pain. "You didn't never know that, did you?"

"No," I said, "I never knew that," and I watched her face.

"Oh, yes," she said, "your Daddy had a brother." She looked out of the window again. "I know you never saw your Daddy cry. But *I* did—many a time, through all these years."

I asked her, "What happened to his brother? How come nobody's ever talked about him?"

This was the first time I ever saw my mother look old.

"His brother got killed," she said, "when he was just a little younger than you are now. I knew him. He was a fine boy. He was maybe a little full of the devil, but he didn't mean nobody no harm."

Then she stopped and the room was silent, exactly as it had sometimes been on those Sunday afternoons. Mama kept looking out into the streets.

"He used to have a job in the mill," she said, "and, like all young folks, he just liked to perform on Saturday nights. Saturday nights, him and your father would drift around to different places, go to dances and things like that, or just sit around with people they knew, and your father's brother would sing, he had a fine voice, and play along with himself on his guitar. Well, this particular Saturday night, him and your father was coming home from some place, and they were both a little drunk and there was a moon that night, it was bright like day. Your father's brother was feeling kind of good, and he was whistling to himself, and he had his guitar slung over his shoulder. They was coming down a hill and beneath them was a road that turned off from the highway. Well, your father's brother, being always kind of frisky, decided to run down this hill, and he did, with that guitar banging and clanging behind him, and he ran across the road, and he was making water behind a tree. And your father was sort of amused at him and he was still coming down the hill, kind of slow. Then he heard a car motor and that same minute his brother stepped from behind the tree, into the road, in the moonlight. And he started to cross the road. And your father started to run down the hill, he says he don't know why. This car was full of white men. They was all drunk, and when they seen your father's brother they let out a great whoop and holler and they aimed the car straight at him. They was having fun, they just wanted to scare him, the way they do sometimes, you know. But they was drunk. And I guess the boy, being drunk, too, and scared, kind of lost his head. By the time he jumped it was too late. Your father says he heard his brother scream when the car rolled over him, and he heard the wood of that guitar when it give, and he heard them strings go flying, and he heard them white men shouting, and the car kept on a-going and it ain't stopped till this day. And, time your father got down the hill, his brother weren't nothing but blood and pulp."

Tears were gleaming on my mother's face. There wasn't anything I could say.

"He never mentioned it," she said, "because I never let him mention it before you children. Your Daddy was like a crazy man that night and for many a night thereafter. He says he never in his life seen anything as dark as that road after the lights of that car had gone away. Weren't nothing, weren't nobody on that road, just your Daddy and his brother and that busted guitar. Oh, yes. Your Daddy never did really get right again. Till the day he died he weren't sure but that every white man he saw was the man that killed his brother."

She stopped and took out her handkerchief and dried her eyes and looked at me.

"I ain't telling you all this," she said, "to make you scared or bitter or to make you hate nobody. I'm telling you this because you got a brother. And the world ain't changed."

I guess I didn't want to believe this. I guess she saw this in my face. She turned away from me, toward the window again, searching those streets.

"But I praise my Redeemer," she said at last, "that He called your Daddy home before me. I ain't saying it to throw no flowers at myself, but, I declare, it keeps me from feeling too cast down to know I helped your father get safely through this world. Your father always acted like he was the roughest, strongest man on earth. And everybody took him to be like that. But if he hadn't had me there—to see his tears!"

She was crying again. Still, I couldn't move. I said, "Lord, Lord, Mama, I didn't know it was like that."

"Oh, honey," she said, "there's a lot that you don't know. But you are going to find out." She stood up from the window and came over to me. "You got to hold on to your brother," she said, "and don't let him fall, no matter what it looks like is happening to him and no matter how evil you gets with him. You going to be evil with him many a time. But don't you forget what I told you, you hear?"

"I won't forget," I said. "Don't you worry, I won't forget. I won't let nothing happen to Sonny."

My mother smiled as though she was amused at something she saw in my face. Then, "You may not be able to stop nothing from happening. But you got to let him know you's *there.*"

Two days later I was married, and then I was gone. And I had a lot of things on my mind and I pretty well forgot my promise to Mama until I got shipped home on a special furlough for her funeral.

And, after the funeral, with just Sonny and me alone in the empty kitchen, I tried to find out something about him.

"What do you want to do?" I asked him.

"I'm going to be a musician," he said.

For he had graduated, in the time I had been away, from dancing to the juke box to finding out who was playing what, and what they were doing with it, and he had bought himself a set of drums.

"You mean, you want to be a drummer?" I somehow had the feeling that being a drummer might be all right for other people but not for my brother Sonny.

"I don't think," he said, looking at me very gravely, "that I'll ever be a good drummer. But I think I can play a piano."

I frowned. I'd never played the role of the oldest brother quite so seriously before, had scarcely ever, in fact, *asked* Sonny a damn thing. I sensed myself in the presence of something I didn't really know how to handle, didn't understand. So I made my frown a little deeper as I asked: "What kind of musician do you want to be?"

He grinned. "How many kinds do you think there are?"

"Be *serious,*" I said.

He laughed, throwing his head back, and then looked at me. "I *am* serious."

"Well, then, for Christ's sake, stop kidding around and answer a serious question. I mean, do you want to be a concert pianist, you want to play classical music and all that, or—or what?" Long before I finished he was laughing again. "For Christ's *sake,* Sonny!"

He sobered, but with difficulty. "I'm sorry. But you sound so—*scared!*" and he was off again.

"Well, you may think it's funny now, baby, but it's not going to be so funny when you have to make your living at it, let me tell you *that.*" I was furious because I knew he was laughing at me and I didn't know why.

"No," he said, very sober now, and afraid, perhaps, that he'd hurt me, "I don't want to be a classical pianist. That isn't what interests me. I mean"—he paused, looking hard at me, as though his eyes would help me to understand, and then gestured helplessly, as though perhaps his hand would help—"I mean, I'll have a lot of studying to do, and I'll have to study *everything,* but, I mean, I want to play *with*—jazz musicians." He stopped. "I want to play jazz," he said.

Well, the word had never before sounded as heavy, as real, as it sounded that afternoon in Sonny's mouth. I just looked at him and I was probably frowning a real frown by this time. I simply couldn't see why on earth he'd want to spend his time hanging around nightclubs, clowning around on bandstands, while people pushed each other around a dance floor. It seemed—beneath him, somehow. I had never thought about it before, had never been forced to, but I suppose I had always put jazz musicians in a class with what Daddy called "good-time people."

"Are you *serious?*"

"Hell, *yes*, I'm serious."

He looked more helpless than ever, and annoyed, and deeply hurt.

I suggested, helpfully: "You mean—like Louis Armstrong?"

His face closed as though I'd struck him. "No. I'm not talking about none of that old-time, down home crap."

"Well, look, Sonny, I'm sorry, don't get mad. I just don't altogether get it, that's all. Name somebody—you know, a jazz musician you admire."

"Bird."

"Who?"

"Bird! Charlie Parker![4] Don't they teach you nothing in the goddamn army?"

I lit a cigarette. I was surprised and then a little amused to discover that I was trembling. "I've been out of touch," I said. "You'll have to be patient with me. Now. Who's this Parker character?"

"He's just one of the greatest jazz musicians alive," said Sonny, sullenly, his hands in his pockets, his back to me. "Maybe *the* greatest," he added, bitterly, "that's probably why *you* never heard of him."

"All right," I said, "I'm ignorant. I'm sorry. I'll go out and buy all the cat's records right away, all right?"

"It don't," said Sonny, with dignity, "make any difference to me. I don't care what you listen to. Don't do me no favors."

I was beginning to realize that I'd never seen him so upset before. With another part of my mind I was thinking that this would probably turn out to be one of those things kids go through and that I shouldn't make it seem important by pushing it too hard. Still, I didn't think it would do any harm to ask: "Doesn't all this take a lot of time? Can you make a living at it?"

He turned back to me and half leaned, half sat, on the kitchen table. "Everything takes time," he said, "and—well, yes, sure, I can make a living at it. But what I don't seem to be able to make you understand is that it's the only thing I want to do."

"Well, Sonny," I said gently, "you know people can't always do exactly what they *want* to do—"

"*No,* I don't know that," said Sonny, surprising me. "I think people *ought* to do what they want to do, what else are they alive for?"

"You getting to be a big boy," I said desperately, "it's time you started thinking about your future."

4. Charlie "Bird" Parker (1920–1955), musician for whom Birdland ballroom in New York was named. A founder of the new jazz that began to flourish in the 1940s.

"I'm thinking about my future," said Sonny, grimly. "I think about it all the time."

I gave up. I decided, if he didn't change his mind, that we could always talk about it later. "In the meantime," I said, "you got to finish school." We had already decided that he'd have to move in with Isabel and her folks. I knew this wasn't the ideal arrangement because Isabel's folks are inclined to be dicty[5] and they hadn't especially wanted Isabel to marry me. But I didn't know what else to do. "And we have to get you fixed up at Isabel's."

There was a long silence. He moved from the kitchen table to the window. "That's a terrible idea. You know it yourself."

"Do you have a *better* idea?"

He just walked up and down the kitchen for a minute. He was as tall as I was. He had started to shave. I suddenly had the feeling that I didn't know him at all.

He stopped at the kitchen table and picked up my cigarettes. Looking at me with a kind of mocking, amused defiance, he put one between his lips. "You mind?"

"You smoking already?"

He lit the cigarette and nodded, watching me through the smoke. "I just wanted to see if I'd have the courage to smoke in front of you." He grinned and blew a great cloud of smoke to the ceiling. "It was easy." He looked at my face. "Come on, now. I bet you was smoking at my age, tell the truth."

I didn't say anything but the truth was on my face, and he laughed. But now there was something very strained in his laugh. "Sure. And I bet that ain't all you was doing."

He was frightening me a little. "Cut the crap," I said. "We already decided that you was going to go and live at Isabel's. Now what's got into you all of a sudden?"

"*You* decided it," he pointed out. "*I* didn't decide nothing." He stopped in front of me, leaning against the stove, arms loosely folded. "Look, brother. I don't want to stay in Harlem no more, I really don't." He was very earnest. He looked at me, then over toward the kitchen window. There was something in his eyes I'd never seen before, some thoughtfulness, some worry all his own. He rubbed the muscle of one arm. "It's time I was getting out of here."

"Where do you want to *go*, Sonny?"

"I want to join the army. Or the navy, I don't care. If I say I'm old enough, they'll believe me."

Then I got mad. It was because I was so scared. "You must be crazy. You goddamn fool, what the hell do you want to go and join the *army* for?"

"I just told you. To get out of Harlem."

"Sonny, you haven't even finished *school.* And if you really want to be a musician, how do you expect to study if you're in the *army*?"

He looked at me, trapped, and in anguish. "There's ways. I might be able to work out some kind of deal. Anyway, I'll have the G.I. Bill when I come out."

5. Dictatorial, overbearing.

"*If* you come out." We stared at each other. "Sonny, please. Be reasonable. I know the setup is far from perfect. But we got to do the best we can."

"I ain't learning nothing in school," he said. "Even when I go." He turned away from me and opened the window and threw his cigarette out into the narrow alley. I watched his back. "At least, I ain't learning nothing you'd want me to learn." He slammed the window so hard I thought the glass would fly out, and turned back to me. "And I'm sick of the stink of these garbage cans!"

"Sonny," I said, "I know how you feel. But if you don't finish school now, you're going to be sorry later that you didn't." I grabbed him by the shoulders. "And you only got another year. It ain't so bad. And I'll come back and I swear I'll help you do *whatever* you want to do. Just try to put up with it till I come back. Will you please do that? For me?"

He didn't answer and he wouldn't look at me.

"Sonny. You hear me?"

He pulled away. "I hear you. But you never hear anything *I* say."

I didn't know what to say to that. He looked out of the window and then back at me. "OK," he said, and sighed. "I'll try."

Then I said, trying to cheer him up a little, "They got a piano at Isabel's. You can practice on it."

And as a matter of fact, it did cheer him up for a minute. "That's right," he said to himself. "I forgot that." His face relaxed a little. But the worry, the thoughtfulness, played on it still, the way shadows play on a face which is staring into the fire.

But I thought I'd never hear the end of that piano. At first, Isabel would write me, saying how nice it was that Sonny was so serious about his music and how, as soon as he came in from school, or wherever he had been when he was supposed to be at school, he went straight to that piano and stayed there until suppertime. And, after supper, he went back to that piano and stayed there until everybody went to bed. He was at the piano all day Saturday and all day Sunday. Then he bought a record player and started playing records. He'd play one record over and over again, all day long sometimes, and he'd improvise along with it on the piano. Or he'd play one section of the record, one chord, one change, one progression, then he'd do it on the piano. Then back to the record. Then back to the piano.

Well, I really don't know how they stood it. Isabel finally confessed that it wasn't like living with a person at all, it was like living with sound. And the sound didn't make any sense to her, didn't make any sense to any of them—naturally. They began, in a way, to be afflicted by this presence that was living in their home. It was as though Sonny were some sort of god, or monster. He moved in an atmosphere which wasn't like theirs at all. They fed him and he ate, he washed himself, he walked in and out of their door; he certainly wasn't nasty or unpleasant or rude, Sonny isn't any of those things; but it was as though he were all wrapped up in some cloud, some fire, some vision all his own; and there wasn't any way to reach him.

At the same time, he wasn't really a man yet, he was still a child, and they had to watch out for him in all kinds of ways. They certainly couldn't throw him out. Neither did they dare to make a great scene about that piano because even they dimly sensed, as I sensed, from so many thousands of miles away, that Sonny was at that piano playing for his life.

But he hadn't been going to school. One day a letter came from the school board and Isabel's mother got it—there had, apparently, been other letters but Sonny had torn them up. This day, when Sonny came in, Isabel's mother showed him the letter and asked where he'd been spending his time. And she finally got it out of him that he'd been down in Greenwich Village, with musicians and other characters, in a white girl's apartment. And this scared her and she started to scream at him and what came up, once she began—though she denies it to this day—was what sacrifices they were making to give Sonny a decent home and how little he appreciated it.

Sonny didn't play the piano that day. By evening, Isabel's mother had calmed down but then there was the old man to deal with, and Isabel herself. Isabel says she did her best to be calm but she broke down and started crying. She says she just watched Sonny's face. She could tell, by watching him, what was happening with him. And what was happening was that they penetrated his cloud, they had reached him. Even if their fingers had been a thousand times more gentle than human fingers ever are, he could hardly help feeling that they had stripped him naked and were spitting on that nakedness. For he also had to see that his presence, that music, which was life or death to him, had been torture for them and that they had endured it, not at all for his sake, but only for mine. And Sonny couldn't take that. He can take it a little better today than he could then but he's still not very good at it and, frankly, I don't know anybody who is.

The silence of the next few days must have been louder than the sound of all the music ever played since time began. One morning, before she went to work, Isabel was in his room for something and she suddenly realized that all of his records were gone. And she knew for certain that he was gone. And he was. He went as far as the navy would carry him. He finally sent me a postcard from some place in Greece and that was the first I knew that Sonny was still alive. I didn't see him any more until we were both back in New York and the war had long been over.

He was a man by then, of course, but I wasn't willing to see it. He came by the house from time to time, but we fought almost every time we met. I didn't like the way he carried himself, loose and dreamlike all the time, and I didn't like his friends, and his music seemed to be merely an excuse for the life he led. It sounded just that weird and disordered.

Then we had a fight, a pretty awful fight, and I didn't see him for months. By and by I looked him up, where he was living, in a furnished room in the Village, and I tried to make it up. But there were lots of other people in the room and Sonny just lay on his bed, and he wouldn't come downstairs with me, and he treated these other people as though they were his family and I weren't. So I got mad and then he got mad, and then I told him that he might just as well be dead as live the way he was living. Then he stood up and he told me not to worry about him any more in life, that he *was* dead as far as I was concerned. Then he pushed me to the door and the other people looked on as though nothing were happening, and he slammed the door behind me. I stood in the hallway, staring at the door. I heard somebody laugh in the room and then the tears came to my eyes. I started down the steps, whistling to keep from crying, I kept whistling to myself, *You going to need me, baby, one of these cold, rainy days.*

I read about Sonny's trouble in the spring. Little Grace died in the fall. She was a beautiful little girl. But she only lived a little over two years. She died of polio and she suffered. She had a slight fever for a couple of days, but it didn't seem like anything and we just kept her in bed. And we would certainly have called the doctor, but the fever dropped, she seemed to be all right. So we thought it had just been a cold. Then, one day, she was up, playing, Isabel was in the kitchen fixing lunch for the two boys when they'd come in from school, and she heard Grace fall down in the living room. When you have a lot of children you don't always start running when one of them falls, unless they start screaming or something. And, this time, Gracie was quiet. Yet, Isabel says that when she heard that *thump* and then that silence, something happened to her to make her afraid. And she ran to the living room and there was little Grace on the floor, all twisted up, and the reason she hadn't screamed was that she couldn't get her breath. And when she did scream, it was the worst sound, Isabel says, that she'd ever heard in all her life, and she still hears it sometimes in her dreams. Isabel will sometimes wake me up with a low, moaning, strangling sound and I have to be quick to awaken her and hold her to me and where Isabel is weeping against me seems a mortal wound.

I think I may have written Sonny the very day that little Grace was buried. I was sitting in the living room in the dark, by myself, and I suddenly thought of Sonny. My trouble made his real.

One Saturday afternoon, when Sonny had been living with us, or anyway, been in our house, for nearly two weeks, I found myself wandering aimlessly about the living room, drinking from a can of beer, and trying to work up courage to search Sonny's room. He was out, he was usually out whenever I was home, and Isabel had taken the children to see their grandparents. Suddenly I was standing still in front of the living room window, watching Seventh Avenue. The idea of searching Sonny's room made me still. I scarcely dared to admit to myself what I'd be searching for. I didn't know what I'd do if I found it. Or if I didn't.

On the sidewalk across from me, near the entrance to a barbecue joint, some people were holding an old-fashioned revival meeting. The barbecue cook, wearing a dirty white apron, his conked[6] hair reddish and metallic in the pale sun, and a cigarette between his lips, stood in the doorway, watching them. Kids and older people paused in their errands and stood there, along with some older men and a couple of very tough-looking women who watched everything that happened on the avenue, as though they owned it, or were maybe owned by it. Well, they were watching this, too. The revival was being carried on by three sisters in black, and a brother. All they had were their voices and their

6. Straightened and greased.

# Toni Cade Bambara

*Bambara (1939–1995) was born in New York City. Early in life she was enlisted by a militant tradition and in high school years learned that writing is a splendid means of doing battle. She began to publish short stories in 1960, and in 1972 many of these were collected in her first book,* Gorilla, My Love. *This was followed by other collections:* The Sea Birds Are Still Alive *(1977),* The Salt Eaters *(1980),* If Blessings Come *(1987), and* Raymond's Run *(1990). Over the years of her career she wrote screenplays and compiled anthologies.*

## Gorilla, My Love

That was the year Hunca Bubba changed his name. Not a change up, but a change back, since Jefferson Winston Vale was the name in the first place. Which was news to me cause he'd been my Hunca Bubba my whole lifetime, since I couldn't manage Uncle to save my life. So far as I was concerned it was a change completely to somethin soundin very geographical weatherlike to me, like somethin you'd find in a almanac. Or somethin you'd run across when you sittin in the navigator seat with a wet thumb on the map crinkly in your lap, watchin the roads and signs so when Granddaddy Vale say "Which way, Scout," you got sense enough to say take the next exit or take a left or whatever it is. Not that Scout's my name. Just the name Grandaddy call whoever sittin in the navigator seat. Which is usually me cause I don't feature sittin in the back with the pecans. Now, you figure pecans all right to be sittin with. If you thinks so, that's your business. But they dusty sometime and make you cough. And they got a way of slidin around and dippin down sudden, like maybe a rat in the buckets. So if you scary like me, you sleep with the lights on and blame it on Baby Jason and, so as not to waste good electric, you study the maps. And that's how come I'm in the navigator seat most times and get to be called Scout.

So Hunca Bubba in the back with the pecans and Baby Jason, and he in love. And we got to hear all this stuff about this woman he in love with and all. Which really ain't enough to keep the mind alive, though Baby Jason got no better sense than to give his undivided attention and keep grabbin at the photograph which is just a picture of some skinny woman in a countrified dress with her hand shot up to her face like she shame fore cameras. But there's a movie house in the background which I ax about. Cause I am a movie freak from way back, even though it do get me in trouble sometime.

Like when me and Big Brood and Baby Jason was on our own last Easter and couldn't go to the Dorset cause we'd seen all the Three Stooges they was. And the RKO Hamilton was closed readying up for the Easter Pageant that night. And the West End, the Regun and the Sunset was too far, less we had grownups with us which we didn't. So we walk up Amsterdam Avenue to the Washington and *Gorilla, My Love* playin, they say, which suit me just fine, though the "my love" part kinda drag Big Brood some. As for Baby Jason, shoot, like Granddaddy say, he'd follow me into the fiery furnace if I say come on. So we go in and get three bags of Havmore potato chips which not only are the best potato chips but the best bags for blowin up and bustin real loud so the matron come trottin down the aisle with her chunky self, flashin that flashlight dead in your eye so you can give her some lip, and if she answer back and you already finish seein the show anyway, why then you just turn the place out. Which I love to do, no lie. With Baby Jason kickin at the seat in front, egging me on, and Big Brood mumblin bout what fiercesome things we goin do. Which means me. Like when the big boys come up on us talkin bout Lemme a nickel. It's me that hide the money. Or when the bad boys in the park take Big Brood's Spaudeen way from him. It's me that jump on they back and fight awhile. And it's me that turns out the show if the matron get too salty.

So the movie come on and right away it's this churchy music and clearly not about no gorilla. Bout Jesus. And I am ready to kill, not cause I got anything gainst Jesus. Just that when you fixed to watch a gorilla picture you don't wanna get messed around with Sunday School stuff. So I am mad. Besides, we see this raggedy old brown film *King of Kings*[1] every year and enough's enough. Grownups figure they can treat you just anyhow. Which burns me up. There I am, my feet up and my Havmore potato chips really salty and crispy and two jawbreakers in my lap and the money safe in my shoe from the big boys, and there comes this Jesus stuff. So we all go wild. Yellin, booin, stompin and carrying on. Really to wake the man in the booth up there who musta went to sleep and put on the wrong reels. But no, cause he holler down to shut up and then he turn the sound up so we really gotta holler like crazy to even hear ourselves good. And the matron ropes off the children section and flashes her light all over the place and we yell some more and some kids slip under the rope and run up and down the aisle just to show it take more than some dusty ole velvet rope to tie us down. And I'm flingin the kid in front of me's popcorn. And Baby Jason kickin seats. And it's really somethin. Then here come the big and bad matron, the one they let out in case of emergency. This here the colored matron Brandy and her friends call Thunderbuns. She do not play. She do not smile. So we shut up and watch the simple ass picture.

Which is not so simple as it is stupid. Cause I realized that just about anybody in my family is better than this god they always talkin about. My daddy wouldn't stand for nobody treatin any of us that way. My mama specially. And I can just see it now, Big Brood up there on the cross talkin bout Forgive them Daddy cause they don't know what they doin. And my Mama say Get on down

1. Silent movie depicting the life of Christ.

from there you big fool, whatcha think this is, playtime? And my Daddy yellin to Granddaddy to get him a ladder cause Big Brood actin the fool, his mother side of the family showin up. And my mama and her sister Daisy jumpin on them Romans beatin them with they pocketbooks. And Hunca Bubba tellin them folks on they knees they better get out the way and go get some help or they goin to get trampled on. And Granddaddy Val sayin Leave the boy alone, if that's what he wants to do with his life we ain't got nothin to say about it. Then Aunt Daisy givin him a taste of that pocketbook, fussin bout what a damn fool old man Grandaddy is. Then everybody jumpin in his chest like the time Uncle Clayton went in the army and come back with only one leg and Granddaddy say somethin stupid about that's life. And by this time Big Brood off the cross and in the park playin handball or skully or somethin. And the family in the kitchen throwin dishes at each other, screamin bout if you hadn't done this I wouldn't had to do that. And me in the parlor trying to do my arithmetic yellin Shut it off.

Which is what I was yellin all by myself which make me a sittin target for Thunderbuns. But when I yell We want our money back, that gets everybody in chorus. And the movie windin up with this heavenly cloud music and the smart-ass up there in his hole in the wall turns up the sound again to drown us out. Then there comes Bugs Bunny which we already seen so we know we been had. No gorilla my nuthin. And Big Brood say Awwww sheeet, we goin to see the manager and get our money back. And I know from this we business. So I brush the potato chips out of my hair which is where Baby Jason like to put em, and I march myself up the aisle to deal with the manager who is a crook in the first place for lyin out there sayin *Gorilla, My Love* playin. And I never did like the man cause he oily and pasty at the same time like the bad guy in the serial, the one that got a hideout behind a push-button bookcase and play "Moonlight Sonata" with gloves on. I knock on the door and I am furious. And I am alone, too. Cause Big Brood suddenly got to go so bad even though my mama told us bout goin in them nasty bathrooms. And I hear him sigh like he disgusted when he get to the door and see only a little kid there. And now I'm really furious cause I get so tired grownups messin over kids cause they little and can't take em to court. What is it, he say to me like I lost my mittens or wet myself or am somebody's retarded child. When in reality I am the smartest kid P.S. 186 ever had in its whole lifetime and you can ax anybody. Even them teachers that don't like me cause I won't sing them Southern songs or back off when they tell me my questions are out of order. And cause my Mama come up there in a minute when them teachers start playin the dozens[2] behind colored folks. She stalks in with her hat pulled down bad and that Persian lamb coat draped back over one hip on account of she got her fist planted there so she can talk that talk which gets us all hypnotized, and teacher be comin undone cause she know this could be her job and her behind cause Mama got pull with the Board and bad by her own self anyhow.

So I kick the door open wider and just walk right by him and sit down and tell the man about himself and that I want my money back and that goes for

2. Trading insults about each others' parents.

Baby Jason and Big Brood too. And he still trying to shuffle me out the door even though I'm sittin which shows him for the fool he is. Just like them teachers do fore they realize Mama like a stone on that spot and ain't backin up. So he ain't gettin up off the money. So I was forced to leave, takin the matches from under his ashtray, and set a fire under the candy stand, which closed the raggedy ole Washington down for a week. My Daddy had the suspect it was me cause Big Brood got a big mouth. But I explained right quick what the whole thing was about and I figured it was even-steven. Cause if you say Gorilla, My Love, you supposed to mean it. Just like when you say you goin to give me a party on my birthday, you gotta mean it. And if you say me and Baby Jason can go South pecan haulin with Grandaddy Vale, you better not be comin up with no stuff about the weather look uncertain or did you mop the bathroom or any other trickified business. I mean even gangsters in the movies say My word is my bond. So don't nobody get away with nothin far as I'm concerned. So Daddy put his belt back on. Cause that's the way I was raised. Like my Mama say in one of them situations when I won't back down, Okay Badbird, you right. Your point is well-taken. Not that Badbird my name, just what she say when she tired arguin and know I'm right. And Aunt Jo, who is the hardest head in the family and worse even than Aunt Daisy, she say, You absolutely right Miss Muffin, which also ain't my real name but the name she gave me one time when I got some medicine shot in my behind and wouldn't get up off her pillows for nothin. And even Grandaddy Vale—who got no memory to speak of, so sometime you can just plain lie to him, if you want to be like that—he say, Well if that's what I said, then that's it. But this name business was different they said. It wasn't like Hunca Bubba had gone back on his word or anything. Just that he was thinkin bout gettin married and was usin his real name now. Which ain't the way I saw it at all.

So there I am in the navigator seat. And I turned to him and just plain ole ax him. I mean I come right on out with it. No sense goin all around that barn the old folks talk about. And like my mama say, Hazel—which is my real name and what she remembers to call me when she bein serious—when you got somethin on your mind, speak up and let the chips fall where they may. And if anybody don't like it, tell em to come see your mama. And Daddy look up from the paper and say, You hear your Mama good, Hazel. And tell em to come see me first. Like that. That's how I was raised.

So I turn clear round in the navigator seat and say, "Look here, Hunca Bubba or Jefferson Windsong Vale or whatever your name is, you gonna marry this girl?"

"Sure am," he say, all grins.

And I say, "Member that time you was baby-sittin me when we lived at four-o-nine and there was this big snow and Mama and Daddy got held up in the country so you had to stay for two days?"

And he say, "Sure do."

"Well. You remember how you told me I was the cutest thing that ever walked the earth?"

"Oh, you were real cute when you were little," he say, which is supposed to be funny. I am not laughin.

"Well. You remember what you said?"

And Grandaddy Vale squintin over the wheel and axin Which way, Scout. But Scout is busy and don't care if we all get lost for days.

"Watcha mean, Peaches?"

"My name is Hazel. And what I mean is you said you were going to marry *me* when I grew up. You were going to wait. That's what I mean, my dear Uncle Jefferson." And he don't say nuthin. Just look at me real strange like he never saw me before in life. Like he lost in some weird town in the middle of night and lookin for directions and there's no one to ask. Like it was me that messed up the maps and turned the road posts round. "Well, you said it, didn't you?" And Baby Jason lookin back and forth like we playin ping-pong. Only I ain't playin. I'm hurtin and I can hear that I am screamin. And Grandaddy Vale mumblin how we never gonna get to where we goin if I don't turn around and take my navigator job serious.

"Well, for cryin out loud, Hazel, you just a little girl. And I was just teasin."

"And I was just teasin,' " I say back just how he said it so he can hear what a terrible thing it is. Then I don't say nuthin. And he don't say nuthin. And Baby Jason don't say nuthin nohow. Then Granddaddy Vale speak up. "Look here, Precious, it was Hunca Bubba what told you them things. This here, Jefferson Winston Vale." And Hunca Bubba say, "That's right. That was somebody else. I'm a new somebody."

"You a lyin dawg," I say, when I meant to say treacherous dog, but just couldn't get hold of the word. It slipped away from me. And I'm crying and crumplin down in the seat and just don't care. And Granddaddy say to hush and steps on the gas. And I'm losin my bearins and don't even know where to look on the map cause I can't see for cryin. And Baby Jason cryin too. Cause he is my blood brother and understands that we must stick together or be forever lost, what with grown-ups playin change-up and turnin you round every which way so bad. And don't even say they sorry.

# Andrea Barrett

*Barrett (1954– ) was born in Massachusetts and received her higher education at Union College, Schenectady, New York. She is the recipient of a National Book Award in Fiction in 1996 for* Ship Fever *and a Guggenheim Fellowship in 1997. Her most recent book is* The Voyage of the Narwhal *(1998).*

## The Littoral Zone

When they met, fifteen years ago, Jonathan had a job teaching botany at a small college near Albany, and Ruby was teaching invertebrate zoology at a college in the Berkshires. Both of them, along with an ornithologist, an ichthyologist, and an oceanographer, had agreed to spend three weeks of their summer break at a marine biology research station on an island off the New Hampshire coast. They had spouses, children, mortgages, bills; they went, they later told each other, because the pay was too good to refuse. Two-thirds of the way through the course, they agreed that the pay was not enough.

How they reached that first agreement is a story they've repeated to each other again and again and told, separately, to their closest friends. Ruby thinks they had this conversation on the second Friday of the course, after Frank Kenary's slide show on the abyssal fish and before Carol Dagliesh's lecture on the courting behavior of herring gulls. Jonathan maintains that they had it earlier—that Wednesday, maybe, when they were still recovering from Gunnar Erickson's trawling expedition. The days before they became so aware of each other have blurred in their minds, but they agree that their first real conversation took place on the afternoon devoted to the littoral zone.

The tide was all the way out. The students were clumped on the rocky, pitted apron between the water and the ledges, peering into the tidal pools and listing the species they found. Gunnar was in the equipment room, repairing one of the sampling claws. Frank was setting up dissections in the tiny lab; Carol had gone back to the mainland on the supply boat, hoping to replace the camera one of the students had dropped. And so the two of them, Jonathan and Ruby, were left alone for a little while.

They both remember the granite ledge where they sat, and the raucous quarrels of the nesting gulls. They agree that Ruby was scratching furiously at her calves and that Jonathan said, "Take it easy, okay? You'll draw blood."

Her calves were slim and tan, Jonathan remembers. Covered with blotches and scrapes.

I folded my fingers, Ruby remembers. Then I blushed. My throat felt sunburned.

Ruby said, "I know, it's so embarrassing. But all this salt on my poison ivy—God, what I wouldn't give for a bath! They never told me there wouldn't be any *water* here. . . ."

Jonathan gestured at the ocean surrounding them and then they started laughing. *Hysteria*, they have told each other since. They were so tired by then, twelve days into the course, and so dirty and overworked and strained by pretending to the students that these things didn't matter, that neither of them could understand that they were also lonely. Their shared laughter felt like pure relief.

"No water?" Jonathan said. "I haven't been dry since we got here. My clothes are damp, my sneakers are damp, my hair never dries. . . ."

His hair was beautiful, Ruby remembers. Thick, a little too long. Part blond and part brown.

"I know," she said. "But you know what I mean. I didn't realize they'd have to bring our drinking water over on a boat."

"Or that they'd expect us to wash in the ocean," Jonathan said. Her forearms were dusted with salt, he remembers. The down along them sparkled in the sun.

"And those cots," Ruby said. "Does yours have a sag in it like a hammock?"

"Like a slingshot," Jonathan said.

For half an hour they sat on their ledge and compared their bubbling patches of poison ivy and the barnacle wounds that scored their hands and feet. Nothing healed out here, they told each other. Everything got infected. When one of the students called, "Look what I found!" Jonathan rose and held his hand out to Ruby. She took it easily and hauled herself up and they walked down to the water together. Jonathan's hand was thick and blunt-fingered, with nails bitten down so far that the skin around them was raw. Odd, Ruby remembers thinking. Those bitten stumps attached to such a good-looking man.

They have always agreed that the worst moment, for each of them, was when they stepped from the boat to the dock on the final day of the course and saw their families waiting in the parking lot. Jonathan's wife had their four-year-old daughter balanced on her shoulders. Their two older children were leaning perilously over the guardrails and shrieking at the sight of him. Jessie had turned nine in Jonathan's absence, and Jonathan can't think of her eager face without remembering the starfish he brought as his sole, guilty gift.

Ruby's husband had parked their car just a few yards from Jonathan's family. Her sons were wearing baseball caps, and what Ruby remembers is the way the yellow linings lit their faces. For a minute she saw the children squealing near her sons as faceless, inconsequential; Jonathan later told her that her children had been similarly blurred for him. Then Jonathan said, "That's my family, there," and Ruby said, "That's mine, right next to yours," and all the faces leapt into focus for both of them.

Nothing that was to come—not the days in court, nor the days they moved, nor the losses of jobs and homes—would ever seem so awful to them as that moment when they first saw their families standing there, unaware and hopeful. Deceitfully, treacherously, Ruby and Jonathan separated and walked to the people awaiting them. They didn't introduce each other to their spouses. They didn't look at each other—although, they later admitted, they cast covert looks at each other's families. They thought they were invisible, that no one could see what had happened between them. They thought their families would not remember how they had stepped off the boat and stood, for an instant, together.

On that boat, sitting dumb and miserable in the litter of nets and equipment, they had each pretended to be resigned to going home. Each foresaw (or so they later told each other) the hysterical phone calls and the frenzied, secret meetings. Neither foresaw how much the sight of each other's family would hurt. "Sweetie," Jonathan remembers Ruby's husband saying. "You've lost so much weight." Ruby remembers staring over her husband's shoulder and watching Jessie butt her head like a dog under Jonathan's hand.

For the first twelve days on the island, Jonathan and Ruby were so busy that they hardly noticed each other. For the next few days, after their conversation on the ledge, they sat near each other during faculty lectures and student presentations. These were held in the library, a ramshackle building separated from the bunkhouse and the dining hall by a stretch of wild roses and poison ivy.

Jonathan had talked about algae in there, holding up samples of *Fucus* and *Hildenbrandtia*[1] Ruby had talked about the littoral zone, that space between high and low watermarks where organisms struggled to adapt to the daily rhythm of immersion and exposure. They had drawn on the blackboard in colored chalk while the students, itchy and hot and tired, scratched their arms and legs and feigned attention.

Neither of them, they admitted much later, had focused fully on the other's lecture. "It was *before*," Ruby has said ruefully. "I didn't know that I was going to want to have listened." And Jonathan has laughed and confessed that he was studying the shells and skulls on the walls while Ruby was drawing on the board.

The library was exceedingly hot, they agreed, and the chairs remarkably uncomfortable; the only good spot was the sofa in front of the fireplace. That was the spot they commandeered on the evening after their first conversation, when dinner led to a walk and then the walk led them into the library a few minutes before the scheduled lecture.

Erika Moorhead, Ruby remembers. Talking about the tensile strength of byssus threads.[2]

Walter Schank, Jonathan remembers. Something to do with hydrozoans.[3]

They both remember feeling comfortable for the first time since their arrival. And for the next few days—three by Ruby's accounting; four by

1. Common seaweeds found on rocky coasts. 2. Long, tough filaments by which some mollusks, such as mussels, bind themselves to rocks or to each other. 3. A class of jellyfish that includes the Portuguese Man-of-War. The Man-of-War tentacles are covered with stinging polyps, which cause intense pain and paralysis in its victims.

Jonathan's—one of them came early for every lecture and saved a seat on the sofa for the other.

They giggled at Frank Kenary's slides, which he'd arranged like a creepy fashion show: abyssal fish sporting varied blobs of luminescent flesh. When Gunnar talked for two hours about subduction zones and the calcium carbonate cycle, they amused themselves exchanging doodles. They can't remember, now, whether Gunnar's endless lecture came before Carol Dagliesh's filmstrip on the herring gulls, or which of the students tipped over the dissecting scope and sent the dish of copepods[4] to their deaths. But both of them remember those days and nights as being almost purely happy. They swam in that odd, indefinite zone where they were more than friends, not yet lovers, still able to deny to themselves that they were headed where they were headed.

Ruby made the first phone call, a week after they left the island. At eleven o'clock on a Sunday night, she told her husband she'd left something in her office that she needed to prepare the next day's class. She drove to campus, unlocked her door, picked up the phone and called Jonathan at his house. One of his children—Jessie, she thinks—answered the phone. Ruby remembers how, even through the turmoil of her emotions, she'd been shocked at the idea of a child staying up so late.

There was a horrible moment while Jessie went to find her father; another when Jonathan, hearing Ruby's voice, said, "Wait, hang on, I'll just be a minute," and then negotiated Jessie into bed. Ruby waited, dreading his anger, knowing she'd been wrong to call him at home. But Jonathan, when he finally returned, said, "Ruby. You got my letter."

"What letter?" she asked. He wrote to tell me good-bye, she remembers thinking.

"My *letter*," he said. "I wrote you, I have to see you. I can't stand this."

Ruby released the breath she hadn't known she was holding.

"You didn't get it?" he said. "You just called?" It wasn't only me, he remembers thinking. She feels it too.

"I had to hear your voice," she said.

Ruby called, but Jonathan wrote. And so when Jonathan's youngest daughter, Cora, later fell in love and confided in Ruby, and then asked her, "Was it like this with you two? Who started it—you or Dad?" all Ruby could say was, "It happened to both of us."

Sometimes, when Ruby and Jonathan sit on the patio looking out at the hills above Palmyra, they will turn and see their children watching them through the kitchen window. Before the children went off to college, the house bulged with them on weekends and holidays and seemed empty in between; Jonathan's wife had custody of Jessie and Gordon and Cora, and Ruby's husband took her sons, Mickey and Ryan, when he remarried. Now that the children are old enough to come and go as they please, the house is silent almost all the time.

4. Small, very common ocean crustaceans; the chief component of the mass of organisms floating passively with the water currents and forming marine plankton.

Jessie is twenty-four, and Gordon is twenty-two; Mickey is twenty-one, and Cora and Ryan are both nineteen. When they visit Jonathan and Ruby they spend an unhealthy amount of time talking about their past. In their conversations they seem to split their lives into three epochs: the years when what they think of as their real families were whole; the years right after Jonathan and Ruby met, when their parents were coming and going, fighting and making up, separating and divorcing; and the years since Jonathan and Ruby's marriage, when they were forced into a reconstituted family. Which epoch they decide to explore depends on who's visiting and who's getting along with whom.

"But we were happy," Mickey may say to Ruby, if he and Ryan are visiting and Jonathan's children are absent. "We were, we were fine."

"It wasn't like you and Mom ever fought," Cora may say to Jonathan, if Ruby's sons aren't around. "You could have worked it out if you'd tried."

When they are all together, they tend to avoid the first two epochs and to talk about their first strained weekends and holidays together. They've learned to tolerate each other, despite their forced introductions; Cora and Ryan, whose birthdays are less than three months apart, seem especially close. Ruby and Jonathan know that much of what draws their youngest children together is shared speculation about what happened on that island.

They look old to their children, they know. Both of them are nearing fifty. Jonathan has grown quite heavy and has lost much of his hair; Ruby's fine-boned figure has gone gaunt and stringy. They know their children can't imagine them young and strong and wrung by passion. The children can't think—can't stand to think—about what happened on the island, but they can't stop themselves from asking questions.

"Did you have other girlfriends?" Cora asks Jonathan. "Were you so unhappy with Mom?"

"Did you know him before?" Ryan asks Ruby. "Did you go there to be with him?"

"We met there," Jonathan and Ruby say. "We had never seen each other before. We fell in love." That is all they will say, they never give details, they say "yes" or "no" to the easy questions and evade the hard ones. They worry that even the little they offer may be too much.

Jonathan and Ruby tell each other the stories of their talk by the tidal pool, their walks and meals, the sagging sofa, the moment in the parking lot, and the evening Ruby made her call. They tell these to console themselves when their children chide them or when, alone in the house, they sit quietly near each other and struggle to conceal their disappointments.

Of course they have expected some of these. Mickey and Gordon have both had trouble in school, and Jessie has grown much too close to her mother; neither Jonathan nor Ruby has found jobs as good as the ones they lost, and their new home in Palmyra still doesn't feel quite like home. But all they have lost in order to be together would seem bearable had they continued to feel the way they felt on the island.

They're sensible people, and very well-mannered; they remind themselves that they were young then and are middle-aged now, and that their fierce attraction would naturally ebb with time. Neither likes to think about how much of the thrill of their early days together came from the obstacles they had to overcome. Some days, when Ruby pulls into the driveway still thinking about her last class and catches sight of Jonathan out in the garden, she can't believe the heavyset figure pruning shrubs so meticulously is the man for whom she fought such battles. Jonathan, who often wakes very early, sometimes stares at Ruby's sleeping face and thinks how much more gracefully his ex-wife is aging.

They never reproach each other. When the tension builds in the house and the silence becomes overwhelming, one or the other will say, "Do you remember . . . ?" and then launch into one of the myths on which they have founded their lives. But there is one story they never tell each other, because they can't bear to talk about what they have lost. This is the one about the evening that has shaped their life together.

Jonathan's hand on Ruby's back, Ruby's hand on Jonathan's thigh, a shirt unbuttoned, a belt undone. They never mention this moment, or the moments that followed it, because that would mean discussing who seduced whom, and any resolution of that would mean assigning blame. Guilt they can handle; they've been living with guilt for fifteen years. But blame? It would be more than either of them could bear, to know the exact moment when one of them precipitated all that has happened to them. The most either of them has ever said is, "How could we have known?"

But the night in the library is what they both think about, when they lie silently next to each other and listen to the wind. It must be summer for them to think about it; the children must be with their other parents and the rain must be falling on the cedar shingles overhead. A candle must be burning on the mantel above the bed and the maple branches outside their window must be tossing against each other. Then they think of the story they know so well and never say out loud.

There was a huge storm three nights before they left the island, the tail end of a hurricane passing farther out to sea. The cedar trees creaked and swayed in the wind beyond the library windows. The students had staggered off to bed, after the visitor from Woods Hole had finished his lecture on the explorations of the *Alvin* in the Cayman Trough, and Frank and Gunnar and Carol had shrouded themselves in their rain gear and left as well, sheltering the visitor between them. Ruby sat at one end of the long table, preparing bottles of fixative[5] for their expedition the following morning, and Jonathan lay on the sofa writing notes. The boat was leaving just after dawn and they knew they ought to go to bed.

The wind picked up outside, sweeping the branches against the walls. The windows rattled. Jonathan shivered and said, "Do you suppose we could get a fire going in that old fireplace?"

"I bet we could," said Ruby, which gave both of them the pretext they needed to crouch side by side on the cracked tiles, brushing elbows as they

5. A substance used to preserve living tissue.

opened the flue and crumpled paper and laid kindling in the form of a grid. The logs Jonathan found near the lobster traps were dry and the fire caught quickly.

Who found the green candle in the drawer below the microscope? Who lit the candle and turned off the lights? And who found the remains of the jug of wine that Frank had brought in honor of the visitor? They sat there side by side, poking at the burning logs and pretending they weren't doing what they were doing. The wind pushed through the window they'd opened a crack, and the tan window shade lifted and then fell back against the frame. The noise was soothing at first; later it seemed irritating.

Jonathan, whose fingernails were bitten to the quick, admired the long nail on Ruby's right little finger and then said, half-seriously, how much he'd love to bite a nail like that. When Ruby held her hand to his mouth he took the nail between his teeth and nibbled through the white tip, which days in the water had softened. Ruby slipped her other hand inside his shirt and ran it up his back. Jonathan ran his mouth up her arm and down her neck.

They started in front of the fire and worked their way across the floor, breaking a glass, knocking the table askew. Ruby rubbed her back raw against the rug and Jonathan scraped his knees, and twice they paused and laughed at their wild excesses. They moved across the floor from east to west and later from west to east, and between those two journeys, during the time when they heaped their clothes and the sofa cushions into a nest in front of the fire, they talked.

This was not the kind of conversation they'd had during walks and meals since that first time on the rocks: who they were, where they'd come from, how they'd made it here. This was the talk where they instinctively edited out the daily pleasures of their lives on the mainland and spliced together the hard times, the dark times, until they'd constructed versions of themselves that could make sense of what they'd just done.

For months after this, as they lay in stolen, secret rooms between houses and divorces and jobs and lives, Jonathan would tell Ruby that he swallowed her nail. The nail dissolved in his stomach, he'd say. It passed into his villi[6] and out to his blood and then flowed to bone and muscle and nerve, where the molecules that had once been part of her became part of him. Ruby, who always seemed to know more acutely than Jonathan that they'd have to leave whatever room this was in an hour or a day, would argue with him.

"Nails are keratin," she'd tell him. "Like hooves and hair. Like wool. We can't digest wool."

"Moths can," Jonathan would tell her. "Moths eat sweaters."

"Moths have a special enzyme in their saliva," Ruby would say. This was true, she knew it for a fact. She'd been so taken by Jonathan's tale that she'd gone to the library to check out the details and discovered he was wrong.

But Jonathan didn't care what the biochemists said. He held her against his chest and said, "I have an enzyme for you."

That night, after the fire burned out, they slept for a couple of hours. Ruby

6. Tiny projections on the small intestine, which absorb nutrients.

woke first and watched Jonathan sleep for a while. He slept like a child, with his knees bent toward his chest and his hands clasped between his thighs. Ruby picked up the tipped-over chair and swept the fragments of broken glass onto a sheet of paper. Then she woke Jonathan and they tiptoed back to the rooms where they were supposed to be.

# Donald Barthelme

*Barthelme (1931–1989) was born in Philadelphia and grew up in Texas, where he worked as a reporter and editor before settling in New York City. His pictorial collages were frequently published in newspapers and magazines, and his characteristic fiction often seems to be constructed as collage—a pasting together of fragments gathered from the chaotic verbiage of our culture, set in comic and unexpected juxtapositions. Advertising slogans, street slang, sociological jargon, clichés, and faded jokes appear in patterns that expose their usually ignored significance. His novels are* Snow White *(1967),* The Dead Father *(1975), and* The King *(1990). His stories are collected in* Come Back, Dr. Caligari *(1964),* Unspeakable Practices, Unnatural Acts *(1968),* City Life *(1970), and* Amateurs *(1976). His more recent books include* Overnight to Many Distant Cities *(1983) and* Paradise *(1986).*

## Me and Miss Mandible

*13 September*

Miss Mandible wants to make love to me but she hesitates because I am officially a child; I am, according to the records, according to the gradebook on her desk, according to the card index in the principal's office, eleven years old. There is a misconception here, one that I haven't quite managed to get cleared up yet. I am in fact thirty-five, I've been in the Army, I am six feet one, I have hair in the appropriate places, my voice is a baritone, I know very well what to do with Miss Mandible if she ever makes up her mind.

In the meantime we are studying common fractions. I could, of course, answer all the questions, or at least most of them (there are things I don't remember). But I prefer to sit in this too-small seat with the desktop cramping my thighs and examine the life around me. There are thirty-two in the class, which is launched every morning with the pledge of allegiance to the flag. My own allegiance, at the moment, is divided between Miss Mandible and Sue Ann Brownly, who sits across the aisle from me all day long and is, like Miss Mandible, a fool for love. Of the two I prefer, today, Sue Ann; although between eleven and eleven and a half (she refuses to reveal her exact age) she is clearly a woman, with a woman's disguised aggression and a woman's peculiar contradictions.

*15 September*

Happily our geography text, which contains maps of all the principal landmasses of the world, is large enough to conceal my clandestine journal-keeping, accomplished in an ordinary black composition book. Every day I must wait until Geography to put down such thoughts as I may have had during the morning about my situation and my fellows. I have tried writing at other times and it does not work. Either the teacher is walking up and down the aisles (during this period, luckily, she sticks close to the map rack in the front of the room) or Bobby Vanderbilt, who sits behind me, is punching me in the kidneys and wanting to know what I am doing. Vanderbilt, I have found out from certain desultory conversations on the playground, is hung up on sports cars, a veteran consumer of *Road & Track*. This explains the continual roaring sounds which seem to emanate from his desk; he is reproducing a record album called *Sounds of Sebring*.

*19 September*

Only I, at times (only at times), understand that somehow a mistake has been made, that I am in a place where I don't belong. It may be that Miss Mandible also knows this, at some level, but for reasons not fully understood by me she is going along with the game. When I was first assigned to this room I wanted to protest, the error seemed obvious, the stupidest principal could have seen it; but I have come to believe it was deliberate, that I have been betrayed again.

Now it seems to make little difference. This life-role is as interesting as my former life-role, which was that of a claims adjuster for the Great Northern Insurance Company, a position which compelled me to spend my time amid the debris of our civilization: rumpled fenders, roofless sheds, gutted warehouses, smashed arms and legs. After ten years of this one has a tendency to see the world as a vast junkyard, looking at a man and seeing only his (potentially) mangled parts, entering a house only to trace the path of the inevitable fire. Therefore when I was installed here, although I knew an error had been made, I countenanced it, I was shrewd; I was aware that there might well be some kind of advantage to be gained from what seemed a disaster. The role of The Adjuster teaches one much.

*22 September*

I am being solicited for the volleyball team. I decline, refusing to take unfair profit from my height.

*23 September*

Every morning the roll is called: Bestvina, Bokenfohr, Broan, Brownly, Cone, Coyle, Crecelius, Darin, Durbin, Geiger, Guiswite, Heckler, Jacobs, Kleinschmidt, Lay, Logan, Masei, Mitgang, Pfeilsticker. It is like the litany chanted in the dim miserable dawns of Texas by the cadre sergeant of our basic training company.

In the Army, too, I was ever so slightly awry. It took me a fantastically long time to realize what the others grasped almost at once: that much of what we were doing was absolutely pointless, to no purpose. I kept wondering why. Then something happened that proposed a new question. One day we were commanded to whitewash, from the ground to the topmost leaves, all of the trees in our training area. The corporal who relayed the order was nervous and apologetic. Later an off-duty captain sauntered by and watched us, white-splashed and totally weary, strung out among the freakish shapes we had created. He walked away swearing. I understood the principle (orders are orders), but I wondered: Who decides?

*29 September*

Sue Ann is a wonder. Yesterday she viciously kicked my ankle for not paying attention when she was attempting to pass me a note during History. It is swollen still. But Miss Mandible was watching me, there was nothing I could do. Oddly enough Sue Ann reminds me of the wife I had in my former role, while Miss Mandible seems to be a child. She watches me constantly, trying to keep sexual significance out of her look; I am afraid the other children have noticed. I have already heard, on that ghostly frequency that is the medium of classroom communication, the words *"Teacher's pet!"*

*2 October*

Sometimes I speculate on the exact nature of the conspiracy which brought me here. At times I believe it was instigated by my wife of former days, whose name was . . . I am only pretending to forget. I know her name very well, as well as I know the name of my former motor oil (Quaker State) or my old Army serial number (US 54109268). Her name was Brenda.

*7 October*

Today I tiptoed up to Miss Mandible's desk (when there was no one else in the room) and examined its surface. Miss Mandible is a clean-desk teacher, I discovered. There was nothing except her gradebook (the one in which I exist as a sixth-grader) and a text, which was open at a page headed *Making the Processes Meaningful.* I read: "Many pupils enjoy working fractions when they understand what they are doing. They have confidence in their ability to take the right steps and to obtain correct answers. However, to give the subject full social significance, it is necessary that many realistic situations requiring the processes be found. Many interesting and lifelike problems involving the use of fractions should be solved . . . "

*8 October*

I am not irritated by the feeling of having been through all this before. Things are done differently now. The children, moreover, are in some ways different from those who accompanied me on my first voyage through the elementary schools: *"They have confidence in their ability to take the right steps and to obtain correct answers."* This is surely true. When Bobby Vanderbilt, who sits behind me and has the great tactical advantage of being able to maneuver in my disproportionate shadow, wishes to bust a classmate in the mouth he first asks Miss Mandible to lower the blind, saying that the sun hurts his eyes. When she does so, *bip!* My generation would never have been able to con authority so easily.

*13 October*

I misread a clue. Do not misunderstand me: it was a tragedy only from the point of view of the authorities. I conceived that it was my duty to obtain satisfaction for the injured, for an elderly lady (not even one of our policy-holders, but a claimant against Big Ben Transfer & Storage, Inc.) from the company. The settlement was $165,000; the claim, I still believe, was just. But without my encouragement Mrs. Bichek would never have had the self-love to prize her injury so highly. The company paid, but its faith in me, in my efficacy in the role, was broken. Henry Goodykind, the district manager, expressed this thought in a few not altogether unsympathetic words, and told me at the same time that I was to have a new role. The next thing I knew I was here, at Horace Greeley Elementary, under the lubricious eye of Miss Mandible.

*17 October*

Today we are to have a fire drill. I know this because I am a Fire Marshal, not only for our room but for the entire right wing of the second floor. This distinction, which was awarded shortly after my arrival, is interpreted by some as another mark of my somewhat dubious relations with our teacher. My armband, which is red and decorated with white felt letters reading FIRE, sits on the little shelf under my desk, next to the brown paper bag containing the lunch I carefully make for myself each morning. One of the advantages of packing my own lunch (I have no one to pack it for me) is that I am able to fill it with things I enjoy. The peanut butter sandwiches that my mother made in my former existence, many years ago, have been banished in favor of ham and cheese. I have found that my diet has mysteriously adjusted to my new situation; I no longer drink, for instance, and when I smoke, it is in the boys' john, like everybody else. When school is out I hardly smoke at all. It is only in the matter of sex that I feel my own true age; this is apparently something that, once learned, can never be forgotten. I live in fear that Miss Mandible will one day keep me after school, and when we are alone, create a compromising situation. To avoid this I have become a model pupil: another reason for the pronounced dislike I have encountered in certain quarters. But I cannot deny that I am singed by those long glances from the vicinity of the chalkboard; Miss Mandible is in many ways, notably about the bust, a very tasty piece.

*24 October*

There are isolated challenges to my largeness, to my dimly realized position in the class as Gulliver.[1] Most of my classmates are polite about this matter, as they would be if I had only one eye, or wasted, metal-wrapped legs. I am viewed as a mutation of some sort but essentially a peer. However Harry Broan, whose

1. Hero and central character of *Gulliver's Travels* by Jonathan Swift (1667–1745), Anglo-Irish novelist, poet, and satirist.

father has made himself rich manufacturing the Broan Bathroom Vent (with which Harry is frequently reproached; he is always being asked how things are in Ventsville), today inquired if I wanted to fight. An interested group of his followers had gathered to observe this suicidal undertaking. I replied that I didn't feel quite up to it, for which he was obviously grateful. We are now friends forever. He has given me to understand privately that he can get me all the bathroom vents I will ever need, at a ridiculously modest figure.

*25 October*

*"Many interesting and lifelike problems involving the use of fractions should be solved . . ."* The theorists fail to realize that everything that is either interesting or lifelike in the classroom proceeds from what they would probably call interpersonal relations: Sue Ann Brownly kicking me in the ankle. How lifelike, how womanlike, is her tender solicitude after the deed! Her pride in my newly acquired limp is transparent; everyone knows that she has set her mark upon me, that it is a victory in her unequal struggle with Miss Mandible for my great, overgrown heart. Even Miss Mandible knows, and counters in perhaps the only way she can, with sarcasm. "Are you wounded, Joseph?" Conflagrations smolder behind her eyelids, yearning for the Fire Marshal clouds her eyes. I mumble that I have bumped my leg.

*30 October*

I return again and again to the problem of my future.

*4 November*

The underground circulating library has brought me a copy of *Movie-TV Secrets,* the multicolor cover blazoned with the headline "Debbie's Date Insults Liz!" It is a gift from Frankie Randolph, a rather plain girl who until today has had not one word for me, passed on via Bobby Vanderbilt. I nod and smile over my shoulder in acknowledgment; Frankie hides her head under her desk. I have seen these magazines being passed around among the girls (sometimes one of the boys will condescend to inspect a particularly lurid cover). Miss Mandible confiscates them whenever she finds one. I leaf through *Movie-TV Secrets* and gets an eyeful. "The exclusive picture on these pages isn't what it seems. We know how it looks and we know what the gossipers will do. So in the interests of a nice guy, we're publishing the facts first. Here's what really happened!" The picture shows a rising young movie idol in bed, pajama-ed and bleary-eyed, while an equally blowzy young woman looks startled beside him. I am happy to know that the picture is not really what it seems; it seems to be nothing less than divorce evidence.

What do these hipless eleven-year-olds think when they come across, in the same magazine, the full-page ad for Maurice de Paree, which features "Hip Helpers" or what appear to be padded rumps? ("A real undercover agent that adds appeal to those hips and derriere, both!") If they cannot decipher the language the illustrations leave nothing to the imagination. "Drive him frantic . . ." the copy continues. Perhaps this explains Bobby Vanderbilt's preoccupation with Lancias and Maseratis; it is a defense against being driven frantic.

Sue Ann has observed Frankie Randolph's overture, and catching my eyes, she pulls from her satchel no less than seventeen of these magazines, thrusting them at me as if to prove that anything any of her rivals has to offer, she can top. I shuffle through them quickly, noting the broad editorial perspective:

"Debbie's Kids Are Crying"
"Eddie Asks Debbie: Will You?"
"The Nightmares Liz Has About Eddie!"
"The Things Debbie Can Tell About Eddie"
"The Private Life of Eddie and Liz"
"Debbie Gets Her Man Back?"
"A New Life for Liz"
"Love Is a Tricky Affair"
"Eddie's Taylor-Made Love Nest"
"How Liz Made a Man of Eddie"
"Are They Planning to Live Together?"
"Isn't It Time to Stop Kicking Debbie Around?"
"Debbie's Dilemma"
"Eddie Becomes a Father Again"
"Is Debbie Planning to Re-wed?"
"Can Liz Fulfill Herself?"
"Why Debbie Is Sick of Hollywood"

Who are these people, Debbie, Eddie, Liz, and how did they get themselves in such a terrible predicament? Sue Ann knows, I am sure; it is obvious that she has been studying their history as a guide to what she may expect when she is suddenly freed from this drab, flat classroom.

I am angry and I shove the magazines back at her with not even a whisper of thanks.

*5 November*

The sixth grade at Horace Greeley Elementary is a furnace of love, love, love. Today it is raining, but inside the air is heavy and tense with passion. Sue Ann is absent; I suspect that yesterday's exchange has driven her to her bed. Guilt hangs about me. She is not responsible, I know, for what she reads, for the models proposed to her by a venal publishing industry; I should not have been so harsh. Perhaps it is only the flu.

Nowhere have I encountered an atmosphere as charged with aborted sexuality as this. Miss Mandible is helpless; nothing goes right today. Amos Darin has been found drawing a dirty picture in the cloakroom. Sad and inaccurate, it was offered not as a sign of something else but as an act of love in itself. It has excited even those who have not seen it, even those who saw but understood only that it was dirty. The room buzzes with imperfectly comprehended titillation. Amos stands by the door, waiting to be taken to the principal's office. He wavers between fear and enjoyment of his temporary celebrity. From time to time Miss Mandible looks at me reproachfully, as if blaming me for the uproar. But I did not create this atmosphere, I am caught in it like all the others.

*8 November*

Everything is promised my classmates and me, most of all the future. We accept the outrageous assurances without blinking.

*9 November*

I have finally found the nerve to petition for a larger desk. At recess I can hardly walk; my legs do not wish to uncoil themselves. Miss Mandible says she will take it up with the custodian. She is worried about the excellence of my themes. Have I, she asks, been receiving help? For an instant I am on the brink of telling her my story. Something, however, warns me not to attempt it. Here I am safe, I have a place; I do not wish to entrust myself once more to the whimsy of authority. I resolve to make my themes less excellent in the future.

*11 November*

A ruined marriage, a ruined adjusting career, a grim interlude in the Army when I was almost not a person. This is the sum of my existence to date, a dismal total. Small wonder that re-education seemed my only hope. It is clear even to me that I need reworking in some fundamental way. How efficient is the society that provides thus for the salvage of its clinkers!

*14 November*

The distinction between children and adults, while probably useful for some purposes, is at bottom a specious one, I feel. There are only individual egos, crazy for love.

*15 November*

The custodian has informed Miss Mandible that our desks are all the correct size for sixth-graders, as specified by the Board of Estimate and furnished the schools by the Nu-Art Educational Supply Corporation of Englewood, California. He has pointed out that if the desk size is correct, then the pupil size must be incorrect. Miss Mandible, who has already arrived at this conclusion, refuses to press the matter further. I think I know why. An appeal to the administration might result in my removal from the class, in a transfer to some sort of setup for "exceptional children." This would be a disaster of the first magnitude. To sit in a room with child geniuses (or, more likely, children who are "retarded") would shrivel me in a week. Let my experience here be that of the common run, I say; let me be, please God, typical.

*20 November*

We read signs as promises. Miss Mandible understands by my great height, by my resonant vowels, that I will one day carry her off to bed. Sue Ann interprets these same signs to mean that I am unique among her male acquaintances, therefore most desirable, therefore her special property as is everything that is

Most Desirable. If neither of these propositions works out then life has broken faith with them.

I myself, in my former existence, read the company motto ("Here to Help in Time of Need") as a description of the duty of the adjuster, drastically mislocating the company's deepest concerns. I believed that because I had obtained a wife who was made up of wife-signs (beauty, charm, softness, perfume, cookery) I had found love. Brenda, reading the same signs that have now misled Miss Mandible and Sue Ann Brownly, felt she had been promised that she would never be bored again. All of us, Miss Mandible, Sue Ann, myself, Brenda, Mr. Goodykind, still believe that the American flag betokens a kind of general righteousness.

But I say, looking about me in this incubator of future citizens, that signs are signs, and some of them are lies.

*23 November*

It may be that my experience as a child will save me after all. If only I can remain quietly in this classroom, making my notes while Napoleon plods through Russia in the droning voice of Harry Broan, reading aloud from our History text. All of the mysteries that perplexed me as an adult have their origins here. But Miss Mandible will not permit me to remain ungrown. Her hands rest on my shoulders too warmly, and for too long.

*7 December*

It is the pledges that this place makes to me, pledges that cannot be redeemed, that will confuse me later and make me feel I am not *getting anywhere.* Everything is presented as the result of some knowable process; if I wish to arrive at four I get there by way of two and two. If I wish to burn Moscow the route I must travel has already been marked out by another visitor. If, like Bobby Vanderbilt, I yearn for the wheel of the Lancia 2.4-liter coupé, I have only to go through the appropriate process, that is, get the money. And if it is money itself that I desire, I have only to *make* it. All of these goals are equally beautiful in the sight of the Board of Estimate; the proof is all around us, in the no-nonsense ugliness of this steel and glass building, in the straightline matter-of-factness with which Miss Mandible handles some of our less reputable wars. Who points out that arrangements sometimes slip, that errors are made, that signs are misread? *"They have confidence in their ability to take the right steps and to obtain correct answers."*

*8 December*

My enlightenment is proceeding wonderfully.

*9 December*

Disaster once again. Tomorrow I am to be sent to a doctor, for observation. Sue Ann Brownly caught Miss Mandible and me in the cloakroom, during recess, Miss Mandible's naked legs in a scissors around my waist. For a moment I thought Sue Ann was going to choke. She ran out of the room weeping, straight for the principal's office, certain now which of us was Debbie, which

Eddie, which Liz. I am sorry to be the cause of her disillusionment, but I know that she will recover. Miss Mandible is ruined but fulfilled. Although she will be charged with contributing to the delinquency of a minor, she seems at peace; *her* promise has been kept. She knows now that everything she has been told about life, about America, is true.

I have tried to convince the school authorities that I am a minor only in a very special sense, that I am in fact mostly to blame—but it does no good. They are as dense as ever. My contemporaries are astounded that I present myself as anything other than an innocent victim. Like the Old Guard[2] marching through the Russian drifts, the class marches to the conclusion that truth is punishment.

Bobby Vanderbilt has given me his copy of *Sounds of Sebring*, in farewell.

2. Napoleon's soldiers retreating from Moscow through the snow.

# CHARLES BAXTER

*Baxter (1947– ) was born in Minneapolis. He directs the writing program at the University of Michigan at Ann Arbor. He has published the short-story collections* Harmony of the World *(1984),* Through the Safety Net *(1985),* A Relative Stranger *(1990), and* Believers *(1997); the novels* First Light *(1987),* Imaginary Paintings *(1990), and* Shadow Play *(1993); and a volume of essays on fiction,* Burning Down *(1997).*

## The Disappeared

What he first noticed about Detroit and therefore America was the smell. Almost as soon as he walked off the plane, he caught it: an acrid odor of wood ash. The smell seemed to go through his nostrils and take up residence in his head. In Sweden, his own country, he associated this smell with autumn, and the first family fires of winter, the smoke chuffing out of chimneys and settling familiarly over the neighborhood. But here it was midsummer, and he couldn't see anything burning.

On the way in from the airport, with the windows of the cab open and hot stony summer air blowing over his face, he asked the driver about it.

"You're smelling Detroit," the driver said.

Anders, who spoke very precise school English, thought that perhaps he hadn't made himself understood. "No," he said. "I am sorry. I mean the burning smell. What is it?"

The cab driver glanced in the rearview mirror. He was wearing a knitted beret, and his deadlocks flapped in the breeze. "Where you from?"

"Sweden."

The driver nodded to himself. "Explains why," he said. The cab took a sharp right turn on the freeway and entered the Detroit city limits. The driver gestured with his left hand toward an electronic signboard, a small windowless factory at its base, and a clustered group of cramped clapboard houses nearby. When he gestured, the cab wobbled on the freeway. "Fires here most all the time," he said. "Day in and day out. You get so you don't notice. Or maybe you get so you do notice and you like it."

"I don't see any fires," Anders said.

"That's right."

Feeling that he was missing the point somehow, Anders decided to change the subject. "I see a saxophone and a baseball bat next to you," he said, in his best English. "Do you like to play baseball?"

"Not in this cab, I don't," the driver said quietly. "It's no game then, you understand?"

The young man sat back, feeling that he had been defeated by the American idiom in his first native encounter with it. An engineer, he was in Detroit to discuss his work in metal alloys that resist oxidation. The company that had invited him had suggested that he might agree to become a consultant on an exclusive contract, for what seemed to him an enormous, American-sized fee. But the money meant little to him. It was America he was curious about, attracted by, especially its colorful disorderliness.

Disorder, of which there was very little in Sweden, seemed sexy to him: the disorder of a disheveled woman who has rushed down two flights of stairs to offer a last long kiss. Anders was single, and before he left the country he hoped to sleep with an American woman in an American bed. It was his ambition. He wondered if the experience would have any distinction. He had an idea that he might be able to go home and tell one or two friends about it.

At the hotel, he was met by a representative of the automobile company, a gray-haired man with thick glasses who, to Anders's surprise, spoke rather good Swedish. Later that afternoon, and for the next two days, he was taken down silent carpeted hallways and shown into plush windowless rooms with recessed lighting. He showed them his slides and metal samples, cited chemical formulas, and made cost projections; he looked at the faces looking back at him. They were interested, friendly, but oddly blank, like faces he had seen in the military. He saw corridor after corridor. The building seemed more expressive than the people in it. The lighting was both bright and diffuse, and a low-frequency hum of power and secrecy seemed to flow out from the ventilators. Everyone complimented him on his English. A tall woman in a tailored suit, flashing him a secretive smile, asked him if he intended to stay in this country for long. Anders smiled, said that his plans on that particular point were open, and managed to work the name of his hotel into his conversation.

At the end of the third day, the division head once again shook Anders's hand in the foyer of the hotel lobby and said they'd be getting in touch with him very soon. Finally free, Anders stepped outside the hotel and sniffed the air. All the rooms he had been in since he had arrived had had no windows, or windows so blocked by drapes or blinds that he couldn't see out.

He felt restless and excited, with three days free for sightseeing in a wide-open American city, not quite in the wild West but close enough to it to suit him. He returned to his room and changed into a pair of jeans, a light cotton shirt, and a pair of running shoes. In the mirror, he thought he looked relaxed and handsome. His vanity amused him, but he felt lucky to look the way he did. Back out on the sidewalk, he asked the doorman which direction he would recommend for a walk.

The doorman, who had curly gray hair and sagging pouches under his eyes, removed his cap and rubbed his forehead. He did not look back at Anders. "You want my recommendation? Don't walk anywhere. I would not recommend a walk. Sit in the bar and watch the soaps." The doorman stared at a fire hydrant as he spoke.

"What about running?"

The doorman suddenly glanced at Anders, sizing him up. "It's a chance. You might be okay. But to be safe, stay inside. There's movies on the cable, you want them."

"Is there a park here?"

"Sure, there's parks. There's always parks. There's Belle Isle. You could go there. People do. I don't recommend it. Still and all you might enjoy it if you run fast enough. What're you planning to do?"

Anders shrugged. "Relax. See your city."

"You're seeing it," the doorman said. "Ain't nobody relaxed, seeing this place. Buy some postcards, you want sights. This place ain't built for tourists and amateurs."

Anders thought that perhaps he had misunderstood again and took a cab out to Belle Isle; as soon as he had entered the park, he saw a large municipal fountain and asked the cabbie to drop him off in front of it. On its rim, children were shouting and dangling their legs in the water. The ornamentation of the stone lions was both solemn and whimsical and reminded him of forced humor of Danish public sculpture. Behind the fountain he saw families grouped in evening picnics on the grass, and many citizens, of various apparent ethnic types, running, bicycling, and walking. Anders liked the way Americans walked, a sort of busyness in their step, as if, having no particular goal, they still had an unconscious urgency to get somewhere, to seem purposeful.

He began to jog, and found himself passing a yacht club of some sort, and then a small zoo, and more landscaped areas where solitaries and couples sat on the grass listening to the evening baseball game on their radios. Other couples were stretched out by themselves, self-absorbed. The light had a bluish-gold quality. It looked like almost any city park to him, placid and decorative, a bit hushed.

He found his way to an old building with a concession stand inside. After admiring the building's fake Corinthian architecture, he bought a hot dog an a cola. Thinking himself disguised as a native—America was full of forei anyway—he walked to the west windows of the dining area to chec unattached women. He wanted to praise, to an American, this evenin park.

There were several couples on this side of the room, and what be several unattached men and women standing near the open w listening to their various earphones. One of these women, with her pinned up, was sipping a lemonade. She had just the right faraway thought he recognized this look. It meant that she was in a kind c between engagements.

He put himself in her line of sight and said, in his heaviest evening!"

"What?" She removed the earphones and looked at him. say?"

"I said the evening was beautiful." He tried to sound as fo

the way Germans in Sweden did. “I am a visitor here,” he added quickly, “and not familiar with any of this.” He motioned his arm to indicate the park.

“Not familiar?” she asked. “Not familiar with what?”

“Well, with this park. With the sky here. The people.”

“Parks are the same everywhere,” the woman said, leaning her hip against the wall. She looked at him with a vague interest. “The sky is the same. Only the people are different.”

“Yes? How?”

“Where are you from?”

He explained, and she looked out the window toward the Canadian side of the Detroit River, at the city of Windsor. “That’s Canada, you know,” she said, pointing a finger at the river. “They make Canadian whiskey right over there.” She pointed at some high buildings and what seemed to be a grain elevator. “I’ve never drunk the whiskey. They say it tastes of acid rain. I’ve never been to Canada. I mean, I’ve seen it, but I’ve never been there. If I can see it from here, why should I go there?”

“To be in Canada,” Anders suggested. “Another country.”

“But I’m *here*,” she said suddenly, turning to him and looking at him directly. Her eyes were so dark they were almost colorless. “Why should I be anywhere else? Why are *you* here?”

“I came to Detroit for business,” he said. “Now I’m sightseeing.”

“Sightseeing?” She laughed out loud, and Anders saw her arch her back. Her breasts seemed to flare in front of him. Her body had distinct athletic lines. “No one sightsees here. Didn’t anyone tell you?”

“Yes. The doorman at the hotel. He told me not to come.”

“But you did. How did you get here?”

“I came by taxi.”

“You’re joking,” she said. Then she reached out and put her hand momentarily on his shoulder. “You took a taxi to this park? How do you expect to get back to your hotel?”

“I suppose,” he shrugged, “I will get another taxi.”

“Oh no you won’t,” she said, and Anders felt himself pleased that things were working out so well. He noticed again her pinned-up hair and its intense black. Her skin was deeply tanned or naturally dark, and he thought that she herself might be black or Hispanic, he didn’t know which, being unpracticed in making such distinctions. Outside he saw fireflies. No one had ever mentioned fireflies in Detroit. Night was coming on. He gazed up at the sky. Same tars, same moon.

“You’re here *alone?*” she asked. “In America? And in this city?”

“Yes,” he said. “Why not?”

‘People shouldn’t be left alone in this country,” she said, leaning toward ith a kind of vehemence. “They shouldn’t have left you here. It can get weird, what happens to people. Didn’t they tell you?”

miled and said that they hadn’t told him anything to that effect.

they should have.” She dropped her cup into a trash can, and he aw the beginning of a scar, a white line, traveling up the underside ward her shoulder.

"Who do you mean?" he asked. "You said, 'they.' Who is 'they'?"

"Any they at all," she said. "Your guardians." She sighed. "All right. Come on. Follow me." She went outside and broke into a run. For a moment he thought that she was running away from him, then realized that he was expected to run *with* her; it was what people did now, instead of holding hands, to get acquainted. He sprinted up next to her, and as she ran, she asked him, "Who are you?"

Being careful not to tire—she wouldn't like it if his endurance was poor—he told her his name, his professional interests, and he patched together a narrative about his mother, father, two sisters, and his Aunt Ingrid. Running past a slower couple, he told her that his aunt was eccentric and broke china by throwing it on the floor on Fridays, which she called "the devil's day."

"Years ago, they would have branded her a witch," Anders said. "But she isn't a witch. She's just moody."

He watched her reactions and noticed that she didn't seem at all interested in his family, or any sort of background. "Do you run a lot?" she asked. "You look as if you're in pretty good shape."

He admitted that, yes, he ran, but that people in Sweden didn't do this as much as they did in America.

"You look a little like that tennis star, that Swede," she said. "By the way, I'm Lauren." Still running, she held out her hand, and, still running, he shook it. "Which god do you believe in?"

"Excuse me?"

"Which god?" she asked. "Which god do you think is in control?"

"I had not thought about it."

"You'd better," she said. "Because one of them is." She stopped suddenly and put her hands on her hips and walked in a small circle. She put her hand to her neck and took her pulse, timing it on her wristwatch. Then she placed her fingers on Ander's neck and took his pulse. "One hundred fourteen," she said. "Pretty good." Again she walked away from him and again he found himself following her. In the growing darkness he noticed other men, standing in the parking lot, watching her, this American with pinned-up hair, dressed in a running outfit. He thought she was pretty, but maybe Americans had other standards so that here, in fact, she wasn't pretty, and it was some kind of optical illusion.

When he caught up with her, she was unlocking the door of a blue Chevrolet rusting near the hubcaps. He gazed down at the rust with professional interest—it had the characteristic blister pattern of rust caused by salt. She slipped inside the car and reached across to unlock the passenger side, and when he got in—he hadn't been invited to get in, but he thought it was all right—he sat down on several small plastic tape cassette cases. He picked them out from underneath him and tried to read their labels. She was taking off her shoes. Debussy, Bach, 10,000 Maniacs, Screamin' Jay Hawkins.

"Where are we going?" he asked. He glanced down at her bare foot on the accelerator. She put the car into reverse. "Wait a minute," he said. "Stop this car." She put on the brake and turned off the ignition. "I just want to look at you," he said.

"Okay, look." She turned on the interior light and kept her face turned so that he was looking at her in profile. Something about her suggested a lovely disorder, a ragged brightness toward the back of her face.

"Are we going to do things?" he asked, touching her on the arm.

"Of course," she said. "Strangers should always do things."

She said that she would drop him off at his hotel, that he must change clothes. This was important. She would then pick him up. On the way over, he saw almost no one downtown. For some reason, it was quite empty of shoppers, strollers, or pedestrians of any kind. "I'm going to tell you some things you should know," she said. He settled back. He was used to this kind of talk on dates: everyone, everywhere, liked to reveal intimate details. It was an international convention.

They were slowing for a red light. "God is love," she said, downshifting, her bare left foot on the clutch. "At least I think so. It's my hope. In the world we have left, only love matters. Do you understand? I'm one of the Last Ones. Maybe you've heard of us."

"No, I have not. What do you do?"

"We do what everyone else does. We work and we go home and have dinner and go to bed. There is only one thing we do that is special."

"What is that?" he asked.

"We don't make plans," she said. "No big plans at all."

"That is not so unusual," he said, trying to normalize what she was saying. "Many people don't like to make—"

"It's not liking," she said. "It doesn't have anything to do with liking or not liking. It's a faith. Look at those buildings." She pointed toward several abandoned multistoried buildings with broken or vacant windows. "What face is moving behind all that? Something is. I live and work here. I'm not blind. *Anyone* can see what's taking place here. You're not blind either. Our church is over on the east side, off Van Dyke Avenue. It's not a good part of town but we want to be near where the face is doing its work."

"Your church?"

"The Church of the Millennium," she said. "Where they preach the Gospel of Last Things." They were now on the freeway, heading up toward the General Motors Building and his hotel. "Do you understand me?"

"Of course," he said. He had heard of American cult religions but thought they were all in California. He didn't mind her talk of religion. It was like talk of the sunset or childhood; it kept things going. "Of course I have been listening."

"Because I won't sleep with you unless you listen to me," she said. "It's the one thing I care about, that people listen. It's so damn rare, listening I mean, that you might as well care about it. I don't sleep with strangers too often. Almost never." She turned to look at him. "Anders," she said, "what do you pray to?"

He laughed. "I don't."

"Okay, then, what do you plan for?"

"A few things," he said.

"Like what?"

"My dinner every night. My job. My friends."

"You don't let accidents happen? You should. Things reveal themselves in accidents."

"Are there many people like you?" he asked.

"What do you think?" He looked again at her face, taken over by the darkness in the car but dimly lit by the dashboard lights and the oncoming flare of traffic. "Do you think there are many people like me?"

"Not very many," he said. "But maybe more than there used to be."

"Any of us in Sweden?"

"I don't think so. It's not a religion over there. People don't . . . They didn't tell us in Sweden about American girls who listen to Debussy and 10,000 Maniacs in their automobiles and who believe in gods and accidents."

"They don't say 'girls' here," she told him. "They say 'women.' "

She dropped him off at the hotel and said that she would pick him up in forty-five minutes. In his room, as he chose a clean shirt and a sport coat and a pair of trousers, he found himself laughing happily. He felt giddy. It was all happening so fast; he could hardly believe his luck. I am a very lucky man, he thought.

He looked out his hotel window at the streetlights. They had an amber glow, the color of gemstones. This city, this American city, was unlike any he had ever seen. A downtown area emptied of people; a river with huge ships going by silently; a park with girls who believe in the millennium. No, not girls: women. He had learned his lesson.

He wanted to open the hotel window to smell the air, but the casement frames were welded shut.

After walking down the stairs to the lobby, he stood out in front of the hotel doorway. He felt a warm breeze against his face. He told the doorman, Luis, that he had met a woman on Belle Isle who was going to pick him up in a few minutes. She was going to take him dancing. The doorman nodded, rubbing his chin with his hand. Anders said that she was friendly and wanted to show him, a foreigner, things. The doorman shook his head. "Yes, I agree," Luis said. "Dancing. Make sure that this is what you do."

"What?"

"Dancing," Luis said, "yes. Go dancing. You know this woman?"

"I just met her."

"Ah," Luis said, and stepped back to observe Anders, as if to remember his face. "Dangerous fun." When her car appeared in front of the hotel, she was wearing a light summer dress, and when she smiled, she looked like the melancholy baby he had heard about in an American song. As they pulled away from the hotel, he looked back at Luis, who was watching them closely, and then Anders realized that Luis was reading the numbers on Lauren's license plate. To break the mood, he leaned over to kiss her on the cheek. She smelled of cigarettes and something else—soap or cut flowers.

She took him uptown to a club where a trio played soft rock and some jazz. Some of this music was slow enough to dance to, in the slow way he wanted to dance. Her hand in his felt bony and muscular; physically, she was direct and immediate. He wondered, now, looking at her face, whether she might be an American Indian, and again he was frustrated because he couldn't tell one race in this country from another. He knew it was improper to ask. When he sat at the table, holding hands with her and sipping from his drink, he began to feel as if he had known her for a long time and was related to her in some obscure way.

Suddenly he asked her, "Why are you so interested in me?"

"Interested?" She laughed, and her long black hair, no longer pinned up, shook in quick thick waves. "Well, all right. I have an interest. I like it that you're so foreign that you take cabs to the park. I like the way you look. You're kind of cute. And the other thing is, your soul is so raw and new, Anders, it's like an oyster."

"What?" He looked at her near him at the table. Their drinks were half finished. "My soul?"

"Yeah, your soul. I can almost see it."

"Where is it?"

She leaned forward, friendly and sexual and now slightly elegant. "You want me to show you?"

"Yes," Anders said. "Sure."

"It's in two places," she said. "One part is up here." She released his hand and put her thumb on his forehead. "And the other part is down here." She touched him in the middle of his stomach. "Right there. And they're connected."

"What are they like?" he asked, playing along.

"Yours? Raw and shiny, just like I said."

"And what about your soul?" he asked.

She looked at him. "My soul is radioactive," she said. "It's like plutonium. Don't say you weren't warned."

He thought that this was another American idiom he hadn't heard before, and he decided not to spoil things by asking her about it. In Sweden, people didn't talk much about the soul, at least not in conjunction with oysters or plutonium. It was probably some local metaphor he had never heard in Sweden.

In the dark he couldn't make out much about her building, except that it was several floors high and at least fifty years old. Her living-room window looked out distantly at the river—once upstairs, he could see the lights of another passing freighter—and through the left side of the window he could see an electrical billboard. The name of the product was made out of hundreds of small incandescent bulbs, which went on and off from left to right. One of the letters was missing.

It's today's CHEVR LET!

All around her living-room walls were brightly framed watercolors, almost celebratory and Matisse-like, but in vague shapes. She went down the hallway, tapped on one of the doors, and said, "I'm home." Then she returned to the living room and kicked off her shoes. "My grandmother," she said. "She has her own room."

"Are these your pictures?" he asked. "Did you draw them?"

"Yes."

"I can't tell what they are. What are they?"

"They're abstract. You use wet paper to get that effect. They're abstract because God has gotten abstract. God used to have a form but now He's dissolving into pure light. That's what you see in those pictures. They're pictures of the trails that God leaves behind."

"Like the vapor trails," he smiled, "behind jets."

"Yes," she said. "Like that."

He went over to her in the dark and drew her to him and kissed her. Her breath was layered with smoke, apparently from cigarettes. Immediately he felt an unusual physical sensation inside his skin, like something heating up on a frypan.

She drew back. He heard another siren go by on the street outside. He wondered whether they should talk some more in the living room—share a few more verbal intimacies—to be really civilized about this and decided, no, it was not necessary, not when strangers make love, as they do, sometimes, in strange cities, away from home. They went into her bedroom and undressed each other. Her body, by the light of a dim bedside lamp, was as beautiful and as exotic as he hoped it would be, darker than his own skin in the dark room, native somehow to this continent. She had the flared shoulders and hips of a dancer. She bent down and snapped off the bedside light, and as he approached her, she was lit from behind by the billboard. Her skin felt vaguely electrical to him.

They stood in the middle of her bedroom, arms around each other, swaying, and he knew, in his arousal, that something odd was about to occur: he had no words for it in either his own language or in English.

They moved over and under each other, changing positions to stay in the breeze created by the window fan. They were both lively and attentive, and at first he thought it would be just the usual fun, this time with an almost anonymous American woman. He looked at her in the bed and saw her dark leg alongside his own, and he saw that same scar line running up her arm to her shoulder, where it disappeared.

"Where did you get that?" he asked.

"That?" She looked at it. "That was an accident that was done to me."

Half an hour later, resting with her, his hands on her back, he felt a wave of happiness; he felt it was a wave of color traveling through his body, surging from his forehead down to his stomach. It took him over again, and then a third time, with such force that he almost sat up.

"What is it?" she asked.

"I don't know. It is like . . . I felt a color moving through my body."

"Oh, that?" She smiled at him in the dark. "It's your soul, Anders. That's all. That's all it is. Never felt it before, huh?"

"I must be very drunk," he said.

She put her hand up into his hair. "Call it anything you want to. Didn't you feel it before? Our souls were curled together."

"You're crazy," he said. "You are a crazy woman."

"Oh yeah?" she whispered. "Is that what you think? Watch. Watch what happens now. You think this is all physical. Guess what. You're the crazy one. Watch. Watch."

She went to work on him, and at first it was pleasurable, but as she moved over him it became a succession of waves that had specific colorations, even when he turned her and thought he was taking charge. Soon he felt some substance, some glossy blue possession entangled in the air above him.

"I bet you're going to say that you're imagining all this," she said, her hand skidding across him.

"Who are you?" he said. "Who in the world are you?"

"I warned you," she whispered, her mouth directly over his ear. "I warned you. You people with your things, your rusty things, you suffer so bad when you come into where *we* live. Did they tell you we were all soulless here? Did they say that?"

He put his hands on her. "This is not love, but it—"

"Of course not," she said. "It's something else. Do you know the word? Do you know the word for something that opens your soul at once? Like that?" She snapped her fingers on the pillow. Her tongue was touching his ear. "Do you?" The words were almost inaudible.

"No."

"Addiction." She waited. "Do you understand?"

"Yes."

In the middle of the night he rose up and went to the window. He felt like a stump, amputated from the physical body of the woman. At the window he looked down, to the right of the billboard, and saw another apartment building with heavy decorations with human forms near the roof's edge, and on the third floor he saw a man at the window, as naked as he himself was but almost completely in shadow, gazing out at the street. There were so far away from each other that being unclothed didn't matter. It was vague and small and impersonal.

"Do you always stand at the window without clothes on?" she asked, from the bed.

"Not in Sweden," he said. He turned around. "This is odd," he said. "At night no one walks out on the streets. But there, over on that block, there's a man like me, at the window, and he is looking out, too. Do people stand everywhere at the windows here?"

"Come to bed."

"When I was in the army, the Swedish army," he said, still looking out, "they taught us to think that we could *decide* to do anything. They talked about the will. Your word 'willpower.' All Sweden believes this—choice, will, willpower. Maybe not so much now. I wonder if they talk about it here."

"You're funny," she said. She had moved up from behind him and embraced him.

In the morning he watched her as she dressed. His eyes hurt from sleeplessness. "I have to go," she said. "I'm already late." She was putting on a light blue skirt. As she did, she smiled. "You're a lovely lover," she said. "I like your body very much."

"What are we going to do?" he asked.

"We? There is no 'we,' Anders. There's you and then there's me. We're not a couple. I'm going to work. You're going back to your country soon. What are you planning to do?"

"May I stay here?"

"For an hour," she said, "and then you should go back to your hotel. I don't think you should stay. You don't live here."

"May I take you to dinner tonight?" he asked, trying not to watch her as he watched her. "What can we do tonight?"

"There's that 'we' again. Well, maybe. You can teach me a few words of Swedish. Why don't you hang around at your hotel and maybe I'll come by around six and get you, but don't call me if I don t come by, because if I don't, I don't."

"I can't call you," he said. "I don't know your last name."

"Oh, that's right," she said. "Well, listen. I ll probably come at six." She looked at him lying in the bed. "I don't believe this," she said.

"What?"

"You think you're in love, don't you?"

"No," he said. "Not exactly." He waited. "Oh, I don't know."

"I get the point," she said. "Well, you'd better get used to it. Welcome to our town. We're not always good at love but we are good at that." She bent to kiss him and then was gone. Happiness and agony simultaneously reached down and pressed against his chest. They, too, were like colors, but when you mixed the two together, you got something greenish-pink, excruciating.

He stood up, put on his trousers, and began looking into her dresser drawers. He expected to find trinkets and whatnot, but all she had were folded clothes, and, in the corner of the top drawer, a small turquoise heart for a charm bracelet. He put it into his pocket.

In the bathroom, he examined the labels on her medicines and facial creams before washing his face. He wanted evidence but didn't know for what. He looked, to himself, like a slightly different version of what he had once been. In the mirror his face had a puffy look and a passive expression, as if he had been assaulted during the night.

After he had dressed and entered the living room, he saw Lauren's grandmother sitting at a small dining-room table. She was eating a piece of toast and looking out of the window toward the river. The apartment, in daylight, had an aggressively scrubbed and mopped look. On the kitchen counter a small black-and-white television was blaring, but the old woman wasn't watching it. Her black hair was streaked with gray, and she wore a ragged pink bathrobe decorated with pictures of orchids. She was very frail. Her skin was as dark as her granddaughter's. Looking at her, Anders was once again unable to guess what race she was. She might be Arabic, or a Native American, or Hispanic, or black. Because he couldn't tell, he didn't care.

Without even looking at him, she motioned at him to sit down.

"Want anything?" she asked. She had a high, distant voice, as if it had come into the room over wires. "There are bananas over there." She made no gesture. "And grapefruit, I think, in the refrigerator."

"That's all right." He sat down on the other side of the table and folded his hands together, studying his fingers. The sound of traffic came up from the street outside.

"You're from somewhere," she said. "Scandinavia?"

"Yes," he said. "How can you tell?" Talking had become a terrible effort.

"Vowels," she said. "You sound like one of those Finns up north of here. When will you go back? To your country?"

"I don't know," he said. "Perhaps a few days. Perhaps not. My name is Anders." He held out his hand.

"Nice to meet you." She touched but did not shake his hand. "Why don't you know when you're going back?" She turned to look at him at last. It was a face on which curiosity still registered. She observed him as if he were an example of a certain kind of human being in whom she still had an interest.

"I don't know . . . I am not sure. Last night, I . . ."

"You don't finish your sentences," the old woman said.

"I am trying to. I don't want to leave your granddaughter," he said. "She is"—he tried to think of the right adjective—"amazing to me."

"Yes, she is." The old woman peered at him. "You don't think you're in love, do you?"

"I don't know."

"Well, don't be. She won't ever be married, so there's no point in being in love with her. There's no point in being married *here*. I see them, you know."

"Who?"

"All the young men. Well, there aren't many. A few. Every so often. They come and sleep here with her and then in the morning they come out for breakfast with me and then they go away. We sit and talk. They're usually very pleasant. Men are, in the morning. They should be. She's a beautiful girl."

"Yes, she is."

"But there's no future in her, you know," the old woman said. "Sure you don't want a grapefruit? You should eat something."

"No, thank you. What do you mean, 'no future'?"

"Well, the young men usually understand that." The old woman looked at the television set, scowled, and shifted her eyes to the window. She rubbed her hands together. "You can't invest in her. You can't do that at all. She won't let you. I know. I know how she thinks."

"We have women like that in my country," Anders said. "They are—"

"Oh no you don't," the old woman said. "Sooner or later they want to get married, don't they?"

"I suppose most of them."

She glanced out the window toward the Detroit River and the city of Windsor on the opposite shore. Just when he thought that she had forgotten all about him, he felt her hand, dry as a winter leaf, taking hold of his own. Another siren went by outside. He felt a weight descending in his stomach. The touch of the old woman's hand made him feel worse than before, and he stood up quickly, looking around the room as if there were some object nearby he had to pick up and take away immediately. Her hand dropped away from his.

"No plans," she said. "Didn't she tell you?" the old woman asked. "It's what she believes." She shrugged. "It makes her happy."

"I am not sure I understand."

The old woman lifted her right hand and made a dismissive wave in his direction. She pursed her mouth; he knew she had stopped speaking to him. He called a cab, and in half an hour he was back in his hotel room. In the shower he realized that he had forgotten to write down her address or phone number.

He felt itchy: he went out running, returned to his room, and took another shower. He did thirty push-ups and jogged in place. He groaned and shouted, knowing that no one would hear. How would he explain this to anyone? He was feeling passionate puzzlement. He went down to the hotel's dining room for lunch and ordered Dover sole and white wine but found himself unable to eat much of anything. He stared at his plate and at the other men and women consuming their meals calmly, and he was suddenly filled with wonder at ordinary life.

He couldn't stand to be by himself, and after lunch he had the doorman hail a cab. He gave the cabdriver a fifty and asked him to drive him around the city until all the money was used up.

"You want to see the nice parts?" the cabbie asked.

"No."

"What is it you want to see then?"

"The city."

"You tryin' to score, man? That it?"

Anders didn't know what he meant. He was certain that no sport was intended. He decided to play it safe. "No," he said.

The cabdriver shook his head and whistled. They drove east and then south; Anders watched the water-ball compass stuck to the front window. Along Jefferson Avenue they went past the shells of apartment buildings, and then, heading north, they passed block after block of vacated or boarded-up properties. One old building with Doric[1] columns was draped with a banner.

PROGRESS! THE OLD MUST MAKE WAY
FOR THE NEW
Acme Wrecking Company

The banner was worn and tattered. Anders noticed broken beer bottles, sharp brown glass, on sidewalks and vacant lots, and the glass, in the sun, seemed

1. A style of classical Greek architecture.

perversely beautiful. Men were sleeping on sidewalks and in front stairwells; one man, wearing a hat, urinated against the corner of a burned-out building. He saw other men—there were very few women out here in the light of day—in groups gazing at him with cold slow deadly expressions. In his state of mind, he understood it all; he identified with it. All of it, the ruins and the remnants, made perfect sense.

At six o'clock she picked him up and took him to a Greek restaurant. All the way over, he watched her. He examined her with the puzzled curiosity of someone who wants to know how another person who looks rather attractive but also rather ordinary could have such power. Her physical features didn't explain anything.

"Did you miss me today?" she asked, half-jokingly.

"Yes," he said. He started to say more but didn't know how to begin. "It was hard to breathe," he said at last.

"I know," she said. "It's the air."

"No, it isn't. Not the air."

"Well, what then?"

He looked at her.

"Oh, come on, Anders. We're just two blind people who staggered into each other and we're about to stagger off in different directions. That's all."

Sentences struggled in his mind, then vanished before he could say them. He watched the pavement pass underneath the car.

In the restaurant, a crowded and lively place smelling of beer and roasted meat and cigars, they sat in a booth and ordered an antipasto plate. He leaned over and took her hands. "Tell me, please, who and what you are."

She seemed surprised that he had asked. "I've explained," she said. She waited, then started up again. "When I was younger I had an idea that I wanted to be a dancer. I had to give that up. My timing was off." She smiled. "Onstage, I looked like a memory of what had already happened. The other girls would do something and then *I'd* do it. I come in late on a lot of things. That's good for me. I've told you where I work. I live with my grandmother. I go with her into the parks in the fall and we watch for birds. And you know what else I believe." He gazed at the gold hoops of her earrings. "What else do you want to know?"

"I feel happy and terrible," he said. "Is it you? Did you do this?"

"I guess I did," she said, smiling faintly. "Tell me some words in Swedish."

"Which ones?"

"House."

"Hus."

"Pain."

"Smärta."

She leaned back. "Face."

"Ansikte."

"Light."

"Ljus."

"Never."

"Aldrig."

"I don't like it," she said. "I don't like the sound of those words at all. They're too cold. They're cold-weather words."

"Cold? Try another one."

"Soul."

"Själ."

"No, I don't like it." She raised her hand to the top of his head, grabbed a bit of his hair, and laughed. "Too bad."

"Do you do this to everyone?" he asked. "I feel such confusion."

He saw her stiffen. "You want to know too much. You're too messed up. Too messed up with plans. You and your rust. All that isn't important. Not here. We don't do all that explaining. I've told you *everything* about me. We re just supposed to be enjoying ourselves. Nobody has to explain. That's freedom, Anders. Never telling why." She leaned over toward him so that her shoulders touched his, and with a sense of shock and desperation, he felt himself becoming aroused. She kissed him, and her lips tasted slightly of garlic. "Just say hi to the New World," she said.

"You feel like a drug to me," he said. "You feel experimental."

"We don't use that word that way," she said. Then she said, "Oh," as if she had understood something, or remembered another engagement. "Okay. I'll explain all this in a minute. Excuse me." She rose and disappeared behind a corner of the restaurant, and Anders looked out the window at a Catholic church the color of sandstone, on whose front steps a group of boys sat, eating popsicles. One of the boys got up and began to ask passersby for money; this went on until a policeman came and sent the boys away. Anders looked at his watch. Ten minutes had gone by since she had left. He looked up. He knew without thinking about it that she wasn't coming back.

He put a ten-dollar bill on the table and left the restaurant, jogging into the parking structure where she had left the car. Although he wasn't particularly surprised to see that it wasn't there, he sat down on the concrete and felt the floor of the structure shaking. He ran his hands through his hair, where she had grabbed at it. He waited as long as he could stand to do so, then returned to the hotel.

Luis was back on duty. Anders told him what had happened.

"Ah," Luis said. "She is disappeared."

"Yes. Do you think I should call the police?"

"No," Luis said. "I do not think so. They have too many disappeared already."

"Too many disappeared?"

"Yes. All over this city. Many many disappeared. For how many times do you take this lady out?"

"Once. No, twice."

"And this time is the time she leave you?"

Anders nodded.

"I have done that," Luis said. "When I get sick of a woman, I too have disappeared. Maybe," he said suddenly, "she will reappear. Sometimes they do."

"I don't think she will." He sat down on the sidewalk in front of the hotel and cupped his chin in his hands.

"No, no," Luis said. "You cannot do that in front of the hotel. This looks very bad. Please stand up." He felt Luis reaching around his shoulders and pulling him to his feet. "What you are acting is impossible after one night," Luis said. "Be like everyone else. Have another night." He took off his doorman's cap and combed his hair with precision. "Many men and women also disappear from each other. It is one thing to do. You had a good time?"

Anders nodded.

"Have another good time," Luis suggested, "with someone else. Beer, pizza, go to bed. Women who have not disappeared will talk to you, I am sure."

"I think I'll call the police," Anders said.

"Myself, no, I would not do that."

He dialed a number he found in the telephone book for a local precinct station. As soon as the station officer understood what Anders was saying to him, he became angry, said it wasn't a police matter, and hung up on him. Anders sat for a moment in the phone booth, then looked up the Church of the Millennium in the directory. He wrote down its address. Someone there would know about her, and explain.

The cab let him out in front. It was like no other church he had ever seen before. Even the smallest places of worship in his own country had vaulted roofs, steeples, and stained glass. This building seemed to be someone's remodeled house. On either side of it, two lots down, were two skeletal homes, one of which had been burned and which now stood with charcoal windows and a charcoal portal where the front door had once been. The other house was boarded-up; in the evening wind, sheets of newspaper were stuck to its south wall. Across the street was an almost deserted playground. The saddles had been removed from the swing set, and the chains hung down from the upper bar and moved slightly in the wind. Four men stood together under a basketball hoop, talking together. One of the men bounced a basketball occasionally.

A signboard had been planted into the ground in front of the church, but so many letters had been removed from it that Anders couldn't make out what it was supposed to say.

Ch r ch of e Mill n i m
Rev. H r old T. oodst th, Pas or
Everyo e elco e!
"Love on other, lest ye f ll to d t le for r le m!"

On the steps leading up to the front door, he turned around and saw, to the south, the lights of the office buildings of downtown Detroit suspended like enlarged stars in the darkness. After hearing what he thought was some sound in the bushes, he opened the front doors of the church and went inside.

Over a bare wood floor, folding chairs were lined up in five straight rows, facing toward a front chest intended as an altar, and everywhere there was a smell of incense, of ashy pine. Above the chest, and nailed to the far wall where a crucifix might be located in a Protestant church, was a polished brass circle with a nimbus of rays projecting out from its top. The rays were extended along the wall for a distance of four feet. One spotlight from a corner behind him lit up the brass circle, which in the gloom looked either like a deity-sun or some kind of explosion. The bare walls had been painted with flames: buildings of the city, some he had already seen, painted in flames, the earth in flames. There was an open Bible on the chest, and in one of the folding chairs a deck of playing cards. Otherwise, the room was completely empty. Glancing at a side door, he decided that he had never seen a church so small, or one that filled him with a greater sense of desolation. Behind him, near the door, was a bench. He had the feeling that the bench was filled with the disappeared. He sat down on it, and as he looked at the folding chairs it occurred to him that the disappeared were in fact here now, in front of him, sitting or standing or kneeling.

He composed himself and went back out onto the street, thinking that perhaps a cab would go by, but he saw neither cabs nor cars, not even pedestrians. After deciding that he had better begin walking toward the downtown area, he made his way down two blocks, past a boarded-up grocery store and a vacated apartment building, when he heard what he thought was the sound of footsteps behind him.

He felt the blow at the back of his head; it came to him not as a sensation of pain but as an instant crashing explosion of light in his brain, a bursting circle with a shooting aura irradiating from it. As he turned to fall, he felt hands touching his chest and his trousers; they moved with speed and almost with tenderness, until they found what they were looking for and took it away from him.

He lay on the sidewalk in a state somewhere between consciousness and unconsciousness, hearing the wind through the trees overhead and feeling some blood trickling out of the back of his scalp, until he felt the hands again, perhaps the same hands, lifting him up, putting him into something, taking him somewhere. Inside the darkness he now inhabited, he found that at some level he could still think: *Someone hit me and I've been robbed*. At another, later, point, he understood that he could open his eyes; he had that kind of permission. He was sitting in a wheelchair in what was clearly a hospital emergency room. It felt as though someone were pushing him toward a planetary corridor. They asked him questions, which he answered in Swedish. "Det gör ont,"[2] he said, puzzled that they didn't understand him. "Var är jag?"[3] he asked. They didn't know. English was what they wanted. He tried to give them some.

They X-rayed him and examined his cut; he would need four stitches, they said. He found that he could walk. They told him he was lucky, that he had not been badly hurt. A doctor, and then a nurse, and then another nurse, told him that he might have been killed—shot or knifed—and that victims of this type, strangers who wandered into the wrong parts of the city, were not unknown.

2. It hurts. 3. Where am I?

He mentioned the disappeared. They were polite, but said that there was no such phrase in English. When he mentioned the name of his hotel, they said, once again, that he was lucky: it was only a few blocks away, walking distance. They smiled. You're a lucky man, they said, grinning oddly. They knew something but weren't saying it.

As the smaller debris of consciousness returned to him, he found himself sitting in a brightly lit room, like a waiting room, near the entryway for emergency medicine. From where he sat, he could see, through his fluent tidal headache, the patients arriving, directed to the Triage[4] Desk, where their condition was judged.

They brought in a man on a gurney, who was hoarsely shouting. They rushed him through. He was bleeding, and they were holding him down as his feet kicked sideways.

They brought in someone else, a girl, who was stumbling, held up on both sides by friends. Anders heard something that sounded like Odie. Who was Odie? Her boyfriend? Odie, she screamed. Get me Odie.

Anders stood up, unable to watch any more. He shuffled through two doorways and found himself standing near an elevator. From a side window, he saw light from the sun rising. He hadn't realized that it was day. The sun made the inside of his head shriek. To escape the light, he stepped on the elevator and pressed the button for the fifth floor.

As the elevator rose, he felt his knees weakening. In order to clear his head, he began to count the other people on the elevator: seven. They seemed normal to him. The signs of this were coats and ties on the men, white frocks and a stethoscope on one of the women, and blouses and jeans on the other women. None of them looked like her. From now on, none of them ever would.

He felt that he must get home to Sweden quickly, before he became a very different person, unrecognizable even to himself.

At the fifth floor the doors opened and he stepped out. Close to the elevators was a nurses' station, and beyond it a long hallway leading to an alcove. He walked down this hallway, turned the corner, and heard small squalling sounds ahead. At the same time, he saw the windows in the hallway and understood that he had wandered onto the maternity floor. He made his way to the viewer's window and looked inside. He counted twenty-five newborns, each one in its own clear plastic crib. He stared down at the babies, hearing, through the glass, the cries of those who were awake.

He was about to turn around and go back to his hotel when one of the nurses saw him. She raised her eyebrows quizzically and spread her hands over the children. He shook his head to indicate no. Still she persisted. She pointed to a baby with white skin and a head of already-blond hair. He shook his head no once again. He would need to get back to the hotel, call his bank in Sweden, get money for the return trip. He touched his pants pocket and found that the wallet was still there. What had they taken? The nurse, smiling, nodded as if she understood, and motioned toward the newborns with darker skin, the

4. The process of determining priorities for emergency medical treatment

Hispanics and light-skinned blacks and all the others, babies of a kind he never saw in Sweden.

Well, he thought, why not? Now that they had done this to him.

He felt himself nodding. Sure. That American word. His right arm rose. He pointed at a baby whose skin was the color of clay, the color of polished bronze, or flames. Now the nurse was wheeling the baby he had pointed to closer to the window. When it was directly in front of him, she left it there, returning to the back of the nursery. Standing on the other side of the glass, staring down at the sleeping infant, he tapped on the panel twice and waved, as he thought fathers should. The baby did not awaken. Anders put his hand in his pocket and touched the little turquoise heart, then pressed his forehead against the glass of the window and recovered himself. He stood for what seemed to him a long time, before taking the elevator down to the ground floor and stepping out onto the front sidewalk, and to the air, which smelled as it always had, of powerful combustible materials and their traces, fire and ash.

# Ann Beattie

*Beattie (1947– ) was born in Washington, D.C. She attended American University and the University of Connecticut. Subsequently, she taught at Harvard and the University of Virginia. She has received a Guggenheim Fellowship and has built a broad reputation for the many stories she has published in* The New Yorker. *These stories have made her the spokesperson for the generation of the 1960s as they adapt to or are baffled and worn down by the oncoming years. She writes of those who took the 1960s to be a Golden Age and cannot free themselves from the enchantment laid on them in their youth. Her books of short stories include* Distortions *(1976),* Secrets and Surprises *(1979),* The Burning House *(1982),* Where You'll Find Me *(1986),* "What Was Mine" and Other Stories *(1991), and* Park City: New and Selected Stories *(1998). Her novels are* Chilly Scenes of Winter *(1976),* Falling in Place *(1980),* Love Always *(1985),* Picturing Will *(1990), and* My Life, Starring Dara Falcon *(1997).*

## Snow

I remember the cold night you brought in a pile of logs and a chipmunk jumped off as you lowered your arms. "What do you think *you're* doing in here?" you said, as it ran through the living room. It went through the library and stopped at the front door as though it knew the house well. This would be difficult for anyone to believe, except perhaps as the subject of a poem. Our first week in the house was spent scraping, finding some of the house's secrets, like wallpaper underneath wallpaper. In the kitchen, a pattern of white-gold trellises supported purple grapes as big and round as Ping-Pong balls. When we painted the walls yellow, I thought of the bits of grape that remained underneath and imagined the vine popping through, the way some plants can tenaciously push through anything. The day of the big snow, when you had to shovel the walk and couldn't find your cap and asked me how to wind a towel so that it would stay on your head—you, in the white towel turban, like a crazy king of snow. People liked the idea of our being together, leaving the city for the country. So many people visited, and the fireplace made all of them want to tell amazing stories: the child who happened to be standing on the right corner when the door of the ice-cream truck came open and hundreds of Popsicles crashed out; the man standing on the beach, sand sparkling in the sun, one bit glinting more than the rest, stooping to find a diamond ring. Did they talk about amazing things because they thought we'd turn into one of them? Now I think they probably guessed it wouldn't work. It was as hopeless as giving a child a matched cup and saucer. Remember the night, out on the lawn, knee-deep in snow, chins pointed at the sky as the wind whirled down all that whiteness? It seemed that the world had been turned upside down, and we were looking into an enormous field of Queen Anne's lace.[1] Later, headlights off, our car was the first to ride through the newly fallen snow. The world outside the car looked solarized.

You remember it differently. You remember that the cold settled in stages, that a small curve of light was shaved from the moon night after night, until you were no longer surprised the sky was black, that the chipmunk ran to hide in the dark, not simply to a door that led to its escape. Our visitors told the same stories people always tell. One night, giving me a lesson in storytelling, you said, "Any life will seem dramatic if you omit mention of most of it."

This, then, for drama: I drove back to that house not long ago. It was April, and Allen had died. In spite of all the visitors, Allen, next door, had been the good friend in bad times. I sat with his wife in their living room, looking out the glass doors to the backyard, and there was Allen's pool, still covered with black plastic that had been stretched across it for winter. It had rained, and as the rain fell, the cover collected more and more water until it finally spilled onto the concrete. When I left that day, I drove past what had been our house. Three or four crocuses were blooming in the front—just a few dots of white, no field of snow. I felt embarrassed for them. They couldn't compete.

This is a story, told the way you say stories should be told: Somebody grew up, fell in love, and spent a winter with her lover in the country. This, of course, is the barest outline, and futile to discuss. It's as pointless as throwing birdseed on the ground while snow still falls fast. Who expects small things to survive when even the largest get lost? People forget years and remember moments. Seconds and symbols are left to sum things up: the black shroud over the pool. Love, in its shortest form, becomes a word. What I remember about all that time is one winter. The snow. Even now, saying "snow," my lips move so that they kiss the air.

No mention has been made of the snowplow that seemed always to be there, scraping snow off our narrow road—an artery cleared, though neither of us could have said where the heart was.

1. *Daucaus carota*, the wild form of the carrot.

# Madison Smartt Bell

*Bell (1957– ) was born in Tennessee and received his B.A. from Princeton and his M.F.A. from Hollins College. He has taught writing at the University of Iowa, the Bennington Writing Workshop, Johns Hopkins University, and Vassar College and currently teaches at Goucher College. His short stories are collected in* Barking Man *(1990). His most recent novels include* Save Me, Joe Lewis *(1993),* All Souls Rising *(1995), and* Ten Indians *(1996).*

## Witness

The day he heard that Paxton Morgan was released, Wilson had been planning to revise a will. It was a slack period for him and he didn't expect to be in court until late in the following week, but he'd come in early just the same. The door to his inner office was open on the lateral hallway, and he could hear the whisk of a letter opener as Mrs. Veech, behind the front desk, sliced into the morning mail. Mostly bills or offers of subscriptions, he'd glanced through it quickly on his way in.

There was a jingle as the front door opened and Wilson raised his head to listen, but it was a man he didn't want to see, and Mrs. Veech denied his presence. A grumble, sound of pacing, scrape of a match and a faint distant odor of tobacco. Mrs. Veech coughed. The voice grudgingly inquired if the smoke bothered her. Mrs. Veech said nothing but coughed again, more significantly. Her allergy to cigarettes was highly selective—Wilson, for instance, smoked himself. When the front door released a jangle of departure, he picked up his pencil and went back to the will. Mrs. Veech, he could hear, was dealing with the remains of the mail.

"Mr. Wilson, did you know they were letting Pax Morgan go?"

He heard her voice without immediately understanding it, registering only the anxiously rising note at the end. The task in his hand was complicated, though almost entirely frivolous: the testament of a women some forty years old who would probably live at least forty more, revising her bequests more or less semiannually. Still, it was an amusement she could afford if it pleased her, harmless enough, and he had use for the fee.

He drafted another line or two on the long yellow pad and broke the point of his pencil. Then the sense of Mrs. Veech's question reached him and he stood up, taking a cigarette from his shirt pocket as he stepped into the hall. Mrs. Veech sat bolt upright in her desk chair, clamping some sort of form in both her hands. Wilson took it from her and walked to the front window, setting the unlit cigarette in the corner of his mouth as he moved. It was a slick gray photocopy of a release form from Central State, with the name of Paxton Morgan typed along with other information and the illegibly scrawled signature of some doctor or official in the lower right-hand corner. He noted that the box for the date was not filled in.

"They might have already turned him out," Mrs. Veech said.

"Or they might just still be thinking about it." Wilson turned to face her. Round, plain and comfortable, she was a clean fifteen years older than he and normally unfazeable, though now she seemed perceptibly disturbed.

"I wonder who sent us this," he said.

"There wasn't any cover letter." Mrs. Veech frowned.

Wilson stepped across and picked up the slit envelope from the stack of circulars on the desk and paced back to the window, turning it over in his hands. It was letterhead stationery from the hospital, with his own address unremarkably typed and a postmark from two days before. Absently he folded it in three and peered out the window, around the hanging vines of the plants Mrs. Veech had insisted on stringing up there. The office was on the ground floor at the corner of the square, and sighting through the letter *O* of his own reversed name on the glass, Wilson could see a couple of cars and one mud-splattered pickup truck revolving lazily around the concrete Confederate soldier on his high pedestal at the center. Opposite, the usual complement of idlers lounged around the courthouse steps. The office had a southern exposure, and he could feel a slight sunny warmth on the side of his face through the pane.

"Well, damn their eyes," he said, and then, as he noticed Mrs. Veech again, "Excuse me."

Back in his inner office, Wilson lit the cigarette and set it in an ashtray to burn itself out, then began dialing the phone with the butt end of his pencil. In some fifteen minutes he had variously heard that Pax Morgan had already been released, was not going to be released at all, or had never been admitted. He hadn't expected to discover who had sent the anonymous notification, and so was not surprised when he didn't. Although he did learn that a Dr. Meagrum was supposed to be presiding over the case, he could not get through to him. He left a message asking that his call be returned. The central spring of his revolving chair squealed slightly as he leaned back, away from the phone. On the rear wall of the room, behind the triangle of clients' chairs, bookshelves rose all the way to the high ceiling, bearing about half of Wilson's law library. Hands laced behind his head, he scanned the top row of heavy books as though looking for something, though he was not. After a moment he tightened his lips and leaned forward again and made the call he had been postponing.

He had the number by heart already because it had once been his own, the Nashville law firm where he'd formerly worked. In those days Sharon

Morgan would likely have answered the phone herself, but they used her more as a researcher now, and had hired a different receptionist. She was good at the work, and with the two children there was no doubt the better pay made a difference. Still studying for her own law degree, part time; Pax had never liked that much. Wilson asked for her and waited till she came on the line, her voice brisk, as he remembered it. It had been some months since they had spoken and the first few exchanges passed in pleasantries, inquiries about each other's children and the like. Then, a pause.

"Well, you never called just to pass the time," Sharon said. "Not if I know you."

Wilson hesitated, thinking, What would she look like now? The same. Phone pinched between her chin and shoulder, a tail of her longish dark hair involved with the cord some way. Chances were she'd be doing something on her desk while she waited for him to continue, brown eyes sharp on some document, wasting no time.

"Right," he said. "Have you heard anything of Pax lately?"

"And don't care to," she said, her tone still easy. "Why would you ask?"

The chair spring squeaked as Wilson shifted position. The distant sound of a typewriter came to him over the line. He flicked his pencil with a fingernail and watched its bevels turning over the lines of the yellow pad. "And not the hospital either, I don't suppose."

"Oh-*ho*," Sharon said. He could hear her voice tightening down, homing in. She took the same grim satisfaction in any discovery, no matter its purport, which was part of what made her good at her job. "Is that what it is?"

"I'm afraid," Wilson said, "they're letting him out, if they haven't already."

"And never even let me know. There ought to be a law . . ."

". . . but there doesn't appear to be one," Wilson said. He picked up the hospital form and read off to her its most salient details. A stall, he thought, even before he was through with it. "The morning mail," he said. "No date, and I don't even know who sent it."

"Then what are you thinking to do?" she said.

"I've been calling the hospital," Wilson said. "If I ever get through to the right doctor, maybe I can convince them to hold him, if he's not already gone."

"*If*," Sharon said sharply. "All up to them, is it?"

"I would call it a case for persuasion," Wilson said. "So, did you have any plans for the weekend? I should be able to get in touch . . ."

"I'm taking the children out to the lake."

Wilson plucked another cigarette from his breast pocket and began to tamp it rhythmically on the old green desktop blotter. "I don't know," he said. "Why not go to your brother's, say? Instead."

"What would we want to do that for?"

"Look, Sharon," he said. "You know, it's to hell and gone from anywhere, that house on the lake. And nobody even out there this time of year."

"I will *not* run from that—" She interrupted herself, but he thought the calm of her voice was artificial when she went on. "The kids are packed for it. They're counting on it. I don't see any reason to change our plans."

"You don't, do you?" Wilson said without sarcasm, and put a match to his cigarette. He supposed he'd been expecting this, or something a whole lot like it.

"Why don't you get a peace bond on him?" Sharon said. "If he really is out, I mean. Something. Because it ought to be *his* problem. Not mine."

"I could do that," Wilson said. "Try to, anyway. You know what good it'll do, too. You know it better than I do."

There was silence in the receiver, the phantom typewriter had stopped. Pax Morgan had been under a restraining order that night back before the divorce decree when he'd appeared at the house in Nashville he and Sharon had shared and smashed out all the ground-floor windows with the butt end of his deer rifle; he'd made it all the way around the house before the police arrived.

"Well, devil take the hindmost," Wilson said. "I'll let you know what I can find out. And you take care."

"Thanks for letting me know."

"Take care, Sharon," Wilson said, but she had already hung up, so he did too.

Shifting the cigarette to his left hand, he picked up the pencil and began jotting a list at the foot of the pad with the blunted tip. Often he did his thinking with the pencil point; he'd discovered that sometimes a solution would appear in the interstices of what he wrote. There were only two items on the list.

—Judge Oldfield injunction P.M.
—Dr. Meagrum Central State

He added a third.

—call back S.M.

The pencil doodled away from the last initial. The list was obvious and complete, and after he acted on it nothing would be solved. A long ash was sprouting from his cigarette, but he didn't notice until the spark crawled far enough to burn his knuckle.

For the rest of the morning he worked abstractedly on the will with imperfect concentration. Every twenty minutes or so he interrupted himself to make some fruitless call. Dr. Meagrum was perpetually "on rounds" or "in consultation." Judge Oldfield was spending his morning on the bench. Wilson's own phone rang occasionally, but always over something trivial. When he called Oldfield's chambers again around noon, he found that the judge was gone to lunch. He tightened his tie, got his seersucker suit coat down from the hat rack and, with a word or two to Mrs. Veech, went out himself.

Circling the square counterclockwise, he passed the Standard Farm Store, the bank and the courthouse steps, where one man or another raised a broad flat palm to greet him. It was warm out, an Indian summer heat wave, though it was late October and the leaves had already turned. A new asphalt path on the southbound street felt tacky on his shoes as he crossed. A couple of blocks west of the square he was already verging on the edge of time; beyond the long low roof of Dotson's Restaurant there were woods, turned fired-clay red patched with sere yellow, with a few deep green cedars standing anomalously among the other trees.

The fans were on inside the restaurant, revolving on tall poles, fluttering the corners of the checked oilcloths on the small square tables. Judge Oldfield sat toward the rear—alone, for a wonder—behind a plate of fried catfish, hush-puppies and boiled greens. As Wilson approached he put down his newspaper and smiled. "What wind blows you here, young fellow my lad?"

"An ill one, I'd say." Wilson sat down on a ladder-back chair. "Do you remember Sharon Morgan? A Lawrence, she was, before she married."

"Married that crazy fellow, didn't she?"

"That's the one." Wilson ordered an iced tea from the waitress who'd appeared at his elbow, and turned back to the judge. "They're letting him out of Central State, at least that's what it looks like." He ran down the brief of the morning's activity while Oldfield grazed on his catfish and nodded.

"It worrying you personally?" the judge said when he was done. "For yourself, I mean?"

"Oh no," Wilson said. "Not hardly. It wasn't me he said he'd kill, was it? I doubt he'd remember much about me. I never knew him any too well. Even while the divorce was going on it was just her he was mad at."

"So it's the wife—ex-wife, I mean. She's the one with the worry."

"She's the one." Wilson frowned down at his hands. There was a small watery blister where the cigarette had burned him, surprisingly painful for its size. He turned the cold curve of the iced tea glass against it. "She asked me to get an injunction on him. That's why I came hunting you."

Oldfield took off his fragile rimless glasses, rubbed them with a handkerchief and put them back on. "That's tricky, old son," he said, "when you don't know for sure if he's loose or he's not."

"Hard to get good information out of that place, don't you know?" Wilson said. "Seems like a lot of them are crazy, doctors and patients alike."

"Must be that's why they call it a madhouse," Oldfield said with a faint smile. "Well. She does live in the county now? Full time?"

"She moved here right after the divorce," Wilson said.

"Just to oblige you, now," Oldfield said, "I could sign you a paper. You draw it up. It happens he *is* out, you let me know and we'll sign it and serve it right away. It won't be much of a help to her, though."

"Don't I know it," Wilson said. "But what else do you do?"

"Not a whole lot that you *can*," said Oldfield. "You really think she's got call to worry? Not just fretful, is she?"

"Not her," Wilson said. "I'm the one fretting. I'm wondering, how can I get a deputy to watch over them for a couple of days?"

"You know you can't set them on her," Oldfield said. "Not without she asks for it herself."

"She won't."

"She was a pretty thing, as I recall," Oldfield said irrelevantly. He took off his glasses and rubbed at the bridge of his nose. "And knew her own mind, or seemed to."

"You mean she's stubborn."

"Yes, that's right."

Wilson stood up. "I thank you," he said.

Oldfield smiled myopically up at him, his eyes a light watery blue. "You ought to stay and try the catfish."

"Well, I believe not," Wilson said. "Not much of an appetite today."

"A young man like you?" The judge shook his head. "Must be this heat."

"Your wife called," Mrs. Veech reported. "She'll call you back. And that man from Central State, he called. Dr. Meagrum."

"He would have, wouldn't he?" Wilson said, shrugging out of his jacket. "Wait till I was gone, I mean."

Mrs. Veech sniffed. "In a tearing-down hurry, too," she said. "He was right cross to find you not here."

"He'll get over it," Wilson said. "All right, then, would you make sure for me that Pax Morgan still has his house in Brentwood? We might want to serve a paper on him a little later in the day."

In the inner office it was a little too warm, though not quite oppressive. He put his coat on the hat rack, cracked the single window and paced for a moment at the far side of his desk. It was a shallow room and the high wall of dark bookbindings seemed uncomfortably close. With a sigh he went back to his seat, lit a cigarette, picked up the will, put it down, lifted a list of the other items on his immediate agenda and then let that drop too.

The urge to pick at the blister seemed irresistible. He tore loose an edge of it, reviewing, in spite of himself, what little he really knew about Pax Morgan. They'd gone to the same high school, but two years apart; Wilson was the younger. Pax had played football—he remembered that—indifferently, in the line. Later on he had inherited money and started dabbling in real estate, or insurance, neither making nor losing much at whatever it might have been. Grown, he was a loud bluff fellow with a ruddy face and crinkly, almost yellow hair. At the large parties where Wilson would occasionally run into him, he w known for drinking too much and becoming not just mush-mouthed but cra incoherent. The drinking was said to be a factor in his later, more se breakdowns.

Wilson had gone to Sharon's wedding but he couldn't think if it was or after it that he'd had the one brush with Pax he remembered with real Another party, undoubtedly some Christmas gathering, for Pax was we incongruous Santa Claus tie and had managed to get quite drunk or Shuffled together by the crowd, they somehow became embroiled i ment over deer hunting. Wilson shot duck and dove, rabbit and so on his father's farm he might shoot what he had to, to protect the li he had no taste for shooting deer, which now appeared to be Pax's sion. Wilson was trying to get off the subject, but Pax wouldn't le

"You've never been blooded," he said thickly. "That's your t never been *blooded.*" He grasped Wilson's lapel and twisted it, drawing himself unpleasantly near, and Wilson was a little startled by what he himself did next, a trick someone had showed him in the Army. He took hold of Pax's thumb and squeezed the joints of it together, so that the sudden sharp pain made Pax flinch and let go. Reflexively, Wilson took a step backward, jostling someone behind him in the crowded room, but Pax's face went from surprise to a total blank, like a television switched to an empty channel, and so the whole episode was amputated.

Real craziness there, or an early sign of it. Wilson pulled the dead skin back from the blister, creating a small red-rimmed sore. By the time of the divorce, there were many worse examples, enough to fill a dossier. Wilson had never cared for divorce work much, but Sharon was both a colleague and a sort of distant friend, and also it was in the first thin stage of his independent practice. But once it was over he swore off friends' divorces altogether, no matter how bad he might need the work. It had been an easy case in the sense that the outcome was not in real doubt, but it was angry and ugly on Pax's side, and there'd been some bitter squabbling over property. Sharon had held out for the house on the lake—impractically, as Wilson thought—surrendering the Nashville residence to Pax, who'd later sold it. Reaching for the phone to call the hospital one more time, he wished again she hadn't done that.

His game of telephone tag with Central State went on for a couple more hours, unpromisingly. When the phone finally rang back around two-thirty, it was his wife.

"Not interrupting, I hope," she said. "Is it busy?"

"Not so you'd notice," he said. "It's been pretty quiet."

"Well, we need a gallon of milk," she said, "and cornmeal. Would you stop on the way home?"

"I'll do it," Wilson said, scribbling on the pad. "Lisa driving you crazy today?" Their daughter was four years old, and frantic.

"How should I describe it?" she said, and laughed. "This time next year she'll be in school . . . . I'll miss her, though."

"That's the spirit," Wilson said. The light on his phone began to flash and Mrs. Veech called down the hall, "It's that Dr. Meagrum!"

"I've got to take this call," Wilson said. "I'll be home on time, I think . . ." He pushed the button.

Dr. Meagrum seemed to be already *in medias res.*[1] "—there's an issue of doctor-patient confidentiality here, Mr., uh, Wilson. I don't know who could ave sent you that form but they did so without my authorization."

"Did they?" Wilson said, catching his breath. "As you may know, I represent Morgan's ex-wife, and given the circumstances of the case, it seems to me priate that *both* of us should have been informed."

can't agree with you there," Dr. Meagrum snapped.

due respect to your point of view," Wilson said, trying to collect him-

1. *Lat* chronolog middle of things; used especially of a narrative that opens in the middle rather than at the inning.

self. The conversation had taken an adversarial turn too soon. "I take it that Mr. Morgan *has*, in fact, been released from your, ah, custodial care."

"My records show that Mr. Morgan has been responding favorably to a course of medication and was transferred to outpatient status two days ago."

"I see," Wilson said. "What medication, may I ask?"

"I'm sorry, but that's confidential."

"And what assurance do we have that he will actually *take* this medication?"

"He's in our outpatient program now, and we'll be monitoring him on a biweekly basis."

"Biweekly, you say. That's *every two weeks*?" Wilson creaked back in his chair, gazing up at the join of his bookcase and the ceiling. "Dr. Meagrum, I would like you to consider"—he paused, thinking over the jargon as if fumbling for a key—"consider returning Mr. Morgan to *inpatient status*. Temporarily, shall we say. In the interests of the safety of his ex-wife and family."

"Our file shows that any such step would be contraindicated," the doctor said. "Not in the patient's best interests."

A white flash of light, something like heat lightning, burst over Wilson's mental horizon, obscuring his view of the bookcases. He found he was clenching the receiver in a strangle grip and talking much louder than before "Sir, you are describing a *piece of paper* to me, and I am talking to you about a man who has threatened to kill his wife, not once but many times—"

Dr. Meagrum harrumphed. "Yes, someone with this type of pathology might make such a threat, but I wouldn't suggest that you take it too seriously . . ."

"He came to her house with a thirty-ought-six rifle," Wilson said. "A *loaded* rifle—I'm now referring to the police report. They found him and the gun and they found her barricaded in an upstairs bedroom. With her two children, I should say. The boy is six now, Dr. Meagrum, and the little girl is seven. Your *outpatient* has threatened to kill them too."

Dr. Meagrum resorted to the imperial "we": "We have no record that this patient is violent. We see no reason to alter the treatment program at this time."

With a mighty effort, Wilson established a greater degree of control over his voice. "Very well," he said frostily. "I do sincerely hope you'll see no reason to regret the course you've taken."

By dumb luck his next call caught Judge Oldfield in his chambers, between cases, on the fly.

"I'm asking the impossible now," Wilson said. "Let's have him picked up. An APB. Lock him up and have a look at him. Just for a day or so."

"You're right," Oldfield said. "That's impossible. I couldn't do it if I wanted to. This is Williamson County. We haven't got a police state here."

"It's a free country, isn't it?" Wilson said. "Well, I had to ask."

"I wonder if you did, at that," Oldfield said. "You're acting mighty worked up about this, old son. Don't you think you might be making a little much of it all? He's been out two days already, so you say, and what happened? Nothing. The lady didn't even know until you called her. Simmer down some, think it over. Go home early. It's Friday, after all."

"All right," Wilson said. "Might give it a try."

"You get me that injunction and I'll pass it on to the sheriff direct," Oldfield said. "I can't do any more than that."

"I know," Wilson said. "Not until something happens. Well, I appreciate it."

He hung up and dialed Sharon Morgan at the office but she was gone, gone for the weekend, had left half an hour before to pick up the children from school. He plopped down the phone and tried, forcibly, to relax. Try it. Judge Oldfield was no fool, after all. Wilson picked up the pencil with a fleeting idea of listing off what he was thinking, feeling, but that was a ridiculous notion; probably that was how they spent their time at Central State. Possibly nothing would happen anyway. Possibly. He looked up Sharon's home number and dialed it, but there was no answer, though it rang twenty times.

In ten minutes he had scratched out the requisite injunction and handed it to Mrs. Veech with instructions to type it and walk it over to the courthouse when she was done. After she had gone out, he sat doing nothing but covering the phone, which didn't ring. The jingle of Mrs. Veech's return moved him to at least pretend to work. But he'd had it with the will for the day, though it still wasn't quite finished. He scraped his agenda toward him across the desk and ran his pencil point down item by item. There were two boundary disputes and a zoning complaint. A piece of frivolous litigation to do with somebody's unleashed dog. There was a murder case where the defendant would plead, draw two-to-ten and count himself lucky. A foregone conclusion, Wilson thought in his present skeptical mood, though matters had not yet reached that stage. At the foot of the list was a patent case that would make him and his client rich if he could win it. This one was the most remote, no court date even set for it yet, but at the same time the most intriguing, as much for its intricacy as its promise. He swiveled and dug in the cabinet for the file.

At four he called Sharon Morgan at the lake and got no answer. For another half hour he studied the patent case, though he was losing interest at an exponential rate. When he next called there was still no answer, and he was out of the chair and snatching his coat down from its peg before he even knew he meant to leave. On the highway bound for Keyhole Lake he began to feel a little foolish. He'd been presuming, counting the time from three o'clock, when school let out. It was not more than an hour from Nashville to the lake house, but he hadn't considered that she might have stopped to shop on the way, or taken the children to a movie or simply for a drive. Now it appeared to him that his every move that day had been an error. It was unlike him to have lost his temper with that doctor. Patience had always been his strength; he left it to his opponents to make mistakes in anger. Then too, that last call to Judge Oldfield was something he'd have to live down, and on top of all that he had wasted the day, and would need to come back in Saturday morning to recover the lost time.

All foolishness, and yet the thought did not comfort him. He drove carefully, a hair under the speed limit, sighting through the windshield across the burn mark on his knuckle. For no reason he could think of, he let the car roll past the Morgan mailbox and coast to a stop on the shoulder, where he got softly out. There was a little lip to climb before he could see down the driveway to the steeply pitched roof of the A-frame house and the blue lake distantly visible out past it. It was cooler here; the weather was turning, or else it was a chill coming off the water.

Below him, the drive was matted with fallen leaves. A staining fall of sunset light came slanting through the tree trunks on either side as the wind rose and combed the red leaves back, bringing a few more falling from the branches. Except for the wind it was utterly still; only across the lake the dogs in Jackson's kennel were barking, their voices echoing off the flat expanse of the water. But probably they were barking all the time. That was not the problem. What was wrong was that the passenger door of Sharon's orange Volkswagen had been left hanging open, sticking out stiffly like a broken arm. The car was pulled around parallel to the back porch, and over its roof he saw that the sliding glass door to the house had been left open too.

He walked to the dangling car door and stopped. Just past the edge of the drive, not more than three yards from him, there lay a child's blue tennis shoe, a Ked, with maple leaves spread around it like the prints of a large hand. Some twenty paces farther on he found the second shoe and then the little boy, barefoot, lying face down in a pile of sloppily raked leaves. Wilson thought that his name had been Billy, but he couldn't be quite certain of it, which bothered him unreasonably. The child had been shot in the base of the neck; the entry wound was rather small. Beyond the leaf pile a wide swath of dun lawn swept down to the lake shore where a canoe, tethered to a little dock, rocked softly on the water.

A strip of almost total darkness fit into the gap of the glass door. The porch floor moaned as Wilson crossed it, and glancing down he saw a brass shell casing caught in a crack between two boards. He bent to pick it up, then stopped himself and put both hands in his pockets. Through the door was a large living room with no ceiling, only the peaked roof and the rafters. At this time of day it was very dim within and it took Wilson's eyes a moment to adjust. The daughter (he was almost sure her name was Jill) was sprawled on a high-backed wicker chair as if flung there by some strong force. There was a single wound in her chest. Her mouth was open slightly and her eyes showed a little white. Wilson thought it more than likely that Pax had shot her from a standing position on the porch.

It took him only a quarter turn of his head to locate Sharon's body at the far end of the long room, lying across a wide flight of steps that rose to the kitchen and dining area. Pax might well have shot her from the doorway; he was a marksman, the proof was plain, and efficient with his shells. Wilson crossed the room to the steps and paused. He couldn't tell just where she'd been hit, though she'd bled very heavily. She lay crooked, twisted over at the waist, the fingers of one hand folded over the overhang of a step. Her hair had fallen full over her face, and Wilson was grateful for that, but her position looked so uncomfortable that he was tempted to turn and straighten her. His hands were still jammed in his pockets, however, and he left them there.

He went up the steps almost on tiptoe, careful to avoid bloodying his shoes, and made a turn to the left that brought him up against the metal kitchen cabinets. His breath was coming very short, each intake arrested as though by a punch in the midsection. He was aware of the tick of his wristwatch, and that was all. There was a telephone on the kitchen counter, and presently he detached a paper towel from a roll neatly suspended beneath the line of cabinets, wrapped it around the receiver and called the sheriff's office.

At the opposite end of the kitchen, a smaller set of sliding doors opened onto a deck overlooking the lawn and the lake. With the help of another paper towel, he slid back the door and went out and sat on a bench to wait. The lake's surface had a painful metallic glitter, with the sunset colors spreading across it like corrosion. He had left his sunglasses in the car, and being in no mood to retrieve them, he simply shut his eyes. In Korea, where the Army had sent him, he had *seen some action*, as they say, but afterward he had thought very little about what he had seen. In some quietly ticking corner of his mind a speculation was going forward as to how the bodies had come to be positioned as they were, and now it came to him that after they were all inside the house the boy must have missed his shoes and gone back to the car—He opened his eyes with a jerk and looked up. A solitary, premature firefly detached itself from the treetops on one side of the yard and floated dreamily across and into the treetops on the other.

It was twilight by the time he had parked his car behind the square, and for some reason he bypassed his office and walked on down Main Street as far as Saint Paul's Episcopal Church. More leaves had carpeted the white stone steps, and Wilson stood looking at them, one hand curved around a spear of the iron fence, and then turned back. The sidewalk was empty but for him, and he could hear the dry leaves crisping under his every footfall.

The street lights were coming on by the time he had returned to the square. The windows of his office were dark, but he could hear the telephone ringing as he came up the steps. Mrs. Veech had, of course, looked up before she left, and while he was searching out his key the phone stopped ringing. He went inside and pressed the light switch. Again the phone began to jangle, and he reached across Mrs. Veech's typewriter to pick it up.

"Mr. Wilson? It's Sam Trimble here. I had your paper to serve on Paxton Morgan?"

"Yes," Wilson said.

The deputy cleared his throat. "I thought you might like to know we picked him up. He'd gone straight back to his own house, you know, like they do."

"Yes," Wilson said again.

"We got him cold, if it's any comfort," Trimble said. "The gun still warm and blood on his shoes."

"That's all right," Wilson said. "He'll plead insanity."

He was not often here at night, and the overhead fixture was harsh and bright, bouncing blurred reflections from the flat black of the window panes, making his inner office look too much like a cell. But if he used only the desk lamp, the shadows reached toward him so. And yet he was still afraid to go home! He shouldn't have said what he had to Trimble, though at the moment he could hardly bring himself to feel regret for it. And he was late by now; he'd better call.

"Daddy, you're late," Lisa said.

"That's right, kiddo," Wilson said. "Where's your mother?"

"She's outside," Lisa said. "We were, both of us. I'll go call her."

"No, you don't need to," Wilson said. "Just tell her I'll be home shortly. Say I still have to stop by the store, though." Hanging up, he glanced at his watch. A fine evening like this, his wife would certainly spend outdoors, not bothering to watch the evening news.

Flushed with relief, he pictured their long curving yard, thick with fireflies, as it would be now, green pinpoints flashing and hovering in the dark. The lights of the house glowed warm behind the calm silhouettes of his wife and his daughter, and inside, the kitchen steamed with the scent of supper waiting. Upstairs, beside his bedside lamp, lay the copy of *War and Peace*[2] he'd been rereading this fall; at a half hour or so a night, it would last him to Christmas or longer. He thought now of Prince Andrey lying wounded on the battlefield, looking up into the reaches of the sky, that radical change in his perspective.

Still, he was not quite ready to leave. He picked up his pencil and tapped the butt of the dried eraser on the pad. At home, tonight or tomorrow or whenever he finally had to tell the story there, then the murders would be absolutely realized and the alternative of their somehow not having happened would be permanently shut off. Above, the fluorescent fixture made a sort of whining sound; Wilson thought that he could feel it in his teeth.

He turned the pencil over in his hand and set the point on the pad, but there was nothing much to write. The yellow paper was down at the bottom of a long pale shaft, stroked with faint parallel lines which signified nothing. If he could note down all the ingredients of the episode, then they could be comprehended, wrapped in a parcel of law and so managed. Wilson was a believer in due process. Without meaning to, he had become a bystander in this case.

It was only dizziness because he had skipped lunch, undoubtedly, and when he remembered that, the pad came floating back up toward him and the desk flattened and held still. There were some scratch marks on the paper, as if during his vertigo he had been trying unsuccessfully to draw a picture. Now he wondered if he had *known* what would happen, and if he had *known*, what then? He had left no legitimate measure untried but still he could picture himself crossing the lip above the lake house with a gun in his own hand, seeing the Volkswagen door still closed, the glass door of the house pulled to and Pax Morgan outlined against the glimmer of the lake like a paper silhouette.

The pencil slipped from his fingers and hit the desk with a clacking report that broke the fantasy. Pax was alive and the others were dead. His freedom was better protected than their safety—that would be one way of putting it. Simple. It was time to go home. Wilson turned off the desk lamp, stood up and

2. Novel by Russian writer Leo Tolstoy (1828–1910).

pulled his coat down from the hat rack. Safer and better to have no freedom maybe, but no, you wouldn't say that. The humming stopped when he flicked the light switch by the door. No, you wouldn't say that, would you? In the dark of the hall he could not see his way; he went toward the vague light of the front window with one hand on the wall. No, you wouldn't, but what would you say?

# Gina Berriault

*Berriault (1926–1999) was born the first day of 1926 in Long Beach, California. After graduating from high school she worked as a clerk, a waitress, and a news reporter. She taught creative writing at San Francisco State University. Her awards included the Aga Khan Prize from* The Paris Review *and the O'Henry Award. Among her published novels are* The Lights of Earth, Afterwards, The Son, *and* The Descent. *Her short stories are collected in* The Mistress and Other Stories *(1965),* The Infinite Passion of Expectation: Twenty-five Stories *(1982), and* Women in Their Beds, New and Selected Stories *(1996).*

## Who Is It Can Tell Me Who I Am?

Alberto Perera, librarian, granted no credibility to police profiles of dangerous persons. Writers, down through the centuries, had that look of being up to no good and were often mistaken for assassins, smugglers, fugitives from justice—criminals of all sorts. But the young man invading his sanctum, hands hidden in the pockets of his badly soiled green parka, could possibly be another lunatic out to kill another librarian. Up in Sacramento, two librarians were shot dead while on duty, and, down in Los Angeles, the main library was sent up in flames by an arsonist. Perera loved life and wished to participate in it further.

"You got a minute?"

"I do not."

"Can I read you something?"

"Please don't." Recalling some emergency advice as to how to dissuade a man from a violent deed—*Engage him in conversation*—he said, "Go ahead," regretting his permission even as he gave it. Was he to hear, as the last words he'd ever hear, a denunciation of all librarians for their heinous liberalism, a damnation for all the lies, the deceptions, the swindles, the sins preserved within the thousands of books they so zealously guarded, even with their lives?

With bafflement in his grainy voice, the fellow read from a scrap of paper.

*Greet the sun, spider. Show no rancor.*
*Give God your thanks, O toad, that you exist.*
*The crab has such thorns as the rose.*
*In the mollusc are reminiscences of women.*

*Know what you are, enigmas in forms.*
*Leave the responsibility to the norms,*
*Which they in turn leave to the Almighty's care.*
*Chirp on, cricket, to the moonlight. Dance on, bear.*

The fellow granted his listener a moment to think about what he'd just heard. Then, "What do you make of it?"

"What do I make of it?"

"What I make of it," said the intruder, "is you're supposed to feel great if you're an animal. Like if you're talking about a spider or a toad. Am I supposed to do that?"

"Do what?"

"Like thank God because I'm me?"

"That's for you to decide. Take your time with it." Shuffling papers on his desk. "Take your time but not in here."

Watch your step with anybody playing dumb, Perera cautioned himself. They sneak up on you from behind. This fellow knew just what he was doing, pulling out a poem by Rubén Darío,[1] reading it aloud to a librarian so proud of his Spanish ancestry he kept the name his dear mother had called him, Alberto, and there it was, his foreign name in a narrow frame on his desk for all who passed his open door to see. Maybe this fellow had been stabbed in prison by a Chicano with the name Perera, and now Perera, the librarian, a man of goodwill, a humanitarian, was singled out among his fellow librarians.

"What do you figure this guy's saying? Wake up every day feeling great you're you?"

"If that's what you figure he's saying, that's what he's saying. That's the best you can do with a poem."

Out in fistfuls from his parka pockets, more scraps of paper. So many, some fluttered to the floor. Cigarette packets inside out, gum wrappers, scavenged street papers of many colors that are slipped along underfoot by the winds of traffic, scraps become transcendentally unfamiliar by the use they'd been put to: Lines of poetry in a fixatedly careful, cramped handwriting.

"That spider, you take that spider." Entranced by a spider that only he could see, swinging between himself and Perera. "That spider is in its web where it belongs. Made it himself, swinging away. Sun comes out, strands all shiny, spider feels the warm sun on his back. Okay, glad he's a spider. I can see that. Same with the cricket. Makes chirpity-chirp to the moon. I can accept that. That toad, too. I can see he likes the mud, they're born in mud. It's the bear I can't figure out. Would you know if bears dance in their natural state?"

"Would I know if bears dance?"

"When they're on their own?" A cough, probably incited by some highly pleasurable secret excitement from tormenting a librarian. "What I know about bears," answering himself before his cough was over, "is bears do not dance. It is not in their genetic code. I'll tell you when they dance. They dance when

1. Nicaraguan poet and diplomat (1867–1916).

they got a rope around their neck. That poet slipped up there. A bear with a rope around his neck, do you see him waking up happy, hallooing the sun? Same thing."

"Same thing as what?"

No answer, only another cough, probably called up to cover his amusement over an obtuse librarian with a silk tie around his stiff neck.

"You know anything about the guy who wrote it? The bear didn't write it, that I know."

"No, the bear did not write it. Darío wrote it. A modernist, brought Spanish poetry into the modern age. Born in Chile. No, Nicaragua. Myself, I like Lorca.[2] Lorca, you know, was assassinated by Franco's[3] Guardia Civil." Why that note? Because, if it happened to him, Alberto Perera, here and now, his death might possess a similar meaning. An enlightened heart snuffed out.

"When he says like, Spider, greet the sun, where do you figure he was lying?" Slyly, the fellow waited.

"Was he lying?" Always the assumption that poets lie. Why else do they deliberately twist things around?

"What I mean is," grudgingly patient, "where was he lying when the sun came up?"

"The spider, you mean?" asked Perera. "Lying in wait?"

"The poet."

"The spider was in its web. I don't know where the poet was."

"I'll tell you. The poet was lying in his own bed."

"That's a thought."

"That's not a thought. That's the truth."

"A poem can come to you wherever you are," Perera explained. "Whatever you're doing. Sleeping, eating, even looking in the fridge, or when you think you're dying. I imagine that in his case he wakes up one morning after a bad night, takes a look at the sun, and accepts who he is. He accepts the enigma of himself."

"Are you?"

"Am I what? An enigma?"

"Are you glad you wake up who you are?"

"I can say yes to that."

"You give thanks to God?"

"More or less."

"Great. I bet you wake up in your own bed. That's what I'm saying. What's-his-name wouldn't've thought up that poem if he woke up where he was lying on the sidewalk."

"Darío," said Perera, "could very well have waked up on a sidewalk. He pursued that sort of life. Opium, absinthe. Quite possibly he was visited by that poem while lying on the sidewalk."

"Then he went back to his own bed and slept it off."

With trembling fingers the fellow gathered up his scraps from the desk.

2. Federico García Lorca (1899–1936), Spanish poet and dramatist. 3. Francisco Franco (1892–1975), Spanish military leader and dictator; chief of state (1939–47); regent of the Kingdom of Spain (1947–75).

Trembling with what? With timidity, if this was a confrontation with a guardian of the virtues of every book in the place? As he bent to the floor to pick up his scraps, the crown of his head was revealed, the hair sprinkled with a scintilla of the stuff of the streets and the culture. How old was he, this fellow? Not more than thirty, maybe younger. Young, with no staying power.

By the door a coughing spell took hold of him. With his back to Perera he drew out from yet another pocket in the murky interior of the parka one of those large Palestinian scarves that Arafat wore around his head and were to be seen in the windows of used-clothing stores, and brought up into it whatever he had tried to keep down. Voiceless, he left, his bare ankles slapped by the grimy cuffs of his pants.

Perera imagined him shuffling down the hall, then down the wide white marble stairs, the grandiose interior stairs, centerpiece of this eternal granite edifice. As for Darío's admonition to the spider to show no rancor, that fellow's rancor was showing all over him. Yet his voice was scratchily respectful and his fingers trembled. Anybody who inquires so relentlessly into the meaning of a poem, and presses the words of poets into the ephemerae of the streets, would surely return, borne up the marble stairs by all those uplifting thoughts in his pockets.

Alberto Perera, a librarian if for just a few months more, shortly to be retired, went out into the cold and misty evening. A rarity, in this time when librarians' ranks were shrinking down as his own head had shrunk while bent for so many years over the invaluable minutiae of his responsibilities, including the selection of belles lettres, of poetry, of literary fiction. The cranium shrinks no matter how much knowledge is crammed inside it. A rarity for another reason—a librarian who did not look like one, who wore a Borsalino fedora, his a classic of thirty years, a Bogart raincoat, English boots John Major would covet, a black silk shirt, a vintage tie.

Never as dashing as he wished to appear, however. Slight, short, and for several years now the bronze-color curls gone gray and the romantically drooping eyelids of his youth now faded flags at half-mast. Dashing, though, in the literary realm, numbering among his pen pals, most dead now: Hemingway, a letter to Perera, the youth, on the Spanish Civil War; Samuel Beckett, on critics mired up to their necks in his plays; Neruda, handwritten lines in green ink of two of his poems. What a prize! Also a note from the lovely British actress Vanessa Redgrave, with whom he'd spent an hour in London when he'd delivered to her an obscure little book of letters by Isadora Duncan,[4] whom she'd portrayed in a film. And more, so much more. Everything kept in a bank vault and to be carried away in their black leather attaché case with double locks when he left this city for warmer climes. It was time to donate it all to an auction of literary memorabilia, on condition that the proceeds be used to establish a fund for down-and-out librarians, himself among them soon enough.

Further, he was a rarity for choosing to reside in what he called the broken heart of the city, or the spleen of it, the Tenderloin, and choosing not to move

4. Modern dance pioneer (1878–1927).

when the scene worsened. Born into a family of refugees from Franco's Spain, Brooklyn their alien soil, he felt a kinship with the dispossessed everywhere in the world, this kinship deepening with the novels he'd read in his youth. Dostoevski's insulted and injured, Dickens' downtrodden. Eighteen years ago he'd found a fourth-floor apartment, the top, in a tentatively respectable building, a walking distance to the main library in the civic center and to the affordable restaurants on Geary Street. Soon after he moved in, the sidewalks and entrances on every block began to fill up with a surge of outcasts of all kinds. The shaven heads, the never-shaven faces, the battle-maimed, the dope-possessed, the jobless, the homeless, the immigrants, and not far from his own corner six-foot-tall transvestite prostitutes and shorter ones, too, all colors. A wave, gathering momentum, swept around him now as he made his way, mornings and evenings, to and from the library. There was no city in the world that was not inundated in its time, or would be in time to come, by refugees from upheavals of all sorts.

On gray days, as this day was, he was reminded of the poor lunatics, madmen, nuisances, all who were herded out of the towns and onto the ships that carried them up and down the rivers of the Rhineland. An idea! The mayor, having deprived the homeless of their carts and their tents, would welcome an idea to rid the city of the homeless themselves. Herd them aboard one of those World War II battleships, rusting away in drydock or muck, and send them out to sea. The thousands—whole families, loners, runaway kids, all to be dropped off in Galveston or New Orleans, under cover of a medieval night.

He ate his supper at Lefty O'Doul's, at a long table in company of other men his age and a woman who looked even older. Retired souls, he called them, come in from their residence hotels, their winter smells of naphthalene and menthol hovering over the aroma of his roast turkey with dressing. One should not be ashamed of eating a substantial meal while the hungry roamed the streets. He told himself this as he'd told himself so many times before, lifelong. He knew from saintly experiments of his youth that when he fasted in sympathy, punishing himself for what he thought was plenitude, his conscience began to starve, unable to survive for very long without a body.

A brandy at the long bar, and the bartender slapping down the napkin, asking the usual. "When you going to sell me that Borsalino?" Then, "This man's a librarian," to the bulky young man in a broadly striped sweater on the stool to the left of Perera. "He's read every book in the public library. Ever been in there?"

"Never was."

"You can ask him anything," said the bartender, and the man to Perera's right did. "Do you know right off the number of dead both sides in the Civil War?"

"Whose civil war?"

Taken for a tricky intellectual, he was left alone.

A theater critic, that's what he wished to be mistaken for, passing the theaters at the right time as the ticket holders were drifting in and the lines forming at the box office. Women's skirts and coats swinging out, swishing against him, and a woman turning to apologize, granting a close glimpse of her face to this man who appeared deserving of it. A critic, that's who he was, of the musical up there on the stage and of the audience so delightedly acceptive of the banal, lustily sung.

Past the lofty Hilton at the Tenderloin's edge, whose ultra-plush interior he had strolled through a time or two, finding gold beyond an interior decorator's wildest dreams. Its penthouse window the highest light in the Tenderloin sky, a shining blind eye. Around a corner of the hotel, and, lying up against the cyclone fence, the bundled and the unbundled to whom he gave a wide berth as he would to the dead, in fear and respect. Over the sidewalks, those slips of refuse paper he'd always noticed but not so closely as now. Alert to approaching figures, to whatever plans they had in mind for him, and warily friendly with the fraternal clusters, exchanging with them joking curses on the weather, he made his way. Until at last he stood before the mesh gate to his apartment building. A gate from sidewalk to the entrance's upper reaches, requiring a swift turn of the key before an assault. The gate, the lock, the fear—none of which had been there when he moved in.

The only man in the Western world to wear a nightcap, he drew his on. Cashmere, dove color, knitted twelve years ago by his dear friend and lover, Barbara, a librarian herself, a beautiful one. Syracuse, New York. Every year, off they'd go. Archaeological tours, walking tours. Three winters ago he was at her bedside, close by in her last hours. She, too, had corresponded with writers. Hers were women—poets, memoirists—and these letters, too, were in his care. Into his plaid flannel robe, also a gift from her, the seat and the elbows worn away. He always read in this robe in his ample chair or at the kitchen table or in bed. Three books lay on the floor by his bed, among the last he'd ever consider ordering for any library. One had seduced and deceived him, the second was unbearably vain, and he was put to sleep by the third, already asleep itself, face down on the carpet.

When he lay down the inevitable happened. At once he wondered where the poetry stalker might be, the librarian stalker with the excitable cough. Could Darío have imagined that his earnest little attempt to accept God's ways would wind up in the parka pocket of a sidewalk sleeper, trying to accept the same a hundred years later?

At his desk he was always attuned to the life of this library, as he'd been to every library where he'd spent his years, even the vaster ones with more locked doors, tonnages of archives. This morning his mind's eye was a benign sensor, following the patrons to their chosen areas. He saw them rising in the slow, creaky elevator, he saw the meandering ones and the fast ones climbing the broad marble stairs, those stairs like a solid promise to the climber of an ennobling of the self on the higher levels. The largest concentration of patrons was in the newspaper and periodical section, always and forever a refuge for men from lonely rooms and also now for those without a room, all observing the proper silence, except the man asleep, head down on the table, his glottal breathing quivering the newspaper before his face. In the past, empty chairs were always available; now every chair was occupied. And where was the young man whose pockets were filled with scraps of poetry? In the poetry section, of course, copying down what the world saw fit to honor with the printed page. *Anything in books represents the godlike and anything in myself represents the vile.* Who said that? A writer, born into grim poverty, whose name he'd recall later. If you felt vile in the midst of all these godlike volumes, what restless rage!

"Am I butting in here?"

Same parka, grimier perhaps. But look! His hair rose higher and had a reddish cast, an almost washed look from the rain. His eyes not clearer, not calmer, and in his arms four books, which he let fall onto the desk.

"This is not a checkout desk," said Perera.

"That I know. Never check out anything. No address. If you try to sneak something out you get the guillotine. You get it in the neck."

To touch or not to touch the books. Since there was no real reason not to touch, Perera set the four books upright, his hands as bookends.

"Who've we got here? Ah, Rilke,[5] the *Elegies*. Good choice. And here we've got Whitman.[6] You know how to pick them. Bishop,[7] she's up there. And who's this? Pound?[8] Sublime, all of them. But don't let yourself be intimidated. Nothing sacred in this place, just a lot of people whose thoughts were driving them crazy, euphoria crazy or doom crazy, and they had to get it out, see what *you* think about what they're thinking. That's all there is to it. Librarians in here are just to give it a semblance of order. I'm not a high priest."

"Never thought you were."

"Ah," said Perera, and the books between his hands resumed their frayed existence, their common humanity. One, he saw, had a bit of green mildew at the spine's bottom edge. It must have been left out in a misty rain or someone had read it while in the tub.

"Can I get you some coffee?" inquired the visitor.

"Strange that you should ask," said Perera. "Got my thermos here. A thirst for coffee comes over me at this hour." How closely he'd been watched! And now forced to take the plunge into familiarity, a plunge he would not have taken without further consideration if this man were the sole homeless man around. They were empowered by their numbers.

From the bottom drawer he brought up his thermos and his porcelain cup. The plastic thermos cup held no pleasure and he never used it. He'd use it now and not bother to guess why, and bring up also the paper bag of macaroons.

"Suppose I sit down?"

Perera nodded, and the guest sat down in the only other chair, a hard chair with an unwelcoming look, a chair used until now only by Alexa Okula, head librarian, and Amy Peck, chief guard, who often described for him the assaults she had suffered that day and where in the library they had occurred.

With both hands around the cup, the guest had no trouble holding it. "This is like dessert," he said. "This is great. Got sugar and cream in it." He was shy around the macaroons. Crumbs were tripping down the parka and when they

5. Rainer Maria Rilke (1875–1926), Austrian poet, born in Prague; author of *The Duino Elegies*. 6. Walt Whitman (1819–1892), American poet. 7. Elizabeth Bishop (1911–1979), American poet. 8. Ezra Pound (1885–1972), American poet.

reached the floor he covered them with his beat-up jogging shoes.

At that moment Perera recalled the very recent tragedy at the Sacramento library. When did the shooting occur? Right after a little party celebrating the library's expanded hours. And what did the assassin do then? Fled to the rooftop, where he was gunned down by the police. It was simple enough to imagine himself dead on the floor, but not so easy to imagine this fellow fleeing anywhere, hampered by the bone-cold ankles, the flappy shoes, the body's tremble at the core.

"You remember that poem?" his guest asked.

"Not verbatim," said Perera. "I did not memorize it."

"You can remember the bear, can't you, and the spider and the toad, anyway? How they're supposed to greet the sun because they are what they are?"

"That I remember," said Perera.

"What I'd like to know is, what am I?"

"You can figure you're a human being," said Perera.

"That's what I thought you'd say. What else you were going to say is, you're a human being by the sweat of your brow. Beavers, that don't take into account beavers. Beavers are dam builders. Then you take those birds who get stuff together to make a nest for the female of their choice. Other birds, too, I've seen them. Can't stop pulling up weeds or whatever stuff is around for a hundred miles, pull this out, pull that out, and off they go and back in a second. Then there's animals who dig a burrow, one hell of a long tunnel in the ground. They can't sweat but they work. It's work, but that don't make them human."

"Work does not get to the essence, I see your point," said Perera. At a moment's notice he could not get to the essence himself and he wished he had not used that word. It could only mean further trouble.

"Okay, take you," said the visitor. "Would you say you were human?"

"I've been led to believe that I am," said Perera.

"What you base that on," said his guest, "is you get to keep guard over this library and you got every book where it's supposed to be and in addition you got it up on a computer, what is its title, what is its number, who wrote it, and maybe you got in your head the reason why the guy wrote it. So in that way you can say you're human and maybe you're glad about it even if you don't look it. Okay, now let's say you're through work for the day and you walk home. Or you go on and have yourself a turkey or whatever they got there, roast beef, chicken and dumplings. Then you go along by that theater, maybe even drop in yourself at fifty bucks a seat in the balcony. After that you go on to your apartment, which is in a bad, I mean *baaad* neighborhood, and you unlock that gate. And then what?"

"I can't imagine."

"You don't have to imagine. You're in your own bed. Got a mattress that's just right for the shape you're in. Maybe you even got an electric blanket. Got pillows with real feathers inside, maybe even that down stuff from the hind end of a couple hundred ducks. Nighty-night."

"So now I'm sure I'm human?"

"So then the sun comes up and what do you say? You say what that spider says. Halloo, old sun up there, had me a good sleep in my own web and now I get to eat some more fat flies. Halloo, says the toad, now I get to spend the day in this hot mud some more. Halloo, says the bear, now I get to dance some more with this rope around my neck. Halloo, says this guy, Alberto Perera, now I get to go to the library again and talk to this guy who can't figure out why he can't halloo the sun with the rest of them."

A flush had spread over the fellow's face, over the pallor and over the pits, over all that was more appallingly obvious today. From his parka he brought out the Arafat[9] headpiece and hid his face in it, coughing up in there something tormentingly intimate.

Alexa Okula, head librarian, passing by and hearing the commotion, paused a moment to look in and Perera held up his hand to calm her fears for his safety. Nothing escaped her, only all the years of her life in the protective custody of tons of books and tons of granite. Soon to be released, just as he was to be, all she'd have was her stringy emeritus professor of a husband and her poodles. Unlike himself, who'd have the world.

The fellow sat staring at the floor, striving to recover from the losing battle with his cough.

"You suppose I could spend the night in here?"

With *unthinkable* on the tip of his tongue, Perera said nothing. Accommodations ought to be available for queries of every sort at any time in your life.

"Looks like it ought to be safer in here."

"Unsafe in here, too," said Perera. "This fortress is in a state of abject deterioration. The last earthquake did some damage, along with the damage done by the budget cuts, along with the damage by vandals. Time's been creeping around in here, too. The whole place could collapse on you while you slept."

"I can handle it," said the supplicant. "Nobody's going to throw lighter fuel on me and set me on fire in here. Nobody's going to knife me in here, at night anyway. Lost my bedroll. I left my stuff with this woman who's my friend, she got room in her cart. I had a change of shirt in there, I had important papers, had a letter from a guy I worked for up the coast. I was good at hauling in those sea urchins they ship over to Japan, tons of them. They love those things over there, then there wasn't any more. Where the sea urchins were, something else is taking over, messing up the water. I'm telling you this because I don't drink, don't do dope, don't smoke, so I sure would not set this place on fire if I was allowed to sleep in here." He was talking fast, outrunning his cough. "The cops took her stuff, took my stuff, dumped it all into the truck. Ordered by the mayor. She lost family pictures, lost the cat she had tied to the cart that sat on top. She was crying. I was in here talking to you."

"It must be damn cold in here at night," Perera said.

"Maybe, maybe not, and if it's raining maybe the roof don't leak."

"Dark, I imagine," said Perera. "I've never thought about it. I suspect they used to leave a few lights on but now it's dark. Saves money. Let's say that once the lights go out you can't see a thing. Your sense of direction is totally lost, you're blind as a bat, and I'm nowhere around to guide you to the lavatory and

9. Yasir Arafat (1929– ), Palestinian political leader.

I wouldn't know where it was myself. You might be pissing on some of the noblest minds that ever put their thoughts on paper."

"I wouldn't do that."

"They do get pissed on, one time and another, but not by you or me. So let's say you're feeling your way around, looking for a comfortable place. Okula has a rug in her office and it's usually warm in there. She exudes a warmth that might stay the night. But how to get there?"

"I know my way around."

"You do seem to," said Perera.

"What you could do when you take off, like your day is done, see? You just leave me in here and close the door. I wouldn't care if you locked it."

"I can lock it," said Perera, "but not with you inside."

"Is there some of that coffee left?"

Perera, pouring, was planning to wash that porcelain cup thoroughly. If it was pneumonia gripping this young man, it would get a more merciless grip on him, twice as old. Or if it was tuberculosis, it would bring on his end with rapacious haste and just as he was about to embark on his most rewarding years.

This time the guest took longer to drink it down, the hot coffee apparently feeling its way past the throat's lacerations.

"Let's say it's like that darkness upon the face of the deep," Perera said. "That same darkness the Creationists are wanting to take us back to. Dark, dark, and you need to find yourself a comfortable place. Now let's say you're at the top of our marble stairs and you don't know it. You take a step and down you go. Come morning, they open up and find you there."

"You think so?"

"You'll be on the front pages in New York, Paris, Tokyo. A homeless man, seeking shelter in San Francisco's main library, fell down in there and died. A library, imagine it, that monument to mankind's exalted IQ. I'll say you dropped by to chat about poetry. I'll say we spent many pleasant hours discussing Darío's *Filosofía.*"

Contempt in the eyes meeting Perera's. "What're you telling me? You're telling me to lie down and die?"

"Not at all. All I'm saying is you cannot spend the night in this library."

Scornfully careful, the fellow placed the porcelain cup on the desk and stood up. "You want me to tell you what that poem is saying? Same thing you're saying. If you can't halloo the sun, if you can't go chirpity-chirp to the moon, what're you doing around here anyway?"

"That is not what it is saying," said Perera.

"To hell with you is what I'm saying."

Gone, leaving his curse behind. A curse so popular, so spread around, it carried little weight.

Closing time, the staff and lingering patrons all forced out through one side entrance and into the early dark, into the rain. Perera hoisted his umbrella, one slightly larger than the ordinary, bought in London the day he met the actress, years ago. It will never turn inside out, the clerk promised, not even in

Conrad's[1] typhoon. And it hadn't yet. Lives were being turned inside out, but this snob of an umbrella stayed up there. A stance of superiority, that was his problem. A problem he always knew he had and yet that always took him by surprise. And how did he figure he was so smart, this Alberto Perera? Well, he could engage in the jesting the smart ones enjoy when they're in the presence of those they figure are not so smart. He could engage in that jovial thievery, that light-fingered, light-headed trivializing of another person's tragic truth, a practice he abhorred wherever he came upon it.

Onward through this neon-colored rain, this headlight-glittering rain, every light no match for the dark, only a constant contesting. *There is a certainty in degradation.* You can puzzle over lines all your life and never be satisfied with the meanings you get. Until, slushing onward, you've got at last one meaning for sure, because now its time had come, bringing proof by the thousands wherever they were this night in their concrete burrows and dens. There was no certainty in anything else, no matter what you're storing up, say tons of gold, say ten billion library books, and if you think you can elude that certainty it sneaks up on you, it sneaks up the marble stairs and into your sanctum and you're degraded right along with the rest.

For several days at noontime Perera looked for him in the long line at St. Anthony's, men and women moving slowly in for their free meal. After work he climbed the stairs to Hospitality House and looked around at the men in the collection of discarded chairs, each day different men and each man confounded by being among the unwanted many. Here, too, he knew he would not find him. The fellow was a loner, hiding out, probably afraid his cough was reason to arrest him.

A rolled-up wool blanket, a large thermos filled with hot coffee, a dozen packaged handkerchiefs, a thick turtleneck sweater, a package of athletic socks. Perera carried all this into his office, piecemeal, as the days came and went, and these offerings had the same aspect of futility that he saw in the primitive practice of laying out clothing and nourishment for the departed.

He braved the Albatross used-book store not far from the library, trying not to breathe the invisible dust from the high stacks of disintegrating books, and in the dim poetry section came upon some unexpected finds. Ah, hah! Michaux,[2] *My life, you take off without me,* and Trakl,[3] sad, suicidal soul, *Beneath the stars a man alone,* and Anna Akhmatova,[4] *Before this grief the mountains stoop,* and Ah! Machado,[5] *He was seen walking between rifles.* Comments in the margins, someone's own poem on a title page, bus schedules, indecipherable odds and ends of penciled thoughts intermingling with the printed ones. He wanted to keep these thin volumes for himself and instead he did as planned. He bought a green nylon parka in a discount place on Market Street, slid the books into the deep pockets, and folded the parka on top of the pile.

1. Joseph Conrad (1857–1924), English novelist and short-story writer, born in Poland as Josef Konrad Korzenoiwski. See *Heart of Darkness*, p. 269 of this anthology. 2. Henri Michaux (1899–1984), French poet and painter. 3. George Trakl (1887–1914), Austrian poet. 4. Russian poet (1889–1966). 5. Joacuim Maria Machado de Assis (1839–1908), Brazilian writer, generally regarded as the greatest Brazilian writer.

On the morning of the twelfth day, before the hour when the public was admitted, Perera entered by the side door, bringing a pair of black plastic shoes, oxford style, made in China, recommended for their comfort by a street friend wearing a pair. The door guard silently led him to the foot of the marble stairs, where Okula, cops and paramedics and librarians were gathered around a man lying on the lowest step.

Perera had never fainted and was not going to faint now, even though all the strength of his intelligence was leaving the abode of his head to darkness.

"Mr. Perera," Okula was saying but not to him, "was an acquaintance of this man. Wasn't he?"

Nobody was answering, though Perera gave them time.

"Occasionally," he said, "he stepped into my office. My door is usually open." Sweat was rising from his scalp. "Did he fall?"

"More like he lay down and died." The paramedic's voice was inappropriately young. "T. B. Take a look at that rag."

"You say you knew him?" A cop's voice. "Do you know his name? He's got nothing in his pockets."

"No," said Perera.

"Any idea where he concealed himself in here?"

"Hundreds of places." Okula, responding. "We check carefully. However, anyone wishing to stay in can also check carefully."

"What you might be needing is a couple of dogs. German shepherds are good at it. Dobermans, too. A couple of good dogs could cover this whole place in half an hour."

Kneeling by the body, Perera took a closer look at the face, closer than when they sat in the office, discoursing on the animal kingdom. The young man was now no one, as he'd feared he already was when alive. The absolute unwanted, that's who the dead become.

"Did this man bother you?"

It would take many months, he knew, before he'd be able to speak without holding back. Humans speaking were unbearable to hear and abominable to see, himself among the rest. Worse, was all that was written down instead, the never-ending outpouring, given print and given covers, given shelves up and down and everywhere in this warehouse of fathomless darkness.

"He did not bother me," he said.

The door to his office was closed but unlocked, just as he'd left it. Scattered over his desk were what appeared to be the contents of his wastebasket. But unfamiliar, not his. So many kinds of paper scraps, they were the bits and pieces his visitor had brought forth from that green parka. Throwaway ads, envelopes, a discount drugstore's paper bag, business cards tossed away. On each, the cramped handwriting. By copying down all these stirringly strange ideas, had the fellow hoped to impress upon himself his likeness to these other humans? A break-in of a different sort. A young man breaking into a home of his own.

Perera sat down at his desk, slipped his glasses on, and spread the scraps out before him as heedfully as his shaking hands allowed.

# Ambrose Bierce

*Bierce (1842–1913?) was born on a religious campground at Western Reserve, Ohio. The poverty of his family required him early in life to work for a newspaper in a menial capacity before his enlistment with the Indiana Infantry for duty in the Civil War. He rose through the military ranks to become a staff officer and was twice wounded. The horrors of war shaped his attitudes with an enduring pessimism, and his war stories are among the first to treat the subject with detailed realism. In San Francisco after the war he began his literary career by working, along with Mark Twain and Bret Harte, as a journalist. He spent the years between 1872 and 1876 in London, where his boisterous Western mannerisms and savage wit made him a celebrity, first earning him the nickname "Bitter Bierce." Poor health forced him to return in 1876 to his journalistic career in California. In 1891 he published* Tales of Soldiers and Civilians, *followed two years later by another volume of short stories,* Can Such Things Be? *The death of his two sons in 1889 and 1901, along with his divorce in 1891, intensified his prevailing pessimism and resulted at length in his disappearance into Mexico, where he is believed to have died in 1913. His sardonic wit can be sampled in* The Devil's Dictionary *(1911). Twelve volumes of his* Collected Works *(prose and poetry) were published in 1909–12.*

## An Occurrence at Owl Creek Bridge

### I

A man stood upon a railroad bridge in Northern Alabama, looking down into the swift waters twenty feet below. The man's hands were behind his back, the wrists bound with a cord. A rope loosely encircled his neck. It was attached to a stout cross-timber above his head, and the slack fell to the level of his knees. Some loose boards laid upon the sleepers supporting the metals of the railway supplied a footing for him and his executioners—two private soldiers of the Federal army, directed by a sergeant, who in civil life may have been a deputy sheriff. At a short remove upon the same temporary platform was an officer in the uniform of his rank, armed. He was a captain. A sentinel at each end of the bridge stood with his rifle in the position known as "support," that is to say, vertical in front of the left shoulder, the hammer resting on the forearm thrown straight across the chest—a formal and unnatural position, enforcing an erect carriage of the body. It did not appear to be the duty of these two men to know what was occurring at the centre of the bridge; they merely blockaded the two ends of the foot plank which traversed it.

Beyond one of the sentinels nobody was in sight; the railroad ran straight away into a forest for a hundred yards, then, curving, was lost to view. Doubtless there was an outpost further along. The other bank of the stream was open ground—a gentle acclivity crowned with a stockade of vertical tree trunks, loopholed for rifles, with a single embrasure through which protruded the muzzle of a brass cannon commanding the bridge. Midway of the slope between bridge and fort were the spectators—a single company of infantry in line, at "parade rest," the butts of the rifles on the ground, the barrels inclining slightly backward against the right shoulder, the hands crossed upon the stock. A lieutenant stood at the right of the line, the point of his sword upon the ground, his left hand resting upon his right. Excepting the group of four at the centre of the bridge not a man moved. The company faced the bridge, staring stonily, motionless. The sentinels, facing the banks of the stream, might have been statues to adorn the bridge. The captain stood with folded arms, silent, observing the work of his subordinates but making no sign. Death is a dignitary who, when he comes announced, is to be received with formal manifestations of respect, even by those most familiar with him. In the code of military etiquette silence and fixity are forms of deference.

The man who was engaged in being hanged was apparently about thirty-five years of age. He was a civilian, if one might judge from his dress, which was that of a planter. His features were good—a straight nose, firm mouth, broad forehead, from which his long, dark hair was combed straight back, falling behind his ears to the collar of his well-fitting frock coat. He wore a moustache and pointed beard, but no whiskers; his eyes were large and dark grey and had a kindly expression which one would hardly have expected in one whose neck was in the hemp. Evidently this was no vulgar assassin. The liberal military code makes provision for hanging many kinds of people, and gentlemen are not excluded.

The preparations being complete, the two private soldiers stepped aside and each drew away the plank upon which he had been standing. The sergeant turned to the captain, saluted and placed himself immediately behind that officer, who in turn moved apart one pace. These movements left the condemned man and the sergeant standing on the two ends of the same plank, which spanned three of the cross-ties of the bridge. The end upon which the civilian stood almost, but not quite, reached a fourth. This plank had been held in place by the weight of the captain; it was now held by that of the sergeant. At a signal from the former, the latter would step aside, the plank would tilt and the condemned man go down between two ties. The arrangement commended itself to his judgment as simple and effective. His face had not been covered nor his eyes bandaged. He looked a moment at his "unsteadfast footing," then let his gaze wander to the swirling water of the stream racing madly beneath his feet. A piece of dancing driftwood caught his attention and his eyes followed it down the current. How slowly it appeared to move! What a sluggish stream!

He closed his eyes in order to fix his last thoughts upon his wife and children. The water, touched to gold by the early sun, the brooding mists under the banks at some distance down the stream, the fort, the soldiers, the piece of drift—all had distracted him. And now he became conscious of a new disturbance. Striking through the thought of his dear ones was a sound which he could neither ignore nor understand, a sharp, distinct, metallic percussion like the stroke of a blacksmith's hammer upon the anvil; it had the same ringing quality. He wondered what it was, and whether immeasurably distant or near by—it seemed both. Its recurrence was regular, but as slow as the tolling of a death knell. He awaited each stroke with impatience and—he knew not why—apprehension. The intervals of silence grew progressively longer, the delays became maddening. With their greater infrequency the sounds increased in strength and sharpness. They hurt his ear like the thrust of a knife; he feared he would shriek. What he heard was the ticking of his watch.

He unclosed his eyes and saw again the water below him. "If I could free my hands," he thought, "I might throw off the noose and spring into the stream. By diving I could evade the bullets, and, swimming vigorously, reach the bank, take to the woods, and get away home. My home, thank God, is as yet outside their lines; my wife and little ones are still beyond the invader's farthest advance."

As these thoughts, which have here to be set down in words, were flashed into the doomed man's brain rather than evolved from it, the captain nodded to the sergeant. The sergeant stepped aside.

## II

Peyton Farquhar was a well-to-do planter, of an old and highly-respected Alabama family. Being a slave owner, and, like other slave owners, a politician, he was naturally an original secessionist and ardently devoted to the Southern cause. Circumstances of an imperious nature which it is unnecessary to relate here, had prevented him from taking service with the gallant army which had fought the disastrous campaigns ending with the fall of Corinth,[1] and he chafed under the inglorious restraint, longing for the release of his energies, the larger life of the soldier, the opportunity for distinction. That opportunity, he felt, would come, as it comes to all in war time. Meanwhile he did what he could. No service was too humble for him to perform in aid of the South, no adventure too perilous for him to undertake if consistent with the character of a civilian who was at heart a soldier, and who in good faith and without too much qualification assented to at least a part of the frankly villainous dictum that all is fair in love and war.

One evening while Farquhar and his wife were sitting on a rustic bench near the entrance to his grounds, a grey-clad soldier rode up to the gate and asked for a drink of water. Mrs. Farquhar was only too happy to serve him with her own white hands. While she was gone to fetch the water, her husband approached the dusty horseman and inquired eagerly for news from the front.

1. In Mississippi; the main battle for Corinth occurred in 1862 when the Confederates tried to retake the town and were decisively beaten.

"The Yanks are repairing the railroads," said the man, "and are getting ready for another advance. They have reached the Owl Creek bridge, put it in order, and built a stockade on the other bank. The commandant has issued an order, which is posted everywhere, declaring that any civilian caught interfering with the railroad, its bridges, tunnels, or trains, will be summarily hanged. I saw the order."

"How far is it to the Owl Creek bridge?" Farquhar asked.

"About thirty miles."

"Is there no force on this side the creek?"

"Only a picket post half a mile out, on the railroad, and a single sentinel at this end of the bridge."

"Suppose a man—a civilian and student of hanging—should elude the picket post and perhaps get the better of the sentinel," said Farquhar, smiling, "what could he accomplish?"

The soldier reflected. "I was there a month ago," he replied. "I observed that the flood of last winter had lodged a great quantity of driftwood against the wooden pier at this end of the bridge. It is now dry and would burn like tow."

The lady had now brought the water, which the soldier drank. He thanked her ceremoniously, bowed to her husband, and rode away. An hour later, after nightfall, he repassed the plantation, going northward in the direction from which he had come. He was a Federal scout.

## III

As Peyton Farquhar fell straight downward through the bridge, he lost consciousness and was as one already dead. From this state he was awakened—ages later, it seemed to him—by the pain of a sharp pressure upon his throat, followed by a sense of suffocation. Keen, poignant agonies seemed to shoot from his neck downward through every fibre of his body and limbs. These pains appeared to flash along well-defined lines of ramification, and to beat with an inconceivably rapid periodicity. They seemed like streams of pulsating fire heating him to an intolerable temperature. As to his head, he was conscious of nothing but a feeling of fullness—of congestion. These sensations were unaccompanied by thought. The intellectual part of his nature was already effaced; he had power only to feel, and feeling was torment. He was conscious of motion. Encompassed in a luminous cloud, of which he was now merely the fiery heart, without material substance, he swung through unthinkable arcs of oscillation, like a vast pendulum. Then all at once, with terrible suddenness, the light about him shot upward with the noise of a loud plash; a frightful roaring was in his ears, and all was cold and dark. The power of thought was restored; he knew that the rope had broken and he had fallen into the stream. There was no additional strangulation; the noose about his neck was already suffocating him, and kept the water from his lungs. To die of hanging at the bottom of a river!—the idea seemed to him ludicrous. He opened his eyes in the blackness and saw above him a gleam of light, but how distant, how inaccessible! He was still sinking, for the light became fainter and fainter until it was a mere glimmer.

Then it began to grow and brighten, and he knew that he was rising toward the surface—knew it with reluctance, for he was now very comfortable. "To be hanged and drowned," he thought, "that is not so bad; but I do not wish to be shot. No; I will not be shot; that is not fair."

He was not conscious of an effort, but a sharp pain in his wrist apprised him that he was trying to free his hands. He gave the struggle his attention, as an idler might observe the feat of a juggler, without interest in the outcome. What splendid effort!—what magnificent, what superhuman strength! Ah, that was a fine endeavour! Bravo! The cord fell away; his arms parted and floated upward, the hands dimly seen on each side in the growing light. He watched them with a new interest as first one and then the other pounced upon the noose at his neck. They tore it away and thrust it fiercely aside, its undulations resembling those of a water-snake. "Put it back, put it back!" He thought he shouted these words to his hands, for the undoing of the noose had been succeeded by the direst pang which he had yet experienced. His neck ached horribly; his brain was on fire; his heart, which had been fluttering faintly, gave a great leap, trying to force itself out at his mouth. His whole body was racked and wrenched with an insupportable anguish! But his disobedient hands gave no heed to the command. They beat the water vigorously with quick, downward strokes, forcing him to the surface. He felt his head emerge; his eyes were blinded by the sunlight; his chest expanded convulsively, and with a supreme and crowning agony his lungs engulfed a great draught of air, which instantly he expelled in a shriek!

He was now in full possession of his physical senses. They were, indeed, preternaturally keen and alert. Something in the awful disturbance of his organic system had so exalted and refined them that they made record of things never before perceived. He felt the ripples upon his face and heard their separate sounds as they struck. He looked at the forest on the bank of the stream, saw the individual trees, the leaves and the veining of each leaf—the very insects upon them, the locusts, the brilliant-bodied flies, the grey spiders stretching their webs from twig to twig. He noted the prismatic colors in all the dewdrops upon a million blades of grass. The humming of the gnats that danced above the eddies of the stream, the beating of the dragon flies' wings, the strokes of the water spiders' legs, like oars which had lifted their boat—all these made audible music. A fish slid along beneath his eyes and he heard the rush of its body parting the water.

He had come to the surface facing down the stream; in a moment the visible world seemed to wheel slowly round, himself the pivotal point, and he saw the bridge, the fort, the soldiers upon the bridge, the captain, the sergeant, the two privates, his executioners. They were in silhouette against the blue sky. They shouted and gesticulated, pointing at him; the captain had drawn his pistol, but did not fire; the others were unarmed. Their movements were grotesque and horrible, their forms gigantic.

Suddenly he heard a sharp report and something struck the water smartly within a few inches of his head, spattering his face with spray. He heard a second report, and saw one of the sentinels with his rifle at his shoulder, a light cloud of blue smoke rising from the muzzle. The man in the water saw the eye of the man on the bridge gazing into his own through the sights of the rifle. He observed that it was a grey eye, and remembered having read that grey eyes were keenest and that all famous marksmen had them. Nevertheless, this one had missed.

A counter swirl had caught Farquhar and turned him half round; he was again looking into the forest on the bank opposite the fort. The sound of a clear, high voice in a monotonous singsong now rang out behind him and came across the water with a distinctness that pierced and subdued all other sounds, even the beating of the ripples in his ears. Although no soldier, he had frequented camps enough to know the dread significance of that deliberate, drawling, aspirated chant; the lieutenant on shore was taking a part in the morning's work. How coldly and pitilessly—with what an even, calm intonation, presaging and enforcing tranquillity in the men—with what accurately-measured intervals fell those cruel words:

"Attention, company. . . . Shoulder arms. . . . Ready. . . . Aim . . . Fire."

Farquhar dived—dived as deeply as he could. The water roared in his ears like the voice of Niagara, yet he heard the dulled thunder of the volley, and rising again toward the surface, met shining bits of metal, singularly flattened, oscillating slowly downward. Some of them touched him on the face and hands, then fell away, continuing their descent. One lodged between his collar and neck; it was uncomfortably warm, and he snatched it out.

As he rose to the surface, gasping for breath, he saw that he had been a long time under water; he was perceptibly farther down stream—nearer to safety. The soldiers had almost finished reloading; the metal ramrods flashed all at once in the sunshine as they were drawn from the barrels, turned in the air, and thrust into their sockets. The two sentinels fired again, independently and ineffectually.

The hunted man saw all this over his shoulder; he was now swimming vigorously with the current. His brain was as energetic as his arms and legs; he thought with the rapidity of lightning.

"The officer," he reasoned, "will not make that martinet's error a second time. It is as easy to dodge a volley as a single shot. He has probably already given the command to fire at will. God help me, I cannot dodge them all!"

An appalling plash within two yards of him, followed by a loud rushing sound, *diminuendo,*[2] which seemed to travel back through the air to the fort and died in an explosion which stirred the very river to its deeps! A rising sheet of water, which curved over him, fell down upon him, blinded him, strangled him! The cannon had taken a hand in the game. As he shook his head free from the commotion of the smitten water, he heard the deflected shot humming through the air ahead, and in an instant it was cracking and smashing the branches in the forest beyond.

"They will not do that again," he thought; "the next time they will use a charge of grape.[3] I must keep my eye upon the gun; the smoke will apprise me—the report arrives too late; it lags behind the missile. It is a good gun."

Suddenly he felt himself whirled round and round—spinning like a top.

2. Diminishing. 3. I.e., grapeshot, a cluster of small pellets fired from a cannon.

"What do you think of Rose's behavior, Violet?" They did this sometimes. In their manual it must say, If you think the parents are too weird, try talking to the sister.

"I don't know. Maybe she's trying to get you to stop talking about her in the third person."

"Nicely put," my mother said.

"Indeed," my father said.

"Fuckin' A," Rose said.

"Well, this is something that the whole family agrees upon," Mr. Walker said, trying to act as if he understood or even liked us.

"That was not a successful intervention, Ferret Face." Rose tended to function better when she was angry. He did look like a blond ferret, and we all laughed again. Even my father, who tried to give these people a chance, out of some sense of collegiality, had given it up.

After fourteen minutes, Mr. Walker decided that our time was up and walked out, leaving us grinning at each other. Rose was still nuts, but at least we'd all had a little fun.

The day we met our best family therapist started out almost as badly. We scared off a resident and then scared off her supervisor, who sent us Dr. Thorne. Three hundred pounds of Texas chili, cornbread, and Lone Star beer, finished off with big black cowboy boots and a small string tie around the area of his neck.

"O frabjous day, it's Big Nut." Rose was in heaven and stopped massaging her breasts immediately.

"Hey, Little Nut." You have to understand how big a man would have to be to call my sister "little." He christened us all, right away. "And it's the good Doctor Nut, and Madame Hickory Nut, 'cause they are the hardest damn nuts to crack, and over here in the overalls and not much else is No One's Nut"—a name that summed up both my sanity and my loneliness. We all relaxed.

Dr. Thorne was good for us. Rose moved into a halfway house whose director loved Big Nut so much that she kept Rose even when Rose went through a period of having sex with everyone who passed her door. She was in a fever for a while, trying to still the voices by fucking her brains out.

Big Nut said, "Darlin', I can't. I cannot make love to every beautiful woman I meet, and furthermore, I can't do that and be your therapist too. It's a great shame, but I think you might be able to find a really nice guy, someone who treats you just as sweet and kind as I would if I were lucky enough to be your beau. I don't want you to settle for less." And she stopped propositioning the crack addicts and the alcoholics and the guys at the shelter. We loved Dr. Thorne.

My father went back to seeing rich neurotics and helped out one day a week at Dr. Thorne's Walk-In Clinic. My mother finished a recording of Mozart concerti and played at fund-raisers for Rose's halfway house. I went back to college and found a wonderful linebacker from Texas to sleep with. In the dark, I would make him call me "darlin'." Rose took her meds, lost about fifty pounds, and began singing at the A. M. E Zion Church, down the street from the halfway house.

At first they didn't know what do to with this big blond lady, dressed funny and hovering wistfully in the doorway during their rehearsals, but she gave them a few bars of "Precious Lord" and the choir director felt God's hand and saw that with the help of His sweet child Rose, the Prospect Street Choir was going all the way to the Gospel Olympics.

Amidst a sea of beige, umber, cinnamon, and espresso faces, there was Rose, bigger, blonder, and pinker than any two white women could be. And Rose and the choir's contralto, Addie Robicheaux, laid out their gold and silver voices and wove them together in strands as fine as silk, as strong as steel. And we wept as Rose and Addie, in their billowing garnet robes, swayed together, clasping hands until the last perfect note floated up to God, and then they smiled down at us.

Rose would still go off from time to time and the voices would tell her to do bad things, but Dr. Thorne or Addie or my mother could usually bring her back. After five good years, Big Nut died. Stuffing his face with a chili dog, sitting in his unair-conditioned office in the middle of July, he had one big, Texas-sized aneurysm and died.

Rose held on tight for seven days; she took her meds, went to choir practice, and rearranged her room about a hundred times. His funeral was like a Lourdes[7] for the mentally ill. If you were psychotic, borderline, bad-off neurotic, or just very hard to get along with, you were there. People shaking so bad from years of heavy meds that they fell out of the pews. People holding hands, crying, moaning, talking to themselves. The crazy people and the not-so-crazy people were all huddled together, like puppies at the pound.

Rose stopped taking her meds, and the halfway house wouldn't keep her after she pitched another patient down the stairs. My father called the insurance company and found out that Rose's new, improved psychiatric coverage wouldn't begin for forty-five days. I put all of her stuff in a garbage bag, and we walked out of the halfway house, Rose winking at the poor drooling boy on the couch.

"This is going to be difficult—not all bad, but difficult—for the whole family, and I thought we should discuss everybody's expectations. I know I have some concerns." My father had convened a family meeting as soon as Rose finished putting each one of her thirty stuffed bears in its own special place.

"No meds," Rose said, her eyes lowered, her stubby fingers, those fingers that had braided my hair and painted tulips on my cheeks, pulling hard on the hem of her dirty smock.

My father looked in despair at my mother.

"Rosie, do you want to drive the new car?" my mother asked.

Rose's face lit up. "I'd love to drive that car. I'd drive to California, I'd go see the bears at the San Diego Zoo. I would take you, Violet, but you always hated the zoo. Remember how she cried at the Bronx Zoo when she found out that the animals didn't get to go home at closing?" Rose put her damp hand on mine and squeezed it sympathetically. "Poor Vi."

"If you take your medication, after a while you'll be able to drive the car.

7. Roman Catholic shrine in southwest France famed for miraculous cures.

# Amy Bloom

*Bloom (1953– ) was born in New York City and was educated at Wesleyan University. She is a psychotherapist as well as a writer. Her books include the novel* Love Invents Us *(1997) and the short-story collection* Come to Me *(1993). Her stories have also appeared in* The New Yorker, Antaeus, *and* Story.

## Silver Water

My sister's voice was like mountain water in a silver pitcher; the clear blue beauty of it cools you and lifts you up beyond your heat, beyond your body. After we went to see *La Traviata*,[1] when she was fourteen and I was twelve, she elbowed me in the parking lot and said, "Check this out." And she opened her mouth unnaturally wide and her voice came out, so crystalline and bright that all the departing operagoers stood frozen by their cars, unable to take out their keys or open their doors until she had finished, and then they cheered like hell.

That's what I like to remember, and that's the story I told to all of her therapists. I wanted them to know her, to know that who they saw was not all there was to see. That before her constant tinkling of commercials and fast-food jingles there had been Puccini[2] and Mozart[3] and hymns so sweet and mighty you expected Jesus to come down off his cross and clap. That before there was a mountain of Thorazined[4] fat, swaying down the halls in nylon maternity tops and sweatpants, there had been the prettiest girl in Arrandale Elementary School, the belle of Landmark Junior High. Maybe there were other pretty girls, but I didn't see them. To me, Rose, my beautiful blond defender, my guide to Tampax and my mother's moods, was perfect.

She had her first psychotic break when she was fifteen. She had been coming home moody and tearful, then quietly beaming, then she stopped coming home. She would go out into the woods behind our house and not come in until my mother went after her at dusk, and stepped gently into the briars and saplings and pulled her out, blank-faced, her pale blue sweater covered with

1. Italian opera by Giuseppe Verdi (1813–1901). 2. Giacomo Puccini, Italian composer (1858–1924). 3. Wolfgang Amadeus Mozart, Austrian composer (1756–1791) 4. Trademark chlorpromazine, an antipsychotic drug.

crumbled leaves, her white jeans smeared with dirt. After three weeks of this, my mother, who is a musician and widely regarded as eccentric, said to my father, who is a psychiatrist and a kind, sad man, "She's going off."

"What is that, your professional opinion?" He picked up the newspaper and put it down again, sighing. "I'm sorry, I didn't mean to snap at you. I know something's bothering her. Have you talked to her?"

"What's there to say? David, she's going crazy. She doesn't need a heart-to-heart talk with Mom, she needs a hospital."

They went back and forth, and my father sat down with Rose for a few hours, and she sat there licking the hairs on her forearm, first one way, then the other. My mother stood in the hallway, dry-eyed and pale, watching the two of them. She had already packed, and when three of my father's friends dropped by to offer free consultations and recommendations, my mother and Rose's suitcase were already in the car. My mother hugged me and told me that they would be back that night, but not with Rose. She also said, divining my worst fear, "It won't happen to you, honey. Some people go crazy and some people never do. You never will." She smiled and stroked my hair. "Not even when you want to."

Rose was in hospitals, great and small, for the next ten years. She had lots of terrible therapists and a few good ones. One place had no pictures on the walls, no windows, and the patients all wore slippers with the hospital crest on them. My mother didn't even bother to go to Admissions. She turned Rose around and the two of them marched out, my father walking behind them, apologizing to his colleagues. My mother ignored the psychiatrists, the social workers, and the nurses, and played Handel[5] and Bessie Smith[6] for the patients on whatever was available. At some places, she had a Steinway donated by a grateful, or optimistic, family; at others, she banged out "Gimme a Pigfoot and a Bottle of Beer" on an old, scarred box that hadn't been tuned since there'd been English-speaking physicians on the grounds. My father talked in serious, appreciative tones to the administrators and unit chiefs and tried to be friendly with whoever was managing Rose's case. We all hated the family therapists.

The worst family therapist we ever had sat in a pale green room with us, visibly taking stock of my mother's ethereal beauty and her faded blue t-shirt and girl-sized jeans, my father's rumpled suit and stained tie, and my own unreadable seventeen-year-old fashion statement. Rose was beyond fashion that year, in one of her dancing teddybear smocks and extra-extra-large Celtics sweatpants. Mr. Walker read Rose's file in front of us and then watched in alarm as Rose began crooning, beautifully, and slowly massaging her breasts. My mother and I laughed, and even my father started to smile. This was Rose's usual opening salvo for new therapists.

Mr. Walker said, "I wonder why it is that everyone is so entertained by Rose behaving inappropriately."

Rose burped, and then we all laughed. This was the seventh family therapist we had seen, and none of them had lasted very long. Mr. Walker, unfortunately, was determined to do right by us.

5. George Frederick Handel, German composer (1685–1759). 6. American blues singer (1894?–1937).

garments; his wife, looking fresh and cool and sweet, steps down from the verandah to meet him. At the bottom of the steps she stands waiting, with a smile of ineffable joy, an attitude of matchless grace and dignity. Ah, how beautiful she is! He springs forward with extended arms. As he is about to clasp her, he feels a stunning blow upon the back of the neck; a blinding white light blazes all about him, with a sound like the shock of a cannon—then all is darkness and silence!

Peyton Farquhar was dead; his body, with a broken neck, swung gently from side to side beneath the timbers of the Owl Creek bridge.

The water, the banks, the forest, the now distant bridge, fort and men—all were commingled and blurred. Objects were represented by their colors only; circular horizontal streaks of color—that was all he saw. He had been caught in a vortex and was being whirled on with a velocity of advance and gyration which made him giddy and sick. In a few moments he was flung upon the gravel at the foot of the left bank of the stream—the southern bank—and behind a projecting point which concealed him from his enemies. The sudden arrest of his motion, the abrasion of one of his hands on the gravel, restored him and he wept with delight. He dug his fingers into the sand, threw it over himself in handfuls and audibly blessed it. It looked like gold, like diamonds, rubies, emeralds; he could think of nothing beautiful which it did not resemble. The trees upon the bank were giant garden plants; he noted a definite order in their arrangement, inhaled the fragrance of their blooms. A strange, roseate light shone through the spaces among their trunks, and the wind made in their branches the music of æolian harps. He had no wish to perfect his escape, was content to remain in that enchanting spot until retaken.

A whizz and rattle of grapeshot among the branches high above his head roused him from his dream. The baffled cannoneer had fired him a random farewell. He sprang to his feet, rushed up the sloping bank, and plunged into the forest.

All that day he travelled, laying his course by the rounding sun. The forest seemed interminable; nowhere did he discover a break in it, not even a woodman's road. He had not known that he lived in so wild a region. There was something uncanny in the revelation.

By nightfall he was fatigued, footsore, famishing. The thought of his wife and children urged him on. At last he found a road which led him in what he knew to be the right direction. It was as wide and straight as a city street, yet it seemed untravelled. No fields bordered it, no dwelling anywhere. Not so much as the barking of a dog suggested human habitation. The black bodies of the great trees formed a straight wall on both sides, terminating on the horizon in a point, like a diagram in a lesson in perspective. Overhead, as he looked up through this rift in the wood, shone great golden stars looking unfamiliar and grouped in strange constellations. He was sure they were arranged in some order which had a secret and malign significance. The wood on either side was full of singular noises, among which—once, twice, and again—he distinctly heard whispers in an unknown tongue.

His neck was in pain, and, lifting his hand to it, he found it horribly swollen. He knew that it had a circle of black where the rope had bruised it. His eyes felt congested; he could no longer close them. His tongue was swollen with thirst; he relieved its fever by thrusting it forward from between his teeth into the cool air. How softly the turf had carpeted the untravelled avenue! He could no longer feel the roadway beneath his feet!

Doubtless, despite his suffering, he fell asleep while walking, for now he sees another scene—perhaps he has merely recovered from a delirium. He stands at the gate of his own home. All is as he left it, and all bright and beautiful in the morning sunshine. He must have travelled the entire night. As he pushes open the gate and passes up the wide white walk, he sees a flutter of female

That's the deal. Meds, car." My mother sounded accommodating but unenthusiastic, careful not to heat up Rose's paranoia.

"You got yourself a deal, darlin'."

I was living about an hour away then, teaching English during the day, writing poetry at night. I went home every few days for dinner. I called every night.

My father said, quietly, "It's very hard. We're doing all right, I think. Rose has been walking in the mornings with your mother, and she watches a lot of TV. She won't go to the day hospital, and she won't go back to the choir. Her friend Mrs. Robicheaux came by a couple of times. What a sweet woman. Rose wouldn't even talk to her. She just sat there, staring at the wall and humming. We're not doing all that well, actually, but I guess we're getting by. I'm sorry, sweetheart, I don't mean to depress you."

My mother said, emphatically, "We're doing fine. We've got our routine and we stick to it and we're fine. You don't need to come home so often, you know. Wait 'til Sunday, just come for the day. Lead your life, Vi. She's leading hers."

I stayed away all week, afraid to pick up my phone, grateful to my mother for her harsh calm and her reticence, the qualities that had enraged me throughout my childhood.

I came on Sunday, in the early afternoon, to help my father garden, something we had always enjoyed together. We weeded and staked tomatoes and killed aphids while my mother and Rose were down at the lake. I didn't even go into the house until four, when I needed a glass of water.

Someone had broken the piano bench into five neatly stacked pieces and placed them where the piano bench usually was.

"We were having such a nice time, I couldn't bear to bring it up," my father said, standing in the doorway, carefully keeping his gardening boots out of the kitchen.

"What did Mommy say?"

"She said, 'Better the bench than the piano.' And your sister lay down on the floor and just wept. Then your mother took her down to the lake. This can't go on, Vi. We have twenty-seven days left, your mother gets no sleep because Rose doesn't sleep, and if I could just pay twenty-seven thousand dollars to keep her in the hospital until the insurance takes over, I'd do it."

"All right. Do it. Pay the money and take her back to Hartley-Rees. It was the prettiest place, and she liked the art therapy there."

"I would if I could. The policy states that she must be symptom-free for at least forty-five days before her coverage begins. Symptom-free means no hospitalization."

"Jesus, Daddy, how could you get that kind of policy? She hasn't been symptom-free for forty-five minutes."

"It's the only one I could get for long-term psychiatric." He put his hand over his mouth, to block whatever he was about to say, and went back out to the garden. I couldn't see if he was crying.

He stayed outside and I stayed inside until Rose and my mother came home from the lake. Rose's soggy sweatpants were rolled up to her knees, and she had a bucketful of shells and seaweed, which my mother persuaded her to leave on the back porch. My mother kissed me lightly and told Rose to go up to her room and change out of her wet pants.

Rose's eyes grew very wide. "Never. I will never . . ." She knelt down and began banging her head on the kitchen floor with rhythmic intensity, throwing all her weight behind each attack. My mother put her arms around Rose's waist and tried to hold her back. Rose shook her off, not even looking around to see what was slowing her down. My mother lay up against the refrigerator.

"Violet, please . . ."

I threw myself onto the kitchen floor, becoming the spot that Rose was smacking her head against. She stopped a fraction of an inch short of my stomach.

"Oh, Vi, Mommy, I'm sorry. I'm sorry, don't hate me." She staggered to her feet and ran wailing to her room.

My mother got up and washed her face brusquely, rubbing it dry with a dishcloth. My father heard the wailing and came running in, slipping his long bare feet out of his rubber boots.

"Galen, Galen, let me see." He held her head and looked closely for bruises on her pale, small face. "What happened?" My mother looked at me. "Violet, what happened? Where's Rose?"

"Rose got upset, and when she went running upstairs she pushed Mommy out of the way." I've only told three lies in my life, and that was my second.

"She must feel terrible, pushing you, of all people. It would have to be you, but I know she didn't want it to be." He made my mother a cup of tea, and all the love he had for her, despite her silent rages and her vague stares, came pouring through the teapot, warming her cup, filling her small, long-fingered hands. She rested her head against his hip, and I looked away.

"Let's make dinner, then I'll call her. Or you call her, David, maybe she'd rather see your face first."

Dinner was filled with all of our starts and stops and Rose's desperate efforts to control herself. She could barely eat and hummed the McDonald's theme song over and over again, pausing only to spill her juice down the front of her smock and begin weeping. My father looked at my mother and handed Rose his napkin. She dabbed at herself listlessly, but the tears stopped.

"I want to go to bed. I want to go to bed and be in my head. I want to go to bed and be in my bed and in my head and just wear red. For red is the color that my baby wore and once more, it's true, yes, it is, it's true. Please don't wear red tonight, oh, oh, please don't wear red tonight, for red is the color—"

"Okay, okay, Rose. It's okay. I'll go upstairs with you and you can get ready for bed. Then Mommy will come up and say good night too. It's okay, Rose." My father reached out his hand and Rose grasped it, and they walked out of the dining room together, his long arm around her middle.

My mother sat at the table for a moment, her face in her hands, and then she began clearing the plates. We cleared without talking, my mother humming Schubert's[8] "Schlummerlied," a lullaby about the woods and the river calling

8. Franz Schubert, Austrian composer (1797–1828).

to the child to go to sleep. She sang it to us every night when we were small.

My father came into the kitchen and signaled to my mother. They went upstairs and came back down together a few minutes later.

"She's asleep," they said, and we went to sit on the porch and listen to the crickets. I don't remember the rest of the evening, but I remember it as quietly sad, and I remember the rare sight of my parents holding hands, sitting on the picnic table, watching the sunset.

I woke up at three o'clock in the morning, feeling the cool night air through my sheet. I went down the hall for a blanket and looked into Rose's room, for no reason. She wasn't there. I put on my jeans and a sweater and went downstairs. I could feel her absence. I went outside and saw her wide, draggy footprints darkening the wet grass into the woods.

"Rosie," I called, too softly, not wanting to wake my parents, not wanting to startle Rose. "Rosie, it's me. Are you here? Are you all right?"

I almost fell over her. Huge and white in the moonlight, her flowered smock bleached in the light and shadow, her sweatpants now completely wet. Her head was flung back, her white, white neck exposed like a lost Greek column.

"Rosie, Rosie—" Her breathing was very slow, and her lips were not as pink as they usually were. Her eyelids fluttered.

"Closing time," she whispered. I believe that's what she said.

I sat with her, uncovering the bottle of Seconal[9] by her hand, and watched the stars fade.

When the stars were invisible and the sun was warming the air, I went back to the house. My mother was standing on the porch, wrapped in a blanket, watching me. Every step I took overwhelmed me; I could picture my mother slapping me, shooting me for letting her favorite die.

"Warrior queens," she said, wrapping her thin strong arms around me. "I raised warrior queens." She kissed me fiercely and went into the woods by herself.

Later in the morning she woke my father, who could not go into the woods, and still later she called the police and the funeral parlor. She hung up the phone, lay down, and didn't get back out of bed until the day of the funeral. My father fed us both and called the people who needed to be called and picked out Rose's coffin by himself.

My mother played the piano and Addie sang her pure gold notes and I closed my eyes and saw my sister, fourteen years old, lion's mane thrown back and eyes tightly closed against the glare of the parking lot lights. That sweet sound held us tight, flowing around us, eddying through our hearts, rising, still rising.

9. Trademark: secobarbital, a sedative drug.

# Jorge Luis Borges

*Borges (1899–1986) was born in Buenos Aires, Argentina, the descendant of middle-class intellectuals. After his education in Geneva and some years in Europe, where he associated with avant garde literary groups, he returned to Buenos Aires in 1921 and became the leader of a South American literary movement based on Surrealism and Imagism. In the early phases of his career, he wrote poetry for the most part, turning to prose as his varied intellectual interests came together to suggest new forms. A vastly erudite man, who directed the National Library until the dictator Perón removed him for political reasons, Borges built a "literature about literature"; his typically brief essays and short narratives are miniature encyclopedias of literary history, mingling gravity with absurdity in a constant exposure of the complexities of human awareness. Though he was blind and a partial invalid in his later years, he lectured and taught in the United States. His books available in English include* Labyrinths *(1962),* Ficciones *(1962),* Dreamtigers *(1964),* The Book of Imaginary Beings *(1969),* "The Aleph" and Other Stories *(1970),* Dr. Brodie's Report *(1972), and* The Book of Sand *(1979).*

## Pierre Menard, Author of the *Quixote*[1]

The *visible*[2] work left by this novelist is easily and briefly enumerated. Impardonable therefore, are the omissions and additions perpetrated by Madame Henri Bachelier in a fallacious catalogue which a certain daily, whose *Protestant* tendency is no secret, has had the inconsideration to inflict upon its deplorable readers—though these be few and Calvinist, if not Masonic and circumcised.[3] The true friends of Menard have viewed this catalogue with alarm and even with a certain melancholy. One might say that only yesterday we gathered before his final monument, amidst the lugubrious cypresses, and already Error tries to tarnish his Memory . . . Decidedly, a brief rectification is unavoidable.

I am aware that it is quite easy to challenge my slight authority. I hope,

1. Translated by James E. Irby. This story parodies a scholarly study. It comes complete with footnotes of its own, and these footnotes must be considered an integral part of the parody. So—to avoid confusion—Borges's footnotes are marked with symbols and printed above a ruled line at the bottom of each page. The editor's footnotes are printed below the line. The editor's footnotes are necessarily numerous because Borges's method is to mix an abundance of scholarly allusions to real personalities and literary works with names of fictitious authors and their fictitious works. 2. I.e., that which actually exists on paper. 3. I.e., those who are prejudiced by their Protestant, Free Thinking, or Jewish biases.

however, that I shall not be prohibited from mentioning two eminent testimonies. The Baroness de Bacourt (at whose unforgettable *vendredis*[4] I had the honor of meeting the lamented poet) has seen fit to approve the pages which follow. The Countess de Bagnoregio,[5] one of the most delicate spirits of the Principality of Monaco (and now of Pittsburgh, Pennsylvania, following her recent marriage to the international philanthropist Simon Kautzsch, who has been so inconsiderately slandered, alas! by the victims of his disinterested maneuvers) has sacrificed "to veracity and to death" (such were her words) the stately reserve which is her distinction, and, in an open letter published in the magazine *Luxe*,[6] concedes me her approval as well. These authorizations, I think, are not entirely insufficient.

I have said that Menard's visible work can be easily enumerated. Having examined with care his personal files, I find that they contain the following items:

a) A Symbolist sonnet which appeared twice (with variants) in the review *La conque*[7] (Issues of March and October 1899).

b) A monograph on the possibility of constructing a poetic vocabulary of concepts which would not be synonyms or periphrases of those which make up our everyday language, "but rather ideal objects created according to convention and essentially designed to satisfy poetic needs" (Nîmes,[8] 1901).

c) A monograph on "certain connections or affinities" between the thought of Descartes, Leibniz and John Wilkins[9] (Nîmes, 1903).

d) A monograph on Leibniz's *Characteristica universalis*[1] (Nîmes, 1904).

e) A technical article on the possibility of improving the game of chess, eliminating one of the rook's pawns. Menard proposes, recommends, discusses and finally rejects this innovation.

f) A monograph on Raymond Lully's *Ars magna generalis*[2] (Nîmes, 1906).

g) A translation, with prologue and notes, of Ruy López de Segura's *Libro de la invención liberal y arte del juego del axedrez*[3] (Paris, 1907).

h) The work sheets of a monograph on George Boole's[4] symbolic logic.

i) An examination of the essential metric laws of French prose, illustrated with examples taken from Saint-Simon (*Revue des langues romanes*, Montpellier, October 1909).[5]

j) A reply to Luc Durtain[6] (who had denied the existence of such laws), illustrated with examples from Luc Durtain (*Revue des langues romanes*, Montpellier, December 1909).

4. Regular Friday meetings devoted to a discussion of the arts. 5. Evidently a fictitious patroness of the arts. 6. Luxury. 7. Seashell. In the second half of the 19th century there arose in France what has come to be known as the Symbolist movement. The Symbolists sought to express or suggest ideas and emotions by means of symbols, as by the mention or introduction of things or the use of words and word sounds to convey a meaning, often with mystical or vague effects. 8. A city in southern France. 9. Bishop of Chester (1614–1672). René Descartes (1596–1650), French philosopher and mathematician. Gottfried Wilhelm Leibniz (1646–1716), German philosopher, mathematician, and theologian. 1. Universal characteristics, written in 1679. 2. The great art of the general, Lully (c. 1232–1315). 3. The book of liberal invention and the game of chess, published in 1561. 4. English mathematician, metaphysician, and author (1815–1864). 5. Review of romance languages, published in Montpellier, France. No article on the Duc de Saint-Simon (1675–1755) appears in the issue cited. 6. Durtain (b. 1881) does not appear in the issue cited.

k) A manuscript translation of the *Aguja de navegar cultos* of Quevedo, entitled *La boussole des précieux.*[7]

l) A preface to the Catalogue of an exposition of lithographs by Carolus Hourcade[8] (Nîmes, 1914).

m) The work *Les problèmes d'un problème*[9] (Paris, 1917) which discusses, in chronological order, the different solutions given to the illustrous problem of Achilles and the tortoise.[1] Two editions of this book have appeared so far; the second bears as an epigraph Leibniz's recommendation *"Ne craignez point, monsieur, la tortue"*[2] and revises the chapters dedicated to Russell[3] and Descartes.

n) A determined analysis of the "syntactical customs" of Toulet (N. R. F.,[4] March 1921). Menard—I recall—declared that censure and praise are sentimental operations which have nothing to do with literary criticism.

o) A transposition into alexandrines of Paul Valéry's *Le cimetière marin*[5] (N. R. F., January 1928).

p) An invective against Paul Valéry, in the *Papers for the Suppression of Reality* of Jacques Reboul.[6] (This invective, we might say parenthetically, is the exact opposite of his true opinion of Valéry. The latter understood it as such and their old friendship was not endangered.)

q) A "definition" of the Countess de Bagnoregio, in the "victorious volume"—the locution is Gabriele d'Annunzio's,[7] another of its collaborators—published annually by this lady to rectify the inevitable falsifications of journalists and to present "to the world and to Italy" an authentic image of her person, so often exposed (by very reason of her beauty and her activities) to erroneous or hasty interpretations.

r) A cycle of admirable sonnets for the Baroness de Bacourt (1934).

s) A manuscript list of verses which owe their efficacy to their punctuation.*

This, then, is the *visible* work of Menard, in chronological order (with no omission other than a few vague sonnets of circumstance written for the hospitable, or avid, album of Madame Henri Bachelier). I turn now to his other work: the subterranean, the interminably heroic, the peerless. And—such are

* Madame Henri Bachelier also lists a literal translation of Quevedo's literal translation of the *Introduction à la vie dévote* of St. Francis of Sales [*Introduction to the Devout Life* of St. Francis of Sales (1567–1622) Bishop and prince of Geneva]. There are no traces of such a work in Menard's library. It must have been a jest of our friend, misunderstood by the lady.

---

7. Both titles mean Guide to (or compass for) the Euphuists (or Aesthetes), by Vasco Mousinho Quevedo (d. 1628), Portuguese poet. 8. Unidentified, probably fictitious. 9. Problems of a problem. 1. The Eleatic school of philosophers, including most probably Zeno and Parmenides, flourished in Greece in the 5th century B.C.E It held that being is the only reality and that plurality, change, and motion are illusory. Among Zeno's arguments against motion, e.g., are these paradoxes: motion cannot begin because a body in motion cannot arrive at another place until it has passed through an unlimited number of places intermediate; Achilles cannot overtake a tortoise, because as often as he reaches the place occupied by the tortoise at some previous moment the tortoise has already left it; a flying arrow is at rest, for it is at every moment in only one place. 2. Don't fear, sir, the tortoise (French). 3. Bertrand Russell (1872–1970), English philosopher and mathematician. 4. *La Nouvelle revue Française* (New French review). Pierre-Jean Toulet (1867–1920), French poet. 5. The graveyard by the sea. Valéry (1871–1945), French poet. 6. Unidentified, probably fictitious. 7. Italian poet, novelist, and dramatist (1863–1938).

the capacities of man!—the unfinished. This work, perhaps the most significant of our time, consists of the ninth and thirty-eighth chapters of the first part of *Don Quixote*[8] and a fragment of chapter twenty-two. I know such an affirmation seems an absurdity; to justify this "absurdity" is the primordial object of this note.*

Two texts of unequal value inspired this undertaking. One is that philological fragment by Novalis[9]—the one numbered 2005 in the Dresden edition—which outlines the theme of a *total* identification with a given author. The other is one of those parasitic books which situate Christ on a boulevard, Hamlet on La Cannebière[1] or Don Quixote on Wall Street. Like all men of good taste, Menard abhorred these useless carnivals, fit only—as he would say—to produce the plebeian pleasure of anachronism or (what is worse) to enthrall us with the elementary idea that all epochs are the same or are different. More interesting, though contradictory and superficial of execution, seemed to him the famous plan of Daudet: to conjoin the Ingenious Gentleman and his squire in *one* figure, which was Tartarin[2] . . . Those who have insinuated that Menard dedicated his life to writing a contemporary *Quixote* calumniate his illustrious memory.

He did not want to compose another *Quixote*—which is easy—but *the Quixote itself.* Needless to say, he never contemplated a mechanical transcription of the original; he did not propose to copy it. His admirable intention was to produce a few pages which would coincide—word for word and line for line—with those of Miguel de Cervantes.

"My intent is no more than astonishing," he wrote me the 30th of September, 1934, from Bayonne. "The final term in a theological or metaphysical demonstration—the objective world, God, causality, the forms of the universe—is no less previous and common than my famed novel. The only difference is that the philosophers publish the intermediary stages of their labor in pleasant volumes and I have resolved to do away with those stages." In truth, not one worksheet remains to bear witness to his years of effort.

The first method he conceived was relatively simple. Know Spanish well, recover the Catholic faith, fight against the Moors or the Turk, forget the history of Europe between the years 1602 and 1918, *be* Miguel de Cervantes. Pierre Menard studied this procedure (I know he attained a fairly accurate command of seventeenth-century Spanish) but discarded it as too easy. Rather as impossible! my reader will say. Granted, but the undertaking was impossible from the very beginning and of all the impossible ways of carrying it out, this was the least interesting. To be, in the twentieth century, a popular novelist of the

* I also had the secondary intention of sketching a personal portrait of Pierre Menard. But how could I dare to compete with the golden pages which, I am told, the Baroness de Bacourt is preparing or with the delicate and punctual pencil of Carolus Hourcade?

8. Famous novel by Miguel de Cervantes (1547–1616). 9. Friedrich von (Hardenberg) Novalis (1772–1801), German poet and philosopher. 1. Street in Paris, an incongruous or absurd setting for Hamlet. 2. Chief character in *Tartarin de Tarascon* (1872) and *Tartarin sur les Alpes* (1885), novels by French writer Alphonse Daudet (1840–1897). "Ingenious Gentleman and his squire": a reference to Don Quixote and Sancho Panza in Cervantes' *Don Quixote*. Tartarin is, in Daudet's treatment, alternately practical—like Sancho Panza—and recklessly idealistic—like Don Quixote.

seventeenth seemed to him a diminution. To be, in some way, Cervantes and reach the *Quixote* seemed less arduous to him—and, consequently, less interesting—than to go on being Pierre Menard and reach the *Quixote* through the experiences of Pierre Menard. (This conviction, we might say in passing, made him omit the autobiographical prologue to the second part of *Don Quixote.* To include that prologue would have been to create another character—Cervantes—but it would also have meant presenting the *Quixote* in terms of that character and not of Menard. The latter, naturally, declined that facility.) "My undertaking is not difficult, essentially," I read in another part of his letter. "I should only have to be immortal to carry it out." Shall I confess that I often imagine he did finish it and that I read the *Quixote*—all of it—as if Menard had conceived it? Some nights past, while leafing through chapter XXVI—never essayed by him—I recognized our friend's style and something of his voice in this exceptional phrase: "the river nymphs and the dolorous and humid Echo."[3] This happy conjunction of a spiritual and a physical adjective brought to my mind a verse by Shakespeare which we discussed one afternoon:

> Where a malignant and a turbaned Turk[4] . . .

But why precisely the *Quixote?* our reader will ask. Such a preference, in a Spaniard, would not have been inexplicable; but it is, no doubt, in a Symbolist from Nîmes, essentially a dévoté of Poe, who engendered Baudelaire, who engendered Mallarmé, who engendered Valéry, who engendered Edmond Teste.[5] The aforementioned letter illuminates this point. "The *Quixote,*" clarifies Menard, "interests me deeply, but it does not seem—how shall I say it?—inevitable. I cannot imagine the universe without Edgar Allan Poe's exclamation:

> Ah, bear in mind this garden was enchanted![6]

or without the *Bateau ivre* or the *Ancient Mariner,*[7] but I am quite capable of imagining it without the *Quixote.* (I speak, naturally, of my personal capacity and not of those works' historical resonance.) The *Quixote* is a contingent book; the *Quixote* is unnecessary. I can premeditate writing it, I can write it, without falling into a tautology. When I was ten or twelve years old, I read it, perhaps in its entirety. Later, I have reread closely certain chapters, those which I shall not attempt for the time being. I have also gone through the interludes, the plays, the *Galatea,* the exemplary novels, the undoubtedly laborious tribulations

3. In Greek mythology Hera (Juno), the wife and sister of Zeus, condemned the nymph Echo to never use her tongue again except to repeat what was said to her. 4. Shakespeare's *Othello* 5.2. 5. A fictional character in *Monsieur Teste,* a novel by Valéry. Edgar Allan Poe (1809–1849), American poet and short-story writer. Charles Baudelaire (1821–1867) and Stéphane Mallarmé (1842–1898), French poets. The names in this sequence are said to engender their successors in the sense that they influenced them and, by their work, provided points for new departures. That the sequence ends with a fictional personage, Monsieur Teste, suggests that both Borges and Pierre Menard—his fictional creation—have been "engendered" by the same ancestors. 6. From one of Poe's two poems titled *To Helen.* This, the lesser known one, is dedicated to Mrs. Sarah Helen Whitman. 7. *The Rime of the Ancient Mariner* by the English poet Samuel Taylor Coleridge (1772–1834). *Bateau ivre* (The drunken boat), by Arthur Rimbaud (1854–1891), a Belgian poet. Both poems and both poets are important forerunners of the literary mode that Menard practices.

of Persiles and Segismunda and the *Viaje del Parnaso*[8] . . . My general recollection of the *Quixote,* simplified by forgetfulness and indifference, can well equal the imprecise and prior image of a book not yet written. Once that image (which no one can legitimately deny me) is postulated, it is certain that my problem is a good bit more difficult than Cervantes' was. My obliging predecessor did not refuse the collaboration of chance: he composed his immortal work somewhat *à la diable,*[9] carried along by the inertias of language and invention. I have taken on the mysterious duty of reconstructing literally his spontaneous work. My solitary game is governed by two polar laws. The first permits me to essay variations of a formal or psychological type; the second obliges me to sacrifice these variations to the 'original' text and reason out this annihilation in an irrefutable manner . . . To these artificial hindrances, another—of a congenital kind—must be added. To compose the *Quixote* at the beginning of the seventeenth century was a reasonable undertaking, necessary and perhaps even unavoidable; at the beginning of the twentieth, it is almost impossible. It is not in vain that three hundred years have gone by, filled with exceedingly complex events. Amongst them, to mention only one, is the *Quixote* itself."

In spite of these three obstacles, Menard's fragmentary *Quixote* is more subtle than Cervantes'. The latter, in a clumsy fashion, opposes to the fictions of chivalry the tawdry provincial reality of his country; Menard selects as his "reality" the land of Carmen during the century of Lepanto and Lope de Vega.[1] What a series of *espagnolades* that selection would have suggested to Maurice Barrès or Dr. Rodríguez Larreta![2] Menard eludes them with complete naturalness. In his work there are no gypsy flourishes or conquistadors or mystics or Philip the Seconds or *autos da fé.*[3] He neglects or eliminates local color. This disdain points to a new conception of the historical novel. This disdain condemns *Salammbô,*[4] with no possibility of appeal.

It is no less astounding to consider isolated chapters. For example, let us examine Chapter XXXVIII of the first part, "which treats of the curious discourse of Don Quixote on arms and letters." It is well known that Don Quixote (like Quevedo in an analogous and later passage in *La hora de todos*[5]) decided the debate against letters and in favor of arms. Cervantes was a former soldier: his verdict is understandable. But that Pierre Menard's Don Quixote—a contemporary of *La trahison des clercs*[6] and Bertrand Russell—should fall prey to such nebulous sophistries! Madame Bachelier has seen here an admirable and typical subordination on the part of the author to the hero's psychology; others

8. Voyage to Parnassus. *Galatea* is a poem of Cervantes, first published in 1914. Other allusions in the line are to Cervantes' works. 9. Like the devil (French), i.e., with inspired haste. 1. The Battle of Lepanto, in which a largely Spanish fleet destroyed the Turkish naval power, was fought in 1571. Thus both references are to the century in which Cervantes lived. Carmen is the Gypsy heroine of a novel by Prosper Merimée (1803–1870), French writer. The novel was made into an immensely popular opera by the composer Georges Bizet (1838–1875). 2. Unidentified and possibly fictitious. *"Espagnolades"* a French term for a literary work heavily saturated with the local color of Spain. Barrès (1862–1923), French novelist. 3. Executions by fire of heretics condemned by the Inquisition. Philip the Second (1527–1598) was a Spanish king, sponsor of the Spanish Inquisition and leader of the Counter Reformation, a movement in opposition to the Protestant Reformation. 4. A colorful and detailed historical novel by French writer Gustave Flaubert (1821–1880). 5. *La hora de todos y la fortuna con seso:* everyone's hour (or time) and the wit of fortune (Spanish, literal trans.), roughly equivalent to "every dog has his day by the irony of fortune." 6. The treason of the intellectuals, by Julien Benda (1867–1956), French essayist who in this book attacks European intellectuals for allowing their talents to be exploited for nationalist political ends.

(not at all perspicaciously), a *transcription* of the *Quixote;* the Baroness de Bacourt, the influence of Nietzsche.[7] To this third interpretation (which I judge to be irrefutable) I am not sure I dare to add a fourth, which concords very well with the almost divine modesty of Pierre Menard: his resigned or ironical habit of propagating ideas which were the strict reverse of those he preferred. (Let us recall once more his diatribe against Paul Valéry in Jacques Reboul's ephemeral Surrealist sheet.) Cervantes' text and Menard's are verbally identical, but the second is almost infinitely richer. (More ambiguous, his detractors will say, but ambiguity is richness.)

It is a revelation to compare Menard's *Don Quixote* with Cervantes'. The latter, for example, wrote (part one, chapter nine):

> . . . truth, whose mother is history, rival of time, depository of deeds, witness of the past, exemplar and adviser to the present, and the future's counselor.

Written in the seventeenth century, written by the "lay genius" Cervantes, this enumeration is a mere rhetorical praise of history. Menard, on the other hand, writes:

> . . . truth, whose mother is history, rival of time, depository of deeds, witness of the past, exemplar and adviser to the present, and the future's counselor.

History, the *mother* of truth: the idea is astounding. Menard, a contemporary of William James,[8] does not define history as an inquiry into reality but as its origin. Historical truth, for him, is not what has happened; it is what we judge to have happened. The final phrases—*exemplar and adviser to the present, and the future's counselor*—are brazenly pragmatic.

The contrast in style is also vivid. The archaic style of Menard—quite foreign, after all—suffers from a certain affectation. Not so that of his forerunner, who handles with ease the current Spanish of his time.

There is no exercise of the intellect which is not, in the final analysis, useless. A philosophical doctrine begins as a plausible description of the universe; with the passage of the years it becomes a mere chapter—if not a paragraph or a name—in the history of philosophy. In literature, this eventual caducity is even more notorious. The *Quixote*—Menard told me—was, above all, an entertaining book; now it is the occasion for patriotic toasts, grammatical insolence and obscene de luxe editions. Fame is a form of incomprehension, perhaps the worst.

There is nothing new in these nihilistic verifications; what is singular is the determination Menard derived from them. He decided to anticipate the vanity awaiting all man's efforts; he set himself to an undertaking which was exceedingly complex and, from the very beginning, futile. He dedicated his scruples and his sleepless nights to repeating an already extant book in an alien tongue. He multiplied draft upon draft, revised tenaciously and tore up thousands of

7. Friedrich Nietzsche (1844–1900), German philosopher. The allusion is probably to his idea of "eternal recurrence"—a belief that everything that happens will happen again and again within the frame of eternity, as Menard's *Quixote* recurs after that of Cervantes. 8. American pragmatist philosopher (1842–1910).

manuscript pages.* He did not let anyone examine these drafts and took care they should not survive him. In vain have I tried to reconstruct them.

I have reflected that it is permissible to see in this "final" *Quixote* a kind of palimpsest,[9] through which the traces—tenuous but not indecipherable—of our friend's "previous" writing should be translucently visible. Unfortunately, only a second Pierre Menard, inverting the other's work, would be able to exhume and revive those lost Troys[1] . . .

"Thinking, analyzing, inventing (he also wrote me) are not anomalous acts; they are the normal respiration of the intelligence. To glorify the occasional performance of that function, to hoard ancient and alien thoughts, to recall with incredulous stupor that the *doctor universalis*[2] thought, is to confess our laziness or our barbarity. Every man should be capable of all ideas and I understand that in the future this will be the case."

Menard (perhaps without wanting to) has enriched, by means of a new technique, the halting and rudimentary art of reading: this new technique is that of the deliberate anachronism and the erroneous attribution. This technique, whose applications are infinite, prompts us to go through the *Odyssey* as if it were posterior to the *Aeneid*[3] and the book *Le jardin du Centaure*[4] of Madame Henri Bachelier as if it were by Madame Henri Bachelier. This technique fills the most placid works with adventure. To attribute the *Imitatio Christi* to Louis Ferdinand Céline or to James Joyce,[5] is this not a sufficient renovation of its tenuous spiritual indications?

*For Silvina Ocampo*

* I remember his quadricular notebooks, his black crossed-out passages, his peculiar typographical symbols and his insect-like handwriting. In the afternoons he liked to go out for a walk around the outskirts of Nîmes; he would take a notebook with him and make a merry bonfire.

---

9. A parchment document from which writing has been partially erased to make room for another text. Frequently fragments of the original text are inadvertently combined with the new additions. 1. Troy, which was destroyed by the Greeks in the Trojan War, has become a conventional symbol of lost cultures. 2. The universal doctor or savant; a term sometimes applied to the philosophers Aristotle and Thomas Aquinas. 3. Homer's epic poem *The Odyssey* dates from the 7th or 8th century B.C.E, while Virgil's *Aeneid* was written in the 1st century B.C.E Borges is playing with anachronism. 4. The centaur's garden, obviously a fictitious work by a fictitious author. 5. Céline (pen name for Ferdinand Destouches) (1894–1961) and Joyce (1882–1941) are 20th-century writers. *Imitatio Christi* was written by Thomas à Kempis (1380–1471). More anachronism.

# Ray Bradbury

*Bradbury (1920– ) was born in Waukegan, Illinois. After attending high school in Los Angeles, he joined a little-theater group there and by 1941 had begun to publish the stories that would make him one of the stars among science fiction writers. His concern about the multitude of threats to the imagination in the modern world has led him occasionally to the social criticism that particularly distinguishes his novel* Fahrenheit 451 *(1953) and to serious expositions of the threat inherent in expansionist technology. His other novels include* Something Wicked This Way Comes *(1962),* The Halloween Tree *(1972), and* Driving Blind *(1997). He has written plays and screenplays—including the one for* Moby-Dick *(1954). Among his numerous books of short stories are* The Martian Chronicles *(1950),* The Golden Apples of the Sun *(1953),* Dandelion Wine *(1957),* I Sing the Body Electric! *(1969), and* The Stories of Ray Bradbury *(1980). He has also published a book of poetry:* When Elephants Last in the Dooryard Bloomed *(1972).*

## The Veldt

"George, I wish you'd look at the nursery."

"What's wrong with it?"

"I don't know."

"Well, then."

"I just want you to look at it, is all, or call a psychologist in to look at it."

"What would a psychologist want with a nursery?"

"You know very well what he'd want." His wife paused in the middle of the kitchen and watched the stove busy humming to itself, making supper for four.

"It's just that the nursery is different now than it was."

"All right, let's have a look."

They walked down the hall of their soundproofed, Happylife Home, which had cost them thirty thousand dollars installed, this house which clothed and fed and rocked them to sleep and played and sang and was good to them. Their approach sensitized a switch somewhere and the nursery light flicked on when they came within ten feet of it. Similarly, behind them, in the halls, lights went on and off as they left them behind, with a soft automaticity.

"Well," said George Hadley.

They stood on the thatched floor of the nursery. It was forty feet across by forty feet long and thirty feet high; it had cost half again as much as the rest of the house. "But nothing's too good for our children," George had said.

The nursery was silent. It was empty as a jungle glade at hot high noon. The walls were blank and two dimensional. Now, as George and Lydia Hadley stood in the center of the room, the walls began to purr and recede into crystalline distance, it seemed, and presently an African veldt appeared, in three dimensions; on all sides, in colors reproduced to the final pebble and bit of straw. The ceiling above them became a deep sky with a hot yellow sun.

George Hadley felt the perspiration start on his brow.

"Let's get out of the sun," he said. "This is a little too real. But I don't see anything wrong."

"Wait a moment, you'll see," said his wife.

Now the hidden odorophonics were beginning to blow a wind of odor at the two people in the middle of the baked veldtland. The hot straw smell of lion grass, the cool green smell of the hidden water hole, the great rusty smell of animals, the smell of dust like a red paprika in the hot air. And now the sounds: the thump of distant antelope feet on grassy sod, the papery rustling of vultures. A shadow passed through the sky. The shadow flickered on George Hadley's upturned, sweating face.

"Filthy creatures," he heard his wife say.

"The vultures."

"You see, there are the lions, far over, that way. Now they're on their way to the water hole. They've just been eating," said Lydia. "I don't know what."

"Some animal." Georger Hadley put his hand up to shield off the burning light from his squinted eyes. "A zebra or a baby giraffe, maybe."

"Are you sure?" His wife sounded peculiarly tense.

"No, it's a little late to be sure," he said, amused. "Nothing over there I can see but cleaned bone, and the vultures dropping for what's left."

"Did you hear that scream?" she asked.

"No."

"About a minute ago?"

"Sorry, no."

The lions were coming. And again George Hadley was filled with admiration for the mechanical genius who had conceived this room. A miracle of efficiency selling for an absurdly low price. Every home should have one. Oh, occasionally they frightened you with their clinical accuracy, they startled you, gave you a twinge, but most of the time what fun for everyone, not only your own son and daughter, but for yourself when you felt like a quick jaunt to a foreign land, a quick change of scenery. Well, here it was!

And here were the lions now, fifteen feet away, so real, so feverishly and startlingly real that you could feel the prickling fur on your hand, and your mouth was stuffed with the dusty upholstery smell of their heated pelts, and the yellow of them was in your eyes like the yellow of an exquisite French tapestry, the yellows of lions and summer grass, and the sound of the matted lion lungs exhaling on the silent noontide, and the smell of meat from the panting, dripping mouths.

The lions stood looking at George and Lydia Hadley with terrible green-yellow eyes.

"Watch out!" screamed Lydia.

The lions came running at them.

Lydia bolted and ran. Instinctively, George sprang after her. Outside, in the hall, with the door slammed, he was laughing and she was crying, and they both stood appalled at the other's reaction.

"George!"

"Lydia! Oh, my dear poor sweet Lydia!"

"They almost got us!"

"Walls, Lydia, remember; crystal walls, that's all they are. Oh, they look real, I must admit—Africa in your parlor—but it's all dimensional superreactionary, supersensitive color film and mental tape film behind glass screens. It's all odorophonics and sonics, Lydia. Here's my handkerchief."

"I'm afraid." She came to him and put her body against him and cried steadily. "Did you see? Did you *feel*? It's too real."

"Now, Lydia . . ."

"You've got to tell Wendy and Peter not to read any more on Africa."

"Of course—of course." He patted her.

"Promise?"

"Sure."

"And lock the nursery for a few days until I get my nerves settled."

"You know how difficult Peter is about that. When I punished him a month ago by locking the nursery for even a few hours—the tantrum he threw! And Wendy too. They *live* for the nursery."

"It's got to be locked, that's all there is to it."

"All right." Reluctantly he locked the huge door. "You've been working too hard. You need a rest."

"I don't know—I don't know," she said, blowing her nose, sitting down in a chair that immediately began to rock and comfort her. "Maybe I don't have enough to do. Maybe I have time to think too much. Why don't we shut the whole house off for a few days and take a vacation?"

"You mean you want to fry my eggs for me?"

"Yes." She nodded.

"And darn my socks?"

"Yes." A frantic, watery-eyed nodding.

"And sweep the house?"

"Yes, yes—oh, yes!"

"But I thought that's why we bought this house, so we wouldn't have to do anything?"

"That's just it. I feel like I don't belong here. The house is wife and mother now and nursemaid. Can I compete with an African veldt? Can I give a bath and scrub the children as efficiently or quickly as the automatic scrub bath can? I can not. And it isn't just me. It's you. You've been awfully nervous lately."

"I suppose I have been smoking too much."

"You look as if you didn't know what to do with yourself in this house, either. You smoke a little more every morning and drink a little more every afternoon and need a little more sedative every night. You're beginning to feel unnecessary too."

"Am I?" He paused and tried to feel into himself to see what was really there.

"Oh, George!" She looked beyond him, at the nursery door. "Those lions can't get out of there, can they?"

He looked at the door and saw it tremble as if something had jumped against it from the other side.

"Of course not," he said.

At dinner they ate alone, for Wendy and Peter were at a special plastic carnival across town and had televised home to say they'd be late, to go ahead eating. So George Hadley, bemused, sat watching the dining-room table produce warm dishes of food from its mechanical interior.

"We forgot the ketchup," he said.

"Sorry," said a small voice within the table, and ketchup appeared.

As for the nursery, thought George Hadley, it won't hurt for the children to be locked out of it awhile. Too much of anything isn't good for anyone. And it was clearly indicated that the children had been spending a little too much time on Africa. That sun. He could feel it on his neck, still, like a hot paw. And the lions. And the smell of blood. Remarkable how the nursery caught the telepathic emanations of the children's minds and created life to fill their every desire. The children thought lions, and there were lions. The children thought zebras, and there were zebras. Sun—sun. Giraffes—giraffes. Death and death.

That last. He chewed tastelessly on the meat that the table had cut for him. Death thoughts. They were awfully young, Wendy and Peter, for death thoughts. Or, no, you were never too young, really. Long before you knew what death was you were wishing it on someone else. When you were two years old you were shooting people with cap pistols.

But this—the long, hot African veldt—the awful death in the jaws of a lion. And repeated again and again.

"Where are you going?"

He didn't answer Lydia. Preoccupied, he let the lights glow softly on ahead of him, extinguished behind him as he padded to the nursery door. He listened against it. Far away, a lion roared.

He unlocked the door and opened it. Just before he stepped inside, he heard a faraway scream. And then another roar from the lions, which subsided quickly.

He stepped into Africa. How many times in the last year had he opened this door and found Wonderland, Alice, the Mock Turtle, or Aladdin and his Magical Lamp, or Jack Pumpkinhead of Oz, or Dr. Doolittle, or the cow jumping over a very real-appearing moon[1]—all the delightful contraptions of a make-believe world. How often had he seen Pegasus[2] flying in the sky ceiling, or seen fountains of red fireworks, or heard angel voices singing. But now, this yellow hot Africa, this bake oven with murder in the heat. Perhaps Lydia was right. Perhaps they needed a little vacation from the fantasy which was growing a bit

1. Characters and places from famous children's stories and nursery rhymes. 2. In Greek mythology, the flying horse.

too real for ten-year-old children. It was all right to exercise one's mind with gymnastic fantasies, but when the lively child mind settled on *one* pattern . . . ? It seemed that, at a distance, for the past month, he had heard lions roaring, and smelled their strong odor seeping as far away as his study door. But, being busy, he had paid it no attention.

George Hadley stood on the African grassland alone. The lions looked up from their feeding, watching him. The only flaw to the illusion was the open door through which he could see his wife, far down the dark hall, like a framed picture, eating her dinner abstractedly.

"Go away," he said to the lions.

They did not go.

He knew the principle of the room exactly. You sent out your thoughts. Whatever you thought would appear.

"Let's have Aladdin and his lamp," he snapped.

The veldtland remained; the lions remained.

"Come on, room! I demand Aladdin!" he said.

Nothing happened. The lions mumbled in their baked pelts.

"Aladdin!"

He went back to dinner. "The fool room's out of order," he said. "It won't respond."

"Or——"

"Or what?"

"Or it *can't* respond," said Lydia, "because the children have thought about Africa and lions and killing so many days that the room's in a rut."

"Could be."

"Or Peter's set it to remain that way."

"*Set* it?"

"He may have got into the machinery and fixed something."

"Peter doesn't know machinery."

"He's a wise one for ten. That I.Q. of his——"

"Nevertheless——"

"Hello, Mom. Hello, Dad."

The Hadleys turned. Wendy and Peter were coming in the front door, cheeks like peppermint candy, eyes like bright blue agate marbles, a smell of ozone on their jumpers from their trip in the helicopter.

"You're just in time for supper," said both parents.

"We're full of strawberry ice cream and hot dogs," said the children, holding hands. "But we'll sit and watch."

"Yes, come tell us about the nursery," said George Hadley.

The brother and sister blinked at him and then at each other. "Nursery?"

"All about Africa and everything," said the father with false joviality.

"I don't understand," said Peter.

"Your mother and I were just traveling through Africa with rod and reel; Tom Swift[3] and his Electric Lion," said George Hadley.

3. The hero of a series of adventure novels for boys by Victor Appleton (pseudonym).

"There's no Africa in the nursery," said Peter simply.

"Oh, come now, Peter. We know better."

"I don't remember any Africa," said Peter to Wendy. "Do you?"

"No."

"Run see and come tell."

She obeyed.

"Wendy, come back here!" said George Hadley, but she was gone. The house lights followed her like a flock of fireflies. Too late, he realized he had forgotten to lock the nursery door after his last inspection.

"Wendy'll look and come tell us," said Peter.

"She doesn't have to tell *me.* I've seen it."

"I'm sure you're mistaken, Father."

"I'm not, Peter. Come along now."

But Wendy was back. "It's not Africa," she said breathlessly.

"We'll see about this," said George Hadley, and they all walked down the hall together and opened the nursery door.

There was a green, lovely forest, a lovely river, a purple mountain, high voices singing, and Rima,[4] lovely and mysterious, lurking in the trees with colorful flights of butterflies, like animated bouquets, lingering on her long hair. The African veldtland was gone. The lions were gone. Only Rima was here now, singing a song so beautiful that it brought tears to your eyes.

George Hadley looked in at the changed scene. "Go to bed," he said to the children.

They opened their mouths.

"You heard me," he said.

They went off to the air closet, where a wind sucked them like brown leaves up the flue to their slumber rooms.

George Hadley walked through the singing glade and picked up something that lay in the corner near where the lions had been. He walked slowly back to his wife.

"What is that?" she asked.

"An old wallet of mine," he said.

He showed it to her. The smell of hot grass was on it and the smell of a lion. There were drops of saliva on it, it had been chewed, and there were blood smears on both sides.

He closed the nursery door and locked it, tight.

In the middle of the night he was still awake and he knew his wife was awake. "Do you think Wendy changed it?" she said at last, in the dark room.

"Of course."

"Made it from a veldt into a forest and put Rima there instead of lions?"

"Yes."

"Why?"

"I don't know. But it's staying locked until I find out."

"How did your wallet get there?"

4. Heroine in *Green Mansions* by W. H. Hudson (1841–1922).

"I don't know anything," he said, "except that I'm beginning to be sorry we bought that room for the children. If children are neurotic at all, a room like that——"

"It's supposed to help them work off their neuroses in a healthful way."

"I'm starting to wonder." He stared at the ceiling.

"We've given the children everything they ever wanted. Is this our reward—secrecy, disobedience?"

"Who was it said, 'Children are carpets, they should be stepped on occasionally'? We've never lifted a hand. They're insufferable—let's admit it. They come and go when they like; they treat us as if *we* were offspring. They're spoiled and we're spoiled."

"They've been acting funny ever since you forbade them to take the rocket to New York a few months ago."

"They're not old enough to do that alone, I explained."

"Nevertheless, I've noticed they've been decidedly cool toward us since."

"I think I'll have David McClean come tomorrow morning to have a look at Africa."

"But it's not Africa now, it's Green Mansions country and Rima."

"I have a feeling it'll be Africa again before then."

A moment later they heard the screams.

Two screams. Two people screaming from downstairs. And then a roar of lions.

"Wendy and Peter aren't in their rooms," said his wife.

He lay in his bed with his beating heart. "No," he said. "They've broken into the nursery."

"Those screams—they sound familiar."

"Do they?"

"Yes, awfully."

And although their beds tried very hard, the two adults couldn't be rocked to sleep for another hour. A smell of cats was in the night air.

"Father?" said Peter.

"Yes."

Peter looked at his shoes. He never looked at his father any more, nor at his mother. "You aren't going to lock up the nursery for good, are you?"

"That all depends."

"On what?" snapped Peter.

"On you and your sister. If you intersperse this Africa with a little variety—oh, Sweden perhaps, or Denmark or China——"

"I thought we were free to play as we wished."

"You are, within reasonable bounds."

"What's wrong with Africa, Father?"

"Oh, so now you admit you have been conjuring up Africa, do you?"

"I wouldn't want the nursery locked up," said Peter coldly. "Ever."

"Matter of fact, we're thinking of turning the whole house off for about a month. Live sort of a carefree one-for-all existence."

"That sounds dreadful! Would I have to tie my own shoes instead of letting the shoe tier do it? And brush my own teeth and comb my hair and give myself a bath?"

"It would be fun for a change, don't you think?"

"No, it would be horrid. I didn't like it when you took out the picture painter last month."

"That's because I wanted you to learn to paint all by yourself, son."

"I don't want to do anything but look and listen and smell; what else *is* there to do?"

"All right, go play in Africa."

"Will you shut off the house sometime soon?"

"We're considering it."

"I don't think you'd better consider it any more, Father."

"I won't have any threats from my son!"

"Very well." And Peter strolled off to the nursery.

"Am I on time?" said David McClean.

"Breakfast?" asked George Hadley.

"Thanks, had some. What's the trouble?"

"David, you're a psychologist."

"I should hope so."

"Well, then, have a look at our nursery. You saw it a year ago when you dropped by; did you notice anything peculiar about it then?"

"Can't say I did; the usual violences, a tendency toward a slight paranoia here or there, usual in children because they feel persecuted by parents constantly, but, oh, really nothing."

They walked down the hall. "I locked the nursery up," explained the father, "and the children broke back into it during the night. I let them stay so they could form the patterns for you to see."

There was a terrible screaming from the nursery.

"There it is," said George Hadley. "See what you make of it."

They walked in on the children without rapping.

The screams had faded. The lions were feeding.

"Run outside a moment, children," said George Hadley. "No, don't change the mental combination. Leave the walls as they are. Get!"

With the children gone, the two men stood studying the lions clustered at a distance, eating with great relish whatever it was they had caught.

"I wish I knew what it was," said George Hadley. "Sometimes I can almost see. Do you think if I brought high-powered binoculars here and——"

David McClean laughed dryly. "Hardly." He turned to study all four walls. "How long has this been going on?"

"A little over a month."

"It certainly doesn't *feel* good."

"I want facts, not feelings."

"My dear George, a psychologist never saw a fact in his life. He only hears about feelings; vague things. This doesn't feel good, I tell you. Trust my hunches and my instincts. I have a nose for something bad. This is very bad. My advice to you is to have the whole damn room torn down and your children brought to me every day during the next year for treatment."

"Is it that bad?"

"I'm afraid so. One of the original uses of these nurseries was so that we could study the patterns left on the walls by the child's mind, study at our leisure, and help the child. In this case, however, the room has become a channel toward—destructive thoughts, instead of a release away from them."

"Didn't you sense this before?"

"I sensed only that you had spoiled your children more than most. And now you're letting them down in some way. What way?"

"I wouldn't let them go to New York."

"What else?"

"I've taken a few machines from the house and threatened them, a month ago, with closing up the nursery unless they did their homework. I did close it for a few days to show I meant business."

"Ah, ha!"

"Does that mean anything?"

"Everything. Where before they had a Santa Claus now they have a Scrooge. Children prefer Santas. You've let this room and this house replace you and your wife in your children's affections. This room is their mother and father, far more important in their lives than their real parents. And now you come along and want to shut it off. No wonder there's hatred here. You can feel it coming out of the sky. Feel that sun. George, you'll have to change your life. Like too many others, you've built it around creature comforts. Why, you'd starve tomorrow if something went wrong in your kitchen. You wouldn't know how to tap an egg. Nevertheless, turn everything off. Start new. It'll take time. But we'll make good children out of bad in a year, wait and see."

"But won't the shock be too much for the children, shutting the room up abruptly, for good?"

"I don't want them going any deeper into this, that's all."

The lions were finished with their red feast.

The lions were standing on the edge of the clearing watching the two men.

"Now *I'm* feeling persecuted," said McClean. "Let's get out of here. I never have cared for these damned rooms. Make me nervous."

"The lions look real, don't they?" said George Hadley. "I don't suppose there's any way——"

"What?"

"—that they could *become* real?"

"Not that I know."

"Some flaw in the machinery, a tampering or someting?"

"No."

They went to the door.

"I don't imagine the room will like being turned off," said the father.

"Nothing ever likes to die—even a room."

"I wonder if it hates me for wanting to switch it off?"

"Paranoia is thick around here today," said David McClean. "You can follow it like a spoor. Hello." He bent and picked up a bloody scarf. "This yours?"

"No." George Hadley's face was rigid. "It belongs to Lydia."

They went to the fuse box together and threw the switch that killed the nursery.

The two children were in hysterics. They screamed and pranced and threw things. They yelled and sobbed and swore and jumped at the furniture.

"You can't do that to the nursery, you can't!"

"Now, children."

The children flung themselves onto a couch, weeping.

"George," said Lydia Hadley, "turn on the nursery, just for a few moments. You can't be so abrupt."

"No."

"You can't be so cruel."

"Lydia, it's off, and it stays off. And the whole damn house dies as of here and now. The more I see of the mess we've put ourselves in, the more it sickens me. We've been contemplating our mechanical, electronic navels for too long. My God, how we need a breath of honest air!"

And he marched about the house turning off the voice clocks, the stoves, the heaters, the shoe shiners, the shoe lacers, the body scrubbers and swabbers and massagers, and every other machine he could put his hand to.

The house was full of dead bodies, it seemed. It felt like a mechanical cemetery. So silent. None of the humming hidden energy of machines waiting to function at the tap of a button.

"Don't let them do it!" wailed Peter at the ceiling, as if he was talking to the house, the nursery. "Don't let Father kill everything." He turned to his father. "Oh, I hate you!"

"Insults won't get you anywhere."

"I wish you were dead!"

"We were, for a long while. Now we're going to really start living. Instead of being handled and massaged, we're going to *live*."

Wendy was still crying and Peter joined her again. "Just a moment, just one moment, just another moment of nursery," they wailed.

"Oh, George," said the wife, "it can't hurt."

"All right—all right, if they'll only just shut up. One minute, mind you, and then off forever."

"Daddy, Daddy, Daddy!" sang the children, smiling with wet faces.

"And then we're going on a vacation. David McClean is coming back in half an hour to help us move out and get to the airport. I'm going to dress. You turn the nursery on for a minute, Lydia, just a minute, mind you."

And the three of them went babbling off while he let himself be vacuumed upstairs through the air flue and set about dressing himself. A minute later Lydia appeared.

"I'll be glad when we get away," she sighed.

"Did you leave them in the nursery?"

"I wanted to dress too. Oh, that horrid Africa. What can they see in it?"

"Well, in five minutes we'll be on our way to Iowa. Lord, how did we ever get in this house? What prompted us to buy a nightmare?"

"Pride, money, foolishness."

"I think we'd better get downstairs before those kids get engrossed with those damned beasts again."

Just then they heard the children calling, "Daddy, Mommy, come quick—quick!"

They went downstairs in the air flue and ran down the hall. The children were nowhere in sight. "Wendy? Peter!"

They ran into the nursery. The veldtland was empty save for the lions waiting, looking at them. "Peter, Wendy?"

The door slammed.

"Wendy, Peter!"

George Hadley and his wife whirled and ran back to the door.

"Open the door!" cried George Hadley, trying the knob. "Why, they've locked it from the outside! Peter!" He beat at the door. "Open up!"

He heard Peter's voice outside, against the door.

"Don't let them switch off the nursery and the house," he was saying.

Mr. and Mrs. George Hadley beat at the door. "Now, don't be ridiculous, children. It's time to go. Mr. McClean'll be here in a minute and . . . "

And then they heard the sounds.

The lions on three sides of them, in the yellow veldt grass, padding through the dry straw, rumbling and roaring in their throats.

The lions.

Mr. Hadley looked at his wife and they turned and looked back at the beasts edging slowly forward, crouching, tails stiff.

Mr. and Mrs. Hadley screamed.

And suddenly they realized why those other screams had sounded familiar.

"Well, here I am," said David McClean in the nursery doorway. "Oh, hello." He stared at the two children seated in the center of the open glade eating a little picnic lunch. Beyond them was the water hole and the yellow veldtland; above was the hot sun. He began to perspire. "Where are your father and mother?"

The children looked up and smiled. "Oh, they'll be here directly."

"Good, we must get going." At a distance Mr. McClean saw the lions fighting and clawing and then quieting down to feed in silence under the shady trees.

He squinted at the lions with his hand up to his eyes.

Now the lions were done feeding. They moved to the water hole to drink.

A shadow flickered over Mr. McClean's hot face. Many shadows flickered. The vultures were dropping down the blazing sky.

"A cup of tea?" asked Wendy in the silence.

# Kate Braverman

*Braverman (1950– ) was born in Los Angeles. She was educated at the University of California at Berkeley. Among her publications are the novels* Palm Latitudes *(1988) and* Wonders of the West *(1993) and the short-story collections* Squandering the Blue *(1990) and* Small Craft Warnings *(1998). Her stories have been published in* Best American Stories (1991, 1995) *and the* O'Henry Prize Stories *(1992).*

## Pagan Night

Sometimes they called him Forest or Sky. Sometimes they called him River or Wind. Once, during a week of storms when she could not leave the van at all, not for seven consecutive days, they called him Gray. The baby with the floating name and how she carries him and he keeps crying, has one rash after another, coughs, seems to shudder and choke. It is a baby of spasms, of a twisted face turning colors. You wouldn't want to put his picture on the baby-food jar. You wouldn't want to carry his picture in your wallet, even if you had his photograph and she doesn't.

Of course, Dalton never wanted this baby. Neither did she. The baby was just something that happened and there didn't seem to be the time to make it not happen. They were on tour, two months of one-nighters between San Diego and Seattle and when it was over the band broke up. When it was over, they got drunk and sold the keyboards and video cameras for heroin. Then they were in San Francisco and she still had the apartment. Later, they had Dalton's van.

Then they had to leave San Francisco. Something about the equipment, the amplifiers Dalton insisted were his, that they had accrued to him by a process of decision and sacrifice. Then they had to wind through California with her belly already showing and all they had left were their black leather jackets and the silver-and-turquoise jewelry they had somehow acquired in Gallup or Flagstaff. Dalton kept talking about the drummer's kit, which he claimed was actually his, and they sold it in Reno and lived on the fortieth floor of an old hotel with a view of the mountains. They had room service for three weeks and by then she had stopped throwing up. After that there was more of Nevada and the van broke again on the other side of the state. There was the slow entry into Idaho, after mountains and desert and Utah and the snow had melted and then the baby they had almost forgotten about was born.

Dalton can't stand the baby crying. That's why she leaves the van, walks three miles into town along the river. When she has a dollar-fifty, she buys an espresso in the café where the waitress has heard of her band.

Sunny stays away from the van as long as she can. Sometimes someone will offer her a ride to the park or the zoo or the shopping mall and she takes it. She's let her hair grow out, the purple and magenta streaks are nearly gone, seem an accident that could have happened to anyone, a mislabeled bottle, perhaps. Dalton says it's better to blend in. He's cut his hair, too, and wears a San Diego Padres baseball cap. He says it makes him feel closer to God.

Willow. Cottonwood. Creek. Eagle. She could call the baby Willow. But Dalton refuses to give it a name. He resists the gender, refers to the baby as it, not he. Just it, the creature that makes the noise. But it doesn't cost any money. She still feeds it from her body and the rashes come and go. It's because she doesn't have enough diapers. Sunny puts suntan lotion on the baby's sores, massage oil, whatever is left in her suitcase from the other life. Once she covered the baby's rash with layers of fluorescent orange lipstick, the last of her stage makeup.

Sunny has begun to realize that if she can't keep the baby quiet, Dalton will leave her. It won't always be summer here. There will come a season when she can't just walk all day, or sit in the mall or the lobby of the granite city hall, pretending to read a newspaper. She won't be able to spend the entire winter in the basement of the museum where they have built a replica of the town as it was in the beginning, with its penny-candy store and nickel barber shop and baths for a quarter. She won't be able to spend five or six months attempting to transport herself through time telepathically. She could work in the saloon, find an Indian to watch the baby. Later she could marry the sheriff.

Today, walking by the river, it occurred to Sunny that this landscape was different from any other she had known. It wasn't the punched-awake, intoxicated glow of the tropics, seductive and inflamed. It didn't tease you and make you want to die for it. That's what she thought of Hawaii. And it wasn't the rancid gleam like spoiled lemons that coated everything in a sort of bad childhood waxy veneer flashback. That's what she thought of Los Angeles where they had lived for two years. In Los Angeles, afternoon smelled of ash and some enormous August you could not placate or forget. Los Angeles air reminded her of what happened to children in foster homes at dusk when they took their clothes off, things that were done in stucco added-on garages with ropes and pieces of metal and the freeway rushing in the background like a cheap sound track. It was in sync, but it had no meaning.

This Idaho was an entirely separate area of the spectrum. There was something unstable about it, as if it had risen from a core of some vast, failed caution. It was the end of restlessness. It was what happened when you stopped looking over your shoulder. It was what happened when you dared to catch your breath, when you thought you were safe.

Sunny feels there is some mean streak to this still raw, still frontier, place. This land knows it gets cold, winter stays too long, crops rot, you starve. This land knows about wind, how after storms the clouds continue to assemble every afternoon over the plain, gather and recombine and rain again and this can go on for weeks. Her shoes are always damp. Her feet are encased in white blisters. Always, the thunderheads are congregating and mating and their spawn is a cold rain.

Somedays the clouds are in remission, ringing the plain but staying low. On such afternoons, the three of them go down to the Snake River. They follow a dirt road to another dirt road and they've been instructed where to turn, near the hit-by-lightning willow. They park on a rise above the channel. Dalton leaves his guitar in the van and padlocks it, walks ahead of her and the baby with the fishing pole over his shoulder. They walk beneath black branches, find the path of smooth rocks down to the bank leading to a railroad bridge. It's a trestle over the Snake made from railroad ties with gaps between them and the tracks running down the center. This is how they cross the Snake, reach the other bank where the fishing is supposed to be good. There are tiny grassy islands Dalton can roll up his black jeans and wade out to. Dalton traded somebody in town for a fly-fishing rod. He probably traded drugs for the rod, though she realizes she hasn't seen her black leather jacket for more than a week.

On Sundays yellow with orioles[1] and tiger monarchs[2] and a sun that turns the grasses soft, Dalton takes them fishing on the far bank of the river. One late afternoon he caught four trout. Sunny could see their rainbows when the sun struck their skin. They looked sewed with red sequins. They were supposed to be sixteen inches. That was the rule for the South Fork of the Snake. Their trout were smaller, seven and eight inches, but they kept them anyway, cooked them on a stick over a fire they made near the van. Dalton said the eyes were the best part and he gave her one and it was white as a pried-open moon and she ate it.

Now she is walking into a yellow that makes her feel both restless and invigorated. A yellow of simultaneity and symbols and some arcane celebration she can vaguely sense. When she ate the trout eyes, they were like crisp white stones. She thought of rituals, primitive people, the fundamental meaning of blood. If one mastered these elements, it might be possible to see better in the dark. She shakes her head as if to clear it, but nothing changes. Her entire life is a network of intuitions, the beginning of words, like neon and dome, pine, topaz, shadow, but then the baby starts crying.

Sunny knows it's all a matter of practice, even silence and erasure and absence. What it isn't is also a matter of practice. In the same way you can take piano or voice and train yourself to recognize and exploit your range, you can also teach yourself not to speak, not to remember. That's why when Dalton asks what's she thinking, she says, "Nothing." It's a kind of discipline. What she's really thinking about is what will happen when summer is over. What will happen if she can't make the baby stop crying?

Sometimes when she is frightened, it calms her to think about Marilyn Monroe. Sunny knows all about Marilyn's childhood, the foster homes, the uncles who fondled her breasts, kissed her seven-year-old nipples, and they got hard. Then Marilyn knew she was a bad girl. She would always be a bad girl.

1. Yellow songbirds with black wings and tail. 2. Large orange butterflies with black and white markings.

It was like being at a carnival, a private carnival, just for her. There were balloons and streamers, party hats and birthday cakes with chocolate frosting and her name written in a neon pink. And no one could tell her no. She had liked to think about Marilyn Monroe when they were driving in the van between gigs. The band was in its final incarnation then. Sunny was already pregnant and it was called Pagan Night.

When Dalton asks her what she's thinking and she says, "Nothing," she is really imagining winter and how she is certain there won't be enough to eat. Dalton says he'll shoot a cow. There are cows grazing outside of town, off half the dirt roads and along the banks of the river. Or he'll shoot a deer, an elk, he'll trap rabbits. He's been talking to people in town, at the Rio Bar. He's traded something for the fly-fishing rig, but he still has both guns and the rifle. He'll never trade the weapons, not even for heroin, even if they could find any here.

Today, on this cool morning, Sunny has walked from the river to the zoo. Admission is one dollar, but the woman in the booth knows her and has started to simply wave her in.

Sunny passes through a gate near a willow and she would like to name the baby Willow. It would be an omen and it would survive winter. Then she is entering the zoo, holding her baby without a name. She sits with her baby near the swan pond until someone gives her a quarter, a sandwich, a freshly purchased bag of popcorn. They simply hand it to her.

She has memorized each animal, bird, and fish in this miniature zoo. The birds stand by mossy waterfalls of the sort she imagines adorn the swimming pools of movie stars. She sits nursing her baby that she is pretending is named Willow. If anyone asks, and she knows no one will, she is prepared to say, His name is Willow.

Later, she stands in a patch of sun by an exhibit featuring a glassed-in bluish pool that should contain a penguin or a seal, but is empty. It smells derelict, harsh and sour with something like the residue of trapped wind and the final thoughts of small mammals as they chew off their feet and bleed to death. You can walk down a flight of stairs and look through the glass, but nothing is swimming. She knows. She has climbed down twice.

Sunny likes to look at what isn't there, in the caged water whipped by sun. This is actually the grotto that is most full, with its battered streams of light like hieroglyphics, a language in flux, lost in shifting ripples.

She pauses in front of the golden eagle. It will not look at her, even when she whistles. The information stenciled to the cage says the golden eagle can live thirty years, longer than many movie stars, longer than Hendrix and Janis and Jim Morrison and James Dean. This particular bird will probably outlive her.

Sunny is thinking about how hungry she is, when someone offers her half a peanut butter and jelly sandwich. Actually, the woman has her child do this, reach out a baby arm to her as if she is now some declawed beast you could let your kid near.

Her own baby is wrapped in a shawl, the same shawl she had once laid across the sofa in the living room of her apartment in San Francisco. She had gone there to study modern dancing, tap, and ballet. Her father had wanted her to go to nursing school. If she went to nursing school, her father could believe she had finally forgotten. He could conclude that she was well and whole, and he could sleep without pills. His ulcer would disappear. He could take communion again.

Sunny took singing lessons and began to meet men with rock 'n' roll bands. Nursing school became white and distant. It became a sort of moon you could put between your teeth and swallow. She stopped envisioning herself in a starched cotton uniform with a stethoscope around her neck. What she wanted now was to smoke grass and hash and opium and stare out the window at Alcatraz. What she wanted to do was sniff powder drawn in lines across a wide square of mirror she kept on the side of the sofa, like a sort of magic screen where you could watch your face change forever.

Now, at the zoo, she stands on the wood slats surrounding the fish pond filled with keepers, twenty- and twenty-five- and thirty-inch rainbow trout. This is what keepers look like. On yellow Sundays, she and Dalton and the baby walk across the railroad trestle over the Snake River. But Dalton will never catch a fish this big.

She was afraid the first time they crossed the bridge. Dalton had to grab her hand. He hadn't touched her body since the baby was born. He had to pull her along. The bridge was higher than she had thought. The river was rushing underneath like a sequence of waves, but faster and sharper, without breath or cycles, and she was holding the baby. That day she was secretly calling the baby Sunday. And she was cradling Sunday with one arm and Dalton was holding her other hand, pulling her through the yellow. He was also holding the fishing rod he'd somehow procured at the Rio Bar, traded somebody something for, she is beginning to think it was her black leather jacket with the studs on the cuffs, the special studs sewed on by a woman who claimed she was a gypsy in Portland.

Dalton must think she won't need her leather jacket in winter. He isn't considering what she'll need in winter. Maybe they won't still be in Idaho. Maybe they won't still be together. And the bridge was wider than she had at first imagined. It was like a pier with its set of two railroad tracks down the center, one thinner, the other fatter, one unused set covered with rust. The bridge was made from railroad ties and there were gaps between them where a foot could get caught, something small could fall through. Dalton said, "Make a pattern. Step every other one. Don't look down." That's what she did, stepped every other one, didn't look down, but still she could hear the river in a kind of anguish beneath her and she was shaking.

"It's an abandoned bridge, isn't it?" she asked Dalton.

The first few times he said yes, but when they had crossed the fourth time, he said no. She stopped, found herself staring into sun. "What do you mean?" she demanded.

"Look at the rails. The larger set are clean. Trains do this." He pointed at the tracks. "Or they'd be covered with rust."

"What if the train came now? As we were crossing?" she finally asked.

"There are beams every twenty feet." Dalton pointed to a kind of metal girder. "We'd hang on the side until it passed."

She tries to imagine herself standing on the girder, holding the baby which in her mind is named Sunday in one of her arms. She cannot conceive of this. Instead she remembers, suddenly, a story Dalton once told her years ago, before they had gone on the road, when they first recited their secret information to each other, their collection of shame, where they were truly from, what had happened, what was irrevocable.

Dalton told her about a night in high school when he had been drinking beer with his friends. Perhaps it was spring. They had been drinking since dawn and now it was after midnight. It was Ohio. That's where Dalton was from. His friends had wandered down to the train station. His best friend had tried to hop a train. Johnny Mohawk. That's what they called him, Mohawk, because he said he was part Indian. Johnny Mohawk tried to hop a train and fell. It ran over him, amputating both legs, his right arm, and half of his left.

"He was so drunk, that's what saved him," Dalton explained. It must have been later. They were riding in a tour bus. They had an album out and the company had given them a roadie, a driver, and a bus. Outside was neon and wind and houses you didn't want to live in. "He was so drunk, he didn't feel it," Dalton was saying. "If he'd been more awake, the shock would have killed him."

Dalton glanced out the window, at some in-between stretch of California where there were waist-high grasses and wild flowers and a sense of too much sun, even in the darkness. She asked him what happened. She tried to imagine Johnny Mohawk, but she could not. Her mind refused to accommodate the brutal lack of symmetry, would produce only words like tunnel and agony, suffocate and scream. Even if she had gone to nursing school, even if she went right now, enrolled in the morning, she could do nothing about Johnny Mohawk. It would always be too late.

"It was the best thing ever happened to him," Dalton said. "He was on his way to becoming a professional drunk. Like his father, like his uncles and inbred cousins. After the accident, he got a scholarship to State. They gave him a tutor and a special car. Now he's an engineer for an oil company."

Sunny thinks about Johnny Mohawk as she stands in the zoo, in front of a grotto with grassy sides and a sleeping male and female lion. Their cage seems too small to contain them if they wanted to do anything other than sleep in the damp green grass. She wonders what would happen if she fell in, over the low metal bar.

Near her, a pregnant woman with three blond daughters, each with a different colored ribbon in their long yellow hair, tells her two-year-old, "Don't you climb up on that bar now. You fall in, there'd be no way to get you out. That hungry old lion would eat you right up."

Sunny feels the baby in her arms, how heavy it is, how it could so easily slide from her, through the bar, into the grassy grotto. She could never retrieve it. No one would expect her to.

Then she is walking past the one zebra. When Dalton asks her if she wants to talk about anything, she shakes her head, no. She is considering how filled each no is, glittering and yellow. Each no is a miniature carnival, with curled smiles and balloons on strings and a profusion of names for babies. And in this no are syllables like willow and cottonwood and shadow and Johnny Mohawk. And in this no is the railroad trestle above one hundred thousand rainbow trout.

Sunny's favorite exhibit is the snow leopard. It is strange that a zoo in a tiny town should have such an animal. They are so rare. She reads what the snow leopard eats, mammals and birds. Its social life is solitary. How long does it live? Twenty-five years. Not quite long enough to see its first record go platinum. And it isn't really asleep on the green slope behind its grid of bars as much as it is simply turned away. Perhaps it is thinking about the past, and on its lip is something that isn't quite a smile. Or perhaps he is simply listening to birds.

There are always birds when they cross the railroad trestle on Sunday, the Snake below them, the bald eagles and blue herons and swallows and robins, orioles and magpies, in the air near their shoulders. And there is no schedule for the train. She's called Union Pacific five times, waited for the man in charge to come back from vacation, to come back from the flu, to be at his desk, and there is no way to predict when the train runs over this particular trestle. It's a local. It gets put together at the last moment, no one knows when.

When they cross the bridge on Sunday, she is obsessively listening for trains. And there are so many birds, fat robins, unbelievably red, and orioles, the yellow of chalk from fourth grade when she got an A and her teacher let her write the entire spelling list for the week on the blackboard. And ducks and Canadian geese and loons, all of them stringing their syllables across the afternoon, hanging them near her face like a kind of party streamer. The baby is named Sunday or Sometimes and she feels how heavy it is, how it could just drop from her arms.

It's become obvious that these fishing Sundays are not about catching trout. It's a practice for something else entirely, for leaving, for erasure, silence, and absence. She understands now. It's the end of July. She won't be able to feed the baby from her body indefinitely or walk through town all day, looking for trash cans where she can deposit the diapers she has used over and over again.

Now it is time to rehearse. They are involved in a new show with an agenda they don't mention. It's a rehearsal for abandoning the baby. She practices leaving it on the bank, walking fifty steps away, smoking a cigarette. Then she rushes back to retrieve it, to press it against her. If she simply took a slightly longer path from the bank, permitted herself to smoke a joint, a third or fourth cigarette, she might not remember exactly where she placed the baby, not with all the foliage, the vines and brush, bushes and trees, the whole bank an ache of greenery. Something could have interceded, a sudden aberration in the river current or perhaps a hawk. She wouldn't be blamed.

In the children's petting zoo, a gray rabbit mounts a white one. Another white rabbit eats from a bowl. They eat and mate, eat and mate. In the winter, Dalton says he'll shoot a deer. He's made a deal with somebody at the Rio Bar, something about sharing and storing. There are always cattle, fish, rabbits, beavers, and otters that can be trapped.

During the day, Dalton says he's working on songs. He still has both guitars. He can only write music when the baby isn't crying or coughing. She wants to name the baby Music or Tears. Once she tells Dalton she wants to name the baby Bay. She remembers the apartment they had with the view of the bridge, the way at midnight the wind felt like a scalded blue. It was when everything seemed simultaneously anesthetized and hot. It was a moment she remembers as happy.

"It's not time to name it," Dalton said. He was strumming his twelve-string. He said many African tribes didn't name a baby until it had survived a year. Dalton looked at her and smiled. His lips reminded her of Marilyn Monroe.

That's when she realized each day would have to be distinct and etched. She licks the baby's face. She sits on a bench in the sun at the zoo by a pond with a mossy waterfall in the center. There are swans in this pond. She closes her eyes and smells the baby and decides to name him Swan. She kisses his cheek and whispers in his ear, "Your name is Swan. Your name is Moss. Your name is Bye-Bye."

"What are you thinking?" Dalton asks. It was during the storm two weeks ago. He was drinking tequila. Rain struck the van and she thought of rocks and bullets and time travel.

"Nothing," she replied.

Wind. Hidden networks. The agenda that sparks. You know how night feels without candles, without light bulbs, maps, schedules. This is what we do not speak of Bye-bye-bye, baby. Bye-bye-bye.

Everyday, Dalton says he's going to write songs while she is gone. He has a joint in his mouth, curled on his side in the back of the van on a ridge above the Snake River where they now live. He has a bottle of vodka tucked into his belt. The vodka is gone when she comes back. Sunny has to knock again and again on the side of the van, has to kick it with her foot, has to shout his name, until he wakes up.

Each day must be separate, an entity, like a species, a snow leopard, a zebra, or a rainbow trout. Each one with a distinct evolution and morphology, niches, complex accidents. Last Sunday, she smoked a joint and drank tequila. Then they crossed the river on the railroad ties. She has a pattern, left foot, skip one with the right, left foot, skip one with the right, don't look down.

She knows it will happen on a Sunday, perhaps next Sunday. Dalton will say, "Come over, look at this."

"I can't. I'm feeding the baby," she will answer.

"Put it down a second," he'll say. "You've got to see this."

She'll place the baby in the center of soft weeds. She'll follow the sound of his voice, find Dalton on the bank with a great trout, twenty inches, thirty inches long. It will be their keeper and she will bend down, help him pull it in. Her feet will get wet. She will use her hat for a net, her red hat that says Wyoming Centennial 1990. The seconds will elongate, the minutes will spread into an afternoon, with no one counting or keeping track. When they've pulled the trout in, when they've finished the tequila, it will be dark. They will begin searching for the baby, but there will be only shadow. No one could say they were at fault. No one could say anything. No one knows about them or the baby, and the van has got at least five thousand miles left in it. They could be in New York or Florida in two days.

Perhaps it will be a Sunday when they are crossing the bridge. She'll be holding the baby named Sometimes or Swan or Willow, and they'll have to leap onto the steel girders as the train rushes by. The baby will drop from her arms into the Snake and it will be taken on the current like Moses.

They will never mention the falling. They will not speak of it, not once. It will just be something caught in the edge of their smile, like a private carnival that went through town and maybe you saw it once and too briefly and then it was gone.

She knows Dalton believes they are purer, more muscle and bone, closer to an archetypal winter beyond artifice. That was part of why they called the band Pagan Night. They are animals, barbarians, heathens. They are savage and recognize this, its possibilities and what it costs. In China and India, girl children are often drowned at birth. There are fashions of surviving famines engraved on the nerves.

Maybe this Sunday they will be crossing the bridge when the train erupts from a spoil of foliage and shadow, willows and heron and orioles. Dalton will have left his guitar in the van, padlocked with his paperback myths of primitive people. Perhaps it will be a Sunday after Dalton returned from the Rio Bar with heroin. They will have cooked it up and had it that night, all night, and the next day, all day, until it was finished and there was nothing left, not even in the cotton in the spoon.

When she stands on the Sunday railroad trestle, she will think about ineluctable trajectories. There is a destiny to the direction and journey of all objects, stars and birds, babies and stones and rivers. Who can explain how or why that snow leopard came from Asia to reside in an obsolete grotto in a marginal farming town among barley and potato fields in southern Idaho? What shaped such a voyage, what miscalculations, what shift of wind or currents, what failure of which deity?

Sunny knows exactly what she will be thinking when it happens. There are always acres of sun and their fading. It is all a sequence of erasures and absences. Who is to say flesh into water or flesh into rock is not a form of perfection? What of Moses on the river with an ineluctable destiny to be plucked from reeds by a princess? Perhaps on some fishing Sunday when the baby is named Swallow or Tiger and falls from her arms, someone on a distant bank will look up and say they saw the sudden ascension of a god.

# Ivan Bunin

*Bunin (1870–1953) was born in Voronezh, Russia. While working as a journalist and clerk Bunin wrote and translated poetry; his first volume of verse was published in 1891. For his translations of H. W. Longfellow's* Hiawatha *he was awarded a Pushkin Prize in 1903 by the Russian Academy, which later elected him as honorary fellow (1909). In 1921 he wrote (with Gorky and Kuprin)* Reminiscences of Anton Chekhov. *He also wrote a book about Tolstoy. Bunin knew both writers personally.* The Gentleman from San Francisco *was first published in English in 1922. A later edition appeared in 1975. His selected poems were published in 1978. His last book of stories,* Dark Avenues, *was published in 1943. He was the first Russian to win a Nobel Prize in Literature, in 1933. He received it for "the strict artistry with which he has carried on the classical Russian tradition in prose."*

## The Gentleman from San Francisco

Alas, alas, that great city
Babylon, that mighty city!
For in one hour is thy
judgement come.
—*Apocalypse*

The gentleman from San Francisco—nobody in either Naples or Capri could remember his name—was on his way to the Old World with his wife and daughter, there to spend two whole years devoted entirely to pleasure.

He was firmly convinced that he was entitled to a rest, to pleasure, to a voyage, splendid in every respect. He had his own reasons for being so firmly convinced; first, he was a wealthy man, and second, he was only beginning to live, although he was already fifty-eight. Until then he had not lived, he had merely existed, not badly at all it must be said, but nevertheless it was nothing but existence, for he had centred all his hopes on the days to come. He had worked without a breathing spell—the Chinese, whom he imported in thousands to work for him, well knew what that meant! And at last he saw that he had achieved a great deal, that he had almost come up to the level of those he had once set up as an example to himself; and then he decided to take a holiday. It was a custom with the class of men to which he belonged to start off with a trip to Europe, India and Egypt when they were ready to enjoy life. He decided to do the same. Naturally, his chief concern was to reward himself for his years of toil; however, he was glad for the sake of his wife and daughter, too. His wife was never known to be particularly impressionable, but then all middle-aged American women are passionate travellers. And as for his daughter, a girl no longer young and rather sickly, the trip was an outright necessity for her. To say nothing of the good it would do her health, what of those happy friendships known to have been made on board ship? You sometimes actually find yourself sitting next to a multi-millionaire at dinner or studying frescoes together in the lounge.

The route planned by the gentleman from San Francisco was an extensive one. During the months of December and January he was hoping to bask in the sun of southern Italy, to enjoy the ancient sights, the tarantella,[1] the serenades of the wandering singers, and something that men of his age appreciate with a peculiar subtlety—the love of young Neapolitan girls, even if it isn't entirely disinterested. He proposed to spend Carnival week in Nice and Monte Carlo, where the most select society foregathers at that time—where some plunge excitedly into automobile and yacht races or into roulette, others into what is customarily known as "light flirtation," and still others into shooting pigeons which, released from their cotes, soar beautifully over the emerald-green lawns, against the background of the forget-me-not sea, and instantly drop on the ground like little white balls. He wanted to devote the first part of March to Florence and arrive in Rome for Passion Week in order to hear the *Miserere*[2] sung there. His plans included Venice and Paris, bullfighting in Seville, bathing in the British Isles, then Athens, Constantinople, Palestine, Egypt, and even Japan—on the way back of course . . . And everything began splendidly.

It was the end of November. Icy fogs and slushy snow-storms accompanied them all the way to Gibraltar, but they sailed on quite safely. There were many passengers on board. The famous *Atlantis* was like a huge hotel with so many facilities—an all-night bar, Turkish baths, a newspaper of its own, and life on board ran a rather smooth course. They got up early, roused by the bugles blaring shrilly in the corridors in that dusky hour of the morning when day was just breaking so slowly and glumly over the grey-green expanse of the sea, rolling heavily in the fog; they put on their flannel pyjamas and had coffee, chocolate or cocoa; after that they had their baths, did their morning exercises to work up a good appetite and a feeling of fitness, dressed and went in to breakfast; until eleven they were supposed to walk briskly up and down the deck, breathing in the cool freshness of the ocean, or to play shuffle-board and other games in order to work up their appetites anew, and at eleven they fortified themselves with sandwiches and beef tea; thus fortified, they read the ship's newspaper with relish and calmly awaited lunch, which was even more

1. A rapid whirling dance of southern Italy. 2. Have pity (Latin); Psalm 51 (or 50 in the Douay Bible), a prayer of appeal for mercy.

nourishing with a greater variety of dishes than breakfast; the next two hours were devoted to rest: deck chairs were then ranged along all the decks, and the passengers lay back in them, wrapped in rugs, gazing at the cloudy sky and the frothy waves through the railing, or falling into a sweet doze; between the hours of four and five, refreshed and cheered, they were served strong, fragrant tea and biscuits; at seven, the bugles signalled the approach of the moment that formed the main purpose of this existence, its crowning glory. And, roused by the bugles, the gentleman from San Francisco, rubbing his hands in an access of life and vigour, hurried to his sumptuous cabin de luxe to dress for dinner.

At night the *Atlantis* seemed to gape into the darkness with countless blazing eyes, while a great number of servants worked busily in the kitchens, sculleries and wine cellars below. The ocean, heaving beyond the walls, was awesome, but no one thought about it, firmly believing it to be in the hands of the Captain, a red-haired man of monstrous size and corpulence, who always looked sleepy and resembled an enormous idol in his black coat trimmed with gold braid, and who very seldom emerged from his secret chambers to be among the passengers. In the forecastle the siren kept wailing with infernal gloom or squealing in frantic fury, but not many of the diners heard the siren, for it was drowned out by the splendid string orchestra, playing exquisitely and indefatigably in the two-storeyed marble dining-room, festively flooded with lights, filled with ladies in low-cut evening-gowns and gentlemen in tail-coats or dinner-jackets, with slender waiters, deferential maîtres d'hôtel, and a wine waiter who wore a chain around his neck like a lord mayor. The dinner-coat and starched shirt made the gentleman from San Francisco look very much younger than he was. Lean and not tall, ungainly in build but well-knit, he sat in the pearly-golden halo of this room with a bottle of wine in front of him, an array of glasses of the finest crystal, and a vase with curly hyacinths. His yellowish face with the neatly trimmed silver moustache had something Mongolian in it, gold fillings gleamed in his large teeth, and his strong bald skull shone like old ivory. His wife, a large, broad and serene woman, was dressed expensively but befitting her age; the daughter—tall and slim, with beautiful hair charmingly done, her breath sweetened with violet cachous, and with the faintest of little pink pimples, around her lips and between her shoulder-blades slightly dusted over with powder wore a gown that was elaborate but light and transparent, innocently frank . . . The dinner went on for over an hour, and after that there was dancing in the ballroom, during which the men—the gentleman from San Francisco among them of course—sprawled in arm-chairs with their feet up, smoking themselves red in the face with Havana cigars and filling themselves with liqueurs in the bar attended by red-coated Negroes with eyeballs that looked like shelled hard-boiled eggs. The ocean roared and heaved in black mountains on the other side of the wall, the storm whistled through the sodden, heavy rigging, the ship shuddered and shook as it struggled through the storm and the black mountains, cutting like a plough through their rippling mass which kept swirling into a froth and flinging high its foamy tails. The siren, suffocating in the fog, wailed in mortal agony; the watch up in the crow's-nest froze in the cold, their minds reeling from the unbearable strain on their attention, and the ship's belly below the water-line was like the abyss of hell at its most sinister and sultry, its last ninth circle—the belly in which the giant furnaces roared with laughter as, with their blazing maws, they devoured ton after ton of coal, flung down them with a clatter by men drenched in pungent sweat, dirty, half-naked and purple in the glow of the flames; while up here in the bar, legs were flung carelessly over the arms of chairs, brandy and liqueurs were sipped at leisure, clouds of aromatic smoke hung in the air, and in the ballroom all was brilliance, radiating light, warmth and joy; couples whirled in a waltz or swayed in a tango, and the music, insistently and with a sadness that was voluptuous and shameless, sang its plea, always that one plea . . . Among this brilliant crowd of people there was a certain well-known millionaire, a lanky, clean-shaven man in an old-fashioned dress-coat, there was a famous Spanish author, a world-celebrated beauty, and an elegant pair of lovers watched by all with curiosity, who made no secret of their happiness, for he danced with no one but her, and all this was so exquisitely and charmingly performed that no one but the Captain knew that the couple was hired by Lloyds to play at love for a good wage, and had been sailing on the company's ships for a long time.

Everyone was glad of the sun in Gibraltar, it seemed like early spring. A new passenger appeared on board the *Atlantis*, instantly drawing everyone's attention to himself. He was the crown prince of a certain kingdom in Asia, travelling incognito; a small man, perfectly wooden, broad-faced and narrow-eyed, wearing gold-rimmed spectacles, slightly unpleasant because the coarse black hairs of his moustache were stringy like a corpse's, but a nice, simple and unpresumptuous man on the whole. In the Mediterranean there was once again a breath of winter; the sea billowed in high varicoloured waves like a peacock's tail, blown by the tramontane which came rushing towards the ship madly and merrily in the brilliant light of a perfectly clear day. And then, on the second day, the sky began to pale, the horizon was wrapped in mist: land was nearing, now there was a glimpse of Ischia and Capri, now if you looked through your binoculars you could see the lumps of sugar strewn at the foot of something dusky-blue, Naples. Many of the ladies and gentlemen had already put on their light fur coats; the meek Chinese "boys," who never spoke above a whisper, bow-legged youngsters with pitch-black plaits hanging down to their heels, with thick maidenly eyelashes, were quietly carrying rugs, canes, suitcases and dressing-cases towards the companion-way. The daughter of the gentleman from San Francisco stood on deck next to the prince, introduced to her the night before by a happy chance, and pretended she was following his pointed finger into the distance as he explained something to her hastily and softly; he was so short he looked like a little boy beside the others, seeming quite unprepossessing and odd—with his spectacles, bowler hat and English overcoat, the horsehair coarseness of his stringy moustache, the thin olive skin stretched tight across his flat face which might have been thinly coated with varnish—but the girl stood listening to him and she was so excited that she could not understand a word he was saying; her heart was beating fast, strangely enraptured; everything, every single thing about him was different from everyone else—his slim hands, his clear skin, beneath which coursed the blood of ancient kings, his very clothes—European and quite plain, but somehow exceptionally neat—held an extraordinary fascination for her. And meanwhile, the gentleman from

San Francisco himself, wearing grey spats over his patent-leather shoes, kept glancing at the famous beauty who stood beside him, a tall blonde with a marvellous figure and eyes painted in the latest Parisian fashion, who was talking to a tiny, humpbacked hairless dog which she held on a thin silver chain. And the daughter, feeling vaguely discomfited, tried to take no notice of the father.

He was rather generous when travelling and therefore quite sincerely believed in the solicitude of all those who fed and waited on him from morning till night forestalling his slightest wish, who safeguarded his peace and kept him immaculate, who summoned porters for him and delivered his trunks to hotels. It had been like this everywhere, it had been so on board ship, it had to be so in Naples. The city grew larger and nearer; the ship's band, with brass instruments flashing in the sun, was already crowded on deck and suddenly burst into a deafening and triumphant march; the gigantic Captain appeared on the bridge in his dress uniform and, like a gracious heathen god, waved to the passengers with an affable gesture. When at last the *Atlantis* entered harbour and its many-storeyed bulk, with people clustering at the rails, tied up to the pier and the chains of the gang-planks clattered—countless hotel porters and their assistants in gold-braided caps, all sorts of commissionaires, whistling urchins and hefty beggars with stacks of coloured postcards in their hands, rushed forward offering their services. And the gentleman from San Francisco smiled at these beggars as he walked to the car of the hotel where the prince might also be putting up, and calmly spoke through his teeth first in English, then in Italian:

"Go away! Via!"

Life in Naples instantly took on a clock-work regularity: in the morning there was breakfast in the gloomy dining-room, an overcast sky that held little promise, and a crowd of guides at the lobby doors; then came the first smiles of the warm rosy sun, a view from the high hanging balcony of Mount Vesuvius cloaked entirely in the shimmering vapours of dawn, of the pearly-silver ripples on the bay and the delicate outlines of Capri on the horizon, of tiny donkeys harnessed into dogcarts, tripping along the muddy quay below, and detachments of toy soldiers marching somewhere to the sounds of vigorous and challenging music. After that came the slow drive through the thronged, narrow and damp corridors of streets, between tall, many-windowed houses, visits to the funereally stark and clean museums, lighted evenly and pleasantly but with a snow-like bleakness, or to the churches, cold and smelling of wax, where the same thing was repeated over and over again: a stately entrance hung with a heavy leather curtain, and inside a vast emptiness and silence, the soft lights of the seven-branched candelabrum flickering redly in the depths upon the altar draped in lace, a solitary old woman among the dark wooden pews, slippery gravestones underfoot, and on the wall a *Deposition*[3]—invariably famous. At one, there was lunch on the hill at San Martino, where quite a number of the very first-class people gathered towards noon, and where on one occasion the daughter of the gentleman from San Francisco had nearly fainted: she thought she saw the prince sitting in the room, whereas the newspapers said he was in

3. A work of art depicting Christ being lowered from the Cross.

Rome. At five, tea was served at the hotel in the beautiful drawing-room which was so warm with its thick carpeting and blazing fires; and before long, it was time to dress for dinner, once again the gong boomed sonorously and masterfully through the whole building, once again the stream of ladies in low-cut gowns, rustling down the stairs in their silks, were reflected in the mirrored walls, once again the doors of the palatial dining-room were flung open, the musicians in their red jackets were on their platform, the black crowd of waiters were round the maître d'hôtel who deftly ladled out the creamy pink soup into plates. The dinners were so rich in food, wine and mineral waters, in sweets and fruit, that by eleven o'clock the maids were required to bring hot-water bottles to all the rooms for the guests to warm their stomachs with.

December, however, was not a very good month that year; when one talked to the porters about the weather they merely raised their shoulders guiltily and muttered that as far as they could remember, there had never been a winter like this, although it wasn't the first year they were obliged to mutter this and blame it on the fact that "something awful was happening all over the world." On the Riviera it stormed and rained as never before, in Athens there was snow, Etna, too, was covered with snow and cast a glow at night; and as for Palermo, the tourists were simply running away from the cold, helter-skelter . . . The early-morning sun deceived them every day. At noon, the sky invariably turned grey and fine rain began to fall, becoming colder and harder as the day wore on; and then the palm-trees at the hotel entrance shone with a metallic sheen, the town appeared particularly dirty and cramped, the museums too monotonous, the cigar ends, thrown by the fat cabmen whose rubber capes flapped in the wind like wings, unbearably foul, the vigorous cracks of their whips over the heads of their skinny-necked hacks too obvious a sham, the boots of the men sweeping the tramway lines too awful, and the women, splashing through the mud in the rain with their black heads uncovered, disgustingly short-legged; as for the dampness and the stench of rotting fish coming from the frothing water's edge, the least said about it the better. The gentleman and the lady from San Francisco began to quarrel in the mornings now; their daughter either had a headache and went about looking wan and pale, or all at once she brightened up, was enthusiastic and keen on everything, and then she was both sweet and beautiful; beautiful were the tender and complex feelings awakened in her by the ugly man with the unusual blood coursing through his veins, for after all, what awakens a girl's heart—whether it is wealth, fame, or an illustrious name—is not really of great consequence. Everyone assured them that it was quite different in Sorrento and Capri—there, it was warmer and sunnier, lemon-trees were in bloom, the people more virtuous and the wine better. And so the family from San Francisco decided to proceed to Capri, taking all their trunks along, with the intention of settling down in Sorrento after they had gone all over Capri, had trod the stones where once the palaces of Tiberius[4] stood, visited the fabulous caves of the Azure Grotto, and listened to the Abruzzian bagpipers, who, during the month before Christmas, roamed the island singing praises to the Virgin Mary.

4 Roman emperor (14 B.C.E.–C.E 37).

On the day of departure—a very memorable day for the family from San Francisco—even the usual early morning sun was missing. A heavy fog completely hid Vesuvius, hanging in a low grey cloud over the leaden surface of the sea. There was no sight of Capri—as if it had never existed in the world at all. And the small ship making towards it lurched so heavily from side to side that the family from San Francisco has to lie prone on their sofas in the wretched saloon of this poor ship, their feet wrapped in rugs and their eyes closed from nausea. The lady thought she suffered more than the others; nausea gripped her again and again and she believed that she was dying, while the maid who came running to her with a basin, and who had for many years been sailing this sea day in, day out, in all weathers, hot or cold, but was indefatigable nevertheless, merely laughed. The daughter was dreadfully pale and she held a slice of lemon between her teeth. The father, who lay on his back dressed in a loose overcoat and a large cap, never unclenched his jaws once during the voyage; his face had grown dark, his moustache seemed whiter, and his head ached terribly: what with the miserable weather, he had been drinking too heavily and enjoying too many "living tableaux" in certain haunts during the last nights on shore. And meanwhile the rain lashed at the rattling port-holes, water dripped down on to the sofas, the wind tore through the masts with a howl, and now and again came together with the onslaught of the swell to lay the little ship on its side, and then something could be heard rolling and rumbling below. It was a little quieter at the stops in Castellammare and Sorrento, but even there the swell was awful and the shores with all their precipices, gardens, pineries, pink and white hotels and dusky curly-green hills, flew up and down as though on swings; boats kept knocking against the side of the ship, damp wind blew in at the door and from a boat tossing on the waves and flying the flag of the Royal Hotel a boy with a speech defect screamed shrilly with never a moment's pause "Kgoyal! Hotel Kgoyal!" to entice the passengers there. And the gentleman from San Francisco, feeling very old—which was what he should have felt—now thought with boredom and anger of all these greedy, garlic-stinking little wretches called Italians. Once, during a stop, he opened his eyes and, sitting up on the sofa, saw a pile of such miserable little stone hovels, mouldy through and through, stuck one on top of the other at the foot of a sheer rock close to the water's edge beside some boats, heaps of rags, empty tins and brown fishing nets, that a feeling of despair seized him as he remembered that this was the real Italy which he had come to enjoy . . . At last, when it was already dusk, the black mass of the island, shot through with the little red lights at its foot, began to bear down on them; the wind abated, becoming warmer and more fragrant, and golden snakes, gliding away from the lamp-posts on the quay, came floating on the subdued waves which gleamed like black oil. Then, suddenly, the anchor began to rumble and with a clatter of chains flopped into the water with a splash; the furious cries of boatmen, vying with one another, came from all sides; and instantly one felt one's spirits lifting, the cabin lights shone more brightly, one wanted to eat, drink, smoke and move about. Ten minutes later the family from San Francisco boarded a roomy barge; in a quarter of an hour they disembarked on the quay, and then they were sitting in a bright little car that buzzed as it took them up a sheer mountain-side, past vine poles, crumbling stone walls and wet, gnarled orange-trees protected here and there with matting, their bright-coloured fruit and thick shiny leaves flashing past the open windows of the car and gliding downhill. In Italy the earth smells sweetly after rain, and every one of the islands has its own peculiar smell.

The Island of Capri was damp and dark that night. But now it came to life for a moment and put on lights here and there. A crowd of those whose duty it was to give the gentleman from San Francisco a fitting welcome, were already waiting at the top of the hill on the funicular platform. There were other arrivals, too, but they deserved no attention—a few Russians who had settled down in Capri, absent-minded and untidy men wearing spectacles and beards, the collars of their threadbare overcoats turned up; and a party of long-legged, round-skulled young Germans in Tirolean[5] suits with canvas rucksacks slung on their shoulders, who were in need of no services from anyone and felt at home wherever they happened to be and were not at all generous with their money. As for the gentleman from San Francisco, who calmly shunned both the Russians and the Germans, he was instantly marked down. He and his ladies were hurriedly helped out of the car; men started running ahead of him to show him the way; he was again surrounded by urchins and those stalwart Capri peasant women who carry on their heads the suitcases and trunks of decent tourists. Their wooden clogs clattered down the small square which was like an opera set with its globe of light swinging above in the damp breeze, and its crowd of urchins breaking into bird-like whistling and turning somersaults. And the gentleman from San Francisco strode in their midst as though he were making a stage entrance, through a kind of mediaeval archway formed by the houses, merging together overhead, beyond which lay the noisy little street, climbing up towards the brilliantly lit hotel entrance, with a tuft of palm leaves showing above the flat roofs on the left and a black sky studded with blue stars above and ahead. And once again it seemed that it was in honour of the guests from San Francisco that this damp little stone town on the rocky island in the Mediterranean had come to life, that it was they who had made the owner of the hotel so happy and hospitable, that for them the Chinese gong was waiting to boom all through the building, summoning everyone to dinner the minute they entered the lobby.

The owner who welcomed them with a polite and courtly bow, an exceedingly elegant young man, gave the gentleman from San Francisco a momentary start, for when he saw him he suddenly remembered that among all the other muddled dreams which had thronged his sleep the previous night he had seen the replica of this gentleman, wearing the same roundly cut-away morning coat, his hair plastered down to the same mirror-like gloss. Amazed, he all but stopped in his tracks. But since his soul had been cleansed of any so-called mystical feelings years ago, to the last mustard seed, his amazement instantly faded away; he jokingly mentioned this strange coincidence between dream and reality to his wife and daughter as they walked down the hotel corridor.

5. Of or designating a style of dress of the Tyrol.

His daughter, however, looked up at him in alarm when she heard it; her heart suddenly cringed with a feeling of sadness, of frightening loneliness on this strange, dark island . . .

A person of exalted rank who had been visiting Capri, had just left. And the guests from San Francisco were allotted the suite he had occupied. They had the prettiest and smartest maid appointed to them, a Belgian girl with a tightly corseted and stiffened waistline and a starched cap perched on her head like a small toothed crown; they were given the most imposing of valets, a black-haired fiery-eyed Sicilian, and the nimblest of "boots," a small, plump man called Luigi, who had changed many such jobs in his time. And a minute later, the gentleman from San Francisco heard a light knock on his door, followed by the appearance of the French maître d'hôtel coming in to inquire if the new guests would be dining, and to inform them, should their answer be in the affirmative (of which, however, there was no doubt), that there was lobster, roast beef, asparagus, pheasants, and so on, on the menu. The gentleman from San Francisco still felt the floor heaving under his feet—that's how sea-sick the rotten little Italian ship had made him—but he calmly went and rather clumsily closed the window which had burst open at the maître d'hôtel's entrance, and through which came the smells of a kitchen far away and wet flowers in the garden below. He replied with unhurried precision that they would be dining, that their table was to be placed well back in the room, a good distance away from the doors, that they would be drinking a local wine, and every word he uttered was echoed by the maître d'hôtel in tones of the most varied pitch, all of which, however, had but one meaning: that the rightness of the gentleman's wishes could not be doubted, and that everything would be carried out to the letter. Finally he inclined his head and asked tactfully:

"Will that be all, sir?"

And, hearing a thoughtful "y-yes" in reply, he volunteered the information that after dinner that night a tarantella would be danced in the lounge by Carmella and Giuseppe, well-known all over Italy and to all the "tourist world".

"I've seen her on postcards," said the gentleman from San Francisco in a voice that expressed nothing. "And that Giuseppe fellow—is he her husband?"

"Her cousin Sir," the maître d'hôtel replied.

And after a moment of hesitation, thinking of something but saying nothing, the gentleman from San Francisco dismissed the man with a nod.

After that he started dressing for dinner with as much care as if he were preparing for his wedding. He switched on all the lights flooding all the mirrors in the room with brilliance, glitter and the reflection of furniture and open trunks. He began to shave and to wash, ringing the bell incessantly, while other impatient rings, coming from the rooms of his wife and daughter, clashed with his and assailed the corridor with peals. And Luigi, in his red apron, distorting his face with a grimace of horror which reduced the maids, who were running past with jugs of water, to tears of laughter, bounded along to answer the gentleman's bell with a lightness common to so many fat men. Rapping on the door with his knuckles, he asked with feigned humility, exaggerated to inanity:

*"Ha sonato, signore?"*[6]

And from the other side of the door came a drawling, rasping and sneeringly polite voice:

"Yes, come in . . ."

What did the gentleman from San Francisco feel, what did he think about on that night that was to be so momentous for him? Like anyone else who had just had a rough crossing, he wanted nothing but his dinner and dreamed with relish of his first spoonful of soup, his first sip of wine; he was actually somewhat flurried as he performed his customary ritual of dressing for dinner, so he had no time for thought or feeling.

When he had shaved and washed and neatly fitted his false teeth back into place, he stood before the looking-glass and with a pair of silver brushes put the moistened strands of his remaining pearly-white hair into place on his dark yellow skull; then he pulled his cream-coloured silk underwear on his strong old body, which was growing fat round the middle from overnourishment, put his black silk socks and pumps on his lean flat feet; then bending his knees he adjusted the silk braces that held up his black trousers, tucked in his snow-white shirt with its bulging starched front, fixed a pair of shining links into his cuffs, and began the struggle to force the collar stud into the stiff collar. He still felt the floor was heaving, the tips of his fingers hurt, the stud pinched the sagging skin under his Adam's apple, but he was persevering and at last he got the better of the job; his eyes shining from the exertion, his face livid because the tight collar was strangling him, he sank down exhausted on the stool in front of the dressing-table and faced his full-size reflection which was repeated in all the other mirrors in the room.

"Oh, it's awful!" he muttered, dropping his strong bald head, without trying to understand, without thinking what it was he found so awful. Then, from habit, he keenly inspected his short fingers with their gout-hardened joints, his large almond-shaped, almond-coloured fingernails, and repeated with conviction, "It's awful . . ."

But just then the dinner gong boomed for the second time, sonorously as in a heathen temple. And, getting up hurriedly, the gentleman from San Francisco tightened his collar still more with a tie, drew in his stomach with a waistcoat, put on his coat, straightened his cuffs, and looked himself over in the glass once more. "That Carmella girl, olive-skinned with artifice in her eyes, like a mulatto, in her flowery orange dress, must be an exceptionally good dancer," he mused. And briskly walking out of the room, he went along the carpeted corridor to his wife's room next door and asked in a loud voice if they would be ready soon.

"In five minutes!" his daughter's voice, lilting and already gay, called back.

"Fine," said the gentleman from San Francisco.

And with leisurely steps he started down the corridors and red-carpeted stairs in quest of the reading-room. The servants he met flattened themselves against the wall when they saw him, while he strode by, apparently unaware of

6. You rang, sir? (Italian).

them. There was an old lady, who was late for dinner, hurrying along the corridor in front of him as quickly as she could—an old lady with milky-white hair and a back that was already stooped, but who wore, despite this, a low-cut gown of pale-grey silk. Her gait was funny, like an old hen's, and he had no difficulty in catching up with her and leaving her behind. At the glass doors leading into the dining-room, where everybody was already seated and had begun to eat, he stopped in front of a table loaded with boxes of cigars and Egyptian cigarettes and choosing a large Manila threw three lire down on the table. As he passed through the winter garden he glanced casually out of the open window. A gentle breeze wafted from the darkness, he fancied he saw the top of the old palm-tree spreading its gigantic-looking branches from star to star, he heard the steady wash of the sea in the distance. In the quiet, cosy reading-room, unlighted but for the lamps shining over the tables, was an old grey-haired German who looked like Ibsen, with crazy, bewildered eyes behind round silver-rimmed spectacles who stood reading some rustling newspapers. Eyeing him coldly up and down, the gentleman from San Francisco settled himself in a deep leather armchair in a corner, beside a green-shaded lamp, put on his pince-nez and, twitching his head because the collar was choking him, disappeared entirely behind his newspaper. He quickly ran through some of the headlines, read a few lines about the never ending war in the Balkans, turned the page over with a habitual gesture—and suddenly the lines glazed up before him with a glassy brilliance, his neck strained forward, his eyes bulged, and the pince-nez fell off his nose. He jerked forward, tried to take a gulp of air and began to wheeze terribly; his lower jaw sagged open, so that his whole mouth was aglitter with gold fillings, his head fell back on his shoulder and lolled helplessly, the hard front of his shirt jutted out, and he began to slide down to the floor, writhing and kicking up the carpet with his heels in a desperate struggle with someone.

If it had not been for the presence of the German in the reading-room, the management would have hushed up this shocking occurrence quickly and neatly, instantly whisking away the gentleman from San Francisco by his head and his feet down the back alleys, as far away as possible, and never a soul from among the hotel guests would have known what he had been up to. But the German rushed screaming out of the reading-room, raised a commotion in the dining-room, and roused the whole place. Many of the guests jumped up from their dinner, overturning chairs, many went pale and ran to the reading-room, crying, "What's happened, what's it all about?" in different languages, and no one gave them an answer, no one could make out what had happened because to this day people find death the most amazing thing in the world, and they flatly refuse to believe in it. The hotel-owner dashed from one guest to the other in an effort to hold back the stampede and to calm them with hurried assurances that it was nothing, a mere trifle, a little fainting fit that had seized a certain gentleman from San Francisco. But no one was listening to him, for many had seen the waiters and "boots" tearing off the gentleman's tie, waistcoat and crumpled dinner-jacket, and even, for some unknown reason, dragging the pumps off his black, silk-clad flat feet. But he was still thrashing about. He doggedly struggled with death, he refused to give in to the thing that had borne down on him so unexpectedly and rudely. He jerked his head from side to side, he wheezed as though his throat had been cut, he rolled his eyes drunkenly. When they had hastily carried him in and laid him on the bed of room No. 43—the smallest, poorest, dampest and coldest room at the end of the ground floor corridor—his daughter came running in with her hair streaming, her dressing-gown gaping open to reveal her bare bosom up-lifted by her corsets, and after that came his wife, big and heavy, already fully dressed for dinner, her mouth round with horror. But by that time he had even stopped jerking his head.

Within a quarter of an hour everything more or less settled down to normal at the hotel. But the night was irreparably ruined. Some of the guests came back into the dining-room and finished their dinner, but in silence and with injured expressions, while the owner went from table to table, shrugging in helpless and seemly annoyance, feeling apologetic although none of this was his fault, assuring everyone that he understood perfectly "how unpleasant it all was" and promising to do "everything in his power" to remove this unpleasantness. But the tarantella had to be cancelled, nevertheless; extra lights were turned off, most of the guests left for the beer hall, and everything grew so quiet that you could hear the clock ticking in the lobby which was deserted except for the parrot who muttered woodenly, fussing in its cage before settling down to sleep and finally doing so with one claw flung ridiculously over the top perch. The gentleman from San Francisco lay on a cheap iron bed, covered with coarse woollen blankets, in the dim light of a single bulb close to the ceiling. A rubber ice bag sagged down on to his cold, wet forehead. His livid and already dead face was cooling gradually, and the hoarse rattle, coming from the open mouth with its glitter of gold, was growing weaker. It was no longer the gentleman from San Francisco who was wheezing—he was no more—it was someone else. His wife, his daughter, the doctor and the servants stood and looked at him. Suddenly, the thing they had been waiting for, the thing they dreaded, happened—the wheezing ceased. And slowly, very slowly, before the eyes of all of them, a pallor spread over the face of the deceased, his features grew finer and lighter.

The owner came in. "*Già é morto*,"[7] the doctor told him in a whisper. The owner shrugged, his face impassive. The lady came up to him with tears trickling down her cheeks, and timidly suggested that the deceased should now be taken up to his room.

"*Mais non, madame*,"[8] the owner objected quickly and politely but with no gallantry whatsoever now, and he spoke to her in French and not in English, for he was not interested in those trifles which the visitors from San Francisco might now leave behind in his cash-box. "*Impossible, madame*," he said and added, in explanation, that he valued the suite most highly and that if he agreed to her request, the whole of Capri would come to know of it and tourists would refuse to stay in the rooms.

The daughter, who had been looking strangely at him all this time, dropped into a chair and, smothering her mouth with her handkerchief, burst into sobs.

7. Yes, he's dead (Italian). 8. But no, madam (French).

The mother's tears dried instantly and her face flushed red. She raised her voice, she became insistent, stating her demands in her own language and still unable to believe that all respect for them had been irrevocably lost. The owner checked her in politely dignified tones: if madame disapproved of the hotel's rules, he dared not hold her there; and he declared firmly that the body was to be removed by morning, that the police had been notified and a representative was due immediately to carry out the necessary formalities. Was it possible to get a coffin here, even if it was only a plain ready-made, madame asked. No, he was sorry, it was quite impossible and the time was too short to have one made. Some other way would have to be found. His English soda-water, for instance, was shipped out to him in large, long packing cases . . . the partitions from one of the cases could be taken out . . .

The hotel was plunged in sleep. They opened the window in room No. 43—which faced a corner of the garden where a sickly banana-tree grew in the shadow of the tall stone wall with broken glass stuck on top. They switched off the light, left the room and locked the door. The dead man remained in the darkness. Blue stars gazed down upon him from the sky. A cricket in the wall began to chirp its wistfully carefree song.

Two maids were sitting on the window-still in the dimly lit corridor, darning. Luigi came in with a pile of clothes in his arms and slippers on his feet.

"*Pronto?*" (Ready?), he asked anxiously in a shrill whisper, rolling his eyes at the frightening door at the end of the corridor. And, waving his free hand lightly in that direction, he hissed loudly, "*Partenza!*" which is the usual shout in Italy when a train steams out of a station, and the maids huddled together, choking down their soundless laughter.

And then he ran up to the door with soft leaps, rapped upon the panel lightly and with his head inclined asked in an undertone, in a most deferential manner:

"*Ha sonato, signore?*"

Now, constricting his throat, jutting his lower jaw forward, in a voice that was rasping, sad and drawling, he spoke the answer, as if it was coming from the other side of the door:

"Yes, come in."

At daybreak, when the sky grew light beyond the window of room No. 43 and the damp breeze rustled the ragged leaves of the banana-tree, when the blue sky of morning awakened and spread its cloak over the Island of Capri, and the pure, clear-cut summit of Monte Soliaro turned golden in the reflection of the sun, rising behind the distant blue mountains of Italy, when the road-menders started out on their way to work, repairing the island's paths for tourists to tread, then a long soda-water packing-case was brought to room No. 43. Shortly afterwards it became very heavy and pressed painfully against the knees of the junior porter who was taking it in a one-horse cab at a brisk pace along the white highroad that ran winding between stone walls and vineyards down the mountain-side, all the way down to the sea. The driver, a flabby man with bloodshot eyes, wearing a shabby old coat, short in the sleeves, and down-at-heel boots, had a hangover, for he had been playing dice all night long at a trattoria.[9] He kept whipping his sturdy young horse, which was decked out in the Sicilian fashion with jingling, clamouring bells of different shapes on the bridle, adorned with red wool pompons, as were the tips of the high copper ridge of the pommel, and with a quivering, yard-long feather sticking up from its trimmed forelock. The cabman was silent, crushed by his own dissoluteness and his vices, and the fact that the night before he had lost all he had down to the last copper. But the morning was crisp and with air as fresh as this, the nearness of the sea and the blue skies above, a head is soon cleared of its drunken haze, and light-heartedness is quickly recovered; and then the cabman also found consolation in the unexpected fee he had earned from some gentleman from San Francisco who was rolling his dead head about in the packing-case behind his back. The small ship, lying like a beetle on the bright and delicate blue that filled the Bay of Naples so generously, was already giving its last hoots and these were eagerly echoed over the whole of the island whose every bend, every mountain ridge and every stone was so clearly visible, as if there were no atmosphere at all. At the quay the cab was overtaken by the car in which the senior porter was bringing the mother and daughter, both of them pale, with eyes sunken from tears and a sleepless night. And ten minutes later, the little ship was again chugging away in a swish of water to Sorrento and Castellammare, taking the family from San Francisco away from Capri for ever. And once again peace and quiet was restored to the island.

On this island, two thousand years ago, lived a man who was unutterably vile in gratifying his lust and who for some reason rose to power over millions of people and committed atrocities beyond all measure. And mankind remembered him for ever, and many, many people come here from all over the world to take a look at the remains of his stone house on one of the sheerest sides of the island. That beautiful morning, all those who had come to Capri for this express purpose were still asleep in their hotels, although a string of little mouse-grey donkeys with crimson saddles was already being led up to the hotel entrances, for the Americans and Germans—men and women, young and old—to clamber on to when they got out of bed and had stuffed themselves with food, to be followed at a run along the rocky paths, all the way to the very top of Monte Tiberio, by ragged, old women with sticks in their gnarled hands to urge on the donkeys. The travellers slept in peace, comforted by the thought that the dead man from San Francisco, who had been planning to go with them but had instead just frightened them with a reminder of death, had already been shipped to Naples. And the island was still wrapped in silence, the shops were still shut. The fish and vegetable market in the small square was the only place open to business, and there was no one there but the common people. Among them, idling his time away as usual, stood the tall boatman Lorenzo, a carefree old rake so unusually handsome that he was known all over Italy, where he had often sat for painters; he had brought along a couple of lobsters he had caught in the night and he had already sold them for next to nothing, and now they were rustling in the apron of the cook from the same hotel where the

9. A restaurant or café serving Italian food.

family from San Francisco has spent the night. Lorenzo was now free to stand there till evening if he so wished, glancing about him with a regal air and cutting a figure with his tatters, his clay pipe and his red flannel beret, worn over one ear. Two Abruzzian mountaineers came down the steep Monte Soliaro from Anacapri, down the ancient Phoenician path, with steps hewn out of the rock. One of them had a bagpipe under his leather cloak—a large goatskin bag with two pipes—while the other carried something that looked like a wooden flute. They were coming downhill, and the whole country lay below, joyous, beautiful and fulgent: the rocky humps of the island, almost all of which lay at their feet, the fabulous azure in which it floated, the vapours of morning rising from the sea towards the East, shimmering in the blinding sun which was already hot as it rose higher and higher in the sky, the dimly-blue bulk of Italy with its mountains near and far still vague in the morning haze, the beauty of which man has no words to express. Halfway down the mountain they slowed their pace. There, above the path, in a niche in the rocky wall of Monte Soliaro, stood the Mother of God, bathed in sunlight, warmth and brilliance, clad in snow-white plaster robes, wearing the crown of a queen, rustily-golden from the rains, meek and gracious, with eyes raised heavenward to the eternal and blissful abode of Her thrice blessed Son. They bared their heads and raised their flutes to their lips—and praises poured forth, naïve and humbly joyous, to the sun, to the morning, and to Her, the Immaculate Intercessor for all the suffering in this wicked and beautiful world, and to the One who had been born of Her womb in a cave at Bethlehem, in the poor shepherds' shelter, in the far land of Judea.

And in the meantime, the body of the old man from San Francisco was returning home to its grave on the shores of the New World. After suffering much humiliation, much carelessness at the hands of men, after travelling form one harbour warehouse to another for about a week, it found itself at last on board the same famous ship which had only such a short while ago brought it to the Old World in so stately a manner. But now he was kept hidden from the living—he was lowered in his tarred coffin into the blackness of the hold. And once again the ship sailed off on its long voyage. That night it passed the Island of Capri and its lights, slowly vanishing in the dark sea, seemed sad to those who were watching it from the island. But there, on board, in halls flooded with light and gleaming with marble, a great ball was being held that night, true to custom.

A ball was held on the second and the third night out too—once again a furious storm was raging over the ocean, making it drone like a dirge and roll in mountains that were sombre and black like a funeral pall, edged with a silvery fringe. To the Devil watching from the rock of Gibraltar, the stony gateway between the two worlds, the countless, blazing eyes of the ship were hardly visible behind the curtain of snow as the ship sailed away into the night and the storm. The Devil was as enormous as a rock, but the ship was even more enormous than he was, many-tiered and many-funnelled, created by the arrogance of a New Man with an old heart. The storm tore at its rigging and its wide-mouthed funnels, white with snow, but it was firm, stalwart, majestic and—frightening. On the very top deck, lonely amid the whirling snow, rose the cosy, dimly lighted apartments, where the corpulent Master, so like a heathen god, presided over the whole ship, sleeping lightly and fitfully. He heard the deep howls and the furious squeals of the siren choking in the storm, but he sought reassurance in the proximity of something in the next room that was, in reality, the thing he could understand least of all: that large cabin, armour-clad it seemed, which every now and again was filled with a mysterious roar, a flickering and a dry sputtering of blue lights, which flared up and burst around the pale-faced radio-operator with a half circle of metal round his head. At the very bottom, in the underwater depths of the *Atlantis* where the twenty-ton steel bulks of the boilers and other machinery shone dimly, hissed out steam and dripped boiling oil and water, in that kitchen where the motion of the ship was being cooked over infernal fires heated from below, power was churning, power frightening in its concentration, transmitted to the very keel, to the endlessly long vault, into the rounded and dimly lighted tunnel, where a colossal shaft rotated slowly in its oily bed with a dauntlessness that was crushing to a man's soul, as if it were a live monster stretched out in the muzzle-like tunnel. But the middle part of the *Atlantis,* its dining-rooms and ball-rooms, radiated light and joy; they hummed with the voices of a well-dressed crowd, sang with string orchestras and emanated the fragrance of flowers. And again there was the slender and graceful couple of hired lovers, swaying sinuously or clinging together convulsively, among the crowd, amid the brilliance of lights, silks, diamonds and women's naked shoulders: the sinfully modest girl with downcast eyes and an innocent hairdo, and the tall young man with black hair that seemed glued on, his face pale with powder, dressed in a narrow long-tailed dress-coat and graceful patent-leather pumps, a beautiful man who looked like a huge leech. And no one knew that it had long been nothing but drudgery for this couple to writhe in their sham bliss to the plaints of the shamelessly seductive music, nor did anyone know that a coffin stood on the floor of the dark hold, far, far below them, close to the gloomy, sultry depths of the ship laboriously forging on through the darkness, the ocean and the storm . . .

*Vasilyevskoye, October 1915*

## GINA BERRIAULT on *The Gentleman from San Francisco*

With this story, Ivan Bunin himself seems caught up by a force of nature so strong his very language is borne along by that force. And the thousand and one details whose purpose is to stem that force, divert it, trick it into submission, are instead swept up by it and borne along. And what are these inestimably precious and futile details? Havana cigars, a bottle of amber-colored Johannisberg, goblets, Oriental baths, the great luxurious ship itself all alight on its night crossing, violet-scented tablets that sweeten the breath, cognac, crocodile leather valises, fur coats, opera glasses, hot water bottles and hotel chamber maids rushing them to guests who have dined too well, even an Asian Crown Prince with gold-rimmed spectacles and a long, sparse mustache. Vesuvius from afar, palm trees, and, yes, the tourists themselves, their great numbers whose company assures the Gentleman from San Francisco that all are happily just where they've scheduled themselves to be, here in this grand hotel on this charming island. The Gentleman from San Francisco, who always keeps arrivals in mind, anticipating pleasures, never wonders much about departures, and certainly not on this very night when, in his suite, he's turned on all the lamps, and the mirrors are filled with reflections of light and the sheen of furniture and the opened trunks, and he's dressing for dinner, pulling on a cream-colored silk undershirt, black silk socks, patent leather dancing shoes, a snow white shirt, cuff links, black trousers drawn up by silk suspenders—more and more of those details meant to save him from anonymity, meant to save him from life's strangenesses, meant to save him from the rising tide. And now, exhausted after this complicated struggle with his attire, with his appearance, he sits down before the pier glass and mutters, "It's terrible, terrible," not understanding just what is so terrible, not even trying to know. Ivan Bunin himself was a restless traveler, driven here and there by his writer's nature, and some of his very wonderful short stories tell about lone travelers drawn together by the force of lust that's made beautifully meaningful by their mutual consent to it for an hour or a night. And what's the natural force that's claiming the Gentleman from San Francisco in those few troubled moments alone in his suite, even as he's looking forward to a splendid meal—lobster, pheasants, wine—at his reserved table in the glittering dining hall? Somewhere in his soul he's lying in a long, oblong shipping box that once held bottles of English soda water and that's now hidden away in the dark hold of a ship that's struggling homeward through mountainous waves through the night sea.

# Frederick Busch

*Busch (1941– ) was born in Brooklyn, New York, and attended Muhlenberg College. He has received a Guggenheim and a PEN/Malamud Award for Short Fiction. His most recent publications are* The Children in the Woods *(1994),* Girls *(1997),* A Dangerous Profession *(1998), and* The Night Inspector (1999). *His short fiction is a blend of magical realism with the picture of life in his region.*

## Bread

First I went from room to chilly room, smoke alarm to smoke alarm. I saw little of the dust-fogged furniture or drapes, or the cobwebs blooming with cluster flies—the slatternly housekeeping for which our mother had been celebrated. Later, we discussed our pride in her carelessness. But this was first. I found the one. It was on the wall, near the molding, above the back-room cellar door. It squeaked like a floorboard, where no one had walked for a week, beneath someone's foot. Every minute or so it squeaked. It was the battery. The battery gives out, and the gizmo makes its little I'm-a-ghostly-footfall cry, and you hunt it down and tear the failing battery away: one ghost less.

It was the next day, in the kitchen, in the chill and in the absence, when I thought, *And not even by terrorists*. I heard my *not even* and I snorted with disgust. I was the man who would complain of his parents' death, of their falling and falling out of the sky, that it was insufficiently political. I snorted again. You make enough such noises, in a house quite suddenly scalloped out by death—by deaths—and the other person with you, in another room, a sister, say, might think she hears her brother weep.

"Chuckie," she called.

"What?"

"Are you okay?"

"Yes."

"Huh?"

"*Yes.*"

"Yeah," she said. "Okay." Then: "It sounded—"

"I wasn't," I said.

Kendall had decided that the room she couldn't deal with, among the rooms she couldn't deal with, was the kitchen. I'd volunteered. I was the brother. I did that. I had recently enough cleaned out rooms to be used to raking through what mustn't matter anymore—an apartment in Manhattan, four rooms on Riverside Drive, and not a house formerly employed for the storage of four lives and the spirits of six dogs, six or seven cats, the famous rooster flock, some insect-eating plants, and of course, though briefly, the boy whom Kendall so many years ago had smuggled in for the night.

In the city, I'd cleaned up what I finally saw as debris, the still-smoking rubble of a two-year marriage—service booklets on blender and toaster oven, playbills from hundred-dollar theater evenings, a lacy, boy-man's prayer of crimson negligée, the duplicate books, the checks and their sloppy but balanced ledgers: the finally usual. So, though Kendall was close to thirty and I four years younger, I volunteered. I thought of myself as experienced.

Therefore, in the home of my parents who had driven to Syracuse and flown to Toronto and stayed in a hotel on the lake at Harbourfront and had gone to a sort of theatrical evening that involved some visiting English friends, and then had flown from Toronto in a two-engine prop-driven airplane that had come apart over Lake Ontario, I was being experienced. I was fighting the stiff, dark dough I'd taken on the night of our arrival, when I'd offered to do—to do, to *do*—the kitchen, and I was kneading it. Like a semiprofessional mourner, I was conducting myself with dignity and in a manner governed by logic.

"I'm kneading bread," I answered Kendall, who'd been drawn perhaps by my silence into the kitchen she had vowed to avoid.

She sat with staring eyes that jumped from surfaces like hands from hot handles and she lit a cigarette. "You mind?" she asked. She propped her elbows on the narrow wooden table the top of which, once upon a time, my head had been level with. I had swiped hot cookies that my mother had set there to cool.

"No," I said. "I was married to a smoker."

"She never smoked here. Anytime that I saw."

"She sneaked it."

"Did she, you know, sneak around? On you? With guys?"

Kendall's face was a little square, her features slightly gathered at the center of her face. She missed bearing a man's strong face by virtue of the brown-green lightness of her large eyes. They were also our father's eyes. It was nearly his face, though he diminished as she widened her eyes to mock the innocence with which she hadn't asked her question. I turned my back to her and the rest of the kitchen, and I worked at the dough. It didn't yield gladly to my palms as I pushed, then gathered it toward me, gathered, then pushed.

"She did," Kendall concluded.

"That doesn't matter," I said.

"Chuckie, never mind. I shouldn't have, but never mind anyway."

"It doesn't matter anymore. It almost didn't then. Now it doesn't, and everybody moves along."

"That's right," she said. "Listen. How did you learn about kneading bread. Do guys normally *do* that?"

I planted my legs wider and drove hard at the football-sized wad of dough, still cold, unready to be shaped. I picked it up and slammed it onto the bread-board on the long counter. "I watched her," I said.

"A lot? You sat here and just looked at her?"

"No. I don't know. One time, I watched instead of—I don't know. *Not* watching. Isn't that what kids do with their parents? Not watch them a lot?"

I heard her sigh out the smoke. "You're lucky. To remember that."

"*You* remember things, Ken. They're just other things."

I heard her walk to the sink. I looked over my shoulder as she ran water on her cigarette. When she turned, I'd turned back to stare at the dough I leaned on with my palms. I almost didn't hear her say, "But I want to remember everything."

There isn't much of an answer. I nodded over the dough and closed my eyes. I continued to knead. She left the kitchen, swatting my ass, not hard, as she went.

When the flock happened, ours and the nearest other house, a usually vacant rental place in much disrepair, were the only buildings for three or four miles. The rental house burned or was burned. My father had used to snarl about the trash, as he called them, who rented it. They littered the dooryard with green garbage, they used an outhouse, and their goggle-eyed, shabbily dressed, pale-skinned children offended him. One winter, they burned an unsafe woodstove too hot, or lit the house in revenge for an impending eviction over nonpayment of rent. The roar of the fire, the pumper trucks and police cars sliding on the road, the ceaseless dirty gray smoke, scared us all. My father put smoke alarms—expensive in those days, and considered scientific wonders—into every room as soon as they were sold. He forbade us, on the day of the fire, the cigarettes he knew we sneaked. (I stopped, Kendall didn't.) He put a metal emergency ladder into Kendall's room and mine. He made us practice household fire drills. We used to rush about at *Go!*, crawling to doors, crouching from windows, crying out whom we would wake, and with what precautions, and then how we would run for our lives and wait for our parents to find us.

The day after the fire, I returned from—my mother's description—a twelve-year-old's sulk in the woods. I bore a seared, semi-featherless, small-headed, singed-comb little chicken. I brought it home, my parents said, whenever they told the story, to ask if I could give it someplace to die in peace. "He's the only survivor," I was said to have said, referring to the fire in which no one died. I named the chicken Bunny because I'd never been permitted to own the rabbit my mother had promised me as consolation after she'd shattered my sixth year of life by disclosing that the Easter Bunny did not in fact bring jelly beans and marshmallow chicks the color of radioactive rocks.

So we owned a scarred, small-headed chicken whose name was that of some cute, stupid girl with big breasts in some movie about big breasts on a California beach. My father, tall and broad and square-faced, balder than any egg, was business manager and assistant superintendent of the school district on the outermost edge of which we lived. He brought home one night, eight or nine days later, a cardboard box filled with chicks hatched and nourished in the high school biology lab.

The dough was working, now, and I pushed and gathered and then went in search of dish towels to drape on the three balls of dough I would cut from what I'd kneaded and arrange for rising. I was working from a book I had taken from the cookbook shelves. The page was relaxed in the binding, stained and limp. I'd stared at the stains before I'd focused on the words.

So I fed them the feed our father complained the birds ate too much of. Complaining about the cost of lumber, he built and fenced a little hen house, complete with roosting shelf. And Bunny, grown to something like health, with her mean, crazy eyes and the tattered wattle under her remarkably small head, staggered across the yard with her flock to raid the garden, then wheeled with stupid precision to stop occasional cars in our rutted, dusty, unpaved road.

The others didn't lay, though Bunny did. Kendall and I refused to eat her eggs, of course—that would be like eating *people*, Kendall explained for us. All of the birds, though unproductive, were more than willing to crow—on the occasion of a car with a leaky muffler that passed, for house lights spilling yellow down the yard, and for, as my father put it at two or three one morning, "a goddamned harvest *moon*."

Taking advice from his district's high school biology teacher, my father soon enough determined that with the exception of poor, exhausted Bunny, we owned a flock of roosters. "Guys!" Kendall had cried, on hearing the news. As for me, I was busy in school and bored by them all; I remained devoted to the idea of Bunny, but saw as little of her as possible. The rooster flock, and Bunny, soon enough disappeared. Then our parents disappeared. I saw them spilling from the plane. I sent that away. No: he would have reached for her. She would have reached for him. I saw them, then, clutching at each other. I cut the dough into three smaller balls and draped them with the soft, faded dish towels under which they would rise. I left the house by the side door. I could always work in the barn, I thought. I could always be useful in the barn.

He took the roosters and Bunny to a high school janitor who promised, he lied to us, that he would protect them until they died of old age. We knew. He killed them and cooked them and ate them. That was how they disappeared. Bunny au vin. Bunny sautée Basquaise. Bunny, more than likely, fried in lard.

I didn't go to the barn. I crossed the country road, paved now, and too well traveled, they'd complained. SaraJean, who used to be my wife, had liked to laugh when my mother began grousing about cars in the peaceable kingdom. "Where do they find up here to *travel* to?" SaraJean had enjoyed asking. She liked closure. She relished ending conversations, and pushing the button that shut the automatic door on anyone's garage, and terminating laden relationships. Kendall had said that if SaraJean and I had produced children, my wife would have happily inserted them, one at a time, in the trash compactor.

I went up the steep hill across from the house. The pitch was difficult, the snow still thick in wind-driven patches, and elsewhere the thorny stalks and slippery dead leaves and mostly frozen mud made the walking breathless. I aimed myself at an evergreen, fat in a low cluster of sinuous bushes, on the wind-flattened northern slope. In my father's lined denim chore coat, the collar up and a watch cap from the pocket pulled over my ears, I grew sweaty though the wind gusted on my back, and soon I was gasping into all that air. But I pushed hard if awkwardly to get myself up. I was desperate, heaving though I was, to not stop, to get away.

When I was near the tree, I turned to look down along the hill, and then I saw what I'd wanted to: all of it, the white house and garage, the gray wooden tool shed from which the house for Bunny and her flock of roosters protruded, the dead garden, the brown-green dormant lawns that ran to fields that went along the rocky tan hill below the house. It looked, from where I puffed and panted, manageable. It looked as though, if you stared hard and studied the details of cornice and chimney and gutter and sill, you could hold it confidently and summon it as you needed to.

Walking downhill, I had to dig my heels into snow patches and leaf heaps to keep from falling. My knees ached and my shins felt too tight. I walked stiff-legged across the road and around the side to the door. It was when I took off his watch cap and wiped my sweaty face with it that I remembered about his head inside the blue-black wool, his sweat already on the loosened knots of its weave, his fringe of iron hair that I remembered as surprisingly fine, soft to touch, the first time I dared to touch it as a man. I rubbed my head. I felt a way that reminded me of my discomfort on first seeing my father naked. A necessary distance had been shortened. Well, you've got all the distance, now, you'll need: I would have said that to me if I had been someone else.

In the kitchen, I took the towels from the bread and, with a wooden rolling pin that was like a long dowel slightly swollen in the middle, I pressed and rolled until the balls were long, thin ovals. According to the recipe in the cookbook I was to delicately and precisely gather up the edge nearest me and tautly roll. *Delicately* and *precisely* and *tautly*. I rolled up three long loaves and set them on a metal cooking sheet and stuck them in the oven. I'd forgotten to preheat the oven, but the bread would have to overcome the cold just as it would have to overcome its weeks or months in the freezer and my inability to roll it with sufficient delicacy, precision, and tautness. I turned up the heat.

I went upstairs to see if Kendall had made some progress. I, surely, had not. We'd planned to spend a weekend, then had changed our plans. had called in to work to say we'd need more like a week. It looked like a month to me. It looked like lasting into middle age or Social Security.

Kendall was on the floor, near the foot of their bed. Beside her, almost around her, was an explosion of clothing. She looked red-eyed and sore, very pale, maybe ill.

My turn to ask it: "You all right?"

"Where'd you go, Chuck?"

"I walked up over the hill."

"You son of a bitch."

"You would just as soon I hadn't walked up over the hill, I take it."

"I called you and called you."

"I didn't know, of course. Being—"

"Ha ha. Over the hill. Ha ha. Except I was *calling* you."

"I wouldn't have gone, you know. If I thought you needed me here right then."

She slumped, so that she looked as if she were studying their silk and rayon and cotton and wool. Then she nodded.

"You know that," I said.

She nodded again.

I said, "I am going to jump to the conclusion, Ken, that you're not enjoying the sorting out of their bedroom."

"Christ," she said. "You—I don't want to make any snappy remarks, all right? I feel terrible."

"Sick, you mean, or—you know. About them."

"Them," she said. She gestured at the clothing, then her arm fell on top of it and she went with it, so that she was lying on top of washed-thin half slips and cheap-looking underwear and starchy shirts with cardboard stiffeners and boot socks I knew he'd bought at Agway and slacks she'd ordered from catalogues and shoes that needed to be heeled and cleaned and shined. Kendall said, "I started to take the things out of their drawers and make piles, and I couldn't figure out what I was piling them for. *I'd* never wear her clothes, never mind I couldn't get into a size eight *glove,* much less her dresses. And they're so *cheap*-looking. Ordinary. I thought I learned how to dress from her, and it's all so, I don't know, worn out and faded and not very brilliantly selected. And you hate *his* clothes, don't you? I mean, who wears a suit to work over high-lace insulated *boots*. Let it *be* fucking wintertime: you dress *right*. Right? Or his terrible—they're not terrible. But his ties. That she picked out, with her famous taste.

"So I stopped stacking and I started heaving. It seemed to end up being some kind of revenge thing. So I stopped that, too. I mostly sat here and wailed for you and you couldn't come up and give me a hand, could you? Because you were being Jack and Jill. Whatever you were doing."

The highboy on my father's side of the bed was missing a brass pull on one side of the second drawer down. His bedside table wasn't identical to hers, I noticed for the first time. And they'd never arrested the damp that was ruining the casements of both their windows.

I said, "Whatever I was doing. I'm going to total it up for us, Ken. In about twenty-four hours, we've defrosted a ball of dough and we've made a mound of clothing. I think we're behind our schedule."

"And yet we're both so experienced at this."

"In a manner of speaking," I said.

Kendall propped herself on her elbows and crossed her legs at the ankle. She wore jeans and a cotton sweater, its sleeves pulled up to the elbows, and, despite her pallor and red eyes, she looked young. "Of course," she said, "you're the one used to cleaning up after marriages. I'm the party who slung it all into a duffel bag and two canvas suitcases and moved out in twelve minutes under the standing Olympic record for leaving *any*one. Much less the maniac I *wouldn't* marry."

"No," I said, "I always thought Bobby had a kind of admirable zest. He's the only man I ever knew outside the movies who actually hallucinated at his desk in front of a client."

"The only man," she said, "who ate amphetamines by dropping them into his martini. 'Straight up, babe, no fruits or vegetables in it, and bring me some kind of food with the second drink, all right?' Zest is a fond and stupid word for him. So's admirable."

"From a fond and stupid guy," I admitted.

"You're only stupid, Chuckie."

I sat in the pretty bentwood chair that needed recaning. It leaned as I let my weight down, and I waited for it to collapse, but it held me. I said, hiding behind my closed eyes, "Let's throw it all away."

"Which all?"

"All of it," I said, still hiding. "The clothes, the bedroom slippers, the pajamas—what can we *use*? We don't want to save things—do we?—and put them on like relics. 'Hi, my name's Chuck and I'm wearing a dead man's shirt with sleeves two inches too long.' Let's not do that, Ken. Let's toss it out."

"No," she said. Then she said, "All right. Except, we give it to—I don't know. Somebody. People. The Salvation Army."

"No way. They sell it to rag merchants. *They* sell it to clothing makers. *They* get wage slaves in Hong Kong and Costa Rica to use it for new clothes. So you're walking up Park Avenue South, say, and you see one of those overbred undermuscled types with blond eyelashes and about seventeen years of experience at a good college, and they're wearing a casually wrinkled natural fiber outfit, you know, and you stare at it because you see Daddy's *shirt* in there. You say to the androgyne, 'Excuse me, but aren't you wearing my father's shirt?' You don't want that to happen. You don't *want* them wearing Daddy's clothes and Mommy's clothes, Ken. Toss it. Throw it. All of it. If you want me to, I'll start a big son of a bitch fire outside, in the backyard, and we'll burn it."

"Is that called howdah? When the woman throws herself on top of the man who's burning? Or is that what they call burnoose?"

"You're a cultural swinette, Ken. We'll just throw it away."

"All right."

"You mean it?"

"I should have said it first," Kendall said. "It's just that—you know what I have left from when I lived with Bobby? Zip. No souvenirs, nothing. I left everything of mine behind, pictures of him, pictures of you and Mommy and Daddy, everything I brought in with me in the first place. He never called or anything to ask if I wanted anything back. Or if he could have *me* back."

"He's a junkie, Ken."

"He was *my* junkie," she said. And then: "Are you afraid of going through the *real* stuff? Are you scared, too?"

"Their papers? They probably don't have any papers. I mean, insurance things, bank things, that. Sure. But no *papers.* You know, that prove we were adopted, or stolen from kings and dukes or anything. No secret diaries or anything. No."

"So how come you haven't gone through Daddy's upper right-hand drawer?"

I told her, "Good conduct medal. Infantry badges. Two sets of corporal's stripes. Old handkerchiefs."

"You just remember from before."

"From high school," I admitted. "I used to look."

"You're as scared as I am," she said.

I looked at the sloping pile of our parents' clothes. They had nothing to do with how my mother wore my father's flannel shirts on Sunday to cook in, the sleeves rolled and the tails hanging almost to her knees. His flannel shirts looked like anybody's, now, anybody's green tartan from the Army-Navy in New Hartford, anybody's gray and black and yellow and white from the mail-order store.

I said, "I used to look for secret stuff. Dirty things. Pictures or rubbers, I don't know. He didn't have anything. Or he didn't leave it there for me to find. We won't steal their secrets here."

"Where would they hide them?" Kendall asked.

"Why *would* they, Ken?"

"Everyone does," she said. "That's why you're divorced and I live alone, and they went swimming," she said. She plucked at clothing.

I said, "They were together. They stuck together. They died together."

"Maybe they were better at it than we are," Kendall said, "but everybody's a secret from everybody else."

I pulled garbage bags from the box that Kendall had brought up. They were transparent, but they changed the color of the clothes I forced inside them. A watery tone, like what you see on docks or the footing of wooden bridges, went over everything. I felt as though I were drowning their clothes, which looked ugly, distorted, as I crushed them in. And I thought about robbers who pulled nylon stockings over their heads to change their features, which also looked crushed. This, I thought, is what our parents must look like, underwater.

Kendall had stood to take some bags and fill them. I heard us panting, as I had when I'd climbed the hill. This is real work too, I thought. We opened all but one of the drawers she hadn't got to, and we emptied all but one into the bags. My fingers felt sore from pulling at their clothing. I kneeled on each bag to force the air out before fastening it. Under my weight, the bags sighed like people, and the cloth inside went heavier.

When we were done, when we had without relenting thrown away our parents' only surviving skins, and when the room was ranked with sacks, Kendall said, "Look at us. It's like Hansel and Gretel made it back all the way, carrying the witch's whatever—"

"Gold," I said.

"Gold. Gingerbread cake. Whatever."

"You're just *hungry*, Ken."

"And they find out there's nobody home anyway. You know? The parent bastards tricked them *again*, and nobody's *home*."

I said, stupidly, "Ken. They didn't *mean* to."

"Why would I think that?" she said.

We stood there awhile and then, as if we'd made a decision, we left the bags and walked down the hall to the small room over the porch that had been Kendall's before she moved away and they turned it into a guest room.

She went to the closet and opened the door. It was empty, I thought. But Kendall reached in, her eyes still on mine, and her hand emerged to show her trophy: a chain ladder, suitable for escaping from fires or admitting boys on steep, snowy roofs. I apparently made a noise.

Kendall said, "I hate that. You keep doing that. You never used to. Where'd you pick it up?"

"I'm not really aware," I said, "of any unseemly new habits. But thanks."

"Yeah," she said. "You do sound like somebody who's about to hawk one on the floor. You sound like some kid on the street. Is that what New York did for you? Hee-*yach*. Like that. You really didn't know you were doing that?"

"I think I sometimes snort," I said. "Blow air out my nose—not the way Bobby snorted. Just a little sniff, sometimes, maybe."

"New York City on the street, that's your little sniffy snort."

"Tell me something country, Ken. How'd you ever get that kid in here?"

Holding the ladder, Kendall sat down. I think she'd have sat on the floor and hit hard, but there was an old footstool covered with maroon vinyl or leather, and she landed, clanking, on that. It was most of the furniture in the room, aside from the bed and bureau. The room was narrow and decorated with a chocolate brown carpet and off-white walls on which our mother had hung prints they'd brought home from Europe.

Kendall said, "I forgot." She was blushing, and I was glad to see her pallor overwhelmed.

"Poor son of a bitch," I said. "You forget, and the poor son of a bitch probably goes over it, step by step, every other day of his life. How he went up a porch stanchion and along the front porch roof and into Kendall Beaucamp's window. And—" I waited. She volunteered nothing. She shook her head and looked at the chenille comforter, dusty as the curtains, I'd have bet, and the narrow cherry dresser over which a cherry frame, of a slightly different hue, held a mirror in which I watched us stand, sit, remember and try not to. I said, "Ken: did he or did he not get into the sack with you? And what was his name?"

She shook her head. "I can't remember."

"Was he your, you know—was he the first guy you ever—"

"That's plain goddamned prurient, Chuckie, you know that? Yes. We got so turned on by being outlaws in here, we did stuff we didn't know we knew to *do*."

"I remember his name," I said. "Peter."

"No: Preston. Press. Press Leutens."

"The stud."

"He wasn't bad," Kendall said.

"And?"

"This is not the time for telling stories," Kendall said, with no rancor or conviction.

I said, "This is why they *invented* stories."

She said, "Daddy had grounded me for coming home an hour late, after my curfew. We'd been out. Press had the car, his parents' car, and there was some kind of game. Basketball, it was a basketball game, the last league game, we had to win to get into the tournament. So we won. He played a good game, and we didn't get home until late."

"You were the hero's reward?"

"He was *my* reward. I'd had to sit through the game, after all. *And* clap for our cheerleaders. We had more bent, humped, sickly pale, short-legged cheerleaders that year. So we got home late, Daddy all but put me on bread and water, Mommy said those moral things she always said until I said I would leave home unless she and Daddy did first, and that night, the next night, when it happened, I was in my room and Press just showed up."

"At your window."

"At my window."

"Like the movies," I said.

She said, "Exactly like the movies."

"And you let him in with the fire ladder?"

"He didn't really need it. He'd made it up the roof already, most of the way, but I liked the idea of opening my window and unrolling the ladder Daddy used to make me practice unrolling all the time."

"Right," I said. "And?"

"God, Chuck, you're so vulgar."

"I know. Tell me the story."

"Chuck. We acted like we were in Nazi-occupied France and we took our clothes off and went to bed. I was a normal, healthy child and so was he. We'd been warming up in cars and dark corners, and we did what we'd been trained for."

"And I spent my childhood reading dirty books," I complained.

"Not from what I heard."

"Tell me the rest," I said.

Kendall said: "Like the movies. Like the books. Whispering and touching and kissing and talking and screwing, Chuck, until, as a matter of fact, dawn."

"When Bunny crowed."

"Bunny crowed. The cocks all crowed. Press got dressed and went to the window and he was so nervous about making his escape from the Nazis and the Vichy[1] police, he forgot to kiss me goodbye. He went onto the slippery, snow-covered roof, without benefit of the fire ladder, and I was in bed, you know, not *believing* it, and Bunny and that goddamned flock of roosters must have come wheeling into the front yard. Because all of a sudden—one of those icy dawns? when there's nothing to hear except wind?—all of a sudden, every goddamned rooster, *and* Bunny, started in screaming. Like they all were saying *Aww! Aww! Aww!*

"Naturally, Daddy and Mommy woke up. Daddy went to the front door. And naturally he saw dumb-ass Preston Leutens's car, his parents' car, parked square in front of the front walk. He went out to investigate. By then, I was looking out from between these exact same curtains. There's Daddy, he's in his navy blue watch cap and his bathrobe and his chore jacket over it, and the bedroom slippers we just threw the hell away, and he's standing there, looking at the car. And there's Press on the roof above him. Like a statue on the roof, because he's trying not to slide or be seen. And there's the goddamned cock flock, *Aww! Aww!* I betrayed him in my heart, poor Preston."

1. A city in central France that was the capital of unoccupied France from 1940 to 1944. The puppet government was set up by Marshall Henri Petain after the fall of Paris.

"Sure you did. You're Kendall Beaucamp. You laughed."

"With Preston's heat still rising from the sheets. I laughed like the witch in *The Wizard of Oz.* I couldn't help it. And Daddy, of course, through the window, in the rooster screams and all that wind, he hears me."

"I was sleeping."

"Of course you were."

"So I missed seeing him kill you and Preston and you're both still dead?"

"Oh, Chuckie. He scrunched up his face until I thought he was going to cry."

"Did he?"

"Mommy claimed he did, later on. He said to Press, 'You get down cautiously. I don't want your parents suing me after I send you to jail.' Then he went inside."

"What'd he *say*?"

"That's between him and me."

"No."

"Goddamned *yes.* That's for him and me."

I had to look someplace else. I looked at what was either a castle in a meadow or something eating the meadow, and then I said, "Weren't you a pistol."

"Wasn't I," she said. "You know what? I just might sit in here awhile. If you don't mind. A little while. All right?"

I didn't know what else to do except lean down and kiss the top of her head, which smelled like a morning's work and herbal shampoo. She bumped her head against my lips, and I went out.

Where I went, of course, was back down the hall and into our parents' room and through the ranked plastic bags to the bureau in the top right drawer of which my father kept the secrets. When I opened it, a sweet, soapy smell came up—the soaps with French names that my mother gave the big, booted school executive for birthdays and Christmases. When they were used up thin, he dried the wafers and broke them into chips and scattered them in his drawers. I thought of the first time I had seen him naked, emerging from the shower, his dimpled flanks and long thighs, the dense hair on his chest and belly, the dangerous mystery of his groin.

What I saw first in the drawer was a small, handled and almost limp photograph, about four inches tall. It was of a young girl with pretty legs. She wore a dress over a T-shirt, and the dress was hiked up by her straddling of a bicycle. A familar, shy smile composed her face: you looked from lips to eyes, and you smiled back. It was our mother, aged eight or nine. I had to say "Hello," back through the thirty-six years of their marriage and the long, funny year (as they had often told it) of their courtship—he did the courting, she, as she said, had held her breath and jumped in, trusting (quite incorrectly as it seemed at last) to the probability that everything, after a while, floats to the surface—and back to her childhood in the Korean War, the drills for taking shelter from atomic bomb blasts, and back through World War II, her father in the Pacific, her mother alone with her, chain-smoking Lucky Greens. "Hello," I said, holding the picture he apparently had many times held.

I saw the dark boxes his medals were in, and some wide brown envelopes, an assortment of cuff links and tie clasps presented by us on birthdays, purchased with our mother's money and rarely used. I opened the envelopes, three of them, and found artifacts of children who'd grown older. The envelope on top contained photographs of Kendall in a prom dress, Kendall in her cap and gown at graduation, me in a Cub Scout shirt and jeans, in football uniform, waist-to-heel cast, and my own cap and gown. The envelope in the middle had letters from us: I was ashamed, somehow, of the childish arcs and curves of my hand. And there were pictures of me and SaraJean, or Kendall and Bobby, of New York City and Poughkeepsie, to which Kendall had moved when IBM told her to. I saw that we were happy children. You would call us happy children, if you saw those photographs. And in the envelope on the bottom, there were notes from our mother. I couldn't read them. *Darling,* one of them began, and I folded it shut. There was a drawing signed Kendall in a loopy hand: *My Family,* it said, and there was the vast, big-headed Daddy, with enormous hands and feet and smile, and under him, like shrubs in the shade of a tree, was a labeled *Mommy* with a face-wide smile, and a smaller *Kendall,* her arms spread as if to tell the viewer that here they all were. Under it, folded, was a large Christmas card I had made in elementary school, perhaps in the first or second grade. I could still smell, in the dried smears between the pasted green evergreen shape and the rough construction-paper rectangle, the corrupted vanilla of grade school mucilage. There was more, but I stopped fingering through it. He might have, I thought, hidden cruel, terrible matters deep and far away. But the secrets he had openly kept, in the place a husband and father stores them, where he knows they'll one day be found, had been us.

For punctuation, the smell came up, carried by the draft that went from the kitchen to the stairwell, where it split to go through the dining room and living room toward the back room cellar door, and also to pour upstairs. The odor was dense, and so, then, was the noise. The alarms went off in the kitchen and stairwell, then in the living room—the dining room alarm pitched in late—and I waited for the back room to squeal, then remembered that I'd gutted its alarm.

So much for bread, I thought, running downstairs to a very smoky kitchen. The screaming of the alarms was painful. I turned off the oven, opened the door, and recoiled from the oily black smoke—some of it bread, some the spattered fat our mother wouldn't have cleaned away. I was grinning for her housekeeping, squinting against the smoke, and screaming back at the screaming of the smoke alarms which sounded inside my skull bone like dentist drills.

Kendall, from the doorway, called, "I *told* you that guys don't do bread."

I threw the pan of small black loaves on the floor and retreated to the dining room. She came with me. We stood in the far corner, near a high narrow basket our mother had filled with late autumn grasses, ocher and brown. "It's my mess," I said, "and I will clean it up. It's my fault. I forgot to set the timer. It was cold, you know, frozen, then thawed, then cold, but I knew you didn't do bread *cold*. So I cranked the oven to about 475, and then I forgot."

"You meant well," Kendall said. "I suppose."

I shook my head.

"No," she said, "tell me. You can tell me. I told you."

"You know about yeast," I said.

"In the little envelopes. Mommy always used it."

"They're alive," I said. "Little microscopic plants. Which are alive. Dough rises, the yeast grows. That's what makes the heat. That's why it *needs* heat. So, Mommy freezes the dough. To let the bread rise and bake some other time, she freezes it. So we come here, and it's some other time. So I thawed it. I let it rise. I baked it. Sort of."

Kendall said, "Chuckie."

"That's right. The bread was—well, the yeast in the dough was. You know."

"Alive," Kendall said. "When Mommy was alive."

I nodded.

"Chuckie," she said.

"So of course," I said, "I made sure to take it and kill it, didn't I?"

Kendall was quiet for a long time. I didn't want to look at her, or at the room we'd sat in with company and for Thanksgiving and Christmas dinners. It seemed now such an ordinary room. Like the subsiding smoke as it was drawn through the house to accumulate upstairs and in the back room, then dissipate against the walls and windows there, we were leaving, too.

Kendall, behind me, put her arms around my waist. I felt her along my back. I wanted to turn and pull her in to me, but I didn't. I thought she ought to be as alone with me as she needed to be.

She said, suddenly, with a hoarse, gulping sound, "You know how bad I've been all my life?" She laid her forehead against my back and pushed her head at me as, with her arms, she pulled in.

I said, "I'm going to take you upstairs, Ken. All right? I opened the drawer. I found the secrets. Now I want you to see them, all right?"

I turned, then, and fought her a little until I could take hold of her hand She stopped resisting, and I led her through the thin current of almost invisible smoke toward the stairs.

"I can't do this," she said. "I don't want to do this."

But I kept pulling her. "Yes," I said. "Really." So we climbed toward their room. In the story, you remember, in the dark forest, when something has inevitably eaten all the crumbs, he leads her home by the hand.

# Raymond Carver

*Carver (1939–1988) was born in Clatskanie, Oregon, and attended Humboldt State University in California before going on to graduate work at the University of Iowa. For several years he taught writing at Syracuse University. In the late 1970s his poetry and fiction marked him as one of the more noteworthy talents of his generation, and his reputation continues to soar. His stories are collected in* Will You Please Be Quiet, Please? *(1978);* What We Talk about When We Talk about Love *(1981);* Cathedral *(1983); and* "Where I'm Calling From": New and Selected Stories *(1988).*

## Cathedral

This blind man, an old friend of my wife's, he was on his way to spend the night. His wife had died. So he was visiting the dead wife's relatives in Connecticut. He called my wife from his in-laws'. Arrangements were made. He would come by train, a five-hour trip, and my wife would meet him at the station. She hadn't seen him since she worked for him one summer in Seattle ten years ago. But she and the blind man had kept in touch. They made tapes and mailed them back and forth. I wasn't enthusiastic about his visit. He was no one I knew. And his being blind bothered me. My idea of blindness came from the movies. In the movies, the blind moved slowly and never laughed. Sometimes they were led by seeing-eye dogs. A blind man in my house was not something I looked forward to.

That summer in Seattle she had needed a job. She didn't have any money. The man she was going to marry at the end of the summer was in officers' training school. He didn't have any money, either. But she was in love with the guy, and he was in love with her, etc. She'd seen something in the paper: HELP WANTED—*Reading to Blind Man,* and a telephone number. She phoned and went over, was hired on the spot. She'd worked with this blind man all summer. She read stuff to him, case studies, reports, that sort of thing. She helped him organize his little office in the county social-service department. They'd become good friends, my wife and the blind man. How do I know these things? She told me. And she told me something else. On her last day in the office, the blind man asked if he could touch her face. She agreed to this. She told me he touched his fingers to every part of her face, her nose—even her neck! She never forgot it. She even tried to write a poem about it. She was always trying to write a poem. She wrote a poem or two every year, usually after something really important had happened to her.

When we first started going out together, she showed me the poem. In the poem, she recalled his fingers and the way they had moved around over her face. In the poem, she talked about what she had felt at the time, about what went through her mind when the blind man touched her nose and lips. I can remember I didn't think much of the poem. Of course, I didn't tell her that. Maybe I just don't understand poetry. I admit it's not the first thing I reach for when I pick up something to read.

Anyway, this man who'd first enjoyed her favors, the officer-to-be, he'd been her childhood sweetheart. So okay. I'm saying that at the end of the summer she let the blind man run his hands over her face, said goodbye to him, married her childhood etc., who was now a commissioned officer, and she moved away from Seattle. But they'd kept in touch, she and the blind man. She made the first contact after a year or so. She called him up one night from an Air Force base in Alabama. She wanted to talk. They talked. He asked her to send him a tape and tell him about her life. She did this. She sent the tape. On the tape, she told the blind man about her husband and about their life together in the military. She told the blind man she loved her husband but she didn't like it where they lived and she didn't like it that he was a part of the military-industrial thing. She told the blind man she'd written a poem about what it was like to be an Air Force officer's wife. The poem wasn't finished yet. She was still writing it. The blind man made a tape. He sent her the tape. She made a tape. This went on for years. My wife's officer was posted to one base and then another. She sent tapes from Moody AFB, McGuire, McConnell and finally Travis, near Sacramento, where one night she got to feeling lonely and cut off from people she kept losing in that moving-around life. She got to feeling she couldn't go it another step. She went in and swallowed all the pills and capsules in the medicine chest and washed them down with a bottle of gin. Then she got into a hot bath and passed out.

But instead of dying, she got sick. She threw up. Her officer—why should he have a name? he was the childhood sweetheart, and what more does he want?—came home from somewhere, found her, and called the ambulance. In time, she put it all on a tape and sent the tape to the blind man. Over the years, she put all kinds of stuff on tapes and sent the tapes off lickety-split. Next to writing a poem every year, I think it was her chief means of recreation. On one tape, she told the blind man she'd decided to live away from her officer for a time. On another tape, she told him about her divorce. She and I began going out, and of course she told her blind man about it. She told him everything, or so it seemed to me. Once she asked me if I'd like to hear the latest tape from the blind man. This was a year ago. I was on the tape, she said. So I said okay, I'd listen to it. I got us drinks and we settled down in the living room. We made ready to listen. First she inserted the tape into the player and adjusted a couple of dials. Then she pushed a lever. The tape squeaked and someone began to talk in this loud voice. She lowered the volume. After a few minutes of harmless chitchat, I heard my own name in the mouth of this stranger, this blind man I didn't even know! And then this: "From all you've said about him, I can only conclude—" But we were interrupted, a knock at the door, something, and we didn't ever get back to the tape. Maybe it was just as well. I'd heard all I wanted to.

Now this same blind man was coming to sleep in my house.

"Maybe I could take him bowling," I said to my wife. She was at the draining board doing scalloped potatoes. She put down the knife she was using and turned around.

"If you love me," she said, "you can do this for me. If you don't love me, okay. But if you had a friend, any friend, and the friend came to visit, I'd make him feel comfortable." She wiped her hands with the dish towel.

"I don't have any blind friends," I said.

"You don't have *any* friends," she said. "Period. Besides," she said, "goddamn it, his wife's just died! Don't you understand that? The man's lost his wife!"

I didn't answer. She'd told me a little about the blind man's wife. Her name was Beulah. Beulah! That's a name for a colored woman.

"Was his wife a Negro?" I asked.

"Are you crazy?" my wife said. "Have you just flipped or something?" She picked up a potato. I saw it hit the floor, then roll under the stove. "What's wrong with you?" she said. "Are you drunk?"

"I'm just asking," I said.

Right then my wife filled me in with more detail than I cared to know. I made a drink and sat at the kitchen table to listen. Pieces of the story began to fall into place.

Beulah had gone to work for the blind man the summer after my wife had stopped working for him. Pretty soon Beulah and the blind man had themselves a church wedding. It was a little wedding—who'd want to go to such a wedding in the first place?—just the two of them, plus the minister and the minister's wife. But it was a church wedding just the same. It was what Beulah had wanted, he'd said. But even then Beulah must have been carrying the cancer in her glands. After they had been inseparable for eight years—my wife's word, *inseparable*—Beulah's health went into a rapid decline. She died in a Seattle hospital room, the blind man sitting beside the bed and holding on to her hand. They'd married, lived and worked together, slept together—had sex, sure—and then the blind man had to bury her. All this without his having ever seen what the goddamned woman looked like. It was beyond my understanding. Hearing this, I felt sorry for the blind man for a little bit. And then I found myself thinking what a pitiful life this woman must have led. Imagine a woman who could never see herself as she was seen in the eyes of her loved one. A woman who could go on day after day and never receive the smallest compliment from her beloved. A woman whose husband could never read the expression on her face, be it misery or something better. Someone who could wear makeup or not—what difference to him? She could, if she wanted, wear green eye-shadow around one eye, a straight pin in her nostril, yellow slacks and purple shoes, no matter. And then to slip off into death, the blind man's hand on her hand, his blind eyes streaming tears—I'm imagining now—her last thought maybe this: that he never even knew what she looked like, and she on an express to the grave. Robert was left with a small insurance policy and half of a twenty-peso Mexican coin. The other half of the coin went into the box with her. Pathetic.

So when the time rolled around, my wife went to the depot to pick him up. With nothing to do but wait—sure, I blamed him for that—I was having a drink and watching the TV when I heard the car pull into the drive. I got up from the sofa with my drink and went to the window to have a look.

I saw my wife laughing as she parked the car. I saw her get out of the car and shut the door. She was still wearing a smile. Just amazing. She went around to the other side of the car to where the blind man was already starting to get out. This blind man, feature this, he was wearing a full beard! A beard on a blind man! Too much, I say. The blind man reached into the back seat and dragged out a suitcase. My wife took his arm, shut the car door, and, talking all the way, moved him down the drive and then up the steps to the front porch. I turned off the TV. I finished my drink, rinsed the glass, dried my hands. Then I went to the door.

My wife said, "I want you to meet Robert. Robert, this is my husband. I've told you all about him." She was beaming. She had this blind man by his coat sleeve.

The blind man let go of his suitcase and up came his hand.

I took it. He squeezed hard, held my hand, and then he let it go.

"I feel like we've already met," he boomed.

"Likewise," I said. I didn't know what else to day. Then I said, "Welcome. I've heard a lot about you." We began to move then, a little group, from the porch into the living room, my wife guiding him by the arm. The blind man was carrying his suitcase in his other hand. My wife said things like, "To your left here, Robert. That's right. Now watch it, there's a chair. That's it. Sit down right here. This is the sofa. We just bought this sofa two weeks ago."

I started to say something about the old sofa. I'd liked that old sofa. But I didn't say anything. Then I wanted to say something else, small-talk, about the scenic ride along the Hudson. How going *to* New York, you should sit on the right-hand side of the train, and coming *from* New York, the left-hand side.

"Did you have a good train ride?" I said. "Which side of the train did you sit on, by the way?"

"What a question, which side!" my wife said. "What's it matter which side?" she said.

"I just asked," I said.

"Right side," the blind man said. "I hadn't been on a train in nearly forty years. Not since I was a kid. With my folks. That's been a long time. I'd nearly forgotten the sensation. I have winter in my beard now," he said. "So I've been told, anyway. Do I look distinguished, my dear?" the blind man said to my wife.

"You look distinguished, Robert," she said. "Robert," she said. "Robert, it's just so good to see you."

My wife finally took her eyes off the blind man and looked at me. I had the feeling she didn't like what she saw. I shrugged.

I've never met, or personally known, anyone who was blind. This blind man was late forties, a heavy-set, balding man with stooped shoulders, as if he carried a great weight there. He wore brown slacks, brown shoes, a light-brown shirt, a tie, a sports coat. Spiffy. He also had this full beard. But he didn't use a cane and he didn't wear dark glasses. I'd always thought dark glasses were a must for the blind. Fact was, I wished he had a pair. At first glance, his eyes looked like anyone else's eyes. But if you looked close, there was something different about them. Too much white in the iris, for one thing, and the pupils seemed to move around in the sockets without his knowing it or being able to stop it. Creepy. As I stared at his face, I saw the left pupil turn in toward his nose while the other made an effort to keep in one place. But it was only an effort, for that eye was on the roam without his knowing it or wanting it to be.

I said, "Let me get you a drink. What's your pleasure? We have a little of everything. It's one of our pastimes."

"Bub, I'm a Scotch man myself," he said fast enough in this big voice.

"Right," I said. Bub! "Sure you are. I knew it."

He let his fingers touch his suitcase, which was sitting alongside the sofa. He was taking his bearings. I didn't blame him for that.

"I'll move that up to your room," my wife said.

"No, that's fine," the blind man said loudly. "It can go up when I go up."

"A little water with the Scotch?" I said.

"Very little," he said.

"I knew it," I said.

He said, "Just a tad. The Irish actor, Barry Fitzgerald? I'm like that fellow. When I drink water, Fitzgerald said, I drink water. When I drink whiskey, I drink whiskey." My wife laughed. The blind man brought his hand up under his beard. He lifted his beard slowly and let it drop.

I did the drinks, three big glasses of Scotch with a splash of water in each. Then we made ourselves comfortable and talked about Robert's travels. First the long flight from the West Coast to Connecticut, we covered that. Then from Connecticut up here by train. We had another drink concerning that leg of the trip.

I remembered having read somewhere that the blind didn't smoke because, as speculation had it, they couldn't see the smoke they exhaled. I thought I knew that much and that much only about blind people. But this blind man smoked his cigarette down to the nubbin and then lit another one. This blind man filled his ashtray and my wife emptied it.

When we sat down at the table for dinner, we had another drink. My wife heaped Robert's plate with cube steak, scalloped potatoes, green beans. I buttered him up two slices of bread. I said, "Here's bread and butter for you." I swallowed some of my drink. "Now let us pray," I said, and the blind man lowered his head. My wife looked at me, her mouth agape. "Pray the phone won't ring and the food doesn't get cold," I said.

We dug in. We ate everything there was to eat on the table. We ate like there was no tomorrow. We didn't talk. We ate. We scarfed. We grazed that table. We were into serious eating. The blind man had right away located his foods, he knew just where everything was on his plate. I watched with admiration as he used his knife and fork on the meat. He'd cut two pieces of meat, fork the meat into his mouth, and then go all out for the scalloped potatoes, the beans next, and then he'd tear off a hunk of buttered bread and eat that.

He'd follow this up with a big drink of milk. It didn't seem to bother him to use his fingers once in a while, either.

We finished everything, including half a strawberry pie. For a few moments, we sat as if stunned. Sweat beaded on our faces. Finally, we got up from the table and left the dirty plates. We didn't look back. We took ourselves into the living room and sank into our places again. Robert and my wife sat on the sofa. I took the big chair. We had us two or three more drinks while they talked about the major things that had come to pass for them in the past ten years. For the most part, I just listened. Now and then I joined in. I didn't want him to think I'd left the room, and I didn't want her to think I was feeling left out. They talked of things that had happened to them—to them!—these past ten years. I waited in vain to hear my name on my wife's sweet lips: "And then my dear husband came into my life"—something like that. But I heard nothing of the sort. More talk of Robert. Robert had done a little of everything, it seemed, a regular blind jack-of-all-trades. But most recently he and his wife had had an Amway distributorship, from which, I gathered, they'd earned their living, such as it was. The blind man was also a ham radio operator. He talked in his loud voice about conversations he'd had with fellow operators in Guam, in the Philippines, in Alaska, and even in Tahiti. He said he'd have a lot of friends there if he ever wanted to go visit those places. From time to time, he'd turn his blind face toward me, put his hand under his beard, ask me something. How long had I been in my present position? (Three years.) Did I like my work? (I didn't.) Was I going to stay with it? (What were the options?) Finally, when I thought he was beginning to run down, I got up and turned on the TV.

My wife looked at me with irritation. She was heading toward a boil. Then she looked at the blind man and said, "Robert, do you have a TV?"

The blind man said, "My dear, I have two TVs. I have a color set and a black-and-white thing, an old relic. It's funny, but if I turn the TV on, and I'm always turning it on, I turn on the color set. It's funny, don't you think?"

I didn't know what to say to that. I had absolutely nothing to say to that. No opinion. So I watched the news program and tried to listen to what the announcer was saying.

"This is a color TV," the blind man said. "Don't ask me how, but I can tell."

"We traded up a while ago," I said.

The blind man had another taste of his drink. He lifted his beard, sniffed it, and let it fall. He leaned forward on the sofa. He positioned his ashtray on the coffee table, then put the lighter to his cigarette. He leaned back on the sofa and crossed his legs at the ankles.

My wife covered her mouth, and then she yawned. She stretched. She said, "I think I'll go upstairs and put on my robe. I think I'll change into something else. Robert, you make yourself comfortable," she said.

"I'm comfortable," the blind man said.

"I want you to feel comfortable in this house," she said.

"I am comfortable," the blind man said.

After she'd left the room, he and I listened to the weather report and then to the sports roundup. By that time, she'd been gone so long I didn't know if she was going to come back. I thought she might have gone to bed. I wished she'd come back downstairs. I didn't want to be left alone with a blind man. I asked him if he wanted to smoke some dope with me. I said I'd just rolled a number. I hadn't, but I planned to do so in about two shakes.

"I'll try some with you," he said.

"Damn right," I said. "That's the stuff."

I got our drinks and sat down on the sofa with him. Then I rolled us two fat numbers. I lit one and passed it. I brought it to his fingers. He took it and inhaled.

"Hold it as long as you can," I said. I could tell he didn't know the first thing.

My wife came back downstairs wearing her pink robe and her pink slippers.

"What do I smell?" she said.

"We thought we'd have us some cannabis," I said.

My wife gave me a savage look. Then she looked at the blind man and said, "Robert, I didn't know you smoked."

He said, "I do now, my dear. There's a first time for everything. But I don't feel anything yet."

"This stuff is pretty mellow," I said. "This stuff is mild. It's dope you can reason with," I said. "It doesn't mess you up."

"Not much it doesn't, bub," he said, and laughed.

My wife sat on the sofa between the blind man and me. I passed her the number. She took it and toked and then passed it back to me. "Which way is this going?" she said. Then she said, "I shouldn't be smoking this. I can hardly keep my eyes open as it is. That dinner did me in. I shouldn't have eaten so much."

"It was the strawberry pie," the blind man said. "That's what did it," he said, and he laughed his big laugh. Then he shook his head.

"There's more strawberry pie," I said.

"Do you want some more, Robert?" my wife said.

"Maybe in a little while," he said.

We gave our attention to the TV. My wife yawned again. She said, "Your bed is made up when you feel like going to bed, Robert. I know you must have had a long day. When you're ready to go to bed, say so." She pulled his arm. "Robert?"

He came to and said, "I've had a real nice time. This beats tapes, doesn't it?"

I said, "Coming at you," and I put the number between his fingers. He inhaled, held the smoke, and then let it go. It was like he'd been doing it since he was nine years old.

"Thanks, bub," he said. "But I think this is all for me. I think I'm beginning to feel it," he said. He held the burning roach out for my wife.

"Same here," she said. "Ditto. Me, too." She took the roach and passed it to me. "I may just sit here for a while between you two guys with my eyes closed. But don't let me bother you, okay? Either one of you. If it bothers you, say so. Otherwise, I may just sit here with my eyes closed until you're ready to go to bed," she said. "Your bed's made up, Robert, when you're ready. It's right next to our room at the top of the stairs. We'll show you up when you're ready. You wake me up now, you guys, if I fall asleep." She said that and then she closed her eyes and went to sleep.

The news program ended. I got up and changed the channel. I sat back down on the sofa. I wished my wife hadn't pooped out. Her head lay across the back of the sofa, her mouth open. She'd turned so that her robe had slipped away from her legs, exposing a juicy thigh. I reached to draw her robe back over her, and it was then that I glanced at the blind man. What the hell! I flipped the robe open again.

"You say when you want some strawberry pie," I said.

"I will," he said.

I said, "Are you tired? Do you want me to take you up to your bed? Are you ready to hit the hay?"

"Not yet," he said. "No, I'll stay up with you, bub. If that's all right. I'll stay up until you're ready to turn in. We haven't had a chance to talk. Know what I mean? I feel like me and her monopolized the evening." He lifted his beard and he let it fall. He picked up his cigarettes and lighter.

"That's all right," I said. Then I said, "I'm glad for the company."

And I guess I was. Every night I smoked dope and stayed up as long as I could before I fell asleep. My wife and I hardly ever went to bed at the same time. When I did go to sleep, I had these dreams. Sometimes I'd wake up from one of them, my heart going crazy.

Something about the church and the Middle Ages was on the TV. Not your run-of-the-mill TV fare. I wanted to watch something else. I turned to the other channels. But there was nothing on them, either. So I turned back to the first channel and apologized.

"Bub, it's all right," the blind man said. "It's fine with me. Whatever you want to watch is okay. I'm always learning something. Learning never ends. It won't hurt me to learn something tonight. I got ears," he said.

We didn't say anything for a time. He was leaning forward with his head turned at me, his right ear aimed in the direction of the set. Very disconcerting. Now and then his eyelids dropped and then they snapped open again. Now and then he put his fingers into his beard and tugged, like he was thinking about something he was hearing on the television.

On the screen, a group of men wearing cowls was being set upon and tormented by men dressed in skeleton costumes and men dressed as devils. The men dressed as devils wore devil masks, horns, and long tails. This pageant was part of a procession. The Englishman who was narrating the thing said it took place in Spain once a year. I tried to explain to the blind man what was happening.

"Skeletons," he said. "I know about skeletons," he said, and he nodded.

The TV showed this one cathedral. Then there was a long, slow look at another one. Finally, the picture switched to the famous one in Paris,[1] with its flying buttresses and its spires reaching up to the clouds. The camera pulled

1. Notre Dame de Paris.

away to show the whole of the cathedral rising above the skyline.

There were times when the Englishman who was telling the thing would shut up, would simply let the camera move around over the cathedrals. Or else the camera would tour the countryside, men in fields walking behind oxen. I waited as long as I could. Then I felt I had to say something. I said, "They're showing the outside of this cathedral now. Gargoyles. Little statues carved to look like monsters. Now I guess they're in Italy. Yeah, they're in Italy. There's paintings on the walls of this one church."

"Are those fresco paintings, bub?" he asked, and he sipped from his drink.

I reached for my glass. But it was empty. I tried to remember what I could remember. "You're asking me are those frescoes?" I said. "That's a good question. I don't know."

The camera moved to a cathedral outside Lisbon. The differences in the Portuguese cathedral compared with the French and Italian were not that great. But they were there. Mostly the interior stuff. Then something occurred to me, and I said, "Something has occurred to me. Do you have any idea what a cathedral is? What they look like, that is? Do you follow me? If somebody says cathedral to you, do you have any notion what they're talking about? Do you know the difference between that and a Baptist church, say?"

He let the smoke dribble from his mouth. "I know they took hundreds of workers fifty or a hundred years to build," he said. "I just heard the man say that, of course. I know generations of the same families worked on a cathedral. I heard him say that, too. The men who began their life's work on them, they never lived to see the completion of their work. In that wise, bub, they're no different from the rest of us, right?" He laughed. Then his eyelids drooped again. His head nodded. He seemed to be snoozing. Maybe he was imagining himself in Portugal. The TV was showing another cathedral now. This one was in Germany. The Englishman's voice droned on. "Cathedrals," the blind man said. He sat up and rolled his head back and forth. "If you want the truth, bub, that's about all I know. What I just said. What I heard him say. But maybe you could describe one to me? I wish you'd do it. I'd like that. If you want to know, I really don't have a good idea."

I stared hard at the shot of the cathedral on the TV. How could I even begin to describe it? But say my life depended on it. Say my life was being threatened by an insane guy who said I had to do it or else.

I stared some more at the cathedral before the picture flipped off into the countryside. There was no use. I turned to the blind man and said, "To begin with, they're very tall." I was looking around the room for clues. "They reach way up. Up and up. Toward the sky. They're so big, some of them, they have to have these supports. To help hold them up, so to speak. These supports are called buttresses. They remind me of viaducts, for some reason. But maybe you don't know viaducts, either? Sometimes the cathedrals have devils and such carved into the front. Sometimes lords and ladies. Don't ask me why this is," I said.

He was nodding. The whole upper part of his body seemed to be moving back and forth.

"I'm not doing so good, am I?" I said.

He stopped nodding and leaned forward on the edge of the sofa. As he listened to me, he was running his fingers through his beard. I wasn't getting through to him, I could see that. But he waited for me to go on just the same. He nodded, like he was trying to encourage me. I tried to think what else to say. "They're really big," I said. "They're massive. They're built of stone. Marble, too, sometimes. In those olden days, when they built cathedrals, men wanted to be close to God. In those olden days, God was an important part of everyone's life. You could tell this from their cathedral-building. I'm sorry," I said, "but it looks like that's the best I can do for you. I'm just no good at it."

"That's all right, bub," the blind man said. "Hey, listen. I hope you don't mind my asking you. Can I ask you something? Let me ask you a simple question, yes or no. I'm just curious and there's no offense. You're my host. But let me ask if you are in any way religious? You don't mind my asking?"

I shook my head. He couldn't see that, though. A wink is the same as a nod to a blind man. "I guess I don't believe in it. In anything. Sometimes it's hard. You know what I'm saying?"

"Sure, I do," he said.

"Right," I said.

The Englishman was still holding forth. My wife sighed in her sleep. She drew a long breath and went on with her sleeping.

"You'll have to forgive me," I said. "But I can't tell you what a cathedral looks like. It just isn't in me to do it. I can't do any more than I've done."

The blind man sat very still, his head down, as he listened to me.

I said, "The truth is, cathedrals don't mean anything special to me. Nothing. Cathedrals. They're something to look at on late-night TV. That's all they are."

It was then that the blind man cleared his throat. He brought something up. He took a handkerchief from his back pocket. Then he said, "I get it, bub. It's okay. It happens. Don't worry about it," he said. "Hey, listen to me. Will you do me a favor? I got an idea. Why don't you find us some heavy paper? And a pen. We'll do something. We'll draw one together. Get us a pen and some heavy paper. Go on, bub, get the stuff," he said.

So I went upstairs. My legs felt like they didn't have any strength in them. They felt like they did after I'd done some running. In my wife's room, I looked around. I found some ballpoints in a little basket on her table. And then I tried to think where to look for the kind of paper he was talking about.

Downstairs, in the kitchen, I found a shopping bag with onion skins at the bottom of the bag. I emptied the bag and shook it. I brought it into the living room and sat down with it near his legs. I moved some things, smoothed the wrinkles from the bag, spread it out on the coffee table.

The blind man got down from the sofa and sat next to me on the carpet.

He ran his fingers over the paper. He went up and down the sides of the paper. The edges, even the edges. He fingered the corners.

"All right," he said. "All right, let's do her."

He found my hand, the hand with the pen. He closed his hand over my hand. "Go ahead, bub, draw," he said. "Draw. You'll see. I'll follow along with you. It'll be okay. Just begin now like I'm telling you. You'll see. Draw," the blind man said.

So I began. First I drew a box that looked like a house. It could have been the house I lived in. Then I put a roof on it. At either end of the roof, I drew spires. Crazy.

"Swell," he said. "Terrific. You're doing fine," he said. "Never thought anything like this could happen in your lifetime, did you, bub? Well, it's a strange life, we all know that. Go on now. Keep it up."

I put in windows with arches. I drew flying buttresses. I hung great doors. I couldn't stop. The TV station went off the air. I put down the pen and closed and opened my fingers. The blind man felt around over the paper. He moved the tips of his fingers over the paper, all over what I had drawn, and he nodded.

"Doing fine," the blind man said.

I took up the pen again, and he found my hand. I kept at it. I'm no artist. But I kept drawing just the same.

My wife opened up her eyes and gazed at us. She sat up on the sofa, her robe hanging open. She said, "What are you doing? Tell me, I want to know."

I didn't answer her.

The blind man said, "We're drawing a cathedral. Me and him are working on it. Press hard," he said to me. "That's right. That's good," he said. "Sure. You got it, bub. I can tell. You didn't think you could. But you can, can't you? You're cooking with gas now. You know what I'm saying? We're going to really have us something here in a minute. How's the old arm?" he said. "Put some people in there now. What's a cathedral without people?"

My wife said, "What's going on? Robert, what are you doing? What's going on?"

"It's all right," he said to her. "Close your eyes now," the blind man said to me.

I did it. I closed them just like he said.

"Are they closed?" he said. "Don't fudge."

"They're closed," I said.

"Keep them that way," he said. He said, "Don't stop now. Draw."

So we kept on with it. His fingers rode my fingers as my hand went over the paper. It was like nothing else in my life up to now.

Then he said, "I think that's it. I think you got it," he said. "Take a look. What do you think?"

But I had my eyes closed. I thought I'd keep them that way for a little longer. I thought it was something I ought to do.

"Well?" he said. "Are you looking?"

My eyes were still closed. I was in my house. I knew that. But I didn't feel like I was inside anything.

"It's really something," I said.

# R. V. CASSILL

*Cassill (1919– ) was born in Cedar Falls, Iowa. As a young man he studied art with the intention of becoming a painter, but after army service in the South Pacific during World II, he began to write and publish fiction. As a teacher of writing at the University of Iowa, Purdue, Columbia, Harvard, and Brown, he numbers many novelists and short-story writers among his former students. His themes range from the little wars of childhood to the clashes of political ideologies, and several of his works deal with the role of the artist in our times. His novels include* Clem Anderson *(1961),* The President *(1964),* The Goss Women *(1974),* Hoyt's Child *(1976),* Labors of Love *(1980),* After Goliath *(1985), and* The Unknown Soldier *(1991). Several of his stories have been collected in* The Father *(1965),* The Happy Marriage *(1967),* Patrimonies *(1987), and* Late Stories *(1995). His* Collected Stories *appeared in 1989.*

## The Rationing of Love

For more than twenty years I was sure my father made too much of the coffee episode. Really, I told him whenever he mentioned the matter it was nothing, nothing, nothing. I wished he would put it out of his mind. I hadn't taken it seriously to begin with and would long ago have forgotten it if he had.

"But it was only one darn little cup of coffee and you were going *over there,*" he always insisted, blaming himself. "I told myself so many times, why, it was only a nickel's worth, but there was all that wartime rationing, you know."

Of course I knew. Had I ever, even for the blink of an eye, refused to accept his first explanation?

The day I went to be drafted in 1942 he refused me a second cup of coffee with my breakfast. He was working as a counterman at the Bolton & Hay Restaurant in Des Moines, having come up from Gath to attend the summer session at Drake University. He was after the master's degree required for his job as superintendent of the consolidated school in Gath.

I had not seen him since my wedding day. For more than a year I had been serious—giving up my college notions of being a painter so I could support a wife by selling farm implements in her hometown of Waterloo. I mean my first wife, and how odd it seems to think of her as "first wife" in the context of these memories, how odd not to think simply of her name. Ora McGilvery. "Ora means gold," my father told me solemnly at the wedding, implying that I should treat her accordingly.

I had come down alone by bus from Waterloo the evening before I was to be inducted at Camp Dodge. I'd stayed the night in the old Victoria Hotel, a rearing and raffish building whose corridors held some scent of illicit arrivals and departures, some stirring premonition of the worldwide turbulence into which I was being drawn. In my little room I had wakened intermittently at three and four in the morning to hear prowling footsteps outside my door, and when I woke I wondered if my wife was crying in the newness of our first separation. Before daybreak I had made myself think that she was all right, and from that it seemed to follow that everything about to happen to me was going to be all right.

So I felt really good as I walked down from the hotel to meet my father at the Bolton & Hay Restaurant. The hot morning seemed as snappy as the ruffle of drums. The capitol dome gleamed in the radiance of my self-confidence, and the shafts of the Civil War monuments there across the river on the capitol grounds held up their testimony to the bravery of us Midwestern heroes.

A cinder-skinned news butcher was shouting, "Tommies can't stop Rommel!"[1] Maybe the Tommies couldn't, but I was on my way that morning, in the nick of time. Look out, Hitler, here comes Ioway! I guess I really felt a little impatient that I had to stop to see my father at all before I took a bus out to Camp Dodge.

Fortunately my father was ready to share my mood. He wasn't taking the fall of Tobruk very hard. Most of the news he had to tell me was about my mother, brothers, and sister, and the folks in Gath. He wasn't bothered that I'd never "got back to painting" since I left college. He was glad Ora could stay with her parents while I was away. But mostly he was eager to tell me about himself.

There was a countryman's twinkle in his eyes and a conspiratorial lowering of his voice as he told how he had euchred his fellow waiters into letting him have the earliest shift at the lunch counter. "You take a lot of these city people aren't used to getting up till maybe six or seven in the morning. So I told them I'd just as soon come down and open the place up and get the coffee urns going and bring in the bakery stuff and milk. And, shoot, there's hardly anything doing here until after seven. So I have time to read the papers and go over my lessons. . . ."

For his job he wore a white dickey and jacket and a limp little bow tie, innocent as the rags that children wrap around their puppies. He was still deeply tanned from working in his garden at home before the summer-school session had started.

He said, "You take these other fellows who don't come on duty before seven-thirty, why they miss the best part of the day. By the time they have their four hours in, why, I'm back up on the campus and I've had a shower at the field house and a swim if I want to, and I'm out under a shade tree with my

1. Eric Rommel (the "Desert Fox"), World War II German field marshall (1891–1944).

books." Four hours of work each day earned him his meals and a dollar in cash that went to help pay his room rent.

While he was watching me eat eggs, bacon, and toast and drink my coffee, he said, "Now you just keep your money in your pocket, son. You may not get civilian food like this for a while, and it's my treat."

Of course I made no argument about that, and since I didn't want any sentimentality to edge in, I kept us talking about his summer. "You've got a pretty soft deal, Dad."

I hadn't meant at all to criticize, but my remark shifted him ever so slightly onto the defensive. "Your mother thinks I just come up to the University to loaf." Well, yes, it was true that my mother kept enforcing a family attitude that he was always too soft to take advantage of his opportunities. "Why," he said, "I'm taking nine hours credit this summer, and with what I've accumulated at Ames and Cedar Falls these last few years I'll get my degree. . . ."

"This summer?"

He didn't even bother to shake his head. ". . . with a little more extension work and making up my education credits, in nineteen forty-five. I'll bet the war will last at least that long, and the school board won't be likely to push me too hard for my degree as long as all those fellows are in the service and teachers hard to find."

"It won't take us till forty-five, Dad," I said, with the first queasy tremor of doubt I'd felt all morning.

"Who knows? You know, Buddy, your mother even said it didn't seem very dignified for a man my age to be working a board job like you boys did when you went to college. But shoot, I don't know what dignified is if it isn't being willing to do what has to be done."

I was glad then and later that he had said this to me before I left. For too many years while I was a kid at home I'd sided with the other children and my mother in a disrespectful tolerance of his weakness in the face of the school boards who sent us packing every three or four years from town to town, of his kid-glove treatment of the schoolmate bullies who used to knock my brothers and me around for no better reason than that we were the "superintendent's kids." We had blamed him—not too harshly, but persistently—when he let himself be cheated by the small-town garagemen and merchants who took advantage of him because he was a public employee dependent on their good will. We were used to resenting him—a little—because he didn't "stand up to people" and show off his dignity.

I liked him awfully much for telling me his side of all that old misery, but I only said, "I've got to run, Dad. Can I have another cup of coffee before I go to camp?" In a sort of embarrassment I waved my empty cup at him. It's funny how I remember that cup—a big awkward piece of restaurant crockery with two thin green bands painted around it.

He hesitated a minute, thinking. "Well, I'd like to son. . . ." He tried to grin when he shook his head and his grin began to hurt us both.

"I don't really want any," I said quickly.

"You know we're trying to do our bit with coffee rationing."

"I *know.*"

"It's only that the boss says. . . ."

"It was an awfully good breakfast, Dad."

"Now, you keep that money in your pocket. No sir, I'm paying for this. Do you need anything? You're going?" He was out from behind the counter quicker than I ever saw him move. As he walked to the door he put his arm over my shoulder, and as we stepped into the explosive sunlight of the street he kissed me quickly on the forehead. He hadn't kissed me since I was five.

He had unbuckled his wristwatch and was trying to fasten the old, sweated band around my arm. "Noticed you weren't wearing one," he said. I let him fasten it, looked at the time, said I'd have to run now to catch the right bus to Camp Dodge.

"Come on back," he said. "Please, come on now, you've got time for one more cup of coffee with me."

But I said I hadn't and that I really, really had drunk all the coffee I needed for a while.

## II

In a bad war, in my own worst phases of it, I lucked out with a consistency just short of miraculous. I mean, the miracles were there to be remembered when I had the heart to poke under the garbage for them.

For one thing, on a rain-drenched island as far from combat as it was from any place fit for human habitation, I started painting again while I was convalescing from a rare Asiatic type of diphtheria. It wasn't the throat kind of diphtheria. It spread big colonies of ulcers all over my skin and poisoned me internally so that I was weeks in getting my strength back after the sores cleared up.

Two cultivated ladies named Fitch and Helspur ran the Red Cross hut at the hospital. When they found out I'd had "art training" they not only rummaged out a fine set of oil paints and canvas, they even wanted me to start classes for the other patients. I was too tired for that. Mostly I sat on the back steps of the New Zealand hut they occupied and painted a banana tree on which the bananas were ripening as my abused cell structure mended.

"You're a regular Van Gogh with those yellows," Miss Fitch told me. It was her profession to be flattering.

I put the lovely, creamy brushful of yellow paint back down on the palette, lit a cigarette, and grinned at her through the rising goblin shapes of smoke. I had learned how important it was in my condition and at the juncture of the war in the Pacific to take things easy and slow when you could. She sat down with me and compared the painted yellows with the real bananas.

I said, "You know the first time I ever saw a banana tree? Understand, I always lived in small towns, but my father was a teacher, and he was always going to some college to summer school. . . ."

I'd set her off now. Her father and her uncle and her two great uncles had all been teachers. At Amherst, Smith, and Duke. She herself had been working on her doctorate at Columbia before she joined the Red Cross. She understood *exactly* what it meant to come from "a family of educators."

While she was running on enthusiastically I shook my head slow and steady. "No, no, no. It wasn't like that for us. My father only went into teaching to raise enough money to buy a farm. He kept on because the family kept growing, that's all. He started out a long time ago with not much more than an eighth-grade education. It took him almost twenty years of summer schools to get his B.A. Anyhow, depending on which college we lived nearest, he used to go off to Cedar Falls, or Ames, or Drake. From the time I was very small I remember his bringing the whole family over to see where he was going to college. Next to the stuffed zebras and whale skeletons in the natural history collections, what I remember best is the greenhouse at the college in Cedar Falls where they had a banana tree just like that one."

"Wonderful!" Miss Fitch said. I could tell she was picturing my father as some grave and stately academician teaching us kids the Latin names of the rare flora—while what my father had said was, "Imagine that! Bananas growing right here in Iowa! Look at 'em growing upside down!"

Because she was such an enthusiastic listener, I told Miss Fitch, "Once when he was in summer school at Ames he took me to see the great, wonderful indoor swimming pool they had there. Imagine that! But it *was* great and wonderful to me. I'd never seen anything like it. The reverberations of the boards in there when the guys dived, the color of the water . . . the color of that chlorinated water was just like the water up around Ulithi, and the mortar shells around us when we were wading in . . . I tell you I'd heard them before when Dad took me to that swimming pool and the diving boards rumbled."

I picked up my brush again from the palette and my hand was trembling. I wasn't any Van Gogh and I didn't any longer expect to be, but the painting—and the associations between one banana tree here and another back there—were making a bridge I needed to live by.

"It makes all the difference if you come from a family of educators," Miss Fitch said, far away in her dream of an Amherst girlhood. It didn't matter that I could never explain to her the petty quarrels in my "family of educators"—about how much of our homemade furniture we'd take with us when we moved from one rinky-dink town to another; whether they should sell my mother's piano after she forgot how to play it; whether the school board hadn't promised to find Dad a lot to keep our cow in when they hired him.

"I'm sure you came by your interest in art from *them*," Miss Fitch said.

"Sure. My mother was a frustrated artiste of the piano," I said lightly. "Naturally, at least one kid had to carry on the yokel dream of busting out of the small town. What does it matter? All that's in the bag now, anyway. Next week or the week after—whenever they cut my orders and there's a ship going that way—I'll go up to Okinawa to join my outfit."

Now knowing how much she'd helped with a miracle, Miss Fitch promised that when I left she and Miss Helspur would pack my new canvases and see that they got home to my wife.

I lucked out, too, when I fell off a troopship in Buckner Bay at Okinawa. The war was over then and we were loading to go home. We were loading from a small boat onto the S. S. Sherman. Tom Hartman was ahead of me on the ladder. I suppose our weird, larking gratitude for surviving the war had become a kind of hysteria. So we were horsing around and it was my own foolish fault that I lunged for the guard rope, missed it, and pitched into the bay.

It happened, too, that I was wearing a field pack full of souvenirs as I fell. That made a bad outfit for swimming. So when I went down headfirst past the small boat, I thought the surprised faces of the boatmen might be the last ones I would ever see.

I went deep before I could get the pack off my shoulders. First I couldn't understand that I had to let it go. Then, as the green of the water got darker around me, the pack clung as if it owned me—that bag full of Okinawa pottery, Japanese pistols, a stained battle flag, and a wooden Buddha I'd looted from a house split open by shellfire. It held onto me like someone drowning who was afraid to let me live if I couldn't take him back up with me.

I don't remember shaking loose from it. All at once I was rising fast and the weight was gone. The strangling water fell away from my face. I saw the boatmen's hands reaching down for mine.

So far so good, but in the same glance I saw my father's wristwatch streaming bright droplets. My first coherent thought as the Navy men were hauling me into their boat was: I finally ruined it for him.

Then all the superstitions I'd been nourishing for three years of war began to concentrate on that ruined watch. I remember how wildly I talked about it to Tom Hartman that night as the ship wallowed east toward home. "I should have got it back to him in the condition he gave it to me."

"Does your father make a lot out of little gestures like that?" he wanted to know.

"I do, whether he does nor not." Then I remembered and laughed. "He's as bad as I am. He'll want to buy me a cup of coffee the minute he sees me." I told Tom what had happened the day I was inducted.

He said, "Well, you better let him buy it for you."

All at once I went morose. I suppose the aftereffects of nearly drowning were coming up on me the way a pain in the jaw comes when the Novocaine wears off. "No, that's silly," I said. "Nothing's going to put things back the way they were before we left. It's too late for some of the things we missed. Are you scared about going home?"

I wish he had said he wasn't. All too easily he knew what I was talking about. "Everybody our age, everybody who's been over as long as we have is a little bit scared. You hear it from everybody," he said. After a while he said, "That's silly. What's to be scared of? Lights, music, girls . . . ?"

We didn't say it, but we were afraid of having permanently lost the track of our lives. Mine—up to the day I'd been drafted—had been nothing but fooling around, as if I'd just been killing time until the war came and a use was found for me. "I found a job just so I could get married," I said. "I wasn't even good at it, or at anything else. So what now?"

"So you might as well have drowned this afternoon." I didn't blame him at all for saying it. He was a man with worries of his own.

I had the mental, moral shakes that night, trying to add up the score of my life in the world as I'd seen it—and coming out with a big round goose egg as of that hour. Coming out with a kind of sad contempt for what I'd grown up trusting. I remembered one time when my father gave the commencement address at Chesterfield for a graduating class of twelve. I had to go to all his public speeches when I was little. Usually I hadn't listened. This time, though, I'd listened because he was talking about Grandpa, whom I'd loved more than anybody. Grandpa, he said, had got in some land dispute with a neighbor. There had been talk among the farmers about how the quarrel could come to a knifing. This neighbor—who must have been a wild man in a generally peaceable community—actually got to carrying a pig sticker with him and showing it at the country store and saying what he meant to do with it.

One day he came by on the road in a spring wagon while my father and Grandpa were raking hay. My father told how Grandpa climbed the fence, went to the middle of the road, and stopped this wild guy, then walked up to him and put out his hand to shake.

That's all there was to the story, and there was my dad up in front of that squirming audience that couldn't care less, him with his bow tie and his soft little grin, holding out his hand to show how it was done. That was his idea of how all problems, domestic and foreign, could probably be handled.

Ah, but behind our ship as I recalled this were the dead cities of Okinawa and Japan. By now the first snow had fallen on the flat cinders of Hiroshima, Nagoya, and the rest. There was Naha blasted into rubble and Shuri Castle where the artillery had blown away everything but the foundations of the ancient walls. With things like that right behind us, who could take seriously a little quarrel so easily mended on a dirt road in southern Iowa?

There was no connection anymore. Before I slept that night I took my father's watch topside and threw it into the froth of our wake. I could be as superstitious as any man in the Army—and believe that watch was the charm that had seen me through. The same superstitions, and a lot more besides, told me it was useless from here on out.

## III

The real miracle of those years was what had happened to Ora. She had grown up while I was away. Without any such melodramatic gesture as tossing a watch into the ocean, she had loosened the ties with her parents. She made it instantly clear to me that I wasn't going back to a futureless job in Waterloo. She had moved to Chicago before I shipped up to Okinawa, and the first thing that faced me when I walked into her apartment on Dearborn Street were some of the banana-tree paintings Miss Fitch and Miss Helspur had sent home. She had also hung up some older things I had done in college.

There was only a sundown light in the room when we came in from the taxi, a poor light that made the paintings look better than they were. The yellow bananas glowed like candle flames against a green background more mysterious than the jungle around the Red Cross hut on the island I'd never see again.

"They're not exactly works of genius," I said when I had switched on the apartment lights.

Ora shook her dark head stubbornly. "All right. Not yet. They're going to be."

I said, "Sure. Turn out the lights again. That improves them."

"We're going to New York," she said. "You're going to study at the Art Students League. Of course you are. You've got the GI bill and you've got me. I'm an economic asset. I've got a job there already. I mean I'm almost sure I have. We might, we just might even have a place to live, though that's tougher in New York than here, even."

"A decent job?" I asked.

She made a face at me, a good-natured grimace, but she was disappointed by my caution. "Oh, don't talk like your father or my father or we'll never get anywhere. If New York won't have us, we'll keep going. We'll go on to Paris. Why not?"

"Now you're talking worse than my mother," I said. "There's no use in that."

"I'm not talking like anybody. I'm talking about *us*."

Let it be understood that our conversation was taking place almost the instant I had returned from twenty-eight months overseas. We had not even kissed yet since we came into the apartment, though we had kissed hard and well when she met me at the station and in the taxi that brought us to the North Side. All the anxiety and hope of my return had avalanched into this moment of decision.

And though we had much more to figure out before we left, I knew from then on that we would go. She had challenged me to put up or shut up about all I knew had fallen short in my parents' lives. I said, "O.K."

Then Ora was kneeling beside me in the wide easy chair, kissing me and rubbing her tears all over my face. "You're going to have your chance. You'll be a great painter," she said. Beyond the fringe of her hair I saw the charcoal velvet silhouette of buildings beyond our little window, a sky the color of a wonderful slice of melon. I had a painter's eye, all right. But it took Ora to show me that even Chicago was not a big enough town to hold us.

Paris was our city. New York didn't seem to have room for us that year. We went past it with a lordly air and borrowed boat fare. Paris was home for several years, and I keep thinking we should have been happy there, since we both loved it so much. But we weren't. Our years there provided "the foundation of my career," as it says in the brochure printed just last year by the gallery in Chicago that handles my painting, now that I've come back to work and teach in the Midwest. There never was a young couple in Paris who got more excitement and pleasure in discovering the fine parks, the old splendors of cathedrals and chateaux, places to eat and buy things, the displays of weather over the Seine, and the way the trees would darken secretly in the Luxembourg Gardens after the steel gates were closed for the night across the street from our apartment.

Too rich for our blood? There was a fault somewhere.

Ora worked first for an American oil company and later for the American Embassy. In the first years I walked alongside the Luxembourg Gardens every morning on my way to the Grande Chaumiere where I was painting with Leger. Paris was very poor in those years just after the war, and we weren't. We had a sports car pretty soon for summer trips into the Loire valley and the Dordogne. When Ora went to the embassy we had PX[2] privileges, American goodies for ourselves and for the black market. Happy or not, we lived the big life, and we stayed long enough to see Paris change again into the prospering capital of the world. Among the Fulbright students and other new waves of young Americans we were accepted as old settlers. I was painting pretty well. I was making contacts with people who could do me some good.

Letters from my parents in those years came like drafts from a window one has forgotten to close before lying down for a warm nap. My mother's indicated she thought we were living an idealist missionary life—presumably weaning the French away from their bad habits of drinking wine, making love indiscriminately, and abusing their colonial peoples. She hoped we would not have children until we got back to the shelter of American sanitation.

My father, who only wrote short notes at Christmas or for our birthdays, seemed to make no distinction between my being "over there" among the Bohemians and my having been "over there" with the Army. I used to read his letters in my favorite cafe on the square at St. Sulpice and parody them for my friends. I would remember them with a kind of terrible nostalgia while I was getting stewed in the *caves* around St. Germain—or at the Select, in the winter of Eleanor. One night when the police picked me up for riotous behavior in Montparnasse I went into a yelling fit in the back of the *salade panier*, the police van. The next day I could remember only that I had been trying to tell my father I was a long time out of the Army and the damned South Pacific and nobody was giving me orders anymore.

If there ever was a chance to clear up such truths for him, I had it when I came back to Iowa in 1954 to tell my parents why Ora divorced me. They hadn't known her well, but they cared about her and knew that I had, too.

So my efforts to be scrupulous in my explanations only confused them further. They wouldn't believe me. They wouldn't comprehend that it had been all my fault instead of the fault of the corrupt French environment. They couldn't quite see why, just because I took some initial interest in the paintings of a Fulbright student named Eleanor Marshall, I should have run off to Africa with her. Or why, when the intoxications of novelty wore off with the drugs we got from the Algerians, Eleanor and I had begun a hesitant, slow circling back toward Paris. I could recall the nastiness and despair of those weeks in Alexandria and the days in Naples, but I just lacked the language to tell the old folks our great sin excursion collapsed because we had used up the money I stole from Ora and saved from black-marketing PX goods.

I heard my own voice tell them these things. I doubt if they heard much. They were living now in another small Iowa town where again my father was teaching. The house to which I had come was excruciatingly like the other houses I remembered living in while I was growing up. The same dark, small living room, the same softwood floors varnished dark, the same high school graduation pictures of my brothers, sister, and me on the piano that had been moved so often and played so little.

2. Post exchange.

It was early summer and the kitchen windows were open as we sat at supper. A light rain was falling on the potted flowers my mother had set on a shelf outside the windows to get some fresh air. My mother said, "I suppose that Eleanor will be coming back soon to join you."

I shook my head carefully, as if I might spatter filth over her clean kitchen if I shook too hard. "She's not going to join me, Mama. She came to New York before I did. I'm not going to see her, didn't I make that clear?"

It was lucky my fingernails were chewed short or I might have drawn blood from the clenching of my hands. The last thing I'd wanted from this visit was the kind of dull sympathy I was getting. Maybe in some dream I had expected I was going to be punished here, like the time I was punished for shooting at the Alleman girl with my air rifle when we lived in Chesterfield.

"I don't understand much about divorces," my mother said, still resisting, still sure things could be arranged for the best, "but it seems to me there's no reason you and she can't be married if you wanted to as bad as all that."

I remembered Eleanor and me lying side by side on a bed in a bad hotel in Rome. It was raining outside that room, too, but it was very cold there so the chill came right through the walls. We'd lain fully dressed with nothing to say to each other, merely passing a rare cigarette back and forth, waiting for the day to be over. The moisture of our lips on the cigarette paper was the only intimacy between us by then.

"At least we'll be spared marriage, whatever other payment we still have to make."

I'm not sure my mother caught the full savagery of what I'd said. My father did. He'd never been stretched past the point of endurance by the untouchable loveliness of my Paris, never seen with a painter's hopeless eye the high white clouds over Oran in the inexpressible Mediterranean light. How could he imagine Eleanor's strange mouth ready to be kissed? He only thought my paintings were "all right if there's people want to buy such things." But he knew what counted.

While I had been talking to my mother he had risen from the supper table. He stood at the window and his hands reached outside, fumbling with or caressing the wet geranium leaves.

After a while he said, "Darn it, I've thought so many times, why didn't I give you that second cup of coffee when you were going away?"

As if that one thing alone might have saved me from all my delinquencies! As if without this one default of courage he might have kept me true!

## IV

My mother nearly died last fall. She dwindled and grew dull through the spring and summer. Each time I drove over from Illinois with my wife and three young children she seemed progressively less interested in finding toys from the attic for the little ones, even less sure of their names. Getting old, we said.

Then she fell down the basement stairs while she was bringing in flower bulbs from the garden about to freeze. She may have hit her head in the fall.

She was very confused and dazed afterward. But when she was taken to the hospital in Des Moines the main source of her trouble was diagnosed as a tumor of the spleen, which had been seriously affecting her blood-sugar level. This had been going on long enough to suggest there might have been brain damage before her tumble.

Occasionally, when we visited her in the hospital, she would seem like her old self. These were times when she had been given medicine to counter the insulin surplus and had taken a lot of extra sugar in her orange juice. When my father, brothers, and sister hovered around her bed she could still beam and chatter and press our hands and thank us for "coming all that way" to be with her at such a time. "All that way. . . ." Perhaps she still thought I was living in Paris. At any rate, her quaint manner of putting it made me remember all my travels as if they were a single journey toward this time of anguish.

With extraordinary effort she could remember each of her grandchildren. When I prompted her, she asked about my children individually and by name. Were they anxious for snow? Did they like kindergarten and school?

But she was frightened, too. Sometimes, even at her most lucid moments and even when all of us were with her, she would ignore her children and speak only to my father. She questioned him about insurance, about the burial plot they had arranged for in the yard of the church where they were married, and about whether someone was taking care of her plants while she was away.

We saw that she always scared him with such talk. "You're not going to die, Mother," he told her over and over again—while the rest of us resolutely avoided any mention of death in her presence.

Often we found her out of her head—when the level of her blood sugar was not being artificially maintained—and she raved her distrust of the doctors who came several times a day to "bother her" and "wasted so much time" in getting it over with.

Her operation, when it took place, was mercifully briefer and luckier than we had been led to expect by the doctors. Her tumor was benign. Very little exploratory surgery was needed to locate it, though it had not showed in the x-rays.

Nonetheless, some ultimate transformation had been wrought on her in those hours when she was under anaesthetic. I was alone with her in the recovery room—we were permitted to go in to her only one at a time—when the fog of ether was leaving her. She was discovering that her right arm was bound to a board to keep the intravenous tube in place, and she fought the bondage piteously, trying to tear the tube out of the vein. Another tube was taped over her forehead and into her right nostril. I restrained her as gently as I could. She hated me for siding with all her other persecutors.

"They have no right to an old lady," she said. "Cut her all open. Bring her in here and cut her body." There was a horrifying strength in the free hand that wrestled against mine to get at the IV tube. Then she became aware of the other tube in her nose. "What's that for, too?" she said, and clawed for it.

I had to call a nurse, and we tied both hands down to make her leave the tubes alone.

She hadn't the strength to raise her head, of course. The hatred in her eyes was like the blow of a fist. She glared at me as if I were her murderer. "You have no right," she said.

"It won't be long now, Mama," I said. "I know you're very uncomfortable right now. They'll give you something for the pain and to make you sleep."

"Oh, the pain," she said. "Untie me. Let me loose."

"No. I won't."

*"Let me loose!"* Her voice was like a man's, compelling and brutal. Perhaps if the nurses had not been working nearby I might have done what she demanded.

"I can't let you loose," I said. "You'll be all right. You'll sleep. You'll rest. You'll sleep."

She turned her head to the side. Her crepey cheek was almost as crimson as blood from the great effort she was making. The tears on her cheek were tears of anger. "Why didn't they get it over with?"

"It's not going to be over," I said. "Don't you understand? You didn't have cancer. You'll be all right. It will take a while to get your strength back, but you're going to be fine."

"Why?"

I'm not certain she meant anything by this syllable. Surely I shouldn't have tried to answer then. But I said, "Why, because we need you. We all need you. My children, too. They've been wanting to come and see Grandma and go up into the attic with her again. Play the piano with her. . . ."

Now she knew exactly what she had to say. It was as if she had always been trying to clarify it. She said it now with a last, hoarded emphasis of deliberation. "No one has any right to bring children into the world." She meant me. She meant my sons. Our wickedness and our suffering had been from her, and she repented us. "Where's Ora? Where's your wife?" she asked with awful scorn. "Ora had no children. What have you done with her?"

I said nothing.

She smiled a little, a smile of terrible cruelty. "We have no right," she said tiredly. Then—perhaps she was sinking back into the vision or dream that had deviled her while she was on the operating table.

"The children are burning everywhere," she said vaguely.

It was less than an hour after that when my father and I walked down the hill from the hospital in the November sun. I saw that my shadow was longer than his on the concrete slope ahead of us, but his step was jauntier than mine. As if he didn't know yet—as if he was never going to find out—the truth my mother had just told me.

"The doctor said it was no bigger than a fingertip," he said of the tumor that had been removed from her. "Boy, the doctor said it was certainly good luck they found it so quick when the x-ray couldn't find it."

"We've been very lucky."

"Well, we sure have." He took a long trembling breath. It sounded like my youngest boy when he has been crying hard and is trying to reestablish a normal rhythm of breathing. "And you know, lucky with the Blue Cross and all. Just couldn't have been luckier."

He had a right to his relief, but I was suspicious of its excess and warned him, "She's not going to be the same, Dad."

"Why," he said, "why, I know that. Why, *of course not*. We're getting older, and all."

"She's in her seventies. It isn't going to be easy for her to make a comeback."

"*Of course* it won't. And I don't know what's the best thing to plan. The doctor said that, well, maybe the best thing for me to count on is to put her in a nursing home awhile because her convalescence might be months, and he thought I wouldn't be much of a hand for taking care of her."

It might well be more than a matter of months. The doctors to whom I had spoken avoided the word *convalescence*. She was too old. There was no return from the descent she had begun. "We ought to consider a nursing home," I said cautiously.

"Why, why, I told him *no*! Why I'd crawl on my hands and knees to take care of her before I'd let them take her away."

He tossed that off as a matter of fact. So jauntily. I doubted if he had even weighed the realities of what might be still to come. He just knew what he had to do—and I envied him for that as I never expected to envy another human being. All his life with us we had thought him too soft, gentle but a little foolish—and he had nursed his courage in the shade of soft foolishness until the time to use it well had come. I knew that, and the wonderful thing is that I think he knew it too.

"Well," I said, "well. We better turn and go back to the hospital."

"Just down that next block. All right?"

I had supposed we were merely getting a breath of fresh air before we rejoined the rest of the family in the vigil at the hospital.

No. He had known exactly where he was leading me. In the next block was the Bolton & Hay Restaurant where I'd said goodbye to him when I went in the Army. Suddenly there we were, in front of it.

"You know, son," he said with his old easy, floppy smile, "you know there's something that's bothered me. . . ."

Of course I knew what was coming, and I wanted no part of it. He had no trick to play except a sentimental one, and that was not nearly enough. The things we had done wrong with our lives were signed, sealed and irretrievable. Ora was gone; I had my new wife and children. My mother was going to live, but her faith in life had not lasted quite as long as her outraged body. I had paid more than a man should choose to pay for my small share of success. My mother had not touched her piano for thirty years. We had been lucky to come this far with a divided verdict.

We had been lucky. My father said so and I believed him. But I saw now that the reckless old fool wanted still to gamble for more. I caught my breath as if watching a clownish acrobat preparing to challenge the trim, athletic professionals on the high wire. He was going to insist you *could* go back, in spite of time, and make the past all right.

"Now," he said, rather formally. "I could just as well have given you that cup of coffee you asked for that morning. Just as well as not."

His trick depended on just one thing—on my willingness to believe in it, at the price of all I'd paid so much to learn. I guessed I could if I wanted to. Nothing was stopping me.

I said, "Well, since we're here, why don't you get it for me now?" The worst had been ahead of us. Now it was behind us. Both of us could claim that much victory.

He said that to give me the coffee I had asked for was just exactly what he intended to do.

Like a boy, I followed him into the restaurant.

# WILLA CATHER

*Cather (1873–1947) was born of Anglo-Irish parents in Back Creek Valley, Virginia. At ten she moved with her family to Red Cloud, Nebraska, where she grew up, exploring the prairies on horseback and making friends with the immigrant farmers of the area. While she worked her way through the University of Nebraska, she acquired an enduring passion for music and determined to devote her energies to writing. From 1896 to 1905 she worked for a newspaper in Pittsburgh, and she later held editorial positions in New York, but her poetry and fiction looked to the Midwest and Southwest for their subject matter and to the depths of the American past for their values. She never married. The last part of her life was spent in New York, with occasional European travels that never swayed her from nostalgia or the conservatism of her views. Once she declared that the world had "broken apart" about 1922; unmistakably, she preferred the manners, styles, and virtues that prevailed before that date. Among her novels are* My Antonía *(1918),* A Lost Lady *(1923),* The Professor's House *(1925), and* Death Comes for the Archbishop *(1927).* Not under Forty *(1936) contains many of her essays. Her collections of short stories are* Youth and the Bright Medusa *(1920),* Obscure Destinies *(1932), and* The Old Beauty and Others *(1948).*

## Paul's Case

### A Study in Temperament

It was Paul's afternoon to appear before the faculty of the Pittsburgh High School to account for his various misdemeanors. He had been suspended a week ago, and his father had called at the Principal's office and confessed his perplexity about his son. Paul entered the faculty room suave and smiling. His clothes were a trifle outgrown, and the tan velvet on the collar of his open overcoat was frayed and worn; but for all that there was something of the dandy about him, and he wore an opal pin in his neatly knotted black four-in-hand,[1] and a red carnation in his buttonhole. This latter adornment the faculty somehow felt was not properly significant of the contrite spirit befitting a boy under the ban of suspension.

Paul was tall for his age and very thin, with high, cramped shoulders and a narrow chest. His eyes were remarkable for a certain hysterical brilliancy, and he continually used them in a conscious, theatrical sort of way, peculiarly offensive in a boy. The pupils were abnormally large, as though he were addicted to

1. The long necktie we are now familiar with.

belladonna, but there was a glassy glitter about them which that drug does not produce.

When questioned by the Principal as to why he was there Paul stated, politely enough, that he wanted to come back to school. This was a lie, but Paul was quite accustomed to lying; found it, indeed, indispensable for overcoming friction. His teachers were asked to state their respective charges against him, which they did with such a rancor and aggrievedness as evinced that this was not a usual case. Disorder and impertinence were among the offenses named, yet each of his instructors felt that it was scarcely possible to put into words the real cause of the trouble, which lay in a sort of hysterically defiant manner of the boy's; in the contempt which they all knew he felt for them, and which he seemingly made not the least effort to conceal. Once, when he had been making a synopsis of a paragraph at the blackboard, his English teacher had stepped to his side and attempted to guide his hand. Paul had started back with a shudder and thrust his hands violently behind him. The astonished woman could scarcely have been more hurt and embarrassed had he struck at her. The insult was so involuntary and definitely personal as to be unforgettable. In one way and another he had made all his teachers, men and women alike, conscious of the same feeling of physical aversion. In one class he habitually sat with his hand shading his eyes; in another he always looked out of the window during the recitation; in another he made a running commentary on the lecture, with humorous intention.

His teachers felt this afternoon that his whole attitude was symbolized by his shrug and his flippantly red carnation flower, and they fell upon him without mercy, his English teacher leading the pack. He stood through it smiling, his pale lips parted over his white teeth. (His lips were continually twitching, and he had a habit of raising his eyebrows that was contemptuous and irritating to the last degree.) Older boys than Paul had broken down and shed tears under that baptism of fire, but his set smile did not once desert him, and his only sign of discomfort was the nervous trembling of the fingers that toyed with the buttons of his overcoat, and an occasional jerking of the other hand that held his hat. Paul was always smiling, always glancing about him, seeming to feel that people might be watching him and trying to detect something. This conscious expression, since it was as far as possible from boyish mirthfulness, was usually attributed to insolence or "smartness."

As the inquisition proceeded one of his instructors repeated an impertinent remark of the boy's, and the Principal asked him whether he thought that a courteous speech to have made a woman. Paul shrugged his shoulders slightly and his eyebrows twitched.

"I don't know," he replied. "I didn't mean to be polite or impolite, either. I guess it's a sort of way I have of saying things regardless."

The Principal, who was a sympathetic man, asked him whether he didn't think that a way it would be well to get rid of. Paul grinned and said he guessed so. When he was told that he could go he bowed gracefully and went out. His bow was but a repetition of the scandalous red carnation.

His teachers were in despair, and his drawing master voiced the feeling of them all when he declared there was something about the boy which none of them understood. He added: "I don't really believe that smile of his comes altogether from insolence; there's something sort of haunted about it. The boy is not strong, for one thing. I happen to know that he was born in Colorado, only a few months before his mother died out there of a long illness. There is something wrong about the fellow."

The drawing master had come to realize that, in looking at Paul, one saw only his white teeth and the forced animation of his eyes. One warm afternoon the boy had gone to sleep at his drawing board, and his master had noted with amazement what a white, blue-veined face it was; drawn and wrinkled like an old man's about the eyes, the lips twitching even in his sleep, and stiff with a nervous tension that drew them back from his teeth.

His teachers left the building dissatisfied and unhappy; humiliated to have felt so vindictive toward a mere boy, to have uttered this feeling in cutting terms, and to have set each other on, as it were, in the gruesome game of intemperate reproach. Some of them remembered having seen a miserable street cat set at bay by a ring of tormentors.

As for Paul, he ran down the hill whistling the "Soldiers' Chorus" from *Faust*,[2] looking wildly behind him now and then to see whether some of his teachers were not there to writhe under his lightheartedness. As it was now late in the afternoon and Paul was on duty that evening as usher at Carnegie Hall,[3] he decided that he would not go home to supper. When he reached the concert hall the doors were not yet open and, as it was chilly outside, he decided to go up into the picture gallery—always deserted at this hour—where there were some of Raffaelli's[4] gay studies of Paris streets and an airy blue Venetian scene or two that always exhilarated him. He was delighted to find no one in the gallery but the old guard, who sat in one corner, a newspaper on his knee, a black patch over one eye and the other closed. Paul possessed himself of the place and walked confidently up and down, whistling under his breath. After a while he sat down before a blue Rico[5] and lost himself. When he bethought him to look at his watch, it was after seven o'clock, and he rose with a start and ran downstairs, making a face at Augustus, peering out from the cast room, and an evil gesture at the Venus de Milo[6] as he passed her on the stairway.

When Paul reached the ushers' dressing room half a dozen boys were there already, and he began excitedly to tumble into his uniform. It was one of the few that at all approached fitting, and Paul thought it very becoming—though he knew that the tight, straight coat accentuated his narrow chest, about which he was exceedingly sensitive. He was always considerably excited while he dressed, twanging all over to the tuning of the strings and the preliminary flourishes of the horns in the music room; but tonight he seemed quite beside himself, and he teased and plagued the boys until, telling him that he was crazy, they put him down on the floor and sat on him.

Somewhat calmed by his suppression, Paul dashed out to the front of the

2. Opera by Charles Gounod (1818–1893). 3. Named for Andrew Carnegie (1835–1919), famous industrialist and philanthropist. 4. Jean-François Raffaelli (1850–1924), French painter, sculptor, and etcher. 5. Andreas Rico (1500–1550), Cretan-Italian painter. 6. A famous Greek statue; the original is in the Louvre, Paris. Augustus (63 B.C.E.–C.E. 14) was the first Roman emperor.

house to seat the early comers. He was a model usher; gracious and smiling he ran up and down the aisles; nothing was too much trouble for him; he carried messages and brought programs as though it were his greatest pleasure in life, and all the people in his section thought him a charming boy, feeling that he remembered and admired them. As the house filled, he grew more and more vivacious and animated, and the color came to his cheeks and lips. It was very much as though this were a great reception and Paul were the host. Just as the musicians came out to take their places, his English teacher arrived with checks for the seats which a prominent manufacturer had taken for the season. She betrayed some embarrassment when she handed Paul the tickets, and a hauteur which subsequently made her feel very foolish. Paul was startled for a moment, and had the feeling of wanting to put her out; what business had she here among all these fine people and gay colors? He looked her over and decided that she was not appropriately dressed and must be a fool to sit downstairs in such togs. The tickets had probably been sent her out of kindness, he reflected as he put down a seat for her, and she had about as much right to sit there as he had.

When the symphony began Paul sank into one of the rear seats with a long sigh of relief, and lost himself, as he had done before the Rico. It was not that symphonies, as such, meant anything in particular to Paul, but the first sigh of the instruments seemed to free some hilarious and potent spirit within him; something that struggled there like the genie in the bottle found by the Arab fisherman.[7] He felt a sudden zest of life; the lights danced before his eyes and the concert hall blazed into unimaginable splendor. When the soprano soloist came on Paul forgot even the nastiness of his teacher's being there and gave himself up to the peculiar stimulus such personages always had for him. The soloist chanced to be a German woman, by no means in her first youth, and the mother of many children; but she wore an elaborate gown and tiara, and above all she had that indefinable air of achievement, that worldshine upon her, which, in Paul's eyes, made her a veritable queen of Romance.

After a concert was over Paul was always irritable and wretched until he got to sleep, and tonight he was even more than usually restless. He had the feeling of not being able to let down, of its being impossible to give up this delicious excitement which was the only thing that could be called living at all. During the last number he withdrew and, after hastily changing his clothes in the dressing room, slipped out to the side door where the soprano's carriage stood. Here he began pacing rapidly up and down the walk, waiting to see her come out.

Over yonder, the Schenley, in its vacant stretch, loomed big and square through the fine rain, the windows of its twelve stories glowing like those of a lighted cardboard house under a Christmas tree. All the actors and singers of the better class stayed there when they were in the city, and a number of the big manufacturers of the place lived there in the winter. Paul had often hung

7. In one of the tales of the *Arabian Nights* (also called *Thousand and One Nights*), the fisherman Ali Baba finds a genie imprisoned in a bottle who is able to perform miracles.

offspring, and interspersed their legends of the iron kings[4] with remarks about their sons' progress at school, their grades in arithmetic, and the amounts they had saved in their toy banks.

On this last Sunday of November Paul sat all the afternoon on the lowest step of his stoop, staring into the street, while his sisters, in their rockers, were talking to the minister's daughters next door about how many shirtwaists they had made in the last week, and how many waffles someone had eaten at the last church supper. When the weather was warm, and his father was in a particularly jovial frame of mind, the girls made lemonade, which was always brought out in a red-glass pitcher, ornamented with forget-me-nots in blue enamel. This the girls thought very fine, and the neighbors always joked about the suspicious color of the pitcher.

Today Paul's father sat on the top step, talking to a young man who shifted a restless baby from knee to knee. He happened to be the young man who was daily held up to Paul as a model, and after whom it was his father's dearest hope that he would pattern. This young man was of a ruddy complexion, with a compressed, red mouth, and faded, nearsighted eyes, over which he wore thick spectacles, with gold bows that curved about his ears. He was clerk to one of the magnates of a great steel corporation, and was looked upon in Cordelia Street as a young man with a future. There was a story that, some five years ago—he was now barely twenty-six—he had been a trifle dissipated, but in order to curb his appetites and save the loss of time and strength that a sowing of wild oats might have entailed, he had taken his chief's advice, oft reiterated to his employees, and at twenty-one had married the first woman whom he could persuade to share his fortunes. She happened to be an angular schoolmistress, much older than he, who also wore thick glasses, and who had now borne him four children, all nearsighted, like herself.

The young man was relating how his chief, now cruising in the Mediterranean, kept in touch with all the details of the business, arranging his office hours on his yacht just as though he were at home, and "knocking off work enough to keep two stenographers busy." His father told, in turn, the plan his corporation was considering, of putting in an electric railway plant in Cairo. Paul snapped his teeth; he had an awful apprehension that they might spoil it all before he got there. Yet he rather liked to hear these legends of the iron kings that were told and retold on Sundays and holidays; these stories of palaces in Venice, yachts on the Mediterranean, and high play at Monte Carlo appealed to his fancy, and he was interested in the triumphs of these cash boys who had become famous, though he had no mind for the cash-boy stage.

After supper was over and he had helped to dry the dishes, Paul nervously asked his father whether he could go to George's to get some help in his geometry, and still more nervously asked for carfare. This latter request he had to repeat, as his father, on principle, did not like to hear requests for money, whether much or little. He asked Paul whether he could not go to some boy who lived nearer, and told him that he ought not to leave his schoolwork until

4. Tycoons of the iron and steel industry.

Sunday; but he gave him the dime. He was not a poor man, but he had a worthy ambition to come up in the world. His only reason for allowing Paul to usher was that he thought a boy ought to be earning a little.

Paul bounded upstairs, scrubbed the greasy odor of the dishwater from his hands with the ill-smelling soap he hated, and then shook over his fingers a few drops of violet water from the bottle he kept hidden in his drawer. He left the house with his geometry conspicuously under his arm, and the moment he got out of Cordelia Street and boarded a downtown car, he shook off the lethargy of two deadening days and began to live again.

The leading juvenile[5] of the permanent stock company which played at one of the downtown theaters was an acquaintance of Paul's, and the boy had been invited to drop in at the Sunday-night rehearsals whenever he could. For more than a year Paul had spent every available moment loitering about Charley Edwards's dressing room. He had won a place among Edwards's following not only because the young actor, who could not afford to employ a dresser, often found him useful, but because he recognized in Paul something akin to what churchmen term "vocation."

It was at the theater and at Carnegie Hall that Paul really lived; the rest was but a sleep and a forgetting. This was Paul's fairy tale, and it had for him all the allurement of a secret love. The moment he inhaled the gassy, painty, dusty odor behind the scenes, he breathed like a prisoner set free, and felt within him the possibility of doing or saying splendid, brilliant, poetic things. The moment the cracked orchestra beat out the overture from *Martha,* or jerked at the serenade from *Rigoletto,*[6] all stupid and ugly things slid from him, and his senses were deliciously, yet delicately fired.

Perhaps it was because, in Paul's world, the natural nearly always wore the guise of ugliness, that a certain element of artificiality seemed to him necessary in beauty. Perhaps it was because his experience of life elsewhere was so full of Sabbath-school picnics, petty economies, wholesome advice as to how to succeed in life, and the inescapable odors of cooking, that he found this existence so alluring, these smartly clad men and women so attractive, that he was so moved by these starry apple orchards that bloomed perennially under the limelight.

It would be difficult to put it strongly enough how convincingly the stage entrance of that theater was for Paul the actual portal of Romance. Certainly none of the company ever suspected it, least of all Charley Edwards. It was very like the old stories that used to float about London of fabulously rich Jews, who had subterranean halls there, with palms, and fountains, and soft lamps and richly appareled women who never saw the disenchanting light of London day. So, in the midst of that smoke-palled city, enamored of figures and grimy toil, Paul had his secret temple, his wishing carpet, his bit of blue-and-white Mediterranean shore bathed in perpetual sunshine.

Several of Paul's teachers had a theory that his imagination had been perverted by garish fiction but the truth was that he scarcely ever read at all. The

5. Youthful male actor. 6. Operas by Friedrich von Flotow (1812–1883) and Giuseppe Verdi (1813–1901).

books at home were not such as would either tempt or corrupt a youthful mind, and as for reading the novels that some of his friends urged upon him—well, he got what he wanted much more quickly from music; any sort of music, from an orchestra to a barrel organ. He needed only the spark, the indescribable thrill that made his imagination master of his senses, and he could make plots and pictures enough of his own. It was equally true that he was not stage-struck—not, at any rate, in the usual acceptation of that expression. He had no desire to become an actor, any more than he had to become a musician. He felt no necessity to do any of these things; what he wanted was to see, to be in the atmosphere, float on the wave of it, to be carried out, blue league after blue league, away from everything.

After a night behind the scenes Paul found the schoolroom more than ever repulsive; the bare floors and naked walls; the prosy men who never wore frock coats, or violets in their bottonholes; the women with their dull gowns, shrill voices, and pitiful seriousness about prepositions that govern the dative. He could not bear to have the other pupils think, for a moment, that he took these people seriously; he must convey to them that he considered it all trivial, and was there only by way of a jest, anyway. He had autographed pictures of all the members of the stock company which he showed his classmates, telling them the most incredible stories of his familiarity with these people, of his acquaintance with the soloists who came to Carnegie Hall, his suppers with them and the flowers he sent them. When these stories lost their effect, and his audience grew listless, he became desperate and would bid all the boys good-by, announcing that he was going to travel for a while; going to Naples, to Venice, to Egypt. Then, next Monday, he would slip back, conscious and nervously smiling; his sister was ill, and he should have to defer his voyage until spring.

Matters went steadily worse with Paul at school. In the itch to let his instructors know how heartily he despised them and their homilies, and how thoroughly he was appreciated elsewhere, he mentioned once or twice that he had no time to fool with theorems; adding—with a twitch of the eyebrows and a touch of that nervous bravado which so perplexed them—that he was helping the people down at the stock company; they were old friends of his.

The upshot of the matter was that the Principal went to Paul's father, and Paul was taken out of school and put to work. The manager at Carnegie Hall was told to get another usher in his stead; the doorkeeper at the theater was warned not to admit him to the house; and Charley Edwards remorsefully promised the boy's father not to see him again.

The members of the stock company were vastly amused when some of Paul's stories reached them—especially the women. They were hard-working women, most of them supporting indigent husbands or brothers, and they laughed rather bitterly at having stirred the boy to such fervid and florid inventions. They agreed with the faculty and with his father that Paul's was a bad case.

The eastbound train was plowing through a January snowstorm; the dull dawn was beginning to show gray when the engine whistled a mile out of

Newark.[7] Paul started up from the seat where he had lain curled in uneasy slumber, rubbed the breath-misted window glass with his hand, and peered out. The snow was whirling in curling eddies above the white bottom lands, and the drifts lay already deep in the fields and along the fences, while here and there the long dead grass and dried weed stalks protruded black above it. Lights shone from the scattered houses, and a gang of laborers who stood beside the track waved their lanterns.

Paul had slept very little, and he felt grimy and uncomfortable. He had made the all-night journey in a day coach, partly because he was ashamed, dressed as he was, to go into a Pullman, and partly because he was afraid of being seen there by some Pittsburgh businessman, who might have noticed him in Denny & Carson's office. When the whistle awoke him, he clutched quickly at his breast pocket, glancing about him with an uncertain smile. But the little, clay-bespattered Italians were still sleeping, the slatternly women across the aisle were in open-mouthed oblivion, and even the crumby, crying babies were for the nonce stilled. Paul settled back to struggle with his impatience as best he could.

When he arrived at the Jersey City station he hurried through his breakfast, manifestly ill at ease and keeping a sharp eye about him. After he reached the Twenty-third Street station,[8] he consulted a cabman and had himself driven to a men's-furnishings establishment that was just opening for the day. He spent upward of two hours, buying with endless reconsidering and great care. His new street suit he put on in the fitting room; the frock coat and dress clothes he had bundled into the cab with his linen. Then he drove to a hatter's and a shoe house. His next errand was at Tiffany's, where he selected his silver and a new scarf pin. He would not wait to have his silver marked,[9] he said. Lastly, he stopped at a trunk shop on Broadway and had his purchases packed into various traveling bags.

It was a little after one o'clock when he drove up to the Waldorf,[1] and after settling with the cabman, went into the office. He registered from Washington; said his mother and father had been abroad, and that he had come down to await the arrival of their steamer. He told his story plausibly and had no trouble, since he volunteered to pay for them in advance, in engaging his rooms; a sleeping room, sitting room, and bath.

Not once, but a hundred times, Paul had planned this entry into New York. He had gone over every detail of it with Charley Edwards, and in his scrapbook at home there were pages of description about New York hotels, cut from the Sunday papers. When he was shown to his sitting room on the eighth floor he saw at a glance that everything was as it should be; there was but one detail in his mental picture that the place did not realize, so he rang for the bellboy and sent him down for flowers. He moved about nervously until the boy returned, putting away his new linen and fingering it delightedly as he did so. When the

7. City in New Jersey just outside New York City. 8. Railway terminal in Manhattan. 9. Monogrammed. Tiffany's is a fashionable jewelry store in Manhattan. "Silver": a comb and brush set. 1. Fashionable hotel in Manhattan.

flowers came he put them hastily into water, and then tumbled into a hot bath. Presently he came out of his white bathroom, resplendent in his new silk underwear, and playing with the tassels of his red robe. The snow was whirling so fiercely outside his windows that he could scarcely see across the street, but within the air was deliciously soft and fragrant. He put the violets and jonquils on the taboret beside the couch, and threw himself down, with a long sigh, covering himself with a Roman blanket. He was thoroughly tired; he had been in such haste, he had stood up to such a strain, covered so much ground in the last twenty-four hours, that he wanted to think how it had all come about. Lulled by the sound of the wind, the warm air, and the cool fragrance of the flowers, he sank into deep, drowsy retrospection.

It had been wonderfully simple; when they had shut him out of the theater and concert hall, when they had taken away his bone, the whole thing was virtually determined. The rest was a mere matter of opportunity. The only thing that at all surprised him was his own courage—for he realized well enough that he had always been tormented by fear, a sort of apprehensive dread that, of late years, as the meshes of the lies he had told closed about him, had been pulling the muscles of his body tighter and tighter. Until now he could not remember the time when he had not been dreading something. Even when he was a little boy it was always there—behind him, or before, or on either side. There had always been the shadowed corner, the dark place into which he dared not look, but from which something seemed always to be watching him—and Paul had done things that were not pretty to watch, he knew.

But now he had a curious sense of relief, as though he had at last thrown down the gauntlet to the thing in the corner.

Yet it was but a day since he had been sulking in the traces; but yesterday afternoon that he had been sent to the bank with Denny & Carson's deposit, as usual—but this time he was instructed to leave the book to be balanced. There was above two thousand dollars in checks, and nearly a thousand in the bank notes which he had taken from the book and quietly transferred to his pocket. At the bank he had made out a new deposit slip. His nerves had been steady enough to permit of his returning to the office, where he had finished his work and asked for a full day's holiday tomorrow, Saturday, giving a perfectly reasonable pretext. The bankbook, he knew, would not be returned before Monday or Tuesday, and his father would be out of town for the next week. From the time he slipped the bank notes into his pocket until he boarded the night train for New York, he had not known a moment's hesitation. It was not the first time Paul had steered through treacherous waters.

How astonishingly easy it had all been; here he was, the thing done; and this time there would be no awakening, no figure at the top of the stairs. He watched the snowflakes whirling by his window until he fell asleep.

When he awoke, it was three o'clock in the afternoon. He bounded up with a start; half of one of his precious days gone already! He spent more than an hour in dressing, watching every stage of his toilet carefully in the mirror. Everything was quite perfect; he was exactly the kind of boy he had always wanted to be.

When he went downstairs Paul took a carriage and drove up Fifth Avenue toward the Park.[2] The snow had somewhat abated; carriages and tradesmen's wagons were hurrying soundlessly to and fro in the winter twilight; boys in woolen mufflers were shoveling off the doorsteps; the avenue stages[3] made fine spots of color against the white street. Here and there on the corners were stands, with whole flower gardens blooming under glass cases, against the sides of which the snowflakes stuck and melted; violets, roses, carnations, lilies of the valley—somehow vastly more lovely and alluring that they blossomed thus unnaturally in the snow. The Park itself was a wonderful stage winterpiece.

When he returned, the pause of the twilight had ceased and the tune of the streets had changed. The snow was falling faster, lights streamed from the hotels that reared their dozen stories fearlessly up into the storm, defying the raging Atlantic winds. A long, black stream of carriages poured down the avenue, intersected here and there by other streams, tending horizontally. There were a score of cabs about the entrance of this hotel, and his driver had to wait. Boys in livery were running in and out of the awning stretched across the sidewalk, up and down the red velvet carpet laid from the door to the street. Above, about, within it all was the rumble and roar, the hurry and toss of thousands of human beings as hot for pleasure as himself, and on every side of him towered the glaring affirmation of the omnipotence of wealth.

The boy set his teeth and drew his shoulders together in a spasm of realization; the plot of all dramas, the text of all romances, the nerve-stuff of all sensations was whirling about him like the snowflakes. He burnt like a faggot in a tempest.

When Paul went down to dinner the music of the orchestra came floating up the elevator shaft to greet him. His head whirled as he stepped into the thronged corridor, and he sank back into one of the chairs against the wall to get his breath. The lights, the chatter, the perfumes, the bewildering medley of color—he had, for a moment, the feeling of not being able to stand it. But only for a moment; these were his own people, he told himself. He went slowly about the corridors, through the writing rooms, smoking rooms, reception rooms, as though he were exploring the chambers of an enchanted palace, built and peopled for him alone.

When he reached the dining room he sat down at a table near a window. The flowers, the white linen, the many-colored wineglasses, the gay toilettes of the women, the low popping of corks, the undulating repetitions of the *Blue Danube*[4] from the orchestra, all flooded Paul's dream with bewildering radiance. When the roseate tinge of his champagne was added—that cold, precious, bubbling stuff that creamed and foamed in his glass—Paul wondered that there were honest men in the world at all. This was what all the world was fighting for, he reflected; this was what all the struggle was about. He doubted the reality of his past. Had he ever known a place called Cordelia Street, a place where fagged-looking businessmen got on the early car; mere rivets in a machine they seemed to Paul,—sickening men, with combings of children's

2. I.e., Central Park, the principal park in Manhattan. 3. Window displays. 4. Waltz by Johann Strauss (1825–1899), Austrian composer.

hair always hanging to their coats, and the smell of cooking in their clothes. Cordelia Street—Ah, that belonged to another time and country; had he not always been thus, had he not sat here night after night, from as far back as he could remember, looking pensively over just such shimmering textures and slowly twirling the stem of a glass like this one between his thumb and middle finger? He rather thought he had.

He was not the least abashed or lonely. He had no especial desire to meet or to know any of these people; all he demanded was the right to look on and conjecture, to watch the pageant. The mere stage properties were all he contended for. Nor was he lonely later in the evening, in his lodge at the Metropolitan.[5] He was now entirely rid of his nervous misgivings, of his forced aggressiveness, of the imperative desire to show himself different from his surroundings. He felt now that his surroundings explained him. Nobody questioned the purple,[6] he had only to wear it passively. He had only to glance down at his attire to reassure himself that here it would be impossible for anyone to humiliate him.

He found it hard to leave his beautiful sitting room to go to bed that night, and sat long watching the raging storm from his turret window. When he went to sleep it was with the lights turned on in his bedroom; partly because of his old timidity, and partly so that, if he should wake in the night, there would be no wretched moment of doubt, no horrible suspicion of yellow wallpaper, or of Washington and Calvin above his bed.

Sunday morning the city was practically snowbound. Paul breakfasted late, and in the afternoon he fell in with a wild San Francisco boy, a freshman at Yale, who said he had run down for a "little flyer" over Sunday. The young man offered to show Paul the night side of the town, and the two boys went out together after dinner, not returning to the hotel until seven o'clock the next morning. They had started out in the confiding warmth of a champagne friendship, but their parting in the elevator was singularly cool. The freshman pulled himself together to make his train, and Paul went to bed. He awoke at two o'clock in the afternoon, very thirsty and dizzy, and rang for ice-water, coffee, and the Pittsburgh papers.

On the part of the hotel management, Paul excited no suspicion. There was this to be said for him, that he wore his spoils with dignity and in no way made himself conspicuous. Even under the glow of his wine he was never boisterous, though he found the stuff like a magician's wand for wonder-building. His chief greediness lay in his ears and eyes, and his excesses were not offensive ones. His dearest pleasures were the gray winter twilights in his sitting room; his quiet enjoyment of his flowers, his clothes, his wide divan, his cigarette, and his sense of power. He could not remember a time when he had felt so at peace with himself. The mere release from the necessity of petty lying, lying every day and every day, restored his self-respect. He had never lied for pleasure, even at school; but to be noticed and admired, to assert his difference from other Cordelia Street boys; and he felt a good deal more manly, more honest, even, now that he had no need for boastful pretensions, now that he

5. His box at the Metropolitan Opera House. 6. I.e., his assumption of a royal robe.

could, as his actor friends used to say, "dress the part." It was characteristic that remorse did not occur to him. His golden days went by without a shadow, and he made each as perfect as he could.

On the eighth day after his arrival in New York he found the whole affair exploited in the Pittsburgh papers, exploited with a wealth of detail which indicated that local news of a sensational nature was at a low ebb. The firm of Denny & Carson announced that the boy's father had refunded the full amount of the theft and that they had no intention of prosecuting. The Cumberland minister had been interviewed, and expressed his hope of yet reclaiming the motherless lad, and his Sabbath-school teacher declared that she would spare no effort to that end. The rumor had reached Pittsburgh that the boy had been seen in a New York hotel, and his father had gone East to find him and bring him home.

Paul had just come in to dress for dinner; he sank into a chair, weak to the knees, and clasped his head in his hands. It was to be worse than jail, even; the tepid waters of Cordelia Street were to close over him finally and forever. The gray monotony stretched before him in hopeless, unrelieved years; Sabbath school, Young People's Meeting, the yellow-papered room, the damp dishtowels; it all rushed back upon him with a sickening vividness. He had the old feeling that the orchestra had suddenly stopped, the sinking sensation that the play was over. The sweat broke out on his face, and he sprang to his feet, looked about him with his white, conscious smile, and winked at himself in the mirror. With something of the old childish belief in miracles with which he had so often gone to class, all his lessons unlearned, Paul dressed and dashed whistling down the corridor to the elevator.

He had no sooner entered the dining room and caught the measure of the music than his remembrance was lightened by his old elastic power of claiming the moment, mounting with it, and finding it all-sufficient. The glare and glitter about him, the mere scenic accessories had again, and for the last time, their old potency. He would show himself that he was game, he would finish the thing splendidly. He doubted, more than ever, the existence of Cordelia Street, and for the first time he drank his wine recklessly. Was he not, after all, one of those fortunate beings born to the purple, was he not still himself and in his own place? He drummed a nervous accompaniment to the Pagliacci[7] music and looked about him, telling himself over and over that it had paid.

He reflected drowsily, to the swell of the music and the chill sweetness of his wine, that he might have done it more wisely. He might have caught an outbound steamer and been well out of their clutches before now. But the other side of the world had seemed too far away and too uncertain then; he could not have waited for it; his need had been too sharp. If he had to choose over again, he would do the same thing tomorrow. He looked affectionately about the dining room, now gilded with a soft mist. Ah, it had paid indeed!

Paul was awakened next morning by a painful throbbing in his head and feet. He had thrown himself across the bed without undressing, and had slept with his shoes on. His limbs and hands were lead heavy, and his tongue and

7. Opera by Ruggiero Leoncavallo (1858–1919).

throat were parched and burnt. There came upon him one of those fateful attacks of clearheadedness that never occurred except when he was physically exhausted and his nerves hung loose. He lay still, closed his eyes, and let the tide of things wash over him.

His father was in New York; "stopping at some joint or other," he told himself. The memory of successive summers on the front stoop fell upon him like a weight of black water. He had not a hundred dollars left; and he knew now, more than ever, that money was everything, the wall that stood between all he loathed and all he wanted. The thing was winding itself up; he had thought of that on his first glorious day in New York, and had even provided a way to snap the thread. It lay on his dressing table now; he had got it out last night when he came blindly up from dinner, but the shiny metal hurt his eyes, and he disliked the looks of it.

He rose and moved about with a painful effort, succumbing now and again to attacks of nausea. It was the old depression exaggerated; all the world had become Cordelia Street. Yet somehow he was not afraid of anything, was absolutely calm; perhaps because he had looked into the dark corner at last and knew. It was bad enough, what he saw there, but somehow not so bad as his long fear of it had been. He saw everything clearly now. He had a feeling that he had made the best of it, that he had lived the sort of life he was meant to live, and for half an hour he sat staring at the revolver. But he told himself that was not the way, so he went downstairs and took a cab to the ferry.

When Paul arrived in Newark he got off the train and took another cab, directing the driver to follow the Pennsylvania tracks out of the town. The snow lay heavy on the roadways and had drifted deep in the open fields. Only here and there the dead grass or dried weed stalks projected, singularly black, above it. Once well into the country, Paul dismissed the carriage and walked, floundering along the tracks, his mind a medley of irrelevant things. He seemed to hold in his brain an actual picture of everything he had seen that morning. He remembered every feature of both his drivers, of the toothless old woman from whom he had bought the red flowers in his coat, the agent from whom he had got his ticket, and all of his fellow passengers on the ferry. His mind, unable to cope with vital matters near at hand, worked feverishly and deftly at sorting and grouping these images. They made for him a part of the ugliness of the world, of the ache in his head, and the bitter burning on his tongue. He stooped and put a handful of snow into his mouth as he walked, but that, too, seemed hot. When he reached a little hillside, where the tracks ran through a cut some twenty feet below him, he stopped and sat down.

The carnations in his coat were drooping with the cold, he noticed, their red glory all over. It occurred to him that all the flowers he had seen in the glass cases that first night must have gone the same way, long before this. It was only one splendid breath they had, in spite of their brave mockery at the winter outside the glass; and it was a losing game in the end, it seemed, this revolt against the homilies by which the world is run. Paul took one of the blossoms carefully from his coat and scooped a little hole in the snow, where he covered it up. Then he dozed awhile, from his weak condition, seemingly insensible to the cold.

The sound of an approaching train awoke him, and he started to his feet, remembering only his resolution, and afraid lest he should be too late. He stood watching the approaching locomotive, his teeth chattering, his lips drawn away from them in a frightened smile; once or twice he glanced nervously sidewise, as though he were being watched. When the right moment came, he jumped. As he fell, the folly of his haste occurred to him with merciless clearness, the vastness of what he had left undone. There flashed through his brain, clearer than ever before, the blue of Adriatic water, the yellow of Algerian sands.

He felt something strike his chest, and that his body was being thrown swiftly through the air, on and on, immeasurably far and fast, while his limbs were gently relaxed. Then, because the picturemaking mechanism was crushed, the disturbing visions flashed into black, and Paul dropped back into the immense design of things.

## ANDREA BARRETT on *Paul's Case*

"His eyes were remarkable for a certain hysterical brilliancy"—there is Willa Cather's Paul, defiantly himself, easy enough not to like. Lonely, motherless, sporting his hopeless red carnation, he's cursed with a vivid imagination and a febrile sensibility, no apparent talent, and no one to show him the way. He's vain and shallow and oversensitive, sentimental and provincial despite his hatred for things provincial; he can't distinguish true art from false, and he confuses the aristocracy of money with that of the spirit.

Yet he speaks to me, as he does to many writers. Perhaps he is who we most dread being. He sees what we all see—that horrifying vision of the world as "Cordelia Street"—but he can do nothing with that knowledge. Through his eyes, that "highly respectable street, where all the houses were exactly alike, and where business men of moderate means begot and reared large families of children" becomes an increasingly potent symbol for the aspects of bourgeois life that an adolescent, or an artist, might despise. Those respectable beds and kitchen odors and smug, pot-bellied householders; the endless chatter of getting and spending and the swarms of children doomed to reproduce their parents' lives exactly—those are what Paul fights, and flees. When his attempt to build another life fails, what he feels is "the old depression exaggerated; all the world had become Cordelia Street."

Another character might have made something from that disgust and despair. Paul makes what he can, within his limitations, with the materials he has at hand. If he can't make art, and can only buy what he desires for a few days, with stolen money: still he can make of his life an artful (if wasteful and violent) shape. And so he does.

I love Cather's astonishing, painful, truthful rendition of Paul's flawed being; I love the story's economy, its swift deep descriptions, and its concentration on Paul's powerful longing for Paradise. If it's a flawed Paradise, misconceived from tawdry elements, misunderstood in its very nature—still it is Paradise to him. That drive toward transformation, that falling into fate, is what makes the story so moving: along with our simultaneous understanding that the narrowness of Paul's surroundings and upbringing has caused him to hurl himself away.

# John Cheever

*Cheever (1912–1982) was born in Quincy, Massachusetts. His formal education ended when he was expelled from Thayer Academy at the age of seventeen—a circumstance that gave him subject matter for his first publication. Thereafter, he devoted himself completely to writing, except for brief interludes of teaching at Barnard and the University of Iowa. He wrote television scripts and four novels, but his fame rests on the large number of short stories, many appearing in* The New Yorker, *that he published in a steady stream beginning in the 1940s. Built around a strong moral core and tinged with melancholy nostalgia for the past, these stories form a running commentary on the tensions, manners, and crippled aspirations of urban and suburban life. Many of his stories have been collected in* The Enormous Radio and Other Stories *(1953),* The Housebreaker of Shady Hill and Other Stories *(1958),* The Brigadier and the Golf Widow *(1964), and* The World of Apples *(1973). His novels are* The Wapshot Chronicle *(1957),* The Wapshot Scandal *(1964),* Bullet Park *(1969), and* Falconer *(1977).* The Stories of John Cheever *(1978) won the Pulitzer Prize.*

## The Enormous Radio

Jim and Irene Westcott were the kind of people who seem to strike that satisfactory average of income, endeavor, and respectability that is reached by the statistical reports in college alumni bulletins. They were the parents of two young children, they had been married nine years, they lived on the twelfth floor of an apartment house near Sutton Place,[1] they went to the theatre on an average of 10.3 times a year, and they hoped someday to live in Westchester.[2] Irene Westcott was a pleasant, rather plain girl with soft brown hair and a wide, fine forehead upon which nothing at all had been written, and in the cold weather she wore a coat of fitch skins dyed to resemble mink. You could not say that Jim Westcott looked younger than he was, but you could at least say of him that he seemed to feel younger. He wore his graying hair cut very short, he dressed in the kind of clothes his class had worn at Andover,[3] and his manner was earnest, vehement, and intentionally naïve. The Westcotts differed from their friends, their classmates, and their neighbors only in an interest they shared in serious music. They went to a great many concerts—although they

1. Fashionable area on New York City's East Side. 2. Affluent suburban county outside New York City. 3. Elite boarding school.

seldom mentioned this to anyone—and they spent a good deal of time listening to music on the radio.

Their radio was an old instrument, sensitive, unpredictable, and beyond repair. Neither of them understood the mechanics of radio—or of any of the other appliances that surrounded them—and when the instrument faltered, Jim would strike the side of the cabinet with his hand. This sometimes helped. One Sunday afternoon, in the middle of a Schubert[4] quartet, the music faded away altogether. Jim struck the cabinet repeatedly, but there was no response; the Schubert was lost to them forever. He promised to buy Irene a new radio, and on Monday when he came home from work he told her that he had got one. He refused to describe it, and said it would be a surprise for her when it came.

The radio was delivered at the kitchen door the following afternoon, and with the assistance of her maid and the handyman Irene uncrated it and brought it into the living room. She was struck at once with the physical ugliness of the large gumwood cabinet. Irene was proud of her living room, she had chosen its furnishings and colors as carefully as she chose her clothes, and now it seemed to her that the new radio stood among her intimate possessions like an aggressive intruder. She was confounded by the number of dials and switches on the instrument panel, and she studied them thoroughly before she put the plug into a wall socket and turned the radio on. The dials flooded with a malevolent green light, and in the distance she heard the music of a piano quintet. The quintet was in the distance for only an instant; it bore down upon her with a speed greater than light and filled the apartment with the noise of music amplified so mightily that it knocked a china ornament from a table to the floor. She rushed to the instrument and reduced the volume. The violent forces that were snared in the ugly gumwood cabinet made her uneasy. Her children came home from school then, and she took them to the Park. It was not until later in the afternoon that she was able to return to the radio.

The maid had given the children their suppers and was supervising their baths when Irene turned on the radio, reduced the volume, and sat down to listen to a Mozart[5] quintet that she knew and enjoyed. The music came through clearly. The new instrument had a much purer tone, she thought, than the old one. She decided that tone was most important and that she could conceal the cabinet behind a sofa. But as soon as she had made her peace with the radio, the interference began. A crackling sound like the noise of a burning powder fuse began to accompany the singing of the strings. Beyond the music, there was a rustling that reminded Irene unpleasantly of the sea, and as the quintet progressed, these noises were joined by many others. She tried all the dials and switches but nothing dimmed the interference, and she sat down, disappointed and bewildered, and tried to trace the flight of the melody. The elevator shaft in her building ran beside the living-room wall, and it was the noise of the elevator that gave her a clue to the character of the static. The rattling of the elevator cables and the opening and closing of the elevator doors were repro-

4. Franz Peter Schubert (1797–1828), Austrian composer. 5. Wolfgang Amadeus Mozart (1756–1791), Austrian composer.

duced in her loudspeaker, and, realizing that the radio was sensitive to electrical currents of all sorts, she began to discern through the Mozart the ringing of telephone bells, the dialing of phones, and the lamentation of a vacuum cleaner. By listening more carefully, she was able to distinguish doorbells, elevator bells, electric razors, and Waring mixers, whose sounds had been picked up from the apartments that surrounded hers and transmitted through her loudspeaker. The powerful and ugly instrument, with its mistaken sensitivity to discord, was more than she could hope to master, so she turned the thing off and went into the nursery to see her children.

When Jim Westcott came home that night, he went to the radio confidently and worked the controls. He had the same sort of experience Irene had had. A man was speaking on the station Jim had chosen, and his voice swung instantly from the distance into a force so powerful that it shook the apartment. Jim turned the volume control and reduced the voice. Then, a minute or two later, the interference began. The ringing of telephones and doorbells set in, joined by the rasp of the elevator doors and the whir of cooking appliances. The character of the noise had changed since Irene had tried the radio earlier; the last of the electric razors was being unplugged, the vacuum cleaners had all been returned to their closets, and the static reflected that change in pace that overtakes the city after the sun goes down. He fiddled with the knobs but couldn't get rid of the noises, so he turned the radio off and told Irene that in the morning he'd call the people who had sold it to him and give them hell.

The following afternoon, when Irene returned to the apartment from a luncheon date, the maid told her that a man had come and fixed the radio. Irene went into the living room before she took off her hat or her furs and tried the instrument. From the loudspeaker came a recording of the "Missouri Waltz."[6] It reminded her of the thin, scratchy music from an old-fashioned phonograph that she sometimes heard across the lake where she spent her summers. She waited until the waltz had finished, expecting an explanation of the recording, but there was none. The music was followed by silence, and then the plaintive and scratchy record was repeated. She turned the dial and got a satisfactory burst of Caucasian music—the thump of bare feet in the dust and the rattle of coin jewelry—but in the background she could hear the ringing of bells and a confusion of voices. Her children came home from school then, and she turned off the radio and went to the nursery.

When Jim came home that night, he was tired, and he took a bath and changed his clothes. Then he joined Irene in the living room. He had just turned on the radio when the maid announced dinner, so he left it on, and he and Irene went to the table.

Jim was too tired to make even pretense of sociability, and there was nothing about the dinner to hold Irene's interest, so her attention wandered from the food to the deposits of silver polish on the candlesticks and from there to the music in the other room. She listened for a few minutes to a Chopin[7]

6. Popular tune of 1916 by J. R. Shannon and Frederick Knight Logan. It was made popular again in the 1940s by President Harry Truman. 7. Frédéric François Chopin (1810–1849), Polish-French composer and pianist.

prelude and then was surprised to hear a man's voice break in. "For Christ's sake, Kathy," he said, "do you always have to play the piano when I get home?" The music stopped abruptly. "It's the only chance I have," a woman said. "I'm at the office all day." "So am I," the man said. He added something obscene about an upright piano, and slammed a door. The passionate and melancholy music began again.

"Did you hear that?" Irene asked.

"What?" Jim was eating his dessert.

"The radio. A man said something while the music was still going on—something dirty."

"It's probably a play."

"I don't think it *is* a play," Irene said.

They left the table and took their coffee into the living room. Irene asked Jim to try another station. He turned the knob. "Have you seen my garters?" a man asked. "Button me up," a woman said. "Have you seen my garters?" the man said again. "Just button me up and I'll find your garters," the woman said. Jim shifted to another station. "I wish you wouldn't leave apple cores in the ashtrays," a man said. "I hate the smell."

"This is strange," Jim said.

"Isn't it?" Irene said.

Jim turned the knob again. " 'On the coast of Coromandel where the early pumpkins blow,' " a woman with a pronounced English accent said, " 'in the middle of the woods lived the Yonghy-Bonghy-Bò. Two old chairs, and half a candle, one old jug without a handle . . .' "[8]

"My God!" Irene cried. "That's the Sweeneys' nurse."

" 'These were all his worldly goods,' " the British voice continued.

"Turn that thing off," Irene said. "Maybe they can hear *us*." Jim switched the radio off. "That was Miss Armstrong, the Sweeneys' nurse," Irene said. "She must be reading to the little girl. They live in 17-B. I've talked with Miss Armstrong in the Park. I know her voice very well. We must be getting other people's apartments."

"That's impossible," Jim said.

"Well, that was the Sweeneys' nurse," Irene said hotly. "I know her voice. I know it very well. I'm wondering if they can hear us."

Jim turned the switch. First from a distance and then nearer, nearer, as if borne on the wind, came the pure accents of the Sweeneys' nurse again: " '*Lady Jingly! Lady Jingly!*' " she said, " '*sitting where the pumpkins blow, will you come and be my wife?* said the Yonghy-Bonghy-Bò . . .' "

Jim went over to the radio and said "Hello" loudly into the speaker.

" '*I am tired of living singly,*" the nurse went on, " '*on this coast so wild and shingly, I'm a-weary of my life; if you'll come and be my wife, quite serene would be my life* . . .' "

"I guess she can't hear us," Irene said. "Try something else."

Jim turned to another station, and the living room was filled with the uproar

8. From *The Courtship of the Yonghy-Bonghy-Bò* by Edward Lear (1812–1888), English nonsense poet.

of a cocktail party that had overshot its mark. Someone was playing the piano and singing the "Whiffenpoof Song,"[9] and the voices that surrounded the piano were vehement and happy. "Eat some more sandwiches," a woman shrieked. There were screams of laughter and a dish of some sort crashed to the floor.

"Those must be the Fullers, in 11-E," Irene said. "I knew they were giving a party this afternoon. I saw her in the liquor store. Isn't this too divine? Try something else. See if you can get those people in 18-C."

The Westcotts overheard that evening a monologue on salmon fishing in Canada, a bridge game, running comments on home movies of what had apparently been a fortnight at Sea Island, and a bitter family quarrel about an overdraft at the bank. They turned off their radio at midnight and went to bed, weak with laughter. Sometime in the night, their son began to call for a glass of water and Irene got one and took it to his room. It was very early. All the lights in the neighborhood were extinguished, and from the boy's window she could see the empty street. She went into the living room and tried the radio. There was some faint coughing, a moan, and then a man spoke. "Are you all right, darling?" he asked. "Yes," a woman said wearily. "Yes, I'm all right, I guess," and then she added with great feeling, "But, you know, Charlie, I don't feel like myself any more. Sometimes there are about fifteen or twenty minutes in the week when I feel like myself. I don't like to go to another doctor, because the doctor's bills are so awful already, but I just don't feel like myself, Charlie. I just never feel like myself." They were not young, Irene thought. She guessed from the timbre of their voices that they were middle-aged. The restrained melancholy of the dialogue and the draft from the bedroom window made her shiver, and she went back to bed.

The following morning, Irene cooked breakfast for the family—the maid didn't come up from her room in the basement until ten—braided her daughter's hair, and waited at the door until her children and her husband had been carried away in the elevator. Then she went into the living room and tried the radio. "I don't want to go to school," a child screamed. "I hate school. I won't go to school. I hate school." "You will go to school," an enraged woman said. "We paid eight hundred dollars to get you into that school and you'll go if it kills you." The next number on the dial produced the worn record of the "Missouri Waltz." Irene shifted the control and invaded the privacy of several breakfast tables. She overheard demonstrations of indigestion, carnal love, abysmal vanity, faith, and despair. Irene's life was nearly as simple and sheltered as it appeared to be, and the forthright and sometimes brutal language that came from the loudspeaker that morning astonished and troubled her. She continued to listen until her maid came in. Then she turned off the radio quickly, since this insight, she realized, was a furtive one.

Irene had a luncheon date with a friend that day, and she left her apartment at a little after twelve. There were a number of women in the elevator when it stopped at her floor. She stared at their handsome and impassive faces, their furs, and the cloth flowers in their hats. Which one of them had been to Sea

9. Famous Yale drinking song.

Island? she wondered. Which one had overdrawn her bank account. The elevator stopped at the tenth floor and a woman with a pair of Skye terriers joined them. Her hair was rigged high on her head and she wore a mink cape. She was humming the "Missouri Waltz."

Irene had two Martinis at lunch, and she looked searchingly at her friend and wondered what her secrets were. They had intended to go shopping after lunch, but Irene excused herself and went home. She told the maid that she was not to be disturbed; then she went into the living room, closed the doors, and switched on the radio. She heard, in the course of the afternoon, the halting conversation of a woman entertaining her aunt, the hysterical conclusion of a luncheon party, and a hostess briefing her maid about some cocktail guests. "Don't give the best Scotch to anyone who hasn't white hair," the hostess said. "See if you can get rid of that liver paste before you pass those hot things, and could you lend me five dollars? I want to tip the elevator man."

As the afternoon waned, the conversations increased in intensity. From where Irene sat, she could see the open sky above the East River. There were hundreds of clouds in the sky, as though the south wind had broken the winter into pieces and were blowing it north, and on her radio she could hear the arrival of cocktail guests and the return of children and businessmen from their schools and offices. "I found a good-sized diamond on the bathroom floor this morning," a woman said. "It must have fallen out of that bracelet Mrs. Dunston was wearing last night." "We'll sell it," a man said. "Take it down to the jeweler on Madison Avenue and sell it. Mrs. Dunston won't know the difference, and we could use a couple of hundred bucks . . . " " 'Oranges and lemons, say the bells of St. Clement's,' " the Sweeneys' nurse sang. " 'Halfpence and farthings, say the bells of St. Martin's. When will you pay me? say the bells at old Bailey . . .' "[1] "It's not a hat," a woman cried, and at her back roared a cocktail party. "It's not a hat, it's a love affair. That's what Walter Florell said. He said it's not a hat, it's a love affair," and then, in a lower voice, the same woman added, "Talk to somebody, for Christ's sake, honey, talk to somebody. If she catches you standing here not talking to anybody, she'll take us off her invitation list, and I love these parties."

The Westcotts were going out for dinner that night, and when Jim came home, Irene was dressing. She seemed sad and vague, and he brought her a drink. They were dining with friends in the neighborhood, and they walked to where they were going. The sky was broad and filled with light. It was one of those splendid spring evenings that excite memory and desire, and the air that touched their hands and faces felt very soft. A Salvation Army band was on the corner playing "Jesus Is Sweeter." Irene drew on her husband's arm and held him there for a minute, to hear the music. "They're really such nice people, aren't they?" she said. "They have such nice faces. Actually, they're so much nicer than a lot of the people we know." She took a bill from her purse and walked over and dropped it into the tambourine. There was in her face, when she returned to her husband, a look of radiant melancholy that he was not familiar with. And her conduct at the dinner party that night seemed strange

1. From a British folk song.

to him, too. She interrupted her hostess rudely and stared at the people across the table from her with an intensity for which she would have punished her children.

It was still mild when they walked home from the party, and Irene looked up at the spring stars. " 'How far that little candle throws its beams,' " she exclaimed. " 'So shines a good deed in a naughty world.' "[2] She waited that night until Jim had fallen asleep, and then went into the living room and turned on the radio.

Jim came home at about six the next night. Emma, the maid, let him in, and he had taken off his hat and was taking off his coat when Irene ran into the hall. Her face was shining with tears and her hair was disordered. "Go up to 16-C, Jim!" she screamed. "Don't take off your coat. Go up to 16-C. Mr. Osborn's beating his wife. They've been quarreling since four o'clock, and now he's hitting her. Go up there and stop him."

From the radio in the living room, Jim heards screams, obscenities, and thuds. "You know you don't have to listen to this sort of thing," he said. He strode into the living room and turned the switch. "It's indecent," he said. "It's like looking in windows. You know you don't have to listen to this sort of thing. You can turn it off."

"Oh, it's so horrible, it's so dreadful," Irene was sobbing. "I've been listening all day, and it's so depressing."

"Well, if it's so depressing, why do you listen to it? I bought this damned radio to give you some pleasure," he said. "I paid a great deal of money for it. I thought it might make you happy. I wanted to make you happy."

"Don't, don't, don't, don't quarrel with me," she moaned, and laid her head on his shoulder. "All the others have been quarreling all day. Everybody's been quarreling. They're all worried about money. Mrs. Hutchinson's mother is dying of cancer in Florida and they don't have enough money to send her to the Mayo Clinic.[3] At least, Mr. Hutchinson says they don't have enough money. And some woman in this building is having an affair with the handyman—with that hideous handyman. It's too disgusting. And Mrs. Melville has heart trouble, and Mr. Hendricks is going to lose his job in April and Mrs. Hendricks is horrid about the whole thing and that girl who plays the 'Missouri Waltz' is a whore, a common whore, and the elevator man has tuberculosis and Mr. Osborn has been beating Mrs. Osborn." She wailed, she trembled with grief and checked the stream of tears down her face with the heel of her palm.

"Well, why do you have to listen?" Jim asked again. "Why do you have to listen to this stuff if it makes you so miserable?"

"Oh, don't, don't, don't," she cried. "Life is too terrible, too sordid and awful. But we've never been like that, have we, darling? Have we? I mean, we've always been good and decent and loving to one another, haven't we? And we have two children, two beautiful children. Our lives aren't sordid, are they, darling? Are they?" She flung her arms around his neck and drew his face down to hers. "We're happy, aren't we, darling? We are happy, aren't we?"

2. Shakespeare's *Merchant of Venice* 5.1. 3. Internationally famous hospital and diagnostic center in Rochester, Minnesota.

"Of course we're happy," he said tiredly. He began to surrender his resentment. "Of course we're happy. I'll have that damned radio fixed or taken away tomorrow." He stroked her soft hair. "My poor girl," he said.

"You love me, don't you? she asked. "And we're not hypercritical or worried about money or dishonest, are we?"

"No, darling," he said.

A man came in the morning and fixed the radio. Irene turned it on cautiously and was happy to hear a California-wine commercial and a recording of Beethoven's Ninth Symphony, including Schiller's[4] "Ode to Joy." She kept the radio on all day and nothing untoward came from the speaker.

A Spanish suite was being played when Jim came home. "Is everything all right?" he asked. His face was pale, she thought. They had some cocktails and went in to dinner to the "Anvil Chorus" from *Il Trovatore.* This was followed by Debussy's[5] "La Mer."

"I paid the bill for the radio today," Jim said. "It cost four hundred dollars. I hope you'll get some enjoyment out of it."

"Oh, I'm sure I will," Irene said.

"Four hundred dollars is a good deal more than I can afford," he went on. "I wanted to get something that you'd enjoy. It's the last extravagance we'll be able to indulge in this year. I see that you haven't paid your clothing bills yet. I saw them on your dressing table." He looked directly at her "Why did you tell me you'd paid them? Why did you lie to me?"

"I just didn't want you to worry, Jim," she said. She drank some water. "I'll be able to pay my bills out of this month's allowance. There were the slipcovers last month, and that party."

"You've got to learn to handle the money I give you a little more intelligently, Irene," he said. "You've got to understand that we don't have as much money this year as we had last. I had a very sobering talk with Mitchell today. No one is buying anything. We're spending all our time promoting new issues, and you know how long that takes. I'm not getting any younger, you know. I'm thirty-seven. My hair will be gray next year. I haven't done as well as I'd hoped to do. And I don't suppose things will get any better."

"Yes, dear," she said.

"We've got to start cutting down," Jim said. "We've got to think of the children. To be perfectly frank with you, I worry about money a great deal. I'm not at all sure of the future. No one is. If anything should happen to me, there's the insurance, but that wouldn't go very far today. I've worked awfully hard to give you and the children a comfortable life," he said bitterly. "I don't like to see all my energies, all of my youth, wasted in fur coats and radios and slipcovers and—"

"Please, Jim," she said. "Please. They'll hear us."

"*Who'll hear us?* Emma can't hear us."

"The radio."

4. Johann Christoph Friedrich von Schiller (1759–1805), German poet and dramatist. Ludwig van Beethoven (1770–1827), German composer. 5. Claude Achille Debussy (1862–1918), French composer. "*Il Trovatore*": opera by Giuseppe Verdi (1813–1901), Italian composer.

"Oh, I'm sick!" he shouted. "I'm sick to death of your apprehensiveness. The radio can't hear us. Nobody can hear us. And what if they can hear us? Who cares?"

Irene got up from the table and went into the living room. Jim went to the door and shouted at her from there. "Why are you so Christly all of a sudden? What's turned you overnight into a convent girl? You stole your mother's jewelry before they probated her will. You never gave your sister a cent of that money that was intended for her—not even when she needed it. You made Grace Howland's life miserable, and where was all your piety and your virtue when you went to that abortionist? I'll never forget how cool you were. You packed your bag and went off to have that child murdered as if you were going to Nassau. If you'd had any reasons, if you'd had any good reasons—"

Irene stood for a minute before the hideous cabinet, disgraced and sickened, but she held her hand on the switch before she extinguished the music and the voices, hoping that the instrument might speak to her kindly, that she might hear the Sweeneys' nurse. Jim continued to shout at her from the door. The voice on the radio was suave and noncommital. "An early-morning railroad disaster in Tokyo," the loudspeaker said, "killed twenty-nine people. A fire in a Catholic hospital near Buffalo for the care of blind children was extinguished early this morning by nuns. The temperature is forty-seven. The humidity is eighty-nine."

# Anton Chekhov

*Chekhov (1860–1904) was born in Taganrog, Russia, the son of a despotic, dishonest, and rough-grained father—who was nevertheless eager to impart to his children his love for music and art. Trained as a physician at Moscow University, Chekhov practiced medicine only intermittently, although he credited his scientific training with conditioning him to be a realistic observer of society and individual behavior. While still a medical student he began to write short pieces for humorous magazines; the popularity of these sketches roused his determination to become a serious artist. In 1890 he visited the Russian penal island of Sakhalin and without fanfare or special pleading wrote a moving account of convict life as he saw it there. He was at the height of his literary powers and his fame in 1901 when he married a young actress, but the state of his health by then was disastrous. In the short time remaining to him, he was confined mostly to the house he had built from his literary earnings at Yalta in southern Russia, infrequently able to accompany his wife to Moscow to watch her performances in his plays. Those plays—among them* The Seagull *(1896),* Uncle Vanya *(1899),* The Three Sisters *(1901), and* The Cherry Orchard *(1904)—established him as one of the great dramatists of modern times, while his hundreds of short stories and novellas have immensely influenced the art of fiction since his death. In tribute to the humanity and responsibility of his work, Leo Tolstoy called him "an artist of life."*

## The Lady with the Dog[1]

### I

People were telling one another that a newcomer had been seen on the promenade—a lady with a dog. Dmitry Dmitrich Gurov had been a fortnight in Yalta,[2] and was accustomed to its ways, and he, too, had begun to take an interest in fresh arrivals. From his seat in Vernet's outdoor café, he caught sight of a young woman in a toque, passing along the promenade; she was fair and not very tall; after her trotted a white Pomeranian.

Later he encountered her in the municipal park and in the square several times a day. She was always alone, wearing the same toque, and the Pomeranian always trotted at her side. Nobody knew who she was, and people referred to her simply as "the lady with the dog."

"If she's here without her husband, and without any friends," thought Gurov, "it wouldn't be a bad idea to make her acquaintance."

1. Translated by Ivy Litvinov. 2. Russian city on the Black Sea, a resort for southern vacations.

He was not yet forty but had a twelve-year-old daughter and two sons in high school. He had been talked into marrying in his third year at college, and his wife now looked nearly twice as old as he did. She was a tall woman with dark eyebrows, erect, dignified, imposing, and, as she said of herself, a "thinker." She was a great reader, omitted the "hard sign"[3] at the end of words in her letters, and called her husband "Dimitry" instead of Dmitry; and though he secretly considered her shallow, narrow-minded, and dowdy, he stood in awe of her, and disliked being at home. He had first begun deceiving her long ago and he was now constantly unfaithful to her, and this was no doubt why he spoke slightingly of women, to whom he referred as *the lower race.*

He considered that the ample lessons he had received from bitter experience entitled him to call them whatever he liked, but without this "lower race" he could not have existed a single day. He was bored and ill-at-ease in the company of men, with whom he was always cold and reserved, but felt quite at home among women, and knew exactly what to say to them, and how to behave; he could even be silent in their company without feeling the slightest awkwardness. There was an elusive charm in his appearance and disposition which attracted women and caught their sympathies. He knew this and was himself attracted to them by some invisible force.

Repeated and bitter experience had taught him that every fresh intimacy, while at first introducing such pleasant variety into everyday life, and offering itself as a charming, light adventure, inevitably developed, among decent people (especially in Moscow, where they are so irresolute and slow to move), into a problem of excessive complication leading to an intolerably irksome situation. But every time he encountered an attractive woman he forgot all about this experience, the desire for life surged up in him, and everything suddenly seemed simple and amusing.

One evening, then, while he was dining at the restaurant in the park, the lady in the toque came strolling up and took a seat at a neighboring table. Her expression, gait, dress, coiffure, all told him that she was from the upper classes, that she was married, that she was in Yalta for the first time, alone and bored. . . . The accounts of the laxity of morals among visitors to Yalta are greatly exaggerated, and he paid no heed to them, knowing that for the most part they were invented by people who would gladly have transgressed themselves, had they known how to set about it. But when the lady sat down at a neighboring table a few yards away from him, these stories of easy conquests, of excursions to the mountains, came back to him, and the seductive idea of a brisk transitory liaison, an affair with a woman whose very name he did not know, suddenly took possession of his mind.

He snapped his fingers at the Pomeranian and, when it trotted up to him, shook his forefinger at it. The Pomeranian growled. Gurov shook his finger again.

The lady glanced at him and instantly lowered her eyes.

"He doesn't bite," she said, and blushed.

3. Certain progressive intellectuals omitted the hard sign after consonants in writing, anticipating the later reform in the Russian alphabet. Here used rather as emancipated affectation.

"May I give him a bone?" he asked, and on her nod of consent added in friendly tones: "Have you been long in Yalta?"

"About five days."

"And I am dragging out my second week here."

Neither spoke for a few minutes.

"The days pass quickly, and yet one is so bored here," she said, not looking at him.

"It's the thing to say it's boring here. People never complain of boredom in godforsaken holes like Belyev or Zhizdra,[4] but when they get here it's: 'Oh, the dullness! Oh, the dust!' You'd think they'd come from Granada[5] to say the least."

She laughed. Then they both went on eating in silence, like complete strangers. But after dinner they left the restaurant together, and embarked upon the light, jesting talk of people free and contented, for whom it is all the same where they go, or what they talk about. They strolled along, remarking on the strange light over the sea. The water was a warm, tender purple, the moonlight lay on its surface in a golden strip. They said how close it was, after the hot day. Gurov told her he was from Moscow, had a degree in literature but worked in a bank; that he had at one time trained himself to sing in a private opera company, but had given up the idea; that he owned two houses in Moscow. . . . And from her he learned that she had grown up in Petersburg, but had gotten married in the town of S., where she had been living two years, that she would stay another month in Yalta, and that perhaps her husband, who also needed a rest, would join her. She was quite unable to explain whether her husband was a member of the province council, or on the board of the *zemstvo*,[6] and was greatly amused at herself for this. Further, Gurov learned that her name was Anna Sergeyevna.

Back in his own room he thought about her, and felt sure he would meet her the next day. It was inevitable. As he went to bed he reminded himself that only a very short time ago she had been a schoolgirl, like his own daughter, learning her lessons, he remembered how much there was of shyness and constraint in her laughter, in her way of conversing with a stranger—it was probably the first time in her life that she found herself alone, and in a situation in which men could follow her and watch her, and speak to her, all the time with a secret aim she could not fail to divine. He recalled her slender, delicate neck, her fine gray eyes.

"And yet there's something pathetic about her," he thought to himself as he fell asleep.

## II

A week had passed since the beginning of their acquaintance. It was a holiday. Indoors it was stuffy, but the dust rose in clouds out of doors, and people's hats blew off. It was a parching day and Gurov kept going to the outdoor café for fruit drinks and ices to offer Anna Sergeyevna. The heat was overpowering.

4. Dull, provincial Russian cities. 5. City in southern Spain, legendary for its charm. 6. A county council (Russian).

In the evening, when the wind had dropped, they walked to the pier to see the steamer come in. There were a great many people strolling about the landing-place; some, bunches of flowers in their hands, were meeting friends. Two peculiarities of the smart Yalta crowd stood out distinctly—the elderly ladies all tried to dress very youthfully, and there seemed to be an inordinate number of generals about.

Owing to the roughness of the sea the steamer arrived late, after the sun had gone down, and it had to maneuver for some time before it could get alongside the pier. Anna Sergeyevna scanned the steamer and passengers through her lorgnette, as if looking for someone she knew, and when she turned to Gurov her eyes were glistening. She talked a great deal, firing off abrupt questions and forgetting immediately what it was she had wanted to know. Then she lost her lorgnette in the crush.

The smart crowd began dispersing, features could no longer be made out, the wind had quite dropped, and Gurov and Anna Sergeyevna stood there as if waiting for someone else to come off the steamer. Anna Sergeyevna had fallen silent, every now and then smelling her flowers, but not looking at Gurov.

"It's turning out a fine evening," he said. "What shall we do? We might go for a drive."

She made no reply.

He looked steadily at her and suddenly took her in his arms and kissed her lips, and the fragrance and dampness of the flowers closed round him, but the next moment he looked behind him in alarm—had anyone seen them?

"Let's go to your room," he murmured.

And they walked off together, very quickly.

Her room was stuffy and smelt of some scent she had bought in the Japanese shop. Gurov looked at her, thinking to himself: "How full of strange encounters life is!" He could remember carefree, good-natured women who were exhilarated by love-making and grateful to him for the happiness he gave them, however short-lived; and there had been others—his wife among them—whose caresses were insincere, affected, hysterical, mixed up with a great deal of quite unnecessary talk, and whose expression seemed to say that all this was not just love-making or passion, but something much more significant; then there had been two or three beautiful, cold women, over whose features flitted a predatory expression, betraying a determination to wring from life more than it could give, women no longer in their first youth, capricious, irrational, despotic, brainless, and when Gurov had cooled to these, their beauty aroused in him nothing but repulsion, and the lace trimming on their underclothes reminded him of fish-scales.

But here the timidity and awkwardness of youth and inexperience were still apparent; and there was a feeling of embarrassment in the atmosphere, as if someone had just knocked at the door. Anna Sergeyevna, "the lady with the dog," seemed to regard the affair as something very special, very serious, as if she had become a fallen woman, an attitude he found odd and disconcerting. Her features lengthened and drooped, and her long hair hung mournfully on either side of her face. She assumed a pose of dismal meditation, like a repentant sinner in some classical painting.

"It isn't right," she said. "You will never respect me anymore."

On the table was a watermelon. Gurov cut himself a slice from it and began slowly eating it. At least half an hour passed in silence.

Anna Sergeyevna was very touching, revealing the purity of a decent, naïve woman who had seen very little of life. The solitary candle burning on the table scarcely lit up her face, but it was obvious that her heart was heavy.

"Why should I stop respecting you?" asked Gurov. "You don't know what you're saying."

"May God forgive me!" she exclaimed, and her eyes filled with tears. "It's terrible."

"No need to seek to justify yourself."

"How can I justify myself? I'm a wicked, fallen woman, I despise myself and have not the least thought of self-justification. It isn't my husband I have deceived, it's myself. And not only now, I have been deceiving myself for ever so long. My husband is no doubt an honest, worthy man, but he's a flunky. I don't know what it is he does at his office, but I know he's a flunky. I was only twenty when I married him, and I was devoured by curiosity, I wanted something higher. I told myself that there must be a different kind of life I wanted to live, to live. . . . I was burning with curiosity . . . you'll never understand that, but I swear to God I could no longer control myself, nothing could hold me back, I told my husband I was ill, and I came here. . . . And I started going about like one possessed, like a madwoman . . . and now I have become an ordinary, worthless woman, and everyone has a right to despise me."

Gurov listened to her, bored to death. The naïve accents, the remorse, all was so unexpected, so out of place. But for the tears in her eyes, she might have been jesting or play-acting.

"I don't understand," he said gently. "What is it you want?"

She hid her face against his breast and pressed closer to him.

"Do believe me, I implore you to believe me," she said. "I love all that is honest and pure in life, vice is revolting to me, I don't know what I'm doing. The common people say they are snared by the Devil. And now I can say that I have been snared by the Devil, too."

"Come, come," he murmured.

He gazed into her fixed, terrified eyes, kissed her, and soothed her with gentle affectionate words, and gradually she calmed down and regained her cheerfulness. Soon they were laughing together again.

When, a little later, they went out, there was not a soul on the promenade, the town and its cypresses looked dead, but the sea was still roaring as it dashed against the beach. A solitary fishing-boat tossed on the waves, its lamp blinking sleepily.

They found a carriage and drove to Oreanda.

"I discovered your name in the hall, just now," said Gurov, "written up on the board. Von Diederitz. Is your husband a German?"

"No. His grandfather was, I think, but he belongs to the Orthodox Church himself."

When they got out of the carriage at Oreanda they sat down on a bench not far from the church, and looked down at the sea, without talking. Yalta could be dimly discerned through the morning mist, and white clouds rested motionless on the summits of the mountains. Not a leaf stirred, the grasshoppers chirruped, and the monotonous hollow roar of the sea came up to them, speaking of peace, of the eternal sleep lying in wait for us all. The sea had roared like this long before there was any Yalta or Oreanda, it was roaring now, and it would go on roaring, just as indifferently and hollowly, when we had passed away. And it may be that in this continuity, this utter indifference to the life and death of each of us lies hidden the pledge of our eternal salvation, of the continuous movement of life on earth, of the continuous movement toward perfection.

Side by side with a young woman, who looked so exquisite in the early light, soothed and enchanted by the sight of all this magical beauty—sea, mountains, clouds and the vast expanse of the sky—Gurov told himself that, when you came to think of it, everything in the world is beautiful really, everything but our own thoughts and actions, when we lose sight of the higher aims of life, and of our dignity as human beings.

Someone approached them—a watchman, probably—looked at them and went away. And there was something mysterious and beautiful even in this. The steamer from Feodosia could be seen coming towards the pier, lit up by the dawn, its lamps out.

"There's dew on the grass," said Anna Sergeyevna, breaking the silence.

"Yes. Time to go home."

They went back to the town.

After this they met every day at noon on the promenade, lunching and dining together, going for walks, and admiring the sea. She complained of sleeplessness, of palpitations, asked the same questions over and over again, alternately surrendering to jealousy and the fear that he did not really respect her. And often, when there was nobody in sight in the square or the park, he would draw her to him and kiss her passionately. The utter idleness, these kisses in broad daylight, accompanied by furtive glances and the fear of discovery, the heat, the smell of the sea, and the idle, smart, well-fed people continually crossing their field of vision, seemed to have given him a new lease on life. He told Anna Sergeyevna she was beautiful and seductive, made love to her with impetuous passion, and never left her side, while she was always pensive, always trying to force from him the admission that he did not respect her, that he did not love her a bit, and considered her just an ordinary woman. Almost every night they drove out of town, to Oreanda, the waterfall, or some other beauty-spot. And these excursions were invariably a success, each contributing fresh impressions of majestic beauty.

All this time they kept expecting her husband to arrive. But a letter came in which he told his wife that he was having trouble with his eyes, and implored her to come home as soon as possible. Anna Sergeyevna made hasty preparations for leaving.

"It's a good thing I'm going," she said to Gurov. "It's the intervention of fate."

She left Yalta in a carriage, and he went with her as far as the railway station. The drive took nearly a whole day. When she got into the express train, after the second bell had been rung, she said:

"Let me have one more look at you. . . . One last look. That's right."

She did not weep, but was mournful, and seemed ill, the muscles of her cheeks twitching.

"I shall think of you . . . I shall think of you all the time," she said. "God bless you! Think kindly of me. We are parting forever, it must be so, because we ought never to have met. Good-bye—God bless you."

The train steamed rapidly out of the station, its lights soon disappearing, and a minute later even the sound it made was silenced, as if everything were conspiring to bring this sweet oblivion, this madness, to an end as quickly as possible. And Gurov, standing alone on the platform and gazing into the dark distance, listened to the shrilling of the grasshoppers and the humming of the telegraph wires, with a feeling that he had only just awakened. And he told himself that this had been just one more of the many adventures in his life, and that it, too, was over, leaving nothing but a memory. . . . He was moved and sad, and felt a slight remorse. After all, this young woman whom he would never again see had not been really happy with him. He had been friendly and affectionate with her, but in his whole behaviour, in the tones of his voice, in his very caresses, there had been a shade of irony, the insulting indulgence of the fortunate male, who was, moreover, almost twice her age. She had insisted in calling him good, remarkable, high-minded. Evidently he had appeared to her different from his real self, in a word he had involuntarily deceived her. . . .

There was an autumnal feeling in the air, and the evening was chilly.

"It's time for me to be going north, too," thought Gurov, as he walked away from the platform. "High time!"

## III

When he got back to Moscow it was beginning to look like winter; the stoves were heated every day, and it was still dark when the children got up to go to school and drank their tea, so that the nurse had to light the lamp for a short time. Frost had set in. When the first snow falls, and one goes for one's first sleigh-ride, it is pleasant to see the white ground, the white roofs; one breathes freely and lightly, and remembers the days of one's youth. The ancient lime-trees and birches, white with hoarfrost, have a good-natured look, they are closer to the heart than cypresses and palms, and beneath their branches one is no longer haunted by the memory of mountains and the sea.

Gurov had always lived in Moscow, and he returned to Moscow on a fine frosty day, and when he put on his fur-lined overcoat and thick gloves, and sauntered down Petrovka Street, and when, on Saturday evening, he heard the church bells ringing, his recent journey and the places he had visited lost their charm for him. He became gradually immersed in Moscow life, reading with avidity three newspapers a day, while declaring he never read Moscow newspapers on principle. Once more he was caught up in a whirl of restaurants, clubs, banquets, and celebrations, once more glowed with the flattering consciousness that well-known lawyers and actors came to his house, that he played cards in the Medical Club opposite a professor. He could once again eat a whole serving of Moscow Fish Stew served in a pan.

He had believed that in a month's time Anna Sergeyevna would be nothing but a vague memory, and that hereafter, with her wistful smile, she would only occasionally appear to him in dreams, like others before her. But the month was now well over and winter was in full swing, and all was as clear in his memory as if he had parted with Anna Sergeyevna only the day before. And his recollections grew ever more insistent. When the voices of his children at their lessons reached him in his study through the evening stillness, when he heard a song, or the sounds of a music-box in a restaurant, when the wind howled in the chimney, it all came back to him: early morning on the pier, the misty mountains, the steamer from Feodosia, the kisses. He would pace up and down his room for a long time, smiling at his memories, and then memory turned into dreaming, and what had happened mingled in his imagination with what was going to happen. Anna Sergeyevna did not come to him in his dreams, she accompanied him everywhere, like his shadow, following him everywhere he went. When he closed his eyes, she seemed to stand before him in the flesh, still lovelier, younger, tenderer than she had really been, and looking back, he saw himself, too, as better than he had been in Yalta. In the evenings she looked out at him from the bookshelves, the fireplace, the corner, he could hear her breathing, the sweet rustle of her skirts. In the streets he followed women with his eyes, to see if there were any like her. . . .

He began to feel an overwhelming desire to share his memories with someone. But he could not speak of his love at home, and outside his home who was there for him to confide in? Not the tenants living in his house, and certainly not his colleagues at the bank. And what was there to tell? Was it love that he had felt? Had there been anything exquisite, poetic, anything instructive or even amusing about his relations with Anna Sergeyevna? He had to content himself with uttering vague generalizations about love and women, and nobody guessed what he meant, though his wife's dark eyebrows twitched as she said:

"The role of a coxcomb doesn't suit you a bit, Dimitry."

One evening, leaving the Medical Club with one of his card-partners, a government official, he could not refrain from remarking:

"If you only knew what a charming woman I met in Yalta!"

The official got into his sleigh, and just before driving off, turned and called out:

"Dmitry Dmitrich!"

"Yes?"

"You were quite right, you know—the sturgeon was just a *leetle* off."

These words, in themselves so commonplace, for some reason infuriated Gurov, seemed to him humiliating, gross. What savage manners, what people! What wasted evenings, what tedious, empty days! Frantic card-playing, gluttony, drunkenness, perpetual talk always about the same thing. The greater part of one's time and energy went on business that was no use to anyone, and on discussing the same thing over and over again, and there was nothing to show for it all but a stunted wingless existence and a round of trivialities, and there was nowhere to escape to, you might as well be in a madhouse or a convict settlement.

Gurov lay awake all night, raging, and went about the whole of the next day with a headache. He slept badly on the succeeding nights, too, sitting up in bed, thinking, or pacing the floor of his room. He was sick of his children, sick of the bank, felt not the slightest desire to go anywhere or talk about anything.

When the Christmas holidays came, he packed his things, telling his wife he had to go to Petersburg in the interests of a certain young man, and set off for the town of S. To what end? He hardly knew himself. He only knew that he must see Anna Sergeyevna, must speak to her, arrange a meeting, if possible.

He arrived at S. in the morning and engaged the best suite in the hotel, which had a carpet of gray military frieze, and a dusty ink-pot on the table, surmounted by a headless rider, holding his hat in his raised hand. The hall porter told him what he wanted to know: von Diederitz had a house of his own in Staro-Goncharnaya Street. It wasn't far from the hotel, he lived on a grand scale, luxuriously, kept carriage-horses, the whole town knew him. The hall porter pronounced the name "Drideritz."

Gurov strolled over to Staro-Goncharnaya Street and discovered the house. In front of it was a long gray fence with inverted nails hammered into the tops of the palings.

"A fence like that is enough to make anyone want to run away," thought Gurov, looking at the windows of the house and the fence.

He reasoned that since it was a holiday, Anna's husband would probably be at home. In any case it would be tactless to embarrass her by calling at the house. And a note might fall into the hands of the husband, and bring about catastrophe. The best thing would be to wait about on the chance of seeing her. And he walked up and down the street, hovering in the vicinity of the fence, watching for his chance. A beggar entered the gate, only to be attacked by dogs, then, an hour later, the faint, vague sounds of a piano reached his ears. That would be Anna Sergeyevna playing. Suddenly the front door opened and an old woman came out, followed by a familiar white Pomeranian. Gurov tried to call to it, but his heart beat violently, and in his agitation he could not remember its name.

He walked on, hating the gray fence more and more, and now ready to tell himself irately that Anna Sergeyevna had forgotten him, had already, perhaps, found distraction in another—what could be more natural in a young woman who had to look at this accursed fence from morning to night? He went back to his hotel and sat on the sofa in his suite for some time, not knowing what to do, then he ordered dinner, and after dinner, had a long sleep.

"What a foolish, restless business," he thought, waking up and looking towards the dark windowpanes. It was evening by now. "Well, I've had my sleep out. And what am I to do in the night?"

He sat up in bed, covered by the cheap gray quilt, which reminded him of a hospital blanket, and in his vexation he fell to taunting himself

"You and your lady with a dog . . . there's adventure for you! See what you get for your pains."

On his arrival at the station that morning he had noticed a poster announcing in enormous letters the first performance at the local theatre of *The Geisha*.[7] Remembering this, he got up and made for the theatre.

"It's highly probable that she goes to first nights," he told himself.

The theatre was full. It was a typical provincial theatre, with a mist collecting over the chandeliers, and the crowd in the gallery fidgeting noisily. In the first row of the stalls the local dandies stood waiting for the curtain to go up, their hands clasped behind them. There, in the front seat of the governor's box, sat the governor's daughter, wearing a boa, the governor himself hiding modestly behind the drapes, so that only his hands were visible. The curtain stirred, the orchestra took a long time tuning up their instruments. Gurov's eyes roamed eagerly over the audience as they filed in and occupied their seats.

Anna Sergeyevna came in, too. She seated herself in the third row of the stalls, and when Gurov's glance fell on her, his heart seemed to stop, and he knew in a flash that the whole world contained no one nearer or dearer to him, no one more important to his happiness. This little woman, lost in the provincial crowd, in no way remarkable, holding a silly lorgnette in her hand, now filled his whole life, was his grief, his joy, all that he desired. Lulled by the sounds coming from the wretched orchestra, with its feeble, amateurish violinists, he thought how beautiful she was . . . thought and dreamed. . . .

Anna Sergeyevna was accompanied by a tall, round-shouldered young man with small whiskers, who nodded at every step before taking the seat beside her and seemed to be continually bowing to someone. This must be her husband, whom, in a fit of bitterness, at Yalta, she had called a "flunky." And there really was something of a lackey's servility in his lanky figure, his side-whiskers, and the little bald spot on the top of his head. And he smiled sweetly, and the badge of some scientific society gleaming in his buttonhole was like the number on a footman's livery.

The husband went out to smoke in the first interval, and she was left alone in her seat. Gurov, who had taken a seat in the stalls, went up to her and said in a trembling voice, with a forced smile: "How d'you do?"

She glanced up at him and turned pale, then looked at him again in alarm, unable to believe her eyes, squeezing her fan and lorgnette in one hand, evidently struggling to overcome a feeling of faintness. Neither of them said a word. She sat there, and he stood beside her, disconcerted by her embarrassment, and not daring to sit down. The violins and flutes sang out as they were tuned, and there was a tense sensation in the atmosphere, as if they were being watched from all the boxes. At last she got up and moved rapidly towards one of the exits. He followed her and they wandered aimlessly along corridors, up and down stairs; figures flashed by in the uniforms of legal officials, high-school teachers and civil servants, all wearing badges; ladies, coats hanging from pegs flashed by; there was a sharp draft, bringing with it an odor of cigarette butts. And Gurov, whose heart was beating violently, thought:

"What on earth are all these people, this orchestra for? . . ."

The next minute he suddenly remembered how, after seeing Anna Sergeyevna off that evening at the station, he had told himself that all was over,

7. An operetta (1897) by the English composer Sidney Jones.

and they would never meet again. And how far away the end seemed to be now!

She stopped on a dark narrow staircase over which was a notice bearing the inscription "To the upper circle."

"How you frightened me!" she said, breathing heavily, still pale and half-stunned. "Oh, how you frightened me! I'm almost dead! Why did you come? Oh, why?"

"But, Anna," he said, in low, hasty tones. "But, Anna. . . . Try to understand . . . do try. . . ."

She cast him a glance of fear, entreaty, love, and then gazed at him steadily, as if to fix his features firmly in her memory.

"I've been so unhappy," she continued, taking no notice of his words. "I could think of nothing but you the whole time, I lived on the thoughts of you. I tried to forget—why, oh, why did you come?"

On the landing above them were two schoolboys, smoking and looking down, but Gurov did not care, and, drawing Anna Sergeyevna towards him, began kissing her face, her lips, her hands.

"What are you doing, oh, what are you doing?" she said in horror, drawing back. "We have both gone mad. Go away this very night, this moment. . . . By all that is sacred, I implore you. . . . Somebody is coming."

Someone was ascending the stairs.

"You must go away," went on Anna Sergeyevna in a whisper. "D'you hear me, Dmitry Dmitrich? I'll come to you in Moscow. I have never been happy, I am unhappy now, and I shall never be happy—never! Do not make me suffer still more! I will come to you in Moscow, I swear it! And now we must part! My dear one, my kind one, my darling, we must part."

She pressed his hand and hurried down the stairs, looking back at him continually, and her eyes showed that she was in truth unhappy. Gurov stood where he was for a short time, listening, and when all was quiet, went to look for his coat, and left the theatre.

## IV

And Anna Sergeyevna began going to Moscow to see him. Every two or three months she left the town of S., telling her husband that she was going to consult a specialist on female diseases, and her husband believed her and did not believe her. In Moscow she always stayed at the Slavyanski Bazaar, sending a man in a red cap to Gurov the moment she arrived. Gurov went to her, and no one in Moscow knew anything about it.

One winter morning he went to see her as usual (the messenger had been to him the evening before, but had not found him at home). His daughter was with him, for her school was on the way and he thought he might as well see her to it.

"It is forty degrees," said Gurov to his daughter, "and yet it is snowing. You see it is only above freezing close to the ground, the temperature in the upper layers of the atmosphere is quite different."

"Why doesn't it ever thunder in winter, Papa?"

He explained this, too. As he was speaking, he kept reminding himself that he was going to a rendezvous and that not a living soul knew about it, or, probably, ever would. He led a double life—one in public, in the sight of all whom it concerned, full of conventional truth and conventional deception, exactly like the lives of his friends and acquaintances, and another which flowed in secret. And, owing to some strange, possibly quite accidental chain of circumstances, everything that was important, interesting, essential, everything about which he was sincere and never deceived himself, everything that composed the kernel of his life, went on in secret, while everything that was false in him, everything that composed the husk in which he hid himself and the truth which was in him—his work at the bank, discussions at the club, his "lower race," his attendance at anniversary celebrations with his wife—was on the surface. He began to judge others by himself, no longer believing what he saw, and always assuming that the real, the only interesting life of every individual goes on as under cover of night, secretly. Every individual existence revolves around mystery, and perhaps that is the chief reason that all cultivated individuals insisted so strongly on the respect due to personal secrets.

After leaving his daughter at the door of her school Gurov set off for the Slavyanski Bazaar. Taking off his overcoat in the lobby, he went upstairs and knocked softly on the door. Anna Sergeyevna, wearing the gray dress he liked most, exhausted by her journey and by suspense, had been expecting him since the evening before. She was pale and looked at him without smiling, but was in his arms almost before he was fairly in the room. Their kiss was lingering, prolonged, as if they had not met for years.

"Well, how are you?" he asked. "Anything new?"

"Wait, I'll tell you in a minute. . . . I can't. . . ."

She could not speak, because she was crying. Turning away, she held her handkerchief to her eyes.

"I'll wait till she's had her cry out," he thought, and sank into a chair.

He rang for tea, and a little later, while he was drinking it, she was still standing there, her face to the window. She wept from emotion, from her bitter consciousness of the sadness of their life; they could only see one another in secret, hiding from people, as if they were thieves. Was not their life a broken one?

"Don't cry," he said.

It was quite obvious to him that this love of theirs would not soon come to an end, and that no one could say when this end would be. Anna Sergeyevna loved him ever more fondly, worshipped him, and there would have been no point in telling her that one day it must end. Indeed, she would not have believed him.

He moved over and took her by the shoulders, intending to caress her, to make a joke, but suddenly he caught sight of himself in the looking-glass.

His hair was already beginning to turn gray. It struck him as strange that he should have aged so much in the last few years, have lost so much of his looks. The shoulders on which his hands lay were warm and quivering. He felt a pity for this life, still so warm and exquisite, but probably soon to fade and droop like his own. Why did she love him so? Women had always believed him different from what he really was, had loved in him not himself but the man their imagination pictured him, a man they had sought for eagerly all their lives. And afterwards when they discovered their mistake, they went on loving him just the same. And not one of them had ever been happy with him. Time had passed, he had met one woman after another, become intimate with each, parted with each, but had never loved. There had been all sorts of things between them, but never love.

And only now, when he was gray-haired, had he fallen in love properly, thoroughly, for the first time in his life.

He and Anna Sergeyevna loved one another as people who are very close and intimate, as husband and wife, as dear friends love one another. It seemd to them that fate had intended them for one another, and they could not understand why she should have a husband, and he a wife. They were like two migrating birds, the male and the female, who had been caught and put into separate cages. They forgave one another all that they were ashamed of in the past and in the present, and felt that this love of theirs had changed them both.

Formerly, in moments of melancholy, he had consoled himself by the first argument that came into his head, but now arguments were nothing to him, he felt profound pity, desired to be sincere, tender.

"Stop crying, my dearest," he said. "You've had your cry, now stop. . . . Now let us have a talk, let us try and think what we are to do."

Then they discussed their situation for a long time, trying to think how they could get rid of the necessity for hiding, deception, living in different towns, being so long without meeting. How were they to shake off these intolerable fetters?

"How? How?" he repeated, clutching his head. "How?"

And it seemed to them that they were within an inch of arriving at a decision, and that then a new, beautiful life would begin. And they both realized that the end was still far, far away, and that the hardest, the most complicated part was only just beginning.

# Gusev

It is already dark, it will soon be night.

Gusev, a discharged private, half rises in his bunk and says in a low voice: "Do you hear me, Pavel Ivanych? A soldier in Suchan was telling me: while they were sailing, their ship bumped into a big fish and smashed a hole in its bottom."

The individual of uncertain social status whom he is addressing, and whom everyone in the ship infirmary calls Pavel Ivanych, is silent as though he hasn't heard.

And again all is still. The wind is flirting with the rigging, the screw is throbbing, the waves are lashing, the bunks creak, but the ear has long since become used to these sounds, and everything around seems to slumber in silence. It is dull. The three invalids—two soldiers and a sailor—who were playing cards all day are dozing and talking deliriously.

The ship is apparently beginning to roll. The bunk slowly rises and falls under Gusev as though it were breathing, and this occurs once, twice, three times . . . Something hits the floor with a clang: a jug must have dropped.

"The wind has broken loose from its chain," says Gusev, straining his ears.

This time Pavel Ivanych coughs and says irritably:

"One minute a vessel bumps into a fish, the next the wind breaks loose from its chain . . . Is the wind a beast that it breaks loose from its chain?"

"That's what Christian folks say."

"They are as ignorant as you . . . They say all sorts of things. One must have one's head on one's shoulders and reason it out. You have no sense."

Pavel Ivanych is subject to seasickness. When the sea is rough he is usually out of sorts, and the merest trifle irritates him. In Gusev's opinion there is absolutely nothing to be irritated about. What is there that is strange or out of the way about that fish, for instance, or about the wind breaking loose from its chain? Suppose the fish were as big as the mountain and its back as hard as a sturgeon's, and supposing, too, that over yonder at the end of the world stood great stone walls and the fierce winds were chained up to the walls. If they haven't broken loose, why then do they rush all over the sea like madmen and strain like hounds tugging at their leash? If they are not chained up what becomes of them when it is calm?

Gusev ponders for a long time about fishes as big as a mountain and about stout, rusty chains. Then he begins to feel bored and falls to thinking about his home, to which he is returning after five years' service in the Far East. He pictures an immense pond covered with drifts. On one side of the pond is the brick-colored building of the pottery with a tall chimney and clouds of black smoke; on the other side is a village. His brother Alexey drives out of the fifth yard from the end in a sleigh; behind him sits his little son Vanka in big felt boots, and his little girl Akulka also wearing felt boots. Alexey has had a drop, Vanka is laughing, Akulka's face cannot be seen, she is muffled up.

"If he doesn't look out, he will have the children frostbitten," Gusev reflects. "Lord send them sense that they may honor their parents and not be any wiser than their father and mother."

"They need new soles," a delirious sailor says in a bass voice. "Yes, yes!"

Gusev's thoughts abruptly break off and suddenly without rhyme or reason the pond is replaced by a huge bull's head without eyes, and the horse and sleigh are no longer going straight ahead but are whirling round and round, wrapped in black smoke. But still he is glad he has had a glimpse of his people. In fact, he is breathless with joy, and his whole body, down to his fingertips, tingles with it. "Thanks be to God we have seen each other again," he mutters deliriously, but at once opens his eyes and looks for water in the dark.

He drinks and lies down, and again the sleigh is gliding along, then again there is the bull's head without eyes, smoke, clouds . . . And so it goes till daybreak.

about the hotel, watching the people go in and out, longing to enter and leave schoolmasters and dull care behind him forever.

At last the singer came out, accompanied by the conductor, who helped her into her carriage and closed the door with a cordial *auf wiedersehen*[8] which set Paul to wondering whether she were not an old sweetheart of his. Paul followed the carriage over to the hotel, walking so rapidly as not to be far from the entrance when the singer alighted, and disappeared behind the swinging glass doors that were opened by a Negro in a tall hat and a long coat. In the moment that the door was ajar it seemed to Paul that he, too, entered. He seemed to feel himself go after her up the steps, into the warm, lighted building, into an exotic, tropical world of shiny, glistening surfaces and basking ease. He reflected upon the mysterious dishes that were brought into the dining room, the green bottles in buckets of ice, as he had seen them in the supper party pictures of the *Sunday World* supplement. A quick gust of wind brought the rain down with sudden vehemence, and Paul was startled to find that he was still outside in the slush of the gravel driveway; that his boots were letting in the water and his scanty overcoat was clinging wet about him; that the lights in front of the concert hall were out and that the rain was driving in sheets between him and the orange glow of the windows above him. There it was, what he wanted—tangibly before him, like the fairy world of a Christmas pantomime—but mocking spirits stood guard at the doors, and, as the rain beat in his face, Paul wondered whether he were destined always to shiver in the black night outside, looking up at it.

He turned and walked reluctantly toward the car[9] tracks. The end had to come sometime; his father in his nightclothes at the top of the stairs, explanations that did not explain, hastily improvised fictions that were forever tripping him up, his upstairs room and its horrible yellow wallpaper, the creaking bureau with the greasy plush collarbox, and over his painted wooden bed the pictures of George Washington and John Calvin,[1] and the framed motto, "Feed my Lambs," which had been worked in red worsted by his mother.

Half an hour later Paul alighted from his car and went slowly down one of the side streets off the main thoroughfare. It was a highly respectable street, where all the houses were exactly alike, and where businessmen of moderate means begot and reared large families of children, all of whom went to Sabbath school and learned the shorter catechism, and were interested in arithmetic; all of whom were as exactly alike as their homes, and of a piece with the monotony in which they lived. Paul never went up Cordelia Street without a shudder of loathing. His home was next to the house of the Cumberland[2] minister. He approached it tonight with the nerveless sense of defeat, the hopeless feeling of sinking back forever into ugliness and commonness that he had always had when he came home. The moment he turned into Cordelia Street he felt the waters close above his head. After each of these orgies of living he experienced all the physical depression which follows a debauch; the loathing of respectable beds, of common food, of a house penetrated by kitchen odors; a shuddering

8. Good-bye (German). 9. I.e., streetcar. 1. French Protestant reformer who lived in Geneva (1509–1564). 2. A division of the Presbyterian Church in the United States.

repulsion for the flavorless, colorless mass of everyday existence; a morbid desire for cool things and soft lights and fresh flowers.

The nearer he approached the house, the more absolutely unequal Paul felt to the sight of it all: his ugly sleeping chamber; the cold bathroom with the grimy zinc tub, the cracked mirror, the dripping spigots; his father, at the top of the stairs, his hairy legs sticking out from his nightshirt, his feet thrust into carpet slippers. He was so much later than usual that there would certainly be inquiries and reproaches. Paul stopped short before the door. He felt that he could not be accosted by his father tonight; that he could not toss again on that miserable bed. He would not go in. He would tell his father that he had no carfare and it was raining so hard he had gone home with one of the boys and stayed all night.

Meanwhile, he was wet and cold. He went around to the back of the house and tried one of the basement windows, found it open, raised it cautiously, and scrambled down the cellar wall to the floor. There he stood, holding his breath, terrified by the noise he had made, but the floor above him was silent, and there was no creak on the stairs. He found a soapbox, and carried it over to the soft ring of light that streamed from the furnace door, and sat down. He was horribly afraid of rats, so he did not try to sleep, but sat looking distrustfully at the dark, still terrified lest he might have awakened his father. In such reactions, after one of the experiences which made days and nights out of the dreary blanks of the calendar, when his senses were deadened, Paul's head was always singularly clear. Suppose his father had heard him getting in at the window and had come down and shot him for a burglar? Then, again, suppose his father had come down, pistol in hand, and he had cried out in time to save himself, and his father had been horrified to think how nearly he had killed him? Then, again, suppose a day should come when his father would remember that night, and wish there had been no warning cry to stay his hand? With this last supposition Paul entertained himself until daybreak.

The following Sunday was fine; the sodden November chill was broken by the last flash of autumnal summer. In the morning Paul had to go to church and Sabbath school, as always. On seasonable Sunday afternoons the burghers of Cordelia Street always sat out on their front stoops and talked to their neighbors on the next stoop, or called to those across the street in neighborly fashion. The men usually sat on gay cushions placed upon the steps that led down to the sidewalk, while the women, in their Sunday "waists,"[3] sat in rockers on the cramped porches, pretending to be greatly at their ease. The children played in the streets; there were so many of them that the place resembled the recreation grounds of a kindergarten. The men on the steps—all in their shirt sleeves their vests unbuttoned—sat with their legs well apart, their stomachs comfortably protruding, and talked of the prices of things, or told anecdotes of the sagacity of their various chiefs and overlords. They occasionally looked over the multitude of squabbling children, listened affectionately to their high-pitched, nasal voices, smiling to see their own proclivities reproduced in their

3. Bodices or blouses.

## II

A blue circle is the first thing to become visible in the darkness—it is the porthole; then, little by little, Gusev makes out the man in the next bunk, Pavel Ivanych. The man sleeps sitting up, as he cannot breathe lying down. His face is gray, his nose long and sharp, his eyes look huge because he is terribly emaciated, his temples are sunken, his beard skimpy, his hair long. His face does not reveal his social status: you cannot tell whether he is a gentleman, a merchant, or a peasant. Judging from his expression and his long hair, he may be an assiduous churchgoer or a lay brother, but his manner of speaking does not seem to be that of a monk. He is utterly worn out by his cough, by the stifling heat, his illness, and he breathes with difficulty, moving his parched lips. Noticing that Gusev is looking at him he turns his face toward him and says:

"I begin to guess . . . Yes, I understand it all perfectly now."

"What do you understand, Pavel Ivanych?"

"Here's how it is . . . It has always seemed strange to me that terribly ill as you fellows are, you should be on a steamer where the stifling air, the heavy seas, in fact everything, threatens you with death; but now it is all clear to me . . . Yes . . . The doctors put you on the steamer to get rid of you. They got tired of bothering with you, cattle . . . You don't pay them any money, you are a nuisance, and you spoil their statistics with your deaths . . . So, of course, you are just cattle. And it's not hard to get rid of you . . . All that's necessary is, in the first place, to have no conscience or humanity, and, secondly, to deceive the ship authorities. The first requirement need hardly be given a thought—in that respect we are virtuosos, and as for the second condition, it can always be fulfilled with a little practice. In a crowd of four hundred healthy soldiers and sailors, five sick ones are not conspicuous; well, they got you all onto the steamer, mixed you with the healthy ones, hurriedly counted you over, and in the confusion nothing untoward was noticed, and when the steamer was on the way, people discovered that there were paralytics and consumptives on their last legs lying about the deck . . ."

Gusev does not understand Pavel Ivanych; thinking that he is being reprimanded, he says in self-justification:

"I lay on the deck because I was so sick; when we were being unloaded from the barge onto the steamer, I caught a bad chill."

"It's revolting," Pavel Ivanych continues. "The main thing is, they know perfectly well that you can't stand the long journey and yet they put you here. Suppose you last as far as the Indian Ocean, and then what? It's horrible to think of . . . And that's the gratitude for your faithful, irreproachable service!"

Pavel Ivanych's eyes flash with anger. He frowns fastidiously and says, gasping for breath, "Those are the people who ought to be given a drubbing in the newspapers till the feathers fly in all directions."

The two sick soldiers and the sailor have waked up and are already playing cards. The sailor is half reclining in his bunk, the soldiers are sitting near by on the floor in most uncomfortable positions. One of the soldiers has his right arm bandaged and his wrist is heavily swathed in wrappings that look like a cap, so that he holds his cards under his right arm or in the crook of his elbow while he plays with his left. The ship is rolling heavily. It is impossible to stand up, or have tea, or take medicine.

"Were you an orderly?" Pavel Ivanych asks Gusev.

"Yes, sir, an orderly."

"My God, my God!" says Pavel Ivanych and shakes his head sadly. "To tear a man from his home, drag him a distance of ten thousand miles, then wear him out till he gets consumption and . . . and what is it all for, one asks? To turn him into an orderly for some Captain Kopeykin or Midshipman Dyrka! How reasonable!"

"It's not hard work, Pavel Ivanych. You get up in the morning and polish the boots, start the samovars going, tidy the rooms, and then you have nothing more to do. The lieutenant drafts plans all day, and if you like, you can say your prayers, or read a book or go out on the street. God grant everyone such a life."

"Yes, very good! The lieutenant drafts plans all day long, and you sit in the kitchen and long for home . . . Plans, indeed! . . . It's not plans that matter but human life. You have only one life to live and it mustn't be wronged."

"Of course, Pavel Ivanych, a bad man gets no break anywhere, either at home or in the service, but if you live as you ought and obey orders, who will want to wrong you? The officers are educated gentlemen, they understand . . . In five years I have never once been in the guard house, and I was struck, if I remember right, only once."

"What for?"

"For fighting. I have a heavy hand, Pavel Ivanych. Four Chinks came into our yard; they were bringing firewood or something, I forget. Well, I was bored and I knocked them about a bit, the nose of one of them, damn him, began bleeding . . . The lieutenant saw it all through the window, got angry, and boxed me on the ear."

"You are a poor, foolish fellow . . ." whispers Pavel Ivanych. "You don't understand anything."

He is utterly exhausted by the rolling of the ship and shuts his eyes; now his head drops back, now it sinks forward on his chest. Several times he tries to lie down but nothing comes of it: he finds it difficult to breathe.

"And what did you beat up the four Chinks for?" he asks after a while.

"Oh, just like that. They came into the yard and I hit them."

There is silence . . . The card-players play for two hours, eagerly, swearing sometimes, but the rolling and pitching of the ship overcomes them, too; they throw aside the cards and lie down. Again Gusev has a vision: the big pond, the pottery, the village . . . Once more the sleigh is gliding along, once more Vanka is laughing and Akulka, the silly thing, throws open her fur coat and thrusts out her feet, as much as to say: "Look, good people, my felt boots are not like Vanka's, they're new ones."

"Going on six, and she has no sense yet," Gusev mutters in his delirium. "Instead of showing off your boots you had better come and get your soldier uncle a drink. I'll give you a present."

And here is Andron with a flintlock on his shoulder, carrying a hare he has killed, and behind him is the decrepit old Jew Isaychik, who offers him a piece of soap in exchange for the hare; and here is the black calf in the entry, and

Domna sewing a shirt and crying about something, and then again the bull's head without eyes, black smoke . . .

Someone shouts overhead, several sailors run by; it seems that something bulky is being dragged over the deck, something falls with a crash. Again some people run by. . . . Has there been an accident? Gusev raises his head, listens, and sees that the two soldiers and the sailor are playing cards again; Pavel Ivanych is sitting up and moving his lips. It is stifling, you haven't the strength to breathe, you are thirsty, the water is warm, disgusting. The ship is still rolling and pitching.

Suddenly something strange happens to one of the soldiers playing cards. He calls hearts diamonds, gets muddled over his score, and drops his cards, then with a frightened, foolish smile looks round at all of them.

"I shan't be a minute, fellows . . ." he says, and lies down on the floor.

Everybody is nonplussed. They call to him, he does not answer.

"Stepan, maybe you are feeling bad, eh?" the soldier with the bandaged arm asks him. "Perhaps we had better call the priest, eh?"

"Have a drink of water, Stepan . . ." says the sailor. "Here, brother, drink."

"Why are you knocking the jug against his teeth?" says Gusev angrily. "Don't you see, you cabbage-head?"

"What?"

"What?" Gusev mimicks him. "There is no breath in him, he's dead! That's what! Such stupid people, Lord God!"

## III

The ship has stopped rolling and Pavel Ivanych is cheerful. He is no longer cross. His face wears a boastful, challenging, mocking expression. It is as though he wants to say: "Yes, right away I'll tell you something that will make you burst with laughter." The round porthole is open and a soft breeze is blowing on Pavel Ivanych. There is a sound of voices, the splash of oars in the water . . . Just under the porthole someone is droning in a thin, disgusting voice; must be a Chinaman singing.

"Here we are in the harbor," says Pavel Ivanych with a mocking smile. "Only another month or so and we shall be in Russia. M'yes, messieurs of the armed forces! I'll arrive in Odessa and from there go straight to Kharkov. In Kharkov I have a friend, a man of letters. I'll go to him and say, 'Come, brother, put aside your vile subjects, women's amours and the beauties of Nature, and show up the two-legged vermin' . . . There's a subject for you."

For a while he reflects, then says:

"Gusev, do you know how I tricked them?"

"Tricked who, Pavel Ivanych?"

"Why, these people . . . You understand, on this steamer there is only a first class and a third class, and they only allow peasants, that is, the common herd, to go in the third. If you have got a jacket on and even at a distance look like a gentleman or a bourgeois,[1] you have to go first class, if you please. You must

1. A member of the middle class.

fork out five hundred rubles if it kills you. 'Why do you have such a regulation?' I ask them. 'Do you mean to raise the prestige of the Russian intelligentsia thereby?' 'Not a bit of it. We don't let you simply because a decent person can't go third class; it is too horrible and disgusting there.' 'Yes, sir? Thank you for being so solicitous about decent people's welfare. But in any case, whether it's nasty there or nice, I haven't got five hundred rubles. I didn't loot the Treasury, I didn't exploit the natives, I didn't traffic in contraband I flogged nobody to death, so judge for yourselves if I have the right to occupy a first class cabin and even to reckon myself among the Russian intelligentsia.' But logic means nothing to them. So I had to resort to fraud. I put on a peasant coat and high boots, I pulled a face so that I looked like a common drunk, and went to the agents: 'Give us a little ticket, your Excellency,' said I—"

"You're not of the gentry, are you?" asked the sailor.

"I come of a clerical family. My father was a priest, and an honest one; he always told the high and mighty the truth to their faces and, as a result, he suffered a great deal."

Pavel Ivanych is exhausted from talking and gasps for breath, but still continues:

"Yes, I always tell people the truth to their faces. I'm not afraid of anyone or anything. In this respect, there is a great difference between me and all of you, men. You are dark people, blind, crushed; you see nothing and what you do see, you don't understand . . . You are told that the wind breaks loose from its chain, that you are beasts, savages, and you believe it; someone gives it to you in the neck—you kiss his hand; some animal in a racoon coat robs you and then tosses you a fifteen-kopeck tip and you say: 'Let me kiss your hand, sir.' You are outcasts, pitiful wretches. I am different, my mind is clear. I see it all plainly like a hawk or an eagle when it hovers over the earth, and I understand everything. I am protest personified. I see tyranny—I protest. I see a hypocrite—I protest, I see a triumphant swine—I protest. And I cannot be put down, no Spanish Inquisition[2] can silence me. No. Cut out my tongue and I will protest with gestures. Wall me up in a cellar—I will shout so that you will hear me half a mile away, or will starve myself to death, so that they may have another weight on their black consciences. Kill me and I will haunt them. All my acquaintances say to me: 'You are a most insufferable person, Pavel Ivanych.' I am proud of such a reputation. I served three years in the Far East and I shall be remembered there a hundred years. I had rows there with everybody. My friends wrote to me from Russia: 'Don't come back,' but here I am going back to spite them . . . Yes . . . That's life as I understand it. That's what one can call life."

Gusev is not listening; he is looking at the porthole. A junk, flooded with dazzling hot sunshine, is swaying on the transparent turquoise water. In it stand naked Chinamen, holding up cages with canaries in them and calling out: "It sings, it sings!"

Another boat knocks against it; a steam cutter glides past. Then there is

2. The state tribunal of the Roman Catholic Church, established in Spain in 1480 to eradicate heresy, infamous for its cruelty and capriciousness. Joseph Bonaparte abolished it in 1808.

another boat: a fat Chinaman sits in it, eating rice with chopsticks. The water sways lazily, white sea gulls languidly hover over it.

"Would be fine to give that fat fellow one in the neck," reflects Gusev, looking at the stout Chinaman and yawning.

He dozes off and it seems to him that all nature is dozing too. Time flies swiftly by. Imperceptibly the day passes. Imperceptibly darkness descends . . . The steamer is no longer standing still but is on the move again.

## IV

Two days pass. Pavel Ivanych no longer sits up but is lying down. His eyes are closed, his nose seems to have grown sharper.

"Pavel Ivanych," Gusev calls to him. "Hey, Pavel Ivanych."

Pavel Ivanych opens his eyes and moves his lips.

"Are you feeling bad?"

"No . . . It's nothing . . ." answers Pavel Ivanych gasping for breath. "Nothing, on the contrary . . . I am better . . . You see, I can lie down now . . . I have improved . . ."

"Well, thank God for that, Pavel Ivanych."

"When I compare myself to you, I am sorry for you, poor fellows. My lungs are healthy, mine is a stomach cough . . . I can stand hell, let alone the Red Sea. Besides, I take a critical attitude toward my illness and the medicines. While you—Your minds are dark . . . It's hard on you, very, very hard!"

The ship is not rolling, it is quiet, but as hot and stifling as a Turkish bath; it is hard, not only to speak, but even to listen. Gusev hugs his knees, lays his head on them and thinks of his home. God, in this stifling heat, what a relief it is to think of snow and cold! You're driving in a sleigh; all of a sudden, the horses take fright at something and bolt. Careless of the road, the ditches, the gullies, they tear like mad things right through the village, across the pond, past the pottery, across the open fields. "Hold them!" the pottery hands and the peasants they meet shout at the top of their voices. "Hold them!" But why hold them? Let the keen cold wind beat in your face and bite your hands; let the lumps of snow, kicked up by the horses, slide down your collar, your neck, your chest; let the runners sing, and the traces and the whippletrees break, the devil take them. And what delight when the sleigh upsets and you go flying full tilt into a drift, face right in the snow, and then you get up, white all over with icicles on your mustache, no cap, no gloves, your belt undone . . . People laugh, dogs bark . . .

Pavel Ivanych half opens one eye, fixes Gusev with it and asks softly:

"Gusev, did your commanding officer steal?"

"Who can tell, Pavel Ivanych? We can't say, we didn't hear about it."

And after that, a long time passes in silence. Gusev broods, his mind wanders, and he keeps drinking water: it is hard for him to talk and hard for him to listen, and he is afraid of being talked to. An hour passes, a second, a third; evening comes, then night, but he doesn't notice it; he sits up and keeps dreaming of the frost.

There is a sound as though someone were coming into the infirmary, voices are heard, but five minutes pass and all is quiet again.

"The kingdom of Heaven be his and eternal peace," says the soldier with a bandaged arm. "He was an uneasy chap."

"What?" asks Gusev. "Who?"

"He died, they have just carried him up."

"Oh, well," mutters Gusev, yawning, "the kingdom of Heaven be his."

"What do you think, Gusev?" the soldier with the bandaged arm says after a while. "Will he be in the kingdom of Heaven or not?"

"Who do you mean?"

"Pavel Ivanych."

"He will . . . He suffered so long. Then again, he belonged to the clergy and priests have a lot of relatives. Their prayers will get him there."

The soldier with the bandage sits down on Gusev's bunk and says in an undertone:

"You too, Gusev, aren't long for this world. You will never get to Russia."

"Did the doctor or the nurse say so?" asks Gusev.

"It isn't that they said so, but one can see it. It's plain when a man will die soon. You don't eat, you don't drink, you've got so thin it's dreadful to look at you. It's consumption, in a word. I say it not to worry you, but because maybe you would like to receive the sacrament and extreme unction. And if you have any money, you had better turn it over to the senior officer."

"I haven't written home," Gusev sighs: "I shall die and they won't know."

"They will," the sick sailor says in a bass voice. "When you die, they will put it down in the ship's log, in Odessa they will send a copy of the entry to the army authorities, and they will notify your district board or somebody like that."

Such a conversation makes Gusev uneasy and a vague craving begins to torment him. He takes a drink—it isn't that; he drags himself to the porthole and breathes the hot, moist air—it isn't that; he tries to think of home, of the frost—it isn't that . . . At last it seems to him that if he stays in the infirmary another minute, he will certainly choke to death.

"It's stifling, brother," he says. "I'll go on deck. Take me there, for Christ's sake."

"All right," the soldier with the bandage agrees. "You can't walk, I'll carry you. Hold on to my neck."

Gusev puts his arm around the soldier's neck, the latter places his uninjured arm round him and carries him up. On the deck, discharged soldiers and sailors are lying asleep side by side; there are so many of them it is difficult to pass.

"Get down on the floor," the soldier with the bandage says softly. "Follow me quietly, hold on to my shirt."

It is dark, there are no lights on deck or on the masts or anywhere on the sea around. On the prow the seaman on watch stands perfectly still like a statue, and it looks as though he, too, were asleep. The steamer seems to be left to its own devices and to be going where it pleases.

"Now they'll throw Pavel Ivanych into the sea," says the soldier with the bandage, "in a sack and then into the water."

"Yes, that's the regulation."

"At home, it's better to lie in the earth. Anyway, your mother will come to the grave and shed a tear."

"Sure."

There is a smell of dung and hay. With drooping heads, steers stand at the ship's rail. One, two, three—eight of them! And there's a pony. Gusev puts out his hand to stroke it, but it shakes its head, shows its teeth, and tries to bite his sleeve.

"Damn brute!" says Gusev crossly.

The two of them thread their way to the prow, then stand at the rail, peering. Overhead there is deep sky, bright stars, peace and quiet, exactly as at home in the village. But below there is darkness and disorder. Tall waves are making an uproar for no reason. Each one of them as you look at it is trying to rise higher than all the rest and to chase and crush its neighbor; it is thunderously attacked by a third wave that has a gleaming white mane and is just as ferocious and ugly.

The sea has neither sense nor pity. If the steamer had been smaller, not made of thick iron plates, the waves would have crushed it without the slightest remorse, and would have devoured all the people in it without distinguishing between saints and sinners. The steamer's expression was equally senseless and cruel. This beaked monster presses forward, cutting millions of waves in its path; it fears neither darkness nor the wind, nor space, nor solitude—it's all child's play for it, and if the ocean had its population, this monster would crush it, too, without distinguishing between saints and sinners.

"Where are we now?" asks Gusev.

"I don't know. Must be the ocean."

"You can't see land . . ."

"No chance of it! They say we'll see it only in seven days."

The two men stare silently at the white phosphorescent foam and brood. Gusev is first to break the silence.

"There is nothing frightening here," he says. "Only you feel queer as if you were in a dark forest; but if, let's say, they lowered the boat this minute and an officer ordered me to go fifty miles across the sea to catch fish, I'll go. Or, let's say, if a Christian were to fall into the water right now, I'd jump in after him. A German or a Chink I wouldn't try to save, but I'd go in after a Christian."

"And are you afraid to die?"

"I am. I am sorry about the farm. My brother at home, you know, isn't steady; he drinks, he beats his wife for no reason, he doesn't honor his father and mother. Without me everything will go to rack and ruin, and before long it's my fear that my father and old mother will be begging their bread. But my legs won't hold me up, brother, and it's stifling here. Let's go to sleep."

## V

Gusev goes back to the infirmary and gets into his bunk. He is again tormented by a vague desire and he can't make out what it is that he wants. There is a weight on his chest, a throbbing in his head, his mouth is so dry that it is difficult for him to move his tongue. He dozes and talks in his sleep and, worn out with nightmares, with coughing and the stifling heat, towards morning he falls into a heavy sleep. He dreams that they have just taken the bread out of the oven in the barracks and that he has climbed into the oven and is having a steam bath there, lashing himself with a besom of birch twigs. He sleeps for two days and on the third at noon two sailors come down and carry him out of the infirmary. He is sewn up in sailcloth and to make him heavier, they put two gridirons in with him. Sewn up in sailcloth, he looks like a carrot or a radish: broad at the head and narrow at the feet. Before sunset, they carry him on deck and put him on a plank. One end of the plank lies on the ship's rail, the other on a box placed on a stool. Round him stand the discharged soldiers and the crew with heads bared.

"Blessed is our God," the priest begins, "now, and ever, and unto ages of ages."

"Amen," three sailors chant.

The discharged men and the crew cross themselves and look off at the waves. It is strange that a man should be sewn up in sailcloth and should soon be flying into the sea. Is it possible that such a thing can happen to anyone?

The priest strews earth upon Gusev and makes obeisance to him. The men sing "Memory Eternal."

The seaman on watch duty raises the end of the plank, Gusev slides off it slowly and then flying, head foremost, turns over in the air and—plop! Foam covers him, and for a moment, he seems to be wrapped in lace, but the instant passes and he disappears in the waves.

He plunges rapidly downward. Will he reach the bottom? At this spot the ocean is said to be three miles deep. After sinking sixty or seventy feet, he begins to descend more and more slowly, swaying rhythmically as though in hesitation, and, carried along by the current, moves faster laterally than vertically.

And now he runs into a school of fish called pilot fish. Seeing the dark body, the little fish stop as though petrified and suddenly all turn round together and disappear. In less than a minute they rush back at Gusev, swift as arrows and begin zigzagging round him in the water. Then another dark body appears. It is a shark. With dignity and reluctance, seeming not to notice Gusev, as it were, it swims under him; then while he, moving downward, sinks upon its back, the shark turns, belly upward, basks in the warm transparent water and languidly opens its jaws with two rows of teeth. The pilot fish are in ecstasy; they stop to see what will happen next. After playing a little with the body, the shark nonchalantly puts his jaws under it, cautiously touches it with his teeth and the sailcloth is ripped the full length of the body, from head to foot; one of the gridirons falls out, frightens the pilot fish and striking the shark on the flank, sinks rapidly to the bottom.

Meanwhile, up above, in that part of the sky where the sun is about to set, clouds are massing, one resembling a triumphal arch, another a lion, a third a pair of scissors. A broad shaft of green light issues from the clouds and reaches to the middle of the sky; a while later, a violet beam appears alongside of it and then a golden one and a pink one . . . The heavens turn a soft lilac tint. Looking at this magnificent enchanting sky, the ocean frowns at first, but soon it, too, takes on tender, joyous, passionate colors for which it is hard to find a name in the language of man.

## RICHARD BAUSCH on *Gusev*

The unusual thing about this story—even as a story of Chekhov's—is its point of view: the radical way it shifts in the last paragraphs, from the limited omniscience of Gusev's consciousness, to a kind of omniscience that includes even the sea and the sky. The way it leaves the province of human thought and action, as Gusev is dropped into the ocean, and enters the animal kingdom. The pilot fish are "in ecstacy," and the shark "languidly opens its jaws with two rows of teeth." The sailcloth that contains Gusev is torn open, the gridiron that was to carry him to the bottom of the sea falls out, and "frightens" the pilot fish. All of this after we have been privy to Gusev's dreams of home, his frustrations with his fellow passengers, his delirium.

Those dreams, his present life as a sick man returning with other sick men to the motherland, a passenger among other passengers, who argue and contend with each other and express strong opinions and speculations about the fate of all of them—this is all delivered with such acute specificity, such fidelity to objects and shapes, personalities and appearances, that we are drawn into it completely: real things in a real world, the palpable world, Gusev's personal life as he sees it in memory and fever:

> Gusev . . . pictures an immense pond covered with drifts. On one side of the pond is the brick-colored building of the pottery with a tall chimney and clouds of black smoke; on the other side is a village. His brother Alexey drives out of the fifth yard from the end in a sleigh; behind him sits his little son Vanka in big felt boots, and his little girl Akulka also wearing felt boots. Alexey has had a drop, Vanka is laughing, Akulka can't be seen, she is muffled up. . . . Gusev's thoughts abruptly break off and suddenly without rhyme or reason the pond is replaced by a huge bull's head without eyes, and the horse and sleigh are no longer going straight ahead but are whirling round and round, wrapped in black smoke.

We are deceived into thinking the story is about Gusev, because most of the world's good stories—indeed, most of its great ones, too—when they make such gestures, follow them out. Chekhov is using the particulars of this character to lead us into a perception we do not want: the enormity of the world and the universe, and our puny place in it. Yet the seeds of what he is about are in the very first line of the story: "It is already dark, it will soon be night." And there are things the men say to each other that carry the story toward its fantastic shift from the reasonable world of men in the hold of a ship to the unreasonable world itself, the unhuman world of matter:

> "One minute a vessel bumps into a fish, the next the wind breaks loose from its chain . . . Is the wind a beast that it breaks loose from its chain? . . . One must have one's head on one's shoulders and reason it out. You have no sense."

When Gusev dies, Chekhov doesn't even mention it. We are told that he sleeps for two days and that at noon on the third day two sailors come and carry him up on deck, where he is wrapped in sailcloth, with two gridirons for weight; they pray over him, and he is dropped overboard, "plop!" into the sea. And the point of view continues to move from him, like a movie camera backing away to an enormous distance. As he performs this feat, Chekhov ends up using an antique literary device, *personification,* which modern writers discarded long ago, and which one of the characters in this very story has questioned ("Is the wind a beast that breaks loose from its chain?") in that astonishing last paragraph, the ocean *looks* at the sky, it actually *frowns*. "But soon it, too, takes on tender, joyous, passionate colors for which it is hard to find a name in the language of man." A modern reader, coming upon this last line, might feel as if an amateur had written it, were it not for the power and richness of detail that precedes it and the turn it makes on what has been, after all, the story of one humble man's death.

There is no more audacious or shocking short story in the world, and it is very great writing indeed, for although it does express, with what is the equivalent of a jolt to the nervous system, the frailty of human life and hope, it also lends this one man's death a strange majesty, even a dignity, in the middle of the tremendous indignity of dying in the hold of a steamer, at sea, among strangers.

# Kate Chopin

*Chopin (1851–1904) was born in St. Louis. On a visit to New Orleans she met her husband-to-be and returned there to live with him when she married at twenty. After her husband's early death, she went back to St. Louis and began to write, largely drawing on the experiences of her years in the Deep South. She contributed to many of the popular periodicals of her time, but her writing career came to an end with the publication of her novel* The Awakening *(1899), which was sharply condemned for its frank representation of adultery and mixed marriage. This book has subsequently been praised for its sensitive portrayal of a woman in quest of her individuality. Several of Chopin's stories were collected in* Bayou Folk *(1894).*

## The Story of an Hour

Knowing that Mrs. Mallard was afflicted with a heart trouble, great care was taken to break to her as gently as possible the news of her husband's death.

It was her sister Josephine who told her, in broken sentences; veiled hints that revealed in half concealing. Her husband's friend Richards was there, too, near her. It was he who had been in the newspaper office when intelligence of the railroad disaster was received, with Brently Mallard's name leading the list of "killed." He had only taken the time to assure himself of its truth by a second telegram, and had hastened to forestall any less careful, less tender friend in bearing the sad message.

She did not hear the story as many women have heard the same, with a paralyzed inability to accept its significance. She wept at once, with sudden, wild abandonment, in her sister's arms. When the storm of grief had spent itself she went away to her room alone. She would have no one follow her.

There stood, facing the open window, a comfortable, roomy armchair. Into this she sank, pressed down by a physical exhaustion that haunted her body and seemed to reach into her soul.

She could see in the open square before her house the tops of trees that were all aquiver with the new spring life. The delicious breath of rain was in the air. In the street below a peddler was crying his wares. The notes of a distant song which some one was singing reached her faintly, and countless sparrows were twittering in the eaves.

There were patches of blue sky showing here and there through the clouds that had met and piled one above the other in the west facing her window.

She sat with her head thrown back upon the cushion of the chair, quite motionless, except when a sob came up into her throat and shook her, as a child who has cried itself to sleep continues to sob in its dreams.

She was young, with a fair, calm face, whose lines bespoke repression and even a certain strength. But now there was a dull stare in her eyes, whose gaze was fixed away off yonder on one of those patches of blue sky. It was not a glance of reflection, but rather indicated a suspension of intelligent thought.

There was something coming to her and she was waiting for it, fearfully. What was it? She did not know; it was too subtle and elusive to name. But she felt it, creeping out of the sky, reaching toward her through the sounds, the scents, the color that filled the air.

Now her bosom rose and fell tumultuously. She was beginning to recognize this thing that was approaching to possess her, and she was striving to beat it back with her will—as powerless as her two white slender hands would have been.

When she abandoned herself a little whispered word escaped her slightly parted lips. She said it over and over under her breath: "free, free, free!" The vacant stare and the look of terror that had followed it went from her eyes. They stayed keen and bright. Her pulses beat fast, and the coursing blood warmed and relaxed every inch of her body.

She did not stop to ask if it were or were not a monstrous joy that held her. A clear and exalted perception enabled her to dismiss the suggestion as trivial.

She knew that she would weep again when she saw the kind, tender hands folded in death; the face that had never looked save with love upon her, fixed and gray and dead. But she saw beyond that bitter moment a long procession of years to come that would belong to her absolutely. And she opened and spread her arms out to them in welcome.

There would be no one to live for her during those coming years; she would live for herself. There would be no powerful will bending hers in that blind persistence with which men and women believe they have a right to impose a private will upon a fellow-creature. A kind intention or a cruel intention made the act seem no less a crime as she looked upon it in that brief moment of illumination.

And yet she had loved him—sometimes. Often she had not. What did it matter! What could love, the unsolved mystery, count for in face of this possession of self-assertion which she suddenly recognized as the strongest impulse of her being!

"Free! Body and soul free!" she kept whispering.

Josephine was kneeling before the closed door with her lips to the keyhold, imploring for admission. "Louise, open the door! I beg; open the door—you will make yourself ill. What are you doing, Louise? For heaven's sake open the door."

"Go away. I am not making myself ill." No; she was drinking in a very elixir of life through that open window.

Her fancy was running riot along those days ahead of her. Spring days, and summer days, and all sorts of days that would be her own. She breathed a quick prayer that life might be long. It was only yesterday she had thought with a shudder that life might be long.

She arose at length and opened the door to her sister's importunities. There was a feverish triumph in her eyes, and she carried herself unwittingly like a goddess of Victory. She clasped her sister's waist, and together they descended the stairs. Richards stood waiting for them at the bottom.

Some one was opening the front door with a latchkey. It was Brently Mallard who entered, a little travel-stained, composedly carrying his grip-sack and umbrella. He had been far from the scene of accident, and did not even know there had been one. He stood amazed at Josephine's piercing cry; at Richards' quick motion to screen him from the view of his wife.

But Richards was too late.

When the doctors came they said she had died of heart disease—of joy that kills.

# Samuel Clemens (Mark Twain)

*Clemens (1835–1910) was born in Florida, Missouri. When he was four, his family took him to the town of Hannibal in the same state, where he experienced some of the adventures described in his novels* The Adventures of Tom Sawyer *(1876) and* Adventures of Huckleberry Finn *(1884). In his twenties he was an apprentice pilot on a Mississippi River steamer, and in "learning the river" he discovered that his true teacher would be the American land itself, with its western reaches just then opening to the surge of farmers, hunters, traders, and gold seekers. He went to California and with his readings and journalism won literary success in the mining camps upriver from San Francisco before the East caught on to his vivid and earthy style or the significance of his subject matter. In San Francisco he began his career as a lecturer—so successfully that in years to come he delighted audiences around the world with his platform manner and the astounding turns of his wit. By the late 1860s, when he went to travel in Europe and the Holy Land, he was looked on by his compatriots as their natural emissary to the Old World, and his report on these travels in* The Innocents Abroad *(1869) gave a new definition to the uniqueness of the American way of looking at things. After two decades of prosperity and popularity he lost his fortune in bad investments, but after 1895 his unceasing work as writer and lecturer enabled him to recoup his losses and build a mansion (now a museum) in Redding, Connecticut, where he died at the height of his fame. The darker, pessimistic side of his outlook was hardly stressed or noted before the publication in 1916 of his novel* The Mysterious Stranger. *Best known among his other works are* Roughing It *(1872),* Life on the Mississippi *(1883), and* A Connecticut Yankee in King Arthur's Court *(1889).*

## The Notorious Jumping Frog of Calaveras County

In compliance with the request of a friend of mine, who wrote me from the East, I called on good-natured, garrulous old Simon Wheeler, and inquired about my friend's friend, Leonidas W. Smiley, as requested to do, and I hereunto append the result. I have a lurking suspicion that *Leonidas* W. Smiley is a myth; that my friend never knew such a personage; and that he only conjectured that if I asked old Wheeler about him, it would remind him of his infamous *Jim* Smiley, and he would go to work and bore me to death with some exasperating reminiscence of him as long and as tedious as it should be useless to me. If that was the design, it succeeded.

I found Simon Wheeler dozing comfortably by the bar-room stove of the dilapidated tavern in the decayed mining camp of Angel's, and I noticed that he was fat and bald-headed, and had an expression of winning gentleness and simplicity upon his tranquil countenance. He roused up, and gave me good-day. I told him that a friend of mine had commissioned me to make some inquiries about a cherished companion of his boyhood named *Leonidas* W. Smiley—*Rev. Leonidas* W. Smiley, a young minister of the Gospel, who he had heard was at one time a resident of Angel's Camp. I added that if Mr. Wheeler could tell me anything about this Rev. Leonidas W. Smiley, I would feel under many obligations to him.

Simon Wheeler backed me into a corner and blockaded me there with his chair, and then sat down and reeled off the monotonous narrative which follows this paragraph. He never smiled, he never frowned, he never changed his voice from the gentle-flowing key to which he tuned his initial sentence, he never betrayed the slightest suspicion of enthusiasm; but all through the interminable narrative there ran a vein of impressive earnestness and sincerity, which showed me plainly that, so far from his imagining that there was anything ridiculous or funny about his story, he regarded it as a really important matter, and admired its two heroes as men of transcendent genius in *finesse*.[1] I let him go on in his own way, and never interrrupted him once.

"Rev. Leonidas W. H'm, Reverend Le—well, there was a feller here once by the name of *Jim* Smiley, in the winter of '49—or maybe it was the spring of '50—I don't recollect exactly, somehow, though what makes me think it was one or the other is because I remember the big flume[2] warn't finished when he first came to the camp; but anyway, he was the curiousest man about always betting on anything that turned up you ever see, if he could get anybody to bet on the other side; and if he couldn't he'd change sides. Any way that suited the other man would suit *him*—any way just so's he got a bet, *he* was satisfied. But still he was lucky, uncommon lucky; he most always come out winner. He was always ready and laying for a chance; there couldn't be no solit'ry thing mentioned but that feller'd offer to bet on it, and take ary side you please, as I was just telling you. If there was a horse-race, you'd find him flush or you'd find him busted at the end of it; if there was a dog-fight, he'd bet on it; if there was a cat-fight, he'd bet on it; if there was a chicken-fight, he'd bet on it; why, if there was two birds setting on a fence, he would bet you which one would fly first; or if there was a camp-meeting,[3] he would be there reg'lar to bet on Parson Walker, which he judged to be the best exhorter about here, and so he was too, and a good man. If he even see a straddle-bug start to go anywheres, he would bet you how long it would take him to get to—to wherever he was going to, and if you took him up, he would foller that straddle-bug to Mexico but what he would find out where he was bound for and how long he was on the road. Lots of the boys here has seen that Smiley, and can tell you about him. Why,

1. Subtle, discriminating skill. 2. Artificial channel to carry water to gold diggings. 3. Outdoor religious meeting.

it never made no difference to *him*—he'd bet on *any* thing—the dangdest feller. Parson Walker's wife laid very sick once, for a good while, and it seemed as if they warn't going to save her; but one morning he come in, and Smiley up and asked him how she was, and he said she was considerable better—thank the Lord for his inf'nite mercy—and coming on so smart that with the blessing of Prov'dence she'd get well yet; and Smiley, before he thought, says, 'Well, I'll resk two-and-a-half she don't anyway.'

"Thish-yer Smiley had a mare—the boys called her the fifteen-minute nag, but that was only in fun, you know, because of course she was faster than that—and he used to win money on that horse, for all she was so slow and always had the asthma, or the distemper, or the consumption, or something of that kind. They used to give her two or three hundred yards' start, and then pass her under way; but always at the fag end of the race she'd get excited and desperate like, and come cavorting and straddling up, and scattering her legs around limber, sometimes in the air, and sometimes out to one side among the fences, and kicking up m-o-r-e dust and raising m-o-r-e racket with her coughing and sneezing and blowing her nose—and *always* fetch up at the stand just about a neck ahead, as near as you could cipher it down.

"And he had a little small bull-pup, that to look at him you'd think he warn't worth a cent but to set around and look ornery and lay for a chance to steal something. But as soon as money was up on him he was a different dog; his under-jaw'd begin to stick out like the fo'castle of a steamboat, and his teeth would uncover and shine like the furnaces. And a dog might tackle him and bully-rag him, and bite him, and throw him over his shoulder two or three times, and Andrew Jackson[4]—which was the name of the pup—Andrew Jackson would never let on but what *he* was satisfied, and hadn't expected nothing else—and the bets being doubled and doubled on the other side all the time, till the money was all up; and then all of a sudden he would grab that other dog jest by the j'int of his hind leg and freeze to it—not chaw, you understand, but only just grip and hang on till they throwed up the sponge, if it was a year. Smiley always come out winner on that pup, till he harnessed a dog once that didn't have no hind legs, because they'd been sawed off in a circular saw, and when the thing had gone along far enough, and the money was all up, and he come to make a snatch for his pet holt, he see in a minute how he'd been imposed on, and how the other dog had him in the door, so to speak, and he 'peared surprised, and then he looked sorter discouraged-like, and didn't try no more to win the fight, and so he got shucked out bad. He give Smiley a look, as much as to say his heart was broke, and it was *his* fault, for putting up a dog that hadn't no hind legs for him to take holt of, which was his main dependence in a fight, and then he limped off a piece and laid down and died. It was a good pup, was that Andrew Jackson, and would have made a name for hisself if he'd lived, for the stuff was in him and he had genius—I know it, because he hadn't no opportunities to speak of, and it don't stand to reason that a dog could make such a fight as he could under them circumstances if he hadn't no talent. It

4. Seventh president of the United States (1767–1845), famous in legend for his iron will.

always makes me feel sorry when I think of that last fight of his'n, and the way it turned out.

"Well, thish-yer Smiley had rat-tarriers, and chicken cocks, and tom-cats and all them kind of things, till you couldn't rest, and you couldn't fetch nothing for him to bet on but he'd match you. He ketched a frog one day, and took him home, and said he cal'lated to educate him; and so he never done nothing for three months but set in his back yard and learn that frog to jump. And you bet you he *did* learn him, too. He'd give him a little punch behind, and the next minute you'd see that frog whirling in the air like a doughnut—see him turn one summerset, or maybe a couple, if he got a good start, and come down flat-footed and all right, like a cat. He got him up so in the matter of ketching flies, and kep' him in practice so constant, that he'd nail a fly every time as fur as he could see him. Smiley said all a frog wanted was education, and he could do 'most anything—and I believe him. Why, I've seen him set Dan'l Webster[5] down here on this floor—Dan'l Webster was the name of the frog—and sing out, 'Flies, Dan'l, flies!' and quicker'n you could wink he'd spring straight up and snake a fly off'n the counter there, and flop down on the floor ag'in as solid as a gob of mud, and fall to scratching the side of his head with his hind foot as indifferent as if he hadn't no idea he'd been doin' any more'n any frog might do. You never see a frog so modest and straightfor'ard as he was, for all he was so gifted. And when it come to fair and square jumping on a dead level, he could get over more ground at one straddle than any animal of his breed you ever see. Jumping on a dead level was his strong suit, you understand; and when it come to that, Smiley would ante up money on him as long as he had a red.[6] Smiley was monstrous proud of his frog, and well he might be, for fellers that had traveled and been everywheres, all said he laid over any frog that ever *they* see.

"Well, Smiley kep' the beast in a little lattice box, and he used to fetch him down-town sometimes and lay for a bet. One day a feller—a stranger in the camp, he was—come acrost him with his box, and says:

" 'What might it be that you've got in the box?'

"And Smiley says, sorter indifferent-like, 'It might be a parrot, or it might be a canary, maybe, but it ain't—it's only just a frog.'

"And the feller took it, and looked at it careful, and turned it round this way and that, and says, 'H'm—so 'tis. Well, what's *he* good for?'

" 'Well,' Smiley says, easy and careless, 'he's good enough for *one* thing, I should judge—he can outjump any frog in Calaveras County.'

"The feller took the box again, and took another long, particular look, and give it back to Smiley, and says, very deliberate, 'Well,' he says, 'I don't see no p'ints about that frog that's any better'n any other frog.'

" 'Maybe you don't,' Smiley says. 'Maybe you understand frogs and maybe you don't understand 'em; maybe you've had experience, and maybe you ain't only a amature, as it were. Anyways, I've got *my* opinion, and I'll resk forty

5. The frog is named for Daniel Webster (1782–1852), distinguished American statesman and orator. 6. A red cent, i.e., any money whatsoever.

dollars that he can outjump any frog in Calaveras County.'

"And the feller studied a minute, and then says, kinder sadlike 'Well, I'm only a stranger here, and I ain't got no frog; but if I had a frog, I'd bet you.'

"And then Smiley says, 'That's all right—that's all right—if you'll hold my box a minute, I'll go and get you a frog.' And so the feller took the box, and put up his forty dollars along with Smiley's, and set down to wait.

"So he set there a good while thinking and thinking to himself, and then he got the frog out and prized his mouth open and took a teaspoon and filled him full of quail shot—filled him pretty near up to his chin—and set him on the floor. Smiley he went to the swamp and slopped around in the mud for a long time, and finally he ketched a frog, and fetched him in, and give him to this feller, and says:

" 'Now, if you're ready, set him alongside of Dan'l, with his fore paws just even with Dan'l's, and I'll give the word.' Then he says, 'One—two—three—*git!*' and him and the feller touched up the frogs from behind, and the new frog hopped off lively, but Dan'l give a heave, and hysted up his shoulders—so—like a Frenchman, but it warn't no use—he couldn't budge; he was planted as solid as a church, and he couldn't no more stir than if he was anchored out. Smiley was a good deal surprised, and he was disgusted too, but he didn't have no idea what the matter was, of course.

"The feller took the money and started away; and when he was going out at the door, he sorter jerked his thumb over his shoulder—so—at Dan'l, and says again, very deliberate, 'Well,' he says, '*I* don't see no p'ints about that frog that's any better'n any other frog.'

"Smiley he stood scratching his head and looking down at Dan'l a long time, and at last he says, 'I do wonder what in the nation that frog throw'd off for—I wonder if there ain't something the matter with him—he 'pears to look mighty baggy, somehow.' And he ketched Dan'l by the nap of the neck, and hefted him, and says, 'Why blame my cats if he don't weigh five pound! " and turned him upside down and he belched out a double handful of shot. And then he see how it was, and he was the maddest man—he set the frog down and took out after that feller, but he never ketched him. And—"

[Here Simon Wheeler heard his name called from the front yard, and got up to see what was wanted.] And turning to me as he moved away, he said: "Just set where you are, stranger, and rest easy—I ain't going to be gone a second."

But, by your leave, I did not think that a continuation of the history of the enterprising vagabond *Jim* Smiley would be likely to afford me much information concerning the Rev. *Leonidas* W. Smiley, and so I started away.

At the door I met the sociable Wheeler returning, and he button-holed me and recommenced:

"Well, thish-yer Smiley had a yaller one-eyed cow that didn't have no tail, only just a short stump like a bannanner, and—"

However, lacking both time and inclination, I did not wait to hear about the afflicted cow, but took my leave.

# Joseph Conrad

*Conrad (1857–1924) (christened Jozef Teodor Konrad Nalecz Korzeniowski) was born in Polish Ukraine to a family of landed gentry. In 1863 his hotheaded father was exiled for revolutionary activities to an area northeast of Moscow. He took his family with him to this inhospitable region, where the climate proved too much for both parents. The orphaned Conrad at seventeen persuaded his guardian uncle to let him join the French merchant navy, and for about twenty years he sailed to many exotic places, surviving shipwrecks and (probably) an attempted suicide, running guns at intervals in his more respectable occupations and rising, finally, to the rank of master (captain) in the British merchant fleet. He began to write before he gave up his seagoing career; and some of his early work led to his friendship with such literary figures as Henry James, Stephen Crane, and Ford Madox Ford. With their encouragement he not only devoted himself full time to fiction but developed the style and form of narration that are so much his own. (One of the marvels is that so fine a stylist should have written in English when Polish was his native tongue and French his "second language.") Though he was respected from the beginning of his writing career and critically acclaimed after the publication of* The Nigger of the "Narcissus" *(1897), he had small popular success before his novel* Chance *was brought out in 1914. In his later years, after World War I, he was one of the most venerated of English novelists. He was working on a novel of Napoleon's escape from Elba when he died. His novels include* Lord Jim *(1900),* Nostromo *(1904),* Under Western Eyes *(1910), and* Victory *(1915). Three works of medium length were published in* Youth *(1902).*

## Heart of Darkness

### I

The *Nellie*, a cruising yawl, swung to her anchor without a flutter of the sails, and was at rest. The flood had made, the wind was nearly calm, and being bound down the river, the only thing for it was to come to and wait for the turn of the tide.

The sea-reach[1] of the Thames stretched before us like the beginning of an interminable waterway. In the offing[2] the sea and the sky were welded together without a joint, and in the luminous space the tanned sails of the barges drifting up with the tide seemed to stand still in red clusters of canvas sharply peaked, with gleams of varnished sprits. A haze rested on the low shores that ran out to sea in vanishing flatness. The air was dark above Gravesend,[3] and farther

1. Tidal part of the river as it broadens toward the sea. 2. Part of the sea visible from the river's mouth. 3. City on the Thames, twenty-six miles east of London.

back still seemed condensed into a mournful gloom, brooding motionless over the biggest, and the greatest, town on earth.

The Director of Companies was our captain and our host. We four affectionately watched his back as he stood in the bows looking to seaward. On the whole river there was nothing that looked half so nautical. He resembled a pilot, which to a seaman is trustworthiness personified. It was difficult to realize his work was not out there in the luminous estuary, but behind him, within the brooding gloom.

Between us there was, as I have already said somewhere, the bond of the sea. Besides holding our hearts together through long periods of separation, it had the effect of making us tolerant of each other's yarns—and even convictions. The Lawyer—the best of old fellows—had, because of his many years and many virtues, the only cushion on deck, and was lying on the only rug. The accountant had brought out already a box of dominoes, and was toying architecturally with the bones. Marlow sat cross-legged right aft, leaning against the mizzen-mast. He had sunken cheeks, a yellow complexion, a straight back, and ascetic aspect, and, with his arms dropped, the palms of hands outwards, resembled an idol. The director, satisfied the anchor had good hold, made his way aft and sat down amongst us. We exchanged a few words lazily. Afterwards there was silence on board the yacht. For some reason or other we did not begin that game of dominoes. We felt meditative, and fit for nothing but placid staring. The day was ending in a serenity of still and exquisite brilliance. The water shone pacifically; the sky, without a speck, was a benign immensity of unstained light; the very mist on the Essex marshes[4] was like a gauzy and radiant fabric, hung from the wooded rises inland, and draping the low shores in diaphanous folds. Only the gloom to the west, brooding over the upper reaches, became more somber every minute, as if angered by the approach of the sun.

And at last, in its curved and imperceptible fall, the sun sank low, and from glowing white changed to a dull red without rays and without heat, as if about to go out suddenly, stricken to death by the touch of that gloom brooding over a crowd of men.

Forthwith a change came over the waters, and the serenity became less brilliant but more profound. The old river in its broad reach rested unruffled at the decline of day, after ages of good service done to the race that peopled its banks, spread out in the tranquil dignity of a waterway leading to the uttermost ends of the earth. We looked at the venerable stream not in the vivid flush of a short day that comes and departs forever, but in the august light of abiding memories. And indeed nothing is easier for a man who has, as the phrase goes, "followed the sea" with reverence and affection, than to evoke the great spirit of the past upon the lower reaches of the Thames. The tidal current runs to and fro in its unceasing service, crowded with memories of men and ships it had borne to the rest of home or to the battles of the sea. It had known and served all the men of whom the nation is proud, from Sir Francis Drake to Sir John Franklin,[5] knights all, titled and untitled—the great knights-errant of the

4. On the north bank of the Thames. 5. An arctic explorer (1786–1847) who commanded an expedition, including the ships *Erebus* and *Terror*, and was lost in a search for the Northwest Passage. Drake (1540–1596) sailed around the world (1577–80) and defeated the Spanish Armada (1588).

sea. It had borne all the ships whose names are like jewels flashing in the night of time, from the *Golden Hind* returning with her round flanks full of treasure, to be visited by the Queen's Highness and thus pass out of the gigantic tale, to the *Erebus* and *Terror,* bound on other conquests—and that never returned. It had known the ships and the men. They had sailed from Deptford, from Greenwich, from Erith—the adventurers and the settlers; kings' ships and the ships of men on 'Change; captains, admirals, the dark "interlopers"[6] of the Eastern trade, and the commissioned "Generals" of East India fleets. Hunters for gold or pursuers of fame, they all had gone out on that stream, bearing the sword, and often the torch, messengers of the might within the land, bearers of a spark from the sacred fire. What greatness had not floated on the ebb of that river into the mystery of an unknown earth! . . . The dreams of men, the seed of commonwealths, the germs of empires.

The sun set; the dusk fell on the stream, and lights began to appear along the shore. The Chapman lighthouse, a three-legged thing erect on a mud-flat, shone strongly. Lights of ships moved in the fairway—a great stir of lights going up and going down. And farther west on the upper reaches the place of the monstrous town was still marked ominously on the sky, a brooding gloom in sunshine, a lurid glare under the stars.

"And this also," said Marlow suddenly, "has been one of the dark places on the earth."

He was the only man of us who still "followed the sea." The worst that could be said of him was that he did not represent his class. He was a seaman, but he was a wanderer, too, while most seamen lead, if one may so express it, a sedentary life. Their minds are of the stay-at-home order, and their home is always with them—the ship; and so is their country—the sea. One ship is very much like another, and the sea is always the same. In the immutability of their surroundings the foreign shores, the foreign faces, the changing immensity of life, glide past, veiled not by a sense of mystery but by a slightly disdainful ignorance; for there is nothing mysterious to a seaman unless it be the sea itself, which is the mistress of his existence and as inscrutable as Destiny. For the rest, after his hours of work, a casual stroll or a casual spree on shore suffices to unfold for him the secret of a whole continent, and generally he finds the secret not worth knowing. The yarns of seamen have a direct simplicity, the whole meaning of which lies within the shell of a cracked nut. But Marlow was not typical (if his propensity to spin yarns be excepted), and to him the meaning of an episode was not inside like a kernel but outside, enveloping the tale which brought it out only as a glow brings out a haze, in the likeness of one of these misty halos that sometimes are made visible by the spectral illumination of moonshine.

His remark did not seem at all surprising. It was just like Marlow. It was accepted in silence. No one took the trouble to grunt even; and presently he said, very slow—

"I was thinking of very old times, when the Romans first came here, nine-

6. Unauthorized competitors of the East India Company, chartered by the British Crown, in the reign of Charles II, who were given the right to maintain troops in India and thus to appoint "generals." Deptford, Greenwich, and Erith are seaports on the Thames. " 'Change": i.e., Exchange, the financial district of London.

teen hundred years ago—the other day. . . . Light came out of this river since—you say Knights? Yes; but it is like a running blaze on a plain, like a flash of lightning in the clouds. We live in the flicker—may it last as long as the old earth keeps rolling! But darkness was here yesterday. Imagine the feelings of a commander of a fine—what d'ye call 'em?—trireme[7] in the Mediterranean, ordered suddenly to the north; run overland across the Gauls[8] in a hurry; put in charge of one of these craft the legionaries—a wonderful lot of handy men they must have been, too—used to build, apparently by the hundred, in a month or two, if we may believe what we read. Imagine him here—the very end of the world, a sea the color of lead, a sky the color of smoke, a kind of ship about as rigid as a concertina—and going up this river with stores, or orders, or what you like. Sand-banks, marshes, forests, savages,—precious little to eat fit for a civilized man, nothing but Thames water to drink. No Falernian wine[9] here, no going ashore. Here and there a military camp lost in a wilderness, like a needle in a bundle of hay—cold, fog, tempests, disease, exile, and death,—death skulking in the air, in the water, in the bush. They must have been dying like flies here. Oh yes—he did it. Did it very well, too, no doubt, and without thinking much about it either, except afterwards to brag of what he had gone through in his time, perhaps. They were men enough to face the darkness. And perhaps he was cheered by keeping his eye on a chance of promotion to the fleet at Ravenna[1] by and by, if he had good friends in Rome and survived the awful climate. Or think of a decent young citizen in a toga—perhaps too much dice, you know—coming out here in the train of some prefect,[2] or taxgatherer, or trader even, to mend his fortunes. Land in a swamp, march through the woods, and in some inland post feel the savagery, the utter savagery, had closed round him,—all that mysterious life of the wilderness that stirs in the forest, in the jungles, in the hearts of wild men. There's no initiation either into such mysteries. He has to live in the midst of the incomprehensible, which is also detestable. And it has a fascination, too, that goes to work upon him. The fascination of the abomination—you know, imagine the growing regrets, the longing to escape, the powerless disgust, the surrender, the hate."

He paused.

"Mind," he began again, lifting one arm from the elbow, the palm of the hand outwards, so that, with his legs folded before him, he had the pose of a Buddha preaching in European clothes and without a lotus-flower—"Mind, none of us would feel exactly like this. What saves us is efficiency—the devotion to efficiency. But these chaps were not much account, really. They were no colonists; their administration was merely a squeeze, and nothing more, I suspect. They were conquerors, and for that you want only brute force—nothing to boast of, when you have it, since your strength is just an accident arising from the weakness of others. They grabbed what they could get for the sake of what was to be got. It was just robbery with violence, aggravated murder on a great scale, and men going at it blind—as is very proper for those who tackle

7. Roman galley propelled by three banks of oars. 8. Inhabitants of France in Roman times. 9. Legendary Roman wine. 1. Base on the Adriatic in northern Italy—a comfortable assignment. 2. High official.

a darkness. The conquest of the earth, which mostly means the taking it away from those who have a different complexion or slightly flatter noses than ourselves, is not a pretty thing when you look into it too much. What redeems it is the idea only. An idea at the back of it; not a sentimental pretense but an idea; and an unselfish belief in the idea—something you can set up, and bow down before, and offer a sacrifice to. . . ."

He broke off. Flames glided in the river, small green flames, red flames, white flames, pursuing, overtaking, joining, crossing each other—then separating slowly or hastily. The traffic of the great city went on in the deepening night upon the sleepless river. We looked on, waiting patiently—there was nothing else to do till the end of the flood; but it was only after a long silence, when he said, in a hesitating voice, "I suppose you fellows remember I did once turn fresh-water sailor for a bit," that we knew we were fated, before the ebb began to run, to hear one of Marlow's inconclusive experiences.

"I don't want to bother you much with what happened to me personally," he began, showing in this remark the weakness of many tellers of tales who seem so often unaware of what their audience would best like to hear; "yet to understand the effect of it on me you ought to know how I got out there, what I saw, how I went up that river to the place where I first met the poor chap. It was the farthest point of navigation and the culminating point of my experience. It seemed somehow to throw a kind of light on everything about me—and into my thoughts. It was somber enough, too—and pitiful—not extraordinary in any way—not very clear either. No, not very clear. And yet it seemed to throw a kind of light.

"I had then, as you remember, just returned to London after a lot of Indian Ocean, Pacific, China Seas—a regular dose of the East—six years or so, and I was loafing about, hindering you fellows in your work and invading your homes, just as though I had got a heavenly mission to civilize you. It was very fine for a time, but after a bit I did get tired of resting. Then I began to look for a ship—I should think the hardest work on earth. But the ships wouldn't even look at me. And I got tired of that game too.

"Now when I was a little chap I had a passion for maps. I would look for hours at South America, or Africa, or Australia, and lose myself in all the glories of exploration. At that time there were many blank spaces on the earth, and when I saw one that looked particularly inviting on a map (but they all look that) I would put my finger on it and say, When I grow up I will go there. The North Pole was one of these places, I remember. Well, I haven't been there yet, and shall not try now. The glamour's off. Other places were scattered about the Equator, and in every sort of latitude all over the two hemispheres. I have been in some of them, and . . . well, we won't talk about that. But there was one[3] yet—the biggest, the most blank, so to speak—that I had a hankering after.

"True, by this time it was not a blank space any more. It had got filled since

3. Congo Free State (now Democratic Republic of the Congo). At the time of the story it was a colony owned personally, in effect, by Leopold II, king of Belgium; it consisted of the Congo River basin and some adjacent territories.

my childhood with rivers and lakes and names. It had ceased to be a blank space of delightful mystery—a white patch for a boy to dream gloriously over. It had become a place of darkness. But there was in it one river especially, a mighty big river, that you could see on the map, resembling an immense snake uncoiled, with its head in the sea, its body at rest curving afar over a vast country, and its tail lost in the depths of the land. And as I looked at the map of it in a shop-window, it fascinated me as a snake would a bird—a silly little bird. Then I remembered there was a big concern, a Company for trade on that river. Dash it all! I thought to myself, they can't trade without using some kind of craft on that lot of fresh water—steamboats! Why shouldn't I try to get charge of one? I went on along Fleet Street, but could not shake off the idea. The snake had charmed me.

"You understand it was a Continental concern, that Trading society; but I have a lot of relations living on the Continent, because it's cheap and not so nasty as it looks, they say.

"I am sorry to own I began to worry them. This was already a fresh departure for me. I was not used to getting things that way, you know. I always went my own road and on my own legs where I had a mind to go. I wouldn't have believed it of myself; but, then—you see—I felt somehow I must get there by hook or by crook. So I worried them. The men said, 'My dear fellow,' and did nothing. Then—would you believe it?—I tried the women. I, Charlie Marlow, set the women to work—to get a job. Heavens! Well, you see, the notion drove me. I had an aunt, a dear enthusiastic soul. She wrote: 'It will be delightful. I am ready to do anything, anything for you. It is a glorious idea. I know the wife of a very high personage in the Administration, and also a man who has lots of influence with,' etc. etc. She was determined to make no end of fuss to get me appointed skipper of a river steamboat, if such was my fancy.

"I got my appointment—of course; and I got it very quick. It appears the Company had received news that one of their captains had been killed in a scuffle with the natives. This was my chance, and it made me the more anxious to go. It was only months and months afterwards, when I made the attempt to recover what was left of the body, that I heard the original quarrel arose from a misunderstanding about some hens. Yes, two black hens. Fresleven—that was the fellow's name, a Dane—thought himself wronged somehow in the bargain, so he went ashore and started to hammer the chief of the village with a stick. Oh, it didn't surprise me in the least to hear this, and at the same time to be told that Fresleven was the gentlest, quietest creature that ever walked on two legs. No doubt he was; but he had been a couple of years already out there engaged in the noble cause, you know, and he probably felt the need at last of asserting his self-respect in some way. Therefore he whacked the old nigger mercilessly, while a big crowd of his people watched him, thunderstruck, till some man—I was told the chief's son—in desperation at hearing the old chap yell, made a tentative jab with a spear at the white man—and of course it went quite easy between the shoulder blades. Then the whole population cleared into the forest, expecting all kinds of calamities to happen, while, on the other hand, the steamer Fresleven commanded left also in a bad panic, in charge of the engineer, I believe. Afterwards nobody seemed to trouble much about Fresleven's remains, till I got out and stepped into his shoes. I couldn't let it rest, though; but when an opportunity offered at last to meet my predecessor, the grass growing through his ribs was tall enough to hide his bones. They were all there. The supernatural being had not been touched after he fell. And the village was deserted, the huts gaped black, rotting, all askew within the fallen enclosures. A calamity had come to it, sure enough. The people had vanished. Mad terror had scattered them, men, women, and children, through the bush, and they had never returned. What became of the hens I don't know either. I should think the cause of progress got them, anyhow. However, through this glorious affair I got my appointment, before I had fairly begun to hope for it.

"I flew around like mad to get ready, and before forty-eight hours I was crossing the Channel to show myself to my employers, and sign the contract. In a very few hours I arrived in a city[4] that always makes me think of a whited sepulcher. Prejudice no doubt. I had no difficulty in finding the Company's offices. It was the biggest thing in the town, and everybody I met was full of it. They were going to run an oversea empire, and make no end of coin by trade.

"A narrow and deserted street in deep shadow, high houses, innumerable windows with venetian blinds, a dead silence, grass sprouting between the stones, imposing carriage archways right and left, immense double doors standing ponderously ajar. I slipped through one of these cracks, went up a swept and ungarnished staircase, as arid as a desert, and opened the first door I came to. Two women, one fat and the other slim, sat on straw-bottomed chairs, knitting black wool. The slim one got up and walked straight at me—still knitting with downcast eyes—and only just as I began to think of getting out of her way, as you would for a somnambulist, stood still, and looked up. Her dress was as plain as an umbrella-cover, and she turned round without a word and preceded me into a waiting-room. I gave my name, and looked about. Deal table in the middle, plain chairs all around the walls, on one end a large shining map, marked with all the colors of a rainbow. There was a vast amount of red—good to see at any time, because one knows that some real work is done in there, a deuce of a lot of blue, a little green, smears of orange, and, on the East Coast, a purple patch,[5] to show where the jolly pioneers of progress drink the jolly lager-beer. However, I wasn't going into any of these. I was going into the yellow. Dead in the center. And the river was there—fascinating—deadly—like a snake. Ough! A door opened, a white-haired secretarial head, but wearing a compassionate expression, appeared, and a skinny forefinger beckoned me into the sanctuary. Its light was dim, and a heavy writing-desk squatted in the middle. From behind that structure came out an impression of pale plumpness in a frock-coat. The great man himself. He was five feet six, I should judge, and had his grip on the handle-end of ever so many millions. He shook hands, I fancy, murmured vaguely, was satisfied with my French. *Bon voyage.*[6]

"In about forty-five seconds I found myself again in the waiting-room with

4. Brussels, Belgium. 5. The red areas on the map were British colonies; blue, French; green, Italian; orange, Portuguese; and purple, German East Africa. 6. Have a good trip (French).

the compassionate secretary, who, full of desolation and sympathy, made me sign some document. I believe I undertook amongst other things not to disclose any trade secrets. Well, I am not going to.

"I began to feel slightly uneasy. You know I am not used to such ceremonies, and there was something ominous in the atmosphere. It was just as though I had been let into some conspiracy—I don't know—something not quite right; and I was glad to get out. In the outer room the two women knitted black wool feverishly. People were arriving, and the younger one was walking back and forth introducing them. The old one sat on her chair. Her flat cloth slippers were propped up on a footwarmer, and a cat reposed on her lap. She wore a starched white affair on her head, had a wart on one cheek, and silver-rimmed spectacles hung on the tip of her nose. She glanced at me above the glasses. The swift and indifferent placidity of that look troubled me. Two youths with foolish and cheery countenances were being piloted over, and she threw at them the same quick glance of unconcerned wisdom. She seemed to know all about them and about me, too. An eerie feeling came over me. She seemed uncanny and fateful. Often far away there I thought of these two, guarding the door of Darkness, knitting black wool as for a warm pall, one introducing, introducing continuously to the unknown, the other scrutinizing the cheery and foolish faces with unconcerned old eyes. *Ave!* Old knitter of black wool. *Morituri te salutant.*[7] Not many of those she looked at ever saw her again—not half, by a long way.

"There was yet a visit to the doctor. 'A simple formality,' assured me the secretary, with an air of taking an immense part in all my sorrows. Accordingly a young chap wearing his hat over the left eyebrow, some clerk I suppose—there must have been clerks in the business, though the house was as still as a house in a city of the dead—came from somewhere upstairs, and led me forth. He was shabby and careless, with inkstains on the sleeves of his jacket, and his cravat was large and billowy, under a chin shaped like the toe of an old boot. It was a little too early for the doctor, so I proposed a drink, and thereupon he developed a vein of joviality. As we sat over our vermouths he glorified the Company's business, and by and by I expressed casually my surprise at him not going out there. He became very cool and collected all at once. 'I am not such a fool as I look, quoth Plato to his disciples,' he said sententiously, emptied his glass with great resolution, and we rose.

"The old doctor felt my pulse, evidently thinking of something else the while. 'Good, good for there,' he mumbled, and then with a certain eagerness asked me whether I would let him measure my head.[8] Rather surprised, I said Yes, when he produced a thing like calipers and got the dimensions back and front and every way, taking notes carefully. He was an unshaven little man in a threadbare coat like a gaberdine, with his feet in slippers, and I thought him a harmless fool. 'I always ask leave, in the interests of science, to measure the crania of those going out there,' he said. 'And when they come back, too?' I asked. 'Oh, I never see them,' he remarked; 'and, moreover, the changes take

7. Hail! . . . They who are about to die salute you (Latin). 8. Phrenology, the study of skull conformation as an index of mind and personality, was a more or less respectable part of nineteenth-century medical study.

place inside, you know.' He smiled, as if at some quiet joke. 'So you are going out there. Famous. Interesting too.' He gave me a searching glance, and made another note. 'Ever any madness in your family?' he asked, in a matter-of-fact tone. I felt very annoyed. 'Is that question in the interests of science, too?' 'It would be,' he said, without taking notice of my irritation, 'interesting for science to watch the mental changes of individuals, on the spot, but . . . ' 'Are you an alienist?'[9] I interrupted. 'Every doctor should be—a little,' answered that original, imperturbably. 'I have a little theory which you Messieurs who go out there must help me to prove. This is my share in the advantages my country shall reap from the possession of such a magnificent dependency. The mere wealth I leave to others. Pardon my questions, but you are the first Englishman coming under my observation . . . ' I hastened to assure him I was not in the least typical. 'If I were,' said I, 'I wouldn't be talking like this with you.' 'What you say is rather profound, and probably erroneous,' he said, with a laugh. 'Avoid irritation more than exposure to the sun. Adieu. How do you English say, eh? Good-by. Ah! Good-by. Adieu. In the tropics one must before everything keep calm.' . . . He lifted a warning forefinger. . . . '*Du calme, du calme. Adieu.*'[1]

"One thing more remained to do—say good-by to my excellent aunt. I found her triumphant. I had a cup of tea—the last decent cup of tea for many days—and in a room that most soothingly looked just as you would expect a lady's drawing-room to look, we had a long quiet chat by the fireside. In the course of these confidences it became quite plain to me I had been represented to the wife of the high dignitary, and goodness knows to how many more people besides, as an exceptional and gifted creature—a piece of good fortune for the Company—a man you don't get hold of every day. Good heavens! and I was going to take charge of a two-penny-half-penny river-steamboat with a penny whistle attached! It appeared, however, I was also one of the Workers, with a capital—you know. Something like an emissary of light, something like a lower sort of apostle. There had been a lot of such rot let loose in print and talk just about that time, and the excellent woman, living right in the rush of all that humbug, got carried off her feet. She talked about 'weaning those ignorant millions from their horrid ways,' till, upon my word, she made me quite uncomfortable. I ventured to hint that the Company was run for profit.

" 'You forget, dear Charlie, that the laborer is worthy of his hire,'[2] she said, brightly. It's queer how out of touch with truth women are. They live in a world of their own, and there has never been anything like it, and never can be. It is too beautiful altogether, and if they were to set it up it would go to pieces before the first sunset. Some confounded fact we men have been living contentedly with ever since the day of creation would start up and knock the whole thing over.

"After this I got embraced, told to wear flannel, be sure to write often, and so on—and I left. In the street—I don't know why—a queer feeling came to me that I was an impostor. Odd thing that I, who used to clear out for any part

9. Doctor who treats mental disease. 1. Keep calm, keep calm. Good-bye (French). 2. Words of Christ (Luke 10.7).

of the world at twenty-four hours' notice, with less thought than most men give to the crossing of a street, had a moment—I won't say of hesitation, but of startled pause, before this commonplace affair. The best way I can explain it to you is by saying that, for a second or two, I felt as though, instead of going to the center of a continent, I were about to set off for the center of the earth.

"I left in a French steamer, and she called in every blamed port they have out there,[3] for, as far as I could see, the sole purpose of landing soldiers and custom-house officers. I watched the coast. Watching a coast as it slips by the ship is like thinking about an enigma. There it is before you—smiling, frowning, inviting, grand, mean, insipid, or savage, and always mute with an air of whispering, Come and find out. This one was almost featureless, as if still in the making, with an aspect of monotonous grimness. The edge of a colossal jungle, so dark-green as to be almost black, fringed with white surf, ran straight, like a ruled line, far, far away along a blue sea whose glitter was blurred by a creeping mist. The sun was fierce, the land seemed to glisten and drip with steam. Here and there grayish-whitish specks showed up clustered inside the white surf, with a flag flying above them perhaps. Settlements some centuries old, and still no bigger than pinheads on the untouched expanse of their background. We pounded along, stopped, landed soldiers; went on, landed custom-house clerks to levy toll in what looked like a God-forsaken wilderness, with a tin shed and a flag-pole lost in it; landed more soldiers—to take care of the custom-house clerks, presumably. Some, I heard, got drowned in the surf; but whether they did or not, nobody seemed particularly to care. They were just flung out there, and on we went. Every day the coast looked the same, as though we had not moved; but we passed various places—trading places—with names like Gran' Bassam, Little Popo; names that seemed to belong to some sordid farce acted in front of a sinister backcloth. The idleness of a passenger, my isolation amongst all these men with whom I had no point of contact, the oily and languid sea, the uniform somberness of the coast, seemed to keep me away from the truth of things, within the toil of a mournful and senseless delusion. The voice of the surf heard now and then was a positive pleasure, like the speech of a brother. It was something natural, that had its reason, that had a meaning. Now and then a boat from the shore gave one a momentary contact with reality. It was paddled by black fellows. You could see from afar the white of their eyeballs glistening. They shouted, sang; their bodies streamed with perspiration; they had faces like grotesque masks—these chaps; but they had bone, muscle, a wild vitality, an intense energy of movement, that was as natural and true as the surf along their coast. They wanted no excuse for being there. They were a great comfort to look at. For a time I would feel I belonged still to a world of straightforward facts, but the feeling would not last long. Something would turn up to scare it away. Once, I remember, we came upon a man-of-war anchored off the coast. There wasn't even a shed there, and she was shelling the bush. It appears the French had one of their wars going on

3. French colonies stretched down most of the West African coast to the mouth of the Congo, with major ports at Casablanca and Dakar.

thereabouts. Her ensign[4] dropped limp like a rag; the muzzles of the long six-inch guns stuck out all over the low hull; the greasy, slimy swell swung her up lazily and let her down, swaying her thin masts. In the empty immensity of earth, sky, and water, there she was, incomprehensible, firing into a continent. Pop, would go one of the six-inch guns; a small flame would dart and vanish, a little white smoke would disappear, a tiny projectile would give a feeble screech—and nothing happened. Nothing could happen. There was a touch of insanity in the proceeding, a sense of lugubrious drollery in the sight; and it was not dissipated by somebody on board assuring me earnestly there was a camp of natives—he called them enemies!—hidden out of sight somewhere.

"We gave her her letters (I heard the men in that lonely ship were dying of fever at the rate of three a day) and went on. We called at some more places with farcical names, where the merry dance of death and trade goes on in a still and earthy atmosphere as of an overheated catacomb; all along the formless coast bordered by dangerous surf, as if Nature herself had tried to ward off intruders; in and out of rivers, streams of death in life, whose banks were rotting into mud, whose waters, thickened into slime, invaded the contorted mangroves, that seemed to writhe at us in the extremity of an impotent despair. Nowhere did we stop long enough to get a particularized impression, but the general sense of vague and oppressive wonder grew upon me. It was like a weary pilgrimage amongst hints for nightmares.

"It was upward of thirty days before I saw the mouth of the big river. We anchored off the seat of the government.[5] But my work would not begin till some two hundred miles farther on. So as soon as I could I made a start for a place thirty miles higher up.

"I had my passage on a little sea-going steamer. Her captain was a Swede, and knowing me for a seaman, invited me on the bridge. He was a young man, lean, fair, and morose, with lanky hair and a shuffling gait. As we left the miserable little wharf, he tossed his head contemptuously at the shore. 'Been living there?' he asked. I said, 'Yes.' 'Fine lot these government chaps—are they not?' he went on, speaking English with great precision and considerable bitterness. 'It is funny what some people will do for a few francs a month. I wonder what becomes of that kind when it goes up-country?' I said to him I expected to see that soon. 'So-o-o!' he exclaimed. He shuffled athwart, keeping one eye ahead vigilantly. 'Don't be too sure,' he continued. 'The other day I took up a man who hanged himself on the road. He was a Swede, too.' 'Hanged himself! Why, in God's name?' I cried. He kept on looking out watchfully. 'Who knows? The sun was too much for him, or the country perhaps.'

"At last we opened a reach.[6] A rocky cliff appeared, mounds of turned-up earth by the shore, houses on a hill, others with iron roofs, amongst a waste of excavations, or hanging to the declivity.[7] A continuous noise of the rapids above hovered over this scene of inhabited devastation. A lot of people, mostly black and naked, moved about like ants. A jetty projected into the river. A blinding

4. Flag. 5. Boma, in the mouth of the Congo River. 6. I.e., came to a clear stretch of the river. 7. Town of Matadi.

sunlight drowned all this at times in a sudden recrudescence of glare. 'There's your Company's station,' said the Swede, pointing to three wooden barrack-like structures on the rocky slope. 'I will send your things up. Four boxes did you say? So. Farewell.'

"I came upon a boiler wallowing in the grass, then found a path leading up the hill. It turned aside for the boulders, and also for an undersized railway-truck lying there on its back with its wheels in the air. One was off. The thing looked as dead as the carcass of some animal. I came upon more pieces of decaying machinery, a stack of rusty nails. To the left a clump of trees made a shady spot, where dark things seemed to stir feebly. I blinked, the path was steep. A horn tooted to the right, and I saw the black people run. A heavy and dull detonation shook the ground, a puff of smoke came out of the cliff, and that was all. No change appeared on the face of the rock. They were building a railway. The cliff was not in the way or anything; but this objectless blasting was all the work going on.

"A slight clinking behind me made me turn my head. Six black men advanced in a file, toiling up the path. They walked erect and slow, balancing small baskets full of earth on their heads, and the clink kept time with their footsteps. Black rags were wound round their loins, and the short ends behind waggled to and fro like tails. I could see every rib, the joints of their limbs were like knots in a rope; each had an iron collar on his neck, and all were connected together with a chain whose bights[8] swung between them, rhythmically clinking. Another report from the cliff made me think suddenly of that ship of war I had seen firing into a continent. It was the same kind of ominous voice; but these men could by no stretch of imagination be called enemies. They were called criminals, and the outraged law, like the bursting shells, had come to them, an insoluble mystery from the sea. All their meager breasts panted together, the violently dilated nostrils quivered, the eyes stared stonily up-hill. They passed me within six inches, without a glance, with that complete, deathlike indifference of unhappy savages. Behind this raw matter one of the reclaimed, the product of the new forces at work, strolled despondently, carrying a rifle by its middle. He had a uniform jacket with one button off, and seeing a white man on the path, hoisted his weapon to his shoulder with alacrity. This was simple prudence, white men being so much alike at a distance that he could not tell who I might be. He was speedily reassured, and with a large, white, rascally grin, and a glance at his charge, seemed to take me into partnership in his exalted trust. After all, I also was a part of the great cause of these high and just proceedings.

"Instead of going up, I turned and descended to the left. My idea was to let that chain-gang get out of sight before I climbed the hill. You know I am not particularly tender; I've had to strike and to fend off. I've had to resist and to attack sometimes—that's only one way of resisting—without counting the exact cost, according to the demands of such sort of life as I had blundered into. I've seen the devil of violence, and the devil of greed, and the devil of hot desire; but, by all the stars! these were strong, lusty, red-eyed devils, that swayed

8. Loops.

and drove men—men, I tell you. But as I stood on this hillside, I foresaw that in the blinding sunshine of that land I would become acquainted with a flabby, pretending, weak-eyed devil of a rapacious and pitiless folly. How insidious he could be, too, I was only to find out several months later and a thousand miles farther. For a moment I stood appalled, as though by a warning. Finally I descended the hill, obliquely, towards the trees I had seen.

"I avoided a vast artificial hole somebody had been digging on the slope, the purpose of which I found it impossible to divine. It wasn't a quarry or a sandpit, anyhow. It was just a hole. It might have been connected with the philanthropic desire of giving the criminals something to do. I don't know. Then I nearly fell into a very narrow ravine, almost no more than a scar in the hillside. I discovered that a lot of imported drainage-pipes for the settlement had been tumbled in there. There wasn't one that was not broken. It was a wanton smash-up. At last I got under the trees. My purpose was to stroll into the shade for a moment; but no sooner within than it seemed to me I had stepped into the gloomy circle of some Inferno. The rapids were near, and an uninterrupted, uniform, headlong, rushing noise filled the mournful stillness of the grove, where not a breath stirred, not a leaf moved, with a mysterious sound—as though the tearing pace of the launched earth had suddenly become audible.

"Black shapes crouched, lay, sat between the trees, leaning against the trunks, clinging to the earth, half coming out, half effaced within the dim light, in all the attitudes of pain, abandonment, and despair. Another mine[9] on the cliff went off, followed by a slight shudder of the soil under my feet. The work was going on. The work! And this was the place where some of the helpers had withdrawn to die.

"They were dying slowly—it was very clear. They were not enemies, they were not criminals, they were nothing earthly now,—nothing but black shadows of disease and starvation, lying confusedly in the greenish gloom. Brought from all the recesses of the coast in all the legality of time contracts, lost in uncongenial surroundings, fed on unfamiliar food, they sickened, became inefficient, and were then allowed to crawl away and rest. These moribund shapes were free as air—and nearly as thin. I began to distinguish the gleam of the eyes under the trees. Then, glancing down, I saw a face near my hand. The black bones reclined at full length with one shoulder against the tree, and slowly the eyelids rose and the sunken eyes looked up at me, enormous and vacant, a kind of blind, white flicker in the depths of the orbs, which died out slowly. The man seemed young—almost a boy—but you know with them it's hard to tell. I found nothing else to do but to offer him one of my good Swede's ship's biscuits I had in my pocket. The fingers closed slowly on it and held—there was no other movement and no other glance. He had tied a bit of white worsted round his neck—Why? Where did he get it? Was it a badge—an ornament—a charm—a propitiatory act? Was there any idea at all connected with it? It looked startling round his black neck, this bit of white thread from beyond the seas.

"Near the same tree two more bundles of acute angles sat with their legs

9. Explosive charge.

drawn up. One, with his chin propped on his knees, stared at nothing, in an intolerable and appalling manner: his brother phantom rested its forehead, as if overcome with a great weariness; and all about others were scattered in every pose of contorted collapse, as in some picture of a massacre or a pestilence. While I stood horror-struck, one of these creatures rose to his hands and knees, and went off on all-fours towards the river to drink. He lapped out of his hand, then sat up in the sunlight, crossing his shins in front of him, and after a time let his woolly head fall on his breastbone.

"I didn't want any more loitering in the shade, and I made haste towards the station. When near the buildings I met a white man, in such an unexpected elegance of get-up that in the first moment I took him for a sort of vision. I saw a high starched collar, white cuffs, a light alpaca jacket, snowy trousers, a clear necktie, and varnished boots. No hat. Hair parted, brushed, oiled, under a green-lined parasol held in a big white hand. He was amazing, and had a penholder behind his ear.

"I shook hands with this miracle, and I learned he was the Company's chief accountant, and that all the bookkeeping was done at this station. He had come out for a moment, he said, 'to get a breath of fresh air.' The expression sounded wonderfully odd, with its suggestion of sedentary desk-life. I wouldn't have mentioned the fellow to you at all, only it was from his lips that I first heard the name of the man who is so indissolubly connected with the memories of that time. Moreover, I respected the fellow. Yes; I respected his collars, his vast cuffs, his brushed hair. His appearance was certainly that of a hairdresser's dummy; but in the great demoralization of the land he kept up his appearance. That's backbone. His starched collars and got-up shirt-fronts were achievements of character. He had been out nearly three years; and, later, I could not help asking him how he managed to sport such linen. He had just the faintest blush, and said modestly, 'I've been teaching one of the native women about the station. It was difficult. She had a distaste for the work.' Thus this man had verily accomplished something. And he was devoted to his books, which were in apple-pie order.

"Everything else in the station was in a muddle,—heads, things, buildings. Strings of dusty niggers with splay feet arrived and departed; a stream of manufactured goods, rubbishy cottons, beads, and brass-wire set into the depths of darkness, and in return came a precious trickle of ivory.

"I had to wait in the station for ten days—an eternity. I lived in a hut in the yard, but to be out of the chaos I would sometimes get into the accountant's office. It was built of horizontal planks, and so badly put together that, as he bent over his high desk, he was barred from neck to heels with narrow strips of sunlight. There was no need to open the big shutter to see. It was hot there, too; big flies buzzed fiendishly, and did not sting, but stabbed. I sat generally on the floor, while, of faultless appearance (and even slightly scented), perching on a high stool, he wrote, he wrote. Sometimes he stood up for exercise. When a trucklebed with a sick man (some invalid agent from up-country) was put in there, he exhibited a gentle annoyance. 'The groans of this sick person,' he said, 'distract my attention. And without that it is extremely difficult to guard against clerical errors in this climate.'

"One day he remarked, without lifting his head, 'In the interior you will no doubt meet Mr. Kurtz.' On my asking who Mr. Kurtz was, he said he was a first-class agent; and seeing my disappointment at this information, he added slowly, laying down his pen, 'He is a very remarkable person.' Further questions elicited from him that Mr. Kurtz was at present in charge of a trading post, a very important one, in the true ivory-country, at 'the very bottom of there. Sends in as much ivory[1] as all the others put together. . . . ' He began to write again. The sick man was too ill to groan. The flies buzzed in a great peace.

"Suddenly there was a growing murmur of voices and a great tramping of feet. A caravan had come in. A violent babble of uncouth sounds burst out on the other side of the planks. All the carriers were speaking together, and in the midst of the uproar the lamentable voice of the chief agent was heard 'giving it up' tearfully for the twentieth time that day. . . . He rose slowly. 'What a frightful row,' he said. He crossed the room gently to look at the sick man, and returning, said to me, 'He does not hear.' 'What! Dead?' I asked, startled. 'No, not yet,' he answered, with great composure. Then, alluding with a toss of the head to the tumult in the station-yard, 'When one has got to make correct entries, one comes to hate those savages—hate them to the death.' He remained thoughtful for a moment. 'When you see Mr. Kurtz,' he went on, 'tell him for me that everything here'—he glanced at the desk—'is very satisfactory. I don't like to write to him—with those messengers of ours you never know who may get hold of your letter—at that Central Station.' He stared at me for a moment with his mild, bulging eyes. 'Oh, he will go far, very far,' he began again. 'He will be a somebody in the Administration before long. They, above—the Council in Europe, you know—mean him to be.'

"He turned to his work. The noise outside had ceased, and presently in going out I stopped at the door. In the steady buzz of flies the homeward-bound agent was lying flushed and insensible; the other, bent over his books, was making correct entries of perfectly correct transactions; and fifty feet below the doorstep I could see the still tree-tops of the grove of death.

"Next day I left that station at last, with a caravan of sixty men, for a two-hundred-mile tramp.

"No use telling you much about that. Paths, paths, everywhere; a stamped-in network of paths spreading over the empty land, through long grass, through burnt grass, through thickets, down and up chilly ravines, up and down stony hills ablaze with heat; and a solitude, a solitude, nobody, not a hut. The population had cleared out a long time ago. Well, if a lot of mysterious niggers armed with all kinds of fearful weapons suddenly took to traveling on the road between Deal and Gravesend,[2] catching the yokels right and left to carry heavy loads for them, I fancy every farm and cottage thereabouts would get empty very soon. Only here the dwellings were gone, too. Still I passed through several abandoned villages. There's something pathetically childish in the ruins of grass walls. Day after day, with the stamp and shuffle of sixty pair of bare feet behind me, each pair under a sixty-pound load. Camp, cook, sleep, strike camp, march.

1. Ivory and rubber were the main commercial resources traded from the Congo Free State. Ivory was used for billiard balls, piano keys, and carved art objects. 2. English coastal cities.

Now and then a carrier dead in harness, at rest in the long grass near the path, with an empty water-gourd and his long staff lying by his side. A great silence around and above. Perhaps on some quiet night the tremor of far-off drums, sinking, swelling, a tremor vast, faint; a sound weird, appealing, suggestive, and wild—and perhaps with as profound a meaning as the sound of bells in a Christian country. Once a white man in an unbuttoned uniform, camping on the path with an armed escort of lank Zanzibaris,[3] very hospitable and festive—not to say drunk. Was looking after the upkeep of the road, he declared. Can't say I saw any road or any upkeep, unless the body of a middle-aged Negro, with a bullet-hole in the forehead, upon which I absolutely stumbled three miles farther on, may be considered as a permanent improvement. I had a white companion, too, not a bad chap, but rather too fleshy and with the exasperating habit of fainting on the hot hillsides, miles away from the least bit of shade and water. Annoying, you know, to hold your own coat like a parasol over a man's head while he is coming-to. I couldn't help asking him once what he meant by coming there at all. 'To make money, of course. What do you think?' he said, scornfully. Then he got fever, and had to be carried in a hammock slung under a pole. As he weighed sixteen stone[4] I had no end of rows with the carriers. They jibbed, ran away, sneaked off with their loads in the night—quite a mutiny. So, one evening, I made a speech in English with gestures, not one of which was lost to the sixty pairs of eyes before me, and the next morning I started the hammock off in front all right. An hour afterwards I came upon the whole concern wrecked in a bush—man, hammock, groans, blankets, horrors. The heavy pole had skinned his poor nose. He was very anxious for me to kill somebody, but there wasn't the shadow of a carrier near. I remembered the old doctor—'It would be interesting for science to watch the mental changes of individuals, on the spot.' I felt I was becoming scientifically interesting. However, all that is to no purpose. On the fifteenth day I came in sight of the big river again, and hobbled into the Central Station. It was on a backwater surrounded by scrub and forest, with a pretty border of smelly mud on one side, and on the three others enclosed by a crazy fence of rushes. A neglected gap was all the gate it had, and the first glance at the place was enough to let you see the flabby devil was running that show. White men with long staves in their hands appeared languidly from amongst the buildings, strolling up to take a look at me, and then retired out of sight somewhere. One of them, a stout, excitable chap with black mustaches, informed me with great volubility and many digressions, as soon as I told him who I was, that my steamer was at the bottom of the river. I was thunderstruck. What, how, why? Oh, it was 'all right.' The 'manager himself' was there. All quite correct. 'Everybody had behaved splendidly! splendidly!'—'you must,' he said in agitation, 'go and see the general manager at once. He is waiting!'

"I did not see the real significance of that wreck at once. I fancy I see it now, but I am not sure—not at all. Certainly the affair was too stupid—when

3. Mercenary soldiers from Zanzibar, an island off the east coast of Africa. 4. British unit of weight equaling 14 pounds—hence he weighed 224 pounds.

I think of it—to be altogether natural. Still . . . . But at the moment it presented itself simply as a confounded nuisance. The steamer was sunk. They had started two days before in a sudden hurry up the river with the manager on board, in charge of some volunteer skipper, and before they had been out three hours they tore the bottom out of her on stones, and she sank near the south bank. I asked myself what I was to do there, now my boat was lost. As a matter of fact, I had plenty to do in fishing my command out of the river. I had to set about it the very next day. That, and the repairs when I brought the pieces to the station, took some months.

"My first interview with the manager was curious. He did not ask me to sit down after my twenty-mile walk that morning. He was commonplace in complexion, in feature, in manners, and in voice. He was of middle size and of ordinary build. His eyes, of the usual blue, were perhaps remarkably cold, and he certainly could make his glance fall on one as trenchant and heavy as an ax. But even at these times the rest of his person seemed to disclaim the intention. Otherwise there was only an indefinable, faint expression of his lips, something stealthy—a smile—not a smile—I remember it, but I can't explain. It was unconscious, this smile was, though just after he had said something it got intensified for an instant. It came at the end of his speeches like a seal applied on the words to make the meaning of the commonest phrase appear absolutely inscrutable. He was a common trader, from his youth up employed in these parts—nothing more. He was obeyed, yet he inspired neither love nor fear, nor even respect. He inspired uneasiness. That was it! Uneasiness. Not a definite mistrust—just uneasiness—nothing more. You have no idea how effective such a . . . a . . . faculty can be. He had no genius for organizing, for initiative, or for order even. That was evident in such things as the deplorable state of the station. He had no learning, and no intelligence. His position had come to him—why? Perhaps because he was never ill. . . . He had served three terms of three years out there. . . . Because triumphant health in the general rout of constitutions is a kind of power in itself. When he went home on leave he rioted on a large scale—pompously. Jack ashore[5]—with a difference—in externals only. This one could gather from his casual talk. He originated nothing, he could keep the routine going—that's all. But he was great. He was great by this little thing that it was impossible to tell what could control such a man. He never gave that secret away. Perhaps there was nothing within him. Such a suspicion made one pause—for out there there were no external checks. Once when various tropical diseases had laid low almost every 'agent' in the station, he was heard to say, 'Men who come out here should have no entrails.' He sealed the utterance with that smile of his, as though it had been a door opening into a darkness he had in his keeping. You fancied you had seen things—but the seal was on. When annoyed at meal-times by the constant quarrels of the white men about precedence, he ordered an immense round table to be made, for which a special house had to be built. This was the station's messroom. Where he sat was the first place—the rest were nowhere. One felt this to be

5. I.e., like a sailor on shore leave.

his unalterable conviction. He was neither civil nor uncivil. He was quiet. He allowed his 'boy'—an overfed young Negro from the coast—to treat the white men, under his very eyes, with provoking insolence.

"He began to speak as soon as he saw me. I had been very long on the road. He could not wait. Had to start without me. The upriver stations had to be relieved. There had been so many delays already that he did not know who was dead and who was alive, and how they got on—and so on, and so on. He paid no attention to my explanations, and, playing with a stick of sealing-wax, repeated several times that the situation was 'very grave, very grave.' There were rumors that a very important station was in jeopardy, and its chief, Mr. Kurtz, was ill. Hoped it was not true. Mr. Kurtz was . . . I felt weary and irritable. Hang Kurtz, I thought. I interrupted him by saying I had heard of Mr. Kurtz on the coast. 'Ah! So they talk of him down there,' he murmured to himself. Then he began again, assuring me Mr. Kurtz was the best agent he had, an exceptional man, of the greatest importance to the Company; therefore I could understand his anxiety. He was, he said, 'very, very uneasy.' Certainly he fidgeted on his chair a good deal, exclaimed, 'Ah, Mr. Kurtz!' broke the stick of sealing-wax and seemed dumfounded by the accident. Next thing he wanted to know 'how long it would take to . . . ' I interrupted him again. Being hungry, you know, and kept on my feet too, I was getting savage. 'How can I tell?' I said, 'I haven't even seen the wreck yet—some months, no doubt.' All this talk seemed to me so futile. 'Some months,' he said. 'Well, let us say three months before we can make a start. Yes. That ought to do the affair.' I flung out of his hut (he lived all alone in a clay hut with a sort of veranda) muttering to myself my opinion of him. He was a chattering idiot. Afterwards I took it back when it was borne in upon me startlingly with what extreme nicety he had estimated the time requisite for the 'affair.'

"I went to work the next day, turning, so to speak, my back on that station. In that way only it seemed to me I could keep my hold on the redeeming facts of life. Still, one must look about sometimes; and then I saw this station, these men strolling aimlessly about in the sunshine of the yard. I asked myself sometimes what it all meant. They wandered here and there with their absurd long staves in their hands, like a lot of faithless pilgrims bewitched inside a rotten fence. The word 'ivory' rang in the air, was whispered, was sighed. You would think they were praying to it. A taint of imbecile rapacity blew through it all, like a whiff from some corpse. By Jove! I've never seen anything so unreal in my life. And outside, the silent wilderness surrounding this cleared speck on the earth struck me as something great and invincible, like evil or truth, waiting patiently for the passing away of this fantastic invasion.

"Oh, these months! Well, never mind. Various things happened. One evening a grass shed full of calico, cotton prints, beads, and I don't know what else, burst into a blaze so suddenly that you would have thought the earth had opened to let an avenging fire consume all that trash. I was smoking my pipe quietly by my dismantled steamer, and saw them all cutting capers in the light, with their arms lifted high, when the stout man with mustaches came tearing down to the river, a tin pail in his hand, assured me that everybody was 'behaving splendidly, splendidly,' dipped about a quart of water and tore back again. I noticed there was a hole in the bottom of his pail.

"I strolled up. There was no hurry. You see the thing had gone off like a box of matches. It had been hopeless from the very first. The flame had leaped high, driven everybody back, lighted up everything—and collapsed. The shed was already a heap of embers glowing fiercely. A nigger was being beaten near by. They said he had caused the fire in some way; be that as it may, he was screeching most horribly. I saw him, later, for several days, sitting in a bit of shade looking very sick and trying to recover himself: afterwards he arose and went out—and the wilderness without a sound took him into its bosom again. As I approached the glow from the dark I found myself at the back of two men, talking. I heard the name of Kurtz pronounced, then the words, 'take advantage of this unfortunate accident.' One of the men was the manager. I wished him a good evening. 'Did you ever see anything like it—eh? it is incredible,' he said, and walked off. The other man remained. He was a first-class agent, young, gentlemanly, a bit reserved, with a forked little beard and a hooked nose. He was standoffish with the other agents, and they on their side said he was the manager's spy among them. As to me, I had hardly ever spoken to him before. We got into talk, and by and by we strolled away from the hissing ruins. Then he asked me to his room, which was in the main building of the station. He struck a match, and I perceived that this young aristocrat had not only a silver-mounted dressing-case but also a whole candle all to himself. Just at that time the manager was the only man supposed to have any right to candles. Native mats covered the clay walls; a collection of spears, assegais,[6] shields, knives was hung up in trophies. The business intrusted to this fellow was the making of bricks—so I had been informed; but there wasn't a fragment of a brick anywhere in the station, and he had been there more than a year—waiting. It seems he could not make bricks without something, I don't know what—straw, maybe. Anyways, it could not be found there, and as it was not likely to be sent from Europe, it did not appear clear to me what he was waiting for. An act of special creation perhaps. However, they were all waiting—all the sixteen or twenty pilgrims of them—for something; and upon my word it did not seem an uncongenial occupation, from the way they took it, though the only thing that ever came to them was disease—as far as I could see. They beguiled the time by backbiting and intriguing against each other in a foolish kind of way. There was an air of plotting about that station, but nothing came of it, of course. It was as unreal as everything else—as the philanthropic pretense of the whole concern, as their talk, as their government, as their show of work. The only real feeling was a desire to get appointed to a trading-post where ivory was to be had, so that they could earn percentages. They intrigued and slandered and hated each other only on that account,—but as to effectually lifting a little finger—oh, no. By heavens! there is something after all in the world allowing one man to steal a horse while another must not look at the halter. Steal a horse straight out. Very well. He has done it. Perhaps he can ride. But there is a way

6. Slender South African throwing spears.

of looking at a halter that would provoke the most charitable of saints into a kick.

"I had no idea why he wanted to be sociable, but as we chatted in there it suddenly occurred to me the fellow was trying to get at something—in fact, pumping me. He alluded constantly to Europe, to the people I was supposed to know there—putting leading questions as to my acquaintances in the sepulchral city, and so on. His little eyes glittered like mica discs—with curiosity—though he tried to keep up a bit of superciliousness. At first I was astonished, but very soon I became awfully curious to see what he would find out from me. I couldn't possibly imagine what I had in me to make it worth his while. It was very pretty to see how he baffled himself, for in truth my body was full only of chills, and my head had nothing in it but that wretched steamboat business. It was evident he took me for a perfectly shameless prevaricator. At last he got angry, and, to conceal a movement of furious annoyance, he yawned. I rose. Then I noticed a small sketch in oils, on a panel, representing a woman, draped and blindfolded, carrying a lighted torch. The background was somber—almost black. The movement of the woman was stately, and the effect of the torchlight on the face was sinister.

"It arrested me, and he stood by civilly, holding an empty half-pint champagne bottle (medical comforts) with the candle stuck in it. To my question he said Mr. Kurtz had painted this—in this very station more than a year ago—while waiting for means to go to his trading-post. 'Tell me, pray,' said I, 'who is this Mr. Kurtz?'

" 'The chief of the Inner Station,' he answered in a short tone, looking away. 'Much obliged,' I said, laughing. 'And you are the brickmaker of the Central Station. Everyone knows that.' He was silent for a while. 'He is a prodigy,' he said at last. 'He is an emissary of pity, and science, and progress, and devil knows what else. We want,' he began to declaim suddenly, 'for the guidance of the cause intrusted to us by Europe, so to speak, higher intelligence, wide sympathies, a singleness of purpose.' 'Who says that?' I asked. 'Lots of them,' he replied. 'Some even write that; and so *he* comes here, a special being, as you ought to know.' 'Why ought I to know?' I interrupted, really surprised. He paid no attention. 'Yes. Today he is chief of the best station, next year he will be assistant-manager, two years more and . . . but I daresay you know what he will be in two years' time. You are of the new gang—the gang of virtue. The same people who sent him specially also recommended you. Oh, don't say no. I've my own eyes to trust.' Light dawned upon me. My dear aunt's influential acquaintances were producing an unexpected effect upon that young man. I nearly burst into a laugh. 'Do you read the Company's confidential correspondence?' I asked. He hadn't a word to say. It was great fun. 'When Mr. Kurtz,' I continued, severely, 'is General Manager, you won't have the opportunity.'

"He blew the candle out suddenly, and we went outside. The moon had risen. Black figures strolled about listlessly, pouring water on the glow, whence proceeded a sound of hissing; steam ascended in the moonlight, the beaten nigger groaned somewhere. 'What a row the brute makes!' said the indefatigable man with the mustaches, appearing near us. 'Serves him right. Transgression—punishment—bang! Pitiless, pitiless. That's the only way. This will prevent all conflagrations for the future. I was just telling the manager. . . .' He noticed my companion, and became crestfallen all at once. 'Not in bed yet,' he said, with a kind of servile heartiness; 'it's so natural. Ha! Danger—agitation.' He vanished. I went on to the river-side, and the other followed me. I heard a scathing murmur at my ear, 'Heap of muffs[7]—go to.' The pilgrims could be seen in knots gesticulating, discussing. Several had still their staves in their hands. I verily believe they took these sticks to bed with them. Beyond the fence the forest stood up spectrally in the moonlight, and through the dim stir, through the faint sounds of that lamentable courtyard, the silence of the land went home to one's very heart—its mystery, its greatness, the amazing reality of its concealed life. The hurt nigger moaned feebly somewhere near by, and then fetched a deep sigh that made me mend my pace away from there. I felt a hand introducing itself under my arm. 'My dear sir,' said the fellow, 'I don't want to be misunderstood, and especially by you, who will see Mr. Kurtz long before I can have that pleasure. I wouldn't like him to get a false idea of my disposition. . . .'

"I let him run on, this papier-mâché Mephistopheles,[8] and it seemed to me that if I tried I could poke my forefinger through him, and would find nothing inside but a little loose dirt, maybe. He, don't you see, had been planning to be assistant-manager by and by under the present man, and I could see that the coming of that Kurtz had upset them both not a little. He talked precipitately, and I did not try to stop him. I had my shoulders against the wreck of my steamer, hauled up on the slope like a carcass of some big river animal. The smell of mud, of primeval mud, by Jove! was in my nostrils, the high stillness of primeval forest was before my eyes; there were shiny patches on the black creek. The moon had spread over everything a thin layer of silver—over the rank grass, over the mud, upon the wall of matted vegetation standing higher than the wall of a temple, over the great river I could see through a somber gap glittering, glittering, as it flowed broadly by without a murmur. All this was great, expectant, mute, while the man jabbered about himself. I wondered whether the stillness on the face of the immensity looking at us two were meant as an appeal or as a menace. What were we who had strayed in here? Could we handle that dumb thing, or would it handle us? I felt how big, how confoundedly big, was that thing that couldn't talk, and perhaps was deaf as well. What was in there? I could see a little ivory coming out from there, and I had heard Mr. Kurtz was in there. I had heard enough about it, too—God knows! Yet somehow it didn't bring any image with it—no more than if I had been told an angel or a fiend was in there. I believed it in the same way one of you might believe there are inhabitants in the planet Mars. I knew once a Scotch sailmaker who was certain, dead sure, there were people in Mars. If you asked him for some idea how they looked and behaved, he would get shy and mutter something about 'walking on all-fours.' If you as much as smiled, he would—though a man of sixty—offer to fight you. I would not have gone so far as to fight for Kurtz, but I went for him near enough to a lie. You know I hate, detest, and can't bear a lie, not because I am straighter than the rest of us, but simply

7. Gang of bunglers. 8. I.e., devil made of pasteboard.

because it appalls me. There is a taint of death, a flavor of mortality in lies—which is exactly what I hate and detest in the world—what I want to forget. It makes me miserable and sick, like biting something rotten would do. Temperament, I suppose. Well, I went near enough to it by letting the young fool there believe anything he liked to imagine as to my influence in Europe. I became in an instant as much of a pretence as the rest of the bewitched pilgrims. This simply because I had a notion it somehow would be of help to that Kurtz whom at the time I did not see—you understand. He was just a word for me. I did not see the man in the name any more than you do. Do you see him? Do you see the story? Do you see anything? It seems to me I am trying to tell you a dream—making a vain attempt, because no relation of a dream can convey the dream-sensation, that commingling of absurdity, surprise, and bewilderment in a tremor of struggling revolt, that notion of being captured by the incredible which is of the very essence of dreams. . . ."

He was silent for a while.

" . . . No, it is impossible; it is impossible to convey the life-sensation of any given epoch of one's existence—that which makes its truth, its meaning—its subtle and penetrating essence. It is impossible. We live, as we dream—alone. . . ."

He paused again as if reflecting, then added—

"Of course in this you fellows see more than I could then. You see me, whom you know. . . ."

It had become so pitch dark that we listeners could hardly see one another. For a long time already he, sitting apart, had been no more to us than a voice. There was not a word from anybody. The others might have been asleep, but I was awake. I listened, I listened on the watch for the sentence, for the word, that would give me the clew to the faint uneasiness inspired by this narrative that seemed to shape itself without human lips in the heavy night-air of the river.

" . . . Yes—I let him run on," Marlow began again, "and think what he pleased about the powers that were behind me. I did! And there was nothing behind me! There was nothing but that wretched, old, mangled steamboat I was leaning against, while he talked fluently about 'the necessity for every man to get on.' 'And when one comes out here, you conceive, it is not to gaze at the moon.' Mr. Kurtz was a 'universal genius,' but even a genius would find it easier to work with 'adequate tools—intelligent men.' He did not make bricks—why, there was a physical impossibility in the way—as I was well aware; and if he did secretarial work for the manager, it was because 'no sensible man rejects wantonly the confidence of his superiors.' Did I see it? I saw it. What more did I want? What I really wanted was rivets, by heaven! Rivets. To get on with the work—to stop the hole. Rivets I wanted. There were cases of them down at the coast—cases—piled up—burst—split! You kicked a loose rivet at every second step in that station yard on the hillside. Rivets had rolled into the grove of death. You could fill your pockets with rivets for the trouble of stooping down—and there wasn't one rivet to be found where it was wanted. We had plates that would do, but nothing to fasten them with. And every week the messenger, a lone Negro, letter-bag on shoulder and staff in hand, left our station for the coast. And several times a week a coast caravan came in with trade goods—ghastly glazed calico that made you shudder only to look at it; glass beads, valued about a penny a quart, confounded spotted cotton handkerchiefs. And no rivets. Three carriers could have brought all that was wanted to set that steamboat afloat.

"He was becoming confidential now, but I fancy my unresponsive attitude must have exasperated him at last, for he judged it necessary to inform me he feared neither God nor devil, let alone any mere man. I said I could see that very well, but what I wanted was a certain quantity of rivets—and rivets were what really Mr. Kurtz wanted, if he had only known it. Now letters went to the coast every week. . . . 'My dear sir,' he cried, 'I write from dictation.' I demanded rivets. There was a way—for an intelligent man. He changed his manner; became very cold, and suddenly began to talk about a hippopotamus; wondered whether sleeping on board the steamer (I stuck to my salvage night and day) I wasn't disturbed. There was an old hippo that had the bad habit of getting out on the bank and roaming at night over the station grounds. The pilgrims used to turn out in a body and empty every rifle they could lay hands on at him. Some even had sat up o' nights for him. All this energy was wasted, though. 'That animal has a charmed life,' he said; 'but you can say this only of brutes in this country. No man—you apprehend me?—no man here bears a charmed life.' He stood there for a moment in the moonlight with his delicate hooked nose set a little askew, and his mica eyes glittering without a wink, then, with a curt good night, he strode off. I could see he was disturbed and considerably puzzled, which made me feel more hopeful than I had been for days. It was a great comfort to turn from that chap to my influential friend, the battered, twisted, ruined, tin-pot steamboat. I clambered on board. She rang under my feet like an empty Huntley & Palmer biscuit-tin kicked along a gutter; she was nothing so solid in make, and rather less pretty in shape, but I had expended enough hard work on her to make me love her. No influential friend would have served me better. She had given me a chance to come out a bit—to find out what I could do. No, I don't like work. I had rather laze about and think of all the fine things that can be done. I don't like work—no man does—but I like what is in the work,—the chance to find yourself. Your own reality—for yourself, not for others—what no other man can ever know. They can only see the mere show, and never can tell what it really means.

"I was not surprised to see somebody sitting aft, on the deck, with his legs dangling over the mud. You see I rather chummed with the few mechanics there were in that station, whom the other pilgrims naturally despised—on account of their imperfect manners, I suppose. This was the foreman—a boiler-maker by trade—a good worker. He was a lank, bony, yellow-faced man, with big intense eyes. His aspect was worried, and his head was as bald as the palm of my hand; but his hair in falling seemed to have stuck to his chin, and had prospered in the new locality, for his beard hung down to his waist. He was a widower with six young children (he had left them in charge of a sister of his to come out there), and the passion of his life was pigeon-flying. He was an enthusiast and a connoisseur. He would rave about pigeons. After work hours he used sometimes to come over from his hut for a talk about his children and his pigeons; at work, when he had to crawl in the mud under the bottom of the steamboat, he would tie up that beard of his in a kind of white serviette[9] he brought for the purpose. It had loops to go over his ears. In the evening he could be seen squatted on the bank rinsing that wrapper in the creek with great care, then spreading it solemnly on a bush to dry.

"I slapped him on the back and shouted, 'We shall have rivets!' He scrambled to his feet exclaiming, 'No! Rivets!' as though he couldn't believe his ears. Then in a low voice, 'You . . . eh?' I don't know why we behaved like lunatics. I put my finger to the side of my nose and nodded mysteriously. 'Good for you!' he cried, snapped his fingers above his head, lifting one foot. I tried a jig. We capered on the iron deck. A frightful clatter came out of that hulk, and the virgin forest on the other bank of the creek sent it back in a thundering roll upon the sleeping station. It must have made some of the pilgrims sit up in their hovels. A dark figure obscured the lighted doorway of the manager's hut, vanished, then, a second or so after, the doorway itself vanished, too. We stopped, and the silence driven away by the stamping of our feet flowed back again from the recesses of the land. The great wall of vegetation, an exuberant and entangled mass of trunks, branches, leaves, boughs, festoons, motionless in the moonlight, was like a rioting invasion of soundless life, a rolling wave of plants, piled up, crested, ready to topple over the creek, to sweep every little man of us out of his little existence. And it moved not. A deadened burst of mighty splashes and snorts reached us from afar as though an ichthyosaurus[1] had been taking a bath of glitter in the great river. 'After all,' said the boiler-maker in a reasonable tone, 'why shouldn't we get the rivets?' Why not, indeed! I did not know of any reason why we shouldn't. 'They'll come in three weeks,' I said, confidently.

"But they didn't. Instead of rivets there came an invasion, an in-fliction, a visitation. It came in sections during the next three weeks, each section headed by a donkey carrying a white man in new clothes and tan shoes, bowing from that elevation right and left to the impressed pilgrims. A quarrelsome band of footsore sulky niggers trod on the heels of the donkeys; a lot of tents, camp-stools, tin boxes, white cases, brown bales would be shot down in the courtyard, and the air of mystery would deepen a little over the muddle of the station. Five such installments came, with their absurd air of disorderly flight with the loot of innumerable outfit shops and provision stores, that, one would think, they were lugging, after a raid, into the wilderness for equitable division. It was an extricable mess of things decent in themselves but that human folly made look like the spoils of thieving.

"This devoted band called itself the Eldorado Exploring Expedition, and I believe they were sworn to secrecy. Their talk, however, was the talk of sordid buccaneers: it was reckless without hardihood, greedy without audacity, and cruel without courage; there was not an atom of foresight or of serious intention in the whole batch of them, and they did not seem aware these things are wanted for the work of the world. To tear treasure out of the bowels of the land was their desire, with no more moral purpose at the back of it than there

9. Napkin. 1. Prehistoric marine reptile.

is in burglars breaking into a safe. Who paid the expenses of the noble enterprise I don't know; but the uncle of our manager was leader of that lot.

"In exterior he resembled a butcher in a poor neighborhood, and his eyes had a look of sleepy cunning. He carried his fat paunch with ostentation on his short legs, and during the time his gang infested the station spoke to no one but his nephew. You could see these two roaming about all day long with their heads close together in an everlasting confab.

"I had given up worrying myself about the rivets. One's capacity for that kind of folly is more limited than you would suppose. I said Hang!—and let things slide. I had plenty of time for meditation, and now and then I would give some thought to Kurtz. I wasn't very interested in him. No. Still, I was curious to see whether this man, who had come out equipped with moral ideas of some sort, would climb to the top after all and how he would set about his work when there."

## II

"One evening as I was lying flat on the deck of my steamboat, I heard voices approaching—and there were the nephew and the uncle strolling along the bank. I laid my head on my arm again, and had nearly lost myself in a doze, when somebody said in my ear, as it were: 'I am as harmless as a little child, but I don't like to be dictated to. Am I the manager—or am I not? I was ordered to send him there. It's incredible.' . . . I became aware that the two were standing on the shore alongside the forepart of the steamboat, just below my head. I did not move; it did not occur to me to move: I was sleepy. 'It *is* unpleasant,' grunted the uncle. 'He has asked the Administration to be sent there,' said the other, 'with the idea of showing what he could do; and I was instructed accordingly. Look at the influence that man must have. Is it not frightful?' They both agreed it was frightful, then made several bizarre remarks: 'Make rain and fine weather—one man—the Council—by the nose'—bits of absurd sentences that got the better of my drowsiness, so that I had pretty near the whole of my wits about me when the uncle said, 'The climate may do away with this difficulty for you. Is he alone there?' 'Yes,' answered the manager; 'he sent his assistant down the river with a note to me in these terms: "Clear this poor devil out of the country, and don't bother sending more of that sort. I had rather be alone than have the kind of men you can dispose of with me." It was more than a year ago. Can you imagine such impudence?' 'Anything since then?' asked the other, hoarsely. 'Ivory,' jerked the nephew; 'lots of it—prime sort—lots—most annoying, from him.' 'And with that?' questioned the heavy rumble. 'Invoice,' was the reply fired out, so to speak. Then silence. They had been talking about Kurtz.

"I was broad awake by this time, but, lying perfectly at ease, remained still, having no inducement to change my position. 'How did that ivory come all this way?' growled the elder man, who seemed very vexed. The other explained that it had come with a fleet of canoes in charge of an English half-caste clerk Kurtz had with him; that Kurtz had apparently intended to return himself, the station being by that time bare of goods and stores, but after coming three hundred miles, had suddenly decided to go back, which he started to do alone in a small dugout with four paddlers, leaving the half-caste to continue down the river with the ivory. The two fellows there seemed astounded at anybody attempting such a thing. They were at a loss for an adequate motive. As to me, I seemed to see Kurtz for the first time. It was a distinct glimpse: the dugout, four paddling savages, and the lone white man turning his back suddenly on the headquarters, on relief, on thoughts of home—perhaps; setting his face towards the depths of the wilderness, towards his empty and desolate station. I did not know the motive. Perhaps he was just simply a fine fellow who stuck to his work for its own sake. His name, you understand, had not been pronounced once. He was 'that man.' The half-caste, who, as far as I could see, had conducted a difficult trip with great prudence and pluck, was invariably alluded to as 'that scoundrel.' The 'scoundrel' had reported that the 'man' had been very ill—had recovered imperfectly. . . . The two below me moved away then a few paces, and strolled back and forth at some little distance. I heard: 'Military post—doctor—two hundred miles—quite alone now—unavoidable delays—nine months—no news—strange rumors.' They approached again, just as the manager was saying, 'No one, as far as I know, unless a species of wandering trader—a pestilential fellow, snapping ivory from the natives.' Who was it they were talking about now? I gathered in snatches that this was some man supposed to be in Kurtz's district, and of whom the manager did not approve. 'We will not be free from unfair competition till one of these fellows is hanged for an example,' he said. 'Certainly,' grunted the other; 'get him hanged! Why not? Anything—anything can be done in this country. That's what I say; nobody here, you understand, *here,* can endanger your position. And why? You stand the climate—you outlast them all. The danger is in Europe; but there before I left I took care to—' They moved off and whispered, then their voices rose again. 'The extraordinary series of delays is not my fault. I did my best.' The fat man sighed. 'Very sad.' 'And the pestiferous absurdity of his talk,' continued the other; 'he bothered me enough when he was here. "Each station should be like a beacon on the road towards better things, a center for trade, of course, but also for humanizing, improving, instructing." Conceive you—that ass! And he wants to be manager! No, it's—' Here he got choked by excessive indignation, and I lifted my head the least bit. I was surprised to see how near they were—right under me. I could have spat upon their hats. They were looking on the ground, absorbed in thought. The manager was switching his leg with a slender twig: his sagacious relative lifted his head. 'You have been well since you came out this time?' he asked. The other gave a start. 'Who? I? Oh! Like a charm—like a charm. But the rest—oh, my goodness! All sick. They die so quick, too, that I haven't the time to send them out of the country—it's incredible!' 'H'm. Just so,' grunted the uncle. 'Ah! my boy, trust to this—I say, trust to this.' I saw him extend his short flipper of an arm for a gesture that took in the forest, the creek, the mud, the river,—seemed to beckon with a dishonoring flourish before the sunlit face of the land a treacherous appeal to the lurking death, to the hidden evil, to the profound darkness of its heart. It was so startling that I leaped to my feet and looked back at the edge of the forest, as though I had expected an answer of some sort to that black display of confidence. You know the foolish notions that come to one sometimes. The high stillness confronted these two figures with its ominous patience, waiting for the passing away of a fantastic invasion.

"They swore aloud together—out of sheer fright, I believe—then pretending not to know anything of my existence, turned back to the station. The sun was low; and leaning forward side by side, they seemed to be tugging painfully uphill their two ridiculous shadows of unequal length, that trailed behind them slowly over the tall grass without bending a single blade.

"In a few days the Eldorado Expedition went into the patient wilderness, that closed upon it as the sea closes over a diver. Long afterwards the news came that all the donkeys were dead. I know nothing as to the fate of the less valuable animals. They, no doubt, like the rest of us, found what they deserved. I did not inquire. I was then rather excited at the prospect of meeting Kurtz very soon. When I say very soon I mean it comparatively. It was just two months from the day we left the creek when we came to the bank below Kurtz's station.

"Going up that river was like traveling back to the earliest beginnings of the world, when vegetation rioted on the earth and the big trees were kings. An empty stream, a great silence, an impenetrable forest. The air was warm, thick, heavy, sluggish. There was no joy in the brilliance of sunshine. The long stretches of the waterway ran on, deserted, into the gloom of overshadowed distances. On silvery sandbanks hippos and alligators sunned themselves side by side. The broadening waters flowed through a mob of wooded islands; you lost your way on that river as you would in a desert, and butted all day long against shoals, trying to find the channel, till you thought yourself bewitched and cut off forever from everything you had known once—somewhere—far away—in another existence perhaps. There were moments when one's past came back to one, as it will sometimes when you have not a moment to spare to yourself; but it came in the shape of an unrestful and noisy dream, remembered with wonder amongst the overwhelming realities of this strange world of plants, and water, and silence. And this stillness of life did not in the least resemble a peace. It was the stillness of an implacable force brooding over an inscrutable intention. It looked at you with a vengeful aspect. I got used to it afterwards; I did not see it any more; I had no time. I had to keep guessing at the channel; I had to discern, mostly by inspiration, the signs of hidden banks; I watched for sunken stones; I was learning to clap my teeth smartly before my heart flew out, when I shaved by a fluke some infernal sly old snag that would have ripped the life out of the tin-pot steamboat and drowned all the pilgrims; I had to keep a lookout for the signs of dead wood we could cut up in the night for next day's steaming. When you have to attend to things of that sort, to the mere incidents of the surface, the reality—the reality, I tell you—fades. The inner truth is hidden—luckily, luckily. But I felt it all the same; I felt often its mysterious stillness watching me at my monkey tricks, just as it watches you fellows performing on your respective tight-ropes for—what is it? half-a-crown a tumble—"

"Try to be civil, Marlow," growled a voice, and I knew there was at least one listener awake besides myself.

"I beg your pardon. I forgot the heartache which makes up the rest of the price. And indeed what does the price matter, if the trick be well done? You do your tricks very well. And I didn't do badly either, since I managed not to sink that steamboat on my first trip. It's a wonder to me yet. Imagine a blindfolded man set to drive a van over a bad road. I sweated and shivered over that business considerably, I can tell you. After all, for a seaman, to scrape the bottom of the thing that's supposed to float all the time under his care is the unpardonable sin. No one may know of it, but you never forget the thump—eh? A blow on the very heart. You remember it, you dream of it, you wake up at night and think of it—years after—and go hot and cold all over. I don't pretend to say that steamboat floated all the time. More than once she had to wade for a bit, with twenty cannibals splashing around and pushing. We had enlisted some of these chaps on the way for a crew. Fine fellows—cannibals—in their place. They were men one could work with, and I am grateful to them. And, after all, they did not eat each other before my face: they had brought along a provision of hippo-meat which went rotten, and made the mystery of the wilderness stink in my nostrils. Phoo! I can sniff it now. I had the manager on board and three or four pilgrims with their staves—all complete. Sometimes we came upon a station close by the bank, clinging to the skirts of the unknown, and the white men rushing out of a tumble-down hovel, with great gestures of joy and surprise and welcome, seemed very strange—had the appearance of being held there captive by a spell. The word ivory would ring in the air for a while—and on we went again into the silence, along empty reaches, round the still bends, between the high walls of our winding way, reverberating in hollow claps the ponderous beat of the stern-wheel. Trees, trees, millions of trees, massive, immense, running up high; and at their foot, hugging the bank against the stream, crept the little begrimed steamboat, like a sluggish beetle crawling on the floor of a lofty portico. It made you feel very small, very lost, and yet it was not altogether depressing, that feeling. After all, if you were small, the grimy beetle crawled on—which was just what you wanted it to do. Where the pilgrims imagined it crawled to I don't know. To some place where they expected to get something, I bet! For me it crawled towards Kurtz—exclusively; but when the steam-pipes started leaking we crawled very slow. The reaches opened before us and closed behind, as if the forest had stepped leisurely across the water to bar the way for our return. We penetrated deeper and deeper into the heart of darkness. It was very quiet there. At night sometimes the roll of drums behind the curtain of trees would run up the river and remain sustained faintly, as if hovering in the air high over our heads, till the first break of day. Whether it meant war, peace, or prayer we could not tell. The dawns were heralded by the descent of a chill stillness; the woodcutters slept, their fires burned low; the snapping of a twig would make you start. We were wanderers on a prehistoric earth, on an earth that wore the aspect of an unknown planet. We could have fancied ourselves the first men taking possession of an accursed inheritance, to be subdued at the cost of profound anguish and of excessive toil. But suddenly, as we struggled round a bend, there would be a glimpse of rush walls, of peaked grass-roofs, a burst of yells, a whirl of black limbs, a mass of hands clapping, of feet stamping, of bodies swaying, of eyes rolling, under the droop of heavy and motionless foliage. The steamer toiled along slowly on the edge of a black and incomprehensible frenzy. The prehistoric man was cursing us, praying to us, welcoming us—who could tell? We were cut off from the comprehension of our surroundings; we glided past like phantoms, wondering and secretly appalled, as sane men would be before an enthusiastic outbreak in a madhouse. We could not understand because we were too far and could not remember, because we were traveling in the night of first ages, of those ages that are gone, leaving hardly a sign—and no memories.

"The earth seemed unearthly. We are accustomed to look upon the shackled form of a conquered monster, but there—there you could look at a thing monstrous and free. It was unearthly, and the men were—No, they were not inhuman. Well, you know, that was the worst of it—this suspicion of their not being inhuman. It would come slowly to one. They howled and leaped, and spun, and made horrid faces; but what thrilled you was just the thought of their humanity—like yours—the thought of your remote kinship with this wild and passionate uproar. Ugly. Yes, it was ugly enough; but if you were man enough you would admit to yourself that there was in you just the faintest trace of a response to the terrible frankness of that noise, a dim suspicion of there being a meaning in it which you—you so remote from the night of first ages—could comprehend. And why not? The mind of man is capable of anything—because everything is in it, all the past as well as all the future. What was there after all? Joy, fear, sorrow, devotion, valor, rage—who can tell?—but truth—truth stripped of its cloak of time. Let the fool gape and shudder—the man knows, and can look on without a wink. But he must at least be as much of a man as these on the shore. He must meet that truth with his own true stuff—with his own inborn strength. Principles won't do. Acquisitions, clothes, pretty rags—rags that would fly off at the first good shake. No; you want a deliberate belief. An appeal to me in this fiendish row—is there? Very well; I hear; I admit, but I have a voice too, and for good or evil mine is the speech that cannot be silenced. Of course, a fool, what with sheer fright and fine sentiments, is always safe. Who's that grunting? You wonder I didn't go ashore for a howl and a dance? Well, no—I didn't. Fine sentiments, you say? Fine sentiments, be hanged! I had no time. I had to mess about with white-lead and strips of woolen blanket helping to put bandages on those leaky steam-pipes—I tell you. I had to watch the steering, and circumvent those snags, and get the tin-pot along by hook or by crook. There was surface-truth enough in these things to save a wiser man. And between whiles I had to look after the savage who was fireman. He was an improved specimen; he could fire up a vertical boiler.[2] He was there below me, and, upon my word, to look at him was as edifying as seeing a dog in a parody of breeches and a feather hat, walking on his hindlegs. A few months of training had done for that really fine chap. He squinted at the steam-gauge and at the water-gauge with an evident effort of intrepidity—and he had filed teeth, too, the poor devil, and the wool of his pate shaved into queer patterns, and three ornamental scars on each of his cheeks. He ought to have been clapping his hands and stamping his feet on the bank, instead of which he was hard at work, a thrall to strange witchcraft, full of improving knowledge. He

2. Simple, easily fired boiler, typical of the primitive machinery on Marlow's "tin-pot" boat.

was useful because he had been instructed; and what he knew was this—that should the water in that transparent thing disappear, the evil spirit inside the boiler would get angry through the greatness of his thirst, and take a terrible vengeance. So he sweated and fired up and watched the glass fearfully (with an impromptu charm, made of rags, tied to his arm, and a piece of polished bone, as big as a watch, stuck flatways through his lower lip), while the wooden banks slipped past us slowly, the short noise was left behind, the interminable miles of silence—and we crept on, towards Kurtz. But the snags were thick, the water was treacherous and shallow, the boiler seemed indeed to have a sulky devil in it, and thus neither that fireman nor I had any time to peer into our creepy thoughts.

"Some fifty miles below the Inner Station we came upon a hut of reeds, an inclined and melancholy pole, with the unrecognizable tatters of what had been a flag of some sort flying from it, and a neatly stacked woodpile. This was unexpected. We came to the bank, and on the stack of firewood found a flat piece of board with some faded pencil-writing on it. When deciphered it said: 'Wood for you. Hurry up. Approach cautiously.' There was a signature, but it was illegible—not Kurtz—a much longer word. 'Hurry up.' Where? Up the river? 'Approach cautiously.' We had not done so. But the warning could not have been meant for the place where it could be only found after approach. Something was wrong above. But what—and how much? That was the question. We commented adversely upon the imbecility of that telegraphic style. The bush around said nothing, and would not let us look very far, either. A torn curtain of red twill hung in the doorway of the hut, and flapped sadly in our faces. The dwelling was dismantled; but we could see a white man had lived there not very long ago. There remained a rude table—a plank on two posts; a heap of rubbish reposed in a dark corner, and by the door I picked up a book. It had lost its covers, and the pages had been thumbed into a state of extremely dirty softness; but the back had been lovingly stitched afresh with white cotton thread, which looked clean yet. It was an extraordinary find. Its title was, *An Inquiry into some Points of Seamanship,* by a man Towser, Towson—some such name—Master in his Majesty's Navy. The matter looked dreary reading enough, with illustrative diagrams and repulsive tables of figures, and the copy was sixty years old. I handled this amazing antiquity with the greatest possible tenderness, lest it should dissolve in my hands. Within, Towson or Towser was inquiring earnestly into the breaking strain of ships' chains and tackle, and other such matters. Not a very enthralling book; but at the first glance you could see there a singleness of intention, an honest concern for the right way of going to work, which made these humble pages, thought out so many years ago, luminous with another than a professional light. The simple old sailor, with his talk of chains and purchases,[3] made me forget the jungle and the pilgrims in a delicious sensation of having come upon something unmistakably real. Such a book being there was wonderful enough; but still more astounding were the notes penciled in the margin, and plainly referring to the text. I couldn't believe my eyes! They were in cipher! Yes, it looked like cipher. Fancy a man lugging

3. Leverages.

with him a book of that description into this nowhere and studying it—and making notes—in cipher at that! It was an extravagant mystery.

"I had been dimly aware for some time of a worrying noise, and when I lifted my eyes I saw the woodpile was gone, and the manager, aided by all the pilgrims, was shouting at me from the river-side. I slipped the book into my pocket. I assure you to leave off reading was like tearing myself away from the shelter of an old and solid friendship.

"I started the lame engine ahead. 'It must be this miserable trader—this intruder,' exclaimed the manager, looking back malevolently at the place we had left. 'He must be English,' I said. 'It will not save him from getting into trouble if he is not careful,' muttered the manager darkly. I observed with assumed innocence that no man was safe from trouble in this world.

"The current was more rapid now, the steamer seemed at her last gasp, the stern-wheel flopped languidly, and I caught myself listening on tiptoe for the next beat of the float,[4] for in sober truth I expected the wretched thing to give up every moment. It was like watching the last flickers of a life. But still we crawled. Sometimes I would pick out a tree a little way ahead to measure our progress towards Kurtz by, but I lost it invariably before we got abreast. To keep the eyes so long on one thing was too much for human patience. The manager displayed a beautiful resignation. I fretted and fumed and took to arguing with myself whether or no I would talk openly with Kurtz; but before I could come to any conclusion it occurred to me that my speech or my silence, indeed any action of mine, would be a mere futility. What did it matter what anyone knew or ignored? What did it matter who was manager? One gets sometimes such a flash of insight. The essentials of this affair lay deep under the surface, beyond my reach, and beyond my power of meddling.

"Towards the evening of the second day we judged ourselves about eight miles from Kurtz's station. I wanted to push on; but the manager looked grave, and told me the navigation up there was so dangerous that it would be advisable, the sun being very low already, to wait where we were till next morning. Moreover, he pointed out that if the warning to approach cautiously were to be followed, we must approach in daylight—not at dusk, or in the dark. This was sensible enough. Eight miles meant nearly three hours' steaming for us, and I could also see suspicious ripples at the upper end of the reach. Nevertheless, I was annoyed beyond expression at the delay, and most unreasonably, too, since one night more could not matter much after so many months. As we had plenty of wood, and caution was the word, I brought up in the middle of the stream. The reach was narrow, straight, with high sides like a railway cutting. The dusk came gliding into it long before the sun had set. The current ran smooth and swift, but a dumb immobility sat on the banks. The living trees, lashed together by the creepers and every living bush of the undergrowth, might have been changed into stone, even to the slenderest twig, to the lightest leaf. It was not sleep—it seemed unnatural, like a state of trance. Not the faintest sound of any kind could be heard. You looked on amazed, and began to suspect yourself of being deaf—then the night came suddenly, and struck you blind as

4. A blade of the multibladed paddle wheel.

well. About three in the morning some large fish leaped, and the loud splash made me jump as though a gun had been fired. When the sun rose there was a white fog, very warm and clammy, and more blinding than the night. It did not shift or drive; it was just there, standing all around you like something solid. At eight or nine, perhaps, it lifted as a shutter lifts. We had a glimpse of the towering multitude of trees, of the immense matted jungle, with the blazing little ball of the sun hanging over it—all perfectly still—and then the white shutter came down again, smoothly, as if sliding in greased grooves. I ordered the chain, which we had begun to heave in, to be paid out again. Before it stopped running with a muffled rattle, a cry, a very loud cry, as of infinite desolation, soared slowly in the opaque air. It ceased. A complaining clamor, modulated in savage discords, filled our ears. The sheer unexpectedness of it made my hair stir under my cap. I don't know how it struck the others: to me it seemed as though the mist itself had screamed, so suddenly, and apparently from all sides at once, did this tumultuous and mournful uproar arise. It culminated in a hurried outbreak of almost intolerably excessive shrieking, which stopped short, leaving us stiffened in a variety of silly attitudes, and obstinately listening to the nearly as appalling and excessive silence. 'Good God! What is the meaning—' stammered at my elbow one of the pilgrims,—a little fat man, with sandy hair and red whiskers, who wore side-spring boots, and pink pajamas tucked into his socks. Two others remained open-mouthed a whole minute, then dashed into the little cabin, to rush out incontinently and stand darting scared glances, with Winchesters[5] at 'ready' in their hands. What we could see was just the steamer we were on, her outlines blurred as though she had been on the point of dissolving, and a misty strip of water, perhaps two feet broad, around her—and that was all. The rest of the world was nowhere, as far as our eyes and ears were concerned. Just nowhere. Gone, disappeared; swept off without leaving a whisper or a shadow behind.

"I went forward, and ordered the chain to be hauled in short, so as to be ready to trip the anchor and move the steamboat at once if necessary. 'Will they attack?' whispered an awed voice. 'We will be all butchered in this fog,' murmured another. The faces twitched with the strain, the hands trembling slightly, the eyes forgot to wink. It was very curious to see the contrast of expressions of the white men and of the black fellows of our crew, who were as much strangers to that part of the river as we, though their homes were only eight hundred miles away. The whites, of course, greatly discomposed, had besides a curious look of being painfully shocked by such an outrageous row. The others had an alert, naturally interested expression; but their faces were essentially quiet, even those of the one or two who grinned as they hauled at the chain. Several exchanged short, grunting phrases, which seemed to settle the matter to their satisfaction. Their headman, a young, broad-chested black, severely draped in dark-blue fringed cloths, with fierce nostrils and his hair all done up artfully in oily ringlets, stood near me. 'Aha!' I said, just for good fellowship's sake. 'Catch 'em,' he snapped, with a bloodshot widening of his eyes and a flash of sharp teeth—'catch 'im. Give 'im to us.' 'To you, eh?' I asked;

5. American repeating rifles.

'what would you do with them?' 'Eat 'em!' he said, curtly, and, leaning his elbow on the rail, looked out into the fog in a dignified and profoundly pensive attitude. I would no doubt have been properly horrified, had it not occurred to me that he and his chaps must be very hungry: that they must have been growing increasingly hungry for at least this month past. They had been engaged for six months (I don't think a single one of them had any clear idea of time, as we at the end of countless ages have. They still belonged to the beginnings of time—had no inherited experience to teach them as it were), and of course, as long as there was a piece of paper written over in accordance with some farcical law or other made down the river, it didn't enter anybody's head to trouble how they would live. Certainly they had brought with them some rotten hippo-meat, which couldn't have lasted very long, anyway, even if the pilgrims hadn't, in the midst of a shocking hullabaloo, thrown a considerable quantity of it overboard. It looked like a high-handed proceeding; but it was really a case of legitimate self-defense. You can't breathe dead hippo waking, sleeping, and eating, and at the same time keep your precarious grip on existence. Besides that, they had given them every week three pieces of brass wire, each about nine inches long; and the theory was they were to buy their provisions with that currency in riverside villages. You can see how *that* worked. There were either no villages, or the people were hostile, or the director, who like the rest of us fed out of tins, with an occasional old he-goat thrown in, didn't want to stop the steamer for some more or less recondite reason. So, unless they swallowed the wire itself, or made loops of it to snare the fishes with, I don't see what good their extravagant salary could be to them. I must say it was paid with a regularity worthy of a large and honorable trading company. For the rest, the only thing to eat—though it didn't look eatable in the least—I saw in their possession was a few lumps of some stuff like half-cooked dough, of a dirty lavender color, they kept wrapped in leaves, and now and then swallowed a piece of, but so small that it seemed done more for the looks of the thing than for any serious purpose of sustenance. Why in the name of all the gnawing devils of hunger they didn't go for us—they were thirty to five—and have a good tuck-in[6] for once, amazes me now when I think of it. They were big powerful men, with not much capacity to weigh the consequences, with courage, with strength, even yet, though their skins were no longer glossy and their muscles no longer hard. And I saw that something restraining, one of those human secrets that baffle probability, had come into play there. I looked at them with a swift quickening of interest—not because it occurred to me I might be eaten by them before very long, though I own to you that just then I perceived—in a new light, as it were—how unwholesome the pilgrims looked, and I hoped, yes, I positively hoped, that my aspect was not so—what shall I say?—so—unappetizing: a touch of fantastic vanity which fitted well with the dream-sensation that pervaded all my days at that time. Perhaps I had a little fever, too. One can't live with one's finger everlastingly on one's pulse. I had often 'a little fever,' or a little touch of other things—the playful paw-strokes of the wilderness, the preliminary trifling before the more serious onslaught which

6. British slang for a good meal.

came in due course. Yes; I looked at them as you would on any human being, with a curiosity of their impulses, motives, capacities, weaknesses, when brought to the test of an inexorable physical necessity. Restraint! What possible restraint? Was it superstition, disgust, patience, fear—or some kind of primitive honor? No fear can stand up to hunger, no patience can wear it out, disgust simply does not exist where hunger is; and as to superstition, beliefs, and what you may call principles, they are less than chaff in a breeze. Don't you know the devilry of lingering starvation, its exasperating torment, its black thoughts, its somber and brooding ferocity? Well, I do. It takes a man all his inborn strength to fight hunger properly. It's really easier to face bereavement, dishonor, and the perdition of one's soul—than this kind of prolonged hunger. Sad, but true. And these chaps, too, had no earthly reason for any kind of scruple. Restraint! I would just as soon have expected restraint from a hyena prowling amongst the corpses of a battlefield. But there was the fact facing me—the fact dazzling, to be seen, like the foam on the depths of the sea, like a ripple on an unfathomable enigma, a mystery greater—when I thought of it—than the curious, inexplicable note of desperate grief in this savage clamor that had swept by us on the river-bank, behind the blind whiteness of the fog.

"Two pilgrims were quarreling in hurried whispers as to which bank. 'Left.' 'No, no; how can you? Right, right, of course.' 'It is very serious,' said the manager's voice behind me; 'I would be desolated if anything should happen to Mr. Kurtz before we came up.' I looked at him, and had not the slightest doubt he was sincere. He was just the kind of man who would wish to preserve appearances. That was his restraint. But when he muttered something about going on at once, I did not even take the trouble to answer him. I knew, and he knew, that it was impossible. Were we to let go our hold of the bottom, we would be absolutely in the air—in space. We wouldn't be able to tell where we were going to—whether up or down stream, or across—till we fetched against one bank or the other,—and then we wouldn't know at first which it was. Of course I made no move. I had no mind for a smash-up. You couldn't imagine a more deadly place for a shipwreck. Whether drowned at once or not, we were sure to perish speedily in one way or another. 'I authorize you to take all the risks,' he said, after a short silence. 'I refuse to take any,' I said, shortly; which was just the answer he expected, though its tone might have surprised him. 'Well, I must defer to your judgment. You are captain,' he said, with marked civility. I turned my shoulder to him in sign of my appreciation, and looked into the fog. How long would it last? It was the most hopeless lookout. The approach to this Kurtz grubbing for ivory in the wretched bush was beset by as many dangers as though he had been an enchanted princess sleeping in a fabulous castle. 'Will they attack, do you think?' asked the manager, in a confidential tone.

"I did not think they would attack, for several obvious reasons. The thick fog was one. If they left the bank in their canoes they would get lost in it, as we would be if we attempted to move. Still, I had also judged the jungle of both banks quite impenetrable—and yet eyes were in it, eyes that had seen us. The river-side bushes were certainly very thick; but the undergrowth behind was evidently penetrable. However, during the short lift I had seen no canoes anywhere in the reach—certainly not abreast of the steamer. But what made the idea of attack inconceivable to me was the nature of the noise—of the cries we had heard. They had not the fierce character boding immediate hostile intention. Unexpected, wild, and violent as they had been, they had given me an irresistible impression of sorrow. The glimpse of the steamboat had for some reason filled those savages with unrestrained grief. The danger, if any, I expounded, was from our proximity to a great human passion let loose. Even extreme grief may ultimately vent itself in violence—but more generally takes the form of apathy. . . .

"You should have seen the pilgrims stare! They had no heart to grin, or even to revile me: but I believe they thought me gone mad—with fright, maybe. I delivered a regular lecture. My dear boys, it was no good bothering. Keep a look-out? Well, you may guess I watched the fog for the signs of lifting as a cat watches a mouse; but for anything else our eyes were of no more use to us than if we had been buried miles deep in a heap of cotton-wool. It felt like it, too—choking, warm, stifling. Besides, all I said, though it sounded extravagant, was absolutely true to fact. What we afterwards alluded to as an attack was really an attempt at repulse. The action was very far from being aggressive—it was not even defensive, in the usual sense: it was undertaken under the stress of desperation, and in its essence was purely protective.

"It developed itself, I should say, two hours after the fog lifted, and its commencement was at a spot, roughly speaking, about a mile and a half below Kurtz's station. We had just floundered and flopped round a bend, when I saw an islet, a mere grassy hummock of bright green, in the middle of the stream. It was the only thing of the kind; but as we opened the reach more, I perceived it was the head of a long sandbank, or rather of a chain of shallow patches stretching down the middle of the river. They were discolored, just awash, and the whole lot was seen just under the water, exactly as a man's backbone is seen running down the middle of his back under the skin. Now, as far as I did see, I could go to the right or to the left of this. I didn't know either channel, of course. The banks looked pretty well alike, the depth appeared the same; but as I had been informed the station was on the west side, I naturally headed for the western passage.

"No sooner had we fairly entered it than I became aware it was much narrower than I had supposed. To the left of us there was the long uninterrupted shoal, and to the right a high, steep bank heavily overgrown with bushes. Above the bush the trees stood in serried ranks. The twigs overhung the current thickly, and from distance to distance a large limb of some tree projected rigidly over the stream. It was then well on in the afternoon, the face of the forest was gloomy, and a broad strip of shadow had already fallen on the water. In this shadow we steamed up—very slowly, as you may imagine. I sheered her well inshore—the water being deepest near the bank, as the sounding-pole informed me.

"One of my hungry and forbearing friends was sounding[7] in the bows just below me. This steamboat was exactly like a decked scow. On the deck, there

7. Measuring water depth with a sounding line.

were two little teak-wood houses, with doors and windows. The boiler was in the fore-end, and the machinery right astern. Over the whole there was a light roof, supported on stanchions. The funnel projected through that roof, and in front of the funnel a small cabin built of light planks served for a pilot-house. It contained a couch, two campstools, a loaded Martini-Henry[8] leaning in one corner, a tiny table, and the steering-wheel. It had a wide door in front and a broad shutter at each side. All these were always thrown open, of course. I spent my days perched up there on the extreme fore-end of that roof, before the door. At night I slept, or tried to, on the couch. An athletic black belonging to some coast tribe, and educated by my poor predecessor, was the helmsman. He sported a pair of brass earrings, wore a blue cloth wrapper from the waist to the ankles, and thought all the world of himself. He was the most unstable kind of fool I had ever seen. He steered with no end of a swagger while you were by; but if he lost sight of you, he became instantly the prey of an abject funk, and would let that cripple of a steamboat get the upper hand of him in a minute.

"I was looking down at the sounding-pole, and feeling much annoyed to see at each try a little more of it stick out of that river, when I saw my poleman give up the business suddenly, and stretch himself flat on the deck, without even taking the trouble to haul his pole in. He kept hold on it though, and it trailed in the water. At the same time the fireman, whom I could also see below me, sat down abruptly before his furnace and ducked his head. I was amazed. Then I had to look at the river mighty quick, because there was a snag in the fairway. Sticks, little sticks, were flying about—thick: they were whizzing before my nose, dropping below me, striking behind me against my pilot-house. All this time the river, the shore, the woods, were very quiet—perfectly quiet. I could only hear the heavy splashing thump of the stern-wheel and the patter of these things. We cleared the snag clumsily. Arrows, by Jove! We were being shot at! I stepped in quickly to close the shutter on the land-side. That fool-helmsman, his hands on the spokes, was lifting his knees high, stamping his feet, champing his mouth, like a reined-in horse. Confound him! And we were staggering within ten feet of the bank. I had to lean right out to swing the heavy shutter, and I saw a face amongst the leaves on the level with my own, looking at me very fierce and steady; and then suddenly, as though a veil had been removed from my eyes, I made out, deep in the tangled gloom, naked breasts, arms, legs, glaring eyes,—the bush was swarming with human limbs in movement, glistening, of bronze color. The twigs shook, swayed, and rustled, the arrows flew out of them, and then the shutter came to. 'Steer her straight,' I said to the helmsman. He held his head rigid, face forward; but his eyes rolled, he kept on lifting and setting down his feet gently, his mouth foamed a little. 'Keep quiet!' I said in a fury. I might just as well have ordered a tree not to sway in the wind. I darted out. Below me there was a great scuffle of feet on the iron deck; confused exclamations; a voice screamed, 'Can you turn back?' I caught sight of a V-shaped ripple on the water ahead. What? Another snag! A fusillade burst out under my feet. The pilgrims had opened with their Win-

8. Heavy military rifle.

chesters, and were simply squirting lead into that bush. A deuce of a lot of smoke came up and drove slowly forward. I swore at it. Now I couldn't see the ripple or the snag either. I stood in the doorway, peering, and the arrows came in swarms. They might have been poisoned, but they looked as though they wouldn't kill a cat. The bush began to howl. Our wood-cutters raised a warlike whoop; the report of a rifle just at my back deafened me. I glanced over my shoulder, and the pilot-house was yet full of noise and smoke when I made a dash at the wheel. The fool-nigger had dropped everything to throw the shutter open and let off[9] that Martini-Henry. He stood before the wide opening, glaring, and I yelled at him to come back, while I straightened the sudden twist out of that steamboat. There was no room to turn even if I had wanted to, the snag was somewhere very near ahead in that confounded smoke, there was no time to lose, so I just crowded her into the bank—right into the bank, where I knew the water was deep.

"We tore slowly along the overhanging bushes in a whirl of broken twigs and flying leaves. The fusillade below stopped short, as I had foreseen it would when the squirts got empty. I threw my head back to a glinting whizz that traversed the pilot-house, in at one shutter-hole and out at the other. Looking past that mad helmsman, who was shaking the empty rifle and yelling at the shore, I saw vague forms of men running bent double, leaping, gliding, distinct, incomplete, evanescent. Something big appeared in the air before the shutter, the rifle went overboard, and the man stepped back swiftly, looked at me over his shoulder in an extraordinary, profound, familiar manner, and fell upon my feet. The side of his head hit the wheel twice, and the end of what appeared a long cane clattered round and knocked over a little campstool. It looked as though after wrenching that thing from somebody ashore he had lost his balance in the effort. The thin smoke had blown away, we were clear of the snag, and looking ahead I could see that in another hundred yards or so I would be free to sheer off, away from the bank; but my feet felt so very warm and wet that I had to look down. The man had rolled on his back and stared straight up at me; both his hands clutched that cane. It was the shaft of a spear that, either thrown or lunged through the opening, had caught him in the side just below the ribs; the blade had gone in out of sight, after making a frightful gash; my shoes were full; a pool of blood lay very still, gleaming dark-red under the wheel; his eyes shone with an amazing luster. The fusillade burst out again. He looked at me anxiously, gripping the spear like something precious, with an air of being afraid I would try to take it away from him. I had to make an effort to free my eyes from his gaze and attend to steering. With one hand I felt above my head for the line of the steam-whistle, and jerked out screech after screech hurriedly. The tumult of angry and warlike yells was checked instantly, and then from the depths of the woods went out such a tremulous and prolonged wail of mournful fear and utter despair as may be imagined to follow the flight of the last hope from the earth. There was a great commotion in the bush; the shower of arrows stopped, a few dropping shots rang out sharply—then silence, in which the languid beat of the stern-wheel came plainly to my ears. I put the helm hard

9. Fire.

a-starboard at the moment when the pilgrim in pink pajamas, very hot and agitated, appeared in the doorway. 'The manager sends me—' he began in an official tone, and stopped short. 'Good God!' he said, glaring at the wounded man.

"We two whites stood over him, and his lustrous and inquiring glance enveloped us both. I declare it looked as though he would presently put to us some question in an understandable language; but he died without uttering a sound, without moving a limb, without twitching a muscle. Only in the very last moment, as though in response to some sign we could not see, to some whisper we could not hear, he frowned heavily, and that frown gave to his black death-mask an inconceivably somber, brooding, and menacing expression. The luster of inquiring glance faded swiftly into vacant glassiness. 'Can you steer?' I asked the agent eagerly. He looked very dubious; but I made a grab at his arm, and he understood at once I meant him to steer whether or no. To tell you the truth, I was morbidly anxious to change my shoes and socks. 'He is dead,' murmured the fellow, immensely impressed. 'No doubt about it,' said I tugging like mad at the shoe-laces. 'And by the way, I suppose Mr. Kurtz is dead as well by this time.'

"For the moment that was the dominant thought. There was a sense of extreme disappointment, as though I had found out I had been striving after something altogether without a substance. I couldn't have been more disgusted if I had traveled all this way for the sole purpose of talking with Mr. Kurtz. Talking with . . . I flung one shoe overboard, and became aware that that was exactly what I had been looking forward to—a talk with Kurtz. I made the strange discovery that I had never imagined him as doing, you know, but as discoursing. I didn't say to myself, 'Now I will never see him,' or 'Now I will never shake him by the hand,' but, 'Now I will never hear him.' The man presented himself as a voice. Not of course that I did not connect him with some sort of action. Hadn't I been told in all the tones of jealousy and admiration that he had collected, bartered, swindled, or stolen more ivory than all the other agents together? That was not the point. The point was in his being a gifted creature, and that of all his gifts the one that stood out preeminently, that carried with it a sense of real presence, was his ability to talk, his words—the gift of expression, the bewildering, the illuminating, the most exalted and the most contemptible, the pulsating stream of light, or the deceitful flow from the heart of an impenetrable darkness.

"The other shoe went flying unto the devil-god of that river. I thought, by Jove! it's all over. We are too late; he has vanished—the gift has vanished, by means of some spear, arrow, or club. I will never hear that chap speak after all,—and my sorrow had a startling extravagance of emotion, even such as I had noticed in the howling sorrow of these savages in the bush. I couldn't have felt more lonely desolation somehow, had I been robbed of a belief or had missed my destiny in life. . . . Why do you sigh in this beastly way, somebody? Absurd? Well, absurd. Good Lord! mustn't a man ever—Here, give me some tobacco." . . .

There was a pause of profound stillness, then a match flared, and Marlow's lean face appeared, worn, hollow, with downward folds and drooped eyelids, with an aspect of concentrated attention; and as he took vigorous draws at his pipe, it seemed to retreat and advance out of the night in the regular flicker of the tiny flame. The match went out.

"Absurd!" he cried. "This is the worst of trying to tell. . . . Here you all are, each moored with two good addresses, like a hulk with two anchors, a butcher round one corner, a policeman round another, excellent appetites, and temperature normal—you hear—normal from year's end to year's end. And you say, Absurd! Absurd be—exploded! Absurd! My dear boys, what can you expect from a man who out of sheer nervousness had just flung overboard a pair of new shoes? Now I think of it, it is amazing I did not shed tears. I am, upon the whole, proud of my fortitude. I was cut to the quick at the idea of having lost the inestimable privilege of listening to the gifted Kurtz. Of course I was wrong. The privilege was waiting for me. Oh yes, I heard more than enough. And I was right, too. A voice. He was very little more than a voice. And I heard—him—it—this voice—other voices—all of them were so little more than voices—and the memory of that time itself lingers around me, impalpable, like a dying vibration of one immense jabber, silly, atrocious, sordid, savage, or simply mean, without any kind of sense. Voices, voices—even the girl herself—now—"

He was silent for a long time.

"I laid the ghost of his gifts at last with a lie," he began, suddenly. "Girl! What? Did I mention a girl? Oh, she is out of it—completely. They—the women I mean—are out of it—should be out of it. We must help them to stay in that beautiful world of their own, lest ours gets worse. Oh, she had to be out of it. You should have heard the disinterred body of Mr. Kurtz saying, 'My Intended.' You would have perceived directly then how completely she was out of it. And the lofty frontal bone of Mr. Kurtz! They say the hair goes on growing sometimes, but this—ah—specimen, was impressively bald. The wilderness had patted him on the head, and, behold, it was like a ball—an ivory ball; it had caressed him, and—lo!—he had withered; it had taken him, loved him, embraced him, got into his veins, consumed his flesh, and sealed his soul to its own by the inconceivable ceremonies of some devilish initiation. He was its spoiled and pampered favorite. Ivory? I should think so. Heaps of it, stacks of it. The old mud shanty was bursting with it. You would think here was not a single tusk left either above or below the ground in the whole country. 'Mostly fossil,' the manager had remarked, disparagingly. It was no more fossil than I am; but they call it fossil when it is dug up. It appears these niggers do bury the tusks sometimes—but evidently they couldn't bury this parcel deep enough to save the gifted Mr. Kurtz from his fate. We filled the steamboat with it, and had to pile a lot on the deck. Thus he could see and enjoy as long as he could see, because the appreciation of this favor had remained with him to the last. You should have heard him say, 'My ivory.' Oh yes, I heard him. 'My Intended, my ivory, my station, my river, my—' everything belonged to him. It made me hold my breath in expectation of hearing the wilderness burst into a prodigious peal of laughter that would shake the fixed stars in their places. Everything belonged to him—but that was a trifle. The thing was to know what he belonged to, how many powers of darkness claimed him for their own. That was the reflection that made you creepy all over. It was impossible—it was not good for one either—trying to imagine. He had taken a high seat amongst the devils of the land—I mean literally. You can't understand. How could you?—with solid pavement under your feet, surrounded by kind neighbors ready to cheer you or to fall on you, stepping delicately between the butcher and the policeman, in the holy terror of scandal and gallows and lunatic asylums—how can you imagine what particular region of the first ages a man's untrammeled feet may take him into by the way of solitude—utter solitude without a policeman—by the way of silence—utter silence, where no warning voice of a kind neighbor can be heard whispering of public opinion? These little things make all the great difference. When they are gone you must fall back upon your own innate strength, upon your own capacity for faithfulness. Of course you may be too much of a fool to go wrong—too dull even to know you are being assaulted by the powers of darkness. I take it, no fool ever made a bargain for his soul with the devil: the fool is too much of a fool, or the devil too much of a devil—I don't know which. Or you may be such a thunderingly exalted creature as to be altogether deaf and blind to anything but heavenly sights and sounds. Then the earth for you is only a standing place—and whether to be like this is your loss or your gain I won't pretend to say. But most of us are neither one nor the other. The earth for us is a place to live in, where we must put up with sights, with sounds, with smells, too, by Jove!—breathe dead hippo, so to speak, and not be contaminated. And there, don't you see? your strength comes in, the faith in your ability for the digging of unostentatious holes to bury the stuff in—your power of devotion, not to yourself, but to an obscure, back-breaking business. And that's difficult enough. Mind, I am not trying to excuse or even explain—I am trying to account to myself for—for—Mr. Kurtz—for the shade of Mr. Kurtz. This initiated wraith from the back of Nowhere honored me with its amazing confidence before it vanished altogether. This was because it could speak English to me. The original Kurtz had been educated partly in England, and—as he was good enough to say himself—his sympathies were in the right place. His mother was half-English, his father was half-French. All Europe contributed to the making of Kurtz; and by and by I learned that, most appropriately, the International Society for the Suppression of Savage Customs had intrusted him with the making of a report, for its future guidance. And he had written it, too. I've seen it. I've read it. It was eloquent, vibrating with eloquence, but too high-strung, I think. Seventeen pages of close writing he had found time for! But this must have been before his—let us say—nerves, went wrong, and caused him to preside at certain midnight dances ending with unspeakable rites, which—as far as I reluctantly gathered from what I heard at various times—were offered up to him—do you understand?—to Mr. Kurtz himself. But it was a beautiful piece of writing. The opening paragraph, however, in the light of later information, strikes me now as ominous. He began with the argument that we whites, from the point of development we had arrived at, 'must necessarily appear to them [savages] in the nature of supernatural beings—we approach them with the might as of a deity,' and so on, and so on. 'By the simple exercise of our will we can exert a power for good practically unbounded,' etc., etc. From that point he soared and took me with him.

The peroration was magnificent, though difficult to remember, you know. It gave me the notion of an exotic Immensity ruled by an august Benevolence. It made me tingle with enthusiasm. This was the unbounded power of eloquence—of words—of burning noble words. There were no practical hints to interrupt the magic current of phrases, unless a kind of note at the foot of the last page, scrawled evidently much later, in an unsteady hand, may be regarded as the exposition of a method. It was very simple, and at the end of that moving appeal to every altruistic sentiment it blazed at you, luminous and terrifying, like a flash of lightning in a serene sky: 'Exterminate all the brutes!' The curious part was that he had apparently forgotten all about that valuable postscriptum, because, later on, when he in a sense came to himself, he repeatedly entreated me to take good care of 'my pamphlet' (he called it), as it was sure to have in the future a good influence upon his career. I had full information about all these things, and, besides, as it turned out, I was to have the care of his memory. I've done enough for it to give me the indisputable right to lay it, if I choose, for an everlasting rest in the dust-bin of progress, amongst all the sweepings and, figuratively speaking, all the dead cats of civilization. But then, you see, I can't choose. He won't be forgotten. Whatever he was, he was not common. He had the power to charm or frighten rudimentary souls into an aggravated witch-dance in his honor; he could also fill the small souls of the pilgrims with bitter misgivings: he had one devoted friend at least, and he had conquered one soul in the world that was neither rudimentary nor tainted with self-seeking. No; I can't forget him, though I am not prepared to affirm the fellow was exactly worth the life we lost in getting to him. I missed my late helmsman awfully,—I missed him even while his body was still lying in the pilot-house. Perhaps you will think it passing strange this regret for a savage who was no more account than a grain of sand in a black Sahara. Well, don't you see, he had done something, he had steered; for months I had him at my back—a help—an instrument. It was a kind of partnership. He steered for me—I had to look after him, I worried about his deficiencies, and thus a subtle bond had been created, of which I only became aware when it was suddenly broken. And the intimate profundity of that look he gave me when he received his hurt remains to this day in my memory—like a claim of distant kinship affirmed in a supreme moment.

"Poor fool! If he had only left that shutter alone. He had no restraint, no restraint—just like Kurtz—a tree swayed by the wind. As soon as I had put on a dry pair of slippers, I dragged him out, after first jerking the spear out of his side, which operation I confess I performed with my eyes shut tight. His heels leaped together over the little doorstep; his shoulders were pressed to my breast; I hugged him from behind desperately. Oh! he was heavy, heavy; heavier than any man on earth, I should imagine. Then without more ado I tipped him overboard. The current snatched him as though he had been a wisp of grass, and I saw the body roll over twice before I lost sight of it forever. All the pilgrims and the manager were then congregated on the awning-deck about the pilot-house, chattering at each other like a flock of excited magpies, and there was a scandalized murmur at my heartless promptitude. What they wanted to keep that body hanging about for I can't guess. Embalm it, maybe. But I had also heard another, and a very ominous, murmur on the deck below. My friends the wood-cutters were likewise scandalized, and with a better show of reason—though I admit that the reason itself was quite inadmissible. Oh, quite! I had made up my mind that if my late helmsman was to be eaten, the fishes alone should have him. He had been a very second-rate helmsman while alive, but now he was dead he might have become a first-class temptation, and possibly cause some startling trouble. Besides, I was anxious to take the wheel, the man in pink pajamas showing himself a hopeless duffer at the business.

"This I did directly the simple funeral was over. We were going half-speed, keeping right in the middle of the stream, and I listened to the talk about me. They had given up Kurtz, they had given up the station; Kurtz was dead, and the station had been burnt—and so on—and so on. The red-haired pilgrim was beside himself with the thought that at least this poor Kurtz had been properly avenged. 'Say! We must have made a glorious slaughter of them in the bush. Eh? What do you think? Say?' He positively danced, the bloodthirsty little gingery beggar.[1] And he had nearly fainted when he saw the wounded man! I could not help saying, 'You made a glorious lot of smoke, anyhow.' I had seen, from the way the tops of the bushes rustled and flew, that almost all the shots had gone too high. You can't hit anything unless you take aim and fire from the shoulder; but these chaps fired from the hip with their eyes shut. The retreat, I maintained—and I was right—was caused by the screeching of the steam-whistle. Upon this they forgot Kurtz, and began to howl at me with indignant protests.

"The manager stood by the wheel murmuring confidentially about the necessity of getting well away down the river before dark at all events, when I saw in the distance a clearing on the river-side and the outlines of some sort of building. 'What's this?' I asked. He clapped his hands in wonder. 'The station!' he cried. I edged in at once, still going half-speed.

"Through my glasses I saw the slope of a hill interspersed with rare trees and perfectly free from undergrowth. A long decaying building on the summit was half buried in the high grass; the large holes in the peaked roof gaped black from afar; the jungle and the woods made a background. There was no enclosure or fence of any kind; but there had been one apparently, for near the house half-a-dozen slim posts remained in a row, roughly trimmed, and with their upper ends ornamented with round carved balls. The rails, or whatever there had been between, had disappeared. Of course the forest surrounded all that. The river-bank was clear, and on the water-side I saw a white man under a hat like a cart-wheel beckoning persistently with his whole arm. Examining the edge of the forest above and below, I was almost certain I could see movements—human forms gliding here and there. I steamed past prudently, then stopped the engines and let her drift down. The man on the shore began to shout, urging us to land. 'We have been attacked,' screamed the manager. 'I know—I know. It's all right,' yelled back the other, as cheerful as you please. 'Come along. It's all right. I am glad.'

"His aspect reminded me of something I had seen—something funny I

1. British slang for redheaded rascal.

had seen somewhere. As I maneuvered to get alongside, I was asking myself, 'What does this fellow look like?' Suddenly I got it. He looked like a harlequin. His clothes had been made of some stuff that was brown holland probably, but it was covered with patches all over, with bright patches, blue, red, and yellow,—patches on the back, patches on the front, patches on elbows, on knees; colored binding around his jacket, scarlet edging at the bottom of his trousers; and the sunshine made him look extremely gay and wonderfully neat withal, because you could see how beautifully all this patching had been done. A beardless, boyish face, very fair, no features to speak of, nose peeling, little blue eyes, smiles and frowns chasing each other over that open countenance like sunshine and shadow on a windswept plain. 'Look out, captain!' he cried; 'there's a snag lodged in here last night.' What! Another snag? I confess I swore shamefully. I had nearly holed my cripple, to finish off that charming trip. The harlequin on the bank turned his little pug-nose up to me. 'You English?' he asked, all smiles. 'Are you?' I shouted from the wheel. The smiles vanished, and he shook his head as if sorry for my disappointment. Then he brightened up. 'Never mind!' he cried, encouragingly. 'Are we in time?' I asked. 'He is up there,' he replied, with a toss of the head up the hill, and becoming gloomy all of a sudden. His face was like the autumn sky, overcast one moment and bright the next.

"When the manager, escorted by the pilgrims, all of them armed to the teeth, had gone to the house this chap came on board. 'I say, I don't like this. These natives are in the bush,' I said. He assured me earnestly it was all right. 'They are simple people,' he added; 'well, I am glad you came. It took me all my time to keep them off.' 'But you said it was all right,' I cried. 'Oh, they meant no harm,' he said; and as I stared he corrected himself, 'Not exactly.' Then vivaciously, 'My faith, your pilot-house wants a clean-up!' In the next breath he advised me to keep enough steam on the boiler to blow the whistle in case of any trouble. 'One good screech will do more for you than all your rifles. They are simple people,' he repeated. He rattled away at such a rate he quite overwhelmed me. He seemed to be trying to make up for lots of silence, and actually hinted, laughing, that such was the case. 'Don't you talk with Mr. Kurtz?' I said. 'You don't talk with that man—you listen to him,' he exclaimed with severe exaltation. 'But now—' He waved his arm, and in the twinkling of an eye was in the uttermost depths of despondency. In a moment he came up again with a jump, possessed himself of both my hands, shook them continuously, while he gabbled: 'Brother sailor . . . honor . . . pleasure . . . delight . . . introduce myself . . . Russian . . . son of an arch-priest . . . Government of Tambov. . . . What? Tobacco! English tobacco; the excellent English tobacco! Now, that's brotherly. Smoke? Where's a sailor that does not smoke?'

"The pipe soothed him, and gradually I made out he had run away from school, had gone to sea in a Russian ship; ran away again; served some time in English ships; was now reconciled with the arch-priest. He made a point of that. 'But when one is young one must see things, gather experience, ideas; enlarge the mind.' 'Here!' I interrupted. 'You can never tell! Here I met Mr. Kurtz,' he said, youthfully solemn and reproachful. I held my tongue after that. It appears he had persuaded a Dutch trading-house on the coast to fit him out with stores and goods, and had started for the interior with a light heart, and no more idea of what would happen to him than a baby. He had been wandering about that river for nearly two years alone, cut off from everybody and everything. 'I am not so young as I look. I am twenty-five,' he said. 'At first old Van Shuyten would tell me to go to the devil,' he narrated with keen enjoyment; 'but I stuck to him, and talked and talked, till at last he got afraid I would talk the hind-leg off his favorite dog, so he gave me some cheap things and a few guns, and told me he hoped he would never see my face again. Good old Dutchman, Van Shuyten. I've sent him one small lot of ivory a year ago, so that he can't call me a little thief when I get back. I hope he got it. And for the rest I don't care. I had some wood stacked for you. That was my old house. Did you see?'

"I gave him Towson's book. He made as though he would kiss me, but restrained himself. 'The only book I had left, and I thought I had lost it,' he said, looking at it ecstatically. 'So many accidents happen to a man going about alone, you know. Canoes get upset sometimes—and sometimes you've got to clear out so quick when the people get angry.' He thumbed the pages. 'You made notes in Russian?' I asked. He nodded. 'I thought they were written in cipher,' I said. He laughed, then became serious. 'I had lots of trouble to keep these people off,' he said. 'Did they want to kill you?' I asked. 'Oh no!' he cried, and checked himself. 'Why did they attack us?' I pursued. He hesitated, then said shamefacedly, 'They don't want him to go.' 'Don't they?' I said curiously. He nodded a nod full of mystery and wisdom. 'I tell you,' he cried, 'this man has enlarged my mind.' He opened his arms wide, staring at me with his little blue eyes that were perfectly round."

## III

"I looked at him, lost in astonishment. There he was before me, in motley, as though he had absconded from a troupe of mimes, enthusiastic, fabulous. His very existence was improbable, inexplicable, and altogether bewildering. He was an insoluble problem. It was inconceivable how he had existed, how he had succeeded in getting so far, how he had managed to remain—why he did not instantly disappear. 'I went a little farther,' he said, 'then still a little farther—till I had gone so far that I don't know how I'll ever get back. Never mind. Plenty time. I can manage. You take Kurtz away quick—quick—I tell you.' The glamour of youth enveloped his parti-colored rags, his destitution, his loneliness, the essential desolation of his futile wanderings. For months—for years—his life hadn't been worth a day's purchase; and there he was gallantly, thoughtlessly alive, to all appearance indestructible solely by the virtue of his few years and of his unreflecting audacity. I was seduced into something like admiration—like envy. Glamour urged him on, glamour kept him unscathed. He surely wanted nothing from the wilderness but space to breathe in and to push on through. His need was to exist, and to move onwards at the greatest possible risk, and with a maximum of privation. If the absolutely pure, uncalculating, unpractical spirit of adventure had ever ruled a human being, it ruled this be-patched youth. I almost envied him the possession of this modest and clear flame. It seemed to have consumed all thought of self so completely, that even while he was talking to you, you forgot that it was he—the man before your eyes—who had gone through these things. I did not envy him his devotion to Kurtz, though. He had not meditated over it. It came to him and he accepted it with a sort of eager fatalism. I must say that to me it appeared about the most dangerous thing in every way he had come upon so far.

"They had come together unavoidably, like two ships becalmed near each other, and lay rubbing sides at last. I suppose Kurtz wanted an audience, because on a certain occasion, when encamped in the forest, they had talked all night, or more probably Kurtz had talked. 'We talked of everything,' he said, quite transported at the recollection. 'I forgot there was such a thing as sleep. The night did not seem to last an hour. Everything! Everything! . . . Of love, too.' 'Ah, he talked to you of love!' I said, much amused. 'It isn't what you think,' he cried, almost passionately. 'It was in general. He made me see things—things.'

"He threw his arms up. We were on deck at the time, and the headman of my wood-cutters, lounging near by, turned upon him his heavy and glittering eyes. I looked around, and I don't know why, but I assure you that never, never before, did this land, this river, this jungle, the very arch of this blazing sky, appear to me so hopeless and so dark, so impenetrable to human thought, so pitiless to human weakness. 'And, ever since, you have been with him, of course?' I said.

"On the contrary. It appears their intercourse had been very much broken by various causes. He had, as he informed me proudly, managed to nurse Kurtz through two illnesses (he alluded to it as you would to some risky feat), but as a rule Kurtz wandered alone far in the depths of the forest. 'Very often coming to this station, I had to wait days and days before he would turn up,' he said. 'Ah, it was worth waiting for!—sometimes.' 'What was he doing? exploring or what?' I asked. 'Oh, yes, of course'; he had discovered lots of villages, a lake, too—he did not know exactly in what direction; it was dangerous to inquire too much—but mostly his expeditions had been for ivory. 'But he had no goods to trade with by that time,' I objected. 'There's a good lot of cartridges left even yet,' he answered, looking away. 'To speak plainly, he raided the country,' I said. He nodded. 'Not alone, surely!' He muttered something about the villages round that lake. 'Kurtz got the tribe to follow him, did he?' I suggested. He fidgeted a little. 'They adored him,' he said. The tone of these words was so extraordinary that I looked at him searchingly. It was curious to see his mingled eagerness and reluctance to speak of Kurtz. The man filled his life, occupied his thoughts, swayed his emotions. 'What can you expect?' he burst out; 'he came to them with thunder and lightning, you know—and they had never seen anything like it—and very terrible. He could be very terrible. You can't judge Mr. Kurtz as you would an ordinary man. No, no, no! Now—just to give you an idea—I don't mind telling you, he wanted to shoot me, too, one day—but I don't judge him.' 'Shoot you!' I cried. 'What for?' 'Well, I had a small lot of ivory the chief of that village near my house gave me. You see I used to shoot game for them. Well, he wanted it, and wouldn't hear reason. He declared he would shoot me unless I gave him the ivory and then cleared out of the country, because he could do so, and had a fancy for it, and there was nothing on earth to prevent him killing whom he jolly well pleased. And it was true, too. I gave him the ivory. What did I care! But I didn't clear out. No, no. I couldn't leave him. I had to be careful, of course, till we got friendly again for a time. He had his second illness then. Afterwards I had to keep out of the way; but I didn't mind. He was living for the most part in those villages on the lake. When he came down to the river, sometimes he would take to me, and sometimes it was better for me to be careful. This man suffered too much. He hated all this, and somehow he couldn't get away. When I had a chance I begged him to try and leave while there was time; I offered to go back with him. And he would say yes, and then he would remain; go off on another ivory hunt; disappear for weeks; forget himself amongst these people—forget himself—you know.' 'Why! he's mad,' I said. He protested indignantly. Mr. Kurtz couldn't be mad. If I had heard him talk, only two days ago, I wouldn't dare hint at such a thing. . . . I had taken up my binoculars while we talked, and was looking at the shore, sweeping the limit of the forest at each side and at the back of the house. The consciousness of there being people in that bush, so silent, so quiet—as silent and quiet as the ruined house on the hill—made me uneasy. There was no sign on the face of nature of this amazing tale that was not so much told as suggested to me in desolate exclamations, completed by shrugs, in interrupted phrases, in hints ending in deep sighs. The woods were unmoved, like a mask—heavy, like the closed door of a prison—they looked with their air of hidden knowledge, of patient expectation, of unapproachable silence. The Russian was explaining to me that it was only lately that Mr. Kurtz had come down to the river, bringing along with him all the fighting men of that lake tribe. He had been absent for several months—getting himself adored, I suppose—and had come down unexpectedly, with the intention to all appearance of making a raid either across the river or down stream. Evidently the appetite for more ivory had got the better of the—what shall I say?—less material aspirations. However he had got much worse suddenly. 'I heard he was lying helpless, and so I came up—took my chance,' said the Russian. 'Oh, he is bad, very bad.' I directed my glass to the house. There were no signs of life, but there was the ruined roof, the long mud wall peeping above the grass, with three little square window-holes, no two of the same size; all this brought within reach of my hand, as it were. And then I made a brusque movement, and one of the remaining posts of that vanished fence leaped up in the field of my glass. You remember I told you I had been struck at the distance by certain attempts at ornamentation, rather remarkable in the ruinous aspect of the place. Now I had suddenly a nearer view, and its first result was to make me throw my head back as if before a blow. Then I went carefully from post to post with my glass, and I saw my mistake. These round knobs were not ornamental but symbolic; they were expressive and puzzling, striking and disturbing—food for thought and also for vultures if there had been any looking down from the sky; but at all events for such ants as were industrious enough to ascend the pole. They would have been even more impressive, those heads on the stakes, if their faces had not been turned to the house. Only one, the first I had made out, was facing my way. I was not so shocked as you may think. The start back I had given was really nothing but a movement of surprise. I had expected to see a knob of wood there, you know. I returned deliberately to the first I had seen—and there it was, black, dried, sunken, with closed eyelids,—a head that seemed to sleep at the top of that pole, and with the shrunken dry lips showing a narrow white line of the teeth, was smiling, too, smiling continuously at some endless and jocose dream of that eternal slumber.

"I am not disclosing any trade secrets. In fact, the manager said afterwards that Mr. Kurtz's methods had ruined the district. I have no opinion on that point, but I want you clearly to understand that there was nothing exactly profitable in these heads being there. They only showed that Mr. Kurtz lacked restraint in the gratification of his various lusts, that there was something wanting in him—some small matter which, when the pressing need arose, could not be found under his magnificent eloquence. Whether he knew of this deficiency himself I can't say. I think the knowledge came to him at last—only at the very last. But the wilderness had found him out early, and had taken on him a terrible vengeance for the fantastic invasion. I think it had whispered to him things about himself which he did not know, things of which he had no conception till he took counsel with this great solitude—and the whisper had proved irresistibly fascinating. It echoed loudly within him because he was hollow at the core. . . . I put down the glass, and the head that had appeared near enough to be spoken to seemed at once to have leaped away from me into inaccessible distance.

"The admirer of Mr. Kurtz was a bit crestfallen. In a hurried indistinct voice he began to assure me he had not dared to take these—say, symbols—down. He was not afraid of the natives; they would not stir till Mr. Kurtz gave the word. His ascendancy was extraordinary. The camps of these people surrounded the place, and the chiefs came every day to see him. They would crawl. . . . 'I don't want to know anything of the ceremonies used when approaching Mr. Kurtz,' I shouted. Curious, this feeling that came over me that such details would be more intolerable than those heads drying on the stakes under Mr. Kurtz's windows. After all, that was only a savage sight, while I seemed at one bound to have been transported into some lightless region of subtle horrors, where pure, uncomplicated savagery was a positive relief, being something that had a right to exist—obviously—in the sunshine. The young man looked at me with surprise. I suppose it did not occur to him that Mr. Kurtz was no idol of mine. He forgot I hadn't heard any of these splendid monologues on, what was it? on love, justice, conduct of life—or what not. If it had come to crawling before Mr. Kurtz, he crawled as much as the veriest savage of them all. I had no idea of the conditions, he said: these heads were the heads of rebels. I shocked him excessively by laughing. Rebels! What would be the next definition I was to hear? There had been enemies, criminals, workers—and these were rebels. Those rebellious heads looked very subdued to me on their sticks. 'You don't know how such a life tries a man like Kurtz,' cried Kurtz's last disciple. 'Well, and you?' I said. 'I! I! I am a simple man. I have no great thoughts. I want nothing from anybody. How can you compare me to . . . ?' His feelings were too much for speech, and suddenly he broke down. 'I don't understand,' he groaned. 'I've been doing my best to keep him alive, and that's enough. I had no hand in all this. I have no abilities. There hasn't been a drop of medicine or a mouthful of invalid food for months here. He was shamefully abandoned.

A man like this, with such ideas. Shamefully! Shamefully! I—I—haven't slept for the last ten nights. . . .'

"His voice lost itself in the calm of the evening. The long shadows of the forest had slipped downhill while we talked, had gone far beyond the ruined hovel, beyond the symbolic row of stakes. All this was in the gloom, while we down there were yet in the sunshine, and the stretch of the river abreast of the clearing glittered in a still and dazzling splendor, with a murky and overshadowed bend above and below. Not a living soul was seen on the shore. The bushes did not rustle.

"Suddenly round the corner of the house a group of men appeared, as though they had come up from the ground. They waded waist-deep in the grass, in a compact body, bearing an improvised stretcher in their midst. Instantly, in the emptiness of the landscape, a cry arose whose shrillness pierced the still air like a sharp arrow flying straight to the very heart of the land; and, as if by enchantment, streams of human beings—of naked human beings—with spears in their hands, with bows, with shields, with wild glances and savage movements, were poured into the clearing by the dark-faced and pensive forest. The bushes shook, the grass swayed for a time, and then everything stood still in attentive immobility.

" 'Now, if he does not say the right thing to them we are all done for,' said the Russian at my elbow. The knot of men with the stretcher had stopped, too, halfway to the steamer, as if petrified. I saw the man on the stretcher sit up, lank and with an uplifted arm, above the shoulders of the bearers. 'Let us hope that the man who can talk so well of love in general will find some particular reason to spare us this time,' I said. I resented bitterly the absurd danger of our situation, as if to be at the mercy of that atrocious phantom had been a dishonoring necessity. I could not hear a sound, but through my glasses I saw the thin arm extended commandingly, the lower jaw moving, the eyes of that apparition shining darkly far in its bony head that nodded with grotesque jerks. Kurtz—Kurtz—that means short in German—don't it? Well, the name was as true as everything else in his life—and death. He looked at least seven feet long. His covering had fallen off, and his body emerged from it pitiful and appalling as from a winding-sheet. I could see the cage of his ribs all astir, the bones of his arm waving. It was as though an animated image of death carved out of old ivory had been shaking its hand with menaces at a motionless crowd of men made of dark and glittering bronze. I saw him open his mouth wide—it gave him a weirdly voracious aspect, as though he had wanted to swallow all the air, all the earth, all the men before him. A deep voice reached me faintly. He must have been shouting. He fell back suddenly. The stretcher shook as the bearers staggered forward again, and almost at the same time I noticed that the crowd of savages was vanishing without any perceptible movement of retreat, as if the forest that had ejected these beings so suddenly had drawn them in again as the breath is drawn in a long aspiration.

"Some of the pilgrims behind the stretcher carried his arms—two shotguns, a heavy rifle, and a light revolver-carbine[2]—the thunderbolts of that pitiful

2. Short-barreled, lightweight rifle with a revolving, chambered cylinder.

Jupiter. The manager bent over him murmuring as he walked beside his head. They laid him down in one of the little cabins—just a room for a bedplace and a campstool or two, you know. We had brought his belated correspondence, and a lot of torn envelopes and open letters littered his bed. His hand roamed feebly amongst these papers. I was struck by the fire in his eyes and the composed languor of his expression. It was not so much the exhaustion of disease. He did not seem in pain. This shadow looked satiated and calm, as though for the moment it had had its fill of all the emotions.

"He rustled one of the letters, and looking straight in my face said, 'I am glad.' Somebody had been writing to him about me. These special recommendations were turning up again. The volume of tone he emitted without effort, almost without the trouble of moving his lips, amazed me. A voice! a voice! It was grave, profound, vibrating, while the man did not seem capable of a whisper. However, he had enough strength in him—factitious no doubt—to very nearly make an end of us, as you shall hear directly.

"The manager appeared silently in the doorway; I stepped out at once and he drew the curtain after me. The Russian, eyed curiously by the pilgrims, was staring at the shore. I followed the direction of his glance.

"Dark human shapes could be made out in the distance, flitting indistinctly against the gloomy border of the forest, and near the river two bronze figures, leaning on tall spears, stood in the sunlight under fantastic headdresses of spotted skins, war-like and still in statuesque repose. And from right to left along the lighted shore moved a wild and gorgeous apparition of a woman.

"She walked with measured steps, draped in striped and fringed cloths, treading the earth proudly, with a slight jingle and flash of barbarous ornaments. She carried her head high; her hair was done in the shape of a helmet; she had brass leggings to the knee, brass wire gauntlets to the elbow, a crimson spot on her tawny cheek, innumerable necklaces of glass beads on her neck; bizarre things, charms, gifts of witch-men, that hung about her, glittered and trembled at every step. She must have had the value of several elephant tusks upon her. She was savage and superb, wild-eyed and magnificent; there was something ominous and stately in her deliberate progress. And in the hush that had fallen suddenly upon the whole sorrowful land, the immense wilderness, the colossal body of the fecund and mysterious life seemed to look at her, pensive, as though it had been looking at the image of its own tenebrous and passionate soul.

"She came abreast of the steamer, stood still, and faced us. Her long shadow fell to the water's edge. Her face had a tragic and fierce aspect of wild sorrow and of dumb pain mingled with the fear of some struggling, half-shaped resolve. She stood looking at us without a stir, and like the wilderness itself, with an air of brooding over an inscrutable purpose. A whole minute passed, and then she made a step forward. There was a low jingle, a glint of yellow metal, a sway of fringed draperies, and she stopped as if her heart had failed her. The young fellow by my side growled. The pilgrims murmured at my back. She looked at us all as if her life had depended upon the unswerving steadiness of her glance. Suddenly she opened her bared arms and threw them up rigid above her head, as though in an uncontrollable desire to touch the sky, and at the same time the swift shadows darted out on the earth, swept around on the river, gathering the steamer into a shadowy embrace. A formidable silence hung over the scene.

"She turned away slowly, walked on, following the bank, and passed into the bushes to the left. Once only her eyes gleamed back at us in the dusk of the thickets before she disappeared.

" 'If she had offered to come aboard I really think I would have tried to shoot her,' said the man of patches, nervously. 'I have been risking my life every day for the last fortnight to keep her out of the house. She got in one day and kicked up a row about those miserable rags I picked up in the storeroom to mend my clothes with. I wasn't decent. At least it must have been that, for she talked like a fury to Kurtz for an hour, pointing at me now and then. I don't understand the dialect of this tribe. Luckily for me, I fancy Kurtz felt too ill that day to care, or there would have been mischief. I don't understand. . . . No—it's too much for me. Ah, well, it's all over now.'

"At this moment I heard Kurtz's deep voice behind the curtain: 'Save me!—save the ivory, you mean. Don't tell me. Save *me!* Why, I've had to save you. You are interrupting my plans now. Sick! Sick! Not so sick as you would like to believe. Never mind. I'll carry my ideas out yet—I will return. I'll show you what can be done. You with your little peddling notions—you are interfering with me. I will return. I . . .'

"The manager came out. He did me the honor to take me under the arm and lead me aside. 'He is very low, very low,' he said. He considered it necessary to sigh, but neglected to be consistently sorrowful. 'We have done all we could for him—haven't we? But there is no disguising the fact, Mr. Kurtz has done more harm than good to the Company. He did not see the time was not ripe for vigorous action. Cautiously, cautiously—that's my principle. We must be cautious yet. The district is closed to us for a time. Deplorable! Upon the whole, the trade will suffer. I don't deny there is a remarkable quantity of ivory—mostly fossil. We must save it, at all events—but look how precarious the position is—and why? Because the method is unsound.' 'Do you,' said I, looking at the shore, 'call it "unsound method"?' 'Without doubt,' he exclaimed hotly. 'Don't you?' . . . 'No method at all,' I murmured after a while. 'Exactly,' he exulted. 'I anticipated this. Shows a complete want of judgment. It is my duty to point it out in the proper quarter.' 'Oh,' said I, 'that fellow—what's his name?—the brick-maker, will make a readable report for you.' He appeared confounded for a moment. It seemed to me I had never breathed an atmosphere so vile, and I turned mentally to Kurtz for relief—positively for relief. 'Nevertheless I think Mr. Kurtz is a remarkable man,' I said with emphasis. He started, dropped on me a cold heavy glance, said very quietly, 'he *was,*' and turned his back on me. My hour of favor was over; I found myself lumped along with Kurtz as a partisan of methods for which the time was not ripe: I was unsound! Ah! but it was something to have at least a choice of nightmares.

"I had turned to the wilderness really, not to Mr. Kurtz, who, I was ready to admit, was as good as buried. And for a moment it seemed to me as if I also were buried in a vast grave full of unspeakable secrets. I felt an intolerable weight oppressing my breast, the smell of the damp earth, the unseen presence of victorious corruption, the darkness of an impenetrable night. . . . The Russian tapped me on the shoulder. I heard him mumbling and stammering something about 'brother seaman—couldn't conceal—knowledge of matters that would affect Mr. Kurtz's reputation.' I waited. For him evidently Mr. Kurtz was not in his grave; I suspect that for him Mr. Kurtz was one of the immortals. 'Well!' said I at last, 'speak out. As it happens, I am Mr. Kurtz's friend—in a way.'

"He stated with a good deal of formality that had we not been 'of the same profession,' he would have kept the matter to himself without regard to consequences. 'He suspected there was an active ill will towards him on the part of these white men that—' 'You are right,' I said, remembering a certain conversation I had overheard. 'The manager thinks you ought to be hanged.' He showed a concern at this intelligence which amused me at first. 'I had better get out of the way quietly,' he said, earnestly. 'I can do no more for Kurtz now, and they would soon find some excuse. What's to stop them? There's a military post three hundred miles from here.' 'Well, upon my word,' said I, 'perhaps you had better go if you have any friends amongst the savages near by.' 'Plenty,' he said. 'They are simple people—and I want nothing, you know.' He stood biting his lip, then: 'I don't want any harm to happen to these whites here, but of course I was thinking of Mr. Kurtz's reputation—but you are a brother seaman and—' 'All right,' said I, after a time. 'Mr. Kurtz's reputation is safe with me.' I did not know how truly I spoke.

"He informed me, lowering his voice, that it was Kurtz who had ordered the attack to be made on the steamer. 'He hated sometimes the idea of being taken away—and then again . . . But I don't understand these matters. I am a simple man. He thought it would scare you away—that you would give it up, thinking him dead. I could not stop him. Oh, I had an awful time of it this last month.' 'Very well,' I said. 'He is all right now.' 'Ye-e-es,' he muttered, not very convinced apparently. 'Thanks,' said I; 'I shall keep my eyes open.' 'But quiet—eh?' he urged, anxiously. 'It would be awful for his reputation if anybody here—' I promised a complete discretion with great gravity. 'I have a canoe and three black fellows waiting not very far. I am off. Could you give me a few Martini-Henry cartridges?' I could, and did, with proper secrecy. He helped himself, with a wink at me, to a handful of my tobacco. 'Between sailors—you know—good English tobacco.' At the door of the pilot-house he turned round—'I say, haven't you a pair of shoes you could spare?' He raised one leg. 'Look.' The soles were tied with knotted strings sandal-wise under his bare feet. I rooted out an old pair, at which he looked with admiration before tucking them under his left arm. One of his pockets (bright red) was bulging with cartridges, from the other (dark blue) peeped 'Towson's Inquiry,' etc., etc. He seemed to think himself excellently well equipped for a renewed encounter with the wilderness. 'Ah! I'll never, never meet such a man again. You ought to have heard him recite poetry—his own, too, it was, he told me. Poetry!' He rolled his eyes at the recollection of these delights. 'Oh, he enlarged my mind!' 'Good-by,' said I. He shook hands and vanished in the night. Sometimes I ask myself whether I had ever really seen him—whether it was possible to meet such a phenomenon! . . .

"When I woke up shortly after midnight his warning came to my mind with its hint of danger that seemed, in the starred darkness, real enough to make me get up for the purpose of having a look round. On the hill a big fire burned, illuminating fitfully a crooked corner of the station-house. One of the agents with a picket of a few of our blacks, armed for the purpose, was keeping guard over the ivory; but deep within the forest, red gleams that wavered, that seemed to sink and rise from the ground amongst confused columnar shapes of intense blackness, showed the exact position of the camp where Mr. Kurtz's adorers were keeping their uneasy vigil. The monotonous beating of a big drum filled the air with muffled shocks and a lingering vibration. A steady droning sound of many men chanting each to himself some weird incantation came out from the black, flat wall of the woods as the humming of bees comes out of a hive, and had a strange narcotic effect upon my half-awake senses. I believe I dozed off leaning over the rail, till an abrupt burst of yells, an overwhelming outbreak of a pent-up and mysterious frenzy, woke me up in a bewildered wonder. It was cut short all at once, and the low droning went on with an effect of audible and soothing silence. I glanced casually into the little cabin. A light was burning within, but Mr. Kurtz was not there.

"I think I would have raised an outcry if I had believed my eyes. But I didn't believe them at first—the thing seemed so impossible. The fact is I was completely unnerved by a sheer blank fright, pure abstract terror, unconnected with any distinct shape of physical danger. What made this emotion so overpowering was—how shall I define it?—the moral shock I received, as if something altogether monstrous, intolerable to thought and odious to the soul, had been thrust upon me unexpectedly. This lasted of course the merest fraction of a second, and then the usual sense of commonplace, deadly danger, the possibility of a sudden onslaught and massacre, or something of the kind, which I saw impending, was positively welcome and composing. It pacified me, in fact, so much, that I did not raise an alarm.

"There was an agent buttoned up inside an ulster and sleeping on a chair on deck within three feet of me. The yells had not awakened him; he snored very slightly; I left him to his slumbers and leaped ashore. I did not betray Mr. Kurtz—it was ordered I should never betray him—it was written I should be loyal to the nightmare of my choice. I was anxious to deal with this shadow by myself alone,—and to this day I don't know why I was so jealous of sharing with anyone the peculiar blackness of that experience.

"As soon as I got on the bank I saw a trail—a broad trail through the grass. I remember the exultation with which I said to myself, 'He can't walk—he is crawling on all-fours—I've got him.' The grass was wet with dew. I strode rapidly with clenched fists. I fancy I had some vague notion of falling upon him and giving him a drubbing. I don't know. I had some imbecile thoughts. The knitting old woman with the cat obtruded herself upon my memory as a most improper person to be sitting at the other end of such an affair. I saw a row of pilgrims squirting lead in the air out of Winchesters held to the hip. I thought I would never get back to the steamer, and imagined myself living alone and unarmed in the woods to an advanced age. Such silly things—you know. And I remember I confounded the beat of the drum with the beating of my heart, and was pleased at its calm regularity.

"I kept to the track though—then stopped to listen. The night was very clear; a dark blue space, sparkling with dew and starlight, in which black things stood very still. I thought I could see a kind of motion ahead of me. I was strangely cocksure of everything that night. I actually left the track and ran in a wide semicircle (I verily believe chuckling to myself) so as to get in front of that stir, of that motion I had seen—if indeed I had seen anything. I was circumventing Kurtz as though it had been a boyish game.

"I came upon him, and, if he had not heard me coming, I would have fallen over him too, but he got up in time. He rose, unsteady, long, pale, indistinct, like a vapor exhaled by the earth, and swayed slightly, misty and silent before me; while at my back the fires loomed between the trees, and the murmur of many voices issued from the forest. I had cut him off cleverly; but when actually confronting him I seemed to come to my senses, I saw the danger in its right proportion. It was by no means over yet. Suppose he began to shout? Though he could hardly stand, there was still plenty of vigor in his voice. 'Go away—hide yourself,' he said, in that profound tone. It was very awful. I glanced back. We were within thirty yards from the nearest fire. A black figure stood up, strode on long black legs, waving long black arms, across the glow. It had horns—antelope horns, I think—on its head. Some sorcerer, some witchman, no doubt: it looked fiend-like enough. 'Do you know what you are doing?' I whispered. 'Perfectly,' he answered, raising his voice for that single word: it sounded to me far off and yet loud, like a hail through a speaking-trumpet. If he makes a row we are lost, I thought to myself. This clearly was not a case for fisticuffs, even apart from the very natural aversion I had to beat that Shadow—this wandering and tormented thing. 'You will be lost,' I said—'utterly lost.' One gets sometimes such a flash of inspiration, you know. I did say the right thing, though indeed he could not have been more irretrievably lost than he was at this very moment, when the foundations of our intimacy were being laid—to endure—to endure—even to the end—even beyond.

" 'I had immense plans,' he muttered irresolutely. 'Yes,' said I; 'but if you try to shout I'll smash your head with—' There was not a stick or a stone near. 'I will throttle you for good,' I corrected myself. 'I was on the threshold of great things,' he pleaded, in a voice of longing, with a wistfulness of tone that made my blood run cold. 'And now for this stupid scoundrel—' 'Your success in Europe is assured in any case,' I affirmed, steadily. I did not want to have the throttling of him, you understand—and indeed it would have been very little use for any practical purpose. I tried to break the spell—the heavy, mute spell of the wilderness—that seemed to draw him to its pitiless breast by the awakening of forgotten and brutal instincts, by the memory of gratified and monstrous passions. This alone, I was convinced, had driven him out to the edge of the forest, to the bush, towards the gleam of fires, the throb of drums, the drone of weird incantations; this alone had beguiled his unlawful soul beyond the bounds of permitted aspirations. And, don't you see, the terror of the position was not in being knocked on the head—though I had a very lively sense of that danger, too—but in this, that I had to deal with a being to whom I could not appeal in the name of anything high or low. I had, even like the niggers, to invoke him—himself—his own exalted and incredible degradation. There was nothing either above or below him, and I knew it. He had kicked himself loose of the earth. Confound the man! he had kicked the very earth to pieces. He was alone, and I before him did not know whether I stood on the ground or floated in the air. I've been telling you what we said—repeating the phrases we pronounced—but what's the good? They were common everyday words—the familiar, vague sounds exchanged on every waking day of life. But what of that? They had behind them, to my mind, the terrific suggestiveness of words heard in dreams, of phrases spoken in nightmares. Soul! If anybody had ever struggled with a soul, I am the man. And I wasn't arguing with a lunatic either. Believe me or not, his intelligence was perfectly clear—concentrated, it is true, upon himself with horrible intensity, yet clear; and therein was my only chance—barring, of course, the killing him there and then, which wasn't so good, on account of unavoidable noise. But his soul was mad. Being alone in the wilderness, it had looked within itself, and, by heavens! I tell you, it had gone mad. I had—for my sins, I suppose—to go through the ordeal of looking into it myself. No eloquence could have been so withering to one's belief in mankind as his final burst of sincerity. He struggled with himself, too. I saw it,—I heard it. I saw the inconceivable mystery of a soul that knew no restraint, no faith, and no fear, yet struggling blindly with itself. I kept my head pretty well; but when I had him at last stretched on the couch, I wiped my forehead, while my legs shook under me as though I had carried half a ton on my back down that hill. And yet I had only supported him, his bony arm clasped round my neck—and he was not much heavier than a child.

"When next day we left at noon, the crowd, of whose presence behind the curtain of trees I had been acutely conscious all the time, flowed out of the woods again, filled the clearing, covered the slope with a mass of naked, breathing, quivering, bronze bodies. I steamed up a bit, then swung downstream, and two thousand eyes followed the evolutions of the splashing, thumping, fierce river-demon beating the water with its terrible tail and breathing black smoke into the air. In front of the first rank, along the river, three men, plastered with bright red earth from head to foot, strutted to and fro restlessly. When we came abreast again, they faced the river, stamped their feet, nodded their horned heads, swayed their scarlet bodies; they shook towards the fierce river-demon a bunch of black feathers, a mangy skin with a pendent tail—something that looked like a dried gourd; they shouted periodically together strings of amazing words that resembled no sounds of human language; and the deep murmurs of the crowd, interrupted suddenly, were like the responses of some satanic litany.

"We had carried Kurtz into the pilot-house: there was more air there. Lying on the couch, he stared through the open shutter. There was an eddy in the mass of human bodies, and the woman with helmeted head and tawny cheeks rushed out to the very brink of the stream. She put out her hands, shouted something, and all that wild mob took up the shout in a roaring chorus of articulated, rapid, breathless utterance.

" 'Do you understand this?' I asked.

"He kept on looking out past me with fiery, longing eyes, with a mingled expression of wistfulness and hate. He made no answer, but I saw a smile, a smile of indefinable meaning, appear on his colorless lips that a moment after twitched convulsively. 'Do I not?' he said slowly, gasping, as if the words had been torn out of him by a supernatural power.

"I pulled the string of the whistle, and I did this because I saw the pilgrims on deck getting out their rifles with an air of anticipating a jolly lark. At the sudden screech there was a movement of abject terror through that wedged mass of bodies. 'Don't! don't you frighten them away,' cried someone on deck disconsolately. I pulled the string time after time. They broke and ran, they leaped, they crouched, they swerved, they dodged the flying terror of the sound. The three red chaps had fallen flat, face down on the shore, as though they had been shot dead. Only the barbarous and superb woman did not so much as flinch, and stretched tragically her bare arms after us over the somber and glittering river.

"And then that imbecile crowd down on the deck started their little fun, and I could see nothing more for smoke.

"The brown current ran swiftly out of the heart of darkness, bearing us down towards the sea with twice the speed of our upward progress; and Kurtz's life was running swiftly, too, ebbing, ebbing out of his heart into the sea of inexorable time. The manager was very placid, he had no vital anxieties now, he took us both in with a comprehensive and satisfied glance: the 'affair' had come off as well as could be wished. I saw the time approaching when I would be left alone of the party of 'unsound method.' The pilgrims looked upon me with disfavor. I was, so to speak, numbered with the dead. It is strange how I accepted this unforeseen partnership, this choice of nightmares forced upon me in the tenebrous land invaded by these mean and greedy phantoms.

"Kurtz discoursed. A voice! a voice! It rang deep to the very last. It survived his strength to hide in the magnificent folds of eloquence the barren darkness of his heart. Oh, he struggled! he struggled! The wastes of his weary brain were haunted by shadowy images now—images of wealth and fame revolving obsequiously round his unextinguishable gift of noble and lofty expression. My Intended, my station, my career, my ideas—these were the subjects for the occasional utterances of elevated sentiments. The shade of the original Kurtz frequented the bedside of the hollow sham, whose fate it was to be buried presently in the mold of primeval earth. But both the diabolic love and the unearthly hate of the mysteries it had penetrated fought for the possession of that soul satiated with primitive emotions, avid of lying fame, of sham distinction, of all the appearances of success and power.

"Sometimes he was contemptibly childish. He desired to have kings meet him at railway stations on his return from some ghastly Nowhere, where he intended to accomplish great things. 'You show them you have in you something that is really profitable, and then there will be no limits to the recognition of your ability,' he would say. 'Of course you must take care of the motives—right motives—always.' The long reaches that were like one and the same reach, monotonous bends that were exactly alike, slipped past the steamer with their multitude of secular[3] trees looking patiently after this grimy fragment of another world, the forerunner of change, of conquest, of trade, of massacres, of blessings. I looked ahead—piloting. 'Close the shutter,' said Kurtz suddenly one day; 'I can't bear to look at this.' I did so. There was a silence. 'Oh, but I will wring your heart yet!' he cried at the invisible wilderness.

"We broke down—as I had expected—and had to lie up for repairs at the head of an island. This delay was the first thing that shook Kurtz's confidence. One morning he gave me a packet of papers and a photograph—the lot tied together with a shoestring. 'Keep this for me,' he said. 'This noxious fool' (meaning the manager) 'is capable of prying into my boxes when I am not looking.' In the afternoon I saw him. He was lying on his back with closed eyes, and I withdrew quietly, but I heard him mutter, 'Live rightly, die, die. . . .' I listened. There was nothing more. Was he rehearsing some speech in his sleep, or was it a fragment of a phrase from some newspaper article? He had been writing for the papers and meant to do so again, 'for the furthering of my ideas. It's a duty.'

"His was an impenetrable darkness. I looked at him as you peer down at a man who is lying at the bottom of a precipice where the sun never shines. But I had not much time to give him, because I was helping the engine-driver to take to pieces the leaky cylinders, to straighten a bent connecting-rod, and in other such matters. I lived in an infernal mess of rust, filings, nuts, bolts, spanners, hammers, ratchet-drills—things I abominate, because I don't get on with them. I tended the little forge we fortunately had aboard; I toiled wearily in a wretched scrap-heap—unless I had the shakes too bad to stand.

"One evening coming in with a candle I was startled to hear him say a little tremulously, 'I am lying here in the dark waiting for death.' The light was within a foot of his eyes. I forced myself to murmur, 'Oh, nonsense!' and stood over him as if transfixed.

"Anything approaching the change that came over his features I have never seen before, and hope never to see again. Oh, I wasn't touched. I was fascinated. It was as though a veil had been rent. I saw on that ivory face the expression of somber pride, of ruthless power, of craven terror—of an intense and hopeless despair. Did he live his life again in every detail of desire, temptation, and surrender during that supreme moment of complete knowledge? He cried in a whisper at some image, at some vision—he cried out twice, a cry that was no more than a breath—

" 'The horror! The horror!'

"I blew the candle out and left the cabin. The pilgrims were dining in the mess-room, and I took my place opposite the manager, who lifted his eyes to give me a questioning glance, which I successfully ignored. He leaned back, serene, with that peculiar smile of his sealing the unexpressed depths of his meanness. A continuous shower of small flies streamed upon the lamp, upon the cloth, upon our hands and faces. Suddenly the manager's boy put his insolent black head in the doorway, and said in a tone of scathing contempt—

" 'Mistah Kurtz—he dead.'

3. Centuries-old.

"All the pilgrims rushed out to see. I remained, and went on with my dinner. I believe I was considered brutally callous. However, I did not eat much. There was a lamp in there—light, don't you know—and outside it was so beastly, beastly dark. I went no more near the remarkable man who had pronounced a judgment upon the adventures of his soul on this earth. The voice was gone. What else had been there? But I am of course aware that next day the pilgrims buried something in a muddy hole.

"And then they very nearly buried me.

"However, as you see, I did not go to join Kurtz there and then. I did not. I remained to dream the nightmare out to the end, and to show my loyalty to Kurtz once more. Destiny. My destiny! Droll thing life is—that mysterious arrangement of merciless logic for a futile purpose. The most you can hope from it is some knowledge of yourself—that comes too late—a crop of unextinguishable regrets. I have wrestled with death. It is the most unexciting contest you can imagine. It takes place in an impalpable grayness, with nothing underfoot, with nothing around, without spectators, without clamor, without glory, without the great desire of victory, without the great fear of defeat, in a sickly atmosphere of tepid skepticism, without much belief in your own right, and still less in that of your adversary. If such is the form of ultimate wisdom, then life is a greater riddle than some of us think it to be. I was within a hair's breadth of the last opportunity for pronouncement, and I found with humiliation that probably I would have nothing to say. This is the reason why I affirm that Kurtz was a remarkable man. He had something to say. He said it. Since I had peeped over the edge myself, I understand better the meaning of his stare, that could not see the flame of the candle, but was wide enough to embrace the whole universe, piercing enough to penetrate all the hearts that beat in the darkness. He had summed up—he had judged. 'The horror!' He was a remarkable man. After all, this was the expression of some sort of belief; it had candor, it had conviction, it had a vibrating note of revolt in its whisper, it had the appalling face of a glimpsed truth—the strange commingling of desire and hate. And it is not my own extremity I remember best—a vision of grayness without form filled with physical pain, and a careless contempt for the evanescence of all things—even of this pain itself. No! It is his extremity that I seem to have lived through. True, he had made that last stride, he had stepped over the edge, while I had been permitted to draw back my hesitating foot. And perhaps in this is the whole difference; perhaps all the wisdom, and all truth, and all sincerity, are just compressed into that inappreciable moment of time in which we step over the threshold of the invisible. Perhaps! I like to think my summing-up would not have been a word of careless contempt. Better his cry—much better. It was an affirmation, a moral victory paid for by innumerable defeats, by abominable terrors, by abominable satisfactions. But it was a victory! That is why I have remained loyal to Kurtz to the last, and even beyond, when a long time after I heard once more, not his own voice, but the echo of his magnificent eloquence thrown to me from a soul as translucently pure as a cliff of crystal.

"No, they did not bury me, though there is a period of time which I remember mistily, with a shuddering wonder, like a passage through some inconceivable world that had no hope in it and no desire. I found myself back in the sepulchral city resenting the sight of people hurrying through the streets to filch a little money from each other, to devour their infamous cookery, to gulp their unwholesome beer, to dream their insignificant and silly dreams. They trespassed upon my thoughts. They were intruders whose knowledge of life was to me an irritating pretense, because I felt so sure they could not possibly know the things I knew. Their bearing, which was simply the bearing of commonplace individuals going about their business in the assurance of perfect safety, was offensive to me like the outrageous flauntings of folly in the face of a danger it is unable to comprehend. I had no particular desire to enlighten them, but I had some difficulty in restraining myself from laughing in their faces, so full of stupid importance. I daresay I was not very well at that time. I tottered about the streets—there were various affairs to settle—grinning bitterly at perfectly respectable persons. I admit my behavior was inexcusable, but then my temperature was seldom normal in these days. My dear aunt's endeavors to 'nurse up my strength' seemed altogether beside the mark. It was not my strength that wanted nursing, it was my imagination that wanted soothing. I kept the bundle of papers given me by Kurtz, not knowing exactly what to do with it. His mother had died lately, watched over, as I was told, by his Intended. A clean-shaven man, with an official manner and wearing gold-rimmed spectacles, called on me one day and made inquiries, at first circuitous, afterwards suavely pressing, about what he was pleased to denominate certain 'documents.' I was not surprised, because I had had two rows with the manager on the subject out there. I had refused to give up the smallest scrap out of that package, and I took the same attitude with the spectacled man. He became darkly menacing at last, and with much heat argued that the Company had the right to every bit of information about its 'territories.' And said he, 'Mr. Kurtz's knowledge of unexplored regions must have been necessarily extensive and peculiar—owing to his great abilities and to the deplorable circumstances in which he had been placed: therefore—' I assured him Mr. Kurtz's knowledge, however extensive, did not bear upon the problems of commerce or administration. He invoked then the name of science. 'It would be an incalculable loss if,' etc., etc. I offered him the report on the 'Suppression of Savage Customs,' with the postscriptum torn off. He took it up eagerly, but ended by sniffing at it with an air of contempt. 'This is not what we had a right to expect,' he remarked. 'Expect nothing else,' I said. 'There are only private letters.' He withdrew upon some threat of legal proceedings, and I saw him no more; but another fellow, calling himself Kurtz's cousin, appeared two days later, and was anxious to hear all the details about his dear relative's last moments. Incidentally he gave me to understand that Kurtz had been essentially a great musician. 'There was the making of an immense success,' said the man, who was an organist, I believe, with lank gray hair flowing over a greasy coat-collar. I had no reason to doubt his statement; and to this day I am unable to say what was Kurtz's profession, whether he ever had any—which was the greatest of his talents. I had taken him for a painter who wrote for the papers, or else for a journalist who could paint—but even the cousin (who took snuff during the interview) could not tell me what he had been—exactly. He was a universal genius—on that point I agreed with the old chap, who thereupon blew his nose noisily into a large cotton handkerchief and withdrew in senile agitation, bearing off some family letters and memoranda without importance. Ultimately a journalist anxious to know something of the fate of his 'dear colleague' turned up. This visitor informed me Kurtz's proper sphere ought to have been politics 'on the popular side.' He had furry straight eyebrows, bristly hair cropped short, an eye-glass on a broad ribbon, and, becoming expansive, confessed his opinion that Kurtz really couldn't write a bit—'But heavens! how that man could talk. He electrified large meetings. He had faith—don't you see?—he had the faith. He could get himself to believe anything—anything. He would have been a splendid leader of an extreme party.' 'What party?' I asked. 'Any party,' answered the other. 'He was an—an—extremist.' Did I not think so? I assented. Did I know, he asked, with a sudden flash of curiosity, 'what it was that had induced him to go out there?' 'Yes,' said I, and forthwith handed him the famous Report for publication, if he thought fit. He glanced through it hurriedly, mumbling all the time, judged 'it would do,' and took himself off with this plunder.

"Thus I was left at last with a slim packet of letters and the girl's portrait. She struck me as beautiful—I mean she had a beautiful expression. I know that the sunlight can be made to lie, too, yet one felt that no manipulation of light and pose could have conveyed the delicate shade of truthfulness upon those features. She seemed ready to listen without mental reservation, without suspicion, without a thought for herself. I concluded I would go and give her back her portrait and those letters myself. Curiosity? Yes; and also some other feeling perhaps. All that had been Kurtz's had passed out of my hands: his soul, his body, his station, his plans, his ivory, his career. There remained only this memory and his Intended—and I wanted to give that up, too, to the past, in a way—to surrender personally all that remained of him with me to that oblivion which is the last word of our common fate. I don't defend myself. I had no clear perception of what it was I really wanted. Perhaps it was an impulse of unconscious loyalty, or the fulfillment of one of those ironic necessities, that lurk in the facts of human existence. I don't know. I can't tell. But I went.

"I thought his memory was like the other memories of the dead that accumulate in every man's life—a vague impress on the brain of shadows that had fallen on it in their swift and final passage; but before the high and ponderous door, between the tall houses of a street as still and decorous as a well-kept alley in a cemetery, I had a vision of him on the stretcher, opening his mouth voraciously, as if to devour all the earth with all its mankind. He lived then before me; he lived as much as he had ever lived—a shadow insatiable of splendid appearances, of frightful realities; a shadow darker than the shadow of the night, and draped nobly in the folds of a gorgeous eloquence. The vision seemed to enter the house with me—the stretcher, the phantom-bearers, the wild crowd of obedient worshipers, the gloom of the forests, the glitter of the reach between the murky bends, the beat of the drum, regular and muffled like the beating of a heart—the heart of a conquering darkness. It was a moment of triumph for the wilderness, an invading and vengeful rush which, it seemed to me, I would have to keep back alone for the salvation of another soul. And the memory of what I had heard him say afar there, with the horned shapes stirring at my back, in the glow of fires, within the patient woods, those broken phrases came back to me, were heard again in their ominous and terrifying simplicity. I remembered his abject pleading, his abject threats, the colossal scale of his vile desires, the meanness, the torment, the tempestuous anguish of his soul. And later on I seem to see his collected languid manner, when he said one day, 'This lot of ivory now is really mine. The Company did not pay for it. I collected it myself at a very great personal risk. I am afraid they will try to claim it as theirs though. H'm. It is a difficult case. What do you think I ought to do—resist? Eh? I want no more than justice.' . . . He wanted no more than justice—no more than justice. I rang the bell before a mahogany door on the first floor, and while I waited he seemed to stare at me out of the glossy panel—stare with that wide and immense stare embracing, condemning, loathing all the universe. I seemed to hear the whispered cry, 'The horror! The horror!'

"The dusk was falling. I had to wait in a lofty drawing-room with three long windows from floor to ceiling that were like three luminous and bedraped columns. The bent gilt legs and backs of the furniture shone in indistinct curves. The tall marble fireplace had a cold and monumental whiteness. A grand piano stood massively in a corner; with dark gleams on the flat surfaces like a somber and polished sarcophagus. A high door opened—closed. I rose.

"She came forward, all in black, with a pale head, floating towards me in the dusk. She was in mourning. It was more than a year since his death, more than a year since the news came; she seemed as though she would remember and mourn forever. She took both my hands in hers and murmured, 'I had heard you were coming.' I noticed she was not very young—I mean not girlish. She had a mature capacity for fidelity, for belief, for suffering. The room seemed to have grown darker, as if all the sad light of the cloudy evening had taken refuge on her forehead. This fair hair, this pale visage, this pure brow, seemed surrounded by an ashy halo from which the dark eyes looked out at me. Their glance was guileless, profound, confident, and trustful. She carried her sorrowful head as though she were proud of that sorrow, as though she would say, I—I alone know how to mourn him as he deserves. But while we were still shaking hands, such a look of awful desolation came upon her face that I perceived she was one of those creatures that are not the playthings of Time. For her he had died only yesterday. And, by Jove! the impression was so powerful that for me, too, he seemed to have died only yesterday—nay, this very minute. I saw her and him in the same instant of time—his death and her sorrow—I saw her sorrow in the very moment of his death. Do you understand? I saw them together—I heard them together. She had said, with a deep catch of the breath, 'I have survived' while my strained ears seemed to hear distinctly, mingled with her tone of despairing regret, the summing up whisper of his eternal condemnation. I asked myself what I was doing there, with a sensation of panic in my heart as though I had blundered into a place of cruel and absurd mysteries not fit for a human being to behold. She motioned me to a chair. We sat down. I laid the packet gently on the little table, and she put her hand over it. . . . 'You knew him well,' she murmured, after a moment of mourning silence.

" 'Intimacy grows quickly out there,' I said. 'I knew him as well as it is possible for one man to know another.'

" 'And you admired him,' she said. 'It was impossible to know him and not to admire him. Was it?'

" 'He was a remarkable man,' I said, unsteadily. Then before the appealing fixity of her gaze, that seemed to watch for more words on my lips, I went on, 'It was impossible not to—'

" 'Love him,' she finished eagerly, silencing me into an appalled dumbness. 'How true! how true! But when you think that no one knew him so well as I! I had all his noble confidence. I knew him best.'

" 'You knew him best,' I repeated. And perhaps she did. But with every word spoken the room was growing darker, and only her forehead, smooth and white, remained illumined by the unextinguishable light of belief and love.

" 'You were his friend,' she went on. 'His friend,' she repeated, a little louder. 'You must have been, if he had given you this, and sent you to me. I feel I can speak to you—and oh! I must speak. I want you—you have heard his last words—to know I have been worthy of him. . . . It is not pride. . . . Yes! I am proud to know I understood him better than anyone on earth—he told me so himself. And since his mother died I have had no one—no one—to—to—'

"I listened. The darkness deepened. I was not even sure whether he had given me the right bundle. I rather suspect he wanted me to take care of another batch of his papers which, after his death, I saw the manager examining under the lamp. And the girl talked, easing her pain in the certitude of my sympathy; she talked as thirsty men drink. I had heard that her engagement with Kurtz had been disapproved by her people. He wasn't rich enough or something. And indeed I don't know whether he had not been a pauper all his life. He had given me some reason to infer that it was his impatience of comparative poverty that drove him out there.

" ' . . . Who was not his friend who had heard him speak once?' she was saying. 'He drew men towards him by what was best in them.' She looked at me with intensity. 'It is the gift of the great,' she went on, and the sound of her low voice seemed to have the accompaniment of all the other sounds, full of mystery, desolation, and sorrow, I had ever heard—the ripple of the river, the soughing of the trees swayed by the wind, the murmurs of the crowds, the faint ring of incomprehensible words cried from afar, the whisper of a voice speaking from beyond the threshold of an eternal darkness. 'But you have heard him! You know!' she cried.

" 'Yes, I know,' I said with something like despair in my heart, but bowing my head before the faith that was in her, before that great and saving illusion that shone with an unearthly glow in the darkness, in the triumphant darkness from which I could not have defended her—from which I could not even defend myself.

" 'What a loss to me—to us!'—she corrected herself with beautiful generosity; then added in a murmur, 'To the world.' By the last gleams of twilight I could see the glitter of her eyes, full of tears—of tears that would not fall.

" 'I have been very happy—very fortunate—very proud,' she went on. 'Too fortunate. Too happy for a little while. And now I am unhappy for—for life.'

"She stood up; her fair hair seemed to catch all the remaining light in a glimmer of gold. I rose, too.

" 'And of all this,' she went on, mournfully, 'of all his promise, and of all his greatness, of his generous mind, of his noble heart, nothing remains—nothing but a memory. You and I—'

" 'We shall always remember him,' I said, hastily.

" 'No!' she cried. 'It is impossible that all this should be lost—that such a life should be sacrificed to leave nothing—but sorrow. You know what vast plans he had. I knew of them, too—I could not perhaps understand—but others knew of them. Something must remain. His words, at least, have not died.'

" 'His words will remain,' I said.

" 'And his example,' she whispered to herself. 'Men looked up to him—his goodness shone in every act. His example—'

" 'True,' I said; 'his example too. Yes, his example. I forgot that.'

" 'But I do not. I cannot—I cannot believe—not yet. I cannot believe that I shall never see him again, that nobody will see him again, never, never, never.'

"She put out her arms as if after a retreating figure, stretching them black and with clasped pale hands across the fading and narrow sheen of the window. Never see him! I saw him clearly enough then. I shall see this eloquent phantom as long as I live, and I shall see her, too, a tragic and familiar Shade, resembling in this gesture another one, tragic also, and bedecked with powerless charms, stretching bare brown arms over the glitter of the infernal stream, the stream of darkness. She said suddenly very low, 'He died as he lived.'

" 'His end,' said I, with dull anger stirring in me, 'was in every way worthy of his life.'

" 'And I was not with him,' she murmured. My anger subsided before a feeling of infinite pity.

" 'Everything that could be done—' I mumbled.

" 'Ah, but I believed in him more than anyone on earth—more than his own mother, more than—himself. He needed me! Me! I would have treasured every sigh, every word, every sign, every glance.'

"I felt like a chill grip on my chest. 'Don't,' I said, in a muffled voice.

" 'Forgive me. I—I—have mourned so long in silence—in silence. . . . You were with him—to the last? I think of his loneliness. Nobody near to understand him as I would have understood. Perhaps no one to hear. . . .'

" 'To the very end,' I said shakily. 'I heard his very last words. . . .' I stopped in a fright.

" 'Repeat them,' she murmured in a heart-broken tone. 'I want—I want—something—something—to—live with.'

"I was on the point of crying at her, 'Don't you hear them?' The dusk was repeating them in a persistent whisper all around us, in a whisper that seemed to swell menacingly like the first whisper of a rising wind. 'The horror! The horror!'

" 'His last word—to live with,' she insisted. 'Don't you understand I loved him—I loved him—I loved him!'

"I pulled myself together and spoke slowly.

" 'The last word he pronounced was—your name.'

"I heard a light sigh and then my heart stood still, stopped dead short by an exulting and terrible cry, by the cry of inconceivable triumph and of unspeakable pain. 'I knew it—I was sure!' . . . She knew. She was sure. I heard her weeping, she had hidden her face in her hands. It seemed to me that the house would collapse before I could escape, that the heavens would fall upon my head. But nothing happened. The heavens do not fall for such a trifle. Would they have fallen, I wonder, if I had rendered Kurtz that justice which was his due? Hadn't he said he wanted only justice? But I couldn't. I could not tell her. It would have been too dark—too dark altogether. . . ."

Marlow ceased, and sat apart, indistinct and silent, in the pose of a meditating Buddha. Nobody moved for a time. "We have lost the first of the ebb," said the Director, suddenly. I raised my head. The offing was barred by a black bank of clouds, and the tranquil waterway leading to the uttermost ends of the earth flowed somber under an overcast sky—seemed to lead into the heart of an immense darkness.

## BARRY HANNAH on *Heart of Darkness*

There were plenty of nineteenth-century authors to study but just a handful of real writers, among whom Joseph Conrad stood tallest, to my mind. High adventure, high art, high wisdom. In fact, he belongs to the Modernists of our times, with their tentative connection to this earth and its events. The narrator of Modernist fiction is characteristically sick, diminished, or shocked, barely able to express the special grief and ecstasies of our century, which Milan Kundera has aptly described as one of "massacres and optimism." He might have been speaking directly of "Heart of Darkness," which sounds often like an organ played by a malaria victim—fulsome, shrill, then muffled, then suddenly lucid. Marlow's conclusions on Kurtz seem fevered and strange, very. For he calls Kurtz's final insight "a victory." Would we speak of Hitler, Stalin, or Pol Pot as *victorious* had they uttered "the horror, the horror"—at last seeing it all clear—at the end of their lives? How happy for them as they move on in their growth.

T. S. Eliot, the High Modernist, might enlist "Mistah Kurtz—he dead" as a rubric for the Hollow Man, but the horror was that Kurtz was *not* hollow. He was cultured (he painted), efficient, a man of "ideas." Conrad tells us all Europe had gone into his making. And he becomes a genocidal, homicidal maniac, once threatening to kill even his young ragtag Russian sycophant but settling for merely driving him mad—"He showed me love!" (cf. the Hale-Bopp comet cult in San Diego at the end of the twentieth century).

The best of Modernism's tales seem fuller than rational linear discourse. Conrad's best forms proceed from the gut and head, as all good experimental writing does (see Samuel Beckett, who told Harold Pinter that the only form in his work was that of a *scream*). They are not brain work merely, as post-Modernists might have it. Conrad hardly ever told a tale that didn't seem urgent and necessary. In this he ranks with Twain and Dostoevsky, two other great natural writers of the nineteenth century. His themes were honor, sacrifice, grace, duty, shame, greed, and redemption. A Pole, he was a ship's captain who began writing at age thirty-two, in his third language, English. His parents perished in revolutionary action for Poland when he was a child, and he experienced dark depressions all his life. In his early twenties he had a brush with suicide. We might think of him finding family on the seas. The sea is solid and sweet: "The voice of the surf heard now and then was a positive pleasure, like the speech of a brother." But the riverside Congo is vicious and grim: "The air was warm, thick, heavy, sluggish. There was no joy in the brilliance of sunshine." He reports from a trip that almost killed him, a journey into the heart of the land the Belgians "settled" at a cost of three million native lives. He, like Marlow, changed from a young adventurer to the Ancient Mariner, unable to quit his tale, even though—ever the gentleman—Marlow lies about its end to the heartbroken fiancée of Kurtz. Women, Marlow says, "can't handle the truth." The deeper fact is Marlow is not certain yet what his tale means either. He himself is stricken with contagious moral sickness, and behaves like a fever patient wandering the halls of London. Elliptical, oblique, nearly opaque often, his measured raving reveals only glances of the truth, which is what the Modernist claims is all we ever get.

Rimbaud, the proto-Modernist, surrendered his talent to posterity and quit poetry at age twenty-one, then plunged into North Africa, a money belt constantly around his ribs, and sank into vilest commerce, dying early of fever. A bundle of poems of Rimbaud, "Heart of Darkness," *The Sound and the Fury, The Stranger*—one could claim a pocket education in Modernism with knowledge of these four works. It is significant, though probably not deeply important, that Africa figures as a source in all of the prose. (Dilsey in Faulkner's work, transported from Africa to no paradise in Oxford, Mississippi, is the Christian ballast for the degenerate white Compson's.) Marlow may have found Rimbaud in the person of the raving harlequin who is the acolyte of Kurtz. Conrad disliked Russians, but this young man has Marlow's sympathy. He worshiped England and English, lucky for us. But better for the world, his Africa, almost silent, always dark, was revealed as a holocaust brought in by Europe, the results of which continue in modern Rwanda at century's end. Conrad may not be the fullest humanitarian required by contemporary black intellectuals, but he was the best artist of his day to even glance at the Heart of Darkness that lurked in Western Colonial powers.

We recall the little French ship lobbing shells into the continent of Africa, as Marlow reports early on in the adventure. A silly and ridiculous and puny exercise for the viewer—say we on the television side of the "conflict"—but not to the target of the shells in, and for whom they are all the Armageddon ever predicted. As we get in close to the country, down the sick regions and past the bodies, Conrad gives us one of the most memorable hells of our era.

# ROBERT COOVER

*Coover (1932– ) was born in Charles City, Iowa. He was educated at Southern Illinois University, Indiana University, and the University of Chicago, with intervening service as an officer in the navy. An author of plays as well as a writer of fiction, he has fused stylistic innovations with an exposure of new forms of consciousness emerging from our technological civilization. Some of his shorter work is based on the structure of fairy tales scrambled and recomposed by the television medium. Absurdity as a metaphysical principle combines with absurdity as a device for entertainment. His novels are* The Origin of the Brunists *(1966),*The Universal Baseball Association, Inc., J. Henry Waugh, Prop. *(1968),* The Public Burning *(1977),* Spanking the Maid *(1981),* Gerald's Party *(1987),* Pinocchio in Venice *(1991),* John's Wife *(1996), and* Ghost Town *(1998). Several of his best stories are collected in* Pricksongs & Descants *(1969). He has also published two novellas:* A Political Fable *(1980) and* Briar Rose *(1997).*

## The Babysitter

She arrives at 7:40, ten minutes late, but the children, Jimmy and Bitsy, are still eating supper, and their parents are not ready to go yet. From other rooms come the sounds of a baby screaming, water running, a television musical (no words: probably a dance number—patterns of gliding figures come to mind). Mrs. Tucker sweeps into the kitchen, fussing with her hair, and snatches a baby bottle full of milk out of a pan of warm water, rushes out again. "Harry!" she calls. "The babysitter's here already!"

• • •

That's My Desire? I'll Be Around?[1] He smiles toothily, beckons faintly with his head, rubs his fast balding pate. Bewitched, maybe? Or, What's the Reason? He pulls on his shorts, gives his hips a slap. The baby goes silent in mid-scream. Isn't this the one who used their tub last time? Who's Sorry Now, that's it.

• • •

Jack is wandering around town, not knowing what to do. His girlfriend is babysitting at the Tuckers', and later, when she's got the kids in bed, maybe he'll drop over there. Sometimes he watches TV with her when she's babysitting, it's about the only chance he gets to make out a little since he doesn't own wheels, but they have to be careful because most people don't like their sitters

1. Titles of popular songs, as are "What's the Reason" and "Who's Sorry Now," below.

to have boyfriends over. Just kissing her makes her nervous. She won't close her eyes because she has to be watching the door all the time. Married people really have it good, he thinks.

• • •

"Hi," the babysitter says to the children, and puts her books on top of the refrigerator. "What's for supper?" The little girl, Bitsy, only stares at her obliquely. She joins them at the end of the kitchen table. "I don't have to go to bed until nine," the boy announces flatly, and stuffs his mouth full of potato chips. The babysitter catches a glimpse of Mr. Tucker hurrying out of the bathroom in his underwear.

• • •

Her tummy. Under her arms. And her feet. Those are the best places. She'll spank him, she says sometimes. Let her.

• • •

That sweet odor that girls have. The softness of her blouse. He catches a glimpse of the gentle shadows amid her thighs, as she curls her legs up under her. He stares hard at her. He has a lot of meaning packed into that stare, but she's not even looking. She's popping her gum and watching television. She's sitting right there, inches away, soft, fragrant, and ready: but what's his next move? He notices his buddy Mark in the drugstore, playing the pinball machine, and joins him. "Hey, this mama's cold, Jack baby! She needs your touch!"

• • •

Mrs. Tucker appears at the kitchen doorway, holding a rolled-up diaper. "Now, don't just eat potato chips, Jimmy! See that he eats his hamburger, dear." She hurried away to the bathroom. The boy glares sullenly at the babysitter, silently daring her to carry out the order. "How about a little of that good hamburger now, Jimmy?" she says perfunctorily. He lets half of it drop to the floor. The baby is silent and a man is singing a love song on the TV. The children crunch chips.

• • •

He loves her. She loves him. They whirl airily, stirring a light breeze, through a magical landscape of rose and emerald and deep blue. Her light brown hair coils and wisps softly in the breeze, and the soft folds of her white gown tug at her body and then float away. He smiles in a pulsing crescendo of sincerity and song.

• • •

"You mean she's alone?" Mark asks. "Well, there's two or three kids," Jack says. He slides the coin in. There's a rumble of steel balls tumbling, lining up. He pushes a plunger with his thumb, and one ball pops up in place, hard and glittering with promise. His stare? to say he loves her. That he cares for her and would protect her, would shield her, if need be, with his own body. Grinning, he bends over the ball to take careful aim: he and Mark have studied this machine and have it figured out, but still it's not that easy to beat.

• • •

On the drive to the party, his mind is partly on the girl, partly on his own high-school days, long past. Sitting at the end of the kitchen table there with his children, she had seemed to be self-consciously arching her back, jutting her pert breasts, twitching her thighs: and for whom if not for him? So she'd seen him coming out of there, after all. He smiles. Yet what could he ever do about it? Those good times are gone, old man. He glances over at his wife, who, readjusting a garter, asks: "What do you think of our babysitter?"

• • •

He loves her. She loves him. And then the babies come. And dirty diapers and one goddamn meal after another. Dishes. Noise. Clutter. And fat. Not just tight, her girdle actually hurts. Somewhere recently she's read about women getting heart attacks or cancer or something from too-tight girdles. Dolly pulls the car door shut with a grunt, strangely irritated, not knowing why. Party mood. Why is her husband humming, "Who's Sorry Now?" Pulling out of the drive, she glances back at the lighted kitchen window. "What do you think of our babysitter?" she asks. While her husband stumbles all over himself trying to answer, she pulls a stocking tight, biting deeper with the garters.

• • •

"Stop it!" she laughs. Bitsy is pulling on her skirt and he is tickling her in the ribs. "Jimmy! Don't!" But she is laughing too much to stop him. He leaps on her, wrapping his legs around her waist, and they all fall to the carpet in front of the TV, where just now a man in a tuxedo and a little girl in a flouncy white dress are doing a tapdance together. The babysitter's blouse is pulling out of her skirt, showing a patch of bare tummy: the target. "I'll spank!"

• • •

Jack pushes the plunger, thrusting up a steel ball, and bends studiously over the machine. "You getting any off her?" Mark asks, and clears his throat, flicks ash from his cigarette. "Well, not exactly, not yet," Jack says, grinning awkwardly, but trying to suggest more than he admits to, and fires. He heaves his weight gently against the machine as the ball bounds off a rubber bumper. He can feel her warming up under his hands, the flippers suddenly coming alive, delicate rapid-fire patterns emerging in the flashing of the lights. 1000 WHEN LIT: *now!* "Got my hand on it, that's about all." Mark glances up from the machine, cigarette dangling from his lip. "Maybe you need some help," he suggests with a wry one-sided grin. "Like maybe together, man, we could do it."

• • •

She likes the big tub. She uses the Tuckers' bath salts, and loves to sink into the hot fragrant suds. She can stretch out, submerged, up to her chin. It gives her a good sleepy tingly feeling.

• • •

"What do you think of our babysitter?" Dolly asks, adjusting a garter. "Oh, I hardly noticed," he says, "Cute girl. She seems to get along fine with the kids. Why?" "I don't know." His wife tugs her skirt down, glances at a lighted window they are passing, adding: "I'm not sure I trust her completely, that's all. With the baby, I mean. She seems a little careless. And the other time, I'm almost sure she had a boyfriend over." He grins, claps one hand on his wife's broad gartered thigh. "What's wrong with that?" he asks. Still in anklets, too. Bare thighs, no girdles, nothing up there but a flimsy pair of panties and soft adolescent flesh. He's flooded with vague remembrances of football rallies and movie balconies.

• • •

How tiny and rubbery it is! she thinks, soaping between the boy's legs, giving him his bath. Just a funny jiggly little thing that looks like it shouldn't even be there at all. Is that what all the songs are about?

• • •

Jack watches Mark lunge and twist against the machine. Got her running now, racked them up. He's not too excited about the idea of Mark fooling around with his girlfriend, but Mark's a cooler operator than he is, and maybe, doing it together this once, he'd get over his own timidity. And if she didn't like it, there were other girls around. If Mark went too far, he could cut him off too. He feels his shoulders tense: enough's enough, man . . . but sees the flesh, too. "Maybe I'll call her later," he says.

• • •

"Hey, Harry! Dolly! Glad you could make it!" "I hope we're not late." "No, no, you're one of the first, come on in! By golly, Dolly, you're looking younger every day! How do you do it? Give my wife your secret, will you?" He pats her on her girdled bottom behind Mr. Tucker's back, leads them in for drinks.

• • •

8:00. The babysitter runs water in the tub, combs her hair in front of the bathroom mirror. There's a western on television, so she lets Jimmy watch it while she gives Bitsy her bath. But Bitsy doesn't want a bath. She's angry and crying because she has to be first. The babysitter tells her if she'll take her bath quickly, she'll let her watch television while Jimmy takes his bath, but it does no good. The little girl fights to get out of the bathroom, and the babysitter has to squat with her back against the door and forcibly undress the child. There are better places to babysit. Both children mind badly, and then, sooner or later, the baby is sure to wake up for a diaper change and more bottle. The Tuckers do have a good color TV, though, and she hopes things will be settled down enough to catch the 8:30 program. She thrusts the child into the tub, but she's still screaming and thrashing around. "Stop it now, Bitsy, or you'll wake the baby!" "I have to go potty!" the child wails, switching tactics. The babysitter sighs, lifts the girl out of the tub and onto the toilet, getting her skirt and blouse all wet in the process. She glances at herself in the mirror. Before she knows it, the girl is off the seat and out of the bathroom. "Bitsy! Come back here!"

• • •

"Okay, that's enough!" Her skirt is ripped and she's flushed and crying. "Who says?" "I do, man!" The bastard goes for her, but she tackles him. They roll and tumble. Tables tip, lights topple, the TV crashes to the floor. He slams a hard right to the guy's gut, clips his chin with a rolling left.

• • •

"We hope it's a girl." That's hardly surprising, since they already have four boys. Dolly congratulates the woman like everybody else, but she doesn't envy her, not a bit. That's all she needs about now. She stares across the room at Harry, who is slapping backs and getting loud, as usual. He's spreading out through the middle, so why the hell does he have to complain about her all the time? "Dolly, you're looking younger every day!" was the nice greeting she got tonight. "What's your secret?" And Harry: "It's all those calories. She's getting back her baby fat." "Haw haw! Harry, have a heart!"

• • •

"Get her feet" he hollers at Bitsy, his fingers in her ribs, running over her naked tummy, tangling in the underbrush of straps and strange clothing. "Get her shoes off!" He holds her pinned by pressing his head against her soft chest. "No! No, Jimmy! Bitsy, stop!" But though she kicks and twists and rolls around, she doesn't get up, she can't get up, she's laughing too hard, and the shoes come off, and he grabs a stockinged foot and scratches the sole ruthlessly, and she raises up her legs, trying to pitch him off, she's wild, boy, but he hangs on, and she's laughing, and on the screen there's a rattle of hooves, and he and Bitsy are rolling around and around on the floor in a crazy rodeo of long bucking legs.

• • •

He slips the coin in. There's a metallic fall and a sharp click as the dial tone begins. "I hope the Tuckers have gone," he says. "Don't worry, they're at our place," Mark says. "They're always the first ones to come and the last ones to go home. My old man's always bitching about them." Jack laughs nervously and dials the number. "Tell her we're coming over to protect her from getting raped," Mark suggests, and lights a cigarette. Jack grins, leaning casually against the door jamb of the phonebooth, chewing gum, one hand in his pocket. He's really pretty uneasy, though. He has the feeling he's somehow messing up a good thing.

• • •

Bitsy runs naked into the livingroom, keeping a hassock between herself and the babysitter. "Bitsy . . . !" the babysitter threatens. Artificial reds and greens and purples flicker over the child's wet body, as hooves clatter, guns crackle, and stagecoach wheels thunder over rutted terrain. "Get outa the way, Bitsy!" the boy complains. "I can't see!" Bitsy streaks past and the babysitter chases, cornering the girl in the back bedroom. Bitsy throws something that hits her softly in the face: a pair of men's undershorts. She grabs the girl scampering by, carries her struggling to the bathroom, and with a smart crack on her glistening bottom, pops her back into the tub. In spite, Bitsy peepees in the bathwater.

• • •

Mr. Tucker stirs a little water into his bourbon and kids with his host and another man, just arrived, about their golf games. They set up a match for the weekend, a threesome looking for a fourth. Holding his drink in his right hand, Mr. Tucker swings his left through the motion of a tee-shot. "You'll have to give me a stroke a hole," he says. "I'll give you a stroke!" says his host: "Bend over!" Laughing, the other man asks: "Where's your boy Mark tonight?" "I don't know," replies the host, gathering up a trayful of drinks. Then he adds in a low growl: "Out chasing tail probably." They chuckle loosely at that, then shrug in commiseration and return to the livingroom to join their women.

• • •

Shades pulled. Door locked. Watching the TV. Under a blanket maybe. Yes, that's right, under a blanket. Her eyes close when he kisses her. Her breasts, under both their hands, are soft and yielding.

• • •

A hard blow to the belly. The face. The dark beardy one staggers, the lean-jawed sheriff moves in, but gets a spurred boot in his face. The dark one hurls himself forward, drives his shoulder into the sheriff's hard midriff, her own tummy tightens, withstands, as the sheriff smashes the dark man's nose, slams him up against a wall, slugs him again! and again! The dark man grunts rhythmically, backs off, then plunges suicidally forward—her own knees draw up protectively—the sheriff staggers! caught low! but instead of following through, the other man steps back—a pistol! the dark one has a pistol! the sheriff draws! shoots from the hip! explosions! she clutches her hands between her thighs—no! the sheriff spins! wounded! the dark man hesitates, aims, her legs stiffen toward the set, the sheriff rolls desperately in the straw, fires: dead! the dark man is dead! groans, crumples, his pistol drooping in his collapsing hand, dropping, he drops. The sheriff, spent, nicked, watches weakly from the floor where he lies. Oh, to be whole! to be good and strong and right! to embrace and be embraced by harmony and wholeness! The sheriff, drawing himself painfully up on one elbow, rubs his bruised mouth with the back of his other hand.

• • •

"Well, we just sorta thought we'd drop over," he says, and winks broadly at Mark. "Who's we?" "Oh, me and Mark here." "Tell her, good thing like her, gotta pass it around," whispers Mark, dragging on his smoke, then flicking the butt over under the pinball machine. "What's that?" she asks. "Oh, Mark and I were just saying, like two's company, three's an orgy," Jack says, and winks again. She giggles. "Oh Jack!" Behind her, he can hear shouts and gunfire. "Well, okay, for just a little while, if you'll both be good." Way to go, man.

• • •

Probably some damn kid over there right now. Wrestling around on the couch in front of his TV. Maybe he should drop back to the house. Just to check. None of that stuff, she was there to do a job! Park the car a couple doors down, slip in the front door before she knows it. He sees the disarray of clothing, the young thighs exposed to the flickering television light, hears his baby crying. "Hey, what's going on here! Get outa here, son, before I call the police!" Of course, they haven't really been doing anything. They probably don't even know how. He stares benignly down upon the girl, her skirt rumpled loosely around her thighs. Flushed, frightened, yet excited, she stares back at him. He smiles. His finger touches a knee, approaches the hem. Another couple arrives. Filling up here with people. He wouldn't be missed. Just slip out, stop back casually to pick up something or other he forgot, never mind what. He remembers that the other time they had this babysitter, she took a bath in their house. She had a date afterwards, and she'd come from cheerleading practice or something. Aspirin maybe. Just drop quietly and casually into the bathroom to pick up some aspirin. "Oh, excuse me, dear! I only . . . !" She gazes back at him, astonished, yet strangely moved. Her soft wet breasts rise and fall in the water, and her tummy looks pale and ripply. He recalls that her pubic hairs, left in the tub, were brown. Light brown.

• • •

She's no more than stepped into the tub for a quick bath, when Jimmy announces from outside the door that he has to go to the bathroom. She sighs: just an excuse, she knows. "You'll have to wait." The little nuisance. "I can't wait." "Okay, then come ahead, but I'm taking a bath." She supposes that will stop him, but it doesn't. In he comes. She slides down into the suds until she's eye-level with the edge of the tub. He hesitates. "Go ahead, if you have to," she says, a little awkwardly, "but I'm not getting out." "Don't look," he says. She: "I will if I want to."

• • •

She's crying. Mark is rubbing his jaw where he's just slugged him. A lamp lies shattered. "Enough's enough. Mark! Now get outa here!" Her skirt is ripped to the waist, her bare hip bruised. Her panties lie on the floor like a broken balloon. Later, he'll wash her wounds, help her dress, he'll take care of her. Pity washes through him, giving him a sudden hard-on. Mark laughs at it, pointing. Jack crouches, waiting, ready for anything.

• • •

Laughing, they roll and tumble. Their little hands are all over her, digging and pinching. She struggles to her hands and knees, but Bitsy leaps astride her neck, bowing her head to the carpet. "Spank her, Jimmy!" His swats sting: is her skirt up? The phone rings. "The cavalry to the rescue!" she laughs, and throws them off to go answer.

• • •

Kissing Mark, her eyes closed, her hips nudge toward Jack. He stares at the TV screen, unsure of himself, one hand slipping cautiously under her skirt. Her hand touches his arm as though to resist, then brushes on by to rub his leg. This blanket they're under was a good idea. "Hi! This is Jack!"

• • •

Bitsy's out and the water's running. "Come on, Jimmy, your turn!" Last time, he told her he took his own baths, but she came in anyway. "I'm not gonna take a bath," he announces, eyes glued on the set. He readies for the struggle. "But I've already run your water. Come on, Jimmy, please!" He shakes his head. She can't make him, he's sure he's as strong as she is. She sighs. "Well, it's up to you. I'll use the water myself then," she says. He waits until he's pretty sure she's not going to change her mind, then sneaks in and peeks through the keyhole in the bathroom door: just in time to see her big bottom as she bends over to stir in the bubblebath. Then she disappears. Trying to see as far down as the keyhole will allow, he bumps his head on the knob. "Jimmy, is that you?" "I—I have to go to the bathroom!" he stammers.

• • •

Not actually in the tub, just getting in. One foot on the mat, the other in the water. Bent over slightly, buttocks flexed, teats swaying, holding on to the edge of the tub. "Oh, excuse me! I only wanted. . . . !" He passes over her astonishment, the awkward excuses, moves quickly to the part where he reaches out to— "What on earth are you doing, Harry?" his wife asks, staring at his hand. His host, passing, laughs. "He's practicing his swing for Sunday, Dolly, but it's not going to do him a damn bit of good!" Mr. Tucker laughs, sweeps his right hand on through the air as though lifting a seven-iron shot onto the green. He makes a *dok!* sound with his tongue. "In there!"

• • •

"No, Jack, I don't think you'd better." "Well, we just called, we just, uh, thought we'd, you know, stop by for a minute, watch television for thirty minutes, or, or something." "Who's we?" "Well, Mark's here, I'm with him, and he said he'd like to, you know, like if it's all right, just—" "Well, it's *not* all right. The Tuckers said no." "Yeah, but if we only—" "And they seemed awfully suspicious about last time." "Why? We didn't—I mean, I just thought—" "No, Jack, and that's period." She hangs up. She returns to the TV, but the commercial is on. Anyway, she's missed most of the show. She decides maybe she'll take a quick bath. Jack might come by anyway, it'd make her mad, that'd be the end as far as he was concerned, but if he should, she doesn't want to be all sweaty. And besides, she likes the big tub the Tuckers have.

• • •

He is self-conscious and stands with his back to her, his little neck flushed. It takes him forever to get started, and when it finally does come, it's just a tiny trickle. "See, it was just an excuse," she scolds, but she's giggling inwardly at the boy's embarrassment. "You're just a nuisance, Jimmy." At the door, his hand on the knob, he hesitates, staring timidly down on his shoes. "Jimmy?" She peeks at him over the edge of the tub, trying to keep a straight face, as he sneaks a nervous glance back over his shoulder. "As long as you bothered me," she says, "you might as well soap my back."

• • •

"The aspirin . . . " They embrace. She huddles in his arms like a child. Lovingly, paternally, knowledgeably, he wraps her nakedness. How compact, how tight and small her body is! Kissing her ear, he stares down past her rump at the still clear water. "I'll join you," he whispers hoarsely.

• • •

She picks up the shorts Bitsy threw at her. Men's underwear. She holds them in front of her, looks at herself in the bedroom mirror. About twenty sizes too big for her, of course. She runs her hand inside the opening in front, pulls out her thumb. How funny it must feel!

• • •

"Well, man, I say we just go rape her," Mark says flatly, and swings his weight against the pinball machine. "Uff! Ahh! Get in there, you mother! Look at that! Hah! Man, I'm gonna turn this baby over!" Jack is embarrassed about the phone conversation. Mark just snorted in disgust when he hung up. He cracks down hard on his gum, angry that he's such a chicken. "Well, I'm game if you are," he says coldly.

• • •

8:30 "Okay, come on, Jimmy, it's time." He ignores her. The western gives way to a spy show. Bitsy, in pajamas, pads into the livingroom. "No, Bitsy, it's time to go to bed." "You said I could watch!" the girl whines, and starts to throw another tantrum. "But you were too slow and it's late. Jimmy, you get in that bathroom, and right now!" Jimmy stares sullenly at the set, unmoving. The babysitter tries to catch the opening scene of the television program so she can follow it later, since Jimmy gives himself his own baths. When the commercial interrupts, she turns off the sound, stands in front of the screen. "Okay, into the tub, Jimmy Tucker, or I'll take you in there and give you your bath myself!" "Just try it," he says, "and see what happens."

• • •

They stand outside, in the dark, crouched in the bushes, peeking in. She's on the floor, playing with the kids. Too early. They seem to be tickling her. She gets to her hands and knees, but the little girl leaps on her head, pressing her face to the floor. There's an obvious target, and the little boy proceeds to beat on it. "Hey, look at that kid go!" whispers Mark, laughing and snapping his fingers softly. Jack feels uneasy out here. Too many neighbors, too many cars going by, too many people in the world. That little boy in there is one up on him, though: he's never thought about tickling her as a starter.

• • •

His little hand, clutching the bar of soap, lathers shyly a narrow space between her shoulderblades. She is doubled forward against her knees, buried in rich suds, peeking at him over the edge of her shoulder. The soap slithers out of his grip and plunks into the water. "I . . . I dropped the soap," he whispers. She: "Find it."

• • •

"I dream of Jeannie with the light brown pubic hair!"[2] "Harry! Stop that! You're drunk!" But they're laughing, they're all laughing, damn! he's feeling pretty goddamn good at that, and now he just knows he needs that aspirin. Watching her there, her thighs spread for him, on the couch, in the tub, hell, on the kitchen table for that matter, he tees off on Number Nine, and —*whap!*— swats his host's wife on the bottom. "Hole in one!" he shouts. "Harry!" Why can't his goddamn wife Dolly ever get happy-drunk instead of sour-drunk all the time? "Gonna be tough Sunday, old buddy!" "You're pretty tough right now, Harry," says his host.

• • •

The babysitter lunges forward, grabs the boy by the arms and hauls him off the couch, pulling two cushions with him, and drags him toward the bathroom. He lashes out, knocking over an endtable full of magazines and ashtrays. "You leave my brother alone!" Bitsy cries and grabs the sitter around the waist. Jimmy jumps on her and down they all go. On the silent screen, there's a fade-in to a dark passageway in an old apartment building in some foreign country. She kicks out and somebody falls between her legs. Somebody else is sitting on her face. "Jimmy! Stop that!" the babysitter laughs, her voice muffled.

• • •

She's watching television. All alone. It seems like a good time to go in. Just remember: really, no matter what she says, she wants it. They're standing in the bushes, trying to get up the nerve. "We'll tell her to be good," Mark whis-

2. Parody of actual song title "I Dream of Jeannie with the Light Brown Hair."

pers, "and if she's not good, we'll spank her." Jack giggles softly, but his knees are weak. She stands. They freeze. She looks right at them. "She can't see us." Mark whispers tensely. "Is she coming out?" "No," says Mark, "she's going into—that must be the bathroom!" Jack takes a deep breath, his heart pounding. "Hey, is there a window back there?" Mark asks.

• • •

The phone rings. She leaves the tub, wrapped in a towel. Bitsy gives a tug on the towel. "Hey, Jimmy, get the towel!" she squeals. "Now stop that, Bitsy!" the babysitter hisses, but too late: with one hand on the phone, the other isn't enough to hang on to the towel. Her sudden nakedness awes them and it takes them a moment to remember about tickling her. By then, she's in the towel again. "I hope you got a good look," she says angrily. She feels chilled and oddly a little frightened. "Hello?" No answer. She glances at the window—is somebody out there? Something, she saw something, and a rustling—footsteps?

• • •

"Okay, I don't care, Jimmy, don't take a bath," she says irritably. Her blouse is pulled out and wrinkled, her hair is all mussed, and she feels sweaty. There's about a million things she'd rather be doing than babysitting with these two. Three: at least the baby's sleeping. She knocks on the overturned endtable for luck, rights it, replaces the magazines and ashtrays. The one thing that really makes her sick is a dirty diaper. "Just go on to bed." "I don't have to go to bed until nine," he reminds her. Really, she couldn't care less. She turns up the volume on the TV, settles down on the couch, poking her blouse back into her skirt, pushing her hair out of her eyes. Jimmy and Bitsy watch from the floor. Maybe, once they're in bed, she'll take a quick bath. She wishes Jack would come by. The man, no doubt the spy, is following a woman, but she doesn't know why. The woman passes another man. Something seems to happen, but it's not clear what. She's probably already missed too much. The phone rings.

• • •

Mark is kissing her. Jack is under the blanket, easing her panties down over her squirming hips. Her hand is in his pants, pulling it out, pulling it toward her, pulling it hard. She knew just where it was! Mark is stripping, too. God, it's really happening! he thinks with a kind of pious joy, and notices the open door. "Hey! What's going on here?"

• • •

He soaps her back, smooth and slippery under his hand. She is doubled over, against her knees, between his legs. Her light brown hair, reaching to her gleaming shoulders, is wet at the edges. The soap slips, falls between his legs. He fishes for it, finds it, slips it behind him. "Help me find it," he whispers in her ear. "Sure Harry," says his host, going around behind him. "What'd you lose?"

• • •

Soon be nine, time to pack the kids off to bed. She clears the table, dumps paper plates and leftover hamburgers into the garbage, puts glasses and silverware into the sink, and the mayonnaise, mustard, and ketchup in the refrigerator. Neither child has eaten much supper finally, mostly potato chips and ice cream, but it's really not her problem. She glances at the books on the refrigerator. Not much chance she'll get to them, she's already pretty worn out. Maybe she'd feel better if she had a quick bath. She runs water into the tub, tosses in bubblebath salts, undresses. Before pushing down her panties, she stares for a moment at the smooth silken panel across her tummy, fingers the place where the opening would be if there were one. Then she steps quickly out of them, feeling somehow ashamed, unhooks her brassiere. She weighs her breasts in the palms of her hands, watching herself in the bathroom mirror, where, in the open window behind her, she sees a face. She screams.

• • •

She screams: "Jimmy! Give me that!" "What's the matter?" asks Jack on the other end. "Jimmy! Give me my towel! Right now!" "Hello? Hey, are you still there?" "I'm sorry, Jack," she says, panting. "You caught me in the tub. I'm just wrapped in a towel and these silly kids grabbed it away!" "Gee, I wish I'd been there!" "Jack—!" "To protect you, I mean." "Oh, sure," she says, giggling. "Well, what do you think, can I come over and watch TV with you?" "Well, not right this minute," she says. He laughs lightly. He feels very cool. "Jack?" "Yeah?" "Jack, I . . . I think there's somebody outside the window!"

• • •

She carries him, fighting all the way, to the tub, Bitsy pummeling her in the back and kicking her ankles. She can't hang on to him and undress him at the same time. "I'll throw you in, clothes and all, Jimmy Tucker!" she gasps. "You better not!" he cries. She sits on the toilet seat, locks her legs around him, whips his shirt up over his head before he knows what's happening. The pants are easier. Like all little boys his age, he has almost no hips at all. He hangs on desperately to his underpants, but when she succeeds in snapping these down out of his grip, too, he gives up, starts to bawl, and beats her wildly in the face with his fists. She ducks her head, laughing hysterically, oddly entranced by the spectacle of that pale little thing down there, bobbing and bouncing rubberlike about the boy's helpless fury and anguish.

• • •

"Aspirin? Whaddaya want aspirin for, Harry? I'm sure they got aspirin here, if you—" "Did I say aspirin? I meant uh, my glasses. And, you know, I thought, well, I'd sorta check to see if everything was okay at home." Why the hell is it his mouth feels like it's got about six sets of teeth packed in there, and a tongue the size of that liverwurst his host's wife is passing around? "Whaddaya want your glasses for, Harry? I don't understand you at all?" "Aw, well, honey, I was feeling kind of dizzy or something, and I thought—" "Dizzy is right. If you want to check on the kids, why don't you just call on the phone?"

• • •

They can tell she's naked and about to get into the tub, but the bathroom window is frosted glass, and they can't see anything clearly. "I got an idea," Mark whispers. "One of us goes and calls her on the phone, and the other watches when she comes out." "Okay, but who calls?" "Both of us, we'll do it twice. Or more."

• • •

Down forbidden alleys. Into secret passageways. Unlocking the world's terrible secrets. Sudden shocks: a trapdoor! a fall! or the stunning report of a rifle shot, the *whaaii-ii-ing!* of the bullet biting concrete by your ear! Careful! Then edge forward once more, avoiding the light, inch at a time, now a quick dash for an open doorway—*look out!* there's a knife! a struggle! no! the long blade glistens! jerks! thrusts! *stabbed!* No, no, it missed! The assailant's down, yes! the spy's on top, pinning him, a terrific thrashing about, the spy rips off the assailant's mask: *a woman!*

• • •

Fumbling behind her, she finds it, wraps her hands around it, tugs. "Oh!" she gasps, pulling her hand back quickly, her ears turning crimson. "I . . . I thought it was the soap!" He squeezes her close between his thighs, pulls her back toward him, one hand sliding down her tummy between her legs. I Dream of Jeannie— "I have to go to the bathroom!" says someone outside the door.

• • •

She's combing her hair in the bathroom when the phone rings. She hurries to answer it before it wakes the baby. "Hello, Tuckers." There's no answer. "Hello?" A soft click. Strange. She feels suddenly alone in the big house, and goes in to watch TV with the children.

• • •

"Stop it!" she screams, "Please stop!" She's on her hands and knees, trying to get up, but they're too strong for her. Mark holds her head down. "Now, baby, we're gonna teach you how to be a nice girl," he says coldly, and nods at Jack. When she's doubled over like that, her skirt rides up her thighs to the leg bands of her panties. "C'mon, man, go! This baby's cold! She needs your touch!"

• • •

Parks the car a couple blocks away. Slips up to the house, glances in his window. Just like he's expected. Her blouse is off and the kid's shirt is unbuttoned. He watches, while slowly, clumsily, childishly, they fumble with each other's clothes. My God, it takes them forever. "Some party!" "You said it!" When they're more or less naked, he walks in. "Hey! What's going on here?" They go white as bleu cheese. Haw haw! "What's the little thing you got sticking out there, boy?" "Harry, behave yourself!" No, he doesn't let the kid get dressed, he sends him home bareassed. "Bareassed!" He drinks to that. "Promises, promises," says his host's wife. "I'll mail you your clothes, son!" He gazes down on the naked little girl on his couch. "Looks like you and me, we got a little secret to keep, honey," he says coolly. "Less you wanna go home the same way your boyfriend did!" He chuckles at his easy wit, leans down over her, and unbuckles his belt. "Might as well make it two secrets, right?" "What in God's name are you talking about, Harry?" He staggers out of there, drink in hand, and goes to look for his car.

• • •

"Hey! What's going on here?" They huddle half-naked under the blanket, caught utterly unawares. On television: the clickety-click of frightened running feet on foreign pavements. Jack is fumbling for his shorts, tangled somehow around his ankles. The blanket is snatched away. "On your feet there!" Mr. Tucker, Mrs. Tucker, and Mark's mom and dad, the police, the neighbors, everybody comes crowding in. Hopelessly, he has a terrific erection. So hard it hurts. Everybody stares down at it.

• • •

Bitsy's sleeping on the floor. The babysitter is taking a bath. For more than an hour now, he'd had to use the bathroom. He doesn't know how much longer he can wait. Finally, he goes to knock on the bathroom door. "I have to use the bathroom." "Well, come ahead, if you have to." "Not while you're in there." She sighs loudly. "Okay, okay, just a minute," she says, "but you're a real nuisance, Jimmy!" He's holding on, pinching it as tight as he can. *"Hurry!"* He holds his breath, squeezing shut his eyes. No. Too late. At last, she opens the door. "Jimmy!" "I *told* you to hurry!" he sobs. She drags him into the bathroom and pulls his pants down.

• • •

He arrives just in time to see her emerge from the bathroom, wrapped in a towel, to answer the phone. His two kids sneak up behind her and pull the towel away. She's trying to hang onto the phone and get the towel back at the same time. It's quite a picture. She's got a sweet ass. Standing there in the bushes, pawing himself with one hand, he lifts his glass with the other and toasts her sweet ass, which his son now swats. Haw haw, maybe that boy's gonna shape up, after all.

• • •

They're in the bushes, arguing about their next move, when she comes out of the bathroom, wrapped in a towel. They can hear the baby crying. Then it stops. They see her running, naked, back to the bathroom like she's scared or something. "I'm going in after her, man, whether you're with me or not!" Mark whispers, and he starts out of the bushes. But just then, a light comes sweeping up through the yard, as a car swings in the drive. They hit the dirt, hearts pounding. "Is it the cops?" "I don't know!" "Do you think they saw us?" "Sshh!" A man comes staggering up the walk from the drive, a drink in his hand, stumbles on in the kitchen door and then straight into the bathroom. "It's Mr. Tucker!" Mark whispers. A scream. "Let's get outa here, man!"

• • •

9:00. Having missed most of the spy show anyway and having little else to do, the babysitter has washed the dishes and cleaned the kitchen up a little. The books on the refrigerator remind her of her better intentions, but she decides that first she'll see what's next on TV. In the livingroom, she finds little Bitsy sound asleep on the floor. She lifts her gently, carries her into her bed, and tucks her in. "Okay, Jimmy, it's nine o'clock, I've let you stay up, now be a good boy." Sullenly, his sleepy eyes glued still to the set, the boy backs out of the room toward his bedroom. A drama comes on. She switches channels. A ballgame and a murder mystery. She switches back to the drama. It's a love story of some kind. A man married to an aging invalid wife, but in love with a younger girl. "Use the bathroom and brush your teeth before going to bed, Jimmy!" she calls, but as quickly regrets it, for she hears the baby stir in its crib.

• • •

Two of them are talking about mothers they've salted away in rest homes. Oh boy, that's just wonderful, this is one helluva party. She leaves them to use the john, takes advantage of the retreat to ease her girdle down awhile, get a few good deep breaths. She has this picture of her three kids carting her off to a rest home. In a wheelbarrow. That sure is something to look forward to, all right. When she pulls her girdle back up, she can't seem to squeeze into it. The host looks in. "Hey, Dolly, are you all right?" "Yeah, I just can't get into my damn girdle, that's all." "Here, let me help."

• • •

She pulls them on, over her own, standing in front of the bedroom mirror, holding her skirt bundled up around the waist. About twenty sizes too big for her, of course. She pulls them tight from behind, runs her hand inside the opening in front, pulls out her thumb. "And what a good boy am I!" She giggles: how funny it must feel! Then, in the mirror, she sees him: in the doorway behind her, sullenly watching. "Jimmy! You're supposed to be in bed!" "Those are my daddy's!" the boy says. "I'm gonna tell!"

• • •

"Jimmy!" she drags him into the bathroom and pulls his pants down. "Even your shoes are wet! Get them off!" She soaps up a warm washcloth she's had with her in the bathtub, scrubs him from the waist down with it. Bitsy stands in the doorway, staring. "Get out! Get out!" the boy screams at his sister. "Go back to bed, Bitsy. It's just an accident." "Get out!" The baby wakes and starts to howl.

• • •

The young lover feels sorry for her rival, the invalid wife; she believes the man has a duty toward the poor woman and insists she is willing to wait. But the man argues that he also has a duty toward himself: his life, too, is short, and he could not love his wife now even were she well. He embraces the young girl feverishly; she twists away in anguish. The door opens. They stand there grinning, looking devilish, but pretty silly at the same time. "Jack! I thought I told you not to come!" She's angry, but she's also glad in a way: she was beginning to feel a little too alone in the big house, with the children all sleeping. She should have taken that bath, after all. "We just came by to see if you were being a good girl," Jack says and blushes. The boys glance at each other nervously.

• • •

She's just sunk down into the tubful of warm fragrant suds, ready for a nice long soaking, when the phone rings. Wrapping a towel around her, she goes to answer: no one there. But now the baby's awake and bawling. She wonders if that's Jack bothering her all the time. If it is, brother, that's the end. Maybe it's the end anyway. She tries to calm the baby with the half-empty bottle, not wanting to change it until she's finished her bath. The bathroom's where the diapers go dirty, and they make it stink to high heaven. "Shush, shush!" she whispers, rocking the crib. The towel slips away, leaving an airy empty tingle up and down her backside. Even before she stoops for the towel, even before she turns around, she knows there's somebody behind her.

• • •

"We just came by to see if you were being a good girl," Jack says, grinning down at her. She's flushed and silent, her mouth half open. "Lean over," says Mark amiably. "We'll soap your back, as long as we're here." But she just huddles there, down in the suds, staring up at them with big eyes.

• • •

"Hey! What's going on here?" It's Mr. Tucker, stumbling through the door with a drink in his hand. She looks up from the TV. "What's the matter, Mr. Tucker?" "Oh, uh, I'm sorry, I got lost—no, I mean, I had to get some aspirin. Excuse me!" And he rushes past her into the bathroom, caroming off the livingroom door jamb on the way. The baby awakes.

• • •

"Okay, get off her, Mr. Tucker!" "Jack!" she cries, "what are *you* doing here?" He stares hard at them a moment: so that's where it goes. Then, as Mr. Tucker swings heavily off, he leans into the bastard with a hard right to the belly. Next thing he knows, though, he's got a face full of an old man's fist. He's not sure, as the lights go out, if that's his girlfriend screaming or the baby . . .

• • •

Her host pushes down on her fat fanny and tugs with all his might on her girdle, while she bawls on his shoulder: "I don't *wanna* go to a rest home!" "Now, now take it easy, Dolly, nobody's gonna make you—" "Ouch! Hey, you're hurting!" "You should buy a bigger girdle, Dolly." "You're telling me?" Some other guy pokes his head in. "Whatsa-matter? Dolly fall in?" "No, she fell out. Give me a hand."

• • •

By the time she's chased Jack and Mark out of there, she's lost track of the program she's been watching on television. There's another woman in the story now for some reason. That guy lives a very complicated life. Impatiently, she switches channels. She hates ballgames, so she settles for the murder mystery. She switches just in time, too: there's a dead man sprawled out on the floor of what looks like an office or a study or something. A heavyset detective gazes up from his crouch over the body: "He's been strangled." Maybe she'll take that bath, after all.

• • •

She drags him into the bathroom and pulls his pants down. She soaps up a warm washcloth she's had in the tub with her, but just as she reaches between his legs, it starts to spurt, spraying her arms and hands. "Oh, Jimmy! I thought you were done!" she cries, pulling him toward the toilet and aiming it into the bowl. How moist and rubbery it is! And you can turn it every which way. How funny it must feel!

• • •

"Stop it!" she screams. "Please stop!" She's on her hands and knees and Jack is holding her head down. "Now we're gonna teach you how to be a nice girl," Mark says and lifts her skirt. "Well, I'll be damned!" "What's the matter?" asks Jack, his heart pounding. "Look at this big pair of men's underpants she's got on!" "Those are my daddy's!" says Jimmy, watching them from the doorway. "I'm gonna tell!"

• • •

People are shooting at each other in the murder mystery, but she's so mixed up, she doesn't know which ones are the good guys. She switches back to the love story. Something seems to have happened, because now the man is kissing his invalid wife tenderly. Maybe she's finally dying. The baby wakes, begins to scream. Let it. She turns up the volume on the TV.

• • •

Leaning down over her, unbuckling his belt. It's all happening just like he's known it would. Beautiful! The kid is gone, though his pants, poor lad, remain. "Looks like you and me, we got a secret to keep, child!" But he's cramped on the couch and everything is too slippery and small. "Lift your legs up, honey. Put them around my back." But instead, she screams. He rolls off, crashing to the floor. There they all come, through the front door. On television, somebody is saying: "Am I a burden to you, darling?" "Dolly! My God! Dolly, I can explain . . . !"

• • •

The game of the night is Get Dolly Tucker Back in Her Girdle Again. They've got her down on her belly in the livingroom and the whole damn crowd is working on her. Several of them are stretching the girdle, while others try to jam the fat inside. "I think we made a couple inches on this side! Roll her over!" Harry?

• • •

She's just stepped into the tub, when the phone rings, waking the baby. She sinks down in the suds, trying not to hear. But that baby doesn't cry, it screams. Angrily, she wraps a towel around herself, stamps peevishly into the baby's room, just letting the phone jangle. She tosses the baby down on its back, unpins its diapers hastily, and gets yellowish baby stool all over her hands. Her towel drops away. She turns to find Jimmy staring at her like a little idiot. She slaps him in the face with her dirty hand, while the baby screams, the phone rings, and nagging voices argue on the TV. There are better things she might be doing.

• • •

What's happening? Now there's a young guy in it. Is he after the young girl or the old invalid? To tell the truth, it looks like he's after the same man the women are. In disgust, she switches channels. "The strangler again," growls the fat detective, hands on hips, staring down at the body of a half-naked girl. She's considering either switching back to the love story or taking a quick bath, when a hand suddenly clutches her mouth.

• • •

"You're both chicken," she says, staring up at them. "But what if Mr. Tucker comes home?" Mark asks nervously.

• • •

How did he get here? He's standing pissing in his own goddamn bathroom, his wife is still back at the party, the three of them are, like good kids, sitting in there in the livingroom watching TV. One of them is his host's boy Mark. "It's a good murder mystery, Mr. Tucker," Mark said, when he came staggering in on them a minute ago. "Sit still!" he shouted, "I am just home for a moment!" Then whump thump on into the bathroom. Long hike for a wee-wee, Mister. But something keeps bothering him. Then it hits him: the girl's panties hanging like a broken balloon from the rabbit-ear antennae on the TV! He barges back in there, giving his shoulder a helluva crack on the livingroom door jamb on the way—but they're not hanging there any more. Maybe he's only imagined it. "Hey, Mr. Tucker," Mark says flatly. "Your fly's open."

• • •

The baby's dirty. Stinks to high heaven. She hurries back to the livingroom, hearing sirens and gunshots. The detective is crouched outside a house, peering in. Already, she's completely lost. The baby screams at the top of its lungs. She turns up the volume. But it's all confused. She hurries back in there, claps an angry hand to the baby's mouth. "Shut up!" she cries. She throws the baby down on its back, starts to unpin the diaper, as the baby tunes up again. The phone rings. She answers it, one eye on the TV. *"What?"* The baby cries so hard it starts to choke. Let it. "I said, hi, this is Jack!" Then it hits her: oh no! the diaper pin!

• • •

"The aspirin . . . " But she's already in the tub. Way down in the tub. Staring at him through the water. Her tummy looks pale and ripply. He hears sirens, people on the porch.

• • •

Jimmy gets up to go to the bathroom and gets his face slapped and smeared with baby poop. Then she hauls him off to the bathroom, yanks off his pajamas, and throws him into the tub. That's okay, but next she gets naked and acts like she's gonna get in the tub, too. The baby's screaming and the phone's ringing like crazy and in walks his dad. Saved! he thinks, but, no, his dad grabs him right back out of the tub and whales the dickens out of him, no questions asked, while she watches, then sends him—*whack!*—back to bed. So he's lying there, wet and dirty and naked and sore, and he still has to go to the bathroom, and outside his window he hears two older guys talking. "Listen, you know where to do it if we get her pinned?" "No! Don't you?"

• • •

"Yo ho heave ho! *Ugh!"* Dolly's on her back and they're working on the belly side. Somebody got the great idea of buttering her down first. Not to lose the ground they've gained, they've shot it inside with a basting syringe. But now suddenly there's this big tug-of-war under way between those who want to stuff her in and those who want to let her out. Something rips, but she feels better. The odor of hot butter makes her think of movie theaters and popcorn. "Hey, has anybody seen Harry?" she asks. "Where's Harry?"

• • •

Somebody's getting chased. She switches back to the love story, and now the man's back kissing the young lover again. What's going on? She gives it up, decides to take a quick bath. She's just stepping into the tub, one foot in, one foot out, when Mr. Tucker walks in. "Oh, excuse me! I only wanted some aspirin . . . " She grabs for a towel, but he yanks it away. "Now, that's not how it's supposed to happen, child," he scolds. "Please! Mr. Tucker . . . !" He embraces her savagely, his calloused old hands clutching roughly at her backside. "Mr. Tucker!" she cries, squirming. "Your wife called—!" He's pushing something between her legs, hurting her. She slips, they both slip—something cold and hard slams her in the back, cracks her skull, she seems to be sinking into a sea . . .

• • •

They've got her over the hassock, skirt up and pants down. "Give her a little lesson there, Jack baby!" The television lights flicker and flash over her glossy flesh, 1000 WHEN LIT. Whack! Slap! Bumper to bumper! He leans into her, feeling her come alive.

• • •

The phone rings, waking the baby. "Jack, is that you? Now, you listen to me—" "No, dear, this is Mrs. Tucker. Isn't the TV awfully loud?" "Oh, I'm sorry, Mrs. Tucker! I've been getting—" "I tried to call you before, but I couldn't hang on. To the phone, I mean. I'm sorry, dear." "Just a minute, Mrs. Tucker, the baby's—" "Honey, listen! Is Harry there? Is Mr. Tucker there, dear?"

• • •

"Stop it!" she screams and claps a hand over the baby's mouth. "Stop it! Stop it! *Stop it!"* Her other hand is full of baby stool and she's afraid she's going to be sick. The phone rings. "No!" she cries. She's hanging on to the baby, leaning woozily away, listening to the phone ring. "Okay, okay," she sighs, getting ahold of herself. But when she lets go of the baby, it isn't screaming any more. She shakes it. Oh no . . .

• • •

"Hello?" No answer. Strange. She hangs up and, wrapped only in a towel, stares out the window at the cold face staring in—she screams!

• • •

She screams, scaring the hell out of him. He leaps out of the tub, glances up at the window she's gaping at just in time to see two faces duck away, then slips on the bathroom tiles, and crashes to his ass, whacking his head on the sink on the way down. She stares down at him, trembling, a towel over her narrow shoulders. "Mr. Tucker! Mr. Tucker, are you all right . . . ?" Who's Sorry Now? Yessir, who's back is breaking with each . . . He stares up at the little tufted locus of all his woes, and passes out, dreaming of Jeannie . . .

• • •

The phone rings. "Dolly! It's for you!" "Hello?" "Hello, Mrs. Tucker?" "Yes, speaking." "Mrs. Tucker, this is the police calling . . ."

• • •

It's cramped and awkward and slippery, but he's pretty sure he got it in her, once anyway. When he gets the suds out of his eyes, he sees her staring up at them. Through the water. "Hey, Mark! Let her up!"

• • •

Down in the suds. Feeling sleepy. The phone rings, startling her. Wrapped in a towel, she goes to answer. "No, he's not here, Mrs. Tucker." Strange. Married people act pretty funny sometimes. The baby is awake and screaming. Dirty, a real mess. Oh boy, there's a lot of things she'd rather be doing than babysitting in this madhouse. She decides to wash the baby off in her own bathwater. She removes her towel, unplugs the tub, lowers the water level so the baby can sit. Glancing back over her shoulder, she sees Jimmy staring at her. "Go back to bed, Jimmy." "I have to go to the bathroom." "Good grief, Jimmy! It looks like you already have!" The phone rings. She doesn't bother with the towel—what can Jimmy see he hasn't already seen?—and goes to answer. "No, Jack, and that's final." Sirens, on the TV, as the police move in. But wasn't that the channel with the love story? Ambulance maybe. Get this over with so she can at least catch the news. "Get those wet pajamas off, Jimmy, and I'll find clean ones. Maybe you better get in the tub, too." "I think something's wrong with the baby," he says. "It's down in the water and it's not swimming or anything."

• • •

She's staring up at them from the rug. They slap her. Nothing happens. "You just tilted her, man!" Mark says softly. "We gotta get outa here!" Two little kids are standing wide-eyed in the doorway. Mark looks hard at Jack. "No, Mark, they're just little kids . . . !" "We gotta, man, or we're dead."

• • •

"Dolly! My God! Dolly, I can explain!" She glowers down at them, her ripped girdle around her ankles. "What the four of you are doing in the bathtub with *my* babysitter?" she says sourly. "I can hardly wait!"

• • •

Police sirens wail, lights flash. "I heard the scream!" somebody shouts. "There were two boys!" "I saw a man!" "She was running with the baby!" "My God!" somebody screams, "they're *all* dead!" Crowds come running. Spotlights probe the bushes.

• • •

"Harry, where the hell you been?" his wife whines, glaring blearily up at him from the carpet. "I can explain," he says. "Hey, whatsamatter, Harry?" his host asks, smeared with butter for some goddamn reason. "You look like you just seen a ghost!" Where did he leave his drink? Everybody's laughing, everybody except Dolly, whose cheeks are streaked with tears. "Hey, Harry, you won't let them take me to a rest home, will you, Harry?"

• • •

10:00. The dishes done, children to bed, her books read, she watches the news on television. Sleepy. The man's voice is gentle, soothing. She dozes—awakes with a start: a babysitter? Did the announcer say something about a babysitter?

• • •

"Just want to catch the weather," the host says, switching on the TV. Most of the guests are leaving, but the Tuckers stay to watch the news. As it comes on, the announcer is saying something about a babysitter. The host switches channels. "They got a better weatherman on four," he explains. "Wait!" says Mrs. Tucker. "There was something about a babysitter . . . !" The host switches back. "Details have not yet been released by the police," the announcer says. "Harry, maybe we'd better go . . ."

• • •

They stroll casually out of the drugstore, run into a buddy of theirs. "Hey! Did you hear about the babysitter?" the guy asks. Mark grunts, glances at Jack. "Got a smoke?" he asks the guy.

• • •

"I think I hear the baby screaming!" Mrs. Tucker cries, running across the lawn from the drive.

• • •

She wakes, startled, to find Mr. Tucker hovering over her. "I must have dozed off!" she exclaims. "Did you hear the news about the babysitter?" Mr. Tucker asks. "Part of it," she says, rising. "Too bad, wasn't it?" Mr. Tucker is watching the report of the ball scores and golf tournaments. "I'll drive you home in just a minute, dear," he says. "Why, how nice!" Mrs. Tucker exclaims from the kitchen. "The dishes are all done!"

• • •

"What can I say, Dolly?" the host says with a sigh, twisting the buttered strands of her ripped girdle between his fingers. "Your children are murdered, your husband gone, a corpse in your bathtub, and your house is wrecked. I'm sorry. But what can I say?" On the TV, the news is over, and they're selling aspirin. "Hell, *I* don't know," she says. "Let's see what's on the late late movie."

# Julio Cortázar

*Cortázar (1914–1984) was born in Brussels. He lived and began his work in Argentina. After 1951, he was established in Paris until his death. He was influenced first by his fellow Argentinean Jorge Luis Borges and later by French Surrealists. As a political activist he made his mark on left-wing theorists of Latin America; as a writer of fiction and verse he moved with the international avant-garde after World War II. Driven by a restless and wide-ranging imagination he produced a multitude of short stories, some of them collected in* The End of the Game *(1965),* We Love Glenda So Much *(1980), and* Unreasonable Hours *(1995).*

## A Continuity of Parks[1]

He had begun to read the novel a few days before. He had put it down because of some urgent business conferences, opened it again on his way back to the estate by train; he permitted himself a slowly growing interest in the plot, in the characterizations. That afternoon, after writing a letter giving his power of attorney and discussing a matter of joint ownership with the manager of his estate, he returned to the book in the tranquillity of his study which looked out upon the park with its oaks. Sprawled in his favorite armchair, its back toward the door—even the possibility of an intrusion would have irritated him, had he thought of it—he let his left hand caress repeatedly the green velvet upholstery and set to reading the final chapters. He remembered effortlessly the names and his mental image of the characters; the novel spread its glamour over him almost at once. He tasted the almost perverse pleasure of disengaging himself line by line from the things around him, and at the same time feeling his head rest comfortably on the green velvet of the chair with its high back, sensing that the cigarettes rested within reach of his hand, that beyond the great windows the air of afternoon danced under the oak trees in the park. Word by word, caught up in the sordid dilemma of the hero and heroine, letting himself be absorbed to the point where the images settled down and took on color and movement, he was witness to the final encounter in the mountain cabin. The woman arrived first, apprehensive; now the lover came in, his face cut by the backlash of a branch. Admirably, she stanched the blood

1. Translated by Paul Blackburn.

with her kisses, but he rebuffed her caresses, he had not come to perform again the ceremonies of a secret passion, protected by a world of dry leaves and furtive paths through the forest. The dagger warmed itself against his chest, and underneath liberty pounded, hidden close. A lustful, panting dialogue raced down the pages like a rivulet of snakes, and one felt it had all been decided from eternity. Even to those caresses which writhed about the lover's body, as though wishing to keep him there, to dissuade him from it; they sketched abominably the frame of that other body it was necessary to destroy. Nothing had been forgotten: alibis, unforeseen hazards, possible mistakes. From this hour on, each instant had its use minutely assigned. The cold-blooded, twice-gone-over reexamination of the details was barely broken off so that a hand could caress a cheek. It was beginning to get dark.

Not looking at one another now, rigidly fixed upon the task which awaited them, they separated at the cabin door. She was to follow the trail that led north. On the path leading in the opposite direction, he turned for a moment to watch her running, her hair loosened and flying. He ran in turn, crouching among the trees and hedges until, in the yellowish fog of dusk, he could distinguish the avenue of trees which led up to the house. The dogs were not supposed to bark, they did not bark. The estate manager would not be there at this hour, and he was not there. He went up the three porch steps and entered. The woman's words reached him over the thudding of blood in his ears: first a blue chamber, then a hall, then a carpeted stairway. At the top, two doors. No one in the first room, no one in the second. The door of the salon, and then, the knife in hand, the light from the great windows, the high back of an armchair covered in green velvet, the head of the man in the chair reading a novel.

# STEPHEN CRANE

*Crane (1871–1900) was born in Newark, New Jersey, the son of a Methodist minister. After schooling at Lafayette College and Syracuse University, he worked in New York as a freelance journalist. In 1893 he published at his own expense* Maggie: A Girl of the Streets, *a pioneering work of sociological realism. Two years later he brought out his famous short novel about the Civil War,* The Red Badge of Courage, *which in theme and technique foreshadows the war novels of the twentieth century. His short stories and experimental poetry also anticipate the ironic realism of the decades ahead. In his brief and energetic life he published fourteen books while acting out, in his personal adventures, the legend of the writer as soldier of fortune. On his way to Cuba for the first time he picked up a mistress at the Hotel de Dream in Jacksonville, Florida—a woman who accompanied him when he went on to Greece as a war correspondent. Malicious gossip about his private life subsequently drove him from America to England, where he settled in 1897 and made friends with leading English writers. In his travels he had accumulated a malignant tangle of debts. He was trying to free himself of them by writing when tuberculosis killed him, his promise only partially fulfilled. His short stories were collected in* "The Open Boat" and Other Tales of Adventure *(1898),* "The Monster" and Other Stories *(1899), and* Wounds in the Rain *(1900). His complete works in prose and verse were published in 1925–26.*

## The Open Boat

### A Tale Intended to Be after the Fact:[1] Being the Experience of Four Men from the Sunk Steamer COMMODORE

#### I

None of them knew the color of the sky. Their eyes glanced level and were fastened upon the waves that swept toward them. These waves were of the hue of slate, save for the tops, which were of foaming white, and all of the men knew the colors of the sea. The horizon narrowed and widened, and dipped and rose, and at all times its edge was jagged with waves that seemed thrust up in points like rocks.

Many a man ought to have a bathtub larger than the boat which here rode upon the sea. These waves were most wrongfully and barbarously abrupt and tall, and each froth-top was a problem in small-boat navigation.

1. Crane underwent the adventure that is here re-created in fiction. He also wrote a journalistic account of it, published in the New York *Press* (January 7, 1897).

The cook squatted in the bottom, and looked with both eyes at the six inches of gunwale which separated him from the ocean. His sleeves were rolled over his fat forearms, and the two flaps of his unbuttoned vest dangled as he bent to bail out the boat. Often he said, "Gawd! that was a narrow clip." As he remarked it he invariably gazed eastward over the broken sea.

The oiler, steering with one of the two oars in the boat, sometimes raised himself suddenly to keep clear of water that swirled in over the stern. It was a thin little oar, and it seemed often ready to snap.

The correspondent, pulling at the other oar, watched the waves and wondered why he was there.

The injured captain, lying in the bow, was at this time buried in that profound dejection and indifference which comes, temporarily at least, to even the bravest and most enduring when, willy-nilly, the firm fails, the army loses, the ship goes down. The mind of the master of a vessel is rooted deep in the timbers of her, though he command for a day or a decade; and this captain had on him the stern impression of a scene in the grays of dawn of seven turned faces, and later a stump of a topmast with a white ball on it, that slashed to and fro at the waves, went low and lower, and down. Thereafter there was something strange in his voice. Although steady, it was deep with mourning, and of a quality beyond oration or tears.

"Keep'er a little more south, Billie," said he.

"A little more south, sir," said the oiler in the stern.

A seat in his boat was not unlike a seat upon a bucking broncho, and by the same token a broncho is not much smaller. The craft pranced and reared and plunged like an animal. As each wave came, and she rose for it, she seemed like a horse making at a fence outrageously high. The manner of her scramble over these walls of water is a mystic thing, and, moreover, at the top of them were ordinarily these problems in white water, the foam racing down from the summit of each wave requiring a new leap, and a leap from the air. Then, after scornfully bumping a crest, she would slide and race and splash down a long incline, and arrive bobbing and nodding in front of the next menace.

A singular disadvantage of the sea lies in the fact that after successfully surmounting one wave you discover that there is another behind it just as important and just as nervously anxious to do something effective in the way of swamping boats. In a ten-foot dinghy one can get an idea of the resources of the sea in the line of waves that is not probable to the average experience, which is never at sea in a dinghy. As each slaty wall of water approached, it shut all else from the view of the men in the boat, and it was not difficult to imagine that this particular wave was the final outburst of the ocean, the last effort of the grim water. There was a terrible grace in the move of the waves, and they came in silence, save for the snarling of the crests.

In the wan light the faces of the men must have been gray. Their eyes must have glinted in strange ways as they gazed steadily astern. Viewed from a balcony, the whole thing would, doubtless, have been weirdly picturesque. But the men in the boat had no time to see it, and if they had had leisure, there were other things to occupy their minds. The sun swung steadily up the sky, and they knew it was broad day because the color of the sea changed from slate to emerald-green streaked with amber lights, and the foam was like tumbling snow. The process of the breaking day was unknown to them. They were aware only of this effect upon the color of the waves that rolled toward them.

In disjointed sentences the cook and the correspondent argued as to the difference between a life-saving station and a house of refuge. The cook had said: "There's a house of refuge just north of the Mosquito Inlet Light, and as soon as they see us they'll come off in their boat and pick us up."

"As soon as who see us?" said the correspondent.

"The crew," said the cook.

"Houses of refuge don't have crews," said the correspondent. "As I understand them, they are only places where clothes and grub are stored for the benefit of shipwrecked people. They don't carry crews."

"Oh, yes, they do," said the cook.

"No, they don't," said the correspondent.

"Well, we're not there yet, anyhow," said the oiler, in the stern.

"Well," said the cook, "perhaps it's not a house of refuge that I'm thinking of as being near Mosquito Inlet Light; perhaps it's a life-saving station."

"We're not there yet," said the oiler in the stern.

## II

As the boat bounced from the top of each wave the wind tore through the hair of the hatless men, and as the craft plopped her stern down again the spray slashed past them. The crest of each of these waves was a hill, from the top of which the men surveyed for a moment a broad tumultuous expanse, shining and wind-riven. It was probably splendid, it was probably glorious, this play of the free sea, wild with lights of emerald and white and amber.

"Bully good thing it's an on-shore wind," said the cook. "If not, where would we be? Wouldn't have a show."

"That's right," said the correspondent.

The busy oiler nodded his assent.

Then the captain, in the bow, chuckled in a way that expressed humor, contempt, tragedy, all in one. "Do you think we've got much of a show now, boys?" said he.

Whereupon the three were silent, save for a trifle of hemming and hawing. To express any particular optimism at this time they felt to be childish and stupid, but they all doubtless possessed this sense of the situation in their minds. A young man thinks doggedly at such times. On the other hand, the ethics of their condition was decidedly against any open suggestion of hopelessness. So they were silent.

"Oh, well," said the captain, soothing his children, "we'll get ashore all right."

But there was that in his tone which made them think; so the oiler quoth, "Yes! if this wind holds."

The cook was bailing. "Yes! if we don't catch hell in the surf."

Canton-flannel[2] gulls flew near and far. Sometimes they sat down on the

2. Actually a plain-weave cotton fabric.

sea, near patches of brown seaweed that rolled over the waves with a movement like carpets on a line in a gale. The birds sat comfortably in groups, and they were envied by some in the dinghy, for the wrath of the sea was no more to them than it was to a covey of prairie chickens a thousand miles inland. Often they came very close and stared at the men with black bead-like eyes. At these times they were uncanny and sinister in their unblinking scrutiny, and the men hooted angrily at them, telling them to be gone. One came, and evidently decided to alight on the top of the captain's head. The bird flew parallel to the boat and did not circle, but made short sidelong jumps in the air in chicken fashion. His black eyes were wistfully fixed upon the captain's head. "Ugly brute," said the oiler to the bird. "You look as if you were made with a jackknife." The cook and the correspondent swore darkly at the creature. The captain naturally wished to knock it away with the end of the heavy painter, but he did not dare do it, because anything resembling an emphatic gesture would have capsized this freighted boat; and so, with his open hand, the captain gently and carefully waved the gull away. After it had been discouraged from the pursuit the captain breathed easier on account of his hair, and others breathed easier because the bird struck their minds at this time as being somehow gruesome and ominous.

In the meantime the oiler and the correspondent rowed; and also they rowed. They sat together in the same seat, and each rowed an oar. Then the oiler took both oars; then the correspondent took both oars, then the oiler; then the correspondent. They rowed and they rowed. The very ticklish part of the business was when the time came for the reclining one in the stern to take his turn at the oars. By the very last star of truth, it is easier to steal eggs from under a hen than it was to change seats in the dinghy. First the man in the stern slid his hand along the thwart and moved with care, as if he were of Sèvres.[3] Then the man in the rowing-seat slid his hand along the other thwart. It was all done with the most extraordinary care. As the two sidled past each other, the whole party kept watchful eyes on the coming wave, and the captain cried: "Look out, now! Steady, there!"

The brown mats of seaweed that appeared from time to time were like islands, bits of earth. They were travelling, apparently, neither one way nor the other. They were, to all intents, stationary. They informed the men in the boat that it was making progress slowly toward the land.

The captain, rearing cautiously in the bow after the dinghy soared on a great swell, said that he had seen the lighthouse at Mosquito Inlet. Presently the cook remarked that he had seen it. The correspondent was at the oars then, and for some reason he too wished to look at the lighthouse, but his back was toward the far shore, and the waves were important, and for some time he could not seize an opportunity to turn his head. But at last there came a wave more gentle than the others, and when at the crest of it he swiftly scoured the western horizon.

"See it?" said the captain.

"No," said the correspondent, slowly; "I didn't see anything."

"Look again," said the captain. He pointed. "It's exactly in that direction."

3. A type of fine china.

At the top of another wave the correspondent did as he was bid, and this time his eyes chanced on a small, still thing on the edge of the swaying horizon. It was precisely like the point of a pin. It took an anxious eye to find a lighthouse so tiny.

"Think we'll make it, Captain?"

"If this wind holds and the boat don't swamp, we can't do much else," said the captain.

The little boat, lifted by each towering sea and splashed viciously by the crests, made progress that in the absence of seaweed was not apparent to those in her. She seemed just a wee thing wallowing, miraculously top up, at the mercy of five oceans. Occasionally a great spread of water, like white flames, swarmed into her.

"Bail her, cook," said the captain, serenely.

"All right, Captain," said the cheerful cook.

## III

It would be difficult to describe the subtle brotherhood of men that was here established on the seas. No one said that it was so. No one mentioned it. But it dwelt in the boat, and each man felt it warm him. They were a captain, an oiler, a cook, and a correspondent, and they were friends—friends in a more curiously iron-bound degree than may be common. The hurt captain, lying against the water jar in the bow, spoke always in a low voice and calmly; but he could never command a more ready and swiftly obedient crew than the motley three of the dinghy. It was more than a mere recognition of what was best for the common safety. There was surely in it a quality that was personal and heart-felt. And after this devotion to the commander of the boat, there was this comradeship, that the correspondent, for instance, who had been taught to be cynical of men, knew even at the time was the best experience of his life. But no one said that it was so. No one mentioned it.

"I wish we had a sail," remarked the captain. "We might try my overcoat on the end of an oar, and give you two boys a chance to rest." So the cook and the correspondent held the mast and spread wide the overcoat; the oiler steered; and the little boat made good way with her new rig. Sometimes the oiler had to scull sharply to keep a sea from breaking into the boat, but otherwise sailing was a success.

Meanwhile the lighthouse had been growing slowly larger. It had now almost assumed color, and appeared like a little gray shadow on the sky. The man at the oars could not be prevented from turning his head rather often to try for a glimpse of this little gray shadow.

At last, from the top of each wave, the men in the tossing boat could see land. Even as the lighthouse was an upright shadow on the sky, this land seemed but a long black shadow on the sea. It certainly was thinner than paper. "We must be about opposite New Smyrna,"[4] said the cook, who had coasted this shore often in schooners. "Captain, by the way, I believe they abandoned that life-saving station there about a year ago."

4. Town on the Florida coast.

"Did they?" said the captain.

The wind slowly died away. The cook and the correspondent were not now obliged to slave in order to hold high the oar. But the waves continued their old impetuous swooping at the dinghy, and the little craft, no longer underway, struggled woundily over them. The oiler or the correspondent took the oars again.

Shipwrecks are *apropos* of nothing. If men could only train for them and have them occur when the men had reached pink condition, there would be less drowning at sea. Of the four in the dinghy none had slept any time worth mentioning for two days and two nights previous to embarking in the dinghy, and in the excitement of clambering about the deck of a foundering ship they had also forgotten to eat heartily.

For these reasons, and for others, neither the oiler nor the correspondent was fond of rowing at this time. The correspondent wondered ingenuously how in the name of all that was sane could there be people who thought it amusing to row a boat. It was not an amusement; it was a diabolical punishment, and even a genius of mental aberrations could never conclude that it was anything but a horror to the muscles and a crime against the back. He mentioned to the boat in general how the amusement of rowing struck him, and the weary-faced oiler smiled in full sympathy. Previously to the foundering, by the way, the oiler had worked a double watch in the engine-room of the ship.

"Take her easy, now, boys," said the captain. "Don't spend yourselves. If we have to run a surf you'll need all your strength, because we'll sure have to swim for it. Take your time."

Slowly the land arose from the sea. From a black line it became a line of black and a line of white—trees and sand. Finally the captain said that he could make out a house on the shore. "That's the house of refuge, sure," said the cook. "They'll see us before long, and come out after us."

The distant lighthouse reared high. "The keeper ought to be able to make us out now, if he's looking through a glass," said the captain. "He'll notify the life-saving people."

"None of those other boats could have got ashore to give word of the wreck," said the oiler, in a low voice, "else the life-boat would be out hunting us."

Slowly and beautifully the land loomed out of the sea. The wind came again. It had veered from the northeast to the southeast. Finally a new sound struck the ears of the men in the boat. It was the low thunder of the surf on the shore. "We'll never be able to make the lighthouse now," said the captain. "Swing her head a little more north, Billie."

"A little more north, sir," said the oiler.

Whereupon the little boat turned her nose once more down the wind, and all but the oarsman watched the shore grow. Under the influence of this expansion doubt and direful apprehension were leaving the minds of the men. The management of the boat was still most absorbing, but it could not prevent a quiet cheerfulness. In an hour, perhaps, they would be ashore.

Their backbones had become thoroughly used to balancing in the boat, and they now rode this wild colt of a dinghy like circus men. The correspondent thought that he had been drenched to the skin, but happening to feel in the top pocket of his coat, he found therein eight cigars. Four of them were soaked with sea-water; four were perfectly scatheless. After a search, somebody produced three dry matches; and thereupon the four waifs rode impudently in their little boat and, with an assurance of an impending rescue shining in their eyes, puffed at the big cigars, and judged well and ill of all men. Everybody took a drink of water.

## IV

"Cook," remarked the captain, "there don't seem to be any signs of life about your house of refuge."

"No," replied the cook. "Funny they don't see us!"

A broad stretch of lowly coast lay before the eyes of the men. It was of low dunes topped with dark vegetation. The roar of the surf was plain, and sometimes they could see the white lip of a wave as it spun up the beach. A tiny house was blocked out black upon the sky. Southward, the slim lighthouse lifted its little gray length.

Tide, wind, and waves were swinging the dinghy northward. "Funny they don't see us," said the men.

The surf's roar was here dulled, but its tone was nevertheless thunderous and mighty. As the boat swam over the great rollers the men sat listening to this roar. "We'll swamp sure," said everybody.

It is fair to say here that there was not a life-saving station within twenty miles in either direction; but the men did not know this fact, and in consequence they made dark and opprobrious remarks concerning the eyesight of the nation's life-savers. Four scowling men sat in the dinghy and surpassed records in the invention of epithets.

"Funny they don't see us."

The light-heartedness of a former time had completely faded. To their sharpened minds it was easy to conjure pictures of all kinds of incompetency and blindness and, indeed, cowardice. There was the shore of the populous land, and it was bitter and bitter to them that from it came no sign.

"Well," said the captain, ultimately, "I suppose we'll have to make a try for ourselves. If we stay out here too long, we'll none of us have strength left to swim after the boat swamps."

And so the oiler, who was at the oars, turned the boat straight for the shore. There was a sudden tightening of muscles. There was some thinking.

"If we don't all get ashore," said the captain—"if we don't all get ashore, I suppose you fellows know where to send news of my finish?"

They then briefly exchanged some addresses and admonitions. As for the reflections of the men, there was a great deal of rage in them. Perchance they might be formulated thus: "If I am going to be drowned—if I am going to be drowned—if I am going to be drowned, why, in the name of the seven mad gods who rule the sea, was I allowed to come thus far and contemplate sand and trees? Was I brought here merely to have my nose dragged away as I was about to nibble the sacred cheese of life? It is preposterous. If this old ninny-woman, Fate, cannot do better than this, she should be deprived of the management of men's fortunes. She is an old hen who knows not her intention. If she has decided to drown me, why did she not do it in the beginning and save me all this trouble? The whole affair is absurd. . . . But no; she cannot mean to drown me. She dare not drown me. She cannot drown me. Not after all this work." Afterward the man might have had an impulse to shake his fist at the clouds. "Just you drown me, now, and then hear what I call you!"

The billows that came at this time were more formidable. They seemed always just about to break and roll over the little boat in a turmoil of foam. There was a preparatory and long growl in the speech of them. No mind unused to the sea would have concluded that the dinghy could ascend these sheer heights in time. The shore was still afar. The oiler was a wily surfman. "Boys," he said, swiftly, "she won't live three minutes more, and we're too far out to swim. Shall I take her to sea again, Captain?"

"Yes; go ahead!" said the captain.

This oiler, by a series of quick miracles and fast and steady oarsmanship, turned the boat in the middle of the surf and took her safely to sea again.

There was a considerable silence as the boat bumped over the furrowed sea to deeper water. Then somebody in gloom spoke: "Well, anyhow, they must have seen us from the shore by now."

The gulls went in slanting flight up the wind toward the gray, desolate east. A squall, marked by dingy clouds and clouds brick-red, like smoke from a burning building, appeared from the southeast.

"What do you think of those life-saving people? Ain't they peaches?"

"Funny they haven't seen us."

"Maybe they think we're out here for sport! Maybe they think we're fishin'. Maybe they think we're damned fools."

It was a long afternoon. A changed tide tried to force them southward, but wind and wave said northward. Far ahead, where coast-line, sea, and sky formed their mighty angle, there were little dots which seemed to indicate a city on the shore.

"St. Augustine?"

The captain shook his head. "Too near Mosquito Inlet."

And the oiler rowed, and then the correspondent rowed; then the oiler rowed. It was a weary business. The human back can become the seat of more aches and pains than are registered in books for the composite anatomy of a regiment. It is a limited area, but it can become the theatre of innumerable muscular conflicts, tangles, wrenches, knots, and other comforts.

"Did you ever like to row, Billie?" asked the correspondent.

"No," said the oiler; "hang it!"

When one exchanged the rowing-seat for a place in the bottom of the boat, he suffered a bodily depression that caused him to be careless of everything save an obligation to wiggle one finger. There was cold sea-water swashing to and fro in the boat, and he lay in it. His head, pillowed on a thwart, was within an inch of the swirl of a wave-crest, and sometimes a particularly obstreperous sea came inboard and drenched him once more. But these matters did not annoy him. It is almost certain that if the boat had capsized he would have tumbled comfortably out upon the ocean as if he felt sure that it was a great soft mattress.

"Look! There's a man on the shore!"

"Where?"

"There? See 'im? See 'im?"

"Yes, sure! He's walking along."

"Now he's stopped. Look! He's facing us!"

"He's waving at us!"

"So he is! By thunder!"

"Ah, now we're all right! Now we're all right! There'll be a boat out here for us in half an hour."

"He's going on. He's running. He's going up to that house there."

The remote beach seemed lower than the sea, and it required a searching glance to discern the little black figure. The captain saw a floating stick, and they rowed to it. A bath towel was by some weird chance in the boat, and, tying this on the stick, the captain waved it. The oarsman did not dare turn his head, so he was obliged to ask questions.

"What's he doing now?"

"He's standing still again. He's looking, I think. . . . There he goes again—toward the house. . . . Now he's stopped again."

"Is he waving at us?"

"No, not now; he was, though."

"Look! There comes another man!"

"He's running."

"Look at him go, would you!"

"Why, he's on a bicycle. Now he's met the other man. They're both waving at us. Look!"

"There comes something up the beach."

"What the devil is that thing?"

"Why, it looks like a boat."

"Why, certainly, it's a boat."

"No; it's on wheels."

"Yes, so it is. Well, that must be the life-boat. They drag them along shore on a wagon."

"That's the life-boat, sure."

"No, by God, it's—it's an omnibus."

"I tell you it's a life-boat."

"It is not! It's an omnibus. I can see it plain. See? One of these big hotel omnibuses."

"By thunder, you're right. It's an omnibus, sure as fate. What do you suppose they are doing with an omnibus? Maybe they are going around collecting the life-crew, hey?"

"That's it, likely. Look! There's a fellow waving a little black flag. He's standing on the steps of the omnibus. There come those other two fellows. Now they're all talking together. Look at the fellow with the flag. Maybe he ain't waving it!"

"That ain't a flag, is it? That's his coat. Why, certainly, that's his coat."

"So it is; it's his coat. He's taken it off and is waving it around his head. But would you look at him swing it!"

"Oh, say, there isn't any life-saving station there. That's just a winter-resort hotel omnibus that has brought over some of the boarders to see us drown."

"What's that idiot with the coat mean? What's he signaling, anyhow?"

"It looks as if he were trying to tell us to go north. There must be a life-saving station up there."

"No; he thinks we're fishing. Just giving us a merry hand. See? Ah, there, Willie!"

"Well, I wish I could make something out of those signals. What do you suppose he means?"

"He don't mean anything; he's just playing."

"Well, if he'd just signal us to try the surf again, or to go to sea and wait, or go north, or go south, or go to hell, there would be some reason in it. But look at him! He just stands there and keeps his coat revolving like a wheel. The ass!"

"There come more people."

"Now there's quite a mob. Look! Isn't that a boat?"

"Where? Oh, I see where you mean. No, that's no boat."

"That fellow is still waving his coat."

"He must think we like to see him do that. Why don't he quit it? It don't mean anything."

"I don't know. I think he is trying to make us go north. It must be that there's a life-saving station there somewhere."

"Say, he ain't tired yet. Look at 'im wave!"

"Wonder how long he can keep that up. He's been revolving his coat ever since he caught sight of us. He's an idiot. Why aren't they getting men to bring a boat out? A fishing boat—one of those big yawls—could come out here all right. Why don't he do something?"

"Oh, it's all right now."

"They'll have a boat out here for us in less than no time, now that they've seen us."

A faint yellow tone came into the sky over the low land. The shadows on the sea slowly deepened. The wind bore coldness with it, and the men began to shiver.

"Holy smoke!" said one, allowing his voice to express his impious mood, "if we keep on monkeying out here! If we've got to flounder out here all night!"

"Oh, we'll never have to stay here all night! Don't you worry. They've seen us now, and it won't be long before they'll come chasing out after us."

The shore grew dusky. The man waving a coat blended gradually into this gloom, and it swallowed in the same manner the omnibus and the group of people. The spray, when it dashed uproariously over the side, made the voyagers shrink and swear like men who were being branded.

"I'd like to catch the chump who waved the coat. I feel like socking him one, just for luck."

"Why? What did he do?"

"Oh, nothing, but then he seemed so damned cheerful."

In the meantime the oiler rowed, and then the correspondent rowed, and then the oiler rowed. Gray-faced and bowed forward, they mechanically, turn by turn, plied the leaden oars. The form of the lighthouse had vanished from the southern horizon, but finally a pale star appeared, just lifting from the sea. The streaked saffron in the west passed before the all-merging darkness, and the sea to the east was black. The land had vanished, and was expressed only by the low and drear thunder of the surf.

"If I am going to be drowned—if I am going to be drowned—if I am going to be drowned, why, in the name of the seven mad gods who rule the sea, was I allowed to come thus far and contemplate sand and trees? Was I brought here merely to have my nose dragged away as I was about to nibble the sacred cheese of life?"

The patient captain, drooped over the water-jar, was sometimes obliged to speak to the oarsman.

"Keep her head up! Keep her head up!"

"Keep her head up, sir." The voices were weary and low.

This was surely a quiet evening. All save the oarsman lay heavily and listlessly in the boat's bottom. As for him, his eyes were just capable of noting the tall black waves that swept forward in a most sinister silence, save for an occasional subdued growl of a crest.

The cook's head was on a thwart, and he looked without interest at the water under his nose. He was deep in other scenes. Finally he spoke. "Billie," he murmured, dreamfully, "what kind of pie do you like best?"

## V

"Pie!" said the oiler and the correspondent, agitatedly. "Don't talk about those things, blast you!"

"Well," said the cook, "I was just thinking about ham sandwiches, and——"

A night on the sea in an open boat is a long night. As darkness settled finally, the shine of the light, lifting from the sea in the south, changed to full gold. On the northern horizon a new light appeared, a small bluish gleam on the edge of the waters. These two lights were the furniture of the world. Otherwise there was nothing but waves.

Two men huddled in the stern, and distances were so magnificent in the dinghy that the rower was enabled to keep his feet partly warm by thrusting them under his companions. Their legs indeed extended far under the rowing-seat until they touched the feet of the captain forward. Sometimes, despite the efforts of the tired oarsman, a wave came piling into the boat, an icy wave of the night, and the chilling water soaked them anew. They would twist their bodies for a moment and groan, and sleep the dead sleep once more, while the water in the boat gurgled about them as the craft rocked.

The plan of the oiler and the correspondent was for one to row until he lost the ability, and then arouse the other from his sea-water couch in the bottom of the boat.

The oiler plied the oars until his head drooped forward and the overpowering sleep blinded him; and he rowed yet afterward. Then he touched a man in the bottom of the boat, and called his name. "Will you spell me for a little while?" he said meekly.

"Sure, Billie," said the correspondent, awaking and dragging himself to a sitting position. They exchanged places carefully, and the oiler, cuddling down in the sea-water at the cook's side, seemed to go to sleep instantly.

The particular violence of the sea had ceased. The waves came without snarling. The obligation of the man at the oars was to keep the boat headed so that the tilt of the rollers would not capsize her, and to preserve her from filling when the crests rushed past. The black waves were silent and hard to be seen in the darkness. Often one was almost upon the boat before the oarsman was aware.

In a low voice the correspondent addressed the captain. He was not sure that the captain was awake, although this iron man seemed to be always awake. "Captain, shall I keep her making for that light north, sir?"

The same steady voice answered him. "Yes. Keep it about two points off the port bow."

The cook had tied a life-belt around himself in order to get even the warmth which this clumsy cork contrivance could donate, and he seemed almost stove-like when a rower, whose teeth invariably chattered wildly as soon as he ceased his labor, dropped down to sleep.

The correspondent, as he rowed, looked down at the two men sleeping underfoot. The cook's arm was around the oiler's shoulders, and, with their fragmentary clothing and haggard faces, they were the babes of the sea—a grotesque rendering of the old babes in the wood.

Later he must have grown stupid at his work, for suddenly there was a growling of water, and a crest came with a roar and a swash into the boat, and it was a wonder that it did not set the cook afloat in his life-belt. The cook continued to sleep, but the oiler sat up, blinking his eyes and shaking with the new cold.

"Oh, I'm awful sorry, Billie," said the correspondent, contritely.

"That's all right, old boy," said the oiler, and lay down again and was asleep.

Presently it seemed that even the captain dozed, and the correspondent thought that he was the one man afloat on all the ocean. The wind had a voice as it came over the waves, and it was sadder than the end.

There was a long, loud swishing astern of the boat, and a gleaming trail of phosphorescence, like blue flame, was furrowed on the black waters. It might have been made by a monstrous knife.

Then there came a stillness, while the correspondent breathed with open mouth and looked at the sea.

Suddenly there was another swish and another long flash of bluish light, and this time it was alongside the boat, and might almost have been reached with an oar. The correspondent saw an enormous fin speed like a shadow through the water, hurling the crystalline spray and leaving the long glowing trail.

The correspondent looked over his shoulder at the captain. His face was hidden, and he seemed to be asleep. He looked at the babes of the sea. They certainly were asleep. So, being bereft of sympathy, he leaned a little way to one side and swore softly into the sea.

But the thing did not then leave the vicinity of the boat. Ahead or astern, on one side or the other, at intervals long or short, fled the long sparkling streak, and there was to be heard the *whirroo* of the dark fin. The speed and power of the thing was greatly to be admired. It cut the water like a gigantic and keen projectile.

The presence of this biding thing did not affect the man with the same horror that it would if he had been a picnicker. He simply looked at the sea dully and swore in an undertone.

Nevertheless, it is true that he did not wish to be alone with the thing. He wished one of his companions to awake by chance and keep him company with it. But the captain hung motionless over the water-jar and the oiler and the cook in the bottom of the boat were plunged in slumber.

## VI

"If I am going to be drowned—if I am going to be drowned—if I am going to be drowned, why, in the name of the seven mad gods who rule the sea, was I allowed to come thus far and contemplate sand and trees?"

During this dismal night, it may be remarked that a man would conclude that it was really the intention of the seven mad gods to drown him, despite the abominable injustice of it. For it was certainly an abominable injustice to drown a man who had worked so hard, so hard. The man felt it would be a crime most unnatural. Other people had drowned at sea since galleys swarmed with painted sails, but still——

When it occurs to a man that nature does not regard him as important, and that she feels she would not maim the universe by disposing of him, he at first wishes to throw bricks at the temple, and he hates deeply the fact that there are no bricks and no temples. Any visible expression of nature would surely be pelleted with his jeers.

Then, if there be no tangible thing to hoot, he feels, perhaps, the desire to confront a personification and indulge in pleas, bowed to one knee, and with hands supplicant, saying, "Yes, but I love myself."

A high cold star on a winter's night is the word he feels that she says to him. Thereafter he knows the pathos of his situation.

The men in the dinghy had not discussed these matters, but each had, no doubt, reflected upon them in silence and according to his mind. There was seldom any expression upon their faces save the general one of complete weariness. Speech was devoted to the business of the boat.

To chime the notes of his emotions, a verse mysteriously entered the correspondent's head. He had even forgotten that he had forgotten this verse, but it suddenly was in his mind.

A soldier of the Legion lay dying in Algiers;
There was lack of woman's nursing,
    there was dearth of woman's tears;
But a comrade stood beside him,
    and he took the comrade's hand,
And he said, "I never more shall see
    my own, my native land."[5]

5. From "Bingen on the Rhine," a sentimental poem by Caroline Norton (1808–1877).

In his childhood the correspondent had been made acquainted with the fact that a soldier of the Legion lay dying in Algiers, but he had never regarded it as important. Myriads of his schoolfellows had informed him of the soldier's plight, but the dinning had naturally ended by making him perfectly indifferent. He had never considered it his affair that a soldier of the Legion lay dying in Algiers, nor had it appeared to him as a matter for sorrow. It was less to him than the breaking of a pencil's point.

Now, however, it quaintly came to him as a human, living thing. It was no longer merely a picture of a few throes in the breast of a poet, meanwhile drinking tea and warming his feet at the grate; it was an actuality—stern, mournful, and fine.

The correspondent plainly saw the soldier. He lay on the sand with his feet out straight and still. While his pale left hand was upon his chest in an attempt to thwart the going of his life, the blood came between his fingers. In the far Algerian distance, a city of low square forms was set against a sky that was faint with the last sunset hues. The correspondent, plying the oars and dreaming of the slow and slower movements of the lips of the soldier, was moved by a profound and perfectly impersonal comprehension. He was sorry for the soldier of the Legion who lay dying in Algiers.

The thing which had followed the boat and waited had evidently grown bored at the delay. There was no longer to be heard the slash of the cutwater, and there was no longer the flame of the long trail. The light in the north still glimmered, but it was apparently no nearer to the boat. Sometimes the boom of the surf rang in the correspondent's ears, and he turned the craft seaward then and rowed harder. Southward, some one had evidently built a watch-fire on the beach. It was too low and too far to be seen, but it made a shimmering, roseate reflection upon the bluff in back of it, and this could be discerned from the boat. The wind came stronger, and sometimes a wave suddenly raged out like a mountain-cat, and there was to be seen the sheen and sparkle of a broken crest.

The captain, in the bow, moved on his water-jar and sat erect. "Pretty long night," he observed to the correspondent. He looked at the shore. "Those life-saving people take their time."

"Did you see that shark playing around?"

"Yes, I saw him. He was a big fellow, all right."

"Wish I had known you were awake."

Later the correspondent spoke into the bottom of the boat. "Billie!" There was a slow and gradual disentanglement. "Billie, will you spell me?"

"Sure," said the oiler.

As soon as the correspondent touched the cold, comfortable seawater in the bottom of the boat and had huddled close to the cook's life-belt he was deep in sleep, despite the fact that his teeth played all the popular airs. This sleep was so good to him that it was but a moment before he heard a voice call his name in a tone that demonstrated the last stages of exhaustion. "Will you spell me?"

"Sure, Billie."

The light in the north had mysteriously vanished, but the correspondent took his course from the wide-awake captain.

Later in the night they took the boat farther out to sea, and the captain directed the cook to take one oar at the stern and keep the boat facing the seas. He was to call out if he should hear the thunder of the surf. This plan enabled the oiler and the correspondent to get respite together. "We'll give those boys a chance to get into shape again," said the captain. They curled down and, after a few preliminary chatterings and trembles, slept once more the dead sleep. Neither knew they had bequeathed to the cook the company of another shark, or perhaps the same shark.

As the boat caroused on the waves, spray occasionally bumped over the side and gave them a fresh soaking, but this had no power to break their repose. The ominous slash of the wind and the water affected them as it would have affected mummies.

"Boys," said the cook, with the notes of every reluctance in his voice, "she's drifted in pretty close. I guess one of you had better take her to sea again." The correspondent, aroused, heard the crash of the toppled crests.

As he was rowing, the captain gave him some whiskey-and-water, and this steadied the chills out of him. "If I ever get ashore and anybody shows me even a photograph of an oar——"

At last there was a short conversation.

"Billie! . . . Billie, will you spell me?"

"Sure," said the oiler.

## VII

When the correspondent again opened his eyes, the sea and the sky were each of the gray hue of the dawning. Later, carmine and gold was painted upon the waters. The morning appeared finally, in its splendor, with a sky of pure blue, and the sunlight flamed on the tips of the waves.

On the distant dunes were set many little black cottages, and a tall white windmill reared above them. No man, nor dog, nor bicycle appeared on the beach. The cottages might have formed a deserted village.

The voyagers scanned the shore. A conference was held in the boat. "Well," said the captain, "if no help is coming, we might better try a run through the surf right away. If we stay out here much longer we will be too weak to do anything for ourselves at all." The others silently acquiesced in this reasoning. The boat was headed for the beach. The correspondent wondered if none ever ascended the tall wind-tower, and if then they never looked seaward. This tower was a giant, standing with its back to the plight of the ants. It represented in a degree, to the correspondent, the serenity of nature amid the struggles of the individual—nature in the wind, and nature in the vision of men. She did not seem cruel to him then, nor beneficent, nor treacherous, nor wise. But she was indifferent, flatly indifferent. It is, perhaps, plausible that a man in this situation, impressed with the unconcern of the universe, should see the innumerable flaws of his life, and have them taste wickedly in his mind, and wish for another chance. A distinction between right and wrong seems absurdly clear to him, then, in this new ignorance of the grave-edge, and he understands that if he were given another opportunity he would mend his conduct and his words, and be better and brighter during an introduction or at a tea.

"Now, boys," said the captain, "she is going to swamp sure. All we can do is to work her in as far as possible, and then when she swamps, pile out and scramble for the beach. Keep cool now, and don't jump until she swamps sure."

The oiler took the oars. Over his shoulders he scanned the surf. "Captain," he said, "I think I'd better bring her about and keep her head-on to the seas and back her in."

"All right, Billie," said the captain. "Back her in." The oiler swung the boat then, and, seated in the stern, the cook and the correspondent were obliged to look over their shoulders to contemplate the lonely and indifferent shore.

The monstrous inshore rollers heaved the boat high until the men were again enabled to see the white sheets of water scudding up the slanted beach. "We won't get in very close," said the captain. Each time a man could wrest his attention from the rollers, he turned his glance toward the shore, and in the expression of the eyes during this contemplation there was a singular quality. The correspondent, observing the others, knew that they were not afraid, but the full meaning of their glances was shrouded.

As for himself, he was too tired to grapple fundamentally with the fact. He tried to coerce his mind into thinking of it, but the mind was dominated at this time by the muscles, and the muscles said they did not care. It merely occurred to him that if he should drown it would be a shame.

There were no hurried words, no pallor, no plain agitation. The men simply looked at the shore. "Now, remember to get well clear of the boat when you jump," said the captain.

Seaward the crest of a roller suddenly fell with a thunderous crash, and the long white comber came roaring down upon the boat.

"Steady now," said the captain. The men were silent. They turned their eyes from the shore to the comber and waited. The boat slid up the incline, leaped at the furious top, bounced over it, and swung down the long back of the wave. Some water had been shipped, and the cook bailed it out.

But the next crest crashed also. The tumbling, boiling flood of white water caught the boat and whirled it almost perpendicular. Water swarmed in from all sides. The correspondent had his hands on the gunwale at this time, and when the water entered at that place he swiftly withdrew his fingers, as if he objected to wetting them.

The little boat, drunken with this weight of water, reeled and snuggled deeper into the sea.

"Bail her out, cook! Bail her out!" said the captain.

"All right, Captain," said the cook.

"Now, boys, the next one will do for us sure," said the oiler. "Mind to jump clear of the boat."

The third wave moved forward, huge, furious, implacable. It fairly swallowed the dinghy, and almost simultaneously the men tumbled into the sea. A piece of life-belt had lain in the bottom of the boat, and as the correspondent went overboard he held this to his chest with his left hand.

The January water was icy, and reflected immediately that it was colder than he had expected to find it off the coast of Florida. This appeared to his dazed mind as a fact important enough to be noted at the time. The coldness of the water was sad; it was tragic. This fact was somehow mixed and confused with his opinion of his own situation, so that it seemed almost a proper reason for tears. The water was cold.

When he came to the surface he was conscious of little but the noisy water. Afterward he saw his companions in the sea. The oiler was ahead in the race. He was swimming strongly and rapidly. Off to the correspondent's left, the cook's great white and corked back bulged out of the water, and in the rear the captain was hanging with his one good hand to the keel of the overturned dinghy.

There is a certain immovable quality to a shore, and the correspondent wondered at it amid the confusion of the sea.

It seemed also very attractive; but the correspondent knew that it was a long journey, and he paddled leisurely. The piece of life-preserver lay under him, and sometimes he whirled down the incline of a wave as if he were on a hand-sled.

But finally he arrived at a place in the sea where travel was beset with difficulty. He did not pause swimming to inquire what manner of current had caught him, but there his progress ceased. The shore was set before him like a bit of scenery on a stage, and he looked at it and understood with his eyes each detail of it.

As the cook passed, much farther to the left, the captain was calling to him, "Turn over on your back, cook! Turn over on your back and use the oar."

"All right, sir." The cook turned on his back, and, paddling with an oar, went ahead as if he were a canoe.

Presently the boat also passed to the left of the correspondent, with the captain clinging with one hand to the keel. He would have appeared like a man raising himself to look over a board fence if it were not for the extraordinary gymnastics of the boat. The correspondent marvelled that the captain could still hold to it.

They passed on nearer to shore—the oiler, the cook, the captain—and following them went the water-jar, bouncing gaily over the seas.

The correspondent remained in the grip of this strange new enemy, a current. The shore, with its white slope of sand and its green bluff topped with little silent cottages, was spread like a picture before him. It was very near to him then, but he was impressed as one who, in a gallery, looks at a scene from Brittany or Algiers.

He thought: "I am going to drown? Can it be possible? Can it be possible? Can it be possible?" Perhaps an individual must consider his own death to be the final phenomenon of nature.

But later a wave perhaps whirled him out of this small deadly current, for he found suddenly that he could again make progress toward the shore. Later still he was aware that the captain, clinging with one hand to the keel of the dinghy, had his face turned away from the shore and toward him, and was calling his name. "Come to the boat! Come to the boat!"

In his struggle to reach the captain and the boat, he reflected that when one gets properly wearied drowning must really be a comfortable arrangement—a cessation of hostilities accompanied by a large degree of relief; and he was glad of it, for the main thing in his mind for some moments had been horror of the temporary agony; he did not wish to be hurt.

Presently he saw a man running along the shore. He was undressing with most remarkable speed. Coat, trousers, shirt, everything flew magically off him.

"Come to the boat!" called the captain.

"All right, Captain." As the correspondent paddled, he saw the captain let himself down to bottom and leave the boat. Then the correspondent performed his one little marvel of the voyage. A large wave caught him and flung him with ease and supreme speed completely over the boat and far beyond it. It struck him even then as an event in gymnastics and a true miracle of the sea. An overturned boat in the surf is not a plaything to a swimming man.

The correspondent arrived in water that reached only to his waist, but his condition did not enable him to stand for more than a moment. Each wave knocked him into a heap, and the undertow pulled at him.

Then he saw the man who had been running and undressing, and undressing and running, come bounding into the water. He dragged ashore the cook, and then waded toward the captain; but the captain waved him away and sent him to the correspondent. He was naked—naked as a tree in winter; but a halo was about his head, and he shone like a saint. He gave a strong pull, and a long drag, and a bully heave at the correspondent's hand. The correspondent, schooled in the minor formulae, said, "Thanks, old man." But suddenly the man cried, "What's that?" He pointed a swift finger. The correspondent said, "Go."

In the shallows, face downward, lay the oiler. His forehead touched sand that was periodically, between each wave, clear of the sea.

The correspondent did not know all that transpired afterward. When he achieved safe ground he fell, striking the sand with each particular part of his body. It was as if he had dropped from a roof, but the thud was grateful to him.

It seems that instantly the beach was populated with men with blankets, clothes, and flasks, and women with coffee-pots and all the remedies sacred to their minds. The welcome of the land to the men from the sea was warm and generous; but a still and dripping shape was carried slowly up the beach, and the land's welcome for it could only be the different and sinister hospitality of the grave.

When it came night, the white waves paced to and fro in the moonlight, and the wind brought the sound of the great sea's voice to the men on the shore, and they felt that they could then be interpreters.

## ALLAN GURGANUS on *The Open Boat*

Few people are inconvenienced by shipwrecks. And fiction faces problems even tougher than your average sailing accident: how to elevate an ordinary landlocked day—its carpooling, its comparative shopping—into drama as life-and-death urgent as all those sharks aimed openmouthed toward your little lifeboat.

Great fiction requires more skill and spirit than simply "writing up" some endured disaster. If that alone made for major works of art, *Titanic* survivors and the bombardiers over Hiroshima would be modern letters' ruling geniuses. Happily for us surburbanites and mall-rats, they are not.

(In a double-parked station wagon, one mom slumps, waiting till her daughter, fourteen, completes the hundredth lesson on a clarinet this same girl will, by age eighteen, have cleanly forgotten: now that takes heroism.)

Stephen Crane, a Methodist preacher's hell-raising youngest son, would die of tuberculosis before age twenty-nine. Weaned on the Bible he resisted, Crane still dragged that book's undertow—its ethics and solemn sweetness—into baseball parks, pool halls, battle zones, Manhattan's darkest slums. The boy compacted into his fraction of a life many an ancient mariner's reckless quest.

The first day of 1897, a young newspaper reporter, seeking stories from the Spanish-American War, boarded *The Commodore,* a Cuba-bound ship. Loaded with rifles, rebels, and ammo, the vessel ran aground, then set to sea anyway. Mistake. A fast leak soon flooded the engine room. On deck, hysteria. One sailor fell to his knees before the captain, begging to be thrown overboard. Of our handsome correspondent, the captain would later say, "That man Crane is the spunkiest fellow out. . . . Many got sick but Crane was like an old sailor. . . . He was the first to volunteer to help. In the dinghy, he suggested putting up his overcoat for a sail. . . . He took his turn at the oars . . . he's a thoroughbred."

We now know that our narrative guide behaved well; we know he survived events not unlike those he shaped (that first week ashore) into "The Open Boat." But, how did young Stephen Crane transform this anecdotal mishap into a shape so fully mythic? Genius always helps. Crane bypasses the usual glamorous spectacle of a sinking ship; he understands which guys to include, and where to start his tale (40 percent of the way in). He riddles the raw experience with all five senses' awe.

"None of them knew the color of the sky." So our story begins, sensually, in living color, but with the horizon's usual twenty-twenty orientation suspended, withheld. We already feel adrift, hungry for news, eager for some fable's shoreline of hard-earned wisdom. Crane presents his voyage in prose as brisk and water clear as superb journalism. And yet, the language of this preacher's kid (all those Sundays, he was listening to Dad) grows rhythmically fulfilling and stained-glass pure as the King James Bible. Crane renders his waterlogged survivors as Everymen, while providing just enough identity to make each fellow count.

A favorite nineteenth-century theme pitted brutal Nature against innocent Mankind. Sir Edwin Landseer, the period's best-loved animal painter, depicted polar bears patrolling icy shipwrecks, seeking tasty human victims. What makes Crane's account so everlastingly contemporary? His natural world is not personified—not moralistically ajudged "red in tooth and claw" as Tennyson, Queen Victoria's favorite poet, quaintly described nature's simple ruthlessness. Instead, Crane's ocean seems amoral, as terrifyingly cool and neutral as cyberspace itself. His castaways might be unmoored shuttle astronauts—spun past voice range of any Mission Control—strangers adrift in some nebula unmapped. Their only true relation now is to themselves and to each other. The whole harsh universe seems abruptly masterminded as a great single theological test.

(Hemingway's telegraphic style and man-of-action stance is so prefigured in Crane, it looks cribbed. Hemingway's entire technique and subject matter might be summarized in one sentence written two years before his birth: "A night on the sea in an open boat is a long night.")

Crane's narrative, set down three years before 1900, prophesied and helped found the twentieth century's great theme: how the human psyche, having conquered so much of nature, finally settles into cannibalizing itself. How can sharks ever really scare a species that invented the Holocaust?

As if to predict twentieth-century powerlessness by eliminating the nineteenth century's pride in capacity, Stephen Crane deletes from the record his actual personal heroism.

When the real dinghy, sweeping ashore off Daytona, Florida, capsized, it crushed the first mate. Crane, trying to swim and save this man, sacrificed to the Atlantic his own heavy money belt; it had been laden with gold enough to see him through a long stay in Cuba. Despite his efforts, the other sailor drowned. Next day's newspaper, bearing all the vainglory of its age, read, "YOUNG NEW YORK WRITER ASTONISHED THE SEA DOGS BY HIS COURAGE IN THE FACE OF DEATH." This headline sounds as dated and comically old-fashioned as Crane's fiction still feels briney and immediate, as adaptable and oddly futuristic as the Bible itself.

What twenty-six-year-old man could bear—in his own tale of high-sea adventure—to hide his singular and noble acts? Answer: A great artist.

Crane neutralizes his own crazy physical courage to make room in his open boat for the rest of us sensible cowards. He admits mainly to his solidarity with others and his own quiet terror. Our narrator finally accepts the "serenity of nature amid the struggle of the individual. . . . She did not seem cruel to him then, nor beneficent, nor treacherous, nor wise. But she was indifferent, flatly indifferent."

How to lend heroism to an undifferentiated, carpooling weekday ashore? And how to render as natural, psychological, almost routine, some event harrowing and extreme as a shipwreck?

For all writers and readers, these constitute literature's twin capitals. What percentage of the mundane, how much of the heroic, can we honorably cargo from one into the other, and back and forth all day? Great works of art make peril at sea feel familiar as flossing; they can reveal one mom's carpooling to be headline worthy, brave, and pirate fierce.

Between these harbors, Port Heroic and Bay Mundane, we all commute. Scared to death ourselves, we still guard and reassure each another. Like Crane, we make a mainsail of our overcoat. And somehow—in our art and our acts—we briefly outwit the depths' indifference. Through almost any setback, we somehow tell, tell, tell ourselves to go ahead and row, row, row our little boat.

# The Blue Hotel

## I

The Palace Hotel at Fort Romper was painted a light blue, a shade that is on the legs of a kind of heron, causing the bird to declare its position against any background. The Palace Hotel, then, was always screaming and howling in a way that made the dazzling winter landscape of Nebraska seem only a gray swampish hush. It stood alone on the prairie, and when the snow was falling the town two hundred yards away was not visible. But when the traveler alighted at the railway station he was obliged to pass the Palace Hotel before he could come upon the company of low clapboard houses which composed Fort Romper, and it was not to be thought that any traveler could pass the Palace Hotel without looking at it. Pat Scully, the proprietor, had proved himself a master of strategy when he chose his paints. It is true that on clear days, when the great transcontinental express, long lines of swaying Pullmans, swept through Fort Romper, passengers were overcome at the sight, and the cult that knows the brown-reds and the subdivisions of the dark greens of the East expressed shame, pity, horror, in a laugh. But to the citizens of this prairie town and to the people who would naturally stop there, Pat Scully had performed a feat. With this opulence and splendor, these creeds, classes, egotisms, that streamed through Romper on the rails day after day, they had no color in common.

As if the display delights of such a blue hotel were not sufficiently enticing, it was Scully's habit to go every morning and evening to meet the leisurely trains that stopped at Romper and work his seductions upon any man that he might see wavering, gripsack in hand.

One morning, when a snow-crusted engine dragged its long string of freight cars and its one passenger coach to the station, Scully performed the marvel of catching three men. One was a shaky and quick-eyed Swede, with a great shining cheap valise; one was a tall bronzed cowboy, who was on his way to a ranch near the Dakota line; one was a little silent man from the East, who didn't look it, and didn't announce it. Scully practically made them prisoners. He was so nimble and merry and kindly that each probably felt it would be the height of brutality to try to escape. They trudged off over the creaking board sidewalks in the wake of the eager little Irishman. He wore a heavy fur cap squeezed tightly down on his head. It caused his two red ears to stick out stiffly, as if they were made of tin.

At last, Scully, elaborately, with boisterous hospitality, conducted them through the portals of the blue hotel. The room which they entered was small. It seemed to be merely a proper temple for an enormous stove, which, in the center, was humming with godlike violence. At various points on its surface the iron had become luminous and glowed yellow from the heat. Beside the stove Scully's son Johnnie was playing High-Five with an old farmer who had whiskers both gray and sandy. They were quarrelling. Frequently the old farmer turned his face toward a box of sawdust—colored brown from tobacco juice—that was behind the stove, and spat with an air of great impatience and irritation. With a loud flourish of words Scully destroyed the game of cards, and bustled his son upstairs with part of the baggage of the new guests. He himself conducted them to three basins of the coldest water in the world. The cowboy and the Easterner burnished themselves fiery red with this water, until it seemed to be some kind of metal polish. The Swede, however, merely dipped his fingers gingerly and with trepidation. It was notable that throughout this series of small ceremonies the three travelers were made to feel that Scully was very benevolent. He was conferring great favors upon them. He handed the towel from one to another with an air of philanthropic impulse.

Afterward they went to the first room, and sitting about the stove, listened to Scully's officious clamor at his daughters, who were preparing the midday meal. They reflected in the silence of experienced men who tread carefully amid new people. Nevertheless, the old farmer, stationary, invincible in his chair near the warmest part of the stove, turned his face from the sawdust-box frequently and addressed a glowing commonplace to the strangers. Usually he was answered in short but adequate sentences by either the cowboy or the Easterner. The Swede said nothing. He seemed to be occupied in making furtive estimates of each man in the room. One might have thought that he had the sense of silly suspicion which comes to guilt. He resembled a badly frightened man.

Later, at dinner, he spoke a little, addressing his conversation entirely to Scully. He volunteered that he had come from New York, where for ten years he had worked as a tailor. These facts seemed to strike Scully as fascinating, and afterward he volunteered that he had lived at Romper for fourteen years. The Swede asked about the crops and the price of labor. He seemed barely to listen to Scully's extended replies. His eyes continued to rove from man to man.

Finally, with a laugh and a wink, he said that some of these Western communities were very dangerous; and after his statement he straightened his legs under the table, tilted his head, and laughed again, loudly. It was plain that the demonstration had no meaning to the others. They looked at him wondering and in silence.

## II

As the men trooped heavily back into the front room, the two little windows presented views of a turmoiling sea of snow. The huge arms of the wind were making attempts—mighty, circular, futile—to embrace the flakes as they sped. A gate-post like a still man with a blanched face stood aghast amid this profligate fury. In a hearty voice Scully announced the presence of a blizzard. The guests of the blue hotel, lighting their pipes, assented with grunts of lazy masculine contentment. No island of the sea could be exempt in the degree of this little room with its humming stove. Johnnie, son of Scully, in a tone which defined his opinion of his ability as a card-player, challenged the old farmer of both gray and sandy whiskers to a game of High-Five. The farmer agreed with a contemptuous and bitter scoff. They sat close to the stove, and squared their knees under a wide board. The cowboy and the Easterner watched the game with interest. The Swede remained near the window, aloof, but with a countenance that showed signs of an inexplicable excitement.

The play of Johnnie and the gray-beard was suddenly ended by another quarrel. The old man arose while casting a look of heated scorn at his adversary. He slowly buttoned his coat, and then stalked with fabulous dignity from the room. In the discreet silence of all the other men the Swede laughed. His laughter rang somehow childish. Men by this time had begun to look at him askance, as if they wished to inquire what ailed him.

A new game was formed jocosely. The cowboy volunteered to become the partner of Johnnie, and they all then turned to ask the Swede to throw in his lot with the little Easterner. He asked some questions about the game, and, learning that it wore many names, and that he had played it when it was under an alias, he accepted the invitation. He strode toward the men nervously, as if he expected to be assaulted. Finally, seated, he gazed from face to face and laughed shrilly. This laugh was so strange that the Easterner looked up quickly, the cowboy sat intent and with his mouth open, and Johnnie paused, holding the cards with still fingers.

Afterward there was a short silence. Then Johnnie said, "Well, let's get at it. Come on now!" They pulled their chairs forward until their knees were bunched under the board. They began to play, and their interest in the game caused the others to forget the manner of the Swede.

The cowboy was a board-whacker. Each time that he held superior cards he whanged them, one by one, with exceeding force, down upon the improvised table, and took the tricks with a glowing air of prowess and pride that sent thrills of indignation into the hearts of his opponents. A game with a board-whacker in it is sure to become intense. The countenances of the Easterner and the Swede were miserable whenever the cowboy thundered down his aces and kings, while Johnnie, his eyes gleaming with joy, chuckled and chuckled.

Because of the absorbing play none considered the strange ways of the Swede. They paid strict heed to the game. Finally, during a lull caused by a new deal, the Swede suddenly addressed Johnnie: "I suppose there have been a good many men killed in this room." The jaws of the others dropped and they looked at him.

"What in hell are you talking about?" asked Johnnie.

The Swede laughed again his blatant laugh, full of a kind of false courage and defiance. "Oh, you know what I mean all right," he answered.

"I'm a liar if I do!" Johnnie protested. The card was halted, and the men stared at the Swede. Johnnie evidently felt that as the son of the proprietor he should make a direct inquiry. "Now, what might you be drivin' at, mister?" he asked. The Swede winked at him. It was a wink full of cunning. His fingers shook on the edge of the board. "Oh, maybe you think I have been to nowheres. Maybe you think I'm a tenderfoot?"

"I don't know nothin' about you," answered Johnnie, "and I don't give a damn where you've been. All I got to say is that I don't know what you're driving at. There hain't never been nobody killed in this room."

The cowboy, who had been steadily gazing at the Swede, then spoke: "What's wrong with you, mister?"

Apparently it seemed to the Swede that he was formidably menaced. He shivered and turned white near the corners of his mouth. He sent an appealing glance in the direction of the little Easterner. During these moments he did not forget to wear his air of advanced pot-valor. "They say they don't know what I mean," he remarked mockingly to the Easterner.

The latter answered after prolonged and cautious reflection. "I don't understand you," he said, impassively.

The Swede made a movement then which announced that he thought he had encountered treachery from the only quarter where he had expected sympathy, if not help. "Oh, I see you are all against me. I see—"

The cowboy was in a state of deep stupefaction. "Say," he cried, as he tumbled the deck violently down upon the board, "say, what are you gittin' at, hey?"

The Swede sprang up with the celerity of a man escaping from a snake on the floor. "I don't want to fight!" he shouted. "I don't want to fight!"

The cowboy stretched his long legs indolently and deliberately. His hands were in his pockets. He spat into the sawdust box. "Well, who the hell thought you did?" he inquired.

The Swede backed rapidly toward a corner of the room. His hands were out protectingly in front of his chest, but he was making an obvious struggle to control his fright. "Gentlemen," he quavered, "I suppose I am going to be killed before I can leave this house! I suppose I am going to be killed before I can leave this house!" In his eyes was the dying-swan look. Through the windows could be seen the snow turning blue in the shadow of dusk. The wind tore at the house, and some loose thing beat regularly against the clapboards like a spirit tapping.

A door opened, and Scully himself entered. He paused in surprise as he noted the tragic attitude of the Swede. Then he said, "What's the matter here?"

The Swede answered him swiftly and eagerly: "These men are going to kill me."

"Kill you!" ejaculated Scully. "Kill you! What are you talkin'?"

The Swede made the gesture of a martyr.

Scully wheeled sternly upon his son. "What is this, Johnnie?"

The lad had grown sullen. "Damned if I know," he answered. "I can't make no sense to it." He began to shuffle the cards, fluttering them together with an angry snap. "He says a good many men have been killed in this room, or something like that. And he says he's goin' to be killed here too. I don't know what ails him. He's crazy, I shouldn't wonder."

Scully then looked for explanation to the cowboy, but the cowboy simply shrugged his shoulders.

"Kill you?" said Scully again to the Swede. "Kill you? Man, you're off your nut."

"Oh, I know," burst out the Swede. "I know what will happen. Yes, I'm crazy—yes. Yes, of course, I'm crazy—yes. But I know one thing—" There was a sort of sweat of misery and terror upon his face. "I know I won't get out of here alive."

The cowboy drew a deep breath, as if his mind was passing into the last stages of dissolution. "Well, I'm doggoned," he whispered to himself.

Scully wheeled suddenly and faced his son. "You've been troublin' this man!"

Johnnie's voice was loud with its burden of grievance. "Why, good Gawd, I ain't done nothin' to 'im."

The Swede broke in. "Gentlemen, do not disturb yourselves. I will leave this house. I will go away, because"—he accused them dramatically with his glance—"because I do not want to be killed."

Scully was furious with his son. "Will you tell me what is the matter, you young divil? What's the matter, anyhow? Speak out!"

"Blame it!" cried Johnnie in despair, "don't I tell you I don't know? He—he says we want to kill him, and that's all I know. I can't tell what ails him."

The Swede continued to repeat: "Never mind, Mr. Scully; never mind. I will leave this house. I will go away, because I do not wish to be killed. Yes, of course, I am crazy—yes. But I know one thing! I will go away. I will leave this house. Never mind, Mr. Scully; never mind. I will go away."

"You will not go 'way," said Scully. "You will not go 'way until I hear the reason of this business. If anybody has troubled you I will take care of him. This is my house. You are under my roof, and I will not allow any peaceable man to be troubled here." He cast a terrible eye upon Johnnie, the cowboy, and the Easterner.

"Never mind, Mr. Scully, never mind. I will go away. I do not wish to be killed." The Swede moved toward the door which opened upon the stairs. It was evidently his intention to go at once for his baggage.

"No, no," shouted Scully peremptorily; but the white-faced man slid by him and disappeared. "Now," said Scully severely, "what does this mane?"

Johnnie and the cowboy cried together: "Why, we didn't do nothin' to 'im!"

Scully's eyes were cold. "No," he said, "you didn't?"

Johnnie swore a deep oath. "Why, this is the wildest loon I ever see. We didn't do nothin' at all. We were jest sittin' here playin' cards, and he—"

The father suddenly spoke to the Easterner. "Mr. Blanc," he asked, "what has these boys been doin'?"

The Easterner reflected again. "I didn't see anything wrong at all," he said at last, slowly.

Scully began to howl. "But what does it mane?" He stared ferociously at his son. "I have a mind to lather you for this, my boy."

Johnnie was frantic. "Well, what have I done?" he bawled at his father.

## III

"I think you are tongue-tied," said Scully finally to his son, the cowboy, and the Easterner; and at the end of this scornful sentence he left the room.

Upstairs the Swede was swiftly fastening the straps of his great valise. Once his back happened to be half turned toward the door, and, hearing a noise there, he wheeled and sprang up, uttering a loud cry. Scully's wrinkled visage showed grimly in the light of the small lamp he carried. This yellow effulgence, streaming upward, colored only his prominent features, and left his eyes, for instance, in mysterious shadow. He resembled a murderer.

"Man! man!" he exclaimed, "have you gone daffy?"

"Oh, no! Oh, no!" rejoined the other. "There are people in this world who know pretty nearly as much as you do—understand?"

For a moment they stood gazing at each other. Upon the Swede's deathly pale cheeks were two spots brightly crimson and sharply edged, as if they had been carefully painted. Scully placed the light on the table and sat himself on the edge of the bed. He spoke ruminatively. "By cracky, I never heard of such a thing in my life. It's a complete muddle. I can't, for the soul of me, think how you ever got this idea into your head." Presently he lifted his eyes and asked: "And did you sure think they were going to kill you?"

The Swede scanned the old man as if he wished to see into his mind. "I did," he said at last. He obviously suspected that this answer might precipitate an outbreak. As he pulled on a strap his whole arm shook, the elbow wavering like a bit of paper.

Scully banged his hand impressively on the footboard of the bed. "Why, man, we're goin' to have a line of ilictric street-cars in this town next spring."

" 'A line of electric street-cars,' " repeated the Swede, stupidly.

"And," said Scully, "there's a new railroad goin' to be built down from Broken Arm to here. Not to mintion the four churches and the smashin' big brick schoolhouse. Then there's the big factory, too. Why, in two years Romper'll be a met-tro-*pol*-is."

Having finished the preparation of his baggage, the Swede straightened himself. "Mr. Scully," he said, with sudden hardihood, "how much do I owe you?"

"You don't owe me anythin'," said the old man, angrily.

"Yes, I do," retorted the Swede. He took seventy-five cents from his pocket and tendered it to Scully; but the latter snapped his fingers in disdainful refusal. However, it happened that they both stood gazing in a strange fashion at three silver pieces on the Swede's open palm.

"I'll not take your money," said Scully at last. "Not after what's been goin' on here." Then a plan seemed to strike him. "Here," he cried, picking up his lamp and moving toward the door. "Here! Come with me a minute."

"No," said the Swede, in overwhelming alarm.

"Yes," urged the old man. "Come on! I want you to come and see a picter—just across the hall—in my room."

The Swede must have concluded that his hour was come. His jaw dropped and his teeth showed like a dead man's. He ultimately followed Scully across the corridor, but he had the step of one hung in chains.

Scully flashed the light high on the wall of his own chamber. There was revealed a ridiculous photograph of a little girl. She was leaning against a balustrade of gorgeous decoration, and the formidable bang to her hair was prominent. The figure was as graceful as an upright sled-stake, and, withal, it was the hue of lead. "There," said Scully tenderly, "that's the picter of my little girl that died. Her name was Carrie. She had the purtiest hair you ever saw! I was that fond of her, she—"

Turning then, he saw that the Swede was not contemplating the picture at all, but, instead, was keeping keen watch on the gloom in the rear.

"Look, man!" cried Scully, heartily. "That's the picter of my little gal that died. Her name was Carrie. And then here's the picter of my oldest boy, Michael. He's a lawyer in Lincoln, an' doin' well. I gave that boy a grand eddication, and I'm glad for it now. He's a fine boy. Look at 'im now. Ain't he bold as blazes, him there in Lincoln, an honored an' respicted gintleman! An honored and respected gintleman," concluded Scully with a flourish. And, so saying, he smote the Swede jovially on the back.

The Swede faintly smiled.

"Now," said the old man, "there's only one more thing." He dropped suddenly to the floor and thrust his head beneath the bed. The Swede could hear his muffled voice. "I'd keep it under me piller if it wasn't for that boy Johnnie.

Then there's the old woman—Where is it now? I never put it twice in the same place. Ah, now come out with you!"

Presently he backed clumsily from under the bed, dragging with him an old coat rolled into a bundle. "I've fetched him," he muttered. Kneeling on the floor, he unrolled the coat and extracted from its heart a large yellow-brown whiskey-bottle.

His first manoeuver was to hold the bottle up to the light. Reassured, apparently, that nobody had been tampering with it, he thrust it with a generous movement toward the Swede.

The weak-kneed Swede was about to eagerly clutch this element of strength, but he suddenly jerked his hand away and cast a look of horror upon Scully.

"Drink," said the old man affectionately. He had risen to his feet, and now stood facing the Swede.

There was a silence. Then again Scully said: "Drink!"

The Swede laughed wildly. He grabbed the bottle, put it to his mouth; and as his lips curled absurdly around the opening and his throat worked, he kept his glance, burning with hatred, upon the old man's face.

## IV

After the departure of Scully the three men, with the cardboard still upon their knees, preserved for a long time an astounded silence. Then Johnnie said: "That's the doddangedest Swede I ever see."

"He ain't no Swede," said the cowboy, scornfully.

"Well, what is he then?" cried Johnnie. "What is he then?"

"It's my opinion," replied the cowboy deliberately, "he's some kind of a Dutchman." It was a venerable custom of the country to entitle as Swedes all light-haired men who spoke with a heavy tongue. In consequence the idea of the cowboy was not without its daring. "Yes, sir," he repeated. "It's my opinion this feller is some kind of a Dutchman."

"Well, he says he's a Swede, anyhow," muttered Johnnie, sulkily. He turned to the Easterner: "What do you think, Mr. Blanc?"

"Oh, I don't know," replied the Easterner.

"Well, what do you think makes him act that way?" asked the cowboy.

"Why, he's frightened." The Easterner knocked his pipe against a rim of the stove. "He's clear frightened out of his boots."

"What at?" cried Johnnie and the cowboy together.

The Easterner reflected over his answer.

"What at?" cried the others again.

"Oh, I don't know, but it seems to me this man has been reading dime novels, and he thinks he's right out in the middle of it—the shootin' and stabbin' and all."

"But," said the cowboy, deeply scandalized, "this ain't Wyoming, ner none of them places. This is Nebrasker."

"Yes," added Johnnie, "an' why don't he wait till he gits *out West*?"

The travelled Easterner laughed. "It isn't different there even—not in these days. But he thinks he's right in the middle of hell."

Johnnie and the cowboy mused long.

"It's awful funny," remarked Johnnie at last.

"Yes," said the cowboy. "This is a queer game. I hope we don't git snowed in, because then we'd have to stand this here man bein' around with us all the time. That wouldn't be no good."

"I wish pop would throw him out," said Johnnie.

Presently they heard a loud stamping on the stairs, accompanied by ringing jokes in the voice of old Scully, and laughter, evidently from the Swede. The men around the stove stared vacantly at each other. "Gosh!" said the cowboy. The door flew open, and old Scully, flushed and anecdotal, came into the room. He was jabbering at the Swede, who followed him, laughing bravely. It was the entry of two roisterers from a banquet ball.

"Come now," said Scully sharply to the three seated men, "move up and give us a chance at the stove." The cowboy and the Easterner obediently sidled their chairs to make room for the newcomers. Johnnie, however, simply arranged himself in a more indolent attitude, and then remained motionless.

"Come! Git over, there," said Scully.

"Plenty of room on the other side of the stove," said Johnnie.

"Do you think we want to sit in the draught?" roared the father.

But the Swede here interposed with a grandeur of confidence. "No, no. Let the boy sit where he likes," he cried in a bullying voice to the father.

"All right! All right!" said Scully, deferentially. The cowboy and the Easterner exchanged glances of wonder.

The five chairs were formed in a crescent about one side of the stove. The Swede began to talk; he talked arrogantly, profanely, angrily. Johnnie, the cowboy, and the Easterner maintained a morose silence, while old Scully appeared to be receptive and eager, breaking in constantly with sympathetic ejaculations.

Finally the Swede announced that he was thirsty. He moved in his chair, and said that he would go for a drink of water.

"I'll git it for you," cried Scully at once.

"No," said the Swede, contemptuously. "I'll get it for myself." He arose and stalked with the air of an owner off into the executive parts of the hotel.

As soon as the Swede was out of hearing Scully sprang to his feet and whispered intensely to the others: "Up-stairs he thought I was tryin' to poison 'im."

"Say," said Johnnie, "this makes me sick. Why don't you throw 'im out in the snow?"

"Why, he's all right now," declared Scully. "It was only that he was from the East, and he thought this was a tough place. That's all. He's all right now."

The cowboy looked with admiration upon the Easterner. "You were straight," he said. "You were on to that there Dutchman."

"Well," said Johnnie to his father, "he may be all right now, but I don't see it. Other time he was scared, but now he's too fresh."

Scully's speech was always a combination of Irish brogue and idiom, Western twang and idiom, and scraps of curiously formal diction taken from the story-books and newspapers. He now hurled a strange mass of language at the at do I keep? What do I keep? What do I keep?" he ... thunder. He slapped his knee impressively, to indicate ...oing to make reply, and that all should heed. "I keep a ... A hotel, do you mind? A guest under my roof has sacred ...e intimidated by none. Not one word shall he hear that ... in favor of goin' away. I'll not have it. There's no place in ...re they can say they iver took in a guest of mine because he ...ere." He wheeled suddenly upon the cowboy and the East-...

...ally," said the cowboy, "I think you're right."

...ully," said the Easterner, "I think you're right."

## V

...lock supper, the Swede fizzed like a fire-wheel. He sometimes ... the point of bursting into riotous song, and in all his madness he ...couraged by old Scully. The Easterner was encased in reserve; the cow-...y sat in wide-mouthed amazement, forgetting to eat, while Johnnie wrathily demolished great plates of food. The daughters of the house, when they were obliged to replenish the biscuits, approached as warily as Indians, and, having succeeded in their purposes, fled with ill-concealed trepidation. The Swede domineered the whole feast, and he gave it the appearance of a cruel bacchanal. He seemed to have grown suddenly taller; he gazed, brutally disdainful, into every face. His voice rang through the room. Once when he jabbed out harpoon-fashion with his fork to pinion a biscuit, the weapon nearly impaled the hand of the Easterner, which had been stretched quietly out for the same biscuit.

After supper, as the men filed toward the other room, the Swede smote Scully ruthlessly on the shoulder. "Well, old boy, that was a good, square meal." Johnnie looked hopefully at his father; he knew that shoulder was tender from an old fall; and, indeed, it appeared for a moment as if Scully was going to flame out over the matter, but in the end he smiled a sickly smile and remained silent. The others understood from his manner that he was admitting his responsibility for the Swede's new view-point.

Johnnie, however, addressed his parent in an aside. "Why don't you license somebody to kick you downstairs?" Scully scowled darkly by way of reply.

When they were gathered about the stove, the Swede insisted on another game of High-Five. Scully gently deprecated the plan at first, but the Swede turned a wolfish glare upon him. The old man subsided, and the Swede canvassed the others. In his tone there was always a great threat. The cowboy and the Easterner both remarked indifferently that they would play. Scully said that he would presently have to go to meet the 6.58 train, and so the Swede turned menacingly upon Johnnie. For a moment their glances crossed like blades, and then Johnnie smiled and said, "Yes, I'll play."

They formed a square, with the little board on their knees. The Easterner and the Swede were again partners. As the play went on, it was noticeable that the cowboy was not board-whacking as usual. Meanwhile, Scully, near the lamp, had put on his spectacles and, with an appearance curiousl was reading a newspaper. In time he went out to meet th despite his precautions, a gust of polar wind whirled into the r the door. Besides scattering the cards, it chilled the players to th Swede cursed frightfully. When Scully returned, his entrance di and friendly scene. The Swede again cursed. But presently they we intent, their heads bent forward and their hands moving swiftly. had adopted the fashion of board-whacking.

Scully took up his paper and for a long time remained immersed in which were extraordinarily remote from him. The lamp burned badly, an he stopped to adjust the wick. The newspaper, as he turned from page to rustled with a slow and comfortable sound. Then suddenly he heard th terrible words: "You are cheatin'!"

Such scenes often prove that there can be little of dramatic import in environment. Any room can present a tragic front; any room can be comic. This little den was now hideous as a torture-chamber. The new faces of the men themselves had changed it upon the instant. The Swede held a huge fist in front of Johnnie's face, while the latter looked steadily over it into the blazing orbs of his accuser. The Easterner had grown pallid; the cowboy's jaw had dropped in that expression of bovine amazement which was one of his important mannerisms. After the three words, the first sound in the room was made by Scully's paper as it floated forgotten to his feet. His spectacles had also fallen from his nose, but by a clutch he had saved them in air. His hand, grasping the spectacles, now remained poised awkwardly and near his shoulder. He stared at the card-players.

Probably the silence was while a second elapsed. Then, if the floor had been suddenly twitched out from under the men they could not have moved quicker. The five had projected themselves headlong toward a common point. It happened that Johnnie, in rising to hurl himself upon the Swede, had stumbled slightly because of his curiously instinctive care for the cards and the board. The loss of the moment allowed time for the arrival of Scully, and also allowed the cowboy time to give the Swede a great push which sent him staggering back. The men found tongue together, and hoarse shouts of rage, appeal, or fear burst from every throat. The cowboy pushed and jostled feverishly at the Swede, and the Easterner and Scully clung wildly to Johnnie; but through the smoky air, above the swaying bodies of the peace-compellers, the eyes of the two warriors ever sought each other in glances of challenge that were at once hot and steely.

Of course the board had been overturned, and now the whole company of cards was scattered over the floor, where the boots of the men trampled the fat and painted kings and queens as they gazed with their silly eyes at the war that was waging above them.

Scully's voice was dominating the yells. "Stop now! Stop, I say! Stop, now—"

Johnnie, as he struggled to burst through the rank formed by Scully and the Easterner, was crying, "Well, he says I cheated! He says I cheated! I won't allow no man to say I cheated! If he says I cheated, he's a——!"

The cowboy was telling the Swede, "Quit, now! Quit, d'ye hear—"

The screams of the Swede never ceased: "He did cheat! I saw him! I saw him—"

As for the Easterner, he was importuning in a voice that was not heeded: "Wait a moment, can't you? Oh, wait a moment. What's the good of a fight over a game of cards? Wait a moment—"

In this tumult no complete sentences were clear. "Cheat"—"Quit"—"He says"—these fragments pierced the uproar and rang out sharply. It was remarkable that, whereas Scully undoubtedly made the most noise, he was the least heard of any of the riotous band.

Then suddenly there was a great cessation. It was as if each man had paused for breath; and although the room was still lighted with the anger of men, it could be seen that there was no danger of immediate conflict, and at once Johnnie, shouldering his way forward, almost succeeded in confronting the Swede. "What did you say I cheated for? What did you say I cheated for? I don't cheat, and I won't let no man say I do!"

The Swede said, "I saw you! I saw you!"

"Well," cried Johnnie, "I'll fight any man what says I cheat!"

"No, you won't," said the cowboy. "Not here."

"Ah, be still, can't you?" said Scully, coming between them.

The quiet was sufficient to allow the Easterner's voice to be heard. He was repeating, "Oh, wait a moment, can't you? What's the good of a fight over a game of cards? Wait a moment!"

Johnnie, his red face appearing above his father's shoulder, hailed the Swede again. "Did you say I cheated?"

The Swede showed his teeth. "Yes."

"Then," said Johnnie, "we must fight."

"Yes, fight," roared the Swede. He was like a demoniac. "Yes, fight! I'll show you what kind of a man I am! I'll show you who you want to fight! Maybe you think I can't fight! Maybe you think I can't! I'll show you, you skin, you card-sharp! Yes, you cheated! You cheated! You cheated!"

"Well, let's go at it, then, mister," said Johnnie, coolly.

The cowboy's brow was beaded with sweat from his efforts in intercepting all sorts of raids. He turned in despair to Scully. "What are you goin' to do now?"

A change had come over the Celtic visage of the old man. He now seemed all eagerness; his eyes glowed.

"We'll let them fight," he answered stalwartly. "I can't put up with it any longer. I've stood this damned Swede till I'm sick. We'll let them fight."

## VI

The men prepared to go out-of-doors. The Easterner was so nervous that he had great difficulty in getting his arms into the sleeves of his new leather coat. As the cowboy drew his fur cap down over his ears his hands trembled. In fact, Johnnie and old Scully were the only ones who displayed no agitation. These preliminaries were conducted without words.

Scully threw open the door. "Well, come on," he said. Instantly a terrific wind caused the flame of the lamp to struggle at its wick, while a puff of black smoke sprang from the chimney-top. The stove was in mid-current of the blast, and its voice swelled to equal the roar of the storm. Some of the scarred and bedabbled cards were caught up from the floor and dashed helplessly against the further wall. The men lowered their heads and plunged into the tempest as into a sea.

No snow was falling, but great whirls and clouds of flakes, swept up from the ground by the frantic winds, were streaming southward with the speed of bullets. The covered land was blue with the sheen of an unearthly satin, and there was no other hue save where, at the low, black railway station—which seemed incredibly distant—one light gleamed like a tiny jewel. As the men floundered into a thigh-deep drift, it was known that the Swede was bawling out something. Scully went to him, put a hand on his shoulder, and projected an ear. "What's that you say?" he shouted.

"I say," bawled the Swede again, "I won't stand much show against this gang. I know you'll all pitch on me."

Scully smote him reproachfully on the arm. "Tut, man!" he yelled. The wind tore the words from Scully's lips and scattered them far a-lee.

"You are all a gang of—" boomed the Swede, but the storm also seized the remainder of this sentence.

Immediately turning their backs upon the wind, the men had swung around a corner to the sheltered side of the hotel. It was the function of the little house to preserve here, amid this great devastation of snow, an irregular V-shape of heavily encrusted grass, which crackled beneath the feet. One could imagine the great drifts piled against the windward side. When the party reached the comparative peace of this spot it was found that the Swede was still bellowing.

"Oh, I know what kind of a thing this is! I know you'll all pitch on me. I can't lick you all!"

Scully turned upon him panther-fashion. "You'll not have to whip all of us. You'll have to whip my son Johnnie. An' the man what troubles you durin' that time will have me to dale with."

The arrangements were swiftly made. The two men faced each other, obedient to the harsh commands of Scully, whose face, in the subtly luminous gloom, could be seen set in the austere impersonal lines that are pictured on the countenances of the Roman veterans. The Easterner's teeth were chattering, and he was hopping up and down like a mechanical toy. The cowboy stood rocklike.

The contestants had not stripped off any clothing. Each was in his ordinary attire. Their fists were up, and they eyed each other in a calm that had the elements of leonine cruelty in it.

During this pause, the Easterner's mind, like a film, took lasting impressions of three men—the iron-nerved master of the ceremony; the Swede, pale, motionless, terrible; and Johnnie, serene yet ferocious, brutish yet heroic. The entire prelude had in it a tragedy greater than the tragedy of action, and this aspect was accentuated by the long, mellow cry of the blizzard, as it sped the tumbling and wailing flakes into the black abyss of the south.

"Now!" said Scully.

The two combatants leaped forward and crashed together like bullocks. There was heard the cushioned sound of blows, and of a curse squeezing out from between the tight teeth of one.

As for the spectators, the Easterner's pent-up breath exploded from him with a pop of relief, absolute relief from the tension of the preliminaries. The cowboy bounded into the air with a yowl. Scully was immovable as from supreme amazement and fear at the fury of the fight which he himself had permitted and arranged.

For a time the encounter in the darkness was such a perplexity of flying arms that it presented no more detail than would a swiftly revolving wheel. Occasionally a face, as if illumined by a flash of light, would shine out, ghastly and marked with pink spots. A moment later, the men might have been known as shadows, if it were not for the involuntary utterance of oaths that came from them in whispers.

Suddenly a holocaust of warlike desire caught the cowboy, and he bolted forward with the speed of a broncho. "Go it, Johnnie! Go it! Kill him! Kill him!"

Scully confronted him. "Kape back," he said; and by his glance the cowboy could tell that this man was Johnnie's father.

To the Easterner there was a monotony of unchangeable fighting that was an abomination. This confused mingling was eternal to his sense, which was concentrated in a longing for the end, the priceless end. Once the fighters lurched near him, and as he scrambled hastily backward he heard them breathe like men on the rack.

"Kill him, Johnnie! Kill him! Kill him! Kill him!" The cowboy's face was contorted like one of those agony masks in museums.

"Keep still," said Scully, icily.

Then there was a sudden loud grunt, incomplete, cut short, and Johnnie's body swung away from the Swede and fell with sickening heaviness to the grass. The cowboy was barely in time to prevent the mad Swede from flinging himself upon his prone adversary. "No, you don't," said the cowboy, interposing an arm. "Wait a second."

Scully was at his son's side. "Johnnie! Johnnie, me boy!" His voice had a quality of melancholy tenderness. "Johnnie! Can you go on with it?" He looked anxiously down into the bloody, pulpy face of his son.

There was a moment of silence, and then Johnnie answered in his ordinary voice, "Yes, I—it—yes."

Assisted by his father he struggled to his feet. "Wait a bit now till you git your wind," said the old man.

A few paces away the cowboy was lecturing the Swede. "No, you don't! Wait a second!"

The Easterner was plucking at Scully's sleeve. "Oh, this is enough," he pleaded. "This is enough! Let it go as it stands. This is enough!"

"Bill," said Scully, "git out of the road." The cowboy stepped aside. "Now." The combatants were actuated by a new caution as they advanced toward collision. They glared at each other, and then the Swede aimed a lightning blow that carried with it his entire weight. Johnnie was evidently half stupid from weakness, but he miraculously dodged, and his fist sent the overbalanced Swede sprawling.

The cowboy, Scully, and the Easterner burst into a cheer that was like a chorus of triumphant soldiery, but before its conclusion the Swede had scuffled agilely to his feet and come in berserk abandon at his foe. There was another perplexity of flying arms, and Johnnie's body again swung away and fell, even as a bundle might fall from a roof. The Swede instantly staggered to a little wind-waved tree and leaned upon it, breathing like an engine, while his savage and flame-lit eyes roamed from face to face as the men bent over Johnnie. There was a splendor of isolation in his situation at this time which the Easterner felt once when, lifting his eyes from the man on the ground, he beheld that mysterious and lonely figure, waiting.

"Are you any good yet, Johnnie?" asked Scully in a broken voice.

The son gasped and opened his eyes languidly. After a moment he answered, "No—I ain't—any good—any—more." Then, from shame and bodily ill, he began to weep, the tears furrowing down through the blood-stains on his face. "He was too—too—too heavy for me."

Scully straightened and addressed the waiting figure. "Stranger," he said, evenly, "it's all up with our side." Then his voice changed into that vibrant huskiness which is commonly the tone of the most simple and deadly announcements. "Johnnie is whipped."

Without replying, the victor moved off on the route to the front door of the hotel.

The cowboy was formulating new and unspellable blasphemies. The Easterner was startled to find that they were out in a wind that seemed to come direct from the shadowed arctic floes. He heard again the wail of the snow as it was flung to its grave in the south. He knew now that all this time the cold had been sinking into him deeper and deeper, and he wondered that he had not perished. He felt indifferent to the condition of the vanquished man.

"Johnnie, can you walk?" asked Scully.

"Did I hurt—hurt him any?" asked the son.

"Can you walk, boy? Can you walk?"

Johnnie's voice was suddenly strong. There was a robust impatience in it. "I asked you whether I hurt him any!"

"Yes, yes, Johnnie," answered the cowboy, consolingly; "he's hurt a good deal."

They raised him from the ground, and as soon as he was on his feet he went tottering off, rebuffing all attempts at assistance. When the party rounded the corner they were fairly blinded by the pelting of the snow. It burned their faces like fire. The cowboy carried Johnnie through the drift to the door. As they entered, some cards again rose from the floor and beat against the wall.

The Easterner rushed to the stove. He was so profoundly chilled that he almost dared to embrace the glowing iron. The Swede was not in the room. Johnnie sank into a chair and, folding his arms on his knees, buried his face in them. Scully, warming one foot and then the other at a rim of the stove, muttered to himself with Celtic mournfulness. The cowboy had removed his fur cap, and with a dazed and rueful air he was running one hand through his tousled locks. From overhead they could hear the creaking of boards, as the Swede tramped here and there in his room.

The sad quiet was broken by the sudden flinging open of a door that led toward the kitchen. It was instantly followed by an inrush of women. They precipitated themselves upon Johnnie amid a chorus of lamentation. Before they carried their prey off to the kitchen, there to be bathed and harangued with that mixture of sympathy and abuse which is a feat of their sex, the mother straightened herself and fixed old Scully with an eye of stern reproach. "Shame be upon you, Patrick Scully!" she cried. "Your own son, too. Shame be upon you!"

"There, now! Be quiet, now!" said the old man, weakly.

"Shame be upon you, Patrick Scully!" The girls, rallying to this slogan, sniffed disdainfully in the direction of those trembling accomplices, the cowboy and the Easterner. Presently they bore Johnnie away, and left the three men to dismal reflection.

## VII

"I'd like to fight this here Dutchman myself," said the cowboy, breaking a long silence.

Scully wagged his head sadly. "No, that wouldn't do. It wouldn't be right. It wouldn't be right."

"Well, why wouldn't it?" argued the cowboy. "I don't see no harm in it."

"No," answered Scully, with mournful heroism. "It wouldn't be right. It was Johnnie's fight, and now we mustn't whip the man just because he whipped Johnnie."

"Yes, that's true enough," said the cowboy; "but—he better not get fresh with me, because I couldn't stand no more of it."

"You'll not say a word to him," commanded Scully, and even then they heard the tread of the Swede on the stairs. His entrance was made theatric. He swept the door back with a bang and swaggered to the middle of the room. No one looked at him. "Well," he cried, insolently, at Scully, "I s'pose you'll tell me now how much I owe you?"

The old man remained stolid. "You don't owe me nothin'."

"Huh!" said the Swede, "huh! Don't owe 'im nothin'."

The cowboy addressed the Swede. "Stranger, I don't see how you come to be so gay around here."

Old Scully was instantly alert. "Stop!" he shouted, holding his hand forth, fingers upward. "Bill, you shut up!"

The cowboy spat carelessly into the sawdust-box. "I didn't say a word, did I?" he asked.

"Mr. Scully," called the Swede, "how much do I owe you?" It was seen that he was attired for departure, and that he had his valise in his hand.

"You don't owe me nothin'," repeated Scully in his same imperturbable way.

"Huh!" said the Swede. "I guess you're right. I guess if it was any way at all, you'd owe me somethin'. That's what I guess." He turned to the cowboy.

" 'Kill him! Kill him! Kill him!' " he mimicked, and then guffawed victoriously. " 'Kill him!' " He was convulsed with ironical humor.

But he might have been jeering the dead. The three men were immovable and silent, staring with glassy eyes at the stove.

The Swede opened the door and passed into the storm, one derisive glance backward at the still group.

As soon as the door was closed, Scully and the cowboy leaped to their feet and began to curse. They trampled to and fro, waving their arms and smashing into the air with their fists. "Oh, but that was a hard minute!" wailed Scully. "That was a hard minute! Him there leerin' and scoffin'! One bang at his nose was worth forty dollars to me that minute! How did you stand it, Bill?"

"How did I stand it?" cried the cowboy in a quivering voice. "How did I stand it? Oh!"

The old man burst into sudden brogue. "I'd loike to take that Swade," he wailed, "and hould 'im down on a shtone flure and bate 'im to a jelly wid a shtick!"

The cowboy groaned in sympathy. "I'd like to git him by the neck and hammer him"—he brought his hand down on a chair with a noise like a pistol-shot—"hammer that there Dutchman until he couldn't tell himself from a dead coyote!"

"I'd bate 'im until he—"

"I'd show *him* some things—"

And then together they raised a yearning, fanatic cry— "Oh-o-oh! if we only could—"

"Yes!"

"Yes!"

"And then I'd—"

"O-o-oh!"

## VIII

The Swede, tightly gripping his valise, tacked across the face of the storm as if he carried sails. He was following a line of little naked, gasping trees which, he knew, must mark the way of the road. His face, fresh from the pounding of Johnnie's fists, felt more pleasure than pain in the wind and the driving snow. A number of square shapes loomed upon him finally, and he knew them as the houses of the main body of the town. He found a street and made travel along it, leaning heavily upon the wind whenever, at a corner, a terrific blast caught him.

He might have been in a deserted village. We picture the world as thick with conquering and elate humanity, but here, with the bugles of the tempest pealing, it was hard to imagine a peopled earth. One viewed the existence of man then as a marvel, and conceded a glamor of wonder to these lice which were caused to cling to a whirling, fire-smitten, ice-locked, disease-stricken, space-lost bulb. The conceit of man was explained by this storm to be the very engine of life. One was a coxcomb not to die in it. However, the Swede found a saloon.

In front of it an indomitable red light was burning, and the snowflakes were made blood-color as they flew through the circumscribed territory of the lamp's shining. The Swede pushed open the door of the saloon and entered. A sanded expanse was before him, and at the end of it four men sat about a table drinking. Down one side of the room extended a radiant bar, and its guardian was leaning upon his elbows listening to the talk of the men at the table. The Swede dropped his valise upon the floor and, smiling fraternally upon the barkeeper, said, "Gimme some whiskey, will you?" The man placed a bottle, a whiskey-glass, and a glass of ice-thick water upon the bar. The Swede poured himself an abnormal portion of whiskey and drank it in three gulps. "Pretty bad night," remarked the bartender, indifferently. He was making the pretension of blindness which is usually a distinction of his class; but it could have been seen that he was furtively studying the half-erased bloodstains on the face of the Swede. "Bad night," he said again.

"Oh, it's good enough for me," replied the Swede, hardily, as he poured himself more whiskey. The barkeeper took his coin and maneuvered it through its reception by the highly nickelled cash-machine. A bell rang; a card labeled "20 cts." had appeared.

"No," continued the Swede, "this isn't too bad weather. It's good enough for me."

"So?" murmured the barkeeper, languidly.

The copious drams made the Swede's eyes swim, and he breathed a trifle heavier. "Yes, I like this weather. I like it. It suits me." It was apparently his design to impart a deep significance to these words.

"So?" murmured the bartender again. He turned to gaze dreamily at the scroll-like birds and bird-like scrolls which had been drawn with soap upon the mirrors in back of the bar.

"Well, I guess I'll take another drink," said the Swede, presently. "Have something?"

"No, thanks; I'm not drinkin'," answered the bartender. Afterward he asked, "How did you hurt your face?"

The Swede immediately began to boast loudly. "Why, in a fight. I thumped the soul out of a man down here at Scully's hotel."

The interest of the four men at the table was at last aroused.

"Who was it?" said one.

"Johnnie Scully," blustered the Swede. "Son of the man what runs it. He will be pretty near dead for some weeks, I can tell you. I made a nice thing of him, I did. He couldn't get up. They carried him in the house. Have a drink?"

Instantly the men in some subtle way encased themselves in reserve. "No, thanks," said one. The group was of curious formation. Two were prominent local business men; one was the district attorney; and one was a professional gambler of the kind known as "square."[1] But a scrutiny of the group would not have enabled an observer to pick the gambler from the men of more reputable pursuits. He was, in fact, a man so delicate in manner, when among people of fair class, and so judicious in his choice of victims, that in the strictly masculine

1. Honest.

part of the town's life he had come to be explicitly trusted and admired. People called him a thoroughbred. The fear and contempt with which his craft was regarded were undoubtedly the reason why his quiet dignity shone conspicuous above the quiet dignity of men who might be merely hatters, billiard-markers, or grocery clerks. Beyond an occasional unwary traveller who came by rail, this gambler was supposed to prey solely upon reckless and senile farmers, who, when flush with good crops, drove into town in all the pride and confidence of an absolutely invulnerable stupidity. Hearing at times in circuitous fashion of the despoilment of such a farmer, the important men of Romper invariably laughed in contempt of the victim, and if they thought of the wolf at all, it was a kind of pride at the knowledge that he would never dare think of attacking their wisdom and courage. Besides, it was popular that this gambler had a real wife and two real children in a neat cottage in a suburb, where he led an exemplary home life; and when any one even suggested a discrepancy in his character, the crowd immediately vociferated descriptions of this virtuous family circle. Then men who led exemplary home lives, and men who did not lead exemplary home lives, all subsided in a bunch, remarking that there was nothing more to be said.

However, when a restriction was placed upon him—as, for instance, when a strong clique of members of the new Pollywog Club refused to permit him, even as a spectator, to appear in the rooms of the organization—the candor and gentleness with which he accepted the judgment disarmed many of his foes and made his friends more desperately partisan. He invariably distinguished between himself and a respectable Romper man so quickly and frankly that his manner actually appeared to be a continual broadcast compliment.

And one must not forget to declare the fundamental fact of his entire position in Romper. It is irrefutable that in all affairs outside his business, in all matters that occur eternally and commonly between man and man, this thieving card-player was so generous, so just, so moral, that, in a contest, he could have put to flight the consciences of nine tenths of the citizens of Romper.

And so it happened that he was seated in this saloon with the two prominent local merchants and the district attorney.

The Swede continued to drink raw whiskey, meanwhile babbling at the barkeeper and trying to induce him to indulge in potations. "Come on. Have a drink. Come on. What—no? Well, have a little one, then. By gawd, I've whipped a man tonight, and I want to celebrate. I whipped him good, too. Gentlemen," the Swede cried to the men at the table, "have a drink?"

"Ssh!" said the barkeeper.

The group at the table, although furtively attentive, had been pretending to be deep in talk, but now a man lifted his eyes toward the Swede and said, shortly, "Thanks. We don't want any more."

At this reply the Swede ruffled out his chest like a rooster. "Well," he exploded, "it seems I can't get anybody to drink with me in this town. Seems so, don't it? Well!"

"Ssh!" said the barkeeper.

"Say," snarled the Swede, "don't you try to shut me up. I won't have it. I'm a gentleman, and I want people to drink with me. And I want 'em to drink with me now. *Now*—do you understand?" He rapped the bar with his knuckles.

Years of experience had calloused the bartender. He merely grew sulky. "I hear you," he answered.

"Well," cried the Swede, "listen hard then. See those men over there? Well, they're going to drink with me, and don't you forget it. Now you watch."

"Hi!" yelled the barkeeper, "this won't do!"

"Why won't it?" demanded the Swede. He stalked over to the table, and by chance laid his hand upon the shoulder of the gambler. "How about this?" he asked wrathfully. "I asked you to drink with me."

The gambler simply twisted his head and spoke over his shoulder. "My friend, I don't know you."

"Oh, hell!" answered the Swede, "come and have a drink."

"Now, my boy," advised the gambler, kindly, "take your hand off my shoulder and go 'way and mind your own business." He was a little, slim man, and it seemed strange to hear him use this tone of heroic patronage to the burly Swede. The other men at the table said nothing.

"What! You won't drink with me, you little dude? I'll make you, then! I'll make you!" The Swede had grasped the gambler frenziedly at the throat, and was dragging him from his chair. The other men sprang up. The barkeeper dashed around the corner of his bar. There was a great tumult, and then was seen a long blade in the hand of the gambler. It shot forward, and a human body, this citadel of virtue, wisdom, power, was pierced as easily as if it had been a melon. The Swede fell with a cry of supreme astonishment.

The prominent merchants and the district attorney must have at once tumbled out of the place backward. The bartender found himself hanging limply to the arm of a chair and gazing into the eyes of a murderer.

"Henry," said the latter, as he wiped his knife on one of the towels that hung beneath the bar rail, "you tell 'em where to find me. I'll be home, waiting for 'em." Then he vanished. A moment afterward the barkeeper was in the street dinning through the storm for help and, moreover, companionship.

The corpse of the Swede, alone in the saloon, had its eye fixed upon a dreadful legend that dwelt atop of the cash-machine: "This registers the amount of your purchase."

## IX

Months later, the cowboy was frying pork over the stove of a little ranch near the Dakota line, when there was a quick thud of hoofs outside, and presently the Easterner entered with the letters and the papers.

"Well," said the Easterner at once, "the chap that killed the Swede has got three years? Wasn't much, was it?"

"He has? Three years?" The cowboy poised his pan of pork, while he ruminated upon the news. "Three years. That ain't much."

"No. It was a light sentence," replied the Easterner as he unbuckled his spurs. "Seems there was a good deal of sympathy for him in Romper."

"If the bartender had been any good," observed the cowboy, thoughtfully, "he would have gone in and cracked that there Dutchman on the head with a bottle in the beginnin' of it and stopped all this here murderin'."

"Yes, a thousand things might have happened," said the Easterner, tartly.

The cowboy returned his pan of pork to the fire, but his philosophy continued. "It's funny, ain't it? If he hadn't said Johnnie was cheatin' he'd be alive this minute. He was an awful fool. Game played for fun, too. Not for money. I believe he was crazy."

"I feel sorry for that gambler," said the Easterner.

"Oh, so do I," said the cowboy. "He don't deserve none of it for killin' who he did."

"The Swede might not have been killed if everything had been square."

"Might not have been killed?" exclaimed the cowboy. "Everythin' square? Why, when he said that Johnnie was cheatin' and acted like such a jackass? And then in the saloon he fairly walked up to git hurt?" With these arguments the cowboy browbeat the Easterner and reduced him to rage.

"You're a fool!" cried the Easterner, viciously. "You're a bigger jackass than the Swede by a million majority. Now let me tell you one thing. Let me tell you something. Listen! Johnnie *was* cheating!"

" 'Johnnie,' " said the cowboy, blankly. There was a minute of silence, and then he said, robustly, "Why, no. The game was only for fun."

"Fun or not," said the Easterner, "Johnnie was cheating. I saw him. I know it. I saw him. And I refused to stand up and be a man. I let the Swede fight it out alone. And you—you were simply puffing around the place and wanting to fight. And then old Scully himself! We are all in it! This poor gambler isn't even a noun. He is kind of an adverb. Every sin is the result of a collaboration. We, five of us, have collaborated in the murder of this Swede. Usually there are from a dozen to forty women really involved in every murder, but in this case it seems to be only five men—you, I, Johnnie, old Scully; and that fool of an unfortunate gambler came merely as a culmination, the apex of a human movement, and gets all the punishment."

The cowboy, injured and rebellious, cried out blindly into this fog of mysterious theory: "Well, I didn't do anythin', did I?"

# H. L. Davis

*Davis (1894–1960) was born north of Roseburg, Oregon, at Rone's Mill in the Cascade foothills. His father, an itinerant teacher, moved the family east to Antelope and then to The Dalles on the Columbia River. His father became a school principal, and Davis lived in The Dalles for the next twenty years. As a young man Davis won the Levinson prize for poetry. He later turned to prose and published* Winds of Morning *(1952),* The Distant Music *(1957), and many stories in* Team Bells Woke Me *(1958). He was noted for deflating the sentimental, debunking the myths of noble pioneers and old families. He won the Pulitzer Prize for Literature in 1936 for* Honey in the Horn.

## Open Winter

The drying east wind, which always brought hard luck to Eastern Oregon at whatever season it blew, had combed down the plateau grasslands through so much of the winter that it was hard to see any sign of grass ever having grown on them. Even though March had come, it still blew, drying the ground deep, shrinking the watercourses, beating back the clouds that might have delivered rain, and grinding coarse dust against the fifty-odd head of work horses that Pop Apling, with young Beech Cartwright helping, had brought down from his homestead to turn back into their home pasture while there was still something left of them.

The two men, one past sixty and the other around sixteen, shouldered the horses through the gate of the home pasture about dark, with lights beginning to shine out from the little freighting town across Three Notch Valley, and then they rode for the ranch house, knowing even before they drew up outside the yard that they had picked the wrong time to come. The house was too dark, and the corrals and outbuildings too still, for a place that anybody lived in.

There were sounds, but they were of shingles flapping in the wind, a windmill running loose and sucking noisily at a well that it had already pumped empty, a door that kept banging shut and dragging open again. The haystacks were gone, the stackyard fence had dwindled to a few naked posts, and the entire pasture was as bare and as hard as a floor all the way down into the valley.

The prospect looked so hopeless that the herd horses refused even to explore it, and merely stood with their tails turned to the wind, waiting to see what was to happen to them next.

Old Apling went poking inside the house, thinking somebody might have left a note or that the men might have run down to the saloon in town for an hour or two. He came back, having used up all his matches and stopped the door from banging, and said the place appeared to have been handed back to the Government, or maybe the mortgage company.

"You can trust old Ream Gervais not to be any place where anybody wants him," Beech said. He had hired out to herd for Ream Gervais over the winter. That entitled him to be more critical than old Apling, who had merely contracted to supply the horse herd with feed and pasture for the season at so much per head. "Well, my job was to help herd these steeds while you had 'em, and to help deliver 'em back when you got through with 'em, and here they are. I've put in a week on 'em that I won't ever git paid for, and it won't help anything to set around and watch 'em try to live on fence pickets. Let's git out."

Old Apling looked at the huddle of horses, at the naked slope with a glimmer of light still on it, and at the lights of the town twinkling in the wind. He said it wasn't his place to tell any man what to do, but that he wouldn't feel quite right to dump the horses and leave.

"I agreed to see that they got delivered back here, and I'd feel better about it if I could locate somebody to deliver 'em to," he said. "I'd like to ride across to town yonder, and see if there ain't somebody that knows something about 'em. You could hold 'em together here till I git back. We ought to look the fences over before we pull out, and you can wait here as well as anywhere else."

"I can't, but go ahead," Beech said. "I don't like to have 'em stand around and look at me when I can't do anything to help 'em out. They'd have been better off if we'd turned 'em out of your homestead and let 'em run loose on the country. There was more grass up there than there is here."

"There wasn't enough to feed 'em, and I'd have had all my neighbors down on me for it," old Apling said. "You'll find out one of these days that if a man aims to live in this world he's got to git along with the people in it. I'd start a fire and thaw out a little and git that pack horse unloaded, if I was you."

He rode down the slope, leaning low and foward to ease the drag of the wind on his tired horse. Beech heard the sound of the road gate being let down and put up again, the beat of hoofs in the hard road, and then nothing but the noises around him as the wind went through its usual process of easing down for the night to make room for the frost. Loose boards settled into place, the windmill clacked to a stop and began to drip water into a puddle, and the herd horses shifted around facing Beech, as if anxious not to miss anything he did.

He pulled off some fence pickets and built a fire, unsaddled his pony and unloaded the pack horse, and got out what was left of a sack of grain and fed them both, standing the herd horses off with a fence picket until they had finished eating.

That was strictly fair, for the pack horse and the saddle pony had worked harder and carried more weight than any of the herd animals, and the grain was little enough to even them up for it. Nevertheless, he felt mean at having to club animals away from food when they were hungry, and they crowded back and eyed the grain sack so wistfully that he carried it inside the yard and stored it down in the root cellar behind the house, so it wouldn't prey on their minds. Then he dumped another armload of fence pickets onto the fire and sat down to wait for old Apling.

The original mistake, he reflected, had been when old Apling took the Gervais horses to feed at the beginning of winter. Contracting to feed them had been well enough, for he had nursed up a stand of bunch grass on his homestead that would have carried an ordinary pack of horses with only a little extra feeding to help out in the roughest weather. But the Gervais horses were all big harness stock, they had pulled in half starved, and they had taken not much over three weeks to clean off the pasture that old Apling had expected would last them at least two months. Nobody would have blamed him for backing out on his agreement then, since he had only undertaken to feed the horses, not to treat them for malnutrition.

Beech wanted him to back out of it, but he refused to, said the stockmen had enough troubles without having that added to them, and started feeding out his hay and insisting that the dry wind couldn't possibly keep up much longer, because it wasn't in Nature.

By the time it became clear that Nature had decided to take in a little extra territory, the hay was all fed out, and, since there couldn't be any accommodation about letting the horses starve to death, he consented to throw the contract over and bring them back where they belonged.

The trouble with most of old Apling's efforts to be accommodating was that they did nobody any good. His neighbors would have been spared all their uneasiness if he had never brought in the horses to begin with. Gervais wouldn't have been any worse off, since he stood to lose them anyway; the horses could have starved to death as gracefully in November as in March, and old Apling would have been ahead a great deal of carefully accumulated bunch grass and two big stacks of extortionately valuable hay. Nobody had gained by his chivalrousness; he had lost by it, and yet he liked it so well that he couldn't stand to leave the horses until he had raked the country for somebody to hand the worthless brutes over to.

Beech fed sticks into the fire and felt out of patience with a man who could stick to his mistakes even after he had been cleaned out by them. He heard the road gate open and shut, and he knew by the draggy-sounding plod of old Apling's horse that the news from town was going to be bad.

Old Apling rode past the fire and over to the picket fence, got off as if he was trying to make it last, tied his horse carefully as if he expected the knot to last a month, and unsaddled and did up his latigo and folded his saddle blanket as if he was fixing them to put in a show window. He remarked that his horse had been given a bait of grain in town and wouldn't need feeding again, and then he began to work down to what he had found out.

"If you think things look bad along this road, you ought to see that town," he said. "All the sheep gone and all the ranches deserted and no trade to run on and their water threatenin' to give out. They've got a little herd of milk cows that they keep up for their children, and to hear 'em talk you'd think it was an ammunition supply that they expected to stand off hostile Indians with. They said Gervais pulled out of here around a month ago. All his men quit him, so he bunched his sheep and took 'em to the railroad, where he could ship in hay for 'em. Sheep will be a price this year, and you won't be able to buy a lamb for under twelve dollars except at a fire sale. Horses ain't in much demand. There's been a lot of 'em turned out wild, and everybody wants to git rid of 'em."

"I didn't drive this bunch of pelters any eighty miles against the wind to git a market report," Beech said. "You didn't find anybody to turn 'em over to, and Gervais didn't leave any word about what he wanted done with 'em. You've probably got it figured out that you ought to trail 'em a hundred and eighty miles to the railroad, so his feelings won't be hurt, and you're probably tryin' to study how you can work me in on it, and you might as well save your time. I've helped you with your accommodation jobs long enough. I've quit, and it would have been a whole lot better for you if I'd quit sooner."

Old Apling said he could understand that state of feeling, which didn't mean that he shared it.

"It wouldn't be as much of a trail down to the railroad as a man might think," he said, merely to settle a question of fact. "We couldn't make it by the road in a starve-out year like this, but there's old Indian trails back on the ridge where any man has got a right to take livestock whenever he feels like it. Still, as long as you're set against it, I'll meet you halfway. We'll trail these horses down the ridge to a grass patch where I used to corral cattle when I was in the business, and we'll leave 'em there. It'll be enough so they won't starve, and I'll ride on down and notify Gervais where they are, and you can go where you please. It wouldn't be fair to do less than that, to my notion."

"Ream Gervais triggered me out of a week's pay," Beech said. "It ain't much, but he swindled you on that pasture contract too. If you expect me to trail his broken-down horses ninety miles down this ridge when they ain't worth anything, you've turned in a poor guess. You'll have to think of a better argument than that if you aim to gain any ground with me."

"Ream Gervais don't count in this," old Apling said. "What does he care about these horses, when he ain't even left word what he wants done with 'em? What counts is you, and I don't have to think up any better argument, because I've already got one. You may not realize it, but you and me are responsible for these horses till they're delivered to their owner, and if we turn 'em loose here to bust fences and overrun that town and starve to death in the middle of it, we'll land in the pen. It's against the law to let horses starve to death, did you know that? If you pull out of here I'll pull out right along with you, and I'll have every man in that town after you before the week's out. You'll have a chance to git some action on that pistol of yours, if you're careful."

Beech said he wasn't intimidated by that kind of talk, and threw a couple of handfuls of dirt on the fire, so it wouldn't look so conspicuous. His pistol was an old single-action relic with its grips tied on with fish line and no trigger, so that it had to be operated by flipping the hammer. The spring was weak, so that sometimes it took several flips to get off one shot. Suggesting that he might use such a thing to stand off any pack of grim-faced pursuers was about the same as saying that he was simple-minded. As far as he could see, his stand was entirely sensible, and even humane.

"It ain't that I don't feel sorry for these horses, but they ain't fit to travel," he said. "They wouldn't last twenty miles. I don't see how it's any worse to let 'em stay here than to walk 'em to death down that ridge."

"They make less trouble for people if you keep 'em on the move," old Apling said. "It's something you can't be cinched for in court, and it makes you feel better afterwards to know that you tried everything you could. Suit yourself about it, though. I ain't beggin' you to do it. If you'd sooner pull out and stand the consequences, it's you for it. Before you go, what did you do with that sack of grain?"

Beech had half a notion to leave, just to see how much of that dark threatening would come to pass. He decided that it wouldn't be worth it. "I'll help you trail the blamed skates as far as they'll last, if you've got to be childish about it," he said. "I put the grain in a root cellar behind the house, so the rats wouldn't git into it. It looked like the only safe place around here. There was about a half a ton of old sprouted potatoes ricked up in it that didn't look like they'd been bothered for twenty years. They had sprouts on 'em—" He stopped, noticing that old Apling kept staring at him as if something was wrong. "Good Lord, potatoes ain't good for horse feed, are they? They had sprouts on 'em a foot long!"

Old Apling shook his head resignedly and got up. "We wouldn't ever find anything if it wasn't for you," he said. "We wouldn't ever git any good out of it if it wasn't for me, so maybe we make a team. Show me where that root cellar is, and we'll pack them spuds out and spread 'em around so the horses can git started on 'em. We'll git this herd through to grassland yet, and it'll be something you'll never be ashamed of. It ain't everybody your age gits a chance to do a thing like this, and you'll thank me for holdin' you to it before you're through."

## II

They climbed up by an Indian trail onto a high stretch of tableland, so stony and scored with rock breaks that nobody had ever tried to cultivate it, but so high that it sometimes caught moisture from the atmosphere that the lower elevations missed. Part of it had been doled out among the Indians as allotment lands, which none of them ever bothered to lay claim to, but the main spread of it belonged to the nation, which was too busy to notice it.

The pasture was thin, though reliable, and it was so scantily watered and so rough and broken that in ordinary years nobody bothered to bring stock onto it. The open winter had spoiled most of that seclusion. There was no part of the trail that didn't have at least a dozen new bed grounds for lambed ewes in plain view, easily picked out of the landscape because of the little white flags stuck up around them to keep sheep from straying out and coyotes from straying in during the night. The sheep were pasturing down the draws out of the wind, where they couldn't be seen. There were no herders visible, not any startling amount of grass, and no water except a mud tank thrown up to catch a little spring for one of the camps.

They tried to water the horses in it, but it had taken up the flavor of sheep, so that not a horse in the herd would touch it. It was too near dark to waste time reasoning with them about it, so old Apling headed them down into a long rock break and across it to a tangle of wild cherry and mountain mahogany that lasted for several miles and ended in a grass clearing among some dwarf cottonwoods with a mud puddle in the center of it.

The grass had been grazed over, though not closely, and there were sheep tracks around the puddle that seemed to be fresh, for the horses, after sniffing the water, decided that they could wait a while longer. They spread out to graze, and Beech remarked that he couldn't see where it was any improvement over the tickle-grass homesteads.

"The grass may be better, but there ain't so much of it, and the water ain't any good if they won't drink it," he said. "Well, do you intend to leave 'em here, or have you got some wrinkle figured out to make me help trail 'em on down to the railroad?"

Old Apling stood the sarcasm unresistingly. "It would be better to trail 'em to the railroad, now that we've got this far," he said. "I won't ask you to do that much, because it's outside of what you agreed to. This place has changed since I was here last, but we'll make it do, and that water ought to clear up fit to drink before long. You can settle down here for a few days while I ride around and fix it up with the sheep camps to let the horses stay here. We've got to do that, or they're liable to think it's some wild bunch and start shootin' 'em. Somebody's got to stay with 'em, and I can git along with these herders better than you can."

"If you've got any sense, you'll let them sheep outfits alone," Beech said. "They don't like tame horses on this grass any better than they do wild ones, and they won't make any more bones about shootin' 'em if they find out they're in here. It's a hard place to find, and they'll stay close on account of the water, and you'd better pull out and let 'em have it to themselves. That's what I aim to do."

"You've done what you agreed to, and I ain't got any right to hold you any longer," old Apling said. "I wish I could. You're wrong about them sheep outfits. I've got as much right to pasture this ridge as they have, and they know it, and nobody ever lost anything by actin' sociable with people."

"Somebody will before very long," Beech said. "I've got relatives in the sheep business, and I know what they're like. You'll land yourself in trouble, and I don't want to be around when you do it. I'm pullin' out of here in the morning, and if you had any sense you'd pull out along with me."

There were several things that kept Beech from getting much sleep during the night. One was the attachment that the horses showed for his sleeping place; they stuck so close that he could almost feel their breath on him, could hear the soft breaking sound that the grass made as they pulled it, the sound of their swallowing, the jar of the ground under him when one of the horses changed ground, the peaceful regularity of their eating, as if they didn't have to bother about anything so long as they kept old Apling in sight.

Another irritating thing was old Apling's complete freedom from uneasiness. He ought by rights to have felt more worried about the future than Beech did, but he slept, with the hard ground for a bed and his hard saddle for a pillow and the horses almost stepping on him every minute or two, as soundly as if the entire trip had come out exactly to suit him and there was nothing ahead but plain sailing.

His restfulness was so hearty and so unjustifiable that Beech couldn't sleep for feeling indignant about it, and got up and left about daylight to keep from being exposed to any more of it. He left without waking old Apling, because he saw no sense in a leave-taking that would consist merely in repeating his common-sense warnings and having them ignored, and he was so anxious to get clear of the whole layout that he didn't even take along anything to eat. The only thing he took from the pack was his ramshackle old pistol; there was no holster for it, and, in the hope that he might get a chance to use it on a loose quail or prairie chicken, he stowed it in an empty flour sack and hung it on his saddle horn, a good deal like an old squaw heading for the far blue distances with a bundle of diapers.

## III

There was never anything recreational about traveling a rock desert at any season of the year, and the combination of spring gales, winter chilliness and summer drought all striking at once brought it fairly close to hard punishment. Beech's saddle pony, being jaded at the start with overwork and underfeeding and no water, broke down in the first couple of miles, and got so feeble and tottery that Beech had to climb off and lead him, searching likely-looking thickets all the way down the gully in the hope of finding some little trickle that he wouldn't be too finicky to drink.

The nearest he came to it was a fair-sized rock sink under some big half-budded cottonwoods that looked, by its dampness and the abundance of fresh animal tracks around it, as if it might have held water recently, but of water there was none, and even digging a hole in the center of the basin failed to fetch a drop.

The work of digging, hill climbing and scrambling through brush piles raised Beech's appetite so powerfully that he could scarcely hold up, and, a little above where the gully opened into the flat sagebrush plateau, he threw away his pride, pistoled himself a jack rabbit, and took it down into the sagebrush to cook, where his fire wouldn't give away which gully old Apling was camped in.

Jack rabbit didn't stand high as a food. It was considered an excellent thing to give men in the last stages of famine, because they weren't likely to injure themselves by eating too much of it, but for ordinary occasions it was looked down on, and Beech covered his trail out of the gully and built his cooking fire in the middle of a high stand of sagebrush, so as not to be embarrassed by inquisitive visitors.

The meat cooked up strong, as it always did, but he ate what he needed of it, and he was wrapping the remainder in his flour sack to take along with him when a couple of men rode past, saw his pony, and turned in to look him over.

They looked him over so closely and with so little concern for his privacy that he felt insulted before they even spoke.

He studied them less openly, judging by their big gallon canteens that they were out on some long scout.

One of them was some sort of hired hand, by his looks; he was broad-faced and gloomy-looking with a fine white horse, a flower-stamped saddle, an expensive rifle scabbarded under his knee, and a fifteen-dollar saddle blanket, while his own manly form was set off by a yellow hotel blanket and a ninety-cent pair of overalls.

The other man had on a store suit, a plain black hat, fancy stitched boots, and a white shirt and necktie, and rode a burrtailed Indian pony and an old wrangling saddle with a loose horn. He carried no weapons in sight, but there was a narrow strap across the lower spread of his necktie which indicated the presence of a shoulder holster somewhere within reach.

He opened the conversation by inquiring where Beech had come from, what his business was, where he was going and why he hadn't taken the country road to go there, and why he had to eat jack rabbit when the country was littered with sheep camps where he could get a decent meal by asking for it?

"I come from the upper country," Beech said, being purposely vague about it. "I'm travelin', and I stopped here because my horse give out. He won't drink out of any place that's had sheep in it, and he's gone short of water till he breaks down easy."

"There's a place corralled in for horses to drink at down at my lower camp," the man said, and studied Beech's pony. "There's no reason for you to bum through the country on jack rabbit in a time like this. My herder can take you down to our water hole and see that you get fed and put to work till you can make a stake for yourself. I'll give you a note. That pony looks like he had Ream Gervais' brand on him. Do you know anything about that herd of old work horses he's been pasturing around?"

"I don't know anything about him," Beech said, sidestepping the actual question while he thought over the offer of employment. He could have used a stake, but the location didn't strike him favorably. It was too close to old Apling's camp, he could see trouble ahead over the horse herd, and he didn't want to be around when it started. "If you'll direct me how to find your water, I'll ride on down there, but I don't need anybody to go with me, and I don't need any stake. I'm travelin'."

The man said there wasn't anybody so well off that he couldn't use a stake, and that it would be hardly any trouble at all for Beech to get one. "I want you to understand how we're situated around here, so you won't think we're any bunch of stranglers," he said. "You can see what kind of a year this has been, when we have to run lambed ewes in a rock patch like this. We've got five thousand lambs in here that we're trying to bring through, and we've had to fight the blamed wild horses for this pasture since the day we moved in. A horse that ain't worth hell room will eat as much as two dozen sheep worth twenty dollars, with the lambs, so you can see how it figures out. We've got 'em pretty well thinned out, but one of my packers found a trail of a new bunch that came up from around Three Notch within the last day or two, and we don't want them to feel as if we'd neglected them. We'd like to find out where they lit. You wouldn't have any information about 'em?"

"None that would do you any good to know," Beech said. "I know the man with that horse herd, and it ain't any use to let on that I don't, but it wouldn't be any use to try to deal with him. He don't sell out on a man he works for."

"He might be induced to," the man said. "We'll find him anyhow, but I don't like to take too much time to do it. Just for instance, now, suppose you knew that pony of yours would have to go thirsty till you gave us a few directions about that horse herd? You'd be stuck here for quite a spell, wouldn't you?"

He was so pleasant about it that it took Beech a full minute to realize that he was being threatened. The heavy-set herder brought that home to him by edging out into a flank position and hoisting his rifle scabbard so it could be reached in a hurry. Beech removed the cooked jack rabbit from his flour sack carefully, a piece at a time, and, with the same mechanical thoughtfulness, brought out his triggerless old pistol, cut down on the pleasant-spoken man, and hauled back on the hammer and held it poised.

"The herder of yours had better go easy on his rifle," he said, trying to keep his voice from trembling. "This pistol shoots if I don't hold back the hammer, and if he knocks me out I'll have to let go of it. You'd better watch him, if you don't want your tack drove. I won't give you no directions about that horse herd, and this pony of mine won't go thirsty for it, either. Loosen them canteens of yours and let 'em drop on the ground. Drop that rifle scabbard back where it belongs, and unbuckle the straps and let go of it. If either of you tries any funny business, there'll be one of you to pack home, heels first."

The quaver in his voice sounded childish and undignified to him, but it had a more businesslike ring to them than any amount of manly gruffness. The herder unbuckled his rifle scabbard, and they both cast loose their canteen straps, making it last as long as they could while they argued with him, not angrily, but as if he was a dull stripling whom they wanted to save from some foolishness that he was sure to regret. They argued ethics, justice, common sense, his future prospects, and the fact that what he was doing amounted to robbery by force and arms and that it was his first fatal step into a probably unsuccessful career of crime. They worried over him, they explained themselves to him, and they ridiculed him.

The managed to make him feel like several kinds of a fool, and they were so pleasant and concerned about it that they came close to breaking him down. What held him steady was the thought of old Apling waiting up the gully.

"That herder with the horses never sold out on any man, and I won't sell out on him," he said. "You've said your say and I'm tired of holdin' this pistol on cock for you, so move along out of here. Keep to open ground, so I can be sure you're gone, and don't be in too much of a hurry to come back. I've got a lot of things I want to think over, and I want to be let alone while I do it."

## IV

He did have some thinking that needed tending to, but he didn't take time for it. When the men were well out of range, he emptied their canteens into his hat and let his pony drink. Then he hung the canteens and the scabbarded rifle on a bush and rode back up the gully where the horse camp was, keeping to shaly ground so as not to leave any tracks. It was harder going up than it had been coming down.

He had turned back from the scene of his run-in with the two sheepmen about noon, and he was still a good two miles from the camp when the sun went down, the wind lulled and the night frost began to bite at him so hard that he dismounted and walked to get warm. That raised his appetite again, and, as if by some special considerateness of Nature, the cottonwoods around him seemed to be alive with jack rabbits heading down into the pitch-dark gully where he had fooled away valuable time trying to find water that morning.

They didn't stimulate his hunger much; for a time they even made him feel less like eating anything. Then his pony gave out and had to rest, and, noticing that the cottonwoods around him were beginning to bud out, he remembered that peeling the bark off in the budding season would fetch out a foamy, sweet-tasting sap which, among children of the plateau country, was considered something of a delicacy.

He cut a blaze on a fair-sized sapling, waited ten minutes or so, and touched his finger to it to see how much sap had accumulated. None had; the blaze was moist to his touch, but scarcely more so than when he had whittled it.

It wasn't important enough to do any bothering about, and yet a whole set of observed things began to draw together in his mind and form themselves into an explanation of something he had puzzled over: the fresh animal tracks he had seen around the rock sink when there wasn't any water; the rabbits going down into the gully; the cottonwoods in which the sap rose enough during the day to produce buds and got driven back at night when the frost set in. During the day, the cottonwoods had drawn the water out of the ground for themselves; at night they stopped drawing it, and it drained out into the rock sink for the rabbits.

It all worked out so simply that he led his pony down into the gully to see how much there was in it, and, losing his footing on the steep slope, coasted down into the rock sink in the dark and landed in water and thin mud up to his knees. He led his pony down into it to drink, which seemed little enough to get back for the time he had fooled away on it, and then he headed for the horse camp, which was all too easily discernible by the plume of smoke rising, white and ostentatious, against the dark sky from old Apling's campfire.

He made the same kind of entrance that old Apling usually affected when bringing some important item of news. He rode past the campfire and pulled up at a tree, got off deliberately, knocked an accumulation of dead twigs from his hat, took off his saddle and bridle and balanced them painstakingly in the tree fork, and said it was affecting to see how widespread the shortage of pasture was.

"It generally is," old Apling said. "I had a kind of a notion you'd be back after you'd had time to study things over. I suppose you got into some kind of a rumpus with some of them sheep outfits. What was it? Couldn't you git along with them, or couldn't they hit it off with you?"

"There wasn't any trouble between them and me," Beech said. "The only point we had words over was you, They wanted to know where you was camped, so they could shoot you up, and I didn't think it was right to tell 'em. I had to put a gun on a couple of 'em before they'd believe I meant business, and that was all there was to it. They're out after you now, and they can see the smoke of this fire of yours for twenty miles, so they ought to be along almost any time now. I thought I'd come back and see you work your sociability on 'em."

"You probably kicked up a squabble with 'em yourself," old Apling said. He looked a little uneasy. "You talked right up to 'em, I'll bet, and slapped their noses with your hat to show 'em that they couldn't run over you. Well, what's done is done. You did come back, and maybe they'd have jumped us anyway. There ain't much that we can do. The horses have got to have water before they can travel, and they won't touch that seep. It ain't cleared up a particle."

"You can put that fire out, not but what the whole country has probably seen the smoke from it already," Beech said. "If you've got to tag after these horses, you can run 'em off down the draw and keep 'em to the brush where they won't leave a trail. There's some young cottonwood bark that they can eat if they have to, and there's water in a rock sink under some big cottonwood trees. I'll stay here and hold off anybody that shows up, so you'll have time to git your tracks covered."

Old Apling went over and untied the flour-sacked pistol from Beech's saddle, rolled it into his blankets, and sat down on it. "If there's any holdin' off to be done, I'll do it," he said. "You're a little too high-spirited to suit me, and a little too hasty about your conclusions. I looked over that rock sink down the draw today, and there wasn't anything in it but mud, and blamed little of that. Somebody had dug for water, and there wasn't none."

"There is now," Beech said. He tugged off one of his wet boots and poured about a pint of the disputed fluid on the ground. "There wasn't any in the daytime because the cottonwoods took it all. They let up when it turns cold, and it runs back in. I waded in it."

He started to put his boot back on. Old Apling reached out and took it, felt of it inside and out, and handed it over as if performing some ceremonial presentation.

"I'd never have figured out a thing like that in this world," he said. "If we git them horses out of here, it'll be you that done it. We'll bunch 'em and work 'em down there. It won't be no picnic, but we'll make out to handle it somehow. We've got to, after a thing like this."

Beech remembered what had occasioned the discovery, and said he would have to have something to eat first. "I want you to keep in mind that it's you I'm doin' this for," he said. "I don't owe that old groundhog of a Ream Gervais anything. The only thing I hate about this is that it'll look like I'd done him a favor."

"He won't take it for one, I guess," old Apling said. "We've got to git these horses out because it'll be a favor to you. You wouldn't want to have it told around that you'd done a thing like findin' that water, and then have to admit that we'd lost all the horses anyhow. We can't lose 'em. You've acted like a man tonight, and I'll be blamed if I'll let you spoil it for any childish spite."

They got the horses out none too soon. Watering them took a long time, and when they finally did consent to call it enough and climb back up the side hill, Beech and old Apling heard a couple of signal shots from the direction of their old camping place, and saw a big glare mount up into the sky from it as the visitors built up their campfire to look the locality over. The sight was almost comforting; if they had to keep away from a pursuit, it was at least something to know where it was.

## V

From then on they followed a grab-and-run policy, scouting ahead before they moved, holding to the draws by day and crossing open ground only after dark, never pasturing over a couple of hours in any one place, and discovering food value in outlandish substances—rock lichens, the sprouts of wild plum and serviceberry, the moss of old trees and the bark of some young ones—that neither they nor the horses had ever considered fit to eat before. When they struck Boulder River Canyon they dropped down and toenailed their way along one side of it where they could find grass and water with less likelihood of having trouble about it.

The breaks of the canyon were too rough to run new-lambed sheep in, and they met with so few signs of occupancy that old Apling got overconfident, neglected his scouting to tie back a break they had been obliged to make in a line fence, and ran the horse herd right over the top of a camp where some men were branding calves, tearing down a cook tent and part of a corral and scattering cattle and bedding from the river all the way to the top of the canyon.

By rights, they should have sustained some damage for that piece of carelessness, but they drove through fast, and they were out of sight around a shoulder of rimrock before any of the men could get themselves picked up. Somebody did throw a couple of shots after them as they were pulling into a thicket of mock orange and chokecherry, but it was only with a pistol, and he probably did it more to relieve his feelings than with any hope of hitting anything.

They were so far out of range that they couldn't even hear where the bullets landed.

Neither of them mentioned that unlucky run-in all the rest of that day. They drove hard, punished the horses savagely when they lagged, and kept them at it until, a long time after dark, they struck an old rope ferry that crossed Boulder River at a place called, in memory of its original founders, Robbers' Roost.

The ferry wasn't a public carrier, and there was not even any main road down to it. It was used by the ranches in the neighborhood as the only means of crossing the river for fifty miles in either direction, and it was tied in to a log with a good solid chain and padlock. It was a way to cross, and neither of them could see anything else but to take it.

Beech favored waiting for daylight for it, pointing out that there was a ranch light half a mile up the slope, and that if anybody caught them hustling a private ferry in the dead of night they would probably be taken for criminals on the dodge. Old Apling said it was altogether likely, and drew Beech's pistol and shot the padlock apart with it.

"They could hear that up at that ranch house," Beech said. "What if they come pokin' down here to see what we're up to?"

Old Apling tossed the fragments of padlock into the river and hung the pistol in the waistband of his trousers. "Let 'em come," he said. "They'll go back again with their fingers in their mouths. This is your trip, and you put in good work on it, and I like to ruined the whole thing stoppin' to patch an eighty-cent fence so some scissorbill wouldn't have his feelings hurt, and that's the last accommodation anybody gits out of me till this is over with. I can take about six horses at a trip, it looks like. Help me to bunch 'em."

Six horses at a trip proved to be an overestimate. The best they could do was five, and the boat rode so deep with them that Beech refused to risk handling it. He stayed with the herd, and old Apling cut it loose, let the current sweep it across into slack water, and hauled it in to the far bank by winding in its cable on an old homemade capstan. Then he turned the horses into a counting pen and came back for another load.

He worked at it fiercely, as if he had a bet up that he could wear the whole ferry rig out, but it went with infernal slowness, and when the wind began to move for daylight there were a dozen horses still to cross and no place to hide them in case the ferry had other customers.

Beech waited and fidgeted over small noises until, hearing voices and the clatter of hoofs on shale far up the canyon behind him, he gave way, drove the remaining horses into the river, and swam them across, letting himself be towed along by his saddle horn and floating his clothes ahead of him on a board.

He paid for that flurry of nervousness before he got out. The water was so cold it paralyzed him, and so swift it whisked him a mile downstream before he could get his pony turned to breast it. He grounded on a gravel bar in a thicket of dwarf willows, with numbness striking clear to the center of his diaphragm and deadening his arms so he couldn't pick his clothes loose from the bundle to put on. He managed it, by using his teeth and elbows, and warmed himself a little by driving the horses afoot through the brush till he struck the ferry landing.

It had got light enough to see things in outline, and old Apling was getting ready to shove off for another crossing when the procession came lumbering at him out of the shadows. He came ashore, counted the horses into the corral to make sure none had drowned, and laid Beech under all the blankets and built up a fire to limber him out by. He got breakfast and got packed to leave, and he did some rapid expounding about the iniquity of risking the whole trip on such a wild piece of foolhardiness.

"That was the reason I wanted you to work this boat," he said. "I could have stood up to anybody that come projectin' around, and if they wanted trouble I could have filled their order for 'em. They won't bother us now, anyhow; it don't matter how bad they want to."

"I could have stood up to 'em if I'd had anything to do it with," Beech said. "You've got that pistol of mine, and I couldn't see to throw rocks. What makes you think they won't bother us? You know it was that brandin' crew comin' after us, don't you?"

"I expect that's who it was," old Apling agreed. "They ought to be out after the cattle we scattered, but you can trust a bunch of cowboys to pick out the most useless things to tend to first. I've got that pistol of yours because I don't aim for you to git in trouble with it while this trip is on. There won't anybody bother us because I've cut all the cables on the ferry, and it's lodged downstream on a gravel spit. If anybody crosses after us within fifty miles of here, he'll swim, and the people around here ain't as reckless around cold water as you are."

Beech sat up. "We got to git out of here," he said. "There's people on this side of the river that use that ferry, you old fool, and they'll have us up before every jury in the country from now on. The horses ain't worth it."

"What the horses is worth ain't everything," old Apling said. "There's part of this trip ahead that you'll be glad you went through. You're entitled to that much out of it, after the work you've put in, and I aim to see that you git it. It ain't any use tryin' to explain to you what it is. You'll notice it when the time comes."

## VI

They worked north, following the breaks of the river canyon, finding the rock breaks hard to travel, but easy to avoid observation in, and the grass fair in stand, but so poor and washy in body that the horses had to spent most of their time eating enough to keep up their strength so they could move.

They struck a series of gorges, too deep and precipitous to be crossed at all, and had to edge back into milder country where there were patches of plowed ground, some being harrowed over for summer fallow and others venturing out with a bright new stand of dark-green wheat.

The pasture was patchy and scoured by the wind, and all the best parts of it were under fence, which they didn't dare cut for fear of getting in trouble with the natives. Visibility was high in that section; the ground lay open to the north as far as they could see, the wind kept the air so clear that it hurt to look at the sky, and they were never out of sight of wheat ranchers harrowing down summer fallow.

A good many of the ranchers pulled up and stared after the horse herd as it went past, and two or three times they waved and rode down toward the road, as if they wanted to make it an excuse for stopping work. Old Apling surmised that they had some warning they wanted to deliver against trespassing, and he drove on without waiting to hear it.

They were unable to find a camping place anywhere among those wheat fields, so they drove clear through to open country and spread down for the night alongside a shallow pond in the middle of some new grass not far enough along to be pastured, though the horses made what they could out of it. There were no trees or shrubs anywhere around, not even sagebrush. Lacking fuel for a fire, they camped without one, and since there was no grass anywhere except around the pond, they left the horses unguarded, rolled in to catch up sleep, and were awakened about daylight by the whole herd stampeding past them at a gallop.

They both got up and moved fast. Beech ran for his pony, which was trying to pull loose from its picket rope to go with the bunch. Old Apling ran out into the dust afoot, waggling the triggerless old pistol and trying to make out objects in the half-light by hard squinting. The herd horses fetched a long circle and came back past him, with a couple of riders clouting along behind trying to turn them back into open country. One of the riders opened up a rope and swung it, the other turned in and slapped the inside flankers with his hat, and old Apling hauled up the old pistol, flipped the hammer a couple of rounds to get it warmed up, and let go at them twice.

The half darkness held noise as if it had been a cellar. The two shots banged monstrously, Beech yelled to old Apling to be careful who he shot at, and the two men shied off sideways and rode away into the open country. One of them yelled something that sounded threatening in tone as they went out of sight, but neither of them seemed in the least inclined to bring on any general engagement. The dust blew clear, the herd horses came back to grass, old Apling looked at the pistol and punched the two exploded shells out of it, and Beech ordered him to hand it over before he got in trouble with it.

"How do you know but what them men had a right here?" he demanded sternly. "We'd be in a fine jack pot if you'd shot one of 'em and it turned out he owned this land we're on, wouldn't we?"

Old Apling looked at him, holding the old pistol poised as if he was getting ready to lead a band with it. The light strengthened and shed a rose-colored radiance over him, so he looked flushed and joyous and lifted up. With some of the dust knocked off him, he could have filled in easily as a day star and son of the morning, whiskers and all.

"I wouldn't have shot them men for anything you could buy me!" he said, and faced north to a blue line of bluffs that came up out of the shadows, a blue gleam of water that moved under them, a white steamboat that moved upstream, glittering as the first light struck it. "Them men wasn't here because we was trespassers. Them was horse thieves, boy! We've brought these horses to a place where they're worth stealin', and we've brought 'em through! The railroad is under them bluffs, and that water down there is the old Columbia River!"

They might have made it down to the river that day, but having it in sight and knowing that nothing could stop them from reaching it, there no longer seemed any object in driving so unsparingly. They ate breakfast and talked about starting, and they even got partly packed up for it. Then they got occupied with talking to a couple of wheat ranchers who pulled in to inquire about buying some of the horse herd; the drought had run up wheat prices at a time when the country's livestock had been allowed to run down, and so many horses had been shot and starved out that they were having to take pretty much anything they could get.

Old Apling swapped them a couple of the most jaded herd horses for part of a haystack, referred other applicants to Gervais down at the railroad, and spent the remainder of the day washing, patching clothes and saddlery, and watching the horses get acquainted once more with a conventional diet.

The next morning a rancher dropped off a note from Gervais urging them to come right on down, and adding a kind but firm admonition against running up any feed bills without his express permission. He made it sound as if there might be some hurry about catching the horse market on the rise, so they got ready to leave, and Beech looked back over the road they had come, thinking of all that had happened on it.

"I'd like it better if old Gervais didn't have to work himself in on the end of it," he said. "I'd like to step out on the whole business right now."

"You'd be a fool to do that," old Apling said. "This is outside your work contract, so we can make the old gopher pay you what it's worth. I'll want to go in ahead and see about that and about the money that he owes me and about corral space and feed and one thing and another, so I'll want you to bring 'em in alone. You ain't seen everything there is to a trip like this, and you won't unless you stay with it."

## VII

There would be no ending to this story without an understanding of what that little river town looked like at the hour, a little before sundown of a windy spring day, when Beech brought the desert horse herd down into it. On the wharf below town, some men were unloading baled hay from a steamboat, with some passengers watching from the saloon deck, and the river beyond them hoisting into white-capped peaks that shone and shed dazzling spray over the darkening water.

A switch engine was handling stock cars on a spur track, and the brakeman flagged it to a stop and stood watching the horses, leaning into the wind to keep his balance while the engineer climbed out on the tender to see what was going on.

The street of the town was lined with big leafless poplars that looked as if they hadn't gone short of moisture a day of their lives; the grass under them was bright green, and there were women working around flower beds and pulling up weeds, enough of them so that a horse could have lived on them for two days.

There was a Chinaman clipping grass with a pair of sheep shears to keep it from growing too tall, and there were lawn sprinklers running clean water on the ground in streams. There were stores with windows full of new clothes, and stores with bright hardware, and stores with strings of bananas and piles of oranges, bread and crackers and candy and rows of hams, and there were groups of anxious-faced men sitting around stoves inside who came out to watch Beech pass and told one another hopefully that the back country might make a good year out of it yet, if a youngster could bring that herd of horses through it.

There were women who hauled back their children and cautioned them not to get in the man's way, and there were boys and girls, some near Beech's own age, who watched him and stood looking after him, knowing that he had been through more than they had ever seen and not suspecting that it had taught him something that they didn't know about the things they saw every day. None of them knew what it meant to be in a place where there were delicacies to eat and new clothes to wear and look at, what it meant to be warm and out of the wind for a change, what it could mean merely to have water enough to pour on the ground and grass enough to cut down and throw away.

For the first time, seeing how the youngsters looked at him, he understood what that amounted to. There wasn't a one of them who wouldn't have traded places with him. There wasn't one that he would have traded places with, for all the haberdashery and fancy groceries in town. He turned down to the corrals, and old Apling held the gate open for him and remarked that he hadn't taken much time to it.

"You're sure you had enough of that ridin' through town?" he said. "It ain't the same when you do it a second time, remember."

"It'll last me," Beech said. "I wouldn't have missed it, and I wouldn't want it to be the same again. I'd sooner have things the way they run with us out in the high country. I'd sooner not have anything be the same a second time."

# Isak Dinesen

*Dinesen (pseudonym for Baroness Karen Blixen) (1885–1962) was born near Elsinore, Denmark, the descendant of an old and cultivated Danish family. She married a cousin and in 1914 went with him to British East Africa, where she remained for seventeen busy years acting as counselor, judge, teacher, and doctor for natives and settlers alike. The color and detail of her experiences there flavor the reminiscences in* Out of Africa *(1937). Several years after her divorce she returned to Denmark and began to write—in English—the spellbinding stories that made her world famous in the 1930s. Her first collection was* Seven Gothic Tales *(1934), an immensely popular book that was a Book-of-the-Month Club selection, as was her* Winter's Tales *(1942). No literary or ideological formula fits her fiction, which seems to spring from a pure impulse to fascinate the reader by a tour among marvels and enchantments. While she was living under the Nazi occupation of Denmark during World War II, she wrote a novel, using the name of Pierre Andrézel, published in 1946 as* The Angelic Avengers. *Later publications are* Last Tales *(1957) and* Anecdotes of Destiny *(1958).*

## Sorrow-Acre

The low, undulating Danish landscape was silent and serene, mysteriously wide-awake in the hour before sunrise. There was not a cloud in the pale sky, not a shadow along the dim, pearly fields, hills and woods. The mist was lifting from the valleys and hollows, the air was cool, the grass and the foliage dripping wet with morning-dew. Unwatched by the eyes of man, and undisturbed by his activity, the country breathed a timeless life, to which language was inadequate.

All the same, a human race had lived on this land for a thousand years, had been formed by its soil and weather, and had marked it with its thoughts, so that now no one could tell where the existence of the one ceased and the other began. The thin grey line of a road, winding across the plain and up and down hills, was the fixed materialisation of human longing, and of the human notion that it is better to be in one place than another.

A child of the country would read this open landscape like a book. The irregular mosaic of meadows and cornlands was a picture, in timid green and yellow, of the people's struggle for its daily bread; the centuries had taught it to plough and sow in this way. On a distant hill the immovable wings of a windmill, in a small blue cross against the sky, delineated a later stage in the career of bread. The blurred outline of thatched roofs—a low, brown growth of the earth—where the huts of the village thronged together, told the history, from his cradle to his grave, of the peasant, the creature nearest to the soil and dependent on it, prospering in a fertile year and dying in years of drought and pests.

A little higher up, with the faint horizontal line of the white cemetery wall round it, and the vertical contour of tall poplars by its side, the red-tiled church bore witness, as far as the eye reached, that this was a Christian country. The child of the land knew it as a strange house, inhabited only for a few hours every seventh day, but with a strong, clear voice in it to give out the joys and sorrows of the land: a plain, square embodiment of the nation's trust in the justice and mercy of heaven. But where, amongst cupular woods and groves, the lordly, pyramidal silhouette of the cut lime avenues rose in the air, there a big country house lay.

The child of the land would read much within these elegant, geometrical ciphers on the hazy blue. They spoke of power, the lime trees paraded round a stronghold. Up here was decided the destiny of the surrounding land and of the men and beasts upon it, and the peasant lifted his eyes to the green pyramids with awe. They spoke of dignity, decorum and taste. Danish soil grew no finer flower than the mansion to which the long avenue led. In its lofty rooms life and death bore themselves with stately grace. The country house did not gaze upward, like the church, nor down to the ground like the huts; it had a wider earthly horizon than they, and was related to much noble architecture all over Europe. Foreign artisans had been called in to panel and stucco it, and its own inhabitants travelled and brought back ideas, fashions and things of beauty. Paintings, tapestries, silver and glass from distant countries had been made to feel at home here, and now formed part of Danish country life.

The big house stood as firmly rooted in the soil of Denmark as the peasants' huts, and was as faithfully allied to her four winds and her changing seasons, to her animal life, trees and flowers. Only its interests lay in a higher plane. Within the domain of the lime trees it was no longer cows, goats, and pigs on which the minds and the talk ran, but horses and dogs. The wild fauna, the game of the land, that the peasant shook his fist at, when he saw it on his young green rye or in his ripening wheat field, to the residents of the country houses were the main pursuit and the joy of existence.

The writing in the sky solemnly proclaimed continuance, a worldly immortality. The great country houses had held their ground through many generations. The families who lived in them revered the past as they honoured themselves, for the history of Denmark was their own history.

A Rosenkrantz had sat at Rosenholm, a Juel at Hverringe, a Skeel at Gammel-Estrup as long as people remembered. They had seen kings and schools of style succeed one another and, proudly and humbly, had made over their personal existence to that of their land, so that amongst their equals and with the peasants they passed by its name: Rosenholm, Hverringe, Gammel-Estrup. To the King and the country, to his family and to the individual lord of the manor himself it was a matter of minor consequence which particular Rosenkrantz, Juel or Skeel, out of a long row of fathers and sons, at the moment in his person incarnated the fields and woods, the peasants, cattle and game of the estate. Many duties rested on the shoulders of the big landowners—towards God in heaven, towards the King, his neighbour and himself—and they were all harmoniously consolidated into the idea of his duties towards his land. Highest amongst these ranked his obligation to uphold the sacred continuance, and to produce a new Rosenkrantz, Juel or Skeel for the service of Rosenholm, Hverringe and Gammel-Estrup.

Female grace was prized in the manors. Together with good hunting and fine wine it was the flower and emblem of the higher existence led there, and in many ways the families prided themselves more on their daughters than on their sons.

The ladies who promenaded in the lime avenues, or drove through them in heavy coaches with four horses, carried the future of the name in their laps and were, like dignified and debonair caryatides,[1] holding up the houses. They were themselves conscious of their value, kept up their price, and moved in a sphere of pretty worship and self-worship. They might even be thought to add to it, on their own, a graceful, arch, paradoxical haughtiness. For how free were they, how powerful! Their lords might rule the country, and allow themselves many liberties, but when it came to that supreme matter of legitimacy which was the vital principle of their world, the centre of gravity lay with them.

The lime trees were in bloom. But in the early morning only a faint fragrance drifted through the garden, an airy message, an aromatic echo of the dreams during the short summer night.

In a long avenue that led from the house all the way to the end of the garden, where, from a small white pavilion in the classic style, there was a great view over the fields, a young man walked. He was plainly dressed in brown, with pretty linen and lace, bare-headed, with his hair tied by a ribbon. He was dark, a strong and sturdy figure with fine eyes and hands; he limped a little on one leg.

The big house at the top of the avenue, the garden and the fields had been his childhood's paradise. But he had travelled and lived out of Denmark, in Rome and Paris, and he was at present appointed to the Danish Legation to the Court of King George, the brother of the late, unfortunate young Danish Queen.[2] He had not seen his ancestral home for nine years. It made him laugh to find, now, everything so much smaller than he remembered it, and at the same time he was strangely moved by meeting it again. Dead people came towards him and smiled at him; a small boy in a ruff ran past him with his hoop and kite, in passing gave him a clear glance and laughingly asked: "Do you mean to tell me that you are I?" He tried to catch him in the flight, and to answer him: "Yes, I assure you that I am you," but the light figure did not wait for a reply.

The young man, whose name was Adam, stood in a particular relation to the house and the land. For six months he had been heir to it all; nominally he was so even at this moment. It was this circumstance which had brought him

1. Carvings of draped female figures supporting upper sections of walls in Greek architecture. 2. Apparently a reference to George II of England. George was the father, not the brother, of Louisa, queen of Denmark (1724–1751).

from England, and on which his mind was dwelling, as he walked along slowly.

The old lord up at the manor, his father's brother, had had much misfortune in his domestic life. His wife had died young, and two of his children in infancy. The one son then left to him, his cousin's playmate, was a sickly and morose boy. For ten years the father travelled with him from one watering place to another, in Germany and Italy, hardly ever in other company than that of his silent, dying child, sheltering the faint flame of life with both hands, until such time as it could be passed over to a new bearer of the name. At the same time another misfortune had struck him: he fell into disfavour at Court, where till now he had held a fine position. He was about to rehabilitate his family's prestige through the marriage which he had arranged for his son, when before it could take place the bridegroom died, not yet twenty years old.

Adam learned of his cousin's death, and his own changed fortune, in England, through his ambitious and triumphant mother. He sat with her letter in his hand and did not know what to think about it.

If this, he reflected, had happened to him while he was still a boy, in Denmark, it would have meant all the world to him. It would be so now with his friends and schoolfellows, if they were in his place, and they would, at this moment, be congratulating or envying him. But he was neither covetous nor vain by nature; he had faith in his own talents and had been content to know that his success in life depended on his personal ability. His slight infirmity had always set him a little apart from other boys; it had, perhaps, given him a keener sensibility of many things in life, and he did not, now, deem it quite right that the head of the family should limp on one leg. He did not even see his prospects in the same light as his people at home. In England he had met with greater wealth and magnificence than they dreamed of; he had been in love with, and made happy by, an English lady of such rank and fortune that to her, he felt, the finest estate of Denmark would look but like a child's toy farm.

And in England, too, he had come in touch with the great new ideas of the age: of nature, of the right and freedom of man, of justice and beauty. The universe, through them, had become infinitely wider to him; he wanted to find out still more about it and was planning to travel to America, to the new world. For a moment he felt trapped and imprisoned, as if the dead people of his name, from the family vault at home, were stretching out their parched arms for him.

But at the same time he began to dream at night of the old house and garden. He had walked in these avenues in dream, and had smelled the scent of the flowering limes. When at Ranelagh an old gypsy woman looked at his hand and told him that a son of his was to sit in the seat of his father, he felt a sudden, deep satisfaction, queer in a young man who till now had never given his sons a thought.

Then, six months later, his mother again wrote to tell him that his uncle had himself married the girl intended for his dead son. The head of the family was still in his best age, not over sixty, and although Adam remembered him as a small, slight man, he was a vigorous person; it was likely that his young wife would bear him sons.

Adam's mother in her disappointment lay the blame on him. If he had returned to Denmark, she told him, his uncle might have come to look upon him as a son, and would not have married; nay, he might have handed the bride over to him. Adam knew better. The family estate, differing from the neighbouring properties, had gone down from father to son ever since a man of their name first sat there. The tradition of direct succession was the pride of the clan and a sacred dogma to his uncle; he would surely call for a son of his own flesh and bone.

But at the news the young man was seized by a strange, deep, aching remorse towards his old home in Denmark. It was as if he had been making light of a friendly and generous gesture, and disloyal to someone unfailingly loyal to him. It would be but just, he thought, if from now the place should disown and forget him. Nostalgia, which before he had never known, caught hold of him; for the first time he walked in the streets and parks of London as a stranger.

He wrote to his uncle and asked if he might come and stay with him, begged leave from the Legation and took ship for Denmark. He had come to the house to make his peace with it; he had slept little in the night, and was up so early and walking in the garden, to explain himself, and to be forgiven.

While he walked, the still garden slowly took up its day's work. A big snail, of the kind that his grandfather had brought back from France, and which he remembered eating in the house as a child, was already, with dignity, dragging a silver train down the avenue. The birds began to sing; in an old tree under which he stopped a number of them were worrying an owl; the rule of the night was over.

He stood at the end of the avenue and saw the sky lightening. An ecstatic clarity filled the world; in half an hour the sun would rise. A rye field here ran along the garden; two roe-deer were moving in it and looked roseate in the dawn. He gazed out over the fields, where as a small boy he had ridden his pony, and towards the wood where he had killed his first stag. He remembered the old servants who had taught him; some of them were now in their graves.

The ties which bound him to this place, he reflected, were of a mystic nature. He might never again come back to it, and it would make no difference. As long as a man of his own blood and name should sit in the house, hunt in the fields and be obeyed by the people in the huts, wherever he travelled on earth, in England or amongst the red Indians of America, he himself would still be safe, would still have a home, and would carry weight in the world.

His eyes rested on the church. In old days, before the time of Martin Luther,[3] younger sons of great families, he knew, had entered the Church of Rome, and had given up individual wealth and happiness to serve the greater ideals. They, too, had bestowed honour upon their homes and were remembered in its registers. In the solitude of the morning half in jest he let his mind run as it listed; it seemed to him that he might speak to the land as to a person, as to the mother of his race. "Is it only my body that you want," he asked her, "while you reject my imagination, energy and emotions? If the world might be brought to acknowledge that the virtue of our name does not belong to the past

3. Leader of the Protestant break from the Roman Catholic Church (1483–1546).

only, will it give you no satisfaction?" The landscape was so still that he could not tell whether it answered him yes or no.

After a while he walked on, and came to the new French rose garden laid out for the young mistress of the house. In England he had acquired a freer taste in gardening, and he wondered if he could liberate these blushing captives, and make them thrive outside their cut hedges. Perhaps, he meditated, the elegantly conventional garden would be a floral portrait of his young aunt from Court, whom he had not yet seen.

As once more he came to the pavilion at the end of the avenue his eyes were caught by a bouquet of delicate colours which could not possibly belong to the Danish summer morning. It was in fact his uncle himself, powdered and silk-stockinged, but still in a brocade dressing-gown, and obviously sunk in deep thought. "And what business, or what meditations," Adam asked himself, "drags a connoisseur of the beautiful, but three months married to a wife of seventeen, from his bed into his garden before sunrise?" He walked up to the small, slim, straight figure.

His uncle on his side showed no surprise at seeing him, but then he rarely seemed surprised at anything. He greeted him, with a compliment on his matunality,[4] as kindly as he had done on his arrival last evening. After a moment he looked to the sky, and solemnly proclaimed: "It will be a hot day." Adam, as a child, had often been impressed by the grand, ceremonial manner in which the old lord would state the common happenings of existence; it looked as if nothing had changed here, but all was what it used to be.

The uncle offered the nephew a pinch of snuff. "No, thank you, Uncle," said Adam, "it would ruin my nose to the scent of your garden, which is as fresh as the Garden of Eden, newly created." "From every tree of which," said his uncle, smiling, "thou, my Adam, mayest freely eat." They slowly walked up the avenue together.

The hidden sun was now already gilding the top of the tallest trees. Adam talked of the beauties of nature, and of the greatness of Nordic scenery, less marked by the hand of man than that of Italy. His uncle took the praise of the landscape as a personal compliment, and congratulated him because he had not, in likeness to many young travellers in foreign countries, learned to despise his native land. No, said Adam, he had lately in England longed for the fields and woods of his Danish home. And he had there become acquainted with a new piece of Danish poetry which had enchanted him more than any English or French work. He named the author, Johannes Ewald,[5] and quoted a few of the mighty, turbulent verses.

"And I have wondered, while I read," he went on after a pause, still moved by the lines he himself had declaimed, "that we have not till now understood how much our Nordic mythology in moral greatness surpasses that of Greece and Rome. If it had not been for the physical beauty of the ancient gods, which has come down to us in marble, no modern mind could hold them worthy of worship. They were mean, capricious and treacherous. The gods of our Danish forefathers are as much more divine than they as the Druid is nobler than the

4. Morning appearance. 5. Denmark's greatest lyric poet (1743–1781).

Augur.[6] For the fair gods of Asgaard[7] did possess the sublime human virtues; they were righteous, trustworthy, benevolent and even, within a barbaric age, chivalrous." His uncle here for the first time appeared to take any real interest in the conversation. He stopped, his majestic nose a little in the air. "Ah, it was easier to them," he said.

"What do you mean, Uncle?" Adam asked. "It was a great deal easier," said his uncle, "to the northern gods than to those of Greece to be, as you will have it, righteous and benevolent. To my mind it even reveals a weakness in the souls of our ancient Danes that they should consent to adore such divinities." "My dear uncle," said Adam, smiling, "I have always felt that you would be familiar with the modes of Olympus. Now please let me share your insight, and tell me why virtue should come easier to our Danish gods than to those of milder climates." "They were not as powerful," said his uncle.

"And does power," Adam again asked, "stand in the way of virtue?" "Nay," said his uncle gravely. "Nay, power is in itself the supreme virtue. But the gods of which you speak were never all-powerful. They had, at all times, by their side those darker powers which they named the Jotuns,[8] and who worked the suffering, the disasters, the ruin of our world. They might safely give themselves up to temperance and kindness. The omnipotent gods," he went on, "have no such facilitation. With their omnipotence they take over the woe of the universe."

They had walked up the avenue till they were in view of the house. The old lord stopped and ran his eyes over it. The stately building was the same as ever; behind the two tall front windows, Adam knew, was now his young aunt's room. His uncle turned and walked back.

"Chivalry," he said, "chivalry, of which you were speaking, is not a virtue of the omnipotent. It must needs imply mighty rival powers for the knight to defy. With a dragon inferior to him in strength, what figure will St. George[9] cut? The knight who finds no superior forces ready to hand must invent them, and combat wind-mills; his knighthood itself stipulates dangers, vileness, darkness on all sides of him. Nay, believe me, my nephew, in spite of his moral worth, your chivalrous Odin of Asgaard as a Regent must take rank below that of Jove[1] who avowed his sovereignty, and accepted the world which he ruled. But you are young," he added, "and the experience of the aged to you will sound pedantic."

He stood immovable for a moment and then with deep gravity proclaimed: "The sun is up."

The sun did indeed rise above the horizon. The wide landscape was suddenly animated by its splendour, and the dewy grass shone in a thousand gleams.

"I have listened to you, Uncle," said Adam, "with great interest. But while we have talked you yourself have seemed to me preoccupied; your eyes have rested on the field outside the garden, as if something of great moment, a matter

6. I.e., as an ancient Celtic wizard-priest is nobler than an ancient Roman soothsayer. 7. In Teutonic mythology the celestial dwelling place. 8. Race of giants. 9. In religious allegory the slayer of the dragon; patron saint of England, Aragon, and Portugal. 1. The chief of Roman gods, as Odin is chief of Norse gods.

of life and death, was going on there. Now that the sun is up, I see the mowers in the rye and hear them whetting their sickles. It is, I remember you telling me, the first day of the harvest. That is a great day to a landowner and enough to take his mind away from the gods. It is very fine weather, and I wish you a full barn."

The elder man stood still, his hands on his walking-stick. "There is indeed," he said at last, "something going on in that field, a matter of life and death. Come, let us sit down here, and I will tell you the whole story." They sat down on the seat that ran all along the pavilion, and while he spoke the old lord of the land did not take his eyes off the rye field.

"A week ago, on Thursday night," he said, "someone set fire to my barn at Rødmosegaard—you know the place, close to the moor—and burned it all down. For two or three days we could not lay hands on the offender. Then on Monday morning the keeper at Rødmose, with the wheelwright over there, came up to the house; they dragged with them a boy, Goske Piil, a widow's son, and they made their Bible oath that he had done it; they had themselves seen him sneaking round the barn by nightfall on Thursday. Goske had no good name on the farm; the keeper bore him a grudge upon an old matter of poaching, and the wheelwright did not like him either, for he did, I believe, suspect him with his young wife. The boy, when I talked to him, swore to his innocence, but he could not hold his own against the two old men. So I had him locked up, and meant to send him in to our judge of the district, with a letter.

"The judge is a fool, and would naturally do nothing but what he thought I wished him to do. He might have the boy sent to the convict prison for arson, or put amongst the soldiers as a bad character and a poacher. Or again, if he thought that that was what I wanted, he could let him off.

"I was out riding in the fields, looking at the corn that was soon ripe to be mowed, when a woman, the widow, Goske's mother, was brought up before me, and begged to speak to me. Anne-Marie is her name. You will remember her; she lives in the small house east of the village. She has not got a good name in the place either. They tell as a girl she had a child and did away with it.

"From five days' weeping her voice was so cracked that it was difficult for me to understand what she said. Her son, she told me at last, had indeed been over at Rødmose on Thursday, but for no ill purpose; he had gone to see someone. He was her only son, she called the Lord God to witness on his innocence, and she wrung her hands to me that I should save the boy for her.

"We were in the rye field that you and I are looking at now. That gave me an idea. I said to the widow: 'If in one day, between sunrise and sunset, with your own hands you can mow this field, and it be well done, I will let the case drop and you shall keep your son. But if you cannot do it, he must go, and it is not likely that you will then ever see him again.'

"She stood up then and gazed over the field. She kissed my riding boot in gratitude for the favour shown to her.

The old lord here made a pause, and Adam said: "Her son meant much to her?" "He is her only child," said his uncle. "He means to her her daily bread and support in old age. It may be said that she holds him as dear as her own life. As," he added, "within a higher order of life, a son to his father means the name and the race, and he holds him as dear as life everlasting. Yes, her son means much to her. For the mowing of that field is a day's work to three men, or three days' work to one man. Today, as the sun rose, she set to her task. And down there, by the end of the field, you will see her now, in a blue head-cloth, with the man I have set to follow her and to ascertain that she does the work unassisted, and with two or three friends by her, who are comforting her."

Adam looked down, and did indeed see a woman in a blue head-cloth, and a few other figures in the corn.

They sat for a while in silence. "Do you yourself," Adam then said, "believe the boy to be innocent?" "I cannot tell," said his uncle. "There is no proof. The word of the keeper and the wheelwright stand against the boy's word. If indeed I did believe the one thing or the other, it would be merely a matter of chance, or maybe of sympathy. The boy," he said after a moment, "was my son's playmate, the only other child that I ever knew him to like or to get on with." "Do you," Adam again asked, "hold it possible to her to fulfill your condition?" "Nay, I cannot tell," said the old lord. "To an ordinary person it would not be possible. No ordinary person would ever have taken it on at all. I chose it so. We are not quibbling with the law, Anne-Marie and I."

Adam for a few minutes followed the movement of the small group in the rye. "Will you walk back?" he asked. "No," said his uncle, "I think that I shall stay here till I have seen the end of the thing." "Until sunset?" Adam asked with surprise. "Yes," said the old lord. Adam said: "It will be a long day." "Yes," said his uncle, "a long day. But," he added, as Adam rose to walk away, "if, as you said, you have got that tragedy of which you spoke in your pocket, be as kind as to leave it here, to keep me company." Adam handed him the book.

In the avenue he met two footmen who carried the old lord's morning chocolate down to the pavilion on large silver trays.

As now the sun rose in the sky, and the day grew hot, the lime trees gave forth their exuberance of scent, and the garden was filled with unsurpassed, unbelievable sweetness. Towards the still hour of midday the long avenue reverberated like a soundboard with a low, incessant murmur: the humming of a million bees that clung to the pendulous, thronging clusters of blossoms and were drunk with bliss.

In all the short lifetime of Danish summer there is no richer or more luscious moment than that week wherein the lime trees flower. The heavenly scent goes to the head and to the heart; it seems to unite the fields of Denmark with those of Elysium;[2] it contains both hay, honey and holy incense, and is half fairy-land and half apothecary's locker. The avenue was changed into a mystic edifice, a dryad's cathedral, outward from summit to base lavishly adorned, set with multitudinous ornaments, and golden in the sun. But behind the walls the vaults were benignly cool and sombre, like ambrosial sanctuaries in a dazzling and burning world, and in here the ground was still moist.

Up in the house, behind the silk curtains of the two front windows, the young mistress of the estate from the wide bed stuck her feet into two little high-heeled slippers. Her lace-trimmed nightgown had slid up above her knee

2. In classic mythology the abode of the good after death.

and down from the shoulder; her hair, done up in curling-pins for the night, was still frosty with the powder of yesterday, her round face flushed with sleep. She stepped out to the middle of the floor and stood there, looking extremely grave and thoughtful, yet she did not think at all. But through her head a long procession of pictures marched, and she was unconsciously endeavouring to put them in order, as the pictures of her existence had used to be.

She had grown up at Court; it was her world, and there was probably not in the whole country a small creature more exquisitely and innocently drilled to the stately measure of a palace. By favour of the old Dowager Queen she bore her name and that of the King's sister, the Queen of Sweden: Sophie Magdalena. It was with a view to these things that her husband, when he wished to restore his status in high places, had chosen her as a bride, first for his son and then for himself. But her own father, who held an Office in the Royal Household and belonged to the new Court aristocracy, in his day had done the same thing the other way round, and had married a country lady, to get a foothold within the old nobility of Denmark. The little girl had her mother's blood in her veins. The country to her had been an immense surprise and delight.

To get into her castle-court she must drive through the farm yard, through the heavy stone gateway in the barn itself, wherein the rolling of her coach for a few seconds re-echoed like thunder. She must drive past the stables and the timber-mare,[3] from which sometimes a miscreant would follow her with sad eyes, and might here startle a long string of squalling geese, or pass the heavy, scowling bull, led on by a ring in his nose and kneading the earth in dumb fury. At first this had been to her, every time, a slight shock and a jest. But after a while all these creatures and things, which belonged to her, seemed to become part of herself. Her mothers, the old Danish country ladies, were robust persons, undismayed by any kind of weather; now she herself had walked in the rain and had laughed and glowed in it like a green tree.

She had taken her great new home in possession at a time when all the world was unfolding, mating and propagating. Flowers, which she had known only in bouquets and festoons, sprung from the earth round her; birds sang in all the trees. The new-born lambs seemed to her daintier than her dolls had been. From her husband's Hanoverian[4] stud, foals were brought to her to give names; she stood and watched as they poked their soft noses into their mothers' bellies to drink. Of this strange process she had till now only vaguely heard. She had happened to witness, from a path in the park, the rearing and screeching stallion on the mare. All this luxuriance, lust and fecundity was displayed before her eyes, as for her pleasure.

And for her own part, in the midst of it, she was given an old husband who treated her with punctilious respect because she was to bear him a son. Such was the compact; she had known of it from the beginning. Her husband, she found, was doing his best to fulfill his part of it, and she herself was loyal by nature and strictly brought up. She would not shirk her obligation. Only she

3. A crude wooden horse on which soldiers—or sometimes servants—were tied for punishment. 4. Hanover, in north-central Germany, was one of the states of the Holy Roman Empire.

was vaguely aware of a discord or an incompatibility within her majestic existence, which prevented her from being as happy as she had expected to be.

After a time her chagrin took a strange form: as the consciousness of an absence. Someone ought to have been with her who was not. She had no experience in analysing her feelings; there had not been time for that at Court. Now, as she was more often left to herself, she vaguely probed her own mind. She tried to set her father in that void place, her sisters, her music master, an Italian singer whom she had admired; but none of them would fill it for her. At times she felt lighter at heart, and believed the misfortune to have left her. And then again it would happen, if she were alone, or in her husband's company, and even within his embrace, that everything round her would cry out: Where? Where? so that she let her wild eyes run about the room in search for the being who should have been there, and who had not come.

When, six months ago, she was informed that her first young bridegroom had died and that she was to marry his father in his place, she had not been sorry. Her youthful suitor, the one time she had seen him, had appeared to her infantile and insipid; the father would make a statelier consort. Now she had sometimes thought of the dead boy, and wondered whether with him life would have been more joyful. But she soon again dismissed the picture, and that was the sad youth's last recall to the stage of this world.

Upon one wall of her room there hung a long mirror. As she gazed into it new images came along. The day before, driving with her husband, she had seen, at a distance, a party of village girls bathing in the river, and the sun shining on them. All her life she had moved amongst naked marble deities, but it had till now never occurred to her that the people she knew should themselves be naked under their bodices and trains, waistcoats and satin breeches, that indeed she herself felt naked within her clothes. Now, in front of the looking-glass, she tardily untied the ribbons of her nightgown, and let it drop to the floor.

The room was dim behind the drawn curtains. In the mirror her body was silvery like a white rose; only her cheeks and mouth, and the tips of her fingers and breasts had a faint carmine. Her slender torso was formed by the whalebones that had clasped it tightly from her childhood; above the slim, dimpled knee a gentle narrowness marked the place of the garter. Her limbs were rounded as if, at whatever place they might be cut through with a sharp knife, a perfectly circular transverse incision would be obtained. The side and belly were so smooth that her own gaze slipped and glided, and grasped for a hold. She was not altogether like a statue, she found, and lifted her arms above her head. She turned to get a view of her back, the curves below the waistline were still blushing from the pressure of the bed. She called to mind a few tales about nymphs and goddesses, but they all seemed a long way off, so her mind returned to the peasant girls in the river. They were, for a few minutes, idealized into playmates, or sisters even, since they belonged to her as did the meadow and the blue river itself. And within the next moment the sense of forlornness once more came upon her, a *horror vacui*[5] like a physical pain. Surely, surely some-

5. Abhorrence of emptiness (Latin).

one should have been with her now, her other self, like the image in the glass, but nearer, stronger, alive. There was no one, the universe was empty round her.

A sudden, keen itching under her knee took her out of her reveries, and awoke in her the hunting instincts of her breed. She wetted a finger on her tongue, slowly brought it down and quickly slapped it to the spot. She felt the diminutive, sharp body of the insect against the silky skin, pressed the thumb to it, and triumphantly lifted up the small prisoner between her fingertips. She stood quite still, as if meditating upon the fact that a flea was the only creature risking its life for her smoothness and sweet blood.

Her maid opened the door and came in, loaded with the attire of the day—shift, stays, hoop and petticoats. She remembered that she had a guest in the house, the new nephew arrived from England. Her husband had instructed her to be kind to their young kinsman, disinherited, so to say, by her presence in the house. They would ride out on the land together.

In the afternoon the sky was no longer blue as in the morning. Large clouds slowly towered up on it, and the great vault itself was colourless, as if diffused into vapours round the white-hot sun in zenith. A low thunder ran along the western horizon; once or twice the dust of the roads rose in tall spirals. But the fields, the hills and the woods were as still as a painted landscape.

Adam walked down the avenue to the pavilion, and found his uncle there, fully dressed, his hands upon his walking-stick and his eyes on the rye field. The book that Adam had given him lay by his side. The field now seemed alive with people. Small groups stood here and there in it, and a long row of men and women were slowly advancing towards the garden in the line of the swath.

The old lord nodded to his nephew, but did not speak or change his position. Adam stood by him as still as himself.

The day to him had been strangely disquieting. At the meeting again with old places the sweet melodies of the past had filled his senses and his mind, and had mingled with new, bewitching tunes of the present. He was back in Denmark, no longer a child but a youth, with a keener sense of the beautiful, with tales of other countries to tell, and still a true son of his own land and enchanted by its loveliness as he had never been before.

But through all these harmonies the tragic and cruel tale which the old lord had told him in the morning, and the sad contest which he knew to be going on so near by, in the corn field, had re-echoed, like the recurrent, hollow throbbing of a muffled drum, a redoubtable sound. It came back time after time, so that he had felt himself to change colour and to answer absently. It brought with it a deeper sense of pity with all that lived than he had ever known. When he had been riding with his young aunt, and their road ran along the scene of the drama, he had taken care to ride between her and the field, so that she should not see what was going on there, or question him about it. He had chosen the way home through the deep, green wood for the same reason.

More dominantly even than the figure of the woman struggling with her sickle for her son's life, the old man's figure, as he had seen it at sunrise, kept him company through the day. He came to ponder on the part which that lonely, determinate form had played in his own life. From the time when his father died, it had impersonated to the boy law and order, wisdom of life and kind guardianship. What was he to do, he thought, if after eighteen years these filial feelings must change, and his second father's figure take on to him a horrible aspect, as a symbol of the tyranny and oppression of the world? What was he to do if ever the two should come to stand in opposition to each other as adversaries?

At the same time an unaccountable, a sinister alarm and dread on behalf of the old man himself took hold of him. For surely here the Goddess Nemesis[6] could not be far away. This man had ruled the world round him for a longer period than Adam's own lifetime and had never been gainsaid by anyone. During the years when he had wandered through Europe with a sick boy of his own blood as his sole companion he had learned to set himself apart from his surroundings, and to close himself up to all outer life, and he had become insusceptible to the ideas and feelings of other human beings. Strange fancies might there have run in his mind, so that in the end he had seen himself as the only person really existing, and the world as a poor and vain shadow-play, which had no substance to it.

Now, in senile wilfullness, he would take in his hand the life of those simpler and weaker than himself, of a woman, using it to his own ends, and he feared of no retributive justice. Did he not know, the young man thought, that there were powers in the world, different from and more formidable than the short-lived might of a despot?

With the sultry heat of the day this foreboding of impending disaster grew upon him, until he felt ruin threatening not the old lord only, but the house, the name and himself with him. It seemed to him that he must cry out a warning to the man he had loved, before it was too late.

But as now he was once more in his uncle's company, the green calm of the garden was so deep that he did not find his voice to cry out. Instead a little French air which his aunt had sung to him up in the house kept running in his mind.—"*C'est un trop doux effort*[7] . . ." He had good knowledge of music; he had heard the air before, in Paris, but not so sweetly sung.

After a time he asked: "Will the woman fulfill her bargain?" His uncle unfolded his hands. "It is an extraordinary thing," he said animatedly, "that it looks as if she might fulfill it. If you count the hours from sunrise till now, and from now till sunset, you will find the time left her to be half of that already gone. And see! She has now mowed two-thirds of the field. But then we will naturally have to reckon with her strength declining as she works on. All in all, it is an idle pursuit in you or me to bet on the issue of the matter; we must wait and see. Sit down, and keep me company in my watch." In two minds Adam sat down.

"And here," said his uncle, and took up the book from the seat, "is your book, which has passed the time finely. It is great poetry, ambrosia to the ear and the heart. And it has, with our discourse on divinity this morning, given me stuff for thought. I have been reflecting upon the law of retributive justice." He took a pinch of snuff, and went on. "A new age," he said, "has made to itself

6. Greek goddess of retribution. 7. It is too sweet an effort (French).

a god in its own image, an emotional god. And now you are already writing a tragedy on your god."

Adam had no wish to begin a debate on poetry with his uncle, but he also somehow dreaded a silence, and said: "It may be, then, that we hold tragedy to be, in the scheme of life, a noble, a divine phenomenon."

"Aye," said his uncle solemnly, "a noble phenomenon, the noblest on earth. But of the earth only, and never divine. Tragedy is the privilege of man, his highest privilege. The God of the Christian Church Himself, when He wished to experience tragedy, had to assume human form. And even at that," he added thoughtfully, "the tragedy was not wholly valid, as it would have become had the hero of it been, in very truth, a man. The divinity of Christ conveyed to it a divine note, the moment of comedy. The real tragic part, by the nature of things, fell to the executors, not to the victim. Nay, my nephew, we should not adulterate the pure elements of the cosmos. Tragedy should remain the right of human beings, subject, in their conditions or in their own nature, to the dire law of necessity. To them it is salvation and beatification. But the gods, whom we must believe to be unacquainted with and incomprehensive of necessity, can have no knowledge of the tragic. When they are brought face to face with it they will, according to my experience, have the good taste and decorum to keep still, and not interfere.

"No," he said after a pause, "the true art of the gods is the comic. The comic is a condescension of the divine to the world of man; it is the sublime vision, which cannot be studied, but must ever be celestially granted. In the comic the gods see their own being reflected as in a mirror, and while the tragic poet is bound by strict laws, they will allow the comic artist a freedom as unlimited as their own. They do not even withhold their own existence from his sports. Jove may favour Lucianos of Samosata.[8] As long as your mockery is in true godly taste you may mock at the gods and still remain a sound devotee. But in pitying, or condoling with your god, you deny and annihilate him, and such is the most horrible of atheisms.

"And here on earth, too," he went on, "we, who stand in lieu of the gods and have emancipated ourselves from the tyranny of necessity, should leave to our vassals their monopoly of tragedy, and for ourselves accept the comic with grace. Only a boorish and cruel master—a parvenu, in fact—will make a jest of his servants' necessity, or force the comic upon them. Only a timid and pedantic ruler, a *petit-maître,*[9] will fear the ludicrous on his own behalf. Indeed," he finished his long speech, "the very same fatality, which, in striking the burgher or peasant, will become tragedy, with the aristocrat is exalted to the comic. By the grace and wit of our acceptance hereof our aristocracy is known."

Adam could not help smiling a little as he heard the apotheosis of the comic on the lips of the erect, ceremonious prophet. In this ironic smile he was, for the first time, estranging himself from the head of his house.

A shadow fell across the landscape. A cloud had crept over the sun; the

8. Greek satirist (C.E. 120–180). Jove would tolerate his satire because of its excellence. 9. Minor master (French).

country changed colour beneath it, faded and bleached, and even all sounds for a minute seemed to die out of it.

"Ah, now," said the old lord, "if it is going to rain, and the rye gets wet, Anne-Marie will not be able to finish in time. And who comes there?" he added, and turned his head a little.

Preceded by a lackey a man in riding boots and a striped waistcoat with silver buttons, and with his hat in his hand, came down the avenue. He bowed deeply, first to the old lord and then to Adam.

"My bailiff," said the old lord. "Good afternoon, Bailiff. What news have you to bring?" The bailiff made a sad gesture. "Poor news only, my lord," he said. "And how poor news?" asked his master. "There is," said the bailiff with weight, "not a soul at work on the land, and not a sickle going except that of Anne-Marie in this rye field. The mowing has stopped; they are all at her heels. It is a poor day for a first day of the harvest." "Yes, I see," said the old lord. The bailiff went on. "I have spoken kindly to them," he said, "and I have sworn at them; it is all one. They might as well all be deaf."

"Good bailiff," said the old lord, "leave them in peace; let them do as they like. This day may, all the same, do them more good than many others. Where is Goske, the boy, Anne-Marie's son?" "We have set him in the small room by the barn," said the bailiff. "Nay, let him be brought down," said the old lord; "let him see his mother at work. But what do you say—will she get the field mowed in time?" "If you ask me, my lord," said the bailiff, "I believe that she will. Who would have thought so? She is only a small woman. It is as hot a day today as, well, as I do ever remember. I myself, you yourself, my lord, could not have done what Anne-Marie has done today." "Nay, nay, we could not, Bailiff," said the old lord.

The bailiff pulled out a red handkerchief and wiped his brow, somewhat calmed by venting his wrath. "If," he remarked with bitterness, "they would all work as the widow works now, we would make a profit on the land." "Yes," said the old lord, and fell into thought, as if calculating the profit it might make. "Still," he said, "as to the question of profit and loss, that is more intricate than it looks. I will tell you something that you may not know: The most famous tissue ever woven was ravelled out again every night.[1] But come," he added, "she is close by now. We will go and have a look at her work ourselves." With these words he rose and set his hat on.

The cloud had drawn away again; the rays of the sun once more burned the wide landscape, and as the small party walked out from under the shade of the trees the dead-still heat was heavy as lead; the sweat sprang out on their faces and their eyelids smarted. On the narrow path they had to go one by one, the old lord stepping along first, all black, and the footman, in his bright livery, bringing up the rear.

The field was indeed filled with people like a marketplace; there were probably a hundred or more men and women in it. To Adam the scene recalled pictures from his Bible: the meeting between Esau and Jacob in Edom, or

1. An allusion to Penelope's weaving, which she unraveled every night to delay suitors while her husband, Odysseus, was away (Homer's *Odyssey*).

Boas' reapers in his barley field near Bethlehem.[2] Some were standing by the side of the field, others pressed in small groups close to the mowing woman, and a few followed in her wake, binding up sheaves where she had cut the corn, as if thereby they thought to help her, or as if by all means they meant to have part in her work. A younger woman with a pail on her head kept close to her side, and with her a number of half-grown children. One of these first caught sight of the lord of the estate and his suite, and pointed to him. The binders let their sheaves drop, and as the old man stood still many of the onlookers drew close round him.

The woman on whom till now the eyes of the whole field had rested—a small figure on the large stage—was advancing slowly and unevenly, bent double as if she were walking on her knees, and stumbling as she walked. His blue head-cloth had slipped back from her head; the grey hair was plastered to the skull with sweat, dusty and stuck with straw. She was obviously totally unaware of the multitude round her; neither did she now once turn her head or her gaze towards the new arrivals.

Absorbed in her work she again and again stretched out her left hand to grasp a handful of corn, and her right hand with the sickle in it to cut it off close to the soil, in wavering, groping pulls, like a tired swimmer's strokes. Her course took her so close to the feet of the old lord that his shadow fell on her. Just then she staggered and swayed sideways, and the woman who followed her lifted the pail from her head and held it to her lips. Anne-Marie drank without leaving her hold on her sickle, and the water ran from the corners of her mouth. A boy, close to her, quickly bent one knee, seized her hands in his own and, steadying and guiding them, cut off a gripe of rye. "No, no," said the old lord, "you must not do that, boy. Leave Anne-Marie in peace to her work." At the sound of his voice the woman, falteringly, lifted her face in his direction.

The bony and tanned face was streaked with sweat and dust; the eyes were dimmed. But there was not in its expression the slightest trace of fear or pain. Indeed amongst all the grave and concerned faces of the field hers was the only one perfectly calm, peaceful and mild. The mouth was drawn together in a thin line, a prim, keen, patient little smile, such as will be seen in the face of an old woman at her spinning-wheel or her knitting, eager on her work, and happy in it. And as the younger woman lifted back the pail, she immediately again fell to her mowing, with an ardent, tender craving, like that of a mother who lays a baby to the nipple. Like an insect that bustles along in high grass, or like a small vessel in a heavy sea, she butted her way on, her quiet face once more bent upon her task.

The whole throng of onlookers, and with them the small group from the pavilion, advanced as she advanced, slowly and as if drawn by a string. The bailiff, who felt the intense silence of the field heavy on him, said to the old lord: "The rye will yield better this year than last," and got no reply. He repeated his remark to Adam, and at last to the footman, who felt himself above a discussion on agriculture, and only cleared his throat in answer. In a while the bailiff again broke the silence. "There is the boy," he said and pointed with his

2. References to Genesis 32 and Ruth 2.

thumb. "They have brought him down." At that moment the woman fell forward on her face and was lifted up by those nearest to her.

Adam suddenly stopped on the path, and covered his eyes with his hand. The old lord without turning asked him if he felt incommoded by the heat. "No," said Adam, "but stay. Let me speak to you." His uncle stopped, with his hand on the stick and looking ahead, as if regretful of being held back.

"In the name of God," cried the young man in French, "force not this woman to continue." There was a short pause. "But I force her not, my friend," said his uncle in the same language. "She is free to finish at any moment." "At the cost of her child only," again cried Adam. "Do you not see that she is dying? You know not what you are doing, or what it may bring upon you."

The old lord, perplexed by this unexpected animadversion, after a second turned all round, and his pale, clear eyes sought his nephew's face with stately surprise. His long, waxen face, with two symmetrical curls at the sides, had something of the mien of an idealized and ennobled old sheep or ram. He made sign to the bailiff to go on. The footman also withdrew a little, and the uncle and nephew were, so to say, alone on the path. For a minute neither of them spoke.

"In this very place where we now stand," said the old lord, then, with hauteur, "I gave Anne-Marie my word."

"My uncle!" said Adam. "A life is a greater thing even than a word. Recall that word, I beseech you, which was given in caprice, as a whim. I am praying you more for your sake than for my own, yet I shall be grateful to you all my life if you will grant me my prayer."

"You will have learned in school," said his uncle, "that in the beginning was the word.[3] It may have been pronounced in caprice, as a whim, the Scripture tells me nothing about it. It is still the principle of our world, its law of gravitation. My own humble word has been the principle of the land on which we stand, for an age of man. My father's word was the same, before my day."

"You are mistaken," cried Adam. "The word is creative—it is imagination, daring and passion. By it the world was made. How much greater are these powers which bring into being than any restricting or controlling law! You wish the land on which we look to produce and propagate; you should not banish from it the forces which cause, and which keep up life, nor turn it into a desert by dominance of law. And when you look at the people, simpler than we and nearer to the heart of nature, who do not analyse their feelings, whose life is one with the life of the earth, do they not inspire in you a tenderness, respect, reverence even? This woman is ready to die for her son; will it ever happen to you or me that a woman willingly gives up her life for us? And if it did indeed come to pass, should we make so light of it as not to give up a dogma in return?"

"You are young," said the old lord. "A new age will undoubtedly applaud you. I am old-fashioned, I have been quoting to you texts a thousand years old. We do not, perhaps, quite understand one another. But with my own people I am, I believe, in good understanding. Anne-Marie might well feel that I am making light of her exploit, if now, at the eleventh hour, I did nullify it by a

3. John 1.1.

second word. I myself should feel so in her place. Yes, my nephew, it is possible, did I grant you your prayer and pronounce such an amnesty, that I should find it void against her faithfulness, and that we would still see her at her work, unable to give it up, as a shuttle in the rye field, until she had it all mowed. But she would then be a shocking, a horrible sight, a figure of unseemly fun, like a small planet running wild in the sky, when the law of gravitation had been done away with."

"And if she dies at her task," Adam exclaimed, "her death, and its consequences will come upon your head."

The old lord took off his hat and gently ran his hand over his powdered head. "Upon my head?" he said. "I have kept up my head in many weathers. Even," he added proudly, "against the cold wind from high places. In what shape will it come upon my head, my nephew?" "I cannot tell," cried Adam in despair. "I have spoken to warn you. God only knows." "Amen," said the old lord with a little delicate smile. "Come, we will walk on." Adam drew in his breath deeply.

"No," he said in Danish. "I cannot come with you. This field is yours; things will happen here as you decide. But I myself must go away. I beg you to let me have, this evening, a coach as far as town. For I could not sleep another night under your roof, which I have honoured beyond any on earth." So many conflicting feelings at his own speech thronged in his breast that it would have been impossible for him to give them words.

The old lord, who had already begun to walk on, stood still, and with him the lackey. He did not speak for a minute, as if to give Adam time to collect his mind. But the young man's mind was in uproar and would not be collected.

"Must we," the old man asked, in Danish, "take leave here, in the rye field? I have held you dear, next to my own son. I have followed your career in life from year to year, and have been proud of you. I was happy when you wrote to say that you were coming back. If now you will go away, I wish you well." He shifted his walking-stick from the right hand to the left and gravely looked his nephew in the face.

Adam did not meet his eyes. He was gazing out over the landscape. In the late mellow afternoon it was resuming its colours, like a painting brought into proper light; in the meadows the little black stacks of peat stood gravely distinct upon the green sward. On this same morning he had greeted it all, like a child running laughingly to its mother's bosom; now already he must tear himself from it, in discordance, and forever. And at the moment of parting it seemed infinitely dearer than any time before, so much beautified and solemnized by the coming separation that it looked like the place in a dream, a landscape out of paradise, and he wondered if it was really the same. But, yes—there before him was, once more, the hunting-ground of long ago. And there was the road on which he had ridden today.

"But tell me where you mean to go from here," said the old lord slowly. "I myself have travelled a good deal in my days. I know the word of leaving, the wish to go away. But I have learned by experience that, in reality, the word has a meaning only to the place and the people which one leaves. When you have left my house—although it will see you go with sadness—as far as it is concerned the matter is finished and done with. But to the person who goes away it is a different thing, and not so simple. At the moment that he leaves one place he will be already, by the laws of life, on his way to another, upon this earth. Let me know, then, for the sake of our old acquaintance, to which place you are going when you leave here. To England?"

"No," said Adam. He felt in his heart that he could never again go back to England or to his easy and carefree life there. It was not far enough away; deeper waters than the North Sea must now be laid between him and Denmark. "No, not to England," he said. "I shall go to America, to the new world." For a moment he shut his eyes, trying to form to himself a picture of existence in America, with the grey Atlantic Ocean between him and these fields and woods.

"To America?" said his uncle and drew up his eyebrows. "Yes, I have heard of America. They have got freedom there, a big waterfall, savage red men. They shoot turkeys, I have read, as we shoot partridges. Well, if it be your wish, go to America, Adam, and be happy in the new world."

He stood for some time, sunk in thought, as if he had already sent off the young man to America, and had done with him. When at last he spoke, his words had the character of a monologue, enunciated by the person who watches things come and go, and himself stays on.

"Take service, there," he said, "with the power which will give you an easier bargain than this: That with your own life you may buy the life of your son."

Adam had not listened to his uncle's remarks about America, but the conclusive, solemn words caught his ear. He looked up. As if for the first time in his life, he saw the old man's figure as a whole, and conceived how small it was, so much smaller than himself, pale, a thin black anchorite upon his own land. A thought ran through his head: "How terrible to be old!" The abhorrence of the tyrant, and the sinister dread on his behalf, which had followed him all day, seemed to die out of him, and his pity with all creation to extend even to the sombre form before him.

His whole being had cried out for harmony. Now, with the possibility of forgiving, of a reconciliation, a sense of relief went through him; confusedly he bethought himself of Anne-Marie drinking the water held to her lips. He took off his hat, as his uncle had done a moment ago, so that to a beholder at a distance it would seem that the two dark-clad gentlemen on the path were repeatedly and respectfully saluting one another, and brushed the hair from his forehead. Once more the tune of the garden-room rang in his mind:

> *"Mourir pour ce qu'on aime*
> *C'est un trop doux effort*[4] *. . ."*

He stood for a long time immobile and dumb. He broke off a few ears of rye, kept them in his hand and looked at them.

He saw the ways of life, he thought, as a twined and tangled design, complicated and mazy; it was not given him or any mortal to command or control it. Life and death, happiness and woe, the past and present, were interlaced

4. To die for one you love / Is too sweet an effort (French).

within the pattern. Yet to the initiated it might be read as easily as our ciphers—which to the savage must seem confused and incomprehensible—will be read by the schoolboy. And out of the contrasting elements concord rose. All that lived must suffer; the old man, whom he had judged hardly, had suffered, as he had watched his son die, and had dreaded the obliteration of his being. He himself would come to know ache, tears and remorse, and, even through these, the fullness of life. So might now, to the woman in the rye field, her ordeal be a triumphant procession. For to die for the one you loved was an effort too sweet for words.

As now he thought of it, he knew that all his life he had sought the unity of things, the secret which connects the phenomena of existence. It was this strife, this dim presage, which had sometimes made him stand still and inert in the midst of the games of his playfellows, or which had, at other moments—on moonlight nights, or in his little boat on the sea—lifted the boy to ecstatic happiness. Where other young people, in their pleasures or their amours, had searched for contrast and variety, he himself had yearned only to comprehend in full the oneness of the world. If things had come differently to him, if his young cousin had not died, and the events that followed his death had not brought him to Denmark, his search for understanding and harmony might have taken him to America, and he might have found them there, in the virgin forests of a new world. Now they have been disclosed to him today, in the place where he had played as a child. As the song is one with the voice that sings it, as the road is one with the goal, as lovers are made one in their embrace, so is man one with his destiny, and he shall love it as himself.[5]

He looked up again, towards the horizon. If he wished to, he felt, he might find out what it was that had brought to him, here, the sudden conception of the unity of the universe. When this same morning he had philosophized, lightly and for his own sake, on his feeling of belonging to this land and soil, it had been the beginning of it. But since then it had grown; it had become a mightier thing, a revelation to his soul. Some time he would look into it, for the law of cause and effect was a wonderful and fascinating study. But not now. This hour was consecrated to greater emotions, to a surrender to fate and to the will of life.

"No," he said at last. "If you wish it I shall not go. I shall stay here."

At that moment a long, loud roll of thunder broke the stillness of the afternoon. It re-echoed for a while amongst the low hills, and it reverberated within the young man's breast as powerfully as if he had been seized and shaken by hands. The landscape had spoken. He remembered that twelve hours ago he had put a question to it, half in jest, and not knowing what he did. Here it gave him its answer.

What it contained he did not know; neither did he inquire. In his promise to his uncle he had given himself over to the mightier powers of the world. Now what must come must come.

"I thank you," said the old lord, and made a little stiff gesture with his hand.

5. Here Dinesen paraphrases a Roman motto revived by Friedrich Nietzsche (1844–1900), German philosopher: Love your fate.

"I am happy to hear you say so. We should not let the difference in our ages, or of our views, separate us. In our family we have been wont to keep peace and faith with one another. You have made my heart lighter."

Something within his uncle's speech faintly recalled to Adam the misgivings of the afternoon. He rejected them; he would not let them trouble the new, sweet felicity which his resolution to stay had brought him.

"I shall go on now," said the old lord. "But there is no need for you to follow me. I will tell you tomorrow how the matter has ended." "No," said Adam, "I shall come back by sunset, to see the end of it myself."

All the same he did not come back. He kept the hour in his mind, and all through the evening the consciousness of the drama, and the profound concern and compassion with which, in his thoughts, he followed it, gave to his speech, glance and movements a grave and pathetic substance. But he felt that he was, in the rooms of the manor, and even by the harpsichord on which he accompanied his aunt to her air from *Alceste*,[6] as much in the centre of things as if he had stood in the rye field itself, and as near to those human beings whose fate was now decided there. Anne-Marie and he were both in the hands of destiny, and destiny would, by different ways, bring each to the designated end.

Later on he remembered what he had thought that evening.

But the old lord stayed on. Late in the afternoon he even had an idea; he called down his valet to the pavilion and made him shift his clothes on him and dress him up in a brocaded suit that he had worn at Court. He let a lace-trimmed shirt be drawn over his head and stuck out his slim legs to have them put into thin silk stockings and buckled shoes. In this majestic attire he dined alone, of a frugal meal, but took a bottle of Rhenish wine with it, to keep up his strength. He sat on for a while, a little sunk in his seat; then, as the sun neared the earth, he straightened himself, and took the way down to the field.

The shadows were now lengthening, azure blue along all the eastern slopes. The lonely trees in the corn marked their site by narrow blue pools running out from their feet, and as the old man walked a thin, immensely elongated reflection stirred behind him on the path. Once he stood still; he thought he heard a lark singing over his head, a spring-like sound; his tired head held no clear perception of the season; he seemed to be walking, and standing, in a kind of eternity.

The people in the field were no longer silent, as they had been in the afternoon. Many of them talked loudly among themselves, and a little farther away a woman was weeping.

When the bailiff saw his master, he came up to him. He told him, in great agitation, that the widow would, in all likelihood, finish the mowing of the field within a quarter of an hour.

"Are the keeper and the wheelwright here?" the old lord asked him. "They have been here," said the bailiff, "and have gone away, five times. Each time they have said that they would not come back. But they have come back again, all the same, and they are here now." "And where is the boy?" the old lord

6. Opera by Christoph Willibald Gluck (1714–1787), Austrian composer. From the Greek myth of Alcestis, who died in her husband's place and was rescued from Hades by Hercules.

asked again. "He is with her," said the bailiff. "I have given him leave to follow her. He has walked close to his mother all the afternoon, and you will see him now by her side, down there."

Anne-Marie was now working her way up towards them more evenly than before, but with extreme slowness, as if at any moment she might come to a standstill. This excessive tardiness, the old lord reflected, if it had been purposely performed, would have been an inimitable, dignified exhibition of skilled art; one might fancy the Emperor of China advancing in like manner on a divine procession or rite. He shaded his eyes with his hand, for the sun was now just beyond the horizon, and its last rays made light, wild, many-coloured specks dance before his sight. With such splendour did the sunset emblazon the earth and the air that the landscape was turned into a melting-pot of glorious metals. The meadows and the grasslands became pure gold; the barley field near by, with its long ears, was a live lake of shining silver.

There was only a small patch of straw standing in the rye field, when the woman, alarmed by the change in the light, turned her head a little to get a look at the sun. The while she did not stop her work, but grasped one handful of corn and cut it off, then another, and another. A great stir, and a sound like a manifold, deep sigh, ran through the crowd. The field was now mowed from one end to the other. Only the mower herself did not realize the fact; she stretched out her hand anew, and when she found nothing in it, she seemed puzzled or disappointed. Then she let her arms drop, and slowly sank to her knees.

Many of the women burst out weeping, and the swarm drew close round her, leaving only a small open space at the side where the old lord stood. Their sudden nearness frightened Anne-Marie; she made a slight, uneasy movement, as if terrified that they should put their hands on her.

The boy, who had kept by her all day, now fell on his knees beside her. Even he dared not touch her, but held one arm low behind her back and the other before her, level with her collar-bone, to catch hold of her if she should fall, and all the time he cried aloud. At that moment the sun went down.

The old lord stepped forward and solemnly took off his hat. The crowd became silent, waiting for him to speak. But for a minute or two he said nothing. Then he addressed her, very slowly.

"Your son is free, Anne-Marie," he said. He again waited a little, and added: "You have done a good day's work, which will long be remembered."

Anne-Marie raised her gaze only as high as his knees, and he understood that she had not heard what he said. He turned to the boy. "You tell your mother, Goske," he said, gently, "what I have told her."

The boy had been sobbing wildly, in raucous, broken moans. It took him some time to collect and control himself. But when at last he spoke, straight into his mother's face, his voice was low, a little impatient, as if he were conveying an everyday message to her. "I am free, Mother," he said. "You have done a good day's work that will long be remembered."

At the sound of his voice she lifted her face to him. A faint, bland shadow of surprise ran over it, but still she gave no sign of having heard what he said, so that the people round them began to wonder if the exhaustion had turned her deaf. But after a moment she slowly and waveringly raised her hand, fumbling in the air as she aimed at his face, and with her fingers touched his cheek. The cheek was wet with tears, so that at the contact her fingertips lightly stuck to it, and she seemed unable to overcome the infinitely slight resistance, or to withdraw her hand. For a minute the two looked each other in the face. Then, softly and lingeringly, like a sheaf of corn that falls to the ground, she sank forward onto the boy's shoulder, and he closed his arms round her.

He held her thus, pressed against him, his own face buried in her hair and head-cloth, for such a long time that those nearest to them, frightened because her body looked so small in his embrace, drew closer, bent down and loosened his grip. The boy let them do so without a word or a movement. But the woman who held Anne-Marie, in her arms to lift her up, turned her face to the old lord. "She is dead," she said.

The people who had followed Anne-Marie all through the day kept standing and stirring in the field for many hours, as long as the evening light lasted, and longer. Long after some of them had made a stretcher from branches of the trees and had carried away the dead woman, others wandered on, up and down the stubble, imitating and measuring her course from one end of the rye field to the other, and binding up the last sheaves, where she had finished her mowing.

The old lord stayed with them for a long time, stepping along a little, and again standing still.

In the place where the woman had died the old lord later on had a stone set up, with a sickle engraved in it. The peasants on the land then named the rye field "Sorrow-Acre." By this name it was known a long time after the story of the woman and her son had itself been forgotten.

## TOBIAS WOLFF on *Sorrow-Acre*

"Sorrow-Acre" is one of those stories, like the parable of the Prodigal Son, that scalds us to attention by insulting our sense of justice. Why should the wastrel be feasted, while the good brother's faithfulness is taken for granted? How can the feudal lord, with all his wealth and power, justify refusing to pardon a poor old woman's son, and release her from the crushing task he has set her to win back the boy's life?

The biblical parable finally soothes us with the promise of mercy when we ourselves have need of it. "Sorrow-Acre" does not soothe; no, it takes its outrageous premise even further by suggesting that mercy itself can be a form of evil and that the ideas of justice that prompt our indignation are sentimental, unnatural, and fatal to human dignity. Those are the ideas expressed by the landowner; and the story itself, with its sensuous evocation of the natural order and the tragic condition of man within that order, seems to confirm his view. Not for nothing is the protagonist named Adam, and his uncle referred to as "the old lord"; but the temptation this Adam must resist is the modern idea that power should always be used to prevent human struggle and suffering. The old lord, who knows plenty about both power and suffering, proposes a different, perhaps longer view of the question: he suggests that effort and pain give meaning to life and that power has no business interfering, that to take desperation out of human existence is to render it a hollow farce.

These ideas are an affront to our customary assumptions; that doesn't mean they're not true. It doesn't mean they *are* true, either; but the force of their expression in this story makes us look again at the ground where we stand, which no longer seems quite so firm. That which before seemed natural appears, in this new light, peculiar, and that which seemed peculiar appears natural. We see the world in a new way. Only the greatest of stories can do this.

# Susan Dodd

*Dodd (1946– ) was born in Chicago, Illinois, and attended Georgetown University, where she received her B.A., the University of Louisville for her M.S., and Vermont College for her M.F.A. Her awards include the Iowa Award for Short Fiction (1984), Pirate's Alley Faulkner Prize for Novella (1995), and an NEA Literary Fellowship (1992). She has published, among others,* Old Wives' Tales *(1984),* Mamaw *(1988),* Hell-Bent Men and Their Cities *(1990), and* The Mourners' Bench (1998).

## Public Appearances

The Governor's wife thought the Governor was looking especially well this evening. As she stood before the mirror in the hotel suite bedroom, fastening her pearls, he appeared next to her in the gilt frame. The force of his presence, more than the width of his shoulders, shifted her into the lower corner of the composition. She became a detail.

"How do I look, do you think?" the Governor asked his wife.

"You're looking especially well this evening," she said.

The Governor nodded into the mirror.

The Governor's wife had taken particular pains with her own appearance. She knew this was an important occasion, although she could not remember precisely what or why. Something to do with the Governor's campaign—kickoff, victory—she had trouble keeping them straight. One campaign bled into another, like the lines in Madras cloth. Odd, she thought, that nobody else seemed to notice this.

"They cut my hair too short," the Governor muttered.

"Oh, no," she said. He needed her before major public appearances. "It's just right," she said.

"It doesn't look plastic?" His hair had turned silver, although he was still young. It called attention to the boyishness of his face.

"Plastic? Not a bit. It's perfect." The Governor's wife smiled at her husband, trying to reassure him. The mirror served as intermediary for their eyes.

"I was afraid of that. I hate it when my hair looks perfect."

She moved further into her bevelled corner. "I didn't mean it that way. I only meant it looks just . . . right."

The Governor sighed, squinted at his image and carefully disarranged the front of his hair. "Better?"

"Just . . . fine," she said. He needed her.

The Governor's wife slipped out of the frame. She felt worried. It seemed to her, now, that she had not taken enough trouble with her own appearance: she was a disappointment. Downstairs the great banquet hall would already be filling with people who wanted a look at her. There would be photographers. She had read somewhere that certain tribes of Indians never permitted themselves to be photographed, convinced that the camera captured the spirit and bore it off. The Governor's wife understood this belief. She frequently stared at imprecise gray and black images of herself in the morning paper and felt horrified at her own lifelessness. Her husband, she thought, must be of a different tribe. The flashes and shutters enlivened and enlarged him. He acquired a natural glossiness in public.

She edged back into the mirror to glance at her hair. Because the occasion was important to her husband, she had gone to a beauty salon, her own hair a responsibility she couldn't manage. The dryer, a fierce metal helmet, was lowered on her for forty minutes; it gave her a headache and burned her ears. When they were finished with her, she thought her head looked lopsided and oversized, as if she had borrowed it. Her husband preferred her hair, unlike his own, to look perfect. It did not.

Still worried, the Governor's wife turned her attention to her dress. She wished the mirror allowed her skirt to be seen, but the frame cut her off at the waist. Although she was wearing the best dress she had, she suspected it wasn't good enough. She turned and went into the bathroom, shutting the door behind her without a sound.

It was bad luck, worse than walking under a ladder, to see herself in fluorescent lighting before important occasions. The uncompromising illumination was a bad omen, a hex on her morale. But the full-length mirror on the bathroom door persuaded her to risk exposure to the unlucky light. She turned to face her reflection and inspect her dress.

It was finer than any dress she had ever owned, not counting her wedding gown. It was made of real silk, the color of winter wheat, and it had cost more than a hundred dollars. She had gone to New York to buy it, so that her husband and his constituents would be unlikely to learn the details of her extravagance. It was the one and only time she had crossed state lines to commit an indiscretion. The money she spent was her own, a birthday check from her parents. But that didn't excuse her. She told her husband the dress was a bargain. He said, very nice. The first time she wore it, an important occasion last year, the Commissioner of Motor Vehicles had burned a hole in her skirt with his cigar while she was dancing with him.

The Governor's wife had mourned her dress for a full year, keeping it in a scented garment bag in the back of her closet. It was a shameful secret, the small charred perforation like an evil eye on her lap. She wore the dress in her dreams, which admitted no flaws or superstitions. She danced in it. Awake, she grieved irreparably.

Finally, two weeks ago, she had taken the ruined dress to a seamstress who was said to be a wizard. The old Hungarian woman, Magda Bogner, had consoled the Governor's wife with her shiny pins and deft hands. "I make like new," she promised. "Nobody even guess." Her throaty voice and thick accent suggested the unassailable authority of a fortuneteller to the Governor's wife, who rather believed in magic. It was a belief her parents had encouraged in her as a child. She had learned in adulthood to call it by other names and, eventually, not to mention it. But the belief itself was intact.

Mrs. Bogner had detached the skirt from the bodice, excised a narrow strip from it, and reassembled the garment with tiny stitches. When the Governor's wife returned for her dress, the burn was gone, like magic. She and the old seamstress had embraced in mutual delight at the fitting. For the first time in a year, the Governor's wife felt like dancing. The older woman considered her own dexterity commonplace. But the Governor's wife was sure there were rhapsodies and gypsy spells in the clever aged fingers. Impulsively, she touched them with her own, and the seamstress smiled at her, as if confirming a suspicion.

No money changed hands. Mrs. Bogner would not hear of it. "My honor," she said, "to do for you. I tell my grandchildren—I sew for wife of Governor. Maybe someday President." For a moment, the Governor's wife turned pale. When she recovered herself, she planned how she'd invite the needlewoman to the Executive Mansion for tea. Sometime when the Governor was out of town.

Now, the Governor's wife stared into the hotel bathroom mirror and reexamined the dress. It was fine, a perfect fit. The gypsy fortune held up under scrutiny: no one would ever guess. But the dress was not like new. The rustle of silk when she moved was not quite as gay or generous as it once had been. Magic no longer clung to her skirt. The Governor's wife switched off the harsh overhead light and returned to the bedroom.

The Governor had remained in front of the mirror, but now he was looking over the notes for his speech. They were typed in capital letters on buff-colored index cards. He looked up as his wife reentered the room, and she smiled at him hopefully.

"You're sure I look all right?" he asked.

They went downstairs a half-hour later than they were expected. Impact, he said, was largely a matter of timing.

There were twelve hundred people in the convention center banquet hall. Or so the Governor's press secretary had told the Governor's wife, who had cultivated the sensible habit of accepting the word of staff members on such matters. Nevertheless, tonight, as she was plunged into the crowd, she found herself wondering how many people were really there—exactly how many. Twelve hundred and six, perhaps? Or maybe less than a thousand? She couldn't guess. She would never know.

There were certain things the Governor's wife had come to accept. Never knowing was one. Entering banquet halls by way of service elevators and institutional kitchens was another. She had learned to anticipate sudden explosions of light and sound when she followed her husband over thresholds. Experience had taught her not to wear rings on her right hand and to carry small purses with shoulder straps when she was placed in receiving lines. She willed herself to develop tolerance for embraces and personal questions from total strangers. She had a whole bag of tricks for remembering names and faces. She had her smile down to a science.

The Governor's wife frequently went out in public holding hands with younger men, something the Governor himself had suggested and even arranged. His wife was not "a natural," not even "a quick study." During his first campaign, staff members had tactfully brought it to his attention that his wife, who was small and rather timid, had an unfortunate proclivity for getting lost. Or *looking* lost, which was worse. The matter was discussed frankly—the Governor believed in treating staff like family. Eventually, it was decided that an aide should be assigned to the Governor's wife in crowds. The solution proved sensible. It was good training for the junior assistants. And the crowds, looking at the Governor, never seemed to notice the succession of pin-striped young men to whose hands the Governor's wife clung in public. Over the years, the handholding and her own determination not to slow her husband down had helped her to mask her misplaced look. In fact, she had acquired a small following of her own. Underdogs, particularly, looked up to her.

Now, flanked by aides, the Governor was moving briskly into the packed hall. The crowd parted for him, but closed quickly over his wake so that the young man holding the Governor's wife's hand had to fight to make a path for her. As always, the first moment of entering a crowd made the Governor's wife feel she was drowning. Hands grasped at her husband. Some of them, missing him, closed around her, as if she might be a rung by which to reach him. Yearning for air, she smiled and tightened her grip on the only familiar fingers she could reach.

"Kevin?" She said the boy's name to calm herself, as a stocky man shouldered his way between them.

"We won't lose him," the young aide reassured her grimly. His face was creased by the pressure of responsibility. He was twenty-three years old, and this was his first job. The Governor's wife wanted to tell him it would be all right.

"You are so skinny!" a lady in purple chiffon exclaimed, filling a momentary gap in the crowd. She pressed the Governor's wife to her bosom, where yards of violet fabric struggled against moist flesh. "I wish I looked like you. I'm going to send you a coffee cake."

The Governor's wife moved her lips graciously, knowing her voice was useless in the noisy room.

The woman turned to throw herself on the Governor. "Your wife needs to put some meat on her bones."

"She works too hard," he said, pulling his wife forward and circling her with his arm as he smiled into a bank of cameras. She lost her balance for a moment, and leaned against him.

"One more picture, Governor . . . this way. . . ." Her husband was pulled away and Kevin stepped smartly into the intervening space, providing equilibrium.

The dais was raised six feet above the floor, a head table of more than twenty places. The over-starched tablecloths, crudely mended in a random design, hung down low in front so that the feet of the dignitaries would not be exposed to public scrutiny. The Governor's wife, taking her place, kept her knees pressed together anyway. Whenever she accompanied her husband on platforms, she had a feeling that people could see up her dress.

Each place at the head table was set with heavy white dishes and dented cutlery. On each dinner plate, under a napkin folded like a fan, was a program with her husband's likeness on the cover. It was his official portrait, for which he had worn an expression she found forbidding. Above his head, embossed in gold lettering, it said, "Favorite Son." Each time she ran across the phrase, she wondered how it made the Governor's brother, a periodontist, feel.

"Handsome program," the Governor's wife said, but her husband did not hear her. He was going over his notes. She turned to her other side and smiled at the Majority Leader of the State Senate, who smiled back and said something she could not hear.

The Senate Majority Leader was in love with her. The Governor's wife didn't realize this, and the Governor didn't, either. In fact, the Senator was hardly aware of it himself. He was, after all, a happily married man with four children. An able politician. A hard-working legislator. He had a law practice to maintain, in addition to his legislative duties and family obligations. His star, the state's major papers all predicted, was on the rise. But none of this precluded the Senate Majority Leader from being a bit in love with the Governor's wife. He had fallen in love with her, slowly and surely, over a period of years, over a series of daises and platforms and lecturns and podia. The Governor's wife had a fragile, wounded look which attracted the Senate Majority Leader powerfully. He had not declared himself; he never would. He genuinely cherished his own wife and family, the law, and his rising star. But the Senator could not keep his eyes off the Governor's wife. He had no appetite when she sat beside him at head tables. He witnessed her fear and bravery across oceans of smoke and sweaty faces and watered drinks, and he wished that he could adopt her.

Tonight he was seated especially close to her at the center of the oversubscribed banquet table. Although their elbows were only inches apart, an arrangement of red and white carnations with miniature silk flags sprouting from them like unseemly pistils made a barrier between them. The Senator leaned around the flowers.

"You look very beautiful," he said.

The Governor's wife, picking the pleats in her napkin, looked up with startled eyes.

"A lovely dress."

Her smile wavered with pleasure, surprise, and disapproval. "Thank you." It was the most personal thing she had ever said to him.

At her right, the Governor speared a fragment of canned pineapple from his fruit cup as he looked over his notes. His wife turned to him as if he had spoken to her. The Majority Leader, who was Master of Ceremonies for the evening, picked up his own notes. This was an important occasion for him, too, a good opportunity for exposure. He had no business thinking about the Governor's wife.

How thin she is, thought the wife of the Lieutenant Governor, leaning forward from her chair at the far end of the table. Cool and thin and above it all and that dress must have cost an arm and a leg. Some people have everything. And she promised herself then and there that she would be better at it, better at all of it, than this Governor's wife. Her own time was coming, her place in the middle. She noticed that the Governor had begun to eat and she picked up her spoon.

A sour cream coffee cake, the lady in purple said to herself. With apples and walnuts. Vinny can deliver it in his cab. There was a vacant place next to her at the table. No one was looking. She quickly exchanged her empty sherbet glass for the extra one and began to eat the fruit. Hundred dollars a plate, damned if she wasn't entitled. Anyway, at least she had a good table, a clear view of the Governor and all them. Thin as a rail, that wife of his . . . no wonder. Look how she picked at her food.

At the rear of the hall, the Governor's staff had gathered at the bar. They knew better than to eat—canned fruit, rubber chicken, chemical ice cream. Everything according to schedule so far. The Governor's press secretary relaxed, sipping his first Scotch of the evening. His suit was rumpled and there were deep circles under his eyes. No one ever believed he was not yet forty: he was a veteran.

"Not a bad crowd," he said.

"Better than we thought, anyway," the speechwriter answered, taking a notebook from his pocket, pausing, then putting it back again.

"How many, you think?"

"Nine-fifty?" The speechwriter's guess was wary. Estimating crowds was not one of his talents.

"Close." The press secretary smiled enigmatically, trying to convince the junior assistants that he knew more than round figures.

"All the papers here?" the executive assistant asked.

"Every last one, the buggers."

"The networks?"

"Present and accounted for."

"Good. We've reeled 'em in. Now let's just hope the old man puts on a show."

"Don't worry, he will." Smiling again, the press secretary turned to the junior assistant assigned to the Governor's wife. "How is *she*, by the way?"

Kevin pushed his horn-rimmed glasses higher on the bridge of his patrician nose. "Seems fine."

"Knock wood."

At the note of derision in the older man's voice, Kevin turned and asked the bartender for a Coke. Then, noticing the press secretary's sardonic expression, he abruptly changed his order to a beer. An attitude of disrespect for the Governor's wife was something he took personally. Besides, he could not understand it. She was very kind to him, and he was proud that he could look after her. Several years earlier, however, while Kevin was still studying political science at Princeton, the Governor's wife had fled from the press corps. On two separate occasions. Her blatant panic had caused talk. The more experienced staff members had kept uneasy eyes on her ever since, regarding her as a problem which might crop up any second if they weren't on their toes.

"She looks good," the Governor's personal secretary said with a grimace of envy. "Nice dress." Her own dress, a plain navy knit, had been pulling across her hips since seven-thirty that morning. She had never made it back to her apartment to change. Retyping his damn note cards. She wondered if she had time, now, to dash to the ladies room and put on some make-up before the speeches got underway. Probably. On the other hand, another vodka might put more color in her face.

The press secretary was staring at her speculatively. "I don't know . . . ," he said.

"Whaddya mean?"

"The dress."

"Hers? It's beautiful . . . what's wrong with it?"

"Maybe a little too . . . rich."

"Shit, she's the Governor's wife! If I were the Governor's wife, I'd sure as hell wear rich clothes. I'd buy out Saks."

The press secretary laughed. "Then you wouldn't be his wife for long, sweetheart."

"Christ, they're serving slower than usual tonight. . . ." The Governor's secretary was still squinting at the wheat-colored blur beside her boss on the dais. Everything must look different from up there, she thought.

"Time flies when you're having—."

"Think dinner's slow, wait 'til the speeches start," the press secretary said, aiming a razor-sharp grin at the speechwriter.

Up on the platform, the Governor's wife abandoned her modest pretenses of eating. She had an irrepressible dread of being kissed, questioned, or photographed with her mouth full. To her left, the Majority Leader jotted a note on the back of his placecard. To her right, the Governor studied his speech. The Governor's wife gazed out over the huge hall and smiled vaguely toward the bandstand, where an awkward transition from "Yankee Doodle Dandy" to "Happy Days Are Here Again" was in progress. She could hardly wait for "Goodnight, Ladies."

*"Governor, Lieutenant Governor, Other Distinguished Guests at the Dais, Reverend Clergy, Ladies and Gentlemen, and Fellow—."*

The Majority Leader's vibrant voice competed confidently with the clatter of coffee cups and dessert plates. The Governor's wife looked down. A block of red, white, and blue ice cream was melting to a lavender pool before her. She pushed the dish aside and sipped her coffee.

"Should I start with a joke, do you think?" her husband whispered.

*"He has done right by us and he has done us proud . . . we have given him our votes and our trust, and he has given us his all . . . we have—."*

"A joke, yes. They always like it when you start with a joke."

"How about the preacher and the farmer—that one?"

"Oh, that's a wonderful story."

"Some of them have heard it before . . . listen, do I look all right?"

*"So we come here tonight, my friends, to say thank-you, Governor . . . we come here to say well-done, Governor . . . we come here, in short, to—."*

"You look wonderful. Just straighten your tie a bit."

*"Ladies and Gentlemen, it is my honor and my privilege to present to you our distinguished Governor, our dear friend and our favorite son, The Honorable—."*

The crowd, bellowing and stamping and clapping, lumbered to its feet like a bull. Smiling, the Governor began to move toward the podium. Then, pausing, a look of boyish embarrassment on his face, he leaned down to kiss his wife. The roaring and stamping intensified. The Governor's wife smiled shyly and applauded her husband along with the others.

*"My friends—."*

For a moment, the public address system emitted a piercing whine. Without missing a beat, the Governor adjusted his tone and the angle of the microphone to a perfect balance.

*"A few minutes ago, my lovely wife suggested to me that I begin by telling you a joke—a joke that is a particular favorite of hers. . . ."*

The Governor's wife lowered her gaze to her lap, where her right hand, naked without the opal ring her parents had given her for her twenty-first birthday, lay on a silk field of winter wheat. Her fingers looked bluish, slightly swollen with too much handling.

*"But then, I said to myself—and those of you who know me know how rarely I disregard my wife's advice—but I thought, no . . . this is no time for a joke."*

The folds of her skirt fell gently open as she sat. The Governor's wife could see the tiny hand-sewn seam where the scorched silk had been cut from her once-perfect dress. Nobody else would notice, it was true. But she knew: there was no longer an allowance in the skirt for gypsy magic, for dream-dancing. The dress was *not* like new anymore. The fullness of luxury had been trimmed from it.

*". . . no jokes tonight, my friends, for this is to me a solemn occasion. . . . Yes, we have a victory to celebrate . . . and yes, we have another campaign ahead . . . but in this interlude between them, we face. . . ."*

The Governor's wife circled her coffee cup with her hands, warming them briefly. From the corner of his eye, the Senate Majority Leader observed the gesture and wondered how her fingers would feel against his cheek. He thought about walking around the State Capitol at night in the snow with the Governor's wife. He would offer her his gloves, and when she refused them, he would pull her hands into his overcoat pockets. Then she wouldn't be the Governor's wife anymore.

*"Now, I don't think I'm an alarmist . . . and I hope I am not a pessimist . . . but I must tell the people of this great State that I am very deeply concerned. For we see all around us the—."*

She watched her husband with studied absorption, her eyes solemn, her lips slightly parted. She noticed, once again, that he was looking especially well this evening. Klieg lights: they were already collecting footage for the next campaign . . . ten-and twenty- and thirty-second daubs of her husband, from which they would fashion pointillist portraits of him for mass viewing. The klieg lights shone on his head, making a halo of his near-perfect hair. His face was suffused with the rich coloration of health, the clarity of intelligence. The Governor's wife watched him, her expression almost rapt. She could feel the intensity of the crowd's assent in the air and in the marrow of her bones. He still amazed her.

In the back of the hall, the Governor's aides stood in a restless cluster by the door. The press secretary held a stop-watch in one hand, a drink in the other.

"The old man's really on tonight," the executive assistant muttered from one side of his mouth.

"You think everybody can hear all right?"

"We can, can't we?"

"Yeah. . . ."

"Damn, that's a great dress!" The Governor's personal secretary sighed. The two men looked at her as if she had mouthed an obscenity, and she grinned at them sourly. "I've heard the speech before," she said.

*"And so I come before you tonight . . . not jubilant in victory . . . not swollen with success . . . but not weighed down, either, by the responsibility with which you have entrusted me. . . . I am full of optimism, my friends . . . inspired by your—."*

Really knows how to reach in and pull it out of them, the Senate Majority Leader thought. He wasn't jealous, only eager to learn. Watching the subtle gestures of the Governor's hands, he denied himself a glance at the small, attentive woman above whose head the Governor addressed his following.

*"I was telling my wife on our way down here this evening. . . ."*

Under the table her chilled fingers probed the invisible repair in her dress, pressing the seam as if it were a wound, deliberately seeking to confirm its existence. Though she realized her husband was talking about her, the substance made little difference. Nothing he said would ever be quite like new again. But he needed her. Her hand stopped moving across her mended lap and lay still.

*"And I am going to tell you, my friends, exactly what I told her, for this is what I truly—."*

The lady in the purple dress looked longingly at the plate of pastries in the center of the table. No one had even touched them, the plate was too far to reach without standing up. They always put the best things in the middle, she thought, where you couldn't get your hands on them.

"He's getting ready to wind 'er up," the press secretary murmured, looking approvingly at the stopwatch. "Right on schedule."

That dress is no color at all, the Lieutenant Governor's wife thought. Cost a fortune, though. When her day came, hers and Bernie's, she'd wear red. Red would stand out in a crowd.

*"And I promise you. . . ."*

Lost, the Senate Majority Leader thought. She looks absolutely lost. His hands rested, helpless, on the edge of the table.

Gathering speed and scattering power like sparks, the Governor raised his hands and his voice together, sending them out to meet the crowd more than halfway. Flashbulbs popped in a vehement, almost steady string of explosions. The Governor's wife saw red, a shower of red blotting out the room and the ocean of hands and mouths. She was lost.

*"And I promise you. . . ."*

She swallowed hard, a foretaste of disaster on her tongue. It always came at such moments: she would hear the crack of a single shot, see her husband fall. Red would bloom on his shirt front, a bouquet of blood-roses clutched to his chest, pearl studs glistening among them like dewdrops. His eyes, full of promise still, would struggle to stay open, to find her. Wide and blue with the true believer's sudden disbelief, her husband's mortally wounded eyes. He needed her, beside him. But she wouldn't be able to find her way to him. She would be long lost. No help at all.

*"The day will come. . . ."*

The Governor's wife shut her eyes. Above her the familiar voice, amplified, rose unharmed, stronger than ever. The hot white lights beat down on her face as she opened her eyes again and gazed up into the aura of promise surrounding her husband's near-perfect hair.

He possessed magical powers. She knew about magic. She understood it was that he was giving them, and why. They needed him. Their need was one of those things she had come to accept. And she understood that her premonition of mayhem was simply another of those false directions in which she constantly seemed to be getting lost. She steadied her sight, now, in her husband's direction.

*". . . moving forward . . . together . . . toward tomorrow."*

Twelve hundred people—she no longer questioned the figure—jumped to their feet with one deafening roar, a sound that seemed to swell, threatening to burst the hall like a huge balloon. Beneath her, the platform bucked and swayed with the pounding.

The Governor bowed his head under the barrage of adulation, a half-smile on his face. As the ovation mounted, he remained perfectly still, almost as if he were resting. Then he turned to his left and held out a hand to his wife, pulling her in to join him inside the circle of blinding light.

As she was captured in a dozen camera lenses, the Governor's wife felt something leave her, something she realized she simply could not hold onto anymore. Magic . . . she could no longer keep a place for it. It was, like mayhem, a belief she could no longer afford to indulge.

As the band struck up "Goodnight, Ladies," and the cameras clicked, the Governor's wife was presented with a spray of deep red roses. Carefully, she held the flowers so that they concealed the flaw in her dress.

While the photographers were still shooting, the Governor leaned toward his wife, bringing his lips close to her cheek.

"How was I, do you think?" he whispered.

"Perfect," she said. "Just perfect."

# Andre Dubus

*Born in Lake Charles, Louisiana, Dubus (1936–1999) is widely regarded for his fiction, which portrays the decline of postwar America, and for his moral responsibility as an author. His titles include* The Lieutenant *(1967), a novel;* We Don't Live Here Any More *(1984), a collected trilogy of novellas;* Separate Flights *(1975),* Land Where My Fathers Died *(1984),* The Last Worthless Evening *(1986), and* Dancing After Hours *(1996), all short-story collections;* Blood Vessels *(1991), a book of personal essays; and* Meditations from a Movable Chair *(1998).*

## The Intruder

Because Kenneth Girard loved his parents and his sister and because he could not tell them why he went to the woods, his first moments there were always uncomfortable ones, as if he had left the house to commit a sin. But he was thirteen and he could not say that he was going to sit on a hill and wait for the silence and trees and sky to close in on him, wait until they all became a part of him and thought and memory ceased and the voices began. He could only say that he was going for a walk and, since there was so much more to say, he felt cowardly and deceitful and more lonely than before.

He could not say that on the hill he became great, that he had saved a beautiful girl from a river (the voice then had been gentle and serious and she had loved him), or that he had ridden into town, his clothes dusty, his black hat pulled low over his sunburned face, and an hour later had ridden away with four fresh notches on the butt of his six-gun, or that with the count three-and-two and the bases loaded, he had driven the ball so far and high that the outfielders did not even move, or that he had waded through surf and sprinted over sand, firing his Tommy gun and shouting to his soldiers behind him.

Now he was capturing a farmhouse. In the late movie the night before, the farmhouse had been very important, though no one ever said why, and sitting there in the summer dusk, he watched the backs of his soldiers as they advanced through the woods below him and crossed the clear, shallow creek and climbed the hill that he faced. Occasionally, he lifted his twenty-two-caliber rifle and fired at a rusty tin can across the creek, the can becoming a Nazi face in a window as he squeezed the trigger and the voices filled him: *You got him, Captain. You got him.* For half an hour he sat and fired at the can, and anyone who might have seen him could never know that he was doing anything else, that he had been wounded in the shoulder and lost half his men but had captured the farmhouse.

Kenneth looked up through the trees, which were darker green now. While he had been watching his battle, the earth, too, had become darker, shadowed, with patches of late sun on the grass and brown fallen pine needles. He stood up, then looked down at the creek, and across it, at the hill on the other side. His soldiers were gone. He was hungry, and he turned and walked back through the woods.

Then he remembered that his mother and father were going to a party in town that night and he would be alone with Connie. He liked being alone, but, even more, he liked being alone with his sister. She was nearly seventeen; her skin was fair, her cheeks colored, and she had long black hair that came down to her shoulders; on the right side of her face, a wave of it reached the corner of her eye. She was the most beautiful girl he knew. She was also the only person with whom, for his entire life, he had been nearly perfectly at ease. He could be silent with her or he could say whatever occurred to him and he never had to think about it first to assure himself that it was not foolish or, worse, uninteresting.

Leaving the woods, he climbed the last gentle slope and entered the house. He leaned his rifle in a corner of his room, which faced the quiet blacktop road, and went to the bathroom and washed his hands. Standing at the lavatory, he looked into the mirror. He suddenly felt as if he had told a lie. He was looking at his face and, as he did several times each day, telling himself, without words, that it was a handsome face. His skin was fair, as Connie's was, and he had color in his cheeks; but his hair, carefully parted and combed, was more brown than black. He believed that Connie thought he was exactly like her, that he was talkative and well liked. But she never saw him with his classmates. He felt that he was deceiving her.

He left the house and went into the outdoor kitchen and sat on a bench at the long, uncovered table and folded his arms on it.

"Did you kill anything?" Connie said.

"Tin cans."

His father turned from the stove with a skillet of white perch in his hand. "They're good ones," he said.

"Mine are the best," Kenneth said.

"You didn't catch but two."

"They're the best."

His mother put a plate in front of him, then opened a can of beer and sat beside him. He sat quietly, watching his father at the stove. Then he looked at his mother's hand holding the beer can. There were veins and several freckles on the back of it. Farther up her forearm was a small yellow bruise; the flesh at her elbow was wrinkled. He looked at her face. People said that he and Connie looked like her, so he supposed it was true, but he could not see the resemblance.

"Daddy and I are going to the Gossetts' tonight," she said.

"I know."

"I wrote the phone number down," his father said. "It's under the phone."

"Okay."

His father was not tall either, but his shoulders were broad. Kenneth wondered if his would be like that when he grew older. His father was the only one in the family who tanned in the sun.

"And *please*, Connie," his mother said, "will you go to sleep at a reasonable hour? It's hard enough to get you up for Mass when you've had a good night's sleep."

"Why don't we go into town for the evening Mass?"

"No. I don't like it hanging over my head all day."

"All right. When will y'all be home?"

"About two. And that doesn't mean read in bed till then. You need your sleep."

"We'll go to bed early," Connie said.

His father served fried perch and hush puppies onto their plates and they had French bread and catsup and Tabasco sauce and iced tea. After dinner, his father read the newspaper and his mother read a Reader's Digest condensation, then they showered and dressed, and at seven-thirty, they left. He and Connie followed them to the door. Connie kissed them; then he did. His mother and father looked happy, and he felt good about that.

"We'll be back about two," his mother said. "Keep the doors locked."

"Definitely," Connie said. "And we'll bar the windows."

"Well, you never know. Y'all be good. G'night."

"Hold down the fort, son," his father said.

"I will."

Then they were gone, the screen door slamming behind them, and Connie left the sunporch, but he stood at the door, listening to the car starting and watching its headlights as it backed down the trail through the yard, then turned into the road and drove away. Still he did not move. He loved the nights at the camp when they were left alone. At home, there was a disturbing climate about their evenings alone, for distant voices of boys in the neighborhood reminded him that he was not alone entirely by choice. Here, there were no sounds.

He latched the screen and went into the living room. Connie was sitting in the rocking chair near the fireplace, smoking a cigarette. She looked at him, then flicked ashes into an ashtray on her lap.

"Now don't you tell on me."

"I didn't know you did that."

"Please don't tell. Daddy would skin me alive."

"I won't."

He could not watch her. He looked around the room for a book.

"Douglas is coming tonight," she said.

"Oh." He picked up the Reader's Digest book and pretended to look at it. "Y'all going to watch TV?" he said.

"Not if you want to."

"It doesn't matter."

"You watch it. You like Saturday nights."

She looked as if she had been smoking for a long time, all during the summer and possibly the school year, too, for months or even a year without his knowing it. He was hurt. He laid down the book.

"Think I'll go outside for a while," he said.

He went onto the sunporch and out the door and walked down the sloping car trail that led to the road. He stopped at the gate, which was open, and leaned on it. Forgetting Connie, he looked over his shoulder at the camp, thinking that he would never tire of it. They had been there for six weeks, since early June, his father coming on Friday evenings and leaving early Monday mornings, driving sixty miles to their home in southern Louisiana. Kenneth fished during the day, swam with Connie in the creeks, read novels about baseball, and watched the major league games on television. He thought winter at the camp was better, though. They came on weekends and hunted squirrels, and there was a fireplace.

He looked down the road. The closest camp was half a mile away, on the opposite side of the road, and he could see its yellow-lighted windows through the trees. *That's the house. Quiet now. We'll sneak through the woods and get the guard, then charge the house. Come on.* Leaning against the gate, he stared into the trees across the road and saw himself leading his soldiers through the woods. They reached the guard. His back was turned and Kenneth crawled close to him, then stood up and slapped a hand over the guard's mouth and stabbed him in the back. They rushed the house and Kenneth reached the door first and kicked it open. The general looked up from his desk, then tried to get his pistol from his holster. Kenneth shot him with his Tommy gun. *Grab those papers, men. Let's get out of here.* They got the papers and ran outside and Kenneth stopped to throw a hand grenade through the door. He reached the woods before it exploded.

He turned from the gate and walked toward the house, looking around him at the dark pines. He entered the sunporch and latched the screen; then he smelled chocolate, and he went to the kitchen. Connie was stirring a pot of fudge on the stove. She had changed to a fresh pale blue shirt, the tails of it hanging almost to the bottom of her white shorts.

"It'll be a while," she said.

He nodded, watching her hand and the spoon. He thought of Douglas coming and began to feel nervous.

"What time's Douglas coming?"

"Any minute now. Let me know if you hear his car."

"All right."

He went to his room and picked up his rifle; then he saw the magazine on the chest of drawers and he leaned the rifle in the corner again. Suddenly his mouth was dry. He got the magazine and quickly turned the pages until he found her: she was stepping out of the surf on the French Riviera, laughing, as if the man with her had just said something funny. She was blond and very tan and she wore a bikini. The photograph was in color. For several moments he looked at it; then he got the rifle and cleaning kit and sat in the rocking chair in the living room, with the rifle across his lap. He put a patch on the cleaning rod and dipped it in bore cleaner and pushed it down the barrel, the handle of the rod clanging against the muzzle. He worked slowly, pausing often to listen for Douglas's car, because he wanted to be cleaning the rifle when Douglas came. Because Douglas was a tackle on the high school football team in the town, and Kenneth had never been on a football team, and never would be.

The football players made him more uncomfortable than the others. They walked into the living room and firmly shook his father's hand, then his hand, beginning to talk as soon as they entered, and they sat and waited for Connie, their talking never ceasing, their big chests and shoulders leaned forward, their faces slowly turning as they looked at each picture on the wall, at the designs on the rug, at the furniture, passing over Kenneth as if he were another chair, filling the room with a feeling of strength and self-confidence that defeated him, paralyzing his tongue and even his mind, so that he merely sat in thoughtless anxiety, hoping they would not speak to him, hoping especially that they would not ask: *You play football?* Two of them had, and he never forgot it. He had answered with a mute, affirming nod.

He had always been shy and, because of it, he had stayed on the periphery of sports for as long as he could remember. When his teachers forced him to play, he spent an anxious hour trying not to become involved, praying in right field that no balls would come his way, lingering on the outside of the huddle so that no one would look up and see his face and decide to throw him a pass on the next play.

But he found that there was one thing he could do and he did it alone, or with his father: he could shoot and he could hunt. He felt that shooting was the only thing that had ever been easy for him. Schoolwork was, too, but he considered that a curse.

He was not disturbed by the boys who were not athletes, unless, for some reason, they were confident anyway. While they sat and waited for Connie, he was cheerful and teasing, and they seemed to like him. The girls were best. He walked into the living room and they stopped their talking and laughing and all of them greeted him and sometimes they said: "Connie, he's so cute," or "I wish you were three years older," and he said: "Me, too," and tried to be witty and usually was.

He heard a car outside.

"Douglas is here," he called.

Connie came through the living room, one hand arranging the wave of hair near her right eye, and went into the sunporch. Slowly, Kenneth wiped the rifle with an oily rag. He heard Douglas's loud voice and laughter and heavy footsteps on the sunporch; then they came into the living room. Kenneth raised his face.

"Hi," he said.

"How's it going?"

"All right."

Douglas Bakewell was not tall. He had blond hair, cut so short on top that you could see his scalp, and a reddish face, and sunburned arms, covered with bleached hair. A polo shirt fit tightly over his chest and shoulders and biceps.

"Whatcha got there?" Douglas said.

"Twenty-two."

"Let's see."

"Better dry it."

He briskly wiped it with a dry cloth and handed it to Douglas. Quickly, Douglas worked the bolt, aimed at the ceiling, and pulled the trigger.

"Nice trigger," he said.

He held it in front of his waist and looked at it, then gave it to Kenneth.

"Well, girl," he said, turning to Connie, "where's the beer?"

"Sit down and I'll get you one."

She went to the kitchen. Douglas sat on the couch and Kenneth picked up his cleaning kit and, not looking at Douglas, walked into his bedroom. He stayed there until Connie returned from the kitchen; then he went into the living room. They were sitting on the couch. Connie was smoking again. Kenneth kept walking toward the sunporch.

"I'll let you know when the fudge is ready," Connie said.

"All right."

On the sunporch, he turned on the television and sat in front of it. He watched ten minutes of a Western before he was relaxed again, before he settled in his chair, oblivious to the quiet talking in the living room, his mind beginning to wander happily as a gunfighter in dark clothes moved across the screen.

By the time the fudge was ready, he was watching a detective story, and when Connie called him, he said: "Okay, in a minute," but did not move, and finally she came to the sunporch with a saucer of fudge and set it on a small table beside his chair.

"When that's over, you better go to bed," she said.

"I'm not sleepy."

"You know what Mother said."

"*You're* staying up."

"Course I am. I'm also a little older than you."

"I want to see the late show."

"No!"

"Yes, I am."

"I'll tell Daddy."

"He doesn't care."

"I'll tell him you wouldn't listen to me."

"I'll tell him you smoke."

"Oh, I could *wring* your neck!"

She went to the living room. He tried to concentrate on the Western, but it was ruined. The late show came on and he had seen it several months before and did not want to see it again, but he would not go to bed. He watched absently. Then he had to urinate. He got up and went into the living room, walking quickly, only glancing at them once, but when he did, Connie smiled and, with her voice friendly again, said: "What is it?"

He stopped and looked at her.

"*Red River.*"

He smiled.

"I already saw it," he said.

"You watching it again?"

"Maybe so."

"Okay."

He went to the bathroom and when he came back, they were gone. He went to the sunporch. Connie and Douglas were standing near the back door. The television was turned off. Kenneth wondered if Connie had seen *Red River*. If she had not, he could tell her what had happened during the part she missed. Douglas was whispering to Connie, his face close to hers. Then he looked at Kenneth.

"Night," he said.

"G'night," Kenneth said.

He was gone. Kenneth picked up the saucer his fudge had been on and took it to the kitchen and put it in the sink. He heard Douglas's car backing down the trail, and he went to the sunporch, but Connie was not there, so he went to the bathroom door and said: "You seen *Red River*?"

"Yes."

"You taking a bath?"

"Just washing my face. I'm going to bed."

He stood quietly for a moment. Then he went into the living room and got a magazine and sat in the rocking chair, looking at the people in the advertisements. Connie came in, wearing a robe. She leaned over his chair and he looked up and she kissed him.

"Good night," she said.

"G'night."

"You going to bed soon?"

"In a minute."

She got her cigarettes and an ashtray from the coffee table and went to her room and closed the door. After a while, he heard her getting into bed.

He looked at half the magazine, then laid it on the floor. Being awake in a house where everyone else was sleeping made him lonely. He went to the sunporch and latched the screen, then closed the door and locked it. He left the light on but turned out the one in the living room. Then he went to his room and took off everything but his shorts. He was about to turn out the light when he looked at the chest of drawers and saw the magazine. He hesitated. Then he picked it up and found the girl and looked at the exposed tops of her breasts and at her navel and below it. Suddenly he closed the magazine and raised his eyes to the ceiling, then closed them and said three Hail Mary's. Without looking at it, he picked up the magazine and took it to the living room, and went back to his bedroom and lay on his belly on the floor and started doing push-ups. He had no trouble with the first eight; then they became harder, and by the fifteenth he was breathing fast and his whole body was trembling as he pushed himself up from the floor. He did one more, then stood up and turned out the light and got into bed.

His room extended forward of the rest of the house, so that, from his bed, he could look through the window to his left and see the living room and Connie's bedroom. He rolled on his back and pulled the sheet up to his chest. He could hear crickets outside his window.

He flexed his right arm and felt the bicep. It seemed firmer than it had in June, when he started doing push-ups every night. He closed his eyes and began the Lord's Prayer and got as far as *Thy kingdom come* before he heard it.

Now it was not the crickets that he heard. He heard his own breathing and the bedsprings as his body tensed; then he heard it again, somewhere in front of the house: a cracking twig, a rustle of dried leaves, a foot on hard earth. Slowly, he rolled on his left side and looked out the window. He waited to be sure, but he did not have to; then he waited to decide what he would do, and he did not have to wait for that either, because he already knew, and he looked at the far corner of the room where his rifle was, though he could not see it, and he looked out the window again, staring at the windows of the living room and Connie's room, forcing himself to keep his eyes there, as if it would be all right if the prowler did not come into his vision, did not come close to the house; but listening to the slow footsteps, Kenneth knew that he would.

*Get up. Get up and get the rifle. If you don't do it now, he might come to this window and look in and then it'll be too late.*

For a moment, he did not breathe. Then, slowly, stopping at each sound of the bedsprings, he rolled out of bed and crouched on the floor beneath the window. He did not move. He listened to his breathing, for there was no other sound, not even crickets, and he began to tremble, thinking the prowler might be standing above him, looking through his window at the empty bed. He held his breath. Then he heard the footsteps again, in front of the house, closer now, and he thought: *He's by the pines in front of Connie's room.* He crawled away from the window, thinking of a large, bearded man standing in the pine trees thirty yards from Connie's room, studying the house and deciding which window to use; then he stood up and walked on tiptoes to the chest of drawers and moved his hand over the top of it until he touched the handful of bullets, his fingers quickly closing on them, and he picked up the rifle and took out the magazine and loaded it, then inserted it again and laid the extra bullets on the chest of drawers. Now he had to work the bolt. He pulled it up and back and eased it forward again.

Staying close to the wall, he tiptoed back to the window, stopping at the edge of it, afraid to look out and see a face looking in. He heard nothing. He looked through the windows in the opposite wall, thinking that if the prowler had heard him getting the rifle, he could have run back to the road, back to wherever he had come from, or he could still be hiding in the pines, or he could have circled to the rear of the house to hide again and listen, but there was no way of knowing, and he would have to stand in the room, listening, until his father came home. He thought of going to wake Connie, but he was afraid to move. Then he heard him again, near the pines, coming toward the house. He kneeled and pressed his shoulder against the wall, moving his face slightly, just enough to look out the screen and see the prowler walking toward Connie's window, stopping there and looking over his shoulder at the front yard and the road, then reaching out and touching the screen.

Kenneth rose and moved away from the wall, standing close to his bed now; he aimed through the screen, found the side of the man's head, then fired. A scream filled the house, the yard, his mind, and he thought at first it was the prowler, who was lying on the ground now, but it was a high, shrieking scream; it was Connie, and he ran into the living room, but she was already on the sunporch, unlocking the back door, not screaming now, but crying, pulling open the wooden door and hitting the screen with both hands, then stopping to unlatch it, and he yelled: "Connie!"

She turned, her hair swinging around her cheek.

"Get away from me!"

Then she ran outside, the screen door slamming, the shriek starting again, a long, high wail, ending in front of the house with *"Douglas, Douglas, Douglas!"* Then he knew.

Afterward, it seemed that the events of a year had occurred in an hour, and, to Kenneth, even that hour seemed to have a quality of neither speed nor slowness, but a kind of suspension, as if time were not passing at all. He remembered somehow calling his father and crying into the phone: "I shot Douglas Bakewell," and because of the crying, his father kept saying: "What's that, son? What did you say?" and then he lay facedown on his bed and cried, thinking of Connie outside with Douglas, hearing her sometimes when his own sounds lulled, and sometimes thinking of Connie inside with Douglas, if he had not shot him. He remembered the siren when it was far away and their voices as they brought Connie into the house. The doctor had come first, then his mother and father, then the sheriff; but, remembering, it was as if they had all come at once, for there was always a soothing or questioning face over his bed. He remembered the footsteps and hushed voices as they carried the body past his window, while his mother sat on the bed and stroked his forehead and cheek. He would never forget that.

Now the doctor and sheriff were gone and it seemed terribly late, almost sunrise. His father came into the room, carrying a glass of water, and sat on the bed.

"Take this," he said. "It'll make you sleep."

Kenneth sat up and took the pill from his father's palm and placed it on his tongue, then drank the water. He lay on his back and looked at his father's face. Then he began to cry.

"I thought it was a prowler," he said.

"It was, son. A prowler. We've told you that."

"But Connie went out there and she stayed all that time and she kept saying *'Douglas'* over and over; I heard her—"

"She wasn't out there with *him.* She was just out in the yard. She was in shock. She meant she wanted Douglas to be there with her. To help."

"No, *no*. It was *him*."

"It was a prowler. You did right. There's no telling what he might have done."

Kenneth looked away.

"He was going in her room," he said. "That's why she went to bed early. So I'd go to bed."

"It was a prowler," his father said.

Now Kenneth was sleepy. He closed his eyes and the night ran together in his mind and he remembered the rifle in the corner and thought: *I'll throw it in the creek tomorrow. I never want to see it again.* He would be asleep soon.

He saw himself standing on the hill and throwing his rifle into the creek; then the creek became an ocean, and he stood on a high cliff and for a moment he was a mighty angel, throwing all guns and cruelty and sex and tears into the sea.

# Stuart Dybek

*Dybek (1942– ) was born and raised in Chicago and lives in Kalamazoo, Michigan, where he teaches literature and writing at Western Michigan University. He has published two collections of short stories,* Childhood and Other Neighborhoods *(1980) and* The Coast of Chicago *(1990), and one book of poetry,* Brass Knuckles *(1979). He is the recipient of a PEN/Malamud Prize for "distinctive achievement in the short story form."*

## We Didn't

We did it in front of the mirror
And in the light. We did it in darkness,
In water, and in the high grass.
—*"We Did It," Yehuda Amichai*

We didn't in the light; we didn't in darkness. We didn't in the fresh-cut summer grass or in the mounds of autumn leaves or on the snow where moonlight threw down our shadows. We didn't in your room on the canopy bed you slept in, the bed you'd slept in as a child, or in the back seat of my father's rusted Rambler which smelled of the smoked chubs and kielbasa[1] that he delivered on weekends from my Uncle Vincent's meat market. We didn't in your mother's Buick Eight where a rosary twined the rearview mirror like a beaded black snake with silver, cruciform fangs.

At the dead end of our lovers' lane—a side street of abandoned factories—where I perfected the pinch that springs open a bra; behind the lilac bushes in Marquette Park[2] where you first touched me through my jeans and your nipples, swollen against transparent cotton, seemed the shade of lilacs; in the balcony of the now defunct Clark Theater where I wiped popcorn salt from my palms and slid them up your thighs and you whispered, "I feel like Doris Day is watching us," we didn't.

How adept we were at fumbling, how perfectly mistimed our timing, how utterly we confused energy with ecstasy.

Remember that night becalmed by heat, and the two of us, fused by sweat, trembling as if a wind from outer space that only we could feel was gusting

1. A Polish smoked sausage. 2. In Chicago.

across Oak Street Beach? Wound in your faded Navajo blanket, we lay soul kissing until you wept with wanting.

We'd been kissing all day—all summer—kisses tasting of different shades of lip gloss and too many Cokes. The lake had turned hot pink, rose rapture, pearl amethyst with dusk, then washed in night black with a ruff of silver foam. Beyond a momentary horizon, silent bolts of heat lightning throbbed, perhaps setting barns on fire somewhere in Indiana. The beach that had been so crowded was deserted as if there was a curfew. Only the bodies of lovers remained behind, visible in lightning flashes, scattered like the fallen on a battlefield, a few of them moaning, waiting for the gulls to pick them clean.

On my fingers your slick scent mixed with the coconut musk of the suntan lotion we'd repeatedly smeared over one another's bodies. When your bikini top fell away, my hands caught your breasts, memorizing their delicate weight, my palms cupped as if bringing water to parched lips.

Along the Gold Coast,[3] high-rises began to glow, window added to window, against the dark. In every lighted bedroom, couples home from work were stripping off their business suits, falling to the bed, and doing it. They did it before mirrors and pressed against the glass in streaming shower stalls, they did it against walls and on the furniture in ways that required previously unimagined gymnastics which they invented on the spot. They did it in honor of man and woman, in honor of beast, in honor of God. They did it because they'd been released, because they were home free, alive, and private, because they couldn't wait any longer, couldn't wait for the appointed hour, for the right time or temperature, couldn't wait for the future, for messiahs, for peace on earth and justice for all. They did it because of the Bomb, because of pollution, because of the Four Horsemen of the Apocalypse,[4] because extinction might be just a blink away. They did it because it was Friday night. It was Friday night and somewhere delirious music was playing—flutter-tongued flutes, muted trumpets meowing like tomcats in heat, feverish plucking and twanging, tom-toms, congas, and gongs all pounding the same pulsebeat.

I stripped your bikini bottom down the skinny rails of your legs and you tugged my swimsuit past my tan. Swimsuits at our ankles, we kicked like swimmers to free our legs, almost expecting a tide to wash over us the way the tide rushes in on Burt Lancaster and Deborah Kerr in their famous love scene on the beach in *From Here to Eternity*—a scene so famous that although neither of us had seen the movie, our bodies assumed the exact position of movie stars on the sand and you whispered to me softly, "I'm afraid of getting pregnant," and I whispered back, "Don't worry, I have protection," then, still kissing you, felt for my discarded cutoffs and the wallet in which for the last several months I had carried a Trojan as if it was a talisman. Still kissing, I tore its flattened, dried-out wrapper and it sprang through my fingers like a spring from a clock and dropped to the sand between our legs. My hands were shaking. In a panic, I groped for it, found it, tried to dust it off, tried, as Burt Lancaster never had to, to slip it on without breaking the mood, felt the grains of sand inside it, a

3. A district in Chicago of luxury hotels, apartments, and shops on Michigan Avenue and Lake Shore Drive. 4. Four horsemen symbolizing pestilence, war, famine, and death in the Book of Revelation 6.2–8.

throb of lightning, and the Great Lake behind us became, for all practical purposes, the Pacific and your skin tasted of salt and to the insistent question that my hips were asking, your body answered yes, your thighs opened like wings from my waist as we surfaced panting from a kiss that left you pleading *oh Christ yes,* a yes gasped sharply as a cry of pain so that for a moment I thought that we *were* already doing it and that somehow I had missed the instant when I entered you, entered you in the bloodless way in which a young man discards his own virginity, entered you as if passing through a gateway into the rest of my life, into a life as I wanted it to be lived *yes* but O then I realized that we were still floundering unconnected in the slick between us and there was sand in the Trojan as we slammed together still feeling for that perfect fit, still in the *Here* groping for an *Eternity* that was only a fine adjustment away, just a millimeter to the left or a fraction of an inch further south though with all the adjusting the sandy Trojan was slipping off and then it was gone but yes you kept repeating although your head was shaking no-not-quite-almost and our hearts were going like mad and you said yes Yes wait . . . Stop!

"What?" I asked, still futilely thrusting as if I hadn't quite heard you.

"Oh, God!" you gasped, pushing yourself up. "What's coming?"

"Julie, what's the matter?" I asked, confused, and then the beam of a spotlight swept over us and I glanced into its blinding eye.

All around us lights were coming, speeding across the sand. Blinking blindness away, I rolled from your body to my knees, feeling utterly defenseless in the way that only nakedness can leave one feeling. Headlights bounded toward us, spotlights crisscrossing, blue dome lights revolving as squad cars converged. I could see other lovers, caught in the beams, fleeing bare-assed through the litter of garbage that daytime hordes had left behind and that night had deceptively concealed. You were crying, clutching the Navajo blanket to your breasts with one hand and clawing for your bikini with the other, and I was trying to calm your terror with reassuring phrases such as, "Holy shit! I don't fucking believe this!"

Swerving and fishtailing in the sand, police calls pouring from their radios, the squad cars were on us, and then they were by us while we sat struggling on our clothes.

They braked at the water's edge, and cops slammed out brandishing huge flashlights, their beams deflecting over the dark water. Beyond the darting of those beams, the far-off throbs of lightning seemed faint by comparison.

"Over there, goddamn it!" one of them hollered, and two cops sloshed out into the shallow water without even pausing to kick off their shoes, huffing aloud for breath, their leather cartridge belts creaking against their bellies.

"Grab the son of a bitch! It ain't gonna bite!" one of them yelled, then they came sloshing back to shore with a body slung between them.

It was a woman—young, naked, her body limp and bluish beneath the play of flashlight beams. They set her on the sand just past the ring of drying, washed-up alewives.[5] Her face was almost totally concealed by her hair. Her hair was brown and tangled in a way that even wind or sleep can't tangle hair,

5. A North American fish; *Alosa pseudoharengus*.

tangled as if it had absorbed the ripples of water—thick strands, slimy-looking like dead seaweed.

"She's been in there a while, that's for sure," a cop with a beer belly said to a younger, crew-cut cop who had knelt beside the body and removed his hat as if he might be considering the kiss of life.

The crew-cut officer brushed the hair away from her face and the flashlight beams settled there. Her eyes were closed. A bruise or a birthmark stained the side of one eye. Her features appeared swollen—her lower lip protruding as if she was pouting.

An ambulance siren echoed across the sand, its revolving red light rapidly approaching.

"Might as well take their sweet-ass time," the beer-bellied cop said.

We had joined the circle of police surrounding the drowned woman almost without realizing that we had. You were back in your bikini, robed in the Navajo blanket, and I had slipped on my cutoffs, my underwear still dangling out of a back pocket.

Their flashlight beams explored her body, causing its whiteness to gleam. Her breasts were floppy; her nipples looked shriveled. Her belly appeared inflated by gallons of water. For a moment, a beam focused on her mound of pubic hair which was overlapped by the swell of her belly, and then moved almost shyly away down her legs, and the cops all glanced at us—at you, especially—above their lights, and you hugged your blanket closer as if they might confiscate it as evidence or to use as a shroud.

When the ambulance pulled up, one of the black attendants immediately put a stethoscope to the drowned woman's swollen belly and announced, "Drowned the baby, too."

Without saying anything, we turned from the group, as unconsciously as we'd joined them, and walked off across the sand, stopping only long enough at the spot where we had lain together like lovers in order to stuff the rest of our gear into a beach bag, to gather our shoes, and for me to find my wallet and kick sand over the forlorn, deflated-looking Trojan that you pretended not to notice. I was grateful for that.

Behind us, the police were snapping photos, flashbulbs throbbing like lightning flashes, and the lightning itself still distant but moving in closer, thunder rumbling audibly now, driving a lake wind before it so that gusts of sand tingled against the metal sides of the ambulance.

Squinting, we walked toward the lighted windows of the Gold Coast, while the shadows of gapers attracted by the whirling emergency lights hurried past up toward the shore.

"What happened? What's going on?" they asked us as they passed without waiting for an answer, and we didn't offer one, just continued walking silently in the dark.

It was only later that we talked about it, and once we began talking about the drowned woman it seemed we couldn't stop.

"She was pregnant," you said. "I mean I don't want to sound morbid, but I can't help thinking how the whole time we were, we almost—you know—there was this poor dead woman and her unborn child washing in and out behind us."

"It's not like we could have done anything for her even if we had known she was there."

"But what if we *had* found her? What if after we had—you know," you said, your eyes glancing away from mine and your voice tailing into a whisper, "what if after we did it, we went for a night swim and found her in the water?"

"But, Jules, we didn't," I tried to reason, though it was no more a matter of reason than anything else between us had ever been.

It began to seem as if each time we went somewhere to make out—on the back porch of your half-deaf, whiskery Italian grandmother who sat in the front of the apartment cackling before *I Love Lucy* reruns; or in your girlfriend Ginny's basement rec room when her parents were away on bowling league nights and Ginny was upstairs with her current crush, Brad; or way off in the burbs, at the Giant Twin Drive-In during the weekend they called Elvis Fest—the drowned woman was with us.

We would kiss, your mouth would open, and when your tongue flicked repeatedly after mine, I would unbutton the first button of your blouse, revealing the beauty spot at the base of your throat which matched a smaller spot I loved above a corner of your lips, and then the second button that opened on a delicate gold cross—that I had always tried to regard as merely a fashion statement—dangling above the cleft of your breasts. The third button exposed the lacy swell of your bra, and I would slide my hand over the patterned mesh, feeling for the firmness of your nipple rising to my fingertip, but you would pull slightly away, and behind your rapid breath your kiss would grow distant, and I would kiss harder trying to lure you back from wherever you had gone, and finally, holding you as if only consoling a friend, I'd ask, "What are you thinking?" although, of course, I knew.

"I don't want to think about her but I can't help it. I mean it seems like some kind of weird omen or something, you know?"

"No, I don't know," I said. "It was just a coincidence."

"Maybe if she'd been further away down the beach, but she was so close to us. A good wave could have washed her up right beside us."

"Great, then we could have had a *ménage à trois*."[6]

"Gross! I don't believe you just said that! Just because you said it in French doesn't make it less disgusting."

"You're driving me to it. Come on, Jules, I'm sorry," I said, "I was just making a dumb joke to get a little different perspective on things."

"What's so goddamn funny about a woman who drowned herself and her baby?"

"We don't even know for sure she did."

"Yeah, right, it was just an accident. Like she just happened to be going for a walk pregnant and naked, and she fell in."

"She could have been on a sailboat or something. Accidents happen; so do murders."

"Oh, like murder makes it less horrible? Don't think that hasn't occurred to me. Maybe the bastard who knocked her up killed her, huh?"

"How should I know? You're the one who says you don't want to talk about

6. Household of three (French); a living arrangement shared by three people who have sexual relations.

it and then gets obsessed with all kinds of theories and scenarios. Why are we arguing about a woman we don't even know, who doesn't have the slightest thing to do with us?"

"I *do* know about her," you said. "I dream about her."

"You dream about her?" I repeated, surprised. "Dreams you remember?"

"Sometimes they wake me up. Like I dreamed I was at my nonna's cottage in Michigan. Off her beach they've got a raft for swimming and in my dream I'm swimming out to it, but it keeps drifting further away until it's way out on the water and I'm so tired that if I don't get to it I'm going to drown. Then, I notice there's a naked person sunning on it and I start yelling, 'Help!' and she looks up, brushes her hair out of her face, and offers me a hand, but I'm too afraid to take it even though I'm drowning because it's her."

"God! Jules, that's creepy."

"I dreamed you and I were at the beach and you bring us a couple hot dogs but forget the mustard, so you have to go all the way back to the stand for it."

"Hot dogs, no mustard—a little too Freudian, isn't it?"

"Honest to God, I dreamed it. You go off for mustard and I'm wondering why you're gone so long, then a woman screams a kid has drowned and immediately the entire crowd stampedes for the water and sweeps me along with it. It's like one time when I was little and got lost at the beach, wandering in a panic through this forest of hairy legs and pouchy crotches, crying for my mother. Anyway, I'm carried into the water by the mob and forced under, and I think, this is it, I'm going to drown, but I'm able to hold my breath longer than could ever be possible. It feels like a flying dream—flying under water—and then I see this baby down there flying, too, and realize it's the kid everyone thinks has drowned, but he's no more drowned than I am. He looks like Cupid or one of those baby angels that cluster around the face of God."

"Pretty weird. What do you think it means? Something to do with drowning maybe, or panic?"

"It means the baby who drowned inside her that night was a love child—a boy—and his soul was released there to wander through the water."

"You really believe that?"

We argued about the interpretation of dreams, about whether dreams were symbolic or psychic, prophetic or just plain nonsense, until you said, "Look, you can believe what you want about your dreams, but keep your nose out of mine, O.K.?"

We argued about the drowned woman, about whether her death was a suicide or a murder, about whether her appearance that night was an omen or a coincidence, which, you argued, is what an omen is anyway: a coincidence that means something. By the end of summer, even if we were no longer arguing about the woman, we had acquired the habit of arguing about everything else. What was better: dogs or cats, rock or jazz, Cubs or Sox, tacos or egg rolls, right or left, night or day—we could argue about anything.

It no longer required arguing or necking to summon the drowned woman; everywhere we went she surfaced by her own volition: at Rocky's Italian Beef, at Lindo Mexico, at the House of Dong, our favorite Chinese restaurant, a place we still frequented because they had let us sit and talk until late over tiny cups of jasmine tea and broken fortune cookies earlier in the year, when it was winter and we had first started going together. We would always kid about going there. "Are you in the mood for Dong tonight?" I'd ask. It was a dopey joke, and you'd break up at its repeated dopiness. Back then, in winter, if one of us ordered the garlic shrimp, we would both be sure to eat them so that later our mouths tasted the same when we kissed.

Even when she wasn't mentioned, she was there with her drowned body—so dumpy next to yours—and her sad breasts with their wrinkled nipples and sour milk—so saggy beside yours which were still budding—with her swollen belly and her pubic bush colorless in the glare of electric light, with her tangled, slimy hair and her pouting, placid face—so lifeless beside yours—and her skin a pallid white, lightning-flash white, flashbulb white, a whiteness that couldn't be duplicated in daylight—how I'd come to hate that pallor, so cold beside the flush of your skin.

There wasn't a particular night when we finally broke up, just as there wasn't a particular night when we began going together, but I do remember a night in fall when I guessed that it was over. We were parked in the Rambler at the dead end of the street of factories that had been our lovers' lane, listening to a drizzle of rain and dry leaves sprinkle the hood. As always, rain revitalized the smells of the smoked fish and kielbasa in the upholstery. The radio was on too low to hear, the windshield wipers swished at intervals as if we were driving, and the windows were steamed as if we'd been making out. But we'd been arguing as usual, this time about a woman poet who had committed suicide, whose work you were reading. We were sitting, no longer talking or touching, and I remember thinking that I didn't want to argue with you anymore. I didn't want to sit like this in silence; I wanted to talk excitedly all night as we once had, I wanted to find some way that wasn't corny-sounding to tell you how much fun I'd had in your company, how much knowing you had meant to me, and how I had suddenly realized that I'd been so intent on becoming lovers that I'd overlooked how close we'd been as friends. I wanted you to know that. I wanted you to like me again.

"It's sad," I started to say, meaning that I was sorry we had reached a point of sitting silently together, but before I could continue, you challenged the statement.

"What makes you so sure it's sad?"

"What do you mean, what makes me so sure?" I asked, confused by your question, and surprised there could be anything to argue over no matter what you thought I was talking about.

You looked at me as if what was sad was that I would never understand. "For all either one of us knows," you said, "she could have been triumphant!"

Maybe when it really ended was that night when I felt we had just reached the beginning, that one time on the beach in the summer between high school and college, when our bodies rammed together so desperately that for a moment I thought we did it, and maybe in our hearts we had, although for me, then, doing it in one's heart didn't quite count. If it did, I supposed we'd all be Casanovas.[7]

I remember riding home together on the El[8] that night, feeling sick and defeated in a way I was embarrassed to mention. Our mute reflections emerged like negative exposures on the dark, greasy window of the train. Lightning branched over the city and when the train entered the subway tunnel, the lights inside flickered as if the power was disrupted although the train continued rocketing beneath the Loop.[9]

When the train emerged again we were on the South Side and it was pouring, a deluge as if the sky had opened to drown the innocent and guilty alike. We hurried from the El station to your house, holding the Navajo blanket over our heads until, soaked, it collapsed. In the dripping doorway of your apartment building, we said goodnight. You were shivering. Your bra showed through the thin blouse plastered to your skin. I swept the wet hair away from your face and kissed you lightly on the lips, then you turned and went inside. I stepped into the rain and you came back out calling after me.

"What?" I asked, feeling a surge of gladness to be summoned back into the doorway with you.

"Want an umbrella?"

I didn't. The downpour was letting up. It felt better to walk back to the El feeling the rain rinse the sand out of my hair, off my legs, until the only places where I could still feel its grit was the crotch of my cutoffs and in each squish of my shoes. A block down the street, I passed a pair of Jockey shorts lying in a puddle and realized they were mine, dropped from my back pocket as we ran to your house. I left them behind, wondering if you'd see them and recognize them the next day.

By the time I had climbed the stairs back to the El platform, the rain had stopped. Your scent still hadn't washed from my fingers. The station—the entire city, it seemed—dripped and steamed. The summer sound of crickets and nighthawks echoed from the drenched neighborhood. Alone, I could admit how sick I felt. For you, it was a night that would haunt your dreams. For me, it was another night when I waited, swollen and aching, for what I had secretly nicknamed the Blue Ball Express.

Literally lovesick, groaning inwardly with each lurch of the train and worried that I was damaged for good, I peered out at the passing yellow-lit stations where lonely men stood posted before giant advertisements, pictures of glamorous models defaced by graffiti—the same old scrawled insults and pleas: FUCK YOU, EAT ME. At his late hour the world seemed given over to men without women, men waiting in abject patience for something indeterminate, the way I waited for our next times. I avoided their eyes so that they wouldn't see the pity in mine, pity for them because I'd just been with you, your scent was still on my hands, and there seemed to be so much future ahead.

For me it was another night like that, and by the time I reached my stop I knew I would be feeling better, recovered enough to walk the dark street

7. Men known for their amorous adventures; from Giovanni Jacopo Casanova (1725–1798), Italian writer.
8. The elevated train. 9. The hub of Chicago's business district.

home making up poems of longing that I never wrote down. I was the D. H. Lawrence of not doing it, the voice of all the would-be lovers who ached and squirmed but still hadn't. From our contortions in doorways, on stairwells, and in the bucket seats of cars we could have composed a *Kama Sutra*[1] of interrupted bliss. It must have been that might when I recalled all the other times of walking home after seeing you, so that it seemed as if I was falling into step behind a parade of my former selves—myself walking home on the night we first kissed, myself on the night when I unbuttoned your blouse and kissed your breasts, myself on the night that I lifted your skirt above your thighs and dropped to my knees—each succeeding self another step closer to that irrevocable moment for which our lives seemed poised.

But we didn't, not in the moonlight, or by the phosphorescent lanterns of lightning bugs in your backyard, not beneath the constellations that we couldn't see, let alone decipher, nor in the dark glow that had replaced the real darkness of night, a darkness already stolen from us; not with the skyline rising behind us while the city gradually decayed, not in the heat of summer while a Cold War raged; despite the freedom of youth and the license of first love—because of fate, karma, luck, what does it matter?—we made not doing it a wonder, and yet we didn't, we didn't, we never did.

1. A book of Hindu aphorisms relating to the erotic life.

# Ralph Ellison

*Ellison (1914–1994) was born in Oklahoma City and educated at Tuskegee Institute. Though his publications were few, his novel* Invisible Man *(1952) is one of the most discussed and praised books published in America since World War II. While it announces no program for the liberation of blacks, it presents in an almost definitive way the moral, political, and psychological considerations involved in the enduring struggle. In his other writings, including the essay collection* Shadow and Act *(1964) and the novel* Juneteenth *(1999), Ellison continued his exploration of the problem of identity within the context of black culture. He brought to a culmination the double consciousness of blacks who also know themselves to be American.*

## King of the Bingo Game

The woman in front of him was eating roasted peanuts that smelled so good that he could barely contain his hunger. He could not even sleep and wished they'd hurry and begin the bingo game. There, on his right, two fellows were drinking wine out of a bottle wrapped in a paper bag, and he could hear soft gurgling in the dark. His stomach gave a low, gnawing growl. "If this was down South," he thought, "all I'd have to do is lean over and say, 'Lady, gimme a few of those peanuts, please ma'am,' and she'd pass me the bag and never think nothing of it." Or he could ask the fellows for a drink in the same way. Folks down South stuck together that way; they didn't even have to know you. But up here it was different. Ask somebody for something, and they'd think you were crazy. Well, I ain't crazy. I'm just broke, 'cause I got no birth certificate to get a job, and Laura 'bout to die 'cause we got no money for a doctor. But I ain't crazy. And yet a pinpoint of doubt was focused in his mind as he glanced toward the screen and saw the hero stealthily entering a dark room and sending the beam of a flashlight along a wall of bookcases. This is where he finds the trapdoor, he remembered. The man would pass abruptly through the wall and find the girl tied to a bed, her legs and arms spread wide, and her clothing torn to rags. He laughed softly to himself. He had seen the picture three times, and this was one of the best scenes.

On his right the fellow whispered wide-eyed to his companion, "Man, look ayonder!"

"Damn!"

"Wouldn't I like to have her tied up like that . . ."

"Hey! That fool's letting her loose!"

"Aw, man, he loves her."

"Love or no love!"

The man moved impatiently beside him, and he tried to involve himself in the scene. But Laura was on his mind. Tiring quickly of watching the picture he looked back to where the white beam filtered from the projection room above the balcony. It started small and grew large, specks of dust dancing in its whiteness as it reached the screen. It was strange how the beam always landed right on the screen and didn't mess up and fall somewhere else. But they had it all fixed. Everything was fixed. Now suppose when they showed that girl with her dress torn the girl started taking off the rest of her clothes, and when the guy came in he didn't untie her but kept her there and went to taking off his own clothes? *That* would be something to see. If a picture got out of hand like that those guys up there would go nuts. Yeah, and there'd be so many folks in here you couldn't find a seat for nine months! A strange sensation played over his skin. He shuddered. Yesterday he'd seen a bedbug on a woman's neck as they walked out into the bright street. But exploring his thigh through a hole in his pocket he found only goose pimples and old scars.

The bottle gurgled again. He closed his eyes. Now a dreamy music was accompanying the film and train whistles were sounding in the distance, and he was a boy again walking along a railroad trestle down South, and seeing the train coming, and running back as fast as he could go, and hearing the whistle blowing, and getting off the trestle to solid ground just in time, with the earth trembling beneath his feet, and feeling relieved as he ran down the cinder-strewn embankment onto the highway, and looking back and seeing with terror that the train had left the track and was following him right down the middle of the street, and all the white people laughing as he ran screaming . . .

"Wake up there, buddy! What the hell do you mean hollering like that? Can't you see we trying to enjoy this here picture?"

He stared at the man with gratitude.

"I'm sorry, old man," he said. "I musta been dreaming."

"Well, here, have a drink. And don't be making no noise like that, damn!"

His hands trembled as he tilted his head. It was not wine, but whiskey. Cold rye whiskey. He took a deep swoller, decided it was better not to take another, and handed the bottle back to its owner.

"Thanks, old man," he said.

Now he felt the cold whiskey breaking a warm path straight through the middle of him, growing hotter and sharper as it moved. He had not eaten all day, and it made him light-headed. The smell of the peanuts stabbed him like a knife, and he got up and found a seat in the middle aisle. But no sooner did he sit than he saw a row of intense-faced young girls, and got up again, thinking, "You chicks musta been Lindy-hopping[1] somewhere." He found a seat several

1. Dancing.

rows ahead as the lights came on, and he saw the screen disappear behind a heavy red and gold curtain; then the curtain rising, and the man with the microphone and a uniformed attendant coming on the stage.

He felt for his bingo cards, smiling. The guy at the door wouldn't like it if he knew about his having *five* cards. Well, not everyone played the bingo game; and even with five cards he didn't have much of a chance. For Laura, though, he had to have faith. He studied the cards, each with its different numerals, punching the free center hole in each and spreading them neatly across his lap; and when the lights faded he sat slouched in his seat so that he could look from his cards to the bingo wheel with but a quick shifting of his eyes.

Ahead, at the end of the darkness, the man with the microphone was pressing a button attached to a long cord and spinning the bingo wheel and calling out the number each time the wheel came to rest. And each time the voice rang out his finger raced over the cards for the number. With five cards he had to move fast. He became nervous; there were too many cards, and the man went too fast with his grating voice. Perhaps he should just select one and throw the others away. But he was afraid. He became warm. Wonder how much Laura's doctor would cost? Damn that, watch the cards! And with despair he heard the man call three in a row which he missed on all five cards. This way he'd never win . . .

When he saw the row of holes punched across the third card, he sat paralyzed and heard the man call three more numbers before he stumbled forward, screaming,

"Bingo! Bingo!"

"Let that fool up there," someone called.

"Get up there, man!"

He stumbled down the aisle and up the steps to the stage into a light so sharp and bright that for a moment it blinded him, and he felt that he had moved into the spell of some strange, mysterious power. Yet it was as familiar as the sun, and he knew it was the perfectly familiar bingo.

The man with the microphone was saying something to the audience as he held out his card. A cold light flashed from the man's finger as the card left his hand. His knees trembled. The man stepped closer, checking the card against the numbers chalked on the board. Suppose he had made a mistake? The pomade on the man's hair made him feel faint, and he backed away. But the man was checking the card over the microphone now, and he had to stay. He stood tense, listening.

"Under the O, forty-four," the man chanted. "Under the I, seven. Under the G, three. Under the B, ninety-six. Under the N, thirteen!"

His breath came easier as the man smiled at the audience.

"Yes sir, ladies and gentlemen, he's one of the chosen people!"

The audience rippled with laughter and applause.

"Step right up to the front of the stage."

He moved slowly forward, wishing that the light was not so bright.

"To win tonight's jackpot of $36.90 the wheel must stop between the double zero, understand?"

He nodded, knowing the ritual from the many days and nights he had watched the winners march across the stage to press the button that controlled the spinning wheel and receive the prizes. And now he followed the instructions as though he'd crossed the slippery stage a million prize-winning times.

The man was making some kind of joke, and he nodded vacantly. So tense had he become that he felt a sudden desire to cry and shook it away. He felt vaguely that his whole life was determined by the bingo wheel; not only that which would happen now that he was at last before it, but all that had gone before, since his birth, and his mother's birth and the birth of his father. It had always been there, even though he had not been aware of it, handing out the unlucky cards and numbers of his days. The feeling persisted, and he started quickly away. I better get down from here before I make a fool of myself, he thought.

"Here, boy," the man called. "You haven't started yet."

Someone laughed as he went hesitantly back.

"Are you all reet?"

He grinned at the man's jive talk, but no words would come, and he knew it was not a convincing grin. For suddenly he knew that he stood on the slippery brink of some terrible embarrassment.

"Where are you from, boy?" the man asked.

"Down South."

"He's from down South, ladies and gentlemen," the man said. "Where from? Speak right into the mike."

"Rocky Mont," he said. "Rock' Mont, North Car'lina."

"So you decided to come down off that mountain to the U.S.," the man laughed. He felt that the man was making a fool of him, but then something cold was placed in his hand, and the lights were no longer behind him.

Standing before the wheel he felt alone, but that was somehow right, and he remembered his plan. He would give the wheel a short quick twirl. Just a touch of the button. He had watched it many times, and always it came close to double zero when it was short and quick. He steeled himself; the fear had left, and he felt a profound sense of promise, as though he were about to be repaid for all the things he'd suffered all his life. Trembling, he pressed the button. There was a whirl of lights, and in a second he realized with finality that though he wanted to, he could not stop. It was as though he held a high-powered line in his naked hand. His nerves tightened. As the wheel increased its speed it seemed to draw him more and more into its power, as though it held his fate; and with it came a deep need to submit, to whirl, to lose himself in its swirl of color. He could not stop it now. So let it be.

The button rested snugly in his palm where the man had placed it. And now he became aware of the man beside him, advising him through the microphone, while behind the shadowy audience hummed with noisy voices. He shifted his feet. There was still that feeling of helplessness within him, making part of him desire to turn back, even now that the jackpot was right in his hand. He squeezed the button until his fist ached. Then, like the sudden shriek of a subway whistle, a doubt tore through his head. Suppose he did not spin the wheel long enough? What could he do, and how could he tell? And then he knew, even as he wondered, that as long as he pressed the button, he could control the jackpot. He and only he could determine whether or not it was to be his. Not even the man with the microphone could do anything about it now. He felt drunk. Then, as though he had come down from a high hill into a valley of people, he heard the audience yelling.

"Come down from there, you jerk!"

"Let somebody else have a chance . . ."

"Ole Jack thinks he done found the end of the rainbow . . ."

The last voice was not unfriendly, and he turned and smiled dreamily into the yelling mouths. Then he turned his back squarely on them.

"Don't take too long, boy," a voice said.

He nodded. They were yelling behind him. Those folks did not understand what had happened to him. They had been playing the bingo game day in and night out for years, trying to win rent money or hamburger change. But not one of those wise guys had discovered this wonderful thing. He watched the wheel whirling past the numbers and experienced a burst of exaltation: This is God! This is the really truly God! He said it aloud, "This is God!"

He said it with such absolute conviction that he feared he would fall fainting into the footlights. But the crowd yelled so loud that they could not hear. These fools, he thought. I'm here trying to tell them the most wonderful secret in the world, and they're yelling like they gone crazy. A hand fell upon his shoulder.

"You'll have to make a choice now, boy. You've taken too long."

He brushed the hand violently away.

"Leave me alone, man. I know what I'm doing!"

The man looked surprised and held on to the microphone for support. And because he did not wish to hurt the man's feelings he smiled, realizing with a sudden pang that there was no way of explaining to the man just why he had to stand there pressing the button forever.

"Come here," he called tiredly.

The man approached, rolling the heavy microphone across the stage.

"Anybody can play this bingo game, right?" he said.

"Sure, but . . ."

He smiled, feeling inclined to be patient with this slick looking white man with his blue shirt and his sharp gabardine suit.

"That's what I thought," he said. "Anybody can win the jackpot as long as they get the lucky number, right?"

"That's the rule, but after all . . ."

"That's what I thought," he said. "And the big prize goes to the man who knows how to win it?"

The man nodded speechlessly.

"Well then, go on over there and watch me win like I want to. I ain't going to hurt nobody," he said, "and I'll show you how to win. I mean to show the whole world how it's got to be done."

And because he understood, he smiled again to let the man know that he held nothing against him for being white and impatient. Then he refused to see the man any longer and stood pressing the button, the voices of the crowd reaching him like sounds in distant streets. Let them yell. All the Negroes down there were just ashamed because he was black like them. He smiled inwardly, knowing how it was. Most of the time he was ashamed of what Negroes did himself. Well, let them be ashamed for something this time. Like him. He was like a long thin black wire that was being stretched and wound upon the bingo wheel; wound until he wanted to scream; wound, but this time himself controlling the winding and the sadness and the shame, and because he did, Laura would be all right. Suddenly the lights flickered. He staggered backwards. Had something gone wrong? All this noise. Didn't they know that although he controlled the wheel, it also controlled him, and unless he pressed the button forever and forever and ever it would stop, leaving him high and dry, dry and high on this hard high slippery hill and Laura dead? There was only one chance; he had to do whatever the wheel demanded. And gripping the button in despair, he discovered with surprise that it imparted a nervous energy. His spine tingled. He felt a certain power.

Now he faced the raging crowd with defiance, its screams penetrating his eardrums like trumpets shrieking from a juke-box. The vague faces glowing in the bingo lights gave him a sense of himself that he had never known before. He was running the show, by God! They had to react to him, for he was their luck. This is *me*, he thought. Let the bastards yell. Then someone was laughing inside him, and he realized that somehow he had forgotten his own name. It was a sad, lost feeling to lose your name, and a crazy thing to do. That name had been given him by the white man who had owned his grandfather a long lost time ago down South. But maybe those wise guys knew his name.

"Who am I?" he screamed.

"Hurry up and bingo, you jerk!"

They didn't know either, he thought sadly. They didn't even know their own names, they were all poor nameless bastards. Well, he didn't need that old name; he was reborn. For as long as he pressed the button he was The-man-who-pressed-the-button-who-held-the-prize-who-was-the-King-of-Bingo. That was the way it was, and he'd have to press the button even if nobody understood, even though Laura did not understand.

"Live!" he shouted.

The audience quieted like the dying of a huge fan.

"Live, Laura, baby. I got holt of it now, sugar. Live!"

He screamed it, tears streaming down his face. "I got nobody but YOU!"

The screams tore from his very guts. He felt as though the rush of blood to his head would burst out in baseball seams of small red droplets, like a head beaten by police clubs. Bending over he saw a trickle of blood splashing the toe of his shoe. With his free hand he searched his head. It was his nose. God, suppose something has gone wrong? He felt that the whole audience had somehow entered him and was stamping its feet in his stomach and he was unable to throw them out. They wanted the prize, that was it. They wanted the secret for themselves. But they'd never get it; he would keep the bingo wheel whirling forever, and Laura would be safe in the wheel. But would she? It had to be, because if she were not safe the wheel would cease to turn; it could not go on. He had to get away, *vomit* all, and his mind formed an image of himself running with Laura in his arms down the tracks of the subway just ahead of an A train, running desperately *vomit* with people screaming for him to come out but knowing no way of leaving the tracks because to stop would bring the train crushing down upon him and to attempt to leave across the other tracks would mean to run into a hot third rail as high as his waist which threw blue sparks that blinded his eyes until he could hardly see.

He heard singing and the audience was clapping its hands.

Shoot the liquor to him, Jim, boy!
Clap-clap-clap
Well a-calla the cop
He's blowing his top!
Shoot the liquor to him, Jim, boy!

Bitter anger grew within him at the singing. They think I'm crazy. Well let 'em laugh. I'll do what I got to do.

He was standing in an attitude of intense listening when he saw that they were watching something on the stage behind him. He felt weak. But when he turned he saw no one. If only his thumb did not ache so. Now they were applauding. And for a moment he thought that the wheel had stopped. But that was impossible, his thumb still pressed the button. Then he saw them. Two men in uniform beckoned from the end of the stage. They were coming toward him, walking in step, slowly, like a tap-dance team returning for a third encore. But their shoulders shot forward, and he backed away, looking wildly about. There was nothing to fight them with. He had only the long black cord which led to a plug somewhere back stage, and he couldn't use that because it operated the bingo wheel. He backed slowly, fixing the men with his eyes as his lips stretched over his teeth in a tight, fixed grin; moved toward the end of the stage and realizing that he couldn't go much further, for suddenly the cord became taut and he couldn't afford to break the cord. But he had to do something. The audience was howling. Suddenly he stopped dead, seeing the men halt, their legs lifted as in an interrupted step of a slow-motion dance. There was nothing to do but run in the other direction and he dashed forward, slipping and sliding. The men fell back, surprised. He struck out violently going past.

"Grab him!"

He ran, but all too quickly the cord tightened, resistingly, and he turned and ran back again. This time he slipped them, and discovered by running in a circle before the wheel he could keep the cord from tightening. But this way he had to flail his arms to keep the men away. Why couldn't they leave a man alone? He ran, circling.

"Ring down the curtain," someone yelled. But they couldn't do that. If they did the wheel flashing from the projection room would be cut off. But they had him before he could tell them so, trying to pry open his fist, and he was wrestling and trying to bring his knees into the fight and holding on to the button, for it was his life. And now he was down, seeing a foot coming down, crushing his wrist cruelly, down, as he saw the wheel whirling serenely above.

"I can't give it up," he screamed. Then quietly, in a confidential tone, "Boys, I really can't give it up."

It landed hard against his head. And in the blank moment they had it away from him, completely now. He fought them trying to pull him up from the stage as he watched the wheel spin slowly to a stop. Without surprise he saw it rest at double-zero.

"You see," he pointed bitterly.

"Sure, boy, sure, it's O.K.," one of the men said smiling.

And seeing the man bow his head to someone he could not see, he felt very, very happy; he would receive what all the winners received.

But as he warmed in the justice of the man's tight smile he did not see the man's slow wink, nor see the bow-legged man behind him step clear of the swiftly descending curtain and set himself for a blow. He only felt the dull pain exploding in his skull, and he knew even as it slipped out of him that his luck had run out on the stage.

# Louise Erdrich

*Erdrich (1954– ) was born in Little Falls, Minnesota, of German-American and Chippewa descent. She grew up in Wahpeton, North Dakota, and graduated from Dartmouth College. Her thriving literary career has included the publication of two books of poems,* Jacklight *(1984) and* Baptism of Desire *(1989), and the novels* Love Medicine *(1984),* The Beet Queen *(1986),* Tracks *(1988), and* The Crown of Columbus *(1991), which she coauthored with Michael Dorris. A novel,* The Antelope Wife, *was published in 1998. She has received ample recognition for the quality of her work, including a fellowship from the National Endowment for the Arts and a Guggenheim Fellowship.* Love Medicine *was the winner of the National Book Critics Circle Award for fiction.*

## Matchimanito

We started dying before the snow, and, like the snow, we continued to fall. We were surprised that so many of us were left to die. For those who survived the spotted sickness from the south and our long fight west to Dakota land, where we signed the treaty, and then a wind from the east, bringing exile in a storm of government papers, what descended from the north in 1914 seemed terrible, and unjust.

By then we thought disaster must surely have spent its force, that disease must have claimed all of the Anishinabe that the earth could hold and bury.

But along with the first bitter punishments of early winter a new sickness swept down. The consumption, it was called by young Father Damien, who came in that year to replace the priest who had succumbed to the same devastation as his flock. This disease was different from the pox and fever, for it came on slowly. The outcome, however, was just as certain. Whole families of Anishinabe lay ill and helpless in its breath. On the reservation, where we were forced close together, the clans dwindled. Our tribe unraveled like a coarse rope, frayed at either end as the old and new among us were taken. My own family was wiped out one by one. I was the only Nanapush who lived. And after, although I had seen no more than fifty winters, I was considered an old man.

I guided the last buffalo hunt. I saw the last bear shot. I trapped the last beaver with a pelt of more than two years' growth. I spoke aloud the words of the government treaty and refused to sign the settlement papers that would take away our woods and lake. I axed the last birch that was older than I, and I saved the last of the Pillager family.

Fleur.

We found her on a cold afternoon in late winter, out in her family's cabin near Matchimanito Lake, where my companion, Edgar Pukwan, of the tribal police, was afraid to go. The water there was surrounded by the highest oaks, by woods inhabited by ghosts and roamed by Pillagers, who knew the secret ways to cure or kill, until their art deserted them. Dragging our sled into the clearing, we saw two things: the smokeless tin chimney spout jutting from the roof, and the empty hole in the door where the string was drawn inside. Pukwan did not want to enter, fearing that the unburied Pillager spirits might seize him by the throat and turn him windigo.[1] So I was the one who broke the thin-scraped hide that made a window. I was the one who lowered himself into the stinking silence, onto the floor. I was also the one to find the old man and woman, the little brother and two sisters, stone cold and wrapped in gray horse blankets, their faces turned to the west.

Afraid as I was, stilled by their quiet forms, I touched each bundle in the gloom of the cabin, and wished each spirit a good journey on the three-day road, the old-time road, so well trampled by our people this deadly season. Then something in the corner knocked. I flung the door wide. It was the eldest daughter, Fleur, so feverish that she'd thrown off her covers. She huddled against the cold wood range, staring and shaking. She was wild as a filthy wolf, a big bony girl whose sudden bursts of strength and snarling cries terrified the listening Pukwan. I was the one who struggled to lash her to the sacks of supplies and to the boards of the sled. I wrapped blankets over her and tied them down as well.

Pukwan kept us back, convinced that he should carry out the agency's instructions to the letter: he carefully nailed up the official quarantine sign, and then, without removing the bodies, he tried to burn down the house. But though he threw kerosene repeatedly against the logs and even started a blaze with birch bark and chips of wood, the flames narrowed and shrank, went out in puffs of smoke. Pukwan cursed and looked desperate, caught between his official duties and his fear of Pillagers. The fear won out. He finally dropped the tinders and helped me drag Fleur along the trail.

And so we left five dead at Matchimanito, frozen behind their cabin door.

Some say that Pukwan and I should have done right and buried the Pillagers first thing. They say the unrest and curse of trouble that struck our people in the years that followed was the doing of dissatisfied spirits. I know what's fact, and have never been afraid of talking. Our trouble came from the living, from liquor and the dollar bill. We stumbled toward the government bait, never looking down, never noticing how the land was snatched from under us at every step.

When Edgar Pukwan's turn came to draw the sled, he took off like devils chased him, bounced Fleur over potholes as if she were a log, and tipped her twice into the snow. I followed the sled, encouraged Fleur with songs, cried at

1. In Algonquin lore someone transformed into a cannibalistic giant by tasting human flesh.

Pukwan to watch for hidden branches and deceptive drops, and finally got her to my cabin, a small, tightly tamped box overlooking the crossroads.

"Help me," I cried, cutting at the ropes, not even bothering with knots. Fleur closed her eyes, panted, and tossed her head from side to side. Her chest rattled as she strained for air; she grabbed me around the neck. Still weak from my own bout with the sickness, I staggered, fell, lurched into my cabin, wrestling the strong girl inside with me. I had no wind left over to curse Pukwan, who watched but refused to touch her, turned away, and vanished with the whole sled of supplies. I was neither surprised nor caused enduring sorrow later when Pukwan's son, also named Edgar and also of the tribal police, told me that his father came home, crawled into bed, and took no food from that moment until his last breath passed.

As for Fleur, each day she improved in small changes. First her gaze focused, and the next night her skin was cool and damp. She was clearheaded, and after a week she remembered what had befallen her family, how they had taken sick so suddenly, gone under. With her memory mine came back, only too sharply. I was not prepared to think of the people I had lost, or to speak of them, although we did, carefully, without letting their names loose in the wind that would reach their ears.

We feared that they would hear us and never rest, come back out of pity for the loneliness we felt. They would sit in the snow outside the door, waiting until from longing we joined them. We would all be together on the journey then, our destination the village at the end of the road, where people gamble day and night but never lose their money, eat but never fill their stomachs, drink but never leave their minds.

The snow receded enough for us to dig the ground with picks. As a tribal policeman, Pukwan's son was forced by regulation to help bury the dead. So again we took the dark road to Matchimanito, the son leading rather than the father. We spent the day chipping at the earth until we had a hole long and deep enough to lay the Pillagers shoulder to shoulder. We covered them and built five small board houses. I scratched out their clan markers, four crosshatched bears and a marten; then Pukwan Junior shouldered the government's tools and took off down the path. I settled myself near the graves.

I asked those Pillagers, as I had asked my own children and wives, to leave us now and never come back. I offered tobacco, smoked a pipe of red willow for the old man. I told them not to pester their daughter just because she had survived, or to blame me for finding them, or Pukwan Junior for leaving too soon. I told them that I was sorry, but they must abandon us. I insisted. But the Pillagers were as stubborn as the Nanapush clan and would not leave my thoughts. I think they followed me home. All the way down the trail, just beyond the edges of my sight, they flickered, thin as needles, shadows piercing shadows.

The sun had set by the time I got back, but Fleur was awake, sitting in the dark as if she knew. She never moved to build up the fire, never asked where I had been. I never told her about it either, and as the days passed we spoke rarely, always with roundabout caution. We felt the spirits of the dead so near that at length we just stopped talking.

This made it worse.

Their names grew within us, swelled to the brink of our lips, forced our eyes open in the middle of the night. We were filled with the water of the drowned, cold and black—airless water that lapped against the seal of our tongues or leaked slowly from the corners of our eyes. Within us, like ice shards, their names bobbed and shifted. Then the slivers of ice began to collect and cover us. We became so heavy, weighted down with the lead-gray frost, that we could not move. Our hands lay on the table like cloudy blocks. The blood within us grew thick. We needed no food. And little warmth. Days passed, weeks, and we didn't leave the cabin for fear we'd crack our cold and fragile bodies. We had gone half windigo. I learned later that this was common, that many of our people died in this manner, of the invisible sickness. Some could not swallow another bite of food because the names of their dead thickened on their tongues. Some let their blood stop, took the road west after all.

One day the new priest—just a boy, really—opened our door. A dazzling and painful light flooded through and surrounded Fleur and me. Numb, stupid as bears in a winter den, we blinked at the priest's slight silhouette. Our lips were parched, stuck together. We could hardly utter a greeting, but we were saved by one thought: a guest must eat. Fleur gave Father Damien her chair and put wood on the gray coals. She found flour for gaulette. I went to fetch snow to boil for tea water, but to my amazement the ground was bare. I was so surprised that I bent over and touched the soft, wet earth.

My voice rasped at first when I tried to speak, but then, oiled by strong tea, lard, and bread, I was off and talking. You could not stop me with a sledgehammer, once I started. Father Damien looked astonished, and then wary, as I began to creak and roll. I gathered speed. I talked both languages in streams that ran alongside each other, over every rock, around every obstacle. The sound of my voice convinced me I was alive. I kept Father Damien listening all night, his green eyes round, his thin face straining to understand, his odd brown hair in curls and clipped knots. Occasionally he took in air, as if to add observations of his own, but I pushed him under with my words.

I don't know when Fleur slipped out.

She was too young and had no stories or depth of life to rely upon. All she had was raw power, and the names of the dead that filled her. I can speak them now. They have no more interest in any of us. Old Pillager. Ogimaakwe, Boss Woman, his wife. Asasaweminikwesens, Chokecherry Girl. Bineshii, Small Bird, also known as Josette. And the last, the boy Ombaashi, He Is Lifted by Wind.

They are gone, but sometimes I don't know where they are anymore—this place of reservation surveys or the other place, boundless, where the dead sit talking, see too much, and regard the living as fools.

And we were. Starvation makes fools of anyone. In the past some had sold their allotment land for a hundred pound weight of flour. Others, who were desperate to hold on, now urged that we get together and buy back our land, or at least pay a tax and refuse the settlement money that would sweep the marks of our boundaries off the map like a pattern of straws. Many were determined not to allow the hired surveyors, or even our own people, to enter the deepest bush.

But that spring outsiders went in as before, permitted by the agent, a short round man with hair blond as chaff. The purpose of these people was to measure the lake. Only now they walked upon the fresh graves of Pillagers, crossed death roads to plot out the deepest water where the lake monster, Misshepeshu, hid and waited.

"Stay here with me," I said to Fleur when she came to visit.

She refused.

"The land will go," I told her. "The land will be sold and measured."

But she tossed back her hair and walked off, down the path, with nothing to eat till thaw but a bag of my onions and a sack of oats.

Who knows what happened? She returned to Matchimanito and stayed there alone in the cabin that even fire did not want. A young girl had never done such a thing before. I heard that in those months she was asked for fee money for the land. The agent went out there and got lost, spent a whole night following the moving lights and lamps of people who would not answer him but talked and laughed among themselves. They let him go, at dawn, only because he was so stupid. Yet he went out there to ask Fleur for money again, and the next thing we heard he was living in the woods and eating roots, gambling with ghosts.

Some had ideas. You know how old chickens scratch and gabble. That's how the tales started, all the gossip, the wondering, all the things people said without knowing and then believed, since they heard it with their own ears, from their own lips, each word.

I am not one to take notice of the talk of those who fatten in the shade of the new agent's storehouse. But I watched the old agent, the one who was never found, take the rutted turnoff to Matchimanito. He was replaced by a darker man who spoke long and hard with many of our own about a money settlement. But nothing changed my mind. I've seen too much go by—unturned grass below my feet, and overhead the great white cranes flung south forever.

I am a holdout, like the Pillagers, and I told the agent, in good English, what I thought of his treaty paper. I could have written my name, and much more too, in script. I had a Jesuit education in the halls of Saint John before I ran back to the woods and forgot all my prayers.

Since I had saved Fleur from the sickness, I was entangled with her. Not that I knew it at first. Only when I look back do I see a pattern. I was the vine of a wild grape that twined the timbers and drew them close. I was a branch that lived long enough to touch the next tree over, which was Pillagers. The story, like all stories, is never visible while it is happening. Only after, when an old man sits dreaming and talking in his chair, does the design spring clear.

There was so much I saw, and never knew.

When Fleur came down onto the reservation, walking right through town, no one guessed what she hid in that green rag of a dress. I do remember that it was too small, split down the back and strained across the front. That's what I noticed when I greeted her. Not whether she had money in the dress, or a child.

Other people speculated.

They added up the money she used now to buy supplies and how the agent disappeared from his post, and came out betting she would have a baby. He could have paid cash to Fleur and then run off in shame. She could even have stolen cash from him, cursed him dead, and hidden his remains. Everybody would have known, they thought, in nine months or less, if young Eli Kashpaw hadn't gone out and muddied the waters.

This Eli never cared to figure out business, politics, or church. He never applied for a chunk of land or registered himself. Eli hid from authorities, never saw the inside of a classroom, and although his mother, Margaret, got baptized in the church and tried to collar him for Mass, the best he could do was sit outside the big pine door and whittle pegs. For money Eli chopped wood, pitched hay, harvested potatoes or cranberry bark. He wanted to be a hunter, though, like me, and he had asked to partner that winter before the sickness.

I think like animals, have perfect understanding for where they hide. I can track a deer back through time and brush and cleared field to the place where it was born. Only one thing is wrong with teaching these things, however. I showed Eli how to hunt and trap from such an early age that he lived too much in the company of trees and wind. At fifteen he was uncomfortable around human beings. Especially women. So I had to help him out some.

I'm a Nanapush, remember. That's as good as saying I knew what interested Eli Kashpaw. He wanted something other than what I could teach him about the woods. He was no longer curious only about where a mink will fish or burrow, or when pike will lie low or bite. He wanted to hear how, in the days before the priest's ban and the sickness, I had satisfied three wives.

"Nanapush," Eli said, appearing at my door one day, "I have to ask you something."

"Come on in here, then," I said. "I won't bite you like the little girls do."

He was steadier, more serious, than he was the winter we went out together on the trapline. I was going to wonder what the different thing about him was when he said, "Fleur Pillager."

"She's no little girl," I answered, motioning toward the table. He told me his story.

It began when Eli got himself good and lost up near Matchimanito. He was hunting a doe in a light rain, having no luck until he rounded a slough and shot badly, which wasn't unusual. She was wounded to death but not crippled. She might walk all day, which shamed him, so he dabbed a bit of her blood on the barrel of his gun, the charm I taught him, and he followed her trail.

He had a time of it. She sawed through the woods, took the worst way, moved into heavy brush like a ghost. For hours Eli blazed his passage with snapped branches and clumps of leaves, scuffed the ground, or left a bootprint. But the trail and the day wore on, and for some reason that he did not understand, he gave up and quit leaving sign.

"That was when you should have turned back," I told him. "You should have known. It's no accident people don't like to go there. Those trees are too big, thick, and twisted at the top like bent arms. In the wind their limbs cast, creak against each other, snap. The leaves speak a cold language that overfills your brain. You want to lie down. You want never to get up. You hunger. You rake black chokecherries off their stems and stuff them down, and then you shit like a bird. Your blood thins. You're too close to where the Lake Man lives. And you're too close to where I buried the Pillagers during the long sickness that claimed them like it claimed the Nanapush clan."

I said this to Eli Kashpaw: "I understand Fleur. I am alone in this. I know that was no ordinary doe drawing you out there."

But the doe was real enough, he told me, and it was gut-shot and weakening. The blood dropped fresher, darker, until he thought he heard her just ahead and bent to the ground, desperate to see in the falling dusk, and looked ahead to catch a glimpse, and instead saw the glow of fire. He started toward it, then stopped just outside the circle of light. The deer hung, already split, turning back and forth on a rope. When he saw the woman, gutting with long quick movements, her arms bloody and bare, he stepped into the clearing.

"That's mine," he said.

I hid my face, shook my head.

"You should have turned back," I told him. "Stupid! You should have left it."

But he was stubborn, a vein of Kashpaw that held out for what it had coming. He couldn't have taken the carcass home anyway, couldn't have lugged it back, even if he had known his direction. Yet he stood his ground with the woman and said he'd tracked that deer too far to let it go. She did not respond. "Or maybe half," he thought, studying her back, uncomfortable. Even so, that was as generous as he could get.

She kept working. Never noticed him. He was so ignorant that he reached out and tapped her on the shoulder. She never even twitched. He walked around her, watched the knife cut, trespassed into her line of vision.

At last she saw him, he said, but then scorned him as though he were nothing.

"Little fly"—she straightened her back, the knife loose and casual in her hand—"quit buzzing."

Eli said she looked so wild her beauty didn't throw him, and I leaned closer, worried as he said this, worried as he reported how her hair was clumped with dirt, her face thin as a bony bitch's, her dress a rag that hung, and no curve to her except her breasts.

He noticed some things.

"No curve?" I said, thinking of the rumors.

He shook his head, impatient to continue his story. He felt sorry for her, he said. I told him the last man who was interested in Fleur Pillager had vanished, never to be found. She made us all uneasy, out there so alone. I was a friend to the Pillagers before they died off, I said, and I was safe from Fleur because the two of us had mourned the dead together. She was almost a relative. But that wasn't the case with him.

Eli looked at me with an unbelieving frown. Then he said he didn't see where she was so dangerous. After a while he had recognized her manner as exhaustion more than anger. She made no protest when he took out his own knife and helped her work. Halfway through the job she allowed him to finish, and then Eli hoisted most of the meat into the tree. He took the choice parts into the cabin. She let him in, hardly noticed him, and he helped her start the small range and even took it on himself to melt lard. She ate the whole heart, fell on it like a starved animal, and then her eyes shut.

From the way he described her actions, I was sure she was pregnant. I'm familiar with the signs, and I can talk about this since I'm an old man, far past anything a woman can do to weaken me. I was more certain still when Eli said that he took her in his arms, helped her to a pile of blankets on a willow bed. And then—hard to believe, even though it was, for the first time, the right thing to do—Eli rolled up in a coat on the other side of the cabin floor and lay there all night, and slept alone.

"So," I said, "why have you come to me now? You got away, you survived, she even let you find your way home. You learned your lesson and none the worse."

"I want her," Eli said.

I could not believe that I heard right, but we were sitting by the stove, face to face, so there was no doubt. I rose and turned away. Maybe I was less than generous, having lost my own girls. Maybe I wanted to keep Fleur as my daughter, who would visit me, joke with me, beat me at cards. But I believe it was only for Eli's own good that I was harsh.

"Forget that thing so heavy in our pocket," I said, "or put it somewhere else. Go town way and find yourself a tamer woman."

He brooded at my tabletop and then spoke. "I want know-how, not warnings, not my mother's caution."

"You don't want instruction!" I was pushed too far. "Love medicine is what you're after. A Nanapush never needed any, but Old Lady Aintapi or the Pillagers, they sell it. Go ask Moses for a medicine and pay your price."

"I don't want anything that can wear off," the boy said. He was determined. Maybe his new, steady coolness was the thing that turned my mind, the quiet of him. He was different, sitting there so still. It struck me that he had come into his growth, and who was I to hold him back from going to a Pillager, since someone had to, since the whole tribe had got to thinking that she couldn't be left alone out there, a girl ready to go wild, a woman whose family would not leave her, even dead, but stayed close to her, whispered, passed on their power. People said that she had to be harnessed. Maybe, I thought, Eli was the young man to do it, even though he couldn't rub two words together and get a spark.

So I gave in. I told him what he wanted to know. He asked me the old-time way to make a woman love him, and I went into detail so that he would make no disgraceful error. I told him about the first woman who had given herself to me. Sanawashonekek, her name was, The Lying-Down Grass, for the place where a deer has spent the night. I described the finicky taste of Omiimii, The Dove, and the trials I'd gone through to keep my second wife pleasured. Zezikaaikwe, The Unexpected, was a woman whose name was the exact prediction of her desires. I gave him a few things from the French trunk my third wife left—a white woman's fan, bead leggings, a little girl's soft doll made of fawn skin.

When Eli Kashpaw stroked their beauty and asked where these things had come from, I remembered the old days, opened my mouth.

Talk is an old man's last vice.

I wore out the boy's ears, but that is not my fault. I shouldn't have been caused to live so long, been shown so much of death, had to squeeze so many stories into the corners of my brain. They're all attached, and once I start, the telling doesn't end, because they're hooked from one side to the other, mouth to tail.

During the year of sickness, when I was the last one left, I saved myself by starting a story. One night I was ready to bring to the other side the fawn-skin doll I now gave Eli. My wife had sewn it together after our daughter died, and I held it in my hands when I fainted, lost breath so that I could hardly keep moving my lips. But I did continue and recovered. I got well by talking. Death could not get a word in edgewise, grew discouraged, and traveled on.

Eli returned to Fleur, and stopped badgering me, which I took as a sign she liked the fan, the bead leggings, and maybe the rest of Eli, the part where he was on his own. The thing I've found about women is that you must use every instinct to confuse.

"Look here," I told Eli, before he went out my door. "It's like you're a log in a stream. Along comes this bear. She jumps on. Don't let her dig in her claws."

So keeping Fleur off balance was what I presumed Eli was doing. But, as I learned in time, he was further along than that, way off and running beyond the reach of anything I said.

His mother was the one who gave me the news.

Margaret Kashpaw was a woman who had sunk her claws in the log and peeled it to a toothpick, and she wasn't going to let any man forget it. Especially me, her dead husband's partner in some youthful pursuits.

"Aneesh," she said, slamming my door shut. Margaret never knocked, because with warning you might get your breath, or escape. She was headlong, bossy, scared of nobody, and full of vinegar. She was a little woman, but so blinded by irritation that she'd take on anyone. She was thin on the top and plump as a turnip below, with a face like a round molasses cake. On each side of it gray plaits hung. With age her part had widened down the middle so that it looked as though the braids were slipping off her head. Her eyes were harsh, bright, and her tongue was honed keen. She sat right down.

"Would you care to know what you have my son doing?"

I mumbled, kept reading by the window, tucked my spectacles from Father Damien more comfortably around my ears. My newspaper came from Grand Forks once a week, and I wasn't about to let Margaret spoil my pleasure or get past my hiding place.

*"Sah!"* She swiped at the sheets with her hand, grazed the print, but never quite dared to flip it aside. This was not for any fear of me, however. She didn't

want the tracks rubbing off on her skin. She never learned to read, and the mystery troubled her.

I took advantage of that, snapped the paper in front of my face and sat for a moment. But she won, of course, because she knew I'd get curious. I felt her eyes glittering beyond the paper, and when I put the pages down, she continued.

"Who learned my Eli to make love standing up? Who learned him to have a woman against a tree in clear daylight? Who learned him to . . ."

"Wait," I said. "How'd you get to know this?"

She shrugged it off, and said in a smaller voice, "Boy Lazarre."

And I, who knew that the dirty Lazarres don't spy for nothing, just smiled.

"How much did you pay the fat-bellied dog?"

"The Lazarres are like animals in their season! No sense of shame!" But the wind was out of her. "Against the wall of the cabin," she said. "Down beside it. In grass and up in trees. Who'd he learn that from?"

"Maybe my late partner Kashpaw."

She puffed her cheeks out, fumed. "Not from him!"

"Not that you knew." I put my spectacles carefully upon the windowsill. Her hand could snake out quickly.

She hissed. The words flew like razor grass between her teeth. "Old man," she said with scorn. "Two wrinkled berries and a twig."

"A twig can grow," I offered.

"But only in the spring."

Then she was gone, out the door, leaving my tongue tingling for the last word, and still ignorant of the full effect of my advice. I didn't wonder until later if it didn't go both ways, though—if Fleur had wound her private hairs around the buttons of Eli's shirt, if she had stirred smoky powders or crushed snakeroot into his tea. Perhaps she had bitten his nails in sleep and swallowed the ends, snipped threads from his clothing and made a doll of them to wear between her legs. For they got bolder, until the whole reservation gossiped.

Then one day the big, unsteady Lazarre, an Indian on whose birth certificate was recorded simply "Boy," returned from the woods talking backwards, garbled, mixing his words. At first people thought the sights of passion had cleft his mind. Then they figured otherwise, imagined that Fleur had caught Lazarre watching and tied him up, cut his tongue out, and sewn it in reversed.

The same day I heard this, Margaret burst into my house a second time.

"Take me out to their place, you four-eyes," she said. "And be ready with the boat tomorrow, sunup!"

She stamped through the door and vanished, leaving me with hardly time enough to patch the seams and holes of the old-time boat I kept, dragged up in a brush shelter on the quieter inlet, the south end of the lake. I took some boiled pine gum to the seams that afternoon, and did my best. I was drawn to the situation, curious myself, and though I didn't want to spy either on the girl whose life I'd saved or on the boy I'd advised on courting, I was down by the water with the paddles at dawn.

The light was chill and green, the waves on the lake were small, confused ripples, and no steady wind had gathered. The water could be deceptive, set snares for the careless young or for withered-up and eager fools like ourselves. I put my hand in the current.

"Margaret," I said, "the lake's too cold. I never could swim, either, not that well."

But Margaret had set her mind, and made her peace, too.

"If he wants me"—she was talking about the lake spirit but, out of caution, using no names—"I'll give him good as I get."

"Oh," I said, "has it been that long, Margaret?"

Her eyes lit and I wished I had kept my mouth shut. But she only commented, later, after we had launched, "Not so long that I would consider the dregs."

I handed her the lard can I kept my bait in. "You better take this, Margaret. You better bail."

So at least on that long trip across I had the satisfaction of seeing her bend to the dipping and pouring with a sour but desperate will. We rode low. The water covered our ankles by the time we beached on shore, but Margaret was forced to shut her mouth in a firm line. The whole idea had been hers. She was so relieved to stand finally upon solid ground that she helped me haul the boat and wedge it in a pile of mangled roots. She wrung her skirt and sat beside me, panting. She shared some dried meat from the pocket of her dress, tore at it like a young snapping turtle. How I envied her sharp, strong teeth.

"Go on, eat," she said, "or I'll take an insult."

I put the jerky into my mouth.

"That's right," she sneered. "Suck long enough and it will soften."

I had no choice. I could think of no other way to get any of it down.

"Go now," I said, after a while. "I was thinking. I had this old barren she-dog once. She'd back up to anything. But the only satisfaction she could get was from watching the young."

Margaret jumped to her feet, skirts flapping. I had said too much. Her claws gave my ears too fast, furious jerks that set me whirling, sickening me so that I couldn't balance or even keep track of time. She took herself up the bank and into the Pillager woods, but I don't know when she went there or how long she stayed, and I had barely set myself to rights before she returned.

By then the sky had gone dead gray, the waves rolled white and fitful. Margaret took tobacco from a pouch in her pocket, threw it on the water, and said a few distracted, imploring words. We jumped into the boat, which leaked worse than ever, and pushed off. The wind blew harsh, in heavy circular gusts, and I was hard put. I never saw the bailing can move so fast, before or since. The old woman made it flash and dip, and hardly even broke the rhythm when, halfway across, she reached into her pocket again and this time dumped the whole pouch into the pounding waves. From then on she alternated between working her arms and addressing different Manitous[2] along with the Blessed Virgin and Her heart, the sacred bloody lump that the blue-robed woman held in the awful picture Margaret kept nailed to her wall. We made it back by the time rain poured down, and hoisted ourselves over the edge of the boat. When

2. Great spirits.

we got back to my house, after she'd swallowed some warm broth and her clothes had begun to steam dry upon her, Margaret told me what she had seen with her own eyes.

Fleur Pillager was pregnant, going to have a child in spring. At least that's what Margaret had decided with her measuring gaze. I stirred the fire with my walking stick. Maybe I had a shiver, a feeling, a worry. I was close as a relative, closer perhaps. Maybe I knew already that when spring did come, the ice milky, porous, and broken, Margaret and I were the ones who would have to save Fleur a second time.

Margaret, however, had no such premonition. The child would turn out fork-footed, she predicted, with straw for hair, yellow as the agent's. Its eyes would glow blue, its skin shine white. As she sipped from her cup, Margaret's memory of the agent made a monster, and she savored the variations the child might reveal: red, flapping ears, a strange birthmark, chicken lips, an extra finger, by which the taint of its conception would be certain and people convinced, at last, that it did not belong to her son.

The morning we got word, the water had just opened for a boat, if you dared to travel that way so early in spring. Fleur was in trouble with her baby. That's all I heard, as the women kept the particulars to themselves. Out of desperation Eli had run to Margaret on the way to the midwife's. He wanted us to take the shortcut and stay with Fleur until he brought back the woman whose hands held the wisdom, who wore the dried caul of a rabbit in a little belt around her waist.

Margaret was puffed up, full of satisfaction, until she saw the boat, leaking even more than usual after another winter of neglect. On the ride, bailing for her life, Margaret raged at me between her prayers and muttered strict assurances that her reasons for helping in this matter were not ties of kinship. Her presence did not count as acknowledgment, she said. It was her duty to see the evidence, whatever that turned out to be—the hair gold as straw, the blazing eyes.

But the child had none of those markings.

She was born on the day we shot the last bear, drunk, on the reservation. The midwife was the one who shot it, and the bear was drunk, not her. That she-bear had broken into the trader's wine I had brought across the lake beneath my jacket and then stowed in a rotten stump off in the woods behind the house. She bit the cork and emptied the white clay jug. Then she lost her mind and stumbled into the beaten grass of Fleur's yard.

By then we were a day in the waiting. In all that time we heard not a sound from Fleur's cabin, just crushing silence, like the inside of a drum before the stick drops. Eli and I slumped against the woodpile. We made a fire, swaddled ourselves in blankets. My stomach creaked with the lack of food, for Eli was starving himself from worry and I hated to eat in front of him. His eyes were rimmed with blood as he moaned and talked and prayed beneath the burden, which grew heavier.

On the second day we leaned to the fire, strained for the sound of the cry a baby makes. Our ears picked up everything in the woods, the rustle of birds, the crack of dead spring leaves and twigs. Our hearing had by then grown so keen that we heard the muffled sounds the women made inside the house. Now we heard other activity, which gave us hope. The stove lid clanked, pans rang together. Margaret came to the door and we heard the tear of water splashing on the ground. Eli moved then, fetched more. But not until the afternoon of that second day did the stillness finally break, and then the Manitous all through the woods seemed to speak through Fleur, loose, arguing. I recognized them. Turtle's quavering scratch, Eagle's high shriek, Loon's crazy bitterness, Otter, the howl of Wolf, Bear's low rasp.

Perhaps the bear heard Fleur calling, and answered.

I was alone when it happened, because Eli had broken when the silence shattered, slashed his arm with his hunting knife, and run out of the clearing, straight north. I sat quietly after he was gone, and sampled the food that he had refused. I drew close to the fire, settled my back against the split logs, and was just about to have a second helping when the drunk bear rambled past. She sniffed the ground, rolled over in an odor that pleased her, drew up and sat, addled, on her haunches like a dog. I jumped straight onto the top of the woodpile—I don't know how, since my limbs were so stiff from the wet cold. I crouched, yelled at the house, screamed for the gun, but only attracted the bear. She dragged herself over, gave a drawn-out whine, a cough, and fixed me with a long patient stare.

Margaret flung the door open. "Shoot it, you old fool," she hollered. But I was empty-handed. Margaret was irritated with this trifle, put out that I had not obeyed her, anxious to get rid of the nuisance and go back to Fleur. She marched straight toward us. Her face was pinched with exhaustion, her pace furious. Her arms moved like pistons, and she came so fast that she and the bear were face to face before she realized that she had nothing with which to attack. She was sensible, Margaret Kashpaw, and turned straight around. Fleur kept her gun above the flour cupboard in a rack of antlers. The bear followed, heeling Margaret like a puppy, and at the door to the house, when Margaret turned, arms spread to bar the way, it swatted her aside with one sharp, dreamy blow. Then it ambled in and reared on its hind legs.

I am a man, so I don't know exactly what happened when the bear came into the birth house, but they talk among themselves, the women, and sometimes they forget I'm listening. So I know that when Fleur saw the bear in the house she was filled with such fear and power that she raised herself on the mound of blankets and gave birth. Then the midwife took down the gun and shot point-blank, filling the bear's heart. She says so, anyway. But Margaret says that the lead only gave the bear strength, and I'll support that. For I heard the gun go off and then saw the creature whirl and roar from the house. It barreled past me, crashed through the brush into the woods, and was not seen after. It left no trail, either, so it could have been a spirit bear. I don't know. I was still on the woodpile.

I took the precaution of finishing my meal there. From what I overheard later, they were sure Fleur was dead, she was so cold and still after giving birth. But then the baby cried. That I heard with my own ears. At that sound, they say, Fleur opened her eyes and breathed. That was when the women went to work and saved her, packed moss between her legs, wrapped her in blankets heated with stones, kneaded Fleur's stomach and forced her to drink cup after cup of boiled raspberry leaf, until at last Fleur groaned, drew the baby against her breast, and lived.

# WILLIAM FAULKNER

*Faulkner (1897–1962) was born in New Albany, Mississippi. His family had included wealthy and powerful people ruined by the Civil War. His great-grandfather was a popular novelist; and this ancestor served, like other family members, as a model from whom Faulkner drew traits used in composing the characters in his fiction. He attended the University of Mississippi in Oxford before and after his service in the Royal Canadian Air Force in World War I. Thereafter, he lived in Oxford most of his life, though he spent much time in Hollywood as a screenwriter. It was in New Orleans that his literary career began. There he met Sherwood Anderson, who encouraged him to turn from poetry to fiction and helped him get his first novel published. His work, which won Faulkner a Nobel Prize in 1950, is largely a depiction of life in his fictional Yoknapatawpha County, an imaginative reconstruction of the area adjacent to Oxford. Faulkner was a passionately devoted hunter, and his love of the disappearing wilderness is expressed in many of his tales. He sought out the honor and courage of people balked by circumstance, and the sum of his writing testifies to his faith that these virtues will prevail through the corruptions of modern life. His major novels were mostly the product of a prodigious decade of creative effort. They include* The Sound and the Fury *(1929),* As I Lay Dying *(1930),* Sanctuary *(1931),* Light in August *(1932),* Absalom, Absalom! *(1936),* Wild Palms *(1939), and* The Hamlet *(1940). His books of short stories include* These Thirteen *(1931),* Go Down, Moses *(1942), and the* Collected Stories of William Faulkner *(1950).*

## Barn Burning

The store in which the Justice of the Peace's court was sitting smelled of cheese. The boy, crouched on his nail keg at the back of the crowded room, knew he smelled cheese, and more: from where he sat he could see the ranked shelves close-packed with the solid, squat, dynamic shapes of tin cans whose labels his stomach read, not from the lettering which meant nothing to his mind but from the scarlet devils and the silver curve of fish—this, the cheese which he knew he smelled and the hermetic meat[1] which his intestines believed he smelled coming in intermittent gusts momentary and brief between the other constant one, the smell and sense just a little of fear because mostly of despair and grief, the old fierce pull of blood. He could not see the table where the Justice sat and before which his father and his father's enemy *(our enemy* he thought in that despair; *ourn! mine and hisn both! He's my father!)* stood, but

1. Canned meat.

he could hear them, the two of them that is, because his father had said no word yet:

"But what proof have you, Mr. Harris?"

"I told you. The hog got into my corn. I caught it up and sent it back to him. He had no fence that would hold it. I told him so, warned him. The next time I put the hog in my pen. When he came to get it I gave him enough wire to patch up his pen. The next time I put the hog up and kept it. I rode down to his house and saw the wire I gave him still rolled on to the spool in his yard. I told him he could have the hog when he paid me a dollar pound fee. That evening a nigger came with the dollar and got the hog. He was a strange nigger. He said, 'He say to tell you wood and hay kin burn.' I said, 'What?' 'That whut he say to tell you,' the nigger said. 'Wood and hay kin burn.' That night my barn burned. I got the stock out but I lost the barn."

"Where is the nigger? Have you got him?"

"He was a strange nigger, I tell you. I don't know what became of him."

"But that's not proof. Don't you see that's not proof?"

"Get that boy up here. He knows." For a moment the boy thought too that the man meant his older brother until Harris said, "Not him. The little one. The boy," and, crouching, small for his age, small and wiry like his father, in patched and faded jeans even too small for him, with straight, uncombed, brown hair and eyes gray and wild as storm scud, he saw the men between himself and the table part and become a lane of grim faces, at the end of which he saw the Justice, a shabby, collarless, graying man in spectacles, beckoning him. He felt no floor under his bare feet; he seemed to walk beneath the palpable weight of the grim turning faces. His father, stiff in his black Sunday coat donned not for the trial but for the moving, did not even look at him. *He aims for me to lie,* he thought, again with that frantic grief and despair. *And I will have to do hit.*

"What's your name, boy?" the Justice said.

"Colonel Sartoris Snopes,"[2] the boy whispered.

"Hey?" the Justice said. "Talk louder. Colonel Sartoris? I reckon anybody named for Colonel Sartoris in this country can't help but tell the truth, can they?" The boy said nothing. *Enemy! Enemy!* he thought; for a moment he could not even see, could not see that the Justice's face was kindly nor discern that his voice was troubled when he spoke to the man named Harris: "Do you want me to question this boy?" But he could hear, and during those subsequent long seconds while there was absolutely no sound in the crowded little room save that of quiet and intent breathing it was as if he had swung outward at the end of a grape vine, over a ravine, and at the top of the swing had been caught in a prolonged instant of mesmerized gravity, weightless in time.

"No!" Harris said violently, explosively. "Damnation! Send him out of here!" Now time, the fluid world, rushed beneath him again, the voices coming to him again through the smell of cheese and sealed meat, the fear and despair and the old grief of blood:

2. The Snopes family figures in many Faulkner stories and novels. Colonel Sartoris is a major personage among Faulkner's fictional inhabitants of Yoknapatawpha County.

"This case is closed. I can't find against you, Snopes, but I can give you advice. Leave this country and don't come back to it."

His father spoke for the first time, his voice cold and harsh, level, without emphasis: "I aim to. I don't figure to stay in a country among people who . . ." he said something unprintable and vile, addressed to no one.

"That'll do," the Justice said. "Take your wagon and get out of this country before dark. Case dismissed."

His father turned, and he followed the stiff black coat, the wiry figure walking a little stiffly from where a Confederate provost's man's[3] musket ball had taken him in the heel on a stolen horse thirty years ago, followed the two backs now, since his older brother had appeared from somewhere in the crowd, no taller than the father but thicker, chewing tobacco steadily, between the two lines of grim-faced men and out of the store and across the worn gallery and down the sagging steps and among the dogs and half-grown boys in the mild May dust, where as he passed a voice hissed:

"Barn burner!"

Again he could not see, whirling; there was a face in a red haze, moonlike, bigger than the full moon, the owner of it half again his size, he leaping in the red haze toward the face, feeling no blow, feeling no shock when his head struck the earth, scrabbling up and leaping again, feeling no blow this time either and tasting no blood, scrabbling up to see the other boy in full flight and himself already leaping into pursuit as his father's hand jerked him back, the harsh, cold voice speaking above him: "Go get in the wagon."

It stood in a grove of locusts and mulberries across the road. His two hulking sisters in their Sunday dresses and his mother and her sister in calico and sunbonnets were already in it, sitting on and among the sorry residue of the dozen and more movings which even the boy could remember—the battered stove, the broken beds and chairs, the clock inlaid with mother-of-pearl, which would not run, stopped at some fourteen minutes past two o'clock of a dead and forgotten day and time, which had been his mother's dowry. She was crying, though when she saw him she drew her sleeve across her face and began to descend from the wagon. "Get back," the father said.

"He's hurt. I got to get some water and wash his . . ."

"Get back in the wagon," his father said. He got in too, over the tail-gate. His father mounted to the seat where the older brother already sat and struck the gaunt mules two savage blows with the peeled willow, but without heat. It was not even sadistic; it was exactly that same quality which in later years would cause his descendants to overrun the engine before putting a motor car into motion, striking and reining back in the same movement. The wagon went on, the store with its quiet crowd of grimly watching men dropped behind; a curve in the road hid it. *Forever* he thought. *Maybe he's done satisfied now, now that he has* . . . stopping himself, not to say it aloud even to himself. His mother's hand touched his shoulder.

"Does hit hurt?" she said.

3. Military policeman's.

"Naw," he said. "Hit don't hurt. Lemme be."

"Can't you wipe some of the blood off before hit dries?"

"I'll wash to-night," he said. "Lemme be, I tell you."

The wagon went on. He did not know where they were going. None of them ever did or ever asked, because it was always somewhere, always a house of sorts waiting for them a day or two days or even three days away. Likely his father had already arranged to make a crop on another farm before he . . . Again he had to stop himself. He (the father) always did. There was something about his wolf-like independence and even courage when the advantage was at least neutral which impressed strangers, as if they got from his latent ravening ferocity not so much a sense of dependability as a feeling that his ferocious conviction in the rightness of his own actions would be of advantage to all whose interest lay with his.

That night they camped, in a grove of oaks and beeches where a spring ran. The nights were still cool and they had a fire against it, of a rail lifted from a nearby fence and cut into lengths—a small fire, neat, niggard almost, a shrewd fire; such fires were his father's habit and custom always, even in freezing weather. Older, the boy might have remarked this and wondered why not a big one; why should not a man who had not only seen the waste and extravagance of war, but who had in his blood an inherent voracious prodigality with material not his own, have burned everything in sight? Then he might have gone a step farther and thought that that was the reason: that niggard blaze was the living fruit of nights passed during those four years in the woods hiding from all men, blue or gray, with his strings of horses (captured horses, he called them). And older still, he might have divined the true reason: that the element of fire spoke to some deep mainspring of his father's being, as the element of steel or of powder spoke to other men, as the one weapon for the preservation of integrity, else breath were not worth the breathing, and hence to be regarded with respect and used with discretion.

But he did not think this now and he had seen those same niggard blazes all his life. He merely ate his supper beside it and was already half asleep over his iron plate when his father called him, and once more he followed the stiff back, the stiff and ruthless limp, up the slope and on to the starlit road where, turning, he could see his father against the stars but without face or depth—a shape black, flat, and bloodless as though cut from tin in the iron folds of the frockcoat which had not been made for him, the voice harsh like tin and without heat like tin:

"You were fixing to tell them. You would have told him." He didn't answer. His father struck him with the flat of his hand on the side of the head, hard but without heat, exactly as he had struck the two mules at the store, exactly as he would strike either of them with any stick in order to kill a horse fly, his voice still without heat or anger: "You're getting to be a man. You got to learn. You got to learn to stick to your own blood or you ain't going to have any blood to stick to you. Do you think either of them, any man there this morning, would? Don't you know all they wanted was a chance to get at me because they knew I had them beat? Eh?" Later, twenty years later, he was to tell himself, "If I had said they wanted only truth, justice, he would have hit me again." But now he said nothing. He was not crying. He just stood there. "Answer me," his father said.

"Yes," he whispered. His father turned.

"Get on to bed. We'll be there tomorrow."

Tomorrow they were there. In the early afternoon the wagon stopped before a paintless two-room house identical almost with the dozen others it had stopped before even in the boy's ten years, and again, as on the other dozen occasions, his mother and aunt got down and began to unload the wagon, although his two sisters and his father and brother had not moved.

"Likely hit ain't fitten for hawgs," one of the sisters said.

"Nevertheless, fit it will and you'll hog it and like it," his father said. "Get out of them chairs and help your Ma unload."

The two sisters got down, big, bovine, in a flutter of cheap ribbons; one of them drew from the jumbled wagon bed a battered lantern, the other a worn broom. His father handed the reins to the older son and began to climb stiffly over the wheel. "When they get unloaded, take the team to the barn and feed them." Then he said, and at first the boy thought he was still speaking to his brother: "Come with me."

"Me?" he said.

"Yes," his father said. "You."

"Abner," his mother said. His father paused and looked back—the harsh level stare beneath the shaggy, graying, irascible brows.

"I reckon I'll have a word with the man that aims to begin to-morrow owning me body and soul for the next eight months."

They went back up the road. A week ago—or before last night, that is—he would have asked where they were going, but not now. His father had struck him before last night but never before had he paused afterward to explain why; it was as if the blow and the following calm, outrageous voice still rang, repercussed, divulging nothing to him save the terrible handicap of being young, the light weight of his few years, just heavy enough to prevent his soaring free of the world as it seemed to be ordered but not heavy enough to keep him footed solid in it, to resist it and try to change the course of its events.

Presently he could see the grove of oaks and cedars and the other flowering trees and shrubs, where the house would be, though not the house yet. They walked beside a fence massed with honeysuckle and Cherokee roses and came to a gate swinging open between two brick pillars, and now, beyond a sweep of drive, he saw the house for the first time and at that instant he forgot his father and the terror and despair both, and even when he remembered his father again (who had not stopped) the terror and despair did not return. Because, for all the twelve movings, they had sojourned until now in a poor country, a land of small farms and fields and houses, and he had never seen a house like this before. *Hit's big as a courthouse* he thought quietly, with a surge of peace and joy whose reason he could not have thought into words, being too young for that: *They are safe from him. People whose lives are a part of this peace and dignity are beyond his touch, he no more to them than a buzzing wasp: capable of stinging for a little moment but that's all; the spell of this peace and dignity rendering even the barns and stable and cribs which belong to it impervious to the puny flames he might contrive* . . . this, the peace and joy, ebbing for an instant as he looked again at the stiff black back, the stiff and implacable limp of the figure which was not dwarfed by the house, for the reason that it had never looked big anywhere and which now, against the serene columned backdrop, had more than ever that impervious quality of something cut ruthlessly from tin, depthless, as though, sidewise to the sun, it would cast no shadow. Watching him, the boy remarked the absolutely undeviating course which his father held and saw the stiff foot come squarely down in a pile of fresh droppings where a horse had stood in the drive and which his father could have avoided by a simple change of stride. But it ebbed only for a moment, though he could not have thought this into words either, walking on in the spell of the house, which he could even want but without envy, without sorrow, certainly never with that ravening and jealous rage which unknown to him walked in the ironlike black coat before him: *Maybe he will feel it too. Maybe it will even change him now from what maybe he couldn't help but be.*

They crossed the portico. Now he could hear his father's stiff foot as it came down on the boards with clocklike finality, a sound out of all proportion to the displacement of the body it bore and which was not dwarfed either by the white door before it, as though it had attained to a sort of vicious and ravening minimum not to be dwarfed by anything—the flat, wide, black hat, the formal coat of broadcloth which had once been black but which had now that friction-glazed greenish cast of the bodies of old house flies, the lifted sleeve which was too large, the lifted hand like a curled claw. The door opened so promptly that the boy knew the Negro must have been watching them all the time, an old man with neat grizzled hair, in a linen jacket, who stood barring the door with his body, saying, "Wipe yo foots, white man, fo you come in here. Major ain't home nohow."

"Get out of my way, nigger," his father said, without heat too, flinging the door back and the Negro also and entering, his hat still on his head. And now the boy saw the prints of the stiff foot on the doorjamb and saw them appear on the pale rug behind the machinelike deliberation of the foot which seemed to bear (or transmit) twice the weight which the body compassed. The Negro was shouting "Miss Lula! Miss Lula!" somewhere behind them, then the boy, deluged as though by a warm wave by a suave turn of carpeted stair and a pendant glitter of chandeliers and a mute gleam of gold frames, heard the swift feet and saw her too, a lady—perhaps he had never seen her like before either—in a gray, smooth gown with lace at the throat and an apron tied at the waist and the sleeves turned back, wiping cake or biscuit dough from her hands with a towel as she came up the hall, looking not at his father at all but at the tracks on the blond rug with an expression of incredulous amazement.

"I tried," the Negro cried. "I tole him to . . ."

"Will you please go away?" she said in a shaking voice. "Major de Spain is not at home. Will you please go away?"

His father had not spoken again. He did not speak again. He did not even look at her. He just stood stiff in the center of the rug, in his hat, the shaggy iron-gray brows twitching slightly above the pebble-colored eyes as he appeared to examine the house with brief deliberation. Then with the same deliberation he turned; the boy watched him pivot on the good leg and saw the stiff foot drag round the arc of the turning, leaving a final long and fading smear. His father never looked at it, he never once looked down at the rug. The Negro held the door. It closed behind them, upon the hysteric and indistinguishable woman-wail. His father stopped at the top of the steps and scraped his boot clean on the edge of it. At the gate he stopped again. He stood for a moment, planted stiffly on the stiff foot, looking back at the house. "Pretty and white, ain't it?" he said. "That's sweat. Nigger sweat. Maybe it ain't white enough yet to suit him. Maybe he wants to mix some white sweat with it."

Two hours later the boy was chopping wood behind the house within which his mother and aunt and the two sisters (the mother and aunt, not the two girls, he knew that; even at this distance and muffled by walls the flat loud voices of the two girls emanated an incorrigible idle inertia) were setting up the stove to prepare a meal, when he heard the hooves and saw the linen-clad man on a fine sorrel mare, whom he recognized even before he saw the rolled rug in front of the Negro youth following on a fat bay carriage horse—a suffused, angry face vanishing, still at full gallop, beyond the corner of the house where his father and brother were sitting in the two tilted chairs; and a moment later, almost before he could have put the axe down, he heard the hooves again and watched the sorrel mare go back out of the yard, already galloping again. Then his father began to shout one of the sisters' names, who presently emerged backward from the kitchen door dragging the rolled rug along the ground by one end while the other sister walked behind it.

"If you ain't going to tote, go on and set up the wash pot," the first said.

"You, Sarty!" the second shouted. "Set up the wash pot!" His father appeared at the door, framed against that shabbiness, as he had been against that other bland perfection, impervious to either, the mother's anxious face at his shoulder.

"Go on," the father said. "Pick it up." The two sisters stooped, broad, lethargic; stooping, they presented an incredible expanse of pale cloth and a flutter of tawdry ribbons.

"If I thought enough of a rug to have to git hit all the way from France I wouldn't keep hit where folks coming in would have to tromp on hit," the first said. They raised the rug.

"Abner," the mother said. "Let me do it."

"You go back and git dinner," his father said. "I'll tend to this."

From the woodpile through the rest of the afternoon the boy watched them, the rug spread flat in the dust beside the bubbling wash pot, the two sisters stooping over it with that profound and lethargic reluctance, while the father stood over them in turn, implacable and grim, driving them though never raising his voice again. He could smell the harsh homemade lye[4] they were using; he saw his mother come to the door once and look toward them with an expression not anxious now but very like despair; he saw his father turn, and he fell to with the axe and saw from the corner of his eye his father raise from

4. A caustic, unsuitable for cleaning fine fabrics.

the ground a flattish fragment of field stone and examine it and return to the pot, and this time his mother actually spoke: "Abner. Abner. Please don't. Please, Abner."

Then he was done too. It was dusk; the whippoorwills had already begun. He could smell coffee from the room where they would presently eat the cold food remaining from the mid-afternoon meal, though when he entered the house he realized they were having coffee again probably because there was a fire on the hearth, before which the rug now lay spread over the backs of the two chairs. The tracks of his father's foot were gone. Where they had been were now long, water-cloudy scoriations resembling the sporadic course of a Lilliputian mowing machine.

It still hung there while they ate the cold food and then went to bed, scattered without order or claim up and down the two rooms, his mother in one bed, where his father would later lie, the older brother in the other, himself, the aunt, and the two sisters on pallets on the floor. But his father was not in bed yet. The last thing the boy remembered was the depthless, harsh silhouette of the hat and coat bending over the rug and it seemed to him that he had not even closed his eyes when the silhouette was standing over him, the fire almost dead behind it, the stiff foot prodding him awake. "Catch up the mule," his father said.

When he returned with the mule his father was standing in the black door, the rolled rug over his shoulder. "Ain't you going to ride?" he said.

"No. Give me your foot."

He bent his knee into his father's hand, the wiry, surprising power flowed smoothly, rising, he rising with it, on to the mule's bare back (they had owned a saddle once; the boy could remember it though not when or where) and with the same effortlessness his father swung the rug up in front of him. Now in the starlight they retraced the afternoon's path, up the dusty road rife with honeysuckle, through the gate and up the black tunnel of the drive to the lightless house, where he sat on the mule and felt the rough warp of the rug drag across his thighs and vanish.

"Don't you want me to help?" he whispered. His father did not answer and now he heard again that stiff foot striking the hollow portico with that wooden and clocklike deliberation, that outrageous overstatement of the weight it carried. The rug, hunched, not flung (the boy could tell that even in the darkness) from his father's shoulder struck the angle of wall and floor with a sound unbelievably loud, thunderous, then the foot again, unhurried and enormous; a light came on in the house and the boy sat, tense, breathing steadily and quietly and just a little fast, though the foot itself did not increase its beat at all, descending the steps now; now the boy could see him.

"Don't you want to ride now?" he whispered. "We kin both ride now," the light within the house altering now, flaring up and sinking. *He's coming down the stairs now,* he thought. He had already ridden the mule up beside the horse block; presently his father was up behind him and he doubled the reins over and slashed the mule across the neck, but before the animal could begin to trot the hard, thin arm came round him, the hard, knotted hand jerking the mule back to a walk.

In the first red rays of the sun they were in the lot, putting plow gear on the mules. This time the sorrel mare was in the lot before he heard it at all, the rider collarless and even bareheaded, trembling, speaking in a shaking voice as the woman in the house had done, his father merely looking up once before stooping again to the hame he was buckling, so that the man on the mare spoke to his stooping back:

"You must realize you have ruined that rug. Wasn't there anybody here, any of your women . . . " he ceased, shaking, the boy watching him, the older brother leaning now in the stable door, chewing, blinking slowly and steadily at nothing apparently. "It cost a hundred dollars. But you never had a hundred dollars. You never will. So I'm going to charge you twenty bushels of corn against your crop. I'll add it in your contract and when you come to the commissary you can sign it. That won't keep Mrs. de Spain quiet but maybe it will teach you to wipe your feet off before you enter her house again."

Then he was gone. The boy looked at his father, who still had not spoken or even looked up again, who was now adjusting the logger-head in the hame.

"Pap," he said. His father looked at him—the inscrutable face, the shaggy brows beneath which the gray eyes glinted coldly. Suddenly the boy went toward him, fast, stopping as suddenly. "You done the best you could!" he cried. "If he wanted hit done different why didn't he wait and tell you how? He won't git no twenty bushels! He won't git none! We'll gether hit and hide hit! I kin watch . . ."

"Did you put the cutter back in that straight stock like I told you?"

"No, sir," he said.

"Then go do it."

That was Wednesday. During the rest of that week he worked steadily, at what was within his scope and some which was beyond it, with an industry that did not need to be driven nor even commanded twice; he had this from his mother, with the difference that some at least of what he did he liked to do, such as splitting wood with the half-size axe which his mother and aunt had earned, or saved money somehow, to present him with at Christmas. In company with the two older women (and on one afternoon, even one of the sisters), he built pens for the shoat and the cow which were a part of his father's contract with the landlord, and one afternoon, his father being absent, gone somewhere on one of the mules, he went to the field.

They were running a middle buster now, his brother holding the plow straight while he handled the reins, and walking beside the straining mule, the rich black soil shearing cool and damp against his bare ankles, he thought *Maybe this is the end of it. Maybe even that twenty bushels that seems hard to have to pay for just a rug will be a cheap price for him to stop forever and always from being what he used to be;* thinking, dreaming now, so that his brother had to speak sharply to him to mind the mule: *Maybe he even won't collect the twenty bushels. Maybe it will all add up and balance and vanish—corn, rug, fire; the terror and grief, the being pulled two ways like between two teams of horses—gone, done with for ever and ever.*

Then it was Saturday; he looked up from beneath the mule he was harnessing and saw his father in the black coat and hat. "Not that," his father said.

"The wagon gear." And then, two hours later, sitting in the wagon bed behind his father and brother on the seat, the wagon accomplished a final curve, and he saw the weathered paintless store with its tattered tobacco- and patent-medicine posters and the tethered wagons and saddle animals below the gallery. He mounted the gnawed steps behind his father and brother, and there again was the lane of quiet, watching faces for the three of them to walk through. He saw the man in spectacles sitting at the plank table and he did not need to be told this was a Justice of the Peace; he sent one glare of fierce, exultant, partisan defiance at the man in collar and cravat now, whom he had seen but twice before in his life, and that on a galloping horse, who now wore on his face an expression not of rage but of amazed unbelief which the boy could not have known was at the incredible circumstance of being sued by one of his own tenants, and came and stood against his father and cried at the Justice: "He ain't done it! He ain't burnt . . ."

"Go back to the wagon," his father said.

"Burnt?" the Justice said. "Do I understand this rug was burned too?"

"Does anybody here claim it was?" his father said. "Go back to the wagon." But he did not, he merely retreated to the rear of the room, crowded as that other had been, but not to sit down this time, instead, to stand pressing among the motionless bodies, listening to the voices:

"And you claim twenty bushels of corn is too high for the damage you did to the rug?"

"He brought the rug to me and said he wanted the tracks washed out of it. I washed the tracks out and took the rug back to him."

"But you didn't carry the rug back to him in the same condition it was in before you made the tracks on it."

His father did not answer, and now for perhaps half a minute there was no sound at all save that of breathing, the faint, steady suspiration of complete and intent listening.

"You decline to answer that, Mr. Snopes?" Again his father did not answer. "I'm going to find against you, Mr. Snopes. I'm going to find that you were responsible for the injury to Major de Spain's rug and hold you liable for it. But twenty bushels of corn seems a little high for a man in your circumstances to have to pay. Major de Spain claims it cost a hundred dollars. October corn will be worth about fifty cents. I figure that if Major de Spain can stand a ninety-five dollar loss on something he paid cash for, you can stand a five-dollar loss you haven't earned yet. I hold you in damages to Major de Spain to the amount of ten bushels of corn over and above your contract with him, to be paid to him out of your crop at gathering time. Court adjourned."

It had taken no time hardly, the morning was but half begun. He thought they would return home and perhaps back to the field, since they were late, far behind all other farmers. But instead his father passed on behind the wagon, merely indicating with his hand for the older brother to follow with it, and crossed the road toward the blacksmith shop opposite, pressing on after his father, overtaking him, speaking, whispering up at the harsh, calm face beneath the weathered hat: "He won't git no ten bushels neither. He won't git one. We'll . . . " until his father glanced for an instant down at him, the face absolutely calm, the grizzled eyebrows tangled above the cold eyes, the voice almost pleasant, almost gentle:

"You think so? Well, we'll wait till October anyway."

The matter of the wagon—the setting of a spoke or two and the tightening of the tires—did not take long either, the business of the tires accomplished by driving the wagon into the spring branch behind the shop and letting it stand there, the mules nuzzling into the water from time to time, and the boy on the seat with the idle reins, looking up the slope and through the sooty tunnel of the shed where the slow hammer rang and where his father sat on an upended cypress bolt, easily, either talking or listening, still sitting there when the boy brought the dripping wagon up out of the branch and halted it before the door.

"Take them on to the shade and hitch," his father said. He did so and returned. His father and the smith and a third man squatting on his heels inside the door were talking, about crops and animals; the boy, squatting too in the ammoniac dust and hoof-parings and scales of rust, heard his father tell a long and unhurried story out of the time before the birth of the older brother even when he had been a professional horsetrader. And then his father came up beside him where he stood before a tattered last year's circus poster on the other side of the store, gazing rapt and quiet at the scarlet horses, the incredible poisings and convolutions of tulle and tights and the painted leers of comedians, and said, "It's time to eat."

But not at home. Squatting beside his brother against the front wall, he watched his father emerge from the store and produce from a paper sack a segment of cheese and divide it carefully and deliberately into three with his pocket knife and produce crackers from the same sack. They all three squatted on the gallery and ate, slowly, without talking; then in the store again, they drank from a tin dipper tepid water smelling of the cedar bucket and of living beech trees. And still they did not go home. It was a horse lot this time, a tall rail fence upon and along which men stood and sat and out of which one by one horses were led, to be walked and trotted and then cantered back and forth along the road while the slow swapping and buying went on and the sun began to slant westward, they—the three of them—watching and listening, the older brother with his muddy eyes and his steady, inevitable tobacco, the father commenting now and then on certain of the animals, to no one in particular.

It was after sundown when they reached home. They ate supper by lamplight, then, sitting on the doorstep, the boy watched the night fully accomplish, listening to the whippoorwills and the frogs, when he heard his mother's voice: "Abner! No! No! Oh, God. Oh, God. Abner!" and he rose, whirled, and saw the altered light through the door where a candle stub now burned in a bottle neck on the table and his father, still in the hat and coat, at once formal and burlesque as though dressed carefully for some shabby and ceremonial violence, emptying the reservoir of the lamp back into the five-gallon kerosene can from which it had been filled, while the mother tugged at his arm until he shifted the lamp to the other hand and flung her back, not savagely or viciously, just hard, into the wall, her hands flung out against the wall for balance, her mouth open and in her face the same quality of hopeless despair as had been in her voice. Then his father saw him standing in the door.

"Go to the barn and get that can of oil we were oiling the wagon with," he said. The boy did not move. Then he could speak.

"What . . . " he cried. "What are you . . ."

"Go get that oil," his father said. "Go."

Then he was moving, running, outside the house, toward the stable: this the old habit, the old blood which he had not been permitted to choose for himself, which had been bequeathed him willy nilly and which had run for so long (and who knew where, battening on what of outrage and savagery and lust) before it came to him. *I could keep on,* he thought. *I could run on and on and never look back, never need to see his face again. Only I can't. I can't,* the rusted can in his hand now, the liquid sploshing in it as he ran back to the house and into it, into the sound of his mother's weeping in the next room, and handed the can to his father.

"Ain't you going to even send a nigger?" he cried. "At least you sent a nigger before!"

This time his father didn't strike him. The hand came even faster than the blow had, the same hand which had set the can on the table with almost excruciating care flashing from the can toward him too quick for him to follow it, gripping him by the back of his shirt and on to tiptoe before he had seen it quit the can, the face stooping at him in breathless and frozen ferocity, the cold, dead voice speaking over him to the older brother, who leaned against the table, chewing with that steady, curious, sidewise motion of cows:

"Empty the can into the big one and go on. I'll catch up with you."

"Better tie him up to the bedpost," the brother said.

"Do like I told you," the father said. Then the boy was moving, his bunched shirt and the hard, bony hand between his shoulder-blades, his toes just touching the floor, across the room and into the other one, past the sisters sitting with spread heavy thighs in the two chairs over the cold hearth, and to where his mother and aunt sat side by side on the bed, the aunt's arms about his mother's shoulders.

"Hold him," the father said. The aunt made a startled movement. "Not you," the father said. "Lennie. Take hold of him. I want to see you do it." His mother took him by the wrist. "You'll hold him better than that. If he gets loose don't you know what he is going to do? He will go up yonder." He jerked his head toward the road. "Maybe I'd better tie him."

"I'll hold him," his mother whispered.

"See you do then." Then his father was gone, the stiff foot heavy and measured upon the boards, ceasing at last.

Then he began to struggle. His mother caught him in both arms, he jerking and wrenching at them. He would be stronger in the end, he knew that. But he had no time to wait for it. "Lemme go!" he cried. "I don't want to have to hit you!"

"Let him go!" the aunt said. "If he don't go, before God, I am going up there myself."

"Don't you see I can't?" his mother cried. "Sarty! Sarty! No! No! Help me, Lizzie!"

Then he was free. His aunt grasped at him but it was too late. He whirled, running, his mother stumbled forward on to her knees behind him, crying to the nearer sister: "Catch him, Net! Catch him!" But that was too late too, the sister (the sisters were twins, born at the same time, yet either of them now gave the impression of being, encompassing as much living meat and volume and weight as any other two of the family) not yet having begun to rise from the chair, her head, face, alone merely turned, presenting to him in the flying instant an astonishing expanse of young female features untroubled by any surprise even, wearing only an expression of bovine interest. Then he was out of the room, out of the house, in the mild dust of the starlit road and the heavy rifeness of honeysuckle, the pale ribbon unspooling with terrific slowness under his running feet, reaching the gate at last and turning in, running, his heart and lungs drumming, on up the drive toward the lighted house, the lighted door. He did not knock, he burst in, sobbing for breath, incapable for the moment of speech; he saw the astonished face of the Negro in the linen jacket without knowing when the Negro had appeared.

"De Spain!" he cried, panted. "Where's . . ." then he saw the white man too emerging from a white door down the hall. "Barn!" he cried. "Barn!"

"What?" the white man said. "Barn?"

"Yes!" the boy cried. "Barn!"

"Catch him!" the white man shouted.

But it was too late this time too. The Negro grasped his shirt, but the entire sleeve, rotten with washing, carried away, and he was out that door too and in the drive again, and had actually never ceased to run even while he was screaming into the white man's face.

Behind him the white man was shouting, "My horse! Fetch my horse!" and he thought for an instant of cutting across the park and climbing the fence into the road, but he did not know the park nor how high the vine-massed fence might be and he dared not risk it. So he ran on down the drive, blood and breath roaring; presently he was in the road again though he could not see it. He could not hear either: the galloping mare was almost upon him before he heard her, and even then he held his course, as if the very urgency of his wild grief and need must in a moment more find his wings, waiting until the ultimate instant to hurl himself aside and into the weed-choked roadside ditch as the horse thundered past and on, for an instant in furious silhouette against the stars, the tranquil early summer night sky which, even before the shape of the horse and rider vanished, stained abruptly and violently upward: a long, swirling roar incredible and soundless, blotting the stars, and he springing up and into the road again, running again, knowing it was too late yet still running even after he heard the shot and, an instant later, two shots, pausing now without knowing he had ceased to run, crying "Pap! Pap!", running again before he knew he had begun to run, stumbling, tripping over something and scrabbling up again without ceasing to run, looking backward over his shoulder at the glare as he got up, running on among the invisible trees, panting, sobbing, "Father! Father!"

At midnight he was sitting on the crest of a hill. He did not know it was midnight and he did not know how far he had come. But there was no glare behind him now and he sat now, his back toward what he had called home for four days anyhow, his face toward the dark woods which he would enter when breath was strong again, small, shaking steadily in the chill darkness, hugging himself into the remainder of his thin, rotten shirt, the grief and despair now no longer terror and fear but just grief and despair. *Father. My father,* he thought. "He was brave!" he cried suddenly, aloud but not loud, no more than a whisper: "He was! He was in the war! He was in Colonel Sartoris' cav'ry!" not knowing that his father had gone to that war a private in the fine old European sense, wearing no uniform, admitting the authority of and giving fidelity to no man or army or flag, going to war as Malbrouck[5] himself did: for booty—it meant nothing and less than nothing to him if it were enemy booty or his own.

The slow constellations wheeled on. It would be dawn and then sun-up after a while and he would be hungry. But that would be to-morrow and now he was only cold, and walking would cure that. His breathing was easier now and he decided to get up and go on, and then he found that he had been asleep because he knew it was almost dawn, the night almost over. He could tell that from the whippoorwills. They were everywhere now among the dark trees below him, constant and inflectioned and ceaseless, so that, as the instant for giving over to the day birds drew nearer and nearer, there was no interval at all between them. He got up. He was a little stiff, but walking would cure that too as it would the cold, and soon there would be the sun. He went on down the hill, toward the dark woods within which the liquid silver voices of the birds called unceasing—the rapid and urgent beating of the urgent and quiring heart of the late spring night. He did not look back.

# The Bear

## I

There was a man and a dog too this time. Two beasts, counting Old Ben, the bear, and two men, counting Boon Hogganbeck, in whom some of the same blood ran which ran in Sam Fathers, even though Boon's was a plebeian strain of it and only Sam and Old Ben and the mongrel Lion were taintless and incorruptible.

Isaac McCaslin was sixteen. For six years now he had been a man's hunter. For six years now he had heard the best of all talking. It was of the wilderness, the big woods, bigger and older than any recorded document—of white man fatuous enough to believe he had bought any fragment of it, of Indian ruthless enough to pretend that any fragment of it had been his to convey; bigger than Major de Spain and the scrap he pretended to, knowing better; older than old Thomas Sutpen of whom Major de Spain had had it and who knew better; older even than old Ikkemoutubbe, the Chickasaw chief, of whom old Sutpen had

5. The chief character in a popular and pervasive eighteenth-century nursery ditty about a legendary warrior. Originally, this warrior figure may have derived from the character and exploits of John Churchill (1650–1722), duke of Marlborough.

had it and who knew better in his turn. It was of the men, not white nor black nor red, but men, hunters, with the will and hardihood to endure and the humility and skill to survive, and the dogs and the bear and deer juxtaposed and reliefed against it, ordered and compelled by and within the wilderness in the ancient and unremitting contest according to the ancient and immitigable rules which voided all regrets and brooked no quarter;—the best game of all, the best of all breathing and forever the best of all listening, the voices quiet and weighty and deliberate for retrospection and recollection and exactitude among the concrete trophies—the racked guns and the heads and skins—in the libraries of town houses or the offices of plantation houses or (and best of all) in the camps themselves where the intact and still-warm meat yet hung, the men who had slain it sitting before the burning logs on hearths, when there were houses and hearths, or about the smoky blazing of piled wood in front of stretched tarpaulins when there were not. There was always a bottle present, so that it would seem to him that those fine fierce instants of heart and brain and courage and wiliness and speed were concentrated and distilled into that brown liquor which not women, not boys and children, but only hunters drank, drinking not of the blood they spilled but some condensation of the wild immortal spirit, drinking it moderately, humbly even, not with the pagan's base and baseless hope of acquiring thereby the virtues of cunning and strength and speed but in salute to them. Thus it seemed to him on this December morning not only natural but actually fitting that this should have begun with whiskey.

He realized later that it had begun long before that. It had already begun on that day when he first wrote his age in two ciphers and his cousin McCaslin[1] brought him for the first time to the camp, the big woods, to earn for himself from the wilderness the name and state of hunter provided he in his turn were humble and enduring enough. He had already inherited then, without ever having seen it, the big old bear with one trap-ruined foot that in an area almost a hundred miles square had earned for himself a name, a definite designation like a living man:—the long legend of corncribs broken down and rifled, of shoats and grown pigs and even calves carried bodily into the woods and devoured, and traps and deadfalls overthrown and dogs mangled and slain, and shotgun and even rifle shots delivered at point-blank range yet with no more effect than so many peas blown through a tube by a child—a corridor of wreckage and destruction beginning back before the boy was born, through which sped, not fast but rather with the ruthless and irresistible deliberation of a locomotive, the shaggy tremendous shape. It ran in his knowledge before he ever saw it. It loomed and towered in his dreams before he even saw the unaxed woods where it left its crooked print, shaggy, tremendous, red-eyed, not malevolent but just big, too big for the dogs which tried to bay it, for the horses which tried to ride it down, for the men and the bullets they fired into it; too big for the very country which was its constricting scope. It was as if the boy had already divined what his senses and intellect had not encompassed yet: that doomed wilderness whose edges were being constantly and punily gnawed at by men with plows and axes who feared it because it was wilderness, men

1. Carothers McCaslin Edmonds, called "Cass" later in the story.

myriad and nameless even to one another in the land where the old bear had earned a name, and through which ran not even a mortal beast but an anachronism indomitable and invincible out of an old, dead time, a phantom, epitome and apotheosis of the old, wild life which the little puny humans swarmed and hacked at in a fury of abhorrence and fear, like pygmies about the ankles of a drowsing elephant;—the old bear, solitary, indomitable, and alone; widowered, childless, and absolved of mortality—old Priam[2] reft of his old wife and outlived all his sons.

Still a child, with three years, then two years, then one year yet before he too could make one of them, each November he would watch the wagon containing the dogs and the bedding and food and guns and his cousin McCaslin and Tennie's Jim and Sam Fathers too, until Sam moved to the camp to live, depart for the Big Bottom, the big woods. To him, they were going not to hunt bear and deer but to keep yearly rendezvous with the bear which they did not even intend to kill. Two weeks later they would return, with no trophy, no skin. He had not expected it. He had not even feared that it might be in the wagon this time with the other skins and heads. He did not even tell himself that in three years or two years or one year more he would be present and that it might even be his gun. He believed that only after he had served his apprenticeship in the woods which would prove him worthy to be a hunter, would he even be permitted to distinguish the crooked print, and that even then for two November weeks he would merely make another minor one, along with his cousin and Major de Spain and General Compson and Walter Ewell and Boon and the dogs which feared to bay it, and the shotguns and rifles which failed even to bleed it, in the yearly pageant-rite of the old bear's furious immortality.

His day came at last. In the surrey with his cousin and Major de Spain and General Compson he saw the wilderness through a slow drizzle of November rain just above the ice point, as it seemed to him later he always saw it or at least always remembered it—the tall and endless wall of dense November woods under the dissolving afternoon and the year's death, sombre, impenetrable (he could not even discern yet how, at what point they could possibly hope to enter it even though he knew that Sam Fathers was waiting there with the wagon), the surrey moving through the skeleton stalks of cotton and corn in the last of open country, the last trace of man's puny gnawing at the immemorial flank, until, dwarfed by that perspective into an almost ridiculous diminishment, the surrey itself seemed to have ceased to move (this too to be completed later, years later, after he had grown to a man and had seen the sea) as a solitary small boat hangs in lonely immobility, merely tossing up and down, in the infinite waste of the ocean, while the water and then the apparently impenetrable land which it nears without appreciable progress, swings slowly and opens the widening inlet which is the anchorage. He entered it. Sam was waiting, wrapped in a quilt on the wagon seat behind the patient and steaming mules. He entered his novitiate to the true wilderness with Sam beside him as he had begun his apprenticeship in miniature to manhood after the rabbits and such with Sam beside him, the two of them wrapped in the damp, warm, Negro-

2. King of Troy at the time it was conquered by the Greeks.

rank quilt, while the wilderness closed behind his entrance as it had opened momentarily to accept him, opening before his advancement as it closed behind his progress, no fixed path the wagon followed but a channel nonexistent ten yards ahead of it and ceasing to exist ten yards after it had passed, the wagon progressing not by its own volition but by attrition of their intact yet fluid circumambience, drowsing, earless, almost lightless.

It seemed to him that at the age of ten he was witnessing his own birth. It was not even strange to him. He had experienced it all before, and not merely in dreams. He saw the camp—a paintless six-room bungalow set on piles above the spring high-water—and he knew already how it was going to look. He helped in the rapid orderly disorder of their establishment in it, and even his motions were familiar to him, foreknown. Then for two weeks he ate the coarse, rapid food—the shapeless sour bread, the wild strange meat, venison and bear and turkey and coon which he had never tasted before—which men ate, cooked by men who were hunters first and cooks afterward; he slept in harsh sheetless blankets as hunters slept. Each morning the gray of dawn found him and Sam Fathers on the stand, the crossing, which had been allotted him. It was the poorest one, the most barren. He had expected that; he had not dared yet to hope even to himself that he would even hear the running dogs this first time. But he did hear them. It was on the third morning—a murmur, sourceless, almost indistinguishable, yet he knew what it was although he had never before heard that many dogs running at once, the murmur swelling into separate and distinct voices until he could call the five dogs which his cousin owned from among the others. "Now," Sam said, "slant your gun up a little and draw back the hammers and then stand still."

But it was not for him, not yet. The humility was there; he had learned that. And he could learn the patience. He was only ten, only one week. The instant had passed. It seemed to him that he could actually see the deer, the buck, smoke-colored, elongated with speed, vanished, the woods, the gray solitude still ringing even when the voices of the dogs had died away; from far away across the sombre woods and the gray half-liquid morning there came two shots. "Now let your hammers down," Sam said.

He did so. "You knew it too," he said.

"Yes," Sam said. "I want you to learn how to do when you didn't shoot. It's after the chance for the bear or the deer has done already come and gone that men and dogs get killed."

"Anyway, it wasn't him," the boy said. "It wasn't even a bear. It was just a deer."

"Yes," Sam said, "it was just a deer."

Then one morning, it was in the second week, he heard the dogs again. This time before Sam even spoke he readied the too-long, too-heavy, man-size gun as Sam had taught him, even though this time he knew the dogs and the deer were coming less close than ever, hardly within hearing even. They didn't sound like any running dogs he had ever heard before even. Then he found that Sam, who had taught him first of all to cock the gun and take position where he could see best in all directions and then never to move again, had himself moved up beside him. "There," he said. "Listen." The boy listened, to no ringing chorus strong and fast on a free scent but, a moiling yapping an octave too high and with something more than indecision and even abjectness in it which he could not yet recognize, reluctant, not even moving very fast, taking a long time to pass out of hearing, leaving even then in the air that echo of thin and almost human hysteria, abject, almost humanly grieving, with this time nothing ahead of it, no sense of a fleeing unseen smoke-colored shape. He could hear Sam breathing at his shoulder. He saw the arched curve of the old man's inhaling nostrils.

"It's Old Ben!" he cried, whispering.

Sam didn't move save for the slow gradual turning of his head as the voices faded on and the faint steady rapid arch and collapse of his nostrils. "Hah," he said. "Not even running. Walking."

"But up here!" the boy cried. "Way up here!"

"He do it every year," Sam said. "Once. Ash and Boon say he comes up here to run the other little bears away. Tell them to get to hell out of here and stay out until the hunters are gone. Maybe." The boy no longer heard anything at all, yet still Sam's head continued to turn gradually and steadily until the back of it was toward him. Then it turned back and looked down at him—the same face, grave, familiar, expressionless until it smiled, the same old man's eyes from which as he watched there faded slowly a quality darkly and fiercely lambent, passionate and proud. "He don't care no more for bears than he does for dogs or men neither. He come to see who's here, who's new in camp this year, whether he can shoot or not. Whether we got the dog yet that can bay and hold him until a man gets there with a gun. Because he's the head bear. He's the man." It faded, was gone; again they were the eyes as he had known them all his life. "He'll let them follow him to the river. Then he'll send them home. We might as well go too; see how they look when they get back to camp."

The dogs were there first, ten of them huddled back under the kitchen, himself and Sam squatting to peer back into the obscurity where they crouched, quiet, the eyes rolling and luminous, vanishing, and no sound, only that effluvium which the boy could not quite place yet, of something more than dog, stronger than dog and not just animal, just beast even. Because there had been nothing in front of the abject and painful yapping except the solitude, the wilderness, so that when the eleventh hound got back about midafternoon and he and Tennie's Jim held the passive and still trembling bitch while Sam daubed her tattered ear and raked shoulder with turpentine and axle-grease, it was still no living creature but only the wilderness which, leaning for a moment, had patted lightly once her temerity. "Just like a man," Sam said. "Just like folks. Put off as long as she could having to be brave, knowing all the time that sooner or later she would have to be brave once so she could keep on calling herself a dog, and knowing beforehand what was going to happen when she done it."

He did not know just when Sam left. He only knew that he was gone. For the next three mornings he rose and ate breakfast and Sam was not waiting for him. He went to his stand alone; he found it without help now and stood on it as Sam had taught him. On the third morning he heard the dogs again, running strong and free on a true scent again, and he readied the gun as he had learned to do and heard the hunt sweep past on since he was not ready yet, had not deserved other yet in just one short period of two weeks as compared to all the long life which he had already dedicated to the wilderness with patience and humility; he heard the shot again, one shot, the single clapping report of Walter Ewell's rifle. By now he could not only find his stand and then return to camp without guidance, by using the compass his cousin had given him he reached Walter, waiting beside the buck and the moiling of dogs over the cast entrails, before any of the other except Major de Spain and Tennie's Jim on the horses, even before Uncle Ash arrived with the one-eyed wagon-mule which did not mind the smell of blood or even, so they said, of bear.

It was not Uncle Ash on the mule. It was Sam, returned. And Sam was waiting when he finished his dinner and, himself on the one-eyed mule and Sam on the other one of the wagon team, they rode for more than three hours through the rapid shortening sunless afternoon, following no path, no trail even that he could discern, into a section of country he had never seen before. Then he understood why Sam had made him ride the one-eyed mule which would not spook at the smell of blood, of wild animals. The other one, the sound one, stopped short and tried to whirl and bolt even as Sam got down, jerking and wrenching at the rein while Sam held it, coaxing it forward with his voice since he did not dare risk hitching it, drawing it forward while the boy dismounted from the marred one which would stand. Then, standing beside Sam in the thick great gloom of ancient woods and the winter's dying afternoon, he looked quietly down at the rotted log scored and gutted with clawmarks and, in the wet earth beside it, the print of the enormous warped two-toed foot. Now he knew what he had heard in the hounds' voices in the woods that morning and what he had smelled when he peered under the kitchen where they huddled. It was in him too, a little different because they were brute beasts and he was not, but only a little different—an eagerness, passive; an abjectness, a sense of his own fragility and impotence against the timeless woods, yet without doubt or dread; a flavor like brass in the sudden run of saliva in his mouth, a hard sharp constriction either in his brain or his stomach, he could not tell which and it did not matter; he knew only that for the first time he realized that the bear which had run in his listening and loomed in his dreams since before he could remember and which therefore must have existed in the listening and the dreams of his cousin and Major de Spain and even old General Compson before they began to remember in their turn, was a mortal animal and that they had departed for the camp each November with no actual intention of slaying it, not because it could not be slain but because so far they had no actual hope of being able to. "It will be tomorrow," he said.

"You mean we will try tomorrow," Sam said. "We ain't got the dog yet."

"We've got eleven," he said. "They ran him Monday."

"And you heard them," Sam said. "Saw them too. We ain't got the dog yet. It won't take but one. But he ain't there. Maybe he ain't nowhere. The only other way will be for him to run by accident over somebody that had a gun and knowed how to shoot it."

"That wouldn't be me," the boy said. "It would be Walter or Major or——"

"It might," Sam said. "You watch close tomorrow. Because he's smart.

That's how come he has lived this long. If he gets hemmed up and has got to pick out somebody to run over, he will pick out you."

"How?" he said. "How will he know. . . ." He ceased. "You mean he already knows me, that I ain't never been to the big bottom before, ain't had time to find out yet whether I . . . " He ceased again, staring at Sam; he said humbly, not even amazed: "It was me he was watching. I don't reckon he did need to come but once."

"You watch tomorrow," Sam said. "I reckon we better start back. It'll be long after dark now before we get to camp."

The next morning they started three hours earlier than they had ever done. Even Uncle Ash went, the cook, who called himself by profession a camp cook and who did little else save cook for Major de Spain's hunting and camping parties, yet who had been marked by the wilderness from simple juxtaposition to it until he responded as they all did, even the boy who until two weeks ago had never even seen the wilderness, to a hound's ripped ear and shoulder and the print of a crooked foot in a patch of wet earth. They rode. It was too far to walk: the boy and Sam and Uncle Ash in the wagon with the dogs, his cousin and Major de Spain and General Compson and Boon and Walter and Tennie's Jim riding double on the horses; again the first gray light found him, as on that first morning two weeks ago, on the stand where Sam had placed and left him. With the gun which was too big for him, the breech-loader which did not even belong to him but to Major de Spain and which he had fired only once, at a stump on the first day to learn the recoil and how to reload it with the paper shells, he stood against a big gum tree beside a little bayou whose black still water crept without motion out of a cane-break, across a small clearing and into the cane again, where, invisible, a bird, the big woodpecker called Lord-to-God by Negroes, clattered at a dead trunk. It was a stand like any other stand, dissimilar only in incidentals to the one where he had stood each morning for two weeks; a territory new to him yet no less familiar than that other one which after two weeks he had come to believe he knew a little—the same solitude, the same loneliness through which frail and timorous man had merely passed without altering it, leaving no mark nor scar, which looked exactly as it must have looked when the first ancestor of Sam Fathers' Chickasaw predecessors crept into it and looked about him, club or stone axe or bone arrow drawn and ready, different only because, squatting at the edge of the kitchen, he had smelled the dogs huddled and cringing beneath it and saw the raked ear and side of the bitch that, as Sam had said, had to be brave once in order to keep on calling herself a dog and saw yesterday in the earth beside the gutted log the print of the living foot. He heard no dogs at all. He never did certainly hear them. He only heard the drumming of the woodpecker stop short off, and knew that the bear was looking at him. He never saw it. He did not know whether it was facing him from the cane or behind him. He did not move, holding the useless gun which he knew now he would never fire at it, now or ever, tasting in his saliva that taint of brass which he had smelled in the huddled dogs when he peered under the kitchen.

Then it was gone. As abruptly as it had stopped, the woodpecker's dry hammering set up again, and after a while he believed he even heard the dogs—a murmur, scarce a sound even, which he had probably been hearing for a time, perhaps a minute or two, before he remarked it, drifting into hearing and then out again, dying away. They came nowhere near him. If it was dogs he heard, he could not have sworn to it; if it was a bear they ran, it was another bear. It was Sam himself who emerged from the cane and crossed the bayou, the injured bitch following at heel as a bird dog is taught to walk. She came and crouched against his leg, trembling. "I didn't see him," he said. "I didn't, Sam."

"I know it," Sam said. "He done the looking. You didn't hear him neither, did you?"

"No," the boy said. "I——"

"He's smart," Sam said. "Too smart." Again the boy saw in his eyes that quality of dark and brooding lambence as Sam looked down at the bitch trembling faintly and steadily against the boy's leg. From her raked shoulder a few drops of fresh blood clung like bright berries. "Too big. We ain't got the dog yet. But maybe some day."

Because there would be a next time, after and after. He was only ten. It seemed to him that he could see them, the two of them, shadowy in the limbo from which time emerged and became time: the old bear absolved of mortality and himself who shared a little of it. Because he recognized now what he had smelled in the huddled dogs and tasted in his own saliva, recognized fear as a boy, a youth, recognizes the existence of love and passion and experience which is his heritage but not yet his patrimony, from entering by chance the presence or perhaps even merely the bedroom of a woman who has loved and been loved by many men. *So I will have to see him,* he thought, without dread or even hope. *I will have to look at him.* So it was in June of the next summer. They were at the camp again, celebrating Major de Spain's and General Compson's birthdays. Although the one had been born in September and the other in the depth of winter and almost thirty years earlier, each June the two of them and McCaslin and Boon and Walter Ewell (and the boy too from now on) spent two weeks at the camp, fishing and shooting squirrels and turkey and running coons and wildcats with the dogs at night. That is, Boon and the Negroes (and the boy too now) fished and shot squirrels and ran the coons and cats, because the proven hunters, not only Major de Spain and old General Compson (who spent those two weeks sitting in a rocking chair before a tremendous iron pot of Brunswick stew, stirring and tasting, with Uncle Ash to quarrel with about how he was making it and Tennie's Jim to pour whiskey into the tin dipper from which he drank it), but even McCaslin and Walter Ewell who were still young enough, scorned such, other than shooting the wild gobblers with pistols for wagers or to test their marksmanship.

That is, his cousin McCaslin and the others thought he was hunting squirrels. Until the third evening he believed that Sam Fathers thought so too. Each morning he would leave the camp right after breakfast. He had his own gun now, a new breech-loader, a Christmas gift; he would own and shoot it for almost seventy years, through two new pairs of barrels and locks and one new stock, until all that remained of the original gun was the silver-inlaid trigger-guard with his and McCaslin's engraved names and the date in 1878. He found the tree beside the little bayou where he had stood that morning. Using the compass he ranged from that point; he was teaching himself to be better than a fair woodsman without even knowing he was doing it. On the third day he even found the gutted log where he had first seen the print. It was almost completely crumbled now, healing with unbelievable speed, a passionate and almost visible relinquishment, back into the earth from which the tree had grown. He ranged the summer woods now, green with gloom, if anything actually dimmer than they had been in November's gray dissolution, where even at noon the sun fell only in windless dappling upon the earth which never completely dried and which crawled with snakes—moccasins and watersnakes and rattlers, themselves the color of the dappled gloom so that he would not always see them until they moved; returning to camp later and later and later, first day, second day, passing in the twilight of the third evening the little log pen enclosing the log barn where Sam was putting up the stock for the night. "You ain't looked right yet," Sam said.

He stopped. For a moment he didn't answer. Then he said peacefully, in a peaceful rushing burst, as when a boy's miniature dam in a little brook gives way: "All right. Yes. But how? I went to the bayou. I even found that log again. I——"

"I reckon that was all right. Likely he's been watching you. You never saw his foot?"

"I . . ." the boy said, "I didn't . . . I never thought . . ."

"It's the gun," Sam said. He stood beside the fence, motionless, the old man, son of a Negro slave and a Chickasaw chief, in the battered and faded overalls and the frayed five-cent straw hat which had been the badge of the Negro's slavery and was now the regalia of his freedom. The camp—the clearing, the house, the barn and its tiny lot with which Major de Spain in his turn had scratched punily and evanescently at the wilderness—faded in the dusk, back into the immemorial darkness of the woods. *The gun*, the boy thought. *The gun.* "You will have to choose," Sam said.

He left the next morning before light, without breakfast, long before Uncle Ash would wake in his quilts on the kitchen floor and start the fire. He had only the compass and a stick for the snakes. He could go almost a mile before he would need to see the compass. He sat on a log, the invisible compass in his hand, while the secret night-sounds which had ceased at his movements, scurried again and then fell still for good and the owls ceased and gave over to the waking day birds and there was light in the gray wet woods and he could see the compass. He went fast yet still quietly, becoming steadily better and better as a woodsman without yet having time to realize it; he jumped a doe and a fawn, walked them out of the bed, close enough to see them—the crash of undergrowth, the white scut, the fawn scudding along behind her, faster than he had known it could have run. He was hunting right, upwind, as Sam had taught him, but that didn't matter now. He had left the gun; by his own will and relinquishment he had accepted not a gambit, not a choice, but a condition in which not only the bear's heretofore inviolable anonymity but all the ancient rules and balances of hunter and hunted had been abrogated. He would not even be afraid, not even in the moment when the fear would take him completely: blood, skin, bowels, bones, memory from the long time before it even became his memory—all save that thin clear quenchless lucidity which alone differed him from this bear and from all the other bears and bucks he would follow during almost seventy years, to which Sam had said: "Be scared. You can't help that. But don't be afraid. Ain't nothing in the woods going to hurt you if you don't corner it or it don't smell that you are afraid. A bear or a deer has got to be scared of a coward the same as a brave man has got to be."

By noon he was far beyond the crossing on the little bayou, farther into the new and alien country than he had ever been, traveling now not only by the compass but by the old, heavy, biscuit-thick silver watch which had been his father's. He had left the camp nine hours ago; nine hours from now, dark would already have been an hour old. He stopped, for the first time since he had risen from the log when he could see the compass face at last, and looked about, mopping his sweating face on his sleeve. He had already relinquished, of his will, because of his need, in humility and peace and without regret, yet apparently that had not been enough, the leaving of the gun was not enough. He stood for a moment—a child, alien and lost in the green and soaring gloom of the markless wilderness. Then he relinquished completely to it. It was the watch and the compass. He was still tainted. He removed the linked chain of the one and the looped thong of the other from his overalls and hung them on a bush and leaned the stick beside them and entered it.

When he realized he was lost, he did as Sam had coached and drilled him: made a cast to cross his backtrack. He had not been going very fast for the last two or three hours, and he had gone even less fast since he left the compass and watch on the bush. So he went slower still now, since the tree could not be very far; in fact, he found it before he really expected to and turned and went to it. But there was no bush beneath it, no compass nor watch, so he did next as Sam had coached and drilled him: made this next circle in the opposite direction and much larger, so that the pattern of the two of them would bisect his track somewhere, but crossing no trace nor mark anywhere of his feet or any feet, and now he was going faster though still not panicked, his heart beating a little more rapidly but strong and steady enough, and this time it was not even the tree because there was a down log beside it which he had never seen before and beyond the log a little swamp, a seepage of moisture somewhere between earth and water, and he did what Sam had coached and drilled him as the next and the last, seeing as he sat down on the log the crooked print, the warped indentation in the wet ground which while he looked at it continued to fill with water until it was level full and the water began to overflow and the sides of the print began to dissolve away. Even as he looked up he saw the next one, and moving, the one beyond it; moving, not hurrying, running, but merely keeping pace with them as they appeared before him as though they were being shaped out of thin air just one constant pace short of where he would lose them forever and be lost forever himself, tireless, eager, without doubt or dread, panting a little above the strong rapid little hammer of his heart, emerging suddenly into a little glade, and the wilderness coalesced. It rushed, soundless, and solidified—the tree, the bush, the compass and the watch glinting where a ray of sunlight touched them. Then he saw the bear. It did not emerge, appear:

it was just there, immobile, fixed in the green and windless noon's hot dappling, not as big as he had dreamed it but as big as he had expected, bigger, dimensionless against the dappled obscurity, looking at him. Then it moved. It crossed the glade without haste, walking for an instant into the sun's full glare and out of it, and stopped again and looked back at him across one shoulder. Then it was gone. It didn't walk into the woods. It faded, sank back into the wilderness without motion as he had watched a fish, a huge old bass, sink back into the dark depths of its pool and vanish without even any movement of its fins.

## II

So he should have hated and feared Lion. He was thirteen then. He had killed his buck and Sam Fathers had marked his face with the hot blood,[3] and in the next November he killed a bear. But before that accolade he had become as competent in the woods as many grown men with the same experience. By now he was a better woodsman than most grown men with more. There was no territory within twenty-five miles of the camp that he did not know—bayou, ridge, landmark trees and path; he could have led anyone direct to any spot in it and brought him back. He knew game trails that even Sam Fathers had never seen; in the third fall he found a buck's bedding-place by himself and unbeknown to his cousin he borrowed Walter Ewell's rifle and lay in wait for the buck at dawn and killed it when it walked back to the bed as Sam had told him how the old Chickasaw fathers did.

By now he knew the old bear's footprint better than he did his own, and not only the crooked one. He could see any one of the three sound prints and distinguished it at once from any other, and not only because of its size. There were other bears within that fifty miles which left tracks almost as large, or at least so near that the one would have appeared larger only by juxtaposition. It was more than that. If Sam Fathers had been his mentor and the backyard rabbits and squirrels his kindergarten, then the wilderness the old bear ran was his college and the old male bear itself, so long unwifed and childless as to have become its own ungendered progenitor, was his alma mater.

He could find the crooked print now whenever he wished, ten miles or five miles or sometimes closer than that, to the camp. Twice while on stand during the next three years he heard the dogs strike its trail and once even jump it by chance, the voices high, abject, almost human in their hysteria. Once, still-hunting with Walter Ewell's rifle, he saw it cross a long corridor of down timber where a tornado had passed. It rushed through rather than across the tangle of trunks and branches as a locomotive would, faster than he had ever believed it could have moved, almost as fast as a deer even because the deer would have spent most of that distance in the air; he realized then why it would take a dog not only of abnormal courage but size and speed too ever to bring it to bay. He had a little dog at home, a mongrel, of the sort called fyce by Negroes, a ratter, itself not much bigger than a rat and possessing that sort of courage which had long since stopped being bravery and had become fool-

3. Traditional ceremony of initiation, performed when a boy kills his first big game.

hardiness. He brought it with him one June and, timing them as if they were meeting an appointment with another human being, himself carrying the fyce with a sack over its head and Sam Fathers with a brace of the hounds on a rope leash, they lay downwind of the trail and actually ambushed the bear. They were so close that it turned at bay although he realized later this might have been from surprise and amazement at the shrill and frantic uproar of the fyce. It turned at bay against the trunk of a big cypress, on its hind feet; it seemed to the boy that it would never stop rising, taller and taller, and even the two hounds seemed to have taken a kind of desperate and despairing courage from the fyce. Then he realized that the fyce was actually not going to stop. He flung the gun down and ran. When he overtook and grasped the shrill, frantically pinwheeling little dog, it seemed to him that he was directly under the bear. He could smell it, strong and hot and rank. Sprawling, he looked up where it loomed and towered over him like a thunderclap. It was quite familiar, until he remembered: this was the way he had used to dream about it.

Then it was gone. He didn't see it go. He knelt, holding the frantic fyce with both hands, hearing the abased wailing of the two hounds drawing further and further away, until Sam came up, carrying the gun. He laid it quietly down beside the boy and stood looking down at him. "You've done seed him twice now, with a gun in your hands," he said. "This time you couldn't have missed him."

The boy rose. He still held the fyce. Even in his arms it continued to yap frantically, surging and straining toward the fading sound of the hounds like a collection of live-wire springs. The boy was panting a little. "Neither could you," he said. "You had the gun. Why didn't you shoot him?"

Sam didn't seem to have heard. He put out his hand and touched the little dog in the boy's arms which still yapped and strained even though the two hounds were out of hearing now. "He's done gone," Sam said. "You can slack off and rest now, until next time." He stroked the little dog until it began to grow quiet under his hand. "You's almost the one we wants," he said. "You just ain't big enough. We ain't got that one yet. He will need to be just a little bigger than smart, and a little braver than either." He withdrew his hand from the fyce's head and stood looking into the woods where the bear and the hounds had vanished. "Somebody is going to, some day."

"I know it," the boy said. "That's why it must be one of us. So it won't be until the last day. When even he don't want it to last any longer."

So he should have hated and feared Lion. It was in the fourth summer, the fourth time he had made one in the celebration of Major de Spain's and General Compson's birthday. In the early spring Major de Spain's mare had foaled a horse colt. One evening when Sam brought the horses and mules up to stable them for the night, the colt was missing and it was all he could do to get the frantic mare into the lot. He had thought at first to let the mare lead him back to where she had become separated from the foal. But she would not do it. She would not even feint toward any particular part of the woods or even in any particular direction. She merely ran, as if she couldn't see, still frantic with terror. She whirled and ran at Sam once, as if to attack him in some ultimate desperation, as if she could not for the moment realize that he was a man and a long-familiar one. He got her into the lot at last. It was too dark by that time to back-track her, to unravel the erratic course she had doubtless pursued.

He came to the house and told Major de Spain. It was an animal, of course, a big one, and the colt was dead now, wherever it was. They all knew that. "It's a panther," General Compson said at once. "The same one. That doe and fawn last March." Sam had sent Major de Spain word of it when Boon Hogganbeck came to the camp on a routine visit to see how the stock had wintered—the doe's throat torn out, and the beast had run down the helpless fawn and killed it too.

"Sam never did say that was a panther," Major de Spain said. Sam said nothing now, standing behind Major de Spain where they sat at supper, inscrutable, as if he were just waiting for them to stop talking so he could go home. He didn't even seem to be looking at anything. "A panther might jump a doe, and he wouldn't have much trouble catching the fawn afterward. But no panther would have jumped that colt with the dam right there with it. It was Old Ben," Major de Spain said. "I'm disappointed in him. He has broken the rules. I didn't think he would have done that. He has killed mine and McCaslin's dogs, but that was all right. We gambled the dogs against him; we gave each other warning. But now he has come into my house and destroyed my property, out of season too. He broke the rules. It was Old Ben, Sam." Still Sam said nothing, standing there until Major de Spain should stop talking. "We'll back-track her tomorrow and see," Major de Spain said.

Sam departed. He would not live in the camp; he had built himself a little hut something like Joe Baker's, only stouter, tighter, on the bayou a quarter-mile away, and a stout log crib where he stored a little corn for the shoat he raised each year. The next morning he was waiting when they waked. He had already found the colt. They did not even wait for breakfast. It was not far, not five hundred yards from the stable—the three-months' colt lying on its side, its throat torn out and the entrails and one ham partly eaten. It lay not as if it had been dropped but as if it had been struck and hurled, and no cat-mark, no claw-mark where a panther would have gripped it while finding its throat. They read the tracks where the frantic mare had circled and at last rushed in with that same ultimate desperation with which she had whirled on Sam Fathers yesterday evening, and the long tracks of dead and terrified running and those of the beast which had not even rushed at her when she advanced but had merely walked three or four paces toward her until she broke, and General Compson said, "Good God, what a wolf!"

Still Sam said nothing. The boy watched him while the men knelt, measuring the tracks. There was something in Sam's face now. It was neither exultation nor joy nor hope. Later, a man, the boy realized what it had been, and that Sam had known all the time what had made the tracks and what had torn the throat out of the doe in the spring and killed the fawn. It had been foreknowledge in Sam's face that morning. *And he was glad,* he told himself. *He was old. He had no children, no people, none of his blood anywhere above earth that he would ever meet again. And even if he were to, he could not have touched it, spoken to it, because for seventy years now he had had to be a Negro. It was almost over now and he was glad.*

They returned to camp and had breakfast and came back with guns and the hounds. Afterward the boy realized that they also should have known then what killed the colt as well as Sam Fathers did. But that was neither the first nor the last time he had seen men rationalize from and even act upon their misconceptions. After Boon, standing astride the colt, had whipped the dogs away from it with his belt, they snuffed at the tracks. One of them, a young dog hound without judgment yet, bayed once, and they ran for a few feet on what seemed to be a trail. Then they stopped, looking back at the men, eager enough, not baffled, merely questioning, as if they were asking "Now what?" Then they rushed back to the colt, where Boon, still astride it, slashed at them with the belt.

"I never knew a trail to get cold that quick," General Compson said.

"Maybe a single wolf big enough to kill a colt with the dam right there beside it don't leave scent," Major de Spain said.

"Maybe it was a hant,"[4] Walter Ewell said. He looked at Tennie's Jim. "Hah, Jim?"

Because the hounds would not run it, Major de Spain had Sam hunt out and find the tracks a hundred yards farther on and they put the dogs on it again and again the young one bayed and not one of them realized then that the hound was not baying like a dog striking game but was merely bellowing like a country dog whose yard has been invaded. General Compson spoke to the boy and Boon and Tennie's Jim: to the squirrel hunters. "You boys keep the dogs with you this morning. He's probably hanging around somewhere, waiting to get his breakfast off the colt. You might strike him."

But they did not. The boy remembered how Sam stood watching them as they went into the woods with the leashed hounds—the Indian face in which he had never seen anything until it smiled, except that faint arching of the nostrils on that first morning when the hounds had found Old Ben. They took the hounds with them on the next day, though when they reached the place where they hoped to strike a fresh trail, the carcass of the colt was gone. Then on the third morning Sam was waiting again, this time until they had finished breakfast. He said, "Come." He led them to his house, his little hut, to the corn-crib beyond it. He had removed the corn and had made a deadfall of the door, baiting it with the colt's carcass; peering between the logs, they saw an animal almost the color of a gun or pistol barrel, what little time they had to examine its color or shape. It was not crouched nor even standing. It was in motion, in the air, coming toward them—a heavy body crashing with tremendous force against the door so that the thick door jumped and clattered in its frame, the animal, whatever it was, hurling itself against the door again seemingly before it could have touched the floor and got a new purchase to spring from. "Come away," Sam said, "fore he break his neck." Even when they retreated the heavy and measured crashes continued, the stout door jumping

4. I.e., haunt, a supernatural creature.

and clattering each time, and still no sound from the beast itself—no snarl, no cry.

"What in hell's name is it?" Major de Spain said.

"It's a dog," Sam said, his nostrils arching and collapsing faintly and steadily and that faint, fierce milkiness in his eyes again as on that first morning when the hounds had struck the old bear. "It's the dog."

*"The dog?"* Major de Spain said.

"That's gonter hold Old Ben."

"Dog the devil," Major de Spain said. "I'd rather have Old Ben himself in my pack than that brute. Shoot him."

"No," Sam said.

"You'll never tame him. How do you ever expect to make an animal like that afraid of you?"

"I don't want him tame," Sam said; again the boy watched his nostrils and the fierce milky light in his eyes. "But I almost rather he be tame than scared, of me or any man or any thing. But he won't be neither, of nothing."

"Then what are you going to do with it?"

"You can watch," Sam said.

Each morning through the second week they would go to Sam's crib. He had removed a few shingles from the roof and had put a rope on the colt's carcass and had drawn it out when the trap fell. Each morning they would watch him lower a pail of water into the crib while the dog hurled itself tirelessly against the door and dropped back and leaped again. It never made any sound and there was nothing frenzied in the act but only a cold and grim indomitable determination. Toward the end of the week it stopped jumping at the door. Yet it had not weakened appreciably and it was not as if it had rationalized the fact that the door was not going to give. It was as if for that time it simply disdained to jump any longer. It was not down. None of them had ever seen it down. It stood, and they could see it now—part mastiff, something of Airedale and something of a dozen other strains probably, better than thirty inches at the shoulders and weighing as they guessed almost ninety pounds, with cold yellow eyes and a tremendous chest and over all that strange color like a blued gun-barrel.

Then the two weeks were up. They prepared to break camp. The boy begged to remain and his cousin let him. He moved into the little hut with Sam Fathers. Each morning he watched Sam lower the pail of water into the crib. By the end of that week the dog was down. It would rise and half stagger, half crawl to the water and drink and collapse again. One morning it could not even reach the water, could not raise its forequarters even from the floor. Sam took a short stick and prepared to enter the crib. "Wait," the boy said. "Let me get the gun——"

"No," Sam said. "He can't move now." Nor could it. It lay on its side while Sam touched it, its head and the gaunted body, the dog lying motionless, the yellow eyes open. They were not fierce and there was nothing of petty malevolence in them, but a cold and almost impersonal malignance like some natural force. It was not even looking at Sam nor at the boy peering at it between the logs.

Sam began to feed it again. The first time he had to raise its head so it could lap the broth. That night he left a bowl of broth containing lumps of meat where the dog could reach it. The next morning the bowl was empty and the dog was lying on its belly, its head up, the cold yellow eyes watching the door as Sam entered, no change whatever in the cold yellow eyes and still no sound from it even when it sprang, its aim and coordination still bad from weakness so that Sam had time to strike it down with the stick and leap from the crib and slam the door as the dog, still without having had time to get its feet under it to jump again seemingly, hurled itself against the door as if the two weeks of starving had never been.

At noon that day someone came whooping through the woods from the direction of the camp. It was Boon. He came and looked for a while between the logs, at the tremendous dog lying again on its belly, its head up, the yellow eyes blinking sleepily at nothing: the indomitable and unbroken spirit. "What we better do," Boon said, "is to let that sonofabitch go and catch Old Ben and run him on the dog." He turned to the boy his weather-reddened and beetling face. "Get your traps together. Cass says for you to come on home. You been in here fooling with that horse-eating varmint long enough."

Boon had a borrowed mule at the camp; the buggy was waiting at the edge of the bottom. He was at home that night. He told McCaslin about it. "Sam's going to starve him again until he can go in and touch him. Then he will feed him again. Then he will starve him again, if he has to."

"But why?" McCaslin said. "What for? Even Sam will never tame that brute."

"We don't want him tame. We want him like he is. We just want him to find out at last that the only way he can get out of that crib and stay out of it is to do what Sam or somebody tells him to do. He's the dog that's going to stop Old Ben and hold him. We've already named him. His name is Lion."

Then November came at last. They returned to the camp. With General Compson and Major de Spain and his cousin and Walter and Boon he stood in the yard among the guns and bedding and boxes of food and watched Sam Fathers and Lion come up the lane from the lot—the Indian, the old man in battered overalls and rubber boots and a worn sheepskin coat and a hat which had belonged to the boy's father; the tremendous dog pacing gravely beside him. The hounds rushed out to meet them and stopped, except the young one which still had but little of judgment. It ran up to Lion, fawning. Lion didn't snap at it. He didn't even pause. He struck it rolling and yelping for five or six feet with a blow of one paw as a bear would have done and came on into the yard and stood, blinking sleepily at nothing, looking at no one, while Boon said, "Jesus. Jesus.—Will he let me touch him?"

"You can touch him," Sam said. "He don't care. He don't care about nothing or nobody."

The boy watched that too. He watched it for the next two years from that moment when Boon touched Lion's head and then knelt beside him, feeling the bones and muscles, the power. It was as if Lion were a woman—or perhaps Boon was the woman. That was more like it—the big, grave, sleepy-seeming dog which, as Sam Fathers said, cared about no man and no thing; and the violent, insensitive, hard-faced man with his touch of remote Indian blood and the mind almost of a child. He watched Boon take over Lion's feeding from Sam and Uncle Ash both. He would see Boon squatting in the cold rain beside the kitchen while Lion ate. Because Lion neither slept nor ate with the other dogs though none of them knew where he did sleep until in the second November, thinking until then that Lion slept in his kennel beside Sam Fathers' hut, when the boy's cousin McCaslin said something about it to Sam by sheer chance and Sam told him. And that night the boy and Major de Spain and McCaslin with a lamp entered the back room where Boon slept—the little, tight, airless room rank with the smell of Boon's unwashed body and his wet hunting-clothes—where Boon, snoring on his back, choked and waked and Lion raised his head beside him and looked back at them from his cold, slumbrous yellow eyes.

"Damn it, Boon," McCaslin said. "Get that dog out of here. He's got to run Old Ben tomorrow morning. How in hell do you expect him to smell anything fainter than a skunk after breathing you all night?"

"The way I smell ain't hurt my nose none that I ever noticed," Boon said.

"It wouldn't matter if it had," Major de Spain said. "We're not depending on you to trail a bear. Put him outside. Put him under the house with the other dogs."

Boon began to get up. "He'll kill the first one that happens to yawn or sneeze in his face or touches him."

"I reckon not," Major de Spain said. "None of them are going to risk yawning in his face or touching him either, even asleep. Put him outside. I want his nose right tomorrow. Old Ben fooled him last year. I don't think he will do it again."

Boon put on his shoes without lacing them; in his long soiled underwear, his hair still tousled from sleep, he and Lion went out. The others returned to the front room and the poker game where McCaslin's and Major de Spain's hands waited for them on the table. After a while McCaslin said, "Do you want me to go back and look again?"

"No," Major de Spain said. "I call," he said to Walter Ewell. He spoke to McCaslin again. "If you do, don't tell me. I am beginning to see the first sign of my increasing age: I don't like to know that my orders have been disobeyed, even when I knew when I gave them that they would be.—A small pair," he said to Walter Ewell.

"How small?" Walter said.

"Very small," Major de Spain said.

And the boy, lying beneath his piled quilts and blankets waiting for sleep, knew likewise that Lion was already back in Boon's bed, for the rest of that night and the next one and during all the nights of the next November and the next one. He thought then: *I wonder what Sam thinks. He could have Lion with him, even if Boon is a white man. He could ask Major or McCaslin either. And more than that. It was Sam's hand that touched Lion first and Lion knows it.* Then he became a man and he knew that too. It had been all right. That was the way it should have been. Sam was the chief, the prince; Boon, the plebeian, was his huntsman. Boon should have nursed the dogs.

On the first morning that Lion led the pack after Old Ben, seven strangers appeared in the camp. They were swampers: gaunt, malaria-ridden men appearing from nowhere, who ran trap-lines for coons or perhaps farmed little patches of cotton and corn along the edge of the bottom, in clothes but little better than Sam Fathers' and nowhere near as good as Tennie's Jim's, with worn shotguns and rifles, already squatting patiently in the cold drizzle in the side yard when day broke. They had a spokesman; afterward Sam Fathers told Major de Spain how all during the past summer and fall they had drifted into the camp singly or in pairs and threes, to look quietly at Lion for a while and then go away: "Mawnin, Major. We heerd you was aimin to put that ere blue dawg on that old two-toed bear this mawnin. We figgered we'd come up and watch, if you don't mind. We won't do no shooting, lessen he runs over us."

"You are welcome," Major de Spain said. "You are welcome to shoot. He's more your bear than ours."

"I reckon that ain't no lie. I done fed him enough cawn to have a sheer in him. Not to mention a shoat three years ago."

"I reckon I got a sheer too," another said. "Only it ain't in the bear." Major de Spain looked at him. He was chewing tobacco. He spat. "Hit was a heifer calf. Nice un too. Last year. When I finally found her, I reckon she looked about like that colt of yourn looked last June."

"Oh," Major de Spain said. "Be welcome. If you see game in front of my dogs, shoot it."

Nobody shot Old Ben that day. No man saw him. The dogs jumped him within a hundred yards of the glade where the boy had seen him that day in the summer of his eleventh year. The boy was less than a quarter-mile away. He heard the jump but he could distinguish no voice among the dogs that he did not know and therefore would be Lion's, and he thought, believed, that Lion was not among them. Even the fact that they were going much faster than he had ever heard them run behind Old Ben before and that the high thin note of hysteria was missing now from their voices was not enough to disabuse him. He didn't comprehend until that night, when Sam told him that Lion would never cry on a trail. "He gonter growl when he catches Old Ben's throat," Sam said. "But he ain't gonter never holler, no more than he ever done when he was jumping at that two-inch door. It's that blue dog in him. What you call it?"

"Airedale," the boy said.

Lion was there; the jump was just too close to the river. When Boon returned with Lion about eleven that night, he swore that Lion had stopped Old Ben once but that the hounds would not go in and Old Ben broke away and took to the river and swam for miles down it and he and Lion went down one bank for about ten miles and crossed and came up the other but it had begun to get dark before they struck any trail where Old Ben had come up out of the water, unless he was still in the water when he passed the ford where they crossed. Then he fell to cursing the hounds and ate the supper Uncle Ash had saved for him and went off to bed and after a while the boy opened the door of the little stale room thunderous with snoring and the great grave dog raised its head from Boon's pillow and blinked at him for a moment and lowered its head again.

When the next November came and the last day, the day which it was now becoming traditional to save for Old Ben, there were more than a dozen strangers waiting. They were not all swampers this time. Some of them were townsmen, from other county seats like Jefferson, who had heard about Lion and Old Ben and had come to watch the great blue dog keep his yearly rendezvous with the old two-toed bear. Some of them didn't even have guns and the hunting-clothes and boots they wore had been on a store shelf yesterday.

This time Lion jumped Old Ben more than five miles from the river and bayed and held him and this time the hounds went in, in a sort of desperate emulation. The boy heard them; he was that near. He heard Boon whooping; he heard the two shots when General Compson delivered both barrels, one containing five buckshot, the other a single ball, into the bear from as close as he could force his almost unmanageable horse. He heard the dogs when the bear broke free again. He was running now; panting, stumbling, his lungs bursting, he reached the place where General Compson had fired and where Old Ben had killed two of the hounds. He saw the blood from General Compson's shots, but he could go no further. He stopped, leaning against a tree for his breathing to ease and his heart to slow, hearing the sound of the dogs as it faded on and died away.

In camp that night—they had as guests five of the still terrified strangers in new hunting coats and boots who had been lost all day until Sam Fathers went out and got them—he heard the rest of it: how Lion had stopped and held the bear again but only the one-eyed mule which did not mind the smell of wild blood would approach and Boon was riding the mule and Boon had never been known to hit anything. He shot at the bear five times with his pump gun,[5] touching nothing, and Old Ben killed another hound and broke free once more and reached the river and was gone. Again Boon and Lion hunted as far down one bank as they dared. Too far; they crossed in the first of dusk and dark overtook them within a mile. And this time Lion found the broken trail, the blood perhaps, in the darkness where Old Ben had come up out of the water, but Boon had him on a rope, luckily, and he got down from the mule and fought Lion hand-to-hand until he got him back to camp. This time Boon didn't even curse. He stood in the door, muddy, spent, his huge gargoyle's face tragic and still amazed. "I missed him," he said. "I was in twenty-five feet of him and I missed him five times."

"But we have drawn blood," Major de Spain said. "General Compson drew blood. We have never done that before."

"But I missed him," Boon said. "I missed him five times. With Lion looking right at me."

"Never mind," Major de Spain said. "It was a damned fine race. And we drew blood. Next year we'll let General Compson or Walter ride Katie, and we'll get him."

Then McCaslin said, "Where is Lion, Boon?"

"I left him at Sam's," Boon said. He was already turning away. "I ain't fit to sleep with him."

5. Repeating shotgun with a slide action.

So he should have hated and feared Lion. Yet he did not. It seemed to him that there was a fatality in it. It seemed to him that something, he didn't know what, was beginning; had already begun. It was like the last act on a set stage. It was the beginning of the end of something, he didn't know what except that he would not grieve. He would be humble and proud that he had been found worthy to be a part of it too or even just to see it too.

## III

It was December. It was the coldest December he had ever remembered. They had been in camp four days over two weeks, waiting for the weather to soften so that Lion and Old Ben could run their yearly race. Then they would break camp and go home. Because of these unforeseen additional days which they had had to pass waiting on the weather, with nothing to do but play poker, the whiskey had given out and he and Boon were being sent to Memphis with a suitcase and a note from Major de Spain to Mr. Semmes, the distiller, to get more. That is, Major de Spain and McCaslin were sending Boon to get the whiskey and sending him to see that Boon got back with it or most of it or at least some of it.

Tennie's Jim waked him at three. He dressed rapidly, shivering, not so much from the cold because a fresh fire already boomed and roared on the hearth, but in that dead winter hour when the blood and the heart are slow and sleep is incomplete. He crossed the gap between house and kitchen, the gap of iron earth beneath the brilliant and rigid night where dawn would not begin for three hours yet, tasting, tongue, palate, and to the very bottom of his lungs, the searing dark, and entered the kitchen, the lamplit warmth where the stove glowed, fogging the windows, and where Boon already sat at the table at breakfast, hunched over his plate, almost in his plate, his working jaws blue with stubble and his face innocent of water and his coarse, horse-mane hair innocent of comb—the quarter Indian, grandson of a Chickasaw squaw, who on occasion resented with his hard and furious fists the intimation of one single drop of alien blood and on others, usually after whiskey, affirmed with the same fists and the same fury that his father had been the full-blood Chickasaw and even a chief and that even his mother had been only half white. He was four inches over six feet; he had the mind of a child, the heart of a horse, and little hard shoe-button eyes without depth or meanness or generosity or viciousness or gentleness or anything else, in the ugliest face the boy had ever seen. It looked like somebody had found a walnut a little larger than a football and with a machinist's hammer had shaped features into it and then painted it, mostly red; not Indian red but a fine bright ruddy color which whiskey might have had something to do with but which was most just happy and violent out-of-doors, the wrinkles in it not the residue of the forty years it had survived but from squinting into the sun or into the gloom of cane-brakes where game had run, baked into it by the camp fires before which he had lain trying to sleep on the cold November or December ground while waiting for daylight so he could rise and hunt again, as though time were merely something he walked through as he did through air, aging him no more than air did. He was brave, faithful, improvident and unreliable; he had neither profession job nor trade and owned one vice and one virtue: whiskey, and that absolute and unquestioning fidelity to Major de Spain and the boy's cousin McCaslin. "Sometimes I'd call them both virtues," Major de Spain said once. "Or both vices," McCaslin said.

He ate his breakfast, hearing the dogs under the kitchen, wakened by the smell of frying meat or perhaps by the feet overhead. He heard Lion once, short and peremptory, as the best hunter in any camp has only to speak once to all save the fools, and none other of Major de Spain's and McCaslin's dogs were Lion's equal in size and strength and perhaps even in courage, but they were not fools; Old Ben had killed the last fool among them last year.

Tennie's Jim came in as they finished. The wagon was outside. Ash decided he would drive them over to the log-line where they would flag the outbound log-train and let Tennie's Jim wash the dishes. The boy knew why. It would not be the first time he had listened to old Ash badgering Boon.

It was cold. The wagon wheels banged and clattered on the frozen ground; the sky was fixed and brilliant. He was not shivering, he was shaking, slow and steady and hard, the food he had just eaten still warm and solid inside him while his outside shook slow and steady around it as though his stomach floated loose. "They won't run this morning," he said. "No dog will have any nose today."

"Cep Lion," Ash said. "Lion don't need no nose. All he need is a bear." He had wrapped his feet in towsacks and he had a quilt from his pallet bed on the kitchen floor drawn over his head and wrapped around him until in the thin brilliant starlight he looked like nothing at all that the boy had ever seen before. "He run a bear through a thousand-acre ice-house. Catch him too. Them other dogs don't matter because they ain't going to keep up with Lion nohow, long as he got a bear in front of him."

"What's wrong with the other dogs?" Boon said. "What the hell do you know about it anyway? This is the first time you've had your tail out of that kitchen since we got here except to chop a little wood."

"Ain't nothing wrong with them," Ash said. "And long as it's up to them, ain't nothing going to be. I just wish I had knowed all my life how to take care of my health good as them hounds knows."

"Well, they ain't going to run this morning," Boon said. His voice was harsh and positive. "Major promised they wouldn't until me and Ike get back."

"Weather gonter break today. Gonter soft up. Rain by night." Then Ash laughed, chuckled, somewhere inside the quilt which concealed even his face. "Hum up here, mules!" he said, jerking the reins so that the mules leaped forward and snatched the lurching and banging wagon for several feet before they slowed again into their quick, short-paced, rapid plodding. "Sides, I like to know why Major need to wait on you. It's Lion he aiming to use. I ain't never heard tell of you bringing no bear nor no other kind of meat into this camp."

*Now Boon's going to curse Ash or maybe even hit him,* the boy thought. But Boon never did, never had; the boy knew he never would even though four years ago Boon had shot five times with a borrowed pistol at a Negro on the street in Jefferson, with the same result as when he had shot five times at Old Ben last fall. "By God," Boon said, "he ain't going to put Lion or no other dog on nothing until I get back tonight. Because he promised me. Whip up them mules and keep them whipped up. Do you want me to freeze to death?"

They reached the log-line and built a fire. After a while the log-train came up out of the woods under the paling east and Boon flagged it. Then in the warm caboose the boy slept again while Boon and the conductor and brakemen talked about Lion and Old Ben as people later would talk about Sullivan and Kilrain and, later still, about Dempsey and Tunney.[6] Dozing, swaying as the springless caboose lurched and clattered, he would hear them still talking, about the shoats and calves Old Ben had killed and the cribs he had rifled and the traps and deadfalls he had wrecked and the lead he probably carried under his hide—Old Ben, the two-toed bear in a land where bears with trap-ruined feet had been called Two-Toe or Three-Toe or Cripple-Foot for fifty years, only Old Ben was an extra bear (the head bear, General Compson called him) and so had earned a name such as a human man could have worn and not been sorry.

They reached Hoke's at sunup. They emerged from the warm caboose in their hunting clothes, the muddy boots and stained khaki and Boon's blue unshaven jowls. But that was all right. Hoke's was a sawmill and commissary and two stores and a loading-chute on a sidetrack from the main line, and all the men in it wore boots and khaki too. Presently the Memphis train came. Boon bought three packages of popcorn-and-molasses and a bottle of beer from the news butch and the boy went to sleep again to the sound of his chewing.

But in Memphis it was not all right. It was as if the high buildings and the hard pavements, the fine carriages and the horse cars and the men in starched collars and neckties made their boots and khaki look a little rougher and a little muddier and made Boon's beard look worse and more unshaven and his face look more and more like he should never have brought it out of the woods at all or at least out of reach of Major de Spain or McCaslin or someone who knew it and could have said, "Don't be afraid. He won't hurt you." He walked through the station, on the slick floor, his face moving as he worked the popcorn out of his teeth with his tongue, his legs spraddled and stiff in the hips as if he were walking on buttered glass, and that blue stubble on his face like the filings from a new gun barrel. They passed the first saloon. Even through the closed doors the boy could seem to smell the sawdust and the reek of old drink. Boon began to cough. He coughed for something less than a minute. "Damn this cold," he said. "I'd sure like to know where I got it."

"Back there in the station," the boy said.

Boon had started to cough again. He stopped. He looked at the boy. "What?" he said.

"You never had it when we left camp nor on the train either." Boon looked at him, blinking. Then he stopped blinking. He didn't cough again. He said quietly:

"Lend me a dollar. Come on. You've got it. If you ever had one, you've still got it. I don't mean you are tight with your money because you ain't. You just

6. Prizefighters of the nineteenth and early twentieth centuries.

don't never seem to ever think of nothing you want. When I was sixteen a dollar bill melted off of me before I ever had time to read the name of the bank that issued it." He said quietly: "Let me have a dollar, Ike."

"You promised Major. You promised McCaslin. Not till we get back to camp."

"All right," Boon said in that quiet and patient voice. "What can I do on just one dollar? You ain't going to lend me another."

"You're damn right I ain't," the boy said, his voice quiet too, cold with rage which was not at Boon, remembering: Boon snoring in a hard chair in the kitchen so he could watch the clock and wake him and McCaslin and drive them the seventeen miles in to Jefferson to catch the train to Memphis; the wild, never-bridled Texas paint pony[7] which he had persuaded McCaslin to let him buy and which he and Boon had bought at auction for four dollars and seventy-five cents and fetched home wired between two gentle old mares with pieces of barbed wire and which had never even seen shelled corn before and didn't even know what it was unless the grains were bugs maybe, and at last (he was ten and Boon had been ten all his life) Boon said the pony was gentled and with a towsack over its head and four Negroes to hold it they backed it into an old two-wheeled cart and hooked up the gear and he and Boon got up and Boon said, "All right, boys. Let him go" and one of the Negroes—it was Tennie's Jim—snatched the towsack off and leaped for his life and they lost the first wheel against a post of the open gate only at that moment Boon caught him by the scruff of the neck and flung him into the roadside ditch so he only saw the rest of it in fragments: the other wheel as it slammed through the side gate and crossed the back yard and leaped up onto the gallery and scraps of the cart here and there along the road and Boon vanishing rapidly on his stomach in the leaping and spurting dust and still holding the reins until they broke too and two days later they finally caught the pony seven miles away still wearing the hames and the headstall of the bridle around its neck like a duchess with two necklaces at one time. He gave Boon the dollar.

"All right," Boon said. "Come on in out of the cold."

"I ain't cold," he said.

"You can have some lemonade."

"I don't want any lemonade."

The door closed behind him. The sun was well up now. It was a brilliant day, though Ash had said it would rain before night. Already it was warmer; they could run tomorrow. He felt the old lift of the heart, as pristine as ever, as on the first day; he would never lose it, no matter how old the hunting and pursuit: the best, the best of all breathing, the humility and the pride. He must stop thinking about it. Already it seemed to him that he was running, back to the station, to the tracks themselves: the first train going south; he must stop thinking about it. The street was busy. He watched the big Norman draft horses, the Percherons; the trim carriages from which the men in the fine overcoats and the ladies rosy in furs descended and entered the station. (They were still

7. Spotted horse. "Paint" is a translation of the Spanish *pinto*.

next door to it but one.) Twenty years ago his father had ridden into Memphis as a member of Colonel Sartoris' horse in Forrest's[8] command, up Main street and (the tale told) into the lobby of the Gayoso Hotel where the Yankee officers sat in the leather chairs spitting into the tall bright cuspidors and then out again, scot-free—

The door opened behind him. Boon was wiping his mouth on the back of his hand. "All right," he said. "Let's go tend to it and get the hell out of here."

They went and had the suitcase packed. He never knew where or when Boon got the other bottle. Doubtless Mr. Semmes gave it to him. When they reached Hoke's again at sundown, it was empty. They could get a return train to Hoke's in two hours; they went straight back to the station as Major de Spain and then McCaslin had told Boon to do and then ordered him to do and had sent the boy along to see that he did. Boon took the first drink from his bottle in the washroom. A man in a uniform cap came to tell him he couldn't drink there and looked at Boon's face once and said nothing. The next time he was pouring into his water glass beneath the edge of a table in the restaurant when the manager (she was a woman) did tell him he couldn't drink there and he went back to the washroom. He had been telling the Negro waiter and all the other people in the restaurant who couldn't help but hear him and who had never heard of Lion and didn't want to, about Lion and Old Ben. Then he happened to think of the zoo. He had found out that there was another train to Hoke's at three o'clock and so they would spend the time at the zoo and take the three o'clock train until he came back from the washroom for the third time. Then they would take the first train back to camp, get Lion and come back to the zoo where, he said, the bears were fed on ice cream and lady fingers and he would match Lion against them all.

So they missed the first train, the one they were supposed to take, but he got Boon onto the three o'clock train and they were all right again, with Boon not even going to the washroom now but drinking in the aisle and talking about Lion and the men he buttonholed no more daring to tell Boon he couldn't drink there than the man in the station had dared.

When they reached Hoke's at sundown, Boon was asleep. The boy waked him at last and got him and the suitcase off the train and he even persuaded him to eat some supper at the sawmill commissary. So he was all right when they got in the caboose of the log-train to go back into the woods, with the sun going down red and the sky already overcast and the ground would not freeze tonight. It was the boy who slept now, sitting behind the ruby stove while the springless caboose jumped and clattered and Boon and the brakeman and the conductor talked about Lion and Old Ben because they knew what Boon was talking about because this was home. "Overcast and already thawing," Boon said. "Lion will get him tomorrow."

It would have to be Lion, or somebody. It would not be Boon. He had never hit anything bigger than a squirrel that anybody ever knew, except the Negro woman that day when he was shooting at the Negro man. He was a big Negro and not ten feet away but Boon shot five times with the pistol he had

8. Nathan Bedford Forrest (1821–1877), Confederate general.

borrowed from Major de Spain's Negro coachman and the Negro he was shooting at outed with a dollar-and-a-half mail-order pistol and would have burned Boon down with it only it never went off, it just went snicksnicksnicksnicksnick five times and Boon still blasting away and he broke a plate-glass window that cost McCaslin forty-five dollars and hit a Negro woman who happened to be passing in the leg only Major de Spain paid for that; he and McCaslin cut cards, the plate-glass window against the Negro woman's leg. And the first day on stand this year, the first morning in camp, the buck ran right over Boon; he heard Boon's old pump gun go whow. whow. whow. whow. whow. and then his voice: "God damn, here he comes! Head him! Head him!" and when he got there the buck's tracks and the five exploded shells were not twenty paces apart.

There were five guests in camp that night from Jefferson: Mr. Bayard Sartoris and his son and General Compson's son and two others. And the next morning he looked out the window, into the gray thin drizzle of daybreak which Ash had predicted, and there they were, standing and squatting beneath the thin rain, almost two dozen of them who had fed Old Ben corn and shoats and even calves for ten years, in their worn hats and hunting coats and overalls which any town Negro would have thrown away or burned and only the rubber boots strong and sound, and the worn and blueless guns,[9] and some even without guns. While they ate breakfast a dozen more arrived, mounted and on foot: loggers from the camp thirteen miles below and sawmill men from Hoke's and the only gun among them that one which the long-train conductor carried: so that when they went into the woods this morning Major de Spain led a party almost as strong, excepting that some of them were not armed, as some he had led in the last darkening days of '64 and '65.[1] The little yard would not hold them. They overflowed it, into the lane where Major de Spain sat his mare while Ash in his dirty apron thrust the greasy cartridges into his carbine and passed it up to him and the great grave blue dog stood at his stirrup not as a dog stands but as a horse stands, blinking his sleepy topaz eyes at nothing, deaf even to the yelling of the hounds which Boon and Tennie's Jim held on leash.

"We'll put General Compson on Katie this morning," Major de Spain said. "He drew blood last year; if he'd had a mule then that would have stood, he would have—"

"No," General Compson said. "I'm too old to go helling through the woods on a mule or a horse or anything else any more. Besides, I had my chance last year and missed it. I'm going on a stand this morning. I'm going to let the boy ride Katie."

"No, wait," McCaslin said. "Ike's got the rest of his life to hunt bears in. Let somebody else—"

"No," General Compson said. "I want Ike to ride Katie. He's already a better woodsman than you or me either and in another ten years he'll be as good as Walter."

At first he couldn't believe it, not until Major de Spain spoke to him. Then he was up, on the one-eyed mule which would not spook at wild blood, looking

9. Guns so worn with use that the dark blue finish has been rubbed off the metal. 1. Near the end of the Civil War, when Southern forces were numerically depleted.

down at the dog motionless at Major de Spain's stirrup, looking in the gray streaming light bigger than a calf, bigger than he knew it actually was—the big head, the chest almost as big as his own, the blue hide beneath which the muscles flinched or quivered to no touch since the heart which drove blood to them loved no man and no thing, standing as a horse stands yet different from a horse which infers only weight and speed while Lion inferred not only courage and all else that went to make up the will and desire to pursue and kill, but endurance, the will and desire to endure beyond all imaginable limits of flesh in order to overtake and slay. Then the dog looked at him. It moved its head and looked at him across the trivial uproar of the hounds, out of the yellow eyes as depthless as Boon's, as free as Boon's of meanness or generosity or gentleness or viciousness. They were just cold and sleepy. Then it blinked, and he knew it was not looking at him and never had been, without even bothering to turn its head away.

That morning he heard the first cry. Lion had already vanished while Sam and Tennie's Jim were putting saddles on the mule and horse which had drawn the wagon and he watched the hounds as they crossed and cast, snuffing and whimpering, until they too disappeared. Then he and Major de Spain and Sam and Tennie's Jim rode after them and heard the first cry out of the wet and thawing woods not two hundred yards ahead, high, with that abject, almost human quality he had come to know, and the other hounds joining in until the gloomed woods rang and clamored. They rode then. It seemed to him that he could actually see the big blue dog boring on, silent, and the bear too: the thick, locomotive-like shape which he had seen that day four years ago crossing the blow-down, crashing on ahead of the dogs faster than he had believed it could have moved, drawing away even from the running mules. He heard a shotgun, once. The woods had opened, they were going fast, the clamor faint and fading on ahead; they passed the man who had fired—a swamper, a pointing arm, a gaunt face, the small black orifice of his yelling studded with rotten teeth.

He heard the changed note in the hounds' uproar and two hundred yards ahead he saw them. The bear had turned. He saw Lion drive in without pausing and saw the bear strike him aside and lunge into the yelling hounds and kill one of them almost in its tracks and whirl and run again. Then they were in a streaming tide of dogs. He heard Major de Spain and Tennie's Jim shouting and the pistol sound of Tennie's Jim's leather thong as he tried to turn them. Then he and Sam Fathers were riding alone. One of the hounds had kept on with Lion though. He recognized its voice. It was the young hound which even a year ago had had no judgment and which, by the lights of the other hounds anyway, still had none. *Maybe that's what courage is,* he thought. "Right," Sam said behind him. "Right. We got to turn him from the river if we can."

Now they were in cane: a brake. He knew the path through it as well as Sam did. They came out of the undergrowth and struck the entrance almost exactly. It would traverse the brake and come out onto a high open ridge above the river. He heard the flat clap of Walter Ewell's rifle, then two more. "No," Sam said. "I can hear the hound. Go on."

They emerged from the narrow roofless tunnel of snapping and hissing cane, still galloping, onto the open ridge below which the thick yellow river, reflectionless in the gray and streaming light, seemed not to move. Now he could hear the hound too. It was not running. The cry was a high frantic yapping and Boon was running along the edge of the bluff, his old gun leaping and jouncing against his back on its sling made of a piece of cotton plowline. He whirled and ran up to them, wild-faced, and flung himself onto the mule behind the boy. "That damn boat!" he cried. "It's on the other side! He went straight across! Lion was too close to him! That little hound too! Lion was so close I couldn't shoot! Go on!" he cried, beating his heels into the mule's flanks. "Go on!"

They plunged down the bank, slipping and sliding in the thawed earth, crashing through the willows and into the water. He felt no shock, no cold, he on one side of the swimming mule, grasping the pommel with one hand and holding his gun above the water with the other, Boon opposite him. Sam was behind them somewhere, and then the river, the water about them, was full of dogs. They swam faster than the mules; they were scrabbling up the bank before the mules touched bottom. Major de Spain was whooping from the bank they had just left and, looking back, he saw Tennie's Jim and the horse as they went into the water.

Now the woods ahead of them and the rain-heavy air were one uproar. It rang and clamored; it echoed and broke against the bank behind them and reformed and clamored and rang until it seemed to the boy that all the hounds which had ever bayed game in this land were yelling down at him. He got his leg over the mule as it came up out of the water. Boon didn't try to mount again. He grasped one stirrup as they went up the bank and crashed through the undergrowth which fringed the bluff and saw the bear, on its hind feet, its back against a tree while the bellowing hounds swirled around it and once more Lion drove it, leaping clear of the ground.

This time the bear didn't strike him down. It caught the dog in both arms, almost loverlike, and they both went down. He was off the mule now. He drew back both hammers of the gun but he could see nothing but moiling spotted houndbodies until the bear surged up again. Boon was yelling something, he could not tell what; he could see Lion still clinging to the bear's throat and he saw the bear, half erect, strike one of the hounds with one paw and hurl it five or six feet and then, rising and rising as though it would never stop, stand erect again and begin to rake at Lion's belly with its forepaws. Then Boon was running. The boy saw the gleam of the blade in his hand and watched him leap among the hounds, hurling them, kicking them aside as he ran, and fling himself astride the bear as he had hurled himself onto the mule, his legs locked around the bear's belly, his left arm under the bear's throat where Lion clung, and the glint of the knife as it rose and fell.

It fell just once. For an instant they almost resembled a piece of statuary: the clinging dog, the bear, the man astride its back, working and probing the buried blade. Then they went down, pulled over backward by Boon's weight, Boon underneath. It was the bear's back which reappeared first but at once Boon was astride it again. He had never released the knife and again the boy saw the almost infinitesimal movement of his arm and shoulder as he probed and sought; then the bear surged erect, raising with it the man and the dog too, and turned and still carrying the man and the dog it took two or three steps toward the woods on its hind feet as a man would have walked and crashed down. It didn't collapse, crumple. It fell all of a piece, as a tree falls, so that all three of them, man dog and bear, seemed to bounce once.

He and Tennie's Jim ran forward. Boon was kneeling at the bear's head. His left ear was shredded, his left coat sleeve was completely gone, his right boot had been ripped from knee to instep; the bright blood thinned in the thin rain down his leg and hand and arm and down the side of his face which was no longer wild but was quite calm. Together they prized Lion's jaws from the bear's throat. "Easy, goddamn it," Boon said. "Can't you see his guts are all out of him?" He began to remove his coat. He spoke to Tennie's Jim in that calm voice: "Bring the boat up. It's about a hundred yards down the bank there. I saw it." Tennie's Jim rose and went away. Then, and he could not remember if it had been a call or an exclamation from Tennie's Jim or if he had glanced up by chance, he saw Tennie's Jim stooping and saw Sam Fathers lying motionless on his face in the trampled mud.

The mule had not thrown him. He remembered that Sam was down too even before Boon began to run. There was no mark on him whatever and when he and Boon turned him over, his eyes were open and he said something in that tongue which he and Joe Baker had used to speak together. But he couldn't move. Tennie's Jim brought the skiff up; they could hear him shouting to Major de Spain across the river. Boon wrapped Lion in his hunting coat and carried him down to the skiff and they carried Sam down and returned and hitched the bear to the one-eyed mule's saddle-bow with Tennie's Jim's leash-thong and dragged him down to the skiff and got him into it and left Tennie's Jim to swim the horse and the two mules back across. Major de Spain caught the bow of the skiff as Boon jumped out and past him before it touched the bank. He looked at Old Ben and said quietly: "Well." Then he walked into the water and leaned down and touched Sam and Sam looked up at him and said something in that old tongue he and Joe Baker spoke. "You don't know what happened?" Major de Spain said.

"No, sir," the boy said. "It wasn't the mule. It wasn't anything. He was off the mule when Boon ran in on the bear. Then we looked up and he was lying on the ground." Boon was shouting at Tennie's Jim, still in the middle of the river.

"Come on, goddamn it!" he said. "Bring me that mule!"

"What do you want with a mule?" Major de Spain said.

Boon didn't even look at him. "I'm going to Hoke's to get the doctor," he said in that calm voice, his face quite calm beneath the steady thinning of the bright blood.

"You need a doctor yourself," Major de Spain said. "Tennie's Jim—"

"Damn that," Boon said. He turned on Major de Spain. His face was still calm, only his voice was a pitch higher. "Can't you see his goddamn guts are all out of him?"

"Boon!" Major de Spain said. They looked at one another. Boon was a good head taller than Major de Spain; even the boy was taller now than Major de Spain.

"I've got to get the doctor," Boon said. "His goddamn guts—"

"All right," Major de Spain said. Tennie's Jim came up out of the water. The horse and the sound mule had already scented Old Ben; they surged and plunged all the way up to the top of the bluff, dragging Tennie's Jim with them, before he could stop them and tie them and come back. Major de Spain unlooped the leather thong of his compass from his buttonhole and gave it to Tennie's Jim. "Go straight to Hoke's," he said. "Bring Doctor Crawford back with you. Tell him there are two men to be looked at. Take my mare. Can you find the road from here?"

"Yes, sir," Tennie's Jim said.

"All right," Major de Spain said. "Go on." He turned to the boy. "Take the mules and the horse and go back and get the wagon. We'll go on down the river in the boat to Coon bridge. Meet us there. Can you find it again?"

"Yes, sir," the boy said.

"All right. Get started."

He went back to the wagon. He realized then how far they had run. It was already afternoon when he put the mules into the traces and tied the horse's lead-rope to the tail-gate. He reached Coon bridge at dusk. The skiff was already there. Before he could see it and almost before he could see the water he had to leap from the tilting wagon, still holding the reins, and work around to where he could grasp the bit and then the ear of the plunging sound mule and dig his heels and hold it until Boon came up the bank. The rope of the lead horse had already snapped and it had already disappeared up the road toward camp. They turned the wagon around and took the mules out and he led the sound mule a hundred yards up the road and tied it. Boon had already brought Lion up to the wagon and Sam was sitting up in the skiff now and when they raised him he tried to walk, up the bank and to the wagon and he tried to climb into the wagon but Boon did not wait; he picked Sam up bodily and set him on the seat. Then they hitched Old Ben to the one-eyed mule's saddle again and dragged him up the bank and set two skid-poles into the open tail-gate and got him into the wagon and he went and got the sound mule and Boon fought it into the traces, striking it across its hard hollow-sounding face until it came into position and stood trembling. Then the rain came down, as though it had held off all day waiting on them.

They returned to camp through it, through the streaming and sightless dark, hearing long before they saw any light the horn and the spaced shots to guide them. When they came to Sam's dark little hut he tried to stand up. He spoke again in the tongue of the old fathers; then he said clearly: "Let me out. Let me out."

"He hasn't got any fire," Major said. "Go on!" he said sharply.

But Sam was struggling now, trying to stand up. "Let me out, master," he said. "Let me go home."

So he stopped the wagon and Boon got down and lifted Sam out. He did not wait to let Sam try to walk this time. He carried him into the hut and Major de Spain got light on a paper spill from the buried embers on the hearth and lit the lamp and Boon put Sam on his bunk and drew off his boots and Major de Spain covered him and the boy was not there, he was holding the mules, the sound one which was trying again to bolt since when the wagon stopped Old Ben's scent drifted forward again along the streaming blackness of air, but Sam's eyes were probably open again on that profound look which saw further than them or the hut, further than the death of a bear and the dying of a dog. Then they went on, toward the long wailing of the horn and the shots which seemed each to linger intact somewhere in the thick streaming air until the next spaced report joined and blended with it, to the lighted house, the bright streaming windows, the quiet faces as Boon entered, bloody and quite calm, carrying the bundled coat. He laid Lion, blood coat and all, on his stale sheetless pallet bed which not even Ash, as deft in the house as a woman, could ever make smooth.

The sawmill doctor from Hoke's was already there. Boon would not let the doctor touch him until he had seen to Lion. He wouldn't risk giving Lion chloroform. He put the entrails back and sewed him up without it while Major de Spain held his head and Boon his feet. But he never tried to move. He lay there, the yellow eyes open upon nothing while the quiet men in the new hunting clothes and in the old ones crowded into the little airless room rank with the smell of Boon's body and garments, and watched. Then the doctor cleaned and disinfected Boon's face and arm and leg and bandaged them and, the boy in front with a lantern and the doctor and McCaslin and Major de Spain and General Compson following, they went to Sam Fathers' hut. Tennie's Jim had built up the fire; he squatted before it, dozing. Sam had not moved since Boon had put him in the bunk and Major de Spain had covered him with the blankets, yet he opened his eyes and looked from one to another of the faces and when McCaslin touched his shoulder and said, "Sam. The doctor wants to look at you," he even drew his hands out of the blanket and began to fumble at his shirt buttons until McCaslin said, "Wait. We'll do it." They undressed him. He lay there—the copper-brown, almost hairless body, the old man's body, the old man, the wild man not even one generation from the woods, childless, kinless, peopleless—motionless, his eyes open but no longer looking at any of them, while the doctor examined him and drew the blankets up and put the stethoscope back into his bag and snapped the bag and only the boy knew that Sam too was going to die.

"Exhaustion," the doctor said. "Shock maybe. A man his age swimming rivers in December. He'll be all right. Just make him stay in bed for a day or two. Will there be somebody here with him?"

"There will be somebody here," Major de Spain said.

They went back to the house, to the rank little room where Boon still sat on the pallet bed with Lion's head under his hand while the men, the ones who had hunted behind Lion and the ones who had never seen him before today, came quietly in to look at him and went away. Then it was dawn and they all went out into the yard to look at Old Ben, with his eyes open too and his lips snarled back from his worn teeth and his mutilated foot and the little hard lumps under his skin which were the old bullets (there were fifty-two of them, buckshot rifle and ball) and the single almost invisible slit under his left shoulder where Boon's blade had finally found his life. Then Ash began to beat on the bottom of the dishpan to call them to breakfast and it was the first time he could remember hearing no sound from the dogs under the kitchen while they were eating. It was as if the old bear, even dead there in the yard, was a more potent terror still than they could face without Lion between them.

The rain had stopped during the night. By midmorning the thin sun appeared, rapidly burning away mist and cloud, warming the air and the earth; it would be one of those windless Mississippi December days which are a sort of Indian summer's Indian summer. They moved Lion out to the front gallery, into the sun. It was Boon's idea. "Goddamn it," he said, "he never did want to stay in the house until I made him. You know that." He took a crowbar and loosened the floor boards under his pallet bed so it could be raised, mattress and all, without disturbing Lion's position, and they carried him out to the gallery and put him down facing the woods.

Then he and the doctor and McCaslin and Major de Spain went to Sam's hut. This time Sam didn't open his eyes and his breathing was so quiet, so peaceful that they could hardly see that he breathed. The doctor didn't even take out his stethoscope nor even touch him. "He's all right," the doctor said. "He didn't even catch cold. He just quit."

"Quit?" McCaslin said.

"Yes. Old people do that sometimes. Then they get a good night's sleep or maybe it's just a drink of whiskey, and they change their minds."

They returned to the house. And then they began to arrive—the swamp-dwellers, the gaunt men who ran trap-lines and lived on quinine and coons and river water, the farmers of little corn and cotton-patches along the bottom's edge whose fields and cribs and pigpens the old bear had rifled, the loggers from the camp, and the sawmill men from Hoke's, and the town men from further away than that, whose hounds the old bear had slain and whose traps and deadfalls he had wrecked and whose lead he carried. They came up mounted and on foot and in wagons, to enter the yard and look at him and then go on to the front porch where Lion lay, filling the little yard and overflowing it until there were almost a hundred of them squatting and standing in the warm and drowsing sunlight, talking quietly of hunting, of the game and the dogs which ran it, of hounds and bear and deer and men of yesterday vanished from the earth, while from time to time the great blue dog would open his eyes, not as if he were listening to them but as though to look at the woods for a moment before closing his eyes again, to remember the woods or to see that they were still there. He died at sundown.

Major de Spain broke camp that night. They carried Lion into the woods, or Boon carried him that is, wrapped in a quilt from his bed, just as he had refused to let anyone else touch Lion yesterday until the doctor got there; Boon carrying Lion, and the boy and General Compson and Walter and still almost fifty of them following with lanterns and lighted pine-knots—men from Hoke's and even further, who would have to ride out of the bottom in the dark, and swampers and trappers who would have to walk even, scattering toward the little hidden huts where they lived. And Boon would let nobody else dig the grave either and lay Lion in it and cover him, and then General Compson stood at the head of it while the blaze and smoke of the pine-knots streamed away among the winter branches and spoke as he would have spoken over a man.

Then they returned to camp. Major de Spain and McCaslin and Ash had rolled and tied all the bedding. The mules were hitched to the wagon and pointed out of the bottom and the wagon was already loaded and the stove in the kitchen was cold and the table was set with scraps of cold food and bread and only the coffee was hot when the boy ran into the kitchen where Major de Spain and McCaslin had already eaten. "What?" he cried. "What? I'm not going."

"Yes," McCaslin said, "we're going out tonight. Major wants to get on back home."

"No!" he said. "I'm going to stay."

"You've got to be back in school Monday. You've already missed a week more than I intended. It will take you from now until Monday to catch up. Sam's all right. You heard Doctor Crawford. I'm going to leave Boon and Tennie's Jim both to stay with him until he feels like getting up."

He was panting. The others had come in. He looked rapidly and almost frantically around at the other faces. Boon had a fresh bottle. He upended it and started the cork by striking the bottom of the bottle with the heel of his hand and drew the cork with his teeth and spat it out and drank. "You're damn right you're going back to school," Boon said. "Or I'll burn the tail off you myself if Cass don't, whether you are sixteen or sixty. Where in hell do you expect to get without education? Where would Cass be? Where in hell would I be if I hadn't never went to school?"

He looked at McCaslin again. He could feel his breath coming shorter and shorter and shallower and shallower, as if there were not enough air in the kitchen for that many to breathe. "This is just Thursday. I'll come home Sunday night on one of the horses. I'll come home Sunday, then. I'll make up time I lost studying Sunday night, McCaslin," he said, without even despair.

"No, I tell you," McCaslin said. "Sit down here and eat your supper. We're going out to—"

"Hold up, Cass," General Compson said. The boy did not know General Compson had moved until he put his hand on his shoulder. "What is it, bud?" he said.

"I've got to stay," he said. "I've got to."

"All right," General Compson said. "You can stay. If missing an extra week of school is going to throw you so far behind you'll have to sweat to find out what some hired pedagogue put between the covers of a book, you better quit altogether.—And you shut up, Cass," he said, though McCaslin had not spoken. "You've got one foot straddled into a farm and the other foot straddled into a bank; you ain't even got a good hand-hold where this boy was already an old man long before you damned Sartorises and Edmondses invented farms and banks to keep yourselves from having to find out what this boy was born knowing, and fearing too maybe, but without being afraid, that could go ten miles on a compass because he wanted to look at a bear none of us had ever got near enough to put a bullet in and looked at the bear and came the ten miles back on the compass in the dark; maybe by God that's the why and the wherefore of farms and banks.—I reckon you still ain't going to tell what it is?"

But still he could not. "I've got to stay," he said.

"All right," General Compson said. "There's plenty of grub left. And you'll come home Sunday, like you promised McCaslin? Not Sunday night: Sunday."

"Yes, sir," he said.

"All right," General Compson said. "Sit down and eat, boys," he said. "Let's get started. It's going to be cold before we get home."

They ate. The wagon was already loaded and ready to depart; all they had to do was to get into it. Boon would drive them out to the road, to the farmer's stable where the surrey had been left. He stood beside the wagon, in silhouette on the sky, turbaned like a Paythan[2] and taller than any there, the bottle tilted. Then he flung the bottle from his lips without even lowering it, spinning and glinting in the faint starlight, empty. "Them that's going," he said, "get in the goddamn wagon. Them that ain't, get out of the goddamn way." The others got in. Boon mounted to the seat beside General Compson and the wagon moved, on into the obscurity until the boy could no longer see it, even the moving density of it amid the greater night. But he could still hear it, for a long while: the slow, deliberate banging of the wooden frame as it lurched from rut to rut. And he could hear Boon even when he could no longer hear the wagon. He was singing, harsh, tuneless, loud.

That was Thursday. On Saturday morning Tennie's Jim left on McCaslin's woods-horse which had not been out of the bottom one time now in six years, and late that afternoon rode through the gate on the spent horse and on to the commissary where McCaslin was rationing the tenants and the wage-hands for the coming week, and this time McCaslin forestalled any necessity or risk of having to wait while Major de Spain's surrey was being horsed and harnessed. He took their own, and with Tennie's Jim already asleep in the back seat he drove in to Jefferson and waited while Major de Spain changed to boots and put on his overcoat, and they drove the thirty miles in the dark of that night and at daybreak on Sunday morning they swapped to the waiting mare and mule and as the sun rose they rode out of the jungle and onto the low ridge where they had buried Lion: the low mound of unannealed earth where Boon's spade-marks still showed, and beyond the grave the platform of freshly cut saplings bound between four posts and the blanket-wrapped bundle upon the platform[3] and Boon and the boy squatting between the platform and the grave until Boon, the bandage removed, ripped from his head so that the long scoriations of Old Ben's claws resembled crusted tar in the sunlight, sprang up and threw down upon them with the old gun[4] with which he had never been known to hit anything although McCaslin was already off the mule, kicked both feet free of the irons and vaulted down before the mule had stopped, walking toward Boon.

"Stand back," Boon said. "By God, you won't touch him. Stand back, McCaslin." Still McCaslin came on, fast yet without haste.

"Cass!" Major de Spain said. Then he said, "Boon! You, Boon!" and he was down too and the boy rose too, quickly, and still McCaslin came on not fast but steady and walked up to the grave and reached his hand steadily out, quickly

2. I.e., the bandages on his head resembled the turban headdress worn in India. 3. An alternative to burying a dead person; generally practiced by American Indian groups of the southeastern United States. 4. I.e., pointed his gun at them.

yet still not fast, and took hold the gun by the middle so that he and Boon faced one another across Lion's grave, both holding the gun, Boon's spent indomitable amazed and frantic face almost a head higher than McCaslin's beneath the black scoriations of beast's claws and then Boon's chest began to heave as though there were not enough air in all the woods, in all the wilderness, for all of them, for him and anyone else, even for him alone.

"Turn it loose, Boon," McCaslin said.

"You damn little spindling—" Boon said. "Don't you know I can take it away from you? Don't you know I can tie it around your neck like a damn cravat?"

"Yes," McCaslin said. "Turn it loose, Boon."

"This is the way he wanted it. He told us. He told us exactly how to do it. And by God you ain't going to move him. So we did it like he said, and I been sitting here ever since to keep the damn wildcats and varmits away from him and by God—" Then McCaslin had the gun, down-slanted while he pumped the slide, the five shells snicking out of it so fast that the last one was almost out before the first one touched the ground and McCaslin dropped the gun behind him without once having taken his eyes from Boon's.

"Did you kill him, Boon?" he said. Then Boon moved. He turned, he moved like he was still drunk and then for a moment blind too, one hand out as he blundered toward the big tree and seemed to stop walking before he reached the tree so that he plunged, fell toward it, flinging up both hands and catching himself against the tree and turning until his back was against it, backing with the tree's trunk his wild spent scoriated face and the tremendous heave and collapse of his chest, McCaslin following, facing him again, never once having moved his eyes from Boon's eyes. "Did you kill him, Boon?"

"No!" Boon said. "No!"

"Tell the truth," McCaslin said. "I would have done it if he had asked me to." Then the boy moved. He was between them, facing McCaslin; the water felt as if it had burst and sprung not from his eyes alone but from his whole face, like sweat.

"Leave him alone!" he cried. "Goddamn it! Leave him alone!"

## IV

then he was twenty-one. He could say it, himself and his cousin juxtaposed not against the wilderness but against the tamed land[5] which was to have been his heritage, the land which old Carothers McCaslin, his grandfather, had bought with white man's money from the wild men whose grandfathers without guns hunted it, and tamed and ordered, or believed he had tamed and ordered it, for the reason that the human beings he held in bondage and in the power

5. In this long and clouded section of the story Isaac and his cousin McCaslin Edmonds are "juxtaposed" against the problems of the "tamed land," i.e., the land that has been taken from the wilderness by settlement and cultivation, claimed as property to be bought and sold, and passed along from one generation to another by legal inheritance. Because the legality of such transfer is complicated by changing patterns of race relations and tainted by the past enslavement of black people, Isaac declines to accept any share of the land coming to him from his grandfather Lucius Quintus Carothers McCaslin.

of life and death had removed the forest from it and in their sweat scratched the surface of it to a depth of perhaps fourteen inches in order to grow something out of it which had not been there before, and which could be translated back into the money he who believed he had bought it had had to pay to get it and hold it, and a reasonable profit too: and for which reason old Carothers McCaslin, knowing better, could raise his children, his descendants and heirs, to believe the land was his to hold and bequeath, since the strong and ruthless man has a cynical foreknowledge of his own vanity and pride and strength and a contempt for all his get: just as, knowing better, Major de Spain had his fragment of that wilderness which was bigger and older than any recorded deed: just as, knowing better, old Thomas Sutpen, from whom Major de Spain had had his fragment for money: just as Ikkemotubbe, the Chickasaw chief, from whom Thomas Sutpen had had the fragment for money or rum or whatever it was, knew in his turn that not even a fragment of it had been his to relinquish or sell

not against the wilderness but against the land, not in pursuit and lust but in relinquishment; and in the commissary as it should have been, not the heart perhaps but certainly the solarplexus of the repudiated and relinquished: the square, galleried, wooden building squatting like a portent above the fields whose laborers it still held in thrall, '65[6] or no, and placarded over with advertisements for snuff and cures for chills and salves and potions manufactured and sold by white men to bleach the pigment and straighten the hair of Negroes that they might resemble the very race which for two hundred years had held them in bondage and from which for another hundred years not even a bloody civil war would have set them completely free

himself and his cousin amid the old smells of cheese and salt meat and kerosene and harness, the ranked shelves of tobacco and overalls and bottled medicine and thread and plow-bolts, the barrels and kegs of flour and meal and molasses and nails, the wall pegs dependant with plowlines and plow-collars and hames and trace-chains, and the desk and the shelf above it on which rested the ledgers in which McCaslin recorded the slow outward trickle of food and supplies and equipment which returned each fall as cotton made and ginned and sold (two threads frail as truth and impalpable as equators yet cable-strong to bind for life them who made the cotton to the land their sweat fell on), and the older ledgers, clumsy and archaic in size and shape, on the yellowed pages of which were recorded in the faded hand of his father Theophilus and his uncle Amodeus during the two decades before the Civil War the manumission,[7] in title at least, of Carothers McCaslin's slaves:

'Relinquish,' McCaslin said. 'Relinquish. You, the direct male descendant of him who saw the opportunity and took it, bought the land, took the land, got the land no matter how, held it to bequeath, no matter how, out of the old grant, the first patent, when it was a wilderness of wild beasts and wilder men, and cleared it, translated it into something to bequeath to his children, worthy

6. I.e., 1865, year when the South surrendered, marking the end of the Civil War. 7. Freeing of black slaves. "Theophilus and his uncle Amodeus": twin brothers, also called Uncle Buck and Uncle Buddy in the story.

of bequeathment for his descendants' ease and security and pride, and to perpetuate his name and accomplishments. Not only the male descendant but the only and last descendant in the male line and in the third generation, while I am not only four generations from old Carothers, I derived through a woman and the very McCaslin in my name is mine only by sufferance and courtesy and my grandmother's pride in what that man accomplished, whose legacy and monument you think you can repudiate.' and he

'I can't repudiate it. It was never mine to repudiate. It was never Father's and Uncle Buddy's to bequeath me to repudiate, because it was never Grandfather's to bequeath them to bequeath me to repudiate, because it was never old Ikkemotubbe's to sell to Grandfather for bequeathment and repudiation. Because it was never Ikkemotubbe's fathers' fathers' to bequeath Ikkemotubbe to sell to Grandfather or any man because on the instant when Ikkemotubbe discovered, realized, that he could sell it for money, on that instant it ceased ever to have been his forever, father to father to father, and the man who bought it bought nothing.'

'Bought nothing?' and he

'Bought nothing. Because He told in the Book how He created the earth, made it and looked at it and said it was all right, and then He made man. He made the earth first and peopled it with dumb creatures, and then He created man to be His overseer on the earth and to hold suzerainty over the earth and the animals on it in His name, not to hold for himself and his descendants inviolable title forever, generation after generation, to the oblongs and squares of the earth, but to hold the earth mutual and intact in the communal anonymity of brotherhood, and all the fee He asked was pity and humility and sufferance and endurance and the sweat of his face for bread. And I know what you are going to say,' he said: 'That nevertheless Grandfather—' and McCaslin

'—did own it. And not the first. Not alone and not the first since, as your Authority states, man was dispossessed of Eden. Nor yet the second and still not alone, on down through the tedious and shabby chronicle of His chosen sprung from Abraham; and of the sons of them who dispossessed Abraham,[8] and of the five hundred years during which half the known world and all it contained was chattel to one city, as this plantation and all the life it contained was chattel and revokeless thrall to this commissary store and those ledgers yonder during your grandfather's life; and the next thousand years while men fought over the fragments of that collapse until at last even the fragments were exhausted and men snarled over the gnawed bones of the old world's worthless evening until an accidental egg discovered to them a new hemisphere.[9] So let me say it: That nevertheless and notwithstanding old Carothers did own it. Bought it, got it, no matter; kept it, held it, no matter; bequeathed it: else why do you stand here relinquishing and repudiating? Held it, kept it for fifty years until you could repudiate it, while He—this Arbiter, this Architect, this Umpire—condoned—or did He? looked down and saw—or did He? Or at

8. See Genesis 25.5–8. 9. According to legend, Columbus demonstrated the mental tactics that led him to find the New World by making an egg stand on end. He accomplished this almost impossibly difficult trick by slightly crushing the end of the eggshell.

least did nothing: saw, and could not, or did not see; saw, and would not, or perhaps He would not see—perverse, impotent, or blind: which?' and he

'Dispossessed.' and McCaslin

'What?' and he

'Dispossessed. Not impotent: He didn't condone; not blind, because He watched it. And let me say it. Dispossessed of Canaan, and those who dispossessed him dispossessed, and the five hundred years of absentee landlords in the Roman bagnios, and the thousand years of wild men from the northern woods who dispossessed them and devoured their ravished substance ravished in turn again and then snarled in what you call the old world's worthless twilight over the old world's gnawed bones, blasphemous in His name until He used a simple egg to discover to them a new world where a nation of people could be found in humility and pity and sufferance and pride of one to another. And Grandfather did own the land nevertheless and notwithstanding because He permitted it, not impotent and not condoning and not blind, because He ordered and watched it. He saw the land already accursed even as Ikkemotubbe and Ikkemotubbe's father old Issetibbeha and old Issetibbeha's fathers too held it, already tainted even before any white man owned it by what Grandfather and his kind, his fathers, had brought into the new land which He had vouchsafed them out of pity and sufferance, on condition, from that old world's corrupt and worthless twilight as though in the sailfuls of the old world's tainted wind which drove the ships—' and McCaslin

'Ah.'

'—and no hope for the land anywhere so long as Ikkemotubbe and Ikkemotubbe's descendants held it in unbroken succession. Maybe He saw that only by voiding the land for a time of Ikkemotubbe's blood and substituting for it another blood, could He accomplish His purpose. Maybe He knew already what that other blood would be, maybe it was more than justice that only the white man's blood was available and capable to raise the white man's curse, more than vengeance when—' and McCaslin

'Ah.'

'—when He used the blood which had brought in the evil to destroy the evil as doctors use fever to burn up fever, poison to slay poison. Maybe He chose Grandfather out of all of them He might have picked. Maybe He knew that Grandfather himself would not serve His purpose because Grandfather was born too soon too, but that Grandfather would have descendants, the right descendants; maybe He had foreseen already the descendants Grandfather would have, maybe He saw already in Grandfather the seed progenitive of the three generations He saw it would take to set at least some of His lowly people free—' and McCaslin

'The sons of Ham. You who quote the Book:[1] the sons of Ham.' and he

'There are some things He said in the Book, and some things reported of Him that He did not say. And I know what you will say now: That if truth is one thing to me and another thing to you, how will we choose which is truth?

1. See Genesis 9.25. Blacks were said to be descended from Canaan (son of Ham) and relegated by Noah to be servants forever.

You don't need to choose. The heart already knows. He didn't have His Book written to be read by what must elect and choose, but by the heart, not by the wise of the earth because maybe they don't need it or maybe the wise no longer have any heart, but by the doomed and lowly of the earth who have nothing else to read with but the heart. Because the men who wrote His Book for Him were writing about truth and there is only one truth and it covers all things that touch the heart.' and McCaslin

'So these men who transcribed His Book for Him were sometimes liars.' and he

'Yes. Because they were human men. They were trying to write down the heart's truth out of the heart's driving complexity, for all the complex and troubled hearts which would beat after them. What they were trying to tell, what He wanted said, was too simple. Those for whom they transcribed His words could not have believed them. It had to be expounded in the everyday terms which they were familiar with and could comprehend, not only those who listened but those who told it too, because if they who were that near to Him as to have been elected from among all who breathed and spoke language to transcribe and relay His words, could comprehend truth only through the complexity of passion and lust and hate and fear which drives the heart, what distance back to truth must they traverse whom truth could only reach by word-of-mouth?' and McCaslin

'I might answer that, since you have taken to proving your points and disproving mine by the same text, I don't know. But I don't say that, because you have answered yourself: No time at all if, as you say, the heart knows truth, the infallible and unerring heart. And perhaps you are right, since although you admitted three generations from old Carothers to you, there were not three. There were not even completely two. Uncle Buck and Uncle Buddy. And they not the first and not alone. A thousand other Bucks and Buddies in less than two generations and sometimes less than one in this land which so you claim God created and man himself cursed and tainted. Not to mention 1865.' and he

'Yes. More men than Father and Uncle Buddy,' not even glancing toward the shelf above the desk, nor did McCaslin. They did not need to. To him it was as though the ledgers in their scarred cracked leather bindings were being lifted down one by one in their fading sequence and spread open on the desk or perhaps upon some apocryphal Bench, or even Altar, or perhaps before the Throne Itself for a last perusal and contemplation and refreshment of the All-knowledgeable, before the yellowed pages and the brown thin ink in which was recorded the injustice and a little at least of its amelioration and restitution faded back forever into the anonymous communal original dust

the yellowed pages scrawled in fading ink by the hand first of his grandfather and then of his father and uncle, bachelors up to and past fifty and then sixty, the one who ran the plantation and the farming of it, and the other who did the housework and the cooking and continued to do it even after his twin married and the boy himself was born

the two brothers who as soon as their father was buried moved out of the tremendously-conceived, the almost barnlike edifice which he had not even completed, into a one-room log cabin which the two of them built themselves and added other rooms to while they lived in it, refusing to allow any slave to touch any timber of it other than the actual raising into place the logs which two men alone could not handle, and domiciled all the slaves in the big house some of the windows of which were still merely boarded up with odds and ends of plank or with the skins of bear and deer nailed over the empty frames: each sundown the brother who superintended the farming would parade the negroes as a first sergeant dismisses a company, and herd them willy-nilly, man woman and child, without question protest or recourse, into the tremendous abortive edifice scarcely yet out of embryo, as if even old Carothers McCaslin had paused aghast at the concrete indication of his own vanity's boundless conceiving: he would call his mental roll and herd them in and with a hand-wrought nail as long as a flenching-knife and suspended from a short deer-hide thong attached to the door-jamb for that purpose, he would nail to the door of that house which lacked half its windows and had no hinged back door at all, so that presently, and for fifty years afterward, when the boy himself was big to hear and remember it, there was in the land a sort of folk-tale: of the countryside all night long full of skulking McCaslin slaves dodging the moonlit roads and the Patrol-riders to visit other plantations, and of the unspoken gentlemen's agreement between the two white men and the two dozen black ones that, after the white man had counted them and driven the home-made nail into the front door at sundown, neither of the white men would go around behind the house and look at the back door, provided that all the negroes were behind the front one when the brother who drove it drew out the nail again at daybreak

the twins who were identical even in their handwriting, unless you had specimens side by side to compare, and even when both hands appeared on the same page (as often happened, as if, long since past any oral intercourse, they had used the diurnally advancing pages to conduct the unavoidable business of the compulsion which had traversed all the waste wilderness of North Mississippi in 1830 and '40 and singled them out to drive) they both looked as though they had been written by the same perfectly normal ten-year-old boy, even to the spelling, except that the spelling did not improve as one by one the slaves which Carothers McCaslin had inherited and purchased—Roscius and Phoebe and Thucydides and Eunice and their descendants, and Sam Fathers and his mother for both of whom he had swapped an underbred trotting gelding to old Ikkemotubbe, the Chickasaw chief, from whom he had likewise bought the land, and Tennie Beauchamp whom the twin Amodeus had won from a neighbor in a poker-game, and the anomaly calling itself Percival Brownlee which the twin Theophilus had purchased, neither he nor his brother ever knew why apparently, from Bedford Forrest while he was still only a slave-dealer and not yet a general (It was a single page, not long and covering less than a year, not seven months in fact, begun in the hand which the boy had learned to distinguish as that of his father:

*Percavil Brownly 26yr Old. cleark @ Bookepper, bought from N.B.Forest at Cold Water 3 Mar 1856 $265. dolars* and beneath that, in the same hand:

*5 mar 1856 No bookepper any way Cant read. Can write his Name but I already put that down My self Says he can Plough but dont look like it to Me. sent to Feild to day Mar 5 1856*

and the same hand:

*6 Mar 1856 Cant plough either Says he aims to be a Precher so may be he can lead live stock to Crick to Drink*

and this time it was the other, the hand which he now recognized as his uncle's when he could see them both on the same page:

*Mar 23th 1856 Cant do that either Except one at a Time Get shut of him*

then the first again:

*24 Mar 1856 Who in hell would buy him*

then the second:

*19th of Apr 1856 Nobody You put yourself out of Market at Cold Water two months ago I never said sell him Free him*

the first:

*22 Apr 1856 Ill get it out of him*

the second:

*Jun 13th 1856 How $1 per yr 265$ 265 yrs Wholl sign his Free paper*

then the first again:

*1 Oct 1856 Mule josephine Broke Leg @ shot Wrong stall wrong niger everything $100. dolars*

and the same:

*2 Oct 1856 Freed Debit McCaslin @ McCaslin $265. dolars*

then the second again:

*Oct 3th Debit Theophilus McCaslin Niger 265$ Mule 100$ 365$ He hasnt gone yet Father should be here*

then the first:

*3 Oct 1856 Son of a bitch wont leave What would father done*

the second:

*29th of Oct 1856 Renamed him*

the first:

*31 Oct 1856 Renamed him what*

the second:

*Chrstms 1856 Spintrius*

) took substance and even a sort of shadowy life with their passions and complexities too, as page followed page and year year; all there, not only the general and condoned injustice and its slow amortization by the specific tragedy which had not been condoned and could never be amortized; the new page and the new ledger, the hand which he could now recognize at first glance as his father's:

*Father dide Lucius Quintus Carothers McCaslin, Callina 1772 Missippy 1837. Dide and burid 27 June 1837*
*Roskus. rased by Granfather in Callina Dont know how old. Freed 27 June 1837 Dont want to leave. Dide and Burid 12 Jan 1841*
*Fibby Roskus Wife. bought by granfather in Callina say Fifty Freed 27 June 1837 Dont want to leave. Dide and burd 1 Aug 1849*
*Thucydus Roskus @ Fibby Son born in Callina 1779. Refused 10acre peace fathers Will 28 Jun 1837 Refused Cash offer $200. dolars from A. @ T. McCaslin 28 Jun 1837 Wants to stay and work it out*

and beneath this and covering the next five pages and almost that many years, the slow, day-by-day accrument of the wages allowed him and the food and clothing—the molasses and meat and meal, the cheap durable shirts and jeans and shoes, and now and then a coat against rain and cold—charged against the slowly yet steadily mounting sum of balance (and it would seem to the boy that he could actually see the black man, the slave whom his white owner had forever manumitted by the very act from which the black man could never be free so long as memory lasted, entering the commissary, asking permission perhaps of the white man's son to see the ledger-page which he could not even read, not even asking for the white man's word, which he would have had to accept for the reason that there was absolutely no way under the sun for him to test it, as to how the account stood, how much longer before he could go and never return, even if only as far as Jefferson seventeen miles away), on to the double pen-stroke closing the final entry:

*3 Nov 1841 By Cash to Thucydus McCaslin $200. dolars Set Up blaksmith in J. Dec 1841 Dide and burid in J. 17 feb 1854*
*Eunice Bought by Father in New Orleans 1807 $650. dolars. Marrid to Thucydus 1809 Drownd in Crick Cristmas Day 1832*[2]

and then the other hand appeared, the first time he had seen it in the ledger to distinguish it as his uncle's, the cook and housekeeper whom even McCaslin, who had known him and the boy's father for sixteen years before the boy was born, remembered as sitting all day long in the rocking chair from which he

2. This ledger entry introduces a special complication in the genealogy descending from the grandfather Lucius Quintus Carothers McCaslin, obscurely picked up by later allusions. Old McCaslin had an adulterous sexual relation with the slave Eunice. She bore him a daughter, Tomasina, with whom he had an incestuous relation, resulting in the birth of a son named Terrel (also called Tomey's Turl). Thus the partly black descendants of Terrel are blood relations of Isaac McCaslin.

cooked the food, before the kitchen fire on which he cooked it:

*June 21th 1833 Drownd herself*

and the first:

*23 June 1833 Who in hell ever heard of a niger drownding him self*

and the second, unhurried, with a complete finality; the two identical entries might have been made with a rubber stamp save for the date:

*Aug 13th 1833 Drownd herself*

and he thought *But why? But why?* He was sixteen then. It was neither the first time he had been alone in the commissary nor the first time he had taken down the old ledgers familiar on their shelf above the desk ever since he could remember. As a child and even after nine and ten and eleven, when he had learned to read, he would look up at the scarred and cracked backs and ends but with no particular desire to open them, and though he intended to examine them someday because he realized that they probably contained a chronological and much more comprehensive though doubtless tedious record than he would ever get from any other source, not alone of his own flesh and blood but of all his people, not only the whites but the black ones too, who were as much a part of his ancestry as his white progenitors, and of the land which they had all held and used in common and fed from and on and would continue to use in common without regard to color or titular ownership, it would only be on some idle day when he was old and perhaps even bored a little, since what the old books contained would be after all these years fixed immutably, finished, unalterable, harmless. Then he was sixteen. He knew what he was going to find before he found it. He got the commissary key from McCaslin's room after midnight while McCaslin was asleep and with the commissary door shut and locked behind him and the forgotten lantern stinking anew the rank dead icy air, he leaned above the yellowed page and thought not Why drowned herself, but thinking what he believed his father had thought when he found his brother's first comment: Why did Uncle Buddy think she had drowned herself? finding, beginning to find on the next succeeding page what he knew he would find, only this was still not it because he already knew this:

*Tomasina called Tomy Daughter of Thucydus @ Eunice Born 1810 dide in Child bed June 1833 and Burd. Yr stars fell*

nor the next:

*Turl Son of Thucydus @ Eunice Tomy born Jun 1833 yr stars fell Fathers will*

and nothing more, no tedious recording filling this page of wages, day by day, and food and clothing charged against them, no entry of his death and burial because he had outlived his white half-brothers and the books which McCaslin kept did not include obituaries: just *Fathers will* and he had seen that too: old Carothers' bold cramped hand far less legible than his sons' even and not much better in spelling, who while capitalizing almost every noun and verb, made no effort to punctuate or construct whatever, just as he made no effort either to explain or obfuscate the thousand-dollar legacy to the son of an unmarried slave-girl, to be paid only at the child's coming-of-age, bearing the consequence of the act of which there was still no definite incontrovertible proof that he acknowledged, not out of his own substance, but penalizing his sons with it, charging them a cash forfeit on the accident of their own paternity; not even a bribe for silence toward his own fame since his fame would suffer only after he was no longer present to defend it, flinging almost contemptuously, as he might a cast-off hat or pair of shoes, the thousand dollars which could have had no more reality to him under those conditions than it would have to the Negro, the slave who would not even see it until he came of age, twenty-one years too late to begin to learn what money was. *So I reckon that was cheaper than saying My son to a nigger,* he thought. *Even if My son wasn't but just two words. But there must have been love,* he thought. *Some sort of love. Even what he would have called love: not just an afternoon's or a night's spittoon.* There was the old man, old, within five years of his life's end, long a widower and, since his sons were not only bachelors but were approaching middleage, lonely in the house and doubtless even bored, since his plantation was established now and functioning and there was enough money now, too much of it probably for a man whose vices even apparently remained below his means; there was the girl, husbandless and young, only twenty-three when the child was born: perhaps he had sent for her at first out of loneliness, to have a young voice and movement in the house, summoned her, bade her mother send her each morning to sweep the floors and make the beds and the mother acquiescing since that was probably already understood, already planned: the only child of a couple who were not field hands and who held themselves something above the other slaves, not alone for that reason but because the husband and his father and mother too had been inherited by the white man from his father, and the white man himself had travelled three hundred miles and better to New Orleans in a day when men travelled by horseback or steamboat, and bought the girl's mother as a wife for him

and that was all. The old frail pages seemed to turn of their own accord even while he thought, *His own daughter His own daughter. No. No Not even him,* back to that one where the white man (not even a widower then) who never went anywhere, any more than his sons in their time ever did, and who did not need another slave, had gone all the way to New Orleans and bought one. And Tomey's Terrel was still alive when the boy was ten years old and he knew from his own observation and memory that there had already been some white in Tomey's Terrel's blood before his father gave him the rest of it; and looking down at the yellowed page spread beneath the yellow glow of the lantern smoking and stinking in that rank chill midnight room fifty years later, he seemed to see her actually walking into the icy creek on that Christmas day six months before her daughter's and her lover's *(Her first lover's,* he thought. *Her first)* child was born, solitary, inflexible, griefless, ceremonial, in formal and succinct repudiation of grief and despair, who had already had to repudiate belief and hope

that was all. He would never need look at the ledgers again nor did he; the yellowed pages in their fading and implacable succession were as much a part of his consciousness and would remain so forever, as the fact of his own nativity:

> *Tennie Beauchamp 21yrs Won by Amodeus McCaslin from Hubert Beauchamp Esqre Possible Strait against three Treys in sigt Not called 1859 Marrid to Tomys Turl 1859*

and no date of freedom because her freedom, as well as that of her first surviving child, derived not from Buck and Buddy McCaslin in the commissary but from a stranger in Washington, and no date of death and burial, not only because McCaslin kept no obituaries in his books, but because in this year 1883 she was still alive and would remain so to see a grandson by her last surviving child:

> *Amodeus McCaslin Beauchamp Son of tomys Turl @ Tennie Beauchamp 1859 died 1859*

then his uncle's hand entire, because his father was now a member of the cavalry command of that man whose name as a slave-dealer he could not even spell: and not even a page and not even a full line:

> *Dauter Tomes Turl and tenny 1862*

and not even a line and not even a sex and no cause given though the boy could guess it because McCaslin was thirteen then and he remembered how there was always enough to eat in more places than Vicksburg:

> *Child of tomes Turl and Tenny 1863*

and the same hand again and this one lived, as though Tennie's perseverance and the fading and diluted ghost of old Carothers' ruthlessness had at last conquered even starvation: and clear, fuller, more carefully written and spelled than the boy had yet seen it, as if the old man, who should have been a woman to begin with, trying to run what was left of the plantation in his brother's absence in the intervals of cooking and caring for himself and the fourteen-year-old orphan, had taken as an omen for renewed hope the fact that this nameless inheritor of slaves was at least remaining alive long enough to receive a name:

> *James Thucydus Beauchamp Son of Tomes Turl and Tenny Beauchamp Born 29th december 1864 and both Well Wanted to call him Theophilus but Tride Amodeus McCaslin and Callina McCaslin and both dide so Disswaded Them Born at Two clock A,m, both Well*

but no more, nothing; it would be another two years yet before the boy, almost a man now, would return from the abortive trip into Tennessee with the still-intact third of old Carothers' legacy to his Negro son and his descendants, which as the three surviving children established at last one by one their apparent intention of surviving, their white half-uncles had increased to a thousand dollars each, conditions permitting, as they came of age, and completed the page himself as far as it would even be completed when that day was long passed beyond which a man born in 1864 (or 1867 either, when he himself saw light) could have expected or himself hoped or even wanted to be still alive; his own hand now, queerly enough resembling neither his father's nor his uncle's nor even McCaslin's, but like that of his grandfather's save for the spelling:

> *Vanished sometime on night of his twenty-first birthday Dec 29 1885. Traced by Isaac McCaslin to Jackson Tenn. and there lost. His third of legacy $1000.00 returned to McCaslin Edmonds Trustee this day Jan 12 1886*

but not yet: that would be two years yet, and now his father's again, whose old commander was now quit of soldiering and slave-trading both; once more in the ledger and then not again, and more illegible than ever, almost indecipherable at all from the rheumatism which now crippled him, and almost completely innocent now even of any sort of spelling as well as punctuation, as if the four years during which he had followed the sword of the only man ever breathing who ever sold him a Negro, let alone beat him in a trade, had convinced him not only of the vanity of faith and hope, but of orthography too:

> *Miss sophonsiba b drt t t @ t 1869*

but not of belief and will because it was there, written, as McCaslin had told him, with the left hand, but there in the ledger one time more and then not again, for the boy himself was a year old, and when Lucas was born six years later, his father and uncle had been dead inside the same twelve-months almost five years; his own hand again, who was there and saw it, 1886, she was just seventeen, two years younger than himself, and he was in the commissary when McCaslin entered out of the first of dusk and said, 'He wants to marry Fonsiba, like that: and he looked past McCaslin and saw the man, the stranger, taller than McCaslin and wearing better clothes than McCaslin and most of the other white men the boy knew habitually wore, who entered the room like a white man and stood in it like a white man, as though he had let McCaslin precede him into it not because McCaslin's skin was white but simply because McCaslin lived there and knew the way, and who talked like a white man too, looking at him past McCaslin's shoulder rapidly and keenly once and then no more, without further interest, as a mature and contained white man not impatient but just pressed for time might have looked. 'Marry Fonsiba?' he cried. 'Marry Fonsiba?' and then no more either, just watching and listening while McCaslin and the Negro talked:

'To live in Arkansas, I believe you said.'

'Yes. I have property there. A farm.'

'Property? A farm? You own it?'

'Yes.'

'You don't say Sir, do you?'

'To my elders, yes.'

'I see. You are from the North.'

'Yes. Since a child.'

'Then your father was a slave.'

'Yes. Once.'

'Then how do you own a farm in Arkansas?'

'I have a grant. It was my father's. From the United States. For military service.'

'I see,' McCaslin said. 'The Yankee army.'

'The United States army,' the stranger said; and then himself again, crying it at McCaslin's back:

'Call aunt Tennie! I'll go get her! I'll—' But McCaslin was not even including him; the stranger did not even glance back toward his voice, the two of them speaking to one another again as if he were not even there:

'Since you seem to have it all settled,' McCaslin said, 'why have you bothered to consult my authority at all?'

'I don't,' the stranger said. 'I acknowledge your authority only so far as you admit your responsibility toward her as a female member of the family of which you are the head. I don't ask your permission. I—'

'That will do!' McCaslin said. But the stranger did not falter. It was neither as if he were ignoring McCaslin nor as if he had failed to hear him. It was as though he were making, not at all an excuse and not exactly a justification, but simply a statement which the situation absolutely required and demanded should be made in McCaslin's hearing whether McCaslin listened to it or not. It was as if he were talking to himself, for himself to hear the words spoken aloud. They faced one another, not close yet at slightly less than foils' distance, erect, their voices not raised, not impactive, just succinct:

'—I inform you, notify you in advance as chief of her family. No man of honor could do less. Besides, you have, in your way, according to your lights and upbringing——'

'That's enough, I said,' McCaslin said. 'Be off this place by full dark. Go.' But for another moment the other did not move, contemplating McCaslin with that detached and heatless look, as if he were watching reflected in McCaslin's pupils the tiny image of the figure he was sustaining.

'Yes,' he said. 'After all, this is your house. And in your fashion you have. . . . But no matter. You are right. This is enough.' He turned back toward the door; he paused again but only for a second, already moving while he spoke: 'Be easy. I will be good to her.' Then he was gone.

'But how did she ever know him?' the boy cried. 'I never even heard of him before! And Fonsiba, that's never been off this place except to go to church since she was born——'

'Ha,' McCaslin said. 'Even their parents don't know until too late how seventeen-year-old girls ever met the men who marry them too, if they are lucky.' And the next morning they were both gone, Fonsiba too. McCaslin never saw her again, nor did he, because the woman he found at last, five months later, was no one he had ever known. He carried a third of the three-thousand-dollar fund in gold in a money-belt, as when he had vainly traced Tennie's Jim into Tennessee a year ago. They—the man—had left an address of some sort with Tennie, and three months later a letter came, written by the man although McCaslin's wife, Alice, had taught Fonsiba to read and write too a little. But it bore a different postmark from the address the man had left with Tennie, and he travelled by rail as far as he could and then by contracted stage and then by a hired livery rig and then by rail again for a distance: an experienced traveller by now and an experienced bloodhound too, and a successful one this time because he would have to be; as the slow interminable empty muddy December miles crawled and crawled and night followed night in hotels, in roadside taverns of rough logs and containing little else but a bar, and in the cabins of strangers, and the hay of lonely barns, in none of which he dared undress because of his secret golden girdle like that of a disguised one of the Magi travelling incognito and not even hope to draw him, but only determination and desperation, he would tell himself: *I will have to find her. I will have to. We have already lost one of them. I will have to find her this time.* He did. Hunched in the slow and icy rain, on a spent hired horse splashed to the chest and higher, he saw it—a single log edifice with a clay chimney, which seemed in process of being flattened by the rain to a nameless and valueless rubble of dissolution in that roadless and even pathless waste of unfenced fallow and wilderness jungle—no barn, no stable, not so much as a hen-coop: just a log cabin built by hand and no clever hand either, a meagre pile of clumsily-cut firewood sufficient for about one day and not even a gaunt hound to come bellowing out from under the house when he rode up—a farm only in embryo, perhaps a good farm, maybe even a plantation someday, but not now, not for years yet and only then with labor, hard and enduring and unflagging work and sacrifice; he shoved open the crazy kitchen door in its awry frame and entered an icy gloom where not even a fire for cooking burned, and after another moment saw, crouched into the wall's angle behind a crude table, the coffee-colored face which he had known all his life but knew no more, the body which had been born within a hundred yards of the room that he was born in and in which some of his own blood ran, but which was now completely inheritor of generation after generation to whom an unannounced white man on a horse was a white man's hired Patroller wearing a pistol sometimes and a blacksnake whip always; he entered the next room, the only other room the cabin owned, and found, sitting in a rocking chair before the hearth, the man himself reading—sitting there in the only chair in the house, before that miserable fire for which there was not wood sufficient to last twenty-four hours, in the same ministerial clothing in which he had entered the commissary five months ago and a pair of gold-framed spectacles which, when he looked up and then rose to his feet, the boy saw did not even contain lenses, reading a book in the midst of that desolation, that muddy waste, fenceless and even pathless and without even a walled shed for stock to stand beneath: and over all, permanent, clinging to the man's very clothing and exuding from his skin itself, that rank stink of baseless and imbecile delusion, that boundless rapacity and folly, of the carpet-bagger followers of victorious armies.

'Don't you see?' he cried. 'Don't you see? This whole land, the whole South, is cursed, and all of us who derive from it, whom it ever suckled, white and black both, lie under the curse? Granted that my people brought the curse onto the land: maybe for that reason their descendants alone can—not resist it, not combat it—maybe just endure and outlast it until the curse is lifted. Then your peoples' turn will come because we have forfeited ours. But not now. Not yet. Don't you see?'

The other side stood now, the unfrayed garments still ministerial even if not quite so fine, the book closed upon one finger to keep the place, the lenseless spectacles held like a music master's wand in the other workless hand while the owner of it spoke his measured and sonorous imbecility of the boundless folly and the baseless hope: 'You're wrong. The curse you whites brought into this land has been lifted. It has been voided and discharged. We are seeing a new era, an era dedicated, as our founders intended it, to freedom, liberty and equality for all, to which this country will be the new Canaan[3]—'

'Freedom from what? From work? Canaan?' He jerked his arm, comprehensive, almost violent: whereupon it all seemed to stand there about them, intact and complete and visible in the drafty, damp, heatless, Negro-stale Negro-rank sorry room—the empty fields without plow or seed to work them, fenceless against the stock which did not exist within or without the walled stable which likewise was not there. 'What corner of Canaan is this?'

'You are seeing it at a bad time. This is winter. No man farms this time of year.'

'I see. And of course her need for food and clothing will stand while the land lies fallow.'

'I have a pension,' the other said. He said it as a man might say *I have grace or I own a gold mine.* 'I have my father's pension too. It will arrive on the first of the month. What day is this?'

'The eleventh,' he said. 'Twenty days more. And until then?'

'I have a few groceries in the house from my credit account with the merchant in Midnight who banks my pension check for me. I have executed to him a power of attorney to handle it for me as a matter of mutual—'

'I see. And if the groceries don't last the twenty days?'

'I still have one more hog.'

'Where?'

'Outside,' the other said. 'It is customary in this country to allow stock to range free during the winter for food. It comes up from time to time. But no matter if it doesn't; I can probably trace its footprints when the need—'

'Yes!' he cried. 'Because no matter: you still have the pension check. And the man in Midnight will cash it and pay himself out of it for what you have already eaten and if there is any left over, it is yours. And the hog will be eaten by then or you still can't catch it, and then what will you do?'

'It will be almost spring then,' the other said. 'I am planning in the spring—'

'It will be January,' he said. 'And then February. And then more than half of March—' and when he stopped again in the kitchen she had not moved, she did not even seem to breathe or to be alive except her eyes watching him; when he took a step toward her it was still not movement because she could have retreated no further: only the tremendous, fathomless, ink-colored eyes in the narrow, thin, coffee-colored face watching him without alarm, without recognition, without hope, 'Fonsiba,' he said. 'Fonsiba. Are you all right?'

'I'm free,' she said. Midnight was a tavern, a livery stable, a big store (that would be where the pension check banked itself as a matter of mutual elimi-

3. The Promised Land of the Israelites.

nation of bother and fret, he thought) and a little one, a saloon and a blacksmith shop. But there was a bank there too. The president (the owner, for all practical purposes) of it was a translated Mississippian who had been one of Forrest's men too: and his body lightened of the golden belt for the first time since he left home eight days ago, with pencil and paper he multiplied three dollars by twelve months and divided it into one thousand dollars; it would stretch that way over almost twenty-eight years and for twenty-eight years at least she would not starve, the banker promising to send the three dollars himself by a trusty messenger on the fifteenth of each month and put it into her actual hand, and he returned home and that was all because in 1874 his father and his uncle were both dead and the old ledgers never again came down from the shelf above the desk to which his father had returned them for the last time that day in 1869. But he could have completed it:

*Lucas Quintus Carothers McCaslin Beauchamp. Last surviving son and child of Tomey's Terrel and Tennie Beauchamp. March 17, 1874*

except that there was no need: not *Lucius Quintus* @c@c@c, but *Lucas Quintus,* not refusing to be called Lucius, because he simply eliminated that word from the name; not denying, declining the name itself, because he used three quarters of it; but simply taking the name and changing, altering it, making it no longer the white man's but his own, by himself composed, himself selfprogenitive and nominate, by himself ancestored, as, for all the old ledgers recorded to the contrary, old Carothers himself was

and that was all: 1874 the boy; 1888 the man, repudiated denied and free; 1895 and husband but no father, unwidowered but without a wife, and found long since that no man is ever free and probably could not bear it if he were; married then and living in Jefferson in the little jerrybuilt bungalow which his wife's father had given them: and one morning Lucas stood suddenly in the doorway of the room where he was reading the Memphis paper and he looked at the paper's dateline and thought *It's his birthday. He's twenty-one today* and Lucas said: 'Whar's the rest of that money old Carothers left? I wants it. All of it.'

that was all: and McCaslin

'More men than that one Buck and Buddy to fumble-heed that truth so mazed for them that spoke it and so confused for them that heard yet still there was 1865:' and he

'But not enough. Not enough of even Father and Uncle Buddy to fumble-heed in even three generations not even three generations fathered by Grandfather not even if there had been nowhere beneath His sight any but Grandfather and so He would not even have needed to elect and choose. But He tried and I know what you will say. That having Himself created them He could have known no more of hope than He could have pride and grief, but He didn't hope He just waited because He had made them: not just because He had set them alive and in motion but because He had already worried with them so long: worried with them so long because He had seen how in individual cases they were capable of anything, any height or depth remembered in mazed incomprehension out of heaven where hell was created too, and so He must admit them or else admit his equal somewhere and so be no longer God and therefore must accept responsibility for what He Himself had done in order to live with Himself in His lonely and paramount heaven. And He probably knew it was vain but He had created them and knew them capable of all things because He had shaped them out of the primal Absolute which contained all and had watched them since in their individual exaltation and baseness, and they themselves not knowing why nor how nor even when: until at last He saw that they were all Grandfather all of them and that even from them the elected and chosen the best the very best He could expect (not hope mind: not hope) would be Bucks and Buddies and not even enough of them and in the third generation not even Bucks and Buddies but—' and McCaslin

'Ah:' and he

'Yes. If He could see Father and Uncle Buddy in Grandfather He must have seen me too. —an Isaac born into a later life than Abraham's and repudiating immolation: fatherless and therefore safe declining the altar because maybe this time the exasperated Hand might not supply the kid—' and McCaslin

'Escape:' and he

'All right. Escape.—Until one day He said what you told Fonsiba's husband that afternoon here in this room: *This will do. This is enough:* not in exasperation or rage or even just sick to death as you were sick that day: just *This is enough* and looked about for one last time, for one time more since He had created them, upon this land this South for which He had done so much with woods for game and streams for fish and deep rich soil for seed and lush springs to sprout it and long summers to mature it and serene falls to harvest it and short mild winters for men and animals, and saw no hope anywhere and looked beyond it where hope should have been, where to East North and West lay illimitable that whole hopeful continent dedicated as a refuge and sanctuary of liberty and freedom from what you called the old world's worthless evening, and saw the rich descendants of slavers, females of both sexes, to whom the black they shrieked of was another specimen another example like the Brazilian macaw brought home in a cage by a traveller, passing resolutions about horror and outrage in warm and air-proof halls: and the thundering cannonade of politicians earning votes and the medicine-shows of pulpiteers earning Chatauqua fees, to whom the outrage and the injustice were as much abstractions as Tariff or Silver or Immortality and who employed the very shackles of its servitude and the sorry rags of its regalia as they did the other beer and banners and mottoes, redfire and brimstone and sleight-of-hand and musical handsaws: and the whirling wheels which manufactured for a profit the pristine replacements of the shackles and shoddy garments as they wore out, and spun the cotton and made the gins which ginned it and the cars and ships which hauled it, and the men who ran the wheels for that profit and established and collected the taxes it was taxed with and the rates for hauling it and the commissions for selling it: and He could have repudiated them since they were his creation now and forever more throughout all their generations, until not only that old world from which He had rescued them but this new one too which He had revealed and led them to as a sanctuary and refuge were become the same worthless tideless rock cooling in the last crimson evening, except that out of all that empty sound and bootless fury one silence, among that loud and moiling all of them just one simple enough to believe that horror and outrage were first and last simply horror and outrage and crude enough to act upon that, illiterate and had no words for talking or perhaps was just busy and had no time to, one out of them all who did not bother Him with cajolery and adjuration then pleading then threat, and had not even bothered to inform Him in advance what he was about so that a lesser than He might have even missed the simple act of lifting the long ancestral musket down from the deerhorns above the door, whereupon He said *My name is Brown too* and the other *So is mine* and He *Then mine or yours can't be because I am against it* and the other *So am I* and He triumphantly *Then where are you going with that gun?* and the other told him in one sentence one word and He: amazed: Who knew neither hope nor pride nor grief *But your Association, your Committee, your Officers. Where are your Minutes, your Motions, your Parliamentary Procedures?* and the other *I ain't against them. They are all right I reckon for them that have the time. I am just against the weak because they are niggers being held in bondage by the strong just because they are white.* So He turned once more to this land which He still intended to save because He had done so much for it—' and McCaslin

'What?' and he

'—to these people He was still committed to because they were his creations—' and McCaslin

'Turned back to us? His face to us?' and he

'—whose wives and daughters at least made soups and jellies for them when they were sick, and carried the trays through the mud and the winter too into the stinking cabins, and sat in the stinking cabins and kept fires going until crises came and passed, but that was not enough: and when they were very sick had them carried into the big house itself into the company room itself maybe and nursed them there, which the white man would have done too for any other of his cattle that was sick but at least the man who hired one from a livery wouldn't have, and still that was not enough: so that He said and not in grief either, Who had made them and so could know no more of grief than He could of pride or hope: *Apparently they can learn nothing save through suffering, remember nothing save when underlined in blood—'* and McCaslin

'Ashby[4] on an afternoon's ride, to call on some remote maiden cousins of his mother or maybe just acquaintances of hers, comes by chance upon a minor engagement of outposts and dismounts and with his crimson-lined cloak for target leads a handful of troops he never saw before against an entrenched position of backwoods-trained riflemen. Lee's[5] battle-order, wrapped maybe about a handful of cigars and doubtless thrown away when the last cigar was smoked, found by a Yankee Intelligence officer on the floor of a saloon behind the Yankee lines after Lee had already divided his forces before Sharpsburg.[6] Jackson on the Plank Road, already rolled up the flank which Hooker believed

4. Colonel Turner Ashby (1828–1862), Confederate leader of guerrilla raiders. 5. Robert E. Lee (1807–1870), commander in chief of Confederate forces. 6. Name of a major battle, also called the battle of Antietam (September 17, 1862).

could not be turned and, waiting only for night to pass to continue the brutal and incessant slogging which would fling that whole wing back into Hooker's lap where he sat on a front gallery in Chancellorsville drinking rum toddies and telegraphing Lincoln that he had defeated Lee, is shot from among a whole covey of minor officers and in the blind night by one of his own patrols, leaving as next by seniority Stuart,[7] that gallant man born apparently already horsed and sabred and already knowing all there was to know about war except the slogging and brutal stupidity of it: and that same Stuart off raiding Pennsylvania hen-roosts when Lee should have known of all of Meade just where Hancock was on Cemetery Ridge: and Longstreet too at Gettysburg[8] and that same Longstreet shot out of saddle by his own men in the dark by mistake just as Jackson was. His face to us? His face to us?' and he

'How else have made them fight? Who else but Jacksons and Stuarts and Ashbys and Morgans[9] and Forrests?—the farmers of the central and middle-west, holding land by the acre instead of the tens or maybe even the hundreds, farming it themselves and to no single crop of cotton or tobacco or cane, owning no slaves and needing and wanting none, and already looking toward the Pacific coast, not always as long as two generations there and having stopped where they did stop only through the fortuitous mischance that an ox died or a wagon-axle broke. And the New England mechanics who didn't even own land and measured all things by the weight of water and the cost of turning wheels, and the narrow fringe of traders and shipowners still looking backward across the Atlantic and attached to the continent only by their counting-houses. And those who should have had the alertness to see: the wildcat manipulators of mythical wilderness townsites; and the astuteness to rationalize: the bankers who held the mortgages on the land which the first were only waiting to abandon, and on the railroads and steamboats to carry them still further west, and on the factories and the wheels and the rented tenements those who ran them lived in; and the leisure and scope to comprehend and fear in time and even anticipate: the Boston-bred (even when not born in Boston) spinster, descendants of long lines of similarly-bred and likewise spinster aunts and uncles whose hands knew no callus except that of the indicting pen, to whom the wilderness itself began at the top of tide and who looked, if at anything other than Beacon Hill, only toward heaven—not to mention all the loud rabble of the camp-followers of pioneers: the bellowing of politicians, the mellifluous choiring of self-styled men of God, the—' and McCaslin

'Here, here. Wait a minute:' And he

'Let me talk now. I'm trying to explain to the head of my family something which I have got to do which I don't quite understand myself, not in justification

7. J. E. B. ("Jeb") Stuart (1833–1864), Confederate general. This passage describes the events and personalities involved in the battle of Chancellorsville (May 1–5, 1863). Joseph Hooker (1814–1879), Union general, was opposed by Thomas Jonathan (Stonewall) Jackson (1824–1863), who had ensured a Confederate victory before he was mistakenly shot by his own men. 8. Battle of Gettysburg (July 1–3, 1863). George Gordon Meade (1815–1872), Union general, was in overall command of Northern forces. His subordinate General Winfield Scott Hancock (1824–1886) distinguished himself in the battle by holding the line along Cemetery Ridge against the main thrust of the Confederate attack. James Longstreet (1821–1904), Confederate general, was sometimes blamed in the South for delay in executing Lee's orders. Longstreet was later wounded in the battle of the Wilderness (May 5–6, 1864). 9. John Hunt Morgan (1826–1864), Confederate general.

of it but to explain it if I can. I could say I don't know why I must do it but that I do know I have got to because I have got myself to have to live with for the rest of my life and all I want is peace to do it in. But you are the head of my family. More. I knew a long time ago that I would never have to miss my father, even if you are just finding out that you have missed your son—the drawers of bills and the shavers of notes and the schoolmasters and the self-ordained to teach and lead and all that horde of the semi-literate with a white shirt but no change for it, with one eye on themselves and watching each other with the other one. Who else could have made them fight: could have struck them so aghast with fear and dread as to turn shoulder to shoulder and face one way and even stop talking for a while and even after two years of it keep them still so wrung with terror that some among them would seriously propose moving their very capital into a foreign country lest it be ravaged and pillaged by a people whose entire white male population would have little more than filled any one of their larger cities: except Jackson in the Valley[1] and three separate armies trying to catch him and none of them ever knowing whether they were just retreating from a battle or just running into one, and Stuart riding his whole command entirely around the biggest single armed force[2] this continent ever saw in order to see what it looked like from behind, and Morgan leading a cavalry charge against a stranded man-of-war. Who else could have declared a war against a power with ten times the area and a hundred times the men and a thousand times the resources, except men who could believe that all necessary to conduct a successful war was not acumen nor shrewdness nor politics nor diplomacy nor money nor even integrity and simple arithmetic, but just love of land and courage—'

'And an unblemished and gallant ancestry and the ability to ride a horse,' McCaslin said. 'Don't leave that out.' It was evening now, the tranquil sunset of October mazy with windless woodsmoke. The cotton was long since picked and ginned, and all day now the wagons loaded with gathered corn moved between field and crib, processional across the enduring land. 'Well, maybe that's what He wanted. At least, that's what He got.' This time there was no yellowed procession of fading and harmless ledger-pages. This was chronicled in a harsher book, and McCaslin, fourteen and fifteen and sixteen, had seen it and the boy himself had inherited it as Noah's grandchildren had inherited the Flood although they had not been there to see the deluge: that dark corrupt and bloody time while three separate peoples had tried to adjust not only to another but to the new land which they had created and inherited too and must live in for the reason that those who had lost it were no less free to quit it than those who had gained it were:—those upon whom freedom and equality had been dumped overnight and without warning or preparation or any training in how to employ it or even just endure it and who misused it, not as children would nor yet because they had been so long in bondage and then so suddenly freed, but misused it as human beings always misuse freedom, so that he

1. I.e., the Shenandoah Valley in Virginia. 2. Before the Seven Days' Battle (June 26–July 2, 1862), Stuart led his cavalry all the way around the Union Army, which was then commanded by General George McClellan (1826–1885).

thought *Apparently there is a wisdom beyond even that learned through suffering necessary for a man to distinguish between liberty and license;* those who had fought for four years and lost to preserve a condition under which that franchisement was anomaly and paradox, not because they were opposed to freedom as freedom but for the old reasons for which man (not the generals and politicians but man) has always fought and died in wars: to preserve a status quo or to establish a better future one to endure for his children; and lastly, as if that were not enough for bitterness and hatred and fear, that third race even more alien to the people whom they resembled in pigment and in whom even the same blood ran, than to the people whom they did not,—that race threefold in one and alien even among themselves save for a single fierce will for rapine and pillage, composed of the sons of middleaged Quartermaster lieutenants and Army sutlers and contractors in military blankets and shoes and transport mules, who followed the battles they themselves had not fought and inherited the conquest they themselves had not helped to gain, sanctioned and protected even if not blessed, and left their bones and in another generation would be engaged in a fierce economic competition of small sloven farms with the black men they were supposed to have freed and the white descendants of fathers who had owned no slaves anyway whom they were supposed to have disinherited, and in the third generation would be back once more in the little lost county seats as barbers and garage mechanics and deputy sheriffs and mill- and gin-hands and power-plant firemen, leading, first in mufti[3] then later in an actual formalized regalia of hooded sheets and passwords and fiery Christian symbols, lynching mobs against the race their ancestors had come to save: and of all that other nameless horde of speculators in human misery, manipulators of money and politics and land, who follow catastrophe and are their own protection as grasshoppers are and need no blessing and sweat no plow or axe-helve and batten and vanish and leave no bones, just as they derived apparently from no ancestry, no mortal flesh, no act even of passion or even of lust: and the Jew who came without protection too, since after two thousand years he had got out of the habit of being or needing it, and solitary, without even the solidarity of the locusts, and in this a sort of courage since he had come thinking not in terms of simple pillage but in terms of his great-grandchildren, seeking yet some place to establish them to endure even though forever alien: and unblessed: a pariah about the face of the Western earth which twenty centuries later was still taking revenge on him for the fairy tale with which he had conquered it. McCaslin had actually seen it, and the boy even at almost eighty would never be able to distinguish certainly between what he had seen and what had been told him: a lightless and gutted and empty land where women crouched with the huddled children behind locked doors and men armed in sheets and masks rode the silent roads and the bodies of white and black both, victims not so much of hate as of desperation and despair, swung from lonely limbs: and men shot dead in polling-booths with the still wet pen in one hand and the unblotted ballot in the other: and a United States marshal in Jefferson who signed his official papers with a crude cross, an ex-slave called Sickymo,

3. Civilian clothes.

not at all because his ex-owner was a doctor and apothecary but because, still a slave, he would steal his master's grain alcohol and dilute it with water and peddle it in pint bottles from a cache beneath the roots of a big sycamore tree behind the drug store, who had attained his high office because his half-white sister was the concubine of the Federal A.P.M.:[4] and this time McCaslin did not even say Look but merely lifted one hand, not even pointing, not even specifically toward the shelf of ledgers but toward the desk, toward the corner where it sat beside the scuffed patch on the floor where two decades of heavy shoes had stood while the white man at the desk added and multiplied and subtracted. And again he did not need to look because he had seen this himself and, twenty-three years after the Surrender and twenty-four after the Proclamation,[5] was still watching it: the ledgers, new ones now and filled rapidly, succeeding one another rapidly and containing more names than old Carothers or even his father and Uncle Buddy had ever dreamed of; new names and new faces to go with them, among which the old names and faces that even his father and uncle would have recognized, were lost, vanished—Tomey's Terrel dead, and even the tragic and miscast Percival Brownlee, who couldn't keep books and couldn't farm either, found his true niche at last, reappeared in 1862 during the boy's father's absence and had apparently been living on the plantation for at least a month before his uncle found out about it, conducting impromptu revival meetings among Negroes, preaching and leading the singing also in his high sweet true soprano voice and disappeared again on foot and at top speed, not behind but ahead of a body of raiding Federal horse and reappeared for the third and last time in the entourage of a travelling Army paymaster, the two of them passing through Jefferson in a surrey at the exact moment when the boy's father (it was 1866) also happened to be crossing the Square, the surrey and its occupants traversing rapidly that quiet and bucolic scene and even in that fleeting moment, and to others beside the boy's father, giving an illusion of flight and illicit holiday like a man on an excursion during his wife's absence with his wife's personal maid, until Brownlee glanced up and saw his late co-master and gave him one defiant female glance and then broke again, leaped from the surrey and disappeared this time for good, and it was only by chance that McCaslin, twenty years later, heard of him again, an old man now and quite fat, as the well-to-do proprietor of a select New Orleans brothel; and Tennie's Jim gone, nobody knew where, and Fonsiba in Arkansas with her three dollars each month and the scholar-husband with his lenseless spectacles and frock coat and his plans for the spring; and only Lucas was left, the baby, the last save himself of old Carothers' doomed and fatal blood which in the male derivation seemed to destroy all it touched, and even he was repudiating and at least hoping to escape it;—Lucas, the boy of fourteen whose name would not even appear for six years yet among those rapid pages in the bindings new and dustless too since McCaslin lifted them down daily now to write into them the continuation of that record which two hundred years had

4. Army provost marshal. 5. The Emancipation Proclamation had been issued by President Abraham Lincoln (1809–1865) in 1862. General Lee surrendered the Confederate armies at Appomattox Court House on April 9, 1865.

not been enough to complete, and another hundred would not be enough to discharge; that chronicle which was a whole land in miniature, which multiplied and compounded was the entire South, twenty-three years after surrender and twenty-four from emancipation—that slow trickle of molasses and meal and meat, of shoes and straw hats and overalls, of plowlines and collars and heel-bolts and buckheads and clevises, which returned each fall as cotton—the two threads frail as truth and impalpable as equators yet cable-strong to bind for life them who made the cotton to the land their sweat fell on: and he

'Yes. Binding them for a while yet, a little while yet. Through and beyond that life and maybe through and beyond the life of that life's sons and maybe even through and beyond that of the sons of those sons. But not always, because they will endure. They will outlast us because they are—' it was not a pause, barely a falter even, possibly appreciable only to himself, as if he couldn't speak even to McCaslin, even to explain his repudiation, that which to him too, even in the act of escaping (and maybe this was the reality and the truth of his need to escape), was heresy: so that even in escaping he was taking with him more of that evil and unregenerate old man who could summon, because she was his property, a human being because she was old enough and female, to his widower's house and get a child on her and then dismiss her because she was of an inferior race, and then bequeath a thousand dollars to the infant because he would be dead then and wouldn't have to pay it, than even he had feared. 'Yes. He didn't want to. He had to. Because they will endure. They are better than we are. Stronger than we are. Their vices are vices aped from white men or that white men and bondage have taught them: improvidence and intemperance and evasion—not laziness: evasion: of what white men had set them to, not for their aggrandizement or even comfort but his own—' and McCaslin

'All right. Go on: Promiscuity. Violence. Instability and lack of control. Inability to distinguish between mine and thine—' and he

'How distinguish, when for two hundred years mine did not even exist for them?' and McCaslin.

'All right. Go on. And their virtues—' and he

'Yes. Their own. Endurance—' and McCaslin

'So have dogs:' and he

'—and pity and tolerance and forbearance and fidelity and love of children—' and McCaslin

'So have dogs:' and he

'—whether their own or not or black or not. And more: what they got not only not from white people but not even despite white people because they had it already from the old free fathers a longer time free than us because we have never been free—' and it was in McCaslin's eyes too, he had only to look at McCaslin's eyes and it was there, that summer twilight seven years ago, almost a week after they had returned from the camp before he discovered that Sam Fathers had told McCaslin: an old bear, fierce and ruthless not just to stay alive but ruthless with the fierce pride of liberty and freedom, jealous and proud enough of liberty and freedom to see it threatened not with fear nor even alarm but almost with joy, seeming deliberately to put it into jeopardy in order to savor it and keep his old strong bones and flesh supple and quick to defend and preserve it; an old man, son of a Negro slave and an Indian king, inheritor on the one hand of the long chronicle of a people who had learned humility through suffering and learned pride through the endurance which survived the suffering, and on the other side the chronicle of a people even longer in the land than the first, yet who now existed there only in the solitary brotherhood of an old and childless Negro's alien blood and the wild and invincible spirit of an old bear; a boy who wished to learn humility and pride in order to become skillful and worthy in the woods but found himself becoming so skillful so fast that he feared he would never become worthy, because he had not learned humility and pride though he had tried, until one day an old man, who could not have defined either, led him as though by the hand to where an old bear and a little mongrel dog showed him that, by possessing one thing other, he would possess them both; and a little dog, nameless and mongrel and many-feathered, grown yet weighing less than six pounds, who couldn't be dangerous because there was nothing anywhere much smaller, not fierce because that would have been called just noise, not humble because it was already too near the ground to genuflect, and not proud because it would not have been close enough for anyone to discern what was casting that shadow, and which didn't even know it was not going to heaven since they had already decided it had no immortal soul, so that all it could be was brave, even though they would probably call that too just noise. *'And you didn't shoot,' McCaslin said. 'How close were you?'*

*'I don't know,' he said. 'There was a big wood tick just inside his off hind leg. I saw that. But I didn't have the gun then.'*

*'But you didn't shoot when you had the gun,' McCaslin said. 'Why?' But McCaslin didn't wait, rising and crossing the room, across the pelt of the bear he had killed two years ago and the bigger one McCaslin had killed before he was born, to the bookcase beneath the mounted head of his first buck, and returned with the book and sat down again and opened it. 'Listen,' he said. He read the five stanzas aloud and closed the book on his finger and looked up. 'All right,' he said. 'Listen,' and read again, but only one stanza this time and closed the book and laid it on the table. 'She cannot fade, though thou hast not thy bliss,' McCaslin said: 'Forever wilt thou love, and she be fair.'*[6]

*'He's talking about a girl,' he said.*

*'He had to talk about something,' McCaslin said. Then he said, 'He was talking about truth. Truth is one. It doesn't change. It covers all things which touch the heart—honor and pride and pity and justice and courage and love. Do you see now?' He didn't know. Somehow it had seemed simpler than that, simpler than somebody talking in a book about a young man and a girl he would never need to grieve over because he could never approach any nearer and would never have to get any further away. He had heard about an old bear and finally got big enough to hunt it and he hunted it four years and at last met it with a gun in his hands and he didn't shoot. Because a little dog—But he could have shot long before the fyce covered the twenty yards to where the bear waited, and Sam Fathers could have shot at any time during the inter-*

6. From "Ode on a Grecian Urn" by English poet John Keats (1795–1821).

*minable minute while Old Ben stood on his hind legs over them. . . . He ceased. McCaslin watched him, still speaking, the voice, the words as quiet as the twilight itself was: 'Courage and honor and pride, and pity and love of justice and of liberty. They all touch the heart, and what the heart holds to becomes truth, as far as we know truth. Do you see now?'*

and he could still hear them, intact in this twilight as in that one seven years ago, no louder still because they did not need to be because they would endure: and he had only to look at McCaslin's eyes beyond the thin and bitter smiling, the faint lip-lift which would have had to be called smiling;—his kinsman, his father almost, who had been born too late into the old time and too soon for the new, the two of them juxtaposed and alien now to each other against their ravaged patrimony, the dark and ravaged fatherland still prone and panting from its etherless operation:

'Habet[7] then.—So this land is, indubitably, of and by itself cursed:' and he

'Cursed:' and again McCaslin merely lifted one hand, not even speaking and not even toward the ledgers: so that, as the stereopticon condenses into one instantaneous field the myriad minutiae of its scope, so did that slight and rapid gesture establish in the small cramped and cluttered twilit room not only the ledgers but the whole plantation in its mazed and intricate entirety—the land, the fields and what they represented in terms of cotton ginned and sold, the men and women whom they fed and clothed and even paid a little cash money at Christmas-time in return for the labor which planted and raised and picked and ginned the cotton, the machinery and mules and gear with which they raised it and their cost and upkeep and replacement—that whole edifice intricate and complex and founded upon injustice and erected by ruthless rapacity and carried on even yet with at times downright savagery not only to the human beings but the valuable animals too, yet solvent and efficient and, more than that: not only still intact but enlarged, increased; brought still intact by McCaslin, himself little more than a child then, through and out of the debacle and chaos of twenty years ago where hardly one in ten survived, and enlarged and increased and would continue so, solvent and efficient and intact and still increasing so long as McCaslin and his McCaslin successors lasted, even though their surnames might not even be Edmonds then: and he

'Habet too. Because that's it: not the land, but us. Not only the blood, but the name too; not only its color but its designation: Edmonds, white, but, a female line, could have no other but the name his father bore; Beauchamp, the elder line and the male one, but black, could have had any name his father bore who had no name—' and McCaslin

'And since I know too what you know I will say now, once more let me say it: And one other, and in the third generation too, and the male, the eldest, the direct and sole and white and still McCaslin even, father to son to son—' and he

'I am free:' and this time McCaslin did not even gesture, no inference of fading pages, no postulation of the stereoptic whole, but the frail and iron thread strong as truth and impervious as evil and longer than life itself and

7. Consider, or take into account.

reaching beyond record and patrimony both to join him with the lusts and passions, the hopes and dreams and griefs, of bones whose names while still fleshed and capable even old Carothers' grandfather had never heard: and he:

'And of that too:' and McCaslin

'Chosen, I suppose (I will concede it) out of all your time by Him, as you say Buck and Buddy were from theirs. And it took Him a bear and an old man and four years just for you. And it took you fourteen years to reach that point and about that many, maybe more, for Old Ben, and more than seventy for Sam Fathers. And you are just one. How long then? How long?' and he

'It will be long. I have never said otherwise. But it will be all right because they will endure—' and McCaslin

'And anyway, you will be free.—No, not now nor ever, we from them nor they from us. So I repudiate too. I would deny even if I knew it were true. I would have to. Even you can see that I could do no else. I am what I am; I will be always what I was born and have always been. And more than me. More than me, just as there were more than Buck and Buddy in what you called His first plan which failed:' and he,

'And more than me:' and McCaslin

'No. Not even you. Because mark. You said how on that instant when Ikkemotubbe realized that he could sell the land to Grandfather, it ceased forever to have been his. All right; go on: Then it belonged to Sam Fathers, old Ikkemotubbe's son. And who inherited from Sam Fathers, if not you? co-heir perhaps with Boon, if not of his life maybe, at least of his quitting it?" and he

'Yes. Sam Fathers set me free.'

and Isaac McCaslin, not yet Uncle Ike, a long time yet before he would be uncle to half a county and still father to none, living in one small cramped fireless rented room in a Jefferson boardinghouse where petit juries were domiciled during court terms and itinerant horse- and mule-traders stayed, with his kit of brand-new carpenter's tools and the shotgun McCaslin had given him with his name engraved in silver and old General Compson's compass (and, when the General died, his silver-mounted horn too) and the iron cot and mattress and the blankets which he would take each fall into the woods for more than sixty years and the bright tin coffee-pot

there had been a legacy, from his Uncle Hubert Beauchamp, his godfather, that bluff burly roaring childlike man from whom Uncle Buddy had won Tomey's Terrel's wife Tennie in the poker-game in 1859—'posible strait against three Treys in sigt Not called'—; no pale sentence or paragraph scrawled in cringing fear of death by a weak and trembling hand as a last desperate sop flung backward at retribution, but a Legacy, a Thing, possessing weight to the hand and bulk to the eye and even audible: a silver cup filled with gold pieces and wrapped in burlap and sealed with his godfather's ring in the hot wax, which (intact still) even before his Uncle Hubert's death and long before his own majority, when it would be his, had become not only a legend but one of the family lares.[8] After his father's and his Uncle Hubert's sister's marriage they

8. Spirits watching over a house.

moved back into the big house, the tremendous cavern which old Carothers had started and never finished, cleared the remaining Negroes out of it and with his mother's dowry completed it, at least the rest of the windows and doors and moved into it, all of them save Uncle Buddy who declined to leave the cabin he and his twin had built, the move being the bride's notion and more than just a notion, and none ever to know if she really wanted to live in the big house or if she knew beforehand that Uncle Buddy would refuse to move: and two weeks after his birth in 1867, the first time he and his mother came down stairs one night, and the silver cup sitting on the cleared dining-room table beneath the bright lamp, and while his mother and his father and McCaslin and Tennie (his nurse: carrying him)—all of them again but Uncle Buddy—watched, his Uncle Hubert rang one by one into the cup the bright and glinting mintage and wrapped it into the burlap envelope and heated the wax and sealed it and carried it back home with him where he lived alone now without even his sister either to hold him down as McCaslin said or to try to raise him up as Uncle Buddy said, and (dark times then in Mississippi) Uncle Buddy said most of the niggers gone and the ones that didn't go even Hub Beauchamp could not have wanted: but the dogs remained and Uncle Buddy said Beauchamp fiddled while Nero fox-hunted.[9]

they would go and see it there; at last his mother would prevail and they would depart in the surrey, once more all save Uncle Buddy and McCaslin to keep Uncle Buddy company, until one winter Uncle Buddy began to fail and from then on it was himself, beginning to remember now, and his mother and Tennie and Tomey's Terrel to drive: the twenty-two miles into the next county, the twin gateposts on one of which McCaslin could remember the half-grown boy blowing a fox-horn at breakfast, dinner, and suppertime and jumping down to open to any passer who happened to hear it, but where there were no gates at all now, the shabby and overgrown entrance to what his mother still insisted that people call Warwick because her brother was, if truth but triumphed and justice but prevailed, the rightful earl of it, the paintless house which outwardly did not change but which on the inside seemed each time larger because he was too little to realize then that there was less and less of it of the fine furnishings, the rosewood and mahogany and walnut, which for him had never existed anywhere anyway save in his mother's tearful lamentations, and the occasional piece small enough to be roped somehow onto the rear or the top of the carriage on their return (And he remembered this, he had seen it: an instant, a flash, his mother's soprano 'Even my dress! Even my dress!' loud and outraged in the barren unswept hall; a face young and female and even lighter in color than Tomey's Terrel's for an instant in a closing door; a swirl, a glimpse of the silk gown and the flick and glint of an ear-ring: an apparition rapid and tawdry and illicit, yet somehow even to the child, the infant still almost, breathless and exciting and evocative: as though, like two limpid and pellucid streams meeting, the child which he still was had made serene and absolute and perfect rapport and contact through that glimpsed nameless illicit hybrid female flesh with the boy which had existed at that stage of inviolable and immortal adoles-

9. A scrambled allusion to the legend that the Roman emperor Nero fiddled while Rome burned.

cence in his uncle for almost sixty years; the dress, the face, the ear-rings gone in that same aghast flash and his uncle's voice: 'She's my cook! She's my new cook! I had to have a cook, didn't I?' then the uncle himself, the face alarmed and aghast too yet still innocently and somehow even indomitably of a boy, they retreating in their turn now, back to the front gallery, and his uncle again, pained and still amazed, in a sort of desperate resurgence if not of courage at least of self-assertion: 'They're free now; They're folks too just like we are!' and his mother: 'That's why! That's why! My mother's house! Defiled! Defiled!' and his uncle: 'Damn it, Sibbey, at least give her time to pack her grip:' then over, finished, the loud uproar and all, himself and Tennie and he remembered Tennie's inscrutable face at the broken shutterless window of the bare room which had once been the parlor while they watched, hurrying down the lane at a stumbling trot, the routed compounder of his uncle's uxory: the back, the nameless face which he had seen only for a moment, the once-hooped dress ballooning and flapping below a man's overcoat, the worn heavy carpet-bag jouncing and banging against her knee, routed and in retreat true enough and in the empty lane, solitary, young-looking, and forlorn, yet withal still exciting and evocative and wearing still the silken banner captured inside the very citadel of respectability, and unforgettable.)

the cup, the sealed inscrutable burlap, sitting on the shelf in the locked closet, Uncle Hubert unlocking the door and lifting it down and passing it from hand to hand: his mother, his father, McCaslin and even Tennie, insisting that each take it in turn and heft it for weight and shake it again to prove the sound, Uncle Hubert himself standing spraddled before the cold unswept hearth in which the very bricks themselves were crumbling into a litter of soot and dust and mortar and the droppings of chimney-sweeps, still roaring and still innocent and still indomitable: and for a long time he believed nobody but himself had noticed that his uncle now put the cup only into his hands, unlocked the door and lifted it down and put it into his hands and stood over him until he had shaken it obediently until it sounded then took it from him and locked it back into the closet before anyone else could have offered to touch it, and even later, when competent not only to remember but to rationalize, he could not say what it was or even if it had been anything because the parcel was still heavy and still rattled, not even when, Uncle Buddy dead and his father, at last and after almost seventy-five years in bed after the sun rose, said: 'Go get that damn cup. Bring that damn Hub Beauchamp too if you have to:' because it still rattled though his uncle no longer put it even into his hands now but carried it himself from one to the other, his mother, McCaslin, Tennie, shaking it before each in turn, saying: 'Hear it? Hear it?' his face still innocent, not quite baffled but only amazed and not very amazed and still indomitable:

and, his father and Uncle Buddy both gone now, one day without reason or any warning the almost completely empty house in which his uncle and Tennie's ancient and quarrelsome great-grandfather (who claimed to have seen Lafayette and McCaslin said in another ten years would be remembering God) lived, cooked and slept in one single room, burst into peaceful conflagration, a tranquil instantaneous sourceless unanimity of combustion, walls floors and roof: at sunup it stood where his uncle's father had built it sixty years ago, at sundown the four blackened and smokeless chimneys rose from a light white powder of ashes and a few charred ends of planks which did not even appear to have been very hot: and out of the last of evening, the last one of the twenty-two miles, on the old white mare which was the last of that stable which McCaslin remembered, the two old men riding double up to the sister's door, the one wearing his fox-horn on its braided deerhide thong and the other carrying the burlap parcel wrapped in a shirt, the tawny wax-daubed shapeless lump sitting again and on an almost identical shelf and his uncle holding the half-opened door now, his hand not only on the knob but one foot against it and the key waiting in the other hand, the face urgent and still not baffled but still and even indomitably not very amazed and himself standing in the half-opened door looking quietly up at the burlap shape, become almost three times its original height and a good half less than its original thickness, and turning away, and he would remember not his mother's look this time nor yet Tennie's inscrutable expression but McCaslin's dark and aquiline face grave insufferable and bemused:

then one night they waked him and fetched him still half-asleep into the lamp light, the smell of medicine which was familiar by now in that room and the smell of something else which he had not smelled before and knew at once and would never forget, the pillow, the worn and ravaged face from which looked out still the boy innocent and immortal and amazed and urgent, looking at him and trying to tell him until McCaslin moved and leaned over the bed and drew from the top of the night shirt the big iron key on the greasy cord which suspended it, the eyes saying Yes Yes Yes now, and cut the cord and unlocked the closet and brought the parcel to the bed, the eyes still trying to tell him even when he took the parcel so that was still not it, the hands still clinging to the parcel even while relinquishing it, the eyes more urgent than ever trying to tell him but they never did; and he was ten and his mother was dead too and McCaslin said, 'You are almost half-way now. You might as well open it:' and he: 'No. He said twenty-one:' and he was twenty-one and McCaslin shifted the bright lamp to the center of the cleared dining-room table and set the parcel beside it and laid his open knife beside the parcel and stood back with that expression of old grave intolerant and repudiating and he lifted it, the burlap lump which fifteen years ago had changed its shape completely overnight, which shaken gave forth a thin weightless not-quite-musical curiously muffled clatter, the bright knife-blade hunting amid the mazed intricacy of string, the knobby gouts of wax bearing his uncle's Beauchamp seal rattling onto the table's polished top and, standing amid the collapse of burlap folds, the unstained tin coffee-pot still brand new, the handful of copper coins and now he knew what had given them the muffled sound: a collection of minutely folded scraps of paper sufficient almost for a rat's nest, of good linen bond, of the crude ruled paper such as Negroes use, of raggedly-torn ledger-pages and the margins of newspapers and once the paper label from a new pair of overalls all dated and all signed, beginning with the first one not six months after they had watched him seal the silver cup into the burlap on this same table in this same room by the light even of this same lamp almost twenty-one years ago:

*I owe my Nephew Isaac Beauchamp McCaslin five (5) pieces Gold which,*
*I,O.U constitutes My note of hand with Interest at 5 percent.*
*Hubert Fitz-Hubert Beauchamp*
*at Warwick 27 Nov 1867*

and he: 'Anyway he called it Warwick:' once at least, even if no more. But there was more:

*Isaac 24 Dec 1867 I.O.U. 2 pieces Gold H.Fh.B. I.O.U. Isaac 1 piece Gold 1 Jan 1868 H.Fh.B.*

then five again then three then one then one then a long time and what dream, what dreamed splendid recoup, not of any injury or betrayal of trust because it had been merely a loan: nay, a partnership:

*I.O.U. Beauchamp McCaslin or his heirs twenty-five (25) pieces Gold This & All preceeding constituting My notes of hand at twenty (20) percentum compounded annually. This date of 19th January 1873*
*Beauchamp*

no location save that in time and signed by the single not name but word as the old proud earl himself might have scrawled Nevile:[1] and that made forty-three and he could not remember himself of course but the legend had it at fifty, which balanced: one: then one: then one: then one and then the last three and then the last chit, dated after he came to live in the house with them and written in the shaky hand not of a beaten old man because he had never been beaten to know it but of a tired old man maybe and even at that tired only on the outside and still indomitable, the simplicity of the last one the simplicity not of resignation but merely of amazement, like a simple comment or remark, and not very much of that:

*One silver cup. Hubert Beauchamp*

and McCaslin: 'So you have plenty of coppers anyway. But they are still not old enough yet to be either rarities or heirlooms. So you will have to take the money:' except that he didn't hear McCaslin, standing quietly beside the table and looking peacefully at the coffee-pot and the pot sitting one night later on the mantel above what was not even a fireplace in the little cramped ice-like room in Jefferson as McCaslin tossed the folded banknotes onto the bed and, still standing (there was nowhere to sit save on the bed) did not even remove his hat and overcoat: and he

'As a loan. From you. This one:' and McCaslin

'You can't. I have no money that I can lend to you. And you will have to go to the bank and get it next month because I won't bring it to you:' and he could not hear McCaslin now either, looking peacefully at McCaslin, his kinsman, his father almost yet no kin now as, at the last, even fathers and sons are no kin: and he

1. Richard Neville (1428–1471), earl of Warwick, who inherited the earldom through marriage to Anne de Beauchamp.

'It's seventeen miles, horseback and in the cold. We could both sleep here:' and McCaslin

'Why should I sleep here in my house when you won't sleep yonder in yours?' and gone, and he looking at the bright rustless unstained tin and thinking, and not for the first time, how much it takes to compound a man (Isaac McCaslin for instance) and of the devious intricate choosing yet unerring path that man's (Isaac McCaslin's for instance) spirit takes among all that mass to make him at last what he is to be, not only to the astonishment of them (the ones who sired the McCaslin who sired his father and Uncle Buddy and their sister, and the ones who sired the Beauchamp who sired his Uncle Hubert and his Uncle Hubert's sister) who believed they had shaped him, but to Isaac McCaslin too

as a loan and used it though he would not have had to: Major de Spain offered him a room in his house as long as he wanted it and asked nor would ever ask any question, and his old General Compson more than that, to take him into his own room, to sleep in half of his own bed and more than Major de Spain because he told him baldly why: 'You sleep with me and before this winter is out, I'll know the reason. You'll tell me. Because I don't believe you just quit. It looks like you just quit but I have watched you in the woods too much and I don't believe you just quit even if it does look damn like it:' using it as a loan, paid his board and rent for a month and bought the tools, not simply because he was good with his hands because he had intended to use his hands and it could have been with horses, and not in mere static and hopeful emulation of the Nazarene,[2] as the young gambler buys a spotted shirt because the old gambler won in one yesterday, but (without the arrogance of false humility and without the false humbleness of pride, who intended to earn his bread, didn't especially want to earn it but had to earn it and for more than just bread) because if the Nazarene had found carpentering good for the life and ends He had assumed and elected to serve, it would be all right too for Isaac McCaslin even though Isaac McCaslin's ends, although simple enough in their apparent motivation, were and would be always incomprehensible to him, and his life, invincible enough in its needs, if he could have helped himself, not being the Nazarene, he would not have chosen it: and paid it back. He had forgotten the thirty dollars which McCaslin put into the bank in his name each month, fetched it in to him and flung it onto the bed that first one time but no more; he had a partner now or rather he was the partner: a blasphemous profane clever old dipsomaniac who had built blockade-runners in Charleston in '62 and '63 and had been a ship's carpenter since and appeared in Jefferson two years ago, nobody knew from where nor why, and spent a good part of his time since recovering from delirium tremens in the jail; they had put a new roof on the stable of the bank's president and (the old man in jail again still celebrating that job) he went to the bank to collect for it and the president said, 'I should borrow from you instead of paying you:' and it had been seven months now and he remembered for the first time, two-hundred-and-ten dollars, and this was the first job of any size and when he left the bank the account stood at

2. I.e., Jesus of Nazareth.

two-twenty, two-forty to balance, only twenty dollars more to go, then it did balance though by then the total had increased to three hundred and thirty and he said, 'I will transfer it now:' and the president said, 'I can't do that. McCaslin told me not to. Haven't you got another initial you could use and open another account?' but that was all right, the coins the silver and the bills as they accumulated knotted into a handkerchief and the coffee-pot wrapped in an old shirt as when Tennie's great-grandfather had fetched it from Warwick eighteen years ago, in the bottom of the iron-bound trunk which old Carothers had brought from Carolina and his landlady said, 'Not even a lock! And you don't even lock your door, not even when you leave!' and himself looking at her as peacefully as he had looked at McCaslin that first night in this same room, no kin to him at all yet more than kin as those who serve you even for pay are your kin and those who injure you are more than brother or wife

and he had the wife now; got the old man out of jail and fetched him to the rented room and sobered him by superior strength, did not even remove his own shoes for twenty-four hours, got him up and got food into him and they built the barn this time from the ground up and he married her: an only child, a small girl yet curiously bigger than she seemed at first, solider perhaps, with dark eyes and a passionate heart-shaped face, who had time even on that farm to watch most of the day while he sawed timbers to the old man's measurements: and she: 'Papa told me about you. That farm is really yours, isn't it?' and he

'And McCaslin's:' and she

'Was there a will leaving half of it to him?' and he

'There didn't need to be a will. His grandmother was my father's sister. We were the same as brothers:' and she

'You are the same as second cousins and that's all you ever will be. But I don't suppose it matters:' and they were married, they were married and it was the new country, his heritage too as it was the heritage of all, out of the earth, beyond the earth yet of the earth because his too was of the earth's long chronicle, his too because each must share with another in order to come into it, and in the sharing they become one: for that while, one: for that while at least, one: indivisible, that while at least irrevocable and unrecoverable, living in a rented room still but for just a little while and that room wall-less and topless and floorless in glory for him to leave each morning and return to at night; her father already owned the lot in town and furnished the material and he and his partner would build it, her dowry from one: her wedding-present from three, she not to know it until the bungalow was finished and ready to be moved into and he never knew who told her, not her father and not his partner and not even in drink though for a while he believed that, himself coming home from work and just time to wash and rest a moment before going down to supper, entering no rented cubicle since it would still partake of glory even after they would have grown old and lost it: and he saw her face then, just before she spoke: 'Sit down:' the two of them sitting on the bed's edge, not even touching yet, her face strained and terrible, her voice a passionate and expiring whisper of immeasurable promise: 'I love you. You know I love you. When are we going to move?' and he

'I didn't—I didn't know—Who told you—' the hot fierce palm clapped over his mouth, crushing his lips into his teeth, the fierce curve of fingers digging into his cheek and only the palm slacked off enough for him to answer:

'The farm. Our farm. Your farm:' and he

'I——' then the hand again, finger and palm, the whole enveloping weight of her although she still was not touching him save the hand, the voice: 'No! No!' and the fingers themselves seeming to follow through the cheek the impulse to speech as it died in his mouth, then the whisper, the breath again, of love and of incredible promise, the palm slackening again to let him answer:

'When?' and he

'——' then she was gone, the hand too, standing, her back to him and her head bent, the voice so calm now that for an instant it seemed no voice of hers that he ever remembered: 'Stand up and turn your back and shut your eyes:' and repeated before he understood and stood himself with his eyes shut and heard the bell ring for supper below stairs, and the calm voice again: 'Lock the door:' and he did so and leaned his forehead against the cold wood, his eyes closed, hearing his heart and the sound he had begun to hear before he moved until it ceased and the bell rang again below stairs and he knew it was time for them this time, and he heard the bed and turned and he had never seen her naked before, he had asked her to once, and why: that he wanted to see her naked because he loved her and he wanted to see her looking at him naked because he loved her, but after that he never mentioned it again, even turning his face when she put the nightgown on over her dress to undress at night and putting the dress on over the gown to remove it in the morning, and she would not let him get into bed beside her until the lamp was out and even in the heat of summer she would draw the sheet up over them both before she would let him turn to her: and the landlady came up the stairs up the hall and rapped on the door and then called their names but she didn't move, lying still on the bed outside the covers, her face turned away on the pillow, listening to nothing, thinking of nothing, not of him anyway he thought: then the landlady went away and she said, 'Take off your clothes:' her head still turned away, looking at nothing, thinking of nothing, waiting for nothing, not even him, her hand moving as though with volition and vision of its own, catching his wrist at the exact moment when he paused beside the bed so that he never paused but merely changed the direction of moving, downward now, the hand drawing him and she moved at last, shifted, a movement one single complete inherent not practiced and one time older than man, looking at him now, drawing him still downward with the one hand down and down and he neither saw nor felt it shift, palm flat against his chest now and holding him away with the same apparent lack of any effort or any need for strength, and not looking at him now, she didn't need to, the chaste woman, the wife, already looked upon all the men who ever rutted and now her whole body had changed, altered, he had never seen it but once and now it was not even the one he had seen but composite of all woman-flesh since man that ever of its own will reclined on its back and opened, and out of it somewhere, without any movement of lips even, the dying and invincible whisper: 'Promise:' and he

'Promise?'

'The farm.' He moved. He had moved, the hand shifting from his chest once more to his wrist, grasping it, the arm still lax and only the light increasing pressure of the fingers as though arm and hand were a piece of wire cable with one looped end, only the hand tightening as he pulled against it. 'No,' he said. 'No:' and she was not looking at him still but not like the other, but still the hand: 'No, I tell you. I won't. I can't. Never:' and still the hand and he said, for the last time, he tried to speak clearly and he knew it was still gently and he thought, *She already knows more than I with all the man-listening in camps where there was nothing to read ever even heard of. They are born already bored with what a boy approaches only at fourteen and fifteen with blundering and aghast trembling:* 'I can't. Not ever. Remember:' and still the steady and invincible hand and he said 'Yes' and he thought, *She is lost. She was born lost. We were all born lost* then he stopped thinking and even saying Yes, it was like nothing he had ever dreamed, let alone heard in mere man-talking until after a no-time he returned and lay spent on the insatiate immemorial beach and again with a movement one time more older than man she turned and freed herself and on their wedding night she had cried and he thought she was crying now at first, into the tossed and wadded pillow, the voice coming from somewhere between the pillow and the cachinnation: 'And that's all. That's all from me. If this don't get you that son you talk about, it won't be mine:' lying on her side, her back to the empty rented room, laughing and laughing

## V

He went back to the camp one more time before the lumber company moved in and began to cut the timber. Major de Spain himself never saw it again. But he made them welcome to use the house and hunt the land whenever they liked, and in the winter following the last hunt when Sam Fathers and Lion died, General Compson and Walter Ewell invented a plan to corporate themselves, the old group, into a club and lease the camp and the hunting privileges of the woods—an invention doubtless of the somewhat childish old General but actually worthy of Boon Hogganbeck himself. Even the boy, listening, recognizing it for the subterfuge it was: to change the leopard's spots when they could not alter the leopard, a baseless and illusory hope to which even McCaslin seemed to subscribe for a while, that once they had persuaded Major de Spain to return to the camp he might revoke himself, which even the boy knew he would not do. And he did not. The boy never knew what occurred when Major de Spain declined. He was not present when the subject was broached and McCaslin never told him. But when June came and the time for the double birthday celebration there was no mention of it and when November came no one spoke of using Major de Spain's house and he never knew whether or not Major de Spain knew they were going on the hunt though without doubt old Ash probably told him: he and McCaslin and General Compson (and that one was the General's last hunt too) and Walter and Boon and Tennie's Jim and old Ash loaded two wagons and drove two days and almost forty miles beyond any country the boy had ever seen before and lived in tents for the two weeks. And the next spring they heard (not from Major de Spain) that he had sold the timber-rights to a Memphis lumber company and in June the boy came to town with McCaslin one Saturday and went to Major de Spain's office—the big, airy, book-lined, second-storey room with windows at one end opening upon the shabby hinder purlieus of stores and at the other a door giving onto the railed balcony above the Square, with its curtained alcove where sat a cedar water-bucket and a sugar-bowl and spoon and tumbler and a wicker-covered demijohn of whiskey, and the bamboo-and-paper punkah[3] swinging back and forth above the desk while old Ash in a tilted chair beside the entrance pulled the cord.

"Of course," Major de Spain said. "Ash will probably like to get off in the woods himself for a while, where he won't have to eat Daisy's cooking. Complain about it, anyway. Are you going to take anybody with you?"

"No sir," he said. "I thought that maybe Boon—" For six months now Boon had been town-marshal at Hoke's; Major de Spain had compounded with the lumber company—or perhaps compromised was closer, since it was the lumber company who had decided that Boon might be better as a town-marshal than head of a logging gang.

"Yes," Major de Spain said. "I'll wire him today. He can meet you at Hoke's. I'll send Ash on by the train and they can take some food in and all you will have to do will be to mount your horse and ride over."

"Yes sir," he said. "Thank you." And he heard his voice again. He didn't know he was going to say it yet he did know, he had known it all the time: "Maybe if you . . . " His voice died. It was stopped, he never knew how because Major de Spain did not speak and it was not until his voice ceased that Major de Spain moved, turned back to the desk and the papers spread on it and even that without moving because he was sitting at the desk with a paper in his hand when the boy entered, the boy standing there looking down at the short plumpish gray-haired man in sober fine broadcloth and an immaculate glazed shirt whom he was used to seeing in boots and muddy corduroy, unshaven, sitting the shaggy powerful long-hocked mare with the worn Winchester carbine across the saddlebow and the great blue dog standing motionless as bronze at the stirrup, the two of them in that last year and to the boy anyway coming to resemble one another somehow as two people competent for love or for business who have been in love or in business together for a long time sometimes do. Major de Spain did not look up again.

"No. I will be too busy. But good luck to you. If you have it, you might bring me a young squirrel."

"Yes sir," he said. "I will."

He rode his mare, the three-year-old filly he had bred and raised and broken himself. He left home a little after midnight and six hours later, without even having sweated her, he rode into Hoke's, the tiny log-line junction which he had always thought of as Major de Spain's property too although Major de Spain had merely sold the company (and that many years ago) the land on which the sidetracks and loading-platforms and the commissary store stood, and looked about in shocked and grieved amazement even though he had had

3. Fan suspended from the ceiling, operated by tugging on an attached rope. "Demijohn": large, wicker-covered bottle.

forewarning and had believed himself prepared: a new planing-mill already half completed which would cover two or three acres and what looked like miles and miles of stacked steel rails red with the light bright rust of newness and of piled crossties sharp with creosote, and wire corrals and feeding-troughs for two hundred mules at least and the tents for the men who drove them; so that he arranged for the care and stabling of his mare as rapidly as he could and did not look any more, mounted into the log-train caboose with his gun and climbed into the cupola and looked no more save toward the wall of wilderness ahead within which he would be able to hide himself from it once more anyway.

Then the little locomotive shrieked and began to move: a rapid churning of exhaust, a lethargic deliberate clashing of slack couplings travelling backward along the train, the exhaust changing to the deep slow clapping bites of power as the caboose too began to move and from the cupola he watched the train's head complete the first and only curve in the entire line's length and vanish into the wilderness, dragging its length of train behind it so that it resembled a small dingy harmless snake vanishing into weeds, drawing him with it too until soon it ran once more at its maximum clattering speed between the twin walls of unaxed wilderness as of old. It had been harmless once. Not five years ago Walter Ewell had shot a six-point buck from this same moving caboose, and there was the story of the half-grown bear: the train's first trip in to the cutting thirty miles away, the bear between the rails, its rear end elevated like that of a playing puppy while it dug to see what sort of ants or bugs they might contain or perhaps just to examine the curious symmetrical squared barkless logs which had appeared apparently from nowhere in one endless mathematical line overnight, still digging until the driver on the braked engine not fifty feet away blew the whistle at it, whereupon it broke frantically and took the first tree it came to: an ash sapling not much bigger than a man's thigh and climbed as high as it could and clung there, its head ducked between its arms as a man (a woman perhaps) might have done while the brakeman threw chunks of ballast at it, and when the engine returned three hours later with the first load of outbound logs the bear was halfway down the tree and once more scrambled back up as high as it could and clung again while the train passed and was still there when the engine went in again in the afternoon and still there when it came back out at dusk; and Boon had been in Hoke's with the wagon after a barrel of flour that noon when the train-crew told about it and Boon and Ash, both twenty years younger then, sat under the tree all that night to keep anybody from shooting it and the next morning Major de Spain had the log-train held at Hoke's and just before sundown on the second day, with not only Boon and Ash but Major de Spain and General Compson and Walter and McCaslin, twelve then, watching, it came down the tree after almost thirty-six hours without even water and McCaslin told him how for a minute they thought it was going to stop right there at the barrow-pit where they were standing and drink, how it looked at the water and paused and looked at them and at the water again, but did not, gone, running, as bears run, the two sets of feet, front and back, tracking two separate though parallel courses.

It had been harmless then. They would hear the passing log-train sometimes from the camp; sometimes, because nobody bothered to listen for it or not. They would hear it going in, running light and fast, the light clatter of the trucks, the exhaust of the diminutive locomotive and its shrill peanut-parcher whistle flung for one petty moment and absorbed by the brooding and inattentive wilderness without even an echo. They would hear it going out, loaded, not quite so fast now yet giving its frantic and toylike illusion of crawling speed, not whistling now to conserve steam, flinging its bitten laboring miniature puffing into the immemorial woodsface with frantic and bootless vainglory, empty and noisy and puerile, carrying to no destination or purpose sticks which left nowhere any scar or stump, as the child's toy loads and transports and unloads its dead sand and rushes back for more, tireless and unceasing and rapid yet never quite so fast as the hand which plays with it moves the toy burden back to load the toy again. But it was different now. It was the same train, engine cars and caboose, even the same enginemen brakeman and conductor to whom Boon, drunk then sober then drunk again then fairly sober once more all in the space of fourteen hours, had bragged that day two years ago about what they were going to do to Old Ben tomorrow, running with its same illusion of frantic rapidity between the same twin walls of impenetrable and impervious woods, passing the old landmarks, the old game crossings over which he had trailed bucks wounded and not wounded and more than once seen them, anything but wounded, bolt out of the woods and up and across the embankment which bore the rails and ties then down and into the woods again as the earth-bound supposedly move but crossing as arrows travel, groundless, elongated, three times its actual length and even paler, different in color, as if there were a point between immobility and absolute motion where even mass chemically altered, changing without pain or agony not only in bulk and shape but in color too, approaching the color of wind, yet this time it was as though the train (and not only the train but himself, not only his vision which had seen it and his memory which remembered it but his clothes too, as garments carry back into the clean edgeless blowing of air the lingering effluvium of a sick-room or of death) had brought with it into the doomed wilderness, even before the actual axe, the shadow and portent of the new mill not even finished yet and the rails and ties which were not even laid; and he knew now what he had known as soon as he saw Hoke's this morning but had not yet thought into words: why Major de Spain had not come back, and that after this time he himself, who had had to see it one time other, would return no more.

Now they were near. He knew it before the engine-driver whistled to warn him. Then he saw Ash and the wagon, the reins without doubt wrapped once more about the brake-lever as within the boy's own memory Major de Spain had been forbidding him for eight years to do, the train slowing, the slackened couplings jolting and clashing again from car to car, the caboose slowing past the wagon as he swung down with his gun, the conductor leaning out above him to signal the engine, the caboose still slowing, creeping, although the engine's exhaust was already slatting in mounting tempo against the unechoing wilderness, the crashing of drawbars once more travelling backward along the train, the caboose picking up speed at last. Then it was gone. It had not been. He could no longer hear it. The wilderness soared, musing, inattentive, myriad, eternal, green; older than any mill-shed, longer than any spur-line. "Mr. Boon here yet?" he said.

"He beat me in," Ash said. "Had the wagon loaded and ready for me at Hoke's yistiddy when I got there and setting on the front steps at camp last night when I got in. He already been in the woods since fo daylight this morning. Said he gwine up to the Gum tree and for you to hunt up that way and meet him." He knew where that was: a single big sweet-gum just outside the woods, in an old clearing; if you crept up to it very quietly this time of year and then ran suddenly into the clearing, sometimes you caught as many as a dozen squirrels in it, trapped, since there was no other tree near they could jump to. So he didn't get into the wagon at all.

"I will," he said.

"I figured you would," Ash said. "I fotch you a box of shells." He passed the shells down and began to unwrap the lines from the brake-pole.

"How many times up to now do you reckon Major has told you not to do that?" the boy said.

"Do which?" Ash said. Then he said: "And tell Boon Hogganbeck dinner gonter be on the table in a hour and if yawl want any to come on and eat it."

"In an hour?" he said. "It ain't nine o'clock yet." He drew out his watch and extended it face-toward Ash. "Look." Ash didn't even look at the watch.

"That's town time. You ain't in town now. You in the woods."

"Look at the sun then."

"Nemmine the sun too," Ash said. "If you and Boon Hogganbeck want any dinner, you better come on in and get it when I tole you. I aim to get done in that kitchen because I got my wood to chop. And watch your feet. They're crawling."[4]

"I will," he said.

Then he was in the woods, not alone but solitary; the solitude closed about him, green with summer. They did not change, and, timeless, would not, any more than would the green of summer and the fire and rain of fall and the iron cold and sometimes even snow

*the day, the morning when he killed the buck and Sam marked his face with its hot blood, they returned to camp and he remembered old Ash's blinking and disgruntled and even outraged disbelief until at last McCaslin had had to affirm the fact that he had really killed it: and that night Ash sat snarling and unapproachable behind the stove so that Tennie's Jim had to serve the supper and waked them with breakfast already on the table the next morning and it was only half-past one o'clock and at last out of Major de Spain's angry cursing and Ash's snarling and sullen rejoinders the fact emerged that Ash not only wanted to go into the woods and shoot a deer also but he intended to and Major de Spain said, 'By God, if we don't let him we will probably have to do the cooking from now on:' and Walter Ewell said, 'Or get up at midnight to eat what Ash cooks:' and since he had already killed his buck for this hunt and was not to shoot again unless they needed meat, he offered his gun to Ash until*

4. I.e., there are many snakes in the woods.

*Major de Spain took command and allotted that gun to Boon for the day and gave Boon's unpredictable pump gun to Ash, with two buckshot shells but Ash said, 'I got shells:' and showed them, four: one buck, one of number three shot for rabbits, two of bird-shot and told one by one their history and their origin and he remembered not Ash's face alone but Major de Spain's and Walter's and General Compson's too, and Ash's voice: 'Shoot? In course they'll shoot! Genl Cawmpson guv me this un'—the buckshot—'right outen the same gun he kilt that big buck with eight years ago. And this un'—it was the rabbit shell: triumphantly—'is oldern thisyer boy!' And that morning he loaded the gun himself, reversing the order: the bird-shot, the rabbit, then the buck so that the buck-shot would feed first into the chamber, and himself without a gun, he and Ash walked beside Major de Spain's and Tennie's Jim's horses and the dogs (that was the snow) until they cast and struck, the sweet strong cries ringing away into the muffled falling air and gone almost immediately, as if the constant and unmurmuring flakes had already buried even the unformed echoes beneath their myriad and weightless falling, Major de Spain and Tennie's Jim gone too, whooping on into the woods; and then it was all right, he knew as plainly as if Ash had told him that Ash had now hunted his deer and that even his tender years had been forgiven for having killed one, and they turned back toward home through the falling snow—that is, Ash said, 'Now whut?' and he said. 'This way'—himself in front because, although they were less than a mile from camp, he knew that Ash, who had spent two weeks of his life in the camp each year for the last twenty, had no idea whatever where they were, until quite soon the manner in which Ash carried Boon's gun was making him a good deal more than just nervous and he made Ash walk in front, striding on, talking now, an old man's garrulous monologue beginning with where he was at the moment then of the woods and of camping in the woods and of eating in camps then of eating then of cooking it and of his wife's cooking then briefly of his old wife and almost at once and at length of a new light-colored woman who nursed next door to Major de Spain's and if she didn't watch out who she was switching her tail at he would show her how old was an old man or not if his wife just didn't watch him all the time, the two of them in a game trail through a dense brake of cane and brier which would bring them out within a quarter-mile of camp, approaching a big fallen tree-trunk lying athwart the path and just as Ash, still talking, was about to step over it the bear, the yearling, rose suddenly beyond the log, sitting up, its forearms against its chest and its wrists limply arrested as if it had been surprised in the act of covering its face to pray: and after a certain time Ash's gun yawed jerkily up and he said, 'You haven't got a shell in the barrel yet. Pump it:' but the gun already snicked and he said, 'Pump it. You haven't got a shell in the barrel yet:' and Ash pumped the action[5] and in a certain time the gun steadied again and snicked and he said, 'Pump it:' and watched the buckshot shell jerk, spinning heavily, into the cane. This is the rabbit shot: he thought and the gun snicked and he thought: The next is bird-shot: and he didn't have to say Pump it; he cried, 'Don't shoot! Don't shoot!' but that was already too late too, the light dry vicious snick! before he could*

5. The part of the gun that locks the shell in the barrel.

*speak and the bear turned and dropped to all-fours and then was gone and there was only the log, the cane, the velvet and constant snow and Ash said, 'Now whut?' and he said, 'This way. Come on:' and began to back away down the path and Ash said, 'I got to find my shells:' and he said, 'Goddamn it, goddamn it, come on:' but Ash leaned the gun against the log and returned and stooped and fumbled among the cane roots until he came back and stooped and found the shells and they rose and at that moment the gun, untouched, leaning against the log six feet away and for that while even forgotten by both of them, roared, bellowed and flamed, and ceased: and he carried it now, pumped out the last mummified shell and gave that one also to Ash and, the action still open, himself carried the gun until he stood it in the corner behind Boon's bed at the camp*

—; summer, and fall, and snow, and wet and saprife spring in their ordered immortal sequence, the deathless and immemorial phases of the mother who had shaped him if any had toward the man he almost was, mother and father both to the old man born of a Negro slave and a Chickasaw chief who had been his spirit's father if any had, whom he had revered and harkened to and loved and lost and grieved: and he would marry someday and they too would own for their brief while that brief unsubstanced glory which inherently of itself cannot last and hence why glory: and they would, might, carry even the remembrance of it into the time when flesh no longer talks to flesh because memory at least does last: but still the woods would be his mistress and his wife.

He was not going toward the Gum Tree. Actually he was getting farther from it. Time was and not so long ago either when he would not have been allowed here without someone with him, and a little later, when he had begun to learn how much he did not know, he would not have dared be here without someone with him, and later still, beginning to ascertain, even if only dimly, the limits of what he did not know, he could have attempted and carried it through with a compass, not because of any increased belief in himself but because McCaslin and Major de Spain and Walter and General Compson too had taught him at last to believe the compass regardless of what it seemed to state. Now he did not even use the compass but merely the sun and that only subconsciously, yet he could have taken a scaled map and plotted at any time to within a hundred feet of where he actually was; and sure enough, at almost the exact moment when he expected it, the earth began to rise faintly, he passed one of the four concrete markers set down by the lumber company's surveyor to establish the four corners of the plot which Major de Spain had reserved out of the sale, then he stood on the crest of the knoll itself, the four corner-markers all visible now, blanched still even beneath the winter's weathering, lifeless and shockingly alien in that place where dissolution itself was a seething turmoil of ejaculation tumescence conception and birth, and death did not even exist. After two winters' blanketings of leaves and the flood-waters of two springs, there was no trace of the two graves any more at all. But those who would have come this far to find them would not need headstones but would have found them as Sam Fathers himself had taught him to find such: by bearings on trees: and did, almost the first thrust of the hunting knife finding (but only to see if it was still there) the round tin box manufactured for axle-grease and containing now Old Ben's dried mutilated paw, resting above Lion's bones.

He didn't disturb it. He didn't even look for the other grave where he and McCaslin and Major de Spain and Boon had laid Sam's body, along with his hunting horn and his knife and his tobacco-pipe, that Sunday morning two years ago; he didn't have to. He had stepped over it, perhaps on it. But that was all right. *He probably knew I was in the woods this morning long before I got here,* he thought, going on to the tree which had supported one end of the platform where Sam lay when McCaslin and Major de Spain found them—the tree, the other axle-grease tin nailed to the trunk, but weathered, rusted, alien too yet healed already into the wilderness' concordant generality, raising no tuneless note, and empty, long since empty of the food and tobacco he had put into it that day, as empty of that as it would presently be of this which he drew from his pocket—the twist of tobacco, the new bandanna handkerchief, the small paper sack of the peppermint candy which Sam had used to love; that gone too, almost before he had turned his back, not vanished but merely translated into the myriad life which printed the dark mold of these secret and sunless places with delicate fairy tracks; which, breathing and biding and immobile, watched him from beyond every twig and leaf until he moved, moving again, walking on; he had not stopped, he had only paused, quitting the knoll which was no abode of the dead because there was no death, not Lion and not Sam: not held fast in earth but free in earth and not in earth but of earth, myriad yet undiffused of every myriad part, leaf and twig and particle, air and sun and rain and dew and night, acorn oak and leaf and acorn again, dark and dawn and dark and dawn again in their immutable progression, and, being myriad, one: and Old Ben too. Old Ben too; they would give him his paw back even, certainly they would give him his paw back: then the long challenge and the long chase, no heart to be driven and outraged, no flesh to be mauled and bled—Even as he froze himself, he seemed to hear Ash's parting admonition. He could even hear the voice as he froze, immobile, one foot just taking his weight, the toe of the other just lifted behind him, not breathing, feeling again and as always the sharp shocking inrush from when Isaac McCaslin long yet was not, and so it was fear all right but not fright as he looked down at it. It had not coiled yet and the buzzer had not sounded either, only one thick rapid contraction, one loop cast sideways as though merely for purchase from which the raised head might start slightly backward, not in fright either, not in threat quite yet, more than six feet of it, the head raised higher than his knee and less than his knee's length away, and old, the once-bright markings of its youth dulled now to a monotone concordant too with the wilderness it crawled and lurked: the old one, the ancient and accursed about the earth, fatal and solitary and he could smell it now: the thin sick smell of rotting cucumbers and something else which had no name, evocative of all knowledge and an old weariness and of pariahhood and of death. At last it moved. Not the head. The elevation of the head did not change as it began to glide away from him, moving erect yet off the perpendicular as if the head and that elevated third were complete and all: an entity walking on two feet and free of all laws of mass and balance, and should have been because even now he could not quite believe that all that shift and flow of shadow behind that walking head could have been one snake: going and then gone; he put the other foot down at last and didn't know it, standing with one hand raised as Sam had stood that afternoon six years ago when Sam led him into the wilderness and showed him and he ceased to be a child, speaking the old tongue which Sam had spoken that day without premeditation either: "Chief," he said: "Grandfather."

He couldn't tell when he first began to hear the sound, because when he became aware of it, it seemed to him that he had been already hearing it for several seconds—a sound as though someone were hammering a gun-barrel against a piece of railroad iron, a sound loud and heavy and not rapid yet with something frenzied about it, as if the hammerer were not only a strong man and an earnest one but a little hysterical too. Yet it couldn't be on the log-line because, although the track lay in that direction, it was at least two miles from him and this sound was not three hundred yards away. But even as he thought that, he realized where the sound must be coming from: whoever the man was and whatever he was doing, he was somewhere near the edge of the clearing where the Gum Tree was and where he was to meet Boon. So far, he had been hunting as he advanced, moving slowly and quietly and watching the ground and the trees both. Now he went on, his gun unloaded and the barrel slanted up and back to facilitate its passage through brier and undergrowth, approaching as it grew louder and louder that steady savage somehow queerly hysterical beating of metal on metal, emerging from the woods, into the old clearing, with the solitary gum tree directly before him. At first glance the tree seemed to be alive with frantic squirrels. There appeared to be forty or fifty of them leaping and darting from branch to branch until the whole tree had become one green maelstrom of mad leaves, while from time to time, singly or in twos and threes, squirrels would dart down the trunk then whirl without stopping and rush back up again as though sucked violently back by the vacuum of their fellows' frenzied vortex. Then he saw Boon, sitting, his back against the trunk, his head bent, hammering furiously at something on his lap. What he hammered with was the barrel of his dismembered gun, what he hammered at was the breech of it. The rest of the gun lay scattered about him in a half-dozen pieces while he bent over the piece on his lap his scarlet and streaming walnut face, hammering the disjointed barrel against the gun-breech with the frantic abandon of a madman. He didn't even look up to see who it was. Still hammering, he merely shouted back at the boy in a hoarse strangled voice:

"Get out of here! Dont touch them! Dont touch a one of them! They're mine!"

*Editor's Note*

Even experienced readers familiar with Faulkner's subject matter and literary devices may have major difficulty in keeping clear the line of the story in *The Bear*. Therefore, we are offering this chronology as an aid in reading the story as it should be read. For this illumination we are indebted to a book of essays called *Bear, Man and God*, eds. F. Utley, L. Bloom, and A. Kinney (1964).

**Chronology**

| | |
|---|---|
| 1772 | Lucius Quintus CAROTHERS McCASLIN is born in Carolina. |
| 1779 | Thucydides ("Thucydus") is born to the McCaslin slaves Roscius ("Roskus") and Phoebe ("Fibby"). |
| 1787? | Carothers McCaslin brings his wife and slaves to Mississippi, buys land for a farm from Chickasaw Chief Ikkemotubbe. |
| ? | A girl is born to Carothers McCaslin and his wife. She is to become the grandmother of McCaslin Edmonds. |
| 1799? | Twin boys, Theophilus and Amodeus ("BUCK" and "BUDDY") McCaslin, are born to Carothers McCaslin and his wife. |
| 1807 | Eunice, a slave girl, is bought by Carothers McCaslin in New Orleans for $650. |
| 1809? | Sam Fathers, son of Ikkemotubbe and a Negro woman, is born and traded with his mother by the chief to Carothers McCaslin for a gelding. |
| 1809 | Eunice is married to the McCaslin slave Thucydides. |
| 1810 | Tomasina ("Tomey" or "Tomy") is born to Eunice. The father is Carothers McCaslin. |
| Dec. 25, 1832 | Eunice, learning that her daughter is pregnant by Carothers McCaslin, drowns herself in a creek. |
| June 1833 | Terrel ("Tomy's Turl") is born to Tomasina. The father is Carothers McCaslin. Tomasina dies in childbirth. |
| June 27, 1837 | Carothers McCaslin dies. His will frees the old slaves Roscius and Phoebe and their son Thucydides, but none leave. Thucydides refuses 10 acres of land, refuses $200 cash, stays on to earn his legacy. The will leaves $1000 to Tomey's Terrel upon his coming of age. Buck and Buddy McCaslin, now running the farm, build a log cabin to live in, move the slaves into the big house. |
| 1838 | Tennie (Beauchamp) is born, a slave of Hubert Beauchamp and his sister Sophonsiba, distant neighbors of the McCaslins. |

| | |
|---|---|
| Nov. 3, 1841 | Thucydides, having earned his $200 from the McCaslins, sets up a blacksmith shop in Jefferson. |
| 1843 ? | Boon Hogganbeck, quarter-Indian, is born. |
| 1851 ? | Carothers McCaslin Edmonds ("Cass") is born, a grandson of the sister of Buck and Buddy. Before he is 14 he is orphaned and comes under care of the McCaslins. |
| 1852 ? | Buck and Buddy McCaslin establish a $1000 legacy for Tomey's Terrel in accordance with Carothers McCaslin's will. |
| Feb. 17, 1854 | Thucydides dies. |
| June 1854 | Tomey's Terrel comes of age, ignores his $1000 legacy, stays on. |
| Mar. 3, 1856 | Buck McCaslin buys the slave Percival Brownlee from slave dealer (later General) Nathan Bedford Forrest at Cold Water for $265. |
| Oct. 3, 1856 | Brownlee, having done $100 damage, is freed, refuses to leave, later disappears. |
| 1859 | Buddy McCaslin wins the slave girl (Tennie Beauchamp) from neighbor Hubert Beauchamp in a poker game, to be married to Tomey's Terrel. |
| 1861 | The Civil War begins. Buck McCaslin joins Col. Sartoris's cavalry, under command of General (formerly slave dealer) Nathan Bedford Forrest. |
| 1862 | Percival Brownlee reappears, conducting revival meetings on the McCaslin farm. |
| 1863 | Buck McCaslin, a Confederate cavalryman, is said to have ridden into Jefferson and out. |
| Dec. 29, 1864 | After 3 children have died in infancy, James Thucydides ("Tennie's Jim") is born to Terrel and Tennie. |
| 1865 | The Civil War ends. Buck McCaslin returns to the farm. Sophonsiba Beauchamp ("Sibbey"), Hubert's sister, is married to Buck McCaslin. They move into the big house on the McCaslin farm. |
| 1865 ? | Hunting parties begin on land in the Big Bottom of the Tallahatchie River bought by Major Cassius de Spain from Thomas Sutpen.<br>Participants with the major are:<br>General Compson, the major's friend<br>Walter Ewell, a crack shot<br>Uncle Ash, the major's camp cook<br>McCaslin Edmonds<br>Sam Fathers<br>Boon Hogganbeck<br>Tennie's Jim |
| 1865 | The logging train makes its first trips into the Big Bottom on Major de Spain's land. It is halted to let a frightened bear escape from a tree. |

| | |
|---|---|
| 1866 | Brownlee reappears in Jefferson, is seen by Buck McCaslin. |

**Ike's Age**

| | |
|---|---|
| 0 Oct./Nov. 1867 | Isaac Beauchamp McCaslin ("Ike") is born to Buck and Sibbey McCaslin. |
| | Hubert Beauchamp, Ike's uncle and godfather, seals 50 gold pieces in a silver cup as a legacy for Ike at 21. |
| 1½ 1869 | Sophonsiba ("Fonsiba") is born to Terrel and Tennie. |
| 1870 ? | Buck and Buddy McCaslin decide to let the legacy under Carothers McCaslin's will accrue to provide $1000 each to the surviving children of Terrel and Tennie as they come of age. |
| 3 Winter 1871 ? | Uncle Buddy's health begins to fail; Ike accompanies his mother on visits to Uncle Hubert at "Warwick." |
| 4 1872 ? | Sibbey McCaslin makes Hubert dismiss his new "cook." |
| 5 1873 ? | First Buddy, then Buck McCaslin dies within the year. Management of the farm passes to McCaslin Edmonds. |
| 5 1873 ? | "Warwick" burns to the ground. Hubert and one Negro (Tennie's great-grandfather) come to live on the McCaslin farm. |
| 6 1874 ? | The silver cup, wrapped in burlap and kept in a closet, changes shape overnight. |
| 7 1875 ? | Hubert Beauchamp dies. |
| 7 1875 ? | Sam Fathers's Indian companion Joe Baker ("Jobaker") dies. |
| 7 1875 ? | Young Ike McCaslin shoots rabbits near the McCaslin farm. |
| 9 Mar. 1877 | Sam Fathers goes to live on Major de Spain's land in the Big Bottom. |
| 9 1877 | Sibbey McCaslin, Ike's mother, dies. |
| 10 Nov. 1877 | Ike McCaslin is taken to the Big Bottom on his first deer-bear hunt. |
| 10 1878 ? | Ike, with Boon, buys a wild pony at an auction. The pony breaks away. |
| 10½ June 1878 | Ike goes alone into the woods, discards his gun, watch, and compass, sees Old Ben. |
| 11 Nov. 1878 | With Sam Fathers, Ike kills his first buck. Ash, jealous, goes hunting with Ike, surprises a bear. His gun misfires. |
| 11 1878 | Boon Hogganbeck shoots at Negro in Jefferson 5 times with a pistol, wounds a bystander. |
| 12 Nov. 1879 | Ike kills his first bear. |
| | Ike kills a buck after waiting at its bedding place. |
| | Ike sees Old Ben crossing a corridor of down timber. |

| | |
|---|---|
| 12½ June 1880 ? | With Sam, Ike and his little dog (a "fyce") corner Old Ben but let him escape. |
| 13 Nov. 1880 | Walter Ewell shoots a buck from the caboose of the logging train. |
| 13 Mar. 1881 | A doe and fawn are found killed; later one of Major de Spain's colts is found killed. At first Old Ben is suspected. |
| 13⅓ June 1881 | Sam captures the killer, a wild mongrel Airedale, whom he trains and names "Lion." |
| 14 Nov. 1881 | Lion participates in the hunt for Old Ben as 7 strangers watch; the bear escapes. |
| 15 Nov. 1882 | Lion is found to be sleeping on Boon's bed. With Lion the hunters twice corner Old Ben. Boon shoots 5 times and misses. General Compson "draws blood." |
| 16 Dec. 1883 | Ike accompanies Boon on an errand to Memphis for whiskey. The hunters close in on Old Ben. With Lion, Boon kills the bear. Lion dies. Sam Fathers "quits" and dies, probably with Boon's help. |
| 16 Dec. 1883 ? | Ike reads the ledgers in the commissary on the McCaslin farm. |
| | The hunters (without Major de Spain) plan to incorporate and lease hunting rights on the land. |
| 17 Nov. 1884 | The hunters (without Major de Spain) go farther into the woods to hunt. |
| 17 Dec. 1884 | Major de Spain leases the timber rights on his land to a Memphis lumber company. |
| | Boon Hogganbeck becomes town marshal at Hoke's. |
| 17½ June 1885 | Ike revisits Major de Spain's land, meets Ash, visits the graves of Sam and Lion, finds Boon under a gum tree. |
| 18 Dec. 29, 1885 | Tennie's Jim disappears on his 21st birthday. Ike traces him to Tennessee to give him his $1000 but loses him. |
| 18½ Summer 1886 | A Negro man takes Fonsiba to Arkansas to be his wife. |
| 1886 | McCaslin Edmonds hears that Percival Brownlee is now proprietor of a brothel in New Orleans. |
| 19 Dec. 1886 | Ike carries Fonsiba's $1000 to Arkansas, deposits it in a bank at midnight, orders her paid $3 a month. |
| 21 Oct./Nov. 1888 | In the commissary on his 21st birthday, in conversation with his cousin McCaslin Edmonds, Ike relinquishes his title to the McCaslin farm. Ike also opens his Uncle Hubert's "legacy," finds a tin coffee pot stuffed with coppers and I.O.U.'s. The next day Ike goes to Jefferson, accepts as a loan a "pension" of $30 a month from McCaslin Edmonds. |
| 21½ June 1889 | Ike, now a carpenter, repays to the bank his "loan." |
| 22 1890 ? | Ike marries a girl who has been living on a farm where he and his partner have rebuilt the barn. |

# Timothy Findley

*Findley (1930– ) was born in Toronto, Ontario, Canada. His formal education was interrupted by illness, and his first career was in the theater. He began his full-time writing career in 1963 and has published eight novels and two collections of short fiction. His novel* The Last of the Crazy People *appeared in 1967. His third novel,* The Wars *(1977), won a Governor-General's Award and became a Canadian classic. Most recent novels include* Headhunter *(1993),* The Piano Man's Daughter *(1995), and* You Went Away *(1996). His stories are collected in* Dust to Dust *(1997).*

## Dreams

Doctor Menlo was having a problem: he could not sleep and his wife—the other Doctor Menlo—was secretly staying awake in order to keep an eye on him. The trouble was that, in spite of her concern and in spite of all her efforts, Doctor Menlo—whose name was Mimi—was always nodding off because of her exhaustion.

She had tried drinking coffee, but this had no effect. She detested coffee and her system had a built-in rejection mechanism. She also prescribed herself a week's worth of Dexedrine to see if that would do the trick. *Five mg at bedtime*—all to no avail. And even though she put the plastic bottle of small orange hearts beneath her pillow and kept augmenting her intake, she would wake half an hour later with a dreadful start to discover the night was moving on to morning.

Everett Menlo had not yet declared the source of his problem. His restless condition had begun about ten days ago and had barely raised his interest. Soon, however, the time spent lying awake had increased from one to several hours and then, on Monday last, to all-night sessions. Now he lay in a state of rigid apprehension—eyes wide open, arms above his head, his hands in fists—like a man in pain unable to shut it out. His neck, his back and his shoulders constantly harried him with cramps and spasms. Everett Menlo had become a full-blown insomniac.

Clearly, Mimi Menlo concluded, her husband was refusing to sleep because he believed something dreadful was going to happen the moment he closed his eyes. She had encountered this sort of fear in one or two of her patients. Everett, on the other hand, would not discuss the subject. If the problem had been hers, he would have said *such things cannot occur if you have gained control of yourself.*

Mimi began to watch for the dawn. She would calculate its approach by listening for the increase of traffic down below the bedroom window. The Menlos' home was across the road from The Manulife Centre—corner of Bloor and Bay streets. Mimi's first sight of daylight always revealed the high, white shape of its terraced storeys. Their own apartment building was of a modest height and colour—twenty floors of smoky glass and polished brick. The shadow of the Manulife would crawl across the bedroom floor and climb the wall behind her, grey with fatigue and cold.

The Menlo beds were an arm's length apart, and lying like a rug between them was the shape of a large, black dog of unknown breed. All night long, in the dark of his well, the dog would dream and he would tell the content of his dreams the way that victims in a trance will tell of being pursued by posses of their nameless fears. He whimpered, he cried and sometimes he howled. His legs and his paws would jerk and flail and his claws would scrabble desperately against the parquet floor. Mimi—who loved this dog—would lay her hand against his side and let her fingers dabble in his coat in vain attempts to soothe him. Sometimes, she had to call his name in order to rouse him from his dreams because his heart would be racing. Other times, she smiled and thought: *at least there's one of us getting some sleep.* The dog's name was Thurber and he dreamed in beige and white.

Everett and Mimi Menlo were both psychiatrists. His field was schizophrenia; hers was autistic children. Mimi's venue was the Parkin Institute at the University of Toronto; Everett's was the Queen Street Mental Health Centre. Early in their marriage they had decided never to work as a team and not—unless it was a matter of financial life and death—to accept employment in the same institution. Both had always worked with the kind of physical intensity that kills, and yet they gave the impression this was the only tolerable way in which to function. It meant there was always a sense of peril in what they did, but the peril—according to Everett—made their lives worth living. This, at least, had been the theory twenty years ago when they were young.

Now, for whatever unnamed reason, peril had become his enemy and Everett Menlo had begun to look and behave and lose his sleep like a haunted man. But he refused to comment when Mimi asked him what was wrong. Instead, he gave the worst of all possible answers a psychiatrist can hear who seeks an explanation of a patient's silence: he said there was *absolutely nothing wrong.*

"You're sure you're not coming down with something?"

"Yes."

"And you wouldn't like a massage?"

"I've already told you: no."

"Can I get you anything?"

"No."

"And you don't want to talk?"

"That's right."

"Okay, Everett . . ."

"Okay, what?"

"Okay, nothing. I only hope you get some sleep tonight."

Everett stood up. "Have you been spying on me, Mimi?"

"What do you mean by *spying*?"

"Watching me all night long."

"Well, Everett, I don't see how I can fail to be aware you aren't asleep when we share this bedroom. I mean—I can hear you grinding your teeth. I can see you lying there wide awake."

"When?"

"All the time. You're staring at the ceiling."

"I've never stared at the ceiling in my whole life. I sleep on my stomach."

"You sleep on your stomach *if* you sleep. But you have not been sleeping. Period. No argument."

Everett Menlo went to his dresser and got out a pair of clean pyjamas. Turning his back on Mimi, he put them on.

Somewhat amused at the coyness of this gesture, Mimi asked what he was hiding.

"Nothing!" he shouted at her.

Mimi's mouth fell open. Everett never yelled. His anger wasn't like that; it manifested itself in other ways, in silence and withdrawal, never shouts.

Everett was staring at her defiantly. He had slammed the bottom drawer of his dresser. Now he was fumbling with the wrapper of a pack of cigarettes.

Mimi's stomach tied a knot.

Everett hadn't touched a cigarette for weeks.

"Please don't smoke those," she said. "You'll only be sorry if you do."

"And you," he said, "will be sorry if I don't."

"But, dear . . ." said Mimi.

"Leave me for Christ's sake alone!" Everett yelled.

Mimi gave up and sighed and then she said: "All right. Thurber and I will go and sleep in the living room. Good-night."

Everett sat on the edge of his bed. His hands were shaking.

"Please," he said—apparently addressing the floor. "Don't leave me here alone. I couldn't bear that."

This was perhaps the most chilling thing he could have said to her. Mimi was alarmed; her husband was genuinely terrified of something and he would not say what it was. If she had not been who she was—if she had not known what she knew—if her years of training had not prepared her to watch for signs like this, she might have been better off. As it was, she had to face the possibility the strongest, most sensible man on earth was having a nervous breakdown of major proportions. Lots of people have breakdowns, of course; but not, she had thought, the gods of reason.

"All right," she said—her voice maintaining the kind of calm she knew a child afraid of the dark would appreciate. "In a minute I'll get us something to drink. But first, I'll go and change . . ."

Mimi went into the sanctum of the bathroom, where her nightgown waited for her—a portable hiding-place hanging on the back of the door. "You stay there," she said to Thurber, who had padded after her. "Mama will be out in just a moment."

Even in the dark, she could gauge Everett's tension. His shadow—all she could see of him—twitched from time to time and the twitching took on a kind of lurching rhythm, something like the broken clock in their living room.

Mimi lay on her side and tried to close her eyes. But her eyes were tied to a will of their own and would not obey her. Now she, too, was caught in the same irreversible tide of sleeplessness that bore her husband backward through the night. Four or five times she watched him lighting cigarettes—blowing out the matches, courting disaster in the bedclothes—conjuring the worst of deaths for the three of them: a flaming pyre on the twentieth floor.

All this behaviour was utterly unlike him; foreign to his code of disciplines and ethics; alien to everything he said and believed. *Openness, directness, sharing of ideas, encouraging imaginative response to every problem. Never hide troubles. Never allow despair* . . . These were his directives in everything he did. Now, he had thrown them over.

One thing was certain. She was not the cause of his sleeplessness. She didn't have affairs and neither did he. He might be ill—but whenever he'd been ill before, there had been no trauma; never a trauma like this one, at any rate. Perhaps it was something about a patient—one of his tougher cases; a wall in the patient's condition they could not break through; some circumstance of someone's lack of progress—a sudden veering towards a catatonic state, for instance—something that Everett had not foreseen that had stymied him and was slowly . . . what? Destroying his sense of professional control? His self-esteem? His scientific certainty? If only he would speak.

Mimi thought about her own worst case: a child whose obstinate refusal to communicate was currently breaking her heart and, thus, her ability to help. If ever she had needed Everett to talk to, it was now. All her fellow doctors were locked in a battle over this child: they wanted to take him away from her. Mimi refused to give him up; he might as well have been her own flesh and blood. Everything had been done—from gentle holding sessions to violent bouts of manufactured anger—in her attempt to make the child react. She was staying with him every day from the moment he was roused to the moment he was induced to sleep with drugs.

His name was Brian Bassett and he was eight years old. He sat on the floor in the furthest corner he could achieve in one of the observation-isolation rooms where all the autistic children were placed when nothing else in their treatment—nothing of love or expertise—had managed to break their silence. Mostly, this was a signal they were coming to the end of life.

There in his four-square, glass-box room, surrounded by all that can tempt a child if a child can be tempted—toys and food and story book companions—Brian Bassett was in the process, now, of fading away. His eyes were never closed and his arms were restrained. He was attached to three machines that nurtured him with all that science can offer. But of course, the spirit and the will to live cannot be fed by force to those who do not want to feed.

Now, in the light of Brian Bassett's utter lack of willing contact with the world around him—his utter refusal to communicate—Mimi watched her husband through the night. Everett stared at the ceiling, lit by the Manulife building's distant lamps, borne on his back further and further out to sea. She had lost him, she was certain.

When, at last, he saw that Mimi had drifted into her own and welcome sleep, Everett rose from his bed and went out into the hall, past the simulated jungle of the solarium, until he reached the dining room. There, all the way till dawn, he amused himself with two decks of cards and endless games of Dead Man's Solitaire.

Thurber rose and shuffled after him. The dining room was one of Thurber's favourite places in all his confined but privileged world, for it was here—as in the kitchen—that from time to time a hand descended filled with the miracle of food. But whatever it was that his master was doing up there above him on the table-top, it wasn't anything to do with feeding or with being fed. The playing cards had an old and dusty dryness to their scent and they held no appeal for the dog. So he once again lay down and he took up his dreams, which at least gave his paws some exercise. This way, he failed to hear the advent of a new dimension to his master's problem. This occurred precisely at 5.45 a.m. when the telephone rang and Everett Menlo, having rushed to answer it, waited breathless for a minute while he listened and then said: "yes" in a curious, strangulated fashion. Thurber—had he been awake—would have recognized in his master's voice the signal for disaster.

For weeks now, Everett had been working with a patient who was severely and uniquely schizophrenic. This patient's name was Kenneth Albright, and while he was deeply suspicious, he was also oddly caring. Kenneth Albright loved the detritus of life, such as bits of woolly dust and wads of discarded paper. He loved all dried-up leaves that had drifted from their parent trees and he loved the dead bees that had curled up to die along the window-sills of his ward. He also loved the spiderwebs seen high up in the corners of the rooms where he sat on plastic chairs and ate with plastic spoons.

Kenneth Albright talked a lot about his dreams. But his dreams had become, of late, a major stumbling block in the process of his recovery. Back in the days when Kenneth had first become Doctor Menlo's patient, the dreams had been overburdened with detail: "over-cast", he would say, "with characters" and over-produced, again in Kenneth's phrase, "as if I were dreaming the dreams of Cecil B. DeMille."[1]

Then he had said: "But a person can't really dream someone else's dreams. Or can they, Doctor Menlo?"

"No" had been Everett's answer—definite and certain.

Everett Menlo had been delighted, at first, with Kenneth Albright's dreams. They had been immensely entertaining—complex and filled with intriguing detail. Kenneth himself was at a loss to explain the meaning of these dreams, but as Everett had said, it wasn't Kenneth's job to explain. That was

1. American producer of film extravaganzas (1881–1959).

Everett's job. His job and his pleasure. For quite a long while, during these early sessions, Everett had written out the dreams, taken them home and recounted them to Mimi.

Kenneth Albright was a paranoid schizophrenic. Four times now, he had attempted suicide. He was a fiercely angry man at times—and at other times as gentle and as pleasant as a docile child. He had suffered so greatly, in the very worst moments of his disease, that he could no longer work. His job—it was almost an incidental detail in his life and had no importance for him, so it seemed—was returning reference books, in the Metro Library, to their places in the stacks. Sometimes—mostly late of an afternoon—he might begin a psychotic episode of such profound dimensions that he would attempt his suicide right behind the counter and even once, in the full view of everyone, while riding in the glass-walled elevator. It was after this last occasion that he was brought, in restraints, to be a resident patient at the Queen Street Mental Health Centre. He had slashed his wrists with a razor—but not before he had also slashed and destroyed an antique copy of *Don Quixote,* the pages of which he pasted to the walls with blood.

For a week thereafter, Kenneth Albright—just like Brian Bassett—had refused to speak or to move. Everett had him kept in an isolation cell, force-fed and drugged. Slowly, by dint of patience, encouragement and caring even Kenneth could recognize as genuine, Everett Menlo had broken through the barrier. Kenneth was removed from isolation, pampered with food and cigarettes, and he began relating his dreams.

At first there seemed to be only the dreams and nothing else in Kenneth's memory. Broken pencils, discarded toys and the telephone directory all had roles to play in these dreams but there were never any people. All the weather was bleak and all the landscapes were empty. Houses, motor cars and office buildings never made an appearance. Sounds and smells had some importance; the wind would blow, the scent of unseen fires was often described. Stairwells were plentiful, leading nowhere, all of them rising from a subterranean world that Kenneth either did not dare to visit or would not describe.

The dreams had little variation, one from another. The themes had mostly to do with loss and with being lost. The broken pencils were all given names and the discarded toys were given to one another as companions. The telephone books were the sources of recitations—hours and hours of repeated names and numbers, some of which—Everett had noted with surprise—were absolutely accurate.

All of this held fast until an incident one morning that changed the face of Kenneth Albright's schizophrenia forever: an incident that stemmed—so it seemed—from something he had dreamed the night before.

Bearing in mind his previous attempts at suicide, it will be obvious that Kenneth Albright was never far from sight at the Queen Street Mental Health Centre. He was, in fact, under constant observation: constant that is, as human beings and modern technology can manage. In the ward to which he was ultimately consigned, for instance, the toilet cabinets had no doors and the shower-rooms had no locks. Therefore, a person could not ever be alone with water, glass or shaving utensils. (All the razors were cordless automatics.) Scissors and knives were banned, as were pieces of string and rubber bands. A person could not even kill his feet and hands by binding up his wrists or ankles. Nothing poisonous was anywhere available. All the windows were barred. All the double doors between this ward and the corridors beyond were doors with triple locks and a guard was always near at hand.

Still, if people want to die, they will find a way. Mimi Menlo would discover this to her everlasting sorrow with Brian Bassett. Everett Menlo would discover this to his everlasting horror with Kenneth Albright.

On the morning of 19 April, a Tuesday, Everett Menlo, in the best of health, had welcomed a brand-new patient into his office. This was Anne Marie Wilson, a young and brilliant pianist whose promising career had been halted mid-flight by a schizophrenic incident involving her ambition. She was, it seemed, no longer able to play and all her dreams were shattered. The cause was simple, to all appearances: Anne Marie had a sense of how, precisely, the music should be and she had not been able to master it accordingly. "Everything I attempt is terrible," she had said—in spite of all her critical accolades and all her professional success. Other doctors had tried and failed to break the barriers in Anne Marie, whose hands had taken on a life of their own, refusing altogether to work for her. Now it was Menlo's turn and hope was high.

Everett had been looking forward to his session with this prodigy. He loved all music and had thought to find some means within its discipline to reach her. She seemed so fragile, sitting there in the sunlight, and he had just begun to take his first notes when the door flew open and Louise, his secretary, had said: "I'm sorry, Doctor Menlo. There's a problem. Can you come with me at once?"

Everett excused himself.

Anne Marie was left in the sunlight to bide her time. Her fingers were moving around in her lap and she put them in her mouth to make them quiet.

Even as he'd heard his secretary speak, Everett had known the problem would be Kenneth Albright. Something in Kenneth's eyes had warned him there was trouble on the way: a certain wariness that indicated all was not as placid as it should have been, given his regimen of drugs. He had stayed long hours in one position, moving his fingers over his thighs as if to dry them on his trousers; watching his fellow patients come and go with abnormal interest—never, however, rising from his chair. An incident was on the horizon and Everett had been waiting for it, hoping it would not come.

Louise had said that Doctor Menlo was to go at once to Kenneth Albright's ward. Everett had run the whole way. Only after the attendant had let him in past the double doors did he slow his pace to a hurried walk and wipe his brow. He didn't want Kenneth to know how alarmed he had been.

Coming to the appointed place, he paused before he entered, closing his eyes, preparing himself for whatever he might have to see. *Other people have killed themselves: I've seen it often enough,* he was thinking. *I simply won't let it affect me.* Then he went in.

The room was small and white—a dining room—and Kenneth was sitting down in a corner, his back pressed out against the walls on either side of him.

His head was bowed and his legs drawn up and he was obviously trying to hide without much success. An intern was standing above him and a nurse was kneeling down beside him. Several pieces of bandaging with blood on them were scattered near Kenneth's feet and there was a white enamel basin filled with pinkish water on the floor beside the nurse.

"Morowetz," Everett said to the intern. "Tell me what has happened here." He said this just the way he posed such questions when he took the interns through the wards at examination time, quizzing them on symptoms and prognoses.

But Morowetz the intern had no answer. He was puzzled. What had happened had no sane explanation.

Everett turned to Charterhouse, the nurse.

"On the morning of 19 April, at roughly ten-fifteen, I found Kenneth Albright covered with blood," Ms Charterhouse was to write in her report. "His hands, his arms, his face and neck were stained. I would say the blood was fresh and the patient's clothing—mostly his shirt—was wet with it. Some—a very small amount of it—had dried on his forehead. The rest was uniformly the kind of blood you expect to find free-flowing from a wound. I called for assistance and meanwhile attempted to ascertain where Mister Albright might have been injured. I performed this examination without success. I could find no source of bleeding anywhere on Mister Albright's body."

Morowetz concurred.

The blood was someone else's.

"Was there a weapon of any kind?" Doctor Menlo had wanted to know.

"No, sir. Nothing," said Charterhouse.

"And was he alone when you found him?"

"Yes sir. Just like this in the corner."

"And the others?"

"All the patients in the ward were examined," Morowetz told him.

"And?"

"Not one of them was bleeding."

Everett said: "I see."

He looked down at Kenneth.

"This is Doctor Menlo, Kenneth. Have you anything to tell me?"

Kenneth did not reply.

Everett said: "When you've got him back in his room and tranquillized, will you call me, please?"

Morowetz nodded.

The call never came. Kenneth had fallen asleep. Either the drugs he was given had knocked him out cold, or he had opted for silence. Either way, he was incommunicado.

No one was discovered bleeding. Nothing was found to indicate an accident, a violent attack, an epileptic seizure. A weapon was not located. Kenneth Albright had not a single scratch on his flesh from stem, as Everett put it, to gudgeon. The blood, it seemed, had fallen like the rain from heaven: unexplained and inexplicable.

Later, as the day was ending, Everett Menlo left the Queen Street Mental

Health Centre. He made his way home on the Queen streetcar and the Bay bus. When he reached the apartment, Thurber was waiting for him. Mimi was at a goddamned meeting.

That was the night Everett Menlo suffered the first of his failures to sleep. It was occasioned by the fact that, when he wakened sometime after three, he had just been dreaming. This, of course, was not unusual—but the dream itself was perturbing. There was someone lying there, in the bright white landscape of a hospital dining room. Whether it was a man or a woman could not be told, it was just a human body, lying down in a pool of blood.

Kenneth Albright was kneeling beside this body, pulling it open the way a child will pull a Christmas present open—yanking at its strings and ribbons, wanting only to see the contents. Everett saw this scene from several angles, never speaking, never being spoken to. In all the time he watched—the usual dream eternity—the silence was broken only by the sound of water dripping from an unseen tap. Then, Kenneth Albright rose and was covered with blood, the way he had been that morning. He stared at Doctor Menlo, looked right through him and departed. Nothing remained in the dining room but plastic tables and plastic chairs and the bright red thing on the floor that once had been a person. Everett Menlo did not know and could not guess who this person might have been. He only knew that Kenneth Albright had left this person's body in Everett Menlo's dream.

Three nights running, the corpse remained in its place and every time that Everett entered the dining room in the nightmare he was certain he would find out who it was. On the fourth night, fully expecting to discover he himself was the victim, he beheld the face and saw it was a stranger.

*But there are no strangers in dreams;* he knew that now after twenty years of practice. *There are no strangers; there are only people in disguise.*

Mimi made one final attempt in Brian Bassett's behalf to turn away the fate to which his other doctors—both medical and psychiatric—had consigned him. Not that, as a group, they had failed to expend the full weight of all they knew and all they could do to save him. One of his medical doctors—a woman whose name was Juliet Bateman—had moved a cot into his isolation room and stayed with him twenty-four hours a day for over a week. But her health had been undermined by this and when she succumbed to the Shanghai flu she removed herself for fear of infecting Brian Bassett.

The parents had come and gone on a daily basis for months in a killing routine of visits. But parents, their presence and their loving, are not the answer when a child has fallen into an autistic state. They might as well have been strangers. And so they had been advised to stay away.

Brian Bassett was eight years old—*unlucky eight,* as one of his therapists had said—and in every other way, in terms of physical development and mental capability, he had always been a perfectly normal child. Now, in the final moments of his life, he weighed a scant thirty pounds, when he should have weighed twice that much.

Brian had not been heard to speak a single word in over a year of constant observation. Earlier—long ago as seven months—a few expressions would visit his face from time to time. Never a smile—but often a kind of sneer, a passing of judgement, terrifying in its intensity. Other times, a pinched expression would appear—a signal of the shyness peculiar to austic children, who think of light as being unfriendly.

Mimi's militant efforts in behalf of Brian had been exemplary. Her fellow doctors thought of her as *Bassett's crazy guardian angel.* They begged her to remove herself in order to preserve her health. Being wise, being practical, they saw that all her efforts would not save him. But Mimi's version of being a guardian angel was more like being a surrogate warrior: a hired gun or a samurai. Her cold determination to thwart the enemies of silence, stillness and starvation gave her strengths that even she had been unaware were hers to command.

Brian Bassett, seated in his corner on the floor, maintained a solemn composure that lent his features a kind of unearthly beauty. His back was straight, his hands were poised, his hair was so fine he looked the very picture of a spirit waiting to enter a newborn creature. Sometimes Mimi wondered if this creature Brian Bassett waited to inhabit could be human. She thought of all the animals she had ever seen in all her travels and she fell upon the image of a newborn fawn as being the most tranquil and the most in need of stillness in order to survive. If only all the natural energy and curiosity of a newborn beast could have entered into Brian Bassett, surely, they would have transformed the boy in the corner into a vibrant, joyous human being. But it was not to be.

On 29 April—one week and three days after Everett had entered into his crisis of insomnia—Mimi sat on the floor in Brian Bassett's isolation room, gently massaging his arms and legs as she held him in her lap.

His weight, by now, was shocking—and his skin had become translucent. His eyes had not been closed for days—for weeks—and their expression might have been carved in stone.

"Speak to me. Speak to me," she whispered to him as she cradled his head beneath her chin. "Please at least speak before you die."

Nothing happened. Only silence.

Juliet Bateman—wrapped in a blanket—was watching through the observation glass as Mimi lifted up Brian Bassett and placed him in his cot. The cot had metal sides—and the sides were raised. Juliet Bateman could see Brian Bassett's eyes and his hands as Mimi stepped away.

Mimi looked at Juliet and shook her head. Juliet closed her eyes and pulled her blanket tighter like a skin that might protect her from the next five minutes.

Mimi went around the cot to the other side and dragged the IV stand in closer to the head. She fumbled for a moment with the long plastic lifelines—anti-dehydrants, nutrients—and she adjusted the needles and brought them down inside the nest of the cot where Brian Bassett lay and she lifted up his arm in order to insert the tubes and bind them into place with tape.

This was when it happened—just as Mimi Menlo was preparing to insert the second tube.

Brian Bassett looked at her and spoke.

"No," he said. "Don't."

*Don't* meant death.

Mimi paused—considered—and set the tube aside. Then she withdrew the tube already in place and she hung them both on the IV stand.

*All right,* she said to Brian Bassett in her mind, *you win.*

She looked down then with her arm along the side of the cot—and one hand trailing down so Brian Bassett could touch it if he wanted to. She smiled at him and said to him: "Not to worry. Not to worry. None of us is ever going to trouble you again." He watched her carefully. "Goodbye, Brian," she said. "I love you."

Juliet Bateman saw Mimi Menlo say all this and was fairly sure she had read the words in Mimi's lips just as they had been spoken.

Mimi started out of the room. She was determined now there was no turning back and that Brian Bassett was free to go his way. But just as she was turning the handle and pressing her weight against the door—she heard Brian Bassett speak again.

"Goodbye," he said.

And died.

Mimi went back and Juliet Bateman, too, and they stayed with him another hour before they turned out his lights. "Someone else can cover his face," said Mimi. "I'm not going to do it." Juliet agreed and they came back out to tell the nurse on duty that their ward had died and their work with him was over.

On 30 April—a Saturday—Mimi stayed home and made her notes and she wondered if and when she would weep for Brian Bassett. Her hand, as she wrote, was steady and her throat was not constricted and her eyes had no sensation beyond the burning itch of fatigue. She wondered what she looked like in the mirror, but resisted that discovery. Some things could wait. Outside it rained. Thurber dreamed in the corner. Bay Street rumbled in the basement.

Everett, in the meantime, had reached his own crisis and because of his desperate straits a part of Mimi Menlo's mind was on her husband. Now he had not slept for almost ten days. *We really ought to consign ourselves to hospital beds,* she thought. Somehow, the idea held no persuasion. It occurred to her that laughter might do a better job, if only they could find it. The brain, when over-extended, gives us the most surprisingly simple propositions, she concluded. *Stop,* it says to us. *Lie down and sleep.*

Five minutes later, Mimi found herself still sitting at the desk, with her fountain pen capped and her fingers raised to her lips in an attitude of gentle prayer. It required some effort to re-adjust her gaze and re-establish her focus on the surface of the window glass beyond which her mind had wandered. Sitting up, she had been asleep.

Thurber muttered something and stretched his legs and yawned, still asleep. Mimi glanced in his direction. *We've both been dreaming,* she thought, *but his dream continues.*

Somewhere behind her, the broken clock was attempting to strike the hour of three. Its voice was dull and rusty, needing oil.

Looking down, she saw the words *BRIAN BASSETT* written on the page before her and it occurred to her that, without his person, the words were nothing more than extrapolations from the alphabet—something fanciful we call a "name" in the hope that, one day, it will take on meaning.

She thought of Brian Bassett with his building blocks—pushing the letters around on the floor and coming up with more acceptable arrangements: *TINA STERABBS . . . IAN BRETT BASS . . . BEST STAB the RAIN:* a sentence. He had known all along, of course, that *BRIAN BASSETT* wasn't what he wanted because it wasn't what he was. He had come here against his will, was held here against his better judgement, fought against his captors and finally escaped.

But where was here to Ian Brett Bass? Where was here to Tina Sterabbs? Like Brian Bassett, they had all been here in someone else's dreams, and had to wait for someone else to wake before they could make their getaway.

Slowly, Mimi uncapped her fountain pen and drew a firm, black line through Brian Bassett's name. *We dreamed him,* she wrote, *that's all. And then we let him go.*

Seeing Everett standing in the doorway, knowing he had just returned from another Kenneth Albright crisis, she had no sense of apprehension. All this was only as it should be. Given the way that everything was going, it stood to reason Kenneth Albright's crisis had to come in this moment. If he managed, at last, to kill himself then at least her husband might begin to sleep again.

Far in the back of her mind a carping, critical voice remarked that any such thoughts were *deeply unfeeling and verging on the barbaric.* But Mimi dismissed this voice and another part of her brain stepped forward in her defence. *I will weep for Kenneth Albright,* she thought, *when I can weep for Brian Bassett. Now, all that matters is that Everett and I survive.*

Then she strode forward and put out her hand for Everett's briefcase, set the briefcase down and helped him out of his topcoat. She was playing wife. It seemed to be the thing to do.

For the next twenty minutes Everett had nothing to say, and after he had poured himself a drink and after Mimi had done the same, they sat in their chairs and waited for Everett to catch his breath.

The first thing he said when he finally spoke was: "Finish your notes?"

"Just about," Mimi told him. "I've written everything I can for now." She did not elaborate. "You're home early," she said, hoping to goad him into saying something new about Kenneth Albright.

"Yes," he said. "I am." But that was all.

Then he stood up—threw back the last of his drink and poured another. He lighted a cigarette and Mimi didn't even wince. He had been smoking now three days. The atmosphere between them had been, since then, enlivened with a magnetic kind of tension. But it was a moribund tension, slowly beginning to dissipate.

Mimi watched her husband's silent torment now with a kind of clinical detachment. This was the result, she liked to tell herself, of her training and her discipline. The lover in her could regard Everett warmly and with concern, but the psychiatrist in her could also watch him as someone suffering a nervous breakdown, someone who could not be helped until the symptoms had multiplied and declared themselves more openly.

Everett went into the darkest corner of the room and sat down hard in one of Mimi's straight-backed chairs: the ones inherited from her mother. He sat, prim, like a patient in a doctor's office, totally unrelaxed and nervy; expressionless. Either he had come to receive a deadly diagnosis, or he would get a clean bill of health.

Mimi glided over to the sofa in the window, plush and red and deeply comfortable; a place to recuperate. The view—if she chose to turn only slightly sideways—was one of the gentle rain that was falling on to Bay Street. Sopping-wet pigeons huddled on the window-sill; people across the street in the Manulife building were turning on their lights.

A renegade robin, nesting in their eaves, began to sing.

Everett Menlo began to talk.

"Please don't interrupt," he said at first.

"You know I won't," said Mimi. It was a rule that neither one should interrupt the telling of a case until they had been invited to do so.

Mimi put her fingers into her glass so the ice-cubes wouldn't click. She waited.

Everett spoke—but he spoke as if in someone else's voice, perhaps the voice of Kenneth Albright. This was not entirely unusual. Often, both Mimi and Everett Menlo spoke in the voices of their patients. What was unusual, this time, was that, speaking in Kenneth's voice, Everett began to sweat profusely—so profusely that Mimi was able to watch his shirt front darkening with perspiration.

"As you know," he said, "I have not been sleeping."

This was the understatement of the year. Mimi was silent.

"I have not been sleeping because—to put it in a nutshell—I have been afraid to dream."

Mimi was somewhat startled by this. Not by the fact that Everett was afraid to dream, but only because she had just been thinking of dreams herself.

"I have been afraid to dream, because in all my dreams there have been bodies. Corpses. Murder victims."

Mimi—not really listening—idly wondered if she had been one of them.

"In all my dreams, there have been corpses," Everett repeated. "But I am not the murderer. Kenneth Albright is the murderer, and, up to this moment, he had left behind him fifteen bodies: none of them people I recognize."

Mimi nodded. The ice-cubes in her drink were beginning to freeze her fingers. Any minute now, she prayed, they would surely melt.

"I gave up dreaming almost a week ago," said Everett, "thinking that if I did, the killing pattern might be altered; broken." Then he said tersely: "It was not. The killings have continued . . ."

"How do you know the killings have continued, Everett, if you've given up your dreaming? Wouldn't this mean he had no place to hide the bodies?"

In spite of the fact she had disobeyed their rule about not speaking, Everett answered her.

"I know they are being continued because I have seen the blood."

"Ah, yes. I see."

"No, Mimi. No. You do not see. The blood is not a figment of my imagination. The blood, in fact, is the only thing not dreamed." He explained the stains on Kenneth Albright's hands and arms and clothes and he said: "It happens every day. We have searched his person for signs of cuts and gashes—even for internal and rectal bleeding. Nothing. We have searched his quarters and all the other quarters in his ward. His ward is locked. His ward is isolated in the extreme. None of his fellow patients was ever found bleeding—never had cause to bleed. There were no injuries—no self-inflicted wounds. We thought of animals. Perhaps a mouse—a rat. But nothing. Nothing. Nothing . . . We also went so far as to strip-search all the members of the staff who entered that ward and I, too, offered myself for this experiment. Still nothing. Nothing. No one had bled."

Everett was now beginning to perspire so heavily he removed his jacket and threw it on the floor. Thurber woke and stared at it, startled. At first, it appeared to be the beast that had just pursued him through the woods and down the road. But, then, it sighed and settled and was just a coat; a rumpled jacket lying down on the rug.

Everett said: "We had taken samples of the blood on the patient's hands—on Kenneth Albright's hands and on his clothing and we had these samples analysed. No. It was not his own blood. No, it was not the blood of an animal. No, it was not the blood of a fellow patient. No, it was not the blood of any members of the staff . . ."

Everett's voice had risen.

"Whose blood was it?" he almost cried. "Whose the hell was it?"

Mimi waited.

Everett Menlo lighted another cigarette. He took a great gulp of his drink.

"Well . . ." He was calmer now; calmer of necessity. He had to marshal the evidence. He had to put it all in order—bring it into line with reason. "Did this mean that—somehow—the patient had managed to leave the premises—do some bloody deed and return without our knowledge of it? That is, after all, the only possible explanation. Isn't it?"

Mimi waited.

"Isn't it?" he repeated.

"Yes," she said. "It's the only possible explanation."

"Except there is no way out of that place. There is absolutely no way out."

Now there was a pause.

"But one," he added—his voice, again, a whisper.

Mimi was silent. Fearful—watching his twisted face.

"Tell me," Everett Menlo said—the perfect innocent, almost the perfect child in quest of forbidden knowledge. "Answer me this—be honest: is there blood in dreams?"

Mimi could not respond. She felt herself go pale. Her husband—after all, the sanest man alive—had just suggested something so completely mad he might as well have handed over his reason in a paper bag and said to her, *burn this.*

"The only place that Kenneth Albright goes, I tell you, is into dreams," Everett said. "That is the only place beyond the ward into which the patient can or does escape."

Another—briefer—pause.

"It is real blood, Mimi. Real. And he gets it all from dreams. *My dreams.*"

They waited for this to settle.

Everett said: "I'm tired. I'm tired. I cannot bear this any more. I'm tired . . ."

Mimi thought, *good. No matter what else happens, he will sleep tonight.*

He did. And so, at last, did she.

Mimi's dreams were rarely of the kind that engender fear. She dreamed more gentle scenes with open spaces that did not intimidate. She would dream quite often of water and of animals. Always, she was nothing more than an observer; roles were not assigned her; often, this was sad. Somehow, she seemed at times locked out, unable to participate. These were the dreams she endured when Brian Bassett died: field trips to see him in some desert setting; underwater excursions to watch him float amongst the seaweed. He never spoke, and, indeed, he never appeared to be aware of her presence.

That night, when Everett fell into his bed exhausted and she did likewise, Mimi's dream of Brian Bassett was the last she would ever have of him and somehow, in the dream, she knew this. What she saw was what, in magical terms, would be called a disappearing act. Brian Bassett vanished. Gone.

Sometime after midnight on May Day morning, Mimi Menlo awoke from her dream of Brian to the sound of Thurber thumping the floor in a dream of his own.

Everett was not in his bed and Mimi cursed. She put on her wrapper and her slippers and went beyond the bedroom into the hall.

No lights were shining but the street lamps far below and the windows gave no sign of stars.

Mimi made her way past the jungle, searching for Everett in the living room. He was not there. She would dream of this one day; it was a certainty.

"Everett?"

He did not reply.

Mimi turned and went back through the bedroom.

"Everett?"

She heard him. He was in the bathroom and she went in through the door.

"Oh," she said, when she saw him. "Oh, my God." Everett Menlo was standing in the bathtub, removing his pyjamas. They were soaking wet, but not with perspiration. They were soaking wet with blood.

For a moment, holding his jacket, letting its arms hang down across his belly and his groin, Everett stared at Mimi, blank-eyed from his nightmare.

Mimi raised her hands to her mouth. She felt as one must feel, if helpless, watching someone burn alive.

Everett threw the jacket down and started to remove his trousers. His pyjamas, made of cotton, had been green. His eyes were blinded now with blood and his hands reached out to find the shower taps.

"Please don't look at me," he said. "I . . . Please go away."

Mimi said: "No." She sat on the toilet seat. "I'm waiting here," she told him, "until we both wake up."

# F. Scott Fitzgerald

*Fitzgerald (1896–1940) was born in St. Paul, Minnesota. After a glamorous undergraduate career at Princeton, he entered the army as a second lieutenant and while he was in training camp met the beautiful young woman who was to become his wife. He married Zelda Sayre as his literary career got off to a meteoric start in 1920. Through the 1920s when money seemed plentiful and postwar morality encouraged a reckless pursuit of happiness, he and Zelda traveled with a well-heeled crowd in Europe and New York, acting out the glamorous lifestyle he wrote of in his most popular magazine fiction. He was a spokesman for the so-called Jazz Age, setting a personal as well as a literary example for a generation whose first commandment was Do what you will. The tempo of his life slackened as his marriage was shredded by Zelda's insanity and his own self-destructive alcoholism. He fell from favor as a writer when the indulgent decade of his triumph went down under the impact of the Great Depression. Through years of emotional and physical collapse he struggled to repair his life by writing for Hollywood—producing at the same time a series of stories that exposed his humiliations there. His last three novels,* The Great Gatsby *(1925),* Tender Is the Night *(1934), and* The Last Tycoon *(1941), amplify the melancholy he discovered beneath the glitter of American-style success. In his pathetically candid book* The Crack-up *(1945) Fitzgerald documents the shattering of his personal ambitions. His stories were collected in* Flappers and Philosophers *(1921),* Tales of the Jazz Age *(1922),* All the Sad Young Men *(1926), and* Taps at Reveille *(1935).*

## Babylon[1] Revisited

### I

And where's Mr. Campbell?" Charlie asked.

"Gone to Switzerland. Mr. Campbell's a pretty sick man, Mr. Wales."

"I'm sorry to hear that. And George Hardt?" Charlie inquired.

"Back in America, gone to work."

"And where is the Snow Bird?"

"He was in here last week. Anyway, his friend, Mr. Schaeffer, is in Paris."

Two familiar names from the long list of a year and a half ago. Charlie scribbled an address in his notebook and tore out the page.

"If you see Mr. Schaeffer, give him this," he said. "It's my brother-in-law's address. I haven't settled on a hotel yet."

1. This ancient city is a symbol of orgiastic decadence.

He was not really disappointed to find Paris was so empty. But the stillness in the Ritz bar[2] was strange and portentous. It was not an American bar any more—he felt polite in it, and not as if he owned it. It had gone back into France. He felt the stillness from the moment he got out of the taxi and saw the doorman, usually in a frenzy of activity at this hour, gossiping with a *chasseur*[3] by the servants' entrance.

Passing through the corridor, he heard only a single, bored voice in the once-clamorous women's room. When he turned into the bar he traveled the twenty feet of green carpet with his eyes fixed straight ahead by old habit; and then, with his foot firmly on the rail, he turned and surveyed the room, encountering only a single pair of eyes that fluttered up from a newspaper in the corner. Charlie asked for the head barman, Paul, who in the latter days of the bull market[4] had come to work in his own custom-built car—disembarking, however, with due nicety at the nearest corner. But Paul was at his country house today and Alix giving him information.

"No, no more," Charlie said, "I'm going slow these days."

Alix congratulated him: "You were going pretty strong a couple of years ago."

"I'll stick to it all right," Charlie assured him. "I've stuck to it for over a year and a half now."

"How do you find conditions in America?"

"I haven't been to America for months. I'm in business in Prague, representing a couple of concerns there. They don't know about me down there."

Alix smiled.

"Remember the night of George Hardt's bachelor dinner here?" said Charlie. "By the way, what's become of Claude Fessenden?"

Alix lowered his voice confidentially: "He's in Paris, but he doesn't come here any more. Paul doesn't allow it. He ran up a bill of thirty thousand francs, charging all his drinks and his lunches, and usually his dinner, for more than a year. And when Paul finally told him he had to pay, he gave him a bad check."

Alix shook his head sadly.

"I don't understand it, such a dandy fellow. Now he's all bloated up—" He made a plump apple of his hands.

Charlie watched a group of strident queens installing themselves in a corner.

"Nothing affects them," he thought. "Stocks rise and fall, people loaf or work, but they go on forever." The place oppressed him. He called for the dice and shook with Alix for the drink.

"Here for long, Mr. Wales?"

"I'm here for four or five days to see my little girl."

"Oh-h! You have a little girl?"

Outside, the fire-red, gas-blue, ghost-green signs shone smokily through the tranquil rain. It was late afternoon and the streets were in movement; the *bistros*[5] gleamed. At the corner of the Boulevard des Capucines he took a taxi.

2. Hangout for wealthy and glamorous Americans. 3. Hotel servant who runs various errands (French). 4. The period of prosperity for players of the stock market that immediately preceded the crash of 1929, which was the beginning of the Great Depression. 5. Small cafés.

The Place de la Concorde moved by in pink majesty; they crossed the logical Seine, and Charlie felt the sudden provincial quality of the Left Bank.[6]

Charlie directed his taxi to the Avenue de l'Opéra, which was out of his way. But he wanted to see the blue hour spread over the magnificent façade, and imagine that the cab horns, playing endlessly the first few bars of *Le Plus que Lent,* were the trumpets of the Second Empire.[7] They were closing the iron grill in front of Brentano's Book-store, and people were already at dinner behind the trim little bourgeois hedge of Duval's. He had never eaten at a really cheap restaurant in Paris. Five-course dinner, four francs fifty, eighteen cents, wine included. For some odd reason he wished that he had.

As they rolled on to the Left Bank and he felt its sudden provincialism, he thought, "I spoiled this city for myself. I didn't realize it, but the days came along one after another, and then two years were gone, and everything was gone, and I was gone."

He was thirty-five, and good to look at. The Irish mobility of his face was sobered by a deep wrinkle between his eyes. As he rang his brother-in-law's bell in the Rue Palatine, the wrinkle deepened till it pulled down his brows; he felt a cramping sensation in his belly. From behind the maid who opened the door darted a lovely little girl of nine who shrieked "Daddy!" and flew up, struggling like a fish, into his arms. She pulled his head around by one ear and set her cheek against his.

"My old pie," he said.

"Oh, daddy, daddy, daddy, daddy, dads, dads, dads!"

She drew him into the salon, where the family waited, a boy and a girl his daughter's age, his sister-in-law and her husband. He greeted Marion with his voice pitched carefully to avoid either feigned enthusiasm or dislike, but her response was more frankly tepid, though she minimized her expression of unalterable distrust by directing her regard toward his child. The two men clasped hands in a friendly way and Lincoln Peters rested his for a moment on Charlie's shoulder.

The room was warm and comfortably American. The three children moved intimately about, playing through the yellow oblongs that led to other rooms; the cheer of six o'clock spoke in the eager smacks of the fire and the sounds of French activity in the kitchen. But Charlie did not relax; his heart sat up rigidly in his body and he drew confidence from his daughter, who from time to time came close to him, holding in her arms the doll he had brought.

"Really extremely well," he declared in answer to Lincoln's question. "There's a lot of business there that isn't moving at all, but we're doing even better than ever. In fact, damn well. I'm bringing my sister over from America next month to keep house for me. My income last year was bigger than it was when I had money. You see, the Czechs——"

His boasting was for a specific purpose; but after a moment, seeing a faint restiveness in Lincoln's eye, he changed the subject:

"Those are fine children of yours, well brought up, good manners."

6. South side of the Seine River; site of the student quarter and in recent tradition the Bohemian part of Paris.
7. I.e., that of Louis Napoleon of France (1852–70), a period of bourgeois ostentation, which seemed, in retrospect, glamorous. *"Le Plus que Lent"*: slower than slow (French); refers to the parodistic piano composition *(La Plus que Lente)* by Claude Debussy (1862–1918).

"We think Honoria's a great little girl too."

Marion Peters came back from the kitchen. She was a tall woman with worried eyes, who had once possessed a fresh American loveliness. Charlie had never been sensitive to it and was always surprised when people spoke of how pretty she had been. From the first there had been an instinctive antipathy between them.

"Well, how do you find Honoria?" she asked.

"Wonderful. I was astonished how much she's grown in ten months. All the children are looking well."

"We haven't had a doctor for a year. How do you like being back in Paris?"

"It seems very funny to see so few Americans around."

"I'm delighted," Marion said vehemently. "Now at least you can go into a store without their assuming you're a millionaire. We've suffered like everybody, but on the whole it's a good deal pleasanter."

"But it was nice while it lasted," Charlie said. "We were a sort of royalty, almost infallible, with a sort of magic around us. In the bar this afternoon"—he stumbled, seeing his mistake—"there wasn't a man I knew."

She looked at him keenly. "I should think you'd have had enough of bars."

"I only stayed a minute. I take one drink every afternoon, and no more."

"Don't you want a cocktail before dinner?" Lincoln asked.

"I take only one drink every afternoon, and I've had that."

"I hope you keep to it," said Marion.

Her dislike was evident in the coldness with which she spoke, but Charlie only smiled; he had larger plans. Her very aggressiveness gave him an advantage, and he knew enough to wait. He wanted them to initiate the discussion of what they knew had brought him to Paris.

At dinner he couldn't decide whether Honoria was most like him or her mother. Fortunate if she didn't combine the traits of both that had brought them to disaster. A great wave of protectiveness went over him. He thought he knew what to do for her. He believed in character; he wanted to jump back a whole generation and trust in character again as the eternally valuable element. Everything else wore out.

He left soon after dinner, but not to go home. He was curious to see Paris by night with clearer and more judicious eyes than those of other days. He bought a *strapontin* for the Casino and watched Josephine Baker[8] go through her chocolate arabesques.

After an hour he left and strolled toward Montmartre, up the Rue Pigalle into the Place Blanche. The rain had stopped and there were a few people in evening clothes disembarking from taxis in front of cabarets, and *cocottes*[9] prowling singly or in pairs, and many Negroes. He passed a lighted door from which issued music, and stopped with the sense of familiarity; it was Bricktop's, where he had parted with so many hours and so much money. A few doors farther on he found another ancient rendezvous and incautiously put his head

8. A celebrated black dancer of the epoch. *"Strapontin"*: a bracket seat in the aisle, cheaper than regular seats.
9. Prostitutes who flourish on the Boulevard Clichy between Pigalle and Place Blanche. Montmartre is a district in northern Paris.

inside. Immediately an eager orchestra burst into sound, a pair of professional dancers leaped to their feet and a maître d'hôtel swooped toward him, crying, "Crowd just arriving, sir!" But he withdrew quickly.

"You have to be damn drunk," he thought.

Zelli's was closed, the bleak and sinister cheap hotels surrounding it were dark; up in the Rue Blanche there was more light and a local, colloquial French crowd. The Poet's Cave had disappeared, but the two great mouths of the Café of Heaven and the Café of Hell still yawned—even devoured, as he watched, the meager contents of a tourist bus—a German, a Japanese, and an American couple who glanced at him with frightened eyes.

So much for the effort and ingenuity of Montmartre. All the catering to vice and waste was on an utterly childish scale, and he suddenly realized the meaning of the word "dissipate"—to dissipate into thin air; to make nothing out of something. In the little hours of the night every move from place to place was an enormous human jump, an increase of paying for the privilege of slower and slower motion.

He remembered thousand-franc notes given to an orchestra for playing a single number, hundred-franc notes tossed to a doorman for calling a cab.

But it hadn't been given for nothing.

It had been given, even the most wildly squandered sum, as an offering to destiny that he might not remember the things most worth remembering, the things that now he would always remember—his child taken from his control, his wife escaped to a grave in Vermont.

In the glare of a *brasserie*[1] a woman spoke to him. He bought her some eggs and coffee, and then, eluding her encouraging stare, gave her a twenty-franc note and took a taxi to his hotel.

## II

He woke upon a fine fall day—football weather. The depression of yesterday was gone and he liked the people on the streets. At noon he sat opposite Honoria at Le Grand Vatel, the only restaurant he could think of not reminiscent of champagne dinners and long luncheons that began at two and ended in a blurred and vague twilight.

"Now, how about vegetables? Oughtn't you to have some vegetables?"

"Well, yes."

"Here's *épinards* and *chou-fleur* and carrots and *haricots*."[2]

"I'd like *chou-fleur*."

"Wouldn't you like to have two vegetables?"

"I usually only have one at lunch."

The waiter was pretending to be inordinately fond of children. *"Qu'elle est mignonne la petite! Elle parle exactement comme une Française."*[3]

"How about dessert? Shall we wait and see?"

1. Small restaurant (French) that also serves drinks. 2. Beans (French). *"Épinards"*: spinach (French) *"Chou-fleur"*: cauliflower (French). 3. What a darling little girl! She speaks exactly like a French girl (French).

The waiter disappeared. Honoria looked at her father expectantly. "What are we going to do?"

"First, we're going to that toy store in the Rue Saint-Honoré and buy you anything you like. And then we're going to the vaudeville at the Empire."

She hesitated. "I like it about the vaudeville, but not the toy store."

"Why not?"

"Well, you brought me this doll." She had it with her. "And I've got lots of things. And we're not rich any more, are we?"

"We never were. But today you are to have anything you want."

"All right," she agreed resignedly.

When there had been her mother and a French nurse he had been inclined to be strict; now he extended himself, reached out for a new tolerance; he must be both parents to her and not shut any of her out of communication.

"I want to get to know you," he said gravely. "First let me introduce myself. My name is Charles J. Wales, of Prague."

"Oh, daddy!" her voice cracked with laughter.

"And who are you, please?" he persisted, and she accepted a rôle immediately: "Honoria Wales, Rue Palatine, Paris."

"Married or single?"

"No, not married. Single."

He indicated the doll. "But I see you have a child, madame."

Unwilling to disinherit it, she took it to her heart and thought quickly: "Yes, I've been married, but I'm not married now. My husband is dead."

He went on quickly, "And the child's name?"

"Simone. That's after my best friend at school."

"I'm very pleased that you're doing so well at school."

"I'm third this month," she boasted. "Elsie"—that was her cousin—"is only about eighteenth, and Richard is about at the bottom."

"You like Richard and Elsie, don't you?"

"Oh, yes. I like Richard quite well and I like her all right."

Cautiously and casually he asked: "And Aunt Marion and Uncle Lincoln—which do you like best?"

"Oh, Uncle Lincoln, I guess."

He was increasingly aware of her presence. As they came in, a murmur of " . . . adorable" followed them, and now the people at the next table bent all their silences upon her, staring as if she were something no more conscious than a flower.

"Why don't I live with you?" she asked suddenly. "Because mamma's dead?"

"You must stay here and learn more French. It would have been hard for daddy to take care of you so well."

"I don't really need much taking care of any more. I do everything for myself."

Going out of the restaurant, a man and a woman unexpectedly hailed him. "Well, the old Wales!"

"Hello there, Lorraine. . . . Dunc."

Sudden ghosts out of the past: Duncan Schaeffer, a friend from college.

Lorraine Quarrles, a lovely, pale blonde of thirty; one of a crowd who had helped them make months into days in the lavish times of three years ago.

"My husband couldn't come this year," she said, in answer to his question. "We're poor as hell. So he gave me two hundred a month and told me I could do my worst on that. . . . This your little girl?"

"What about coming back and sitting down?" Duncan asked.

"Can't do it." He was glad for an excuse. As always, he felt Lorraine's passionate, provocative attraction, but his own rhythm was different now.

"Well, how about dinner?" she asked.

"I'm not free. Give me your address and let me call you."

"Charlie, I believe you're sober," she said judicially. "I honestly believe he's sober, Dunc. Pinch him and see if he's sober."

Charlie indicated Honoria with his head. They both laughed.

"What's your address?" said Duncan skeptically.

He hesitated, unwilling to give the name of his hotel.

"I'm not settled yet. I'd better call you. We're going to see the vaudeville at the Empire."

"There! That's what I want to do," Lorraine said. "I want to see some clowns and acrobats and jugglers. That's just what we'll do, Dunc."

"We've got to do an errand first," said Charlie. "Perhaps we'll see you there."

"All right, you snot. . . . Good-by, beautiful little girl."

"Good-by."

Honoria bobbed politely.

Somehow, an unwelcome encounter. They liked him because he was functioning, because he was serious; they wanted to see him, because he was stronger than they were now, because they wanted to draw a certain sustenance from his strength.

At the Empire, Honoria proudly refused to sit upon her father's folded coat. She was already an individual with a code of her own, and Charlie was more and more absorbed by the desire of putting a little of himself into her before she crystallized utterly. It was hopeless to try to know her in so short a time.

Between the acts they came upon Duncan and Lorraine in the lobby where the band was playing.

"Have a drink?"

"All right, but not up at the bar. We'll take a table."

"The perfect father."

Listening abstractedly to Lorraine, Charlie watched Honoria's eyes leave their table, and he followed them wistfully about the room, wondering what they saw. He met her glance and she smiled.

"I liked that lemonade," she said.

What had she said? What had he expected? Going home in a taxi afterward, he pulled her over until her head rested against his chest.

"Darling, do you ever think about your mother?"

"Yes, sometimes," she answered vaguely.

"I don't want you to forget her. Have you got a picture of her?"

"Yes, I think so. Anyhow, Aunt Marion has. Why don't you want me to forget her?"

"She loved you very much."

"I loved her too."

They were silent for a moment.

"Daddy, I want to come and live with you," she said suddenly.

His heart leaped; he had wanted it to come like this.

"Aren't you perfectly happy?"

"Yes, but I love you better than anybody. And you love me better than anybody, don't you, now that mummy's dead?"

"Of course I do. But you won't always like me best, honey. You'll grow up and meet somebody your own age and go marry him and forget you ever had a daddy."

"Yes, that's true," she agreed tranquilly.

He didn't go in. He was coming back at nine o'clock and he wanted to keep himself fresh and new for the thing he must say then.

"When you're safe inside, just show yourself in that window."

"All right. Good-by, dads, dads, dads, dads."

He waited in the dark street until she appeared, all warm and glowing, in the window above and kissed her fingers out into the night.

## III

They were waiting. Marion sat behind the coffee service in a dignified black dinner dress that just faintly suggested mourning. Lincoln was walking up and down with the animation of one who had already been talking. They were as anxious as he was to get into the question. He opened it almost immediately:

"I suppose you know what I want to see you about—why I really came to Paris."

Marion played with the black stars on her necklace and frowned.

"I'm awfully anxious to have a home," he continued. "And I'm awfully anxious to have Honoria in it. I appreciate your taking in Honoria for her mother's sake, but things have changed now"—he hesitated and then continued more forcibly—"changed radically with me, and I want to ask you to reconsider the matter. It would be silly for me to deny that about three years ago I was acting badly——"

Marion looked up at him with hard eyes.

"—but all that's over. As I told you, I haven't had more than a drink a day for over a year, and I take that drink deliberately, so that the idea of alcohol won't get too big in my imagination. You see the idea?"

"No," said Marion succinctly.

"It's a sort of stunt I set myself. It keeps the matter in proportion."

"I get you," said Lincoln. "You don't want to admit it's got any attraction for you."

"Something like that. Sometimes I forget and don't take it. But I try to take it. Anyhow, I couldn't afford to drink in my position. The people I represent are more than satisfied with what I've done, and I'm bringing my sister over from Burlington to keep house for me, and I want awfully to have Honoria too. You know that even when her mother and I weren't getting along well we never let anything that happened touch Honoria. I know she's fond of me and I know I'm able to take care of her and—well, there you are. How do you feel about it?"

He knew that now he would have to take a beating. It would last an hour or two hours, and it would be difficult, but if he modulated his inevitable resentment to the chastened attitude of the reformed sinner, he might win his point in the end.

Keep your temper, he told himself. You don't want to be justified. You want Honoria.

Lincoln spoke first: "We've been talking it over ever since we got your letter last month. We're happy to have Honoria here. She's a dear little thing, and we're glad to be able to help her, but of course that isn't the question——"

Marion interrupted suddenly. "How long are you going to stay sober, Charlie?" she asked.

"Permanently, I hope."

"How can anybody count on that?"

"You know I never did drink heavily until I gave up business and came over here with nothing to do. Then Helen and I began to run around with——"

"Please leave Helen out of it. I can't bear to hear you talk about her like that."

He stared at her grimly; he had never been certain how fond of each other the sisters were in life.

"My drinking only lasted about a year and a half—from the time we came over until I—collapsed."

"It was time enough."

"It was time enough," he agreed.

"My duty is entirely to Helen," she said. "I try to think what she would have wanted me to do. Frankly, from the night you did that terrible thing you haven't really existed for me. I can't help that. She was my sister."

"Yes."

"When she was dying she asked me to look out for Honoria. If you hadn't been in a sanitarium then, it might have helped matters."

He had no answer.

"I'll never in my life be able to forget the morning when Helen knocked at my door, soaked to the skin and shivering, and said you'd locked her out."

Charlie gripped the sides of the chair. This was more difficult than he expected; he wanted to launch out into a long expostulation and explanation, but he only said: "The night I locked her out—" and she interrupted, "I don't feel up to going over that again."

After a moment's silence Lincoln said: "We're getting off the subject. You want Marion to set aside her legal guardianship and give you Honoria. I think the main point for her is whether she has confidence in you or not."

"I don't blame Marion," Charlie said slowly, "but I think she can have entire confidence in me. I had a good record up to three years ago. Of course, it's within human possibilities I might go wrong any time. But if we wait much longer I'll lose Honoria's childhood and my chance for a home." He shook his head, "I'll simply lose her, don't you see?"

"Yes, I see," said Lincoln.

"Why didn't you think of all this before?" Marion asked.

"I suppose I did, from time to time, but Helen and I were getting along badly. When I consented to the guardianship, I was flat on my back in a sanitarium and the market had cleaned me out. I knew I'd acted badly, and I thought if it would bring any peace to Helen, I'd agree to anything. But now it's different. I'm functioning, I'm behaving damn well, so far as——"

"Please don't swear at me," Marion said.

He looked at her, startled. With each remark the force of her dislike became more and more apparent. She had built up all her fear of life into one wall and faced it toward him. This trivial reproof was possibly the result of some trouble with the cook several hours before. Charlie became increasingly alarmed at leaving Honoria in this atmosphere of hostility against himself; sooner or later it would come out, in a word here, a shake of the head there, and some of that distrust would be irrevocably implanted in Honoria. But he pulled his temper down out of his face and shut it up inside him; he had won a point, for Lincoln realized the absurdity of Marion's remark and asked her lightly since when she had objected to the word "damn."

"Another thing," Charlie said: "I'm able to give her certain advantages now. I'm going to take a French governess to Prague with me. I've got a lease on a new apartment——"

He stopped, realizing that he was blundering. They couldn't be expected to accept with equanimity the fact that his income was again twice as large as their own.

"I suppose you can give her more luxuries than we can," said Marion. "When you were throwing away money we were living along watching every ten francs. . . . I suppose you'll start doing it again."

"Oh, no," he said. "I've learned. I worked hard for ten years, you know—until I got lucky in the market, like so many people. Terribly lucky. It won't happen again."

There was a long silence. All of them felt their nerves straining, and for the first time in a year Charlie wanted a drink. He was sure now that Lincoln Peters wanted him to have his child.

Marion shuddered suddenly; part of her saw that Charlie's feet were planted on the earth now, and her own maternal feeling recognized the naturalness of his desire; but she had lived for a long time with a prejudice—a prejudice founded on a curious disbelief in her sister's happiness, and which, in the shock of one terrible night, had turned to hatred for him. It had all happened at a point in her life where the discouragement of ill health and adverse circumstances made it necessary for her to believe in tangible villainy and a tangible villain.

"I can't help what I think!" she cried out suddenly. "How much you were responsible for Helen's death, I don't know. It's something you'll have to square with your own conscience."

An electric current of agony surged through him; for a moment he was almost on his feet, an unuttered sound echoing in his throat. He hung on to himself for a moment, another moment.

"Hold on there," said Lincoln uncomfortably. "I never thought you were responsible for that."

"Helen died of heart trouble," Charlie said dully.

"Yes, heart trouble." Marion spoke as if the phrase had another meaning for her.

Then, in the flatness that followed her outburst, she saw him plainly and she knew he had somehow arrived at control over the situation. Glancing at her husband, she found no help from him, and as abruptly as if it were a matter of no importance, she threw up the sponge.

"Do what you like!" she cried, springing up from her chair. "She's your child. I'm not the person to stand in your way. I think if it were my child I'd rather see her—" She managed to check herself. "You two decide it. I can't stand this. I'm sick. I'm going to bed."

She hurried from the room; after a moment Lincoln said:

"This has been a hard day for her. You know how strongly she feels—" His voice was almost apologetic: "When a woman gets an idea in her head."

"Of course."

"It's going to be all right. I think she sees now that you—can provide for the child, and so we can't very well stand in your way or Honoria's way."

"Thank you, Lincoln."

"I'd better go along and see how she is."

"I'm going."

He was still trembling when he reached the street, but a walk down the Rue Bonaparte to the *quais*[4] set him up, and as he crossed the Seine, fresh and new by the *quai* lamps, he felt exultant. But back in his room he couldn't sleep. The image of Helen haunted him. Helen whom he had loved so until they had senselessly begun to abuse each other's love, tear it into shreds. On that terrible February night that Marion remembered so vividly, a slow quarrel had gone on for hours. There was a scene at the Florida, and then he attempted to take her home, and then she kissed young Webb at a table; after that there was what she had hysterically said. When he arrived home alone he turned the key in the lock in wild anger. How could he know she would arrive an hour later alone, that there would be a snowstorm in which she wandered about in slippers, too confused to find a taxi? Then the aftermath, her escaping pneumonia by a miracle, and all the attendant horror. They were "reconciled," but that was the beginning of the end, and Marion, who had seen with her own eyes and who imagined it to be one of many scenes from her sister's martyrdom, never forgot.

Going over it again brought Helen nearer, and in the white, soft light that steals upon half sleep near morning he found himself talking to her again. She said that he was perfectly right about Honoria and that she wanted Honoria to be with him. She said she was glad he was being good and doing better. She

4. Paved riverbanks (French).

said a lot of other things—very friendly things—but she was in a swing in a white dress, and swinging faster and faster all the time, so that at the end he could not hear clearly all that she said.

## IV

He woke up feeling happy. The door of the world was open again. He made plans, vistas, futures for Honoria and himself, but suddenly he grew sad, remembering all the plans he and Helen had made. She had not planned to die. The present was the thing—work to do and someone to love. But not to love too much, for he knew the injury that a father can do to a daughter or a mother to a son by attaching them too closely: afterward, out in the world, the child would seek in the marriage partner the same blind tenderness and, failing probably to find it, turn against love and life.

It was another bright, crisp day. He called Lincoln Peters at the bank where he worked and asked if he could count on taking Honoria when he left for Prague. Lincoln agreed that there was no reason for delay. One thing—the legal guardianship. Marion wanted to retain that a while longer. She was upset by the whole matter, and it would oil things if she felt that the situation was still in her control for another year. Charlie agreed, wanting only the tangible, visible child.

Then the question of a governess. Charles sat in a gloomy agency and talked to a cross Béarnaise and to a buxom Breton peasant, neither of whom he could have endured. There were others whom he would see tomorrow.

He lunched with Lincoln Peters at Griffons, trying to keep down his exultation.

"There's nothing quite like your own child," Lincoln said. "But you understand how Marion feels too."

"She's forgotten how hard I worked for seven years there," Charlie said. "She just remembers one night."

"There's another thing." Lincoln hesitated. "While you and Helen were tearing around Europe throwing money away, we were just getting along. I didn't touch any of the prosperity because I never got ahead enough to carry anything but my insurance. I think Marion felt there was some kind of injustice in it—you not even working toward the end, and getting richer and richer."

"It went just as quick as it came," said Charlie.

"Yes, a lot of it stayed in the hands of *chasseurs* and saxophone players and maîtres d'hôtel—well, the big party's over now. I just said that to explain Marion's feeling about those crazy years. If you drop in about six o'clock tonight before Marion's too tired, we'll settle the details on the spot."

Back at his hotel, Charlie found a *pneumatique*[5] that had been redirected from the Ritz bar where Charlie had left his address for the purpose of finding a certain man.

> DEAR CHARLIE: You were so strange when we saw you the other day that I wondered if I did something to offend you. If so, I'm not conscious of it. In fact,

5. Message delivered speedily by special Parisian system (French).

I have thought about you too much for the last year, and it's always been in the back of my mind that I might see you if I came over here. We *did* have such good times that crazy spring, like the night you and I stole the butcher's tricycle, and the time we tried to call on the president and you had the old derby rim and the wire cane. Everybody seems so old lately, but I don't feel old a bit. Couldn't we get together some time today for old time's sake? I've got a vile hang-over for the moment, but will be feeling better this afternoon and will look for you about five in the sweatshop at the Ritz.

Always devotedly,
Lorraine

His first feeling was one of awe that he had actually, in his mature years, stolen a tricycle and pedaled Lorraine all over the Étoile between the small hours and dawn. In retrospect it was a nightmare. Locking out Helen didn't fit in with any other act of his life, but the tricycle incident did—it was one of many. How many weeks or months of dissipation to arrive at that condition of utter irresponsibility?

He tried to picture how Lorraine had appeared to him then—very attractive; Helen was unhappy about it, though she said nothing. Yesterday, in the restaurant, Lorraine had seemed trite, blurred, worn away. He emphatically did not want to see her, and he was glad Alix had not given away his hotel address. It was a relief to think, instead, of Honoria, to think of Sundays spent with her and of saying good morning to her and of knowing she was there in his house at night, drawing her breath in the darkness.

At five he took a taxi and bought presents for all the Peters—a piquant cloth doll, a box of Roman soldiers, flowers for Marion, big linen handkerchiefs for Lincoln.

He saw, when he arrived in the apartment, that Marion had accepted the inevitable. She greeted him now as though he were a recalcitrant member of the family, rather than a menacing outsider. Honoria had been told she was going; Charlie was glad to see that her tact made her conceal her excessive happiness. Only on his lap did she whisper her delight and the question "When?" before she slipped away with the other children.

He and Marion were alone for a minute in the room, and on an impulse he spoke out boldly:

"Family quarrels are bitter things. They don't go according to any rules. They're not like aches or wounds; they're more like splits in the skin that won't heal because there's not enough material. I wish you and I could be on better terms."

"Some things are hard to forget," she answered. "It's a question of confidence." There was no answer to this and presently she asked, "When do you propose to take her?"

"As soon as I can get a governess. I hoped the day after tomorrow."

"That's impossible. I've got to get her things in shape. Not before Saturday."

He yielded. Coming back into the room, Lincoln offered him a drink.

"I'll take my daily whisky," he said.

It was warm here, it was a home, people together by a fire. The children felt very safe and important; the mother and father were serious, watchful. They had things to do for the children more important than his visit here. A spoonful of medicine was, after all, more important than the strained relations between Marion and himself. They were not dull people, but they were very much in the grip of life and circumstances. He wondered if he couldn't do something to get Lincoln out of his rut at the bank.

A long peal at the door-bell; the *bonne à tout faire*[6] passed through and went down the corridor. The door opened upon another long ring, and then voices, and the three in the salon looked up expectantly; Richard moved to bring the corridor within his range of vision, and Marion rose. Then the maid came back along the corridor, closely followed by the voices, which developed under the light into Duncan Schaeffer and Lorraine Quarrles.

They were gay, they were hilarious, they were roaring with laughter. For a moment Charlie was astounded; unable to understand how they ferreted out the Peters' address.

"Ah-h-h!" Duncan wagged his finger roguishly at Charlie. "Ah-h-h!"

They both slid down another cascade of laughter. Anxious and at a loss, Charlie shook hands with them quickly and presented them to Lincoln and Marion. Marion nodded, scarcely speaking. She had drawn back a step toward the fire; her little girl stood beside her, and Marion put an arm about her shoulder.

With growing annoyance at the intrusion, Charlie waited for them to explain themselves. After some concentration Duncan said:

"We came to invite you out to dinner. Lorraine and I insist that all this shishi, cagy business 'bout your address got to stop."

Charlie came closer to them, as if to force them backward down the corridor.

"Sorry, but I can't. Tell me where you'll be and I'll phone you in half an hour."

This made no impression. Lorraine sat down suddenly on the side of a chair, and focusing her eyes on Richard, cried, "Oh, what a nice little boy! Come here, little boy." Richard glanced at his mother, but did not move. With a perceptible shrug of her shoulders, Lorraine turned back to Charlie:

"Come and dine. Sure your cousins won' mine. See you so sel'om. Or solemn."

"I can't," said Charlie sharply. "You two have dinner and I'll phone you."

Her voice became suddenly unpleasant. "All right, we'll go. But I remember once when you hammered on my door at four A.M. I was enough of a good sport to give you a drink. Come on, Dunc."

Still in slow motion, with blurred, angry faces, with uncertain feet, they retired along the corridor.

"Good night," Charlie said.

"Good night!" responded Lorraine emphatically.

When he went back into the salon Marion had not moved, only now her son was standing in the circle of her other arm. Lincoln was still swinging

6. Maid of all work (French).

Honoria back and forth like a pendulum from side to side.

"What an outrage!" Charlie broke out. "What an absolute outrage!"

Neither of them answered. Charlie dropped into an armchair, picked up his drink, set it down again and said:

"People I haven't seen for two years having the colossal nerve——"

He broke off. Marion had made the sound "Oh!" in one swift, furious breath, turned her body from him with a jerk and left the room.

Lincoln set down Honoria carefully.

"You children go in and start your soup," he said, and when they obeyed, he said to Charlie:

"Marion's not well and she can't stand shocks. That kind of people make her really physically sick."

"I didn't tell them to come here. They wormed your name out of somebody. They deliberately——"

"Well, it's too bad. It doesn't help matters. Excuse me a minute."

Left alone, Charlie sat tense in his chair. In the next room he could hear the children eating, talking in monosyllables, already oblivious to the scene between their elders. He heard a murmur of conversation from a farther room and then the ticking bell of a telephone receiver picked up, and in a panic he moved to the other side of the room and out of earshot.

In a minute Lincoln came back. "Look here, Charlie. I think we'd better call off dinner for tonight. Marion's in bad shape."

"Is she angry with me?"

"Sort of," he said, almost roughly. "She's not strong and——"

"You mean she's changed her mind about Honoria?"

"She's pretty bitter right now. I don't know. You phone me at the bank tomorrow."

"I wish you'd explain to her I never dreamed these people would come here. I'm just as sore as you are."

"I couldn't explain anything to her now."

Charlie got up. He took his coat and hat and started down the corridor. Then he opened the door of the dining room and said in a strange voice, "Good night, children."

Honoria rose and ran around the table to hug him.

"Good night, sweetheart," he said vaguely, and then trying to make his voice more tender, trying to conciliate something, "Good night, dear children."

## V

Charlie went directly to the Ritz bar with the furious idea of finding Lorraine and Duncan, but they were not there, and he realized that in any case there was nothing he could do. He had not touched his drink at the Peters', and now he ordered a whisky-and-soda. Paul came over to say hello.

"It's a great change," he said sadly. "We do about half the business we did. So many fellows I hear about back in the States lost everything, maybe not in the first crash, but then in the second. Your friend George Hardt lost every cent, I hear. Are you back in the States?"

"No, I'm in business in Prague."

"I heard that you lost a lot in the crash."

"I did," and he added grimly, "but I lost everything I wanted in the boom."

"Selling short."

"Something like that."

Again the memory of those days swept over him like a nightmare—the people they had met travelling; then people who couldn't add a row of figures or speak a coherent sentence. The little man Helen had consented to dance with at the ship's party, who had insulted her ten feet from the table; the women and girls carried screaming with drink or drugs out of public places——

—The men who locked their wives out in the snow, because the snow of twenty-nine wasn't real snow. If you didn't want it to be snow, you just paid some money.

He went to the phone and called the Peters' apartment; Lincoln answered.

"I called up because this thing is on my mind. Has Marion said anything definite?"

"Marion's sick," Lincoln answered shortly. "I know this thing isn't altogether your fault, but I can't have her go to pieces about it. I'm afraid we'll have to let it slide for six months; I can't take the chance of working her up to this state again."

"I see."

"I'm sorry, Charlie."

He went back to his table. His whisky glass was empty, but he shook his head when Alix looked at it questioningly. There wasn't much he could do now except send Honoria some things; he would send her a lot of things tomorrow. He thought rather angrily that this was just money—he had given so many people money. . . .

"No, no more," he said to another waiter. "What do I owe you?"

He would come back some day; they couldn't make him pay forever. But he wanted his child, and nothing was much good now, beside that fact. He wasn't young any more, with a lot of nice thoughts and dreams to have by himself. He was absolutely sure Helen wouldn't have wanted him to be so alone.

# Richard Ford

*Ford (1944– ) was born in Jackson, Mississippi. After a boyhood in Arkansas, he attended Michigan State University, the University of California, and Washington University Law School in St. Louis. He has traveled in the fast lane of American letters since he began to publish stories in* Esquire, The New Yorker, *and* Granta. *For these he has received Guggenheim and National Endowment for the Arts grants, and his reputation puts him in the top rank of young writers. His novels are* A Piece of My Heart *(1976),* The Ultimate Good Luck *(1981),* The Sportswriter *(1986),* Wildlife *(1990), and* Women with Men: Stories *(1997). Among his awards is a Pulitzer Prize (1996) for* Independence Day. *More of his stories can be found in* Rock Springs *(1987).*

## Great Falls

This is not a happy story. I warn you.

My father was a man named Jack Russell, and when I was a young boy in my early teens, we lived with my mother in a house to the east of Great Falls, Montana, near the small town of Highwood and the Highwood Mountains and the Missouri River. It is a flat, treeless benchland there, all of it used for wheat farming, though my father was never a farmer, but was brought up near Tacoma, Washington, in a family that worked for Boeing.

He—my father—had been an Air Force sergeant and had taken his discharge in Great Falls. And instead of going home to Tacoma, where my mother wanted to go, he had taken a civilian's job with the Air Force, working on planes, which was what he liked to do. And he had rented the house out of town from a farmer who did not want it left standing empty.

The house itself is gone now—I have been to the spot. But the double row of Russian olive trees and two of the outbuildings are still standing in the milkweeds. It was a plain, two-story house with a porch on the front and no place for the cars. At the time, I rode the school bus to Great Falls every morning, and my father drove in while my mother stayed home.

My mother was a tall pretty woman, thin, with black hair and slightly sharp features that made her seem to smile when she wasn't smiling. She had grown up in Wallace, Idaho, and gone to college a year in Spokane, then moved out to the coast, which is where she met Jack Russell. She was two years older than he was, and married him, she said to me, because he was young and wonderful looking, and because she thought they could leave the sticks and see the world together—which I suppose they did for a while. That was the life she wanted, even before she knew much about wanting anything else or about the future.

When my father wasn't working on airplanes, he was going hunting or fishing, two things he could do as well as anyone. He had learned to fish, he said, in Iceland, and to hunt ducks up on the DEW[1] line—stations he had visited in the Air Force. And during the time of this—it was 1960—he began to take me with him on what he called his "expeditions." I thought even then, with as little as I knew, that these were opportunities other boys would dream of having but probably never would. And I don't think that I was wrong in that.

It is a true thing that my father did not know limits. In the spring, when we would go east to the Judith River Basin and camp up on the banks, he would catch a hundred fish in a weekend, and sometimes more than that. It was all he did from morning until night, and it was never hard for him. He used yellow corn kernels stacked onto a #4 snelled hook, and he would rattle this rig-up along the bottom of a deep pool below a split-shot sinker, and catch fish. And most of the time, because he knew the Judith River and knew how to feel his bait down deep, he would catch fish of good size.

It was the same with ducks, the other thing he liked. When the northern birds were down, usually by mid-October, he would take me and we would build a cattail and wheat-straw blind on one of the tule ponds or sloughs he knew about down the Missouri, where the water was shallow enough to wade. We would set out his decoys to the leeward side of our blind, and he would sprinkle corn on a hunger-line from the decoys to where we were. In the evenings when he came home from the base, we would go and sit out in the blind until the roosting flights came and put down among the decoys—there was never calling involved. And after a while, sometimes it would be an hour and full dark, the ducks would find the corn, and the whole raft of them—sixty, sometimes—would swim in to us. At the moment he judged they were close enough, my father would say to me, "Shine, Jackie," and I would stand and shine a seal-beam car light out onto the pond, and he would stand up beside me and shoot all the ducks that were there, on the water if he could, but flying and getting up as well. He owned a Model 11 Remington with a long-tube magazine that would hold ten shells, and with that many, and shooting straight over the surface rather than down onto it, he could kill or wound thirty ducks in twenty seconds' time. I remember distinctly the report of that gun and the flash of it over the water into the dark air, one shot after another, not even so fast, but measured in a way to hit as many as he could.

What my father did with the ducks he killed, and the fish, too, was sell them. It was against the law then to sell wild game, and it is against the law now. And though he kept some for us, most he would take—his fish laid on ice, or his ducks still wet and bagged in the burlap corn sacks—down to the Great Northern Hotel, which was still open then on Second Street in Great Falls, and sell them to the Negro caterer who bought them for his wealthy customers and for the dining car passengers who came through. We would

1. Distant early warning line of radar installations established by the United States in northern Canada.

drive in my father's Plymouth to the back of the hotel—always this was after dark—to a concrete loading ramp and lighted door that were close enough to the yards that I could sometimes see passengér trains waiting at the station, their car lights yellow and warm inside, the passengers dressed in suits, all bound for someplace far away from Montana—Milwaukee or Chicago or New York City, unimaginable places to me, a boy fourteen years old, with my father in the cold dark selling illegal game.

The caterer was a tall, stooped-back man in a white jacket, who my father called "Professor Ducks" or "Professor Fish," and the Professor referred to my father as "Sarge." He paid a quarter per pound for trout, a dime for whitefish, a dollar for a mallard duck, two for a speckle or a blue goose, and four dollars for a Canada. I have been with my father when he took away a hundred dollars for fish he'd caught and, in the fall, more than that for ducks and geese. When he had sold game in that way, we would drive out 10th Avenue and stop at a bar called The Mermaid which was by the air base, and he would drink with some friends he knew there, and they would laugh about hunting and fishing while I played pinball and wasted money in the jukebox.

It was on such a night as this that the unhappy things came about. It was in late October. I remember the time because Halloween had not been yet, and in the windows of the houses that I passed every day on the bus to Great Falls, people had put pumpkin lanterns, and set scarecrows in their yards in chairs.

My father and I had been shooting ducks in a slough on the Smith River, upstream from where it enters on the Missouri. He had killed thirty ducks, and we'd driven them down to the Great Northern and sold them there, though my father had kept two back in his corn sack. And when we had driven away, he suddenly said, "Jackie, let's us go back home tonight. Who cares about those hard-dicks at The Mermaid. I'll cook these ducks on the grill. We'll do something different tonight." He smiled at me in an odd way. This was not a thing he usually said, or the way he usually talked. He liked The Mermaid, and my mother—as far as I knew—didn't mind it if he went there.

"That sounds good," I said.

"We'll surprise your mother," he said. "We'll make her happy."

We drove out past the air base on Highway 87, past where there were planes taking off into the night. The darkness was dotted by the green and red beacons, and the tower light swept the sky and trapped planes as they disappeared over the flat landscape toward Canada or Alaska and the Pacific.

"Boy-oh-boy," my father said—just out of the dark. I looked at him and his eyes were narrow, and he seemed to be thinking about something. "You know, Jackie," he said, "your mother said something to me once I've never forgotten. She said, 'Nobody dies of a broken heart.' This was somewhat before you were born. We were living down in Texas and we'd had some big blow-up, and that was the idea she had. I don't know why." He shook his head.

He ran his hand under the seat, found a half-pint bottle of whiskey, and held it up to the lights of the car behind us to see what there was left of it. He unscrewed the cap and took a drink, then held the bottle out to me. "Have a drink, son," he said. "Something oughta be good in life." And I felt that something was wrong. Not because of the whiskey, which I had drunk before and he had reason to know about, but because of some sound in his voice, something I didn't recognize and did not know the importance of, though I was certain it was important.

I took a drink and gave the bottle back to him, holding the whiskey in my mouth until it stopped burning and I could swallow it a little at a time. When we turned out the road to Highwood, the lights of Great Falls sank below the horizon, and I could see the small white lights of farms, burning at wide distances in the dark.

"What do you worry about, Jackie," my father said. "Do you worry about girls? Do you worry about your future sex life? Is that some of it?" He glanced at me, then back at the road.

"I don't worry about that," I said.

"Well, what then?" my father said. "What else is there?"

"I worry if you're going to die before I do," I said, though I hated saying that, "or if Mother is. That worries me."

"It'd be a miracle if we didn't," my father said, with the half-pint held in the same hand he held the steering wheel. I had seen him drive that way before. "Things pass too fast in your life, Jackie. Don't worry about that. If I were you, I'd worry we might not." He smiled at me, and it was not the worried, nervous smile from before, but a smile that meant he was pleased. And I don't remember him ever smiling at me that way again.

We drove on out behind the town of Highwood and onto the flat field roads toward our house. I could see, out on the prairie, a moving light where the farmer who rented our house to us was disking his field for winter wheat. "He's waited too late with that business," my father said and took a drink, then threw the bottle right out the window. "He'll lose that," he said, "the cold'll kill it." I did not answer him, but what I thought was that my father knew nothing about farming, and if he was right it would be an accident. He knew about planes and hunting game, and that seemed all to me.

"I want to respect your privacy," he said then, for no reason at all that I understood. I am not even certain he said it, only that it is in my memory that way. I don't know what he was thinking of. Just words. But I said to him, I remember well, "It's all right. Thank you."

We did not go straight out the Geraldine Road to our house. Instead my father went down another mile and turned, went a mile and turned back again so that we came home from the other direction. "I want to stop and listen now," he said. "The geese should be in the stubble." We stopped and he cut the lights and engine, and we opened the car windows and listened. It was eight o'clock at night and it was getting colder, though it was dry. But I could hear nothing, just the sound of air moving lightly through the cut field, and not a goose sound. Though I could smell the whiskey on my father's breath and on mine, could hear the motor ticking, could hear him breathe, hear the sound we made sitting side by side on the car seat, our clothes, our feet, almost our hearts beating. And I could see out in the night the yellow lights of our house, shining through the olive trees south of us like a ship on the sea. "I hear them, by God," my father said, his head stuck out the window. "But they're high up. They won't stop here now, Jackie. They're high flyers, those boys. Long gone geese."

There was a car parked off the road, down the line of wind-break trees, beside a steel thresher the farmer had left there to rust. You could see moonlight off the taillight chrome. It was a Pontiac, a two-door hardtop. My father said nothing about it and I didn't either, though I think now for different reasons.

The floodlight was on over the side door of our house and lights were on inside, upstairs and down. My mother had a pumpkin on the front porch, and the wind chime she had hung by the door was tinkling. My dog, Major, came out of the quonset shed and stood in the car lights when we drove up.

"Let's see what's happening here," my father said, opening the door and stepping out quickly. He looked at me inside the car, and his eyes were wide and his mouth drawn tight.

We walked in the side door and up the basement steps into the kitchen, and a man was standing there—a man I had never seen before, a young man with blond hair, who might've been twenty or twenty-five. He was tall and was wearing a short-sleeved shirt and beige slacks with pleats. He was on the other side of the breakfast table, his fingertips just touching the wooden tabletop. His blue eyes were on my father, who was dressed in hunting clothes.

"Hello," my father said.

"Hello," the young man said, and nothing else. And for some reason I looked at his arms, which were long and pale. They looked like a young man's arms, like my arms. His short sleeves had each been neatly rolled up, and I could see the bottom of a small green tattoo edging out from underneath. There was a glass of whiskey on the table, but no bottle.

"What's your name?" my father said, standing in the kitchen under the bright ceiling light. He sounded like he might be going to laugh.

"Woody," the young man said and cleared his throat. He looked at me, then he touched the glass of whiskey, just the rim of the glass. He wasn't nervous, I could tell that. He did not seem to be afraid of anything.

"Woody," my father said and looked at the glass of whiskey. He looked at me, then sighed and shook his head. "Where's Mrs. Russell, Woody? I guess you aren't robbing my house, are you?"

Woody smiled. "No," he said. "Upstairs. I think she went upstairs."

"Good," my father said, "that's a good place." And he walked straight out of the room, but came back and stood in the doorway. "Jackie, you and Woody step outside and wait on me. Just stay there and I'll come out." He looked at Woody then in a way I would not have liked him to look at me, a look that meant he was studying Woody. "I guess that's your car," he said.

"That Pontiac." Woody nodded.

"Okay. Right," my father said. Then he went out again and up the stairs. At that moment the phone started to ring in the living room, and I heard my mother say, "Who's that?" And my father say, "It's me. It's Jack." And I decided I wouldn't go answer the phone. Woody looked at me, and I understood he wasn't sure what to do. Run, maybe. But he didn't have run in him. Though I thought he would probably do what I said if I would say it.

"Let's just go outside," I said.

And he said, "All right."

Woody and I walked outside and stood in the light of the floodlamp above the side door. I had on my wool jacket, but Woody was cold and stood with his hands in him pockets, and his arms bare, moving from foot to foot. Inside, the phone was ringing again. Once I looked up and saw my mother come to the window and look down at Woody and me. Woody didn't look up or see her, but I did. I waved at her, and she waved back at me and smiled. She was wearing a powder-blue dress. In another minute the phone stopped ringing.

Woody took a cigarette out of his shirt pocket and lit it. Smoke shot through his nose into the cold air, and he sniffed, looked around the ground and threw his match on the gravel. His blond hair was combed backwards and neat on the sides, and I could smell his aftershave on him, a sweet, lemon smell. And for the first time I noticed his shoes. They were two-tones, black with white tops and black laces. They stuck out below his baggy pants and were long and polished and shiny, as if he had been planning on a big occasion. They looked like shoes some country singer would wear, or a salesman. He was handsome, but only like someone you would see beside you in a dime store and not notice again.

"I like it out here," Woody said, his head down, looking at his shoes. "Nothing to bother you. I bet you'd see Chicago if the world was flat. The Great Plains commence here."

"I don't know," I said.

Woody looked up at me, cupping his smoke with one hand. "Do you play football?"

"No," I said. I thought about asking him something about my mother. But I had no idea what it would be.

"I *have* been drinking," Woody said, "but I'm not drunk now."

The wind rose then, and from behind the house I could hear Major bark once from far away, and I could smell the irrigation ditch, hear it hiss in the field. It ran down from Highwood Creek to the Missouri, twenty miles away. It was nothing Woody knew about, nothing he could hear or smell. He knew nothing about anything that was here. I heard my father say the words, "That's a real joke," from inside the house, then the sound of a drawer being opened and shut, and a door closing. Then nothing else.

Woody turned and looked into the dark toward where the glow of Great Falls rose on the horizon, and we both could see the flashing lights of a plane lowering to land there. "I once passed my brother in the Los Angeles airport and didn't even recognize him," Woody said, staring into the night. "He recognized *me,* though. He said, 'Hey, bro, are you mad at me, or what?' I wasn't mad at him. We both had to laugh."

Woody turned and looked at the house. His hands were still in his pockets, his cigarette clenched between his teeth, his arms taut. They were, I saw, bigger, stronger arms than I had thought. A vein went down the front of each of them. I wondered what Woody knew that I didn't. Not about my mother—I didn't know anything about that and didn't want to—but about a lot of things, about the life out in the dark, about coming out here, about airports, even about me. He and I were not so far apart in age, I knew that. But Woody was one thing, and I was another. And I wondered how I would ever get to be like him, since it didn't necessarily seem so bad a thing to be.

"Did you know your mother was married before?" Woody said.

"Yes," I said. "I knew that."

"It happens to all of them, now," he said. "They can't wait to get divorced."

"I guess so," I said.

Woody dropped his cigarette into the gravel and toed it out with his black-and-white shoe. He looked up at me and smiled the way he had inside the house, a smile that said he knew something he wouldn't tell, a smile to make you feel bad because you weren't Woody and never could be.

It was then that my father came out of the house. He still had on his plaid hunting coat and his wool cap, but his face was as white as snow, as white as I have ever seen a human being's face to be. It was odd. I had the feeling that he might've fallen inside, because he looked roughed up, as though he had hurt himself somehow.

My mother came out the door behind him and stood in the floodlight at the top of the steps. She was wearing the powder-blue dress I'd seen through the window, a dress I had never seen her wear before, though she was also wearing a car coat and carrying a suitcase. She looked at me and shook her head in a way that only I was supposed to notice, as if it was not a good idea to talk now.

My father had his hands in his pockets, and he walked right up to Woody. He did not even look at me. "What do you do for a living?" he said, and he was very close to Woody. His coat was close enough to touch Woody's shirt.

"I'm in the Air Force," Woody said. He looked at me and then at my father. He could tell my father was excited.

"Is this your day off, then?" my father said. He moved even closer to Woody, his hands still in his pockets. He pushed Woody with his chest, and Woody seemed willing to let my father push him.

"No," he said, shaking his head.

I looked at my mother. She was just standing, watching. It was as if someone had given her an order, and she was obeying it. She did not smile at me, though I thought she was thinking about me, which made me feel strange.

"What's the matter with you?" my father said into Woody's face, right into his face—his voice tight, as if it had gotten hard for him to talk. "Whatever in the world is the matter with you? Don't you understand something?" My father took a revolver pistol out of his coat and put it up under Woody's chin, into the soft pocket behind the bone, so that Woody's whole face rose, but his arms stayed at his sides, his hands open. "I don't know what to do with you," my father said. "I don't have any idea what to do with you. I just don't." Though I thought that what he wanted to do was hold Woody there just like that until something important took place, or until he could simply forget about all this.

My father pulled the hammer back on the pistol and raised it tighter under Woody's chin, breathing into Woody's face—my mother in the light with her suitcase, watching them, and me watching them. A half a minute must've gone by.

And then my mother said, "Jack, let's stop now. Let's just stop."

My father stared into Woody's face as if he wanted Woody to consider doing something—moving or turning around or anything on his own to stop this—that my father would then put a stop to. My father's eyes grew narrowed, and his teeth were gritted together, his lips snarling up to resemble a smile. "You're crazy, aren't you?" he said. "You're a goddamned crazy man. Are you in love with her, too? Are you, crazy man? Are you? Do you say you love her? Say you love her! Say you love her so I can blow your fucking brains in the sky."

"All right," Woody said. "No. It's all right."

"He doesn't love me, Jack. For God's sake," my mother said. She seemed so calm. She shook her head at me again. I do not think she thought my father would shoot Woody. And I don't think Woody thought so. Nobody did, I think, except my father himself. But I think he did, and was trying to find out how to.

My father turned suddenly and glared at my mother, his eyes shiny and moving, but with the gun still on Woody's skin. I think he was afraid, afraid he was doing this wrong and could mess all of it up and make matters worse without accomplishing anything.

"You're leaving," he yelled at her. "That's why you're packed. Get out. Go on."

"Jackie has to be at school in the morning," my mother said in just her normal voice. And without another word to any one of us, she walked out of the floodlamp light carrying her bag, turned the corner at the front porch steps and disappeared toward the olive trees that ran in rows back into the wheat.

My father looked back at me where I was standing in the gravel, as if he expected to see me go with my mother toward Woody's car. But I hadn't thought about that—though later I would. Later I would think I should have gone with her, and that things between them might've been different. But that isn't how it happened.

"You're sure you're going to get away now, aren't you, mister?" my father said into Woody's face. He was crazy himself, then. Anyone would've been. Everything must have seemed out of hand to him.

"I'd like to," Woody said. "I'd like to get away from here."

"And I'd like to think of some way to hurt you," my father said and blinked his eyes. "I feel helpless about it." We all heard the door to Woody's car close in the dark. "Do you think that I'm a fool?" my father said.

"No," Woody said. "I don't think that."

"Do you think you're important?"

"No," Woody said. "I'm not."

My father blinked again. He seemed to be becoming someone else at that moment, someone I didn't know. "Where are you from?"

And Woody closed his eyes. He breathed in, then out, a long sigh. It was as if this was somehow the hardest part, something he hadn't expected to be asked to say.

"Chicago," Woody said. "A suburb of there."

"Are your parents alive?" my father said, all the time with his blue magnum pistol pushed under Woody's chin.

"Yes," Woody said. "Yessir."

"That's too bad," my father said. "Too bad they have to know what you are. I'm sure you stopped meaning anything to them a long time ago. I'm sure they both wish you were dead. You didn't know that. But I know it. I can't help them out, though. Somebody else'll have to kill you. I don't want to have to think about you anymore. I guess that's it."

My father brought the gun down to his side and stood looking at Woody. He did not back away, just stood, waiting for what I don't know to happen. Woody stood a moment, then he cut his eyes at me uncomfortably. And I know that I looked down. That's all I could do. Though I remember wondering if Woody's heart was broken and what any of this meant to him. Not to me, or my mother, or my father. But to him, since he seemed to be the one left out somehow, the one who would be lonely soon, the one who had done something he would someday wish he hadn't and would have no one to tell him that it was all right, that they forgave him, that these things happen in the world.

Woody took a step back, looked at my father and at me again as if he intended to speak, then stepped aside and walked away toward the front of our house, where the wind chime made a noise in the new cold air.

My father looked at me, his big pistol in his hand. "Does this seem stupid to you?" he said. "All this? Yelling and threatening and going nuts? I wouldn't blame you if it did. You shouldn't even see this. I'm sorry. I don't know what to do now."

"It'll be all right," I said. And I walked out to the road. Woody's car started up behind the olive trees. I stood and watched it back out, its red taillights clouded by exhaust. I could see their two heads inside, with the headlights shining behind them. When they got into the road, Woody touched his brakes, and for a moment I could see that they were talking, their heads turned toward each other, nodding. Woody's head and my mother's. They sat that way for a few seconds, then drove slowly off. And I wondered what they had to say to each other, something important enough that they had to stop right at that moment and say it. Did she say, *I love you?* Did she say, *This is not what I expected to happen?* Did she say, *This is what I've wanted all along?* And did he say, *I'm sorry for all this,* or *I'm glad,* or *None of this matters to me?* These are not the kinds of things you can know if you were not there. And I was not there and did not want to be. It did not seem like I should be there. I heard the door slam when my father went inside, and I turned back from the road where I could still see their taillights disappearing, and went back into the house where I was to be alone with my father.

Things seldom end in one event. In the morning I went to school on the bus as usual, and my father drove in to the air base in his car. We had not said very much about all that had happened. Harsh words, in a sense, are all alike. You can make them up yourself and be right. I think we both believed that we were in a fog we couldn't see through yet, though in a while, maybe not even a long while, we would see lights and know something.

In my third-period class that day a messenger brought a note for me that said I was excused from school at noon, and I should meet my mother at a motel down 10th Avenue South—a place not so far from my school—and we would eat lunch together.

It was a gray day in Great Falls that day. The leaves were off the trees and the mountains to the east of town were obscured by a low sky. The night before had been cold and clear, but today it seemed as if it would rain. It was the beginning of winter in earnest. In a few days there would be snow everywhere.

The motel where my mother was staying was called the Tropicana, and was beside the city golf course. There was a neon parrot on the sign out front, and the cabins made a U shape behind a little white office building. Only a couple of cars were parked in front of cabins, and no car was in front of my mother's cabin. I wondered if Woody would be here, or if he was at the air base. I wondered if my father would see him there, and what they would say.

I walked back to cabin 9. The door was open, though a DO NOT DISTURB sign was hung on the knob outside. I looked through the screen and saw my mother sitting on the bed alone. The television was on, but she was looking at me. She was wearing the powder-blue dress she had had on the night before. She was smiling at me, and I liked the way she looked at that moment, through the screen, in shadows. Her features did not seem as sharp as they had before. She looked comfortable where she was, and I felt like we were going to get along, no matter what had happened, and that I wasn't mad at her—that I had never been mad at her.

She sat forward and turned the television off. "Come in, Jackie," she said, and I opened the screen door and came inside. "It's the height of grandeur in here, isn't it?" My mother looked around the room. Her suitcase was open on the floor by the bathroom door, which I could see through and out the window onto the golf course, where three men were playing under the milky sky. "Privacy can be a burden, sometimes," she said, and reached down and put on her high-heeled shoes. "I didn't sleep very well last night, did you?"

"No," I said, though I had slept all night. I wanted to ask her where Woody was, but it occurred to me at that moment that he was gone now and wouldn't be back, that she wasn't thinking in terms of him and didn't care where he was or ever would be.

"I'd like a nice compliment from you," she said. "Do you have one of those to spend?"

"Yes," I said. "I'm glad to see you."

"That's a nice one," she said and nodded. She had both her shoes on now. "Would you like to go have lunch? We can walk across the street to the cafeteria. You can get hot food."

"No," I said. "I'm not really hungry now."

"That's okay," she said and smiled at me again. And, as I said before, I liked the way she looked. She looked pretty in a way I didn't remember seeing her, as if something that had had a hold on her had let her go, and she could be different about things. Even about me.

"Sometimes, you know," she said, "I'll think about something I did. Just anything. Years ago in Idaho, or last week, even. And it's as if I'd read it. Like a story. Isn't that strange?"

"Yes," I said. And it did seem strange to me because I was certain then what the difference was between what had happened and what hadn't, and knew I always would be.

"Sometimes," she said, and she folded her hands in her lap and stared out the little side window of her cabin at the parking lot and the curving row of other cabins. "Sometimes I even have a moment when I completely forget what life's like. Just altogether." She smiled. "That's not so bad, finally. Maybe it's a disease I have. Do you think I'm just sick and I'll get well?"

"No. I don't know," I said. "Maybe. I hope so." I looked out the bathroom window and saw the three men walking down the golf course fairway carrying golf clubs.

"I'm not very good at sharing things right now," my mother said. "I'm sorry." She cleared her throat, and then she didn't say anything for almost a minute while I stood there. "I *will* answer anything you'd like me to answer, though. Just ask me anything, and I'll answer it the truth, whether I want to or not. Okay? I will. You don't even have to trust me. That's not a big issue with us. We're both grown-ups now."

And I said, "Were you ever married before?"

My mother looked at me strangely. Her eyes got small, and for a moment she looked the way I was used to seeing her—sharp-faced, her mouth set and taut. "No," she said. "Who told you that? That isn't true. I never was. Did Jack say that to you? Did your father say that? That's an awful thing to say. I haven't been that bad."

"He didn't say that," I said.

"Oh, of course he did," my mother said. "He doesn't know just to let things go when they're bad enough."

"I wanted to know that," I said. "I just thought about it. It doesn't matter."

"No, it doesn't," my mother said. "I could've been married eight times. I'm just sorry he said that to you. He's not generous sometimes."

"He didn't say that," I said. But I'd said it enough, and I didn't care if she believed me or didn't. It was true that trust was not a big issue between us then. And in any event, I know now that the whole truth of anything is an idea that stops existing finally.

"Is that all you want to know, then?" my mother said. She seemed mad, but not at me, I didn't think. Just at things in general. And I sympathized with her. "Your life's your own business, Jackie," she said. "Sometimes it scares you to death it's so much your own business. You just want to run."

"I guess so," I said.

"I'd like a less domestic life, is all." She looked at me, but I didn't say anything. I didn't see what she meant by that, though I knew there was nothing I could say to change the way her life would be from then on. And I kept quiet.

In a while we walked across 10th Avenue and ate lunch in the cafeteria. When she paid for the meal I saw that she had my father's silver-dollar money clip in her purse and that there was money in it. And I understood that he had been to see her already that day, and no one cared if I knew it. We were all of us on our own in this.

When we walked out onto the street, it was colder and the wind was blowing. Car exhausts were visible and some drivers had their lights on, though it was only two o'clock in the afternoon. My mother had called a taxi, and we stood and waited for it. I didn't know where she was going, but I wasn't going with her.

"Your father won't let me come back," she said, standing on the curb. It was just a fact to her, not that she hoped I would talk to him or stand up for her or take her part. But I did wish then that I had never let her go the night before. Things can be fixed by staying; but to go out into the night and not come back hazards life, and everything can get out of hand.

My mother's taxi came. She kissed me and hugged me very hard, then got inside the cab in her powder-blue dress and high heels and her car coat. I smelled her perfume on my cheeks as I stood watching her. "I used to be afraid of more things than I am now," she said, looking up at me, and smiled. "I've got a knot in my stomach, of all things." And she closed the cab door, waved at me, and rode away.

I walked back toward my school. I thought I could take the bus home if I got there by three. I walked a long way down 10th Avenue to Second Street, beside the Missouri River, then over to town. I walked by the Great Northern Hotel, where my father had sold ducks and geese and fish of all kinds. There were no passenger trains in the yard and the loading dock looked small. Garbage cans were lined along the edge of it, and the door was closed and locked.

As I walked toward school I thought to myself that my life had turned suddenly, and that I might not know exactly how or which way for possibly a long time. Maybe, in fact, I might never know. It was a thing that happened to you—I knew that—and it had happened to me in this way now. And as I walked on up the cold street that afternoon in Great Falls, the questions I asked myself were these: why wouldn't my father let my mother come back? Why would Woody stand in the cold with me outside my house and risk being killed? Why would he say my mother had been married before, if she hadn't been? And my mother herself—why would she do what she did? In five years my father had gone off to Ely, Nevada, to ride out the oil strike there, and been killed by accident. And in the years since then I have seen my mother from time to time—in one place or another, with one man or other—and I can say, at least, that we know each other. But I have never known the answer to these questions, have never asked anyone their answers. Though possibly it—the answer—is simple: it is just low-life, some coldness in us all, some helplessness that causes us to misunderstand life when it is pure and plain, makes our existence seem like a border between two nothings, and makes us no more or less than animals who meet on the road—watchful, unforgiving, without patience or desire.

# E. M. FORSTER

*Forster (1879–1970) was born in London. After completing his education at Cambridge, he traveled in Italy and Greece, forming impressions that were often to recur in the settings and themes of his fiction. In 1905 he began to publish a group of novels, which appeared in quick succession until 1910. These early novels are structured on conflicts between the stifling pettiness of conventional English life and the impulses of youth toward a larger and freer manner of living. After his first burst of productivity Forster published no more novels until 1924, when* A Passage to India *appeared, and thereafter produced no more major fiction. (A novel,* Maurice, *which had evidently been withheld by its author because of its homosexual subject matter, was published posthumously in 1971.) During the latter decades of his life Forster remained quietly at home in Cambridge, reading happily at his own pace; refraining from literary or political controversies; and occasionally publishing criticism and essays, which reflect his skeptical, good-natured humanism. The rich common sense of* Aspects of the Novel *(1927) makes it an invaluable primer for the critic of fiction.* Abinger-Harvest *(1927) and* Two Cheers for Democracy *(1951) range widely over the culture of our times. Forster's novels include* The Longest Journey *(1907),* A Room with a View *(1908), and* Howards End *(1910). His short stories can be found in* The Collected Tales of E. M. Forster *(1947) and* The Life to Come and Other Stories *(1972).*

## The Road from Colonus[1]

### I

For no very intelligible reason, Mr. Lucas had hurried ahead of his party. He was perhaps reaching the age at which independence becomes valuable, because it is so soon to be lost. Tired of attention and consideration, he liked breaking away from the younger members, to ride by himself, and to dismount unassisted. Perhaps he also relished that more subtle pleasure of being kept waiting for lunch, and of telling the others on their arrival that it was of no consequence.

So, with childish impatience, he battered the animal's sides with his heels, and made the muleteer bang it with a thick stick and prick it with a sharp one,

1. After blinding himself and fleeing Thebes when he learned he had killed his father and married his mother, Oedipus wandered with his daughters until he came to Colonus. There, in a sacred grove, he sat down and refused to leave. Presently, amid rumblings of the earth, the gods carried him off to his rest. See Sophocles' play *Oedipus at Colonus.*

and jolted down the hillsides through clumps of flowering shrubs and stretches of anemones and asphodel, till he heard the sound of running water, and came in sight of the group of plane trees where they were to have their meal.

Even in England those trees would have been remarkable, so huge were they, so interlaced, so magnificently clothed in quivering green. And here in Greece they were unique, the one cool spot in that hard brilliant landscape, already scorched by the heat of an April sun. In their midst was hidden a tiny Khan or country inn, a frail mud building with a broad wooden balcony in which sat an old woman spinning, while a small brown pig, eating orange peel, stood beside her. On the wet earth below squatted two children, playing some primeval game with their fingers; and their mother, none too clean either, was messing with some rice inside. As Mrs. Forman would have said, it was all very Greek, and the fastidious Mr. Lucas felt thankful that they were bringing their own food with them, and should eat it in the open air.

Still, he was glad to be there—the muleteer had helped him off—and glad that Mrs. Forman was not there to forestall his opinions—glad even that he should not see Ethel for quite half an hour. Ethel was his youngest daughter, still unmarried. She was unselfish and affectionate, and it was generally understood that she was to devote her life to her father, and be the comfort of his old age. Mrs. Forman always referred to her as Antigone,[2] and Mr. Lucas tried to settle down to the role of Oedipus, which seemed the only one that public opinion allowed him.

He had this in common with Oedipus, that he was growing old. Even to himself it had become obvious. He had lost interest in other people's affairs, and seldom attended when they spoke to him. He was fond of talking himself but often forgot what he was going to say, and even when he succeeded, it seldom seemed worth the effort. His phrases and gestures had become stiff and set, his anecdotes, once so successful, fell flat, his silence was as meaningless as his speech. Yet he had led a healthy, active life, had worked steadily, made money, educated his children. There was nothing and no one to blame: he was simply growing old.

At the present moment, here he was in Greece, and one of the dreams of his life was realized. Forty years ago he had caught the fever of Hellenism,[3] and all his life he had felt that could he but visit that land, he would not have lived in vain. But Athens had been dusty, Delphi wet, Thermopylae[4] flat, and he had listened with amazement and cynicism to the rapturous exclamations of his companions. Greece was like England: it was a man who was growing old, and it made no difference whether that man looked at the Thames or the Eurotas.[5] It was his last hope of contradicting that logic of experience, and it was failing.

Yet Greece had done something for him, though he did not know it. It had made him discontented, and there are stirrings of life in discontent. He knew that he was not the victim of continual ill-luck. Something great was wrong, and he was pitted against no mediocre or accidental enemy. For the last month a strange desire had possessed him to die fighting.

2. Daughter of Oedipus. 3. Spirit and culture of Greece. 4. Pass in eastern Greece where Persians defeated Spartans in 480 B.C. "Delphi": ancient Greek city famous for its oracle. 5. Rivers in England and Greece.

"Greece is the land for young people," he said to himself as he stood under the plane trees, "but I will enter into it, I will possess it. Leaves shall be green again, water shall be sweet, the sky shall be blue. They were so forty years ago, and I will win them back. I do mind being old, and I will pretend no longer."

He took two steps forward, and immediately cold waters were gurgling over his ankle.

"Where does the water come from?" he asked himself. "I do not even know that." He remembered that all the hillsides were dry; yet here the road was suddenly covered with flowing streams.

He stopped still in amazement, saying: "Water out of a tree—out of a hollow tree? I never saw nor thought of that before."

For the enormous plane that leant towards the Khan was hollow—it had been burnt out for charcoal—and from its living trunk there gushed an impetuous spring, coating the bark with fern and moss, and flowing over the mule track to create fertile meadows beyond. The simple country folk had paid to beauty and mystery such tribute as they could, for in the rind of the tree a shrine was cut, holding a lamp and a little picture of the Virgin, inheritor of the Naiad's and Dryad's[6] joint abode.

"I never saw anything so marvellous before," said Mr. Lucas. "I could even step inside the trunk and see where the water comes from."

For a moment he hesitated to violate the shrine. Then he remembered with a smile his own thought—"the place shall be mine; I will enter it and possess it"—and leapt almost aggressively onto a stone within.

The water pressed up steadily and noiselessly from the hollow roots and hidden crevices of the plane, forming a wonderful amber pool ere it spilt over the lip of bark on to the earth outside. Mr. Lucas tasted it and it was sweet, and when he looked up the black funnel of the trunk he saw sky which was blue, and some leaves which were green; and he remembered, without smiling, another of his thoughts.

Others had been before him—indeed he had a curious sense of companionship. Little votive offerings to the presiding Power were fastened on to the bark—tiny arms and legs and eyes in tin, grotesque models of the brain or the heart—all tokens of some recovery of strength or wisdom or love. There was no such thing as the solitude of nature, for the sorrows and joys of humanity had pressed even into the bosom of a tree. He spread out his arms and steadied himself against the soft charred wood, and then slowly leant back, till his body was resting on the trunk behind. His eyes closed, and he had the strange feeling of one who is moving, yet at peace—the feeling of the swimmer, who, after long struggling with chopping seas, finds that after all the tide will sweep him to his goal.

So he lay motionless, conscious only of the stream below his feet, and that all things were a stream, in which he was moving.

He was aroused at last by a shock—the shock of an arrival perhaps, for when he opened his eyes, something unimagined, indefinable, had passed over all things, and made them intelligible and good.

6. Wood nymph. "Naiad": a water nymph.

There was meaning in the stoop of the old woman over her work, and in the quick motions of the little pig, and in her diminishing globe of wool. A young man came singing over the streams on a mule, and there was beauty in his pose and sincerity in his greeting. The sun made no accidental patterns upon the spreading roots of the trees, and there was intention in the nodding clumps of asphodel, and in the music of the water. To Mr. Lucas, who, in a brief space of time, had discovered not only Greece, but England and all the world and life, there seemed nothing ludicrous in the desire to hang within the tree another votive offering—a little model of an entire man.

"Why, here's papa, playing at being Merlin."[7]

All unnoticed they had arrived—Ethel, Mrs. Forman, Mr. Graham, and the English-speaking dragoman.[8] Mr. Lucas peered out at them suspiciously. They had suddenly become unfamiliar, and all that they did seemed strained and coarse.

"Allow me to give you a hand," said Mr. Graham, a young man who was always polite to his elders.

Mr. Lucas felt annoyed. "Thank you, I can manage perfectly well by myself," he replied. His foot slipped as he stepped out of the tree, and went into the spring.

"Oh papa, my papa!" said Ethel, "what are you doing? Thank goodness I have got a change for you on the mule."

She tended him carefully, giving him clean socks and dry boots, and then sat him down on the rug beside the lunch basket, while she went with the others to explore the grove.

They came back in ecstasies, in which Mr. Lucas tried to join. But he found them intolerable. Their enthusiasm was superficial, commonplace, and spasmodic. They had no perception of the coherent beauty that was flowering around them. He tried at least to explain his feelings, and what he said was:

"I am altogether pleased with the appearance of this place. It impresses me very favourably. The trees are fine, remarkably fine for Greece, and there is something very poetic in the spring of clear running water. The people too seem kindly and civil. It is decidedly an attractive place."

Mrs. Forman upbraided him for his tepid praise.

"Oh, it is a place in a thousand!" she cried, "I could live and die here! I really would stop if I had not to be back at Athens! It reminds me of the Colonus of Sophocles."

"Well, *I* must stop," said Ethel. "I positively must."

"Yes, do! You and your father! Antigone and Oedipus. Of course you must stop at Colonus!"

Mr. Lucas was almost breathless with excitement. When he stood within the tree, he had believed that his happiness would be independent of locality. But these few minutes' conversation had undeceived him. He no longer trusted himself to journey through the world, for old thoughts, old wearinesses might be waiting to rejoin him as soon as he left the shade of the planes, and the music of the virgin water. To sleep in the Khan with the gracious, kind-eyed

7. Legendary English magician associated with King Arthur's court. 8. Interpreter.

country people, to watch the bats flit about within the globe of shade, and see the moon turn the golden patterns into silver—one such night would place him beyond relapse, and confirm him forever in the kingdom he had regained. But all his lips could say was: "I should be willing to put in a night here."

"You mean a week, papa! It would be sacrilege to put in less."

"A week then, a week," said his lips, irritated at being corrected, while his heart was leaping with joy. All through lunch he spoke to them no more, but watched the place he should know so well, and the people who would so soon be his companions and friends. The inmates of the Khan only consisted of an old woman, a middle-aged woman, a young man and two children, and to none of them had he spoken, yet he loved them as he loved everything that moved or breathed or existed beneath the benedictory shade of the planes.

"En route!"[9] said the shrill voice of Mrs. Forman. "Ethel! Mr. Graham! The best of things must end."

"Tonight," thought Mr. Lucas, "they will light the little lamp by the shrine. And when we all sit together on the balcony, perhaps they will tell me which offerings they put up."

"I beg your pardon, Mr. Lucas," said Graham, "but they want to fold up the rug you are sitting on."

Mr. Lucas got up, saying to himself: "Ethel shall go to bed first, and then I will try to tell them about my offering too—for it is a thing I must do. I think they will understand if I am left with them alone."

Ethel touched him on the cheek. "Papa! I've called you three times. All the mules are here."

"Mules? What mules?"

"Our mules. We're all waiting. Oh, Mr. Graham, do help my father on."

"I don't know what you're talking about, Ethel."

"My dearest papa, we must start. You know we have to get to Olympia tonight."

Mr. Lucas in pompous, confident tones replied: "I always did wish, Ethel, that you had a better head for plans. You know perfectly well that we are putting in a week here. It is your own suggestion."

Ethel was startled into impoliteness. "What a perfectly ridiculous idea. You must have known I was joking. Of course I meant I wished we could."

"Ah! if we could only do what we wished!" sighed Mrs. Forman, already seated on her mule.

"Surely," Ethel continued in calmer tones, "you didn't think I meant it."

"Most certainly I did. I have made all my plans on the supposition that we are stopping here, and it will be extremely inconvenient, indeed, impossible for me to start."

He delivered this remark with an air of great conviction, and Mrs. Forman and Mr. Graham had to turn away to hide their smiles.

"I am sorry I spoke so carelessly; it was wrong of me. But, you know, we can't break up our party, and even one night here would make us miss the boat at Patras."

9. On our way! (French).

Mrs. Forman, in an aside, called Mr. Graham's attention to the excellent way in which Ethel managed her father.

"I don't mind about the Patras boat. You said that we should stop here, and we are stopping."

It seemed as if the inhabitants of the Khan had divined in some mysterious way that the altercation touched them. The old woman stopped her spinning, while the young man and the two children stood behind Mr. Lucas, as if supporting him.

Neither arguments nor entreaties moved him. He said little, but he was absolutely determined, because for the first time he saw his daily life aright. What need had he to return to England? Who would miss him? His friends were dead or cold. Ethel loved him in a way, but, as was right, she had other interests. His other children he seldom saw. He had only one other relative, his sister Julia, whom he both feared and hated. It was no effort to struggle. He would be a fool as well as a coward if he stirred from the place which brought him happiness and peace.

At last Ethel, to humour him, and not disinclined to air her modern Greek, went into the Khan with the astonished dragoman to look at the rooms. The woman inside received them with loud welcomes, and the young man, when no one was looking, began to lead Mr. Lucas' mule to the stable.

"Drop it, you brigand!" shouted Graham, who always declared that foreigners could understand English if they chose. He was right, for the man obeyed, and they all stood waiting for Ethel's return.

She emerged at last, with close-gathered skirts, followed by the dragoman bearing the little pig, which he had bought at a bargain.

"My dear papa, I will do all I can for you, but stop in that Khan—no."

"Are there—fleas?" asked Mrs. Forman.

Ethel intimated that "fleas" was not the word.

"Well, I am afraid that settles it," said Mrs. Forman, "I know how particular Mr. Lucas is."

"It does not settle it," said Mr. Lucas. "Ethel, you go on. I do not want you. I don't know why I ever consulted you. I shall stop here alone."

"That is absolute nonsense," said Ethel, losing her temper. "How can you be left alone at your age? How would you get your meals or your bath? All your letters are waiting for you at Patras. You'll miss the boat. That means missing the London operas, and upsetting all your engagements for the month. And as if you could travel by yourself!"

"They might knife you," was Mr. Graham's contribution.

The Greeks said nothing; but whenever Mr. Lucas looked their way, they beckoned him towards the Khan. The children would even have drawn him by the coat, and the old woman on the balcony stopped her almost completed spinning, and fixed him with mysterious appealing eyes. As he fought, the issue assumed gigantic proportions, and he believed that he was not merely stopping because he had regained youth or seen beauty or found happiness, but because in that place and with those people a supreme event was awaiting him which would transfigure the face of the world. The moment was so tremendous that he abandoned words and arguments as useless, and rested on the strength of his mighty unrevealed allies: silent men, murmuring water, and whispering trees. For the whole place called with one voice, articulate to him, and his garrulous opponents became every minute more meaningless and absurd. Soon they would be tired and go chattering away into the sun, leaving him to the cool grove and the moonlight and the destiny he foresaw.

Mrs. Forman and the dragoman had indeed already started, amid the piercing screams of the little pig, and the struggle might have gone on indefinitely if Ethel had not called in Mr. Graham.

"Can you help me?" she whispered. "He is absolutely unmanageable."

"I'm no good at arguing—but if I could help you in any other way—" and he looked down complacently at his well-made figure.

Ethel hesitated. Then she said: "Help me in any way you can. After all, it is for his good that we do it."

"Then have his mule led up behind him."

So when Mr. Lucas thought he had gained the day, he suddenly felt himself lifted off the ground, and set sideways on the saddle, and at the same time the mule started off at a trot. He said nothing, for he had nothing to say, and even his face showed little emotion as he felt the shade pass and heard the sound of the water cease. Mr. Graham was running at his side, hat in hand, apologizing.

"I know I had no business to do it, and I do beg your pardon awfully. But I do hope that some day you too will feel that I was—damn!"

A stone had caught him in the middle of the back. It was thrown by the little boy, who was pursuing them along the mule track. He was followed by his sister, also throwing stones.

Ethel screamed to the dragoman, who was some way ahead with Mrs. Forman, but before he could rejoin them, another adversary appeared. It was the young Greek, who had cut them off in front, and now dashed down at Mr. Lucas' bridle. Fortunately Graham was an expert boxer, and it did not take him a moment to beat down the youth's feeble defense, and to send him sprawling with a bleeding mouth into the asphodel. By this time the dragoman had arrived, the children, alarmed at the fate of their brother, had desisted, and the rescue party, if such it is to be considered, retired in disorder to the trees.

"Little devils!" said Graham, laughing with triumph. "That's the modern Greek all over. Your father meant money if he stopped, and they consider we were taking it out of their pocket."

"Oh, they are terrible—simple savages! I don't know how I shall ever thank you. You've saved my father."

"I only hope you didn't think me brutal."

"No," replied Ethel with a little sigh. "I admire strength."

Meanwhile the cavalcade reformed, and Mr. Lucas, who, as Mrs. Forman said, bore his disappointment wonderfully well, was put comfortably on to his mule. They hurried up the opposite hillside, fearful of another attack, and it was not until they had left the eventful place far behind that Ethel found an opportunity to speak to her father and ask his pardon for the way she had treated him.

"You seemed so different, dear father, and you quite frightened me. Now I feel that you are your old self again."

He did not answer, and she concluded that he was not unnaturally offended at her behaviour.

By one of those curious tricks of mountain scenery, the place they had left an hour before suddenly reappeared far below them. The Khan was hidden under the green dome, but in the open there still stood three figures, and through the pure air rose up a faint cry of defiance or farewell.

Mr. Lucas stopped irresolutely, and let the reins fall from his hand.

"Come, father dear," said Ethel gently.

He obeyed, and in another moment a spur of the hill hid the dangerous scene forever.

## II

It was breakfast time, but the gas was alight, owing to the fog. Mr. Lucas was in the middle of an account of a bad night he had spent. Ethel, who was to be married in a few weeks, had her arms on the table, listening.

"First the door bell rang, then you came back from the theater. Then the dog started, and after the dog the cat. And at three in the morning a young hooligan passed by singing. Oh yes: then there was the water gurgling in the pipe above my head."

"I think that was only the bath water running away," said Ethel, looking rather worn.

"Well, there's nothing I dislike more than running water. It's perfectly impossible to sleep in the house. I shall give it up. I shall give notice next quarter. I shall tell the landlord plainly, 'The reason I am giving up the house is this: it is perfectly impossible to sleep in it.' If he says—says—well, what has he got to say?"

"Some more toast, father?"

"Thank you, my dear." He took it, and there was an interval of peace.

But he soon recommenced. "I'm not going to submit to the practicing next door as tamely as they think. I wrote and told them so—didn't I?"

"Yes," said Ethel, who had taken care that the letter should not reach. "I have seen the governess, and she has promised to arrange it differently. And Aunt Julia hates noise. It will be sure to be all right."

Her aunt, being the only unattached member of the family, was coming to keep house for her father when she left him. The reference was not a happy one, and Mr. Lucas commenced a series of half articulate sighs, which was only stopped by the arrival of the post.

"Oh, what a parcel!" cried Ethel. "For me! What can it be! Greek stamps. This is most exciting!"

It proved to be some asphodel bulbs, sent by Mrs. Forman from Athens for planting in the conservatory.

"Doesn't it bring it all back! You remember the asphodels, father. And all wrapped up in Greek newspapers. I wonder if I can read them still. I used to be able to, you know."

She rattled on, hoping to conceal the laughter of the children next door—a favorite source of querulousness at breakfast time.

"Listen to me! 'A rural disaster.' Oh, I've hit on something sad. But never mind. 'Last Tuesday at Plataniste, in the province of Messenia, a shocking tragedy occurred. A large tree'—aren't I getting on well?—'blew down in the night and'—wait a minute—oh, dear! 'crushed to death the five occupants of the little Khan there, who had apparently been sitting in the balcony. The bodies of Maria Rhomaides, the aged proprietress, and of her daughter, aged forty-six, were easily recognizable, whereas that of her grandson'—oh, the rest is really too horrid; I wish I had never tried it, and what's more I feel to have heard the name Plataniste before. We didn't stop there, did we, in the spring?"

"We had lunch," said Mr. Lucas, with a faint expression of trouble on his vacant face. "Perhaps it was where the dragoman bought the pig."

"Of course," said Ethel in a nervous voice. "Where the dragoman bought the little pig. How terrible!"

"Very terrible!" said her father, whose attention was wandering to the noisy children next door. Ethel suddenly started to her feet with genuine interest.

"Good gracious!" she exclaimed. "This is an old paper. It happened not lately but in April—the night of Tuesday the eighteenth—and we—we must have been there in the afternoon."

"So we were," said Mr. Lucas. She put her hand to her heart, scarcely able to speak.

"Father, dear father, I must say it: you wanted to stop there. All those people, those poor half savage people, tried to keep you, they're dead. The whole place, it says, is in ruins, and even the stream has changed its course. Father, dear, if it had not been for me, and if Arthur had not helped me, you must have been killed."

Mr. Lucas waved his hand irritably. "It is not a bit of good speaking to the governess, I shall write to the landlord and say, 'The reason I am giving up the house is this: the dog barks, the children next door are intolerable, and I cannot stand the noise of running water.' "

Ethel did not check his babbling. She was aghast at the narrowness of the escape, and for a long time kept silence. At last she said: "Such a marvelous deliverance does make one believe in Providence."

Mr. Lucas, who was still composing his letter to the landlord, did not reply.

# Mary E. Wilkins Freeman

*Freeman (1852–1930) was born in Randolph, Massachusetts. As a child she was too frail to lead a normal life, and her schooling was irregular. When her immediate family died, she began to write in the hope of supporting herself and an aunt, publishing children's stories first, before she found a more lucrative market with fiction for adults. For a time she was secretary to Oliver Wendell Holmes, Sr., the celebrated writer, and it was through this position that she made the acquaintance of established writers of her time. She left New England in 1902 when she married a doctor from New Jersey, but the majority of her two hundred and thirty stories and twelve novels dealt with characters in New England villages and the remnants of the Puritan culture. Among her novels are* Jane Field *(1893),* Pembroke *(1894),* The Portion of Labor *(1901), and* The Shoulders of Atlas *(1908). Her books of short stories include* A New England Nun and Other Stories *(1891),* Young Lucretia *(1892), and* The Green Door *(1910).*

## A New England Nun

It was late in the afternoon, and the light was waning. There was a difference in the look of the tree shadows out in the yard. Somewhere in the distance cows were lowing and a little bell was tinkling; now and then a farm-wagon tilted by, and the dust flew; some blue-shirted laborers with shovels over their shoulders plodded past; little swarms of flies were dancing up and down before the people's faces in the soft air. There seemed to be a gentle stir arising over everything for the mere sake of subsidence—a very premonition of rest and hush and night.

This soft diurnal commotion was over Louisa Ellis also. She had been peacefully sewing at her sitting-room window all the afternoon. Now she quilted her needle carefully into her work, which she folded precisely, and laid in a basket with her thimble and thread and scissors. Louisa Ellis could not remember that ever in her life she had mislaid one of these little feminine appurtenances, which had become, from long use and constant association, a very part of her personality.

Louisa tied a green apron round her waist, and got out a flat straw hat with a green ribbon. Then she went into the garden with a little blue crockery bowl, to pick some currants for her tea. After the currants were picked she sat on the back door-step and stemmed them, collecting the stems carefully in her apron, and afterwards throwing them into the hen-coop. She looked sharply at the grass beside the step to see if any had fallen there.

Louisa was slow and still in her movements; it took her a long time to prepare her tea; but when ready it was set forth with as much grace as if she had been a veritable guest to her own self. The little square table stood exactly in the centre of the kitchen, and was covered with a starched linen cloth whose border pattern of flowers glistened. Louisa had a damask napkin on her tea-tray, where were arranged a cut-glass tumbler full of teaspoons, a silver cream-pitcher, a china sugar-bowl, and one pink china cup and saucer. Louisa used china every day—something which none of her neighbors did. They whispered about it among themselves. Their daily tables were laid with common crockery, their sets of best china stayed in the parlor closet, and Louisa Ellis was no richer nor better bred than they. Still she would use the china. She had for her supper a glass dish full of sugared currants, a plate of little cakes, and one of light white biscuits. Also a leaf or two of lettuce, which she cut up daintily. Louisa was very fond of lettuce, which she raised to perfection in her little garden. She ate quite heartily, though in a delicate, pecking way; it seemed almost surprising that any considerable bulk of the food should vanish.

After tea she filled a plate with nicely baked thin corn-cakes, and carried them out into the back-yard.

"Caesar!" she called. "Caesar! Caesar!"

There was a little rush, and the clank of a chain, and a large yellow-and-white dog appeared at the door of his tiny hut, which was half hidden among the tall grasses and flowers. Louisa patted him and gave him the corn-cakes. Then she returned to the house and washed the tea-things, polishing the china carefully. The twilight had deepened; the chorus of the frogs floated in at the open window wonderfully loud and shrill, and once in a while a long sharp drone from a tree-toad pierced it. Louisa took off her green gingham apron, disclosing a shorter one of pink and white print. She lighted her lamp, and sat down again with her sewing.

In about half an hour Joe Dagget came. She heard his heavy step on the walk, and rose and took off her pink-and-white apron. Under that was still another—white linen with a little cambric edging on the bottom; that was Louisa's company apron. She never wore it without her calico sewing apron over it unless she had a guest. She had barely folded the pink and white one with methodical haste and laid it in a table-drawer when the door opened and Joe Dagget entered.

He seemed to fill up the whole room. A little yellow canary that had been asleep in his green cage at the south window woke up and fluttered wildly, beating his little yellow wings against the wires. He always did so when Joe Dagget came into the room.

"Good-evening," said Louisa. She extended her hand with a kind of solemn cordiality.

"Good-evening, Louisa," returned the man, in a loud voice.

She placed a chair for him, and they sat facing each other, with the table between them. He sat bolt-upright, toeing out his heavy feet squarely, glancing with a good-humored uneasiness around the room. She sat gently erect, folding her slender hands in her white-linen lap.

"Been a pleasant day," remarked Dagget.

"Real pleasant," Louisa assented, softly. "Have you been haying?" she asked, after a little while.

"Yes, I've been haying all day, down in the ten-acre lot. Pretty hot work."

"It must be."

"Yes, it's pretty hot work in the sun."

"Is your mother well to-day?"

"Yes, mother's pretty well."

"I suppose Lily Dyer's with her now?"

Dagget colored. "Yes, she's with her," he answered, slowly.

He was not very young, but there was a boyish look about his large face. Louisa was not quite as old as he, her face was fairer and smoother, but she gave people the impression of being older.

"I suppose she's a good deal of help to your mother," she said, further.

"I guess she is; I don't know how mother'd get along without her," said Dagget, with a sort of embarrassed warmth.

"She looks like a real capable girl. She's pretty-looking too," remarked Louisa.

"Yes, she is pretty fair looking."

Presently Dagget began fingering the books on the table. There was a square red autograph album, and a Young Lady's Gift-Book which had belonged to Louisa's mother. He took them up one after the other and opened them; then laid them down again, the album on the Gift-Book.

Louisa kept eying them with mild uneasiness. Finally she rose and changed the position of the books, putting the album underneath. That was the way they had been arranged in the first place.

Dagget gave an awkward little laugh. "Now what difference did it make which book was on top?" said he.

Louisa looked at him with a deprecating smile. "I always keep them that way," murmured she.

"You do beat everything," said Dagget, trying to laugh again. His large face was flushed.

He remained about an hour longer, then rose to take leave. Going out, he stumbled over a rug, and trying to recover himself, hit Louisa's work-basket on the table, and knocked it on the floor.

He looked at Louisa, then at the rolling spools; he ducked himself awkwardly toward them, but she stopped him. "Never mind," said she; "I'll pick them up after you're gone."

She spoke with a mild stiffness. Either she was a little disturbed, or his nervousness affected her, and made her seem constrained in her effort to reassure him.

When Joe Dagget was outside he drew in the sweet evening air with a sigh, and felt much as an innocent and perfectly well-intentioned bear might after his exit from a china shop.

Louisa, on her part, felt much as the kind-hearted, long-suffering owner of the china shop might have done after the exit of the bear.

She tied on the pink, then the green apron, picked up all the scattered treasures and replaced them in her work-basket, and straightened the rug. Then she set the lamp on the floor, and began sharply examining the carpet. She even rubbed her fingers over it, and looked at them.

"He's tracked in a good deal of dust," she murmured. "I thought he must have."

Louisa got a dust-pan and brush, and swept Joe Dagget's track carefully.

If he could have known it, it would have increased his perplexity and uneasiness, although it would not have disturbed his loyalty in the least. He came twice a week to see Louisa Ellis, and every time, sitting there in her delicately sweet room, he felt as if surrounded by a hedge of lace. He was afraid to stir lest he should put a clumsy foot or hand through the fairy web, and he had always the consciousness that Louisa was watching fearfully lest he should.

Still the lace and Louisa commanded perforce his perfect respect and patience and loyalty. They were to be married in a month, after a singular courtship which had lasted for a matter of fifteen years. For fourteen out of the fifteen years the two had not once seen each other, and they had seldom exchanged letters. Joe had been all those years in Australia, where he had gone to make his fortune, and where he had stayed until he made it. He would have stayed fifty years if it had taken so long, and come home feeble and tottering, or never come home at all, to marry Louisa.

But the fortune had been made in the fourteen years, and he had come home now to marry the woman who had been patiently and unquestioningly waiting for him all that time.

Shortly after they were engaged he had announced to Louisa his determination to strike out into new fields, and secure a competency before they should be married. She had listened and assented with the sweet serenity which never failed her, not even when her lover set forth on that long and uncertain journey. Joe, buoyed up as he was by his sturdy determination, broke down a little at the last, but Louisa kissed him with a mild blush, and said good-by.

"It won't be for long," poor Joe had said, huskily; but it was for fourteen years.

In that length of time much had happened. Louisa's mother and brother had died, and she was all alone in the world. But greatest happening of all—a subtle happening which both were too simple to understand—Louisa's feet had turned into a path, smooth maybe under a calm, serene sky, but so straight and unswerving that it could only meet a check at her grave, and so narrow that there was no room for any one at her side.

Louisa's first emotion when Joe Dagget came home (he had not apprised her of his coming) was consternation, although she would not admit it to herself, and he never dreamed of it. Fifteen years ago she had been in love with him—at least she considered herself to be. Just at that time, gently acquiescing with and falling into the natural drift of girlhood, she had seen marriage ahead as a reasonable feature and a probable desirability of life. She had listened with calm docility to her mother's views upon the subject. Her mother was remarkable for her cool sense and sweet, even temperament. She talked wisely to her daughter when Joe Dagget presented himself, and Louisa accepted him with no hesitation. He was the first lover she had ever had.

She had been faithful to him all these years. She had never dreamed of the possibility of marrying any one else. Her life, especially for the last seven years, had been full of a pleasant peace, she had never felt discontented nor impatient over her lover's absence; still she had always looked forward to his return and their marriage as the inevitable conclusion of things. However, she had fallen into a way of placing it so far in the future that it was almost equal to placing it over the boundaries of another life.

When Joe came she had been expecting him, and expecting to be married for fourteen years, but she was as much surprised and taken aback as if she had never thought of it.

Joe's consternation came later. He eyed Louisa with an instant confirmation of his old admiration. She had changed but little. She still kept her pretty manner and soft grace, and was, he considered, every whit as attractive as ever. As for himself, his stent was done; he had turned his face away from fortune-seeking, and the old winds of romance whistled as loud and sweet as ever through his ears. All the song which he had been wont to hear in them was Louisa; he had for a long time a loyal belief that he heard it still, but finally it seemed to him that although the winds sang always that one song, it had another name. But for Louisa the wind had never more than murmured; now it had gone down, and everything was still. She listened for a little while with half-wistful attention; then she turned quietly away and went to work on her wedding clothes.

Joe had made some extensive and quite magnificent alterations in his house. It was the old homestead; the newly-married couple would live there, for Joe could not desert his mother, who refused to leave her old home. So Louisa must leave hers. Every morning, rising and going about among her neat maidenly possessions, she felt as one looking her last upon the faces of dear friends. It was true that in a measure she could take them with her, but, robbed of their old environments, they would appear in such new guises that they would almost cease to be themselves. Then there were some peculiar features of her happy solitary life which she would probably be obliged to relinquish altogether. Sterner tasks than these graceful but half-needless ones would probably devolve upon her. There would be a large house to care for; there would be company to entertain; there would be Joe's rigorous and feeble old mother to wait upon; and it would be contrary to all thrifty village traditions for her to keep more than one servant. Louisa had a little still, and she used to occupy herself pleasantly in summer weather with distilling the sweet and aromatic essences from roses and peppermint and spearmint. By-and-by her still must be laid away. Her store of essences was already considerable, and there would be no time for her to distil for the mere pleasure of it. Then Joe's mother would think it foolishness; she had already hinted her opinion in the matter. Louisa dearly loved to sew a linen seam, not always for use, but for the simple, mild pleasure which she took in it. She would have been loath to confess how more than once she had ripped a seam for the mere delight of sewing it together again. Sitting at her window during long sweet afternoons, drawing her needle gently through the dainty fabric, she was peace itself. But there was small chance of such foolish comfort in the future. Joe's mother, domineering, shrewd old matron that she was even in her old age, and very likely even Joe himself, with his honest masculine rudeness, would laugh and frown down all these pretty but senseless old maiden ways.

Louisa had almost the enthusiasm of an artist over the mere order and cleanliness of her solitary home. She had throbs of genuine triumph at the sight of the window-panes which she had polished until they shone like jewels. She gloated gently over her orderly bureau-drawers, with their exquisitely folded contents redolent with lavender and sweet clover and very purity. Could she be sure of the endurance of even this? She had visions, so startling that she half repudiated them as indelicate, of coarse masculine belongings strewn about in endless litter; of dust and disorder arising necessarily from a coarse masculine presence in the midst of all this delicate harmony.

Among her forebodings of disturbance, not the least was with regard to Caesar. Caesar was a veritable hermit of a dog. For the greater part of his life he had dwelt in his secluded hut, shut out from the society of his kind and all innocent canine joys. Never had Caesar since his early youth watched at a woodchuck's hole; never had he known the delights of a stray bone at a neighbor's kitchen door. And it was all on account of a sin committed when hardly out of his puppyhood. No one knew the possible depth of remorse of which this mild-visaged, altogether innocent-looking old dog might be capable; but whether or not he had encountered remorse, he had encountered a full measure of righteous retribution. Old Caesar seldom lifted up his voice in a growl or a bark; he was fat and sleepy; there were yellow rings which looked like spectacles around his dim old eyes; but there was a neighbor who bore on his hand the imprint of several of Caesar's sharp white youthful teeth, and for that he had lived at the end of a chain, all alone in a little hut, for fourteen years. The neighbor, who was choleric and smarting with the pain of his wound, had demanded either Caesar's death or complete ostracism. So Louisa's brother, to whom the dog had belonged, had built him his little kennel and tied him up. It was now fourteen years since, in a flood of youthful spirits, he had inflicted that memorable bite, and with the exception of short excursions, always at the end of the chain, under the strict guardianship of his master or Louisa, the old dog had remained a close prisoner. It is doubtful if, with his limited ambition, he took much pride in the fact, but it is certain that he was possessed of considerable cheap fame. He was regarded by all the children in the village and by many adults as a very monster of ferocity. St. George's dragon could hardly have surpassed in evil repute Louisa Ellis's old yellow dog. Mothers charged their children with solemn emphasis not to go too near him, and the children listened and believed greedily, with a fascinated appetite for terror, and ran by Louisa's house stealthily, with many sidelong and backward glances at the terrible dog. If perchance he sounded a hoarse bark, there was a panic. Wayfarers chancing into Louisa's yard eyed him with respect, and inquired if the chain were stout. Caesar at large might have seemed a very ordinary dog, and excited no comment whatever; chained, his reputation overshadowed him, so that he lost his own proper outlines and looked darkly vague and enormous. Joe Dagget, however, with his good-humored sense and shrewdness, saw him as he was. He strode valiantly up to him and patted him on the head, in spite of Louisa's soft clamor of warning, and even attempted to set him loose. Louisa grew so alarmed that he desisted, but kept announcing his opinion in the matter quite forcibly at intervals. "There ain't a better-natured dog in town," he would say, "and it's downright cruel to keep him tied up there. Some day I'm going to take him out."

Louisa had very little hope that he would not, one of these days, when their interests and possessions should be more completely fused in one. She pictured to herself Caesar on the rampage through the quiet and unguarded village. She saw innocent children bleeding in his path. She was herself very fond of the old dog, because he had belonged to her dead brother, and he was always very gentle with her; still she had great faith in his ferocity. She always warned people not to go too near him. She fed him on ascetic fare of corn-mush and cakes, and never fired his dangerous temper with heating and sanguinary diet of flesh and bones. Louisa looked at the old dog munching his simple fare, and thought of her approaching marriage and trembled. Still no anticipation of disorder and confusion in lieu of sweet peace and harmony, no forebodings of Caesar on the rampage, no wild fluttering of her little yellow canary, were sufficient to turn her a hair's-breadth. Joe Dagget had been fond of her and working for her all these years. It was not for her, whatever came to pass, to prove untrue and break his heart. She put the exquisite little stitches into her wedding-garments, and the time went on until it was only a week before her wedding-day. It was a Tuesday evening, and the wedding was to be a week from Wednesday.

There was a full moon that night. About nine o'clock Louisa strolled down the road a little way. There were harvest-fields on either hand, bordered by low stone walls. Luxuriant clumps of bushes grew beside the wall, and trees—wild cherry and old apple-trees—at intervals. Presently Louisa sat down on the wall and looked about her with mildly sorrowful reflectiveness. Tall shrubs of blueberry and meadow-sweet, all woven together and tangled with blackberry vines and horsebriers, shut her in on either side. She had a little clear space between them. Opposite her, on the other side of the road, was a spreading tree; the moon shone between its boughs, and the leaves twinkled like silver. The road was bespread with a beautiful shifting dapple of silver and shadow; the air was full of a mysterious sweetness. "I wonder if it's wild grapes?" murmured Louisa. She sat there some time. She was just thinking of rising, when she heard footsteps and low voices, and remained quiet. It was a lonely place, and she felt a little timid. She thought she would keep still in the shadow and let the persons, whoever they might be, pass her.

But just before they reached her the voices ceased, and the footsteps. She understood that their owners had also found seats upon the stone wall. She was wondering if she could not steal away unobserved, when the voice broke the stillness. It was Joe Dagget's. She sat still and listened.

The voice was announced by a loud sigh, which was as familiar as itself. "Well," said Dagget, "you've made up your mind, then, I suppose?"

"Yes," returned another voice; "I'm going day after to-morrow."

"That's Lily Dyer," thought Louisa to herself. The voice embodied itself in her mind. She saw a girl tall and full-figured, with a firm, fair face, looking fairer and firmer in the moonlight, her strong yellow hair braided in a close knot. A girl full of a calm rustic strength and bloom, with a masterful way which might have beseemed a princess. Lily Dyer was a favorite with the village folk; she had just the qualities to arouse the admiration. She was good and handsome and smart. Louisa had often heard her praises sounded.

"Well," said Joe Dagget, "I ain't got a word to say."

"I don't know what you could say," returned Lily Dyer.

"Not a word to say," repeated Joe, drawing out the words heavily. Then there was silence. "I ain't sorry," he began at last, "that that happened yesterday—that we kind of let on how we felt to each other. I guess it's just as well we knew. Of course I can't do anything any different. I'm going right on an' get married next week. I ain't going back on a woman that's waited for me fourteen years, an' break her heart."

"If you should jilt her to-morrow, I wouldn't have you," spoke up the girl, with sudden vehemence.

"Well, I ain't going to give you the chance," said he; "but I don't believe you would, either."

"You'd see I wouldn't. Honor's honor, an' right's right. An' I'd never think anything of any man that went against 'em for me or any other girl; you'd find that out, Joe Dagget."

"Well, you'll find out fast enough that I ain't going against 'em for you or any other girl," returned he. Their voices sounded almost as if they were angry with each other. Louisa was listening eagerly.

"I'm sorry you feel as if you must go away," said Joe, "but I don't know but it's best."

"Of course it's best. I hope you and I have got common-sense."

"Well, I suppose you're right." Suddenly Joe's voice got an undertone of tenderness. "Say, Lily," said he, "I'll get along well enough myself, but I can't bear to think—You don't suppose you're going to fret much over it?"

"I guess you'll find out I sha'n't fret much over a married man."

"Well, I hope you won't—I hope you won't, Lily. God knows I do. And—I hope—one of these days—you'll—come across somebody else—"

"I don't see any reason why I shouldn't." Suddenly her tone changed. She spoke in a sweet, clear voice, so loud that she could have been heard across the street. "No, Joe Dagget," said she, "I'll never marry any other man as long as I live. I've got good sense, an' I ain't going to break my heart nor make a fool of myself; but I'm never going to be married, you can be sure of that. I ain't that sort of a girl to feel this way twice."

Louisa heard an exclamation and a soft commotion behind the bushes; then Lily spoke again—the voice sounded as if she had risen. "This must be put a stop to," said she. "We've stayed here long enough. I'm going home."

Louisa sat there in a daze, listening to their retreating steps. After a while she got up and slunk softly home herself. The next day she did her housework methodically; that was as much a matter of course as breathing; but she did not sew on her wedding-clothes. She sat at her window and meditated. In the evening Joe came. Louisa Ellis had never known that she had any diplomacy in her, but when she came to look for it that night she found it, although meek of its kind, among her little feminine weapons. Even now she could hardly believe that she had heard aright, and that she would not do Joe a terrible injury should she break her troth-plight. She wanted to sound him without betraying too soon her own inclinations in the matter. She did it successfully, and they finally came to an understanding; but it was a difficult thing, for he was as afraid of betraying himself as she.

She never mentioned Lily Dyer. She simply said that while she had no cause of complaint against him, she had lived so long in one way that she shrank from making a change.

"Well, I never shrank, Louisa," said Dagget. "I'm going to be honest enough to say that I think maybe it's better this way; but if you'd wanted to keep on, I'd have stuck to you till my dying day. I hope you know that."

"Yes, I do," said she.

That night she and Joe parted more tenderly than they had done for a long time. Standing in the door, holding each other's hands, a last great wave of regretful memory swept over them.

"Well, this ain't the way we've thought it was all going to end, is it, Louisa?" said Joe.

She shook her head. There was a little quiver on her placid face.

"You let me know if there's ever anything I can do for you," said he. "I ain't ever going to forget you, Louisa." Then he kissed her, and went down the path.

Louisa, all alone by herself that night, wept a little, she hardly knew why; but the next morning, on waking, she felt like a queen who, after fearing lest her domain be wrested away from her, sees it firmly insured in her possession.

Now the tall weeds and grasses might cluster around Caesar's little hermit hut, the snow might fall on its roof year in and year out, but he never would go on a rampage through the unguarded village. Now the little canary might turn itself into a peaceful yellow ball night after night, and have no need to wake and flutter with wild terror against its bars. Louisa could sew linen seams, and distil roses, and dust and polish and fold away in lavender, as long as she listed. That afternoon she sat with her needle-work at the window, and felt fairly steeped in peace. Lily Dyer, tall and erect and blooming, went past; but she felt no qualm. If Louisa Ellis had sold her birthright she did not know it, the taste of the pottage[1] was so delicious, and had been her sole satisfaction for so long. Serenity and placid narrowness had become to her as the birthright itself. She gazed ahead through a long reach of future days strung together like pearls in a rosary, every one like the others, and all smooth and flawless and innocent, and her heart went up in thankfulness. Outside was the fervid summer afternoon; the air was filled with the sounds of the busy harvest of men and birds and bees; there were halloos, metallic clatterings, sweet calls, and long hummings. Louisa sat, prayerfully numbering her days, like an uncloistered nun.

1. See Genesis 25.30–34. Esau sold his birthright to his brother for a mess of pottage.

# Mavis Gallant

*Gallant (1922– ) was born in Montreal, Canada, and by virtue of her early contacts with the French-speaking people of Quebec has been bilingual from childhood. This early virtuosity is reflected in much of her later work, which explores the tangled customs, sensibilities, and expectations of characters from diverse origins meeting in a European setting. She began to write poems at five, and attendance at a strictly disciplined French convent school sharpened her eye for ironies of character and circumstance. From France, where she has spent many of her adult years, she has contributed a long string of stories to* The New Yorker. *Her novels are* Green Water, Green Sky *(1959), and* A Fairly Good Time *(1970). Her stories have been collected in* The Other Paris *(1956),* My Heart Is Broken *(1964),* The Pegnitz Junction *(1973),* From the Fifteenth District *(1979),* Home Truths *(1985),* Overhead in a Balloon *(1987),* Across the Bridge *(1993), and* Selected Stories *(1996).*

## Bernadette

On the hundred and twenty-sixth day, Bernadette could no longer pretend not to be sure. She got the calendar out from her bureau drawer—a kitchen calendar, with the Sundays and saints' days in fat red figures, under a brilliant view of Alps. Across the Alps was the name of a hardware store and its address on the other side of Montreal. From the beginning of October the calendar was smudged and grubby, so often had Bernadette with moistened forefinger counted off the days: thirty-four, thirty-five, thirty-six . . . That had been October, the beginning of fear, with the trees in the garden and on the suburban street a blaze of red and yellow. Bernadette had scrubbed floors and washed walls in a frenzy of bending and stretching that alarmed her employers, the kindly, liberal Knights.

"She's used to hard work—you can see that, of course," Robbie Knight had remarked, one Sunday, almost apologizing for the fact that they employed anyone in the house at all. Bernadette had chosen to wash the stairs and woodwork that day, instead of resting. It disturbed the atmosphere of the house, but neither of the Knights knew how to deal with a servant who wanted to work too much. He sat by the window, enjoying the warm October sunlight, trying to get on with the Sunday papers but feeling guilty because his wife was worried about Bernadette.

"She *will* keep on working," Nora said. "I've told her to leave that hard work for the char, but she insists. I suppose it's her way of showing gratitude, because we've treated her like a human being instead of a slave. Don't you agree?"

"I suppose so."

"I'm so tired," Nora said. She lay back in her chair with her eyes closed, the picture of total exhaustion. She had broken one of her nails clean across, that morning, helping Bernadette with something Bernadette might easily have done alone. "You're right about her being used to hard work. She's probably been working all her life." Robbie tried not answering this one. "It's so much the sort of thing I've battled," Nora said.

He gave up. He let his paper slide to the floor. Compelled to think about his wife's battles, he found it impossible to concentrate on anything else. Nora's weapons were kept sharp for two dragons: crooked politics and the Roman Catholic Church. She had battled for birth control, clean milk, vaccination, homes for mothers, homes for old people, homes for cats and dogs. She fought against censorship, and for votes for cloistered nuns, and for the provincial income tax.

"Good old Nora," said Robbie absently. Nora accepted this tribute without opening her eyes. Robbie looked at her, at the thin, nervous hand with the broken nail.

"She's not exciting, exactly," he had once told one of his mistresses. "But she's an awfully good sort, if you know what I mean. I mean, she's really a good sort. I honestly couldn't imagine not living with Nora." The girl to whom this was addressed had instantly burst into tears, but Robbie was used to that. Unreasonable emotional behaviour on the part of other women only reinforced his respect for his wife.

The Knights had been married nearly sixteen years. They considered themselves solidly united. Like many people no longer in love, they cemented their relationship with opinions, pet prejudices, secret meanings, a private vocabulary that enabled them to exchange amused glances over a dinner-table and made them feel a shade superior to the world outside the house. Their home held them, and their two daughters, now in boarding school. Private schools were out of line with the Knights' social beliefs, but in the case of their own children they had judged a private school essential.

"Selfish, they were," Robbie liked to explain. "Selfish, like their father." Here he would laugh a little, and so would his listeners. He was fond of assuming a boyish air of self-deprecation—a manner which, like his boyish nickname, had clung to him since school. "Nora slapped them both in St. Margaret's, and it cleared up in a year."

On three occasions, Nora had discovered Robbie in an affair. Each time, she had faced him bravely and made him discuss it, a process she called "working things out." Their talks would be formal, at first—a frigid question-and-answer period, with Robbie frightened and almost sick and Nora depressingly unreproachful. For a few nights, she would sleep in another room. She said that this enabled her to think. Thinking all night, she was fresh and ready for talk the next day. She would analyse their marriage, their lives, their childhoods, and their uncommon characters. She would tell Robbie what a Don Juan[1] complex was, and tell him what he was trying to prove. Finally, reconciled, they were able to talk all night, usually in the kitchen, the most neutral room of the house, slowly and congenially sharing a bottle of Scotch. Robbie would begin avoiding his mistress's telephone calls and at last would write her a letter saying that his marriage had been rocked from top to bottom and that but for the great tolerance shown by his wife they would all of them have been involved in something disagreeable. He and his wife had now arrived at a newer, fuller, truer, richer, deeper understanding. The long affection they held for each other would enable them to start life again on a different basis, the letter would conclude.

The basic notion of the letter was true. After such upheavals his marriage went swimmingly. He would feel flattened, but not unpleasantly, and it was Nora's practice to treat him with tolerance and good humour, like an ailing child.

He looked at the paper lying at his feet and tried to read the review of a film. It was hopeless. Nora's silence demanded his attention. He got up, kissed her lightly, and started out.

"Off to work?" said Nora, without opening her eyes.

"Well, yes," he said.

"I'll keep the house quiet. Would you like your lunch on a tray?"

"No, I'll come down."

"Just as you like, darling. It's no trouble."

He escaped.

Robbie was a partner in a firm of consulting engineers. He had, at one time, wanted to be a playwright. It was this interest that had, with other things, attracted Nora when they had been at university together. Robbie had been taking a course in writing for the stage—a sideline to his main degree. His family had insisted on engineering; he spoke of defying them, and going to London or New York. Nora had known, even then, that she was a born struggler and fighter. She often wished she had been a man. She believed that to balance this overassertive side of her nature she should marry someone essentially feminine, an artist of some description. At the same time, a burning fear of poverty pushed her in the direction of someone with stability, background, and a profession outside the arts. Both she and Robbie were campus liberals; they met at a gathering that had something to do with the Spanish war—the sort of party where, as Nora later described it, you all sat on the floor and drank beer out of old pickle jars. There had been a homogeneous quality about the group that was quite deceptive; political feeling was a great leveller. For Nora, who came from a poor and an ugly lower-middle-class home, political action was a leg up. It brought her in contact with people she would not otherwise have known. Her snobbishness moved to a different level; she spoke of herself as working-class, which was not strictly true. Robbie, in revolt against his family, who were well-to-do, conservative, and had no idea of the injurious things he said about

1. A legendary figure famous for his many seductions and his dissolute life.

them behind their backs, was, for want of a gentler expression, slumming around. He drifted into a beer-drinking Left Wing movement, where he was welcomed for his money, his good looks, and the respectable tone he lent the group. His favourite phrase at that time was "of the people." He mistook Nora for someone of the people, and married her almost before he had discovered his mistake. Nora then did an extraordinary about-face. She reconciled Robbie with his family. She encouraged him to go into his father's firm. She dampened, ever so gently, the idea of London and New York.

Still, she continued to encourage his interest in theatre. More, she managed to create such a positive atmosphere of playwriting in the house that many of their casual acquaintances thought he *was* a playwright, and were astonished to learn he was the Knight of Turnbull, Knight & Beardsley. Robbie had begun and abandoned many plays since college. He had not consciously studied since the creative-writing course, but he read, and criticized, and had reached the point where he condemned everything that had to do with the English-language stage.

Nora agreed with everything he believed. She doggedly shared his passion for the theatre—which had long since ceased to be real, except when she insisted—and she talked to him about his work, sharing his problems and trying to help. She knew that his trouble arose from the fact that he had to spend his daytime hours in the offices of the firm. She agreed that his real life was the theatre, with the firm a practical adjunct. She was sensible: she did not ask that he sell his partnership and hurl himself into uncertainty and insecurity—a prospect that would have frightened him very much indeed. She understood that it was the firm that kept them going, that paid for the girls at St. Margaret's and the trip to Europe every second summer. It was the firm that gave Nora leisure and scope for her tireless battles with the political and ecclesiastical authorities of Quebec. She encouraged Robbie to write in his spare time. Every day, or nearly, during his "good" periods, she mentioned his work. She rarely accepted an invitation without calling Robbie at his office and asking if he wanted to shut himself up and work that particular night. She could talk about his work, without boredom or exhaustion, just as she could discuss his love affairs. The only difference was that when they were mutually explaining Robbie's infidelity, they drank whisky. When they talked about his play and his inability to get on with it, Nora would go to the refrigerator and bring out a bottle of milk. She was honest and painstaking; she had at the tip of her tongue the vocabulary needed to turn their relationship and marriage inside out. After listening to Nora for a whole evening, agreeing all the way, Robbie would go to bed subdued with truth and totally empty. He felt that they had drained everything they would ever have to say. After too much talk, he would think, a couple should part; just part, without another word, full of kind thoughts and mutual understanding. He was afraid of words. That was why, that Sunday morning toward the end of October, the simple act of leaving the living-room took on the dramatic feeling of escape.

He started up the stairs, free. Bernadette was on her knees, washing the painted baseboard. Her hair, matted with a cheap permanent, had been flattened into curls that looked like snails, each snail held with two crossed bobby pins. She was young, with a touching attractiveness that owed everything to youth.

*"Bonjour, Bernadette."*

*" 'Jour."*

Bending, she plunged her hands into the bucket of soapy water. A moment earlier, she had thought of throwing herself down the stairs and making it seem an accident. Robbie's sudden appearance had frightened her into stillness. She wiped her forehead, waiting until he had closed the door behind him. Then she flung herself at the baseboard, cloth in hand. Did she feel something—a tugging, a pain? *"Merci, mon Dieu,"*[2] she whispered. But there was nothing to be thankful for, in spite of the walls and the buckets of water and the bending and the stretching.

Now it was late December, the hundred and twenty-sixth day, and Bernadette could no longer pretend not to be certain. The Knights were giving a party. Bernadette put the calendar back in the drawer, under her folded slips. She had counted on it so much that she felt it bore witness to her fears; anyone seeing it would know at once.

For weeks she had lived in a black sea of nausea and fear. The Knights had offered to send her home to Abitibi[3] for Christmas, had even wanted to pay her fare. But she knew that her father would know the instant he saw her, and would kill her. She preferred going on among familiar things, as if the normality, the repeated routine of getting up in the morning and putting on Mr. Knight's coffee and Mrs. Knight's tea would, by force of pattern, cause things to be the way they had been before October. So far, the Knights had noticed nothing, although the girls, home for Christmas, teased her about getting fat. Thanks to St. Joseph, the girls had now been sent north to ski with friends, and there was no longer any danger of their drawing attention to Bernadette's waist.

Because of the party, Bernadette was to wear a uniform, which she had not done for some time. She pressed it and put it back on its hanger without trying it on, numb with apprehension, frightened beyond all thought. She had spent the morning cleaning the livingroom. Now it was neat, unreal, like a room prepared for a colour photo in a magazine. There were flowers and plenty of ashtrays. It was a room waiting for disorder to set in.

"Thank you, Bernadette," Nora had said, taking, as always, the attitude that Bernadette had done her an unexpected service. "It looks lovely."

Nora liked the room; it was comfortable and fitted in with her horror of ostentation. Early in her marriage she had decided that her taste was uncertain; confusing elegance with luxury, she had avoided both. Later, she had discovered French Canadian furniture, which enabled her to refer to her rooms in terms of the simple, the charming, even the amusing. The bar, for example, was a *prie-dieu*[4] Nora had discovered during one of her forays into rural Quebec just after the war, before American tourists with a nose for a bargain had (as she

2. Thank you, God (French). 3. A lake in eastern Ontario and western Quebec, Canada. 4. A piece of furniture for kneeling on during prayer (French).

said) cleaned out the province of its greatest heritage. She had found the *prie-dieu* in a barn and had bought it for three dollars. Sandpapered, waxed, its interior recess deepened to hold bottles, it was considered one of Nora's best *trouvailles.*[5] The party that evening was being given in honour of a priest—a liberal priest from Belgium, a champion of modern ecclesiastical art, and another of Nora's finds. (Who but Nora would have dreamed of throwing a party for a priest?)

Robbie wondered if the *prie-dieu* might not offend him. "Maybe you ought to keep the lid up, so he won't see the cross," he said.

But Nora felt that would be cheating. If the priest accepted her hospitality, he must also accept her views.

"He doesn't know your views," Robbie said. "If he did, he probably wouldn't come." He had a cold, and was spending the day at home, in order to be well for the party. The cold made him interfering and quarrelsome.

"Go to bed, Robbie," said Nora kindly. "Haven't you anything to read? What about all the books you got for Christmas?"

Considering him dismissed, she coached Bernadette for the evening. They rehearsed the handing around of the tray, the unobtrusive clearing of ashtrays. Nora noticed that Bernadette seemed less shy. She kept a blank, hypnotized stare, concentrating hard. After a whole year in the household, she was just beginning to grasp what was expected. She understood work, she had worked all her life, but she did not always understand what these terrifying, well-meaning people wanted. If, dusting a bookcase, she slowed her arm, lingering, thinking of nothing in particular, one of them would be there, like a phantom, frightening her out of her wits.

"Would you like to borrow one of these books, Bernadette?"

Gentle, tolerant, infinitely baffling, Mr. or Mrs. Knight would offer her a book in French.

"For me?"

"Yes. You can read in the afternoon, while you are resting."

Read while resting? How could you do both? During her afternoon rest periods, Bernadette would lie on the bed, looking out the window. When she had a whole day to herself, she went downtown in a bus and looked in the windows of stores. Often, by the end of the afternoon, she had met someone, a stranger, a man who would take her for a drive in a car or up to his room. She accepted these adventures as inevitable; she had been so overwarned before leaving home. Cunning prevented her giving her address or name, and if one of her partners wanted to see her again, and named a time and a street number, she was likely to forget or to meet someone else on the way. She was just as happy in the cinema, alone, or looking at displays of eau de cologne in shops.

Reduced to perplexity, she would glance again at the book. Read?

"I might get it dirty."

"But books are to be read, Bernadette."

She would hang her head, wondering what they wanted, wishing they

5. Discoveries (French); lucky finds.

woul[d] [go] away. At last she had given in. It was in the autumn, the start of [h]er per[iod] of fear. She had been dusting in Robbie's room. Unexpectedly, in that [gh]ostly way they had, he was beside her at the bookcase. Blindly shy, she [remem]bered what Mrs. Knight, all tact and kindness and firm common sense, [had s]aid that morning: that Bernadette sometimes smelled of perspiration, and this was unpleasant. Probably Mr. Knight was thinking this now. In a pan[icky] motion her hand flew to *L'Amant de Lady Chatterley*,[6] which Nora had [bro]ught from Paris so that she could test the blundering ways of censorship. [(T]he English version had been held at customs, the French let through, which [g]ave Nora ammunition for a whole winter.)

"You won't like that," Robbie had said. "Still . . ." He pulled it out of the bookcase. She took the book to her room, wrapped it carefully in newspaper, and placed it in a drawer. A few days later she knocked on the door of Robbie's room and returned *L'Amant de Lady Chatterley*.

"You enjoyed it?"

*"Oui. Merci."*[7]

He gave her *La Porte Etroite*.[8] She wrapped it in newspaper and placed it in a drawer for five days. When she gave it back, he chose for her one of the Claudine series, and then, rather doubtfully, *Le Rouge et le Noir*.[9]

"Did you like the book by Stendhal, Bernadette?"

*"Oui. Merci."*

To dinner guests, Nora now said, "Oh, our Bernadette! Not a year out of Abitibi, and she was reading Gide and Colette.[1] She knows more about French literature than we do. She goes through Stendhal like a breeze. She adores Giraudoux."[2] When Bernadette, grim with the effort of remembering what to do next, entered the room, everyone would look at her and she would wonder what she had done wrong.

During the party rehearsal, Robbie, snubbed, went up to bed. He knew that Nora would never forgive him if he hadn't recovered by evening. She regarded a cold in the head as something that could be turned off with a little effort; indeed, she considered any symptom of illness in her husband an act of aggression directed against herself. He sat up in bed, bitterly cold in spite of three blankets and a bathrobe. It was the chill of grippe, in the centre of his bones; no external warmth could reach it. He heard Nora go out for some last-minute shopping, and he heard Bernadette's radio in the kitchen.

"*Sans amour, on est rien du tout*,"[3] Edith Piaf sang. The song ended and a commercial came on. He tried not to hear.

On the table by his bed were books Nora had given him for Christmas. He had decided, that winter, to reread some of the writers who had influenced him as a young man. He began this project with the rather large idea of summing himself up as a person, trying to find out what had determined the direction of his life. In college, he remembered, he had promised himself a life of action and freedom and political adventure. Perhaps everyone had then. But surely

6. A novel by D. H. Lawrence, (1885–1930). 7. Yes, thank you (French). 8. The narrow door; a novel by André Gide (1869–1951). 9. The red and the black; a novel by Marie Henri Beyle Stendhal (1783–1842). 1. Sidonie-Gabrielle Colette (1873–1954); author of *Cheri*, *Gigi*, and many other novels. 2. Jean Giraudoux (1882–1944). 3. Without love, one is nothing at all (French).

he, Robbie Knight, should have moved on to something other than a p Tudor house in a suburb of Montreal. He had been considered promisin attractive young man with a middling-good brain, a useful background, u pected opinions, and considerable charm. He did not consider himself unhap but he was beginning to wonder what he was doing, and why. He had decid to carry out his reassessment program in secret. Unfortunately, he could no help telling Nora, who promptly gave him the complete Orwell[4] bound in green.

He read with the conviction of habit. There was Orwell's Spain, the Spain of action and his university days. There was also the Spain he and Nora knew as tourists, a poor and dusty country where tourists became colicky because of the oil. For the moment, he forgot what he had seen, just as he could sometimes forget he had not become a playwright. He regretted the Spain he had missed, but the death of a cause no longer moved him. So far, the only result of his project was a feeling of loss. Leaving Spain, he turned to an essay on England. It was an essay he had not read until now. He skipped about, restless, and suddenly stopped at this: "I have often been struck by the peculiar easy completeness, the perfect symmetry as it were, of a working-class interior at its best. Especially on winter evenings after tea, when the fire glows in the open range and dances mirrored in the steel fender, when Father, in shirt-sleeves, sits in the rocking chair at one side of the fire reading the racing finals, and Mother sits on the other with her sewing, and the children are happy with a penn'orth of mint humbugs, and the dog lolls roasting himself on the rag mat."

Because he had a cold and Nora had gone out and left him on a snowy miserable afternoon, he saw in this picture everything missing in his life. He felt frozen and left out. Robbie had never been inside the kitchen of a working-class home; it did not occur to him that the image he had just been given might be idyllic or sentimental. He felt only that he and Nora had missed something, and that he ought to tell her so; but he knew that it would lead to a long bout of analytical talk, and he didn't feel up to that. He blew his nose, pulled the collar of his dressing-gown up around his ears, and settled back on the pillows.

Bernadette knocked at the door. Nora had told her to prepare a tray of tea, rum, and aspirin at four o'clock. It was now half past four, and Bernadette wondered if Mr. Knight would betray her to Mrs. Knight. Bernadette's sleeves were rolled up, and she brought with her an aura of warmth and good food. She had, in fact, been cooking a ham for the party. Her hair was up in the hideous snails again, but it gave her, Robbie thought, the look of a hard-working woman—a look his own wife achieved only by seeming totally exhausted.

"*Y a un* book, too," said Bernadette, in her coarse, flat little voice. She put the tray down with care. "*Je l'ai mis sur le* tray." She indicated the new Prix Goncourt,[5] which, Robbie had lent her the day it arrived. He saw at once that the pages were still uncut.

"You didn't like it?"

"Oh, *oui*," she said automatically. "*Merci.*"

Never before had a lie seemed to him more pathetic, or more justified. Instead of taking the book, or his tea, he gripped Bernadette's plump, strong

4. George Orwell (1903–1950), author of the novel *1984*, among many others. 5. An award for literary excellence. "*Je l'ai mis sur le* tray": I have put it on the tray (French).

forearm. The room was full of warmth and comfort. Bernadette had brought this atmosphere with her; it was her native element. She was the world they had missed sixteen years before, and they, stupidly, had been trying to make her read books. He held her arm, gripping it. She stared back at him, and he saw that she was frightened. He let her go, furious with himself, and said, rather coldly, "Do you ever think about your home in Abitibi?"

*"Oui,"* she said flatly.

"Some of the farms up there are very modern now, I believe," he said, sounding as if he were angry with her. "Was yours?"

She shrugged. *"On a pas la* television, *nous,"*[6] she said.

"I didn't think you had. What about your kitchen. What was your kitchen like at home, Bernadette?"

*"Sais pas,"*[7] said Bernadette, rubbing the released arm on the back of her dress. "It's big," she offered, after some thought.

"Thank you," said Robbie. He went back to his book, still furious, and upset. She stood still, uncertain, a fat dark little creature not much older than his own elder daughter. He turned a page, not reading, and at last she went away.

Deeply bewildered, Bernadette returned to the kitchen and contemplated the cooling ham. She seldom thought about home. Now her memory, set in motion, brought up the image of a large, crowded room. The prevailing smell was the odour of the men's boots as they came in from the outbuildings. The table, masked with oilcloth, was always set between meals, the thick plates turned upside down, the spoons in a glass jar. At the centre of the table, never removed, were the essentials: butter, vinegar, canned jam with the lid of the can half opened and wrenched back, ketchup, a tin of molasses glued to its saucer. In winter, the washing hung over the stove. By the stove, every year but the last two or three, had stood a basket containing a baby—a wailing, swaddled baby, smelling sad and sour. Only a few of Bernadette's mother's children had straggled up past the infant stage. Death and small children were inextricably knotted in Bernadette's consciousness. As a child she had watched an infant brother turn blue and choke to death. She had watched two others die of diphtheria. The innocent dead became angels; there was no reason to grieve. Bernadette's mother did all she could; terrified of injections and vaccines, she barred the door to the district nurse. She bound her infants tightly to prevent excess motion, she kept them by the flaming heat of the stove, she fed them a bouillon of warm water and cornstarch to make them fat. When Bernadette thought of the kitchen at home, she thought of her mother's pregnant figure, and her swollen feet, in unlaced tennis shoes.

Now she herself was pregnant. Perhaps Mr. Knight knew, and that was why he had asked about her mother's kitchen. Sensing a connection between her mother and herself, she believed he had seen it as well. Nothing was too farfetched, no wisdom, no perception, for these people. Their mental leaps and guesses were as mysterious to her as those of saints, or of ghosts.

Nora returned and, soon afterward, Robbie wandered downstairs. His wife had told him to get up (obviously forgetting that it was she who had sent him

6. We had no television (French). 7. I don't know (French).

to bed) so that she could tidy the room. She did not ask how he felt and seemed to take it for granted that he had recovered. He could not help comparing her indifference with the solicitude of Bernadette, who had brought him tea and rum. He began comparing Bernadette with other women he had known well. His mistresses, *faute de mieux,* had been girls with jobs and little apartments. They had in common with Nora a desire to discuss the situation; they were alarmingly likely to burst into tears after love-making because Robbie didn't love them enough or because he had to go home for dinner. He had never known a working-class girl, other than the women his wife employed. (Even privately, he no longer used the expression "of the people.") As far as he could determine now, girls of Bernadette's sort were highly moral, usually lived with their parents until marriage, and then disappeared from sight, like Moslem women. He might have achieved an interesting union, gratifying a laudable social curiosity, during his college days, but he had met Nora straightaway. He had been disappointed to learn that her father did not work in a factory. There was an unbridgeable gap, he had since discovered, between the girl whose father went off to work with a lunch pail and the daughter of a man who ate macaroni-and-cheese in the company cafeteria. In the midst of all her solicitude for the underprivileged, Nora never let him forget it. On the three occasions when she had caught him out in a love affair, among her first questions had been "Where does she come from? What does she do?"

Robbie decided to apologize to Bernadette. He had frightened her, which he had no right to do. He no longer liked the classic role he had set for himself, the kindly educator of young servant girls. It had taken only a glimpse of his thin, busy wife to put the picture into perspective. He allowed himself one last, uncharitable thought, savouring it: Compared with Bernadette, Nora looked exactly like a furled umbrella.

Bernadette was sitting at the kitchen table. The ham had been put away, the room aired. She was polishing silver for the party, using a smelly antiseptic pink paste. He no longer felt the atmosphere of warmth and food and comfort Bernadette had brought up to his room. She did not look up. She regarded her own upside-down image in the bowl of a spoon. Her hands moved slowly, then stopped. What did he want now?

Before coming to Montreal, Bernadette had been warned about the licentious English—reserved on the surface, hypocritical, infinitely wicked underneath—and she had, in a sense, accepted it as inevitable that Mr. Knight would try to seduce her. When it was over, she would have another sin to account for. Mr. Knight, a Protestant, would not have sinned at all. Unique in her sin, she felt already lonely. His apology sent her off into the strange swamp world again, a world in which there was no footing; she had the same feeling as when they tried to make her read books. What was he sorry about? She looked dumbly around the kitchen. She could hear Nora upstairs, talking on the telephone.

Robbie also heard her and thought: Bernadette is afraid of Nora. The idea that the girl might say something to his wife crossed his mind, and he was annoyed to realize that Nora's first concern would be for Bernadette's feelings. His motives and his behaviour they would discuss later, over a drink. He no longer knew what he wanted to say to Bernadette. He made a great show of drinking a glass of water and went out.

By evening, Robbie's temperature was over ninety-nine. Nora did not consider it serious. She felt that he was deliberately trying to ruin the party, and said so. "Take one good stiff drink," she said. "That's all you need."

He saw the party through a feverish haze. Nora was on top of the world, controlling the room, clergy-baiting, but in the most charming manner. No priest could possibly have taken offense, particularly a nice young priest from Belgium, interested in modern art and preceded by a liberal reputation. He could not reply; his English was limited. Besides, as Nora kept pointing out, he didn't know the situation in Quebec. He could only make little grimaces, acknowledging her thrusts, comically chewing the stem of a cold pipe.

"Until you know this part of the world, you don't know your own Church," Nora told him, smiling, not aggressive.

The English Canadians in the room agreed, glancing nervously at the French. French Canada was represented by three journalists huddled on a couch. (Nora had promised the priest, as if offering hors d' oeuvres, representatives of what she called "our chief ethnic groups.") The three journalists supported Nora, once it was made plain that clergy-baiting and French-baiting were not going to be combined. Had their wives been there, they might not have concurred so brightly; but Nora could seldom persuade her French Canadian finds to bring their wives along. The drinking of Anglo-Saxon women rather alarmed them, and they felt that their wives, genteel, fluffy-haired, in good little dresses and strings of pearls, would disappoint and be disappointed. Nora never insisted. She believed in emancipation, but no one was more vocal in deploring the French Canadian who spoke hard, flat English and had become anglicized out of all recognition. Robbie, feverish and disloyal, almost expected her to sweep the room with her hand and, pointing to the trio of journalists, announce, "I found them in an old barn and bought them for five dollars each. I've sandpapered and waxed them, and there they are."

From the Church she went on to Bernadette. She followed the familiar pattern, explaining how environment had in a few months overcome generations of intellectual poverty.

"Bernadette reads Gide and Lawrence," she said, choosing writers the young priest was bound to disapprove of. "She adores Colette."

"Excellent," he said, tepid.

Bernadette came in, walking with care, as if on a tightrope. She had had difficulty with her party uniform and she wondered if it showed.

"Bernadette," Nora said, "how many children did your mother have?"

"Thirteen, Madame," said the girl. Accustomed to this interrogation, she continued to move around the room, remembering Nora's instructions during the rehearsal.

"In how many years?" Nora said.

"Fifteen."

"And how many are living?"

"Six, Madame."

The young priest stopped chewing his pipe and said quietly, in French, "Are you sorry that your seven brothers and sisters died, Bernadette?"

Jolted out of her routine, Bernadette replied at once, as if she had often thought about it, "Oh, no. If they had lived, they would have had to grow up and work hard, and the boys would have to go to war, when there is war, to fight—" About to say "fight for the English," she halted. "Now they are little angels, praying for their mother," she said.

"Where?" said the priest.

"In Heaven."

"What does an angel look like, Bernadette?" he said.

She gave him her hypnotized gaze and said, "They are very small. They have small golden heads and little wings. Some are tall and wear pink and blue dresses. You don't see them because of the clouds."

"I see. Thank you," said Nora, cutting in, and the student of Gide and Colette moved off to the kitchen with her tray.

It ruined the evening. The party got out of hand. People stopped talking about the things Nora wanted them to talk about, and the ethnic groups got drunk and began to shout. Nora heard someone talking about the fluctuating dollar, and someone else said to her, of television, "Well, Nora, still holding out?"—when only a few months ago anyone buying a set had been sheepish and embarrassed and had said it was really for the maid.

When it was all over and Nora was running the vacuum so that there would be less for Bernadette to do the next day, she frowned and looked tired and rather old. The party had gone wrong. The guest of honour had slipped away early. Robbie had gone to bed before midnight without a word to anybody. Nora had felt outside the party, bored and disappointed, wishing to God they would all clear out. She had stood alone by the fireplace, wondering at the access of generosity that had led her to invite these ill-matched and noisy people to her home. Her parties in the past had been so different: everyone had praised her hospitality, applauded her leadership, exclaimed at her good sense. Indignant with her over some new piece of political or religious chicanery, they had been grateful for her combativeness, and had said so—more and more as the evening wore on. Tonight, they seemed to have come just as they went everywhere else, for the liquor and good food. A rot, a feeling of complacency, had set in. She had looked around the room and thought, with an odd little shock: How old they all seem! Just then one of her ethnic treasures—a recently immigrated German doctor—had come up to her and said, "That little girl is pregnant."

"What?"

"The little servant girl. One has only to look."

Afterward, she wondered how she could have failed to notice. Everything gave Bernadette away: her eyes, her skin, the characteristic thickening of her waist. There were the intangible signs, too, the signs that were not quite physical. In spite of her own motherhood, Nora detested, with a sort of fastidious horror, any of the common references to pregnancy. But even to herself, now, she could think of Bernadette only in terms of the most vulgar expressions, the terminology her own family (long discarded, never invited here) had employed. Owing to a "mistake," Bernadette was probably "caught." She was beginning to "show." She was at least four months "gone." It seemed to Nora that she had better go straight to the point with Bernadette. The girl was under twenty-one.

It was quite possible that the Knights would be considered responsible. If the doctor had been mistaken, then Bernadette could correct her. If Bernadette were to tell Nora to mind her own business, so much the better, because it would mean that Bernadette had more character than she seemed to have. Nora had no objection to apologizing in either instance.

Because of the party and the extra work involved, Bernadette had been given the next afternoon off. She spent the morning cleaning. Nora kept out of the way, Robbie stayed in bed, mulishly maintaining that he wasn't feeling well. It was after lunch, and Bernadette was dressed and ready to go downtown to a movie, when Nora decided not to wait any longer. She cornered Bernadette in the kitchen and, facing her, suddenly remembered how, as a child, she had cornered field mice with a flashlight and then drowned them. Bernadette seemed to know what was coming; she exuded fear. She faced her tormentor with a beating, animal heart.

Nora sat down at the kitchen table and began, as she frequently had done with Robbie, with the words "I think we ought to talk about a certain situation." Bernadette stared. "Is there anything you'd like to tell me?" Nora said.

"No," said Bernadette, shaking her head.

"But you're worried about something. Something is wrong. Isn't that true?"

"No."

"Bernadette, I want to help you. Sit down. Tell me, are you pregnant?"

"I don't understand."

"Yes, you do. *Un enfant. Un bébé.* Am I right?"

*"Sais pas,"* said Bernadette. She looked at the clock over Nora's head.

*"Bernadette."*

It was getting late. Bernadette said, "Yes, I think so. Yes."

"You poor little mutt," said Nora. "Don't keep standing there like that. Sit down here, by the table. Take off your coat. We must talk about it. This is much more important than a movie." Bernadette remained standing, in hat and coat. "Who is it?" asked Nora. "I didn't know you had . . . I mean, I didn't know you knew anyone here. Tell me. It's most important. I'm not angry." Bernadette continued to look up at the clock, as if there were no other point in the room on which she dared fix her eyes. "Bern*adette!*" Nora said. "I've just asked you a question. Who is the boy?"

*"Un monsieur,"* said Bernadette.

Did she mean by that an older man, or was Bernadette, in using the word *"monsieur,"* implying a social category? *"Quel monsieur?"*[8] said Nora.

Bernadette shrugged. She stole a glance at Nora, and something about the oblique look suggested more than fear or evasiveness. A word came into Nora's mind: sly.

"Can you . . . I mean, is it someone you're going to marry?" But no. In that case, he would have been a nice young boy, someone of Bernadette's own background. Nora would have met him. He would have been caught in the kitchen drinking Robbie's beer. He would have come every Sunday and every

8. What man? (French).

Thursday afternoon to call for Bernadette. "Is it someone you *can* marry?" Nora said. Silence. "Don't be afraid," said Nora, deliberately making her voice kind. She longed to shake the girl, even slap her face. It was idiotic; here was Bernadette in a terrible predicament, and all she could do was stand, shuffling from one foot to the other, as if a movie were the most important thing in the world. "If he isn't already married," Nora said, "which I'm beginning to suspect is the case, he'll marry you. You needn't worry about that. I'll deal with it, or Mr. Knight will."

*"Pas possible,"* said Bernadette, low.

"Then I was right. He *is* married." Bernadette looked up at the clock, desperate. She wanted the conversation to stop. "A married man," Nora repeated. *"Un monsieur."* An unfounded and wholly outrageous idea rushed into her mind. Dismissing it, she said, "When did it happen?"

*"Sais pas."*

"Don't be silly. That really is a very silly reply. Of course you know. You've only had certain hours out of this house."

The truth of it was that Bernadette did not know. She didn't know his name or whether he was married or even where she could find him again, even if she had desired such a thing. He seemed the least essential factor. Lacking words, she gave Nora the sidelong glance that made her seem coarse and deceitful. She is so uninnocent, Nora thought, surprised and a little repelled. It occurred to her that in spite of her long marriage and her two children, she knew less than Bernadette. While she was thinking about Bernadette and her lover, there came into her mind the language of the street. She remembered words that had shocked and fascinated her as a child. That was Bernadette's fault. It was Bernadette's atmosphere, Nora thought, excusing herself to an imaginary censor. She said, "We must know when your baby will be born. Don't you think so?" Silence. She tried again: "How long has it been since you . . . I mean, since you missed . . ."

"One hundred and twenty-seven days," said Bernadette. She was so relieved to have, at last, a question that she could answer that she brought it out in a kind of shout.

"My God. What are you going to do?"

*"Sais pas."*

"Oh, Bernadette!" Nora cried. "But you must think." The naming of a number of days made the whole situation so much more immediate. Nora felt that they ought to be doing something—telephoning, writing letters, putting some plan into motion. "We shall have to think for you," she said. "I shall speak to Mr. Knight."

"No," said Bernadette, trembling, suddenly coming to life. "Not Mr. Knight."

Nora leaned forward on the table. She clasped her hands together, hard. She looked at Bernadette. "Is there a special reason why I shouldn't speak to Mr. Knight?" she said.

*"Oui."* Bernadette had lived for so many days now in her sea of nausea and fear that it had become a familiar element. There were greater fears and humiliations, among them that Mr. Knight, who was even more baffling and

dangerous than his wife, should try to discuss this thing with Bernadette. She remembered what he had said the day before, and how he had held her arm. "He must know," said Bernadette. "I think he must already know."

"You had better go on," said Nora, after a moment. "You'll miss your bus. She sat quite still and watched Bernadette's progress down the drive. She looked at the second-hand imitation-seal coat that had been Bernadette's first purchase (and Nora's despair) and the black velveteen snow boots trimmed with dyed fur and tied with tasselled cords. Bernadette's purse hung over her arm. She had the walk of a fat girl—the short steps, the ungainly little trot

It was unreasonable, Nora knew it was unreasonable; but there was so much to reinforce the idea—*"Un monsieur,"* and the fact that he already knew ("He must know," Bernadette had said)—and then there was Bernadette's terror when she said she was going to discuss it with him. She thought of Robbie's interest in Bernadette's education. She thought of Robbie in the past, his unwillingness to remain faithful, his absence of courage and common sense. Recalling Bernadette's expression, prepared now to call it corrupt rather than sly, she felt that the girl had considered herself deeply involved with Nora; that she knew Nora much better than she should.

Robbie had decided to come downstairs, and was sitting by the living-room fire. He was reading a detective novel. Beside him was a drink.

"Get you a drink?" he said, without lifting his eyes, when Nora came in.

"Don't bother."

He went on reading. He looked so innocent, so unaware that his life was shattered. Nora remembered how he had been when she had first known him, so pleasant and dependent and good-looking and stupid. She remembered how he had been going to write a play, and how she had wanted to change the world, or at least Quebec. Tears of fatigue and strain came into her eyes. She felt that the failure of last night's party had been a symbol of the end. Robbie had done something cheap and dishonourable, but he reflected their world. The world was ugly, Montreal was ugly, the street outside the window contained houses of surpassing ugliness. There was nothing left to discuss but television and the fluctuating dollar; that was what the world had become. The children were in boarding school because Nora didn't trust herself to bring them up. The living-room was full of amusing peasant furniture because she didn't trust her own taste. Robbie was afraid of her and liked humiliating her by demonstrating again and again that he preferred nearly any other woman in bed. That was the truth of things. Why had she never faced it until now?

She said, "Robbie, can I talk to you?" Reluctant, he looked away from his book. She said, "I just wanted to tell you about a dream. Last night I dreamed you died. I dreamed that there was nothing I could do to bring you back, and that I had to adjust all my thoughts to the idea of going on without you. It was a terrible, shattering feeling." She intended this to be devastating, a prelude to the end. Unfortunately, she had had this dream before, and Robbie was bored with it. They had already discussed what it might mean, and he had no desire to go into it now.

"I wish to God you wouldn't keep on dreaming I died," he said.

She waited. There was nothing more. She blinked back her tears and said,

"Well, listen to this, then. I want to talk about Bernadette. What do you know, exactly, about Bernadette's difficulties?"

"Has Bernadette got difficulties?" The floor under his feet heaved and settled. He had never been so frightened in his life. Part of his mind told him that nothing had happened. He had been ill, a young girl had brought warmth and comfort into his room, and he wanted to touch her. What was wrong with that? Why should it frighten him so much that Nora knew? He closed his eyes. It was hopeless; Nora was not going to let him get on with the book. Nora looked without any sentiment at all at the twin points where his hairline was moving back. "Does she seem sort of unsettled?" he asked.

"That's a way of putting it. Sometimes you have a genuine talent for irony."

"Oh, hell," said Robbie, suddenly fed up with Nora's cat-and-mouse. "I don't feel like talking about anything. Let's skip it for now. It's not important."

"Perhaps you'd better tell me what you consider important," Nora said. "Then we'll see what we can skip." She wondered how he could sit there, concerned with his mild grippe, or his hangover, when the whole structure of their marriage was falling apart. Already, she saw the bare bones of the room they sat in, the rugs rolled, the cracks that would show in the walls when they took the pictures down.

He sighed, giving in. He closed the book and put it beside his drink. "It was just that yesterday when I was feeling so lousy she brought me—she brought me a book. One of those books we keep lending her. She hadn't even cut the pages. The whole thing's a farce. She doesn't even look at them."

"Probably not," said Nora. "Or else she does and that's the whole trouble. To get straight to the point, which I can see you don't want to do, Bernadette has told me she's having a baby. She takes it for granted that you already know. She's about four months under way, which makes yesterday seem rather pointless."

Robbie said impatiently, "We're not talking about the same thing." He had not really absorbed what Nora was saying; she spoke so quickly, and got so many things in all at once. His first reaction was astonishment, and a curious feeling that Bernadette had deceived him. Then the whole import of Nora's speech entered his mind and became clear. He said, "Are you crazy? Are you out of your mind? Are you completely crazy?" Anger paralysed him. He was unable to think of words or form them on his tongue. At last he said, "It's too bad that when I'm angry I can't do anything except feel sick. Or maybe it's just as well. You're crazy, Nora. You get these—I don't know—you get these ideas." He said, "If I'd hit you then, I might have killed you."

It had so seldom occurred in their life together that Robbie was in the right morally that Nora had no resources. She had always triumphed. Robbie's position had always been indefensible. His last remark was so completely out of character that she scarcely heard it. He had spoken in an ordinary tone of voice. She was frightened, but only because she had made an insane mistake and it was too late to take it back. Bravely, because there was nothing else to do, she went on about Bernadette. "She doesn't seem to know what to do. She's a minor, so I'm afraid it rather falls on us. There is a place in Vermont, a private place, where they take these girls and treat them well, rather like a boarding school. I can get her in, I think. Having her admitted to the States could be your end of it."

"I suppose you think that's going to be easy," Robbie said bitterly. "I suppose you think they admit pregnant unmarried minors every day of the year."

"None of it is easy!" Nora cried, losing control. "Whose fault is it?"

"It's got nothing to do with me!" said Robbie, shouting at her. "Christ Almighty, get that through your head!"

They let silence settle again. Robbie found that he was trembling. As he had said, it was physically difficult for him to be angry.

Nora said, "Yes, Vermont," as if she were making notes. She was determined to behave as if everything were normal. She knew that unless she established the tone quickly, nothing would ever be normal again.

"What will she do with it? Give it out for adoption?" said Robbie, in spite of himself diverted by details.

"She'll send it north, to her family," said Nora. "There's always room on a farm. It will make up for the babies that died. They look on those things, on birth and on death, as acts of nature, like the changing of the seasons. They don't think of them as catastrophes."

Robbie wanted to say, You're talking about something you've read, now. They'll be too ashamed to have Bernadette or the baby around; this is Quebec. But he was too tired to offer a new field of discussion. He was as tired as if they had been talking for hours. He said, "I suppose this Vermont place, this school or whatever it is, has got to be paid for."

"It certainly does." Nora looked tight and cold at this hint of stinginess. It was unnatural for her to be in the wrong, still less to remain on the defensive. She had taken the position now that even if Robbie were not responsible, he had somehow upset Bernadette. In some manner, he could be found guilty and made to admit it. She would find out about it later. Meanwhile, she felt morally bound to make him pay.

"Will it be expensive, do you think?"

She gave him a look, and he said nothing more.

Bernadette sat in the comforting dark of the cinema. It was her favourite kind of film, a musical comedy in full colour. They had reached the final scene. The hero and heroine, separated because of a stupid quarrel for more than thirty years, suddenly found themselves in the same night club, singing the same song. They had grey hair but youthful faces. All the people around them were happy to see them together. They clapped and smiled. Bernadette smiled, too. She did not identify herself with the heroine, but with the people looking on. She would have liked to have gone to a night club in a low-cut dress and applauded such a scene. She believed in love and in uncomplicated stories of love, even though it was something she had never experienced or seen around her. She did not really expect it to happen to her, or to anyone she knew.

For the first time, her child moved. She was so astonished that she looked at the people sitting on either side of her, wondering if they had noticed. They were looking at the screen. For the first time, then, she thought of it as a child, here, alive—not a state of terror but something to be given a name, clothed, fed, and baptized. Where and how and when it would be born she did not question. Mrs. Knight would do something. Somebody would. It would be born, and it would die. That it would die she never doubted. She was uncertain of so much else; her own body was a mystery, nothing had ever been explained. At home, in spite of her mother's pregnancies, the birth of the infants was shrouded in secrecy and, like their conception, suspicion of sin. This baby was Bernadette's own; when it died, it would pray for her, and her alone, for all of eternity. No matter what she did with the rest of her life, she would have an angel of her own, praying for her. Oddly secure in the dark, the dark of the cinema, the dark of her personal fear, she felt protected. She thought: *Il prie pour moi.*[9] She saw, as plainly as if it had been laid in her arms, her child, her personal angel, white and swaddled, baptized, innocent, ready for death.

9. He prays for me (French).

# Gabriel García Márquez

*García Márquez (1928– ) was born in Aracataca, Colombia; moved to Mexico in 1954; and in 1967 took up permanent residence in Barcelona, Catalonia. His first novel,* La hojarasca, *was written when he was nineteen but was not published until eight years later, in 1955 (translated as* Leaf Storm, *1972). Many of his short stories as well as his most ambitious novel,* One Hundred Years of Solitude *(1967, trans. 1970), are drawn from the fictional town of Macondo, which some critics have seen as a counterpart of Faulkner's Yoknapatawpha County. This renowned novel presents six generations of one family, fusing magic, reality, fable, and fantasy in a fashion that expands the family saga into a panorama of civilization. His other novels include* In Evil Hour *(1962, trans. 1979),* The Autumn of the Patriarch *(1975, trans. 1976),* Chronicle of a Death Foretold *(1981, trans. 1982), and* Love in the Time of Cholera *(1987, trans. 1988). His stories are most easily found in* Collected Stories *(1984) and in a newer collection of stories,* Strange Pilgrims *(1973). In 1982 he was awarded the Nobel Prize for Literature.*

## The Handsomest Drowned Man in the World[1]

### A Tale for Children

The first children who saw the dark and slinky bulge approaching through the sea let themselves think it was an empty ship. Then they saw it had no flags or masts and they thought it was a whale. But when it washed up on the beach, they removed the clumps of seaweed, the jellyfish tentacles, and the remains of fish and flotsam, and only then did they see that it was a drowned man.

They had been playing with him all afternoon, burying him in the sand and digging him up again, when someone chanced to see them and spread the alarm in the village. The men who carried him to the nearest house noticed that he weighed more than any dead man they had ever known, almost as much as a horse, and they said to each other that maybe he'd been floating too long and the water had got into his bones. When they laid him on the floor they said he'd been taller than all other men because there was barely enough room for

1. Translated by Gregory Rabassa.

him in the house, but they thought that maybe the ability to keep on growing after death was part of the nature of certain drowned men. He had the smell of the sea about him and only his shape gave one to suppose that it was the corpse of a human being, because the skin was covered with a crust of mud and scales.

They did not even have to clean off his face to know that the dead man was a stranger. The village was made up of only twenty-odd wooden houses that had stone courtyards with no flowers and which were spread about on the end of a desertlike cape. There was so little land that mothers always went about with the fear that the wind would carry off their children and the few dead that the years had caused among them had to be thrown off the cliffs. But the sea was calm and bountiful and all the men fit into seven boats. So when they found the drowned man they simply had to look at one another to see that they were all there. That night they did not go out to work at sea. While the men went to find out if anyone was missing in neighboring villages, the women stayed behind to care for the drowned man. They took the mud off with grass swabs, they removed the underwater stones entangled in his hair, and they scraped the crust off with tools used for scaling fish. As they were doing that they noticed that the vegetation on him came from faraway oceans and deep water and that his clothes were in tatters, as if he had sailed through labyrinths of coral. They noticed too that he bore his death with pride, for he did not have the lonely look of other drowned men who came out of the sea or that haggard, needy look of men who drowned in rivers. But only when they finished cleaning him off did they become aware of the kind of man he was and it left them breathless. Not only was he the tallest, strongest, most virile, and best built man they had ever seen, but even though they were looking at him there was no room for him in their imagination.

They could not find a bed in the village large enough to lay him on nor was there a table solid enough to use for his wake. The tallest men's holiday pants would not fit him, nor the fattest ones' Sunday shirts, nor the shoes of the one with the biggest feet. Fascinated by his huge size and his beauty, the women then decided to make him some pants from a large piece of sail and a shirt from some bridal brabant linen so that he could continue through his death with dignity. As they sewed, sitting in a circle and gazing at the corpse between stitches, it seemed to them that the wind had never been so steady nor the sea so restless as on that night and they supposed that the change had something to do with the dead man. They thought that if that magnificent man had lived in the village, his house would have had the widest doors, the highest ceiling, and the strongest floor, his bedstead would have been made from a midship frame held together by iron bolts, and his wife would have been the happiest woman. They thought that he would have had so much authority that he could have drawn fish out of the sea simply by calling their names and that he would have put so much work into his land that springs would have burst forth from among the rocks so that he would have been able to plant flowers on the cliffs. They secretly compared him to their own men, thinking that for all their lives theirs were incapable of doing what he could do in one night, and they ended up dismissing them deep in their hearts as the weakest, meanest, and most useless creatures on earth. They were wandering through that maze of fantasy when the oldest woman, who as the oldest had looked upon the drowned man with more compassion than passion, sighed:

"He has the face of someone called Esteban."

It was true. Most of them had only to take another look at him to see that he could not have any other name. The more stubborn among them, who were the youngest, still lived for a few hours with the illusion that when they put his clothes on and he lay among the flowers in patent leather shoes his name might be Lautaro. But it was a vain illusion. There had not been enough canvas, the poorly cut and worse sewn pants were too tight, and the hidden strength of his heart popped the buttons on his shirt. After midnight the whistling of the wind died down and the sea fell into its Wednesday drowsiness. The silence put an end to any last doubts: he was Esteban. The women who had dressed him, who had combed his hair, had cut his nails and shaved him were unable to hold back a shudder of pity when they had to resign themselves to his being dragged along the ground. It was then that they understood how unhappy he must have been with that huge body since it bothered him even after death. They could see him in life, condemned to going through doors sideways, cracking his head on crossbeams, remaining on his feet during visits, not knowing what to do with his soft, pink, sea lion hands while the lady of the house looked for her most resistant chair and begged him, frightened to death, sit here, Esteban, please, and he, leaning against the wall, smiling, don't bother, ma'am, I'm fine where I am, his heels raw and his back roasted from having done the same thing so many times whenever he paid a visit, don't bother, ma'am, I'm fine where I am, just to avoid the embarrassment of breaking up the chair, and never knowing perhaps that the ones who said don't go, Esteban, at least wait till the coffee's ready, were the ones who later on would whisper the big boob finally left, how nice, the handsome fool has gone. That was what the women were thinking beside the body a little before dawn. Later, when they covered his face with a handkerchief so that the light would not bother him, he looked so forever dead, so defenseless, so much like their men that the first furrows of tears opened in their hearts. It was one of the younger ones who began the weeping. The others, coming to, went from sighs to wails, and the more they sobbed the more they felt like weeping, because the drowned man was becoming all the more Esteban for them, and so they wept so much, for he was the most destitute, most peaceful, and most obliging man on earth, poor Esteban. So when the men returned with the news that the drowned man was not from the neighboring villages either, the women felt an opening of jubilation in the midst of their tears.

"Praise the Lord," they sighed, "he's ours!"

The men thought the fuss was only womanish frivolity. Fatigued because of the difficult nighttime inquiries, all they wanted was to get rid of the bother of the newcomer once and for all before the sun grew strong on that arid, windless day. They improvised a litter with the remains of foremasts and gaffs, tying it together with rigging so that it would bear the weight of the body until they reached the cliffs. They wanted to tie the anchor from a cargo ship to him so that he would sink easily into the deepest waves, where fish are blind and divers die of nostalgia, and bad currents would not bring him back to shore, as had happened with other bodies. But the more they hurried, the more the women thought of ways to waste time. They walked about like startled hens, pecking with the sea charms on their breasts, some interfering on one side to put a scapular of the good wind on the drowned man, some on the other side to put a wrist compass on him, and after a great deal of *get away from there, woman, stay out of the way, look, you almost made me fall on top of the dead man,* the men began to feel mistrust in their livers and started grumbling about why so many main-altar decorations for a stranger, because no matter how many nails and holy-water jars he had on him, the sharks would chew him all the same, but the women kept piling on their junk relics, running back and forth, stumbling, while they released in sighs what they did not in tears, so that the men finally exploded with *since when has there ever been such a fuss over a drifting corpse, a drowned nobody, a piece of cold Wednesday meat.* One of the women, mortified by so much lack of care, then removed the handkerchief from the dead man's face and the men were left breathless too.

He was Esteban. It was not necessary to repeat it for them to recognize him. If they had been told Sir Walter Raleigh,[2] even they might have been impressed with his gringo accent, the macaw on his shoulder, his cannibal-killing blunderbuss, but there could be only one Esteban in the world and there he was, stretched out like a sperm whale, shoeless, wearing the pants of an undersized child, and with those stony nails that had to be cut with a knife. They only had to take the handkerchief off his face to see that he was ashamed, that it was not his fault that he was so big or so heavy or so handsome, and if he had known that this was going to happen, he would have looked for a more discreet place to drown in, seriously, I even would have tied the anchor off a galleon around my neck and staggered off a cliff like someone who doesn't like things in order not to be upsetting people now with this Wednesday dead body, as you people say, in order not to be bothering anyone with this filthy piece of cold meat that doesn't have anything to do with me. There was so much truth in his manner that even the most mistrustful men, the ones who felt the bitterness of endless nights at sea fearing that their women would tire of dreaming about them and begin to dream of drowned men, even they and others who were harder still shuddered in the marrow of their bones at Esteban's sincerity.

That was how they came to hold the most splendid funeral they could conceive of for an abandoned drowned man. Some women who had gone to get flowers in the neighboring villages returned with other women who could not believe what they had been told, and those women went back for more flowers when they saw the dead man, and they brought more and more until there were so many flowers and so many people that it was hard to walk about. At the final moment it pained them to return him to the waters as an orphan and they chose a father and mother from among the best people, and aunts and uncles and cousins, so that through him all the inhabitants of the village became kinsmen. Some sailors who heard weeping from a distance went off

2. English navigator, statesman, courtier, and author (1552–1618).

course and people heard of one who had himself tied to the mainmast, remembering ancient fables about sirens.[3] While they fought for the privilege of carrying him on their shoulders along the steep escarpment by the cliffs, men and women became aware for the first time of the desolation of their streets, the dryness of their courtyards, the narrowness of their dreams as they faced the splendor and beauty of their drowned man. They let him go without an anchor so that he could come back if he wished and whenever he wished, and they all held their breath for the fraction of centuries the body took to fall into the abyss. They did not need to look at one another to realize that they were no longer all present, that they would never be. But they also knew that everything would be different from then on, that their houses would have wider doors, higher ceilings, and stronger floors so that Esteban's memory could go everywhere without bumping into beams and so that no one in the future would dare whisper the big boob finally died, too bad, the handsome fool has finally died, because they were going to paint their house fronts gay colors to make Esteban's memory eternal and they were going to break their backs digging for springs among the stones and planting flowers on the cliffs so that in future years at dawn the passengers on great liners would awaken, suffocated by the smell of gardens on the high seas, and the captain would have to come down from the bridge in his dress uniform, with his astrolabe, his pole star, and his row of war medals and, pointing to the promontory of roses on the horizon, he would say in fourteen languages, look there, where the wind is so peaceful now that it's gone to sleep beneath the beds, over there, where the sun's so bright that the sunflowers don't know which way to turn, yes, that's Esteban's village.

3. Sea nymphs who lured mariners to their destruction, in Greek and Roman mythology.

# George Garrett

*Garrett (1929– ) was born in Orlando, Florida. After some years of schooling at the Sewanee Military Academy he went on to Princeton for his B.A. and M.A. degrees. Ever since, his prodigious output has included verse as well as fiction, satires, reviews, and assorted commentary on the literary scene. He has taught at and directed a number of prestigious writing programs and is an indefatigable traveler as he goes forth year-round to read his work to audiences across the country. At the core of his protean achievement is a trilogy of "Elizabethan" novels,* Death of the Fox *(1971),* The Succession *(1983), and* Entered from the Sun *(1990), which are not only historical novels but also imaginative verbal and fictive explorations of the dimensions of human understanding. Though the main characters are nominally Sir Walter Raleigh, Queen Elizabeth, and Christopher Marlowe—plus innumerable courtiers and servants in their retinues—they are all new creatures on display in multiple and interpenetrating layers of creative pageantry. His other novels include* Which Ones Are the Enemy? *(1961),* Do Lord, Remember Me *(1965), and* The Magic Strip Tease *(1973). Other short stories by Garrett can be found in* A Wreath for Garibaldi *(1969) and* An Evening Performance *(1985). His latest publications include* Days of Our Lives Lie in Fragments: Poems *(1998) and* Bad Man Blues *(1998). His many awards include the Award in Literature from the American Academy of Arts and Letters (1985).*

## Wounded Soldier

**(Cartoon Strip)**

When the time came at last and they removed the wealth of bandages from his head and face, all with the greatest of care as if they were unwinding a precious mummy, the Doctor—he of the waxed, theatrical, upswept mustache and the wet sad eyes of a beagle hound—turned away. Orderlies and aides coughed, looked at floor and ceiling, busied themselves with other tasks. Only the Head Nurse, a fury stiff with starch and smelling of strong soap, looked, pink-cheeked and pale white as fresh flour, over the Veteran's shoulders. She stared back at him, unflinching and expressionless, from the swimming light of the mirror.

No question. It was a terrible wound.

—I am so sorry, the Doctor said.—It's the best we can do for you.

But the Veteran barely heard his words. The Veteran looked deeply into the mirror and stared at the stranger who was now to be himself with an inward wincing that was nearer to the sudden gnawing of love at first sight than of self-pity. It was like being born again. He had, after all, not seen himself since the blinding, burning instant when he was wounded. Ever since then he had been a mystery to himself. How many times he had stared into the mirror through the neat little slits left for his eyes and seen only a snowy skull of gauze and bandages! He imagined himself as a statue waiting to be unveiled. And now he regretted that there was no real audience for the occasion except for the Doctor, who would not look, and the Head Nurse—she for whom no truth could be veiled anyway and hence for whom there could never be any system or subtle aesthetic of exposure or disclosure by any clever series of gradual deceptions. She carried the heavy burden of one who was familiar with every imaginable kind of wound and deformity.

—You're lucky to be alive, she said. —Really lucky.

—I don't know what you will want to do with yourself, the Doctor said. —Of course, you understand that you are welcome to remain here.

—That might be the best thing for any number of good reasons, the Head Nurse said. Then to the Doctor: —Ordinarily cases like this one elect to remain in the hospital.

—Are there others? the Veteran asked.

—Well . . . the Head Nurse admitted, there are none quite like you.

—I should hope not, the Veteran said, suddenly laughing at himself in the mirror. —Under the circumstances it's only fair that I should be able to feel unique.

—I am so sorry, the Doctor said.

Over the Veteran's shoulder in the mirror the Head Nurse smiled back at him.

That same afternoon a High-ranking Officer came to call on him. The Officer kept his eyes fixed on the glossy shine of his boots. After mumbled amenities he explained to the Veteran that while the law certainly allowed him to be a free man, free to come and go as he might choose, he ought to give consideration to the idea that his patriotic duty had not ended with the misfortune of his being stricken in combat. There were, the Officer explained, certain abstract obligations which clearly transcended those written down as statute law and explicitly demanded by the State.

—There are duties, he continued, waxing briefly poetic, which like certain of the cardinal virtues, are deeply disguised. Some of these are truly sublime. Some are rare and splendid like the aroma of a dying arrangement of flowers or the persistent haunting of half-remembered melodies.

The Veteran, who knew something about the music of groans and howls, and something about odors, including, quite recently, the stink of festering and healing, was not to be deceived by this sleight of hand.

—Get to the point, he said.

The High-ranking Officer was flustered, for he was not often addressed by anyone in this fashion. He stammered, spluttered as he offered the Veteran a bonus to his regular pension, a large sum of money, should he freely choose to remain here in the hospital. After all, his care and maintenance would be excellent and he would be free of many commonplace anxieties. Moreover, he need never feel that his situation was anything like being a prisoner. The basic truth about any prisoner is—is it not?—that he is to be deliberately deprived, insofar as possible, of all the usual objects of desire. The large bonus would enable the

Veteran to live well, even lavishly in the hospital if he wanted to.

—Why?

Patiently the Officer pointed out that his appearance in public, in the city or the country, would probably serve to arouse the anguish of the civilian population. So many among the military personnel had been killed or wounded in this most recent war. Wasn't it better for everyone concerned, especially the dependents, the friends and relatives of these unfortunate men, that they be permitted to keep their innocent delusions of swirling battle flags and dimly echoing bugle calls, rather than being forced to confront in fact and flesh the elemental brute ugliness of modern warfare? As an old soldier, or as one old soldier to another, surely the Veteran must and would acknowledge the validity of this argument.

The Veteran nodded and replied that he guessed the Officer also hadn't overlooked the effect his appearance might have on the young men of the nation. Most likely a considerable cooling of patriotic ardor. Probably a noticeable, indeed a measurable, decline in the number of enlistments.

—Just imagine for a moment, the Veteran said, what it would be like if I went out there and stood right next to the recruiting poster at the Post Office. Sort of like a "before and after" advertisement.

At this point the Officer stiffened, scolded, and threatened. He ended by reminding the Veteran that no man, save the One,[1] had ever been perfect and blameless. He suggested to him that, under the strictest scrutiny, his service record would no doubt reveal some error or other, perhaps some offense committed while he was a soldier on active duty which would still render him liable to a court-martial prosecution.

Safe for the time being with his terrible wound, the Veteran laughed out loud and told the Officer that nothing they could do or think of doing to him could ever equal this. That he might as well waste his time trying to frighten a dead man or violate a corpse.

Then the Officer pleaded with the Veteran. He explained that his professional career as a leader of men might be ruined if he failed in the fairly simple assignment of convincing one ordinary common soldier to do as he was told to.

The Veteran, pitying this display of naked weakness, said that he would think about it very seriously. With that much accomplished, the Officer brightened and recovered his official demeanor.

—I imagine it would have been so much more convenient for everyone if I had simply been killed, wouldn't it? the Veteran asked as the Officer was leaving.

Still bowed, still unable to look at him directly, the Officer shrugged his epauleted shoulders and closed the door very quietly behind him.

Nevertheless the Veteran had made up his mind to leave the sanctuary of the hospital. Despite his wound and appearance he was in excellent health, young still and full of energy. And the tiptoeing routine of this place was inef-

1. Jesus Christ.

fably depressing. Yet even though he had decided to leave, even though he was certain he was going soon, he lingered, he delayed, he hesitated. Days went by quietly and calmly, and in the evening when she was off duty, the Head Nurse often came to his room to talk to him about things. Often they played cards. A curious and easy intimacy developed. It seemed almost as if they were husband and wife. On one occasion he spoke to her candidly about this.

—You better be careful, he said. —I'm not sexless.

—No, I guess not, she said. —But I am.

She told him that she thought his plan of going out into the world again was dangerous and foolish.

—Go ahead. Try it and you'll be back here in no time at all, beating on the door with bloody knuckles and begging us to be readmitted, to get back in. You are too young and inexperienced to understand anything about people. Human beings are the foulest things in all creation. They will smell your blood and go mad like sharks. They will kill you if they can. They can't allow you to be out there among them. They will tear you limb from limb. They will strip the meat off your bones and trample your bones to dust. They will turn you into dust and a fine powder and scatter you to the four winds!

—I can see you have been deeply wounded, too, the Veteran said.

At that the Head Nurse laughed out loud. Her whole white mountainous body shook with laughter.

When the Veteran left the hospital he wore a mask. He wanted to find a job and wearing the mask seemed to him to be an act of discretion which would be appreciated. But this, as he soon discovered, was not the case at all. A mask is somehow intolerable. A mask becomes an unbearable challenge. When he became aware of this, when he had considered it, only the greatest exercise of self-discipline checked within him the impulse to gratify their curiosity. It would have been so easy. He could so easily have peeled off his protective mask and thereby given to the ignorant and innocent a new creature for their bad dreams.

One day he came upon a small traveling circus and applied for a job with them.

—What can you do? the Manager asked.

This Manager was a man so bowed down by the weight of weariness and boredom that he seemed at first glance to be a hunchback. He had lived so long and so closely with the oddly gifted and with natural freaks that his lips were pursed as if to spit in contempt at everything under the sun.

—I can be a clown, the Veteran said.

—I have enough clowns, the Manager said. Frankly, I am sick to death of clowns.

—I'll be different from any other clown you have ever seen, the Veteran said.

And then and there he took off his mask.

—Well, this is highly original, the Manager said, studying the crude configuration of the wound with a careful, pitiless interest. This has some definite possibilities.

—I suppose the real question is, will the people laugh?

—Without a doubt. Believe me. Remember this—a man is just as apt to giggle when he is introduced to his executioner as he is to melt into a mess of piss and fear. The real and true talent, the exquisite thing, is of course to be able to raise tears to the throat and to the rims of the eyes, and then suddenly to convert those tears into laughter.

—I could play "The Wounded Soldier."

—Well, we'll try it, the Manager said. I think it's worth a try.

And so that same night he first appeared in his new role. He entered with all the other clowns. The other clowns were conventional. They wore masks and elaborate makeup, sported baggy trousers and long, upturned shoes. They smoked exploding cigars. They flashed red electric noses on and off. They gamboled like a blithe flock of stray lambs, unshepherded. The Veteran, however, merely entered with them and then walked slowly around the ring. He wore a battered tin helmet and a uniform a generation out of date with its old-fashioned, badly wrapped puttees and a high, choker collar. He carried a broken stub of a rifle, hanging in two pieces like an open shotgun. A touch of genius, the Manager had attached a large clump of barbed wire to the seat of his pants.

The Veteran was seriously worried that people would not laugh at him and that he wouldn't be able to keep his job. Slowly, apprehensively he strolled around the enormous circle and turned his wound toward them. He could see nothing at all outside of the zone of light surrounding him. But it was not long before he heard a great gasp from the outer darkness, a shocked intaking of breath so palpable that it was like a sudden breeze. And then he heard the single, high-pitched, hysterical giggle of a woman. And next came all that indrawn air returning, rich and warm. The whole crowd laughed at once. The crowd laughed loudly and the tent seemed to swell like a full sail from their laughter. He could see the circus bandsmen puffing like bullfrogs as they played their instruments and could see the sweat-stained leader waving his baton in a quick, strict, martial time. But he could not hear the least sound of their music. It was engulfed, drowned out, swallowed up by the raging storm of laughter.

Soon afterwards the Veteran signed a contract with the circus. His name was placed prominently on all the advertising posters and materials together with such luminaries as the Highwire Walker, the Trapeze Artists, the Lion Tamer, and the Bareback Riders. He worked only at night. For he soon discovered that by daylight he could see his audience, and they knew that and either refused to laugh or were unable to do so under the circumstances. He concluded that only when they were in the relative safety of the dark would they give themselves over to the impulse of laughter.

His fellow clowns, far from being envious of him, treated him with the greatest respect and admiration. And before much time had passed, he had received the highest compliment from a colleague in that vocation. A clown in a rival circus attempted an imitation of his art. But this clown was not well received. In fact, he was pelted with peanuts and hotdogs, with vegetables and fruit and rotten eggs and bottles. He was jeered at and cat-called out of the ring. Because no amount of clever makeup could rival or compete with the Veteran's unfortunate appearance.

Once a beautiful young woman came to the trailer where he lived and prepared for his performance. She told him that she loved him.

—I have seen every single performance since the first night, she said. I want to be with you always.

The Veteran was not unmoved by her beauty and her naïveté. Besides, he had been alone for quite a long time.

—I'm afraid you don't realize what you are saying, he told her.

—If you won't let me be your mistress, I am going to kill myself, she said.

—That would be a pity.

She told him that more than anything else she wanted to have a child by him.

—If we have a child, then I'll have to marry you.

—Do you think, she asked, that our child would look like you?

—I don't believe that is scientifically possible, he said.

Later when she bore his child, it was a fine healthy baby, handsome and glowing. And then, as inexplicably as she had first come to him, the young woman left him.

After a few successful seasons, the Veteran began to lose some of his ability to arouse laughter from the public. By that time almost all of them had seen him at least once already, and the shock had numbed their responses. Perhaps some of them had begun to pity him.

The Manager was concerned about his future.

—Maybe you should take a rest, go into a temporary retirement, he said. People forget everything very quickly nowadays. You could come back to clowning in no time.

—But what would I ever do with myself?

The Manager shrugged.

—You could live comfortably on your savings and your pension, he said. Don't you have any hobbies or outside interests?

—But I really like it here, the Veteran said. Couldn't I wear a disguise and be one of the regular clowns?

—It would take much too long to learn the tricks of the trade, the Manager said. Besides which your real clowns are truly in hiding. Their whole skill lies in the concealment of anguish. And your talent is all a matter of revelation.

It was not long after this conversation that the Veteran received a letter from the Doctor.

—Your case has haunted me and troubled me, night and day, the Doctor wrote. I have been studying the problem incessantly. And now I think I may be able to do something for you. I make no promises, but I think I can help you. Could you return to the hospital for a thorough examination?

While he waited for the results of all the tests, the Veteran lived in his old room. It was clean and bright and quiet as before. Daily the Head Nurse put a bouquet of fresh flowers in a vase by his bed.

—You may be making a big mistake, she told him. You have lived too long with your wound. Even if the Doctor is successful—and he may be, for he is extremely skillful—you'll never be happy with yourself again.

—Do you know? he began. I was very happy being a clown. For the first and only time in my life all that I had to do was to be myself. But, of course, like everything else, it couldn't last for long.

—You can always come back here. You can stay just as you are now.

—Would you be happy, he asked her, if I came back to the hospital for good just as I am now?

—Oh yes, she said. I believe I would be very happy.

Nevertheless the Veteran submitted to the Doctor's treatment. Once again he became a creature to be wheeled into the glaring of harsh lights, to be surrounded and hovered over by intense masked figures. Once again he was swathed in white bandages and had to suffer through a long time of healing, waiting for the day when he would see himself again. Once again the momentous day arrived, and he stood staring into a mirror as they unwound his bandages.

This time, when the ceremony was completed, he looked into the eyes of a handsome stranger.

—You cannot possibly imagine, the Doctor said, what this moment means to me.

The Head Nurse turned away and could not speak to him.

When he was finally ready to leave the hospital, the Veteran found the High-ranking Officer waiting for him. A gleaming staff car was parked at the curb, and the Veteran noticed by his insignia that the Officer had been promoted.

—We all hope, the Officer said, that you will seriously consider returning to active duty. We need experienced men more than ever now.

—That's a very kind offer, the Veteran said. And I'll certainly consider it in all seriousness.

## MADISON SMARTT BELL on *Wounded Soldier*

"Beauty is only skin-deep," whines the old saw. But what about ugliness?

George Garrett served as an artilleryman late in World War II, but his "Wounded Soldier" bears virtually no resemblance to any other fiction from the postwar period and none whatsoever to the hyperrealistic war novels of Norman Mailer or James Jones, whose narratives center on the careers of very well specified individuals. By contrast, the characters of Garrett's tale are intentionally deployed as *types,* thus named not for their selves but for their roles: Doctor, Nurse, Officer, Veteran, and so on. Furthermore, the important elements of the background situation—war, wounding, circuses, military and medical hierarchies—have been present in human experience, in one form or another, for many centuries. This generalization of both character and situation gives "Wounded Soldier" a timeless, eternal quality. From this point of view the story has less in common with the prevalent trends of late-twentieth-century American fiction than with medieval allegories and morality plays.

But despite its allegorical feeling, the story does not decode itself according to a simple pattern of correspondence with elements on some other plane of religious or philosophical abstraction, as medieval texts like *The Canterbury Tales* and *The Faerie Queen* are supposed to do. Indeed, it is not very easy to decode in any way. There is no easy or obvious moral to be extracted from it, nor can its meaning be very readily restated in the form of abstract paraphrase. That rather obstinate resistance to paraphrase is a modern, twentieth-century quality of "Wounded Soldier." Like a poem—and Garrett is also a significant poet—it cannot be reduced to any other form.

Despite their namelessness and typicality, the characters of "Wounded Soldier" are endowed with some specific qualities that make them look like modern individuals. In the High-ranking Officer and the Doctor we feel personalities mostly shaped by ambition; in the case of the Officer, ambition is tempered by fear. From her treatment of the Veteran, and especially from her deeply cynical pronouncement on human nature when the Veteran tells her he is leaving the hospital, we deduce that she has her own unique inner life, though little of it is reported to the reader. Although the Veteran is to a large extent an "Everyman" figure, so loosely specified that he readily stands for you or for me in the same situation, his inward reactions to that situation are more fully reported (in the first half of the story) and his inner life is noticeably more present to the reader than that of any other character. At the same time he is always masked in one way or another: by bandages, by the disfigurement of the wound itself, by the actual mask he wears out of the hospital, and finally by the medically reconstructed face "of a handsome stranger" he wears at the story's conclusion.

At the end of the story the reader is likely to notice that the Veteran's inner responses are no longer forthcoming. How does he *feel* about his new face? No answer to this question is provided. In fact the reporting of the Veteran's inward reactions tapers off at an earlier point, soon after the first circus audience's burst of laughter echoes and confirms the earlier laughing fit of the Head Nurse.

Despite its surface context, "Wounded Soldier" does not by any means seem to be a paean to pacifism or an allegorical argument against war. Rather, its overtly symbolical manner seems meant to address the relations between the inner and outer self—realms of private and public identity—which theme runs powerfully through most of George Garrett's vast body of work. Correspondences between inward and outward wounds, both direct and inverse, are suggested everywhere in the story, but whether such wounds can ever be healed is left entirely to the reader to decide.

# Charlotte Perkins Gilman

*Gilman (1860–1935) was born in Hartford, Connecticut. Aspiring to be an artist, she briefly attended the Rhode Island School of Design and married a man working in the same field. After the birth of her daughter she went into a deep and long-drawn depression. The medical treatment available not only failed to help her, it angered her. From that anger sprang her famous story "The Yellow Wallpaper" and a long career as a lecturer and a writer of tracts and books expounding feminist causes. Her second marriage, when she had regained her mental health, was a solid and productive one. Among her writings are two novels,* What Diantha Did *(1910) and* The Crux *(1911).*

## The Yellow Wallpaper[1]

It is very seldom that mere ordinary people like John and myself secure ancestral halls for the summer.

A colonial mansion, a hereditary estate, I would say a haunted house and reach the height of romantic felicity—but that would be asking too much of fate!

Still I will proudly declare that there is something queer about it.

Else, why should it be let so cheaply? And why have stood so long untenanted?

John laughs at me, of course, but one expects that.

John is practical in the extreme. He has no patience with faith, an intense horror of superstition, and he scoffs openly at any talk of things not to be felt and seen and put down in figures.

John is a physician, and *perhaps*—(I would not say it to a living soul, of course, but this is dead paper and a great relief to my mind)—*perhaps* that is one reason I do not get well faster.

You see, he does not believe I am sick! And what can one do?

If a physician of high standing, and one's own husband, assures friends and

1. This story was first published in the *New England Magazine* in January 1892. Alfred Bendixen, to whom we are indebted for information concerning the publication history of this story, is preparing a version using the manuscript as copy text. The only change we have made in the magazine text is to make *wallpaper* one word; in the magazine it appears both as one word and as a hypenated compound.

relatives that there is really nothing the matter with one but temporary nervous depression—a slight hysterical tendency[2]—what is one to do?

My brother is also a physician, and also of high standing, and he says the same thing.

So I take phosphates or phosphites—whichever it is—and tonics, and air and exercise, and journeys, and am absolutely forbidden to "work" until I am well again.

Personally, I disagree with their ideas.

Personally, I believe that congenial work, with excitement and change, would do me good.

But what is one to do?

I did write for a while in spite of them; but it *does* exhaust me a good deal—having to be so sly about it, or else meet with heavy opposition.

I sometimes fancy that in my condition, if I had less opposition and more society and stimulus—but John says the very worst thing I can do is to think about my condition, and I confess it always makes me feel bad.

So I will let it alone and talk about the house.

The most beautiful place! It is quite alone, standing well back from the road, quite three miles from the village. It makes me think of English places that you read about, for there are hedges and walls and gates that lock, and lots of separate little houses for the gardeners and people.

There is a *delicious* garden! I never saw such a garden—large and shady, full of box-bordered paths, and lined with long grape-covered arbors with seats under them.

There were greenhouses, but they are all broken now.

There was some legal trouble, I believe, something about the heirs and co-heirs; anyhow, the place has been empty for years.

That spoils my ghostliness, I am afraid, but I don't care—there is something strange about the house—I can feel it.

I even said so to John one moonlight evening, but he said what I felt was a draught, and shut the window.

I get unreasonably angry with John sometimes. I'm sure I never used to be so sensitive. I think it is due to this nervous condition.

But John says if I feel so, I shall neglect proper self-control; so I take pains to control myself—before him, at least, and that makes me very tired.

I don't like our room a bit. I wanted one downstairs that opened on the piazza and had roses all over the window, and such pretty old-fashioned chintz hangings! But John would not hear of it.

He said there was only one window and not room for two beds, and no near room for him if he took another.

He is very careful and loving, and hardly lets me stir without special direction.

I have a schedule prescription for each hour in the day; he takes all care

2. At the time this story was written, *hysteria* was a term used loosely to describe a wide variety of symptoms, thought to be particularly prevalent among women, that indicated emotional disturbance or dysfunction. Depression, anxiety, excitability, and vague somatic complaints were among the conditions treated as "hysteria."

from me, and so I feel basely ungrateful not to value it more.

He said we came here solely on my account, that I was to have perfect rest and all the air I could get. "Your exercise depends on your strength, my dear," said he, "and your food somewhat on your appetite; but air you can absorb all the time." So we took the nursery at the top of the house.

It is a big, airy room, the whole floor nearly, with windows that look all ways, and air and sunshine galore. It was nursery first and then playroom and gymnasium, I should judge; for the windows are barred for little children, and there are rings and things in the walls.

The paint and paper look as if a boys' school had used it. It is stripped off—the paper—in great patches all around the head of my bed, about as far as I can reach, and in a great place on the other side of the room low down. I never saw a worse paper in my life. One of those sprawling flamboyant patterns committing every artistic sin.

It is dull enough to confuse the eye in following, pronounced enough to constantly irritate and provoke study, and when you follow the lame uncertain curves for a little distance they suddenly commit suicide—plunge off at outrageous angles, destroy themselves in unheard-of contradictions.

The color is repellant, almost revolting; a smouldering unclean yellow, strangely faded by the slow-turning sunlight. It is a dull yet lurid orange in some places, a sickly sulphur tint in others.

No wonder the children hated it! I should hate it myself if I had to live in this room long.

There comes John, and I must put this away—he hates to have me write a word.

• • • • • •

We have been here two weeks, and I haven't felt like writing before, since that first day.

I am sitting by the window now, up in this atrocious nursery, and there is nothing to hinder my writing as much as I please, save lack of strength.

John is away all day, and even some nights when his cases are serious.

I am glad my case is not serious!

But these nervous troubles are dreadfully depressing.

John does not know how much I really suffer. He knows there is no reason to suffer, and that satisfies him.

Of course it is only nervousness. It does weigh on me so not to do my duty in any way!

I mean to be such a help to John, such a real rest and comfort, and here I am a comparative burden already!

Nobody would believe what an effort it is to do what little I am able—to dress and entertain, and order things.

It is fortunate Mary is so good with the baby. Such a dear baby!

And yet I *cannot* be with him, it makes me so nervous.

I suppose John never was nervous in his life. He laughs at me so about this wallpaper!

At first he meant to repaper the room, but afterwards he said that I was letting it get the better of me, and that nothing was worse for a nervous patient than to give way to such fancies.

He said that after the wallpaper was changed it would be the heavy bedstead, and then the barred windows, and then that gate at the head of the stairs, and so on.

"You know the place is doing you good," he said, "and really, dear, I don't care to renovate the house just for a three months' rental."

"Then do let us go downstairs," I said. "There are such pretty rooms there."

Then he took me in his arms and called me a blessed little goose, and said he would go down cellar, if I wished, and have it whitewashed into the bargain.

But he is right enough about the beds and windows and things.

It is as airy and comfortable a room as anyone need wish, and, of course, I would not be so silly as to make him uncomfortable just for a whim.

I'm really getting quite fond of the big room, all but that horrid paper.

Out of one window I can see the garden—those mysterious deep-shaded arbors, the riotous old-fashioned flowers, and bushes and gnarly trees.

Out of another I get a lovely view of the bay and a little private wharf belonging to the estate. There is a beautiful shaded lane that runs down there from the house. I always fancy I see people walking in these numerous paths and arbors, but John has cautioned me not to give way to fancy in the least. He says that with my imaginative power and habit of story-making, a nervous weakness like mine is sure to lead to all manner of excited fancies, and that I ought to use my will and good sense to check the tendency. So I try.

I think sometimes that if I were only well enough to write a little it would relieve the press of ideas and rest me.

But I find I get pretty tired when I try.

It is so discouraging not to have any advice and companionship about my work. When I get really well, John says we will ask Cousin Henry and Julia down for a long visit; but he says he would as soon put fireworks in my pillowcase as to let me have those stimulating people about now.

I wish I could get well faster.

But I must not think about that. This paper looks to me as if it *knew* what a vicious influence it had!

There is a recurrent spot where the pattern lolls like a broken neck and two bulbous eyes stare at you upside down.

I get positively angry with the impertinence of it and the everlastingness. Up and down and sideways they crawl, and those absurd unblinking eyes are everywhere. There is one place where two breadths didn't match, and the eyes go all up and down the line, one a little higher than the other.

I never saw so much expression in an inanimate thing before, and we all know how much expression they have! I used to lie awake as a child and get more entertainment and terror out of blank walls and plain furniture than most children could find in a toy-store.

I remember what a kindly wink the knobs of our big old bureau used to have, and there was one chair that always seemed like a strong friend.

I used to feel that if any of the other things looked too fierce I could always hop into that chair and be safe.

The furniture in this room is no worse than inharmonious, however, for we had to bring it all from downstairs. I suppose when this was used as a playroom they had to take the nursery things out, and no wonder! I never saw such ravages as the children have made here.

The wallpaper, as I said before, is torn off in spots, and it sticketh closer than a brother—they must have had perseverance as well as hatred.

Then the floor is scratched and gouged and splintered, the plaster itself is dug out here and there, and this great heavy bed which is all we found in the room, looks as if it had been through the wars.

But I don't mind it a bit—only the paper.

There comes John's sister. Such a dear girl as she is, and so careful of me! I must not let her find me writing.

She is a perfect and enthusiastic housekeeper, and hopes for no better profession. I verily believe she thinks it is the writing which made me sick!

But I can write when she is out, and see her a long way off from these windows.

There is one that commands the road, a lovely shaded winding road, and one that just looks off over the country. A lovely country, too, full of great elms and velvet meadows.

This wallpaper has a kind of sub-pattern in a different shade, a particularly irritating one, for you can only see it in certain lights, and not clearly then.

But in the places where it isn't faded and where the sun is just so—I can see a strange, provoking, formless sort of figure that seems to skulk about behind that silly and conspicuous front design.

There's sister on the stairs!

• • • • • •

Well, the Fourth of July is over! The people are all gone, and I am tired out. John thought it might do me good to see a little company, so we just had Mother and Nellie and the children down for a week.

Of course I didn't do a thing. Jennie sees to everything now.

But it tired me all the same.

John says if I don't pick up faster he shall send me to Weir Mitchell[3] in the fall.

But I don't want to go there at all. I had a friend who was in his hands once, and she says he is just like John and my brother, only more so!

Besides, it is such an undertaking to go so far.

I don't feel as if it was worthwhile to turn my hand over for anything, and I'm getting dreadfully fretful and querulous.

I cry at nothing, and cry most of the time.

Of course I don't when John is here, or anybody else, but when I am alone.

And I am alone a good deal just now. John is kept in town very often by serious cases, and Jennie is good and lets me alone when I want her to.

3. Silas Weir Mitchell (1829–1914), American physician, novelist, and specialist in nerve disorders, popularized the "rest cure" in the management of hysteria, nervous breakdowns, and related disorders. A friend of W. D. Howells (1837–1920), he was the model for the nerve specialist in Howells's *The Shadow of a Dream* (1890).

So I walk a little in the garden or down that lovely lane, sit on the porch under the roses, and lie down up here a good deal.

I'm getting really fond of the room in spite of the wallpaper. Perhaps *because* of the wallpaper.

It dwells in my mind so!

I lie here on this great immovable bed—it is nailed down, I believe—and follow that pattern about by the hour. It is as good as gymnastics, I assure you. I start, we'll say, at the bottom, down in the corner over there where it has not been touched, and I determine for the thousandth time that I *will* follow that pointless pattern to some sort of conclusion.

I know a little of the principle of design, and I know this thing was not arranged on any laws of radiation, or alternation, or repetition, or symmetry, or anything else that I ever heard of.

It is repeated, of course, by the breadths, but not otherwise.

Looked at in one way, each breadth stands alone; the bloated curves and flourishes—a kind of "debased Romanesque"[4] with delirium tremens—go waddling up and down in isolated columns of fatuity.

But, on the other hand, they connect diagonally, and the sprawling outlines run off in great slanting waves of optic horror, like a lot of wallowing sea-weeds in full chase.

The whole thing goes horizontally, too, at least it seems so, and I exhaust myself trying to distinguish the order of its going in that direction.

They have used a horizontal breadth for a frieze,[5] and that adds wonderfully to the confusion.

There is one end of the room where it is almost intact, and there, when the crosslights fade and the low sun shines directly upon it, I can almost fancy radiation after all—the interminable grotesque seems to form around a common center and rush off in headlong plunges of equal distraction.

It makes me tired to follow it. I will take a nap, I guess.

• • • • • • •

I don't know why I should write this.

I don't want to.

I don't feel able.

And I know John would think it absurd. But I *must* say what I feel and think in some way—it is such a relief!

But the effort is getting to be greater than the relief.

Half the time now I am awfully lazy, and lie down ever so much.

John says I mustn't lose my strength, and has me take cod liver oil and lots of tonics and things, to say nothing of ale and wine and rare meat.

Dear John! He loves me very dearly, and hates to have me sick. I tried to have a real earnest reasonable talk with him the other day, and tell him how I wish he would let me go and make a visit to Cousin Henry and Julia.

But he said I wasn't able to go, nor able to stand it after I got there; and I

4. Romanesque style is here associated with ornamental complexity and repeated motifs and figures. 5. An ornamental band used as a border at the top of the wall.

did not make out a very good case for myself, for I was crying before I had finished.

It is getting to be a great effort for me to think straight. Just this nervous weakness, I suppose.

And dear John gathered me up in his arms, and just carried me upstairs and laid me on the bed, and sat by me and read to me till it tired my head.

He said I was his darling and his comfort and all he had, and that I must take care of myself for his sake, and keep well.

He says no one but myself can help me out of it, that I must use my will and self-control and not let any silly fancies run away with me.

There's one comfort—the baby is well and happy, and does not have to occupy this nursery with the horrid wallpaper.

If we had not used it, that blessed child would have! What a fortunate escape! Why, I wouldn't have a child of mine, an impressionable little thing, live in such a room for worlds.

I never thought of it before, but it is lucky that John kept me here after all, I can stand it so much easier than a baby, you see.

Of course I never mention it to them any more—I am too wise—but I keep watch for it all the same.

There are things in that paper that nobody knows about but me, or ever will.

Behind that outside pattern the dim shapes get clearer every day.

It is always the same shape, only very numerous.

And it is like a woman stooping down and creeping about behind that pattern. I don't like it a bit. I wonder—I begin to think—I wish John would take me away from here!

• • • • • •

It is so hard to talk with John about my case, because he is so wise, and because he loves me so.

But I tried it last night.

It was moonlight. The moon shines in all around just as the sun does.

I hate to see it sometimes, it creeps so slowly, and always comes in by one window or another.

John was asleep and I hated to waken him, so I kept still and watched the moonlight on that undulating wallpaper till I felt creepy.

The faint figure behind seemed to shake the pattern, just as if she wanted to get out.

I got up softly and went to feel and see if the paper *did* move, and when I came back John was awake.

"What is it, little girl?" he said. "Don't go walking about like that—you'll get cold."

I thought it was a good time to talk, so I told him that I really was not gaining here, and that I wished he would take me away.

"Why, darling!" said he. "Our lease will be up in three weeks, and I can't see how to leave before.

"The repairs are not done at home, and I cannot possibly leave town just now. Of course if you were in any danger, I could and would, but you really are better, dear, whether you can see it or not. I am a doctor, dear, and I know. You are gaining flesh and color, your appetite is better, I feel really much easier about you."

"I don't weigh a bit more," said I, "nor as much; and my appetite may be better in the evening when you are here but it is worse in the morning when you are away!"

"Bless her little heart!" said he with a big hug. "She shall be as sick as she pleases! But now let's improve the shining hours by going to sleep, and talk about it in the morning!"

"And you won't go away?" I asked gloomily.

"Why, how can I, dear? It is only three weeks more and then we will take a nice little trip of a few days while Jennie is getting the house ready. Really, dear, you are better!"

"Better in body perhaps—" I began, and stopped short, for he sat up straight and looked at me with such a stern, reproachful look that I could not say another word.

"My darling," said he, "I beg of you, for my sake and for our child's sake, as well as for your own, that you will never for one instant let that idea enter your mind! There is nothing so dangerous, so fascinating, to a temperament like yours. It is a false and foolish fancy. Can you not trust me as a physician when I tell you so?"

So of course I said no more on that score, and we went to sleep before long. He thought I was asleep first, but I wasn't, and lay there for hours trying to decide whether that front pattern and the back pattern really did move together or separately.

• • • • • •

On a pattern like this, by daylight, there is a lack of sequence, a defiance of law, that is a constant irritant to a normal mind.

The color is hideous enough, and unreliable enough, and infuriating enough, but the pattern is torturing.

You think you have mastered it, but just as you get well under way in following, it turns a back-somersault and there you are. It slaps you in the face, knocks you down, and tramples upon you. It is like a bad dream.

The outside pattern is a florid arabesque, reminding one of a fungus. If you can imagine a toadstool in joints, an interminable string of toadstools, budding and sprouting in endless convolutions—why, that is something like it.

That is, sometimes!

There is one marked peculiarity about this paper, a thing nobody seems to notice but myself, and that is that it changes as the light changes.

When the sun shoots in through the east window—I always watch for that first long, straight ray—it changes so quickly that I never can quite believe it.

That is why I watch it always.

By moonlight—the moon shines in all night when there is a moon—I wouldn't know it was the same paper.

At night in any kind of light, in twilight, candlelight, lamplight, and worst of all by moonlight, it becomes bars! The outside pattern, I mean, and the woman behind it is as plain as can be.

I didn't realize for a long time what the thing was that showed behind, that dim sub-pattern, but now I am quite sure it is a woman.

By daylight she is subdued, quiet. I fancy it is the pattern that keeps her so still. It is so puzzling. It keeps me quiet by the hour.

I lie down ever so much now. John says it is good for me, and to sleep all I can.

Indeed he started the habit by making me lie down for an hour after each meal.

It is a very bad habit I am convinced, for you see, I don't sleep.

And that cultivates deceit, for I don't tell them I'm awake—O no!

The fact is I am getting a little afraid of John.

He seems very queer sometimes, and even Jennie has an inexplicable look.

It strikes me occasionally, just as a scientific hypothesis, that perhaps it is the paper!

I have watched John when he did not know I was looking, and come into the room suddenly on the most innocent excuses, and I've caught him several times *looking at the paper!* And Jennie too. I caught Jennie with her hand on it once.

She didn't know I was in the room, and when I asked her in a quiet, a very quiet voice, with the most restrained manner possible, what she was doing with the paper—she turned around as if she had been caught stealing, and looked quite angry—asked me why I should frighten her so!

Then she said that the paper stained everything it touched, that she had found yellow smooches on all my clothes and John's, and she wished we would be more careful!

Did not that sound innocent? But I know she was studying that pattern, and I am determined that nobody shall find it out but myself!

• • • • • •

Life is very much more exciting now than it used to be. You see I have something more to expect, to look forward to, to watch. I really do eat better, and am more quiet than I was.

John is so pleased to see me improve! He laughed a little the other day, and said I seemed to be flourishing in spite of my wallpaper.

I turned it off with a laugh. I had no intention of telling him it was *because* of the wallpaper—he would make fun of me. He might even want to take me away.

I don't want to leave now until I have found it out. There is a week more, and I think that will be enough.

• • • • • •

I'm feeling so much better!

I don't sleep much at night, for it is so interesting to watch developments; but I sleep a good deal during the daytime.

In the daytime it is tiresome and perplexing.

There are always new shoots on the fungus, and new shades of yellow all over it. I cannot keep count of them, though I have tried conscientiously.

It is the strangest yellow, that wallpaper! It makes me think of all the yellow things I ever saw—not beautiful ones like buttercups, but old, foul, bad yellow things.

But there is something else about that paper—the smell! I noticed it the moment we came into the room, but with so much air and sun it was not bad. Now we have had a week of fog and rain, and whether the windows are open or not, the smell is here.

It creeps all over the house.

I find it hovering in the dining-room, skulking in the parlor, hiding in the hall, lying in wait for me on the stairs.

It gets into my hair.

Even when I go to ride, if I turn my head suddenly and surprise it—there is that smell!

Such a peculiar odor, too! I have spent hours in trying to analyze it, to find what it smelled like.

It is not bad—at first—and very gentle, but quite the subtlest, most enduring odor I ever met.

In this damp weather it is awful, I wake up in the night and find it hanging over me.

It used to disturb me at first. I thought seriously of burning the house—to reach the smell.

But now I am used to it. The only thing I can think of that it is like is the *color* of the paper! A yellow smell.

There is a very funny mark on this wall, low down, near the mopboard. A streak that runs round the room. It goes behind every piece of furniture, except the bed, a long, straight, even *smooch,* as if it had been rubbed over and over.

I wonder how it was done and who did it, and what they did it for. Round and round and round—round and round and round—it makes me dizzy!

• • • • • •

I really have discovered something at last.

Through watching so much at night, when it changes so, I have finally found out.

The front pattern *does* move—and no wonder! The woman behind shakes it!

Sometimes I think there are a great many women behind, and sometimes only one, and she crawls around fast, and her crawling shakes it all over.

Then in the very bright spots she keeps still, and in the very shady spots she just takes hold of the bars and shakes them hard.

And she is all the time trying to climb through. But nobody could climb through that pattern—it strangles so; I think that is why it has so many heads.

They get through, and then the pattern strangles them off and turns them upside down, and makes their eyes white!

If those heads were covered or taken off it would not be half so bad.

. . . . . . .

I think that woman gets out in the daytime!

And I'll tell you why—privately—I've seen her!

I can see her out of every one of my windows!

It is the same woman, I know, for she is always creeping, and most women do not creep by daylight.

I see her in that long shaded lane, creeping up and down. I see her in those dark grape arbors, creeping all around the garden.

I see her on that long road under the trees, creeping along, and when a carriage comes she hides under the blackberry vines.

I don't blame her a bit. It must be very humiliating to be caught creeping by daylight!

I always lock the door when I creep by daylight. I can't do it at night, for I know John would suspect something at once.

And John is so queer now that I don't want to irritate him. I wish he would take another room! Besides, I don't want anybody to get that woman out at night but myself.

I often wonder if I could see her out of all the windows at once.

But, turn as fast as I can, I can only see out of one at one time.

And though I always see her, she *may* be able to creep faster than I can turn! I have watched her sometimes away off in the open country, creeping as fast as a cloud shadow in a wind.

. . . . . . .

If only that top pattern could be gotten off from the under one! I mean to try it, little by little.

I have found out another funny thing, but I shan't tell it this time! It does not do to trust people too much.

There are only two more days to get this paper off, and I believe John is beginning to notice. I don't like the look in his eyes.

And I heard him ask Jennie a lot of professional questions about me. She had a very good report to give.

She said I slept a good deal in the daytime.

John knows I don't sleep very well at night, for all I'm so quiet!

He asked me all sorts of questions, too, and pretended to be very loving and kind.

As if I couldn't see through him!

Still, I don't wonder he acts so, sleeping under this paper for three months.

It only interests me, but I feel sure John and Jennie are affected by it.

. . . . . . .

Hurrah! This is the last day, but it is enough. John is to stay in town over night, and won't be out until this evening.

Jennie wanted to sleep with me—the sly thing; but I told her I should undoubtedly rest better for a night all alone.

That was clever, for really I wasn't alone a bit! As soon as it was moonlight and that poor thing began to crawl and shake the pattern, I got up and ran to help her.

I pulled and she shook, I shook and she pulled, and before morning we had peeled off yards of that paper.

A strip about as high as my head and half around the room.

And then when the sun came and that awful pattern began to laugh at me, I declared I would finish it today!

We go away tomorrow, and they are moving all my furniture down again to leave things as they were before.

Jennie looked at the wall in amazement, but I told her merrily that I did it out of pure spite at the vicious thing.

She laughed and said she wouldn't mind doing it herself, but I must not get tired.

How she betrayed herself that time!

But I am here, and no person touches this paper but Me—not *alive!*

She tried to get me out of the room—it was too patent! But I said it was so quiet and empty and clean now that I believed I would lie down again and sleep all I could; and not to wake me even for dinner—I would call when I woke.

So now she is gone, and the servants are gone, and the things are gone, and there is nothing left but that great bedstead nailed down, with the canvas mattress we found on it.

We shall sleep downstairs tonight, and take the boat home tomorrow.

I quite enjoy the room, now it is bare again.

How those children did tear about here!

This bedstead is fairly gnawed!

But I must get to work.

I have locked the door and thrown the key down into the front path.

I don't want to go out, and I don't want to have anybody come in, till John comes.

I want to astonish him.

I've got a rope up here that even Jennie did not find. If that woman does get out, and tries to get away, I can tie her!

But I forgot I could not reach far without anything to stand on!

This bed will *not* move!

I tried to lift and push it until I was lame, and then I got so angry I bit off a little piece at one corner—but it hurt my teeth.

Then I peeled off all the paper I could reach standing on the floor. It sticks horribly and the pattern just enjoys it! All those strangled heads and bulbous eyes and waddling fungus growths just shriek with derision!

I am getting angry enough to do something desperate. To jump out of the window would be admirable exercise, but the bars are too strong even to try.

Besides I wouldn't do it. Of course not. I know well enough that a step like that is improper and might be misconstrued.

I don't like to *look* out of the windows even—there are so many of those creeping women, and they creep so fast.

I wonder if they all come out of that wallpaper as I did?

But I am securely fastened now by my well-hidden rope—you don't get *me* out in the road there!

I suppose I shall have to get back behind the pattern when it comes night, and that is hard!

It is so pleasant to be out in this great room and creep around as I please!

I don't want to go outside. I won't, even if Jennie asks me to.

For outside you have to creep on the ground, and everything is green instead of yellow.

But here I can creep smoothly on the floor, and my shoulder just fits in that long smooch around the wall, so I cannot lose my way.

Why there's John at the door!

It is no use, young man, you can't open it!

How he does call and pound!

Now he's crying to Jennie for an axe.

It would be a shame to break down that beautiful door!

"John dear!" said I in the gentlest voice. "The key is down by the front steps, under a plantain leaf!"

That silenced him for a few moments.

Then he said—very quietly indeed, "Open the door, my darling!"

"I can't," said I. "The key is down by the front door under a plantain leaf!"

And then I said it again, several times, very gently and slowly, and said it so often that he had to go and see, and he got it of course, and came in. He stopped short by the door.

"What is the matter?" he cried. "For God's sake, what are you doing!"

I kept on creeping just the same, but I looked at him over my shoulder.

"I've got out at last," said I, "in spite of you and Jane! And I've pulled off most of the paper, so you can't put me back!"

Now why should that man have fainted? But he did, and right across my path by the wall, so that I had to creep over him every time!

# Nadine Gordimer

*Gordimer (1923– ) was born in Springs, South Africa, where her parents had immigrated from Europe. By her own account, her formal education was uneven and minimal, but the reading she did outside of school led to an auspicious beginning of her career as a writer when she began to publish in distinguished American magazines in the late 1940s. Her first collection of these stories was* Face to Face *(1949) followed soon after by* The Soft Voice of the Serpent *(1952). Her first novel* The Lying Days *was published the following year. Her first work tended to be lyrical and personal. As the social and political crisis in South Africa deepened, so did her concern with it. The ferment and violence of repression and the onrushing surge for independence became increasingly the subject of her fiction. Throughout the world she was recognized as the conscience of her troubled homeland. Her primary focus is on the middle class and the terror they encounter in their attempts to come to terms with a history of social injustice. Among her other novels are* A World of Strangers *(1976),* Burger's Daughter *(1979),* A Sport of Nature *(1987),* My Son's Story *(1990), and* None to Accompany Me *(1994). More of her short stories can be found in* Six Feet of the Country *(1956),* A Soldier's Embrace *(1980),* Something Out There *(1984),* Jump *(1991), and* The House Gun *(1998). In 1991 she was awarded the Nobel Prize.*

## A Soldier's Embrace

The day the cease-fire was signed she was caught in a crowd. Peasant boys from Europe who had made up the colonial army and freedom fighters whose column had marched into town were staggering about together outside the barracks, not three blocks from her house in whose rooms, for ten years, she had heard the blurred parade-ground bellow of colonial troops being trained to kill and be killed.

The men weren't drunk. They linked and swayed across the street; because all that had come to a stop, everything *had* to come to a stop: they surrounded cars, bicycles, vans, nannies with children, women with loaves of bread or basins of mangoes on their heads, a road gang with picks and shovels, a Coca-Cola truck, an old man with a barrow who bought bottles and bones. They were grinning and laughing amazement. That it could be: there they were, bumping into each other's bodies in joy, looking into each other's rough faces, all eyes crescent-shaped, brimming greeting. The words were in languages not mutually comprehensible, but the cries were new, a whooping and crowing all understood. She was bumped and jostled and she let go, stopped trying to move in any self-determined direction. There were two soldiers in front of her, blocking her off by their clumsy embrace (how do you do it, how do you do what you've never done before) and the embrace opened like a door and took her in—a pink hand with bitten nails grasping her right arm, a black hand with a big-dialled watch and thong bracelet pulling at her left elbow. Their three heads collided gaily, musk of sweat and tang of strong sweet soap clapped a mask to her nose and mouth. They all gasped with delicious shock. They were saying things to each other. She put up an arm round each neck, the rough pile of an army haircut on one side, the soft negro hair on the other, and kissed them both on the cheek. The embrace broke. The crowd wove her away behind backs, arms, jogging heads; she was returned to and took up the will of her direction again—she was walking home from the post office, where she had just sent a telegram to relatives abroad: ALL CALM DON'T WORRY.

The lawyer came back early from his offices because the courts were not sitting although the official celebration holiday was not until next day. He described to his wife the rally before the Town Hall, which he had watched from the office-building balcony. One of the guerilla leaders (not the most important; he on whose head the biggest price had been laid would not venture so soon and deep into the territory so newly won) had spoken for two hours from the balcony of the Town Hall. "Brilliant. Their jaws dropped. Brilliant. They've never heard anything on that level: precise, reasoned—none of them would ever have believed it possible, out of the bush. You should have seen de Poorteer's[1] face. He'd like to be able to get up and open his mouth like that. And be listened to like that . . . " The Governor's handicap did not even bring the sympathy accorded to a stammer; he paused and gulped between words. The blacks had always used a portmanteau name for him that meant the-crane-who-is-trying-to-swallow-the-bullfrog.

One of the members of the black underground organization that could now come out in brass-band support of the freedom fighters had recognized the lawyer across from the official balcony and given him the freedom fighters' salute. The lawyer joked about it, miming, full of pride. "You should have been there—should have seen him, up there in the official party. I told you—really—you ought to have come to town with me this morning."

"And what did you do?" She wanted to assemble all details.

"Oh I gave the salute in return, chaps in the street saluted *me* . . . everybody was doing it. *It was marvellous.* And the police standing by; just to think, last month—only last week—you'd have been arrested."

"Like thumbing your nose at them," she said, smiling.

"Did anything go on around here?"

"Muchanga was afraid to go out all day. He wouldn't even run up to the post office for me!" Their servant had come to them many years ago, from service in the house of her father, a colonial official in the Treasury.

"But there was no excitement?"

1. The governor's.

She told him: "The soldiers and some freedom fighters mingled outside the barracks. I got caught for a minute or two. They were dancing about; you couldn't get through. All very good-natured.—Oh, I sent the cable."

An accolade, one side a white cheek, the other a black. The white one she kissed on the left cheek, the black one on the right cheek, as if these were two sides of one face.

That vision, version, was like a poster; the sort of thing that was soon peeling off dirty shopfronts and bus shelters while the months of wrangling talks preliminary to the take-over by the black government went by.

To begin with, the cheek was not white but pale or rather sallow, the poor boy's pallor of winter in Europe (that draft must have only just arrived and not yet seen service) with homesick pimples sliced off by the discipline of an army razor. And the cheek was not black but opaque peat-dark, waxed with sweat round the plump contours of the nostril. As if she could return to the moment again, she saw what she had not consciously noted: there had been a narrow pink strip in the darkness near the ear, the sort of tender stripe of healed flesh revealed when a scab is nicked off a little before it is ripe. The scab must have come away that morning: the young man picked at it in the troop carrier or truck (whatever it was the freedom fighters had; the colony had been told for years that they were supplied by the Chinese and Russians indiscriminately) on the way to enter the capital in triumph.

According to newspaper reports, the day would have ended for the two young soldiers in drunkenness and whoring. She was, apparently, not yet too old to belong to the soldier's embrace of all that a land-mine in the bush might have exploded for ever. That was one version of the incident. Another: the opportunity taken by a woman not young enough to be clasped in the arms of the one who (same newspaper, while the war was on, expressing the fears of the colonists for their women) would be expected to rape her.

She considered this version.

She had not kissed on the mouth, she had not sought anonymous lips and tongues in the licence of festival. Yet she had kissed. Watching herself again, she knew that. She had—god knows why—kissed them on either cheek, his left, his right. It was deliberate, if a swift impulse: she had distinctly made the move.

She did not tell what happened not because her husband would suspect licence in her, but because he would see her—born and brought up in the country as the daughter of an enlightened white colonial official, married to a white liberal lawyer well known for his defence of blacks in political trials—as giving free expression to liberal principles.

She had not told, she did not know what had happened.

She thought of a time long ago when a school camp had gone to the sea and immediately on arrival everyone had run down to the beach from the train, tripping and tearing over sand dunes of wild fig, aghast with ecstatic shock at the meeting with the water.

De Poorteer was recalled and the lawyer remarked to one of their black friends, "The crane has choked on the bullfrog. I hear that's what they're saying in the Quarter."

The priest who came from the black slum that had always been known simply by that anonymous term did not respond with any sort of glee. His reserve implied it was easy to celebrate; there were people who "shouted freedom too loud all of a sudden."

The lawyer and his wife understood: Father Mulumbua was one who had shouted freedom when it was dangerous to do so, and gone to prison several times for it, while certain people, now on the Interim Council set up to run the country until the new government took over, had kept silent. He named a few, but reluctantly. Enough to confirm their own suspicions—men who perhaps had made some deal with the colonial power to place its interests first, no matter what sort of government might emerge from the new constitution? Yet when the couple plunged into discussion their friend left them talking to each other while he drank his beer and gazed, frowning as if at a headache or because the sunset light hurt his eyes behind his spectacles, round her huge-leaved tropical plants that bowered the terrace in cool humidity.

They had always been rather proud of their friendship with him, this man in a cassock who wore a clenched fist carved of local ebony as well as a silver cross round his neck. His black face was habitually stern—a high seriousness balanced by sudden splurting laughter when they used to tease him over the fist—but never inattentively ill-at-ease.

"What was the matter?" She answered herself; "I had the feeling he didn't want to come here." She was using a paper handkerchief dipped in gin to wipe greenfly off the back of a pale new leaf that had shaken itself from its folds like a cut-out paper lantern.

"Good lord, he's been here hundreds of times."

"—Before, yes."

What things were they saying?

With the shouting in the street and the swaying of the crowd, the sweet powerful presence that confused the senses so that sound, sight, stink (sweat, cheap soap) ran into one tremendous sensation, she could not make out words that came so easily.

Not even what she herself must have said.

A few wealthy white men who had been boastful in their support of the colonial war and knew they would be marked down by the blacks as arch exploiters, left at once. Good riddance, as the lawyer and his wife remarked. Many ordinary white people who had lived contentedly, without questioning its actions, under the colonial government, now expressed an enthusiastic intention to help build a nation, as the newspapers put it. The lawyer's wife's neighbourhood butcher was one. "I don't mind blacks." He was expansive with her, in his shop that he had occupied for twelve years on a licence available only to white people. "Makes no difference to me who you are so long as you're honest." Next to a chart showing a beast mapped according to the cuts of meat it provided, he had hung a picture of the most important leader of the freedom fighters, expected to be first President. People like the butcher turned out with their babies clutching pennants when the leader drove through the town from the airport.

There were incidents (newspaper euphemism again) in the Quarter. It was to be expected. Political fractions, tribally based, who had not fought the war, wanted to share power with the freedom fighters' Party. Muchanga no longer went down to the Quarter on his day off. His friends came to see him and sat privately on their hunkers near the garden compost heap. The ugly mansions of the rich who had fled stood empty on the bluff above the sea, but it was said they would make money out of them yet—they would be bought as ambassadorial residences when independence came, and with it many black and yellow diplomats. Zealots who claimed they belonged to the Party burned shops and houses of the poorer whites who lived, as the lawyer said, "in the inevitable echelon of colonial society," closest to the Quarter. A house in the lawyer's street was noticed by his wife to be accommodating what was certainly one of those families, in the outhouses; green nylon curtains had appeared at the garage window, she reported. The suburb was pleasantly overgrown and well-to-do; no one rich, just white professional people and professors from the university. The barracks was empty now, except for an old man with a stump and a police uniform stripped of insignia, a friend of Muchanga, it turned out, who sat on a beer-crate at the gates. He had lost his job as night-watchman when one of the rich people went away, and was glad to have work.

The street had been perfectly quiet; except for that first day.

The fingernails she sometimes still saw clearly were bitten down until embedded in a thin line of dirt all round, in the pink blunt fingers. The thumb and thick fingertips were turned back coarsely even while grasping her. Such hands had never been allowed to take possession. They were permanently raw, so young, from unloading coal, digging potatoes from the frozen Northern Hemisphere, washing hotel dishes. He had not been killed, and now that day of the cease-fire was over he would be delivered back across the sea to the docks, the stony farm, the scullery of the grand hotel. He would have to do anything he could get. There was unemployment in Europe where he had returned, the army didn't need all the young men any more.

A great friend of the lawyer and his wife, Chipande, was coming home from exile. They heard over the radio he was expected, accompanying the future President as confidential secretary, and they waited to hear from him.

The lawyer put up his feet on the empty chair where the priest had sat, shifting it to a comfortable position by hooking his toes, free in sandals, through the slats. "Imagine, Chipande!" Chipande had been almost a protégé—but they didn't like the term, it smacked of patronage. Tall, cocky, casual Chipande, a boy from the slummiest part of the Quarter, was recommended by the White Fathers' Mission (was it by Father Mulumbua himself?—the lawyer thought so, his wife was not sure they remembered correctly) as a bright kid who wanted to be articled to a lawyer. That was asking a lot, in those days—nine years ago. He never finished his apprenticeship because while he and his employer were soon close friends, and the kid picked up political theories from the books in the house he made free of, he became so involved in politics that he had to skip the country one jump ahead of a detention order signed by the crane-who-was-trying-to-swallow-the-bullfrog.

After two weeks, the lawyer phoned the offices the guerilla-movement-become-Party had set up openly in the town but apparently Chipande had an office in the former colonial secretariat. There he had a secretary of his own; he wasn't easy to reach. The lawyer left a message. The lawyer and his wife saw from the newspaper pictures he hadn't changed much: he had a beard and had adopted the Muslim cap favoured by political circles in exile on the East Coast.

He did come to the house eventually. He had the distracted, insistent friendliness of one who has no time to re-establish intimacy; it must be taken as read. And it must not be displayed. When he remarked on a shortage of accommodation for exiles now become officials, and the lawyer said the house was far too big for two people, he was welcome to move in and regard a self-contained part of it as his private living quarters, he did not answer but went on talking generalities. The lawyer's wife mentioned Father Mulumbua, whom they had not seen since just after the cease-fire. The lawyer added, "There's obviously some sort of big struggle going on, he's fighting for his political life there in the Quarter." "Again," she said, drawing them into a reminder of what had only just become their past.

But Chipande was restlessly following with his gaze the movements of old Muchanga, dragging the hose from plant to plant, careless of the spray; "You remember who this is, Muchanga?" she had said when the visitor arrived, yet although the old man had given, in their own language, the sort of respectful greeting even an elder gives a young man whose clothes and bearing denote rank and authority, he was not in any way overwhelmed nor enthusiastic—perhaps he secretly supported one of the rival factions?

The lawyer spoke of the latest whites to leave the country—people who had got themselves quickly involved in the sort of currency swindle that draws more outrage than any other kind of crime, in a new state fearing the flight of capital.[2] "Let them go, let them go. Good riddance." And he turned to talk of other things—there were so many more important questions to occupy the attention of the three old friends.

But Chipande couldn't stay. Chipande could not stay for supper; his beautiful long velvety black hands with their pale lining (as she thought of the palms) hung impatiently between his knees while he sat forward in the chair, explaining, adamant against persuasion. He should not have been there, even now; he had official business waiting, sometimes he drafted correspondence until one or two in the morning. The lawyer remarked how there hadn't been a proper chance to talk; he wanted to discuss those fellows in the Interim Council Mulumbua was so warily distrustful of—what did Chipande know?

Chipande, already on his feet, said something dismissing and very slightly disparaging, not about the Council members but of Mulumbua—a reference to his connection with the Jesuit missionaries as an influence that "comes through." "But I must make a note to see him sometime."

It seemed that even black men who presented a threat to the Party could be discussed only among black men themselves, now. Chipande put an arm around each of his friends as for the brief official moment of a photograph, left

2. Exportation of financial resources necessary to the economy of a new government.

them; he who used to sprawl on the couch arguing half the night before dossing down in the lawyer's pyjamas. "As soon as I'm settled I'll contact you. You'll be around, ay?"

"Oh we'll be around." The lawyer laughed, referring, for his part, to those who were no longer. "Glad to see you're not driving a Mercedes!" he called with reassured affection at the sight of Chipande getting into a modest car. How many times, in the old days, had they agreed on the necessity for African leaders to live simply when they came to power!

On the terrace to which he turned back, Muchanga was doing something extraordinary—wetting a dirty rag with Gilbey's. It was supposed to be his day off, anyway; why was he messing about with the plants when one wanted peace to talk undisturbed?

"Is those things again, those thing is killing the leaves."

"For heaven's sake, he could use methylated for that! Any kind of alcohol will do! Why don't you get him some?"

There were shortages of one kind and another in the country, and gin happened to be something in short supply.

Whatever the hand had done in the bush had not coarsened it. It, too, was suède-black, and elegant. The pale lining was hidden against her own skin where the hand grasped her left elbow. Strangely, black does not show toil—she remarked this as one remarks the quality of a fabric. The hand was not as long but as distinguished by beauty as Chipande's. The watch a fine piece of equipment for a fighter. There was something next to it, in fact looped over the strap by the angle of the wrist as the hand grasped. A bit of thong with a few beads knotted where it was joined as a bracelet. Or amulet. Their babies wore such things; often their first and only garment. Grandmothers or mothers attached it as protection. It had worked; he was alive at cease-fire. Some had been too deep in the bush to know, and had been killed after the fighting was over. He had pumped his head wildly and laughingly at whatever it was she—they—had been babbling.

The lawyer had more free time than he'd ever remembered. So many of his clients had left; he was deputed to collect their rents and pay their taxes for them, in the hope that their property wasn't going to be confiscated—there had been alarmist rumours among such people since the day of the cease-fire. But without the rich whites there was little litigation over possessions, whether in the form of the children of dissolved marriages or the houses and cars claimed by divorced wives. The Africans had their own ways of resolving such redistribution of goods. And a gathering of elders under a tree was sufficient to settle a dispute over boundaries or argue for and against the guilt of a woman accused of adultery. He had had a message, in a round-about way, that he might be asked to be consultant on constitutional law to the Party, but nothing seemed to come of it. He took home with him the proposals for the draft constitution he had managed to get hold of. He spent whole afternoons in his study making notes for counter or improved proposals he thought he would send to Chipande or one of the other people he knew in high positions: every time he glanced up, there through his open windows was Muchanga's little company at the bottom of the garden. Once, when he saw they had straggled off, he wandered down himself to clear his head (he got drowsy, as he never did when he used to work twelve hours a day at the office). They ate dried shrimps, from the market: that's what they were doing! The ground was full of bitten-off heads and black eyes on stalks. His wife smiled. "They bring them. Muchanga won't go near the market since the riot." "It's ridiculous. Who's going to harm him?"

There was even a suggestion that the lawyer might apply for a professorship at the university. The chair of the Faculty of Law was vacant, since the students had demanded the expulsion of certain professors engaged during the colonial regime—in particular of the fuddy-duddy (good riddance) who had gathered dust in the Law chair, and the quite decent young man (pity about him) who had had Political Science. But what professor of Political Science could expect to survive both a colonial regime and the revolutionary regime that defeated it? The lawyer and his wife decided that since he might still be appointed in some consultative capacity to the new government it would be better to keep out of the university context, where the students were shouting for Africanization, and even an appointee with his credentials as a fighter of legal battles for blacks against the colonial regime in the past might not escape their ire.

Newspapers sent by friends from over the border gave statistics for the number of what they termed "refugees" who were entering the neighbouring country. The papers from outside also featured sensationally the inevitable mistakes and misunderstandings, in a new administration, that led to several foreign businessmen being held for investigation by the new regime. For the last fifteen years of colonial rule, Gulf[3] had been drilling for oil in the territory, and just as inevitably it was certain that all sorts of questionable people, from the point of view of the regime's determination not to be exploited preferentially, below the open market for the highest bidder in ideological as well as economic terms, would try to gain concessions.

His wife said, "The butcher's gone."

He was home, reading at his desk; he could spend the day more usefully there than at the office, most of the time. She had left after breakfast with her fisherman's basket that she liked to use for shopping, she wasn't away twenty minutes. "You mean the shop's closed?" There was nothing in the basket. She must have turned and come straight home.

"Gone. It's empty. He's cleared out over the weekend."

She sat down suddenly on the edge of the desk; and after a moment of silence, both laughed shortly, a strange, secret, complicit laugh. "Why, do you think?" "Can't say. He certainly charged, if you wanted a decent cut. But meat's so hard to get, now; I thought it was worth it—justified."

The lawyer raised his eyebrows and pulled down his mouth: "Exactly." They understood; the man probably knew he was marked to run into trouble for profiteering—he must have been paying through the nose for his supplies on the black market, anyway, didn't have much choice.

Shops were being looted by the unemployed and loafers (there had always

3. Gulf Oil Company, an international giant of the industry.

been a lot of unemployed hanging around for the pickings of the town) who felt the new regime should entitle them to take what they dared not before. Radio and television shops were the most favoured objective for gangs who adopted the freedom fighters' slogans. Transistor radios were the portable luxuries of street life; the new regime issued solemn warnings, over those same radios, that looting and violence would be firmly dealt with but it was difficult for the police to be everywhere at once. Sometimes their actions became street battles, since the struggle with the looters changed character as supporters of the Party's rival political factions joined in with the thieves against the police. It was necessary to be ready to reverse direction, quickly turning down a side street in detour if one encountered such disturbances while driving around town. There were bodies sometimes; both husband and wife had been fortunate enough not to see any close up, so far. A company of the freedom fighters' army was brought down from the north and installed in the barracks to supplement the police force; they patrolled the Quarter, mainly. Muchanga's friend kept his job as gatekeeper although there were armed sentries on guard: the lawyer's wife found that a light touch to mention in letters to relatives in Europe.

"Where'll you go now?"

She slid off the desk and picked up her basket. "Supermarket, I suppose. Or turn vegetarian." He knew that she left the room, smiling, because she didn't want him to suggest Muchanga ought to be sent to look for fish in the markets along the wharf in the Quarter. Muchanga was being allowed to indulge in all manner of eccentric refusals; for no reason, unless out of some curious sentiment about her father?

She avoided walking past the barracks because of the machine guns the young sentries had in place of rifles. Rifles pointed into the air but machine guns pointed to the street at the level of different parts of people's bodies, short and tall, the backsides of babies slung on mothers' backs, the round heads of children, her fisherman's basket—she knew she was getting like the others; what she felt was afraid. She wondered what the butcher and his wife had said to each other. Because he was at least one whom she had known. He had sold the meat she had bought that these women and their babies passing her in the street didn't have the money to buy.

It was something quite unexpected and outside their own efforts that decided it. A friend over the border telephoned and offered a place in a lawyers' firm of highest repute there, and some prestige in the world at large, since the team had defended individuals fighting for freedom of the press and militant churchmen upholding freedom of conscience on political issues. A telephone call; as simple as that. The friend said (and the lawyer did not repeat this even to his wife) they would be proud to have a man of his courage and convictions in the firm. He could be satisfied he would be able to uphold the liberal principles everyone knew he had always stood for; there were many whites, in that country still ruled by a white minority, who deplored the injustices under which their black population suffered etc. and believed you couldn't ignore the need for peaceful change etc.

His offices presented no problem; something called Africa Seabeds (Formosan Chinese who had gained a concession to ship seaweed and dried shrimps in exchange for rice) took over the lease and the typists. The senior clerks and the current articled clerk (the lawyer had always given a chance to young blacks, long before other people had come round to it—it wasn't only the secretary to the President who owed his start to him) he managed to get employed by the new Trades Union Council; he still knew a few blacks who remembered the times he had acted for black workers in disputes with the colonial government. The house would just have to stand empty, for the time being. It wasn't imposing enough to attract an embassy but maybe it would do for a Chargé d'Affaires—it was left in the hands of a half-caste letting agent who was likely to stay put: only whites were allowed in, at the country over the border. Getting money out was going to be much more difficult than disposing of the house. The lawyer would have to keep coming back, so long as this remained practicable, hoping to find a loophole in exchange control regulations.

She was deputed to engage the movers. In their innocence, they had thought it as easy as that! Every large vehicle, let alone a pantechnicon,[4] was commandeered for months ahead. She had no choice but to grease a palm,[5] although it went against her principles, it was condoning a practice they believed a young black state must stamp out before corruption took hold. He would take his entire legal library, for a start; that was the most important possession, to him. Neither was particularly attached to furniture. She did not know what there was she felt she really could not do without. Except the plants. And that was out of the question. She could not even mention it. She did not want to leave her towering plants, mostly natives of South America and not Africa, she supposed, whose aerial tubes pushed along the terrace brick erect tips extending hourly in the growth of the rainy season, whose great leaves turned shields to the spatter of Muchanga's hose glancing off in a shower of harmless arrows, whose two-hand-span trunks were smooth and grooved in one sculptural sweep down their length, or carved by the drop of each dead leaf-stem with concave medallions marking the place and building a pattern at once bold and exquisite. Such things would not travel; they were too big to give away.

The evening she was beginning to pack the books, the telephone rang in the study. Chipande—and he called her by her name, urgently, commandingly—"What is this all about? Is it true, what I hear? Let me just talk to him—"

"Our friend," she said, making a long arm, receiver at the end of it, towards her husband.

"But you can't leave!" Chipande shouted down the phone. "*You* can't go! I'm coming round. *Now.*"

She went on packing the legal books while Chipande and her husband were shut up together in the living-room.

"He cried. You know, he actually cried." Her husband stood in the doorway alone.

"I know—that's what I've always liked so much about them, whatever they do. They feel."

The lawyer made a face: there it is, it happened; hard to believe.

4. Large moving van. 5. To give bribes.

"Rushing in here, after nearly a year! I said, but we haven't seen you, all this time . . . he took no notice. Suddenly he starts pressing me to take the university job, raising all sorts of objections, why not this . . . that. And then he really wept, for a moment."

They got on with packing books like builder and mate deftly handling and catching bricks.

And the morning they were to leave it was all done; twenty-one years of life in that house gone quite easily into one pantechnicon. They were quiet with each other, perhaps out of apprehension of the tedious search of their possessions that would take place at the border; it was said that if you struck over-conscientious or officious freedom fighter patrols they would even make you unload a piano, a refrigerator or washing machine. She had bought Muchanga a hawker's licence, a hand-cart, and stocks of small commodities. Now that many small shops owned by white shopkeepers had disappeared, there was an opportunity for humble itinerant black traders. Muchanga had lost his fear of the town. He was proud of what she had done for him and she knew he saw himself as a rich merchant; this was the only sort of freedom he understood, after so many years as a servant. But she also knew, and the lawyer sitting beside her in the car knew she knew, that the shortages of the goods Muchanga could sell from his cart, the sugar and soap and matches and pomade and sunglasses, would soon put him out of business. He promised to come back to the house and look after the plants every week; and he stood waving, as he had done every year when they set off on holiday. She did not know what to call out to him as they drove away. The right words would not come again; whatever they were, she left them behind.

# William Goyen

*Goyen (1915–1983) was a native of Texas and attended Rice University in that state. Among his books are* Ghost and Flesh *(1952), a collection of stories, and* Faces of Blood Kindred *(1960), a collection of ten stories plus a novella. His last book was* Half a Look of Cain, *published in 1994.*

# Ghost and Flesh, Water and Dirt

Was somebody here while ago acallin for you . . .

*O don't say that, don't tell me who . . . was he fair and had a wrinkle in his chin? I wonder was he the one . . . describe me his look, whether the eyes were pale light-colored and swimmin and wild and shifty; did he bend a little at the shoulders was his face agrievin what did he say where did he go, which-away, hush don't tell me; wish I could keep him but I cain't, so go, go (but come back).*

Cause you know honey there's a time to go roun and tell and there's a time to set still (and let a ghost grieve ya); so listen to me while I tell, cause I'm in my time a tellin and you better run fast if you don wanna hear what I tell, cause I'm goin ta tell . . .

Dreamt last night again I saw pore Raymon Emmons, all last night seen im plain as day. There uz tears in iz glassy eyes and iz face uz all meltin away. O I was broken of my sleep and of my night disturbed, for I dreamt of pore Raymon Emmons live as ever.

He came on the sleepin porch where I was sleepin (and he's there to stay) ridin a purple horse (like King was), and then he got off and tied im to the bedstead and come and stood over me and commenced iz talkin. All night long he uz talkin and talkin, his speech (whatever he uz sayin) uz like steam streamin outa the mouth of a kettle, streamin and streamin and streamin. At first I said in my dream, "Will you do me the favor of tellin me just who in the world you can be, will you please show the kindness to tell me who you can be, breakin my sleep and disturbin my rest?" "I'm Raymon Emmons," the steamin voice said, "and I'm here to stay; putt out my things that you've putt away, putt out my oatmeal bowl and putt hot oatmeal in it, get out my rubberboots when it rains, iron my clothes and fix my supper . . . I never died and I'm here to stay."

*(Oh go way ole ghost of Raymon Emmons, whisperin in my ear on the pilla at night; go way ole ghost and lemme be! Quit standin over me like that, all night standin there sayin somethin to me . . . behave ghost of Raymon Emmons, behave yoself and lemme be! Lemme get out and go roun, lemme put on those big ole rubberboots and go clompin. . . . )*

Now you shoulda known that Raymon Emmons. *There* was *somebody,* I'm tellin you. Oh he uz a bright thang, quick 'n fair, tall, about six feet, real lean and a devlish face full of snappin eyes, he had eyes all over his face, didn't miss a thang, that man, saw everythang; and a clean brow. He was a rayroad man, worked for the Guff Coast Lines all iz life, our house always smelt like a train.

When I first knew of him he was livin at the Boardinhouse acrost from the depot (oh that uz years and years ago), and I uz in town and wearin my first pumps when he stopped me on the corner and ast me to do him the favor of tellin him the size a my foot. I was not afraid atall to look at him and say the size a my foot uz my own affair and would he show the kindness to not be so fresh. But when he said I only want to know because there's somebody livin up in New Waverley about your size and age and I want to send a birthday present of some houseshoes to, I said that's different; and we went into Richardson's store, to the back where the shoes were, and tried on shoes till he found the kind and size to fit me and this person in New Waverley. I didn't tell im that the pumps I'uz wearin were Sistah's and not my size (when I got home and Mama said why'd it take you so long? I said it uz because I had to walk so slow in Sistah's pumps).

Next time I saw im in town (and I made it a point to look for im, was why I come to town), I went up to im and said do you want to measure my foot again Raymon Emmons, ha! And he said any day in the week I'd measure that pretty foot; and we went into Richardson's and he bought *me* a pair of white summer pumps with a pink tie (and I gave Sistah's pumps back to her). Miz Richardson said my lands Margy you buyin lotsa shoes lately, are you goin to take a trip (O I took a trip, and one I come back from, too).

We had other meetins and was plainly in love; and when we married, runnin off to Groveton to do it, everybody in town said things about the marriage because he uz thirty and I uz seventeen.

We moved to this house owned by the Picketts, with a good big clothesyard and a swing on the porch, and I made it real nice for me and Raymon Emmons, made curtains with fringe, putt jar-dinears on the front bannisters and painted the fern buckets. We furnished those unfurnished rooms with our brand new lives, and started goin along.

Between those years and this one I'm tellin about them in, there seems a space as wide and vacant and silent as the Neches River, with my life *then* standin on one bank and my life *now* standin on the other, lookin acrost at each other like two diffrent people wonderin who the other can really be.

How did Raymon Emmons die? Walked right through a winda and tore hisself all to smithereens. Walked right through a second-story winda at the depot and fell broken on the tracks—nothin much left a Raymon Emmons after he walked through that winda—broken his crown, hon, broken his crown. But he lingered for three days in Victry Hospital and then passed, sayin just before he passed away, turnin towards me, "I hope you're satisfied. . . ."

Why did he die? From grievin over his daughter and mine, Chitta was her name, that fell off a horse they uz both ridin on the Emmonses' farm. Horse's name was King and we had im shot.

Buried im next to Chitta's grave with iz insurance, two funerals in as many weeks, then set aroun blue in our house, cryin all day and cryin half the night, sleep all broken and disturbed of my rest, thinkin oh if he'd come knockin at that door right now I'd let him in, oh I'd let Raymon Emmons in! After he died, I set aroun sayin who's gonna meet all the hours in a day with me, whatever is in each one—*all those hours*—who's gonna be with me in the mornin, in the ashy afternoons that we always have here, in the nights of lightnin who's goan be lyin there, seen in the flashes and makin me feel as safe as if he uz a lightnin rod (and honey he *wuz*); who's gonna be like a light turned on in a dark room when I go in, who's gonna be at the door when I open it, who's goin to be there when I wake up or when I go to sleep, who's goin to call my name? I cain't stand a life of just me and our furniture in a room, who's gonna *be* with me? Honey it's true that you never miss water till the well runs dry, tiz truly true.

Went to talk to the preacher, but he uz no earthly help, regalin me with iz pretty talk, he's got a tongue that will trill out a story pretty as a bird on a bobwire fence—but meanin what?—sayin "the wicked walk on every hand when the vilest men are exalted"—now what uz that mean?—; went to set and talk with Fursta Evans in her Millinary Shop (who's had her share of tumult in her sad life, but never shows it) but she uz no good, sayin "Girl pick up the pieces and go on . . . here try on this real cute hat" (that woman had nothin but hats on her mind—even though she taught me *my* life, grant cha *that*—for brains she's got hats). Went to the graves on Sundays carryin potplants and cryin over the mounds, one long wide one and one little un—how sad are the little graves a childrun, childrun ought not to have to die it's not right to bring death to childrun, they're just little toys grownups play with or neglect (thas how some of em die, too, honey, but won't say no more bout that); but all childrun go to Heaven so guess it's best—the grasshoppers flyin all roun me (they say graveyard grasshoppers spit tobacco juice and if it gets in your eye it'll putt your eye out) and an armadilla diggin in the crepemyrtle bushes—sayin "dirt lay light on Raymon Emmons and iz child," and thinkin "all my life is dirt I've got a famly of dirt." And then I come back to set and scratch aroun like an armadilla myself in these rooms, alone; but honey that uz no good either.

And then one day, I guess it uz a year after my famly died, there uz a knock on my door and it uz Fursta Evans knockin when I opened it to see. And she said "honey now listen I've come to visit with you and to try to tell you somethin: why are you so glued to Raymon Emmonses memry when you never cared a hoot bout him while he was on earth, you despised all the Emmonses, said they was just trash, wouldn't go to the farm on Christmas or Thanksgivin, wouldn't set next to em in church, broke pore Raymon Emmons's heart because you'd never let Chitta stay with her grandparents and when you finely did the Lord purnished you for bein so hateful by takin Chitta. Then you blamed it on Raymon Emmons, hounded im night and day, said he killed Chitta, drove im stark ravin mad. While Raymon Emmons was live you'd never even give him the time a day, wouldn't lift a hand for im, you never would cross the street for im, to you he uz just a dog in the yard, and you know it, and now that he's dead you grieve yo life away and suddenly fall in love with im." Oh she tole me good and proper—said, "you never loved im till you lost im, till it uz too late, said now set up and listen to me and get some brains in yo head, chile." Said, "cause listen honey, I've had four husbands in my time, two of em died and two of em quit me, but each one of em I thought was goin to be the *only* one, and I took each one for that, then let im go when he uz gone, kept goin roun, kept ready, we got to honey, left the gate wide open for anybody to come through, friend or stranger, ran with the hare and hunted with the hound, honey we got to *greet* life not grieve life," is what she said.

"Well," I said, "I guess that's the way life is, you don't know what you have till you don't have it any longer, till you've lost it, till it's too late."

"Anyway," Fursta said, "little cattle little care—you're beginnin again now, fresh and empty handed, it's later and it's shorter, yo life, but go on from *here* not *there*," she said. "You've had one kind of a life, had a husband, putt im in iz grave (now leave im there!), had a child and putt her away, too; start over, hon, the world don't know it, the world's fresh as ever—it's a new day, putt some powder on yo face and start goin roun. Get you a job, and try that; or take you a trip. . . ."

"But I got to stay in this house," I said. "Feel like I cain't budge. Raymon Emmons is here, live as ever, and I cain't get away from im. He keeps me fastened to this house."

"Oh poot," Fursta said, lightin a cigarette. "Honey you're losin ya mine. Now listen here, put on those big ole rubberboots and go clompin, go steppin high and wide—cause listen here, if ya don't they'll have ya up in the Asylum at Rusk sure's as shootin, specially if you go on talkin about this ghost of Raymon Emmons the way you do."

"But if I started goin roun, what would people say?"

"You can tell em it's none of their beeswax. Cause listen honey, the years uv passed and are passin and you in ever one of em, passin too, and not gettin any younger—yo hair's gettin bunchy and the lines clawed roun yo mouth and eyes by the glassy claws of cryin sharp tears. We got to paint ourselves up and go on, young *outside,* anyway—cause listen honey the sun comes up and the sun crosses over and *goes down*—and while the sun's up we got to get on that fence and crow. Cause night muss fall—and then thas all. Come on, les go roun; have us a Sataday night weddin ever Sataday night; forget this ole patched-faced ghost I hear you talkin about. . . ."

"In this town?" I said. "I hate this ole town, always rain fallin—'cept this ain't rain it's rainin, Fursta, it's rainin mildew. . . ."

"O deliver me!" Fursta shouted out, and putt out her cigarette, "you won't do. Are you afraid you'll *melt?*"

"I wish I'd melt—and run down the drains. Wish I uz rain, fallin on the dirt of certain graves I know and seepin down into the dirt, could lie in the dirt with Raymon Emmons on one side and Chitta on the other. Wish I uz dirt. . . ."

"I wish you are just crazy," Fursta said. "Come on, you're gonna take a trip. You're gonna get on a train and take a nonstop trip and get off at the end a the line and start all over again new as a New Year's Baby, baby. I'm gonna see to that."

"Not on no train, all the king's men couldn't get me to ride a train again, no siree. . . ."

"Oh no train my foot," said Fursta.

"But what'll I use for money please tell me," I said.

"With Raymon Emmons's insurance of course—it didn't take all of it to bury im, I know. Put some acreage tween you and yo past life, and maybe some new friends and scenery too, and pull down the shade on all the water that's gone under the bridge; and come back here a new woman. Then if ya want new you can come into my millinary shop with me."

"Oh," I said, "is the world still there? Since Raymon Emmons walked through that winda seems the whole world's gone, the whole world went out through that winda when he walked through it."

Closed the house, sayin 'goodbye ghost of Raymon Emmons,' bought my ticket at the depot, deafenin my ears to the sound of the tickin telegraph machine, got on a train and headed west to California. Day and night the trainwheels on the traintracks said *Raymon Emmons Raymon Emmons Raymon Emmons*, and I looked through the winda at dirt and desert, miles and miles of dirt, thinkin I wish I uz dirt I wish I uz dirt. O I uz vile with grief.

In California the sun was out, wide, and everybody and everything lighted up; and oh honey the world *was* still there. I decided to stay awhile. I started my new life with Raymon Emmons's insurance money. It uz in San Diego, by the ocean and with mountains of dirt standin gold in the blue waters. A war had come. I was alone for awhile, but not for long. Got me a job in an airplane factory, met a lotta girls, met a lotta men. I worked in fusilodges.

There uz this Nick Natowski, a brown clean Pollock from Chicargo, real wile, real Satanish. What kind of a life did he start me into? I don't know how it started, but it did, and in a flash we uz everwhere together, dancin and swimmin and *everthing*. He uz in the war and in the U.S. Navy, but we didn't think of the war or of water. I just liked him tight as a glove in iz uniform, I just liked him laughin, honey, I just liked him *ever* way he was, and that uz all I knew. And then one night he said, "Margy I'm goin to tell you somethin, goin on a boat, be gone a long long time, goin in a week." Oh I cried and had a nervous fit and said, 'Why do you have to go when there's these thousands of others all aroun San Diego that could go?' and he said, "We're goin away to Coronada for that week, you and me, and what happens there will be enough to keep and save for the whole time we're apart." We went, honey, Nick and me, to Coronada, I mean we really *went.* Lived like a king and queen—where uz my life behind me that I thought of onct and a while like a story somebody was whisperin to me?—laughed and loved and I cried; and after that week at Coronada, Nick left for sea on his boat, to the war, sayin I want you to know baby I'm leavin you my allotment.

I was blue, so blue, all over again, but this time it uz diffrent someway.

guess cause I uz blue for somethin live this time and not dead under dirt, I don't know; anyway I kept goin roun, kept my job in fusilodges and kept goin roun. There was this friend of Nick Natowski's called George, and we went together some. "But why doesn't Nick Natowski write me, George?" I said. "Because he cain't yet," George said, "but just wait and he'll write." I kept waitin but no letter ever came, and the reason he didn't write when he could of, finely, was because his boat was sunk and Nick Natowski in it.

Oh what have I ever done in this world, I said, to send my soul to torment? Lost one to dirt and one to water, makes my life a life of mud, why was I ever put to such a test as this O Lord, I said. I'm goin back home to where I started, gonna get on that train and backtrack to where I started from, want to look at dirt awhile, can't stand to look at water. I rode the train back. Somethin drew me back like I'd been pastured on a rope in California.

Come back to this house, opened it up and aired it all out, and when I got back you know who was there in that house? That ole faithful ghost of Raymon Emmons. He'd been there, waitin, while I went aroun, in my goin roun time, and was there to have me back. While I uz gone he'd covered everythin in our house with the breath a ghosts, fine ghost dust over the tables and chairs and a curtain of ghost lace over my bed on the sleepinporch.

Took me this job in Richardson's Shoe Shop (this town's big now and got money in it, the war 'n oil made it rich, ud never know it as the same if you hadn't known it before; and Fursta Evans married to a rich widower), set there fittin shoes on measured feet all day—it all started in a shoestore measurin feet and it ended that way—can you feature that? Went home at night to my you-know-what.

Comes ridin onto the sleepinporch ever night regular as clockwork, ties iz horse to the bedstead and I say hello Raymon Emmons and we start our conversation. Don't ask me what he says or what I say, but ever night is a night full of talkin, and it lasts the whole night through. Oh onct in a while I get real blue and want to hide away and just set with Raymon Emmons in my house, cain't budge, don't see daylight nor dark, putt away my wearin clothes, couldn't walk outa that door if my life depended on it. But I set real still and let it all be, claimed by that ghost until he unclaims me—and then I get up and go roun, free, and that's why I'm here, settin with you here in the Pass Time Club, drinkin this beer and tellin you all I've told.

Honey, why am I tellin all this? Oh all our lives! So many things to tell. And I keep em to myself a long long time, tight as a drum, won't open my mouth, just set in my blue house with that ole ghost agrievin me, until there comes a time of tellin, a time to tell, a time to putt on those big ole rubberboots.

Now I believe in *tellin,* while we're live and goin roun; when the tellin times comes I say spew it out, we just got to tell things, things in our lives, things that've happened, things we've fancied and things we dream about or are haunted by. Cause you know honey the time to shut you mouth and set moultin and mildewed in yo room, grieved by a ghost and fastened to a chair, comes back roun again, don't worry honey, it comes roun again. There's a time ta tell and a time ta set still ta let a ghost grieve ya. So listen to me while I tell, cause I'm in my time atellin, and you better run fast if you don wanna hear what I tell, cause I'm goin ta tell. . . .

The world is changed, let's drink ower beer and have us a time, tell and tell and tell, let's get that hot bird in a cole bottle tonight. Cause next time you think you'll see me and hear me tell, you won't: I'll be flat where I cain't budge again, like I wuz all that year, settin and hidin way . . . until the time comes roun again when I can say oh go way ole ghost of Raymon Emmons, go way ole ghost and lemme be!

Cause I've learned this and I'm gonna tell ya: there's a time for live things and a time for dead, for ghosts and for flesh 'n bones: all life is just a sharin of ghosts and flesh. Us humans are part ghost and part flesh—part fire and part ash—but I think maybe the ghost part is the longest lastin, the fire blazes out the ashes last forever. I had fire in California (and water putt it out) and ash in Texis (and it went to dirt); but I say now, while I'm tellin you, there's a world both places, a world where there's ghosts and a world where there's flesh, and I believe the real right way is to take our worlds, of ghosts or of flesh, take each one as they come and take what comes in em: take a ghost and grieve with im, settin still; and take the flesh 'n bones and go roun; and even run out to meet what worlds come in to our lives, strangers (like you), and ghosts (like Raymon Emmons) and lovers (like Nick Natowski) . . . and be what each world wants us to be.

And I think that ghosts, if you set still with em long enough, can give you over to flesh 'n bones; and that flesh 'n bones, if you go roun when it's time, can send you back to a faithful ghost. One provides the other.

Saw pore Raymon Emmons all last night, all last night seen im plain as day.

## GEORGE GARRETT on *Ghost and Flesh, Water and Dust*

William Goyen was probably the most original story writer of my lifetime—certainly in my language and of my nation. His stories are strange at first to the reader (or writer) coming to them without any warning. After experience and engagement and pleasure, they are wonderful and strange. They are also, at one and the same time, deeply simple, as a child's fairy tale can be simple yet highly sophisticated, impeccable line by line.

I love his people, the ordinary folks riddled with extraordinary thoughts and feelings, of his east Texas home place; and I love the language he first borrows from them, then returns reduced to its essential poetry.

But of all the many large and small things that capture and delight me in the fiction of William Goyen, and in this story especially, it is the music that moves me most. Not surprising—he was, after all, a prize-winning composer; and in several interviews he compared his kind of fiction to folk music. In his preface to *The Collected Stories of William Goyen* he said it again and aptly: "For me, story telling is a rhythm, a charged movement, a chain of pulses or beats. . . . Mostly, then, I've cared about the buried song in somebody, and sought it passionately; or the music in what happened. And so I have thought of my stories as folk song, as ballad, or rhapsody."

More than most story writers, then, Goyen created a language, what he called "a lyric speech," and used it in forms of fiction that demand to be listened to. I often play for my students a tape recording of Goyen reading this very story and even before they have seen the text of it. The text serves only to confirm what they have heard. Here lipreading, even reading out loud, is a good thing to do. Listen and you will find this Goyen story rich with melodies and motifs. See how, later, long after you have finished reading, this story will continue to haunt you like a persistent, remembered tune.

# Allan Gurganus

*Gurganus (1947– ) was born in Rocky Mount, North Carolina, and attended Sarah Lawrence and the Iowa Writer's Workshop. His novels include* Oldest Living Confederate Widow Tells All *(1989),* White People *(1992), and* Plays Well with Others *(1997). He is the recipient of the Sue Kaufman Prize, given by the American Academy of Arts and Letters (1989), and the Los Angeles Times Book Prize (1992).*

## Nativity, Caucasian

*For Ethel Mae Morris*

("What's wrong with you?" my wife asks. She already knows. I tell her anyway.)

I was born at a bridge party.

This explains certain frills and soft spots in my character. I sometimes picture my own genes as so many crustless multicolored canapés spread upon a silver oval tray.

Mother'd just turned thirty and was eight-and-one-half months gone. A colonel's daughter, she could boast a laudable IQ plus a smallish independent income. She loved gardening but, pregnant, couldn't stoop or weed. She loved swimming but felt too modest to appear at the Club in a bathing suit. "I walk like a duck," she told her husband, laughing. "Like six ducks trying to keep in line. I *hate* ducks."

Her best friend, Chloe, local grand master, tournament organizer, was a perfect whiz at stuffing compatible women into borrowed seaside cottages for marathon contract bridge.

"Helen precious?" Chloe phoned. "I know you're incommoded, but listen, dear. We're short a person over here at my house. Saundra Harper Briggs finally checked into Duke for that radical rice diet? And not one minute too soon. They say her husband had to drive the poor thing up there in the station wagon, in the *back* of the station wagon. I refuse to discriminate against you because of your condition. We keep talking about you, still ga-ga over that grand slam of yours in Hilton Head. I could send somebody around to fetch you in, say, fifteen minutes? No, yes? Will that be time enough to throw something on? Unless, of course, you feel too shaky."

Hobbyists often leap at compliments with an eagerness unknown to pros. And Helen Larkin Grafton was the classic amateur, product of a Richmond that deftly and early on espaliers, topiaries, and bonsais its young ladies, pruning this and that, preparing them for decorative root-bound existences either in or very near the home. Helen, unmistakably a white girl, a postdeb, was most accustomed to kind comments concerning clothes or looks or her special ability to foxtrot. And any talk about the mind itself, even mention of her well-known flair for cards, delighted her. So, dodging natural duty, bored with being treated as if pregnancy were some debilitating terminal disease, she said, "I'd adore to come. See you shortly, Chloe. And God love you for thinking of me. I've been sitting here feeling like . . . well, like one great big mudpie."

The other women applauded when she strolled in wearing a loose-cut frock of unbleached linen, hands thrust into front patch pockets piped with chocolate brown. (All this I have on hearsay from my godmother, Irma Stythe, a fashion-conscious former war nurse and sometime movie critic for the local paper.)

With much hoopla, two velvet pillows were placed on a folding chair, the new guest settled. They dealt her in. Young Helen Larkin Grafton. Phrases floated into the smoky air: Darling girl. Somewhat birdlike. Miscarried her first two, you know? Oh yes. Wonderful organizer—good with a garden. School up north but it didn't spoil her outlook or even her accent: pure Richmond. Good bones. Fine little game player. Looking fresh as a bride.

These women liked each other, mostly. At least they *knew* each other, which maybe matters more. Their children carried family secrets, cross-pollinating, house to house. Their husbands owned shares of the same things and golfed in groups. If the women knew about each other first, *then* either liked one another or not, husbands liked each other (till proven wrong) but didn't always *know* each other deeply. Anyway, it was a community. Shelter, shared maids, assured Christmas cards, to be greeted on the street by your full name.

One yard above the Persian and Caucasian rugs, temporary tabletops paved a whole new level. Surfaces glided along halls and on the second-story landing. Women huddled from four edges toward each other. That season's mandatory pastels, shoulder padding. Handbags propped on every level ledge. Mantels, banisters. Cloisonné[1] ashtrays glutted with half-smoked cigarettes. Refreshments—aspics, watercress, cucumber—waiting in the kitchen. The serving lady late, Chloe, our hostess, a plumpish blond woman, discreetly glancing at her watch. Such nice chatting. Exclamations over bad hands and good. Forty belles and semi-belles. Junior guilded. All rooms musical with voices, the great gift of Southern women, knowing how to coax out sounds, all ringing like this. Queen Anne furniture, ancestral portraits, actual Audubon[2] prints thanks to forebears who underwrote the project actually, Moroccan-bound books, maroon and gilt. Williamsburgy knickknacks, beiges, muted olive greens. A charming house chock full of lovely noise, and smokers not inhaling but hooked anyway.

Chloe's prize Pekingese, Mikado, snorted under card tables as through a

1. Enamelware in which colored areas are separated by thin bands of metal. 2. John J. Audubon (1785–1851), naturalist, who wrote about and painted the birds of North America.

tunnel ridged with nyloned columns. He edged, grimly interested, toward this new arrival's scent. An ancient wheezy male animal, Mikado took the liberty en route of sniffing up as high on women's limbs as he could reach, of rubbing languidly against the swishy silk and hazy shins of every woman there. Chloe had tied a yellow bow around his topknot; he tolerated this on bridge days, a fair trade for the cozy sense of being underneath a long playhouse of gaming tables, cards fatly snapping overhead. His path lay strewn with kicked-off shoes. Dainty aromatic feet to nudge. Mikado, the Blankenships' cranky one time ribbon winner, is only mentioned here because he suspected—before any other living creature in this murmurous house—that something was about to give.

He sauntered to a halt, stood under her table, stared—proprietary and enraptured—up at the area (dare I go through with this grisly sequence and its raunchy aftermath, my life?) between the young Helen's barely opened knees.

Mikado's flat face was mostly nose, very wet, chill as the jellyish aspic now gleaming on a kitchen counter. Cataracts had silvered over both his popping goldfish eyes. Smell, swollen to exciting new dimensions, remained the one great jolt and consolation left him. He nuzzled near enough and quite almost against the silk to get a better sample scent of something rich and decidedly awry here. The placing of his wide cool snout upon her shinbone made Helen, who'd just spread her cards, shudder with a little flinch. The subtlest sort of pelvic twist, then a serene smile of recognition: "Oh, Mikado," she whispered to her geisha fan of cards. For this was a society where ladies knew the names of other ladies' gardeners and maids and lapdogs.

Next . . . into this party cubicle of china shop small talk and play-it-safe decor, Nature lunged fairly bullishly. Intent on clobbering mere taste, it went right for a trigger spot and let loose one deep-seated wallop. It happened Now.

The Peke got hit by falling waters, about a bucket's worth. He yelped and scrambled down the hallway through a grove of table legs and female feet, skidding to safety under a favorite sideboard's shadow. Once there, Mikado collapsed and was panting when Helen, mouth a perfect O, bellowed forth in some voice totally unladylike and three full octaves deeper than her usual musical lilt, "Oh my Gawd, I've stawrted!"

Cards scattered atop the table, some teetered onto her steep lap, fell to dampened Persians. Her three tablemates stood, overturned the Samsonite. With it went a coaster full of lipsticked butts. Table to table, downstairs then up, news darted at the speed of sound. Three women moved to help Helen stand but she'd stretched out all her limbs. She was less seated on the chair than propped against it, semi-rigid as a starfish, muttering some Latin from her convent days.

First they dragged her toward the velvet chair. But Chloe, who'd just spent a fortune having that piece reupholstered, dissuaded them by backing, beckoning, through the kitchen's swinging portholed door. The cluster veered in there and, for want of a better spot, laid Helen on the central counter, under a panel of humming fluorescent tubes. Her shoulder bumped a wooden salad bowl filled with party mix (pretzel sticks, nuts, crackers, sprinkled salts, and Worcestershire sauce) and sent this shooting across linoleum's fake brick. Other dishes toppled, too. Pink and green mints rattled everywhere, the silver compote clanged toward a corner. One red aspic fell, splitting to sheeny smithereens before the Spicer twins took charge and set the other party foods along shelves or on the floor around the waist-high counter where Helen lay, distended.

Friends bustled to hold her hands, trying to dry her skirt with paper toweling. Pat Smiley quickly phoned the hospital for advice, forgetting to request an ambulance. Others listened in on two upstairs extensions, scolding her when she hung up. Then someone just as flustered dialed the fire department. Irma, my godmother, the movie reviewer, a short sensible woman who'd seen more films more times than practically anyone, now did what they would do in movies at such moments, on sea voyages, at Western waystations: she put water on to boil and fetched some string plus a bottle of Jack Daniel's (still in last year's Christmas gift box). She spread what seemed to be a sheet under my poor mother, rocking her from side to side. Helen, chewing knuckles, apologized to Chloe. "Really ruined your party. If I'd only guessed . . . Richard will be absolutely livid. Oh, this is so *unlike* me."

"Hush," Chloe said. "You couldn't know. It's Nature's doing, darling. Keep calm. Help's coming. We all love you."

Others, timing her contractions by the kitchen's sunburst wall clock, mumbled Yes, they did. They patted her wrist, pressed cool terry cloth scented with wintergreen across her dead-white forehead. Irma said, "Forgive me, dear. I hate to, but—" and boldly flapped back Helen's dress, took a look, mumbled, "Uh-oh. Somebody did call someone, an ambulance or something, right?" Others gathered behind Irma, stooped, shook heads sideways, held onto one another. Mavis DeWitt gave an empathetic moan, recalling her twins' forty-nine-hour delivery. She whispered, "I think I'm going home. I feel . . . I feel . . . Good-bye."

At the corner of Elm Avenue and Country Club Drive, the ambulance, ignoring a stoplight, overcome by the power of its siren and right of way, bisected the route of a northbound fire truck headed to the same address, and each vehicle, similarly entranced and headstrong with mission-of-mercy noise, mistook the other for its potent echo. They collided. Nobody was hurt but the vehicles got pretty well smashed up. A medic shunted about applying first aid to firemen all in black rubber raincoats and seated on someone's lawn. The assistant fire chief lifted the ambulance's hood and sniffed for smoldering.

Women fought to peek through the kitchen door's porthole. Helen was thrashing now and Irma, a squat level-headed person, ordered all potential fainters to the living room. Then Pat Smiley barged in with news that sirens had been heard from an upstairs window and, grinning at her own alertness, saw my mother laid upon the work counter, legs apart, surrounded by floored platters of party foods set like offerings around some sacrificial altar—my demure mother spread-eagled where the light refreshments should be, now writhing, gasping rhythmically, some heady severance already evident—and Pat, usually so stalwart, tottered toward the sink, blacking out en route, grabbing a hanging split-leaf philodendron, taking this down and falling in a ripe blur of store-bought dirt and looping greenery. Irma promptly shooed the others out, all but the hostess and the reliable Spicer twins, who, for twenty-nine years, had locally team-taught Home Ec. These lanky sisters hoisted Pat from either end and crunched toward the living room, shuffling through broken crockery, vines, aspic scattered here and there like wobbly carnage. They'd revived her when Mikado waddled in, having licked himself clean of perfectly respectable waters. He sniffed at the damp towels blotting Chloe's rug. A beast, wet to the size of a rat, white in the eyes, still licking his dark chops, sent poor Pat Smiley out again with one sleepy shriek. The Spicers simply lifted her legs back onto the furniture.

"Where *are* those ambulances?" Chloe got out ice tongs, any tool that looked silvery and surgical. "Sirens have been at it for ten darn minutes." Mother's wails now filled the house. Thirty acquaintances took up handbags, met at the front door, faces wary as if Helen's fate had befallen each and all of them. They told one another in lowered voices, "We'll only be underfoot," and, once assured of their basic good sense, fled.

Young Helen pleaded, between quickening seizures, to be gagged for decency's sake. She kept screeching personal charges against her husband, saying this mess was all his fault, his fault, his fault. Irma cradled Mother's head, lifted a water tumbler of Jack Daniel's, tried to tip some between the victim's lips. But Helen kept choking. So instead they doubled over a tulip-shaped potholder and simply stuffed this between chattery teeth. "Bite down," Irma told her. "It's risky to move you, dear. We hear them, hold on tight."

At the phone, Chloe was barking orders to the manager of the country club two blocks away. "Preston, listen and listen good: you get into a cart right now. You ride out and grab any doctor on the course. A dentist, a vet, anybody. But, Preston? Hurry. The poor little thing's head is out already."

A fringe-topped golf cart wobbled into the driveway. Two young doctors, one podiatrist plus everybody's dermatologist, wearing three-toned golf shoes and flashy shirts, barged in without knocking, found a fainted woman sprawled on the living-room chaise, hurried over, peeled back her skirt, yanked down panties. Elvyra Spicer, unmarried and long aware of men's baser drives, flew enraged across the room, slapped Dr. Kenilworth's head and sports cap, shrilling, "Not her. Not her, you. In there!"

The kitchen was an epic mess. Cereal, pretzels, soils, shards of aspic, stepped-on mints both pink and green—all this litter split and crackled under their spiked shoes, which sent Chloe swooping through the kitchen door to check on her inherited Orientals. But the kitchen did smell wonderful: good bourbon. Someone with nothing better to do perked coffee.

A wet Pekingese sat on hind legs in the pantry doorway, panting, a soggy yellow ribbon draped across its head. The doctors' caddy, a handsome black kid of fourteen, now jangled in from the cart, heaving forward two golf bags. In his excitement, he stood braced, as if expecting players to choose a proper putter for this situation.

Young doctors studied the event with an old amazement, some wonder missing from their hospital routine. They studied the committee of busy improvising women, studied a red rabbit-sized and wholly uninvited little wriggler aim out toward fluorescent light, looped to a pink cord that spiraled downward.

Irma Stythe (God bless her sane and civil heart) guided the creature, eased it—still trailing slick residues and varnishes—up into general view. Just now, Irma, recognizing the doctors, grinned wanly over at them, said, "You want to slap it?" proferring the ankles.

"No." Kenilworth shook his head, took his cap off, modest at the sight of women in such complete control. "No. Please. You—" and he lifted one hand as if offering the option of a waltz.

So Irma hauled off and smacked it smartly. She did this again. And once more, until It squalled into Me. They all smiled to hear a new human voice in the room. As recognition, the caddy clapped. Applause, but just a smattering.

The ambulance driver, nose bloodied, rushed in to explain the delay, chatted with a doctor who dabbed at the guy's upper lip. Pattie Smiley, coming to, hearing the cries, insisted on getting up. The door swung open just long enough for the company to see her grin, glimpse the coral-colored cord, blanch of human coloration and drop backward to the carpet as the door fell closed. They wrapped the baby in monogrammed towels and laid him in his mother's arms. Helen's face was puffed, glossy with tears. Her bun had come undone some time ago, brown hair a wooly pagan mess. She gazed down at the purplish child, still bawling, his fists already pounding air in spastic if determined blows, the infant's flop-eared ugliness a final indignity in a series of such. Helen really sobbed now. Concerned, Elmira Spicer tugged the potholder from the sudden mother's mouth but she groaned, "You put that back."

A new siren, then the fire chief lumbered in, wearing full regalia. Helen and the infant, both wailing in different registers, were carried past the card tables, borne over the prone Pattie Smiley and her attendant, Elvyra, who bent across her, pressing down the hem, sure the men had come back for a second try.

Irma phoned Richard's insurance office to make sure he knew. Somehow, no one had thought to call him. His best business voice: "Yes Irma? Actually I'm in the middle of a group life conference. But what can I do for you?"

She gave one croupy giggle, then leaned against the wall, fatigued. Irma, midwife, clamped a hand over the receiver as if to smother, told Chloe, "Richard's asking what *he* can do for *me*."

Chloe was wandering around, palms pressed to her cheeks, surveying the remains of her model kitchen.

"You heard right. Go to her, Richard, take flowers. She was so brave. The baby has real lung power. No, have your *secretary* send the flowers. You get moving."

Chloe stumbled into the front room and collapsed on the beleaguered chaise. Irma followed, stood looking down at today's hostess, Grand Master Chloe, rubbing her neck and shoulders, eyes mashed shut.

The twins had dragged Pat Smiley home a few doors down. Abandoned handbags lay scattered under chairs. Cards and party favors, a set of keys, one ashtray smoldering.

"Irma." Chloe lifted her head. "You're still standing? Could I ask you for one more thing? That damask tablecloth on the counter, the one that was under her? Would you just maybe toss it into the washer? Put in about a pound of

Oxydol. I can clean up the rest later. I'll just call Fatima and her sister and their whole neighborhood to come over here and work for a solid week. But I don't think I can quite abide the sight of that cloth just yet."

"You mean the sheet?"

"Yes, it was a tablecloth, actually. Damask. You couldn't have known, Irma. It was Grandmother Halsey's, 1870 or so. Not to fret, darling."

Irma Stythe leaned back into the kitchen. Cloth's pattern of wheat sheaves, bounty, harvest home, was now spread with urgent gloss and gore. Mikado trotted after her toward the laundry room. Upstaged all afternoon, antsy for attention, he now rolled over, played dead dog, sat on his haunches, then—tentatively—pranced.

Irma held a tumbler full of bourbon above the chaise. Chloe sniffed, opened one eye. The big house was oddly silent now. A few yards away, some lawn mower hissed and yammered, reassuring. Chloe sat up, took the glass in both hands as a child might, and tossed back three adult swallows. Mikado circled the heaped towels, smelling them. "No," Chloe called, halfhearted, "bad dog." But the animal climbed onto the pile, gave a huffy sigh and, head resting on crossed paws, closed his eyes.

"How about a toast?" Irma retrieved the glass. "Here's to it, to the baby. To the neighborhood's newest. Some start, hunh? And here's to our dear ole alcoholic neighborhood, God help us all."

Then both of them glanced at the closed kitchen door. They'd just decided without words, to go back in and start the cleaning job themselves. It would be wrong to burden the maid and her sister. Those two women had lives and troubles of their own. Besides, this was probably some sort of tribal duty, a task too ludicrous and personal to inflict on anybody else.

Chloe stood with difficulty, then stretched a bit, seemed steadied. "Well, my dear, are you ready?"

Irma nodded, then punched open the swinging door and lightly draped one arm around her friend's shoulder. They lingered here on the threshold for a moment, two well-meaning white women, childhood friends, lots nearer their deaths than their births. They studied the whole mess realistically.

"You know?" Irma cheered herself. "It's not nearly so bad as I remembered."

Then they scuffed straight into ankle-deep debris, waded toward the broom closet, got boldly back to it, got on with it, with life as it is practiced on this particular handsome side street in this particular dwindling country, ladies getting on with business as usual.

World without end. Amen.

# Barry Hannah

*Hannah (1942– ) was born in Meridian, Mississippi. He completed his higher education at Mississippi College and the University of Arkansas. Like many writers of his generation, he has taught in the writing programs of various universities and been the writer-in-residence at as many more. His reputation as a bold, rambunctious novelist was established by his first novel,* Geronimo Rex *(1972), about the turmoil of the 1960s. In an exuberant carnival of violence, despair, and longing his collegiate hero barely grabs a purchase on values by which he can live. In the fiction that has followed, Hannah has not abated his frenzied pace nor settled into the stereotypes that have seduced so many of his contemporaries. His other novels include* Nightwatchmen *(1973),* Ray *(1980),* The Tennis Handsome *(1983), and* Never Die *(1991). More of his short stories can be found in* Airships *(1978),* Bats Out of Hell *(1993), and* High Lonesome *(1996). In 1983 he published the novella* Power and Light.

## Testimony of Pilot

When I was ten, eleven and twelve, I did a good bit of my play in the backyard of a three-story wooden house my father had bought and rented out, his first venture into real estate. We lived right across the street from it, but over here was the place to do your real play. Here there was a harrowed but overgrown garden, a vine-swallowed fence at the back end, and beyond the fence a cornfield which belonged to someone else. This was not the country. This was the town, Clinton, Mississippi, between Jackson on the east and Vicksburg on the west. On this lot stood a few water oaks, a few plum bushes, and much overgrowth of honeysuckle vine. At the very back end, at the fence, stood three strong nude chinaberry trees.

In Mississippi it is difficult to achieve a vista. But my friends and I had one here at the back corner of the garden. We could see across the cornfield, see the one lone tin-roofed house this side of the railroad tracks, then on across the tracks many other bleaker houses with rustier tin roofs, smoke coming out of the chimneys in the late fall. This was niggertown. We had binoculars and could see the colored children hustling about and perhaps a hopeless sow or two with her brood enclosed in a tiny boarded-up area. Through the binoculars one afternoon in October we watched some men corner and beat a large hog on the brain. They used an ax and the thing kept running around, head leaning toward the ground, for several minutes before it lay down. I thought I saw the men laughing when it finally did. One of them was staggering, plainly drunk to my sight from three hundred yards away. He had the long knife. Because of that scene I considered Negroes savage cowards for a good five more years of my life. Our maid brought some sausage to my mother and when it was put in the pan to fry, I made a point of running out of the house.

I went directly across the street and to the back end of the garden behind the apartment house we owned, without my breakfast. That was Saturday. Eventually, Radcleve saw me. His parents had him mowing the yard that ran alongside my dad's property. He clicked off the power mower and I went over to his fence, which was storm wire. His mother maintained handsome flowery grounds at all costs; she had a leaf mold bin and St. Augustine grass as solid as a rug.

Radcleve himself was a violent experimental chemist. When Radcleve was eight, he threw a whole package of .22 shells against the sidewalk in front of his house until one of them went off, driving lead fragments into has calf, most of them still deep in there where the surgeons never dared tamper. Radcleve knew about the sulfur, potassium nitrate and charcoal mixture for gunpowder when he was ten. He bought things through the mail when he ran out of ingredients in his chemistry sets. When he was an infant, his father, a quiet man who owned the Chevrolet agency in town, bought an entire bankrupt sporting-goods store, and in the middle of their backyard he built a house, plain-painted and neat, one room and a heater, where Radcleve's redundant toys forevermore were kept—all the possible toys he would need for boyhood. There were things in there that Radcleve and I were not mature enough for and did not know the real use of. When we were eleven, we uncrated the new Dunlop golf balls and went on up on a shelf for the tennis rackets, went out in the middle of his yard, and served new golf ball after golf ball with blasts of the rackets over the cornfield, out of sight. When the strings busted we just went in and got another racket. We were absorbed by how a good smack would set the heavy little pills on an endless flight. Then Radcleve's father came down. He simply dismissed me. He took Radcleve into the house and covered his whole body with a belt. But within the week Radcleve had invented the mortar. It was a steel pipe into which a flashlight battery fit perfectly, like a bullet into a muzzle. He had drilled a hole for the fuse of an M-80 firecracker at the base, for the charge. It was a grand cannon, set up on a stack of bricks at the back of my dad's property, which was the free place to play. When it shot, it would back up violently with thick smoke and you could hear the flashlight battery whistling off. So that morning when I ran out of the house protesting the hog sausage, I told Radcleve to bring over the mortar. His ma and dad were in Jackson for the day, and he came right over with the pipe, the batteries and the M-80 explosives. He had two gross of them.

Before, we'd shot off towards the woods to the right of niggertown. I turned the bricks to the left; I made us a very fine cannon carriage pointing toward niggertown. When Radcleve appeared, he had two pairs of binoculars around his neck, one pair a newly plundered German unit as big as a brace of whiskey bottles. I told him I wanted to shoot for that house where we saw them killing the pig. Radcleve loved the idea. We singled out the house with heavy use of the binoculars.

There were children in the yard. Then they all went in. Two men came out of the back door. I thought I recognized the drunkard from the other afternoon. I helped Radcleve fix the direction of the cannon. We estimated the altitude we needed to get down there. Radcleve put the M-80 in the breech with its fuse standing out of the hole. I dropped the flashlight battery in. I lit the fuse. We backed off. The M-80 blasted off deafeningly, smoke rose, but my concentration was on that particular house over there. I brought the binoculars. We waited six or seven seconds. I heard a great joyful wallop on tin. "We've hit him on the first try, the first try!" I yelled. Radcleve was ecstatic. "Right on his roof!" We bolstered up the brick carriage. Radcleve remembered the correct height of the cannon exactly. So we fixed it, loaded it, lit it and backed off. The battery landed on the roof, blat, again, louder. I looked to see if there wasn't a great dent or hole in the roof. I could not understand why niggers weren't pouring out distraught from that house. We shot the mortar again and again, and always our battery hit the tin roof. Sometimes there was only a dull thud, but other times there was a wild distress of tin. I was still looking through the binoculars, amazed that the niggers wouldn't even come out of their house to see what was hitting their roof. Radcleve was on to it better than me. I looked over at him and he had the huge German binocs much lower than I did. He was looking straight through the cornfield, which was all bare and open, with nothing left but rotten stalks. "What we've been hitting is the roof of that house just this side of the tracks. White people live in there," he said.

I took up my binoculars again. I looked around the yard of that white wooden house on this side of the tracks, almost next to the railroad. When I found the tin roof, I saw four significant dents in it. I saw one of our batteries lying in the middle of a sort of crater. I took the binoculars down into the yard and saw a blond middle-aged woman looking our way.

"Somebody's coming up toward us. He's from that house and he's got, I think, some sort of fancy gun with him. It might be an automatic weapon."

I ran my binoculars all over the cornfield. Then, in a line with the house, I saw him. He was coming our way but having some trouble with the rows and dead stalks of the cornfield.

"That is just a boy like us. All he's got is a saxophone with him," I told Radcleve. I had recently got in the school band, playing drums, and had seen all the weird horns that made up a band.

I watched this boy with the saxophone through the binoculars until he was ten feet from us. This was Quadberry. His name was Ard, short for Arden. His shoes were foot-square wads of mud from the cornfield. When he saw us across the fence and above him, he stuck out his arm in my direction.

"My dad says stop it!"

"We weren't doing anything," says Radcleve.

"Mother saw the smoke puff up from here. Dad has a hangover."

"A what?"

"It's a headache from indiscretion. You're lucky he does. He's picked up the poker to rap on you, but he can't move further the way his head is."

"What's your name? You're not in the band," I said, focusing on the saxophone.

"It's Ard Quadberry. Why do you keep looking at me through the binoculars?"

It was because he was odd, with his hair and its white ends, and his Arab nose, and now his name. Add to that the saxophone.

"My dad's a doctor at the college. Mother's a musician. You better quit what you're doing. . . . I was out practicing in the garage. I saw one of those flashlight batteries roll off the roof. Could I see what you shoot 'em with?"

"No," said Radcleve. Then he said: "If you'll play that horn."

Quadberry stood out there ten feet below us in the field, skinny, feet and pants booted with black mud, and at his chest the slung-on, very complex, radiant horn.

Quadberry began sucking and licking the reed. I didn't care much for this act, and there was too much desperate oralness in his face when he began playing. That was why I chose the drums. One had to engage himself like suck's revenge with a horn. But what Quadberry was playing was pleasant and intricate. I was sure it was advanced, and there was no squawking, as from the other eleven-year-olds on sax in the band room. He made the end with a clean upward riff, holding the final note high, pure and unwavering.

"Good!" I called to him.

Quadberry was trying to move out of the sunken row toward us, but his heavy shoes were impending him.

"Sounded like a duck. Sounded like a girl duck," said Radcleve, who was kneeling down and packing a mudball around one of the M-80s. I saw and I was an accomplice, because I did nothing. Radcleve lit the fuse and heaved the mudball over the fence. An M-80 is a very serious firecracker; it is like the charge they use to shoot up those sprays six hundred feet on July Fourth at country clubs. It went off, this one, even bigger than most M-80s.

When we looked over the fence, we saw Quadberry all muck specks and fragments of stalks. He was covering the mouthpiece of his horn with both hands. Then I saw there was blood pouring out of, it seemed, his right eye. I thought he was bleeding directly out of his eye.

"Quadberry?" I called.

He turned around and never said a word to me until I was eighteen. He walked back holding his eye and staggering through the cornstalks. Radcleve had him in the binoculars. Radcleve was trembling . . . but intrigued.

"His mother just screamed. She's running out in the field to get him."

I thought we'd blinded him, but we hadn't. I thought the Quadberrys would get the police or call my father, but they didn't. The upshot of this is that Quadberry had a permanent white space next to his right eye, a spot that looked like a tiny upset crown.

I went from sixth through half of twelfth grade ignoring him and that wound. I was coming on as a drummer and a lover, but if Quadberry happened to appear within fifty feet of me and my most tender, intimate sweetheart, I would duck out. Quadberry grew up just like the rest of us. His father was still a doctor—professor of history—at the town college; his mother was still blond, and a musician. She was organist at an Episcopalian church in Jackson, the big capital city ten miles east of us.

As for Radcleve, he still had no ear for music, but he was there, my buddy. He was repentant about Quadberry, although not so much as I. He'd thrown the mud grenade over the fence only to see what would happen. He had not really wanted to maim. Quadberry had played his tune on the sax, Radcleve had played his tune on the mud grenade. It was just a shame they happened to cross talents.

Radcleve went into a long period of nearly nothing after he gave up violent explosives. Then he trained himself to copy the comic strips, *Steve Canyon* to *Major Hoople,* until he became quite a versatile cartoonist with some very provocative new faces and bodies that were gesturing intriguingly. He could never fill in the speech balloons with the smart words they needed. Sometimes he would pencil in "Err" or "What?" in the empty speech places. I saw him a great deal. Radcleve was not spooked by Quadberry. He even once asked Quadberry what his opinion was of his future as a cartoonist. Quadberry told Radcleve that if he took all his cartoons and stuffed himself with them, he would make an interesting dead man. After that, Radcleve was shy of him too.

When I was a senior we had an extraordinary band. Word was we had outplayed all the big A.A.A. division bands last April in the state contest. Then came news that a new blazing saxophone player was coming into the band as first chair. This person had spent summers in Vermont in music camps, and he was coming in with us for the concert season. Our director, a lovable aesthete named Richard Prender, announced to us in a proud silent moment that the boy was joining us tomorrow night. The effect was that everybody should push over a seat or two and make room for this boy and his talent. I was annoyed. Here I'd been with the band and had kept hold of the taste among the whole percussion section. I could play rock and jazz drum and didn't even really need to be here. I could be in Vermont too, give me a piano and a bass. I looked at the kid on first sax, who was going to be supplanted tomorrow. For two years he had thought he was the star, then suddenly enters this boy who's three times better.

The new boy was Quadberry. He came in, but he was meek, and when he tuned up he put his head almost on the floor, bending over trying to be inconspicuous. The girls in the band had wanted him to be handsome, but Quadberry refused and kept himself in such hiding among the sax section that he was neither handsome, ugly, cute or anything. What he was was pretty near invisible, except for the bell of his horn, the all-but-closed eyes, the Arabian nose, the brown hair with its halo of white ends, the desperate oralness, the giant reed punched into his face, and hazy Quadberry, loving the wound in a private dignified ecstasy.

I say dignified because of what came out of the end of his horn. He was more than what Prender had told us he would be. Because of Quadberry, we could take the band arrangement of Ravel's[1] *Bolero* with us to the state contest Quadberry would do the saxophone solo. He would switch to alto sax, he would do the sly Moorish ride. When he played, I heard the sweetness, I heard the horn which finally brought human *talk* into the realm of music. It could sound like the mutterings of a field nigger, and then it could get up into inhumanly careless beauty, it could get among mutinous helium bursts around Saturn. I already loved *Bolero* for the constant drum part. The percussion was always there, driving along with the subtly increasing triplets, insistent, insistent, at last outraged and trying to steal the whole show from the horns and the others. I knew a large boy with dirty blond hair, name of Wyatt, who played viola in the Jackson Symphony and sousaphone in our band—one of the rare closet transmutations of my time—who was forever claiming to have discovered the central *Bolero* one Sunday afternoon over FM radio as he had seven distinct sexual moments with a certain B., girl flutist with black bangs and skin like mayonnaise, while the drums of Ravel carried them on and on in a ceremony of Spanish sex. It was agreed by all the canny in the band that *Bolero* was exactly the piece to make the band soar—now especially as we had Quadberry, who made his walk into the piece like an actual lean Spanish bandit. This boy could blow his horn. He was, as I had suspected, a genius. His solo was not quite the same as the New York Phil's saxophonist's, but it was better. It came in and was with us. It entered my spine and, I am sure, went up the skirts of the girls. I had almost deafened myself playing drums in the most famous rock and jazz band in the state, but I could hear the voice that went through and out that horn. It sounded like a very troubled forty-year-old man, a man who had had his brow in his hands a long time.

The next time I saw Quadberry up close, in fact the first time I had seen him up close since we were eleven and he was bleeding in the cornfield, was in late February. I had only three classes this last semester, and went up to the band room often, to loaf and complain and keep up my touch on the drums. Prender let me keep my set in one of the instrument rooms, with a tarpaulin thrown over it, and I would drag it out to the practice room and whale away. Sometimes a group of sophomores would come up and I would make them marvel, whaling away as if not only deaf but blind to them, although I wasn't at all. If I saw a sophomore girl with exceptional bod or face, I would do miracles of technique I never knew were in me. I would amaze myself. I would be threatening Buddy Rich and Sam Morello.[2] But this time when I went into the instrument room, there was Quadberry on one side, and, back in a dark corner, a small ninth-grade euphonium player whose face was all red. The little boy was weeping and grinning at the same time.

"Queerberry," the boy said softly.

Quadberry flew upon him like a demon. He grabbed the boy's collar, slapped his face, and yanked his arm behind him in a merciless wrestler's grip, the one that made them bawl on TV. Then the boy broke it and slugged Quadberry in the lips and ran across to my side of the room. He said "Queerberry"

1. French composer (1875–1937). 2. Jazz drummers of the era.

softly again and jumped for the door. Quadberry plunged across the room and tackled him on the threshold. Now that the boy was under him, Quadberry pounded the top of his head with his fist made like a mallet. The boy kept calling him "Queerberry" throughout this. He had not learned his lesson. The boy seemed to be going into concussion, so I stepped over and touched Quadberry, telling him to quit. Quadberry obeyed and stood up off the boy, who crawled on out into the band room. But once more the boy looked back with a bruised grin, saying "Queerberry." Quadberry made a move toward him, but I blocked it.

"Why are you beating up on this little guy?" I said. Quadberry was sweating and his eyes were wild with hate; he was a big fellow now, though lean. He was, at six feet tall, bigger than me.

"He kept calling me Queerberry."

"What do you care?" I asked.

"I care," Quadberry said, and left me standing there.

We were to play at Millsaps College Auditorium for the concert. It was April. We got on the buses, a few took their cars, and were a big tense crowd, getting over there. To Jackson was only a twenty-minute trip. The director, Prender, followed the bus in his Volkswagen. There was a thick fog. A flashing ambulance, snaking the lanes, piled into him head on. Prender, who I would imagine was thinking of *Bolero* and hearing the young horn voices in his band—perhaps he was dwelling on Quadberry's spectacular gypsy entrance, or perhaps he was meditating on the percussion section, of which I was the king—passed into the airs of band-director heaven. We were told by the student director as we set up on the stage. The student director was a senior from the town college, very much afflicted, almost to the point of drooling, by a love and respect for Dick Prender, and now afflicted by a heartbreaking esteem for his ghost. As were we all.

I loved the tough and tender director awesomely and never knew it until I found myself bawling along with all the rest of the boys of the percussion. I told them to keep setting up, keep tuning, keep screwing the stands together, keep hauling in the kettledrums. To just quit and bawl seemed a betrayal to Prender. I caught some girl clarinetists trying to flee the stage and go have their cry. I told them to get the hell back to their section. They obeyed me. Then I found the student director. I had to have my say.

"Look. I say we just play *Bolero* and junk the rest. That's our horse. We can't play *Brighton Beach* and *Neptune's Daughter*.[3] We'll never make it through them. And they're too happy."

"We aren't going to play anything," he said. "Man, to play is filthy. Did you ever hear Prender play piano? Do you know what a cool man he was in all things?"

"We play. He got us ready, and we play."

"Man, you can't play any more than I can direct. You're bawling your face off. Look out there at the rest of them. Man, it's a herd, it's a weeping herd."

3. Popular musical pieces for high school bands.

"What's wrong? Why aren't you pulling this crowd together?" This was Quadberry, who had come up urgently. "I got those little brats in my section sitting down, but we've got people abandoning the stage, tearful little finks throwing their horns on the floor."

"I'm not directing," said the mustached college man.

"Then get out of here. You're weak, weak!"

"Man, we've got teen-agers in ruin here, we got sorrowville. Nobody can—"

"Go ahead. Do your number. Weak out on us."

"Man, I—"

Quadberry was already up on the podium, shaking his arms.

"We're right here! The band is right here! Tell your friends to get back in their seats. We're doing *Bolero.* Just put *Bolero* up and start tuning. *I'm* directing. I'll be right here in front of you. You look at *me!* Don't you dare quit on Prender. Don't you dare quit on me. You've got to be heard. *I've* got to be heard. Prender wanted me to be heard. I am the star, and I say we sit down and blow."

And so we did. We all tuned and were burning low for the advent into *Bolero,* though we couldn't believe that Quadberry was going to remain with his saxophone strapped to him and conduct us as well as play his solo. The judges, who apparently hadn't heard about Prender's death, walked down to their balcony desks.

One of them called out "Ready" and Quadberry's hand was instantly up in the air, his fingers hard as if around the stem of something like a torch. This was not Prender's way, but it had to do. We went into the number cleanly and Quadberry one-armed it in the conducting. He kept his face, this look of hostility, at the reeds and trumpets. I was glad he did not look toward me and the percussion boys like that. But he must have known we would be constant and tasteful because I was the king there. As for the others, the soloists especially, he was scaring them into excellence. Prender had never got quite this from them. Boys became men and girls became women as Quadberry directed us through *Bolero.* I even became a bit better of a man myself, though Quadberry did not look my way. When he turned away toward the people in the auditorium to enter on his solo, I knew it was my baby. I and the drums were the metronome. That was no trouble. It was talent to keep the metronome ticking amidst any given chaos of sound.

But this keeps one's mind occupied and I have no idea what Quadberry sounded like on his sax ride. All I know is that he looked grief-stricken and pale, and small. Sweat had popped out on his forehead. He bent over extremely. He was wearing the red brass-button jacket and black pants, black bow tie at the throat, just like the rest of us. In this outfit he bent over his horn almost out of sight. For a moment, before I caught the glint of his horn through the music stands, I thought he had pitched forward off the stage. He went down so far to do his deep oral thing, his conducting arm had disappeared so quickly, I didn't know but what he was having a seizure.

When *Bolero* was over, the audience stood up and made meat out of their hands applauding. The judges themselves applauded. The band stood up, bawling again, for Prender and because we had done so well. The student director rushed out crying to embrace Quadberry, who eluded him with his dipping shoulders. The crowd was still clapping insanely. I wanted to see Quadberry myself. I waded through the red backs, through the bow ties, over the white bucks. Here was the first-chair clarinetist, who had done his bit like an angel; he sat close to the podium and could hear Quadberry.

"Was Quadberry good?" I asked him.

"Are you kidding? These tears in my eyes, they're for how good he was. He was too good. I'll never touch my clarinet again." The clarinetist slung the pieces of his horn into their case like underwear and a toothbrush.

I found Quadberry fitting the sections of his alto in the velvet holds of his case.

"Hooray," I said. "Hip damn hooray for you."

Arden was smiling too, showing a lot of teeth I had never seen. His smile was sly. He knew he had pulled off a monster unlikelihood.

"Hip, hip hooray for me," he said. "Look at her. I had the bell of the horn almost smack in her face."

There was a woman of about thirty sitting in the front row of the auditorium. She wore a sundress with a drastic cleavage up front; looked like something that hung around New Orleans and kneaded your heart to death with her feet. She was still mesmerized by Quadberry. She bore on him with a stare and there was moisture in her cleavage.

"You played well."

"Well? Play well? Yes."

He was trying not to look at her directly. Look at *me,* I beckoned to her with full face: I was the *drums.* She arose and left.

"I was walking downhill in a valley, is all I was doing," said Quadberry. "Another man, a wizard, was playing my horn." He locked his sax case. "I feel nasty for not being able to cry like the rest of them. Look at them. Look at them crying."

True, the children of the band were still weeping, standing around the stage. Several moms and dads had come up among them, and they were misty-eyed too. The mixture of grief and superb music had been unbearable.

A girl in tears appeared next to Quadberry. She was a majorette in football season and played third-chair sax during the concert season. Not even her violent sorrow could take the beauty out of the face of this girl. I had watched her for a number of years—her alertness to her own beauty, the pride of her legs in the majorette outfit—and had taken out her younger sister, a second-rate version of her and a wayward overcompensating nymphomaniac whom several of us made a hobby out of pitying. Well, here was Lilian herself crying in Quadberry's face. She told him that she'd run off the stage when she heard about Prender, dropped her horn and everything, and had thrown herself into a tavern across the street and drunk two beers quickly for some kind of relief. But she had come back through the front doors of the auditorium and sat down, dizzy with beer, and seen Quadberry, the miraculous way he had gone on with *Bolero.* And now she was eaten up by feelings of guilt, weakness, cowardice.

"We didn't miss you," said Quadberry.

"Please forgive me. Tell me to do something to make up for it."

"Don't breathe my way, then. You've got beer all over your breath."

"I want to talk to you."

"Take my horn case and go out, get in my car, and wait for me. It's the ugly Plymouth in front of the school bus."

"I know," she said.

Lilian Field, this lovely teary thing, with the rather pious grace of her carriage, with the voice full of imminent swoon, picked up Quadberry's horn case and her own and walked off the stage.

I told the percussion boys to wrap up the packing. Into my suitcase I put my own gear and also managed to steal drum keys, two pairs of brushes, a twenty-inch Turkish cymbal, a Gretsch snare drum that I desired for my collection, a wood block, kettledrum mallets, a tuning harp and a score sheet of *Bolero* full of marginal notes I'd written down straight from the mouth of Dick Prender, thinking I might want to look at the score sheet sometime in the future when I was having a fit of nostalgia such as I am having right now as I write this. I had never done any serious stealing before, and I was stealing for my art. Prender was dead, the band had done its last thing of the year, I was a senior. Things were finished at the high school. I was just looting a sinking ship. I could hardly lift the suitcase. As I was pushing it across the stage, Quadberry was there again.

"You can ride back with me if you want to."

"But you've got Lilian."

"Please ride back with me . . . us. Please."

"Why?"

"To help me get rid of her. Her breath is full of beer. My father always had that breath. Every time he was friendly, he had that breath. And she looks a great deal like my mother." We were interrupted by the Tupelo band director. He put his baton against Quadberry's arm.

"You were big with *Bolero,* son, but that doesn't mean you own the stage."

Quadberry caught the end of the suitcase and helped me with it out to the steps beyond the auditorium. The buses were gone. There sat his ugly ocher Plymouth; it was a failed, gay, experimental shade from the Chrysler people. Lilian was sitting in the front seat wearing her shirt and bow tie, her coat off.

"Are you going to ride back with me?" Quadberry said to me.

"I think I would spoil something. You never saw her when she was a majorette. She's not stupid, either. She likes to show off a little, but she's not stupid. She's in the History Club."

"My father has a doctorate in history. She smells of beer."

I said, "She drank two cans of beer when she heard about Prender."

"There are a lot of other things to do when you hear about death. What I did, for example. She ran away. She fell to pieces."

"She's waiting for us," I said.

"One damned thing I am never going to do is drink."

"I've never seen your mother up close, but Lilian doesn't look like your mother. She doesn't look like anybody's mother."

I rode with them silently to Clinton. Lilian made no bones about being disappointed I was in the car, though she said nothing. I knew it would be like this and I hated it. Other girls in town would not be so unhappy that I was in the car with them. I looked for flaws in Lilian's face and neck and hair, but there weren't any. Couldn't there be a mole, an enlarged pore, too much gum on a tooth, a single awkward hair around the ear? No. Memory, the whole lying opera of it, is killing me now. Lilian was faultless beauty, even sweating, even and especially in the white man's shirt and the bow tie clamping together her collar, when one knew her uncomfortable bosoms, her poor nipples. . . .

"Don't take me back to the band room. Turn off here and let me off at my house," I said to Quadberry. He didn't turn off.

"Don't tell Arden what to do. He can do what he wants to," said Lilian, ignoring me and speaking to me at the same time. I couldn't bear her hatred. I asked Quadberry to please just stop the car and let me out here, wherever he was: this front yard of the mobile home would do. I was so earnest that he stopped the car. He handed back the keys and I dragged my suitcase out of the trunk, then flung the keys back at him and kicked the car to get it going again.

My band came together in the summer. We were the Bop Fiends . . . that was our name. Two of them were from Ole Miss, our bass player was from Memphis State, but when we got together this time, I didn't call the tenor sax, who went to Mississippi Southern, because Quadberry wanted to play with us. During the school year the college boys and I fell into minor groups to pick up twenty dollars on a weekend, playing dances for the Moose Lodge, medical-student fraternities in Jackson, teen-age recreation centers in Greenwood, and such as that. But come summer we were the Bop Fiends again, and the price for us went up to $1,200 a gig. Where they wanted the best rock and bop and they had some bread, we were called. The summer after I was a senior, we played in Alabama, Louisiana, and Arkansas. Our fame was getting out there on the interstate route.

This was the summer that I made myself deaf.

Years ago Prender had invited down an old friend from a high school in Michigan. He asked me over to meet the friend, who had been a drummer with Stan Kenton at one time and was now a band director just like Prender. This fellow was almost totally deaf and he warned me very sincerely about deafing myself. He said there would come a point when you had to lean over and concentrate all your hearing on what the band was doing and that was the time to quit for a while, because if you didn't you would be irrevocably deaf like him in a month or two. I listened to him but could not take him seriously. Here was an oldish man who had his problems. My ears had ages of hearing left. Not so. I played the drums so loud the summer after I graduated from high school that I made myself, eventually, stone deaf.

We were at, say, the National Guard Armory in Lake Village, Arkansas, Quadberry out in front of us on the stage they'd built. Down on the floor were hundreds of sweaty teen-agers. Four girls in sundresses, showing what they could, were leaning on the stage with broad ignorant lust on their minds. I'd play so loud for one particular chick, I'd get absolutely out of control. The guitar boys would have to turn the volume up full blast to compensate. Thus I went deaf. Anyhow, the dramatic idea was to release Quadberry on a very soft sweet ballad right in the middle of a long ear-piercing run of rock-and-roll tunes. I'd get out the brushes and we would astonish the crowd with our tenderness. By August, I was so deaf I had to watch Quadberry's fingers changing notes on the saxophone, had to use my eyes to keep time. The other members of the Bop Fiends told me I was hitting out of time. I pretended I was trying to do experimental things with rhythm when the truth was I simply could no longer hear I was no longer a tasteful drummer, either. I had become deaf through lack of taste.

Which was—taste—exactly the quality that made Quadberry wicked on the saxophone. During the howling, during the churning, Quadberry had taste. The noise did not affect his personality; he was solid as a brick. He could blend. Oh, he could hoot through his horn when the right time came, but he could do supporting roles for an hour. Then, when we brought him out front for his solo on something like "Take Five," he would play with such light blissful technique that he even eclipsed Paul Desmond. The girls around the stage did not cause him to enter into excessive loudness or vibrato.

Quadberry had his own girl friend now, Lilian back at Clinton, who put all the sundressed things around the stage in the shade. In my mind I had congratulated him for getting up next to this beauty, but in June and July, when I was still hearing things a little, he never said a word about her. It was one night in August, when I could hear nothing and was driving him to his house, that he asked me to turn off the inside light and spoke in a retarded deliberate way. He knew I was deaf and counted on my being able to read lips.

"Don't . . . make fun . . . of her . . . or me. . . . We . . . think . . . she . . . is . . . in trouble."

I wagged my head. Never would I make fun of him or her. She detested me because I had taken out her helpless little sister for a few weeks, but I would never think there was anything funny about Lilian, for all her haughtiness. I only thought of this event as monumentally curious.

"No one except you knows," he said.

"Why did you tell me?"

"Because I'm going away and you have to take care of her. I wouldn't trust her with anybody but you."

"She hates the sight of my face. Where are you going?"

"Annapolis."

"You aren't going to any damned Annapolis."

"That was the only school that wanted me."

"You're going to play your saxophone on a boat?"

"I don't know what I'm going to do."

"How . . . how can you just leave her?"

"She wants me to. She's very excited about me at Annapolis. William [this is my name], there is no girl I could imagine who has more inner sweetness than Lilian."

I entered the town college, as did Lilian. She was in the same chemistry class I was. But she sat rows away. It was difficult to learn anything, being deaf.

The professor wasn't a pantomimer—but finally he went to the blackboard with the formulas and the algebra of problems, to my happiness. I hung in and made a B. At the end of the semester I was swaggering around the grade sheet he'd posted. I happened to see Lilian's grade. She'd only made a C. Beautiful Lilian got only a C while I, with my handicap, had made a B.

It had been a very difficult chemistry class. I had watched Lilian's stomach the whole way through. It was not growing. I wanted to see her look like a watermelon, make herself an amazing mother shape.

When I made the B and Lilian made the C, I got up my courage and finally went to see her. She answered the door. Her parents weren't home. I'd never wanted this office of watching over her as Quadberry wanted me to, and this is what I told her. She asked me into the house. The rooms smelled of nail polish and pipe smoke. I was hoping her little sister wasn't in the house, and my wish came true. We were alone.

"You can quit watching over me."

"Are you pregnant?"

"No." Then she started crying. "I wanted to be. But I'm not."

"What do you hear from Quadberry?"

She said something, but she had her back to me. She looked to me for an answer, but I had nothing to say. I knew she'd said something, but I hadn't heard it.

"He doesn't play the saxophone anymore," she said.

This made me angry.

"Why not?"

"Too much math and science and navigation. He wants to fly. That's what his dream is now. He wants to get into an F-something jet."

I asked her to say this over and she did. Lilian really was full of inner sweetness, as Quadberry had said. She understood that I was deaf. Perhaps Quadberry had told her.

The rest of the time in her house I simply witnessed her beauty and her mouth moving.

I went through college. To me it is interesting that I kept a B average and did it all deaf, though I know that isn't interesting to people who aren't deaf. I loved music, and never heard it. I loved poetry, and never heard a word that came out of the mouths of the visiting poets who read at the campus. I loved my mother and dad, but never heard a sound they made. One Christmas Eve, Radcleve was back from Ole Miss and threw an M-80 out in the street for old times' sake. I saw it explode, but there was only a pressure in my ears. I was at parties when lusts were raging and I went home with two girls (I am medium handsome) who lived in apartments of the old two-story 1920 vintage, and I took my shirt off and made love to them. But I have no real idea what their reaction was. They were stunned and all smiles when I got up, but I have no idea whether I gave them the least pleasure or not. I hope I did. I've always been partial to women and have always wanted to see them satisfied till their eyes popped out.

Through Lilian I got the word that Quadberry was out of Annapolis and now flying jets off the *Bonhomme Richard,* an aircraft carrier headed for Vietnam. He telegrammed her that he would set down at the Jackson airport at ten o'clock one night. So Lilian and I were out there waiting. It was a familiar place to her. She was a stewardess and her loops were mainly in the South. She wore a beige raincoat, had red sandals on her feet; I was in a black turtleneck and corduroy jacket, feeling significant, so significant I could barely stand it. I'd already made myself the lead writer at Gordon-Marx Advertising in Jackson. I hadn't seen Lilian in a year. Her eyes were strained, no longer the bright blue things they were when she was a pious beauty. We drank coffee together. I loved her. As far as I knew, she'd been faithful to Quadberry.

He came down in an F-something Navy jet right on the dot of ten. She ran out on the airport pavement to meet him. I saw her crawl up the ladder. Quadberry never got out of the plane. I could see him in his blue helmet. Lilian backed down the ladder. Then Quadberry had the cockpit cover him again. He turned the plane around so its flaming red end was at us. He took it down the runway. We saw him leap into the night at the middle of the runway going west, toward San Diego and the *Bonhomme Richard.* Lilian was crying.

"What did he say?" I asked.

"He said. 'I am a dragon. America the beautiful, like you will never know.' He wanted to give you a message. He was glad you were here."

"What was the message?"

"The same thing. 'I am a dragon. America the beautiful, like you will never know.' "

"Did he say anything else?"

"Not a thing."

"Did he express any love toward you?"

"He wasn't Ard. He was somebody with a sneer in a helmet."

"He's going to war, Lilian."

"I asked him to kiss me and he told me to get off the plane, he was firing up and it was dangerous."

"Arden is going to war. He's just on his way to Vietnam and he wanted us to know that. It wasn't just him he wanted us to see. It was him in the jet he wanted us to see. He *is* that black jet. You can't kiss an airplane."

"And what are we supposed to do?" cried sweet Lilian.

"We've just got to hang around. He didn't have to lift off and disappear straight up like that. That was to tell us how he isn't with us anymore."

Lilian asked me what she was supposed to do now. I told her she was supposed to come with me to my apartment in the old 1920 Clinton place where I was. I was supposed to take care of her. Quadberry had said so. His six-year-old directive was still working.

She slept on the fold-out bed of the sofa for a while. This was the only bed in my place. I stood in the dark in the kitchen and drank a quarter bottle of gin on ice. I would not turn on the light and spoil her sleep. The prospect of Lilian asleep in my apartment made me feel like a chaplain on a visit to the Holy Land; I stood there getting drunk, biting my tongue when dreams of lust burst on me. That black jet Quadberry wanted us to see him in, its flaming rear end, his blasting straight up into the night at mid-runway—what precisely was he wanting to say in this stunt? Was he saying remember him forever or forget him forever? But I had my own life and was neither going to mother-hen it over his memory nor his old sweetheart. What did he mean, *America the beautiful, like you will never know*? I, William Howly, knew a goddamn good bit about America the beautiful, even as a deaf man. Being deaf had brought me up closer to people. There were only about five I knew, but I knew their mouth movements, the perspiration under their noses, their tongues moving over the crowns of their teeth, their fingers on their lips. Quadberry, I said, you don't have to get up next to the stars in your black jet to see America the beautiful.

I was deciding to lie down on the kitchen floor and sleep the night, when Lilian turned on the light and appeared in her panties and bra. Her body was perfect except for a tiny bit of fat on her upper thighs. She'd sunbathed herself so her limbs were brown, and her stomach, and the instinct was to rip off the white underwear and lick, suck, say something terrific into the flesh that you discovered.

She was moving her mouth.

"Say it again slowly."

"I'm lonely. When he took off in his jet, I think it meant he wasn't ever going to see me again. I think it meant he was laughing at both of us. He's an astronaut and he spits on us."

"You want me on the bed with you?" I asked.

"I know you're an intellectual. We could keep on the lights so you'd know what I said."

"You want to say things? This isn't going to be just sex?"

"It could never be just sex."

"I agree. Go to sleep. Let me make up my mind whether to come in there. Turn out the lights."

Again the dark, and I thought I would cheat not only Quadberry but the entire Quadberry family if I did what was natural.

I fell asleep.

Quadberry escorted B-52s on bombing missions into North Vietnam. He was catapulted off the *Bonhomme Richard* in his suit at 100 degrees temperature, often at night, and put on the F-8 on all it could get—the tiny cockpit, the immense long two-million-dollar fuselage, wings, tail and jet engine, Quadberry, the genius master of his dragon, going up to twenty thousand feet to be cool. He'd meet with the big B-52 turtle of the air and get in a position, his cockpit glowing with green and orange lights, and turn on his transistor radio. There was only one really good band, never mind the old American rock-and-roll from Cambodia, and that was Red Chinese opera. Quadberry loved it. He loved the nasal horde in the finale, when the peasants won over the old fat dilettante mayor. Then he'd turn the jet around when he saw the squatty abrupt little fires way down there after the B-52s had dropped their diet. It was a seven-hour trip. Sometimes he slept, but his body knew when to wake up. Another thirty minutes and there was his ship waiting for him out in the waves.

All his trips weren't this easy. He'd have to blast out in daytime and get with the B-52s, and a SAM missile would come up among them. Two of his mates were taken down by these missiles. But Quadberry, as on saxophone, had endless learned technique. He'd put his jet perpendicular in the air and make the SAMs look silly. He even shot down two of them. Then, one day in daylight, a MIG came floating up level with him and his squadron. Quadberry couldn't believe it. Others in the squadron were shy, but Quadberry knew where and how the MIG could shoot. He flew below the cannons and then came in behind it. He knew the MIG wanted one of the B-52s and not mainly him. The MIG was so concentrated on the fat B-52 that he forgot about Quadberry. It was really an amateur suicide pilot in the MIG. Quadberry got on top of him and let down a missile, rising out of the way of it. The missile blew off the tail of the MIG. But then Quadberry wanted to see if the man got safely out of the cockpit. He thought it would be pleasant if the fellow got out with his parachute working. Then Quadberry saw that the fellow wanted to collide his wreckage with the B-52, so Quadberry turned himself over and cannoned, evaporated the pilot and cockpit. It was the first man he'd killed.

The next trip out, Quadberry was hit by a ground missile. But his jet kept flying. He flew it a hundred miles and got to the sea. There was the *Bonhomme Richard,* so he ejected. His back was snapped but, by God, he landed right on the deck. His mates caught him in their arms and cut the parachute off him. His back hurt for weeks, but he was all right. He rested and recuperated in Hawaii for a month.

Then he sent off the front of the ship. Just like that, his F-6 plopped in the ocean and sank like a rock. Quadberry saw the ship go over him. He knew he shouldn't eject just yet. If he ejected now he'd knock his head on the bottom and get chewed up in the motor blades. So Quadberry waited. His plane was sinking in the green and he could see the hull of the aircraft carrier getting smaller, but he had oxygen through his mask and it didn't seem that urgent a decision. Just let the big ship get over. Down what later proved to be sixty feet, he pushed the ejection button. It fired him away, bless it, and he woke up ten feet under the surface swimming against an almost overwhelming body of underwater parachute. But two of his mates were in a helicopter, one of them on the ladder to lift him out.

Now Quadberry's back was really hurt. He was out of this war and all wars for good.

Lilian, the stewardess, was killed in a crash. Her jet exploded with a hijacker's bomb, an inept bomb which wasn't supposed to go off, fifteen miles out of Havana; the poor pilot, the poor passengers, the poor stewardesses were all splattered like flesh sparklers over the water just out of Cuba. A fisherman found one seat of the airplane. Castro expressed regrets.

Quadberry came back to Clinton two weeks after Lilian and the others bound for Tampa were dead. He hadn't heard about her. So I told him Lilian was dead when I met him at the airport. Quadberry was thin and rather meek in his civvies—a gray suit and an out-of-style tie. The white ends of his hair were not there—the halo had disappeared—because his hair was cut short.

The Arab nose seemed a pitiable defect in an ash-whiskered face that was beyond anemic now. He looked shorter, stooped. The truth was he was sick, his back was killing him. His breath was heavy-laden with airplane martinis and in his limp right hand he held a wet cigar. I told him about Lilian. He mumbled something sideways that I could not possibly make out.

"You've got to speak right at me, remember? Remember me, Quadberry?"

"Mom and Dad of course aren't here."

"No. Why aren't they?"

"He wrote me a letter after we bombed Hué.[4] Said he hadn't sent me to Annapolis to bomb the architecture of Hué. He had been there once and had some important experience—French-kissed the queen of Hué or the like. Anyway, he said I'd have to do a hell of a lot of repentance for that. But he and Mom are separate people. Why isn't *she* here?"

"I don't know."

"I'm not asking you the question. The question is to God."

He shook his head. Then he sat down on the floor of the terminal. People had to walk around. I asked him to get up.

"No. How is old Clinton?"

"Horrible. Aluminum subdivisions, cigar boxes with four thin columns in front, thick as a hive. We got a turquoise water tank; got a shopping center, a monster Jitney Jungle, fifth-rate teeny-boppers covering the place like ants." Why was I being so frank just now, as Quadberry sat on the floor downcast, drooped over like a long weak candle? "It's not our town anymore, Ard. It's going to hurt to drive back into it. Hurts me every day. Please get up."

"And Lilian's not even over there now."

"No. She's a cloud over the Gulf of Mexico. You flew out of Pensacola once. You know what beauty those pink and blue clouds are. That's how I think of her."

"Was there a funeral?"

"Oh, yes. Her Methodist preacher and a big crowd over at Wright Ferguson funeral home. Your mother and father were there. Your father shouldn't have come. He could barely walk. Please get up."

"Why? What am I going to do, where am I going?"

"You've got your saxophone."

"Was there a coffin? Did you all go by and see the pink or blue cloud in it?" He was sneering now as he had done when he was eleven and fourteen and seventeen.

"Yes, they had a very ornate coffin."

"Lilian was the Unknown Stewardess. I'm not getting up."

"I said you still have your saxophone."

"No, I don't. I tried to play it on the ship after the last time I hurt my back. No go. I can't bend my neck or spine to play it. The pain kills me."

"Well, *don't* get up, then. Why am I asking you to get up? I'm just a deaf drummer, too vain to buy a hearing aid. Can't stand to write the ad copy I do. Wasn't I a good drummer?"

4. Ancient Vietnamese city and the scene of heavy fighting during the Vietnam War.

"Superb."

"But we can't be in this condition forever. The police are going to come and make you get up if we do it much longer."

The police didn't come. It was Quadberry's mother who came. She looked me in the face and grabbed my shoulders before she saw Ard on the floor. When she saw him she yanked him off the floor, hugging him passionately. She was shaking with sobs. Quadberry was gathered to her as if he were a rope she was trying to wrap around herself. Her mouth was all over him. Quadberry's mother was a good-looking woman of fifty. I simply held her purse. He cried out that his back was hurting. At last she let him go.

"So now we walk," I said.

"Dad's in the car trying to quit crying," said his mother.

"This is nice," Quadberry said. "I thought everything and everybody was dead around here." He put his arms around his mother. "Let's all go off and kill some time together." His mother's hair was on his lips. "You?" he asked me.

"Murder the devil out of it," I said.

I pretended to follow their car back to their house in Clinton. But when we were going through Jackson, I took the North 55 exit and disappeared from them, exhibiting a great amount of taste, I thought. I would get in their way in this reunion. I had an unimprovable apartment on Old Canton Road in a huge plaster house, Spanish style, with a terrace and ferns and yucca plants, and a green door where I went in. When I woke up I didn't have to make my coffee or fry my egg. The girl who slept in my bed did that. She was Lilian's little sister, Esther Field. Esther was pretty in a minor way and I was proud how I had tamed her to clean and cook around the place. The Field family would appreciate how I lived with her. I showed her the broom and the skillet, and she loved them. She also learned to speak very slowly when she had to say something.

Esther answered the phone when Quadberry called me seven months later. She gave me his message. He wanted to know my opinion on a decision he had to make. There was this Dr. Gordon, a surgeon at Emory Hospital in Atlanta, who said he could cure Quadberry's back problem. Quadberry's back was killing him. He was in torture even holding up the phone to say this. The surgeon said there was a seventy-five/twenty-five chance. Seventy-five that it would be successful, twenty-five that it would be fatal. Esther waited for my opinion. I told her to tell Quadberry to go over to Emory. He'd got through with luck in Vietnam, and now he should ride it out in this petty back operation.

Esther delivered the message and hung up.

"He said the surgeon's just his age; he's some genius from Johns Hopkins Hospital. He said this Gordon guy has published a lot of articles on spinal operations," said Esther.

"Fine and good. All is happy. Come to bed."

I felt her mouth and her voice on my ears, but I could hear only a sort of loud pulse from the girl. All I could do was move toward moisture and nipples and hair.

Quadberry lost his gamble at Emory Hospital in Atlanta. The brilliant surgeon his age lost him. Quadberry died. He died with his Arabian nose up in the air.

That is why I told this story and will never tell another.

# Tom Hawkins

*Hawkins (1946– ) was born and grew up in Park Ridge, Illinois. He received his Bachelor of Journalism degree from the University of Missouri and his Master of Fine Arts degree from the University of North Carolina at Greensboro. His book of short and short-short fiction,* Paper Crown *(1989), contains pieces that had been published in distinguished literary magazines over the preceding decade.*

## Wedding Night

I have worked at this bus station magazine stand since nineteen fifty three, waiting for the right girl to come along. When I took this job, the paint on that wall over there was new; it was a light green color then. The servicemen from the Korean War would stop and buy cigarettes, and I learned the insignia from the Army, Coast Guard, Navy, and Marines.

Once I was held up by a stocky white man in a brown jacket. Showed me the two teeth he had left in his head and the barrel of a little tape-wrapped automatic pointed at my heart. I gave him all the dough but never felt scared. Way I saw it, he was just like me, and I could die behind that counter and just walk away inside his skin, with a few dollars to spend. We were all one thing. So I handed him the money, feeling richer right away—three hundred twenty-three dollars—and let him get away before I called the cops.

I heard they never caught him, then I heard they caught him in another state—Utah I think—and then I heard they found him dead in an airport parking lot in Kansas. I don't know. He may be out there yet. He may be back. May hold me up tonight, or just shoot me dead, or both.

Anything can happen in the bus station. In the nineteen-sixties, we had what we called the hippies, young people in ragged get-ups. They used to sleep all over the furniture in sleeping bags, with packs and rolled-up tents.

That's when I began to think that the right girl might come along after all, some girl who'd grown tired of the long-haired boys, and tired of the road, and walk home with me and hold my hand, and curl up with me in my bed and on my squeaky springs. I kept an eye out. One day I saw a young lady: she looked so long-tired and in need of a friend. I bought her a sandwich and coffee and a peanut-butter cup. I bought her some aspirin and a pint of milk, fingernail clippers and a souvenir shirt.

I told her I had a place where she could come to rest and stay, as long as she might want. I told her it wasn't fancy and wasn't but one room, but what was mine was hers. I knew it was clean. I'd cleaned it up the day before when I saw this girl hanging around.

She stroked my hair and said my heart was full of love. She said she had to sleep about twelve hours and then she'd go away. I took her home. She slumped down on the bed and cried—told me I was "so very kind." And then she slept like the dead. I lay down on the floor beside her, where I said I'd stay. In the middle of the night I woke up on fire, and the room was turning. I couldn't think. The air turned furry, where I crept up and slid in bed beside her, that girl still completely dressed. She breathed like the sea. I touched her skin, just her skin inside her clothes. She really never woke, just sighed and turned. In the morning when I woke up in the bed, she was gone.

I've worked here since nineteen fifty three, waiting for the right girl to come along. I guess she did. Some good marriages don't last long.

# Nathaniel Hawthorne

*Hawthorne (1804–1864) was born in Salem, Massachusetts, where he lived in quiet seclusion before and after his four years of attendance at Bowdoin College. Seldom leaving his room by daylight, he read, meditated, and wrote the stories and sketches that first appeared in 1837 in* Twice-Told Tales. *They brought him neither renown nor money, so in 1839 he took a job in the Boston Custom House and, when he lost it, spent some time at Brook Farm, an experiment in communal living, which provided him with background for his novel* The Blithedale Romance *(1852). At the time of his marriage in 1842 he took his wife to live in a historic house called the Old Manse in Concord, publishing more short pieces in 1846 in a volume called* Mosses from an Old Manse. The Scarlet Letter, *his greatest novel, published in 1850, brought him recognition as a major literary figure. In 1853 he was appointed consul to Liverpool by his college friend Franklin Pierce, who had become president of the United States. After four years of service in his post, Hawthorne traveled in England and Italy until his return to America in 1860. Much of his work is colored by romanticism, while the weight of his Puritan heritage, with its ethical biases and emphasis on sin, radically shaped his themes. The allegorical strain in much of his imaginative work is compensated by the clear and realistic picture of daily experience in his notebooks and in many travel sketches. His novels include* The House of Seven Gables *(1851) and* The Marble Faun *(1860). His books of short stories are two volumes of* Twice-Told Tales *(1837 and 1842) and* Mosses from an Old Manse *(1846).*

## Young Goodman Brown

Young Goodman[1] Brown came forth at sunset into the street of Salem village; but put his head back, after crossing the threshold, to exchange a parting kiss with his young wife. And Faith, as the wife was aptly named, thrust her own pretty head into the street, letting the wind play with the pink ribbons of her cap while she called to Goodman Brown.

"Dearest heart," whispered she, softly and rather sadly, when her lips were close to his ear, "prithee put off your journey until sunrise and sleep in your own bed to-night. A lone woman is troubled with such dreams and such thoughts that she's afeard of herself sometimes. Pray tarry with me this night, dear husband, of all nights in the year!"

1. Title of respect for those below the rank of gentleman.

"My love and my Faith," replied young Goodman Brown, "of all nights in the year, this one night must I tarry away from thee. My journey, as thou callest it, forth and back again, must needs be done 'twixt now and sunrise. What, my sweet, pretty wife, dost thou doubt me already, and we but three months married?"

"Then God bless you!" said Faith, with the pink ribbons; "and may you find all well when you come back."

"Amen!" cried Goodman Brown. "Say thy prayers, dear Faith, and go to bed at dusk, and no harm will come to thee."

So they parted; and the young man pursued his way until, being about to turn the corner by the meeting-house, he looked back and saw the head of Faith still peeping after him with a melancholy air, in spite of her pink ribbons.

"Poor little Faith!" thought he, for his heart smote him. "What a wretch am I to leave her on such an errand! She talks of dreams, too. Methought as she spoke there was trouble in her face, as if a dream had warned her what work is to be done to-night. But no, no; 't would kill her to think it. Well, she's a blessed angel on earth; and after this one night I'll cling to her skirts and follow her to heaven."

With this excellent resolve for the future, Goodman Brown felt himself justified in making more haste on his present evil purpose. He had taken a dreary road, darkened by all the gloomiest trees of the forest, which barely stood aside to let the narrow path creep through, and closed immediately behind. It was all as lonely as could be; and there is this peculiarity in such a solitude, that the traveler knows not who may be concealed by the innumerable trunks and the thick boughs overhead; so that with lonely footsteps he may yet be passing through an unseen multitude.

"There may be a devilish Indian behind every tree," said Goodman Brown to himself; and he glanced fearfully behind him as he added, "What if the devil himself should be at my very elbow!"

His head being turned back, he passed a crook of the road, and, looking forward again, beheld the figure of a man, in grave and decent attire, seated at the foot of an old tree. He arose at Goodman Brown's approach and walked onward side by side with him.

"You are late, Goodman Brown," said he. "The clock of the Old South was striking as I came through Boston,[2] and that is full fifteen minutes agone."

"Faith kept me back a while," replied the young man, with a tremor in his voice, caused by the sudden appearance of his companion, though not wholly unexpected.

It was now deep dusk in the forest, and deepest in that part of it where these two were journeying. As nearly as could be discerned, the second traveller was about fifty years old, apparently in the same rank of life as Goodman Brown, and bearing a considerable resemblance to him, though perhaps more in expression than features. Still they might have been taken for father and son.

2. Boston is some fifteen miles from Salem—perhaps an indication of the supernatural speed of the speaker's travel.

And yet, though the elder person was as simply clad as the younger, and as simple in manner too, he had an indescribable air of one who knew the world, and would not have felt abashed at the governor's dinner table or in King William's[3] court, were it possible that his affairs should call him thither. But the only thing about him that could be fixed upon as remarkable was his staff, which bore the likeness of a great black snake, so curiously wrought that it might almost be seen to twist and wriggle itself like a living serpent. This, of course, must have been an ocular deception, assisted by the uncertain light.

"Come, Goodman Brown!" cried his fellow-traveller, "this is a dull pace for the beginning of a journey. Take my staff, if you are so soon weary."

"Friend," said the other, exchanging his slow pace for a full stop, "having kept covenant by meeting thee here, it is my purpose now to return whence I came. I have scruples touching the matter thou wot'st of."

"Sayest thou so?" replied he of the serpent, smiling apart. "Let us walk on, nevertheless, reasoning as we go; and if I convince thee not thou shalt turn back. We are but a little way in the forest yet."

"Too far, too far!" exclaimed the goodman, unconsciously resuming his walk. "My father never went into the woods on such an errand, nor his father before him. We have been a race of honest men and good Christians since the days of the martyrs; and shall I be the first of the name of Brown that ever took this path and kept—"

"Such company, thou wouldst say," observed the elder person, interpreting his pause. "Well said, Goodman Brown! I have been as well acquainted with your family as with ever a one among the Puritans; and that's no trifle to say. I helped your grandfather, the constable, when he lashed the Quaker woman so smartly through the streets of Salem; and it was I that brought your father a pitch-pine knot, kindled at my own hearth, to set fire to an Indian village in King Philip's war.[4] They were my good friends, both; and many a pleasant walk have we had along this path, and returned merrily after midnight. I would fain be friends with you for their sake."

"If it be as thou sayest," replied Goodman Brown, "I marvel they never spoke of these matters; or, verily, I marvel not, seeing that the least rumor of the sort would have driven them from New England. We are a people of prayer, and good works to boot, and abide no such wickedness."

"Wickedness or not," said the traveler with the twisted staff, "I have a very general acquaintance here in New England. The deacons of many a church have drunk the communion wine with me; the selectmen of divers towns make me their chairman; and a majority of the Great and General Court are firm supporters of my interest. The governor and I, too—But these are state secrets."

"Can this be so?" cried Goodman Brown, with a stare of amazement at his undisturbed companion. "Howbeit, I have nothing to do with the governor and council; they have their own ways, and are no rule for a simple husbandman

3. King William III of England (ruled 1689–1702). 4. Rebellion by Native Americans against white settlers (1675–76).

like me. But, were I to go on with thee, how should I meet the eye of that good old man, our minister, at Salem village? Oh, his voice would make me tremble both Sabbath day and lecture day."

Thus far the elder traveller had listened with due gravity; but now burst into a fit of irrepressible mirth, shaking himself so violently that his snake-like staff actually seemed to wriggle in sympathy.

"Ha! ha! ha!" shouted he again and again; then composing himself, "Well, go on, Goodman Brown, go on; but, prithee, don't kill me with laughing."

"Well, then, to end the matter at once," said Goodman Brown, considerably nettled, "there is my wife, Faith. It would break her dear little heart; and I'd rather break my own."

"Nay, if that be the case," answered the other, "e'en go thy ways, Goodman Brown. I would not for twenty old women like the one hobbling before us that Faith should come to any harm."

As he spoke he pointed his staff at a female figure on the path, in whom Goodman Brown recognized a very pious and exemplary dame, who had taught him his catechism in youth, and was still his moral and spiritual adviser, jointly with the minister and Deacon Gookin.

"A marvel, truly, that Goody Cloyse should be so far in the wilderness at nightfall," said he. "But with your leave, friend, I shall take a cut through the woods until we have left this Christian woman behind. Being a stranger to you, she might ask whom I was consorting with and whither I was going."

"Be it so," said his fellow-traveller. "Betake you to the woods, and let me keep the path."

Accordingly the young man turned aside, but took care to watch his companion, who advanced softly along the road until he had come within a staff's length of the old dame. She, meanwhile, was making the best of her way, with singular speed for so aged a woman, and mumbling some indistinct words—a prayer, doubtless—as she went. The traveller put forth his staff and touched her withered neck with what seemed the serpent's tail.

"The devil!" screamed the pious old lady.

"Then Goody Cloyse knows her old friend?" observed the traveller, confronting her and leaning on his writhing stick.

"Ah, forsooth, and is it your worship indeed?" cried the good dame. "Yea, truly is it, and in the very image of my old gossip,[5] Goodman Brown, the grandfather of the silly fellow that now is. But—would your worship believe it?—my broomstick hath strangely disappeared, stolen, as I suspect, by that unhanged witch, Goody Cory, and that, too, when I was all anointed with the juice of smallage, and cinquefoil, and wolf's-bane—"[6]

"Mingled with fine wheat and the fat of a new-born babe," said the shape of old Goodman Brown.

"Ah, your worship knows the recipe," cried the old lady, cackling aloud. "So, as I was saying, being all ready for the meeting, and no horse to ride on, I made up my mind to foot it; for they tell me there is a nice young man to be

5. Friend. 6. Plants used in witchcraft.

taken into communion to-night. But now your good worship will lend me your arm, and we shall be there in a twinkling."

"That can hardly be," answered her friend. "I may not spare you my arm, Goody Cloyse; but here is my staff, if you will."

So saying, he threw it down at her feet, where, perhaps, it assumed life, being one of the rods which its owner had formerly lent to the Egyptian magi. Of this fact, however, Goodman Brown could not take cognizance. He had cast up his eyes in astonishment, and, looking down again, beheld neither Goody Cloyse nor the serpentine staff, but this fellow-traveller alone, who waited for him as calmly as if nothing had happened.

"That old woman taught me my catechism," said the young man; and there was a world of meaning in this simple comment.

They continued to walk onward, while the elder traveller exhorted his companion to make good speed and persevere in the path, discoursing so aptly that his arguments seemed rather to spring up in the bosom of his auditor than to be suggested by himself. As they went, he plucked a branch of maple, to serve for a walking stick, and began to strip it of the twigs and little boughs, which were wet with evening dew. The moment his fingers touched them they became strangely withered and dried up as with a week's sunshine. Thus the pair proceeded, at a good free pace, until suddenly, in a gloomy hollow of the road, Goodman Brown sat himself down on the stump of a tree and refused to go any farther.

"Friend," said he, stubbornly, "my mind is made up. Not another step will I budge on this errand. What if a wretched old woman do choose to go to the devil when I thought she was going to heaven: is that any reason why I should quit my dear Faith and go after her?"

"You will think better of this by and by," said his acquaintance, composedly. "Sit here and rest yourself a while; and when you feel like moving again, there is my staff to help you along."

Without more words, he threw his companion the maple stick, and was as speedily out of sight as if he had vanished into the deepening gloom. The young man sat a few moments by the roadside, applauding himself greatly, and thinking with how clear a conscience he should meet the minister in his morning walk, nor shrink from the eye of good old Deacon Gookin. And what calm sleep would be his that very night, which was to have been spent so wickedly, but so purely and sweetly now, in the arms of Faith! Amidst these pleasant and praiseworthy meditations, Goodman Brown heard the tramp of horses along the road, and deemed it advisable to conceal himself within the verge of the forest, conscious of the guilty purpose that had brought him thither, though now so happily turned from it.

On came the hoof tramps and the voices of the riders, two grave old voices, conversing soberly as they drew near. These mingled sounds appeared to pass along the road, within a few yards of the young man's hiding-place; but, owing doubtless to the depth of the gloom at that particular spot, neither the travellers nor their steeds were visible. Though their figures brushed the small boughs by the wayside, it could not be seen that they intercepted, even for a moment, the faint gleam from the strip of bright sky athwart which they must have passed. Goodman Brown alternately crouched and stood on tiptoe, pulling aside the branches and thrusting forth his head as far as he durst without discerning so much as a shadow. It vexed him the more, because he could have sworn, were such a thing possible, that he recognized the voices of the minister and Deacon Gookin, jogging along quietly, as they were wont to do, when bound to some ordination or ecclesiastical council. While yet within hearing, one of the riders stopped to pluck a switch.

"Of the two, reverend sir," said the voice like the deacon's, "I had rather miss an ordination dinner than to-night's meeting. They tell me that some of our community are to be here from Falmouth and beyond, and others from Connecticut and Rhode Island, besides several of the Indian powwows, who, after their fashion, know almost as much deviltry as the best of us. Moreover, there is a goodly young woman to be taken into communion."

"Mighty well, Deacon Gookin!" replied the solemn old tones of the minister. "Spur up, or we shall be late. Nothing can be done, you know, until I get on the ground."

The hoofs clattered again; and the voices, talking so strangely in the empty air, passed on through the forest, where no church had ever been gathered or solitary Christian prayed. Whither, then, could these holy men be journeying so deep into the heathen wilderness? Young Goodman Brown caught hold of a tree for support, being ready to sink down on the ground, faint and overburdened with the heavy sickness of his heart. He looked up to the sky, doubting whether there really was a heaven above him. Yet there was the blue arch, and the stars brightening in it.

"With heaven above and Faith below, I will yet stand firm against the devil!" cried Goodman Brown.

While he still gazed upward into the deep arch of the firmament and had lifted his hands to pray, a cloud, though no wind was stirring, hurried across the zenith and hid the brightening stars. The blue sky was still visible, except directly overhead, where this black mass of cloud was sweeping swiftly northward. Aloft in the air, as if from the depths of the cloud, came a confused and doubtful sound of voices. Once the listener fancied that he could distinguish the accents of towns-people of his own, men and women, both pious and ungodly, many of whom he had met at the communion table, and had seen others rioting at the tavern. The next moment, so indistinct were the sounds, he doubted whether he had heard aught but the murmur of the old forest, whispering without a wind. Then came a stronger swell of those familiar tones, heard daily in the sunshine at Salem village, but never until now from a cloud of night. There was one voice, of a young woman, uttering lamentations, yet with an uncertain sorrow, and entreating for some favor, which, perhaps, it would grieve her to obtain; and all the unseen multitude, both saints and sinners, seemed to encourage her onward.

"Faith!" shouted Goodman Brown, in a voice of agony and desperation; and the echoes of the forest mocked him, crying, "Faith! Faith!" as if bewildered wretches were seeking her all through the wilderness.

The cry of grief, rage, and terror was yet piercing the night, when the unhappy husband held his breath for a response. There was a scream, drowned immediately in a louder murmur of voices, fading into far-off laughter, as the dark cloud swept away, leaving the clear and silent sky above Goodman Brown. But something fluttered lightly down through the air and caught on the branch of a tree. The young man seized it, and beheld a pink ribbon.

"My Faith is gone!" cried he, after one stupefied moment. "There is no good on earth; and sin is but a name. Come, devil; for to thee is this world given."

And, maddened with despair, so that he laughed loud and long, did Goodman Brown grasp his staff and set forth again, at such a rate that he seemed to fly along the forest path rather than to walk or run. The road grew wilder and drearier and more faintly traced, and vanished at length, leaving him in the heart of the dark wilderness, still rushing onward with the instinct that guides mortal man to evil. The whole forest was peopled with frightful sounds—the creaking of the trees, the howling of wild beasts, and the yell of Indians; while sometimes the wind tolled like a distant church bell, and sometimes gave a broad roar around the traveller, as if all Nature were laughing him to scorn. But he was himself the chief horror of the scene, and shrank not from its other horrors.

"Ha! ha! ha!" roared Goodman Brown when the wind laughed at him. "Let us hear which will laugh loudest. Think not to frighten me with your deviltry. Come witch, come wizard, come Indian powwow, come devil himself, and here comes Goodman Brown. You may as well fear him as he fear you."

In truth, all through the haunted forest, there could be nothing more frightful than the figure of Goodman Brown. On he flew among the black pines, brandishing his staff with frenzied gestures, now giving vent to an inspiration of horrid blasphemy, and now shouting forth such laughter as set all the echoes of the forest laughing like demons around him. The fiend in his own shape is less hideous than when he rages in the breast of man. Thus sped the demoniac on his course, until, quivering among the trees, he saw a red light before him, as when the felled trunks and branches of a clearing have been set on fire, and throw up their lurid blaze against the sky, at the hour of midnight. He paused, in a lull of the tempest that had driven him onward, and heard the swell of what seemed a hymn, rolling solemnly from a distance with the weight of many voices. He knew the tune; it was a familiar one in the choir of the village meeting-house. The verse died heavily away, and was lengthened by a chorus, not of human voices, but of all the sounds of the benighted wilderness pealing in awful harmony together. Goodman Brown cried out, and his cry was lost to his own ear, by its unison with the cry of the desert.

In the interval of silence he stole forward until the light glared full upon his eyes. At one extremity of an open space, hemmed in by the dark wall of the forest, arose a rock, bearing some rude, natural resemblance either to an altar or a pulpit, and surrounded by four blazing pines, their tops aflame, their stems untouched, like candles at an evening meeting. The mass of foliage that had overgrown the summit of the rock was all on fire, blazing high into the night and fitfully illuminating the whole field. Each pendent twig and leafy festoon was in a blaze. As the red light arose and fell, a numerous congregation alternately shone forth, then disappeared in shadow, and again grew, as it were, out of the darkness, peopling the heart of the solitary woods at once.

"A grave and dark-clad company," quoth Goodman Brown.

In truth they were such. Among them, quivering to and fro between gloom and splendor, appeared faces that would be seen next day at the council board of the province, and others which, Sabbath after Sabbath, looked devoutly heavenward, and benignantly over the crowded pews, from the holiest pulpits in the land. Some affirm that the lady of the governor was there. At least there were high dames well known to her, and wives of honored husbands, and widows, a great multitude, and ancient maidens, all of excellent repute, and fair young girls, who trembled lest their mothers should espy them. Either the sudden gleams of light flashing over the obscure field bedazzled Goodman Brown, or he recognized a score of the church members of Salem village famous for their especial sanctity. Good old Deacon Gookin had arrived, and waited at the skirts of that venerable saint, his revered pastor. But, irreverently consorting with these grave, reputable, and pious people, these elders of the church, these chaste dames and dewy virgins, there were men of dissolute lives and women of spotted fame, wretches given over to all mean and filthy vice, and suspected even of horrid crimes. It was strange to see that the good shrank not from the wicked, nor were the sinners abashed by the saints. Scattered also among their pale-faced enemies were the Indian priests, or powwows, who had often scared their native forest with more hideous incantations than any known to English witchcraft.

"But where is Faith?" thought Goodman Brown; and, as hope came into his heart, he trembled.

Another verse of the hymn arose, a slow and mournful strain, such as the pious love, but joined to words which expressed all that our nature can conceive of sin, and darkly hinted at far more. Unfathomable to mere mortals is the lore of fiends. Verse after verse was sung, and still the chorus of the desert swelled between like the deepest tone of a mighty organ; and with the final peal of that dreadful anthem there came a sound, as if the roaring wind, the rushing streams, the howling beasts, and every other voice of the unconverted wilderness were mingling and according with the voice of guilty man in homage to the prince of all. The four blazing pines threw up a loftier flame, and obscurely discovered shapes and visages of horror on the smoke wreaths above the impious assembly. At the same moment the fire on the rock shot redly forth and formed a glowing arch above its base, where now appeared a figure. With reverence be it spoken, the apparition bore no slight similitude, both in garb and manner, to some grave divine of the New England churches.

"Bring forth the converts!" cried a voice that echoed through the field and rolled into the forest.

At the word, Goodman Brown stepped forth from the shadow of the trees and approached the congregation, with whom he felt a loathful brotherhood by the sympathy of all that was wicked in his heart. He could have well-nigh sworn that the shape of his own dead father beckoned him to advance, looking downward from a smoke wreath, while a woman, with dim features of despair, threw out her hand to warn him back. Was it his mother? But he had no power to retreat one step, nor to resist, even in thought, when the minister and good old Deacon Gookin seized his arms and led him to the blazing rock. Thither came also the slender form of a veiled female, led between Goody Cloyse, that pious teacher of the catechism, and Martha Carrier, who had received the devil's promise to be queen of hell. A rampant hag was she. And there stood the proselytes beneath the canopy of fire.

"Welcome, my children," said the dark figure, "to the communion of your race. Ye have found thus young your nature and your destiny. My children, look behind you!"

They turned; and flashing forth, as it were, in a sheet of flame, the fiend worshippers were seen; the smile of welcome gleamed darkly on every visage.

"There," resumed the sable form, "are all whom ye have reverenced from youth. Ye deemed them holier than yourselves, and shrank from your own sin, contrasting it with their lives of righteousness and prayerful aspirations heavenward. Yet here are they all in my worshipping assembly. This night it shall be granted you to know their secret deeds: how hoary-bearded elders of the church have whispered wanton words to the young maids of their households; how many a woman, eager for widows' weeds, has given her husband a drink at bedtime and let him sleep his last sleep in her bosom; how beardless youths have made haste to inherit their fathers' wealth; and how fair damsels—blush not, sweet ones—have dug little graves in the garden, and bidden me, the sole guest, to an infant's funeral. By the sympathy of your human hearts for sin ye shall scent out all the places—whether in church, bed-chamber, street, field, or forest—where crime has been committed, and shall exult to behold the whole earth one stain of guilt, one mighty blood spot. Far more than this. It shall be yours to penetrate, in every bosom, the deep mystery of sin, the fountain of all wicked arts, and which inexhaustibly supplies more evil impulses than human power—than my power at its utmost—can make manifest in deeds. And now, my children, look upon each other."

They did so; and, by the blaze of the hell-kindled torches, the wretched man beheld his Faith, and the wife her husband, trembling before that unhallowed altar.

"Lo, there ye stand, my children," said the figure, in a deep and solemn tone, almost sad with its despairing awfulness, as if his once angelic nature could yet mourn for our miserable race. "Depending upon one another's hearts, ye had still hoped that virtue were not all a dream. Now are ye undeceived. Evil is the nature of mankind. Evil must be your only happiness. Welcome again, my children, to the communion of your race."

"Welcome," repeated the fiend worshippers, in one cry of despair and triumph.

And there they stood, the only pair, as it seemed, who were yet hesitating on the verge of wickedness in this dark world. A basin was hollowed, naturally, in the rock. Did it contain water, reddened by the lurid light? or was it blood? or, perchance, a liquid flame? Herein did the shape of evil dip his hand and prepare to lay the mark of baptism upon their foreheads, that they might be partakers of the mystery of sin, more conscious of the secret guilt of others, both in deed and thought, than they could now be of their own. The husband cast one look at his pale wife, and Faith at him. What polluted wretches would the next glance show them to each other, shuddering alike at what they disclosed and what they saw!

"Faith! Faith!" cried the husband, "look up to Heaven, and resist the wicked one."

Whether Faith obeyed he knew not. Hardly had he spoken when he found himself amid calm night and solitude, listening to a roar of the wind which died heavily away through the forest. He staggered against the rock and felt it chill and damp, while a hanging twig, that had been all on fire, besprinkled his cheek with the coldest dew.

The next morning young Goodman Brown came slowly into the street of Salem village, staring around him like a bewildered man. The good old minister was taking a walk along the graveyard, to get an appetite for breakfast and meditate his sermon, and bestowed a blessing, as he passed, on Goodman Brown. He shrank from the venerable saint as if to avoid an anathema. Old Deacon Gookin was at domestic worship, and the holy words of his prayer were heard through the open window. "What God doth the wizard pray to?" quoth Goodman Brown. Goody Cloyse, that excellent old Christian, stood in the early sunshine, at her own lattice, catechizing a little girl who had brought her a pint of morning's milk. Goodman Brown snatched away the child as from the grasp of the fiend himself. Turning the corner by the meeting-house, he spied the head of Faith, with the pink ribbons, gazing anxiously forth, and bursting into such joy at sight of him that she skipped along the street and almost kissed her husband before the whole village. But Goodman Brown looked sternly and sadly into her face, and passed on without a greeting.

Had Goodman Brown fallen asleep in the forest, and only dreamed a wild dream of a witch-meeting?

Be it so if you will; but, alas! it was a dream of evil omen for young Goodman Brown. A stern, a sad, a darkly meditative, a distrustful, if not a desperate man did he become from the night of that fearful dream. On the Sabbath day, when the congregation were singing a holy psalm, he could not listen because an anthem of sin rushed loudly upon his ear and drowned all the blessed strain. When the minister spoke from the pulpit with power and fervid eloquence, and, with his hand on the open Bible, of the sacred truths of our religion, and of saint-like lives and triumphant deaths, and of future bliss or misery unutterable, then did Goodman Brown turn pale, dreading lest the roof should thunder down upon the gray blasphemer and his hearers. Often, awaking suddenly at midnight, he shrank from the bosom of Faith; and at morning or eventide, when the family knelt down at prayer, he scowled and muttered to himself, and gazed sternly at his wife, and turned away. And when he had lived long, and was borne to his grave a hoary corpse, followed by Faith, an aged woman, and children and grandchildren, a goodly procession, besides neighbors not a few, they carved no hopeful verse upon his tombstone, for his dying hour was gloom.

# The Birthmark

In the latter part of the last century there lived a man of science, an eminent proficient in every branch of natural philosophy, who not long before our story opens had made experience of a spiritual affinity more attractive than any chemical one. He had left his laboratory to the care of an assistant, cleared his fine countenance from the furnace smoke, washed the stain of acids from his fingers, and persuaded a beautiful woman to become his wife. In those days when the comparatively recent discovery of electricity and other kindred mysteries of Nature seemed to open paths into the region of miracle, it was not unusual for the love of science to rival the love of woman in its depth and absorbing energy. The higher intellect, the imagination, the spirit, and even the heart might all find their congenial aliment in pursuits which, as some of their ardent votaries believed, would ascend from one step of powerful intelligence to another, until the philosopher should lay his hand on the secret of creative force and perhaps make new worlds for himself. We know not whether Aylmer possessed this degree of faith in man's ultimate control over Nature. He had devoted himself, however, too unreservedly to scientific studies ever to be weaned from them by any second passion. His love for his young wife might prove the stronger of the two; but it could only be by intertwining itself with his love of science, and uniting the strength of the latter to his own.

Such a union accordingly took place, and was attended with truly remarkable consequences and a deeply impressive moral. One day, very soon after their marriage, Aylmer sat gazing at his wife with a trouble in his countenance that grew stronger until he spoke.

"Georgiana," said he, "has it never occurred to you that the mark upon your cheek might be removed?"

"No, indeed," said she, smiling; but perceiving the seriousness of his manner, she blushed deeply. "To tell the truth it has been so often called a charm that I was simple enough to imagine it might be so."

"Ah, upon another face perhaps it might," replied her husband; "but never on yours. No, dearest Georgiana, you came so nearly perfect from the hand of Nature that this slightest possible defect, which we hesitate whether to term a defect or a beauty, shocks me, as being the visible mark of earthly imperfection."

"Shocks you, my husband!" cried Georgiana, deeply hurt; at first reddening with momentary anger, but then bursting into tears. "Then why did you take me from my mother's side? You cannot love what shocks you!"

To explain this conversation it must be mentioned that in the centre of Georgiana's left cheek there was a singular mark, deeply interwoven, as it were, with the texture and substance of her face. In the usual state of her complexion—a healthy though delicate bloom—the mark wore a tint of deeper crimson, which imperfectly defined its shape amid the surrounding rosiness. When she blushed it gradually became more indistinct, and finally vanished amid the triumphant rush of blood that bathed the whole cheek with its brilliant glow. But if any shifting motion caused her to turn pale there was the mark again, a crimson stain upon the snow, in what Aylmer sometimes deemed an almost fearful distinctness. Its shape bore not a little similarity to the human hand, though of the smallest pygmy size. Georgiana's lovers were wont to say that some fairy at her birth hour had laid her tiny hand upon the infant's cheek, and left this impress there in token of the magic endowments that were to give her such sway over all hearts. Many a desperate swain would have risked life for the privilege of pressing his lips to the mysterious hand. It must not be concealed, however, that the impression wrought by this fairy sign manual varied exceedingly, according to the difference of temperament in the beholders. Some fastidious persons—but they were exclusively of her own sex—affirmed that the bloody hand, as they chose to call it, quite destroyed the effect of Georgiana's beauty, and rendered her countenance even hideous. But it would be as reasonable to say that one of those small blue stains which sometimes occur in the purest statuary marble would convert the Eve of Powers[1] to a monster. Masculine observers, if the birthmark did not heighten their admiration, contented themselves with wishing it away, that the world might possess one living specimen of ideal loveliness without the semblance of a flaw. After his marriage,—for he thought little or nothing of the matter before,—Aylmer discovered that this was the case with himself.

Had she been less beautiful,—if Envy's self could have found aught else to sneer at,—he might have felt his affection heightened by the prettiness of this mimic hand, now vaguely portrayed, now lost, now stealing forth again and glimmering to and fro with every pulse of emotion that throbbed within her heart; but seeing her otherwise so perfect, he found this one defect grow more and more intolerable with every moment of their united lives. It was the fatal flaw of humanity which Nature, in one shape or another, stamps ineffaceably on all her productions, either to imply that they are temporary and finite, or that their perfection must be wrought by toil and pain. The crimson hand expressed the ineludible gripe[2] in which mortality clutches the highest and purest of earthly mould, degrading them into kindred with the lowest, and even with the very brutes, like whom their visible frames return to dust. In this manner, selecting it as the symbol of his wife's liability to sin, sorrow, decay, and death, Aylmer's sombre imagination was not long in rendering the birthmark a frightful object, causing him more trouble and horror than ever Georgiana's beauty, whether of soul or sense, had given him delight.

At all the seasons which should have been their happiest, he invariably and without intending it, nay, in spite of a purpose to the contrary, reverted to this one disastrous topic. Trifling as it at first appeared, it so connected itself with innumerable trains of thought and modes of feeling that it became the central point of all. With the morning twilight Aylmer opened his eyes upon his wife's face and recognized the symbol of imperfection; and when they sat together at the evening hearth his eyes wandered stealthily to her cheek, and beheld, flickering with the blaze of the wood fire, the spectral hand that wrote mortality

1. Hiram Powers (1805–1873), American sculptor. 2. Grip.

where he would fain have worshipped. Georgiana soon learned to shudder at his gaze. It needed but a glance with the peculiar expression that his face often wore to change the roses of her cheek into a deathlike paleness, amid which the crimson hand was brought strongly out, like a bas-relief of ruby on the whitest marble.

Late one night when the lights were growing dim, so as hardly to betray the stain on the poor wife's cheek, she herself, for the first time, voluntarily took up the subject.

"Do you remember, my dear Aylmer," said she, with a feeble attempt at a smile, "have you any recollection of a dream last night about this odious hand?"

"None! none whatever!" replied Aylmer, starting; but then he added, in a dry, cold tone, affected for the sake of concealing the real depth of his emotion, "I might well dream of it; for before I fell asleep it had taken a pretty firm hold of my fancy."

"And you did dream of it?" continued Georgiana, hastily; for she dreaded lest a gush of tears should interrupt what she had to say. "A terrible dream! I wonder that you forget it. Is it possible to forget this one expression?—'It is in her heart now; we must have it out!' Reflect, my husband; for by all means I would have you recall that dream."

The mind is in a sad state when Sleep, the all-involving, cannot confine her spectres within the dim region of her sway, but suffers them to break forth, affrighting this actual life with secrets that perchance belong to a deeper one. Aylmer now remembered his dream. He had fancied himself with his servant Aminadab, attempting an operation for the removal of the birthmark; but the deeper went the knife, the deeper sank the hand, until at length its tiny grasp appeared to have caught hold of Georgiana's heart; whence, however, her husband was inexorably resolved to cut or wrench it away.

When the dream had shaped itself perfectly in his memory, Aylmer sat in his wife's presence with a guilty feeling. Truth often finds its way to the mind close muffled in robes of sleep, and then speaks with uncompromising directness of matters in regard to which we practise an unconscious self-deception during our waking moments. Until now he had not been aware of the tyrannizing influence acquired by one idea over his mind, and of the lengths which he might find in his heart to go for the sake of giving himself peace.

"Aylmer," resumed Georgiana, solemnly, "I know not what may be the cost to both of us to rid me of this fatal birthmark. Perhaps its removal may cause cureless deformity; or it may be the stain goes as deep as life itself. Again: do we know that there is a possibility, on any terms, of unclasping the firm gripe of this little hand which was laid upon me before I came into the world?"

"Dearest Georgiana, I have spent much thought upon the subject," hastily interrupted Aylmer. "I am convinced of the perfect practicability of its removal."

"If there be the remotest possibility of it," continued Georgiana, "let the attempt be made at whatever risk. Danger is nothing to me; for life, while this hateful mark makes me the object of your horror and disgust,—life is a burden which I would fling down with joy. Either remove this dreadful hand, or take my wretched life! You have deep science. All the world bears witness of it. You have achieved great wonders. Cannot you remove this little, little mark, which I cover with the tips of two small fingers? Is this beyond your power, for the sake of your own peace, and to save your poor wife from madness?"

"Noblest, dearest, tenderest wife," cried Aylmer, rapturously, "doubt not my power. I have already given this matter the deepest thought—thought which might almost have enlightened me to create a being less perfect than yourself. Georgiana, you have led me deeper than ever into the heart of science. I feel myself fully competent to render this dear cheek as faultless as its fellow; and then, most beloved, what will be my triumph when I shall have corrected what Nature left imperfect in her fairest work! Even Pygmalion,[3] when his sculptured woman assumed life, felt not greater ecstasy than mine will be."

"It is resolved, then," said Georgiana, faintly smiling. "And, Aylmer, spare me not, though you should find the birthmark take refuge in my heart at last."

Her husband tenderly kissed her cheek—her right cheek—not that which bore the impress of the crimson hand.

The next day Aylmer apprised his wife of a plan that he had formed whereby he might have opportunity for the intense thought and constant watchfulness which the proposed operation would require; while Georgiana, likewise, would enjoy the perfect repose essential to its success. They were to seclude themselves in the extensive apartments occupied by Aylmer as a laboratory, and where, during his toilsome youth, he had made discoveries in the elemental powers of Nature that had roused the admiration of all the learned societies in Europe. Seated calmly in this laboratory, the pale philosopher had investigated the secrets of the highest cloud region and of the profoundest mines; he had satisfied himself of the causes that kindled and kept alive the fires of the volcano; and had explained the mystery of fountains, and how it is that they gush forth, some so bright and pure, and others with such rich medicinal virtues, from the dark bosom of the earth. Here, too, at an earlier period, he had studied the wonders of the human frame, and attempted to fathom the very process by which Nature assimilates all her precious influences from earth and air, and from the spiritual world, to create and foster man, her masterpiece. The latter pursuit, however, Aylmer had long laid aside in unwilling recognition of the truth—against which all seekers sooner or later stumble—that our great creative Mother, while she amuses us with apparently working in the broadest sunshine, is yet severely careful to keep her own secrets, and, in spite of her pretended openness, shows us nothing but results. She permits us, indeed, to mar, but seldom to mend, and, like a jealous patentee, on no account to make. Now, however, Aylmer resumed these half-forgotten investigations; not, of course, with such hopes or wishes as first suggest them; but because they involved much physiological truth and lay in the path of his proposed scheme for the treatment of Georgiana.

As he led her over the threshold of the laboratory, Georgiana was cold and tremulous. Aylmer looked cheerfully into her face, with intent to reassure her, but was so startled with the intense glow of the birthmark upon the whiteness

3. King of Cyprus who fell in love with a female statue he had made. Aphrodite, goddess of love, made the statue live.

of her cheek that he could not restrain a strong convulsive shudder. His wife fainted.

"Aminadab! Aminadab!" shouted Aylmer, stamping violently on the floor.

Forthwith there issued from an inner apartment a man of low stature but bulky frame, with shaggy hair hanging about his visage, which was grimed with the vapors of the furnace. This personage had been Aylmer's underworker during his whole scientific career, and was admirably fitted for that office by his great mechanical readiness, and the skill with which, while incapable of comprehending a single principle, he executed all the details of his master's experiments. With his vast strength, his shaggy hair, his smoky aspect, and the indescribable earthiness that incrusted him, he seemed to represent man's physical nature; while Aylmer's slender figure, and pale, intellectual face, were no less apt a type of the spiritual element.

"Throw open the door of the boudoir, Aminadab," said Aylmer, "and burn a pastil."[4]

"Yes, master," answered Aminadab, looking intently at the lifeless form of Georgiana; and then he muttered to himself, "If she were my wife, I'd never part with that birthmark."

When Georgiana recovered consciousness she found herself breathing an atmosphere of penetrating fragrance, the gentle potency of which had recalled her from her deathlike faintness. The scene around her looked like enchantment. Aylmer had converted those smoky, dingy, sombre rooms, where he had spent his brightest years in recondite pursuits, into a series of beautiful apartments not unfit to be the secluded abode of a lovely woman. The walls were hung with gorgeous curtains, which imparted the combination of grandeur and grace that no other species of adornment can achieve; and as they fell from the ceiling to the floor, their rich and ponderous folds, concealing all angles and straight lines, appeared to shut in the scene from infinite space. For aught Georgiana knew, it might be a pavilion among the clouds. And Aylmer, excluding the sunshine, which would have interfered with his chemical processes, had supplied its place with perfumed lamps, emitting flames of various hue, but all uniting in a soft, impurpled radiance. He now knelt by his wife's side, watching her earnestly, but without alarm; for he was confident in his science, and felt that he could draw a magic circle round her within which no evil might intrude.

"Where am I? Ah, I remember," said Georgiana, faintly; and she placed her hand over her cheek to hide the terrible mark from her husband's eyes.

"Fear not, dearest!" exclaimed he. "Do not shrink from me! Believe me, Georgiana, I even rejoice in this single imperfection, since it will be such a rapture to remove it."

"Oh, spare me!" sadly replied his wife. "Pray do not look at it again. I never can forget that convulsive shudder."

In order to soothe Georgiana, and, as it were, to release her mind from the burden of actual things, Aylmer now put in practice some of the light and playful secrets which science had taught him among its profounder lore. Airy figures, absolutely bodiless ideas, and forms of unsubstantial beauty came and

4. Aromatic paste used in fumigation.

danced before her, imprinting their momentary footsteps on beams of light. Though she had some indistinct idea of the method of these optical phenomena, still the illusion was almost perfect enough to warrant the belief that her husband possessed sway over the spiritual world. Then again, when she felt a wish to look forth from her seclusion, immediately, as if her thoughts were answered, the procession of external existence flitted across a screen. The scenery and the figures of actual life were perfectly represented, but with that bewitching, yet indescribable difference which always makes a picture, an image, or a shadow so much more attractive than the original. When wearied of this, Aylmer bade her cast her eyes upon a vessel containing a quantity of earth. She did so, with little interest at first; but was soon startled to perceive the germ of a plant shooting upward from the soil. Then came the slender stalk; the leaves gradually unfolded themselves; and amid them was a perfect and lovely flower.

"It is magical!" cried Georgiana. "I dare not touch it."

"Nay, pluck it," answered Aylmer,—"pluck it, and inhale its brief perfume while you may. The flower will wither in a few moments and leave nothing save its brown seed vessels; but thence may be perpetuated a race as ephemeral as itself."

But Georgiana had no sooner touched the flower than the whole plant suffered a blight, its leaves turning coal-black as if by the agency of fire.

"There was too powerful a stimulus," said Aylmer, thoughtfully.

To make up for this abortive experiment, he proposed to take her portrait by a scientific process of his own invention. It was to be effected by rays of light striking upon a polished plate of metal. Georgiana assented; but, on looking at the result, was affrighted to find the features of the portrait blurred and indefinable; while the minute figure of a hand appeared where the cheek should have been. Aylmer snatched the metallic plate and threw it into a jar of corrosive acid.

Soon, however, he forgot these mortifying failures. In the intervals of study and chemical experiment he came to her flushed and exhausted, but seemed invigorated by her presence, and spoke in glowing language of the resources of his art. He gave a history of the long dynasty of the alchemists, who spent so many ages in quest of the universal solvent by which the golden principle might be elicited from all things vile and base. Aylmer appeared to believe that, by the plainest scientific logic, it was altogether within the limits of possibility to discover this long-sought medium; "but," he added, "a philosopher who should go deep enough to acquire the power would attain too lofty a wisdom to stoop to the exercise of it." Not less singular were his opinions in regard to the elixir vitae.[5] He more than intimated that it was at his option to concoct a liquid that should prolong life for years, perhaps interminably; but that it would produce a discord in Nature which all the world, and chiefly the quaffer of the immortal nostrum, would find cause to curse.

"Aylmer, are you in earnest?" asked Georgiana, looking at him with amazement and fear. "It is terrible to possess such power, or even dream of possessing it."

"Oh, do not tremble, my love," said her husband. "I would not wrong either

5. Substance supposed capable of prolonging life.

you or myself by working such inharmonious effects upon our lives; but I would have you consider how trifling, in comparison, is the skill requisite to remove this little hand."

At the mention of the birthmark, Georgiana, as usual, shrank as if a redhot iron had touched her cheek.

Again Aylmer applied himself to his labors. She could hear his voice in the distant furnace room giving directions to Aminadab, whose harsh, uncouth, misshapen tones were audible in response, more like the grunt or growl of a brute than human speech. After hours of absence, Aylmer reappeared and proposed that she should now examine his cabinet of chemical products and natural treasures of the earth. Among the former he showed her a small vial, in which, he remarked, was contained a gentle yet most powerful fragrance, capable of impregnating all the breezes that blow across a kingdom. They were of inestimable value, the contents of that little vial; and, as he said so, he threw some of the perfume into the air and filled the room with piercing and invigorating delight.

"And what is this?" asked Georgiana, pointing to a small crystal globe containing a gold-colored liquid. "It is so beautiful to the eye that I could imagine it the elixir of life."

"In one sense it is," replied Aylmer; "or, rather, the elixir of immortality. It is the most precious poison that ever was concocted in this world. By its aid I could apportion the lifetime of any mortal at whom you might point your finger. The strength of the dose would determine whether he were to linger out years, or drop dead in the midst of a breath. No king on his guarded throne could keep his life if I, in my private station, should deem that the welfare of millions justified me in depriving him of it."

"Why do you keep such a terrific drug?" inquired Georgiana in horror.

"Do not mistrust me, dearest," said her husband, smiling; "its virtuous potency is yet greater than its harmful one. But see! here is a powerful cosmetic. With a few drops of this in a vase of water, freckles may be washed away as easily as the hands are cleansed. A stronger infusion would take the blood out of the cheek, and leave the rosiest beauty a pale ghost."

"Is it with this lotion that you intend to bathe my cheek?" asked Georgiana, anxiously.

"Oh, no," hastily replied her husband; "this is merely superficial. Your case demands a remedy that shall go deeper."

In his interviews with Georgiana, Aylmer generally made minute inquiries as to her sensations and whether the confinement of the rooms and the temperature of the atmosphere agreed with her. These questions had such a particular drift that Georgiana began to conjecture that she was already subjected to certain physical influences, either breathed in with the fragrant air or taken with her food. She fancied likewise, but it might be altogether fancy, that there was a stirring up of her system—a strange, indefinite sensation creeping through her veins, and tingling, half painfully, half pleasurably, at her heart. Still, whenever she dared to look into the mirror, there she beheld herself pale as a white rose and with the crimson birthmark stamped upon her cheek. Not even Aylmer now hated it so much as she.

To dispel the tedium of the hours which her husband found it necessary to devote to the processes of combination and analysis, Georgiana turned over the volumes of his scientific library. In many dark old tomes she met with chapters full of romance and poetry. They were the works of the philosophers of the middle ages, such as Albertus Magnus, Cornelius Agrippa, Paracelsus, and the famous friar who created the prophetic Brazen Head.[6] All these antique naturalists stood in advance of their centuries, yet were imbued with some of their credulity, and therefore were believed, and perhaps imagined themselves to have acquired from the investigation of Nature a power above Nature, and from physics a sway over the spiritual world. Hardly less curious and imaginative were the early volumes of the Transactions of the Royal Society, in which the members, knowing little of the limits of natural possibility, were continually recording wonders or proposing methods whereby wonders might be wrought.

But to Georgiana the most engrossing volume was a large folio from her husband's own hand, in which he had recorded every experiment of his scientific career, its original aim, the methods adopted for its development, and its final success or failure, with the circumstances to which either event was attributable. The book, in truth, was both the history and emblem of his ardent, ambitious, imaginative, yet practical and laborious life. He handled physical details as if there were nothing beyond them; yet spiritualized them all, and redeemed himself from materialism by his strong and eager aspiration towards the infinite. In his grasp the veriest clod of earth assumed a soul. Georgiana, as she read, reverenced Aylmer and loved him more profoundly than ever, but with a less entire dependence on his judgment than heretofore. Much as he had accomplished, she could not but observe that his most splendid successes were almost invariably failures, if compared with the ideal at which he aimed. His brightest diamonds were the merest pebbles, and felt to be so by himself, in comparison with the inestimable gems which lay hidden beyond his reach. The volume, rich with achievements that had won renown for its author, was yet as melancholy a record as ever mortal hand had penned. It was the sad confession and continual exemplification of the shortcomings of the composite man, the spirit burdened with clay and working in matter, and of the despair that assails the higher nature at finding itself so miserably thwarted by the earthly part. Perhaps every man of genius in whatever sphere might recognize the image of his own experience in Aylmer's journal.

So deeply did these reflections affect Georgiana that she laid her face upon the open volume and burst into tears. In this situation she was found by her husband.

"It is dangerous to read in a sorcerer's books," said he, with a smile, though his countenance was uneasy and displeased. "Georgiana, there are pages in that volume which I can scarcely glance over and keep my senses. Take heed lest it prove as detrimental to you."

"It has made me worship you more than ever," said she.

"Ah, wait for this one success," rejoined he, "then worship me if you will. I shall deem myself hardly unworthy of it. But come, I have sought you for the luxury of your voice. Sing to me, dearest."

6. All alchemists and philosophers who prepared the way for modern science.

So she poured out the liquid music of her voice to quench the thirst of his spirit. He then took his leave with a boyish exuberance of gayety, assuring her that her seclusion would endure but a little longer, and that the result was already certain. Scarcely had he departed when Georgiana felt irresistibly impelled to follow him. She had forgotten to inform Aylmer of a symptom which for two or three hours past had begun to excite her attention. It was a sensation in the fatal birthmark, not painful, but which induced a restlessness throughout her system. Hastening after her husband, she intruded for the first time into the laboratory.

The first thing that struck her eye was the furnace, that hot and feverish worker, with the intense glow of its fire, which by the quantities of soot clustered above it seemed to have been burning for ages. There was a distilling apparatus in full operation. Around the room were retorts, tubes, cylinders, crucibles, and other apparatus of chemical research. An electrical machine stood ready for immediate use. The atmosphere felt oppressively close, and was tainted with gaseous odors which had been tormented forth by the processes of science. The severe and homely simplicity of the apartment, with its naked walls and brick pavement, looked strange, accustomed as Georgiana had become to the fantastic elegance of her boudoir. But what chiefly, indeed almost solely, drew her attention, was the aspect of Aylmer himself.

He was pale as death, anxious and absorbed, and hung over the furnace as if it depended upon his utmost watchfulness whether the liquid which it was distilling should be the draught of immortal happiness or misery. How different from the sanguine and joyous mien that he had assumed for Georgiana's encouragement!

"Carefully now, Aminadab; carefully, thou human machine; carefully, thou man of clay!" muttered Aylmer, more to himself than his assistant. "Now, if there be a thought too much or too little, it is all over."

"Ho! ho!" mumbled Aminadab. "Look, master! look!"

Aylmer raised his eyes hastily, and at first reddened, then grew paler than ever, on beholding Georgiana. He rushed towards her and seized her arm with a gripe that left the print of his fingers upon it.

"Why do you come hither? Have you no trust in your husband?" cried he, impetuously. "Would you throw the blight of that fatal birthmark over my labors? It is not well done. Go, prying woman, go!"

"Nay, Aylmer," said Georgiana with the firmness of which she possessed no stinted endowment, "it is not you that have a right to complain. You mistrust your wife; you have concealed the anxiety with which you watch the development of this experiment. Think not so unworthily of me, my husband. Tell me all the risk we run, and fear not that I shall shrink; for my share in it is far less than your own."

"No, no, Georgiana!" said Aylmer, impatiently; "it must not be."

"I submit," replied she calmly. "And Aylmer, I shall quaff whatever draught you bring me; but it will be on the same principle that would induce me to take a dose of poison if offered by your hand."

"My noble wife," said Aylmer, deeply moved, "I knew not the height and depth of your nature until now. Nothing shall be concealed. Know, then, that this crimson hand, superficial as it seems, has clutched its grasp into your being with a strength of which I had no previous conception. I have already administered agents powerful enough to do aught except to change your entire physical system. Only one thing remains to be tried. If that fail us we are ruined."

"Why did you hesitate to tell me this?" asked she.

"Because, Georgiana," said Aylmer, in a low voice, "there is danger."

"Danger? There is but one danger—that this horrible stigma shall be left upon my cheek!" cried Georgiana. "Remove it, remove it, whatever be the cost, or we shall both go mad!"

"Heaven knows your words are too true," said Aylmer, sadly. "And now, dearest, return to your boudoir. In a little while all will be tested."

He conducted her back and took leave of her with a solemn tenderness which spoke far more than his words how much was now at stake. After his departure Georgiana became rapt in musings. She considered the character of Aylmer, and did it completer justice than at any previous moment. Her heart exulted, while it trembled, at his honorable love—so pure and lofty that it would accept nothing less than perfection nor miserably make itself contented with an earthlier nature than he had dreamed of. She felt how much more precious was such a sentiment than that meaner kind which would have borne with the imperfection for her sake, and have been guilty of treason to holy love by degrading its perfect idea to the level of the actual; and with her whole spirit she prayed that, for a single moment, she might satisfy his highest and deepest conception. Longer than one moment she well knew it could not be; for his spirit was ever on the march, ever ascending, and each instant required something that was beyond the scope of the instant before.

The sound of her husband's footsteps aroused her. He bore a crystal goblet containing a liquor colorless as water, but bright enough to be the draught of immortality. Aylmer was pale; but it seemed rather the consequence of a highly-wrought state of mind and tension of spirit than of fear or doubt.

"The concoction of the draught has been perfect," said he, in answer to Georgiana's look. "Unless all my science have deceived me, it cannot fail."

"Save on your account, my dearest Aylmer," observed his wife, "I might wish to put off this birthmark of mortality by relinquishing mortality itself in preference to any other mode. Life is but a sad possession to those who have attained precisely the degree of moral advancement at which I stand. Were I weaker and blinder it might be happiness. Were I stronger, it might be endured hopefully. But, being what I find myself, methinks I am of all mortals the most fit to die."

"You are fit for heaven without tasting death!" replied her husband. "But why do we speak of dying? The draught cannot fail. Behold its effect upon this plant."

On the window seat there stood a geranium diseased with yellow blotches, which had overspread all its leaves. Aylmer poured a small quantity of the liquid upon the soil in which it grew. In a little time, when the roots of the plant had taken up the moisture, the unsightly blotches began to be extinguished in a living verdure.

"There needed no proof," said Georgiana, quietly. "Give me the goblet. I joyfully stake all upon your word."

"Drink, then, thou lofty creature!" exclaimed Aylmer, with fervid admiration. "There is no taint of imperfection on thy spirit. Thy sensible frame, too, shall soon be all perfect."

She quaffed the liquid and returned the goblet to his hand.

"It is grateful," said she with a placid smile. "Methinks it is like water from a heavenly fountain; for it contains I know not what of unobtrusive fragrance and deliciousness. It allays a feverish thirst that had parched me for many days. Now, dearest, let me sleep. My earthly senses are closing over my spirit like the leaves around the heart of a rose at sunset."

She spoke the last words with a gentle reluctance, as if it required almost more energy than she could command to pronounce the faint and lingering syllables. Scarcely had they loitered through her lips ere she was lost in slumber. Aylmer sat by her side, watching her aspect with the emotions proper to a man the whole value of whose existence was involved in the process now to be tested. Mingled with this mood, however, was the philosophic investigation characteristic of the man of science. Not the minutest symptom escaped him. A heightened flush of the cheek, a slight irregularity of breath, a quiver of the eyelid, a hardly perceptible tremor through the frame,—such were the details which, as the moments passed, he wrote down in his folio volume. Intense thought had set its stamp upon every previous page of that volume, but the thoughts of years were all concentrated upon the last.

While thus employed, he failed not to gaze often at the fatal hand, and not without a shudder. Yet once, by a strange and unaccountable impulse, he pressed it with his lips. His spirit recoiled, however, in the very act; and Georgiana, out of the midst of her deep sleep, moved uneasily and murmured as if in remonstrance. Again Aylmer resumed his watch. Nor was it without avail. The crimson hand, which at first had been strongly visible upon the marble paleness of Georgiana's cheek, now grew more faintly outlined. She remained not less pale than ever; but the birthmark, with every breath that came and went, lost somewhat of its former distinctness. Its presence had been awful; its departure was more awful still. Watch the stain of the rainbow fading out of the sky, and you will know how that mysterious symbol passed away.

"By Heaven! it is well-nigh gone!" said Aylmer to himself, in almost irrepressible ecstasy. "I can scarcely trace it now. Success! success! And now it is like the faintest rose color. The lightest flush of blood across her cheek would overcome it. But she is so pale!"

He drew aside the window curtain and suffered the light of natural day to fall into the room and rest upon her cheek. At the same time he heard a gross, hoarse chuckle, which he had long known as his servant Aminadab's expression of delight.

"Ah, clod! ah, earthly mass!" cried Aylmer, laughing in a sort of frenzy, "you have served me well! Matter and spirit—earth and heaven—have both done their part in this! Laugh, thing of the senses! You have earned the right to laugh."

These exclamations broke Georgiana's sleep. She slowly unclosed her eyes and gazed into the mirror which her husband had arranged for that purpose. A faint smile flitted over her lips when she recognized how barely perceptible was now that crimson hand which had once blazed forth with such disastrous brilliancy as to scare away all their happiness. But then her eyes sought Aylmer's face with a trouble and anxiety that he could by no means account for.

"My poor Aylmer!" murmured she.

"Poor? Nay, richest, happiest, most favored!" exclaimed he. "My peerless bride, it is successful! You are perfect!"

"My poor Aylmer," she repeated, with a more than human tenderness, "you have aimed loftily; you have done nobly. Do not repent that with so high and pure a feeling, you have rejected the best the earth could offer. Aylmer, dearest Aylmer, I am dying!"

Alas! it was too true! The fatal hand had grappled with the mystery of life, and was the bond by which an angelic spirit kept itself in union with a mortal frame. As the last crimson tint of the birthmark—that sole token of human imperfection—faded from her cheek, the parting breath of the now perfect woman passed into the atmosphere, and her soul, lingering a moment near her husband, took its heavenward flight. Then a hoarse, chuckling laugh was heard again! Thus ever does the gross fatality of earth exult in its invariable triumph over the immortal essence which, in this dim sphere of half development, demands the completeness of a higher state. Yet, had Aylmer reached a profounder wisdom, he need not thus have flung away the happiness which would have woven his mortal life of the selfsame texture with the celestial. The momentary circumstance was too strong for him; he failed to look beyond the shadowy scope of time, and, living once for all in eternity, to find the perfect future in the present.

# Ernest Hemingway

*Hemingway (1899–1961) was born in Oak Park, Illinois, the son of a doctor, who gave him an enduring enthusiasm for the outdoor life. As a boy Hemingway spent summer vacations in the woods of northern Michigan, which became the setting for some of his best-known stories. He volunteered for service as an ambulance driver with the Italian Army and was seriously wounded in the fighting on the Austrian front toward the end of World War I. Recovering from his wounds, he went to Paris as a correspondent for the Toronto* Star *and there met, among other writers, Ezra Pound and Gertrude Stein. They encouraged him in the invention of his own style, and by twenty-five he was well on his way to mastery of the craft of fiction. From the publication of his first books he was acclaimed as a spokesman for the "Lost Generation"—the young who had been disillusioned and cast adrift by the murderous blunders of those who had plunged the world into war. The Hemingway hero and his code of conduct—living with "grace under pressure"—were as widely emulated and admired as the style of his short stories and novels. He was an enthusiastic and discriminating bullfight fan, big-game hunter, and fisherman, whose personal exploits kept him often in the limelight. During the Spanish Civil War he went to Spain as a war correspondent and wrote one of his best novels,* For Whom the Bell Tolls *(1940), about that conflict. Later he followed the U.S. Army in Europe as a correspondent before returning to peacetime life at his home in Cuba. He was awarded the Nobel Prize in 1954. At a time when he seemed to be falling out of fashion and his old vigor was waning, he killed himself with a shotgun. His novels include* The Sun Also Rises *(1926),* A Farewell to Arms *(1929),* To Have and Have Not *(1937), and* The Old Man and the Sea *(1952). In* A Moveable Feast *(1964) he re-creates the Paris of his earlier years. His story collections include* In Our Time *(1925),* Men without Women *(1927), and* Winner Take Nothing *(1933).*

## Hills Like White Elephants

The hills across the valley of the Ebro[1] were long and white. On this side there was no shade and no trees and the station was between two lines of rails in the sun. Close against the side of the station there was the warm shadow of the building and a curtain, made of strings of bamboo beads, hung across the open door into the bar, to keep out flies. The American and the girl with him sat at a table in the shade, outside the building. It was very hot and the express from Barcelona would come in forty minutes. It stopped at this junction for two minutes and went on to Madrid.

1. River in northern Spain.

"What should we drink?" the girl asked. She had taken off her hat and put it on the table.

"It's pretty hot," the man said.

"Let's drink beer."

"Dos cervezas," the man said into the curtain.

"Big ones?" a woman asked from the doorway.

"Yes. Two big ones."

The woman brought two glasses of beer and two felt pads. She put the felt pads and the beer glasses on the table and looked at the man and the girl. The girl was looking off at the line of hills. They were white in the sun and the country was brown and dry.

"They look like white elephants," she said.

"I've never seen one," the man drank his beer.

"No, you wouldn't have."

"I might have," the man said. "Just because you say I wouldn't have doesn't prove anything."

The girl looked at the bead curtain. "They've painted something on it," she said. "What does it say?"

"Anis del Toro. It's a drink."

"Could we try it?"

The man called "Listen" through the curtain. The woman came out from the bar.

"Four reales."[2]

"We want two Anis del Toro."

"With water?"

"Do you want it with water?"

"I don't know," the girl said. "Is it good with water?"

"It's all right."

"You want them with water?" asked the woman.

"Yes, with water."

"It tastes like licorice," the girl said and put the glass down.

"That's the way with everything."

"Yes," said the girl. "Everything tastes of licorice. Especially all the things you've waited so long for, like absinthe."

"Oh, cut it out."

"You started it," the girl said. "I was being amused. I was having a fine time."

"Well, let's try and have a fine time."

"All right. I was trying. I said the mountains looked like white elephants. Wasn't that bright?"

"That was bright."

"I wanted to try this new drink. That's all we do, isn't it—look at things and try new drinks?"

"I guess so."

The girl looked across at the hills.

2. Spanish coins.

"They're lovely hills," she said. "They don't really look like white elephants. I just meant the coloring of their skin through the trees."

"Should we have another drink?"

"All right."

The warm wind blew the bead curtain against the table.

"The beer's nice and cool," the man said.

"It's lovely," the girl said.

"It's really an awfully simple operation, Jig," the man said. "It's not really an operation at all."

The girl looked at the ground the table legs rested on.

"I know you wouldn't mind it, Jig. It's really not anything. It's just to let the air in."

The girl did not say anything.

"I'll go with you and I'll stay with you all the time. They just let the air in and then it's all perfectly natural."

"Then what will we do afterward?"

"We'll be fine afterward. Just like we were before."

"What makes you think so?"

"That's the only thing that bothers us. It's the only thing that's made us unhappy."

The girl looked at the bead curtain, put her hand out and took hold of two of the strings of beads.

"And you think then we'll be all right and be happy."

"I know we will. You don't have to be afraid. I've known lots of people that have done it."

"So have I," said the girl. "And afterward they were all so happy."

"Well," the man said, "if you don't want to you don't have to. I wouldn't have you do it if you didn't want to. But I know it's perfectly simple."

"And you really want to?"

"I think it's the best thing to do. But I don't want you to do it if you don't really want to."

"And if I do it you'll be happy and things will be like they were and you'll love me?"

"I love you now. You know I love you."

"I know. But if I do it, then it will be nice again if I say things are like white elephants, and you'll like it?"

"I'll love it. I love it now but I just can't think about it. You know how I get when I worry."

"If I do it you won't ever worry?"

"I won't worry about that because it's perfectly simple."

"Then I'll do it. Because I don't care about me."

"What do you mean?"

"I don't care about me."

"Well, I care about you."

"Oh, yes. But I don't care about me. And I'll do it and then everything will be fine."

"I don't want you to do it if you feel that way."

The girl stood up and walked to the end of the station. Across, on the other side, were fields of grain and trees along the banks of the Ebro. Far away, beyond the river, were mountains. The shadow of a cloud moved across the field of grain and she saw the river through the trees.

"And we could have all this," she said. "And we could have everything and every day we make it more impossible."

"What did you say?"

"I said we could have everything."

"We can have everything."

"No, we can't."

"We can have the whole world."

"No, we can't."

"We can go everywhere."

"No, we can't. It isn't ours any more."

"It's ours."

"No, it isn't. And once they take it away, you never get it back."

"But they haven't taken it away."

"We'll wait and see."

"Come on back in the shade," he said. "You mustn't feel that way."

"I don't feel any way," the girl said. "I just know things."

"I don't want you to do anything that you don't want to do—"

"Nor that isn't good for me," she said. "I know. Could we have another beer?"

"All right. But you've got to realize—"

"I realize," the girl said. "Can't we maybe stop talking?"

They sat down at the table and the girl looked across at the hills on the dry side of the valley and the man looked at her and at the table.

"You've got to realize," he said, "that I don't want you to do it if you don't want to. I'm perfectly willing to go through with it if it means anything to you."

"Doesn't it mean anything to you? We could get along."

"Of course it does. But I don't want anybody but you. I don't want any one else. And I know it's perfectly simple."

"Yes, you know it's perfectly simple."

"It's all right for you to say that, but I do know it."

"Would you do something for me now?"

"I'd do anything for you."

"Would you please please please please please please please stop talking?"

He did not say anything but looked at the bags against the wall of the station. There were labels on them from all the hotels where they had spent nights.

"But I don't want you to," he said, "I don't care anything about it."

"I'll scream," the girl said.

The woman came out through the curtains with two glasses of beer and put them down on the damp felt pads. "The train comes in five minutes," she said.

"What did she say?" asked the girl.

"That the train is coming in five minutes."

The girl smiled brightly at the woman, to thank her.

"I'd better take the bags over to the other side of the station," the man said. She smiled at him.

"All right. Then come back and we'll finish the beer."

He picked up the two heavy bags and carried them around the station to the other tracks. He looked up the tracks but could not see the train. Coming back, he walked through the barroom, where people waiting for the train were drinking. He drank an Anis at the bar and looked at the people. They were all waiting reasonably for the train. He went out through the bead curtain. She was sitting at the table and smiled at him.

"Do you feel better?" he asked.

"I feel fine," she said. "There's nothing wrong with me. I feel fine."

## FREDERICK BUSCH on *Hills Like White Elephants*

It's the story to which I send students who want to learn how to write dialogue, and it's the story to which I return when I want to read about selfishness, disputation, and the fragility of the imagination. In this story, the imagination—the ability to see in metaphors, as opposed to the strength that crushes them, that insists on seeing, say, a hill as a hill and as nothing else—is linked, in its pregnancy, to the body of a pregnant woman. Her lover or husband wants the fetus aborted, and she wants to keep him. He will win.

We have just seen the Spanish countryside: the hills "were white in the sun and the country was brown and dry." But she sees the landscape this way: "They look like white elephants." He replies, with the bullying facticity of a country-club Babbit, that he's never seen one, and they proceed to squabble. Eventually, she dismantles her vision in an effort to win his approval. "They don't really look like white elephants," she explains, "I just meant the coloring of their skin through the trees."

But the hills, and her analogy, bear the weight of their real subject—her will, and her body, which Hemingway sets in opposition to her lover's plans for her body in spite of her will. When he stands in the bar, he notices the waiting passengers: "They are all waiting reasonably for the train." She, then, is not waiting "reasonably"; she wants them to live with regard for one another and in such a way that "if I say things are like white elephants . . . you'll like it." He swears that he does, that he will; but you know that he won't, for his notion of behaving "reasonably" has to do with pleasure, with self-aggrandizement, but not with birth of any sort.

He becomes a force for death as she, now wooing him, buries her way of seeing as she will bury her child. He asks if she feels "better," as if the way one viewed the world were an illness, or a misbehavior, from which one recovers. And she cooperates, betraying herself, to reply in the terms he has dictated: "There's nothing wrong with me," she says. Imagination and the pulse of life are "wrong," or are an illness, a deviation from his definition of health. "I feel fine," she lies.

We can feel the energy of coercion and the weight of despair in the awful white spaces that separate the lines, the paragraphs, the words.

# Amy Hempel

*Hempel (1951– ) was born in Chicago and educated in California, with further study at Columbia University. Several of her short stories are collected in* Reasons to Live *(1985) and* At the Gates of the Animal Kingdom *(1990); a novella and short stories are published in* Tumble Home *(1997).*

## In the Cemetery Where Al Jolson[1] Is Buried

*for Jessica*

Tell me things I won't mind forgetting," she said. "Make it useless stuff or skip it."

I began. I told her insects fly through rain, missing every drop, never getting wet. I told her no one in America owned a tape recorder before Bing Crosby did. I told her the shape of the moon is like a banana—you see it looking full, you're seeing it end-on.

The camera made me self-conscious and I stopped. It was trained on us from a ceiling mount—the kind of camera banks use to photograph robbers. It played our image to the nurses down the hall in Intensive Care.

"Go on, girl," she said, "you get used to it."

I had my audience. I went on. Did she know that Tammy Wynette had changed her tune? Really. That now she sings "Stand By Your *Friends*"? Paul Anka did it too, I said. Does "You're Having *Our* Baby." He got sick of all that feminist bitching.

"What else?" she said. "Have you got something else?"

Oh yes. For her I would always have something else.

"Did you know when they taught the first chimp to talk, it lied? When they asked her who did it on the desk, she signed back Max, the janitor. And when they pressed her, she said she was sorry, that it was really the project director. But she was a mother, so I guess she had her reasons."

"Oh, that's good," she said. "A parable."

1. American entertainer and film actor (1886–1950).

"There's more about the chimp," I said. "But it will break your heart."
"No thanks," she says, and scratches at her mask.

We look like good-guy outlaws. Good or bad, I am not used to the mask yet. I keep touching the warm spot where my breath, thank God, comes out. She is used to hers. She only ties the strings on top. The other ones—a pro by now—she lets hang loose.

We call this place the Marcus Welby[2] Hospital. It's the white one with the palm trees under the opening credits of all those shows. A Hollywood hospital, though in fact it is several miles west. Off camera, there is a beach across the street.

She introduces me to a nurse as "the Best Friend." The impersonal article is more intimate. It tells me that *they* are intimate, my friend and her nurse.

"I was telling her we used to drink Canada Dry Ginger Ale and pretend we were in Canada."

"That's how dumb *we* were," I say.

"You could be sisters," the nurse says.

So how come, I'll bet they are wondering, it took me so long to get to such a glamorous place? But do they ask?

They do not ask.

Two months, and how long is the drive?

The best I can explain it is this—I have a friend who worked one summer in a mortuary. He used to tell me stories. The one that really got to me was not the grisliest, but it's the one that did. A man wrecked his car on 101 going south. He did not lose consciousness. But his arm was taken down to the wet bone—and when he looked at it—it scared him to death. I mean, he died.

So I didn't dare look any closer. But now I'm doing it—and hoping I won't be scared to death.

She shakes out a summer-weight blanket, showing a leg you did not want to see. Except for that, you look at her and understand the law that requires *two* people to be with the body at all times.

"I thought of something," she says. "I thought of it last night. I think there is a real and present need here. You know," she says, "like for someone to do it for you when you can't do it yourself. You call them up whenever you want—like when push comes to shove."

She grabs the bedside phone and loops the cord around her neck.

"Hey," she says, "the End o' the Line."

She keeps on, giddy with something. But I don't know with what.

"The giveaway was the solarium," she says. "That's where Marcus Welby broke the news to his patients. Then here's the real doctor suggesting we talk in the solarium. So I knew I was going to die.

"I can't remember," she says, "what does Kübler-Ross[3] say comes after Denial?"

2. Title character in a long-running TV hospital drama. 3. Elisabeth Kübler-Ross (b. 1926), author of popular books on death and dying.

It seems to me Anger must be next. Then Bargaining, Depression, and so on and so forth. But I keep my guesses to myself.

"The only thing is," she says, "is where's Resurrection? God knows I want to do it by the book. But she left out Resurrection."

She laughs, and I cling to the sound the way someone dangling above a ravine holds fast to the thrown rope.

We could have cried then, but when we didn't, we couldn't.

"Tell me," she says, "about that chimp with the talking hands. What do they do when the thing ends and the chimp says, 'I don't want to go back to the zoo'?"

When I don't say anything, she says, "O.K.—then tell me another animal story. I like animal stories. But not a sick one—I don't want to know about all the Seeing Eye dogs going blind."

No, I would not tell her a sick one.

"How about the hearing-ear dogs?" I say. "They're not going deaf, but they are getting very judgmental. For instance, there's this golden retriever in Jersey, he wakes up the deaf mother and drags her into the daughter's room because the kid has got a flashlight and is reading under the covers."

"Oh, you're killing me," she says. "Yes, you're definitely killing me."

"They say the smart dog obeys, but the smarter dog knows when to *disobey*."

"Yes," she says, "the smarter *anything* knows when to disobey. Now, for example."

She is flirting with the Good Doctor, who has just appeared. Unlike the Bad Doctor, who checks the I.V. drip before saying good morning, the Good Doctor says things like "God didn't give epileptics a fair shake." He awards himself points for the cripples he could have hit in the parking lot. Because the Good Doctor is a little in love with her he says maybe a year. He pulls a chair up to her bed and suggests I might like to spend an hour on the beach.

"Bring me something back," she says. "Anything from the beach. Or the gift shop. Taste is no object."

The doctor slowly draws the curtain around her bed.

"Wait!" she cries.

I look in at her.

"Anything," she says, "except a magazine subscription."

The doctor turns away.

I watch her mouth laugh.

What seems dangerous often is not—black snakes, for example, or clear-air turbulence. While things that just lie there, like this beach, are loaded with jeopardy. A yellow dust rising from the ground, the heat that ripens melons overnight—this is earthquake weather. You can sit here braiding the fringe on your towel and the sand will all of a sudden suck down like an hourglass. The air roars. In the cheap apartments onshore, bathtubs fill themselves and gardens roll up and over like green waves. If nothing happens, the dust will drift and the heat deepen till fear turns to desire. Nerves like that are only bought off by catastrophe.

"It never happens when you're thinking about it," she observed once.

"Earthquake, earthquake, earthquake," she said.

"Earthquake, earthquake, earthquake," I said.

Like the aviaphobe who keeps the plane aloft with prayer, we kept it up till an aftershock cracked the ceiling.

That was after the big one in '72. We were in college; our dormitory was five miles from the epicenter. When the ride was over and my jabbering pulse began to slow, she served five parts champagne to one part orange juice and joked about living in Ocean View, Kansas. I offered to drive her to Hawaii on the new world psychics predicted would surface the next time, or the next.

I could not say that now—next. *Whose* next? she could ask.

Was I the only one who noticed that the experts had stopped saying *if* and now spoke of *when?* Of course not; the fearful ran to thousands. We watched the traffic of Japanese beetles for deviation. Deviation might mean more natural violence.

I wanted her to be afraid with me, but she said, "I don't know. I'm just not."

She was afraid of nothing, not even of flying.

I have this dream before a flight where we buckle in and the plane moves down the runway. It takes off at thirty-five miles an hour, and then we're airborne, skimming on tree tops. Still, we arrive in New York on time. It is so pleasant. One night I flew to Moscow this way.

She flew with me once. That time she flew with me she ate macadamia nuts while the wings bounced. She knows the wing tips can bend thirty feet up and thirty feet down without coming off. She believes it. She trusts the laws of aerodynamics. My mind stampedes. I can almost accept that a battleship floats, and everybody knows steel sinks.

I see fear in her now and am not going to try to talk her out of it. She is right to be afraid.

After a quake, the six o'clock news airs a film clip of first-graders yelling at the broken playground per their teacher's instructions.

"*Bad* earth!" they shout, because anger is stronger than fear.

But the beach is standing still today. Everyone on it is tranquilized, numb or asleep. Teenaged girls rub coconut oil on each other's hard-to-reach places. They smell like macaroons. They pry open compacts like clamshells; mirrors catch the sun and throw a spray of white rays across glazed shoulders. The girls arrange their wet hair with silk flowers the way they learned in *Seventeen.* They pose.

A formation of low-riders[4] pulls over to watch with a six-pack. They get vocal when the girls check their tan lines. When the beer is gone, so are they—flexing their cars on up the boulevard.

Above this aggressive health are the twin wrought-iron terraces, painted flamingo pink, of the Palm Royale. Someone dies there every time the sheets

4. Drivers of rebuilt, underslung cars.

are changed. There's an ambulance in the driveway, so the remaining residents line the balconies, rocking and not talking, one-upped.

The ocean they stare at is dangerous, and not just the undertow. You can almost see the slapping tails of sand sharks keeping cruising bodies alive.

If she looked, she could see this, some of it, from her window. She would be the first to say how little it takes to make a thing all wrong.

There was a second bed in the room when I returned. For two beats I didn't get it. Then it hit me like an open coffin.

She wants every minute, I thought. She wants my life.

"You missed Gussie," she said.

Gussie is her parents' 300-pound narcoleptic maid. Her attacks often come at the ironing board. The pillowcases in that family are all bordered with scorch.

"It's a hard trip for her," I said. "How is she?"

"Well, she didn't fall asleep, if that's what you mean. Gussie's great—you know what she said? She said, 'Darlin' just keep prayin', down on your knees.' "

She shrugged, "See anybody good?"

"No," I said, "just the new Charlie's Angel.[5] And I saw Cher's car down near the Arcade."

"Cher's car is worth *three* Charlie's Angels," she said. "What else am I missing?"

"It's earthquake weather," I told her.

"The best thing to do about earthquakes," she said, "is not to live in California."

"That's useful," I said. "You sound like Reverend Ike: 'The best thing to do for the poor is not be one of them.' "

We're crazy about Reverend Ike.

I noticed her face was bloated.

"You know," she said, "I feel like hell. I'm about to stop having fun."

"The ancients have a saying," I said. " 'There are times when the wolves are silent; there are times when the moon howls.' "

"What's that, Navajo?"

"Palm Royale lobby graffiti," I said. "I bought a paper there. I'll read to you."

"Even though I care about nothing?" she said.

I turned to page three, to a UPI filler datelined Mexico City. I read her "Man Robs Bank with Chicken," about a man who bought a barbecued chicken at a stand down the block from a bank. Passing the bank, he got the idea. He walked in and approached a teller. He pointed the brown paper bag at her and she handed over the day's receipts. It was the smell of barbecue sauce that eventually led to his capture.

The story made her hungry, she said, so I took the elevator down six floors to the cafeteria and brought back all the ice cream she wanted. We lay side by side, adjustable beds cranked up for optimal TV viewing, littering the sheets

5. A rotation of pretty young women in the TV series *Charlie's Angels*.

with Good Humor wrappers, picking toasted almonds out of the gauze. We were Lucy and Ethel, Mary and Rhoda[6] in extremis. The blinds were closed to keep light off the screen.

We watched a movie starring men we used to think we wanted to sleep with. Hers was a tough cop out to stop mine, a vicious rapist who went after cocktail waitresses.

"This is a good movie," she said, when snipers felled them both.

I missed her already; my straight man, my diary.

A Filipino nurse tiptoed in and gave her an injection. She removed the pile of Popsicle sticks from the nightstand—-enough to splint a small animal.

The injection made us sleepy—me in the way I picked up her inflection till her mother couldn't tell us apart on the phone. We slept.

I dreamed she was a decorator, come to furnish my house. She worked in secret, singing to herself. When she finished, she guided me proudly to the door. "How do you like it?" she asked, easing me inside.

Every beam and sill and shelf and knob was draped in black bunting, with streamers and black crepe looped around darkened mirrors.

"I have to go home," I said when she woke up.

She thought I meant home to her house in the Canyon, and I had to say, No, *home* home. I twisted my hands in the hackneyed fashion of people in pain. I was supposed to offer something. The Best Friend. I could not even offer to come back.

I felt weak and small and failed. Also exhilarated. I had a convertible in the parking lot. Once out of that room, I would drive it too fast down the coast highway through the crab-smelling air. A stop in Malibu for sangria. The music in the place would be sexy and loud. They would serve papaya and shrimp and watermelon ice. After dinner I would pick up beach boys. I would shimmer with life, buzz with heat, vibrate with health, stay up all night with one and then the other.

Without a word, she yanked off her mask and threw it on the floor. She kicked at the blankets and moved to the door. She must have hated having to pause for breath and balance before slamming out of Isolation, and out of the second room, the one where you scrub and tie on the white masks.

A voice shouted her name in alarm, and people ran down the corridor. The Good Doctor was paged over the intercom. I opened the door and the nurses at the station stared hard, as if this flight had been my idea.

"Where is she?" I asked, and they nodded to the supply closet.

I looked in. Two nurses were kneeling beside her on the floor, talking to her in low voices. One held a mask over her nose and mouth, the other rubbed her back in slow circles. The nurses glanced up to see if I was the doctor, and when they saw I wasn't, they went back to what they were doing.

"There, there, honey," they cooed.

6. Principal characters in *The Mary Tyler Moore* TV series. "Lucy and Ethel": principal characters in the *I Love Lucy* TV series.

On the morning she was moved to the cemetery, the one where Al Jolson is buried, I enrolled in a Fear of Flying class. "What is your worst fear?" the instructor asked, and I answered, "That I will finish this course and still be afraid."

I sleep with a glass of water on the nightstand so I can see by its level if the coastal earth is trembling or if the shaking is still me.

What do I remember? I remember only the useless things I hear—that Bob Dylan's mother invented Wite-out, that twenty-three people must be in a room before there is a fifty-fifty chance two will have the same birthdate. Who cares whether or not it's true? In my head there are bath towels swaddling this stuff. Nothing else seeps through.

I review those things that will figure in the retelling: a kiss through surgical gauze, the pale hand correcting the position of the wig. I noted these gestures as they happened, not in any retrospect. Though I don't know why looking *back* should show us more than looking *at.* It is just possible I will say I stayed the night. And who is there that can say I did not?

Nothing else gets through until I think of the chimp, the one with the talking hands.

In the course of the experiment, that chimp had a baby. Imagine how her trainers must have thrilled when the mother, without prompting, began to sign to the newborn. Baby, drink milk. Baby, play ball. And when the baby died, the mother stood over the body, her wrinkled hands moving with animal grace, forming again and again the words, Baby, come hug, Baby, come hug, fluent now in the language of grief.

# Zora Neale Hurston

*Hurston (1903–1960) was born in Eatonville, Florida. She became a vigorous activist in the cultural, social, and literary awakening that converged in the Harlem Renaissance of the 1920s and 1930s. Her gifts as a writer helped her absorb the rich diversities of black folklore in Haiti, Jamaica, and Bermuda, as well as in rural and urban areas of the United States. At various times she was a journalist and librarian, and wherever she could make herself heard she bore witness against the stereotyping that denied the multifarious heritage of blacks. She was a trained anthropologist whose personal insights enlarged that discipline, giving it depth and liveliness. Her appreciation of the subtleties and ambiguities of the vernacular influenced the generation of writers who followed her. The thematic core of her work is the love blacks bear for one another rather than the hostilities they feel against their oppressors. Her stories and articles appeared in several distinguished magazines, and she published four novels:* Jonah's Gourd Vine *(1934),* Their Eyes Were Watching God *(1937),* Moses, Man of the Mountain *(1939), and* Seraph on the Suwanee *(1948).*

## The Conscience of the Court

The clerk of the court took a good look at the tall brown-skinned woman with the head rag on. She sat on the third bench back with a husky officer beside her.

"The People versus Laura Lee Kimble!"

The policeman nudged the woman to get to her feet and led her up to the broad rail. She stood there, looking straight ahead. The hostility in the room reached her without her seeking to find it.

Unpleasant things were ahead of Laura Lee Kimble, but she was ready for this moment. It might be the electric chair or the rest of her life in some big lonesome jail house, or even torn to pieces by a mob, but she had passed three long weeks in jail. She had come to the place where she could turn her face to the wall and feel neither fear nor anguish. So this here so-called trial was nothing to her but a form and a fashion and an outside show to the world. She could stand apart and look on calmly. She stood erect and looked up at the judge.

"Charged with felonious and aggravated assault. Mayhem. Premeditated attempted murder on the person of one Clement Beasley. Obscene and abusive language. Laura Lee Kimble, how do you plead?"

Laura Lee was so fascinated by the long-named things that they were accusing her of that she stood there tasting over the words. *Lawdy me!* she mused inside herself. *Look like I done every crime excepting habeas corpus and stealing a mule.*

"Answer the clerk!" The officer nudged Laura Lee. "Tell him how you plead."

"Plead? Don't reckon I make out just what you all mean by that." She looked from face to face and at last up at the judge, with bewilderment in her eyes. She found him looking her over studiously.

The judge understood the look in her face, but he did not interfere so promptly as he ordinarily would have. This was the man-killing bear cat of a woman that he had heard so much about. Though spare of fat, she was built strongly enough, all right. An odd Negro type. Gray-green eyes, large and striking, looking out of a chestnut-brown face. A great abundance of almost straight hair only partially hidden by the high-knotted colored kerchief about her head. Somehow this woman did not look fierce to him at all. Yet she had beaten a man within an inch of his life. Here was a riddle to solve. With the proud, erect way she held herself, she might be some savage queen. The shabby housedress she had on detracted nothing from this impression. She was a challenge to him somehow or other.

"Perhaps you don't understand what the clerk means, Laura," the judge found himself saying to her in a gentle voice. "He wants you to say whether you are guilty of the charges or not."

"Oh, I didn't know. Didn't even know if he was talking to me or not. Much obliged to you, sir." Laura Lee sent His Honor a shy smile. " 'Deed I don't know if I'm guilty or not. I hit the man after he hit me, to be sure, Mister Judge, but if I'm guilty I don't know for sure. All them big words and all."

The clerk shook his head in exasperation and quickly wrote something down. Laura Lee turned her head and saw the man on the hospital cot swaddled all up in bandage rags. Yes, that was the very man who caused her to be here where she was.

"All right, Laura Lee," the judge said. "You can take your seat now until you are called on."

The prosecutor looked a question at the judge and said, "We can proceed." The judge nodded, then halted things as he looked down at Laura Lee.

"The defendant seems to have no lawyer to represent her." Now he leaned forward and spoke to Laura Lee directly. "If you have no money to hire yourself a lawyer to look out for your interests, the court will appoint one for you."

There was a pause, during which Laura Lee covered a lot of ground. Then she smiled faintly at the judge and answered him. "Naw sir, I thank you, Mister Judge. Not to turn you no short answer, but I don't reckon it would do me a bit of good. I'm mighty much obliged to you just the same."

The implications penetrated instantly and the judge flushed. This unlettered woman had called up something that he had not thought about for quite some time. The campus of the University of Virginia and himself as a very young man there, filled with a reverence for his profession amounting to an almost holy dedication. His fascination and awe as a professor traced the more than two thousand years of growth of the concepts of human rights and justice. That brought him to his greatest hero, John Marshall, and his inner resolve to follow in the great man's steps, and even add to interpretations of human rights if his abilities allowed. No, he had not thought about all this for quite some time. The judge flushed slowly and deeply.

Below him there, the prosecutor was moving swiftly, but somehow his brisk cynicism offended the judge. He heard twelve names called, and just like that the jury box was filled and sworn in.

Rapidly now, witnesses took the stand, and their testimony was all damaging to Laura Lee. The doctor who told how terribly Clement Beasley had been hurt. Left arm broken above the elbow, compound fracture of the forearm, two ribs cracked, concussion of the brain and various internal injuries. Two neighbors who had heard the commotion and arrived before the house in time to see Laura Lee fling the plaintiff over the gate into the street. The six arresting officers all got up and had their say, and it was very bad for Laura Lee. A two-legged she-devil no less.

Clement Beasley was borne from his cot to the witness stand, and he made things look a hundred times blacker. His very appearance aroused a bumble of pity, and anger against the defendant. The judge had to demand quiet repeatedly. Beasley's testimony blew strongly on the hot coals.

His story was that he had come in conflict with this defendant by loaning a sizable sum of money to her employer. The money was to be repaid at his office. When the date was long past due, he had gone to the house near the river, just off Riverside Drive, to inquire why Mrs. Clairborne had not paid him, nor even come to see him and explain. Imagine his shock when he wormed it out of the defendant that Mrs. Clairborne had left Jacksonville. Further, he detected evidence that the defendant was picking up the things in the house. The loan had been made, six hundred dollars, on the furnishings of the entire house. He had doubted that the furnishings were worth enough for the amount loaned, but he had wanted to be generous to a widow lady. Seeing the defendant packing away the silver, he was naturally alarmed, and the next morning went to the house with a moving van to seize the furniture and protect the loan. The defendant, surprised, attacked him as soon as he appeared at the front door, injured him as he was, and would have killed him if help had not arrived in time.

Laura Lee was no longer a spectator at her own trial. Now she was in a flaming rage. She would have leaped to her feet as the man pictured Miz' Celestine as a cheat and a crook, and again as he sat up there and calmly lied about the worth of the furniture. All of those wonderful antiques, this man making out that they did not equal his minching six hundred dollars! That lie was a sin and a shame! The People was a meddlesome and unfriendly passel and had no use for the truth. It brought back to her in a taunting way what her husband, Tom, had told her over and over again. This world had no use for the love and friending that she was ever trying to give.

It looked now that Tom could be right. Even Miz' Celestine had turnt her back on her. She was here in this place, the house of The People, all by herself. She had ever disbelieved Tom and had to get to be forty-nine before she found out the truth. Well, just as the old folks said, "It's never too long for a bull frog to wear a stiff-bosom shirt. He's bound to get it dirtied some time or other."

"You have testified," Laura Lee heard the judge talking, "that you came in contact with the defendant through a loan to Mrs. J. Stuart Clairborne, her employer, did you not?"

"Yes, Your Honor," Beasley answered promptly and glibly.

"That being true, the court cannot understand why that note was not offered in evidence."

Beasley glanced quickly at the prosecutor and lowered his eyes. "I—I just didn't see why it was necessary, Your Honor. I have it, but—"

"It is not only pertinent, it is of the utmost importance to this case. I order it sent for immediately and placed in evidence."

The tall, lean, black-haired prosecutor hurled a surprised and betrayed look at the bench, then, after a pause, said in a flat voice, "The State rests."

What was in the atmosphere crawled all over Laura Lee like reptiles. The silence shouted that her goose was cooked. But even if the sentence was death, she didn't mind. Celestine Beaufort Clairborne had failed her. Her husband and all her folks had gone on before. What was there to be so happy to live for any more? She had writ that letter to Miz' Celestine the very first day that she had been placed in jail. Three weeks had gone by on their rusty ankles, and never one word from her Celestine. Laura Lee choked back a sob and gritted her teeth. You had to bear what was placed on your back for you to tote.

"Laura Lee Kimble," the judge was saying, "you are charged with serious felonies, and the law must take its course according to the evidence. You refused the lawyer that the court offered to provide for you, and that was a mistake on your part. However, you have a right to be sworn and tell the jury your side of the story. Tell them anything that might help you, so long as you tell the truth."

Laura Lee made no move to get to her feet and nearly a minute passed. Then the judge leaned forward.

"Believe it or not, Laura Lee, this is a court of law. It is needful to hear both sides of every question before the court can reach a conclusion and know what to do. Now, you don't strike me as a person that is unobliging at all. I believe if you knew you would be helping me out a great deal by telling your side of the story, you would do it."

Involuntarily Laura Lee smiled. She stood up. "Yes, sir, Mister Judge. If I can be of some help to you, I sure will. And I thank you for asking me."

Being duly sworn, Laura Lee sat in the chair to face the jury as she had been told to do.

"You jury-gentlemens, they asked me if I was guilty or no, and I still don't know whether I is or not. I am a unlearnt woman and common-clad.[1] It don't surprise me to find out I'm ignorant about a whole heap of things. I ain't never rubbed the hair off of my head against no college walls and schooled out nowhere at all. All I'm able to do is to tell you gentlemens how it was and then you can tell me if I'm guilty or no.

"I would not wish to set up here and lie and make out that I never hit this plaintive back. Gentlemens, I ain't had no malice in my heart against the plaintive. I seen him only one time before he come there and commenced that

1. Lower class.

fracas with me. That was three months ago, the day after Tom, my husband, died. Miz' Celestine called up the funeral home and they come and got Tom to fix him up so we could take him back to Georgia to lay him to rest. That's where us all come from, Chatham County—Savannah, that is.

"Then now, Miz' Celestine done something I have never knowed her to do be-fore. She put on her things and went off from home without letting me know where she was bound for. She come back afterwhile with this plaintive, which I had never seen before in all my borned days. I glimpsed him good from the kitchen where I was at, walking all over the dining room and the living room with Miz' Celestine and looking at things, but they was talking sort of low like, and I couldn't make out a word what they was talking about. I figgered that Miz' Celestine must of been kind of beside herself, showing somebody look like this plaintive all her fine things like that. Her things is fine and very scarce old antiques, and I know that she have been offered vast sums of money for 'em, but she would never agree to part with none. Things that been handed down in both the Beaufort and the Clairborne families from way back. That little old minching six hundred dollars that the plaintive mentioned wouldn't even be worth one piece of her things, not to mention her silver. After a while they went off and when Miz' Celestine come back, she told me that everything had been taken care of and she had the tickets to Savannah in her purse.

"Bright and soon next morning we boarded the train for Savannah to bury Tom. Miz' Celestine done even more than she had promised Tom. She took him back like she had promised, so that he could be buried in our family lot, and he was covered with flowers, and his church and his lodges turned out with him, and he was put away like some big mogul of a king. Miz' Celestine was there sitting right along by my side all the time. Then me and Miz' Celestine come on back down here to Jacksonville by ourselves.

"And Mrs. Clairborne didn't run off to keep from paying nobody. She's a Clairborne, and before that, she was born a Beaufort. They don't owe nobody, and they don't run away. That ain't the kind of raising they gets. Miz' Clairborne's got money of her own, and lives off of the interest which she receives regular every six months. She went off down there to Miami Beach to sort of refresh herself and rest up her nerves. What with being off down here in Florida, away from all the folks she used to know, for three whole years, and cooped up there in her house, and remembering her dear husband being dead, and now Tom gone, and nobody left of the old family around excepting her and me, she was nervous and peaked like. It wasn't her, it was me that put her up to going off down there for a couple of months so maybe she would come back to herself. She never cheeped to me about borrowing no money from nobody, and I sure wasn't packing nothing up to move off when this plaintive come to the door. I was just gleaming up the silver to kill time whilst I was there by myself.

"And gentlemens, I never tackled the plaintive just as soon as he mounted the porch like he said. The day before that, he had come there and asked-ed me if Miz' Clairborne was at home. I told him no, and then he asked-ed me just when I expected her back. I told him she was down at Miami Beach, and got the letter that she had sent me so he could get her right address. He thanked me and went off. Then the next morning, here he was back with a great big moving wagon, rapped on the door and didn't use a bit of manners and politeness this time. Without even a 'Good morning' he says for me to git out of his way because he come to haul off all the furniture and things in the house and he is short for time.

"You jury-gentlemens, I told him in the nicest way that I knowed how that he must of been crazy. Miz' Celestine was off from home and she had left me there as a kind of guardeen to look after her house and things, and I sure couldn't so handy leave nobody touch a thing in Mrs. Clairborne's house unlessen she was there and said so.

"He just looked at me like I was something that the buzzards laid and the sun hatched out, and told me to move out of his way so he could come on in and get his property. I propped myself and braced one arm across the doorway to bar him out, reckoning he would have manners enough to go on off. But, no! He flew just as hot as Tucker when the mule kicked his mammy and begun to cuss and double-cuss me, and call me all out of my name, something nobody had never done be-fore in all my borned days. I took it to keep from tearing up peace and agreement. Then he balled up his fistes and demanded me to move 'cause he was coming in.

" 'Aw, naw you ain't,' I told him. 'You might think that you's going to grow horns, but I'm here to tell you you'll die butt-headed.'

"His mouth slewed one-sided and he hauled off and hit me in my chest with his fist two times. Hollered that nothing in the drugstore would kill me no quicker than he would if I didn't git out of his way. I didn't, and then he upped and kicked me.

"I jumped as salty as the 'gator when the pond went dry. I stretched out my arm and he hit the floor on a prone. Then, that truck with the two men on it took off from there in a big hurry. All I did next was to grab him by his heels and frail[2] the pillar of the porch with him a few times. I let him go, but he just laid there like a log.

" 'Don't you lay there, making out you's dead, sir!' I told him. 'Git up from there, even if you is dead, and git on off this place!'

"The contrary scamp laid right there, so I reached down and muscled him up on acrost my shoulder and toted him to the gate, and heaved him over the fence out into the street. None of my business what become of him and his dirty mouth after that.

"I figgered I done right not to leave him come in there and haul off Miz' Celestine's things which she had left there under my trust and care. But Tom, my husband, would have said I was wrong for taking too much on myself. Tom claimed that he ever loved me harder than the thunder could bump a stump, but I had one habit that he ever wished he could break me of. Claimed that I always placed other folks's cares in front of my own, and more expecially Miz' Celestine. Said that I made out of myself a wishbone shining in the sun. Just something for folks to come along and pick up and rub and pull and get their wishes and good luck on. Never looked out for nothing for my ownself.

2. Hit.

"I never took a bit of stock in what Tom said like that until I come to be in this trouble. I felt right and good, looking out for Miz' Celestine's interest and standing true and strong, till they took me off to jail and I writ Miz' Celestine a letter to please come see 'bout me and help me out, and give it to the folks there at the jail to mail off for me."

A sob wrestled inside Laura Lee and she struck silence for a full minute before she could go on.

"Maybe it reached her, and then maybe again it didn't. Anyhow, I ain't had a single scratch from Miz' Celestine, and here I is. But I love her so hard, and I reckon I can't help myself. Look, gentlemens, Celestine was give to me when I was going on five—"

The prosecutor shot up like a striking trout and waved his long arm. "If the court please, this is not a street corner. This is a court of law. The witness cannot be allowed to ramble—"

The judge started as if he had been shaken out of a dream. He looked at the prosecutor and shook his head. "The object of a trial, I need not remind you, is to get at the whole truth of a case. The defendant is unlearned, as she has said. She has no counsel to guide her along the lines of procedure. It is important to find out why an act was committed, as you well know. Please humor the court by allowing the witness to tell her story in her own way." The judge looked at Laura Lee and told her to go ahead. A murmur of approval followed this from all over the room.

"I don't mean that her mama and papa throwed her away. You know how it used to be the style when a baby was born to place it under the special care of a older brother or sister, or somebody that had worked on the place for a long time and was apt to stay. That's what I mean by Celestine was give to me.

"Just going on five, I wasn't yet old enough to have no baby give to me, but that I didn't understand. All I did know that some way I loved babies. I had me a old rag doll-baby that my mama had made for me, and I loved it better'n anything I can mention.

"Never will forget the morning mama said she was going to take me upstairs to Miz' Beaufort's bedroom to lemme see the new baby. Mama was borned on the Beaufort place just like I was. She was the cook, and everything around the place was sort of under her care. Papa was the houseman and drove for the family when they went out anywhere.

"Well, I seen that tee-ninchy baby laying there in a pink crib all trimmed with a lot of ribbons. Gentlemens, it was the prettiest thing I had ever laid my eyes on. I thought that it was a big-size doll-baby laying there, and right away I wanted it. I carried on so till afterwhile Miz' Beaufort said that I could have it for mine if I wanted it. I was so took with it that I went plumb crazy with joy. I asked her again, and she still said that she was giving it to me. My mama said so too. So, for fear they might change they minds, I said right off that I better take my baby home with me so that I could feed it my ownself and make it something to put on and do for it in general.

"I cried and carried on something terrible when they wouldn't leave me take it on out to the little house where we lived on the place. They pacified me by telling me I better leave it with Miz' Beaufort until it was weaned.

"That couldn't keep me from being around Celestine every chance I got. Later on I found out how they all took my carrying-on for jokes. Made out they was serious to my face, but laughing fit to kill behind my back. They wouldn't of done it if they had knowed how I felt inside. I lived just to see and touch Celestine—my baby, I thought. And she took to me right away.

"When Celestine was two, going on three, I found out that they had been funning with me, and that Celestine was not my child at all. I was too little to have a baby, and then again, how could a colored child be the mother of a white child? Celestine belonged to her papa and mama. It was all right for me to play with her all I wanted to, but forget the notion that she was mine.

"Jury-gentlemens, it was mighty hard, but as I growed on and understood more things I knowed what they was talking about. But Celestine wouldn't allow me to quit loving her. She ever leaned on me, and cried after me, and run to me first for every little thing.

"When I was going on sixteen, papa died and Tom Kimble, a young man, got the job that papa used to have. Right off he put in to court me, even though he was twelve years older than me. But lots of fellows around Savannah was pulling after me too. One wanted to marry me that I liked extra fine, but he was settling in Birmingham, and mama was aginst me marrying and settling way off somewhere. She ruthered for me to marry Tom. When Celestine begin to hang on me and beg and beg me not to leave her, I give in and said that I would have Tom, but for the sake of my feelings, I put the marriage off for a whole year. That was my first good chance to break off from Celestine, but I couldn't.

"General Beaufort, the old gentleman, was so proud for me to stay and pacify Celestine, that he built us a nice house on the place and made it over to us for life. Miz' Beaufort give me the finest wedding that any colored folks had ever seen around Savannah. We stood on the floor in the Beaufort parlor with all the trimmings.

"Celestine, the baby, was a young lady by then, and real pretty with reddish-gold hair and blue eyes. The young bloods was hanging after her in swarms. It was me that propped her up when she wanted to marry young J. Stuart Clairborne, a lawyer just out of school, with a heap of good looks, a smiling disposition, a fine family name and no money to mention. He did have some noble old family furniture and silver. So Celestine had her heart's desire, but little money. They was so happy together that it was like a play.

"Then things begin to change. Mama and Miz' Beaufort passed on in a year of each other. The old gentleman lingered around kind of lonesome, then one night he passed away in his sleep, leaving all he had to Celestine and her husband. Things went on fine for five years like that. He was building up a fine practice and things went lovely.

"Then, it seemed all of a sudden, he took to coughing, and soon he was too tired all the time to go to his office and do around like he used to. Celestine spent her money like water, sending her husband and taking him to different places from one end of the nation to the other, and keeping him under every kind of a doctor's care.

"Four years of trying and doing like that, and then even Celestine had to acknowledge that it never did a bit of good. Come a night when Clairborne laid his dark curly head in her lap like a trusting child and breathed his last.

"Inside our own house of nights, Tom would rear and pitch like a mule in a tin stable, trying to get me to consent to pull out with him and find us better-paying jobs elsewhere. I wouldn't hear to that kind of a talk at all. We had been there when times was extra good, and I didn't aim to tear out and leave Miz' Celestine by herself at low water. This was another time I passed up my chance to cut aloose.

"The third chance wasn't too long a-coming. A year after her husband died, Miz' Celestine come to me and told me that the big Beaufort place was too much for her to keep up with the money she had on hand now. She had been seeking around, and she had found a lovely smaller house down at Jacksonville, Florida. No big grounds to keep up and all. She choosed that instead of a smaller place around Savannah because she could not bear to sing small where she had always led off. An' now she had got hold of a family who was willing to buy the Beaufort estate at a very good price.

"Then she told me that she wanted me to move to Florida with her. She realized that she had no right to ask me no such a thing, but she just could not bear to go off down there with none of her family with her. Would I please consent to go? If I would not go with her, she would give Tom and me the worth of our property in cash money and we could do as we pleased. She had no call to ask us to go with her at all, excepting for old-time love and affection.

"Right then, jury-gentlemens, I knowed that I was going. But Tom had ever been a good husband to me, and I wanted him to feel that he was considered, so I told her that I must consult my pillow. Give her my word one way or another the next day.

"Tom pitched a acre of fits the moment that it was mentioned in his hearing. Hollered that we ought to grab the cash and, with what we had put away, buy us a nice home of our own. What was wrong with me nohow? Did I aim to be a wishbone all my days? Didn't I see that he was getting old? He craved to end his days among his old friends, his lodges and his churches. We had a fine cemetery lot, and there was where he aimed to rest.

"Miz' Celestine cried when he told her. Then she put in to meet all of Tom's complaints. Sure, we was all getting on in years, but that was the very reason why we ought not to part now. Cling together and share and lean and depend on one another. Then when Tom still held out, she made a oath. If Tom died before she did, she would fetch him back and put him away right at her own expense. And if she died before either of us, we was to do the same for her. Anything she left was willed to me to do with as I saw fit.

"So we put in to pack up all the finest pieces, enough and plenty to furnish up our new home in Florida, and moved on down here to live. We passed three peaceful years like that, then Tom died."

Laura Lee paused, shifted so that she faced the jury more directly, then summed up.

"Maybe I is guilty sure enough. I could be wrong for staying all them years and making Miz' Celestine's cares my own. You gentlemens is got more book-learning than me, so you would know more than I do. So far as this fracas is concerned, yeah, I hurted this plaintive, but with him acting the way he was, it just couldn't be helped. And 'tain't nary one of you gentlemens but what wouldn't of done the same."

There was a minute of dead silence. Then the judge sent the prosecutor a cut-eye look and asked. "Care to cross-examine?"

"That's all!" the prosecutor mumbled, and waved Laura Lee to her seat.

"I have here," the judge began with great deliberation, "the note made by Mrs. J. Stuart Clairborne with the plaintiff. It specifies that the purpose of the loan was to finance the burial of Thomas Kimble." The judge paused and looked directly at Laura Lee to call her attention to this point. "The importance to this trial, however, is the due date, which is still more than three months away."

The court officers silenced the gasps and mumbles that followed this announcement.

"It is therefore obvious why the plaintiff has suppressed this valuable piece of evidence. It is equally clear to the court that the plaintiff knew that he had no justification whatsoever for being upon the premises of Mrs. Clairborne."

His Honor folded the paper and put it aside, and regarded the plaintiff with cold gray eyes.

"This is the most insulting instance in the memory of the court of an attempt to prostitute the very machinery of justice for an individual's own nefarious ends. The plaintiff first attempts burglary with forceful entry and violence and, when thoroughly beaten for his pains, brazenly calls upon the law to punish the faithful watch-dog who bit him while he was attempting his trespass. Further, it seems apparent that he has taken steps to prevent any word from the defendant reaching Mrs. Clairborne, who certainly would have moved heaven and earth in the defendant's behalf, and rightfully so."

The judge laced the fingers of his hands and rested them on the polished wood before him and went on.

The protection of women and children, he said, was inherent, implicit in Anglo-Saxon civilization, and here in these United States it had become a sacred trust. He reviewed the long, slow climb of humanity from the rule of the club and the stone hatchet to the Constitution of the United States. The English-speaking people had given the world its highest concepts of the rights of the individual, and they were not gong to be made a mock of, and nullified by this court.

"The defendant did no more than resist the plaintiff's attempted burglary. Valuable assets of her employer were trusted in her care, and she placed her very life in jeopardy in defending that trust, setting an example which no decent citizen need blush to follow. The jury is directed to find for the defendant."

Laura Lee made her way diffidently to the judge and thanked him over and over again.

"That will do, Laura Lee. I am the one who should be thanking you."

Laura Lee could see no reason why, and wandered off, bewildered. She was instantly surrounded by smiling, congratulating strangers, many of whom made her ever so welcome if ever she needed a home. She was rubbed and polished to a high glow.

Back at the house, Laura Lee did not enter at once. Like a pilgrim before a shrine, she stood and bowed her head. "I ain't fitten to enter. For a time, I allowed myself to doubt my Celestine. But maybe nobody ain't as pure in heart as they aim to be. The cock crowed on Apostle Peter.[3] Old Maker, please take my guilt away and cast it into the sea of forgetfulness where it won't never rise to accuse me in this world, nor condemn me in the next."

Laura Lee entered and opened all the windows with a ceremonial air. She was hungry, but before she would eat, she made a ritual of atonement by serving. She took a finely wrought silver platter from the massive old sideboard and gleamed it to perfection. So the platter, so she wanted her love to shine.

3. Apostle Peter denied Christ before the cock crowed.

# Shirley Jackson

*Jackson (1919–1965) was born in San Francisco. Shortly after completing her undergraduate education at Syracuse University she married the literary critic Stanley Edgar Hyman, and when he became a teacher at Bennington College in Vermont, they settled permanently there. She is a master of the gothic horror tale refurbished in the modern manner, rousing terror from situations that initially appear normal and even dull. Her novels include* Hangsaman *(1951),* The Bird's Nest *(1954), and* We Have Always Lived in the Castle *(1962). Her short stories are collected in* The Lottery *(1944) and* The Magic of Shirley Jackson *(1966).*

## The Lottery

The morning of June 27th was clear and sunny, with the fresh warmth of a full-summer day; the flowers were blossoming profusely and the grass was richly green. The people of the village began to gather in the square, between the post office and the bank, around ten o'clock; in some towns there were so many people that the lottery took two days and had to be started on June 26th, but in this village, where there were only about three hundred people, the whole lottery took less than two hours, so it could begin at ten o'clock in the morning and still be through in time to allow the villagers to get home for noon dinner.

The children assembled first, of course. School was recently over for the summer, and the feeling of liberty sat uneasily on most of them; they tended to gather together quietly for a while before they broke into boisterous play, and their talk was still of the classroom and the teacher, of books and reprimands. Bobby Martin had already stuffed his pockets full of stones, and the other boys soon followed his example, selecting the smoothest and roundest stones; Bobby and Harry Jones and Dickie Delacroix—the villagers pronounced this name "Dellacroy"—eventually made a great pile of stones in one corner of the square and guarded it against the raids of the other boys. The girls stood aside, talking among themselves, looking over their shoulders at the boys, and the very small children rolled in the dust or clung to the hands of their older brothers or sisters.

Soon the men began to gather, surveying their own children, speaking of planting and rain, tractors and taxes. They stood together, away from the pile of stones in the corner, and their jokes were quiet and they smiled rather than laughed. The women, wearing faded house dresses and sweaters, came shortly after their menfolk. They greeted one another and exchanged bits of gossip as they went to join their husbands. Soon the women, standing by their husbands, began to call to their children, and the children came reluctantly, having to be called four or five times. Bobby Martin ducked under his mother's grasping hand and ran, laughing, back to the pile of stones. His father spoke up sharply, and Bobby came quickly and took his place between his father and his oldest brother.

The lottery was conducted—as were the square dances, the teenage club, the Halloween program—by Mr. Summers, who had time and energy to devote to civic activities. He was a round-faced, jovial man and he ran the coal business, and people were sorry for him, because he had no children and his wife was a scold. When he arrived in the square, carrying the black wooden box, there was a murmur of conversation among the villagers, and he waved and called, "Little late today, folks." The postmaster, Mr. Graves, followed him, carrying a three-legged stool, and the stool was put in the center of the square and Mr. Summers set the black box down on it. The villagers kept their distance, leaving a space between themselves and the stool, and when Mr. Summers said, "Some of you fellows want to give me a hand?" there was a hesitation before two men, Mr. Martin and his oldest son, Baxter, came forward to hold the box steady on the stool while Mr. Summers stirred up the papers inside it.

The original paraphernalia for the lottery had been lost long ago, and the black box now resting on the stool had been put into use even before Old Man Warner, the oldest man in town, was born. Mr. Summers spoke frequently to the villagers about making a new box, but no one liked to upset even as much tradition as was represented by the black box. There was a story that the present box had been made with some pieces of the box that had preceded it, the one that had been constructed when the first people settled down to make a village here. Every year, after the lottery, Mr. Summers began talking again about a new box, but every year the subject was allowed to fade off without anything's being done. The black box grew shabbier each year; by now it was no longer completely black but splintered badly along one side to show the original wood color, and in some places faded or stained.

Mr. Martin and his oldest son, Baxter, held the black box securely on the stool until Mr. Summers had stirred the papers thoroughly with his hand. Because so much of the ritual had been forgotten or discarded, Mr. Summers had been successful in having slips of paper substituted for the chips of wood that had been used for generations. Chips of wood, Mr. Summers had argued, had been all very well when the village was tiny, but now that the population was more than three hundred and likely to keep on growing, it was necessary to use something that would fit more easily into the black box. The night before the lottery, Mr. Summers and Mr. Graves made up the slips of paper and put them in the box, and it was then taken to the safe of Mr. Summers' coal company and locked up until Mr. Summers was ready to take it to the square next morning. The rest of the year, the box was put away, sometimes one place, sometimes another; it had spent one year in Mr. Graves's barn and another year underfoot in the post office, and sometimes it was set on a shelf in the Martin grocery and left there.

There was a great deal of fussing to be done before Mr. Summers declared the lottery open. There were the lists to make up—of heads of families, heads of households in each family, members of each household in each family. There was the proper swearing-in of Mr. Summers by the postmaster, as the official of the lottery; at one time, some people remembered, there had been a recital of some sort, performed by the official of the lottery, a perfunctory, tuneless chant that had been rattled off duly each year; some people believed that the official of the lottery used to stand just so when he said or sang it, others believed that he was supposed to walk among the people, but years and years ago this part of the ritual had been allowed to lapse. There had been, also, a ritual salute, which the official of the lottery had had to use in addressing each person who came up to draw from the box, but this also had changed with time, until now it was felt necessary only for the official to speak to each person approaching. Mr. Summers was very good at all this; in his clean white shirt and blue jeans, with one hand resting carelessly on the black box, he seemed very proper and important as he talked interminably to Mr. Graves and the Martins.

Just as Mr. Summers finally left off talking and turned to the assembled villagers, Mrs. Hutchinson came hurriedly along the path to the square, her sweater thrown over her shoulders, and slid into place in the back of the crowd. "Clean forgot what day it was," she said to Mrs. Delacroix, who stood next to her, and they both laughed softly. "Thought my old man was out back stacking wood," Mrs. Hutchinson went on, "and then I looked out the window and the kids was gone, and then I remembered it was the twenty-seventh and came a-running." She dried her hands on her apron, and Mrs. Delacroix said, "You're in time, though. They're still talking away up there."

Mrs. Hutchinson craned her neck to see through the crowd and found her husband and children standing near the front. She tapped Mrs. Delacroix on the arm as a farewell and began to make her way through the crowd. The people separated good-humoredly to let her through; two or three people said, in voices just loud enough to be heard across the crowd, "Here comes your Missus, Hutchinson," and "Bill, she made it after all." Mrs. Hutchinson reached her husband, and Mr. Summers, who had been waiting, said cheerfully, "Thought we were going to have to get on without you, Tessie." Mrs. Hutchinson said, grinning, "Wouldn't have me leave m'dishes in the sink, now, would you, Joe?," and soft laughter ran through the crowd as the people stirred back into position after Mrs. Hutchinson's arrival.

"Well, now," Mr. Summers said soberly, "guess we better get started, get this over with, so's we can go back to work. Anybody ain't here?"

"Dunbar," several people said, "Dunbar, Dunbar."

Mr. Summers consulted his list. "Clyde Dunbar," he said. "That's right. He's broke his leg, hasn't he? Who's drawing for him?"

"Me, I guess," a woman said, and Mr. Summers turned to look at her. "Wife draws for her husband," Mr. Summers said. "Don't you have a grown boy to do it for you, Janey?" Although Mr. Summers and everyone else in the village knew the answer perfectly well, it was the business of the official of the lottery to ask such questions formally. Mr. Summers waited with an expression of polite interest while Mrs. Dunbar answered.

"Horace's not but sixteen yet," Mrs. Dunbar said regretfully. "Guess I gotta fill in for the old man this year."

"Right," Mr. Summers said. He made a note on the list he was holding. Then he asked, "Watson boy drawing this year?"

A tall boy in the crowd raised his hand. "Here," he said. "I'm drawing for m'mother and me." He blinked his eyes nervously and ducked his head as several voices in the crowd said things like "Good fellow, Jack," and "Glad to see your mother's got a man to do it."

"Well," Mr. Summers said, "guess that's everyone. Old Man Warner make it?"

"Here," a voice said, and Mr. Summers nodded.

A sudden hush fell on the crowd as Mr. Summers cleared his throat and looked at the list. "All ready?" he called. "Now, I'll read the names—heads of families first—and the men come up and take a paper out of the box. Keep the paper folded in your hand without looking at it until everyone has had a turn. Everything clear?"

The people had done it so many times that they only half listened to the directions; most of them were quiet, wetting their lips, not looking around. Then Mr. Summers raised one hand high and said, "Adams." A man disengaged himself from the crowd and came forward. "Hi, Steve," Mr. Summers said, and Mr. Adams said, "Hi, Joe." They grinned at one another humorlessly and nervously. Then Mr. Adams reached into the black box and took out a folded paper. He held it firmly by one corner as he turned and went hastily back to his place in the crowd, where he stood a little apart from his family, not looking down at his hand.

"Allen," Mr. Summers said. "Anderson. . . . Bentham."

"Seems like there's no time at all between lotteries any more," Mrs. Delacroix said to Mrs. Graves in the back row. "Seems like we got through with the last one only last week."

"Time sure goes fast," Mrs. Graves said.

"Clark. . . . Delacroix."

"There goes my old man," Mrs. Delacroix said. She held her breath while her husband went forward.

"Dunbar," Mr. Summers said, and Mrs. Dunbar went steadily to the box while one of the women said, "Go on, Janey," and another said, "There she goes."

"We're next," Mrs. Graves said. She watched while Mr. Graves came around from the side of the box, greeted Mr. Summers gravely, and selected a slip of paper from the box. By now, all through the crowd there were men holding the small folded papers in their large hands, turning them over and over nervously. Mrs. Dunbar and her two sons stood together, Mrs. Dunbar holding the slip of paper.

"Harburt. . . . Hutchinson."

"Get up there, Bill," Mrs. Hutchinson said, and the people near her laughed.

"Jones."

"They do say," Mr. Adams said to Old Man Warner, who stood next to him, "that over in the north village they're talking of giving up the lottery."

Old Man Warner snorted. "Pack of crazy fools," he said. "Listening to the young folks, nothing's good enough for *them.* Next thing you know, they'll be wanting to go back to living in caves, nobody work any more, live *that* way for a while. Used to be a saying about 'Lottery in June, corn be heavy soon.' First thing you know, we'd all be eating stewed chickweed and acorns. There's *always* been a lottery," he added petulantly. "Bad enough to see young Joe Summers up there joking with everybody."

"Some places have already quit lotteries," Mrs. Adams said.

"Nothing but trouble in *that,*" Old Man Warner said stoutly. "Pack of young fools."

"Martin." And Bobby Martin watched his father go forward. "Overdyke. . . . Percy."

"I wish they'd hurry," Mrs. Dunbar said to her older son. "I wish they'd hurry."

"They're almost through," her son said.

"You get ready to run tell Dad," Mrs. Dunbar said.

Mr. Summers called his own name and then stepped forward precisely and selected a slip from the box. Then he called, "Warner."

"Seventy-seventh year I been in the lottery," Old Man Warner said as he went through the crowd. "Seventy-seventh time."

"Watson." The tall boy came awkwardly through the crowd. Someone said, "Don't be nervous, Jack," and Mr. Summers said, "Take your time, son."

"Zanini."

After that, there was a long pause, a breathless pause, until Mr. Summers, holding his slip of paper in the air, said, "All right, fellows." For a minute, no one moved, and then all the slips of paper were opened. Suddenly, all the women began to speak at once, saying, "Who is it?," "Who's got it?," "Is it the Dunbars?," "Is it the Watsons?" Then the voices began to say, "It's Hutchinson. It's Bill," "Bill Hutchinson's got it."

"Go tell your father," Mrs. Dunbar said to her older son.

People began to look around to see the Hutchinsons. Bill Hutchinson was standing quiet staring down at the paper in his hand. Suddenly, Tessie Hutchinson shouted to Mr. Summers, "You didn't give him time enough to take any paper he wanted. I saw you. It wasn't fair."

"Be a good sport, Tessie," Mrs. Delacroix called, and Mrs. Graves said, "All of us took the same chance."

"Shut up, Tessie," Bill Hutchinson said.

"Well, everyone," Mr. Summers said, "that was done pretty fast, and now we've got to be hurrying a little more to get done in time." He consulted his next list. "Bill," he said, "you draw for the Hutchinson family. You got any other households in the Hutchinsons?"

"There's Don and Eva," Mrs. Hutchinson yelled. "Make *them* take their chance!"

"Daughters draw for their husbands' families, Tessie," Mr. Summers said gently. "You know that as well as anyone else."

"It wasn't *fair,*" Tessie said.

"I guess not, Joe," Bill Hutchinson said regretfully. "My daughter draws with her husband's family, that's only fair. And I've got no other family except the kids."

"Then, as far as drawing for families is concerned, it's you," Mr. Summers said in explanation, "and as far as drawing for households is concerned, that's you, too. Right?"

"Right," Bill Hutchinson said.

"How many kids, Bill?" Mr. Summers asked formally.

"Three," Bill Hutchinson said. "There's Bill, Jr., and Nancy, and little Dave. And Tessie and me."

"All right, then," Mr. Summers said. "Harry, you got their tickets back?"

Mr. Graves nodded and held up the slips of paper. "Put them in the box, then," Mr. Summers directed. "Take Bill's and put it in."

"I think we ought to start over," Mrs. Hutchinson said, as quietly as she could, "I tell you it wasn't *fair.* You didn't give him time enough to choose. *Every*body saw that."

Mr. Graves had selected the five slips and put them in the box, and he dropped all the papers but those onto the ground, where the breeze caught them and lifted them off.

"Listen, everybody," Mrs. Hutchinson was saying to the people around her.

"Ready, Bill?" Mr. Summers asked, and Bill Hutchinson, with one quick glance around at his wife and children, nodded.

"Remember," Mr. Summers said, "take the slips and keep them folded until each person has taken one. Harry, you help little Dave." Mr. Graves took the hand of the little boy, who came willingly with him up to the box. "Take a paper out of the box, Davy," Mr. Summers said. Davy put his hand into the box and laughed. "Take just *one* paper," Mr. Summers said. "Harry, you hold it for him." Mr. Graves took the child's hand and removed the folded paper from the tight fist and held it while little Dave stood next to him and looked up at him wonderingly.

"Nancy next," Mr. Summers said. Nancy was twelve, and her school friends breathed heavily as she went forward, switching her skirt, and took a slip daintily from the box. "Bill, Jr.," Mr. Summers said, and Billy, his face red and his feet over-large, nearly knocked the box over as he got a paper out. "Tessie," Mr. Summers said. She hesitated for a minute, looking around defiantly, and then set her lips and went up to the box. She snatched a paper out and held it behind her.

"Bill," Mr. Summers said, and Bill Hutchinson reached into the box and felt around, bringing his hand out at last with the slip of paper in it.

The crowd was quiet. A girl whispered, "I hope it's not Nancy," and the sound of the whisper reached the edges of the crowd.

"It's not the way it used to be," Old Man Warner said clearly. "People ain't the way they used to be."

"All right," Mr. Summers said. "Open the papers. Harry, you open little Dave's."

Mr. Graves opened the slip of paper and there was a general sigh through the crowd as he held it up and everyone could see that it was blank. Nancy and Bill, Jr., opened theirs at the same time, and both beamed and laughed, turning around to the crowd and holding their slips of paper above their heads.

"Tessie," Mr. Summers said. There was a pause, and then Mr. Summers looked at Bill Hutchinson, and Bill unfolded his paper and showed it. It was blank.

"It's Tessie," Mr. Summers said, and his voice was hushed. "Show us her paper, Bill."

Bill Hutchinson went over to his wife and forced the slip of paper out of her hand. It had a black spot on it, the black spot Mr. Summers had made the night before with the heavy pencil in the coal-company office. Bill Hutchinson held it up, and there was a stir in the crowd.

"All right, folks," Mr. Summers said. "Let's finish quickly."

Although the villagers had forgotten the ritual and lost the original black box, they still remembered to use stones. The pile of stones the boys had made earlier was ready; there were stones on the ground with the blowing scraps of paper that had come out of the box. Mrs. Delacroix selected a stone so large she had to pick it up with both hands and turned to Mrs. Dunbar. "Come on," she said. "Hurry up."

Mrs. Dunbar had small stones in both hands, and she said, gasping for breath, "I can't run at all. You'll have to go ahead and I'll catch up with you."

The children had stones already, and someone gave little Davy Hutchinson a few pebbles.

Tessie Hutchinson was in the center of a cleared space by now, and she held her hands out desperately as the villagers moved in on her. "It isn't fair," she said. A stone hit her on the side of the head.

Old Man Warner was saying, "Come on, come on, everyone." Steve Adams was in the front of the crowd of villagers, with Mrs. Graves beside him.

"It isn't fair, it isn't right," Mrs. Hutchinson screamed, and then they were upon her.

# Henry James

*James (1843–1916) was born in New York City. His father was a writer and religious philosopher; his brother was William James, the philosopher and psychologist. James's father chose to have him educated chiefly in Europe by tutors in several countries, and his foreign education culminated in his acquaintance with several European writers, among them Turgenev, Flaubert, and de Maupassant. James's familiarity with life on both sides of the Atlantic led him, in much of his writing, to contrast European and American cultures and, above all, to show the effects of their mingling. In 1875 he took up permanent residence in England, becoming a naturalized citizen of that country in 1915 in protest against the initial neutrality of the United States in World War I. Throughout his later life James was the model of the professional writer, experimenting with ways of making his writing more pictorial, developing refinements in the handling of point of view, and commenting in many essays on these practices so that his theories of the art have been instructive to many later writers. He wrote several rather unsuccessful plays and more than seventy stories, which are most readily found in collected editions of his work or in paperback selections. Among his novels are* The American *(1877),* The Portrait of a Lady *(1881),* The Ambassadors *(1903), and* The Golden Bowl *(1904).*

## Greville Fane

Coming in to dress for dinner I found a telegram: "Mrs. Stormer dying; can you give us half a column for tomorrow evening? Let her down easily, but not too easily." I was late; I was in a hurry; I had very little time to think; but at a venture I despatched a reply: "Will do what I can." It was not till I had dressed and was rolling away to dinner that, in the hansom, I bethought myself of the difficulty of the condition attached. The difficulty was not of course in letting her down easily but in qualifying that indulgence. "So I simply won't qualify it," I said. I didn't admire but liked her, and had known her so long that I almost felt heartless in sitting down at such an hour to a feast of indifference. I must have seemed abstracted, for the early years of my acquaintance with her came back to me. I spoke of her to the lady I had taken down, but the lady I had taken down had never heard of Greville Fane. I tried my other neighbour, who pronounced her books "too vile." I had never thought them very good, but I should let her down more easily than that.

I came away early, for the express purpose of driving to ask about her. The journey took time, for she lived in the northwest district, in the neighbourhood of Primrose Hill. My apprehension that I should be too late was justified in a fuller sense than I had attached to it—I had only feared that the house would be shut up. There were lights in the windows, and the temperate tinkle of my bell brought a servant immediately to the door; but poor Mrs. Stormer had passed into a state in which the resonance of no earthly knocker was to be feared. A lady hovering behind the servant came forward into the hall when she heard my voice. I recognised Lady Luard, but she had mistaken me for the doctor.

"Pardon my appearing at such an hour," I said; "it was the first possible moment after I heard."

"It's all over," Lady Luard replied. "Dearest mamma!"

She stood there under the lamp with her eyes on me; she was very tall, very stiff, very cold, and always looked as if these things, and some others beside, in her dress, in her manner and even in her name, were an implication that she was very admirable. I had never been able to follow the argument, but that's a detail. I expressed briefly and frankly what I felt, while the little mottled maid-servant flattened herself against the wall of the narrow passage and tried to look detached without looking indifferent. It was not a moment to make a visit, and I was on the point of retreating when Lady Luard arrested me with a queer casual drawling "Would you—a—would you perhaps be *writing* something?" I felt for the instant like an infamous interviewer, which I wasn't. But I pleaded guilty to this intention, on which she returned: "I'm so very glad—but I think my brother would like to see you." I detested her brother, but it wasn't an occasion to act this out; so I suffered myself to be inducted, to my surprise, into a small back room which I immediately recognised as the scene, during the later years, of Mrs. Stormer's imperturbable industry. Her table was there, the battered and blotted accessory to innumerable literary lapses, with its contracted space for the arms (she wrote only from the elbow down) and the confusion of scrappy scribbled sheets which had already become literary remains. Leolin was also there, smoking a cigarette before the fire and looking impudent even in his grief, sincere as it well might have been.

To meet him, to greet him, I had to make a sharp effort; for the air he wore to me as he stood before me was quite that of his mother's murderer. She lay silent for ever upstairs—as dead as an unsuccessful book, and his swaggering erectness was a kind of symbol of his having killed her. I wondered if he had already, with his sister, been calculating what they could get for the poor papers on the table; but I hadn't long to wait to learn, since in reply to the few words of sympathy I addressed him he puffed out: "It's miserable, miserable, yes; but she has left three books complete." His words had the oddest effect; they converted the cramped little room into a seat of trade and made the "book" wonderfully feasible. He would certainly get all that could be got for the three. Lady Luard explained to me that her husband had been with them, but had had to go down to the House. To her brother she mentioned that I was going to write something, and to me again made it clear that she hoped I would "do mamma justice." She added that she didn't think this had ever been done. She said to her brother: "Don't you think there are some things he ought thoroughly to understand?" and on his instantly exclaiming "Oh thoroughly, thoroughly!" went on rather austerely: "I mean about mamma's birth."

"Yes and her connexions," Leolin added.

I professed every willingness, and for five minutes I listened; but it would be too much to say I clearly understood. I don't even now, but it's not important. My vision was of other matters than those they put before me, and while they desired there should be no mistake about their ancestors I became keener and keener about themselves. I got away as soon as possible and walked home through the great dusky empty London—the best of all conditions for thought. By the time I reached my door my little article was practically composed—ready to be transferred on the morrow from the polished plate of fancy. I believe it attracted some notice, was thought "graceful" and was said to be by some one else. I had to be pointed without being lively, and it took some doing. But what I said was much less interesting than what I thought—especially during the half-hour I spent in my armchair by the fire, smoking the cigar I always light before going to bed. I went to sleep there, I believe; but I continued to moralise about Greville Fane. I'm reluctant to lose that retrospect altogether, and this is a dim little memory of it, a document not to "serve." The dear woman had written a hundred stories, but none so curious as her own.

When first I knew her she had published half a dozen fictions, and I believe I had also perpetrated a novel. She was more than a dozen years my elder, but a person who always acknowledged her comparative state. It wasn't so very long ago, but in London, amid the big waves of the present, even a near horizon gets hidden. I met her at some dinner and took her down, rather flattered at offering my arm to a celebrity. She didn't look like one, with her matronly mild inanimate face, but I supposed her greatness would come out in her conversation. I gave it all the opportunities I could, but was nevertheless not disappointed when I found her only a dull kind woman. This was why I liked her—she rested me so from literature. To myself literature was an irritation, a torment; but Greville Fane slumbered in the intellectual part of it even as a cat on a hearthrug or a Creole in a hammock. She wasn't a woman of genius, but her faculty was so special, so much a gift out of hand, that I've often wondered why she fell below that distinction. This was doubtless because the transaction, in her case, had remained incomplete; genius always pays for the gift, feels the debt, and she was placidly unconscious of a call. She could invent stories by the yard, but couldn't write a page of English. She went down to her grave without suspecting that though she had contributed volumes to the diversion of her contemporaries she hadn't contributed a sentence to the language. This hadn't prevented bushels of criticism from being heaped on her head; she was worth a couple of columns any day to the weekly papers, in which it was shown that her pictures of life were dreadful but her style superior. She asked me to come and see her and I complied. She lived then in Montpellier Square; which helped me to see how dissociated her imagination was from her character.

An industrious widow, devoted to her daily stint, to meeting the butcher and baker and making a home for her son and daughter, from the moment she took her pen in her hand she became a creature of passion. She thought the English novel deplorably wanting in that element, and the task she had cut out for herself was to supply the deficiency. Passion in high life was the general formula of this work, for her imagination was at home only in the most exalted circles. She adored in truth the aristocracy, and they constituted for her the romance of the world or what is more to the point, the prime material of fiction. Their beauty and luxury, their loves and revenges, their temptations and surrenders, their immoralities and diamonds were as familiar to her as the blots on her writing-table. She was not a belated producer of the old fashionable novel, but, with a cleverness and a modernness of her own, had freshened up the fly-blown tinsel. She turned off plots by the hundred and—so far as her flying quill could convey her—was perpetually going abroad. Her types, her illustrations, her tone were nothing if not cosmopolitan. She recognised nothing less provincial than European society, and her fine folk knew each other and made love to each other from Doncaster to Bucharest. She had an idea that she resembled Balzac, and her favourite historical characters were Lucien de Rubempré[1] and the Vidame de Pamiers. I must add that when I once asked her who the latter personage was she was unable to tell me. She was very brave and healthy and cheerful, very abundant and innocent and wicked. She was expert and vulgar and snobbish, and never so intensely British as when she was particularly foreign.

This combination of qualities had brought her early success, and I remember having heard with wonder and envy of what she "got," in those days, for a novel. The revelation gave me a pang: it was such a proof that, practising a totally different style, I should never make my fortune. And yet when, as I knew her better she told me her real tariff and I saw how rumour had quadrupled it, I liked her enough to be sorry. After a while I discovered too that if she got less it was not that *I* was to get any more. My failure never had what Mrs. Stormer would have called the banality of being relative—it was always admirably absolute. She lived at ease however in those days—ease is exactly the word, though she produced three novels a year. She scorned me when I spoke of difficulty—it was the only thing that made her angry. If I hinted at the grand licking into shape that a work of art required she thought it a pretension and a *pose*. She never recognised the "torment of form"; the furthest she went was to introduce into one of her books (in satire her hand was heavy) a young poet who was always talking about it. I couldn't quite understand her irritation on this score, for she had nothing at stake in the matter. She had a shrewd perception that form, in prose at least, never recommended any one to the public we were condemned to address; according to which she lost nothing (her private humiliation not counted) by having none to show. She made no pretence of producing works of art, but had comfortable tea-drinking hours in which she freely confessed herself a common pastrycook, dealing in such tarts and puddings as would bring customers to the shop. She put in plenty of sugar and of cochineal, or whatever it is that gives these articles a rich and attractive colour. She had a calm independence of observation and opportunity which constituted an inexpugnable strength and would enable her to go on indefinitely. It's only real success that wanes, it's only solid things that melt. Greville Fane's ignorance of life was a resource still more unfailing than the most approved receipt. On

1. A fictional character in the novel *A Distinguished Provincial at Paris* by Honoré de Balzac (1799–1850).

her saying once that the day would come when she should have written herself out I answered: "Ah you open straight into fairyland, and the fairies love you and *they* never change. Fairyland's always there; it always was from the beginning of time and always will be to the end. They've given you the key and you can always open the door. With me it's different; I try, in my clumsy way, to be in some direct relation to life." "Oh bother your direct relation to life!" she used to reply, for she was always annoyed by the phrase—which wouldn't in the least prevent her using it as a note of elegance. With no more prejudices than an old sausage-mill, she would give forth again with patient punctuality any poor verbal scrap that had been dropped into her. I cheered her with saying that the dark day, at the end, would be for the "likes" of *me*; since, proceeding in our small way by experience and study—priggish we!—we depended not on a revelation but on a little tiresome process. Attention depended on occasion, and where should we be when occasion failed?

One day she told me that as the novelist's life was so delightful and, during the good years at least, such a comfortable support—she had these staggering optimisms—she meant to train up her boy to follow it. She took the ingenious view that it was a profession like another and that therefore everything was to be gained by beginning young and serving an apprenticeship. Moreover the education would be less expensive than any other special course, inasmuch as she could herself administer it. She didn't profess to keep a school, but she could at least teach her own child. It wasn't that she had such a gift, but—she confessed to me as if she were afraid I should laugh at her—that *he* had. I didn't laugh at her for that, because I thought the boy sharp—I had seen him sundry times. He was well-grown and good-looking and unabashed, and both he and his sister made me wonder about their defunct papa, concerning whom the little I knew was that he had been a country vicar and brother to a small squire. I explained them to myself by suppositions and imputations possibly unjust to the departed; so little were they—superficially at least—the children of their mother. There used to be on an easel in her drawing-room an enlarged photograph of her husband, done by some horrible posthumous "process" and draped, as to its florid frame, with a silken scarf which testified to the candour of Greville Fane's bad taste. It made him look like an unsuccessful tragedian, but it wasn't a thing to trust. He may have been a successful comedian. Of the two children the girl was the elder, and struck me in all her younger years as singularly colourless. She was only long, very long, like an undecipherable letter. It wasn't till Mrs. Stormer came back from a protracted residence abroad that Ethel (which was this young lady's name) began to produce the effect, large and stiff and afterwards eminent in her, of a certain kind of resolution, something as public and important as if a meeting and a chairman had passed it. She gave one to understand she meant to do all she could for herself. She was long-necked and near-sighted and striking, and I thought I had never seen sweet seventeen in a form so hard and high and dry. She was cold and affected and ambitious, and she carried an eyeglass with a long handle, which she put up whenever she wanted not to see. She had come out, as the phrase is, immensely; and yet I felt as if she were surrounded with a spiked iron railing. What she meant to do for herself was to marry, and it was the only thing, I think, that she meant to do for any one else; yet who would be inspired to clamber over that bristling barrier? What flower of tenderness or of intimacy would such an adventurer conceive as his reward?

This was for Sir Baldwin Luard to say; but he naturally never confided me the secret. He was a joyless jokeless young man, with the air of having other secrets as well, and a determination to get on politically that was indicated by his never having been known to commit himself—as regards any proposition whatever—beyond an unchallengeable "Oh!" His wife and he must have conversed mainly in prim ejaculations, but they understood sufficiently that they were kindred spirits. I remember being angry with Greville Fane when she announced these nuptials to me as magnificent; I remember asking her what splendour there was in the union of the daughter of a woman of genius with an irredeemable mediocrity. "Oh he has immense ability," she said; but she blushed for the maternal fib. What she meant was that though Sir Baldwin's estates were not vast—he had a dreary house in South Kensington and a still drearier "Hall" somewhere in Essex, which was let—the connexion was a "smarter" one than a child of hers could have aspired to form. In spite of the social bravery of her novels she took a very humble and dingy view of herself, so that of all her productions "my daughter Lady Luard" was quite the one she was proudest of. That personage thought our authoress vulgar and was distressed and perplexed by the frequent freedoms of her pen, but had a complicated attitude for this indirect connexion with literature. So far as it was lucrative her ladyship approved of it and could compound with the inferiority of the pursuit by practical justice to some of its advantages. I had reason to know—my reason was simply that poor Mrs. Stormer told me—how she suffered the inky fingers to press an occasional banknote into her palm. On the other hand she deplored the "peculiar style" to which Greville Fane had devoted herself, and wondered where a spectator with the advantage of so ladylike a daughter could have picked up such views about the best society. "She might know better, with Leolin and me," Lady Luard had been heard to remark; but it appeared that some of Greville Fane's superstitions were incurable. She didn't live in Lady Luard's society, and the best wasn't good enough for her—she must improve on it so prodigiously.

I could see this necessity increase in her during the years she spent abroad, when I had glimpses of her in the shifting sojourns that lay in the path of my annual ramble. She betook herself from Germany to Switzerland and from Switzerland to Italy; she favoured cheap places and set up her desk in the smaller capitals. I took a look at her whenever I could, and I always asked how Leolin was getting on. She gave me beautiful accounts of him, and, occasion favouring, the boy was produced for my advantage. I had entered from the first into the joke of his career—I pretended to regard him as a consecrated child. It had been a joke for Mrs. Stormer at first, but the youth himself had been shrewd enough to make the matter serious. If his parent accepted the principle that the intending novelist can't begin too early to see life, Leolin wasn't interested in hanging back from the application of it. He was eager to qualify himself and took to cigarettes at ten on the highest literary grounds. His fond mother gazed at him with extravagant envy and, like Desdemona, wished heaven had made *her* such a man. She explained to me more than once that in her profession she had found her sex a dreadful drawback. She loved the story of Madame George Sand's early rebellion against this hindrance, and believed that if she had worn trousers she could have written as well as that lady. Leolin had for the career at least the qualification of trousers, and as he grew older he recognised its importance by laying in ever so many pair. He grew up thus in gorgeous apparel, which was his way of interpreting his mother's system. Whenever I met her, accordingly, I found her still under the impression that she was carrying this system out and that the sacrifices made him were bearing heavy fruit. She was giving him experience, she was giving him impressions, she was putting a *gagne-pain*[2] into his hand. It was another name for spoiling him with the best conscience in the world. The queerest pictures come back to me of this period of the good lady's life and of the extraordinarily virtuous muddled bewildering tenor of it. She had an idea she was seeing foreign manners as well as her petticoats would allow; but in reality she wasn't seeing anything, least of all, fortunately, how much she was laughed at. She drove her whimsical pen at Dresden and at Florence—she produced in all places and at all times the same romantic and ridiculous fictions. She carried about her box of properties, tumbling out promptly the familiar tarnished old puppets. She believed in them when others couldn't, and as they were like nothing that was to be seen under the sun it was impossible to prove by comparison that they were wrong. You can't compare birds and fishes; you could only feel that, as Greville Fane's characters had the fine plumage of the former species, human beings must be of the latter.

It would have been droll if it hadn't been so exemplary to see her tracing the loves of the duchesses beside the innocent cribs of her children. The immoral and the maternal lived together, in her diligent days, on the most comfortable terms, and she stopped curling the moustaches of her Guardsmen to pat the heads of her babes. She was haunted by solemn spinsters who came to tea from Continental pensions,[3] and by unsophisticated Americans who told her she was just loved in *their* country. "I had rather be just paid there," she usually replied; for this tribute of transatlantic opinion was the only thing that galled her. The Americans went away thinking her coarse; though as the author of so many beautiful love-stories she was disappointing to most of these pilgrims, who hadn't expected to find a shy stout ruddy lady in a cap like a crumbled pyramid. She wrote about the affections and the impossibility of controlling them, but she talked of the price of pension and the convenience of an English chemist. She devoted much thought and many thousands of francs to the education of her daughter, who spent three years at a very superior school at Dresden, receiving wonderful instruction in sciences, arts and tongues, and who, taking a different line from Leolin, was to be brought up wholly as a *femme du monde.*[4] The girl was musical and philological; she went in for several languages and learned enough about them to be inspired with a great contempt for her mother's artless accents. Greville Fane's French and Italian were droll;

2. Earning his bread (French); i.e., making a living. 3. Boarding houses or small hotels. 4. Woman of the world (French).

the imitative faculty had been denied her, and she had an unequalled gift, especially pen in hand, of squeezing big mistakes into small opportunities. She knew it but didn't care; correctness was the virtue in the world that, like her heroes and heroines, she valued least. Ethel, who had noted in her pages some remarkable lapses, undertook at one time to revise her proofs; but I remember her telling me a year after the girl had left school that this function had been very briefly exercised. "She can't read me," said Mrs. Stormer; "I offend her taste. She tells me that at Dresden—at school—I was never allowed." The good lady seemed surprised at this, having the best conscience in the world about her lucubrations. She had never meant to fly in the face of anything, and considered that she grovelled before the Rhadamanthus[5] of the English literary tribunal, the celebrated and awful Young Person. I assured her, as a joke, that she was frightfully indecent (she hadn't in fact that reality any more than any other) my purpose being solely to prevent her from guessing that her daughter had dropped her not because she was immoral but because she was vulgar. I used to figure her children closeted together and asking each other while they exchanged a gaze of dismay: "Why should she *be* so—and so *fearfully* so—when she has the advantage of our society? Shouldn't *we* have taught her better?" Then I imagined their recognising with a blush and a shrug that she was unteachable, irreformable. Indeed she was, poor lady; but it is never fair to read by the light of taste things that were not written by it. Greville Fane had, in the topsy-turvy, a serene good faith that ought to have been safe from allusion, like a stutter or a *faux pas*.

She didn't make her son ashamed of the profession to which he was destined, however; she only made him ashamed of the way she herself exercised it. But he bore his humiliation much better than his sister, for he was ready to take for granted that he should one day restore the balance. He was a canny and far-seeing youth, with appetites and aspirations, and he had not a scruple in his composition. His mother's theory of the happy knack he could pick up deprived him of the wholesome discipline required to prevent young idlers from becoming cads. He had, abroad, a casual tutor and a snatch or two of a Swiss school, but no consecutive study, no prospect of a university or a degree. It may be imagined with what zeal, as the years went on, he entered into the pleasantry of there being no manual so important to him as the massive book of life. It was an expensive volume to peruse, but Mrs. Stormer was willing to lay out a sum in what she would have called her *premiers frais*.[6] Ethel disapproved—she thought this education far too unconventional for an English gentleman. Her voice was for Eton and Oxford, or for any public school (she would have resigned herself) with the army to follow. But Leolin never was afraid of his sister, and they visibly disliked, though they sometimes agreed to assist, each other. They could combine to work the oracle—to keep their mother at her desk.

When she reappeared in England, telling me she had "secured" all the Continent could give her, Leolin was a broad-shouldered red-faced young man

5. In Greek mythology, the son of Zeus and Europa, who was rewarded for his stern justice by being made judge of the dead in the underworld. 6. Primary expense (French).

with an immense wardrobe and an extraordinary assurance of manner. She was fondly, quite aggressively certain she had taken the right course with him, and addicted to boasting of all he knew and had seen. He was now quite ready to embark on the family profession, to commence author, as they used to say, and a little while later she told me he had started. He had written something tremendously clever which was coming out in the *Cheapside.* I believe it came out; I had no time to look for it; I never heard anything about it. I took for granted that if this contribution had passed through his mother's hands it would virtually rather illustrate *her* fine facility, and it was interesting to consider the poor lady's future in the light of her having to write her son's novels as well as her own. This wasn't the way she looked at it herself—she took the charming ground that he'd help her to write hers. She used to assure me he supplied passages of the greatest value to these last—all sorts of telling technical things, happy touches about hunting and yachting and cigars and wine, about City slang and the way men talk at clubs—that she couldn't be expected to get very straight. It was all so much practice for him and so much alleviation for herself. I was unable to identify such pages, for I had long since ceased to "keep up" with Greville Fane; but I could quite believe at least that the wine-question had been put by Leolin's good offices on a better footing, for the dear woman used to mix her drinks—she was perpetually serving the most splendid suppers—in the queerest fashion. I could see him quite ripe to embrace regularly that care. It occurred to me indeed, when she settled in England again, that she might by a shrewd use of both her children be able to rejuvenate her style. Ethel had come back to wreak her native, her social yearning, and if she couldn't take her mother into company would at least go into it herself. Silently, stiffly, almost grimly, this young lady reared her head, clenched her long teeth, squared her lean elbows and found her way up the staircases she had marked. The only communication she ever made, the only effusion of confidence with which she ever honoured me, was when she said "I don't want to know the people mamma knows, I mean to know others." I took due note of the remark, for I wasn't one of the "others." I couldn't trace therefore the steps and stages of her climb; I could only admire it at a distance and congratulate her mother in due course on the results. The results, the gradual, the final, the wonderful, were that Ethel went to "big" parties and got people to take her. Some of them were people she had met abroad, and others people the people she had met abroad had met. They ministered alike to Miss Ethel's convenience, and I wondered how she extracted so many favours without the expenditure of a smile. Her smile was the dimmest thing in nature, diluted, unsweetened, inexpensive lemonade, and she had arrived precociously at social wisdom, recognising that if she was neither pretty enough nor rich enough nor clever enough, she could at least, in her muscular youth, be rude enough. Therefore, so placed to give her parent tips, to let her know what really occurred in the mansions of the great, to supply her with local colour, with *data* to work from, she promoted the driving of the well-worn quill, over the brave old battered blotting book, to a still lustier measure and precisely at the moment when most was to depend on this labour. But if she became a great critic it appeared that the labourer herself was constitutionally inapt for the lesson. It was late in the day for Greville Fane to learn, and I heard nothing of her having developed a new manner. She was to have had only one manner, as Leolin would have said, from start to finish.

She was weary and spent at last, but confided to me that she couldn't afford to pause. She continued to speak of her son's work as the great hope of their future—she had saved no money—though the young man wore to my sense an air more and more professional if you like, but less and less literary. There was at the end of a couple of years something rare in the impudence of his playing of his part in the comedy. When I wondered how she could play hers it was to feel afresh the fatuity of her fondness, which was proof, I believed—I indeed saw to the end—against any interference of reason. She loved the young impostor with a simple blind benighted love, and of all the heroes of romance who had passed before her eyes he was by far the brightest. He was at any rate the most real—she could touch him, pay for him, suffer for him, worship him. He made her think of her princes and dukes, and when she wished to fix these figures in her mind's eye she thought of her boy. She had often told me she was herself carried away by her creations, and she was certainly carried away by Leolin. He vivified—by what romantically might have been at least—the whole question of youth and passion. She held, not unjustly, that the sincere novelist should feel the whole flood of life; she acknowledged with regret that she hadn't had time to feel it herself, and the lapse in her history was in a manner made up by the sight of its rush through this magnificent young man. She exhorted him, I suppose, to encourage the rush; she wrung her own flaccid little sponge into the torrent. What passed between them in her pedagogic hours was naturally a blank to me, but I gathered that she mainly impressed on him that the great thing was to live, because that gave you material. He asked nothing better; he collected material, and the recipe served as a universal pretext. You had only to look at him to see that, with his rings and breastpins, his crossbarred jackets, his early *embonpoint*,[7] his eyes that looked like imitation jewels, his various indications of a dense full-blown temperament, his idea of life was singularly vulgar; but he was so far auspicious as that his response to his mother's expectations was in a high degree practical. If she had imposed a profession on him from his tenderest years it was exactly a profession that he followed. The two were not quite the same, inasmuch as the one he had adopted was simply to live at her expense; but at least she couldn't say he hadn't taken a line. If she insisted on believing in him he offered himself to the sacrifice. My impression is that her secret dream was that he should have a *liaison* with a countess, and he persuaded her without difficulty that he had one. I don't know what countesses are capable of, but I've a clear notion of what Leolin was.

He didn't persuade his sister, who despised him—she wished to work her mother in her own way; so that I asked myself why the girl's judgment of him didn't make me like her better. It was because it didn't save her after all from the mute agreement with him to go halves. There were moments when I couldn't help looking hard into his atrocious young eyes, challenging him to confess his fantastic fraud and give it up. Not a little tacit conversation passed

7. Stoutness (French).

between us in this way, but he had always the best of the business. If I said: "Oh come now, with *me* you needn't keep it up; plead guilty and I'll let you off," he wore the most ingenuous, the most candid expression, in the depths of which I could read: "Ah yes, I know it exasperates you—that's just why I do it." He took the line of earnest enquiry, talked about Balzac and Flaubert, asked me if I thought Dickens *did* exaggerate and Thackeray *ought* to be called a pessimist. Once he came to see me, at his mother's suggestion he declared, on purpose to ask me how far, in my opinion, in the English novel, one really might venture to "go." He wasn't resigned to the usual pruderies, the worship of childish twaddle; he suffered already from too much bread and butter. He struck out the brilliant idea that nobody knew how far we might go, since nobody had ever tried. Did I think *he* might safely try—would it injure his mother if he did? He would rather disgrace himself by his timidities than injure his mother, but certainly some one ought to try. Wouldn't *I* try—couldn't I be prevailed upon to look at it as a duty? Surely the ultimate point ought to be fixed—he was worried, haunted by the question. He patronised me unblushingly, made me feel a foolish amateur, a helpless novice, inquired into my habits of work and conveyed to me that I was utterly *vieux jeu*[8] and hadn't had the advantage of an early training. I hadn't been brought up from the egg, I knew nothing of life—didn't go at it on *his* system. He had dipped into French feuilletons[9] and picked up plenty of phrases, and he made a much better show in talk than his poor mother, who never had time to read anything and could only be showy with her pen. If I didn't kick him downstairs it was because he would have landed on her at the bottom.

When she went to live at Primrose Hill I called there and found her wasted and wan. It had visibly dropped, the elation caused the year before by Ethel's marriage; the foam on the cup had subsided and there was bitterness in the draught. She had had to take a cheaper house—and now had to work still harder to pay even for that. Sir Baldwin was obliged to be close; his charges were fearful, and the dream of her living with her daughter—a vision she had never mentioned to me—must be renounced. "I'd have helped them with things, and could have lived perfectly in one room," she said; "I'd have paid for everything, and—after all—I'm some one, ain't I? But I don't fit in, and Ethel tells me there are tiresome people she *must* receive. I can help them from here, no doubt, better than from there. She told me once, you know, what she thinks of my picture of life. 'Mamma, your picture of life's preposterous!' No doubt it is, but she's vexed with me for letting my prices go down; and I had to write three novels to pay for all her marriage cost me. I did it very well—I mean the outfit and the wedding; but that's why I'm here. At any rate she doesn't want a dingy old woman at Blicket. I should give the place an atmosphere of literary prestige, but literary prestige is only the eminence of nobodies. Besides, she knows what to think of my glory—she knows I'm glorious only at Peckham and Hackney. She doesn't want her friends to ask if I've never known nice people. She can't tell them I've never been in society. She tried to teach me better once, but I

8. Old game (French). 9. A part of a European newspaper devoted to light literature; the feature pages or tabloids.

couldn't catch on. It would seem too as if Peckham and Hackney had had enough of me; for (don't tell any one) I've had to take less for my last than I ever took for anything." I asked her how little this had been, not from curiosity, but in order to upbraid her, more disinterestedly than Lady Luard had done, for such concessions. She answered "I'm ashamed to tell you" and then began to cry.

I had never seen her break down and I was proportionately moved; she sobbed like a frightened child over the extinction of her vogue and the exhaustion of her vein. Her little workroom seemed indeed a barren place to grow flowers for the market, and I wondered in the after years (for she continued to produce and publish) by what desperate and heroic process she dragged them out of the soil. I remember asking her on that occasion what had become of Leolin and how much longer she intended to allow him to amuse himself at her cost. She retorted with spirit, wiping her eyes, that he was down at Brighton hard at work—he was in the midst of a novel—and that he *felt* life so, in all its misery and mystery, that it was cruel to speak of such experiences as a pleasure. "He goes beneath the surface," she said, "and he *forces* himself to look at things from which he'd rather turn away. Do you call that amusing yourself? You should see his face sometimes! And he does it for me as much as for himself. He tells me everything—he comes home to me with his *trouvailles.*[1] We're artists together, and to the artist all things are pure. I've often heard you say so yourself." The novel Leolin was engaged in at Brighton never saw the light, but a friend of mine and of Mrs. Stormer's who was staying there happened to mention to me later that he had seen the young apprentice to fiction driving, in a dog-cart, a young lady with a very pink face. When I suggested that she was perhaps a woman of title with whom he was conscientiously flirting my informant replied: "She is indeed, but do you know what her title is?" He pronounced it—it was familiar and descriptive—but I won't reproduce it here. I don't know whether Leolin mentioned it to his mother: she would have needed all the purity of the artist to forgive him. I hated so to come across him that in the very last years I went rarely to see her, though I knew she had come pretty well to the end of her rope. I didn't want her to tell me she had fairly to give her books away; I didn't want to see her old and abandoned and derided; I didn't want, in a word, to see her terribly cry. She still, however, kept it up amazingly, and every few months, at my club, I saw three new volumes, in green, in crimson, in blue, on the booktable that groaned with light literature. Once I met her at the Academy soirée, where you meet people you thought were dead, and she vouchsafed the information, as if she owed it to me in candour, that Leolin had been obliged to recognise the insuperable difficulties of the question of *form*—he was so fastidious; but that she had now arrived at a definite understanding with him (it was such a comfort!) that *she* would do the form if he would bring home the substance. That was now his employ—he foraged for her in the great world at a salary. "He's my 'devil,' don't you see? as if I were a great lawyer: he gets up the case and I argue it." She mentioned further that in addition to his salary he was paid by the piece: he got so much

1. Discoveries, lucky finds (French).

for a striking character, so much for a pretty name, so much for a plot, so much for an incident, and had so much promised him if he would invent a new crime.

"He *has* invented one," I said, "and he's paid every day of his life."

"What is it?" she asked, looking hard at the picture of the year, "Baby's Tub," near which we happened to be standing.

I hesitated a moment. "I myself will write a little story about it, and then you'll see."

But she never saw; she had never seen anything, and she passed away with her fine blindness unimpaired. Her son published every scrap of scribbled paper that could be extracted from her table-drawers, and his sister quarrelled with him mortally about the proceeds, which showed her only to have wanted a pretext, for they can't have been great. I don't know what Leolin lives on unless on a queer lady many years older than himself, whom he lately married. The last time I met him he said to me with his infuriating smile: "*Don't* you think we can go a little further still—just a little?" *He* really—with me at least—goes too far.

# Ruth Prawer Jhabvala

*Jhabvala (1927– ) was born in Germany and was educated at London University. Among her awards is a MacArthur Fellowship (1986–89). She has published twelve novels, including* Shards of Memory *(1995) and* In Search of Love and Beauty *(1999), and four volumes of short stories, including* East into Upper East *(1998).*

## Passion

Apart from the fact that they had both been in India for about a year and both had well-paid jobs with British cultural organizations, Christine and Betsy had very little in common. Nevertheless they shared a flat. Their friends—Christine's friends especially, Betsy didn't have all that many—were surprised when they first decided on this step and wondered how it would ever work out; but in fact it worked very well, perhaps just because they were so different, and led different lives, and so never got in each other's way.

The mantelpiece in their flat was always full of invitations, and they were almost all Christine's. She was tall, slim, and good-looking. She had a number of Indian boy-friends, who would call for her at the flat in the evenings in order to take her out in their cars. Sometimes she wasn't quite ready and she would trill from out of the bathroom that she wouldn't be a second; Betsy in the meantime invited them to make themselves comfortable in the sitting-room and have a drink. Sometimes they had several before Christine finally appeared, and then they jumped smartly to their feet while she, laughing and breathless and tying a gauze scarf round her hair, flippantly apologized for keeping them waiting.

Her favourite escort was a tall, handsome officer of the President's body-guard called Captain Manohar Singh ("Manny" to his friends). Betsy too was glad when it was Manny who was taking Christine out, and the longer he was kept waiting the better Betsy liked it. She felt good sitting next to the handsome Manny on the sofa and talking to him. She talked to him about India—Indian philosophy or music, or about the current political situation—while he drank one whisky after the other and sat at his ease with his large legs apart and a good-natured, listening expression on his face. Betsy sometimes had reason to believe that he wasn't really listening, for he never made any kind of remark that could be construed as a comment on what she was telling him. Indeed, he hardly said anything at all, and when he did, it was something completely unexpected like, "Boy, did we have a party last night! Wow!" But for Betsy it was really enough to be allowed to talk to him and look at him at such close quarters to her heart's content. Manny was a Sikh,[1] and he had an exquisitely barbered, shining black beard and wore a dark blue turban; his eyes were not dark but surprisingly light-coloured, a pellucid grey shining like a lake between the heavy fringe of his black lashes.

Once Manny kissed Betsy. It was entirely unexpected. They were sitting on the sofa and Betsy was telling him about her preference for the Kangra school of painting over that of Basohli, when suddenly he jumped on her. Really, there was no other word for it—he *jumped*, took a leap from where he was sitting and snatched her into his arms. She gave a short cry of shock, but next moment his lips were pressed weightily on hers, his tongue—strong, pulsing, muscled like some animal alive in its own right—pushed its way into her mouth; beneath his silk shirt she could feel his chest and his ribs as strong as steel. Waves of rapture passed over her like a fainting fit. But it seemed he was more collected than she was. As suddenly as he had seized her, he pushed her away, hastily adjusted his turban and got to his feet as Christine came breezing in, wafting scent and shouting "Darling!" "Darling!" he answered with his great boom of a laugh. "Again you are late, ho-ho, darling!" He was quite unembarrassed, while Betsy was left sitting stunned on the sofa with her hair dishevelled and her skirt slipped high up on her thighs.

With few friends and few entertainments, Betsy had very little to do in her spare time and spent most of it reading. She often went to the American library and became well known to the local staff there. One member of the staff was particularly assiduous in finding the books she wanted and keeping back those she had asked for. He was a slim, shy young Indian who, like a thousand other clerks, was always dressed in a clean but rather old white shirt and Western-style trousers. In the evenings, when she took a taxi home from the office, Betsy often saw him standing in a bus queue. The queue was always immensely long, and many of the buses that passed were crowded and did not even stop. He looked very patient standing there, holding a small, worn brass tiffin-carrier in his hand. Once it was raining, and she saw him trying to protect himself by placing the tiffin-carrier on his head. She stopped her taxi and offered him a lift; he got in without a word.

"Where can I drop you?" she asked.

"Where you are going."

"But that may be miles out of your way."

"It is all right."

That was all she could get out of him: "It is all right." For the rest, he sat straight and silent on the edge of the seat, holding his arms close to his sides; he was very wet and exuded vapours of dampness and discomfort. When the

1. A religious sect founded ca. 1500 as an offshoot of Hinduism. The Sikhs refused to acknowledge the caste system in India.

taxi stopped at her house and she got out, he got out with her, without a word. "Do you live near here?" she asked; she felt quite guilty about him by this time. "It is all right," he said, and stood and waited. Perhaps he was waiting to be asked up, but Betsy couldn't do that because Christine was having people in. She fumbled in her bag for her bag for her keys and, in the process, feeling nervous and hurried, dropped many things on the pavement. He stooped to pick them up, and she cried out in alarm, "No, don't bother!" She crouched down with him on the pavement, and they both scrabbled for her things and got wet in the rain. When she had found her keys, she stuffed everything back into her bag and tucked it bulging under her arm and ran inside, leaving him standing. She had a bad conscience about him for hours afterwards.

A few days later she passed him again at the bus stand. Feeling embarrassed, she looked quickly the other way, but he had seen her, and without a moment's hesitation he ran into the road and signalled her taxi to a halt; he waved both arms like a person in distress. But he wasn't in distress at all, he only wanted a ride with her. Again he came to her door and stood there, waiting expectantly. When she asked him up, he agreed at once. He sat down on a chair and looked round him with undisguised curiosity, up and down the walls, across the ceiling, at all the furniture. Betsy said, "Would you like a drink?" Now that she had brought him here, she didn't know what to do with him.

When she had mixed him his drink, he held the glass as if it were some strange object and then he asked: "It is alcohol?"

"Oh dear." She bit her lip and stared at him in consternation. "Don't you drink? I'm so sorry—"

But he took a big gulp and, after coughing a bit, another; then he finished the glass. She looked at him apprehensively. "It doesn't taste very nice," he said.

"No, if you're not used to it. It never occurred to me that you might not—everybody seems to drink such a lot. I mean, all the people one meets—" She stopped herself, for she realized she was saying he was not the sort of person one met. She sought desperately for something to say to cancel this out. But he did not seem to have noticed. He was smiling: "It is a funny taste."

"Would you like some more?"

"Yes."

This time too he drank it down very quickly, as if it were water or tea. She would have liked to warn him but was afraid of hurting his feelings. When he had finished, he was smiling again; he seemed happy.

"Once we drank beer," he said. "It was at my friend's sister's wedding. We hid behind the cowshed, but afterwards one of the uncles found the empty bottle, and how angry everyone was with us!" He giggled. Betsy realized to her dismay that he was drunk. "We were very mischievous boys. I could tell you other stories also. . . . It is a nice place here. Who else lives here? There are many rooms?" He got up and began to walk round the room as if he owned it. He picked up objects and asked their price, and peeped into cupboard doors. "I think you must be getting a lot of salary. How much? More than 1,000 rupees? More? How much more? Tell me, please. Only for my information."

Suddenly and without any warning he was sick all over the off-white rug.

He stood there and retched, and held his stomach and groaned. Betsy laid her hand on his forehead. "Don't worry," she said. "It doesn't matter." She had to turn her head away, but she felt terribly sorry for him.

And afterwards she blamed herself severely. She disliked herself for having mismanaged the not overwhelmingly difficult task of inviting an unsophisticated young man up to her flat and making him welcome. She longed to make amends, to invite him again and see to it that the occasion went off with dignity on both sides. Yet at the same time she felt that she could not bear to have him here again, indeed ever to see him again; and what she would really have liked to do was to forget the whole incident and the person who had caused it.

A day or two later she heard an altercation at the door. Angry voices were raised, and then her servant came in. "He says he wants to see you," said the servant accusingly. The young librarian had followed him into the room, looking indignant and like a man determined to stand on his rights.

"Your servant was rude to me," he said as soon as they were alone. He waved aside her explanation and apologies. "I am not very much used to being treated rudely by servants."

"Betsy!" called Christine from inside her bedroom. "Has Manny come?"

"Not yet!"

"Who is that?" asked the young man sternly, but before Betsy could explain, Christine stood in the doorway. She was wearing a pink flowered wrap which she held shut with one hand. "Hallo," she told the young man.

Betsy said, "This is—" and realized she didn't know her visitor's name. He was too stunned by Christine's appearance to help her out.

"I'm Christine," Christine said. She waited politely for him to introduce himself, but when he didn't, she smiled at him in her friendly way and disappeared again inside. She could be heard, a moment later, singing in her bath. The young man remained staring at the spot where she had stood.

Betsy explained, "We share this flat." She smiled: "I don't even know your name, how silly."

"Har Gopal. She is English also?"

"Oh yes. She works for the British Council." For want of anything better to say, she began to tell him about Christine's job. But he did not listen. He looked rather distraught, glancing now round the room, now at the spot where Christine had stood. Betsy noticed how refined his face was, with a delicately chiselled nose and sad eyes. Every now and again he brought his hand up to his open collar, pressing the two ends together over his throat as if wanting thereby to improve his appearance; it was a movement at once modest and self-protective. Betsy found herself feeling very tender towards this young man.

Then Manny came to fetch Christine. He was in uniform and all his buttons shone and so did his beautiful, brown, hard-leather boots. He strode up and down the room, waiting for Christine, immensely tall and exuding a smell of whisky and eau-de-Cologne. His eyes had merely swept for a second over the top of Har Gopal's head—it did not need more than that for him to sum up a fellow-countryman. With Betsy he was, as usual, absently affable. He had never, after the event, given a sign that he remembered having kissed her. Probably he didn't remember. He strode about the room, thinking of other things, and only became alert when Christine entered. She was no longer in her negligee but in a primrose-yellow dress, and golden sandals with high heels which made her even taller than she was. The room seemed very small with these two in it, and when they had gone, it seemed very empty.

Har Gopal spoke bitterly: "Are they your friends? I don't like that Sikh. I know his type very well." When she made no comment, he spoke harshly to her, as if she had dared to contradict him: "I tell you I have seen hundreds like him. What do you know about it?" Neither of them in the least questioned his right to speak to her in this manner.

"I am B.A. Kurukshetra University," he said next. "Yes, now you are surprised. You thought I was just anyone, isn't it? B.A. in history and philosophy. And my wife is a matriculate. Come here." He beckoned to her with his slender, fine-boned hand, displaying a surprising authority, and she went.

He jumped on her in the same sudden way Manny had done. Betsy thought, do all Indian men make love like this? In spite of his frail appearance, Har Gopal was strong. Not with Manny's massive body-strength, but he had a sort of sharp, incisive, relentless quality which rode down opposition. He went straight ahead without question, not skilful but resolute, steely. He commanded respect.

Betsy was in love with Har Gopal. If she hadn't been, the situation might have become embarrassing. He came every day to the flat, and when any of Christine's friends was there, he sat in a corner like a poor relation and looked at them with burning, hungry eyes. Afterwards he was angry with Betsy and blamed her for any lack of respect he felt had been shown to him. Christine was always very nice and tactful with him, and in return he went to some pains to make serious conversation with her. He would tell her about the unemployment problem in Uttar Pradesh, or the number of light aircraft manufactured by the Hindustan aircraft factory per year. She would appear to be listening and would say "No really?" and "How fascinating!" in between, without irony. She might be doing her nails, daubing on the varnish with exquisite little brushstrokes, and he would look on in fascination. He loved seeing her do her nails. Sometimes he asked Betsy why she didn't paint hers, and he clicked his tongue in disapproval when she held them out to him, clipped very short and one or two of them bitten down at the end of her short, squarish fingers.

But she took a lot of trouble for him. She brushed and brushed her hair till it shone, and then she slipped a red band round it. She wore white frilly blouses and short skirts and white ballet shoes and a gold locket round her neck. She loved going out for walks with him and would tuck her hand proudly under his arm. He allowed her to keep it there and walked by her side in a stately manner, with his head held stiffly. Many people looked at them. They were both about the same height, both short, but he was thin and she was rather stocky with very muscular legs. Once or twice they met people he knew—some friend or neighbour—and he would stop to exchange a few words in a rather formal, self-conscious way, and though her hand remained tucked under his arm, he made no attempt to introduce her. But if they met anyone she knew, some fellow-countrymen from her office or the High Commission, she made a point of introducing Har Gopal at once, flaunting him and clinging to him in such a way that her acquaintances became embarrassed and looked away and parted from her as quickly as possible. But Har Gopal always behaved correctly and said "Very happy to meet you," and shook hands all round the way he knew foreigners did.

Betsy confided a lot in Christine. She needed to have someone to talk to about Har Gopal. "I know it's ridiculous, ridiculous," she said and buried her head in her arms, overwhelmed with laughter and happiness. "He's all wrong—of course he is—*and* he's married, *and* three children." She hid her face again and her shoulders shook laughing. She tried to but could never quite explain to Christine what it was she loved so much about Har Gopal. His finely drawn features, yes, his dark, dreaming eyes, his sadness, his sensitivity: and also—but how could she tell Christine this?—she loved the shabby clothes he wore, his badly cut cotton trousers and his frequently washed shirt with his thin wrists coming out of the buttoned cuffs. She was positively proud of the fact that he looked so much like everybody else—like hundreds and thousands of other Indian clerks going to offices every morning on the bus and coming home again with their empty tiffin-carriers in the evenings: people who worked for small salaries and supported their families and worried. She frowned with the effort of trying to express all this to Christine and said finally that well, she supposed she loved him for being so typically Indian.

Christine laughed: "But that's why I like Manny too."

Betsy had to admit that Manny too was typically Indian—but in a very different way. Manny was the India one read about in childhood, coloured with tigers, sunsets, and princes; but Har Gopal was *real*, he was everyday, urban, suffering India that people in the West didn't know about.

Har Gopal often asked her: "Do you talk about me with Christine?" He wanted to know everything that they said. When she teased and wouldn't tell, he twisted her wrist or squeezed her muscles till she screamed. He loved practicing these boyhood tortures on her; it was the only way he knew of being playful, for that was how he had played with his friends at school and college. He had never had a woman friend before. But he had had many male friends, and they had had grand times together. He often told Betsy about his friends, and it always put him in a good mood. He had a serious, even melancholy nature, but when he recollected his student days, he became gay and laughed at all the mad pranks they had played together. One of his friends, Chandu, had been a great joker, and how he had teased the masters at school! No one could do anything to him, because his father was an important man in town. Another friend had had the ability to chew up newspapers and even razor blades. They were all crazy about the cinema and went to see the same film over and over again till they knew the lyrics and dialogues by heart. He could still recite great chunks of old films and he did so for Betsy, and he sang the songs for her. She loved his voice, which was sweet and girlish, and the soft expression which came into his eyes when he sang; but he said no no, his voice was nothing, she should have heard Mohan, then she would have known what good singing was. They had all thought that Mohan would surely go into films and become a playback singer, but instead he had got a job in the life insurance corporation. There had been so many friends, and they had all been so close and had thought their friendship was eternal; but now Har Gopal didn't even know where most of them were. Everyone was married, like himself, and had their own worries and no more time for their friends. But he still thought about them often and wished for the old days back again, or at least to have one friend left with him in whom to confide his thoughts and have a good time together.

"Well you've got me now," said Betsy, putting her arm round his neck, tender and comradely.

But he could not feel about her the way he did about his friends. He was, she knew, less fond of her. She excited him, and he was proud to have her, but he did not really, she often suspected, *like* her. All the loving came from her side, and he accepted it as his due but made no attempt to return it. There was something lordly, almost tyrannical in his attitude to her. When he lounged at his ease in her room, all his shyness and shabbiness—that *depressed* quality that was so evident in him when he stood with his tiffin-carrier at the bus-stop—left him completely, and he became what, as a Brahmin, he perhaps was by nature: an aristocrat for whom the goods and riches of this world were created and whose right it was to be served by others. Betsy was the one who served, and the goods and riches were the things she gave him for which he had developed a taste: English biscuits, raspberry syrup (he never again drank alcohol), tinned peaches.

He kept some clothes in her room, and when he came to her straight from the office, as he usually did, he would take off his trousers and carefully fold them and then put on his dhoti. He dressed and undressed with delicate precaution, so as never to be seen naked by any human eye, not even his own. Although his lovemaking left nothing to be desired, he never lost his reticence: his manner was always controlled and fastidious, and never for a moment was there any abandon in it. Betsy, on the other hand, was all abandon. She would fling off her clothes, leaving them just where they dropped, and walk round the room naked. Very often she forgot to lock the door, so that the servant or Christine or anyone who came to the flat could have walked in at any time. She didn't care. Her attitude shocked and at the same time pleased him. In the beginning he could only watch her undressing with his face averted and his eyes half lowered, ashamed of himself and of her, but as time went on, he looked at her boldly and with a strange smile which was perhaps partly appreciation and partly, she sometimes suspected, contempt.

He never spoke to her about his family. She wanted to know so much about them, but he always completely evaded her questions. If she insisted too much, he became annoyed and refused to speak to her at all and perhaps even went home earlier than usual. So she dared not ask much. But it tortured her to have all this area of his life concealed from her with a deliberateness which suggested she was not worthy to approach it. Why should he feel that way? He was *proud* of her—she knew he was—otherwise would he parade through the town with her on his arm and greet people he met on the way with such a superior air?

Sometimes, when she found he was relaxed and in a good mood, she tried to coax him into talking: "Is your wife taller than me? Shorter? The same? Say!" But at once his good mood would disappear and he turned away from her, frowning. Once she asked him half jokingly, "What's the matter? You don't think I'm good enough to hear about your family?" But at that he took on such a strange, closed expression that she realized she had stumbled on something near the truth. But she wouldn't at first believe it; she even laughed at it and said, "My God, what am I—a fallen woman or something?" Still he made no answer, but the expression on his face did not change nor did he make any attempt to contradict or deny. She laughed again, more harshly, even though by now she felt far from laughing. It was ridiculous, something out of Victorian melodrama, but still it was true, it was the way he saw her. She felt so humiliated that she could speak nothing further and tears flowed silently from her eyes: but even as they rolled down her cheeks and her heart heaved with pain at the thought of her humiliation, at the same time—so bizarre were her feelings for him—this very humiliation actually increased, exacerbated her passion for him.

One day she went secretly to see the place where he lived. She found blocks of tenements set out side by side and surrounded by an area of waste land on which had sprung up a dusty little bazaar and a shanty colony of thatched huts. As soon as she got out of her taxi, she found herself the centre of a group of children who laughed and marvelled at her strangeness and followed her closely. She looked round her for a time, then plucked up courage and walked through the doorway that led into the compound of the first block of buildings. It was as lively here as in any street. Children played, and there were some men repairing string-beds and a number of itinerant vegetable-sellers and a fish-seller, all of whom were bargaining with women who suspiciously untied their bundles of money from the end of their saris and complained to one another about dishonest traders; other women called down from the windows that opened in tiers and rows from the tall buildings. Betsy, with her little cluster of attendant children, looked around her and did not know what to do next. Suddenly she wondered what would happen if he were to come now out of one of those dark doorways and find her standing there. She could almost see the expression of panic and fury that would instantly transform his face, and at the thought of it, she began to panic a little herself and to wish she had not come.

But then it was too late to retreat. A round little man in an English-style suit came running up to her, calling in an excited voice, "Yes, please, yes, please! You have come to see Mr. Har Gopal?" Betsy did not recognize him, but guessed at once that he must be someone whom they had met and Har Gopal had talked to on one of their evening walks.

"This way, please," said the little man, pushing aside all the children and leading her out of the compound. To curious bystanders he explained importantly, "For Har Gopal in C Block." He strutted in front while the children surged after him and Betsy found herself swept along in the procession. Behind her the women nudged and talked. The little man led her along the street and then turned into the next compound, waving a plump hand over his shoulder at her and calling, "This way, please!"

Then she saw that the little procession had brought her back to the street where her taxi was waiting. Murmuring apologies which no one heard, she suddenly climbed into it and sat down, and the driver skilfully flicked away the children who at once surrounded the car. Betsy did not dare look out of the window, as she was driven away, and she even put her handkerchief up to her face as if she hoped thereby neither to see nor be seen.

The next time Har Gopal came to the flat he did not talk to her at all but straightaway took his dhoti and a pair of slippers and bottle of hair-oil he kept in her bedroom and, grimly determined, wrapped them up in a bundle. "What are you doing?" she cried out in distress. He did not answer but made for the door. She clung to him to prevent him. She begged him to stay.

"Let me go, please," he said, but standing quite still and making no effort to release himself.

"It's only that I wanted to *see* where you were."

"You came to spy on me. Yes, and now you will laugh at me with your friends because my house is poor and I am poor." Suddenly he shrieked: "I don't care! You can laugh, what do I care!"

"Please don't," she said and clung to him tighter, but he shook her off and shouted at her, "And my position? That's nothing to you what people will say that you come openly to my home—" He sank down to sit on the edge of her bed and covered his eyes with his hands in grief and shame. And Betsy sank down beside him, and she too covered her eyes. What followed was a loud scene, echoing all over the flat, in which he spoke a lot about his position in the world and she lacerated herself with accusations regarding her own selfishness and insensitivity; and when this had gone on for a long time, and she had again and again begged his forgiveness, they were at last reconciled, and she dissolved in tears of gratitude while he was proud and gracious with her.

Then it was time for him to go home, and on his way out, they had to pass through the sitting-room where Christine sat playing ludo with Manny. These two must have heard every word of what had passed in the other room. Christine delicately kept her eyes fixed on the ludo-board, and Manny hummed a tune to himself. Har Gopal's face took on a tight expression, and his thin body seemed to shrink as he walked through the room; he looked as he did waiting at the bus-stop. Only Betsy was entirely free from embarrassment as she ushered her lover out of the flat.

That night Christine knocked timidly on Betsy's door. Betsy was lying stark naked on her rumpled bed, reading the Katha-Upanishad.[2] She was wearing her reading-glasses and thoughtfully twisting a lock of hair round her finger. She didn't seem to be a bit shy to be found naked. Her breasts were very much heavier than one would have expected from seeing her dressed. "Yes, come in," she said and shut her book with her finger inside to hold the page. "I'm sorry, we made an awful lot of noise today, didn't we?" she said cheerfully.

Christine sat on the edge of a chair. She was wearing a flowered wrap and looked crisp and fresh and a contrast to Betsy's room which was rather untidy.

"I know it's none of my business," said Christine, talking very quickly so as to get it over with, "but I do think you ought to be a bit more careful."

Betsy laughed and said, "I wish I were the sort of person who *could* be careful."

2. One of the speculative Hindu treatises (Upanishads) composed between the 8th and 6th centuries B.C. and first written down around C.E. 1300.

"Everyone's talking you know, Betsy, in the office and everywhere. I mean, good heavens, not that anyone cares about your having an Indian boy-friend—don't we all?—but he's so . . . *different* from the other Indians we all know."

"You mean he's poor."

"It's not that," Christine said miserably. "But he's—I don't know, odd. And there's something unhealthy about it all—of course it's absolutely terrible of me to be saying all this and do tell me to shut up if you want to."

There was a moment's pause. Then Betsy said, "It *is* unhealthy." She tried to sound detached and dispassionate, but could not keep it up for long. "I suppose all passion is unhealthy. Sometimes I tell you I feel *insane*—and what's more—what's terrible: I revel in it! I glory in it!" She rolled over on to her side to face Christine, and her big breasts fell to that side and her eyes shone behind her flesh-coloured glasses.

Christine was not the only person who tried to warn Betsy. One day her office chief invited her to lunch at his house, and in the kindest manner possible, full of embarrassment and apologies, told her that unless she behaved in what he called a more conventional way he would have to have her sent home. Betsy understood that he had to tell her this and that he was right, but she had no intention of changing. Instead she began to make plans what to do if she were really posted back home. Of course, she would resign immediately; she would stay and get a job locally. She was vague as to what kind of job and did not stop much to wonder whether anyone would employ her; but she knew that, whatever she did, her salary would only be a fraction of what it was now and she would have to change her whole way of life. She didn't mind that; in fact, she rather looked forward to it. She would have to move out of the flat and go somewhere much cheaper. She thought of herself in some small room in a crowded locality; to get to her, one would have to cross a courtyard and climb up a very dark, very narrow winding staircase. She would be the only European living in the house. Every day Har Gopal would come to visit her. Actually Betsy couldn't cook, but now she had visions of herself squatting over a little bucket of coal and preparing a meal for him and serving him just like an Indian wife. She might take to wearing a sari. Perhaps she would have a baby, a boy, who would grow up dark and delicate like Har Gopal.

She neglected her work in the office and was distant with her colleagues. She realized vaguely that something was going on around her and that perhaps steps were being taken against her, but she did not bother to find out what they were. Christine told her that she would be moving out of their joint flat soon; she made up some polite lies that the flat was getting too expensive for her and that she had found another smaller one elsewhere, but Betsy cut her short and said it didn't matter, that she herself would be moving out too, very soon. She already saw herself in her small room in the house with the winding staircase.

She even began to make inquiries about the rents to be paid for such places, and about how much money would be needed for the simple, Indian-style life she intended to adopt. All her thoughts were concentrated on this problem. Once, finding herself alone with Manny who was waiting for Christine to get ready, she even asked him, very seriously, "Supposing you only eat dal and rice twice a day—how much would that come to a week?"

"Only dal and rice!" exclaimed Manny humorously. "And what about a peg of whisky?"

"I'm being serious, Manny," Betsy said impatiently, but it was impossible to make him be serious with her. Ever since she had started her affair with Har Gopal, Manny's attitude to her had become strange and ambivalent: on the one hand, he was rather more brusque, and even rude with her than he had been before; on the other, he indulged in sudden spurts of familiarity which extended to, whenever they found themselves alone in a room, pinching her in intimate places.

He did this now, and at the same time he joked with her: "My two-three pegs a day I must have, otherwise I'm like my car without petrol. Hm? Han?" He encouraged her to laugh with him and drew her close, and his beard nuzzled against her cheek. She struggled to get free, but that made him hold her all the more tightly. She stared into his face, and she saw his light-coloured eyes and his red, moist, healthy mouth smiling inside his black beard. She let out a cry. He released her immediately and even gave her a push to get her farther away from him. Christine, zipping her dress, came in and said, "Whatever's the matter?"

"It is Betsy," said Manny. "She thought she saw a snake." He laughed uproariously.

Betsy did not speak to Har Gopal about her future plans. She was afraid. She knew that the idea of anyone giving up a job, an assured livelihood, was not one he would ever be able to understand. He himself was very timid about his own job and took good care never to give cause for complaint to his superiors. Not only was he very polite, even deferential, to them in their presence, but he also spoke of them in tones of the highest respect when they were not there and had no chance of ever knowing what he was saying about them. Once, when Betsy spoke with lighthearted disdain of one or two of the top people in her own organization, he rebuked her for doing so, and when she laughed at the rebuke, he frowned and became annoyed with her and said that she had no respect in her nature. The very least, he said, that one owed one's superiors was respect; and quite apart from that, one should be careful what one said about them because who knew what might not get back to them. But how *could* anything get back to them, asked Betsy, amused, when there was no one there but he and she, and surely he wasn't going to go and tell on her, was he? He refused to smile at the idea but only said that in these matters one could never be careful enough. His eyes even roved solemnly for a moment round the room—her bedroom—as if he feared someone might be be lurking somewhere listening.

One Sunday afternoon he was reclining on her bed in his rather lordly way, wearing his vest and dhoti, his feet crossed comfortably at the ankle; he had his arms folded behind his head and was staring into space with melancholy eyes. He looked noble and sensitive and gave the impression of being sunk in deep philosophic thought. This impression, however, was false, for when he finally broke his silence it was to say nothing more significant than, "Just see, I have had this blister for two days. It is very painful." He plaintively held up his finger to her.

She burst out laughing and, overcome with tenderness for him, threw herself on his reclining figure. "Oh, you're so sweet, so *sweet*!" she cried, and crushed him as tight as she could as if she hoped thereby to relieve her overwhelming feelings. He cried out and struggled to get free—unsuccessfully, till she released him of her own accord. He smoothed down his hair with one hand and his dhoti with the other and said indignantly, "How rough you are."

She laughed again and settled herself happily on the floor, leaning her head against the edge of the bed on which he lay. She felt exquisitely comfortable and domestic and knew that this was the way she wanted her life to go on for ever. And then she blurted it out, about giving up her job and staying in India so as to be always near him.

Har Gopal was appalled. He quite genuinely thought she was mad. He argued with her, pointed out that even if she managed to get some kind of job in India, which was in itself unlikely, she would never be able to live on the salary she would be paid. But Betsy said no, she wanted to live on it; she was tired of living the way she did here, as a foreigner, as a privileged person.

"I want to live in India like an Indian," she said, "like everyone else, like you. Exactly like you," and she seized his fine, frail hand and kissed it.

He drew it away from her. "You don't know anything," he said. "If you had to live in a place where there is never enough water and the neighbours quarrel and you clean and clean but still the cockroaches come—"

"I don't care," Betsy said.

"Yes, it is so easy to talk," he said bitterly. He got up from the bed and began to get dressed, though it was not yet his usual time for departure.

"I want to give up everything for you," Betsy said. "To lay my whole life at your feet and say: here, take it." She shut her eyes, carried away by the passion with which she spoke.

He uttered a short sound of impatience and turned his back on her. He began to comb his hair in the mirror. She came up behind him and put her arms round his waist and laid her cheek caressingly against his back. He continued to comb his hair very carefully; he was always careful of his appearance before going out into the street.

"I'm not 'sacrificing' anything" she said. "Don't think that. Good heavens, what do you think I care for my job, or this flat, or money, or anything?"

He could hold himself no longer: "No, you don't care! You are like that. You have everything in life and you throw it all away. Aren't you ashamed? There are others who would give God knows what to have something, to live nicely, but for them—no, there's nothing, not even in their dreams . . ." His voice failed him, and he could not go on. It was as if all the frustrations of his life had risen up and formed a hard ball in his chest and left him unable to speak. He waved his hand in her direction, dismissing her, not wanting her, and turned to the door.

"Don't go," she pleaded and held on to his arm. He attempted to free himself but she held on tightly. Suddenly he became vicious. He thumped his fist on the hand holding on to his arm and cursed her in Hindi: "*Hath mat lagao, besharm kahin Ki!*" He left the room, with her running after him.

Christine and Manny were having drinks in the sitting-room. Manny put down his glass and got up and strode over to Har Gopal. He seized him by the front of his shirt and shook him to and fro, and Har Gopal allowed this to be done without offering resistance. His face was frozen with fright while his body was being shaken, and the oiled, stiff hair on his head flopped up and down.

"Let him go, Manny," Christine said in a low, embarrassed voice.

Manny gave one last shake and then flung him towards the door. Har Gopal fell down but he picked himself up again and patiently dusted off his knees and hands. Without looking back at anyone, he walked down the stairs, slowly and with dignity. Betsy followed him.

When he reached the bottom of the stairs, he told her in a tone of cold command, "Get my things."

"What things?"

"My things. My dhoti and my slippers, and don't forget my bottle of hair-oil."

He stood very straight and thin and proud. But suddenly he sat down on the bottom stair. He hid his face in his arms and his shoulders shook with sobbing. She sat down next to him; she held him and murmured to him, words of the sweetest comfort.

After a while he raised his face which was smeared with tears. He cut across her murmuring and said, "You must leave this place. I don't want you to stay with these people one day more."

Betsy said that they would look for a place for her together; somewhere very cheap, very Indian. She glanced at him to note his reaction, but he gave no sign of having heard her and remained staring gloomily in front of him. She allowed herself to believe that his silence meant assent. At this her heart leaped in joy and her mind shone with visions of the new life that was about to begin for her.

# Charles Johnson

*Johnson (1948– ) was born in Evanston, Illinois. A novelist, short-story writer, cartoonist, and critic, he teaches literature at the University of Washington. Author of the novels* Oxherding Tale *(1974),* Middle Passage *(1990), and* Dreamer *(1997), a fictionalized version of the life of Martin Luther King Jr., he has also published a story collection,* The Sorcerer's Apprentice *(1986); a book of cartoons,* Black Humor *(1970); and a critical study,* Being and Race *(1983). He is the recipient of a MacArthur Fellowship.*

## Moving Pictures

You sit in the Neptune Theatre waiting for the thin, overhead lights to dim with a sense of respect, perhaps even reverence, for American movie houses are, as everyone knows, the new cathedrals, their stories better remembered than legends, totems, or mythologies, their directors more popular than novelists, more influential than saints—enough people, you've been told, have seen the James Bond adventures to fill the entire country of Argentina. Perhaps you have written this movie. Perhaps not. Regardless, you come to it as everyone does, as a seeker groping in the darkness for light, hoping something magical will be beamed from above, and no matter how bad this matinee is, or silly, something deep and maybe even too dangerous to talk loudly about will indeed happen to you and the others before this drama reels to its last transparent frame.

Naturally, you have left your life outside the door. Like any life, it's a messy thing, hardly as orderly as art, what some call life in the fast lane—: the Sanka and sugar-donut breakfasts, bumper-to-bumper traffic downtown, the business lunches, and a breakneck schedule not to get ahead but simply to stay in one place, which is peculiar, because you grew up in the sixties speeding on Methadone and despising all this, knowing your Age (Aquarian) was made for finer stuff. But no matter. Outside, across town, you have put away for ninety minutes the tedious, repetitive job that is, obviously, beneath your talents, sensitivity, and education (a degree in English), the once beautiful woman—or wife—a former model (local), college dancer, or semiprofessional actress named Megan or Daphne, who has grown tired of you, or you of her, and talks now of legal separation and finding herself, the children from a former, frighteningly brief marriage whom you don't want to lose, the mortgage, alimony, IRS audit, the aging, gin-fattened face that once favored a rock star's but now frowns back at you in the bathroom mirror, the young woman at work, born in 1960 and unable to recall John Kennedy, who after the Christmas party took you to bed in her spacious downtown loft, perhaps out of pity because your mother, God bless her, died and left you with a thousand dollars in debt before you could get the old family house clear—all that shelved, mercifully, as the film starts: first that frosty mountaintop ringed by stars, or a lion roaring, or floodlights bathing the tips of buildings in a Hollywood skyline: stable trademarks in a world of flux, you think, sure-fire signs that whatever follows—tragedy or farce—is made by people who are accomplished dream-merchants. Perhaps more: masters of vision, geniuses of the epistemological Murphy.

If you have written this film, which is possible, you look for your name in the credits, and probably frown at the names of the Crew, each recalling some disaster during the production, first at the studio, then later on location for five weeks in Oklahoma cowtowns during the winter, which was worse than living on the moon, the days boiling and nights so cold. Nevertheless, you'd seen it as a miracle, an act of God when the director, having read your novel, called, offering you the project—a historical romance—then walked you patiently through the first eight drafts, suspicious of you at first (there was real money riding on this, it wasn't poetry), of your dreary, novelistic pretensions to Deep Profundity, and you equally suspicious of him, his background in sitcoms, obsession with "keeping it sexy," and love of Laurel and Hardy films. For this you wrote a dissertation on Derrida?[1] Yet, you'd listened. He was right, in the end. He was good, you admitted, grudgingly. He knew, as you—with your liberal arts degree—didn't, the meaning of Entertainment. You'd learned. With his help, you got good, too. You gloated. And lost friends. "A movie?" said your poet friends, "that's wonderful, it's happening for you," and then they avoided you as if you had AIDS. What *was* happening was this:

You'd shelved the novel, the Big Book, for bucks monitored by the Writers Guild (West), threw yourself into fast-and-dirty scripts, the instant gratification of quick deadlines and fat checks because the Book, with its complexity and promise of critical praise, the Book with its long-distance demands and no financial reward whatsoever, was impossible, and besides, you didn't have it anymore, not really, the gift for narrative or language, while the scripts were easy, like writing shorthand, and soon—way sooner than you thought—the films, with their lifespan shorter than a mayfly's, were all you could do. It's a living, you said. Nothing lasts forever. And you pushed on.

The credits crawl up against a montage of Oklahoma farmlife, and in this you read a story, too, even before the film begins. For the audience, the actors are stars, the new Olympians, but oh, you know them, this one—the male lead—whose range is boundless, who could be a Brando, but who hadn't seen work in two years before this role and survived by doing voice-overs for a cartoon villain in *The Smurfs*; that one—the female supporting role—who can play the full scale of emotions, but whose last memorable performance was a

1. Jacques Derrida (1930– ), contemporary French philosopher and literary critic.

commercial for Rolaids, all of them; all, including you, fighting for life in a city where the air is so corrupt joggers spit black after a two-mile run; failing, trying desperately to keep up the front of doing-well, these actors, treating you shabbily sometimes because your salary was bigger than theirs, even larger than the producer's, though he wasn't exactly hurting—no, he was richer than a medieval king, a complex man of remarkable charm and cunning, someone to both admire for his Horatio Alger[2] orphan-boy success and fear for his worship at the altar of power. You won't forget the evening he asked you to his home after a long conference, served you Scotch, and then, from inside a drawer in his desk removed an envelope, dumped its contents out, and you saw maybe fifty snapshots of beautiful, naked women on his bed—all of them second-rate actresses, though the female supporting role was there, too—and he watched you closely for your reaction, sipping his drink, smiling, then asked, "You ever sleep with a woman like that?" No, you hadn't. And, no, you didn't trust him either. You didn't turn your back. But, then again, nobody in this business did, and in some ways he was, you knew, better than most.

You'd compromised, given up ground, won a few artistic points, but generally you agreed to the producer's ideas—it *was* his show—and then the small army of badly-paid performers and production people took over, you trailing behind them in Oklahoma, trying to look writerly, wearing a Panama hat, holding your notepad ready for rewrites, surviving the tedium of eight or nine takes for difficult scenes, the fights, fallings-out, bad catered food, and midnight affairs, watching your script change at each level of interpretation—director, actor—until it was unrecognizable, a new thing entirely, a celebration of the Crew. Not you. Does anyone suspect how bad this thing really looked in rough-cut? How miraculous it is that its rags of shots, conflicting ideas, and scraps of footage actually cohere? You sneak a look around at the audience, the faces lit by the glow of the screen. No one suspects. You've managed to fool them again, you old fox.

No matter whether the film is yours or not, it pulls you in, reels in your perception like a trout. On the narrow screen, the story begins with an establishing wideshot of an Oklahoma farm, then in close-up shows the face of a big towheaded, brown-freckled boy named Bret, and finally settles on a two-shot of Bret and his blonde, bosomy girlfriend, Bess. No margin for failure in a formula like that. In the opening funeral scene at a tiny, whitewashed church, camera favors Bret, whose father has died. Our hero must seek his fortune in the city. Bess just hates to see him go. Dissolve to cemetery gate. As they leave the cemetery, and the coffin is lowered, she squeezes his hand, and something inside you shivers, the sense of ruin you felt at your own mother's funeral, the irreversible feeling of abandonment. There was no girl with you, but you wished to heaven there had been, the one named Sondra you knew in high school who wouldn't see you for squat, preferring basketball players to weird little wimps and geeks, which is pretty much what you were back then, a washout to those who knew you, but you give all that to Bret and Bess, the pain of parental loss,

2. U.S. author (1834–1889), known for his novels about poor boys who become rich through their earnest attitudes and hard work.

the hopeless, quiet love never to be, which thickens the screen so thoroughly that when Bess kisses Bret your nose is clogged with tears and mucus, and then you have your handkerchief out, honking shamelessly, your eyes streaming, locked—even you—in a cycle of emotion (yours), which their images have borrowed, intensified, then given back to you, not because the images or sensations are sad, but because, at bottom, all you have known these last few minutes are the workings of your own nervous system. You yourself have been supplying the grief and satisfaction all along, from within. But even that is not the true magic of film.

As Bret rides away, you remember sitting in the studio's tiny editing room amidst reels of film hanging like stockings in a bathroom, the editor, a fat, friendly man named Coates, tolerating your curiosity, letting you peer into his viewer as he patched the first reel together, figuring he owed you, a semifamous scriptwriter, that much. Each frame, you recall, was a single, frozen image, like an individual thought, complete in itself, with no connection to the others, as if time stood still; but then the frames came faster as the viewer sped up, chasing each other, surging forward and creating finance their lives at a job that is a ghastly joke, given your talents, where you can't slow down and at least four competitors stand waiting for you to step aside, fall on your face, or die, and the injustice of all this, what you see in the narrow range of radiation you call vision, in the velocity of ideation, is necessary and sufficient—as some logicians say—to bring your fists down again and again on the Fiat's roof. You climb inside, sit, furiously cranking the starter, then swear and lower your forehead to the steering wheel, which is, as anyone in Hollywood can tell you, conduct unbecoming a triple-threat talent like yourself: producer, star, and director in the longest, most fabulous show of all.

# Edward P. Jones

*Jones (1950– ) was born in Washington, D.C., and was educated at Holy Cross College and the University of Virginia. His book* Lost in the City *was published in 1992. He has received a National Book Award for Fiction and the PEN/Hemingway Award for Best First Fiction.*

## A New Man

One day in late October, Woodrow L. Cunningham came home early with his bad heart and found his daughter with the two boys. He was then fifty-two years old, a conscientious deacon at Rising Star AME Zion, a paid-up lifetime member of the NAACP and the Urban League, a twenty-five-year member of the Elks. For ten years he had been the chief engineer at the Sheraton Park Hotel, where practically every employee knew his name. For longer than he could recall, his friends and lodge members had been telling him that he was capable of being more than just the number-one maintenance man. But he always told them that he was contented in the job, that it was all he needed, and this was true for the most part. He would be in that same position some thirteen years later, when death happened upon him as he bent down over a hotel bathroom sink, about to do a job a younger engineer claimed he could not handle.

The afternoon he came home early and discovered his daughter with the boys, he found a letter in the mailbox from his father in Georgia. He read the letter while standing in the hall of the apartment building. He expected nothing of importance, as usual, and that was what he found. "Alice took me to Buddy Wilson funeral just last week," Woodrow read. "I loaned him the shirt they buried him in. And that tie he had on was one that I give him too. I thought I would miss him but I do not miss him very much. Checkers was never Buddy Wilsons game." As he read, he massaged the area around his heart, an old habit, something he did even when his heart was not giving him trouble. "I hope you and the family can come down before the winter months set in. Company is never the same after winter get here."

He put the letter back in the envelope, and as he absently looked at the upside-down stamp taped in the vicinity of the corner, the pain in his heart eased. He could picture his father sitting at the kitchen table, writing the letter, occasionally touching the pencil point to his tongue. A new mongrel's head would be resting across his lap, across thin legs that could still carry the old man five miles down the road and back. Woodrow, feeling better, considered returning to work, but he knew his heart was deceitful. He folded the envelope and stuck it in his back pocket, and out of the pocket it would fall late that night as he prepared for bed after returning from the police station.

Several feet before he reached his apartment door he could hear the boys' laughter and bits and pieces of their man-child conquer-the-world talk. He could not hear his daughter at first. He stopped at his door and listened for nearly five minutes, and in that time he became so fascinated by what the boys were saying that he would not have cared if someone walking in the hall found him listening. It was only when he heard his daughter's laughter, familiar, known, that he put his key in the door. She stood just inside the door when he entered, her eyes accusing but her mouth set in a small O of surprise. Beyond her he could see the boys with their legs draped over the arms of the couch and gray smoke above their heads wafting toward the open window.

He asked his daughter, "Why ain't you in school?"

"They let us out early today," she said. "The teachers had some kinda meetin."

He did not listen to her, because he had found that she lived to lie. Woodrow watched the boys as they took their time straightening themselves up, and he knew that their deliberateness was the result of something his daughter had said about him. Without taking his eyes from the boys, he asked his daughter again why she wasn't in school. When he finally looked at her, he saw that she was holding the stump of a thin cigarette. The smoke he smelled was unfamiliar, and at first he thought that they were smoking very stale cigarettes, or cigarettes that had gotten wet and been dried. He slapped her. "I told you not to smoke in my house," he said.

She was fifteen, and up until six months or so before, she would have collapsed into the chair, collapsed into a fit of crying. But now she picked up the fallen cigarette from the floor and stamped it out in the ashtray on the tiny table beside the easy chair. Her hand shook, the only reminder of the old days. "We just talkin. We ain't doin nothin wrong," she said quietly.

He shouted to the boys, "Get outta my house!" They stood up quickly, and Woodrow could tell that whatever she had told them about him, such anger was not part of it. They looked once at the girl.

"They my guests, Daddy," she said, sitting in the easy chair and crossing her legs. "I invited em over here."

Woodrow took two steps to the boy nearest him—the tall light-skinned one he would spot from a bus window a year or so later—and grabbed him with one hand by the jacket collar, shook him until the boy raised his hands as if to protect his face from a blow. The boy's eyes widened and Woodrow shook him some more. He had been living a black man's civilized life in Washington and had not felt so coiled and bristled since the days when he worked with wild men in the turpentine camps in Florida. "I ain't done nothin," the boy said. The words sounded familiar, similar to those of a wild man ready to slink away into his cabin with his tail between his legs. Woodrow relaxed. "I swear. I don't want no trouble, Mr. Cunningham." The boy had no other smell but that peculiar cigarette smoke, and it was a shock to Woodrow that a body with that smell should know something that seemed as personal as his name. The other, smaller boy had tiptoed around Woodrow and was having trouble opening the door. After the small boy had gone out, Woodrow flung the light-skinned boy out behind him. Woodrow locked the door, and the boys stood for several minutes, pounding on the door, mouthing off.

"Why you treat my guests like that?" Elaine Cunningham had not moved from the chair.

"Clean up this mess," he told her, "and I don't wanna see one ash when you done."

She said nothing more, but busied herself tidying the couch cushions. Then Woodrow, after flicking the cushions a few times with his handkerchief, sat in the middle of the couch, and the couch sagged with the familiarity of this weight.

When Elaine had returned the room to what it was, her father said, "I want to know what you was doin in here with them boys."

"Nothin. We wasn't doin nothin. Just talkin, thas all, Daddy." She sat in the easy chair, leaned toward him with her elbows on her knees.

"You can do your talkin down on the stoop," he said.

"Why don't you just say you tryin to cuse me a somethin? Why don't you just come out and say it?"

"If you didn't do things, you wouldn't get accused," he said. He talked without thought, because those words and words like them had been spoken so much to her that he was able to parrot himself. "If you start actin like a young lady should, start studyin and what not, and tryin to make somethin of yourself . . ." Woodrow L. Cunningham bein Woodrow L. Cunningham, he thought.

She stood up quickly, and he was sickened to see her breasts bounce. "I could study them stupid books half the damn day and sit in church the other half, and I'd still get the same stuff thrown in my face bout how I ain't doin right."

"Okay, thas anough a that." He felt a familiar rumbling in his heart. "I done heard anough."

"I wanna go out," she stood with her arms folded. "I wanna go out."

"Go on back to your room. Thas the only goin out you gonna be doin. I don't wanna hear another word outta your mouth till your mother get home." He closed his eyes to wait her out, for he knew she was now capable of standing there till doomsday to sulk. When he heard her going down the hall, he waited for the door to slam. But there was no sound and he gradually opened his eyes. He put a cushion at one end of the couch and took off his shoes and lay down, his hands resting on the large mound that was his stomach. All his friends told him that if he lost thirty or forty pounds he would be a new man, but he did not think that was true. He considered asking Elaine to bring his pills from his bedroom, for he had left the vial he traveled with at work. But he suffered the pain rather than suffer her stirring about. He watched his wife's curtains flap gently with the breeze and the movement soothed him.

"I would not say anything bad about marriage," his father had written to Woodrow after Woodrow called to say he was considering marrying Rita Hadley.

"It is easier to pick up and walk away from a wife and a family if you don't like it then you can walk away from your own bad cooking." Woodrow had never been inclined to marry anyone, was able, as he would tell his lodge brothers, to get all the trim he wanted without buying some woman a ring and walking down the aisle with her. "Doin it to a woman for a few months was all right," he would say, sounding like his father, "cause that only put the idea of marryin in their heads. Doin it to them any more than that and the idea take root."

It had never crossed his mind to sleep with any of the women at Rising Star AME, for he had discovered in Georgia that the wrath of church women was greater than that of all others, even old whores. He only went out with Rita because the preacher took him aside one Sunday and told him it was unnatural to go about unmarried and that he should give some thought to promenading with Sister Rita sometime. And, too, he was thirty-six and it was beginning to occur to him that women might not go on forever laying down and opening their legs for him. The second time they went out, he put his arm around Rita and pulled her to him there in the Booker-T Theater. She smacked his hand and that made his johnson hard. "I ain't like that, Mr. Cunningham." He had heard those words before. But when he pulled her to him again, she twisted his finger until it hurt. And that was something he had not experienced before.

His father suffered a mild stroke a week before the wedding. "Do not take this sicknes to mean that I do not send my blessing to your mariage to Miss Rita Hadley," his father said in a letter he had dictated to Alice, his oldest daughter. "God took pity on you when he send her your way." Even in the unfamiliarity of Alice's handwriting, the familiarity of his father was there in all the lines, right down to the misspelled words. Until some of his father's children learned in their teens, his father had been the only one in the family who could read and write. "This," he said of his reading and writing, "makes me as good as a white man." And before some of his children learned, discovered there was no magic to it, he enjoyed reading aloud at the supper table to his family, his voice stringing out a long monotone of words that often meant nothing to him and even less to his family because the man read so quickly.

His father read anything he could get his hands on—the words on feed bags, on medicine bottles, on years-old magazine pages they used for wallpaper, just about everything except the Bible. He had a fondness for weeks-old newspapers he would find in the streets when he went to town. No one—not even the squirming small kids—was allowed to move from the supper table until he had finished reading, hooking one word to another until it all became babble. Indeed, it was such a babble that some of his sons would joke behind his back that he was lying about knowing how to read. "Few white men can do what I'm doin right now," he would say. "You go bring ten white men in here and I bet nine couldn't read this. Couldn't read it if God commanded em to." Sometimes, to torment his wife, he would hold a scrap of newspaper close to her face and tell her to read the headlines. "I cain't," she would say. "You know I cain't." No matter how many times he did this, his father would laugh with the pleasure of the very first time. Then he would pass the newspaper among his children and tell them to read him the headlines, and each one would hold it uncomfortably and repeat what their mother had said.

When Woodrow woke, it was nearly five o'clock and his wife was sitting on the side of the couch, asking where Elaine was. "She ain't in her room," his wife said and kissed his forehead. A school cafeteria worker, Rita was a very thin woman who, before she met Woodrow, had lived only for her job and her church activities. She was five years older than he was and had resigned herself to the fact that she was not the type of woman men wanted to marry. "I've put it all in God's hands," she once said to a friend before Woodrow came along, "and left it there."

Rita waited until seven o'clock before she began calling her daughter's friends. "Stop worryin," Woodrow told her after the tenth call, "you know how that girl is." At eight-thirty, they put on light coats and went in search, visiting the same houses and apartments that Rita had called. They returned home about ten and waited until eleven, when they put on their coats again and went to the police station at 16th and V Northwest. They did not call the station because somewhere Woodrow had heard that the law wouldn't begin to hear a complaint unless you stood before it in person.

At the station, the man at the front desk did not look up until they had been standing there for some two minutes. Woodrow wanted to tell him that the police chief and the mayor were now black men and that they couldn't be ignored, but when the man behind the desk looked up, Woodrow could see in his eyes that none of that would have mattered to him.

"Our daughter is missing," Rita said.

"How long?" said the man, a sergeant with an unpronounceable name on his name tag. He pulled a form from a pile to his left and then he took up a pen, loudly clicking out the point to write.

"We haven't seen her since this afternoon," Woodrow says.

The sergeant clicked the pen again and set it on the desk, then put the form back on top with the others. "Not long enough," he said. "Has to be gone forty-eight hours. Till then she's missing, but she's not a missing person."

"She only a baby."

"How old?"

"Fifteen," Woodrow said.

"She's just a runaway," the sergeant said.

"She never run away before," Woodrow said. "This ain't like her, sergeant." Woodrow felt that like all white men, the man enjoyed having attention paid to his rank.

"Don't matter. She's probably waiting for you at home right now, wondering where you two buggied off to. Go home. If she isn't home, then come back when she's a missing person."

Woodrow took Rita's arm as they went back, because he sensed that she was near collapsing. "What happened?" she asked as they turned the corner of U and 10th streets. "Did you say somethin bad to her?"

He told her everything that he could remember, even what Elaine was wearing when he last saw her. Answering was not difficult because no blame had yet been assigned. Despite the time nearing midnight, they became confident with each step that Elaine was just at a friend's they did not know about, that the friend's mother, like any good mother, would soon send their daughter home. Rita, in the last blocks before their apartment, leaned into her husband and his warmth helped to put her at ease.

They waited up until about four in the morning, and then they undressed without words in the dark. Rita began to cry the moment her head hit the pillow, for she was afraid to see the sun come up and find that a new day had arrived without Elaine being home. She asked him again what happened, and he told her again, even things that he had forgotten—the logo of the football team on the light-skinned boy's jacket, the fact that the other boy was bald except for a half-dollar-sized spot of hair carved on the back of his head. He was still talking when she dozed off with him holding her.

Before they had coffee later that morning, about seven thirty, they called their jobs to say they would not be in. Work had always occupied a place at the center of their lives, and there was initially something eerie about being home when it was not a holiday or the weekend. They spent the rest of the morning searching the streets together, and in the afternoon, they separated to cover more ground. They did the same thing after dinner, each spreading out farther and farther from their apartment on R Street. That evening, they called neighbors and friends, church and lodge members, to tell them that their child was missing and that they needed their help and their prayers. Their friends and neighbors began searching that evening, and a few went with Woodrow and Rita the next day to the police station to file a missing person's report. A different sergeant was at the desk, and though he was a white man, Woodrow felt that he understood their trouble.

For nearly three months, Woodrow and Rita searched after they came from work, and each evening after they and their friends had been out, the pastor of Rising Star spoke to a small group that gathered in the Cunninghams' living room. "The world is cold and not hospitable," he would conclude, holding his hat in both hands, "but we know our God to be a kind God and that he has provided our little sister with a place of comfort and warmth until she returns to her parents and to all of us who love and treasure her."

In the kitchen beside the refrigerator, Rita tacked up a giant map of Washington, on which she noted where she and others had searched. "I didn't know the city was this big," she said the day she put it up, her fingertips touching the neighborhoods that she had never heard of or had heard of only in passing—foreign lands she thought she would never set eyes on. Petworth. Anacostia Lincoln Park. And in the beginning, the very size of the city lifted her spirits, for in a place so big, there was certainly a spot that held something as small as her child, and if they just kept looking long enough, they would come upon that place.

"What happened?" Rita would ask as they prepared for bed. What he told her and her listening replaced everything they had ever done in that bed—discussing what future they wanted for Elaine, lovemaking, sharing what the world had done to them that workday. "What happened?" It was just about the only thing she ever asked Woodrow as the months grew colder. "What happened? Whatcha say to her?" By late February, when fewer and fewer people were going out to search, he had told the whole story, but then he began to tell her things that had not happened. There were three boys, he said at one point, for example. Or, he could see a gun sticking out of the jacket pocket of the light-skinned one, and he could see the outline of a knife in the back pants pocket of the third. Or he would say that the record player was playing so loudly he could hear it from the street. They were small embellishments at first, and if his wife noticed that the story of what happened was changing, she said nothing. In time, with winter disappearing, he was adding more and more so that it was no longer a falseness here and there that was embedded in the whole of the truth, but the truth itself, an ever-diminishing kernel, that was contained in the whole of falseness. And, like some kind of bedtime story, she listened and drifted with his words into a sleep where the things he was telling her were sometimes happening.

By March, Woodrow had written countless letters to his father telling the old man it was not necessary to come to Washington to help look for the girl. "I got a sign from God," the old man kept writing, "that I could help find her." Then, with spring, he began writing that he had received signs that he was not long for the world, that finding the girl was the last thing God wanted him to do. In the longest letters the old man had ever written to the one child of his who responded, he would go on and on about the signs he saw signaling his own death: The mongrel would no longer take food from his hand; the dead visited him at night, sitting down on the side of his bed and telling him things about himself; the rising sun now touched his house last in the morning, though there were houses to the left and right of his.

"You keep telling me that I'll be hurt or lost," the old man wrote Woodrow. "But I know the way that Washinton, D.C. is set up. I came there once maybe twice. How could I get lost. Take a chance on me, and we'll have that child home before you can blink one eye. I can bring Sparky he got some bloodhound in him."

In late April, Rita took down the map in the kitchen. The tacks fell to the floor and she left them there. She put the map in the bottom drawer of her daughter's dresser, among the blouses and blue jeans and a diary she would not find the strength to read for another three months. Her days of searching during the week dwindled down to two, then to one. She returned the car a church member had lent her to drive around the city in. Each evening when she got home, Woodrow would be out and she left his dinner in the oven to stay warm. Every now and again, when the hour was late, she went out to look for him, often for no other reason than that there was nothing worth watching on the television. As she put on more and more weight, it became difficult for her to stand and dish out food to the students at lunchtime. Her supervisor and fellow workers sympathized, and, after a week of perfunctory training, she was allowed to sit and work at the cash register.

As he continued going about the city, sometimes on foot, Woodrow told himself and everyone else that he was hunting for his daughter, but this was only a piece of the truth. "I'm lookin for my daughter, who's run away," he said to those opening the doors where he knocked. "She's been gone a long time, and her mama and me are about to lose our minds." He sometimes presented a picture of his daughter, smiling radiantly, that was taken only months before she disappeared. But just as often, he would pull out a photograph of the girl when she was five, standing one Easter between her parents in front of Rising Star. All who looked at the photograph, even the drunks half-blind with alcohol, were touched by the picture of the little girl in her Easter dress who had now gone away from her parents, parents who were now worried sick. Many people invited Woodrow into their homes.

The Easter picture became a passport, and the more places he visited the more places he wanted to see. On U Street, a woman of twenty-five or so with three children put down the child she was holding to get a better look at the picture of the five-year-old girl. Woodrow, in the doorway, noted just over her shoulder that on her wall there was a calendar with a snow-covered mountain, hung with the prominence others would have given a landscape painting. An old woman on Harvard Street, tsk-tsking as she looked at the picture, invited him in for coffee and cake. "My prayers go out to you." Nearly everything in her apartment was covered in plastic, even the pictures on the walls. The old woman sat him on her plastic-covered couch and placed the food on a coffee table covered with a plastic cloth. "And such a sweet-lookin child, too, son." When he asked to use the bathroom (more out of curiosity than for relief), she pointed to a plastic path leading away down the hall. "Stay on the mat, son."

A tottering man in a place on 21st Street just off Benning Road began to cry when Woodrow told him his story. "Dora, Dora," the man called to a woman. "Come see this little angel." The woman, who was also tottering, pulled Woodrow into their house with one hand, while the other hand pressed the picture to her bosom. The man and Woodrow sat on the couch. The woman stood in front of them, swaying trancelike, her eyes closed, the picture still pressed to her. The man put his arm around Woodrow and breathed a sour wine smell into his face. "Let's me and you pray about this situation," he said.

• • • • • •

One April evening, a little more than a year and a half after their daughter disappeared, Rita was standing in front of their building, waiting for him. "We have fish tonight. It's in the stove waitin," she said, in the same way she would have said, "I know what you been doin. And who you been doin it with." "We have fish to eat," she said again. She turned around and went back inside. "We have fish, and we have to move from this place," she said.

Woodrow's father died nearly seven years after Elaine Cunningham disappeared. Of the eight children he had had with Woodrow's mother and the five he had had with other women, only Woodrow, Alice, and a half-brother who lived down the road from the old man came to the funeral. It was a frozen day in January, and the gravediggers broke two picks before they had even gone down one foot. They labored seven hours to make a hole for the old man. "Even the ground don't want him," said one of the old man's friends standing at the gravesite.

There was not much in the old man's place to divide among his heirs. In a wooden trunk in one of the back rooms, Woodrow found several pictures of his mother. He had been kneeling down, going through the trunk, and when he saw the pictures, he cried out as if he had been struck. He had not seen his mother's face in more than forty years, had thought his father had destroyed all the pictures of her. "You always looked like her," Alice said, coming up behind him. "Even when you sat at the right hand of the father, you looked like her."

Though he was younger than three other brothers, Woodrow had worked hardest of his father's children. At first, his father had sat his children about the supper table according to their ages, but then he began to seat them according to who did the most work. His best workers sat closest to him, and by the time he was seven, Woodrow had worked his way to the right hand of his father. Woodrow's mother sat at the far end of the table, between two of her daughters. Most of his brothers and sisters, unable to pick the amount of cotton Woodrow could, never forgave him for living only to be close to their father. But he learned to pay them no mind and even learned to enjoy their hostility. He never moved from that right-hand place until the day he went off down the road to work in the turpentine camps.

He also found in the trunk some letters he wrote his father from the camps and from railroad yards and from the places he worked as he made his way up to Washington. They were all of one page or less, and they were all about work, work from sunnup to sundown. There were no friends mentioned, there were no descriptions of places where he lived, there were no names of women courted, loved. "I got a two-week job tanning hides," he wrote from a nameless place in South Carolina. "I got work cureing tobacco. I may stay on after the season," he wrote from somewhere near Raleigh. "I have been working in the stables outside Charlotesvile. The pay is good. I got used to the smell. and the work goes easy."

Woodrow and Rita took the train back to Washington, bringing back a few of the pictures and none of the letters, which he burned in a barrel outside his father's house. Everything along the way back to D.C. was as frozen as Georgia. It was as if the cold had separated the world into three unrelated and distinct parts—the earth, what was on the earth, and the sky above. Nothing moved. Flying birds seemed to freeze in midair, and then the cold would nail them there.

Rita and Woodrow were back in the apartment on Independence Avenue in Southeast by ten o'clock that night. Rita took her usual place at an easy chair near the window. On a table beside the chair was all she needed—the television guide, snacks, the telephone. The chair was very large and had had to be specially ordered, because she could not fit into the regular ones in the store.

Woodrow, even though the hour was late and the weather people were predicting even colder temperatures, quietly put on his heaviest coat and left the apartment. He said nothing to Rita, and she did not look up when the door locked behind him. At the corner of Independence and 15th, Woodrow looked into the grocery store window at the owner he had become friends with since moving to Southeast. No customers went into the store, and the owner was dozing behind the counter, his head back, his mouth open. Woodrow watched him for a very long time. By now he knew everything about the man and his store and the sons who helped the man, and there was no urgency to be inside with him. Having lost so much weight, Woodrow felt that even more of the world had opened up to him. And so he wondered if he should go on down 15th Street, try to find a house he had not visited before, and bring out the picture of the child in her Easter dress.

# THOM JONES

*Jones (1945– ) was born in Aurora, Illinois, and was educated at the Universities of Hawaii, Washington, and Iowa. A former Marine and an amateur boxer, Jones currently teaches at the University of Iowa. He is the author of the highly regarded story collections* The Pugilist at Rest *(1993) and* Cold Snap *(1995). His latest novel,* Sonny Liston Was a Friend of Mine, *was published in 1999. He is the recipient of a Guggenheim Fellowship (1994–95). His work is included in* The Best American Short Stories of the Century *(1999), edited by John Updike.*

## The Pugilist at Rest

Hey Baby got caught writing a letter to his girl when he was supposed to be taking notes on the specs of the M-14 rifle. We were sitting in a stifling hot Quonset hut during the first weeks of boot camp, August 1966, at the Marine Corps Recruit Depot in San Diego. Sergeant Wright snatched the letter out of Hey Baby's hand, and later that night in the squad bay he read the letter to the Marine recruits of Platoon 263, his voice laden with sarcasm. *"Hey, Baby!"* he began, and then as he went into the body of the letter he worked himself into a state of outrage and disgust. It was a letter to *Rosie Rottencrotch,* he said at the end, and what really mattered, what was really at issue and what was of utter importance was not *Rosie Rottencrotch* and her steaming-hot panties but rather the muzzle velocity of the M-14 rifle.

Hey Baby paid for the letter by doing a hundred squat thrusts on the concrete floor of the squad bay, but the main prize he won that night was that he became forever known as Hey Baby to the recruits of Platoon 263—in addition to being a shitbird, a faggot, a turd, a maggot, and other such standard appellations. To top it all off, shortly after the incident, Hey Baby got a Dear John from this girl back in Chicago, of whom Sergeant Wright, myself, and seventy-eight other Marine recruits had come to know just a little.

Hey Baby was not in the Marine Corps for very long. The reason for this was that he started in on my buddy, Jorgeson. Jorgeson was my main man, and Hey Baby started calling him Jorge-pussy and began harassing him and pushing him around. He was down on Jorgeson because whenever we were taught some sort of combat maneuver or tactic, Jorgeson would say, under his breath, "You could get *killed* if you try that." Or, "Your ass is *had,* if you do that." You got the feeling that Jorgeson didn't think loving the American flag and defending democratic ideals in Southeast Asia were all that important. He told me that what he really wanted to do was have an artist's loft in the SoHo district of New York City, wear a beret, eat liver sausage sandwiches made with stale baguettes, drink Tokay wine, smoke dope, paint pictures, and listen to the wailing, sorrowful songs of that French singer Edith Piaf, otherwise known as "The Little Sparrow."

After the first half hour of boot camp most of the other recruits wanted to get out, too, but they nourished dreams of surfboards, Corvettes, and blond babes. Jorgeson wanted to be a beatnik and hang out with Jack Kerouac and Neal Cassady,[1] slam down burning shots of amber whiskey, and hear Charles Mingus play real cool jazz on the bass fiddle. He wanted to practice Zen Buddhism, throw the I Ching, eat couscous, and study astrology charts. All of this was foreign territory to me. I had grown up in Aurora, Illinois, and had never heard of such things. Jorgeson had a sharp tongue and was so supercilious in his remarks that I didn't know quite how seriously I should take this talk, but I enjoyed his humor and I did believe he had the sensibilities of an artist. It was not some vague yearning. I believed very much that he could become a painter of pictures. At that point he wasn't putting his heart and soul into becoming a Marine. He wasn't a true believer like me.

Some weeks after Hey Baby began hassling Jorgeson, Sergeant Wright gave us his best speech: "You men are going off to war, and it's not a pretty thing," etc. & etc., "and if Luke the Gook knocks down one of your buddies, a fellow Marine, you are going to risk your life and go in and get that Marine and you are going to bring him out. Not because I said so. No! You are going after that Marine because *you* are a Marine, a member of the most elite fighting force in the world, and that man out there who's gone down is a Marine, and he's your *buddy*. He is your brother! Once you are a Marine, you are *always* a Marine and you will never let another Marine down." Etc. & etc. "You can take a Marine out of the Corps but you can't take the Corps out of a Marine." Etc. & etc. At the time it seemed to me a very good speech, and it stirred me deeply. Sergeant Wright was no candy ass. He was one squared-away dude, and he could call cadence. Man, it puts a lump in my throat when I remember how that man could sing cadence. Apart from Jorgeson, I think all of the recruits in Platoon 263 were proud of Sergeant Wright. He was the real thing, the genuine article. He was a crackerjack Marine.

In the course of training, lots of the recruits dropped out of the original platoon. Some couldn't pass the physical fitness tests and had to go to a special camp for pussies. This was a particularly shameful shortcoming, the most humiliating apart from bed-wetting. Other recruits would get pneumonia, strep throat, infected foot blisters, or whatever, and lose time that way. Some didn't qualify at the rifle range. One would break a leg. Another would have a nervous breakdown (and this was also deplorable). People dropped out right and left. When the recruit corrected whatever deficiency he had, or when he got better, he would be picked up by another platoon that was in the stage of basic training

1. Friend and inspiration to Kerouac; his *Grace Beats Karma, Letters from Prison, 1958–1960* was published in 1993. Kerouac (1922–1969) was a U.S. novelist of the so-called Beat generation.

that he had been in when his training was interrupted. Platoon 263 picked up dozens of recruits in this fashion. If everything went well, however, you got through with the whole business in twelve weeks. That's not a long time, but it seemed like a long time. You did not see a female in all that time. You did not see a newspaper or a television set. You did not eat a candy bar. Another thing was the fact that you had someone on top of you, watching every move you made. When it was time to "shit, shower, and shave," you were given just ten minutes, and had to confront lines and so on to complete the entire affair. Head calls were so infrequent that I spent a lot of time that might otherwise have been neutral or painless in the eye-watering anxiety that I was going to piss my pants. We *ran* to chow, where we were faced with enormous steam vents that spewed out a sickening smell of rancid, superheated grease. Still, we entered the mess hall with ravenous appetites, ate a huge tray of food in just a few minutes, and then *ran* back to our company area in formation, choking back the burning bile of a meal too big to be eaten so fast. God forbid that you would lose control and vomit.

If all had gone well in the preceding hours, Sergeant Wright would permit us to smoke one cigarette after each meal. Jorgeson had shown me the wisdom of switching from Camels to Pall Malls—they were much longer, packed a pretty good jolt, and when we snapped open our brushed-chrome Zippos, torched up, and inhaled the first few drags, we shared the overmastering pleasure that tobacco can bring if you use it seldom and judiciously. These were always the best moments of the day—brief respites from the tyrannical repression of recruit training. As we got close to the end of it all Jorgeson liked to play a little game. He used to say to me (with fragrant blue smoke curling out of his nostrils), "If someone said, 'I'll give you ten thousand dollars to do all of this again,' what would you say?" "No way, Jack!" He would keep on upping it until he had John Beresford Tipton, the guy from "The Millionaire," offering me a check for a million bucks. "Not for any money," I'd say.

While they were all smoldering under various pressures, the recruits were also getting pretty "salty"—they were beginning to believe. They were beginning to think of themselves as Marines. If you could make it through this, the reasoning went, you wouldn't crack in combat. So I remember that I had tears in my eyes when Sergeant Wright gave us the spiel about how a Marine would charge a machine-gun nest to save his buddies, dive on a hand grenade, do whatever it takes—and yet I was ashamed when Jorgeson caught me wiping them away. All of the recruits were teary except Jorgeson. He had these very clear cobalt blue eyes. They were so remarkable that they caused you to notice Jorgeson in a crowd. There was unusual beauty in these eyes, and there was an extraordinary power in them. Apart from having a pleasant enough face, Jorgeson was small and unassuming except for these eyes. Anyhow, when he caught me getting sentimental he gave me this look that penetrated to the core of my being. It was the icy look of absolute contempt, and it caused me to doubt myself. I said, "Man! Can't you get into it? For Christ's sake!"

"I'm not like you," he said. "But I am into it, more than you could ever know. I never told you this before, but I am Kal-El, born on the planet Krypton and rocketed to Earth as an infant, moments before my world exploded. Disguised as a mild-mannered Marine, I have resolved to use my powers for the good of mankind. Whenever danger appears on the scene, truth and justice will be served as I slip into the green U.S.M.C.[2] utility uniform and become Earth's greatest hero."

I got highly pissed and didn't talk to him for a couple of days after this. Then, about two weeks before boot camp was over, when we were running out to the parade field for drill with our rifles at port arms, all assholes and elbows, I saw Hey Baby give Jorgeson a nasty shove with his M-14. Hey Baby was a large and fairly tough young man who liked to displace his aggressive impulses on Jorgeson, but he wasn't as big or as tough as I.

Jorgeson nearly fell down as the other recruits scrambled out to the parade field, and Hey Baby gave a short, malicious laugh. I ran past Jorgeson and caught up to Hey Baby; he picked me up in his peripheral vision, but by then it was too late. I set my body so that I could put everything into it, and with one deft stroke I hammered him in the temple with the sharp edge of the steel butt plate of my M-14. It was not exactly a premeditated crime, although I had been laying to get him. My idea before this had simply been to lay my hands on him, but now I had blood in my eye. I was a skilled boxer, and I knew the temple was a vulnerable spot; the human skull is otherwise hard and durable, except at its base. There was a sickening crunch, and Hey Baby dropped into the ice plants along the side of the company street.

The entire platoon was out on the parade field when the house mouse screamed at the assistant D.I.,[3] who rushed back to the scene of the crime to find Hey Baby crumpled in a fetal position in the ice plants with blood all over the place. There was blood from the scalp wound as well as a froth of blood emitting from his nostrils and his mouth. Blood was leaking from his right ear. Did I see skull fragments and brain tissue? It seemed that I did. To tell you the truth, I wouldn't have cared in the least if I had killed him, but like most criminals I was very much afraid of getting caught. It suddenly occurred to me that I could be headed for the brig for a long time. My heart was pounding out of my chest. Yet the larger part of me didn't care. Jorgeson was my buddy, and I wasn't going to stand still and let someone fuck him over.

The platoon waited at parade rest while Sergeant Wright came out of the duty hut and took command of the situation. An ambulance was called, and it came almost immediately. A number of corpsmen squatted down alongside the fallen man for what seemed an eternity. Eventually they took Hey Baby off with a fractured skull. It would be the last we ever saw of him. Three evenings later, in the squad bay, the assistant D.I. told us rather ominously that Hey Baby had recovered consciousness. That's all he said. What did *that* mean? I was worried, because Hey Baby had seen me make my move, but, as it turned out, when he came to he had forgotten the incident and all events of the preceding two weeks. Retrograde amnesia. Lucky for me. I also knew that at least three other recruits had seen what I did, but none of them reported me. Every member of the platoon was called in and grilled by a team of hard-ass captains

2. The United States Marine Corps.
3. Drill instructor.

and a light colonel from the Criminal Investigation Detachment. It took a certain amount of balls to lie to them, yet none of my fellow jarheads reported me. I was well liked and Hey Baby was not. Indeed, many felt that he got exactly what was coming to him.

The other day—Memorial Day, as it happened—I was cleaning some stuff out of the attic when I came upon my old dress-blue uniform. It's a beautiful uniform, easily the most handsome worn by any of the U.S. armed forces. The rich color recalled Jorgeson's eyes for me—not that the color matched, but in the sense that the color of each was so startling. The tunic does not have lapels, of course, but a high collar with red piping and the traditional golden eagle, globe, and anchor insignia on either side of the neck clasp. The tunic buttons are not brassy—although they are in fact made of brass—but are a delicate gold in color, like Florentine gold. On the sleeves of the tunic my staff sergeant's chevrons are gold on red. High on the left breast is a rainbow display of fruit salad representing my various combat citations. Just below these are my marksmanship badges; I shot Expert in rifle as well as pistol.

I opened a sandalwood box and took my various medals out of the large plastic bag I had packed them in to prevent them from tarnishing. The Navy Cross and the two Silver Stars are the best; they are such pretty things they dazzle you. I found a couple of Thai sticks in the sandalwood box as well. I took a whiff of the box and smelled the smells of Saigon—the whores, the dope, the saffron, cloves, jasmine, and patchouli oil. I put the Thai sticks back, recalling the three-day hangover that particular batch of dope had given me more than twenty-three years before. Again I looked at my dress-blue tunic. My most distinctive badge, the crowning glory, and the one of which I am most proud is the set of Airborne wings. I remember how it was, walking around Oceanside, California—the Airborne wings and the high-and-tight haircut were recognized by all the Marines; they meant you were the crème de la crème, you were a recon Marine.

Recon was all Jorgeson's idea. We had lost touch with each other after boot camp. I was sent to com school in San Diego, where I had to sit in a hot Class A wool uniform all day and learn the Morse code. I deliberately flunked out, and when I was given the perfunctory option for a second shot, I told the colonel, "Hell no, sir. I want to go 003—infantry. I want to be a ground-pounder. I didn't join the service to sit at a desk all day."

I was on a bus to Camp Pendleton three days later, and when I got there I ran into Jorgeson. I had been thinking of him a lot. He was a clerk in headquarters company. Much to my astonishment, he was fifteen pounds heavier, and had grown two inches, and he told me he was hitting the weight pile every night after running seven miles up and down the foothills of Pendleton in combat boots, carrying a rifle and a full field pack. After the usual what's-been-happening? b.s., he got down to business and said, "They need people in Force Recon, what do you think? Headquarters is one boring motherfucker."

I said, "Recon? Paratrooper? You got to be shittin' me! When did you get so gung-ho, man?"

He said, "Hey, you were the one who *bought* the program. Don't fade on me now, God damn it! Look, we pass the physical fitness test and then they send us to jump school at Benning. If we pass that, we're in. And we'll pass. Those doggies ain't got jack. Semper fi, motherfucker! Let's do it."

There was no more talk of Neal Cassady, Edith Piaf, or the artist's loft in SoHo. I said, "If Sergeant Wright could only see you now!"

We were just three days in country when we got dropped in somewhere in the western highlands of the Quang Tri province. It was a routine reconnaissance patrol. It was not supposed to be any kind of big deal at all—just acclimation. The morning after our drop we approached a clear field. I recall that it gave me a funny feeling, but I was too new to fully trust my instincts. *Everything* was spooky; I was fresh meat, F.N.G.—a Fucking New Guy.

Before moving into the field, our team leader sent Hanes—a lance corporal, a short-timer, with only twelve days left before his rotation was over—across the field as a point man. This was a bad omen and everyone knew it. Hanes had two Purple Hearts. He followed the order with no hesitation and crossed the field without drawing fire. The team leader signaled for us to fan out and told me to circumvent the field and hump through the jungle to investigate a small mound of loose red dirt that I had missed completely but that he had picked up with his trained eye. I remember I kept saying, "Where?" He pointed to a heap of earth about thirty yards along the tree line and about ten feet back in the bushes. Most likely it was an anthill, but you never knew—it could have been an N.V.A. tunnel. "Over there," he hissed. "God damn it, do I have to draw pictures for you?"

I moved smartly in the direction of the mound while the rest of the team reconverged to discuss something. As I approached the mound I saw that it was in fact an anthill, and I looked back at the team and saw they were already halfway across the field, moving very fast.

Suddenly there were several loud hollow pops and the cry "Incoming!" Seconds later the first of a half-dozen mortar rounds landed in the loose earth surrounding the anthill. For a millisecond, everything went black. I was blown back and lifted up on a cushion of warm air. At first it was like the thrill of a carnival ride, but it was quickly followed by that stunned, jangly, electric feeling you get when you hit your crazy bone. Like that, but not confined to a small area like the elbow. I felt it shoot through my spine and into all four limbs. A thick plaster of sand and red clay plugged up my nostrils and ears. Grit was blown in between my teeth. If I hadn't been wearing a pair of Ray-Ban aviator shades, I would certainly have been blinded permanently—as it was, my eyes were loaded with grit. (I later discovered that fine red earth was somehow blown in behind the crystal of my pressure-tested Rolex Submariner, underneath my fingernails and toenails, and deep into the pores of my skin.) When I was able to, I pulled out a canteen filled with lemon-lime Kool-Aid and tried to flood my eyes clean. This helped a little, but my eyes still felt like they were on fire. I rinsed them again and blinked furiously.

I rolled over on my stomach in the prone position and leveled my field-issue M-16. A company of screaming N.V.A. soldiers ran into the field, firing as they came—I saw their green tracer rounds blanket the position where the team had quickly congregated to lay out a perimeter, but none of our own red tracers were going out. Several of the Marines had been killed outright by the mortar rounds. Jorgeson was all right, and I saw him cast a nervous glance in my direction. Then he turned to the enemy and began to fire his M-16. I clicked my rifle on to automatic and pulled the trigger, but the gun was loaded with dirt and it wouldn't fire.

Apart from Jorgeson, the only other American putting out any fire was Second Lieutenant Milton, also a fairly new guy, a "cherry," who was down on one knee firing his .45, an exercise in almost complete futility. I assumed that Milton's 16 had jammed, like mine, and watched as AK-47 rounds, having penetrated his flak jacket and then his chest, ripped through the back of his field pack and buzzed into the jungle beyond like a deadly swarm of bees. A few seconds later, I heard the swoosh of an R.P.G. rocket, a dud round that dinged the lieutenant's left shoulder before it flew off in the bush behind him. It took off his whole arm, and for an instant I could see the white bone and ligaments of his shoulder, and the red flesh of muscle tissue, looking very much like fresh prime beef, well marbled and encased in a thin layer of yellowish white adipose tissue that quickly became saturated with dark red blood. What a lot of blood there was. Still, Milton continued to fire his .45. When he emptied his clip, I watched him remove a fresh one from his web gear and attempt to load the pistol with one hand. He seemed to fumble with the fresh clip for a long time, until at last he dropped it, along with his .45. The lieutenant's head slowly sagged forward, but he stayed up on one knee with his remaining arm extended out to the enemy, palm upward in the soulful, heartrending gesture of Al Jolson doing a rendition of "Mammy."

A hail of green tracer rounds buzzed past Jorgeson, but he coolly returned fire in short, controlled bursts. The light, tinny pops from his M-16 did not sound very reassuring, but I saw several N.V.A. go down. AK-47 fire kicked up red dust all around Jorgeson's feet. He was basically out in the open, and if ever a man was totally alone it was Jorgeson. He was dead meat and he had to know it. It was very strange that he wasn't hit immediately.

Jorgeson zigged his way over to the body of a large black Marine who carried an M-60 machine gun. Most of the recon Marines carried grease guns or Swedish Ks; an M-60 was too heavy for traveling light and fast, but this Marine had been big and he had been paranoid. I had known him least of anyone in the squad. In three days he had said nothing to me, I suppose because I was F.N.G., and had spooked him. Indeed, now he was dead. That august seeker of truth, Schopenhauer,[4] was correct: *We are like lambs in a field, disporting themselves under the eye of the butcher, who chooses out first one and then another for his prey. So it is that in our good days we are all unconscious of the evil Fate may have presently in store for us—sickness, poverty, mutilation, loss of sight or reason.*

It was difficult to judge how quickly time was moving. Although my senses had been stunned by the concussion of the mortar rounds, they were, however paradoxical this may seem, more acute than ever before. I watched Jorgeson

4. German philopher (1788–1860).

pick up the machine gun and begin to spread an impressive field of fire back at the enemy. Thuk thuk thuk, thuk thuk thuk, thuk thuk thuk! I saw several more bodies fall, and began to think that things might turn out all right after all. The N.V.A. dropped for cover, and many of them turned back and headed for the tree line. Jorgeson fired off a couple of bandoliers, and after he stopped to load another, he turned back and looked at me with those blue eyes and a smile like "How am I doing?" Then I heard the steel-cork pop of an M-79 launcher and saw a rocket grenade explode through Jorgeson's upper abdomen, causing him to do something like a back flip. His M-60 machine gun flew straight up into the air. The barrel was glowing red like a hot poker, and continued to fire in a "cook off" until the entire bandolier had run through.

In the meantime I had pulled a cleaning rod out of my pack and worked it through the barrel of my M-16. When I next tried to shoot, the Tonka-toy son of a bitch remained jammed, and at last I frantically broke it down to find the source of the problem. I had a dirty bolt. Fucking dirt everywhere. With numbed fingers I removed the firing pin and worked it over with a toothbrush, dropping it in the red dirt, picking it up, cleaning it, and dropping it again. My fingers felt like Novocain, and while I could see far away, I was unable to see up close. I poured some more Kool-Aid over my eyes. It was impossible for me to get my weapon clean. Lucky for me, ultimately.

Suddenly N.V.A. soldiers were running through the field shoving bayonets into the bodies of the downed Marines. It was not until an N.V.A. trooper kicked Lieutenant Milton out of his tripod position that he finally fell to the ground. Then the soldiers started going through the dead Marines' gear. I was still frantically struggling with my weapon when it began to dawn on me that the enemy had forgotten me in the excitement of the firefight. I wondered what had happened to Hanes and if he had gotten clear. I doubted it, and hopped on my survival radio to call in an air strike when finally a canny N.V.A. trooper did remember me and headed in my direction most ricky-tick.

With a tight grip on the spoon, I pulled the pin on a fragmentation grenade and then unsheathed my K-bar. About this time Jorgeson let off a horrendous shriek—a gut shot is worse than anything. Or did Jorgeson scream to save my life? The N.V.A. moving in my direction turned back to him, studied him for a moment, and then thrust a bayonet into his heart. As badly as my own eyes hurt, I was able to see Jorgeson's eyes—a final flash of glorious azure before they faded into the unfocused and glazed gray of death. I repinned the grenade, got up on my knees, and scrambled away until finally I was on my feet with a useless and incomplete handful of M-16 parts, and I was running as fast and as hard as I have ever run in my life. A pair of Phantom F-4s came in very low with delayed-action high-explosive rounds and napalm. I could feel the almost unbearable heat waves of the latter, volley after volley. I can still feel it and smell it to this day.

Concerning Lance Corporal Hanes: they found him later, fried to a crisp by the napalm, but it was nonetheless ascertained that he had been mutilated while alive. He was like the rest of us—eighteen, nineteen, twenty years old. What did we know of life? Before Vietnam, Hanes didn't think he would ever die. I mean, yes, he knew that in theory he would die, but he *felt* like he was going to live forever. I know that I felt that way. Hanes was down to twelve days and a wake-up. When other Marines saw a short-timer get greased, it devastated their morale. However, when I saw them zip up the body bag on Hanes I became incensed. Why hadn't Milton sent him back to the rear to burn shit or something when he got so short? Twelve days to go and then mutilated. Fucking Milton! Fucking Second Lieutenant!

Theogenes was the greatest of gladiators. He was a boxer who served under the patronage of a cruel nobleman, a prince who took great delight in bloody spectacles. Although this was several hundred years before the times of those most enlightened of men Socrates, Plato, and Aristotle, and well after the Minoans of Crete, it still remains a high point in the history of Western civilization and culture. It was the approximate time of Homer, the greatest poet who ever lived. Then, as now, violence, suffering, and the cheapness of life were the rule.

The sort of boxing Theogenes practiced was not like modern-day boxing with those kindergarten Queensberry Rules. The two contestants were not permitted the freedom of a ring. Instead, they were strapped to flat stones, facing each other nose-to-nose. When the signal was given they would begin hammering each other with fists encased in heavy leather thongs. It was a fight to the death. Fourteen hundred and twenty-five times Theogenes was strapped to the stone and fourteen hundred and twenty-five times he emerged a victor.

Perhaps it is Theogenes who is depicted in the famous Roman statue (based on the earlier Greek original) of "The Pugilist at Rest." I keep a grainy black-and-white photograph of it in my room. The statue depicts a muscular athlete approaching his middle age. He has a thick beard and a full head of curly hair. In addition to the telltale broken nose and cauliflower ears of a boxer, the pugilist has the slanted, drooping brows that bespeak torn nerves. Also, the forehead is piled with scar tissue. As may be expected, the pugilist has the musculature of a fighter. His neck and trapezius muscles are well developed. His shoulders are enormous; his chest is thick and flat, without the bulging pectorals of the bodybuilder. His back, oblique, and abdominal muscles are highly pronounced, and he has that greatest asset of the modern boxer—sturdy legs. The arms are large, particularly the forearms, which are reinforced with the leather wrappings of the cestus. It is the body of a small heavyweight—lithe rather than bulky, but by no means lacking in power: a Jack Johnson or a Dempsey, say. If you see the authentic statue at the Terme Museum, in Rome, you will see that the seated boxer is really not much more than a light heavyweight. People were small in those days. The important thing was that he was perfectly proportioned.

The pugilist is sitting on a rock with his forearms balanced on his thighs. That he is seated and not pacing implies that he has been through all this many times before. It appears that he is conserving his strength. His head is turned as if he were looking over his shoulder—as if someone had just whispered something to him. It is in this that the "art" of the sculpture is conveyed to the viewer. Could it be that someone has just summoned him to the arena? There is a slight look of befuddlement on his face, but there is no trace of fear. There is an air about him that suggests that he is eager to proceed and does not wish to cause anyone any trouble or to create a delay, even though his life will soon be on the line. Besides the deformities on his noble face, there is also the suggestion of weariness and philosophical resignation. *All the world's a stage, and all the men and women merely players*. Exactly! He knew this more than two thousand years before Shakespeare penned the line. How did he come to be at this place in space and time? Would he rather be safely removed to the countryside—an obscure, stinking peasant shoving a plow behind a mule? Would that be better? Or does he revel in his role? Perhaps he once did, but surely not now. Is this the great Theogenes or merely a journeyman fighter, a former slave or criminal bought by one of the many contractors who for months trained the condemned for their brief moment in the arena? I wonder if Marcus Aurelius loved the "Pugilist" as I do, and came to study it and to meditate before it?

I cut and ran from that field in Southeast Asia. I've read that Davy Crockett, hero of the American frontier, was cowering under a bed when Santa Anna[5] and his soldiers stormed into the Alamo. What is the truth? Jack Dempsey used to get so scared before his fights that he sometimes wet his pants. But look what he did to Willard and to Luis Firpo, the Wild Bull of the Pampas! It was something close to homicide. What is courage? What is cowardice? The magnificent Roberto Duran gave us "*No más,*" but who had a greater fighting heart than Duran?

I got over that first scare and saw that I was something quite other than that which I had known myself to be. Hey Baby proved only my warm-up act. There was a reservoir of malice, poison, and vicious sadism in my soul, and it poured forth freely in the jungles and rice paddies of Vietnam. I pulled three tours. I wanted some payback for Jorgeson. I grieved for Lance Corporal Hanes. I grieved for myself and what I had lost. I committed unspeakable crimes and got medals for it.

It was only fair that I got a head injury myself. I never got a scratch in Vietnam, but I got tagged in a boxing smoker at Pendleton. Fought a bad-ass light heavyweight from artillery. Nobody would fight this guy. He could box. He had all the moves. But mainly he was a puncher—it was said that he could punch with either hand. It was said that his hand speed was superb. I had finished off at least a half rack of Hamm's before I went in with him and started getting hit with head shots I didn't even see coming. They were right. His hand speed *was* superb.

I was twenty-seven years old, smoked two packs a day, was a borderline alcoholic. I shouldn't have fought him—I knew that—but he had been making noise. A very long time before, I had been the middleweight champion of the First Marine Division. I had been a so-called war hero. I had been a recon Marine. But now I was a garrison Marine and in no kind of shape.

He put me down almost immediately, and when I got up I was terribly afraid. I was tight and I could not breathe. It felt like he was hitting me in the

5. Mexican general and president (1795?–1876).

face with a ball peen hammer. It felt like he was busting light bulbs in my face. Rather than one opponent, I saw three. I was convinced his gloves were loaded, and a wave of self-pity ran through me.

I began to move. He made a mistake by expending a lot of energy trying to put me away quickly. I had no intention of going down again, and I knew I wouldn't. My buddies were watching, and I had to give them a good show. While I was afraid, I was also exhilarated; I had not felt this alive since Vietnam. I began to score with my left jab, and because of this I was able to withstand his bull charges and divert them. I thought he would throw his bolt, but in the beginning he was tireless. I must have hit him with four hundred left jabs. It got so that I could score at will, with either hand, but he would counter, trap me on the ropes, and pound. He was the better puncher and was truly hurting me, but I was scoring, and as the fight went on the momentum shifted and I took over. I staggered him again and again. The Marines at ringside were screaming for me to put him away, but however much I tried, I could not. Although I could barely stand by the end, I was sorry that the fight was over. Who had won? The referee raised my arm in victory, but I think it was pretty much a draw. Judging a prizefight is a very subjective thing.

About an hour after the bout, when the adrenaline had subsided, I realized I had a terrible headache. It kept getting worse, and I rushed out of the N.C.O. Club, where I had gone with my buddies to get loaded.

I stumbled outside, struggling to breathe, and I headed away from the company area toward Sheepshit Hill, one of the many low brown foothills in the vicinity. Like a dog who wants to die alone, so it was with me. Everything got swirly, and I dropped in the bushes.

I was unconscious for nearly an hour, and for the next two weeks I walked around like I was drunk, with double vision. I had constant headaches and seemed to have grown old overnight. My health was gone.

I became a very timid individual. I became introspective. I wondered what had made me act the way I had acted. Why had I killed my fellowmen in war, without any feeling, remorse, or regret? And when the war was over, why did I continue to drink and swagger around and get into fistfights? Why did I like to dish out pain, and why did I take positive delight in the suffering of others? Was I insane? Was it too much testosterone? Women don't do things like that. The rapacious Will to Power lost its hold on me. Suddenly I began to feel sympathetic to the cares and sufferings of all living creatures. You lose your health and you start thinking this way.

Has man become any better since the times of Theogenes? The world is replete with badness. I'm not talking about that old routine where you drag out the Spanish Inquisition, the Holocaust, Joseph Stalin, the Khmer Rouge, etc. It happens in our own back yard. Twentieth-century America is one of the most materially prosperous nations in history. But take a walk through an American prison, a nursing home, the slums where the homeless live in cardboard boxes, a cancer ward. Go to a Vietnam vets' meeting, or an A.A. meeting, or an Overeaters Anonymous meeting. *How hollow and unreal a thing is life, how deceitful are its pleasures, what horrible aspects it possesses*. Is the world not rather like a hell, as Schopenhauer, that clearheaded seer—who has helped me transform my suffering into an object of understanding—was so quick to point out? They called him a pessimist and dismissed him with a word, but it is peace and self-renewal that I have found in his pages.

About a year after my fight with the guy from artillery I started having seizures. I suffered from a form of left-temporal-lobe seizure which is sometimes called Dostoyevski's epilepsy. It's so rare as to be almost unknown. Freud, himself a neurologist, speculated that Dostoyevski was a hysterical epileptic, and that his fits were unrelated to brain damage—psychogenic in origin. Dostoyevski did not have his first attack until the age of twenty-five, when he was imprisoned in Siberia and received fifty lashes after complaining about the food. Freud figured that after Dostoyevski's mock execution, the four years' imprisonment in Siberia, the tormented childhood, the murder of his tyrannical father, etc. & etc.—he had all the earmarks of hysteria, of grave psychological trauma. And Dostoyevski had displayed the trademark features of the psychomotor epileptic long before his first attack. These days physicians insist there is no such thing as the "epileptic personality." I think they say this because they do not want to add to the burden of the epileptic's suffering with an extra stigma. Privately they do believe in these traits. Dostoyevski was nervous and depressed, a tormented hypochondriac, a compulsive writer obsessed with religious and philosophic themes. He was hyperloquacious, raving, etc. & etc. His gambling addiction is well known. By most accounts he was a sick soul.

The peculiar and most distinctive thing about his epilepsy was that in the split second before his fit—in the aura, which is in fact officially a part of the attack—Dostoyevski experienced a sense of felicity, of ecstatic well-being unlike anything an ordinary mortal could hope to imagine. It was the experience of satori. Not the nickel-and-dime satori of Abraham Maslow,[6] but the Supreme. He said that he wouldn't trade ten years of life for this feeling, and I, who have had it, too, would have to agree. I can't explain it, I don't understand it—it becomes slippery and elusive when it gets any distance on you—but I have felt this down to the core of my being. Yes, God exists! But then it slides away and I lose it. I become a doubter. Even Dostoyevski, the fervent Christian, makes an almost airtight case against the possibility of the existence of God in the Grand Inquisitor digression in *The Brothers Karamazov.* It is probably the greatest passage in all of world literature, and it tilts you to the court of the atheist. This is what happens when you approach Him with the intellect.

It is thought that St. Paul had a temporal-lobe fit on the road to Damascus. Paul warns us in First Corinthians that God will confound the intellectuals. It is known that Muhammad composed the Koran after attacks of epilepsy. Black Elk experienced fits before his grand "buffalo" vision. Joan of Arc is thought to have been a left-temporal-lobe epileptic. Each of these in a terrible flash of brain lightning was able to pierce the murky veil of illusion which is spread over all things. Just so did the scales fall from my eyes. It is called the "sacred disease."

But what a price. I rarely leave the house anymore. To avoid falling injuries,

6. U.S. psychologist and author (1908–1970), regarded as the founder of humanistic psychology.

I always wear my old boxer's headgear, and I always carry my mouthpiece. Rather more often than the aura where "every common bush is afire with God," I have the typical epileptic aura, which is that of terror and impending doom. If I can keep my head and think of it, and if there is time, I slip the mouthpiece in and thus avoid biting my tongue. I bit it in half once, and when they sewed it back together it swelled enormously, like a huge red-and-black sausage. I was unable to close my mouth for more than two weeks.

The fits are coming more and more. I'm loaded on Depakene, phenobarbital, Tegretol, Dilantin—the whole shitload. A nurse from the V.A. bought a pair of Staffordshire terriers for me and trained them to watch me as I sleep, in case I have a fit and smother face down in my bedding. What delightful companions these dogs are! One of them, Gloria, is especially intrepid and clever. Inevitably, when I come to I find that the dogs have dragged me into the kitchen, away from blankets and pillows, rugs, and objects that might suffocate me, and that they have turned me on my back. There's Gloria, barking in my face. Isn't this incredible?

My sister brought a neurosurgeon over to my place around Christmas—not some V.A. butcher but a guy from the university hospital. He was a slick dude in a nine-hundred-dollar suit. He came down on me hard, like a used-car salesman. He wants to cauterize a small spot in a nerve bundle in my brain. "It's not a lobotomy, it's a *cingulotomy,*" he said.

Reckless, desperate, last-ditch psychosurgery is still pretty much unthinkable in the conservative medical establishment. That's why he made a personal visit to my place. A house call. Drumming up some action to make himself a name. "See that bottle of Thorazine?" he said. "You can throw that poison away," he said. "All that amitriptyline. That's garbage, you can toss that, too." He said, "Tell me something. How can you take all of that shit and still walk?" He said, "You take enough drugs to drop an elephant."

He wants to cut me. He said that the feelings of guilt and worthlessness, and the heaviness of a heart blackened by sin, will go away. "It is *not* a lobotomy," he said.

I don't like the guy. I don't trust him. I'm not convinced, but I can't go on like this. If I am not having a panic attack I am engulfed in tedious, unrelenting depression. I am overcome with a deadening sense of languor; I can't *do* anything. I wanted to give my buddies a good show! What a goddam fool. I am a goddam fool!

It has taken me six months to put my thoughts in order, but I wanted to do it in case I am a vegetable after the operation. I know that my buddy Jorgeson was a real American hero. I wish that he had lived to be something else, if not a painter of pictures then even some kind of fuckup with a factory job and four divorces, bankruptcy petitions, in and out of jail. I wish he had been that. I wish he had been *anything* rather than a real American hero. So, then, if I am to feel somewhat *indifferent* to life after the operation, all the better. If not, not.

If I had a more conventional sense of morality I would shitcan those dress blues, and I'd send that Navy Cross to Jorgeson's brother. Jorgeson was the one who won it, who pulled the John Wayne number up there near Khe Sanh and saved my life, although I lied and took the credit for all of those dead N.V.A. He had created a stunning body count—nothing like Theogenes, but Jorgeson only had something like twelve minutes total in the theater of war.

The high command almost awarded me the Medal of Honor, but of course there were no witnesses to what I claimed I had done, and I had saved no one's life. When I think back on it, my tale probably did not sound as credible as I thought it had at the time. I was only nineteen years old and not all that practiced a liar. I figure if they *had* given me the Medal of Honor, I would have stood in the ring up at Camp Las Pulgas in Pendleton and let that light heavyweight from artillery fucking kill me.

Now I'm thinking I might call Hey Baby and ask how he's doing. No shit, a couple of neuropsyches—we probably have a lot in common. I could apologize to him. But I learned from my fits that you don't have to do that. Good and evil are only illusions. Still, I cannot help but wonder sometimes if my vision of the Supreme Reality was any more real than the demons visited upon schizophrenics and madmen. Has it all been just a stupid neurochemical event? Is there no God at all? The human heart rebels against this.

If they fuck up the operation, I hope I get to keep my dogs somehow—maybe stay at my sister's place. If they send me to the nuthouse I lose the dogs for sure.

# James Joyce

*Joyce (1882–1941) was born in Dublin; and though he fled the narrowness of Catholic Ireland for the broader cultural horizons of Europe, the Dublin of his experience and imagination was the setting for all his major work. In 1904 he went to live permanently on the Continent, supporting himself—badly—by teaching in language schools in Trieste and Zurich. The fear of censorship, coupled with the timidity of his publisher, delayed until 1914 the publication of his short stories in* Dubliners. *Soon after this, however, Joyce came to the attention of the energetic American poet Ezra Pound, who arranged for the first publication of* A Portrait of the Artist as a Young Man *(1916), Joyce's semiautobiographical novel. Pound's support continued through the following years while Joyce was writing what is generally acknowledged as his masterpiece, the novel* Ulysses *(1922). When parts of it began to appear in a literary magazine, it touched off a storm of controversy that brought him both notoriety and lasting fame. On the one hand, this work experimented more boldly with language and devices of narration, including use of the stream of consciousness, than any work in English that preceded it. On the other, some of the sexual passages were so candid that censors banned it from the United States until 1933. Joyce continued to explore the resources of language in his years of fame, these experiments reaching their height in* Finnegans Wake *(1939).*

## Araby

North Richmond Street, being blind, was a quiet street except at the hour when the Christian Brothers' School set the boys free. An uninhabited house of two storeys stood at the blind end, detached from its neighbours in a square ground. The other houses of the street, conscious of decent lives within them, gazed at one another with brown imperturbable faces.

The former tenant of our house, a priest, had died in the back drawing-room. Air, musty from having been long enclosed, hung in all the rooms, and the waste room behind the kitchen was littered with old useless papers. Among these I found a few paper-covered books, the pages of which were curled and damp: *The Abbot*, by Walter Scott, *The Devout Communicant* and *The Memoirs of Vidocq*. I liked the last best because its leaves were yellow. The wild garden behind the house contained a central apple-tree and a few straggling bushes under one of which I found the late tenant's rusty bicycle-pump. He had been a very charitable priest; in his will he had left all his money to institutions and the furniture of his house to his sister.

When the short days of winter came dusk fell before we had well eaten our dinners. When we met in the street the houses had grown sombre. The space of sky above us was the colour of ever-changing violet and towards it the lamps of the street lifted their feeble lanterns. The cold air stung us and we played till our bodies glowed. Our shouts echoed in the silent street. The career of our play brought us through the dark muddy lanes behind the houses where we ran the gantlet of the rough tribes from the cottages, to the back doors of the dark dripping gardens where odours arose from the ashpits, to the dark odorous stables where a coachman smoothed and combed the horse or shook music from the buckled harness. When we returned to the street light from the kitchen windows had filled the areas. If my uncle was seen turning the corner we hid in the shadow until we had seen him safely housed. Or if Mangan's sister came out on the doorstep to call her brother in to his tea we watched her from our shadow peer up and down the street. We waited to see whether she would remain or go in and, if she remained, we left our shadow and walked up to Mangan's steps resignedly. She was waiting for us, her figure defined by the light from the half-opened door. Her brother always teased her before he obeyed and I stood by the railings looking at her. Her dress swung as she moved her body and the soft rope of her hair tossed from side to side.

Every morning I lay on the floor in the front parlour watching her door. The blind was pulled down to within an inch of the sash so that I could not be seen. When she came out on the doorstep my heart leaped. I ran to the hall, seized my books and followed her. I kept her brown figure always in my eye and, when we came near the point at which our ways diverged, I quickened my pace and passed her. This happened morning after morning. I had never spoken to her, except for a few casual words, and yet her name was like a summons to all my foolish blood.

Her image accompanied me even in places the most hostile to romance. On Saturday evenings when my aunt went marketing I had to go to carry some of the parcels. We walked through the flaring streets, jostled by drunken men and bargaining women, amid the curses of labourers, the shrill litanies of shop-boys who stood on guard by the barrels of pigs' cheeks, the nasal chanting of street-singers, who sang a *come-all-you* about O'Donovan Rossa,[1] or a ballad about the troubles in our native land. These noises converged in a single sensation of life for me: I imagined that I bore my chalice safely through a throng of foes. Her name sprang to my lips at moments in strange prayers and praises which I myself did not understand. My eyes were often full of tears (I could not tell why) and at times a flood from my heart seemed to pour itself out into my bosom. I thought little of the future. I did not know whether I would ever speak to her or not or, if I spoke to her, how I could tell her of my confused adoration. But my body was like a harp and her words and gestures were like fingers running upon the wires.

One evening I went into the back drawing-room in which the priest had died. It was a dark rainy evening and there was no sound in the house. Through one of the broken panes I heard the rain impinge upon the earth, the fine

1. Jeremiah O'Donovan ("Dynamite Rossa") (1831–1915), an Irish nationalist banished to the United States in 1870 for revolutionary activities. "Come-all-you": any popular song beginning "Come all you Irishmen."

incessant needles of water playing in the sodden beds. Some distant lamp or lighted window gleamed below me. I was thankful that I could see so little. All my senses seemed to desire to veil themselves and, feeling that I was about to slip from them, I pressed the palms of my hands together until they trembled, murmuring: *O love! O love!* many times.

At last she spoke to me. When she addressed the first words to me I was so confused that I did not know what to answer. She asked me was I going to *Araby*.[2] I forget whether I answered yes or no. It would be a splendid bazaar, she said; she would love to go.

—And why can't you? I asked.

While she spoke she turned a silver bracelet round and round her wrist. She could not go, she said, because there would be a retreat[3] that week in her convent. Her brother and two other boys were fighting for their caps and I was alone at the railings. She held one of the spikes, bowing her head towards me. The light from the lamp opposite our door caught the white curve of her neck, lit up her hair that rested there and, falling, lit up the hand upon the railing. It fell over one side of her dress and caught the white border of a petticoat, just visible as she stood at ease.

—It's well for you, she said.

—If I go, I said, I will bring you something.

What innumerable follies laid waste my waking and sleeping thoughts after that evening! I wished to annihilate the tedious intervening days. I chafed against the work of school. At night in my bedroom and by day in the classroom her image came between me and the page I strove to read. The syllables of the word *Araby* were called to me through the silence in which my soul luxuriated and cast an Eastern enchantment over me. I asked for leave to go to the bazaar on Saturday night. My aunt was surprised and hoped it was not some Freemason[4] affair. I answered few questions in class. I watched my master's face pass from amiability to sternness; he hoped I was not beginning to idle. I could not call my wandering thoughts together. I had hardly any patience with the serious work of life which, now that it stood between me and my desire, seemed to me child's play, ugly monotonous child's play.

On Saturday morning I reminded my uncle that I wished to go to the bazaar in the evening. He was fussing at the hallstand, looking for the hat-brush, and answered me curtly:

—Yes, boy, I know.

As he was in the hall I could not go into the front parlour and lie at the window. I left the house in bad humour and walked slowly towards the school. The air was pitilessly raw and already my heart misgave me.

When I came home to dinner my uncle had not yet been home. Still it was early. I sat staring at the clock for some time and, when its ticking began to irritate me, I left the room. I mounted the staircase and gained the upper part of the house. The high cold empty gloomy rooms liberated me and I went from

2. A billboard sign of the time actually reads: "ARABY in DUBLIN Official Catalogue GRAND ORIENTAL FÊTE May 14th to 19th in aid of Jervis St. Hospital. Admission one shilling." 3. A gathering for prayer and meditation in her convent school. 4. The Masonic Order was felt by Catholics to be an enemy of the Church.

room to room singing. From the front window I saw my companions playing below in the street. Their cries reached me weakened and indistinct and, leaning my forehead against the cool glass, I looked over at the dark house where she lived. I may have stood there for an hour, seeing nothing but the brown-clad figure cast by my imagination, touched discreetly by the lamplight at the curved neck, at the hand upon the railings and at the border below the dress.

When I came downstairs again I found Mrs. Mercer sitting at the fire. She was an old garrulous woman, a pawnbroker's widow, who collected used stamps for some pious purpose. I had to endure the gossip of the tea-table. The meal was prolonged beyond an hour and still my uncle did not come. Mrs. Mercer stood up to go: she was sorry she couldn't wait any longer, but it was after eight o'clock and she did not like to be out late, as the night air was bad for her. When she had gone I began to walk up and down the room, clenching my fists. My aunt said:

—I'm afraid you may put off your bazaar for this night of Our Lord.

At nine o'clock I heard my uncle's latchkey in the halldoor. I heard him talking to himself and heard the hallstand rocking when it had received the weight of his overcoat. I could interpret these signs. When he was midway through his dinner I asked him to give me the money to go to the bazaar. He had forgotten.

—The people are in bed and after their first sleep now, he said.

I did not smile. My aunt said to him energetically:

—Can't you give him the money and let him go? You've kept him late enough as it is.

My uncle said he was very sorry he had forgotten. He said he believed in the old saying: *All work and no play makes Jack a dull boy*. He asked me where I was going and, when I had told him a second time he asked me did I know *The Arab's Farewell to his Steed*.[5] When I left the kitchen he was about to recite the opening lines of the piece to my aunt.

I held a florin tightly in my hand as I strode down Buckingham Street towards the station. The sight of the streets thronged with buyers and glaring with gas recalled to me the purpose of my journey. I took my seat in a third-class carriage of a deserted train. After an intolerable delay the train moved out of the station slowly. It crept onward among ruinous houses and over the twinkling river. At Westland Row Station a crowd of people pressed to the carriage doors; but the porters moved them back, saying that it was a special train for the bazaar. I remained alone in the bare carriage. In a few minutes the train drew up beside an improvised wooden platform. I passed out on to the road and saw by the lighted dial of a clock that it was ten minutes to ten. In front of me was a large building which displayed the magical name.

I could not find any sixpenny entrance and, fearing that the bazaar would be closed, I passed in quickly through a turnstile, handing a shilling to a weary-looking man. I found myself in a big hall girdled at half its height by a gallery. Nearly all the stalls were closed and the greater part of the hall was in darkness.

5. Sentimental poem by Caroline Norton (1808–1877). The Arab imagines his heartbreak after selling his favorite horse.

I recognised a silence like that which pervades a church after a service. I walked into the centre of the bazaar timidly. A few people were gathered about the stalls which were still open. Before a curtain, over which the words *Café Chantant*[6] were written in coloured lamps, two men were counting money on a salver. I listened to the fall of the coins.

Remembering with difficulty why I had come I went over to one of the stalls and examined porcelain vases and flowered tea-sets. At the door of the stall a young lady was talking and laughing with two young gentlemen. I remarked their English accents and listened vaguely to their conversation.

—O, I never said such a thing!

—O, but you did!

—O, but I didn't!

—Didn't she say that?

—Yes. I heard her.

—O, there's a . . . fib!

Observing me the young lady came over and asked me did I wish to buy anything. The tone of her voice was not encouraging; she seemed to have spoken to me out of a sense of duty. I looked humbly at the great jars that stood like eastern guards at either side of the dark entrance to the stall and murmured:

—No, thank you.

The young lady changed the position of one of the vases and went back to the two young men. They began to talk of the same subject. Once or twice the young lady glanced at me over her shoulder.

I lingered before her stall, though I knew my stay was useless, to make my interest in her wares seem the more real. Then I turned away slowly and walked down the middle of the bazaar. I allowed the two pennies to fall against the sixpence in my pocket. I heard a voice call from one end of the gallery that the light was out. The upper part of the hall was now completely dark.

Gazing up into the darkness I saw myself as a creature driven and derided by vanity; and my eyes burned with anguish and anger.

# A Little Cloud

Eight years before he had seen his friend off at the North Wall[1] and wished him godspeed. Gallaher had got on. You could tell that at once by his travelled air, his well-cut tweed suit and fearless accent. Few fellows had talents like his and fewer still could remain unspoiled by such success. Gallaher's heart was in the right place and he had deserved to win. It was something to have a friend like that.

Little Chandler's thoughts ever since lunch-time had been of his meeting with Gallaher, of Gallaher's invitation and of the great city London where Gal-

6. Café offering musical entertainment. 1. Cluster of docks and railway stations in Dublin.

laher lived. He was called Little Chandler because, though he was but slightly under the average stature, he gave one the idea of being a little man. His hands were white and small, his frame was fragile, his voice was quiet and his manners were refined. He took the greatest care of his fair silken hair and moustache and used perfume discreetly on his handkerchief. The half-moons of his nails were perfect and when he smiled you caught a glimpse of a row of childish white teeth.

As he sat at his desk in the King's Inns[2] he thought what changes those eight years had brought. The friend whom he had known under a shabby and necessitous guise had become a brilliant figure on the London Press. He turned often from his tiresome writing to gaze out of the office window. The glow of a late autumn sunset covered the grass plots and walks. It cast a shower of kindly golden dust on the untidy nurses and decrepit old men who drowsed on the benches; it flickered upon all the moving figures—on the children who ran screaming along the gravel paths and on everyone who passed through the gardens. He watched the scene and thought of life; and (as always happened when he thought of life) he became sad. A gentle melancholy took possession of him. He felt how useless it was to struggle against fortune, this being the burden of wisdom which the ages had bequeathed to him.

He remembered the books of poetry upon his shelves at home. He had bought them in his bachelor days and many an evening, as he sat in the little room off the hall, he had been tempted to take one down from the bookshelf and read out something to his wife. But shyness had always held him back; and so the books had remained on their shelves. At times he repeated lines to himself and this consoled him.

When his hour had struck he stood up and took leave of his desk and of his fellow-clerks punctiliously. He emerged from under the feudal arch of the King's Inns, a neat modest figure, and walked swiftly down Henrietta Street. The golden sunset was waning and the air had grown sharp. A horde of grimy children populated the street. They stood or ran in the roadway or crawled up the steps before the gaping doors or squatted like mice upon the thresholds. Little Chandler gave them no thought. He picked his way deftly through all that minute vermin-like life and under the shadow of the gaunt spectral mansions in which the old nobility of Dublin had roistered. No memory of the past touched him, for his mind was full of a present joy.

He had never been in Corless's but he knew the value of the name. He knew that people went there after the theatre to eat oysters and drink liqueurs; and he had heard that the waiters there spoke French and German. Walking swiftly by at night he had seen cabs drawn up before the door and richly dressed ladies, escorted by cavaliers, alight and enter quickly. They wore noisy dresses and many wraps. Their faces were powdered and they caught up their dresses, when they touched earth, like alarmed Atalantas.[3] He had always passed without turning his head to look. It was his habit to walk swiftly in the street even by day and whenever he found himself in the city late at night he hurried on his way apprehensively and excitedly. Sometimes, however, he courted the causes

2. Offices and residences for lawyers comparable to London's Inns of Court. 3. Atalanta was a virgin huntress of classic mythology, who promised to marry the first man who could beat her in a footrace.

of his fear. He chose the darkest and narrowest streets and, as he walked boldly forward, the silence that was spread about his footsteps troubled him, the wandering silent figures troubled him; and at times a sound of low fugitive laughter made him tremble like a leaf.

He turned to the right towards Capel Street. Ignatius Gallaher on the London Press! Who would have thought it possible eight years before? Still, now that he reviewed the past, Little Chandler could remember many signs of future greatness in his friend. People used to say that Ignatius Gallaher was wild. Of course, he did mix with a rakish set of fellows at that time, drank freely and borrowed money on all sides. In the end he had got mixed up in some shady affair, some money transaction: at least, that was one version of his flight. But nobody denied him talent. There was always a certain . . . something in Ignatius Gallaher that impressed you in spite of yourself. Even when he was out at elbows and at his wits' end for money he kept up a bold face. Little Chandler remembered (and the remembrance brought a slight flush of pride to his cheek) one of Ignatius Gallaher's sayings when he was in a tight corner:

—Half time, now, boys, he used to say lightheartedly. Where's my considering cap?

That was Ignatius Gallaher all out, and, damn it, you couldn't but admire him for it.

Little Chandler quickened his pace. For the first time in his life he felt himself superior to the people he passed. For the first time his soul revolted against the dull inelegance of Capel Street. There was no doubt about it: if you wanted to succeed you had to go away. You could do nothing in Dublin. As he crossed Grattan Bridge he looked down the river towards the lower quays and pitied the poor stunted houses. They seemed to him a band of tramps, huddled together along the river-banks, their old coats covered with dust and soot, stupefied by the panorama of sunset and waiting for the first chill of night to bid them arise, shake themselves and begone. He wondered whether he could write a poem to express his idea. Perhaps Gallaher might be able to get it into some London paper for him. Could he write something original? He was not sure what idea he wished to express but the thought that a poetic moment had touched him took life within him like an infant hope. He stepped onward bravely.

Every step brought him nearer to London, farther from his own sober inartistic life. A light began to tremble on the horizon of his mind. He was not so old—thirty-two. His temperament might be said to be just at the point of maturity. There were so many different moods and impressions that he wished to express in verse. He felt them within him. He tried to weigh his soul to see if it was a poet's soul. Melancholy was the dominant note of his temperament, he thought, but it was a melancholy tempered by recurrences of faith and resignation and simple joy. If he could give expression to it in a book of poems perhaps men would listen. He would never be popular: he saw that. He could not sway the crowd but he might appeal to a little circle of kindred minds. The English critics, perhaps, would recognise him as one of the Celtic school[4] by

4. Term applied by critics to Irish poets of the turn of the century who drew on Irish legend for their subject matter.

reason of the melancholy tone of his poems; besides that, he would put in allusions. He began to invent sentences and phrases from the notices which his book would get. *Mr. Chandler has the gift of easy and graceful verse. . . . A wistful sadness pervades these poems . . . The Celtic note*. It was a pity his name was not more Irish-looking. Perhaps it would be better to insert his mother's name before the surname: Thomas Malone Chandler, or better still: T. Malone Chandler. He would speak to Gallaher about it.

He pursued his revery so ardently that he passed his street and had to turn back. As he came near Corless's his former agitation began to overmaster him and he halted before the door in indecision. Finally he opened the door and entered.

The light and noise of the bar held him at the doorway for a few moments. He looked about him, but his sight was confused by the shining of many red and green wineglasses. The bar seemed to him to be full of people and he felt that the people were observing him curiously. He glanced quickly to right and left (frowning slightly to make his errand appear serious), but when his sight cleared a little he saw that nobody had turned to look at him: and there, sure enough, was Ignatius Gallaher leaning with his back against the counter and his feet planted far apart.

—Hallo, Tommy, old hero, here you are! What is it to be? What will you have? I'm taking whisky: better stuff than we get across the water. Soda? Lithia?[5] No mineral? I'm the same. Spoils the flavour. . . . Here, *garçon,*[6] bring us two halves of malt whisky, like a good fellow. . . . Well, and how have you been pulling along since I saw you last? Dear God, how old we're getting! Do you see any signs of aging in me—eh, what? A little grey and thin on the top—what?

Ignatius Gallaher took off his hat and displayed a large closely cropped head. His face was heavy, pale and clean-shaven. His eyes, which were of bluish slate-colour, relieved his unhealthy pallor and shone out plainly above the vivid orange tie he wore.[7] Between these rival features the lips appeared very long and shapeless and colourless. He bent his head and felt with two sympathetic fingers the thin hair at the crown. Little Chandler shook his head as a denial. Ignatius Gallaher put on his hat again.

—It pulls you down, he said, Press life. Always hurry and scurry, looking for copy and sometimes not finding it: and then, always to have something new in your stuff. Damn proofs and printers, I say, for a few days. I'm deuced glad, I can tell you, to get back to the old country. Does a fellow good, a bit of a holiday. I feel a ton better since I landed again in dear dirty Dublin. . . . Here you are, Tommy. Water? Say when.

Little Chandler allowed his whisky to be very much diluted.

—You don't know what's good for you, my boy, said Ignatius Gallaher. I drink mine neat.

—I drink very little as a rule, said Little Chandler modestly. An old half-one or so when I meet any of the old crowd: that's all.

5. Mineral Water. 6. Waiter (French). 7. Wearing an orange tie, Gallaher seems to be flaunting his allegiance to England. Orangemen (called after William of Orange, last British conqueror of Ireland) were supporters of Anglo-Irish Protestantism.

—Ah, well, said Ignatius Gallaher, cheerfully, here's to us and to old times and old acquaintance.

They clinked glasses and drank the toast.

—I met some of the old gang to-day, said Ignatius Gallaher. O'Hara seems to be in a bad way. What's he doing?

—Nothing, said Little Chandler. He's gone to the dogs.

—But Hogan has a good sit,[8] hasn't he?

—Yes; he's in the Land Commission.

—I met him one night in London and he seemed to be very flush. . . . Poor O'Hara! Boose, I suppose?

—Other things, too, said Little Chandler shortly.

Ignatius Gallaher laughed.

—Tommy, he said, I see you haven't changed an atom. You're the very same serious person that used to lecture me on Sunday mornings when I had a sore head and a fur on my tongue. You'd want to knock about a bit in the world. Have you never been anywhere, even for a trip?

—I've been to the Isle of Man,[9] said Little Chandler.

Ignatius Gallaher laughed.

—The Isle of Man! he said. Go to London or Paris: Paris, for choice. That'd do you good.

—Have you seen Paris?

—I should think I have! I've knocked about there a little.

—And is it really so beautiful as they say? asked Little Chandler.

He sipped a little of his drink while Ignatius Gallaher finished his boldly.

—Beautiful? said Ignatius Gallaher, pausing on the word and on the flavour of his drink. It's not so beautiful, you know. Of course, it is beautiful. . . . But it's the life of Paris; that's the thing. Ah, there's no city like Paris for gaiety, movement, excitement. . . .

Little Chandler finished his whisky and, after some trouble, succeeded in catching the barman's eye. He ordered the same again.

—I've been to the Moulin Rouge,[1] Ignatius Gallaher continued when the barman had removed their glasses, and I've been to all the Bohemian cafés. Hot stuff! Not for a pious chap like you, Tommy.

Little Chandler said nothing until the barman returned with the two glasses: then he touched his friend's glass lightly and reciprocated the former toast. He was beginning to feel somewhat disillusioned. Gallaher's accent and way of expressing himself did not please him. There was something vulgar in his friend which he had not observed before. But perhaps it was only the result of living in London amid the bustle and competition of the Press. The old personal charm was still there under this new gaudy manner. And, after all, Gallaher had lived, he had seen the world. Little Chandler looked at his friend enviously.

—Everything in Paris is gay, said Ignatius Gallaher. They believe in enjoying life—and don't you think they're right? If you want to enjoy yourself properly you must go to Paris. And, mind you, they've a great feeling for the Irish there. When they heard I was from Ireland they were ready to eat me, man.

8. Situation. 9. In the Irish Sea, not far from Dublin. 1. Famous Parisian dance hall.

Little Chandler took four or five sips from his glass.

—Tell me, he said, is it true that Paris is so . . . immoral as they say?

Ignatius Gallaher made a catholic gesture with his right arm.

—Every place is immoral, he said. Of course you do find spicy bits in Paris. Go to one of the students' balls for instance. That's lively, if you like, when the *cocottes*[2] begin to let themselves loose. You know what they are, I suppose?

—I've heard of them, said Little Chandler.

Ignatius Gallaher drank off his whisky and shook his head.

—Ah, he said, you may say what you like. There's no woman like the Parisienne—for style, for go.

—Then it is an immoral city, said Little Chandler, with timid insistence—I mean, compared with London or Dublin?

—London! said Ignatius Gallaher. It's six of one and half-a-dozen of the other. You ask Hogan, my boy. I showed him a bit about London when he was over there. He'd open your eye. . . . I say, Tommy, don't make punch of that whisky: liquor up.

—No, really. . . .

—O, come on, another one won't do you any harm. What is it? The same again, I suppose?

—Well . . . all right.

—*François,* the same again. . . . Will you smoke, Tommy?

Ignatius Gallaher produced his cigar-case. The two friends lit their cigars and puffed at them in silence until their drinks were served.

—I'll tell you my opinion, said Ignatius Gallaher, emerging after some time from the clouds of smoke in which he had taken refuge, it's a rum world. Talk of immorality! I've heard of cases—what am I saying?—I've known them: cases of . . . immorality. . . .

Ignatius Gallaher puffed thoughtfully at his cigar and then, in a calm historian's tone, he proceeded to sketch for his friend some pictures of the corruption which was rife abroad. He summarised the vices of many capitals and seemed inclined to award the palm to Berlin. Some things he could not vouch for (his friends had told him), but of others he had had personal experience. He spared neither rank nor caste. He revealed many of the secrets of religious houses on the Continent and described some of the practices which were fashionable in high society and ended by telling, with details, a story about an English duchess—a story which he knew to be true. Little Chandler was astonished.

—Ah, well, said Ignatius Gallaher, here we are in old jog-along Dublin where nothing is known of such things.

—How dull you must find it, said Little Chandler, after all the other places you've seen!

—Well, said Ignatius Gallaher, it's a relaxation to come over here, you know. And, after all, it's the old country, as they say, isn't it? You can't help having a certain feeling for it. That's human nature. . . . But tell me something about yourself. Hogan told me you had . . . tasted the joys of connubial bliss. Two years ago, wasn't it?

2. Prostitutes (French).

Little Chandler blushed and smiled.

—Yes, he said. I was married last May twelve months.

—I hope it's not too late in the day to offer my best wishes, said Ignatius Gallaher. I didn't know your address or I'd have done so at the time.

He extended his hand, which Little Chandler took.

—Well, Tommy, he said, I wish you and yours every joy in life, old chap, and tons of money, and may you never die till I shoot you. And that's the wish of a sincere friend, an old friend. You know that?

—I know that, said Little Chandler.

—Any youngsters? said Ignatius Gallaher.

Little Chandler blushed again.

—We have one child, he said.

—Son or daughter?

—A little boy.

Ignatius Gallaher slapped his friend sonorously on the back.

—Bravo, he said, I wouldn't doubt you, Tommy.

Little Chandler smiled, looked confusedly at his glass and bit his lower lip with three childishly white front teeth.

—I hope you'll spend an evening with us, he said, before you go back. My wife will be delighted to meet you. We can have a little music and—

—Thanks awfully, old chap, said Ignatius Gallaher, I'm sorry we didn't meet earlier. But I must leave tomorrow night.

—To-night, perhaps . . . ?

—I'm awfully sorry, old man. You see I'm over here with another fellow, clever young chap he is too, and we arranged to go to a little card-party. Only for that . . .

—O, in that case. . . .

—But who knows? said Ignatius Gallaher considerately. Next year I may take a little skip over here now that I've broken the ice. It's only a pleasure deferred.

—Very well, said Little Chandler, the next time you come we must have an evening together. That's agreed now, isn't it?

—Yes, that's agreed, said Ignatius Gallaher. Next year if I come, *parole d'honneur.*[3]

—And to clinch the bargain, said Little Chandler, we'll just have one more now.

Ignatius Gallaher took out a large gold watch and looked at it.

—Is it to be the last? he said. Because you know, I have an a.p.[4]

—O, yes, positively, said Little Chandler.

—Very well, then, said Ignatius Gallaher, let us have another one as a *deoc an doruis*[5]—that's good vernacular for a small whisky, I believe.

Little Chandler ordered the drinks. The blush which had risen to his face a few moments before was establishing itself. A trifle made him blush at any time: and now he felt warm and excited. Three small whiskies had gone to his head and Gallaher's strong cigar had confused his mind, for he was a delicate and abstinent person. The adventure of meeting Gallaher after eight years, of

3. My word of honor (French). 4. Author's proof, i.e., trial printing that Gallaher, as journalist, would have to correct before sending it to press. 5. A door drink (Gaelic, literal trans.); a drink as one departs.

finding himself with Gallaher in Corless's surrounded by lights and noise, of listening to Gallaher's stories and of sharing for a brief space Gallaher's vagrant and triumphant life, upset the equipoise of his sensitive nature. He felt acutely the contrast between his own life and his friend's, and it seemed to him unjust. Gallaher was his inferior in birth and education. He was sure that he could do something better than his friend had ever done, or could ever do, something higher than mere tawdry journalism if he only got the chance. What was it that stood in his way? His unfortunate timidity! He wished to vindicate himself in some way, to assert his manhood. He saw behind Gallaher's refusal of his invitation. Gallaher was only patronising him by his friendliness just as he was patronising Ireland by his visit.

The barman brought their drinks. Little Chandler pushed one glass towards his friend and took up the other boldly.

—Who knows? he said, as they lifted their glasses. When you come next year I may have the pleasure of wishing long life and happiness to Mr. and Mrs. Ignatius Gallaher.

Ignatius Gallaher in the act of drinking closed one eye expressively over the rim of his glass. When he had drunk he smacked his lips decisively, set down his glass and said:

—No blooming fear of that, my boy. I'm going to have my fling first and see a bit of life and the world before I put my head in the sack—if I ever do.

—Some day you will, said Little Chandler calmly.

Ignatius Gallaher turned his orange tie and slate-blue eyes full upon his friend.

—You think so? he said.

—You'll put your head in the sack, repeated Little Chandler stoutly, like everyone else if you can find the girl.

He had slightly emphasised his tone and he was aware that he had betrayed himself; but, though the colour had heightened in his cheek, he did not flinch from his friend's gaze. Ignatius Gallaher watched him for a few moments and then said:

—If ever it occurs, you may bet your bottom dollar there'll be no mooning and spooning about it. I mean to marry money. She'll have a good fat account at the bank or she won't do for me.

Little Chandler shook his head.

—Why, man alive, said Ignatius Gallaher, vehemently, do you know what it is? I've only to say the word and tomorrow I can have the woman and the cash. You don't believe it? Well, I know it. There are hundreds—what am I saying?—thousands of rich Germans and Jews, rotten with money, that'd only be too glad. . . . You wait a while, my boy. See if I don't play my cards properly. When I go about a thing I mean business, I tell you. You just wait.

He tossed his glass to his mouth, finished his drink and laughed loudly. Then he looked thoughtfully before him and said in a calmer tone:

—But I'm in no hurry. They can wait. I don't fancy tying myself up to one woman, you know.

He imitated with his mouth the act of tasting and made a wry face.

—Must get a bit stale, I should think, he said.

• • • • • • • • • • •

Little Chandler sat in the room off the hall, holding a child in his arms. To save money they kept no servant but Annie's young sister Monica came for an hour or so in the morning and an hour or so in the evening to help. But Monica had gone home long ago. It was a quarter to nine. Little Chandler had come home late for tea and, moreover, he had forgotten to bring Annie home the parcel of coffee from Bewley's. Of course she was in a bad humour and gave him short answers. She said she would do without any tea but when it came near the time at which the shop at the corner closed she decided to go out herself for a quarter of a pound of tea and two pounds of sugar. She put the sleeping child deftly in his arms and said:

—Here. Don't waken him.

A little lamp with a white china shade stood upon the table and its light fell over a photograph which was enclosed in a frame of crumpled horn. It was Annie's photograph. Little Chandler looked at it, pausing at the thin tight lips. She wore the pale blue summer blouse which he had brought her home as a present one Saturday. It had cost him ten and elevenpence; but what an agony of nervousness it had cost him! How he had suffered that day, waiting at the shop door until the shop was empty, standing at the counter and trying to appear at his ease while the girl piled ladies' blouses before him, paying at the desk and forgetting to take up the odd penny of his change, being called back by the cashier, and, finally, striving to hide his blushes as he left the shop by examining the parcel to see if it was securely tied. When he brought the blouse home Annie kissed him and said it was very pretty and stylish; but when she heard the price she threw the blouse on the table and said it was a regular swindle to charge ten and elevenpence for that. At first she wanted to take it back but when she tried it on she was delighted with it, especially with the make of the sleeves, and kissed him and said he was very good to think of her.

Hm! . . .

He looked coldly into the eyes of the photograph and they answered coldly. Certainly they were pretty and the face itself was pretty. But he found something mean in it. Why was it so unconscious and lady-like? The composure of the eyes irritated him. They repelled him and defied him: there was no passion in them, no rapture. He thought of what Gallaher had said about rich Jewesses. Those dark Oriental eyes, he thought, how full they are of passion, of voluptuous longing! . . . Why had he married the eyes in the photograph?

He caught himself up at the question and glanced nervously round the room. He found something mean in the pretty furniture which he had bought for his house on the hire system.[6] Annie had chosen it herself and it reminded him of her. It too was prim and pretty. A dull resentment against his life awoke within him. Could he not escape from his little house? Was it too late for him to try to live bravely like Gallaher? Could he go to London? There was the furniture still to be paid for. If he could only write a book and get it published, that might open the way for him.

6. The installment plan.

A volume of Byron's[7] poems lay before him on the table. He opened it cautiously with his left hand lest he should waken the child and began to read the first poem in the book:

*Hushed are the winds and still the evening gloom,*
*Not e'en a Zephyr wanders through the grove,*
*Whilst I return to view my Margaret's tomb*
*And scatter flowers on the dust I love.*

He paused. He felt the rhythm of the verse about him in the room. How melancholy it was! Could he, too, write like that, express the melancholy of his soul in verse? There were so many things he wanted to describe: his sensation of a few hours before on Grattan Bridge, for example. If he could get back again into that mood. . .

The child awoke and began to cry. He turned from the page and tried to hush it: but it would not be hushed. He began to rock it to and fro in his arms but its wailing cry grew keener. He rocked it faster while his eyes began to read the second stanza:

*Within this narrow cell reclines her clay,*
*That clay where once . . .*

It was useless. He couldn't read. He couldn't do anything. The wailing of the child pierced the drum of his ear. It was useless, useless! He was a prisoner for life. His arms trembled with anger and suddenly bending to the child's face he shouted:

—Stop!

The child stopped for an instant, had a spasm of fright and began to scream. He jumped up from his chair and walked hastily up and down the room with the child in his arms. It began to sob piteously, losing its breath for four or five seconds, and then bursting out anew. The thin walls of the room echoed the sound. He tried to soothe it but it sobbed more convulsively. He looked at the contracted and quivering face of the child and began to be alarmed. He counted seven sobs without a break between them and caught the child to his breast in fright. If it died! . . .

The door was burst open and a young woman ran in, panting.

—What is it? What is it? she cried.

The child, hearing its mother's voice, broke out into a paroxysm of sobbing.

—It's nothing, Annie . . . it's nothing. . . . He began to cry . . .

She flung her parcels on the floor and snatched the child from him.

—What have you done to him? she cried, glaring into his face.

Little Chandler sustained for one moment the gaze of her eyes and his heart closed together as he met the hatred in them. He began to stammer:

7. George Gordon, Lord Byron (1788–1824), English Romantic poet. The stanza is from Byron's *On the Death of a Young Lady*.

—It's nothing. . . . He . . . he began to cry. . . . I couldn't . . . I didn't do anything. . . . What?

Giving no heed to him she began to walk up and down the room, clasping the child tightly in her arms and murmuring:

—My little man! My little mannie! Was 'ou frightened, love? . . . There now, love! There now! . . . Lambabaun! Mamma's little lamb of the world! . . . There now!

Little Chandler felt his cheeks suffused with shame and he stood back out of the lamplight. He listened while the paroxysm of the child's sobbing grew less and less; and tears of remorse started to his eyes.

# The Dead

Lily, the caretaker's daughter, was literally run off her feet. Hardly had she brought one gentleman into the little pantry behind the office on the ground floor and helped him off with his overcoat than the wheezy hall-door bell clanged again and she had to scamper along the bare hallway to let in another guest. It was well for her she had not to attend to the ladies also. But Miss Kate and Miss Julia had thought of that and had converted the bathroom upstairs into a ladies' dressing-room. Miss Kate and Miss Julia were there, gossiping and laughing and fussing, walking after each other to the head of the stairs, peering down over the banisters and calling down to Lily to ask her who had come.

It was always a great affair, the Misses Morkan's annual dance. Everybody who knew them came to it, members of the family, old friends of the family, the members of Julia's choir, any of Kate's pupils that were grown up enough and even some of Mary Jane's pupils too. Never once had it fallen flat. For years and years it had gone off in splendid style as long as anyone could remember; ever since Kate and Julia, after the death of their brother Pat, had left the house in Stoney Batter and taken Mary Jane, their only niece, to live with them in the dark gaunt house on Usher's Island, the upper part of which they had rented from Mr. Fulham, the cornfactor[1] on the ground floor. That was a good thirty years ago if it was a day. Mary Jane, who was then a little girl in short clothes, was now the main prop of the household for she had the organ in Haddington Road. She had been through the Academy and gave a pupils' concert every year in the upper room of the Antient Concert Rooms.[2] Many of her pupils belonged to better-class families on the Kingstown and Dalkey line. Old as they were, her aunts also did their share. Julia, though she was quite grey, was still the leading soprano in Adam and Eve's,[3] and Kate, being too feeble to go about much, gave music lessons to beginners on the old square piano in

1. Agent or broker dealing in grain. 2. A building in which rooms could be rented for musical or dramatic productions. "The Academy": the Royal Academy of Music. 3. A Dublin church.

the back room. Lily, the caretaker's daughter, did housemaid's work for them. Though their life was modest they believed in eating well; the best of everything: diamond-bone sirloins, three-shilling tea and the best bottled stout. But Lily seldom made a mistake in the orders so that she got on well with her three mistresses. They were fussy, that was all. But the only thing they would not stand was back answers.

Of course they had good reason to be fussy on such a night. And then it was long after ten o'clock and yet there was no sign of Gabriel and his wife. Besides they were dreadfully afraid that Freddy Malins might turn up screwed.[4] They would not wish for worlds that any of Mary Jane's pupils should see him under the influence; and when he was like that it was sometimes very hard to manage him. Freddy Malins always came late but they wondered what could be keeping Gabriel: and that was what brought them every two minutes to the banisters to ask Lily had Gabriel or Freddy come.

—O, Mr. Conroy, said Lily to Gabriel when she opened the door for him, Miss Kate and Miss Julia thought you were never coming. Good-night, Mrs. Conroy.

—I'll engage they did, said Gabriel, but they forget that my wife here takes three mortal hours to dress herself.

He stood on the mat, scraping the snow from his goloshes, while Lily led his wife to the foot of the stairs and called out:

—Miss Kate, here's Mrs. Conroy.

Kate and Julia came toddling down the dark stairs at once. Both of them kissed Gabriel's wife, said she must be perished alive and asked was Gabriel with her.

—Here I am as right as the mail, Aunt Kate! Go on up. I'll follow, called out Gabriel from the dark.

He continued scraping his feet vigorously while the three women went upstairs, laughing, to the ladies' dressing-room. A light fringe of snow lay like a cape on the shoulders of his overcoat and like toecaps on the toes of his goloshes; and, as the buttons of his overcoat slipped with a squeaking noise through the snow-stiffened frieze, a cold fragrant air from out-of-doors escaped from crevices and folds.

—Is it snowing again, Mr. Conroy? asked Lily.

She had preceded him into the pantry to help him off with his overcoat. Gabriel smiled at the three syllables she had given his surname and glanced at her. She was a slim, growing girl, pale in complexion and with hay-coloured hair. The gas in the pantry made her look still paler. Gabriel had known her when she was a child and used to sit on the lowest step nursing a rag doll.

—Yes, Lily, he answered, and I think we're in for a night of it.

He looked up at the pantry ceiling, which was shaking with the stamping and shuffling of feet on the floor above, listened for a moment to the piano and then glanced at the girl, who was folding his overcoat carefully at the end of a shelf.

—Tell me, Lily, he said in a friendly tone, do you still go to school?

4. Drunk.

—O no, sir, she answered. I'm done schooling this year and more.

—O, then, said Gabriel gaily, I suppose we'll be going to your wedding one of these fine days with your young man, eh?

The girl glanced back at him over her shoulder and said with great bitterness:

—The men that is now is only all palaver and what they can get out of you.

Gabriel coloured as if he felt he had made a mistake and, without looking at her, kicked off his goloshes and flicked actively with his muffler at his patent-leather shoes.

He was a stout tallish young man. The high colour of his cheeks pushed upwards even to his forehead where it scattered itself in a few formless patches of pale red; and on his hairless face there scintillated restlessly the polished lenses and the bright gilt rims of the glasses which screened his delicate and restless eyes. His glossy black hair was parted in the middle and brushed in a long curve behind his ears where it curled slightly beneath the groove left by his hat.

When he had flicked lustre into his shoes he stood up and pulled his waistcoat down more tightly on his plump body. Then he took a coin rapidly from his pocket.

—O Lily, he said, thrusting it into her hands, it's Christmas-time, isn't it? Just . . . here's a little. . . .

He walked rapidly towards the door.

—O no, sir! cried the girl, following him. Really, sir, I wouldn't take it.

—Christmas-time! Christmas-time! said Gabriel, almost trotting to the stairs and waving his hand to her in deprecation.

The girl, seeing that he had gained the stairs, called out after him:

—Well, thank you, sir.

He waited outside the drawing-room door until the waltz should finish, listening to the skirts that swept against it and to the shuffling of feet. He was still discomposed by the girl's bitter and sudden retort. It had cast a gloom over him which he tried to dispel by arranging his cuffs and the bows of his tie. Then he took from his waistcoat pocket a little paper and glanced at the headings he had made for his speech. He was undecided about the lines from Robert Browning[5] for he feared they would be above the heads of his hearers. Some quotation that they could recognise from Shakespeare or from the Melodies[6] would be better. The indelicate clacking of the men's heels and the shuffling of their soles reminded him that their grade of culture differed from his. He would only make himself ridiculous by quoting poetry to them which they could not understand. They would think that he was airing his superior education. He would fail with them just as he had failed with the girl in the pantry. He had taken up a wrong tone. His whole speech was a mistake from first to last, an utter failure.

Just then his aunts and his wife came out of the ladies' dressing-room. His aunts were two small plainly dressed old women. Aunt Julia was an inch or so the taller. Her hair, drawn low over the tops of her ears, was grey; and grey

5. English poet (1812–1889). 6. The *Irish Melodies* by Thomas Moore (1779–1852), Irish poet.

also, with darker shadows, was her large flaccid face. Though she was stout in build and stood erect her slow eyes and parted lips gave her the appearance of a woman who did not know where she was or where she was going. Aunt Kate was more vivacious. Her face, healthier than her sister's, was all puckers and creases, like a shrivelled red apple, and her hair, braided in the same old-fashioned way, had not lost its ripe nut colour.

They both kissed Gabriel frankly. He was their favourite nephew, the son of their dead elder sister, Ellen, who had married T. J. Conroy of the Port and Docks.[7]

—Gretta tells me you're not going to take a cab back to Monkstown to-night, Gabriel, said Aunt Kate.

—No, said Gabriel, turning to his wife, we had quite enough of that last year, hadn't we? Don't you remember, Aunt Kate, what a cold Gretta got out of it? Cab windows rattling all the way, and the east wind blowing in after we passed Merrion. Very jolly it was. Gretta caught a dreadful cold.

Aunt Kate frowned severely and nodded her head at every word.

—Quite right, Gabriel, quite right, she said. You can't be too careful.

—But as for Gretta there, said Gabriel, she'd walk home in the snow if she were let.

Mrs. Conroy laughed.

—Don't mind him, Aunt Kate, she said. He's really an awful bother, what with green shades for Tom's eyes at night and making him do the dumb-bells, and forcing Eva to eat the stirabout.[8] The poor child! And she simply hates the sight of it! . . . O, but you'll never guess what he makes me wear now!

She broke out into a peal of laughter and glanced at her husband, whose admiring and happy eyes had been wandering from her dress to her face and hair. The two aunts laughed heartily too, for Gabriel's solicitude was a standing joke with them.

—Goloshes! said Mrs. Conroy. That's the latest. Whenever it's wet under-foot I must put on my goloshes. To-night even he wanted me to put them on, but I wouldn't. The next thing he'll buy me will be a diving suit.

Gabriel laughed nervously and patted his tie reassuringly while Aunt Kate nearly doubled herself, so heartily did she enjoy the joke. The smile soon faded from Aunt Julia's face and her mirthless eyes were directed towards her nephew's face. After a pause she asked:

—And what are goloshes, Gabriel?

—Goloshes, Julia! exclaimed her sister. Goodness me, don't you know what goloshes are? You wear them over your . . . over your boots, Gretta, isn't it?

—Yes, said Mrs. Conroy. Guttapercha[9] things. We both have a pair now. Gabriel says everyone wears them on the continent.

—O, on the continent, murmured Aunt Julia, nodding her head slowly.

Gabriel knitted his brows and said, as if he were slightly angered:

—It's nothing very wonderful but Gretta thinks it very funny because she says the word reminds her of Christy Minstrels.[1]

7. Government bureau. 8. Porridge. 9. Similar to rubber. 1. Well-known nineteenth-century minstrel show organized by Edwin T. Christy.

—But tell me, Gabriel, said Aunt Kate, with brisk tact. Of course, you've seen about the room. Gretta was saying . . .

—O, the room is all right, replied Gabriel. I've taken one in the Gresham.

—To be sure, said Aunt Kate, by far the best thing to do. And the children, Gretta, you're not anxious about them?

—O, for one night, said Mrs. Conroy. Besides, Bessie will look after them.

—To be sure, said Aunt Kate again. What a comfort it is to have a girl like that, one you can depend on! There's that Lily, I'm sure I don't know what has come over her lately. She's not the girl she was at all.

Gabriel was about to ask his aunt some questions on this point but she broke off suddenly to gaze after her sister who had wandered down the stairs and was craning her neck over the banisters.

—Now, I ask you, she said, almost testily, where is Julia going? Julia! Julia! Where are you going?

Julia, who had gone halfway down one flight, came back and announced blandly:

—Here's Freddy.

At the same moment a clapping of hands and a final flourish of the pianist told that the waltz had ended. The drawing-room door was opened from within and some couples came out. Aunt Kate drew Gabriel aside hurriedly and whispered into his ear:

—Slip down, Gabriel, like a good fellow and see if he's all right, and don't let him up if he's screwed. I'm sure he's screwed. I'm sure he is.

Gabriel went to the stairs and listened over the banisters. He could hear two persons talking in the pantry. Then he recognised Freddy Malins' laugh. He went down the stairs noisily.

—It's such a relief, said Aunt Kate to Mrs. Conroy, that Gabriel is here. I always feel easier in my mind when he's here. . . . Julia, there's Miss Daly and Miss Power will take some refreshment. Thanks for your beautiful waltz, Miss Daly. It made lovely time.

A tall wizen-faced man, with a stiff grizzled moustache and swarthy skin, who was passing out with his partner said:

—And may we have some refreshment, too, Miss Morkan?

—Julia, said Aunt Kate summarily, and here's Mr. Browne and Miss Furlong. Take them in, Julia, with Miss Daly and Miss Power.

—I'm the man for the ladies, said Mr. Browne, pursing his lips until his moustache bristled and smiling in all his wrinkles. You know, Miss Morkan, the reason they are so fond of me is—

He did not finish his sentence, but, seeing that Aunt Kate was out of earshot, at once led the three young ladies into the back room. The middle of the room was occupied by two square tables placed end to end, and on these Aunt Julia and the caretaker were straightening and smoothing a large cloth. On the sideboard were arrayed dishes and plates, and glasses and bundles of knives and forks and spoons. The top of the closed square piano served also as a sideboard for viands and sweets. At a smaller sideboard in one corner two young men were standing, drinking hop-bitters.

Mr. Browne led his charges thither and invited them all, in jest, to some ladies' punch, hot, strong and sweet. As they said they never took anything strong he opened three bottles of lemonade for them. Then he asked one of the young men to move aside, and, taking hold of the decanter, filled out for himself a goodly measure of whisky. The young men eyed him respectfully while he took a trial sip.

—God help me, he said, smiling, it's the doctor's orders.

His wizened face broke into a broader smile, and the three young ladies laughed in musical echo to his pleasantry, swaying their bodies to and fro, with nervous jerks of their shoulders. The boldest said:

—O, now, Mr. Browne, I'm sure the doctor never ordered anything of the kind.

Mr. Browne took another sip of his whisky and said, with sidling mimicry:

—Well, you see, I'm like the famous Mrs. Cassidy, who is reported to have said: *Now, Mary Grimes, if I don't take it, make me take it, for I feel I want it.*

His hot face had leaned forward a little too confidentially and he had assumed a very low Dublin accent so that the young ladies, with one instinct, received his speech in silence. Miss Furlong, who was one of Mary Jane's pupils, asked Miss Daly what was the name of the pretty waltz she had played; and Mr. Browne, seeing that he was ignored, turned promptly to the two young men who were more appreciative.

A red-faced young woman, dressed in pansy, came into the room, excitedly clapping her hands and crying:

—Quadrilles![2] Quadrilles!

Close on her heels came Aunt Kate, crying:

—Two gentlemen and three ladies, Mary Jane!

—O, here's Mr. Bergin and Mr. Kerrigan, said Mary Jane. Mr. Kerrigan, will you take Miss Power? Miss Furlong, may I get you a partner, Mr. Bergin. O, that'll just do now.

—Three ladies, Mary Jane, said Aunt Kate.

The two young gentlemen asked the ladies if they might have the pleasure, and Mary Jane turned to Miss Daly.

—O, Miss Daly, you're really awfully good, after playing for the last two dances, but really we're so short of ladies to-night.

—I don't mind in the least, Miss Morkan.

—But I've a nice partner for you, Mr. Bartell D'Arcy, the tenor. I'll get him to sing later on. All Dublin is raving about him.

—Lovely voice, lovely voice! said Aunt Kate.

As the piano had twice begun the prelude to the first figure Mary Jane led her recruits quickly from the room. They had hardly gone when Aunt Julia wandered slowly into the room, looking behind her at something.

—What is the matter, Julia? asked Aunt Kate anxiously. Who is it?

Julia, who was carrying in a column of table-napkins, turned to her sister and said, simply, as if the question had surprised her:

—It's only Freddy, Kate, and Gabriel with him.

2. Square dances.

In fact right behind her Gabriel could be seen piloting Freddy Malins across the landing. The latter, a young man of about forty, was of Gabriel's size and build, with very round shoulders. His face was fleshy and pallid, touched with colour only at the thick hanging lobes of his ears and at the wide wings of his nose. He had coarse features, a blunt nose, a convex and receding brow, tumid and protruded lips. His heavy-lidded eyes and the disorder of his scanty hair made him look sleepy. He was laughing heartily in a high key at a story which he had been telling Gabriel on the stairs and at the same time rubbing the knuckles of his left fist backwards and forwards into his left eye.

—Good-evening, Freddy, said Aunt Julia.

Freddy Malins bade the Misses Morkan good-evening in what seemed an offhand fashion by reason of the habitual catch in his voice and then, seeing that Mr. Browne was grinning at him from the sideboard, crossed the room on rather shaky legs and began to repeat in an undertone the story he had just told to Gabriel.

—He's not so bad, is he? said Aunt Kate to Gabriel.

Gabriel's brows were dark but he raised them quickly and answered:

—O no, hardly noticeable.

—Now, isn't he a terrible fellow! she said. And his poor mother made him take the pledge[3] on New Year's Eve. But come on, Gabriel, into the drawing-room.

Before leaving the room with Gabriel she signalled to Mr. Browne by frowning and shaking her forefinger in warning to and fro. Mr. Browne nodded in answer and, when she had gone, said to Freddy Malins:

—Now, then, Teddy, I'm going to fill you out a good glass of lemonade just to buck you up.

Freddy Malins, who was nearing the climax of his story, waved the offer aside impatiently but Mr. Browne, having first called Freddy Malins' attention to a disarray in his dress, filled out and handed him a full glass of lemonade. Freddy Malins' left hand accepted the glass mechanically, his right hand being engaged in the mechanical readjustment of his dress. Mr. Browne, whose face was once more wrinkling with mirth, poured out for himself a glass of whisky while Freddy Malins exploded, before he had well reached the climax of his story, in a kink of high-pitched bronchitic laughter and, setting down his untasted and overflowing glass, began to rub the knuckles of his left fist backwards and forwards into his left eye, repeating words of his last phrase as well as his fit of laughter would allow him.

• • • • • •

Gabriel could not listen while Mary Jane was playing her Academy piece, full of runs and difficult passages, to the hushed drawing-room. He liked music but the piece she was playing had no melody for him and he doubted whether it had any melody for the other listeners, though they had begged Mary Jane to play something. Four young men, who had come from the refreshment-room to stand in the doorway at the sound of the piano, had gone away quietly in couples after a few minutes. The only persons who seemed to follow the

3. A formal pledge not to drink.

music were Mary Jane herself, her hands racing along the key-board or lifted from it at the pauses like those of a priestess in momentary imprecation, and Aunt Kate standing at her elbow to turn the page.

Gabriel's eyes, irritated by the floor, which glittered with beeswax under the heavy chandelier, wandered to the wall above the piano. A picture of the balcony scene in *Romeo and Juliet* hung there and beside it was a picture of the two murdered princes[4] in the Tower which Aunt Julia had worked in red, blue and brown wools when she was a girl. Probably in the school they had gone to as girls that kind of work had been taught, for one year his mother had worked for him as a birthday present a waistcoat of purple tabinet, with little foxes' heads upon it, lined with brown satin and having round mulberry buttons. It was strange that his mother had had no musical talent though Aunt Kate used to call her the brains carrier of the Morkan family. Both she and Julia had always seemed a little proud of their serious and matronly sister. Her photograph stood before the pierglass.[5] She held an open book on her knees and was pointing out something in it to Constantine who, dressed in a man-o'-war suit,[6] lay at her feet. It was she who had chosen the names for her sons for she was very sensible of the dignity of family life. Thanks to her, Constantine was now senior curate in Balbriggan and, thanks to her, Gabriel himself had taken his degree in the Royal University. A shadow passed over his face as he remembered her sullen opposition to his marriage. Some slighting phrases she had used still rankled in his memory; she had once spoken of Gretta as being country cute and that was not true of Gretta at all. It was Gretta who had nursed her during all her last long illness in their house at Monkstown.

He knew that Mary Jane must be near the end of her piece for she was playing again the opening melody with runs of scales after every bar and while he waited for the end the resentment died down in his heart. The piece ended with a trill of octaves in the treble and a final deep octave in the bass. Great applause greeted Mary Jane as, blushing and rolling up her music nervously, she escaped from the room. The most vigorous clapping came from the four young men in the doorway who had gone away to the refreshment-room at the beginning of the piece but had come back when the piano had stopped.

Lancers[7] were arranged. Gabriel found himself partnered with Miss Ivors. She was a frank-mannered talkative young lady, with a freckled face and prominent brown eyes. She did not wear a low-cut bodice and the large brooch which was fixed in the front of her collar bore on it an Irish device.

When they had taken their places she said abruptly:

—I have a crow to pluck with you.[8]

—With me? said Gabriel.

She nodded her head gravely.

—What is it? asked Gabriel, smiling at her solemn manner.

—Who is G. C.? answered Miss Ivors, turning her eyes upon him.

Gabriel coloured and was about to knit his brows, as if he did not understand, when she said bluntly:

4. Edward and Richard, sons of King Edward IV of England. The two princes were murdered reputedly by order of King Richard III. 5. A tall mirror. 6. Sailor suit. 7. A set of quadrilles, danced in sequence. 8. Equivalent of "I have a bone to pick."

—O, innocent Amy! I have found out that you write for *The Daily Express*.[9] Now, aren't you ashamed of yourself?

—Why should I be ashamed of myself? asked Gabriel, blinking his eyes and trying to smile.

—Well, I'm ashamed of you, said Miss Ivors frankly. To say you'd write for a rag like that. I didn't think you were a West Briton.[1]

A look of perplexity appeared on Gabriel's face. It was true that he wrote a literary column every Wednesday in *The Daily Express*, for which he was paid fifteen shillings. But that did not make him a West Briton surely. The books he received for review were almost more welcome than the paltry cheque. He loved to feel the covers and turn over the pages of newly printed books. Nearly every day when his teaching in the college was ended he used to wander down the quays to the second-hand booksellers, to Hickey's on Bachelor's Walk, to Webb's or Massey's on Aston's Quay, or to O'Clohissey's in the by-street. He did not know how to meet her charge. He wanted to say that literature was above politics. But they were friends of many years' standing and their careers had been parallel, first at the University and then as teachers: he could not risk a grandiose phrase with her. He continued blinking his eyes and trying to smile and murmured lamely that he saw nothing political in writing reviews of books.

When their turn to cross had come he was still perplexed and inattentive. Miss Ivors promptly took his hand in a warm grasp and said in a soft friendly tone:

—Of course, I was only joking. Come, we cross now.

When they were together again she spoke of the University question[2] and Gabriel felt more at ease. A friend of hers had shown her his review of Browning's poems. That was how she had found out the secret: but she liked the review immensely. Then she said suddenly:

—O, Mr. Conroy, will you come for an excursion to the Aran Isles[3] this summer? We're going to stay there a whole month. It will be splendid out in the Atlantic. You ought to come. Mr. Clancy is coming, and Mr. Kilkelly and Kathleen Kearney. It would be splendid for Gretta too if she'd come. She's from Connacht,[4] isn't she?

—Her people are, said Gabriel shortly.

—But you will come, won't you? said Miss Ivors, laying her warm hand eagerly on his arm.

—The fact is, said Gabriel, I have already arranged to go—

—Go where? asked Miss Ivors.

—Well, you know every year I go for a cycling tour with some fellows and so—

—But where? asked Miss Ivors.

—Well, we usually go to France or Belgium or perhaps Germany, said Gabriel awkwardly.

9. A newspaper opposed to Irish liberation. 1. In context this means he considers himself British rather than Irish. 2. The issue was whether to provide equal educational opportunities for Roman Catholic students at the overwhelmingly Protestant Trinity College in Dublin. 3. Off the west coast of Ireland. Irish traditions were preserved by their Gaelic-speaking natives. 4. Province in northwest Ireland. Probably considered backwoods by Dubliners.

—And why do you go to France and Belgium, said Miss Ivors, instead of visiting your own land?

—Well, said Gabriel, it's partly to keep in touch with the languages and partly for a change.

—And haven't you your own language to keep in touch with—Irish? asked Miss Ivors.

—Well, said Gabriel, if it comes to that, you know, Irish is not my language.

Their neighbours had turned to listen to the cross-examination. Gabriel glanced right and left nervously and tried to keep his good humour under the ordeal which was making a blush invade his forehead.

—And haven't you your own land to visit, continued Miss Ivors, that you know nothing of, your own people, and your own country?

—O, to tell you the truth, retorted Gabriel suddenly, I'm sick of my own country, sick of it!

—Why? asked Miss Ivors.

Gabriel did not answer for his retort had heated him.

—Why? repeated Miss Ivors.

They had to go visiting together and, as he had not answered her, Miss Ivors said warmly:

—Of course, you've no answer.

Gabriel tried to cover his agitation by taking part in the dance with great energy. He avoided her eyes for he had seen a sour expression on her face. But when they met in the long chain he was surprised to feel his hand firmly pressed. She looked at him from under her brows for a moment quizzically until he smiled. Then, just as the chain was about to start again, she stood on tiptoe and whispered into his ear:

—West Briton!

When the lancers were over Gabriel went away to a remote corner of the room where Freddy Malins' mother was sitting. She was a stout feeble old woman with white hair. Her voice had a catch in it like her son's and she stuttered slightly. She had been told that Freddy had come and that he was nearly all right. Gabriel asked her whether she had had a good crossing. She lived with her married daughter in Glasgow and came to Dublin on a visit once a year. She answered placidly that she had had a beautiful crossing and that the captain had been most attentive to her. She spoke also of the beautiful house her daughter kept in Glasgow, and of all the nice friends they had there. While her tongue rambled on Gabriel tried to banish from his mind all memory of the unpleasant incident with Miss Ivors. Of course the girl or woman, or whatever she was, was an enthusiast but there was a time for all things. Perhaps he ought not to have answered her like that. But she had no right to call him a West Briton before people, even in joke. She had tried to make him ridiculous before people, heckling him and staring at him with her rabbit's eyes.

He saw his wife making her way towards him through the waltzing couples. When she reached him she said into his ear:

—Gabriel, Aunt Kate wants to know won't you carve the goose as usual. Miss Daly will carve the ham and I'll do the pudding.

—All right, said Gabriel.

—She's sending in the younger ones first as soon as this waltz is over so that we'll have the table to ourselves.

—Were you dancing? asked Gabriel.

—Of course I was. Didn't you see me? What words had you with Molly Ivors?

—No words. Why? Did she say so?

—Something like that. I'm trying to get that Mr. D'Arcy to sing. He's full of conceit, I think.

—There were no words, said Gabriel moodily, only she wanted me to go for a trip to the west of Ireland and I said I wouldn't.

His wife clasped her hands excitedly and gave a little jump.

—O, do go, Gabriel, she cried. I'd love to see Galway[5] again.

—You can go if you like, said Gabriel coldly.

She looked at him for a moment, then turned to Mrs. Malins and said:

—There's a nice husband for you, Mrs. Malins.

While she was threading her way back across the room Mrs. Malins, without adverting to the interruption, went on to tell Gabriel what beautiful places there were in Scotland and beautiful scenery. Her son-in-law brought them every year to the lakes and they used to go fishing. Her son-in-law was a splendid fisher. One day he caught a fish, a beautiful big big fish, and the man in the hotel boiled it for their dinner.

Gabriel hardly heard what she said. Now that supper was coming near he began to think again about his speech and about the quotation. When he saw Freddy Malins coming across the room to visit his mother Gabriel left the chair free for him and retired into the embrasure of the window. The room had already cleared and from the back room came the clatter of plates and knives. Those who still remained in the drawing-room seemed tired of dancing and were conversing quietly in little groups. Gabriel's warm trembling fingers tapped the cold pane of the window. How cool it must be outside! How pleasant it would be to walk out alone, first along by the river and then through the park! The snow would be lying on the branches of the trees and forming a bright cap on the top of the Wellington Monument.[6] How much more pleasant it would be there than at the supper-table!

He ran over the headings of his speech: Irish hospitality, sad memories, the Three Graces, Paris,[7] the quotation from Browning. He repeated to himself a phrase he had written in his review: *One feels that one is listening to a thought-tormented music.* Miss Ivors had praised the review. Was she sincere? Had she really any life of her own behind all her propagandism? There had never been any ill-feeling between them until that night. It unnerved him to think that she would be at the supper-table, looking up at him while he spoke with her critical quizzing eyes. Perhaps she would not be sorry to see him fail in his speech. An idea came into his mind and gave him courage. He would say, alluding to Aunt

5. Capital of Connacht. 6. Monument to the duke of Wellington (1769–1852), Irish-born hero of the Napoleonic Wars. 7. The Trojan prince who was obliged to choose among the goddesses Hera, Athena, and Aphrodite. He awarded the prize (the apple of discord) to Aphrodite, who then helped him carry off Helen. "Three Graces": goddesses representing aspects of beauty—Aglaia (Brilliance), Euphrosyne (Joy), and Thalia (Bloom).

Kate and Aunt Julia: *Ladies and Gentlemen, the generation which is now on the wane among us may have had its faults but for my part I think it had certain qualities of hospitality, of humour, of humanity, which the new and very serious and hypereducated generation that is growing up around us seems to me to lack.* Very good: that was one for Miss Ivors. What did he care that his aunts were only two ignorant old women?

A murmur in the room attracted his attention. Mr. Browne was advancing from the door, gallantly escorting Aunt Julia, who leaned upon his arm, smiling and hanging her head. An irregular musketry of applause escorted her also as far as the piano and then, as Mary Jane seated herself on the stool, and Aunt Julia, no longer smiling, half turned so as to pitch her voice fairly into the room, gradually ceased. Gabriel recognised the prelude. It was that of an old song of Aunt Julia's—*Arrayed for the Bridal.* Her voice, strong and clear in tone, attacked with great spirit the runs which embellish the air and though she sang very rapidly she did not miss even the smallest of the grace notes. To follow the voice, without looking at the singer's face, was to feel and share the excitement of swift and secure flight. Gabriel applauded loudly with all the others at the close of the song and loud applause was borne in from the invisible supper-table. It sounded so genuine that a little colour struggled into Aunt Julia's face as she bent to replace in the music-stand the old leather-bound song-book that had her initials on the cover. Freddy Malins, who had listened with his head perched sideways to hear her better, was still applauding when everyone else had ceased and talking animatedly to his mother who nodded her head gravely and slowly in acquiescence. At last, when he could clap no more, he stood up suddenly and hurried across the room to Aunt Julia whose hand he seized and held in both his hands, shaking it when words failed him or the catch in his voice proved too much for him.

—I was just telling my mother, he said, I never heard you sing so well, never. No, I never heard your voice so good as it is to-night. Now! Would you believe that now? That's the truth. Upon my word and honour that's the truth. I never heard your voice sound so fresh and so . . . so clear and fresh, never.

Aunt Julia smiled broadly and murmured something about compliments as she released her hand from his grasp. Mr. Browne extended his open hand towards her and said to those who were near him in the manner of a showman introducing a prodigy to an audience:

—Miss Julia Morkan, my latest discovery!

He was laughing very heartily at this himself when Freddy Malins turned to him and said:

—Well, Browne, if you're serious you might make a worse discovery. All I can say is I never heard her sing half so well as long as I am coming here. And that's the honest truth.

—Neither did I, said Mr. Browne. I think her voice has greatly improved.

Aunt Julia shrugged her shoulders and said with meek pride:

—Thirty years ago I hadn't a bad voice as voices go.

—I often told Julia, said Aunt Kate emphatically, that she was simply thrown away in that choir. But she never would be said by me.

She turned as if to appeal to the good sense of the others against a refractory child while Aunt Julia gazed in front of her, a vague smile of reminiscence playing on her face.

—No, continued Aunt Kate, she wouldn't be said or led by anyone, slaving there in that choir night and day, night and day. Six o'clock on Christmas morning! And all for what?

—Well, isn't it for the honour of God, Aunt Kate? asked Mary Jane, twisting round on the piano-stool and smiling.

Aunt Kate turned fiercely on her niece and said:

—I know all about the honour of God, Mary Jane, but I think it's not at all honourable for the pope to turn out the women out of the choirs that have slaved there all their lives and put little whipper-snappers of boys over their heads. I suppose it is for the good of the Church if the pope does it. But it's not just, Mary Jane, and it's not right.

She had worked herself into a passion and would have continued in defence of her sister for it was a sore subject with her but Mary Jane, seeing that all the dancers had come back, intervened pacifically:

—Now, Aunt Kate, you're giving scandal to Mr. Browne who is of the other persuasion.

Aunt Kate turned to Mr. Browne, who was grinning at this allusion to his religion, and said hastily:

—O, I don't question the pope's being right. I'm only a stupid old woman and I wouldn't presume to do such a thing. But there's such a thing as common everyday politeness and gratitude. And if I were in Julia's place I'd tell that Father Healy straight up to his face . . .

—And besides, Aunt Kate, said Mary Jane, we really are all hungry and when we are hungry we are all very quarrelsome.

—And when we are thirsty we are also quarrelsome, added Mr. Browne.

—So that we had better go to supper, said Mary Jane, and finish the discussion afterwards.

On the landing outside the drawing-room Gabriel found his wife and Mary Jane trying to persuade Miss Ivors to stay for supper. But Miss Ivors, who had put on her hat and was buttoning her cloak, would not stay. She did not feel in the least hungry and she had already overstayed her time.

—But only for ten minutes, Molly, said Mrs. Conroy. That won't delay you.

—To take a pick itself, said Mary Jane, after all your dancing.

—I really couldn't, said Miss Ivors.

—I am afraid you didn't enjoy yourself at all, said Mary Jane hopelessly.

—Ever so much, I assure you, said Miss Ivors, but you really must let me run off now.

—But how can you get home? asked Mrs. Conroy.

—O, it's only two steps up the quay.

Gabriel hesitated a moment and said:

—If you will allow me, Miss Ivors, I'll see you home if you really are obliged to go.

But Miss Ivors broke away from them.

—I won't hear of it, she cried. For goodness sake go in to your suppers and don't mind me. I'm quite well able to take care of myself.

—Well, you're the comical girl, Molly, said Mrs. Conroy frankly.

—*Beannacht libh,*[8] cried Miss Ivors, with a laugh, as she ran down the staircase.

Mary Jane gazed after her, a moody puzzled expression on her face, while Mrs. Conroy leaned over the banisters to listen for the hall-door. Gabriel asked himself was he the cause of her abrupt departure. But she did not seem to be in ill humour: she had gone away laughing. He stared blankly down the staircase.

At that moment Aunt Kate came toddling out of the supper-room, almost wringing her hands in despair.

—Where is Gabriel? she cried. Where on earth is Gabriel? There's everyone waiting in there, stage to let, and nobody to carve the goose!

—Here I am, Aunt Kate! cried Gabriel, with sudden animation, ready to carve a flock of geese, if necessary.

A fat brown goose lay at one end of the table and at the other end, on a bed of creased paper strewn with sprigs of parsley, lay a great ham, stripped of its outer skin and peppered over with crust crumbs, a neat paper frill round its shin and beside this was a round of spiced beef. Between these rival ends ran parallel lines of side-dishes: two little minsters of jelly, red and yellow; a shallow dish full of blocks of blancmange and red jam, a large green leaf-shaped dish with a stalk-shaped handle, on which lay bunches of purple raisins and peeled almonds, a companion dish on which lay a solid rectangle of Smyrna figs, a dish of custard topped with grated nutmeg, a small bowl full of chocolates and sweets wrapped in gold and silver papers and a glass vase in which stood some tall celery stalks. In the centre of the table there stood, as sentries to a fruit-stand which upheld a pyramid of oranges and American apples, two squat old-fashioned decanters of cut glass, one containing port and the other dark sherry. On the closed square piano a pudding in a huge yellow dish lay in waiting and behind it were three squads of bottles of stout and ale and minerals, drawn up according to the colours of their uniforms, the first two black, with brown and red labels, the third and smallest squad white, with transverse green sashes.

Gabriel took his seat boldly at the head of the table and, having looked to the edge of the carver, plunged his fork firmly into the goose. He felt quite at ease now for he was an expert carver and liked nothing better than to find himself at the head of a well-laden table.

—Miss Furlong, what shall I send you? he asked. A wing or a slice of the breast?

—Just a small slice of the breast.

—Miss Higgins, what for you?

—O, anything at all, Mr. Conroy.

While Gabriel and Miss Daly exchanged plates of goose and plates of ham and spiced beef Lily went from guest to guest with a dish of hot floury potatoes wrapped in a white napkin. This was Mary Jane's idea and she had also suggested apple sauce for the goose but Aunt Kate had said that plain roast goose without apple sauce had always been good enough for her and she hoped

8. Blessings on you (Gaelic).

she might never eat worse. Mary Jane waited on her pupils and saw that they got the best slices and Aunt Kate and Aunt Julia opened and carried across from the piano bottles of stout and ale for the gentlemen and bottles of minerals for the ladies. There was a great deal of confusion and laughter and noise, the noise of orders and counter-orders, of knives and forks, of corks and glass-stoppers. Gabriel began to carve second helpings as soon as he had finished the first round without serving himself. Everyone protested loudly so that he compromised by taking a long draught of stout for he had found the carving hot work. Mary Jane settled down quietly to her supper but Aunt Kate and Aunt Julia were still toddling round the table, walking on each other's heels, getting in each other's way and giving each other unheeded orders. Mr. Browne begged of them to sit down and eat their suppers and so did Gabriel but they said there was time enough so that, at last, Freddy Malins stood up and, capturing Aunt Kate, plumped her down on her chair amid general laughter.

When everyone had been well served Gabriel said, smiling:

—Now, if anyone wants a little more of what vulgar people call stuffing let him or her speak.

A chorus of voices invited him to begin his own supper and Lily came forward with three potatoes which she had reserved for him.

—Very well, said Gabriel amiably, as he took another preparatory draught, kindly forget my existence, ladies and gentlemen, for a few minutes.

He set to his supper and took no part in the conversation with which the table covered Lily's removal of the plates. The subject of talk was the opera company which was then at the Theatre Royal. Mr. Bartell D'Arcy, the tenor, a dark-complexioned young man with a smart moustache, praised very highly the leading contralto of the company but Miss Furlong thought she had a rather vulgar style of production. Freddy Malins said there was a negro chieftain singing in the second part of the Gaiety pantomime who had one of the finest tenor voices he had ever heard.

—Have you heard him? he asked Mr. Bartell D'Arcy across the table.

—No, answered Mr. Bartell D'Arcy carelessly.

—Because, Freddy Malins explained, now I'd be curious to hear your opinion of him. I think he has a grand voice.

—It takes Teddy to find out the really good things, said Mr. Browne familiarly to the table.

—And why couldn't he have a voice too? asked Freddy Malins sharply. Is it because he's only a black?

Nobody answered this question and Mary Jane led the table back to the legitimate opera. One of her pupils had given her a pass for *Mignon.*[9] Of course it was very fine, she said, but it made her think of poor Georgina Burns. Mr. Browne could go back farther still, to the old Italian companies that used to come to Dublin—Tietjens, Ilma de Murzka, Campanini, the great Trebelli, Giuglini, Ravelli, Aramburo.[1] Those were the days, he said, when there was

9. Opera by Ambroise Thomas, French composer (1811–1896). 1. Some nineteenth-century singing stars: Therese Tietjens (1831–1877), Ilma di Murzka (1836–1889), Italo Campanini (1845–1896), Zelia Trebelli (1838–1892), and Antonio Giuglini (1827–1865). Others not identified.

something like singing to be heard in Dublin. He told too of how the top gallery of the old Royal used to be packed night after night, of how one night an Italian tenor had sung five encores to *Let Me Like a Soldier Fall,*[2] introducing a high C every time, and of how the gallery boys would sometimes in their enthusiasm unyoke the horses from the carriage of some great *prima donna* and pull her themselves through the streets to her hotel. Why did they never play the grand old operas now, he asked, *Dinorah, Lucrezia Borgia?*[3] Because they could not get the voices to sing them: that was why.

—O, well, said Mr. Bartell D'Arcy, I presume there are as good singers to-day as there were then.

—Where are they? asked Mr. Browne defiantly.

—In London, Paris, Milan, said Mr. Bartell D'Arcy warmly. I suppose Caruso,[4] for example, is quite as good, if not better than any of the men you have mentioned.

—Maybe so, said Mr. Browne. But I may tell you I doubt it strongly.

—O, I'd give anything to hear Caruso sing, said Mary Jane.

—For me, said Aunt Kate, who had been picking a bone, there was only one tenor. To please me, I mean. But I suppose none of you ever heard of him.

—Who was he, Miss Morkan? asked Mr. Bartell D'Arcy politely.

—His name, said Aunt Kate, was Parkinson.[5] I heard him when he was in his prime and I think he had then the purest tenor voice that was ever put into a man's throat.

—Strange, said Mr. Bartell D'Arcy. I never even heard of him.

—Yes, yes, Miss Morkan is right, said Mr. Browne. I remember hearing of old Parkinson but he's too far back for me.

—A beautiful pure sweet mellow English tenor, said Aunt Kate with enthusiasm.

Gabriel having finished, the huge pudding was transferred to the table. The clatter of forks and spoons began again. Gabriel's wife served out spoonfuls of the pudding and passed the plates down the table. Midway down they were held up by Mary Jane, who replenished them with raspberry or orange jelly or with blancmange and jam. The pudding was of Aunt Julia's making and she received praises for it from all quarters. She herself said that it was not quite brown enough.

—Well, I hope, Miss Morkan, said Mr. Browne, that I'm brown enough for you because, you know, I'm all brown.

All the gentlemen, except Gabriel, ate some of the pudding out of compliment to Aunt Julia. As Gabriel never ate sweets the celery had been left for him. Freddy Malins also took a stalk of celery and ate it with his pudding. He had been told that celery was a capital thing for the blood and he was just then under doctor's care. Mrs. Malins, who had been silent all through the supper, said that her son was going down to Mount Melleray,[6] in a week or so. The table then spoke of Mount Melleray, how bracing the air was down there, how

2. From *Maritana* by Brunn, Fitzball, and Wallace. 3. Operas by Giacomo Meyerbeer, German composer (1791–1864), and by Gaetano Donizetti, Italian composer (1797–1848). 4. Enrico Caruso, operatic tenor (1873–1921). 5. Not identified; perhaps fictional. 6. Trappist monastery in the south of Ireland.

hospitable the monks were and how they never asked for a penny-piece from their guests.

—And do you mean to say, asked Mr. Browne incredulously, that a chap can go down there and put up there as if it were a hotel and live on the fat of the land and then come away without paying a farthing?

—O, most people give some donation to the monastery when they leave, said Mary Jane.

—I wish we had an institution like that in our Church, said Mr. Browne candidly.

He was astonished to hear that the monks never spoke, got up at two in the morning and slept in their coffins. He asked what they did it for.

—That's the rule of the order, said Aunt Kate firmly.

—Yes, but why? asked Mr. Browne.

Aunt Kate repeated that it was the rule, that was all. Mr. Browne still seemed not to understand. Freddy Malins explained to him, as best he could, that the monks were trying to make up for the sins committed by all the sinners in the outside world. The explanation was not very clear for Mr. Browne grinned and said:

—I like that idea very much but wouldn't a comfortable spring bed do them as well as a coffin?

—The coffin, said Mary Jane, is to remind them of their last end.

As the subject had grown lugubrious it was buried in a silence of the table during which Mrs. Malins could be heard saying to her neighbour in an indistinct undertone:

—They are very good men, the monks, very pious men.

The raisins and almonds and figs and apples and oranges and chocolates and sweets were now passed about the table and Aunt Julia invited all the guests to have either port or sherry. At first Mr. Bartell D'Arcy refused to take either but one of his neighbours nudged him and whispered something to him upon which he allowed his glass to be filled. Gradually as the last glasses were being filled the conversation ceased. A pause followed, broken only by the noise of the wine and by unsettlings of chairs. The Misses Morkan, all three, looked down at the tablecloth. Someone coughed once or twice and then a few gentlemen patted the table gently as a signal for silence. The silence came and Gabriel pushed back his chair and stood up.

The patting at once grew louder in encouragement and then ceased altogether. Gabriel leaned his ten trembling fingers on the tablecloth and smiled nervously at the company. Meeting a row of upturned faces he raised his eyes to the chandelier. The piano was playing a waltz tune and he could hear the skirts sweeping against the drawing-room door. People, perhaps, were standing in the snow on the quay outside, gazing up at the lighted windows and listening to the waltz music. The air was pure there. In the distance lay the park where the trees were weighted with snow. The Wellington Monument wore a gleaming cap of snow that flashed westward over the white field of Fifteen Acres.[7]

He began:

7. Section of Phoenix Park in which the Wellington Monument stands.

—Ladies and Gentlemen.

—It has fallen to my lot this evening, as in years past, to perform a very pleasing task but a task for which I am afraid my poor powers as a speaker are all too inadequate.

—No, no! said Mr. Browne.

—But, however that may be, I can only ask you to-night to take the will for the deed and to lend me your attention for a few moments while I endeavour to express to you in words what my feelings are on this occasion.

—Ladies and Gentlemen. It is not the first time that we have gathered together under this hospitable roof, around this hospitable board. It is not the first time that we have been the recipients—or perhaps, I had better say, the victims—of the hospitality of certain good ladies.

He made a circle in the air with his arm and paused. Everyone laughed or smiled at Aunt Kate and Aunt Julia and Mary Jane who all turned crimson with pleasure. Gabriel went on more boldly:

—I feel more strongly with every recurring year that our country has no tradition which does it so much honour and which it should guard so jealously as that of its hospitality. It is a tradition that is unique as far as my experience goes (and I have visited not a few places abroad) among the modern nations. Some would say, perhaps, that with us it is rather a failing than anything to be boasted of. But granted even that, it is, to my mind, a princely failing, and one that I trust will long be cultivated among us. Of one thing, at least, I am sure. As long as this one roof shelters the good ladies aforesaid—and I wish from my heart it may do so for many and many a long year to come—the tradition of genuine warm-hearted courteous Irish hospitality, which our forefathers have handed down to us and which we in turn must hand down to our descendants, is still alive among us.

A hearty murmur of assent ran round the table. It shot through Gabriel's mind that Miss Ivors was not there and that she had gone away discourteously: and he said with confidence in himself:

—Ladies and Gentlemen.

—A new generation is growing up in our midst, a generation actuated by new ideas and new principles. It is serious and enthusiastic for these new ideas and its enthusiasm, even when it is misdirected, is, I believe, in the main sincere. But we are living in a sceptical and, if I may use the phrase, a thought-tormented age: and sometimes I fear that this new generation, educated or hypereducated as it is, will lack those qualities of humanity, of hospitality, of kindly humour which belonged to an older day. Listening to-night to the names of all those great singers of the past it seemed to me, I must confess, that we were living in a less spacious age. Those days might, without exaggeration, be called spacious days: and if they are gone beyond recall let us hope, at least, that in gatherings such as this we shall still speak of them with pride and affection, still cherish in our hearts the memory of those dead and gone great ones whose fame the world will not willingly let die.

—Hear, hear! said Mr. Browne loudly.

—But yet, continued Gabriel, his voice falling into a softer inflection, there are always in gatherings such as this sadder thoughts that will recur to our minds: thoughts of the past, of youth, of changes, of absent faces that we miss here to-night. Our path through life is strewn with many such sad memories: and were we to brood upon them always we could not find the heart to go on bravely with our work among the living. We have all of us living duties and living affections which claim, and rightly claim, our strenuous endeavours.

—Therefore, I will not linger on the past. I will not let any gloomy moralising intrude upon us here to-night. Here we are gathered together for a brief moment from the bustle and rush of our everyday routine. We are met here as friends, in the spirit of good-fellowship, as colleagues, also to a certain extent, in the true spirit of *camaraderie*, and as the guests of—what shall I call them?—the Three Graces of the Dublin musical world.

The table burst into applause and laughter at this sally. Aunt Julia vainly asked each of her neighbours in turn to tell her what Gabriel had said.

—He says we are the Three Graces, Aunt Julia, said Mary Jane.

Aunt Julia did not understand but she looked up, smiling, at Gabriel, who continued in the same vein:

—Ladies and Gentlemen.

—I will not attempt to play to-night the part that Paris played on another occasion. I will not attempt to choose between them. The task would be an invidious one and one beyond my poor powers. For when I view them in turn whether it be our chief hostess herself, whose good heart, whose too good heart has become a byword with all who know her, or her sister, who seems to be gifted with perennial youth and whose singing must have been a surprise and a revelation to us all to-night, or, last but not least, when I consider our youngest hostess, talented, cheerful, hard-working and the best of nieces, I confess, Ladies and Gentlemen, that I do not know to which of them I should award the prize.

Gabriel glanced down at his aunts and, seeing the large smile on Aunt Julia's face and the tears which had risen to Aunt Kate's eyes, hastened to his close. He raised his glass of port gallantly, while every member of the company fingered a glass expectantly, and said loudly:

—Let us toast them all three together. Let us drink to their health, wealth, long life, happiness and prosperity and may they long continue to hold the proud and self-won position which they hold in their profession and the position of honour and affection which they hold in our hearts.

All the guests stood up, glass in hand, and, turning towards the three seated ladies, sang in unison, with Mr. Browne as leader:

*For they are jolly gay fellows,*
*For they are jolly gay fellows,*
*For they are jolly gay fellows,*
*Which nobody can deny.*

Aunt Kate was making frank use of her handkerchief and even Aunt Julia seemed moved. Freddy Malins beat time with his pudding-fork and the singers turned towards one another, as if in melodious conference, while they sang, with emphasis:

*Unless he tells a lie,*
*Unless he tells a lie.*

Then, turning once more towards their hostesses, they sang:

*For they are jolly gay fellows,*
*For they are jolly gay fellows,*
*For they are jolly gay fellows,*
*Which nobody can deny.*

The acclamation which followed was taken up beyond the door of the supper-room by many of the other guests and renewed time after time, Freddy Malins acting as officer with his fork on high.

• • • • • • •

The piercing morning air came into the hall where they were standing so that Aunt Kate said:

—Close the door, somebody. Mrs. Malins will get her death of cold.

—Browne is out there, Aunt Kate, said Mary Jane.

—Browne is everywhere, said Aunt Kate, lowering her voice.

Mary Jane laughed at her tone.

—Really, she said archly, he is very attentive.

—He has been laid on[8] here like the gas, said Aunt Kate in the same tone, all during the Christmas.

She laughed herself this time good-humouredly and then added quickly:

—But tell him to come in, Mary Jane, and close the door. I hope to goodness he didn't hear me.

At that moment the hall-door was opened and Mr. Browne came in from the doorstep, laughing as if his heart would break. He was dressed in a long green overcoat with mock astrakhan cuffs and collar and wore on his head an oval fur cap. He pointed down the snow-covered quay from where the sound of shrill prolonged whistling was borne in.

—Teddy will have all the cabs in Dublin out, he said.

Gabriel advanced from the little pantry behind the office, struggling into his overcoat and, looking round the hall, said:

—Gretta not down yet?

—She's getting on her things, Gabriel, said Aunt Kate.

—Who's playing up there? asked Gabriel.

—Nobody. They're all gone.

—O no, Aunt Kate, said Mary Jane. Bartell D'Arcy and Miss O'Callaghan aren't gone yet.

—Someone is strumming at the piano, anyhow, said Gabriel.

Mary Jane glanced at Gabriel and Mr. Browne and said with a shiver:

—It makes me feel cold to look at you two gentlemen muffled up like that. I wouldn't like to face your journey home at this hour.

—I'd like nothing better this minute, said Mr. Browne stoutly, than a rattling fine walk in the country or a fast drive with a good spanking goer between the shafts.

8. Supplied.

—We used to have a very good horse and trap[9] at home, said Aunt Julia sadly.

—The never-to-be-forgotten Johnny, said Mary Jane, laughing.

Aunt Kate and Gabriel laughed too.

—Why, what was wonderful about Johnny? asked Mr. Browne.

—The late lamented Patrick Morkan, our grandfather, that is, explained Gabriel, commonly known in his later years as the old gentleman, was a glue-boiler.

—O, now, Gabriel, said Aunt Kate, laughing, he had a starch mill.

—Well, glue or starch, said Gabriel, the old gentleman had a horse by the name of Johnny. And Johnny used to work in the old gentleman's mill, walking round and round in order to drive the mill. That was all very well; but now comes the tragic part about Johnny. One fine day the old gentleman thought he'd like to drive out with the quality[1] to a military review in the park.

—The Lord have mercy on his soul, said Aunt Kate compassionately.

—Amen, said Gabriel. So the old gentleman, as I said, harnessed Johnny and put on his very best tall hat and his very best stock collar and drove out in grand style from his ancestral mansion somewhere near Back Lane, I think.

Everyone laughed, even Mrs. Malins, at Gabriel's manner and Aunt Kate said:

—O now, Gabriel, he didn't live in Back Lane, really. Only the mill was there.

—Out from the mansion of his forefathers, continued Gabriel, he drove with Johnny. And everything went on beautifully until Johnny came in sight of King Billy's statue:[2] and whether he fell in love with the horse King Billy sits on or whether he thought he was back again in the mill, anyhow he began to walk round the statue.

Gabriel paced in a circle round the hall in his goloshes amid the laughter of the others.

—Round and round he went, said Gabriel, and the old gentleman, who was a very pompous old gentleman, was highly indignant. *Go on, sir! What do you mean, sir? Johnny! Johnny! Most extraordinary conduct! Can't understand the horse!*

The peals of laughter which followed Gabriel's imitation of the incident were interrupted by a resounding knock at the hall-door. Mary Jane ran to open it and let in Freddy Malins. Freddy Malins, with his hat well back on his head and his shoulders humped with cold, was puffing and steaming after his exertions.

—I could only get one cab, he said.

—O, we'll find another along the quay, said Gabriel.

—Yes, said Aunt Kate. Better not keep Mrs. Malins standing in the draught.

Mrs. Malins was helped down the front steps by her son and Mr. Browne and, after many manoeuvres, hoisted into the cab. Freddy Malins clambered in after her and spent a long time settling her on the seat, Mr. Browne helping him

9. One-horse carriage. 1. Upper classes. 2. Equestrian statue of King William III of England, last military conquerer of Ireland (in 1690).

with advice. At last she was settled comfortably and Freddy Malins invited Mr. Browne into the cab. There was a good deal of confused talk, and then Mr. Browne got into the cab. The cabman settled his rug over his knees, and bent down for the address. The confusion grew greater and the cabman was directed differently by Freddy Malins and Mr. Browne, each of whom had his head out through a window of the cab. The difficulty was to know where to drop Mr. Browne along the route and Aunt Kate, Aunt Julia and Mary Jane helped the discussion from the doorstep with cross-directions and contradictions and abundance of laughter. As for Freddy Malins he was speechless with laughter. He popped his head in and out of the window every moment, to the great danger of his hat, and told his mother how the discussion was progressing till at last Mr. Browne shouted to the bewildered cabman above the din of everybody's laughter:

—Do you know Trinity College?

—Yes, sir, said the cabman.

—Well, drive bang up against Trinity College gates, said Mr. Browne, and then we'll tell you where to go. You understand now?

—Yes, sir, said the cabman.

—Make like a bird for Trinity College.

—Right, sir, cried the cabman.

The horse was whipped up and the cab rattled off along the quay amid a chorus of laughter and adieus.

Gabriel had not gone to the door with the others. He was in a dark part of the hall gazing up the staircase. A woman was standing near the top of the first flight, in the shadow also. He could not see her face but he could see the terracotta and salmonpink panels of her skirt which the shadow made appear black and white. It was his wife. She was leaning on the banisters, listening to something. Gabriel was surprised at her stillness and strained his ear to listen also. But he could hear little save the noise of laughter and dispute on the front steps, a few chords struck on the piano and a few notes of a man's voice singing.

He stood still in the gloom of the hall, trying to catch the air that the voice was singing and gazing up at his wife. There was grace and mystery in her attitude as if she were a symbol of something. He asked himself what is a woman standing on the stairs in the shadow, listening to distant music, a symbol of. If he were a painter he would paint her in that attitude. Her blue felt hat would show off the bronze of her hair against the darkness and the dark panels of her skirt would show off the light ones. *Distant Music* he would call the picture if he were a painter.

The hall-door was closed; and Aunt Kate, Aunt Julia and Mary Jane came down the hall, still laughing.

—Well, isn't Freddy terrible? said Mary Jane. He's really terrible.

Gabriel said nothing but pointed up the stairs towards where his wife was standing. Now that the hall-door was closed the voice and the piano could be heard more clearly. Gabriel held up his hand for them to be silent. The song seemed to be in the old Irish tonality and the singer seemed uncertain both of his words and of his voice. The voice, made plaintive by distance and by the singer's hoarseness, faintly illuminated the cadence of the air with words expressing grief:

*O, the rain falls on my heavy locks*
*And the dew wets my skin,*
*My babe lies cold . . .*

—O, exclaimed Mary Jane. It's Bartell D'Arcy singing and he wouldn't sing all the night. O, I'll get him to sing a song before he goes.

—O do, Mary Jane, said Aunt Kate.

Mary Jane brushed past the others and ran to the staircase but before she reached it the singing stopped and the piano was closed abruptly.

—O, what a pity! she cried. Is he coming down, Gretta?

Gabriel heard his wife answer yes and saw her come down towards them. A few steps behind her were Mr. Bartell D'Arcy and Miss O'Callaghan.

—O, Mr. D'Arcy, cried Mary Jane, it's downright mean of you to break off like that when we were all in raptures listening to you.

—I have been at him all the evening, said Miss O'Callaghan, and Mrs. Conroy too and he told us he had a dreadful cold and couldn't sing.

—O, Mr. D'Arcy, said Aunt Kate, now that was a great fib to tell.

—Can't you see that I'm as hoarse as a crow? said Mr. D'Arcy roughly.

He went into the pantry hastily and put on his overcoat. The others, taken aback by his rude speech, could find nothing to say. Aunt Kate wrinkled her brows and made signs to the others to drop the subject. Mr. D'Arcy stood swathing his neck carefully and frowning.

—It's the weather, said Aunt Julia, after a pause.

—Yes, everybody has colds, said Aunt Kate readily, everybody.

—They say, said Mary Jane, we haven't had snow like it for thirty years; and I read this morning in the newspapers that the snow is general all over Ireland.

—I love the look of snow, said Aunt Julia sadly.

—So do I, said Miss O'Callaghan. I think Christmas is never really Christmas unless we have the snow on the ground.

—But poor Mr. D'Arcy doesn't like the snow, said Aunt Kate, smiling.

Mr. D'Arcy came from the pantry, fully swathed and buttoned, and in a repentant tone told them the history of his cold. Everyone gave him advice and said it was a great pity and urged him to be very careful of his throat in the night air. Gabriel watched his wife who did not join in the conversation. She was standing right under the dusty fanlight and the flame of the gas lit up the rich bronze of her hair which he had seen her drying at the fire a few days before. She was in the same attitude and seemed unaware of the talk about her. At last she turned towards them and Gabriel saw that there was colour on her cheeks and that her eyes were shining. A sudden tide of joy went leaping out of his heart.

—Mr. D'Arcy, she said, what is the name of that song you were singing?

—It's called *The Lass of Aughrim*,[3] said Mr. D'Arcy, but I couldn't remember it properly. Why? Do you know it?

—*The Lass of Aughrim*, she repeated. I couldn't think of the name.

3. Variant of *The Lass of Loch Royal*, Child's ballad No. 76. It tells of a girl seduced and abandoned. She stands in the rain outside the house of her seducer with her baby in her arms.

—It's a very nice air, said Mary Jane. I'm sorry you were not in voice to-night.

—Now, Mary Jane, said Aunt Kate, don't annoy Mr. D'Arcy. I won't have him annoyed.

Seeing that all were ready to start she shepherded them to the door where good-night was said:

—Well, good-night, Aunt Kate, and thanks for the pleasant evening.

—Good-night, Gabriel. Good-night, Gretta!

—Good-night, Aunt Kate, and thanks ever so much. Good-night, Aunt Julia.

—O, good-night, Gretta, I didn't see you.

—Good-night, Mr. D'Arcy. Good-night, Miss O'Callaghan.

—Good-night, Miss Morkan.

—Good-night, again.

—Good-night, all. Safe home.

—Good-night. Good-night.

The morning was still dark. A dull yellow light brooded over the houses and the river; and the sky seemed to be descending. It was slushy underfoot; and only streaks and patches of snow lay on the roofs, on the parapets of the quay and on the area railings. The lamps were still burning redly in the murky air and, across the river, the palace of the Four Courts stood out menacingly against the heavy sky.

She was walking on before him with Mr. Bartell D'Arcy, her shoes in a brown parcel tucked under one arm and her hands holding her skirt up from the slush. She had no longer any grace of attitude but Gabriel's eyes were still bright with happiness. The blood went bounding along his veins; and the thoughts went rioting through his brain, proud, joyful, tender, valorous.

She was walking on before him so lightly and so erect that he longed to run after her noiselessly, catch her by the shoulders and say something foolish and affectionate into her ear. She seemed to him so frail that he longed to defend her against something and then to be alone with her. Moments of their secret life together burst like stars upon his memory. A heliotrope envelope was lying beside his breakfast-cup and he was caressing it with his hand. Birds were twittering in the ivy and the sunny web of the curtain was shimmering along the floor: he could not eat for happiness. They were standing on the crowded platform and he was placing a ticket inside the warm palm of her glove. He was standing with her in the cold, looking in through a grated window at a man making bottles in a roaring furnace. It was very cold. Her face, fragrant in the cold air, was quite close to his; and suddenly she called out to the man at the furnace:

—Is the fire hot, sir?

But the man could not hear her with the noise of the furnace. It was just as well. He might have answered rudely.

A wave of yet more tender joy escaped from his heart and went coursing in warm flood along his arteries. Like the tender fires of stars moments of their life together, that no one knew of or would ever know of, broke upon and illumined his memory. He longed to recall to her those moments, to make her forget the years of their dull existence together and remember only their moments of ecstasy. For the years, he felt, had not quenched his soul or hers. Their children, his writing, her household cares had not quenched all their souls' tender fire. In one letter that he had written to her then he had said: *Why is it that words like these seem to me so dull and cold? Is it because there is no word tender enough to be your name?*

Like distant music these words that he had written years before were borne towards him from the past. He longed to be alone with her. When the others had gone away, when he and she were in their room in the hotel, then they would be alone together. He would call her softly:

—Gretta!

Perhaps she would not hear at once: she would be undressing. Then something in his voice would strike her. She would turn and look at him. . . .

At the corner of Winetavern Street they met a cab. He was glad of its rattling noise as it saved him from conversation. She was looking out of the window and seemed tired. The others spoke only a few words, pointing out some building or street. The horse galloped along wearily under the murky morning sky, dragging his old rattling box after his heels, and Gabriel was again in a cab with her, galloping to catch the boat, galloping to their honeymoon.

As the cab drove across O'Connell Bridge Miss O'Callaghan said:

—They say you never cross O'Connell Bridge without seeing a white horse.

—I see a white man this time, said Gabriel.

Where? asked Mr. Bartell D'Arcy.

Gabriel pointed to the statue, on which lay patches of snow. Then he nodded familiarly to it and waved his hand.

—Good-night, Dan,[4] he said gaily.

When the cab drew up before the hotel Gabriel jumped out and, in spite of Mr. Bartell D'Arcy's protest, paid the driver. He gave the man a shilling over his fare. The man saluted and said:

—A prosperous New Year to you, sir.

—The same to you, said Gabriel cordially.

She leaned for a moment on his arm in getting out of the cab and while standing at the curbstone, bidding the others good-night. She leaned lightly on his arm, as lightly as when she had danced with him a few hours before. He had felt proud and happy then, happy that she was his, proud of her grace and wifely carriage. But now, after the kindling again of so many memories, the first touch of her body, musical and strange and perfumed, sent through him a keen pang of lust. Under cover of her silence he pressed her arm closely to his side; and, as they stood at the hotel door, he felt that they had escaped from their lives and duties, escaped from home and friends and run away together with wild and radiant hearts to a new adventure.

An old man was dozing in a great hooded chair in the hall. He lit a candle in the office and went before them to the stairs. They followed him in silence, their feet falling in soft thuds on the thickly carpeted stairs. She mounted the stairs behind the porter, her head bowed in the ascent, her frail shoulders

4. The statue is of Daniel O'Connell (1775–1847), Irish patriot for whom the bridge is named.

curved as with a burden, her skirt girt tightly about her. He could have flung his arms about her hips and held her still for his arms were trembling with desire to seize her and only the stress of his nails against the palms of his hands held the wild impulse of his body in check. The porter halted on the stairs to settle his guttering candle. They halted too on the steps below him. In the silence Gabriel could hear the falling of the molten wax into the tray and the thumping of his own heart against his ribs.

The porter led them along a corridor and opened a door. Then he set his unstable candle down on a toilet-table and asked at what hour they were to be called in the morning.

—Eight, said Gabriel.

The porter pointed to the tap of the electric-light and began a muttered apology but Gabriel cut him short.

—We don't want any light. We have light enough from the street. And I say, he added, pointing to the candle, you might remove that handsome article, like a good man.

The porter took up his candle again, but slowly for he was surprised by such a novel idea. Then he mumbled good-night and went out. Gabriel shot the lock to.

A ghostly light from the street lamp lay in a long shaft from one window to the door. Gabriel threw his overcoat and hat on a couch and crossed the room towards the window. He looked down into the street in order that his emotion might calm a little. Then he turned and leaned against a chest of drawers with his back to the light. She had taken off her hat and cloak and was standing before a large swinging mirror, unhooking her waist. Gabriel paused for a few moments, watching her, and then said:

—Gretta!

She turned away from the mirror slowly and walked along the shaft of light towards him. Her face looked so serious and weary that the words would not pass Gabriel's lips. No, it was not the moment yet.

—You looked tired, he said.

—I am a little, she answered.

—You don't feel ill or weak?

—No, tired: that's all.

She went on to the window and stood there, looking out. Gabriel waited again and then, fearing that diffidence was about to conquer him, he said abruptly:

—By the way, Gretta!

—What is it?

—You know that poor fellow Malins? he said quickly.

—Yes. What about him?

—Well, poor fellow, he's a decent sort of chap after all, continued Gabriel in a false voice. He gave me back that sovereign[5] I lent him and I didn't expect it really. It's a pity he wouldn't keep away from that Browne, because he's not a bad fellow at heart.

He was trembling now with annoyance. Why did she seem so abstracted?

5. Gold coin worth one pound.

He did not know how he could begin. Was she annoyed, too, about something? If she would only turn to him or come to him of her own accord! To take her as she was would be brutal. No, he must see some ardour in her eyes first. He longed to be master of her strange mood.

—When did you lend him the pound? she asked, after a pause.

Gabriel strove to restrain himself from breaking out into brutal language about the sottish Malins and his pound. He longed to cry to her from his soul, to crush her body against his, to overmaster her. But he said:

—O, at Christmas, when he opened that little Christmas-card shop in Henry Street.

He was in such a fever of rage and desire that he did not hear her come from the window. She stood before him for an instant, looking at him strangely. Then, suddenly raising herself on tiptoe and resting her hands lightly on his shoulders, she kissed him.

—You are a very generous person, Gabriel, she said.

Gabriel, trembling with delight at her sudden kiss and at the quaintness of her phrase, put his hands on her hair and began smoothing it back, scarcely touching it with his fingers. The washing had made it fine and brilliant. His heart was brimming over with happiness. Just when he was wishing for it she had come to him of her own accord. Perhaps her thoughts had been running with his. Perhaps she had felt the impetuous desire that was in him and then the yielding mood had come upon her. Now that she had fallen to him so easily he wondered why he had been so diffident.

He stood, holding her head between his hands. Then, slipping one arm swiftly about her body and drawing her towards him, he said softly:

—Gretta dear, what are you thinking about?

She did not answer nor yield wholly to his arm. He said again, softly:

—Tell me what it is, Gretta. I think I know what is the matter. Do I know?

She did not answer at once. Then she said in an outburst of tears:

—O, I am thinking about that song, *The Lass of Aughrim*.

She broke loose from him and ran to the bed and, throwing her arms across the bed-rail, hid her face. Gabriel stood stock-still for a moment in astonishment and then followed her. As he passed in the way of the cheval-glass he caught sight of himself in full length, his broad, well-filled shirt-front, the face whose expression always puzzled him when he saw it in a mirror and his glimmering gilt-rimmed eyeglasses. He halted a few paces from her and said:

—What about the song? Why does that make you cry?

She raised her head from her arms and dried her eyes with the back of her hand like a child. A kinder note than he had intended went into his voice.

—Why, Gretta? he asked.

—I am thinking about a person long ago who used to sing that song.

—And who was the person long ago? asked Gabriel, smiling.

—It was a person I used to know in Galway when I was living with my grandmother, she said.

The smile passed away from Gabriel's face. A dull anger began to gather again at the back of his mind and the dull fires of his lust began to glow angrily in his veins.

—Someone you were in love with? he asked ironically.

—It was a young boy I used to know, she answered, named Michael Furey. He used to sing that song, *The Lass of Aughrim*. He was very delicate.

Gabriel was silent. He did not wish her to think that he was interested in this delicate boy.

—I can see him so plainly, she said after a moment. Such eyes as he had: big dark eyes! And such an expression in them—an expression!

—O then, you were in love with him? said Gabriel.

—I used to go out walking with him, she said, when I was in Galway.

A thought flew across Gabriel's mind.

—Perhaps that was why you wanted to go to Galway with that Ivors girl? he said coldly.

She looked at him and asked in surprise:

—What for?

Her eyes made Gabriel feel awkward. He shrugged his shoulders and said:

—How do I know? To see him perhaps.

She looked away from him along the shaft of light towards the window in silence.

—He is dead, she said at length. He died when he was only seventeen. Isn't it a terrible thing to die so young as that?

—What was he? asked Gabriel, still ironically.

—He was in the gasworks, she said.

Gabriel felt humiliated by the failure of his irony and by the evocation of this figure from the dead, a boy in the gasworks. While he had been full of memories of their secret life together, full of tenderness and joy and desire, she had been comparing him in her mind with another. A shameful consciousness of his own person assailed him. He saw himself as a ludicrous figure, acting as a pennyboy[6] for his aunts, a nervous well-meaning sentimentalist, orating to vulgarians and idealising his own clownish lusts, the pitiable fatuous fellow he had caught a glimpse of in the mirror. Instinctively he turned his back more to the light lest she might see the shame that burned upon his forehead.

He tried to keep up his tone of cold interrogation but his voice when he spoke was humble and indifferent.

—I suppose you were in love with this Michael Furey, Gretta, he said.

—I was great with him at that time, she said.

Her voice was veiled and sad. Gabriel, feeling now how vain it would be to try to lead her whither he had purposed, caressed one of her hands and said, also sadly:

—And what did he die of so young, Gretta? Consumption, was it?

—I think he died for me, she answered.

A vague terror seized Gabriel at this answer as if, at that hour when he had hoped to triumph, some impalpable and vindictive being was coming against him, gathering forces against him in its vague world. But he shook himself free of it with an effort of reason and continued to caress her hand. He did not question her again for he felt that she would tell him of herself. Her hand was warm and moist: it did not respond to his touch but he continued to

6. Errand boy.

caress it just as he had caressed her first letter to him that spring morning.

—It was in the winter, she said, about the beginning of the winter when I was going to leave my grandmother's and come up here to the convent. And he was ill at the time in his lodgings in Galway and wouldn't be let out and his people in Oughterard[7] were written to. He was in decline, they said, or something like that. I never knew rightly.

She paused for a moment and sighed.

—Poor fellow, she said. He was very fond of me and he was such a gentle boy. We used to go out together, walking, you know, Gabriel, like the way they do in the country. He was going to study singing only for his health. He had a very good voice, poor Michael Furey.

—Well; and then? asked Gabriel.

—And then when it came to the time for me to leave Galway and come up to the convent he was much worse and I wouldn't be let see him so I wrote a letter saying I was going up to Dublin and would be back in the summer and hoping he would be better then.

She paused for a moment to get her voice under control and then went on:

—Then the night before I left I was in my grandmother's house in Nuns' Island, packing up, and I heard gravel thrown up against the window. The window was so wet I couldn't see so I ran downstairs as I was and slipped out the back into the garden and there was the poor fellow at the end of the garden, shivering.

—And did you not tell him to go back? asked Gabriel.

—I implored of him to go home at once and told him he would get his death in the rain. But he said he did not want to live. I can see his eyes as well as well! He was standing at the end of the wall where there was a tree.

—And did he go home? asked Gabriel.

—Yes, he went home. And when I was only a week in the convent he died and he was buried in Oughterard where his people came from. O, the day I heard that, that he was dead!

She stopped, choking with sobs, and, overcome by emotion, flung herself face downward on the bed, sobbing in the quilt. Gabriel held her hand for a moment longer, irresolutely, and then, shy of intruding on her grief, let it fall gently and walked quietly to the window.

She was fast asleep.

Gabriel, leaning on his elbow, looked for a few moments unresentfully on her tangled hair and half-open mouth, listening to her deep-drawn breath. So she had had that romance in her life: a man had died for her sake. It hardly pained him now to think how poor a part he, her husband, had played in her life. He watched her while she slept as though he and she had never lived together as man and wife. His curious eyes rested long upon her face and on her hair: and, as he thought of what she must have been then, in that time of her first girlish beauty, a strange friendly pity for her entered his soul. He did

7. Town in Connacht, twenty miles north of Galway.

not like to say even to himself that her face was no longer beautiful but he knew that it was no longer the face for which Michael Furey had braved death.

Perhaps she had not told him all the story. His eyes moved to the chair over which she had thrown some of her clothes. A petticoat string dangled to the floor. One boot stood upright, its limp upper fallen down: the fellow of it lay upon its side. He wondered at his riot of emotions of an hour before. From what had it proceeded? From his aunt's supper, from his own foolish speech, from the wine and dancing, the merry-making when saying good-night in the hall, the pleasure of the walk along the river in the snow. Poor Aunt Julia! She, too, would soon be a shade with the shade of Patrick Morkan and his horse. He had caught that haggard look upon her face for a moment when she was singing *Arrayed for the Bridal.* Soon, perhaps, he would be sitting in that same drawing-room, dressed in black, his silk hat on his knees. The blinds would be drawn down and Aunt Kate would be sitting beside him, crying and blowing her nose and telling him how Julia had died. He would cast about in his mind for some words that might console her, and would find only lame and useless ones. Yes, yes: that would happen very soon.

The air of the room chilled his shoulders. He stretched himself cautiously along under the sheets and lay down beside his wife. One by one they were all becoming shades. Better pass boldly into that other world, in the full glory of some passion, than fade and wither dismally with age. He thought of how she who lay beside him had locked in her heart for so many years that image of her lover's eyes when he had told her that he did not wish to live.

Generous tears filled Gabriel's eyes. He had never felt like that himself towards any woman but he knew that such a feeling must be love. The tears gathered more thickly in his eyes and in the partial darkness he imagined he saw the form of a young man standing under a dripping tree. Other forms were near. His soul had approached that region where dwell the vast hosts of the dead. He was conscious of, but could not apprehend, their wayward and flickering existence. His own identity was fading out into a grey impalpable world: the solid world itself which these dead had one time reared and lived in was dissolving and dwindling.

A few light taps upon the pane made him turn to the window. It had begun to snow again. He watched sleepily the flakes, silver and dark, falling obliquely against the lamplight. The time had come for him to set out on his journey westward. Yes, the newspapers were right: snow was general all over Ireland. It was falling on every part of the dark central plain, on the treeless hills, falling softly upon the Bog of Allen and, farther westward, softly falling into the dark mutinous Shannon[8] waves. It was falling, too, upon every part of the lonely churchyard on the hill where Michael Furey lay buried. It lay thickly drifted on the crooked crosses and headstones, on the spears of the little gate, on the barren thorns. His soul swooned slowly as he heard the snow falling faintly through the universe and faintly falling, like the descent of their last end, upon all the living and the dead.

8. River flowing westward through Ireland. The Bog of Allen is southwest of Dublin.

# Franz Kafka

*Kafka (1883–1924) was born in Prague, the son of a middle-class Jewish family. After obtaining a law degree at the German University in Prague, he held an inconspicuous position in the civil service for many years. His few intimates remembered him as a warmly humorous man; however, his deep sense of inferiority to his father, the frailty of his health, his indecisive and prolonged engagement that never led to marriage, his preoccupation with suicide, and his last years of struggle against the tuberculosis that killed him suggest some origins of the great anxiety that pervades his literary production. He was not altogether a pessimist but was tormented by the conviction that goodness is very remote and nearly impossible to attain. Though he considered his writing the major task of his life, he had completed very few of his projects at the time of his death and published even fewer. He directed his friend Max Brod to burn his remaining manuscripts when he died. Brod ignored the command and saw that many of them were published. Three unfinished novels—*The Trial *(1925),* The Castle *(1926), and* Amerika *(1927)—brought Kafka his first posthumous fame, but the fairly large body of stories published under Brod's sponsorship show the complexity of the author's imagination and metaphysical irony perhaps more comprehensively than the novels that earned him his place as a major spokesman for the Age of Anxiety. His stories in English translation can be found in* The Great Wall of China *(1933),* The Penal Colony *(1948), and* The Complete Stories *(1976).*

## The Metamorphosis[1]

### I

One morning, upon awakening from agitated dreams, Gregor Samsa found himself, in his bed, transformed into a monstrous vermin. He lay on his hard, armorlike back, and when lifting his head slightly, he could view his brown, vaulted belly partitioned by arching ridges, while on top of it, the blanket, about to slide off altogether, could barely hold. His many legs, wretchedly thin compared with his overall girth, danced helplessly before his eyes.

"What's happened to me?" he wondered. It was no dream. His room, a normal if somewhat tiny human room, lay quietly between the four familiar walls. Above the table, on which a line of fabric samples had been unpacked and spread out (Samsa was a traveling salesman), hung the picture that he had recently clipped from an illustrated magazine and inserted in a pretty gilt frame

1. Translated by Joachim Neugroschel.

The picture showed a lady sitting there upright, bedizened in a fur hat and fur boa, with her entire forearm vanishing inside a heavy fur muff that she held out toward the viewer.

Gregor's eyes then focused on the window, and the dismal weather—raindrops could be heard splattering on the metal ledge—made him feel quite melancholy.

"What if I slept a little more and forgot all about this nonsense," he thought. But his idea was impossible to carry out, for while he was accustomed to sleeping on his right side, his current state prevented him from getting into that position. No matter how forcefully he attempted to wrench himself over on his right side, he kept rocking back into his supine state. He must have tried it a hundred times, closing his eyes to avoid having to look at those wriggling legs, and he gave up only when he started feeling a mild, dull ache in his side such as he had never felt before.

"Oh, God," he thought, "what a strenuous profession I've picked! Day in, day out on the road. It's a lot more stressful than the work in the home office, and along with everything else I also have to put up with these agonies of traveling—worrying about making trains, having bad, irregular meals, meeting new people all the time, but never forming any lasting friendships that mellow into anything intimate. To hell with it all!"

Feeling a slight itch on his belly, he slowly squirmed along on his back toward the bedpost in order to raise his head more easily. Upon locating the itchy place, which was dotted with lots of tiny white specks that he could not fathom, he tried to touch the area with one of his legs, but promptly withdrew it, for the contact sent icy shudders through his body.

He slipped back into his former position.

"Getting up so early all the time," he thought, "makes you totally stupid. A man has to have his sleep. Other traveling salesmen live like harem women. For instance, whenever I return to the hotel during the morning to write up my orders, those men are still having breakfast. Just let me try that with my boss; I'd be kicked out on the spot. And anyway, who knows, that might be very good for me. If I weren't holding back because of my parents, I would have given notice long ago, I would have marched straight up to the boss and told him off from the bottom of my heart. He would have toppled from his desk! Besides, it's so peculiar the way he seats himself on it and talks down to the employees from his great height, and we also have to get right up close because he's so hard of hearing. Well, I haven't abandoned all hope; once I've saved enough to pay off my parents' debt to him—that should take another five or six years—I'll go through with it no matter what. I'll make a big, clean break! But for now, I've got to get up, my train is leaving at five A.M."

And he glanced at the alarm clock ticking on the wardrobe. "God Almighty!" he thought. It was six-thirty, and the hands of the clock were calmly inching forward, it was even past the half hour, it was almost a quarter to. Could the alarm have failed to go off? From the bed, you could see that it was correctly set at four o'clock; it must have gone off. Yes, but was it possible to sleep peacefully through that furniture-quaking jangle? Well, fine, he had not slept peacefully, though probably all the more soundly. But what should he do now?

The next train would be leaving at seven; and to catch it, he would have to rush like mad, and the samples weren't packed up yet, and he felt anything but fresh or sprightly. And even if he did catch the train, there would be no avoiding the boss's fulminations, for the errand boy must have waited at the five A.M. train and long since reported Gregor's failure to show up. The boy was the director's creature, spineless and mindless. Now what if Gregor reported sick? But that would be extremely embarrassing and suspect, for throughout his five years with the firm he had never been sick even once. The boss was bound to come over with the medical-plan doctor, upbraid the parents about their lazy son, and cut off all objections by referring to the doctor, for whom everybody in the world was in the best of health but work-shy. And besides, would the doctor be all that wrong in this case? Aside from his drowsiness, which was really superfluous after his long sleep, Gregor actually felt fine and was even ravenous

As he speedily turned all these things over in his mind, but could not resolve to get out of bed—the alarm clock was just striking a quarter to seven—there was a cautious rap on the door near the top end of his bed.

"Gregor," a voice called—it was his mother—"it's a quarter to seven. Didn't you have a train to catch?"

The gentle voice! Gregor was shocked to hear his own response; it was unmistakably his earlier voice, but with a painful and insuppressible squeal blending in as if from below, virtually leaving words in their full clarity for just a moment, only to garble them in their resonance, so that you could not tell whether you had heard right. Gregor had meant to reply in detail and explain everything, but, under the circumstances, he limited himself to saying, "Yes, yes, thank you, Mother, I'm getting up."

Because of the wooden door, the change in Gregor's voice was probably not audible on the other side, for the mother was put at ease by his reassurance and she shuffled away. However, their brief exchange had made the rest of the family realize that Gregor, unexpectedly, was still at home, and the father was already at one side door, knocking weakly though with his fist: "Gregor, Gregor," he called, "what's wrong?" And after a short pause, he admonished him again, though in a deeper voice, "Gregor! Gregor!"

At the other side door, however, the sister plaintively murmured, "Gregor? Aren't you well? Do you need anything?"

Gregor replied to both sides, "I'm ready now," and by enunciating fastidiously with drawn-out pauses between words, he tried to eliminate anything abnormal from his voice. Indeed, the father returned to his breakfast; but the sister whispered, "Gregor, open up, I beg you." However, Gregor had absolutely no intention of opening up; instead, he praised the cautious habit he had developed during his travels of locking all doors at night, even in his home.

For now, he wanted to get up calmly and without being nagged, put on his clothes, above all have breakfast, and only then think about what to do next; for he realized he would come to no sensible conclusion by pondering in bed. He remembered that often, perhaps from lying awkwardly, he had felt a slight ache, which, upon his getting up, had turned out to be purely imaginary, and he looked forward to seeing today's fancies gradually fading away. He had no doubt whatsoever that the change in his voice was nothing but the harbinger of a severe cold, an occupational hazard of traveling salesmen.

Throwing off the blanket was quite simple; all he had to do was puff himself up a little, and it dropped away by itself. Doing anything else, however, was difficult, especially since he was so uncommonly broad. He would have needed arms and hands to prop himself up, and all he had was the numerous tiny legs that kept perpetually moving every which way but without his managing to control them. If he tried to bend a leg, it first straightened out; and if he finally succeeded in taking charge of it, the other legs meanwhile all kept carrying on, as if emancipated, in extreme and painful agitation. "Just don't dawdle in bed," Gregor told himself.

To start with, he wanted to get out of bed with the lower part of his body; but this portion, which, incidentally, he had not yet seen and could not properly visualize, proved too cumbersome to move—it went so slowly. And when eventually, having grown almost frantic, he gathered all his strength and recklessly thrust forward, he chose the wrong direction and slammed violently into the lower bedpost, whereupon the burning pain he then felt made him realize that the lower part of his body might be precisely the most sensitive, at least for now.

He therefore first tried to get his upper portion out of the bed, and to do so he cautiously turned his head toward the side of the mattress. This actually proved easy; and eventually, despite its breadth and weight, his body bulk slowly followed the twisting of his head. But when his head was finally looming over the edge of the bed, in the free air, he was scared of advancing any further in this manner; for if he ultimately let himself plunge down like this, only an outright miracle would prevent injury to his head. And no matter what, he must not lose consciousness now of all times; he would be better off remaining in bed.

But when, sighing after repeating this exertion, he still lay there as before, watching his tiny legs battle each other perhaps even more fiercely and finding no way to bring peace and order to this idiosyncratic condition, he again mused that he could not possibly stay there. The most logical recourse would be to make any sacrifice whatsoever if there was even the slightest hope of his freeing himself from the bed. Yet at the same time, he did not neglect to keep reminding himself that a calm, indeed the calmest reflection was far superior to desperate resolves. In such moments, he fixed his eyes as sharply as he could on the window; but unfortunately, little comfort or encouragement could be drawn from the sight of the morning fog, which shrouded even the other side of the narrow street. "Already seven o'clock," he said to himself when the alarm clock struck again, "already seven o'clock and still such a thick fog." And for a short while, he lay quietly, breathing faintly, as if perhaps expecting the silence to restore real and normal circumstances.

But then he told himself, "I absolutely must be out of bed completely before the clock strikes seven-fifteen. Besides, by then someone from work will come to inquire about me, since the office opens before seven." And he now began seesawing the full length of his body at an altogether even rhythm in order to rock it from the bed. If he could get himself to tumble from the bed in this way, then he would no doubt prevent injury to his head by lifting it sharply while falling. His back seemed hard; nothing was likely to happen to it during the landing on the carpet. His greatest misgiving was about the loud crash that was sure to ensue, probably causing anxiety if not terror behind all the doors. Still, this risk had to be run.

By the time Gregor was already sticking halfway out of the bed (this new method was more of a game than a struggle, all he had to do was keep seesawing and wrenching himself along), it occurred to him how easy everything would be if someone lent him a hand. It would take only two strong people (he thought of his father and the maid); they would only have to slip their arms under his vaulted back, slide him out of the bed, crouch down with their burden, and then just wait patiently and cautiously as he flipped over to the floor, where he hoped his tiny legs would have some purpose. Now quite aside from the fact that the doors were locked, should he really call for assistance? Despite his misery, he could not help smiling at the very idea.

By now he was already seesawing so intensely that he barely managed to keep his balance, and so he would have to make up his mind very soon, for it was already ten after seven—when the doorbell rang. "It's someone from the office," he told himself, almost petrified, while his tiny legs only danced all the more hastily. For an instant, there was total hush. "They're not answering," Gregor said to himself, prey to some absurd hope. But then of course, the maid, as usual, strode firmly to the door and opened it. Gregor only had to hear the visitor's first word of greeting and he knew who it was—the office manager himself. Why oh why was Gregor condemned to working for a company where the slightest tardiness aroused the murkiest suspicions? Was every last employee a scoundrel, wasn't there a single loyal and dedicated person among them, a man who, if he failed to devote even a few morning hours to the firm, would go crazy with remorse, becoming absolutely incapable of leaving his bed? Wouldn't it suffice to send an office boy to inquire—if indeed this snooping were at all necessary? Did the office manager himself have to come, did the entire innocent family have to be shown that this was the only person who had enough brains to be entrusted with investigating this suspicious affair? And more because of these agitating reflections than because of any concrete decision, Gregor swung himself out of bed with all his might. There was a loud thud, but not really a crash. His fall was slightly cushioned by the carpet; and also, his back was more pliable than he had thought. Hence the dull thud was not so blatant. However, by not holding his head carefully enough, he had banged it; now he twisted it, rubbing it on the carpet in annoyance and pain.

"Something fell in there," said the office manager in the left-hand room. Gregor tried to imagine whether something similar to what had happened to him today might not someday happen to the office manager. After all, the possibility had to be granted. However, as if in brusque response to this question, the office manager now took a few resolute steps in the next room, causing his patent-leather boots to creak.

From the right-hand room, the sister informed Gregor in a whisper, "Gregor, the office manager is here."

"I know," said Gregor to himself, not daring to speak loudly enough for the sister to hear.

"Gregor," the father now said from the left-hand room, "the office manager has come to inquire why you didn't catch the early train. We have no idea what to tell him. Besides, he would like to speak to you personally. So please open the door. I'm sure he will be kind enough to overlook the disorder in the room."

"Good morning, Mr. Samsa," the office manager was calling amiably.

"He's not well," the mother said to the office manager while the father kept talking through the door, "he's not well, believe me, sir. Why else would Gregor miss a train! I mean, the boy thinks of nothing but his job. I'm almost annoyed that he never goes out in the evening; goodness, he's been back in town for a whole week now, but he's stayed in every single night. He just sits here at the table, quietly reading the newspaper or poring over timetables. The only fun he has is when he does some fretsawing. For instance, he spent two or three evenings carving out a small picture frame; you'd be amazed how pretty it is. It's hanging inside, in his room; you'll see it in a moment when Gregor opens the door. By the way, sir, I'm delighted that you're here; we could never have gotten Gregor to unlock the door by ourselves—he's so stubborn; and he must be under the weather, even though he denied it this morning."

"I'll be right there," said Gregor slowly and deliberately, but not stirring so as not to miss one word of the conversation.

"I can think of no other explanation either, Mrs. Samsa," said the manager, "I do hope it is nothing serious. Though still and all, I must say that for business reasons we businessmen—unfortunately or fortunately, as you will—very often must simply overcome a minor indisposition."

"Well, can the manager come into your room now?" asked the impatient father, knocking on the door again.

"No," said Gregor. In the left-hand room there was an embarrassed silence, in the right-hand room the sister began sobbing.

Why didn't she join the others? She had probably only just gotten out of bed and not yet started dressing. And what was she crying about? Because Gregor wouldn't get up and let the manager in, because he was in danger of losing his job, and because the boss would then go back to dunning Gregor's parents with his old claims? For the time being, those were most likely pointless worries. Gregor was still here and had no intention whatsoever of running out on his family. True, at this moment he was simply lying on the carpet, and no one aware of his condition would have seriously expected him to let in the manager. Indeed, Gregor could hardly be dismissed on the spot for this petty discourtesy, for which he would easily hit on an appropriate excuse later on. He felt it would make far more sense if they left him alone for now instead of pestering him with tears and coaxing. However, the others were in a state of suspense, which justified their behavior.

"Mr. Samsa," the manager now called out, raising his voice, "what is wrong? You are barricading yourself in your room, answering only 'yes' or 'no,' causing your parents serious and unnecessary anxieties, and—I only mention this in passing—neglecting your professional duties in a truly outrageous manner. I am speaking on behalf of your parents and the director of the firm and I am quite earnestly requesting an immediate and cogent explanation. I am dumbfounded, dumbfounded. I believed you to be a quiet, reasonable person, and now you suddenly seem intent on flaunting bizarre moods. This morning the director hinted at a possible explanation for your tardiness—it pertained to the cash collections that you were recently entrusted with—but in fact I practically gave him my word of honor that this explanation could not be valid. Now, however, I am witnessing your incomprehensible stubbornness, which makes me lose any and all desire to speak up for you in any way whatsoever. And your job is by no means rock solid. My original intention was to tell you all this in private, but since you are forcing me to waste my time here needlessly, I see no reason why your parents should not find out as well. Frankly, your recent work has been highly unsatisfactory. We do appreciate that this is not the season for doing a lot of business; still, there is no season whatsoever, there can be no season for doing no business at all, Mr. Samsa."

"But, sir," Gregor exclaimed, beside himself, forgetting everything else in his agitation, "I'll open the door immediately, this very instant. A slight indisposition, a dizzy spell have prevented me from getting up. I am still lying in bed. But now I am quite fresh again. I am getting out of bed this very second. Please be patient for another moment or two! It is not going as well as I expected. But I do feel fine. How suddenly it can overcome a person! Just last night I was quite well, my parents know I was—or rather, last night I did have a slight foreboding. It must have been obvious to anyone else. Just why didn't I report it at the office!? But one always thinks one can get over an illness without staying home. Sir! Please spare my parents! There are no grounds for any of the things you are accusing me of—in fact, no one has ever so much as breathed a word to me. Perhaps you have not seen the latest orders that I sent in. Anyhow, I *will* be catching the eight A.M. train, these several hours of rest have revitalized me. Do not waste any more of your time, sir; I'll be in the office myself instantly—please be kind enough to inform them of this and to give my best to the director!"

And while hastily blurting out all these things, barely knowing what he was saying, Gregor, most likely because of his practice in bed, had managed to get closer to the wardrobe and was now trying to pull himself up against it. He truly wanted to open the door, truly show himself and speak to the office manager; he was eager to learn what the others, who were so keen on his presence now, would say upon seeing him. If they were shocked, then Gregor would bear no further responsibility and could hold his peace. But if they accepted everything calmly, then he likewise had no reason to get upset, and could, if he stepped on it, actually be in the station by eight. At first, he kept sliding down the smooth side of the wardrobe, but eventually he gave himself a final swing and stood there ignoring the burning pains in his abdomen, distressful as they were. Next he let himself keel over against the back of a nearby chair, his tiny legs clinging to the edges. In this way, he gained control of himself and he kept silent, for now he could listen to the office manager.

"Did you understand a single word of that?" the office manager asked the parents. "He's not trying to make fools of us, is he?!"

"For goodness' sake," the mother exclaimed, already weeping, "he may be seriously ill and we're torturing him. Grete! Grete!" she then shouted.

"Mother?" the sister called from the other side. They were communicating across Gregor's room. "You have to go to the doctor immediately. Gregor is sick. Hurry, get the doctor. Did you hear Gregor talking just now?"

"That was an animal's voice," said the manager, his tone noticeably soft compared with the mother's shouting.

"Anna! Anna!" the father called through the vestibule into the kitchen, clapping his hands, "Get a locksmith immediately!" And the two girls, their skirts rustling, were already dashing through the vestibule (how could the sister have dressed so quickly?) and tearing the apartment door open. No one heard it slamming; they must have left it open, as is common in homes that are struck by disaster.

Gregor, however, had grown much calmer. True, the others no longer understood what he said even though it sounded clear enough to him, clearer than before, perhaps because his ears had gotten used to it. But nevertheless, the others now believed there was something not quite right about him, and they were willing to help. His spirits were brightened by the aplomb and assurance with which their first few instructions had been carried out. He felt included once again in human society and, without really drawing a sharp distinction between the doctor and the locksmith, he expected magnificent and astonishing feats from both. Trying to make his voice as audible as he could for the crucial discussions about to take place, he coughed up a little, though taking pains to do so quite softly, since this noise too might sound different from human coughing, which he no longer felt capable of judging for himself. Meanwhile, the next room had become utterly hushed. Perhaps the parents and the office manager were sitting and whispering at the table, perhaps they were all leaning against the doors and eavesdropping.

Gregor slowly lumbered toward the door, shoving the chair along, let go of it upon arriving, tackled the door, held himself erect against it—the pads on his tiny feet were a bit sticky—and for a moment he rested from the strain. But then, using his mouth, he began twisting the key in the lock. Unfortunately he appeared to have no real teeth—now with what should he grasp the key?—but to make up for it his jaws were, of course, very powerful. They actually enabled him to get the key moving, whereby he ignored the likelihood of his harming himself in some way, for a brown liquid oozed from his mouth, flowing over the key and dripping to the floor.

"Listen," said the office manager in the next room, "he's turning the key." This was very encouraging for Gregor; but everyone should have cheered him on, including the father and the mother. "Attaboy, Gregor!" they should have shouted. "Don't let go, get that lock!" And imagining them all as suspensefully following his efforts, he obliviously bit into the key with all the strength he could muster. In tune with his progress in turning the key, he kept dancing around the lock, holding himself upright purely by his mouth and, as need be, either dangling from the key or pushing it down again with the full heft of his body. It was the sharper click of the lock finally snapping back that literally brought Gregor to. Sighing in relief, he told himself, "So I didn't need the locksmith after all," and he put his head on the handle in order to pull one wing of the double door all the way in.

Since he had to stay on the same side as the key, the door actually swung back quite far without his becoming visible. He had to twist slowly around the one wing, and very gingerly at that, to avoid plopping over on his back before entering the next room. He was still busy performing this tricky maneuver, with no time to heed anything else, when he heard the office manager blurt out a loud "Oh!"—it sounded like a whoosh of wind—and now he also saw him, the person nearest to the door, pressing his hand to his open mouth and slowly shrinking back as if he were being ousted by some unseeable but relentless force. The mother, who, despite the office manager's presence, stood there with her hair still undone and bristling, first gaped at the father, clasping her hands, then took two steps toward Gregor and collapsed, her petticoats flouncing out all around her and her face sinking quite undetectably into her breasts. The father clenched his fist, glaring at Gregor as if trying to shove him back into his room, then peered unsteadily around the parlor before covering his eyes with his hands and weeping so hard that his powerful chest began to quake.

Gregor did not step into the parlor after all; instead he leaned against his side of the firmly bolted second wing of the door, so that only half his body could be seen along with his head, which tilted sideways above it, peeping out at the others. Meanwhile the day had grown much lighter. Across the street, a portion of the endless, grayish black building (it was a hospital) stood out clearly with its regular windows harshly disrupting the façade. The rain was still falling, but only in large, visibly separate drops that were also literally hurled separately to the ground. The breakfast dishes still abundantly covered the table because breakfast was the most important meal of the day for Gregor's father; and he would draw it out for hours on end by reading various newspapers. The opposite wall sported a photograph of Gregor from his military days: it showed him as a lieutenant, hand on sword, with a carefree smile, demanding respect for his bearing and his uniform. The vestibule door was open, and since the apartment door was open too, one could see all the way out to the landing and the top of the descending stairs.

"Well," said Gregor, quite aware of being the only one who had kept calm, "I'll be dressed in a minute, pack up my samples, and catch my train. Would you all, would you all let me go on the road? Well, sir, you can see I am not stubborn and I enjoy working. Traveling is arduous, but I could not live without it. Why, where are you going, sir? To the office? Right? Will you report all this accurately? A man may be temporarily incapacitated, but that is precisely the proper time to remember his past achievements and to bear in mind that later on, once the obstacle is eliminated, he is sure to work all the harder and more intently. After all, I am so deeply obligated to the director, you know that very well. And then, I have to take care of my parents and my sister. I'm in a tight spot, but still I'll work my way out again. So please don't make things more difficult for me than they already are. Put in a good word for me at the office! People don't like a traveling salesman, I know. They think he makes barrels of money and has a wonderful life. They simply have no special reason to examine their prejudice. But you, sir, you have a better notion of what it's all about than the rest of the staff, why, than even—this is strictly between us—a better notion than even the director, who, as owner of the firm, is easily swayed against an employee. You also know very well that a traveling salesman, being away from the office most of the year, can so easily fall victim to gossip, coincidences, and unwarranted complaints, and he cannot possibly defend himself since he almost never finds out about them, except perhaps when he returns from a trip, exhausted, and personally suffers their awful consequences at home without fathoming their inscrutable causes. Sir, please do not leave without saying something to show that you agree with me at least to some small extent!"

But the office manager had already turned away at Gregor's very first words, and he only looked back at him over his twitching shoulder and with gaping lips. Indeed during Gregor's speech, the manager did not halt for even an instant. Rather, without losing sight of Gregor, he retreated toward the door, but only very gradually, as if there were some secret ban on leaving the room. He was already in the vestibule, and to judge by his abrupt movement when he finally pulled his leg out of the parlor, one might have thought he had just burned the sole of his foot. In the vestibule, however, he stretched out his right hand very far, toward the staircase, as if some unearthly redemption were awaiting him there.

Gregor realized he must on no account allow the office manager to leave in this frame of mind; if he did, Gregor's position at the office would be thoroughly compromised. The parents did not quite understand this. During these long years, they had become convinced that he was set up for life at this firm, and besides they were so preoccupied with their immediate problems as to have lost all sense of foresight. Gregor, however, did possess such foresight. The office manager had to be held back, calmed down, cajoled, and finally won over; Gregor's future and that of his family hinged on it! If only the sister had been here! She was intelligent; she had already started to cry when Gregor was still lying calmly on his back. And the office manager, that ladies' man, would certainly have let her take him in hand: she would have shut the apartment door, kept him in the vestibule, and talked him out of his terror. But the sister was not there, so Gregor had to act on his own. Forgetting that he was as yet unacquainted with his current powers of movement and also that once again his words had possibly, indeed probably, not been understood, he left the wing of the door and lumbered through the opening. He intended to head toward the office manager, who was ludicrously clutching the banister on the landing with both hands. But Gregor, fumbling for support, yelped as he flopped down upon his many tiny legs. The instant this happened, he felt a physical ease and comfort for the first time that morning. His tiny legs had solid ground underneath, and he was delighted to note that they were utterly obedient—they even strove to carry him off to wherever he wished; and he already believed that the final recovery from all sufferings was at hand. He lay on the floor, wobbling because of his checked movement, not that far from his mother, who seemed altogether self-absorbed. But at that same moment, she unexpectedly leaped up, stretched her arms far apart, splayed her fingers, and cried, "Help! For God's sake, help!" Next she lowered her head as if to see Gregor more clearly, but then, in self-contradiction, she senselessly backed away, forgetting the covered table behind her, hurriedly sat down upon it without thinking, and apparently failed to notice that next to her the large coffeepot had been knocked over and was discharging a torrent of coffee full force upon the carpet.

"Mother, Mother," Gregor murmured, looking up at her. For an instant, the office manager had entirely slipped his mind; on the other hand, Gregor could not help snapping his jaws a few times at the sight of the flowing coffee. This prompted the mother to scream again, flee from the table, and collapse into the father's arms as he came dashing up to her. But Gregor had no time for his parents: the office manager was already on the stairs; with his chin on the banister, he took one final look back. Gregor broke into a run, doing his best to catch up with him. The office manager must have had an inkling of this, for he jumped down several steps at a time and disappeared. However, he did shout, "Ugh!" and his shout rang through the entire stairwell.

Unfortunately, the father, who so far had stayed relatively composed, seemed thoroughly bewildered by the office manager's flight. For, instead of rushing after him or at least not preventing Gregor from pursuing him, the father, with his right hand, grabbed the cane that the office manager, together with a hat and overcoat, had forgotten on a chair and, with his left hand, took a large newspaper from the table. Stamping his feet, he brandished the cane and the newspaper at Gregor in order to drive him back into his room. No pleading from Gregor helped, indeed no pleading was understood; no matter how humbly Gregor turned his head, the father merely stamped his feet all the more forcefully. Across the room, the mother had flung open a window despite the cool weather, and leaning way out, she buried her face in her hands. A strong draft arose between the street and the stairwell, the window curtains flew up, the newspapers rustled on the table, stray pages wafted across the floor. The father charged pitilessly, spewing hisses like a savage. Since Gregor as yet had no practice in moving backwards, it was really slow going. Had he only been permitted to wheel around, he would have been inside his room at once. But he was afraid it would take too long, trying the father's patience even more—and at any moment now the cane in the father's hand threatened to deal the lethal blow to Gregor's back or head. Ultimately, however, Gregor had no choice, for he realized with dismay that he did not even know how to stay the course when backing up. And so, while constantly darting fearful side glances at his father, he began rotating as swiftly as he could, though he was actually very slow. Perhaps the father sensed Gregor's good intention, for he did not interfere—instead, he occasionally even steered the pivoting motion from a distance with the tip of his cane. If only the father would stop that unbearable hissing! It made Gregor lose his head altogether. He had swung around almost fully when, constantly distracted by those hisses, he actually miscalculated and briefly shifted the wrong way. And then, as soon as he finally managed to get his head to the doorway, his body proved too broad to squeeze through all that readily. Naturally, in the father's present mood, it never even remotely crossed his mind to push back the other wing of the door and create a passage wide enough for Gregor. He was obsessed simply with forcing Gregor back into his room as fast as possible. Nor would he ever have stood for the intricate preparations that Gregor needed for hoisting himself on end and perhaps passing through the doorway in that posture. Instead, as if there were no hindrance, the father drove Gregor forward with a great uproar: behind Gregor the yelling no longer sounded like the voice of merely one father. Now it was do or die, and Gregor—come what might—jammed into the doorway. With one side of his body heaving up, he sprawled lopsided in the opening. His one flank was bruised raw, ugly splotches remained on the white door, and he was soon wedged in and unable to budge on his own. The tiny legs on his one side were dangling and trembling in midair and the tiny legs on his other side were painfully crushed against the floor. But now the father gave him a powerful shove from behind—a true deliverance. And Gregor, bleeding heavily, flew far into his room. The door was slammed shut with the cane, and then the apartment was still at last.

## II

It was almost dusk by the time Gregor emerged from his comatose sleep. He would certainly have awoken not much later even without being disturbed, for he felt sufficiently well rested; yet it seemed to him as if he had been aroused by fleeting steps and a cautious shutting of the vestibule door. The glow from the electric streetlamps produced pallid spots on the ceiling and the higher parts of the furniture, but down by Gregor it was dark. Slowly, still clumsily groping with his feelers, which he was just learning to appreciate, he lumbered toward the door to see what had been going on. His left side appeared to be one long, unpleasantly tightening scar, and he actually had to limp on his two rows of legs. One tiny leg, moreover, had been badly hurt during that morning's events (it was almost miraculous that only one had been hurt) and it dragged along lifelessly.

Only upon reaching the door did Gregor discover what had actually enticed him: it was the smell of something edible. For there stood a bowl full of fresh milk with tiny slices of white bread floating in it. He practically chortled for joy, being even hungrier now than in the morning, and he promptly dunked his head into the milk until it was nearly over his eyes. Soon, however, he withdrew his head in disappointment. Not only did the bruises on his left side make it difficult for him to eat—he could eat only if his entire wheezing body joined in—but he did not care for the milk, even though it had always been his favorite beverage, which was no doubt why his sister had placed it in his room. As a matter of fact, he turned away from the bowl almost with loathing and crawled back to the middle of the room.

In the parlor, as Gregor could see through the door crack, the gaslight was lit. But while at this time of day his father would usually take up his newspaper, an afternoon daily, and read it in a raised voice to the mother and sometimes also to the sister, not a sound was to be heard. Well, perhaps this practice of reading aloud, which the sister had always told Gregor about and written him about, had recently been discarded altogether. Yet while the entire apartment was hushed, it was anything but deserted.

"My, what a quiet life the family used to lead," Gregor thought to himself, and as he peered into the darkness, he felt a certain pride that he had managed to provide his parents and his sister with such a life in such a beautiful apartment. What if now all calm, all prosperity, all contentment should come to a horrifying end? Rather than lose himself in such ruminations, Gregor preferred to start moving, and so he crept up and down the room.

Once, during the long evening, one side door and then the other was opened a tiny crack and quickly shut again: somebody had apparently felt an urge to come in, but had then thought the better of it. Gregor halted right at the parlor door, determined to somehow bring in the hesitant visitor or at least find out who it was. But the door was not reopened, and Gregor waited in vain. That morning, when the doors had been locked, everybody had wanted to come in; but now that he had opened one door, and the rest had clearly been opened during the day, nobody came, and the keys were on the other side.

It was not until late at night that the light in the parlor was put out. Gregor could easily tell that the parents and the sister had stayed up this long, for, as he could clearly discern, all three of them were tiptoeing off. Since nobody would be visiting Gregor until morning, he had lots of time to reflect undisturbed and to figure out how to restructure his life. But the free, high-ceilinged room where he was forced to lie flat on the floor terrified him without his being able to pinpoint the cause; after all, it was his room and he had been living there for the last five years. Turning half involuntarily and not without a faint sense of embarrassment, he scurried under the settee, where, even though his back was a bit squashed and he could not lift his head, he instantly felt very cozy, regretting only that his body was too broad to squeeze in all the way.

There he remained for the rest of the night, either drowsing and repeatedly yanked awake by his hunger, or else fretting amid vague hopes, all of which, however, led to his concluding that for now he would have to lie low and, by being patient and utterly considerate, help the family endure the inconveniences that, as it happened, he was forced to cause them in his present state.

By early morning—it was still almost night—Gregor had a chance to test the strength of the resolutions he had just made, for the sister, almost fully dressed, opened the vestibule door and suspensefully peered in. She did not find him right away, but when she noticed him under the settee (goodness, he had to be somewhere, he couldn't just have flown away), she was so startled that unable to control herself she slammed the door from the outside. But, apparently regretting her behavior, she instantly reopened the door and tiptoed in as if visiting a very sick patient or even a stranger. Gregor, having pushed his head forward to the very edge of the settee, was watching her. Would she notice that he had barely touched the milk, though by no means for lack of hunger, and would she bring in some other kind of food more to his taste? If she did not do so on her own, he would rather starve to death than point it out to her, even while he felt a tremendous urge to scoot out from under the settee, throw himself at her feet, and beg her for some good food. But the sister, with some surprise, instantly noticed the full bowl, from which only a little milk had splattered all around. She promptly picked up the bowl, though not with her bare hands, but with a rag, and carried it away. Gregor was extremely curious as to what she would replace it with, and all sorts of conjectures ran through his mind. But he would never have hit on what the sister actually did in the goodness of her heart. Hoping to check his likes and dislikes, she brought him a whole array of food, all spread out on an old newspaper. There were old, half-rotten vegetables, some bones left over from supper and coated with a solidified white sauce, a few raisins and almonds, some cheese that Gregor had declared inedible two days ago, dry bread, bread and butter, and salted bread and butter. Furthermore, along with all those things, she brought some water in the bowl, which had probably been assigned to Gregor for good. And sensing that Gregor would not eat in front of her, she discreetly hurried away, even turning the key, just to show him that he could make himself as comfortable as he wished. Gregor's tiny legs whirred as he charged toward the food. His wounds, incidentally, must have healed up by now, he felt no handicap anymore, which was astonishing; for, as he recalled, after he had nicked his finger with a knife over a month ago, the injury had still been hurting the day before yesterday. "Am I less sensitive now?" he wondered, greedily sucking at the cheese, which had promptly exerted a more emphatic attraction on him than any of the other food. His eyes watered with contentment as he gulped down the cheese, the vegetables, and the sauce in rapid succession. By contrast, he did not relish the fresh foods, he could not even stand their smells, and he actually dragged the things he wanted to eat a short distance away. He was already done long since and was simply lazing in the same spot when the sister, to signal that he should withdraw, slowly turned the key. Startled, he jumped up though he was almost dozing, and scuttered back under the settee. However, it took a lot of self-control to remain there even during the few short moments that the sister spent in the room, for his body was slightly bloated from the ample food and he could scarcely breathe in that cramped space. Amid short fits of suffocation, he stared with somewhat bulging eyes while the unsuspecting sister, wielding a broom, swept up not only the leftovers but also the untouched food, as if this too were now unusable; she then hastily dumped everything into a pail, shutting its wooden lid and carrying everything out. No sooner had she turned her back than he skulked out from under the settee and began stretching and puffing up.

That was how Gregor received his food every day: once in the morning, when the parents and the maid were still asleep, and the second time after the family lunch, for the parents would then take a brief nap while the sister would send the maid out on some errand. While the parents certainly did not want Gregor to starve either, they may not have endured knowing more about his eating than from hearsay, or the sister may have wished to spare them some—perhaps only slight—grief, for they were really suffering enough as it was.

Gregor could not find out what excuses they had come up with to get the doctor and the locksmith out of the apartment; for since he was not understood, no one, including the sister, assumed that he could understand them. And so, whenever she was in his room, he had to content himself with occasionally hearing her sighs and her appeals to the saints. It was only later, when she had gotten a bit accustomed to everything (naturally there could be no question of her ever becoming fully accustomed), Gregor sometimes caught a remark that was meant to be friendly or might be interpreted as such. "He certainly enjoyed it today," she would say when Gregor had polished off a good portion of the food; while in the opposite event, which was gradually becoming more and more frequent, she would say almost sadly: "Now once again nothing's been touched."

But while Gregor could learn no news directly, he would eavesdrop, picking up a few things from the adjacent rooms, and the instant he heard voices, he would promptly scuttle over to the appropriate door, squeezing his entire body against it. During the early period in particular, no conversation took place that was not somehow about him, even if only in secret. For two whole days, every single meal was filled with discussions about what they ought to do; but even between meals, they kept harping on the same theme, for there were always at least two family members in the apartment, since plainly nobody wished to stay home alone and they could by no means all go out at the same time. Furthermore, on the very first day, the maid—it was not quite clear how much she knew about what had occurred—had implored the mother on bended knees to dismiss her immediately. Then, saying goodbye a quarter hour later, she had tearfully thanked them for the dismissal as if it were the most benevolent deed that they had ever done for her; and without being asked, she had sworn a dreadful oath that she would never breathe a single word to anyone.

So now the sister, together with the mother, also had to do the cooking; but this was not much of a bother, for they ate next to nothing. Over and over, Gregor heard them urging one another to eat, though in vain, receiving no other answer than, "Thanks, I've had enough," or something similar. They may not have drunk anything either. The sister would often ask the father if he would like some beer and she warmly offered to go and get it herself; when he failed to respond, she anticipated any misgivings on his part by saying she could also send the janitor's wife. But then the father would finally utter an emphatic "No," and the subject was no longer broached.

In the course of the very first day, the father laid out their overall financial circumstances and prospects to both the mother and the sister. From time to time, he rose from the table to fetch some document or notebook from his small strongbox, which he had salvaged after the collapse of his business five years earlier. They heard him opening the complicated lock and then shutting it again after removing whatever he had been looking for. The father's explanations were to some extent the first pleasant news that Gregor got to hear since his imprisonment. He had been under the impression that the father had failed to rescue anything from his business—at least, the father had told him nothing to the contrary, nor, admittedly, had Gregor ever asked him. Gregor's sole concern at that time had been to do whatever he could to make the family forget as quickly as possible the business catastrophe that had plunged them all into utter despair. And so he had thrown himself into his job with tremendous fervor, working his way up, almost overnight, from minor clerk to traveling salesman, who, naturally, had an altogether different earning potential and whose professional triumphs were instantly translated, by way of commissions, into cash, which could be placed on the table at home for the astonished and delighted family. Those had been lovely times, and they had never recurred, at least not with that same luster, even though Gregor was eventually earning so much money that he was able to cover and indeed did cover all the expenditures of the family. They had simply grown accustomed to this, both the family and Gregor; they accepted the money gratefully, he was glad to hand it over, but no great warmth came of it. Only the sister had remained close to Gregor; and since she, unlike Gregor, loved music and could play the violin poignantly, he was secretly planning to send her to the conservatory next year regardless of the great expense that it was bound to entail and that would certainly be made up for in some other way. During Gregor's brief stays in the city, the conservatory was often mentioned in his talks with the sister, but only as a lovely dream that could never possibly be realized; nor did the parents care to hear these innocent references. But Gregor's ideas on the subject were very definite and he intended to make the solemn announcement on Christmas Eve.

Such were the thoughts, quite futile in his present condition, that ran through his mind as he clung upright to the door, eavesdropping. Sometimes he was so thoroughly exhausted that he could no longer listen. His head would then inadvertently bump against the door, but he promptly pulled it erect again; for even that slight tap had been heard in the next room, causing everyone to stop talking. "What's he up to now!?" the father would say after a while, obviously turning toward the door, and only then did the interrupted conversation gradually resume.

Gregor now learned precisely enough (for the father would often repeat his explanations, partly because he himself had not dealt with these matters in a long time and partly because the mother did not always understand everything right off) that despite the disaster, some assets, albeit a very tiny sum, had survived from the old days, growing bit by bit because of the untouched interest. Furthermore, since the money that Gregor had brought home every month (keeping only a little for himself) had never been fully spent, it had accumulated into a small principal. Gregor, behind his door, nodded eagerly, delighted at this unexpected thrift and prudence. Actually, he could have applied this surplus toward settling the father's debt to the director, thereby bringing the day when he could have been rid of that job a lot closer; but now, the way the father had arranged things was better, no doubt.

Of course this sum was by no means large enough for the family to live off the interest; it might suffice to keep them going for one, at most two years, and that was all. It was simply money that really should not be drawn on and that ought to be put aside for emergencies, while the money to live on had to be earned. But the father, though still healthy, was an old man, who had not done a lick of work in five years and in any case could not be expected to take on very much. During those five years, his first vacation in an arduous and yet unsuccessful life, he had grown very fat, becoming rather clumsy. And should perhaps the old mother go to work—she, who suffered from asthma, who found it strenuous just walking through the apartment, and who spent every other day on the sofa, gasping for air by the open window? Or should the sister go to work—she, who was still a child at seventeen and should certainly keep enjoying her lifestyle, which consisted of dressing nicely, sleeping late, lending a hand with the housekeeping, going out to a few modest amusements, and above all, playing the violin? At first, whenever the conversation turned to this need to earn money, Gregor would always let go of the door and throw himself on the cool leather sofa nearby, for he felt quite hot with shame and grief.

Often he would lie there all through the long night, not getting a wink of sleep and merely scrabbling on the leather for hours on end. Or else, undaunted by the great effort, he would shove a chair over to the window, clamber up to the sill, and, propped on the chair, lean against the panes, obviously indulging in some vague memory of the freedom he had once found by gazing out the window. For actually, from day to day, even the things that were rather close were growing hazier and hazier; he could no longer even make out the hospital across the street, the all-too-frequent sight of which he used to curse. And if he had not known for sure that he lived on Charlotte Street, a quiet but entirely urban thoroughfare, he might have believed that he was staring at a wasteland in which gray sky and gray earth blurred together indistinguishably. Only twice had the observant sister needed to see the chair standing by the window; now, whenever she tidied up the room she would push the chair back to the window—indeed, from then on she would even leave the inside casement ajar.

If only Gregor could have spoken to her and thanked her for everything she had to do for him, he would have endured her kind actions more readily; but instead they caused him great suffering. Of course, she tried to surmount the overall embarrassment as much as possible, and naturally, as time wore by, she succeeded more and more. However, Gregor too eventually gained a sharper sense of things. Her very entrance was already terrible for him. No sooner had she stepped in than, without even taking time to close the door—careful as she usually was to protect everyone else from seeing Gregor's room—she charged straight over to the window and, as if almost suffocating, yanked it open with hasty hands, lingering there briefly no matter how chilly the weather and inhaling deeply. This din and dashing terrified Gregor twice a day. Throughout her visits he would cower under the settee, fully realizing that she would certainly have preferred to spare him this disturbance if only she had been able to keep the window shut while staying in the same room with him.

Once—something like a month had passed since Gregor's metamorphosis, and there was truly no special reason why the sister should still be alarmed by his appearance—she turned up a bit earlier than usual and caught Gregor staring out the window, motionless and terrifyingly erect. He would not have been surprised if she had refused to come in, since his position prevented her from opening the window immediately. But not only did she not come in, she actually recoiled and closed the door; an outsider might have honestly thought that Gregor had meant to ambush her and bite her. Naturally he hid under the settee at once, but then had to wait until noon for his sister to return, and she seemed far more upset than usual. It thus dawned on him that his looks were still unbearable to her and were bound to remain unbearable, which meant that it must have taken a lot of self-control for her not to run away upon glimpsing even the tiny scrap of his body that protruded from under the settee. So one day, hoping to spare her even this sight—the job took him four hours—he got the sheet on his back and lugged it over to the settee, arranging it in such a way that it concealed him entirely, thereby preventing the sister from seeing him even when she stooped down. After all, if she considered the sheet unnecessary, she could have removed it, for it was plain that Gregor could not possibly enjoy cutting himself off so thoroughly. But she left the sheet just as it was, and once, he even believed he caught a grateful glance when he cautiously lifted it a smidgen with his head to see how his sister was taking this innovation.

During the first two weeks, the parents could not get themselves to come into his room, and he often heard them expressing their great appreciation of the sister's efforts, whereas earlier they had often been cross with her for being, they felt, a somewhat useless girl. But now both the father and the mother would frequently wait outside Gregor's door while the sister tidied up inside, and upon reemerging, she promptly had to render a detailed account of what the room looked like, what Gregor had eaten, how he had behaved this time, and whether he was perhaps showing some slight improvement. The mother, incidentally, wanted to visit Gregor relatively soon. At first, the father and the sister tried to reason with her, and Gregor paid very close attention to their arguments, approving of them wholeheartedly. Later, however, the mother had to be held back forcibly, and when she then cried out, "Let me go to Gregor, he's my unhappy son! Don't you understand I have to go to him?" Gregor felt it might be a good idea if she did come in after all—not every day, naturally, but perhaps once a week: she was much better at everything than the sister, who, for all her courage, was still a child and might ultimately have taken on such a demanding task purely out of teenage capriciousness.

Gregor's wish to see his mother came true shortly. During the day, if only out of consideration for his parents, he did not want to appear at the window. On the other hand, he could not creep very far around the few square meters of the floor, he found it hard to lie still even at night, and eating soon gave him no pleasure whatsoever. So, for amusement, he got into the habit of prowling crisscross over the walls and ceiling. He particularly liked hanging from the ceiling. It was quite different from lying on the floor: he could breathe more freely and a faint tingle quivered through his body. In his almost blissful woolgathering up there, Gregor might, to his own surprise, let go and crash down on the floor. But since he naturally now controlled his body far more effectively than before, he was never harmed by that great plunge. The sister instantly noticed the new entertainment that Gregor had found for himself—after all, when creeping, he occasionally left traces of his sticky substance behind. And so, taking it into her head to enable Gregor to crawl over the widest possible area, she decided to remove the obstructive furniture—especially the wardrobe and the desk. However, there was no way she could manage this alone. She did not dare ask her father for help, and the maid would most certainly not have pitched in; for while this girl, who was about sixteen, had been valiantly sticking it out since the cook's departure, she had asked for the special favor of keeping the kitchen door locked all the time and opening it only when specifically called. As a result, the sister had no choice but to approach the mother one day during the father's absence. And indeed, with cries of joyful excitement, the mother came over, although falling silent at the door to Gregor's room. First, naturally, the sister checked inside to make sure everything was in order; only then did she let the mother enter. Gregor had hurriedly pulled the sheet lower and in tighter folds, truly making it look as if it had been tossed casually over the settee. This time, Gregor also refrained from peeping out from under the sheet:

he would go without seeing the mother for now and was simply glad that she had come despite everything.

"Come on, he's out of sight," said the sister, evidently leading the mother by the hand. Gregor now heard the two delicate women pushing the very heavy old wardrobe from its place and the sister constantly insisting on doing the major share of the work, ignoring the warnings from the mother, who was afraid she would overexert herself. It took a very long time. After probably just a quarter hour of drudging, the mother said it would be better if they left the wardrobe here. For one thing, it was too heavy—they would not be done before the father's arrival; and if the wardrobe stood in the middle of the room, it would block Gregor's movements in all directions. Secondly, it was not at all certain that they were doing Gregor a favor by removing the furniture. She said that the opposite seemed to be the case, the sight of the bare wall literally made her heart bleed. And why wouldn't Gregor respond in the same way since he was long accustomed to the furniture and would therefore feel desolate in the empty room? "And isn't that," the mother concluded very softly (in fact, she persistently almost whispered, as if, not knowing Gregor's precise whereabouts, she wanted to keep him from hearing the very sound of her voice, convinced as she was that he did not understand the words), "and if we remove the furniture, isn't that like showing him that we've given up all hope of his improvement and that we're callously leaving him to his own devices? I believe it would be best if we tried to keep the room just as it was, so that when Gregor comes back to us he will find that nothing's been changed and it will be much easier for him to forget what happened."

Upon hearing the mother's words, Gregor realized that in the course of these two months the lack of having anyone to converse with, plus the monotonous life in the midst of the family, must have befuddled his mind, for there was no other way to account for how he could have seriously longed to have his room emptied out. Did he really want the warm room, so cozily appointed with heirlooms, transformed into a lair, where he might, of course, be able to creep, unimpeded, in any direction, though forgetting his human past swiftly and totally? By now, he was already on the verge of forgetting, and had been brought up sharply only by the mother's voice after not hearing it for a long time. Nothing should be removed, everything had to remain: he could not do without the positive effects of the furniture on his state of mind. And if the furniture interfered with his senselessly crawling about, then it was a great asset and no loss.

Unfortunately, the sister was of a different mind; in the discussions concerning Gregor, she had gotten into the habit—not without some justification, to be sure—of acting the great expert in front of the parents. So now the mother's advice was again reason enough for the sister to demand that they remove not only the wardrobe and the desk, in line with her original plan, but all the furniture except for the indispensable settee. Her resoluteness was, naturally, prompted not just by childish defiance and the unexpected self-confidence she had recently gained at such great cost. After all, she had observed that while he needed a lot of space to creep around in, Gregor, so far as could be seen, made no use whatsoever of the furniture. Perhaps, however, the enthusiasm of girls her age also played its part—an exuberance that they try to indulge every chance they get. It now inveigled Grete into making Gregor's situation even more terrifying, so she could do even more for him than previously. For most likely no one but Grete would ever dare venture into a room where Gregor ruled the bare walls all alone.

And so she dug in her heels, refusing to give in to the mother, who, apparently quite anxious and uncertain of herself in this room, soon held her tongue and, to the best of her ability, helped the sister push out the wardrobe. Well, Gregor could, if necessary, do without the wardrobe, but the desk had to remain. And no sooner had the squeezing, groaning women shoved the wardrobe through the doorway than Gregor poked his head out from under the settee to judge how he could intervene as cautiously and considerately as possible. But alas, it was precisely the mother who was the first to return while Grete was still in the next room, holding her arms around the wardrobe and rocking it back and forth by herself without, of course, getting it to budge from the spot. The mother, however, was not used to the sight of Gregor—it might sicken her. And so Gregor, terrified, scuttered backwards to the other end of the settee, but was unable to prevent the front of the sheet from stirring slightly. That was enough to catch the mother's eye. She halted, stood still for an instant, then went back to Grete.

Gregor kept telling himself that nothing out of the ordinary was happening, it was just some furniture being moved. But these comings and goings of the women, their soft calls to one another, the scraping of the furniture along the floor was, as he soon had to admit, like a huge rumpus pouring in on all sides. And no matter how snugly he pulled in his head and legs and pressed his body against the floor, he inevitably had to own up that he would not endure the hubbub much longer. They were clearing out his room, stripping him of everything he loved. They had already dragged away the wardrobe, which contained the fretsaw and other tools, and they were now unprying the solidly embedded desk, where he had done his assignments for business college, high school, why, even elementary school—and he really had no time to delve into the good intentions of the two women, whom, incidentally, he had almost forgotten about, for they were so exhausted that they were already laboring in silence, and all that could be heard was the heavy plodding of their feet.

And so, while the women were in the next room, leaning against the desk to catch their breath, he broke out, changing direction four times, for he was truly at a loss about what to rescue first—when he saw the picture of the woman clad in nothing but furs hanging blatantly on the otherwise empty wall. He quickly scrambled up to it and squeezed against the glass, which held him fast, soothing his hot belly. At least, with Gregor now covering it up, this picture would certainly not be carried off by anyone. He turned his head toward the parlor door, hoping to observe the women upon their return.

After granting themselves little rest, they were already coming back; Grete had put her arm around her mother, almost carrying her. "Well, what should we take next?" said Grete, looking around. At this point, her eyes met those of Gregor on the wall. It was no doubt only because of the mother's presence that she maintained her composure. Bending her face toward the mother to keep her from peering about, she said, although trembling and without thinking: "Come on, why don't we go back to the parlor for a moment?" It was obvious to Gregor that she wanted to get the mother to safety and then chase him down from the wall. Well, just let her try! He clung to his picture, refusing to surrender it. He would rather jump into Grete's face.

But Grete's words had truly unnerved the mother, who stepped aside, glimpsed the huge brown splotch on the flowered wallpaper, and cried out in a harsh, shrieking voice before actually realizing that this was Gregor, "Oh God, oh God!" With outspread arms as if giving up everything, she collapsed across the settee and remained motionless.

"Hey, Gregor!" the sister shouted with a raised fist and a penetrating glare. These were her first direct words to him since his metamorphosis. She ran into the next room to get some sort of essence for reviving the mother from her faint. Gregor also wanted to help (there was time enough to salvage the picture later), but he was stuck fast to the glass and had to wrench himself loose. He then also scurried into the next room as if he could give the sister some kind of advice as in earlier times, but then had to stand idly behind her while she rummaged through an array of vials. Upon spinning around, she was startled by the sight of him. A vial fell on the floor and shattered. A sliver of glass injured Gregor's face, and some corrosive medicine oozed from the sliver. Grete, without further delay, grabbed as many vials as she could hold and dashed over to the mother, slamming the door with her foot. Gregor was thus cut off from the mother, who might have been dying because of him; he had to refrain from opening the door lest he frighten away the sister, who had to remain with the mother. There was nothing he could do but wait, and so, tortured by self-rebukes and worries, he began to creep about—he crept over everything, walls, furniture, and ceiling, and finally, in his despair, when the entire room began whirling around him, he plunged down to the middle of the large table.

A short while passed, with Gregor lying there worn out. The entire apartment was still, which was possibly a good sign. Then the doorbell rang. The maid was, naturally, locked up in her kitchen, and so Grete had to go and answer the door. The father had come.

"What's happened?" were his first words; Grete's face must have revealed everything. She replied in a muffled voice, obviously pressing her face into his chest: "Mother fainted, but she's feeling better now. Gregor broke out."

"I expected it," said the father, "I kept telling you both, but you women refuse to listen."

It was clear to Gregor that the father had misinterpreted Grete's all-too-brief statement and leaped to the conclusion that Gregor had perpetrated some kind of violence. That was why he now had to try and placate the father, for he had neither the time nor the chance to enlighten him. He therefore fled to the door of his room, squeezing against it, so that the father, upon entering from the vestibule, could instantly see that Gregor had every intention of promptly returning to his room and that there was no need to force him back. All they had to do was open the door and he would vanish on the spot.

But the father was in no mood to catch such niceties. "Ah!" he roared upon entering, and his tone sounded both furious and elated. Gregor drew his head back from the door and raised it toward the father. He had really not pictured him as he was standing there now; naturally, because of his new habit of creeping around, Gregor had lately failed to concern himself with anything else going on in the apartment and he should actually have been prepared for some changes. And yet, and yet, was this still his father? The same man who used to lie buried in bed, exhausted, whenever Gregor started out on a business trip; who, whenever Gregor came home in the evening, would greet him, wearing a robe, in the armchair; who, being quite incapable of standing up, would only raise his arms as a sign of joy; and who, bundled up in his old overcoat, laboriously shuffled along during rare family strolls on a few Sundays during the year and on the highest holidays, always cautiously planting his cane, trudging a bit more slowly between Gregor and the mother (they were walking slowly as it was), and who, whenever he was about to say anything, nearly always halted and gathered the others around him? But now the father stood quite steady, in a snug blue uniform with gold buttons, such as attendants in banks wear; his heavy double chin unfurled over the high stiff collar of the jacket. From under his bushy eyebrows, the black eyes gazed fresh and alert; the once disheveled hair was now glossy, combed down, and meticulously parted. Removing his cap with its gold monogram, probably that of a bank, and pitching it in an arc the full length of the room over to the settee, he lunged toward Gregor, his face grim, his hands in his trouser pockets, the tails of his long uniform jacket swinging back. He himself most likely did not know what he had in mind; nevertheless he lifted his feet unusually high, and Gregor marveled at the gigantic size of his boot soles. But he did not dwell on this; after all, from the very first day of his new life, he had known that the father viewed only the utmost severity as appropriate for dealing with him. And so now Gregor scooted away, stopping only when the father halted, and skittering forward again the instant the father moved. In this way, they circled the room several times with nothing decisive happening; in fact, because of its slow tempo, the whole business did not even resemble a chase. That was why Gregor kept to the floor for now, especially since he feared that the father might view an escape to the walls or the ceiling as particularly wicked. Nevertheless, Gregor had to admit that he could not endure even this scurrying much longer, because for every step the father took, Gregor had to carry out an endless string of movements. He was already panting noticeably, just as his lungs had never been altogether reliable even in his earlier days. He was just barely staggering along, trying to focus all his strength on running, scarcely keeping his eyes open, feeling so numb that he could think of no other possible recourse than running, and almost forgetting that he was free to use the walls, which, however, were blocked here by intricately carved furniture bristling with sharp points and notches—when all at once a lightly tossed something flew down right next to him, barely missing him, and rolled on ahead of him. It was an apple. Instantly a second one flew after the first. Gregor halted, petrified. Any more running would be useless, for the father was dead set on bombarding him. He had filled his pockets with fruit from the bowl on the sideboard and, not taking sharp aim for the moment, was hurling apple after apple. Those small red apples ricocheted around the floor as if galvanized, colliding with one another. A weakly thrown apple grazed Gregor's back, sliding off harmlessly. Another one, however, promptly following it, actually dug right into his back. Gregor wanted to keep dragging himself along as though this startling and incredible pain would vanish with a change of location, yet he felt nailed to the spot and so he stretched out with all his senses in utter derangement. It was only with his final glance that he saw the door to his room burst open. The mother, wearing only a chemise (for the sister had undressed her to let her breathe more freely while unconscious), hurried out in front of the screaming sister and dashed toward the father. Stumbling over her unfastened petticoats as they glided to the floor one by one, she pressed against the father, flung her arms around his neck in total union with him—but now Gregor's eyesight failed entirely—and, with her hands clutching the back of the father's head, she begged him to spare Gregor's life.

## III

Gregor's serious injury, from which he suffered for over a month (since no one had the nerve to remove the apple, it stayed lodged in his flesh as a visible memento), apparently reminded even the father that Gregor, despite his now dismal and disgusting shape, was a member of the family and could not be treated like an enemy. Instead, familial obligations dictated that they swallow their repulsion and endure, simply endure.

Now Gregor's injury may have cost him some mobility, no doubt for good, impelling him to take long, long minutes to shuffle across his room like an old war invalid (there was no question of his creeping up the walls). Still, this worsening of his condition was, to his mind, more than made up for by the fact that every evening the parlor door, which he would watch sharply for one or two hours in advance, was opened, so that he, lying in the darkness of his room and invisible from the parlor, was allowed to see the entire family at the illuminated table and, by general consent as it were, listen to their talks—rather, that is, than eavesdropping as before.

Of course, these were no longer the lively exchanges of earlier days, which Gregor had always somewhat wistfully mused about in the tiny hotel rooms whenever he had wearily collapsed into the damp bedding. Now, the evenings were usually very hushed. The father would doze off in his armchair shortly after supper; the mother and the sister would urge one another to keep still. The mother, hunched way over beneath the light, would be sewing fine lingerie for a fashion boutique; the sister, having found a job as salesgirl, was studying shorthand and French every evening in hopes of perhaps eventually obtaining a better position. Sometimes the father would wake up and, as if unaware that he had been sleeping, would say to the mother: "How long you've been sewing again today!" and doze off again while mother and sister smiled wearily at each other.

In a kind of obstinacy, the father refused to take off his attendant's uniform at home; and while his robe dangled uselessly on the clothes hook, he would slumber in his chair, fully dressed, as if always on duty and at his superior's beck and call even here. And so, despite all the painstaking efforts of mother and sister, the uniform, which had not been brand-new in the first place, grew less and less tidy, and Gregor would often spend entire evenings gazing at this soiled and spotted garment, which shone with its always polished gold buttons, while the old man slept a very uncomfortable and yet peaceful sleep.

The instant the clock struck ten, the mother, by speaking softly to the father, tried to awaken him and talk him into going to bed, for after all, this was no way to get proper sleep, which the father, who had to start work at six A.M., badly needed. But with the obstinacy that had gotten hold of him upon his becoming a bank attendant, he would always insist on remaining at the table a bit longer even though he invariably nodded out and, moreover, could then be coaxed only with the greatest difficulty to trade the chair for the bed. No matter how much the mother and the sister cajoled and gently admonished him, he would shake his head slowly for a quarter of an hour, keeping his eyes shut and refusing to stand up. The mother would tug at his sleeve, whispering honeyed words into his ear, and the sister would leave her homework to help the mother; but none of this had any effect on the father. He would merely sink deeper into his chair. It was only when the women lifted him under his armpits that he would open his eyes, glance to and fro between mother and sister, and say: "What a life. This is my rest in my old days." And supporting himself on the two women, he would ponderously struggle to his feet as if being the greatest burden on himself, let the two women steer him to the door, wave them off upon arriving and trudge on unaided, while the mother hastily discarded her sewing and the daughter her pen in order to run after him and continue being helpful.

Who in this overworked and exhausted family had time to look after Gregor any more than was absolutely necessary? The household was reduced further; the maid was now dismissed after all, and a gigantic bony charwoman with white hair fluttering around her head would come every morning and evening to do the heaviest chores. Everything else was taken care of by the mother along with her great amount of needlework. It even happened that various items of family jewelry, which mother and sister had once blissfully sported at celebrations and festivities, were now being sold off, as Gregor learned in the evenings from the general discussions of the prices they had obtained. Their greatest persistent complaint, though, was that since they could hit on no way of moving Gregor, they could not give up this apartment, which was much too large for their present circumstances. Gregor, however, realized it was not just their consideration for him that held them back, for they could have easily transported him in a suitable crate with a couple of air holes in it. The main obstacle to the family's relocation was their utter despair and their sense of being struck by a misfortune like no one else among their friends and relatives. Whatever the world demands of poor people, they carried out to an extreme: the father fetched breakfast for the minor bank tellers, the mother sacrificed herself to underwear for strangers, the sister, ordered around by customers, ran back and forth behind the counter. But those were the limits of the family's strength. And the injury in Gregor's back started hurting again whenever mother and sister, having returned from getting the father to bed, ignored their work as they huddled together cheek to cheek, and the mother, pointing toward Gregor's room, now said: "Close that door, Grete," so that Gregor was back in the dark, while the women in the next room mingled their tears or peered dry-eyed at the table.

Gregor spent his nights and days almost entirely without sleep. Occasionally he decided that the next time the door opened, he would take over the family's affairs as in the past. Now, after a long absence, the director and the office manager reappeared in his thoughts, the clerks and the trainees, the dim-witted errand boy, two or three friends from other companies, a chambermaid in a provincial hotel, a dear, fleeting memory, a milliner's cashier whom he had courted earnestly but too slowly—they all reappeared, mingling with strangers or forgotten people. Yet rather than helping him and his family, they were all unapproachable, and he was glad when they dwindled away. At other moments, he was in no mood to worry about his family—he was filled with sheer rage at being poorly looked after; and although unable to picture anything that might tempt his appetite, he did try to devise ways of getting into the pantry and, while not hungry, taking what was ultimately his due. No longer paying any heed to what might be a special treat for Gregor, the sister, before hurrying off to work in the morning and after lunch, would use her foot to shove some random food into Gregor's room. Then, in the evening, indifferent as to whether the food had been merely tasted or—most often the case—left entirely untouched, she would sweep it out with a swing of the broom. She would now tidy up the room in the evening, and she could not have done it any faster. Grimy streaks lined the walls, knots of dust and filth littered the floor. In the beginning, when the sister arrived, Gregor would station himself in such particularly offensive corners as if to chide her. But he could have waited there for weeks on end without her making any improvement; she certainly saw the dirt as clearly as he did, but she had simply made up her mind to leave it there. Nevertheless, with a touchiness that aside from being quite novel for her had actually seized hold of the entire family, she made sure that this tidying-up remained her bailiwick. Once, the mother had subjected Gregor's room to a major cleansing, which had required several buckets of water (the great dampness, of course, made Gregor ill, and afterwards he sprawled on the settee, embittered and immobile). But the mother's punishment was not long in coming. For that evening, the instant the sister noticed the change in Gregor's room, she ran, deeply offended, into the parlor, and even though the mother raised her hands beseechingly, the sister had a crying fit. The father was, naturally, startled out of his armchair, and both parents gaped, at first in helpless astonishment, until they too started in: the father upbraided the mother, on his right, for not leaving the cleaning to the sister and he yelled at the sister, on his left, warning her that she would never again be allowed to clean Gregor's room. The mother tried to drag the father, who was beside himself with rage, into the bedroom; the sister, quaking with sobs, kept hammering the table with her little fists; and Gregor hissed loudly in his fury because no one thought of closing his door to shield him from this spectacle and commotion.

But even if the sister, exhausted from her work at the shop, was fed up with looking after Gregor as before, by no means did the mother have to step in to keep Gregor from being neglected. For now the charwoman was here. This old widow, who, with the help of her strong bone structure, must have managed to overcome the worst things in her long life, felt no actual repugnance toward Gregor. While not really snooping, she had once happened to open the door to his room and, at the sight of Gregor, who, completely caught off guard, began scrambling every which way even though no one was chasing him, she had halted in astonishment with her hands folded on her abdomen. Since then, she had never failed to quickly open the door a crack every morning and evening and peep in on him. Initially, she would even summon him with phrases that she must have considered friendly, like "C'mon over, you old dung beetle!" or "Just look at the old dung beetle!" But Gregor refused to respond to such overtures; he stayed motionless in his place as though the door had not been opened. If only they had ordered this charwoman to clean his room daily instead of letting her gratuitously disturb him whenever the mood struck her! Early one morning, when a violent rain, perhaps a sign of the coming spring, was pelting against the windowpanes, the charwoman launched into her phrases again. Gregor felt so bitterly provoked that he charged toward her as if to attack, albeit slowly and feebly. But the charwoman, undaunted, merely heaved up a chair by the door and stood there with her mouth wide open, obviously intending to close it only when the chair in her hand smashed down into Gregor's back. "So that's as far as you're going?" she asked when he shifted away, and she calmly returned the chair to the corner.

Gregor was now eating next to nothing. It was only when he happened to pass the food left for him that he would playfully take a morsel into his mouth, keep it in for hours and hours, and then usually spit it out again. At first, he thought that his anguish about the condition of his room was what kept him from eating, but he very soon came to terms with those very changes. The family had gotten used to storing things here that could not be put anywhere else, and now there were many such items here, for they had rented out one room of the apartment to three boarders. These earnest gentlemen—all three had full beards, as Gregor once ascertained through the crack of the door—were sticklers for order, not only in their room, but also, since they were lodging here, throughout the apartment, especially the kitchen. They could not endure useless, much less dirty refuse. Moreover, they had largely brought in their own household goods. For this reason, many of the family's belongings had become superfluous; but while they had no prospects of selling them, they did not want to throw them out either. All these items wound up in Gregor's room—as did the ash bucket and the garbage can from the kitchen. If anything was unusable at the moment, the charwoman, who was always in a mad rush, would simply toss it into Gregor's room; luckily, he mostly saw only the object in question and the hand that held it. She may have intended to come for these things in her own good time or dump them all out in one fell swoop; but instead, they remained wherever they happened to land, unless Gregor twisted his way through the clutter, making it shift. At first, he had no choice, there being nowhere else for him to crawl; but later on it got to be more and more fun, even if, dead-tired and mournful after such treks, he would lie unstirring for hours on end.

Since the boarders sometimes also ate their supper at home in the common parlor, the door between that room and Gregor's would remain shut on those evenings. But Gregor easily did without the open door—after all, there had been evenings when he had not even taken advantage of it; instead, unnoticed by the family, he had crouched in the darkest nook of his room. Once, however the charwoman had left the parlor door ajar, and it remained ajar even when the boarders came in that evening and the light was turned on. Settling down at the head of the table, where the father, the mother, and Gregor had eaten in earlier times, they unfolded their napkins and took hold of their knives and forks. Instantly the mother appeared in the kitchen doorway with a platter of meat and, right behind her, the sister with a heaping platter of potatoes. The steaming food gave off thick fumes. The platters were set down in front of the boarders, who bent over them as if to test the food before eating it; and indeed the man sitting in the middle, and apparently looked up to as an authority by the two others, cut up a piece of meat on the platter, clearly in order to determine whether it was tender enough or should perhaps be sent back to the kitchen. He was satisfied, and so mother and sister, who had been watching in suspense, began to smile with sighs of relief.

The family itself ate in the kitchen. Nevertheless, before heading there, the father would stop off in the parlor, bowing once, with his cap in his hand, and circle the table. The boarders would all rise and mumble something into their beards. Then, by themselves again, they would eat in almost total silence. It struck Gregor as bizarre that amid all the various and sundry noises of eating, he kept making out the noise of their chewing as if he were being shown that one needed teeth for eating and that one could accomplish nothing with even the most wonderful toothless jaws. "I do have an appetite," Gregor told himself, "but not for these foods. How well these boarders eat, and I'm starving to death!"

That very evening (Gregor could not recall hearing it all this time), the sound of the violin came from the kitchen. The boarders had already finished their supper. The middle one had pulled out a newspaper, giving the other two one page each; and now they were leaning back, reading and smoking. When the violin began to play, the boarders pricked up their ears, got to their feet, and tiptoed over to the vestibule doorway, crowding into it and remaining there.

They must have been overheard from the kitchen, for the father called: "Do you gentlemen mind the violin? We can stop it immediately."

"Quite the contrary," said the middle gentleman, "would the young lady care to come and play in this room, which is far more convenient and comfortable?"

"Oh, thank you," called the father as if he were the violinist. The gentlemen came back into the parlor and waited. Soon the father arrived with the music stand, the mother with the sheet music, and the sister with the violin. The sister calmly prepared everything for the playing. The parents, having never rented out rooms before, which was why they were being so overly courteous to the boarders, did not dare sit in their own chairs. The father leaned against the door, slipping his right hand between two buttons of his buttoned-up uniform jacket; the mother, however, was offered a chair by one gentleman and, leaving it where he happened to place it, she sat off to the side, in a corner.

The sister began to play; the father and the mother, on either side, closely followed the motions of her hands. Gregor, drawn to the playing, had ventured a bit further out, so that his head was already sticking into the parlor. He was hardly aware of his recent lack of consideration toward the others, although earlier he had prided himself on being considerate. For now more than ever he had reason to hide, thoroughly coated as he was with the dust that shrouded everything in his room, flurrying about at the vaguest movement. Furthermore, threads, hairs, and scraps of leftover food were sticking to his back and his sides, for he had become much too apathetic to turn over and scour his back on the carpet as he used to do several times a day. And so, despite his present state, he had no qualms about advancing a bit across the spotless parlor floor.

Nor, to be sure, did anyone take any notice of him. The family was engrossed in the violin playing; the boarders, in contrast, their hands in their trouser pockets, had initially placed themselves much too close to the sister's music stand so they could all read the score, which was bound to fluster her. As a result, half muttering with lowered heads, they soon retreated to the window, where they remained, with the father eyeing them uneasily. It now truly seemed more than obvious that their hope of listening to a lovely or entertaining violin recital had been dashed, that they had had enough of the performance, and that it was only out of sheer courtesy that they were allowing themselves to be put upon in their leisure. It was especially the manner in which they all blew their cigar smoke aloft through their mouths and noses that hinted at how fidgety they were. And yet the sister was playing so beautifully. Her face was leaning to the side, her sad, probing eyes were following the lines of notes. Gregor crawled a bit farther out, keeping his head close to the floor, so that their eyes might possibly meet. Was he a beast to be so moved by music? He felt as if he were being shown the path to the unknown food he was yearning for. He was determined to creep all the way over to the sister, tug at her skirt to suggest that she take her violin and come into his room, for no one here would reward her playing as he intended to reward it. He wanted to keep her there and never let her out, at least not in his lifetime. For once, his terrifying shape would be useful to him; he would be at all the doors of his room simultaneously, hissing at the attackers. His sister, however, should remain with him not by force, but of her own free will. She should sit next to him on the settee, leaning down to him and listening to him confide that he had been intent on sending her to the conservatory, and that if the misfortune had not interfered, he would have announced his plan to everyone last Christmas (Christmas was already past, wasn't it?), absolutely refusing to take "no" for an answer. After his declaration, the sister would burst into tears of emotion, and Gregor would lift himself all the way up to her shoulder and kiss her throat, which she had been keeping free of any ribbon or collar since she had first started working.

"Mr. Samsa!" the middle gentleman called to the father and, not wasting another word, pointed his index finger at Gregor, who was slowly edging forward. The violin broke off, the middle gentleman first smiled at his friends, shaking his head, and then looked back at Gregor. The father, instead of driving Gregor out, evidently considered it imperative first to calm the boarders, even though they were not the least bit upset and appeared to find Gregor more entertaining than the violin playing. The father hurried over to them and, with outspread arms, tried to push them into their room while simultaneously blocking their view of Gregor with his body. They now in fact began to grow a bit irate, though there was no telling whether it was due to the father's behavior or to their gradual realization that they had unknowingly had a neighbor like Gregor in the next room. They demanded explanations from the father, raised their arms like him, plucked at their beards, and only very slowly backed away toward their room. Meanwhile the sister had managed to overcome her bewilderment, caused by the abrupt end to her playing, and after a time of holding the violin and the bow in her slackly dangling hands and gazing at the score as if still playing, she suddenly pulled herself together, left the instrument in the mother's lap (she was still in her chair, her lungs heaving violently), and rushed into the next room, toward which the father was more and more forcefully herding the boarders. One could see the blankets and pillows in the beds flying aloft, then being neatly arranged under the sister's practiced hands. Before the gentlemen ever reached the room, she had finished making up the beds and slipped out. The father seemed once again so thoroughly overcome by his obstinacy that he neglected to pay the tenants the respect nevertheless due them. He merely kept shoving until the middle gentleman, who was already in the doorway of the room, brought him to a halt by thunderously stamping his foot. "I hereby declare," said the middle gentleman, raising his hand and looking around for the mother and the sister as well, "that in consideration of the repulsive conditions" (here he abruptly spit on the floor) "prevailing in this apartment and in this family, I am giving immediate notice in regard to my room. Naturally, I will not pay a single penny for the days I have resided here; on the other hand, I will give serious thought to the eventuality of pursuing some sort of claims against you, for which—believe me—excellent grounds can easily be shown." He paused and peered straight ahead as if expecting something. And indeed, his two friends promptly chimed in, saying, "We are giving immediate notice too." Thereupon he grabbed the doorknob and slammed the door with a crash.

The father, groping and staggering along, collapsed into his chair; he looked as if he were stretching out for his usual evening nap, but his head, dangling as if unsupported, revealed that he was anything but asleep. All this, while, Gregor had been lying right where the boarders had first spotted him. His frustration at the failure of his plan, and perhaps also the feebleness caused by his persistent hunger, made it impossible for him to move. Dreading with some certainty that at any moment now he would have to bear the blame for the overall disaster, he waited. He was not even startled when the violin, sliding away from the mother's trembling fingers, plunged from her lap with a reverberating thud.

"My dear parents," said the sister, pounding her hand on the table by way of introduction, "things cannot go on like this. You may not realize it, but I do. I will not pronounce my brother's name in front of this monstrosity, and so all I will say is: We must try to get rid of it. We have done everything humanly possible to look after it and put up with it; I do not believe there is anything we can be reproached for."

"She couldn't be more right," said the father to himself. The mother, still struggling to catch her breath and with an insane look in her eyes, began to cough into her muffling hand.

The sister hurried over to the mother and held her forehead. The father, apparently steered to more concrete thoughts by the sister's words, sat bolt upright now, toying with his attendant's cap, which lay on the table, among the borders' leftover supper dishes. Every so often he glanced at Gregor, who kept silent.

"We've got to get rid of it," the sister now said exclusively to the father, for the mother heard nothing through her coughing, "it will kill the both of you, I can see it coming. People who have to work as hard as we do can't also endure this nonstop torture at home. I can't stand it anymore either." And she began sobbing so violently that her tears flowed down to the mother's face, from which she wiped them with mechanical gestures.

"But, child," said the father with compassion and marked understanding, "what should we do?"

The sister merely shrugged her shoulders to convey the perplexity that, in contrast with her earlier self-assurance, had overcome her as she wept.

"If he understood us," said the father, half wondering. The sister, in the thick of her weeping, wildly flapped her hand to signal that this was inconceivable.

"If he understood us," the father repeated, closing his eyes in order to take in the sister's conviction that this was impossible, "then perhaps we might come to some sort of terms with him. But as things are now—"

"It has to go," exclaimed the sister, "that's the only way, Father. You simply have to try and get rid of the idea that it is Gregor. Our real misfortune is that we believed it for such a long time. Just how can that possibly be Gregor? If that were Gregor, he would have realized long ago that human beings can't possibly live with such an animal and he would have left of his own accord. We might have no brother then, but we could go on living and honor his memory. Instead, this animal harries us, it drives out the boarders, it obviously wants to take over the whole apartment and make us sleep in the gutter. Look, Father," she suddenly screamed, "he's starting again!" And in a panic that Gregor could not for the life of him fathom, the sister actually deserted the mother. Literally thrusting away from her chair as if she would rather sacrifice her mother than remain near Gregor, she dashed behind the father, who, made frantic only by the sister's behavior, stood up, half raising his hands to shield her.

Yet Gregor never even dreamed of scaring anyone, least of all his sister. He had merely started wheeling around in order to lumber back to his room, although because of his sickly condition his movements did look peculiar, for he had to execute the intricate turns by repeatedly raising his head and banging it against the floor. He paused and looked around. His good intention seemed to have been recognized; the panic had only been momentary. Now they all gazed at him in dismal silence. The mother, stretching out her legs and pressing them together, sprawled in her chair, her eyes almost shut in exhaustion; the father and the sister sat side by side, she with her arm around his neck.

"Now maybe I can turn around," Gregor thought, resuming his labor. He could not help panting from the strain and he also had to rest intermittently.

At least, no one was bullying him, and he was left to his own devices. Upon completing the turn, he headed straight back. Amazed that his room was far away, he could not understand how, given his feebleness, he had come this great distance almost unwittingly. But, absorbed in creeping rapidly, he scarcely noticed that no interfering word or outcry came from his family. It was only upon reaching the door that he turned his head—not all the way for he felt his neck stiffening; nevertheless, he did see that nothing had changed behind him, except that the sister had gotten to her feet. His final look grazed the mother, who was fast asleep by now.

No sooner was he inside his room than the door was hastily slammed, bolted, and locked. Gregor was so terrified by the sudden racket behind him that his tiny legs buckled. It was the sister who had been in such a rush. She had been standing there, waiting, and had then nimbly jumped forward, before Gregor had even heard her coming. "Finally!" she yelled to the parents while turning the key in the lock.

"What now?" Gregor wondered, peering around in the dark. He soon discovered that he could no longer budge at all. He was not surprised, it even struck him as unnatural that he had ever succeeded in moving on these skinny little legs. Otherwise he felt relatively comfortable. His entire body was aching, but it seemed to him as if the pains were gradually fading and would ultimately vanish altogether. He could barely feel the rotting apple in his back or the inflamed area around it, which were thoroughly cloaked with soft dust. He recalled his family with tenderness and love. His conviction that he would have to disappear was, if possible, even firmer than his sister's. He lingered in this state of blank and peaceful musing until the tower clock struck three in the morning. He held on long enough to glimpse the start of the overall brightening outside the window. Then his head involuntarily sank to the floor, and his final breath came feebly from his nostrils.

When the charwoman showed up early that morning (in her haste and sheer energy, and no matter how often she had been asked not to do it, she slammed all the doors so hard that once she walked in no peaceful sleep was possible anywhere in the apartment), and peeked in on Gregor as usual, she at first found nothing odd about him. Having credited him with goodness knows what brain power, she thought he was deliberately lying there so motionless, pretending to sulk. Since she happened to be clutching the long broom, she tried to tickle him from the doorway. This had no effect, and so she grew annoyed and began poking Gregor. It was only upon shoving him from his place but meeting no resistance that she became alert. When the true state of affairs now dawned on the charwoman, her eyes bulged in amazement and she whistled to herself. But instead of dawdling there, she yanked the bedroom door open and hollered into the darkness: "Go and look, it's croaked; it's lying there, absolutely croaked!"

Mr. and Mrs. Samsa sat upright in their matrimonial bed, trying to cope with the shock caused by the charwoman. When they managed to grasp what she meant, the two of them, one on either side, hastily clambered out of bed. Mr. Samsa threw the blanket over his shoulders, while Mrs. Samsa emerged in her nightgown; that was how they entered Gregor's room. Meanwhile, the door to the parlor, where Grete had been sleeping since the arrival of the boarders, had likewise opened; she was fully dressed and her face was pale as if she had not slept.

"Dead?" said Mrs. Samsa, quizzically eyeing the charwoman even though she could have gone to check everything for herself, or could have surmised it without checking.

"You bet," said the charwoman and by way of proof she thrust out the broom and pushed Gregor's corpse somewhat further to the side. Mrs. Samsa made as if to hold back the broom, but then let it be.

"Well," said Mr. Samsa, "now we can thank the Lord." He crossed himself and the three women imitated his example. Grete, her eyes glued to the corpse, said: "Just look how skinny he was. Well, he stopped eating such a long time ago. The food came back out exactly as it went in." And indeed, Gregor's body was utterly flat and dry; they realized this only now when it was no longer raised on its tiny legs and nothing else diverted their eyes.

"Grete, come into our room for a bit," said Mrs. Samsa, smiling wistfully, and Grete, not without looking back at the corpse, followed her parents into the bedroom. The charwoman closed the door to Gregor's room and opened the window all the way. Though it was still early morning, there was a touch of warmth in the fresh air. It was already late March, after all.

The three boarders stepped out of their room and, astonished, cast about for their breakfast; they had been forgotten. "Where is breakfast?" the middle gentleman peevishly asked the charwoman. But putting her finger on her lips, she hastily and silently beckoned for the gentlemen to come into Gregor's room. And come they did, and with their hands in the pockets of their somewhat threadbare jackets, they stood around Gregor's corpse in the now sunlit room.

Next, the bedroom door opened, and Mr. Samsa, in his livery, appeared with his wife on one arm and his daughter on the other. Their eyes were all slightly tearstained; now and then, Grete pressed her face into the father's arm.

"Leave my home at once!" Mr. Samsa told the three gentlemen, pointing at the door without releasing the women.

"What do you mean?" asked the middle gentleman, somewhat dismayed and with a sugary smile. The two other gentlemen held their hands behind their backs, incessantly rubbing them together as if gleefully looking forward to a grand argument that they were bound to win.

"I mean exactly what I said," replied Mr. Samsa, and with his two companions he made a beeline toward the tenant. The latter at first stood his ground, eyeing the floor as if his thoughts were being rearranged to form a new pattern in his head.

"Well, then we'll go," he said, looking up at Mr. Samsa as if, in a sudden burst of humility, he were requesting sanction even for this decision. Mr. Samsa, with bulging eyes, merely vouchsafed him a few brief nods. Thereupon the gentleman strode right into the vestibule. His two friends, who had been listening for a short while with utterly calm hands, now quite literally hopped after him as if fearing that Mr. Samsa might precede them into the vestibule and might thrust himself between them and their leader. Once in the vestibule, all three boarders pulled their hats from the coat rack, their canes from the umbrella stand, bowed wordlessly, and left the apartment. Impelled by a suspicion that proved to be thoroughly groundless, Mr. Samsa and the two women stepped out on the landing. As they leaned on the banister, they watched the three gentlemen marching down the long stairway slowly but steadily, vanishing on every floor in the regular twist of the staircase, and popping up again several moments later. The lower the gentlemen got, the more the Samsa family lost interest in them, and as a butcher's boy, proudly balancing a basket on his head, came toward the gentlemen and then mounted well beyond them, Mr. Samsa and the women left the banister, and as if relieved, they all returned to their apartment.

They decided to spend this day resting and strolling; not only had they earned this break from work, they absolutely needed it. And so they sat down at the table to write three letters of explanation: Mr. Samsa to his superiors, Mrs. Samsa to her customer, and Grete to her employer. As they were writing, the charwoman came in to tell them she was leaving, for her morning's work was done. The three letter writers at first merely nodded without glancing up; it was only when she kept hovering that they looked up in annoyance. "Well?" asked Mr. Samsa. The charwoman stood beaming in the doorway as if she were about to announce some great windfall for the family, but would do so only if they dragged it out of her. On her hat, the small, almost erect ostrich plume, which had annoyed Mr. Samsa throughout her service here, swayed lightly in all directions. "What can we do for you?" asked Mrs. Samsa, whom the charwoman respected the most.

"Well," the charwoman replied with such friendly chuckling that she had to break off, "listen, you don't have to worry about getting rid of that stuff in the next room. It's all been taken care of."

Mrs. Samsa and Grete huddled over their letters as if to keep writing; Mr. Samsa, aware that the charwoman was on the verge of launching into a blow-by-blow description, resolutely stretched out his arm to ward her off. Not being allowed to tell her story, she suddenly remembered that she was in an awful hurry, and clearly offended, she called out: "So long, everybody." She then vehemently whirled around and charged out of the apartment with a horrible slam of the door.

"She'll be dismissed tonight," said Mr. Samsa, receiving no answer from his wife or his daughter, for the charwoman had ruffled the peace and quiet that they had barely gained. Standing up, the two women went over to the window and remained there, clasped in each other's arms. Mr. Samsa looked back from his chair and silently watched them for a while. Then he exclaimed: "Come on, get over here. Forget about the past once and for all. And show me a little consideration." The women, promptly obeying him, hurried over, caressed him, and swiftly finished their letters.

Then all three of them left the apartment together, which they had not done in months, and took the trolley out to the countryside beyond the town. The streetcar, where they were the only passengers, was flooded with warm sunshine. Leaning back comfortably in their seats, they discussed their future prospects and concluded that, upon closer perusal, these were anything but bad; for while they had never actually asked one another for any details, their jobs were all exceedingly advantageous and also promising. Naturally, the greatest immediate improvement in their situation could easily be brought about by their moving; they hoped to rent a smaller and cheaper apartment, but with a better location and altogether more practical than their current place, which had been found by Gregor. As they were conversing, both Mr. and Mrs. Samsa, upon seeing the daughter becoming more and more vivacious, realized almost in unison that lately, despite all the sorrows that had left her cheeks pale, she had blossomed into a lovely and shapely girl. Lapsing into silence and communicating almost unconsciously with their eyes, they reflected that it was high time they found a decent husband for her. And it was like a confirmation of their new dreams and good intentions that at the end of their ride the daughter was the first to get up, stretching her young body.

# A Hunger Artist[1]

During these last decades the interest in professional fasting has markedly diminished. It used to pay very well to stage such great performances under one's own management, but today that is quite impossible. We live in a different world now. At one time the whole town took a lively interest in the hunger artist; from day to day of his fast the excitement mounted; everybody wanted to see him at least once a day; there were people who bought season tickets for the last few days and sat from morning till night in front of his small barred cage; even in the nighttime there were visiting hours, when the whole effect was heightened by torch flares; on fine days the cage was set out in the open air, and then it was the children's special treat to see the hunger artist; for their elders he was often just a joke that happened to be in fashion, but the children stood open-mouthed, holding each other's hands for greater security, marveling at him as he sat there pallid in black tights, with his ribs sticking out so prominently, not even on a seat but down among straw on the ground, sometimes giving a courteous nod, answering questions with a constrained smile, or perhaps stretching an arm through the bars so that one might feel how thin it was, and then again withdrawing deep into himself, paying no attention to anyone or anything, not even to the all-important striking of the clock that was the only piece of furniture in his cage, but merely staring into vacancy with half shut eyes, now and then taking a sip from a tiny glass of water to moisten his lips.

Besides casual onlookers there were also relays of permanent watchers selected by the public, usually butchers, strangely enough, and it was their task to watch the hunger artist day and night, three of them at a time, in case he should have some secret recourse to nourishment. This was nothing but a formality, instituted to reassure the masses, for the initiates knew well enough that during his fast the artist would never in any circumstances, not even under

1. Translated by Edwin and Willa Muir.

forcible compulsion, swallow the smallest morsel of food: the honor of his profession forbade it. Not every watcher, of course, was capable of understanding this, there were often groups of night watchers who were very lax in carrying out their duties and deliberately huddled together in a retired corner to play cards with great absorption, obviously intending to give the hunger artist the chance of a little refreshment, which they supposed he could draw from some private hoard. Nothing annoyed the artist more than such watchers; they made him miserable; they made his fast seem unendurable; sometimes he mastered his feebleness sufficiently to sing during their watch for as long as he could keep going, to show them how unjust their suspicions were. But that was of little use; they only wondered at his cleverness in being able to fill his mouth even while singing. Much more to his taste were the watchers who sat close up to the bars, who were not content with the dim night lighting of the hall but focused him in the full glare of the electric pocket torch given them by the impresario. The harsh light did not trouble him at all, in any case he could never sleep properly, and he could always drowse a little, whatever the light, at any hour, even when the hall was thronged with noisy onlookers. He was quite happy at the prospect of spending a sleepless night with such watchers; he was ready to exchange jokes with them, to tell them stories out of his nomadic life, anything at all to keep them awake and demonstrate to them again that he had no eatables in his cage and that he was fasting as not one of them could fast. But his happiest moment was when the morning came and an enormous breakfast was brought them, at his expense, on which they flung themselves with the keen appetite of healthy men after a weary night of wakefulness. Of course there were people who argued that this breakfast was an unfair attempt to bribe the watchers, but that was going rather too far, and when they were invited to take on a night's vigil without a breakfast, merely for the sake of the cause, they made themselves scarce, although they stuck stubbornly to their suspicions.

Such suspicions, anyhow, were a necessary accompaniment to the profession of fasting. No one could possibly watch the hunger artist continuously, day and night, and so no one could produce first-hand evidence that the fast had really been rigorous and continuous; only the artist himself could know that, he was therefore bound to be the sole completely satisfied spectator of his own fast. Yet for other reasons he was never satisfied; it was not perhaps mere fasting that had brought him to such skeleton thinness that many people had regretfully to keep away from his exhibitions, because the sight of him was too much for them, perhaps it was dissatisfaction with himself that had worn him down. For he alone knew, what no other initiate knew, how easy it was to fast. It was the easiest thing in the world. He made no secret of this, yet people did not believe him, at the best they set him down as modest, most of them, however, thought he was out for publicity or else was some kind of cheat who found it easy to fast because he had discovered a way of making it easy, and then had the impudence to admit the fact, more or less. He had to put up with all that, and in the course of time had got used to it, but his inner dissatisfaction always rankled, and never yet, after any term of fasting—this must be granted to his credit—had he left the cage of his own free will. The longest period of fasting was fixed by his impresario at forty days, beyond that term he was not allowed to go, not even in great cities, and there was good reason for it, too. Experience had proved that for about forty days the interest of the public could be stimulated by a steadily increasing pressure of advertisement, but after that the town began to lose interest, sympathetic support began notably to fall off; there were of course local variations as between one town and another or one country and another, but as a general rule forty days marked the limit. So on the fortieth day the flower-bedecked cage was opened, enthusiastic spectators filled the hall, a military band played, two doctors entered the cage to measure the results of the fast, which were announced through a megaphone, and finally two young ladies appeared, blissful at having been selected for the honor, to help the hunger artist down the few steps leading to a small table on which was spread a carefully chosen invalid repast. And at this very moment the artist always turned stubborn. True, he would entrust his bony arms to the outstretched helping hands of the ladies bending over him, but stand up he would not. Why stop fasting at this particular moment, after forty days of it? He had held out for a long time, an illimitably long time; why stop now, when he was in his best fasting form, or rather, not yet quite in his best fasting form? Why should he be cheated of the fame he would get for fasting longer, for being not only the record hunger artist of all time, which presumably he was already, but for beating his own record by a performance beyond human imagination, since he felt that there were no limits to his capacity for fasting? His public pretended to admire him so much, why should it have so little patience with him; if he could endure fasting longer, why shouldn't the public endure it? Besides, he was tired, he was comfortable sitting in the straw, and now he was supposed to lift himself to his full height and go down to a meal the very thought of which gave him a nausea that only the presence of the ladies kept him from betraying, and even that with an effort. And he looked up into the eyes of the ladies who were apparently so friendly and in reality so cruel, and shook his head, which felt too heavy on its strengthless neck. But then there happened yet again what always happened. The impresario came forward, without a word—for the band made speech impossible—lifted his arms in the air above the artist, as if inviting Heaven to look down upon its creature here in the straw, this suffering martyr, which indeed he was, although in quite another sense; grasped him round the emaciated waist, with exaggerated caution, so that the frail condition he was in might be appreciated; and committed him to the care of the blenching ladies, not without secretly giving him a shaking so that his legs and body tottered and swayed. The artist now submitted completely; his head lolled on his breast as if it had landed there by chance; his body was hollowed out; his legs in a spasm of self-preservation clung close to each other at the knees, yet scraped on the ground as if it were not really solid ground, as if they were only trying to find solid ground; and the whole weight of his body, a feather-weight after all, relapsed onto one of the ladies, who, looking round for help and panting a little—this post of honor was not at all what she had expected it to be—first stretched her neck as far as she could to keep her face at least free from contact with the artist, when finding this impossible, and her more fortunate companion not coming to her aid but merely holding extended on her own trembling hand the little bunch of knucklebones that was the artist's, to the great delight of the spectators burst into tears and had to be replaced by an attendant who had long been stationed in readiness. Then came the food, a little of which the impresario managed to get between the artist's lips, while he sat in a kind of half-fainting trance, to the accompaniment of cheerful patter designed to distract the public's attention from the artist's condition; after that, a toast was drunk to the public, supposedly prompted by a whisper from the artist in the impresario's ear; the band confirmed it with a mighty flourish, the spectators melted away, and no one had any cause to be dissatisfied with the proceedings, no one except the hunger artist himself, he only, as always.

So he lived for many years, with small regular intervals of recuperation, in visible glory, honored by the world, yet in spite of that troubled in spirit, and all the more troubled because no one would take his trouble seriously. What comfort could he possibly need? What more could he possibly wish for? And if some good-natured person, feeling sorry for him, tried to console him by pointing out that his melancholy was probably caused by fasting, it could happen, especially when he had been fasting for some time, that he reacted with an outburst of fury and to the general alarm began to shake the bars of his cage like a wild animal. Yet the impresario had a way of punishing these outbreaks which he rather enjoyed putting into operation. He would apologize publicly for the artist's behavior, which was only to be excused, he admitted, because of the irritability caused by fasting; a condition hardly to be understood by well-fed people; then by natural transition he went on to mention the artist's equally incomprehensible boast that he could fast for much longer than he was doing; he praised the high ambition, the good will, the great self-denial undoubtedly implicit in such a statement; and then quite simply countered it by bringing out photographs, which were also on sale to the public, showing the artist on the fortieth day of a fast lying in bed almost dead from exhaustion. This perversion of the truth, familiar to the artist though it was, always unnerved him afresh and proved too much for him. What was a consequence of the premature ending of his fast was here presented as the cause of it! To fight against this lack of understanding, against a whole world of non-understanding, was impossible. Time and again in good faith he stood by the bars listening to the impresario, but as soon as the photographs appeared he always let go and sank with a groan back on to his straw, and the reassured public could once more come close and gaze at him.

A few years later when the witnesses of such scenes called them to mind, they often failed to understand themselves at all. For meanwhile the aforementioned change in public interest had set in; it seemed to happen almost overnight; there may have been profound causes for it, but who was going to bother about that; at any rate the pampered hunger artist suddenly found himself deserted one fine day by the amusement seekers, who went streaming past him to other more favored attractions. For the last time the impresario hurried him over half Europe to discover whether the old interest might still survive here and there; all in vain; everywhere, as if by secret agreement, a positive revulsion from professional fasting was in evidence. Of course it could not really have sprung up so suddenly as all that, and many premonitory symptoms which had not been sufficiently remarked or suppressed during the rush and glitter of success now came retrospectively to mind, but it was now too late to take any countermeasures. Fasting would surely come into fashion again at some future date, yet that was no comfort for those living in the present. What, then, was the hunger artist to do? He had been applauded by thousands in his time and could hardly come down to showing himself in a street booth at village fairs, and as for adopting another profession, he was not only too old for that but too fanatically devoted to fasting. So he took leave of the impresario, his partner in an unparalleled career, and hired himself to a large circus; in order to spare his own feelings he avoided reading the conditions of his contract.

A large circus with its enormous traffic in replacing and recruiting men, animals and apparatus can always find a use for people at any time, even for a hunger artist, provided of course that he does not ask too much, and in this particular case anyhow it was not only the artist who was taken on but his famous and long-known name as well, indeed considering the peculiar nature of his performance, which was not impaired by advancing age, it could not be objected that here was an artist past his prime, no longer at the height of his professional skill, seeking a refuge in some quiet corner of a circus; on the contrary, the hunger artist averred that he could fast as well as ever, which was entirely credible, he even alleged that if he were allowed to fast as he liked, and this was at once promised him without more ado, he could astound the world by establishing a record never yet achieved, a statement which certainly provoked a smile among the other professionals, since it left out of account the change in public opinion, which the hunger artist in his zeal conveniently forgot.

He had not, however, actually lost his sense of the real situation and took it as a matter of course that he and his cage should be stationed, not in the middle of the ring as a main attraction, but outside, near the animal cages, on a site that was after all easily accessible. Large and gaily painted placards made a frame for the cage and announced what was to be seen inside it. When the public came thronging out in the intervals to see the animals, they could hardly avoid passing the hunger artist's cage and stopping there for a moment, perhaps they might even have stayed longer had not those pressing behind them in the narrow gangway, who did not understand why they should be held up on their way toward the excitements of the menagerie, made it impossible for anyone to stand gazing quietly for any length of time. And that was the reason why the hunger artist, who had of course been looking forward to these visiting hours as the main achievement of his life, began instead to shrink from them. At first he could hardly wait for the intervals; it was exhilarating to watch the crowds come streaming his way, until only too soon—not even the most obstinate self-deception, clung to almost consciously, could hold out against the fact—the conviction was borne in upon him that these people, most of them, to judge from their actions, again and again, without exception, were all on their way to the menagerie. And the first sight of them from the distance remained the best. For when they reached his cage he was at once deafened by the storm of shouting and abuse that arose from the two contending factions, which renewed themselves continuously, of those who wanted to stop and stare at him—he soon began to dislike them more than the others—not out of real interest but only out of obstinate self-assertiveness, and those who wanted to go straight on to the animals. When the first great rush was past, the stragglers came along, and these, whom nothing could have prevented from stopping to look at him as long as they had breath, raced past with long strides, hardly even glancing at him, in their haste to get to the menagerie in time. And all too rarely did it happen that he had a stroke of luck, when some father of a family fetched up before him with his children, pointed a finger at the hunger artist and explained at length what the phenomenon meant, telling stories of earlier years when he himself had watched similar but much more thrilling performances, and the children, still rather uncomprehending, since neither inside nor outside school had they been sufficiently prepared for this lesson—what did they care about fasting?—yet showed by the brightness of their intent eyes that new and better times might be coming. Perhaps, said the hunger artist to himself many a time, things would be a little better if his cage were set not quite so near the menagerie. That made it too easy for people to make their choice, to say nothing of what he suffered from the stench of the menagerie, the animals' restlessness by night, the carrying past of raw lumps of flesh for the beasts of prey, the roaring at feeding times, which depressed him continually. But he did not dare to lodge a complaint with the management; after all, he had the animals to thank for the troops of people who passed his cage, among whom there might always be one here and there to take an interest in him, and who could tell where they might seclude him if he called attention to his existence and thereby to the fact that, strictly speaking, he was only an impediment on the way to the menagerie.

A small impediment, to be sure, one that grew steadily less. People grew familiar with the strange idea that they could be expected, in times like these, to take an interest in a hunger artist, and with this familiarity the verdict went out against him. He might fast as much as he could, and he did so; but nothing could save him now, people passed him by. Just try to explain to anyone the art of fasting! Anyone who has no feeling for it cannot be made to understand it. The fine placards grew dirty and illegible, they were torn down; the little notice board telling the number of fast days achieved, which at first was changed carefully every day, had long stayed at the same figure, for after the first few weeks even this small task seemed pointless to the staff; and so the artist simply fasted on and on, as he had once dreamed of doing, and it was no trouble to him, just as he had always foretold, but no one counted the days, no one, not even the artist himself, knew what records he was already breaking, and his heart grew heavy. And when once in a time some leisurely passer-by stopped, made merry over the old figure on the board and spoke of swindling, that was in its way the stupidest lie ever invented by indifference and inborn malice, since it was not the hunger artist who was cheating; he was working honestly, but the world was cheating him of his reward.

Many more days went by, however, and that too came to an end. An overseer's eye fell on the cage one day and he asked the attendants why this perfectly good cage should be left standing there unused with dirty straw inside it; nobody knew, until one man, helped out by the notice board, remembered about the hunger artist. They poked into the straw with sticks and found him in it. "Are you still fasting?" asked the overseer. "When on earth do you mean to stop?" "Forgive me, everybody," whispered the hunger artist; only the overseer, who had his ear to the bars, understood him. "Of course," said the overseer, and tapped his forehead with a finger to let the attendants know what state the man was in, "we forgive you." "I always wanted you to admire my fasting," said the hunger artist. "We do admire it," said the overseer, affably. "But you shouldn't admire it," said the hunger artist. "Well, then we don't admire it," said the overseer, "but why shouldn't we admire it?" "Because I have to fast, I can't help it," said the hunger artist. "What a fellow you are," said the overseer, "and why can't you help it?" "Because," said the hunger artist, lifting his head a little and speaking, with his lips pursed, as if for a kiss, right into the overseer's ear, so that no syllable might be lost, "because I couldn't find the food I liked. If I had found it, believe me, I should have made no fuss and stuffed myself like you or anyone else." These were his last words, but in his dimming eyes remained the firm though no longer proud persuasion that he was still continuing to fast.

"Well, clear this out now!" said the overseer, and they buried the hunger artist, straw and all. Into the cage they put a young panther. Even the most insensitive felt it refreshing to see this wild creature leaping around the cage that had so long been dreary. The panther was all right. The food he liked was brought him without hesitation by the attendants; he seemed not even to miss his freedom; his noble body, furnished almost to the bursting point with all that it needed, seemed to carry freedom around with it too; somewhere in his jaws it seemed to lurk; and the joy of life streamed with such ardent passion from his throat that for the onlookers it was not easy to stand the shock of it. But they braced themselves, crowded round the cage, and did not want ever to move away.

# Jamaica Kincaid

*Kincaid (1946– ) was born in St. Johns, Antigua, West Indies, but is now a naturalized U.S. citizen. From the time of her first publication of stories about life on Antigua she was acclaimed not only for the vividness of her portrayal of that milieu but also for her mixture of fantasy and reality and the acuity of her style. Her first book,* At the Bottom of the River *(1983), was a collection of short stories, and her second,* Annie John *(1985), was a group of interrelated stories that some critics saw as a novel.* A Small Place *won her further praise in 1988.* Lucy *was published in 1990;* The Autobiography of My Mother, *in 1996; and* My Brother, *in 1997.*

## Girl

Wash the white clothes on Monday and put them on the stone heap; wash the color clothes on Tuesday and put them on the clothesline to dry; don't walk barehead in the hot sun; cook pumpkin fritters in very hot sweet oil; soak your little cloths right after you take them off; when buying cotton to make yourself a nice blouse, be sure that it doesn't have gum on it, because that way it won't hold up well after a wash; soak salt fish overnight before you cook it; is it true that you sing benna[1] in Sunday school?; always eat your food in such a way that it won't turn someone else's stomach; on Sundays try to walk like a lady and not like the slut you are so bent on becoming; don't sing benna in Sunday school; you mustn't speak to wharf-rat boys, not even to give directions; don't eat fruits on the street—flies will follow you; *but I don't sing benna on Sundays at all and never in Sunday school*; this is how to sew on a button; this is how to make a buttonhole for the button you have just sewed on; this is how to hem a dress when you see the hem coming down and so to prevent yourself from looking like the slut I know you are so bent on becoming; this is how you iron your father's khaki shirt so that it doesn't have a crease; this is how you iron your father's khaki pants so that they don't have a crease; this is how you grow okra—far from the house, because okra tree harbors red ants; when you are growing dasheen, make sure it gets plenty of water or else it makes your throat itch when you are eating it; this is how you sweep a corner; this is how you sweep a whole house; this is how you sweep a yard; this is how

1. Calypso songs.

you smile to someone you don't like very much; this is how you smile to someone you don't like at all; this is how you smile to someone you like completely; this is how you set a table for tea; this is how you set a table for dinner; this is how you set a table for dinner with an important guest; this is how you set a table for lunch; this is how you set a table for breakfast; this is how to behave in the presence of men who don't know you very well, and this way they won't recognize immediately the slut I have warned you against becoming; be sure to wash every day, even if it is with your own spit; don't squat down to play marbles—you are not a boy, you know; don't pick people's flowers—you might catch something; don't throw stones at blackbirds, because it might not be a blackbird at all; this is how to make a bread pudding; this is how to make doukona;[2] this is how to make pepper pot; this is how to make a good medicine for a cold; this is how to make a good medicine to throw away a child before it even becomes a child; this is how to catch a fish; this is how to throw back a fish you don't like, and that way something bad won't fall on you; this is how to bully a man; this is how a man bullies you; this is how to love a man, and if this doesn't work there are other ways, and if they don't work don't feel too bad about giving up; this is how to spit up in the air if you feel like it, and this is how to move quick so that it doesn't fall on you; this is how to make ends meet; always squeeze bread to make sure it's fresh; *but what if the baker won't let me feel the bread?*; you mean to say that after all you are really going to be the kind of woman who the baker won't let near the bread?

2. Another kind of pudding.

# RUDYARD KIPLING

*Kipling (1865–1936) was born in Bombay, India, and after spending his youth in England returned to Bombay at seventeen to work as a reporter and editor. Struck by the color, variety, and exoticism of Indian and military life, he soon began to write poems and short stories that expressed the vividness of what went on before his eyes. His first books of poems were* Departmental Ditties *(1886) and* Barrack Room Ballads *(1892), and the stories of that epoch were collected in* Plain Tales from the Hills *(1888) and* Soldiers Three *(1888). From the first, these spirited tales and poems were extremely popular; the meteoric energy of his mind elicited worldwide admiration. His romanticizing of British imperialism fitted the spirit of an age of expansion. His rendition of soldier slang struck many readers as a charming novelty.*

*Kipling returned to London in 1889 and there published a novel,* The Light That Failed *(1889), which fell somewhat short of the popularity of his first works. Subsequently, he migrated to the United States and lived here for four years while he wrote overwhelmingly successful children's books:* The Jungle Book *(1894),* The Second Jungle Book *(1895),* Kim *(1901),* Just So Stories *(1902), and* Captains Courageous *(1904). In the long life remaining to him Kipling's productivity waned, and with the disasters of imperialism before and during World War I, his popularity dimmed. Nevertheless, while it was still at its peak he became in 1907 the first Englishman to win the Nobel Prize.*

## The Man Who Would Be King

**"Brother to a Prince and Fellow to a Beggar if He Be Found Worthy."**

The law, as quoted, lays down a fair conduct of life, and one not easy to follow. I have been fellow to a beggar again and again under circumstances which prevented either of us finding out whether the other was worthy. I have still to be brother to a Prince, though I once came near to kinship with what might have been a veritable King and was promised the reversion of a Kingdom—army, law courts, revenue and policy all complete. But, today, I greatly fear that my King is dead, and if I want a crown I must go and hunt it for myself.

The beginning of everything was in a railway train upon the road to Mhow from Ajmir.[1] There had been a Deficit in the Budget, which necessitated traveling, not Second-class, which is only half as dear as First-class, but by Intermediate, which is very awful indeed. There are no cushions in the Intermediate-class, and the population are either Intermediate, which is Eura-

1. Cities in northwestern India.

sian, or native, which for a long night journey is nasty, or Loafer, which is amusing though intoxicated. Intermediates do not patronize refreshment rooms. They carry their food in bundles and pots, and buy sweets from the native sweetmeat-sellers, and drink the roadside water. That is why in the hot weather Intermediates are taken out of the carriages dead, and in all weathers are most properly looked down upon.

My particular Intermediate happened to be empty till I reached Nasirabad, when a huge gentleman in shirt sleeves entered, and, following the custom of Intermediates, passed the time of day. He was a wanderer and a vagabond like myself, but with an educated taste for whisky. He told tales of things he had seen and done, of out-of-the-way corners of the Empire into which he had penetrated, and of adventures in which he risked his life for a few days' food. "If India was filled with men like you and me, not knowing more than the crows where they'd get their next day's rations, it isn't seventy millions of revenue the land would be paying—it's seven hundred millions," said he; and as I looked at his mouth and chin I was disposed to agree with him. We talked politics—the politics of Loaferdom that sees things from the underside where the lath and plaster is not smoothed off—and we talked postal arrangements because my friend wanted to send a telegram back from the next station to Ajmir, which is the turning-off place from the Bombay to the Mhow line as you travel westward. My friend had no money beyond eight annas which he wanted for dinner, and I had no money at all, owing to the hitch in the Budget before-mentioned. Further, I was going into a wilderness where, though I should resume touch with the Treasury, there were no telegraph offices. I was, therefore, unable to help him in any way.

"We might threaten a Stationmaster, and make him send a wire on tick," said my friend, "but that'd mean inquiries for you and for me, and I've got my hands full these days. Did you say you are traveling back along this line within any days?"

"Within ten," I said.

"Can't you make it eight?" said he. "Mine is rather urgent business."

"I can send your telegram within ten days if that will serve you," I said.

"I couldn't trust the wire to fetch him now I think of it. It's this way. He leaves Delhi on the twenty-third for Bombay. That means he'll be running through Ajmir about the night of the twenty-third."

"But I'm going into the Indian Desert," I explained.

"Well *and* good," said he. "You'll be changing at Marwar Junction to get into Jodhpore territory—you must do that—and he'll be coming through Marwar Junction in the early morning of the twenty-fourth by the Bombay Mail. Can you be at Marwar Junction on that time? 'Twon't be inconveniencing you because I know that there's precious few pickings to be got out of these Central India States—even though you pretend to be correspondent of the *Backwoodsman.*"

"Have you ever tried that trick?" I asked.

"Again and again, but the Residents find you out, and then you get escorted to the Border before you've time to get your knife into them. But about my friend here. I *must* give him a word o' mouth to tell him what's come to me or else he won't know where to go. I would take it more than kind of you if you was to come out of Central India in time to catch him at Marwar Junction, and say to him, 'He has gone South for the week.' He'll know what that means. He's a big man with a red beard, and a great swell he is. You'll find him sleeping like a gentleman with all his luggage round him in a Second-class compartment. But don't you be afraid. Slip down the window, and say, 'He has gone South for the week,' and he'll tumble. It's only cutting your time of stay in those parts by two days. I ask you as a stranger—going to the West," he said, with emphasis.

"Where have *you* come from?" said I.

"From the East," said he, "and I am hoping that you will give him the message on the Square—for the sake of my Mother as well as your own."

Englishmen are not usually softened by appeals to the memory of their mothers, but for certain reasons, which will be fully apparent, I saw fit to agree.

"It's more than a little matter," said he, "and that's why I ask you to do it—and now I know that I can depend on you doing it. A Second-class carriage at Marwar Junction, and a red-haired man asleep in it. You'll be sure to remember. I get out at the next station, and I must hold on there till he comes or sends me what I want."

"I'll give the message if I catch him," I said, "and for the sake of your Mother as well as mine I'll give you a word of advice. Don't try to run the Central India States just now as the correspondent of the *Backwoodsman*. There's a real one knocking about here, and it might lead to trouble."

"Thank you," said he, simply, "and when will the swine be gone? I can't starve because he's ruining my work. I wanted to get hold of the Degumber Rajah down here about his father's widow, and give him a jump."

"What did he do to his father's widow, then?"

"Filled her up with red pepper and slippered her to death as she hung from a beam. I found that out myself, and I'm the only man that would dare going into the State to get hush money for it. They'll try to poison me, same as they did in Chortumna when I went on the loot there. But you'll give the man at Marwar Junction my message?"

He got out at a little roadside station, and I reflected. I had heard, more than once, of men personating correspondents of newspapers and bleeding small Native States with threats of exposure, but I had never met any of the caste before. They lead a hard life, and generally die with great suddenness. The Native States have a wholesome horror of English newspapers, which may throw light on their peculiar methods of government, and do their best to choke correspondents with champagne, or drive them out of their mind with four-in-hand barouches. They do not understand that nobody cares a straw for the internal administration of Native States so long as oppression and crime are kept within decent limits, and the ruler is not drugged, drunk, or diseased from one end of the year to the other. Native States were created by Providence in order to supply picturesque scenery, tigers, and tall writing. They are the dark places of the earth, full of unimaginable cruelty, touching the Railway and the Telegraph on one side, and, on the other, the days of Harun-al-Raschid.[2] When

2. Great caliph of Baghdad (ca. 764–809).

I left the train I did business with divers Kings, and in eight days passed through many changes of life. Sometimes I wore dress clothes and consorted with Princes and Politicals, drinking from crystal and eating from silver. Sometimes I lay out upon the ground and devoured what I could get, from a plate made of a flapjack, and drank the running water, and slept under the same rug as my servant. It was all in the day's work.

Then I headed for the Great Indian Desert upon the proper date, as I had promised, and the night Mail set me down at Marwar Junction, where a funny little, happy-go-lucky, native-managed railway runs to Jodhpore. The Bombay Mail from Delhi makes a short halt at Marwar. She arrived as I got in, and I had just time to hurry to her platform and go down the carriages. There was only one Second-class on the train. I slipped the window, and looked down upon a flaming red beard, half covered by a railway rug. That was my man, fast asleep, and I dug him gently in the ribs. He woke with a grunt, and I saw his face in the light of the lamps. It was a great and shining face.

"Tickets again?" said he.

"No," said I. "I am to tell you that he is gone South for the week. He is gone South for the week!"

The train had begun to move out. The red man rubbed his eyes. "He has gone South for the week," he repeated. "Now that's just like his impidence. Did he say that I was to give you anything?—'Cause I won't."

"He didn't," I said, and dropped away, and watched the red lights die out in the dark. It was horribly cold, because the wind was blowing off the sands. I climbed into my own train—not an Intermediate Carriage this time—and went to sleep.

If the man with the beard had given me a rupee I should have kept it as a memento of a rather curious affair. But the consciousness of having done my duty was my only reward.

Later on I reflected that two gentlemen like my friends could not do any good if they foregathered and personated correspondents of newspapers, and might, if they "stuck up" one of the little rat-trap states of Central India or Southern Rajputana, get themselves into serious difficulties. I therefore took some trouble to describe them as accurately as I could remember to people who would be interested in deporting them; and succeeded, so I was later informed, in having them headed back from Degumber borders.

Then I became respectable, and returned to an Office where there were no Kings and no incidents except the daily manufacture of a newspaper. A newspaper office seems to attract every conceivable sort of person, to the prejudice of discipline. Zenana-mission ladies arrive, and beg that the Editor will instantly abandon all his duties to describe a Christian prize-giving in a back-slum of a perfectly inaccessible village; Colonels who have been overpassed for commands sit down and sketch the outline of a series of ten, twelve, or twenty-four leading articles on Seniority *versus* Selection; missionaries wish to know why they have not been permitted to escape from their regular vehicles of abuse and swear at a brother missionary under special patronage of the editorial We; stranded theatrical companies troop up to explain that they cannot pay for their advertisements, but on their return from New Zealand or Tahiti will do so with interest; inventors of patent punkah-pulling machines, carriage couplings, and unbreakable swords and axletrees call with specifications in their pockets and hours at their disposal; tea companies enter and elaborate their prospectuses with the office pens; secretaries of ball committees clamor to have the glories of their last dance more fully expounded; strange ladies rustle in and say, "I want a hundred lady's cards printed *at once,* please," which is manifestly part of an Editor's duty; and every dissolute ruffian that ever tramped the Grand Trunk Road makes it his business to ask for employment as a proofreader. And, all the time, the telephone bell is ringing madly, and Kings are being killed on the Continent, and Empires are saying—"You're another," and Mister Gladstone is calling down brimstone upon the British Dominions, and the little black copy boys are whining, *"kaa-pi chay-ha-yeh"* (copy wanted) like tired bees, and most of the paper is as blank as Modred's[3] shield.

But that is the amusing part of the year. There are other six months wherein none ever come to call, and the thermometer walks inch by inch up to the top of the glass, and the office is darkened to just above reading light, and the press machines are red-hot of touch, and nobody writes anything but accounts of amusements in the Hill stations or obituary notices. Then the telephone becomes a tinkling terror, because it tells you of the sudden deaths of men and women that you knew intimately, and the prickly heat covers you as with a garment, and you sit down and write: "A slight increase of sickness is reported from the Khuda Janta Khan District. The outbreak is purely sporadic in its nature, and, thanks to the energetic efforts of the District authorities, is now almost at an end. It is, however, with deep regret we record the death, etc."

Then the sickness really breaks out, and the less recording and reporting the better for the peace of the subscribers. But the Empires and the Kings continue to divert themselves as selfishly as before, and the Foreman thinks that a daily paper really ought to come out once in twenty-four hours, and all the people at the Hill stations in the middle of their amusements say, "Good gracious! Why can't the paper be sparkling? I'm sure there's plenty going on up here."

That is the dark half of the moon, and, as the advertisements say, "must be experienced to be appreciated."

It was in that season, and a remarkably evil season, that the paper began running the last issue of the week on Saturday night, which is to say, Sunday morning, after the custom of a London paper. This was a great convenience, for immediately after the paper was put to bed, the dawn would lower the thermometer from 96° to almost 84° for half an hour, and in that chill—you have no idea how cold is 84° on the grass until you begin to pray for it—a very tired man could set off to sleep ere the heat roused him.

One Saturday night it was my pleasant duty to put the paper to bed alone. A King or courtier or a courtesan or a community was going to die or get a new Constitution, or do something that was important on the other side of the world, and the paper was to be held open till the latest possible minute in order to

3. Son, nephew, and betrayer of King Arthur in Arthurian legend. William Ewart Gladstone (1809–1898), four times prime minister of England.

catch the telegram. It was a pitchy black night, as stifling as a June night can be, and the *loo,* the red-hot wind from the westward, was booming among the tinder-dry trees and pretending that the rain was on its heels. Now and again a spot of almost boiling water would fall on the dust with the flop of a frog, but all our weary world knew that was only pretense. It was a shade cooler in the press room than the office, so I sat there, while the type clicked and clicked and the nightjars hooted at the windows, and the all but naked compositors wiped the sweat from their foreheads and called for water. The thing that was keeping us back, whatever it was, would not come off, though the *loo* dropped and the last type was set, and the whole round earth stood still in the choking heat, with its finger on its lip, to wait the event. I drowsed, and wondered whether the telegraph was a blessing, and whether this dying man, or struggling people, was aware of the inconvenience the delay was causing. There was no special reason beyond the heat and worry to make tension, but, as the clock hands crept up to three o'clock and the machines spun their flywheels two or three times to see that all was in order, before I said the word that would set them off, I could have shrieked aloud.

Then the roar and rattle of the wheels shivered the quiet into little bits. I rose to go away, but two men in white clothes stood in front of me. The first one said, "It's him!" The second said, "So it is!" And they both laughed almost as loudly as the machinery roared, and mopped their foreheads. "We see there was a light burning across the road and we were sleeping in that ditch there for coolness, and I said to my friend here, 'The office is open. Let's come along and speak to him as turned us back from the Degumber State,' " said the smaller of the two. He was the man I had met in the Mhow train, and his fellow was the red-bearded man of Marwar Junction. There was no mistaking the eyebrows of the one or the beard of the other.

I was not pleased, because I wished to go to sleep, not to squabble with Loafers. "What do you want?" I asked.

"Half an hour's talk with you cool and comfortable, in the office," said the red-bearded man. "We'd *like* some drink—the Contrack doesn't begin yet, Peachey, so you needn't look—but what we really want is advice. We don't want money. We ask you as a favor, because you did us a bad turn about Degumber."

I led from the press room to the stifling office with the maps on the walls, and the red-haired man rubbed his hands. "That's something like," said he. "This was the proper shop to come to. Now, Sir, let me introduce to you Brother Peachey Carnehan, that's him, and Brother Daniel Dravot, that is *me,* and the less said about our professions the better, for we have been most things in our time. Soldier, sailor, compositor, photographer, proofreader, street preacher, and correspondents of the *Backwoodsman* when we thought the paper wanted one. Carnehan is sober, and so am I. Look at us first and see that's sure. It will save you cutting into my talk. We'll take one of your cigars apiece, and you shall see us light."

I watched the test. The men were absolutely sober, so I gave them each a tepid peg.

"Well *and* good," said Carnehan of the eyebrows, wiping the froth from his mustache. "Let me talk now, Dan. We have been all over India, mostly on foot. We have been boiler-fitters, engine-drivers, petty contractors, and all that, and we have decided that India isn't big enough for such as us."

They certainly were too big for the office. Dravot's beard seemed to fill half the room and Carnehan's shoulders the other half, as they sat on the big table. Carnehan continued: "The country isn't half worked out because they that governs it won't let you touch it. They spend all their blessed time in governing it, and you can't lift a spade, nor chip a rock, nor look for oil, nor anything like that without all the Government saying, 'Leave it alone and let us govern.' Therefore, such as it is, we will let it alone, and go away to some other place where a man isn't crowded and can come to his own. We are not little men, and there is nothing that we are afraid of except Drink, and we have signed a Contrack on that. *Therefore,* we are going away to be Kings."

"Kings in our own right," muttered Dravot.

"Yes, of course," I said. "You've been tramping in the sun, and it's a very warm night, and hadn't you better sleep over the notion? Come tomorrow."

"Neither drunk nor sunstruck," said Dravot. "We have slept over the notion half a year, and require to see Books and Atlases, and we have decided that there is only one place now in the world that two strong men can Sar-a-*whack.*[4] They call it Kafiristan. By my reckoning it's the top right-hand corner of Afghanistan, not more than three hundred miles from Peshawur. They have two and thirty heathen idols there, and we'll be the thirty-third. It's a mountainous country, and the women of those parts are very beautiful."

"But that is provided against in the Contrack," said Carnehan. "Neither Women nor Liqu-or, Daniel."

"And that's all we know, except that no one has gone there, and they fight, and in any place where they fight, a man who knows how to drill men can always be a King. We shall go to those parts and say to any King we find, 'D'you want to vanquish your foes?' and we will show him how to drill men; for that we know better than anything else. Then we will subvert that King and seize his Throne and establish a Dy-nasty."

"You'll be cut to pieces before you're fifty miles across the Border," I said. "You have to travel through Afghanistan to get to that country. It's one mass of mountains and peaks and glaciers, and no Englishman has been through it. The people are utter brutes, and even if you reached them you couldn't do anything."

"That's more like," said Carnehan. "If you could think us a little more mad we would be more pleased. We have come to you to know about this country, to read a book about it, and be shown maps. We want you to tell us that we are fools and to show us your books." He turned to the bookcases.

"Are you at all in earnest?" I said.

"A little," said Dravot, sweetly. "As big a map as you have got, even if it's all blank where Kafiristan is, and any books you've got. We can read, though we aren't very educated."

4. The sultan of Sarawak, on the island of Borneo, had named an adventuring Englishman raja of the country.

I uncased the big thirty-two-miles-to-the-inch map of India, and two smaller Frontier maps, hauled down volume INF-KAN of the *Encyclopaedia Britannica,* and the men consulted them.

"See here!" said Dravot, his thumb on the map. "Up to Jagdallak, Peachey and me know the road. We was there with Robert's Army. We'll have to turn off to the right at Jagdallak through Laghmann territory. Then we get among the hills—fourteen thousand feet—fifteen thousand—it will be cold work there, but it don't look very far on the map."

I handed him Wood on the *Sources of the Oxus.* Carnehan was deep in the *Encyclopaedia.*

"They're a mixed lot," said Dravot, reflectively; "and it won't help us to know the names of their tribes. The more tribes the more they'll fight, and the better for us. From Jagdallak to Ashang. H'mm!"

"But all the information about the country is as sketchy and inaccurate as can be," I protested. "No one knows anything about it really. Here's the file of the *United Services' Institute.* Read what Bellew says."

"Blow Bellew!" said Carnehan. "Dan, they're an all-fired lot of heathens, but this book here says they think they're related to us English."

I smoked while the men pored over *Raverty, Wood,* the maps, and the *Encyclopaedia.*

"There is no use of your waiting," said Dravot, politely. "It's about four o'clock now. We'll go before six o'clock if you want to sleep, and we won't steal any of the papers. Don't you sit up. We're two harmless lunatics and if you come, tomorrow evening, down to the Serai we'll say good-by to you."

"You *are* two fools," I answered. "You'll be turned back at the Frontier or cut up the minute you set foot in Afghanistan. Do you want any money or a recommendation down-country? I can help you to the chance of work next week."

"Next week we shall be hard at work ourselves, thank you," said Dravot. "It isn't so easy being a King as it looks. When we've got our Kingdom in going order we'll let you know, and you can come up and help us to govern it."

"Would two lunatics make a Contrack like that?" said Carnehan, with subdued pride, showing me a greasy half sheet of note paper on which was written the following. I copied it, then and there, as a curiosity:

*This Contract between me and you pursuing witnesseth in the name of God—Amen and so forth.*

(ONE) *That me and you will settle this matter together:* i.e., *to be Kings of Kafiristan.*

(TWO) *That you and me will not, while this matter is being settled, look at any Liquor, nor any Woman, black, white or brown, so as to get mixed up with one or the other harmful.*

(THREE) *That we conduct ourselves with dignity and discretion and if one of us gets into trouble the other will stay by him.*

*Signed by you and me this day.*

PEACHEY TALIAFERRO CARNEHAN.

DANIEL DRAVOT.

*Both Gentlemen at Large.*

"There was no need for the last article," said Carnehan, blushing modestly; "but it looks regular. Now you know the sort of men that Loafers are—we *are* Loafers, Dan, until we get out of India—and *do* you think that we would sign a Contrack like that unless we was in earnest? We have kept away from the two things that make life worth having."

"You won't enjoy your lives much longer if you are going to try this idiotic adventure. Don't set the office on fire," I said, "and go away before nine o'clock."

I left them still poring over the maps and making notes on the back of the "Contrack." "Be sure to come down to the Serai tomorrow," were their parting words.

The Kumharsen Serai is the great four-square sink of humanity where the strings of camels and horses from the North load and unload. All the nationalities of Central Asia may be found there, and most of the folk of India proper. Balkh and Bokhara there meet Bengal and Bombay, and try to draw eyeteeth. You can buy ponies, turquoises, Persian pussy cats, saddlebags, fat-tailed sheep, and musk in the Kumharsen Serai, and get many strange things for nothing. In the afternoon I went down there to see whether my friends intended to keep their word or were lying about drunk.

A priest attired in fragments of ribbons and rags stalked up to me, gravely twisting a child's paper whirligig. Behind was his servant bending under the load of a crate of mud toys. The two were loading up two camels, and the inhabitants of the Serai watched them with shrieks of laughter.

"The priest is mad," said a horse-dealer to me. "He is going up to Kabul to sell toys to the Amir. He will either be raised to honor or have his head cut off. He came in here this morning and has been behaving madly ever since."

"The witless are under the protection of God," stammered a flat-cheeked Usbeg in broken Hindi. "They foretell future events."

"Would they could have foretold that my caravan would have been cut up by the Shinwaris almost within shadow of the Pass!" grunted the Eusufzai agent of a Rajputana trading house whose goods had been feloniously diverted into the hands of other robbers just across the Border, and whose misfortunes were the laughingstock of the bazaar. "Ohé, priest, whence come you and whither do you go?"

"From Roum have I come," shouted the priest, waving his whirligig; "from Roum, blown by the breath of a hundred devils across the sea! O thieves, robbers, liars, the blessing of Pir Khan on pigs, dogs, and perjurers! Who will take the Protected of God to the North to sell charms that are never still to the Amir? The camels shall not gall, the sons shall not fall sick, and the wives shall remain faithful while they are away, of the men who give me place in their caravan. Who will assist me to slipper the King of the Roos with a golden slipper with a silver heel? The protection of Pir Khan be upon his labors!" He spread out the skirts of his garberdine and pirouetted between the lines of tethered horses.

"There starts a caravan from Peshawur to Kabul in twenty days, *Huzrut*," said the Eusufzai trader. "My camels go therewith. Do thou also go and bring us good luck."

"I will go even now!" shouted the priest. "I will depart upon my winged camels, and be at Peshawur in a day! Ho! Hazar Mir Khan," he yelled to his servant, "drive out the camels, but let me first mount my own."

He leaped on the back of his beast as it knelt, and, turning round to me, cried, "Come thou also, Sahib, a little along the road, and I will sell thee a charm—an amulet that shall make thee King of Kafiristan."

Then the light broke upon me, and I followed the two camels out of the Serai till we reached open road and the priest halted.

"What d'you think o' that?" said he in English. "Carnehan can't talk their patter, so I've made him my servant. He makes a handsome servant. 'Tisn't for nothing that I've been knocking about the country for fourteen years. Didn't I do that talk neat? We'll hitch on to a caravan at Peshawur till we get to Jagdallak, and then we'll see if we can get donkeys for our camels, and strike into Kafiristan. Whirligigs for the Amir, O Lor'! Put your hand under the camel bags and tell me what you feel."

I felt the butt of a Martini,[5] and another and another.

"Twenty of 'em," said Dravot, placidly. "Twenty of 'em, and ammunition to correspond, under the whirligigs and the mud dolls."

"Heaven help you if you are caught with those things!" I said. "A Martini is worth her weight in silver among the Pathans."

"Fifteen hundred rupees of capital—every rupee we could beg, borrow, or steal—are invested on these two camels," said Dravot. "We won't get caught. We're going through the Khyber with a regular caravan. Who'd touch a poor mad priest?"

"Have you got everything you want?" I asked, overcome with astonishment.

"Not yet, but we shall soon. Give us a memento of your kindness, *Brother*. You did me a service yesterday, and that time in Marwar. Half my Kingdom shall you have, as the saying is." I slipped a small charm compass from my watch chain and handed it up to the priest.

"Good-bye," said Dravot, giving me hand cautiously. "It's the last time we'll shake hands with an Englishman these many days. Shake hands with him, Carnehan," he cried, as the second camel passed me.

Carnehan leaned down and shook hands. Then the camels passed away along the dusty road, and I was left alone to wonder. My eye could detect no failure in the disguises. The scene in Serai attested that they were complete to the native mind. There was just the chance, therefore, that Carnehan and Dravot would be able to wander through Afghanistan without detection. But, beyond, they would find death, certain and awful death.

Ten days later a native friend of mine, giving me the news of the day from Peshawur, wound up his letter with:—"There has been much laughter here on account of a certain mad priest who is going in his estimation to sell petty gauds and insignificant trinkets which he ascribes as great charms to H. H. the Amir of Bokhara. He passed through Peshawur and associated himself to the Second Summer caravan that goes to Kabul. The merchants are pleased, because through superstition they imagine that such mad fellows bring good fortune."

5. Military rifle.

The two, then, were beyond the Border. I would have prayed for them, but, that night, a real King died in Europe, and demanded an obituary notice.

The wheel of the world swings through the same phases again and again. Summer passed and winter thereafter, and came and passed again. The daily paper continued and I with it, and upon the third summer there fell a hot night, a night issue, and a strained waiting for something to be telegraphed from the other side of the world, exactly as had happened before. A few great men had died in the past two years, the machines worked with more clatter, and some of the trees in the Office garden were a few feet taller. But that was all the difference.

I passed over to the press room, and went through just such a scene as I have already described. The nervous tension was stronger than it had been two years before, and I felt the heat more acutely. At three o'clock I cried, "Print off," and turned to go, when there crept to my chair what was left of a man. He was bent into a circle, his head was sunk between his shoulders, and he moved his feet one over the other like a bear. I could hardly see whether he walked or crawled—this rag-wrapped, whining cripple who addressed me by name, crying that he was come back. "Can you give me a drink?" he whimpered. "For the Lord's sake, give me a drink!"

I went back to the office, the man followed with groans of pain, and I turned up the lamp.

"Don't you know me?" he gasped, dropping into a chair, and he turned his drawn face, surmounted by a shock of gray hair, to the light.

I looked at him intently. Once before had I seen eyebrows that met over the nose in an inch-broad black band, but for the life of me I could not tell where.

"I don't know you," I said, handing him the whisky. "What can I do for you?"

He took a gulp of the spirit raw, and shivered in spite of the suffocating heat.

"I've come back," he repeated; "and I was the King of Kafiristan—me and Dravot—crowned Kings we was! In this office we settled it—you setting there and giving us the books. I am Peachey—Peachey Taliaferro Carnehan, and you've been setting here ever since—O Lord!"

I was more than a little astonished, and expressed my feelings accordingly.

"It's true," said Carnehan, with a dry cackle, nursing his feet, which were wrapped in rags. "True as gospel. Kings we were, with crowns upon our heads—me and Dravot—poor Dan—oh, poor, poor Dan, that would never take advice, not though I begged of him!"

"Take the whisky," I said, "and take your own time. Tell me all you can recollect of everything from beginning to end. You got across the border on your camels, Dravot dressed as a mad priest and you his servant. Do you remember that?"

"I ain't mad—yet, but I shall be that way soon. Of course I remember. Keep looking at me, or maybe my words will go all to pieces. Keep looking at me in my eyes and don't say anything."

I leaned forward and looked into his face as steadily as I could. He dropped one hand upon the table and I grasped it by the wrist. It was twisted like a bird's claw, and upon the back was a ragged, red, diamond-shaped scar.

"No, don't look there. Look at *me,*" said Carnehan. "That comes afterward, but for the Lord's sake don't distrack me. We left with that caravan, me and Dravot playing all sorts of antics to amuse the people we were with. Dravot used to make us laugh in the evenings when all the people was cooking their dinners—cooking their dinners, and . . . what did they do then? They lit little fires with sparks that went into Dravot's beard, and we all laughed—fit to die. Little red fires they was, going into Dravot's big red beard—so funny." His eyes left mine and he smiled foolishly.

"You went as far as Jagdallak with that caravan," I said, at a venture, "after you had lit those fires. To Jagdallak, where you turned off to try to get into Kafiristan."

"No, we didn't neither. What are you talking about? We turned off before Jagdallak, because we heard the roads was good. But they wasn't good enough for our two camels—mine and Dravot's. When we left the caravan, Dravot took off all his clothes and mine too, and said we would be heathen, because the Kafirs didn't allow Mohammedans to talk to them. So we dressed betwixt and between, and such a sight as Daniel Dravot I never saw yet nor expect to see again. He burned half his beard, and slung a sheepskin over his shoulder, and shaved his head into patterns. He shaved mine, too, and made me wear outrageous things to look like a heathen. That was in a most mountaineous country, and our camels couldn't go along any more because of the mountains. They were tall and black, and coming home I saw them fight like wild goats—there are lots of goats in Kafiristan. And these mountains, they never keep still, no more than goats. Always fighting they are, and don't let you sleep at night."

"Take some more whisky," I said, very slowly. "What did you and Daniel Dravot do when the camels could go no further because of the rough roads that led into Kafiristan?"

"What did which do? There was a party called Peachey Taliaferro Carnehan that was with Dravot. Shall I tell you about him? He died out there in the cold. Slap from the bridge fell old Peachey, turning and twisting in the air like a penny whirligig that you can sell to the Amir—No; they was two for three ha'pence, those whirligigs, or I am much mistaken and woeful sore. And then these camels were no use, and Peachey said to Dravot—'For the Lord's sake, let's get out of this before our heads are chopped off,' and with that they killed the camels all among the mountains, not having anything in particular to eat, but first they took off the boxes with the guns and the ammunition, till two men came along driving four mules. Dravot up and dances in front of them, singing,—'Sell me four mules.' Says the first man,—'If you are rich enough to buy, you are rich enough to rob'; but before ever he could put his hand to his knife, Dravot breaks his neck over his knee, and the other party runs away. So Carnehan loaded the mules with the rifles that was taken off the camels, and together we starts forward into those bitter cold mountaineous parts, and never a road broader than the back of your hand."

He paused for a moment, while I asked him if he could remember the nature of the country through which he had journeyed.

"I am telling you as straight as I can, but my head isn't as good as it might be. They drove nails through it to make me hear better how Dravot died. The country was mountaineous and the mules were most contrary, and the inhabitants was dispersed and solitary. They went up and up, and down and down, and that other party, Carnehan, was imploring of Dravot not to sing and whistle so loud, for fear of bringing down the tremenjus avalanches. But Dravot says that if a King couldn't sing it wasn't worth being King, and whacked the mules over the rump, and never took no heed for ten cold days. We came to a big level valley all among the mountains, and the mules were near dead, so we killed them, not having anything in special for them or us to eat. We sat upon the boxes, and played odd and even with the cartridges that was jolted out.

"Then ten men with bows and arrows ran down that valley, chasing twenty men with bows and arrows, and the row was tremenjus. They was fair men—fairer than you or more—with yellow hair and remarkable well built. Says Dravot, unpacking the guns—'This is the beginning of the business. We'll fight for the ten men,' and with that he fires two rifles at the twenty men, and drops one of them at two hundred yards from the rock where we was sitting. The other men began to run, but Carnehan and Dravot sits on the boxes picking them off at all ranges, up and down the valley. Then we goes up to the ten men that had run across the snow too, and they fires a footy little arrow at us. Dravot he shoots above their heads and they all falls down flat. Then he walks over and kicks them, and then he lifts them up and shakes hands all around to make them friendly like. He calls them and gives them the boxes to carry, and waves his hand for all the world as though he was King already. They takes the boxes and him across the valley and up the hill into a pine wood on the top, where there was half a dozen big stone idols. Dravot he goes to the biggest—a fellow they call Imbra—and lays a rifle and a cartridge at his feet, rubbing his nose respectful with his own nose, patting him on the head, and saluting in front of it. He turns round to the men and nods his head, and says, 'That's all right. I'm in the know too, and all these old jim-jams are my friends.' Then he opens his mouth and points down it, and when the first man brings him food, he says 'No'; and when the second man brings him food, he says 'No'; but when one of the old priests and the boss of the village brings him food, he says 'Yes'; very haughty, and eats it slow. That was how we came to our first village, without any trouble, just as though we had tumbled from the skies. But we tumbled from one of those damned rope bridges, you see, and you couldn't expect a man to laugh much after that."

"Take some more whisky and go on," I said. "That was the first village you came into. How did you get to be King?"

"I wasn't King," said Carnehan. "Dravot he was the King, and a handsome man he looked with the gold crown on his head and all. Him and the other party stayed in that village, and every morning Dravot sat by the side of old Imbra, and the people came and worshiped. That was Dravot's order. Then a lot of men came into the valley, and Carnehan and Dravot picks them off with the rifles before they knew where they was, and runs down into the valley and up again the other side, and finds another village, same as the first one, and the people all falls down flat on their faces, and Dravot says, 'Now what is the trouble between you two villages?' and the people points to a woman, as fair as you or me, that was carried off, and Dravot takes her back to the first village and counts up the dead—eight there was. For each dead man Dravot pours a little milk on the ground and waves his arms like a whirligig and 'That's all right,' says he. Then he and Carnehan takes the big boss of each village by the arm and walks them down into the valley, and shows them how to scratch a line with a spear right down the valley, and gives each a sod of turf from both sides o' the line. Then all the people comes down and shouts like the devil and all, and Dravot says, 'Go and dig the land, and be fruitful and multiply,' which they did, though they didn't understand. Then we asks the names of things in their lingo—bread and water and fire and idols and such, and Dravot leads the priest of each village up to the idol, and says he must sit there and judge the people, and if anything goes wrong he is to be shot.

"Next week they was all turning up the land in the valley as quiet as bees and much prettier, and the priests heard all the complaints and told Dravot in dumb show what it was about. 'That's just the beginning,' says Dravot. 'They think we're Gods.' He and Carnehan picks out twenty good men and shows them how to click off a rifle, and form fours, and advance in line, and they was very pleased to do so, and clever to see the hang of it. Then he takes out his pipe and his 'baccy pouch and leaves one at one village and one at the other, and off we two goes to see what was to be done in the next valley. That was all rock, and there was a little village there, and Carnehan says, 'Send 'em to the old valley to plant,' and takes 'em there and gives 'em some land that wasn't took before. They were a poor lot, and we blooded 'em with a kid before letting 'em into the new Kingdom. That was to impress the people, and then they settled down quiet, and Carnehan went back to Dravot, who had got into another valley, all snow and ice and most mountaineous. There was no people there, and the Army got afraid, so Dravot shoots one of them, and goes on till he finds some people in a village, and the Army explains that unless the people wants to be killed they had better not shoot their little matchlocks; for they had matchlocks. We makes friends with the priest and I stays there alone with two of the Army, teaching the men how to drill, and a thundering big Chief comes across the snow with kettledrums and horns twanging, because he heard there was a new God kicking about. Carnehan sights for the brown of the men half a mile across the snow and wings one of them. Then he sends a message to the Chief that, unless he wished to be killed, he must come and shake hands with me and leave his arms behind. The Chief comes alone first, and Carnehan shakes hands with him and whirls his arms about, same as Dravot used, and very much surprised that Chief was, and strokes my eyebrows. Then Carnehan goes alone to the Chief, and asks him in dumb show if he had an enemy he hated. 'I have,' says the Chief. So Carnehan weeds out the pick of his men, and sets the two of the Army to show them drill, and at the end of two weeks the men can maneuver about as well as Volunteers. So he marches with the Chief to a great big plain on the top of a mountain, and the Chief's men rushes into a village and takes it; we three Martinis firing into the brown of the enemy. So we took that village too, and I gives the Chief a rag from my coat and says, 'Occupy till I come'; which was scriptural. By way of a reminder, when me and the Army was eighteen hundred yards away, I drops a bullet near him standing on the snow, and all the people falls flat on their faces. Then I sends a letter to Dravot, wherever he be by land or by sea."

At the risk of throwing the creature out of train I interrupted, "How could you write a letter up yonder?"

"The letter?—Oh!—The letter! Keep looking at me between the eyes, please. It was a string-talk letter, that we'd learned the way of it from a blind beggar in the Punjab."

I remember that there had once come to the office a blind man with a knotted twig and a piece of string which he wound round the twig according to some cipher of his own. He could, after the lapse of days or hours, repeat the sentence which he had reeled up. He had reduced the alphabet to eleven primitive sounds; and tried to teach me his method, but failed.

"I sent that letter to Dravot," said Carnehan; "and told him to come back because this Kingdom was growing too big for me to handle, and then I struck for the first valley, to see how the priests were working. They called the village we took along with the Chief, Bashkai, and the first village we took, Er-Heb. The priests at Er-Heb was doing all right, but they had a lot of pending cases about land to show me, and some men from another village had been firing arrows at night. I went out and looked for that village and fired four rounds at it from a thousand yards. That used all the cartridges I cared to spend, and I waited for Dravot, who had been away two or three months, and I kept my people quiet.

"One morning I heard the devil's own noise of drums and horns, and Dan Dravot marches down the hill with his Army and a tail of hundreds of men, and, which was the most amazing—a great gold crown on his head. 'My Gord, Carnehan,' says Daniel, 'this is a tremenjus business, and we've got the whole country as far as it's worth having. I am the son of Alexander by Queen Semiramis, and you're my younger brother and a God too! It's the biggest thing we've ever seen. I've been marching and fighting for six weeks with the Army, and every footy little village for fifty miles has come in rejoiceful; and more than that, I've got the key of the whole show, as you'll see, and I've got a crown for you! I told 'em to make two of 'em at a place called Shu, where the gold lies in the rock like suet in mutton. Gold I've seen, and turquoise I've kicked out of the cliffs, and there's garnets in the sands of the river, and here's a chunk of amber that a man brought me. Call up all the priests and, here, take your crown.'

"One of the men opens a black hair bag and I slips the crown on. It was too small and too heavy, but I wore it for the glory. Hammered gold it was—five pound weight, like a hoop of a barrel.

" 'Peachey,' says Dravot, 'we don't want to fight no more. The Craft's[6] the trick, so help me!' and he brings forward that same Chief that I left at Bashkai—

6. Masonic rituals and emblems.

Billy Fish we called him afterward, because he was so like Billy Fish that drove the big tank engine at Mach on the Bolan in the old days. 'Shake hands with him,' says Dravot, and I shook hands and nearly dropped, for Billy Fish gave me the Grip. I said nothing, but tried him with the Fellow Craft Grip. He answers, all right, and I tried the Master's Grip, but that was a slip. 'A Fellow Craft he is!' I says to Dan. 'Does he know the word?' 'He does,' says Dan, 'and all the priests know. It's a miracle! The Chiefs and the priests can work a Fellow Craft Lodge in a way that's very like ours, and they've cut the marks on the rocks, but they don't know the Third Degree, and they've come to find out. It's Gord's Truth. I've known these long years that the Afghans knew up to the Fellow Craft Degree, but this is a miracle. A God and a Grand Master of the Craft am I, and a Lodge in the Third Degree I will open, and we'll raise the head priests and the Chiefs of the villages.'

" 'It's against all the law,' I says, 'holding a Lodge without warrant from anyone; and we never held office in any Lodge.'

" 'It's a master stroke of policy,' says Dravot. 'It means running the country as easy as a four-wheeled bogy on a down grade. We can't stop to inquire now, or they'll turn against us. I've forty Chiefs at my heel, and passed and raised according to their merit they shall be. Billet these men on the villages and see that we run up a Lodge of some kind. The temple of Imbra will do for the Lodge room. The women must make aprons as you show them. I'll hold a levee of Chiefs tonight and Lodge tomorrow.'

"I was fair run off my legs, but I wasn't such a fool as not to see what a pull this Craft business gave us. I showed the priests' families how to make aprons of the degrees, but for Dravot's apron the blue border and marks was made of turquoise lumps on white hide, not cloth. We took a great square stone in the temple for the Master's chair, and little stones for the officers' chairs, and painted the black pavement with white squares, and did what we could to make things regular.

"At the levee which was held that night on the hillside with big bonfires, Dravot gives out that him and me were Gods and sons of Alexander, and Past Grand Masters in the Craft, and was come to make Kafiristan a country where every man should eat in peace and drink in quiet, and specially obey us. Then the Chiefs come round to shake hands, and they was so hairy and white and fair it was just shaking hands with old friends. We gave them names according as they was like men we had known in India—Billy Fish, Holly Wilworth, Pikky Kergan that was Bazaar-master when I was at Mhow, and so on and so on.

"*The* most amazing miracle was at Lodge next night. One of the old priests was watching us continuous, and I felt uneasy, for I knew we'd have to fudge the Ritual, and I didn't know what the men knew. The old priest was a stranger come in from beyond the village of Bashkai. The minute Dravot puts on the Master's apron that the girls had made for him, the priest fetches a whoop and a howl, and tried to overturn the stone that Dravot was sitting on. 'It's all up now,' I says. 'That comes of meddling with the Craft without warrant!' Dravot never winked an eye, not when ten priests took and tilted over the Grand Master's chair—which was to say the stone of Imbra. The priest begins rubbing the bottom end of it to clear away the black dirt, and presently he shows all the other priests the Master's Mark, same as was on Dravot's apron, cut into the stone. Not even the priests of the temple of Imbra knew it was there. The old chap falls flat on his face at Dravot's feet and kisses 'em. 'Luck again,' says Dravot, across the Lodge to me, 'they say it's the missing Mark that no one could understand the why of. We're more than safe now.' Then he bangs the butt of his gun for a gavel and says, 'By virtue of the authority vested in me by my own right hand and the help of Peachey, I declare myself Grand Master of all Freemasonry in Kafiristan in this the Mother Lodge o' the country, and King of Kafiristan equally with Peachey!' At that he puts on his crown and I puts on mine—I was doing Senior Warden—and we opens the Lodge in most ample form. It was a amazing miracle! The priests moved in Lodge through the first two degrees almost without telling, as if the memory was coming back to them. After that, Peachey and Dravot raised such as was worthy—high priests and Chiefs of far-off villages. Billy Fish was the first, and I can tell you we scared the soul out of him. It was not in any way according to Ritual, but it served our turn. We didn't raise more than ten of the biggest men, because we didn't want to make the Degree common. And they was clamoring to be raised.

" 'In another six months,' says Dravot, 'we'll hold another Communication and see how you are working.' Then he asks them about their villages, and learns that they was fighting one against the other and were fair sick and tired of it. And when they wasn't doing that they was fighting with the Mohammedans. 'You can fight those when they come into our country,' says Dravot. 'Tell off every tenth man of your tribes for a Frontier guard, and send two hundred at a time to this valley to be drilled. Nobody is going to be shot or speared any more so long as he does well, and I know that you won't cheat me because you're white people—sons of Alexander—and not like common, black Mohammedans. You are *my* people and by God,' says he, running off into English at the end—'I'll make a damned fine Nation of you, or I'll die in the making!'

"I can't tell all we did for the next six months because Dravot did a lot I couldn't see the hang of, and he learned their lingo in a way I never could. My work was to help the people plow, and now and again go out with some of the Army and see what the other villages were doing, and make 'em throw rope bridges across the ravines which cut up the country horrid. Dravot was very kind to me, but when he walked up and down in the pine wood pulling that bloody red beard of his with both fists I knew he was thinking plans I could not advise him about, and I just waited for orders.

"But Dravot never showed me disrespect before the people. They were afraid of me and the Army, but they loved Dan. He was the best of friends with the priests and the Chiefs; but anyone could come across the hills with a complaint and Dravot would hear him out fair, and call four priests together and say what was to be done. He used to call in Billy Fish from Bashkai, and Pikky Kergan from Shu, and an old Chief we called Kafuzelum—it was like enough to his real name—and hold councils with 'em when there was any fighting to be done in small villages. That was his Council of War, and the four priests of Bashkai, Shu, Khawak, and Madora was his Privy Council. Between the lot of 'em they sent me, with forty men and twenty rifles, and sixty men carrying turquoises, into the Ghorband country to buy those hand-made Martini rifles, that come out of the Amir's workshops at Kabul, from one of the Amir's Herati regiments that would have sold the very teeth out of their mouths for turquoises.

"I stayed in Ghorband a month, and gave the Governor there the pick of my baskets for hush money, and bribed the Colonel of the regiment some more, and, between the two and the tribespeople, we got more than a hundred hand-made Martinis, a hundred good Kohat Jezails that'll throw to six hundred yards, and forty manloads of very bad ammunition for the rifles. I came back with what I had, and distributed 'em among the men that the Chiefs sent to me to drill. Dravot was too busy to attend to those things, but the old Army that we first made helped me, and we turned out five hundred men that could drill, and two hundred that knew how to hold arms pretty straight. Even those cork-screwed, hand-made guns was a miracle to them. Dravot talked big about powder shops and factories, walking up and down in the pine wood when the winter was coming on.

" 'I won't make a Nation,' says he. 'I'll make an Empire! These men aren't niggers; they're English! Look at their eyes—look at their mouths. Look at the way they stand up. They sit on chairs in their own houses. They're the Lost Tribes, or something like it, and they've grown to be English. I'll take a census in the spring if the priests don't get frightened. There must be a fair two million of 'em in these hills. The villages are full o' little children. Two million people—two hundred and fifty thousand fighting men—and all English! They only want the rifles and a little drilling. Two hundred and fifty thousand men, ready to cut in on Russia's right flank when she tries for India! Peachey, man,' he says, chewing his beard in great hunks, 'we shall be Emperors—Emperors of the Earth! Rajah Brooke[7] will be a suckling to us. I'll treat with the Vice-roy on equal terms. I'll ask him to send me twelve picked English—twelve that I know of—to help us govern a bit. There's Mackray, Sergeant-pensioner at Segowli—many's the good dinner he's given me, and his wife a pair of trousers. There's Donkin, the Warder of Tounghoo Jail; there's hundreds that I could lay my hand on if I was in India. The Vice-roy shall do it for me. I'll send a man through in the spring for those men, and I'll write for a dispensation from the Grand Lodge for what I've done as Grand Master. That—and all the Sniders[8] that'll be thrown out when the native troops in India take up the Martini. They'll be worn smooth, but they'll do for fighting in these hills. Twelve English, a hundred thousand Sniders run through the Amir's country in driblets—I'd be content with twenty thousand in one year—and we'd be an Empire. When everything was shipshape, I'd hand over the crown—this crown I'm wearing now—to Queen Victoria on my knees, and she'd say: "Rise up, Sir Daniel Dravot." Oh, it's big! It's big, I tell you! But there's so much to be done in every place—Bashkai, Khawak, Shu, and everywhere else.'

" 'What is it?' I says. 'There are no more men coming in to be drilled this autumn. Look at those fat, black clouds. They're bringing the snow.'

" 'It isn't that,' says Daniel, putting his hand very hard on my shoulder;

7. Sir Charles Brooke (1829–1917), one of three members of the family who governed Sarawak from 1841 to 1942. 8. Obsolete military rifles.

'and I don't wish to say anything that's against you, for no other living man would have followed me and made me what I am as you have done. You're a first-class Commander-in-Chief, and the people know you; but—it's a big country, and somehow you can't help me, Peachey, in the way I want to be helped.'

" 'Go to your blasted priests, then!' I said, and I was sorry when I made that remark, but it did hurt me sore to find Daniel talking so superior when I'd drilled all the men, and done all he told me.

" 'Don't let's quarrel, Peachey,' says Daniel, without cursing. 'You're a King, too, and the half of this Kingdom is yours; but can't you see, Peachey, we want cleverer men than us now—three or four of 'em, that we can scatter about for our Deputies. It's a hugeous great State, and I can't always tell the right thing to do, and I haven't time for all I want to do, and here's the winter coming on and all.' He put half his beard into his mouth, and it was as red as the gold of his crown.

" 'I'm sorry, Daniel,' says I. 'I've done all I could. I've drilled the men and shown the people how to stack their oats better; and I've brought in those tinware rifles from Ghorband—but I know what you're driving at. I take it Kings always feel oppressed that way.'

" 'There's another thing too,' says Dravot, walking up and down. 'The winter's coming and these people won't be giving much trouble and if they do we can't move about. I want a wife.'

" 'For Gord's sake leave the women alone!' I says. 'We've both got all the work we can, though I *am* a fool. Remember the Contrack, and keep clear o' women.'

" 'The Contrack only lasted till such time as we was Kings; and Kings we have been these months past,' says Dravot, weighing his crown in his hand. 'You go get a wife too, Peachey—a nice, strappin', plump girl that'll keep you warm in the winter. They're prettier than English girls, and we can take the pick of 'em. Boil 'em once or twice in hot water, and they'll come as fair as chicken and ham.'

" 'Don't tempt me!' I says. 'I will not have any dealings with a woman not till we are a dam' side more settled than we are now. I've been doing the work o' two men, and you've been doing the work o' three. Let's lie off a bit, and see if we can get some better tobacco from Afghan country and run in some good liquor; but no women.'

" 'Who's talking o' *women*?' says Dravot. 'I said *wife*—a Queen to breed a King's son for the King. A Queen out of the strongest tribe, that'll make them your blood brothers, and that'll lie by your side and tell you all the people thinks about you and their own affairs. That's what I want.'

" 'Do you remember that Bengali woman I kept at Mogul Serai when I was a plate layer?' says I. 'A fat lot o' good she was to me. She taught me the lingo and one or two other things; but what happened? She ran away with the Stationmaster's servant and half my month's pay. Then she turned up at Dadur Junction in tow of a half-caste, and had the impidence to say I was her husband—all among the drivers in the running shed!'

" 'We've done with that,' says Dravot. 'These women are whiter than you or me, and a Queen I will have for the winter months.'

" 'For the last time o' asking, Dan, do *not*,' I says. 'It'll only bring us harm. The Bible says that Kings ain't to waste their strength on women, 'specially when they've got a new raw Kingdom to work over.'

" 'For the last time of answering, I will,' said Dravot, and he went away through the pine trees looking like a big red devil. The low sun hit his crown and beard on one side and the two blazed like hot coals.

"But getting a wife was not as easy as Dan thought. He put it before the Council, and there was no answer till Billy Fish said that he'd better ask the girls. Dravot damned them all around. 'What's wrong with me?' he shouts, standing by the idol Imbra. 'Am I a dog or am I not enough of a man for your wenches? Haven't I put the shadow of my hand over this country? Who stopped the last Afghan raid?' It was me really, but Dravot was too angry to remember. 'Who brought your guns? Who repaired the bridges? Who's the Grand Master of the sign cut in the stone?' and he thumped his hand on the block that he used to sit on in Lodge, and at Council, which opened like Lodge always. Billy Fish said nothing, and no more did the others. 'Keep your hair on, Dan,' said I; 'and ask the girls. That's how it's done at Home, and these people are quite English.'

" 'The marriage of the King is a matter of State,' says Dan, in a white-hot rage, for he could feel, I hope, that he was going against his better mind. He walked out of the Council room, and the others sat still, looking at the ground.

" 'Billy Fish,' says I to the Chief of Bashkai, 'what's the difficulty here? A straight answer to a true friend.' 'You know,' says Billy Fish. 'How should a man tell you who know everything? How can daughters of men marry Gods or Devils? It's not proper.'

"I remembered something like that in the Bible; but if, after seeing us as long as they had, they still believed we were Gods, it wasn't for me to undeceive them.

" 'A God can do anything,' says I. 'If the King is fond of a girl he'll not let her die.' 'She'll have to,' said Billy Fish. 'There are all sorts of Gods and Devils in these mountains, and now and again a girl marries one of them and isn't seen any more. Besides, you two know the Mark cut in the stone. Only the Gods know that. We thought you were men till you showed the sign of the Master.'

"I wished then that we had explained about the loss of the genuine secrets of a Master Mason at the first go-off; but I said nothing. All that night there was a blowing of horns in a little dark temple halfway down the hill, and I heard a girl crying fit to die. One of the priests told us that she was being prepared to marry the King.

" 'I'll have no nonsense of that kind,' says Dan. 'I don't want to interfere with your customs, but I'll take my own wife.' 'The girl's a little bit afraid,' says the priest. 'She thinks she's going to die, and they are a-heartening of her up down in the temple.'

" 'Hearten her very tender, then,' says Dravot, 'or I'll hearten you with the butt of a gun so that you'll never want to be heartened again.' He licked his lips, did Dan, and stayed up walking about more than half the night, thinking of the wife that he was going to get in the morning. I wasn't any means comfortable, for I knew that dealings with a woman in foreign parts, though you was a crowned King twenty times over, could not but be risky. I got up very early in the morning while Dravot was asleep, and I saw the priests talking together in whispers, and the Chiefs talking together too, and they looked at me out of the corners of their eyes.

" 'What is up, Fish?' I says to the Bashkai man, who was wrapped up in his furs and looking splendid to behold.

" 'I can't rightly say,' says he; 'but if you can induce the King to drop all this nonsense about marriage, you'll be doing him and me and yourself a great service.'

" 'That I do believe,' says I. 'But sure, you know, Billy, as well as me, having fought against and for us, that the King and me are nothing more than two of the finest men that God Almighty ever made. Nothing more, I do assure you.'

" 'That may be,' says Billy Fish, 'and yet I should be sorry if it was.' He sinks his head upon his great fur cloak for a minute and thinks. 'King,' says he, 'be you man or God or Devil, I'll stick by you today. I have twenty of my men with me, and they will follow me. We'll go to Bashkai until the storm blows over.'

"A little snow had fallen in the night, and everything was white except the greasy fat clouds that blew down and down from the north. Dravot came out with his crown on his head, swinging his arms and stamping his feet, and looking more pleased than Punch.

" 'For the last time, drop it, Dan,' says I, in a whisper. 'Billy Fish here says that there will be a row.'

" 'A row among my people!' says Dravot. 'Not much. Peachey, you're a fool not to get a wife too. Where's the girl?' says he, with a voice as loud as the braying of a jackass. 'Call up all the Chiefs and priests, and let the Emperor see if his wife suits him.'

"There was no need to call anyone. They were all there leaning on their guns and spears round the clearing in the center of the pine wood. A deputation of priests went down to the little temple to bring up the girl, and the horns blew up fit to wake the dead. Billy Fish saunters round and gets as close to Daniel as he could, and behind him stood his twenty men with matchlocks. Not a man of them under six feet. I was next to Dravot, and behind me was twenty men of the regular Army. Up comes the girl, and a strapping wench she was, covered with silver and turquoises, but white as death, and looking back every minute at the priests.

" 'She'll do,' said Dan, looking her over. 'What's to be afraid of, lass? Come and kiss me.' He puts his arm round her. She shuts her eyes, gives a bit of a squeak, and down goes her face in the side of Dan's flaming red beard.

" 'The slut's bitten me!' says he, clapping his hand to his neck, and, sure enough, his hand was red with blood. Billy Fish and two of his matchlock men catches hold of Dan by his shoulders and drags him into the Bashkai lot, while the priests howl in their lingo, 'Neither God nor Devil, but a man!' I was all taken aback, for a priest cut at me in front, and the Army behind began firing into the Bashkai men.

" 'God A-mighty!' says Dan. 'What is the meaning o' this?'

" 'Come back! Come away!' says Billy Fish, 'Ruin and Mutiny is the matter. We'll break for Bashkai if we can.'

"I tried to give some sort of orders to my men—the men o' the regular Army—but it was no use, so I fired into the brown of 'em with an English Martini and drilled three beggars in a line. The valley was full of shouting, howling creatures, and every soul was shrieking, 'Not a God not a Devil, but only a man!' The Bashkai troops stuck to Billy Fish all they were worth, but their matchlocks wasn't half as good as the Kabul breechloaders, and four of them dropped. Dan was bellowing like a bull, for he was very wrathy; and Billy Fish had a hard job to prevent him running out at the crowd.

" 'We can't stand,' says Billy Fish. 'Make a run for it down the valley! The whole place is against us.' The matchlock men ran, and we went down the valley in spite of Dravot's protestations. He was swearing horribly and crying out that he was a King. The priests rolled great stones on us, and the regular Army fired hard, and there wasn't more than six men, not counting Dan, Billy Fish, and Me, that came down to the bottom of the valley alive.

"Then they stopped firing and the horns in the temple blew again. 'Come away—for Gord's sake come away!' says Billy Fish. 'They'll send runners out to all the villages before ever we get to Bashkai. I can protect you there, but I can't do anything now.'

"My own notion is that Dan began to go mad in his head from that hour. He stared up and down like a stuck pig. Then he was all for walking back alone and killing the priests with his bare hands; which he could have done. 'An Emperor am I,' says Daniel, 'and next year I shall be a Knight of the Queen.'

" 'All right, Dan,' says I; 'but come along now while there's time.'

" 'It's your fault,' says he, 'for not looking after your Army better. There was mutiny in the midst and you didn't know—you damned engine-driving, plate-laying, missionary's-pass-hunting hound!' He sat upon a rock and called me every foul name he could lay tongue to. I was too heartsick to care, though it was all his foolishness that brought the smash.

" 'I'm sorry, Dan,' says I, 'but there's no accounting for natives. This business is our Fifty-Seven.[9] Maybe we'll make something out of it yet, when we've got to Bashkai.'

" 'Let's get to Bashkai, then,' says Dan, 'and, by God, when I come back here again I'll sweep the valley so there isn't a bug in a blanket left!'

"We walked all that day, and all that night Dan was stumping up and down on the snow, chewing his beard and muttering to himself.

" 'There's no hope o' getting clear,' said Billy Fish. 'The priests will have sent runners to the villages to say that you are only men. Why didn't you stick on as Gods till things was more settled? I'm a dead man,' says Billy Fish, and he throws himself down on the snow and begins to pray to his Gods.

"Next morning we was in a cruel bad country—all up and down, no level ground at all, and no food either. The six Bashkai men looked at Billy Fish

9. The Indian Mutiny of 1857–58, in which a revolt of Indian soldiers serving the British led to a widespread uprising against British rule.

hungrywise as if they wanted to ask something, but they said never a word. At noon we came to the top of a flat mountain all covered with snow, and when we climbed up into it, behold, there was an Army in position waiting in the middle!

" 'The runners have been very quick,' says Billy Fish, with a little bit of a laugh. 'They are waiting for us.'

"Three or four men began to fire from the enemy's side, and a chance shot took Daniel in the calf of the leg. That brought him to his senses. He looks across the snow at the Army, and sees the rifles that we had brought into the country.

" 'We're done for,' says he. 'They are Englishmen, these people—and it's my blasted nonsense that has brought you to this. Get back, Billy Fish, and take your men away; you've done what you could, and now cut for it. Carnehan,' says he, 'shake hands with me and go along with Billy. Maybe they won't kill you. I'll go and meet 'em alone. It's me that did it. Me, the King!'

" 'Go!' says I. 'Go to Hell, Dan. I'm with you here. Billy Fish, you clear out, and we two will meet those folk.'

" 'I'm a Chief,' says Billy Fish, quite quiet. 'I stay with you. My men can go.'

"The Bashkai fellows didn't wait for a second word, but ran off, and Dan and Me and Billy Fish walked across to where the drums were drumming and the horns were horning. It was cold—awful cold. I've got that cold in the back of my head now. There's a lump of it there."

The punkah coolies had gone to sleep. Two kerosene lamps were blazing in the office, and the perspiration poured down my face and splashed on the blotter as I leaned forward. Carnehan was shivering, and I feared that his mind might go. I wiped my face, took a fresh grip of the piteously mangled hands, and said, "What happened after that?"

The momentary shift of my eyes had broken the clear current.

"What was you pleased to say?" whined Carnehan. "They took them without any sound. Not a little whisper all along the snow, not though the King knocked down the first man that set hand on him—not though old Peachey fired his last cartridge into the brown of 'em. Not a single solitary sound did those swines make. They just closed up tight, and I tell you their furs stunk. There was a man called Billy Fish, a good friend of us all, and they cut his throat, Sir, then and there, like a jig; and the King kicks up the bloody snow and says, 'We've had a dashed fine run for our money. What's coming next?' But Peachey, Peachey Taliaferro, I tell you, Sir, in confidence as betwixt two friends, he lost his head, Sir. No, he didn't neither. The King lost his head, so he did, all along o' one of those cunning rope bridges. Kindly let me have the paper cutter, Sir. It tilted this way. They marched him a mile across that snow to a rope bridge over a ravine with a river at the bottom. You may have seen such. They prodded him behind like an ox. 'Damn your eyes!' says the King. 'D'you suppose I can't die like a gentleman?' He turns to Peachey—Peachey that was crying like a child. 'I've brought you to this, Peachey,' says he. 'Brought you out of your happy life to be killed in Kafiristan, where you was late Commander-in-Chief of the Emperor's forces. Say you forgive me, Peachey.'

'I do,' says Peachey. 'Fully and freely do I forgive you, Dan.' 'Shake hands, Peachey,' says he. 'I'm going now.' Out he goes, looking neither right nor left, and when he was plumb in the middle of those dizzy dancing ropes, 'Cut, you beggars,' he shouts; and they cut, and old Dan fell, turning round and round and round twenty thousand miles, for he took half an hour to fall till he struck the water, and I could see his body caught on a rock with the gold crown close beside.

"But do you know what they did to Peachey between two pine trees? They crucified him, Sir, as Peachey's hand will show. They used wooden pegs for his hands and his feet; and he didn't die. He hung there and screamed, and they took him down next day, and said it was a miracle that he wasn't dead. They took him down—poor old Peachey that hadn't done them any harm—that hadn't done them any . . ."

He rocked to and fro and wept bitterly, wiping his eyes with the back of his scarred hands and moaning like a child for some ten minutes.

"They was cruel enough to feed him up in the temple, because they said he was more of a God than old Daniel that was a man. Then they turned him out on the snow, and told him to go home, and Peachey came home in about a year, begging along the roads quite safe; for Daniel Dravot he walked before and said, 'Come along, Peachey. It's a big thing we're doing.' The mountains they danced at night, and the mountains they tried to fall on Peachey's head, but Dan he held up his hand, and Peachey came along bent double. He never let go of Dan's hand, and he never let go of Dan's head. They gave it to him as a present in the temple, to remind him not to come again, and though the crown was pure gold, and Peachey was starving, never would Peachey sell the same. You knew Dravot, Sir! You knew Right Worshipful Brother Dravot! Look at him now!"

He fumbled in the mass of rags round his bent waist; brought out a black horsehair bag embroidered with silver thread; and shook therefrom on to my table—the dried, withered head of Daniel Dravot! The morning sun that had long been paling the lamps struck the red beard and blind sunken eyes; struck, too, a heavy circlet of gold studded with raw turquoises, that Carnehan placed tenderly on the battered temples.

"You behold now," said Carnehan, "the Emperor in his habit as he lived—the King of Kafiristan with his crown upon his head. Poor old Daniel that was a monarch once!"

I shuddered, for, in spite of defacements manifold, I recognized the head of the man of Marwar Junction. Carnehan rose to go. I attempted to stop him. He was not fit to walk abroad. "Let me take away the whisky, and give me a little money," he gasped. "I was a King once. I'll go to the Deputy Commissioner and ask to set in the Poorhouse till I get my health. No, thank you, I can't wait till you get a carriage for me. I've urgent private affairs—in the South—at Marwar."

He shambled out of the office and departed in the direction of the Deputy Commissioner's house. That day at noon I had occasion to go down the blinding hot Mall, and I saw a crooked man crawling along the white dust of the roadside, his hat in his hand, quavering dolorously after the fashion of street-singers at

Home. There was not a soul in sight, and he was out of all possible earshot of the houses. And he sang through his nose, turning his head from right to left:

> The Son of Man goes forth to war,
> A golden crown to gain;
> His blood-red banner streams afar—
> Who follows in his train?

I waited to hear no more, but put the poor wretch into my carriage and drove him off to the nearest missionary for eventual transfer to the Asylum. He repeated the hymn twice while he was with me, whom he did not in the least recognize, and I left him singing it to the missionary.

Two days later I inquired after his welfare of the Superintendent of the Asylum.

"He was admitted suffering from sunstroke. He died early yesterday morning," said the Superintendent. "Is it true that he was half an hour bareheaded in the sun at midday?"

"Yes," said I, "but do you happen to know if he had anything upon him by any chance when he died?"

"Not to my knowledge," said the Superintendent.

And there the matter rests.

# William Kotzwinkle

*Kotzwinkle (1938– ) was born in Pennsylvania and received his education at Rider College and Pennsylvania State University. His first book publications were juvenile fiction, but since 1971 he has brought out novels as well as short stories that have attracted attention for their varied stylistic resources and imaginative reconstructions of the familiar world. Now supporting himself as a writer, he lives in New Brunswick, Canada. Many of his short stories were collected in* Elephant Bangs Train *(1971) and* Jewel of the Moon *(1986). His novels include* The Fan Man *(1974),* Hermes Three Thousand *(1975),* Doctor Rat *(1976), and* The Bear Went over the Mountain *(1996).*

## Jewel of the Moon

She and Mother watched through the curtains as the handsome stranger and Father discussed her marriage. The stranger offered money, which Father said was too little. Then they smoked and Father grew poetic, calling her Jewel of the Moon, and she was afraid the bargaining would never finish. She desperately hoped it would, for the stranger was fine-looking and the frog-faced rug-seller of the village was also seeking her hand. Take me away, whispered her heart, and perhaps the stranger felt its delicate beat, for he suddenly doubled his offer of gold and Father agreed.

On the day of their marriage a celebration was held in the village. The drums spoke their hollow song, she danced, the sun was bright. Then as afternoon grew late, he took her away, onto the country road, toward his own village.

Confused, frightened, delighted, mad with anxiety, a virgin, she did not know what to say to him, though her thighs spoke silken words through her gown as she walked along the dirt road, aflame.

The setting sun cast her husband's face in deep red. His eyes burned through her and she grew too red, her stomach flip-flopping, young and silly, but her breasts were moving sweetly as she walked, her hips were full and swayed and how pretty were her bare painted toes. Her ears dangled with earrings and through their jingling she heard the sound of a distant flute.

"That is the musician of my village, welcoming you," said her husband.

She fell into sadness. To strange music, into a strange town, with childhood gone, Jewel of the Moon is letting herself be led. But circling, dancing in the air, the song enticed her, set her dreaming. Soon she would let her black hair down.

Ahead she saw the trees and rooftops of his village, and doubt ruined her again. Afraid to look at him now, she pulled her veil over her head, to hide, to die. How cruel of Father to abandon her, to trade Jewel of the Moon for two bags of gold to this stranger.

"Here we are," he said, turning onto a narrow dirt path.

At the end of the path she saw a small house. Slowly she walked toward it, numb with fear. Still she kept dignity, which Mother had taught her to maintain always, whatever the situation. She did not slouch, tremble, or faint crossing the strange threshold to the cool gloom of the living room. Out of the corner of her eye, through a small doorway, she saw the rattan foot of a bed.

Her husband pointed toward that room and she walked to the doorway, heart thundering.

A purple lamp hung there, and her skin turned to pale moon shades as she walked through the opening. My husband is an exotic, she thought, inspecting the ornate shade of the lamp, on which a thousand-armed God[1] was embracing his naked purple-skinned wife. Will I be sophisticated or will I scream? In the purple den of love, she turned to face him.

He unwrapped the white marriage turban from his head and dark hair fell to his shoulders. Tenderness? Or will he ravish me with bloody sword? Her body played possibilities as he lit incense on the tiny altar by the bed

She looked down at her toes, wanting to conceal the rest of herself from him, wanting also to reveal what he hadn't seen, wanting this and wanting that, frozen flame in a purple place. The window was near and she could escape, but she longed to surprise him with the fullness of her thighs.

"Sit down," he said. She sat on the edge of the bed, dropping her hips into the soft embrace of the mattress. I am ready.

He knelt before her, looked into her eyes. This is the moment.

"I'll sleep down here," he said, stretching himself out on the floor at her feet.

I must awake, she thought, trying to escape the silly dream.

"Perhaps you would like a glass of milk with a piece of toast?" he asked, raising himself on one elbow.

She looked dumbly at the far wall of the bedroom, as her husband hustled off to the kitchen. Nervously, she opened the ribbon on her hair and let her long black head-cloak fall, scented and shimmering. I am Jewel of the Moon. Why does he talk of milk and toast?

"Here I am," he said, coming toward her on his knees, holding the milk and toast.

She took the plate. He turned back down at her feet. "Just kick me if you want anything else."

I have married a madman. Jewel of the Moon peered over the edge of the bed.

Her husband's eyes quickly opened. "Anything else, Perfect One?"

Unable to speak, she shook her head, and though she was not hungry she ate the toast. Then she stretched out on the wedding bed and stared at the

1. The Hindu deity Lord Shiva, whose many arms represent his ability to embrace every aspect of the world

ceiling. I must escape. She waited until she was sure he was asleep, but as soon as her foot touched the floor, he was up, like a watchdog, watching her.

Frightened, she lay back down. She would look for another chance, but sleep overtook her, and she spent the night dreaming of a powerful horse who galloped her to freedom.

"Here is your breakfast, Daughter of the Sun," said her ridiculous husband in the morning, coming toward her on his knees with a silver tray of food.

She ate and he sat at her feet, watching the window, heedless of her morning beauty, as if his fearful bargaining for her had never been. She was truly miserable, for it was real, had been no dream, she'd married an imbecile. That is what he looks like, sitting there. He looks like an incredible idiot and I hate him.

"Here," she said, contemptuously, "I'm done."

"At once." Taking away her cup and plate, he scurried off to the kitchen. She watched him return, to the doorway only, where he lay down, and she covered her tearful eyes. Peeking through her fingers she saw him lying there, doglike, eyes on her, bright, stupid. She wanted to wave her tail at him, give him something to growl about.

"I'm going for a walk," she said, defiantly stepping over the crumpled man on the floor. Perhaps he will bite me, seek to hold me somehow.

"I'll just walk a few paces behind you," he said. "If you want anything, just spit on me."

They walked through the streets of his strange village. She knew no one there, except the shadowy dog at her heels. He lapped along behind her to the well. Women were fetching water and they gave her inquiring looks, as her husband curled up at her feet in the sand. They know I've been tricked by a weak-kneed fiend. Looking down she wanted to spit on him, but the women would love that too much.

She left the well and walked on through the village, curling her toes in the hot sand as the men of this new village eyed her bare feet and a bit more, perhaps, for her hips were expressing themselves, too enthusiastically for a married woman, but her so-called husband was licking along at the ground. I'll give him one more chance this afternoon.

She sat upon the bed, brushing her long hair over her heart. Her ankles were smooth and bare and she wriggled her toes as he entered the room, bathed in the gold of afternoon. But there came no spicy kiss upon her toes, only curried peas, served on a tray which he placed on her thighs.

Night. Beneath purple light he gave her milk and toast and curled down again on the floor. The milk and toast made her brain sleepy, but her pale thighs wanted something indescribably nice, and it wasn't milk toast.

She tossed on her pillow, recalling the passages from the Holy Sutra on Love.[2] I studied the book faithfully, yet here I am, perspiring on an empty bed.

2. The Sanskrit treatise containing rules for sensual pleasure in accordance with Hindu law.

She rose up and with her bare foot gave her husband a kick.

He rolled over, looking up from the floor like a whipped mongrel.

"Stop snoring," she said, angrily.

"I will stop breathing," he said, and wrapped a strip of linen around his nose.

The moon crossed her pillow. Slowly her passion subsided, like a body fallen away, and she moved in dreams, a queen with many servants, all of them her idiot husband.

As the wedding month went by, she grew tense. Her husband was silent, devoted, treated her like a queen, and she loathed him and his entire line of ancestors. She thrust her foot out, so that he might remove her sandals, which he did, handling her foot as carefully as a dish of precious rice, except that he did not taste or swallow the delight and it soon grew cold.

She raised her feet on the barren marriage bed, drawing her knees up to her breasts. I am so young. There are other men. They would not treat me like this. They would torture me with glances, drive me mad with their eyes. I will die soon of dullness. Neglect can end woman's life, so says the Holy Sutra.

She felt the end of the mattress suddenly sink down with unusual force. "What are you doing?" she cried, for the impudent servant was sitting on the foot of the bed.

"If you want anything," he said, curling up at her feet, "just kick me in the face."

She pulled herself into a fetal ball, wishing she could be reborn in some hidden world. The night bird blew his flute, she lay in purple moon-robe, and dreams of mating came to her. A shining man held her, ghostly thin he was, and she stretched herself out beneath him, at the same time touching with her toe accidentally the face of the vile sleeper at her feet.

"Yes, Tower of Grace," said her husband sitting up quickly, "have you bad dreams? I will make a cup of tea which relaxes the mind."

He left and returned with a silver tray, surrounded by steam. He poured the tea and she let the sheet fall away from her, moonlight coming on her breasts, bare behind her thin midnight gown.

"This will help," he said, handing her a cup of the tea, not even glancing at the pale cups she had so immodestly revealed. She drew the sheet around herself again, hating him, and drank the tea, a gentle herb, which soon brought the charm of sleep.

Each night, following milk and toast, he slipped onto the foot of the bed, like a dog trained to warm the feet of his mistress. Silently, while he slept, she felt over his face lightly with her toe. The second month of their marriage passed this way, with her body inflamed by his nearness. Though his canine countenance expressed no more than a stupid smile, his simple animal nature inspired her, and in dreams she attacked him. *It has grown hot in this lagoon. I shall swim with him. She slipped into the warm water, where his silver face shined. Into his heat she swam.*

She woke, feverish. Her husband's hot breath was on her feet. Unable to resist, she tiptoed on the warm waves from his tongue, dancing there.

In the third month, the dog became a tortoise, crawling slowly up the mattress toward her. Each night she felt his shell coming closer. When she looked in the dark purple toward him, he seemed wrinkled as an ancient. His faithful dog-eye was gone and in its place was a wiser, if somewhat frightening beak, and two gleaming eyes, accustomed to the night sea.

She wanted to hide inside the pillow, to shrink into nothingness, to keep herself apart from his breathing on her knees, and from his devious turtle-eyes coldly haunting her.

Daytime brought her release from the illusion. She went to the temple and begged Kali[3] to advise her. The beautiful altar goddess danced on the head of a slave. If only I could be fierce as you, Goddess. The statue was mute. The distraught girl rose and left the temple. Her husband was kneeling in the sand of the temple garden, the sun upon his dark curling hair. If he weren't so shifty, he might almost be good-looking, she thought, walking slowly toward him.

That night he came slowly toward her, to her thighs with his head. What fiendish ticklement is this, she wondered in a moment of clarity, before the warm cream of his breath poured over her thighs. She pressed them together to stop the sensation and it grew more intense. She spread them apart trying to cool them and her soft leg-flesh touched his nose.

"Yes, Queen," he said in a whisper.

"Please," she said, softly.

"What would you have me do?" asked the turtle.

Could she tell him her thighs were milk? She raised her hips just a little.

"Is there a lump in the mattress, Gracious Saint?"

"Oh, the dog!" she cried and turned quickly away, but her gown rose up so that perhaps he could see the soft underness of her thighs. What an immodesty, she thought, quickly pulling down her gown.

The fourth month of marriage brought the face of her husband directly in line with her secret. His breath upon her toes had been inflaming; his breathing on her rose was driving her insane. Streams of air reached between her thighs, gently handling her flower. She tried always to sleep on her stomach, so she would not be subjected to warm southern winds, but in dreams she soon rolled over again, into the tropic breeze from his nose, which played over the hot little island between her thighs.

Later, when they walked outside, she went head down, deep in confusion. Caught in the rain, she made no attempt to take cover. The cloudburst ran along her hot flesh and her husband stood with her in the rain, and the village women no doubt thought them mad.

At five months, his face lay by her stomach. His breath blew her gown lightly; she touched him with her belly, upon his hooked nose.

His eagle-eye saw through her gown, to the soul in her rolling ocean of jelly, to the eye in her navel. Into that canyon of time went his nose, filling it

3. A fierce female goddess, commonly depicted wearing a necklace of skulls, dancing on a dead man.

with warmth. She lay perspiring like a holy woman on a bed of coals, though she did not feel holy, in fact, quite the opposite.

When six months ended, the wandering slave in her bed had lodged at her breasts. His eyes gleamed in the dark like an idol's. The purple light played on his face. She tried to cover her breasts, to hide them from his dark look, but they are so tender, they hurt me, let him look if he dares to. His breath touched her lightly on her soft little island tops, her red-peaked nipples. Excited as if she were dancing in the village, her breasts heaved and touched him. In the crevice of dreams where her heart lay concealed, she enclosed his nose.

It tickled ridiculously. That was its strange power. She was ten-thousand-times-over afraid of it, yet somehow withstood the invasion. Encircle his nose again, my breasts, smother him with your sweetness, drive him mad too.

He remained calm. Yet in the seventh month he was stretched out entirely beside her. Kinglike he slept, lightly, staring sometimes at the ceiling for long hours. Around her body was an envelope of heat, as if she were afloat in a warm cloud. His breath seemed to have lingered all over her body, gathering around it like a mist. His elbow touched her. Quickly she drew her arm away. This bed is far too small for two people. She withdrew to the farthest corner. But in curling up she bumped him with her backside and he, amazingly, returned the bump.

This shocking demonstration was repeated on the following night and on many nights afterward. Like wandering taxis they bumped each other, bumper to bumper they lay pressed together in the street of feathers. It is mad play, but what pleasure. Later she rose up and looked at the impertinent fellow, naked to the waist in the moonlight.

"Yes, Lotus?" He woke and rose to her.

"I'm so thirsty," she said.

"At once," he said, and leapt out of the bed.

He returned with a cool drink of water. She drank it slowly and extended the glass back to him. As he retrieved it, his hand brushed light as a wing-tip across her breast. He put the glass down and crawled into bed beside her. Reaching for the thin sheet, the devil's finger touched her again. Her red breasts heaved to meet his hands, wanting that and wanting more.

On the following night, as he served her milk, she leaned in a most favorable angle and his palm touched underneath her breasts, in the softness, and lingered there.

Next night, she was seated on a cushion by the window. He came from the kitchen on his knees, bearing a tray on which a glass of red wine was balanced. He bowed. His black curling hair was like snakes in a dance. His hand came forward. All night he held the threads of her shoulder straps in his fingertips, and toward dawn he let them drop and half awake, half dreaming, she watched her left moon appear, naked, round, full.

Earlier, in the fashion of the slave girls, she had made herself up, reddening the nipple, tanning the round globe, even underneath, where the sun never came. Now, she dared not move, the silence was all around them. He stared at her breast like a devotee at a statue and she accepted his stare.

For days he stared at it, through the passing light of morning, afternoon, and evening. He pondered it from every angle, looking all around it and underneath it, like a monkey with a problem. She did not know what to do. Her thoughts were jumbled, her head was spinning, for they spent so much time in bed these days. Slowly his hand came forward. Was it an age or an instant that passed, she'd lost touch with time. Suddenly he was touching her on the left breast and fondling it.

So she spent the ninth month, one breast out. Each time she tried to tie her gown up, he untied it again. She felt so odd sitting eating dinner with one breast bare. Shortly after dinner he began stroking the other one, and each night it was the same, until the tenth month came and he slipped the knot on her right shoulder, rendering both breasts bare.

She sat, naked to the waist. All night he sat looking at her, and she at him. She nodded off to sleep finally, and her dreams were filled with insanity. She'd lost sight of father, mother, dignity, the world, except for two moons in the air. She felt a cloudy field all around her and she ran through a ghostly mist, awaking to his lips upon the tiny crater of her right moon.

Then he revolved both moons in his hands, until she was thrashing back and forth on the bed, most indecorously. She begged him to stop revolving them but he laughed and went on revolving them.

That morning she rose early and since she was in the kitchen before him, she prepared her own breakfast, and as an afterthought, prepared his too, and served it to him.

She knelt by the bed and slipped the tray over the covers. He opened his eyes and she lowered her own. He ate quietly and the sunlight came, turning the bed to a gold palanquin on which he seemed to float, looking down on her. She had covered her bosom to serve him. With a gesture of perfect sovereignty, he slipped the knots of her gown and bared her breasts again. He digested his breakfast, fondling them.

About noontime, after five hours of feeling her breasts, he began sucking them, first one, then the other, alternating on the hour. At dinnertime she could not help but scream, so tender had they grown from his feasting. This incredibly idiotic child is draining my soul, sucking it into himself, but she welcomed him nonetheless and in fact offered up to him with her hands the twin fruits.

By night he continued lowering her gown. Inch by inch he pulled it, a little each evening, until her stomach heaved up into the moonlight. Like a vast continent it came into view, but she did not feel continent, in fact, just the opposite, ravished as she was by feverish grindings in her stomach. He squeezed her moons and licked across the land of her belly, his moustache trailing in her navel.

Finally the gown was down to the edge of her secret. In a dream she was taken down the night to an ancient forest altar, a cave in which a priestess dwelled. It was a shimmering red crack in the mountain and she entered. The shining man was sitting on a throne, deep inside the cave.

She woke, moved her legs, felt suddenly free; her gown was gone. He was looking at her dark scented place, which sparkled as if with dewdrops. She felt older, parting her legs, then demurely closed them, feeling childish. He stared at it all night, and continued to stare at it throughout the morning, as the sun rose upon her little tangled grove. He ate lunch looking at it and spent the evening with his nose practically next to it. She felt herself burning alive.

She had to leave the bed. She ran naked through the house. He caught her in the kitchen, in a most peculiar position, putting his hand directly into her forest. She sank to her knees and bowed her head, worshipping him as he ran his finger all along the crack in the forest floor.

For the entire eleventh month he investigated that mysterious forest. He parted the underbrush so that the altar was plainly visible, and then like a blind man feeling letters, he ran his fingers along the sacred tabernacle, reading every wrinkle and fold. The altar streamed with the precious nectar. His finger slipped just the slightest bit inside it and remained there, all day, every day, for a month. She screamed, beating him about the head with her hands.

Silently, day by day, he worked like a hermit drawing with his finger on a cave wall. Then, by night, he brought his head to the cave and spoke a wordless whisper. She pressed her forest lips to his in silent answer and they kissed softly. All night, hour after hour, he kissed her there, while she squirmed, kicking her legs, beating her hands upon the mattress. For a month she writhed, groaning, in and out of delightful anguish.

From the devil he had learned to take in his lips the tiny turned-out root that hung from the mouth of her sacred cave. Known to no one, guarded and carefully hidden by her through all her years, it was now in the man's lips and he was humming on it. The tune was crazy, mad bees swarmed through her, but each time, just as she felt herself about to turn into sweetest honey, he stopped, leaving her hovering, dying, frantic.

They did not go out any longer. When he tried to lift his head away to bring food, she held him by the ears. The food grew cold and she grew hotter, running her fingers through his curly hair.

By day she followed him around the house, served him on her knees, washed his body, made his bed. He had enslaved her with his tongue. Her will was gone, sucked out in the night. Standing by the kitchen doorway, she moved aside to let him pass. His sleeping gown was loose and some devil played it open and she saw the outline of his manhood. He brushed past her and the hot organ touched her thigh.

Later in the day, as she bent over to pick up his slippers, he pressed it against her backside. Day after day then, she encountered it, and in her dreams she saw it standing on the throne inside the altar, shining, one-eyed, on fire.

Unable to resist any longer, she touched it, thinking he was asleep. He was not. He opened his eyes, fully awake.

"Please," she said. It was the twelfth month and she stretched out on the bed and spread her legs like a courtesan. Her forest stream was flowing, she was made of liquid, her body was undone, the veils of her passion unknotted.

"Please," she said, taking his member in her hand. He rose and knelt between her legs. Then he braced himself over her and slowly, like a man falling in a dream, lowered himself.

The night fell upon her. His thighs rested on hers and against her altar she felt the hot hard pressing, not of a fist or a finger, but of a finer thing, a more distinguished tool, of shape divine, like the shining thing in her dreams, and she longed to take it into herself. She pressed her forest crack against the fleshy head, feeling its wet eyedrop. She nibbled with her clumsy forest lips, dumbly trying to swallow the burning Godhead.

Each night for a week it played at her melting doorway, and just when she thought she could stand its presence, it entered the buttery folds and she gasped with amazement for she could not stand it, so painful and terrible was it, at last. She gave her hips just the slightest move, to appreciate her agony better.

"Don't move," he said in a dark voice beside her ear, and she didn't.

They lay that way each night for a week, like trees fallen together in a storm. Her legs entangled his, locking at the ankles, and her tiny cave-root was engaged.

Pressing deeper each night, he soon reached the tiny red curtain across her virgin altar. He pressed harder, but the way was small, the pressure unbearable. The space is too tight, she thought, weeping. I can never fit this thing into me, it is unendurable, it . . . seems to be going in a little farther.

No longer a virgin, she howled, for the jewel of the moon was red with blood. The veil is burning, the veil is gone. God's body slipped slowly into her.

Wheels of flame revolved in her brain and in the forest cave the Godhead reigned, solemn, still, supreme, and she felt the beat of his burning heart-shape.

All night they lay that way, he did not allow her to move, but surreptitiously she managed to, flexing the tiny muscles of her secret mouth. Each time she did lights appeared to her and her warm tears flowed. The dreams of mating danced round her, encircling her, and she was their center and her hair was entwined with his. There was a beat, it is slow, this coming of beauty, and their locked bodies brought it nearer, so that by dawn it had almost arrived.

The need for nourishment finally overtook them and that afternoon he withdrew the Godhead from her and her cave closed shut. This is reality, she thought, stumbling naked toward the kitchen. She fried them lunch, a festival of grains, and naked they ate, lightly.

At sundown she lay down again and parted her legs. We are on the mountain of pleasure. It goes into me again. I am reassured of its constancy. I am . . . quite full, dearest, come closer.

When it was fully lodged in her, she spread her legs into a wide V, and raising them into the air, kicked them about, laughing madly, with elephants dancing, serpents too, and she walked in her brain, room by room, through waking dreams, down the road of joy, tossing, turning, coming closer, to the mysterious presence. Panting, sweating, she held his buttocks, tried to make him move, to take them closer.

Not until the thirteenth month did he move, but that movement was definitive, marking a farther outpost of bliss. To feel his tool run in and out of me, that is the deep truth. Could there be more? She suspected another door.

Each night he stroked her once, so slowly, the entire night was needed for the length of his thousand-armed shaft to move in and out. At times she thought it was not moving at all, but it was, and in the extremities of slowness she saw concealed worlds.

Time changed; in a single second she saw great lengths of his organ. Breathless, afire, stupefied, she too learned to move slowly. Here the moment opens. In it are contained like tiny seeds a million more divisions. And she grew smaller.

It was the end of the thirteenth month. She loved him but wanted to reach their plateau, the resting spot. I am so hot. He is boiling me. Still they went more slowly. She fell through enormous canyons of time, down the deep pocket of pleasure, swooning ever more slowly into the depths of delight. She heard dragons roaring, such a slow grinding noise, such a slow turning.

They ate only liquids, some ethereal force seeming to sustain them now, for they lost no weight, but grew light as lamps. His countenance became magical. In his face she saw blue God-masks, jewels, crowns. The sound, the sound of their divine grinding surrounded them. No longer human, they lived outside of time.

The beautiful presence came, as he touched her in the womb, and like spring burst forth. I am creation. From her came the universe, that was the roar. From her came worlds, she was their door. Spread across the galaxies, she moved her body slowly, coming everywhere, at once, very wise.

In the beat of moons, not seconds, he stroked her, so say the Scriptures.

# Patricia Landers

*Landers (1929– ) was born in Evanston, Illinois. She graduated from Portland State University in Oregon. Currently she teaches creative writing at Portland Community College. Along with her fiction, she has published poems in various little magazines. She has received a Burnham Award for Fiction.*

## My Life as a Mollusk

For a long time now I've been telling myself, he's probably dead. Black men don't live all that long in Chicago. But Maddox stays with me, alive in the layers of my past as if time doesn't exist. He came into my life like a tide, walking toward me as if he poured himself forward. In 1947. Then I heard him speak with the inflection that made everything seem a question even when it wasn't, and I recognized him as mine.

I was eighteen and living with a roommate in her South Side apartment, going to the university and acquiring words like *empirical, syllogism, a priori*. Maddox was a thirty-year-old Army veteran working at the Post Office, dreaming of going, but not going to college and reading things like Ovid and Sappho's[1] poems and ancient history. Hemingway. The pack I was roaming with—two grad students, a professor's wife who was the girlfriend of one of them, and two musicians (bebop, blues)—was at Hattie's Cafe, a ribs joint, when Maddox came in. He knew one of the musicians, but he pulled up his chair beside me. The next day I missed him and weeks later I moved in with him—it happened so naturally—into his West Side apartment a block from the El, in a part of the city I'd always thought barren, a kind of dingy no-account part of town between the prim suburb where I'd grown up and the macho extravagance of the Loop.

We were sitting at the kitchen table sharing the Sunday *Tribune* when I read that Judith Anderson was coming to town in *Medea*.[2] I rose and laid the ad in front of Maddox. I wanted to see the play. Maddox was apprehensive about going downtown. We'd never gone there together. "It's not a good idea,"

1. Greek poet of Lesbos (ca. 620–ca. 565 B.C.E.), known for her love lyrics. Ovid (43 B.C.E.–C.E. 17?), Roman poet. 2. A play by Euripides, produced in 431 B.C.E., about Medea, sorceress wife of Jason. In a jealous rage, she kills their children. Dame Judith Anderson, (1898–1992), Australian actress chiefly popular in the United States.

he said. "Why should we see this play? Will I like it? Will you?"

I put my forehead against his and stared into his eyes—they swam out of focus. "Oh, yes, I think so."

"How do you *know?*" he said, peering back at me from glittering brown pools.

He knew who Judith Anderson was—she had appeared in a lot of movies. I sat back down. "She's stern, powerful, don't you think?" I said, trying not to be too kittenish. "Medea is one tough woman. Not like me."

One black eyebrow rose.

"Well, but she's like me in the way she loves Jason," I said. "You'll see."

It would be good for him to see how powerful a woman could be, I thought. When I had read the play for my humanities class, I couldn't imagine anyone so vengeful toward her husband that she could destroy her own children. But I saw that she and I had something in common when she said to Jason, *Father and home of my free will, I left and came with thee . . . for my love was stronger than my prudence.* Learning there were seats available we could afford, I had ordered tickets. We would arrive at the theater forty minutes early, as I had done often, pick up the tickets, then wander outside.

We walked to the El. I had dressed up my black dress with a rhinestone pin. Maddox wore a shirt I had pressed that day, slacks and sport coat fresh from the cleaner and a crisp fedora fit for the occasion. I took his arm. His neat appearance, mustache trimmed to a precise slash and shoes buffed to winking, mollified my uneasiness at riding the El with a man whose skin wasn't pink like mine. He held himself erect, walking with his gaze fixed upon the street before him.

When Maddox held open the theater door, I stepped into the yellow light of the lobby where cigarette smoke ribboned above a chattering few who had gathered early. A man with a pinched face sat in the box office. He looked at me, then at Maddox. "There are no tickets under the name of *Temple*."

"Look again," I told him, thinking he'd made a mistake.

He tilted up his chin and staring at Maddox said, "There are *no* tickets under *Temple* and *no* tickets left for sale."

We rode home, Maddox sitting on the cane seat beside me, tight lipped and silent, hands in his trench coat pockets. I seethed. "He was so rude!" I said. I didn't understand then that Maddox folded up his rage like dollar bills and pocketed and saved it.

"Mm-hmn," he said and bent his head down, the pulse at his forehead throbbing, then he turned up his eyes and scanned the overhead ads for Bryl-Cream and Ovaltine.

"How could he make a mistake like that?" I went on. "It was unforgivable."

"Mistake? Shoot." He faced me. "If the Man don't let us, then we don't get in the door. Baby, if you gonna stay with me, you'll have to get used to that, because that's the way it's gonna be."

When we got back to the West Side, he bought a pint of gin to take to the gray stone building and his flat on the second floor. He put records on his phonograph—Dizzy, Lady, Bird. We drank at the yellow enameled kitchen table, speaking of things that weren't really on our minds—his job at the Post

Office, a temporary one, and how it would end soon—avoiding the scene at the theater.

Finally Maddox said, "You think the Man's gonna treat me like he does you just because we're together? Shit. I told you, when you got me at your elbow, you're gonna be treated same as me."

"I didn't know," I said, "I thought you'd like to see the play."

"I would." Puzzling changes flickered over his face.

"Maybe we could read the play togeth . . ."

"That's not the point. You should have listened when I told you, Hope."

What had he told me? Had he told me?

"You're crazy to stay with me."

"But I need you," I said. "Don't you need me?"

His gloom deepened. He stood and the hanging naked light bulb clapped a violet shadow around his neck. "You *like* to keep me on edge, don't you, Hope? You're asking for something, begging for it, aren't you? Does it excite you when people stare at us? Do you *want* pain. . . . Are you getting excited now, Hope?"

I smiled and tried to play his game. "What do you mean?"

His eyes flashed and then grew inky. I saw his fist coming just before lightning cracked behind my eyes, blinding me. He hit again. I screamed and fell to the floor, crying. Then he kicked over a chair and banged the door as he flung it open and lurched out of the apartment.

I waited for more than an hour in bed, eyes wide open and head aching, until he returned and undressed. He didn't speak. I pretended to be asleep.

When morning came, my nose thumped and felt large as my knee. He looked at it and said softly, "Oh, baby, how could I have done that to you?" And he held me against his chest, kissed my bruises, and stroked me tenderly with his big hands.

We lay in bed, entangled. His black hair, tight waves, stiffly pomaded. My pale hair, awry. I loved his body and his butter smooth skin. And I loved my body, because he did. I loved him more that morning than I had before. I didn't worry about him hitting me again—I couldn't believe he would.

When I was small, I found baby dresses in my mother's cedar chest on our sun porch, some mine and one my sister wore for her only birthday. And a picture book of famous paintings with a reproduction of a painting I liked of Venus in a giant shell, rising from ocean waves, rosy lips and locks like scrolls blown on the wind. There was a fat album filled with photographs mounted on black pages soft as lawn handkerchiefs. One of me as a baby, seated on a blanket like a little Buddha with dimpled knees, wearing only a tiny hair ribbon and a studious expression. Other photos showed my grandparents, Sophie and Jacob, perched astride the tandem bike they rode on their honeymoon and on a different page, my mother, when she was small, holding her pretty porcelain doll. On other pages she was a flapper with bobbed hair, skirt above her knees, sitting cross-legged on a wooden porch-swing beside my father, cocky in his rakish knickers and white sweater. Those were the important events in our family history, the births and marriages.

That's what you did when you grew up—you got married. Until you got married, you dreamed about it when you cut out Brenda Starr[3] paper dolls or read Nancy Drew mysteries or went to the movies. During Saturday matinees you dreamed about it when you watched Jean Arthur find true love with Mister Right or Carole Lombard walk out on but return to Mister Wrong—either way, they couldn't live without him, and they married him. I would put one of Papa's love songs on the Victrola and Nelson Eddy would sing: *Ah sweet mystery of life, at last I've found you!* To my mind, married people lived in a shimmering love dream fragrant with lilacs in spring and baking bread in winter. All my female life was commended to Marriage and living happily ever after.

We sat in the Club Delisa,[4] scents of Tigress Cologne and Fleur de Nuit floating all around us, and talked about our coming marriage. Plum-color shadows of dancers undulated high on the wall beside us, brown cheeks shone with triangles of refracted light, and Maddox sat close to me, appearing burnished in his tan sport coat and emerald green shirt. He put his arm behind me along the back of the seat, the curve of his arm like a wing I leaned into. *Mrs. Hope Temple.* I savored the sound. I was stunned with love for Maddox.

We toasted each other with gin poured from the half-pint he had brought in his overcoat pocket. Bobby T. Williams sang "Everything I Have Is Yours" in his chocolate-malt baritone. "Your hair is shinier than a shower of Christmas tinsel," Maddox said, stroking it.

When we left the club, we stepped from the moan of the blues into sudden silence. We burrowed into the pocket of a rattling taxi. As it lumbered through the dark, putty-colored beams from the streetlights crossed our faces. The broad-nosed driver turned his head in profile to us and spoke now and then; Maddox would nod and answer, "Yeah, that's right, man," and hug and draw me to him, pressing our bodies together.

Two weeks later we were married at the courthouse. There was no fanfare. I had wondered if the sky would break open or mirrors crack and fall, but nothing happened. Nothing.

We drew our world closer around us.

Rain washed the winter slush away. Maddox's job at the Post Office ended. At breakfast, we watched each other from over the rims of our coffee cups, the black kitten he'd brought home for me weaving between our ankles. More than anything, I wanted to go downtown to walk in the jostling crowds. But I didn't tell him. I sensed the terrible weight of the rage he carried. He leaned back in his chair, pulled a cigarette from the pack in his shirt pocket, and tilted his head sideways.

"If we had the money to go to Brazil to live," he said, "we could be free. Like in Germany. When I was there, Hope, the people treated me the same as they did the white GIs."

"Intoxicating stuff, freedom," I said, suddenly realizing I had given up mine. But I loved him, and it seemed like I never had a choice.

His gaze meandered, the cigarette still perched between two fingers, unlit. He sat brooding and staring at the wall.

White men owned the West Side apartments. Ours was a front room and

3. Comic-strip character of the 1930s and 1940s. 4. An African-American nightclub in Chicago.

a kitchen; but this can be said for it, we never saw a rat. Invasions of roaches were few and easily vanquished from around the sink. The stove stood on bowed iron legs and had a pilot that I lit with a match. We had no refrigerator at first. We stood our quart bottle of milk on the sill outside the kitchen window in the shadowy air shaft, the heart of the building and the coolest place. A neighbor family in the flat behind ours shared the bathroom with us. The tan paint in the musty hall and on the stairs had peeled, leaving green and yellow patches, but Maddox painted our apartment. "The landlord should hire someone to do that," I told him. "Baby, the Man don't wanna spend a *dime* on any of these places."

When we thought I was pregnant, I was panicky, but I didn't say so. Maddox was pleased. I just couldn't imagine myself with a baby. It would be so . . . final, like locking the door to the life I'd left behind and throwing the key in the river.

The janitor, Bill, so dark he was the color of prunes, had a pale wife, Shirley. They lived in a basement apartment. A plain woman with hair a natural wheat shade and what seemed to me a simple mind (maybe because she seemed content with her life, and I couldn't understand that), she had a country drawl and was a checker at the A&P. Ours were the only two white faces in the neighborhood. Bill and Shirley had bought a television set, the first in the building and the first we would see. When they invited us to watch wrestling with them.

I dressed for our visit. After a hot bath, I passed a clot. My mood lightened. I might even be able to enjoy our night out. I didn't mention the clot to Maddox.

We sat on the sofa across from the tiny screen. The only windows in the apartment were higher than my head—squatty ones at sidewalk level. Shirley and Bill said it gave them more wall space. Their two bashful little girls came into the living room in their pajamas and stood with their backs against their mother's knees, first one and then the other, to let her brush their frizzy hair. "We may have one of our own before too long," Maddox said as he watched the girls roll their eyes at him every now and then. Smiling, he glanced at me. "A girl, eh? Wouldn't she be beautiful?"

"Won't that be fine? You must be happy about that," Shirley said watching me. I grinned at her. (Or maybe I grimaced.) Maddox was proud. Maybe to him a child meant stability; we would be a family, extend ourselves into the future, and beat the Man that way.

Shirley chirped about the girls, then asked about my job. Timidly I told her, "I waited on Elizabeth Taylor last week . . . she was in town with Nicky Hilton, you know, shopping for her trousseau."

"Glory! What a thrill that must've been," Shirley said. Repose shone on her face, illuminated by the television when she turned toward it. She seemed so easy with her husband and so confident and happy with the little brown girls.

Later, lying in our bed . . . windows open and the juke box in the tavern downstairs whining, I told Maddox I wasn't pregnant after all and watched disappointment settle over his face like sleep.

"If we had a little girl, we wouldn't be able to keep to ourselves any longer,"

I said. "We'd have to go out, take her to school, you know, the doctor, downtown even."

When we did sleep that night, it was like a small death.

In July, the heat slunk thickly up and down the walls in the unforgiving air. The cool stone of the building and the airy height of the bay windows helped only a little. Maddox had a construction job with a road crew, and he would come home, shirt stuck to his back, and go down the hall with a towel and clean clothes over his arm.

Once after a breakfast of eggs and fried potatoes we went to the A&P—the only time we went there together—to buy cornmeal, bread, greens, things like that, carefully counting before we approached the cash register. One black woman stood right in my way in the aisle, mercilessly staring when I tried to reach the oatmeal. That as well as the scornful glances from other shoppers and darting eyes of the checker were too much for us to want to go back again. We trudged home with the cumbrous sacks to unload them onto a sagging wall shelf next to the nook where I washed dishes in a sink not much larger than a bathroom basin.

He washed the kitchen floor—he had enameled it with a high-gloss pine green and stippled it pale yellow—while I sat studying at the little spinet desk he had bought at Goodwill. When I took my book and moved to the sofa, he came to sit beside me with one he'd found at the library about Egyptian history. He had one of Hemingway's, too, about bullfights. I was reading Katherine Ann Porter. I let myself sink against him, and his arm wrapped around me. He looked up from the page, light perspiration glistening on his forehead. "What shall we do this afternoon?"

I longed to go to the big theater with gold goddesses in wall niches, and the wide, wide staircase with curving banisters. I leaned forward and looked at him. "Go downtown to a movie?"

"No, no, no. We already tried one theater. What makes you think a movie house will be different?"

"What will we do then?"

"Come here."

"What for?"

"Sugar." He undid the buttons of my shirt.

With the windows open, a radio buzzing from some other apartment, and the heat clinging to the walls, we lay on our sides in the opened out sofa bed, pressed together belly to belly. My sweat trickled down my neck. His stood on his face in beads. We moved together, and I was a river in which he swam.

Reed, an old friend, stopped by once. He and I had spent a lot of time together and had done some tentative touching . . . but that was before I married Maddox; none of it meant anything. Mr. Summers knocked one time, too, surprising us. He had been my freshman English Lit professor. When I opened the door there he was, his full lips moving a little in his thin pale face as if he were about to speak, while I yammered something meant as a greeting. I was mortified that he saw the way we had to live. Maddox was stiff with him and condescending to me. I wondered if that was for Mr. Summers's benefit. All I can remember of that visit was how awkward we all were.

On another night, Eddie was sitting on our sofa when Maddox came from work. Eddie and I had been friends since I had first met him at the university. I'd had sex two times with Eddie, but we were never more than friends. I could see that Maddox didn't want him there; didn't want Eddie telling me about the jazz combo he played in; didn't want me to go on talking to him, animated and glad to have someone listening to me. Maddox left and brought back a bottle of gin for the three of us. Eddie stayed for dinner.

As night crept over the building and in through the bay windows, Eddie and I stopped but Maddox continued to drink, growing aloof and rigid as steel. When he and I were alone again I told him, "Eddie doesn't mean a thing to me—he's a friend, that's all." I raised my arms, inviting him to take me in his.

He swept me aside. "Hope, you act like some high-stepper twirling her baton, leading your parade of men through here any time, any day." He strode toward the bay windows, whirled, and came back to stand in front of me. "Expect you can blow your whistle and I'm gonna follow right along to your tune with all the others, do you?" Spittle flew as he talked. "Well, life ain't no parade, baby!" He slapped me with the back of his hand, knocking me away from him. Then he grabbed my shoulders and banged my head on the wall.

The next morning, Maddox sat on the edge of the bed, his head hung down. "You know I don't want to hurt you, baby."

He said his love was uncontrollable. There were happy times for us. And there were times when I left him.

Like one Saturday night when he bought a pint of gin and some lime soda. After I fed the cat, we had a drink at the kitchen table. Over the greens and ham hocks I'd fixed for our dinner, we watched each other. A week earlier I had made a cake for his thirty-second birthday. A month before, I had turned twenty. I felt old.

Maddox leaned back in his chair, pulled a Lucky Strike from his shirt pocket, lit it, and blew a long ruffle of smoke. The air drifting in on my shoulders cooled suddenly. When I rose to close the window I knocked the milk off the sill. I couldn't see where it had landed and could only imagine it souring while basement rats fed on it. I wondered what else might have been lost there. Maddox wasn't listening. He finished his third drink, poured another, and patiently concentrated on the glass before drinking.

His eyes widened, and his face changed eerily. A fugitive fear clamped around me.

"Have you seen any of your old boyfriends, lately, baby?"

"Just once in a while . . . someone from school now and then, you know . . . friends."

"Friends, my ass! Friends like an insurance policy. Isn't that what you mean, Hope?" One ink-black eyebrow rose. He nearly knocked his drink over when he stood. Grabbing a handful of my shirt, he yanked me up to stand in front of him, tearing off one of the buttons. It ticked across the floor. "Don't want to close off your options, do you?"

I didn't see his fist coming. I heard it.

He banged the door shut, leaving me stupefied in a heap on the floor. I sat up, sobbing. Maybe he'd gone to buy another bottle. It gave me time enough to scoop up a few overnight things, get out the door and down the stairs, and hurry to Charlotte's apartment where I'd lived before marrying Maddox. She let me stay.

The next day I went back to him. When he saw the purple thundercloud below my eye, he looked as though he might cry. He cupped my face in his palms. "Baby, baby, what did I do to you?"

"Maybe you have to stop drinking," I told him. "It might be that."

He pulled me with him into bed, and I withheld myself from him until he had caressed all my secret places. But I knew what limits he set for me and didn't refuse him for long.

And when I lay my head on his chest and his lips fumbled at my neck I forgot my aching eye, and when the small of his back yielded to my hand and the fanatical penis, warm as blood, ventured against my thigh, I understood what it was I couldn't live without.

I grew thin. Every night I'd wait at the window for him to come into view, hoping his walk would be steady. And I'd listen, holding my breath, for his step on the hall stairs. One night after he beat me and when he'd fallen a sleep, I caught an El and clattered to the other side of the city to stay with my aunt. But when I heard his voice the next day on the phone, the way he made everything sound like a question, I went back, drunk with love for him. He needed me. And without him, I didn't know what I might do.

In the cool of morning, I rose and put on my robe and made coffee while he slept. With our black cat curled in my lap I sat sipping coffee in the moving air from the windows. The sun rose over the glistening street, and the pavement steamed from a rainstorm. The moving curtain cast shadows on my hand that grew sharp then faded. Just as the shadows of elm leaves did when I was small and sat in the living room of my grandfather's house, enclosed in the rose brocade of the sofa with a crocheted doily rough against my arm. There were no elm leaves here. No lawns. Nor were there fragrant lilacs or baking bread.

Maddox gasped. I turned to him. "I can't breathe," he said. I'd never seen him look like that, the cords in his arms and neck so taut. Terror shone in his eyes. I helped prop him up on pillows. "Get help," he whispered. I moved fast. I ran to the neighbors' phone to call the fire department and hurried back to him. I wasn't thinking, just moving, then waiting, my heart pounding. It seemed like time froze and could not move forward. "Heart attack," he managed to say. He couldn't breathe. I didn't know what to do. Then an emergency vehicle pulled up in front of the building.

Two white men came up the stairs. One set a tank on the floor, glancing at me as he did, and fixed a mask over Maddox's mouth and nose; the other set down a stretcher nearby and stared. The first one laid a hand on Maddox's shoulder and spoke quietly to him, setting a steady rhythm for his breathing. He took his blood pressure. I could feel the other man's icy stare. I waited while the men, in coats hanging like stiff robes, tended Maddox. They would take him to County Hospital; I could come too. I went quickly to the closet to get my forest green wool, the sensible dress I wore on campus, then to the kitchen to put it on. I remembered that I hadn't washed my stockings—the only clean pair I owned had a run and a hole so large the edge cut into my knee. I put on the dress, left my feet bare, working them into my loafers. Then I put on my aunt's mink jacket that she had let me wear. I followed the men out into the musty hall. They threaded the stretcher with Maddox on it down the stairwell and into the waiting vehicle. I stepped into the rear too and sat with one of the firemen on a side seat, while the other clambered into the front. Shivering in the dank air, I nestled into the jacket as the ambulance swayed. The fireman took Maddox's pulse again.

We pulled up at the emergency entrance of a dingy, gray stone building. The firemen took Maddox to the admitting desk. Then someone wheeled Maddox down the hall, while I answered a nurse's questions. "He did construction work over the summer, but he's not working now," I said. Service record? "He was in the army." Another nurse came, her eyes on mine, cold as iron. I stared back just as hard, daring her to say what she was thinking. She bent and spoke to the nurse questioning me, then beckoned me. The heels of my loafers clopping, I followed her down a hall reeking of ether and PineSol.

Tucking my bare legs beneath my chair to hide them, I waited in a small office. I wished I had combed my hair more carefully.

A white-coated doctor rustled into the room as if blown on a wind, and closed the door swiftly. He stared straight at me as he sat down at the desk and spread a manila folder. His scrubbed fingers held a pen, his straight ash-blond hair was slicked back. I felt unkempt. He told me that Maddox would be in the "Psych Ward"; that he had had an anxiety attack; that they would keep him for psychiatric evaluation; and that I should bring his toilet articles but nothing sharp, his pajamas, robe, his street clothes but no belt. Then he told me that he had scheduled an appointment for me to visit with the social worker, Mrs. Hewett, at 10:30. Meanwhile, I could see Maddox if I wished.

Maybe all Maddox needed was some pills or something.

The nurse showed me into the ward, a large room that resembled a bus depot: wooden benches, black linoleum floor, and two-story windows covered with chain link. One white man stood against a wall, empty-eyed, rumpled hair on end, his hand moving as if he were working a yo-yo. Men sat at small tables playing cards; other men sat on benches, legs stretched in front of them. Maddox was among them. He didn't rise when he saw me, and he didn't smile. He kept silent when I sat beside him.

"I'll bring your shaving things and clothes," I said. I avoided talking much—I didn't want to upset him. And I didn't want to think about the place we were sitting in. I sat as close to him as I could, our hips touching. A burly man at the other end of the room began yelling. I didn't want to think Maddox might belong there.

"If I wasn't crazy when I came, I will be before I leave," Maddox said, ruefully. He looked around the room. "Look at these people. Do I look like them? The Man's just fuckin' me over."

At 10:25 I left Maddox to find the social worker. At the reception area I gave my name and waited. Mrs. Hewett opened her door. "Mrs. Temple?" she asked. She was plump with full breasts and short, sausage arms. I had expected her to be startled when she saw I was white, but she wasn't. I followed her into the office and sat in the chair she indicated.

I answered her questions about our marriage, then she wanted to know about my parents.

"I don't under any circumstances want my parents to be contacted," I told her.

She peered at me without any visible reaction. "How long have you lived away from your parents?"

"Since I was seventeen. While I've been in college."

"Are you still in school?"

"I go part time . . . and I work."

"Do you know of anything that might have led to your husband's anxiety this morning?"

"Not really." I remembered how fast the change would come over him when he drank. I told her about the time we tried to go to the theater, and how rude the man in the box office had been. I told her about the people in the A&P. After each incident, Maddox had seemed edgier. "We have disagreements sometimes."

She was looking into my eyes. "Disagreements about what kinds of things?"

I didn't like the way she looked in my eyes all the time. I shifted my gaze to the Utrillo print on the wall across from her desk. "Well, he's jealous a lot."

"Is there a reason for him to be?" She smiled faintly, as if she were encouraging me to trust her.

"Not since we've been married," I told her. "I've been completely faithful to him." I looked down at my bare feet in the loafers. I felt scruffy. "We love each other," I added. I crossed my legs at the ankles and pulled them under the chair as tight as I could.

That afternoon when I brought his clothes I told Maddox I was too scared to stay alone at night. I would leave the cat with Bill and Shirley and I'd stay with my old roommate, Charlotte. I'd call every day and come to see him on my days off.

"I suppose I can call you at Charlotte's then?"

I nodded.

"You wouldn't lie to me, would you, Hope?"

"No."

"Course you would."

"Please . . . there's no reason to worry." I handed him the library books I'd brought, then left.

I took the Illinois Central to the South Side, staring sightlessly out the window. I sighed and swallowed all the way to campus. I slept the night in a narrow bed next to Charlotte. By Sunday night I was bereft; I ached for Maddox to be lying beside me. Monday night was no better. Then Tuesday night I stepped out of the cafe on Ellis Avenue and ran into Eddie.

He was short—his eyes met mine straight on. I told him about Maddox.

We went back inside and sat at the counter drinking Cokes. Eddie teased, and soon I was giggling. He tilted his head and looked at me devilishly. When Eddie laughed, the tip of his tongue peeked from his mouth. I watched, fascinated. He looked in my eyes and leaned close, letting his shoulder touch mine, his chin brush against my hair. I only meant to stay a short while.

When I sank into the front seat of his Studebaker, I realized that I hadn't ridden in a car for a year. I only meant to go with him for one drink. And then, I was lying beside him in his bed. I wasn't happy, but I wasn't quite as lonely anymore. Afterwards he said, "You're crazy. You claim you love Maddox. What the devil are you doing here, anyway? Are your heels so round, you drop your pants just to pass the time?"

"But you and I are friends, Eddie. I'll always be your friend."

"God, I hope not," Eddie said.

I was angry. I flung myself out of his bed. I hadn't intended anything with Eddie.

It wasn't sex I wanted. It was comfort.

I loved Maddox. But I had such a ponderous rock of disappointment locked inside—I hated him. My fear of him had sunk me to my shins in soft river mud from which I couldn't wrench free. No one, not even my mother-in-law, would help me. No police would come (I'd called them once). No neighbor would come to help me when Maddox banged me against the wall. No one would hold out a life-saving branch to me. I was spurned wherever I turned.

There was no comfort for me. None. Eddie was there. I was grateful.

I wasn't sleeping well.

On my day off, I stopped in the ward to tell Maddox I'd be back to see him after my appointment with Mrs. Hewett.

Mrs. Hewett told me that Maddox would be kept in the hospital for at least another ten days and was getting psychotherapy everyday. She asked me more about our marriage.

"He'd be willing to change anything that makes me unhappy. He just doesn't understand," I said, looking at the floor.

"What should he change?"

I glanced up at her—her eyes sought mine—then I looked at the floor again. "You know, the jealousy." My voice dropped. She made me repeat it.

She waited for me to say more. When I didn't she asked, "Has Maddox had a loss in his life?"

What kind of question was that? I looked at her.

"Do you know if he's lost someone close to him?"

"You'll have to ask him, I guess."

"What about you, Hope?" Her gaze never left my face. She asked questions about my family and what kind of child I'd been. She asked, "Were you an only child, then?" I told her no, not really. There was my baby sister. "What happened to your sister?" Her voice was gentle.

"She died. She was two years old. She had a high temperature, too high. My mother held her in water in the bathroom basin, but she died." I stopped. I'd said too much.

Mrs. Hewett laid down her pad and pen. "That must have been very sad for you. And for your mother, too."

"I tried to help her . . . I made the beds, picked some flowers for her, made a picture. She didn't see them."

"You took care of Mother . . . and who took care of you?" she asked gently.

A ticking wall clock was the only sound. If I had spoken then, I would have cried.

Finally, I said, "Look, I think Maddox might do a lot better if I had some . . . I mean if *he* had some help. He really does get crazy jealous. I think we would both be better off, if . . . he had some help."

"Tell me what he does when he gets 'crazy jealous?' "

"He changes so fast. He flies into a rage."

"Then what does he do?"

"He hits me."

"Oh-h-h." She seemed truly sorry. "What do you do then?"

"I leave, if I can."

"And if you can't?"

I didn't answer.

Mrs. Hewett waited. When some time had passed, she said, "All right, Hope. Is there anything else you want to tell me?"

I shook my head.

"I'll talk with the doctor. Can you come back in an hour?"

I murmured something and left, found the cafeteria, and bought a sandwich and coffee. When I picked up the saucer, the cup rattled against it. I sat down near a window and looked out at the street, swarming with noon traffic, then at the faces of the people sitting around me, the stiff backs of the nurses, their hats like folded paper boats. I turned back to the window. A murky October sun tried to shine through the city's air-born detritus, then faded like a ghost. I ate some of the sandwich, then smoked a cigarette while I drank my coffee and thought of my sister in her coffin in our living room. No one had been in the room. I stood in front of her, wondering what death was like. I reached out to touch her . . . Later, in my bedroom, I cut out pictures for my scrapbook. . . . My father called. *Hope*. I pasted and cut. I took all those things in like an oyster. *Hope. . . . Hope*. He kept calling. I wondered why I hadn't died and she did?

At the cashier's counter I bought three packs of Lucky Strikes for Maddox.

When I opened the ward door, the nurse at the desk took the cigarettes. She wouldn't let me see Maddox. "Visiting hours are from 2:00 to 4:00," she said, turning her back.

I went to see Mrs. Hewett again. I stared at the print on the wall, then looked at her as she explained that Maddox had considerable anxiety, and needed to see a psychiatrist—his army benefits would cover the bill. Maybe he wouldn't hit me anymore, I thought. "We can't be sure how long it will take," she said, "or even how much he can be helped."

"I know he'll try hard," I said. "He loves me too much not to." I'd said more than I usually would. I burrowed down again.

"Hope, have you thought about therapy, for yourself?" she asked.

"There's no money."

"You have a job. We can find a therapist who will let you pay according to your income." She paused, watching me quietly.

The ticking of the clock grew loud. I kept my eyes lowered, but I knew her eyes were on me. I was in deep water, sinking to the bottom. The room was full of pressure, like waves breaking over my head. Then she asked, "Hope. . . . Do you need help?" and something raw and sore spilled from me. Could I reach the surface? I looked up through tears.

She didn't speak.

I was suprised to hear myself say, "Yes. I do."

Maddox and I sat on the bench, amid the ward patients. Rain rushed at the window, sounding like crumpling newspaper. His face was soft and full of tenderness. "I want to be home with you, baby," he said. "I love you more than anything in the world." Then the muscles around his eyes tightened, and his heavy eyebrows drew together. "Don't ever leave me."

"I won't leave." We sat quietly, close enough to touch. "Mrs. Hewett thinks I should see a therapist, too," I said.

He raised one eyebrow. "Oh? Do you want to?"

"I can pay for it from my salary." In the days we had been apart, I had seen that there really were no limits set for me, except those I set for myself. Suddenly, I became afraid, knowing how free I really was.

Maddox pulled a cigarette from his shirt pocket and watched me. "What are you thinking, Hope?"

"I'm wondering what you want to do."

"Today? I don't have much choice, do I?"

"I mean with the rest of our lives."

He tilted his head sideways. "What do you want me to do?" he asked.

*Take care of me*, I thought. *I'm afraid of what I might do*.

"What do you want me to do, Hope?" he asked again.

"How would I know."

For the first time, I pictured how he would look years and years in the future, his hair like gray lambs wool, wrinkles where worry lines now crossed his brow. He would brood and stare at the walls while I would still love him with this hopeless love. All the years between, nothing would have happened, even though our whole lives would have happened!

Maddox lit the cigarette, and smoke streamed through his nostrils. "If you go into therapy . . . you'll leave me," he said.

"No, I won't. I need you!" I pleaded.

Maddox stared at the floor. "Shoot." he said. "I'd give anything, my left hand and foot, for what you wanna throw away. I'd take that Freedom." He scowled. "The *good* life, yeah, baby! And you wanna turn your back on it?"

He chuckled deep in his throat. "If that ain't somethin.' "

Then he flung back his head and laughed.

We were together for three years. We didn't know then that more than a year of therapy would follow for both of us, or that he would be treated with phenobarbital, and it would bend and break him more. I grew to understand that when he hit me, it was because I stood for something more than just me. Then, just as I had run from freedom, I abandoned him too. When that part of my life closed, I didn't look back.

Except for one day. "Hope?" he said over the phone.

Though I'd been gone a year, in that moment my heart tore cpen, but I kept my voice even. "I can't come back to you," I said. Didn't he know that I needed to expect something more of each dawn than only the gray seeping in at the window?

Still, in the deepest part of some nights I hear his voice, how it rose as if everything were a question. For a long time now I've been telling myself, he's probably dead.

# D. H. Lawrence

*Lawrence (1885–1930) was born in Eastwood, Nottinghamshire, England. His father was a coal miner, his mother a former schoolteacher whose thwarted life and fierce ambition for her son pushed him to struggle up into the world of culture. The anguish of this effort amid family tensions is the subject of the novel* Sons and Lovers *(1913), which established him as a major literary figure. Before World War I he eloped to the Continent with the wife of a Nottingham professor, but spent the war years miserably in England, suspected of disloyalty because his wife was of German origin, oppressed by disgust at what was happening to his country. Through all the years of his maturity he was harassed by efforts to censor his books and paintings. His distaste for the industrialization and commercialism of English life in his time sent him wandering to Italy, Australia, Mexico, and the mountains of New Mexico in search of an alternative. As he continued to outrage the guardians of public morals—and to reply to them in many of his works with polemic attacks and warnings of the disasters they were brewing—he attracted passionate disciples. His stature as prophet and critic of modern culture has always been a matter of controversy; his explorations of the dark strata of the unconscious, his shrewdly intuitive revisions of conventional notions of human motivation, and the vital energy of his style place him unarguably among the great poets and novelists of his age. His life has inspired a flood of biographies; his remarkable marriage and his death by tuberculosis in the south of France seem hardly distinguishable from his creations in prose and verse. Some of his best-known novels are* The Rainbow *(1915),* Women in Love *(1920), and* Lady Chatterley's Lover *(1928). His shorter works and poems are most easily found in* The Complete Stories *(1961),* Four Short Novels *(1965), and* Complete Poems *(1964).*

## The Horse Dealer's Daughter

Well, Mabel, and what are you going to do with yourself?" asked Joe, with foolish flippancy. He felt quite safe himself. Without listening for an answer, he turned aside, worked a grain of tobacco to the tip of his tongue, and spat it out. He did not care about anything, since he felt safe himself.

The three brothers and the sister sat round the desolate breakfast-table, attempting some sort of desultory consultation. The morning's post had given the final tap to the family fortunes, and all was over. The dreary dining-room itself, with its heavy mahogany furniture, looked as if it were waiting to be done away with.

But the consultation amounted to nothing. There was a strange air of ineffectuality about the three men, as they sprawled at table, smoking and reflecting vaguely on their own condition. The girl was alone, a rather short, sullen-looking young woman of twenty-seven. She did not share the same life as her brothers. She would have been good-looking, save for the impressive fixity of her face, "bull-dog," as her brothers called it.

There was a confused tramping of horses' feet outside. The three men all sprawled round in their chairs to watch. Beyond the dark holly bushes that separated the strip of lawn from the high-road, they could see a cavalcade of shire horses swinging out of their own yard, being taken for exercise. This was the last time. These were the last horses that would go through their hands. The young men watched with critical, callous look. They were all frightened at the collapse of their lives, and the sense of disaster in which they were involved left them no inner freedom.

Yet they were three fine, well-set fellows enough. Joe, the eldest, was a man of thirty-three, broad and handsome in a hot, flushed way. His face was red, he twisted his black moustache over a thick finger, his eyes were shallow and restless. He had a sensual way of uncovering his teeth when he laughed, and his bearing was stupid. Now he watched the horses with a glazed look of helplessness in his eyes, a certain stupor of downfall.

The great draught-horses swung past. They were tied head to tail, four of them, and they heaved along to where a lane branched off from the high-road, planting their great hoofs floutingly in the fine black mud, swinging their great rounded haunches sumptuously, and trotting a few sudden steps as they were led into the lane, round the corner. Every movement showed a massive, slumbrous strength, and a stupidity which held them in subjection. The groom at the head looked back, jerking the leading rope. And the cavalcade moved out of sight up the lane, the tail of the last horse, bobbed up tight and stiff, held out taut from the swinging great haunches as they rocked behind the hedges in a motion-like sleep.

Joe watched with glazed hopeless eyes. The horses were almost like his own body to him. He felt he was done for now. Luckily he was engaged to a woman as old as himself, and therefore her father, who was steward of a neighbouring estate, would provide him with a job. He would marry and go into harness. His life was over, he would be a subject animal now.

He turned uneasily aside, the retreating steps of the horses echoing in his ears. Then, with foolish restlessness, he reached for the scraps of bacon-rind from the plates, and making a faint whistling sound, flung them to the terrier that lay against the fender. He watched the dog swallow them, and waited till the creature looked into his eyes. Then a faint grin came on his face, and in a high, foolish voice he said:

"You won't get much more bacon, shall you, you little b——?"

The dog faintly and dismally wagged its tail, then lowered its haunches, circled round, and lay down again.

There was another helpless silence at the table. Joe sprawled uneasily in his seat, not willing to go till the family conclave was dissolved. Fred Henry, the second brother, was erect, clean-limbed, alert. He had watched the passing of the horses with more *sang-froid*.[1] If he was an animal, like Joe, he was an animal which controls, not one which is controlled. He was master of any horse, and he carried himself with a well-tempered air of mastery. But he was not master of the situations of life. He pushed his coarse brown moustache upwards, off his lip, and glanced irritably at his sister, who sat impassive and inscrutable.

"You'll go and stop with Lucy for a bit, shan't you?" he asked. The girl did not answer.

"I don't see what else you can do," persisted Fred Henry.

"Go as a skivvy,"[2] Joe interpolated laconically.

The girl did not move a muscle.

"If I was her, I should go in for training for a nurse," said Malcolm, the youngest of them all. He was the baby of the family, a young man of twenty-two, with a fresh, jaunty *museau*.[3]

But Mabel did not take any notice of him. They had talked at her and round her for so many years, that she hardly heard them at all.

The marble clock on the mantelpiece softly chimed the half-hour, the dog rose uneasily from the hearth-rug and looked at the party at the breakfast-table. But still they sat in an ineffectual conclave.

"Oh, all right," said Joe suddenly, apropos of nothing. "I'll get a move on."

He pushed back his chair, straddled his knees with a downward jerk, to get them free, in horsey fashion, and went to the fire. Still he did not go out of the room; he was curious to know what the others would do or say. He began to charge his pipe, looking down at the dog and saying in a high, affected voice:

"Going wi' me? Going wi' me are ter? Tha'rt goin' further than tha counts on just now, dost hear?"

The dog faintly wagged his tail, the man stuck out his jaw and covered his pipe with his hands, and puffed intently, losing himself in the tobacco, looking down all the while at the dog with an absent brown eye. The dog looked up at him in mournful distrust. Joe stood with his knees stuck out, in real horsey fashion.

"Have you had a letter from Lucy?" Fred Henry asked of his sister.

"Last week," came the neutral reply.

"And what does she say?"

There was no answer.

"Does she *ask* you to go and stop there?" persisted Fred Henry.

"She says I can if I like."

"Well, then, you'd better. Tell her you'll come on Monday."

This was received in silence.

"That's what you'll do then, is it?" said Fred Henry, in some exasperation.

But she made no answer. There was a silence of futility and irritation in the room. Malcolm grinned fatuously.

"You'll have to make up your mind between now and next Wednesday," said Joe loudly, "or else find yourself lodgings on the kerbstone."

The face of the young woman darkened, but she sat on immutable.

1. Coolness (French). 2. Menial worker. 3. Face (French).

"Here's Jack Ferguson!" exclaimed Malcolm, who was looking aimlessly out of the window.

"Where?" exclaimed Joe loudly.

"Just gone past."

"Coming in?"

Malcolm craned his neck to see the gate.

"Yes," he said.

There was a silence. Mabel sat on like one condemned, at the head of the table. Then a whistle was heard from the kitchen. The dog got up and barked sharply. Joe opened the door and shouted:

"Come on."

After a moment a young man entered. He was muffled up in overcoat and a purple woollen scarf, and his tweed cap, which he did not remove, was pulled down on his head. He was of medium height, his face was rather long and pale, his eyes looked tired.

"Hello, Jack! Well, Jack!" exclaimed Malcolm and Joe. Fred Henry merely said: "Jack."

"What's doing?" asked the newcomer, evidently addressing Fred Henry.

"Same. We've got to be out by Wednesday. Got a cold?"

"I have—got it bad, too."

"Why don't you stop in?"

"*Me* stop in? When I can't stand on my legs, perhaps I shall have a chance." The young man spoke huskily. He had a slight Scotch accent.

"It's a knock-out, isn't it," said Joe, boisterously, "if a doctor goes round croaking with a cold. Looks bad for the patients, doesn't it?"

The young doctor looked at him slowly.

"Anything the matter with *you,* then?" he asked sarcastically.

"Not as I know of. Damn your eyes, I hope not. Why?"

"I thought you were very concerned about the patients, wondered if you might be one yourself."

"Damn it, no, I've never been patient to no flaming doctor, and hope I never shall be," returned Joe.

At this point Mabel rose from the table, and they all seemed to become aware of her existence. She began putting the dishes together. The young doctor looked at her, but did not address her. He had not greeted her. She went out of the room with the tray, her face impassive and unchanged.

"When are you off then, all of you?" asked the doctor.

"I'm catching the eleven-forty," replied Malcolm. "Are you goin' down wi' th' trap, Joe?"

"Yes, I've told you I'm going down wi' th' trap, haven't I?"

"We'd better be getting her in then. So long Jack, if I don't see you before I go," said Malcolm, shaking hands.

He went out, followed by Joe, who seemed to have his tail between his legs.

"Well, this is the devil's own," exclaimed the doctor, when he was left alone with Fred Henry. "Going before Wednesday, are you?"

"That's the orders," replied the other.

"Where, to Northampton?"

"That's it."

"The devil!" exclaimed Ferguson, with quiet chagrin.

And there was silence between the two.

"All settled up, are you?" asked Ferguson.

"About."

There was another pause.

"Well, I shall miss yer, Freddy, boy," said the young doctor.

"And I shall miss thee, Jack," returned the other.

"Miss you like hell," mused the doctor.

Fred Henry turned aside. There was nothing to say. Mabel came in again, to finish clearing the table.

"What are *you* going to do, then, Miss Pervin?" asked Ferguson. "Going to your sister's, are you?"

Mabel looked at him with her steady, dangerous eyes, that always made him uncomfortable, unsettling his superficial ease.

"No," she said.

"Well, what in the name of fortune *are* you going to do? Say what you mean to do," cried Fred Henry, with futile intensity.

But she only averted her head, and continued her work. She folded the white table-cloth, and put on the chenille cloth.

"The sulkiest bitch that ever trod!" muttered her brother.

But she finished her task with perfectly impassive face, the young doctor watching her interestedly all the while. Then she went out.

Fred Henry stared after her, clenching his lips, his blue eyes fixing in sharp antagonism, as he made a grimace of sour exasperation.

"You could bray her into bits, and that's all you'd get out of her," he said, in a small, narrowed tone.

The doctor smiled faintly.

"What's she *going* to do, then?" he asked.

"Strike me if *I* know!" returned the other.

There was a pause. Then the doctor stirred.

"I'll be seeing you tonight, shall I?" he said to his friend.

"Ay—where's it to be? Are we going over to Jessdale?"

"I don't know. I've got such a cold on me. I'll come round to the 'Moon and Stars', anyway."

"Let Lizzie and May miss their night for once, eh?"

"That's it—if I feel as I do now."

"All's one——"

The two young men went through the passage and down to the back door together. The house was large, but it was servantless now, and desolate. At the back was a small brick house-yard and beyond that a big square, graveled fine and red, and having stables on two sides. Sloping, dank, winter-dark fields stretched away on the open sides.

But the stables were empty. Joseph Pervin, the father of the family, had been a man of no education, who had become a fairly large horse dealer. The stables had been full of horses, there was a great turmoil and come-and-go of horses and of dealers and grooms. Then the kitchen was full of servants. But of late things had declined. The old man had married a second time, to retrieve his fortunes. Now he was dead and everything was gone to the dogs, there was nothing but debt and threatening.

For months, Mabel had been servantless in the big house, keeping the home together in penury for her ineffectual brothers. She had kept house for ten years. But previously it was with unstinted means. Then, however brutal and coarse everything was, the sense of money had kept her proud, confident. The men might be foul-mouthed, the women in the kitchen might have bad reputations, her brothers might have illegitimate children. But so long as there was money, the girl felt herself established, and brutally proud, reserved.

No company came to the house, save dealers and coarse men. Mabel had no associates of her own sex, after her sister went away. But she did not mind. She went regularly to church, she attended to her father. And she lived in the memory of her mother, who had died when she was fourteen, and whom she had loved. She had loved her father, too, in a different way, depending upon him, and feeling secure in him, until at the age of fifty-four he married again. And then she had set hard against him. Now he had died and left them all hopelessly in debt.

She had suffered badly during the period of poverty. Nothing, however, could shake the curious, sullen, animal pride that dominated each member of the family. Now, for Mabel, the end had come. Still she would not cast about her. She would follow her own way just the same. She would always hold the keys of her own situation. Mindless and persistent, she endured from day to day. Why should she think? Why should she answer anybody? It was enough that this was the end, and there was no way out. She need not pass any more darkly along the main street of the small town, avoiding every eye. She need not demean herself any more, going into the shops and buying the cheapest food. This was at an end. She thought of nobody, not even of herself. Mindless and persistent, she seemed in a sort of ecstasy to be coming nearer to her fulfilment, her own glorification, approaching her dead mother, who was glorified.

In the afternoon, she took a little bag, with shears and sponge and a small scrubbing-brush, and went out. It was a grey, wintry day, with saddened, dark green fields and an atmosphere blackened by the smoke of foundries not far off. She went quickly, darkly along the causeway, heeding nobody, through the town to the churchyard.

There she always felt secure, as if no one could see her, although as a matter of fact she was exposed to the stare of everyone who passed along under the churchyard wall. Nevertheless, once under the shadow of the great looming church, among the graves, she felt immune from the world, reserved within the thick churchyard wall as in another country.

Carefully she clipped the grass from the grave, and arranged the pinky white, small chrysanthemums in the tin cross. When this was done, she took an empty jar from a neighbouring grave, brought water, and carefully, most scrupulously sponged the marble headstone and the coping-stone.

It gave her sincere satisfaction to do this. She felt in immediate contact with the world of her mother. She took minute pains, went through the park in a state bordering on pure happiness, as if in performing this task she came into a subtle, intimate connection with her mother. For the life she followed here in the world was far less real than the world of death she inherited from her mother.

The doctor's house was just by the church. Ferguson, being a mere hired assistant, was slave to the country-side. As he hurried now to attend to the out-patients in the surgery, glancing across the graveyard with his quick eye, he saw the girl at her task at the grave. She seemed so intent and remote, it was like looking into another world. Some mystical element was touched in him. He slowed down as he walked, watching her as if spellbound.

She lifted her eyes, feeling him looking. Their eyes met. And each looked away again at once, each feeling, in some way, found out by the other. He lifted his cap and passed on down the road. There remained distinct in his consciousness, like a vision, the memory of her face, lifted from the tombstone in the churchyard, and looking at him with slow, large, portentous eyes. It *was* portentous, her face. It seemed to mesmerize him. There was a heavy power in her eyes which laid hold of his whole being, as if he had drunk some powerful drug. He had been feeling weak and done before. Now the life came back into him, he felt delivered from his own fretted, daily self.

He finished his duties at the surgery as quickly as might be, hastily filling up the bottles of the waiting people with cheap drugs. Then, in perpetual haste, he set off again to visit several cases in another part of his round, before tea-time. At all times he preferred to walk if he could, but particularly when he was not well. He fancied the motion restored him.

The afternoon was falling. It was grey, deadened, and wintry, with a slow, moist, heavy coldness sinking in and deadening all the faculties. But why should he think or notice? He hastily climbed the hill and turned across the dark green fields, following the black cinder-track. In the distance, across a shallow dip in the country, the small town was clustered like smouldering ash, a tower, a spire, a heap of low, raw, extinct houses. And on the nearest fringe of the town, sloping into the dip, was Oldmeadow, the Pervins' house. He could see the stables and the outbuildings distinctly, as they lay towards him on the slope. Well, he would not go there many more times! Another resource would be lost to him, another place gone: the only company he cared for in the alien, ugly little town he was losing. Nothing but work, drudgery, constant hastening from dwelling to dwelling among the colliers and the iron-workers. It wore him out, but at the same time he had a craving for it. It was a stimulant to him to be in the homes of the working people, moving, as it were, through the innermost body of their life. His nerves were excited and gratified. He could come so near, into the very lives of the rough, inarticulate, powerfully emotional men and women. He grumbled, he said he hated the hellish hole. But as a matter of fact it excited him, the contact with the rough, strongly-feeling people was a stimultant applied direct to his nerves.

Below Oldmeadow, in the green, shallow, soddened hollow of fields, lay a square, deep pond. Roving across the landscape, the doctor's quick eye detected a figure in black passing through the gate of the field, down towards the pond.

He looked again. It would be Mabel Pervin. His mind suddenly became alive and attentive.

Why was she going down there? He pulled up on the path on the slope above, and stood staring. He could just make sure of the small black figure moving in the hollow of the failing day. He seemed to see her in the midst of such obscurity, that he was like a clairvoyant, seeing rather with the mind's eye than with ordinary sight. Yet he could see her positively enough, whilst he kept his eye attentive. He felt, if he looked away from her, in the thick, ugly falling dusk, he would lose her altogether.

He followed her minutely as she moved, direct and intent, like something transmitted rather than stirring in voluntary activity, straight down the field towards the pond. There she stood on the bank for a moment. She never raised her head. Then she waded slowly into the water.

He stood motionless as the small black figure walked slowly and deliberately towards the center of the pond, very slowly, gradually moving deeper into the motionless water, and still moving forward as the water got up to her breast. Then he could see her no more in the dusk of the dead afternoon.

"There!" he exclaimed. "Would you believe it?"

And he hastened straight down, running over the wet, soddened fields, pushing through the hedges, down into the depression of callous wintry obscurity. It took him several minutes to come to the pond. He stood on the bank, breathing heavily. He could see nothing. His eyes seemed to penetrate the dead water. Yes, perhaps that was the dark shadow of her black clothing beneath the surface of the water.

He slowly ventured into the pond. The bottom was deep, soft clay, he sank in, and the water clasped dead cold round his legs. As he stirred he could smell the cold, rotten clay that fouled up into the water. It was objectionable in his lungs. Still, repelled and yet not heeding, he moved deeper into the pond. The cold water rose over his thighs, over his loins, upon his abdomen. The lower part of his body was all sunk in the hideous cold element. And the bottom was so deeply soft and uncertain, he was afraid of pitching with his mouth underneath. He could not swim, and was afraid.

He crouched a little, spreading his hands under the water and moving them round, trying to feel for her. The dead cold pond swayed upon his chest. He moved again, a little deeper, and again, with his hands underneath, he felt all around under the water. And he touched her clothing. But it evaded his fingers. He made a desperate effort to grasp it.

And so doing he lost his balance and went under, horribly, suffocating in the foul earthy water, struggling madly for a few moments. At last, after what seemed an eternity, he got his footing, rose again into the air and looked around. He gasped, and knew he was in the world. Then he looked at the water. She had risen near him. He grasped her clothing, and drawing her nearer, turned to take his way to land again.

He went very slowly, carefully, absorbed in the slow progress. He rose higher, climbing out of the pond. The water was now only about his legs; he was thankful, full of relief to be out of the clutches of the pond. He lifted her and staggered onto the bank, out of the horror of wet, grey clay.

He laid her down on the bank. She was quite unconscious and running with water. He made the water come from her mouth, he worked to restore her. He did not have to work very long before he could feel the breathing begin again in her; she was breathing naturally. He worked a little longer. He could feel her live beneath his hands; she was coming back. He wiped her face, wrapped her in his overcoat, looked round into the dim, dark grey world, then lifted her and staggered down the bank and across the fields.

It seemed an unthinkably long way, and his burden so heavy he felt he would never get to the house. But at last he was in the stable-yard, and then in the house-yard. He opened the door and went into the house. In the kitchen he laid her down on the hearth-rug and called. The house was empty. But the fire was burning in the grate.

Then again he kneeled to attend to her. She was breathing regularly, her eyes were wide open and as if conscious, but there seemed something missing in her look. She was conscious in herself, but unconscious of her surroundings.

He ran upstairs, took blankets from a bed, and put them before the fire to warm. Then he removed her saturated, earthy-smelling clothing, rubbed her dry with a towel, and wrapped her naked in the blankets. Then he went into the dining-room, to look for spirits. There was a little whisky. He drank a gulp himself, and put some into her mouth.

The effect was instantaneous. She looked full into his face, as if she had been seeing him for some time, and yet had only just become conscious of him.

"Dr. Ferguson?" she said.

"What?" he answered.

He was divesting himself of his coat, intending to find some dry clothing upstairs. He could not bear the smell of the dead, clayey water, and he was mortally afraid for his own health.

"What did I do?" she asked.

"Walked into the pond," he replied. He had begun to shudder like one sick, and could hardly attend to her. Her eyes remained full on him, he seemed to be going dark in his mind, looking back at her helplessly. The shuddering became quieter in him, his life came back to him, dark and unknowing, but strong again.

"Was I out of my mind?" she asked, while her eyes were fixed on him all the time.

"Maybe, for the moment," he replied. He felt quiet, because his strength had come back. The strange fretful strain had left him.

"Am I out of my mind now?" she asked.

"Are you?" he reflected a moment. "No," he answered truthfully. "I don't see that you are." He turned his face aside. He was afraid now, because he felt dazed, and felt dimly that her power was stronger than his, in this issue. And she continued to look at him fixedly all the time. "Can you tell me where I shall find some dry things to put on?" he asked.

"Did you dive into the pond for me?" she asked.

"No," he answered. "I walked in. But I went in over head as well."

There was silence for a moment. He hesitated. He very much wanted to go upstairs to get into dry clothing. But there was another desire in him. And she seemed to hold him. His will seemed to have gone to sleep, and left him, standing there slack before her. But he felt warm inside himself. He did not shudder at all, though his clothes were sodden on him.

"Why did you?" she asked.

"Because I didn't want you to do such a foolish thing," he said.

"It wasn't foolish," she said, still gazing at him as she lay on the floor, with a sofa cushion under her head. "It was the right thing to do. *I* knew best, then."

"I'll go and shift these wet things," he said. But still he had not the power to move out of her presence, until she sent him. It was as if she had the life of his body in her hands, and he could not extricate himself. Or perhaps he did not want to.

Suddenly she sat up. Then she became aware of her own immediate condition. She felt the blankets about her, she knew her own limbs. For a moment it seemed as if her reason were going. She looked round, with wild eye, as if seeking something. He stood still with fear. She saw her clothing lying scattered.

"Who undressed me?" she asked, her eyes resting full and inevitable on his face.

"I did," he replied, "to bring you round."

For some moments she sat and gazed at him awfully, her lips parted.

"Do you love me, then?" she asked.

He only stood and stared at her, fascinated. His soul seemed to melt.

She shuffled forward on her knees, and put her arms round him, round his legs, as he stood there, pressing her breasts against his knees and thighs, clutching him with strange, convulsive certainty, pressing his thighs against her, drawing him to her face, her throat, as she looked up at him with flaring, humble eyes of transfiguration, triumphant in first possession.

"You love me," she murmured, in strange transport, yearning and triumphant and confident. "You love me. I know you love me, I know."

And she was passionately kissing his knees, through the wet clothing, passionately and indiscriminately kissing his knees, his legs, as if unaware of everything.

He looked down at the tangled wet hair, the wild, bare, animal shoulders. He was amazed, bewildered, and afraid. He had never thought of loving her. He had never wanted to love her. When he rescued her and restored her, he was a doctor, and she was a patient. He had had no single personal thought of her. Nay, this introduction of the personal element was very distasteful to him, a violation of his professional honour. It was horrible to have her there embracing his knees. It was horrible. He revolted from it, violently. And yet—and yet—he had not the power to break away.

She looked at him again, with the same supplication of powerful love, and that same transcendent, frightening light of triumph. In view of the delicate flame which seemed to come from her face like a light, he was powerless. And yet he had never intended to love her. He had never intended. And something stubborn in him could not give way.

"You love me," she repeated, in a murmur of deep, rhapsodic assurance. "You love me."

Her hands were drawing him, drawing him down to her. He was afraid, even a little horrified. For he had, really, no intention of loving her. Yet her hands were drawing him towards her. He put out his hand quickly to steady himself, and grasped her bare shoulder. A flame seemed to burn the hand that grasped her soft shoulder. He had no intention of loving her: his whole will was against his yielding. It was horrible. And yet wonderful was the touch of her shoulders, beautiful the shining of her face. Was she perhaps mad? He had a horror of yielding to her. Yet something in him ached also.

He had been staring away at the door, away from her. But his hand remained on her shoulder. She had gone suddenly very still. He looked down at her. Her eyes were now wide with fear, with doubt, the light was dying from her face, a shadow of terrible greyness was returning. He could not bear the touch of her eyes' question upon him, and the look of death behind the question.

With an inward groan he gave way, and let his heart yield towards her. A sudden gentle smile came on his face. And her eyes, which never left his face, slowly, slowly filled with tears. He watched the strange water rise in her eyes, like some slow fountain coming up. And his heart seemed to burn and melt away in his breast.

He could not bear to look at her any more. He dropped on his knees and caught her head with his arms and pressed her face against his throat. She was very still. His heart, which seemed to have broken, was burning with a kind of agony in his breast. And he felt her slow, hot tears wetting his throat. But he could not move.

He felt the hot tears wet his neck and the hollows of his neck, and he remained motionless, suspended through one of man's eternities. Only now it had become indispensable to him to have her face pressed close to him; he could never let her go again. He could never let her head go away from the close clutch of his arm. He wanted to remain like that for ever, with his heart hurting him in a pain that was also life to him. Without knowing, he was looking down on her damp, soft brown hair.

Then, as it were suddenly, he smelt the horrid stagnant smell of that water. And at the same moment she drew away from him and looked at him. Her eyes were wistful and unfathomable. He was afraid of them, and he fell to kissing her, not knowing what he was doing. He wanted her eyes not to have that terrible, wistful, unfathomable look.

When she turned her face to him again, a faint delicate flush was glowing, and there was again dawning that terrible shining of joy in her eyes, which really terrified him, and yet which he now wanted to see, because he feared the look of doubt still more.

"You love me?" she said, rather faltering.

"Yes." The word cost him a painful effort. Not because it wasn't true. But because it was too newly true, the *saying* seemed to tear open again his newly-torn heart. And he hardly wanted it to be true, even now.

She lifted her face to him, and he bent forward and kissed her on the mouth, gently, with the one kiss that is an eternal pledge. And as he kissed her his heart strained again in his breast. He never intended to love her. But now it was over. He had crossed over the gulf to her, and all that he had left behind had shrivelled and become void.

After the kiss, her eyes again slowly filled with tears. She sat still, away from him, with her face drooped aside, and her hands folded in her lap. The tears fell very slowly. There was complete silence. He too sat there motionless and silent on the hearth-rug. The strange pain of his heart that was broken seemed to consume him. That he should love her? That this was love! That he should be ripped open in this way! Him, a doctor! How they would all jeer if they knew! It was agony to him to think they might know.

In the curious naked pain of the thought he looked again to her. She was sitting there drooped into a muse. He saw a tear fall, and his heart flared hot. He saw for the first time that one of her shoulders was quite uncovered, one arm bare, he could see one of her small breasts; dimly, because it had become almost dark in the room.

"Why are you crying?" he asked, in an altered voice.

She looked up at him, and behind her tears the consciousness of her situation for the first time brought a dark look of shame to her eyes.

"I'm not crying, really," she said, watching him, half frightened.

He reached his hand, and softly closed it on her bare arm.

"I love you! I love you!" he said in a soft, low vibrating voice, unlike himself.

She shrank, and dropped her head. The soft, penetrating grip of his hand on her arm distressed her. She looked up at him.

"I want to go," she said. "I want to go and get you some dry things."

"Why?" he said. "I'm all right."

"But I want to go," she said. "And I want you to change your things."

He released her arm, and she wrapped herself in the blanket, looking at him rather frightened. And still she did not rise.

"Kiss me," she said wistfully.

He kissed her, but briefly, half in anger.

Then, after a second, she rose nervously, all mixed up in the blanket. He watched her in her confusion as she tried to extricate herself and wrap herself up so that she could walk. He watched her relentlessly, as she knew. And as she went, the blanket trailing, and as he saw a glimpse of her feet and her white leg, he tried to remember her as she was when he had wrapped her in the blanket. But then he didn't want to remember, because she had been nothing to him then, and his nature revolted from remembering her as she was when she was nothing to him.

A tumbling, muffled noise from within the dark house startled him. Then he heard her voice: "There are clothes." He rose and went to the foot of the stairs, and gathered up the garments she had thrown down. Then he came back to the fire, to rub himself down and dress. He grinned at his own appearance when he had finished.

The fire was sinking, so he put on coal. The house was now quite dark, save for the light of a street-lamp that shone in faintly from beyond the holly trees. He lit the gas with matches he found on the mantelpiece. Then he emptied the pockets of his own clothes, and threw all his wet things in a heap into the scullery. After which he gathered up her sodden clothes, gently, and put them in a separate heap on the copper-top in the scullery.

It was six o'clock on the clock. His own watch had stopped. He ought to go back to the surgery. He waited, and still she did not come down. So he went to the foot of the stairs and called:

"I shall have to go."

Almost immediately he heard her coming down. She had on her best dress of black voile, and her hair was tidy, but still damp. She looked at him—and in spite of herself, smiled.

"I don't like you in those clothes," she said.

"Do I look a sight?" he answered.

They were shy of one another.

"I'll make you some tea," she said.

"No, I must go."

"Must you?" And she looked at him again with the wide, strained, doubtful eyes. And again, from the pain of his breast, he knew how he loved her. He went and bent to kiss her, gently, passionately, with his heart's painful kiss.

"And my hair smells so horrible," she murmured in distraction. "And I'm so awful, I'm so awful! Oh no, I'm too awful." And she broke into bitter, heart-broken sobbing. "You can't want to love me, I'm horrible."

"Don't be silly, don't be silly," he said, trying to comfort her, kissing her, holding her in his arms. "I want you, I want to marry you, we're going to be married, quickly, quickly—to-morrow if I can."

But she only sobbed terribly, and cried:

"I feel awful. I feel awful. I feel I'm horrible to you."

"No, I want you, I want you," was all he answered, blindly, with that terrible intonation which frightened her almost more than her horror lest he should *not* want her.

# Sharyn Layfield

*Layfield was born in 1949 in the United States. She received her undergraduate education at Temple University and a Master of Fine Arts degree at Goddard College. She has primarily published essays and stories. She received the Vermont Council on the Arts Grant in 1986.*

## The Coggios

It is spring, and flamingoes return to the Coggios' lawn, along with the virgin in her sky-blue robe. Inside the miniature picket fence, daisy pinwheels are spinning; a pair of young deer graze and listen. I listen too, imagining the voices of the Coggios calling to me from out behind the house where they take their afternoon leisure.

The Coggio house is lemon yellow, large but not too large. Mr. Coggio is old and bowlegged, and he wears a straw hat when he works outside. In the early days of spring, two of his boys are out with him, hauling manure, mowing and raking while Mr. Coggio, on his hands and knees, trims the edges and collects clippings, talking softly to himself or maybe to the ground. You never see a dandelion on the Coggio property. No clover, no weeds. The grasses are plush, untangled, as tempting to walk on as those golf courses you see.

As lunchtime approaches, two large Coggio daughters emerge from the house carrying first rags and buckets of soapy water, then linens, china and silverware. They move across the lawn through sunlight and shade to the screened-in-picnic pavilion which has the same yellow roof as the house and bird-houses, perched high over the garden on long poles. Daughters scour the picnic table, the benches, the cement floor. Now they lay out a clean white linen table cloth. The cloth and the table may be ten, twenty, thirty years old. It's hard to tell the age of things the Coggios own, because they take such good care of them. The white cloth, for instance: if anything is spilled on it the women run boiling water through the stain, soak it, scrub it, and hang it on the clothes line in the sun. I have seen them circle the yard in the evenings gathering up garden tools, lawn chairs. Their knives are sharpened on a stone, their tools oiled, paint brushes rinsed and rinsed. Rust never forms on the hedge clippers. Nothing is left out in the rain or snow.

It is time to eat, and Mrs. Coggio steps grandly out of the house carrying before her a deep dish pie with an intricate lattice-work crust on top. The ruffles on her flowered apron, stiff and shiny with starch, are unmoving in the breeze. All the Coggio clothes are crisp, their colors bright with bluing, ironed with great patience by daughters on the sunporch. Tuesday afternoons they take turns at the ironing board, singing with the radio and sipping lemonade while they work. When they sweat, they pat their faces with real handkerchiefs.

The Coggios have settled at the table, crossing themselves and saying the words. Plates are passed and napkins raised and lowered. The boys and their father eat fast, buttering rolls and popping them into their mouths. The women chew steadily, rhythmically, watching the youngest boy as he talks. Mr. Coggio listens but does not look up from his plate.

The ceremony reverses itself, and the women rise to collect remnants of the meal, returning to the house in a silent procession. Now that I know them so well I can almost see the Coggios through the walls of their house, working in the kitchen. They are placing empty soda bottles under the sink in order of size. They are twisting the tops of large plastic trash bags. Someone is bent over the oven replacing the perfectly clean tin foil liner. I can see white, gold-flecked formica countertops, gleaming chrome and stainless steel, a toaster cover made to look like a cat.

Outside Mr. Coggio takes up his bag of clippings. The boys poke each other, returning to their rakes. Then there are sounds: dishes tinkling, a bird that alternates melodies, one high shrill call followed by another that sounds like a crow. The oldest Coggio boy is smoking a cigarette behind the shed, leaning against the wall and staring off into the woods.

It is late afternoon. I can see them from here, taking the sun out back. The girls sit across from one another in the swing, the sun in their hair. The Mr. and Mrs. sit close by in lawn chairs. She knits and he, like his son, gazes toward the woods, smoking his pipe. The girls talk softly. Mr. Coggio nods, is sleepy. The pipe in his lap, he sleeps. The girls whisper. Nothing is moving but the wisps of loose hair that flutter around the faces of the women in the sunlight. This is my favorite way of seeing them.

I survey the house, the grounds, and imagine the Coggios' future. I know the girls will never marry. Why should they? But the boys are restless. They will go, and come back with women carrying babies in white baptismal clothes, and the Coggios will add a high chair, swing sets and a wading pool to their collection. Sunday afternoon gatherings will be bigger and louder. The girls will play with toddlers in the green grass, first urging them to walk, then holding them back as they chase one another in and out among the adults, screaming happily.

At this hour of day, when the sun is low and strong, the Coggios will stand at the end of the driveway waving and smiling as the sons and wives and children back away from them onto the highway and disappear. It is then they will see me. I am patient, knowing that if I wait long enough I will be welcome in this yard. I will be ready, having learned their cleanliness and their order; ready, when I hear them call me from across the yard.

Come to us, the women will sing sweetly. Come, come! The old man will speak roughly but with a hint of a smile. Mrs. Coggio will hold up a peach pie for me to see.

I'm coming! I'll call back, and stepping lightly onto the grass, past the pinwheels, past the virgin and the flamingoes, I will take my place.

# DAVID LEAVITT

*Leavitt (1961– ) is a native of California and a graduate of Yale. His early years, however, were spent around Stanford University, where his father was on the faculty. He worked in New York as he started to publish his stories. In 1984 he was awarded an O'Henry Prize. His collection of stories* Family Dancing *appeared the same year. Among his books are* A Place I've Never Been *(1990),* Arkansas: Three Novellas *(1997), and* The Page Turner *(1998).*

## Gravity

Theo had a choice between a drug that would save his sight and a drug that would keep him alive, so he chose not to go blind. He stopped the pills and started the injections—these required the implantation of an unpleasant and painful catheter just above his heart—and within a few days the clouds in his eyes started to clear up; he could see again. He remembered going into New York City to a show with his mother, when he was twelve and didn't want to admit he needed glasses. "Can you read that?" she'd shouted, pointing to a Broadway marquee, and when he'd squinted, making out only one or two letters, she'd taken off her own glasses—harlequins with tiny rhinestones in the corners—and shoved them onto his face. The world came into focus, and he gasped, astonished at the precision around the edges of things, the legibility, the hard, sharp, colorful landscape. Sylvia had to squint through *Fiddler on the Roof* that day, but for Theo, his face masked by his mother's huge glasses, everything was as bright and vivid as a comic book. Even though people stared at him, and muttered things, Sylvia didn't care; he could *see.*

Because he was dying again, Theo moved back to his mother's house in New Jersey. The DHPG injections she took in stride—she'd seen her own mother through *her* dying, after all. Four times a day, with the equanimity of a nurse, she cleaned out the plastic tube implanted in his chest, inserted a sterilized hypodermic and slowly dripped the bag of sight-giving liquid into his veins. They endured this procedure silently, Sylvia sitting on the side of the hospital bed she'd rented for the duration of Theo's stay—his life, he sometimes thought—watching reruns of *I Love Lucy* or the news, while he tried not to think about the hard piece of pipe stuck into him, even though it was a constant reminder of how wide and unswimmable the gulf was becoming between him and the ever-receding shoreline of the well. And Sylvia was intricately cheerful. Each day she urged him to go out with her somewhere—to the library, or the little museum with the dinosaur replicas he'd been fond of as a child—and when his thinness and the cane drew stares, she'd maneuver him around the people who were staring, determined to shield him from whatever they might say or do. It had been the same that afternoon so many years ago, when she'd pushed him through a lobbyful of curious and laughing faces, determined that nothing should interfere with the spectacle of his seeing. What a pair they must have made, a boy in ugly glasses and a mother daring the world to say a word about it!

This warm, breezy afternoon in May they were shopping for revenge. "Your cousin Howard's engagement party is next month," Sylvia explained in the car. "A very nice girl from Livingston. I met her a few weeks ago, and really, she's a superior person."

"I'm glad," Theo said. "Congratulate Howie for me."

"Do you think you'll be up to going to the party?"

"I'm not sure. Would it be okay for me just to give him a gift?"

"You already have. A lovely silver tray, if I say so myself. The thank-you note's in the living room."

"Mom," Theo said, "why do you always have to—"

Sylvia honked her horn at a truck making an illegal left turn. "Better they should get something than no present at all, is what I say," she said. "But now, the problem is, *I* have to give Howie something, to be from me, and it better be good. It better be very, very good."

"Why?"

"Don't you remember that cheap little nothing Bibi gave you for your graduation? It was disgusting."

"I can't remember what she gave me."

"Of course you can't. It was a tacky pen-and-pencil set. Not even a real leather box. So naturally, it stands to reason that I have to get something truly spectacular for Howard's engagement. Something that will make Bibi blanch. Anyway, I think I've found just the thing, but I need your advice."

"Advice? Well, when my old roommate Nick got married, I gave him a garlic press. It cost five dollars and reflected exactly how much I felt, at that moment, our friendship was worth."

Sylvia laughed. "Clever. But my idea is much more brilliant, because it makes it possible for me to get back at Bibi *and* give Howard the nice gift he and his girl deserve." She smiled, clearly pleased with herself. "Ah, you live and learn."

"You live," Theo said.

Sylvia blinked. "Well, look, here we are." She pulled the car into a handicapped-parking place on Morris Avenue and got out to help Theo, but he was already hoisting himself up out of his seat, using the door handle for leverage. "I can manage myself," he said with some irritation. Sylvia stepped back.

"Clearly one advantage to all this for you," Theo said, balancing on his cane, "is that it's suddenly so much easier to get a parking place."

"Oh Theo, please," Sylvia said. "Look, here's where we're going."

She leaned him into a gift shop filled with porcelain statuettes of Snow White and all seven of the dwarves, music boxes which, when you opened them, played "The Shadow of Your Smile," complicated-smelling potpourris in purple wallpapered boxes, and stuffed snakes you were supposed to push up against drafty windows and doors.

"Mrs. Greenman," said an expansive, gray-haired man in a cream-colored cardigan sweater. "Look who's here, Archie, it's Mrs. Greenman."

Another man, this one thinner and balding, but dressed in an identical cardigan, peered out from the back of the shop. "Hello there!" he said, smiling. He looked at Theo, and his expression changed.

"Mr. Sherman, Mr. Baker. This is my son, Theo."

"Hello," Mr. Sherman and Mr. Baker said. They didn't offer to shake hands.

"Are you here for that item we discussed last week?" Mr. Sherman asked.

"Yes," Sylvia said. "I want advice from my son here." She walked over to a large ridged crystal bowl, a very fifties sort of bowl, stalwart and square-jawed. "What do you think? Beautiful, isn't it?"

"Mom, to tell the truth, I think it's kind of ugly."

"Four hundred and twenty-five dollars," Sylvia said admiringly. "You have to feel it."

Then she picked up the big bowl and tossed it to Theo, like a football.

The gentlemen in the cardigan sweaters gasped and did not exhale. When Theo caught it, it sank his hands. His cane rattled as it hit the floor.

"That's heavy," Sylvia said, observing with satisfaction how the bowl had weighted Theo's arms down. "And where crystal is concerned, heavy is impressive."

She took the bowl back from him and carried it to the counter. Mr. Sherman was mopping his brow. Theo looked at the floor, still surprised not to see shards of glass around his feet.

Since no one else seemed to be volunteering, he bent over and picked up the cane.

"Four hundred and fifty-nine, with tax," Mr. Sherman said, his voice still a bit shaky, and a look of relish came over Sylvia's face as she pulled out her checkbook to pay. Behind the counter, Theo could see Mr. Baker put his hand on his forehead and cast his eyes to the ceiling.

It seemed Sylvia had been looking a long time for something like this, something heavy enough to leave an impression, yet so fragile it could make you sorry.

They headed back out to the car.

"Where can we go now?" Sylvia asked, as she got in. "There must be someplace else to go."

"Home," Theo said. "It's almost time for my medicine."

"Really? Oh. All right." She pulled on her seat belt, inserted the car key in the ignition and sat there.

For just a moment, but perceptibly, her face broke. She squeezed her eyes shut so tight the blue shadow on the lids cracked.

Almost as quickly she was back to normal again, and they were driving.

"It's getting hotter," Sylvia said. "Shall I put on the air?"

"Sure," Theo said. He was thinking about the bowl, or more specifically, about how surprising its weight had been, pulling his hands down. For a while now he'd been worried about his mother, worried about what damage his illness might secretly be doing to her that of course she would never admit. On the surface things seemed all right. She still broiled herself a skinned chicken breast for dinner every night, still swam a mile and a half a day, still kept used teabags wrapped in foil in the refrigerator. Yet she had also, at about three o'clock one morning, woken him up to tell him she was going to the twenty-four-hour supermarket, and was there anything he wanted. Then there was the gift shop: She had literally pitched that bowl toward him, pitched it like a ball, and as that great gleam of flight and potential regret came sailing in his direction, it had occurred to him that she was trusting his two feeble hands, out of the whole world, to keep it from shattering. What was she trying to test? Was it his newly regained vision? Was it the assurance that he was there, alive, that he hadn't yet slipped past all her caring, a little lost boy in rhinestone-studded glasses? There are certain things you've already done before you even think how to do them—a child pulled from in front of a car, for instance, or the bowl, which Theo was holding before he could even begin to calculate its brief trajectory. It had pulled his arms down, and from that apish posture he'd looked at his mother, who smiled broadly, as if, in the war between heaviness and shattering, he'd just helped her win some small but sustaining victory.

# Ursula K. Le Guin

*Le Guin (1929– ) was born in Berkeley, California. She was educated at Radcliffe College and Columbia University and spent a year as a Fulbright student in Paris, where she married the historian Charles Le Guin. She has won an extraordinary number of science fiction prizes, and her thematically charged use of the medium caught the mood of concerned readers of the 1970s and 1980s. Some of her novels are* A Wizard of Earthsea *(1968),* The Tombs of Atuan *(1971),* The Farthest Shore *(1972) (which comprise the* Earthsea Trilogy*),* The Left Hand of Darkness *(1969),* The Dispossessed *(1974),* The Beginning Place *(1980), and* Always Coming Home *(1985). Her most recent titles include* Unlocking the Air and Others Stories *(1996) and* Lao Tzu: Tao Te Ching *(1997). Some of her shorter works have been collected in* The Wind's Twelve Quarters *(1975) and* Orsinian Tales *(1976).*

## The Ones Who Walk Away from Omelas

**(Variations on a Theme by William James)**[1]

With a clamor of bells that set the swallows soaring, the Festival of Summer came to the city Omelas, bright-towered by the sea. The rigging of the boats in harbor sparkled with flags. In the streets between houses with red roofs and painted walls, between old moss-grown gardens and under avenues of trees, past great parks and public buildings, processions moved. Some were decorous: old people in long stiff robes of mauve and grey, grave master workmen, quiet, merry women carrying their babies and chatting as they walked. In other streets the music beat faster, a shimmering of gong and tambourine, and the people went dancing, the procession was a dance. Children dodged in and out, their high calls rising like the swallows' crossing flights over the music and the singing. All the processions wound towards the north side of the city, where on the great water-meadow called the Green Fields boys and girls, naked in the bright air, with mud-stained feet and ankles and long, lithe arms, exercised their restive horses before the race. The horses wore no gear at all but a halter without bit. Their manes were braided with streamers of silver, gold, and green. They flared their nostrils and pranced and boasted to one another; they were vastly

1. American philosopher and experimental psychologist (1842–1910).

excited, the horse being the only animal who has adopted our ceremonies as his own. Far off to the north and west the mountains stood up half encircling Omelas on her bay. The air of morning was so clear that the snow still crowning the Eighteen Peaks burned with white-gold fire across the miles of sunlit air, under the dark blue of the sky. There was just enough wind to make the banners that marked the racecourse snap and flutter now and then. In the silence of the broad green meadows one could hear the music winding through the city streets, farther and nearer and ever approaching, a cheerful faint sweetness of the air that from time to time trembled and gathered together and broke out into the great joyous clanging of the bells.

Joyous! How is one to tell about joy? How describe the citizens of Omelas?

They were not simple folk, you see, though they were happy. But we do not say the words of cheer much any more. All smiles have become archaic. Given a description such as this one tends to make certain assumptions. Given a description such as this one tends to look next for the King, mounted on a splendid stallion and surrounded by his noble knights, or perhaps in a golden litter borne by great-muscled slaves. But there was no king. They did not use swords, or keep slaves. They were not barbarians. I do not know the rules and laws of their society, but I suspect that they were singularly few. As they did without monarchy and slavery, so they also got on without the stock exchange, the advertisement, the secret police, and the bomb. Yet I repeat that these were not simple folk, not dulcet shepherds, noble savages, bland utopians. They were not less complex than us. The trouble is that we have a bad habit, encouraged by pedants and sophisticates, of considering happiness as something rather stupid. Only pain is intellectual, only evil interesting. This is the treason of the artist: a refusal to admit the banality of evil and the terrible boredom of pain. If you can't lick 'em, join 'em. If it hurts, repeat it. But to praise despair is to condemn delight, to embrace violence is to lose hold of everything else. We have almost lost hold, we can no longer describe a happy man, nor make any celebration of joy. How can I tell you about the people of Omelas? They were not naïve and happy children—though their children were, in fact, happy. They were mature, intelligent, passionate adults whose lives were not wretched. O miracle! but I wish I could describe it better. I wish I could convince you. Omelas sounds in my words like a city in a fairy tale, long ago and far away, once upon a time. Perhaps it would be best if you imagined it as your own fancy bids, assuming it will rise to the occasion, for certainly I cannot suit you all. For instance, how about technology? I think that there would be no cars or helicopters in and above the streets; this follows from the fact that the people of Omelas are happy people. Happiness is based on a just discrimination of what is necessary, what is neither necessary nor destructive, and what is destructive. In the middle category, however—that of the unnecessary but undestructive, that of comfort, luxury, exuberance, etc.—they could perfectly well have central heating, subway trains, washing machines, and all kinds of marvelous devices not yet invented here, floating light-sources, fuelless power, a cure for the common cold. Or they could have none of that: it doesn't matter. As you like it. I incline to think that people from towns up and down the coast have been coming in to Omelas during the last days before the Festival on very fast little trains and double-decked trams, and that the train station of Omelas is actually the handsomest building in town, though plainer than the magnificent Farmers' Market. But even granted trains, I fear that Omelas so far strikes some of you as goody-goody. Smiles, bells, parades, horses, bleh. If so, please add an orgy. If an orgy would help, don't hesitate. Let us not, however, have temples from which issue beautiful nude priests and priestesses already half in ecstasy and ready to copulate with any man or woman, lover or stranger, who desires union with the deep godhead of the blood, although that was my first idea. But really it would be better not to have any temples in Omelas—at least, not manned temples. Religion yes, clergy no. Surely the beautiful nudes can just wander about, offering themselves like divine soufflés to the hunger of the needy and the rapture of the flesh. Let them join the processions. Let tambourines be struck above the copulations, and the glory of desire be proclaimed upon the gongs, and (a not unimportant point) let the offspring of these delightful rituals be beloved and looked after by all. One thing I know there is none of in Omelas is guilt. But what else should there be? I thought at first there were no drugs, but that is puritanical. For those who like it, the faint insistent sweetness of *drooz* may perfume the ways of the city, *drooz* which first brings a great lightness and brilliance to the mind and limbs, and then after some hours a dreamy languor, and wonderful visions at last of the very arcana and inmost secrets of the Universe, as well as exciting the pleasure of sex beyond all belief; and it is not habit-forming. For more modest tastes I think there ought to be beer. What else, what else belongs in the joyous city? The sense of victory, surely, the celebration of courage. But as we did without clergy, let us do without soldiers. The joy built upon successful slaughter is not the right kind of joy; it will not do; it is fearful and it is trivial. A boundless and generous contentment, a magnanimous triumph felt not against some outer enemy but in communion with the finest and fairest in the souls of all men everywhere and the splendor of the world's summer: this is what swells the hearts of the people of Omelas, and the victory they celebrate is that of life. I really don't think many of them need to take *drooz*.

Most of the procession have reached the Green Fields by now. A marvelous smell of cooking goes forth from the red and blue tents of the provisioners. The faces of small children are amiably sticky; in the benign grey beard of a man a couple of crumbs of rich pastry are entangled. The youths and girls have mounted their horses and are beginning to group around the starting line of the course. An old woman, small, fat, and laughing, is passing out flowers from a basket, and tall young men wear her flowers in their shining hair. A child of nine or ten sits at the edge of the crowd, alone, playing on a wooden flute. People pause to listen, and they smile, but they do not speak to him, for he never ceases playing and never sees them, his dark eyes wholly rapt in the sweet, thin magic of the tune.

He finishes, and slowly lowers his hands holding the wooden flute.

As if that little private silence were the signal, all at once a trumpet sounds from the pavilion near the starting line: imperious, melancholy, piercing. The horses rear on their slender legs, and some of them neigh in answer. Sober-faced, the young riders stroke the horses' necks and soothe them, whispering,

"Quiet, quiet, there my beauty, my hope. . . ." They begin to form in rank along the starting line. The crowds along the racecourse are like a field of grass and flowers in the wind. The Festival of Summer has begun.

Do you believe? Do you accept the festival, the city, the joy? No? Then let me describe one more thing.

In a basement under one of the beautiful public buildings of Omelas, or perhaps in the cellar of one of its more spacious private homes, there is a room. It has one locked door, and no window. A little light seeps in dustily between cracks in the boards, secondhand from a cobwebbed window somewhere across the cellar. In one corner of the little room a couple of mops, with stiff, clotted, foul-smelling heads, stand near a rusty bucket. The floor is dirt, a little damp to the touch, as cellar dirt usually is. The room is about three paces long and two wide: a mere broom closet or disused tool room. In the room a child is sitting. It could be a boy or a girl. It looks about six, but actually is nearly ten. It is feeble-minded. Perhaps it was born defective, or perhaps it has become imbecile through fear, malnutrition, and neglect. It picks its nose and occasionally fumbles vaguely with its toes or genitals, as it sits hunched in the corner farthest from the bucket and the two mops. It is afraid of the mops. It finds them horrible. It shuts its eyes, but it knows the mops are still standing there; and the door is locked; and nobody will come. The door is always locked; and nobody ever comes, except that sometimes—the child has no understanding of time or interval—sometimes the door rattles terribly and opens, and a person, or several people, are there. One of them may come in and kick the child to make it stand up. The others never come close, but peer in at it with frightened, disgusted eyes. The food bowl and the water jug are hastily filled, the door is locked, the eyes disappear. The people at the door never say anything, but the child, who has not always lived in the tool room, and can remember sunlight and its mother's voice, sometimes speaks. "I will be good," it says. "Please let me out. I will be good!" They never answer. The child used to scream for help at night, and cry a good deal, but now it only makes a kind of whining, "eh-haa, eh-haa," and it speaks less and less often. It is so thin there are no calves to its legs; its belly protrudes; it lives on a half-bowl of corn meal and grease a day. It is naked. Its buttocks and thighs are a mass of festered sores, as it sits in its own excrement continually.

They all know it is there, all the people of Omelas. Some of them have come to see it, others are content merely to know it is there. They all know that it has to be there. Some of them understand why, and some do not, but they all understand that their happiness, the beauty of their city, the tenderness of their friendships, the health of their children, the wisdom of their scholars, the skill of their makers, even the abundance of their harvest and the kindly weathers of their skies, depend wholly on this child's abominable misery.

This is usually explained to children when they are between eight and twelve, whenever they seem capable of understanding; and most of those who come to see the child are young people, though often enough an adult comes, or comes back, to see the child. No matter how well the matter has been explained to them, these young spectators are always shocked and sickened at the sight. They feel disgust, which they had thought themselves superior to.

They feel anger, outrage, impotence, despite all the explanations. They would like to do something for the child. But there is nothing they can do. If the child were brought up into the sunlight out of the vile place, if it were cleaned and fed and comforted, that would be a good thing, indeed; but if it were done, in that day and hour all the prosperity and beauty and delight of Omelas would wither and be destroyed. Those are the terms. To exchange all the goodness and grace of every life in Omelas for that single, small improvement: to throw away the happiness of thousands for the chance of the happiness of one: that would be to let guilt within the walls indeed.

The terms are strict and absolute; there may not even be a kind word spoken to the child.

Often the young people go home in tears, or in a tearless rage, when they have seen the child and faced this terrible paradox. They may brood over it for weeks or years. But as time goes on they begin to realize that even if the child could be released, it would not get much good of its freedom: a little vague pleasure of warmth and food, no doubt, but little more. It is too degraded and imbecile to know any real joy. It has been afraid too long ever to be free of fear. Its habits are too uncouth for it to respond to humane treatment. Indeed, after so long it would probably be wretched without walls about it to protect it, and darkness for its eyes, and its own excrement to sit in. Their tears at the bitter injustice dry when they begin to perceive the terrible justice of reality, and to accept it. Yet it is their tears and anger, the trying of their generosity and the acceptance of their helplessness, which are perhaps the true source of the splendor of their lives. Theirs is no vapid, irresponsible happiness. They know that they, like the child, are not free. They know compassion. It is the existence of the child, and their knowledge of its existence, that makes possible the nobility of their architecture, the poignancy of their music, the profundity of their science. It is because of the child that they are so gentle with children. They know that if the wretched one were not there snivelling in the dark, the other one, the flute-player, could make no joyful music as the young riders line up in their beauty for the race in the sunlight of the first morning of summer.

Now do you believe in them? Are they not more credible? But there is one more thing to tell, and this is quite incredible.

At times one of the adolescent girls or boys who go to see the child does not go home to weep or rage, does not, in fact, go home at all. Sometimes also a man or woman much older falls silent for a day or two, and then leaves home. These people go out into the street, and walk down the street alone. They keep walking, and walk straight out of the city of Omelas, through the beautiful gates. They keep walking across the farmlands of Omelas. Each one goes alone, youth or girl, man or woman. Night falls; the traveler must pass down village streets, between the houses with yellow-lit windows, and on out into the darkness of the fields. Each alone, they go west or north, towards the mountains. They go on. They leave Omelas, they walk ahead into the darkness, and they do not come back. The place they go towards is a place even less imaginable to most of us than the city of happiness. I cannot describe it at all. It is possible that it does not exist. But they seem to know where they are going, the ones who walk away from Omelas.

# Doris Lessing

*Lessing (1919– ) was born in Kermanshah, Persia (now Iran), the daughter of a bank manager, and was taken by her family to Rhodesia (now Zimbabwe) in 1924. Fleeing the loneliness of an unhappy childhood, she went to the capital of Salisbury (Harare) at eighteen and there involved herself in politics and the intellectual life. She became a Communist and retained her party affiliation until she moved to London, where disillusion led her to break with the party. She was twice married and twice divorced before her departure from Africa. She published a well-made, conventional novel,* The Grass Is Singing, *in 1950, and soon thereafter began to experiment more freely with work that combines autobiography and fiction in an unorthodox attempt to come at the dilemmas of the modern woman struggling for emancipation. Following this vein she published five novels between 1952 and 1969 under the general title* Children of Violence. The Golden Notebook *(1962) has the form of several overlapping notebooks prepared by a writer simultaneously preparing and postponing the composition of a novel. In her despair of rational solutions to political and sexual disorders of our times, Lessing has entertained the possibilities for reorientation that lie in extrasensory perception and in the visions of the insane. Among her novels are* Briefing for a Descent into Hell *(1971),* The Summer before the Dark *(1973), the tetralogy* Canopus in Argos: Archives *(1981), two novels collected under the title* The Diaries of Jane Somers *(1984),* The Good Terrorist *(1985),* The Fifth Child *(1988), and* Love, Again *(1996).* Under My Skin *(1994) and* Walking in the Shade *(1997) are volumes one and two of her autobiography. Many of her stories are collected in* African Stories *(1964) and* Stories *(1978). An anthology of her work,* The Doris Lessing Reader, *was published in 1989.*

## To Room Nineteen

This is a story, I suppose, about a failure in intelligence: the Rawlings' marriage was grounded in intelligence.

They were older when they married than most of their married friends: in their well-seasoned late twenties. Both had had a number of affairs, sweet rather than bitter; and when they fell in love—for they did fall in love—had known each other for some time. They joked that they had saved each other "for the real thing." That they had waited so long (but not too long) for this real thing was to them a proof of their sensible discrimination. A good many of their friends had married young, and now (they felt) probably regretted lost opportunities; while others, still unmarried, seemed to them arid, self-doubting, and likely to make desperate or romantic marriages.

Not only they, but others, felt they were well-matched: their friends' delight was an additional proof of their happiness. They had played the same roles, male and female, in this group or set, if such a wide, loosely connected, constantly changing constellation of people could be called a set. They had both become, by virtue of their moderation, their humour, and their abstinence from painful experience, people to whom others came for advice. They could be, and were, relied on. It was one of those cases of a man and a woman linking themselves whom no one else had ever thought of linking, probably because of their similarities. But then everyone exclaimed: Of course! How right! How was it we never thought of it before!

And so they married amid general rejoicing, and because of their foresight and their sense for what was probable, nothing was a surprise to them.

Both had well-paid jobs. Matthew was a subeditor on a large London newspaper, and Susan worked in an advertising firm. He was not the stuff of which editors or publicised journalists are made, but he was much more than "a subeditor," being one of the essential background people who in fact steady, inspire and make possible the people in the limelight. He was content with this position. Susan had a talent for commercial drawing. She was humorous about the advertisements she was responsible for, but she did not feel strongly about them one way or the other.

Both, before they married, had had pleasant flats, but they felt it unwise to base a marriage on either flat, because it might seem like a submission of personality on the part of the one whose flat it was not. They moved into a new flat in South Kensington[1] on the clear understanding that when their marriage had settled down (a process they knew would not take long, and was in fact more a humorous concession to popular wisdom than what was due to themselves) they would buy a house and start a family.

And this is what happened. They lived in their charming flat for two years, giving parties and going to them, being a popular young married couple, and then Susan became pregnant, she gave up her job, and they bought a house in Richmond.[2] It was typical of this couple that they had a son first, then a daughter, then twins, son and daughter. Everything right, appropriate, and what everyone would wish for, if they could choose. But people did feel these two had chosen; this balanced and sensible family was no more than what was due to them because of their infallible sense for *choosing* right.

And so they lived with their four children in their gardened house in Richmond and were happy. They had everything they had wanted and had planned for.

*And yet . . .*

Well, even this was expected, that there must be a certain flatness. . . .

Yes, yes, of course, it was natural they sometimes felt like this. Like what?

Their life seemed to be like a snake biting its tail. Matthew's job for the sake of Susan, children, house, and garden—which caravanserai needed a well-paid job to maintain it. And Susan's practical intelligence for the sake of Matthew, the children, the house and the garden—which unit would have collapsed in a week without her.

1. Part of the fashionable west end of London. 2. One of the outer boroughs of greater London.

But there was no point about which either could say: "For the sake of *this* is all the rest." Children? But children can't be a centre of life and a reason for being. They can be a thousand things that are delightful, interesting, satisfying, but they can't be a wellspring to live from. Or they shouldn't be. Susan and Matthew knew that well enough.

Matthew's job? Ridiculous. It was an interesting job, but scarcely a reason for living. Matthew took pride in doing it well, but he could hardly be expected to be proud of the newspaper; the newspaper he read, *his* newspaper, was not the one he worked for.

Their love for each other? Well, that was nearest it. If this wasn't a centre, what was? Yes, it was around this point, their love, that the whole extraordinary structure revolved. For extraordinary it certainly was. Both Susan and Matthew had moments of thinking so, of looking in secret disbelief at this thing they had created: marriage, four children, big house, garden, charwoman, friends, cars . . . and this *thing,* this entity, all of it had come into existence, been blown into being out of nowhere, because Susan loved Matthew and Matthew loved Susan. Extraordinary. So that was the central point, the wellspring.

And if one felt that it simply was not strong enough, important enough, to support it all, well whose fault was that? Certainly neither Susan's nor Matthew's. It was in the nature of things. And they sensibly blamed neither themselves nor each other.

On the contrary, they used their intelligence to preserve what they had created from a painful and explosive world: they looked around them, and took lessons. All around them, marriages collapsing, or breaking, or rubbing along (even worse, they felt). They must not make the same mistakes, they must not.

They had avoided the pitfall so many of their friends had fallen into—of buying a house in the country *for the sake of the children,* so that the husband became a weekend husband, a weekend father, and the wife always careful not to ask what went on in the town flat which they called (in joke) a bachelor flat. No, Matthew was a full-time husband, a full-time father, and at night, in the big married bed in the big married bedroom (which had an attractive view of the river), they lay beside each other talking and he told her about his day, and what he had done, and whom he had met; and she told him about her day (not as interesting, but that was not her fault), for both knew of the hidden resentments and deprivations of the woman who has lived her own life—and above all, has earned her own living—and is now dependent on a husband for outside interests and money.

Nor did Susan make the mistake of taking a job for the sake of her independence, which she might very well have done, since her old firm, missing her qualities of humour, balance, and sense, invited her often to go back. Children needed their mother to a certain age, that both parents knew and agreed on; and when these four healthy wisely brought up children were of the right age, Susan would work again, because she knew, and so did he, what happened to women of fifty at the height of their energy and ability, with grownup children who no longer needed their full devotion.

So here was this couple, testing their marriage, looking after it, treating it like a small boat full of helpless people in a very stormy sea. Well, of course, so it was. . . . The storms of the world were bad, but not too close—which is not to say they were selfishly felt: Susan and Matthew were both well-informed and responsible people. And the inner storms and quicksands were understood and charted. So everything was all right. Everything was in order. Yes, things were under control.

So what did it matter if they felt dry, flat? People like themselves, fed on a hundred books (psychological, anthropological, sociological), could scarcely be unprepared for the dry, controlled wistfulness which is the distinguishing mark of the intelligent marriage. Two people, endowed with education, with discrimination, with judgement, linked together voluntarily from their will to be happy together and to be of use to others—one sees them everywhere, one knows them, one even is that thing oneself: sadness because so much is after all so little. These two, unsurprised, turned towards each other with even more courtesy and gentle love: this was life, that two people, no matter how carefully chosen, could not be everything to each other. In fact, even to say so, to think in such a way, was banal; they were ashamed to do it.

It was banal, too, when one night Matthew came home late and confessed he had been to a party, taken a girl home and slept with her. Susan forgave him, of course. Except that forgiveness is hardly the word. Understanding, yes. But if you understand something, you don't forgive it, you are the thing itself: forgiveness is for what you *don't* understand. Nor had he *confessed*—what sort of word is that?

The whole thing was not important. After all, years ago they had joked: Of course I'm not going to be faithful to you, no one can be faithful to one other person for a whole lifetime. (And there was the word "faithful"—stupid, all these words, stupid, belonging to a savage old world.) But the incident left both of them irritable. Strange, but they were both bad-tempered, annoyed. There was something unassimilable about it.

Making love splendidly after he had come home that night, both had felt that the idea that Myra Jenkins, a pretty girl met at a party, could be even relevant was ridiculous. They had loved each other for over a decade, would love each other for years more. Who, then, was Myra Jenkins?

Except, thought Susan, unaccountably bad-tempered, she was (is?) the first. In ten years. So either the ten years' fidelity was not important, or she isn't. (No, no, there is something wrong with this way of thinking, there must be.) But if she isn't important, presumably it wasn't important either when Matthew and I first went to bed with each other that afternoon whose delight even now (like a very long shadow at sundown) lays a long, wandlike finger over us. (Why did I say sundown?) Well, if what we felt that afternoon was not important, nothing is important, because if it hadn't been for what we felt, we wouldn't be Mr. and Mrs. Rawlings with four children, et cetera, et cetera. The whole thing is *absurd*—for him to have come home and told me was absurd. For him not to have told me was absurd. For me to care or, for that matter, not to care, is absurd . . . and who is Myra Jenkins? Why, no one at all.

There was only one thing to do, and of course these sensible people did it; they put the thing behind them, and consciously, knowing what they were doing, moved forward into a different phase of their marriage, giving thanks for past good fortune as they did so.

For it was inevitable that the handsome, blond, attractive, manly man, Matthew Rawlings, should be at times tempted (oh, what a word!) by the attractive girls at parties she could not attend because of the four children; and that sometimes he would succumb (a word even more repulsive, if possible) and that she, a goodlooking woman in the big well-tended garden at Richmond, would sometimes be pierced as by an arrow from the sky with bitterness. Except that bitterness was not in order, it was out of court. Did the casual girls touch the marriage? They did not. Rather it was they who knew defeat because of the handsome Matthew Rawlings' marriage body and soul to Susan Rawlings.

In that case why did Susan feel (though luckily not for longer than a few seconds at a time) as if life had become a desert, and that nothing mattered, and that her children were not her own?

Meanwhile her intelligence continued to assert that all was well. What if her Matthew did have an occasional sweet afternoon, the odd affair? For she knew quite well, except in her moments of aridity, that they were very happy, that the affairs were not important.

Perhaps that was the trouble? It was in the nature of things that the adventures and delights could no longer be hers, because of the four children and the big house that needed so much attention. But perhaps she was secretly wishing, and even knowing that she did, that the wildness and the beauty could be his. But he was married to her. She was married to him. They were married inextricably. And therefore the gods could not strike him with the real magic, not really. Well, was it Susan's fault that after he came home from an adventure he looked harassed rather than fulfilled? (In fact, that was how she knew he had been *unfaithful*, because of his sullen air, and his glances at her, similar to hers at him: What is it that I share with this person that shields all delight from me?) But none of it by anybody's fault. (But what did they feel ought to be somebody's fault?) Nobody's fault, nothing to be at fault, no one to blame, no one to offer or to take it . . . and nothing wrong, either, except that Matthew never was really struck, as he wanted to be, by joy; and that Susan was more and more often threatened by emptiness. (It was usually in the garden that she was invaded by this feeling: she was coming to avoid the garden, unless the children or Matthew were with her.) There was no need to use the dramatic words "unfaithful," "forgive," and the rest: intelligence forbade them. Intelligence barred, too, quarrelling, sulking, anger, silences of withdrawal, accusations and tears. Above all, intelligence forbids tears.

A high price has to be paid for the happy marriage with the four healthy children in the large white gardened house.

And they were paying it, willingly, knowing what they were doing. When they lay side by side or breast to breast in the big civilised bedroom overlooking the wild sullied river, they laughed, often, for no particular reason; but they knew it was really because of these two small people, Susan and Matthew, supporting such an edifice on their intelligent love. The laugh comforted them; it saved them both, though from what, they did not know.

They were now both fortyish. The older children, boy and girl, were ten and eight, at school. The twins, six, were still at home. Susan did not have nurses or girls to help her: childhood is short; and she did not regret the hard work. Often enough she was bored, since small children can be boring; she was often very tired; but she regretted nothing. In another decade, she would turn herself back into being a woman with a life of her own.

Soon the twins would go to school, and they would be away from home from nine until four. These hours, so Susan saw it, would be the preparation for her own slow emancipation away from the role of hub-of-the-family into woman-with-her-own-life. She was already planning for the hours of freedom when all the children would be "off her hands." That was the phrase used by Matthew and by Susan and by their friends, for the moment when the youngest child went off to school. "They'll be off your hands, darling Susan, and you'll have time to yourself." So said Matthew, the intelligent husband, who had often enough commended and consoled Susan, standing by her in spirit during the years when her soul was not her own, as she said, but her children's.

What it amounted to was that Susan saw herself as she had been at twenty-eight, unmarried; and then again somewhere about fifty, blossoming from the root of what she had been twenty years before. As if the essential Susan were in abeyance, as if she were in cold storage. Matthew said something like this to Susan one night: and she agreed that it was true—she did feel something like that. What, then, was this essential Susan? She did not know. Put like that it sounded ridiculous, and she did not really feel it. Anyway, they had a long discussion about the whole thing before going off to sleep in each other's arms.

So the twins went off to their school, two bright affectionate children who had no problems about it, since their older brother and sister had trodden this path so successfully before them. And now Susan was going to be alone in the big house, every day of the school term, except for the daily woman who came in to clean.

It was now, for the first time in this marriage, that something happened which neither of them had foreseen.

This is what happened. She returned, at nine-thirty, from taking the twins to the school by car, looking forward to seven blissful hours of freedom. On the first morning she was simply restless, worrying about the twins "naturally enough" since this was their first day away at school. She was hardly able to contain herself until they came back. Which they did happily, excited by the world of school, looking forward to the next day. And the next day Susan took them, dropped them, came back, and found herself reluctant to enter her big and beautiful home because it was as if something was waiting for her there that she did not wish to confront. Sensibly, however, she parked the car in the garage, entered the house, spoke to Mrs. Parkes, the daily woman, about her duties, and went up to her bedroom. She was possessed by a fever which drove her out again, downstairs, into the kitchen, where Mrs. Parkes was making cake and did not need her, and into the garden. There she sat on a bench and tried to calm herself looking at trees, at a brown glimpse of the river. But she was filled with tension, like a panic: as if an enemy was in the garden with her. She spoke to herself severely, thus: All this is quite natural. First, I spent twelve years of my adult life working, *living my own life.* Then I married, and from the moment I became pregnant for the first time I signed myself over, so to speak, to other people. To the children. Not for one moment in twelve years have I been alone, had time to myself. So now I have to learn to be myself again. That's all.

And she went indoors to help Mrs. Parkes cook and clean, and found some sewing to do for the children. She kept herself occupied every day. At the end of the first term she understood she felt two contrary emotions. First: secret astonishment and dismay that during those weeks when the house was empty of children she had in fact been more occupied (had been careful to keep herself occupied) than ever she had been when the children were around her needing her continual attention. Second: that now she knew the house would be full of them, and for five weeks, she resented the fact she would never be alone. She was already looking back at those hours of sewing, cooking (but by herself) as at a lost freedom which would not be hers for five long weeks. And the two months of term which would succeed the five weeks stretched alluringly open to her—freedom. But what freedom—when in fact she had been so careful *not* to be free of small duties during the last weeks? She looked at herself, Susan Rawlings, sitting in a big chair by the window in the bedroom, sewing shirts or dresses, which she might just as well have bought. She saw herself making cakes for hours at a time in the big family kitchen: yet usually she bought cakes. What she saw was a woman alone, that was true, but she had not felt alone. For instance, Mrs. Parkes was always somewhere in the house. And she did not like being in the garden at all, because of the closeness there of the enemy—irritation, restlessness, emptiness, whatever it was—which keeping her hands occupied made less dangerous for some reason.

Susan did not tell Matthew of these thoughts. They were not sensible. She did not recognize herself in them. What should she say to her dear friend and husband, Matthew? "When I go into the garden, that is, if the children are not there, I feel as if there is an enemy there waiting to invade me." "What enemy, Susan darling?" "Well I don't know, really. . . ." "Perhaps you should see a doctor?"

No, clearly this conversation should not take place. The holidays began and Susan welcomed them. Four children, lively, energetic, intelligent, demanding: she was never, not for a moment of her day, alone. If she was in a room, they would be in the next room, or waiting for her to do something for them; or it would soon be time for lunch or tea, or to take one of them to the dentist. Something to do: five weeks of it, thank goodness.

On the fourth day of these so welcome holidays, she found she was storming with anger at the twins; two shrinking beautiful children who (and this is what checked her) stood hand in hand looking at her with sheer dismayed disbelief. This was their calm mother, shouting at them. And for what? They had come to her with some game, some bit of nonsense. They looked at each other, moved closer for support, and went off hand in hand, leaving Susan holding on to the windowsill of the livingroom, breathing deep, feeling sick. She went to lie down, telling the older children she had a headache. She heard the boy Harry telling the little ones: "It's all right, Mother's got a headache." She heard that *It's all right* with pain.

That night she said to her husband: "Today I shouted at the twins, quite unfairly." She sounded miserable, and he said gently: "Well, what of it?"

"It's more of an adjustment than I thought, their going to school."

"But Susie, Susie darling. . . ." For she was crouched weeping on the bed. He comforted her: "Susan, what is all this about? You shouted at them? What of it? If you shouted at them fifty times a day it wouldn't be more than the little devils deserve." But she wouldn't laugh. She wept. Soon he comforted her with his body. She became calm. Calm, she wondered what was wrong with her, and why she should mind so much that she might, just once, have behaved unjustly with the children. What did it matter? They had forgotten it all long ago: Mother had a headache and everything was all right.

It was a long time later that Susan understood that that night, when she had wept and Matthew had driven the misery out of her with his big solid body, was the last time, ever in their married life, that they had been—to use their mutual language—with each other. And even that was a lie, because she had not told him of her real fears at all.

The five weeks passed, and Susan was in control of herself, and good and kind, and she looked forward to the end of the holidays with a mixture of fear and longing. She did not know what to expect. She took the twins off to school (the elder children took themselves to school) and she returned to the house determined to face the enemy wherever he was, in the house, or the garden or—where?

She was again restless, she was possessed by restlessness. She cooked and sewed and worked as before, day after day, while Mrs. Parkes remonstrated: "Mrs. Rawlings, what's the need for it? I can do that, it's what you pay me for."

And it was so irrational that she checked herself. She would put the car into the garage, go up to her bedroom, and sit, hands in her lap, forcing herself to be quiet. She listened to Mrs. Parkes moving around the house. She looked out into the garden and saw the branches shake the trees. She sat defeating the enemy, restlessness. Emptiness. She ought to be thinking about her life, about herself. But she did not. Or perhaps she could not. As soon as she forced her mind to think about Susan (for what else did she want to be alone for?), it skipped off to thoughts of butter or school clothes. Or it thought of Mrs. Parkes. She realised that she sat listening for the movements of the cleaning woman, following her every turn, bend, thought. She followed her in her mind from kitchen to bathroom, from table to oven, and it was as if the duster, the cleaning cloth, the saucepan, were in her own hand. She would hear herself saying: No, not like that, don't put that there. . . . Yet she did not give a damn what Mrs. Parkes did, or if she did it at all. Yet she could not prevent herself from being conscious of her, every minute. Yes, this was what was wrong with her: she needed, when she was alone, to be really alone, with no one near. She could not endure the knowledge that in ten minutes or in half an hour Mrs. Parkes would call up the stairs: "Mrs. Rawlings, there's no silver polish. Madam, we're out of flour."

So she left the house and went to sit in the garden where she was screened from the house by trees. She waited for the demon to appear and claim her, but he did not.

She was keeping him off, because she had not, after all, come to an end of arranging herself.

She was planning how to be somewhere where Mrs. Parkes would not come after her with a cup of tea, or a demand to be allowed to telephone (always irritating, since Susan did not care who she telephoned or how often), or just a nice talk about something. Yes, she needed a place, or a state of affairs, where it would not be necessary to keep reminding herself: In ten minutes I must telephone Matthew about . . . and at half past three I must leave early for the children because the car needs cleaning. And at ten o'clock tomorrow I must remember. . . . She was possessed with resentment that the seven hours of freedom in every day (during weekdays in the school term) were not free, that never, not for one second, ever, was she free from the pressure of time, from having to remember this or that. She could never forget herself; never really let herself go into forgetfulness.

Resentment. It was poisoning her. (She looked at this emotion and thought it was absurd. Yet she felt it.) She was a prisoner. (She looked at this thought too, and it was no good telling herself it was a ridiculous one.) She must tell Matthew—but what? She was filled with emotions that were utterly ridiculous, that she despised, yet that nevertheless she was feeling so strongly she could not shake them off.

The school holidays came round, and this time they were for nearly two months, and she behaved with a conscious controlled decency that nearly drove her crazy. She would lock herself in the bathroom, and sit on the edge of the bath, breathing deep, trying to let go into some kind of calm. Or she went up into the spare room, usually empty, where no one would expect her to be. She heard the children calling "Mother, Mother," and kept silent, feeling guilty. Or she went to the very end of the garden, by herself, and looked at the slow-moving brown river; she looked at the river and closed her eyes and breathed slow and deep, taking it into her being, into her veins.

Then she returned to the family, wife and mother, smiling and responsible, feeling as if the pressure of these people—four lively children and her husband—were a painful pressure on the surface of her skin, a hand pressing on her brain. She did not once break down into irritation during these holidays, but it was like living out a prison sentence, and when the children went back to school, she sat on a white stone seat near the flowing river, and she thought: It is not even a year since the twins went to school, since *they were off my hands* (What on earth did I think I meant when I used that stupid phrase?), and yet I'm a different person. I'm simply not myself. I don't understand it.

Yet she had to understand it. For she knew that this structure—big white house, on which the mortgage still cost four hundred[3] a year, a husband, so good and kind and insightful; four children, all doing so nicely; and the garden where she sat; and Mrs. Parkes, the cleaning woman—all this depended on her, and yet she could not understand why, or even what it was she contributed to it.

She said to Matthew in their bedroom: "I think there must be something wrong with me."

And he said: "Surely not, Susan? You look marvellous—you're as lovely as ever."

She looked at the handsome blond man, with his clear, intelligent, blue-

3. I.e., four hundred pounds.

eyed face, and thought: Why is it I can't tell him? Why not? And she said: "I need to be alone more than I am."

At which he swung his slow blue gaze at her, and she saw what she had been dreading: Incredulity. Disbelief. And fear. An incredulous blue stare from a stranger who was her husband, as close to her as her own breath.

He said: "But the children are at school and off your hands."

She said to herself: I've got to force myself to say: Yes, but do you realize that I never feel free? There's never a moment I can say to myself: There's nothing I have to remind myself about, nothing I have to do in half an hour, or an hour, or two hours. . . .

But she said: "I don't feel well."

He said: "Perhaps you need a holiday."

She said, appalled: "But not without you, surely?" For she could not imagine herself going off without him. Yet that was what he meant. Seeing her face, he laughed, and opened his arms, and she went into them, thinking: Yes, yes, but why can't I say it? And what is it I have to say?

She tried to tell him, about never being free. And he listened and said: "But Susan, what sort of freedom can you possibly want—short of being dead! Am I ever free? I go to the office, and I have to be there at ten—all right, half past ten, sometimes. And I have to do this or that, don't I? Then I've got to come home at a certain time—I don't mean it, you know I don't—but if I'm not going to be back home at six I telephone you. When can I ever say to myself: I have nothing to be responsible for in the next six hours?"

Susan, hearing this, was remorseful. Because it was true. The good marriage, the house, the children, depended just as much on his voluntary bondage as it did on hers. But why did he not feel bound? Why didn't he chafe and become restless? No, there was something really wrong with her and this proved it.

And that word "bondage"—why had she used it? She had never felt marriage, or the children, as bondage. Neither had he, or surely they wouldn't be together lying in each other's arms content after twelve years of marriage.

No, her state (whatever it was) was irrelevant, nothing to do with her real good life with her family. She had to accept the fact that, after all, she was an irrational person and to live with it. Some people had to live with crippled arms, or stammers, or being deaf. She would have to live knowing she was subject to a state of mind she could not own.

Nevertheless, as a result of this conversation with her husband, there was a new regime next holidays.

The spare room at the top of the house now had a cardboard sign saying: PRIVATE! DO NOT DISTURB! on it. (This sign had been drawn in coloured chalks by the children, after a discussion between the parents in which it was decided this was psychologically the right thing.) The family and Mrs. Parkes knew this was "Mother's Room" and that she was entitled to her privacy. Many serious conversations took place between Matthew and the children about not taking Mother for granted. Susan overheard the first, between father and Harry, the older boy, and was surprised at her irritation over it. Surely she could have a room somewhere in that big house and retire into it without such a fuss being made? Without it being so solemnly discussed? Why couldn't she simply have announced: "I'm going to fit out the little top room for myself, and when I'm in it I'm not to be disturbed for anything short of fire"? Just that, and finished; instead of long earnest discussions. When she heard Harry and Matthew explaining it to the twins with Mrs. Parkes coming in—"Yes, well, a family sometimes gets on top of a woman"—she had to go right away to the bottom of the garden until the devils of exasperation had finished their dance in her blood.

But now there was a room, and she could go there when she liked, she used it seldom: she felt even more caged there than in her bedroom. One day she had gone up there after a lunch for ten children she had cooked and served because Mrs. Parkes was not there, and had sat alone for a while looking into the garden. She saw the children stream out from the kitchen and stand looking up at the window where she sat behind the curtains. They were all—her children and their friends—discussing Mother's Room. A few minutes later, the chase of children in some game came pounding up the stairs, but ended as abruptly as if they had fallen over a ravine, so sudden was the silence. They had remembered she was there, and had gone silent in a great gale of "Hush! Shhhhhh! Quiet, you'll disturb her. . . . " And they went tiptoeing downstairs like criminal conspirators. When she came down to make tea for them, they all apologised. The twins put their arms around her, from front and back, making a human cage of loving limbs, and promised it would never occur again. "We forgot, Mummy, we forgot all about it!"

What it amounted to was that Mother's Room, and her need for privacy, had become a valuable lesson in respect for other people's rights. Quite soon Susan was going up to the room only because it was a lesson it was a pity to drop. Then she took sewing up there, and the children and Mrs. Parkes came in and out: it had become another family room.

She sighed, and smiled, and resigned herself—she made jokes at her own expense with Matthew over the room. That is, she did from the self she liked, she respected. But at the same time, something inside her howled with impatience, with rage. . . . And she was frightened. One day she found herself kneeling by her bed and praying: "Dear God, keep it away from me, keep him away from me." She meant the devil, for she now thought of it, not caring if she was irrational, as some sort of demon. She imagined him, or it, as a youngish man, or perhaps a middleaged man pretending to be young. Or a man young-looking from immaturity? At any rate, she saw the young-looking face which, when she drew closer, had dry lines about mouth and eyes. He was thinnish, meagre in build. And he had a reddish complexion, and ginger hair. That was he—a gingery, energetic man, and he wore a reddish hairy jacket, unpleasant to the touch.

Well, one day she saw him. She was standing at the bottom of the garden, watching the river ebb past, when she raised her eyes and saw this person, or being, sitting on the white stone bench. He was looking at her, and grinning. In his hand was a long crooked stick, which he had picked off the ground, or broken off the tree above him. He was absent-mindedly, out of an absent-minded or freakish impulse of spite, using the stick to stir around in the coils of a blindworm or a grass snake (or some kind of snakelike creature: it was whitish and unhealthy to look at, unpleasant). The snake was twisting about, flinging its coils from side to side in a kind of dance of protest against the teasing prodding stick.

Susan looked at him thinking: Who is the stranger? What is he doing in our garden? Then she recognised the man around whom her terrors had crystallised. As she did so, he vanished. She made herself walk over to the bench. A shadow from a branch lay across thin emerald grass, moving jerkily over its roughness, and she could see why she had taken it for a snake, lashing and twisting. She went back to the house thinking: Right, then, so I've seen him with my own eyes, so I'm not crazy after all—there *is* a danger because I've seen him. He is lurking in the garden and sometimes even in the house, and he wants to *get into me and to take me over*.

She dreamed of having a room or a place, anywhere, where she could go and sit, by herself, no one knowing where she was.

Once, near Victoria,[4] she found herself outside a news agent that had Rooms to Let advertised. She decided to rent a room, telling no one. Sometimes she could take the train into Richmond and sit alone in it for an hour or two. Yet how could she? A room would cost three or four pounds a week, and she earned no money, and how could she explain to Matthew that she needed such a sum? What for? It did not occur to her that she was taking it for granted she wasn't going to tell him about the room.

Well, it was out of the question, having a room; yet she knew she must.

One day, when a school term was well established, and none of the children had measles or other ailments, and everything seemed in order, she did the shopping early, explained to Mrs. Parkes she was meeting an old school friend, took the train to Victoria, searched until she found a small quiet hotel, and asked for a room for the day. They did not let rooms by the day, the manageress said, looking doubtful, since Susan so obviously was not the kind of woman who needed a room for unrespectable reasons. Susan made a long explanation about not being well, being unable to shop without frequent rests for lying down. At last she was allowed to rent the room provided she paid a full night's price for it. She was taken up by the manageress and a maid, both concerned over the state of her health . . . which must be pretty bad if, living at Richmond (she had signed her name and address in the register), she needed a shelter at Victoria.

The room was ordinary and anonymous, and was just what Susan needed. She put a shilling in the gas fire, and sat, eyes shut, in a dingy armchair with her back to a dingy window. She was alone. She was alone. She was alone. She could feel pressures lifting off her. First the sounds of traffic came very loud; then they seemed to vanish; she might even have slept a little. A knock on the door: it was Miss Townsend, the manageress, bringing her a cup of tea with her own hands, so concerned was she over Susan's long silence and possible illness.

Miss Townsend was a lonely woman of fifty, running this hotel with all the rectitude expected of her, and she sensed in Susan the possibility of under-

4. One of the main railway stations in central London.

standing companionship. She stayed to talk. Susan found herself in the middle of a fantastic story about her illness, which got more and more improbable as she tried to make it tally with the large house at Richmond, well-off husband, and four children. Suppose she said instead: Miss Townsend, I'm here in your hotel because I need to be alone for a few hours, above all *alone and with no one knowing where I am.* She said it mentally, and saw, mentally, the look that would inevitably come on Miss Townsend's elderly maiden's face. "Miss Townsend, my four children and my husband are driving me insane, do you understand that? Yes, I can see from the gleam of hysteria in your eyes that comes from loneliness controlled but only just contained that I've got everything in the world you've ever longed for. Well, Miss Townsend, I don't want any of it. You can have it, Miss Townsend. I wish I was absolutely alone in the world, like you. Miss Townsend, I'm besieged by seven devils, Miss Townsend, Miss Townsend, let me stay here in your hotel where the devils can't get me. . . ." Instead of saying all this, she described her anaemia, agreed to try Miss Townsend's remedy for it, which was raw liver, minced, between whole-meal bread, and said yes, perhaps it would be better if she stayed at home and let a friend do shopping for her. She paid her bill and left the hotel, defeated.

At home Mrs. Parkes said she didn't really like it, no, not really, when Mrs. Rawlings was away from nine in the morning until five. The teacher had telephoned from school to say Joan's teeth were paining her, and she hadn't known what to say; and what was she to make for the children's tea, Mrs. Rawlings hadn't said.

All this was nonsense, of course. Mrs. Parkes's complaint was that Susan had withdrawn herself spiritually, leaving the burden of the big house on her.

Susan looked back at her day of "freedom" which had resulted in her becoming a friend of the lonely Miss Townsend, and in Mrs. Parkes's remonstrances. Yet she remembered the short blissful hour of being alone, really alone. She was determined to arrange her life, no matter what it cost, so that she could have that solitude more often. An absolute solitude, where no one knew her or cared about her.

But how? She thought of saying to her old employer: I want you to back me up in a story with Matthew that I am doing part-time work for you. The truth is that . . . But she would have to tell him a lie too, and which lie? She could not say: I want to sit by myself three or four times a week in a rented room. And besides, he knew Matthew, and she could not really ask him to tell lies on her behalf, apart from being bound to think it meant a lover.

Suppose she really took a part-time job, which she could get through fast and efficiently, leaving time for herself. What job? Addressing envelopes? Canvassing?

And there was Mrs. Parkes, working widow, who knew exactly what she was prepared to give to the house, who knew by instinct when her mistress withdrew in spirit from her responsibilities. Mrs. Parkes was one of the servers of this world, but she needed someone to serve. She had to have Mrs. Rawlings, her madam, at the top of the house or in the garden, so that she could come and get support from her: "Yes, the bread's not what it was when I was a girl. . . . Yes, Harry's got a wonderful appetite, I wonder where he puts it all. . . .

Yes, it's lucky the twins are so much of a size, they can wear each other's shoes, that's a saving in these hard times. . . . Yes, the cherry jam from Switzerland is not a patch on the jam from Poland, and three times the price . . ." And so on. That sort of talk Mrs. Parkes must have, every day, or she would leave, not knowing herself why she left.

Susan Rawlings, thinking these thoughts, found that she was prowling through the great thicketed garden like a wild cat: she was walking up the stairs, down the stairs, through the rooms into the garden, along the brown running river, back, up through the house, down again. . . . It was a wonder Mrs. Parkes did not think it strange. But, on the contrary, Mrs. Rawlings could do what she liked, she could stand on her head if she wanted, provided she was *there*. Susan Rawlings prowled and muttered through her house, hating Mrs. Parkes, hating poor Miss Townsend, dreaming of her hour of solitude in the dingy respectability of Miss Townsend's hotel bedroom, and she knew quite well she was mad. Yes, she was mad.

She said to Matthew that she must have a holiday. Matthew agreed with her. This was not as things had been once—how they had talked in each other's arms in the marriage bed. He had, she knew, diagnosed her finally as *unreasonable.* She had become someone outside himself that he had to manage. They were living side by side in this house like two tolerably friendly strangers.

Having told Mrs. Parkes—or rather, asked for her permission—she went off on a walking holiday in Wales. She chose the remotest place she knew of. Every morning the children telephoned her before they went off to school, to encourage and support her, just as they had over Mother's Room. Every evening she telephoned them, spoke to each child in turn, and then to Matthew. Mrs. Parkes, given permission to telephone for instructions or advice, did so every day at lunchtime. When, as happened three times, Mrs. Rawlings was out on the mountainside, Mrs. Parkes asked that she should ring back at such-and-such a time, for she would not be happy in what she was doing without Mrs. Rawlings' blessing.

Susan prowled over wild country with the telephone wire holding her to her duty like a leash. The next time she must telephone, or wait to be telephoned, nailed her to her cross. The mountains themselves seemed trammelled by her unfreedom. Everywhere on the mountains, where she met no one at all, from breakfast time to dusk, excepting sheep, or a shepherd, she came face to face with her own craziness, which might attack her in the broadest valleys, so that they seemed too small, or on a mountaintop from which she could see a hundred other mountains and valleys, so that they seemed too low, too small, with the sky pressing down too close. She would stand gazing at a hillside brilliant with ferns and bracken, jewelled with running water, and see nothing but her devil, who lifted inhuman eyes at her from where he leaned negligently on a rock, switching at his ugly yellow boots with a leafy twig.

She returned to her home and family, with the Welsh emptiness at the back of her mind like a promise of freedom.

She told her husband she wanted to have an *au pair* girl.[5]

5. Young woman, usually foreign, who lives in with a family, doing housework and baby-sitting in exchange for room and board (French).

They were in their bedroom, it was late at night, the children slept. He sat, shirted and slippered, in a chair by the window, looking out. She sat brushing her hair and watching him in the mirror. A time-hallowed scene in the connubial bedroom. He said nothing, while she heard the arguments coming into his mind, only to be rejected because every one was *reasonable*.

"It seems strange to get one now; after all, the children are in school most of the day. Surely the time for you to have help was when you were stuck with them day and night. Why don't you ask Mrs. Parkes to cook for you? She's even offered to—I can understand if you are tired of cooking for six people. But you know that an *au pair* girl means all kinds of problems, it's not like having an ordinary char in during the day. . . ."

Finally he said carefully: "Are you thinking of going back to work?"

"No," she said, "no, not really," She made herself sound vague, rather stupid. She went on brushing her black hair and peering at herself so as to be oblivious of the short uneasy glances her Matthew kept giving her. "Do you think we can't afford it?" she went on vaguely, not at all the old efficient Susan who knew exactly what they could afford.

"It's not that," he said, looking out of the window at dark trees, so as not to look at her. Meanwhile she examined a round, candid, pleasant face with clear dark brows and clear grey eyes. A sensible face. She brushed thick healthy black hair and thought: Yet that's the reflection of a madwoman. How very strange! Much more to the point if what looked back at me was the gingery green-eyed demon with his dry meagre smile. . . . Why wasn't Matthew agreeing? After all, what else could he do? She was breaking her part of the bargain and there was no way of forcing her to keep it: that her spirit, her soul, should live in this house, so that the people in it could grow like plants in water, and Mrs. Parkes remain content in their service. In return for this, he would be a good loving husband, and responsible towards the children. Well, nothing like this had been true of either of them for a long time. He did his duty, perfunctorily; she did not even pretend to do hers. And he had become like other husbands, with his real life in his work and the people he met there, and very likely a serious affair. All this was her fault.

At last he drew heavy curtains, blotting out the trees, and turned to force her attention: "Susan, are you really sure we need a girl?" But she would not meet his appeal at all. She was running the brush over her hair again and again, lifting fine black clouds in a small hiss of electricity. She was peering in and smiling as if she were amused at the clinging hissing hair that followed the brush.

"Yes, I think it would be a good idea, on the whole," she said, with the cunning of a madwoman evading the real point.

In the mirror she could see her Matthew lying on his back, his hands behind his head, staring upwards, his face sad and hard. She felt her heart (the old heart of Susan Rawlings) soften and call out to him. But she set it to be indifferent.

He said: "Susan, the children?" It was an appeal that *almost* reached her. He opened his arms, lifting them palms up, empty. She had only to run across and fling herself into them, onto his hard, warm chest, and melt into herself, into Susan. But she could not. She would not see his lifted arms. She said vaguely: "Well, surely it'll be even better for them? We'll get a French or a German girl and they'll learn the language."

In the dark she lay beside him, feeling frozen, a stranger. She felt as if Susan had been spirited away. She disliked very much this woman who lay here, cold and indifferent beside a suffering man, but she could not change her.

Next morning she set about getting a girl, and very soon came Sophie Traub from Hamburg, a girl of twenty, laughing, healthy, blue-eyed, intending to learn English. Indeed, she already spoke a good deal. In return for a room—"Mother's Room"—and her food, she undertook to do some light cooking, and to be with the children when Mrs. Rawlings asked. She was an intelligent girl and understood perfectly what was needed. Susan said: "I go off sometimes, for the morning or for the day—well, sometimes the children run home from school, or they ring up, or a teacher rings up. I should be here, really. And there's the daily woman. . . ." And Sophie laughed her deep fruity *Fräulein*'s laugh, showed her fine white teeth and her dimples, and said: "You want some person to play mistress of the house sometimes, not so?"

"Yes, that is just so," said Susan, a bit dry, despite herself, thinking in secret fear how easy it was, how much nearer to the end she was than she thought. Healthy Fräulein Traub's instant understanding of their position proved this to be true.

The *au pair* girl, because of her own commonsense, or (as Susan said to herself, with her new inward shudder) because she had been *chosen* so well by Susan, was a success with everyone, the children liking her, Mrs. Parkes forgetting almost at once that she was German, and Matthew finding her "nice to have around the house." For he was now taking things as they came, from the surface of life, withdrawn both as a husband and a father from the household.

One day Susan saw how Sophie and Mrs. Parkes were talking and laughing in the kitchen, and she announced that she would be away until tea time. She knew exactly where to go and what she must look for. She took the District Line to South Kensington, changed to the Circle, got off at Paddington,[6] and walked around looking at the smaller hotels until she was satisfied with one which had FRED'S HOTEL painted on windowpanes that needed cleaning. The facade was a faded shiny yellow, like unhealthy skin. A door at the end of a passage said she must knock; she did, and Fred appeared. He was not at all attractive, not in any way, being fattish, and run-down, and wearing a tasteless striped suit. He had small sharp eyes in a white creased face, and was quite prepared to let Mrs. Jones (she chose the farcical name deliberately, staring him out) have a room three days a week from ten until six. Provided of course that she paid in advance each time she came? Susan produced fifteen shillings (no price had been set by him) and held it out, still fixing him with a bold unblinking challenge she had not known until then she could use at will. Looking at her still, he took up a ten-shilling note from her palm between thumb and forefinger, fingered it; then shuffled up two half-crowns,[7] held out his own palm with these bits of money displayed thereon, and let his gaze lower brood-

6. Railway and subway station in London. The Circle is the Circle Line of the subway. 7. Coins worth five shillings each.

ingly at them. They were standing in the passage, a red-shaded light above, bare boards beneath, and a strong smell of floor polish rising about them. He shot his gaze up at her over the still-extended palm, and smiled as if to say: What do you take me for? "I shan't," said Susan, "be using this room for the purposes of making money." He still waited. She added another five shillings, at which he nodded and said: "You pay, and I ask no questions." "Good," said Susan. He now went past her to the stairs, and there waited a moment: the light from the street door being in her eyes, she lost sight of him momentarily. Then she saw a sober-suited, white-faced, white-balding little man trotting up the stairs like a waiter, and she went after him. They proceeded in utter silence up the stairs of this house where no questions were asked—Fred's Hotel, which could afford the freedom for its visitors that poor Miss Townsend's hotel could not. The room was hideous. It had a single window, with thin green brocade curtains, a three-quarter bed that had a cheap green satin bedspread on it, a fireplace with a gas fire and a shilling meter by it, a chest of drawers, and a green wicker armchair.

"Thank you," said Susan, knowing that Fred (if this was Fred, and not George, or Herbert or Charlie) was looking at her, not so much with curiosity, an emotion he would not own to, for professional reasons, but with a philosophical sense of what was appropriate. Having taken her money and shown her up and agreed to everything, he was clearly disapproving of her for coming here. She did not belong here at all, so his look said. (But she knew, already, how very much she did belong: the room had been waiting for her to join it.) "Would you have me called at five o'clock, please?" and he nodded and went downstairs.

It was twelve in the morning. She was free. She sat in the armchair, she simply sat, she closed her eyes and sat and let herself be alone. She was alone and no one knew where she was. When a knock came on the door she was annoyed, and prepared to show it: but it was Fred himself, it was five o'clock and he was calling her as ordered. He flicked his sharp little eyes over the room—bed, first. It was undisturbed. She might never have been in the room at all. She thanked him, said she would be returning the day after tomorrow, and left. She was back home in time to cook supper, to put the children to bed, to cook a second supper for her husband and herself later. And to welcome Sophie back from the pictures where she had gone with a friend. All these things she did cheerfully, willingly. But she was thinking all the time of the hotel room; she was longing for it with her whole being.

Three times a week. She arrived promptly at ten, looked Fred in the eyes, gave him twenty shillings, followed him up the stairs, went into the room, and shut the door on him with gentle firmness. For Fred, disapproving of her being here at all, was quite ready to let friendship, or at least acquaintanceship, follow his disapproval, if only she would let him. But he was content to go off on her dismissing nod, with the twenty shillings in his hand.

She sat in the armchair and shut her eyes.

What did she *do* in the room? Why, nothing at all. From the chair, when it had rested her, she went to the window, stretching her arms, smiling, treasuring her anonymity, to look out. She was no longer Susan Rawlings, mother of four, wife of Matthew, employer of Mrs. Parkes and of Sophie Traub, with these and those relations with friends, school-teachers, tradesmen. She no longer was mistress of the big white house and garden, owning clothes suitable for this and that activity or occasion. She was Mrs. Jones, and she was alone, and she had no past and no future. Here I am, she thought, after all these years of being married and having children and playing those roles of responsibility—and I'm just the same. Yet there have been times I thought that nothing existed of me except the roles that went with being Mrs. Matthew Rawlings. Yes, here I am, and if I never saw any of my family again, here I would still be . . . how very strange that is! And she leaned on the sill, and looked into the street, loving the men and women who passed, because she did not know them. She looked at the downtrodden buildings over the street, and at the sky, wet and dingy, or sometimes blue, and she felt she had never seen buildings or sky before. And then she went back to the chair, empty, her mind a blank. Sometimes she talked aloud, saying nothing—an exclamation, meaningless, followed by a comment about the floral pattern on the thin rug, or a stain on the green satin coverlet. For the most part, she wool-gathered—what word is there for it?—brooded, wandered, simply went dark, feeling emptiness run deliciously through her veins like the movement of her blood.

This room had become more her own than the house she lived in. One morning she found Fred taking her a flight higher than usual. She stopped, refusing to go up, and demanded her usual room, Number 19. "Well, you'll have to wait half an hour, then," he said. Willingly she descended to the dark disinfectant-smelling hall, and sat waiting until the two, man and woman, came down the stairs, giving her swift indifferent glances before they hurried out into the street, separating at the door. She went up to the room, *her* room, which they had just vacated. It was no less hers, though the windows were set wide open, and a maid was straightening the bed as she came in.

After these days of solitude, it was both easy to play her part as mother and wife, and difficult—because it was so easy: she felt an impostor. She felt as if her shell moved here, with her family, answering to Mummy, Mother, Susan, Mrs. Rawlings. She was surprised no one saw through her, that she wasn't turned out of doors, as a fake. On the contrary, it seemed the children loved her more; Matthew and she "got on" pleasantly, and Mrs. Parkes was happy in her work under (for the most part, it must be confessed) Sophie Traub. At night she lay beside her husband, and they made love again, apparently just as they used to, when they were really married. But she, Susan, or the being who answered so readily and improbably to the name of Susan, was not there: she was in Fred's Hotel, in Paddington, waiting for the easing hours of solitude to begin.

Soon she made a new arrangement with Fred and with Sophie. It was for five days a week. As for the money, five pounds, she simply asked Matthew for it. She saw that she was not even frightened he might ask what for: he would give it to her, she knew that, and yet it was terrifying it could be so, for this close couple, these partners, had once known the destination of every shilling they must spend. He agreed to give her five pounds a week. She asked for just so much, not a penny more. He sounded indifferent about it. It was as if he were paying her, she thought: *paying her off*—yes, that was it. Terror came back for a moment when she understood this, but she stilled it: things had gone too far for that. Now, every week, on Sunday nights, he gave her five pounds, turning away from her before their eyes could meet on the transaction. As for Sophie Traub, she was to be somewhere in or near the house until six at night, after which she was free. She was not to cook, or to clean; she was simply to be there. So she gardened or sewed, and asked friends in, being a person who was bound to have a lot of friends. If the children were sick, she nursed them. If teachers telephoned, she answered them sensibly. For the five daytimes in the school week, she was altogether the mistress of the house.

One night in the bedroom, Matthew asked: "Susan, I don't want to interfere—don't think that, please—but are you sure you are well?"

She was brushing her hair at the mirror. She made two more strokes on either side of her head, before she replied: "Yes, dear, I am sure I am well."

He was again lying on his back, his blond head on his hands, his elbows angled up and part-concealing his face. He said: "Then Susan, I have to ask you this question, though you must understand, I'm not putting any sort of pressure on you." (Susan heard the word "pressure" with dismay, because this was inevitable; of course she could not go on like this.) "Are things going to go on like this?"

"Well," she said, going vague and bright and idiotic again, so as to escape: "Well, I don't see why not."

He was jerking his elbows up and down, in annoyance or in pain, and, looking at him, she saw he had got thin, even gaunt; and restless angry movements were not what she remembered of him. He said: "Do you want a divorce, is that it?"

At this, Susan only with the greatest difficulty stopped herself from laughing: she could hear the bright bubbling laughter she *would* have emitted, had she let herself. He could only mean one thing: she had a lover, and that was why she spent her days in London, as lost to him as if she had vanished to another continent.

Then the small panic set in again: she understood that he hoped she did have a lover, he was begging her to say so, because otherwise it would be too terrifying.

She thought this out as she brushed her hair, watching the fine black stuff fly up to make its little clouds of electricity, hiss, hiss, hiss. Behind her head, across the room, was a blue wall. She realised she was absorbed in watching the black hair making shapes against the blue. She should be answering him. "Do *you* want a divorce, Matthew?"

He said: "That surely isn't the point, is it?"

"You brought it up, I didn't," she said, brightly, suppressing meaningless tinkling laughter.

Next day she asked Fred: "Have enquiries been made for me?"

He hesitated, and she said: "I've been coming here a year now. I've made no trouble, and you've been paid every day. I have a right to be told."

"As a matter of fact, Mrs. Jones, a man did come asking."

"A man from a detective agency?"

"Well, he could have been, couldn't he?"

"I was asking you. . . . Well, what did you tell him?"

"I told him a Mrs. Jones came every weekday from ten until five or six and stayed in Number 19 by herself."

"Describing me?"

"Well, Mrs. Jones, I had no alternative. Put yourself in my place."

"By rights I should deduct what that man gave you for the information."

He raised shocked eyes: she was not the sort of person to make jokes like this! Then he chose to laugh: a pinkish wet slit appeared across his white crinkled face; his eyes positively begged her to laugh, otherwise he might lose some money. She remained grave, looking at him.

He stopped laughing and said: "You want to go up now?"—returning to the familiarity, the comradeship, of the country where no questions are asked, on which (and he knew it) she depended completely.

She went up to sit in her wicker chair. But it was not the same. Her husband had searched her out. (The world had searched her out.) The pressures were on her. She was here with his connivance. He might walk in at any moment, here, into Room 19. She imagined the report from the detective agency: "A woman calling herself Mrs. Jones, fitting the description of your wife (et cetera, et cetera, et cetera), stays alone all day in Room No. 19. She insists on this room, waits for it if it is engaged. As far as the proprietor knows, she receives no visitors there, male or female." A report something on these lines Matthew must have received.

Well, of course he was right: things couldn't go on like this. He had put an end to it all simply by sending the detective after her.

She tried to shrink herself back into the shelter of the room, a snail pecked out of its shell and trying to squirm back. But the peace of the room had gone. She was trying consciously to revive it, trying to let go into the dark creative trance (or whatever it was) that she had found there. It was no use, yet she craved for it, she was as ill as a suddenly deprived addict.

Several times she returned to the room, to look for herself there, but instead she found the unnamed spirit of restlessness, a pricking fevered hunger for movement, an irritable self-consciousness that made her brain feel as if it had coloured lights going on and off inside it. Instead of the soft dark that had been the room's air, were now waiting for her demons that made her dash blindly about, muttering words of hate; she was impelling herself from point to point like a moth dashing itself against a windowpane, sliding to the bottom, fluttering off on broken wings, then crashing into the invisible barrier again. And again and again. Soon she was exhausted, and she told Fred that for a while she would not be needing the room, she was going on holiday. Home she went, to the big white house by the river. The middle of a weekday, and she felt guilty at returning to her own home when not expected. She stood unseen, looking in at the kitchen window. Mrs. Parkes, wearing a discarded floral overall of Susan's, was stooping to slide something into the oven. Sophie, arms folded, was leaning her back against a cupboard and laughing at some joke made by a girl not seen before by Susan—a dark foreign girl, Sophie's visitor. In an armchair Molly, one of the twins, lay curled, sucking her thumb and watching the grownups. She must have some sickness, to be kept from school. The child's listless face, the dark circles under her eyes, hurt Susan: Molly was looking at the three grownups working and talking in exactly the same way Susan looked at the four through the kitchen window: she was remote, shut off from them.

But then, just as Susan imagined herself going in, picking up the little girl, and sitting in an armchair with her, stroking her probably heated forehead, Sophie did just that: she had been standing on one leg, the other knee flexed, its foot set against the wall. Now she let her foot in its ribbon-tied red shoe slide down the wall, stood solid on two feet, clapping her hands before and behind her, and sang a couple of lines in German, so that the child lifted her heavy eyes at her and began to smile. Then she walked, or rather skipped, over to the child, swung her up, and let her fall into her lap at the same moment she sat herself. She said "Hopla! Hopla! Molly . . . " and began stroking the dark untidy young head that Molly laid on her shoulder for comfort.

*Well.* . . . Susan blinked the tears of farewell out of her eyes, and went quietly up through the house to her bedroom. There she sat looking at the river through the trees. She felt at peace, but in a way that was new to her. She had no desire to move, to talk, to do anything at all. The devils that had haunted the house, the garden, were not there; but she knew it was because her soul was in Room 19 in Fred's Hotel; she was not really here at all. It was a sensation that should have been frightening: to sit at her own bedroom window, listening to Sophie's rich young voice sing German nursery songs to her child, listening to Mrs. Parkes clatter and move below, and to know that all this had nothing to do with her: she was already out of it.

Later, she made herself go down and say she was home: it was unfair to be here unannounced. She took lunch with Mrs. Parkes, Sophie, Sophie's Italian friend Maria, and her daughter Molly, and felt like a visitor.

A few days later, at bedtime, Matthew said: "Here's your five pounds," and pushed them over at her. Yet he must have known she had not been leaving the house at all.

She shook her head, gave it back to him, and said, in explanation, not in accusation: "As soon as you knew where I was, there was no point."

He nodded, not looking at her. He was turned away from her: thinking, she knew, how best to handle this wife who terrified him.

He said: "I wasn't trying to . . . It's just that I was worried."

"Yes, I know."

"I must confess that I was beginning to wonder . . ."

"You thought I had a lover?"

"Yes, I am afraid I did."

She knew that he wished she had. She sat wondering how to say. "For a year now I've been spending all my days in a very sordid hotel room. It's the place where I'm happy. In fact, without it I don't exist." She heard herself saying this, and understood how terrified he was that she might. So instead she said: "Well, perhaps you're not far wrong."

Probably Matthew would think the hotel proprietor lied: he would want to think so.

"Well," he said, and she could hear his voice spring up, so to speak, with relief, "in that case I must confess I've got a bit of an affair on myself."

She said, detached and interested: "Really? Who is she?" and saw Matthew's startled look because of this reaction.

"It's Phil. Phil Hunt."

She had known Phil Hunt well in the old unmarried days. She was thinking: No, she won't do, she's too neurotic and difficult. She's never been happy yet. Sophie's much better. Well, Matthew will see that himself, as sensible as he is.

This line of thought went on in silence, while she said aloud: "It's no point in telling you about mine, because you don't know him."

Quick, quick, invent, she thought. Remember how you invented all that nonsense for Miss Townsend.

She began slowly, careful not to contradict herself: "His name is Michael" *(Michael What?)*—"Michael Plant." (What a silly name!) "He's rather like you—in looks, I mean." And indeed, she could imagine herself being touched by no one but Matthew himself. "He's a publisher." (Really? Why?) "He's got a wife already and two children."

She brought out this fantasy, proud of herself.

Matthew said: "Are you two thinking of marrying?"

She said, before she could stop herself: "Good God, *no!*"

She realised, if Matthew wanted to marry Phil Hunt, that this was too emphatic, but apparently it was all right, for his voice sounded relieved as he said: "It is a bit impossible to imagine oneself married to anyone else, isn't it?" With which he pulled her to him, so that her head lay on his shoulder. She turned her face into the dark of his flesh, and listened to the blood pounding through her ears saying: I am alone, I am alone, I am alone.

In the morning Susan lay in bed while he dressed.

He had been thinking things out in the night, because now he said: "Susan, why don't we make a foursome?"

Of course, she said to herself, of course he would be bound to say that. If one is sensible, if one is reasonable, if one never allows oneself a base thought or an envious emotion, naturally one says: Let's make a foursome!

"Why not?" she said.

"We could all meet for lunch. I mean, it's ridiculous, you sneaking off to filthy hotels, and me staying late at the office, and all the lies everyone has to tell."

What on earth did I say his name was?—she panicked, then said: "I think it's a good idea, but Michael is away at the moment. When he comes back, though—and I'm sure you two would like each other."

"He's away, is he? So that's why you've been . . ." Her husband put his hand to the knot of his tie in a gesture of male coquetry she would not before have associated with him; and he bent to kiss her cheek with the expression that goes with the words: Oh you naughty little puss! And she felt its answering look, naughty and coy, come onto her face.

Inside she was dissolving in horror at them both, at how far they had both sunk from honesty of emotion.

So now she was saddled with a lover, and he had a mistress! How ordinary, how reassuring, how jolly! And now they would make a foursome of it, and go about to theatres and restaurants. After all, the Rawlings could well afford that sort of thing, and presumably the publisher Michael Plant could afford to do himself and his mistress quite well. No, there was nothing to stop the four of them developing the most intricate relationship of civilised tolerance, all enveloped in a charming afterglow of autumnal passion. Perhaps they would all go off on holidays together? She had known people who did. Or perhaps Matthew would draw the line there? Why should he, though, if he was capable of talking about "foursomes" at all?

She lay in the empty bedroom, listening to the car drive off with Matthew in it, off to work. Then she heard the children clattering off to school to the accompaniment of Sophie's cheerfully ringing voice. She slid down into the hollow of the bed, for shelter against her own irrelevance. And she stretched out her hand to the hollow where her husband's body had lain, but found no comfort there: he was not her husband. She curled herself up in a small tight ball under the clothes: she could stay here all day, all week, indeed, all her life.

But in a few days she must produce Michael Plant, and—but how? She must presumably find some agreeable man prepared to impersonate a publisher called Michael Plant. And in return for which she would—what? Well, for one thing they would make love. The idea made her want to cry with sheer exhaustion. Oh no, she had finished with all that—the proof of it was that the words "make love," or even imagining it, trying hard to revive no more than the pleasures of sensuality, let alone affection, or love, made her want to run away and hide from the sheer effort of the thing. . . . Good Lord, why make love at all? Why make love with anyone? Or if you are going to make love, what does it matter who with? Why shouldn't she simply walk into the street, pick up a man and have a roaring sexual affair with him? Why not? Or even with Fred? What difference did it make?

But she had let herself in for it—an interminable stretch of time with a lover, called Michael, as part of a gallant civilised foursome. Well, she could not, and she would not.

She got up, dressed, went down to find Mrs. Parkes, and asked her for the loan of a pound, since Matthew, she said, had forgotten to leave her money. She exchanged with Mrs. Parkes variations on the theme that husbands are all the same, they don't think, and without saying a word to Sophie, whose voice could be heard upstairs from the telephone, walked to the underground, travelled to South Kensington, changed to the Inner Circle, got out at Paddington, and walked to Fred's Hotel. There she told Fred that she wasn't going on holiday after all, she needed the room. She would have to wait an hour, Fred said. She went to a busy tearoom-cum-restaurant around the corner, and sat watching the people flow in and out the door that kept swinging open and shut, watched them mingle and merge, and separate, felt her being flow into them, into their movement. When the hour was up, she left a half-crown for her pot of tea, and left the place without looking back at it, just as she had left her house, the big, beautiful white house, without another look, but silently dedicating it to Sophie. She returned to Fred, received the key of Number 19, now free, and ascended the grimy stairs slowly, letting floor after floor fall away below her, keeping her eyes lifted, so that floor after floor descended jerkily to her level of vision, and fell away out of sight.

Number 19 was the same. She saw everything with an acute, narrow, checking glance: the cheap shine of the satin spread, which had been replaced carelessly after the two bodies had finished their convulsions under it; a trace of powder on the glass that topped the chest of drawers; an intense green shade in a fold of the curtain. She stood at the window, looking down, watching people pass and pass and pass until her mind went dark from the constant movement. Then she sat in the wicker chair, letting herself go slack. But she had to be careful, because she did not want, today, to be surprised by Fred's knock at five o'clock.

The demons were not here. They had gone forever, because she was buying her freedom from them. She was slipping already into the dark fructifying dream that seemed to caress her inwardly, like the movement of her blood . . . but she had to think about Matthew first. Should she write a letter for the coroner? But what should she say? She would like to leave him with the look on his face she had seen this morning—banal, admittedly, but at least confidently healthy. Well, that was impossible, one did not look like that with a wife dead from suicide. But how to leave him believing she was dying because of a man—because of the fascinating publisher Michael Plant? Oh, how ridiculous! How absurd! How humiliating! But she decided not to trouble about it, simply not to think about the living. If he wanted to believe she had a lover, he would believe it. And he *did* want to believe it. Even when he had found out that there was no publisher in London called Michael Plant, he would think: Oh poor Susan, she was afraid to give me his real name.

And what did it matter whether he married Phil Hunt or Sophie? Though it ought to be Sophie, who was already the mother of those children . . . and what hypocrisy to sit here worrying about the children, when she was going to leave them because she had not got the energy to stay.

She had about four hours. She spent them delightfully, darkly, sweetly, letting herself slide gently, gently, to the edge of the river. Then, with hardly a break in her consciousness, she got up, pushed the thin rug against the door, made sure the windows were tight shut, put two shillings in the meter, and turned on the gas. For the first time since she had been in the room she lay on the hard bed that smelled stale, that smelled of sweat and sex.

She lay on her back on the green satin cover, but her legs were chilly. She got up, found a blanket folded in the bottom of the chest of drawers, and carefully covered her legs with it. She was quite content lying there, listening to the faint soft hiss of the gas that poured into the room, into her lungs, into her brain, as she drifted off into the dark river.

# John L'Heureux

*L'Heureux (1934– ) was born in South Hadley, Massachusetts, and received his education at Boston College and Harvard University. He is currently teaching at Stanford University. His works include* The Comedians *(1990),* An Honorable Profession *(1991),* The Shrine at Altamira *(1992),* The Handmaid of Desire *(1996), and* Having Everything *(1999).*

## Brief Lives in California

Leonora started out pretty and bright.

"She could be a movie star," her mother said, "but I would never do that to my child. I would never allow a child of mine to be in the limelight. I want Leonora to be just normal."

So Leonora took ballet and tap and piano.

"Perhaps she has other gifts," the dance teacher said. "Perhaps she has a gift for music."

The piano teacher was more to the point. "She has nothing," he said. "And she's driving me crazy."

"You could be a movie star," her mother said.

In junior high Leonora was one of the first to grow breasts; the other girls resented her for that. But in high school her breasts made her popular with the boys, so she didn't care about the girls. She became a cheerleader and after every game she and the other cheerleaders crowded into the booths at Dante's and waited for the team to arrive. Then they all drank Cokes and ate cheeseburgers and grabbed at one another in the booths—nothing serious, just good fun—and made out on the way home.

In November of her senior year Leonora was parked in front of her house in Chuckie's car.

"Why won't you do it?" Chuckie asked. "Everybody does."

"I don't know," she said, miserable. "I want to, but I can't. I just can't."

"Nobody saves themselves for marriage anymore. Is that what you think you're doing?"

"I think I was meant for better things," she said, not really knowing what she meant. "I mean, I get straight A's and B's."

"Ah shit," Chuckie said. "Just put your hand here. Feel this."

"No, I was meant for better things."

"But you've got to start somewhere," Chuckie said. "Hell, I'm captain of the team."

But Leonora was already getting out of the car, feeling chosen, feeling—she searched for the word—exalted. Yes, that was it. She was meant for better things.

In the admissions office at Stanford, Leonora was a floater, somebody who hadn't yet sunk to the bottom but somebody who wouldn't get picked out of the pool unless a real Stanford freshman decided to go to Yale or somewhere. That year a lot of freshmen went to Yale and so Leonora, floating almost to the end, was admitted to Stanford.

"You could be a college professor," her mother said. "Or a famous writer. You could win the Nobel Prize, maybe."

"Dry up," Leonora said. "What do you know about it? You never even went to college."

"Oh baby," she said. "Oh sweetheart, don't be mean to your mother, Leonora. I only want what's best for you. I only want you to be happy."

"Then dry up," Leonora said.

The worst part about Stanford was that they made her take freshman English. She had been among the top thirty in high school and now she was back to writing compositions. At first she had just been a little nasty to the teacher in class, to let him know how she felt about being there. But after she had written the first assigned paper, she decided to go see him and demand an explanation. He gave it to her. He explained that it was a requirement of the university that every student demonstrate a basic competence in expository writing and that she had not, in the qualifying tests, demonstrated that. And then he handed her the corrected paper.

It was covered with little red marks—diction? antecedent? obscure, no no no—and there was a large black C at the bottom of the page.

"You gave me a C," Leonora said. "I've never had a C in my life."

"There's nothing wrong with a C," he said. "It's a perfectly acceptable grade. It's average, maybe even above average."

"You gave me a C," she said and, choking on her tears, ran from his office.

Her next two papers came back with C's on them also, so she knew he was out to get her. His name was Lockhardt and he had written a couple of novels and thought he was hot shit.

Leonora went to the ombudsman and complained that she was being discriminated against. She should not have to take freshman English in the first place, and in the second place Lockhardt was guilty of unprofessional conduct in browbeating her and making her feel inferior.

The ombudsman went to the chairman of the English department who called in Lockhardt and then called in Leonora and finally checked her papers himself. The next day he told Leonora that yes, she would have to take freshman English like all the others, that the grades Professor Lockhardt had given her seemed fair enough, that he was sorry Professor Lockhardt had made her feel inferior. He told Lockhardt for God's sake go easy on the girl, she's half-crazy, and whatever you do don't be alone with her in your office. He told the ombudsman that the problem had been settled to everyone's satisfaction and there was no need to take all this to the provost. So everyone was miserable and satisfied.

Leonora's final grade was a C, all because of that bastard Lockhardt.

Patty Hearst was wrestled, struggling, into the trunk of a car in Berkeley and the next day she was headlines in all the papers. Leonora narrowed her thin eyes and thought, Why couldn't they have taken me?

In her junior year she moved in with Horst Kammer. He was clearly one of the better things that she was meant for. He was very smart and spent a lot of time with the housemaster, so that in Horst she had not only a roommate, she had instant acceptance as well. Horst was too intellectual to be much interested in sex, but he didn't mind occasional sex with Leonora and that was enough for her.

Horst dressed in army fatigues and spent a lot of his time protesting Stanford's investments in South Africa. Leonora protested along with him and they were arrested together during the spring sit-in at Old Union. Leonora felt proud to be involved in something historical, something that mattered. There were over a hundred students arrested and they were each fined nearly two hundred dollars. Leonora's mother sent the money, and with it a note saying, "You're like Vanessa Redgrave or Jane Fonda. You're doing your part."

"God, that woman is hopeless," Leonora said.

Two photographs.

One. Leonora is home from college and all the relatives have come over for dinner. Afterwards somebody snaps an Instamatic of Leonora and her mother and father, sitting on the floor in front of the Christmas tree, surrounded by gifts. The mother and father each have an arm around Leonora and they are smiling directly into the camera. Leonora is smiling too, but she is looking off to the right of the camera, as if at the very last minute she decided the picture is not what she wants; she wants something else.

"She could be a photographer's model," her mother says, examining the picture. "She could be on all the covers."

Two. Leonora has just crested the hill on Campus Drive and is about to make the long clear descent on her new ten-speed bike. She passes two professors who are taking a noon walk, looking like anybody else, just enjoying the California spring. Leonora does not notice them, does not see that one of them is Lockhardt. She sees only the long long hill before her, and she feels the warm wind blowing through her hair. She sits high on the seat, no hands, and lifts her arms straight out from the shoulders, surrendering completely to the sun and the wind and being young and pretty, with everything, every wonderful thing ahead of her.

"Look at that girl," Lockhardt says. "God, somebody should photograph that."

In her senior year, her second year with Horst, Leonora was all showered and getting ready to go to a frat party when Horst said, "Come on, let's do it." He wasn't interested in doing it that often, so she said, "I'm all ready for the party, but if you're sure you want to . . ." "I want to," he said. "I'm up for it. Look." And so he chased her from the bedroom into the living room and then back into the bedroom where she collapsed on the bed, laughing and tickling him, and they made love. "Was it wonderful?" she said. "Was it better?" "You're terrific," he said, "you're great. Where the hell is my deodorant?"

At the party everybody drank a lot of beer and tequila sunrises and after a while they got to the subject of how often you ball your roommate. When Horst's turn came, he gave a long and funny speech about the primacy of the intellect and the transitory nature of sexuality. He described the postures you get into and he made them sound new and funny, and he said the real problem is that an hour later you're still hungry for more. He had everybody with him and he was feeling really good about his performance, you could tell, and then he paused and said, anticlimactically, "Let's face it folks, what we're dealing with here is just two mucous membranes rubbing together."

Everybody laughed and applauded and spilled beer. Horst shook his head and smiled sneakily at Leonora.

But then somebody added, "They're sebaceous membranes, actually. Get your membranes straight, Horst."

Everybody laughed even louder and Leonora laughed too and Horst saw her do it.

So he was furious and, on the way home, when Leonora leaned against his side, her head on his shoulder, Horst put his hand on her breast. He felt for the nipple and when he had it firmly between his thumb and forefinger, he twisted it suddenly and violently, pressing down with his thumbnail. Leonora screamed in pain.

"You bitch," he said. "You fucking whore. Why don't you get out of my life? You're just a nothing. You're a noose around my neck."

"No," Leonora said. "No."

Patty Hearst was arrested in an apartment in San Francisco. Her picture appeared in all the papers, laughing like crazy, her fist clenched in the revolutionary salute. She listed her occupation as "urban guerrilla." Leonora was done with all that now that she was done with Horst. And who cared about Patty Hearst anyhow?

Leonora got her diploma in June, but she had to take one more course that summer before she had enough credits to officially graduate. She signed up for creative writing, taught by "staff." But staff turned out to be that bastard Lockhardt. He didn't seem to remember her, and everybody said he was a really good teacher, and she wanted to write a novel someday, so she decided to give him another chance.

Lockhardt wasn't interested in the things that interested her. She wanted to write something different, but Lockhardt kept talking about the initiating incident and the conflict and the characters. Old stuff. She wrote a story about a shoplifter named Horst, following him from the moment he picked up a tie until the moment he got out of the store, and she wrote it completely from within his mind, what he was thinking. Lockhardt said that the reader had no way of knowing that Horst was stealing, and that she should simply say so. But she explained that she was trying to be more subtle than that. She explained that the reader was supposed to find out Horst was stealing only after the fact, after he was outside the shop, otherwise the story would be just like any other story. They argued back and forth for a long time and then Lockhardt just shrugged his shoulders and said, "Well, I guess you've accomplished what you set out to do. Congratulations." The same thing happened with her next two stories. He didn't like them, so he said the reader couldn't follow them. He couldn't seem to understand that she was trying to do something different.

And then in August she got her grade. A flat C. She went straight from the registrar's office to Lockhardt.

"I have to speak to you," she said.

"Sit down," he said. "Have a seat. But I've got to see the dean in five minutes, so if you're going to need more than that . . ."

"You gave me a C."

"Right. I hope you weren't too disappointed."

"You," she said. "You," but the words wouldn't come out.

"Well, your work was not really extraordinary. I mean, I think you'll agree that it wasn't A work."

"It was C work, I suppose. It was only average."

"There's nothing wrong with being average. Most of us are. Most of our work is average."

She stood up and walked to the door. "What do I care," she said. "I can live with a C." And she slammed the door behind her.

She came back late the next afternoon, she was not sure why, but she knew she had to tell him something. Lockhardt was at his desk, typing, his back to the open door, and Leonora stood there in the corridor watching him. Nobody else was around. She could kill him and no one would know she had done it. If she had a knife or a gun, she could do it. That bastard.

He kept on typing and she just stood there watching him, thinking. And then suddenly he turned around and gave a little shout. "My God, you scared me half to death."

Leonora just stared at him, and he stared back, looking confused or maybe frightened. Then she turned and walked away.

She had not told him what he had done to her, but she would someday. She'd let him know. She'd let him know.

Leonora moved to San Francisco to be on her own. She got a studio apartment with a fire escape that looked down onto the roof of the Jack Tarr Hotel and she applied for jobs at Gumps and at the St. Francis—they asked her "doing what?"—and she shrugged and said to hell with them, she had a Stanford education. But her money ran out eventually and she took a job at Dalton's selling books.

Nothing interesting ever happened at Dalton's, and besides you had to press sixty buttons on the computerized register every time you rang up a sale. The worst part was that everybody kept buying a novel called *The Love Hostage,* written by that bastard Lockhardt. After the first four sales, she refused to sell any more. "I'm on my break," she'd say and make the customer go to another register.

Leonora hated her job, hated the people she worked with, hated books. Somewhere there must be something different happening. Even Patty Hearst, who was a zilch, a nothing, even she had things happen to her. With a name like Patty.

One night when she had worked late, Leonora decided to take a walk. She would make something happen. She moped along Polk Street to Geary and then back, but nothing happened. There were a million or so faggots eyeing each other, but nobody eyed Leonora. She went up to her studio and had a beer and then came down again and set off deliberately in the direction of Golden Gate Park. She knew what she was doing. She could be raped. She could be murdered. Lockhardt used to talk all the time about Joyce Carol Oates characters, how they set up situations for themselves, getting trapped, getting murdered, having their pink and gray brains spilled out on the sidewalk. She liked Joyce Carol Oates. She got as far as the Panhandle and was about to turn around and go home when she realized somebody was following her. For a block, then for a second block. She could hear the heels go faster when she went faster, slow down when she did. Her heart began to beat very fast and she could feel the vein in her forehead pulsing. She wanted it to happen, whatever it was. She turned around suddenly, hands on hips, her head thrown back, ready. At once the man following her crossed the street and headed in the opposite direction. Leonora walked for another hour and then went home. Would nothing happen to her, ever?

The next day she quit her job at Dalton's. They were limiting her. They were worse than Stanford.

The Women's Support Group was having a terrible time with Leonora.

"You've got to open up to your feelings as a woman," they said.

"Men have done this to you. They've refused to let you get in touch with your feelings," they said.

"What is it you feel? What is it you want?" they said.

"I want," Leonora said, "I don't know, but I think I want to die."

"No, what do you really want?" they said.

Leonora bought a gun and a copy of *The Love Hostage* on the same day. There was no connection she could see. She wanted them, that was all. It was time.

She loaded the gun with six bullets and hid it in a Kleenex box under a lot of tissues. It was for protection in this crazy city. It was a safeguard. It was just something nice to have around.

And then she sat down to read *The Love Hostage.* From the first page she was fascinated and appalled. The dust jacket said it was a novel about a young heiress who is kidnapped and brainwashed and all the other stuff that would make you think it was about Patty Hearst. But it wasn't about Patty at all; it was about her, it was about Leonora. Lockhardt had changed things to make it look as if it were about Patty, but she knew he meant her. He described her as an ordinary girl, a normal girl, average in every way. So now he had finally done it. He had killed her.

Leonora put the gun to the side of her head and pulled the trigger. There was an awful noise and the gun leaped from her hand and she felt something wet on the side of her face. She had only grazed her scalp, but inside she was dead just the same.

On the night she was committed to Agnew Mental, Leonora had forced down the beef stew her mother served for dinner and then she had gone back to her room to lie down. Almost at once she threw up into the wastebasket by her bed and then she went to the bathroom and threw up again. Back in her room she put on Phoebe Snow's *Poetry Man*. She played the album through twice, though she was not listening. She was thinking—as she had been for these last three weeks—of Lockhardt and how he had ruined everything and how someday she would let him know. But not now. Someday.

And then, as if it were somebody else doing it, she got up and got dressed and drove to the Stanford campus. She found Lockhardt's house with no trouble at all, and it was only when she had rung the doorbell that she realized she didn't know what she was going to say. But it didn't matter; somehow she would just tell him, calmly, with no tears, that he had degraded her, humiliated her, he had ruined her life.

"Yes?"

"I want to talk to you. I want to tell you something."

"Are you a student of mine? A former student?"

And then she realized that this was not Lockhardt at all, this was a much older man with a beard and glasses. The Lockhardts, it turned out, had moved to San Francisco.

Leonora got back into her car. She was frantic now, she would have to find a phone booth and get his address. She drove to Town and Country Shopping Center and found a booth, but there was no San Francisco directory. She drove to Stanford Shopping Center, and again there was no directory. Never mind. She would drive straight to the city, she would find him, he wouldn't get away from her now. She would let him know.

Traffic on 101 was heavy and it had begun to rain. Leonora passed cars that were already doing sixty. She had to get there. She had to tell him. The words were piling up in her brain, like stones, like bullets. Bullets, yes, she should have brought the gun. She should kill the bastard. A car pulled into her lane and then began slowly to brake. Leonora braked too, but not fast enough. Her car fishtailed and, with a short crunching sound, it smashed the side of a Volkswagen. She tore on ahead, though she could see in her mirror that the Volkswagen had ground to a halt, that its lights were blinking on and off. Tough. Yes, she should kill him, she thought, and she pressed her foot harder on the accelerator.

She couldn't find a parking place and so she left the car in a tow zone a block from the Jack Tarr Hotel and ran back in the rain. She found the phone booth, the directory, she opened it to the *L*'s. Lockhardt lived in North Beach. Of course he would, with all that money from *The Love Hostage*. She ran back to her car. A tow truck was backed up to it and a little bald man was kneeling down trying to attach a bar under the front bumper. "No," she shouted. "Stop it. Stop it. Stop." He stood up and looked at her, a screaming woman with her wet hair flying all around, a real crazy. "Okay, lady, okay," he said. "Okay." And then she was in her car again, tearing up Van Ness, running yellow lights, turning right on Pacific. In a few minutes she was there, at Lockhardt's blue and gray Victorian.

Leonora's head was pounding now and her back ached. She wanted to throw up, but there was nothing left to throw up. She wanted a drink. She wanted a pill. She wanted to take Lockhardt by the hair and tear the scalp off him, to expose the pink and gray brain that had written those things, that had done this to her.

She put her finger up to ring the bell, but she was shaking so much she couldn't do it. She began to beat the doorbell with her palm and then with her fist. Still the bell made no sound. She struck the door itself, with her hand, and then with her foot, and then she leaned her entire body against it, beating the door rhythmically with her fist and then with both fists, the rhythm growing faster and faster, the blows harder and harder, until there was blood on her hands and blood on the door and she heard a voice screaming that sounded like her own.

The door opened and Lockhardt, with a book in his hand, stood there looking at the young woman whose wet hair was streaked across her face, a face distorted beyond recognition by her hysteria, and he listened to the screaming, which made no sense to him until her voice broke and he could make out the words. "I am not average," she sobbed. "I am not average. I am not average."

It was nearly a half-hour before the orderlies came and took her away.

The world had gone crazy, that's just the way it was. Leonora's mother stared at the television where for days she had been watching pictures of the 911 corpses in Guyana. They had taken poison mixed with grape Kool-Aid and in five minutes they were dead. Every one of them. And Patty Hearst had been refused parole. And so had Charles Manson. And her own Leonora in that loony bin. Leonora could have been something once. She could have been . . . but nothing came to mind. It was Lockhardt's fault, Leonora was right. It was all Lockhardt's fault. Leonora's mother turned up the volume on the TV. And now somebody had shot Mayor Moscone and that Harvey Milk. It was the way you expressed yourself today, you shot somebody.

She thought of the gun hidden in the Kleenex box and suddenly it was all clear to her. She got in the car and drove to North Beach. She had no trouble finding Lockhardt's house; she had been there three times since Leonora was taken away. She had just parked opposite the house and sat there and watched. But this time she went up the steep wooden stairs and rang the bell. She rang again and as she was about to ring a third time Lockhardt opened the door, laughing. She could hear other people laughing too; he must be having a party.

Over his left shoulder, in the entrance hall, she could see a chandelier, a deep green wall, the corner of a picture. She couldn't make out what it was a picture of, but she could see that he was rich. He had everything. "Yes?" he said, and there was more laughter from that other room. "Yes?" he said again.

"Leonora," she said. "She could have been something."

And then she took the gun from her purse and leveled it at his chest. There were three loud shots and when his body slumped to the floor, Leonora's mother could see that the painting on the green wall was one of those new-fangled things with little blocks of color, all different sizes, that really aren't the picture of anything.

# Sandra Tsing Loh

*Loh (1962– ) was born in Los Angeles, California, and was educated at the California Institute of Technology and the University of Southern California. She published* Depth Takes a Holiday *in 1996 and both* Aliens in America *and* If You Lived Here, You'd Be Home by Now *in 1997. She received a Pushcart Prize in Fiction in 1995.*

## My Father's Chinese Wives

My father doesn't want to alarm us. But then again, it would not be fair to hide anything either. The fact is, at 70, he is going to try and get married again. This time to a Chinese wife. He thinks this would be more suitable than to someone American, given his advanced age.

He has written his family in Shanghai, and is awaiting response. He is hoping to be married within six months.

Let us unpeel this news one layer at a time.

Question: At this point, is my father even what one would consider marriageable?

At age 70, my father—a retired Chinese aerospace engineer—is starting to look more and more like somebody's gardener. His feet shuffle along the patio in their broken sandals. He stoops to pull out one or two stray weeds, coughing phlegmatically. He wears a hideous old crew-neck tennis sweater. Later, he sits in a rattan chair and eats leathery green vegetables in brown sauce, his old eyes slitted wearily.

He is the sort of person one would refer to as "Old Dragon Whiskers." And not just because it is a picturesque Oriental way of speaking.

"I am old now," he started saying, about 10 years after my mother had died of cancer. "I'm just your crazy old Chinese father." He would rock backwards in his chair and sigh. "I am an old, old man . . ."

At times he almost seems to be over-acting this lizardy old part. He milks it. After all, he still does the same vigorous exercise regime—45 minutes of pull-ups, something that looks like the twist and much bellowing—he did 10 years ago. This always performed on the most public beaches possible, in his favorite Speedo—one he found in a dumpster.

"Crazy old Chinese father" is, in truth, a code word, a rationalization for the fact that my father has always had a problem . . . spending money. Why buy a briefcase to carry to work, when an empty Frosted Flakes Cereal box will do? Papers slip down neatly inside, and pens can be clipped conveniently on either side.

Why buy Bounty Paper Towels when, at work, he can just walk down the hall to the washroom, open the dispenser, and lift out a stack? They're free—he can bring home as many as we want!

If you've worn the same sweater for so many years that the elbows wear out, turn it around! Get another decade out of it! Which is why to this day, my father wears only crew neck, not V-neck sweaters . . .

Why drive the car to work when you can take the so-convenient RTD bus? More time to read interesting scientific papers . . . and here they are, in my empty Frosted Flakes Box!

"Terrific!" is my older sister Kaitlin's response when I phone her with the news. Bear in mind that Kaitlin has not seen my father since the mid-'80s, preferring to nurse her bad memories of him independently, via a therapist. She allows herself a laugh, laying aside her customary dull hostility for a moment of more jocular hostility. "So who does he think would want to marry *him*?"

"Someone Chinese," I answer.

"Oh good!" she exclaims. "That narrows down the field . . . to what? Half a billion? Nah, as always, he's doing this to punish us.

"Think about it," Kaitlin continues with her usual chilling logic. "He marries a German woman the first time around. It's a disaster. You and I represent that. Because he's passive aggressive and he's cheap. But no, to him, it's that rebellious Aryan strain that's the problem.

"You take an Asian immigrant just off the boat, on the other hand. This is a person who has just fled a Communist government and a horrible life working in a bicycle factory for 10 cents a month and no public sanitation and repeated floggings every hour on the hour. After that, living with our father might seem like just another bizarre interlude. It could happen."

Kaitlin scores some compelling points, but nonetheless . . .

I'm bothered for a different reason . . .

Perhaps it is because in describing the potential new wife, he has used only that one adjective: *Chinese*. He has not said: "I'm looking for a smart wife," or even "a fat wife," he has picked "Chinese." It is meant to stand for so much.

Asian. Asian women. Asian *ladies*.

I think back to a college writing workshop I once attended. (No credit and perhaps that was appropriate.) It was long before my current "administrative assistant" job at Swanson Films. (Makers of the 10-minute instructional video "Laughterobics! Featuring Meredith Baxter Birney," among other fine titles.)

Anyway, the workshop contained 13 hysterical women—and one Fred. Fred was a wealthy Caucasian sixtysomething urologist; he was always serene and beautifully dressed and insistent upon holding the door open for me "because you're such a lovely lady." I always wore jeans and a USC sweatshirt, sometimes even sweatpants, so at first I did not know what he meant.

We women, on the other hand, were a wildly mixed group—writing anything from wintery Ann Beattie–esque snippets to sci-fi romance/porn novels ("She would be King Zenothar's concubine, whether she liked it or not"). We attacked each other's writing accordingly. People were bursting into tears every week, then making up by emotionally sharing stories about mutual eating disorders.

But there was one moment when all 13 women were of like minds. It was that moment when Fred would enter the classroom, laden with xeroxes, blushing shyly as a new bride. We would all look at each other as if to say, "Oh my God, Fred has brought in work *again*."

As though springing from a murky bottomless well, each week new chapters would appear from this semi-epistolary novel Fred was penning about an elderly doctor named Fred who goes on sabbatical for a year to Japan and there finds love with a 23-year-old Japanese medical student named Aku who smells of cherry blossoms.

There were many awkward scenes in which Fred and Aku were exploring each other's bodies as they lay—as far as I could gather—upon the bare floor, only a *tatami*[1] mat for comfort. (Fred would always italicize the Japanese words, as if to separate and somehow protect them from other, lesser words.) But it was all beautifully pure and unlike the urban squalor we find in America—the rock music, the drugs, the uncouth teenagers.

Anyway, I recall the one line that I have never since been able to blot from my mind. I cannot think of it without a bit of a shiver. Nor the way he read it, in that hoarse tremulous voice . . .

"I put my hand in hers, and her little fingers opened like the petals of a moist flower."

It is a month later and, as in a dream, I sit at the worn formica family dining table with my father, photos and letters spread before us.

Since my father has written to Shanghai, the mail has come pouring in. I have to face the fact that my father is, well, hot. "You see?" he says. "Seven women have written! Ha!" He beams, his gold molar glinting. He is drinking steaming green tea from a beaker, which he handles with a Beauty and the Beast potholder.

Remarkably, my father doesn't make the least effort to mask his delight, no matter how inappropriate. He is old now. *He can do whatever the hell he wants,* is how I now understand it. With a sigh, I turn to the photos. In spite of myself, I am wowed!

Tzau Pa, Ling Ling, Sui Pai, Chong Zhou . . . "28, administrative assistant," "47, owner of a seamstress business," "39, freelance beautician." The words jump off the pages, both in English and Chinese translations. These women are dynamos, achievers, with black curly hair, in turtlenecks, jauntily riding bicycles, seated squarely on cannons before military museums, standing proudly with three grown daughters.

One thing unites them: they're all ready to leap off the mainland at the drop of a hat.

1. A thick woven straw mat used in Asian houses as a floor covering.

And don't think their careers and hobbies are going to keep them from being terrific wives. Quite the opposite. Several already have excellent experience, including one who's been married twice already. The seamstress has sent him two shorts and several pairs of socks; there is much talk of seven-course meals and ironing and terrific expertise in gardening.

Super-achievement is a major theme that applies to all. And the biggest star of all is my father. He clears his throat and gleefully reads from a letter by one Liu Tzun:

> Dr. Chow, your family has told me of your great scientific genius and of your many awards. I respect academic scholarship very highly, and would be honored to meet you on your next visit.

"You see?" my father chuckles. "They have a lot of respect for me in China. When I go there, they treat me like President Bush! Free meals, free drinks . . . I don't pay for anything!"

"He had his chance. He got married once, for 25 years. He was a terrible husband and a worse father."

Kaitlin is weighing in. All jokes are off. Her fury blazes away further aggravated by the fact that she is going through a divorce and hates her $50,000 a year job. Her monthly Nordstrom bills are astronomical. MCI is positively crackling.

"He's a single man," I say. "Mum's been gone for 12 years now—"

"And now he gets a second try—just like that?" Kaitlin exclaims. "Clean slate? Start right over? Buy a wife? It makes me sick. He is totally unqualified to sustain a marriage. A family structure of any kind collapses around him. Do you even remember one happy Christmas?"

Twinkling lights and tinsel suddenly swirl before me and looking deeper, through green foliage, I see my mother looking beautiful and crisp in lipstick and pearls, her wavy auburn hair done . . . except for the fact that she is hysterical, and my father, his face a mask of disgust so extreme it is almost parodic, is holding his overpriced new V-necked tennis sweater from Saks out in front of him like it is a dead animal—

"I try to block it out," is what I say.

"Well I was six years older than you so I can't." Kaitlin's pain is raw. "Why does he deserve to be happy . . . now? He made Mama miserable in her lifetime—he was so cheap! I think she was almost glad to go as soon as she did! A $70 dress, leaving the heater on over night, too much spent on a nice steak dinner—he could never let anything go! He could never just let it go! He just could . . . not . . . let . . . things . . . go!"

Meanwhile . . .

On its own gentle time clock, unsullied by the raging doubts of his two daughters . . .

My father's project bursts into flower.

And 47-year-old Liu—the writer of the magic letter—is the lucky winner!

Within three months, she is flown to Los Angeles. She and my father are married a week later.

I do not get to meet her right away, but my father fills me in on the stats. And I have to confess, I'm a little surprised at how modern she is, how urban. Liu is a divorcee with, well, with ambitions in the entertainment business. Although she speaks no English, she seems to be an expert on American culture. The fact that Los Angeles is near Hollywood has not escaped her. This is made clear to me one Sunday evening, three weeks later, via telephone.

"I know you have friends in the entertainment business," my father declares. He has never fully grasped the fact that I am a typist and that Swanson Films' clients include such Oscar contenders as Kraft Foods and Motorola.

"Aside from having knitted me a new sweater and playing the piano," my father continues, "you should know that Liu is an excellent singer—" Turning away from the phone, he and his new wife exchange a series of staccato reports in Mandarin, which mean nothing to me.

"I'm sure that Liu is quite accomplished," I reply, "it's just that—"

"Oh . . . she's terr-ific!" my father exclaims, shocked that I may be calling Liu's musical talent into question. "You want to hear her sing? Here, here, I will put her on the phone right now . . ."

Creeping into my father's voice is a tremulous note that is sickeningly familiar. How many times had I heard it during my childhood as I was being pushed towards the piano, kicking and screaming? How many times—

But that was 20 years ago. I gulp terror back down. I live in my own apartment now, full of director's chairs, potted fici,[2] and Matisse posters. I will be fine. My father has moved on to a totally new pushee . . .

Who picks up the phone, sighs—then bursts out triumphantly:

"Nee-ee hoo-oo man, tieh-hen see bau-hau jioo . . . !"

I have left you and taken the Toyota, Dr. Chow—so there!

Five weeks later, Liu just packs up her suitcase, makes some sandwiches, and takes off in the family Toyota. She leaves her note on the same formica table at which she'd first won his heart.

My father is in shock. Then again, he is philosophical.

"Liu—she had a lot of problems. She said she had no one to talk to. There were no other Chinese people in Tarzana. She wanted me to give her gifts. She was bored. You know I don't like to go out at night. But I tell her, 'Go! See your friends in Chinatown.' But Liu does not want to take the bus. She wants to drive! But you know me, your cheap father. I don't want to pay her insurance. That Liu—she was a very bad driver—"

"Ha!" is Kaitlin's only comment.

Summer turns to fall in Southern California, causing the palm trees to sway a bit. The divorce is soon final, Liu's settlement including $10,000, the microwave and the Toyota.

2. Fig trees (species: *Ficus*).

Never one to dwell, my father has picked a new bride: Zhou Ping, 37, home-maker from Qang-Zhou province. I groan.

"But no . . . Zhou Ping is very good," my father insists. He has had several phone conversations with her. "And she comes very highly recommended, not, I have to say, like Liu. Liu was bad, that one. Zhou Ping is sensible and hard-working. She has had a tough life. Boy! She worked in a coal mine in Manchuria until she was 25. The winters there were very, very bitter! She had to make her own shoes and clothing. Then she worked on a farming collective, where she raised cattle and grew many different kinds of crops—by herself!"

"I'm sure she's going to fit in really well in Los Angeles," I say.

Zhou Ping is indeed a different sort. The news, to my astonishment, comes from Kaitlin. "I received . . ." her voice trails off, the very words seeming to elude her. "A *birthday card*. From Papa . . . and *Zhou Ping*."

My sister continues in a kind of trance of matter-of-factness, as if describing some curious archaeological artifact. "Let's see, on the front is a picture with flowers on it. It's from Hallmark. Inside is gold lettering, cursive, that says, 'Happy Birthday!' At the bottom, in red pen, it says . . . 'Love, Zhou Ping and *your* Dad.' "

"Your 'Dad'?"

"I think Zhou Ping put him up to this. The envelope is not addressed in his hand-writing. Nonetheless . . ." Kaitlin thinks it over, concurs with herself. "Yes. Yes. I believe this is the first birthday card I've ever received from him in my life. The first. It's totally bizarre."

A week later, Kaitlin receives birthday gifts in the mail: a sweater hand-knit by Zhou Ping, and a box of "mooncakes." She is flipping out. "Oh no," she worries, "Now I really have to call and thank her. I mean, the poor woman probably has no friends in America. Who knows what he's having her do? We may be her only link to society!"

Kaitlin finally does call, managing to catch Zhou Ping when my father is on the beach doing his exercises (which he always does at 11 and at 3). Although Zhou Ping's English is very broken, she somehow convinces Kaitlin to fly down for a visit.

It will be Kaitlin's first trip home since our mother's passing. And my first meeting of either of my step-mothers.

I pull up the familiar driveway in my Geo. Neither Kaitlin nor I say anything. We peer out the windows.

The yard doesn't look too bad. There are new sprinklers, and a kind of irrigation system made by a network of ingenuously placed rain gutters. Soil has been turned, and thoughtfully. Cypresses have been trimmed. Enormous bundles of weeds flank the driveway, as if for some momentous occasion.

We ring the doorbell. Neither of us has had keys to the house in years.

The door opens. A short, somewhat plump Chinese woman, in round glasses and a perfect bowl haircut, beams at us. She is wearing a bright yellow "I hate housework!" apron that my mother was once given as a gag gift—and I think never wore.

"Kat-lin! Jen-na!" she exclaims in what seems like authentic joy, embracing us. She is laughing and almost crying with emotion.

In spite of myself, giggles begin to well up from inside me as if from a spring. I can't help it: I feel warm and euphoric. Authentic joy is contagious. Who cares who this woman is: no one has been this happy to see me in ages.

"Wel-come home," Zhou Ping says, with careful emphasis. She turns to Kaitlin, a shadow falling over her face. "I am glad you finally come home to see your Daddy," she says in a low, sorrowful voice. She looks over her shoulder. "He old now."

Then, as if exhausted by that effort, Zhou Ping collapses into giggles. I sneak a glance over at Kaitlin, whose expression seems to be straining somewhere between joy and nausea. Pleasantries lunge out of my mouth: "It's nice to finally meet you!" "How do you like America?" "I've heard so much about your cooking!"

My father materializes behind a potted plant. He is wearing a new sweater and oddly formal dress pants. His gaze hovers somewhere near the floor.

"Hul-lo," he declares, attempting a smile. "Long time no see!" he exclaims, not making eye contact, but in Kaitlin's general direction.

"Yes!" Kaitlin exclaims back, defiant, a kind of winged Amazon in perfect beige Anne Klein II leisurewear. "It certainly is!"

My father stands stiffly.

Kaitlin blazes.

"It's good to see you!" he finally concludes, as though this were something he learned in English class.

Feeling, perhaps, that we should all leave well enough alone, the Chow family, such as we are, moves on through the house. It is ablaze with color—the sort of eye-popping combinations one associates with Thai restaurants and Hindu shrines. There are big purple couches, peach rugs, a shiny brass trellis and creeping charlies everywhere.

All this redecorating came at no great expense, though. "See this rug?" my father says proudly, while Zhou Ping giggles. "She found it in a dumpster. They were going to throw it away!" "Throw it away!" she exclaims. "See? It very nice."

Over their heads, Kaitlin silently mouths one word to me: "Help."

Beyond, the formica dining room table is set. Oddly. There are little rice bowls, chopsticks, and a sheet of plain white paper at each place setting. It is good to know some definite event has been planned. Kaitlin, my father and I are so unaccustomed to being in a room together that any kind of definite agenda—aka: "We'll eat dinner, and then we'll leave"—is comforting.

My father goes off to put some music on his new CD player. "That bad Liu made me buy it!" he explains. "But it's nice." Zhou Ping bustles into the kitchen. "Dinner ready—in five minute!" she declares.

Kaitlin waits a beat, then pulls me aside into the bathroom and slams the door.

"This is so weird!" she hisses.

We have not stood together in this bathroom for some 15 years. It seems different. I notice that the wallpaper is faded, the towels are new—but no, it's something else. On one wall is my mother's framed reproduction of the brown Da Vinci etching called "Praying Hands" which she had always kept in her sewing room. Right next to it, in shocking juxtaposition, is a green, red, blue and yellow "Bank of Canton" calendar from which a zaftig[3] Asian female chortles.

"I can't go through with this!" Kaitlin continues in stage whisper. "It's too weird! There are so many memories here, and not good ones!"

And like debris from a hurricane, the words tumble out:

"I go by the kitchen and all I can see is me standing before the oven clock at age five with tears in my eyes. He is yelling: 'What time is it? The little hand is most of the way to four and the big hand is on the eight! It was 3:18 twenty-two minutes ago—so what time is it now? What's eighteen plus twenty-two? Come on—you can do it in your head! Come on! Come on!'

"I go by the dining room and I see him hurling my Nancy Drew books across the floor. They slam against the wall and I huddle against Mum, screaming. 'Why do you waste your time on this when your algebra homework isn't finished? You . . . good for nothing! You're nothing, nothing—you'll never amount to anything!'

"I go by the bedroom—"

"Please—" I have this sickening feeling like I'm going to cry, that I'm just going to lose it. I want to just sit down in the middle of the floor and roll myself into a ball. But I can't. Kaitlin's rage is like something uncontainable, a dreadful natural force, and I am the gatekeeper. I feel if I open the door, it will rush out and destroy the house and everyone in it. "Please," is what I end up whispering. "Please. Let's just eat. We'll be done in a hour. Then we can go home. I promise. You won't have to do this again for another 10 years—or maybe ever."

At dinner, endless plates of food twirl their way out of the kitchen, Zhou Ping practically dancing underneath. Spinach, teriyaki-ish chicken, shrimp, some kind of egg thing with peas, dumplings packed with little pillows of pork.

And amazingly, there is no want of conversational material. Photos from Shanghai are being pulled out of envelopes and passed around, of her family, his family . . .

I do recognize three or four Chinese relatives—a cousin, an aunt, a grand-uncle? Their names are impossible for me to remember. We had met them in China during our last trip as a family. I was 15; it was right before our mother started to get sick.

Shanghai is a distant, confused memory for me, of ringing bicycle bells and laundry lines hanging from buildings. What I do remember is how curious my father's family had seemed about Kaitlin and me, his odd American experiment, oohing over our height and touching our auburn hair. There were many smiles but no intelligible conversation, at least to our ears. We probably won't see any of these people again before we die.

Zhou Ping, though, is determined to push through, to forge a bridge between us. She plunges ahead with her bad English, my father almost absent-mindedly correcting her.

Their lives are abuzz with activity. Zhou Ping is taking piano lessons at the

3. Juicy, succulent (Yiddish); pleasantly plump.

community college. My father is learning Italian and French off the Learning Channel—he sets his alarm for four in the morning. "So early!" Zhou Ping hoots. They listen to Karl Haas' "Listening to Good Music" on the classical station at 10. "Mot-sart—he very nice!" They have joined the Bahais, a local quasi-religious group. "I must cook food all the time!" My father suddenly puts his spoon down. He is chewing slowly, a frown growing.

"This meat . . ." he shakes his head, "is very greasy."

He turns to Zhou Ping and the lines at both sides of his mouth deepen. His eyes cloud. He says something to her in Chinese, with a certain sharp cadence that makes my spine stiffen . . .

Zhou Ping's face goes blank for a moment. Her eyes grow big. My stomach turns to ice.

How will she respond? By throwing her napkin down, bursting into tears, running from the room? Will she knock the table over, plates sliding after each other, sauces spilling, crockery breaking? Will we hear the car engine turn over as she drives off into the night, to leave us frightened and panicked?

It is none of these things.

Zhou Ping's head tilts back, her eyes crinkle . . .

And laughter pours out of her, peal after peal after peal. It is a big laugh, an enormous laugh, the laugh of a woman who has birthed calves and hoed crops and seen harsh winters decimate countrysides. Pointing to our father, Zhou Ping turns to us with large glittering eyes and says words which sound incredible to our ears:

"Your Papa—he so funny!"

My jaw drops. No one has ever laughed out loud at this table, ever. We laughed behind closed doors, in our bedrooms, in the bathroom, never before my father. We laughed sometimes with my mother, on those glorious days when he would be off on a trip—

But Kaitlin is not laughing. She is trembling; her face is turning red.

"Why were you always so angry?" Kaitlin cries out in a strangled voice. It is the question that she has waited 30 years to ask. "Why were you so angry?"

There is shocked silence. My father looks weary and embarrassed. He smiles wanly and shrugs his thin shoulders.

"No really," Kaitlin insists. "All those years. With Mama. Why?"

"I don't know," my father murmurs. "People get angry."

And I know, in that moment, that he doesn't have an answer. He literally doesn't. It's as if anger was this chemical which reacted on him for 20 years. Who knows why, but like some kind of spirit, it has left him now. The rage is spent. He is old now. He is old.

Dusk has fallen, and long shadows fall across the worn parquet floor of the dining room. After a moment of silence, my father asks Zhou Ping to sing a song. The hausfrau from Qang Zhou opens her mouth and with an odd dignity, sings simply and slowly. My father translates.

From the four corners of the earth
My lover comes to me

Playing the lute
Like the wind over the water

He recites the words without embarrassment, almost without emotion. And why shouldn't he? The song has nothing to do with him personally: it is from some old Chinese fable. It has to do with missing someone, something, that perhaps one can't even define any more.

As Zhou Ping sings, everyone longs for home. But what home? Zhou Ping—for her bitter winters? My father—for the Shanghai he left 40 years ago? Kaitlin and I? We are even sitting in our home, and we long for it.

# Robie Macauley

*Macauley (1919–1995) was born in Grand Rapids, Michigan. He was educated at Kenyon College and the universities of Iowa and Illinois. During 1942–46 he was in counterintelligence in the U.S. Army. He taught at Bard, University of Iowa, Women's College of the University of North Carolina, and Kenyon. He edited the* Kenyon Review *from 1959 to 1966, was fiction editor at* Playboy *from 1966 to 1977, and was an editor at Houghton Mifflin. His awards include a Rockefeller Fellowship, a Guggenheim Fellowship, and a Fulbright award. He also received an O'Henry Prize in 1967. His books include* The Disguises of Love *(1952),* The End of Pity and Other Stories *(1957), and* A Secret History of Time to Come *(1979).*

## The Chevigny Man

"The last of the Renaissance men," said Paul Teeling, tipping the bottle uncertainly at the jigger as if trying to salt the tail of some elusive bird. "Poet, art critic, novelist, playwright, traveler, officer—he was in the British navy during the war, you know—editor and a dozen other things. Veritably an *uomo universale*."[1] This sounded a little pedantic. "A man of parts. He's had a dozen distinguished careers." That made it better. He now noticed that in his excitement he had given Marian, his wife, a double shot of the good Bourbon and the Dean a single one of the imitation Scotch.

"But will he *live*?" asked Watters from the sofa.

Poor Watters. Paul looked at him and almost smiled. Still sniping from the bushes even after he'd been completely outmaneuvered. Watters' man was Samuel Daniel, who died in 1619—no chance of *his* ever coming to the campus to lecture.

"Not a doubt," said Paul pointedly. "His *Collected Poems* alone make him one of the outstanding figures of the twentieth century." This was cruel, but deserved. Watters blinked behind his spectacles and nervously dipped up a handful of cheese crackers. For the past year or so his greatest apprehension had been that Daniel was fading. He had almost disappeared from PMLA altogether, the Oxford Press man had shown only the mildest interest in Watters' manuscript of the *Life* and a library talk on "Several Themes in the *Civil*

1. Universal man (Latin).

*Wars*," had been saved at the last minute only by the compulsory attendance of Sophomore English classes.

"Do you know Mr. Chevigny?" asked the Dean. "Personally, I mean."

"The crucial question," Paul thought. The question that had galled him so often in the past. He deftly switched the little straw glass holders with their identifying colors between Marian's glass and the Dean's before he answered. "No," he said with just a tinge of smugness. "Not *yet*."

How often he'd seen the look of interest fade. The old lady who approached him after his lecture in Dayton two years ago. The bright students in his modern literature course. The young writer from Chicago who'd called on him. "Do you know . . . personally, I mean?" they'd all asked at various times and, trying to choke back that sense of insufficiency, he'd had to answer, "I must admit . . ." And they had all stared at his apology in the same way: He got it all out of books. The talk ebbing, the questions dying off, people turning away. "Well, nevertheless, it was a very informative discussion." He'd never felt the magic touch, seen the face that appeared so often in the *Times* Sunday book section, couldn't quote a single anecdote that began, "I remember Geoffrey saying to me once, 'Now Paul, I'm astonished at your perception when you say . . .' " Letters to Chevigny had drawn only a brief reply from a secretary.

"Not *yet*," he said again.

"Now aren't we fortunate," Martha Baker, the Dean's wife, said, "to have the greatest authority on Geoffrey Chevigny right here just at the time he decided to make an American lecture tour? I think it's a wonderful coincidence." Martha always babbled on.

"Thank you, Martha," he said with a smile a little broader than genuine and handed her the glass of sherry he had just refilled. "The man and his work have always fascinated me—ever since I discovered one of his plays when I was a junior in college. *The Exiled*—it's about the old age of Prince Charles Stuart. A wealth of material about the Stuart character in it."

"I heard he'll be passed over for the laureateship—that is, when Masefield dies," said Watters rudely.

Didn't the man know when he was demolished? There were so many answers to this that he hardly knew which weapon to choose—or whether it wouldn't be more damning just to keep silent. He wondered if the thought weren't passing through the Dean's mind that a man who had never heard of *The Exiled* and who still thought of the poet laureateship as a great distinction ought not to be teaching English on the college level. Then he suddenly realized that he was mistaken to attribute these fine distinctions of his own to Baker. As a matter of fact, the Dean *did* love Masefield. He remembered hearing him say so.

Confused by the wide range of possibilities, he suddenly realized that they were all coming out in one sentence. "Surely after its history—after Shadwell, Cibber and Austin—you can't take that thing seriously and so Chevigny stands with Milton, Pope, Byron, Yeats . . . he has nothing to do with such faded official honors, or can you imagine the author of *The British Consul* ever *wanting* it and anyway he's quite old, you know, rarely ever stirs from his house in Rome—

can you imagine what satire there'd be in Chevigny's 'Ode to the Youngest Princess on the Occasion of Her Ninth Birthday'?" Seeing that he was going wrong, he stopped. They were looking at him in a slightly puzzled way, he thought. He'd meant to be a load of bricks on Watters, but he'd only succeeded in burying himself.

From his seat in the corner Dr. Dunmeade chuckled at him. For years the head of the English Department had practiced and cultivated that sound until now it was rich, rattly and, more than any other sound in the world, fitted the word "chuckle." It sounded like a pair of oversized dice being rattled around in his throat.

"Teeling, my boy," he said. Whenever Dr. Dunmeade called him that, Paul felt confusedly that it had some reference to his disappearing hairline. Dr. Dunmeade still had an ugly black shock on his head. "Teeling, we understand your natural warmth of interest in Chevigny. Admirable. But I don't think Watters meant anything by his remark. After all, it's an academic question, isn't it, with Masefield still hale and hearty?" Dunmeade was a Wordsworth man—therefore unassailable. Paul was often irritated with his absolute neutrality; as a matter of fact, when the Donne man in the department had been nominated for the headship in opposition to the Shelley man, Dunmeade had finally come out as the compromise choice; Wordsworth was felt to be safe and middle-of-the-road.

"No offense meant," Watters said offensively. "How old *is* this Chevigny? He must be up in his eighties, isn't he?"

He didn't die at the beginning of the seventeenth century—but Paul thought better of saying this.

"He's sixty-nine," said the Dean, "born in 1871." The Dean must have been looking him up in *Who's Who*, or perhaps he had been reading one of Paul's own articles in *The Northeast Review* or *The Journal of Modern Literary Scholarship*.

"I think he owes a debt of gratitude to Paul," Marian said loyally. "In spite of his reputation, he's never had the serious consideration he deserves—outside of Europe, at least. Why, do you know Paul's book will be the first biography to appear in English?" She *had* been listening to him these past ten years, in spite of her distracted looks and frequent interruptions to ask if he'd paid the grocery bill. Good girl.

"I'm dying to meet him," said Mrs. Dunmeade. "I enjoyed his *Brief Encounter* so much." Here was support. Let Watters notice that even Mrs. Dunmeade, who read almost nothing but Lloyd Douglas—even *she* knew something of Chevigny.

"*The Curt Reply*," he said.

"Why, I didn't mean to be," said Mrs. Dunmeade.

"No—that's the name of the play. *The Curt Reply*."

"Of *course*. I *knew* the other was by Bernard Shaw the moment I said it."

He thought Watters was looking sly. Wasn't there some way of reminding him how the conscripted sophomores had hawked and shuffled during his interminable droning about the *Civil Wars*? Teeling had refreshed the last of the drinks and now he sat down again.

"Well, now, tell us something more about Chevigny," said the Dean, who always threw a good deal of heartiness as a kind of makeweight into his most banal remarks. "I know him by his popular reputation, of course [*Who's Who*, Teeling thought again] but I'm not too well acquainted with the details."

Leaning back in his chair, Paul Teeling said, "Geoffrey Chevigny was born of an old family of Norman descent in York, England, in 1871."

"The Dean already gave us that," said Watters.

"I'm sorry, George," Teeling said mildly. Watters looked sheepish.

"No, *I'm* sorry," said Watters. "Shouldn't have interrupted you. It was a very good beginning."

"His father, Sir Manfred Chevigny—named for Byron's hero, by the way—was high in the councils of the Tory party during his lifetime . . ." This oft-told story had now become a part of his life and it was with a sense of satisfaction that he realized while shaving in the morning that he had been thinking of Geoffrey Chevigny ever since he had arisen—that period between 1885 and '87. Weren't there any letters still in existence to account for Chevigny's whereabouts and, more important, his thoughts at that period? In the department store a pretty girl waited on him and he had some trouble in describing the curtains that Marian wanted. He wondered what Chevigny would have thought of the girl. Wasn't she rather like "the sinuous girl with the ivory face" in *Ucalegon*? Perhaps the same one mentioned in the journal as "the jade-and-ivory Jeanette." He read the war headlines in the paper and thought, "Chevigny said that historians have misunderstood the Battle of Jutland. It was actually more than decisive." He had read and mastered every maneuver of that conflict, finding, to his disappointment, however, no mention of Chevigny in the official report and very little mention of his ship, *The Indispensable*, which had, it appeared, arrived a little late and had returned to drydock before the battle was completely over.

What epigram would Chevigny have coined to dispose of Watters at lunch? What was the reason for Chevigny's great attraction to ballet dancers in that 1895 period? Was it that the movement of the classical ballet was very much akin to the kind of movement of his plays and poetry? Teeling had waited anxiously for the appearance of the Ballet Russe in town and then, to his mortification, had fallen asleep in the middle of the second ballet.

As he walked to the bus stop, he wondered what Geoffrey Chevigny had been doing on this sunlit morning thirty years ago. Let's see—he had been living in Venice at the time, working over *The Three Roisterers*. Had he, at this exact time, been walking along the Grand Canal (he had lived two houses away from the one in which Browning had died and Teeling had a map of the neighborhood) signaling for a gondola, just as Teeling, on this fine May morning thirty years later, was signaling for the King Power Co. Trolley Car? What had Chevigny been thinking? Undoubtedly the theme of self-destruction that runs so brilliantly and gloomily through *The Three Roisterers* was more connected with the suicide of his friend Caldwell than himself. Chevigny had always been in favor of life.

And so Chevigny had become almost a part of him. Paul knew considerably more about the man, he reflected, than most of Chevigny's closest friends. It was really amazing how much could be learned—to the minutest detail—about the life of a man who had never come within a thousand miles of you. In fact it was probably true that Paul knew many things that Chevigny had forgotten or had never realized about himself. It would be amazing when they met. He imagined the two of them in his study late at night. "Do you realize," Paul was saying, "that at the same time you were working on *Dead Mansions* a very good friend of yours was writing a poetic drama with the identical idea—stemming from the anecdote about General Burgoyne and the children that you told one evening—June 1, 1905, I believe—at a dinner party at the Byerleys' house in Paris?" "No!" Chevigny would say, starting from his seat, "I never suspected. Not . . . ?" Paul would nod gravely. "I'm afraid so. A brilliant man, but he outlived his genius, don't you agree?"

That recalled a delicate problem, a problem that was actually more one of introduction than accomplishment. How was he going to get Chevigny aside for a long session of tactful questioning that would serve to fill in those baffling gaps in the biography? The truth had to be known, for instance, about that two months in 1907 that Chevigny had spent on an island in the Cyclades.[2] Teeling was absolutely convinced that it had been neither Lady Judith Perrigeau nor the "Turkish girl with odd tastes" that malicious gossips had hinted at—but a long poem on a classical subject that had apparently never been printed. He had a clue to that. And the six months in the Swiss hospital that ensued? And the mysterious Dane with whom Geoffrey had taken that walking trip in North Africa? His opinion of Winston Churchill? The famous quarrel with Yeats? Had he actually called Pound a "damned, dirty, stinking—" as Widdicomb had reported or had he actually been referring to Widdicomb?

But all this had to be approached with the greatest smoothness—it all had to be in context. For the last two months, ever since he had heard from the agent that Chevigny would accept the lecture engagement, he had been wondering about a setting that would induce the reminiscent mood. Nothing seemed to help very much here. At Cambridge, he knew, Chevigny had been known as a "four-bottle man." The encyclopedia was unfortunately blank on this term. Dunmeade, who had been at Oxford, wasn't much help. He had said, "Might be Vichy water. That's all I drank when I was there. Couldn't stand English beer." Then, Chevigny liked long walking trips and mountain climbing—almost out of the question here in Indiana. Brilliant women were supposed to stimulate his conversation—then Paul thought of the faculty wives, a great many of whom, unhappily, seemed to be pregnant just at this moment, and the college girls, most of whom were trying to look like Lana Turner just now and—what was worse—succeeding. There was one pretty girl in the English Department, but, Paul reflected, she was a Swinburne man—in the middle of her thesis about Swinburne. Nothing would enrage Chevigny more than to hear all about *that.*

". . . and so," Paul began to wind up, "at the outbreak of the war he was forced to remove from his house in Rome whence he traveled to Majorca, where he now lives. It's a delightful place, I understand. He has a study over-

2. Group of Greek islands in the Aegean Sea.

looking the 'wine-dark waters' of the Mediterranean where he sits every morning from nine to twelve and writes on his work-in-progress, which is to be a grand critical study of all his literary contemporaries."

There was a brief silence. "It's snowing outside," Watters remarked.

But he had lost the patience of the group. "Illuminating. Most illuminating," said the Dean. "I shall look forward to your biography with the greatest pleasure."

"*Very* interesting. I'm dying to meet him," said Mrs. Dunmeade.

"I hope he won't be too—well, you know how some of those writers are," said Mrs. Baker.

"Please try to be here at six-thirty for a drink or two before dinner. You remember that the lecture is at eight-thirty," said Marian.

They went out into the hall, putting on coats and rubbers. Watters lingered a little behind the others and Paul saw a forlorn look on his face. With a sudden warmth of forgiveness, he helped him on with his coat.

With his hand at the knob, Watters turned and leaned towards him, the wretched look magnified behind the show-windows of his large spectacles. In a low voice he said, "I envy you, Paul. I wish *my* man were alive."

To Paul the next two days were intense but hazy. They spent a lot of their time doing what Marian called "stocking up." At the liquor store Paul took an annoying half hour trying to get several wines he had never tasted, wines famous to literature but nearly unknown in the Dandy-Corner Liquor Store. Claret, Port, Bristol Cream Sherry and sack—no, sack was Falstaff—it must be hock.

"Have you any good hock?" he asked.

"This ain't a pawnshop, mister," said the fat man, laughing heavily.

He laid in an extravagant stock of Benson and Hedges cigarettes and pipe tobacco and Marian made two heavy hauls at the delicatessen. The house was cleaned and their part-time maid was engaged full time for the next three days. After some debate, Marian even bought her a uniform.

Coming into his study the evening before the arrival, Paul saw how thoroughly it had been cleaned—and even rearranged, a bit ostentatiously, he thought. All of the Chevigny books, for instance (his collection was complete), were now on the top shelf of the bookcase along with the magazines containing Paul's articles. *The Manchester Guardians* for the last six months had been brought out of the closet and laid in a neat overlapping file on the lamp table. His big book of newspaper clippings relating to Chevigny, his friends and the places where he had lived for the past twenty years, had been placed on the top of the desk. Over the desk, Paul noticed something missing. On one side always hung the greatly enlarged photograph of Chevigny that Paul had had made from a publisher's publicity picture and on the other side hung a reproduction of a portrait of Landor—an old love from Ph.D days, now forsaken. Landor had been stored away. A small feeling of guilt prickled in his mind and he wondered if Chevigny hadn't taken somewhat of an advantage with him over Landor—a rather unfair advantage simply by being alive.

Watters had made that point, but Paul still wasn't sure of all the ins and outs of it. Until recently he had hardly ever thought of Chevigny as actually being alive; he was still breathing somewhere, of course, and still furnishing material for the last chapter but, in a sense, not really living. He moved the Chevigny picture over to the Landor hook, judging that there it could be seen a little better on first entrance into the room.

He slept badly that night and Marian accused him of mumbling. The next morning in his ten o'clock class he felt a little tired and on edge. He talked about Chevigny's life and read a selection of his poems. There were ten minutes left then and he called for comments or questions. A discouraging silence followed. Finally a boy in the last row raised his hand. "Yes?"

"Did Robert Frost know him?" he asked.

"I doubt if Chevigny would have noticed Frost," Paul snapped, being unfair and knowing it. "Any other questions?"

"You said *Ucalegon* is one of the greatest modern poems," one of the girls said. "It isn't in our textbook and . . ."

"Simply ignorance on the part of the editors," Paul said grimly. "These questions are all pretty frivolous, it seems to me."

Perry Reynolds, a great smoother-over, trying to nurse his athletic scholarship along for another year, said, "Sir, I understand that some critics place it above *The Waste Land* in importance. Isn't that true?"

So the class ended on a sweeter note and after a good lunch, Teeling felt somewhat better. It was just nerves, he told himself as he sat in his office going over the typescript of his little introductory speech. "A modern Odysseus on a voyage of intellectual discovery through . . ." Didn't that phrase sound a little too rhetorical? And the reference to his own work on Chevigny? However modest it might seem here in the quiet of his office, wasn't it possible that it might have another ring when spoken into the microphone in the auditorium? Finally he drew a light pencil line through several sentences, leaving them optional, to be decided on later. From time to time he had glanced out of the window and at last with a feeling of displeasure he went and stood at it, looking out on the snowy campus. It was only three o'clock and already it was becoming alarmingly dark. A sweeping wind coming out of the west kept the deserted walks bare but cast up odd drifts around the bases of the tree boles and at the edges of buildings. One moment, when the wind died, the air seemed salted with granular snow and the next moment was cleared with a vicious new blast. Standing there, Paul had an odd, almost portentous feeling, a half wish that Chevigny wouldn't come or that he had already gone.

But he had to leave; it was already only a half hour before train time. He muffled up and went out to the lot for his car. The streets seemed tortuous with slowly moving traffic, cars looking like monstrous buns with a layer of frosting. As he drove down the long street of gloomy warehouses and wholesale establishments that led to the railway station, he thought how dreary this must be and how strange to a man accustomed to the bright air and colors of the Mediterranean. But he censored that thought quickly; it had no bearing whatsoever, he told himself.

At the station he found that he still had fifteen minutes to wait and so he walked around aimlessly, peering at the magazines on the stand, stopping for a moment to call Marian to let her know everything was all right, getting caught in the middle of two embracing families who were about to be parted.

Five minutes early he got out on the platform in the vicious wind. The light down the tracks was green but the train seemed to take a long time coming into the yards even after its whistle. But finally it was slowing up alongside. The porters were jumping down and beginning to haul bags off. Passengers stood waiting on the steps with money showing between the fingers of their gloves. A great crowd had appeared from somewhere and he was shoved in the legs with suitcases and sideswiped by children, caught in a sudden steambath from beneath the train. How in the world was he going to find Chevigny in this mess? He started down the platform.

Then he suddenly discovered that he had been gazing at the face of an old man without understanding who he was. It was partly the overpowering familiarity of his looks that made him unrecognizable. It was partly that Paul, almost unconsciously, had been hearing the long physical description with which he had begun chapter five: "those eagle eyes beneath the sharp-cut brows . . . the military moustache . . . the clean angle of the cheekbone . . . the clear, reddish tone of the skin." Chevigny was taller than he had imagined, broader in the shoulders. With a gulp, Paul rushed up and spoke to him.

"Eh?" he answered. "No—CHIVingee, CHIVingee. Yes. You're the boy sent down from the school?"

It was a terrible blast for Paul. For years he had been calling him SheVEENye and everybody in college knew it. No time to worry about that now.

"I'm *Paul Teeling*," he said, waiting for the fierce face to soften into a recognitory smile.

It didn't. "Howjado."

"Paul Teeling," he said again with despair, but Chevigny was already getting his bags away from the redcap. "Now, sir, here is my luggage," he said brusquely.

On the ramp, Paul couldn't help staggering under the weight of the three fat bags. Chevigny strode ahead of him like a brigadier leading a charge into the thick-packed but demoralized natives.

Paul finally caught up with him in the middle of the station and panted directions to the car. Once they got there, Paul nearly dropped the luggage. His muscles felt like broken threads. He leaned against the fender and caught his breath. Then he raised the cover of the trunk and slowly and carefully stowed the bags away.

When he turned he saw that Chevigny was still waiting for him to open the car door, though it wasn't locked.

"Inevitable awkwardness at first," Paul thought as they went down the street. "There's a kind of genuine hauteur that surrounds a truly great man." He'd decided that by no means would he ask Chevigny what he thought of America or Indiana—he'd have only scorn for such a hackneyed opening. Better let him speak first.

"Damned depressing place," Chevigny said. "Reminds me of Manchester and the Naples slums scrambled together at the North Pole."

"Yes, it does, rather," said Paul, weakly, trying to accommodate himself.

"I'm used to the bright colors of the Mediterranean, y'know," Chevigny remarked again.

CHIVingee. CHIVingee. CHIVingee. He must drill himself and remember to say it that way. "Mr. CHIVingee, your talk has been much anticipated. I think you'll find that your work is well known and appreciated here."

Wait until he saw the study—he'd tumble then. In the excitement at the station he probably hadn't connected the name with Paul's writing.

"Mph?"

"The weather is nasty but I think we can offer you a little bit of compensation at least with a warm fire and a good glass of Scotch."

"Bawph."

Paul tried once or twice more, but got nothing. When they came to a stoplight he took a quick sideglance at the author. "You look a little pale, Mr. Chevigny. Are you tired?"

"Oh. Quite. That is, not really." He put a fine carved hand to his forehead. "I was a bit dizzy in the train, you know. I had a fall. Nothing, really. I'll soon be right as rain." He seemed to slump even as he said this.

"Some sleep and all's well," he said. Paul thought of the people coming for cocktails, the dinner, the lecture, the Dean's reception after the lecture, and began to pass cars recklessly on the slippery pavement. It would have to be a quick nap. Marian would be firm about that.

At last he turned into the driveway and stopped at the walk. Chevigny seemed to waken from a slight doze. He looked out of the window. "Where are we?" he asked.

"Right here at our house," Paul said heartily, "and only a minute away from a good drink."

"But, my good fellow," Chevigny said abruptly, "those people at the school are expecting me. You'd better take me there at once. I do appreciate your offer, but . . ."

"I should have explained," Paul said in a rush. "You're staying with us. We have the honor . . ."

Chevigny got out of the car somewhat doubtfully, opening the door by himself this time. He followed Paul, who carried the bags. Marian had been waiting. She threw the front door open before he could touch the knob. "Mr. SheVEENye!" she exclaimed. But it was only Paul and the luggage. Chevigny was standing several yards back, looking uncertainly down the street as if wondering whether any rescue was in sight.

They bundled him inside and got his hat and coat away from him. Marian was brisk and forceful and full of bright conversational bits. Chevigny was marched upstairs with the maid to be shown his room. He was given five minutes to wash and then marched down again—this time to the study where Paul had a fantastic battalion of bottles arranged on a silver tray in preparation for "a little drink before they all get here." Chevigny, to Paul's alarm, looked paler than ever and he saw him sink into the easy chair with a feeling of relief—even though his eye had passed blankly over the photograph and the books.

"A Scotch and soda, sir?" Paul asked.

jokester. Is this what a Jewish angel looks like? he asked himself. This I am not convinced.

He asked a last question. "So if God sends to me an angel, why a black? Why not a white that there are so many of them?"

"It was my turn to go next," Levine explained.

Manischevitz could not be persuaded. "I think you are a faker."

Levine slowly rose. His eyes showed disappointment and worry. "Mr. Manischevitz," he said tonelessly, "if you should desire me to be of assistance to you any time in the near future, or possibly before, I can be found"—he glanced at his fingernails—"in Harlem."

He was by then gone.

The next day Manischevitz felt some relief from his backache and was able to work four hours at pressing. The day after, he put in six hours; and the third day four again. Fanny sat up a little and asked for some halvah to suck. But on the fourth day the stabbing, breaking ache afflicted his back, and Fanny again lay supine, breathing with blue-lipped difficulty.

Manischevitz was profoundly disappointed at the return of his active pain and suffering. He had hoped for a longer interval of easement, long enough to have some thought other than of himself and his troubles. Day by day, hour by hour, minute after minute, he lived in pain, pain his only memory, questioning the necessity of it, inveighing against it, also, though with affection, against God. Why *so much*, Gottenyu? If He wanted to teach His servant a lesson for some reason, some cause—the nature of His nature—to teach him, say, for reasons of his weakness, his pride, perhaps, during his years of prosperity, his frequent neglect of God—to give him a little lesson, why then any of the tragedies that had happened to him, any *one* would have sufficed to chasten him. But *all together*—the loss of both his children, his means of livelihood, Fanny's health and his—that was too much to ask one frail-boned man to endure. Who, after all, was Manischevitz that he had been given so much to suffer? A tailor. Certainly not a man of talent. Upon him suffering was largely wasted. It went nowhere, into nothing: into more suffering. His pain did not earn him bread, nor fill the cracks in the wall, nor lift, in the middle of the night, the kitchen table; only lay upon him, sleepless, so sharply, oppressively, that he could many times have cried out yet not heard himself through this thickness of misery.

In this mood he gave no thought to Mr. Alexander Levine, but at moments when the pain waivered, slightly diminishing, he sometimes wondered if he had been mistaken to dismiss him. A black Jew and angel to boot—very hard to believe, but suppose he *had* been sent to succor him, and he, Manischevitz, was in his blindness too blind to comprehend? It was this thought that put him on the knife-point of agony.

Therefore the tailor, after much self-questioning and continuing doubt, decided he would seek the self-styled angel in Harlem. Of course he had great difficulty, because he had not asked for specific directions, and movement was tedious to him. The subway took him to 116th Street, and from there he wandered in the dark world. It was vast and its lights lit nothing. Everywhere were shadows, often moving. Manischevitz hobbled along with the aid of a cane, and not knowing where to seek in the blackened tenement buildings, looked fruitlessly through store windows. In the stores he saw people and *everybody* was black. It was an amazing thing to observe. When he was too tired, too unhappy to go farther, Manischevitz stopped in front of a tailor's store. Out of familiarity with the appearance of it, with some sadness he entered. The tailor, an old skinny Negro with a mop of woolly gray hair, was sitting cross-legged on his workbench, sewing a pair of full-dress pants that had a razor slit all the way down the seat.

"You'll excuse me, please, gentleman," said Manischevitz, admiring the tailor's deft, thimbled fingerwork, "but you know maybe somebody by the name Alexander Levine?"

The tailor, who Manischevitz thought, seemed a little antagonistic to him, scratched his scalp.

"Cain't say I ever heared dat name."

"Alex-ander Lev-ine," Manischevitz repeated it.

The man shook his head. "Cain't say I heared."

About to depart, Manischevitz remembered to say: "He is an angel, maybe."

"Oh *him,*" said the tailor clucking. "He hang out in dat honky tonk down here a ways." He pointed with his skinny finger and returned to the pants.

Manischevitz crossed the street against a red light and was almost run down by a taxi. On the block after the next, the sixth store from the corner was a cabaret, and the name in sparkling lights was Bella's. Ashamed to go in, Manischevitz gazed through the neon-lit window, and when the dancing couples had parted and drifted away, he discovered at a table on the side, towards the rear, Levine.

He was sitting alone, a cigarette butt hanging from the corner of his mouth, playing solitaire with a dirty pack of cards, and Manischevitz felt a touch of pity for him, for Levine had deteriorated in appearance. His derby was dented and had a gray smudge on the side. His ill-fitting suit was shabbier, as if he had been sleeping in it. His shoes and trouser cuffs were muddy, and his face was covered with an impenetrable stubble the color of licorice. Manischevitz, though deeply disappointed, was about to enter, when a big-breasted Negress in a purple evening gown appeared before Levine's table, and with much laughter through many white teeth, broke into a vigorous shimmy. Levine looked straight at Manischevitz with a haunted expression, but the tailor was too paralyzed to move or acknowledge it. As Bella's gyrations continued, Levine rose, his eyes lit in excitement. She embraced him with vigor, both his hands clasped around her big restless buttocks and they tangoed together across the floor, loudly applauded by the noisy customers. She seemed to have lifted Levine off his feet and his large shoes hung limp as they danced. They slid past the windows where Manischevitz, white-faced, stood staring in. Levine winked slyly and the tailor left for home.

Fanny lay at death's door. Through shrunken lips she muttered concerning her childhood, the sorrows of the marriage bed, the loss of her children, yet wept to live. Manischevitz tried not to listen, but even without ears he would have heard. It was not a gift. The doctor panted up the stairs, a broad but bland, unshaven man (it was Sunday), and soon shook his head. A day at most, or two. He left at once, not without pity, to spare himself Manischevitz's multiplied sorrow; the man who never stopped hurting. He would someday get him into a public home.

Manischevitz visited a synagogue and there spoke to God, but God had absented himself. The tailor searched his heart and found no hope. When she died he would live dead. He considered taking his life although he knew he wouldn't. Yet it was something to consider. Considering, you existed. He railed against God—Can you love a rock, a broom, an emptiness? Baring his chest, he smote the naked bones, cursing himself for having believed.

Asleep in a chair that afternoon, he dreamed of Levine. He was standing before a faded mirror, preening small decaying opalescent wings. "This means," mumbled Manischevitz, as he broke out of sleep, "that it is possible he could be an angel." Begging a neighbor lady to look in on Fanny and occasionally wet her lips with a few drops of water, he drew on his thin coat, gripped his walking stick, exchanged some pennies for a subway token, and rode to Harlem. He knew this act was the last desperate one of his woe: to go without belief, seeking a black magician to restore his wife to invalidism. Yet if there was no choice, he did at least what was chosen.

He hobbled to Bella's but the place had changed hands. It was now, as he breathed, a synagogue in a store. In the front, towards him, were several rows of empty wooden benches. In the rear stood the Ark, its portals of rough wood covered with rainbows of sequins; under it a long table on which lay the sacred scroll unrolled, illuminated by the dim light from a bulb on a chain overhead. Around the table, as if frozen to it and the scroll, which they all touched with their fingers, sat four Negroes wearing skullcaps. Now as they read the Holy Word, Manischevitz could, through the plate glass window, hear the singsong chant of their voices. One of them was old, with a gray beard. One was bubble-eyed. One was humpbacked. The fourth was a boy, no older than thirteen. Their heads moved in rhythmic swaying. Touched by this sight from his childhood and youth, Manischevitz entered and stood silent in the rear.

"Neshoma," said bubble eyes, pointing to the word with a stubby finger. "Now what dat mean?"

"That's the word that means soul," said the boy. He wore glasses.

"Let's git on wid de commentary," said the old man.

"Ain't necessary," said the humpback. "Souls is immaterial substance. That's all. The soul is derived in that manner. The immateriality is derived from the substance, and they both, causally an' otherwise, derived from the soul. There can be no higher."

"That's the highest."

"Over de top."

"Wait a minute," said bubble eyes. "I don't see what is dat immaterial substance. How come de one gits hitched up to de odder?" He addressed the humpback.

"Ask me something hard. Because it is substanceless immateriality. It couldn't be closer together, like all the parts of the body under one skin—closer."

"Hear now," said the old man.

"All you done is switched de words."

"It's the primum mobile, the substanceless substance from which comes all things that were incepted in the idea—you, me and everything and body else."

"Now how did all dat happen? Make it sound simple."

"It de speerit," said the old man. "On de face of de water moved de speerit. An' dat was good. It say so in de Book. From de speerit ariz de man."

"But now listen here. How come it become substance if it all de time a spirit?"

"God alone done dat."

"Holy! Holy! Praise His Name."

"But has dis spirit got some kind of a shade or color?" asked bubble eyes, deadpan.

"Man, of course not. A spirit is a spirit."

"Then how come we is colored?" he said with a triumphant glare.

"Ain't got nothing to do wid dat."

"I still like to know."

"God put the spirit in all things," answered the boy. "He put it in the green leaves and the yellow flowers. He put it with the gold in the fishes and the blue in the sky. That's how come it came to us."

"Amen."

"Praise Lawd and utter loud His speechless name."

"Blow de bugle till it bust the sky."

They fell silent, intent upon the next word. Manischevitz approached them.

"You'll excuse me," he said. "I am looking for Alexander Levine. You know him maybe?"

"That's the angel," said the boy.

"Oh, *him,*" snuffed bubble eyes.

"You'll find him at Bella's. It's the establishment right across the street," the humpback said.

Manischevitz said he was sorry that he could not stay, thanked them, and limped across the street. It was already night. The city was dark and he could barely find his way.

But Bella's was bursting with the blues. Through the window Manischevitz recognized the dancing crowd and among them sought Levine. He was sitting loose-lipped at Bella's side table. They were tippling from an almost empty whiskey fifth. Levine had shed his old clothes, wore a shiny new checkered suit, pearl-gray derby, cigar, and big, two-tone button shoes. To the tailor's dismay, a drunken look had settled upon his formerly dignified face. He leaned toward Bella, tickled her ear lobe with his pinky, while whispering words that sent her into gales of raucous laughter. She fondled his knee.

Manischevitz, girding himself, pushed open the door and was not welcomed.

"This place reserved."

"Beat it, pale puss."

"Exit, Yankel, Semitic trash."

But he moved towards the table where Levine sat, the crowd breaking before him as he hobbled forward.

"Mr. Levine," he spoke in a trembly voice. "Is here Manischevitz."

Levine glared blearily. "Speak yo' piece, son."

Manischevitz shuddered. His back plagued him. Cold tremors tormented his crooked legs. He looked around, everybody was all ears.

"You'll excuse me. I would like to talk to you in a private place."

"Speak, Ah is a private pusson."

Bella laughed piercingly. "Stop it, boy, you killin' me."

Manischevitz, no end disturbed, considered fleeing but Levine addressed him:

"Kindly state the pu'pose of yo' communication with yo's truly."

The tailor wet cracked lips. "You are Jewish. This I am sure."

Levine rose, nostrils flaring. "Anythin' else yo' got to say?"

Manischevitz's tongue lay like stone.

"Speak now or fo'ever hold off."

Tears blinded the tailor's eyes. Was ever man so tried? Should he say he believed a half-drunken Negro to be an angel?

The silence slowly petrified.

Manischevitz was recalling scenes of his youth as a wheel in his mind whirred: believe, do not, yes, no, yes, no. The pointer pointed to yes, to between yes and no, to no, no it was yes. He sighed. It moved but one had still to make a choice.

"I think you are an angel from God." He said it in a broken voice, thinking. If you said it it was said. If you believed it you must say it. If you believed, you believed.

The hush broke. Everybody talked but the music began and they went on dancing. Bella, grown bored, picked up the cards and dealt herself a hand.

Levine burst into tears. "How you have humiliated me."

Manischevitz apologized.

"Wait'll I freshen up." Levine went to the men's room and returned in his old clothes.

No one said goodbye as they left.

They rode to the flat via subway. As they walked up the stairs Manischevitz pointed with his cane at his door.

"That's all been taken care of," Levine said. "You best go in while I take off."

Disappointed that it was so soon over but torn by curiosity, Manischevitz followed the angel up three flights to the roof. When he got there the door was already padlocked.

Luckily he could see through a small broken window. He heard an odd noise, as though of a whirring of wings, and when he strained for a wider view, could have sworn he saw a dark figure borne aloft on a pair of magnificent black wings.

A feather drifted down. Manischevitz gasped as it turned white, but it was only snowing.

He rushed downstairs. In the flat Fanny wielded a dust mop under the bed and then upon the cobwebs on the wall.

"A wonderful thing, Fanny," Manischevitz said. "Believe me, there are Jews everywhere."

# Thomas Mann

*Mann (1875–1955) was born in Lübeck, Germany, the son of a distinguished merchant family. His brother Heinrich also became a well-known writer. In 1900, Mann told the story of several generations of this family in his first novel,* Buddenbrooks, *which, upon its appearance, made the author immediately famous. For the remainder of his long life he was something of a literary statesman, whose task was to reconcile the distinctive qualities of the German temperament with the more general currents of European thought and culture. In* The Magic Mountain *(1924) he uses the setting of an isolated sanitarium to stage the encounter of an easygoing and naive young German with representatives of the nationalisms and ideologies competing in Europe on the eve of World War I. Mann's vocal opposition to the Nazis led him to exile after they came to power in 1933. He spent most of the next twelve years in the United States, writing novels and political attacks against the Hitler regime. He became an American citizen in 1944. After the defeat of the Axis powers, he returned to Europe, still painfully concerned about the political situation and the beginnings of the cold war. His novel* Doctor Faustus *(1947) is, among other things, an allegory of the fall of Germany and the cultural crisis manifested in that collapse. Some of his other novels are* The Beloved Returns *(translated in 1940),* Joseph and His Brothers *(1933–44), and* Confessions of Felix Krull, Confidence Man *(1954). His stories are collected in* Stories of Three Decades *(1936).*

## Death in Venice[1]

Gustave Aschenbach—or von Aschenbach, as he had been known officially since his fiftieth birthday[2]—had set out alone from his house in Prince Regent Street, Munich, for an extended walk. It was a spring afternoon in that year of grace 19—, when Europe sat upon the anxious seat beneath a menace that hung over its head for months.[3] Aschenbach had sought the open soon after tea. He was overwrought by a morning of hard, nerve-taxing work, work which had not ceased to exact his uttermost in the way of sustained concentration, conscientiousness, and tact; and after the noon meal found himself powerless to check the onward sweep of the productive mechanism within him, that *motus animi continuus*[4] in which, according to Cicero, eloquence resides. He had sought but not found relaxation in sleep—though the wear and tear upon his

1. Translated by H. T. Lowe-Porter. 2. He has been given the German equivalent of a knighthood. 3. One of the confrontations between Imperial Germany and other colonial powers that led to World War I. 4. Continuous motion of the spirit (Latin).

system had come to make a daily nap more and more imperative—and now undertook a walk, in the hope that air and exercise might send him back refreshed to a good evening's work.

May had begun, and after weeks of cold and wet a mock summer had set in. The English Gardens,[5] though in tenderest leaf, felt as sultry as in August and were full of vehicles and pedestrians near the city. But towards Aumeister the paths were solitary and still, and Aschenbach strolled thither, stopping awhile to watch the lively crowds in the restaurant garden with its fringe of carriages and cabs. Thence he took his homeward way outside the park and across the sunset fields. By the time he reached the North Cemetery, however, he felt tired, and a storm was brewing above Föhring; so he waited at the stopping-place for a tram to carry him back to the city.

He found the neighbourhood quite empty. Not a wagon in sight, either on the paved Ungererstrasse, with its gleaming tramlines stretching off towards Schwabing, nor on the Föhring Highway. Nothing stirred behind the hedge in the stone-mason's yard, where crosses, monuments, and commemorative tablets made a supernumerary and untenanted graveyard opposite the real one. The mortuary chapel, a structure in Byzantine style, stood facing it, silent in the gleam of the ebbing day. Its façade was adorned with Greek crosses and tinted hieratic designs, and displayed a symmetrically arranged selection of scriptural texts in gilded letters, all of them with a bearing upon the future life, such as: "They are entering into the House of the Lord" and "May the Light Everlasting shine upon them." Aschenbach beguiled some minutes of his waiting with reading these formulas and letting his mind's eye lose itself in their mystical meaning. He was brought back to reality by the sight of a man standing in the portico, above the two apocalyptic beasts that guarded the staircase, and something not quite usual in this man's appearance gave his thoughts a fresh turn.

Whether he had come out of the hall through the bronze doors or mounted unnoticed from outside, it was impossible to tell. Aschenbach casually inclined to the first idea. He was of medium height, thin, beardless, and strikingly snub-nosed; he belonged to the red-haired type and possessed its milky, freckled skin. He was obviously not Bavarian; and the broad, straight-brimmed straw hat he had on even made him look distinctly exotic. True, he had the indigenous rucksack buckled on his back, wore a belted suit of yellowish woollen stuff, apparently frieze,[6] and carried a grey mackintosh cape across his left forearm, which was propped against his waist. In his right hand, slantwise to the ground, he held an iron-shod stick, and braced himself against its crook, with his legs crossed. His chin was up, so that the Adam's apple looked very bald in the lean neck rising from the loose shirt; and he stood there sharply peering up into space out of colourless, red-lashed eyes, while two pronounced perpendicular furrows showed on his forehead in curious contrast to his little turned-up nose. Perhaps his heightened and heightening position helped out the impression Aschenbach received. At any rate, standing there as though at survey, the man had a bold and domineering, even a ruthless air, and his lips completed the

5. Large public park in Munich. 6. A coarse cloth.

picture by seeming to curl back, either by reason of some deformity or else because he grimaced, being blinded by the sun in his face; they laid bare the long, white, glistening teeth to the gums.

Aschenbach's gaze, though unawares, had very likely been inquisitive and tactless; for he became suddenly conscious that the stranger was returning it, and indeed so directly, with such hostility, such plain intent to force the withdrawal of the other's eyes, that Aschenbach felt an unpleasant twinge and, turning his back, began to walk along the hedge, hastily resolving to give the man no further heed. He had forgotten him the next minute. Yet whether the pilgrim air the stranger wore kindled his fantasy or whether some other physical or psychical influence came in play, he could not tell; but he felt the most surprising consciousness of a widening of inward barriers, a kind of vaulting unrest, a youthfully ardent thirst for distant scenes—a feeling so lively and so new, or at least so long ago outgrown and forgot, that he stood there rooted to the spot, his eyes on the ground and his hands clasped behind him, exploring these sentiments of his, their bearing and scope.

True, what he felt was no more than a longing to travel; yet coming upon him with such suddenness and passion as to resemble a seizure, almost a hallucination. Desire projected itself visually: his fancy, not quite yet lulled since morning, imaged the marvels and terrors of the manifold earth. He saw. He beheld a landscape, a tropical marshland, beneath a reeking sky, steaming, monstrous, rank—a kind of primeval wilderness-world of islands, morasses, and alluvial channels. Hairy palm-trunks rose near and far out of lush brakes of fern, out of bottoms of crass vegetation, fat, swollen, thick with incredible bloom. There were trees, mis-shapen as a dream, that dropped their naked roots straight through the air into the ground or into water that was stagnant and shadowy and glassy-green, where mammoth milk-white blossoms floated, and strange high-shouldered birds with curious bills stood gazing sidewise without sound or stir. Among the knotted joints of a bamboo thicket the eyes of a crouching tiger gleamed—and he felt his heart throb with terror, yet with a longing inexplicable. Then the vision vanished. Aschenbach, shaking his head, took up his march once more along the hedge of the stone-mason's yard.

He had, at least ever since he commanded means to get about the world at will, regarded travel as a necessary evil, to be endured now and again willy-nilly for the sake of one's health. Too busy with the tasks imposed upon him by his own ego and the European soul, too laden with the care and duty to create, too preoccupied to be an amateur of the gay outer world, he had been content to know as much of the earth's surface as he could without stirring far outside his own sphere—had, indeed, never even been tempted to leave Europe. Now more than ever, since his life was on the wane, since he could no longer brush aside as fanciful his artist fear of not having done, of not being finished before the works ran down, he had confined himself to close range, had hardly stepped outside the charming city which he had made his home and the rude country house he had built in the mountains, whither he went to spend the rainy summers.

And so the new impulse which thus late and suddenly swept over him was speedily made to conform to the pattern of self-discipline he had followed from his youth up. He had meant to bring his work, for which he lived, to a certain point before leaving for the country, and the thought of a leisurely ramble across the globe, which should take him away from his desk for months, was too fantastic and upsetting to be seriously entertained. Yet the source of the unexpected contagion was known to him only too well. This yearning for new and distant scenes, this craving for freedom, release, forgetfulness—they were, he admitted to himself, an impulse towards flight, flight from the spot which was the daily theatre of a rigid, cold, and passionate service. That service he loved, had even almost come to love the enervating daily struggle between a proud, tenacious, well-tried will and this growing fatigue, which no one must suspect, nor the finished product betray by any faintest sign that his inspiration could ever flag or miss fire. On the other hand, it seemed the part of common sense not to span the bow too far, not to suppress summarily a need that so unequivocally asserted itself. He thought of his work, and the place where yesterday and again today he had been forced to lay it down, since it would not yield either to patient effort, or a swift *coup de main.*[7] Again and again he had tried to break or untie the knot—only to retire at last from the attack with a shiver of repugnance. Yet the difficulty was actually not a great one; what sapped his strength was distaste for the task, betrayed by a fastidiousness he could no longer satisfy. In his youth, indeed, the nature and inmost essence of the literary gift had been, to him, this very scrupulosity; for it he had bridled and tempered his sensibilities, knowing full well that feeling is prone to be content with easy gains and blithe half-perfection. So now, perhaps, feeling, thus tyrannized, avenged itself by leaving him, refusing from now on to carry and wing his art and taking away with it all the ecstasy he had known in form and expression. Not that he was doing bad work. So much, at least, the years had brought him, that at any moment he might feel tranquilly assured of mastery. But he got no joy of it—not though a nation paid it homage. To him it seemed his work had ceased to be marked by that fiery play of fancy which is the product of joy, and more, and more potently, than any intrinsic content, forms in turn the joy of the receiving world. He dreaded the summer in the country, alone with the maid who prepared his food and the man who served him; dreaded to see the familiar mountain peaks and walls that would shut him up again with his heavy discontent. What he needed was a break, an interim existence, a means of passing time, other air and a new stock of blood, to make the summer tolerable and productive. Good, then, he would go a journey. Not far—not all the way to the tigers. A night in a *wagon-lit,*[8] three or four weeks of lotus-eating at some one of the gay world's playgrounds in the lovely south. . . .

So ran his thoughts, while the clang of the electric tram drew nearer down the Ungererstrasse; and as he mounted the platform he decided to devote the evening to a study of maps and railway guides. Once in, he bethought him to look back after the man in the straw hat, the companion of this brief interval which had after all been so fruitful. But he was not in his former place, nor in the train itself, nor yet at the next stop; in short, his whereabouts remained a mystery.

7. Single decisive stroke (French). 8. Sleeping car (French).

Gustave Aschenbach was born at L———, a country town in the province of Silesia. He was the son of an upper official in the judicature, and his forebears had all been officers, judges, departmental functionaries—men who lived their strict, decent, sparing lives in the service of king and state. Only once before had a livelier mentality—in the quality of a clergyman—turned up among them; but swifter, more perceptive blood had in the generation before the poet's flowed into the stock from the mother's side, she being the daughter of a Bohemian musical conductor. It was from her he had the foreign traits that betrayed themselves in his appearance. The union of dry, conscientious officialdom and ardent, obscure impulse, produced an artist—and this particular artist: author of the lucid and vigorous prose epic on the life of Frederick the Great; careful, tireless weaver of the richly patterned tapestry entitled *Maia,* a novel that gathers up the threads of many human destinies in the warp of a single idea; creator of that powerful narrative *The Abject,* which taught a whole grateful generation that a man can still be capable of moral resolution even after he has plumbed the depths of knowledge; and lastly—to complete the tale of works of his mature period—the writer of that impassioned discourse on the theme of Mind and Art whose ordered force and antithetic eloquence led serious critics to rank it with Schiller's[9] *Simple and Sentimental Poetry.*

Aschenbach's whole soul, from the very beginning, was bent on fame—and thus, while not precisely precocious, yet thanks to the unmistakable trenchancy of his personal accent he was early ripe and ready for a career. Almost before he was out of high school he had a name. Ten years later he had learned to sit at his desk and sustain and live up to his growing reputation, to write gracious and pregnant phrases in letters that must needs be brief, for many claims press upon the solid and successful man. At forty, worn down by the strains and stresses of his actual task, he had to deal with a daily post heavy with tributes from his own and foreign countries.

Remote on one hand from the banal, on the other from the eccentric, his genius was calculated to win at once the adhesion of the general public and the admiration, both sympathetic and stimulating, of the connoisseur. From childhood up he was pushed on every side to achievement, and achievement of no ordinary kind; and so his young days never knew the sweet idleness and blithe *laissez aller*[1] that belong to youth. A nice observer once said of him in company—it was at the time when he fell ill in Vienna in his thirty-fifth year: "You see, Aschenbach has always lived liked this"—here the speaker closed the fingers of his left hand to a fist—"never like this"—and he let his open hand hang relaxed from the back of his chair. It was apt. And this attitude was the more morally valiant in that Aschenbach was not by nature robust—he was only called to the constant tension of his career, not actually born to it.

By medical advice he had been kept from school and educated at home. He had grown up solitary, without comradeship; yet had early been driven to see that he belonged to those whose talent is not so much out of the common as is the physical basis on which talent relies for its fulfilment. It is a seed that

9. German poet (1759–1805), playwright, and critic. Frederick the Great (1740–1786), king of Prussia. "Maia": in the Hindu religion this is the veil of illusion that hides reality. 1. Letting things slide (French).

gives early of its fruit, whose powers seldom reach a ripe old age. But his favourite motto was "Hold fast"; indeed, in his novel on the life of Frederick the Great he envisaged nothing else than the apotheosis of the old hero's word of command, *"Durchhalten,"* which seemed to him the epitome of fortitude under suffering. Besides, he deeply desired to live to a good old age, for it was his conviction that only the artist to whom it has been granted to be fruitful on all stages of our human scene can be truly great, or universal, or worthy of honor.

Bearing the burden of his genius, then, upon such slender shoulders and resolved to go so far, he had the more need of discipline—and discipline, fortunately, was his native inheritance from the father's side. At forty, at fifty, he was still living as he had commenced to live in the years when others are prone to waste and revel, dream high thoughts and postpone fulfilment. He began his day with a cold shower over chest and back; then, setting a pair of tall wax candles in silver holders at the head of his manuscript, he sacrificed to art, in two or three hours of almost religious fervour, the powers he had assembled in sleep. Outsiders might be pardoned for believing that his *Maia* world and the epic amplitude revealed by the life of Frederick were a manifestation of great power working under high pressure, that they came forth, as it were, all in one breath. It was the more triumph for his morale; for the truth was that they were heaped up to greatness in layer after layer, in long days of work, out of hundreds and hundreds of single inspirations; they owed their excellence, both of mass and detail, to one thing and one alone; that their creator could hold out for years under the strain of the same piece of work, with an endurance and a tenacity of purpose like that which had conquered his native province of Silesia,[2] devoting to actual composition none but his best and freshest hours.

For an intellectual product of any value to exert an immediate influence which shall also be deep and lasting, it must rest on an inner harmony, yes, an affinity, between the personal destiny of its author and that of his contemporaries in general. Men do not know why they award fame to one work of art rather than another. Without being in the faintest connoisseurs, they think to justify the warmth of their commendations by discovering in it a hundred virtues, whereas the real ground of their applause is inexplicable—it is sympathy. Aschenbach had once given direct expression—though in an unobtrusive place—to the idea that almost everything conspicuously great is great in despite: has come into being in defiance of affliction and pain; poverty, destitution, bodily weakness, vice, passion, and a thousand other obstructions. And that was more than observation—it was the fruit of experience, it was precisely the formula of his life and fame, it was the key to his work. What wonder, then, if it was also the fixed character, the outward gesture, of his most individual figures?

The new type of hero favoured by Aschenbach, and recurring many times in his works, had early been analysed by a shrewd critic: "The conception of an intellectual and virginal manliness, which clenches its teeth and stands in modest defiance of the swords and spears that pierce its side." That was beautiful,

2. Frederick's conquest of this province was accomplished over a period of years.

it was *spirituel,* it was exact, despite the suggestion of too great passivity it held. Forbearance in the fact of fate, beauty constant under torture, are not merely passive. They are a positive achievement, an explicit triumph; and the figure of Sebastian[3] is the most beautiful symbol, if not of art as a whole, yet certainly of the art we speak of here. Within that world of Aschenbach's creation were exhibited many phases of this theme: there was the aristocratic self-command that is eaten out within and for as long as it can conceals it biologic decline from the eyes of the world; the sere and ugly outside, hiding the embers of smouldering fire—and having power to fan them to so pure a flame as to challenge supremacy in the domain of beauty itself; the pallid languors of the flesh, contrasted with the fiery ardours of the spirit within, which can fling a whole proud people down at the foot of the Cross, at the feet of its own sheer self-abnegation; the gracious bearing preserved in the stern, stark service of form; the unreal, precarious existence of the born intrigant with its swiftly enervating alternation of schemes and desires—all these human fates and many more of their like one read in Aschenbach's pages, and reading them might doubt the existence of any other kind of heroism than the heroism born of weakness. And, after all, what kind could be truer to the spirit of the times? Gustave Aschenbach was the poet-spokesman of all those who labour at the edge of exhaustion; of the overburdened, of those who are already worn out but still hold themselves upright; of all our modern moralizers of accomplishment, with stunted growth and scanty resources, who yet contrive by skilful husbanding and prodigious spasms of will to produce, at least for a while, the effect of greatness. There are many such, they are the heroes of the age. And in Aschenbach's pages they saw themselves; he justified, he exalted them, he sang their praise—and they, they were grateful, they heralded his fame.

He had been young and crude with the times and by them badly counselled. He had taken false steps, blundered, exposed himself, offended in speech and writing against fact and good sense. But he had attained to honour, and honour, he used to say, is the natural goal towards which every considerable talent presses with whip and spur. Yes, one might put it that his whole career had been one conscious and overweening ascent to honour, which left in the rear all the misgivings or self-derogation which might have hampered him.

What pleases the public is lively and vivid delineation which makes no demands on the intellect; but passionate and absolutist youth can only be enthralled by a problem. And Aschenbach was as absolute, as problematist, as any youth of them all. He had done homage to intellect, had overworked the soil of knowledge and ground up her seed-corn; had turned his back on the "mysteries," called genius itself in question, held up art to scorn—yes, even while his faithful following revelled in the characters he created, he, the young artist, was taking away the breath of the twenty-year-olds with his cynic utterances on the nature of art and the artist life.

But it seems that a noble and active mind blunts itself against nothing so quickly as the sharp and bitter irritant of knowledge. And certain it is that the youth's constancy of purpose, no matter how painfully conscientious, was shal-

3. St. Sebastian was a Roman martyred in the third century A.D.

low beside the mature resolution of the master of his craft, who made a right-about-face, turned his back on the realm of knowledge, and passed it by with averted face, lest it lame his will or power of action, paralyse his feelings or his passions, deprive any of these of their conviction or utility. How else interpret the oft-cited story of *The Abject* than as a rebuke to the excess of a psychology-ridden age, embodied in the delineation of the weak and silly fool who manages to lead fate by the nose; driving his wife, out of sheer innate pusillanimity, into the arms of a beardless youth, and making this disaster an excuse for trifling away the rest of his life?

With rage the author here rejects the rejected, casts out the outcast—and the measure of his fury is the measure of his condemnation of all moral shilly-shallying. Explicitly he renounces sympathy with the abyss, explicitly he refutes the flabby humanitarianism of the phrase: *"Tout comprendre c'est tout pardonner."*[4] What was here unfolding or rather was already in full bloom, was the "miracle of regained detachment," which a little later became the theme of one of the author's dialogues, dwelt upon not without a certain oracular emphasis. Strange sequence of thought! Was it perhaps an intellectual consequence of this rebirth, this new austerity, that from now on his style showed an almost exaggerated sense of beauty, a lofty purity, symmetry, and simplicity, which gave his productions a stamp of the classic, of conscious and deliberate mastery? And yet: this moral fibre, surviving the hampering and disintegrating effect of knowledge, does it not result in its turn in a dangerous simplification, in a tendency to equate the world and the human soul, and thus to strengthen the hold of the evil, the forbidden, and the ethically impossible? And has not form two aspects? Is it not moral and immoral at once: moral in so far as it is the expression and result of discipline, immoral—yes, actually hostile to morality—in that of its very essence it is indifferent to good and evil, and deliberately concerned to make the moral world stoop beneath its proud and undivided sceptre?

Be that as it may. Development is destiny; and why should a career attended by the applause and adulation of the masses necessarily take the same course as one which does not share the glamour and the obligations of fame? Only the incorrigible bohemian smiles or scoffs when a man of transcendent gifts outgrows his carefree prentice stage, recognizes his own worth and forces the world to recognize it too and pay it homage, though he puts on a courtly bearing to hide his bitter struggles and his loneliness. Again, the play of a developing talent must give its possessor joy, if of a wilful, defiant kind. With time, an official note, something almost expository, crept into Gustave Aschenbach's method. His later style gave up the old sheer audacities, the fresh and subtle nuances—it became fixed and exemplary, conservative, formal, even formulated. Like Louis XIV[5]—or as tradition has it of him—Aschenbach, as he went on in years, banished from his style every common word. It was at this time that the school authorities adopted selections from his works into their text-books. And he found it only fitting—and had no thought but to accept—when a German prince signalized his accession to the throne by conferring

4. "To understand all is to forgive all" (French). 5. French king (1638–1715).

upon the poet-author of the life of Frederick the Great on his fiftieth birthday the letters-patent of nobility.

He had roved about for a few years, trying this place and that as a place of residence, before choosing, as he soon did, the city of Munich for his permanent home. And there he lived, enjoying among his fellow-citizens the honour which is in rare cases the reward of intellectual eminence. He married young, the daughter of a university family; but after a brief term of wedded happiness his wife had died. A daughter, already married, remained to him. A son he never had.

Gustave von Aschenbach was somewhat below middle height, dark and smooth-shaven, with a head that looked rather too large for his almost delicate figure. He wore his hair brushed back; it was thin at the parting, bushy and grey on the temples, framing a lofty, rugged, knotty brow—if one may so characterize it. The nose-piece of his rimless gold spectacles cut into the base of his thick, aristocratically hooked nose. The mouth was large, often lax, often suddenly narrow and tense; the cheeks lean and furrowed, the pronounced chin slightly cleft. The vicissitudes of fate, it seemed, must have passed over this head, for he held it, plaintively, rather on one side; yet it was art, not the stern discipline of an active career, that had taken over the office of modelling these features. Behind this brow were born the flashing thrust and parry of the dialogue between Frederick and Voltaire on the theme of war; these eyes, weary and sunken, gazing through their glasses, had beheld the blood-stained inferno of the hospitals in the Seven Years' War.[6] Yes, personally speaking too, art heightens life. She gives deeper joy, she consumes more swiftly. She engraves adventures of the spirit and the mind in the faces of her votaries; let them lead outwardly a life of the most cloistered calm, she will in the end produce in them a fastidiousness, an over-refinement, a nervous fever and exhaustion, such as a career of extravagant passions and pleasures can hardly show.

Eager though he was to be off, Aschenbach was kept in Munich by affairs both literary and practical for some two weeks after that walk of his. But at length he ordered his country home put ready against his return within the next few days, and on a day between the middle and the end of May took the evening train for Trieste, where he stopped only twenty-four hours, embarking for Pola[7] the next morning but one.

What he sought was a fresh scene, without associations, which should yet be not too out-of-the-way; and accordingly he chose an island in the Adriatic, not far off the Istrian coast. It had been well known for some years, for its splendidly rugged cliff formations on the side next the open sea, and its population, clad in a bright flutter of rags and speaking an outlandish tongue. But there was rain and heavy air; the society at the hotel was provincial Austrian, and limited; besides, it annoyed him not to be able to get at the sea—he missed the close and soothing contact which only a gentle sandy slope affords. He could not feel this was the place he sought; an inner impulse made him

6. A war involving European powers on the Continent, in India, and in America (1756–63). François-Marie Arouet de Voltaire (1694–1778), French philosopher and writer. 7. Trieste and Pola were, at the time of the story, Italian cities.

wretched, urging him on he knew not whither; he racked his brains, he looked up boats, then all at once his goal stood plain before his eyes. But of course! When one wanted to arrive overnight at the incomparable, the fabulous, the like-nothing-else-in-the-world, where was it one went? Why, obviously; he had intended to go there, what ever was he doing here? A blunder. He made all haste to correct it, announcing his departure at once. Ten days after his arrival on the island a swift motorboat bore him and his luggage in the misty dawning back across the water to the naval station, where he landed only to pass over the landing-stage and on to the wet decks of a ship lying there with steam up for the passage to Venice.

It was an ancient hulk belonging to an Italian line, obsolete, dingy, grimed with soot. A dirty hunchbacked sailor, smirkingly polite, conducted him at once below-ship to a cavernous, lamplit cabin. There behind a table sat a man with a beard like a goat's; he had his hat on the back of his head, a cigar-stump in the corner of his mouth; he reminded Aschenbach of an old-fashioned circus-director. This person put the usual questions and wrote out a ticket to Venice, which he issued to the traveller with many commercial flourishes.

"A ticket for Venice," repeated he, stretching out his arm to dip the pen into the thick ink in a tilted inkstand. "One first-class to Venice! Here you are, *signore mio.*" He made some scrawls on the paper, strewed bluish sand on it out of a box, thereafter letting the sand run off into an earthen vessel, folded the paper with bony yellow fingers, and wrote on the outside. "An excellent choice," he rattled on. "Ah, Venice! What a glorious city! Irresistibly attractive to the cultured man for her past history as well as her present charm." His copious gesturings and empty phrases gave the odd impression that he feared the traveller might alter his mind. He changed Aschenbach's note, laying the money on the spotted tablecover with the glibness of a croupier. "A pleasant visit to you, signore," he said, with a melodramatic bow. "Delighted to serve you." Then he beckoned and called out: "Next" as though a stream of passengers stood waiting to be served, though in point of fact there was not one. Aschenbach returned to the upper deck.

He leaned an arm on the railing and looked at the idlers lounging along the quay to watch the boat go out. Then he turned his attention to his fellow-passengers. Those of the second class, both men and women, were squatted on their bundles of luggage on the forward deck. The first cabin consisted of a group of lively youths, clerks from Pola, evidently, who had made up a pleasure excursion to Italy and were not a little thrilled at the prospect, bustling about and laughing with satisfaction at the stir they made. They leaned over the railings and shouted, with a glib command of epithet, derisory remarks at such of their fellow-clerks as they saw going to business along the quay; and these in turn shook their sticks and shouted as good back again. One of the party, in a dandified buff suit, a rakish panama with a coloured scarf, and a red cravat, was loudest of the loud: he outcrowed all the rest. Aschenbach's eye dwelt on him, and he was shocked to see that the apparent youth was no youth at all. He was an old man, beyond a doubt, with wrinkles and crow's-feet round eyes and a mouth; the dull carmine of the cheeks was rouge, the brown hair a wig. His neck was shrunken and sinewy, his turned-up moustaches and small imperial were dyed, and the unbroken double row of yellow teeth he showed when he laughed were but too obviously a cheapish false set. He wore a seal ring on each forefinger, but the hands were those of an old man. Aschenbach was moved to shudder as he watched the creature and his association with the rest of the group. Could they not see he was old, that he had no right to wear the clothes they wore or pretend to be one of them? But they were used to him, it seemed; they suffered him among them, they paid back his jokes in kind and the playful pokes in the ribs he gave them. How could they? Aschenbach put his hand to his brow, he covered his eyes, for he had slept little, and they smarted. He felt not quite canny, as though the world were suffering a dream-like distortion of perspective which he might arrest by shutting it all out for a few minutes and then looking at it afresh. But instead he felt a floating sensation, and opened his eyes with unreasoning alarm to find that the ship's dark sluggish bulk was slowly leaving the jetty. Inch by inch, with the to-and-fro motion of her machinery, the strip of iridescent dirty water widened, the boat manœuvred clumsily and turned her bow to the open sea. Aschenbach moved over to the starboard side, where the hunchbacked sailor had set up a deck-chair for him, and a steward in a greasy dress-coat asked for orders.

The sky was grey, the wind humid. Harbour and island dropped behind, all sight of land soon vanished in mist. Flakes of sodden, clammy soot fell upon the still undried deck. Before the boat was an hour out a canvas had to be spread as a shelter from the rain.

Wrapped in his cloak, a book in his lap, our traveller rested; the hours slipped by unawares. It stopped raining, the canvas was taken down. The horizon was visible right round; beneath the sombre dome of the sky stretched the vast plain of empty sea. But immeasurable unarticulated space weakens our power to measure time as well: the time-sense falters and grows dim. Strange, shadowy figures passed and repassed—the elderly cox-comb, the goat-bearded man from the bowels of the ship—with vague gesturings and mutterings through the traveller's mind as he lay. He fell asleep.

At midday he was summoned to luncheon in a corridor-like saloon with the sleeping-cabins giving off it. He ate at the head of the long table; the party of clerks, including the old man, sat with the jolly captain at the other end, where they had been carousing since ten o'clock The meal was wretched, and soon done. Aschenbach was driven to seek the open and look at the sky—perhaps it would lighten presently above Venice.

He had not dreamed it could be otherwise, for the city had ever given him a brilliant welcome. But sky and sea remained leaden, with spurts of fine, mist-like rain; he reconciled himself to the idea of seeing a different Venice from that he had always approached on the landward side. He stood by the foremast, his gaze on the distance, alert for the first glimpse of the coast. And he thought of the melancholy and susceptible poet who had once seen the towers and turrets of his dreams rise out of these waves; repeated the rhythms born of his awe, his mingled emotions of joy and suffering—and easily susceptible to a prescience already shaped within him, he asked his own sober, weary heart if a new enthusiasm, a new preoccupation, some late adventure of the feelings could still be in store for the idle traveller.

The flat coast showed on the right, the sea was soon populous with fishing-boats. The Lido[8] appeared and was left behind as the ship glided at half speed through the narrow harbor of the same name, coming to a full stop on the lagoon in sight of garish, badly built houses. Here it waited for the boat bringing the sanitary inspector.

An hour passed. One had arrived—and yet not. There was no conceivable haste—yet one felt harried. The youths from Pola were on deck, drawn hither by the martial sound of horns coming across the water from the direction of the Public Gardens. They had drunk a good deal of Asti and were moved to shout and hurrah at the drilling *bersaglieri*.[9] But the young-old man was a truly repulsive sight in the condition to which his company with youth had brought him. He could not carry his wine like them: he was pitiably drunk. He swayed as he stood—watery-eyed, a cigarette between his shaking fingers, keeping upright with difficulty. He could not have taken a step without falling and knew better than to stir, but his spirits were deplorably high. He buttonholed anyone who came within reach, he stuttered, he giggled, he leered, he fatuously shook his beringed old forefinger; his tongue kept seeking the corner of his mouth in a suggestive motion ugly to behold. Aschenbach's brow darkened as he looked, and there came over him once more a dazed sense, as though things about him were just slightly losing their ordinary perspective, beginning to show a distortion that might merge into the grotesque. He was prevented from dwelling on the feeling, for now the machinery began to thud again, and the ship took up its passage through the Canale di San Marco which had been interrupted so near the goal.

He saw it once more, that landing-place that takes the breath away, that amazing group of incredible structures the Republic[1] set up to meet the awe-struck eye of the approaching seafarer: the airy splendour of the palace and Bridge of Sighs, the columns of lion and saint on the shore, the glory of the projecting flank of the fairy temple, the vista of gateway and clock. Looking, he thought that to come to Venice by the station is like entering a palace by the back door. No one should approach, save by the high seas as he was doing now, this most improbable of cities.

The engines stopped. Gondolas pressed alongside, the landing-stairs were let down, customs officials came on board and did their office, people began to go ashore. Aschenbach ordered a gondola. He meant to take up his abode by the sea and needed to be conveyed with his luggage to the landing-stage of the little steamers that ply between the city and the Lido. They called down his order to the surface of the water where the gondoliers were quarrelling in dialect. Then came another delay while his trunk was worried down the ladder-like stairs. Thus he was forced to endure the importunities of the ghastly young-old man, whose drunken state obscurely urged him to pay the stranger the honour of a formal farewell. "We wish you a very pleasant sojourn," he babbled, bowing and scraping. "Pray keep us in mind. *Au revoir, excusez et bon jour,*

8. Island lying just beyond the mouths of the canals of Venice. 9. Italian soldiers. 1. Venice was an independent republic before its incorporation into Italy.

*votre Excellence.*"[2] He drooled, he blinked, he licked the corner of his mouth, the little imperial bristled on his elderly chin. He put the tips of two fingers to his mouth and said thickly: "Give her our love, will you, the p-pretty little dear"—here his upper plate came away and fell down on the lower one. . . . Aschenbach escaped. "Little sweety-sweety-sweetheart" he heard behind him, gurgled and stuttered, as he climbed down the rope stair into the boat.

Is there anyone but must repress a secret thrill, on arriving in Venice for the first time—or returning thither after long absence—and stepping into a Venetian gondola? That singular conveyance, come down unchanged from ballad times, black as nothing else on earth except a coffin—what pictures it calls up of lawless, silent adventures in the plashing night; or even more, what visions of death itself, the bier and solemn rites and last soundless voyage! And has anyone remarked that the seat in such a bark, the arm-chair lacquered in coffin-black and dully black-upholstered, is the softest, most luxurious, most relaxing seat in the world? Aschenbach realized it when he had let himself down at the gondolier's feet, opposite his luggage, which lay neatly composed on the vessel's beak. The rowers still gestured fiercely; he heard their harsh, incoherent tones. But the strange stillness of the water-city seemed to take up their voices gently, to disembody and scatter them over the sea. It was warm here in the harbour. The lukewarm air of the sirocco[3] breathed upon him, he leaned back among his cushions and gave himself to the yielding element, closing his eyes for very pleasure in an indolence as unaccustomed as sweet. "The trip will be short," he thought, and wished it might last forever. They gently swayed away from the boat with its bustle and clamour of voices.

It grew still and stiller all about. No sound but the splash of the oars, the hollow slap of the wave against the steep, black, halbert-shaped beak of the vessel, and one sound more—a muttering by fits and starts, expressed as it were by the motion of his arms, from the lips of the gondolier. He was talking to himself, between his teeth. Aschenbach glanced up and saw with surprise that the lagoon was widening, his vessel was headed for the open sea. Evidently it would not do to give himself up to sweet *far niente,*[4] he must see his wishes carried out.

"You are to take me to the steamboat landing, you know," he said, half turning round towards it. The muttering stopped. There was no reply.

"Take me to the steamboat landing," he repeated, and this time turned quite round and looked up into the face of the gondolier as he stood there on his little elevated deck, high against the pale grey sky. The man had an unpleasing, even brutish face, and wore blue clothes like a sailor's, with a yellow sash; a shapeless straw hat with the braid torn at the brim perched rakishly on his head. His facial structure, as well as the curling blond moustache under the short snub nose, showed him to be of non-Italian stock. Physically rather undersized, so that one would not have expected him to be very muscular, he pulled vigorously at the oar, putting all his body-weight behind each stroke. Now and

2. "Goodbye, excuse me, and good day, your Excellence" (French). 3. The sultry and unwholesome south wind. 4. Doing nothing (Italian).

then the effort he made curled back his lips and bared his white teeth to the gums. He spoke in a decided, almost curt voice, looking out to sea over his fare's head: "The signore is going to the Lido."

Aschenbach answered: "Yes, I am. But I only took the gondola to cross over to San Marco. I am using the *vaporetto*[5] from there."

"But the signore cannot use the *vaporetto*."

"And why not?"

"Because the *vaporetto* does not take luggage."

It was true. Aschenbach remembered it. He made no answer. But the man's gruff, overbearing manner, so unlike the usual courtesy of his countrymen towards the stranger, was intolerable. Aschenbach spoke again: "That is my own affair. I may want to give my luggage in deposit. You will turn round."

No answer. The oar splashed, the wave struck dull against the prow. And the muttering began anew, the gondolier talked to himself, between his teeth.

What should the traveller do? Alone on the water with this tongue-tied, obstinate, uncanny man, he saw no way of enforcing his will. And if only he did not excite himself, how pleasantly he might rest! Had he not wished the voyage might last forever? The wisest thing—and how much the pleasantest!—was to let matters take their own course. A spell of indolence was upon him; it came from the chair he sat in—this low, black-upholstered arm-chair, so gently rocked at the hands of the despotic boatman in his rear. The thought passed dreamily through Aschenbach's brain that perhaps he had fallen into the clutches of a criminal; it had not power to rouse him to action. More annoying was the simpler explanation: that the man was only trying to extort money. A sense of duty, a recollection, as it were, that this ought to be prevented, made him collect himself to say:

"How much do you ask for the trip?"

And the gondolier, going out over his head, replied: "The signore will pay."

There was an established reply to this; Aschenbach made it, mechanically: "I will pay nothing whatever if you do not take me where I want to go."

"The signore wants to go to the Lido."

"But not with you."

"I am a good rower, signore. I will row you well."

"So much is true," thought Aschenbach, and again he relaxed. "That is true, you row me well. Even if you mean to rob me, even if you hit me in the back with your oar and send me down to the kingdom of Hades, even then you will have rowed me well."

But nothing of the sort happened. Instead, they fell in with company: a boat came alongside and waylaid them, full of men and women singing to guitar and mandolin. They rowed persistently bow for bow with the gondola and filled the silence that had rested on the waters with their lyric love of gain. Aschenbach tossed money into the hat they held out. The music stopped at once, they rowed away. And once more the gondolier's mutter became audible as he talked to himself in fits and snatches.

Thus they rowed on, rocked by the wash of a steamer returning citywards.

5. Steamboat (Italian).

At the landing two municipal officials were walking up and down with their hands behind their backs and their faces turned towards the lagoon. Aschenbach was helped on shore by the old man with a boat-hook who is the permanent feature of every landing-stage in Venice; and having no small change to pay the boatman, crossed over into the hotel opposite. His wants were supplied in the lobby; but when he came back his possessions were already on a hand-car on the quay, and gondola and gondolier were gone.

"He ran away, signore," said the old boatman. "A bad lot, a man without a licence. He is the only gondolier without one. The others telephoned over, and he knew we were on the look-out, so he made off."

Aschenbach shrugged.

"The signore has had a ride for nothing," said the old man, and held out his hat. Aschenbach dropped some coins. He directed that his luggage be taken to the Hôtel des Bains and followed the hand-car through the avenue, that white-blossoming avenue with taverns, booths, and pensions on either side it, which runs across the island diagonally to the beach.

He entered the hotel from the garden terrace at the back and passed through the vestibule and hall into the office. His arrival was expected, and he was served with courtesy and dispatch. The manager, a small, soft, dapper man with a black moustache and a caressing way with him, wearing a French frock-coat, himself took him up in the lift and showed him his room. It was a pleasant chamber, furnished in cherry-wood, with lofty windows looking out to sea. It was decorated with strong-scented flowers. Aschenbach, as soon as he was alone, and while they brought in his trunk and bags and disposed them in the room, went up to one of the windows and stood looking out upon the beach in its afternoon emptiness, and at the sunless sea, now full and sending long, low waves with rhythmic beat upon the sand.

A solitary, unused to speaking of what he sees and feels, has mental experiences which are at once more intense and less articulate than those of a gregarious man. They are sluggish, yet more wayward, and never without a melancholy tinge. Sights and impressions which others brush aside with a glance, a light comment, a smile, occupy him more than their due; they sink silently in, they take on meaning, they become experience, emotion, adventure. Solitude gives birth to the original in us, to beauty unfamiliar and perilous—to poetry. But also, it gives birth to the opposite: to the perverse, the illicit, the absurd. Thus the traveller's mind still dwelt with disquiet on the episodes of his journey hither: on the horrible old fop with his drivel about a mistress, on the outlaw boatman and his lost tip. They did not offend his reason, they hardly afforded food for thought; yet they seemed by their very nature fundamentally strange, and thereby vaguely disquieting. Yet here was the sea; even in the midst of such thoughts he saluted it with his eyes, exulting that Venice was near and accessible. At length he turned round, disposed his personal belongings and made certain arrangements with the chambermaid for his comfort, washed up, and was conveyed to the ground floor by the green-uniformed Swiss who ran the lift.

He took tea on the terrace facing the sea and afterwards went down and walked some distance along the shore promenade in the direction of Hôtel

Excelsior. When he came back it seemed to be time to change for dinner. He did so, slowly and methodically as his way was, for he was accustomed to work while he dressed; but even so found himself a little early when he entered the hall, where a large number of guests had collected—strangers to each other and affecting mutual indifference, yet united in expectancy of the meal. He picked up a paper, sat down in a leather arm-chair, and took stock of the company, which compared most favourably with that he had just left.

This was a broad and tolerant atmosphere, of wide horizons. Subdued voices were speaking most of the principal European tongues. That uniform of civilization, the conventional evening dress, gave outward conformity to the varied types. There were long, dry Americans, large-familied Russians, English ladies, German children with French *bonnes.* The Slavic element predominated, it seemed. In Aschenbach's neighbourhood Polish was being spoken.

Round a wicker table next to him was gathered a group of young folk in charge of a governess or companion—three young girls, perhaps fifteen to seventeen years old, and a long-haired boy of about fourteen. Aschenbach noticed with astonishment the lad's perfect beauty. His face recalled the noblest moment of Greek sculpture—pale, with a sweet reserve, with clustering honey-coloured ringlets, the brow and nose descending in one line, the winning mouth, the expression of pure and godlike serenity. Yet with all this chaste perfection of form it was of such unique personal charm that the observer thought he had never seen, either in nature or art, anything so utterly happy and consummate. What struck him further was the strange contrast the group afforded, a difference in educational method, so to speak, shown in the way the brother and sisters were clothed and treated. The girls, the eldest of whom was practically grown up, were dressed with an almost disfiguring austerity. All three wore half-length slate-coloured frocks of cloister-like plainness, arbitrarily unbecoming in cut, with white turn-over collars as their only adornment. Every grace of outline was wilfully suppressed; their hair lay smoothly plastered to their heads, giving them a vacant expression, like a nun's. All this could only be by the mother's orders; but there was no trace of the same pedagogic severity in the case of the boy. Tenderness and softness, it was plain, conditioned his existence. No scissors had been put to the lovely hair that (like the Spinnario's)[6] curled about his brows, above his ears, longer still in the neck. He wore an English sailor suit, with quilted sleeves that narrowed round the delicate wrists of his long and slender though still childish hands. And this suit, with its breast-knot, lacings, and embroideries, lent the slight figure something "rich and strange," a spoilt, exquisite air. The observer saw him in half profile, with one foot in its black patent leather advanced, one elbow resting on the arm of his basket-chair, the cheek nestled into the closed hand in a pose of easy grace, quite unlike the stiff subservient mien which was evidently habitual to his sisters. Was he delicate? His facial tint was ivory-white against the golden darkness of his clustering locks. Or was he simply a pampered darling, the object of a self-willed and partial love? Aschenbach inclined to think the latter. For in almost every artist nature is inborn a wanton and treacherous proneness to side

6. Famous Greek statue of a boy (fourth or fifth century B.C.).

with the beauty that breaks hearts, to single out aristocratic pretensions and pay them homage.

A waiter announced, in English, that dinner was served. Gradually the company dispersed through the glass doors into the dining-room. Late-comers entered from the vestibule or the lifts. Inside, dinner was being served; but the young Poles still sat and waited about their wicker table. Aschenbach felt comfortable in his deep arm-chair, he enjoyed the beauty before his eyes, he waited with them.

The governess, a short, stout, red-faced person, at length gave the signal. With lifted brows she pushed back her chair and made a bow to the tall woman, dressed in palest grey, who now entered the hall. This lady's abundant jewels were pearls, her manner was cool and measured; the fashion of her gown and the arrangement of her lightly powdered hair had the simplicity prescribed in certain circles whose piety and aristocracy are equally marked. She might have been, in Germany, the wife of some high official. But there was something faintly fabulous, after all, in her appearance, though lent it solely by the pearls she wore: they were well-nigh priceless, and consisted of earrings and a three-stranded necklace, very long, with gems the size of cherries.

The brother and sisters had risen briskly. They bowed over their mother's hand to kiss it, she turning away from them, with a slight smile on her face, which was carefully preserved but rather sharp-nosed and worn. She addressed a few words in French to the governess, then moved towards the glass door. The children followed, the girls in order of age, then the governess, and last the boy. He chanced to turn before he crossed the threshold, and as there was no one else in the room, his strange, twilit grey eyes met Aschenbach's, as our traveller sat there with the paper on his knee, absorbed in looking after the group.

There was nothing singular, of course, in what he had seen. They had not gone in to dinner before their mother, they had waited, given her a respectful salute, and but observed the right and proper forms on entering the room. Yet they had done all this so expressly, with such self-respecting dignity, discipline, and sense of duty that Aschenbach was impressed. He lingered still a few minutes, then he, too, went into the dining-room, where he was shown a table far off the Polish family, as he noted at once, with a stirring of regret.

Tired, yet mentally alert, he beguiled the long, tedious meal with abstract, even with transcendent matters: pondered the mysterious harmony that must come to subsist between the individual human being and the universal law, in order that human beauty may result; passed on to general problems of form and art, and came at length to the conclusion that what seemed to him fresh and happy thoughts were like the flattering inventions of a dream, which the waking sense proves worthless and insubstantial. He spent the evening in the park, that was sweet with the odours of evening—sitting, smoking, wandering about; went to bed betimes, and passed the night in deep, unbroken sleep, visited, however, by varied and lively dreams.

The weather next day was no more promising. A land breeze blew. Beneath a colourless, overcast sky the sea lay sluggish, and as it were shrunken, so far withdrawn as to leave bare several rows of long sand-banks. The horizon looked close and prosaic. When Aschenbach opened his window he thought he smelt the stagnant odour of the lagoons.

He felt suddenly out of sorts and already began to think of leaving. Once, years before, after weeks of bright spring weather, this wind had found him out; it had been so bad as to force him to flee from the city like a fugitive. And now it seemed beginning again—the same feverish distaste, the pressure on his temples, the heavy eyelids. It would be a nuisance to change again; but if the wind did not turn, this was no place for him. To be on the safe side, he did not entirely unpack. At nine o'clock he went down to the buffet, which lay between the hall and the dining-room and served as breakfast-room.

A solemn stillness reigned here, such as it is the ambition of all large hotels to achieve. The waiters moved on noiseless feet. A rattling of tea-things, a whispered word—and no other sounds. In a corner diagonally to the door, two tables off his own, Aschenbach saw the Polish girls with their governess. They sat there very straight, in their stiff blue linen frocks with little turn-over collars and cuffs, their ash-blond hair newly brushed flat, their eyelids red from sleep; and handed each other the marmalade. They had nearly finished their meal. The boy was not there.

Aschenbach smiled. "Aha, little Phæax," he thought. "It seems you are privileged to keep yourself out." With sudden gaiety he quoted:

*"Oft veränderten Schmuck und warme Bäder und Ruhe."*[7]

He took a leisurely breakfast. The porter came up with his braided cap in his hand, to deliver some letters that had been sent on. Aschenbach lighted a cigarette and opened a few letters and thus was still seated to witness the arrival of the sluggard.

He entered through the glass doors and passed diagonally across the room to his sisters at their table. He walked with extraordinary grace—the carriage of the body, the action of the knee, the way he set down his foot in its white shoe—it was all so light, it was at once dainty and proud, it wore an added charm in the childish shyness which made him twice turn his head as he crossed the room, made him give a quick glance and then drop his eyes. He took his seat, with a smile and a murmured word in his soft and blurry tongue; and Aschenbach, sitting so that he could see him in profile, was astonished anew, yes, startled, at the godlike beauty of the human being. The lad had on a light sailor suit of blue and white striped cotton, with a red silk breast-knot and a simple white standing collar round the neck—a not very elegant effect—yet above this collar the head was poised like a flower, in incomparable loveliness. It was the head of Eros,[8] with the yellowish bloom of Parian marble, with fine serious brows, and dusky clustering ringlets standing out in soft plenteousness over temples and ears.

"Good, oh, very good indeed!" thought Aschenbach, assuming the patron-

7. "Frequent changes of clothes, warm baths, and rest" (German)—a quotation from Homer's *Odyssey.* Phæax is a playful appellation suggesting the boy is a luxury-loving Phaeacian as depicted in the *Odyssey.* 8. The god of love in Greek mythology.

izing air of the connoisseur to hide, as artists will, their ravishment over a masterpiece. "Yes," he went on to himself, "if it were not that sea and beach were waiting for me, I should sit here as long as you do." But he went out on that, passing through the hall, beneath the watchful eye of the functionaries, down the steps and directly across the board walk to the section of the beach reserved for the guests of the hotel. The bathing-master, a barefoot old man in linen trousers and sailor blouse, with a straw hat, showed him the cabin that had been rented for him, and Aschenbach had him set up table and chair on the sandy platform before it. Then he dragged the reclining-chair through the pale yellow sand, closer to the sea, sat down, and composed himself.

He delighted, as always in the scene on the beach, the sight of sophisticated society giving itself over to a simple life at the edge of the element. The shallow grey sea was already gay with children wading, with swimmers, with figures in bright colours lying on the sand-banks with arms behind their heads. Some were rowing in little keelless boats painted red and blue, and laughing when they capsized. A long row of *capanne*[9] ran down the beach, with platforms, where people sat as on verandas, and there was social life, with bustle and with indolent repose; visits were paid, amid much chatter, punctilious morning toilettes hob-nobbed with comfortable and privileged dishabille. On the hard wet sand close to the sea figures in white bath-robes or loose wrappings in garish colours strolled up and down. A mammoth sand-hill had been built up on Aschenbach's right, the work of children, who had stuck it full of tiny flags. Vendors of sea-shells, fruits, and cakes knelt beside their wares spread out on the sand. A row of cabins on the left stood obliquely to the others and to the sea, thus forming the boundary of the enclosure on this side; and on the little veranda in front of one of these a Russian family was encamped; bearded men with strong white teeth, ripe, indolent women, a Fräulein from the Baltic provinces, who sat at an easel painting the sea and tearing her hair in despair; two ugly but good-natured children and an old maidservant in a head-cloth, with the caressing, servile manner of the born dependent. There they sat together in grateful enjoyment of their blessings: constantly shouting at their romping children, who paid not the slightest heed; making jokes in broken Italian to the funny old man who sold them sweetmeats, kissing each other on the cheeks—no jot concerned that their domesticity was overlooked.

"I'll stop," thought Aschenbach. "Where could it be better than here?" With his hands clasped in his lap he let his eyes swim in the wideness of the sea, his gaze lose focus, blur, and grow vague in the misty immensity of space. His love of the ocean had profound sources: the hard-worked artist's longing for rest, his yearning to seek refuge from the thronging manifold shapes of his fancy in the bosom of the simple and vast; and another yearning, opposed to his art and perhaps for that very reason a lure, for the unorganized, the immeasurable, the eternal—in short, for nothingness. He whose preoccupation is with excellence longs fervently to find rest in perfection; and is not nothingness a form of perfection? As he sat there dreaming thus, deep, deep into the void, suddenly the margin line of the shore was cut by a human form. He gathered up his gaze

9. Dressing cabins (Italian).

and withdrew it from the illimitable, and lo, it was the lovely boy who crossed his vision coming from the left along the sand. He was barefoot, ready for wading, the slender legs uncovered above the knee, and moved slowly, yet with such a proud, light tread as to make it seem he had never worn shoes. He looked towards the diagonal row of cabins; and the sight of the Russian family, leading their lives there in joyous simplicity, distorted his features in a spasm of angry disgust. His brow darkened, his lips curled, one corner of the mouth was drawn down in a harsh line that marred the curve of the cheek, his frown was so heavy that the eyes seemed to sink in as they uttered beneath the black and vicious language of hate. He looked down, looked threateningly back once more; then giving it up with a violent and contemptuous shoulder-shrug, he left his enemies in the rear.

A feeling of delicacy, a qualm, almost like a sense of shame, made Aschenbach turn away as though he had not seen, he felt unwilling to take advantage of having been, by chance, privy to this passionate reaction. But he was in truth both moved and exhilarated—that is to say, he was delighted. This childish exhibition of fanaticism, directed against the good-naturedest simplicity in the world—it gave to the godlike and inexpressive the final human touch. The figure of the half-grown lad, a masterpiece from nature's own hand, had been significant enough when it gratified the eye alone; and now it evoked sympathy as well—the little episode had set it off, lent it a dignity in the onlooker's eyes that was beyond its years.

Aschenbach listened with still averted head to the boy's voice announcing his coming to his companions at the sand-heap. The voice was clear, though a little weak, but they answered, shouting his name—or his nickname—again and again. Aschenbach was not without curiosity to learn it, but could make out nothing more exact than two musical syllables, something like Adgio—or, oftener still, Adjiu, with a long-drawn-out *u* at the end. He liked the melodious sound, and found it fitting; said it over to himself a few times and turned back with satisfaction to his papers.

Holding his travelling-pad on his knees, he took his fountain-pen and began to answer various items of his correspondence. But presently he felt it too great a pity to turn his back, and the eyes of his mind, for the sake of mere commonplace correspondence, to this scene which was, after all, the most rewarding one he knew. He put aside his papers and swung round to the sea; in no long time, beguiled by the voices of the children at play, he had turned his head and sat resting it against the chair-back, while he gave himself up to contemplating the activities of the exquisite Adgio.

His eye found him out at once, the red breast-knot was unmistakable. With some nine or ten companions, boys and girls of his own age and younger, he was busy putting in place an old plank to serve as a bridge across the ditches between the sand-piles. He directed the work by shouting and motioning with his head, and they were all chattering in many tongues—French, Polish, and even some of the Balkan languages. But his was the name oftenest on their lips, he was plainly sought after, wooed, admired. One lad in particular, a Pole like himself, with a name that sounded something like Jaschiu, a sturdy lad with brilliantined black hair, in a belted linen suit, was his particular liegeman and friend. Operations at the sand-pile being ended for the time, the two walked away along the beach, with their arms round each other's waists, and once the lad Jaschiu gave Adgio a kiss.

Aschenbach felt like shaking a finger at him. "But you, Critobulus,"[1] he thought with a smile, "you I advise to take a year's leave. That long, at least, you will need for complete recovery." A vendor came by with strawberries, and Aschenbach made his second breakfast of the great luscious, dead-ripe fruit. It had grown very warm, although the sun had not availed to pierce the heavy layer of mist. His mind felt relaxed, his senses revelled in this vast and soothing communion with the silence of the sea. The grave and serious man found sufficient occupation in speculating what name it could be that sounded like Adgio. And with the help of a few Polish memories he at length fixed on Tadzio, a shortened form of Thaddeus, which sounded, when called, like Tadziu or Adziu.

Tadzio was bathing. Aschenbach had lost sight of him for a moment, then descried him far out in the water, which was shallow a very long way—saw his head, and his arm striking out like an oar. But his watchful family were already on the alert; the mother and governess called from the veranda in front of their bathing-cabin, until the lad's name, with its softened consonants and long-drawn *u*-sound, seemed to possess the beach like a rallying-cry; the cadence had something sweet and wild: "Tadziu! Tadziu!" He turned and ran back against the water, churning the waves to a foam, his head flung high. The sight of this living figure, virginally pure and austere, with dripping locks, beautiful as a tender young god, emerging from the depths of sea and sky, outrunning the element—it conjured up mythologies, it was like a primeval legend, handed down from the beginning of time, of the birth of form, of the origin of the gods. With closed lids Aschenbach listened to this poesy hymning itself silently within him, and anon he thought it was good to be here and that he would stop awhile.

Afterwards Tadzio lay on the sand and rested from his bathe, wrapped in his white sheet, which he wore drawn underneath the right shoulder, so that his head was cradled on his bare right arm. And even when Aschenbach read, without looking up, he was conscious that the lad was there; that it would cost him but the slightest turn of the head to have the rewarding vision once more in his purview. Indeed, it was almost as though he sat there to guard the youth's repose; occupied, of course, with his own affairs, yet alive to the presence of that noble human creature close at hand. And his heart was stirred, it felt a father's kindness: such an emotion as the possessor of beauty can inspire in one who has offered himself up in spirit to create beauty.

At midday he left the beach, returned to the hotel, and was carried up in the lift to his room. There he lingered a little time before the glass and looked at his own grey hair, his keen and weary face. And he thought of his fame, and how people gazed respectfully at him in the streets, on account of his unerring gift of words and their power to charm. He called up all the worldly successes his genius had reaped, all he could remember, even his patent of nobility. Then went to luncheon down in the dining-room, sat at his little table and ate. After-

1. Son of a disciple of Socrates (469–399 B.C.), Greek philosopher.

wards he mounted again in the lift, and a group of young folk, Tadzio among them, pressed with him into the little compartment. It was the first time Aschenbach had seen him close at hand, not merely in perspective, and could see and take account of the details of his humanity. Someone spoke to the lad, and he, answering, with indescribably lovely smile, stepped out again, as they had come to the first floor, backwards, with his eyes cast down. "Beauty makes people self-conscious," Aschenbach thought, and considered within himself imperatively why this should be. He had noted, further, that Tadzio's teeth were imperfect, rather jagged and bluish, without a healthy glaze, and of that peculiar brittle transparency which the teeth of chlorotic people often show. "He is delicate, he is sickly," Aschenbach thought. "He will most likely not live to grow old." He did not try to account for the pleasure the idea gave him.

In the afternoon he spent two hours in his room, then took the *vaporetto* to Venice, across the foul-smelling lagoon. He got out at San Marco, had his tea in the Piazza, and then, as his custom was, took a walk through the streets. But this walk of his brought about nothing less than a revolution in his mood and an entire change in all his plans.

There was a hateful sultriness in the narrow streets. The air was so heavy that all the manifold smells wafted out of houses, shops, and cook-shops—smells of oil, perfumery, and so forth—hung low, like exhalations, not dissipating. Cigarette smoke seemed to stand in the air, it drifted so slowly away. Today the crowd in these narrow lanes oppressed the stroller instead of diverting him. The longer he walked, the more was he in tortures under that state, which is the product of the sea air and the sirocco and which excites and enervates at once. He perspired painfully. His eyes rebelled, his chest was heavy, he felt feverish, the blood throbbed in his temples. He fled from the huddled, narrow streets of the commercial city, crossed many bridges, and came into the poor quarter of Venice. Beggars waylaid him, the canals sickened him with their evil exhalations. He reached a quiet square, one of those that exist at the city's heart, forsaken of God and man; there he rested awhile on the margin of a fountain, wiped his brow, and admitted to himself that he must be gone.

For the second time, and now quite definitely, the city proved that in certain weathers it could be directly inimical to his health. Nothing but sheer unreasoning obstinacy would linger on, hoping for an unprophesiable change in the wind. A quick decision was in place. He could not go home at this stage, neither summer nor winter quarters would be ready. But Venice had not a monopoly of sea and shore: there were other spots where these were to be had without the evil concomitants of lagoon and fever-breeding vapours. He remembered a little bathing-place not far from Trieste of which he had had a good report. Why not go thither? At once, of course, in order that this second change might be worth the making. He resolved, he rose to his feet and sought the nearest gondola-landing, where he took a boat and was conveyed to San Marco through the gloomy windings of many canals, beneath balconies of delicate marble traceries flanked by carven lions; round slippery corners of wall, past melancholy facades with ancient business shields reflected in the rocking water. It was not too easy to arrive at his destination, for his gondolier, being in league with various lace-makers and glass-blowers, did his best to persuade his fare to pause, look, and be tempted to buy. Thus the charm of this bizarre passage though the heart of Venice, even while it played upon his spirit, yet was sensibly cooled by the predatory commercial spirit of the fallen queen of the seas.[2]

Once back in his hotel, he announced at the office, even before dinner, that circumstances unforeseen obliged him to leave early next morning. The management expressed its regret, it changed his money and receipted his bill. He dined, and spent the lukewarm evening in a rocking-chair on the rear terrace, reading the newspapers. Before he went to bed, he made his luggage ready against the morning.

His sleep was not of the best, for the prospect of another journey made him restless. When he opened his window next morning, the sky was still overcast, but the air seemed fresher—and there and then his rue began. Had he not given notice too soon? Had he not let himself be swayed by a slight and momentary indisposition? If he had only been patient, not lost heart so quickly, tried to adapt himself to the climate, or even waited for a change in the weather before deciding! Then, instead of the hurry and flurry of departure, he would have before him now a morning like yesterday's on the beach. Too late! He must go on wanting what he had wanted yesterday. He dressed and at eight o'clock went down to breakfast.

When he entered the breakfast-room it was empty. Guests came in while he sat waiting for his order to be filled. As he sipped his tea he saw the Polish girls enter with their governess, chaste and morning-fresh, with sleep-reddened eyelids. They crossed the room and sat down at their table in the window. Behind them came the porter, cap in hand, to announce that it was time for him to go. The car was waiting to convey him and other travellers to the Hôtel Excelsior, whence they would go by motor-boat through the company's private canal to the station. Time pressed. But Aschenbach found it did nothing of the sort. There still lacked more than an hour of train-time. He felt irritated at the hotel habit of getting the guests out of the house earlier than necessary; and requested the porter to let him breakfast in peace. The man hesitated and withdrew, only to come back again five minutes later. The car could wait no longer. Good, then it might go, and take his trunk with it, Aschenbach answered with some heat. He would use the public conveyance, in his own time; he begged them to leave the choice of it to him. The functionary bowed. Aschenbach, pleased to be rid of him, made a leisurely meal, and even had a newspaper of the waiter. When at length he rose, the time was grown very short. And it so happened that at that moment Tadzio came through the glass doors into the room.

To reach his own table he crossed the traveller's path, and modestly cast down his eyes before the grey-haired man of the lofty brows—only to lift them again in that sweet way he had and direct his full soft gaze upon Aschenbach's face. Then he was past. "For the last time, Tadzio," thought the elder man. "It was all too brief!" Quite unusually for him, he shaped a farewell with his lips,

2. Once a preeminent maritime and military power, Venice degenerated into crass commercialism and catering to tourists.

he actually uttered it, and added: "May God bless you!" Then he went out, distributed tips, exchanged farewells with the mild little manager in the frock-coat, and, followed by the porter with his hand-luggage, left the hotel. On foot as he had come, he passed through the white-blossoming avenue, diagonally across the island to the boat-landing. He went on board at once—but the tale of his journey across the lagoon was a tale of woe, a passage through the very valley of regrets.

It was the well-known route: through the lagoon, past San Marco, up the Grand Canal. Aschenbach sat on the circular bench in the bows, with his elbow on the railing, one hand shading his eyes. They passed the Public Gardens, once more the princely charm of the Piazzetta rose up before him and then dropped behind, next came the great row of palaces, the canal curved, and the splendid marble arches of the Rialto came in sight. The traveller gazed—and his bosom was torn. The atmosphere of the city, the faintly rotten scent of swamp and sea, which had driven him to leave—in what deep, tender, almost painful draughts he breathed it in! How was it he had not known, had not thought, how much his heart was set upon it all! What this morning had been slight regret, some little doubt of his own wisdom, turned now to grief, to actual wretchedness, a mental agony so sharp that it repeatedly brought tears to his eyes, while he questioned himself how he could have foreseen it. The hardest part, the part that more than once it seemed he could not bear, was the thought that he should never more see Venice again. Since now for the second time the place had made him ill, since for the second time he had had to flee for his life, he must henceforth regard it as a forbidden spot, to be forever shunned; senseless to try it again, after he had proved himself unfit. Yes, if he fled it now, he felt that wounded pride must prevent his return to this spot where twice he had made actual bodily surrender. And this conflict between inclination and capacity all at once assumed, in this middle-aged man's mind, immense weight and importance; the physical defeat seemed a shameful thing, to be avoided at whatever cost; and he stood amazed at the ease with which on the day before he had yielded to it.

Meanwhile the steamer neared the station landing; his anguish of irresolution amounted almost to panic. To leave seemed to the sufferer impossible, to remain not less so. Torn thus between two alternatives, he entered the station. It was very late, he had not a moment to lose. Time pressed, it scourged him onward. He hastened to buy his ticket and looked round in the crowd to find the hotel porter. The man appeared and said that the trunk had already gone off. "Gone already?" "Yes, it has gone to Como." "To Como?" A hasty exchange of words—angry questions from Aschenbach, and puzzled replies from the porter—at length made it clear that the trunk had been put with the wrong luggage even before leaving the hotel, and in company with other trunks was now well on its way in precisely the wrong direction.

Aschenbach found it hard to wear the right expression as he heard this news. A reckless joy, a deep incredible mirthfulness shook him almost as with a spasm. The porter dashed off after the lost trunk, returning very soon, of course, to announce that his efforts were unavailing. Aschenbach said he would not travel without his luggage; that he would go back and wait at the Hôtel des Bains until it turned up. Was the company's motor-boat still outside? The man said yes, it was at the door. With his native eloquence he prevailed upon the ticket-agent to take back the ticket already purchased; he swore that he would wire, that no pains should be spared, that the trunk would be restored in the twinkling of an eye. And the unbelievable thing came to pass: the traveller, twenty minutes after he had reached the station, found himself once more on the Grand Canal on his way back to the Lido.

What a strange adventure indeed, this right-about face of destiny—incredible, humiliating, whimsical as any dream! To be passing again, within the hour, these scenes from which in profoundest grief he had but now taken leave forever! The little swift-moving vessel, a furrow of foam at its prow, tacking with droll agility between steamboats and gondolas, went like a shot to its goal; and he, its sole passenger, sat hiding the panic and thrills of a truant schoolboy beneath a mask of forced resignation. His breast still heaved from time to time with a burst of laughter over the contretemps. Things could not, he told himself, have fallen out more luckily. There would be the necessary explanations, a few astonished faces—then all would be well once more, a mischance prevented, a grievous error set right; and all he had thought to have left forever was his own once more, his for as long as he liked. . . . And did the boat's swift motion deceive him, or was the wind now coming from the sea?

The waves struck against the tiled sides of the narrow canal. At Hôtel Excelsior the automobile omnibus awaited the returned traveller and bore him along by the crisping waves back to the Hôtel des Bains. The little mustachioed manager in the frock-coat came down the steps to greet him.

In dulcet tones he deplored the mistake, said how painful it was to the management and himself; applauded Aschenbach's resolve to stop on until the errant trunk came back; his former room, alas, was already taken, but another as good awaited his approval. *"Pas de chance, monsieur,"*[3] said the Swiss lift-porter, with a smile as he conveyed him upstairs. And the fugitive was soon quartered in another room which in situation and furnishings almost precisely resembled the first.

He laid out the contents of his hand-bag in their wonted places; then, tired out, dazed by the whirl of the extraordinary forenoon, subsided into the arm-chair by the open window. The sea wore a pale-green cast, the air felt thinner and purer, the beach with its cabins and boats had more colour, notwithstanding the day was still grey. Aschenbach, his hands folded in his lap, looked out. He felt rejoiced to be back, yet displeased with his vacillating moods, his ignorance of his own real desires. Thus for nearly an hour he sat, dreaming, resting, barely thinking. At midday he saw Tadzio, in his striped sailor suit with red breast-knot, coming up from the sea, across the barrier and along the board walk to the hotel. Aschenbach recognized him, even at this height, knew it was he before he actually saw him, had it in mind to say to himself: "Well, Tadzio, so here you are again too!" But the casual greeting died away before it reached

3. "Bad luck, sir" (French).

his lips, slain by the truth in his heart. He felt the rapture of his blood, the poignant pleasure, and realized that it was for Tadzio's sake the leavetaking had been so hard.

He sat quite still, unseen at his high post, and looked within himself. His features were lively, he lifted his brows; a smile, alert, inquiring, vivid, widened the mouth. Then he raised his head, and with both hands, hanging limp over the chair-arms, he described a slow motion, palms outward, a lifting and turning movement, as though to indicate a wide embrace. It was a gesture of welcome, a calm and deliberate acceptance of what might come.

Now daily the naked god[4] with cheeks aflame drove his four fire-breathing steeds through heaven's spaces; and with him streamed the strong east wind that fluttered his yellow locks. A sheen, like white satin, lay over all the idly rolling sea's expanse. The sand was burning hot. Awnings of rust-coloured canvas were spanned before the bathing-huts, under the ether's quivering silver-blue; one spent the morning hours within the small, sharp square of shadow they purveyed. But evening too was rarely lovely: balsamic with the breath of flowers and shrubs from the near-by park, while overhead the constellations circled in their spheres, and the murmuring of the night-girted sea swelled softly up and whispered to the soul. Such nights as these contained the joyful promise of a sunlit morrow, brim-full of sweetly ordered idleness, studded thick with countless precious possibilities.

The guest detained here by so happy a mischance was far from finding the return of his luggage a ground for setting out anew. For two days he had suffered slight inconvenience and had to dine in the large salon in his travelling-clothes. Then the lost trunk was set down in his room, and he hastened to unpack, filling presses and drawers with his possessions. He meant to stay on—and on; he rejoiced in the prospect of wearing a silk suit for the hot morning hours on the beach and appearing in acceptable evening dress at dinner.

He was quick to fall in with the pleasing monotony of this manner of life, readily enchanted by its mild soft brilliance and ease. And what a spot it is, indeed!—uniting the charms of a luxurious bathing-resort by a southern sea with the immediate nearness of a unique and marvellous city. Aschenbach was not pleasure-loving. Always, wherever and whenever it was the order of the day to be merry, to refrain from labour and make glad the heart, he would soon be conscious of the imperative summons—and especially was this so in his youth—back to the high fatigues, the sacred and fasting service that consumed his days. This spot and this alone had power to beguile him, to relax his resolution, to make him glad. At times—of a forenoon perhaps, as he lay in the shadow of his awning, gazing out dreamily over the blue of the southern sea, or in the mildness of the night, beneath the wide starry sky, ensconced among the cushions of the gondola that bore him Lidowards after an evening on the Piazza, while the gay lights faded and the melting music of the serenades died away on his ear—he would think of his mountain home, the theatre of his summer labours. There clouds hung low and trailed through the garden, violent storms

4. Greek god of the sun, called Helios or Apollo.

extinguished the lights of the house at night, and the ravens he fed swung in the tops of the fir trees. And he would feel transported to Elysium,[5] to the ends of the earth, to a spot most carefree for the sons of men, where no snow is, and no winter, no storms or downpours of rain; where Oceanus sends a mild and cooling breath, and days flow on in blissful idleness, without effort or struggle, entirely dedicated to the sun and the feasts of the sun.

Aschenbach saw the boy Tadzio almost constantly. The narrow confines of their world of hotel and beach, the daily round followed by all alike, brought him in close, almost uninterrupted touch with the beautiful lad. He encountered him everywhere—in the salons of the hotel, on the cooling rides to the city and back, among the splendours of the Piazza, and besides all this in many another going and coming as chance vouchsafed. But it was the regular morning hours on the beach which gave him his happiest opportunity to study and admire the lovely apparition. Yes, this immediate happiness, this daily recurring boon at the hand of circumstance, this it was that filled him with content, with joy in life, enriched his stay, and lingered out the row of sunny days that fell into place so pleasantly one behind the other.

He rose early—as early as though he had a panting press of work—and was among the first on the beach, when the sun was still benign and the sea lay dazzling white in its morning slumber. He gave the watchman a friendly good-morning and chatted with the barefoot, white-haired old man who prepared his place, spread the awning, trundled out the chair and table onto the little platform. Then he settled down; he had three or four hours before the sun reached its height and the fearful climax of its power; three or four hours while the sea went deeper and deeper blue; three or four hours in which to watch Tadzio.

He would see him come up, on the left, along the margin of the sea; or from behind, between the cabins; or, with a start of joyful surprise, would discover that he himself was late, and Tadzio already down, in the blue and white bathing-suit that was now his only wear on the beach; there and engrossed in his usual activities in the sand, beneath the sun. It was a sweetly idle, trifling, fitful life, of play and rest, of strolling, wading, digging, fishing, swimming, lying on the sand. Often the women sitting on the platform would call out to him in their high voices: "Tadziu! Tadziu!" and he would come running and waving his arms, eager to tell them what he had done, show them what he had found, what caught—shells, seahorses, jellyfish, and sidewards-running crabs. Aschenbach understood not a word he said; it might be the sheerest commonplace, in his ear it became mingled harmonies. Thus the lad's foreign birth raised his speech to music; a wanton sun showered splendour on him, and the noble distances of the sea formed the background which set off his figure.

Soon the observer knew every line and pose of this form that limned itself so freely against sea and sky; its every loveliness, though conned by heart, yet thrilled him each day afresh; his admiration knew no bounds, the delight of his eye was unending. Once the lad was summoned to speak to a guest who was waiting for his mother at their cabin. He ran up, ran dripping wet out of the

5. Dwelling place of the immortals.

sea, tossing his curls, and put out his hand, standing with his weight on one leg, resting the other foot on the toes; as he stood there in a posture of suspense the turn of his body was enchanting, while his features wore a look half shamefaced, half conscious of the duty breeding laid upon him to please. Or he would lie at full length, with his bath-robe around him, one slender young arm resting on the sand, his chin in the hollow of his hand; the lad they called Jaschiu squatting beside him, paying him court. There could be nothing lovelier on earth than the smile and look with which the playmate thus singled out rewarded his humble friend and vassal. Again, he might be at the water's edge, alone, removed from his family, quite close to Aschenbach; standing erect, his hands clasped at the back of his neck, rocking slowly on the balls of his feet, day-dreaming away into blue space, while little waves ran up and bathed his toes. The ringlets of honey-coloured hair clung to his temples and neck, the fine down along the upper vertebræ was yellow in the sunlight; the thin envelope of flesh covering the torso betrayed the delicate outlines of the ribs and the symmetry of the breast-structure. His armpits were still as smooth as a statue's, smooth the glistening hollows behind the knees, where the blue network of veins suggested that the body was formed of some stuff more transparent than mere flesh. What discipline, what precision of thought were expressed by the tense youthful perfection of this form! And yet the pure, strong will which had laboured in darkness and succeeded in bringing this godlike work of art to the light of day—was it not known and familiar to him, the artist? Was not the same force at work in himself when he strove in cold fury to liberate from the marble mass of language the slender forms of his art which he saw with the eye of his mind and would body forth to men as the mirror and image of spiritual beauty?

Mirror and image! His eyes took in the proud bearing of that figure there at the blue water's edge; with an outburst of rapture he told himself that what he saw was beauty's very essence; form as divine thought, the single and pure perfection which resides in the mind, of which an image and likeness, rare and holy, was here raised up for adoration. This was very frenzy—and without a scruple, nay, eagerly, the aging artist bade it come. His mind was in travail, his whole mental background in a state of flux. Memory flung up in him the primitive thoughts which are youth's inheritance, but which with him had remained latent, never leaping up into a blaze. Has it not been written that the sun beguiles our attention from things of the intellect to fix it on things of the sense? The sun, they say, dazzles; so bewitching reason and memory that the soul for very pleasure forgets its actual state, to cling with doting on the loveliest of all the objects she shines on. Yes, and then it is only through the medium of some corporeal being that it can raise itself again to contemplation of higher things. Amor,[6] in sooth, is like the mathematician who in order to give children a knowledge of pure form must do so in the language of pictures; so, too, the god, in order to make visible the spirit, avails himself of the forms and colours of human youth, gilding it with all imaginable beauty that it may serve memory as a tool, the very sight of which then sets us afire with pain or longing.

6. Another name for the god of love.

Such were the devotee's thoughts, such the power of his emotions. And the sea, so bright with glancing sunbeams, wove in his mind a spell and summoned up a lovely picture: there was the ancient plane-tree outside the walls of Athens, a hallowed, shady spot, fragrant with willow-blossom and adorned with images and votive offerings in honour of the nymphs and Achelous. Clear ran the smooth-pebbled stream at the foot of the spreading tree. Crickets were fiddling. But on the gentle grassy slope, where one could lie yet hold the head erect, and shelter from the scorching heat, two men reclined, an elder with a younger, ugliness paired with beauty and wisdom with grace. Here Socrates held forth to youthful Phædrus upon the nature of virtue and desire, wooing him with insinuating wit and charming turns of phrase. He told him of the shuddering and unwonted heat that come upon him whose heart is open, when his eye beholds an image of eternal beauty; spoke of the impious and corrupt, who cannot conceive beauty though they see its image, and are incapable of awe; and of the fear and reverence felt by the noble soul when he beholds a godlike face or a form which is a good image of beauty: how as he gazes he worships the beautiful one and scarcely dares to look upon him, but would offer sacrifice as to an idol or a god, did he not fear to be thought stark mad. "For beauty, my Phædrus, beauty alone, is lovely and visible at once. For, mark you, it is the sole aspect of the spiritual which we can perceive through our senses, or bear so to perceive. Else what should become of us, if the divine, if reason and virtue and truth, were to speak to us through the senses? Should we not perish and be consumed by love, as Semele[7] aforetime was by Zeus? So beauty, then, is the beauty-lover's way to the spirit—but only the way, only the means, my little Phædrus." . . . And then, sly arch-lover that he was, he said the subtlest thing of all: that the lover was nearer the divine than the beloved; for the god was in the one but not in the other—perhaps the tenderest, most mocking thought that ever was thought, and source of all the guile and secret bliss the lover knows.

Thought that can merge wholly into feeling, feeling that can merge wholly into thought—these are the artist's highest joy. And our solitary felt in himself at this moment power to command and wield a thought that thrilled with emotion, an emotion as precise and concentrated as thought: namely, that nature herself shivers with ecstasy when the mind bows down in homage before beauty. He felt a sudden desire to write. Eros, indeed, we are told, loves idleness, and for idle hours alone was he created. But in this crisis the violence of our sufferer's seizure was directed almost wholly towards production, its occasion almost a matter of indifference. News had reached him on his travels that a certain problem had been raised, the intellectual world challenged for its opinion on a great and burning question of art and taste. By nature and experience the theme was his own; and he could not resist the temptation to set it off in the glistening foil of his words. He would write, and more over he would write in Tadzio's presence. This lad should be in a sense his model, his style should follow the lines of this figure that seemed to him divine; he would snatch

7. Aschenbach is recalling Plato's treatise on love. In Greek myth Semele was consumed by fire when Zeus appeared to her in the guise of lightning.

up this beauty into the realms of the mind, as once the eagle bore the Trojan shepherd[8] aloft. Never had the pride of the word been so sweet to him, never had he known so well that Eros is in the word, as in those perilous and precious hours when he sat at his rude table, within the shade of his awning, his idol full in his view and the music of his voice in his ears, and fashioned his little essay after the model Tadzio's beauty set: that page and a half of choicest prose, so chaste, so lofty, so poignant with feeling, which would shortly be the wonder and admiration of the multitude. Verily it is well for the world that it sees only the beauty of the completed work and not its origins nor the conditions whence it sprang; since knowledge of the artist's inspiration might often but confuse and alarm and so prevent the full effect of its excellence. Strange hours, indeed, these were, and strangely unnerving the labour that filled them! Strangely fruitful intercourse this, between one body and another mind! When Aschenbach put aside his work and left the beach he felt exhausted, he felt broken—conscience reproached him, as it were after a debauch.

Next morning on leaving the hotel he stood at the top of the stairs leading down from the terrace and saw Tadzio in front of him on his way to the beach. The lad had just reached the gate in the railings, and he was alone. Aschenbach felt, quite simply, a wish to overtake him, to address him and have the pleasure of his reply and answering look; to put upon a blithe and friendly footing his relation with this being who all unconsciously had so greatly heightened and quickened his emotions. The lovely youth moved at a loitering pace—he might easily be overtaken; and Aschenbach hastened his own step. He reached him on the board walk that ran behind the bathing-cabins, and all but put out his hand to lay it on shoulder or head, while his lips parted to utter a friendly salutation in French. But—perhaps from the swift pace of his last few steps—he found his heart throbbing unpleasantly fast, while his breath came in such quick pants that he could only have gasped had he tried to speak. He hesitated, sought after self-control, was suddenly panic-stricken lest the boy notice him hanging there behind him and look round. Then he gave up, abandoned his plan, and passed him with bent head and hurried step.

"Too late! Too late!" he thought as he went by. But was it too late? This step he had delayed to take might so easily have put everything in a lighter key, have led to a sane recovery from his folly. But the truth may have been that the aging man did not want to be cured, that his illusion was far too dear to him. Who shall unriddle the puzzle of the artist nature? Who understands that mingling of discipline and licence in which it stands so deeply rooted? For not to be able to want sobriety is licentious folly. Aschenbach was no longer disposed to self-analysis. He had no taste for it; his self-esteem, the attitude of mind proper to his years, his maturity and single-mindedness, disinclined him to look within himself and decide whether it was constant or puerile sensuality that had prevented him from carrying out his project. He felt confused, he was afraid someone, if only the watchman, might have been observing his behaviour and final surrender—very much he feared being ridiculous. And all the time he was laughing at himself for his serio-comic seizure. "Quite crestfallen," he

8. Ganymede, who was ravished by Zeus in the guise of an eagle.

thought. "I was like the gamecock that lets his wings droop in the battle. That must be the Love-God himself, that makes us hang our heads at sight of beauty and weighs our proud spirits low as the ground." Thus he played with the idea—he embroidered upon it, and was too arrogant to admit fear of an emotion.

The term he had set for his holiday passed by unheeded; he had no thought of going home. Ample funds had been sent him. His sole concern was that the Polish family might leave, and a chance question to put to the hotel barber elicited the information that they had come only very shortly before himself. The sun browned his face and hands, the invigorating salty air heightened his emotional energies. Heretofore he had been wont to give out at once, in some new effort, the powers accumulated by sleep or food or outdoor air; but now the strength that flowed in upon him with each day of sun and sea and idleness he let go up in one extravagant gush of emotional intoxication.

His sleep was fitful; the priceless, equable days were divided one from the next by brief nights filled with happy unrest. He went, indeed, early to bed, for at nine o'clock, with the departure of Tadzio from the scene, the day was over for him. But in the faint greyness of the morning a tender pang would go through him as his heart was minded of its adventure; he could no longer bear his pillow and, rising, would wrap himself against the early chill and sit down by the window to await the sunrise. Awe of the miracle filled his soul new-risen from its sleep. Heaven, earth, and its waters yet lay enfolded in the ghostly, glassy pallor of dawn; one paling star still swam in the shadowy vast. But there came a breath, a winged word from far and inaccessible abodes, that Eos[9] was rising from the side of her spouse; and there was that first sweet reddening of the farthest strip of sea and sky that manifests creation to man's sense. She neared, the goddess, ravisher of youth, who stole away Cleitos and Cephalus and, defying all the envious Olympians, tasted beautiful Orion's love.[1] At the world's edge began a strewing of roses, a shining and a blooming ineffably pure; baby cloudlets hung illumined, like attendant amoretti, in the blue and blushful haze; purple effulgence fell upon the sea, that seemed to heave it forward on its welling waves; from horizon to zenith went great quivering thrusts like golden lances, the gleam became a glare; without a sound, with godlike violence, glow and glare and rolling flames streamed upwards, and with flying hoof-beats and steeds of the sun-god mounted the sky. The lonely watcher sat, the splendour of the god shone on him, he closed his eyes and let the glory kiss his lids. Forgotten feelings, precious pangs of his youth, quenched long since by the stern service that had been his life and now returned so strangely metamorphosed—he recognized them with a puzzled, wondering smile. He mused, he dreamed, his lips slowly shaped a name; still smiling, his face turned seawards and his hands lying folded in his lap, he fell asleep once more as he sat.

But that day, which began so fierily and festally, was not like other days; it was transmuted and gilded with mythical significance. For whence could come the breath, so mild and meaningful, like a whisper from higher spheres, that played about temple and ear? Troops of small feathery white clouds ranged over the sky, like grazing herds of the gods. A stronger wind arose, and Posei-

9. Goddess of the dawn. 1. The myth celebrates the seductive power of the dawn.

don's[2] horses ran up, arching their manes, among them too the steers of him with the purpled locks, who lowered their horns and bellowed as they came on; while like prancing goats the waves on the farther strand leaped among the craggy rocks. It was a world possessed, peopled by Pan,[3] that closed round the spellbound man, and his doting heart conceived the most delicate fancies. When the sun was going down behind Venice, he would sometimes sit on a bench in the park and watch Tadzio, white-clad, with gay-coloured sash, at play there on the rolled gravel with his ball; and at such times it was not Tadzio whom he saw, but Hyacinthus,[4] doomed to die because two gods were rivals for his love. Ah, yes, he tasted the envious pangs that Zephyr knew when his rival, bow and cithara, oracle and all forgot, played with the beauteous youth; he watched the discus, guided by torturing jealousy, strike the beloved head; paled as he received the broken body in his arms, and saw the flower spring up, watered by that sweet blood and signed forevermore with his lament.

There can be no relation more strange, more critical, than that between two beings who know each other only with their eyes, who meet daily, yes, even hourly, eye each other with a fixed regard, and yet by some whim or freak of convention feel constrained to act like strangers. Uneasiness rules between them, unslaked curiosity, a hysterical desire to give rein to their suppressed impulse to recognize and address each other; even, actually, a sort of strained but mutual regard. For one human being instinctively feels respect and love for another human being so long as he does not know him well enough to judge him; and that he does not, the craving he feels is evidence.

Some sort of relation and acquaintanceship was perforce set up between Aschenbach and the youthful Tadzio; it was with a thrill of joy the older man perceived that the lad was not entirely unresponsive to all the tender notice lavished on him. For instance, what should move the lovely youth, nowadays when he descended to the beach, always to avoid the board walk behind the bathing-huts and saunter along the sand, passing Aschenbach's tent in front, sometimes so unnecessarily close as almost to graze his table or chair? Could the power of an emotion so beyond his own so draw, so fascinate its innocent object? Daily Aschenbach would wait for Tadzio. Then sometimes, on his approach, he would pretend to be preoccupied and let the charmer pass unregarded by. But sometimes he looked up, and their glances met; when that happened both were profoundly serious. The elder's dignified and cultured mien let nothing appear of his inward state; but in Tadzio's eyes a question lay—he faltered in his step, gazed on the ground, then up again with that ineffably sweet look he had; and when he was past, something in his bearing seemed to say that only good breeding hindered him from turning round.

But once, one evening, it fell out differently. The Polish brother and sisters, with their governess, had missed the evening meal, and Aschenbach had noted the fact with concern. He was restive over their absence, and after dinner walked up and down in front of the hotel, in evening dress and a straw hat; when suddenly he saw the nunlike sisters with their companion appear in the

2. In Greek mythology Poseidon was lord of the sea. 3. The ruler of all natural creatures. 4. Mythological boy of great beauty, loved by Apollo and Boreas, killed by their jealousy.

light of the arc-lamps, and four paces behind them Tadzio. Evidently they came from the steamer-landing, having dined for some reason in Venice. It had been chilly on the lagoon, for Tadzio wore a dark-blue reefer-jacket with gilt buttons, and a cap to match. Sun and sea air could not burn his skin, it was the same creamy marble hue as at first—though he did look a little pale, either from the cold or in the bluish moonlight of the arc-lamps. The shapely brows were so delicately drawn, the eyes so deeply dark—lovelier he was than words could say, and as often the thought visited Aschenbach, and brought its own pang, that language could but extol, not reproduce, the beauties of the sense.

The sight of that dear form was unexpected, it had appeared unhoped-for, without giving him time to compose his features. Joy, surprise, and admiration might have painted themselves quite openly upon his face—and just at this second it happened that Tadzio smiled. Smiled at Aschenbach, unabashed and friendly, a speaking, winning, captivating smile, with slowly parting lips. With such a smile it might be that Narcissus[5] bent over the mirroring pool a smile profound, infatuated, lingering, as he put out his arms to the reflection of his own beauty; the lips just slightly pursed, perhaps half-realizing his own folly in trying to kiss the cold lips of his shadow—with a mingling of coquetry and curiosity and a faint unease, enthralling and enthralled.

Aschenbach received that smile and turned away with it as though entrusted with a fatal gift. So shaken was he that he had to flee from the lighted terrace and front gardens and seek out with hurried steps the darkness of the park at the rear. Reproaches strangely mixed of tenderness and remonstrance burst from him: "How dare you smile like that! No one is allowed to smile like that!" He flung himself on a bench, his composure gone to the winds, and breathed in the nocturnal fragrance of the garden. He leaned back, with hanging arms, quivering from head to foot, and quite unmanned he whispered the hackneyed phrase of love and longing—impossible in these circumstances, absurd, abject, ridiculous enough, yet sacred too, and not unworthy of honour even here: "I love you!"

In the fourth week of his stay on the Lido, Gustave von Aschenbach made certain singular observations touching the world about him. He noticed, in the first place, that though the season was approaching its height, yet the number of guests declined and, in particular, that the German tongue had suffered a rout, being scarcely or never heard in the land. At table and on the beach he caught nothing but foreign words. One day at the barber's—where he was now a frequent visitor—he heard something rather startling. The barber mentioned a German family who had just left the Lido after a brief stay, and rattled on in his obsequious way: "The signore is not leaving—he has no fear of the sickness, has he?" Aschenbach looked at him. "The sickness?" he repeated. Whereat the prattler fell silent, became very busy all at once, affected not to hear. When Aschenbach persisted he said he really knew nothing at all about it, and tried in a fresh burst of eloquence to drown the embarrassing subject.

5. This youth fell in love with his own reflection in the water and was drowned when he leaned to embrace it.

That was one forenoon. After luncheon Aschenbach had himself ferried across to Venice, in a dead calm, under a burning sun; driven by his mania, he was following the Polish young folk, whom he had seen with their companion, taking the way to the landing-stage. He did not find his idol on the Piazza. But as he sat there at tea, at a little round table on the shady side, suddenly he noticed a peculiar odour, which, it seemed to him now, had been in the air for days without his being aware: a sweetish, medicinal smell, associated with wounds and disease and suspect cleanliness. He sniffed and pondered and at length recognized it; finished his tea and left the square at the end facing the cathedral. In the narrow space the stench grew stronger. At the street corners placards were stuck up, in which the city authorities warned the population against the danger of certain infections of the gastric system, prevalent during the heated season; advising them not to eat oysters or other shellfish and not to use the canal waters. The ordinance showed every sign of minimizing an existing situation. Little groups of people stood about silently in the squares and on the bridges; the traveller moved among them, watched and listened and thought.

He spoke to a shopkeeper lounging at his door among dangling coral necklaces and trinkets of artificial amethyst, and asked him about the disagreeable odour. The man looked at him, heavy-eyed, and hastily pulled himself together. "Just a formal precaution, signore," he said, with a gesture. "A police regulation we have to put up with. The air is sultry—the sirocco is not wholesome, as the signore knows. Just a precautionary measure, you understand—probably unnecessary. . . ." Aschenbach thanked him and passed on. And on the boat that bore him back to the Lido he smelt the germicide again.

On reaching his hotel he sought the table in the lobby and buried himself in the newspapers. The foreign-language sheets had nothing. But in the German papers certain rumours were mentioned, statistics given, then officially denied, then the good faith of the denials called in question. The departure of the German and Austrian contingent was thus made plain. As for other nationals, they knew or suspected nothing—they were still undisturbed. Aschenbach tossed the newspapers back on the table. "It ought to be kept quiet," he thought, aroused. "It should not be talked about." And he felt in his heart a curious elation at these events impending in the world about him. Passion is like crime: it does not thrive on the established order and the common round; it welcomes every blow dealt the bourgeois structure, every weakening of the social fabric, because therein it feels a sure hope of its own advantage. These things that were going on in the unclean alleys of Venice, under cover of an official hushing-up policy—they gave Aschenbach a dark satisfaction. The city's evil secret mingled with the one in the depths of his heart—and he would have staked all he possessed to keep it, since in his infatuation he cared for nothing but to keep Tadzio here, and owned to himself not without horror, that he could not exist were the lad to pass from his sight.

He was no longer satisfied to owe his communion with his charmer to chance and the routine of hotel life; he had begun to follow and waylay him. On Sundays, for example, the Polish family never appeared on the beach. Aschenbach guessed they went to mass at San Marco and pursued them thither.

He passed from the glare of the Piazza into the golden twilight of the holy place and found him he sought bowed in worship over a *prie-dieu.*[6] He kept in the background, standing on the fissured mosaic pavement among the devout populace, that knelt and muttered and made the sign of the cross; and the crowded splendour of the oriental temple weighed voluptuously on his sense. A heavily ornate priest intoned and gesticulated before the altar, where little candle-flames flickered helplessly in the reek of incense-breathing smoke; and with that cloying sacrificial smell another seemed to mingle—the odour of the sickened city. But through all the glamour and glitter Aschenbach saw the exquisite creature there in front turn his head, seek out and meet his lover's eye.

The crowd streamed out through the portals into the brilliant square thick with fluttering doves, and the fond fool stood aside in the vestibule on the watch. He saw the Polish family leave the church. The children took ceremonial leave of their mother, and she turned towards the Piazzetta on her way home, while his charmer and the cloistered sisters, with their governess, passed beneath the clock tower into the Merceria.[7] When they were a few paces on, he followed—he stole behind them on their walk through the city. When they paused, he did so too; when they turned round, he fled into inns and courtyards to let them pass. Once he lost them from view, hunted feverishly over bridges and in filthy *culs-de-sac,* only to confront them suddenly in a narrow passage whence there was no escape, and experience a moment of panic fear. Yet it would be untrue to say he suffered. Mind and heart were drunk with passion, his footsteps guided by the dæmonic power whose pastime it is to trample on human reason and dignity.

Tadzio and his sisters at length took a gondola. Aschenbach hid behind a portico or fountain while they embarked, and directly they pushed off did the same. In a furtive whisper he told the boatman he would tip him well to follow at a little distance the other gondola, just rounding a corner, and fairly sickened at the man's quick, sly grasp and ready acceptance of the go-between's rôle.

Leaning back among soft, black cushions he swayed gently in the wake of the other black-snouted bark, to which the strength of his passion chained him. Sometimes it passed from his view, and then he was assailed by an anguish of unrest. But his guide appeared to have long practice in affairs like these; always, by dint of short cuts or deft manœuvres, he contrived to overtake the coveted sight. The air was heavy and foul, the sun burnt down through a slate-coloured haze. Water slapped gurgling against wood and stone. The gondolier's cry, half warning, half salute, was answered with singular accord from far within the silence of the labyrinth. They passed little gardens, high up the crumbling wall, hung with clustering white and purple flowers that sent down an odour of almonds. Moorish lattices showed shadowy in the gloom. The marble steps of a church descended into the canal, and on them a beggar squatted, displaying his misery to view, showing the whites of his eyes, holding out his hat for alms. Farther on a dealer in antiquities cringed before his lair, inviting the passer-by to enter and be duped. Yes, this was Venice, this the fair frailty that fawned and that betrayed, half fairy-tale, half snare; the city in whose stagnating air the

6. Church furniture designed to be knelt on (French). 7. Market quarter (Italian).

art of painting once put forth so lusty a growth, and where musicians were moved to accords so weirdly lulling and lascivious. Our adventurer felt his senses wooed by this voluptuousness of sight and sound, tasted his secret knowledge that the city sickened and hid its sickness for love of gain, and bent an ever more unbridled leer on the gondola that glided on before him.

It came at last to this—that his frenzy left him capacity for nothing else but to pursue his flame; to dream of him absent, to lavish, loverlike, endearing terms on his mere shadow. He was alone, he was a foreigner, he was sunk deep in this belated bliss of his—all which enabled him to pass unblushing through experiences well-nigh unbelievable. One night, returning late from Venice, he paused by his beloved's chamber door in the second storey, leaned his head against the panel, and remained there long, in utter drunkenness, powerless to tear himself away, blind to the danger of being caught in so mad an attitude.

And yet there were not wholly lacking moments when he paused and reflected, when in consternation he asked himself what path was this on which he had set his foot. Like most other men of parts and attainments, he had an aristocratic interest in his forbears, and when he achieved a success he liked to think he had gratified them, compelled their admiration and regard. He thought of them now, involved as he was in this illicit adventure, seized of these exotic excesses of feeling; thought of their stern self-command and decent manliness, and gave a melancholy smile. What would they have said? What, indeed, would they have said to his entire life, that varied to the point of degeneracy from theirs? This life in the bonds of art, had not he himself, in the days of youth and in the very spirit of those bourgeois forefathers, pronounced mocking judgment upon it? And yet, at bottom, it had been so like their own! It had been a service, and he a soldier, like some of them; and art was war—a grilling, exhausting struggle that nowadays wore one out before one could grow old. It had been a life of self-conquest, a life against odds, dour, steadfast, abstinent; he had made it symbolical of the kind of overstrained heroism the time admired, and he was entitled to call it manly, even courageous. He wondered if such a life might not be somehow specially pleasing in the eyes of the god who had him in his power. For Eros had received most countenance among the most valiant nations—yes, were we not told that in their cities prowess made him flourish exceedingly? And many heroes of olden time had willingly borne his yoke, not counting any humiliation such if it happened by the god's decree; vows, prostrations, self-abasements, these were no source of shame to the lover; rather they reaped him praise and honour.

Thus did the fond man's folly condition his thoughts; thus did he seek to hold his dignity upright in his own eyes. And all the while he kept doggedly on the traces of the disreputable secret the city kept hidden at its heart, just as he kept his own—and all that he learned fed his passion with vague, lawless hopes. He turned over newspapers at cafés, bent on finding a report on the progress of the disease; and in the German sheets, which had ceased to appear on the hotel table, he found a series of contradictory statements. The deaths, it was variously asserted, ran to twenty, to forty, to a hundred or more; yet in the next day's issue the existence of the pestilence was, if not roundly denied, reported as a matter of a few sporadic cases as might be brought into a seaport town.

After that the warnings would break out again, and the protests against the unscrupulous game the authorities were playing. No definite information was to be had.

And yet our solitary felt he had a sort of first claim on a share in the unwholesome secret; he took a fantastic satisfaction in putting leading questions to such persons as were interested to conceal it, and forcing them to explicit untruths by way of denial. One day he attacked the manager, that small, soft-stepping man in the French frock-coat, who was moving about among the guests at luncheon, supervising the service and making himself socially agreeable. He paused at Aschenbach's table to exchange a greeting, and the guest put a question, with a negligent, casual air: "Why in the world are they forever disinfecting the city of Venice?" "A police regulation," the adroit one replied; "a precautionary measure, intended to protect the health of the public during this unseasonably warm and sultry weather." "Very praiseworthy of the police," Aschenbach gravely responded. After a further exchange of meteorological commonplaces the manager passed on.

It happened that a band of street musicians came to perform in the hotel gardens that evening after dinner. They grouped themselves beneath an iron stanchion supporting an arc-light, two women and two men, and turned their faces, that shone white in the glare, up towards the guests who sat on the hotel terrace enjoying this popular entertainment along with their coffee and iced drinks. The hotel lift-boys, waiters, and office staff stood in the doorway and listened; the Russian family displayed the usual Russian absorption in their enjoyment—they had their chairs put down into the garden to be nearer the singers and sat there in a half-circle with gratitude painted on their features, the old serf in her turban erect behind their chairs.

These strolling players were adepts at mandolin, guitar, harmonica, even compassing a reedy violin. Vocal numbers alternated with instrumental, the younger woman, who had a high shrill voice, joining in a love-duet with the sweetly falsettoing tenor. The actual head of the company, however, and incontestably its most most gifted member, was the other man, who played the guitar. He was a sort of baritone buffo; with no voice to speak of, but possessed of a pantomimic gift and remarkable burlesque *élan.* Often he stepped out of the group and advanced towards the terrace, guitar in hand, and his audience rewarded his sallies with bursts of laughter. The Russians in their parterre seats were beside themselves with delight over this display of southern vivacity; their shouts and screams of applause encouraged him to bolder and bolder flights.

Aschenbach sat near the balustrade, a glass of pomegranate-juice and soda-water sparkling ruby-red before him, with which he now and then moistened his lips. His nerves drank in thirstily the unlovely sounds, the vulgar and sentimental tunes, for passion paralyses good taste and makes its victim accept with rapture what a man in his senses would either laugh at or turn from with disgust. Idly he sat and watched the antics of the buffoon with his face set in a fixed and painful smile, while inwardly his whole being was rigid with the intensity of the regard he bent on Tadzio, leaning over the railing six paces off.

He lounged there, in the white belted suit he sometimes wore at dinner, in all his innate, inevitable grace, with his left arm on the balustrade, his legs crossed, the right hand on the supporting hip; and looked down on the strolling singers with an expression that was hardly a smile, but rather a distant curiosity and polite toleration. Now and then he straightened himself and with a charming movement of both arms drew down his white blouse through his leather belt, throwing out his chest. And sometimes—Aschenbach saw it with triumph, with horror, and a sense that his reason was tottering—the lad would cast a glance, that might be slow and cautious, or might be sudden and swift, as though to take him by surprise, to the place where his lover sat. Aschenbach did not meet the glance. An ignoble caution made him keep his eyes in leash. For in the rear of the terrace sat Tadzio's mother and governess; and matters had gone so far that he feared to make himself conspicuous. Several times, on the beach, in the hotel lobby, on the Piazza, he had seen, with a stealing numbness, that they called Tadzio away from his neighborhood. And his pride revolted at the affront, even while conscience told him it was deserved.

The performer below presently began a solo, with guitar accompaniment, a street song in several stanzas, just then the rage all over Italy. He delivered it in a striking and dramatic recitative, and his company joined in the refrain. He was a man of slight build, with a thin, undernourished face; his shabby felt hat rested on the back of his neck, a great mop of red hair sticking out in front; and he stood there on the gravel in advance of his troupe, in an impudent, swaggering posture, twanging the strings of his instrument and flinging a witty and rollicking recitative up to the terrace, while the veins of his forehead swelled with the violence of his effort. He was scarcely a Venetian type, belonging rather to the race of Neapolitan jesters, half bully, half comedian, brutal, blustering, an unpleasant customer, and entertaining to the last degree. The words of his song were trivial and silly, but on his lips, accompanied with gestures of head, hands, arms, and body, with leers and winks and the loose play of the tongue in the corner of his mouth, they took on meaning, an equivocal meaning, yet vaguely offensive. He wore a white sports shirt with a suit of ordinary clothes, and strikingly large and naked-looking Adam's apple rose out of the open collar. From that pale, snub-nosed face it was hard to judge of his age; vice sat on it, it was furrowed with grimacing, and two deep wrinkles of defiance and self-will, almost of desperation, stood oddly between the red brows, above the grinning, mobile mouth. But what more than all drew upon him the profound scrutiny of our solitary watcher was that this suspicious figure seemed to carry with it its own suspicious odour. For whenever the refrain occurred and the singer, with waving arms and antic gestures, passed in his grotesque march immediately beneath Aschenbach's seat, a strong smell of carbolic was wafted up to the terrace.

After the song he began to take up money, beginning with the Russian family, who gave liberally, and then mounting the steps to the terrace. But here he became as cringing as he had before been forward. He glided between the tables, bowing and scraping, showing his strong white teeth in a servile smile, though the two deep furrows on the brow were still very marked. His audience looked at the strange creature as he went about collecting his livelihood, and their curiosity was not unmixed with disfavor. They tossed coins with their finger-tips into his hat and took care not to touch it. Let the enjoyment be never so great, a sort of embarrassment always comes when the comedian oversteps the physical distance between himself and respectable people. This man felt it and sought to make his peace by fawning. He came along the railing to Aschenbach, and with him came that smell no one else seemed to notice.

"Listen!" said the solitary, in a low voice, almost mechanically; "they are disinfecting Venice—why?" The mounteback answered hoarsely: "Because of the police. Orders, signore. On account of the heat and the sirocco. The sirocco is oppressive. Not good for the health." He spoke as though surprised that anyone could ask, and with the flat of his hand he demonstrated how oppressive the sirocco was. "So there is no plague in Venice?" Aschenbach asked the question between his teeth, very low. The man's expressive face fell, he put on a look of comical innocence. "A plague? What sort of a plague? Is the sirocco a plague? Or perhaps our police are a plague! You are making fun of us, signore! A plague! Why should there be? The police make regulations on account of the heat and the weather. . . ." He gestured. "Quite," said Aschenbach, once more, soft and low; and dropping an unduly large coin into the man's hat dismissed him with a sign. He bowed very low and left. But he had not reached the steps when two of the hotel servants flung themselves on him and began to whisper, their faces close to his. He shrugged, seemed to be giving assurances, to be swearing he had said nothing. It was not hard to guess the import of his words. They let him go at last and he went back into the garden, where he conferred briefly with his troupe and then stepped forward for a farewell song.

It was one Aschenbach had never to his knowledge heard before, a rowdy air, with words in impossible dialect. It had a laughing-refrain in which the other three artists joined at the top of their lungs. The refrain had neither words nor accompaniment, it was nothing but rhythmical, modulated, natural laughter, which the soloist in particular knew how to render with most deceptive realism. Now that he was farther off his audience, his self-assurance had come back, and this laughter of his rang with a mocking note. He would be overtaken, before he reached the end of the last line of each stanza; he would catch his breath, lay his hand over his mouth, his voice would quaver and his shoulders shake, he would lose power to contain himself longer. Just at the right moment each time, it came whooping, bawling, crashing out of him, with a verisimilitude that never failed to set his audience off in profuse and unpremeditated mirth that seemed to add gusto to his own. He bent his knees, he clapped his thigh, he held his sides, he looked ripe for bursting. He no longer laughed, but yelled, pointing his finger at the company there above as though there could be in all the world nothing so comic as they; until at last they laughed in hotel, terrace, and garden, down to the waiters, lift-boys, and servants—laughed as though possessed.

Aschenbach could no longer rest in his chair, he sat poised for flight. But the combined effect of the laughing, the hospital odour in his nostrils, and the nearness of the beloved was to hold him in a spell; he felt unable to stir. Under cover of the general commotion he looked across at Tadzio and saw that the lovely boy returned his gaze with a seriousness that seemed the copy of his own; the general hilarity, it seemed to say, had no power over him, he kept aloof. The grey-haired man was overpowered, disarmed by this docile, childlike deference; with difficulty he refrained from hiding his face in his hands. Tadzio's habit, too, of drawing himself up and taking a deep sighing breath struck him as being due to an oppression of the chest. "He is sickly, he will never live to grow up," he thought once again, with that dispassionate vision to which his madness of desire sometimes so strangely gave way. And compassion struggled with the reckless exultation of his heart.

The players, meanwhile, had finished and gone; their leader bowing and scraping, kissing his hands and adorning his leave-taking with antics that grew madder with the applause they evoked. After all the others were outside, he pretended to run backwards full tilt against a lamp-post and slunk to the gate apparently doubled over with pain. But there he threw off his buffoon's mask, stood erect, with an elastic straightening of his whole figure, ran out his tongue impudently at the guests on the terrace, and vanished in the night. The company dispersed. Tadzio had long since left the balustrade. But he, the lonely man, sat for long, to the waiters' great annoyance, before the dregs of pomegranate-juice in his glass. Time passed, the night went on. Long ago, in his parental home, he had watched the sand filter through an hourglass—he could still see, as though it stood before him, the fragile, pregnant little toy. Soundless and fine the rust-red streamlet ran through the narrow neck, and made, as it declined in the upper cavity, an exquisite little vortex.

The very next afternoon the solitary took another step in pursuit of his fixed policy of baiting the outer world. This time he had all possible success. He went, that is, into the English travel bureau in the Piazza, changed some money at the desk, and posing as the suspicious foreigner, put his fateful question. The clerk was a tweed-clad young Britisher, with his eyes set close together, his hair parted in the middle, and radiating that steady reliability which makes his like so strange a phenomenon in the *gamin,* agile-witted south. He began: "No ground for alarm, sir. A mere formality. Quite regular in view of the unhealthy climatic conditions." But then, looking up, he chanced to meet with his own blue eyes the stranger's weary, melancholy gaze, fixed on his face. The Englishman coloured. He continued in a lower voice, rather confused: "At least, that is the official explanation, which they see fit to stick to. I may tell you there's a bit more to it than that." And then, in his good, straightforward way, he told the truth.

For the past several years Asiatic cholera had shown a strong tendency to spread. Its source was the hot, moist swamps of the delta of the Ganges, where it bred in the mephitic air of that primeval island-jungle, among whose bamboo thickets the tiger crouches, where life of every sort flourishes in rankest abundance, and only man avoids the spot. Thence the pestilence had spread throughout Hindustan, raging with great violence; moved eastward to China, westward to Afghanistan and Persia; following the great caravan routes, it brought terror to Astrakhan, terror to Moscow. Even while Europe trembled lest the spectre be seen striding westward across country, it was carried by sea from Syrian ports and appeared simultaneously at several points on the Mediterranean littoral; raised its head in Toulon and Malaga, Palermo and Naples, and soon got a firm hold in Calabria and Apulia.[8] Northern Italy had been spared—so far. But in May the horrible vibrions[9] were found on the same day in two bodies: the emaciated, blackened corpses of a bargee and a woman who kept a greengrocer's shop. Both cases were hushed up. But in a week there were ten more—twenty, thirty in different quarters of the town. An Austrian provincial, having come to Venice on a few days' pleasure trip, went home and died with all the symptoms of the plague. Thus was explained the fact that the German-language papers were the first to print the news of the Venetian outbreak. The Venetian authorities published in reply a statement to the effect that the state of the city's health had never been better; at the same time instituting the most necessary precautions. But by that time the food supplies—milk, meat, or vegetables—had probably been contaminated, for death unseen and unacknowledged was devouring and laying waste in the narrow streets, while a brooding, unseasonable heat warmed the waters of the canals and encouraged the spread of the pestilence. Yes, the disease seemed to flourish and wax strong, to redouble its generative powers. Recoveries were rare. Eighty out of every hundred died, and horribly, for the onslaught was of the extremest violence, and not infrequently of the "dry" type, the most malignant form of the contagion. In this form the victim's body loses power to expel the water secreted by the blood-vessels, it shrivels up, he passes with hoarse cries from convulsion to convulsion, his blood grows thick like pitch, and he suffocates in a few hours. He is fortunate indeed, if, as sometimes happens, the disease, after a slight *malaise,* takes the form of a profound unconsciousness, from which the sufferer seldom or never rouses. By the beginning of June the quarantine buildings of the *ospedale civico*[1] had quietly filled up, the two orphan asylums were entirely occupied, and there was a hideously brisk traffic between the *Nuovo Fundamento* and the island of San Michele, where the cemetery was. But the city was not swayed by high-minded motives or regard for international agreements. The authorities were more actuated by fear of being out of pocket, by regard for the new exhibition of paintings just opened in the Public Gardens, or by apprehension of the large losses the hotels and the shops that catered to foreigners would suffer in case of panic and blockade. And the fears of the people supported the persistent official policy of silence and denial. The city's first medical officer, an honest and competent man, had indignantly resigned his office and been privily replaced by a more compliant person. The fact was known; and this corruption in high places played its part, together with the suspense as to where the walking terror might strike next, to demoralize the baser elements in the city and encourage those antisocial forces which shun the light of day. There was intemperance, indecency, increase of crime. Evenings one saw many drunken people, which was unusual. Gangs of men in surly mood made the streets unsafe, theft and assault were said to be frequent, even murder; for in two cases persons supposedly victims of the plague were proved to have been poisoned by their own families. And professional vice was rampant, displaying excesses heretofore unknown and only at home much farther south and in the east.

8. Southern parts of Italy, Spain, and France. 9. Cholera bacteria. 1. Municipal hospital (Italian).

Such was the substance of the Englishman's tale. "You would do well," he concluded, "to leave today instead of tomorrow. The blockade cannot be more than a few days off."

"Thank you," said Aschenbach, and left the office.

The Piazza lay in sweltering sunshine. Innocent foreigners sat before the cafés or stood in front of the cathedral, the centre of clouds of doves that, with fluttering wings, tried to shoulder each other away and pick the kernels of maize from the extended hand. Aschenbach strode up and down the spacious flags, feverishly excited, triumphant in possession of the truth at last, but with a sickening taste in his mouth and a fantastic horror at his heart. One decent, expiatory course lay open to him; he considered it. Tonight, after dinner, he might approach the lady of the pearls and address her in words which he precisely formulated in his mind: "Madame, will you permit an entire stranger to serve you with a word of advice and warning which self-interest prevents others from uttering? Go away. Leave here at once, without delay, with Tadzio and your daughters. Venice is in the grip of pestilence." Then might he lay his hand in farewell upon the head of that instrument of a mocking deity; and thereafter himself flee the accursed morass. But he knew that he was far indeed from any serious desire to take such a step. It would restore him, would give him back himself once more; but he who is beside himself revolts at the idea of self-possession. There crossed his mind the vision of a white building with inscriptions on it, glittering in the sinking sun—he recalled how his mind had dreamed away into their transparent mysticism; recalled the strange pilgrim apparition that had wakened in the aging man a lust for strange countries and fresh sights. And these memories, again, brought in their train the thought of returning home, returning to reason, self-mastery, an ordered existence, to the old life of effort. Alas! the bare thought made him wince with a revulsion that was like physical nausea. "It must be kept quiet," he whispered fiercely. "I will not speak!" The knowledge that he shared the city's secret, the city's guilt—it put him beside himself, intoxicated him as a small quantity of wine will a man suffering from brain-fag. His thoughts dwelt upon the image of the desolate and calamitous city, and he was giddy with fugitive, mad, unreasoning hopes and visions of a monstrous sweetness. That tender sentiment he had a moment ago evoked, what was it compared with such images as these? His art, his moral sense, what were they in the balance beside the boons that chaos might confer? He kept silence, he stopped on.

That night he had a fearful dream—if dream be the right word for a mental and physical experience which did indeed befall him in deep sleep, as a thing quite apart and real to his senses, yet without his seeing himself as present in it. Rather its theatre seemed to be his own soul, and the events burst in from outside, violently overcoming the profound resistance of his spirit; passed him through and left him, left the whole cultural structure of a lifetime trampled on, ravaged, and destroyed.

The beginning was fear; fear and desire, with a shuddering curiosity. Night reigned, and his senses were on the alert; he heard loud, confused noises from far away, clamour and hubbub. There was a rattling, a crashing, a low dull thunder; shrill halloos and a kind of howl with a long-drawn *u*-sound at the end.

And with all these, dominating them all, flute-notes of the cruellest sweetness, deep and cooing, keeping shamelessly on until the listener felt his very entrails bewitched. He heard a voice, naming, though darkly, that which was to come: "The stranger god!"[2] A glow lighted up the surrounding mist and by it he recognized a mountain scene like that about his country home. From the wooded heights, from among the tree-trunks and crumbling moss-covered rocks, a troop came tumbling and raging down, a whirling rout of men and animals, and overflowed the hillside with flames and human forms, with clamour and the reeling dance. The females stumbled over the long, hairy pelts that dangled from their girdles; with heads flung back they uttered loud hoarse cries and shook their tambourines high in air; brandished naked daggers or torches vomiting trails of sparks. They shrieked, holding their breasts in both hands; coiling snakes with quivering tongues they clutched about their waists. Horned and hairy males, girt about the loins with hides, drooped heads and lifted arms and thighs in unison, as they beat on brazen vessels that gave out droning thunder, or thumped madly on drums. There were troops of beardless youths[3] armed with garlanded staves; these ran after goats and thrust their staves against the creatures' flanks, then clung to the plunging horns and let themselves be borne off with triumphant shouts. And one and all the mad rout yelled that cry, composed of soft consonants with a long-drawn *u*-sound at the end, so sweet and wild it was together, and like nothing ever heard before! It would ring through the air like the bellow of a challenging stag, and be given back many-tongued; or they would use it to goad each other on to dance with wild excess of tossing limbs—they never let it die. But the deep, beguiling notes of the flute wove in and out and over all. Beguiling too it was to him who struggled in the grip of these sights and sounds, shamelessly awaiting the coming feast and the uttermost surrender. He trembled, he shrank, his will was steadfast to preserve and uphold his own god against this stranger who was sworn enemy to dignity and self-control. But the mountain wall took up the noise and howling and gave it back manifold; it rose high, swelled to a madness that carried him away. His senses reeled in the steam of panting bodies, the acrid stench from the goats, the odour as of stagnant waters—and another, too familiar smell—of wounds, uncleanness, and disease. His heart throbbed to the drums, his brain reeled, a blind rage seized him, a whirling lust, he craved with all his soul to join the ring that formed about the obscene symbol of the godhead, which they were unveiling and elevating, monstrous and wooden, while from full throats they yelled their rallying-cry. Foam dripped from their lips, they drove each other on with lewd gesturings and beckoning hands. They laughed, they howled, they thrust their pointed staves into each other's flesh and licked the blood as it ran down. But now the dreamer was in them and of them, the stranger god was his own. Yes, it was he who was flinging himself upon the animals, who bit and tore and swallowed smoking gobbets of flesh—while on the trampled moss there now began the rites of honour of the god, an orgy of promiscuous embraces—and in his very soul he tasted the bestial degradation of his fall.

The unhappy man woke from this dream shattered, unhinged, powerless

2. Dionysus, god of disorder and excess. 3. These maddened rioters are votaries of Dionysus.

in the demon's grip. He no longer avoided men's eyes nor cared whether he exposed himself to suspicion. And anyhow, people were leaving; many of the bathing-cabins stood empty, there were many vacant places in the dining-room, scarcely any foreigners were seen in the streets. The truth seemed to have leaked out; despite all efforts to the contrary, panic was in the air. But the lady of the pearls stopped on with her family; whether because the rumours had not reached her on because she was too proud and fearless to heed them. Tadzio remained; and it seemed at times to Aschenbach, in his obsessed state, that death and fear together might clear the island of all other souls and leave him there alone with him he coveted. In the long mornings on the beach his heavy gaze would rest, a fixed and reckless stare, upon the lad; towards nightfall, lost to shame, he would follow him through the city's narrow streets where horrid death stalked too, and at such time it seemed to him as though the moral law were fallen in ruins and only the monstrous and perverse held out a hope.

Like any lover, he desired to please; suffered agonies at the thought of failure, and brightened his dress with smart ties and handkerchiefs and other youthful touches. He added jewellery and perfumes and spent hours each day over his toilette, appearing at dinner elaborately arrayed and tensely excited. The presence of the youthful beauty that had bewitched him filled him with disgust of his own aging body; the sight of his own sharp features and grey hair plunged him in hopeless mortification; he made desperate efforts to recover the appearance and freshness of his youth and began paying frequent visits to the hotel barber. Enveloped in the white sheet, beneath the hands of that garrulous personage, he would lean back in the chair and look at himself in the glass with misgiving.

"Grey," he said, with a grimace.

"Slightly," answered the man. "Entirely due to neglect, to a lack of regard for appearances. Very natural, of course, in men of affairs, but, after all, not very sensible, for it is just such people who ought to be above vulgar prejudice in matters like these. Some folk have very strict ideas about the use of cosmetics; but they never extend them to the teeth, as they logically should. And very disgusted other people would be if they did. No, we are all as old as we feel, but no older, and grey hair can misrepresent a man worse than dyed. You, for instance, signore, have a right to your natural colour. Surely you will permit me to restore what belongs to you?"

"How?" asked Aschenbach.

For answer the oily one washed his client's hair in two waters, one clear and one dark, and lo, it was as black as in the days of his youth. He waved it with the tongs in wide, flat undulations, and stepped back to admire the effect.

"Now if we were just to freshen up the skin a little," he said.

And with that he went on from one thing to another, his enthusiasm waxing with each new idea. Aschenbach sat there comfortably; he was incapable of objecting to the process—rather as it went forward it roused his hopes. He watched it in the mirror and saw his eyebrows grow more even and arching, the eyes gain in size and brilliance, by dint of a little application below the lids. A delicate carmine glowed on his cheeks where the skin had been so brown and leathery. The dry, anæmic lips grew full, they turned the colour of ripe strawberries, the lines round eyes and mouth were treated with a facial cream and gave place to youthful bloom. It was a young man who looked back at him from the glass—Aschenbach's heart leaped at the sight. The artist in cosmetic at last professed himself satisfied; after the manner of such people, he thanked his client profusely for what he had done himself. "The merest trifle, the merest, signore," he said as he added the final touches. "Now the signore can fall in love as soon as he likes." Aschenbach went off as in a dream, dazed between joy and fear, in his red neck-tie and broad straw hat with its gay striped band.

A lukewarm storm-wind had come up. It rained a little now and then, the air was heavy and turbid and smelt of decay. Aschenbach, with fevered cheeks beneath the rouge, seemed to hear rushing and flapping sounds in his ears, as though storm-spirits were abroad—unhallowed ocean harpies who follow those devoted to destruction, snatch away and defile their viands. For the heat took away his appetite and thus he was haunted with the idea that his food was infected.

One afternoon he pursued his charmer deep into the stricken city's huddled heart. The labyrinthine little streets, squares, canals, and bridges, each one so like the next, at length quite made him lose his bearings. He did not even know the points of the compass; all his care was not to lose sight of the figure after which his eyes thirsted. He slunk under walls, he lurked behind buildings or people's backs; and the sustained tension of his senses and emotions exhausted him more and more, though for a long time he was unconscious of fatigue. Tadzio walked behind the others, he let them pass ahead in the narrow alleys, and as he sauntered slowly after, he would turn his head and assure himself with a glance of his strange, twilit grey eyes that his lover was still following. He saw him—and he did not betray him. The knowledge enraptured Aschenbach. Lured by those eyes, led on the leading-string of his own passion and folly, utterly lovesick, he stole upon the footsteps of his unseemly hope—and at the end found himself cheated. The Polish family crossed a small vaulted bridge, the height of whose archway hid them from his sight, and when he climbed it himself they were nowhere to be seen. He hunted in three directions—straight ahead and on both sides the narrow, dirty quay—in vain. Worn quite out and unnerved, he had to give over the search.

His head burned, his body was wet with clammy sweat, he was plagued by intolerable thirst. He looked about for refreshment, of whatever sort, and found a little fruit-shop where he bought some strawberries. They were overripe and soft; he ate them as he went. The street he was on opened out into a little square, one of those charmed, forsaken spots he liked; he recognized it as the very one where he had sat weeks ago and conceived his abortive plan of flight. He sank down on the steps of the well and leaned his head against its stone rim. It was quiet here. Grass grew between the stones, and rubbish lay about. Tall, weather-beaten houses bordered the square, one of them rather palatial, with vaulted windows, gaping now, and little lion balconies. In the ground floor of another was an apothecary's shop. A waft of carbolic acid was borne on a warm gust of wind.

There he sat, the master; this was he who had found a way to reconcile art and honours; who had written *The Abject*, and in a style of classic purity renounced bohemianism and all its works, all sympathy with the abyss and the troubled depths of the outcast human soul. This was he who had put knowledge underfoot to climb so high; who had outgrown the ironic pose and adjusted himself to the burdens and obligations of fame; whose renown had been officially recognized and his name ennobled, whose style was set for a model in the schools. There he sat. His eyelids were closed, there was only a swift, sidelong glint of the eyeballs now and again, something between a question and a leer; while the rouged and flabby mouth uttered single words of the sentences shaped in his disordered brain by the fantastic logic that governs our dreams.

"For mark you, Phædrus, beauty alone is both divine and visible; and so it is the sense way, the artist's way, little Phædrus, to the spirit.[4] But, now tell me, my dear boy, do you believe that such a man can ever attain wisdom and true manly worth, for whom the path to the spirit must lead through the senses? Or do you rather think—for I leave the point to you—that it is a path of perilous sweetness, a way of transgression, and must surely lead him who walks in it astray? For you know that we poets cannot walk the way of beauty without Eros as our companion and guide. We may be heroic after our fashion, disciplined warriors of our craft, yet are we all like women, for we exult in passion, and love is still our desire—our craving and our shame. And from this you will perceive that we poets can be neither wise nor worthy citizens. We must needs be wanton, must needs rove at large in the realm of feeling. Our magisterial style is all folly and pretence, our honourable repute a farce, the crowd's belief in us is merely laughable. And to teach youth, or the populace, by means of art is a dangerous practice and ought to be forbidden. For what good can an artist be as a teacher, when from his birth up he is headed direct for the pit? We may want to shun it and attain to honour in the world; but however we turn, it draws us still. So, then, since knowledge might destroy us, we will have none of it. For knowledge, Phædrus, does not make him who possess it dignified or austere. Knowledge is all-knowing, understanding, forgiving; it takes up no position, sets no store by form. It has compassion with the abyss—it *is* the abyss. So we reject it, firmly, and henceforward our concern shall be with beauty only. And by beauty we mean simplicity, largeness, and renewed severity of discipline; we mean a return to detachment and to form. But detachment, Phædrus, and preoccupation with form lead to intoxication and desire, they may lead the noblest among us to frightful emotional excesses, which his own stern cult of the beautiful would make him the first to condemn. So they too, they too, lead to the bottomless pit. Yes, they lead us thither, I say, us who are poets—who by our natures are prone not to excellence but to excess. And now, Phædrus, I will go. Remain here; and only when you can no longer see me, then do you depart also."

A few days later Gustave Aschenbach left his hotel rather later than usual in the morning. He was not feeling well and had to struggle against spells of giddiness only half physical in their nature, accompanied by a swiftly mounting dread, a sense of futility and hopelessness—but whether this referred to himself or to the outer world he could not tell. In the lobby he saw a quantity of luggage

4. Here, again, Aschenbach is playing the role of Socrates in dialogue with his lover. See Socrates' *Phaedrus*.

lying strapped and ready; asked the porter whose it was, and received in answer the name he already knew he should hear—that of the Polish family. The expression of his ravaged features did not change; he only gave that quick lift of the head with which we sometimes receive the uninteresting answer to a casual query. But he put another: "When?" "After luncheon," the man replied. He nodded, and went down to the beach.

It was an unfriendly scene. Little crisping shivers ran all across the wide stretch of shallow water between the shore and the first sand-bank. The whole beach, once so full of colour and life, looked now autumnal, out of season; it was nearly deserted and not even very clean. A camera on a tripod stood at the edge of the water, apparently abandoned; its black cloth snapped in the freshening wind.

Tadzio was there, in front of his cabin, with the three or four playfellows still left him. Aschenbach set up his chair some half-way between the cabins and the water, spread a rug over his knees, and sat looking on. The game this time was unsupervised, the elders being probably busy with their packing, and it looked rather lawless and out-of-hand. Jaschiu, the sturdy lad in the belted suit, with the black, brilliantined hair, became angry at a handful of sand thrown in his eyes; he challenged Tadzio to a fight, which quickly ended in the downfall of the weaker. And perhaps the coarser nature saw here a chance to avenge himself at last, by one cruel act, for his long weeks of subserviency: the victor would not let the vanquished get up, but remained kneeling on Tadzio's back, pressing Tadzio's face into the sand—for so long a time that it seemed the exhausted lad might even suffocate. He made spasmodic efforts to shake the other off, lay still, and then began a feeble twitching. Just as Aschenbach was about to spring indignantly to the rescue, Jaschiu let his victim go. Tadzio, very pale, half sat up, and remained so, leaning on one arm, for several minutes, with darkening eyes and rumpled hair. Then he rose and walked slowly away. The others called him, at first gaily, then imploringly; he would not hear. Jaschiu was evidently overtaken by swift remorse; he followed his friend and tried to make his peace, but Tadzio motioned him back with a jerk of one shoulder and went down to the water's edge. He was barefoot and wore his striped linen suit with the red breast-knot.

There he stayed a little, with bent head, tracing figures in the wet sand with one toe; then stepped into the shallow water, which at its deepest did not wet his knees; waded idly through it and reached the sand-bar. Now he paused again, with his face turned seaward; and next began to move slowly leftwards along the narrow strip of sand the sea left bare. He paced there, divided by an expanse of water from the shore, from his mates by his moody pride; a remote and isolated figure, with floating locks, out there in sea and wind, against the misty inane. Once more he paused to look: with a sudden recollection, or by an impulse, he turned from the waist up, in an exquisite movement, one hand resting on his hip, and looked over his shoulder at the shore. The watcher sat just as he had sat that time in the lobby of the hotel when first the twilit grey eyes had met his own. He rested his head against the chair-back and followed the movements of the figure out there, then lifted it, as it were in answer to Tadzio's gaze. It sank on his breast, the eyes looked out beneath their lids, while his whole face took on the relaxed and brooding expression of deep slumber. It seemed to him the pale and lovely Summoner out there smiled at him and beckoned; as though, with the hand he lifted from his hip, he pointed outward as he hovered on before into an immensity of richest expectation. And, as so often before, he rose to follow.

Some minutes passed before anyone hastened to the aid of the elderly man sitting there collapsed in his chair. They bore him to his room. And before nightfall a shocked and respectful world received the news of his decease.

# Katherine Mansfield

*Mansfield (1888–1923) was born in Wellington, New Zealand. Though her intention in going to England at the end of her teens was to study music, there she made the acquaintance of literary people—among them D. H. Lawrence, who was for a while a close friend, and John Middleton Murry, whom she later married. Under their influence she began to write, first as a journalist and then as an innovative artist in the short story. The impressionism of many of her stories has led to some comparisons with Chekhov, who was, in any case, an example on whom she meant to model her working life. Her persisting ill health and the death of a beloved brother in World War I were among the circumstances that darkened her personal life more than they influenced the temper of her fiction, which remained eager and venturesome. Her keen satire was often directed at the self-righteousness of the upper classes and the intelligentsia, at the complacencies insulating them from the realities of existence as experienced by ordinary people. Her best-known collections of stories are* Bliss and Other Stories *(1920),* The Garden-Party and Other Stories *(1922), and* The Dove's Nest and Other Stories *(1923).*

## Bliss

Although Bertha Young was thirty she still had moments like this when she wanted to run instead of walk, to take dancing steps on and off the pavement, to bowl a hoop, to throw something up in the air and catch it again, or to stand still and laugh at—nothing—at nothing, simply.

What can you do if you are thirty and, turning the corner of your own street, you are overcome, suddenly, by a feeling of bliss—absolute bliss!—as though you'd suddenly swallowed a bright piece of that late afternoon sun and it burned in your bosom, sending out a little shower of sparks into every particle, into every finger and toe . . . ?

Oh, is there no way you can express it without being "drunk and disorderly"? How idiotic civilization is! Why be given a body if you have to keep it shut up in a case like a rare, rare fiddle?

"No, that about the fiddle is not quite what I mean," she thought, running up the steps and feeling in her bag for the key—she'd forgotten it, as usual—and rattling the letter-box. "It's not what I mean, because—Thank you, Mary"—she went into the hall. "Is nurse back?"

"Yes, M'm."

"And has the fruit come?"

"Yes, M'm. Everything's come."

"Bring the fruit up to the dining-room, will you? I'll arrange it before I go upstairs."

It was dusky in the dining-room and quite chilly. But all the same Bertha threw off her coat; she could not bear the tight clasp of it another moment, and the cold air fell on her arms.

But in her bosom there was still that bright glowing place—that shower of little sparks coming from it. It was almost unbearable. She hardly dared to breath for fear of fanning it higher, and yet she breathed deeply, deeply. She hardly dared to look into the cold mirror—but she did look, and it gave her back a woman, radiant, with smiling, trembling lips, with big, dark eyes and an air of listening, waiting for something . . . divine to happen . . . that she knew must happen . . . infallibly.

Mary brought in the fruit on a tray and with it a glass bowl, and a blue dish, very lovely, with a strange sheen on it as though it had been dipped in milk.

"Shall I turn on the light, M'm?"

"No, thank you. I can see quite well."

There were tangerines and apples stained with strawberry pink. Some yellow pears, smooth as silk, some white grapes covered with a silver bloom and a big cluster of purple ones. These last she had bought to tone in with the new living-room carpet. Yes, that did sound rather far-fetched and absurd, but it was really why she had bought them. She had thought in the shop: "I must have some purple ones to bring the carpet up to the table." And it had seemed quite sense at the time.

When she had finished with them and had made two pyramids of these bright round shapes, she stood away from the table to get the effect—and it really was most curious. For the dark table seemed to melt into the dusky light and the glass dish and the blue bowl to float in the air. This, of course in her present mood, was so incredibly beautiful. . . . She began to laugh.

"No, no. I'm getting hysterical." And she seized her bag and coat and ran upstairs to the nursery.

Nurse sat at a low table giving Little B her supper after her bath. The baby had on a white flannel gown and a blue woollen jacket, and her dark, fine hair was brushed up into a funny little peak. She looked up when she saw her mother and began to jump.

"Now, my lovey, eat it up like a good girl," said Nurse, setting her lips in a way that Bertha knew, and that meant she had come into the nursery at another wrong moment.

"Has she been good, Nanny?"

"She's been a little sweet all the afternoon," whispered Nanny. "We went to the park and I sat down on a chair and took her out of the pram and a big dog came along and put its head on my knee and she clutched its ear, tugged it. Oh, you should have seen her."

Bertha wanted to ask if it wasn't rather dangerous to let her clutch at a strange dog's ear. But she did not dare to. She stood watching them, her hands by her side, like the poor little girl in front of the rich little girl with the doll.

The baby looked up at her again, stared, and then smiled so charmingly that Bertha couldn't help crying:

"Oh, Nanny, do let me finish giving her her supper while you put the bath things away."

"Well, M'm, she oughtn't to be changed hands while she's eating," said Nanny, still whispering. "It unsettles her; it's very likely to upset her."

How absurd it was. Why have a baby if it has to be kept—not in a case like a rare, rare fiddle—but in another woman's arms?

"Oh, I must!" said she.

Very offended, Nanny handed her over.

"Now, don't excite her after her supper. You know you do, M'm. And I have such a time with her after!"

Thank heaven! Nanny went out of the room with the bath towels.

"Now I've got you to myself, my little precious," said Bertha, as the baby leaned against her.

She ate delightfully, holding up her lips for the spoon and then waving her hands. Sometimes she wouldn't let the spoon go; and sometimes, just as Bertha had filled it, she waved it away to the four winds.

When the soup was finished Bertha turned round to the fire.

"You're nice—you're very nice!" said she, kissing her warm baby. "I'm fond of you. I like you."

And, indeed, she loved Little B so much—her neck as she bent forward, her exquisite toes as they shone transparent in the firelight—that all her feeling of bliss came back again, and again she didn't know how to express it—what to do with it.

"You're wanted on the telephone," said Nanny, coming back in triumph and seizing *her* Little B.

Down she flew. It was Harry.

"Oh, is that you, Ber? Look here. I'll be late. I'll take a taxi and come along as quickly as I can, but get dinner put back ten minutes—will you? All right?"

"Yes, perfectly. Oh, Harry!"

"Yes?"

What had she to say? She'd nothing to say. She only wanted to get in touch with him for a moment. She couldn't absurdly cry: "Hasn't it been a divine day!"

"What is it?" rapped out the little voice.

"Nothing. *Entendu*,"[1] said Bertha, and hung up the receiver, thinking how more than idiotic civilization was.

They had people coming to dinner. The Norman Knights—a very sound couple—he was about to start a theatre, and she was awfully keen on interior decoration, a young man, Eddie Warren, who had just published a little book of poems and whom everybody was asking to dine, and a "find" of Bertha's

1. Understood (French).

called Pearl Fulton. What Miss Fulton did, Bertha didn't know. They had met at the club and Bertha had fallen in love with her, as she always did fall in love with beautiful women who had something strange about them.

The provoking thing was that, though they had been about together and met a number of times and really talked, Bertha couldn't yet make her out. Up to a certain point Miss Fulton was rarely, wonderfully frank, but the certain point was there, and beyond that she would not go.

Was there anything beyond it? Harry said "No." Voted her dullish, and "cold like all blond women, with a touch, perhaps, of anæmia of the brain." But Bertha wouldn't agree with him; not yet, at any rate.

"No, the way she has of sitting with her head a little on one side, and smiling, has something behind it, Harry, and I must find out what that something is."

"Most likely it's a good stomach," answered Harry.

He made a point of catching Bertha's heels with replies of that kind . . . "liver frozen, my dear girl," or "pure flatulence," or "kidney disease," . . . and so on. For some strange reason Bertha liked this, and almost admired it in him very much.

She went into the drawing-room and lighted the fire; then, picking up the cushions, one by one, that Mary had disposed so carefully, she threw them back on to the chairs and the couches. That made all the difference; the room came alive at once. As she was about to throw the last one she surprised herself by suddenly hugging it to her, passionately, passionately. But it did not put out the fire in her bosom. Oh, on the contrary!

The windows of the drawing-room opened on to a balcony overlooking the garden. At the far end, against the wall, there was a tall, slender pear tree in fullest, richest bloom; it stood perfect, as though becalmed against the jade-green sky. Bertha couldn't help feeling, even from this distance, that it had not a single bud or a faded petal. Down below, in the garden beds, the red and yellow tulips, heavy with flowers, seemed to lean upon the dusk. A grey cat, dragging its belly, crept across the lawn, and a black one, its shadow, trailed after. The sight of them, so intent and so quick, gave Bertha a curious shiver.

"What creepy things cats are!" she stammered, and she turned away from the window and began walking up and down. . . .

How strong the jonquils smelled in the warm room. Too strong? Oh, no. And yet, as though overcome, she flung down on a couch and pressed her hands to her eyes.

"I'm too happy—too happy!" she murmured.

And she seemed to see on her eyelids the lovely pear tree with its wide open blossoms as a symbol of her own life.

Really—really—she had everything. She was young. Harry and she were as much in love as ever, and they got on together splendidly and were really good pals. She had an adorable baby. They didn't have to worry about money. They had this absolutely satisfactory house and garden. And friends—modern, thrilling friends, writers and painters and poets or people keen on social questions—just the kind of friends they wanted. And then there were books, and there was music, and she had found a wonderful little dressmaker, and they were going abroad in the summer, and their new cook made the most superb omelettes. . . .

"I'm absurd. Absurd!" She sat up; but she felt quite dizzy, quite drunk. It must have been the spring.

Yes, it was the spring. Now she was so tired she could not drag herself upstairs to dress.

A white dress, a string of jade beads, green shoes and stockings. It wasn't intentional. She had thought of this scheme hours before she stood at the drawing-room window.

Her petals rustled softly into the hall, and she kissed Mrs. Norman Knight, who was taking off the most amusing orange coat with a procession of black monkeys round the hem and up the fronts.

". . . Why! Why! Why is the middle-class so stodgy—so utterly without a sense of humour! My dear, it's only by a fluke that I am here at all—Norman being the protective fluke. For my darling monkeys so upset the train that it rose to a man and simply ate me with its eyes. Didn't laugh—wasn't amused—that I should have loved. No, just stared—and bored me through and through."

"But the cream of it was," said Norman, pressing a large tortoise-shell-rimmed monocle into his eye, "you don't mind me telling this, Face, do you?" (In their home and among their friends they called each other Face and Mug.) "The cream of it was when she, being full fed, turned to the woman beside her and said: 'Haven't you ever seen a monkey before?' "

"Oh, yes!" Mrs. Norman Knight joined in the laughter. "Wasn't that too absolutely creamy?"

And a funnier thing still was that now her coat was off she did look like a very intelligent monkey—who had even made that yellow silk dress out of scraped banana skins. And her amber ear-rings; they were like little dangling nuts.

"This is a sad, sad fall!" said Mug, pausing in front of Little B's perambulator. "When the perambulator comes into the hall—" and he waved the rest of the quotation away.

The bell rang. It was lean, pale Eddie Warren (as usual) in a state of acute distress.

"It *is* the right house, *isn't* it?" he pleaded.

"Oh, I think so—I hope so," said Bertha brightly.

"I have had such a *dreadful* experience with a taxi-man; he was *most* sinister. I couldn't get him to *stop.* The *more* I knocked and called the *faster* he went. And *in* the moonlight this *bizarre* figure with the *flattened* head *crouching* over the *lit-tle* wheel. . . ."

He shuddered, taking off an immense white silk scarf. Bertha noticed that his socks were white, too—most charming.

"But how dreadful!" she cried.

"Yes, it really was," said Eddie, following her into the drawing-room. "I saw myself *driving* through Eternity in a *timeless* taxi."

He knew the Norman Knights. In fact, he was going to write a play for N. K. when the theatre scheme came off.

"Well, Warren, how's the play?" said Norman Knight, dropping his monocle and giving his eye a moment in which to rise to the surface before it was screwed down again.

And Mrs. Norman Knight: "Oh, Mr. Warren, what happy socks!"

"I *am* so glad you like them," said he, staring at his feet. "They seem to have got so *much* whiter since the moon rose." And he turned his lean sorrowful young face to Bertha. "There *is* a moon, you know."

She wanted to cry: "I am sure there is—often—often!"

He really was a most attractive person. But so was Face, crouched before the fire in her banana skins, and so was Mug, smoking a cigarette and saying as he flicked the ash: "Why doth the bridegroom tarry?"

"There he is, now."

Bang went the front door open and shut. Harry shouted: "Hullo, you people. Down in five minutes." And they heard him swarm up the stairs. Bertha couldn't help smiling; she knew how he loved doing things at high pressure. What, after all, did an extra five minutes matter? But he would pretend to himself that they mattered beyond measure. And then he would make a great point of coming into the drawing-room, extravagantly cool and collected.

Harry had such a zest for life. Oh, how she appreciated it in him. And his passion for fighting—for seeking in everything that came up against him another test of his power and of his courage—that, too, she understood. Even when it made him just occasionally, to other people, who didn't know him well, a little ridiculous perhaps. . . . For there were moments when he rushed into battle where no battle was. . . . She talked and laughed and positively forgot until he had come in (just as she had imagined) that Pearl Fulton had not turned up.

"I wonder if Miss Fulton has forgotten?"

"I expect so," said Harry. "Is she on the 'phone?"

"Ah! There's a taxi, now." And Bertha smiled with that little air of proprietorship that she always assumed while her women finds were new and mysterious. "She lives in taxis."

"She'll run to fat if she does," said Harry coolly, ringing the bell for dinner. "Frightful danger for blond women."

"Harry—don't," warned Bertha, laughing up at him.

Came another tiny moment, while they waited, laughing and talking, just a trifle too much at their ease, a trifle too unaware. And then Miss Fulton, all in silver, with a silver fillet binding her pale blond hair, came in smiling, her head a little on one side.

"Am I late?"

"No, not at all," said Bertha. "Come along." And she took her arm and they moved into the dining-room.

What was there in the touch of that cool arm that could fan—fan—start blazing—blazing—the fire of bliss that Bertha did not know what to do with?

Miss Fulton did not look at her; but then she seldom did look at people directly. Her heavy eyelids lay upon her eyes and the strange half smile came and went upon her lips as though she lived by listening rather than seeing. But Bertha knew, suddenly, as if the longest, most intimate look had passed between them—as if they had said to each other: "You, too?"—that Pearl Fulton, stirring the beautiful red soup in the grey plate, was feeling just what she was feeling.

And the others? Face and Mug, Eddie and Harry, their spoons rising and falling—dabbing their lips with their napkins, crumbling bread, fiddling with the forks and glasses and talking.

"I met her at the Alpha show—the weirdest little person. She'd not only cut off her hair, but she seemed to have taken a dreadfully good snip off her legs and arms and her neck and her poor little nose as well."

"Isn't she very *liée*[2] with Michael Oat?"

"The man who wrote *Love in False Teeth*?"

"He wants to write a play for me. One act. One man. Decides to commit suicide. Gives all the reasons why he should and why he shouldn't. And just as he has made up his mind either to do it or not to do it—curtain. Not half a bad idea."

"What's he going to call it—'Stomach Trouble'?"

"I *think* I've come across the *same* idea in a lit-tle French review, *quite* unknown in England."

No, they didn't share it. They were dears—dears—and she loved having them there, at her table, and giving them delicious food and wine. In fact, she longed to tell them how delightful they were, and what a decorative group they made, how they seemed to set one another off and how they reminded her of a play by Tchekof![3]

Harry was enjoying his dinner. It was part of his—well, not his nature, exactly, and certainly not his pose—his—something or other—to talk about food and to glory in his "shameless passion for the white flesh of the lobster" and "the green of pistachio ices—green and cold like the eyelids of Egyptian dancers."

When he looked up at her and said: "Bertha, this is a very admirable *soufflé*!" she almost could have wept with child-like pleasure.

Oh, why did she feel so tender towards the whole world tonight? Everything was good—was right. All that happened seemed to fill again her brimming cup of bliss.

And still, in the back of her mind, there was the pear tree. It would be silver now, in the light of poor dear Eddie's moon, silver as Miss Fulton, who sat there turning a tangerine in her slender fingers that were so pale a light seemed to come from them.

What she simply couldn't make out—what was miraculous—was how she should have guessed Miss Fulton's mood so exactly and so instantly. For she never doubted for a moment that she was right, and yet what had she to go on? Less than nothing.

"I believe this does happen very, very rarely between women. Never between men," thought Bertha. "But while I am making the coffee in the drawing-room perhaps she will 'give a sign.'"

What she meant by that she did not know, and what would happen after that she could not imagine.

2. Involved (French). 3. Variant spelling for Chekhov (1860–1904), Russian playwright and short-story writer.

While she thought like this she saw herself talking and laughing. She had to talk because of her desire to laugh.

"I must laugh or die."

But when she noticed Face's funny little habit of tucking something down the front of her bodice—as if she kept a tiny, secret hoard of nuts there, too—Bertha had to dig her nails into her hands—so as not to laugh too much.

It was over at last. And: "Come and see my new coffee machine," said Bertha.

"We only have a new coffee machine once a fortnight," said Harry. Face took her arm this time; Miss Fulton bent her head and followed after.

The fire had died down in the drawing-room to a red, flickering "nest of baby phœnixes," said Face.

"Don't turn up the light for a moment. It is so lovely." And down she crouched by the fire again. She was always cold . . . "without her little red flannel jacket, of course," thought Bertha.

At that moment Miss Fulton "gave the sign."

"Have you a garden?" said the cool, sleepy voice.

This was so exquisite on her part that all Bertha could do was to obey. She crossed the room, pulled the curtains apart, and opened those long windows.

"There!" she breathed.

And the two women stood side by side looking at the slender, flowering tree. Although it was so still it seemed, like the flame of a candle, to stretch up, to point, to quiver in the bright air, to grow taller and taller as they gazed—almost to touch the rim of the round, silver moon.

How long did they stand there? Both, as it were, caught in that circle of unearthly light, understanding each other perfectly, creatures of another world, and wondering what they were to do in this one with all this blissful treasure that burned in their bosoms and dropped, in silver flowers, from their hair and hands?

For ever—for a moment? And did Miss Fulton murmur: "Yes. Just *that.*" Or did Bertha dream it?

Then the light was snapped on and Face made the coffee and Harry said: "My dear Mrs. Knight, don't ask me about my baby. I never see her. I shan't feel the slightest interest in her until she has a lover," and Mug took his eye out of the conservatory for a moment and then put it under glass again and Eddie Warren drank his coffee and set down the cup with a face of anguish as though he had drunk and seen the spider.

"What I want to do is to give the young men a show. I believe London is simply teeming with first-chop, unwritten plays. What I want to say to 'em is: 'Here's the theatre. Fire ahead.' "

"You know, my dear, I am going to decorate a room for the Jacob Nathans. Oh, I am so tempted to do a fried-fish scheme, with the backs of the chairs shaped like frying pans and lovely chip potatoes embroidered all over the curtains."

"The trouble with our young writing men is that they are still too romantic. You can't put out to sea without being seasick and wanting a basin. Well, why won't they have the courage of those basins?"

"A *dreadful* poem about a *girl* who was *violated* by a beggar *without* a nose in a lit-tle wood. . . ."

Miss Fulton sank into the lowest, deepest chair and Harry handed round the cigarettes.

From the way he stood in front of her shaking the silver box and saying abruptly: "Egyptian? Turkish? Virginian? They're all mixed up," Bertha realized that she not only bored him; he really disliked her. And she decided from the way Miss Fulton said: "No, thank you, I won't smoke," that she felt it, too, and was hurt.

"Oh, Harry, don't dislike her. You are quite wrong about her. She's wonderful, wonderful. And, besides, how can you feel so differently about someone who means so much to me. I shall try to tell you when we are in bed to-night what has been happening. What she and I have shared."

At those last words something strange and almost terrifying darted into Bertha's mind. And this something blind and smiling whispered to her: "Soon these people will go. The house will be quiet—quiet. The lights will be out. And you and he will be alone together in the dark room—the warm bed. . . ."

She jumped up from her chair and ran over to the piano.

"What a pity someone does not play!" she cried. "What a pity somebody does not play."

For the first time in her life Bertha Young desired her husband.

Oh, she'd loved him—she'd been in love with him, of course, in every other way, but just not in that way. And, equally, of course, she'd understood that he was different. They'd discussed it so often. It had worried her dreadfully at first to find that she was so cold, but after a time it had not seemed to matter. They were so frank with each other—such good pals. That was the best of being modern.

But now—ardently! ardently! The word ached in her ardent body! Was this what that feeling of bliss had been leading up to? But then, then—

"My dear," said Mrs. Norman Knight, "you know our shame. We are the victims of time and train. We live in Hampstead.[4] It's been so nice."

"I'll come with you into the hall," said Bertha. "I loved having you. But you must not miss the last train. That's so awful, isn't it?"

"Have a whisky, Knight, before you go?" called Harry.

"No, thanks, old chap."

Bertha squeezed his hand for that as she took it.

"Good night, good-bye," she cried from the top step, feeling that this self of hers was taking leave of them for ever.

When she got back into the drawing-room the others were on the move.

" . . . Then you can come part of the way in my taxi."

"I shall be *so* thankful *not* to have to face *another* drive *alone* after my *dreadful* experience."

"You can get a taxi at the rank[5] just at the end of the street. You won't have to walk more than a few yards."

"That's a comfort. I'll go and put on my coat."

4. A suburb of London. 5. Stand.

Miss Fulton moved towards the hall and Bertha was following when Harry almost pushed past.

"Let me help you."

Bertha knew that he was repenting his rudeness—she let him go. What a boy he was in some ways—so impulsive—so—simple.

And Eddie and she were left by the fire.

"I *wonder* if you have seen Bilks' *new* poem called *Table d'Hôte,*" said Eddie softly. "It's *so* wonderful. In the last Anthology. Have you got a copy? I'd *so* like to *show* it to you. It begins with an *incredibly* beautiful line: 'Why Must it Always be Tomato Soup?' "

"Yes," said Bertha. And she moved noiselessly to a table opposite the drawing-room door and Eddie glided noiselessly after her. She picked up the little book and gave it to him; they had not made a sound.

While he looked it up she turned her head towards the hall. And she saw . . . Harry with Miss Fulton's coat in his arms and Miss Fulton with her back turned to him and her head bent. He tossed the coat away, put his hands on her shoulders and turned her violently to him. His lips said: "I adore you," and Miss Fulton laid her moonbeam fingers on his cheeks and smiled her sleepy smile. Harry's nostrils quivered; his lips curled back in a hideous grin while he whispered. "To-morrow," and with her eyelids Miss Fulton said: "Yes."

"Here it is," said Eddie. " 'Why Must it Always be Tomato Soup?' It's so *deeply* true, don't you feel? Tomato soup is so *dreadfully* eternal."

"If you prefer," said Harry's voice, very loud, from the hall. "I can phone you a cab to come to the door."

"Oh, no. It's not necessary," said Miss Fulton, and she came up to Bertha and gave her the slender fingers to hold.

"Good-bye. Thank you so much."

"Good-bye," said Bertha.

Miss Fulton held her hand a moment longer.

"Your lovely pear tree!" she murmured.

And then she was gone, with Eddie following, like the black cat following the grey cat.

"I'll shut up shop," said Harry, extravagantly cool and collected.

"Your lovely pear tree—pear tree—pear tree!"

Bertha simply ran over to the long windows.

"Oh, what is going to happen now?" she cried.

But the pear tree was as lovely as ever and as full of flower and as still.

# Bobbie Ann Mason

*Mason (1940– ) has written for* Movie Stars, Movie Life, *and* T.V. Star Parade, *earned a doctorate, and taught English. She has been awarded a Guggenheim Foundation Fellowship, has had stories in* Best American Short Stories *in 1981 and 1983, and won the Pushcart Prize for fiction in 1983.* Shiloh and Other Stories *(1982), her first collection, earned nominations for both the National Book Critics Circle Award and the American Book Award and won the Ernest Hemingway Foundation Award. She has also written two novels,* In Country *(1985) and* Feather Crowns *(1993); a short novel,* Spence and Lila *(1988); and two more collections of short stories,* Love Life *(1989) and* Midnight Magic *(1998).*

## Shiloh

Leroy Moffitt's wife, Norma Jean, is working on her pectorals. She lifts three-pound dumbbells to warm up, then progresses to a twenty-pound barbell. Standing with her legs apart, she reminds Leroy of Wonder Woman.

"I'd give anything if I could just get these muscles to where they're real hard," says Norma Jean. "Feel this arm. It's not as hard as the other one."

"That's cause you're right-handed," says Leroy, dodging as she swings the barbell in an arc.

"Do you think so?"

"Sure."

Leroy is a truckdriver. He injured his leg in a highway accident four months ago, and his physical therapy, which involves weights and a pulley, prompted Norma Jean to try building herself up. Now she is attending a body-building class. Leroy has been collecting temporary disability since his tractor-trailer jackknifed in Missouri, badly twisting his left leg in its socket. He has a steel pin in his hip. He will probably not be able to drive his rig again. It sits in the backyard, like a gigantic bird that has flown home to roost. Leroy has been home in Kentucky for three months, and his leg is almost healed, but the accident frightened him and he does not want to drive any more long hauls. He is not sure what to do next. In the meantime, he makes things from craft kits. He started by building a miniature log cabin from notched Popsicle sticks. He varnished it and placed it on the TV set, where it remains. It reminds him of a rustic Nativity scene. Then he tried string art (sailing ships on black velvet), a macramé owl kit, a snap-together B-17 Flying Fortress, and a lamp made out of a model truck, with a light fixture screwed in the top of the cab. At first the kits were diversions, something to kill time, but now he is thinking about building a full-scale log house from a kit. It would be considerably cheaper than building a regular house, and besides, Leroy has grown to appreciate how things are put together. He has begun to realize that in all the years he was on the road he never took time to examine anything. He was always flying past scenery.

"They won't let you build a log cabin in any of the new subdivisions," Norma Jean tells him.

"They will if I tell them it's for you," he says, teasing her. Ever since they were married, he has promised Norma Jean he would build her a new home one day. They have always rented, and the house they live in is small and nondescript. It does not even feel like a home, Leroy realizes now.

Norma Jean works at the Rexall drugstore, and she has acquired an amazing amount of information about cosmetics. When she explains to Leroy the three stages of complexion care, involving creams, toners, and moisturizers, he thinks happily of other petroleum products—axle grease, diesel fuel. This is a connection between him and Norma Jean. Since he has been home, he has felt unusually tender about his wife and guilty over his long absences. But he can't tell what she feels about him. Norma Jean has never complained about his traveling; she has never made hurt remarks, like calling his truck a "widowmaker." He is reasonably certain she has been faithful to him, but he wishes she would celebrate his permanent homecoming more happily. Norma Jean is often startled to find Leroy at home, and he thinks she seems a little disappointed about it. Perhaps he reminds her too much of the early days of their marriage, before he went on the road. They had a child who died as an infant, years ago. They never speak about their memories of Randy, which have almost faded, but now that Leroy is home all the time, they sometimes feel awkward around each other, and Leroy wonders if one of them should mention the child. He has the feeling that they are waking up out of a dream together—that they must create a new marriage, start afresh. They are lucky they are still married. Leroy has read that for most people losing a child destroys the marriage—or else he heard this on *Donahue.* He can't always remember where he learns things anymore.

At Christmas, Leroy bought an electric organ for Norma Jean. She used to play the piano when she was in high school. "It don't leave you," she told him once. "It's like riding a bicycle."

The new instrument had so many keys and buttons that she was bewildered by it at first. She touched the keys tentatively, pushed some buttons, then pecked out "Chopsticks." It came out in an amplified fox-trot rhythm, with marimba sounds.

"It's an orchestra!" she cried.

The organ had a pecan-look finish and eighteen preset chords, with optional flute, violin, trumpet, clarinet, and banjo accompaniments. Norma Jean mastered the organ almost immediately. At first she played Christmas songs. Then she bought *The Sixties Songbook* and learned every tune in it, adding variations to each with the rows of brightly colored buttons.

"I didn't like these old songs back then," she said. "But I have this crazy feeling I missed something."

"You didn't miss a thing," said Leroy.

Leroy likes to lie on the couch and smoke a joint and listen to Norma Jean play "Can't Take My Eyes Off You" and "I'll Be Back." He is back again. After fifteen years on the road, he is finally settling down with the woman he loves. She is still pretty. Her skin is flawless. Her frosted curls resemble pencil trimmings.

Now that Leroy has come home to stay, he notices how much the town has changed. Subdivisions are spreading across western Kentucky like an oil slick. The sign at the edge of town says "Pop: 11,500"—only seven hundred more than it said twenty years before. Leroy can't figure out who is living in all the new houses. The farmers who used to gather around the courthouse square on Saturday afternoons to play checkers and spit tobacco juice have gone. It has been years since Leroy has thought about the farmers, and they have disappeared without his noticing.

Leroy meets a kid named Stevie Hamilton in the parking lot at the new shopping center. While they pretend to be strangers meeting over a stalled car, Stevie tosses an ounce of marijuana under the front seat of Leroy's car. Stevie is wearing orange jogging shoes and a T-shirt that says CHATTAHOOCHEE SUPER-RAT. His father is a prominent doctor who lives in one of the expensive subdivisons in a new white-columned brick house that looks like a funeral parlor. In the phone book under his name there is a separate number, with the listing "Teenagers."

"Where do you get this stuff?" asks Leroy. "From your pappy!"

"That's for me to know and you to find out," Stevie says. He is slit-eyed and skinny.

"What else you got?"

"What you interested in?'

"Nothing special. Just wondered."

Leroy used to take speed on the road. Now he has to go slowly. He needs to be mellow. He leans back against the car and says, "I'm aiming to build me a log house, soon as I get time. My wife, though, I don't think she likes the idea."

"Well, let me know when you want me again," Stevie says. He has a cigarette in his cupped palm, as though sheltering it from the wind. He takes a long drag, then stomps it on the asphalt and slouches away.

Stevie's father was two years ahead of Leroy in high school. Leroy is thirty-four. He married Norma Jean when they were both eighteen, and their child Randy was born a few months later, but he died at the age of four months and three days. He would be about Stevie's age now. Norma Jean and Leroy were at the drive-in, watching a double feature (*Dr. Strangelove* and *Lover Come Back*), and the baby was sleeping in the back seat. When the first movie ended, the baby was dead. It was the sudden infant death syndrome. Leroy remembers handing Randy to a nurse at the emergency room, as though he were offering her a large doll as a present. A dead baby feels like a sack of flour. "It just happens sometimes," said the doctor, in what Leroy always recalls as a nonchalant tone. Leroy can hardly remember the child anymore, but he still sees vividly a scene from *Dr. Strangelove* in which the President of the United States was talking in a folksy voice on the hot line to the Soviet premier about the bomber accidentally headed toward Russia. He was in the War Room, and the world map was lit up. Leroy remembers Norma Jean catatonically beside him in the hospital and himself thinking: Who is this strange girl? He had forgotten who she was. Now scientists are saying that crib death is caused by a virus. Nobody knows anything, Leroy thinks. The answers are always changing.

When Leroy gets home from the shopping center, Norma Jean's mother, Mabel Beasley, is there. Until this year, Leroy has not realized how much time she spends with Norma Jean. When she visits, she inspects the closets and then the plants, informing Norma Jean when a plant is droopy or yellow. Mabel calls the plants "flowers," although there are never any blooms. She always notices if Norma Jean's laundry is piling up. Mabel is a short, overweight woman whose tight, brown-dyed curls look more like a wig than the actual wig she sometimes wears. Today she has brought Norma Jean an off-white dust ruffle she made for the bed; Mabel works in a custom-upholstery shop.

"This is the tenth one I made this year," Mabel says. "I got started and couldn't stop."

"It's real pretty," says Norma Jean.

"Now we can hide things under the bed," says Leroy, who gets along with his mother-in-law primarily by joking with her. Mabel has never really forgiven him for disgracing her by getting Norma Jean pregnant. When the baby died, she said that fate was mocking her.

"What's that thing?" Mabel says to Leroy in a loud voice, pointing to a tangle of yarn on a piece of canvas.

Leroy holds it up for Mabel to see. "It's my needlepoint," he explains. "This is a *Star Trek* pillow cover."

"That's what a woman would do," says Mabel. "Great day in the morning!"

"All the big football players on TV do it," he says.

"Why, Leroy, you're always trying to fool me. I don't believe you for one minute. You don't know what to do with yourself—that's the whole trouble. Sewing!"

"I'm aiming to build us a log house," says Leroy. "Soon as my plans come."

"Like *heck* you are," says Norma Jean. She takes Leroy's needlepoint and shoves it into a drawer. "You have to find a job first. Nobody can afford to build now anyway."

Mabel straightens her girdle and says, "I still think before you get tied down y'all ought to take a little run to Shiloh."

"One of these days, Mama," Norma Jean says impatiently.

Mabel is talking about Shiloh, Tennessee. For the past few years, she has been urging Leroy and Norma Jean to visit the Civil War battleground there. Mabel went there on her honeymoon—the only real trip she ever took. Her husband died of a perforated ulcer when Norma Jean was ten, but Mabel, who was accepted into the United Daughters of the Confederacy in 1975, is still preoccupied with going back to Shiloh.

"I've been to kingdom come and back in that truck out yonder," Leroy says to Mabel, "but we never yet set foot in that battleground. Ain't that something? How did I miss it?"

"It's not even that far," Mabel says.

After Mabel leaves, Norma Jean reads to Leroy from a list she has made. "Thing you could do," she announces. "You could get a job as a guard at Union Carbide, where they'd let you set on a stool. You could get on at the lumberyard. You could do a little carpenter work, if you want to build so bad. You could—"

"I can't do something where I'd have to stand up all day."

"You ought to try standing up all day behind a cosmetics counter. It's amazing that I have strong feet, coming from two parents that never had strong feet at all." At the moment Norma Jean is holding on to the kitchen counter, raising her knees one at a time as she talks. She is wearing two-pound ankle weights.

"Don't worry," says Leroy. "I'll do something."

"You could truck calves to slaughter for somebody. You wouldn't have to drive any big old truck for that."

"I'm going to build you this house," says Leroy. "I want to make you a real home."

"I don't want to live in any log cabin."

"It's not a cabin. It's a house."

"I don't care. It looks like a cabin."

"You and me together could lift those logs. It's just like lifting weights."

Norma Jean doesn't answer. Under her breath, she is counting. Now she is marching through the kitchen. She is doing goose steps.

Before his accident, when Leroy came home he used to stay in the house with Norma Jean, watching TV in bed and playing cards. She would cook fried chicken, picnic ham, chocolate pie—all his favorites. Now he is home alone much of the time. In the mornings, Norma Jean disappears, leaving a cooling place in the bed. She eats a cereal called Body Buddies, and she leaves the bowl on the table, with soggy tan balls floating in a milk puddle. He sees things about Norma Jean that he never realized before. When she chops onions, she stares off into a corner, as if she can't bear to look. She puts on her house slippers almost precisely at nine o'clock every evening and nudges her jogging shoes under the couch. She saves bread heels for the birds. Leroy watches the birds at the feeder. He notices the peculiar way goldfinches fly past the window. They close their wings, then fall, then spread their wings to catch and lift themselves. He wonders if they close their eyes when they fall. Norma Jean closes her eyes when they are in bed. She wants the lights turned out. Even then, he is sure she closes her eyes.

He goes for long drives around town. He tends to drive a car rather carelessly. Power steering and an automatic shift make a car feel so small and inconsequential that his body is hardly involved in the driving process. His injured leg stretches out comfortably. Once or twice he has almost hit something, but even the prospect of an accident seems minor in a car. He cruises the new subdivisions, feeling like a criminal rehearsing for a robbery. Norma Jean is probably right about a log house being inappropriate here in the new subdivisions. All the houses look grand and complicated. They depress him.

One day when Leroy comes home from a drive he finds Norma Jean in tears. She is in the kitchen making a potato and mushroom-soup casserole, with grated-cheese topping. She is crying because her mother caught her smoking.

"I didn't hear her coming. I was standing here puffing away pretty as you please," Norma Jean says, wiping her eyes.

"I knew it would happen sooner or later," says Leroy, putting his arm around her.

"She don't know the meaning of the word 'knock,' " says Norma Jean. "It's a wonder she hadn't caught me years ago."

"Think of it this way," Leroy says. "What if she caught me with a joint?"

"You better not let her!" Norma Jean shrieks. "I'm warning you, Leroy Moffitt!"

"I'm just kidding. Here, play me a tune. That'll help you relax."

Norma Jean puts the casserole in the oven and sets the timer. Then she plays a ragtime tune, with horns and banjo, as Leroy lights up a joint and lies on the couch, laughing to himself about Mabel's catching him at it. He thinks of Stevie Hamilton—a doctor's son pushing grass. Everything is funny. The whole town seems crazy and small. He is reminded of Virgil Mathis, a boastful policeman Leroy used to shoot pool with. Virgil recently led a drug bust in a back room at a bowling alley, where he seized ten thousand dollars' worth of marijuana. The newspaper had a picture of him holding up the bags of grass and grinning widely. Right now, Leroy can imagine Virgil breaking down the door and arresting him with a lungful of smoke. Virgil would probably have been alerted to the scene because of all the racket Norma Jean is making. Now she sounds like a hard-rock band. Norma Jean is terrific. When she switches to a latin-rhythm version of "Sunshine Superman," Leroy hums along. Norma Jean's foot goes up and down, up and down.

"Well, what do you think?" Leroy says, when Norma Jean pauses to search through her music.

"What do I think about what?"

His mind has gone blank. Then he says, "I'll sell my rig and build us a house." That wasn't what he wanted to say. He wanted to know what she thought—what she *really* thought—about them.

"Don't start in on that again," says Norma Jean. She begins playing "Who'll Be the Next in Line?"

Leroy used to tell hitchhikers his whole life story—about his travels, his hometown, the baby. He would end with a question: "Well, what do you think?" It was just a rhetorical question. In time, he had the feeling that he'd been telling the same story over and over to the same hitchhikers. He quit talking to hitchhikers when he realized how his voice sounded—whining and self-pitying, like some teenage-tragedy song. Now Leroy has the sudden impulse to tell Norma Jean about himself, as if he had just met her. They have known each other so long they have forgotten a lot about each other. They could become reacquainted. But when the oven timer goes off and she runs to the kitchen, he forgets why he wants to do this.

The next day, Mabel drops by. It is Saturday and Norma Jean is cleaning. Leroy is studying the plans of his log house, which have finally come in the mail. He has them spread out on the table—big sheets of stiff blue paper, with diagrams and numbers printed in white. While Norma Jean runs the vacuum, Mabel drinks coffee. She sets her coffee cup on a blueprint.

"I'm just waiting for time to pass," she says to Leroy, drumming her fingers on the table.

As soon as Norma Jean switches off the vacuum, Mabel says in a loud voice, "Did you hear about the datsun dog that killed the baby?"

Norma Jean says, "The word is 'dachshund.' "

"They put the dog on trial. It chewed the baby's legs off. The mother was in the next room all the time." She raises her voice. "They thought it was neglect."

Norma Jean is holding her ears. Leroy manages to open the refrigerator and get some Diet Pepsi to offer Mabel. Mabel still has some coffee and she waves away the Pepsi.

"Datsuns are like that," Mabel says. "They're jealous dogs. They'll tear a place to pieces if you don't keep an eye on them."

"You better watch out what you're saying, Mabel," says Leroy.

"Well, facts is facts."

Leroy looks out the window at his rig. It is like a huge piece of furniture gathering dust in the backyard. Pretty soon it will be an antique. He hears the vacuum cleaner. Norma Jean seems to be cleaning the living room rug again.

Later, she says to Leroy, "She just said that about the baby because she caught me smoking. She's trying to pay me back."

"What are you talking about?" Leroy says, nervously shuffling blueprints.

"You know good and well," Norma Jean says. She is sitting in a kitchen chair with her feet up and her arms wrapped around her knees. She looks small and helpless. She says, "The very idea, her bringing up a subject like that! Saying it was neglect."

"She didn't mean that," Leroy says.

"She might not have *thought* she meant it. She always says things like that. You don't know how she goes on."

"But she didn't really mean it. She was just talking."

Leroy opens a king-sized bottle of beer and pours it into two glasses, dividing it carefully. He hands a glass to Norma Jean and she takes it from him mechanically. For a long time, they sit by the kitchen window watching the birds at the feeder.

Something is happening. Norma Jean is going to night school. She has graduated from her six-week body-building course and now she is taking an adult-education course in composition at Paducah Community College. She spends her evenings outlining paragraphs.

"First you have a topic sentence," she explains to Leroy. "Then you divide it up. Your secondary topic has to be connected to your primary topic."

To Leroy, this sounds intimidating. "I never was any good in English," he says.

"It makes a lot of sense."

"What are you doing this for, anyhow?"

She shrugs. "It's something to do." She stands up and lifts her dumbbells a few times.

"Driving a rig, nobody cared about my English."

"I'm not criticizing your English."

Norma Jean used to say, "If I lose ten minutes' sleep, I just drag all day." Now she stays up late, writing compositions. She got a B on her first paper—a how-to theme on soup-based casseroles. Recently Norma Jean has been cooking unusual foods—tacos, lasagna, Bombay chicken. She doesn't play the organ anymore, though her second paper was called "Why Music Is Important to Me." She sits at the kitchen table, concentrating on her outlines, while Leroy plays with his log house plans, practicing with a set of Lincoln Logs. The thought of getting a truckload of notched, numbered logs scares him, and he wants to be prepared. As he and Norma Jean work together at the kitchen table, Leroy has the hopeful thought that they are sharing something, but he knows he is a fool to think this. Norma Jean is miles away. He knows he is going to lose her. Like Mabel, he is just waiting for time to pass.

One day, Mabel is there before Norma Jean gets home from work, and Leroy finds himself confiding in her. Mabel, he realizes, must know Norma Jean better than he does.

"I don't know what's got into that girl," Mabel says. "She used to go to bed with the chickens. Now you say she's up all hours. Plus her a-smoking. I like to died."

"I want to make her this beautiful home," Leroy says, indicating the Lincoln Logs. "I don't think she even wants it. Maybe she was happier with me gone."

"She don't know what to make of you, coming home like this."

"Is that it?"

Mabel takes the roof off his Lincoln Log cabin. "You couldn't get *me* in a log cabin," she says. "I was raised in one. It's no picnic, let me tell you."

"They're different now," says Leroy.

"I tell you what," Mabel says, smiling oddly at Leroy.

"What?"

"Take her on down to Shiloh. Y'all need to get out together, stir a little. Her brain's all balled up over them books."

Leroy can see traces of Norma Jean's features in her mother's face. Mabel's face has the texture of crinkled cotton, but suddenly she looks pretty. It occurs to Leroy that Mabel has been hinting all along that she wants them to take her with them to Shiloh.

"Let's all go to Shiloh," he says. "You and me and her. Come Sunday."

Mabel throws up her hands in protest. "Oh, no, not me. Young folks want to be by theirselves."

When Norma Jean comes in with groceries, Leroy says excitedly, "Your mama here's been dying to go to Shiloh for thirty-five years. It's about time we went, don't you think?"

"I'm not going to butt in on anybody's second honeymoon," Mabel says.

"Who's going on a honeymoon, for Christ's sake?" Norma Jean says loudly.

"I never raised no daughter of mine to talk that-a-way," Mabel says.

"You ain't seen nothing yet," says Norma Jean. She starts putting away boxes and cans, slamming cabinet doors.

"There's a log cabin at Shiloh." Mabel says, "It was there during the battle. There's bullet holes in it."

"When are you going to *shut up* about Shiloh, Mama?" asks Norma Jean.

"I always thought Shiloh was the prettiest place, so full of history," Mabel goes on. "I just hoped y'all could see it once before I die, so you could tell me about it." Later, she whispers to Leroy, "You do what I said. A little change is what she needs."

"Your name means 'the king,' " Norma Jean says to Leroy that evening. He is trying to get her to go to Shiloh, and she is reading a book about another century.

"Well, I reckon I ought to be right proud."

"I guess so."

"Am I still king around here?"

Norma Jean flexes her biceps and feels them for hardness. "I'm not fooling around with anybody, if that's what you mean," she says.

"Would you tell me if you were?"

"I don't know."

"What does *your* name mean?"

"It was Marilyn Monroe's real name."

"No kidding!"

"Norma comes from the Normans. They were invaders," she says. She closes her book and looks hard at Leroy. "I'll go to Shiloh with you if you'll stop staring at me."

On Sunday, Norma Jean packs a picnic and they go to Shiloh. To Leroy's relief, Mabel says she does not want to come with them. Norma Jean drives, and Leroy, sitting beside her, feels like some boring hitchhiker she has picked up. He tries some conversation, but she answers him in monosyllables. At Shiloh, she drives aimlessly through the park, past bluffs and trails and steep ravines. Shiloh is an immense place, and Leroy cannot see it as a battleground. It is not what he expected. He thought it would look like a golf course. Monuments are everywhere, showing through the thick clusters of trees. Norma Jean passes the log cabin Mabel mentioned. It is surrounded by tourists looking for bullet holes.

"That's not the kind of log house I've got in mind," says Leroy apologetically.

"I know *that*."

"This is a pretty place. Your mama was right."

"It's O.K.," says Norma Jean. "Well, we've seen it. I hope she's satisfied."

They burst out laughing together.

At the park museum, a movie on Shiloh is shown every half hour, but they decide that they don't want to see it. They buy a souvenir Confederate flag for Mabel, and then they find a picnic spot near the cemetery. Norma Jean has brought a picnic cooler, with pimiento sandwiches, soft drinks, and Yodels. Leroy eats a sandwich and then smokes a joint, hiding it behind the picnic cooler. Norma Jean has quit smoking altogether. She is picking cake crumbs from the cellophane wrapper, like a fussy bird.

Leroy says, "So the boys in gray ended up in Corinth. The Union soldiers zapped 'em finally. April 7, 1862."

They both know that he doesn't know any history. He is just talking about some of the historical plaques they have read. He feels awkward, like a boy on a date with an older girl. They are still just making conversation.

"Corinth is where Mama eloped to," says Norma Jean.

They sit in silence and stare at the cemetery for the Union dead and, beyond, at a tall cluster of trees. Campers are parked nearby, bumper to bumper, and small children in bright clothing are cavorting and squealing. Norma Jean wads up the cake wrapper and squeezes it tightly in her hand. Without looking at Leroy, she says, "I want to leave you."

Leroy takes a bottle of Coke out of the cooler and flips off the cap. He holds the bottle poised near his mouth but cannot remember to take a drink. Finally he says, "No, you don't."

"Yes, I do."

"I won't let you."

"You can't stop me."

"Don't do me that way."

Leroy knows Norma Jean will have her own way. "Didn't I promise to be home from now on?" he says.

"In some ways, a woman prefers a man who wanders," says Norma Jean. "That sounds crazy, I know."

"You're not crazy."

Leroy remembers to drink from his Coke. Then he says, "Yes, you *are* crazy. You and me could start all over again. Right back at the beginning."

"We *have* started all over again," says Norma Jean. "And this is how it turned out."

"What did I do wrong?"

"Nothing."

"Is this one of those women's lib things?" Leroy asks.

"Don't be funny."

The cemetery, a green slope dotted with white markers, looks like a subdivision site. Leroy is trying to comprehend that his marriage is breaking up, but for some reason he is wondering about white slabs in a graveyard.

"Everything was fine till Mama caught me smoking," says Norma Jean, standing up. "That set something off."

"What are you talking about?"

"She won't leave me alone—*you* won't leave me alone." Norma Jean seems to be crying, but she is looking away from him. "I feel eighteen again. I can't face that all over again." She starts walking away. "No, it *wasn't* fine. I don't know what I'm saying. Forget it."

Leroy takes a lungful of smoke and closes his eyes as Norma Jean's words sink in. He tries to focus on the fact that thirty-five hundred soldiers died on the grounds around him. He can only think of that war as a board game with plastic soldiers. Leroy almost smiles, as he compares the Confederates' daring attack on the Union camps and Virgil Mathis's raid on the bowling alley. General Grant, drunk and furious, shoved the Southerners back to Corinth, where Mabel and Jet Beasley were married years later, when Mabel was still thin and good-looking. The next day, Mabel and Jet visited the battleground, and then Norma Jean was born, and then she married Leroy and they had a baby, which they lost, and now Leroy and Norma Jean are here at the same battleground. Leroy knows he is leaving out a lot. He is leaving out the insides of history. History was always just names and dates to him. It occurs to him that building a house out of logs is similarly empty—too simple. And the real inner workings of a marriage, like most of history, have escaped him. Now he sees that building a log house is the dumbest idea he could have had. It was clumsy of him to think Norma Jean would want a log house. It was a crazy idea. He'll have to think of something else, quickly. He will wad the blueprints into tight balls and fling them into the lake. Then he'll get moving again. He opens his eyes. Norma Jean has moved away and is walking through the cemetery, following a serpentine brick path.

Leroy gets up to follow his wife, but his good leg is asleep and his bad leg still hurts him. Norma Jean is far away, walking rapidly toward the bluff by the river, and he tries to hobble toward her. Some children run past him, screaming noisily. Norma Jean has reached the bluff, and she is looking out over the Tennessee River. Now she turns toward Leroy and waves her arms. Is she beckoning to him? She seems to be doing an exercise for her chest muscles. The sky is unusually pale—the color of the dust ruffle Mabel made for their bed.

# Guy de Maupassant

*Maupassant (1850–1893) was born near Dieppe, France. His parents were friends of the novelist Gustave Flaubert, whose views on literature and the artistic life influenced Maupassant even in his early years. Rebellious in school, he accepted army discipline during the Franco-Prussian war of 1870–71, and then for nearly ten years apprenticed himself to Flaubert to learn the craft of fiction, discarding most of what he wrote. In 1880 he became famous with the publication of a single story,* Boule de Suif, *which contrasts the patriotism of a young prostitute with the amorality of middle-class citizens. Maupassant published, during the next ten years, nearly three hundred short stories, half a dozen novels, some plays, verse, and travel books. The short stories, which appeared regularly in popular periodicals, sampled military and peasant life, the decadent world of politics and journalism, prostitution, perversion, the supernatural, and the hypocrisies of solid citizens. Maupassant's income from his prodigious literary output permitted him to indulge the appetites for women and luxury that had always been part of his character, but in his last years syphilis, which he apparently contracted before he was twenty, began to unravel his capacity for concentrated work. He sought relief in drugs and travels on his yacht but became completely insane before he died of paresis. His novels include* Une Vie *(A Life) (1883),* Bel Ami *(Handsome Friend) (1885), and* Pierre et Jean *(1888). His short stories are most readily available in his collected works.*

## Boule de Suif[1]

For several days in succession straggling remnants of the routed French army had been passing through the town. This was not the regular army, but a disjointed rabble, the men unshaven and dirty, their uniforms in tatters, slouching along without regimental colors, without order—worn out, broken down, incapable of thought or resolution, marching from pure habit and dropping with fatigue the moment they stopped. The majority belonged to the militia and were men of peaceful pursuits, retired from business, all sinking under the weight of their accouterments: quick-witted little militiamen as prone to terror as they were to enthusiasm, as ready to attack as they were to fly; here and there a few red trousers, remnants of a company mowed down in one of the big battles; dark-coated artillerymen, side by side with these various uniforms of the infantry, and now and then the glittering helmet of a heavily booted

1. Translated by Ernest Boyd and Storm Jameson. "Boule de Suif": ball of fat (French).

dragoon who followed with difficulty the march of the more light-footed soldiers of the line.

Companies of franc-tireurs,[2] heroically named "Avengers of the Defeat," "Citizens of the Tomb," "Companions in Death," passed in their turn, looking like a horde of bandits.

Their chiefs—formerly drapers or grain-dealers, retired soap-boilers or suet-refiners, temporary heroes, created officers by reason of their wealth or the length of their mustaches, burdened with weapons, flannels, and gold lace—talked loudly, discussed plans of campaign, and gave you to understand that they were the sole support of France in her death-agony; but they were generally in terror of their own soldiers, gallows birds, most of them brave to foolhardiness, all of them given to pillage and debauchery.

Report said that the Prussians[3] were about to enter Rouen. The National Guard, which for two months past had made the most careful reconnoiterings in the neighboring wood, even to the extent of occasionally shooting their own sentries and putting themselves in battle array if a rabbit stirred in the brushwood, had now retired to their domestic hearths; their arms, their uniforms, all the murderous apparatus with which they had been wont to strike terror into the hearts of all beholders for three leagues round, had vanished.

Finally, the last of the French soldiery crossed the Seine on their way to Pont-Audemer by Saint-Severin and Bourg-Achard; and then, last of all, came their despairing general tramping on foot between two orderlies, powerless to attempt any action with these disjointed fragments of his forces, himself utterly dazed and bewildered by the downfall of a people accustomed to victory and now so disastrously beaten in spite of its traditional bravery.

After that a profound calm, the silence of terrified suspense, fell over the city. Many a rotund bourgeois, emasculated by a lifetime of trade, awaited the arrival of the victors with anxiety, trembling lest his meat-skewers and kitchen carving-knives should come under the category of arms.

Life seemed to have come to a standstill, the shops were closed, the streets silent. From time to time an inhabitant, intimidated by their silence, would flit rapidly along the pavement, keeping close to the walls.

In this anguish of suspense, men longed for the coming of the enemy.

Towards the end of the day following the departure of the French troops, some Uhlans, appearing from goodness knows where, traversed the city hastily. A little later, a black mass descended from the direction of Sainte-Catherine, while two more invading torrents poured in over the roads from Darnetal and Boisguillaume. The advance guards of the three corps converged at the same moment into the square of the Hotel de Ville, while battalion after battalion of the German army wound through the adjacent streets, making the pavement ring under their heavy rhythmic tramp.

Orders shouted in strange and guttural tones were echoed back by the apparently dead and deserted houses, while from behind closed shutters eyes peered furtively at the conquerors, masters by right of might, of the city and

2. Army sharpshooters (French). 3. Germans.

the lives and fortunes of its inhabitants. The people in their darkened dwellings fell a prey to the helpless bewilderment which comes over men before the floods, the devastating upheavals of the earth, against which all wisdom and all force are unavailing. The same phenomenon occurs each time that the established order of things is overthrown, when public security is at an end, and when all that the laws of man or of nature protect is at the mercy of some blind elemental force. The earthquake burying an entire population under its falling houses; the flood that carries away the drowned body of the peasant with the carcasses of his cattle and the beams torn from his roof-tree; or the victorious army massacring those who defend their lives, and making prisoners of the rest—pillaging in the name of the sword, and thanking God to the roar of cannon—are so many appalling scourges which overthrow all faith in eternal justice, all the confidence we are taught to place in the protection of Providence and the reason of man.

Small detachments now began knocking at the doors and then disappearing into the houses. It was the occupation after the invasion. It now behooved the vanquished to make themselves agreeable to the victors.

After a while, the first alarms having subsided, a new sense of tranquillity began to establish itself. In many houses the Prussian officer shared the family meals. Not infrequently he was a gentleman, and out of politeness expressed his commiseration with France and his repugnance at having to take part in such a war. They were grateful enough to him for this sentiment—besides, who knew when they might not be glad of his protection? By gaining his good offices one might have fewer men to feed. And why offend a person on whom one was utterly dependent? That would not be bravery but temerity, a quality of which the citizens of Rouen could no longer be accused as in the days of those heroic defenses by which the city had made itself famous. Above all, they said, with the unassailable urbanity of the Frenchman, it was surely permissible to be on politely familiar terms in private, provided one held aloof from the foreign soldier in public. In the street, therefore, they ignored one another's existence, but once indoors they were perfectly ready to be friendly, and each evening found the German staying longer at the family fireside.

The town itself gradually regained its wonted aspect. The French inhabitants did not come out much, but the Prussian soldiers swarmed in the streets. For the rest, the blue hussar officers who trailed their mighty implements of death so arrogantly over the pavement did not appear to entertain a vastly deeper grade of contempt for the simple townsfolk than did the officers of the Chasseurs[4] who had drunk in the same cafés the year before. Nevertheless there was something in the air; something subtle and indefinable, an intolerably unfamiliar atmosphere like a widely diffused odor—the odor of invasion. It filled the private dwellings and the public places, it affected the taste of food, and gave one the impression of being on a journey, far away from home, among barbarous and dangerous tribes.

The conquerors demanded money—a great deal of money. The inhabitants paid and went on paying; for the matter of that, they were rich. But the wealth-

4. Troops, cavalry, or infantry trained for quick deployment or movement (French).

ier a Normandy tradesman becomes, the more keenly he suffers at each sacrifice each time he sees the smallest particle of his fortune pass into the hands of another.

Two or three leagues beyond the town, however, following the course of the river about Croisset, Dieppedalle or Biessard, the sailors and the fishermen would often drag up the swollen corpse of some uniformed German, killed by a knife-thrust or a kick, his head smashed in by a stone, or thrown into the water from some bridge. The slime of the river bed swallowed up many a deed of vengeance, obscure, savage, and legitimate; unknown acts of heroism, silent onslaughts more perilous to the doer than battles in the light of day and without the trumpet-blasts of glory.

For hatred of the alien is always strong enough to arm some intrepid beings who are ready to die for an Idea.

At last, seeing that though the invaders had subjected the city to their inflexible discipline they had not committed any of the horrors with which rumor had credited them throughout the length of their triumphal progress, the public took courage and the commercial spirit began once more to stir in the hearts of the local tradespeople. Some of them who had grave interests at stake at Havre, then occupied by the French army, purposed trying to reach that port by going overland to Dieppe and there taking ship.

They took advantage of the influence of German officers whose acquaintance they had made, and a passport was obtained from the general in command.

Having therefore engaged a large coach with four horses for the journey, and ten persons having entered their names at the livery stable office, they resolved to start on Tuesday morning before daybreak, to avoid all public remark.

For some days already the ground had been hard with frost, and on Monday, about three o'clock in the afternoon, thick dark clouds coming up from the north brought snow, which fell steadily all evening and during the night.

At half-past four the travelers were assembled in the courtyard of the Hotel de Normandie, from whence they were to start.

They were still half asleep, their teeth chattering with cold in spite of their thick wraps. It was difficult to distinguish one from another in the darkness, their heaped-up winter clothing making them look like fat priests in long cassocks. Two of the men, however, recognized each other; they were joined by a third, and they began to talk. "I am taking my wife with me," said one. "So am I." "And I too." The first one added, "We shall not return to Rouen, and if the Prussians come to Havre we shall slip over to England."

They were all like-minded and all had the same plan.

Meanwhile there was no sign of the horses being put in. A small lantern carried by a hostler appeared from time to time out of one dark doorway only to vanish instantly into another. There was a stamping of horses' hoofs deadened by the straw of the litter, and the voice of a man speaking to the animal and cursing sounded from the depths of the stables. A faint tinkle of bells gave evidence of harnessing, and became presently a clear and continual jingle timed by the movement of the beast, now stopping, now going on again with a brisk shake, and accompanied by the dull tramp of hobnailed clogs.

A door slammed sharply. All sound ceased. The frozen travelers were silent, standing stiff and motionless. A continuous curtain of white snowflakes glistened as it fell to the ground, blotting out the shape of things, powdering everything with an icy froth; and in the utter stillness of the town, quiet and buried under its winter pall, nothing was audible but this faint, fluttering, and indefinable rustle of falling snow—more a sensation than a sound—the intermingling of ethereal atoms seeming to fill space, to cover the world.

The man reappeared with his lantern, dragging after him by a rope a dejected and unwilling horse. He pushed it against the pole, fixed the traces, and was occupied for a long time in buckling the harness, having only the use of one hand as he carried the lantern in the other. As he turned away to fetch the other horse he caught sight of the motionless group of travelers, by this time white with snow. "Why don't you get inside the carriage?" he said, "you would at least be under cover."

It had never occurred to them, and they made a rush for it. The three men packed their wives into the upper end and then got in themselves, after which other distinct and veiled forms took the remaining seats without exchanging a word.

The floor of the vehicle was covered with straw into which the feet sank. The ladies at the end, who had brought little copper charcoal foot-warmers, proceeded to light them, and for some time discussed their merits in subdued tones, repeating to one another things which they had known all their lives.

At last, the coach having been furnished with six horses instead of four on account of the difficulties of the road, a voice outside asked, "Is everybody here?" A voice from within answered, "Yes," and they started.

The conveyance advanced slowly—slowly—the wheels sinking in the snow; the whole vehicle groaned and creaked, the horses slipped, wheezed, and smoked, and the driver's gigantic whip cracked incessantly, flying from side to side, twining and untwining like a slender snake, and cutting sharply across one or other of the six humping backs, which would thereupon straighten up with a more violent effort.

Imperceptibly the day advanced. The airy flakes which a traveler—a trueborn Rouennais—likened to a shower of cotton, had ceased to fall; a dirty gray light filtered through the heavy thick clouds which served to heighten the dazzling whiteness of the landscape, where now a long line of trees crusted with icicles would appear, now a cottage with a hood of snow.

In the light of this melancholy dawn the occupants of the diligence began to examine one another curiously.

Right at the end, in the best seats, opposite to one another, dozed Madame and Monsieur Loiseau, wholesale wine merchant of the Rue Grand-Pont.

The former salesman of a master who had become bankrupt, Loiseau had bought up the stock and made his fortune. He sold very bad wine at very low prices to the small country retail dealers, and enjoyed the reputation among his friends and acquaintances of being an unmitigated rogue, a thorough Norman full of trickery and jovial humor.

His character for knavery was so well established that one evening at the

Prefecture, Monsieur Tournel, a man of keen and trenchant wit, author of certain fables and songs—a local celebrity—seeing the ladies growing drowsy, proposed a game of "L'oiseau vole." The pun itself flew through the prefect's reception rooms and afterwards through the town, and for a whole month called up a grin on every face in the province.

Loiseau was himself a noted wag famous for his jokes both good and bad, and nobody ever mentioned him without adding immediately, "That man, Loiseau, is simply priceless!"

He was of medium height with a balloon-like stomach and a rubicund face framed in grizzled whiskers. His wife—tall, strong, resolute, loud in voice and rapid of decision—represented order and arithmetic in the business, which he enlivened by his jollity and bustling activity.

Beside them, in a more dignified attitude as befitted his superior station, sat Monsieur Carré-Lamadon, a man of weight; an authority on cotton, proprietor of three spinning factories, officer of the Legion of Honor and member of the General Council of the *Département.* So long as the Second Empire lasted, he had remained leader of a friendly opposition, for the sole purpose of making a better thing out of it when he decided to come over to the régime which he had fought with polite weapons, to use his own expression. Madame Carré-Lamadon, who was much younger than her husband, was the consolation of all officers of good family who might be quartered at the Rouen garrison. She sat there opposite to her husband, very small, very dainty, very pretty, wrapped in her furs, and staring at the lamentable interior of the vehicle with despairing eyes.

Their neighbors, the Count and Countess Hubert de Bréville, bore one of the most ancient and noble names in Normandy. The Count, an elderly gentleman of dignified appearance, did all in his power to accentuate by every artifice of the toilet his natural resemblance to Henri Quatre, who, according to a legend of the utmost glory to the family, had honored with his royal embraces a Dame de Bréville, whose husband, in consequence, had been made Count and Governor of the province.

A colleague of Monsieur Carré-Lamadon in the General Council, Count Hubert represented the Orleanist faction in the department. The history of his marriage with the daughter of a small tradesman of Nantes had always remained a mystery. But as the Countess had an air of grandeur, understood better than anyone else the art of receiving, passed even for having been beloved by one of the sons of Louis Philippe, the neighboring nobility bowed down to her, and her salon held the first place in the province, the only one which preserved the traditions of old-fashioned gallantry and to which the entrée was difficult.

The fortune of the Brévilles—all in Government bonds—was reported to yield them an income of five hundred thousand francs.

The six passengers who occupied the upper end of the conveyance represented the unearned income stratum of society, serene in the consciousness of its strength—honest well-to-do people possessed of religion and principles.

By some strange chance all the women were seated on the same side, the Countess having two Sisters of Mercy for neighbors, wholly occupied in fingering their long rosaries and mumbling Paters and Aves. One of them was old and so deeply pitted with the smallpox that she looked as if she had received a charge of grapeshot full in the face; the other was very shadowy and frail, with a pretty unhealthy little face, a narrow consumptive chest, consumed by that devouring faith which creates martyrs and ecstatics.

Seated opposite the two nuns were a man and woman who excited a good deal of attention.

The man, who was well known, was Cornudet, "the Democrat," the terror of all respectable, law-abiding people. For twenty years he had dipped his great red beard into the beer mugs of all the democratic cafés. In the company of kindred spirits he had managed to run through a comfortable little fortune inherited from his father, a confectioner, and he looked forward with impatience to the Republic, when he should obtain the well-merited reward for so many revolutionary draughts. On the fourth of September—probably through some practical joke—he understood that he had been appointed prefect, but when he attempted to take office the clerks, who had remained sole masters of the prefecture, refused to recognize him, and he was constrained to retire. For the rest, he was a good fellow, inoffensive and willing, and had busied himself with incomparable industry in organizing the defense of the town; had had holes dug all over the plain, cut down all the young trees in the neighboring woods, scattered pitfalls up and down all the high roads, and at the threatened approach of the enemy—satisfied with his preparations—had fallen back with all haste on the town. He now considered that he would be more useful in Havre, where fresh entrenchments would soon become necessary.

The woman, one of the so-called "gay" sisterhood, was noted for her precocious stoutness, which had gained her the nickname of "Boule de Suif"—"Butter-Ball." She was a little roly-poly creature, cushioned with fat, with podgy fingers squeezed in at the joints like rows of thick, short sausages; her skin tightly stretched and shiny, her bust enormous, and yet she was attractive and much sought after, her freshness was so pleasant. Her face was like a ruddy apple—a peony rose just burst into bloom—and out of it gazed a pair of magnificent dark eyes overshadowed by long thick lashes that deepened their blackness; and lower down, a charming little mouth, dewy to the kiss, and furnished with a row of tiny milk-white teeth. Apart from all this she was said to be a good-hearted creature, full of inestimable qualities.

No sooner was her identity recognized than a whisper ran through the ladies in which the words "prostitute" and "public scandal" were so conspicuously distinct that she raised her head and retaliated by sweeping her companions with such a bold and defiant look that deep silence instantly fell upon them, and they all cast down their eyes with the exception of Loiseau, who watched her with a kindling eye.

However, conversation was soon resumed between the three ladies, whom the presence of this "person" had suddenly rendered friendly—almost intimate. It seemed to them that they must, as it were, raise a rampart of their dignity as spouses between them and this shameless creature who made a traffic of herself; for legalized love always takes a high hand with her unlicensed sister.

The three men too, drawn to one another by a conservative instinct at sight of Cornudet, talked money in a certain tone of contempt for the impecunious.

Count Hubert spoke of the damage inflicted on him by the Prussians, of the losses which would result to him from the seizing of cattle and from ruined crops, but with all the assurance of a great landed proprietor, ten times a millionaire, whom these ravages might inconvenience for the space of a year at most. Monsieur Carré-Lamadon, of great experience in the cotton industry, had taken the precaution to send six hundred thousand francs across to England as provision against a rainy day. As for Loiseau, he had made arrangements to sell all the common wines in his cellars to the French commission of supplies, consequently the government owed him a formidable sum, which he counted upon receiving at Havre.

The three exchanged rapid and amicable glances. Although differing in position they felt themselves brothers in money, and of the great freemasonry of those who possess, of those who can make the gold jingle when they put their hands in their pockets.

The coach went so slowly that by ten o'clock in the morning they had not made ten miles. The men had got out three times to climb hills on foot. They began to grow anxious, for they were to have lunched at Tôtes, and now they despaired of reaching that place before night. Everybody was on the lookout for some inn by the way. Once the vehicle stuck fast in a snowdrift, and it took two hours to get it out.

Meanwhile the pangs of hunger began to affect them severely both in mind and body, and yet not an inn, not a tavern even, was to be seen; the approach of the Prussians and the passage of the famished French troops had frightened away all trade.

The gentlemen foraged diligently for provisions in the farms by the roadside; but they failed to obtain so much as a piece of bread, for the mistrustful peasant hid all reserve stores for fear of being pillaged by the soldiers, who, having no food supplied to them, took by force everything they could lay their hands on.

Towards one o'clock Loiseau announced that he felt a very decided void in his stomach. Everybody had been suffering in the same manner for a long time, and the violent longing for food had extinguished conversation.

From time to time someone would yawn, to be almost immediately imitated by another and then each of the rest in turn, and according to their disposition, manners, or social standing, would open his mouth noisily, or modestly cover with the hand the gaping cavity from which the breath issued in a vapor.

Boule de Suif had several times stooped down as if feeling for something under her skirts. She hesitated a moment, looked at her companions, and then composedly resumed her former position. The faces were pale and drawn. Loiseau declared he would give a thousand francs for a ham. His wife made a faint movement as to protest, but restrained herself. It always affected her painfully to hear of money being thrown away, nor could she ever understand a joke upon the subject.

"To tell the truth," said the Count, "I do not feel quite myself either—how could I have omitted to think of bringing provisions?" And everybody reproached himself with the same neglect.

Cornudet, however, had a flask of rum which he offered round. It was coldly refused. Loiseau alone accepted a mouthful, and handed back the flask with thanks saying, "That's good! That warms you up and keeps the hunger off a bit." The alcohol raised his spirits somewhat, and he proposed that they should do the same as on the little ship in the song—eat the fattest of the passengers. This indirect but obvious allusion to Boule de Suif shocked the gentlefolk. Nobody responded and only Cornudet smiled. The two Sisters of Mercy had ceased to tell their beads and sat motionless, their hands buried in their wide sleeves, their eyes obstinately lowered, doubtless engaged in offering back to Heaven the sacrifice of suffering which it sent them.

At last, at three o'clock, when they were in the middle of an interminable stretch of bare country without a single village in sight, Boule de Suif, stooping hurriedly, drew from under the seat a large basket covered with a white napkin.

Out of it she took, first of all, a little china plate and a delicate silver drinking-cup, and then an immense dish, in which two whole fowls ready carved lay stiffened in their jelly. Other good things were visible in the basket: patties, fruits, pastry—in fact provisions for a three days' journey in order to be independent of inn cookery. The necks of four bottles protruded from between the parcels of food. She took the wing of a fowl and began to eat it daintily with one of those little rolls which they call "Régence" in Normandy.

Every eye was fixed upon her. As the odor of the food spread through the carriage nostrils began to quiver and mouths to water, while the jaws, just below the ears, contracted painfully. The dislike entertained by the ladies for this abandoned young woman grew savage, almost to the point of longing to murder her or at least to turn her out into the snow, her and her drinking-cup and her basket and her provisions.

Loiseau, however, was devouring the dish of chicken with his eyes. "Madame has been more prudent than we," he said. "Some people always think of everything."

She turned her head in his direction. "If you would care for any, Sir—? It is not comfortable to fast for so long."

He bowed. "By Jove!—frankly, I won't refuse. I can't stand this any longer—the fortune of war, is it not, madame?" And with a comprehensive look he added, "In moments such as this we are only too glad to find anyone who will oblige us." He had a newspaper which he spread on his knee to save his trousers, and with the point of a knife which he always carried in his pocket he captured a drumstick all glazed with jelly, tore it with his teeth, and then proceeded to chew it with satisfaction so evident that a deep groan of distress went up from the whole party.

Upon this Boule de Suif in a gentle and humble tone invited the two Sisters to share the collation. They both accepted on the spot, and without raising their eyes began to eat very hurriedly, after stammering a few words of thanks. Nor did Cornudet refuse his neighbor's offer, and with the Sisters they formed a kind of table by spreading out newspapers on their knees.

The jaws opened and shut without a pause, biting, chewing, gulping ferociously. Loiseau, hard at work in his corner, urged his wife in a low voice to follow his example. She resisted for some time, then, after a pang which gripped her very vitals, she gave in. Whereupon her husband, rounding off his phrases, asked if their "charming fellow-traveler" would permit him to offer a little something to Madame Loiseau.

"Why, yes, certainly, Monsieur," she answered with a pleasant smile, and handed him the dish.

There was a moment of embarrassment when the first bottle of claret was uncorked—there was but the one drinking-cup. Each one wiped it before passing it to the rest. Cornudet alone, from an impulse of gallantry no doubt, placed his lips on the spot still wet from the lips of his neighbor.

Then it was that, surrounded by people who were eating, suffocated by the fragrant odor of the viands, the Count and Countess de Bréville and Monsieur and Madame Carré-Lamadon suffered the agonies of that torture which has ever been associated with the name of Tantalus.[5] Suddenly the young wife of the cotton manufacturer gave a deep sigh. Every head turned towards her; she was as white as the snow outside, her eyes closed, her head fell forward—she had fainted. Her husband, distraught with fear, implored assistance of the whole company. All lost their heads till the elder of the two Sisters, who supported the unconscious lady, forced Boule de Suif's drinking-cup between her lips and made her swallow a few drops of wine. The pretty creature stirred, opened her eyes, smiled and then declared in an expiring voice that she felt quite well now. But to prevent her being overcome again in the same manner, the Sister induced her to drink a full cup of wine, adding, "It is simply hunger—nothing else."

At this Boule de Suif, blushing violently, looked at the four starving passengers and faltered shyly, "*Mon Dieu!* If I might make so bold as to offer the ladies and gentlemen—" She stopped short, fearing a rude rebuff.

Loiseau, however, at once threw himself into the breach. "*Parbleu!* Under such circumstances we are all companions in misfortune and bound to help each other. Come, ladies, don't stand on ceremony—take what you can get and be thankful: who knows whether we shall be able to find so much as a house where we can spend the night? At this rate we shall not reach Tôtes till tomorrow afternoon."

They still hesitated, nobody having the courage to take upon themselves the responsibility of the decisive "Yes." Finally the Count seized the bull by the horns. Adopting his grandest air, he turned with a bow to the embarrassed young woman and said, "We accept your offer with thanks, madame."

The first step only was difficult. The Rubicon once crossed, they fell to with a will. They emptied the basket, which contained, besides the provisions already mentioned: a pâté de foie gras, a lark pie, a piece of smoked tongue, some pears, a slab of gingerbread, mixed biscuits, and a cup of pickled onions and gherkins in vinegar—for, like all women, Boule de Suif adored pickles.

They could not well eat the young woman's provisions and not speak to her, so they conversed—stiffly at first, and then, seeing that she showed no

5. In Greek mythology, a king, sometimes believed to be a son of Zeus, who for his crimes was condemned to remain forever in Tartarus, standing in water up to his chin, with branches heavy with fruit above his head. When he attempted to eat or drink, the fruit or water would recede from his reach. The word *tantalize* stems from this myth.

signs of presuming, with less reserve. Mesdames de Bréville and Carré-Lamadon, having a great deal of *savoir vivre,* knew how to make themselves agreeable with tact and delicacy. The Countess, in particular, exhibited the amiable condescension of the extremely high-born lady whom no contact can sully, and was charming. But big Madame Loiseau, who had the soul of a gendarme, remained unmoved, speaking little and eating much.

The conversation naturally turned upon the war. They related horrible deeds committed by the Prussians and examples of the bravery of the French; all these people who were flying rendering full homage to the courage of those who remained behind. Incidents of personal experience soon followed, and Boule de Suif told, with that warmth of coloring which women of her type often employ in expressing their natural feelings, how she had come to leave Rouen.

"I thought at first I should be able to hold out," she said, "for I had plenty of provisions in my house, and would much rather feed a few soldiers than turn out of my home and go goodness knows where. But when I saw them—those Prussians—it was too much for me. They made my blood boil with rage, and I cried the whole day for shame. Oh, if I had only been a man!—well, there! I watched them from my window—fat pigs that they were with their spiked helmets—and my servant had to hold my hands to prevent me throwing the furniture down on the top of them. Then some of them came to be quartered on me, and I flew at the throat of the first one—they are not harder to strangle than anyone else—and would have finished him too if they had not dragged me off by the hair. Of course I had to lie low after that. So as soon as I found an opportunity I left—and here I am."

Everybody congratulated her. She rose considerably in the estimation of her companions, who had not shown themselves of such valiant mettle, and listening to her tale, Cornudet smiled the benignant and approving smile of an apostle—as a priest might on hearing a devout person praise the Almighty. Democrats with long beards have the monopoly of patriotism as the men of the cassock possess that of religion. He then took up the parable in a didactic tone with the phraseology culled from the notices posted each day on the walls, and finished up with a flourish of eloquence in which he scathingly alluded to "that blackguard Badinguet."

But Boule de Suif fired up at this for she was a Bonapartist. She turned upon him with scarlet cheeks and stammering with indignation, "Ah! I should just like to have seen any of you in his place! A nice mess you would have made of it! It is men of your sort that ruined him, poor man. There would be nothing for it but to leave France for good if we were governed by cowards like you!"

Cornudet, nothing daunted, preserved a disdainful and superior smile, but there was a feeling in the air that high words would soon follow, whereupon the Count interposed, and managed, not without difficulty, to quiet the infuriated young woman by asserting authoritatively that every sincere opinion was to be respected. Nevertheless the Countess and the manufacturer's wife, who nourished in their hearts the unreasoning hatred of all well-bred people for the Republic and at the same time that instinctive weakness of all women for uniformed and despotic governments, felt drawn, in spite of themselves, to this woman of the streets who had so much sense of the fitness of things and whose opinions so closely resembled their own.

The basket was empty—this had not been difficult among ten of them—they only regretted it was not larger. The conversation was kept up for some little time longer, although somewhat more coldly after they had finished eating.

The night fell, the darkness grew gradually deeper, and the cold, to which digestion rendered them more sensitive, made even Boule de Suif shiver in spite of her fat. Madame de Bréville thereupon offered her her charcoal foot-warmer, which had been replenished several times since the morning; she accepted with alacrity, for her feet were like ice. Mesdames Carré-Lamadon and Loiseau lent theirs to the two Sisters.

The driver had lit his lanterns, which shed a vivid light over the cloud of vapor that hung above the steaming backs of the horses and over the snow at each side of the road, that seemed to open out under the shifting reflection of the lights.

Inside the conveyance nothing could be distinguished any longer, but there was a sudden movement between Boule de Suif and Cornudet, and Loiseau, peering through the gloom, fancied he saw the man with the beard start back quickly as if he had received a well-directed but noiseless blow.

Tiny points of light appeared upon the road ahead. It was Tôtes. The travelers had been driving for eleven hours, which, with the four half-hours for feeding and resting the horses, made thirteen. They entered the town and stopped in front of the Hôtel du Commerce.

The door opened. A familiar sound caused every passenger to tremble—it was the clink of a scabbard on the stones. At the same moment a German voice called out something.

Although the coach had stopped, nobody attempted to get out, as though they expected to be massacred on setting foot to the ground. The driver then appeared holding up one of the lanterns, which suddenly illumined the vehicle to its farthest corner and revealed the two rows of bewildered faces with their open mouths and startled eyes wide with alarm.

Beside the driver in the full glare of the light stood a German officer, a tall young man excessively slender and blonde, compressed into his uniform like a girl in her stays, and wearing, well over one ear, a flat black wax-cloth cap like the "Boots" of an English hotel. His preposterously long mustache, which was drawn out stiff and straight, and tapered away indefinitely to each side till it finished off in a single thread so thin that it was impossible to say where it ended, seemed to weigh upon the corners of his mouth and form a deep furrow in either cheek.

In Alsatian-French and stern accents he invited the passengers to descend, "Will you get out, gentlemen and ladies?"

The two Sisters were the first to obey with the docility of holy women accustomed to unfaltering submission. The Count and Countess appeared next, followed by the manufacturer and his wife, and after them Loiseau pushing his better half in front of him. As he set foot to the ground he remarked to the officer, more from motives of prudence than politeness, "Good evening, Sir," to which the other with the insolence of the man in possession, vouchsafed no reply but a stare.

Boule de Suif and Cornudet, though the nearest the door, were the last to emerge—grave and haughty in face of the enemy. The buxom young woman struggled hard to command herself and be calm; the democrat tugged at his long rusty beard with a tragic and slightly trembling hand. They sought to preserve their dignity, realizing that in such encounters each one, to a certain extent, represents his country; and the two being similarly disgusted at the ready servility of their companions, she endeavored to show herself prouder than her fellow travelers who were respectable women, while he, feeling that he must set an example, continued in his attitude his mission of resistance begun by digging pitfalls in the high roads.

They entered the huge kitchen of the inn, and the German, having been presented with the passport signed by the general in command—where each traveler's name was accompanied by a personal description and a statement as to his or her profession—he proceeded to scrutinize the party for a long time, comparing the persons with the written notices.

Finally, he exclaimed unceremoniously, "That's all right," and disappeared.

They breathed again more freely. Hunger having reasserted itself, supper was ordered. It would take half an hour to prepare, so while two servants were apparently busied about it the travelers dispersed to look at their rooms. These were all together down each side of a long passage ending in a door marked "Toilet."

At last, just as they were sitting down to table, the innkeeper himself appeared. He was a former horse-dealer, a stout asthmatic man with perpetual wheezings and blowings and rattlings of phlegm in his throat. His father had transmitted to him the name of Follenvie.

"Mademoiselle Elizabeth Rousset?" he said.

Boule de Suif started and turned round. "That is my name."

"Mademoiselle, the Prussian officer wants to speak to you at once."

"To me?"

"Yes, if you really are Mademoiselle Elizabeth Rousset."

She hesitated, thought for a moment, and then declared roundly, "That may be, but I'm not going."

There was a movement round about her—everybody was much exercised as to the reason of this summons. The Count came over to her.

"You may do wrong to refuse, madame, for it may entail considerable annoyance not only to yourself but to the rest of your companions. It is a fatal mistake ever to offer resistance to people who are stronger than ourselves. The step can have no possible danger for you—it is probably about some little formality that has been omitted."

One and all concurred with him, implored and urged and scolded, till they ended by convincing her; for they were all apprehensive of the results of her obstinacy.

"Well, it is only for your sakes that I am doing it!" she said at last. The Countess pressed her hand. "And we are most grateful to you."

She left the room, and the others agreed to wait for her before beginning the meal. Each one lamented that he had not been asked for instead of this hot-headed, violent young woman, and mentally prepared any number of platitudes for the event of being called in his turn.

At the end of ten minutes she returned, crimson with rage, choking, snorting—"Oh, the blackguard; the low blackguard!" she stammered.

They all crowded round her to know what had happened, but she would not say, and the Count becoming insistent, she answered with much dignity, "No, it does not concern anybody! I can't speak of it."

They then seated themselves round a great soup tureen from which steamed a smell of cabbage. In spite of this little incident the supper was a gay one. The cider, of which the Loiseaus and the two nuns partook from motives of economy, was good. The rest ordered wine and Cornudet called for beer. He had a particular way of uncorking the bottle, of making the liquid froth, of gazing at it while he tilted the glass, which he then held up between his eye and the light to enjoy the color; while he drank, his great beard, which had the tints of his favorite beverage, seemed to quiver fondly, his eyes squinting that he might not lose sight of his tankard for a moment, and altogether he had the appearance of fulfilling the sole function for which he had been born. You would have said that he established in his own mind some connection or affinity between the two great passions that monopolized his life—Ale and Revolution—and most assuredly he never tasted the one without thinking of the other.

Monsieur and Madame Follenvie dined at the farther end of the table. The husband—puffing and blowing like a locomotive—had too much cold on the chest to be able to speak and eat at the same time, but his wife never ceased talking. She described her every impression at the arrival of the Prussians and all they did and all they said, execrating them in the first place because they cost so much, and secondly because she had two sons in the army. She addressed herself chiefly to the Countess, as it flattered her to be able to say she had conversed with a lady of quality.

She presently lowered her voice and proceeded to recount some rather delicate matters, her husband breaking in from time to time with—"You had much better hold your tongue, Madame Follenvie,"—to which she paid not the slightest attention, but went on.

"Well, madame, as I was saying—these men, they do nothing but eat potatoes and pork and pork and potatoes from morning till night. And as for their habits—! Saving your presence, they make dirt everywhere. And you should see them exercising for hours and days together out there in the fields. It's forward march and backward march, and turn this way and turn that. If they even worked in the fields or mended the roads in their own country! But, no, madame, these soldiers are no good to anybody, and the poor people have to keep them and feed them simply that they may learn how to murder. I know I am only a poor ignorant old woman, but when I see these men wearing themselves out by tramping up and down from morning till night, I cannot help saying to myself, if there are some people who make a lot of useful discoveries, why should others give themselves so much trouble to do harm? After all, isn't it an abomination to kill anybody, no matter whether they are Prussians, or English, or Poles, or French? If you revenge yourself on someone who has harmed you, that is wicked, for you are punished; but let them shoot down our sons as if they were game, and it is all right, and they give medals to the man who kills the most. No, no, I say, I shall never be able to see any rhyme or reason in that!"

"War is barbarous if one attacks an unoffending neighbor—it is a sacred duty if one defends one's country," remarked Cornudet in a declamatory tone.

The old woman drooped her head. "Yes—defending oneself, of course, that is quite another thing; but wouldn't it be better to kill all these kings who do this for their pleasure?"

Cornudet's eyes flashed. "Bravo, citizeness!" he cried.

Monsieur Carré-Lamadon was lost in thought. Although he was an ardent admirer of famous military men, the sound common sense of this peasant woman made him reflect upon the wealth which would necessarily accrue to the country if all these unemployed and consequently ruinous hands—so much unproductive force—were available for the great industrial works that would take centuries to complete.

Loiseau meanwhile had left his seat and gone over beside the innkeeper, to whom he began talking in a low voice. The fat man laughed, coughed, and spat, his unwieldy stomach shaking with mirth at his neighbor's jokes, and he bought six hogsheads of claret from him for the spring when the Prussians would have cleared out.

Supper was scarcely over when, dropping with fatigue, everybody went off to bed.

Loiseau, however, who had noticed certain things, let his wife go to bed and proceeded to glue first his ear and then his eye to the keyhole, endeavoring to penetrate what he called "the mysteries of the corridor."

After about an hour he heard a rustling, and hurrying to the keyhole, he perceived Boule de Suif looking ampler than ever in a dressing-gown of blue cashmere trimmed with white lace. She had a candle in her hand and was going towards the door at the end of the corridor. Then a door at one side opened cautiously, and when she returned after a few minutes, Cornudet in his shirt-sleeves was following her. They were talking in a low voice and presently stood still; Boule de Suif apparently defending the entrance of her room with much energy. Unfortunately Loiseau was unable to hear what they said, but at last, as they raised their voices somewhat, he caught a word or two. Cornudet was insisting eagerly. "Look here," he said, "you are really very ridiculous—what difference can it make to you?"

And she with an offended air retorted, "No!—let me tell you there are moments when that sort of thing won't do; and besides—here—it would be a crying shame."

He obviously did not understand. "Why?"

At this she grew angry. "Why?" and she raised her voice still more, "you don't see why? and there are Prussians in the house—in the next room for all you know!"

He made no reply. This display of patriotic prudery evidently aroused his failing dignity, for with a brief kiss he made for his own door on tiptoe.

Loiseau, deeply thrilled and amused, executed a double shuffle in the middle of the room, donned his nightcap, slipped into the blankets where the bony figure of his spouse already reposed, and waking her with a kiss he murmured, "Do you love me, darling?"

The whole house sank to silence. But anon there arose from somewhere—it might have been the cellar, it might have been the attic—impossible to determine the direction—a rumbling—sonorous, even, regular, dull, prolonged roar as of a boiler under high pressure: Monsieur Follenvie slept.

It had been decided that they should start at eight o'clock the next morning, so they were all assembled in the kitchen by that hour; but the coach, roofed with snow, stood solitary in the middle of the courtyard without horses or driver. The latter was sought for in vain either in the stables or in the coachhouse. The men of the party then resolved to beat the country round for him, and went out accordingly. They found themselves in the public square with the church at one end, and low-roofed houses down each side in which they caught sight of Prussian soldiers. The first one they came upon was peeling potatoes; farther on another was washing out a barber's shop; while a third, bearded to the eyes, was soothing a crying child and rocking it to and for on his knee to quiet it. The big peasant women whose men were all "with the army in the war" were ordering about their docile conquerors and showing them by signs what work they wanted done—chopping wood, grinding coffee, fetching water; one of them was even doing the washing for his hostess, a helpless old crone.

The Count, much astonished, stopped the beadle, who happened to come out of the priest's house at that moment, and asked the meaning of it all.

"Oh," replied the old church rat, "they are not at all bad. From what I hear they are not Prussians, either; they come from farther off, but where I can't say; and they have all left a wife and children at home. I am very sure their women at home are crying for their men, too, and it will all make a nice lot of misery for them as well as for us. We are not so badly off here for the moment, because they do no harm and are working just as if they were in their own homes. You see, Sir, the poor always help one another; it is the bigwigs who make the wars."

Cornudet, indignant at the friendly understanding established between the victors and the vanquished, retired from the scene, preferring to shut himself up in the inn. Loiseau of course must have his joke. "They are re-populating," he said. Monsieur Carré-Lamadon found a more fitting expression. "They are making reparations."

But the driver was nowhere to be found. At last he was unearthed in the village café hobnobbing fraternally with the officer's orderly.

"Did you not have orders to have the coach ready by eight o'clock?" the Count asked him.

"Oh, yes, but I got another order later on."

"What?"

"Not to put the horses in at all."

"Who gave you that order?"

"Why—the Prussian commandant."

"Why?"

"I don't known—you had better ask him. I am told not to harness the horses, and so I don't harness them—there you are."

"Did he tell you so himself?"

"No, Sir, the innkeeper brought me the message from him."

"When was that?"

"Last night, just as I was going to bed."

The three men returned much disconcerted. They asked for Monsieur Follenvie, but were informed by the servant that on account of his asthma he never got up before ten o'clock—he had even positively forbidden them to awaken him before then except in case of fire.

Then they asked to see the officer, but that was absolutely impossible, although he lodged at the inn.

Monsieur Follenvie alone was authorized to approach him on non-military matters. So they had to wait. The women returned to their rooms and occupied themselves as best they could.

Cornudet installed himself in the high chimney-corner of the kitchen, where a great fire was burning. He had one of the little coffee-room tables brought to him and a can of beer, and puffed away placidly at his pipe, which enjoyed among the democrats almost equal consideration with himself, as if in serving Cornudet it served the country also. The pipe was a superb meerschaum, admirably colored, black as the teeth of its owner, but fragrant, curved, shining, familiar to his hand, and the natural complement to his physiognomy. He sat there motionless, his eyes fixed alternately on the flame of the hearth and the foam on the top of his tankard, and each time after drinking he passed his bony fingers with a self-satisfied gesture through his long greasy hair, while he absorbed the fringe of froth from his mustache.

Under the pretext of stretching his legs, Loiseau went out and palmed off his wines on the country retail dealers. The Count and the manufacturer talked politics. They forecast the future of France, the one putting his faith in the Orleans princes, the other in an unknown savior, a hero who would come to the fore when things were at their very worst—a Du Guesclin, a Joan of Arc perhaps, or even another Napoleon I. Ah, if only the Prince Imperial were not so young! Cornudet listened to them with the smile of a man who could solve the riddle of Fate if he would. His pipe perfumed the whole kitchen with its balmy fragrance.

On the stroke of ten Monsieur Follenvie made his appearance. They instantly attacked him with questions, but he had but one answer which he repeated two or three times without variation. "The officer said to me, 'Monsieur Follenvie, you will forbid them to harness the horses for these travelers tomorrow morning. They are not to leave till I give my permission. You understand?' That is all."

They demanded to see the officer; the Count sent up his card, on which Monsieur Carré-Lamadon added his name and all his titles. The Prussian sent word that he would admit the two men to his presence after he had lunched, that is to say, about one o'clock.

The ladies came down and they all managed to eat a little in spite of their anxiety. Boule de Suif looked quite ill and very much agitated.

They were just finishing coffee when the orderly arrived to fetch the two gentlemen.

Loiseau joined them, but when they proposed to bring Cornudet along to give more solemnity to their proceedings, he declared haughtily that nothing would induce him to enter into any communication whatsoever with the Germans, and he returned to his chimney-corner and ordered another bottle of beer.

The three men went upstairs, and were shown into the best room in the inn, where they were received by the officer lolling in an armchair, his heels on the chimney-piece, smoking a long porcelain pipe, and arrayed in a flamboyant dressing-gown, taken, no doubt, from the abandoned dwelling-house of some bourgeois of inferior taste. He did not rise, he vouchsafed them no greeting of any description, he did not even look at them—a brilliant example of the victorious military cad.

At last after some moments' waiting he said: "What do you want?"

The Count acted as spokesman.

"We wish to leave, Sir."

"No."

"May I take the liberty of asking the reason for this refusal?"

"Because I do not choose."

"With all due respect, Sir, I would draw your attention to the fact that your general gave us a permit for Dieppe, and I cannot see that we have done anything to justify your hard measures."

"I do not choose—that's all—you can go down."

They all bowed and withdrew.

The afternoon was miserable. They could make nothing of this caprice of the German's, and the most far-fetched ideas tortured their minds. The whole party remained in the kitchen engaging in endless discussions, imagining the most improbable things. Were they to be kept as hostages?—but if so, to what end?—or taken prisoners?—or asked a large ransom? This last suggestion threw them into a cold perspiration of fear. The wealthiest were seized with the worst panic and saw themselves forced, if they valued their lives, to empty bags of gold into the rapacious hands of this soldier. They racked their brains for plausible lies to dissemble their riches, to pass themselves off as poor—very poor. Loiseau pulled off his watch-chain and hid it in his pocket. As night fell their apprehensions increased. The lamp was lighted, and as there were still two hours till supper Madame Loiseau proposed a game of cards. It would be some little distraction, at any rate. The plan was accepted; even Cornudet, who had put out his pipe from motives of politeness, taking a hand.

The Count shuffled the cards, dealt, Boule de Suif won the first deal; and very soon the interest in the game allayed the fears that beset their minds. Cornudet, however, observed that the two Loiseaus were in league to cheat.

Just as they were sitting down to the evening meal Monsieur appeared and said in his husky voice, "The Prussian officer wishes to know if Mademoiselle Elizabeth Rousset has not changed her mind yet?"

Boule de Suif remained standing and turned very pale, then suddenly her face flamed and she fell into such a paroxysm of rage that she could not speak. At last she burst out, "You can tell that scoundrel—that low scum of a Prussian—that I won't—and I never will—do you hear?—never! never! never!"

The fat innkeeper retired. They instantly surrounded Boule de Suif, questioning, entreating her to disclose the mystery of her visit. At first she refused, but presently she was carried away by her indignation: "What does he want?—what does he want?—he wants me to go to bed with him!" she shouted.

The general indignation was so violent that nobody was shocked by the words she used. Cornudet brought his beer glass down on the table with such a bang that it broke. There was a perfect babel of invective against the drunken lout, a hurricane of wrath, a union of all for resistance, as if each had been required to contribute a portion of the sacrifice demanded of her. The Count protested with disgust that these people behaved really as if they were early barbarians. The women, in particular, accorded her the most lively and affectionate sympathy. The nuns, who only appeared at meals, dropped their eyes and said nothing.

The first fury of the storm having abated, they sat down to supper, but there was little conversation and a good deal of thoughtful abstraction.

The ladies retired early; the men, while they smoked, got up a game of écarté, which Monsieur Follenvie was invited to join, as they intended pumping him skillfully as to the means that could be employed for overcoming the officer's opposition to their departure. Unfortunately, he would absorb himself wholly in his cards, and neither listened to what they said nor gave any answer to their questions, but repeated incessantly, "Play, gentlemen, play!" His attention was so deeply engaged that he forgot to spit, which caused his chest to wheeze from time to time; his wheezing lungs running through the whole gamut of asthma from notes of the profoundest bass to the shrill, hoarse crow of the young cock.

He refused to go to bed when his wife, who was dropping with sleep, came to fetch him. She therefore departed alone, for on her devolved the "day duty," and she always rose with the sun, while her husband took the "night duty," and was always ready to sit up all night with friends. He merely called out, "Mind you put my egg flip in front of the fire!" and returned to his cards. When they were convinced that there was nothing to be got out of him, they declared that it was high time to go to bed, and left him.

They were up again pretty early the next day, filled with an indefinite hope, a still keener desire to be gone, and a horror of another day to be got through in this horrible little inn.

Alas! The horses were still in the stable and the coachman remained invisible. For lack of something better to do, they sadly wandered round the carriage.

Lunch was very depressing, and a certain chilliness had sprung up with regard to Boule de Suif, for the night—which brings counsel—had somewhat modified their opinions. They were almost vexed with the girl now for not having gone to the Prussian secretly, and thus prepared a pleasant surprise for her companions in the morning. What could be simpler, and, after all, who could have been any the wiser? She might have saved appearances by telling the officer that she could not bear to see their distress any longer. It could make so very little difference to her one way or another!

But, as yet, nobody confessed to these thoughts.

In the afternoon, as they were feeling bored to extinction, the Count proposed a walk round the village. Everybody wrapped up carefully and the little party started, with the exception of Cornudet, who preferred sitting by the fire, and the two Sisters, who passed their days in the church or with the parish priest.

The cold—grown more intense each day—nipped their noses and ears viciously, and the feet hurt so that every step was anguish; but when they caught sight of the open stretch of country it appeared to them so appallingly lugubrious under its illimitable white covering that they turned back with one accord, their hearts constricted, their spirits below zero. The four ladies walked in front, the three men following a little behind.

Loiseau, who thoroughly took in the situation, suddenly broke out, "How long was this damned wench going to keep them hanging on in this hole?" The Count, courteous as ever, observed that one could not demand so painful a sacrifice of any woman—the offer must come from her. Monsieur Carré-Lamadon remarked that if—as there was every reason to believe—the French made an offensive counter-march by way of Dieppe, the collision could only take place at Tôtes. This reflection greatly alarmed the other two. "Why not escape on foot?" suggested Loiseau. The Count shrugged his shoulders. "How can you think of such a thing in this snow—and with our wives? Besides which, we should instantly be pursued, caught in ten minutes, and brought back prisoners at the mercy of these soldiers." This was incontestable—there was nothing more to be said.

The ladies talked dress, but a certain constraint seemed to have risen up among them.

All at once, at the end of the street, the officer came in sight, his tall figure, like a wasp in uniform, silhouetted against the dazzling background of snow. He was walking with his knees well apart, with that movement peculiar to the military when endeavoring to save their carefully polished boots from the mud.

In passing the ladies he bowed, but only stared contemptuously at the men, who, be it said, had the dignity not to lift their hats, though Loiseau made a faint gesture in that direction.

Boule de Suif blushed up to her eyes, and the three married women felt it a deep humiliation to have encountered this soldier while they were in the company of the young woman he had treated so cavalierly.

The conversation then turned upon him, his general appearance, his face. Madame Carré-Lamadon, who had known a great many officers and was competent to judge of them as a connoisseur, considered this one really not half bad—she even regretted that he was not French, he would have made such a fascinating hussar, and would certainly have been much run after.

Once indoors again, they did not know what to do with themselves. Sharp words were exchanged on the most insignificant pretexts. The silent dinner did not last long, and they shortly afterwards went to bed, hoping to kill time by sleeping.

They came down next morning with jaded faces and exasperation in their hearts. The women scarcely addressed a word to Boule de Suif.

Presently the church bell began to ring; it was for a christening. Boule de Suif had a child out at nurse with some peasants near Yvetot. She did not see it once a year and never gave it a thought, but the idea of this baby that was going to be baptized filled her heart with sudden and violent tenderness for her own, and nothing would satisfy her but that she should assist at the ceremony.

No sooner was she gone than they all looked at one another and proceeded to draw up their chairs; for everybody felt that things had come to that point that something must be decided upon. Loiseau had an inspiration: they should propose to the officer to keep Boule de Suif and let the rest go.

Monsieur Follenvie undertook the mission, but returned almost immediately. The German, who had some knowledge of human nature, had simply turned him out of the room. He meant to retain the whole party so long as his desire was unsatisfied.

At this Madame Loiseau's plebeian tendencies got the better of her. "But surely we are not going to sit down calmly here and die of old age! As that is this harlot's trade, I don't see that she has any right to refuse one man more than another. Why, she took anybody she could get in Rouen, down to the very cab drivers. Yes, Madame, the coachman of the Prefecture. I know all about it. He buys his wine at our shop. And now, when it lies with her to get us out of this scrape, she pretends to be particular—the brazen hussy! For my part, I consider the officer has behaved very well! He has probably not had a chance for some time, and there were three here whom, no doubt, he would have preferred; but no—he is content to take the one who is public property. He respects married women. Remember, he is master here. He had only to say 'I will,' and he could have taken us by force with his soldiers!"

A little quiver ran through the other two women. Pretty little Madame Carré-Lamadon's eyes shone and she turned rather pale as though she already felt herself forcibly seized by the officer.

The men, who had been arguing the matter in a corner, now joined them. Loiseau, foaming with rage, was for delivering up "the hussy" bound hand and foot to the enemy. But the Count, coming of three generations of ambassadors, and gifted with the physique of the diplomatist, was on the side of skill as opposed to brute force.

"She must be persuaded," he said. Whereupon they conspired.

The women drew up closer together, voices were lowered, and the discussion became general, each one offering his or her advice. Nothing was said to shock the proprieties. The ladies, in particular, were most expert in felicitous turns of phrase, charming subtleties of speech for expressing the most ticklish things. A foreigner would have understood nothing, the language was so carefully veiled. But as the slight coating of modesty with which every woman of the world is enveloped is hardly more than skin deep, they expanded under the influence of this equivocal adventure, enjoying themselves tremendously at bottom, thoroughly in their element, dabbling in sensuality with the gusto of an epicurean cook preparing a toothsome delicacy for somebody else.

The story finally appeared to them so funny that they quite recovered their spirits. The Count indulged in some rather risky pleasantries, but so well put that they raised a responsive smile; Loiseau, in his turn, rapped out some decidedly strong jokes which nobody took in bad part, and the brutal proposition expressed by his wife swayed all their minds: "As that is her trade, why refuse one man more than another?" Little Madame Carré-Lamadon seemed even to think that in her place she would refuse this one less readily than another.

They were long in preparing the siege, as if against an invested fortress. Each one agreed upon the part they would play, the arguments they would bring forward, the maneuvers they would execute. They arranged the plan of attack, the stratagems to be employed, and the surprises of the assault for forcing this living citadel to receive the enemy within its gates. Cornudet alone held aloof, completely outside the affair.

They were so profoundly occupied with the matter in hand that they never heard Boule de Suif enter the room. But the Count breathed a low warning "Hush!" and they lifted their heads. She was there. The talk ceased abruptly, and a certain feeling of embarrassment prevented them from addressing her at first, till the Countess, more versed than the others in the duplicities of the drawing-room, asked how she had enjoyed the christening.

Still full of emotion at what she had witnessed, Boule de Suif described every detail—the people's faces, their attitudes, even the appearance of the church. It was so nice to pray now and then, she added.

Till luncheon, however, the ladies confined themselves merely to being agreeable to her in order to increase her confidence in them and her acquiescence in their counsels. But once seated at table, the attack began. It first took the form of a desultory conversation on devotion to a cause. Examples from ancient history were cited: Judith and Holofernes, and then, without any apparent connection, Lucretia and Sextus, Cleopatra admitting to her couch all the hostile generals, and reducing them to the servility of slaves. Then began a fantastic history, which had sprung up in the minds of the ignorant millionaires, in which the women of Rome were seen on their way to Capua, to rock Hannibal to sleep in their arms, and his officers along with him, and the phalanxes of the mercenaries. The women were mentioned who had arrested the course of conquerors, made of their bodies a rampart, a means of domination, a weapon; who had vanquished by their heroic embraces beings hideous or repulsive, and sacrificed their chastity to vengeance or patriotism. They even talked in veiled terms of an Englishwoman of good family who had herself inoculated with a horrible contagious disease, in order to give it to Napoleon, who was saved miraculously by a sudden indisposition at the hour of the fatal meeting.

And all this in a discreet and moderate manner, with now and then a little burst of warm enthusiasm, admirably calculated to excite emulation. To hear them you would have come to the conclusion that woman's sole mission here below was perpetually to sacrifice her person, to abandon herself continually to the caprices of the warrior.

The two Sisters appeared to be deaf to it all, sunk in profound thought. Boule de Suif said nothing.

They allowed her all the afternoon for reflection, but instead of calling her "Madame," as they had done up till now, they addressed her as "Mademoiselle"—nobody could have said exactly why—as if to send her down a step in the esteem she had gained, and force her to feel the shame of her position.

In the evening just as the soup was being brought to table Monsieur Follenvie made his appearance again with the same message as before: "The Prussian officer sends to ask Mademoiselle Elizabeth Rousset if she had not changed her mind."

"No, Sir," Boule de Suif replied curtly.

At supper the coalition weakened. Loiseau put his foot in it three times. They all racked their brains for fresh instances to the point, and found none, when the Countess, possibly without premeditation and only from a vague desire to render homage to religion, interrogated the older of the two Sisters on the main incidents in the lives of the saints. Now, several saints had committed acts which would be counted crimes in our eyes, but the Church readily pardons such misdeeds when they are accomplished for the glory of God or the benefit of our neighbors. It was a powerful argument, and the Countess took advantage of it. Then by one of those tacit agreements, those veiled complaisances in which every one who wears ecclesiastical habit excels, or perhaps simply from a happy want of intelligence, a helpful stupidity, the old nun brought formidable support to the conspiracy. They had imagined her timid; she proved herself bold, verbose, violent. She was not troubled by any of the shilly-shallyings of casuistry, her doctrine was like a bar of iron, her faith never wavered, her conscience knew no scruples. She considered Abraham's sacrifice a very simple affair, for she herself would have instantly killed father or mother at an order from above, and nothing, she averred, could displease the Lord if the intention were commendable. The Countess, taking advantage of the sacred authority of her unexpected ally, drew her on to make an edifying paraphrase, as it were, on the well-known moral maxim: "The end justifies the means."

"Then, Sister," she inquired, "you think God approves of every pathway that leads to Him, and pardons the deed if the motive be a pure one?"

"Who can doubt it, Madame? An action blamable in itself is often rendered meritorious by the impulse which inspires it."

And she continued in the same strain, unraveling the intricacies of the will of the Almighty, predicting His decisions, making Him interest Himself in matters which, of a truth, did not concern Him at all.

All this was skillfully and discreetly wrapped up, but each word spoken by the pious woman in the big white cap made a breach in the indignant resistance of the courtesan. The conversation then glancing off slightly, the woman of the rosaries went on to speak of the religious houses of her Order, of her Superior, of herself and her fragile little companion, her dear little Sister St. Nicephora. They had been summoned to Havre to nurse the hundreds of soldiers there down with smallpox. She described the condition of these poor wretches, gave details of their disease; and while they were thus stopped upon the road by the whim of this Prussian, many French soldiers might die whom perhaps they could have saved. That was her specialty—nursing soldiers. She had been in the Crimea, in Italy, in Austria; and relating her campaigns, she suddenly revealed herself as one of those Sisters of the fife and drum who seem made for following the camp, picking up the wounded in the thick of battle, and better than any officer for quelling with a word the great hulking undisciplined louts—her ravaged face all pitted with innumerable holes, calling up an image of the devastations of war.

No one spoke after her for fear of spoiling the excellent effect.

Immediately after dinner they hurried to their rooms, not to reappear till pretty late the next morning.

Luncheon passed off quietly. They allowed time for the seed sown yesterday to grow and bear fruit.

In the afternoon the Countess proposed a walk, whereupon the Count, following the preconcerted arrangement, took Boule de Suif's arm and fell behind with her a little. He adopted that familiar, paternal, somewhat contemptuous tone which elderly men affect towards such girls, calling her "my dear child," talking down to her from the height of his social position and indisputable respectability.

He came to the point without further preamble. "So you prefer to keep us here exposed like yourself to all the violence which must inevitably follow a check to the Prussian arms, rather than consent to accord one of those favors you have so often dispensed in your time?"

Boule de Suif did not reply.

He then appealed to her kindness of heart, her reason, her sentiment. He knew how to remain "Monsieur le Comte," yet showing himself at the same time chivalrous, flattering—in a word, altogether amiable. He exalted the sacrifice she would be making for them, touched upon their gratitude, and with a final flash of roguishness, "Besides, my dear, he may think himself lucky—he will not find many such pretty girls as you in his own country!"

Boule de Suif said nothing and rejoined the rest of the party.

When they returned, she went straight to her room and did not come down again. The anxiety was terrible. What was she going to do? How unspeakably mortifying if she still persisted in her refusal!

The dinner-hour arrived, they waited for her in vain. Monsieur Follenvie, entering presently, announced that Mademoiselle Rousset was indisposed, and that there was consequently no need to delay supper any longer. They all pricked up their ears. The Count approached the innkeeper with a whispered "All right?"

"Yes."

For propriety's sake he said nothing to his companions, but he made them a slight sign of the head. A great sigh of relief went up from every heart, every face lit up with joy.

"*Saperlipopette!*" cried Loiseau, "I will stand champagne if there is such a thing in this establishment!"

Madame Loiseau suffered a pang of anguish when the innkeeper returned with four bottles in his hands. Everybody suddenly turned communicative and cheerful, and their hearts overflowed with prurient delight. The Count seemed all at once to become aware that Madame Carré-Lamadon was charming; the manufacturer paid compliments to the Countess. Conversation became lively, sprightly, and full of sparkle.

Suddenly Loiseau, with an anxious expression, raised his arms and shouted,

"Silence!" They all stopped talking, surprised and already terrified. Then he listened intently, motioning to them to be silent with his two hands, and raising his eyes to the ceiling. He listened again, and resumed in his natural voice, "It is all right. Don't worry."

They did not understand at first, but soon a smile spread over their faces.

A quarter of an hour later he began the same comedy, and repeated it frequently during the evening. He pretended to be questioning someone on the floor above, giving advice in double-meaning phrases which he drew from his repertory as a commercial traveler. At times he would assume an air of sadness, and sigh, "Poor girl"; or he would mutter between his teeth with a furious air: "You swine of a Prussian!"—Sometimes, when least expected, he would shout in resonant tones: "Enough! Enough!" adding, as though speaking to himself, "If only we see her again; if the scoundrel does not kill her!"

Although these jokes were in deplorable taste, they amused every one and hurt nobody, for, like everything else, indignation is qualified by circumstances, and the atmosphere about them had gradually become charged with obscene thoughts.

By the time they reached dessert the women themselves were indulging in decidedly risky witticisms. Eyes grew bright, tongues were loosened, a good deal of wine had been consumed. The Count, who, even in his cups, retained his characteristic air of diplomatic gravity, made some highly spiced comparisons on the subject of the end of the winter season at the Pole and the joy of ice-bound mariners at sight of an opening to the south.

Loiseau, now in full swing, rose, and lifting high his glass of champagne, "To our deliverance!" he cried. Everybody started to their feet with acclamation. Even the two Sisters of Mercy, yielding to the solicitations of the ladies, consented to take a sip of the effervescing wine which they had never tasted before. They pronounced it to be very like lemonade, though the taste was finer.

"What a pity there is no piano," said Loiseau as a crowning point to the situation, "we might have finished up with a quadrille."

Cornudet had not uttered a word, nor made a sign of joining in the general hilarity; he was apparently plunged in the gravest abstractions, only pulling viciously at his great beard from time to time as if to draw it out longer than before. At last, about midnight, when the company was preparing to separate, Loiseau came stumbling over to him, and digging him in the ribs: "You seem rather down in the mouth this evening, citizen—haven't said a word."

Cornudet threw up his head angrily, and sweeping the company with a flashing and terrible look, "I tell you all that what you have done today is infamous!"

He rose, made his way to the door, exclaimed once again, "Infamous!" and vanished.

This somewhat dashed their spirits for the moment. Loiseau, nonplussed at first, soon regained his aplomb and burst into a roar of laughter. "Sour grapes, old man—sour grapes!"

The others not understanding the allusion, he proceeded to relate the "mysteries of the corridor." This was followed by an uproarious revival of gaiety.

The ladies were in a frenzy of delight, the Count and Monsieur Carré-Lamadon laughed till they cried. They could not believe it.

"Do you mean to say he wanted—"

"I tell you I saw it with my own eyes."

"And she refused?"

"Because the Prussian was in the next room."

"It is incredible."

"As true as I stand here!"

The Count nearly choked; the manufacturer held both his sides.

"And you can understand that he does not quite see the joke of the thing this evening—oh, no—not at all!"

And they all three went off again, breathless, choking, sick with laughter.

After that they parted for the night. But Madame Loiseau remarked to her husband when they were alone that that little cat of a Carré-Lamadon had laughed on the wrong side of her mouth all the evening. "You know how it is with those women—they dote upon a uniform, and whether it is French or Prussian matters precious little to them. But, Lord—it seems to me a poor way of looking at things."

All night the darkness of the corridor seemed full of thrills, of slight noises, scarcely audible, the pattering of bare feet, and creaking that was almost imperceptible. Certainly nobody got to sleep until very late, for it was long before the lights ceased to shine under the doors. Champagne, they say, often has that disturbing effect; it makes one restless and wakeful.

Next morning a brilliant winter sun shone on the dazzling snow. The coach was by this time ready and waiting before the door, while a flock of white pigeons, muffled in their thick plumage, strutted solemnly in and out among the feet of the six horses, seeking what they might devour.

The driver, enveloped in his sheepskin, sat on the box smoking his pipe, and the radiant travelers were busily laying in provisions for the rest of the journey.

They had only to wait now for Boule de Suif. She appeared.

She looked agitated and downcast as she advanced timidly towards her fellow travelers, who all, with one movement, turned away their heads as if they had not seen her. The Count, with a dignified movement, took his wife by the arm and drew her away from this contaminating contact.

The poor thing stopped short, bewildered; then gathering up her courage she accosted the wife of the manufacturer with a humble "Good morning, Madame." The other merely replied with an impertinent little nod, accompanied by a stare of outraged virtue. Everybody seemed suddenly extremely busy, and they avoided her as if she had brought the plague in her skirts. They then precipitated themselves into the vehicle, where she arrived the last and by herself, and resumed in silence the seat she had occupied during the first part of the journey.

They affected not to see her, not to recognize her; only Madame Loiseau, glancing round at her with scorn and indignation, said half audibly to her husband, "It's a good thing that I am not sitting beside her!"

The heavy conveyance jolted off, and the journey was resumed.

No one spoke for the first little while. Boule de Suif did not venture to raise her eyes. She felt incensed at her companions, and at the same time deeply humiliated at having yielded to their persuasions, and let herself be sullied by the kisses of this Prussian into whose arms they had hypocritically thrust her.

The Countess was the first to break the uncomfortable silence. Turning to Madame Carré-Lamadon, she said, "You know Madame d'Etrelles, I think?"

"Oh, yes; she is a great friend of mine."

"What a charming woman!"

"Fascinating! So truly refined; very cultivated, too, and an artist to the tips of her fingers—she sings delightfully, and draws to perfection."

The manufacturer was talking to the Count, and through the rattle of the crazy windowpanes one caught a word here and there; shares—dividends—premium—settlement day—and the like. Loiseau, who had appropriated an old pack of cards from the inn, thick with the grease of the five years' rubbing on dirty tables, started a game of bezique with his wife. The two Sisters pulled up the long rosaries hanging at their waists, made the sign of the cross, and suddenly began moving their lips rapidly, faster and faster, hurrying their vague babble as if for a wager; kissing a medal from time to time, crossing themselves again, and then resuming their rapid and monotonous murmur.

Cornudet sat motionless—thinking.

At the end of the three hours' steady traveling Loiseau gathered up his cards and remarked facetiously, "It's turning hungry."

His wife then produced a parcel, which she untied, and brought out a piece of cold veal. This she cut up into thin, firm slices, and both began to eat.

"Supposing we do the same?" said the Countess, and proceeded to unpack the provisions prepared for both couples. In one of those oblong dishes with a china hare upon the cover to indicate that a roast hare lies beneath, was a succulent selection of cold viands—brown slices of juicy venison mingled with other meats. A delicious square of Gruyère cheese wrapped in newspaper still bore imprinted on its dewy surface the words "Latest News."

The two Sisters brought out a sausage smelling of garlic, and Cornudet, plunging his hands into the vast pockets of his loose greatcoat, drew up four hard-boiled eggs from one and a big crust of bread from the other. He peeled off the shells and threw them into the straw under his feet, and proceeded to bite into the egg, dropping pieces of the yolk into his long beard, from whence they shone out like stars.

In the hurry and confusion of the morning Boule de Suif had omitted to take thought for the future, and she looked on, furious, choking with mortification, at these people all munching away so placidly. A storm of rage convulsed her, and she opened her mouth to hurl at them the torrent of abuse that rose to her lips, but she could not speak, suffocated by her indignation.

Nobody looked at her, nobody thought of her. She felt herself drowning in the flood of contempt shown towards her by these respectable scoundrels who had first sacrificed her and then cast her off like some useless and unclean thing. Then her thoughts reverted to her great basket full of good things which they had so greedily devoured—the two fowls in their glittering coat of jelly, her patties, her pears, her four bottles of claret; and her fury suddenly subsided like the breaking of an overstrung chord and she felt that she was on the verge of tears. She made the most strenuous efforts to overcome it—straightened herself up and choked back her sobs as children do, but the tears would rise. They glittered for a moment on her lashes, and presently two big drops rolled slowly over her cheeks. Others gathered in quick succession like water dripping from a rock and splashed onto the ample curve of her bosom. She sat up very straight, her eyes fixed, her face pale and rigid, hoping that nobody would notice.

But the Countess saw her and nudged her husband. He shrugged his shoulders as much as to say, "What can you expect? It is not my fault." Madame Loiseau gave a silent chuckle of triumph and murmured, "She is crying over her shame." The two Sisters had resumed their devotions after carefully wrapping up the remnants of their sausages.

Then Cornudet, while digesting his eggs, stretched his long legs under the opposite seat, leaned back, smiled like a man who has just thought of a capital joke, and began to softly whistle the *Marseillaise.*

The faces clouded; the people's anthem seemed unpleasing to his neighbors; they became nervous—irritable—looking as if they were ready to throw back their heads and howl like dogs at the sound of a barrel organ. He was perfectly aware of this, but did not stop. From time to time he hummed a few of the words:

> *Amour sacré de la patrie,*
> *Conduis, soutiens nos bras vengeurs,*
> *Liberté, liberté chérie,*
> *Combats avec tes défenseurs!*

They drove at a much quicker pace today, the snow being harder; and all the way to Dieppe, during the long, dull hours of the journey, through all the jolting and rattling of the conveyance, in the falling shades of evening and later in the profound darkness of the carriage he continued with unabated persistency his vengeful and monotonous whistling; forcing his wearied and exasperated fellow travelers to follow the song from end to end and to remember every word that corresponded to each note.

And Boule de Suif wept on, and at times a sob which she could not repress broke out between two stanzas in the darkness.

# William Maxwell

*Maxwell (1908– ) was born in Lincoln, Illinois. He attended the University of Illinois and Harvard. He was fiction editor at the* New Yorker *magazine from 1936 to 1976. His publications include a memoir,* Ancestors *(1971),* Bill Dyer and Other Stories *(1992), and his collected stories,* All the Days and Nights *(1995). He has received an American Academy Award (1958) and an American Book Award (1982) and was president of the National Institute of Arts and Letters from 1969 to 1972.*

## The Thistles in Sweden

The brownstone is on Murray Hill, facing south. The year is 1950. We have the top floor-through, and our windows are not as tall as the windows on the lower floors. They are deeply recessed, and almost square, and have divided panes. I know that beauty is in the eye of the beholder and all that, but even so, these windows are romantic. The apartment could be in Leningrad or Innsbruck or Dresden (before the bombs fell on it) or Parma or any place we have never been to. When I come home at night, I look forward to the moment when I turn the corner and raise my eyes to those three lighted windows. Since I was a child, no place has been quite so much home to me. The front windows look out on Thirty-sixth Street, the back windows on an unpainted brick wall (the side of a house on Lexington Avenue) with no break in it on our floor, but on the floor below there is a single window with a potted plant, and when we raise our eyes we see the sky, so the room is neither dark nor prisonlike.

Since we are bothered by street noises, the sensible thing would be to use this room to sleep in, but it seems to want to be our living room, and offers two irresistible arguments: (1) a Victorian white marble fireplace and (2) a stairway. If we have a fireplace it should be in the living room, even though the chimney is blocked up, so we can't have a fire in it. (I spend a good deal of time unblocking it, in my mind.) The stairs are the only access to the roof for the whole building. There is, of course, nothing up there, but it looks as if we are in a house and you can go upstairs to bed, and this is very cozy: a house on the top floor of a brownstone walk-up. I draw the bolt and push the trapdoor up with my shoulder, and Margaret and I stand together, holding the cat, Floribunda, in our arms so she will not escape, and see the stars (when there are any) or the winking lights of an airplane, or sometimes a hallucinatory effect brought about by fog or very fine rain and mist—the lighted windows of midtown skyscrapers set in space, without any surrounding masonry. The living room and the bedroom both have a door opening onto the outer hall, which, since we are on the top floor and nobody else in the building uses it, we regard as part of the apartment. We leave these doors open when we are at home, and the stair railing and the head of the stairs are blocked off with huge pieces of cardboard. The landlord says that this is a violation of the fire laws, but we cannot think of any other way to keep Floribunda from escaping down the stairs, and neither can he.

The living-room curtains are of heavy Swedish linen: life-sized thistles, printed in light blue and charcoal grey, on a white background. They are very beautiful (and so must the thistles in Sweden be) and they also have an emotional context; Margaret made them, and, when they did not hang properly, wept, and ripped them apart and remade them, and now they do hang properly. The bedroom curtains are of a soft ivory material, with seashells—cowries, scallops, sea urchins and sand dollars, turbinates, auriculae—drawn on them in brown indelible ink, with a flowpen. The bedroom floor is black, the walls are sandalwood, the woodwork is white. On the wall above the double bed is a mural in two sections—a hexagonal tower in an imaginary kingdom that resembles Persia. Children are flying kites from the roof. Inside the tower, another child is playing on a musical instrument that is cousin to the lute. The paperhanger hung the panels the wrong way, so the tower is even stranger architecturally than the artist intended. The parapet encloses outer instead of inner space—like a man talking to somebody who is standing behind him, facing the other way. And the fish-shaped kite, where is that being flown from? And by whom? Some other children are flying kites from the roof of the tower next to this one, perhaps, only there wasn't room to show it. (Lying in bed I often, in my mind, correct the paperhanger's mistake.) Next to the mural there is a projection made by a chimney that conducts sounds from the house next door. Or rather, a single sound: a baby crying in the night. The brownstone next door is not divided into apartments, and so much money has been spent on the outside (blue shutters, fresh paint, stucco, polished brass, etc.) that, for this neighborhood, the effect of chic is overdone. We assume there is a nurse, but nobody ever does anything when the baby cries, and the sound that comes through the wall is unbearably sad. (Unable to stand it any longer, Margaret gets up and goes through the brick chimney and picks the baby up and brings it back into our bedroom and rocks it.)

The double chest of drawers came from Macy's unfinished-furniture department, and Margaret gave it nine coats of enamel before she was satisfied with the way it looked. The black lacquered dining table (we have two dining tables and no dining room) is used as a desk. Over it hangs a large engraving of the Spanish Steps, which, two years ago, in the summer of 1948, for a brief time belonged to us—flower stands, big umbrellas, Bernini fountain, English Tea Room, Keats museum, children with no conception of bedtime, everything. At night we drape our clothes over two cheap rush-bottom chairs, from Italy. The mahogany dressing table, with an oval mirror in a lyre-shaped frame and turned legs such as one sees in English furniture of the late seventeenth century, came by express from the West Coast. The express company delivered it to the sidewalk in front of the building, and, notified by telephone that this was about to happen, I rushed home from the office to supervise the uncrating. As I stepped from the taxi, I saw the expressman with the mirror and half the lyre in his huge hands. He was looking at it thoughtfully. The rest of the dressing table was ten feet away, by the entrance to the building. The break does not show unless you look closely. And most old furniture has been mended at one time or another.

When we were shown the apartment for the first time, the outgoing tenant let us in and stood by pleasantly while we tried to imagine what the place would look like if it were not so crowded with his furniture. It was hardly possible to take a step for oak tables and chests and sofas and armoires and armchairs. Those ancestral portraits and Italian landscapes in heavy gilt frames that there was no room for on the walls were leaning against the furniture. To get from one room to the next we had to step over pyramids of books and scientific journals. An inventory of the miscellaneous objects and musical instruments in the living room would have taken days and been full of surprises. (Why did he keep that large soup tureen on the floor?) We thought at first he was packing, but he was not; this was the way he lived. If we had asked him to make a place in his life for us too, he would have. He was a very nice man. The disorder was dignified and somehow enviable, and the overfurnished apartment so remote from what went on down below in the street that it was like a cave deep in the forest.

Now it is underfurnished (we have just barely enough money to manage a small one-story house in the country and this apartment in town), instead, and all light and air. The living-room walls are a pale blue that changes according to the light and the time of day and the season of the year and the color of the sky. The walls are hardly there. The furniture is half old and half new, and there isn't much of it, considering the size of the room: a box couch, a cabinet with sliding doors, a small painted bookcase, an easy chair with its ottoman, a round fruitwood side table with long, thin, spidery legs and a glass tray that fits over the top, the table and chairs we eat on, a lowboy that serves as a sideboard, another chair, a wobbly tea cart, and a canvas stool. The couch has a high wooden back, L-shaped, painted black, with a thin gold line. It was made for an old house in Dover, New Hampshire, and after I don't know how many generations found itself in Minneapolis. I first saw it in Margaret's mother's bedroom in Seattle, and now it is here. It took two big men and a lot of patient maneuvering to get it four times past the turning of the stairs. The shawl that is draped over the back and the large tin tray that serves as a coffee table both came from Mexico—a country I do not regard as romantic, even though we have never been there. The lowboy made the trip from the West Coast with the dressing table, and one of its Chippendale[1] legs got broken in transit, or by that same impetuous expressman. I suppose it is a hundred and fifty or two hundred years old. The man in the furniture-repair shop, after considering the broken leg, asked if we wanted the lowboy refinished. I asked why, and he said,

1. Of or in the style of English cabinetmaker and furniture designer Thomas Chippendale (1718?–1779).

s been painted." We looked, and sure enough it had. "They did that "Becau," he said. "It's painted to simulate mahogany." I asked what was some paint, and he picked up a chisel and took a delicate gouge out of the unde. This time it was his turn to be surprised. "It's mahogany," he uced. The lowboy was painted to simulate what it actually was, it looks hat it is, so we let it be.

he gateleg table we eat on has four legs instead of the usual six. When sides are extended, it looks as if the cabinetmaker had been studying clid's[2] geometry. Margaret found it in an antique shop in Putnam Valley, d asked me to come look at it. I got out of the car and went in and saw the able and knew I could not live without it. The antique dealer said the table had an interesting history that she wasn't free to tell us. (Was it a real Hepplewhite[3] and not just in the style of? Was it stolen?) She was a very old woman and lived alone. The shop was lined with bookshelves, and the books on the shelves and lying around on the tables were so uncommon I had trouble keeping my hands off them. They were not for sale, the old woman said. They had belonged to her husband, and she was keeping them for her grandchildren; she herself read nothing but murder mysteries.

Margaret wanted the table, but she wanted also to talk about whether or not we could afford it. I can always afford what I dearly want—or rather, when I want something very much I would rather not think about whether or not we can afford it. As we drove away without the table, I said coldly, "We won't talk about it." As if she were the kind of wife she isn't. And we did talk about it, all the way home. The next day we were back, nobody had bought the table in the meantime, I wrote out a check for two hundred dollars, and the old woman gave us a big rag rug to wrap around the marvel so it wouldn't be damaged on the drive home. Also heavy twine to tie it with. But then I asked for a knife, and this upset her, to my astonishment. I looked carefully and saw that the expression in her faded blue eyes was terror: She thought I wanted a knife so I could murder her and make off with the table *and* the check. It is disquieting to have one's intentions so misjudged. (Am I a murderer? And is it usual for the murderer to ask for his weapon?) "A pair of scissors will do just as well," I said, and the color came back into her face.

The rug the table now stands on is only slightly larger than the tabletop. It is threadbare, but we cannot find another like it. For some reason, it is the last yellowish beige rug ever made. People with no children have perfectionism to fall back on.

The space between the fireplace and the door to the kitchen is filled by shelves and a shallow cupboard. The tea cart is kept under the stairs. Then comes the door to the coat closet, the inside of which is painted a particularly beautiful shade of Chinese red, and the door to the hall. On the sliding-door cabinet (we have turned the corner now and are moving toward the windows) there is a pottery lamp with a wide perforated grey paper shade and such a long thin neck that it seems to be trying to turn into a crane. Also a record

2. Greek geometrician and educator at Alexandria (ca. 300 B.C.E.). 3. George Hepplewhite (d. 1876), English furniture designer and cabinetmaker.

player that plays only 78s and has to be wound after every recor painting over the couch is of a rock quarry in Maine, and we have dis that it changes according to the time of day and the color of the sk particularly alive after a snowfall.

Here we live, in our modest perfectionism, with two black cats. The o on the mantelpiece is Bastet, the Egyptian goddess of love and joy.[4] The othe is under the impression that she is our child. This is our fault, of course, not hers. Around her neck she wears a scarlet ribbon, or sometimes a turquoise ribbon, or a collar with little bells. Her toys dangle from the tea cart, her kitty litter is in a pan beside the bathtub, and she sleeps on the foot of our bed or curled against the back of Margaret's knees. When she is bored she asks us to remove a piece of the cardboard barricade so she can go tippeting down the stairs and pay a call on the landlord and his wife, Mr. and Mrs. Holmes, who live in the garden apartment and have the rear half of the second floor, with an inside stairs, so they really do go upstairs to bed. The front part of the second floor is the pied-à-terre[5] of the artist who designed the wallpaper mural of the children flying kites from a hexagonal tower in an imaginary kingdom that resembles Persia. It is through the artist's influence (Mr. Holmes is intimidated by her) that we managed to get our rent-controlled apartment, for which we pay a hundred and thirteen dollars and some odd cents. The landlord wishes we paid more, and Mr. and Mrs. Venable, who live under us, wish we'd get a larger rug for the living room. Their bedroom is on the back, and Margaret's heels crossing the ceiling at night keep them awake. Also, in the early morning the Egyptian goddess leaves our bed and chases wooden spools and glass marbles from one end of the living room to the other. The Venables have mentioned this subject of the larger rug to the landlord and he has mentioned it to us. We do nothing about it, except that Margaret puts the spools and marbles out of Floribunda's reach when we go to bed at night, and walks around in her stocking feet after ten o'clock. Some day, when we are kept awake by footsteps crossing our bedroom ceiling, hammering, furniture being moved, and other idiot noises, we will remember the Venables and wish we had been more considerate.

The Venables leave their door open too, and on our way up the stairs I look back over my shoulder and see chintz-covered chairs and Oriental rugs and the lamplight falling discreetly on an Early American this and an Old English that. (No children here, either; Mrs. Venable works in a decorator's shop.) Mrs. Pickering, third floor, keeps her door closed. She is a sweet-faced woman who smiles when we meet her on the stairs. She has a grown son and daughter who come to see her regularly, but her life isn't the same as when they were growing up and Mr. Pickering was alive. (Did she tell us this or have I invented it?) If we met her anywhere but on the stairs we would have racked our brains to find something to say to her. The Holmeses' furniture is nondescript but comfortable. Mrs. Holmes has lovely brown eyes and the voice that goes with them, and it is no wonder that Floribunda likes to sit on her lap. *He*

4. Also called *Bast*; essentially a goddess of the home, she was worshiped in the form of a cat and later equated with the lioness war goddess. 5. A small dwelling maintained for temporary use (French).

wants everybody to be happy, which is not exactly the way to be happy yourself, and he isn't. If we all paid a little more rent, it would make him happier, but we don't feel like it, any of us.

I am happy because we are in town: I don't have to commute in bad weather. I can walk to the office. And after the theater we jump in a cab and are home in five minutes. I stand at the front window listening to the weather report. It is snowing in Westchester, and the driving conditions are very bad. In Thirty-sixth Street it is raining. The middle-aged man who lives on the top floor of the brownstone directly across from us is in the habit of posing at the window with a curtain partly wrapped around his naked body. He keeps guppies or goldfish in a lighted tank, spends the whole day in a kimono ironing, and at odd moments goes to the front window and acts out somebody's sexual dream. If I could only marry him off to the old woman who goes through the trash baskets on Lexington Avenue, talking to herself. What pleasure she would have in showing him the things she has brought home in her string bag—treasures whose value nobody else realizes. And what satisfaction to him it would be to wrap himself in a curtain just for her.

The view to the south is cut off by a big apartment building on Thirty-fifth Street. The only one. If it were not there (I spend a good deal of time demolishing it, with my bare hands) we would have the whole of the sky to look at. Because I have not looked carefully enough at the expression in Margaret's eyes, I go on thinking that she is happy too. When I met her she was working in a publishing house. Shortly after we decided to get married she was offered a job with the *Partisan Review*. If she had taken it, it would have meant commuting with me or even commuting at different hours from when I did. When I was a little boy and came home from school and called out, "Is anybody home?" somebody nearly always was. I took it for granted that the same thing would be true when I married. We didn't talk about it, and should have. I didn't understand that in her mind it was the chance of a fulfilling experience. Because she saw that I could not even imagine her saying yes, she said no, and turned her attention to learning how to cook and keep house. If we had had children right away it would have been different; but then if we had had children we wouldn't have been living on the top floor of a brownstone on Thirty-sixth Street.

The days in town are long and empty for her. The telephone doesn't ring anything like as often as it does when we are in the country. There Hester Gale comes across the road to see how Margaret is, or because she is out of cake flour, and they have coffee together. Margaret sews with Olivia Bingham. There are conversations in the supermarket. And miles of woods to walk in. Old Mrs. Delano, whose front door on Thirty-sixth Street is ten feet west of ours, is no help whatever. Though she knows Margaret's Aunt Caroline, she doesn't know that Margaret is her niece, or even that she exists, probably, and Margaret has no intention of telling her. Any more than she has any intention of telling me that in this place where I am so happy she feels like a prisoner much of the time.

She is accustomed to space, to a part of the country where there is more room than people and buildings to occupy it. In her childhood she woke up in the morning in a big house set on a wide lawn, with towering pine trees behind it, and a copper beech as big as two brownstones, and a snow-capped mountain that mysteriously comes and goes, like an idea in the mind. Every afternoon after school she went cantering through the trees on horseback. Now she is confined to two rooms—the kitchen cannot be called a room; it is hardly bigger than a handkerchief—and these two rooms are not enough. This is a secret she manages to keep from me so I can go on being happy.

There is another secret that cannot be kept from me because, with her head in a frame made by my head, arms, and shoulder, I know when she weeps. She weeps because her period was five days late and she thought something had happened that she now knows is not going to happen. The child is there, and could just as well as not decide to come to us, and doesn't, month after month. Instead, we consult one gynecologist after another, and take embarrassing tests (only they don't really embarrass me, they just seem unreal). And what the doctors do not tell us is why, when there is nothing wrong with either of us, nothing happens. Before we can have a child we must solve a riddle, like Oedipus and the Sphinx.[6] On my forty-second birthday I go to the Spence-Chapin adoption service and explain our situation to a woman who listens attentively. I like her and feel that she understands how terribly much we want a child, and she shocks me by reaching across the desk and taking the application blank out of my hands: Forty-two is the age past which the agency will not consider giving out a child for adoption.

Meanwhile, Margaret herself has been adopted, by the Italian market under the El at Third Avenue and Thirty-fourth Street. Four or five whistling boys with white aprons wrapped around their skinny hips run it. They also appear to own it, but what could be more unlikely? Their faces light up when Margaret walks into the store. They drop what they are doing and come to greet her as if she were their older sister. And whatever she asks for, it turns out they have. Their meat is never tough, their vegetables are not tarnished and limp, their sole is just as good as the fish market's and nothing like as expensive. Now one boy, now another arrives at our door with a carton of groceries balanced on his head, having taken the stairs two steps at a time. Four flights are nothing to them. They are in business for the pure pleasure of it. They don't think or talk about love, they just do it. Or perhaps it isn't love but joy. But over what? Over the fact that they are alive and so are we?

It occurs to the landlord that the tenants could carry their garbage down to the street and then he wouldn't have to. I prepare for a scene, compose angry speeches in the bath. Everybody knows what landlords are like—only he isn't like that. He isn't even a landlord, strictly speaking. He has a good job with an actuarial firm. The building is a hobby. It was very run down when he bought it, and he has had the pleasure of fixing it up. We meet on the front sidewalk as I am on my way to work. Looking up at him—he is a very tall man—I announce that I will not carry our garbage down. Looking down at me,

6. In the Greek tragedian Sophocles' greatest play, *Oedipus the King*, Oedipus saved Thebes by solving the riddle of the Sphinx.

he says that if we don't feel like carrying our garbage down he will go on doing it. What an unsatisfactory man to quarrel with.

I come home from the office and find that Margaret has spent the afternoon drawing: a pewter coffeepot (Nantucket), a Venetian-glass goblet, a white china serving dish with a handle and a cover, two eggs, a lemon, apples, a rumpled napkin with a blue border. Or the view from the living room all the way into the bedroom, through three doorways, involving the kind of foreshortened perspective Italian Renaissance artists were so fond of. Or the view from the bedroom windows (the apartment house on Thirty-fifth Street that I have so often taken down I now see is all right; it belongs there) in sepia wash. Or her own head and shoulders reflected in the dressing-table mirror. Or the goblet, the coffeepot, the lemon, a green pepper, and a brown luster bowl. The luster bowl has a chip in it, and so the old woman in the antique shop in Putnam Valley gave it to us for a dollar, after the table was safely stowed away in the backseat of the car. And some years later, her daughter, sitting next to me at a formal dinner party, said, "You're mistaken. Mother was absolutely fearless." She said it again, perceiving that I did not believe her. Somebody is mistaken, and it could just as well as not be me. Even though I looked quite carefully at the old woman's expression. In any case, there is something I didn't see. Her husband—the man whose books the old woman was unwilling to sell—committed suicide. "I was their only child, and had to deal with sadness all my life—sadness from within as well as from without." If the expression in the old woman's eyes was not terror, what was it?

Floribunda misses the country, and sits at the top of the living-room stairs, clawing at the trapdoor. She refuses to eat, is shedding. Her hairs are on everything. One night we take her across Park Avenue to the Morgan Library and push the big iron gate open like conspirators about to steal the forty-two-line Gutenberg Bible or the three folios of Redouté's roses.[7] Floribunda leaps from Margaret's arms and runs across the sickly grass and climbs a small tree. Ecstatically she sharpens her claws on the bark. I know that we will be arrested, but it is worth it.

Neither the landlord and his wife, nor the artist and her husband, who is Dutch, nor Mrs. Pickering, nor the Venables ever entertain in their apartments, but we have a season of being sociable. We have the Fitzgeralds and Eileen Fitzgerald's father from Dublin for dinner. We celebrate Bastille Day[8] with the Potters. We have Elinor Hinkley's mother to tea. She arrives at the head of the stairs, where she can see into the living room, and exclaims—before she has even caught her breath—"What beautiful horizontal surfaces!" She is incapable of small talk. Instead, she describes the spiritual emanations of a row of huge granite boulders lining the driveway of her house on Martha's Vineyard. And other phenomena that cannot be described very easily, or that, when described,

7. Ancient texts. 8. July 14, a French national holiday, celebrating the fall of the Bastille, a famous fortress prison in Paris, in 1789.

cannot be appreciated by someone who isn't half mad or a Theosophist.[9]

Dean Wilson brings one intelligent, pretty girl after another to meet us. Like the woman in Isak Dinesen's[1] story who sailed the seas looking for the perfect blue, he is looking for a flawless girl. Flawless in whose eyes is the question. And isn't flawlessness itself a serious flaw? "What a charming girl," we say afterward, and he looks in our faces and is not satisfied, and brings still another girl, including, finally, Ivy Sérurier, who is half English and half French. When she was seven years old her nurse took her every day to the Jardin du Luxembourg and there she ran after a hoop. She is attracted to all forms of occult knowledge, and things happen to her that do not happen to anyone who does not have a destiny. The light bulbs respond to her amazing stories by giving off a higher voltage. The expression on our faces is satisfactory. Dean brings her again, and again. He asks Margaret if she thinks they should get married, but he cannot quite bring himself to ask Ivy this question.

On a night when we are expecting Henry Coddington to dinner, Hester and Nick Gale come up the stairs blithely at seven o'clock, having got the invitation wrong. Or perhaps it is our fault. There is plenty of food, and it turns out to be a pleasant evening. The guests get on well, but Henry must have thought we did not want to know why Louise left him and took their little girl, whom he idolizes—that we have insulated ourselves from his catastrophe by asking this couple from the country. Anyway, he never comes or calls again. But other people come. Melissa Lovejoy, from Montgomery, Alabama, comes for Sunday lunch, and her hilarious account of her skirmishes with her mother-in-law make the tears run down my cheeks. Melissa, who loves beautiful china, looks around the living room and sees what no one else has ever seen or commented on—a Meissen[2] plate on the other end of the mantelpiece from the Egyptian cat. It is white, with very small green grape leaves and a wide filigree border. Margaret's brother John had it in his rucksack when he made his way from Geneva to Bordeaux in May 1940. As easily as the plate could have got broken, so he could have ended up in a detention camp and then what? But they are both safe, intact, here in New York. He has his own place, on Lexington Avenue in the Fifties. On Christmas Eve he bends down and selects a present for Margaret and another for me from the pile under the tree at the foot of the stair.

On New Year's Eve, John and Dean and Ivy and Margaret and I sit down to dinner. The champagne cork hits the ceiling. Between courses we take turns getting up and going into the bedroom and waiting behind a closed door until a voice calls "Ready!" If you were a school of Italian painting or a color of the spectrum or a character from fiction, what school of Italian painting or color or character would you be? John is Dostoevski's[3] Idiot, Margaret is lavender blue. Elinor Hinkley joins us for dessert. Just before midnight a couple from the U.N., whom Dean has invited, come up the stairs and an hour later on the dot they leave for another party. It is daylight when we push our chairs back. We

9. A person who believes he has divine revelation or special insight into the nature of the divine. 1. Baroness Karen Blixen (1885–1962), Danish author whose most famous book is *Out of Africa*. 2. A German city famous for fine porcelain. 3. Fyodor Dostoevski (1821–1881), Russian novelist, among whose novels are *Crime and Punishment*, *The Brothers Karamazov*, and *The Idiot*.

have not left the table (except to go into the front room while the questions are being framed) all night long. With our heads out of the window, Margaret and I wait for them to emerge from the building and then we call down to them, "Happy New Year!" But softly, so as not to wake up the neighbors.

Margaret's Uncle James, who is not her uncle but her mother's first cousin, comes to dinner, bringing long-stemmed red roses. He confesses that he has been waiting for this invitation ever since we were married—eight or nine years—and he thoroughly enjoys himself, though he is dying of cancer of the throat. Faced with extinction, you can't just stand and scream; it isn't good manners. And men and women of that generation do not discuss their feelings. Anyway he doesn't. Instead he says, "I like your curtains, Margaret," and we are filled with remorse that we didn't ask him sooner. But still, he did come to dinner. And satisfied his curiosity about the way we live. And we were surprised to discover that we were fond of him—as the rabbit is surprised to discover that he is what was concealed in the magician's hat. *I am not the person you thought I was,* Uncle James as much as says, sitting back in the easy chair but not using the ottoman lest he look ill.

I realize that the air is full of cigarette smoke, and prop the trapdoor open with a couple of books—but only a crack. At eleven-thirty Uncle James rises and puts his coat on and says good night, and tromps down the stairs, waking the Venables, and Mrs. Pickering, and the artist and her husband, and Mr. and Mrs. Holmes. And we lock the doors and say what a nice evening it was, and empty the ashtrays, and carry the liquor glasses out to the kitchen, and suddenly perceive an emptiness, an absence. "Floribunda? . . . Pussy?" She is nowhere. She has slipped through the crack that I thought was too small for her to get through. Fur is deceptive, her bone structure is not what I thought it was, and perhaps cats have something in common with cigarette smoke. I have often seen her attenuate herself alarmingly. Outside, on the roof, I call softly, but no little black cat comes. In the night we both wake and talk about her. The bottom of the bed feels strange when we put our feet out and there is nothing there, no weight. When morning comes I dress and go up to the roof again, and make my way toward Park Avenue, stepping over two-foot-high tile walls and making my way around projections and feeling giddy when I peer down into back gardens.

Margaret, meanwhile, has dressed and gone down the stairs. She rings the Delanos' bell, and the Irish maid opens the door. "A little cat came in through my bedroom window last night and the mistress said to put her on the street, so I did." *On the street* . . . when she could so easily have put her back on the roof she came from! "Here, Puss, Puss, Puss . . . here, Puss!" Up Thirty-sixth Street and down Thirty-fifth. All her life she has known nothing but love, and she is so timid. How will she survive with no home? What will the poor creature do? We meet Rose Bernstein, who has just moved into town from our country road, and just as I am saying "On the street. Did you ever hear of anything so heartless?" there is a faint miaow. Floribunda heard us calling and was too frightened to answer. I find her hiding in an areaway. Margaret gathers her up in her arms and we say good-bye to Rose Bernstein, and, unable to believe our good fortune, take her home. Our love and joy.

In Chicago there is an adoption agency whose policy with respect to age is not so rigid as Spence-Chapin's. We pull strings. (Dean Wilson has a friend whose wife's mother is on the board.) Letters pass back and forth, and finally there we are, in Chicago, nervously waiting in the reception room. Miss Mattie Gessner is susceptible (or so I feel) to the masculine approach. It turns out that she voted for Truman too; and she doesn't reach across the desk and take the application from my hands. Instead she promises to help us. But it isn't as simple as the old song my mother used to sing: Today is not the day they give babies away with a half a pound of tay.[4] The baby that is given to us for adoption must be the child of a couple reasonably like us—that is to say, a man and woman who, in the year 1952, would have a record player that plays only 78s and that you wind by hand; who draw seashells on their bedroom curtains and are made happy by a blocked-up fireplace and a stairway that leads nowhere. And this means we must wait God knows how long.

So we do wait, sometimes in rather odd places for a couple with no children. For example, by the carousel in Central Park. The plunging horses slowly come to a halt with their hoofs in midair. The children get off and more children climb up, take a firm grip on the pole, and look around for their mother or their nurse or their father, in the crowd standing in the open doorway. Slowly the cavalcade begins to move again, and I take the little boy in the plaid snowsuit, with half a pound of English Breakfast, and Margaret takes half a pound of Lipton's and the little girl with blue ribbons in her hair.

We start going to the country weekends. And then we go for the summer, taking suitcases full of clothes, boxes of unread books, drawing materials, the sewing machine, the typewriter. And in September all this is carried up four flights of stairs. And more: flowers, vegetables from the garden, plants we could not bear to have the frost put an end to, even though we know they will not live long in town. And one by one we take up our winter habits. When Saturday night comes around we put on our coats at ten o'clock and go out to buy the Sunday *Times* at the newspaper stand under the El. We rattle the door of the antique shop on Third Avenue that always has something interesting in the window but has never been known to be open at any hour of any day of the week. On three successive nights we go to *Ring Round the Moon*, *King Lear*, and *An Enemy of the People*, after which it seems strange to sit home reading a book. I am so in love with Adlai Stevenson's[5] speeches that, though I am afraid of driving in ordinary traffic in New York City, I get the car out of the garage and we drive right down the center of 125th Street, in a torchlight parade, hemmed in by a flowing river of people, all of whom feel the way we do.

How many years did we live in that apartment on Thirty-sixth Street? From 1950 to—The mere dates are misleading, even if I could get them right, because time was not progressive or in sequence, it was one of Mrs. Hinkley's horizontal surfaces divided into squares. On one square an old woman waters

4. Tea. 5. Politician (1900–1965), who was twice a candidate for president (1952 and 1956) and ambassador to the U.N. (1960–65).

a houseplant in the window of an otherwise blank wall. On another, Albertha, who is black, comes to clean. When she leaves, the apartment looks as if an angel had walked through it. She is the oldest of eleven children. And what she and Margaret say, over a cup of coffee, makes Margaret more able to deal with her solitary life. On another square, we go to the Huguenot Church on Sunday morning, expecting something new and strange, and instead the hymns are perfectly familiar to us from our Presbyterian childhoods: In French they have become more elegant and rhetorical, and it occurs to me that they may not reach all the way to the ear of Heaven. But the old man who then mounts the stairs to the pulpit addresses Seigneur Dieu in a confident voice, as if they are extremely well acquainted, the two of them. On another square we go to Berlitz, and the instructor, a White Russian named Mikhael Miloradovitch, sits by blandly while Margaret and I say things to each other in French that we have managed not to say in English. I am upset when I discover that she prefers the country to the city. The discussion becomes heated, but because it is in French nothing comes of it. We go on living in the city. Until another summer comes and we fill the car, which is now nearly twenty years old, to the canvas top with our possessions; then, locking the doors of the apartment, we drive off to our other life. At which point the shine goes out of this one. The slipcovers fade and so do the seashells and thistles that are exposed to the direct light of the summer sun. Dust gathers on the books, the lampshades, the record player. In the middle of the night, a hand pries at the trapdoor and, finding it securely locked, tries somewhere else. The man out of Krafft-Ebing[6] shows himself seductively to our blank windows. And the intense heat builds up to a violent thunderstorm. After which there is a spell of cooler weather. And a tragedy. For two days there has been no garbage outside Mrs. Pickering's door in the morning. She does not answer her telephone or the landlord's knocking, and she has not said she was going away. The first floor extends farther back than the rest of the house, and he is able to place a ladder on the roof of this extension. From the top of the ladder he stares into the third-floor bedroom at a terrible sight: Mrs. Pickering, sitting in a wing chair, naked. He thinks it is death he is staring at, but he is mistaken; she has had a stroke. He breaks the door down, and she is taken to the hospital in an ambulance. She does not die, but neither does she ever come back to this apartment. Passing her door on our way up the stairs, we are aware of the silence inside, and think uneasily of those two days and nights of helpless waiting. Along with the silence there is the sense of something malign, of trouble of a very serious kind that could spread all through the house. To ward it off, we draw closer to the other tenants, linger talking on the stairs, and speak to them in a more intimate tone of voice. We have the Holmeses and the Venables and the artist and her husband up for a drink. It doesn't do the trick. There *was* something behind Mrs. Pickering's door. My sister's only son turns up and, since we are in the country, we offer him the apartment to live in until he finds a job. He leads a life there that the books and furniture do not approve of. He brings girls home and makes love

6. Baron Von Richard Krafft-Ebing (1840–1902), German neurologist and author of studies about mental illness.

to them in our bed, under the very eyes of the children flying kites. He borrows fifty bucks from me, to eat on, and to get some shirts, so he won't look like a bum when he goes job hunting. He has a check coming from his previous job, in Florida, and will pay me back next week. The check doesn't come, and he borrows some more money, and then some more, and it begins to mount up. Jobs that were as good as promised to him vanish into thin air, and meanwhile we are his sole means of support. I listen attentively to what I more and more suspect are inventions, but his footwork is fast, and what he says could be true; it just isn't what he said before, quite. My bones inform me that I am not the first person these excuses and appeals have been tried out on. He comes to my office to tell me that he has given up the idea of staying in New York and can I let him have the fare home, and I dial my sister's number in Evansville, Indiana, and hand the receiver to him and leave the room.

I give up smoking on one square, and on another I go through all the variant pages of a book I have been writing for four and a half years and reduce it to a single pile of manuscript. This I put in a blue canvas duffel bag that can absentmindedly be left behind on the curbing when we drive off to the country at eleven o'clock of a spring night. At midnight, driving up the Taconic Parkway, I suddenly see in my mind's eye the backseat of the car: The blue duffel bag is not there. Nor, when we come to a stop in front of our house on Thirty-sixth Street at one o'clock in the morning, is it on the sidewalk where I left it. With a dry mouth I describe it to the desk sergeant in the police station, and he gets up and goes into the back room. "No, nothing," he calls. And then, as we are almost at the door, "Wait a minute."

On another square Margaret starts behaving in a way that is not at all like her. Sleepy at ten o'clock in the evening, and when I open my eyes in the morning she is already awake and looking at me. Her face is somehow different. Can it be that she is . . . that we are going to . . . that . . . I study her when she is not aware that I am looking at her, and find in her behavior the answer to that riddle: If we are so longing for a child that we are willing to bring up somebody else's child—anybody's child whatever—then we may as well be allowed to have our own. Margaret comes home from the doctor bringing the news to me that I have not dared break to her.

After boning up on the subject, in a book, she shows me, on her finger, just how long the child in her womb now is. And it is growing larger, very slowly. And so is she. The child is safe inside her, and she is safe so long as she remains a prisoner in this top-floor apartment. The doctor has forbidden her to use the stairs. Everybody comes to see her, instead—including an emanation from the silent apartment two floors below. A black man, a stranger, suddenly appears at the top of the stairs. His intention, unclear but frightening, shows in his face, in his eyes. But the goddess Bastet is at work again, and the man comes on Albertha's day, and she, with a stream of such foulmouthed cursing as Margaret has never heard in her life, sends him running down the stairs. If he had come on a day that was not Albertha's day, when Margaret was there alone—But this holds true for everything, good or bad.

Margaret's face grows rounder, and she no longer has a secret that must be kept from me. The days while I am at the office are not lonely, and time is an unbroken landscape of daydreaming. When I get home at six o'clock, I creep in under the roof of the spell she is under, and am allowed into the daydream. But what shall we tell Miss Mattie Gessner when she comes to investigate the way we live?

The apartment, feeling our inattention, begins to withdraw from us sadly. And then something else unexpected happens. The landlord, having achieved perfection, having created the Peaceable Kingdom on Thirty-sixth Street, is restless and wants to begin all over again. "You'll be sorry," his wife tells him, stroking Floribunda's ear, and he is. But by that time they are living uptown, in a much less handsome house in the Nineties—a house that needs fixing from top to bottom. But it will never have any style, and it is filled with disagreeable tenants who do not pay their rent on time. On Thirty-sixth Street we have a new landlord, and in no time his hand is on everything. He hangs a cheap print of van Gogh's[7] *The Drawbridge* in the downstairs foyer. We are obliged to take down the cardboard barricade and keep our doors closed. Hardly a day passes without some maddening new improvement. The artist is the first to go. Then we give notice; how is Margaret to carry the baby, the stroller, the package from the drugstore, etc., up four flights of stairs? *What better place can there be to bring up a child in?* the marble fireplace asks, remembering the eighteen-eighties, when this was a one-family house and our top-floor living room was the nursery. The stairway to the roof was devoted to the previous tenant (the man who lived in the midst of a monumental clutter) and says bitterly, in the night, when we are not awake to hear, *They seem as much a part of your life as the doors and windows, and then it turns out that they are not a part of your life at all. The moving men come and cart all the furniture away, and the people go down to the street, and that's the last you see of them. . . .*

What will the fireplace and the stairway to the roof say when they discover that they are about to be shut off forever from the front room? The landlord is planning to divide our apartment into two apartments and charge the same for each that he is now getting for the floor-through. For every evil under the sun there is a remedy or there is none. I soak the mural of the children flying kites, hoping to remove it intact and put it up somewhere in the house in the country. The paper tears no matter how gently I pull it loose from the wall, and comes off in little pieces, which end up in the wastebasket.

Now when I walk past that house I look up at the windows that could be in Leningrad or Innsbruck or Dresden or Parma, and I think of the stairway that led only to the trapdoor in the roof, and of the marble fireplace, the bathroom skylight, and the tiny kitchen, and of what school of Italian painting we would have been if we had been a school of Italian painting, and poor Mrs. Pickering sitting in her bedroom chair with her eyes wide open, waiting for help, and the rainy nights on Thirty-sixth Street, and the grey-and-blue thistles, the brown seashells, the Mills Brothers[8] singing *Shine, little glowworm, glimmer, glimmer,* and the guests who came the wrong night, the guest who was going to die and knew it, the sound of my typewriter, and of a paintbrush clinking in a glass of cloudy water, and Floribunda's adventure, and Margaret's

7. Vincent Van Gogh (1853–1890), Dutch painter. 8. Popular singing group of the mid-1900s.

empty days, and how it was settled that, although I wanted to put my head on her breast as I was falling asleep, she needed even more (at that point) to put her head on mine. And of our child's coming, at last, and the black cat who thought *she* was our child, and of the two friends who didn't after all get married, and the old woman who found one treasure after another in the trash baskets all up and down Lexington Avenue, and that other old woman, now dead, who was so driven by the need to describe the inner life of very large granite boulders. I think of how Miss Mattie Gessner's face fell and how she closed her notebook and became a stranger to us, who had been so deeply our friend. I think of the oversexed ironer, and the Holmeses, and the Venables, and the stranger who meant nobody good and was frightened away by Albertha's cursing, and the hissing of the air brakes of the Lexington Avenue bus, and the curtains moving at the open window, and the baby crying on the other side of the wall. I think of that happy grocery store run by boys, and the horse-drawn flower cart that sometimes waited on the corner, and the sound of footsteps in the night, and the sudden no-sound that meant it was snowing, and I think of the unknown man or woman who found the blue duffel bag with the manuscript of my novel in it and took it to the police station, and the musical instrument (not a lute, but that's what the artist must have had in mind, only she no longer bothers to look at objects and draws what she remembers them as being like) played in the dark, over our sleeping bodies, while the children flew their kites, and I think if it is true that we are all in the hands of God, what a capacious hand it must be.

## CHARLES BAXTER on *The Thistles in Sweden*

This wonderful, luminous story practices a harmless deception. It pretends (at first) to be about a couple living in New York City in the early 1950s. Of course, the narrator and his wife inhabit the story; but they are merely two beings in a tale that gradually, by means of an inventory method—naming and describing one by one the objects in a life—envelops the two main characters and enfolds them in a cosmic order.

The domestic details at first seem rather ordinary: tables, chairs, married life, neighbors, a cat. Because these small subjects are greatly beloved, they acquire life, so much so that by the end of the story the bed and the mantelpiece are expressing their own opinions. An inventory in a story can convey bewilderment about what importance anything might have (you make a list when you don't know what else to do), but in William Maxwell's story, the narrator tells us about the particulars of his life almost in the way a survivor of a calamity would set out on a table his most cherished objects, not to display but to bless them by naming them.

The Germans have a phrase—*das Glück im Winkel,* "happiness in a corner"—to refer to the household objects we value and love, the things that make our lives liveable. In this story, we start with the perfection of a city apartment and gradually discover the shadows that cross that perfection: a woman's unhappiness, the couple's childlessness, breakage and loss, cancer, a malevolent intruder, and death. And yet as the shadows darken, the contrasting light becomes stronger. The narrator's love for his world is unshakable, his love so far-seeing, so complete, that his tale can begin with curtains and wallpaper and conclude with the hand of God. The narrative line is constructed to move from small to large, from the life of objects to the life of the spirit, and to conclude with that most mysterious of all conditions, blessedness.

# Herman Melville

*Melville (1819–1891) was born in New York City, the son of a merchant from New England who died when Melville was still young. He took on jobs as clerk, farmhand, and schoolteacher before shipping to the South Seas on the whaler* Acushnet. *In a helter-skelter period of adventure he deserted from his ship, lived among cannibals, took part in a mutiny on an Australian vessel, and then spent almost two years on an American man-of-war returning to his home country. Then he began successfully to romanticize these adventures in fiction. In six years he published seven novels, among them* Moby-Dick *(1851), which is generally regarded as one of the masterworks of American fiction. His popularity was already waning by the time he published this great novel, and it continued to decline until, at his death, he was virtually forgotten. The short stories in* Piazza Tales *(1856) did little to refurbish his reputation. In 1876 he published a long narrative poem,* Clarel, *that received hardly any notice, and his last fictional masterpiece,* Billy Budd, *was not published until 1924, long after his death. As his writing activities declined, Melville made another sea voyage around Cape Horn to San Francisco on a clipper ship commanded by his brother, and for nineteen quiet years he was a customs inspector in New York. It was not until the 1920s that critical interest in his work revived. Since then it has increased in fervor and scope, discovering the richly ambiguous thought structured into his most ambitious work. His novels include* Typee *(1846),* Omoo *(1847),* Mardi *(1849), and* Pierre *(1852).*

## Bartleby, the Scrivener

**A Story of Wall Street**

I am a rather elderly man. The nature of my avocations for the last thirty years has brought me into more than ordinary contact with what would seem an interesting and somewhat singular set of men, of whom as yet nothing that I know of has ever been written:—I mean the law-copyists or scriveners. I have known very many of them, professionally and privately, and if I pleased, could relate divers histories, at which good-natured gentlemen might smile, and sentimental souls might weep. But I waive the biographies of all other scriveners for a few passages in the life of Bartleby, who was a scrivener the strangest I ever saw or heard of. While of other law-copyists I might write the complete life, of Bartleby nothing of that sort can be done. I believe that no materials exist for a full and satisfactory biography of this man. It is an irreparable loss to literature. Bartleby was one of those beings of whom nothing is ascertainable, except from the original sources, and in his case those are very small. What my own astonished eyes saw of Bartleby, *that* is all I know of him, except, indeed, one vague report which will appear in the sequel.

Ere introducing the scrivener, as he first appeared to me, it is fit I make some mention of myself, my *employés*, my business, my chambers, and general surroundings; because some such description is indispensable to an adequate understanding of the chief character about to be presented.

*Imprimis:*[1] I am a man who, from his youth upward, has been filled with a profound conviction that the easiest way of life is the best. Hence, though I belong to a profession proverbially energetic and nervous, even to turbulence, at times, yet nothing of that sort have I ever suffered to invade my peace. I am one of those unambitious lawyers who never addresses a jury, or in any way draws down public applause; but in the cool tranquillity of a snug retreat, do a snug business among rich men's bonds and mortgages and title-deeds. All who know me, consider me an eminently *safe* man. The late John Jacob Astor,[2] a personage little given to poetic enthusiasm, had no hesitation in pronouncing my first grand point to be prudence; my next, method. I do not speak it in vanity, but simply record the fact, that I was notunemployed in my profession by the late John Jacob Astor; a name which, I admit, I love to repeat, for it hath a rounded and orbicular sound to it, and rings like unto bullion. I will freely add, that I was not insensible to the late John Jacob Astor's good opinion.

Some time prior to the period at which this little history begins, my avocations had been largely increased. The good old office, now extinct in the State of New-York, of a Master in Chancery,[3] had been conferred upon me. It was not a very arduous office, but very pleasantly remunerative. I seldom lose my temper; much more seldom indulge in dangerous indignation at wrongs and outrages; but I must be permitted to be rash here and declare, that I consider the sudden and violent abrogation of the office of Master in Chancery, by the new Constitution, as a —— premature act; inasmuch as I had counted upon a life-lease of the profits, whereas I only received those of a few short years. But this is by the way.

My chambers were upstairs at No. —— Wall-street. At one end they looked upon the white wall of the interior of a spacious skylight shaft, penetrating the building from top to bottom. This view might have been considered rather tame than otherwise, deficient in what landscape painters call "life." But if so, the view from the other end of my chambers offered, at least, a contrast, if nothing more. In that direction my windows commanded an unobstructed view of a lofty brick wall, black by age and everlasting shade; which wall required no spy-glass to bring out its lurking beauties, but for the benefit of all near-sighted spectators, was pushed up to within ten feet of my window panes. Owing to the great height of the surrounding buildings, and my chambers being on the second floor, the interval between this wall and mine not a little resembled a huge square cistern.

1. In the first place (Latin). 2. American landowner (1763–1848), capitalist, and fur merchant. His name signified great wealth. 3. The duty of this office was to temper the rigidity of the law with "dictates of conscience."

At the period just preceding the advent of Bartleby, I had two persons as copyists in my employment, and a promising lad as an office-boy. First, Turkey; second, Nippers; third, Ginger Nut. These may seem names, the like of which are not usually found in the Directory.[4] In truth they were nicknames, mutually conferred upon each other by my three clerks, and were deemed expressive of their respective persons or characters. Turkey was a short, pursy Englishman of about my own age, that is, somewhere not far from sixty. In the morning, one might say, his face was of a fine florid hue, but after twelve o'clock, meridian—his dinner hour—it blazed like a grate full of Christmas coals; and continued blazing—but, as it were, with a gradual wane—till 6 o'clock P.M. or thereabouts, after which I saw no more of the proprietor of the face, which, gaining its meridian with the sun, seemed to set with it, to rise, culminate, and decline the following day, with the like regularity and undiminished glory. There are many singular coincidences I have known in the course of my life, not the least among which was the fact, that exactly when Turkey displayed his fullest beams from his red and radiant countenance, just then, too, at that critical moment, began the daily period when I considered his business capacities as seriously disturbed for the remainder of the twenty-four hours. Not that he was absolutely idle, or averse to business then; far from it. The difficulty was, he was apt to be altogether too energetic. There was a strange, inflamed, flurried, flighty recklessness of activity about him. He would be incautious in dipping his pen into his inkstand. All his blots upon my documents, were dropped there after twelve o'clock, meridian. Indeed, not only would he be reckless and sadly given to making blots in the afternoon, but some days he went further, and was rather noisy. At such times, too, his face flamed with augmented blazonry, as if cannel coal had been heaped on anthracite.[5] He made an unpleasant racket with his chair; spilled his sand-box;[6] in mending his pens, impatiently split them all to pieces, and threw them on the floor in a sudden passion; stood up and leaned over his table, boxing his papers about in a most indecorous manner, very sad to behold in an elderly man like him. Nevertheless, as he was in many ways a most valuable person to me, and all the time before twelve o'clock, meridian, was the quickest, steadiest creature, too, accomplishing a great deal of work in a style not easy to be matched—for these reasons, I was willing to overlook his eccentricities, though indeed, occasionally, I remonstrated with him. I did this very gently, however, because, though the civilest, nay, the blandest and most reverential of men in the morning, yet in the afternoon he was disposed, upon provocation, to be slightly rash with his tongue, in fact, insolent. Now, valuing his morning services as I did, and resolved not to lose them—yet, at the same time made uncomfortable by his inflamed ways after twelve o'clock; and being a man of peace, unwilling by my admonitions to call forth unseemly retorts from him—I took upon me, one Saturday noon (he was always worse on Saturdays), to hint to him, very kindly, that perhaps now that he was growing old, it might be well to abridge his labors; in short, he need not come to my chambers after twelve o'clock, but, dinner

4. Post Office directory. 5. Oily, quick-burning coal heaped on slower burning kind. 6. I.e., sand used to dry ink.

over, had best go home to his lodgings and rest himself till tea-time. But no; he insisted upon his afternoon devotions. His countenance became intolerably fervid, as he oratorically assured me—gesticulating with a long ruler at the other end of the room—that if his services in the morning were useful, how indispensable, then, in the afternoon?

"With submission, sir," said Turkey on this occasion, "I consider myself your right-hand man. In the morning I but marshal and deploy my columns; but in the afternoon I put myself at their head, and gallantly charge the foe, thus!"—and he made a violent thrust with the ruler.

"But the blots, Turkey," intimated I.

"True,—but, with submission, sir, behold these hairs! I am getting old. Surely, sir, a blot or two of a warm afternoon is not to be severely urged against gray hairs. Old age—even if it blot the page—is honorable. With submission, sir, we *both* are getting old."

This appeal to my fellow-feeling was hardly to be resisted. At all events, I saw that go he would not. So I made up my mind to let him stay, resolving, nevertheless, to see to it, that during the afternoon he had to do with my less important papers.

Nippers, the second on my list, was a whiskered, sallow, and, upon the whole, rather piratical-looking young man of about five and twenty. I always deemed him the victim of two evil powers—ambition and indigestion. The ambition was evinced by a certain impatience of the duties of a mere copyist—an unwarrantable usurpation of strictly professional affairs, such as the original drawing up of legal documents. The indigestion seemed betokened in an occasional nervous testiness and grinning irritability, causing the teeth to audibly grind together over mistakes committed in copying; unnecessary maledictions, hissed, rather than spoken, in the heat of business; and especially by a continual discontent with the height of the table where he worked. Though of a very ingenious mechanical turn, Nippers could never get this table to suit him. He put chips under it, blocks of various sorts, bits of pasteboard, and at last went so far as to attempt an exquisite adjustment by final pieces of folded blotting-paper. But no invention would answer. If, for the sake of easing his back, he brought the table lid at a sharp angle well up towards his chin, and wrote there like a man using the steep roof of a Dutch house for his desk—then he declared that it stopped the circulation in his arms. If now he lowered the table to his waistbands, and stooped over it in writing, then there was a sore aching in his back. In short, the truth of the matter was, Nippers knew not what he wanted. Or, if he wanted anything, it was to be rid of a scrivener's table altogether. Among the manifestations of his diseased ambition was a fondness he had for receiving visits from certain ambiguous-looking fellows in seedy coats, whom he called his clients. Indeed I was aware that not only was he, at times, considerable of a ward-politician, but he occasionally did a little business at the Justices' courts, and was not unknown on the steps of the Tombs.[7] I have good

7. The Manhattan House of Detention is often called "the Tombs" because of its distinctive Egyptian architecture. As "ward-politician" Nippers was a fixer who seems to have made extralegal arrangements for constituents of his district of the city when they had legal problems.

reason to believe, however, that one individual who called upon him at my chambers, and who, with a grand air, he insisted was his client, was no other than a dun,[8] and the alleged title-deed, a bill. But with all his failings, and the annoyances he caused me, Nippers, like his compatriot Turkey, was a very useful man to me; wrote a neat, swift hand; and, when he chose, was not deficient in a gentlemanly sort of deportment. Added to this, he always dressed in a gentlemanly sort of way; and so, incidentally, reflected credit upon my chambers. Whereas with respect to Turkey, I had much ado to keep him from being a reproach to me. His clothes were apt to look oily and smell of eating-houses. He wore his pantaloons very loose and baggy in summer. His coats were execrable; his hat not to be handled. But while the hat was a thing of indifference to me, inasmuch as his natural civility and deference, as a dependent Englishman, always led him to doff it the moment he entered the room, yet his coat was another matter. Concerning his coats, I reasoned with him; but with no effect. The truth was, I suppose, that a man with so small an income, could not afford to sport such a lustrous face and a lustrous coat at one and the same time. As Nippers once observed, Turkey's money went chiefly for red ink. One winter day I presented Turkey with a highly-respectable looking coat of my own, a padded gray coat, of a most comfortable warmth, and which buttoned straight up from the knee to the neck. I thought Turkey would appreciate the favour, and abate his rashness and obstreperousness of afternoons. But no. I verily believe that buttoning himself up in so downy and blanket-like a coat had a pernicious effect upon him; upon the same principle that too much oats are bad for horses. In fact, precisely as a rash, restive horse is said to feel his oats, so Turkey felt his coat. It made him insolent. He was a man whom prosperity harmed.

Though concerning the self-indulgent habits of Turkey I had my own private surmises, yet touching Nippers I was well persuaded that whatever might be his faults in other respects, he was, at least, a temperate young man. But, indeed, nature herself seemed to have been his vintner, and at his birth charged him so thoroughly with an irritable, brandy-like disposition, that all subsequent potations were needless. When I consider how, amid the stillness of my chambers, Nippers would sometimes impatiently rise from his seat, and stooping over his table, spread his arms wide apart, seize the whole desk, and move it, and jerk it, with a grim, grinding motion on the floor, as if the table were a perverse voluntary agent, intent on thwarting and vexing him; I plainly perceive that for Nippers, brandy and water were altogether superfluous.

It was fortunate for me that, owing to its peculiar cause—indigestion—the irritability and consequent nervousness of Nippers, were mainly observable in the morning, while in the afternoon he was comparatively mild. So that Turkey's paroxysms only coming on about twelve o'clock, I never had to do with their eccentricities at one time. Their fits relieved each other like guards. When Nippers' was on, Turkey's was off; and *vice versa*. This was a good natural arrangement under the circumstances.

Ginger Nut, the third on my list, was a lad some twelve years old. His

8. Bill-collector.

father was a carman,[9] ambitious of seeing his son on the bench instead of a cart, before he died. So he sent him to my office as student at law, errand boy, and cleaner and sweeper, at the rate of one dollar a week. He had a little desk to himself, but he did not use it much. Upon inspection, the drawer exhibited a great array of the shells of various sorts of nuts. Indeed, to this quick-witted youth the whole noble science of the law was contained in a nut-shell. Not the least among the employments of Ginger Nut, as well as one which he discharged with the most alacrity, was his duty as cake and apple purveyor for Turkey and Nippers. Copying law papers being proverbially a dry, husky sort of business, my two scriveners were fain to moisten their mouths very often with Spitzenbergs[1] to be had at the numerous stalls nigh the Custom House and Post Office. Also, they sent Ginger Nut very frequently for that peculiar cake—small, flat, round, and very spicy—after which he had been named by them. Of a cold morning when business was but dull, Turkey would gobble up scores of these cakes, as if they were mere wafers—indeed they sell them at the rate of six or eight for a penny—the scrape of his pen blending with the crunching of the crisp particles in his mouth. Of all the fiery afternoon blunders and flurried rashnesses of Turkey, was his once moistening a ginger-cake between his lips, and clapping it on to a mortgage for a seal. I came within an ace of dismissing him then. But he mollified me by making an oriental bow, and saying—"With submission, sir, it was generous of me to find[2] you in stationery on my own account."

Now my original business—that of a conveyancer and title hunter,[3] and drawer-up of recondite documents of all sorts—was considerably increased by receiving the master's office. There was now great work for scriveners. Not only must I push the clerks already with me, but I must have additional help. In answer to my advertisement, a motionless young man one morning stood upon my office threshold, the door being open, for it was summer. I can see that figure now—pallidly neat, pitiably respectable, incurably forlorn! It was Bartleby.

After a few words touching his qualifications, I engaged him, glad to have among my corps of copyists a man of so singularly sedate an aspect, which I thought might operate beneficially upon the flighty temper of Turkey, and the fiery one of Nippers.

I should have stated before that ground glass folding-doors divided my premises into two parts, one of which was occupied by my scriveners, the other by myself. According to my humour I threw open these doors, or closed them. I resolved to assign Bartleby a corner by the folding-doors, but on my side of them, so as to have this quiet man within easy call, in case any trifling thing was to be done. I placed his desk close up to a small side-window in that part of the room, a window which originally had afforded a lateral view of certain grimy back-yards and bricks, but which, owing to subsequent erections, commanded at present no view at all, though it gave some light. Within three feet of the panes was a wall, and the light came down from far above, between two

9. Driver of a cart. 1. Apples. 2. "To provide you with." 3. I.e., examining the abstract of property deeds. A conveyance is a legal paper for transferring property.

lofty buildings, as from a very small opening in a dome. Still further to a satisfactory arrangement, I procured a high green folding screen, which might entirely isolate Bartleby from my sight, though not remove him from my voice. And thus, in a manner, privacy and society were conjoined.

At first Bartleby did an extraordinary quantity of writing. As if long famishing for something to copy, he seemed to gorge himself on my documents. There was no pause for digestion. He ran a day and night line, copying by sunlight and by candle-light. I should have been quite delighted with his application, had he been cheerfully industrious. But he wrote on silently, palely, mechanically.

It is, of course, an indispensable part of a scrivener's business to verify the accuracy of his copy, word by word. Where there are two or more scriveners in an office, they assist each other in this examination, one reading from the copy, the other holding the original. It is a very dull, wearisome, and lethargic affair. I can readily imagine that to some sanguine temperaments it would be altogether intolerable. For example, I cannot credit that the mettlesome poet Byron would have contentedly sat down with Bartleby to examine a law document of, say five hundred pages, closely written in a crimpy hand.

Now and then, in the haste of business, it had been my habit to assist in comparing some brief document myself, calling Turkey or Nippers for this purpose. One object I had in placing Bartleby so handy to me behind the screen, was to avail myself of his services on such trivial occasions. It was on the third day, I think, of his being with me, and before any necessity had arisen for having his own writing examined, that, being much hurried to complete a small affair I had in hand, I abruptly called to Bartleby. In my haste and natural expectancy of instant compliance, I sat with my head bent over the original on my desk, and my right hand sideways, and somewhat nervously extended with the copy, so that immediately upon emerging from his retreat, Bartleby might snatch it and proceed to business without the least delay.

In this very attitude did I sit when I called to him, rapidly stating what it was I wanted him to do—namely, to examine a small paper with me. Imagine my surprise, nay, my consternation, when without moving from his privacy, Bartleby in a singularly mild, firm voice, replied, "I would prefer not to."

I sat awhile in perfect silence, rallying my stunned faculties. Immediately it occurred to me that my ears had deceived me, or Bartleby had entirely misunderstood my meaning. I repeated my request in the clearest tone I could assume. But in quite as clear a one came the previous reply, "I would prefer not to."

"Prefer not to," echoed I, rising in high excitement, and crossing the room with a stride. "What do you mean? Are you moon-struck?[4] I want you to help me compare this sheet here—take it," and I thrust it toward him.

"I would prefer not to," said he.

I looked at him steadfastly. His face was leanly composed; his gray eye dimly calm. Not a wrinkle of agitation rippled him. Had there been the least

4. This popular synonym for *crazy* incorporates the old belief that the lunatic was affected by phases of the moon (Latin: *luna*).

uneasiness, anger, impatience or impertinence in his manner; in other words, had there been anything ordinarily human about him, doubtless I should have violently dismissed him from the premises. But as it was, I should have as soon thought of turning my pale plaster-of-paris bust of Cicero out of doors. I stood gazing at him awhile, as he went on with his own writing, and then reseated myself at my desk. This is very strange, thought I. What had one best do? But my business hurried me. I concluded to forget the matter for the present, reserving it for my future leisure. So calling Nippers from the other room, the paper was speedily examined.

A few days after this, Bartleby concluded four lengthy documents, being quadruplicates of a week's testimony taken before me in my High Court of Chancery. It became necessary to examine them. It was an important suit, and great accuracy was imperative. Having all things arranged, I called Turkey, Nippers and Ginger Nut from the next room, meaning to place the four copies in the hands of my four clerks, while I should read from the original. Accordingly Turkey, Nippers and Ginger Nut had taken their seats in a row, each with his document in hand, when I called to Bartleby to join this interesting group.

"Bartleby! quick, I am waiting."

I heard a slow scrape of his chair legs on the uncarpeted floor, and soon he appeared standing at the entrance of his hermitage.

"What is wanted?" said he mildly.

"The copies, the copies," said I hurriedly. "We are going to examine them. There"—and I held towards him the fourth quadruplicate.

"I would prefer not to," he said, and gently disappeared behind the screen.

For a few moments I was turned into a pillar of salt,[5] standing at the head of my seated column of clerks. Recovering myself, I advanced toward the screen, and demanded the reason for such extraordinary conduct.

"*Why* do you refuse?"

"I would prefer not to."

With any other man I should have flown outright into a dreadful passion, scorned all further words, and thrust him ignominiously from my presence. But there was something about Bartleby that not only strangely disarmed me, but in a wonderful manner touched and disconcerted me. I began to reason with him.

"These are your own copies we are about to examine. It is labour saving to you, because one examination will answer for your four papers. It is common usage. Every copyist is bound to help examine his copy. Is it not so? Will you not speak? Answer!"

"I prefer not to," he replied in a flute-like tone. It seemed to me that while I had been addressing him, he carefully revolved every statement that I made; fully comprehended the meaning; could not gainsay the irresistible conclusion; but, at the same time, some paramount consideration prevailed with him to reply as he did.

5. I.e., was paralyzed. The allusion is to Genesis 19.26; Lot's wife is turned into a pillar of salt when she looks back at the destruction of Sodom.

"You are decided, then, not to comply with my request—a request made according to common usage and common sense?"

He briefly gave me to understand that on that point my judgment was sound. Yes: his decision was irreversible.

It is not seldom the case that when a man is browbeaten in some unprecedented and violently unreasonable way, he begins to stagger in his own plainest faith. He begins, as it were, vaguely to surmise that, wonderful as it may be, all the justice and all the reason are on the other side. Accordingly, if any disinterested persons are present, he turns to them for some reinforcement for his own faltering mind.

"Turkey," said I, "what do you think of this? Am I not right?"

"With submission, sir," said Turkey, with his blandest tone, "I think that you are."

"Nippers," said I, "what do *you* think of it?"

"I think I should kick him out of the office."

(The reader of nice perceptions will here perceive that, it being morning, Turkey's answer is couched in polite and tranquil terms, but Nippers's reply in ill-tempered ones. Or, to repeat a previous sentence, Nippers's ugly mood was on duty, and Turkey's off.)

"Ginger Nut," said I, willing to enlist the smallest suffrage in my behalf, "what do *you* think of it?"

"I think, sir, he's a little *luny*,"[6] replied Ginger Nut, with a grin.

"You hear what they say," said I, turning towards the screen, "come forth and do your duty."

But he vouchsafed no reply. I pondered a moment in sore perplexity. But once more business hurried me. I determined again to postpone the consideration of this dilemma to my future leisure. With a little trouble we made out to examine the papers without Bartleby, though at every page or two, Turkey deferentially dropped his opinion that this proceeding was quite out of the common; while Nippers, twitching in his chair with a dyspeptic nervousness, ground out between his set teeth occasional hissing maledictions against the stubborn oaf behind the screen. And for his (Nippers's) part, this was the first and the last time he would do another man's business without pay.

Meanwhile Bartleby sat in his hermitage, oblivious to everything but his own peculiar business there.

Some days passed, the scrivener being employed upon another lengthy work. His late remarkable conduct led me to regard his ways narrowly. I observed that he never went to dinner; indeed that he never went any where. As yet I had never of my personal knowledge known him to be outside of my office. He was a perpetual sentry in the corner. At about eleven o'clock though, in the morning, I noticed that Ginger Nut would advance toward the opening in Bartleby's screen, as if silently beckoned thither by a gesture invisible to me where I sat. The boy would then leave the office jingling a few pence, and reappear with a handful of ginger-nuts which he delivered in the hermitage, receiving two of the cakes for his trouble.

6. Loony—here Melville's spelling recalls the word *lunatic*.

He lives, then, on ginger-nuts, thought I; never eats a dinner, properly speaking; he must be a vegetarian then; but no; he never eats even vegetables, he eats nothing but ginger-nuts. My mind then ran on in reveries concerning the probable effects upon the human constitution of living entirely on ginger-nuts. Ginger-nuts are so called because they contain ginger as one of their peculiar constituents, and the final flavoring one. Now what was ginger? A hot, spicy thing. Was Bartleby hot and spicy? Not at all. Ginger, then, had no effect upon Bartleby. Probably he preferred it should have none.

Nothing so aggravates an earnest person as a passive resistance. If the individual so resisted be of a not inhumane temper, and the resisting one perfectly harmless in his passivity; then, in the better moods of the former, he will endeavor charitably to construe to his imagination what proves impossible to be solved by his judgment. Even so, for the most part, I regarded Bartleby and his ways. Poor fellow! thought I, he means no mischief; it is plain he intends no insolence; his aspect sufficiently evinces that his eccentricities are involuntary. He is useful to me. I can get along with him. If I turn him away, the chances are he will fall in with some less indulgent employer, and then he will be rudely treated, and perhaps driven forth miserably to starve. Yes. Here I can cheaply purchase a delicious self-approval. To befriend Bartleby; to humour him in his strange wilfulness, will cost me little or nothing, while I lay up in my soul what will eventually prove a sweet morsel for my conscience. But this mood was not invariable with me. The passiveness of Bartleby sometimes irritated me. I felt strangely goaded on to encounter him in new opposition, to elicit some angry spark from him answerable to my own. But indeed I might as well have essayed to strike fire with my knuckles against a bit of Windsor soap. But one afternoon the evil impulse in me mastered me, and the following little scene ensued:

"Bartleby," said I, "when those papers are all copied, I will compare them with you."

"I would prefer not to."

"How? Surely you do not mean to persist in that mulish vagary?"

No answer.

I threw open the folding-doors near by, and turning upon Turkey and Nippers, exclaimed in an excited manner:

"He says, a second time, he won't examine his papers. What do you think of it, Turkey?"

It was afternoon, be it remembered. Turkey sat glowing like a brass boiler, his bald head steaming, his hands reeling among his blotted papers.

"Think of it?" roared Turkey; "I think I'll just step behind his screen, and black his eyes for him!"

So saying, Turkey rose to his feet and threw his arms into a pugilistic position. He was hurrying away to make good his promise, when I detained him, alarmed at the effect of incautiously rousing Turkey's combativeness after dinner.

"Sit down, Turkey," said I, "and hear what Nippers has to say. What do you think of it, Nippers? Would I not be justified in immediately dismissing Bartleby?"

"Excuse me, that is for you to decide, sir. I think his conduct quite unusual, and indeed unjust, as regards Turkey and myself. But it may only be a passing whim."

"Ah," exclaimed I, "You have strangely changed your mind then—you speak very gently of him now."

"All beer," cried Turkey; "gentleness is effects of beer—Nippers and I dined together to-day. You see how gentle *I* am, sir. Shall I go and black his eyes?"

"You refer to Bartleby, I suppose. No, not to-day, Turkey," I replied; "pray, put up your fists."

I closed the doors, and again advanced towards Bartleby. I felt additional incentives tempting me to my fate. I burned to be rebelled against again. I remembered that Bartleby never left the office.

"Bartleby," said I, "Ginger Nut is away; just step round to the Post Office, won't you? (it was but a three minutes' walk), and see if there is any thing for me."

"I would prefer not to."

"You *will* not?"

"I *prefer* not."

I staggered to my desk, and sat there in a deep study. My blind inveteracy returned. Was there any other thing in which I could procure myself to be ignominiously repulsed by this lean, penniless wight?—my hired clerk? What added thing is there, perfectly reasonable, that he will be sure to refuse to do?

"Bartleby!"

No answer.

"Bartleby," in a louder tone.

No answer.

"Bartleby," I roared.

Like a very ghost, agreeably to the laws of magical invocation, at the third summons, he appeared at the entrance of his hermitage.

"Go to the next room, and tell Nippers to come to me."

"I prefer not to," he respectfully and slowly said, and mildly disappeared.

"Very good, Bartleby," said I, in a quiet sort of serenely severe self-possessed tone, intimating the unalterable purpose of some terrible retribution very close at hand. At the moment I half intended something of the kind. But upon the whole, as it was drawing towards my dinner-hour, I thought it best to put on my hat and walk home for the day, suffering much from perplexity and distress of mind.

Shall I acknowledge it? The conclusion of this whole business was, that it soon became a fixed fact of my chambers, that a pale young scrivener, by the name of Bartleby, had a desk there; that he copied for me at the usual rate of four cents a folio (one hundred words); but he was permanently exempt from examining the work done by him, that duty being transferred to Turkey and Nippers, out of compliment doubtless to their superior acuteness; moreover, said Bartleby was never on any account to be despatched on the most trivial errand of any sort; and that even if entreated to take upon him such a matter, it was generally understood that he would prefer not to—in other words, that he would refuse point-blank.

As days passed on, I became considerably reconciled to Bartleby. His steadiness, his freedom from all dissipation, his incessant industry (except when he chose to throw himself into a standing revery behind his screen), his great stillness, his unalterableness of demeanor under all circumstances, made him a valuable acquisition. One prime thing was this,—*he was always there;*—first in the morning, continually through the day, and the last at night. I had a singular confidence in his honesty. I felt my most precious papers perfectly safe in his hands. Sometimes to be sure I could not, for the very soul of me, avoid falling into sudden spasmodic passions with him. For it was exceeding difficult to bear in mind all the time those strange peculiarities, privileges, and unheard of exemptions, forming the tacit stipulations on Bartleby's part under which he remained in my office. Now and then, in the eagerness of despatching pressing business, I would inadvertently summon Bartleby, in a short, rapid tone, to put his finger, say, on the incipient tie of a bit of red tape with which I was about compressing some papers. Of course, from behind the screen the usual answer, "I prefer not to," was sure to come; and then, how could a human creature with common infirmities of our nature, refrain from bitterly exclaiming upon such perverseness—such unreasonableness. However, every added repulse of this sort which I received only tended to lessen the probability of my repeating the inadvertence.

Here it must be said, that according to the customs of most legal gentlemen occupying chambers in densely-populated law buildings, there were several keys to my door. One was kept by a woman residing in the attic, which person weekly scrubbed and daily swept and dusted my apartments. Another was kept by Turkey for convenience sake. The third I sometimes carried in my own pocket. The fourth I knew not who had.

Now, one Sunday morning I happened to go to Trinity Church,[7] to hear a celebrated preacher, and finding myself rather early on the ground, I thought I would walk round to my chambers for awhile. Luckily I had my key with me; but upon applying it to the lock, I found it resisted by something inserted from the inside. Quite surprised, I called out; when to my consternation a key was turned from within; and thrusting his lean visage at me, and holding the door ajar, the apparition of Bartleby appeared, in his shirt sleeves, and otherwise in a strangely tattered dishabille, saying quietly that he was sorry, but he was deeply engaged just then, and—preferred not admitting me at present. In a brief word or two, he moreover added, that perhaps I had better walk round the block two or three times, and by that time he would probably have concluded his affairs.

Now, the utterly unsurmised appearance of Bartleby, tenanting my law-chambers of a Sunday morning, with his cadaverously gentlemanly *nonchalance*, yet withal firm and self-possessed, had such a strange effect upon me, that incontinently I slunk away from my own door, and did as desired. But not

7. Venerable church in the Wall Street district.

without sundry twinges of impotent rebellion against the mild effrontery of this unaccountable scrivener. Indeed, it was his wonderful mildness chiefly, which not only disarmed me, but unmanned me, as it were. For I consider that one, for the time, is in a way unmanned when he tranquilly permits his hired clerk to dictate to him, and order him away from his own premises. Furthermore, I was full of uneasiness as to what Bartleby could possibly be doing in my office in his shirt sleeves, and in an otherwise dismantled condition of a Sunday morning. Was any thing amiss going on? Nay, that was out of the question. It was not to be thought of for a moment that Bartleby was an immoral person. But what could he be doing there—copying? Nay again, whatever might be his eccentricities, Bartleby was an eminently decorous person. He would be the last man to sit down to his desk in any state approaching to nudity. Besides, it was Sunday; and there was something about Bartleby that forbade the supposition that he would by any secular occupation violate the proprieties of the day.

Nevertheless, my mind was not pacified; and full of a restless curiosity, at last I returned to the door. Without hindrance I inserted my key, opened it, and entered. Bartleby was not to be seen. I looked round anxiously, peeped behind his screen; but it was very plain that he was gone. Upon more closely examining the place, I surmised that for an indefinite period Bartleby must have ate, dressed, and slept in my office, and that too without plate, mirror, or bed. The cushioned seat of a ricketty old sofa in one corner bore the faint impress of a lean, reclining form. Rolled away under his desk, I found a blanket; under the empty grate, a blacking box[8] and brush; on a chair, a tin basin, with soap and a ragged towel; in a newspaper a few crumbs of ginger-nuts and a morsel of cheese. Yes, thought I, it is evident enough that Bartleby has been making his home here, keeping bachelor's hall all by himself. Immediately then the thought came sweeping across me, What miserable friendlessness and loneliness are here revealed! His poverty is great; but his solitude, how horrible! Think of it. Of a Sunday, Wall street is deserted as Petra;[9] and every night of every day it is an emptiness. This building too, which of week-days hums with industry and life, at nightfall echoes with sheer vacancy, and all through Sunday is forlorn. And here Bartleby makes his home; sole spectator of a solitude which he has seen all populous—a sort of innocent and transformed Marius brooding among the ruins of Carthage![1]

For the first time in my life a feeling of overpowering stinging melancholy seized me. Before, I had never experienced aught but a not-unpleasing sadness. The bond of a common humanity now drew me irresistibly to gloom. A fraternal melancholy! For both I and Bartleby were sons of Adam. I remembered the bright silks and sparkling faces I had seen that day, in gala trim, swan-like sailing down the Mississippi of Broadway; and I contrasted them with the pallid copyist, and thought to myself, Ah, happiness courts the light, so we deem the world is gay; but misery hides aloof, so we deem that misery there is none. These sad fancyings—chimeras, doubtless, of a sick and silly brain—led on to

8. Box of shoe polish. 9. Long-ruined and deserted Middle Eastern city. 1. Roman consul and general expelled from Rome and seeking sanctuary in the city Rome had destroyed; i.e., a ruined man in a ruined city.

other and more special thoughts, concerning the eccentricities of Bartleby. Presentiments of strange discoveries hovered round me. The scrivener's pale form appeared to me laid out, among uncaring strangers, in its shivering winding sheet.

Suddenly I was attracted by Bartleby's closed desk, the key in open sight left in the lock.

I mean no mischief, seek the gratification of no heartless curiosity, thought I; besides, the desk is mine, and its contents too, so I will make bold to look within. Everything was methodically arranged, the papers smoothly placed. The pigeon holes were deep, and, removing the files of documents, I groped into their recesses. Presently I felt something there, and dragged it out. It was an old bandanna handkerchief, heavy and knotted. I opened it, and saw it was a savings' bank.

I now recalled all the quiet mysteries which I had noted in the man. I remembered that he never spoke but to answer; that though at intervals he had considerable time to himself, yet I had never seen him reading—no, not even a newspaper; that for long periods he would stand looking out, at his pale window behind the screen, upon the dead brick wall; I was quite sure he never visited any refectory or eating-house; while his pale face clearly indicated that he never drank beer like Turkey, or tea and coffee even, like other men; that he never went anywhere in particular that I could learn; never went out for a walk, unless indeed that was the case at present; that he had declined telling who he was, or whence he came, or whether he had any relatives in the world; that though so thin and pale, he never complained of ill health. And more than all, I remembered a certain unconscious air of pallid—how shall I call it?—of pallid haughtiness, say, or rather an austere reserve about him, which had positively awed me into my tame compliance with his eccentricities, when I had feared to ask him to do the slightest incidental thing for me, even though I might know, from his long-continued motionlessness, that behind his screen he must be standing in one of those dead-wall reveries of his.

Revolving all these things, and coupling them with the recently discovered fact that he made my office his constant abiding place and home, and not forgetful of his morbid moodiness; revolving all these things, a prudential feeling began to steal over me. My first emotions had been those of pure melancholy and sincerest pity; but just in proportion as the forlornness of Bartleby grew and grew to my imagination, did that same melancholy merge into fear, that pity into repulsion. So true it is, and so terrible too, that up to a certain point the thought or sight of misery enlists our best affections; but, in certain special cases, beyond that point it does not. They err who would assert that invariably this is owing to the inherent selfishness of the human heart. It rather proceeds from a certain hopelessness of remedying excessive and organic ill. To a sensitive being, pity is not seldom pain. And when at last it is perceived that such pity cannot lead to effectual succor, common sense bids the soul be rid of it. What I saw that morning persuaded me that the scrivener was the victim of innate and incurable disorder. I might give alms to his body; but his body did not pain him; it was his soul that suffered, and his soul I could not reach.

I did not accomplish the purpose of going to Trinity Church that morning. Somehow, the things I had seen disqualified me for the time from church-going. I walked homeward, thinking what I would do with Bartleby. Finally, I resolved upon this:—I would put certain calm questions to him the next morning, touching his history, &c., and if he declined to answer them openly and unreservedly (and I supposed he would prefer not), then to give him a twenty dollar bill over and above whatever I might owe him, and tell him his services were no longer required; but that if in any other way I could assist him, I would be happy to do so, especially if he desired to return to his native place, wherever that might be, I would willingly help to defray the expenses. Moreover, if, after reaching home, he found himself at any time in want of aid, a letter from him would be sure of a reply.

The next morning came.

"Bartleby," said I, gently calling to him behind his screen.

No reply.

"Bartleby," said I, in a still gentler tone, "come here; I am not going to ask you to do anything you would prefer not to do—I simply wish to speak to you."

Upon this he noiselessly slid into view.

"Will you tell me, Bartleby, where you were born?"

"I would prefer not to."

"Will you tell me *anything* about yourself?"

"I would prefer not to."

"But what reasonable objection can you have to speak to me? I feel friendly towards you."

He did not look at me while I spoke, but kept his glance fixed upon my bust of Cicero, which, as I then sat, was directly behind me, some six inches above my head.

"What is your answer, Bartleby?" said I, after waiting a considerable time for a reply, during which his countenance remained immovable, only there was the faintest conceivable tremor of the white attenuated mouth.

"At present I prefer to give no answer," he said, and retired into his hermitage.

It was rather weak in me I confess, but his manner on this occasion nettled me. Not only did there seem to lurk in it a certain calm disdain, but his perverseness seemed ungrateful, considering the undeniable good usage and indulgence he had received from me.

Again I sat ruminating what I should do. Mortified as I was at his behavior, and resolved as I had been to dismiss him when I entered my office, nevertheless I strangely felt something superstitious knocking at my heart, and forbidding me to carry out my purpose, and denouncing me for a villain if I dared to breathe one bitter word against this forlornest of mankind. At last, familiarly drawing my chair behind his screen, I sat down and said: "Bartleby, never mind then about revealing your history; but let me entreat you, as a friend, to comply as far as may be with the usages of this office. Say now you will help to examine papers to-morrow or next day: in short, say now that in a day or two you will begin to be a little reasonable:—say so, Bartleby."

"At present I would prefer not to be a little reasonable," was his mildly cadaverous reply.

Just then the folding-doors opened, and Nippers approached. He seemed suffering from an unusually bad night's rest, induced by severer indigestion than common. He overheard those final words of Bartleby.

"*Prefer not,* eh?" gritted Nippers—"I'd *prefer* him, if I were you, sir," addressing me—"I'd *prefer* him; I'd give him preferences, the stubborn mule! What is it, sir, pray, that he *prefers* not to do now?"

Bartleby moved not a limb.

"Mr. Nippers," said I, "I'd prefer that you would withdraw for the present."

Somehow, of late I had got into the way of involuntarily using this word "prefer" upon all sorts of not exactly suitable occasions. And I trembled to think that my contact with the scrivener had already and seriously affected me in a mental way. And what further and deeper aberration might it not yet produce? This apprehension had not been without efficacy in determining me to summary means.

As Nippers, looking very sour and sulky, was departing, Turkey blandly and deferentially approached.

"With submission, sir," said he, "yesterday I was thinking about Bartleby here, and I think that if he would but prefer to take a quart of good ale every day, it would do much towards mending him, and enabling him to assist in examining his papers."

"So you have got the word too," said I, slightly excited.

"With submission, what word, sir," asked Turkey, respectfully crowding himself into the contracted space behind the screen, and by so doing, making me jostle the scrivener. "What word, sir?"

"I would prefer to be left alone here," said Bartleby, as if offended at being mobbed in his privacy.

"*That's* the word, Turkey," said I—"*that's* it."

"Oh, *prefer*? oh, yes—queer word. I never use it myself. But, sir, as I was saying, if he would but prefer—"

"Turkey," interrupted I, "you will please withdraw."

"Oh certainly, sir, if you prefer that I should."

As he opened the folding-door to retire, Nippers at his desk caught a glimpse of me, and asked whether I would prefer to have a certain paper copied on blue paper or white. He did not in the least roguishly accent the word prefer. It was plain that it involuntarily rolled from his tongue. I thought to myself, surely I must get rid of a demented man, who already has in some degree turned the tongues, if not the heads, of myself and clerks. But I thought it prudent not to break the dismission at once.

The next day I noticed that Bartleby did nothing but stand at his window in his dead-wall revery. Upon asking him why he did not write, he said that he had decided upon doing no more writing.

"Why, how now? what next?" exclaimed I, "do no more writing?"

"No more."

"And what is the reason?"

"Do you not see the reason for yourself," he indifferently replied.

I looked steadfastly at him, and perceived that his eyes looked dull and glazed. Instantly it occurred to me, that his unexampled diligence in copying by his dim window for the first few weeks of his stay with me might have temporarily impaired his vision.

I was touched. I said something in condolence with him. I hinted that of course he did wisely in abstaining from writing for a while, and urged him to embrace that opportunity of taking wholesome exercise in the open air. This, however, he did not do. A few days after this, my other clerks being absent, and being in a great hurry to dispatch certain letters by the mail, I thought that, having nothing else earthly to do, Bartleby would surely be less inflexible than usual, and carry these letters to the Post Office. But he blankly declined. So, much to my inconvenience, I went myself.

Still added days went by. Whether Bartleby's eyes improved or not, I could not say. To all appearance, I thought they did. But when I asked him if they did, he vouchsafed no answer. At all events, he would do no copying. At last, in reply to my urgings, he informed me that he had permanently given up copying.

"What!" exclaimed I; "suppose your eyes should get entirely well—better than ever before—would you not copy then?"

"I have given up copying," he answered and slid aside.

He remained as ever, a fixture in my chamber. Nay—if that were possible—he became still more of a fixture than before. What was to be done? He would do nothing in the office: why should he stay there? In plain fact, he had now become a millstone[2] to me, not only useless as a necklace, but afflictive to bear. Yet I was sorry for him. I speak less than truth when I say that, on his own account, he occasioned me uneasiness. If he would but have named a single relative or friend, I would instantly have written, and urged their taking the poor fellow away to some convenient retreat. But he seemed alone, absolutely alone in the universe. A bit of wreckage in the mid-Atlantic. At length, necessities connected with my business tyrannized over all other considerations. Decently as I could, I told Bartleby that in six days' time he must unconditionally leave the office. I warned him to take measures, in the interval, for procuring some other abode. I offered to assist him in this endeavor, if he himself would but take the first step towards a removal. "And when you finally quit me, Bartleby," added I, "I shall see that you go away not entirely unprovided. Six days from this hour, remember."

At the expiration of that period, I peeped behind the screen, and lo! Bartleby was there.

I buttoned up my coat, balanced myself; advanced slowly towards him, touched his shoulder, and said, "The time has come; you must quit this place; I am sorry for you; here is money; but you must go."

2. Conventional image of a burden hung on someone. Matthew 18.6: "But whoso shall offend one of these little ones which believe in me, it were better for him that a millstone were hanged about his neck, and that he were drowned in the depths of the sea."

"I would prefer not," he replied, with his back still towards me.

"You *must.*"

He remained silent.

Now I had an unbounded confidence in this man's common honesty. He had frequently restored to me sixpences and shillings carelessly dropped upon the floor, for I am apt to be very reckless in such shirt-button affairs. The proceeding then which followed will not be deemed extraordinary.

"Bartleby," said I, "I owe you twelve dollars on account; here are thirty-two; the odd twenty are yours.—Will you take it?" and I handed the bills towards him.

But he made no motion.

"I will leave them here then," putting them under a weight on the table. Then taking my hat and cane and going to the door, I tranquilly turned and added—"After you have removed your things from these offices, Bartleby, you will of course lock the door—since every one is now gone for the day but you—and if you please, slip your key underneath the mat, so that I may have it in the morning. I shall not see you again; so good-bye to you. If hereafter in your new place of abode I can be of any service to you, do not fail to advise me by letter. Good-bye, Bartleby, and fare you well."

But he answered not a word; like the last column of some ruined temple, he remained standing mute and solitary in the middle of the otherwise deserted room.

As I walked home in a pensive mood, my vanity got the better of my pity. I could not but highly plume myself on my masterly management in getting rid of Bartleby. Masterly I call it, and such it must appear to any dispassionate thinker. The beauty of my procedure seemed to consist in its perfect quietness. There was no vulgar bullying, no bravado of any sort, no choleric hectoring, no striding to and fro across the apartment, jerking out vehement commands for Bartleby to bundle himself off with his beggarly traps.[3] Nothing of the kind. Without loudly bidding Bartleby depart—as an inferior genius might have done—I *assumed* the ground that depart he must; and upon that assumption built all I had to say. The more I thought over my procedure, the more I was charmed with it. Nevertheless, next morning, upon awakening, I had my doubts,—I had somehow slept off the fumes of vanity. One of the coolest and wisest hours a man has, is just after he awakes in the morning. My procedure seemed as sagacious as ever,—but only in theory. How it would prove in practice—there was the rub. It was truly a beautiful thought to have assumed Bartleby's departure; but, after all, that assumption was simply my own, and none of Bartleby's. The great point was, not whether I had assumed that he would quit me, but whether he would prefer so to do. He was more a man of preferences than assumptions.

After breakfast, I walked down town, arguing the probabilities *pro* and *con.* One moment I thought it would prove a miserable failure, and Bartleby would be found all alive at my office as usual; the next moment it seemed certain that

3. Personal belongings.

I should see his chair empty. And so I kept veering about. At the corner of Broadway and Canal Street, I saw quite an excited group of people standing in earnest conversation.

"I'll take odds he doesn't," said a voice as I passed.

"Doesn't go?—done!" said I, "put up your money."

I was instinctively putting my hand in my pocket to produce my own, when I remembered that this was an election day. The words I had overheard bore no reference to Bartleby, but to the success or non-success of some candidate for the mayoralty. In my intent frame of mind, I had, as it were, imagined that all Broadway shared in my excitement, and were debating the same question with me. I passed on, very thankful that the uproar of the street screened my momentary absent-mindedness.

As I had intended, I was earlier than usual at my office door. I stood listening for a moment. All was still. He must be gone. I tried the knob. The door was locked. Yes, my procedure had worked to a charm; he indeed must be vanished. Yet a certain melancholy mixed with this: I was almost sorry for my brilliant success. I was fumbling under the door mat for the key, which Bartleby was to have left there for me, when accidentally my knee knocked against a panel, producing a summoning sound, and in response a voice came to me from within—"Not yet; I am occupied."

It was Bartleby.

I was thunderstruck. For an instant I stood like the man who, pipe in mouth, was killed one cloudless afternoon long ago in Virginia, by summer lightning; at his own warm open window he was killed, and remained leaning out there upon the dreamy afternoon, till some one touched him, and he fell.

"Not gone!" I murmured at last. But again obeying that wondrous ascendancy which the inscrutable scrivener had over me—and from which ascendency, for all my chafing, I could not completely escape—I slowly went down stairs and out into the street, and while walking round the block, considered what I should next do in this unheard-of perplexity. Turn the man out by an actual thrusting I could not; to drive him away by calling him hard names would not do; calling in the police was an unpleasant idea; and yet, permit him to enjoy his cadaverous triumph over me,—this too I could not think of. What was to be done? or, if nothing could be done, was there anything further that I could *assume* in the matter? Yes, as before I had prospectively assumed that Bartleby would depart, so now I might retrospectively assume that departed he was. In the legitimate carrying out of this assumption, I might enter my office in a great hurry, and pretending not to see Bartleby at all, walk straight against him as if he were air. Such a proceeding would in a singular degree have the appearance of a home-thrust.[4] It was hardly possible that Bartleby could withstand such an application of the doctrine of assumptions. But, upon second thought, the success of the plan seemed rather dubious. I resolved to argue the matter over with him again.

"Bartleby," said I, entering the office, with a quietly severe expression, "I am seriously displeased. I am pained, Bartleby. I had thought better of you. I

4. I.e., an action that accomplishes its purpose.

had imagined you of such a gentlemanly organization, that in any delicate dilemma a slight hint would suffice—in short, an assumption. But it appears I am deceived. Why," I added, unaffectedly starting, "you have not even touched that money yet," pointing to it, just where I had left it the evening previous.

He answered nothing.

"Will you, or will you not, quit me?" I now demanded in a sudden passion, advancing close to him.

"I would prefer *not* to quit you," he replied, gently emphasizing the *not*.

"What earthly right have you to stay here? Do you pay any rent? Do you pay my taxes? Or is this property yours?"

He answered nothing.

"Are you ready to go on and write now? Are your eyes recovered? Could you copy a small paper for me this morning? or help examine a few lines? or step round to the Post Office? In a word, will you do any thing at all, to give a colouring to your refusal to depart the premises?"

He silently retired into his hermitage.

I was now in such a state of nervous resentment that I thought it but prudent to check myself, at present, from further demonstrations. Bartleby and I were alone. I remembered the tragedy of the unfortunate Adams and the still more unfortunate Colt[5] in the solitary office of the latter; and how poor Colt, being dreadfully incensed by Adams, and imprudently permitting himself to get wildly excited, was at unawares hurried into his fatal act—an act which certainly no man could possibly deplore more than the actor himself. Often it had occurred to me in my ponderings upon the subject, that had that altercation taken place in the public street, or at a private residence, it would not have terminated as it did. It was the circumstance of being alone in a solitary office, upstairs, of a building entirely unhallowed by humanizing domestic associations—an uncarpeted office, doubtless, of a dusty, haggard sort of appearance; —this it must have been, which greatly helped to enhance the irritable desperation of the hapless Colt.

But when this old Adam[6] of resentment rose in me and tempted me concerning Bartleby, I grappled him and threw him. How? Why, simply by recalling the divine injunction: "A new commandment give I unto you, that ye love one another."[7] Yes, this it was that saved me. Aside from higher considerations, charity often operates as a vastly wise and prudent principle—a great safeguard to its possessor. Men have committed murder for jealousy's sake, and anger's sake, and hatred's sake, and selfishness' sake, and spiritual pride's sake; but no man that ever I heard of, ever committed a diabolical murder for sweet charity's sake. Mere self-interest, then, if no better motive can be enlisted, should, especially with high-tempered men, prompt all beings to charity and philanthropy. At any rate, upon the occasion in question, I strove to drown my exasperated feelings towards the scrivener by benevolently constructing his conduct. Poor fellow, poor fellow! thought I, he doesn't mean any thing; and besides, he has seen hard times, and ought to be indulged.

5. In 1841 John C. Colt, brother of the famous gunmaker, killed Samuel Adams, a printer, when he hit him on the head during a fight. 6. The sinful element in man. 7. John 13.34 and John 15.17.

I endeavored also immediately to occupy myself, and at the same time to comfort my despondency. I tried to fancy that in the course of the morning, at such time as might prove agreeable to him, Bartleby, of his own free accord, would emerge from his hermitage, and take up some decided line of march in the direction of the door. But no. Half-past twelve o'clock came; Turkey began to glow in the face, overturn his inkstand, and become generally obstreperous; Nippers abated down into quietude and courtesy; Ginger Nut munched his noon apple; and Bartleby remained standing at his window in one of his profoundest dead-wall reveries. Will it be credited? Ought I to acknowledge it? That afternoon I left the office without saying one further word to him.

Some days now passed, during which, at leisure intervals I looked a little into "Edwards on the Will," and "Priestley on Necessity."[8] Under the circumstances, those books induced a salutary feeling. Gradually I slid into the persuasion that these troubles of mine, touching the scrivener, had been all predestinated from eternity, and Bartleby was billeted upon me for some mysterious purpose of an all-wise Providence, which it was not for a mere mortal like me to fathom. Yes, Bartleby, stay there behind your screen, thought I; I shall persecute you no more; you are harmless and noiseless as any of these old chairs; in short, I never feel so private as when I know you are here. At least I see it, I feel it; I penetrate to the predestinated purpose of my life. I am content. Others may have loftier parts to enact; but my mission in this world, Bartleby, is to furnish you with office-room for such period as you may see fit to remain.

I believe that this wise and blessed frame of mind would have continued with me, had it not been for the unsolicited and uncharitable remarks obtruded upon me by my professional friends who visited the rooms. But thus it often is, that the constant friction of illiberal minds wears out at last the best resolves of the more generous. Though to be sure, when I reflected upon it, it was not strange that people entering my office should be struck by the peculiar aspect of the unaccountable Bartleby, and so be tempted to throw out some sinister observations concerning him. Sometimes an attorney having business with me, and calling at my office, and finding no one but the scrivener there, would undertake to obtain some sort of precise information from him touching my whereabouts; but without heeding his idle talk, Bartleby would remain standing immovable in the middle of the room. So, after contemplating him in that position for a time, the attorney would depart, no wiser than he came.

Also, when a Reference[9] was going on, and the room full of lawyers and witnesses and business was driving fast, some deeply occupied legal gentleman present, seeing Bartleby wholly unemployed, would request him to run round to his (the legal gentleman's) office and fetch some papers for him. Thereupon, Bartleby would tranquilly decline, and yet remain idle as before. Then the lawyer would give a great stare, and turn to me. And what could I say? At last I was made aware that all through the circle of my professional acquaintance, a whisper of wonder was running round, having reference to the strange crea-

8. The reference is obscure because of the form Melville has given the titles, but the books indicated are probably *The Freedom of the Will* by Jonathan Edwards (1703–1758) and *The Doctrine of Philosophical Necessity* by Joseph Priestley (1733–1804). The theses of these two books conform to the "persuasion" Melville here describes. 9. Conference.

ture I kept at my office. This worried me very much. And as the idea came upon me of his possibly turning out a long-lived man, and keep occupying my chambers, and denying my authority; and perplexing my visitors; and scandalizing my professional reputation; and casting a general gloom over the premises; keeping soul and body together to the last upon his savings (for doubtless he spent but half a dime a day), and in the end perhaps outlive me, and claim possession of my office by right of his perpetual occupancy: as all these dark anticipations crowded upon me more and more, and my friends continually intruded their relentless remarks upon the apparition in my room, a great change was wrought in me. I resolved to gather all my faculties together, and for ever rid me of this intolerable incubus.[1]

Ere revolving any complicated project, however, adapted to this end, I first simply suggested to Bartleby the propriety of his permanent departure. In a calm and serious tone, I commended the idea to his careful and mature consideration. But having taken three days to meditate upon it, he apprised me that his original determination remained the same; in short, that he still preferred to abide with me.

What shall I do? I now said to myself, buttoning up my coat to the last button. What shall I do? what ought I to do? what does conscience say I *should* do with this man, or rather ghost? Rid myself of him, I must; go, he shall. But how? You will not thrust him, the poor, pale, passive mortal,—you will not thrust such a helpless creature out of your door? you will not dishonour yourself by such cruelty? No, I will not, I cannot do that. Rather would I let him live and die here, and then mason up his remains in the wall. What then will you do? For all your coaxing, he will not budge. Bribes he leaves under your own paper-weight on your table; in short, it is quite plain that he prefers to cling to you.

Then something severe, something unusual must be done. What! surely you will not have him collared by a constable, and commit his innocent pallor to the common jail? And upon what ground could you procure such a thing to be done?—a vagrant, is he? What! he a vagrant, a wanderer, who refuses to budge? It is because he will *not* be a vagrant, then, that you seek to count him *as* a vagrant. That is too absurd. No visible means of support: there I have him. Wrong again: for indubitably he *does* support himself, and that is the only unanswerable proof that any man can show of his possessing the means so to do. No more then. Since he will not quit me, I must quit him. I will change my offices; I will move elsewhere; and give him fair notice, that if I find him on my new premises I will then proceed against him as a common trespasser.

Acting accordingly, next day I thus addressed him: "I find these chambers too far from the City Hall; the air is unwholesome. In a word, I propose to remove my offices next week, and shall no longer require your services. I tell you this now, in order that you may seek another place."

He made no reply, and nothing more was said.

On the appointed day I engaged carts and men, proceeded to my chambers, and having but little furniture, every thing was removed in a few hours.

1. Imaginary demon supposed to descend on sleepers.

Throughout all, the scrivener remained standing behind the screen, which I directed to be removed the last thing. It was withdrawn; and being folded up like a huge folio, left him the motionless occupant of a naked room. I stood in the entry watching him a moment, while something from within me upbraided me.

I re-entered, with my hand in my pocket—and—and my heart in my mouth.

"Good-bye, Bartleby; I am going—good-bye, and God some way bless you; and take that," slipping something in his hand. But it dropped upon the floor, and then—strange to say—I tore myself from him whom I had so longed to be rid of.

Established in my new quarters, for a day or two I kept the door locked, and started at every footfall in the passages. When I returned to my rooms after any little absence, I would pause at the threshold for an instant, and attentively listen, ere applying my key. But these fears were needless. Bartleby never came nigh me.

I thought all was going well, when a perturbed looking stranger visited me, inquiring whether I was the person who had recently occupied rooms at No. —— Wall-street.

Full of forebodings, I replied that I was.

"Then sir," said the stranger, who proved a lawyer, "you are responsible for the man you left there. He refuses to do any copying, he refuses to do any thing; he says he prefers not to; and he refuses to quit the premises."

"I am very sorry, sir," said I, with assumed tranquillity, but an inward tremor, "but, really, the man you allude to is nothing to me—he is no relation or apprentice of mine, that you should hold me responsible for him."

"In mercy's name, who is he?"

"I certainly cannot inform you. I know nothing about him. Formerly I employed him as a copyist; but he has done nothing for me now for some time past."

"I shall settle him then,—good morning, sir."

Several days passed, and I heard nothing more; and though I often felt a charitable prompting to call at the place and see poor Bartleby, yet a certain squeamishness of I know not what withheld me.

All is over with him, by this time, thought I at last, when through another week no further intelligence reached me. But coming to my room the day after, I found several persons waiting at my door in a high state of nervous excitement.

"That's the man—here he comes," cried the foremost one, whom I recognized as the lawyer who had previously called upon me alone.

"You must take him away, sir, at once," cried a portly person among them, advancing upon me, and whom I knew to be the landlord of No. —— Wall-street. "These gentlemen, my tenants, cannot stand it any longer; Mr.B——," pointing to the lawyer, "has turned him out of his room, and he now persists in haunting the building generally, sitting upon the banisters of the stairs by day, and sleeping in the entry by night. Everybody is concerned; clients are leaving the offices; some fears are entertained of a mob; something you must do, and that without delay."

Aghast at this torrent, I fell back before it, and would fain have locked myself in my new quarters. In vain I persisted that Bartleby was nothing to me—no more than to any one else. In vain:—I was the last person known to have anything to do with him, and they held me to the terrible account. Fearful then of being exposed in the papers (as one person present obscurely threatened) I considered the matter, and at length said, that if the lawyer would give me a confidential interview with the scrivener, in his (the lawyer's) own room, I would that afternoon strive my best to rid them of the nuisance they complained of.

Going up stairs to my old haunt, there was Bartleby silently sitting upon the banister at the landing.

"What are you doing here, Bartleby?" said I.

"Sitting upon the banister," he mildly replied.

I motioned him into the lawyer's room, who then left us.

"Bartleby," said I, "are you aware that you are the cause of great tribulation to me, by persisting in occupying the entry after being dismissed from the office?"

No answer.

"Now one of two things must take place. Either you must do something, or something must be done to you. Now what sort of business would you like to engage in? Would you like to re-engage in copying for some one?"

"No; I would prefer not to make any change."

"Would you like a clerkship in a dry-goods store?"

"There is too much confinement about that. No, I would not like a clerkship; but I am not particular."

"Too much confinement," I cried, "why you keep yourself confined all the time!"

"I would prefer not to take a clerkship," he rejoined, as if to settle that little item at once.

"How would a bar tender's business suit you? There is no trying of the eyesight in that."

"I would not like it at all; though, as I said before, I am not particular."

His unwonted wordiness inspirited me. I returned to the charge.

"Well then, would you like to travel through the country collecting bills for the merchants? That would improve your health."

"No, I would prefer to be doing something else."

"How then would going as a companion to Europe to entertain some young gentleman with your conversation,—how would that suit you?"

"Not at all. It does not strike me that there is anything definite about that. I like to be stationary. But I am not particular."

"Stationary you shall be then," I cried, now losing all patience, and for the first time in all my exasperating connection with him fairly flying into a passion. "If you do not go away from these premises before night, I shall feel bound—indeed I *am* bound—to—to—to quit the premises myself!" I rather absurdly concluded, knowing not with what possible threat to try to frighten his immobility into compliance. Despairing of all further efforts, I was precipitately leaving him, when a final thought occurred to me—one which had not been wholly unindulged before.

"Bartleby," said I, in the kindest tone I could assume under such exciting circumstances, "will you go home with me now—not to my office, but my dwelling—and remain there till we can conclude upon some convenient arrangement for you at our leisure? Come, let us start now, right away."

"No: at present I would prefer not to make any change at all."

I answered nothing; but effectually dodging every one by the suddenness and rapidity of my flight, rushed from the building, ran up Wall street towards Broadway, and jumping into the first omnibus was soon removed from pursuit. As soon as tranquillity returned I distinctly perceived that I had now done all that I possibly could, both in respect to the demands of the landlord and his tenants, and with regard to my own desire and sense of duty, to benefit Bartleby, and shield him from rude persecution. I now strove to be entirely care-free and quiescent; and my conscience justified me in the attempt; though indeed it was not so successful as I could have wished. So fearful was I of being again hunted out by the incensed landlord and his exasperated tenants, that, surrendering my business to Nippers, for a few days I drove about the upper part of the town and through the suburbs, in my rockaway;[2] crossed over to Jersey City and Hoboken, and paid fugitive visits to Manhattanville and Astoria. In fact I almost lived in my rockaway for the time.

When again I entered my office, lo, a note from the landlord lay upon the desk. I opened it with trembling hands. It informed me that the writer had sent to the police, and had Bartleby removed to the Tombs as a vagrant. Moreover, since I knew more about him than any one else, he wished me to appear at that place, and make a suitable statement of the facts. These tidings had a conflicting effect upon me. At first I was indignant; but at last almost approved. The landlord's energetic, summary disposition had led him to adopt a procedure which I do not think I would have decided upon myself; and yet as a last resort, under such peculiar circumstances, it seemed the only plan.

As I afterwards learned, the poor scrivener, when told that he must be conducted to the Tombs, offered not the slightest obstacle, but in his pale, unmoving way silently acquiesced.

Some of the compassionate and curious bystanders joined the party; and headed by one of the constables, arm in arm with Bartleby the silent procession filed its way through all the noise, and heat, and joy of the roaring thoroughfares at noon.

The same day I received the note I went to the Tombs, or, to speak more properly, the Halls of Justice. Seeking the right officer, I stated the purpose of my call, and was informed that the individual I described was indeed within. I then assured the functionary that Bartleby was a perfectly honest man, and greatly to be a compassionated, (however unaccountable) eccentric. I narrated all I knew, and closed by suggesting the idea of letting him remain in as indulgent confinement as possible till something less harsh might be done—though indeed I hardly knew what. At all events, if nothing else could be decided upon, the alms-house must receive him. I then begged to have an interview.

Being under no disgraceful charge, and quite serene and harmless in all his ways, they had permitted him freely to wander about the prison, and espe-

2. Light, four-wheeled carriage.

cially in the inclosed grass-platted yards thereof. And so I found him there, standing all alone in the quietest of the yards, his face towards a high wall—while all around, from the narrow slits of the jail windows, I thought I saw peering out upon him the eyes of murderers and thieves.

"Bartleby!"

"I know you," he said, without looking round,—"and I want nothing to say to you."

"It was not I that brought you here, Bartleby," said I, keenly pained at his implied suspicion. "And to you, this should not be so vile a place. Nothing reproachful attaches to you by being here. And see, it is not so sad a place as one might think. Look, there is the sky and here is the grass."

"I know where I am," he replied, but would say nothing more, and so I left him.

As I entered the corridor again, a broad, meat-like man, in an apron, accosted me, and jerking his thumb over his shoulder said—"Is that your friend?"

"Yes."

"Does he want to starve? If he does, let him live on the prison fare, that's all."

"Who are you?" asked I, not knowing what to make of such an unofficially speaking person in such a place.

"I am the grub-man. Such gentlemen as have friends here, hire me to provide them with something good to eat."

"Is this so?" said I, turning to the turnkey.

He said it was.

"Well then," said I, slipping some silver into the grub-man's hands (for so they called him), "I want you to give particular attention to my friend there; let him have the best dinner you can get. And you must be as polite to him as possible."

"Introduce me, will you?" said the grub-man, looking at me with an expression which seemed to say he was all impatience for an opportunity to give a specimen of his breeding.

Thinking it would prove of benefit to the scrivener, I acquiesced; and asking the grub-man his name, went up with him to Bartleby.

"Bartleby, this is Mr. Cutlets; you will find him very useful to you."

"Your sarvant, sir, your sarvant," said the grub-man, making a low salutation behind his apron. "Hope you find it pleasant here, sir;—spacious grounds—cool apartments, sir—hope you'll stay with us some time—try to make it agreeable. May Mrs. Cutlets and I have the pleasure of your company to dinner, sir, in Mrs. Cutlets' private room?"

"I prefer not to dine to-day," said Bartleby, turning away. "It would disagree with me; I am unused to dinners." So saying, he slowly moved to the other side of the inclosure and took up a position fronting the dead-wall.

"How's this?" said the grub-man, addressing me with a stare of astonishment. "He's odd, aint he?"

"I think he is a little deranged," said I, sadly.

"Deranged? deranged is it? Well now, upon my word, I thought that friend of yourn was a gentleman forger; they are always pale and genteel-like, them forgers. I can't help pity 'em—can't help it, sir. Did you know Monroe Edwards?" he added touchingly, and paused. Then, laying his hand pityingly on my shoulder, sighed, "he died of consumption at Sing-Sing.[3] So you weren't acquainted with Monroe?"

"No, I was never socially acquainted with any forgers. But I cannot stop longer. Look to my friend yonder. You will not lose by it. I will see you again."

Some few days after this, I again obtained admission to the Tombs, and went through the corridors in quest of Bartleby; but without finding him.

"I saw him coming from his cell not long ago," said a turnkey, "maybe he's gone to loiter in the yards."

So I went in that direction.

"Are you looking for the silent man?" said another turnkey passing me. "Yonder he lies—sleeping in the yard there. 'Tis not twenty minutes since I saw him lie down."

The yard was entirely quiet. It was not accessible to the common prisoners. The surrounding walls, of amazing thickness, kept off all sounds behind them. The Egyptian character of the masonry weighed upon me with its gloom. But a soft imprisoned turf grew under foot. The heart of the eternal pyramids, it seemed, wherein, by some strange magic, through the clefts grass-seed, dropped by birds, had sprung.

Strangely huddled at the base of the wall—his knees drawn up, and lying on his side, his head touching the cold stones—I saw the wasted Bartleby. But nothing stirred. I paused; then went close up to him; stooped over, and saw that his dim eyes were open; otherwise he seemed profoundly sleeping. Something prompted me to touch him. I felt his hand, when a tingling shiver ran up my arm and down my spine to my feet.

The round face of the grub-man peered upon me now. "His dinner is ready. Won't he dine to-day, either? Or does he live without dining?"

"Lives without dining," said I, and closed the eyes.

"Eh!—He's asleep, aint he?"

"With kings and counsellors,"[4] murmured I.

There would seem little need for proceeding further in this history. Imagination will readily supply the meagre recital of poor Bartleby's interment. But ere parting with the reader, let me say, that if this little narrative has sufficiently interested him, to awaken curiosity as to who Bartleby was, and what manner of life he led prior to the present narrator's making his acquaintance, I can only reply, that in such curiosity I fully share—but am wholly unable to gratify it. Yet here I hardly know whether I should divulge one little item of rumour, which came to my ear a few months after the scrivener's decease. Upon what basis it rested, I could never ascertain; and hence, how true it is I cannot now tell. But inasmuch as this vague report has not been without a certain strange suggestive interest to me, however sad, it may prove the same with some others; and so I will briefly mention it. The report was this: that Bartleby had been a

3. State prison at Ossining, New York. 4. Job 3.13–14: "then had I been at rest, With kings and counsellors of the earth, which built desolate places for themselves."

subordinate clerk in the Dead Letter Office[5] at Washington, from which he had been suddenly removed by a change in the administration. When I think over this rumor I cannot adequately express the emotions which seize me. Dead letters! Does it not sound like dead men? Conceive a man by nature and misfortune prone to a pallid hopelessness: can any business seem more fitted to heighten it than that of continually handling these dead letters, and assorting them for the flames? For by the cart-load they are annually burned. Sometimes from out the folded paper the pale clerk takes a ring:—the finger it was meant for, perhaps, moulders in the grave; a bank-note sent in swiftest charity:—he whom it would relieve, nor eats nor hungers any more; pardon for those who died despairing; hope for those who died unhoping; good tidings for those who died stifled by unrelieved calamities. On errands of life, these letters speed to death.

Ah Bartleby! Ah humanity!

5. Place for storage and disposition of undeliverable mail.

# Bharati Mukherjee

*Mukherjee (1940– ) was born in Calcutta. She spent her early years with her family in England but returned to India in her teens to study. She continued her education in the 1960s at the University of Iowa, where she met and married the writer Clark Blaise in 1963. While they were living in Canada for the next ten years, she published her first two novels,* The Tiger's Daughter *(1972) and* Wife *(1975). Later, when the couple traveled in India, they collaborated on two nonfiction books, built from their observations and impressions of Indian life. Her stories are collected in* Darkness *(1985) and* The Middleman and Other Stories *(1988). Her most recent books are* Jasmine *(1989),* The Holder of the World *(1994), and* Leave It To Me *(1997). She now lives in the United States and teaches at the University of California at Berkeley.*

## The Management of Grief

A woman I don't know is boiling tea the Indian way in my kitchen. There are a lot of women I don't know in my kitchen, whispering, and moving tactfully. They open doors, rummage through the pantry, and try not to ask me where things are kept. They remind me of when my sons were small, on Mother's Day or when Vikram and I were tired, and they would make big, sloppy omelettes. I would lie in bed pretending I didn't hear them.

Dr. Sharma, the treasurer of the Indo-Canada Society, pulls me into the hallway. He wants to know if I am worried about money. His wife, who has just come up from the basement with a tray of empty cups and glasses, scolds him. "Don't bother Mrs. Bhave with mundane details." She looks so monstrously pregnant her baby must be days overdue. I tell her she shouldn't be carrying heavy things. "Shaila," she says, smiling, "this is the fifth." Then she grabs a teenager by his shirt-tails. He slips his Walkman off his head. He has to be one of her four children, they have the same domed and dented foreheads. "What's the official word now?" she demands. The boy slips the headphones back on. "They're acting evasive, Ma. They're saying it could be an accident or a terrorist bomb."

All morning, the boys have been muttering, Sikh Bomb, Sikh Bomb. The men, not using the word, bow their heads in agreement. Mrs. Sharma touches her forehead at such a word. At least they've stopped talking about space debris and Russian lasers.

Two radios are going in the dining room. They are tuned to different stations. Someone must have brought the radios down from my boys' bedrooms. I haven't gone into their rooms since Kusum came running across the front lawn in her bathrobe. She looked so funny, I was laughing when I opened the door.

The big TV in the den is being whizzed through American networks and cable channels.

"Damn!" some man swears bitterly. "How can these preachers carry on like nothing's happened?" I want to tell him we're not that important. You look at the audience, and at the preacher in his blue robe with his beautiful white hair, the potted palm trees under a blue sky, and you know they care about nothing.

The phone rings and rings. Dr. Sharma's taken charge. "We're with her," he keeps saying. "Yes, yes, the doctor has given calming pills. Yes, yes, pills are having necessary effect." I wonder if pills alone explain this calm. Not peace, just a deadening quiet. I was always controlled, but never repressed. Sound can reach me, but my body is tensed, ready to scream. I hear their voices all around me. I hear my boys and Vikram cry, "Mommy, Shaila!" and their screams insulate me, like headphones.

The woman boiling water tells her story again and again. "I got the news first. My cousin called from Halifax before six A.M., can you imagine? He'd gotten up for prayers and his son was studying for medical exams and he heard on a rock channel that something had happened to a plane. They said first it had disappeared from the radar, like a giant eraser just reached out. His father called me, so I said to him, what do you mean, 'something bad'? You mean a hijacking? And he said, *behn,*[1] there is no confirmation of anything yet, but check with your neighbors because a lot of them must be on that plane. So I called poor Kusum straightaway. I knew Kusum's husband and daughter were booked to go yesterday."

Kusum lives across the street from me. She and Satish had moved in less than a month ago. They said they needed a bigger place. All these people, the Sharmas and friends from the Indo-Canada Society had been there for the housewarming. Satish and Kusum made homemade tandoori on their big gas grill and even the white neighbors piled their plates high with that luridly red, charred, juicy chicken. Their younger daughter had danced, and even our boys had broken away from the Stanley Cup telecast to put in a reluctant appearance. Everyone took pictures for their albums and for the community newspapers—another of our families had made it big in Toronto—and now I wonder how many of those happy faces are gone. "Why does God give us so much if all along He intends to take it away?" Kusum asks me.

I nod. We sit on carpeted stairs, holding hands like children. "I never once told him that I loved him," I say. I was too much the well brought up woman. I was so well brought up I never felt comfortable calling my husband by his first name.

"It's all right," Kusum says. "He knew. My husband knew. They felt it. Modern young girls have to say it because what they feel is fake."

1. No (Hindi).

Kusum's daughter, Pam, runs in with an overnight case. Pam's in her McDonald's uniform. "Mummy! You have to get dressed!" Panic makes her cranky. "A reporter's on his way here."

"Why?"

"You want to talk to him in your bathrobe?" She starts to brush her mother's long hair. She's the daughter who's always in trouble. She dates Canadian boys and hangs out in the mall, shopping for tight sweaters. The younger one, the goody-goody one according to Pam, the one with a voice so sweet that when she sang *bhajans*[2] for Ethiopian relief even a frugal man like my husband wrote out a hundred dollar check, *she* was on that plane. *She* was going to spend July and August with grandparents because Pam wouldn't go. Pam said she'd rather waitress at McDonald's. "If it's a choice between Bombay and Wonderland, I'm picking Wonderland," she'd said.

"Leave me alone," Kusum yells. "You know what I want to do? If I didn't have to look after you now, I'd hang myself."

Pam's young face goes blotchy with pain. "Thanks," she says, "don't let me stop you."

"Hush," pregnant Mrs. Sharma scolds Pam. "Leave your mother alone. Mr. Sharma will tackle the reporters and fill out the forms. He'll say what has to be said."

Pam stands her ground. "You think I don't know what Mummy's thinking? *Why ever?* that's what. That's sick! Mummy wishes my little sister were alive and I were dead."

Kusum's hand in mine is trembly hot. We continue to sit on the stairs.

She calls before she arrives, wondering if there's anything I need. Her name is Judith Templeton and she's an appointee of the provincial government. "Multiculturalism?" I ask, and she says, "partially," but that her mandate is bigger. "I've been told you knew many of the people on the flight," she says. "Perhaps if you'd agree to help us reach the others . . . ?"

She gives me time at least to put on tea water and pick up the mess in the front room. I have a few *samosas*[3] from Kusum's housewarming that I could fry up, but then I think, why prolong this visit?

Judith Templeton is much younger than she sounded. She wears a blue suit with a white blouse and a polka dot tie. Her blond hair is cut short, her only jewelry is pearl drop earrings. Her briefcase is new and expensive looking, a gleaming cordovan leather. She sits with it across her lap. When she looks out the front windows onto the street, her contact lenses seem to float in front of her light blue eyes.

"What sort of help do you want from me?" I ask. She has refused the tea, out of politeness, but I insist, along with some slightly stale biscuits.

"I have no experience," she admits. "That is, I have an MSW and I've worked in liaison with accident victims, but I mean I have no experience with a tragedy of this scale—"

"Who could?" I ask.

2. Hymns (Hindi). 3. Fried turnovers filled with meat or vegetable mixtures (Hindi).

"—and with the complications of culture, language, and customs. Someone mentioned that Mrs. Bhave is a pillar—because you've taken it more calmly."

At this, perhaps, I frown, for she reaches forward, almost to take my hand. "I hope you understand my meaning, Mrs. Bhave. There are hundreds of people in Metro directly affected, like you, and some of them speak no English. There are some widows who've never handled money or gone on a bus, and there are old parents who still haven't eaten or gone outside their bedrooms. Some houses and apartments have been looted. Some wives are still hysterical. Some husbands are in shock and profound depression. We want to help, but our hands are tied in so many ways. We have to distribute money to some people, and there are legal documents—these things can be done. We have interpreters, but we don't always have the human touch, or maybe the right human touch. We don't want to make mistakes, Mrs. Bhave, and that's why we'd like to ask you to help us."

"More mistakes, you mean," I say.

"Police matters are not in my hands," she answers.

"Nothing I can do will make any difference," I say. "We must all grieve in our own way."

"But you are coping very well. All the people said, Mrs. Bhave is the strongest person of all. Perhaps if the others could see you, talk with you, it would help them."

"By the standards of the people you call hysterical, I am behaving very oddly and very badly, Miss Templeton." I want to say to her, *I wish I could scream, starve, walk into Lake Ontario, jump from a bridge.* "They would not see me as a model. I do not see myself as a model."

I am a freak. No one who has ever known me would think of me reacting this way. This terrible calm will not go away.

She asks me if she may call again, after I get back from a long trip that we all must make. "Of course," I say. "Feel free to call, anytime."

Four days later, I find Kusum squatting on a rock overlooking a bay in Ireland. It isn't a big rock, but it juts sharply out over water. This is close as we'll ever get to them. June breezes balloon out her sari and unpin her knee-length hair. She has the bewildered look of a sea creature whom the tides have stranded.

It's been one hundred hours since Kusum came stumbling and screaming across my lawn. Waiting around the hospital, we've heard many stories. The police, the diplomats, they tell us things thinking that we're strong, that knowledge is helpful to the grieving, and maybe it is. Some, I know, prefer ignorance, or their own versions. The plane broke into two, they say. Unconsciousness was instantaneous. No one suffered. My boys must have just finished their breakfasts. They loved eating on planes, they loved the smallness of plates, knives, and forks. Last year they saved the airline salt and pepper shakers. Half an hour more and they would have made it to Heathrow.

Kusum says that we can't escape our fate. She says that all those people—our husbands, my boys, her girl with the nightingale voice, all those Hindus, Christians, Sikhs, Muslims, Parsis, and atheists on that plane—were fated to die together off this beautiful bay. She learned this from a swami in Toronto.

I have my Valium.

Six of us "relatives"—two widows and four widowers—choose to spend the day today by the waters instead of sitting in a hospital room and scanning photographs of the dead. That's what they call us now: relatives. I've looked through twenty-seven photos in two days. They're very kind to us, the Irish are very understanding. Sometimes understanding means freeing a tourist bus for this trip to the bay, so we can pretend to spy our loved ones through the glassiness of waves or in sunspeckled cloud shapes.

I could die here, too, and be content.

"What is that, out there?" She's standing and flapping her hands and for a moment I see a head shape bobbing in the waves. She's standing in the water, I, on the boulder. The tide is low, and a round, black, headsized rock has just risen from the waves. She returns, her sari end dripping and ruined and her face is a twisted remnant of hope, the way mine was a hundred hours ago, still laughing but inwardly knowing that nothing but the ultimate tragedy could bring two women together at six o'clock on a Sunday morning. I watch her face sag into blankness.

"That water felt warm, Shaila," she says at length.

"You can't," I say. "We have to wait for our turn to come."

I haven't eaten in four days, haven't brushed my teeth.

"I know," she says. "I tell myself I have no right to grieve. They are in a better place than we are. My swami says I should be thrilled for them. My swami says depression is a sign of our selfishness."

Maybe I'm selfish. Selfishly I break away from Kusum and run, sandals slapping against stones, to the water's edge. What if my boys aren't lying pinned under the debris? What if they aren't stuck a mile below that innocent blue chop? What if, given the strong currents. . . .

Now I've ruined my sari, one of my best. Kusum has joined me, knee-deep in water that feels to me like a swimming pool. I could settle in the water, and my husband would take my hand and the boys would slap water in my face just to see me scream.

"Do you remember what good swimmers my boys were, Kusum?"

"I saw the medals," she says.

One of the widowers, Dr. Ranganathan from Montreal, walks out to us, carrying his shoes in one hand. He's an electrical engineer. Someone at the hotel mentioned his work is famous around the world, something about the place where physics and electricity come together. He has lost a huge family, something indescribable. "With some luck," Dr. Ranganathan suggests to me, "a good swimmer could make it safely to some island. It is quite possible that there may be many, many microscopic islets scattered around."

"You're not just saying that?" I tell Dr. Ranganathan about Vinod, my elder son. Last year he took diving as well.

"It's a parent's duty to hope," he says. "It is foolish to rule out possibilities that have not been tested. I myself have not surrendered hope."

Kusum is sobbing once again. "Dear lady," he says, laying his free hand on her arm, and she calms down.

"Vinod is how old?" he asks me. He's very careful, as we all are. *Is,* not was.

"Fourteen. Yesterday he was fourteen. His father and uncle were going to take him down to the Taj and give him a big birthday party. I couldn't go with them because I couldn't get two weeks off from my stupid job in June." I process bills for a travel agent. June is a big travel month.

Dr. Ranganathan whips the pockets of his suit jacked inside out. Squashed roses, in darkening shades of pink, float on the water. He tore the roses off creepers in somebody's garden. He didn't ask anyone if he could pluck the roses, but now there's been an article about it in the local papers. When you see an Indian person, it says, please give him or her flowers.

"A strong youth of fourteen," he says, "can very likely pull to safety a younger one."

My sons, though four years apart, were very close. Vinod wouldn't let Mithun drown. *Electrical engineering,* I think, foolishly perhaps: this man knows important secrets of the universe, things closed to me. Relief spins me lightheaded. No wonder my boys' photographs haven't turned up in the gallery of photos of the recovered dead. "Such pretty roses," I say.

"My wife loved pink roses. Every Friday I had to bring a bunch home. I used to say, why? After twenty odd years of marriage you're still needing proof positive of my love?" He has identified his wife and three of his children. Then others from Montreal, the lucky ones, intact families with no survivors. He chuckles as he wades back to shore. Then he swings around to ask me a question. "Mrs. Bhave, you are wanting to throw in some roses for your loved ones? I have two big ones left."

But I have other things to float: Vinod's pocket calculator; a half-painted model B-52 for my Mithun. They'd want them on their island. And for my husband? For him I let fall into the calm, glassy waters a poem I wrote in the hospital yesterday. Finally he'll know my feelings for him.

"Don't tumble, the rocks are slippery," Dr. Ranganathan cautions. He holds out a hand for me to grab.

Then it's time to get back on the bus, time to rush back to our waiting posts on hospital benches.

Kusum is one of the lucky ones. The lucky ones flew here, identified in multiplicate their loved ones, then will fly to India with the bodies for proper ceremonies. Satish is one of the few males who surfaced. The photos of faces we saw on the walls in an office at Heathrow and here in the hospital are mostly of women. Women have more body fat, a nun said to me matter-of-factly. They float better.

Today I was stopped by a young sailor on the street. He had loaded bodies, he'd gone into the water when—he checks my face for signs of strength—when the sharks were first spotted. I don't blush, and he breaks down. "It's all right," I say. "Thank you." I had heard about the sharks from Dr. Ranganathan. In his orderly mind, science brings understanding, it holds no terror. It is the shark's duty. For every deer there is a hunter, for every fish a fisherman.

The Irish are not shy; they rush to me and give me hugs and some are crying. I cannot imagine reactions like that on the streets of Toronto. Just strangers, and I am touched. Some carry flowers with them and give them to any Indian they see.

After lunch, a policeman I have gotten to know quite well catches hold of me. He says he thinks he has a match for Vinod. I explain what a good swimmer Vinod is.

"You want me with you when you look at photos?" Dr. Ranganathan walks ahead of me into the picture gallery. In these matters, he is a scientist, and I am grateful. It is a new perspective. "They have performed miracles," he says. "We are indebted to them."

The first day or two the policemen showed us relatives only one picture at a time; now they're in a hurry, they're eager to lay out the possibles, and even the probables.

The face on the photo is of a boy much like Vinod; the same intelligent eyes, the same thick brows dipping into a V. But this boy's features, even his cheeks, are puffier, wider, mushier.

"No." My gaze is pulled by other pictures. There are five other boys who look like Vinod.

The nun assigned to console me rubs the first picture with a fingertip. "When they've been in the water for a while, love, they look a little heavier." The bones under the skin are broken, they said on the first day—try to adjust your memories. It's important.

"It's not him. I'm his mother. I'd know."

"I know this one!" Dr. Ranganathan cries out suddenly from the back of the gallery. "And this one!" I think he senses that I don't want to find my boys. "They are the Kutty brothers. They were also from Montreal." I don't mean to be crying. On the contrary, I am ecstatic. My suitcase in the hotel is packed heavy with dry clothes for my boys.

The policeman starts to cry. "I am so sorry, I am so sorry, ma'am. I really thought we had a match."

With the nun ahead of us and the policeman behind, we, the unlucky ones without our children's bodies, file out of the makeshift gallery.

From Ireland most of us go on to India. Kusum and I take the same direct flight to Bombay, so I can help her clear customs quickly. But we have to argue with a man in uniform. He has large boils on his face. The boils swell and glow with sweat as we argue with him. He wants Kusum to wait in line and he refuses to take authority because his boss is on a tea break. But Kusum won't let her coffins out of sight, and I shan't desert her though I know that my parents, elderly and diabetic, must be waiting in a stuffy car in a scorching lot.

"You bastard!" I scream at the man with the popping boils. Other passengers press closer. "You think we're smuggling contraband in those coffins!"

Once upon a time we were well brought up women; we were dutiful wives who kept our heads veiled, our voices shy and sweet.

In India, I become, once again, an only child of rich, ailing parents. Old friends of the family come to pay their respects. Some are Sikh, and inwardly, involuntarily, I cringe. My parents are progressive people; they do not blame communities for a few individuals.

In Canada it is a different story now.

"Stay longer," my mother pleads. "Canada is a cold place. Why would you want to be all by yourself?" I stay.

Three months pass. Then another.

"Vikram wouldn't have wanted you to give up things!" they protest. They call my husband by the name he was born with. In Toronto he'd changed to Vik so the men he worked with at his office would find his name as easy as Rod or Chris. "You know, the dead aren't cut off from us!"

My grandmother, the spoiled daughter of a rich *zamindar*,[4] shaved her head with rusty razor blades when she was widowed at sixteen. My grandfather died of childhood diabetes when he was nineteen, and she saw herself as the harbinger of bad luck. My mother grew up without parents, raised indifferently by an uncle, while her true mother slept in a hut behind the main estate house and took her food with the servants. She grew up a rationalist. My parents abhor mindless mortification.

The zamindar's daughter kept stubborn faith in Vedic rituals; my parents rebelled. I am trapped between two modes of knowledge. At thirty-six, I am too old to start over and too young to give up. Like my husband's spirit, I flutter between worlds.

Courting aphasia, we travel. We travel with our phalanx of servants and poor relatives. To hill stations and to beach resorts. We play contract bridge in dusty gymkhana clubs. We ride stubby ponies up crumbly mountain trails. At tea dances, we let ourselves be twirled twice round the ballroom. We hit the holy spots we hadn't made time for before. In Varanasi, Kalighat, Rishikesh, Hardwar, astrologers and palmists seek me out and for a fee offer me cosmic consolations.

Already the widowers among us are being shown new bride candidates. They cannot resist the call of custom, the authority of their parents and older brothers. They must marry; it is the duty of a man to look after a wife. The new wives will be young widows with children, destitute but of good family. They will make loving wives, but the men will shun them. I've had calls from the men over crackling Indian telephone lines. "Save me," they say, these substantial, educated, successful men of forty. "My parents are arranging a marriage for me." In a month they will have buried one family and returned to Canada with a new bride and partial family.

I am comparatively lucky. No one here thinks of arranging a husband for an unlucky widow.

Then, on the third day of the sixth month into this odyssey, in an abandoned temple in a tiny Himalayan village, as I make my offering of flowers and sweetmeats to the god of a tribe of animists, my husband descends to me. He is squatting next to a scrawny *sadhu* in moth-eaten robes. Vikram wears the vanilla suit he wore the last time I hugged him. The *sadhu* tosses petals on a butter-

4. Landowner (Hindi).

fed flame, reciting Sanskrit mantras and sweeps his face of flies. My husband takes my hands in his.

*You're beautiful,* he starts. Then, *What are you doing here?*

*Shall I stay?* I ask. He only smiles, but already the image is fading. *You must finish alone what we started together.* No seaweed wreathes his mouth. He speaks too fast just as he used to when we were an envied family in our pink split-level. He is gone.

In the windowless altar room, smoky with joss sticks and clarified butter lamps, a sweaty hand gropes for my blouse. I do not shriek. The *sadhu* arranges his robe. The lamps hiss and sputter out.

When we come out of the temple, my mother says, "Did you feel something weird in there?"

My mother has no patience with ghosts, prophetic dreams, holy men, and cults.

"No," I lie. "Nothing."

But she knows that she's lost me. She knows that in days I shall be leaving.

Kusum's put her house up for sale. She wants to live in an ashram in Hardwar. Moving to Hardwar was her swami's idea. Her swami runs two ashrams, the one in Hardwar and another here in Toronto.

"Don't run away," I tell her.

"I'm not running away," she says. "I'm pursuing inner peace. You think you or that Ranganathan fellow are better off?"

Pam's left for California. She wants to do some modelling, she says. She says when she comes into her share of the insurance money she'll open a yoga-cum-aerobics studio in Hollywood. She sends me postcards so naughty I daren't leave them on the coffee table. Her mother has withdrawn from her and the world.

The rest of us don't lose touch, that's the point. Talk is all we have, says Dr. Ranganathan, who has also resisted his relatives and returned to Montreal and to his job, alone. He says, whom better to talk with than other relatives? We've been melted down and recast as a new tribe.

He calls me twice a week from Montreal. Every Wednesday night and every Saturday afternoon. He is changing jobs, going to Ottawa. But Ottawa is over a hundred miles away, and he is forced to drive two hundred and twenty miles a day. He can't bring himself to sell his house. The house is a temple, he says; the king-sized bed in the master bedroom is a shrine. He sleeps on a folding cot. A devotee.

There are still some hysterical relatives. Judith Templeton's list of those needing help and those who've "accepted" is in nearly perfect balance. Acceptance means you speak of your family in the past tense and you make active plans for moving ahead with your life. There are courses at Seneca and Ryerson[5] we could be taking. Her gleaming leather briefcase is full of college catalogues

5. Ryerson Polytechnical Institute, Toronto. Seneca College of Applied Arts and Technology, in Willowdale.

and lists of cultural societies that need our help. She has done impressive work, I tell her.

"In the textbooks on grief management," she replies—I am her confidante, I realize, one of the few whose grief has not sprung bizarre obsessions—"there are stages to pass through: rejection, depression, acceptance, reconstruction." She has compiled a chart and finds that six months after the tragedy, none of us still reject reality, but only a handful are reconstructing. "Depressed Acceptance" is the plateau we've reached. Remarriage is a major step in reconstruction (though she's a little surprised, even shocked, over *how* quickly some of the men have taken on new families). Selling one's house and changing jobs and cities is healthy.

How do I tell Judith Templeton that my family surrounds me, and that like creatures in epics, they've changed shapes? She sees me as calm and accepting but worries that I have no job, no career. My closest friends are worse off than I. I cannot tell her my days, even my nights, are thrilling.

She asks me to help with families she can't reach at all. An elderly couple in Agincourt whose sons were killed just weeks after they had brought their parents over from a village in Punjab. From their names, I know they are Sikh. Judith Templeton and a translator have visited them twice with offers of money for air fare to Ireland, with bank forms, power-of-attorney forms, but they have refused to sign, or to leave their tiny apartment. Their sons' money is frozen in the bank. Their sons' investment apartments have been trashed by tenants, the furnishings sold off. The parents fear that anything they sign or any money they receive will end the company's or the country's obligations to them. They fear they are selling their sons for two airline tickets to a place they've never seen.

The high-rise apartment is a tower of Indians and West Indians, with a sprinkling of Orientals. The nearest bus stop kiosk is lined with women in saris. Boys practice cricket in the parking lot. Inside the building, even I wince a bit from the ferocity of onion fumes, the distinctive and immediate Indianness of frying *ghee,* but Judith Templeton maintains a steady flow of information. These poor old people are in imminent danger of losing their place and all their services.

I say to her, "They are Sikh. They will not open up to a Hindu woman." And what I want to add is, as much as I try not to, I stiffen now at the sight of beards and turbans. I remember a time when we all trusted each other in this new country, it was only the new country we worried about.

The two rooms are dark and stuffy. The lights are off, and an oil lamp sputters on the coffee table. The bent old lady has let us in, and her husband is wrapping a white turban over his oiled, hip-length hair. She immediately goes to the kitchen, and I hear the most familiar sound of an Indian home, tap water hitting and filling a teapot.

They have not paid their utility bills, out of fear and the inability to write a check. The telephone is gone; electricity and gas and water are soon to follow. They have told Judith their sons will provide. They are good boys, and they have always earned and looked after their parents.

We converse a bit in Hindi. They do not ask about the crash and I wonder if I should bring it up. If they think I am here merely as a translator, then they may feel insulted. There are thousands of Punjabi-speakers, Sikhs, in Toronto to do a better job. And so I say to the old lady, "I too have lost my sons, and my husband, in the crash."

Her eyes immediately fill with tears. The man mutters a few words which sound like a blessing. "God provides and God takes away," he says.

I want to say, but only men destroy and give back nothing. "My boys and my husband are not coming back," I say. "We have to understand that."

Now the old woman responds. "But who is to say? Man alone does not decide these things." To this her husband adds his agreement.

Judith asks about the bank papers, the release forms. With a stroke of the pen, they will have a provincial trustee to pay their bills, invest their money, send them a monthly pension.

"Do you know this woman?" I ask them.

The man raises his hand from the table, turns it over and seems to regard each finger separately before he answers. "This young lady is always coming here, we make tea for her and she leaves papers for us to sign." His eyes scan a pile of papers in the corner of the room. "Soon we will be out of tea, then will she go away?"

The old lady adds, "I have asked my neighbors and no one else gets *angrezi*[6] visitors. What have we done?"

"It's her job," I try to explain. "The government is worried. Soon you will have no place to stay, no lights, no gas, no water."

"Government will get its money. Tell her not to worry, we are honorable people."

I try to explain the government wishes to give money, not take. He raises his hand. "Let them take," he says. "We are accustomed to that. That is no problem."

"We are strong people," says the wife. "Tell her that."

"Who needs all this machinery?" demands the husband. "It is unhealthy, the bright lights, the cold air on a hot day, the cold food, the four gas rings. God will provide, not government."

"When our boys return," the mother says. Her husband sucks his teeth. "Enough talk," he says.

Judith breaks in. "Have you convinced them?" The snaps on her cordovan briefcase go off like firecrackers in that quiet apartment. She lays the sheaf of legal papers on the coffee table. "If they can't write their names, an X will do—I've told them that."

Now the old lady has shuffled to the kitchen and soon emerges with a pot of tea and two cups. "I think my bladder will go first on a job like this," Judith says to me, smiling. "If only there was some way of reaching them. Please thank her for the tea. Tell her she's very kind."

I nod in Judith's direction and tell them in Hindi, "She thanks you for the tea. She thinks you are being very hospitable but she doesn't have the slightest idea what it means."

6. English, Anglo (Hindi).

I want to say, humor her. I want to say, my boys and my husband are with me too, more than ever. I look in the old man's eyes and I can read his stubborn, peasant's message: *I have protected this woman as best I can. She is the only person I have left. Give to me or take from me what you will, but I will not sign for it. I will not pretend that I accept.*

In the car, Judith says, "You see what I'm up against? I'm sure they're lovely people, but their stubbornness and ignorance are driving me crazy. They think signing a paper is signing their sons' death warrants, don't they?"

I am looking out the window. I want to say, *In our culture, it is a parent's duty to hope.*

"Now Shaila, this next woman is a real mess. She cries day and night, and she refuses all medical help. We may have to—"

"—Let me out at the subway," I say.

"I beg your pardon?" I can feel those blue eyes staring at me.

It would not be like her to disobey. She merely disapproves, and slows at a corner to let me out. Her voice is plaintive. "Is there anything I said? Anything I did?"

I could answer her suddenly in a dozen ways, but I choose not to. "Shaila? Let's talk about it," I hear, then slam the door.

A wife and mother begins her new life in a new country, and that life is cut short. Yet her husband tells her: Complete what we have started. We, who stayed out of politics and came halfway around the world to avoid religious and political feuding have been the first in the New World to die from it. I no longer know what we started, nor how to complete it. I write letters to the editors of local papers and to members of Parliament. Now at least they admit it was a bomb. One MP answers back, with sympathy, but with a challenge. You want to make a difference? Work on a campaign. Work on mine. Politicize the Indian voter.

My husband's old lawyer helps me set up a trust. Vikram was a saver and a careful investor. He had saved the boys' boarding school and college fees. I sell the pink house at four times what we paid for it and take a small apartment downtown. I am looking for a charity to support.

We are deep in the Toronto winter, gray skies, icy pavements. I stay indoors, watching television. I have tried to assess my situation, how best to live my life, to complete what we began so many years ago. Kusum has written me from Hardwar that her life is now serene. She has seen Satish and has heard her daughter sing again. Kusum was on a pilgrimage, passing through a village when she heard a young girl's voice, singing one of her daughter's favorite *bhajans.* She followed the music through the squalor of a Himalayan village, to a hut where a young girl, an exact replica of her daughter, was fanning coals under the kitchen fire. When she appeared, the girl cried out, "Ma!" and ran away. What did I think of that?

I think I can only envy her.

Pam didn't make it to California, but writes me from Vancouver. She works in a department store, giving make-up hints to Indian and Oriental girls. Dr. Ranganathan has given up his commute, given up his house and job, and accepted an academic position in Texas where no one knows his story and he has vowed not to tell it. He calls me now once a week.

I wait, I listen, and I pray, but Vikram has not returned to me. The voices and the shapes and the nights filled with visions ended abruptly several weeks ago.

I take it as a sign.

One rare, beautiful, sunny day last week, returning from a small errand on Yonge Street, I was walking through the park from the subway to my apartment. I live equidistant from the Ontario Houses of Parliament and the University of Toronto. The day was not cold, but something in the bare trees caught my attention. I looked up from the gravel, into the branches and the clear blue sky beyond. I thought I heard the rustling of larger forms, and I waited a moment for voices. Nothing.

"What?" I asked.

Then as I stood in the path looking north to Queen's Park and west to the university, I heard the voices of my family one last time. *Your time has come,* they said. *Go, be brave.*

I do not know where this voyage I have begun will end. I do not know which direction I will take. I dropped the package on a park bench and started walking.

## RICHARD FORD on *The Management of Grief*

Bharati Mukherjee's "The Management of Grief" is a story of great intelligence, poignant surprise, and elegant simplicity. A jetliner has exploded over the seas off Ireland. All passengers are seemingly lost, including families of those characters who, as grieving survivors, populate the story—most prominently Mrs. Bhave, its narrator, who has lost her husband and two young sons. Dramatizing how these characters and Mrs. Bhave herself feel, express, and indeed manage their awful grief becomes the story's subject and its strategy for revealing those nuances of grief that ordinary experience does not alert us to (that it can be thrilling as well as defeating, for instance). And this also becomes the story's means of assuring us that grief can be withstood.

As in any story—great or otherwise—what provokes and surprises us, and what provides the reader's experience of its primary intellectual *ground,* is the writer's decision about which segment or segments of life to tell us and which to leave untold. Obviously this decision determines what is emphasized, and thus what our notice and curiosity will be sharpened to. Often in great stories, such as Mukherjee's, what is emphasized by being told is different from what conventional understanding has prepared us to believe is important. We admire writers who show us the world in this fresh way—show us what we did not expect to be important. And as we're shown the world newly, our awareness and appreciation of it are redeemed.

Indeed, in Mukherjee's story, human survivorship, the facing of grief, and the obligation to narrate one's stricken life in order to save it are depicted almost entirely separate from the terrible physical devastation—the plane crash—which might seem the indispensable dramatic element if we were to learn of the events in a news story or on TV. But grief, in Mukherjee's story, is experienced in its own vivid, intense, but nearly sealed realm. True, it is a force born of disaster, but in Mukherjee's fine vision, grief is best understood and complexly felt—and most hopefully accommodated—almost entirely by itself.

# Alice Munro

*Munro (1931–    ) was born in Wingham, Ontario, Canada, and was educated at the University of Western Ontario. Her first collection of stories,* Dance of the Happy Shades *(1968), won the Governor-General's Award, and her novel* Lives of Girls and Women *(1971) won the Canadian Bookseller's Award. Munro is the highly acclaimed author of short stories that find the humanity in small-town life. In 1978 and 1986 she once again received the Governor-General's Award for* Who Do You Think You Are?, *published in the United States as* The Beggar Maid, *and* The Progress of Love. *She also received the Pen/Malamud Award in 1997. Her more recent books include* Open Secrets *(1994),* Selected Stories *(1996), and* Love of a Good Woman *(1998).*

## Royal Beatings

R*oyal beating.* That was Flo's promise. You are going to get one Royal Beating.

The word Royal lolled on Flo's tongue, took on trappings. Rose had a need to picture things, to pursue absurdities, that was stronger than the need to stay out of trouble, and instead of taking this threat to heart she pondered: how is a beating royal? She came up with a tree-lined avenue, a crowd of formal spectators, some white horses and black slaves. Someone knelt, and the blood came leaping out like banners. An occasion both savage and splendid. In real life they didn't approach such dignity, and it was only Flo who tried to supply the event with some high air of necessity and regret. Rose and her father soon got beyond anything presentable.

Her father was king of the royal beatings. Those Flo gave never amounted to much; they were quick cuffs and slaps dashed off while her attention remained elsewhere. You get out of my road, she would say. You mind your own business. You take that look off your face.

They lived behind a store in Hanratty, Ontario. There were four of them: Rose, her father, Flo, Rose's young half brother Brian. The store was really a house, bought by Rose's father and mother when they married and set up here in the furniture and upholstery repair business. Her mother could do upholstery. From both parents Rose should have inherited clever hands, a quick sympathy with materials, an eye for the nicest turns of mending, but she hadn't. She was clumsy, and when something broke she couldn't wait to sweep it up and throw it away.

Her mother had died. She said to Rose's father during the afternoon, "I have a feeling that is so hard to describe. It's like a boiled egg in my chest, with the shell left on." She died before night, she had a blood clot on her lung. Rose was a baby in a basket at the time, so of course could not remember any of this. She heard it from Flo, who must have heard it from her father. Flo came along soon afterward, to take over Rose in the basket, marry her father, open up the front room to make a grocery store. Rose, who had known the house only as a store, who had known only Flo for a mother, looked back on the sixteen or so months her parents spent here as an orderly, far gentler and more ceremonious time, with little touches of affluence. She had nothing to go on but some egg cups her mother had bought, with a pattern of vines and birds on them, delicately drawn as if with red ink; the pattern was beginning to wear away. No books or clothes or pictures of her mother remained. Her father must have got rid of them, or else Flo would. Flo's only story about her mother, the one about her death, was oddly grudging. Flo liked the details of a death: the things people said, the way they protested or tried to get out of bed or swore or laughed (some did those things), but when she said that Rose's mother mentioned a hard-boiled egg in her chest she made the comparison sound slightly foolish, as if her mother really was the kind of person who might think you could swallow an egg whole.

Her father had a shed out behind the store, where he worked at his furniture repairing and restoring. He caned chair seats and backs, mended wickerwork, filled cracks, put legs back on, all most admirably and skillfully and cheaply. That was his pride: to startle people with such fine work, such moderate, even ridiculous charges. During the Depression people could not afford to pay more, perhaps, but he continued the practice through the war, through the years of prosperity after the war, until he died. He never discussed with Flo what he charged or what was owing. After he died she had to go out and unlock the shed and take all sorts of scraps of paper and torn envelopes from the big wicked-looking hooks that were his files. Many of these she found were not accounts or receipts at all but records of the weather, bits of information about the garden, things he had been moved to write down.

Ate new potatoes 25th June. Record.
Dark Day, 1880's, nothing supernatural. Clouds of ash from forest fires.
Aug 16, 1938. Giant thunderstorm in evng. Lightning str. Pres. Church, Turberry Twp. Will of God?
Scald strawberries to remove acid.
All things are alive. Spinoza.[1]

Flo thought Spinoza must be some new vegetable he planned to grow, like broccoli or eggplant. He would often try some new thing. She showed the scrap of paper to Rose and asked, did she know what Spinoza was? Rose did know, or had an idea—she was in her teens by that time—but she replied that she did not. She had reached an age where she thought she could not stand to

1. Benedict Spinoza (1632–1677), Dutch philosopher.

know any more, about her father, or about Flo; she pushed any discovery aside with embarrassment and dread.

There was a stove in the shed, and many rough shelves covered with cans of paint and varnish, shellac and turpentine, jars of soaking brushes and also some dark sticky bottles of cough medicine. Why should a man who coughed constantly, whose lungs took in a whiff of gas in the War (called, in Rose's earliest childhood, not the First, but the Last,[2] War) spend all his days breathing fumes of paint and turpentine? At the time, such questions were not asked as often as they are now. On the bench outside Flo's store several old men from the neighborhood sat gossiping, drowsing, in the warm weather, and some of these old men coughed all the time too. The fact is they were dying, slowly and discreetly, of what was called, without any particular sense of grievance, "the foundry disease." They had worked all their lives at the foundry in town, and now they sat still, with their wasted yellow faces, coughing, chuckling, drifting into aimless obscenity on the subject of women walking by, or any young girl on a bicycle.

From the shed came not only coughing, but speech, a continual muttering, reproachful or encouraging, usually just below the level at which separate words could be made out. Slowing down when her father was at a tricky piece of work, taking on a cheerful speed when he was doing something less demanding, sandpapering or painting. Now and then some words would break through and hang clear and nonsensical on the air. When he realized they were out, there would be a quick bit of cover-up coughing, a swallowing, an alert, unusual silence.

"Macaroni, pepperoni, Botticelli,[3] beans—"

What could that mean? Rose used to repeat such things to herself. She could never ask him. The person who spoke these words and the person who spoke to her as her father were not the same, though they seemed to occupy the same space. It would be the worst sort of taste to acknowledge the person who was not supposed to be there; it would not be forgiven. Just the same, she loitered and listened.

The cloud-capped towers, she heard him say once.

"The cloud-capped towers, the gorgeous palaces."[4]

That was like a hand clapped against Rose's chest, not to hurt, but astonish her, to take her breath away. She had to run then, she had to get away. She knew that was enough to hear, and besides, what if he caught her? It would be terrible.

This was something the same as bathroom noises. Flo had saved up, and had a bathroom put in, but there was no place to put it except in a corner of the kitchen. The door did not fit, the walls were only beaver-board. The result was that even the tearing of a piece of toilet paper, the shifting of a haunch, was audible to those working or talking or eating in the kitchen. They were all familiar with each other's nether voices, not only in

2. World War I was euphemistically referred to as "the war to end all wars." 3. Sandro Botticelli (1444?–1510), Italian painter. 4. "The cloud-capped towers, the gorgeous palaces, / The solemn temples, the great globe itself. / Yea, all which it inherit, shall dissolve, / And, like this insubstantial pageant faded, / Leave not a wrack behind." Shakespeare's *Tempest* 4.1.

their more explosive moments but in their intimate sighs and growls and pleas and statements. And they were all most prudish people. So no one ever seemed to hear, or be listening, and no reference was made. The person creating the noises in the bathroom was not connected with the person who walked out.

They lived in a poor part of town. There was Hanratty and West Hanratty, with the river flowing between them. This was West Hanratty. In Hanratty the social structure ran from doctors and dentists and lawyers down to foundry workers and factory workers and draymen; in West Hanratty it ran from factory workers and foundry workers down to large improvident families of casual bootleggers and prostitutes and unsuccessful thieves. Rose thought of her own family as straddling the river, belonging nowhere, but that was not true. West Hanratty was where the store was and they were, on the straggling tail end of the main street. Across the road from them was a blacksmith shop, boarded up about the time the war started, and a house that had been another store at one time. The Salada Tea sign had never been taken out of the front window; it remained as a proud and interesting decoration though there was no Salada Tea for sale inside. There was just a bit of sidewalk, too cracked and tilted for roller-skating, though Rose longed for roller skates and often pictured herself whizzing along in a plaid skirt, agile and fashionable. There was one street light, a tin flower; then the amenities gave up and there were dirt roads and boggy places, front-yard dumps and strange-looking houses. What made the houses strange-looking were the attempts to keep them from going completely to ruin. With some the attempt had never been made. These were gray and rotted and leaning over, falling into a landscape of scrub hollows, frog ponds, cattails and nettles. Most houses, however, had been patched up with tarpaper, a few fresh shingles, sheets of tin, hammered-out stovepipes, even cardboard. This was, of course, in the days before the war, days of what would later be legendary poverty, from which Rose would remember mostly low-down things—serious-looking anthills and wooden steps, and a cloudy, interesting, problematical light on the world.

There was a long truce between Flo and Rose in the beginning. Rose's nature was growing like a prickly pineapple, but slowly, and secretly, hard pride and skepticism overlapping, to make something surprising even to herself. Before she was old enough to go to school, and while Brian was still in the baby carriage, Rose stayed in the store with both of them—Flo sitting on the high stool behind the counter, Brian asleep by the window; Rose knelt or lay on the wide creaky floorboards working with crayons on pieces of brown paper too torn or irregular to be used for wrapping.

People who came to the store were mostly from the houses around. Some country people came too, on their way home from town, and a few people from Hanratty, who walked across the bridge. Some people were always on the main street, in and out of stores, as if it was their duty to be always on display and their right to be welcomed. For instance, Becky Tyde.

Becky Tyde climbed up on Flo's counter, made room for herself beside an open tin of crumbly jam-filled cookies.

"Are these any good?" she said to Flo, and boldly began to eat one. "When are you going to give us a job, Flo?"

"You could go and work in the butcher shop," said Flo innocently. "You could go and work for your brother."

"Roberta?" said Becky with a stagey sort of contempt. "You think I'd work for him?" Her brother who ran the butcher shop was named Robert but often called Roberta, because of his meek and nervous ways. Becky Tyde laughed. Her laugh was loud and noisy like an engine bearing down on you.

She was a big-headed loud-voiced dwarf, with a mascot's sexless swagger, a red velvet tam, a twisted neck that forced her to hold her head on one side, always looking up and sideways. She wore little polished high-heeled shoes, real lady's shoes. Rose watched her shoes, being scared of the rest of her, of her laugh and her neck. She knew from Flo that Becky Tyde had been sick with polio as a child, that was why her neck was twisted and why she had not grown any taller. It was hard to believe that she had started out differently, that she had ever been normal. Flo said she was not cracked, she had as much brains as anybody, but she knew she could get away with anything.

"You know I used to live out here?" Becky said, noticing Rose. "Hey! What's-your-name! Didn't I used to live out here, Flo?"

"If you did it was before my time," said Flo, as if she didn't know anything.

"That was before the neighborhood got so downhill. Excuse me saying so. My father built his house out here and he built his slaughterhouse and we had half an acre of orchard."

"Is that so?" said Flo, using her humoring voice, full of false geniality, humility even. "Then why did you ever move away?"

"I told you, it got to be such a downhill neighborhood," said Becky. She would put a whole cookie in her mouth if she felt like it, let her cheeks puff out like a frog's. She never told any more.

Flo knew anyway, and who didn't. Everyone knew the house, red brick with the veranda pulled off and the orchard, what was left of it, full of the usual outflow—car seats and washing machines and bedsprings and junk. The house would never look sinister, in spite of what had happened in it, because there was so much wreckage and confusion all around.

Becky's old father was a different kind of butcher from her brother according to Flo. A bad-tempered Englishman. And different from Becky in the matter of mouthiness. His was never open. A skinflint, a family tyrant. After Becky had polio he wouldn't let her go back to school. She was seldom seen outside the house, never outside the yard. He didn't want people gloating. That was what Becky said, at the trial. Her mother was dead by that time and her sisters married. Just Becky and Robert at home. People would stop Robert on the road and ask him, "How about your sister, Robert? Is she altogether better now?"

"Yes."

"Does she do the housework? Does she get your supper?"

"Yes."

"And is your father good to her, Robert?"

The story being that the father beat them, had beaten all his children and beaten his wife as well, beat Becky more now because of her deformity, which some people believed he had caused (they did not understand about polio). The stories persisted and got added to. The reason that Becky was kept out of sight was now supposed to be her pregnancy, and the father of the child was supposed to be her own father. Then people said it had been born, and disposed of.

"What?"

"Disposed of," Flo said. "They used to say go and get your lamb chops at Tyde's, get them nice and tender! It was all lies in all probability," she said regretfully.

Rose could be drawn back—from watching the wind shiver along the old torn awning, catch in the tear—by this tone of regret, caution, in Flo's voice. Flo telling a story—and this was not the only one, or even the most lurid one, she knew—would incline her head and let her face go soft and thoughtful, tantalizing, warning.

"I shouldn't even be telling you this stuff."

More was to follow.

Three useless young men, who hung around the livery stable, got together—or were got together, by more influential and respectable men in town—and prepared to give old man Tyde a horsewhipping, in the interests of public morality. They blacked their faces. They were provided with whips and a quart of whiskey apiece, for courage. They were: Jelly Smith, a horse-racer and a drinker; Bob Temple, a ballplayer and strongman; and Hat Nettleton, who worked on the town dray,[5] and had his nickname from a bowler hat he wore, out of vanity as much as for the comic effect. He still worked on the dray, in fact; he had kept the name if not the hat, and could often be seen in public almost as often as Becky Tyde—delivering sacks of coal, which blackened his face and arms. That should have brought to mind his story, but didn't. Present time and past, the shady melodramatic past of Flo's stories, were quite separate, at least for Rose. Present people could not be fitted into the past. Becky herself, town oddity and public pet, harmless and malicious, could never match the butcher's prisoner, the cripple daughter, a white streak at the window: mute, beaten, impregnated. As with the house, only a formal connection could be made.

The young men primed to do the horsewhipping showed up late, outside Tyde's house, after everybody had gone to bed. They had a gun, but they used up their ammunition firing it off in the yard. They yelled for the butcher and beat on the door; finally they broke it down. Tyde concluded they were after his money, so he put some bills in a handkerchief and sent Becky down with them, maybe thinking those men would be touched or scared by the sight of a little wry-necked girl, a dwarf. But that didn't content them. They came upstairs and dragged the butcher out from under his bed, in his nightgown. They dragged him outside and stood him in the snow. The temperature was four below zero, a fact noted later in court. They meant to hold a mock trial but they could not remember how it was done. So they began to beat him and kept

5. Wagon used for carrying heavy loads for hire.

beating him until he fell. They yelled at him, *Butcher's meat!* and continued beating him while his nightgown and the snow he was lying in turned red. His son Robert said in court that he had not watched the beating. Becky said that Robert had watched at first but had run away and hid. She herself had watched all the way through. She watched the men leave at last and her father make his delayed bloody progress through the snow and up the steps of the veranda. She did not go out to help him, or open the door until he got to it. Why not? she was asked in court, and she said she did not go out because she just had her nightgown on, and she did not open the door because she did not want to let the cold into the house.

Old man Tyde then appeared to have recovered his strength. He sent Robert to harness the horse, and made Becky heat water so that he could wash. He dressed and took all the money and with no explanation to his children got into the cutter and drove to Belgrave where he left the horse tied in the cold and took the early morning train to Toronto. On the train he behaved oddly, groaning and cursing as if he was drunk. He was picked up on the streets of Toronto a day later, out of his mind with fever, and was taken to a hospital, where he died. He still had all the money. The cause of death was given as pneumonia.

But the authorities got wind, Flo said. The case came to trial. The three men who did it all received long prison sentences. A farce, said Flo. Within a year they were all free, had all been pardoned, had jobs waiting for them. And why was that? It was because too many higher-ups were in on it. And it seemed as if Becky and Robert had no interest in seeing justice done. They were left well-off. They bought a house in Hanratty. Robert went into the store. Becky after her long seclusion started on a career of public sociability and display.

That was all. Flo put the lid down on the story as if she was sick of it. It reflected no good on anybody.

"Imagine," Flo said.

Flo at this time must have been in her early thirties. A young woman. She wore exactly the same clothes that a woman of fifty, or sixty, or seventy, might wear: print housedresses loose at the neck and sleeves as well as the waist; bib aprons, also of print, which she took off when she came from the kitchen into the store. This was a common costume at the time, for a poor though not absolutely poverty-stricken woman; it was also, in a way, a scornful deliberate choice. Flo scorned slacks, she scorned the outfits of people trying to be in style, she scorned lipstick and permanents. She wore her own black hair cut straight across, just long enough to push behind her ears. She was tall but fine-boned, with narrow wrists and shoulders, a small head, a pale, freckled, mobile, monkeyish face. If she had thought it worthwhile, and had the resources, she might have had a black-and-pale, fragile, nurtured sort of prettiness; Rose realized that later. But she would have to have been a different person altogether; she would have to have learned to resist making faces, at herself and others.

Rose's earliest memories of Flo were of extraordinary softness and hardness. The soft hair, the long, soft, pale cheeks, soft almost invisible fuzz in front of her ears and above her mouth. The sharpness of her knees, hardness of her lap, flatness of her front.

When Flo sang:

Oh the buzzin' of the bees in the cigarette trees
And the soda-*water* fountain . . .[6]

Rose thought of Flo's old life before she married her father, when she worked as a waitress in the coffee shop in Union Station, and went with her girl friends Mavis and Irene to Centre Island,[7] and was followed by men on dark streets and knew how pay phones and elevators worked. Rose heard in her voice the reckless dangerous life of cities, the gum-chewing sharp answers.

And when she sang:

Then slowly, slowly, she got up
And slowly she came nigh him
And all she said, that she ever did say,
Was young man I think, you're dyin'![8]

Rose thought of a life Flo seemed to have had beyond that, earlier than that, crowded and legendary, with Barbara Allen and Becky Tyde's father and all kinds of outrages and sorrows jumbled up together in it.

The royal beatings. What got them started?

Suppose a Saturday, in spring. Leaves not out yet but the doors open to the sunlight. Crows. Ditches full of running water. Hopeful weather. Often on Saturdays Flo left Rose in charge of the store—it's a few years now, these are the years when Rose was nine, ten, eleven, twelve—while she herself went across the bridge to Hanratty (going uptown they called it) to shop and see people, and listen to them. Among the people she listened to were Mrs. Lawyer Davies, Mrs. Anglican Rector Henley-Smith, and Mrs. Horse-Doctor McKay. She came home and imitated their flibberty voices. Monsters, she made them seem; of foolishness, and showiness, and self-approbation.

When she finished shopping she sent into the coffee shop of the Queen's Hotel and had a sundae. What kind? Rose and Brian wanted to know when she got home, and they would be disappointed if it was only pineapple or butterscotch, pleased if it was a Tin Roof, or Black and White. Then she smoked a cigarette. She had some ready-rolled, that she carried with her, so that she wouldn't have to roll one in public. Smoking was the one thing she did that she would have called showing off in anybody else. It was a habit left over from her working days, from Toronto. She knew it was asking for trouble. Once the Catholic priest came over to her right in the Queen's Hotel, and flashed his lighter at her before she could get her matches out. She thanked him but did not enter into conversation, lest he should try to convert her.

Another time, on the way home, she saw at the town end of the bridge a boy in a blue jacket, apparently looking at the water. Eighteen, nineteen years old. Nobody she knew. Skinny, weakly looking, something the matter with him, she saw at once. Was he thinking of jumping? Just as she came up even with him, what does he do but turn and display himself, holding his jacket open,

6. From the ballad *The Big Rock Candy Mountain.* 7. Park in Toronto Harbour. Union Station is the main railroad terminal in Toronto. 8. From the ballad *Barbara Allen.*

also his pants. What he must have suffered from the cold, on a day that had Flo holding her coat collar tight around her throat.

When she first saw what he had in his hand, Flo said, all she could think of was, what is he doing out here with a baloney sausage?

She could say that. It was offered as truth; no joke. She maintained that she despised dirty talk. She would go out and yell at the old men sitting in front of her store.

"If you want to stay where you are you better clean your mouths out!"

Saturday, then. For some reason Flo is not going uptown, has decided to stay home and scrub the kitchen floor. Perhaps this has put her in a bad mood. Perhaps she was in a bad mood anyway, due to people not paying their bills, or the stirring-up of feelings in spring. The wrangle with Rose has already commenced, has been going on forever, like a dream that goes back and back into other dreams, over hills and through doorways, maddeningly dim and populous and familiar and elusive. They are carting all the chairs out of the kitchen preparatory to the scrubbing, and they have also got to move some extra provisions for the store, some cartons of canned goods, tins of maple syrup, coal-oil cans, jars of vinegar. They take these things out to the woodshed. Brian who is five or six by this time is helping drag the tins.

"Yes," says Flo, carrying on from our lost starting point. "Yes, and that filth you taught to Brian."

"What filth?"

"And he doesn't know any better."

There is one step down from the kitchen to the woodshed, a bit of carpet on it so worn Rose can't even remember seeing the pattern. Brian loosens it, dragging a tin.

"Two Vancouvers," she says softly.

Flo is back in the kitchen. Brian looks from Flo to Rose and Rose says again in a slightly louder voice, an encouraging singsong, "Two Vancouvers—"

"Fried in snot!" finishes Brian, not able to control himself any longer.

"Two pickled arseholes—"

"—tied in a knot!"

There it is. The filth.

> Two Vancouvers fried in snot!
> Two pickled arseholes tied in a knot!

Rose has known that for years, learned it when she first went to school. She came home and asked Flo, what is a Vancouver?

"It's a city. It's a long ways away."

"What else besides a city?"

Flo said, what did she mean, what else? How could it be fried, Rose said, approaching the dangerous moment, the delightful moment, when she would have to come out with the whole thing.

"Two Vancouvers fried in snot! / Two pickled arseholes tied in a knot!"

"You're going to get it!" cried Flo in a predictable rage. "Say that again and you'll get a good clout!"

Rose couldn't stop herself. She hummed it tenderly, tried saying the innocent words aloud, humming through the others. It was not just the words snot and arsehole that gave her pleasure, though of course they did. It was the pickling and tying and the unimaginable Vancouvers. She saw them in her mind shaped rather like octopuses, twitching in the pan. The tumble of reason; the spark and spit of craziness.

Lately she has remembered it again and taught it to Brian, to see if it has the same effect on him, and of course it has.

"Oh, I heard you!" says Flo. "I heard that! And I'm warning you!"

So she is. Brian takes the warning. He runs away, out the woodshed door, to do as he likes. Being a boy, free to help or not, involve himself or not. Not committed to the household struggle. They don't need him anyway, except to use against each other, they hardly notice his going. They continue, can't help continuing, can't leave each other alone. When they seem to have given up they really are just waiting and building up steam.

Flo gets out the scrub pail and the brush and the rag and the pad for her knees, a dirty red rubber pad. She starts to work on the floor. Rose sits on the kitchen table, the only place left to sit, swinging her legs. She can feel the cool oilcloth, because she is wearing shorts, last summer's tight faded shorts dug out of the summer-clothes bag. They smell a bit moldy from winter storage.

Flo crawls underneath, scrubbing with the brush, wiping with the rag. Her legs are long, white and muscular, marked all over with blue veins as if somebody had been drawing rivers on them with an indelible pencil. An abnormal energy, a violent disgust, is expressed in the chewing of the brush at the linoleum, the swish of the rag.

What do they have to say to each other? It doesn't really matter. Flo speaks of Rose's smart-aleck behavior, rudeness and sloppiness and conceit. Her willingness to make work for others, her lack of gratitude. She mentions Brian's innocence, Rose's corruption. Oh, don't you think you're somebody, says Flo, and a moment later, Who do you think you are? Rose contradicts and objects with such poisonous reasonableness and mildness, displays theatrical unconcern. Flo goes beyond her ordinary scorn and self-possession and becomes amazingly theatrical herself, saying it was for Rose that she sacrificed her life. She saw her father saddled with a baby daughter and she thought, what is that man going to do? So she married him, and here she is, on her knees.

At that moment the bell rings, to announce a customer in the store. Because the fight is on, Rose is not permitted to go into the store and wait on whoever it is. Flo gets up and throws off her apron, groaning—but not communicatively, it is not a groan whose exasperation Rose is allowed to share—and goes in and serves. Rose hears her using her normal voice.

"About time! Sure is!"

She comes back and ties on her apron and is ready to resume.

"You never have a thought for anybody but your ownself! You never have a thought for what I'm doing."

"I never asked you to do anything. I wish you never had. I would have been a lot better off."

Rose says this smiling directly at Flo, who has not yet gone down on her knees. Flo sees the smile, grabs the scrub rag that is hanging on the side of the pail, and throws it at her. It may be meant to hit her in the face but instead it falls against Rose's leg and she raises her foot and catches it, swinging it negligently against her ankle.

"All right," says Flo. "You've done it this time. All right."

Rose watches her go to the woodshed door, hears her tramp through the woodshed, pause in the doorway, where the screen door hasn't yet been hung, and the storm door is standing open, propped with a brick. She calls Rose's father. She calls him in a warning, summoning voice, as if against her will preparing him for bad news. He will know what this is about.

The kitchen floor has five or six different patterns of linoleum on it. Ends, which Flo got for nothing and ingeniously trimmed and fitted together, bordering them with tin strips and tacks. While Rose sits on the table waiting, she looks at the floor, at this satisfying arrangement of rectangles, triangles, some other shape whose name she is trying to remember. She hears Flo coming back through the woodshed, on the creaky plank walk laid over the dirt floor. She is loitering, waiting, too. She and Rose can carry this no further, by themselves.

Rose hears her father come in. She stiffens, a tremor runs through her legs, she feels them shiver on the oilcloth. Called away from some peaceful, absorbing task, away from the words running in his head, called out of himself, her father has to say something. He says, "Well? What's wrong?"

Now comes another voice of Flo's. Enriched, hurt, apologetic, it seems to have been manufactured on the spot. She is sorry to have called him from his work. Would never have done it, if Rose was not driving her to distraction. How to distraction? With her back talk and impudence and her terrible tongue. The things Rose has said to Flo are such that, if Flo had said them to her mother, she knows her father would have thrashed her into the ground.

Rose tries to butt in, to say this isn't true.

What isn't true?

Her father raises a hand, doesn't look at her, says, "Be quiet."

When she says it isn't true, Rose means that she herself didn't start this, only responded, that she was goaded by Flo, who is now, she believes, telling the grossest sort of lies, twisting everything to suit herself. Rose puts aside her other knowledge that whatever Flo has said or done, whatever she herself has said or done, does not really matter at all. It is the struggle itself that counts, and that can't be stopped, can never be stopped, short of where it has got to, now.

Flo's knees are dirty, in spite of the pad. The scrub rag is still hanging over Rose's foot.

Her father wipes his hands, listening to Flo. He takes his time. He is slow at getting into the spirit of things, tired in advance, maybe, on the verge of rejecting the role he has to play. He won't look at Rose, but at any sound or stirring from Rose, he holds up his hand.

"Well we don't need the public in on this, that's for sure," Flo says, and she goes to lock the door of the store, putting in the store window the sign that says BACK SOON, a sign Rose made for her with a great deal of fancy curving and shading of letters in black and red crayon. When she comes back she shuts the door to the store, then the door to the stairs, then the door to the woodshed.

Her shoes have left marks on the clean wet part of the floor.

"Oh, I don't know," she says now, in a voice worn down from its emotional peak. "I don't know what to do about her." She looks down and sees her dirty knees (following Rose's eyes) and rubs at them viciously with her bare hands, smearing the dirt around.

"She humiliates me," she says, straightening up. There it is, the explanation. "She humiliates me," she repeats with satisfaction. "She has no respect."

"I do not!"

"Quiet, you!" says her father.

"If I hadn't called your father you'd still be sitting there with that grin on your face! What other way is there to manage you?"

Rose detects in her father some objections to Flo's rhetoric, some embarrassment and reluctance. She is wrong, and ought to know she is wrong, in thinking that she can count on this. The fact that she knows about it, and he knows she knows, will not make things any better. He is beginning to warm up. He gives her a look. This look is at first cold and challenging. It informs her of his judgment, of the hopelessness of her position. Then it clears, it begins to fill up with something else, the way a spring fills up when you clear the leaves away. It fills with hatred and pleasure. Rose sees that and knows it. Is that just a description of anger, should she see his eyes filling up with anger? No. Hatred is right. Pleasure is right. His face loosens and changes and grows younger, and he holds up his hand this time to silence Flo.

"All right," he says, meaning that's enough, more than enough, this part is over, things can proceed. He starts to loosen his belt.

Flo has stopped anyway. She has the same difficulty Rose does, a difficulty in believing that what you know must happen really will happen, that there comes a time when you can't draw back.

"Oh, I don't know, don't be too hard on her." She is moving around nervously as if she has thoughts of opening some escape route. "Oh, you don't have to use the belt on her. Do you have to use the belt?"

He doesn't answer. The belt is coming off, not hastily. It is being grasped at the necessary point. *All right you.* He is coming over to Rose. He pushes her off the table. His face, like his voice, is quite out of character. He is like a bad actor, who turns a part grotesque. As if he must savor and insist on just what is shameful and terrible about this. That is not to say he is pretending, that he is acting, and does not mean it. He is acting, and he means it. Rose knows that, she knows everything about him.

She has since wondered about murders, and murderers. Does the thing have to be carried through, in the end, partly for the effect, to prove to the audience of one—who won't be able to report, only register, the lesson—that such a thing can happen, that there is nothing that can't happen, that the most dreadful antic is justified, feelings can be found to match it?

She tries again looking at the kitchen floor, that clever and comforting geometrical arrangement, instead of looking at him or his belt. How can this go on in front of such daily witnesses—the linoleum, the calendar with the mill and creek and autumn trees, the old accommodating pots and pans?

*Hold out your hand!*

Those things aren't going to help her, none of them can rescue her. They turn bland and useless, even unfriendly. Pots can show malice, the patterns of linoleum can leer up at you, treachery is the other side of dailiness.

At the first, or maybe the second, crack of pain, she draws back. She will not accept it. She runs around the room, she tries to get to the doors. Her father blocks her off. Not an ounce of courage or of stoicism in her, it would seem. She runs, she screams, she implores. Her father is after her, cracking the belt at her when he can, then abandoning it and using his hands. Bang over the ear, then bang over the other ear. Back and forth, her head ringing. Bang in the face. Up against the wall and bang in the face again. He shakes her and hits her against the wall, he kicks her legs. She is incoherent, insane, shrieking. *Forgive me! Oh please, forgive me!*

Flo is shrieking too. *Stop, stop!*

Not yet. He throws Rose down. Or perhaps she throws herself down. He kicks her legs again. She has given up on words but is letting out a noise, the sort of noise that makes Flo cry, *Oh, what if people can hear her?* The very last-ditch willing sound of humiliation and defeat it is, for it seems Rose must play her part in this with the same grossness, the same exaggeration, that her father displays, playing his. She plays his victim with a self-indulgence that arouses, and maybe hopes to arouse, his final, sickened contempt.

They will give this anything that is necessary, it seems, they will go to any lengths.

Not quite. He has never managed really to injure her, though there are times, of course, when she prays that he will. He hits her with an open hand, there is some restraint in his kicks.

Now he stops, he is out of breath. He allows Flo to move in, he grabs Rose up and gives her a push in Flo's direction, making a sound of disgust. Flo retrieves her, opens the stair door, shoves her up the stairs.

"Go on up to your room now! Hurry!"

Rose goes up the stairs, stumbling, letting herself stumble, letting herself fall against the steps. She doesn't bang her door because a gesture like that could still bring him after her, and anyway, she is weak. She lies on the bed. She can hear through the stovepipe hole Flo snuffling and remonstrating, her father saying angrily that Flo should have kept quiet then, if she did not want Rose punished she should not have recommended it. Flo says she never recommended a hiding like that.

They argue back and forth on this. Flo's frightened voice is growing stronger, getting its confidence back. By stages, by arguing, they are being drawn back into themselves. Soon it's only Flo talking; he will not talk anymore. Rose has had to fight down her noisy sobbing, so as to listen to them, and when she loses interest in listening, and wants to sob some more, she finds she can't work herself up to it. She has passed into a state of calm, in which outrage is perceived as complete and final. In this state events and possibilities take on a lovely simplicity. Choices are mercifully clear. The words that come to mind are not the quibbling, seldom the conditional. Never is a word to which the right is suddenly established. She will never speak to them, she will never look at them with anything but loathing, she will never forgive them. She will punish them; she will finish them. Encased in these finalities, and in her bodily pain, she floats in curious comfort, beyond herself, beyond responsibility.

Suppose she dies now? Suppose she commits suicide? Suppose she runs away? Any of these things would be appropriate. It is only a matter of choosing, of figuring out the way. She floats in her pure superior state as if kindly drugged.

And just as there is a moment, when you are drugged, in which you feel perfectly safe, sure, unreachable, and then without warning and right next to it a moment in which you know the whole protection has fatally cracked, though it is still pretending to hold soundly together, so there is a moment now—the moment, in fact, when Rose hears Flo step on the stairs—that contains for her both present peace and freedom and a sure knowledge of the whole down-spiraling course of events from now on.

Flo comes into the room without knocking, but with a hesitation that shows it might have occurred to her. She brings a jar of cold cream. Rose is hanging on to advantage as long as she can, lying face down on the bed, refusing to acknowledge or answer.

"Oh come on," Flo says uneasily. "You aren't so bad off, are you? You put some of this on and you'll feel better."

She is bluffing. She doesn't know for sure what damage has been done. She has the lid off the cold cream. Rose can smell it. The intimate, babyish, humiliating smell. She won't allow it near her. But in order to avoid it, the big ready clot of it in Flo's hand, she has to move. She scuffles, resists, loses dignity, and lets Flo see there is not really much the matter.

"All right," Flo says. "You win. I'll leave it here and you can put it on when you like."

Later still a tray will appear. Flo will put it down without a word and go away. A large glass of chocolate milk on it, made with Vita-Malt from the store. Some rich streaks of Vita-Malt around the bottom of the glass. Little sandwiches, neat and appetizing. Canned salmon of the first quality and reddest color, plenty of mayonnaise. A couple of butter tarts from a bakery package, chocolate biscuits with a peppermint filling. Rose's favorites, in the sandwich, tart and cookie line. She will turn away, refuse to look, but left alone with these eatables will be miserably tempted, roused and troubled and drawn back from thoughts of suicide or flight by the smell of salmon, the anticipation of crisp chocolate, she will reach out a finger, just to run it around the edge of one of the sandwiches (crusts cut off!) to get the overflow, get a taste. Then she will decide to eat one, for strength to refuse the rest. One will not be noticed. Soon, in helpless corruption, she will eat them all. She will drink the chocolate milk, eat the tarts, eat the cookies. She will get the malty syrup out of the bottom of the glass with her finger, though she sniffles with shame. Too late.

Flo will come up and get the tray. She may say, "I see you got your appetite still," or, "Did you like the chocolate milk, was it enough syrup in it?" depending on how chastened she is feeling, herself. At any rate, all advantage will be lost. Rose will understand that life has started up again, that they will all sit around the table eating again, listening to the radio news. Tomorrow morning, maybe even tonight. Unseemly and unlikely as that may be. They will be embarrassed, but rather less than you might expect considering how they have behaved. They will feel a queer lassitude, a convalescent indolence, not far off satisfaction.

One night after a scene like this they were all in the kitchen. It must have been summer, or at least warm weather, because her father spoke of the old men who sat on the bench in front of the store.

"Do you know what they're talking about now?" he said, and nodded his head toward the store to show who he meant, though of course they were not there now, they went home at dark.

"Those old coots," said Flo. "What?"

There was about them both a geniality not exactly false but a bit more emphatic than was normal, without company.

Rose's father told them then that the old men had picked up the idea somewhere that what looked like a star in the western sky, the first star that came out after sunset, the evening star, was in reality an airship hovering over Bay City, Michigan, on the other side of Lake Huron. An American invention, sent up to rival the heavenly bodies. They were all in agreement about this, the idea was congenial to them. They believed it to be lit by ten thousand electric light bulbs. Her father had ruthlessly disagreed with them, pointing out that it was the planet Venus they saw, which had appeared in the sky long before the invention of an electric light bulb. They had never heard of the planet Venus.

"Ignoramuses," said Flo. At which Rose knew, and knew her father knew, that Flo had never heard of the planet Venus either. To distract them from this, or even apologize for it, Flo put down her teacup, stretched out with her head resting on the chair she had been sitting on and her feet on another chair (somehow she managed to tuck her dress modestly between her legs at the same time), and lay stiff as a board, so that Brian cried out in delight, "Do that! Do that!"

Flo was double-jointed and very strong. In moments of celebration or emergency she would do tricks.

They were silent while she turned herself around, not using her arms at all but just her strong legs and feet. Then they all cried out in triumph, though they had seen it before.

Just as Flo turned herself Rose got a picture in her mind of that airship, an elongated transparent bubble, with its strings of diamond lights, floating in the miraculous American sky.

"The planet Venus!" her father said, applauding Flo. "Ten thousand electric lights!"

There was a feeling of permission, relaxation, even a current of happiness, in the room.

Years later, many years later, on a Sunday morning, Rose turned on the radio. This was when she was living by herself in Toronto.

*Well Sir.*

*It was a different kind of place in our day. Yes it was.*

*It was all horses then. Horses and buggies. Buggy races up and down the main street on the Saturday nights.*

"Just like the chariot races," says the announcer's, or interviewer's, smooth encouraging voice.

*I never seen a one of them.*

"No sir, that was the old Roman chariot races I was referring to. That was before your time."

*Musta been before my time. I'm a hunerd and two years old.*

"That's a wonderful age, sir."

*It is so.*

She left it on, as she went around the apartment kitchen, making coffee for herself. It seemed to her that this must be a staged interview, a scene from some play, and she wanted to find out what it was. The old man's voice was so vain and belligerent, the interviewer's quite hopeless and alarmed, under its practiced gentleness and ease. You were surely meant to see him holding the microphone up to some toothless, reckless, preening centenarian, wondering what in God's name he was doing here, and what would he say next?

"They must have been fairly dangerous."

*What was dangerous?*

"Those buggy races."

*They was. Dangerous. Used to be the runaway horses. Used to be a-plenty of accidents. Fellows was dragged along on the gravel and cut their face open. Wouldna matter so much if they was dead. Heh.*

*Some of them horses was the high-steppers. Some, they had to have the mustard under their tail. Some wouldn step out for nothin. That's the thing it is with the horses. Some'll work and pull till they drop down dead and some wouldn pull your cock out of a pail of lard. Hehe.*

It must be a real interview after all. Otherwise they wouldn't have put that in, wouldn't have risked it. It's all right if the old man says it. Local color. Anything rendered harmless and delightful by his hundred years.

*Accidents all the time then. In the mill. Foundry. Wasn't the precautions.*

"You didn't have so many strikes then, I don't suppose? You didn't have so many unions?"

*Everybody taking it easy nowadays. We worked and we was glad to get it. Worked and was glad to get it.*

"You didn't have television."

*Didn't have no TV. Didn't have no radio. No picture show.*

"You made your own entertainment."

*That's the way we did.*

"You had a lot of experiences young men growing up today will never have."

*Experiences.*

"Can you recall any of them for us?"

*I eaten groundhog meat one time. One winter. You wouldna cared for it. Heh.*

There was a pause, of appreciation, it would seem, then the announcer's voice saying that the foregoing had been an interview with Mr. Wilfred Nettleton of Hanratty, Ontario, made on his hundred and second birthday, two weeks before his death, last spring. A living link with our past. Mr. Nettleton had been interviewed in the Wawanash County Home for the aged.

Hat Nettleton.

Horsewhipper into centenarian. Photographed on his birthday, fussed over by nurses, kissed no doubt by a girl reporter. Flash bulbs popping at him. Tape recorder drinking in the sound of his voice. Oldest resident. Oldest horsewhipper. Living link with our past.

Looking out from her kitchen window at the cold lake, Rose was longing to tell somebody. It was Flo who would enjoy hearing. She thought of her saying *Imagine!* in a way that meant she was having her worst suspicions gorgeously confirmed. But Flo was in the same place Hat Nettleton had died in, and there wasn't any way Rose could reach her. She had been there even when that interview was recorded, though she would not have heard it, would not have known about it. After Rose put her in the Home, a couple of years earlier, she had stopped talking. She had removed herself, and spent most of her time sitting in a corner of her crib, looking crafty and disagreeable, not answering anybody, though she occasionally showed her feelings by biting a nurse.

# Prue

Prue used to live with Gordon. This was after Gordon left his wife and before he went back to her—a year and four months in all. Some time later, he and his wife were divorced. After that came a period of indecision, of living together off and on; then the wife went away to New Zealand, most likely for good.

Prue did not go back to Vancouver Island, where Gordon had met her when she was working as a dining-room hostess in a resort hotel. She got a job in Toronto, working in a plant shop. She had many friends in Toronto by that time, most of them Gordon's friends and his wife's friends. They liked Prue and were ready to feel sorry for her, but she laughed them out of it. She is very likable. She has what eastern Canadians call an English accent, though she was born in Canada—in Duncan, on Vancouver Island. This accent helps her to say the most cynical things in a winning and light-hearted way. She presents her life in anecdotes, and though it is the point of most of her anecdotes that hopes are dashed, dreams ridiculed, things never turn out as expected, everything is altered in a bizarre way and there is no explanation ever, people always feel cheered up after listening to her; they say of her that it is a relief to meet somebody who doesn't take herself too seriously, who is so unintense, and civilized, and never makes any real demands or complaints.

The only thing she complains about readily is her name. Prue is a schoolgirl, she says, and Prudence is an old virgin; the parents who gave her that name must have been too shortsighted even to take account of puberty. What if she had grown a great bosom, she says, or developed a sultry look? Or was the name itself a guarantee that she wouldn't? In her late forties now, slight and fair, attending to customers with a dutiful vivacity, giving pleasure to dinner guests, she might not be far from what those parents had in mind: bright and thoughtful, a cheerful spectator. It is hard to grant her maturity, maternity, real troubles.

Her grownup children, the products of an early Vancouver Island marriage she calls a cosmic disaster, come to see her, and instead of wanting money, like other people's children, they bring presents, try to do her accounts, arrange to have her house insulated. She is delighted with their presents, listens to their advice, and, like a flighty daughter, neglects to answer their letters.

Her children hope she is not staying on in Toronto because of Gordon. Everybody hopes that. She would laugh at the idea. She gives parties and goes to parties; she goes out sometimes with other men. Her attitude toward sex is very comforting to those of her friends who get into terrible states of passion and jealousy, and feel cut loose from their moorings. She seems to regard sex as a wholesome, slightly silly indulgence, like dancing and nice dinners—something that shouldn't interfere with people's being kind and cheerful to each other.

Now that his wife is gone for good, Gordon comes to see Prue occasionally, and sometimes asks her out for dinner. They may not go to a restaurant; they may go to his house. Gordon is a good cook. When Prue or his wife lived with him he couldn't cook at all, but as soon as he put his mind to it he became—he says truthfully—better than either of them.

Recently he and Prue were having dinner at his house. He had made chicken Kiev, and crème brûlée for dessert. Like most new, serious cooks, he talked about food.

Gordon is rich, by Prue's—and most people's—standards. He is a neurologist. His house is new, built on a hillside north of the city, where there used to be picturesque, unprofitable farms. Now there are one-of-a-kind, architect-designed, very expensive houses on half-acre lots. Prue, describing Gordon's house, will say, "Do you know there are four bathrooms? So that if four people want to have baths at the same time there's no problem. It seems a bit much, but it's very nice, really, and you'd never have to go through the hall."

Gordon's house has a raised dining area—a sort of platform, surrounded by a conversation pit, a music pit, and a bank of heavy greenery under sloping glass. You can't see the entrance area from the dining area, but there are no intervening walls, so that from one area you can hear something of what is going on in the other.

During dinner the doorbell rang. Gordon excused himself and went down the steps. Prue heard a female voice. The person it belonged to was still outside, so she could not hear the words. She heard Gordon's voice, pitched low, cautioning. The door didn't close—it seemed the person had not been invited in—but the voices went on, muted and angry. Suddenly there was a cry from Gordon, and he appeared halfway up the steps, waving his arms.

"The crême brûlée," he said. "Could you?" He ran back down as Prue got up and went into the kitchen to save the dessert. When she returned he was climbing the stairs more slowly, looking both agitated and tired.

"A friend," he said gloomily. "Was it all right?"

Prue realized he was speaking of the crême brûlée, and she said yes, it was perfect, she had got it just in time. He thanked her but did not cheer up. It seemed it was not the dessert he was troubled over but whatever had happened at the door. To take his mind off it, Prue started asking him professional questions about the plants.

"I don't know a thing about them," he said. "You know that."

"I thought you might have picked it up. Like the cooking."

"She takes care of them."

"Mrs. Carr?" said Prue, naming his housekeeper.

"Who did you think?"

Prue blushed. She hated to be thought suspicious.

"The problem is that I think I would like to marry you," said Gordon, with no noticeable lightening of his spirits. Gordon is a large man, with heavy features. He likes to wear thick clothing, bulky sweaters. His blue eyes are often bloodshot, and their expression indicates that there is a helpless, baffled soul squirming around inside this doughty fortress.

"What a problem," said Prue lightly, though she knew Gordon well enough to know that it was.

The doorbell rang again, rang twice, three times, before Gordon could get to it. This time there was a crash, as of something flung and landing hard. The door slammed and Gordon was immediately back in view. He staggered on the steps and held his hand to his head, meanwhile making a gesture with the other hand to signify that nothing serious had happened, Prue was to sit down.

"Bloody overnight bag," he said. "She threw it at me."

"Did it hit you?"

"Glancing."

"It made a hard sound for an overnight bag. Were there rocks in it?"

"Oh."

Prue watched him pour himself a drink. "I'd like some coffee, if I might," she said. She went to the kitchen to put the water on, and Gordon followed her.

"I think I'm in love with this person," he said.

"Who is she?"

"You don't know her. She's quite young."

"Oh."

"But I do think I want to marry you, in a few years' time."

"After you get over being in love?"

"Yes."

"Well. I guess nobody knows what can happen in a few years' time."

When Prue tells about this, she says, "I think he was afraid I was going to laugh. He doesn't know why people laugh or throw their overnight bags at him, but he's noticed they do. He's such a proper person, really. The lovely dinner. Then she comes and throws her overnight bag. And it's quite reasonable to think of marrying me in a few years' time, when he gets over being in love. I think he first thought of telling me to sort of put my mind at rest."

She doesn't mention that the next morning she picked up one of Gordon's cufflinks from his dresser. The cufflinks are made of amber and he bought them in Russia, on the holiday he and wife took when they got back together again. They look like squares of candy, golden, translucent, and this one warms quickly in her hand. She drops it into the pocket of her jacket. Taking one is not a real theft. It could be a reminder, an intimate prank, a piece of nonsense.

She is alone in Gordon's house; he has gone off early, as he always does. The housekeeper does not come till nine. Prue doesn't have to be at the shop until ten; she could make herself breakfast, stay and have coffee with the housekeeper, who is her friend from olden times. But once she has the cufflink in her pocket she doesn't linger. The house seems too bleak a place to spend an extra moment in. It was Prue, actually, who helped choose the building lot. But she's not responsible for approving the plans—the wife was back by that time.

When she gets home she puts the cufflink in an old tobacco tin. The children bought this tobacco tin in a junk shop years ago, and gave it to her for a present. She used to smoke, in those days, and the children were worried about her, so they gave her this tin full off toffees, jelly beans, and gumdrops, with a note saying, "Please get fat instead." That was for her birthday. Now the tin has in it several things besides the cufflink—all small things, not of great value but not worthless, either. A little enamelled dish, a sterling-silver spoon for salt, a crystal fish. These are not sentimental keepsakes. She never looks at them, and often forgets what she has there. They are not booty, they don't have ritualistic significance. She does not take something every time she goes to Gordon's house, or every time she stays over, or to mark what she might call memorable visits. She doesn't do it in a daze and she doesn't seem to be under a compulsion. She just takes something, every now and then, and puts it away in the dark of the old tobacco tin, and more or less forgets about it.

# Vladimir Nabokov

*Nabokov (1899–1977) was born in St. Petersburg, Russia, of rich and cultured parents. At the time of the Communist revolution, he fled with his family into Western Europe. He attended Cambridge University in England and took a degree in modern languages there in 1922. Thereafter, he spent years in Berlin and Paris, supporting himself by coaching tennis and making up chess problems, all the while writing novels in Russian, German, French, and English. Living in France when it was overrun by the Nazis, he escaped with his family to the United States, where he became a citizen and—by a remarkable imaginative transformation—an American writer. He taught Russian literature at Cornell University until* Lolita *(a best-seller in 1955) and subsequent novels gave him enough money to allow him a full-time commitment to writing. He then lived in Montreux, Switzerland. His complete works in all languages would run to thirty or forty volumes, exemplifying the complexity of his life and his interests in language and experience. In most of his fiction, memories of a dissolving past mingle with an ironic sense of the precariousness of the present. Among his novels are* Laughter in the Dark *(translated in 1938),* Lolita *(1955),* Pnin *(1957),* Pale Fire *(1962), and* Ada; Or, Ardor: A Family Chronicle *(1969).* The Stories of Vladimir Nabokov *was published in 1995.*

## Signs and Symbols

### I

For the fourth time in as many years they were confronted with the problem of what birthday present to bring a young man who was incurably deranged in his mind. He had no desires. Man-made objects were to him either hives of evil, vibrant with a malignant activity that he alone could perceive, or gross comforts for which no use could be found in his abstract world. After eliminating a number of articles that might offend him or frighten him (anything in the gadget line for instance was taboo), his parents chose a dainty and innocent trifle: a basket with ten different fruit jellies in ten little jars.

At the time of his birth they had been married already for a long time; a score of years had elapsed, and now they were quite old. Her drab gray hair was done anyhow. She wore cheap black dresses. Unlike other women of her age (such as Mrs. Sol, their next-door neighbor, whose face was all pink and mauve with paint and whose hat was a cluster of brookside flowers), she presented a naked white countenance to the fault-finding light of spring days. Her husband, who in the old country had been a fairly successful businessman, was now wholly dependent on his brother Isaac, a real American of almost forty years standing. They seldom saw him and had nicknamed him "the Prince."

That Friday everything went wrong. The underground train lost its life current between two stations, and for a quarter of an hour one could hear nothing but the dutiful beating of one's heart and the rustling of newspapers. The bus they had to take next kept them waiting for ages; and when it did come, it was crammed with garrulous high-school children. It was raining hard as they walked up the brown path leading to the sanitarium. There they waited again; and instead of their boy shuffling into the room as he usually did (his poor face blotched with acne, ill-shaven, sullen, and confused), a nurse they knew, and did not care for, appeared at last and brightly explained that he had again attempted to take his life. He was all right, she said, but a visit might disturb him. The place was so miserably understaffed, and things got mislaid or mixed up so easily, that they decided not to leave their present in the office but to bring it to him next time they came.

She waited for her husband to open his umbrella and then took his arm. He kept clearing his throat in a special resonant way he had when he was upset. They reached the bus-stop shelter on the other side of the street and he closed his umbrella. A few feet away, under a swaying and dripping tree, a tiny half-dead unfledged bird was helplessly twitching in a puddle.

During the long ride to the subway station, she and her husband did not exchange a word; and every time she glanced at his old hands (swollen veins, brown-spotted skin), clasped and twitching upon the handle of his umbrella, she felt the mounting pressure of tears. As she looked around trying to hook her mind onto something, it gave her a kind of soft shock, a mixture of compassion and wonder, to notice that one of the passengers, a girl with dark hair and grubby red toenails, was weeping on the shoulder of an older woman. Whom did that woman resemble? She resembled Rebecca Borisovna, whose daughter had married one of the Soloveichiks—in Minsk,[1] years ago.

The last time he had tried to do it, his method had been, in the doctor's words, a masterpiece of inventiveness; he would have succeeded, had not an envious fellow patient thought he was learning to fly—and stopped him. What he really wanted to do was to tear a hole in his world and escape.

The system of his delusions had been the subject of an elaborate paper in a scientific monthly, but long before that she and her husband had puzzled it out for themselves. "Referential mania," Herman Brink had called it. In these very rare cases the patient imagines that everything happening around him is a veiled reference to his personality and existence. He excludes real people from the conspiracy—because he considers himself to be so much more intelligent than other men. Phenomenal nature shadows him wherever he goes. Clouds in the staring sky transmit to one another, by means of slow signs, incredibly detailed information regarding him. His inmost thoughts are discussed at nightfall, in manual alphabet,[2] by darkly gesticulating trees. Pebbles or stains or sun flecks form patterns representing in some awful way messages which he must intercept. Everything is a cipher and of everything he is the

1. A city in western Russia. 2. Sign language used by the deaf.

theme. Some of the spies are detached observers, such as glass surfaces and still pools; others, such as coats in store windows, are prejudiced witnesses, lynchers at heart; others again (running water, storms) are hysterical to the point of insanity, have a distorted opinion of him and grotesquely misinterpret his actions. He must be always on his guard and devote every minute and module of life to the decoding of the undulation of things. The very air he exhales is indexed and filed away. If only the interest he provokes were limited to his immediate surroundings—but alas it is not! With distance the torrents of wild scandal increase in volume and volubility. The silhouettes of his blood corpuscles, magnified a million times, flit over vast plains; and still farther, great mountains of unbearable solidity and height sum up in terms of granite and groaning firs the ultimate truth of his being.

## II

When they emerged from the thunder and foul air of the subway, the last dregs of the day were mixed with the street lights. She wanted to buy some fish for supper, so she handed him the basket of jelly jars, telling him to go home. He walked up to the third landing and then remembered he had given her his keys earlier in the day.

In silence he sat down on the steps and in silence rose when some ten minutes later she came, heavily trudging upstairs, wanly smiling, shaking her head in deprecation of her silliness. They entered their two-room flat and he at once went to the mirror. Straining the corners of his mouth apart by means of his thumbs, with a horrible masklike grimace, he removed his new hopelessly uncomfortable dental plate and severed the long tusks of saliva connecting him to it. He read his Russian-language newspaper while she laid the table. Still reading, he ate the pale victuals that needed no teeth. She knew his moods and was also silent.

When he had gone to bed, she remained in the living room with her pack of soiled cards and her old albums. Across the narrow yard where the rain tinkled in the dark against some battered ash cans, windows were blandly alight and in one of them a black-trousered man with his bare elbows raised could be seen lying supine on an untidy bed. She pulled the blind down and examined the photographs. As a baby he looked more surprised than most babies. From a fold in the album, a German maid they had had in Leipzig and her fat-faced fiancé fell out. Minsk, the Revolution, Leipzig,[3] Berlin, Leipzig, a slanting house front badly out of focus. Four years old, in a park: moodily, shyly, with puckered forehead, looking away from an eager squirrel as he would from any other stranger. Aunt Rose, a fussy, angular, wild-eyed old lady, who had lived in a tremulous world of bad news, bankruptcies, train accidents, cancerous growths—until the Germans put her to death, together with all the people she had worried about. Age six—that was when he drew wonderful birds with human hands and feet, and suffered from insomnia like a grown-up man. His cousin, now a famous chess player. He again, aged about eight, already difficult

3. Leipzig is a city in Germany. The Revolution is the Russian Revolution of 1917–22.

to understand, afraid of the wallpaper in the passage, afraid of a certain picture in a book which merely showed an idyllic landscape with rocks on a hillside and an old cart wheel hanging from the branch of a leafless tree. Aged ten: the year they left Europe. The shame, the pity, the humiliating difficulties, the ugly, vicious, backward children he was with in that special school. And then came a time in his life, coinciding with a long convalescence after pneumonia, when those little phobias of his which his parents had stubbornly regarded as the eccentricities of a prodigiously gifted child hardened as it were into a dense tangle of logically interacting illusions, making him totally inaccessible to normal minds.

This, and much more, she accepted—for after all living did mean accepting the loss of one joy after another, not even joys in her case—mere possibilities of improvement. She thought of the endless waves of pain that for some reason or other she and her husband had to endure; of the invisible giants hurting her boy in some unimaginable fashion; of the incalculable amount of tenderness contained in the world; of the fate of this tenderness, which is either crushed, or wasted, or transformed into madness; of neglected children humming to themselves in unswept corners; of beautiful weeds that cannot hide from the farmer and helplessly have to watch the shadow of his simian stoop leave mangled flowers in its wake, as the monstrous darkness approaches.

## III

It was past midnight when from the living room she heard her husband moan; and presently he staggered in, wearing over his nightgown the old overcoat with astrakhan[4] collar which he much preferred to the nice blue bathrobe he had.

"I can't sleep," he cried.

"Why," she asked, "why can't you sleep? You were so tired."

"I can't sleep because I am dying," he said and lay down on the couch.

"Is it your stomach? Do you want me to call Dr. Solov?"

"No doctors, no doctors," he moaned. "To the devil with doctors! We must get him out of there quick. Otherwise we'll be responsible. Responsible!" he repeated and hurled himself into a sitting position, both feet on the floor, thumping his forehead with his clenched fist.

"All right," she said quietly, "we shall bring him home tomorrow morning."

"I would like some tea," said her husband and retired to the bathroom.

Bending with difficulty, she retrieved some playing cards and a photograph or two that had slipped from the couch to the floor: knave of hearts, nine of spades, ace of spades, Elsa and her bestial beau.

He returned in high spirits, saying in a loud voice:

"I have it all figured out. We will give him the bedroom. Each of us will spend part of the night near him and the other part on this couch. By turns. We will have the doctor see him at least twice a week. It does not matter what the Prince says. He won't have to say much anyway because it will come out cheaper."

4. Lustrous, closely curled wool (from Astrakhan, a city in southeast Russia).

The telephone rang. It was an unusual hour for their telephone to ring. His left slipper had come off and he groped for it with his heel and toe as he stood in the middle of the room, and childishly, toothlessly, gaped at his wife. Having more English than he did, it was she who attended to calls.

"Can I speak to Charlie," said a girl's dull little voice.

"What number you want? No. That is not the right number."

The receiver was gently cradled. Her hand went to her old tired heart.

"It frightened me," she said.

He smiled a quick smile and immediately resumed his excited monologue. They would fetch him as soon as it was day. Knives would have to be kept in a locked drawer. Even at his worst he presented no danger to other people.

The telephone rang a second time. The same toneless anxious young voice asked for Charlie.

"You have the incorrect number. I will tell you what you are doing: you are turning the letter O instead of zero."

They sat down to their unexpected festive midnight tea. The birthday present stood on the table. He sipped noisily; his face was flushed; every now and then he imparted a circular motion to his raised glass so as to make the sugar dissolve more thoroughly. The vein on the side of his bald head where there was a large birthmark stood out conspicuously and, although he had shaved that morning, a silvery bristle showed on his chin. While she poured him another glass of tea, he put on his spectacles and re-examined with pleasure the luminous yellow, green, red little jars. His clumsy moist lips spelled out their eloquent labels: apricot, grape, beech plum, quince. He had got to crab apple, when the telephone rang again.

# Hua-ling Nieh

*Nieh (1915– ) was born in China. She received her Master of Fine Arts degree at the University of Iowa Writer's Workshop in 1966. Her publications include* Mulberry and Peach *(1990) and* Tales from the Deer Garden *(1997). Married to the poet Paul Engle, she was the director of the International Writer's Workshop based at the University of Iowa.*

## The Several Blessings of Wang Ta-nien

Having served three "emperors"—his own name for his principals—the teacher Ta-nien became privileged to occupy, with his wife and children, one of the three small rows of houses behind the school. They had lived in a single room as cramped as a chicken coop. Now they had both a kitchen, and a bedroom containing two double beds made of bamboo, a table and two rattan chairs with legs bound with wire, a desk long unpainted, and a bookshelf, built by Ta-nien himself, out of wooden crates.

Taped to the wall mirror a schedule dangled loosely; one of the tapes had come unstuck. Every morning Ta-nien stood with his head cocked, studying his directions to himself for the day's work, his teeth clenched with determination. Yet the tape stayed unstuck and every day hung more loosely.

*Schedule of Ta-nien*

*Morning*

| | |
|---|---|
| 6:30 a.m. | I do fifty push-ups. I do deep breathing. |
| 7:00 a.m. | I listen to English lessons on the radio with English-Chinese dictionary. |
| 7:30 a.m. | I read *Speeches of Chiang Kai-shek*. |

*Evening*

| | |
|---|---|
| 8:00 a.m. | I read *Speeches of Richard Nixon*. |
| 10:00 p.m. | I I listen to English lessons on the radio with Chinese-English dictionary. |
| 11:00 p.m. | I do fifty push-ups before going to bed. |

To the unexpected fortune of these rooms Ta-nien's emperor quickly added two blessings—a bonus and a certificate of merit "for outstanding service":

> *This is to certify to the outstanding service rendered the First High School, Taipei, Taiwan, during the period from September, 1964, to August, 1965 . . .*

"Wen-chin!" Ta-nien cried triumphantly, bearing in his hand the certificate he'd already read aloud to his wife a dozen times, "Wen-chin! Our luck has turned at last! Who knows what fresh fortune awaits tomorrow? Let's invite the Sage to a feed!"

His four-year-old son, Little Oak, wearing a G.I. cap, began goosestepping proudly for no reason except his contentment in seeing his father victorious.

In the house below the palms the windows were steaming. Odors of urine, mild and strong soap that babies give off, mixed with the scent of frying pork, the smoke from Ta-nien's pipe, and of tea brewing.

These odors swirled between ceiling and floor, trying to find some means of escape, while beyond the window the rain, furious then fitful, tried to find some way of getting inside.

"Sage!" said Ta-nien, attempting to cheer up his old friend. "Why so forlorn? Good times are with us once more! Why, the way things are booming here and the way they're going to hell in a handcar over *there,* we'll be back on the mainland by this time next year!"

The Sage shook his head almost imperceptibly; all his movements were nearly imperceptible. The meaninglessness of years in the routine of a small provincial school had left his face meaningless: a face of no particular shape, a voice that had lost its inflection, and a smile that apologized to everyone all day long.

"We can never get those good years back," the Sage murmured, half to himself, yet casting a dulled look at Wen-chin. One of his hopes had long been to invite Ta-nien and Wen-chin to his own home for Peking duck. Every week while dining here, this hope had returned. Yet even now as he was about to say the words, he saw, in raising his wine cup, how frayed his sleeves had become. So all he said was, "To *you,* Wen-chin."

And as he drank, his eyes still upon her, he saw how time had marred this woman; he remembered her face flawless as the moon on a night when the sky is clear. Now crow's-feet had frayed her eyes as time had frayed his sleeves; and her belly was swollen again.

He remembered her walking a bridge between two clusters of willows. One cluster was bright in the morning; the other bright by evening. She had worn a vermilion sweater and a white silk scarf, walking toward him and twirling a twig. They had walked together down Lovebird Road.

"Stop staring at my wife, Sage," Ta-nien teased his friend good-naturedly, "You had your chance and missed it."

"I never deserved her," the Sage acknowledged; "the better man won."

Although Wen-chin was perpetually angry at her husband, she never felt irritated by him; and although the Sage never angered her, everything he did irritated her.

"I can't say that between you two, I had a wide choice," she said.

"I'm eating you out of house and home," Sage apologized as he apologized every Sunday.

"There is always a place for you here, Sage," Ta-nien reassured him as he reassured him every Sunday. "Now—I wish to speak seriously: I have a plan which will make us both independent!"

The Sage wiped his chin and stopped eating out of respect for his host.

"But it is strictly *confidential,*" Ta-nien warned his friend.

"What else?" Wen-chin put in quickly. "Wasn't the prep school *confidential?* Wasn't the chain of correspondence courses *confidential?* Wasn't the plan for a farm *confidential?* Perhaps this time you'd better advertise."

Ta-nien ignored his wife with practiced deliberation. His belly resting upon his crossed legs, he sat in the rattan chair confidently.

"This time we have to be resolute," he declared.

"*Very* resolute," the Sage agreed immediately without the faintest notion of his part in the newest plan. "I'm ready for The Plan," he assured Ta-nien.

*"Breed fish!"* Ta-nien gave his idea to the waiting world.

*"Breed fish?"* the Sage echoed, as though it had just now occurred to him that fish reproduced.

"Fish?" Wen-chin cut in. "Are all fish the same? *What* fish? Eels? Salmon? Mackerel? Carp? *What* fish?"

"Why"—Ta-nien grinned sheepishly; it had apparently not occurred to him that there was more than one kind—"why, *carp,* of *course,*" he added quickly.

"The ducks will finish off the eggs," Wen-chin decided; "hoodlums will electrify the pond to kill off what the ducks won't get. The rest will die for lack of fresh water. Your fish will starve. So will your family."

"Now for the second step," Ta-nien went on, as if his wife hadn't said a word.

"What was the first?" she demanded.

"*First*, we *clean* out the pond. *Second,* we fertilize it. *Third,* we *put* in the eggs. And, finally—our Sage here guards our investment day and night protecting us from ducks, vandals, and all disasters."

The Sage gave a start, paled, and recovered.

"I would have to leave the school," he reminded Ta-nien; "if it didn't work, I'd be jobless. You're asking me to take a great risk, Ta-nien."

"What? Are you going to go about with frayed sleeves *all* your life?"

"But, Ta-nien, I don't know *how* to breed fish," the Sage pleaded weakly.

"It's an age of specialization, old friend," Ta-nien assured him firmly. "Breeding of the fish will be *my* responsibility. Guarding them will be yours. Nothing ventured, nothing gained. OK?"

Behind her husband's back Wen-chin shook her head, slowly, sadly, yet warningly, at the Sage.

"I'll have to have a week to think it over," the Sage told Ta-nien.

"One week—but no more. We're now operating on a tight schedule, Sage," Ta-nien said. "A week is all we can let you have."

The Sage wondered who the "we" could be, but did not press the question for fear of embarrassing Ta-nien.

"Fry cost about seven cents each," Ta-nien went on. "Twenty thousand carp sell for about nineteen each in the market. But we'll sell wholesale at about ten each. Now, tell me, Sage, how many cents shall we take in by selling twenty thousand carp?"

The Sage blinked his eyes with the effort of calculation. *"Two hundred thousand?"*

*"Two hundred thousand* exactly!" Ta-nien slapped him on the shoulder in their common triumph.

"How will you get the fish to the market?" Wen-chin asked.

Ta-nien poured wine into his own cup and then held the bottle. *"One* problem at a time, *Madame."*

"I would do it," the Sage volunteered. "But if we failed, I'd be jobless!"

"When Daddy gets money I want a whole sack of chewing gum," Little Oak said.

"And a dancing monkey as well," Wen-chin said. "You can count on your daddy. 'I do fifty push-ups,' " she mimicked him, " 'I read *Speeches of Richard Nixon.*' "

"Shut the window, woman!" Ta-nien demanded.

"It is not open!" Wen-chin told him.

"Ta-nien." The Sage made him sit down in the creaking rattan chair and patted him on the shoulder. "Don't shout at her. You're a lucky dog. A pretty wife, two lovely kids."

A whimpering came from the bed. Wen-chin dropped her chopsticks and rushed to the baby. "The little devil! Wet your diaper on such an occasion!"

"She has no appreciation of me," Ta-nien complained to the Sage.

"He means he cares for nobody but himself," Wen-chin said.

"If only the world could be more like you," the Sage said as if he really meant it.

"Little Oak!" Ta-nien was encouraged to shout, "One! Two! Three! Four! One! Two! Three! Four!"

The child slipped off the chair. Twisting his head to the right, straightening his shoulders and holding his neck stiff, he began goosestepping past Ta-nien.

"He's reviewing his troops," Wen-chin told the Sage, sitting on the bed as she fed the baby.

The Sage could not refrain from laughing and coughed out the piece of pork rump he had just put in his mouth. Ta-nien, however, said abruptly: "Sage, I was thinking of our school days back on the mainland. You were really quite active."

"He *was* a poet," Wen-chin remembered.

"I knew a little about everything, but now can't claim to be expert in anything," the Sage admitted.

"I didn't like your dandified ways," Ta-nien recalled.

"I felt you were arrogant," the Sage remembered.

"Mama," Little Oak said, "I'm going outside. If Daddy and Uncle come to blows, call me."

"I had a right to be arrogant," Ta-nien said certainly. "Three girls chased me at one time. One was the daughter of a high-ranking official. She used to wait for me at the corner of Lovebird Road."

"How could you know she was waiting for you if you didn't cast a glance at her?" Wen-chin asked. "Turn off the gas!"

"Ho! Look at her. She's jealous. Back then, I tell you, if I'd only given a hint, huh!" Ta-nien stopped and nodded his head vigorously.

"Little Oak, here's a piece of pig ribs for you!" Wen-chin called to the child.

He rushed in, grabbed it, took a bite, and put it down again. "Mama—too cold."

Wen-chin flung it into Ta-nien's bowl.

Ta-nien shook his head, putting on the look of an injured husband. "You see, in my wife's eye, I've become a bear in the zoo and she's the trainer."

Little Oak clapped his hands with delight and shouted: "Daddy's a bear in the zoo! Daddy's a bear in the zoo!"

Ta-nien bellowed with laughter at his own joke. Then he leaned back, and his chair collapsed with a snap. His wife, his son, and his guest rushed to the rescue. Aroused from sleep, the baby began to cry. Ta-nien struggled strenuously to stand up, but to no avail. Finally the Sage got his arms under his shoulders and raised him to his feet.

"Thank you, thank you," Ta-nien said, debating between anger and smile. Then he kicked at the ruins of the chair. "Damn it! Throw it out—I don't want to have another look at it!"

"I'd like to treat you to Peking duck next weekend," the Sage announced suddenly.

"No, Sage," Wen-chin said, holding her crying baby and patting it on the back. "Save your money and buy yourself a new suit."

"You think so little of me! I, Chen Hao . . ." He approached Wen-chin with his forefinger pointing at his own nose. "I'm not a colt, am I? All these years, and nothing to show for it! But I've learned how to get an advance of a month's salary!"

"Ai-yah," Ta-nien complained, "I'm getting old. Just falling off a chair has given me an ache in the back." Ta-nien sat on the edge of the bed, tapping himself above the hips with his fist.

"What difference does it make!" The Sage waved his hand gallantly. "Here's wine, let's sing; for life's short, like the morning dew."

The rain had almost but not quite stopped when the Sage took his leave. Ta-nien and his wife saw him to the door. Under the dim streetlights the couple watched him walk to the turn in the lane.

"Sage!" Wen-chin called after him.

The Sage turned and stood waiting with his hand cocked to his ear.

"Don't let the ducks eat the fish's food!" Wen-chin shouted into the wind—and she hurried back into the house and slammed the door hard behind her.

For a long moment the two men stood looking at one another, too far apart to explain life to one another any longer. The wind in the coco palms above them whispered a warning, but neither seemed to catch its meaning. Finally the Sage turned off down the narrowing road. Ta-nien watched him out of sight.

The wind that once had blown through the bright willows now rose in the coco palms, chilling and cold. Between them Ta-nien saw the first lamps of evening coming on.

And turning into his own house, Ta-nien pretended to feel afraid of nothing in the whole wide windy world.

# Joyce Carol Oates

*Oates (1938– ) was born in Lockport, New York. She received degrees from Syracuse University and the University of Wisconsin before launching one of the more spectacular careers among contemporary writers. Poet and critic as well as fiction writer, she continues to astonish readers with the ingenuity of her formal innovations as with the sheer volume of her production. Violence, madness, and social disorder are frequently her subject matter. The mysteries of psychological and sociological motivation fascinate her; she constructs ingenious theories to explain them and to focus their moral significance. Her novels include* A Garden of Earthly Delights *(1967),* Expensive People *(1968),* Them *(1969),* Childwold *(1976),* Bellefleur *(1980),* Marya: A Life *(1986),* You Must Remember This *(1987),* American Appetites *(1990),* Because It Is Bitter, and Because It Is My Heart *(1990),* Black Water *(1992),* Foxfire: The Story of a Girl Gang *(1993),* What I Lived For *(1994),* Man Crazy *(1997), and* My Heart Laid Bare *(1998). Her short stories are collected in* By the North Gate *(1963),* Upon the Sweeping Flood and Other Stories *(1966),* The Wheel of Love and Other Stories *(1970),* Marriages and Infidelities *(1972),* The Seduction and Other Stories *(1976),* Night-Side *(1977),* A Sentimental Education *(1981),* Last Days: Stories *(1984),* The Assignation *(1988), and* The Collector of Hearts *(1998). She has published thrillers under the pseudonym Rosamond Smith;* Starr Bright Will Be with You Soon *(1999) is the most recent title.*

## How I Contemplated the World from the Detroit House of Correction and Began My Life Over Again

**Notes for an Essay for an English Class at Baldwin Country Day School; Poking Around in Debris; Disgust and Curiosity; A Revelation of the Meaning of Life; A Happy Ending . . .**

### I. Events

The girl (myself) is walking through Branden's, that excellent store. Suburb of a large famous city that is a symbol for large famous American cities. The event sneaks up on the girl, who believes she is herding it along with a small fixed smile, a girl of fifteen, innocently experienced. She dawdles in a certain style by a counter of costume jewelry. Rings, earrings, necklaces. Prices from $5 to $50, all within reach. All ugly. She eases over to the glove counter, where everything is ugly too. In her close-fitted coat with its black fur collar she contemplates the luxury of Branden's, which she has known for many years: its many mild pale lights, easy on the eye and the soul, its elaborate tinkly decorations, its women shoppers with their excellent shoes and coats and hairdos, all dawdling gracefully, in no hurry.

Who was ever in a hurry here?

2. The girl seated at home. A small library, paneled walls of oak. Some one is talking to me. An earnest, husky, female voice drives itself against my ears, nervous, frightened, groping around my heart, saying, "If you wanted gloves, why didn't you say so? Why didn't you ask for them?" That store, Branden's, is owned by Raymond Forrest who lives on Du Maurier Drive. We live on Sioux Drive. Raymond Forrest. A handsome man? An ugly man? A man of fifty or sixty, with gray hair, or a man of forty with earnest, courteous eyes, a good golf game; who is Raymond Forrest, this man who is my salvation? Father has been talking to him. Father is not his physician; Dr. Berg is his physician. Father and Dr. Berg refer patients to each other. There is a connection. Mother plays bridge with . . . On Mondays and Wednesdays our maid Billie works at . . . The strings draw together in a cat's cradle, making a net to save you when you fall. . . .

3. *Harriet Arnold's.* A small shop, better than Branden's. Mother in her black coat, I in my close-fitted blue coat. Shopping. Now look at this, isn't this cute, do you want this, why don't you want this, try this on, take this with you to the fitting room, take this also, what's wrong with you, what can I do for you, why are you so strange . . . ? "I wanted to steal but not to buy," I don't tell her. The girl droops along in her coat and gloves and leather boots, her eyes scan the horizon, which is pastel pink and decorated like Branden's, tasteful walls and modern ceilings with graceful glimmering lights.

4. Weeks later, the girl at a bus stop. Two o'clock in the afternoon, a Tuesday; obviously she has walked out of school.

5. The girl stepping down from a bus. Afternoon, weather changing to colder. Detroit. Pavement and closed-up stores; grillwork over the windows of a pawnshop. What is a pawnshop, exactly?

## II. Characters

1. The girl stands five feet five inches tall. An ordinary height. Baldwin Country Day School draws them up to that height. She dreams along the corridors and presses her face against the Thermoplex glass. No frost or steam can ever form on that glass. A smudge of grease from her forehead . . . could she be boiled down to grease? She wears her hair loose and long and straight in suburban teen-age style, 1968. Eyes smudged with pencil, dark brown. Brown hair. Vague green eyes. A pretty girl? An ugly girl? She sings to herself under

her breath, idling in the corridor, thinking of her many secrets (the thirty dollars she once took from the purse of a friend's mother, just for fun, the basement window she smashed in her own house just for fun) and thinking of her brother who is at Susquehanna Boys' Academy, an excellent preparatory school in Maine, remembering him unclearly . . . he has long manic hair and a squeaking voice and he looks like one of the popular teen-age singers of 1968, one of those in a group, *The Certain Forces, The Way Out, The Maniacs Responsible.* The girl in her turn looks like one of those fieldsful of girls who listen to the boys' singing, dreaming and mooning restlessly, breaking into high sullen laughter, innocently experienced.

2. The mother. A Midwestern woman of Detroit and suburbs. Belongs to the Detroit Athletic Club. Also the Detroit Golf Club. Also the Bloomfield Hills Country Club. The Village Women's Club at which lectures are given each winter on Genet and Sartre and James Baldwin,[1] by the Director of the Adult Education Program at Wayne State University. . . . The Bloomfield Art Association. Also the Founders Society of the Detroit Institute of Arts. Also . . . Oh, she is in perpetual motion, this lady, hair like blown-up gold and finer than gold, hair and fingers and body of inestimable grace. Heavy weighs the gold on the back of her hairbrush and hand mirror. Heavy heavy the candlesticks in the dining room. Very heavy is the big car, a Lincoln, long and black, that on one cool autumn day split a squirrel's body in two unequal parts.

3. The father. Dr. ______. He belongs to the same clubs as #2. A player of squash and golf; he has a golfer's umbrella of stripes. Candy stripes. In his mouth nothing turns to sugar, however; saliva works no miracles here. His doctoring is of the slightly sick. The sick are sent elsewhere (to Dr. Berg?), the deathly sick are sent back for more tests and their bills are sent to their homes, the unsick are sent to Dr. Coronet (Isabel, a lady), an excellent psychiatrist for unsick people who angrily believe they are sick and want to do something about it. If they demand a male psychiatrist, the unsick are sent by Dr. ______ (my father) to Dr. Lowenstein, a male psychiatrist, excellent and expensive, with a limited practice.

4. Clarita. She is twenty, twenty-five, she is thirty or more? Pretty, ugly, what? She is a woman lounging by the side of a road, in jeans and a sweater, hitchhiking, or she is slouched on a stool at a counter in some roadside diner. A hard line of jaw. Curious eyes. Amused eyes. Behind her eyes processions move, funeral pageants, cartoons. She says, "I never can figure out why girls like you bum around down here. What are you looking for anyway?" An odor of tobacco about her. Unwashed underclothes, or no underclothes, unwashed skin, gritty toes, hair long and falling into strands, not recently washed.

5. Simon. In this city the weather changes abruptly, so Simon's weather changes abruptly. He sleeps through the afternoon. He sleeps through the

1. American novelist and essayist (1924–1987). Jean Genet (1910–1986), French novelist and playwright. Jean Paul Sartre (1905–1980), French novelist, dramatist, and philosopher.

morning. Rising, he gropes around for something to get him going, for a cigarette or a pill to drive him out to the street, where the temperature is hovering around 35°. Why doesn't it drop? Why, why doesn't the cold clean air come down from Canada; will he have to go up into Canada to get it? will he have to leave the Country of his Birth and sink into Canada's frosty fields . . . ? Will the F.B.I. (which he dreams about constantly) chase him over the Canadian border on foot, hounded out in a blizzard of broken glass and horns . . . ?

"Once I was Huckleberry Finn," Simon says, "but now I am Roderick Usher."[2] Beset by frenzies and fears, this man who makes my spine go cold, he takes green pills, yellow pills, pills of white and capsules of dark blue and green . . . he takes other things I may not mention, for what if Simon seeks me out and climbs into my girl's bedroom here in Bloomfield Hills and strangles me, what then . . . ? (As I write this I begin to shiver. Why do I shiver? I am now sixteen and sixteen is not an age for shivering.) It comes from Simon, who is always cold.

### III. World Events

Nothing.

### IV. People and Circumstances Contributing to This Delinquency

Nothing.

### V. Sioux Drive

George, Clyde G. 240 Sioux. A manufacturer's representative; children, a dog, a wife. Georgian with the usual columns. You think of the White House, then of Thomas Jefferson, then your mind goes blank on the white pillars and you think of nothing. Norris, Ralph W. 246 Sioux. Public relations. Colonial. Bay window, brick, stone, concrete, wood, green shutters, sidewalk, lantern, grass, trees, blacktop drive, two children, one of them my classmate Esther (Esther Norris) at Baldwin. Wife, cars. Ramsey, Michael D. 250 Sioux. Colonial. Big living room, thirty by twenty-five, fireplaces in living room, library, recreation room, paneled walls wet bar five bathrooms five bedrooms two lavatories central air conditioning automatic sprinkler automatic garage door three children one wife two cars a breakfast room a patio a large fenced lot fourteen trees a front door with a brass knocker never knocked. Next is our house. Classic contemporary. Traditional modern. Attached garage, attached Florida room, attached patio, attached pool and cabana, attached roof. A front door mail slot through which pour *Time Magazine, Fortune, Life, Business Week*, the *Wall Street Journal,* the *New York Times*, the *New Yorker*, the *Saturday Review, M.D., Modern Medicine, Disease of the Month* . . . and also. . . . And in addition to all this, a quiet sealed letter from Baldwin saying: *Your daughter is not doing*

2. I.e., he has changed from a wholesome American boy into a morbid neurotic. Usher is the chief character in Edgar Allan Poe's *Fall of the House of Usher.* Huck Finn is the young hero of Mark Twain's novel *Adventures of Huckleberry Finn.*

*work compatible with her performance on the Stanford-Binet.*[3] . . . And your son is not doing well, not well at all, very sad. Where is your son anyway? Once he stole trick-and-treat candy from some six-year-old kids, he himself being a robust ten. The beginning. Now your daughter steals. In the Village Pharmacy she made off with, yes she did, don't deny it, she made off with a copy of *Pageant Magazine* for no reason, she swiped a roll of Life Savers in a green wrapper and was in no need of saving her life or even in need of sucking candy; when she was no more than eight years old she stole, don't blush, she stole a package of Tums only because it was out on the counter and available, and the nice lady behind the counter (now dead) said nothing. . . . Sioux Drive. Maples, oaks, elms. Diseased elms cut down. Sioux Drive runs into Roosevelt Drive. Slow, turning lanes, not streets, all drives and lanes and ways and passes. A private police force. Quiet private police, in unmarked cars. Cruising on Saturday evenings with paternal smiles for the residents who are streaming in and out of houses, going to and from parties, a thousand parties, slightly staggering, the women in their furs alighting from automobiles bought of Ford and General Motors and Chrysler, very heavy automobiles. No foreign cars. Detroit. In 275 Sioux, down the block in that magnificent French-Normandy mansion, lives ______ himself, who has the C______ account itself, imagine that! Look at where he lives and look at the enormous trees and chimneys, imagine his many fireplaces, imagine his wife and children, imagine his wife's hair, imagine her fingernails, imagine her bathtub of smooth clean glowing pink, imagine their embraces, his trouser pockets filled with odd coins and keys and dust and peanuts, imagine their ecstasy on Sioux Drive, imagine their income tax returns, imagine their little boy's pride in his experimental car, a scaled down C______, as he roars round the neighborhood on the sidewalks frightening dogs and Negro maids, oh imagine all these things, imagine everything, let your mind roar out all over Sioux Drive and Du Maurier Drive and Roosevelt Drive and Ticonderoga Pass and Burning Bush Way and Lincolnshire Pass and Lois Lane.

When spring comes, its winds blow nothing to Sioux Drive, no odors of hollyhocks or forsythia, nothing Sioux Drive doesn't already possess, everything is planted and performing. The weather vanes, had they weather vanes, don't have to turn with the wind, don't have to contend with the weather. There is no weather.

## VI. Detroit

There is always weather in Detroit. Detroit's temperature is always 32°. Fast-falling temperatures. Slow-rising temperatures. Wind from the north-northeast four to forty miles an hour, small-craft warnings, partly cloudy today and Wednesday changing to partly sunny through Thursday . . . small warnings of frost, soot warnings, traffic warnings, hazardous lake conditions for small craft and swimmers, restless Negro gangs, restless cloud formations, restless temperatures aching to fall out the very bottom of the thermometer or shoot up over the top and boil everything over in red mercury.

3. An intelligence test.

Detroit's temperature is 32°. Fast-falling temperatures. Slow-rising temperatures. Wind from the north-northeast four to forty miles an hour. . . .

## VII. Events

1. The girl's heart is pounding. In her pocket is a pair of gloves! In a plastic bag! Airproof breathproof plastic bag, gloves selling for twenty-five dollars on Branden's counter! In her pocket! Shoplifted! . . . In her purse is a blue comb, not very clean. In her purse is a leather billfold (a birthday present from her grandmother in Philadelphia) with snapshots of the family in clean plastic windows, in the billfold are bills, she doesn't know how many bills. . . . In her purse is an ominous note from her friend Tykie *What's this about Joe H. and the kids hanging around at Louise's Sat. night? You heard anything?*. . . passed in French class. In her purse is a lot of dirty yellow Kleenex, her mother's heart would break to see such very dirty Kleenex, and at the bottom of her purse are brown hairpins and safety pins and a broken pencil and a ballpoint pen (blue) stolen from somewhere forgotten and a purse-size compact of Cover Girl Make-Up, Ivory Rose. . . . Her lipstick is Broken Heart, a corrupt pink; her fingers are trembling like crazy; her teeth are beginning to chatter; her insides are alive; her eyes glow in her head; she is saying to her mother's astonished face *I want to steal but not to buy.*

2. At Clarita's. Day or night? What room is this? A bed, a regular bed, and a mattress on the floor nearby. Wallpaper hanging in strips. Clarita says she tore it like that with her teeth. She was fighting a barbaric tribe that night, high from some pills; she was battling for her life with men wearing helmets of heavy iron and their faces no more than Christian crosses to breathe through, every one of those bastards looking like her lover Simon, who seems to breathe with great difficulty through the slits of mouth and nostrils in his face. Clarita has never heard of Sioux Drive. Raymond Forrest cuts no ice with her, nor does the C______ account and its millions; Harvard Business School could be at the corner of Vernor and 12th Street for all she cares, and Vietnam might have sunk by now into the Dead Sea under its tons of debris, for all the amazement she could show . . . her face is overworked, overwrought, at the age of twenty (thirty?) it is already exhausted but fanciful and ready for a laugh. Clarita says mournfully to me *Honey somebody is going to turn you out let me give you warning.* In a movie shown on late television Clarita is not a mess like this but a nurse, with short neat hair and a dedicated look, in love with her doctor and her doctor's patients and their diseases, enamored of needles and sponges and rubbing alcohol. . . . Or no: she is a private secretary. Robert Cummings is her boss. She helps him with fantastic plots, the canned audience laughs, no, the audience doesn't laugh because nothing is funny, instead her boss is Robert Taylor and they are not boss and secretary but husband and wife, she is threatened by a young starlet, she is grim, handsome, wifely, a good companion for a good man. . . . She is Claudette Colbert. Her sister too is Claudette Colbert. They are twins, identical. Her husband Charles Boyer[4] is a very rich handsome

4. Cummings, Taylor, Colbert, and Boyer are romantic film stars of the 1930s to 1950s.

man and her sister, Claudette Colbert, is plotting her death in order to take her place as the rich man's wife, no one will know because they are *twins*. . . . All these marvelous lives Clarita might have lived, but she fell out the bottom at the age of thirteen. At the age when I was packing my overnight case for a slumber party at Toni Deshield's she was tearing filthy sheets off a bed and scratching up a rash on her arms. . . . Thirteen is uncommonly young for a white girl in Detroit, Miss Brock of the Detroit House of Correction said in a sad newspaper interview for the *Detroit News;* fifteen and sixteen are more likely. Eleven, twelve, thirteen are not surprising in colored . . . they are more precocious. What can we do? Taxes are rising and the tax base is falling. The temperature rises slowly but falls rapidly. Everything is falling out the bottom, Woodward Avenue is filthy, Livernois Avenue is filthy! Scraps of paper flutter in the air like pigeons, dirt flies up and hits you right in the eye, oh Detroit is breaking up into dangerous bits of newspaper and dirt, watch out. . . .

Clarita's apartment is over a restaurant. Simon her lover emerges from the cracks at dark. Mrs. Olesko, a neighbor of Clarita's, an aged white wisp of a woman, doesn't complain but sniffs with contentment at Clarita's noisy life and doesn't tell the cops, hating cops, when the cops arrive. I should give more fake names, more blanks, instead of telling all these secrets. I myself am a secret; I am a minor.

3. My father reads a paper at a medical convention in Los Angeles. There he is, on the edge of the North American continent, when the unmarked detective put his hand so gently on my arm in the aisle of Branden's and said, "Miss, would you like to step over here for a minute?"

And where was he when Clarita put her hand on my arm, that wintry dark sulphurous aching day in Detroit, in the company of closed-down barber shops, closed-down diners, closed-down movie houses, homes, windows, basements, faces . . . she put her hand on my arm and said, "Honey, are you looking for somebody down here?"

And was he home worrying about me, gone for two weeks solid, when they carried me off . . . ? It took three of them to get me in the police cruiser, so they said, and they put more than their hands on my arm.

4. I work on this lesson. My English teacher is Mr. Forest, who is from Michigan State. Not handsome, Mr. Forest, and his name is plain, unlike Raymond Forrest's, but he is sweet and rodentlike, he has conferred with the principal and my parents, and everything is fixed . . . treat her as if nothing has happened, a new start, begin again, only sixteen years old, what a shame, how did it happen?—nothing happened, nothing could have happened, a slight physiological modification known only to a gynecologist or to Dr. Coronet. I work on my lesson. I sit in my pink room. I look around the room with my sad pink eyes. I sigh, I dawdle, I pause. I eat up time. I am limp and happy to be home, I am sixteen years old suddenly, my head hangs heavy as a pumpkin on my shoulders, and my hair has just been cut by Mr. Faye at the Crystal Salon and is said to be very becoming.

(Simon too put his hand on my arm and said, "Honey, you have got to come with me," and in his six-by-six room we got to know each other. Would

I go back to Simon again? Would I lie down with him in all that filth and craziness? Over and over again.

a Clarita is being betrayed as in front of a Cunningham Drug Store she is nervously eyeing a colored man who may or may not have money, or a nervous white boy of twenty with sideburns and an Appalachian look, who may or may not have a knife hidden in his jacket pocket, or a husky red-faced man of friendly countenance who may or may not be a member of the Vice Squad out for an early twilight walk.)

I work on my lesson for Mr. Forest. I have filled up eleven pages. Words pour out of me and won't stop. I want to tell everything . . . what was the song Simon was always humming, and who was Simon's friend in a very new trench coat with an old high school graduation ring on his finger . . . ? Simon's bearded friend? When I was down too low for him, Simon kicked me out and gave me to him for three days, I think, on Fourteenth Street in Detroit, an airy room of cold cruel drafts with newspapers on the floor. . . . Do I really remember that or am I piercing it together from what they told me? Did they tell the truth? Did they know much of the truth?

## VIII. Characters

1. Wednesdays after school, at four; Saturday mornings at ten. Mother drives me to Dr. Coronet. Ferns in the office, plastic or real, they look the same. Dr. Coronet is queenly, an elegant nicotine-stained lady who would have studied with Freud had circumstances not prevented it, a bit of a Catholic, ready to offer you some mystery if your teeth will ache too much without it. Highly recommended by Father! Forty dollars an hour, Father's forty dollars! Progress! Looking up! Looking better! That new haircut is so becoming, says Dr. Coronet herself, showing how normal she is for a woman with an I.Q. of 180 and many advanced degrees.

2. Mother. A lady in a brown suede coat. Boots of shiny black material, black gloves, a black fur hat. She would be humiliated could she know that of all the people in the world it is my ex-lover Simon who walks most like her . . . self-conscious and unreal, listening to distant music, a little bowlegged with craftiness. . . .

3. Father. Tying a necktie. In a hurry. On my first evening home he put his hand on my arm and said, "Honey, we're going to forget all about this."

4. Simon. Outside, a plane is crossing the sky, in here we're in a hurry. Morning. It must be morning. The girl is half out of her mind, whimpering and vague; Simon her dear friend is wretched this morning . . . he is wretched with morning itself . . . he forces her to give him an injection with that needle she knows is filthy, she had a dread of needles and surgical instruments and the odor of things that are to be sent into the blood, thinking somehow of her

father. . . . This is a bad morning, Simon says that his mind is being twisted out of shape, and so he submits to the needle that he usually scorns and bites his lip with his yellowish teeth, his face going very pale. *Ah baby!* he says in his soft mocking voice, which with all women is a mockery of love, *do it like this—Slowly*—And the girl, terrified, almost drops the precious needle but manages to turn it up to the light from the window . . . is it an extension of herself then? She can give him this gift then? I *wish you wouldn't do this to me,* she says, wise in her terror, because it seems to her that Simon's danger—in a few minutes he may be dead—is a way of pressing her against him that is more powerful than any other embrace. She has to work over his arm, the knotted corded veins of his am, her forehead wet with perspiration as she pushes and releases the needle, staring at that mixture of liquid now stained with Simon's bright blood. . . . When the drug hits him she can feel it herself, she feels that magic that is more than any woman can give him, striking the back of his head and making his face stretch as if with the impact of a terrible sun. . . . She tries to embrace him but he pushes her aside and stumbles to his feet. *Jesus Christ,* he says. . . .

5. Princess, a Negro girl of eighteen. What is her charge? She is closed-mouthed about it, shrewd and silent, you know that no one had to wrestle her to the sidewalk to get her in here; she came with dignity. In the recreation room she sits reading *Nancy Drew and the Jewel Box Mystery,*[5] which inspires in her face tiny wrinkles of alarm and interest: what a face! Light brown skin, heavy shaded eyes, heavy eyelashes, a serious sinister dark brow, graceful fingers, graceful wristbones, graceful legs, lips, tongue, a sugar-sweet voice, a leggy stride more masculine than Simon's and my mother's, decked out in a dirty white blouse and dirty white slacks; vaguely nautical is Princess' style. . . . At breakfast she is in charge of clearing the table and leans over me, saying, *Honey you sure you ate enough?*

6. The girl lies sleepless, wondering. Why here, why not there? Why Bloomfield Hills and not jail? Why jail and not her pink room? Why downtown Detroit and not Sioux Drive? What is the difference? Is Simon all the difference? The girl's head is a parade of wonders. She is nearly sixteen, her breath is marvelous with wonders, not long ago she was coloring with crayons and now she is smearing the landscape with paints that won't come off and won't come off her fingers either. She says to the matron *I am not talking about anything,* not because everyone has warned her not to talk but because, because she will not talk; because she won't say anything about Simon, who is her secret. And she says to the matron, *I won't go home,* up until that night in the lavatory when everything was changed. . . . "No, I won't go home I want to stay here," she says, listening to her own words with amazement, thinking that weeds might climb everywhere over that marvelous $180,000 house and dinosaurs might return to muddy the beige carpeting, but never never will she reconcile four o'clock in the morning in Detroit with eight o'clock breakfasts in Bloomfield

5. Mystery story for juveniles.

Hills. . . . oh, she aches still for Simon's hands and his caressing breath, though he gave her little pleasure, he took everything from her (five-dollar bills, ten-dollar bills, passed into her numb hands by men and taken out of her hands by Simon) until she herself was passed into the hands of other men, police, when Simon evidently got tired of her and her hysteria. . . . *No, I won't go home, I don't want to be bailed out.* The girl thinks as a *Stubborn and Wayward Child* (one of several charges lodged against her), and the matron understands her crazy white-rimmed eyes that are seeking out some new violence that will keep her in jail, should someone threaten to let her out. Such children try to strangle the matrons, the attendants, or one another . . . they want the locks locked forever, the doors nailed shut . . . and this girl is no different up until that night her mind is changed for her. . . .

## IX. That Night

Princess and Dolly, a little white girl of maybe fifteen, hardy however as a sergeant and in the House of Correction for armed robbery, corner her in the lavatory at the farthest sink and the other girls look away and file out to bed, leaving her. God, how she is beaten up! Why is she beaten up? Why do they pound her, why such hatred? Princess vents all the hatred of a thousand silent Detroit winters on her body, this girl whose body belongs to me, fiercely she rides across the Midwestern plains on this girl's tender bruised body . . . revenge on the oppressed minorities of America! revenge on the slaughtered Indians! revenge on the female sex, on the male sex, revenge on Bloomfield Hills, revenge revenge. . . .

## X. Detroit

In Detroit, weather weighs heavily upon everyone. The sky looms large. The horizon shimmers in smoke. Downtown the buildings are imprecise in the haze. Perpetual haze. Perpetual motion inside the haze. Across the choppy river is the city of Windsor, in Canada. Part of the continent has bunched up here and is bulging outward, at the tip of Detroit; a cold hard rain is forever falling on the expressways. . . . Shoppers shop grimly, their cars are not parked in safe places, their windshields may be smashed and graceful ebony hands may drag them out through their shatterproof smashed windshields, crying, *Revenge of the Indians!* Ah, they all fear leaving Hudson's and being dragged to the very tip of the city and thrown off the parking roof of Cobo Hall, that expensive tomb, into the river. . . .

## XI. Characters We Are Forever Entwined With

1. Simon drew me into his tender rotting arms and breathed gravity into me. Then I came to earth, weighed down. He said, *You are such a little girl,* and he weighed me down with his delight. In the palms of his hands were teeth marks from his previous life experiences. He was thirty-five, they said. Imagine Simon in this room, in my pink room: he is about six feet tall and stoops slightly, in a feline cautious way, always thinking, always on guard, with his scuffed light suede shoes and his clothes that are anyone's clothes, slightly rumpled ordinary

clothes that ordinary men might wear to not-bad jobs. Simon has fair long hair, curly hair, spent languid curls that are like . . . exactly like the curls of wood shavings to the touch, I am trying to be exact . . . and he smells of unheated mornings and coffee and too many pills coating his tongue with a faint green-white scum. . . . Dear Simon, who would be panicked in this room and in this house (right now Billie is vacuuming next door in my parents' room; a vacuum cleaner's roar is a sign of all good things), Simon who is said to have come from a home not much different from this, years ago, fleeing all the carpeting and the polished banisters . . . Simon has a deathly face, only desperate people fall in love with it. His face is bony and cautious, the bones of his cheeks prominent as if with the rigidity of his ceaseless thinking, plotting, for he has to make money out of girls to whom money means nothing, they're so far gone they can hardly count it, and in a sense money means nothing to him either except as a way of keeping on with his life. *Each Day's Proud Struggle,* the title of a novel we could read at jail. . . . Each day he needs a certain amount of money. He devours it. It wasn't love he uncoiled in me with his hollowed-out eyes and his courteous smile, that remnant of a prosperous past, but a dark terror that needed to press itself flat against him, or against another man . . . but he was the first, he came over to me and took my arm, a claim. We struggled on the stairs and I said, *Let me loose, you're hurting my neck, my face,* it was such a surprise that my skin hurt where he rubbed it, and afterward we lay face to face and he breathed everything into me. In the end I think he turned me in.

2. Raymond Forrest. I just read this morning that Raymond Forrest's father, the chairman of the board at ______, died of a heart attack on a plane bound for London. I would like to write Raymond Forrest a note of sympathy. I would like to thank him for not pressing charges against me one hundred years ago, saving me, being so generous . . . well, men like Raymond Forrest are generous men, not like Simon. I would like to write him a letter telling of my love, or of some other emotion that is positive and healthy. Not like Simon and his poetry, which he scrawled down when he was high and never changed a word . . . but when I try to think of something to say, it is Simon's language that comes back to me, caught in my head like a bad song, it is always Simon's language:

> There is no reality only dreams
> Your neck may get snapped when you wake
> My love is drawn to some violent end
> She keeps wanting to get away
> My love is heading downward
> And I am heading upward
> She is going to crash on the sidewalk
> And I am going to dissolve into the clouds

## XII. Events

1. Out of the hospital, bruised and saddened and converted, with Princess' grunts still tangled in my hair . . . and Father in his overcoat, looking like a

prince himself, come to carry me off. Up the expressway and out north to home. Jesus Christ, but the air is thinner and cleaner here. Monumental houses. Heartbreaking sidewalks, so clean.

2. Weeping in the living room. The ceiling is two stories high and two chandeliers hang from it. Weeping, weeping, though Billie the maid is *probably listening.* I will never leave home again. Never. Never leave home. Never leave this home again, never.

3. Sugar doughnuts for breakfast. The toaster is very shiny and my face is distorted in it. Is that my face?

4. The car is turning in the driveway. Father brings me home. Mother embraces me. Sunlight breaks in movieland patches on the roof of our traditional-contemporary home, which was designed for the famous automotive stylist whose identity, if I told you the name of the famous car he designed, you would all know, so I can't tell you because my teeth chatter at the thought of being sued . . . or having someone climb into my bedroom window with a rope to strangle me. . . . The car turns up the blacktop drive. The house opens to me like a doll's house, so lovely in the sunlight, the big living room beckons to me with its walls falling away in a delirium of joy at my return, Billie the maid is *no doubt* listening from the kitchen as I burst into tears and the hysteria Simon got so sick of. Convulsed in Father's arms, I say I will never leave again, never, why did I leave, where did I go, what happened, my mind is gone wrong, my body is one big bruise, my backbone was sucked dry, it wasn't the men who hurt me and Simon never hurt me but only those girls . . . my God, how they hurt me . . . I will never leave home again. . . . The car is perpetually turning up the drive and I am perpetually breaking down in the living room and we are perpetually taking the right exit from the expressway (Lahser Road) and the wall of the rest room is perpetually banging against my head and perpetually are Simon's hands moving across my body and adding everything up and so too are Father's hands on my shaking bruised back, far from the surface of my skin on the surface of my good blue cashmere coat (dry-cleaned for my release). . . . I weep for all the money here, for God in gold and beige carpeting, for the beauty of chandeliers and the miracle of a clean polished gleaming toaster and faucets that run both hot and cold water, and I tell them, *I will never leave home, this is my home, I love everything here, I am in love with everything here. . . .*

I am home.

# Tim O'Brien

*O'Brien (1946– ) was born in Austin, Minnesota, and educated at Macalester College. He served in the U.S. Army in Vietnam and emerged as one of the most brilliant chroniclers of that carnage. Though there is a solid vein of realism in his work, it also has something in common with the "magical realism" of contemporary South American novelists; fantasy is entwined with his reliable reportage. He is the author of* If I Die in a Combat Zone, Box Me Up and Ship Me Home *(1973);* Northern Lights *(1974);* Going after Cacciato *(1978);* The Nuclear Age *(1985);* The Things They Carried *(1990), a collection of his stories;* In the Lake of the Woods *(1994); and* Tomcat in Love *(1998).*

## The Things They Carried

First Lieutenant Jimmy Cross carried letters from a girl named Martha, a junior at Mount Sebastian College in New Jersey. They were not love letters, but Lieutenant Cross was hoping, so he kept them folded in plastic at the bottom of his rucksack. In the late afternoon, after a day's march, he would dig his foxhole, wash his hands under a canteen, unwrap the letters, hold them with the tips of his fingers, and spend the last hour of light pretending. He would imagine romantic camping trips into the White Mountains in New Hampshire. He would sometimes taste the envelope flaps, knowing her tongue had been there. More than anything, he wanted Martha to love him as he loved her, but the letters were mostly chatty, elusive on the matter of love. She was a virgin, he was almost sure. She was an English major at Mount Sebastian, and she wrote beautifully about her professors and roommates and midterm exams, about her respect for Chaucer and her great affection for Virginia Woolf. She often quoted lines of poetry; she never mentioned the war, except to say, Jimmy, take care of yourself. The letters weighed ten ounces. They were signed "Love, Martha," but Lieutenant Cross understood that "Love" was only a way of signing and did not mean what he sometimes pretended it meant. At dusk, he would carefully return the letters to his rucksack. Slowly, a bit distracted, he would get up and move among his men, checking the perimeter, then at full dark he would return to his hole and watch the night and wonder if Martha was a virgin.

The things they carried were largely determined by necessity. Among the necessities or near necessities were P-38 can openers, pocket knives, heat tabs, wrist watches, dog tags, mosquito repellent, chewing gum, candy, cigarettes, salt tablets, packets of Kool-Aid, lighters, matches, sewing kits, Military Payment Certificates, C rations, and two or three canteens of water. Together, these items weighed between fifteen and twenty pounds, depending upon a man's habits or rate of metabolism. Henry Dobbins, who was a big man, carried extra rations; he was especially fond of canned peaches in heavy syrup over pound cake. Dave Jensen, who practiced field hygiene, carried a toothbrush, dental floss, and several hotel-size bars of soap he'd stolen on R&R[1] in Sydney, Australia. Ted Lavender, who was scared, carried tranquilizers until he was shot in the head outside the village of Than Khe in mid-April. By necessity, and because it was SOP,[2] they all carried steel helmets that weighed five pounds including the liner and camouflage cover. They carried the standard fatigue jackets and trousers. Very few carried underwear. On their feet they carried jungle boots—2.1 pounds—and Dave Jensen carried three pairs of socks and a can of Dr. Scholl's foot powder as a precaution against trench foot. Until he was shot, Ted Lavender carried six or seven ounces of premium dope, which for him was a necessity. Mitchell Sanders, the RTO,[3] carried condoms. Norman Bowker carried a diary. Rat Kiley carried comic books. Kiowa, a devout Baptist, carried an illustrated New Testament that had been presented to him by his father, who taught Sunday school in Oklahoma City, Oklahoma. As a hedge against bad times, however, Kiowa also carried his grandmother's distrust of the white man, his grandfather's old hunting hatchet. Necessity dictated. Because the land was mined and booby-trapped, it was SOP for each man to carry a steel-centered, nylon-covered flak jacket, which weighed 6.7 pounds, but which on hot days seemed much heavier. Because you could die so quickly, each man carried at least one large compress bandage, usually in the helmet band for easy access. Because the nights were cold, and because the monsoons were wet, each carried a green plastic poncho that could be used as a raincoat or ground sheet or makeshift tent. With its quilted liner, the poncho weighed almost two pounds, but it was worth every ounce. In April, for instance, when Ted Lavender was shot, they used his poncho to wrap him up, then to carry him across the paddy, then to lift him into the chopper that took him away.

They were called legs or grunts.

To carry something was to "hump" it, as when Lieutenant Jimmy Cross humped his love for Martha up the hills and through the swamps. In its intransitive form, "to hump" meant "to walk," or "to march," but it implied burdens far beyond the intransitive.

Almost everyone humped photographs. In his wallet, Lieutenant Cross carried two photographs of Martha. The first was a Kodachrome snapshot signed "Love," though he knew better. She stood against a brick wall. Her eyes were gray and neutral, her lips slightly open as she stared straight-on at the camera. At night, sometimes, Lieutenant Cross wondered who had taken the picture, because he knew she had boyfriends, because he loved her so much, and because he could see the shadow of the picture taker spreading out against the brick wall. The second photograph had been clipped from the 1968 Mount

1. Rest and rehabilitation leave. 2. Standard operating procedure. 3. Radio and telephone operator.

Sebastian yearbook. It was an action shot—women's volleyball—and Martha was bent horizontal to the floor, reaching, the palms of her hands in sharp focus, the tongue taut, the expression frank and competitive. There was no visible sweat. She wore white gym shorts. Her legs, he thought, were almost certainly the legs of a virgin, dry and without hair, the left knee cocked and carrying her entire weight, which was just over one hundred pounds. Lieutenant Cross remembered touching that left knee. A dark theater, he remembered, and the movie was *Bonnie and Clyde,* and Martha wore a tweed skirt, and during the final scene, when he touched her knee, she turned and looked at him in a sad, sober way that made him pull his hand back, but he would always remember the feel of the tweed skirt and the knee beneath it and the sound of the gunfire that killed Bonnie and Clyde, how embarrassing it was, how slow and oppressive. He remembered kissing her good night at the dorm door. Right then, he thought, he should've done something brave. He should've carried her up the stairs to her room and tied her to the bed and touched that left knee all night long. He should've risked it. Whenever he looked at the photographs, he thought of new things he should've done.

What they carried was partly a function of rank, partly of field specialty.

As a first lieutenant and platoon leader, Jimmy Cross carried a compass, maps, code books, binoculars, and a .45-caliber pistol that weighed 2.9 pounds fully loaded. He carried a strobe light and the responsibility for the lives of his men.

As an RTO, Mitchell Sanders carried the PRC-25 radio, a killer, twenty-six pounds with its battery.

As a medic, Rat Kiley carried a canvas satchel filled with morphine and plasma and malaria tablets and surgical tape and comic books and all the things a medic must carry, including M&M's[4] for especially bad wounds, for a total weight of nearly twenty pounds.

As a big man, therefore a machine gunner, Henry Dobbins carried the M-60, which weighed twenty-three pounds unloaded, but which was almost always loaded. In addition, Dobbins carried between ten and fifteen pounds of ammunition draped in belts across his chest and shoulders.

As PFCs or Spec 4s, most of them were common grunts and carried the standard M-16 gas-operated assault rifle. The weapon weighed 7.5 pounds unloaded, 8.2 pounds with its full twenty-round magazine. Depending on numerous factors, such as topography and psychology, the riflemen carried anywhere from twelve to twenty magazines, usually in cloth bandoliers, adding on another 8.4 pounds at minimum, fourteen pounds at maximum. When it was available, they also carried M-16 maintenance gear—rods and steel brushes and swabs and tubes of LSA oil—all of which weighed about a pound. Among the grunts, some carried the M-79 grenade launcher, 5.9 pounds unloaded, a reasonably light weapon except for the ammunition, which was heavy. A single round weighed ten ounces. The typical load was twenty-five rounds. But Ted Lavender, who was scared, carried thirty-four rounds when he was shot and

4. Apparently this candy was used as a placebo since it would have no other medical value.

killed outside Than Khe, and he went down under an exceptional burden, more than twenty pounds of ammunition, plus the flak jacket and helmet and rations and water and toilet paper and tranquilizers and all the rest, plus the unweighed fear. He was dead weight. There was no twitching or flopping. Kiowa, who saw it happen, said it was like watching a rock fall, or a big sandbag or something—just boom, then down—not like the movies where the dead guy rolls around and does fancy spins and goes ass over teakettle—not like that, Kiowa said, the poor bastard just flat-fuck fell. Boom. Down. Nothing else. It was a bright morning in mid-April. Lieutenant Cross felt the pain. He blamed himself. They stripped off Lavender's canteens and ammo, all the heavy things, and Rat Kiley said the obvious, the guy's dead, and Mitchell Sanders used his radio to report one U.S. KIA[5] and to request a chopper. Then they wrapped Lavender in his poncho. They carried him out to a dry paddy, established security, and sat smoking the dead man's dope until the chopper came. Lieutenant Cross kept to himself. He pictured Martha's smooth young face, thinking he loved her more than anything, more than his men, and now Ted Lavender was dead because he loved her so much and could not stop thinking about her. When the dust-off[6] arrived, they carried Lavender aboard. Afterward they burned Than Khe. They marched until dusk, then dug their holes, and that night Kiowa kept explaining how you had to be there, how fast it was, how the poor guy just dropped like so much concrete. Boom-down, he said. Like cement.

In addition to the three standard weapons—the M-60, M-16, and M-79—they carried whatever presented itself, or whatever seemed appropriate as a means of killing or staying alive. They carried catch-as-catch-can. At various times, in various situations, they carried M-14s and CAR-15s and Swedish Ks and grease guns and captured AK-47s and Chi-Coms and RPGs and Simonov carbines and black-market Uzis and .38-caliber Smith & Wesson handguns and 66 mm LAWs and shotguns and silencers and blackjacks and bayonets and C-4 plastic explosives. Lee Strunk carried a slingshot; a weapon of last resort, he called it. Mitchell Sanders carried brass knuckles. Kiowa carried his grandfather's feathered hatchet. Every third or fourth man carried a Claymore antipersonnel mine—3.5 pounds with its firing device. They all carried fragmentation grenades—fourteen ounces each. They all carried at least one M-18 colored smoke grenade—twenty-four ounces. Some carried CS or tear-gas grenades. Some carried white-phosphorus grenades. They carried all they could bear, and then some, including a silent awe for the terrible power of the things they carried.

In the first week of April, before Lavender died, Lieutenant Jimmy Cross received a good-luck charm from Martha. It was a simple pebble, an ounce at most. Smooth to the touch, it was a milky-white color with flecks of orange and violet, oval-shaped, like a miniature egg. In the accompanying letter, Martha wrote that she had found the pebble on the Jersey shoreline, precisely where the land touched water at high tide, where things came together but also separated. It was this separate-but-together quality, she wrote, that had inspired

5. Killed in action. 6. Helicopter.

her to pick up the pebble and to carry it in her breast pocket for several days, where it seemed weightless, and then to send it through the mail, by air, as a token of her truest feelings for him. Lieutenant Cross found this romantic. But he wondered what her truest feelings were, exactly, and what she meant by separate-but-together. He wondered how the tides and waves had come into play on that afternoon along the Jersey shoreline when Martha saw the pebble and bent down to rescue it from geology. He imagined bare feet. Martha was a poet, with the poet's sensibilities, and her feet would be brown and bare, the toenails unpainted, the eyes chilly and somber like the ocean in March, and though it was painful, he wondered who had been with her that afternoon. He imagined a pair of shadows moving along the strip of sand where things came together but also separated. It was phantom jealousy, he knew, but he couldn't help himself. He loved her so much. On the march, through the hot days of early April, he carried the pebble in his mouth, turning it with his tongue, tasting sea salts and moisture. His mind wandered. He had difficulty keeping his attention on the war. On occasion he would yell at his men to spread out the column, to keep their eyes open, but then he would slip away into daydreams, just pretending, walking barefoot along the Jersey shore, with Martha, carrying nothing. He would feel himself rising. Sun and waves and gentle winds, all love and lightness.

What they carried varied by mission.

When a mission took them to the mountains, they carried mosquito netting, machetes, canvas tarps, and extra bug juice.

If a mission seemed especially hazardous, or if it involved a place they knew to be bad, they carried everything they could. In certain heavily mined AOs,[7] where the land was dense with Toe Poppers and Bouncing Betties, they took turns humping a twenty-eight-pound mine detector. With its headphones and big sensing plate, the equipment was a stress on the lower back and shoulders, awkward to handle, often useless because of the shrapnel in the earth, but they carried it anyway, partly for safety, partly for the illusion of safety.

On ambush, or other night missions, they carried peculiar little odds and ends. Kiowa always took along his New Testament and a pair of moccasins for silence. Dave Jensen carried night-sight vitamins high in carotin. Lee Strunk carried his slingshot; ammo, he claimed, would never be a problem. Rat Kiley carried brandy and M&M's. Until he was shot, Ted Lavender carried the starlight scope, which weighed 6.3 pounds with its aluminum carrying case. Henry Dobbins carried his girlfriend's pantyhose wrapped around his neck as a comforter. They all carried ghosts. When dark came, they would move out single file across the meadows and paddies to their ambush coordinates, where they would quietly set up the Claymores and lie down and spend the night waiting.

Other missions were more complicated and required special equipment. In mid-April, it was their mission to search out and destroy the elaborate tunnel complexes in the Than Khe area south of Chu Lai. To blow the tunnels, they

7. Areas of operations.

carried one-pound blocks of pentrite high explosives, four blocks to a man, sixty-eight pounds in all. They carried wiring, detonators, and battery-powered clackers. Dave Jensen carried earplugs. Most often, before blowing the tunnels, they were ordered by higher command to search them, which was considered bad news, but by and large they just shrugged and carried out orders. Because he was a big man, Henry Dobbins was excused from tunnel duty. The others would draw numbers. Before Lavender died there were seventeen men in the platoon, and whoever drew the number seventeen would strip off his gear and crawl in head first with a flashlight and Lieutenant Cross's .45-caliber pistol. The rest of them would fan out as security. They would sit down or kneel, not facing the hole, listening to the ground beneath them, imagining cobwebs and ghosts, whatever was down there—the tunnel walls squeezing in—how the flashlight seemed impossibly heavy in the hand and how it was tunnel vision in the very strictest sense, compression in all ways, even time, and how you had to wiggle in—ass and elbows—a swallowed-up feeling—and how you found yourself worrying about odd things—will your flashlight go dead? Do rats carry rabies? If you screamed, how far would the sound carry? Would your buddies hear it? Would they have the courage to drag you out? In some respects, though not many, the waiting was worse than the tunnel itself. Imagination was a killer.

On April 16, when Lee Strunk drew the number seventeen, he laughed and muttered something and went down quickly. The morning was hot and very still. Not good, Kiowa said. He looked at the tunnel opening, then out across a dry paddy toward the village of Than Khe. Nothing moved. No clouds or birds or people. As they waited, the men smoked and drank Kool-Aid, not talking much, feeling sympathy for Lee Strunk but also feeling the luck of the draw. You win some, you lose some, said Mitchell Sanders, and sometimes you settle for a rain check. It was a tired line and no one laughed.

Henry Dobbins ate a tropical chocolate bar. Ted Lavender popped a tranquilizer and went off to pee.

After five minutes, Lieutenant Jimmy Cross moved to the tunnel, leaned down, and examined the darkness. Trouble, he thought—a cave-in maybe. And then suddenly, without willing it, he was thinking about Martha. The stresses and fractures, the quick collapse, the two of them buried alive under all that weight. Dense, crushing love. Kneeling, watching the hole, he tried to concentrate on Lee Strunk and the war, all the dangers, but his love was too much for him, he felt paralyzed, he wanted to sleep inside her lungs and breathe her blood and be smothered. He wanted her to be a virgin and not a virgin, all at once. He wanted to know her. Intimate secrets—why poetry? Why so sad? Why that grayness in her eyes? Why so alone? Not lonely, just alone—riding her bike across campus or sitting off by herself in the cafeteria. Even dancing, she danced alone—and it was the aloneness that filled him with love. He remembered telling her that one evening. How she nodded and looked away. And how, later, when he kissed her, she received the kiss without returning it, her eyes wide open, not afraid, not a virgin's eyes, just flat and uninvolved.

Lieutenant Cross gazed at the tunnel. But he was not there. He was buried with Martha under the white sand at the Jersey shore. They were pressed together, and the pebble in his mouth was her tongue. He was smiling. Vaguely, he was aware of how quiet the day was, the sullen paddies, yet he could not bring himself to worry about matters of security. He was beyond that. He was just a kid at war, in love. He was twenty-two years old. He couldn't help it.

A few moments later Lee Strunk crawled out of the tunnel. He came up grinning, filthy but alive. Lieutenant Cross nodded and closed his eyes while the others clapped Strunk on the back and made jokes about rising from the dead.

Worms, Rat Kiley said. Right out of the grave. Fuckin' zombie.

The men laughed. They all felt great relief.

Spook City, said Mitchell Sanders.

Lee Strunk made a funny ghost sound, a kind of moaning, yet very happy, and right then, when Strunk made that high happy moaning sound, when he went *Ahhooooo*, right then Ted Lavender was shot in the head on his way back from peeing. He lay with his mouth open. The teeth were broken. There was a swollen black bruise under his left eye. The cheekbone was gone. Oh shit, Rat Kiley said, the guy's dead. The guy's dead, he kept saying, which seemed profound—the guy's dead. I mean really.

The things they carried were determined to some extent by superstition. Lieutenant Cross carried his good-luck pebble. Dave Jensen carried a rabbit's foot. Norman Bowker, otherwise a very gentle person, carried a thumb that had been presented to him as a gift by Mitchell Sanders. The thumb was dark brown, rubbery to the touch, and weighed four ounces at most. It had been cut from a VC corpse, a boy of fifteen or sixteen. They'd found him at the bottom of an irrigation ditch, badly burned, flies in his mouth and eyes. The boy wore black shorts and sandals. At the time of his death he had been carrying a pouch of rice, rifle, and three magazines of ammunition.

You want my opinion, Mitchell Sanders said, there's a definite moral here.

He put his hand on the dead boy's wrist. He was quiet for a time, as if counting a pulse, then he patted the stomach, almost affectionately, and used Kiowa's hunting hatchet to remove the thumb.

Henry Dobbins asked what the moral was.

Moral?

You know. *Moral.*

Sanders wrapped the thumb in toilet paper and handed it across to Norman Bowker. There was no blood. Smiling, he kicked the boy's head, watched the flies scatter, and said, It's like with that old TV show—Paladin. Have gun, will travel.

Henry Dobbins thought about it.

Yeah, well, he finally said. I don't see no moral.

There it *is*, man.

Fuck off.

They carried USO stationery and pencils and pens. They carried Sterno, safety pins, trip flares, signal flares, spools of wire, razor blades, chewing tobacco, liberated joss sticks and statuettes of the smiling Buddha, candles, grease pencils, *The Stars and Stripes*, fingernail clippers, Psy Ops[8] leaflets, bush hats, bolos, and much more. Twice a week, when the resupply choppers came in, they carried hot chow in green Mermite cans and large canvas bags filled with iced beer and soda pop. They carried plastic water containers, each with a two-gallon capacity. Mitchell Sanders carried a set of starched tiger fatigues for special occasions. Henry Dobbins carried Black Flag insecticide. Dave Jensen carried empty sandbags that could be filled at night for added protection. Lee Strunk carried tanning lotion. Some things they carried in common. Taking turns, they carried the big PRC-77 scrambler radio, which weighed thirty pounds with its battery. They shared the weight of memory. They took up what others could no longer bear. Often, they carried each other, the wounded or weak. They carried infections. They carried chess sets, basketballs, Vietnamese-English dictionaries, insignia of rank, Bronze Stars and Purple Hearts, plastic cards imprinted with the Code of Conduct. They carried diseases, among them malaria and dysentery. They carried lice and ringworm and leeches and paddy algae and various rots and molds. They carried the land itself—Vietnam, the place, the soil—a powdery orange-red dust that covered their boots and fatigues and faces. They carried the sky. The whole atmosphere, they carried it, the humidity, the monsoons, the stink of fungus and decay, all of it, they carried gravity. They moved like mules. By daylight they took sniper fire, at night they were mortared, but it was not battle, it was just the endless march, village to village, without purpose, nothing won or lost. They marched for the sake of the march. They plodded along slowly, dumbly, leaning forward against the heat, unthinking, all blood and bone, simple grunts, soldiering with their legs, toiling up the hills and down into the paddies and across the rivers and up again and down, just humping, one step and then the next and then another, but no volition, no will, because it was automatic, it was anatomy, and the war was entirely a matter of posture and carriage, the hump was everything, a kind of inertia, a kind of emptiness, a dullness of desire and intellect and conscience and hope and human sensibility. Their principles were in their feet. Their calculations were biological. They had no sense of strategy or mission. They searched the villages without knowing what to look for, not caring, kicking over jars of rice, frisking children and old men, blowing tunnels, sometimes setting fires and sometimes not, then forming up and moving on to the next village, then other villages, where it would always be the same. They carried their own lives. The pressures were enormous. In the heat of early afternoon, they would remove their helmets and flak jackets, walking bare, which was dangerous but which helped ease the strain. They would often discard things along the route of march. Purely for comfort, they would throw away rations, blow their Claymores and grenades, no matter, because by nightfall the resupply choppers would arrive with more of the same, then a day or two later still more, fresh watermelons and crates of ammunition and sunglasses and woolen sweaters—the resources were stunning—sparklers for the Fourth of July, colored eggs for Easter. It was the great American war chest—the fruits of science, the

8. Psychological Operations.

smokestacks, the canneries, the arsenals at Hartford, the Minnesota forests, the machine shops, the vast fields of corn and wheat—they carried like freight trains; they carried it on their backs and shoulders—and for all the ambiguities of Vietnam, all the mysteries and unknowns, there was at least the single abiding certainty that they would never be at a loss for things to carry.

After the chopper took Lavender away, Lieutenant Jimmy Cross led his men into the village of Than Khe. They burned everything. They shot chickens and dogs, they trashed the village well, they called in artillery and watched the wreckage, then they marched for several hours through the hot afternoon, and then at dusk, while Kiowa explained how Lavender died, Lieutenant Cross found himself trembling.

He tried not to cry. With his entrenching tool, which weighed five pounds, he began digging a hole in the earth.

He felt shame. He hated himself. He had loved Martha more than his men, and as a consequence Lavender was now dead, and this was something he would have to carry like a stone in his stomach for the rest of the war.

All he could do was dig. He used his entrenching tool like an ax, slashing, feeling both love and hate, and then later, when it was full dark, he sat at the bottom of his foxhole and wept. It went on for a long while. In part, he was grieving for Ted Lavender, but mostly it was for Martha, and for himself, because she belonged to another world, which was not quite real, and because she was a junior at Mount Sebastian College in New Jersey, a poet and a virgin and uninvolved, and because he realized she did not love him and never would.

Like cement, Kiowa whispered in the dark. I swear to God—boom-down. Not a word.

I've heard this, said Norman Bowker.

A pisser, you know? Still zipping himself up. Zapped while zipping.

All right, fine. That's enough.

Yeah, but you had to see it, the guy just—

I *heard*, man. Cement. So why not shut the fuck *up*?

Kiowa shook his head sadly and glanced over at the hole where Lieutenant Jimmy Cross sat watching the night. The air was thick and wet. A warm, dense fog had settled over the paddies and there was the stillness that precedes rain.

After a time Kiowa sighed.

One thing for sure, he said. The Lieutenant's in some deep hurt. I mean that crying jag—the way he was carrying on—it wasn't fake or anything, it was real heavy-duty hurt. The man cares.

Sure, Norman Bowker said.

Say what you want, the man does care.

We all got problems.

Not Lavender.

No, I guess not. Bowker said. Do me a favor, though.

Shut up?

That's a smart Indian. Shut up.

Shrugging, Kiowa pulled off his boots. He wanted to say more, just to lighten up his sleep, but instead he opened his New Testament and arranged it beneath his head as a pillow. The fog made things seem hollow and unattached. He tried not to think about Ted Lavender, but then he was thinking how fast it was, no drama, down and dead, and how it was hard to feel anything except surprise. It seemed un-Christian. He wished he could find some great sadness, or even anger, but the emotion wasn't there and he couldn't make it happen. Mostly he felt pleased to be alive. He liked the smell of the New Testament under his cheek, the leather and ink and paper and glue, whatever the chemicals were. He liked hearing the sounds of night. Even his fatigue, it felt fine, the stiff muscles and the prickly awareness of his own body, a floating feeling. He enjoyed not being dead. Lying there, Kiowa admired Lieutenant Jimmy Cross's capacity for grief. He wanted to share the man's pain, he wanted to care as Jimmy Cross cared. And yet when he closed his eyes, all he could think was Boom-down, and all he could feel was the pleasure of having his boots off and the fog curling in around him and the damp soil and the Bible smells and the plush comfort of night.

After a moment Norman Bowker sat up in the dark.

What the hell, he said. You want to talk, *talk*. Tell it to me.

Forget it.

No, man, go on. One thing I hate, it's a silent Indian.

For the most part they carried themselves with poise, a kind of dignity. Now and then, however, there were times of panic, when they squealed or wanted to squeal but couldn't, when they twitched and made moaning sounds and covered their heads and said Dear Jesus and flopped around on the earth and fired their weapons blindly and cringed and sobbed and begged for the noise to stop and went wild and made stupid promises to themselves and to God and to their mothers and fathers, hoping not to die. In different ways, it happened to all of them. Afterward, when the firing ended, they would blink and peek up. They would touch their bodies, feeling shame, then quickly hiding it. They would force themselves to stand. As if in slow motion, frame by frame, the world would take on the old logic—absolute silence, then the wind, then sunlight, then voices. It was the burden of being alive. Awkwardly, the men would reassemble themselves, first in private, then in groups, becoming soldiers again. They would repair the leaks in their eyes. They would check for casualties, call in dust-offs, light cigarettes, try to smile, clear their throats and spit and begin cleaning their weapons. After a time someone would shake his head and say, No lie, I almost shit my pants, and someone else would laugh, which meant it was bad, yes, but the guy had obviously not shit his pants, it wasn't that bad, and in any case nobody would ever do such a thing and then go ahead and talk about it. They would squint into the dense, oppressive sunlight. For a few moments, perhaps, they would fall silent, lighting a joint and tracking its passage from man to man, inhaling, holding in the humiliation. Scary stuff, one of them might say. But then someone else would grin or flick his eyebrows and say, Roger-dodger, almost cut me a new asshole, *almost*.

There were numerous such poses. Some carried themselves with a sort of wistful resignation, others with pride or stiff soldierly discipline or good humor

l. They were afraid of dying but they were even more afraid to

or macho

show it ound jokes to tell.

Thused a hard vocabulary to contain the terrible softness. *Greased,* y. *Offed, lit up, zapped while zipping.* It wasn't cruelty, just stage the. They were actors and the war came at them in 3-D. When someone t wasn't quite dying, because in a curious way it seemed scripted, and use they had their lines mostly memorized, irony mixed with tragedy, and ey called it by other names, as if to encyst and destroy the reality of n itself. They kicked corpses. They cut off thumbs. They talked grunt lingo. told stories about Ted Lavender's supply of tranquilizers, how the poor idn't feel a thing, how incredibly tranquil he was.

here's a moral here, said Mitchell Sanders.

hey were waiting for Lavender's chopper, smoking the dead man's dope.

he moral's pretty obvious, Sanders said, and winked. Stay away from . No joke, they'll ruin your day every time.

Cute, said Henry Dobbins.

Mind-blower, get it? Talk about wiggy—nothing left, just blood and brains.

They made themselves laugh.

There it is, they'd say, over and over, as if the repetition itself were an act of poise, a balance between crazy and almost crazy, knowing without going. There it is, which meant be cool, let it ride, because oh yeah, man, you can't change what can't be changed, there it is, there it absolutely and positively and fucking well *is*.

They were tough.

They carried all the emotional baggage of men who might die. Grief, terror, love, longing—these were intangibles, but the intangibles had their own mass and specific gravity, they had tangible weight. They carried shameful memories. They carried the common secret of cowardice barely restrained, the instinct to run or freeze or hide, and in many respects this was the heaviest burden of all, for it could never be put down, it required perfect balance and perfect posture. They carried their reputations. They carried the soldier's greatest fear, which was the fear of blushing. Men killed, and died, because they were embarrassed not to. It was what had brought them to the war in the first place, nothing positive, no dreams of glory or honor, just to avoid the blush of dishonor. They died so as not to die of embarrassment. They crawled into tunnels and walked point and advanced under fire. Each morning, despite the unknowns, they made their legs move. They endured. They kept humping. They did not submit to the obvious alternative, which was simply to close the eyes and fall. So easy, really. Go limp and tumble to the ground and let the muscles unwind and not speak and not budge until your buddies picked you up and lifted you into the chopper that would roar and dip its nose and carry you off to the world. A mere matter of falling, yet no one ever fell. It was not courage, exactly; the object was not valor. Rather, they were too frightened to be cowards.

By and large they carried these things inside, maintaining the masks of composure. They sneered at sick call. They spoke bitterly about guys who had found release by shooting off their own toes or fingers. Pussies, they'd say.

Candyasses. It was fierce, mocking talk, with only a trace of envy ve, but even so, the image played itself out behind their eyes.

They imagined the muzzle against flesh. They imagined the quic pain, then the evacuation to Japan, then a hospital with warm beds a et geisha nurses.

They dreamed of freedom birds.

At night, on guard, staring into the dark, they were carried away by jum jets. They felt the rush of takeoff. *Gone*! they yelled. And then ve city, wing and engines, a smiling stewardess—but it was more than a plane, it bird, a big sleek silver bird with feathers and talons and high screeching. Th were flying. The weights fell off, there was nothing to bear. They laughed an held on tight, feeling the cold slap of wind and altitude, soaring, thinking *It over, I'm gone*!—they were naked, they were light and free—it was all lightness, bright and fast and buoyant, light as light, a helium buzz in the brain, a giddy bubbling in the lungs as they were taken up over the clouds and the war, beyond duty, beyond gravity and mortification and global entanglements—*Sin loi*![9] they yelled, *I'm sorry, motherfuckers, but I'm out of it, I'm goofed, I'm on a space cruise, I'm gone*!—and it was a restful, disencumbered sensation, just riding the light waves, sailing that big silver freedom bird over the mountains and oceans, over America, over the farms and great sleeping cities and cemeteries and highways and the golden arches of McDonald's. It was flight, a kind of fleeing, a kind of falling, falling higher and higher, spinning off the edge of the earth and beyond the sun and through the vast, silent vacuum where there were no burdens and were everything weighed exactly nothing. *Gone*! they screamed, *I'm sorry but I'm gone*! And so at night, not quite dreaming, they gave themselves over to lightness, they were carried, they were purely borne.

On the morning after Ted Lavender died, First Lieutenant Jimmy Cross crouched at the bottom of his foxhole and burned Martha's letters. Then he burned the two photographs. There was a steady rain falling, which made it difficult, but he used heat tabs and Sterno to build a small fire, screening it with his body, holding the photographs over the tight blue flame with the tips of his fingers.

He realized it was only a gesture. Stupid, he thought. Sentimental, too, but mostly just stupid.

Lavender was dead. You couldn't burn the blame.

Besides, the letters were in his head. And even now, without photographs, Lieutenant Cross could see Martha playing volleyball in her white gym shorts and yellow T-shirt. He could see her moving in the rain.

When the fire died out, Lieutenant Cross pulled his poncho over his shoulders and ate breakfast from a can.

There was no great mystery, he decided.

In those burned letters Martha had never mentioned the war, except to say, Jimmy, take care of yourself. She wasn't involved. She signed the letters

9. Sorry about that (Vietnamese).

or macho zeal. They were afraid of dying but they were even more afraid to show it.

They found jokes to tell.

They used a hard vocabulary to contain the terrible softness. *Greased*, they'd say. *Offed, lit up, zapped while zipping.* It wasn't cruelty, just stage presence. They were actors and the war came at them in 3-D. When someone died, it wasn't quite dying, because in a curious way it seemed scripted, and because they had their lines mostly memorized, irony mixed with tragedy, and because they called it by other names, as if to encyst and destroy the reality of death itself. They kicked corpses. They cut off thumbs. They talked grunt lingo. They told stories about Ted Lavender's supply of tranquilizers, how the poor guy didn't feel a thing, how incredibly tranquil he was.

There's a moral here, said Mitchell Sanders.

They were waiting for Lavender's chopper, smoking the dead man's dope.

The moral's pretty obvious, Sanders said, and winked. Stay away from drugs. No joke, they'll ruin your day every time.

Cute, said Henry Dobbins.

Mind-blower, get it? Talk about wiggy—nothing left, just blood and brains.

They made themselves laugh.

There it is, they'd say, over and over, as if the repetition itself were an act of poise, a balance between crazy and almost crazy, knowing without going. There it is, which meant be cool, let it ride, because oh yeah, man, you can't change what can't be changed, there it is, there it absolutely and positively and fucking well *is*.

They were tough.

They carried all the emotional baggage of men who might die. Grief, terror, love, longing—these were intangibles, but the intangibles had their own mass and specific gravity, they had tangible weight. They carried shameful memories. They carried the common secret of cowardice barely restrained, the instinct to run or freeze or hide, and in many respects this was the heaviest burden of all, for it could never be put down, it required perfect balance and perfect posture. They carried their reputations. They carried the soldier's greatest fear, which was the fear of blushing. Men killed, and died, because they were embarrassed not to. It was what had brought them to the war in the first place, nothing positive, no dreams of glory or honor, just to avoid the blush of dishonor. They died so as not to die of embarrassment. They crawled into tunnels and walked point and advanced under fire. Each morning, despite the unknowns, they made their legs move. They endured. They kept humping. They did not submit to the obvious alternative, which was simply to close the eyes and fall. So easy, really. Go limp and tumble to the ground and let the muscles unwind and not speak and not budge until your buddies picked you up and lifted you into the chopper that would roar and dip its nose and carry you off to the world. A mere matter of falling, yet no one ever fell. It was not courage, exactly; the object was not valor. Rather, they were too frightened to be cowards.

By and large they carried these things inside, maintaining the masks of composure. They sneered at sick call. They spoke bitterly about guys who had found release by shooting off their own toes or fingers. Pussies, they'd say.

Candyasses. It was fierce, mocking talk, with only a trace of envy or awe, but even so, the image played itself out behind their eyes.

They imagined the muzzle against flesh. They imagined the quick, sweet pain, then the evacuation to Japan, then a hospital with warm beds and cute geisha nurses.

They dreamed of freedom birds.

At night, on guard, staring into the dark, they were carried away by jumbo jets. They felt the rush of takeoff. *Gone*! they yelled. And then velocity, wings and engines, a smiling stewardess—but it was more than a plane, it was a real bird, a big sleek silver bird with feathers and talons and high screeching. They were flying. The weights fell off, there was nothing to bear. They laughed and held on tight, feeling the cold slap of wind and altitude, soaring, thinking *It's over, I'm gone*!—they were naked, they were light and free—it was all lightness, bright and fast and buoyant, light as light, a helium buzz in the brain, a giddy bubbling in the lungs as they were taken up over the clouds and the war, beyond duty, beyond gravity and mortification and global entanglements—*Sin loi*![9] they yelled, *I'm sorry, motherfuckers, but I'm out of it, I'm goofed, I'm on a space cruise, I'm gone*!—and it was a restful, disencumbered sensation, just riding the light waves, sailing that big silver freedom bird over the mountains and oceans, over America, over the farms and great sleeping cities and cemeteries and highways and the golden arches of McDonald's. It was flight, a kind of fleeing, a kind of falling, falling higher and higher, spinning off the edge of the earth and beyond the sun and through the vast, silent vacuum where there were no burdens and were everything weighed exactly nothing. *Gone*! they screamed, *I'm sorry but I'm gone*! And so at night, not quite dreaming, they gave themselves over to lightness, they were carried, they were purely borne.

On the morning after Ted Lavender died, First Lieutenant Jimmy Cross crouched at the bottom of his foxhole and burned Martha's letters. Then he burned the two photographs. There was a steady rain falling, which made it difficult, but he used heat tabs and Sterno to build a small fire, screening it with his body, holding the photographs over the tight blue flame with the tips of his fingers.

He realized it was only a gesture. Stupid, he thought. Sentimental, too, but mostly just stupid.

Lavender was dead. You couldn't burn the blame.

Besides, the letters were in his head. And even now, without photographs, Lieutenant Cross could see Martha playing volleyball in her white gym shorts and yellow T-shirt. He could see her moving in the rain.

When the fire died out, Lieutenant Cross pulled his poncho over his shoulders and ate breakfast from a can.

There was no great mystery, he decided.

In those burned letters Martha had never mentioned the war, except to say, Jimmy, take care of yourself. She wasn't involved. She signed the letters

9. Sorry about that (Vietnamese).

"Love," but it wasn't love, and all the fine lines and technicalities did not matter.

The morning came up wet and blurry. Everything seemed part of everything else, the fog and Martha and the deepening rain.

It was a war, after all.

Half smiling, Lieutenant Jimmy Cross took out his maps. He shook his head hard, as if to clear it, then bent forward and began planning the day's march. In ten minutes, or maybe twenty, he would rouse the men and they would pack up and head west, where the maps showed the country to be green and inviting. They would do what they had always done. The rain might add some weight, but otherwise it would be one more day layered upon all the other days.

He was realistic about it. There was that new hardness in his stomach.

No more fantasies, he told himself.

Henceforth, when he thought about Martha, it would be only to think that she belonged elsewhere. He would shut down the daydreams. This was not Mount Sebastian, it was another world, where there were no pretty poems or midterm exams, a place where men died because of carelessness and gross stupidity. Kiowa was right. Boom-down, and you were dead, never partly dead.

Briefly, in the rain, Lieutenant Cross saw Martha's gray eyes gazing back at him.

He understood.

It was very sad, he thought. The things men carried inside. The things men did or felt they had to do.

He almost nodded at her, but didn't.

Instead he went back to his maps. He was now determined to perform his duties firmly and without negligence. It wouldn't help Lavender, he knew that, but from this point on he would comport himself as a soldier. He would dispose of his good-luck pebble. Swallow it, maybe, or use Lee Strunk's slingshot, or just drop it along the trail. On the march he would impose strict field discipline. He would be careful to send out flank security, to prevent straggling or bunching up, to keep his troops moving at the proper pace and at the proper interval. He would insist on clean weapons. He would confiscate the remainder of Lavender's dope. Later in the day, perhaps, he would call the men together and speak to them plainly. He would accept the blame for what had happened to Ted Lavender. He would be a man about it. He would look them in the eyes, keeping his chin level, and he would issue the new SOPs in a calm, impersonal tone of voice, an officer's voice, leaving no room for argument or discussion. Commencing immediately, he'd tell them, they would no longer abandon equipment along the route of march. They would police up their acts. They would get their shit together, and keep it together, and maintain it neatly and in good working order.

He would not tolerate laxity. He would show strength, distancing himself.

Among the men there would be grumbling, of course, and maybe worse, because their days would seem longer and their loads heavier, but Lieutenant Cross reminded himself that his obligation was not to be loved but to lead. He would dispense with love; it was not now a factor. And if anyone quarreled or complained, he would simply tighten his lips and arrange his shoulders in the correct command posture. He might give a curt little nod. Or he might not. He might just shrug and say Carry on, then they would saddle up and form into a column and move out toward the villages of Than Khe.

# Flannery O'Connor

*O'Connor (1925–1964) was born in Savannah, Georgia. Her undergraduate writing at the Georgia State College for Women won her a fellowship to the Writers' Workshop of the University of Iowa, where she received a Master of Fine Arts degree. She began her professional career with two years in New York, but serious illness forced her to return to Georgia, where she lived with her mother on a farm near Milledgeville, raising peafowls, writing, and painting. For the rest of her life disease restricted her activities, though she traveled occasionally to give lectures and read from her work. She was a devout and uncompromising Christian; the extraordinary violences of her fiction are designed to expose the precarious conditions of the spirit in a temporal world, as the startling comedy disintegrates the pretenses of a facile civilization. During her lifetime she won a number of honors, including three O. Henry first prizes and (posthumously) the National Book Award for* The Complete Stories *(1971). Her novels are* Wise Blood *(1952) and* The Violent Bear It Away *(1960). Her other books of short stories are* A Good Man Is Hard to Find *(1955) and* Everything That Rises Must Converge *(1965). A selection of her letters was edited by Sally Fitzgerald and published in 1979 under the title* The Habit of Being.

## A Good Man Is Hard to Find

The grandmother didn't want to go to Florida. She wanted to visit some of her connections in east Tennessee and she was seizing every chance to change Bailey's mind. Bailey was the son she lived with, her only boy. He was sitting on the edge of his chair at the table, bent over the orange sports section of the *Journal.* "Now look here, Bailey," she said, "see here, read this," and she stood with one hand on her thin hip and the other rattling the newspaper at his bald head. "Here this fellow that calls himself The Misfit is aloose from the Federal Pen and headed toward Florida and you read here what it says he did to these people. Just you read it. I wouldn't take my children in any direction with a criminal like that aloose in it. I couldn't answer to my conscience if I did."

Bailey didn't look up from his reading so she wheeled around then and faced the children's mother; a young woman in slacks, whose face was as broad and innocent as a cabbage and was tied around with a green headkerchief that had two points on the top like rabbit's ears. She was sitting on the sofa, feeding the baby his apricots out of a jar. "The children have been to Florida before," the old lady said. "You all ought to take them somewhere else for a change so they would see different parts of the world and be broad. They never have been to east Tennessee."

The children's mother didn't seem to hear her, but the eight-year-old boy, John Wesley, a stocky child with glasses, said, "If you don't want to go to Florida, why dontcha stay at home?" He and the little girl, June Star, were reading the funny papers on the floor.

"She wouldn't stay at home to be queen for a day," June Star said without raising her yellow head.

"Yes, and what would you do if this fellow, The Misfit, caught you?" the grandmother asked.

"I'd smack his face," John Wesley said.

"She wouldn't stay at home for a million bucks," June Star said. "Afraid she'd miss something. She has to go everywhere we go."

"All right, Miss," the grandmother said. "Just remember that the next time you want me to curl your hair."

June Star said her hair was naturally curly.

The next morning the grandmother was the first one in the car, ready to go. She had her big black valise that looked like the head of a hippopotamus in one corner, and underneath it she was hiding a basket with Pitty Sing,[1] the cat, in it. She didn't intend for the cat to be left alone in the house for three days because he would miss her too much and she was afraid he might brush against one of the gas burners and accidentally asphyxiate himself. Her son, Bailey, didn't like to arrive at a motel with a cat.

She sat in the middle of the back seat with John Wesley and June Star on either side of her. Bailey and the children's mother and the baby sat in the front and they left Atlanta at eight forty-five with the mileage on the car at 55890. The grandmother wrote this down because she thought it would be interesting to say how many miles they had been when they got back. It took them twenty minutes to reach the outskirts of the city.

The old lady settled herself comfortably, removing her white cotton gloves and putting them up with her purse on the shelf in front of the back window. The children's mother still had on slacks and still had her head tied up in a green kerchief, but the grandmother had on a navy blue straw sailor hat with a bunch of white violets on the brim and a navy blue dress with a small white dot in the print. Her collar and cuffs were white organdy trimmed with lace and at her neckline she had pinned a purple spray of cloth violets containing a sachet. In case of an accident, anyone seeing her dead on the highway would know at once that she was a lady.

She said she thought it was going to be a good day for driving, neither too hot nor too cold, and she cautioned Bailey that the speed limit was fifty-five miles an hour and that the patrolmen hid themselves behind billboards and small clumps of trees and sped out after you before you had a chance to slow down. She pointed out interesting details of the scenery: Stone Mountain; the blue granite that in some places came up to both sides of the highway; the brilliant red clay banks slightly streaked with purple; and the various crops that made rows of green lace-work on the ground. The trees were full of silver-white sunlights and the meanest of them sparkled. The children were reading

1. Also the name of a character (Pitti-Sing) in *The Mikado,* an operetta (1885) by Gilbert and Sullivan.

comic magazines and their mother had gone back to sleep.

"Let's go through Georgia fast so we won't have to look at it much," John Wesley said.

"If I were a little boy," said the grandmother, "I wouldn't talk about my native state that way. Tennessee has the mountains and Georgia has the hills."

"Tennessee is just a hillbilly dumping ground," John Wesley said, "and Georgia is a lousy state too."

"You said it," June Star said.

"In my time," said the grandmother, folding her thin veined fingers, "children were more respectful of their native states and their parents and everything else. People did right then. Oh look at the cute little pickaninny!" she said and pointed to a Negro child standing in the door of a shack. "Wouldn't that make a picture, now?" she asked and they all turned and looked at the little Negro out of the back window. He waved.

"He didn't have any britches on," June Star said.

"He probably didn't have any," the grandmother explained. "Little niggers in the country don't have things like we do. If I could paint, I'd paint that picture," she said.

The children exchanged comic books.

The grandmother offered to hold the baby and the children's mother passed him over the front seat to her. She set him on her knee and bounced him and told him about the things they were passing. She rolled her eyes and screwed up her mouth and stuck her leathery thin face into his smooth bland one. Occasionally he gave her a faraway smile. They passed a large cotton field with five or six graves fenced in the middle of it, like a small island. "Look at the graveyard!" the grandmother said, pointing it out. "That was the old family burying ground. That belonged to the plantation."

"Where's the plantation?" John Wesley asked.

"Gone With the Wind,"[2] said the grandmother. "Ha. Ha."

When the children finished all the comic books they had brought, they opened the lunch and ate it. The grandmother ate a peanut butter sandwich and an olive and would not let the children throw the box and the paper napkins out the window. When there was nothing else to do they played a game by choosing a cloud and making the other two guess what shape it suggested. John Wesley took one the shape of a cow and June Star guessed a cow and John Wesley said, no, an automobile, and June Star said he didn't play fair, and they began to slap each other over the grandmother.

The grandmother said she would tell them a story if they would keep quiet. When she told a story, she rolled her eyes and waved her head and was very dramatic. She said once when she was a maiden lady she had been courted by a Mr. Edgar Atkins Teagarden from Jasper, Georgia. She said he was a very good-looking man and a gentleman and that he brought her a watermelon every Saturday afternoon with his initials cut in it, E.A.T. Well, one Saturday, she said, Mr. Teagarden brought the watermelon and there was nobody at home

2. Title of the best-selling novel by Margaret Mitchell about the passing of the old South; published in 1936 and made into a very popular movie in 1939.

and he left it on the front porch and returned in his buggy to Jasper, but she never got the watermelon, she said, because a nigger boy ate it when he saw the initials, E.A.T.! This story tickled John Wesley's funny bone and he giggled and giggled but June Star didn't think it was any good. She said she wouldn't marry a man that just brought her a watermelon on Saturday. The grandmother said she would have done well to marry Mr. Teagarden because he was a gentleman and had bought Coca-Cola stock when it first came out and that he had died only a few years ago, a very wealthy man.

They stopped at The Tower for barbecued sandwiches. The Tower was a part-stucco and part-wood filling station and dance hall set in a clearing outside of Timothy. A fat man named Red Sammy Butts ran it and there were signs stuck here and there on the building and for miles up and down the highway saying, TRY RED SAMMY'S FAMOUS BARBECUE. NONE LIKE FAMOUS RED SAMMY'S! RED SAM! THE FAT BOY WITH THE HAPPY LAUGH. A VETERAN! RED SAMMY'S YOUR MAN!

Red Sammy was lying on the bare ground outside The Tower with his head under a truck while a gray monkey about a foot high, chained to a small chinaberry tree, chattered nearby. The monkey sprang back into the tree and got on the highest limb as soon as he saw the children jump out of the car and run toward him.

Inside, The Tower was a long dark room with a counter at one end and tables at the other and dancing space in the middle. They all sat down at a broad table next to the nickelodeon and Red Sam's wife, a tall burnt-brown woman with hair and eyes lighter than her skin, came and took their order. The children's mother put a dime in the machine and played "The Tennessee Waltz," and the grandmother said that tune always made her want to dance. She asked Bailey if he would like to dance but he only glared at her. He didn't have a naturally sunny disposition like she did and trips made him nervous. The grandmother's brown eyes were very bright. She swayed her head from side to side and pretended she was dancing in her chair. June Star said play something she could tap to so the children's mother put in another dime and played a fast number and June Star stepped out onto the dance floor and did her tap routine.

"Ain't she cute?" Red Sam's wife said, leaning over the counter. "Would you like to come be my little girl?"

"No, I certainly wouldn't," June Star said. "I wouldn't live in a broken-down place like this for a million bucks!" and she ran back to the table.

"Ain't she cute?" the woman repeated, stretching her mouth politely.

"Aren't you ashamed?" hissed the grandmother.

Red Sam came in and told his wife to quit lounging on the counter and hurry up with these people's order. His khaki trousers reached just to his hip bones and his stomach hung over them like a sack of meal swaying under his shirt. He came over and sat down at a table nearby and let out a combination sigh and yodel. "You can't win," he said. "You can't win," and he wiped his sweating red face off with a gray handkerchief. "These days you don't know who to trust," he said. "Ain't that the truth?"

"People are certainly not nice like they used to be," said the grandmother.

"Two fellers come in here last week," Red Sammy said, "driving a Chrysler.

It was an old beat-up car but it was a good one and these boys looked all right to me. Said they worked at the mill and you know I let them fellers charge the gas they bought? Now why did I do that?"

"Because you're a good man!" the grandmother said at once.

"Yes'm, I suppose so," Red Sam said as if he were struck with this answer.

His wife brought the orders, carrying the five plates all at once without a tray, two in each hand and one balanced on her arm. "It isn't a soul in this green world of God's that you can trust," she said. "And I don't count nobody out of that, not nobody," she repeated, looking at Red Sammy.

"Did you read about that criminal, The Misfit, that's escaped?" asked the grandmother.

"I wouldn't be a bit surprised if he didn't attack this place right here," said the woman. "If he hears about it being here, I wouldn't be none surprised to see him. If he hears it's two cent in the cash register, I wouldn't be a tall surprised if he . . ."

"That'll do," Red Sam said. "Go bring these people their Co'-Colas," and the woman went off to get the rest of the order.

"A good man is hard to find," Red Sammy said. "Everything is getting terrible. I remember the day you could go off and leave your screen door unlatched. Not no more."

He and the grandmother discussed better times. The old lady said that in her opinion Europe was entirely to blame for the way things were now. She said the way Europe acted you would think we were made of money and Red Sam said it was no use talking about it, she was exactly right. The children ran outside into the white sunlight and looked at the monkey in the lacy chinaberry tree. He was busy catching fleas on himself and biting each one carefully between his teeth as if it were a delicacy.

They drove off again into the hot afternoon. The grandmother took cat naps and woke up every few minutes with her own snoring. Outside of Toombsboro she woke up and recalled an old plantation that she had visited in this neighborhood once when she was a young lady. She said the house had six white columns across the front and that there was an avenue of oaks leading up to it and two little wooden trellis arbors on either side in front where you sat down with your suitor after a stroll in the garden. She recalled exactly which road to turn off to get to it. She knew that Bailey would not be willing to lose any time looking at an old house, but the more she talked about it, the more she wanted to see it once again and find out if the little twin arbors were still standing. "There was a secret panel in this house," she said craftily, not telling the truth but wishing that she were, "and the story went that all the family silver was hidden in it when Sherman[3] came through but it was never found . . ."

"Hey!" John Wesley said. "Let's go see it! We'll find it! We'll poke all the woodwork and find it! Who lives there? Where do you turn off at? Hey Pop, can't we turn off there?"

"We never have seen a house with a secret panel!" June Star shrieked.

3. In November and December 1864 the Union general William Tecumseh Sherman marched his army from Atlanta to the Atlantic coast, plundering and burning as they went.

"Let's go to the house with the secret panel! Hey, Pop, can't we go see the house with the secret panel!"

"It's not far from here, I know," the grandmother said. "It wouldn't take over twenty minutes."

Bailey was looking straight ahead. His jaw was as rigid as a horseshoe. "No," he said.

The children began to yell and scream that they wanted to see the house with the secret panel. John Wesley kicked the back of the front seat and June Star hung over her mother's shoulder and whined desperately into her ear that they never had any fun even on their vacation, that they could never do what THEY wanted to do. The baby began to scream and John Wesley kicked the back of the seat so hard that his father could feel the blows in his kidney.

"All right!" he shouted and drew the car to a stop at the side of the road. "Will you all shut up? Will you all just shut up for one second? If you don't shut up, we won't go anywhere."

"It would be very educational for them," the grandmother murmured.

"All right," Bailey said, "but get this. This is the only time we're going to stop for anything like this. This is the one and only time."

"The dirt road that you have to turn down is about a mile back," the grandmother directed. "I marked it when we passed."

"A dirt road," Bailey groaned.

After they had turned around and were headed toward the dirt road, the grandmother recalled other points about the house, the beautiful glass over the front doorway and the candle lamp in the hall. John Wesley said that the secret panel was probably in the fireplace.

"You can't go inside this house," Bailey said. "You don't know who lives there."

"While you all talk to the people in front, I'll run around behind and get in a window," John Wesley suggested.

"We'll all stay in the car," his mother said.

They turned onto the dirt road and the car raced roughly along in a swirl of pink dust. The grandmother recalled the times when there were no paved roads and thirty miles was a day's journey. The dirt road was hilly and there were sudden washes in it and sharp curves on dangerous embankments. All at once they would be on a hill, looking down over the blue tops of trees for miles around, then the next minute, they would be in a red depression with the dust-coated trees looking down on them.

"This place had better turn up in a minute," Bailey said, "or I'm going to turn around."

The road looked as if no one had traveled on it in months.

"It's not much farther," the grandmother said and just as she said it, a horrible thought came to her. The thought was so embarrassing that she turned red in the face and her eyes dilated and her feet jumped up, upsetting her valise in the corner. The instant the valise moved, the newspaper top she had over the basket under it rose with a snarl and Pitty Sing, the cat, sprang onto Bailey's shoulder.

The children were thrown to the floor and their mother, clutching the baby, was thrown out the door onto the ground; the old lady was thrown into the front seat. The car turned over once and landed right-side-up in a gulch on the side of the road. Bailey remained in the driver's seat with the cat—gray-striped with a broad white face and an orange nose—clinging to his neck like a caterpillar.

As soon as the children saw they could move their arms and legs, they scrambled out of the car, shouting, "We've had an ACCIDENT!" The grandmother was curled up under the dashboard, hoping she was injured so that Bailey's wrath would not come down on her all at once. The horrible thought she had had before the accident was that the house she had remembered so vividly was not in Georgia but in Tennessee.

Bailey removed the cat from his neck with both hands and flung it out the window against the side of a pine tree. Then he got out of the car and started looking for the children's mother. She was sitting against the side of the red gutted ditch, holding the screaming baby, but she only had a cut down her face and a broken shoulder. "We've had an ACCIDENT!" the children screamed in a frenzy of delight.

"But nobody's killed," June Star said with disappointment as the grandmother limped out of the car, her hat still pinned to her head but the broken front brim standing up at a jaunty angle and the violet spray hanging off the side. They all sat down in the ditch, except the children, to recover from the shock. They were all shaking.

"Maybe a car will come along," said the children's mother hoarsely.

"I believe I have injured an organ," said the grandmother, pressing her side, but no one answered her. Bailey's teeth were clattering. He had on a yellow sport shirt with bright blue parrots designed in it and his face was as yellow as the shirt. The grandmother decided that she would not mention that the house was in Tennessee.

The road was about ten feet above and they could see only the tops of the trees on the other side of it. Behind the ditch they were sitting in there were more woods, tall and dark and deep. In a few minutes they saw a car some distance away on top of a hill, coming slowly as if the occupants were watching them. The grandmother stood up and waved both arms dramatically to attract their attention. The car continued to come on slowly, disappeared around a bend and appeared again, moving even slower, on top of the hill they had gone over. It was a big black battered hearselike automobile. There were three men in it.

It came to a stop over them and for some minutes, the driver looked down with a steady expressionless gaze to where they were sitting, and didn't speak. Then he turned his head and muttered something to the other two and they got out. One was a fat boy in black trousers and a red sweat shirt with a silver stallion embossed on the front of it. He moved around on the right side of them and stood staring, his mouth partly open in a kind of loose grin. The other had on khaki pants and a blue striped coat and a gray hat pulled down very low, hiding most of his face. He came around slowly on the left side. Neither spoke.

The driver got out of the car and stood by the side of it, looking down at them. He was an older man than the other two. His hair was just beginning to gray and he wore silver-rimmed spectacles that gave him a scholarly look. He had a long creased face and didn't have on any shirt or undershirt. He had on blue jeans that were too tight for him and was holding a black hat and a gun. The two boys also had guns.

"We've had an ACCIDENT!" the children screamed.

The grandmother had the peculiar feeling that the bespectacled man was someone she knew. His face was as familiar to her as if she had known him all her life but she could not recall who he was. He moved away from the car and began to come down the embankment, placing his feet carefully so that he wouldn't slip. He had on tan and white shoes and no socks, and his ankles were red and thin. "Good afternoon," he said. "I see you all had you a little spill."

"We turned over twice!" said the grandmother.

"Oncet," he corrected. "We seen it happen. Try their car and see will it run, Hiram," he said quietly to the boy with the gray hat.

"What you got that gun for?" John Wesley asked. "Whatcha gonna do with that gun?"

"Lady," the man said to the children's mother, "would you mind calling them children to sit down by you? Children make me nervous. I want all you all to sit down right together there were you're at."

"What are you telling us what to do for?" June Star asked.

Behind them the line of woods gaped like a dark open mouth. "Come here," said their mother.

"Look here now," Bailey began suddenly, "we're in a predicament! We're in . . ."

The grandmother shrieked. She scrambled to her feet and stood staring.

"You're The Misfit!" she said. "I recognized you at once!"

"Yes'm," the man said, smiling slightly as if he were pleased in spite of himself to be known, "but it would have been better for all of you, lady, if you hadn't of reckernized me."

Bailey turned his head sharply and said something to his mother that shocked even the children. The old lady began to cry and The Misfit reddened.

"Lady," he said, "don't you get upset. Sometimes a man says things he don't mean. I don't reckon he meant to talk to you thataway."

"You wouldn't shoot a lady, would you?" the grandmother said and removed a clean handkerchief from her cuff and began to slap at her eyes with it.

The Misfit pointed the toe of his shoe into the ground and made a little hole and then covered it up again. "I would hate to have to," he said.

"Listen," the grandmother almost screamed, "I know you're a good man. You don't look a bit like you have common blood. I know you must come from nice people!"

"Yes mam," he said, "finest people in the world." When he smiled he showed a row of strong white teeth. "God never made a finer woman than my mother and my daddy's heart was pure gold," he said. The boy with the red sweat shirt had come around behind them and was standing with his gun at his hip. The Misfit squatted down on the ground. "Watch them children, Bobby Lee," he said. "You know they make me nervous." He looked at the six of them huddled together in front of him and he seemed to be embarrassed as if he couldn't think of anything to say. "Ain't a cloud in the sky," he remarked, looking up at it. "Don't see no sun but don't see no cloud neither."

"Yes, it's a beautiful day," said the grandmother. "Listen," she said, "you shouldn't call yourself The Misfit because I know you're a good man at heart. I can just look at you and tell."

"Hush!" Bailey yelled. "Hush! Everybody shut up and let me handle this!" He was squatting in the position of a runner about to spring forward but he didn't move.

"I pre-chate that, lady," The Misfit said and drew a little circle in the ground with the butt of his gun.

"It'll take a half a hour to fix this here car," Hiram called, looking over the raised hood of it.

"Well, first you and Bobby Lee get him and that little boy to step over yonder with you," The Misfit said, pointing to Bailey and John Wesley. "The boys want to ask you something," he said to Bailey. "Would you mind stepping back in them woods there with them?"

"Listen," Bailey began, "we're in a terrible predicament! Nobody realizes what this is," and his voice cracked. His eyes were as blue and intense as the parrots in his shirt and he remained perfectly still.

The grandmother reached up to adjust her hat brim as if she were going to the woods with him but it came off in her hand. She stood staring at it and after a second she let it fall on the ground. Hiram pulled Bailey up by the arm as if he were assisting an old man. John Wesley caught hold of his father's hand and Bobby Lee followed. They went off toward the woods and just as they reached the dark edge, Bailey turned and supporting himself against a gray naked pine trunk, he shouted, "I'll be back in a minute, Mamma, wait on me!"

"Come back this instant!" his mother shrilled but they all disappeared into the woods.

"Bailey Boy!" the grandmother called in a tragic voice but she found she was looking at The Misfit squatting on the ground in front of her. "I just know you're a good man," she said desperately. "You're not a bit common!"

"Nome, I ain't a good man," The Misfit said after a second as if he had considered her statement carefully, "but I ain't the worst in the world neither. My daddy said I was a different breed of dog from my brothers and sisters. 'You know,' Daddy said, 'it's some that can live their whole life out without asking about it and it's others has to know why it is, and this boy is one of the latters. He's going to be into everything!' " He put on his black hat and looked up suddenly and then away deep into the woods as if he were embarrassed again. "I'm sorry I don't have on a shirt before you ladies," he said, hunching his shoulders slightly. "We buried our clothes that we had on when we escaped and we're just making do until we can get better. We borrowed these from some folks we met," he explained.

"That's perfectly all right," the grandmother said. "Maybe Bailey has an extra shirt in his suitcase."

"I'll look and see terrectly," The Misfit said.

"Where are they taking him?" the children's mother screamed.

"Daddy was a card himself," The Misfit said. "You couldn't put anything over on him. He never got in trouble with the Authorities though. Just had the knack of handling them."

"You could be honest too if you'd only try," said the grandmother. "Think how wonderful it would be to settle down and live a comfortable life and not have to think about somebody chasing you all the time."

The Misfit kept scratching in the ground with the butt of his gun as if he were thinking about it. "Yes'm, somebody is always after you," he murmured.

The grandmother noticed how thin his shoulder blades were just behind his hat because she was standing up looking down on him. "Do you ever pray?" she asked.

He shook his head. All she saw was the black hat wiggle between his shoulder blades. "Nome," he said.

There was a pistol shot from the woods, followed closely by another. Then silence. The old lady's head jerked around. She could hear the wind move through the tree tops like a long satisfied insuck of breath. "Bailey Boy!" she called.

"I was a gospel singer for a while," The Misfit said. "I been most everything. Been in the arm service, both land and sea, at home and abroad, been twict married, been an undertaker, been with the railroads, plowed Mother Earth, been in a tornado, seen a man burnt alive oncet," and he looked up at the children's mother and the little girl who were sitting close together, their faces white and their eyes glassy; "I even seen a woman flogged," he said.

"Pray, pray," the grandmother began, "pray, pray . . ."

"I never was a bad boy that I remember of," The Misfit said in an almost dreamy voice, "but somewheres along the line I done something wrong and got sent to the penitentiary. I was buried alive," and he looked up and held her attention to him by a steady stare.

"That's when you should have started to pray," she said. "What did you do to get sent to the penitentiary that first time?"

"Turn to the right, it was a wall," The Misfit said, looking up again at the cloudless sky. "Turn to the left, it was a wall. Look up it was a ceiling, look down it was a floor. I forget what I done, lady. I set there and set there, trying to remember what it was I done and I ain't recalled it to this day. Oncet in a while, I would think it was coming to me, but it never come."

"Maybe they put you in by mistake," the old lady said vaguely.

"Nome," he said. "It wasn't no mistake. They had the papers on me."

"You must have stolen something," she said.

The Misfit sneered slightly. "Nobody had nothing I wanted," he said. "It was a head-doctor at the penitentiary said what I had done was kill my daddy but I known that for a lie. My daddy died in nineteen ought nineteen of the epidemic flu[4] and I never had a thing to do with it. He was buried in the Mount Hopewell Baptist churchyard and you can go there and see for yourself."

"If you would pray," the old lady said, "Jesus would help you."

"That's right," The Misfit said.

4. There was a devastating, worldwide epidemic of influenza in 1919, an aftermath of World War I.

"Well then, why don't you pray?" she asked trembling with delight suddenly.

"I don't want no hep," he said. "I'm doing all right by myself."

Bobby Lee and Hiram came ambling back from the woods. Bobby Lee was dragging a yellow shirt with bright blue parrots in it.

"Throw me that shirt, Bobby Lee," The Misfit said. The shirt came flying at him and landed on his shoulder and he put it on. The grandmother couldn't name what the shirt reminded her of. "No, lady," The Misfit said while he was buttoning up, "I found out the crime don't matter. You can do one thing or you can do another, kill a man or take a tire off his car, because sooner or later you're going to forget what it was you done and just be punished for it."

The children's mother had begun to make heaving noises as if she couldn't get her breath. "Lady," he asked, "would you and that little girl like to step off yonder with Bobby Lee and Hiram and join your husband?"

"Yes, thank you," the mother said faintly. Her left arm dangled helplessly and she was holding the baby, who had gone to sleep, in the other. "Hep that lady up, Hiram," The Misfit said as she struggled to climb out of the ditch, "and Bobby Lee, you hold onto that little girl's hand."

"I don't want to hold hands with him," June Star said. "He reminds me of a pig."

The fat boy blushed and laughed and caught her by the arm and pulled her off into the woods after Hiram and her mother.

Alone with The Misfit, the grandmother found that she had lost her voice. There was not a cloud in the sky nor any sun. There was nothing around her but woods. She wanted to tell him that he must pray. She opened and closed her mouth several times before anything came out. Finally she found herself saying, "Jesus, Jesus," meaning, Jesus will help you, but the way she was saying it, it sounded as if she might be cursing.

"Yes'm," The Misfit said as if he agreed. "Jesus thrown everything off balance. It was the same case with Him as with me except He hadn't committed any crime and they could prove I had committed one because they had the papers on me. Of course," he said, "they never shown me my papers. That's why I sign myself now. I said long ago, you get you a signature and sign everything you do and keep a copy of it. Then you'll know what you done and you can hold up the crime to the punishment and see do they match and in the end you'll have something to prove you ain't been treated right. I call myself The Misfit," he said, "because I can't make what all I done wrong fit what all I gone through in punishment."

There was a piercing scream from the woods, followed closely by a pistol report. "Does it seem right to you, lady, that one is punished a heap and another ain't punished at all?"

"Jesus!" the old lady cried. "You've got good blood! I know you wouldn't shoot a lady! I know you come from nice people! Pray! Jesus, you ought not to shoot a lady. I'll give you all the money I've got!"

"Lady," The Misfit said, looking beyond her far into the woods, "there never was a body that give the undertaker a tip."

There were two more pistol reports and the grandmother raised her head like a parched old turkey hen crying for water and called, "Bailey Boy, Bailey Boy!" as if her heart would break.

"Jesus was the only One that ever raised the dead," The Misfit continued, "and He shouldn't have done it. He thown everything off balance. If He did what He said, then it's nothing for you to do but thow away everything and follow Him, and if He didn't then it's nothing for you to do but enjoy the few minutes you got left the best way you can—by killing somebody or burning down his house or doing some other meanness to him. No pleasure but meanness," he said and his voice had become almost a snarl.

"Maybe He didn't raise the dead," the old lady mumbled, not knowing what she was saying and feeling so dizzy that she sank down in the ditch with her legs twisted under her.

"I wasn't there so I can't say He didn't," The Misfit said. "I wisht I had of been there," he said, hitting the ground with his fist. "It ain't right I wasn't there because if I had of been there I would of known. Listen lady," he said in a high voice, "if I had of been there I would of known and I wouldn't be like I am now." His voice seemed about to crack and the grandmother's head cleared for an instant. She saw the man's face twisted close to her own as if he were going to cry and she murmured, "Why, you're one of my babies. You're one of my own children!" She reached out and touched him on the shoulder. The Misfit sprang back as if a snake had bitten him and shot her three times through the chest. Then he put his gun down on the ground and took off his glasses and began to clean them.

Hiram and Bobby Lee returned from the woods and stood over the ditch, looking down at the grandmother who half sat and half lay in a puddle of blood with her legs crossed under her like a child's and her face smiling up at the cloudless sky.

Without his glasses, The Misfit's eyes were red-rimmed and pale and defenseless-looking. "Take her off and thow her where you thown the others," he said, picking up the cat that was rubbing itself against his leg.

"She was a talker, wasn't she?" Bobby Lee said, sliding down the ditch with a yodel.

"She would of been a good woman," The Misfit said, "if it had been somebody there to shoot her every minute of her life."

"Some fun!" Bobby Lee said.

"Shut up, Bobby Lee," The Misfit said. "It's no real pleasure in life."

## LEE SMITH on *A Good Man Is Hard to Find*

"A Good Man Is Hard to Find" first hit me like a revelation. I was a college student trying to learn to write fiction myself; somehow I had got the idea that a short story should follow a kind of recipe, like a Lady Baltimore cake. Conflict, suspense, resolution; a clear theme; an ending that tied it all up in a neat little bow. Yet when I read that famous line of "A Good Man Is Hard to Find," I realized that *nothing* was wrapped up here—instead, a whole world opened out before my astonished eyes, a world as wild and scary as life itself. I turned back to the beginning and read it straight through again. I felt like the grandmother in the story, clinging desperately to her outworn beliefs: "I know you're a good man . . . You're not a bit common . . . I know you wouldn't shoot a lady . . . I know you come from nice people!" The gun went off in my own head as surely as it went off in those Georgia pines, and a number of my own ideas died instantly along with the grandmother. A story does *not* have to be resolved in the end, I realized. It is enough to glimpse something, momentarily, before it slips back into the dark woods.

Furthermore, a story can be both very funny and deadly serious at the same time. Though she drew a steady bead on salvation and kept it always in her sights, Flannery O'Connor had time for the gross world, too, and for people with all their comic posturing and blundering. The mix of menace and hilarity is evident early on in "A Good Man Is Hard to Find"; the ominous foreshadowing in the line "this fellow that calls himself The Misfit is aloose from the Federal pen and headed toward Florida and you read here what it says he did to these people" is immediately undercut by the humorous description of the children's mother, "whose face was as broad and innocent as a cabbage and was tied around with a green headkerchief that had two points on top like rabbit's ears." This kind of juxtaposition continues throughout the story—in the image of Bobby Lee and Hiram ambling back from the woods, for instance, dragging Bailey's ridiculous yellow shirt with blue parrots on it, just after killing him, or in those children screaming, "We've had an ACCIDENT!" in a frenzy of delight. The world has always struck me as both funny and awful, too, and reading "A Good Man Is Hard to Find" for the first time, I realized that I didn't have to *pick*. What a relief!

The older I get, the more profound this story seems to me. Perhaps the constant presence of death in Flannery O'Connor's life allowed her to see beyond her own years. I never read it now without that deep shock of recognition at the bone, and wonder, and pity for us all.

# Everything That Rises Must Converge

Her doctor had told Julian's mother that she must lose twenty pounds on account of her blood pressure, so on Wednesday nights Julian had to take her downtown on the bus for a reducing class at the Y. The reducing class was designed for working girls over fifty, who weighed from 165 to 200 pounds. His mother was one of the slimmer ones, but she said ladies did not tell their age or weight. She would not ride the buses by herself at night since they had been integrated, and because the reducing class was one of her few pleasures, necessary for her health, and *free,* she said Julian could at least put himself out to take her, considering all she did for him. Julian did not like to consider all she did for him, but every Wednesday night he braced himself and took her.

She was almost ready to go, standing before the hall mirror, putting on her hat, while he, his hands behind him, appeared pinned to the door frame, waiting like Saint Sebastian[1] for the arrows to begin piercing him. The hat was new and had cost her seven dollars and a half. She kept saying, "Maybe I shouldn't have paid that for it. No, I shouldn't have. I'll take it off and return it tomorrow. I shouldn't have bought it."

Julian raised his eyes to heaven. "Yes, you should have bought it," he said. "Put it on and let's go." It was a hideous hat. A purple velvet flap came down on one side of it and stood up on the other; the rest of it was green and looked like a cushion with the stuffing out. He decided it was less comical than jaunty and pathetic. Everything that gave her pleasure was small and depressed him.

She lifted the hat one more time and set it down slowly on top of her head. Two wings of gray hair protruded on either side of her florid face, but her eyes, sky-blue, were as innocent and untouched by experience as they must have been when she was ten. Were it not that she was a widow who had struggled fiercely to feed and clothe and put him through school and who was supporting him still, "until he got on his feet," she might have been a little girl that he had to take to town.

"It's all right, it's all right," he said. "Let's go." He opened the door himself and started down the walk to get her going. The sky was a dying violet and the houses stood out darkly against it, bulbous liver-colored monstrosities of a uniform ugliness though no two were alike. Since this had been a fashionable neighborhood forty years ago, his mother persisted in thinking they did well to have an apartment in it. Each house had a narrow collar of dirt around it in

1. Roman martyr, symbol of calm indifference to suffering.

which sat, usually, a grubby child. Julian walked with his hands in his pockets, his head down and thrust forward and his eyes glazed with the determination to make himself completely numb during the time he would be sacrificed to her pleasure.

The door closed and he turned to find the dumpy figure, surmounted by the atrocious hat, coming toward him. "Well," she said, "you only live once and paying a little more for it, I at least won't meet myself coming and going."

"Some day I'll start making money," Julian said gloomily—he knew he never would—"and you can have one of those jokes whenever you take the fit." But first they would move. He visualized a place where the nearest neighbors would be three miles away on either side.

"I think you're doing fine," she said, drawing on her gloves. "You've only been out of school a year. Rome wasn't built in a day."

She was one of the few members of the Y reducing class who arrived in hat and gloves and who had a son who had been to college. "It takes time," she said, "and the world is in such a mess. This hat looked better on me than any of the others, though when she brought it out I said, 'Take that thing back. I wouldn't have it on my head,' and she said, 'Now wait till you see it on,' and when she put it on me, I said, 'We-ull,' and she said, 'If you ask me, that hat does something for you and you do something for the hat, and besides,' she said, 'with that hat, you won't meet yourself coming and going.' "

Julian thought he could have stood his lot better if she had been selfish, if she had been an old hag who drank and screamed at him. He walked along, saturated in depression, as if in the midst of his martyrdom he had lost his faith. Catching sight of his long, hopeless, irritated face, she stopped suddenly with a grief-stricken look, and pulled back on his arm. "Wait on me," she said. "I'm going back to the house and take this thing off and tomorrow I'm going to return it. I was out of my head. I can pay the gas bill with that seven-fifty."

He caught her arm in a vicious grip. "You are not going to take it back," he said. "I like it."

"Well," she said, "I don't think I ought . . ."

"Shut up and enjoy it," he muttered, more depressed than ever.

"With the world in the mess it's in," she said, "it's a wonder we can enjoy anything. I tell you, the bottom rail is on the top."

Julian sighed.

"Of course," she said, "if you know who are you, you can go anywhere." She said this every time he took her to the reducing class. "Most of them in it are not our kind of people," she said, "but I can be gracious to anybody. I know who I am."

"They don't give a damn for your graciousness," Julian said savagely. "Knowing who you are is good for one generation only. You haven't the foggiest idea where you stand now or who you are."

She stopped and allowed her eyes to flash at him. "I most certainly do know who I am," she said, "and if you don't know who you are, I'm ashamed of you."

"Oh hell," Julian said.

"Your great-grandfather was a former governor of this state," she said. "Your grandfather was a prosperous land-owner. Your grandmother was a Godhigh."

"Will you look around you," he said tensely, "and see where you are now?" and he swept his arm jerkily out to indicate the neighborhood, which the growing darkness at least made less dingy.

"You remain what you are," she said. "Your great-grandfather had a plantation and two hundred slaves."

"There are no more slaves," he said irritably.

"They were better off when they were," she said. He groaned to see that she was off on that topic. She rolled onto it every few days like a train on an open track. He knew every stop, every junction, every swamp along the way, and knew the exact point at which her conclusion would roll majestically into the station: "It's ridiculous. It's simply not realistic. They should rise, yes, but on their own side of the fence."

"Let's skip it," Julian said.

"The ones I feel sorry for," she said, "are the ones that are half white. They're tragic."

"Will you skip it?"

"Suppose we were half white. We would certainly have mixed feelings."

"I have mixed feelings now," he groaned.

"Well let's talk about something pleasant," she said. "I remember going to Grandpa's when I was a little girl. Then the house had double stairways that went up to what was really the second floor—all the cooking was done on the first. I used to like to stay down in the kitchen on account of the way the walls smelled. I would sit with my nose pressed against the plaster and take deep breaths. Actually the place belonged to the Godhighs but your grandfather Chestny paid the mortgage and saved it for them. They were in reduced circumstances," she said, "but reduced or not, they never forgot who they were."

"Doubtless that decayed mansion reminded them," Julian muttered. He never spoke of it without contempt or thought of it without longing. He had seen it once when he was a child before it had been sold. The double stairways had rotted and been torn down. Negroes were living in it. But it remained in his mind as his mother had known it. It appeared in his dreams regularly. He would stand on the wide porch, listening to the rustle of oak leaves, then wander through the high-ceilinged hall into the parlor that opened onto it and gaze at the worn rugs and faded draperies. It occurred to him that it was he, not she, who could have appreciated it. He preferred its threadbare elegance to anything he could name and it was because of it that all the neighborhoods they had lived in had been a torment to him—whereas she had hardly known the difference. She called her insensitivity "being adjustable."

"And I remember the old darky who was my nurse, Caroline. There was no better person in the world. I've always had a great respect for my colored friends," she said. "I'd do anything in the world for them and they'd . . ."

"Will you for God's sake get off that subject?" Julian said. When he got on a bus by himself, he made it a point to sit down beside a Negro, in reparation as it were for his mother's sins.

"You're mighty touchy tonight," she said. "Do you feel all right?"

"Yes I feel all right," he said. "Now lay off."

She pursed her lips. "Well, you certainly are in a vile humor," she observed. "I just won't speak to you at all."

They had reached the bus stop. There was no bus in sight and Julian, his hands still jammed in his pockets and his head thrust forward, scowled down the empty street. The frustration of having to wait on the bus as well as ride on it began to creep up his neck like a hot hand. The presence of his mother was borne in upon him as she gave a pained sigh. He looked at her bleakly. She was holding herself very erect under the preposterous hat, wearing it like a banner of her imaginary dignity. There was in him an evil urge to break her spirit. He suddenly unloosened his tie and pulled it off and put it in his pocket.

She stiffened. "Why must you look like *that* when you take me to town?" she said. "Why must you deliberately embarrass me?"

"If you'll never learn where you are," he said, "you can at least learn where I am."

"You look like a—thug," she said.

"Then I must be one," he murmured.

"I'll just go home," she said. "I will not bother you. If you can't do a little thing like that for me . . ."

Rolling his eyes upward, he put his tie back on. "Restored to my class," he muttered. He thrust his face toward her and hissed, "True culture is in the mind, the *mind,*" he said, and tapped his head, "the mind."

"It's in the heart," she said, "and in how you do things and how you do things is because of who you *are.*"

"Nobody in the damn bus cares who you are."

"I care who I am," she said icily.

The lighted bus appeared on top of the next hill and as it approached, they moved out into the street to meet it. He put his hand under her elbow and hoisted her up on the creaking step. She entered with a little smile, as if she were going into a drawing room where everyone had been waiting for her. While he put in the tokens, she sat down on one of the broad front seats for three which faced the aisle. A thin woman with protruding teeth and long yellow hair was sitting on the end of it. His mother moved up beside her and left room for Julian beside herself. He sat down and looked at the floor across the aisle where a pair of thin feet in red and white canvas sandals were planted.

His mother immediately began a general conversation meant to attract anyone who felt like talking. "Can it get any hotter?" she said and removed from her purse a folding fan, black with a Japanese scene on it, which she began to flutter before her.

"I reckon it might could," the woman with the protruding teeth said, "but I know for a fact my apartment couldn't get no hotter."

"It must get the afternoon sun," his mother said. She sat forward and looked up and down the bus. It was half filled. Everybody was white. "I see we have the bus to ourselves," she said. Julian cringed.

"For a change," said the woman across the aisle, the owner of the red and white canvas sandals. "I come on one the other day and they were thick as fleas—up front and all through."

"The world is in a mess everywhere," his mother said. "I don't know how we've let it get in this fix."

"What gets my goat is all those boys from good families stealing automobile tires," the woman with the protruding teeth said. "I told my boy, I said you may not be rich but you been raised right and if I ever catch you in any such mess, they can send you on to the reformatory. Be exactly where you belong."

"Training tells," his mother said. "Is your boy in high school?"

"Ninth grade," the woman said.

"My son just finished college last year. He wants to write but he's selling typewriters until he gets started," his mother said.

The woman leaned forward and peered at Julian. He threw her such a malevolent look that she subsided against the seat. On the floor across the aisle there was an abandoned newspaper. He got up and got it and opened it out in front of him. His mother discreetly continued the conversation in a lower tone but the woman across the aisle said in a loud voice, "Well that's nice. Selling typewriters is close to writing. He can go right from one to the other."

"I tell him," his mother said, "that Rome wasn't built in a day."

Behind the newspaper Julian was withdrawing into the inner compartment of his mind where he spent most of his time. This was a kind of mental bubble in which he established himself when he could not bear to be a part of what was going on around him. From it he could see out and judge but in it he was safe from any kind of penetration from without. It was the only place where he felt free of the general idiocy of his fellows. His mother had never entered it but from it he could see her with absolute clarity.

The old lady was clever enough and he thought that if she had started from any of the right premises, more might have been expected of her. She lived according to the laws of her own fantasy world, outside of which he had never seen her set foot. The law of it was to sacrifice herself for him after she had first created the necessity to do so by making a mess of things. If he had permitted her sacrifices, it was only because her lack of foresight had made them necessary. All of her life had been a struggle to act like a Chestny without the Chestny goods, and to give him everything she thought a Chestny ought to have; but since, said she, it was fun to struggle, why complain? And when you had won, as she had won, what fun to look back on the hard times! He could not forgive her that she had enjoyed the struggle and that she thought *she* had won.

What she meant when she said she had won was that she had brought him up successfully and had sent him to college and that he had turned out so well—good looking (her teeth had gone unfilled so that his could be straightened), intelligent (he realized he was too intelligent to be a success), and with a future ahead of him (there was of course no future ahead of him). She excused his gloominess on the grounds that he was still growing up and his radical ideas on his lack of practical experience. She said he didn't yet know a thing about "life," that he hadn't even entered the real world—when already he was as disenchanted with it as a man of fifty.

The further irony of all this was that in spite of her, he had turned out so well. In spite of going to only a third-rate college, he had, on his own initiative, come out with a first-rate education; in spite of growing up dominated by a small mind, he had ended up with a large one; in spite of all her foolish views, he was free of prejudice and unafraid to face facts. Most miraculous of all, instead of being blinded by love for her as she was for him, he had cut himself emotionally free of her and could see her with complete objectivity. He was not dominated by his mother.

The bus stopped with a sudden jerk and shook him from his meditation. A woman from the back lurched forward with little steps and barely escaped falling in his newspaper as she righted herself. She got off and a large Negro got on. Julian kept his paper lowered to watch. It gave him a certain satisfaction to see injustice in daily operation. It confirmed his view that with a few exceptions there was no one worth knowing within a radius of three hundred miles. The Negro was well dressed and carried a briefcase. He looked around and then sat down on the other end of the seat where the woman with the red and white canvas sandals was sitting. He immediately unfolded a newspaper and obscured himself behind it. Julian's mother's elbow at once prodded insistently into his ribs. "Now you see why I won't ride on these buses by myself," she whispered.

The woman with the red and white canvas sandals had risen at the same time the Negro sat down and had gone further back in the bus and taken the seat of the woman who had got off. His mother leaned forward and cast her an approving look.

Julian rose, crossed the aisle, and sat down in the place of the woman with the canvas sandals. From this position, he looked serenely across at his mother. Her face had turned an angry red. He stared at her, making his eyes the eyes of a stranger. He felt his tension suddenly lift as if he had openly declared war on her.

He would have liked to get in conversation with the Negro and to talk with him about art or politics or any subject that would be above the comprehension of those around them, but the man remained entrenched behind his paper. He was either ignoring the change of seating or had never noticed it. There was no way for Julian to convey his sympathy.

His mother kept her eyes fixed reproachfully on his face. The woman with the protruding teeth was looking at him avidly as if he were a type of monster new to her.

"Do you have a light?" he asked the Negro.

Without looking away from his paper, the man reached in his pocket and handed him a packet of matches.

"Thanks," Julian said. For a moment he held the matches foolishly. A NO SMOKING sign looked down upon him from over the door. This alone would not have deterred him; he had no cigarettes. He had quit smoking some months before because he could not afford it. "Sorry," he muttered and handed back the matches. The Negro lowered the paper and gave him an annoyed look. He took the matches and raised the paper again.

His mother continued to gaze at him but she did not take advantage of his momentary discomfort. Her eyes retained their battered look. Her face seemed to be unnaturally red, as if her blood pressure had risen. Julian allowed no glimmer of sympathy to show on his face. Having got the advantage, he wanted desperately to keep it and carry it through. He would have liked to teach her a lesson that would last her a while, but there seemed no way to continue the point. The Negro refused to come out from behind his paper.

Julian folded his arms and looked stolidly before him, facing her but as if he did not see her, as if he had ceased to recognize her existence. He visualized a scene in which, the bus having reached their stop, he would remain in his seat and when she said, "Aren't you going to get off?" he would look at her as a stranger who had rashly addressed him. The corner they got off on was usually deserted, but it was well lighted and it would not hurt her to walk by herself the four blocks to the Y. He decided to wait until the time came and then decide whether or not he would let her get off by herself. He would have to be at the Y at ten to bring her back, but he could leave her wondering if he was going to show up. There was no reason for her to think she could always depend on him.

He retired again into the high-ceilinged room sparsely settled with large pieces of antique furniture. His soul expanded momentarily but then he became aware of his mother across from him and the vision shriveled. He studied her coldly. Her feet in little pumps dangled like a child's and did not quite reach the floor. She was training on him an exaggerated look of reproach. He felt completely detached from her. At that moment he could with pleasure have slapped her as he would have slapped a particularly obnoxious child in his charge.

He began to imagine various unlikely ways by which he could teach her a lesson. He might make friends with some distinguished Negro professor or lawyer and bring him home to spend the evening. He would be entirely justified but her blood pressure would rise to 300. He could not push her to the extent of making her have a stroke, and moreover, he had never been successful at making any Negro friends. He had tried to strike up an acquaintance on the bus with some of the better types, with ones that looked like professors or ministers or lawyers. One morning he had sat down next to a distinguished-looking dark brown man who had answered his questions with a sonorous solemnity but who had turned out to be an undertaker. Another day he had sat down beside a cigar-smoking Negro with a diamond ring on his finger, but after a few stilted pleasantries, the Negro had rung the buzzer and risen, slipping two lottery tickets into Julian's hand as he climbed over him to leave.

He imagined his mother lying desperately ill and his being able to secure only a Negro doctor for her. He toyed with that idea for a few minutes and then dropped it for a momentary vision of himself participating as a sympathizer in a sit-in demonstration. This was possible but he did not linger with it. Instead, he approached the ultimate horror. He brought home a beautiful suspiciously Negroid woman. Prepare yourself, he said. There is nothing you can do about it. This is the woman I've chosen. She's intelligent, dignified, even good, and she's suffered and she hasn't thought it *fun.* Now persecute us, go ahead and persecute us. Drive her out of here, but remember, you're driving me too. His eyes were narrowed and through the indignation he had generated, he saw his mother across the aisle, purple-faced, shrunken to the dwarf-like proportions of her moral nature, sitting like a mummy beneath the ridiculous banner of her hat.

He was tilted out of his fantasy again as the bus stopped. The door opened with a sucking hiss and out of the dark a large, gaily dressed, sullen-looking colored woman got on with a little boy. The child, who might have been four, had on a short plaid suit and a Tyrolean hat with a blue feather in it. Julian hoped that he would sit down beside him and that the woman would push in beside his mother. He could think of no better arrangement.

As she waited for her tokens, the woman was surveying the seating possibilities—he hoped with the idea of sitting where she was least wanted. There was something familiar-looking about her but Julian could not place what it was. She was a giant of a woman. Her face was set not only to meet opposition but to seek it out. The downward tilt of her large lower lip was like a warning sign: DON'T TAMPER WITH ME. Her bulging figure was encased in a green crepe dress and her feet overflowed in red shoes. She had on a hideous hat. A purple velvet flap came down on one side of it and stood up on the other; the rest of it was green and looked like a cushion with the stuffing out. She carried a mammoth red pocketbook that bulged throughout as if it were stuffed with rocks.

To Julian's disappointment, the little boy climbed up on the empty seat beside his mother. His mother lumped all children, black and white, into the common category, "cute," and she thought little Negroes were on the whole cuter than little white children. She smiled at the little boy as he climbed on the seat.

Meanwhile the woman was bearing down upon the empty seat beside Julian. To his annoyance, she squeezed herself into it. He saw his mother's face change as the woman settled herself next to him and he realized with satisfaction that this was more objectionable to her than it was to him. Her face seemed almost gray and there was a look of dull recognition in her eyes, as if suddenly she had sickened at some awful confrontation. Julian saw that it was because she and the woman had, in a sense, swapped sons. Though his mother would not realize the symbolic significance of this, she would feel it. His amusement showed plainly on his face.

The woman next to him muttered something unintelligible to herself. He was conscious of a kind of bristling next to him, a muted growling like that of an angry cat. He could not see anything but the red pocketbook upright on the bulging green thighs. He visualized the woman as she had stood waiting for her tokens—the ponderous figure, rising from the red shoes upward over the solid hips, the mammoth bosom, the haughty face, to the green and purple hat.

His eyes widened.

The vision of the two hats, identical, broke upon him with the radiance of a brilliant sunrise. His face was suddenly lit with joy. He could not believe that Fate had thrust upon his mother such a lesson. He gave a loud chuckle so that she would look at him and see that he saw. She turned her eyes on him slowly. The blue in them seemed to have turned a bruised purple. For a moment he had an uncomfortable sense of her innocence, but it lasted only a second before principle rescued him. Justice entitled him to laugh. His grin hardened until it said to her as plainly as if he were saying aloud: Your punishment exactly fits your pettiness. This should teach you a permanent lesson.

Her eyes shifted to the woman. She seemed unable to bear looking at him and to find the woman preferable. He became conscious again of the bristling presence at his side. The woman was rumbling like a volcano about to become active. His mother's mouth began to twitch slightly at one corner. With a sinking heart, he saw incipient signs of recovery on her face and realized that this was going to strike her suddenly as funny and was going to be no lesson at all. She kept her eyes on the woman and an amused smile came over her face as if the woman were a monkey that had stolen her hat. The little Negro was looking up at her with large fascinated eyes. He had been trying to attract her attention for some time.

"Carver!" the woman said suddenly. "Come heah!"

When he saw that the spotlight was on him at last, Carver drew his feet up and turned himself toward Julian's mother and giggled.

"Carver!" the woman said. "You heah me? Come heah!"

Carver slid down from the seat but remained squatting with his back against the base of it, his head turned slyly around toward Julian's mother, who was smiling at him. The woman reached a hand across the aisle and snatched him to her. He righted himself and hung backwards on her knees, grinning at Julian's mother. "Isn't he cute?" Julian's mother said to the woman with the protruding teeth.

"I reckon he is," the woman said without conviction.

The Negress yanked him upright but he eased out of her grip and shot across the aisle and scrambled, giggling wildly, onto the seat beside his love.

"I think he likes me," Julian's mother said, and smiled at the woman. It was the smile she used when she was being particularly gracious to an inferior. Julian saw everything was lost. The lesson had rolled off her like rain on a roof.

The woman stood up and yanked the little boy off the seat as if she were snatching him from contagion. Julian could feel the rage in her at having no weapon like his mother's smile. She gave the child a sharp slap across his leg. He howled once and then thrust his head into her stomach and kicked his feet against her shins. "Behave," she said vehemently.

The bus stopped and the Negro who had been reading the newspaper got off. The woman moved over and set the little boy down with a thump between herself and Julian. She held him firmly by the knee. In a moment he put his hands in front of his face and peeped at Julian's mother through his fingers.

"I see yoooooooo!" she said and put her hand in front of her face and peeped at him.

The woman slapped his hand down. "Quit yo' foolishness," she said, "before I knock the living Jesus out of you!"

Julian was thankful that the next stop was theirs. He reached up and pulled the cord. The woman reached up and pulled it at the same time. Oh my God, he thought. He had the terrible intuition that when they got off the bus together, his mother would open her purse and give the little boy a nickel. The gesture would be as natural to her as breathing. The bus stopped and the woman got up and lunged to the front, dragging the child, who wished to stay on, after her. Julian and his mother got up and followed. As they neared the door, Julian tried to relieve her of her pocketbook.

"No," she murmured, "I want to give the little boy a nickel."

"No!" Julian hissed. "No!"

She smiled down at the child and opened her bag. The bus door opened and the woman picked him up by the arm and descended with him, hanging at her hip. Once in the street she set him down and shook him.

Julian's mother had to close her purse while she got down the bus step but as soon as her feet were on the ground, she opened it again and began to rummage inside. "I can't find but a penny," she whispered, "but it looks like a new one."

"Don't do it!" Julian said fiercely between his teeth. There was a streetlight on the corner and she hurried to get under it so that she could better see into her pocketbook. The woman was heading off rapidly down the street with the child still hanging backward on her hand.

"Oh little boy!" Julian's mother called and took a few quick steps and caught up with them just beyond the lamppost. "Here's a bright new penny for you," and she held out the coin, which shone bronze in the dim light.

The huge woman turned and for a moment stood, her shoulders lifted and her face frozen with frustrated rage, and stared at Julian's mother. Then all at once she seemed to explode like a piece of machinery that had been given one ounce of pressure too much. Julian saw the black fist swing out with the red pocketbook. He shut his eyes and cringed as he heard the woman shout, "He don't take nobody's pennies!" When he opened his eyes, the woman was disappearing down the street with the little boy staring wide-eyed over her shoulder. Julian's mother was sitting on the sidewalk.

"I told you not to do that," Julian said angrily. "I told you not to do that!"

He stood over her for a minute, gritting his teeth. Her legs were stretched out in front of her and her hat was on her lap. He squatted down and looked her in the face. It was totally expressionless. "You got exactly what you deserved," he said. "Now get up."

He picked up her pocketbook and put what had fallen out back in it. He picked the hat up off her lap. The penny caught his eye on the sidewalk and he picked that up and let it drop before her eyes into the purse. Then he stood up and leaned over and held his hands out to pull her up. She remained immobile. He sighed. Rising above them on either side were black apartment buildings, marked with irregular rectangles of light. At the end of the block a man came out of a door and walked off in the opposite direction. "All right," he said, "suppose somebody happens by and wants to know why you're sitting on the sidewalk?"

She took the hand and, breathing hard, pulled heavily up on it and then stood for a moment, swaying slightly as if the spots of light in the darkness were circling around her. Her eyes, shadowed and confused, finally settled on his face. He did not try to conceal his irritation. "I hope this teaches you a lesson," he said. She leaned forward and her eyes raked his face. She seemed trying to determine his identity. Then, as if she found nothing familiar about him, she started off with a headlong movement in the wrong direction.

"Aren't you going on to the Y?" he asked.

"Home," she muttered.

"Well, are we walking?"

For answer she kept going. Julian followed along, his hands behind him. He saw no reason to let the lesson she had had go without backing it up with an explanation of its meaning. She might as well be made to understand what had happened to her. "Don't think that was just an uppity Negro woman," he said. "That was the whole colored race which will no longer take your condescending pennies. That was your black double. She can wear the same hat as you, and to be sure," he added gratuitously (because he thought it was funny), "it looked better on her than it did on you. What all this means," he said, "is that the old world is gone. The old manners are obsolete and your graciousness is not worth a damn." He thought bitterly of the house that had been lost for him. "You aren't who you think you are," he said.

She continued to plow ahead, paying no attention to him. Her hair had come undone on one side. She dropped her pocketbook and took no notice. He stooped and picked it up and handed it to her but she did not take it.

"You needn't act as if the world had come to an end," he said, "because it hasn't. From now on you've got to live in a new world and face a few realities for a change. Buck up," he said, "it won't kill you."

She was breathing fast.

"Let's wait on the bus," he said.

"Home," she said thickly.

"I hate to see you behave like this," he said. "Just like a child. I should be able to expect more of you." He decided to stop where he was and make her stop and wait for a bus. "I'm not going any farther," he said stopping. "We're going on the bus."

She continued to go on as if she had not heard him. He took a few steps and caught her arm and stopped her. He looked into her face and caught his breath. He was looking into a face he had never seen before. "Tell Grandpa to come get me," she said.

He stared, stricken.

"Tell Caroline to come get me," she said.

Stunned, he let her go and she lurched forward again, walking as if one leg were shorter than the other. A tide of darkness seemed to be sweeping her from him. "Mother!" he cried. "Darling, sweetheart, wait!" Crumpling, she fell to the pavement. He dashed forward and fell at her side, crying, "Mamma, Mamma!" He turned her over. Her face was fiercely distorted. One eye, large and staring, moved slightly to the left as if it had become unmoored. The other remained fixed on him, raked his face again, found nothing and closed.

"Wait here, wait here!" he cried and jumped up and began to run for help toward a cluster of lights he saw in the distance ahead of him. "Help, help!" he shouted, but his voice was thin, scarcely a thread of sound. The lights drifted farther away the faster he ran and his feet moved numbly as if they carried him nowhere. The tide of darkness seemed to sweep him back to her, postponing from moment to moment his entry into the world of guilt and sorrow.

# Frank O'Connor

*O'Connor is the pen name of Michael O'Donovan (1903–1966), who was born in Cork, Ireland, of a family too poor to give him a university education. During Ireland's struggle for independence he was briefly a member of the Irish Republican Army. Then he worked as a librarian in Cork and Dublin and for a time was director of the Abbey Theatre before he became established as a writer of short stories. From 1931 on he published regularly in American magazines, and he taught for some years at Harvard and Northwestern Universities. His declared objective was to find the natural rhythms and stresses of the storyteller's voice in shaping his material. He rewrote many of his stories—often after first publication—ten, twenty, or thirty times. The subsequent publication of these revisions makes it hard to pin down the exact scale of his life's work, because some of his books contain pieces that appeared in different form in previous volumes. He was in any event a prolific historian of Irish manners and the Irish character. His titles include* Guests of the Nation *(1931),* Crab Apple Jelly *(1944),* The Stories of Frank O'Connor *(1956), and* A Set of Variations *(1971).*

## Guests of the Nation

### I

At dusk the big Englishman, Belcher, would shift his long legs out of the ashes and say "Well, chums, what about it?" and Noble or me would say "All right, chum" (for we had picked up some of their curious expressions), and the little Englishman, Hawkins, would light the lamp and bring out the cards. Sometimes Jeremiah Donovan would come up and supervise the game and get excited over Hawkins's cards, which he always played badly, and shout at him as if he was one of our own "Ah, you divil, you, why didn't you play the tray?"

But ordinarily Jeremiah was a sober and contented poor devil like the big Englishman, Belcher, and was looked up to only because he was a fair hand at documents, though he was slow enough even with them. He wore a small cloth hat and big gaiters over his long pants, and you seldom saw him with his hands out of his pockets. He reddened when you talked to him, tilting from toe to heel and back, and looking down all the time at his big farmer's feet. Noble and me used to make fun of his broad accent, because we were from the town.

I couldn't at the time see the point of me and Noble guarding Belcher and Hawkins at all, for it was my belief that you could have planted that pair down anywhere from this to Claregalway and they'd have taken root there like a native weed. I never in my short experience seen two men to take to the country as they did.

They were handed on to us by the Second Battalion when the search[1] for them became too hot, and Noble and myself, being young, took over with a natural feeling of responsibility, but Hawkins made us look like fools when he showed that he knew the country better than we did.

"You're the bloke they calls Bonaparte," he says to me. "Mary Brigid O'Connell told me to ask you what you done with the pair of her brother's socks you borrowed."

For it seemed, as they explained it, that the Second used to have little evenings, and some of the girls of the neighbourhood turned in, and, seeing they were such decent chaps, our fellows couldn't leave the two Englishmen out of them. Hawkins learned to dance "The Walls of Limerick," "The Siege of Ennis," and "The Waves of Tory"[2] as well as any of them, though naturally, he couldn't return the compliment, because our lads at that time did not dance foreign dances on principle.

So whatever privileges Belcher and Hawkins had with the Second they just naturally took with us, and after the first day or two we gave up all pretence of keeping a close eye on them. Not that they could have got far, for they had accents you could cut with a knife and wore khaki tunics and overcoats with civilian pants and boots. But it's my belief that they never had any idea of escaping and were quite content to be where they were.

It was a treat to see how Belcher got off with the old woman of the house where we were staying. She was a great warrant to scold, and cranky even with us, but before ever she had a chance to giving our guests, as I may call them, a lick of her tongue, Belcher had made her his friend for life. She was breaking sticks, and Belcher, who hadn't been more than ten minutes in the house, jumped up from his seat and went over to her.

"Allow me, madam," he says, smiling his queer little smile, "please allow me"; and he takes the bloody hatchet. She was struck too paralytic to speak, and after that, Belcher would be at her heels, carrying a bucket, a basket, or a load of turf, as the case might be. As Noble said, he got into looking before she leapt, and hot water, or any little thing she wanted, Belcher would have it ready for her. For such a huge man (and though I am five foot ten myself I had to look up at him) he had an uncommon shortness—or should I say lack?—of speech. It took us some time to get used to him, walking in and out, like a ghost, without a word. Especially because Hawkins talked enough for a platoon, it was strange to hear big Belcher with his toes in the ashes come out with a solitary "Excuse me, chum," or "That's right, chum." His one and only passion was cards, and I will say for him that he was a good card-player. He could have fleeced myself and Noble, but whatever we lost to him Hawkins lost to us, and Hawkins played with the money Belcher gave him.

Hawkins lost to us because he had too much old gab, and we probably lost

1. Belcher and Hawkins are English soldiers, captured during the Irish battle for independence of 1922. The British Army and its collaborators are searching for them. 2. Native Irish dances.

to Belcher for the same reason. Hawkins and Noble would spit at one another about religion into the early hours of the morning, and Hawkins worried the soul out of Noble, whose brother was a priest, with a string of questions that would puzzle a cardinal. To make it worse even in treating of holy subjects, Hawkins had a deplorable tongue. I never in all my career met a man who could mix such a variety of cursing and bad language into an argument. He was a terrible man, and a fright to argue. He never did a stroke of work, and when he had no one else to talk to, he got stuck in the old woman.

He met his match in her, for one day when he tried to get her to complain profanely of the drought, she gave him a great comedown by blaming it entirely on Jupiter Pluvius (a deity neither Hawkins nor I had ever heard of, though Noble said that among the pagans it was believed that he had something to do with the rain).[3] Another day he was swearing at the capitalists for starting the German war[4] when the old lady laid down her iron, puckered up her little crab's mouth, and said: "Mr. Hawkins, you can say what you like about the war, and think you'll deceive me because I'm only a simple poor countrywoman, but I know what started the war. It was the Italian Count that stole the heathen divinity out of the temple in Japan. Believe me, Mr. Hawkins, nothing but sorrow and want can follow the people that disturb the hidden powers."

A queer old girl, all right.

## II

We had our tea one evening, and Hawkins lit the lamp and we all sat into cards. Jeremiah Donovan came in too, and sat down and watched us for a while, and it suddenly struck me that he had no great love for the two Englishmen. It came as a great surprise to me, because I hadn't noticed anything about him before.

Late in the evening a really terrible argument blew up between Hawkins and Noble, about capitalists and priests and love of your country.

"The capitalists," says Hawkins with an angry gulp, "pays the priests to tell you about the next world so as you won't notice what the bastards are up to in this."

"Nonsense, man!" says Noble, losing his temper. "Before ever a capitalist was thought of, people believed in the next world."

Hawkins stood up as though he was preaching a sermon.

"Oh, they did, did they?" he says with a sneer. "They believed all the things you believe, isn't that what you mean? And you believe that God created Adam, and Adam created Shem, and Shem created Jehoshophat.[5] You believe all that silly old fairytale about Eve and Eden and the apple. Well, listen to me, chum. If you're entitled to hold a silly belief like that, I'm entitled to hold my silly belief—which is that the first thing your God created was a bleeding capitalist, with morality and Rolls-Royce complete. Am I right, chum?" he says to Belcher.

3. In fact the Roman god Jupiter had many functions, among them bringing rain for the crops, hence "Pluvius" (rainy). 4. World War I, in which England was at war with Germany. 5. Hawkins's scrambled version of Old Testament lore.

"You're right, chum," says Belcher with his amused smile, and got up from the table to stretch his long legs into the fire and stroke his moustache. So, seeing that Jeremiah Donovan was going, and that there was no knowing when the argument about religion would be over, I went out with him. We strolled down to the village together, and then he stopped and started blushing and mumbling and saying I ought to be behind, keeping guard on the prisoners. I didn't like the tone he took with me, and anyway I was bored with life in the cottage, so I replied by asking him what the hell we wanted guarding them at all for. I told him I'd talked it over with Noble, and that we'd both rather be out with a fighting column.

"What use are those fellows to us?" says I.

He looked at me in surprise and said: "I thought you knew we were keeping them as hostages."

"Hostages?" I said.

"The enemy have prisoners belonging to us," he says, "and now they're talking of shooting them. If they shoot our prisoners, we'll shoot theirs."

"Shoot them?" I said.

"What else did you think we were keeping them for?" he says.

"Wasn't it very unforeseen of you not to warn Noble and myself of that in the beginning?" I said.

"How was it?" says he. "You might have known it."

"We couldn't know it, Jeremiah Donovan," says I. "How could we when they were on our hands so long?"

"The enemy have our prisoners as long and longer," says he.

"That's not the same thing at all," says I.

"What difference is there?" says he.

I couldn't tell him, because I knew he wouldn't understand. If it was only an old dog that was going to the vet's, you'd try and not get too fond of him, but Jeremiah Donovan wasn't a man that would ever be in danger of that.

"And when is this thing going to be decided?" says I.

"We might hear tonight," he says. "Or tomorrow or the next day at latest. So if it's only hanging round here that's a trouble to you, you'll be free soon enough."

It wasn't the hanging round that was a trouble to me at all by this time. I had worse things to worry about. When I got back to the cottage the argument was still on. Hawkins was holding forth in his best style, maintaining that there was no next world, and Noble was maintaining that there was; but I could see that Hawkins had had the best of it.

"Do you know what, chum?" he was saying with a saucy smile. "I think you're just as big a bleeding unbeliever as I am. You say you believe in the next world, and you know just as much about the next world as I do, which is sweet damn-all. What's heaven? You don't know. Where's heaven? You don't know. You know sweet damn-all! I ask you again, do they wear wings?"

"Very well, then," says Noble, "they do. Is that enough for you? They do wear wings."

"Where do they get them, then? Who makes them? Have they a factory for wings? Have they a sort of store where you hands in your chit and takes your bleeding wings?"

"You're an impossible man to argue with," says Noble. "Now, listen to me—" And they were off again.

It was long after midnight when we locked up and went to bed. As I blew out the candle I told Noble what Jeremiah Donovan was after telling me. Noble took it very quietly. When we'd been in bed about an hour he asked me did I think we ought to tell the Englishmen. I didn't think we should, because it was more than likely that the English wouldn't shoot our men, and even if they did, the brigade officers, who were always up and down with the Second Battalion and knew the Englishmen well, wouldn't be likely to want them plugged. "I think so too," says Noble. "It would be great cruelty to put the wind to them now."

"It was very unforeseen of Jeremiah Donovan anyhow," says I.

It was next morning that we found it so hard to face Belcher and Hawkins. We went about the house all day scarcely saying a word. Belcher didn't seem to notice; he was stretched into the ashes as usual, with his look unusual of waiting in quietness for something unforeseen to happen, but Hawkins noticed and put it down to Noble's being beaten in the argument of the night before.

"Why can't you take a discussion in the proper spirit?" he says severely. "You and your Adam and Eve! I'm a Communist, that's what I am. Communist or anarchist, it all comes to much the same thing." And for hours he went round the house, muttering when the fit took him. "Adam and Eve! Adam and Eve! Nothing better to do with their time than picking bleeding apples!"

## III

I don't know how we got through that day, but I was very glad when it was over, the tea things were cleared away, and Belcher said in his peaceable way: "Well, chums, what about it?" We sat round the table and Hawkins took out the cards, and just then I heard Jeremiah Donovan's footstep on the path and a dark presentiment crossed my mind. I rose from the table and caught him before he reached the door.

"What do you want?" I asked.

"I want those two soldier friends of yours," he says, getting red.

"Is that the way, Jeremiah Donovan?" I asked.

"That's the way. There were four of our lads shot this morning, one of them a boy of sixteen."

"That's bad," I said.

At that moment Noble followed me out, and the three of us walked down the path together, talking in whispers. Feeney, the local intelligence officer, was standing by the gate.

"What are you going to do about it?" I asked Jeremiah Donovan.

"I want you and Noble to get them out; tell them they're being shifted again; that'll be the quietest way."

"Leave me out of that," says Noble under his breath.

Jeremiah Donovan looks at him hard.

"All right," he says. "You and Feeney get a few tools from the shed and dig a hole by the far end of the bog. Bonaparte and myself will be after you. Don't let anyone see you with the tools. I wouldn't like it to go beyond ourselves."

We saw Feeney and Noble go round to the shed and went in ourselves. I left Jeremiah Donovan to do the explanations. He told them that he had orders to send them back to the Second Battalion. Hawkins let out a mouthful of curses, and you could see that though Belcher didn't say anything, he was a bit upset too. The old woman was for having them stay in spite of us, and she didn't stop advising them until Jeremiah Donovan lost his temper and turned on her. He had a nasty temper, I noticed. It was pitch-dark in the cottage by this time, but no one thought of lighting the lamp, and in the darkness the two Englishmen fetched their topcoats and said good-bye to the old woman.

"Just as a man makes a home of a bleeding place, some bastard at headquarters thinks you're too cushy and shunts you off," says Hawkins, shaking her hand.

"A thousand thanks, madam," says Belcher. "A thousand thanks for everything"—as though he'd made it up.

We went round to the back of the house and down towards the bog. It was only then that Jeremiah Donovan told them. He was shaking with excitement.

"There were four of our fellows shot in Cork this morning and now you're to be shot as a reprisal."

"What are you talking about?" snaps Hawkins. "It's bad enough being mucked about as we are without having to put up with your funny jokes."

"It isn't a joke," says Donovan. "I'm sorry, Hawkins, but it's true," and begins on the usual rigmarole about duty and how unpleasant it is.

I never noticed that people who talk a lot about duty find it much of a trouble to them.

"Oh, cut it out!" says Hawkins.

"Ask Bonaparte," says Donovan, seeing that Hawkins isn't taking him seriously. "Isn't it true, Bonaparte?"

"It is," I say, and Hawkins stops.

"Ah, for Christ's sake, chum!"

"I mean it, chum," I say.

"You don't sound as if you meant it."

"If he doesn't mean it, I do," says Donovan, working himself up.

"What have you against me, Jeremiah Donovan?"

"I never said I had anything against you. But why did your people take out four of our prisoners and shoot them in cold blood?"

He took Hawkins by the arm and dragged him on, but it was impossible to make him understand that we were in earnest. I had the Smith and Wesson[6] in my pocket and I kept fingering it and wondering what I'd do if they put up a fight for it or ran, and wishing to God they'd do one or the other. I knew if they did run for it, that I'd never fire on them. Hawkins wanted to know was Noble in it, and when we said yes, he asked us why Noble wanted to plug him.

6. Revolver, as is the Webley, below.

Why did any of us want to plug him? What had he done to us? Weren't we all chums? Didn't we understand him and didn't he understand us? Did we imagine for an instant that he'd shoot us for all the so-and-so officers in the so-and-so British Army?

By this time we'd reached the bog, and I was so sick I couldn't even answer him. We walked along the edge of it in the darkness, and every now and then Hawkins would call a halt and begin all over again, as if he was wound up, about our being chums, and I knew that nothing but the sight of the grave would convince him that we had to do it. And all the time I was hoping that something would happen; that they'd run for it or that Noble would take over the responsibility from me. I had the feeling that it was worse on Noble than on me.

## IV

At last we saw the lantern in the distance and made towards it. Noble was carrying it, and Feeney was standing somewhere in the darkness behind him, and the picture of them so still and silent in the bogland brought it home to me that we were in earnest, and banished the last bit of hope I had.

Belcher, on recognizing Noble, said: "Hallo, chum," in his quiet way, but Hawkins flew at him at once, and the argument began all over again, only this time Noble had nothing to say for himself and stood with his head down, holding the lantern between his legs.

It was Jeremiah Donovan who did the answering. For the twentieth time, as though it was haunting his mind, Hawkins asked if anybody thought he'd shoot Noble.

"Yes, you would," says Jeremiah Donovan.

"No, I wouldn't, damn you!"

"You would, because you'd know you'd be shot for not doing it."

"I wouldn't, not if I was to be shot twenty times over. I wouldn't shoot a pal. And Belcher wouldn't—isn't that right, Belcher?"

"That's right, chum," Belcher said, but more by way of answering the question than of joining in the argument. Belcher sounded as though whatever unforeseen thing he'd always been waiting for had come at last.

"Anyway, who says Noble would be shot if I wasn't? What do you think I'd do if I was in his place, out in the middle of a blasted bog?"

"What would you do?" asks Donovan.

"I'd go with him wherever he was going, of course. Share my last bob with him and stick by him through thick and thin. No one can ever say of me that I let down a pal."

"We had enough of this," says Jeremiah Donovan, cocking his revolver. "Is there any message you want to send?"

"No, there isn't."

"Do you want to say your prayers?"

Hawkins came out with a cold-blooded remark that even shocked me and turned on Noble again.

"Listen to me, Noble," he says. "You and me are chums. You can't come over to my side, so I'll come over to your side. That show you I mean what I say? Give me a rifle and I'll go along with you and the other lads."

Nobody answered him. We knew that was no way out.

"Hear what I'm saying?" he says. "I'm through with it. I'm a deserter or anything else you like. I don't believe in your stuff, but it's no worse than mine. That satisfy you?"

Noble raised his head, but Donovan began to speak and he lowered it again without replying.

"For the last time, have you any messages to send?" says Donovan in a cold excited sort of voice.

"Shut up, Donovan! You don't understand me, but these lads do. They're not the sort to make a pal and kill a pal. They're not the tools of any capitalist."

I alone of the crowd saw Donovan raise his Webley to the back of Hawkins's neck, and as he did so I shut my eyes and tried to pray. Hawkins had begun to say something else when Donovan fired, and as I opened my eyes at the bang, I saw Hawkins stagger at the knees and lie out flat at Noble's feet, slowly and as quiet as a kid falling asleep, with the lantern-light on his lean legs and bright farmer's boots. We all stood very still, watching him settle out in the last agony.

Then Belcher took out a handkerchief and began to tie it about his own eyes (in our excitement we'd forgotten to do the same for Hawkins), and, seeing it wasn't big enough, turned and asked for the loan of mine. I gave it to him and he knotted the two together and pointed with his foot at Hawkins.

"He's not quite dead," he says. "Better give him another."

Sure enough, Hawkins's left knee is beginning to rise. I bend down and put my gun to his head; then, recollecting myself, I get up again. Belcher understands what's in my mind.

"Give him his first," he says. "I don't mind. Poor bastard, we don't know what's happening to him now."

I knelt and fired. By this time I didn't seem to know what I was doing. Belcher, who was fumbling a bit awkwardly with the handkerchiefs, came out with a laugh as he heard the shot. It was the first time I heard him laugh and it sent a shudder down my back; it sounded so unnatural.

"Poor bugger!" he said quietly. "And last night he was so curious about it all. It's very queer, chums, I always think. Now he knows as much about it as they'll ever let him know, and last night he was all in the dark."

Donovan helped him to tie the handkerchiefs about his eyes. "Thanks, chum," he said. Donovan asked if there were any messages he wanted sent.

"No, chum," he says. "Not for me. If any of you would like to write to Hawkins's mother, you'll find a letter from her in his pocket. He and his mother were great chums. But my missus left me eight years ago. Went away with another fellow and took the kid with her. I like the feeling of a home, as you may have noticed, but I couldn't start again after that."

It was an extraordinary thing, but in those few minutes Belcher said more than in all the weeks before. It was just as if the sound of the shot had started a flood of talk in him and he could go on the whole night like that, quite happily, talking about himself. We stood round like fools now that he couldn't see us any longer. Donovan looked at Noble, and Noble shook his head. Then Donovan raised his Webley, and at that moment Belcher gives his queer laugh again.

He may have thought we were talking about him, or perhaps he noticed the same thing I'd noticed and couldn't understand it.

"Excuse me, chums," he says. "I feel I'm talking the hell of a lot, and so silly, about my being so handy about a house and things like that. But this thing came on me suddenly. You'll forgive me, I'm sure."

"You don't want to say a prayer?" asks Donovan.

"No, chum," he says. "I don't think it would help. I'm ready, and you boys want to get it over."

"You understand that we're only doing our duty?" says Donovan.

Belcher's head was raised like a blind man's so that you could only see his chin and the tip of his nose in the lantern-light.

"I never could make out what duty was myself," he said. "I think you're all good lads, if that's what you mean. I'm not complaining."

Noble, just as if he couldn't bear any more of it, raised his fist at Donovan, and in a flash Donovan raised his gun and fired. The big man went over like a sack of meal, and this time there was no need for a second shot.

I don't remember much about the burying, but that it was worse than all the rest because we had to carry them to the grave. It was all mad lonely with nothing but a patch of lantern-light between ourselves and the dark, and birds hooting and screeching all round, disturbed by the guns. Noble went through Hawkins's belongings to find the letter from his mother, and then joined his hands together. He did the same with Belcher. Then, when we'd filled in the grave, we separated from Jeremiah Donovan and Feeney and took our tools back to the shed. All the way we didn't speak a word. The kitchen was dark and cold as we'd left it, and the old woman was sitting over the hearth, saying her beads. We walked past her into the room, and Noble struck a match to light the lamp. She rose quietly and came to the doorway with all her cantankerousness gone.

"What did ye do with them?" she asked in a whisper, and Noble started so that the match went out in his hand.

"What's that?" he asked without turning round.

"I heard ye," she said.

"What did you hear?" asked Noble.

"I heard ye. Do ye think I didn't hear ye, putting the spade back in the houseen?"[7]

Noble struck another match and this time the lamp lit for him.

"Was that what ye did to them?" she asked.

Then, by God, in the very doorway, she fell on her knees and began praying, and after looking at her for a minute or two Noble did the same by the fireplace. I pushed my way out past her and left them at it. I stood at the door, watching the stars and listening to the shrieking of the birds dying out over the bogs. It is so strange what you feel at times like that that you can't describe it. Noble says he saw everything ten times the size, as though there were nothing in the whole world but that little patch of bog with the two Englishmen stiffening into it, but with me it was as if the patch of bog where the Englishmen were was a

7. Shed.

million miles away, and even Noble and the old woman, mumbling behind me, and the birds and the bloody stars were all far away, and I was somehow very small and very lost and lonely like a child astray in the snow. And anything that happened to me afterwards, I never felt the same about again.

## EDWARD P. JONES on *Guests of the Nation*

I discovered "Guests of the Nation" some twenty-five years ago at a time when I was—in a creative and just about every other way—young and naive enough to hope that Frank O'Connor would manage some literary sleight of hand to prevent what even the first pages of the story conveyed to me was inevitable. I was never so naive, however, as not to understand that I had come upon a treasure, a small guide of five pages or so to the way I wanted eventually to begin crafting things.

Stories, that me-of-twenty-five-years-ago was beginning to learn, should strive to illuminate that moment or those moments, however grand, however seemingly insignificant, in a character's life when the earth shifts and the world is forever different: Humpty Dumpty falls off the wall reaching for a butterfly and the inconsolable king forsakes his queen and ultimately exhausts all his power in a hopeless effort to put his best friend back together again. . . . I had read very good stories before "Guests of the Nation," but nothing had for a while—and few stories since have—showed what I was coming to believe stories should be.

I go back to the story at least once each year to rediscover the wonders I was able to appreciate after that first, breathless reading: the way, for example, O'Connor seems to dash through the events in the first three sections, then slows down in the last section—which is about twice as long as each of the previous sections—to a nearly minute-by-minute telling of the last hours in the Englishmen's lives.

There is, as well, an appreciation of the things it was almost too easy to overlook with the thunder of the ending: the way O'Connor, in a few strokes, aims to humanize Jeremiah Donovan, who undeservedly lives in some readers' minds as the villain. "He reddened when you talked to him, . . . looking down at his big farmer's feet. Noble and me used to make fun of his broad accent, because we were from the town." The narrator is pulled down just a bit here. And Bonaparte, doing his "duty," falls even farther when he puts the second bullet in his friend's head.

But perhaps the most important reason I am compelled to reread "Guests of the Nation" is that sense of being a witness as the earth shifts for Bonaparte and he is being re-created, even as his friends, in Noble's words, are "stiffening" in that "little patch of bog." Even twenty-five years later, the story continues to unfold for me with a monstrous inevitability that begins with the coziness of the first paragraph when Belcher "shifts his long legs out of the ashes." Even twenty-five years and dozens of readings later, the story continues to amaze and move me, perhaps because, given the world I grew into, it is so inevitable.

# Tillie Olsen

*Olsen (1913–    ) was born in Omaha, Nebraska, the daughter of Russian immigrants. She began to write in the 1930s, but most of her life was committed to working in industry and raising her four children. It wasn't until after they were grown that she began to publish in earnest. When her rare stories began to appear in the 1950s, she attracted a small group of enthusiastic readers who loyally acclaimed her talents until she gained a wider reputation. Although she has quite a small body of work, she has an established reputation as an ardent feminist as well as a writer. Her devotion to social and political causes is also well-known. She has taught or been a writer-in-residence at such colleges and universities as Amherst College, Stanford University, MIT, and Kenyon College. She is the recipient of five honorary degrees, a National Endowment for the Arts fellowship, a Guggenheim fellowship, and the O'Henry Award for best short story. Her stories are collected in* Tell Me a Riddle *(1961).* Silences *(1978) is a collection of essays and meditations. Her novel,* Yonnondio, *was published in 1974. Her work has appeared in over one hundred anthologies.*

## Tell Me a Riddle

**"These Things Shall Be"**

### I

For forty-seven years they had been married. How deep back the stubborn, gnarled roots of the quarrel reached, no one could say—but only now, when tending to the needs of others no longer shackled them together, the roots swelled up visible, split the earth between them, and the tearing shook even to the children, long since grown.

Why now, why now? wailed Hannah.

As if when we grew up weren't enough, said Paul.

Poor Ma. Poor Dad. It hurts so for both of them, said Vivi. They never had very much; at least in old age they should be happy.

Knock their heads together, insisted Sammy; tell 'em: you're too old for this kind of thing; no reason not to get along now.

Lennie wrote to Clara: They've lived over so much together; what could possibly tear them apart?

Something tangible enough.

Arthritic hands, and such work as he got, occasional. Poverty all his life, and there was little breath left for running. He could not, could not turn away from this desire: to have the troubling of responsibility, the fretting with money, over and done with; to be free, to be *care*free where success was not measured by accumulation, and there was use for the vitality still in him.

There was a way. They could sell the house, and with the money join his lodge's Haven, co-operative for the aged. Happy communal life, and was he not already an official; had he not helped organize it, raise funds, served as a trustee?

But she—would not consider it.

"What do we need all this for?" he would ask loudly, for her hearing aid was turned down and the vacuum was shrilling. "Five rooms" (pushing the sofa so she could get into the corner) "furniture" (smoothing down the rug) "floors and surfaces to make work. Tell me, why do we need it?" And he was glad he could ask in a scream.

"Because I'm use't."

"Because you're use't. This is a reason, Mrs. Word Miser? Used to can get unused!"

"Enough unused I have to get used to already. . . . Not enough words?" turning off the vacuum a moment to hear herself answer. "Because soon enough we'll need only a little closet, no windows, no furniture, nothing to make work, but for worms. Because now I want room . . . Screech and blow like you're doing, you'll need that closet even sooner. . . . Ha, again!" for the vacuum bag wailed, puffed half up, hung stubbornly limp. "This time fix it so it stays; quick before the phone rings and you get too important-busy."

But while he struggled with the motor, it seethed in him. Why fix it? Why have to bother? And if it can't be fixed, have to wring the mind with how to pay the repair? At the Haven they come in with their own machines to clean your room or your cottage; you fish, or play cards, or make jokes in the sun, not with knotty fingers fight to mend vacuums.

Over the dishes, coaxingly: "For once in your life, to be free, to have everything done for you, like a queen."

"I never liked queens."

"No dishes, no garbage, no towel to sop, no worry what to buy, what to eat."

"And what else would I do with my empty hands? Better to eat at my own table when I want, and to cook and eat how I want."

"In the cottages they buy what you ask, and cook it how you like. *You* are the one who always used to say: better mankind born without mouths and stomachs than always to worry for money to buy, to shop, to fix, to cook, to wash, to clean."

"How cleverly you hid that you heard. I said it then because eighteen hours a day I ran. And you never scraped a carrot or knew a dish towel sops. Now—for you and me—who cares? A herring out of a jar is enough. But when *I* want, and nobody to bother." And she turned off her ear button, so she would not have to hear.

But as *he* had no peace, juggling and rejuggling the money to figure: how will I pay for this now?; prying out the storm windows (there they take care of this); jolting in the streetcar on errands (there I would not have to ride to take care of this or that); fending the patronizing relatives just back from Florida (there it matters what one is, not what one can afford), he gave *her* no peace.

"Look! In their bulletin. A reading circle. Twice a week it meets."

"Haumm," her answer of not listening.

"A reading circle. Chekhov they read that you like, and Peretz.[1] Cultured people at the Haven that you would enjoy."

"Enjoy!" She tasted the word. "Now, when it pleases you, you find a reading circle for me. And forty years ago when the children were morsels and there was a Circle, did you stay home with them once so I could go? Even once? You trained me well. I do not need others to enjoy. Others!" Her voice trembled. "Because you want to be there with others. Already it makes me sick to think of you always around others. Clown, grimacer, floormat, yesman, entertainer, whatever they want of you."

And now it was he who turned on the television loud so he need not hear.

Old scar tissue ruptured and the wounds festered anew. Chekhov indeed. She thought without softness of that young wife, who in the deep night hours while she nursed the current baby, and perhaps held another in her lap, would try to stay awake for the only time there was to read. She would feel again the weather of the outside on his cheek when, coming late from a meeting, he would find her so, and stimulated and ardent, sniffing her skin, coax: "I'll put the baby to bed, and you—put the book away, don't read, don't read."

That had been the most beguiling of all the "don't read, put your book away" her life had been. Chekhov indeed!

"Money?" She shrugged him off. "Could we get poorer than once we were? And in America, who starves?"

But as still he pressed:

"Let me alone about money. Was there ever enough? Seven little ones—for every penny I had to ask—and sometimes, remember, there was nothing. But always *I* had to manage. Now *you* manage. Rub your nose in it good."

But from those years she had had to manage, old humiliations and terrors rose up, lived again, and forced her to relive them. The children's needings; that grocer's face or this merchant's wife she had had to beg credit from when credit was a disgrace; the scenery of the long blocks walked around when she could not pay; school coming, and the desperate going over the old to see what could yet be remade; the soups of meat bones begged "for-the-dog" one winter. . . .

Enough. Now they had no children. Let *him* wrack his head for how they would live. She would not exchange her solitude for anything. *Never again to be forced to move to the rhythms of others.*

For in this solitude she had won to a reconciled peace.

Tranquillity from having the empty house no longer an enemy, for it stayed clean—not as in the days when it was her family, the life in it, that had seemed the enemy: tracking, smudging, littering, dirtying, engaging her in endless

1. I. L. Peretz (1852–1915), Russian author of poems, plays, and stories in Yiddish, "the Jewish Chekhov." Anton Chekhov, Russian writer (1860–1904).

defeating battle—and on whom her endless defeat had been spewed.

The few old books, memorized from rereading; the pictures to ponder (the magnifying glass superimposed on her heavy eyeglasses). Or if she wishes, when he is gone, the phonograph, that if she turns up very loud and strains, she can hear: the ordered sounds and the struggling.

Out in the garden, growing things to nurture. Birds to be kept out of the pear tree, and when the pears are heavy and ripe, the old fury of work, for all must be canned, nothing wasted.

And her one social duty (for she will not go to luncheons or meetings) the boxes of old clothes left with her, as with a life-practised eye for finding what is still wearable within the worn (again the magnifying glass superimposed on the heavy glasses) she scans and sorts—this for rag or rummage, that for mending and cleaning, and this for sending away.

*Being able at last to live within, and not move to the rhythms of others*, as life had forced her to: denying; removing; isolating; taking the children one by one; then deafening, half-blinding—and at last, presenting her solitude.

And in it she had won to a reconciled peace.

Now he was violating it with his constant campaigning: *Sell the house and move to the Haven.* (You sit, you sit—there too you could sit like a stone.) He was making of her a battleground where old grievances tore. (Turn on your ear button—I am talking.) And stubbornly she resisted—so that from wheedling, reasoning, manipulation, it was bitterness he now started with.

And it came to where every happening lashed up a quarrel.

"I will sell the house anyway," he flung at her one night. "I am putting it up for sale. There will be a way to make you sign."

The television blared, as always it did on the evenings he stayed home, and as always it reached her only as noise. She did not know if the tumult was in her or outside. Snap! she turned the sound off. "Shadows," she whispered to him, pointing to the screen, "look, it is only shadows." And in a scream: "Did you say that you will sell the house? Look at me, not at that. I am no shadow. You cannot sell without me."

"Leave on the television. I am watching."

"Like Paulie, like Jenny, a four-year-old. Staring at shadows. *You cannot sell the house.*"

"I will. We are going to the Haven. There you would not hear the television when you do not want it. I could sit in the social room and watch. You could lock yourself up to smell your unpleasantness in a room by yourself—for who would want to come near you?"

"No, no selling." A whisper now.

"The television is shadows. Mrs. Enlightened! Mrs. Cultured! A world comes into your house—and it is shadows. People you would never meet in a thousand lifetimes. Wonders. When you were four years old, yes, like Paulie, like Jenny, did you know of Indian dances, alligators, how they use bamboo in Malaya? No, you scratched in your dirt with the chickens and thought Olshana[2]

2. Village in Russia.

was the world. Yes, Mrs. Unpleasant, I will sell the house, for there better can we be rid of each other than here."

She did not know if the tumult was outside, or in her. Always a ravening inside, a pull to the bed, to lie down, to succumb.

"Have you thought maybe Ma should let a doctor have a look at her?" asked their son Paul after Sunday dinner, regarding his mother crumpled on the couch, instead of, as was her custom, busying herself in Nancy's kitchen.

"Why not the President too?"

"Seriously, Dad. This is the third Sunday she's lain down like that after dinner. Is she that way at home?"

"A regular love affair with the bed. Every time I start to talk to her."

Good protective reaction, observed Nancy to herself. The workings of hos-til-ity.

"Nancy could take her. I just don't like how she looks. Let's have Nancy arrange an appointment."

"You think she'll go?" regarding his wife gloomily. "All right, we have to have doctor bills, we have to have doctor bills." Loudly: "Something hurts you?"

She startled, looked to his lips. He repeated: "Mrs. Take It Easy, something hurts?"

"Nothing. . . . Only you."

"A woman of honey. That's why you're lying down?"

"Soon I'll get up to do the dishes, Nancy."

"Leave them, Mother, I like it better this way."

"Mrs. Take It Easy, Paul says you should start ballet. You should go to see a doctor and ask: how soon can you start ballet?"

"A doctor?" she begged. "Ballet?"

"We were talking, Ma," explained Paul, "you don't seem any too well. It would be a good idea for you to see a doctor for a checkup."

"I get up now to do the kitchen. Doctors are bills and foolishness, my son. I need no doctors."

"At the Haven," he could not resist pointing out, "a doctor is *not* bills. He lives beside you. You start to sneeze, he is there before you open up a Kleenex. You can be sick there for free, all you want."

"Diarrhea of the mouth, is there a doctor to make you dumb?"

"Ma. Promise me you'll go. Nancy will arrange it."

"It's all of a piece when you think of it," said Nancy, "the way she attacks my kitchen, scrubbing under every cup hook, doing the inside of the oven so I can't enjoy Sunday dinner, knowing that half-blind or not, she's going to find every speck of dirt. . . ."

"Don't Nancy, I've told you—it's the only way she knows to be useful. What did the *doctor* say?"

"A real fatherly lecture. Sixty-nine is young these days. Go out, enjoy life, find interests. Get a new hearing aid, this one is antiquated. Old age is sickness only if one makes it so. Geriatrics, Inc."

"So there was nothing physical."

"Of course there was. How can you live to yourself like she does without there being? Evidence of a kidney disorder, and her blood count is low. He gave her a diet, and she's to come back for follow-up and lab work. . . . But he was clear enough: Number One prescription—start living like a human being. When I think of your dad, who could really play the invalid with that arthritis of his, as active as a teenager, and twice as much fun. . . ."

"You didn't tell me the doctor says your sickness is in you, how you live." He pushed his advantage. "Life and enjoyments you need better than medicine. And this diet, how can you keep it? To weigh each morsel and scrape away each bit of fat, to make this soup, that pudding. There, at the Haven, they have a dietician, they would do it for you."

She is silent.

"You would feel better there, I know it," he says gently. "There there is life and enjoyments all around."

"What is the matter, Mr. Importantbusy, you have no card game or meeting you can go to?"—turning her face to the pillow.

For a while he cut his meetings and going out, fussed over her diet, tried to wheedle her into leaving the house, brought in visitors:

"I should come to a fashion tea. I should sit and look at pretty babies in clothes I cannot buy. This is pleasure?"

"Always you are better than everyone else. The doctor said you should go out. Mrs. Brem comes to you with goodness and you turn her away."

"Because *you* asked her to, she asked me."

"They won't come back. People you need, the doctor said. Your own cousins I asked; they were willing to come and make peace as if nothing had happened. . . ."

"No more crushers of people, pushers, hypocrites, around me. No more in *my* house. You go to them if you like."

"Kind he is to visit. And you, like ice."

"A babbler. All my life around babblers. Enough!"

"She's even worse, Dad? Then let her stew a while," advised Nancy. "You can't let it destroy you; it's a psychological thing, maybe too far gone for any of us to help."

So he let her stew. More and more she lay silent in bed, and sometimes did not even get up to make the meals. No longer was the tongue-lashing inevitable if he left the coffee cup where it did not belong, or forgot to take out the garbage or mislaid the broom. The birds grew bold that summer and for once pocked the pears, undisturbed.

A bellyful of bitterness and every day the same quarrel in a new way and a different old grievance the quarrel forced her to enter and relive. And the new torment: I am not really sick, the doctor said it, then why do I feel so sick?

One night she asked him: "You have a meeting tonight? Do not go. Stay . . . with me."

He had planned to watch "This Is Your Life," but half sick himself from the heavy heat, and sickening therefore the more after the brooks and woods of the Haven, with satisfaction he grated:

"Hah, Mrs. Live Alone And Like It wants company all of a sudden. It doesn't seem so good the time of solitary when she was a girl exile in Siberia. 'Do not go. Stay with me.' A new song for Mrs. Free As A Bird. Yes, I am going out, and while I am gone chew this aloneness good, and think how you keep us both from where if you want people you do not need to be alone."

"Go, go. All your life you have gone without me."

After him she sobbed curses he had not heard in years, old-country curses from their childhood: Grow, oh shall you grow like an onion, with your head in the ground. Like the hide of a drum shall you be, beaten in life, beaten in death. Oh shall you be like a chandelier, to hang, and to burn. . . .

She was not in their bed when he came back. She lay on the cot on the sun-porch. All week she did not speak or come near him; nor did he try to make peace or care for her.

He slept badly, so used to her next to him. After all the years, old harmonies and dependencies deep in their bodies; she curled to him, or he coiled to her, each warmed, warming, turning as the other turned, the nights a long embrace.

It was not the empty bed or the storm that woke him, but a faint singing. *She* was singing. Shaking off the drops of rain, the lightning riving her lifted face, he saw her so; the cot covers on the floor.

"This is a private concert?" he asked. "Come in, you are wet."

"I can breathe now," she answered; "my lungs are rich." Though indeed the sound was hardly a breath.

"Come in, come in." Loosing the bamboo shades. "Look how wet you are." Half helping, half carrying her, still faint-breathing her song.

A Russian love song of fifty years ago.

He had found a buyer, but before he told her, he called together those children who were close enough to come. Paul, of course, Sammy from New Jersey, Hannah from Connecticut, Vivi from Ohio.

With a kindling of energy for her beloved visitors, she arrayed the house, cooked and baked. She was not prepared for the solemn after-dinner conclave, they too probing in and tearing. Her frightened eyes watched from mouth to mouth as each spoke.

His stories were eloquent and funny of her refusal to go back to the doctor; of the scorned invitations; of her stubborn silence or the bile "like a Niagara"; of her contrariness: "If I clean it's no good how I cleaned; if I don't clean, I'm still a master who thinks he has a slave."

(Vinegar he poured on me all his life; I am well marinated; how can I be honey now?)

Deftly he marched in the rightness for moving to the Haven; their money from social security free for visiting the children, not sucked into daily needs and into the house; the activities in the Haven for him; but mostly the Haven for *her*: her health, her need of care, distraction, amusement, friends who shared her interests.

"This does offer an outlet for Dad," said Paul; "he's always been an active person. And economic peace of mind isn't to be sneezed at, either. I could use a little of that myself."

But when they asked: "And you, Ma, how do you feel about it?" could only whisper:

"For him it is good. It is not for me. I can no longer live between people."

"You lived all your life *for* people," Vivi cried.

"Not with." Suffering doubly for the unhappiness on her children's faces.

"You have to find some compromise," Sammy insisted. "Maybe sell the house and buy a trailer. After forty-seven years there's surely some way you can find to live in peace."

"There is no help, my children. Different things we need."

"Then live alone!" He could control himself no longer. "I have a buyer for the house. Half the money for you, half for me. Either alone or with me to the Haven. You think I can live any longer as we are doing now?"

"Ma doesn't have to make a decision this minute, however you feel, Dad," Paul said quickly, "and you wouldn't want her to. Let's let it lay a few months, and then talk some more."

"I think I can work it out to take Mother home with me for a while," Hannah said. "You both look terrible, but especially you, Mother. I'm going to ask Phil to have a look at you."

"Sure," cracked Sammy. "What's the use of a doctor husband if you can't get free service out of him once in a while for the family? And absence might make the heart . . . you know."

"There was something after all," Paul told Nancy in a colorless voice. "That was Hannah's Phil calling. Her gall bladder. . . . Surgery."

"Her *gall* bladder. If that isn't classic. 'Bitter as gall'—talk of psychosom——"

He stepped closer, put his hand over her mouth, and said in the same colorless, plodding voice. "We have to get Dad. They operated at once. The cancer was everywhere, surrounding the liver, everywhere. They did what they could . . . at best she has a year. Dad . . . we have to tell him."

## II

Honest in his weakness when they told him, and that she was not to know. "I'm not an actor. She'll know right away by how I am. Oh that poor woman. I am old too, it will break me into pieces. Oh that poor woman. She will spit on me: 'So my sickness was how I live.' Oh Paulie, how she will be, that poor woman. Only she should not suffer. . . . I can't stand sickness, Paulie, I can't go with you."

But went. And play-acted.

"A grand opening and you did not even wait for me. . . . A good thing Hannah took you with her."

"Fashion teas I needed. They cut out what tore in me; just in my throat something hurts yet. . . . Look! so many flowers, like a funeral. Vivi called, did Hannah tell you? And Lennie from San Francisco, and Clara; and Sammy is coming." Her gnome's face pressed happily into the flowers.

It is impossible to predict in these cases, but once over the immediate effects of the operation, she should have several months of comparative well-being.

*The money, where will come the money?*

Travel with her, Dad. Don't take her home to the old associations. The other children will want to see her.

*The money, where will I wring the money?*

Whatever happens, she is not to know. No, you can't ask her to sign papers to sell the house; nothing to upset her. Borrow instead, then after. . . .

*I had wanted to leave you each a few dollars to make life easier, as other fathers do. There will be nothing left now. (Failure! you and your "business is exploitation." Why didn't you make it when it could be made?—Is that what you're thinking, Sammy?)*

Sure she's unreasonable, Dad—but you have to stay with her. If there's to be any happiness in what's left of her life, it depends on you.

*Prop me up, children, think of me, too. Shuffled, chained with her, bitter woman. No Haven, and the little money going. . . . How happy she looks, poor creature.*

The look of excitement. The straining to hear everything (the new hearing aid turned full). Why are you so happy, dying woman?

How the petals are, fold on fold, and the gladioli color. The autumn air.

Stranger grandsons, tall above the little gnome grandmother, the little spry grandfather. Paul in a frenzy of picture-taking before going.

She, wandering the great house. Feeling the books; laughing at the maple shoemaker's bench of a hundred years ago used as a table. The ear turned to music.

"Let us go home. See how good I walk now." "One step from the hospital," he answers, "and she wants to fly. Wait till Doctor Phil says."

"Look—the birds too are flying home. Very good Phil is and will not show it, but he is sick of sickness by the time he comes home."

"Mrs. Telepathy, to read minds," he answers; "read mine what it says: when the trunks of medicines become a suitcase, then we will go."

The grandboys, they do not know what to say to us. . . . Hannah, she runs around here, there, when is there time for herself?

Let us go home. Let us go home.

Musing; gentleness—*but for the incidents of the rabbi in the hospital, and of the candles of benediction.*

*Of the rabbi in the hospital:*

Now tell me what happened, Mother.

From the sleep I awoke, Hannah's Phil, and he stands there like a devil in a dream and calls me by name. I cannot hear. I think he prays. Go away, please, I tell him, I am not a believer. Still he stands, while my heart knocks with fright.

You scared *him,* Mother. He thought you were delirious.

Who sent him? Why did he come to *me*?

It is a custom. The men of God come to visit those of their religion they might help. The hospital makes up the list for them—race, religion—and you are on the Jewish list.

Not for rabbis. At once go and make them change. Tell them to write: Race, human; Religion, none.

*And of the candles of benediction:*

Look, how you have upset yourself, Mrs. Excited Over Nothing. Pleasant memories you should leave.

Go in, go back to Hannah and the lights. Two weeks I saw candles and said nothing. But she asked me.

So what was so terrible? She forgets you never did, she asks you to light the Friday candles and say the benediction like Phil's mother when she visits. If the candles give her pleasure, why shouldn't she have the pleasure?

Not for pleasure she does it. For emptiness. Because his family does. Because all around her do.

That is not a good reason too? But you did not hear her. For heritage, she told you. For the boys, from the past they should have tradition.

Superstition! From our ancestors, savages, afraid of the dark, of themselves: mumbo words and magic lights to scare away ghosts.

She told you: how it started does not take away the goodness. For centuries, peace in the house it means.

Swindler! does she look back on the dark centuries? Candles bought instead of bread and stuck into a potato for a candlestick? Religion that stifled and said: in Paradise, woman, you will be the footstool of your husband, and in life—poor chosen Jew—ground under, despised, trembling in cellars. And cremated. And cremated.

This is religion's fault? You think you are still an orator of the 1905 revolution?[3] Where are the pills for quieting? Which are they?

Heritage. How have we come from our savage past, how no longer to be savages—this to teach. To look back and learn what humanizes—this to teach. To smash all ghettos that divide us—not to go back, not to go back—this to teach. Learned books in the house, will humankind live or die, and she gives to her boys—superstition.

3. Attempt to establish a democracy in czarist Russia. It was crushed by totalitarian terror.

Hannah that is so good to you. Take your pill, Mrs. Excited For Nothing, swallow.

Heritage! But when did I have time to teach? Of Hannah I asked only hands to help.

Swallow.

Otherwise—musing; gentleness.

Not to travel. To go home.

The children want to see you. We have to show them you are as thorny a flower as ever.

Not to travel.

Vivi wants you should see her new baby. She sent the tickets—airplane tickets—a Mrs. Roosevelt[4] she wants to make of you. To Vivi's we have to go.

A new baby. How many warm, seductive babies. She holds him stiffly, *away* from her, so that he wails. And a long shudder begins, and the sweat beads on her forehead.

"Hush, shush," croons the grandfather, lifting him back. "You should forgive your grandmamma, little prince, she has never held a baby before, only seen them in glass cases. Hush, shush."

"You're tired, Ma," says Vivi. "The travel and the noisy dinner. I'll take you to lie down."

*(A long travel from, to, what the feel of a baby evokes.)*

In the airplane, cunningly designed to encase from motion (no wind, no feel of flight), she had sat severely and still, her face turned to the sky through which they cleaved and left no scar.

So this was how it looked, the determining, the crucial sky, and this was how man moved through it, remote above the dwindled earth, the concealed human life. Vulnerable life, that could scar.

There was a steerage ship[5] of memory that shook across a great, circular sea: clustered, ill human beings; and through the thick-stained air, tiny fretting waters in a window round like the airplane's—sun round, moon round. (The round thatched roofs of Olshana.) Eye round—like the smaller window that framed distance the solitary year of exile when only her eyes could travel, and no voice spoke. And the polar winds hurled themselves across snows trackless and endless and white—like the clouds which had closed together below and hidden the earth.

Now they put a baby in her lap. Do not ask me, she would have liked to beg. Enough the worn face of Vivi, the remembered grandchildren, I cannot, cannot. . . .

*Cannot what?* Unnatural grandmother, not able to make herself embrace a baby.

4. Eleanor Roosevelt (1884–1962), wife of President Franklin D. Roosevelt, was famous for extensive, frequent travels. 5. I.e., a ship having only the lowest class of accommodations.

She lay there in the bed of the two little girls, her new hearing aid turned full, listening to the sound of the children going to sleep, the baby's fretful crying and hushing, the clatter of dishes being washed and put away. They thought she slept. Still she rode on.

It was not that she had not loved her babies, her children. The love—the passion of tending—had risen with the need like a torrent; and like a torrent drowned and immolated all else. But when the need was done—oh the power that was lost in the painful damming back and drying up of what still surged, but had nowhere to go. Only the thin pulsing left that could not quiet, suffering over lives one felt, but could no longer hold nor help.

On that torrent she had borne them to their own lives, and the riverbed was desert long years now. Not there would she dwell, a memoried wraith. Surely that was not all, surely there was more. Still the springs, the springs were in her seeking. Somewhere an older power that beat for life. Somewhere coherence, transport, meaning. If they would but leave her in the air now stilled of clamor, in the reconciled solitude, to journey on.

And they put a baby in her lap. Immediacy to embrace, and the breath of *that* past: warm flesh like this that had claims and nuzzled away all else and with lovely mouths devoured; hot-living like an animal—intensely and now; the turning maze; the long drunkenness; the drowning into needing and being needed. Severely she looked back—and the shudder seized her again, and the sweat. Not that way. Not there, not now could she, not yet. . . .

And all that visit, she could not touch the baby.

"Daddy, is it the . . . sickness she's like that?" asked Vivi. "I was so glad to be having the baby—for her. I told Tim, it'll give her more happiness than anything, being around a baby again. And she hasn't played with him once."

He was not listening. "Aahh little seed of life, little charmer," he crooned, "Hollywood should see you. A heart of ice you would melt. Kick, kick. The future you'll have for a ball. In 2050 still kick. Kick for your grandaddy then."

Attentive with the older children; sat through their performances (command performance; we command you to be the audience); helped Ann sort autumn leaves to find the best for a school program; listened gravely to Richard tell about his rock collection, while her lips mutely formed the words to remember: *igneous, sedimentary, metamorphic;*[6] looked for missing socks, books and bus tickets; watched the children whoop after their grandfather who knew how to tickle, chuck, lift, toss, do tricks, tell secrets, make jokes, match riddle for riddle. (Tell me a riddle, Grammy. I know no riddles, child.) Scrubbed sills and woodwork and furniture in every room; folded the laundry; straightened drawers; emptied the heaped baskets waiting for ironing (while he or Vivi or Tim nagged: You're supposed to rest here, you've been sick) but to none tended or gave food—and could not touch the baby.

After a week she said: "Let us go home. Today call about the tickets."

"You have important business, Mrs. Inahurry? The President waits to

6. Basic types of rocks.

consult with you?" He shouted, for the fear of the future raced in him. "The clothes are still warm from the suitcase, your children cannot show enough how glad they are to see you, and you want home. There is plenty of time for home. We cannot be with the children at home."

"Blind to around you as always: the little ones sleep four in a room because we take their bed. We are two more people in a house with a new baby, and no help."

"Vivi is happy so. The children should have their grandparents a while, she told to me. I should have my mommy and daddy. . . ."

"Babbler and blind. Do you look at her so tired? How she starts to talk and she cries? I am not strong enough yet to help. Let us go home."

(To reconciled solitude.)

*For it seemed to her the crowded noisy house was listening to her, listening for* her. *She could feel it like a great ear pressed under her heart. And everything knocked: quick constant raps: let me in, let me in.*

*How was it that soft reaching tendrils also became blows that knocked?*

C'mon, Grandma, I want to show you. . . .

Tell me a riddle, Grandma. *(I know no riddles.)*

Look, Grammy, he's so dumb he can't even find his hands. (Dody and the baby on a blanket over the fermenting autumn mould.)

I made them—for you. (Ann) (Flat paper dolls with aprons that lifted on scalloped skirts that lifted on flowered pants; hair of yarn and great ringed questioning eyes.)

Watch me, Grandma. (Richard snaking up the tree, hanging exultant, free, with one hand at the top. Below Dody hunching over in pretend-cooking.) *(Climb too, Dody, climb and look.)*

Be my nap bed, Grammy. (The "No!" too late.) Morty's abandoned heaviness, while his fingers ladder up and down her hearing-aid cord to his drowsy chant: eentsiebeentsiespider. *(Children trust.)*

It's to start off your own rock collection, Grandma. That's a trilobite fossil, 200 million years old (millions of years on a boy's mouth) and that one's obsidian, black glass.

*Knocked and knocked.*

Mother, I *told* you the teacher said we had to bring it back all filled out this morning. Didn't you even ask Daddy? Then tell *me* which plan and I'll check it: evacuate or stay in the city or wait for you to come and take me away. (Seeing the look of straining to hear.) It's for Disaster, Grandma.[7] *(Children trust.)*

Vivi in the maze of the long, the lovely drunkenness. The old old noises: baby sounds; screaming of a mother flayed to exasperation; children quarreling; children playing; singing; laughter.

7. During the 1950s, with the encouragement of the federal government, a number of American communities built fallout shelters and drew up evacuation ("disaster") plans to be used in a nuclear attack.

*And Vivi's tears and memories,* spilling so fast, half the words not understood.

She had started remembering out loud deliberately, so her mother would know the past was cherished, still lived in her.

Nursing the baby: My friends marvel, and I tell them, oh it's easy to be such a cow. I remember how beautiful my mother seemed nursing my brother, and the milk just flows. . . . Was that Davy? It must have been Davy. . . .

Lowering a hem: How did you ever . . . when I think how you made everything we wore . . . Tim, just think, seven kids and Mommy sewed everything . . . do I remember you sang while you sewed? That white dress with the red apples on the skirt you fixed over for me, was it Hannah's or Clara's before it was mine?

Washing sweaters: Ma, I'll never forget, one of those days so nice you washed clothes outside; one of the first spring days it must have been. The bubbles just danced up and down while you scrubbed, and we chased after, and you stopped to show us how to blow our own bubbles with green onion stalks . . . you always. . . .

"Strong onion, to still make you cry after so many years," her father said, to turn the tears into laughter.

While Richard bent over his homework: Where is it now, do we still have it, the Book of the Martyrs? It always seemed so, well—exalted, when you'd put it on the round table and we'd all look at it together; there was even a halo from the lamp. The lamp with the beaded fringe you could move up and down; they're in style again, pulley lamps like that, but without the fringe. You know the book I'm talking about, Daddy, the Book of the Martyrs, the first picture was a bust of Spartacus?. . . Socrates? I wish there was something like that for the children, Mommy, to give them what you. . . . (And the tears splashed again.)

(What I intended and did not? Stop it, daughter, stop it, leave that time. And he, the hypocrite, sitting there with tears in his eyes—it was nothing to you then, nothing.)

. . . The time you came to school and I almost died of shame because of your accent and because I knew you knew I was ashamed; how could I?. . . Sammy's harmonica and you danced to it once, yes you did, you and Davy squealing in your arms. . . . That time you bundled us up and walked us down to the railway station to stay the night 'cause it was heated and we didn't have any coal, that winter of the strike, you didn't think I remembered that, did you, Mommy?. . . How you'd call us out to see the sunsets. . . .

Day after day, the spilling memories. Worse now, questions, too. Even the grandchildren: Grandma, in the olden days, when you were little. . . .

It was the afternoons that saved.

While they thought she napped, she would leave the mosaic on the wall (of children's drawings, maps, calendars, pictures, Ann's cardboard dolls with their great ringed questioning eyes) and hunch in the girls' closet, on the low shelf where the shoes stood, and the girls' dresses covered.

For that while she would painfully sheathe against the listening house, the tendrils and noises that knocked, and Vivi's spilling memories. Sometimes it helped to braid and unbraid the sashes that dangled, or to trace the pattern on the hoop slips.

Today she had jacks and children under jet trails to forget. Last night, Ann and Dody silhouetted in the window against a sunset of flaming man-made clouds of jet trail, their jacks ball accenting the peaceful noise of dinner being made. Had she told them, yes she had told them of how they played jacks in her village though there was no ball, no jacks. Six stones, round and flat, toss them out, the seventh on the back of the hand, toss, catch and swoop up as many as possible, toss again. . . .

Of stones (repeating Richard) there are three kinds: earth's fire jetting; rock of layered centuries; crucibled new out of the old (*igneous, sedimentary, metamorphic*). But there was that other—frozen to black glass, never to transform or hold the fossil memory . . . (let not my seed fall on stone). There was an ancient one who fought to heights a great rock that crashed back down eternally—eternal labor, freedom, labor . . . (stone will perish, but the word remain).[8] And you, David, who with a stone slew, screaming: Lord, take my heart of stone and give me flesh.

*Who* was screaming? Why was she back in the common room of the prison, the sun motes dancing in the shafts of light, and the informer being brought in, a prisoner now, like themselves. And Lisa leaping, yes, Lisa, the gentle and tender, biting at the betrayer's jugular. Screaming and screaming.

No, it is the children screaming. Another of Paul and Sammy's terrible fights?

In Vivi's house. Severely: you are in Vivi's house.

Blows, screams, a call: "Grandma!" For her? Oh please not for her. Hide, hunch behind the dresses deeper. But a trembling little body hurls itself beside her—surprised, smothered laughter, arms surround her neck, tears rub dry on her cheek, and words too soft to understand whisper into her ear (Is this where you hide too, Grammy? It's my secret place, we have a secret now).

And the sweat beads, and the long shudder seizes.

It seemed the great ear pressed inside now, and the knocking. "We have to go home," she told him, "I grow ill here."

"It is your own fault, Mrs. Bodybusy, you do not rest, you do too much." He raged, but the fear was in his eyes. "It was a serious operation, they told you to take care. . . . All right, we will go to where you can rest."

But where? Not home to death, not yet. He had thought to Lennie's, to Clara's; beautiful visits with each of the children. She would have to rest first, be stronger. If they could but go to Florida—it glittered before him, the never-realized promise of Florida. California: of course. (The money, the money, dwindling!) Los Angeles first for sun and rest, then to Lennie's in San Francisco.

He told her the next day, "You saw what Nancy wrote: snow and wind back home, a terrible winter. And look at you—all bones and a swollen belly. I called Phil: he said: 'A prescription, Los Angeles sun and rest.' "

8. An allusion to the myth of Sisyphus, who was punished in Tartarus (below Hades) by having to roll a huge stone uphill; each time he approached the top, the stone would roll back.

She watched the words on his lips. "You have sold the house," she cried, "that is why we do not go home. That is why you talk no more of the Haven, why there is money for travel. After the children you will drag me to the Haven."

"The Haven! Who thinks of the Haven any more? Tell her, Vivi, tell Mrs. Suspicious: a prescription, sun and rest, to make you healthy. . . . And how could I sell the house without *you*?"

At the place of farewells and greetings, of winds of coming and winds of going, they say their good-byes.

They look back at her with the eyes of others before them: Richard with her own blue blaze; Ann with the Nordic eyes of Tim; Morty's dreaming brown of a great-grandmother he will never know; Dody with the laughing eyes of him who had been her springtide love (who stands beside her now); Vivi's, all tears.

The baby's eyes are closed in sleep.

*Good-bye, my children.*

## III

It is to the back of the great city he brought her, to the dwelling places of the cast-off old. Bounded by two lines of amusement piers to the north and to the south, and between a long straight paving rimmed with black benches facing the sand—sands so wide the ocean is only a far fluting.

In the brief vacation season, some of the boarded stores fronting the sands open, and families, young people and children, may be seen. A little tasselled tram shuttles between the piers, and the lights of roller coasters prink and tweak over those who come to have sensation made in them.

The rest of the year it is abandoned to the old, all else boarded up and still; seemingly empty, except the occasional days and hours when the sun, like a tide, sucks them out of the low rooming houses, casts them on to the benches and sandy rim of the walk—and sweeps them into decaying enclosures back again.

A few newer apartments glint among the low bleached squares. It is in one of these Lennie's Jeannie has arranged their rooms. "Only a few miles north and south people pay hundreds of dollars a month for just this gorgeous air, Grandaddy, just this ocean closeness."

She had been ill on the plane, lay ill for days in the unfamiliar room. Several times the doctor came by—left medicine she would not take. Several times Jeannie drove in the twenty miles from work, still in her Visiting Nurse uniform, the lightness and brightness of her like a healing.

"Who can believe it is winter?" he asked one morning. "Beautiful it is outside like an ad. Come, Mrs. Invalid, come to taste it. You are well enough to sit in here, you are well enough to sit outside. The doctor said it too."

But the benches were encrusted with people, and the sands at the sidewalk's edge. Besides, she had seen the far ruffle of the sea: "there take me," and though she leaned against him, it was she who led.

Plodding and plodding, sitting often to rest, he grumbling. Patting the sand so warm. Once she scooped up a handful, cradling it close to her better eye;

peered, and flung it back. And as they came almost to the brink and she could see the glistening wet, she sat down, pulled off her shoes and stockings, left him and began to run. "You'll catch cold," he screamed, but the sand in his shoes weighed him down—he who had always been the agile one—and already the white spray creamed her feet.

He pulled her back, took a handkerchief to wipe off the wet and the sand. "Oh no," she said, "the sun will dry," seized the square and smoothed it flat, dropped on it a mound of sand, knotted the kerchief corners and tied it to a bag—"to look at with the strong glass" (for the first time in years explaining an action of hers)—and lay down with the little bag against her cheek, looking toward the shore that nurtured life as it first crawled toward consciousness the millions of years ago.

He took her one Sunday in the evil-smelling bus, past flat miles of blister houses, to the home of relatives. Oh what is this? she cried as the light began to smoke and the houses to dim and recede. Smog, he said, everyone knows but you. . . . Outside he kept his arms about her, but she walked with hands pushing the heavy air as if to open it, whispered: who has done this? sat down suddenly to vomit at the curb and for a long while refused to rise.

*One's age as seen on the altered face of those known in youth.* Is this they he has come to visit? This Max and Rose, smooth and pleasant, introducing them to polite children, disinterested grandchildren, "the whole family, once a month on Sundays. And why not? We have the room, the help, the food."

Talk of cars, of houses, of success: this son that, that daughter this. And *your* children? Hastily skimped over, the intermarriages, the obscure work—"my doctor son-in-law, Phil"—all he has to offer. She silent in a corner. (Car-sick like a baby, he explains.) Years since he has taken her to visit anyone but the children, and old apprehensions prickle: "no incidents," he silently begs, "no incidents." He itched to tell them. "A very sick woman," significantly, indicating her with his eyes, "a very sick women." Their restricted faces did not react. "Have you thought maybe she'd do better at Palm Springs?" Rose asked. "Or at least a nicer section of the beach, nicer people, a pool." Not to have to say "money" he said instead: "would she have sand to look at through a magnifying glass?" and went on, detail after detail, the old habit betraying of parading the queerness of her for laughter.

After dinner—the others into the living-room in men- or women-clusters, or into the den to watch TV—the four of them alone. She sat close to him, and did not speak. Jokes, stories, people they had known, beginning of reminiscence, Russia fifty-sixty years ago. Strange words across the Duncan Phyfe table: *hunger; secret meetings; human rights; spies; betrayals; prison; escape*—interrupted by one of the grandchildren: "Commercial's on; any Coke left? Gee, you're missing a real hair-raiser." And then a granddaughter (Max proudly: "look at her, an American queen") drove them home on her way back to U.C.L.A. No incident—except that there had been no incidents.

The first few mornings she had taken with her the magnifying glass, but he would sit only on the benches, so she rested at the foot, where slatted bench shadows fell, and unless she turned her hearing aid down, other voices invaded.

Now on the days when the sun shone and she felt well enough, he took her on the tram to where the benches ranged in oblongs, some with tables for draughts or cards. Again the blanket on the sand in the striped shadows, but she no longer brought the magnifying glass. He played cards, and she lay in the sun and looked towards the waters; or they walked—two blocks down to the scaling hotel, two blocks back—past chili-hamburger stands, open-doored bars, Next to New and Perpetual Rummage Sale stores.

Once, out of the aimless walkers, slow and shuffling like themselves, someone ran unevenly towards them, embraced, kissed, wept: "dear friends, old friends." A friend of *hers*, not his: Mrs. Mays who had lived next door to them in Denver when the children were small.

Thirty years are compressed into a dozen sentences; and the present, not even in three. All is told the children scattered; the husband dead; she lives in a room two blocks up from the sing hall—and points to the domed auditorium jutting before the pier. The leg? phlebitis; the heavy breathing? that, one does not ask. She, too, comes to the benches each day to sit. And tomorrow, tomorrow, are they going to the community sing? Of course he would have heard of it, everybody goes—the big doings they wait for all week. They have never been? She will come for them to dinner tomorrow and they will all go together.

*So it is that she sits in the wind of the singing, among the thousand various faces of age.*

*She had turned off her hearing aid at once they came into the auditorium—as she would have wished to turn off sight.*

*One by one they streamed by and imprinted on her—and though the savage zest of their singing came voicelessly soft and distant, the faces still roared—the faces densened the air—chorded into*

children-chants, mother-croons, singing of the chained
love serenades, Beethoven storms, mad Lucia's scream
drunken joy-songs, keens for the dead, work-singing

> *while from floor to balcony to dome a bare-footed sore-covered little girl threaded the sound-thronged tumult, danced her ecstasy of grimace to flutes that scratched at a cross-roads village wedding*

*Yes, faces became sound, and the sound became faces; and faces and sound became weight—pushed, pressed*

"Air"—her hands claw his.

"Whenever I enjoy myself. . . ." Then he saw the grey sweat on her face. "Here. Up. Help me, Mrs. Mays," and they support her out to where she can gulp the air in sob after sob.

"A doctor, we should get for her a doctor."

"Tch, it's nothing," says Ellen Mays, "I get it all the time. You've missed the tram; come to my place. Fix your hearing aid, honey . . . close . . . tea. My view. See, she *wants* to come. Steady now, that's how." Adding mysteriously: "Remember your advice, easy to keep your head above water, empty things float. Float."

The singing a fading march for them, tall woman with a swollen leg, weaving little man, and the swollen thinness they help between.

The stench in the hall: mildew? decay? "We sit and rest then climb. My gorgeous view. We help each other and here we are."

The stench along into the slab of room. A wash stand for a sink, a box with oilcloth tacked around for a cupboard, a three-burner gas plate. Artificial flowers, colorless with dust. Everywhere pictures foaming: wedding, baby, party, vacation, graduation, family pictures. From the narrow couch under a slit of window, sure enough the view: lurching rooftops and a scallop of ocean heaving, preening, twitching under the moon.

"While the water heats. Excuse me . . . down the hall." Ellen Mays has gone.

"You'll live?" he asks mechanically, sat down to feel his fright; tried to pull her alongside.

She pushed him away. "For air," she said; stood clinging to the dresser. Then, in a terrible voice:

After a lifetime of room. Of many rooms.

Shhh.

You remember how she lived. Eight children. And now one room like a coffin.

She pays rent!

Shrinking the life of her    into one room    like a coffin    Rooms and rooms like this    I lie on the quilt and hear them talk

Please, Mrs. Orator-without-Breath.

Once you went for coffee    I walked    I saw    A Balzac[9]    a Chekhov to write it    Rummage    Alone    On scraps

Better old here than in the old country!

On scraps    Yet they sang like    like    Wondrous! *Human-kind    one has to believe*    So strong    for what?    To rot    not grow?

Your poor lungs beg you. They sob between each word.

Singing.    Unused    the life in them.    She    in this poor room with her    pictures    Max    You    The children    Everywhere    unused    the life    And who has meaning?    Century after century still all in us    not    to grow?

Coffins, rummage, plants: sick woman. Oh lay down. We will get for you the doctor.

"And when will it end. Oh, *the end.*" *That* nightmare thought, and this time she writhed, crumpled against him, seized his hand (for a moment again the weight, the soft distant roaring of humanity) and on the strangled-for breath, begged: "Man . . . we'll destroy ourselves?"

And looking for answer—in the helpless pity and fear for her (for *her*) that

9. Honoré de Balzac (1799–1850), French writer.

distorted his face—she understood the last months, and knew that she was dying.

## IV

"Let us go home," she said after several days.

"You are in training for a cross-country run? That is why you do not even walk across the room? Here, like a prescription Phil said, till you are stronger from the operation. You want to break doctor's orders?"

She saw the fiction was necessary to him, was silent; then: "At home I will get better. If the doctor here says?"

"And winter? And the visits to Lennie and to Clara? All right," for he saw the tears in her eyes, "I will write Phil, and talk to the doctor."

Days passed. He reported nothing. Jeannie came and took her out for air, past the boarded concessions, the hooded and tented amusement rides, to the end of the pier. They watched the spent waves feeding the new, the gulls in the clouded sky; even up where they sat, the wind-blown sand stung.

She did not ask to go down the crooked steps to the sea.

Back in her bed, while he was gone to the store, she said: "Jeannie, this doctor, he is not one I can ask questions. Ask him for me, can I go home?"

Jeannie looked at her, said quickly: "Of course, poor Granny. You want your own things around you, don't you? I'll call him tonight. . . . Look, I've something to show you," and from her purse unwrapped a large cookie, intricately shaped like a little girl. "Look at the curls—can you hear me well, Granny?—and the darling eyelashes. I just came from a house where they were baking them."

"The dimples, there in the knees," she marvelled, holding it to the better light, turning, studying, "like art. Each singly they cut, or a mold?"

"Singly," said Jeannie, "and if it is a child only the mother can make them. Oh Granny, it's the likeness of a real little girl who died yesterday—Rosita. She was three years old. *Pan del Muerto,* the Bread of the Dead. It was the custom in the part of Mexico they came from."

Still she turned and inspected. "Look, the hollow in the throat, the little cross necklace. . . . I think for the mother it is a good thing to be busy with such bread. You know the family?"

Jeannie nodded. "On my rounds. I nursed. . . . Oh Granny, it is like a party; they play songs she liked to dance to. The coffin is lined with pink velvet and she wears a white dress. There are candles. . . ."

"In the house?" Surprised, "They keep her in the house?"

"Yes," said Jeannie, "and it *is* against the health law. The father said it will be sad to bury her in this country; in Oaxaca they have a feast night with candles each year; everyone picnics on the graves of those they loved until dawn."

"Yes, Jeannie, the living must comfort themselves." And closed her eyes.

"You want to sleep, Granny?"

"Yes, tired from the pleasure of you. I may keep the Rosita? There stand it, on the dresser, where I can see; something of my own around me."

In the kitchenette, helping her grandfather unpack the groceries, Jeannie said in her light voice:

"I'm resigning my job, Grandaddy."

"Ah, the lucky young man. Which one is he?"

"Too late. You're spoken for." She made a pyramid of cans, unstacked, and built again.

"Something is wrong with the job?"

"With me. I can't be"—she searched for the word—"What they call professional enough. I let myself feel things. And tomorrow I have to report a family. . . ." The cans clicked again. "It's not that, either. I just don't know what I want to do, maybe go back to school, maybe go to art school. I thought if you went to San Francisco I'd come along and talk it over with Momma and Daddy. But I don't see how you can go. She wants to go home. She asked me to ask the doctor."

The doctor told her himself. "Next week you may travel, when you are a little stronger." But next week there was the fever of an infection, and by the time that was over, she could not leave the bed—a rented hospital bed that stood beside the double bed he slept in alone now.

Outwardly the days repeated themselves. Every other afternoon and evening he went out to his newfound cronies, to talk and play cards. Twice a week, Mrs. Mays came. And the rest of the time, Jeannie was there.

By the sickbed stood Jeannie's FM radio. Often into the room the shapes of music came. She would lie curled on her side, her knees drawn up, intense in listening (Jeannie sketched her so, coiled, convoluted like an ear), then thresh her hand out and abruptly snap the radio mute—still to lie in her attitude of listening, concealing tears.

Once Jeannie brought in a young Marine to visit, a friend from high-school days she had found wandering near the empty pier. Because Jeannie asked him to, gravely, without self-consciousness, he sat himself cross-legged on the floor and performed for them a dance of his native Samoa.

Long after they left, a tiny thrumming sound could be heard where, in her bed, she strove to repeat the beckon, flight, surrender of his hands, the fluttering footbeats, and his low plaintive calls.

Hannah and Phil sent flowers. To deepen her pleasure, he placed one in her hair. "Like a girl," he said, and brought the hand mirror so she could see. She looked at the pulsing red flower, the yellow skull face; a desolate, excited laugh shuddered from her, and she pushed the mirror away—but let the flower burn.

The week Lennie and Helen came, the fever returned. With it the excited laugh, and incessant words. She, who in her life had spoken but seldom and then only when necessary (never having learned the easy, social uses of words), now in dying, spoke incessantly.

In a half-whisper: "Like Lisa she is, your Jeannie. Have I told you of Lisa who taught me to read? Of the highborn she was, but noble in herself. I was sixteen; they beat me; my father beat me so I would not go to her. It was forbidden, she was a Tolstoyan.[1] At night, past dogs that howled, terrible dogs, my son, in the snows of winter to the road, I to ride in her carriage like a lady, to books. To her, life was holy, knowledge was holy, and she taught me to read. They hung her. Everything that happens one must try to understand why. She killed one who betrayed many. Because of betrayal, betrayed all she lived and believed. In one minute she killed, before my eyes (there is so much blood in a human being, my son), in prison with me. All that happens, one must try to understand.

"The name?" Her lips would work. "The name that was their pole star; the doors of the death houses fixed to open on it; I read of it my year of penal servitude. Thuban!" very excited, "Thuban, in ancient Egypt the pole star. Can you see, look out to see it, Jeannie, if it swings around *our* pole star that seems to *us* not to move.

"Yes, Jeannie, at your age my mother and grandmother had already buried children . . . yes, Jeannie, it is more than oceans between Olshana and you . . . yes, Jeannie, they danced, and for all the bodies they had they might as well be chickens, and indeed, they scratched and flapped their arms and hopped.

"And Andrei Yefimitch, who was twenty years had never known of it and never wanted to know, said as if he wanted to cry: but why my dear friend this malicious laughter?" Telling to herself half-memorized phrases from her few books. "Pain I answer with tears and cries, baseness with indignation, meanness with repulsion . . . for life may be hated or wearied of, but never despised."

Delirious: "Tell me, my neighbor, Mrs. Mays, the pictures never lived, but what of the flowers? Tell them who ask: no rabbis, no ministers, no priests, no speeches, no ceremonies: ah, false—let the living comfort themselves. Tell Sammy's boy, he who flies, tell him to go to Stuttgart[2] and see where Davy has no grave. And what?. . . And what? where millions have no graves—save air."

In delirium or not, wanting the radio on; not seeming to listen, the words still jetting, wanting the music on. Once, silencing it abruptly as of old, she began to cry, unconcealed tears this time. "You have pain, Granny?" Jeannie asked.

"The music," she said, "still it is there and we do not hear; knocks, and our poor human ears too weak. What else, what else we do not hear?"

Once she knocked his hand aside as he gave her a pill, swept the bottles from her bedside table: "no pills, let me feel what I feel," and laughed as on his hands and knees he groped to pick them up.

Nighttimes her hand reached across the bed to hold his.

A constant retching began. Her breath was too faint for sustained speech now, but still the lips moved:

*When no longer necessary    to injure others*
*Pick    pick pick    Blind chicken*
*As a human being    responsibility*

1. I.e., a follower of Leo Tolstoy (1828–1910), Russian novelist, social reformer, and teacher of nonviolence. 2. City in Germany, figuring in World War II.

"David!" imperious, "Basin!" and she would vomit, rinse her mouth, the wasted throat working to swallow, and begin the chant again.

She will be better off in the hospital now, the doctor said.

He sent the telegrams to the children, was packing her suitcase, when her hoarse voice startled. She had roused, was pulling herself to sitting.

"Where now?" she asked. "Where now do you drag me?"

"You do not even have to have a baby to go this time," he soothed, looking for the brush to pack. "Remember, after Davy you told me—worthy to have a baby for the pleasure of the ten-day rest in the hospital?"

"Where now? Not home yet?" Her voice mourned. "Where *is* my home?"

He rose to ease her back. "The doctor, the hospital," he started to explain, but deftly, like a snake, she had slithered out of bed and stood swaying, propped behind the night table.

"Coward," she hissed, "runner."

"You stand," he said senselessly.

"To take me there and run. Afraid of a little vomit."

He reached her as she fell. She struggled against him, half slipped from his arms, pulled herself up again.

"Weakling," she taunted, "to leave me there and run. Betrayer. All your life you have run."

He sobbed, telling Jeannie. "A Marilyn Monroe to run for her virtue. Fifty-nine pounds she weighs, the doctor said, and she beats at me like a Dempsey.[3] Betrayer, she cries, and I running like a dog when she calls; day and night, running to her, her vomit, the bedpan. . . ."

"She needs you, Grandaddy," said Jeannie. "Isn't that what they call love? I'll see if she sleeps, and if she does, poor worn-out darling, we'll have a party, you and I; I brought us rum babas."

They did not move her. By her bed now stood the tall hooked pillar that held the solutions—blood and dextrose—to feed her veins. Jeannie moved down the hall to take over the sickroom, her face so radiant, her grandfather asked her once: "you are in love?" (Shameful the joy, the pure overwhelming joy from being with her grandmother; the peace, the serenity that breathed.) "My darling escape," she answered incoherently, "my darling Granny"—as if that explained.

Now one by one the children came, those that were able. Hannah, Paul, Sammy. Too late to ask: and what did you learn with your living, Mother, and what do we need to know?

Clara, the eldest, clenched:

> *Pay me back, Mother, pay me back for all you took from me. Those others you crowded into your heart. The hands I needed to be for you, the heaviness, the responsibility.*

3. Jack Dempsey, world heavyweight champion boxer in the 1920s.

*Is this she? Noises the dying make, the crablike hands crawling over the covers. The ethereal singing.*

*She hears that music, that singing from childhood; forgotten sound—not heard since, since. . . . And the hardness breaks like a cry: Where did we lose each other, first mother, singing mother?*

*Annulled: the quarrels, the gibing, the harshness between; the fall into silence and the withdrawal.*

*I do not know you, Mother. Mother, I never knew you.*

Lennie, suffering not alone for her who was dying, but for that in her which never lived (for that which in him might never come to live). From him too, unspoken words: *good-bye Mother who taught me to mother myself.*

Not Vivi, who must stay with her children; not Davy, but he is already here, having to die again with *her* this time, for the living take their dead with them when they die.

Light she grew, like a bird, and, like a bird, sound bubbled in her throat while the body fluttered in agony. Night and day, asleep or awake (though indeed there was no difference now) the songs and the phrases leaping.

And he, who had once dreaded a long dying (from fear of himself, from horror of the dwindling money) now desired her quick death profoundly, for *her* sake. He no longer went out, except when Jeannie forced him; no longer laughed, except when, in the bright kitchenette, Jeannie coaxed his laughter (and she, who seemed to hear nothing else, would laugh too, conspiratorial wisps of laughter).

Light, like a bird, the fluttering body, the little claw hands, the beaked shadow on her face; and the throat, bubbling, straining.

He tried not to listen, as he tried not to look on the face in which only the forehead remained familiar, but trapped with her the long nights in that little room, the sounds worked themselves into his consciousness, with their punctuation of death swallows, whimpers, gurglings.

*Even in reality* (swallow) *life's lack of it*

*Slaveships deathtrains clubs eeenough*

*The bell summon what enables*

*78,000*[4] *in one minute* (whisper of a scream) *78,000 human beings we'll destroy ourselves?*

"Aah, Mrs. Miserable," he said, as if she could hear, "all your life working, and now in bed you lie, servants to tend, you do not even need to call to be tended, and still you work. Such hard work it is to die? Such hard work?"

The body threshed, her hand clung in his. A melody, ghost-thin, hovered on her lips, and like a guilty ghost, the vision of her bent in listening to it, silencing the record instantly he was near. Now, heedless of his presence, she floated the melody on and on.

"Hid it from me," he complained, "how many times you listened to remem-

4. The number killed in Hiroshima by the first atomic bomb.

ber it so?" And tried to think when she had first played it, or first begun to silence her few records when he came near—but could reconstruct nothing. There was only this room with its tall hooked pillar and its swarm of sounds.

*No man one except through others*

*Strong with the not yet in the now*

*Dogma dead war dead one country*

"It helps, Mrs. Philosopher, words from books? It helps?" And it seemed to him that for seventy years she had hidden a tape recorder, infinitely microscopic, within her, that it had coiled infinite mile on mile, trapping every song, every melody, every word read, heard, and spoken—and that maliciously she was playing back only what said nothing of him, of the children, of their intimate life together.

"Left us indeed, Mrs. Babbler," he reproached, "you who called others babbler and cunningly saved your words. A lifetime you tended and loved, and now not a word of us, for us. Left us indeed? Left me."

And he took out his solitaire deck, shuffled the cards loudly, slapped them down.

*Lift high banner of reason* (tatter of an orator's voice) *justice freedom light*

*Humankind life worthy capacities*

*Seeks* (blur of shudder) *belong human being*

"Words, words," he accused, "and what human beings did *you* seek around you, Mrs. Live Alone, and what mankind think worthy?"

Though even as he spoke, he remembered she had not always been isolated, had not always to be alone (as he knew there had been a voice before this gossamer one; before the hoarse voice that broke from silence to lash, make incidents, shame him—a girl's voice of eloquence that spoke their holiest dreams). But again he could reconstruct, image, nothing of what had been before, or when, or how, it had changed.

Ace, queen, jack. The pillar shadow fell, so, in two tracks; in the mirror depths glistened a moonlike blob, the empty solution bottle. And it worked in him: *of reason and justice and freedom . . . Dogma dead:* he remembered the full quotation, laughed bitterly. "Hah, good you do not know what you say; good Victor Hugo[5] died and did not see it, his twentieth century."

Deuce, ten, five. Dauntlessly she began a song of their youth of belief:

*These things shall be,[6] a loftier race*
*than e'er the world hath known shall rise*
*with flame of freedom in their souls*
*and light of knowledge in their eyes*

King, four, jack. "In the twentieth century, hah!"

5. Victor Hugo (1802–1885), French writer and champion of liberty; he prophesied the triumph of peace and liberty in the twentieth century. 6. Century-old socialist song, for a United Nations hymn. The first line is a translation of the French Revolutionary slogan "Ça ira."

*They shall be gentle, brave and strong*
*to spill no drop of blood, but dare*
*all . . .*

*on earth and fire and sea and air*

"To spill no drop of blood, hah! So, cadaver, and you too, cadaver Hugo, 'in the twentieth century ignorance will be dead, dogma will be dead, war will be dead, and for all mankind one country—of fulfilment?' Hah!"

*And every life* (long strangling cough) *shall be a song*

The cards fell from his fingers. Without warning, the bereavement and betrayal he had sheltered—compounded through the years—hidden even from himself—revealed itself,

uncoiled,
released,
*sprung*

and with it the monstrous shapes of what had actually happened in the century.

A ravening hunger or thirst seized him. He groped into the kitchenette, switched on all three lights, piled a tray—"you have finished your night snack, Mrs. Cadaver, now I will have mine." And he was shocked at the tears that splashed on the tray.

"Salt tears. For free. I forgot to shake on salt?"

Whispered: "Lost, how much I lost."

Escaped to the grandchildren whose childhoods were childish, who had never hungered, who lived unravaged by disease in warm houses of many rooms, had all the school for which they cared, could walk on any street, stood a head taller than their grandparents, towered above—beautiful skins, straight backs, clear straightforward eyes. "Yes, you in Olshana," he said to the town of sixty years ago, "they would look nobility to you."

And was this not the dream then, come true in ways undreamed? he asked.

*And are there no other children in the world?* he answered, as if in her harsh voice.

*And the flame of freedom, the light of knowledge?*

*And the drop, to spill no drop of blood?*

And he thought that at six Jeannie would get up and it would be his turn to go to her room and sleep, that he could press the buzzer and she would come now; that in the afternoon Ellen Mays was coming, and this time they would play cards and he could marvel at how rouge can stand half an inch on the cheek; that in the evening the doctor would come, and he could beg him to be merciful, to stop the feeding solutions, to let her die.

To let her die, and with her their youth of belief out of which her bright, betrayed words foamed; stained words, that on her working lips came stainless.

Hours yet before Jeannie's turn. He could press the buzzer and wake her to come now; he could take a pill, and with it sleep; he could pour more brandy into his milk glass, though what he had poured was not yet touched.

Instead he went back, checked her pulse, gently tended with his knotty fingers as Jeannie had taught.

She was whimpering; her hand crawled across the covers for his. Compassionately he enfolded it, and with his free hand gathered up the cards again. Still was there thirst or hunger ravening in him.

That world of their youth—dark, ignorant, terrible with hate and disease—how was it that living in it, in the midst of corruption, filth, treachery, degradation, they had not mistrusted man nor themselves; had believed so beautifully, so . . . falsely?

"Aaah, children," he said out loud, "how we believed, how we belonged." And he yearned to package for each of the children, the grandchildren, for everyone, *that joyous certainty, that sense of mattering, of moving and being moved, of being one and indivisible with the great of the past, with all that freed, ennobled.* Package it, stand on corners, in front of stadiums and on crowded beaches, knock on doors, give it as a fabled gift.

"And why not in cereal boxes, in soap packages?" he mocked himself. "Aah. You have taken my senses, cadaver."

Words foamed, died unsounded. Her body writhed; she made kissing motions with her mouth. (Her lips moving as she read, poring over the Book of the Martyrs, the magnifying glass superimposed over the heavy eyeglasses.) *Still she believed?* "Eva!" he whispered. "Still you believed? You lived by it? These Things Shall Be?"

"One pound soup meat," she answered distinctly, "one soup bone."

"My ears heard you. Ellen Mays was witness: 'Humankind . . . one has to believe.' " Imploringly: "Eva!"

"Bread, day-old." She was mumbling. "Please, in a wooden box . . . for kindling. The thread, hah, the thread breaks. Cheap thread"—and a gurgling, enormously loud, began in her throat.

"I ask for stone; she gives me bread—day-old." He pulled his hand away, shouted: "Who wanted questions? Everything you have to wake?" Then dully, "Ah, let me help you turn, poor creature."

Words jumbled, cleared. In a voice of crowded terror:

"Paul, Sammy, don't fight.

"Hannah, have I ten hands?

"How can I give it, Clara, how can I give it if I don't have?"

"You lie," he said sturdily, "there was joy too." Bitterly: "Ah how cheap you speak of us at the last."

As if to rebuke him, as if her voice had no relationship with her flailing body, she sang clearly, beautifully, a school song the children had taught her when they were little; begged:

"Not look   my hair   when they cut. . . ."

(The crown of braids shorn.) And instantly he left the mute old woman poring over the Book of the Martyrs; went past the mother treadling at the sewing machine, singing with the children; past the girl in her wrinkled prison dress, hiding her hair with scarred hands, lifting to him her awkward, shamed, imploring eyes of love; and took her in his arms, dear, personal, fleshed, in all the heavy passion he had loved to rouse from her.

"Eva!"

Her little claw hand beat the covers. How much, how much can a man stand? He took up the cards, put them down, circled the beds, walked to the dresser, opened, shut drawers, brushed his hair, moved his hand bit by bit over the mirror to see what of the reflection he could blot out with each move, and felt that at any moment he would die of what was endurable. Went to press the buzzer to wake Jeannie, looked down, saw on Jeannie's sketch pad the hospital bed, with *her*; the double bed alongside, with him; the tall pillar feeding into her veins, and their hands, his and hers, clasped, feeding each other. And as if he had been instructed he went to his bed, lay down, holding the sketch (as if it could shield against the monstrous shapes of loss, of betrayal, of death) and with his free hand took hers back into his.

So Jeannie found them in the morning.

That last day the agony was perpetual. Time after time it lifted her almost off the bed, so they had to fight to hold her down. He could not endure and left the room; wept as if there never would be tears enough.

Jeannie came to comfort him. In her light voice she said: Grandaddy, Grandaddy don't cry. She is not there, she promised me. On the last day, she said she would go back to when she first heard music, a little girl on the road of the village where she was born. She promised me. It is a wedding and they dance, while the flutes so joyous and vibrant tremble in the air. Leave her there, Grandaddy, it is all right. She promised me. Come back, come back and help her poor body to die.

*For my mother, my father,*
*and*
*Two of that generation*
*Seevya and Genya*
*Infinite, dauntless, incorruptible*

*Death deepens the wonder*

# Luigi Pirandello

*Pirandello (1867–1936) was born in Girgenti, Sicily. As a young man he studied at the University of Rome and in Bonn, Germany. Subsequently, he became a professor of literature but was chiefly famous for his prodigious output as a playwright and as the author of novels and short stories. In all, he wrote forty-three plays, the bulk of them elaborating the conflict between illusion and reality. The best-known and most typical of his imaginative constructions is* Six Characters in Search of an Author, *in which the characters of an unfinished play assert their claims to be more real than the drab existences from which they emerge. Pirandello's inversions of reality and make-believe had a strong influence on modern drama; his practices were often imitated. His extraordinary scrambling of normal expectations led to many charges that he perpetrated hoaxes. Nevertheless, he was awarded the Nobel Prize in 1934.*

## War

The passengers who had left Rome by the night express had had to stop until dawn at the small station of Fabriano in order to continue their journey by the small old-fashioned local joining the main line with Sulmona.

At dawn, in a stuffy and smoky second-class carriage in which five people had already spent the night, a bulky woman in deep mourning was hoisted in—almost like a shapeless bundle. Behind her, puffing and moaning, followed her husband—a tiny man, thin and weakly, his face death-white, his eyes small and bright and looking shy and uneasy.

Having at last taken a seat he politely thanked the passengers who had helped his wife and who had made room for her; then he turned round to the woman trying to pull down the collar of her coat, and politely inquired:

"Are you all right, dear?"

The wife, instead of answering, pulled up her collar again to her eyes, so as to hide her face.

"Nasty world," muttered the husband with a sad smile.

And he felt it his duty to explain to his traveling companions that the poor woman was to be pitied, for the war was taking away from her her only son, a boy of twenty to whom both had devoted their entire life, even breaking up their home at Sulmona to follow him to Rome, where he had to go as a student, then allowing him to volunteer for war with an assurance, however, that at least for six months he would not be sent to the front and now, all of a sudden, receiving a wire saying that he was due to leave in three days' time and asking them to go and see him off.

The woman under the big coat was twisting and wriggling, at times growling like a wild animal, feeling certain that all those explanations would not have aroused even a shadow of sympathy from those people who—most likely—were in the same plight as herself. One of them, who had been listening with particular attention, said:

"You should thank God that your son is only leaving now for the front. Mine has been sent there the first day of the war. He has already come back twice wounded and been sent back again to the front."

"What about me? I have two sons and three nephews at the front," said another passenger.

"Maybe, but in our case it is our *only* son," ventured the husband.

"What difference can it make? You may spoil your only son with excessive attentions, but you cannot love him more than you would all your other children if you had any. Paternal love is not like bread that can be broken into pieces and split amongst the children in equal shares. A father gives *all* his love to each one of his children without discrimination, whether it be one or ten, and if I am suffering now for my two sons, I am not suffering half for each of them but double . . ."

"True . . . true . . ." sighed the embarrassed husband, "but suppose (of course we all hope it will never be your case) a father has two sons at the front and he loses one of them, there is still one left to console him . . . while . . ."

"Yes," answered the other, getting cross, "a son left to console him but also a son left for whom he must survive, while in the case of the father of an only son if the son dies the father can die too and put an end to his distress. Which of the two positions is the worse? Don't you see how my case would be worse than yours?"

"Nonsense," interrupted another traveler, a fat, red-faced man with bloodshot eyes of the palest gray.

He was panting. From his bulging eyes seemed to spurt inner violence of an uncontrolled vitality which his weakened body could hardly contain.

"Nonsense," he repeated, trying to cover his mouth with his hand so as to hide the two missing front teeth. "Nonsense. Do we give life to our children for our own benefit?"

The other travelers stared at him in distress. The one who had had his son at the front since the first day of the war sighed: "You are right. Our children do not belong to us, they belong to the Country. . . ."

"Bosh," retorted the fat traveler. "Do we think of the Country when we give life to our children? Our sons are born because . . . well, because they must be born and when they come to life they take our own life with them. This is the truth. We belong to them but they never belong to us. And when they reach twenty they are exactly what we were at their age. We too had a father and mother, but there were so many other things as well . . . girls, cigarettes, illusions, new ties . . . and the Country, of course, whose call we would have answered—when we were twenty—even if father and mother had said no. Now at our age, the love of our Country is still great, of course, but stronger than it is the love for our children. Is they any one of us here who wouldn't gladly take his son's place at the front if he could?"

There was a silence all round, everybody nodding as to approve.

"Why then," continued the fat man, "shouldn't we consider the feelings of our children when they are twenty? Isn't it natural that at their age they should consider the love for their Country (I am speaking of decent boys, of course) even greater than the love for us? Isn't it natural that it should be so, as after all they must look upon us as upon old boys who cannot move any more and must stay at home? If Country exists, if Country is a natural necessity, like bread, of which each of us must eat in order not to die of hunger, somebody must go to defend it. And our sons go, when they are twenty, and they don't want tears, because if they die, they die inflamed and happy (I am speaking, of course, of decent boys). Now, if one dies young and happy, without having the ugly sides of life, the boredom of it, the pettiness, the bitterness of disillusion . . . what more can we ask for him? Everyone should stop crying; everyone should laugh, as I do . . . or at least thank God—as I do—because my son, before dying, sent me a message saying that he was dying satisfied at having ended his life in the best way he could have wished. That is why, as you see, I do not even wear mourning. . . ."

He shook his light fawn coat as to show it; his livid lip over his missing teeth was trembling, his eyes were watery and motionless, and soon after he ended with a shrill laugh which might well have been a sob.

"Quite so . . . quite so . . ." agreed the others.

The woman who, bundled in a corner under her coat, had been sitting and listening had—for the last three months—tried to find in the words of her husband and her friends something to console her in her deep sorrow, something that might show her how a mother should resign herself to send her son not even to death but to a probably dangerous life. Yet not a word had she found amongst the many which had been said . . . and her grief had been greater in seeing that nobody—as she thought—could share her feelings.

But now the words of the traveler amazed and almost stunned her. She suddenly realized that it wasn't the others who were wrong and could not understand her but herself who could not rise up to the same height of those fathers and mothers willing to resign themselves, without crying, not only to the departure of their sons but even to their death.

She lifted her head, she bent over from her corner trying to listen with great attention to the details which the fat man was giving to his companions about the way his son had fallen as a hero, for his King and his Country, happy and without regrets. It seemed to her that she had stumbled into a world she had never dreamt of, a world so far unknown to her and she was so pleased to hear everyone joining in congratulating that brave father who could so stoically speak of his child's death.

Then suddenly, just as if she had heard nothing of what had been said and almost as if waking up from a dream, she turned to the old man, asking him:

"Then . . . is your son really dead?"

Everybody stared at her. The old man, too, turned to look at her, fixing his great, bulging, horribly watery light gray eyes, deep in her face. For some little time he tried to answer, but words failed him. He looked and looked at her, almost as if only then—at that silly, incongruous question—he had suddenly realized at last that his son was really dead—gone for ever—for ever. His face contracted, became horribly distorted, then he snatched in haste a handkerchief from his pocket and, to the amazement of everyone, broke into harrowing, heart-rending, uncontrollable sobs.

# EDGAR ALLAN POE

*Poe (1809–1849) was born in Boston, the son of itinerant actors who died before he was three years old. He became the ward of a Virginia couple, the Allans, whose name he added to his own. His student days at the University of Virginia were brought to a quick end by his drinking and gambling; but then, enlisting in the army, he served soberly and well from 1827 to 1829. Accepted into West Point in 1830, he quickly ruined his prospects for a military career by more carousing, and that established a pattern he never again escaped. In 1836 he married his cousin Virginia Clemm, then a girl of thirteen, and tried to support her by writing and editing. He was an editor of the Richmond* Southern Literary Messenger, *among other publications, and for a time had his own magazine,* The Stylus. *He won a number of literary prizes early in his writing career, but his earnings remained meager, and alcoholic excesses repeatedly cost him his jobs in journalism. After his wife died in 1847, he became engaged to a wealthy widow; there was hope of relief from his long run of misfortune and poverty. Traveling to meet the widow in 1849, he met some acquaintances and with them set out to celebrate the change in his luck. After this binge he was found unconscious in a Baltimore street and died a few days later. His short fiction, with its effects of terror and its supernatural trappings, made him a household name for American readers, though in fact there are few traces of American experience in his work. Gothic devices and the mood of German romanticism were his specialty. He has been called the inventor of the detective story. His critical writings have deeply influenced literary taste and practice—for example, his insistence on unity of effect in the short story. His poetry has been admired more greatly and persistently abroad, particularly in France, than at home. He is remembered, as well, for the picturesqueness of his career, for his striking personal appearance, his fine manners, his debauchery, and his poverty—the stuff of a romantic legend. His work is most readily available in numerous anthologies and in collected editions.*

## The Fall of the House of Usher

*Son cœur est un luth suspendu;*
*Sitôt qu'on le touche il résonne.*
—De Béranger[1]

During the whole of a dull, dark, and soundless day in the autumn of the year, when the clouds hung oppressively low in the heavens, I had been passing alone, on horseback, through a singularly dreary tract of country; and at length found myself, as the shades of the evening drew on, within view of the melancholy House of Usher. I know not how it was—but, with the first glimpse of

1. His heart is a ready lute / As soon as it is touched it resounds; *Le Refus* (lines 41–42), by Pierre-Jean de Béranger (1780–1857), French poet.

the building, a sense of insufferable gloom pervaded my spirit. I say insufferable; for the feeling was unrelieved by any of that half-pleasurable, because poetic, sentiment, with which the mind usually receives even the sternest natural images of the desolate or terrible. I looked upon the scene before me—upon the mere house, and the simple landscape features of the domain, upon the bleak walls, upon the vacant eye-like windows, upon a few rank sedges, and upon a few white trunks of decayed trees—with an utter depression of soul which I can compare to no earthly sensation more properly than to the after-dream of the reveller upon opium: the bitter lapse into everyday life, the hideous dropping off of the veil. There was an iciness, a sinking, a sickening of the heart, an unredeemed dreariness of thought which no goading of the imagination could torture into aught of the sublime. What was it—I paused to think—what was it that so unnerved me in the contemplation of the House of Usher? It was a mystery all insoluble; nor could I grapple with the shadowy fancies that crowded upon me as I pondered. I was forced to fall back upon the unsatisfactory conclusion, that while, beyond doubt, there *are* combinations of very simple natural objects which have the power of thus affecting us, still the analysis of this power lies among considerations beyond our depth. It was possible, I reflected, that a mere different arrangement of the particulars of the scene, of the details of the picture, would be sufficient to modify, or perhaps to annihilate its capacity for sorrowful impression; and, acting upon this idea, I reined my horse to the precipitous brink of a black and lurid tarn that lay in unruffled lustre by the dwelling, and gazed down—but with a shudder even more thrilling than before—upon the remodelled and inverted images of the gray sedge, and the ghastly tree-stems, and the vacant and eye-like windows.

Nevertheless, in this mansion of gloom I now proposed to myself a sojourn of some weeks. Its proprietor, Roderick Usher, had been one of my boon companions in boyhood; but many years had elapsed since our last meeting. A letter, however, had lately reached me in a distant part of the country—a letter from him—which, in its wildly importunate nature, had admitted of no other than a personal reply. The MS. gave evidence of nervous agitation. The writer spoke of acute bodily illness, of a mental disorder, which oppressed him, and of an earnest desire to see me, as his best, and indeed his only personal friend, with a view of attempting, by the cheerfulness of my society, some alleviation of his malady. It was the manner in which all this, and much more, was said—it was the apparent *heart* that went with his request—which allowed me no room for hesitation; and I accordingly obeyed forthwith what I still considered a very singular summons.

Although, as boys, we had been even intimate associates, yet I really knew little of my friend. His reserve had been always excessive and habitual. I was aware, however, that his very ancient family had been noted, time out of mind, for a peculiar sensibility of temperament, displaying itself, through long ages, in many works of exalted art, and manifested, of late, in repeated deeds of munificent yet unobtrusive charity, as well as in a passionate devotion to the intricacies, perhaps even more than to the orthodox and easily recognizable beauties, of musical science. I had learned, too, the very remarkable fact, that the stem of the Usher race, all time-honored as it was, had put forth, at no period, any enduring branch; in other words, that the entire family lay in the direct line of descent, and had always, with very trifling and very temporary variation, so lain. It was this deficiency, I considered, while running over in thought the perfect keeping of the character of the premises with the accredited character of the people, and while speculating upon the possible influence which the one, in the long lapse of centuries, might have exercised upon the other—it was this deficiency, perhaps, of collateral issue, and the consequent undeviating transmission, from sire to son, of the patrimony with the name, which had, at length, so identified the two as to merge the original title of the estate in the quaint and equivocal appellation of the "House of Usher"—an appellation which seemed to include, in the minds of the peasantry who used it, both the family and the family mansion.

I have said that the sole effect of my somewhat childish experiment, that of looking down within the tarn, had been to deepen the first singular impression. There can be no doubt that the consciousness of the rapid increase of my superstition—for why should I not so term it?—served mainly to accelerate the increase itself. Such, I have long known, is the paradoxical law of all sentiments having terror as a basis. And it might have been for this reason only, that, when I again uplifted my eyes to the house itself, from its image in the pool, there grew in my mind a strange fancy—a fancy so ridiculous, indeed, that I but mention it to show the vivid force of the sensations which oppressed me. I had so worked upon my imagination as really to believe that about the whole mansion and domain there hung an atmosphere peculiar to themselves and their immediate vicinity: an atmosphere which had no affinity with the air of heaven, but which had reeked up from the decayed trees, and the gray wall, and the silent tarn: a pestilent and mystic vapor, dull, sluggish, faintly discernible, and leaden-hued.

Shaking off from my spirit what *must* have been a dream, I scanned more narrowly the real aspect of the building. Its principal feature seemed to be that of an excessive antiquity. The discoloration of ages had been great. Minute fungi overspread the whole exterior, hanging in a fine tangled web-work from the eaves. Yet all this was apart from any extraordinary dilapidation. No portion of the masonry had fallen; and there appeared to be a wild inconsistency between its still perfect adaptation of parts, and the crumbling condition of the individual stones. In this there was much that reminded me of the specious totality of old woodwork which has rotted for long years in some neglected vault, with no disturbance from the breath of the external air. Beyond this indication of extensive decay, however, the fabric gave little token of instability. Perhaps the eye of a scrutinizing observer might have discovered a barely perceptible fissure, which, extending from the roof of the building in front, made its way down the wall in a zigzag direction, until it became lost in the sullen waters of the tarn.

Noticing these things, I rode over a short causeway to the house. A servant in waiting took my horse, and I entered the Gothic archway of the hall. A valet, of stealthy step, thence conducted me, in silence, through many dark and intricate passages in my progress to the *studio* of his master. Much that I encountered on the way contributed, I know not how, to heighten the vague sentiments of which I have already spoken. While the objects around me—while the carvings of the ceilings, the sombre tapestries of the walls, the ebon blackness of the floors, and the phantasmagoric armorial trophies which rattled as I strode, were but matters to which, or to such as which, I had been accustomed from my infancy—while I hesitated not to acknowledge how familiar was all this—I still wondered to find how unfamiliar were the fancies which ordinary images were stirring up. On one of the staircases, I met the physician of the family. His countenance, I thought, wore a mingled expression of low cunning and perplexity. He accosted me with trepidation and passed on. The valet now threw open a door and ushered me into the presence of his master.

The room in which I found myself was very large and lofty. The windows were long, narrow, and pointed, and at so vast a distance from the black oaken floor as to be altogether inaccessible from within. Feeble gleams of encrimsoned light made their way through the trellised panes, and served to render sufficiently distinct the more prominent objects around; the eye, however, struggled in vain to reach the remoter angles of the chamber, or the recesses of the vaulted and fretted ceiling. Dark draperies hung upon the walls. The general furniture was profuse, comfortless, antique, and tattered. Many books and musical instruments lay scattered about, but failed to give any vitality to the scene. I felt that I breathed an atmosphere of sorrow. An air of stern, deep, and irredeemable gloom hung over and pervaded all.

Upon my entrance, Usher arose from a sofa upon which he had been lying at full length, and greeted me with a vivacious warmth which had much in it, I at first thought of an overdone cordiality—of the constrained effort of the *ennuyé*[2] man of the world. A glance, however, at his countenance convinced me of his perfect sincerity. We sat down; and for some moments, while he spoke not, I gazed upon him with a feeling half of pity, half of awe. Surely, man had never before so terribly altered, in so brief a period, as had Roderick Usher! It was with difficulty that I could bring myself to admit the identity of the wan being before me with the companion of my early boyhood. Yet the character of his face had been at all times remarkable. A cadaverousness of complexion; an eye large, liquid, and luminous beyond comparison, lips somewhat thin and very pallid, but of a surpassingly beautiful curve; a nose of a delicate Hebrew model, but with a breadth of nostril unusual in similar formations; a finely moulded chin, speaking, in its want of prominence, of a want of moral energy; hair of a more than web-like softness and tenuity; these features, with an inordinate expansion above the regions of the temple, made up altogether a countenance not easily to be forgotten. And now in the mere exaggeration of the prevailing character of these features, and of the expression they were wont to convey, lay so much of change that I doubted to whom I spoke. The now ghastly pallor of the skin, and the now miraculous lustre of the eye, above all things startled and even awed me. The silken hair, too, had been suffered to grow all unheeded, and as, in its wild gossamer texture, it floated rather than fell about

2. Bored, jaded (French).

the face, I could not, even with effort, connect its Arabesque[3] expression with any idea of simple humanity.

In the manner of my friend I was at once struck with an incoherence—an inconsistency; and I soon found this to arise from a series of feeble and futile struggles to overcome an habitual trepidancy, an excessive nervous agitation. For something of this nature I had indeed been prepared, no less by his letter, than by reminiscences of certain boyish traits, and by conclusions deduced from his peculiar physical conformation and temperament. His action was alternately vivacious and sullen. His voice varied rapidly from a tremulous indecision (when the animal spirits seemed utterly in abeyance) to that species of energetic concision—that abrupt, weighty, unhurried, and hollow-sounding enunciation—that leaden, self-balanced and perfectly modulated gutteral utterance, which may be observed in the lost drunkard, or the irreclaimable eater of opium, during the periods of his most intense excitement.

It was thus that he spoke of the object of my visit, of his earnest desire to see me, and of the solace he expected me to afford him. He entered, at some length, into what he conceived to be the nature of his malady. It was, he said, a constitutional and a family evil, and one for which he despaired to find a remedy—a mere nervous affection, he immediately added, which would undoubtedly soon pass off. It displayed itself in a host of unnatural sensations. Some of these, as he detailed them, interested and bewildered me; although, perhaps, the terms, and the general manner of the narration had their weight. He suffered much from a morbid acuteness of the senses; the most insipid food was alone endurable; he could wear only garments of certain texture; the odors of all flowers were oppressive; his eyes were tortured by even a faint light; and there were but peculiar sounds, and these from stringed instruments, which did not inspire him with horror.

To an anomalous species of terror I found him a bounden slave. "I shall perish," said he, "I *must* perish in this deplorable folly. Thus, thus, and not otherwise, shall I be lost. I dread the events of the future, not in themselves, but in their results. I shudder at the thought of any, even the most trivial, incident, which may operate upon this intolerable agitation of soul. I have, indeed, no abhorrence of danger, except in its absolute effect—in terror. In this unnerved—in this pitiable condition, I feel that I must inevitably abandon life and reason together, in some struggle with the grim phantasm, FEAR."

I learned, moreover, at intervals, and through broken and equivocal hints, another singular feature of his mental condition. He was enchained by certain superstitious impressions in regard to the dwelling which he tenanted, and from whence, for many years, he had never ventured forth—in regard to an influence whose suppositious force was conveyed in terms too shadowy here to be restated—an influence which some peculiarities in the mere form and substance of his family mansion, had, by dint of long sufferance, he said, obtained over his spirit—an effect which the *physique* of the gray walls and turrets, and of the dim tarn into which they all looked down, had, at length, brought about upon the *morale* of his existence.

3. Curving, in the manner of Arab decorations.

He admitted, however, although with hesitation, that much of the peculiar gloom which thus afflicted him could be traced to a more natural and far more palpable origin—to the severe and long-continued illness, indeed to the evidently approaching dissolution, of a tenderly beloved sister—his sole companion for long years, his last and only relative on earth. "Her decease," he said, with a bitterness which I can never forget, "would leave him (him the hopeless and the frail) the last of the ancient race of the Ushers." While he spoke, the lady Madeline (for so was she called) passed slowly through a remote portion of the apartment, and, without having noticed my presence, disappeared. I regarded her with an utter astonishment not unmingled with dread, and yet I found it impossible to account for such feelings. A sensation of stupor oppressed me, as my eyes followed her retreating steps. When a door, at length, closed upon her, my glance sought instinctively and eagerly the countenance of the brother; but he had buried his face in his hands, and I could only perceive that a far more than ordinary wanness had overspread the emaciated fingers through which trickled many passionate tears.

The disease of the lady Madeline had long baffled the skill of her physicians. A settled apathy, a gradual wasting away of the person, and frequent although transient affections of a partially cataleptical[4] character, were the unusual diagnosis. Hitherto she had steadily borne up against the pressure of her malady, and had not betaken herself finally to bed; but, on the closing in of the evening of my arrival at the house, she succumbed (as her brother told me at night with inexpressible agitation) to the prostrating power of the destroyer; and I learned that the glimpse I had obtained of her person would thus probably be the last I should obtain—that the lady, at least while living, would be seen by me no more.

For several days ensuing, her name was unmentioned by either Usher or myself: and, during this period, I was busied in earnest endeavors to alleviate the melancholy of my friend. We painted and read together; or I listened, as if in a dream, to the wild improvisations of his speaking guitar. And thus, as a closer and still closer intimacy admitted me more unreservedly into the recesses of his spirit, the more bitterly did I perceive the futility of all attempt at cheering a mind from which darkness, as if an inherent positive quality, poured forth upon all objects of the moral and physical universe, in one unceasing radiation of gloom.

I shall ever bear about me a memory of the many solemn hours I thus spent alone with the master of the House of Usher. Yet I should fail in any attempt to convey an idea of the exact character of the studies, or of the occupations, in which he involved me, or led me the way. An excited and highly distempered ideality threw a sulphureous lustre over all. His long improvised dirges will ring for ever in my ears. Among other things, I hold painfully in mind a certain singular perversion and amplification of the wild air of the last waltz of Von Weber.[5] From the paintings over which his elaborate fancy

4. Psychological paralysis. 5. Carl Maria von Weber (1786–1826), German composer. Karl Gottlieb Reissiger succeeded Weber as conductor of the German Opera at Dresden. A nondramatic work by Reissiger contains a piece misleadingly known as *Weber's Last Waltz* or, literally, *Weber's Last Thought*

brooded, and which grew, touch by touch, into vaguenesses at which I shuddered the more thrillingly, because I shuddered knowing not why;—from these paintings (vivid as their images now are before me) I would in vain endeavor to educe more than a small portion which should lie within the compass of merely written words. By the utter simplicity, by the nakedness of his designs, he arrested and over-awed attention. If ever mortal painted an idea, that mortal was Roderick Usher. For me at least—in the circumstances then surrounding me, there arose out of the pure abstractions which the hypochondriac contrived to throw upon his canvas, an intensity of intolerable awe, no shadow of which felt I ever yet in the contemplation of the certainly glowing yet too concrete reveries of Fuseli.[6]

One of the phantasmagoric conceptions of my friend, partaking not so rigidly of the spirit of abstraction, may be shadowed forth, although feebly, in words. A small picture presented the interior of an immensely long and rectangular vault or tunnel, with low walls, smooth, white, and without interruption or device. Certain accessory points of the design served well to convey the idea that this excavation lay at an exceeding depth below the surface of the earth. No outlet was observed in any portion of its vast extent, and no torch, or other artificial source of light was discernible; yet a flood of intense rays rolled throughout, and bathed the whole in a ghastly and inappropriate splendor.

I have just spoken of that morbid condition of the auditory nerve which rendered all music intolerable to the sufferer, with the exception of certain effects of stringed instruments. It was, perhaps, the narrow limits to which he thus confined himself upon the guitar, which gave birth, in great measure, to the fantastic character of his performances. But the fervid *facility* of his impromptus could not be so accounted for. They must have been, and were, in the notes, as well as in the words of his wild fantasias (for he not unfrequently accompanied himself with rhymed verbal improvisations), the result of that intense mental collectedness and concentration to which I have previously alluded as observable only in particular moments of the highest artificial excitement. The words of one of these rhapsodies I have easily remembered. I was, perhaps, the more forcibly impressed with it, as he gave it, because, in the under or mystic current of its meaning, I fancied that I perceived, and for the first time, a full consciousness on the part of Usher, of the tottering of his lofty reason upon her throne. The verses, which were entitled "The Haunted Palace," ran very nearly, if not accurately, thus:

In the greenest of our valleys,
By good angels tenanted,
Once a fair and stately palace—
Radiant palace—reared its head.
In the monarch Thought's dominion,
It stood there!
Never seraph spread a pinion
Over fabric half so fair.

6. Henry Fuseli (Johann Heinrich Füssli; 1741–1825), Swiss painter.

Banners yellow, glorious, golden,
    On its roof did float and flow,
(This—all this—was in the olden
    Time long ago)
And every gentle air that dallied,
    In that sweet day,
Along the ramparts plumed and pallid,
    A winged odor went away.

Wanderers in that happy valley
    Through two luminous windows, saw
Spirits moving musically
    To a lute's well-tunèd law,
Round about a throne where, sitting
    Porphyrogene![7]
In state his glory well befitting,
    The ruler of the realm was seen.

And all with pearl and ruby glowing
    Was the fair palace door,
Through which came flowing, flowing, flowing,
    And sparkling evermore,
A troop of Echoes, whose sweet duty
    Was but to sing,
In voices of surpassing beauty,
    The wit and wisdom of their king.

But evil things, in robes of sorrow,
    Assailed the monarch's high estate;
(Ah, let us mourn!—for never morrow
    Shall dawn upon him, desolate!)
And, round about his home, the glory
    That blushed and bloomed
Is but a dim-remembered story
    Of the old time entombed.

And travellers now, within that valley,
    Through the red-litten[8] windows see
Vast forms that move fantastically
    To a discordant melody;
While, like a ghastly rapid river,
    Through the pale door
A hideous throng rush out forever,
    And laugh—but smile no more.

I well remember that suggestions arising from this ballad led us into a train of thought wherein there became manifest an opinion of Usher's which I men-

7. One born to the purple—i.e., of royal blood. 8. Lit with red.

tion not so much on account of its novelty, (for other men have thought thus), as on account of the pertinacity with which he maintained it. This opinion, in its general form, was that of the sentience of all vegetable things. But, in his disordered fancy, the idea had assumed a more daring character, and trespassed, under certain conditions, upon the kingdom of inorganization. I lack words to express the full extent, or the earnest *abandon* of his persuasion. The belief, however, was connected (as I have previously hinted) with the gray stones of the home of his forefathers. The condition of the sentience had been here, he imagined, fulfilled in the method of collocation of these stones—in the order of their arrangement, as well as in that of the many *fungi* which overspread them, and of the decayed trees which stood around—above all, in the long undisturbed endurance of this arrangement, and in its reduplication in the still waters of the tarn. Its evidence—the evidence of the sentience—was to be seen, he said, (and I here started as he spoke), in the gradual yet certain condensation of an atmosphere of their own about the waters and the walls. The result was discoverable, he added, in that silent, yet importunate and terrible influence which for centuries had moulded the destinies of his family, and which made *him* what I now saw him—what he was. Such opinions need no comment, and I will make none.

Our books—the books which, for years, had formed no small portion of the mental existence of the invalid—were, as might be supposed, in strict keeping with this character of phantasm. We pored together over such works as the *Ververt et Chartreuse* of Gresset; the *Belphegor* of Machiavelli; the *Heaven and Hell* of Swedenborg; the *Subterranean Voyage of Nicholas Klimm* by Holberg; the *Chiromancy* of Robert Flud, of Jean d'Indaginé, and of De la Chambre; the *Journey into the Blue Distance* of Tieck; and the *City of the Sun* of Campanella. One favorite volume was a small octavo edition of the *Directorium Inquisitorium,* by the Dominican Eymeric de Gironne; and there were passages in Pomponius Mela, about the old African Satyrs and Aegipans, over which Usher would sit dreaming for hours.[9] His chief delight, however, was found in the perusal of an exceedingly rare and curious book in quarto Gothic—the manual of a forgotten church—the *Vigilae Mortuorum Secundum Chorum Ecclesiæ Maguntinæn.*[1]

I could not help thinking of the wild ritual of this work, and of its probable influence upon the hypochondriac, when, one evening, having informed me abruptly that the lady Madeline was no more, he stated his intention of pre-

9. Exotic and romantic literary works. *Ververt* and *Chartreuse* are anticlerical satires by French poet and dramatist Jean Baptiste Louis Gresset (1709–1777). The novel of Niccolò Machiavelli (1469–1527) concerns a demon come to earth to prove that the damnation of man is woman. Emmanuel Swedenborg (1688–1772), a Swedish scientist and theologian, offers in *Heaven and Hell* (1758) an argument concerning the continuity of spiritual identity. The book of Ludwig Holberg (1684–1754), a German dramatist, concerns a round-trip voyage to the world of the dead. Chiromancy, the art of palm reading, is the concern of Robert Flud (1574–1637), British alchemist, of Jean D'Indaginé (*Chiromantia,* 1522), and of Marin Cureau de la Chambre (*Principes de la Chiromancie,* 1653). The next two titles by the German novelist Johann Ludwig Tieck (1773–1853) and the Italian scientist and philosopher Tommasso Campanella (1568–1639), respectively, are concerned with voyages to other worlds. The Spanish historian Nicolas Eymeric de Girone (1320–1399) in *Inquisitorium Directorium* gives an outline of tortures and appropriate procedures. Satyrs were goatmen of Greek mythology. Pomponius Mela, a Roman of the first century C.E., gives an account of "Aegipans," supposedly goatmen of Africa, in his work *Geography.* 1. Vigil for the Dead, Second Chorus, Church of Maguntinae (Latin).

serving her corpse for a fortnight, (previously to its final interment), in one of the numerous vaults within the main walls of the building. The wordly reason, however, assigned for this singular proceeding, was one which I did not feel at liberty to dispute. The brother had been led to his resolution (so he told me) by considerations of the unusual character of the malady of the deceased, of certain obtrusive and eager inquiries on the part of her medical men,[2] and of the remote and exposed situation of the burial-ground of the family, I will not deny that when I called to mind the sinister countenance of the person whom I met upon the staircase, on the day of my arrival at the house, I had no desire to oppose what I regarded as at best but a harmless, and by no means an unnatural, precaution.

At the request of Usher, I personally aided him in the arrangements for the temporary entombment. The body having been encoffined, we two alone bore it to its rest. The vault in which we placed it (and which had been so long unopened that our torches, half smothered in its oppressive atmosphere, gave us little opportunity for investigation) was small, damp, and entirely without means of admission for light; lying, at great depth, immediately beneath that portion of the building in which was my own sleeping apartment. It had been used, apparently, in remote feudal times, for the worst purposes of a donjon-keep,[3] and, in later days, as a place of deposit for powder, or other highly combustible substance, as a portion of its floor, and the whole interior of a long archway through which we reached it, were carefully sheathed with copper. The door, of massive iron, had been, also, similarly protected. Its immense weight caused an unusually sharp grating sound, as it moved upon its hinges.

Having deposited our mournful burden upon tressels within this region of horror, we partially turned aside the yet unscrewed lid of the coffin, and looked upon the face of the tenant. The exact similitude between the brother and sister now first arrested my attention; and Usher, divining, perhaps, my thoughts, murmured out some few words from which I learned that the deceased and himself had been twins, and that sympathies of a scarcely intelligible nature had always existed between them. Our glances, however, rested not long upon the dead—for we could not regard her unawed. The disease which had thus entombed the lady in the maturity of youth, had left, as usual in all maladies of a strictly cataleptical character, the mockery of a faint blush upon the bosom and the face, and that suspiciously lingering smile upon the lip which is so terrible in death. We replaced and screwed down the lid, and, having secured the door of iron, made our way, with toil, into the scarcely less gloomy apartments of the upper portion of the house.

And now, some days of bitter grief having elapsed, an observable change came over the features of the mental disorder of my friend. His ordinary manner had vanished. His ordinary occupations were neglected or forgotten. He roamed from chamber to chamber with hurried, unequal, and objectless step. The pallor of his countenance had assumed, if possible, a more ghastly hue—but the luminousness of his eye had utterly gone out. The once occasional

2. Usher appears to be afraid the doctors will dig up her corpse to satisfy their professional curiosity about her ailment. 3. Prison.

huskiness of his tone was heard no more; and a tremulous quaver, as if of extreme terror, habitually characterized his utterance. There were times, indeed, when I thought his unceasingly agitated mind was laboring with an oppressive secret, to divulge which he struggled for the necessary courage. At times, again, I was obliged to resolve all into the mere inexplicable vagaries of madness, as I beheld him gazing upon vacancy for long hours, in an attitude of the profoundest attention, as if listening to some imaginary sound. It was no wonder that his condition terrified—that it infected me. I felt creeping upon me, by slow yet certain degrees, the wild influences of his own fantastic yet impressive superstitions.

It was, especially, upon retiring to bed late in the night of the seventh or eighth day after the placing of the lady Madeline within the donjon, that I experienced the full power of such feelings. Sleep came not near my couch—while the hours waned and waned away. I struggled to reason off the nervousness which had dominion over me. I endeavored to believe that much, if not all of what I felt, was due to the bewildering influence of the gloomy furniture of the room—of the dark and tattered draperies, which, tortured into motion by the breath of a rising tempest, swayed fitfully to and fro upon the walls, and rustled uneasily about the decorations of the bed. But my efforts were fruitless. An irrepressible tremor gradually pervaded my frame; and, at length, there sat upon my very heart an incubus of utterly causeless alarm. Shaking this off with a gasp and a struggle, I uplifted myself upon the pillows, and, peering earnestly within the intense darkness of the chamber, harkened—I know not why, except that an instinctive spirit prompted me—to certain low and indefinite sounds which came, through the pauses of the storm, at long intervals I knew not whence. Overpowered by an intense sentiment of horror, unaccountable yet unendurable, I threw on my clothes with haste (for I felt that I should sleep no more during the night), and endeavored to arouse myself from the pitiable condition into which I had fallen, by pacing rapidly to and fro through the apartment.

I had taken but few turns in this manner, when a light step on an adjoining staircase arrested my attention. I presently recognized it as that of Usher. In an instant afterward he rapped, with a gentle touch, at my door, and entered, bearing a lamp. His countenance was, as usually, cadaverously wan—but there was a species of mad hilarity in his eyes—an evidently restrained *hysteria* in his whole demeanor. His air appalled me—but anything was preferable to the solitude which I had so long endured, and I even welcomed his presence as a relief.

"And you have not seen it?" he said abruptly, after having stared about him for some moments in silence—"you have not then seen it?—but, stay! you shall." Thus speaking, and having carefully shaded his lamp, he hurried to one of the casements, and threw it freely open to the storm.

The impetuous fury of the entering gust nearly lifted us from our feet. It was, indeed, a tempestuous yet sternly beautiful night, and one wildly singular in its terror and its beauty. A whirlwind had apparently collected its force in our vicinity; for there were frequent and violent alterations in the direction of the wind; and the exceeding density of the clouds (which hung so low as to press upon the turrets of the house) did not prevent our perceiving the life-like velocity with which they flew careering from all points against each other, without passing away into the distance. I say that even their exceeding density did not prevent our perceiving this; yet we had no glimpse of the moon or stars, nor was there any flashing forth of the lightning. But the under surfaces of the huge masses of agitated vapor, as well as all terrestrial objects immediately around us, were glowing in the unnatural light of a faintly luminous and distinctly visible gaseous exhalation which hung about and enshrouded the mansion.

"You must not—you shall not behold this!" said I, shudderingly, to Usher, as I led him, with a gentle violence, from the window to a seat. "These appearances, which bewilder you, are merely electrical phenomena not uncommon—or it may be that they have their ghastly origin in the rank miasma of the tarn. Let us close this casement; the air is chilling and dangerous to your frame. Here is one of your favorite romances. I will read, and you shall listen; and so we will pass away this terrible night together."

The antique volume which I had taken up was the *Mad Trist* of Sir Launcelot Canning; but I had called it a favorite of Usher's more in sad jest than in earnest; for, in truth, there is little in its uncouth and unimaginative prolixity which could have had interest for the lofty and spiritual ideality of my friend. It was, however, the only book immediately at hand; and I indulged a vague hope that the excitement which now agitated the hypochondriac might find relief (for the history of mental disorder is full of similar anomalies) even in the extremeness of the folly which I should read. Could I have judged, indeed, by the wild, overstrained air of vivacity with which he hearkened, or apparently hearkened, to the words of the tale, I might have well congratulated myself upon the success of my design.

I had arrived at that well-known portion of the story where Ethelred, the hero of the *Trist,* having sought in vain for peaceable admission into the dwelling of the hermit, proceeds to make good an entrance by force. Here, it will be remembered, the words of the narrative run thus:

> And Ethelred, who was by nature of a doughty heart, and who was now mighty withal, on account of the powerfulness of the wine which he had drunken, waited no longer to hold parley with the hermit, who, in sooth, was of an obstinate and maliceful turn, but, feeling the rain upon his shoulders, and fearing the rising of the tempest, uplifted his mace outright, and, with blows, made quickly room in the plankings of the door for his gauntleted hand; and now pulling therewith sturdily, he so cracked, and ripped, and tore all asunder, that the noise of the dry and hollow-sounding wood alarumed and reverberated throughout the forest.

At the termination of this sentence I started, and, for a moment, paused; for it appeared to me (although I at once concluded that my excited fancy had deceived me)—it appeared to me that, from some very remote portion of the mansion, there came, indistinctly, to my ears, what might have been, in its exact similarity of character, the echo (but a stifled and dull one certainly) of the very cracking and ripping sound which Sir Launcelot had so particularly described. It was, beyond doubt, the coincidence alone which had arrested my attention;

for, amid the rattling of the sashes of the casements, and the ordinary commingled noises of the still increasing storm, the sound, in itself, had nothing, surely, which should have interested or disturbed me. I continued the story:

> But the good champion Ethelred, now entering within the door, was sore enraged and amazed to perceive no signal of the maliceful hermit; but, in the stead thereof, a dragon of scaly and prodigious demeanor, and of a fiery tongue, which sate in guard before a palace of gold, with a floor of silver; and upon the wall there hung a shield of shining brass with this legend enwritten—
>
> *Who entereth herein, a conqueror hath bin,*
> *Who slayeth the dragon, the shield he shall win.*
>
> And Ethelred uplifted his mace, and struck upon the head of the dragon, which fell before him, and gave up his pesty breath, with a shriek so horrid and harsh, and withal so piercing, that Ethelred had fain to close his ears with his hands against the dreadful noise of it, the like whereof was never before heard.

Here again I paused abruptly, and now with a feeling of wild amazement—for there could be no doubt whatever that, in this instance, I did actually hear (although from what direction it proceeded I found it impossible to say) a low and apparently distant, but harsh, protracted, and most unusual screaming or grating sound—the exact counterpart of what my fancy had already conjured up as the sound of the dragon's unnatural shriek as described by the romancer.

Oppressed, as I certainly was, upon the occurrence of this second and most extraordinary coincidence, by a thousand conflicting sensations, in which wonder and extreme terror were predominant, I still retained sufficient presence of mind to avoid exciting, by any observation, the sensitive nervousness of my companion. I was by no means certain that he had noticed the sounds in question; although, assuredly, a strange alteration had, during the last few minutes, taken place in his demeanor. From a position fronting my own, he had gradually brought round his chair, so as to sit with his face to the door of the chamber; and thus I could but partially perceive his features, although I saw that his lips trembled as if he were murmuring inaudibly. His head had dropped upon his breast—yet I knew that he was not asleep, from the wide and rigid opening of the eye, as I caught a glance of it in profile. The motion of his body, too, was at variance with this idea—for he rocked from side to side with a gentle yet constant and uniform sway. Having rapidly taken notice of all this, I resumed the narrative of Sir Launcelot, which thus proceeded:

> And now, the champion, having escaped from the terrible fury of the dragon, bethinking himself of the brazen shield, and of the breaking up of the enchantment which was upon it, removed the carcass from out of the way before him, and approached valorously over the silver pavement of the castle to where the shield was upon the wall; which in sooth tarried not for his full coming, but fell down at his feet upon the silver floor, with a mighty great and terrible ringing sound.

No sooner had these syllables passed my lips, than—as if a shield of brass had indeed, at the moment, fallen heavily upon a floor of silver—I became aware of a distinct, hollow, metallic and clangorous yet apparently muffled reverberation. Completely unnerved, I leaped to my feet; but the measured rocking movement of Usher was undisturbed. I rushed to the chair in which he sat. His eyes were bent fixedly before him, and throughout his whole countenance there reigned a more than stony rigidity. But as I laid my hand upon his shoulder, there came a strong shudder over his whole person; a sickly smile quivered about his lips; and I saw that he spoke in a low, hurried, and gibbering murmur, as if unconscious of my presence. Bending closely over him, I at length drank in the hideous import of his words.

"Not hear it?—yes, I hear it, and *have* heard it. Long—long—long—many minutes, many hours, many days, have I heard it—yet I dared not—oh, pity me; miserable wretch that I am!—I dared not—I *dared* not speak! *We have put her living in the tomb!* Said I not that my senses were acute?—I *now* tell you that I heard her first feeble movements in the hollow coffin. I heard them—many, many days ago—yet I dared not—*I dared not speak!* And now—to-night—Ethelred—ha! ha!—the breaking of the hermit's door, and the death-cry of the dragon, and the clangor of the shield!—say, rather, the rending of her coffin, and the grating of the iron hinges of her prison, and her struggles within the coppered archway of the vault! Oh whither shall I fly? Will she not be here anon? Is she not hurrying to upbraid me for my haste? Have I not heard her footstep on the stair? Do I not distinguish that heavy and horrible beating of her heart? MADMAN!" here he sprang violently to his feet, and shrieked out his syllables, as if in the effort he were giving up his soul—*"Madman! I tell you that she now stands without the door!"*

As if in the superhuman energy of his utterance there had been found the potency of a spell, the huge antique panels to which the speaker pointed, threw slowly back, upon the instant, their ponderous and ebony jaws. It was the work of the rushing gust—but then without those doors there DID stand the lofty and enshrouded figure of the lady Madeline of Usher. There was blood upon her white robes, and the evidence of some bitter struggle upon every portion of her emaciated frame. For a moment she remained trembling and reeling to and fro upon the threshold—then, with a low moaning cry, fell heavily inward upon the person of her brother, and in her violent and now final death-agonies, bore him to the floor a corpse, and a victim to the terrors he had anticipated.

From that chamber, and from that mansion, I fled aghast. The storm was still abroad in all its wrath as I found myself crossing the old causeway. Suddenly there shot along the path a wild light, and I turned to see whence a gleam so unusual could have issued; for the vast house and its shadows were alone behind me. The radiance was that of the full, setting, and blood-red moon, which now shone vividly through that once barely-discernible fissure of which I have before spoken as extending from the roof of the building, in a zigzag direction, to the base. While I gazed, this fissure rapidly widened—there came a fierce breath of the whirlwind—the entire orb of the satellite burst at once upon my sight—my brain reeled as I saw the mighty walls rushing asunder—there was a long tumultuous shouting sound like the voice of a thousand waters—and the deep and dank tarn at my feet closed sullenly and silently over the fragments of the HOUSE OF USHER.

# The Purloined Letter

*Nil sapientae odiosius acumine nimio.*
—Seneca[1]

At Paris, just after dark one gusty evening in the autumn of 18—, I was enjoying the twofold luxury of meditation and a meerschaum, in company with my friend C. Auguste Dupin, in his little back library, or book-closet, *au troisième, No. 33, Rue Dunôt, Faubourg St. Germain.*[2] For one hour at least we had maintained a profound silence; while each, to any casual observer, might have seemed intently and exclusively occupied with the curling eddies of smoke that oppressed the atmosphere of the chamber. For myself, however, I was mentally discussing certain topics which had formed matter for conversation between us at an earlier period of the evening; I mean the affair of the Rue Morgue, and the mystery attending the murder of Marie Rogêt.[3] I looked upon it, therefore, as something of coincidence, when the door of our apartment was thrown open and admitted our old acquaintance, Monsieur G——, the Prefect of the Parisian police.

We gave him a hearty welcome; for there was nearly half as much of the entertaining as of the contemptible about the man, and we had not seen him for several years. We had been sitting in the dark, and Dupin now arose for the purpose of lighting a lamp, but sat down again, without doing so, upon G.'s saying that he had called to consult us, or rather to ask the opinion of my friend, about some official business which had occasioned a great deal of trouble.

"If it is any point requiring reflection," observed Dupin, as he forebore to enkindle the wick, "we shall examine it to better purpose in the dark."

"That is another of your odd notions," said the Prefect, who had a fashion of calling every thing "odd" that was beyond his comprehension, and thus lived amid an absolute legion of "oddities."

"Very true," said Dupin, as he supplied his visitor with a pipe, and rolled towards him a very comfortable chair.

"And what is the difficulty now?" I asked. "Nothing more in the assassination way, I hope?"

"Oh no; nothing of that nature. The fact is, the business is *very* simple indeed, and I make no doubt that we can manage it sufficiently well ourselves; but then I thought Dupin would like to hear the details of it, because it is so excessively *odd.*"

"Simple and odd," said Dupin.

"Why, yes; and not exactly that, either. The fact is, we have all been a good deal puzzled because the affair *is* so simple, and yet baffles us altogether."

1. Nothing is more distasteful to good sense than too much cunning (Latin); Lucius Annaeus Seneca (4 B.C.E.–C.E. 65), Roman poet and philosopher. 2. Fashionable quarter of Paris. The "troisième" is literally the third floor, but is equivalent to the fourth floor in North America. 3. *The Mystery of Marie Rogêt* and *The Murders in the Rue Morgue* are titles of earlier Dupin tales by Poe.

"Perhaps it is the very simplicity of the thing which puts you at fault," said my friend.

"What nonsense you *do* talk!" replied the Prefect, laughing heartily.

"Perhaps the mystery is a little *too* plain," said Dupin.

"Oh, good heavens! who ever heard of such an idea?"

"A little *too* self-evident."

"Ha! ha! ha!—ha! ha! ha!—ho! ho! ho!" roared out our visitor, profoundly amused, "oh, Dupin, you will be the death of me yet!"

"And what, after all, *is* the matter on hand?" I asked.

"Why, I will tell you," replied the Prefect, as he gave a long, steady, and contemplative puff, and settled himself in his chair. "I will tell you in a few words; but, before I begin, let me caution you that this is an affair demanding the greatest secrecy, and that I should most probably lose the position I now hold, were it known that I confided it to any one."

"Proceed," said I.

"Or not," said Dupin.

"Well, then; I have received personal information, from a very high quarter, that a certain document of the last importance, has been purloined from the royal apartments. The individual who purloined it is known; this beyond a doubt; he was seen to take it. It is known, also, that it still remains in his possession."

"How is this known?" asked Dupin.

"It is clearly inferred," replied the Prefect, "from the nature of the document, and from the non-appearance of certain results which would at once arise from its passing *out* of the robber's possession;—that is to say, from his employing it as he must design in the end to employ it."

"Be a little more explicit," I said.

"Well, I may venture so far as to say that the paper gives its holder a certain power in a certain quarter where such power is immensely valuable." The Prefect was fond of the cant of diplomacy.

"Still I do not quite understand," said Dupin.

"No? Well; the disclosure of the document to a third person, who shall be nameless, would bring in question the honour of a personage of most exalted station; and this fact gives the holder of the document an ascendancy over the illustrious personage whose honour and peace are so jeopardized."

"But this ascendancy," I interposed, "would depend upon the robber's knowledge of the loser's knowledge of the robber. Who would dare—"

"The thief," said G, "is the Minister D——, who dares all things, those unbecoming as well as those becoming a man. The method of the theft was not less ingenious than bold. The document in question—a letter, to be frank—had been received by the personage robbed while alone in the royal *boudoir*. During its perusal she was suddenly interrupted by the entrance of the other exalted personage from whom especially it was her wish to conceal it. After a hurried and vain endeavour to thrust it in a drawer, she was forced to place it, open as it was, upon a table. The address, however, was uppermost, and the contents thus unexposed, the letter escaped notice. At this juncture enters the Minister D——. His lynx eye immediately perceives the paper, recognises the handwriting of the address, observes the confusion of the personage addressed, and fathoms her secret. After some business transactions, hurried through in his ordinary manner, he produces a letter somewhat similar to the one in question, opens it, pretends to read it, and then places it in close juxtaposition to the other. Again he converses, for some fifteen minutes, upon the public affairs. At length, in taking leave, he takes also from the table the letter to which he had no claim. Its rightful owner saw, but, of course, dared not call attention to the act, in the presence of the third personage who stood at her elbow. The minister decamped; leaving his own letter—one of no importance—upon the table."

"Here, then," said Dupin to me, "you have precisely what you demand to make the ascendancy complete—the robber's knowledge of the loser's knowledge of the robber."

"Yes," replied the Prefect; "and the power thus attained has, for some months past, been wielded, for political purposes, to a very dangerous extent. The personage robbed is more thoroughly convinced, every day, of the necessity of reclaiming her letter. But this, of course, cannot be done openly. In fine, driven to despair, she has committed the matter to me."

"Than whom," said Dupin, amid a perfect whirlwind of smoke, "no more sagacious agent could, I suppose, be desired, or even imagined."

"You flatter me," replied the Prefect; "but it is possible that some such opinion may have been entertained."

"It is clear," said I, "as you observe, that the letter is still in possession of the minister; since it is this possession, and not any employment of the letter, which bestows the power. With the employment the power departs."

"True," said G.; "and upon this conviction I proceeded. My first care was to make thorough search of the minister's hotel;[4] and here my chief embarrassment lay in the necessity of searching without his knowledge. Beyond all things, I have been warned of the danger which would result from giving him reason to suspect our design."

"But," said I, "you are quite *au fait*[5] in these investigations. The Parisian police have done this thing often before."

"O yes; and for this reason I did not despair. The habits of the minister gave me, too, a great advantage. He is frequently absent from home all night. His servants are by no means numerous. They sleep at a distance from their master's apartment, and, being chiefly Neapolitans, are readily made drunk. I have keys, as you know, with which I can open any chamber or cabinet in Paris. For three months a night has not passed, during the greater part of which I have not been engaged, personally, in ransacking the D—— Hôtel. My honour is interested, and, to mention a great secret, the reward is enormous. So I did not abandon the search until I had become fully satisfied that the thief is a more astute man than myself. I fancy that I have investigated every nook and corner of the premises in which it is possible that the paper can be concealed."

"But is it not possible," I suggested, "that although the letter may be in

4. I.e., town house. 5. Adept (French).

possession of the minister, as it unquestionably is, he may have concealed it elsewhere than upon his own premises?"

"This is barely possible," said Dupin. "The present peculiar condition of affairs at court, and especially of those intrigues in which D—— is known to be involved, would render the instant availability of the document—its susceptibility of being produced at a moment's notice—a point of nearly equal importance with its possession."

"Its susceptibility of being produced?" said I.

"That is to say, of being *destroyed,*" said Dupin.

"True," I observed; "the paper is clearly then upon the premises. As for its being upon the person of the minister, we may consider that as out of the question."

"Entirely," said the Prefect. "He has been twice waylaid, as if by footpads, and his person rigorously searched under my own inspection."

"You might have spared yourself this trouble," said Dupin. "D——, I presume, is not altogether a fool, and, if not, must have anticipated these waylayings, as a matter of course."

"Not *altogether* a fool," said G., "but then he's a poet, which I take to be only one remove from a fool."

"True," said Dupin, after a long and thoughtful whiff from his meerschaum, "although I have been guilty of certain doggerel myself."

"Suppose you detail," said I, "the particulars of your search."

"Why the fact is, we took our time, and we searched *every where.* I have had long experience in these affairs. I took the entire building, room by room; devoting the nights of a whole week to each. We examined, first, the furniture of each apartment. We opened every possible drawer; and I presume you know that, to a properly trained police agent, such a thing as a *secret* drawer is impossible. Any man is a dolt who permits a 'secret' drawer to escape him in a search of this kind. The thing is *so* plain. There is a certain amount of bulk—of space—to be accounted for in every cabinet. Then we have accurate rules.[6] The fiftieth part of a line could not escape us. After the cabinets we took the chairs. The cushions we probed with the fine long needles you have seen me employ. From the tables we removed the tops."

"Why so?"

"Sometimes the top of a table, or other similarly arranged piece of furniture, is removed by the person wishing to conceal an article; then the leg is excavated, the article deposited within the cavity, and the top replaced. The bottoms and tops of bedposts are employed in the same way."

"But could not the cavity be detected by sounding?" I asked.

"By no means, if, when the article is deposited, a sufficient wadding of cotton be placed around it. Besides, in our case, we were obliged to proceed without noise."

"But you could not have removed—you could not have taken to pieces *all* articles of furniture in which it would have been possible to make a deposit in

6. Rulers.

the manner you mention. A letter may be compressed into a thin spiral roll, not differing much in shape or bulk from a large knitting-needle, and in this form it might be inserted into the rung of a chair, for example. You did not take to pieces all the chairs?"

"Certainly not; but we did better—we examined the rungs of every chair in the hotel, and, indeed, the jointings of every description of furniture, by the aid of a most powerful microscope.[7] Had there been any traces of recent disturbance we should not have failed to detect it instantly. A single grain of gimlet-dust, for example, would have been as obvious as an apple. Any disorder in the glueing—any unusual gaping in the joints—would have sufficed to insure detection."

"I presume you looked to the mirrors, between the boards and the plates, and you probed the beds and the bed-clothes, as well as the curtains and carpets."

"That of course; and when we had absolutely completed every particle of the furniture in this way, then we examined the house itself. We divided its entire surface into compartments, which we numbered, so that none might be missed; then we scrutinized each individual square inch throughout the premises, including the two houses immediately adjoining, with the microscope, as before."

"The two houses adjoining!" I exclaimed; "you must have had a great deal of trouble."

"We had; but the reward offered is prodigious."

"You include the *grounds* about the houses?"

"All the grounds are paved with brick. They gave us comparatively little trouble. We examined the moss between the bricks, and found it undisturbed."

"You looked among D——'s papers, of course, and into the books of the library?"

"Certainly; we opened every package and parcel; we not only opened every book, but we turned over every leaf in each volume, not contenting ourselves with a mere shake, according to the fashion of some of our police officers. We also measured the thickness of every book-*cover,* with the most accurate admeasurement, and applied to each the most jealous scrutiny of the microscope. Had any of the bindings been recently meddled with, it would have been utterly impossible that the fact should have escaped observation. Some five or six volumes, just from the hands of the binder, we carefully probed, longitudinally, with the needles."

"You explored the floors beneath the carpets?"

"Beyond doubt. We removed every carpet, and examined the boards with the microscope."

"And the paper on the walls?"

"Yes."

"You looked into the cellars?"

"We did."

7. Magnifying glass.

"Then," I said, "you have been making a miscalculation, and the letter is *not* upon the premises, as you suppose."

"I fear you are right there," said the Prefect. "And now, Dupin, what would you advise me to do?"

"To make a thorough re-search of the premises."

"That is absolutely needless," replied G——. "I am not more sure that I breathe than I am that the letter is not at the Hôtel."

"I have no better advice to give you," said Dupin. "You have, of course, an accurate description of the letter?"

"Oh yes!"—And here the Prefect, producing a memorandum-book, proceeded to read aloud a minute account of the internal, and especially of the external, appearance of the missing document. Soon after finishing the perusal of this description, he took his departure, more entirely depressed in spirits than I had ever known the good gentleman before.

In about a month afterwards he paid us another visit, and found us occupied very nearly as before. He took a pipe and a chair and entered into some ordinary conversation. At length I said;—

"Well, but G——, what of the purloined letter? I presume you have at last made up your mind that there is no such thing as overreaching the Minister?"

"Confound him, say I—yes; I made the re-examination, however, as Dupin suggested—but it was all labour lost, as I knew it would be."

"How much was the reward offered, did you say?" asked Dupin.

"Why, a very great deal—a *very* liberal reward—I don't like to say how much, precisely; but one thing I *will* say, that I wouldn't mind giving my individual check for fifty thousand francs to any one who could obtain me that letter. The fact is, it is becoming of more and more importance every day; and the reward has been lately doubled. If it were trebled, however, I could do no more than I have done."

"Why, yes," said Dupin, drawlingly, between the whiffs of his meerschaum, "I really—think, G——, you have not exerted yourself—to the utmost in this matter. You might—do a little more, I think, eh?"

"How?—in what way?"

"Why—puff, puff—you might—puff, puff—employ counsel in the matter, eh?—puff, puff, puff. Do you remember the story they tell of Abernethy?"

"No; hang Abernethy!"

"To be sure! hang him and welcome. But, once upon a time, a certain rich miser conceived the design of spunging upon this Abernethy for a medical opinion. Getting up, for this purpose, an ordinary conversation in a private company, he insinuated his case to the physician, as that of an imaginary individual.

" 'We will suppose,' said the miser, 'that his symptoms are such and such; now, doctor, what would *you* have directed him to take?'

" 'Take!' said Abernethy, 'why, take *advice*, to be sure.' "

"But," said the Prefect, a little discomposed, "I am *perfectly* willing to take advice, and to pay for it. I would *really* give fifty thousand francs to any one who would aid me in the matter."

"In that case," replied Dupin, opening a drawer, and producing a check-book, "you may as well fill me up a check for the amount mentioned. When you have signed it, I will hand you the letter."

I was astounded. The Prefect appeared absolutely thunder-stricken. For some minutes he remained speechless and motionless, looking incredulously at my friend with open mouth, and eyes that seemed starting from their sockets; then, apparently recovering himself in some measure, he seized a pen, and after several pauses and vacant stares, finally filled up and signed a check for fifty thousand francs, and handed it across the table to Dupin. The latter examined it carefully and deposited it in his pocket-book; then, unlocking an *escritoire*,[8] took thence a letter and gave it to the Prefect. This functionary grasped it in a perfect agony of joy, opened it with a trembling hand, cast a rapid glance at its contents, and then, scrambling and struggling to the door, rushed at length unceremoniously from the room and from the house, without having uttered a syllable since Dupin had requested him to fill up the check.

When he had gone, my friend entered into some explanations.

"The Parisian police," he said, "are exceedingly able in their way. They are persevering, ingenious, cunning, and thoroughly versed in the knowledge which their duties seem chiefly to demand. Thus, when G—— detailed to us his mode of searching the premises at the Hôtel D——, I felt the entire confidence in his having made a satisfactory investigation—so far as his labours extended."

"So far as his labours extended?" said I.

"Yes," said Dupin. "The measures adopted were not only the best of their kind, but carried out to absolute perfection. Had the letter been deposited within the range of their search, these fellows would, beyond a question, have found it."

I merely laughed—but he seemed quite serious in all that he said.

"The measures, then," he continued, "were good in their kind, and well executed; their defect lay in their being inapplicable to the case, and to the man. A certain set of highly ingenious resources are, with the Prefect, a sort of Procrustean bed,[9] to which he forcibly adapts his designs. But he perpetually errs by being too deep or too shallow, for the matter in hand; and many a schoolboy is a better reasoner than he. I knew one about eight years of age, whose success at guessing in the game of 'even and odd' attracted universal admiration. This game is simple, and is played with marbles. One player holds in his hand a number of these toys, and demands of another whether that number is even or odd. If the guess is right, the guesser wins one; if wrong, he loses one. The boy to whom I allude won all the marbles of the school. Of course he had some principle of guessing; and this lay in mere observation and admeasurement of the astuteness of his opponents. For example, an arrant simpleton is his opponent, and, holding up his closed hand, asks: 'Are they even or odd?' Our schoolboy replies 'Odd,' and loses; but upon the second trial he wins, for he then says to himself, 'The simpleton had them even upon the first trial, and his amount of cunning is just sufficient to make him have them odd

8. A writing table (French). 9. In Greek mythology the giant Procrustes tied travelers to an iron bed and made them fit it by either stretching or amputating their limbs.

upon the second; I will therefore guess odd;'—he guesses odd, and wins. Now, with a simpleton a degree above the first, he would have reasoned thus: 'This fellow finds that in the first instance I guessed odd, and, in the second, he will propose to himself, upon the first impulse, a simple variation from even to odd, as did the first simpleton; but then a second thought will suggest that this is too simple a variation, and finally he will decide upon putting it even as before. I will therefore guess even';—he guesses even, and wins. Now this mode of reasoning in the schoolboy, whom his fellows termed 'lucky,'—what, in its last analysis, is it?"

"It is merely," I said, "an identification of the reasoner's intellect with that of his opponent."

"It is," said Dupin; "and, upon inquiring of the boy by what means he effected the *thorough* identification in which his success consisted, I received answer as follows: 'When I wish to find out how wise, or how stupid, or how good, or how wicked is any one, or what are his thoughts at the moment, I fashion the expression on my face, as accurately as possible, in accordance with the expression of his, and then wait to see what thoughts or sentiments arise in my mind or heart, as if to match or correspond with the expression.' This response of the schoolboy lies at the bottom of all the spurious profundity which has been attributed to Rochefoucault, to La Bougive, to Machiavelli, and to Campanella."[1]

"And the identification," I said, "of the reasoner's intellect with that of his opponent, depends, if I understand you aright, upon the accuracy with which the opponent's intellect is admeasured."

"For its practical value it depends upon this," replied Dupin; "and the Prefect and his cohort fail so frequently, first, by default of this identification, and, secondly, by ill-admeasurement, or rather through non-admeasurement, of the intellect with which they are engaged. They consider only their *own* ideas of ingenuity; and, in searching for anything hidden, advert only to the modes in which *they* would have hidden it. They are right in this much—that their own ingenuity is a faithful representative of that of *the mass*; but when the cunning of the individual felon is diverse in character from their own, the felon foils them, of course. This always happens when it is above their own, and very usually when it is below. They have no variation of principle in their investigations; at best, when urged by some unusual emergency—by some extraordinary reward—they extend or exaggerate their old modes of *practice,* without touching their principles. What, for example, in this case of D——, has been done to vary the principle of action? What is all this boring, and probing, and sounding, and scrutinizing with the microscope, and dividing the surface of the building into registered square inches—what is it all but an exaggeration *of the application* of the one principle or set of principles of search, which are based upon the one set of notions regarding human ingenuity, to which the Prefect, in the long routine of his duty, has been accustomed? Do you not see he has

1. Italian philosopher and Dominican monk (1568–1639). François, duc de la Rochefoucauld (1613–1680), French moralist and courtier. La Bougive is probably Jean de la Bruyere (1645–1696). Niccolò Machiavelli (1469–1527), Italian statesman and writer.

taken it for granted that *all* men proceed to conceal a letter,—not exactly in a gimlet-hole bored in a chair-leg—but, at least in *some* out-of-the-way hole or corner suggested by the same tenor of thought which would urge a man to secrete a letter in a gimlet-hole bored in a chair-leg? And do you not see also, that such *recherchés*[2] nooks for concealment are adapted only for ordinary occasions, and would be adopted only by ordinary intellects; for, in all cases of concealment, a disposal of the article concealed—a disposal of it in this *recherché* manner—is, in the very first instance, presumable and presumed; and thus its discovery depends, not at all upon the acumen, but altogether upon the mere care, patience, and determination of the seekers; and where the case is of importance—or, what amounts to the same thing in the political eyes, when the reward is of magnitude,—the qualities in question have *never* been known to fail. You will now understand what I meant in suggesting that, had the purloined letter been hidden anywhere within the limits of the Prefect's examination—in other words, had the principle of its concealment been comprehended within the principles of the Prefect—its discovery would have been a matter altogether beyond question. This functionary, however, has been thoroughly mystified; and the remote source of his defeat lies in the supposition that the Minister is a fool, because he has acquired renown as a poet. All fools are poets; this the Prefect *feels*; and he is merely guilty of a *non distributio medii*[3] in thence inferring that all poets are fools."

"But is this really the poet?" I asked. "There are two brothers, I know; and both have attained reputation in letters. The Minister I believe has written learnedly on the Differential Calculus. He is a mathematician, and no poet."

"You are mistaken; I know him well; he is both. As poet *and* mathematician, he would reason well; as mere mathematician, he could not have reasoned at all, and thus would have been at the mercy of the Prefect."

"You surprise me," I said, "by these opinions, which have been contradicted by the voice of the world. You do not mean to set at naught the well-digested idea of centuries. The mathematical reason has long been regarded as *the* reason *par excellence.*"

" '*Il y a à parier,*' " replied Dupin, quoting from Chamfort, " '*que toute idée publique, toute convention reçue, est une sottise, car elle a convenue au plus grand nombre.*'[4] The mathematicians, I grant you, have done their best to promulgate the popular error to which you allude, and which is none the less an error for its promulgation as truth. With an art worthy a better cause, for example, they have insinuated the term 'analysis' into application to algebra. The French are the originators of this particular deception; but if a term is of any importance—if words derive any value from applicability—then 'analysis' conveys 'algebra' about as much as, in Latin, '*ambitus*' implies 'ambition,' '*religio*' 'religion,' or '*homines honesti,*' a set of *honourable* men."

"You have a quarrel on hand, I see," said I, "with some of the algebraists of Paris; but proceed."

2. I.e., excessively cunning (French). 3. The undistributed middle, an error in logic (Latin). 4. The odds are that every popular idea, every accepted convention is nonsense, because it has suited itself to the majority (French); from *Maximes et Pensées* by Sébastian Chamfort (1741–1794).

"I dispute the availability, and thus the value, of that reason which is cultivated in any especial form other than the abstractly logical. I dispute, in particular, the reason educed by mathematical study. The mathematics are the science of form and quantity; mathematical reasoning is merely logic applied to observation upon form and quantity. The great error lies in supposing that even the truths of what is called *pure* algebra, are abstract or general truths. And this error is so egregious that I am confounded at the universality with which it has been received. Mathematical axioms are *not* axioms of general truth. What is true of *relation*—of form and quantity—is often grossly false in regard to morals, for example. In this latter science it is very usually *un*true that the aggregated parts are equal to the whole. In chemistry also the axiom fails. In the consideration of motive it fails; for two motives, each of a given value, have not, necessarily, a value when united, equal to the sum of their values apart. There are numerous other mathematical truths which are only truths within the limits of *relation*. But the mathematician argues, from his *finite truths*, through habit, as if they were of absolutely general applicability—as the world indeed imagines them to be. Bryant, in his very learned 'Mythology,'[5] mentions an analogous source of error, when he says that 'although the Pagan fables are not believed, yet we forget ourselves continually, and make inferences from them as existing realities.' With the algebraists, however, who are Pagans themselves, the 'Pagan fables' *are* believed, and the inferences are made, not so much through lapse of memory, as through an unaccountable addling of the brains. In short, I never yet encountered the mere mathematician who could be trusted out of equal roots, or one who did not clandestinely hold it as a point of his faith $x^2+px$ was absolutely and unconditionally equal to $q$. Say to one of these gentlemen, by way of experiment, if you please, that you believe occasions may occur where $x^2+px$ is *not* altogether equal to $q$, and, having made him understand what you mean, get out of his reach as speedily as convenient, for, beyond doubt, he will endeavour to knock you down.

"I mean to say," continued Dupin, while I merely laughed at his last observations, "that if the Minister had been no more than a mathematician, the Prefect would have been under no necessity of giving me this check. I knew him, however, as both mathematician and poet, and my measures were adapted to his capacity, with reference to the circumstances by which he was surrounded. I knew him as a courtier, too, and as a bold *intriguant.*[6] Such a man, I considered, could not fail to be aware of the ordinary political modes of action. He could not have failed to anticipate—and events have proved that he did not fail to anticipate—the waylayings to which he was subjected. He must have foreseen, I reflected, the secret investigations of his premises. His frequent absences from home at night, which were hailed by the Prefect as certain aids to his success, I regarded only as *ruses*, to afford opportunity for thorough search to the police, and thus the sooner to impress them with the conviction to which G——, in fact, did finally arrive—the conviction that the letter was not upon the premises. I felt, also, that the whole train of thought, which I was

5. *A New System, or an Analysis of Antient Mythology*, by Jacob Bryant (1715–1804), an English scholar.
6. Intriguer (French).

at some pains in detailing to you just now, concerning the invariable principle of political action in searches for articles concealed—I felt that this whole train of thought would necessarily pass through the mind of the Minister. It would imperatively lead him to despise all the ordinary *nooks* of concealment. *He* could not, I reflected, be so weak as not to see that the most intricate and remote recess of his hotel would be as open as his commonest closets to the eyes, to the probes, to the gimlets, and to the microscopes of the Prefect. I saw, in fine, that he would be driven, as a matter of course, to simplicity, if not deliberately induced to it as a matter of choice. You will remember, perhaps how desperately the Prefect laughed when I suggested, upon our first interview, that it was just possible this mystery troubled him so much on account of its being so *very* self-evident."

"Yes," said I, "I remember his merriment well. I really thought he would have fallen into convulsions."

"The material world," continued Dupin, "abounds with very strict analogies to the immaterial; and thus some color of truth has been given to the rhetorical dogma, that metaphor, or simile, may be made to strengthen an argument as well as to embellish a description. The principle of *vis inertiae,*[7] for example, seems to be identical in physics and metaphysics. It is not more true in the former, that a large body is with more difficulty set in motion than a smaller one, and that its subsequent *momentum* is commensurate with this difficulty, than it is, in the latter, that intellects of the vaster capacity, while more forcible, more constant, and more eventful in their movements than those of inferior grade, are yet the less readily moved, and more embarrassed and full of hesitation in the first few steps of their progress. Again: have you ever noticed which of the street signs, over the shop doors, are the most attractive of attention?"

"I have never given the matter a thought," I said.

"There is a game of puzzles," he resumed, "which is played upon a map. One party playing requires another to find a given word—the name of town, river, state, or empire—any word, in short, upon the motley and perplexed surface of the chart. A novice in the game generally seeks to embarrass his opponents by giving them the most minutely lettered names; but the adept selects such words as stretch, in large characters, from one end of the chart to the other. These, like the over-largely lettered signs and placards of the street, escape observation by dint of being excessively obvious; and here the physical oversight is precisely analogous with the moral inapprehension by which the intellect suffers to pass unnoticed those considerations which are too obtrusively and too palpably self-evident. But this is a point, it appears, somewhat above or beneath the understanding of the Prefect. He never once thought it probable, or possible, that the Minister had deposited the letter immediately beneath the nose of the whole world, by way of best preventing any portion of that world from perceiving it.

"But the more I reflected upon the daring, dashing, and discriminating ingenuity of D——; upon the fact that the document must always have been *at hand,* if he intended to use it to good purpose; and upon the decisive evi-

7. The power of inertia (Latin).

dence, obtained by the Prefect, that it was not hidden within the limits of that dignitary's ordinary search—the more satisfied I became that, to conceal this letter, the Minister had resorted to the comprehensive and sagacious expedient of not attempting to conceal it at all.

"Full of these ideas, I prepared myself with a pair of green spectacles, and called one fine morning, quite by accident, at the Ministerial hotel. I found D—— at home, yawning, lounging, and dawdling as usual, and pretending to be in the last extremity of *ennui*. He is, perhaps, the most really energetic human being now alive—but that is only when nobody sees him.

"To be even with him, I complained of my weak eyes, and lamented the necessity of the spectacles, under cover of which I cautiously and thoroughly surveyed the whole apartment, while seemingly intent only upon the conversation of my host.

"I paid especial attention to a large writing-table near which he sat, and upon which lay confusedly, some miscellanous letters and other papers, with one or two musical instruments and a few books. Here, however, after a long and very deliberate scrutiny, I saw nothing to excite particular suspicion.

"At length my eyes, in going the circuit of the room, fell upon a trumpery filigree card-rack of pasteboard, that hung dangling by a dirty blue ribbon, from a little brass knob just beneath the middle of the mantel-piece. In this rack, which had three or four compartments, were five or six visiting cards, and a solitary letter. This last was much soiled and crumpled. It was torn nearly in two, across the middle—as if a design, in the first instance, to tear it entirely up as worthless, had been altered, or stayed, in the second. It had a large black seal, bearing the D—— cipher *very* conspicuously, and was addressed, in a diminutive female hand, to D——, the minister, himself. It was thrust carelessly, and even, as it seemed, contemptuously, into one of the uppermost divisions of the rack.

"No sooner had I glanced at this letter than I concluded it to be that of which I was in search. To be sure, it was, to all appearance, radically different from the one of which the Prefect had read us so minute a description. Here the seal was large and black, with the D—— cipher; there, it was small and red, with the ducal arms of the S—— family. Here, the address, to the minister, was diminutive and feminine; there, the superscription, to a certain royal personage, was markedly bold and decided; the size alone formed a point of correspondence. But, then, the *radicalness* of these differences, which was excessive; the dirt; the soiled and torn condition of the paper, so inconsistent with the *true* methodical habits of D——, and so suggestive of a design to delude the beholder into an idea of the worthlessness of the document; these things, together with the hyperobtrusive situation of this document, full in the view of every visitor, and thus exactly in accordance with the conclusions to which I had previously arrived; these things, I say, were strongly corroborative of suspicion, in one who came with the intention to suspect.

"I protracted my visit as long as possible, and, while I maintained a most animated discussion with the minister, upon a topic which I knew well had never failed to interest and excite him, I kept my attention really riveted upon the letter. In this examination, I committed to memory its external appearance and arrangement in the rack; and also fell, at length, upon a discovery which set at rest whatever trivial doubt I might have entertained. In scrutinizing the edges of the paper, I observed them to be more *chafed* than seemed necessary. They presented the *broken* appearance which is manifested when a stiff paper, having been once folded and pressed with a folder, is refolded in a reversed direction, in the same creases or edges which had formed the original fold. This discovery was sufficient. It was clear to me that the letter had been turned, as a glove, inside out, re-directed, and re-sealed. I bade the Minister good morning and took my departure at once, leaving a gold snuff-box upon the table.

"The next morning I called for the snuff-box, when we resumed, quite eagerly, the conversation of the preceding day. While thus engaged, however, a loud report, as if of a pistol, was heard immediately beneath the windows of the hotel, and was succeeded by a series of fearful screams, and the shoutings of a mob. D—— rushed to a casement, threw it open, and looked out. In the meantime, I stepped to the card-rack, took the letter, put it in my pocket, and replaced it by a *fac-simile,* (so far as regards externals) which I had carefully prepared at my lodgings; imitating the D—— cipher, very readily, by means of a seal formed of bread.

"The disturbance in the street had been occasioned by the frantic behaviour of a man with a musket. He had fired it among a crowd of women and children. It proved, however, to have been without ball, and the fellow was suffered to go his way as a lunatic or a drunkard. When he had gone, D—— came from the window, whither I had followed him immediately upon securing the object in view. Soon afterward I bade him farewell. The pretended lunatic was a man in my own pay."

"But what purpose had you," I asked, "in replacing the letter by a *fac-simile*? Would it not have been better, at the first visit, to have seized it openly, and departed?"

"D——," replied Dupin, "is a desperate man, and a man of nerve. His hotel, too, is not without attendants devoted to his interests. Had I made the wild attempt you suggest, I should never have left the ministerial presence alive. The good people of Paris would have heard of me no more. But I had an object apart from these considerations. You know my political prepossessions. In this matter, I act as a partisan of the lady concerned. For eighteen months the minister has had her in his power. She has now him in hers; since, being unaware that the letter is not in his possession, he will proceed with his exactions as if it was. Thus will he inevitably commit himself, at once, to his political destruction. His downfall, too, will not be more precipitate than awkward. It is all very well to talk about the *facilis descensus Averni;* but in all kinds of climbing, as Catalini[8] said of singing, it is far more easy to get up than to come down. In the present instance I have no sympathy—at least no pity for him who descends. He is that *monstrum horrendum,*[9] an unprincipled man of genius. I confess, however, that I should like very well to know the precise character of

8. Angelica Catalini (1780–1844), Italian singer. "Facilis descensus Averni": Easy is the descent into hell . . . but to recall thy steps and issue to upper air, this is the task, this the burden (Latin); *Aeneid* 6.126, by Virgil (70–19 B.C.E.), Roman poet. 9. The description of Polyphemus the Cyclops after his one eye had been put out by Ulysses (Latin); *Aeneid* 3.658.

his thoughts, when, being defied by her whom the Prefect terms 'a certain personage,' he is reduced to opening the letter which I left for him in the card-rack."

"How? did you put any thing particular in it?"

"Why—it did not seem altogether right to leave the interior blank—that would have been insulting. To be sure, D——, at Vienna once, did me an evil turn, which I told him, quite good-humouredly, that I should remember. So, as I knew he would feel some curiosity in regard to the identity of the person who had outwitted him, I thought it a pity not to give him a clue. He is well acquainted with my MS., and I just copied into the middle of the blank sheet the words—

*—Un dessein si funeste,*
*S'il n'est digne d'Atrée, est digne de Thyeste.*

They are to be found in Crébillon's 'Atrée.' "[1]

1. So baneful a plot, if not worthy of Atreus, is worthy of Thyestes (French); from *Atrée et Thyeste* by Prosper Jolyot de Crébillon (1674–1762).

# Katherine Anne Porter

*Porter (1890–1980) was born in Indian Creek, Texas, and brought up in that state and in Louisiana. She was educated at home, in private schools, and in an Ursuline convent. Though she began to write stories as soon as she could form letters on paper, she made no attempt to publish until she was past thirty, and she associated with no literary people until she had become something of a celebrity with the publication of her first book of stories,* Flowering Judas *(1930). Before and after that date she earned a meager living by journalism, traveling from city to city with little baggage except her manuscripts—trunkfuls of which were destroyed, bit by bit, as she found them inadequate to meet her exacting standards. She lived for a time in Mexico, which provided material for some of her most famous stories. Her novel* Ship of Fools *was begun during the 1930s but not finished for more than two decades. It was at last published in 1962. Her nomadic career took her to Europe to live some of her later years. Her shorter works have been collected also in* Hacienda: A Story of Mexico *(1934),* Pale Horse, Pale Rider *(1939), and* The Leaning Tower and Other Stories *(1944).* The Collected Stories of Katherine Anne Porter *appeared in 1965, winning the Pulitzer Prize and the National Book Award.*

## Flowering Judas

Braggioni sits heaped upon the edge of a straight-backed chair much too small for him, and sings to Laura in a furry, mournful voice. Laura has begun to find reasons for avoiding her own house until the latest possible moment, for Braggioni is there almost every night. No matter how late she is, he will be sitting there with a surly, waiting expression, pulling at his kinky yellow hair, thumbing the strings of his guitar, snarling a tune under his breath. Lupe the Indian maid meets Laura at the door, and says with a flicker of a glance towards the upper room, "He waits."

Laura wishes to lie down, she is tired of her hairpins and the feel of her long tight sleeves, but she says to him, "Have you a new song for me this evening?" If he says yes, she asks him to sing it. If he says no, she remembers his favorite one, and asks him to sing it again. Lupe brings her a cup of chocolate and a plate of rice, and Laura eats at the small table under the lamp, first inviting Braggioni, whose answer is always the same: "I have eaten, and besides, chocolate thickens the voice."

Laura says, "Sing, then," and Braggioni heaves himself into song. He scratches the guitar familiarly as though it were a pet animal, and sings passionately off key, taking the high notes in a prolonged painful squeal. Laura, who haunts the markets listening to the ballad singers, and stops every day to hear the blind boy playing his reed-flute in Sixteenth of September Street,[1] listens to Braggioni with pitiless courtesy, because she dares not smile at his miserable performance. Nobody dares to smile at him. Braggioni is cruel to everyone, with a kind of specialized insolence, but he is so vain of his talents, and so sensitive to slights, it would require a cruelty and vanity greater than his own to lay a finger on the vast cureless wound of his self-esteem. It would require courage, too, for it is dangerous to offend him, and nobody has this courage.

Braggioni loves himself with such tenderness and amplitude and eternal charity that his followers—for he is a leader of men, a skilled revolutionist, and his skin has been punctured in honorable warfare—warm themselves in the reflected glow, and say to each other: "He has a real nobility, a love of humanity raised above mere personal affections." The excess of this self-love has flowed out, inconveniently for her, over Laura, who, with so many others, owes her comfortable situation and her salary to him. When he is in a very good humor, he tells her, "I am tempted to forgive you for being a *gringa, gringita*!"[2] and Laura, burning, imagines herself leaning forward suddenly, and with a sound back-handed slap wiping the suety smile from his face. If he notices her eyes at these moments he gives no sign.

She knows what Braggioni would offer her, and she must resist tenaciously without appearing to resist, and if she could avoid it she would not admit even to herself the slow drift of his intention. During these long evenings which have spoiled a long month for her, she sits in her deep chair with an open book on her knees, resting her eyes on the consoling rigidity of the printed page when the sight and sound of Braggioni singing threaten to identify themselves with all her remembered afflictions and to add their weight to her uneasy premonitions of the future. The gluttonous bulk of Braggioni has become a symbol of her many disillusions, for a revolutionist should be lean, animated by heroic faith, a vessel of abstract virtues. This is nonsense, she knows it now and is ashamed of it. Revolution must have leaders, and leadership is a career for energetic men. She is, her comrades tell her, full of romantic error, for what she defines as cynicism in them is merely "a developed sense of reality." She is almost too willing to say, "I am wrong, I suppose I don't really understand the principles," and afterward she makes a secret truce with herself, determined not to surrender her will to such expedient logic. But she cannot help feeling that she has been betrayed irreparably by the disunion between her way of living and her feeling of what life should be, and at times she is almost contented to rest in this sense of grievance as a private store of consolation. Sometimes she wishes to run away, but she stays. Now she longs to fly out of this room,

1. Street in Mexico City named to commemorate the date of the enactment of a new Mexican constitution in 1857. 2. Diminutive form of *gringa,* a somewhat derogatory term for a fair-haired woman, especially an American (Spanish).

down the narrow stairs, and into the street where the houses lean together like conspirators under a single mottled lamp, and leave Braggioni singing to himself.

Instead she looks at Braggioni, frankly and clearly, like a good child who understands the rules of behavior. Her knees cling together under sound blue serge, and her round white collar is not purposely nun-like. She wears the uniform of an idea, and has renounced vanities. She was born Roman Catholic, and in spite of her fear of being seen by someone who might make a scandal of it, she slips now and again into some crumbling little church, kneels on the chilly stone, and says a Hail Mary on the gold rosary she bought in Tehuantepec.[3] It is no good and she ends by examining the altar with its tinsel flowers and ragged brocades, and feels tender about the battered doll-shape of some male saint whose white, lace-trimmed drawers hang limply around his ankles below the hieratic dignity of his velvet robe. She has encased herself in a set of principles derived from her early training, leaving no detail of gesture or of personal taste untouched, and for this reason she will not wear lace made on machines. This is her private heresy, for in her special group the machine is sacred, and will be the salvation of the workers. She loves fine lace, and there is a tiny edge of fluted cobweb on this collar, which is one of twenty precisely alike, folded in blue tissue paper in the upper drawer of her clothes chest.

Braggioni catches her glance solidly as if he had been waiting for it, leans forward, balancing his paunch between his spread knees, and sings with tremendous emphasis, weighing his words. He has, the song relates, no father and no mother, nor even a friend to console him; lonely as a wave of the sea he comes and goes, lonely as a wave. His mouth opens round and yearns sideways, his balloon cheeks grow oily with the labor of song. He bulges marvelously in his expensive garments. Over his lavender collar, crushed upon a purple necktie, held by a diamond hoop: over his ammunition belt of tooled leather worked in silver, buckled cruelly around his gasping middle: over the tops of his glossy yellow shoes Braggioni swells with ominous ripeness, his mauve silk hose stretched taut, his ankles bound with the stout leather thongs of his shoes.

When he stretches his eyelids at Laura she notes again that his eyes are the true tawny yellow cat's eyes. He is rich, not in money, he tells her, but in power, and this power brings with it the blameless ownership of things, and the right to indulge his love of small luxuries. "I have a taste for the elegant refinements," he said once, flourishing a yellow silk handkerchief before her nose. "Smell that? It is Jockey Club, imported from New York." Nonetheless he is wounded by life. He will say so presently. "It is true everything turns to dust in the hand, to gall on the tongue." He sighs and his leather belt creaks like a saddle girth. "I am disappointed in everything as it comes. Everything." He shakes his head. "You, poor thing, you will be disappointed too. You are born for it. We are more alike than you realize in some things. Wait and see. Some day you will remember what I have told you, you will know that Braggioni was your friend."

Laura feels a slow chill, a purely physical sense of danger, a warning in her

3. City in southern Mexico.

blood that violence, mutilation, a shocking death, wait for her with lessening patience. She has translated this fear into something homely, immediate, and sometimes hesitates before crossing the street. "My personal fate is nothing, except as the testimony of a mental attitude," she reminds herself, quoting from some forgotten philosophic primer, and is sensible enough to add, "Anyhow, I shall not be killed by an automobile if I can help it."

"It may be true I am as corrupt, in another way, as Braggioni," she thinks in spite of herself, "as callous, as incomplete," and if this is so, any kind of death seems preferable. Still she sits quietly, she does not run. Where could she go? Uninvited she has promised herself to this place; she can no longer imagine herself as living in another country, and there is no pleasure in remembering her life before she came here.

Precisely what is the nature of this devotion, its true motives, and what are its obligations? Laura cannot say. She spends part of her days in Xochimilco, near by, teaching Indian children to say in English, "The cat is on the mat." When she appears in the classroom they crowd about her with smiles on their wise, innocent, clay-colored faces, crying, "Good morning, my titcher!" in immaculate voices, and they make of her desk a fresh garden of flowers every day.

During her leisure she goes to union meetings and listens to busy important voices quarreling over tactics, methods, internal politics. She visits the prisoners of her own political faith in their cells, where they entertain themselves with counting cockroaches, repenting of their indiscretions, composing their memoirs, writing out manifestoes and plans for their comrades who are still walking about free, hands in pockets, sniffing fresh air. Laura brings them food and cigarettes and a little money, and she brings messages disguised in equivocal phrases from the men outside who dare not set foot in the prison for fear of disappearing into the cells kept empty for them. If the prisoners confuse night and day, and complain, "Dear little Laura, time doesn't pass in this infernal hole, and I won't know when it is time to sleep unless I have a reminder," she brings them their favorite narcotics, and says in a tone that does not wound them with pity, "Tonight will really be night for you," and though her Spanish amuses them, they find her comforting, useful. If they lose patience and all faith, and curse the slowness of their friends in coming to their rescue with money and influence, they trust her not to repeat everything, and if she inquires, "Where do you think we can find money, or influence?" they are certain to answer, "Well, there is Braggioni, why doesn't he do something?"

She smuggles letters from headquarters to men hiding from firing squads in back streets in mildewed houses, where they sit in tumbled beds and talk bitterly as if all Mexico were at their heels, when Laura knows positively they might appear at the band concert in the Alameda[4] on Sunday morning, and no one would notice them. But Braggioni says, "Let them sweat a little. The next time they may be careful. It is very restful to have them out of the way for a while." She is not afraid to knock on any door in any street after midnight, and enter in the darkness, and say to one of these men who is really in danger:

4. Public square in Mexico City.

"They will be looking for you—seriously—tomorrow morning after six. Here is some money from Vicente. Go to Vera Cruz and wait."

She borrows money from the Roumanian agitator to give to his bitter enemy the Polish agitator. The favor of Braggioni is their disputed territory, and Braggioni holds the balance nicely, for he can use them both. The Polish agitator talks love to her over café tables, hoping to exploit what he believes is her secret sentimental preference for him, and he gives her misinformation which he begs her to repeat as the solemn truth to certain persons. The Roumanian is more adroit. He is generous with his money in all good causes, and lies to her with an air of ingenuous candor, as if he were her good friend and confidant. She never repeats anything they may say. Braggioni never asks questions. He has other ways to discover all that he wishes to know about them.

Nobody touches her, but all praise her gray eyes, and the soft, round under lip which promises gayety, yet is always grave, nearly always firmly closed: and they cannot understand why she is in Mexico. She walks back and forth on her errands, with puzzled eyebrows, carrying her little folder of drawings and music and school papers. No dancer dances more beautifully than Laura walks, and she inspires some amusing, unexpected ardors, which cause little gossip, because nothing comes of them. A young captain who had been a soldier in Zapata's[5] army attempted, during a horseback ride near Cuernavaca, to express his desire for her with the noble simplicity befitting a rude folk-hero: but gently, because he was gentle. This gentleness was his defeat, for when he alighted, and removed her foot from the stirrup, and essayed to draw her down into his arms, her horse, ordinarily a tame one, shied fiercely, reared and plunged away. The young hero's horse careened blindly after his stable-mate, and the hero did not return to the hotel until rather late that evening. At breakfast he came to her table in full charro dress,[6] gray buckskin jacket and trousers with strings of silver buttons down the leg, and he was in a humorous, careless mood. "May I sit with you?" and "You are a wonderful rider. I was terrified that you might be thrown and dragged. I should never have forgiven myself. But I cannot admire you enough for your riding."

"I learned to ride in Arizona," said Laura.

"If you will ride with me again this morning, I promise you a horse that will not shy with you," he said. But Laura remembered that she must return to Mexico City at noon.

Next morning the children made a celebration and spent their playtime writing on the blackboard, "We lov ar ticher," and with tinted chalks they drew wreaths of flowers around the words. The young hero wrote her a letter: "I am a very foolish, wasteful, impulsive man. I should have first said I love you, and then you would not have run away. But you shall see me again." Laura thought, "I must send him a book of colored crayons," but she was trying to forgive herself for having spurred her horse at the wrong moment.

A brown, shock-haired youth came and stood in her patio one night and sang like a lost soul for two hours, but Laura could think of nothing to do about it. The moonlight spread a wash of gauzy silver over the clear spaces of the

5. Emiliano Zapata (1883–1919), Mexican revolutionary general and agrarian reformer. 6. Cowboy dress.

garden, and the shadows were cobalt blue. The scarlet blossoms of the Judas tree[7] were dull purple, and the names of the colors repeated themselves automatically in her mind, while she watched not the boy, but his shadow, fallen like a dark garment across the fountain rim, trailing in the water. Lupe came silently and whispered expert counsel in her ear: "If you will throw him one little flower, he will sing another song or two and go away." Laura threw the flower, and he sang a last song and went away with the flower tucked in the band of his hat. Lupe said, "He is one of the organizers of the Typographers Union, and before that he sold corridos[8] in the Merced market, and before that, he came from Guanajuato, where I was born. I would not trust any man, but I trust least those from Guanajuato."

She did not tell Laura that he would be back again the next night, and the next, nor that he would follow her at a certain fixed distance around the Merced market, through the Zócolo, up Francisco I. Madero Avenue, and so along the Paseo de la Reforma to Chapultepec Park, and into the Philosopher's Footpath,[9] still with that flower withering in his hat, and an indivisible attention in his eyes.

Now Laura is accustomed to him, it means nothing except that he is nineteen years old and is observing a convention with all propriety, as though it were founded on a law of nature, which in the end it might well prove to be. He is beginning to write poems which he prints on a wooden press, and he leaves them stuck like handbills in her door. She is pleasantly disturbed by the abstract, unhurried watchfulness of his black eyes which will in time turn easily towards another object. She tells herself that throwing the flower was a mistake, for she is twenty-two years old and knows better; but she refuses to regret it, and persuades herself that her negation of all external events as they occur is a sign that she is gradually perfecting herself in the stoicism she strives to cultivate against that disaster she fears, though she cannot name it.

She is not at home in the world. Every day she teaches children who remain strangers to her, though she loves their tender round hands and their charming opportunist savagery. She knocks at unfamiliar doors not knowing whether a friend or a stranger shall answer, and even if a known face emerges from the sour gloom of that unknown interior, still it is the face of a stranger. No matter what this stranger says to her, nor what her message to him, the very cells of her flesh reject knowledge and kinship in one monotonous word. No. No. No. She draws her strength from this one holy talismanic word which does not suffer her to be led into evil. Denying everything, she may walk anywhere in safety, she looks at everything without amazement.

No, repeats this firm unchanging voice of her blood; and she looks at Braggioni without amazement. He is a great man, he wishes to impress this simple girl who covers her great round breasts with thick dark cloth, and who hides long, invaluably beautiful legs under a heavy skirt. She is almost thin except for the incomprehensible fullness of her breasts, like a nursing mother's, and Brag-

7. So called because Judas is said to have hanged himself on a tree of this kind. 8. Bullfight tickets (Spanish). 9. Streets and parks in Mexico City. Madero (1873–1913) led the revolution against the dictator Porfirio Diaz (1830–1915).

gioni, who considers himself a judge of women, speculates again on the puzzle of her notorious virginity, and takes the liberty of speech which she permits without a sign of modesty, indeed, without any sort of sign, which is disconcerting.

"You think you are so cold, *gringita*! Wait and see. You will surprise yourself some day! May I be there to advise you!" He stretches his eyelids at her, and his ill-humored cat's eyes waver in a separate glance for the two points of light marking the opposite ends of a smoothly drawn path between the swollen curve of her breasts. He is not put off by that blue serge, nor by her resolutely fixed gaze. There is all the time in the world. His cheeks are bellying with the wind of song. "O girl with the dark eyes," he sings, and reconsiders. "But yours are not dark. I can change all that. O girl with the green eyes, you have stolen my heart away!" Then his mind wanders to the song, and Laura feels the weight of his attention being shifted elsewhere. Singing thus, he seems harmless, he is quite harmless, there is nothing to do but sit patiently and say "No," when the moment comes. She draws a full breath, and her mind wanders also, but not far. She dares not wander too far.

Not for nothing has Braggioni taken pains to be a good revolutionist and a professional lover of humanity. He will never die of it. He has the malice, the cleverness, the wickedness, the sharpness of wit, the hardness of heart, stipulated for loving the world profitably. *He will never die of it.* He will live to see himself kicked out from his feeding trough by other hungry world-saviors. Traditionally he must sing in spite of his life which drives him to bloodshed, he tells Laura, for his father was a Tuscany peasant who drifted to Yucatan and married a Maya woman:[1] a woman of race, an aristocrat. They gave him the love and knowledge of music, thus: and under the rip of his thumbnail, the strings of the instrument complain like exposed nerves.

Once he was called Delgadito by all the girls and married women who ran after him; he was so scrawny all his bones showed under his thin cotton clothing, and he could squeeze his emptiness to the very backbone with his two hands. He was a poet and the revolution was only a dream then; too many women loved him and sapped away his youth, and he could never find enough to eat anywhere, anywhere! Now he is a leader of men, crafty men who whisper in his ear, hungry men who wait for hours outside his office for a word with him, emaciated men with wild faces who waylay him at the street gate with a timid, "Comrade, let me tell you . . ." and they blow the foul breath from their empty stomachs in his face.

He is always sympathetic. He gives them handfuls of small coins from his own pockets, he promises them work, there will be demonstrations, they must join the unions and attend the meetings, above all they must be on the watch for spies. They are closer to him than his own brothers, without them he can do nothing—until tomorrow, comrade!

Until tomorrow. "They are stupid, they are lazy, they are treacherous, they would cut my throat for nothing," he says to Laura. He has good food and abundant drink, he hires an automobile and drives in the Paseo on Sunday

1. I.e., an Indian woman. Tuscany is a region in west central Italy.

morning, and enjoys plenty of sleep in a soft bed beside a wife who dares not disturb him; and he sits pampering his bones in easy billows of fat, singing to Laura, who knows and thinks these things about him. When he was fifteen, he tried to drown himself because he loved a girl, his first love, and she laughed at him. "A thousand women have paid for that," and his tight little mouth turns down at the corners. Now he perfumes his hair with Jockey Club, and confides to Laura: "One woman is really as good as another for me, in the dark. I prefer them all."

His wife organizes unions among the girls in the cigarette factories, and walks in picket lines, and even speaks at meetings in the evening. But she cannot be brought to acknowledge the benefits of true liberty. "I tell her I must have my freedom, net. She does not understand my point of view." Laura has heard this many times. Braggioni scratches the guitar and meditates. "She is an instinctively virtuous woman, pure gold, no doubt of that. If she were not, I should lock her up, and she knows it."

His wife, who works so hard for the good of the factory girls, employs part of her leisure lying on the floor weeping because there are so many women in the world, and only one husband for her, and she never knows where nor when to look for him. He told her: "Unless you can learn to cry when I am not here, I must go away for good." That day he went away and took a room at the Hotel Madrid.

It is this month of separation for the sake of higher principles that has been spoiled not only for Mrs. Braggioni, whose sense of reality is beyond criticism, but for Laura, who feels herself bogged in a nightmare. Tonight Laura envies Mrs. Braggioni, who is alone, and free to weep as much as she pleases about a concrete wrong. Laura has just come from a visit to the prison, and she is waiting for tomorrow with a bitter anxiety as if tomorrow may not come, but time may be caught immovably in this hour, with herself transfixed, Braggioni singing on forever, and Eugenio's body not yet discovered by the guard.

Braggioni says: "Are you going to sleep?" Almost before she can shake her head, he begins telling her about the May-day disturbances coming on in Morelia, for the Catholics hold a festival in honor of the Blessed Virgin, and the Socialists celebrate their martyrs on that day. "There will be two independent processions, starting from either end of town, and they will march until they meet, and the rest depends . . ." He asks her to oil and load his pistols. Standing up, he unbuckles his ammunition belt, and spreads it laden across her knees. Laura sits with the shells slipping through the cleaning cloth dipped in oil, and he says again he cannot understand why she works so hard for the revolutionary idea unless she loves some man who is in it. "Are you not in love with someone?" "No," says Laura. "And no one is in love with you?" "No." "Then it is your own fault. No woman need go begging. Why, what is the matter with you? The legless beggar woman in the Alameda has a perfectly faithful lover. Did you know that?"

Laura peers down the pistol barrel and says nothing, but a long, slow faintness rises and subsides in her; Braggioni curves his swollen fingers around the throat of the guitar and softly smothers the music out of it, and when she hears him again he seems to have forgotten her, and is speaking in the hypnotic voice he uses when talking in small rooms to a listening, close-gathered crowd. Some day this world, now seemingly so composed and eternal, to the edges of every sea shall be merely a tangle of gaping trenches, of crashing walls and broken bodies. Everything must be torn from its accustomed place where it has rotted for centuries, hurled skyward and distributed, cast down again clean as rain, without separate identity. Nothing shall survive that the stiffened hands of poverty have created for the rich and no one shall be left alive except the elect spirits destined to procreate a new world cleansed of cruelty and injustice, ruled by benevolent anarchy: "Pistols are good, I love them, cannon are even better, but in the end I pin my faith to good dynamite," he concludes, and strokes the pistol lying in her hands. "Once I dreamed of destroying this city, in case it offered resistance to General Ortiz,[2] but it fell into his hands like an over-ripe pear."

He is made restless by his own words, rises and stands waiting. Laura holds up the belt to him: "Put that on, and go kill somebody in Morelia, and you will be happier," she says softly. The presence of death in the room makes her bold. "Today, I found Eugenio going into a stupor. He refused to allow me to call the prison doctor. He had taken all the tablets I brought him yesterday. He said he took them because he was bored."

"He is a fool, and his death is his own business," says Braggioni, fastening his belt carefully.

"I told him if he had waited only a little while longer, you would have got him set free," says Laura. "He said he did not want to wait."

"He is a fool and we are well rid of him," says Braggioni, reaching for his hat.

He goes away. Laura knows his mood has changed, she will not see him any more for a while. He will send word when he needs her to go on errands into strange streets, to speak to the strange faces that will appear, like clay masks with the power of human speech, to mutter their thanks to Braggioni for his help. Now she is free, and she thinks, I must run while there is time. But she does not go.

Braggioni enters his own house where for a month his wife has spent many hours every night weeping and tangling her hair upon her pillow. She is weeping now, and she weeps more at the sight of him, the cause of all her sorrows. He looks about the room. Nothing is changed, the smells are good and familiar, he is well acquainted with the woman who comes toward him with no reproach except grief on her face. He says to her tenderly: "You are so good, please don't cry any more, you dear good creature." She says, "Are you tired, my angel? Sit here and I will wash your feet." She brings a bowl of water, and kneeling, unlaces his shoes, and when from her knees she raises her sad eyes under her blackened lids, he is sorry for everything, and bursts into tears. "Ah, yes, I am hungry, I am tired, let us eat something together," he says, between sobs. His wife leans her head on his arm and says, "Forgive me!" and this time he is refreshed by the solemn, endless rain of her tears.

Laura takes off her serge dress and puts on a white linen nightgown and

2. Pascual Ortiz Rubio (1877–1963) was a revolutionary who became president of Mexico.

goes to bed. She turns her head a little to one side, and lying still, reminds herself that it is time to sleep. Numbers tick in her brain like little clocks, soundless doors close of themselves around her. If you would sleep, you must not remember anything, the children will say tomorrow, good morning, my teacher, the poor prisoners who come every day bringing flowers to their jailor. 1-2-3-4-5—it is monstrous to confuse love with revolution, night with day, life with death—ah, Eugenio!

The tolling of the midnight bell is a signal, but what does it mean? Get up, Laura, and follow me: come out of your sleep, out of your bed, out of this strange house. What are you doing in this house? Without a word, without fear she rose and reached for Eugenio's hand, but he eluded her with a sharp, sly smile and drifted away. This is not all, you shall see—Murderer, he said, follow me, I will show you a new country, but it is far away and we must hurry. No, said Laura, not unless you take my hand, no; and she clung first to the stair rail, and then to the topmost branch of the Judas tree that bent down slowly and set her upon the earth, and then to the rocky ledge of a cliff, and then to the jagged wave of a sea that was not water but a desert of crumbling stone. Where are you taking me, she asked in wonder but without fear. To death, and it is a long way off, and we must hurry, said Eugenio. No, said Laura, not unless you take my hand. Then eat these flowers, poor prisoner, said Eugenio in a voice of pity, take and eat: and from the Judas tree he stripped the warm bleeding flowers, and held them to her lips. She saw that his hand was fleshless, a cluster of small white petrified branches, and his eye sockets were without light, but she ate the flowers greedily for they satisfied both hunger and thirst. Murderer! said Eugenio, and Cannibal! This is my body and my blood.[3] Laura cried No! and at the sound of her own voice, she awoke trembling, and was afraid to sleep again.

3. Allusion to Christ's words at the Last Supper. Luke 22.19–20.

# V. S. Pritchett

*Pritchett (1900–1997) was a British writer of prodigious versatility. He was born in Ipswich, Suffolk, England. He attended Alleyn's School, Dulwich, London. Well-known for his literary criticism, especially that which he published in* The New Statesman, *as well as his own writing, he had a sharp ear for dialogue and an eye for detail. He wrote of the extraordinary in the ordinarily middle-class life. He was at his best in his short stories. Two volumes of memoirs,* A Cab at the Door *(1968) and* Midnight Oil *(1972), give a view into his long life. He taught at many colleges in the United States and received numerous awards. He was knighted in 1995. In 1979 a collection of his stories called* On the Edge of the Cliff *appeared. In 1989 another book of stories,* A Careless Widow and Other Stories, *was published. His* Complete Stories *appeared in 1990.*

## The Fall

It was the evening of the Annual Dinner. More than two hundred accountants were at that hour changing into evening clothes, in the flats, villas and hotel rooms of a large, wet, Midland city. At the Royal was Charles Peacock, slender in his shirt, balancing on one leg and gazing with frowns of affection in the wardrobe mirror at the other leg as he pulled his trouser on; and then with a smile of farewell as the second went in. Buttoned up, relieved of nakedness, he visited other mirrors—the one at the dressing table, the two in the bathroom, assembling the scattered aspects of the unsettled being called Peacock "doing"—as he was apt to say—"no so badly" in this city which smelled of coal and where thirty-eight years ago he had been born. When he left his room there were mirrors in the hotel lift and down below in the foyer and outside in the street. Certain shop windows were favourable and assuring. The love affair was taken up again at the Assembly Rooms by the mirrors in the tiled corridor leading towards the bullocky noise of two hundred-odd chartered accountants in black ties, taking their drinks under the chandeliers that seemed to weep above their heads.

Crowds or occasions frightened Peacock. They engaged him, at first sight, in the fundamental battle of his life: the struggle against nakedness, the panic of grabbing for clothes and becoming someone. An acquaintance in a Scottish firm was standing near the door of the packed room as Peacock went in.

"Hullo, laddie," Peacock said, fitting himself out with a Scottish accent, as he went into the crowded, chocolate coloured buffet.

"What's to do?" he said, passing on to a Yorkshireman.

"Are you well now?" he said, in his Irish voice. And, gaining confidence, "Whatcha cock!" to a man up from London, until he was shaking hands in the crowd with the President himself, who was leaning on a stick and had his foot in plaster.

"I hope this is not serious, sir," said Peacock in his best southern English, nodding at the foot.

"Bloody serious," said the President sticking out his peppery beard. "I caught my foot in a grating. Some damn fools here think I've got gout."

No one who saw Peacock in his office, in Board Rooms, on Committees, at meetings, knew the exhausting number of rough sketches that had to be made before the naked Peacock could become Peacock dressed for his part. Now, having spoken to several human beings, the fragments called Peacock closed up. And he had one more trick up his sleeve if he panicked again: he could drop into music hall Negro.

Peacock got a drink at the buffet table and pushed his way to a solitary island of carpet two feet square, in the guffawing corral. He was looking at the back of the President's neck. Almost at once the President, on the crest of a successful joke he had told, turned round with appetite.

"Hah!" he shouted. "Hah! Here's friend Peacock again." "Why 'again'?" thought Peacock.

The President looked Peacock over.

"I saw your brother this afternoon," shouted the President. The President's injured foot could be said to have made his voice sound like a hilarious smash. Peacock's drink jumped and splashed his hand. The President winked at his friends.

"Hah!" said the President. "That gave our friend Peacock a scare!"

"At the Odeon," explained a kinder man.

"Is Shelmerdine Peacock your brother? The actor?" another said, astonished, looking at Peacock from head to foot.

"Shelmerdine Peacock was born and bred in this city," said the President fervently.

"I saw him in *Waste*," someone said. And others recalled him in *The Gun Runner and Doctor Zut*.

Four or five men stood gazing at Peacock with admiration, waiting for him to speak.

"Where is he now?" said the President, stepping forward, beard first. "In Hollywood? Have you seen him lately?"

They all moved forward to hear about the famous man.

Peacock looked to the right—he wanted to do this properly—but there was no mirror in that direction; he looked to the left, but there was no mirror there. He lowered his head gravely and then looked up shaking his head sorrowfully. He brought out the old reliable Negro voice:

"The last time I saw l'il ole brudder Shel," he said, "he was being thrown out of the Orchid Room. He was calling the waiters goatherds."

Peacock looked up at them all and stood, collected, assembled, whole at last, among their shouts of laughter. One man who did not laugh and who asked what the Orchid Room was, was put in his place. And in a moment, a voice bawled from the door, "Gentlemen. Dinner is served." The crowd moved through two ante-rooms into the Great Hall where, from their portraits on the wall, Mayors, Presidents and Justices looked down with the complacent rosiness of those who have dined and died. It was gratifying to Peacock that the President rested his arm on his shoulder for a few steps as they went into the hall.

Shel often cropped up in Peacock's life, especially in clubs and at dinners. It was pleasing. There was always praise; there were always questions. He had seen the posters about Shel's film during the week on his way to his office. They pleased, but they also troubled. Peacock stood at his place at table in the Great Hall and paused to look around, in case there was one more glance of vicarious fame to be collected. He was enjoying one of those pauses of self-possession in which, for a few seconds, he could feel the sensations Shel must feel when he stepped before the curtain to receive the applause of some great audience in London or New York. Then Peacock sat down. More than two hundred soup spoons scraped.

"Sherry, sir?" said the waiter.

Peacock sipped.

He meant no harm to Shel, of course. But in a city like this, with Shel appearing in a big picture, with his name fifteen feet long on the hoardings, talked about by girls in offices, the universal instinct of family disparagement was naturally tickled into life. The President might laugh and the crowd admire, but it was not always agreeable for the family to have Shel roaming loose—and often very loose—in the world. One had to assert the modesty, the anonymity of the ordinary assiduous Peacocks. One way of doing this was to add a touch or two to famous scandals: to enlarge the drunken scrimmages and add to the divorces and the breaches of contract, increase the over-doses taken by flighty girls. One was entitled to a little rake off—an accountant's charges—from the fame that so often annoyed. One was entitled, above all, because one loved Shel.

"Hock, sir?" said the waiter.

Peacock drank. Yes, he loved Shel. Peacock put down his glass and the man opposite to him spoke across the table, a man with an amused mouth, who turned his sallow face sideways so that one had the impression of being inquired into under a loose lock of black hair by one sharp, serious eye only.

"An actor's life is a struggle," the man said. Peacock recognized him: it was the man who had not laughed at his story and who had asked what the Orchid Room was, in a voice that had a sad and puncturing feeling for information sought for its own sake.

Peacock knew this kind of admirer of Shel's and feared him. They were not content to admire, they wanted to advance into intimacy, and collect facts on behalf of some general view of life's mysteriousness. As an accountant Peacock rejected mystery.

"I don't think l'il ole brudder Shel has struggled much," said Peacock, wagging his head from side to side carelessly.

"I mean he has to dedicate himself," said the man.

Peacock looked back mistrustfully.

"I remember some interview he gave about his schooldays—in this city," said the man. "It interested me. I do the books for the Hippodrome."

Peacock stopped wagging his head from side to side. He was alert. What Shel had said about his early life had been damned tactless.

"Shel had a good time," said Peacock sharply. "He always got his own way."

Peacock put on his face of stone. He dared the man to say out loud, in that company, three simple English words. He dared him. The man smiled and did not say them.

"Volnay, sir?" said the waiter as the pheasant was brought. Peacock drank.

Fried Fish Shop, Peacock said to himself as he drank. Those were the words. Shel could have kept his mouth shut about that. I'm not a snob, but why mention it? Why, after they were all doing well, bring ridicule upon the family? Why not say, simply, "Shop." Why not say, if he had to, "Fishmonger"? Why mention "Frying"? Why add "*Bankrupt* Fried Fish Shop"?

It was swinish, disloyal, ungrateful. Bankrupt—all right; but some of that money (Peacock said, hectoring the pheasant on his plate), paid for Shel's years at the Dramatic School. It was unforgiveable.

Peacock looked across at the man opposite, but the man had turned to talk to a neighbour. Peacock finished his glass and chatted with the man sitting to his right, but he felt like telling the whole table a few facts about dedication.

Dedication—he would have said. Let us take a look at the figures. An example of Shel's dedication in those Fried Fish Shop days he is so fond of remembering to make fools of us. Saturday afternoon. Father asleep in the back room. Shel says "Come down the High Street with me, Tom. I want to get a record." Classical, of course. Usual swindle. If we get into the shop he won't have the money and will try and borrow from me. "No," I say. "I haven't got any money." "Well, let's get out of this stink of lard and fish." He wears me down. He wore us all down, the whole family. He would be sixteen, two years older than me. And so we go out and at once I know there is going to be trouble. "I saw the Devil in Cramers," he says. We go down the High Street to Cramers, it's a music shop, and he goes up to the girl to ask if they sell bicycle pumps or rubber heels When the girl says "No," he makes a terrible face at her and shouts out "Bah." At Hooks, the stationers, he stands at the door, and calls to the girl at the cash desk: "You've got the Devil in here. I've reported it," and slams the door. We go on to Bonds, the grocers, and he pretends to be sick when he sees the bacon. Goes out. "Rehearsing," he says. The Bonds are friends of Father's. There is a row. Shel swears he was never anywhere near the place and goes back the following Saturday and falls flat on the floor in front of the Bond daughter groaning, "I've been poisoned. I'm dying. Water! Water!" Falls flat on his back . . .

"Caught his foot in a grating, he told me, and fell," the man opposite was saying. "Isn't that what he told you, Peacock?"

Peacock's imaginary speech came suddenly to an end. The man was smiling as if he had heard every word.

"Who?" said Peacock.

"The President," said the man. "My friend, Mr. McAlister is asking me what happened to the President. Did he fall in the street?"

Peacock collected himself quickly and to hide his nakedness became Scottish.

"Ay, mon," he nodded across the table. "A wee bit of a tumble in the street."

Peacock took up his glass and drank.

"He's a heavy man to fall," said the man called McAlister.

"He carries a lot of weight," said his neighbour. Peacock eyed him. The impression was growing that this man knew too much, too quietly. It struck him that the man was one of those who ask what they know already, a deeply unbelieving man. They have to be crushed.

"Weight makes no difference," said Peacock firmly.

"It's weight and distance," said the Scotsman. "Look at children."

Peacock felt a smile coming over his body from the feet upwards.

"Weight and distance make no difference," Peacock repeated.

"How can you say that?"

An enormous voice, hanging brutally on the air like a sergeant's, suddenly shouted in the hall. It was odd to see the men in the portraits on the wall still sitting down after the voice sounded. It was the voice of the toastmaster.

"Gen—tle—men," it shouted. "I ask you. To rise to. The Toast of Her. Maj—es—ty. The Queen."

Two hundred or more accountants pushed back their chairs and stood up.

"The Queen," they growled. And one or two, Peacock among them, fervently added, "God bless her," and drained his glass.

Two hundred or more accountants sat down. It was the moment Peacock loved. And he loved the Queen.

"Port or brandy, sir?" the waiter asked.

"Brandy," said Peacock.

"You were saying that weight and distance make no difference. How do you make that out?" the sidelong man opposite said in a sympathetic and curious voice that came softly and lazily out.

Peacock felt the brandy burn. The question floated by, answerable if seized as it went and yet, suddenly, unanswerable for the moment. Peacock stared at the question keenly as if it were a fly that he was waiting to swat when it came round again. Ah, there it came. Now! But no, it had gone by once more. It was answerable. He knew the answer. Peacock smiled loosely biding his time. He felt the flame of authority, of absolute knowledge burn in him.

There was a hammering at the President's table, there was hand-clapping. The President was on his feet and his beard had begun to move up and down.

"I'll tell you later," said Peacock curtly across the table. The interest went out of the man's eye.

"Once more," (the President's beard was saying and it seemed sometimes that he had two beards), "Honour," said one beard. "Privilege," said the other. "Old friends," said both beards together. "Speeches . . . brief . . . reminded of story . . . shortest marriage service in the world . . . Tennessee . . ."

"Hah! Hah! Hah!" shouted a pack of wolves, hyenas, hounds in dinner jackets.

Peacock looked across at the unbeliever who sat opposite. The interest in weight and distance had died away in his face.

"Englishman . . . Irishman . . . Scotsman . . . train . . . Englishman said . . . Scotsman said . . . Och, says Paddy . . ."

"Hah! Hah! Hah!" from the pack.

Over the carnations in the silver plated vases on the table, over the heads of the diners, the cigar smoke was rising sweetly and the first level indigo shafts of it were tipping across the middle air and turning the portraits of the Past Masters into day dreams. Peacock gazed at it. Then a bell rang in his ear, so loudly that he looked shyly to see if anyone else had heard it. The voice of Shel was on some line of his memory, a voice richer, more insinuating than the toastmaster's or the President's, a voice utterly flooring.

"Abel?" Shel was saying. "Is that you Abel? This is Cain speaking. How's the smoke? Is it still going up straight to heaven? Not blowing about all over the place . . ."

The man opposite caught Peacock's eye for a second, as if he too had heard the voice and then turned his head away. And, just at the very moment, when once more Peacock could have answered that question about the effect of weight and distance, the man opposite stood up, all the accountants stood up. Peacock was the last. There was another toast to drink. And immediately there was more hammering and another speaker. Peacock's opportunity was lost. The man who sat opposite had moved his chair back from the table and was sitting sideways to it listening, his interest in Peacock gone for good.

Peacock became lonely. Sulkily he played with matchsticks and arranged them in patterns on the tablecloth. There was a point at Annual Dinners when he always did this. It was at that point when one saw the function had become fixed by a flash photograph in the gloss of celebration and when everyone looked sickly and old. Eyes became hollow, temples sank, teeth loosened. Shortly the diners would be carried out in coffins. One waited restlessly for the thing to be over. Ten years of life went by and then, it seemed, there were no more speeches. There was some business talk in groups; then twos and threes left the table. Others filed off into a large chamber next door. Peacock's neighbours got up. He, who feared occasions, feared even more their dissolution. It was like that frightening ten minutes in a theatre when the audience slowly moves out, leaving a hollow stage and row after row, always increasing, of empty seats behind them. In a panic Peacock got up. He was losing all acquaintance. He had even let the man opposite slip away, for that man was walking down the hall with some friends. Peacock hurried down his side of the long table to meet them at the bottom and when he got there he turned and barred their way.

"What we were talking about," he said. "It's an art. Simply a matter of letting the breath go, relaxing the muscles. Any actor can do it. It's the first thing they learn."

"I'm out of my depth," said the Scotsman.

"Falling," said Peacock. "The stage fall." He looked at them with dignity, then he let the expression die on his face. He fell quietly full length to the floor. Before they could speak he was up on his feet.

"My brother weighs two hundred and twenty pounds," he said with condescension to the man opposite. "The ordinary person falls and breaks an arm or a foot, because he doesn't know. It's an art."

His eyes conveyed that if the Peacocks had kept a fried fish shop years ago, they had an art.

"Simple," said Peacock.

And down he went, thump, on the carpet again and lying at their feet he said:

"Painless. Nothing broken. Not a bruise. I said 'an art.' Really one might call it a science. Do you see how I'm lying?"

"What's happened to Peacock?" said two or three men joining the group.

"He's showing us the stage fall."

"Nothing," said Peacock, getting up and brushing his coat sleeve and smoothing back his hair. "It is just a stage trick."

"I wouldn't do it," said a large man, patting his stomach.

"I've just been telling them—weight is nothing. Look." Peacock fell down and got up at once.

"You turn. You crumple. You can go flat on your back. I mean, that is what it looks like," he said.

And Peacock fell.

"Shel and I used to practise it in the bedroom. Father thought the ceiling was coming down," he said.

"Good God, has Peacock passed out?" A group standing by the fireplace in the hall called across. Peacock got up and brushing his jacket again walked up to them. The group he had left watched him. There was a thump.

"He's done it again," the man opposite said.

"Once more. There he goes. Look, he's going to show the President. He's going after him. No, he's missed him. The old boy has slipped out of the door."

Peacock was staring with annoyance at the door. He looked at other groups of two and threes.

"Who was the casualty over there?" someone said to him as he walked past.

Peacock went over to them and explained.

"Like judo," said a man.

"No!" said Peacock indignantly, even grandly. And in Shel's manner. Anyone who had seen Shelmerdine Peacock affronted knew what he looked like. That large white face trod on you. "Nothing to do with judo. This is the theatre . . ."

"Shelmerdine Peacock's brother," a man whispered to a friend.

"Is that so?"

"It's in the blood," someone said.

To the man who had said "Judo," Peacock said, "No throwing, no wrestling, no somersaulting or fancy tricks. That is not theatre. Just . . . simply . . ." said Peacock. And crumpling, as Shel might have done in *Macbeth* or *Hamlet*, or like some gangster shot in the stomach, Peacock once more let his body go down with the cynicism of the skilful corpse. This time he did not get up at once. He looked up at their knees, their waists, at their goggling faces, saw under their double chins and under their hairy eyebrows. He grinned at their absurdity. He saw that he held them. They were obliged to look at him. Shel must always have had this sensation of hundreds of astonished eyes watching him lie, waiting for him to move. Their gaze would never leave him. Peacock never felt less at a loss, never felt more completely himself. Even the air was better at carpet level; it was certainly cooler and he was glad of that. Then he saw two pairs of feet advancing from another group. He saw two faces peep over the shoulders of the others, and heard one of them say:

"It's Peacock—still at it."

He saw the two pairs of boots and trousers go off. Peacock got to his feet at once and resentfully stared after them. He knew something, as they went, that Shel must have known: the desperation, the contempt for the audience that is thinning out. He was still brushing his sleeve and trousers legs when he saw everyone moving away out of the hall. Peacock moved after them into the chamber.

A voice spoke behind him. It was the quiet, intimate voice of the man with the loose lock of black hair who had sat opposite to him.

"You need a drink," the man said.

They were standing in the chamber where the buffet table was. The man had gone into the chamber and, clearly, he had waited for Peacock. A question was going round as fast as a catherine wheel[1] in Peacock's head and there was no need to ask it: it must be so blindingly obvious. He looked for someone to put it to, on the quiet, but there were only three men at the buffet table with their backs turned to him. Why (the question ran) at the end of a bloody good dinner is one always left with some awful drunk, a man you've never liked—an unbeliever?

Peacock mopped his face. The unbeliever was having a short disgusting laugh with the men at the bar and now was coming back with a glass of whisky.

"Sit down. You must be tired," said the unbeliever.

They sat down. The man spoke of the dinner and the speeches. Peacock did not listen. He had just noticed a door leading into a small ante-room and he was wondering how he could get into it.

"There was one thing I don't quite get," the man said. "Perhaps it was the quickness of the hand deceiving the eye. I should say feet. What I mean is—do you first take a step, I mean like in dancing: I mean is the art of falling really a paradox—I mean the art of keeping your balance all the time?"

The word "paradox" sounded offensive to Peacock.

The man looked too damn clever, in Peacock's opinion and didn't sit still. Wearily Peacock got up.

"Hold my drink," he said. "You are standing like this, or facing sideways—on a level floor, of course. On a slope like this . . ."

The man nodded.

"I mean—well, now, watch carefully. Are you watching?"

"Yes," said the man.

"Look at my feet," said Peacock.

"No," said the man, hastily, putting out a free hand and catching Peacock by the arm. "I see what you mean. I was just interested in the theory."

1. A kind of firework that is ignited and revolves on a pin, making a wheel of fire or sparks, often called a pinwheel. The term also designates a spiked wheel used as an instrument of torture (named after Saint Catherine of Alexandria, from the wheel used to torture her.)

Peacock halted. He was offended. He shook the man's arm off.

"Nothing theoretical about it," he said, and shaking his sleeves added, "No paradox."

"No," said the man standing up and grabbing Peacock so that he could not fall. "I've got the idea." He looked at his watch. "Which way are you going? Can I give you a lift?"

Peacock was greatly offended. To be turned down! He nodded to the door of the ante-room: "Thanks," he said. "The President's waiting for me."

"The President's gone," said the man. "Oh well, good night." And he went away. Peacock watched him go. Even the men at the bar had gone. He was alone.

"But thanks," he called after him. "Thanks."

Cautiously Peacock sketched a course into the ante-room. It was a small, high room, quite empty and yet (one would have said), packed with voices, chattering, laughing and mixed with music along the panelled walls, but chiefly coming from behind the heavy green velvet curtains that were drawn across the window at one end. There were no mirrors, but Peacock had no need of them. The effect was ornate—gilded pillars at the corners, a small chandelier rising and falling gracefully from a carven ceiling. On the wall hung what, at first sight, seemed to be two large oil paintings of Queens of England but, on going closer, Peacock saw there was only one oil painting—of Queen Victoria.[2] Peacock considered it. The opportunity was enormous. Loyally, his face went blank. He swayed, loyally fell, and loyally got to his feet. The Queen might or might not have clapped her little hands. So encouraged, he fell again and got up. She was still sitting there.

Shel, said Peacock aloud to the Queen, has often acted before royalty. He's in Hollywood now, having left me to settle all his tax affairs. Hundreds of documents. All lies, of course. And there is this case for alimony going on. He's had four wives, he said to Queen Victoria. That's the side of theatre life I couldn't stand, even when we were boys. I could see it coming. But—watch me, he said.

And delightfully he crumpled, the perfect backwards spin. Leaning up on his elbow from where he was lying he waited for her to speak.

She did not speak, but two or three other queens joined her, all crowding and gossiping together, as Peacock got up. The Royal Box! It was full. Cars hooting outside the window behind the velvet curtains had the effect of an orchestra and then, inevitably, those heavy green curtains were drawn up. A dark, packed and restless auditorium opened itself to him. There was dense applause.

Peacock stepped forward in awe and wholeness. Not to fall, not to fall, this time, he murmured. To bow. One must bow and bow and bow and not fall, to the applause. He set out. It was a strangely long up-hill journey towards the footlights and not until he got there did it occur to him that he did not know how to bow. Shel had never taught him. Indeed, at the first attempt the floor came up and hit him in the face.

2. Victoria (1819–1901) was queen of England from 1837 to 1901.

# PHILIP ROTH

*Roth (1933– ) was born in Newark, New Jersey, and was educated at Bucknell University and the University of Chicago. He attracted serious critical attention from the time his first stories began to appear in magazines, and his first book,* Goodbye, Columbus *(1959), a novella and collection of stories, was a prizewinner that established him as a major writer. Since then he has demonstrated his mastery of form in the well-made novel* When She Was Good *(1967) and his gift for ribald, acid comedy in* Portnoy's Complaint *(1969). Roth has collected many awards and has taught intermittently at a number of universities. His other books include* The Breast *(1972),* My Life as a Man *(1974),* The Professor of Desire *(1977),* The Ghost Writer *(1979),* Zuckerman Unbound *(1981), and* The Anatomy Lesson *(1983). His collection* Zuckerman Bound *(1985) includes the previous three novels plus the novella* The Prague Orgy. *His recent books include* The Counterlife *(1987);* Deception *(1990);* Operation Shylock *(1993);* Sabbath's Theater *(1995), for which he received the National Book Award;* American Pastoral *(1997); and* I Married a Communist *(1998).*

## The Conversion of the Jews

"You're a real one for opening your mouth in the first place," Itzie said. "What do you open your mouth all the time for?"

"I didn't bring it up, Itz, I didn't," Ozzie said.

"What do you care about Jesus Christ for anyway?"

"I didn't bring up Jesus Christ. He did. I didn't even know what he was talking about. Jesus is historical, he kept saying. Jesus is historical." Ozzie mimicked the monumental voice of Rabbi Binder.

"Jesus was a person that lived like you and me," Ozzie continued. "That's what Binder said—"

"Yeah? . . . So what! What do I give two cents whether he lived or not. And what do you gotta open your mouth!" Itzie Lieberman favored closed-mouthedness, especially when it came to Ozzie Freedman's questions. Mrs. Freedman had to see Rabbi Binder twice before about Ozzie's questions and this Wednesday at four-thirty would be the third time. Itzie preferred to keep *his* mother in the kitchen; he settled for behind-the-back subtleties such as gestures, faces, snarls and other less delicate barnyard noises.

"He was a real person, Jesus, but he wasn't like God, and we don't believe he is God." Slowly, Ozzie was explaining Rabbi Binder's position to Itzie, who had been absent from Hebrew School the previous afternoon.

"The Catholics," Itzie said helpfully, "they believe in Jesus Christ, that he's God." Itzie Lieberman used "the Catholics" in its broadest sense—to include the Protestants.

Ozzie received Itzie's remark with a tiny head bob, as though it were a footnote, and went on. "His mother was Mary, and his father probably was Joseph," Ozzie said. "But the New Testament says his real father was God."

"His *real* father?"

"Yeah," Ozzie said, "that's the big thing, his father's supposed to be God."

"Bull."

"That's what Rabbi Binder says, that it's impossible—"

"Sure it's impossible. That stuff's all bull. To have a baby you gotta get laid," Itzie theologized. "Mary hadda get laid."

"That's what Binder says: 'The only way a woman can have a baby is to have intercourse with a man.' "

"He said *that,* Ozz?" For a moment it appeared that Itzie had put the theological question aside. "He said that, intercourse?" A little curled smile shaped itself in the lower half of Itzie's face like a pink mustache. "What you guys do, Ozz, you laugh or something?"

"I raised my hand."

"Yeah? Whatja say?"

"That's when I asked the question."

Itzie's face lit up. "Whatja ask about—intercourse?"

"No, I asked the question about God, how if He could create the heaven and earth in six days, and make all the animals and the fish and the light in six days—the light especially, that's what always gets me, that He could make the light. Making fish and animals, that's pretty good—"

"That's damn good." Itzie's appreciation was honest but unimaginative: it was as though God had just pitched a one-hitter.

"But making light . . . I mean when you think about it, it's really something," Ozzie said. "Anyway, I asked Binder if He could make all that in six days, and He could *pick* the six days he wanted right out of nowhere, why couldn't He let a woman have a baby without having intercourse."

"You said intercourse, Ozz, to Binder?"

"Yeah."

"Right in class?"

"Yeah."

Itzie smacked the side of his head.

"I mean, no kidding around," Ozzie said, "that'd really be nothing. After all that other stuff, that'd practically be nothing."

Itzie considered a moment. "What'd Binder say?"

"He started all over again explaining how Jesus was historical and how he lived like you and me but he wasn't God. So I said I under*stood* that. What I wanted to know was different."

What Ozzie wanted to know was always different. The first time he had wanted to know how Rabbi Binder could call the Jews "The Chosen People" if the Declaration of Independence claimed all men to be created equal. Rabbi

Binder tried to distinguish for him between political equality and spiritual legitimacy, but what Ozzie wanted to know, he insisted vehemently, was different. That was the first time his mother had to come.

Then there was the plane crash. Fifty-eight people had been killed in a plane crash at La Guardia.[1] In studying a casualty list in the newspaper his mother had discovered among the list of those dead eight Jewish names (his grandmother had nine but she counted Miller as a Jewish name); because of the eight she said the plane crash was "a tragedy." During free-discussion time on Wednesday Ozzie had brought to Rabbi Binder's attention this matter of "some of his relations" always picking out the Jewish names. Rabbi Binder had begun to explain cultural unity and some other things when Ozzie stood up at his seat and said that what he wanted to know was different. Rabbi Binder insisted that he sit down and it was then that Ozzie shouted that he wished all fifty-eight were Jews. That was the second time his mother came.

"And he kept explaining about Jesus being historical, and so I kept asking him. No kidding, Itz, he was trying to make me look stupid."

"So what he finally do?"

"Finally he starts screaming that I was deliberately simple-minded and a wise guy, and that my mother had to come, and this was the last time. And that I'd never get bar-mitzvahed[2] if he could help it. Then, Itz, then he starts talking in that voice like a statue, real slow and deep, and he says that I better think over what I said about the Lord. He told me to go to his office and think it over." Ozzie leaned his body towards Itzie. "Itz, I thought it over for a solid hour, and now I'm convinced God could do it."

Ozzie had planned to confess his latest transgression to his mother as soon as she came home from work. But it was a Friday night in November and already dark, and when Mrs. Freedman came through the door she tossed off her coat, kissed Ozzie quickly on the face, and went to the kitchen table to light the three yellow candles, two for the Sabbath and one for Ozzie's father.

When his mother lit the candles she would move her two arms slowly towards her, dragging them through the air, as though persuading people whose minds were half made up. And her eyes would get glassy with tears. Even when his father was alive Ozzie remembered that her eyes had gotten glassy, so it didn't have anything to do with his dying. It had something to do with lighting the candles.

As she touched the flaming match to the unlit wick of a Sabbath candle, the phone rang, and Ozzie, standing only a foot from it, plucked it off the receiver and held it muffled to his chest. When his mother lit candles Ozzie felt there should be no noise; even breathing, if you could manage it, should be softened. Ozzie pressed the phone to his breast and watched his mother dragging whatever she was dragging, and he felt his own eyes get glassy. His mother was a round, tired, gray-haired penguin of a woman whose gray skin had begun to feel the tug of gravity and the weight of her own history. Even

1. Airport in New York City. 2. The bar mitzvah is the Jewish initiation ceremony performed on a boy's thirteenth birthday, recognizing his acceptance of religious responsibility and duties.

when she was dressed up she didn't look like a chosen person. But when she lit candles she looked like something better; like a woman who knew momentarily that God could do anything.

After a few mysterious minutes she was finished. Ozzie hung up the phone and walked to the kitchen table where she was beginning to lay the two places for the four-course Sabbath meal. He told her that she would have to see Rabbi Binder next Wednesday at four-thirty, and then he told her why. For the first time in their life together she hit Ozzie across the face with her hand.

All through the chopped liver and chicken soup part of the dinner Ozzie cried; he didn't have any appetite for the rest.

On Wednesday, in the largest of the three basement classrooms of the synagogue, Rabbi Marvin Binder, a tall, handsome, broad-shouldered man of thirty with thick strong-fibered black hair, removed his watch from his pocket and saw that it was four o'clock. At the rear of the room Yakov Blotnik, the seventy-one-year-old custodian, slowly polished the large window, mumbling to himself, unaware that it was four o'clock or six o'clock, Monday or Wednesday. To most of the students Yakov Blotnik's mumbling, along with his brown curly beard, scythe nose, and two heel-trailing black cats, made of him an object of wonder, a foreigner, a relic, towards whom they were alternately fearful and disrespectful. To Ozzie the mumbling had always seemed a monotonous, curious prayer; what made it curious was the old Blotnik had been mumbling so steadily for so many years, Ozzie suspected he had memorized the prayers and forgotten all about God.

"It is now free-discussion time," Rabbi Binder said. "Feel free to talk about any Jewish matter at all—religion, family, politics, sports—"

There was silence. It was a gusty, clouded November afternoon and it did not seem as though there ever was or could be a thing called baseball. So nobody this week said a word about that hero from the past, Hank Greenberg[3]—which limited free discussion considerably.

And the soul-battering Ozzie Freedman had just received from Rabbi Binder had imposed its limitation. When it was Ozzie's turn to read aloud from the Hebrew book the rabbi had asked him petulantly why he didn't read more rapidly. He was showing no progress. Ozzie said he could read faster but that if he did he was sure not to understand what he was reading. Nevertheless, at the rabbi's repeated suggestion Ozzie tried, and showed a great talent, but in the midst of a long passage he stopped short and said he didn't understand a word he was reading, and started in again at a drag-footed pace. Then came the soul-battering.

Consequently when free-discussion time rolled around none of the students felt too free. The rabbi's invitation was answered only by the mumbling of feeble old Blotnik.

"Isn't there anything at all you would like to discuss?" Rabbi Binder asked again, looking at his watch. "No questions or comments?"

There was a small grumble from the third row. The rabbi requested that

3. Jewish baseball star, with the Detroit Tigers, 1934–45.

Ozzie rise and give the rest of the class the advantage of his thought.

Ozzie rose. "I forget it now," he said, and sat down in his place.

Rabbi Binder advanced a seat towards Ozzie and poised himself on the edge of the desk. It was Itzie's desk and the rabbi's frame only a dagger's-length away from his face snapped him to sitting attention.

"Stand up again, Oscar," Rabbi Binder said calmly, "and try to assemble your thoughts."

Ozzie stood up. All his classmates turned in their seats and watched as he gave an unconvincing scratch to his forehead.

"I can't assemble any," he announced, and plunked himself down.

"Stand up!" Rabbi Binder advanced from Itzie's desk to the one directly in front of Ozzie; when the rabbinical back was turned Itzie gave it five-fingers off the tip of his nose, causing a small titter in the room. Rabbi Binder was too absorbed in squelching Ozzie's nonsense once and for all to bother with titters. "Stand up, Oscar. What's your question about?"

Ozzie pulled a word out of the air. It was the handiest word. "Religion."

"Oh, now you remember?"

"Yes."

"What is it?"

Trapped, Ozzie blurted the first thing that came to him. "Why can't He make anything He wants to make!"

As Rabbi Binder prepared an answer, a final answer, Itzie, ten feet behind him, raised one finger on his left hand, gestured it meaningfully towards the rabbi's back, and brought the house down.

Binder twisted quickly to see what had happened and in the midst of the commotion Ozzie shouted into the rabbi's back what he couldn't have shouted to his face. It was a loud, toneless sound that had the timbre of something stored inside for about six days.

"You don't know! You don't know anything about God!"

The rabbi spun back towards Ozzie. "What?"

"You don't know—you don't—"

"Apologize, Oscar, apologize!" It was a threat.

"You don't—"

Rabbi Binder's hand flicked out at Ozzie's cheek. Perhaps it had only been meant to clamp the boy's mouth shut, but Ozzie ducked and the palm caught him squarely on the nose.

The blood came in a short, red spurt on to Ozzie's shirt front.

The next moment was all confusion. Ozzie screamed, "You bastard, you bastard!" and broke for the classroom door. Rabbi Binder lurched a step backwards, as though his own blood had started flowing violently in the opposite direction, then gave a clumsy lurch forward and bolted out the door after Ozzie. The class followed after the rabbi's huge blue-suited back, and before old Blotnik could turn from his window, the room was empty and everyone was headed full speed up the three flights leading to the roof.

If one should compare the light of day to the life of man: sunrise to birth; sunset—the dropping down over the edge—to death; then as Ozzie Freedman wiggled through the trapdoor of the synagogue roof, his feet kicking backwards bronco-style at Rabbi Binder's outstretched arms—at that moment the day was fifty years old. As a rule, fifty or fifty-five reflects accurately the age of late afternoons in November, for it is in that month, during those hours, that one's awareness of light seems no longer a matter of seeing, but of hearing: light begins clicking away. In fact, as Ozzie locked shut the trapdoor in the rabbi's face, the sharp click of the bolt into the lock might momentarily have been mistaken for the sound of the heavier gray that had just throbbed through the sky.

With all his weight Ozzie kneeled on the locked door; any instant he was certain that Rabbi Binder's shoulder would fling it open, splintering the wood into shrapnel and catapulting his body into the sky. But the door did not move and below him he heard only the rumble of feet, first loud then dim, like thunder rolling away.

A question shot through his brain. "Can this be *me*?" For a thirteen-year-old who had just labeled his religious leader a bastard, twice, it was not an improper question. Louder and louder the question came to him—"Is it me? Is it me?"—until he discovered himself no longer kneeling, but racing crazily towards the edge of the roof, his eyes crying, his throat screaming, and his arms flying everywhichway as though not his own.

"Is it me? Is it me ME ME ME ME! It has to be me—but is it!"

It is the question a thief must ask himself the night he jimmies open his first window, and it is said to be the question with which bridegrooms quiz themselves before the altar.

In the few wild seconds it took Ozzie's body to propel him to the edge of the roof, his self-examination began to grow fuzzy. Gazing down at the street, he became confused as to the problem beneath the question: was it, is-it-me-who-called-Binder-a-bastard? or, is-it-me-prancing-around-on-the-roof? However, the scene below settled all, for there is an instant in any action when whether it is you or somebody else is academic. The thief crams the money in his pockets and scoots out the window. The bridegroom signs the hotel register for two. And the boy on the roof finds a streetful of people gaping at him, necks stretched backwards, faces up, as though he were the ceiling of the Hayden Planetarium.[4] Suddenly you know it's you.

"Oscar! Oscar Freedman!" A voice rose from the center of the crowd, a voice that, could it have been seen, would have looked like the writing on a scroll. "Oscar Freedman, get down from there. Immediately!" Rabbi Binder was pointing one arm stiffly up at him; and at the end of that arm, one finger aimed menacingly. It was the attitude of a dictator, but one—the eyes confessed all—whose personal valet had spit neatly in his face.

Ozzie didn't answer. Only for a blink's length did he look towards Rabbi Binder. Instead his eyes began to fit together the world beneath him, to sort out people from places, friends from enemies, participants from spectators. In little jagged starlike clusters his friends stood around Rabbi Binder, who was

4. An auditorium with a domed ceiling on which movements of stars and constellations are projected with spots of light, in New York City.

still pointing. The topmost point on a star compounded not of angels but of five adolescent boys with Itzie. What a world it was, with those stars below, Rabbi Binder below . . . Ozzie, who a moment earlier hadn't been able to control his own body, started to feel the meaning of the word control: he felt Peace and he felt Power.

"Oscar Freedman, I'll give you three to come down."

Few dictators give their subjects three to do anything; but, as always, Rabbi Binder only looked dictatorial.

"Are you ready, Oscar?"

Ozzie nodded his head yes, although he had no intention in the world—the lower one or the celestial one he'd just entered—of coming down even if Rabbi Binder should give him a million.

"All right then," said Rabbi Binder. He ran a hand through his black Samson hair as though it were the gesture prescribed for uttering the first digit. Then, with his other hand cutting a circle out of the small piece of sky around him, he spoke. "One!"

There was no thunder. On the contrary, at that moment, as though "one" was the cue for which he had been waiting, the world's least thunderous person appeared on the synagogue steps. He did not so much come out the synagogue door as lean out, onto the darkening air. He clutched at the doorknob with one hand and looked up at the roof.

"Oy!"

Yakov Blotnik's old mind hobbled slowly, as if on crutches, and though he couldn't decide precisely what the boy was doing on the roof, he knew it wasn't good—that is, it wasn't-good-for-the-Jews. For Yakov Blotnik life had fractionated itself simply: things were either good-for-the-Jews or no-good-for-the-Jews.

He smacked his free hand to his in-sucked cheek, gently. "Oy, Gut!"[5] And then quickly as he was able, he jacked down his head and surveyed the street. There was Rabbi Binder (like a man at an auction with only three dollars in his pocket, he had just delivered a shaky "Two!"); there were the students, and that was all. So far it-wasn't-so-bad-for-the-Jews. But the boy had to come down immediately, before anybody saw. The problem: how to get the boy off the roof?

Anybody who has ever had a cat on the roof knows how to get him down. You call the fire department. Or first you call the operator and you ask her for the fire department. And the next thing there is great jamming of brakes and clanging of bells and shouting of instructions. And then the cat is off the roof. You do the same thing to get a boy off the roof.

That is, you do the same thing if you are Yakov Blotnik and you once had a cat on the roof.

When the engines, all four of them, arrived, Rabbi Binder had four times given Ozzie the count of three. The big hook-and-ladder swung around the corner and one of the firemen leaped from it, plunging headlong towards the

5. Oh, God! (Yiddish).

yellow fire hydrant in front of the synagogue. With a huge wrench he began to unscrew the top nozzle. Rabbi Binder raced over to him and pulled at his shoulder.

"There's no fire . . ."

The fireman mumbled back over his shoulder and, heatedly, continued working at the nozzle.

"But there's no fire, there's no fire . . ." Binder shouted. When the fireman mumbled again, the rabbi grasped his face with both his hands and pointed it up at the roof.

To Ozzie it looked as though Rabbi Binder was trying to tug the fireman's head out of his body, like a cork from a bottle. He had to giggle at the picture they made: it was a family portrait—rabbi in black skullcap, fireman in red fire hat, and the little yellow hydrant squatting beside like a kid brother, bareheaded. From the edge of the roof Ozzie waved at the portrait, a one-handed, flapping, mocking wave; in doing it his right foot slipped from under him. Rabbi Binder covered his eyes with his hands.

Firemen work fast. Before Ozzie had even regained his balance, a big, round, yellowed net was being held on the synagogue lawn. The firemen who held it looked up at Ozzie with stern, feelingless faces.

One of the firemen turned his head towards Rabbi Binder. "What, is the kid nuts or something?"

Rabbi Binder unpeeled his hands from his eyes, slowly, painfully, as if they were tape. Then he checked: nothing on the sidewalk, no dents in the net.

"Is he gonna jump, or what?" the fireman shouted.

In a voice not at all like a statue, Rabbi Binder finally answered. "Yes, yes, I think so . . . He's been threatening to . . ."

Threatening to? Why, the reason he was on the roof, Ozzie remembered, was to get away; he hadn't even thought about jumping. He had just run to get away, and the truth was that he hadn't really headed for the roof as much as he'd been chased there.

"What's his name, the kid?"

"Freedman," Rabbi Binder answered. "Oscar Freedman."

The fireman looked up at Ozzie. "What is it with you, Oscar? You gonna jump, or what?"

Ozzie did not answer. Frankly, the question had just arisen.

"Look, Oscar, if you're gonna jump, jump—and if you're not gonna jump, don't jump. But don't waste our time, willya?"

Ozzie looked at the fireman and then at Rabbi Binder. He wanted to see Rabbi Binder cover his eyes one more time.

"I'm going to jump."

And then he scampered around the edge of the roof to the corner, where there was no net below, and he flapped his arms at his sides, swishing the air and smacking his palms to his trousers on the downbeat. He began screaming like some kind of engine, "Wheeeee . . . wheeeeee," and leaning way out over the edge with the upper half of his body. The firemen whipped around to cover the ground with the net. Rabbi Binder mumbled a few words to Somebody and covered his eyes. Everything happened quickly, jerkily, as in a silent movie.

The crowd, which had arrived with the fire engines, gave out a long, Fourth-of-July fireworks oooh-aahhh. In the excitement no one had paid the crowd much heed, except, of course, Yakov Blotnik, who swung from the doorknob counting heads. "Fier und tsvansik . . . finf und tsvantsik[6] . . . Oy, Gut!" It wasn't like this with the cat.

Rabbi Binder peeked through his fingers, checked the sidewalk and net. Empty. But there was Ozzie racing to the other corner. The firemen raced with him but were unable to keep up. Whenever Ozzie wanted to he might jump and splatter himself upon the sidewalk, and by the time the firemen scooted to the spot all they could do with their net would be to cover the mess.

"Wheeeee . . . wheeeee . . ."

"Hey, Oscar," the winded fireman yelled, "What the hell is this, a game or something?"

"Wheeeee . . . wheeeee . . ."

"Hey, Oscar—"

But he was off now to the other corner, flapping his wings fiercely. Rabbi Binder couldn't take it any longer—the fire engines from nowhere, the screaming suicidal boy, the net. He fell to his knees, exhausted, and with his hands curled together in front of his chest, like a little dome, he pleaded, "Oscar, stop it, Oscar. Don't jump, Oscar. Please come down . . . Please don't jump."

And further back in the crowd a single voice, a single young voice, shouted a lone word to the boy on the roof.

"Jump!"

It was Itzie. Ozzie momentarily stopped flapping.

"Go ahead, Ozz—jump!"

Itzie broke off his point of the star and courageously, with the inspiration not of a wise-guy but of a disciple, stood alone. "Jump, Ozz, jump!"

Still on his knees, his hands still curled, Rabbi Binder twisted his body back. He looked at Itzie, then, agonizingly, back to Ozzie.

"OSCAR, DON'T JUMP! PLEASE, DON'T JUMP . . . please please . . ."

"Jump!" This time it wasn't Itzie but another point of the star. By the time Mrs. Freedman arrived to keep her four-thirty appointment with Rabbi Binder, the whole little upside down heaven was shouting and pleading for Ozzie to jump, and Rabbi Binder no longer was pleading with him not to jump, but was crying into the dome of his hands.

Understandably Mrs. Freedman couldn't figure out what her son was doing on the roof. So she asked.

"Ozzie, my Ozzie, what are you doing? My Ozzie, what is it?"

Ozzie stopped wheeeeeing and slowed his arms down to a cruising flap, the kind birds use in soft winds, but he did not answer. He stood against the low, clouded, darkening sky—light clicked down swiftly now, as on a small gear—flapping softly and gazing down at the small bundle of a woman who was his mother.

"What are you doing, Ozzie?" She turned towards the kneeling Rabbi

6. Twenty-four . . . twenty-five . . . (Yiddish).

Binder and rushed so close that only a paper-thickness of dusk lay between her stomach and his shoulders.

"What is my baby doing?"

Rabbi Binder gaped up at her but he too was mute. All that moved was the dome of his hands; it shook back and forth like a weak pulse.

"Rabbi, get him down! He'll kill himself. Get him down, my only baby . . ."

"I can't," Rabbi Binder said, "I can't . . ." and he turned his handsome head towards the crowd of boys behind him. "It's them. Listen to them."

And for the first time Mrs. Freedman saw the crowd of boys, and she heard what they were yelling.

"He's doing it for them. He won't listen to me. It's them." Rabbi Binder spoke like one in a trance.

"For them?"

"Yes."

"Why for them?"

"They want him to . . ."

Mrs. Freedman raised her two arms upward as though she were conducting the sky. "For them he's doing it!" And then in a gesture older than pyramids, older than prophets and floods, her arms came slapping down to her sides. "A martyr I have. Look!" She tilted her head to the roof. Ozzie was still flapping softly. "My martyr."

"Oscar, come down, *please,*" Rabbi Binder groaned.

In a startlingly even voice Mrs. Freedman called to the boy on the roof. "Ozzie, come down, Ozzie. Don't be a martyr, my baby."

As though it were a litany, Rabbi Binder repeated her words. "Don't be a martyr, my baby. Don't be a martyr."

"Gawhead, Ozz—*be* a Martin!" It was Itzie. "Be a Martin, be a Martin," and all the voices joined in singing for Martindom, whatever *it* was. "Be a Martin, be a Martin . . ."

Somehow when you're on a roof the darker it gets the less you can hear. All Ozzie knew was that two groups wanted two new things: his friends were spirited and musical about what they wanted; his mother and the rabbi were even-toned, chanting, about what they didn't want. The rabbi's voice was without tears now and so was his mother's.

The big net stared up at Ozzie like a sightless eye. The big, clouded sky pushed down. From beneath it looked like a gray corrugated board. Suddenly, looking up into that unsympathetic sky, Ozzie realized all the strangeness of what these people, his friends, were asking: they wanted him to jump, to kill himself; they were singing about it now—it made them that happy. And there was an even greater strangeness: Rabbi Binder was on his knees, trembling. If there was a question to be asked now it was not "Is it me?" but rather "Is it us?. . . Is it us?"

Being on the roof, it turned out, was a serious thing. If he jumped would the singing become dancing? Would it? What would jumping stop? Yearningly, Ozzie wished he could rip open the sky, plunge his hands through, and pull out the sun; and on the sun, like a coin, would be stamped JUMP OR DON'T JUMP.

Ozzie's knees rocked and sagged a little under him as though they were setting him for a dive. His arms tightened, stiffened, froze, from shoulders to fingernails. He felt as if each part of his body were going to vote as to whether he should kill himself or not—and each part as though it were independent of *him.*

The light took an unexpected click down and the new darkness, like a gag, hushed the friends singing for this and the mother and rabbi chanting for that.

Ozzie stopped counting votes, and in a curiously high voice, like one who wasn't prepared for speech, he spoke.

"Mamma?"

"Yes, Oscar."

"Mamma, get down on your knees, like Rabbi Binder."

"Oscar—"

"Get down on your knees," he said, "or I'll jump."

Ozzie heard a whimper, then a quick rustling, and when he looked down where his mother had stood he saw the top of a head and beneath that a circle of dress. She was kneeling beside Rabbi Binder.

He spoke again. "Everybody kneel." There was the sound of everybody kneeling.

Ozzie looked around. With one hand he pointed towards the synagogue entrance. "Make *him* kneel."

There was a noise, not of kneeling, but of body-and-cloth stretching. Ozzie could hear Rabbi Binder saying in a gruff whisper, ". . . or he'll *kill* himself," and when next he looked there was Yakov Blotnik off the doorknob and for the first time in his life upon his knees in the Gentile posture of prayer.

As for the firemen—it was not as difficult as one might imagine to hold a net taut while you are kneeling.

Ozzie looked around again; and then he called to Rabbi Binder.

"Rabbi?"

"Yes, Oscar."

"Rabbi Binder, do you believe in God?"

"Yes."

"Do you believe God can do Anything?" Ozzie leaned his head out into the darkness. "Anything?"

"Oscar, I think—"

"Tell me you believe God can do Anything."

There was a second's hesitation. Then: "God can do Anything."

"Tell me you believe God can make a child without intercourse."

"He can."

"Tell me!"

"God," Rabbi Binder admitted, "can make a child without intercourse."

"Mamma, you tell me."

"God can make a child without intercourse," his mother said.

"Make *him* tell me." There was no doubt who *him* was.

In a few moments Ozzie heard an old comical voice say something to the increasing darkness about God.

Next, Ozzie made everybody say it. And then he made them all say they believed in Jesus Christ—first one at a time, then all together.

When the catechizing was through it was the beginning of evening. From the street it sounded as if the boy on the roof might have sighed.

"Ozzie?" A woman's voice dared to speak. "You'll come down now?"

There was no answer, but the woman waited, and when a voice finally did speak it was thin and crying, and exhausted as that of an old man who has just finished pulling the bells.

"Mamma, don't you see—you shouldn't hit me. He shouldn't hit me. You shouldn't hit me about God, Mamma. You should never hit anybody about God—"

"Ozzie, please come down now."

"Promise me, promise me you'll never hit anybody about God."

He had asked only his mother, but for some reason everyone kneeling in the street promised he would never hit anybody about God.

Once again there was silence.

"I can come down now, Mamma," the boy on the roof finally said. He turned his head both ways as though checking the traffic lights. "Now I can come down . . ."

And he did, right into the center of the yellow net that glowed in the evening's edge like an overgrown halo.

# Jo Sapp

*Sapp (1944– ) was born in San Antonio, Texas, to a military family. After a nomadic childhood, she moved to Columbia, Missouri, where she currently lives and writes. She is an editor of the* Missouri Review *and coeditor of* The Best of the Missouri Review Fiction: 1978–1990. *In 1997 she edited* Conversations with American Novelists, *published by the University of Missouri Press.*

## Nadine at 35: A Synopsis

The brain cells slip away, one by one by one. One hundred thousand of them a day, departing. If she is very still and concentrates very hard she can feel it happen. One by one by one, the cells descending to her rump. It is an exodus, a relocation. A mass conservation. Her brain is escaping.

And so, she discovers, is her husband.

"All I need is a little time," he says, his brown eyes wet and earnest as a cocker spaniel's. "Kind of a vacation from marriage. A year or two to find myself."

And she didn't even know he was lost.

She bounces back quickly. "So go," she says. "What the hell," her vocabulary impoverished already by virtue of the missing cells. She figures she has lost over twelve billion to date, and counting, but is uneasy about numbers, so might be wrong.

"What the hell," she says again, and helps him pack.

In retrospect she realizes that his defection might be related in cause to her word loss. He, too, is over thirty-five, and has, in fact, been losing cells for six months longer than she. His, at least, did not settle in his rump. She wonders exactly where they went, but cannot summon the energy to look for them. And she cannot ask him, for by the time she thinks of it he is halfway to California.

She sells the house and buys a car, gets a haircut, and prowls the bars. When she has the time. She cannot search for herself because, unlike her husband, she has yet to fully realize that she is lost. She would like to return to school, to become a nuclear engineer, or perhaps a dietitian. There is, however, a problem. Only two worn suits, a set of golf clubs, three monogrammed neckties, and a few billion brain cells were left behind by the vacating husband. The money he took.

So here she is, brain cells oozing out, slipping southward, with three children, a dog, two cats, and a goldfish. Hungry mouths. She does what any other right-thinking thirty-five-year-old American girl would do. She gets a job, subscribes to *Ms.,* deletes the word *girl,* along with *housewife* and *mankind,* from her vocabulary, further limiting it, and decides to take a lover. As for the children, she has an extra key to the apartment made for each of them and tells them to fend for themselves. That is the American way.

Finding a lover is difficult. Lovers for thirty-five-year-old brain-diminished vocabulary-impoverished women are in short supply. Particularly for those with three children and miscellaneous pets, even if they do all fend for themselves. So she resigns herself to celibacy, broken by occasional chance encounters and bouts of masturbation. It is a not altogether satisfactory life, but it has its rewards.

She finds, to her surprise, that she enjoys working, and is good at her job. She is a teller at a savings and loan. So friendly is she, so helpful, and so accurate in tabulating the amount of money in her drawer at day's end—never having to add a penny secretly or take away two—that in time she is promoted to New Accounts. She will go far, they tell her, and she knows they are right.

She makes more money now, and hires a housekeeper. The children and pets are fended for.

She controls the numbers of her life.

The second vice-president of the S&L invites her to dinner.

She accepts.

She is promoted to Business Loans.

The brain cells still escape, but she has no time to notice.

She has found herself without really looking.

And then one day the dog eats the goldfish and the cats get distemper. Her older boy steals a lace bra and the girl gets the measles. The younger boy sulks. The sink backs up in the bathroom and the housekeeper quits. She finds twelve gray hairs at her left temple and her life insurance lapses. Her husband always handled that sort of thing.

The second vice-president's wife calls her a name that she wishes had been deleted from her vocabulary, and she realizes she is no longer thirty-five. Then her husband telephones from Oregon where he has been working on a lumber crew and drinking beer and sleeping around since he left California and tells her he is tired of his vacation and wants to come home. She feels the cells slipping, and her rump widens alarmingly.

"What the hell," she says.

# Irwin Shaw

*Shaw (1913–1984) was born in New York City of Russian Jewish immigrants and educated at Brooklyn College. In the late 1930s he wrote stories for such magazines as* The New Yorker *and* Esquire. *These stories appeared in book form as* The Sailor Off the Bremen *in 1939 and* Welcome to the City *in 1942. The collections contain some of his best works, including* "The Girls in their Summer Dresses" *and* "The Eighty-Yard Run." *They are considered twentieth-century American classics. His stories are also collected in* Stories of Five Decades *(1978). Shaw's novels include* The Young Lions *(1958),* Voices of a Summer Day *(1965),* Rich Man, Poor Man *(1970), and* Evening in Byzantium *(1973). In his heyday Shaw was considered one of the very best American short-story writers and exerted considerable influence on the form.*

## The Eighty-Yard Run

The pass was high and wide and he jumped for it, feeling it slap flatly against his hands, as he shook his hips to throw off the halfback who was diving at him. The center floated by, his hands desperately brushing Darling's knee as Darling picked his feet up high and delicately ran over a blocker and an opposing linesman in a jumble on the ground near the scrimmage line. He had ten yards in the clear and picked up speed, breathing easily, feeling his thigh pads rising and falling against his legs, listening to the sound of cleats behind him, pulling away from them, watching the other backs heading him off toward the sideline, the whole picture, the men closing in on him, the blockers fighting for position, the ground he had to cross, all suddenly clear in his head, for the first time in his life not a meaningless confusion of men, sounds, speed. He smiled a little to himself as he ran, holding the ball lightly in front of him with his two hands, his knees pumping high, his hips twisting in the almost girlish run of a back in a broken field. The first halfback came at him and he fed him his leg, then swung at the last moment, took the shock of the man's shoulder without breaking stride, ran right through him, his cleats biting securely into the turf. There was only the safety man now, coming warily at him, his arms crooked, hands spread. Darling tucked the ball in, spurted at him, driving hard, hurling himself along, his legs pounding, knees high, all two hundred pounds bunched into controlled attack. He was sure he was going to get past the safety man. Without thought, his arms and legs working beautifully together, he headed right for the safety man, stiff-armed him, feeling blood spurt instantaneously from the man's nose onto his hand, seeing his face go awry, head turned, mouth pulled to one side. He pivoted away, keeping the arm locked, dropping the safety man as he ran easily toward the goal line, with the drumming of cleats diminishing behind him.

How long ago? It was autumn then, and the ground was getting hard because the nights were cold and leaves from the maples around the stadium blew across the practice fields in gusts of wind, and the girls were beginning to put polo coats over their sweaters when they came to watch practice in the afternoons. . . . Fifteen years. Darling walked slowly over the same ground in the spring twilight, in his neat shoes, a man of thirty-five dressed in a double-breasted suit, ten pounds heavier in the fifteen years, but not fat, with the years between 1925 and 1940 showing in his face.

The coach was smiling quietly to himself and the assistant coaches were looking at each other with pleasure the way they always did when one of the second stringers suddenly did something fine, bringing credit to them, making their $2,000 a year a tiny bit more secure.

Darling trotted back, smiling, breathing deeply but easily, feeling wonderful, not tired, though this was the tail end of practice and he'd run eighty yards. The sweat poured off his face and soaked his jersey and he liked the feeling, the warm moistness lubricating his skin like oil. Off in a corner of the field some players were punting and the smack of leather against the ball came pleasantly through the afternoon air. The freshmen were running signals on the next field and the quarterback's sharp voice, the pound of the eleven pairs of cleats, the "Dig, now *dig!*" of the coaches, the laughter of the players all somehow made him feel happy as he trotted back to midfield, listening to the applause and shouts of the students along the sidelines, knowing that after that run the coach would have to start him Saturday against Illinois.

Fifteen years, Darling thought, remembering the shower after the workout, the hot water steaming off his skin and the deep soapsuds and all the young voices singing with the water streaming down and towels going and managers running in and out and the sharp sweet smell of oil of wintergreen and everybody clapping him on the back as he dressed and Packard, the captain, who took being captain very seriously, coming over to him and shaking his hand and saying, "Darling, you're going to go places in the next two years."

The assistant manager fussed over him, wiping a cut on his leg with alcohol and iodine, the little sting making him realize suddenly how fresh and whole and solid his body felt. The manager slapped a piece of adhesive tape over the cut, and Darling noticed the sharp clean white of the tape against the ruddiness of the skin, fresh from the shower.

He dressed slowly, the softness of his shirt and the soft warmth of his wool socks and his flannel trousers a reward against his skin after the harsh pressure of the shoulder harness and thigh and hip pads. He drank three glasses of cold water, the liquid reaching down coldly inside of him, soothing the harsh dry places in his throat and belly left by the sweat and running and shouting of practice.

Fifteen years.

The sun had gone down and the sky was green behind the stadium and he laughed quietly to himself as he looked at the stadium, rearing above the trees, and knew that on Saturday when the 70,000 voices roared as the team came running out onto the field, part of that enormous salute would be for him. He walked slowly, listening to the gravel crunch satisfactorily under his shoes in the still twilight, feeling his clothes swing lightly against his skin, breathing the thin evening air, feeling the wind move softly in his damp hair, wonderfully cool behind his ears and at the nape of his neck.

Louise was waiting for him at the road, in her car. The top was down and he noticed all over again, as he always did when he saw her, how pretty she was, the rough blonde hair and the large, inquiring eyes and the bright mouth, smiling now.

She threw the door open. "Were you good today?" she asked.

"Pretty good," he said. He climbed in, sank luxuriously into the soft leather, stretched his legs far out. He smiled, thinking of the eighty yards. "Pretty damn good."

She looked at him seriously for a moment, then scrambled around, like a little girl, kneeling on the seat next to him, grabbed him, her hands along his ears, and kissed him as he sprawled, head back, on the seat cushion. She let go of him, but kept her head close to his, over his. Darling reached up slowly and rubbed the back of his hand against her cheek, lit softly by a street lamp a hundred feet away. They looked at each other, smiling.

Louise drove down to the lake and they sat there silently, watching the moon rise behind the hills on the other side. Finally he reached over, pulled her gently to him, kissed her. Her lips grew soft, her body sank into his, tears formed slowly in her eyes. He knew, for the first time, that he could do whatever he wanted with her.

"Tonight," he said. "I'll call for you at seven-thirty. Can you get out?"

She looked at him. She was smiling, but the tears were still full in her eyes. "All right," she said. "I'll get out. How about you? Won't the coach raise hell?"

Darling grinned. "I got the coach in the palm of my hand," he said. "Can you wait till seven-thirty?"

She grinned back at him. "No," she said.

They kissed and she started the car and they went back to town for dinner. He sang on the way home.

Christian Darling, thirty-five years old, sat on the frail spring grass, greener now than it ever would be again on the practice field, looked thoughtfully up at the stadium, a deserted ruin in the twilight. He had started on the first team that Saturday and every Saturday after that for the next two years, but it had never been as satisfactory as it should have been. He never had broken away, the longest run he'd ever made was thirty-five yards, and that in a game that was already won, and then that kid had come up from the third team, Diederich, a blank-faced German kid from Wisconsin, who ran like a bull, ripping lines to pieces Saturday after Saturday, plowing through, never getting hurt, never changing his expression, scoring more points, gaining more ground than all the rest of the team put together, making everybody's All-American, carrying the ball three times out of four, keeping everybody else out of the headlines. Darling was a good blocker and he spent his Saturday afternoons working on the big Swedes and Polacks who played tackle and end for Michigan, Illinois, Purdue, hurling into huge pile-ups, bobbing his head wildly to elude the great raw hands swinging like meat-cleavers at him as he went charging in to open up holes for Diederich coming through like a locomotive behind him. Still, it wasn't so bad. Everybody liked him and he did his job and he was pointed out on the campus and boys always felt important when they introduced their girls to him at their proms, and Louise loved him and watched him faithfully in the games, even in the mud, when your own mother wouldn't know you, and drove him around in her car keeping the top down because she was proud of him and wanted to show everybody that she was Christian Darling's girl. She bought him crazy presents because her father was rich, watches, pipes, humidors, an icebox for beer for his room, curtains, wallets, a fifty-dollar dictionary.

"You'll spend every cent your old man owns," Darling protested once when she showed up at his rooms with seven different packages in her arms and tossed them onto the couch.

"Kiss me," Louise said, "and shut up."

"Do you want to break your poor old man?"

"I don't mind. I want to buy you presents."

"Why?"

"It makes me feel good. Kiss me. I don't know why. Did you know that you're an important figure?"

"Yes," Darling said gravely.

"When I was waiting for you at the library yesterday two girls saw you coming and one of them said to the other, 'That's Christian Darling. He's an important figure.' "

"You're a liar."

"I'm in love with an important figure."

"Still, why the hell did you have to give me a forty-pound dictionary?"

"I wanted to make sure," Louise said, "that you had a token of my esteem. I want to smother you in tokens of my esteem."

Fifteen years ago.

They'd married when they got out of college. There'd been other women for him, but all casual and secret, more for curiosity's sake, and vanity, women who'd thrown themselves at him and flattered him, a pretty mother at a summer camp for boys, an old girl from his home town who'd suddenly blossomed into a coquette, a friend of Louise's who had dogged him grimly for six months and had taken advantage of the two weeks that Louise went home when her mother died. Perhaps Louise had known, but she'd kept quiet, loving him completely, filling his rooms with presents, religiously watching him battling with the big Swedes and Polacks on the line of scrimmage on Saturday afternoons, making plans for marrying him and living with him in New York and going with him there to the night clubs, the theaters, the good restaurants, being proud of him in advance, tall, white-teethed, smiling, large, yet moving lightly, with an athlete's grace, dressed in evening clothes, approvingly eyed by magnificently dressed and famous women in theater lobbies, with Louise adoringly at his side.

Her father, who manufactured inks, set up a New York office for Darling to manage and presented him with three hundred accounts, and they lived on Beekman Place with a view of the river with fifteen thousand dollars a year between them, because everybody was buying everything in those days, including ink. They saw all the shows and went to all the speakeasies and spent their fifteen thousand dollars a year and in the afternoons Louise went to the art galleries and the matinees of the more serious plays that Darling didn't like to sit through and Darling slept with a girl who danced in the chorus of *Rosalie* and with the wife of a man who owned three copper mines. Darling played squash three times a week and remained as solid as a stone barn and Louise never took her eyes off him when they were in the same room together, watching him with a secret, miser's smile, with a trick of coming over to him in the middle of a crowded room and saying gravely, in a low voice, "You're the handsomest man I've ever seen in my whole life. Want a drink?"

Nineteen twenty-nine came to Darling and to his wife and father-in-law, the maker of inks, just as it came to everyone else. The father-in-law waited until 1933 and then blew his brains out and when Darling went to Chicago to see what the 1933 books of the firm looked like he found out all that was left were debts and three or four gallons of unbought ink.

"Please, Christian," Louise said, sitting in their neat Beekman Place apartment, with a view of the river and prints of paintings by Dufy and Braque and Picasso[1] on the wall, "please, why do you want to start drinking at two o'clock in the afternoon?"

"I have nothing else to do," Darling said, putting down his glass, emptied of its fourth drink. "Please pass the whisky."

Louise filled his glass. "Come take a walk with me," she said. "We'll walk along the river."

"I don't want to walk along the river," Darling said, squinting intensely at the prints of paintings by Dufy, Braque and Picasso.

"We'll walk along Fifth Avenue."

"I don't want to walk along Fifth Avenue."

"Maybe," Louise said gently, "you'd like to come with me to some art galleries. There's an exhibition by a man named Klee.[2]. . ."

"I don't want to go to any art galleries. I want to sit here and drink Scotch whisky," Darling said. "Who the hell hung those goddam pictures up on the wall?"

"I did," Louise said.

"I hate them."

"I'll take them down," Louise said.

"Leave them there. It gives me something to do in the afternoon. I can hate them." Darling took a long swallow. "Is that the way people paint these days?"

"Yes, Christian. Please don't drink any more."

"Do you like painting like that?"

"Yes, dear."

1. Pablo Picasso (1881–1973), Spanish painter and sculptor Roaul Dufy (1877–1953), French painter. Georges Braque, (1882–1963), French painter. 2. Paul Klee (1879–1940), Swiss abstract painter.

"Really?"

"Really."

Darling looked carefully at the prints once more. "Little Louise Tucker. The middle-western beauty. I like pictures with horses in them. Why should you like pictures like that?"

"I just happen to have gone to a lot of galleries in the last few years . . ."

"Is that what you do in the afternoon?"

"That's what I do in the afternoon," Louise said.

"I drink in the afternoon."

Louise kissed him lightly on the top of his head as he sat there squinting at the pictures on the wall, the glass of whisky held firmly in his hand. She put on her coat and went out without saying another word. When she came back in the early evening, she had a job on a woman's fashion magazine.

They moved downtown and Louise went out to work every morning and Darling sat home and drank and Louise paid the bills as they came up. She made believe she was going to quit work as soon as Darling found a job, even though she was taking over more responsibility day by day at the magazine, interviewing authors, picking painters for the illustrations and covers, getting actresses to pose for pictures, going out for drinks with the right people, making a thousand new friends whom she loyally introduced to Darling.

"I don't like your hat," Darling said, once, when she came in in the evening and kissed him, her breath rich with Martinis.

"What's the matter with my hat, Baby?" she asked, running her fingers through his hair. "Everybody says it's very smart."

"It's too damned smart," he said. "It's not for you. It's for a rich, sophisticated woman of thirty-five with admirers."

Louise laughed. "I'm practicing to be a rich, sophisticated woman of thirty-five with admirers," she said. He stared soberly at her. "Now, don't look so grim, Baby. It's still the same simple little wife under the hat." She took the hat off, threw it into a corner, sat on his lap. "See? Homebody Number One."

"Your breath could run a train," Darling said, not wanting to be mean, but talking out of boredom, and sudden shock at seeing his wife curiously a stranger in a new hat, with a new expression in her eyes under the little brim, secret, confident, knowing.

Louise tucked her head under his chin so he couldn't smell her breath. "I had to take an author out for cocktails," she said. "He's a boy from the Ozark Mountains and he drinks like a fish. He's a Communist."

"What the hell is a Communist from the Ozarks doing writing for a woman's fashion magazine?"

Louise chuckled. "The magazine business is getting all mixed up these days. The publishers want to have a foot in every camp. And anyway, you can't find an author under seventy these days who isn't a Communist."

"I don't think I like you to associate with all those people, Louise," Darling said. "Drinking with them."

"He's a very nice, gentle boy," Louise said. "He reads Ernest Dowson."

"Who's Ernest Dowson?"

Louise patted his arm, stood up, fixed her hair. "He's an English poet."

Darling felt that somehow he had disappointed her. "Am I supposed to know who Ernest Dowson is?"

"No, dear. I'd better go in and take a bath."

After she had gone, Darling went over to the corner where the hat was lying and picked it up. It was nothing, a scrap of straw, a red flower, a veil, meaningless on his big hand, but on his wife's head a signal of something . . . big city, smart and knowing women drinking and dining with men other than their husbands, conversation about things a normal man wouldn't know much about, Frenchmen who painted as though they used their elbows instead of brushes, composers who wrote whole symphonies without a single melody in them, writers who knew all about politics and women who knew all about writers, the movement of the proletariat, Marx, somehow mixed up with five-dollar dinners and the best-looking women in America and fairies who made them laugh and half-sentences immediately understood and secretly hilarious and wives who called their husbands "Baby." He put the hat down, a scrap of straw and a red flower, and a little veil. He drank some whisky straight and went into the bathroom where his wife was lying deep in her bath, singing to herself and smiling from time to time like a little girl, paddling the water gently with her hands, sending up a slight spicy fragrance from the bath salts she used.

He stood over her, looking down at her. She smiled up at him, her eyes half closed, her body pink and shimmering in the warm, scented water. All over again, with all the old suddenness, he was hit deep inside him with the knowledge of how beautiful she was, how much he needed her.

"I came in here," he said, "to tell you I wish you wouldn't call me 'Baby.' "

She looked up at him from the bath, her eyes quickly full of sorrow, half-understanding what he meant. He knelt and put his arms around her, his sleeves plunged heedlessly in the water, his shirt and jacket soaking wet as he clutched her wordlessly, holding her crazily tight, crushing her breath from her, kissing her desperately, searchingly, regretfully.

He got jobs after that, selling real estate and automobiles, but somehow, although he had a desk with his name on a wooden wedge on it, and he went to the office religiously at nine each morning, he never managed to sell anything and he never made any money.

Louise was made assistant editor, and the house was always full of strange men and women who talked fast and got angry on abstract subjects like mural painting, novelists, labor unions. Negro short-story writers drank Louise's liquor, and a lot of Jews and big solemn men with scarred faces and knotted hands who talked slowly but clearly about picket lines and battles with guns and leadpipe at mine-shaft-heads and in front of factory gates. And Louise moved among them all, confidently, knowing what they were talking about, with opinions that they listened to and argued about just as though she were a man. She knew everybody, condescended to no one, devoured books that Darling had never heard of, walked along the streets of the city, excited, at home, soaking in all the million tides of New York without fear, with constant wonder.

Her friends liked Darling and sometimes he found a man who wanted to get off in the corner and talk about the new boy who played fullback for Princeton, and the decline of the double wing-back, or even the state of the stock market, but for the most part he sat on the edge of things, solid and quiet in the high storm of words. "The dialectics of the situation . . . The theater has been given over to expert jugglers . . . Picasso? What man has a right to paint old bones and collect ten thousand dollars for them? . . . I stand firmly behind Trotsky[3] . . . Poe was the last American critic. When he died they put lilies on the grave of American criticism. I don't say this because they panned my last book, but . . ."

Once in a while he caught Louise looking soberly and consideringly at him through the cigarette smoke and the noise and he avoided her eyes and found an excuse to get up and go into the kitchen for more ice or to open another bottle.

"Come on," Cathal Flaherty was saying, standing at the door with a girl, "you've got to come down and see this. It's down on Fourteenth Street, in the old Civic Repertory, and you can only see it on Sunday nights and I guarantee you'll come out of the theater singing." Flaherty was a big young Irishman with a broken nose who was the lawyer for a longshoreman's union, and he had been hanging around the house for six months on and off, roaring and shutting everybody else up when he got in an argument. "It's a new play, *Waiting for Lefty;* it's about taxi-drivers."

"Odets,"[4] the girl with Flaherty said. "It's by a guy named Odets."

"I never heard of him," Darling said.

"He's a new one," the girl said.

"It's like watching a bombardment," Flaherty said. "I saw it last Sunday night. You've got to see it."

"Come on, Baby," Louise said to Darling, excitement in her eyes already. "We've been sitting in the Sunday *Times* all day, this'll be a great change."

"I see enough taxi-drivers every day," Darling said, not because he meant that, but because he didn't like to be around Flaherty, who said things that made Louise laugh a lot and whose judgment she accepted on almost every subject.

"Let's go to the movies."

"You've never seen anything like this before," Flaherty said. "He wrote this play with a baseball bat."

"Come on," Louise coaxed, "I bet it's wonderful."

"He has long hair," the girl with Flaherty said. "Odets. I met him at a party. He's an actor. He didn't say a goddam thing all night."

"I don't feel like going down to Fourteenth Street," Darling said, wishing Flaherty and his girl would get out. "It's gloomy."

"Oh, hell!" Louise said loudly. She looked coolly at Darling, as though she'd just been introduced to him and was making up her mind about him, and not very favorably. He saw her looking at him, knowing there was something new and dangerous in her face and he wanted to say something, but Flaherty was there and his damned girl, and anyway, he didn't know what to say.

3. Leon Trotsky (1879–1940), Russian Communist revolutionary. 4. Clifford Odets (1906–1963), U.S. dramatist.

"I'm going," Louise said, getting her coat. "I don't think Fourteenth Street is gloomy."

"I'm telling you," Flaherty was saying, helping her on with her coat, "it's the Battle of Gettysburg, in Brooklynese."

"Nobody could get a word out of him," Flaherty's girl was saying as they went through the door. "He just sat there all night."

The door closed. Louise hadn't said good night to him. Darling walked around the room four times, then sprawled out on the sofa, on top of the Sunday *Times.* He lay there for five minutes looking at the ceiling, thinking of Flaherty walking down the street talking in that booming voice, between the girls, holding their arms.

Louise had looked wonderful. She'd washed her hair in the afternoon and it had been very soft and light and clung close to her head as she stood there angrily putting her coat on. Louise was getting prettier every year, partly because she knew by now how pretty she was, and made the most of it.

"Nuts," Darling said, standing up. "Oh, nuts."

He put on his coat and went down to the nearest bar and had five drinks off by himself in a corner before his money ran out.

The years since then had been foggy and downhill. Louise had been nice to him, and in a way, loving and kind, and they'd fought only once, when he said he was going to vote for Landon. ("Oh, Christ," she'd said, "doesn't *anything* happen inside your head? Don't you read the papers? The penniless Republican!") She'd been sorry later and apologized for hurting him, but apologized as she might to a child. He'd tried hard, had gone grimly to the art galleries, the concert halls, the bookshops, trying to gain on the trail of his wife, but it was no use. He was bored, and none of what he saw or heard or dutifully read made much sense to him and finally he gave it up. He had thought, many nights as he ate dinner alone, knowing that Louise would come home late and drop silently into bed without explanation, of getting a divorce, but he knew the loneliness, the hopelessness, of not seeing her again would be too much to take. So he was good, completely devoted, ready at all times to go any place with her, do anything she wanted. He even got a small job, in a broker's office and paid his own way, bought his own liquor.

Then he'd been offered the job of going from college to college as a tailor's representative. "We want a man," Mr. Rosenberg had said, "who as soon as you look at him, you say, 'There's a university man.' " Rosenberg had looked approvingly at Darling's broad shoulders and well-kept waist, at his carefully brushed hair and his honest, wrinkle-less face. "Frankly, Mr. Darling, I am willing to make you a proposition. I have inquired about you, you are favorably known on your old campus, I understand you were in the backfield with Alfred Diederich."

Darling nodded. "Whatever happened to him?"

"He is walking around in a cast for seven years now. An iron brace. He played professional football and they broke his neck for him."

Darling smiled. That, at least, had turned out well.

"Our suits are an easy product to sell, Mr. Darling," Rosenberg said. "We have a handsome, custom-made garment. What has Brooks Brothers got that we haven't got? A name. No more."

"I can make fifty, sixty dollars a week," Darling said to Louise that night. "And expenses. I can save some money and then come back to New York and really get started here."

"Yes, Baby," Louise said.

"As it is," Darling said carefully, "I can make it back here once a month, and holidays and the summer. We can see each other often."

"Yes, Baby." He looked at her face, lovelier now at thirty-five than it had ever been before, but fogged over now as it had been for five years with a kind of patient, kindly, remote boredom.

"What do you say?" he asked. "Should I take it?" Deep within him he hoped fiercely, longingly, for her to say, "No, Baby, you stay right here," but she said, as he knew she'd say, "I think you'd better take it."

He nodded. He had to get up and stand with his back to her, looking out the window, because there were things plain on his face that she had never seen in the fifteen years she'd known him. "Fifty dollars is a lot of money," he said. "I never thought I'd ever see fifty dollars again." He laughed, Louise laughed, too.

Christian Darling sat on the frail green grass of the practice field. The shadow of the stadium had reached out and covered him. In the distance the lights of the university shone a little mistily in the light haze of evening. Fifteen years. Flaherty even now was calling for his wife, buying her a drink, filling whatever bar they were in with that voice of his and that easy laugh. Darling half-closed his eyes, almost saw the boy fifteen years ago reach for the pass, slip the halfback, go skittering lightly down the field, his knees high and fast and graceful, smiling to himself because he knew he was going to get past the safety man. That was the high point, Darling thought, fifteen years ago, on an autumn afternoon, twenty years old and far from death, with the air coming easily into his lungs, and a deep feeling inside him that he could do anything, knock over anybody, outrun whatever had to be outrun. And the shower after and the three glasses of water and the cool night air on his damp head and Louise sitting hatless in the open car with a smile and the first kiss she ever really meant. The high point, an eighty-yard run in the practice, and a girl's kiss and everything after that a decline. Darling laughed. He had practiced the wrong thing, perhaps. He hadn't practiced for 1929 and New York City and a girl who would turn into a woman. Somewhere, he thought, there must have been a point where she moved up to me, was even with me for a moment, when I could have held her hand, if I'd known, held tight, gone with her. Well, he'd never known. Here he was on a playing field that was fifteen years away and his wife was in another city having dinner with another and better man, speaking with him a different, new language, a language nobody had ever taught him.

Darling stood up, smiled a little, because if he didn't smile he knew the tears would come. He looked around him. This was the spot. O'Connor's pass had come sliding out just to here . . . the high point. Darling put up his hands, felt all over again the flat slap of the ball. He shook his hips to throw off the halfback, cut back inside the center, picked his knees high as he ran gracefully over two men jumbled on the ground at the line of scrimmage, ran easily, gaining speed, for ten yards, holding the ball lightly in his two hands, swung away from the halfback diving at him, ran, swinging his hips in the almost girlish manner of a back in a broken field, tore into the safety man, his shoes drumming heavily on the turf, stiff-armed, elbow locked, pivoted, raced lightly and exultantly for the goal line.

It was only after he had sped over the goal line and slowed to a trot that he saw the boy and girl sitting together on the turf, looking at him wonderingly.

He stopped short, dropping his arms. "I . . ." he said, gasping a little, though his condition was fine and the run hadn't winded him. "I—once I played here."

The boy and the girl said nothing. Darling laughed embarrassedly, looked hard at them sitting there, close to each other, shrugged, turned and went toward his hotel, the sweat breaking out on his face and running down into his collar.

# Isaac Bashevis Singer

*Singer (1904–1991) was born in Radzymin, Poland. His father, a rabbi, was an author, as was his brother, the novelist I. J. Singer. Before he emigrated to the United States in 1935, Singer worked as a journalist in Warsaw, and in New York he resumed similar work with the* Jewish Daily Forward. *As a master of Yiddish, he continued to write in that language. His fiction is characteristically in the tradition of the spoken tale, mingling forthright literalness about the visible world with an equally literal rendition of fantastic and supernatural forms. Flavored with the colorful residue of folk tales, his explorations of Jewish life, past and present, are haunted allegories of the irrationality of history. He wrote a number of books for children. His stories are most easily found in* The Collected Stories of Isaac Bashevis Singer *(1982). Among his novels are* The Family Moskat *(1950),* The Slave *(1962),* The Manor *(1967),* The Estate *(1970),* Enemies: A Love Story *(1972),* Shosha *(1978), and* Meshugah, *published posthumously in 1994. He was awarded the Nobel Prize in 1978.*

## Gimpel the Fool[1]

### I

I am Gimpel the fool. I don't think myself a fool. On the contrary. But that's what folks call me. They gave me the name while I was still in school. I had seven names in all: imbecile, donkey, flax-head, dope, glump, ninny, and fool. The last name stuck. What did my foolishness consist of? I was easy to take in. They said, "Gimpel, you know the rabbi's wife has been brought to childbed?" So I skipped school. Well, it turned out to be a lie. How was I supposed to know? She hadn't had a big belly. But I never looked at her belly. Was that really so foolish? The gang laughed and hee-hawed, stomped and danced and chanted a good-night prayer. And instead of the raisins they give when a woman's lying in, they stuffed my hand full of goat turds. I was no weakling. If I slapped someone he'd see all the way to Cracow. But I'm really not a slugger by nature. I think to myself: Let it pass. So they take advantage of me.

I was coming home from school and heard a dog barking. I'm not afraid

1. Translated by Saul Bellow.

of dogs, but of course I never want to start up with them. One of them may be mad, and if he bites there's not a Tartar[2] in the world who can help you. So I made tracks. Then I looked around and saw the whole market place wild with laughter. It was no dog at all but Wolf-Leib the thief. How was I supposed to know it was he? It sounded like a howling bitch.

When the pranksters and leg-pullers found that I was easy to fool, every one of them tried his luck with me. "Gimpel, the czar is coming to Frampol; Gimpel, the moon fell down in Turbeen; Gimpel, little Hodel Furpiece found a treasure behind the bathhouse." And I like a golem[3] believed everyone. In the first place, everything is possible, as it is written in *The Wisdom of the Fathers*. I've forgotten just how. Second, I had to believe when the whole town came down on me! If I ever dared to say, "Ah, you're kidding!" there was trouble. People got angry. "What do you mean! You want to call everyone a liar?" What was I to do? I believed them, and I hope at least that did them some good.

I was an orphan. My grandfather who brought me up was already bent toward the grave. So they turned me over to a baker, and what a time they gave me there! Every woman or girl who came to bake a batch of noodles had to fool me at least once. "Gimpel, there's a fair in Heaven; Gimpel, the rabbi gave birth to a calf in the seventh month; Gimpel, a cow flew over the roof and laid brass eggs." A student from the yeshiva came once to buy a roll, and he said, "You, Gimpel, while you stand here scraping with your baker's shovel the Messiah has come. The dead have risen." "What do you mean?" I said. "I heard no one blowing the ram's horn!" He said, "Are you deaf?" And all began to cry, "We heard it, we heard!" Then in came Rietze the candle-dipper and called out in her hoarse voice, "Gimpel, your father and mother have stood up from the grave. They're looking for you."

To tell the truth, I knew very well that nothing of the sort had happened, but all the same, as folks were talking, I threw on my wool vest and went out. Maybe something had happened. What did I stand to lose by looking? Well, what a cat music went up! And then I took a vow to believe nothing more. But that was no go either. They confused me so that I didn't know the big end from the small.

I went to the rabbi to get some advice. He said, "It is written, better to be a fool all your days than for one hour to be evil. You are not a fool. They are the fools. For he who causes his neighbor to feel shame loses Paradise himself." Nevertheless, the rabbi's daughter took me in. As I left the rabbinical court she said, "Have you kissed the wall yet?" I said, "No; what for?" She answered, "It's the law; you've got to do it after every visit." Well, there didn't seem to be any harm in it. And she burst out laughing. It was a fine trick. She put one over on me, all right.

I wanted to go off to another town, but then everyone got busy matchmaking, and they were after me so they nearly tore my coat tails off. They talked at me and talked until I got water on the ear. She was no chaste maiden, but they told me she was virgin pure. She had a limp, and they said it was

2. A people with a reputation for fighting. 3. An artificial human being (Hebrew).

deliberate, from coyness. She had a bastard, and they told me the child was her little brother. I cried, "You're wasting your time. I'll never marry that whore." But they said indignantly, "What a way to talk! Aren't you ashamed of yourself? We can take you to the rabbi and have you fined for giving her a bad name." I saw then that I wouldn't escape them so easily and I thought: They're set on making me their butt. But when you're married the husband's the master, and if that's all right with her it's agreeable to me too. Besides, you can't pass through life unscathed, nor expect to.

I went to her clay house, which was built on the sand, and the whole gang, hollering and chorusing, came after me. They acted like bearbaiters. When we came to the well they stopped all the same. They were afraid to start anything with Elka. Her mouth would open as if it were on a hinge, and she had a fierce tongue. I entered the house. Lines were strung from wall to wall and clothes were drying. Barefoot she stood by the tub, doing the wash. She was dressed in a worn hand-me-down gown of plush. She had her hair put up in braids and pinned across her head. It took my breath away, almost, the reek of it all.

Evidently she knew who I was. She took a look at me and said, "Look who's here! He's come, the drip. Grab a seat."

I told her all; I denied nothing. "Tell me the truth," I said, "are you really a virgin, and is that mischievous Yechiel actually your little brother? Don't be deceitful with me, for I'm an orphan."

"I'm an orphan myself," she answered, "and whoever tries to twist you up, may the end of his nose take a twist. But don't let them think they can take advantage of me. I want a dowry of fifty guilders, and let them take up a collection besides. Otherwise they can kiss my you-know-what." She was very plainspoken. I said, "It's the bride and not the groom who gives a dowry." Then she said, "Don't bargain with me. Either a flat yes or a flat no. Go back where you came from."

I thought: No bread will ever be baked from *this* dough. But ours is not a poor town. They consented to everything and proceeded with the wedding. It so happened that there was a dysentery epidemic at the time. The ceremony was held at the cemetery gates, near the little corpse-washing hut. The fellows got drunk. While the marriage contract was being drawn up I heard the most pious high rabbi ask, "Is the bride a widow or a divorced woman?" And the sexton's wife answered for her, "Both a widow and divorced." It was a black moment for me. But what was I to do, run away from under the marriage canopy?

There was singing and dancing. An old granny danced opposite me, hugging a braided white hallah.[4] The master of revels made a "God 'a mercy" in memory of the bride's parents. The schoolboys threw burrs, as on Tishe b'Av fast day. There were a lot of gifts after the sermon: a noodle board, a kneading trough, a bucket, brooms, ladles, household articles galore. Then I took a look and saw two strapping young men carrying a crib. "What do we need this for?" I asked. So they said, "Don't rack your brains about it. It's all right, it'll come in handy." I realized I was going to be rooked. Take it another way though,

4. Or "challah," a kind of bread (Hebrew).

what did I stand to lose? I reflected: I'll see what comes of it. A whole town can't go altogether crazy.

## II

At night I came where my wife lay, but she wouldn't let me in. "Say, look here, is this what they married us for?" I said. And she said, "My monthly has come." "But yesterday they took you to the ritual bath, and that's afterwards, isn't it supposed to be?" "Today isn't yesterday," said she, "and yesterday's not today. You can beat it if you don't like it." In short, I waited.

Not four months later, she was in childbed. The townsfolk hid their laughter with their knuckles. But what could I do? She suffered intolerable pains and clawed at the walls. "Gimpel," she cried, "I'm going. Forgive me!" The house filled with women. They were boiling pans of water. The screams rose to the welkin.

The thing to do was to go to the house of prayer to repeat psalms, and that was what I did.

The townsfolk liked that, all right. I stood in a corner saying psalms and prayers, and they shook their heads at me. "Pray, pray!" they told me. "Prayer never made any woman pregnant." One of the congregation put a straw to my mouth and said, "Hay for the cows." There was something to that too, by God!

She gave birth to a boy. Friday at the synagogue the sexton stood up before the Ark, pounded on the reading table, and announced, "The wealthy Reb Gimpel invites the congregation to a feast in honor of the birth of a son." The whole house of prayer rang with laughter. My face was flaming. But there was nothing I could do. After all, I *was* the one responsible for the circumcision honors and rituals.

Half the town came running. You couldn't wedge another soul in. Women brought peppered chick-peas, and there was a keg of beer from the tavern. I ate and drank as much as anyone, and they all congratulated me. Then there was a circumcision, and I named the boy after my father, may he rest in peace. When all were gone and I was left with my wife alone, she thrust her head through the bed-curtain and called me to her.

"Gimpel," said she, "why are you silent? Has your ship gone and sunk?"

"What shall I say?" I answered. "A fine thing you've done to me! If my mother had known of it she'd have died a second time."

She said, "Are you crazy, or what?"

"How can you make such a fool," I said, "of one who should be the lord and master?"

"What's the matter with you?" she said. "What have you taken it into your head to imagine?"

I saw that I must speak bluntly and openly. "Do you think this is the way to use an orphan?" I said. "You have borne a bastard."

She answered, "Drive this foolishness out of your head. The child is yours."

"How can he be mine?" I argued. "He was born seventeen weeks after the wedding."

She told me then that he was premature. I said, "Isn't he a little too premature?" She said, she had had a grandmother who carried just as short a time and she resembled this grandmother of hers as one drop of water does another. She swore to it with such oaths that you would have believed a peasant at the fair if he had used them. To tell the plain truth, I didn't believe her; but when I talked it over the next day with the schoolmaster, he told me that the very same thing had happened to Adam and Eve. Two they went up to bed, and four they descended.

"There isn't a woman in the world who is not the granddaughter of Eve," he said.

That was how it was; they argued me dumb. But then, who really knows how such things are?

I began to forget my sorrow. I loved the child madly, and he loved me too. As soon as he saw me he'd wave his little hands and want me to pick him up, and when he was colicky I was the only one who could pacify him. I bought him a little bone teething ring and a little gilded cap. He was forever catching the evil eye from someone, and then I had to run to get one of those abracadabras for him that would get him out of it. I worked like an ox. You know how expenses go up when there's an infant in the house. I don't want to lie about it; I didn't dislike Elka either, for that matter. She swore at me and cursed, and I couldn't get enough of her. What strength she had! One of her looks could rob you of the power of speech. And her orations! Pitch and sulphur, that's what they were full of, and yet somehow also full of charm. I adored her every word. She gave me bloody wounds though.

In the evening I brought her a white loaf as well as a dark one, and also poppyseed rolls I baked myself. I thieved because of her and swiped everything I could lay hands on: macaroons, raisins, almonds, cakes. I hoped I may be forgiven for stealing from the Saturday pots the women left to warm in the baker's oven. I would take out scraps of meat, a chunk of pudding, a chicken leg or head, a piece of tripe, whatever I could nip quickly. She ate and became fat and handsome.

I had to sleep away from home all during the week, at the bakery. On Friday nights when I got home she always made an excuse of some sort. Either she had heartburn, or a stitch in the side, or hiccups, or headaches. You know what women's excuses are. I had a bitter time of it. It was rough. To add to it, this little brother of hers, the bastard, was growing bigger. He'd put lumps on me, and when I wanted to hit back she'd open her mouth and curse so powerfully I saw a green haze floating before my eyes. Ten times a day she threatened to divorce me. Another man in my place would have taken French leave and disappeared. But I'm the type that bears it and says nothing. What's one to do? Shoulders are from God, and burdens too.

One night there was a calamity at the bakery; the oven burst, and we almost had a fire. There was nothing to do but go home, so I went home. Let me, I thought, also taste the joy of sleeping in bed in midweek. I didn't want to wake the sleeping mite and tiptoed into the house. Coming in, it seemed to me that I heard not the snoring of one but, as it were, a double snore, one a thin enough snore and the other like the snoring of a slaughtered ox. Oh, I didn't like that! I didn't like it at all. I went up to the bed, and things suddenly turned black.

Next to Elka lay a man's form. Another in my place would have made an uproar, and enough noise to rouse the whole town, but the thought occurred to me that I might wake the child. A little thing like that—why frighten a little swallow, I thought. All right then, I went back to the bakery and stretched out on a sack of flour and till morning I never shut an eye. I shivered as if I had had malaria. "Enough of being a donkey," I said to myself. "Gimpel isn't going to be a sucker all his life. There's a limit even to the foolishness of a fool like Gimpel."

In the morning I went to the rabbi to get advice, and it made a great commotion in the town. They sent the beadle for Elka right away. She came, carrying the child. And what do you think she did? She denied it, denied everything, bone and stone! "He's out of his head," she said. "I know nothing of dreams of divinations." They yelled at her, warned her, hammered on the table, but she stuck to her guns: it was a false accusation, she said.

The butchers and the horse-traders took her part. One of the lads from the slaughterhouse came by and said to me, "We've got our eye on you, you're a marked man." Meanwhile, the child started to bear down and soiled itself. In the rabbinical court there was an Ark of the Covenant, and they couldn't allow that, so they sent Elka away.

I said to the rabbi, "What shall I do?"

"You must divorce her at once," said he.

"And what if she refuses?" I asked.

He said, "You must serve the divorce. That's all you'll have to do."

I said, "Well, all right, Rabbi. Let me think about it."

"There's nothing to think about," said he. "You mustn't remain under the same roof with her."

"And if I want to see the child?" I asked.

"Let her go, the harlot," said he, "and her brood of bastards with her."

The verdict he gave was that I mustn't even cross her threshold—never again, as long as I should live.

During the day it didn't bother me so much. I thought: It was bound to happen, the abscess had to burst. But at night when I stretched out upon the sacks I felt it all very bitterly. A longing took me, for her and for the child. I wanted to be angry, but that's my misfortune exactly, I don't have it in me to be really angry. In the first place—this was how my thoughts went—there's bound to be a slip sometimes. You can't live without errors. Probably that lad who was with her led her on and gave her presents and what not, and women are often long on hair and short on sense, and so he got around her. And then since she denies it so, maybe I was only seeing things? Hallucinations do happen. You see a figure or a mannikin or something, but when you come up closer it's nothing, there's not a thing there. And if that's so, I'm doing her an injustice. And when I got so far in my thoughts I started to weep. I sobbed so that I wet the flour where I lay. In the morning I went to the rabbi and told him that I had made a mistake. The rabbi wrote on with his quill, and he said that if that were so he would have to reconsider the whole case. Until he had finished I wasn't to go near my wife, but I might send her bread and money by messenger.

## III

Nine months passed before all the rabbis could come to an agreement. Letters went back and forth. I hadn't realized that there could be so much erudition about a matter like this.

Meanwhile, Elka gave birth to still another child, a girl this time. On the Sabbath I went to the synagogue and invoked a blessing on her. They called me up to the Torah, and I named the child for my mother-in-law—may she rest in peace. The louts and loudmouths of the town who came into the bakery gave me a going over. All Frampol refreshed its spirits because of my trouble and grief. However, I resolved that I would always believe what I was told. What's the good of *not* believing? Today it's your wife you don't believe; tomorrow it's God Himself you won't take stock in.

By an apprentice who was her neighbor I sent her daily a corn or a wheat loaf, or a piece of pastry, rolls or bagels, or, when I got the chance, a slab of pudding, a slice of honeycake, or wedding strudel—whatever came my way. The apprentice was a goodhearted lad, and more than once he added something on his own. He had formerly annoyed me a lot, plucking my nose and digging me in the ribs, but when he started to be a visitor to my house he became kind and friendly. "Hey, you, Gimpel," he said to me, "you have a very decent little wife and two fine kids. You don't deserve them."

"But the things people say about her," I said.

"Well, they have long tongues," he said, "and nothing to do with them but babble. Ignore it as you ignore the cold of last winter."

One day the rabbi sent for me and said, "Are you certain, Gimpel, that you were wrong about your wife?"

I said, "I'm certain."

"Why, but look here! You yourself saw it."

"It must have been a shadow," I said.

"The shadow of what?"

"Just of one of the beams, I think."

"You can go home then. You owe thanks to the Yanover rabbi. He found an obscure reference in Maimonides[5] that favored you."

I seized the rabbi's hand and kissed it.

I wanted to run home immediately. It's no small thing to be separated for so long a time from wife and child. Then I reflected: I'd better go back to work now, and go home in the evening. I said nothing to anyone, although as far as my heart was concerned it was like one of the Holy Days. The women teased and twitted me as they did every day, but my thought was: Go on, with your loose talk. The truth is out, like the oil upon the water. Maimonides says it's right, and therefore it is right!

At night, when I had covered the dough to let it rise, I took my share of bread and a little sack of flour and started homeward. The moon was full and the stars were glistening, something to terrify the soul. I hurried onward, and before me darted a long shadow. It was winter, and a fresh snow had fallen. I

5. Jewish scholastic philosopher (1135–1204).

had a mind to sing, but it was growing late and I didn't want to wake the householders. Then I felt like whistling, but I remembered that you don't whistle at night because it brings the demons out. So I was silent and walked as fast as I could.

Dogs in the Christian yards barked at me when I passed, but I thought: Bark your teeth out! What are you but mere dogs? Whereas I am a man, the husband of a fine wife, the father of promising children.

As I approached the house my heart started to pound as though it were the heart of a criminal. I felt no fear, but my heart went thump! thump! Well, no drawing back. I quietly lifted the latch and went in. Elka was asleep. I looked at the infant's cradle. The shutter was closed, but the moon forced its way through the cracks. I saw the newborn child's face and loved it as soon as I saw it—immediately—each tiny bone.

Then I came near to the bed. And what did I see but the apprentice lying there beside Elka. The moon went out all at once. It was utterly black, and I trembled. My teeth chattered. The bread fell from my hands, and my wife waked and said, "Who is that, ah?"

I muttered, "It's me."

"Gimpel?" she asked. "How come you're here? I thought it was forbidden."

"The rabbi said," I answered and shook as with a fever.

"Listen to me, Gimpel," she said, "go out to the shed and see if the goat's all right. It seems she's been sick." I have forgotten to say that we had a goat. When I heard she was unwell I went into the yard. The nannygoat was a good little creature. I had nearly human feeling for her.

With hesitant steps I went up to the shed and opened the door. The goat stood there on her four feet. I felt her everywhere, drew her by the horns, examined her udders, and found nothing wrong. She had probably eaten too much bark. "Good night, little goat," I said. "Keep well." And the little beast answered with a "Maa" as though to thank me for the good will.

I went back. The apprentice had vanished.

"Where," I asked, "is the lad?"

"What lad?" my wife answered.

"What do you mean?" I said. "The apprentice. You were sleeping with him."

"The things I have dreamed this night and the night before," she said, "may they come true and lay you low, body and soul! An evil spirit has taken root in you and dazzles your sight." She screamed out, "You hateful creature! You moon calf! You spook! You uncouth man! Get out, or I'll scream all Frampol out of bed!"

Before I could move, her brother sprang out from behind the oven and struck me a blow on the back of the head. I thought he had broken my neck. I felt that something about me was deeply wrong, and I said, "Don't make a scandal. All that's needed now is that people should accuse me of raising spooks and dybbuks."[6] For that was what she had meant. "No one will touch bread of my baking."

In short, I somehow calmed her.

6. Ghosts and wandering souls (Hebrew).

"Well," she said, "that's enough. Lie down, and be shattered by wheels."

Next morning I called the apprentice aside. "Listen here, brother!" I said. And so on and so forth. "What do you say?" He stared at me as though I had dropped from the roof or something.

"I swear," he said, "you'd better go to an herb doctor or some healer. I'm afraid you have a screw loose, but I'll hush it up for you." And that's how the thing stood.

To make a long story short, I lived twenty years with my wife. She bore me six children, four daughters and two sons. All kinds of things happened, but I neither saw nor heard. I believed, and that's all. The rabbi recently said to me, "Belief in itself is beneficial. It is written that a good man lives by his faith."

Suddenly my wife took sick. It began with a trifle, a little growth upon the breast. But she evidently was not destined to live long; she had no years. I spent a fortune on her. I have forgotten to say that by this time I had a bakery of my own and in Frampol was considered to be something of a rich man. Daily the healer came, and every witch doctor in the neighborhood was brought. They decided to use leeches, and after that to try cupping. They even called a doctor from Lublin, but it was too late. Before she died she called me to her bed and said, "Forgive me, Gimpel."

I said, "What is there to forgive? You have been a good and faithful wife."

"Woe, Gimpel!" she said. "It was ugly how I deceived you all these years. I want to go clean to my Maker, and so I have to tell you that the children are not yours."

If I had been clouted on the head with a piece of wood it couldn't have bewildered me more.

"Whose are they?" I asked.

"I don't know," she said. "There were a lot . . . but they're not yours." And as she spoke she tossed her head to the side, her eyes turned glassy, and it was all up to Elka. On her whitened lips there remained a smile.

I imagined that, dead as she was, she was saying, "I deceived Gimpel. That was the meaning of my brief life."

## IV

One night, when the period of mourning was done, as I lay dreaming on the flour sacks, there came the Spirit of Evil himself and said to me, "Gimpel, why do you sleep?"

I said, "What should I be doing? Eating kreplech?"

"The whole world deceives you," he said, "and you ought to deceive the world in your turn."

"How can I deceive all the world?" I asked him.

He answered, "You might accumulate a bucket of urine every day and at night pour it into the dough. Let the sages of Frampol eat filth."

"What about the judgment in the world to come?" I said.

"There is no world to come," he said. "They've sold you a bill of goods and talked you into believing you carried a cat in your belly. What nonsense!"

"Well then," I said, "and is there a God?"

He answered, "There is no God either."

"What," I said, "*is* there, then?"

"A thick mire."

He stood before my eyes with a goatish beard and horn, long-toothed, and with a tail. Hearing such words, I wanted to snatch him by the tail, but I tumbled from the flour sacks and nearly broke a rib. Then it happened that I had to answer the call of nature, and, passing, I saw the risen dough, which seemed to say to me, "Do it!" In brief, I let myself be persuaded.

At dawn the apprentice came. We kneaded the bread, scattered caraway seeds on it, and set it to bake. Then the apprentice went away, and I was left sitting in the little trench by the oven, on a pile of rags. Well, Gimpel, I thought, you've revenged yourself on them for all the shame they've put on you. Outside the frost glittered, but it was warm beside the oven. The flames heated my face. I bent my head and fell into a doze.

I saw in a dream, at once, Elka in her shroud. She called to me, "What have you done, Gimpel?"

I said to her, "It's all your fault," and started to cry.

"You fool!" she said. "You fool! Because I was false is everything false too? I never deceived anyone but myself. I'm paying for it all, Gimpel. They spare you nothing here."

I looked at her face. It was black; I was startled and waked, and remained sitting dumb. I sensed that everything hung in the balance. I seized the long shovel and took out the loaves, carried them into the yard, and started to dig a hole in the frozen earth.

My apprentice came back as I was doing it. "What are you doing, boss?" he said, and grew pale as a corpse.

"I know what I'm doing," I said, and I buried it all before his very eyes.

Then I went home, took my hoard from its hiding place, and divided it among the children. "I saw your mother tonight," I said. "She's turning black, poor thing."

They were so astounded they couldn't speak a word.

"Be well," I said, "and forget that such a one as Gimpel ever existed." I put on my short coat, a pair of boots, took the bag that held my prayer shawl in one hand, my stock in the other, and kissed the mezuzah.[7] When people saw me in the street they were greatly surprised.

"Where are you going?" they said.

I answered, "Into the world." And so I departed from Frampol.

I wandered over the land, and good people did not neglect me. After many years I became old and white; I heard a great deal, many lies and falsehoods, but the longer I lived the more I understood that there were really no lies. Whatever doesn't really happen is dreamed at night. It happens to one if it doesn't happen to another, tomorrow if not today, or a century hence if not

7. A case containing parchment inscribed with Torah quotes attached to the door frame of a Jewish household as a sign of its faith (Hebrew).

next year. What difference can it make? Often I heard tales of which I said, "Now this is a thing that cannot happen." But before a year had elapsed I heard that it actually had come to pass somewhere.

Going from place to place, eating at strange tables, it often happens that I spin yarns—improbable things that could never have happened—about devils, magicians, windmills, and the like. The children run after me, calling, "Grandfather, tell us a story." Sometimes they ask for particular stories, and I try to please them. A fat young boy once said to me, "Grandfather, it's the same story you told us before." The little rogue, he was right.

So it is with dreams too. It is many years since I left Frampol, but as soon as I shut my eyes I am there again. And whom do you think I see? Elka. She is standing by the washtub, as at our first encounter, but her face is shining and her eyes are as radiant as the eyes of a saint, and she speaks outlandish words to me, strange things. When I wake I have forgotten it all. But while the dream lasts I am comforted. She answers all my queries, and what comes out is that all is right. I weep and implore, "Let me be with you." And she consoles me and tells me to be patient. The time is nearer than it is far. Sometimes she strokes and kisses me and weeps upon my face. When I awaken I feel her lips and taste the salt of her tears.

No doubt the world is entirely an imaginary world, but it is only once removed from the true world. At the door of the hovel where I lie, there stands the plank on which the dead are taken away. The grave-digger Jew has his spade ready. The grave waits and the worms are hungry; the shrouds are prepared—I carry them in my beggar's sack. Another *shnorrer*[8] is waiting to inherit my bed of straw. When the time comes I will go joyfully. Whatever may be there, it will be real, without complication, without ridicule, without deception. God be praised: there even Gimpel cannot be deceived.

8. Beggar, sponger (Yiddish).

# Lee Smith

*Smith was born in 1944 in the state of Virginia. She attended Hollins College, where she received her B.A. Among her awards are the Lyndhurst Prize (1990–92), the Robert Penn Warren Prize for Fiction (1991), and the Lila Wallace/Reader's Digest Award (1995–97). Her books include* Oral History *(1983),* Family Linen *(1985),* The Devil's Dream *(1992),* Saving Grace *(1995), and* News of the Spirit *(1997). Stories and articles have appeared in various periodicals and anthologies such as* Southern Review, Redbook, The New York Times, *and* Atlantic. *She presently teaches at North Carolina State University.*

## Intensive Care

Cherry Oxendine is dying now, and everybody knows it. Everybody in town except maybe her new husband, Harold Stikes, although Lord knows he ought to, it's as plain as the nose on your face. And it's not like he hasn't been *told* either, by both Dr. Thacker and Dr. Pinckney and also that hotshot young Jew doctor from Memphis, Dr. Shapiro, who comes over here once a week. "Harold just can't take it in," is what the head nurse in Intensive Care, Lois Hickey, said in the Beauty Nook last week. Lois ought to know. She's been right there during the past six weeks while Cherry Oxendine has been in Intensive Care, writing down Cherry's blood pressure every hour on the hour, changing bags on the IV, checking the stomach tube, moving the bed up and down to prevent bedsores, monitoring the respirator—and calling in Rodney Broadbent, the respiratory therapist, more and more frequently. "Her blood gases is not but twenty-eight," Lois said in the Beauty Nook. "If we was to unhook that respirator, she'd die in a day."

"I would go on and do it then, if I was Harold," said Mrs. Hooker, the Presbyterian minister's wife, who was getting a permanent. "It is the Christian thing."

"You wouldn't either," Lois said, "because she *still knows him.* That's the awful part. She still knows him. In fact she peps right up ever time he comes in, like they are going on a date or something. It's the saddest thing. And ever time we open the doors, here comes Harold, regular as clockwork. Eight o'clock, one o'clock, six o'clock, eight o'clock, why shoot, he'd stay in there all day and all night if we'd let him. Well, she opens her mouth and says *Hi honey,* you can tell what she's saying even if she can't make a sound. And her eyes get real bright and her face looks pretty good too, that's because of the Lasix,[1] only Harold don't know that. He just can't take it all in," Lois said.

"Oh, I feel so sorry for him," said Mrs. Hooker. Her face is as round and flat as a dime.

"Well, I don't." Dot Mains, owner of the Beauty Nook, started cutting Lois Hickey's hair. Lois wears it too short, in Dot's opinion. "I certainly don't feel sorry for Harold Stikes, after what he did." Dot snipped decisively at Lois Hickey's frosted hair. Mrs. Hooker made a sad little sound, half sigh, half words, as Janice stuck her under the dryer, while Miss Berry, the old-maid home demonstration agent waiting for her appointment, snapped the pages of *Cosmopolitan* magazine one by one, blindly, filled with somewhat gratuitous rage against the behavior of Harold Stikes. Miss Berry is Harold Stikes's ex-wife's cousin. So she does not pity him, not one bit. He got what's coming to him, that's all, in Miss Berry's opinion. Most people don't. It's a pleasure to see it, but Miss Berry would never say this out loud since Cherry Oxendine is of course dying. Cherry Oxendine! Like it was yesterday, Miss Berry remembers how Cherry Oxendine acted in high school, wearing her skirts too tight, popping her gum.

"The doctors can't do a thing," said Lois Hickey.

Silence settled like fog then on the Beauty Nook, on Miss Berry and her magazine, on Dot Mains cutting Lois Hickey's hair, on little Janice thinking about her boyfriend Bruce, and on Mrs. Hooker crying gently under the dryer. Suddenly, Dot remembered something her old granny used to say about such moments of sudden absolute quiet: "An angel is passing over."

After a while, Mrs. Hooker said, "It's all in the hands of God, then." She spread out her fingers one by one on the tray, for Janice to give her a manicure.

And as for Harold Stikes, he's not even considering God. Oh, he doesn't interfere when Mr. Hooker comes by the hospital once a day to check on him—Harold was a Presbyterian in his former life—or even when the Baptist preacher from Cherry's mama's church shows up and insists that everybody in the whole waiting room join hands and bow heads in prayer while he raises his big red face and curly gray head straight up to heaven and prays in a loud voice that God will heal these loved ones who walk through the Valley of Death, and comfort these others who watch, through their hour of need. This includes Mrs. Eunice Sprayberry, whose mother has had a stroke, John and Paula Ripman, whose infant son is dying of encephalitis, and different others who drift in and out of Intensive Care following surgery or wrecks. Harold is losing track. He closes his eyes and bows his head, figuring it can't hurt, like taking out insurance. But deep down inside, he knows that if God is worth His salt, He is not impressed by the prayer of Harold Stikes, who knowingly gave up all hope of peace on earth and heaven hereafter for the love of Cherry Oxendine.

Not to mention his family.

He gave them up too.

But this morning when he leaves the hospital after his eight-o'clock visit

1. A medication that facilitates breathing.

to Cherry, Harold finds himself turning left out of the lot instead of right toward Food Lion, his store. Harold finds himself taking 15-501 just south of town and then driving through those ornate marble gates that mark the entrance to Camelot Hills, his old neighborhood. Some lucky instinct makes him pull into the little park and stop there, beside the pond. Here comes his ex-wife, Joan, driving the Honda Accord he paid for last year. Joan looks straight ahead. She's still wearing her shiny blond hair in the pageboy she's worn ever since Harold met her at Mercer College so many years ago. Harold is sure she's wearing low heels and a shirtwaist dress. He knows her briefcase is in the backseat, containing lesson plans for today, yogurt, and a banana. Potassium is important. Harold has heard this a million times. Behind her, the beds are all made, the breakfast dishes stacked in the sink. As a home ec teacher, Joan believes that breakfast is the most important meal of the day. The two younger children, Brenda and Harold Jr., are already on the bus to the Academy. James rides to the high school with his mother, hair wet, face blank, staring straight ahead. They don't see Harold. Joan brakes at the stop sign before entering 15-501. She always comes to a complete stop, even if nothing's coming. Always. She looks both ways. Then she's gone.

Harold drives past well-kept lawn after well-kept lawn and lovely house after lovely house, many of them houses where Harold has attended Cub Scout meetings, eaten barbecue, watched bowl games. Now these houses have a blank, closed look to them, like mean faces. Harold turns left on Oxford, then right on Shrewsbury. He comes to a stop beside the curb at 1105 Cambridge and just sits there with the motor running, looking at the house. His house. The Queen Anne house he and Joan planned so carefully, down to the last detail, the fish-scale siding. The house he is still paying for and will be until his dying day, if Joan has her way about it.

Which she will, of course. Everybody is on her side: *desertion.* Harold Stikes deserted his lovely wife and three children for a redheaded waitress. For a fallen woman with a checkered past. Harold can hear her now. "I fail to see why I and the children should lower our standards of living, Harold, and go to the dogs just because you have chosen to become insane in mid-life." Joan's voice is slow and amiable. It has a down-to-earth quality which used to appeal to Harold but now drives him wild. Harold sits at the curb with the motor running and looks at his house good. It looks fine. It looks just like it did when they picked it out of the pages of *Southern Living* and wrote off for the plans. The only difference is, that house was in Stone Mountain, Georgia, and this house is in Greenwood, Mississippi. Big deal.

Joan's response to Harold's desertion has been a surprise to him. He expected tears, recriminations, fireworks. He did not expect her calm, reasonable manner, treating Harold the way she treats the Mormon missionaries who come to the door in their black suits, for instance, that very calm sweet careful voice. Joan acts like Harold's desertion is nothing much. And nothing much appears to have changed for her except the loss of Harold's actual presence, and this cannot be a very big deal since everything else has remained exactly the same.

What the hell. After a while Harold turns off the motor and walks up the flagstone walk to the front door. His key still fits. All the furniture is arranged exactly the way it was arranged four years ago. The only thing that ever changes here is the display of magazines on the glass coffee table before the fireplace, Joan keeps them up to date. *Newsweek, National Geographic, Good Housekeeping, Gourmet.* It's a mostly educational grouping, unlike what Cherry reads—*Parade, Coronet, National Enquirer.* Now these magazines litter the floor at the side of the bed like little souvenirs of Cherry. Harold can't stand to pick them up.

He sits down heavily on the white sofa and stares at the coffee table. He remembers the quiz and the day he found it, four years ago now although it feels like only yesterday, funny thing though that he can't remember which magazine it was in. Maybe *Reader's Digest.* The quiz was titled "How Good Is Your Marriage?" and Harold noticed that Joan had filled it in carefully. This did not surprise him. Joan was so law-abiding, such a *good girl,* that she always filled in such quizzes when she came across them, as if she *had to,* before she could go ahead and finish the magazine. Usually Harold didn't pay much attention.

This time, he picked the magazine up and started reading. One of the questions said: "What is your idea of the perfect vacation? (a) a romantic getaway for you and your spouse alone; (b) a family trip to the beach; (c) a business convention; (d) an organized tour of a foreign land." Joan had wavered on this one. She had marked and then erased "an organized tour of a foreign land." Finally she had settled on "a family trip to the beach." Harold skimmed along. The final question was: "When you think of the love between yourself and your spouse, do you think of (a) a great passion; (b) a warm, meaningful companionship; (c) an average love; (d) an unsatisfying habit." Joan had marked "(c) an average love." Harold stared at these words, knowing they were true. An average love, nothing great, an average marriage between an average man and woman. Suddenly, strangely, Harold was filled with rage.

"It is not enough!" He thought he actually said these words out loud. Perhaps he *did* say them out loud, into the clean hushed air-conditioned air of his average home. Harold's rage was followed by a brief period, maybe five minutes, of unbearable longing, after which he simply closed the magazine and put it back on the table and got up and poured himself a stiff shot of bourbon. He stood for a while before the picture window in the living room, looking out at his even green grass, his clipped hedge, and the impatiens blooming in its bed, the clematis climbing the mailbox. The colors of the world fairly leaped at him—the sky so blue, the grass so green. A passing jogger's shorts glowed unbearably red. He felt that he had never seen any of these things before. Yet in another way it all seemed so familiar as to be an actual part of his body—his throat, his heart, his breath. Harold took another drink. Then he went out and played nine holes of golf at the country club with Bubba Fields, something he did every Wednesday afternoon. He shot 82.

By the time he came home for dinner he was okay again. He was very tired and a little lightheaded, all his muscles tingling. His face was hot. Yet Harold felt vaguely pleased with himself, as if he had been through something and come out the other side of it, as if he had done a creditable job on a difficult assignment. But right then, during dinner, Harold could not have told you exactly what had happened to him that day, or why he felt this way. Because the mind will forget what it can't stand to remember, and anyway the Stikeses had beef Stroganoff that night, a new recipe that Joan was testing for the Junior League cookbook, and Harold Jr. had written them a funny letter from camp, and for once Brenda did not whine. James, who was twelve that year, actually condescended to talk to his father, with some degree of interest, about baseball, and after supper was over he and Harold went out and pitched to each other until it grew dark and lightning bugs emerged. This is how it's supposed to be, Harold thought, father and son playing catch in the twilight.

Then he went upstairs and joined Joan in bed to watch TV, after which they turned out the light and made love. But Joan had greased herself all over with Oil of Olay, earlier, and right in the middle of doing it, Harold got a crazy terrified feeling that he was losing her, that Joan was slipping, slipping away.

But time passed, as it does, and Harold forgot that whole weird day, forgot it until *right now,* in fact, as he sits on the white sofa in his old house again and stares at the magazines on the coffee table, those magazines so familiar except for the date, which is four years later. Now Harold wonders: If he hadn't picked up that quiz and read it, would he have even *noticed* when Cherry Oxendine spooned out that potato salad for him six months later, in his own Food Lion deli? Would the sight of redheaded Cherry Oxendine, the Food Lion smock mostly obscuring her dynamite figure, have hit him like a bolt out of the blue the way it did?

Cherry herself does not believe there is any such thing as coincidence. Cherry thinks there is a master plan for the universe, and what is *meant* to happen will. She thinks it's all set in the stars. For the first time, Harold thinks maybe she's right. He sees part of a pattern in the works, but dimly, as if he is looking at a constellation hidden by clouds. Mainly, he sees her face.

Harold gets up from the sofa and goes into the kitchen, suddenly aware that he isn't supposed to be here. He could be arrested, probably! He looks back at the living room but there's not a trace of him left, not even an imprint on the soft white cushions of the sofa. Absentmindedly, Harold opens and shuts the refrigerator door. There's no beer, he notices. He can't have a Coke. On the kitchen calendar, he reads:

> Harold Jr to dentist, 3:30 p.m. Tues
> Change furnace filter 2/18/88 (James)

So James is changing the furnace filters now, James is the man of the house. Why not? It's good for him. He's been given too much, kids these days grow up so fast, no responsibilities, they get on drugs, you read about it all the time. But deep down inside, Harold knows that James is not on drugs and he feels something awful, feels the way he felt growing up, that sick little flutter in his stomach that took years to go away.

Harold's dad died of walking pneumonia when he was only three, so his mother raised him alone. She called him her "little man." This made Harold feel proud but also wild, like a boy growing up in a cage. Does James feel this way now? Harold suddenly decides to get James a car for his birthday, and take him hunting.

Hunting is something Harold never did as a boy, but it means a lot to him now. In fact Harold never owned a gun until he was thirty-one, when he bought a shotgun in order to accept the invitation of his regional manager, "Little Jimmy" Fletcher, to go quail hunting in Georgia. He had a great time. Now he's invited back every year, and Little Jimmy is in charge of the company's whole eastern division. Harold has a great future with Food Lion too. He owns three stores, one in downtown Greenwood, one out at the mall, and one over in Indianola. He owned two of them when his mother died, and he's pleased to think that she died proud—proud of the good little boy he'd always been, and the good man he'd become.

Of course she'd wanted him to make a preacher, but Harold never got the call, and she gave that up finally when he was twenty. Harold was not going to pretend to get the call if he never got it, and he held strong to this principle. He *wanted* to see a burning bush, but if this was not vouchsafed to him, he wasn't going to lie about it. He would just major in math instead, which he was good at anyway. Majoring in math at Mercer College, the small Baptist school his mother had chosen for him, Harold came upon Joan Berry, a home ec major from his own hometown who set out single-mindedly to marry him, which wasn't hard. After graduation, Harold got a job as management trainee in the Food Lion store where he had started as a bagboy at fourteen. Joan produced their three children, spaced three years apart, and got her tubes tied. Harold got one promotion, then another. Joan and Harold prospered. They built this house.

Harold looks around and now this house, his house, strikes him as creepy, a wax museum. He lets himself out the back door and walks quickly, almost runs, to his car. It's real cold out, a gray day in February, but Harold's sweating. He starts his car and roars off toward the hospital, driving—as Cherry would say—like a bat out of hell.

They're letting Harold stay with her longer now. He knows it, they know it, but nobody says a word. Lois Hickey just looks the other way when the announcement "Visiting hours are over" crackles across the PA. Is this a good sign or a bad sign? Harold can't tell. He feels slow and confused, like a man underwater. "I think she looks better, don't you?" he said last night to Cherry's son Stan, the TV weatherman, who had driven down from Memphis for the day. Eyes slick and bright with tears, Stan went over to Harold and hugged him tight. This scared Harold to death, he has practically never touched his own sons, and he doesn't even *know* Stan, who's been grown and gone for years. Harold is not used to hugging anybody, especially men. Harold breathed in Stan's strong go-get-'em cologne, he buried his face in Stan's long curly hair. He thinks it is possible that Stan has a permanent. They'll do anything up in Memphis. Then Stan stepped back and put one hand on each of Harold's shoulders, holding him out at arm's length. Stan has his mother's wide, mobile mouth. The bright white light of Intensive Care glinted off the gold chain and the crystal that he wore around his neck. "I'm afraid we're going to lose her, Pop," he said.

But Harold doesn't think so. Today he thinks Cherry looks the best she's looked in weeks, with a bright spot of color in each cheek to match her flaming hair. She's moving around a lot too, she keeps kicking the sheet off.

"She's getting back some of that old energy now," he tells Cherry's daughter, Tammy Lynn Palladino, when she comes by after school. Tammy Lynn and Harold's son James are both members of the senior class, but they aren't friends. Tammy Lynn says James is a "stuck-up jock," a "preppie," and a "country-clubber." Harold can't say a word to defend his own son against these charges, he doesn't even *know* James anymore. It might be true, anyway. Tammy Lynn is real smart, a teenage egghead. She's got a full scholarship to Millsaps College for next year. She applied for it all by herself. As Cherry used to say, Tammy Lynn came into this world with a full deck of cards and an ace or two up her sleeve. Also she looks out for Number One.

In this regard Tammy Lynn is as different from her mama as night from day, because Cherry would give you the shirt off her back and frequently has. That's gotten her into lots of trouble. With Ed Palladino, for instance, her second husband and Tammy Lynn's dad. Just about everybody in this town got took by Ed Palladino, who came in here wearing a seersucker suit and talking big about putting in an outlet mall across the river. A lot of people got burned on that outlet mall deal. But Ed Palladino had a way about him that made you want to cast your lot with his, it is true. You wanted to give Ed Palladino your savings, your time-sharing condo, your cousin, your ticket to the Super Bowl. Cherry gave it all.

She married him and turned over what little inheritance she had from her daddy's death—and that's the only time in her life she ever had *any* money, mind you—and then she just shrugged and smiled her big crooked smile when he left town under cover of night. *"C'est la vie,"* Cherry said. She donated the rest of his clothes to the Salvation Army. *"Que será, será,"* Cherry said, quoting a song that was popular when she was in junior high.

Tammy Lynn sits by her mama's bed and holds Cherry's thin dry hand. "I brought you a Chick-Fil-A," she says to Harold. "It's over there in that bag." She points to the shelf by the door. Harold nods. Tammy Lynn works at Chick-Fil-A. Cherry's eyes are wide and blue and full of meaning as she stares at her daughter. Her mouth moves, both Harold and Tammy Lynn lean forward, but then her mouth falls slack and her eyelids flutter shut. Tammy sits back.

"I think she looks some better today, don't you?" Harold asks.

"No," Tammy Lynn says. She has a flat little redneck voice. She sounds just the way she did last summer when she told Cherry that what she saw in the field was a cotton picker working at night, and not a UFO after all. "I wish I did but I don't, Harold. I'm going to go on home now and heat up some Beanee Weenee for Mamaw. You come on as soon as you can."

"Well," Harold says. He feels like things have gotten all turned around here some way, he feels like he's the kid and Tammy Lynn has turned into a freaky little grown-up. He says, "I'll be along directly."

But they both know he won't leave until Lois Hickey throws him out. And speaking of Lois, as soon as Tammy Lynn takes off, here she comes again, checking something on the respirator, making a little clucking sound with her mouth, then whirling to leave. When Lois walks, her panty girdle goes *swish, swish, swish* at the top of her legs. She comes right back with the young black man named Rodney Broadbent, Respiratory Therapist. It says so on his badge. Rodney wheels a complicated-looking cart ahead of himself. He's all built up, like a weightlifter.

"How you doing tonight, Mr. Stipe?" Rodney says.

"I think she's some better," Harold says.

Lois Hickey and Rodney look at him.

"Well, lessee here," Rodney says. He unhooks the respirator tube at Cherry's throat, sticks the tube from his own machine down the opening, and switches on the machine. It makes a whirring sound. It looks like an electric ice cream mixer. Rodney Broadbent looks at Lois Hickey in a significant way as she turns to leave the room.

They don't have to tell him, Harold knows. Cherry is worse, not better. Harold gets the Chick-Fil-A, unwraps it, eats it, and then goes over to stand by the window. It's already getting dark. The big mercury arc light glows in the hospital parking lot. A little wind blows some trash around on the concrete. He has had Cherry for three years, that's all. One trip to Disney World, two vacations at Gulf Shores Alabama, hundreds of nights in the old metal bed out at the farm with Cherry sleeping naked beside him, her arm thrown over his stomach. They had a million laughs.

"Alrightee," Rodney Broadbent nearly sings, unhooking his machine. Harold turns to look at him. Rodney Broadbent certainly looks more like a middle linebacker than a respiratory therapist. But Harold likes him.

"Well, Rodney?" Harold says.

Rodney starts shadow-boxing in the middle of the room. "Tough times," he says finally. "These is tough times, Mr. Stipe." Harold stares at him. Rodney is light on his feet as can be.

Harold sits down in the chair by the respirator. "What do you mean?" he asks.

"I mean she is drowning, Mr. Stipe," Rodney says. He throws a punch which lands real close to Harold's left ear. "What I'm doing here, see, is suctioning. I'm pulling all the fluid up out of her lungs. But now looka here, Mr. Stipe, they is just too damn much of it. See this little doohickey here I'm measuring it with? This here is the danger zone, man. Now Mrs. Stipe, she has been in the danger zone for some time. They is just too much damn fluid in there. What she got, anyway? Cancer and pneumonia both, am I right? What can I tell you, man? She is *drowning*." Rodney gives Harold a short affectionate punch in the ribs, then wheels his cart away. From the door, apparently struck by some misgivings, he says, "Well, man, if it was me, I'd want to know what the story is, you follow me, man? If it was me, what I'm saying." Harold can't see Rodney anymore, only hear his voice from the open door.

"Thank you, Rodney," Harold says. He sits in the chair. In a way he has known this already, for quite some time. In a way, Rodney's news is no news, to Harold. He just hopes he will be man enough to bear it, to do what will have to be done. Harold has always been scared that he is not man enough for Cherry Oxendine, anyway. This is his worst secret fear. He looks around the little Intensive Care room, searching for a sign, some sign, anything, that he will be man enough. Nothing happens. Cherry lies strapped to the bed, flanked by so many machines that it looks like she's in the cockpit of a jet. Her eyes are closed, eyelids fluttering, red spots on her freckled cheeks. Her chest rises and falls as the respirator pushes air in and out through the tube in her neck. He doesn't see how she can sleep in the bright white light of Intensive Care, where it is always noon. And does she dream? Cherry used to tell him her dreams, which were wild, long Technicolor dreams, like movies. Cherry played different parts in them. If you dream in color, it means you're intelligent, Cherry said. She used to tease him all the time. She thought Harold's own dreams were a stitch, dreams more boring than his life, dreams in which he'd drive to Jackson, say, or be washing his car.

"Harold?" It's Ray Muncey, manager of the Food Lion at the mall.

"Why, what are you doing over here, Ray?" Harold asks, and then in a flash he *knows*, Lois Hickey must have called him, to make Harold go on home.

"I was just driving by and I thought, Hey, maybe Harold and me might run by the Holiday Inn, get a bite to eat." Ray shifts from foot to foot in the doorway. He doesn't come inside, he's not supposed to, nobody but immediate family is allowed in Intensive Care, and Harold's glad—Cherry would just die if people she barely knows, like Ray Muncey, got to see her looking so bad.

"No, Ray, you go on and eat," Harold says. "I already ate. I'm leaving right now, anyway."

"Well, how's the missus doing?" Ray is a big man, afflicted with big, heavy manners.

"She's drowning," Harold says abruptly. Suddenly he remembers Cherry in a water ballet at the town pool, it must have been the summer of junior year, Fourth of July, Cherry and the other girls floating in a circle on their backs to form a giant flower—legs high, toes pointed. Harold doesn't know it when Ray Muncey leaves. Out the window, the parking lot light glows like a big full moon. Lois Hickey comes in. "You've got to go home now, Harold," she says. "I'll call if there's any change." He remembers Cherry at Glass Lake, on the senior class picnic. Cherry's getting real agitated now, she tosses her head back and forth, moves her arms. She'd pull out the tubes if she could. She kicks off the sheet. Her legs are still good, great legs in fact, the legs of a beautiful young woman.

Harold at seventeen was tall and skinny, brown hair in a soft flat crew cut, glasses with heavy black frames. His jeans were too short. He carried a pen-and-pencil set in a clear plastic case in his breast pocket. Harold and his best friend, Ben Hill, looked so much alike that people had trouble telling them apart. They did everything together. They built model rockets, they read every science fiction book they could get their hands on, they collected Lionel train parts and Marvel comics. They loved superheroes with special powers, enormous beings who leaped across rivers and oceans. Harold's friendship with Ben Hill kept the awful loneliness of the only child at bay, and it also kept him from having to talk to girls. You couldn't talk to those two, not seriously. They were giggling and bumping into each other all the time. They were immature.

So it was in Ben's company that Harold experienced the most private, the most *personal* memory he has of Cherry Oxendine in high school. Oh, he also has those other memories you'd expect, the big public memories of Cherry being crowned Miss Greenwood High (for her talent; she surprised everybody by reciting "Abou Ben Adhem" in such a stirring way that there wasn't a dry eye in the whole auditorium when she got through), or running out onto the field ahead of the team with the other cheerleaders, red curls flying, green and white skirt whirling out around her hips like a beach umbrella when she turned a cartwheel. Harold noticed her then, of course. He noticed her when she moved through the crowded halls of the high school with her walk that was almost a prance, she put a little something extra into it, all right. Harold noticed Cherry Oxendine then in the way that he noticed Sandra Dee on the cover of a magazine, or Annette Funicello on *American Bandstand*.

But such girls were not for the likes of Harold, and Harold knew it. Girls like Cherry always had boyfriends like Lamar Peebles, who was hers—a doctor's son with a baby-blue convertible and plenty of money. They used to drive around town in his car, smoking cigarettes. Harold saw them, as he carried out grocery bags. He did not envy Lamar Peebles, or wish he had a girl like Cherry Oxendine. Only something about them made him stand where he was in the Food Lion lot, watching, until they had passed from sight.

So Harold's close-up encounter with Cherry was unexpected. It took place at the senior class picnic, where Harold and Ben had been drinking beer all afternoon. No alcohol was allowed at the senior class picnic, but some of the more enterprising boys had brought out kegs the night before and hidden them in the woods. Anybody could go back there and pay some money and get some beer. The chaperones didn't know, or appeared not to know. In any case, the chaperones all left at six o'clock, when the picnic was officially over. Some of the class members left then too. Then some of them came back with more beer, more blankets. It was a free lake. Nobody could *make* you go home. Normally, Harold and Ben would have been among the first to leave, but because they had had four beers apiece, and because this was the first time they had ever had *any* beer ever, at all, they were still down by the water, skipping rocks and waiting to sober up so that they would not wreck Harold's mother's green Gremlin on the way home. All the cool kids were on the other side of the lake, listening to transistor radios. The sun went down. Bullfrogs started up. A mist came out all around the sides of the lake. It was a cloudy, humid day anyway, not a great day for a picnic.

"If God is really God, how come He let Himself get crucified, is what I want to know," Ben said. Ben's daddy was a Holiness preacher, out in the county.

But Harold heard something. "Hush, Ben," he said.

"If I was God I would go around and really kick some ass," Ben said.

Harold heard it again. It was almost too dark to see.

"Damn." It was a girl's voice, followed by a splash.

All of a sudden, Harold felt sober. "Who's there?" he asked. He stepped forward, right up to the water's edge. Somebody was in the water. Harold was wearing his swim trunks under his jeans, but he had not gone in the water himself. He couldn't stand to show himself in front of people. He thought he was too skinny.

"Well, *do something*." It was the voice of Cherry Oxendine, almost wailing. She stumbled up the bank. Harold reached out and grabbed her arm. Close up, she was a mess, wet and muddy, with her hair all over her head. But the thing that got Harold, of course, was that she didn't have any top on. She didn't even try to cover them up either, just stomped her little foot on the bank and said, "I am going to *kill* Lamar Peebles when I get ahold of him." Harold had never even imagined so much skin.

"What's going on?" asked Ben, from up the bank.

Harold took off his own shirt as fast as he could and handed it over to Cherry Oxendine. "Cover yourself," he said.

"Why, thank you." Cherry didn't bat an eye. She took his shirt and put it on, tying it stylishly at the waist. Harold couldn't believe it. Close up, Cherry was a lot smaller than she looked on the stage or the football field. She looked up at Harold through her dripping hair and gave him her crooked grin.

"Thanks, hey?" she said.

And then she was gone, vanished into the mist and trees before Harold could say another word. He opened his mouth and closed it. Mist obscured his view. From the other side of the lake he could hear "Ramblin' Rose" playing on somebody's radio. He heard a girl's high-pitched giggle, a boy's whooping laugh.

"What's going on?" asked Ben.

"Nothing," Harold said. It was the first time he had ever lied to Ben. Harold never told anybody what had happened that night, not ever. He felt that it was up to him to protect Cherry Oxendine's honor. Later, much later, when he and Cherry were lovers, he was astonished to learn that she couldn't remember any of this, not who she was with or what had happened or what she was doing in the lake like that with her top off, or Harold giving her his shirt. "I think that was sweet, though," Cherry told him.

When Harold and Ben finally got home that night at nine or ten o'clock, Harold's mother was frantic. "You've been drinking," she shrilled at him under the hanging porch light. "And where's your shirt?" It was a new madras shirt which Harold had gotten for graduation. Now Harold's mother is out at the Hillandale Rest Home. Ben died in Vietnam, and Cherry is drowning. This time, and Harold knows it now, he can't help her.

Oh, Cherry! Would she have been so wild if she hadn't been so cute? And what if her parents had been younger when she was born—normal-age parents—couldn't they have controlled her better? As it was, the Oxendines were sober, solid people living in a farmhouse out near the county line, and Cherry lit up their lives like a rocket. Her dad, Martin "Buddy" Oxendine, went to sleep in his chair every night right after supper, woke back up for the eleven-o'clock news, and then went to bed for good. Buddy was an elder in the Baptist church. Cherry's mom, Gladys Oxendine, made drapes for people. She assumed she would never have children at all because of her spastic colitis. Gladys and Buddy had started raising cockapoos when they gave up on children. Imagine Gladys's surprise, then, to find herself pregnant at thirty-eight, when she was already old! They say she didn't even know it when she went to the doctor. She thought she had a tumor.

But then she got so excited, that old farm woman, when Dr. Grimwood told her what was what, and she wouldn't even consider an abortion when he mentioned the chances of a mongoloid. People didn't use to have babies so old then as they do now, so Gladys Oxendine's pregnancy was the talk of the county. Neighbors crocheted little jackets and made receiving blankets. Buddy built a baby room onto the house and made a cradle by hand. During the last two months of the pregnancy, when Gladys had to stay in bed because of toxemia, people brought over casseroles and boiled custard, everything good. Gladys's pregnancy was the only time in her whole life that she was ever pretty, and she loved it, and she loved the attention, neighbors in and out of the house. When the baby was finally born on November 1, 1944, no parents were ever more ready than Gladys and Buddy Oxendine. And the baby was everything they hoped for too, which is not usually the case—the prettiest baby in the world, a baby like a little flower.

They named her Doris Christine which is who she was until eighth grade, when she made junior varsity cheerleader and announced that she was changing her name to Cherry. Cherry! Even her parents had to admit it suited her better than Doris Christine. As a little girl, Doris Christine was redheaded, bouncy, and busy—she was always into something, usually something you'd never thought to tell her not to do. She started talking early and never shut up. Her old dad, old Buddy Oxendine, was so crazy about Doris Christine that he took her everywhere with him in his red pickup truck. You got used to seeing the two of them, Buddy and his curly-headed little daughter, riding the country roads together, going to the seed-and-feed together, sharing a shake at the Dairy Queen. Gladys made all of Doris Christine's clothes, the most beautiful little dresses in the world, with hand-smocking and French seams. They gave Doris Christine everything they could think of—what she asked for, what she didn't. "That child is going to get spoiled," people started to say. And of course she did get spoiled, she couldn't have helped *that,* but she was never spoiled rotten as so many are. She stayed sweet in spite of it all.

Then along about ninth grade, soon after she changed her name to Cherry and got interested in boys, things changed between Cherry and the old Oxendines. Stuff happened. Instead of being the light of their lives, Cherry became the bane of their existence, the curse of their old age. She wanted to wear makeup, she wanted to have car dates. You can't blame her—she was old enough, sixteen. Everybody else did it. But you can't blame Gladys and Buddy either—they were old people by then, all worn out. They were not up to such a daughter. Cherry sneaked out. She wrecked a car. She ran away to Pensacola with a soldier. Finally, Gladys and Buddy just gave up. When Cherry eloped with the disc jockey, Don Westall, right after graduation, they threw up their hands. They did not do a thing about it. They had done the best they could, and everybody knew it. They went back to raising cockapoos.

Cherry, living up in Nashville, Tennessee, had a baby, Stan, the one that's in his twenties now. Cherry sent baby pictures back to Gladys and Buddy, and wrote that she was going to be a singer. Six years later, she came home. She said nothing against Don Westall, who was still a disc jockey on WKIX, Nashville. You could hear him on the radio every night after ten P.M. Cherry said the breakup was all her fault. She said she had made some mistakes, but she didn't say what they were. She was thin and noble. Her kid was cute. She did not go back out to the farm then. She rented an apartment over the hardware store, down by the river, and got a job downtown working in Ginger's Boutique. After a year or so, she started acting more like herself again, although not *quite* like herself, she had grown up somehow in Nashville, and quit being spoiled. She put Stan, her kid, first. And if she did run around a little bit, or if she was the life of the party sometimes out at the country club, so what? Stan didn't want for a thing. By then the Oxendines were failing and she had to take care of them too, she had to drive her daddy up to Grenada for dialysis twice a week. It was not an easy life for Cherry, but if it ever got her down, you couldn't tell it. She was still cute. When her daddy finally died and left her a little money, everybody was real glad. Oh *now*, they said, Cherry Oxendine can quit working so hard and put her mama in a home or something and have a decent life. She can go on a cruise. But then along came Ed Palladino, and the rest is history.

Cherry Oxendine was left with no husband, no money, a little girl, and a mean old mama to take care of. At least by this time Stan was in the Navy. Cherry never complained, though. She moved back out to the farm. When Ginger retired from business and closed her boutique, Cherry got another job, as a receptionist at Wallace, Wallace and Peebles. This was her undoing. Because Lamar Peebles had just moved back to town with his family, to join his father's firm. Lamar had two little girls. He had been married to a tobacco heiress since college. All this time he had run around on her. He was not on the up-and-up. And when he encountered redheaded Cherry Oxendine again after the passage of so many years, all those old fireworks went off again. They got to be a scandal, then a disgrace. Lamar said he was going to marry her, and Cherry believed him. After six months of it, Mrs. Lamar Peebles checked herself into a mental hospital in Silver Hill, Connecticut. First, she called her lawyers.

And then it was all over, not even a year after it began. Mr. and Mrs. Lamar Peebles were reconciled and moved to Winston-Salem, North Carolina, her hometown. Cherry Oxendine lost her job at Wallace, Wallace and Peebles, and was reduced to working in the deli at Food Lion. Why did she do it? Why did she lose all the goodwill she'd built up in this community over so many years? It is because she doesn't know how to look out for Number One. Her own daughter, Tammy Lynn Palladino, is aware of this.

"You have got a fatal flaw, Mama," Tammy said after learning about fatal flaws in English class. "You believe everything everybody tells you."

Still, Tammy loves her mother. Sometimes she writes her mother's whole name, Cherry Oxendine Westall Palladino Stikes, over and over in her Blue Horse notebook. Tammy Lynn will never be half the woman her mother is, and she's so smart she knows it. She gets a kick out of her mother's wild ideas.

"When you get too old to be cute, honey, you get to be eccentric," Cherry told Tammy one time. It's the truest thing she ever said.

It seems to Tammy that the main thing about her mother is, Cherry always has to have *something* going on. If it isn't a man it's something else, such as having her palm read by that woman over in French Camp, or astrology, or the grapefruit diet. Cherry believes in the Bermuda Triangle, Bigfoot, Atlantis, and ghosts. It kills her that she's not psychic. The UFO Club was just the latest in a long string of interests although it has lasted the longest, starting back before Cherry's marriage to Harold Stikes. And then Cherry got cancer, and she kind of forgot about it. But Tammy still remembers the night her mama first got so turned on to UFOs.

Rhonda Ramey, Cherry's best friend, joined the UFO Club first. Rhonda and Cherry are a lot alike, although it's hard to see this at first. While Cherry is short and peppy, Rhonda is tall, thin, and listless. She looks like Cher. Rhonda doesn't have any children. She's crazy about her husband, Bill, but he's a workaholic who runs a string of video rental stores all over northern Mississippi, so he's gone a lot, and Rhonda gets bored. She works out at the spa, but it isn't enough. Maybe this is why she got so interested when the UFO landed at a farm outside her mother's hometown of Como. It was first spotted by sixteen-year-old Donnie Johnson just at sunset, as he was finishing his chores on his parents' farm. He heard a loud rumbling sound "in the direction of the hog house," it said in the paper. Looking up, he suddenly saw a "brilliantly lit mushroom-shaped object" hovering about two feet above the ground, with a shaft of white light below and glowing all over with an intensely bright multicolored light, "like the light of a welder's arc."

Donnie said it sounded like a jet. He was temporarily blinded and paralyzed. He fell down on the ground. When he came back to his senses again, it was gone. Donnie staggered into the kitchen where his parents, Durel, fifty-four, and Erma, forty-nine, were eating supper, and told them what had happened. They all ran back outside to the field, where they found four large imprints and four small imprints in the muddy ground, and a nearby clump of sage grass on fire. The hogs were acting funny, bunching up, looking dazed. Immediately, Durel jumped in his truck and went to get the sheriff, who came right back with two deputies. All in all, six people viewed the site while the bush continued to burn, and who knows how many people—half of Como—saw the imprints the next day. Rhonda saw them too. She drove out to the Johnson farm with her mother, as soon as she heard about it.

It was a close encounter of the second kind, according to Civil Air Patrol head Glenn Raines, who appeared on TV to discuss it, because the UFO "interacted with its surroundings in a significant way." A close encounter of the first kind is simply a close-range sighting, while a close encounter of the third kind is something like the most famous example, of Betty and Barney Hill of Exeter, New Hampshire, who were actually kidnapped by a UFO while they were driving along on a trip. Betty and Barney Hill were taken aboard the alien ship and given physical exams by intelligent humanoid beings. Two hours and thirty-five minutes were missing from their trip, and afterward, Betty had to be treated for acute anxiety. Glenn Raines, wearing his brown Civil Air Patrol uniform, said all this on TV.

His appearance, plus what had happened at the Johnson farm, sparked a rash of sightings all across Mississippi, Louisiana, and Texas for the next two years. Metal disklike objects were seen, and luminous objects appearing as lights at night. In Levelland, Texas, fifteen people called the police to report an egg-shaped UFO appearing over State Road 1173. Overall, the UFOs seemed to show a preference for soybean fields and teenage girl viewers. But a pretty good photograph of a UFO flying over the Gulf was taken by a retired man from Pascagoula, so you can't generalize. Clubs sprang up all over the place. The one that Rhonda and Cherry went to had seventeen members and met once a month at the junior high school.

Tammy recalls exactly how her mama and Rhonda acted the night they came home from Cherry's first meeting. Cherry's eyes sparkled in her face like Brenda Starr's eyes in the comics. She started right in telling Tammy all about it, beginning with the Johnsons from Como and Betty and Barney Hill.

Tammy was not impressed. "I don't believe it," she said. She was president of the Science Club at the junior high school.

"You are the most irritating child!" Cherry said. "*What* don't you believe?"

"Well, any of it," Tammy said then. "All of it," and this has remained her attitude ever since.

"Listen, honey, *Jimmy Carter* saw one," Cherry said triumphantly. "In nineteen seventy-one, at the Executive Mansion in Georgia. He turned in an official report on it."

"How come nobody knows about it, then?" Tammy asked. She was a tough customer.

"Because the government covered it up!" said Rhonda, just dying to tell this part. "People see UFOs all the time, it's common knowledge, they are trying to make contact with us right now, honey, but the government doesn't want the average citizen to know about it. There's a big cover-up going on."

"It's just like Watergate." Cherry opened a beer and handed it over to Rhonda.

"That's right," Rhonda said, "and every time there's a major incident, you know what happens? These men from the government show up at your front door dressed all in black. After they get through with you, you'll wish you never heard the word 'saucer.' You turn pale and get real sick. You can't get anything to stay on your stomach."

Tammy cracked up. But Rhonda and Cherry went on and on. They had official-looking gray notebooks to log their sightings in. At their meetings, they reported these sightings to each other, and studied up on the subject in general. Somebody in the club was responsible for the educational part of each meeting, and somebody else brought the refreshments.

Tammy Lynn learned to keep her mouth shut. It was less embarrassing than belly dancing; she had a friend whose mother took belly dancing at the YMCA. Tammy did not tell her mama about all the rational explanations for UFOs that she found in the school library. They included: (1) hoaxes; (2) natural phenomena, such as fungus causing the so-called fairy rings sometimes found after a landing; (3) real airplanes flying off course; and Tammy's favorite, (4) the Fata Morgana, described as a "rare and beautiful type of mirage, constantly changing, the result of unstable layers of warm and cold air. The Fata Morgana takes its name from fairy lore and is said to evoke in the viewer a profound sense of longing," the book went on to say. Tammy's biology teacher, Mr. Owens, said he thought that the weather patterns in Mississippi might be especially conducive to this phenomenon. But Tammy kept her mouth shut. And after a while, when nobody in the UFO Club saw anything, its membership declined sharply. Then her mama met Harold Stikes, then Harold Stikes left his wife and children and moved out to the farm with them, and sometimes Cherry forgot to attend the meetings, she was so happy with Harold Stikes.

Tammy couldn't see *why,* initially. In her opinion, Harold Stikes was about as interesting as a telephone pole. "But he's so *nice!*" Cherry tried to explain it to Tammy Lynn. Finally Tammy decided that there is nothing in the world that makes somebody as attractive as if they really love you. And Harold Stikes really did love her mama, there was no question. That old man—what a crazy old Romeo! Why, he proposed to Cherry when she was still in the hospital after she had her breast removed (this was back when they thought that was *it,* that the doctors had gotten it all).

"Listen, Cherry," he said solemnly, gripping a dozen red roses. "I want you to marry me."

"What?" Cherry said. She was still groggy.

"I want you to marry me," Harold said. He knelt down heavily beside her bed.

"Harold! Get up from there!" Cherry said. "Somebody will see you."

"Say yes," said Harold.

"I just had my breast removed."

"Say yes," he said again.

"*Yes, yes, yes!*" Cherry said.

And as soon as she got out of the hospital, they were married out in the orchard, on a beautiful April day, by Lew Uggams, a JP from out of town. They couldn't find a local preacher to do it. The sky was bright blue, not a cloud in sight. Nobody was invited except Stan, Tammy, Rhonda and Bill, and Cherry's mother, who wore her dress inside out. Cherry wore a new pink lace dress, the color of cherry blossoms. Tough little Tammy cried and cried. It's the most beautiful wedding she's ever seen, and now she's completely devoted to Harold Stikes.

So Tammy leaves the lights on for Harold when she finally goes to bed that night. She tried to wait up for him, but she has to go to school in the morning, she's got a chemistry test. Her mamaw is sound asleep in the little added-on baby room that Buddy Oxendine built for Cherry. Gladys acts like a baby now, a spoiled baby at that. The only thing she'll drink is Sprite out of a can. She talks mean. She doesn't like anything in the world except George and Tammy, the two remaining cockapoos.

They bark up a storm when Harold finally gets back out to the farm, at one-thirty. The cockapoos are barking, Cherry's mom is snoring like a chain saw. Harold doesn't see how Tammy Lynn can sleep through all of this, but she always does. Teenagers can sleep through anything. Harold himself has started waking up several times a night, his heart pounding. He wonders if he's going to have a heart attack. He almost mentioned his symptoms to Lois Hickey last week, in fact, but then thought, What the hell. His heart is broken. Of course it's going to act up some. And everything, not only his heart, is out of whack. Sometimes he'll break into a sweat for no reason. Often he forgets really crucial things, such as filing his estimated income tax on January 15. Harold is not the kind to forget something this important. He has strange aches that float from joint to joint. He has headaches. He's lost twelve pounds. Sometimes he has no appetite at all. Other times, like right now, he's just starving.

Harold goes in the kitchen and finds a flat rectangular casserole, carefully wrapped in tinfoil, on the counter, along with a Tupperware cake carrier. He lifts off the top of the cake carrier and finds a piña colada cake, his favorite. Then he pulls back the tinfoil on the casserole. Lasagna! Plenty is left over. Harold sticks it in the microwave. He knows that the cake and the lasagna were left here by his ex-wife. Ever since Cherry has been in Intensive Care, Joan has been bringing food out to the farm. She comes when Harold's at work or at the hospital, and leaves it with Gladys or Tammy. She probably figures that Harold would refuse it, if she caught him at home, which he would. She's a great cook, though. Harold takes the lasagna out of the microwave, opens a beer, and sits down at the kitchen table. He loves Joan's lasagna. Cherry's idea of a terrific meal is one she doesn't have to cook. Harold remembers eating in bed with Cherry, tacos from Taco Bell, sour-cream-and-onion chips, beer. He gets some more lasagna and a big wedge of piña colada cake.

Now it's two-thirty, but for some reason Harold is not a bit sleepy. His mind whirls with thoughts of Cherry. He snaps off all the lights and stands in the darkened house. His heart is racing. Moonlight comes in the windows, it falls on the old patterned rug. Outside, it's as bright as day. He puts his coat on and goes out, with the cockapoos scampering along beside him. They are not even surprised. They think it's a fine time for a walk. Harold goes past the mailbox, down the dirt road between the fields. Out here in the country, the sky is both bigger and closer than it is in town. Harold feels like he's in a huge bowl turned upside down, with tiny little pinpoints of light shining through. And everything is silvered by the moonlight—the old fence-posts, the corn stubble in the flat long fields, a distant barn, the highway at the end of the dirt road, his own strange hand when he holds it out to look at it.

He remembers when she waited on him in the Food Lion deli, three years ago. He had asked for a roast beef sandwich, which come prepackaged. Cherry put it on his plate. Then she paused, and cocked her hip, and looked at him. "Can I give you some potato salad to go with that?" she asked. "Some slaw?"

Harold looked at her. Some red curls had escaped the required net. "Nothing else," he said.

But Cherry spooned a generous helping of potato salad onto his plate. "Thank you so much," he said. They looked at each other.

"I know I know you," Cherry said.

It came to him then. "Cherry Oxendine," said Harold. "I remember you from high school."

"Lord, you've got a great memory, then!" Cherry had an easy laugh. "That was a hundred years ago."

"Doesn't seem like it." Harold knew he was holding up the line.

"Depends on who you're talking to," Cherry said.

Later that day, Harold found an excuse to go back over to the deli for coffee and apple pie, then he found an excuse to look through the personnel files. He started eating lunch at the deli every day, without making any conscious decision to do so. In the afternoons, when he went back for coffee, Cherry would take her break and sit at a table with him.

Harold and Cherry talked and talked. They talked about their families, their kids, high school. Cherry told him everything that had happened to her. She was tough and funny, not bitter or self-pitying. They talked and talked. In his whole life, Harold had never had so much to say. During this period, which lasted for several weeks, his whole life took on a heightened aspect. Everything that happened to him seemed significant, a little incident to tell Cherry about. Every song he liked on the radio he remembered, so he could ask Cherry if she liked it too. Then there came the day when they were having coffee and she mentioned she'd left her car at Al's Garage that morning to get a new clutch.

"I'll give you a ride over there to pick it up," said Harold instantly. In his mind he immediately canceled the sales meeting he had scheduled for four o'clock.

"Oh, that's too much trouble," Cherry said.

"But I insist." In his conversations with Cherry, Harold had developed a brand-new gallant manner he had never had before.

"Well, if you're sure it's not any trouble . . ." Cherry grinned at him like she knew he really wanted to do it, and that afternoon when he grabbed her hand suddenly before letting her out at Al's Garage, she did not pull it away.

The next weekend Harold took her up to Memphis and they stayed at the Peabody Hotel, where Cherry got the biggest kick out of the ducks in the lobby, and ordering from room service.

"You're a fool," Harold's friends told him later, when the shit hit the fan.

But Harold didn't think so. He doesn't think so now, walking the old dirt road on the Oxendine farm in the moonlight. He loves his wife. He feels that he has been ennobled and enlarged, by knowing Cherry Oxendine. He feels like he has been specially selected among men, to receive a precious gift. He stepped out of his average life for her, he gave up being a good man, but the rewards have been extraordinary. He's glad he did it. He'd do it all over again.

Still walking, Harold suddenly knows that something is going to happen. But he doesn't stop walking. Only, the whole world around him seems to waver a bit, and intensify. The moonlight shines whiter than ever. A little wind whips up out of nowhere. The stars are twinkling so brightly that they seem to dance, actually dance, in the sky. And then, while Harold watches, one of them detaches itself from the rest of the sky and grows larger, moves closer, until it's clear that it is actually moving across the sky, at an angle to the earth. A falling star, perhaps? A comet?

Harold stops walking. The star moves faster and faster, with an erratic pattern. It's getting real close now. It's no star. Harold hears a high whining noise, like a blender. The cockapoos huddle against his ankles. They don't bark. Now he can see the blinking red lights on the top of it, and the beam of white light shooting out the bottom. His coat is blown straight out behind him by the wind. He feels like he's going blind. He shields his eyes. At first it's as big as a barn, then a tobacco warehouse. It covers the field. Although Harold can't say exactly how it communicates to him or even if it does, suddenly his soul is filled to bursting. The ineffable occurs. And then, more quickly than it came, it's gone, off toward Carrollton, rising into the night, leaving the field, the farm, the road. Harold turns back.

It will take Cherry Oxendine two more weeks to die. She's tough. And even when there's nothing left of her but heart, she will fight all the way. She will go out furious, squeezing Harold's hand at the very moment of death, clinging fast to every minute of this bright, hard life. And although at first he won't want to, Harold will go on living. He will buy another store. Gladys will die. Tammy Lynn will make Phi Beta Kappa. Harold will start attending the Presbyterian church again. Eventually Harold may even go back to his family, but he will love Cherry Oxendine until the day he dies, and he will never, ever, tell anybody what he saw.

# Jean Stafford

*Stafford (1915–1979) was born in Covina, California, the daughter of a writer. She was educated at the University of Colorado and Heidelberg University. Though she wrote of cosmopolitan scenes, at the heart of many stories is a self-conscious, vulnerable child, viewing the promises of the world with an aching mistrust. Her novels include* Boston Adventure *(1944) and* The Mountain Lion *(1947). Her stories have been brought together in* Children Are Bored on Sunday *(1953),* Bad Characters *(1964), and* The Collected Stories *(1969).*

## In the Zoo

Keening harshly in his senility, the blind polar bear slowly and ceaselessly shakes his head in the stark heat of the July and mountain noon. His open eyes are blue. No one stops to look at him; an old farmer, in passing, sums up the old bear's situation by observing, with a ruthless chuckle, that he is a "back number." Patient and despairing, he sits on his yellowed haunches on the central rock of his pool, his huge toy paws wearing short boots of mud.

The grizzlies to the right of him, a conventional family of father and mother and two spring cubs, alternately play the clown and sleep. There is a blustery, scoundrelly, half-likable bravado in the manner of the black bear on the polar's left; his name, according to the legend on his cage, is Clancy, and he is a rough-and-tumble, brawling blowhard, thundering continually as he paces back and forth, or pauses to face his audience of children and mothers and release from his great, gray-tongued mouth a perfectly Vesuvian roar. If he were to be reincarnated in human form, he would be a man of action, possibly a football coach, probably a politician. One expects to see his black hat hanging from a branch of one of his trees; at any moment he will light a cigar.

The polar bear's next-door neighbors are not the only ones who offer so sharp and sad a contrast to him. Across a reach of scrappy grass and litter is the convocation of conceited monkeys, burrowing into each other's necks and chests for fleas, picking their noses with their long, black, finicky fingers, swinging by their gifted tails on the flying trapeze, screaming bloody murder. Even when they mourn—one would think the male orangutan was on the very brink of suicide—they are comedians; they only fake depression, for they are firmly secure in their rambunctious tribalism and in their appalling insight and contempt. Their flibbertigibbet gamboling is a sham, and, stealthily and shiftily, they are really watching the pitiful polar bear ("Back number," they quote the farmer. "That's *his* number all right," they snigger), and the windy black bear ("Life of the party. Gasbag. Low I.Q.," they note scornfully on his dossier), and the stupid, bourgeois grizzlies ("It's feed the face and hit the sack for them," the monkeys say). And they are watching my sister and me, two middle-aged women, as we sit on a bench between the exhibits, eating popcorn, growing thirsty. We are thoughtful.

A chance remark of Daisy's a few minutes before has turned us to memory and meditation. "I don't know why," she said, "but that poor blind bear reminds me of Mr. Murphy." The name "Mr. Murphy" at once returned us both to childhood, and we were floated far and fast, our later lives diminished. So now we eat our popcorn in silence with the ritualistic appetite of childhood, which has little to do with hunger; it is not so much food as a sacrament, and in tribute to our sisterliness and our friendliness I break the silence to say that this is the best popcorn I have ever eaten in my life. The extravagance of my statement instantly makes me feel self-indulgent, and for some time I uneasily avoid looking at the blind bear. My sister does not agree or disagree; she simply says that popcorn is the only food she has ever really liked. For a long time, then, we eat without a word, but I know, because I know her well and know her similarity to me, that Daisy is thinking what I am thinking; both of us are mournfully remembering Mr. Murphy, who, at one time in our lives, was our only friend.

This zoo is in Denver, a city that means nothing to my sister and me except as a place to take or meet trains. Daisy lives two hundred miles farther west, and it is her custom, when my every-other-year visit with her is over, to come across the mountains to see me off on my eastbound train. We know almost no one here, and because our stays are short, we have never bothered to learn the town in more than the most desultory way. We know the Burlington[1] uptown office and the respectable hotels, a restaurant or two, the Union Station, and, beginning today, the zoo in the city park.

But since the moment that Daisy named Mr. Murphy by name our situation in Denver has been only corporeal; our minds and our hearts are in Adams, fifty miles north, and we are seeing, under the white sun at its pitiless meridian, the streets of that ugly town, its parks and trees and bridges, the bandstand in its dreary park, the roads that lead away from it, west to the mountains and east to the plains, its mongrel and multitudinous churches, its high school shaped like a loaf of bread, the campus of its college, an oasis of which we had no experience except to walk through it now and then, eyeing the woodbine on the impressive buildings. These things are engraved forever on our minds with a legibility so insistent that you have only to say the name of the town aloud to us to rip the rinds from our nerves and leave us exposed in terror and humiliation.

We have supposed in later years that Adams was not so bad as all that, and we know that we magnified its ugliness because we looked upon it as the extension of the possessive, unloving, scornful, complacent foster mother, Mrs.

1. Burlington Railway.

Placer, to whom, at the death of our parents within a month of each other, we were sent like Dickensian grotesqueries[2]—cowardly, weak-stomached, given to tears, backward in school. Daisy was ten and I was eight when, unaccompanied, we made the long trip from Marblehead to our benefactress, whom we had never seen and, indeed, never heard of until the pastor of our church came to tell us of the arrangement our father had made on his deathbed, seconded by our mother on hers. This man, whose name and face I have forgotten and whose parting speeches to us I have not forgiven, tried to dry our tears with talk of Indians and of buffaloes; he spoke, however, at much greater length, and in preaching cadences, of the Christian goodness of Mrs. Placer. She was, he said, childless and fond of children, and for many years she had been a widow, after the lingering demise of her tubercular husband, for whose sake she had moved to the Rocky Mountains. For his support and costly medical care, she had run a boarding house, and after his death, since he had left her nothing, she was obliged to continue running it. She had been a girlhood friend of our paternal grandmother, and our father, in the absence of responsible relatives, had made her the beneficiary of his life insurance on the condition that she lodge and rear us. The pastor, with a frankness remarkable considering that he was talking to children, explained to us that our father had left little more than a drop in the bucket for our care, and he enjoined us to give Mrs. Placer, in return for her hospitality and sacrifice, courteous help and eternal thanks. "Sacrifice" was a word we were never allowed to forget.

And thus it was, in grief for our parents, that we came cringing to the dry Western town and to the house where Mrs. Placer lived, a house in which the square, uncushioned furniture was cruel and the pictures on the walls were either dour or dire and the lodgers, who lived in the upper floors among shadowy wardrobes and chiffoniers, had come through the years to resemble their landlady in appearance as well as in deportment.

After their ugly-colored evening meal, Gran—as she bade us call her—and her paying guests would sit, rangy and aquiline, rocking on the front porch on spring and summer and autumn nights, tasting their delicious grievances: those slights delivered by ungrateful sons and daughters, those impudences committed by trolley-car conductors and uppity salesgirls in the ready-to-wear, all those slurs and calculated elbow-jostlings that were their daily crucifixion and their staff of life. We little girls, washing the dishes in the cavernous kitchen, listened to their even, martyred voices, fixed like leeches to their solitary subject and their solitary creed—that life was essentially a matter of being done in, let down, and swindled.

At regular intervals, Mrs. Placer, chairwoman of the victims, would say, "Of course, I don't care; I just have to laugh," and then would tell a shocking tale of an intricate piece of skulduggery perpetrated against her by someone she did not even know. Sometimes, with her avid, partial jury sitting there on the porch behind the bitter hopvines in the heady mountain air, the cases she tried involved Daisy and me, and, listening, we travailed, hugging each other, whispering, "I wish she wouldn't! Oh, how did she find out?" How *did* she?

2. Like the caricaturish characters in Charles Dickens's novels.

Certainly we never told her when we were snubbed or chosen last on teams, never admitted to a teacher's scolding or to the hoots of laughter that greeted us when we bit on silly, unfair jokes. But she knew. She knew about the slumber parties we were not invited to, the beefsteak fries at which we were pointedly left out; she knew that the singing teacher had said in so many words that I could not carry a tune in a basket and that the sewing superintendent had said that Daisy's fingers were all thumbs. With our teeth chattering in the cold of our isolation, we would hear her protestant, litigious voice defending our right to be orphans, paupers, wholly dependent on her—except for the really ridiculous pittance from our father's life insurance—when it was all she could do to make ends meet. She did not care, but she had to laugh that people in general were so small-minded that they looked down on fatherless, motherless waifs like us and, by association, looked down on her. It seemed funny to her that people gave her no credit for taking on these sickly youngsters who were not even kin but only the grandchildren of a friend.

If a child with braces on her teeth came to play with us, she was, according to Gran, slyly lording it over us because our teeth were crooked but there was no money to have them straightened. And what could be the meaning of our being asked to come for supper at the doctor's house? Were the doctor and his la-di-da New York wife and those pert girls with their solid-gold barrettes and their Shetland pony going to shame her poor darlings? Or shame their poor Gran by making them sorry to come home to the plain but honest life that was all she could provide for them?

There was no stratum of society not reeking with the effluvium of fraud and pettifoggery. And the school system was almost the worst of all: if we could not understand fractions, was that not our teacher's fault? And therefore what right had she to give us F? It was as plain as a pikestaff[3] to Gran that the teacher was only covering up her own inability to teach. It was unlikely, too—highly unlikely—that it was by accident that time and time again the free medical clinic was closed for the day just as our names were about to be called out, so that nothing was done about our bad tonsils, which meant that we were repeatedly sick in the winter, with Gran fetching and carrying for us, climbing those stairs a jillion times a day with her game leg and her heart that was none too strong.

Steeped in these mists of accusation and hidden plots and double meanings, Daisy and I grew up like worms. I think no one could have withstood the atmosphere in that house where everyone trod on eggs that a little bird had told them were bad. They spied on one another, whispered behind doors, conjectured, drew parallels beginning "With all due respect . . ." or "It is a matter of indifference to *me* but . . ." The vigilantes patrolled our town by day, and by night returned to lay their goodies at their priestess's feet and wait for her oracular interpretation of the innards of the butcher, the baker, the candlestick maker, the soda jerk's girl, and the barber's unnatural deaf white cat.

Consequently, Daisy and I also became suspicious. But it was suspicion of ourselves that made us mope and weep and grimace with self-judgment. Why

3. Plain as day.

were we not happy when Gran had sacrificed herself to the bone for us? Why did we not cut dead the paper boy who had called her a filthy name? Why did we persist in our willful friendliness with the grocer who had tried, unsuccessfully, to overcharge her on a case of pork and beans?

Our friendships were nervous and surreptitious; we sneaked and lied, and as our hungers sharpened, our debasement deepened; we were pitied; we were shifty-eyed, always on the lookout for Mrs. Placer or one of her tattletale lodgers; we were hypocrites.

Nevertheless, one thin filament of instinct survived, and Daisy and I in time found asylum in a small menagerie down by the railroad tracks. It belonged to a gentle alcoholic ne'er-do-well, who did nothing all day long but drink bathtub gin in rickeys and play solitaire and smile to himself and talk to his animals. He had a little, stunted red vixen and a deodorized skunk, a parrot from Tahiti that spoke Parisian French, a woebegone coyote, and two capuchin monkeys, so serious and humanized, so small and sad and sweet, and so religious-looking with their tonsured heads that it was impossible not to think their gibberish was really an ordered language with the grammar that some day some philologist would understand.

Gran knew about our visits to Mr. Murphy and she did not object, for it gave her keen pleasure to excoriate him when we came home. His vice was not a matter of guesswork; it was an established fact that he was half-seas over from dawn till midnight. "With the black Irish," said Gran, "the taste for drink is taken in with the mother's milk and is never mastered. Oh, I know all about those promises to join the temperance movement and not to touch another drop. The way to hell is paved with good intentions."

We were still little girls when we discovered Mr. Murphy, before the shattering disease of adolescence was to make our bones and brains ache even more painfully than before, and we loved him and we hoped to marry him when we grew up. We loved him, and we loved his monkeys to exactly the same degree and in exactly the same way; they were husbands and fathers and brothers, these three little, ugly, dark, secret men who minded their own business and let us mind ours. If we stuck our fingers through the bars of the cage, the monkeys would sometimes take them in their tight, tiny hands and look into our faces with a tentative, somehow absent-minded sorrow, as if they terribly regretted that they could not place us but were glad to see us all the same. Mr. Murphy, playing a solitaire game of cards called "once in a blue moon" on a kitchen table in his back yard beside the pens, would occasionally look up and blink his beautiful blue eyes and say, "You're peaches to make over my wee friends. I love you for it." There was nothing demanding in his voice, and nothing sticky; on his lips the word "love" was jocose and forthright, it had no strings attached. We would sit on either side of him and watch him regiment his ranks of cards and stop to drink as deeply as if he were dying of thirst and wave to his animals and say to them, "Yes, lads, you're dandies."

Because Mr. Murphy was as reserved with us as the capuchins were, as courteously noncommittal, we were surprised one spring day when he told us that he had a present for us, which he hoped Mrs. Placer would let us keep; it was a puppy, for whom the owner had asked him to find a home—half collie and half Labrador retriever, blue-blooded on both sides.

"You might tell Mrs. Placer—" he said, smiling at the name, for Gran was famous in the town. "You might tell Mrs. Placer," said Mr. Murphy, "that this lad will make a fine watchdog. She'll never have to fear for her spoons again. Or her honor." The last he said to himself, not laughing but tucking his chin into his collar; lines sprang to the corners of his eyes. He would not let us see the dog, whom we could hear yipping and squealing inside his shanty, for he said that our disappointment would weigh on his conscience if we lost our hearts to the fellow and then could not have him for our own.

That evening at supper, we told Gran about Mr. Murphy's present. A dog? In the first place, why a dog? Was it possible that the news had reached Mr. Murphy's ears that Gran had just this very day finished planting her spring garden, the very thing that a rampageous dog would have in his mind to destroy? What sex was it? A male! Females, she had heard, were more trustworthy; males roved and came home smelling of skunk; such a consideration as this, of course, would not have crossed Mr. Murphy's fuddled mind. Was this young male dog housebroken? We had not asked? That was the limit!

Gran appealed to her followers, too raptly fascinated by Mr. Murphy's machinations to eat their Harvard beets. "Am I being farfetched or does it strike you as decidedly queer that Mr. Murphy is trying to fob off on my little girls a young cur that has not been trained?" she asked them. "If it were housebroken, he would have said so, so I feel it is safe to assume that it is not. Perhaps cannot *be* housebroken. I've heard of such cases."

The fantasy spun on, richly and rapidly, with all the skilled helping hands at work at once. The dog was tangibly in the room with us, shedding his hair, scratching his fleas, shaking rain off himself to splatter the walls, dragging some dreadful carcass across the floor, chewing up slippers, knocking over chairs with his tail, gobbling the chops from the platter, barking, biting, fathering, fighting, smelling to high heaven of carrion, staining the rug with his muddy feet, scratching the floor with his claws. He developed rabies; he bit a child, two children! Three! Everyone in town! And Gran and her poor darlings went to jail for harboring this murderous, odoriferous, drunk, Roman Catholic dog.

And yet, astoundingly enough, she came around to agreeing to let us have the dog. It was, as Mr. Murphy had predicted, the word "watchdog" that deflected the course of the trial. The moment Daisy uttered it, Gran halted, marshaling her reverse march; while she rallied and tacked and reconnoitered, she sent us to the kitchen for the dessert. And by the time this couse was under way, the uses of a dog, the enormous potentialities for investigation and law enforcement in a dog trained by Mrs. Placer, were being minutely and passionately scrutinized by the eight upright bloodhounds sitting at the table wolfing their brown Betty as if it were fresh-killed rabbit. The dog now sat at attention beside his mistress, fiercely alert, ears cocked, nose aquiver, the protector of widows, of orphans, of lonely people who had no homes. He made short shrift of burglars, homicidal maniacs, Peeping Toms, gypsies, bogus missionaries, Fuller Brush men with a risqué spiel. He went to the store and brought back groceries, retrieved the evening paper from the awkward place the boy had meanly thrown it, rescued cripples from burning houses, saved children from drowning, heeled at command, begged, lay down, stood up, sat, jumped through a hoop, ratted.

Both times—when he was a ruffian of the blackest delinquency and then a pillar of society—he was full-grown in his prefiguration, and when Laddy appeared on the following day, small, unsteady, and whimpering lonesomely, Gran and her lodgers were taken aback; his infant, clumsy paws embarrassed them, his melting eyes were unapropos. But it could never be said of Mrs. Placer, as Mrs. Placer her own self said, that she was a women who went back on her word, and her darlings were going to have their dog, softheaded and feckless as he might be. All the first night, in his carton in the kitchen, he wailed for his mother, and in the morning, it was true, he had made a shambles of the room—fouled the floor, and pulled off the tablecloth together with a ketchup bottle, so that thick gore lay everywhere. At breakfast, the lodgers confessed they had had a most amusing night, for it had actually been funny the way the dog had been determined not to let anyone get a wink of sleep. After that first night, Laddy slept in our room, receiving from us, all through our delighted, sleepless nights, pats and embraces and kisses and whispers. He was our baby, our best friend, the smartest, prettiest, nicest dog in the entire wide world. Our soft and rapid blandishments excited him to yelp at us in pleased bewilderment, and then we would playfully grasp his muzzle, so that he would snarl, deep in this throat like an adult dog, and shake his head violently, and, when we freed him, nip us smartly with great good will.

He was an intelligent and genial dog and we trained him quickly. He steered clear of Gran's radishes and lettuce after she had several times given him a brisk comeuppance with a strap across the rump, and he soon left off chewing shoes and the laundry on the line, and he outgrew his babyish whining. He grew like a weed; he lost his spherical softness, and his coat, which had been sooty fluff, came in stiff and rusty black; his nose grew aristocratically long, and his clever, pointed ears stood at attention. He was all bronzy, lustrous black except for an Elizabethan ruff[4] of white and a tip of white at the end of his perky tail. No one could deny that he was exceptionally handsome and that he had, as well, great personal charm and style. He escorted Daisy and me to school in the morning, laughing interiorly out of the enormous pleasure of his life as he gracefully cantered ahead of us, distracted occasionally by his private interest in smells or unfamiliar beings in the grass but, on the whole, engrossed in his role of chaperone. He made friends easily with other dogs, and sometimes he went for a long hunting weekend into the mountains with a huge and bossy old red hound named Mess, who had been on the county[5] most of his life and had made a good thing of it, particularly at the fire station.

It was after one of these three-day excursions into the high country that Gran took Laddy in hand. He had come back spent and filthy, his coat a mass of cockleburs and ticks, his eyes bloodshot, loud *râles*[6] in his chest; for half

4. I.e., a collar of thick, marked hair accentuating the head, looking like the collar worn by Elizabethan gentlemen. 5. On welfare. 6. Abnormal sounds accompanying the normal respiratory murmur, as in pulmonary diseases.

a day he lay motionless before the front door like someone in a hangover, his groaning eyes explicitly saying "Oh, for God's sake, leave me be" when we offered him food or bowls of water. Gran was disapproving, then affronted, and finally furious. Not, of course, with Laddy, since all inmates of her house enjoyed immunity, but with Mess, whose caddish character, together with that of his nominal masters, the firemen, she examined closely under a strong light, with an air of detachment, with her not caring but her having, all the same, to laugh. A lodger who occupied the back west room had something to say about the fire chief and his nocturnal visits to a certain house occupied by a certain group of young women, too near the same age to be sisters and too old to be the daughters of the woman who claimed to be their mother. What a story! The exophthalmic librarian—she lived in one of the front rooms—had some interesting insinuations to make about the deputy marshal, who had borrowed, significantly, she thought, a book on hypnotism. She also knew—she was, of course, in a most useful position in the town, and from her authoritative pen in the middle of the library her mammiform and azure eyes and her eager ears missed nothing—that the fire chief's wife was not as scrupulous as she might be when she was keeping score on bridge night at the Sorosis.

There was little at the moment that Mrs. Placer and her disciples could do to save the souls of the Fire Department and their families, and therefore save the town from holocaust (a very timid boarder—a Mr. Beaver, a newcomer who was not to linger long—had sniffed throughout this recitative as if he were smelling burning flesh), but at least the unwholesome bond between Mess and Laddy could and would be severed once and for all. Gran looked across the porch at Laddy, who lay stretched at full length in the darkest corner, shuddering and baying abortively in his throat as he chased jack rabbits in his dreams, and she said, "A dog can have morals like a human." With this declaration Laddy's randy, manly holidays were finished. It may have been telepathy that woke him; he lifted his heavy head from his paws, laboriously got up, hesitated for a moment, and then padded languidly across the porch to Gran. He stood docilely beside her chair, head down, tail drooping as if to say, "O.K., Mrs. Placer, show me how and I'll walk the straight and narrow."

The very next day, Gran changed Laddy's name to Caesar, as being more dignified, and a joke was made at the supper table that he had come, seen, and conquered Mrs. Placer's heart—for within her circle, where the magnanimity she lavished upon her orphans was daily demonstrated, Mrs. Placer's heart was highly thought of. On that day also, although we did not know it yet, Laddy ceased to be our dog. Before many weeks passed, indeed, he ceased to be anyone we had ever known. A week or so after he became Caesar, he took up residence in her room, sleeping alongside her bed. She broke him of the habit of taking us to school (temptation to low living was rife along those streets; there was a chow—well, never mind) by the simple expedient of chaining him to a tree as soon as she got up in the morning. This discipline, together with the stamina building cuffs she gave his sensitive ears from time to time, gradually but certainly remade his character. From a sanguine, affectionate, easy-going Gael (with the fits of melancholy that alternated with the larkiness), he turned into an overbearing, military, efficient, loud-voiced Teuton.[7] His bark, once wide of range, narrowed to one dark, glottal tone.

Soon the paper boy flatly refused to serve our house after Caesar efficiently removed the bicycle clip from his pants leg; the skin was not broken, or even bruised, but it was a matter of principle with the boy. The milkman approached the back door in a seizure of shakes like St. Vitus's dance. The metermen, the coal men, and the garbage collector crossed themselves if they were Catholics and, if they were not, tried whistling in the dark. "Good boy, good Caesar," they caroled, and, unctuously lying, they said they knew his bark was worse than his bite, knowing full well that it was not, considering the very nasty nip, requiring stitches, he had given a representative of the Olson Rug Company, who had had the folly to pat him on the head. Caesar did not molest the lodgers, but he disdained them and he did not brook being personally addressed by anyone except Gran. One night, he wandered into the dining room, appearing to be in search of something he had mislaid, and, for some reason that no one was ever able to divine, suddenly stood stock-still and gave the easily upset Mr. Beaver a long and penetrating look. Mr. Beaver, trembling from head to toe, stammered, "Why—er, hello there, Caesar, old boy, old boy," and Caesar charged. For a moment, it was touch and go, but Gran saved Mr. Beaver, only to lose him an hour later when he departed, bag and baggage, for the Y.M.C.A. This rout and the consequent loss of revenue would more than likely have meant Caesar's downfall and his deportation to the pound if it had not been that a newly widowed druggist, very irascible and very much Gran's style, had applied for a room in her house a week or so before, and now he moved in delightedly, as if he were coming home.

Finally, the police demanded that Caesar be muzzled and they warned that if he committed any major crime again—they cited the case of the Olson man—he would be shot on sight. Mrs. Placer, although she had no respect for the law, knowing as much as she did about its agents, obeyed. She obeyed, that is, in part; she put the muzzle on Caesar for a few hours a day, usually early in the morning when the traffic was light and before the deliveries had started, but the rest of the time his powerful jaws and dazzling white saber teeth were free and snapping. There was between these two such preternatural rapport, such an impressive conjugation of suspicion, that he, sensing the approach of a policeman, could convey instantly to her the immediate necessity of clapping his nose cage on. And the policeman, sent out on the complaint of a terrorized neighbor, would be greeted by this law-abiding pair at the door.

Daisy and I wished we were dead. We were divided between hating Caesar and loving Laddy, and we could not give up the hope that something, some day, would change him back into the loving animal he had been before he was appointed vice-president of the Placerites. Now at the meetings after supper on the porch he took an active part, standing rigidly at Gran's side except when she sent him on an errand. He carried out these assignments not with an air of

7. The terms Gael and Teuton are here used to refer to different kinds of temperament. The author is invoking popularized stereotypes to represent this difference.

a servant but with that of an accomplice. "Get me the paper, Caesar," she would say to him, and he, dismayingly intelligent and a shade smart-alecky, would open the screen door by himself and in a minute come back with the *Bulletin*, from which Mrs. Placer would then read an item, like the Gospel of the day, and then read between the lines of it, scandalized.

In the deepening of our woe and our bereavement and humiliation, we mutely appealed to Mr. Murphy. We did not speak outright to him, for Mr. Murphy lived in a state of indirection, and often when he used the pronoun "I," he seemed to be speaking of someone standing a little to the left of him, but we went to see him and his animals each day during the sad summer, taking what comfort we could from the cozy, quiet indolence of his back yard, where small black eyes encountered ours politely and everyone was half asleep. When Mr. Murphy inquired about Laddy in his bland, inattentive way, looking for a stratagem whereby to shift the queen of hearts into position by the king, we would say, "Oh, he's fine," or "Laddy is a nifty dog." And Mr. Murphy, reverently slaking the thirst that was his talent and his concubine, would murmur, "I'm glad."

We wanted to tell him, we wanted his help, or at least his sympathy, but how could we cloud his sunny world? It was awful to see Mr. Murphy ruffled. Up in the calm clouds as he generally was, he could occasionally be brought to earth with a thud, as we had seen and heard one day. Not far from his house, there lived a bad, troublemaking boy of twelve, who was forever hanging over the fence trying to teach the parrot obscene words. He got nowhere, for she spoke no English and she would flabbergast him with her cold eye and sneer, "*Tant pis.*"[8] One day, this boorish fellow went too far; he suddenly shot his head over the fence like a jack-in-the-box and aimed a water pistol at the skunk's face. Mr. Murphy leaped to his feet in a scarlet rage; he picked up a stone and threw it accurately, hitting the boy square in the back, so hard that he fell right down in a mud puddle and lay there kicking and squalling and, as it turned out, quite badly hurt. "If you ever come back here again, I'll kill you!" roared Mr. Murphy. I think he meant it, for I have seldom seen an anger so resolute, so brilliant, and so voluble. "How dared he!" he cried, scrambling into Mallow's cage to hug and pet and soothe her. "He must be absolutely mad! He must be the Devil!" He did not go back to his game after that but paced the yard, swearing a blue streak and only pausing to croon to his animals, now as frightened by him as they had been by the intruder, and to drink straight from the bottle, not bothering with fixings. We were fascinated by this unfamiliar side of Mr. Murphy, but we did not want to see it ever again, for his face had grown so dangerously purple and the veins of his forehead seemed ready to burst and his eyes looked scorched. He was the closest thing to a maniac we had ever seen. So we did not tell him about Laddy; what he did not know would not hurt him, although it was hurting us, throbbing in us like a great, bleating wound.

But eventually Mr. Murphy heard about our dog's conversion, one night at the pool hall, which he visited from time to time when he was seized with a

8. Too bad (French).

rare but compelling garrulity, and the next afternoon when he asked us how Laddy was and we replied that he was fine, he tranquilly told us, as he deliberated whether to move the jack of clubs now or to bide his time, that we were sweet girls but we were lying in our teeth. He did not seem at all angry but only interested, and all the while he questioned us, he went on about his business with the gin and the hearts and spades and diamonds and clubs. It rarely happened that he won the particular game he was playing, but that day he did, and when he saw all the cards laid out in their ideal pattern, he leaned back, looking disappointed, and he said, "I'm damned." He then scooped up the cards, in a gesture unusually quick and tidy for him, stacked them together, and bound them with a rubber band. Then he began to tell us what he thought of Gran. He grew as loud and apoplectic as he had been that other time, and though he kept repeating that he knew *we* were innocent and he put not a shred of the blame on us, we were afraid he might suddenly change his mind, and, speechless, we cowered against the monkeys' cage. In dread, the monkeys clutched the fingers we offered to them and made soft, protesting noises, as if to say, "Oh, stop it, Murphy! Our nerves!"

As quickly as it had started, the tantrum ended. Mr. Murphy paled to his normal complexion and said calmly that the only practical thing was to go and have it out with Mrs. Placer. "At once," he added, although he said he bitterly feared that it was too late and there would be no exorcising the fiend from Laddy's misused spirit. And because he had given the dog to us and not to her, he required that we go along with him, stick up for our rights, stand on our own mettle, get up our Irish, and give the old bitch something to put in her pipe and smoke.

Oh, it was hot that day! We walked in a kind of delirium through the summer, where only the grasshoppers had the energy to move, and I remember wondering if ether smelled like the gin on Mr. Murphy's breath. Daisy and I, in one way or another, were going to have our gizzards cut out along with our hearts and our souls and our pride, and I wished I were as drunk as Mr. Murphy, who swam effortlessly through the heat, his lips parted comfortably, his eyes half closed. When we turned into the path at Gran's house, my blood began to scald my veins. It was futile and so dangerous and so absurd. Here we were on a high moral mission, two draggletailed, gumptionless little girls and a toper whom no one could take seriously, partly because he was little more than a gurgling bottle of booze and partly because of the clothes he wore. He was a sight, as he always was when he was out of his own yard. There, somehow, in the carefree disorder, his clothes did not look especially strange, but on the streets of the town, in the barbershop or the post office or on Gran's path, they were fantastic. He wore a pair of hound's-tooth pants, old but maintaining a vehement pattern, and with them he wore a collarless blue flannelette shirt. His hat was the silliest of all, because it was a derby three sizes too big. And as if Shannon, too, was a part of his funny-paper costume, the elder capuchin rode on his shoulder, tightly embracing his thin red neck.

Gran and Caesar were standing side by side behind the screen door, looking as if they had been expecting us all along. For a moment, Gran and Mr. Murphy faced each other across the length of weedy brick between the gate and the front porch, and no one spoke. Gran took no notice at all of Daisy and me. She adjusted her eyeglasses, using both hands, and then looked down at Caesar and matter-of-factly asked, "Do you want out?"

Caesar flung himself full-length upon the screen and it sprang open like a jaw. I ran to meet him and head him off, and Daisy threw a library book at his head, but he was on Mr. Murphy in one split second and had his monkey off his shoulder and had broken Shannon's neck in two shakes. He would have gone on nuzzling and mauling and growling over the corpse for hours if Gran had not marched out of the house and down the path and slapped him lightly on the flank and said, in a voice that could not have deceived an idiot, "Why, Caesar, you scamp! You've hurt Mr. Murphy's monkey! Aren't you ashamed!"

Hurt the monkey! In one final, apologetic shudder, the life was extinguished from the little fellow. Bloody and covered with slather, Shannon lay with his arms suppliantly stretched over his head, his leather fingers curled into loose, helpless fists. His hind legs and his tail lay limp and helter-skelter on the path. And Mr. Murphy, all of a sudden reeling drunk, burst into the kind of tears that Daisy and I knew well—the kind that time alone could stop. We stood aghast in the dark-red sunset, killed by our horror and our grief for Shannon and our unforgivable disgrace. We stood upright in a dead faint, and an eon passed before Mr. Murphy picked up Shannon's body and wove away, sobbing, "I don't believe it! I don't *believe* it!"

The very next day, again at morbid, heavy sunset, Caesar died in violent convulsions, knocking down two tall hollyhocks in his throes. Long after his heart had stopped, his right hind leg continued to jerk in aimless reflex. Madly methodical, Mr. Murphy had poisoned some meat for him, had thoroughly envenomed a whole pound of hamburger, and early in the morning, before sunup, when he must have been near collapse with his hangover, he had stolen up to Mrs. Placer's house and put it by the kitchen door. He was so stealthy that Caesar never stirred in his fool's paradise there on the floor by Gran. We knew these to be the facts, for Mr. Murphy made no bones about them. Afterward, he had gone home and said a solemn Requiem for Shannon in so loud a voice that someone sent for the police, and they took him away in the Black Maria to sober him up on strong green tea. By the time he was in the lockup and had confessed what he had done, it was far too late, for Caesar had already gulped down the meat. He suffered an undreamed-of agony in Gran's flower garden, and Daisy and I, unable to bear the sight of it, hiked up to the red rocks and shook there, wretchedly ripping to shreds the sand lilies that grew in the cracks. Flight was the only thing we could think of, but where could we go? We stared west at the mountains and quailed at the look of the stern white glacier; we wildly scanned the prairies for escape. "If only we were something besides kids! Besides girls!" mourned Daisy. I could not speak at all; I huddled in a niche of the rocks and cried.

No one in town, except, of course, her lodgers, had the slightest sympathy for Gran. The townsfolk allowed that Mr. Murphy was a drunk and was fighting Irish, but he had a heart and this was something that could never be said of Mrs. Placer. The neighbor who had called the police when he was chanting the

*Dies Irae*[9] before breakfast in that deafening monotone had said, "The poor guy is having some kind of a spell, so don't be rough on him, hear?" Mr. Murphy became, in fact, a kind of hero; some people, stretching a point, said he was a saint for the way that every day and twice on Sunday he sang a memorial Mass over Shannon's grave, now marked with a chipped, cheap plaster figure of Saint Francis. He withdrew from the world more and more, seldom venturing into the streets at all, except when he went to the bootlegger to get a new bottle to snuggle into. All summer, all fall, we saw him as we passed by his yard, sitting at his dilapidated table, enfeebled with gin, graying, withering, turning his head ever and ever more slowly as he maneuvered the protocol of the kings and the queens and the knaves. Daisy and I could never stop to visit him again.

It went on like this, year after year. Daisy and I lived in a mesh of lies and evasions, baffled and mean, like rats in a maze. When we were old enough for beaux, we connived like sluts to see them, but we would never admit to their existence until Gran caught us out by some trick. Like this one, for example: Once, at the end of a long interrogation, she said to me, "I'm more relieved than I can tell you that you *don't* have anything to do with Jimmy Gilmore, because I happen to know that he is after only one thing in a girl," and then, off guard in the loving memory of sitting in the movies the night before with Jimmy, not even holding hands, I defended him and defeated myself, and Gran, smiling with success, said, "I *thought* you knew him. It's a pretty safe rule of thumb that where there's smoke there's fire." That finished Jimmy and me, for afterward I was nervous with him and I confounded and alarmed and finally bored him by trying to convince him, although the subject had not come up, that I did not doubt his good intentions.

Daisy and I would come home from school, or, later, from our jobs, with a small triumph or an interesting piece of news, and if we forgot ourselves and, in our exuberance, told Gran, we were hustled into court at once for cross-examination. Once, I remember, while I was still in high school, I told her about getting a part in a play. How very nice for me, she said, if that kind of make-believe seemed to me worth while. But what was my role? An old woman! A widow woman believed to be a witch? She did not care a red cent, but she did have to laugh in view of the fact that Miss Eccles, in charge of dramatics, had almost run her down in her car. And I would forgive her, would I not, if she did not come to see the play, and would not think her eccentric for not wanting to see herself ridiculed in public?

My pleasure strangled, I crawled, joy-killed, to our third-floor room. The room was small and its monstrous furniture was too big and the rag rugs were repulsive, but it was bright. We would not hang a blind at the window, and in this day I stood there staring into the mountains that burned with the sun. I feared the mountains, but at times like this their massiveness consoled me; they, at least, could not be gossiped about.

Why did we stay until we were grown? Daisy and I ask ourselves this question as we sit here on the bench in the municipal zoo, reminded of Mr.

9. Latin hymn, *The Day of Wrath* or *The Day of Judgment*.

Murphy by the polar bear, reminded by the monkeys not of Shannon but of Mrs. Placer's insatiable gossips at their post-prandial feast.

"But how could we have left?" says Daisy, wringing her buttery hands. "It was the depression. We had no money. We had nowhere to go."

"All the same, we could have gone," I say, resentful still of the waste of all those years. "We could have come here and got jobs as waitresses. Or prostitutes, for that matter."

"I wouldn't have wanted to be a prostitute," says Daisy.

We agree that under the circumstances it would have been impossible for us to run away. The physical act would have been simple, for the city was not far and we could have stolen the bus fare or hitched a ride. Later, when we began to work as salesgirls in Kress's,[1] it would have been no trick at all to vanish one Saturday afternoon with our week's pay, without so much as going home to say goodbye. But it had been infinitely harder than that, for Gran, as we now see, held us trapped by our sense of guilt. We were vitiated, and we had no choice but to wait, flaccidly, for her to die.

You may be sure we did not unlearn those years as soon as we put her out of sight in the cemetery and sold her house for a song to the first boob who would buy it. Nor did we forget when we left the town for another one, where we had jobs at a dude camp—the town where Daisy now lives with a happy husband and two happy sons. The succubus did not relent for years, and I can still remember, in the beginning of our days at the Lazy S 3, overhearing an edgy millionaire say to his wife, naming my name, "That girl gives me the cold shivers. One would think she had just seen a murder." Well, I had. For years, whenever I woke in the night in fear or pain or loneliness, I would increase my suffering by the memory of Shannon, and my tears were as bitter as poor Mr. Murphy's.

We have never been back to Adams. But we see that house plainly, with the hopvines straggling over the porch. The windows are hung with the cheapest grade of marquisette, dipped into coffee to impart to it an unwilling color, neither white nor tan but individual and spitefully unattractive. We see the wicker rockers and the swing, and through the screen door we dimly make out the slightly veering corridor, along one wall of which stands a glass-doored bookcase; when we were children, it had contained not books but stale old cardboard boxes filled with such things as W.C.T.U.[2] tracts and anti-cigarette literature and newspaper clippings relating to sexual sin in the Christianized islands of the Pacific.

Even if we were able to close our minds' eyes to the past, Mr. Murphy would still be before us in the apotheosis of the polar bear. My pain becomes intolerable, and I am relieved when Daisy rescues us. "We've got to go," she says in a sudden panic. "I've got asthma coming on." We rush to the nearest exit of the city park and hail a cab, and, once inside it, Daisy gives herself an injection of adrenalin and then leans back. We are heartbroken and infuriated, and we cannot speak.

1. Chain of dime stores. 2. Woman's Christian Temperance Union, an association of women formed in the United States in 1874 for the advancement of total abstinence and prohibition by organizing educational, evangelistic, and legal work.

Two hours later, beside my train, we clutch each other as if we were drowning. We ought to go out to the nearest policeman and say, "We are not responsible women. You will have to take care of us because we cannot take care of ourselves." But gradually the storm begins to lull.

"You're sure you've got your ticket?" says Daisy. "You'll surely be able to get a roomette once you're on."

"I don't know about that," I say. "If there are any V.I.P.s on board, I won't have a chance. 'Spinsters and Orphans Last' is the motto of this line."

Daisy smiles. "I didn't care," she says, "but I had to laugh when I saw that woman nab the redcap[3] you had signaled to. I had a good notion to give her a piece of my mind."

"It will be a miracle if I ever see my bags again," I say, mounting the steps of the train. "Do you suppose that blackguardly porter knows about the twenty-dollar gold piece in my little suitcase?"

"Anything's possible!" cries Daisy, and begins to laugh. She is so pretty, standing there in her bright-red linen suit and her black velvet hat. A solitary ray of sunshine comes through a broken pane in the domed vault of the train shed and lies on her shoulder like a silver arrow.

"So long, Daisy!" I call as the train begins to move.

She walks quickly along beside the train. "Watch out for pick-pockets!" she calls.

"You, too!" My voice is thin and lost in the increasing noise of the speeding train wheels. "Goodbye, old dear!"

I go at once to the club car and I appropriate the writing table, to the vexation of a harried priest, who snatches up the telegraph pad and gives me a sharp look. I write Daisy approximately the same letter I always write her under this particular set of circumstances, the burden of which is that nothing for either of us can ever be as bad as the past before Gran mercifully died. In a postscript I add: "There is a Roman Catholic priest (that is to say, he is *dressed* like one) sitting behind me although all the chairs on the opposite side of the car are empty. I can only conclude that he is looking over my shoulder, and while I do not want to cause you any alarm, I think you would be advised to be on the lookout for any appearance of miraculous medals, scapulars, papist booklets, etc., in the shops of your town. It really makes me laugh to see the way he is pretending that all he wants is for me to finish this letter so that he can have the table."

I sign my name and address the envelope, and I give up my place to the priest, who smiles nicely at me, and then I move across the car to watch the fields as they slip by. They are alfalfa fields, but you can bet your bottom dollar that they are chockablock with marijuana.

I begin to laugh. The fit is silent but it is devastating; it surges and rattles in my rib cage, and I turn my face to the window to avoid the narrow gaze of the Filipino bar boy. I must think of something sad to stop this unholy giggle, and I think of the polar bear. But even his bleak tragedy does not sober me. Wildly I fling open the newspaper I have brought and I pretend to be reading

3. Train station porter.

something screamingly funny. The words I see are in a Hollywood gossip column: "How a well-known starlet can get a divorce in Nevada without her crooner husband's consent, nobody knows. It won't be worth a plugged nickel here."

## R. V. CASSILL on *In the Zoo*

Just as she was among the best writers of her generation, she was also the luckiest and unluckiest.

Her father was a writer—of unsalable pulp Western stories—who worked incessantly on them while the modest family fortune dissolved with the failure of his "walnut ranch" in California.

After the family fled to Colorado, Jean soon participated in a writers' conference at Boulder. There, in a fairy-tale manner, her gifts as a writer were discovered by some of the visiting teachers; and for the rest of her life she was the companion and friend of writers of high reputation and influence.

Presently she married one of them, who broke her nose twice, once from his ineptitude as a driver and once from his ineptitude as a human being. She began to publish and to teach in a classy school for girls. Disease and an ugly scandal associated with it quickly terminated her career in the academic world. But by then sales of her novels supported her and her erratic husband. It is from this period of the late forties that her masterpiece of a novel, *The Mountain Lion,* comes. It has much the same mixture of hilarious horror and terrifying comedy that you find in the story published here—"In the Zoo."

Seen in retrospect, the sisters of the story are total victims of their guardian, the vicious and implacable Mrs. Placer. She thwarts every impulse they have to love and to know themselves as individuals. In the transformation of the dog from a fuzzy little companion to a mechanical killer, we see the witchlike power of the woman's disposition.

Her power to corrupt is displayed at its worst in what she does to the girls. As victims sometimes do, they internalize some of her wicked traits and attitudes. They have "seen a murder" and know no way to eradicate its triumph. In adulthood they remain paranoiac and immature. Yet, a kind of gallows humor redeems the whole history of misfortune. We retain the image of a love with shattered wings. This gallantry of hope as it succumbs to the power of Caesar is the signature of Jean Stafford, on a bleak page the sign of a surviving merriment.

# John Steinbeck

*Steinbeck (1902–1968) was born in Salinas, California. His mother was a former schoolteacher, who encouraged him to read widely as a child, but his formal schooling made little impression on him. He attended Stanford University intermittently, leaving in 1926 to drift through an array of odd jobs that educated him in the life of working people. His first, rather romantic novel,* Cup of Gold, *appeared in 1929. By 1936 his involvement with the struggles of migrant workers resulted in his militantly political novel* In Dubious Battle. *In 1937 his short novel* Of Mice and Men *proved immensely popular and provided the base for an equally popular film, as did* The Grapes of Wrath *in 1939. He served as a war correspondent during World War II. In 1962 he was awarded the Nobel Prize. His postwar novels include* East of Eden *(1952) and* The Winter of Our Discontent *(1961). Several of his stories are collected in* The Long Valley *(1938).*

## The Chrysanthemums

The high grey-flannel fog of winter closed off the Salinas Valley from the sky and from all the rest of the world. On every side it sat like a lid on the mountains and made of the great valley a closed pot. On the broad, level land floor the gang ploughs bit deep and left the black earth shining like metal where the shares had cut. On the foot-hill ranches across the Salinas River, the yellow stubble fields seemed to be bathed in pale cold sunshine, but there was no sunshine in the valley now in December. The thick willow scrub along the river flamed with sharp and positive yellow leaves.

It was a time of quiet and of waiting. The air was cold and tender. A light wind blew up from the southwest so that the farmers were mildly hopeful of a good rain before long; but fog and rain do not go together.

Across the river, on Henry Allen's foot-hill ranch there was little work to be done, for the hay was cut and stored and the orchards were ploughed up to receive the rain deeply when it should come. The cattle on the higher slopes were becoming shaggy and rough-coated.

Elisa Allen, working in her flower garden, looked down across the yard and saw Henry, her husband, talking to two men in business suits. The three of them stood by the tractor-shed, each man with one foot on the side of the little Fordson. They smoked cigarettes and studied the machine as they talked.

Elisa watched them for a moment and then went back to her work. She was thirty-five. Her face was lean and strong and her eyes were as clear as water. Her figure looked blocked and heavy in her gardening costume, a man's black hat pulled low down over her eyes, clod-hopper shoes, a figured print dress almost completely covered by a big corduroy apron with four big pockets to hold the snips, the trowel and scratcher, the seeds and the knife she worked with. She wore heavy leather gloves to protect her hands while she worked.

She was cutting down the old year's chrysanthemum stalks with a pair of short and powerful scissors. She looked down toward the men by the tractor-shed now and then. Her face was eager and mature and handsome; even her work with the scissors was overeager, over-powerful. The chrysanthemum stems seemed too small and easy for her energy.

She brushed a cloud of hair out of her eyes with the back of her glove, and left a smudge of earth on her cheek in doing it. Behind her stood the neat white farmhouse with red geraniums close-banked around it as high as the windows. It was a hard-swept-looking little house, with hard-polished windows, and a clean mud-mat on the front steps.

Elisa cast another glance toward the tractor-shed. The strangers were getting into their Ford coupé. She took off a glove and put her strong fingers down into the forest of new green chrysanthemum sprouts that were growing around the old roots. She spread the leaves and looked down among the close-growing stems. No aphids were there, no sow bugs or snails or cutworms. Her terrier fingers destroyed such pests before they could get started.

Elisa started at the sound of her husband's voice. He had come near quietly, and he leaned over the wire fence that protected her flower garden from cattle and dogs and chickens.

"At it again," he said. "You've got a strong new crop coming."

Elisa straightened her back and pulled on the gardening glove again. "Yes. They'll be strong this coming year." In her tone and on her face there was a little smugness.

"You've got a gift with things," Henry observed. "Some of those yellow chrysanthemums you had this year were ten inches across. I wish you'd work out in the orchard and raise some apples that big."

Her eyes sharpened. "Maybe I could do it, too. I've a gift with things, all right. My mother had it. She could stick anything in the ground and make it grow. She said it was having planters' hands that knew how to do it."

"Well, it sure works with flowers," he said.

"Henry, who were those men you were talking to?"

"Why, sure, that's what I came to tell you. They were from the Western Meat Company. I sold those thirty head of three-year-old steers. Got nearly my own price, too."

"Good," she said. "Good for you."

"And I thought," he continued, "I thought how it's Saturday afternoon, and we might go into Salinas for dinner at a restaurant, and then to a picture show—to celebrate, you see."

"Good," she repeated. "Oh, yes. That will be good."

Henry put on his joking tone. "There's fights tonight. How'd you like to go to the fights?"

"Oh, no," she said breathlessly. "No, I wouldn't like fights."

"Just fooling, Elisa. We'll go to a movie. Let's see. It's two now. I'm going to take Scotty and bring down those steers from the hill. It'll take us maybe two hours. We'll go in town about five and have dinner at the Cominos Hotel. Like that?"

"Of course I'll like it. It's good to eat away from home."

"All right, then. I'll go get up a couple of horses."

She said: "I'll have plenty of time to transplant some of these sets, I guess."

She heard her husband calling Scotty down by the barn. And a little later she saw the two men ride up the pale yellow hillside in search of the steers.

There was a little square sandy bed kept for rooting the chrysanthemums. With her trowel she turned the soil over and over, and smoothed it and patted it firm. Then she dug ten parallel trenches to receive the sets. Back at the chrysanthemum bed she pulled out the little crisp shoots, trimmed off the leaves of each one with her scissors and laid it on a small orderly pile.

A squeak of wheels and plod of hoofs came from the road. Elisa looked up. The country road ran along the dense bank of willows and cottonwoods that bordered the river, and up this road came a curious vehicle, curiously drawn. It was an old spring-wagon, with a round canvas top on it like the cover of a prairie schooner. It was drawn by an old bay horse and a little grey-and-white burro. A big stubble-bearded man sat between the cover flaps and drove the crawling team. Underneath the wagon, between the hind wheels, a lean and rangy mongrel dog walked sedately. Words were painted on the canvas, in clumsy, crooked letters. "Pots, pans, knives, sisors, lawn mores, Fixed." Two rows of articles, and the triumphantly definitive "Fixed" below. The black paint had run down in little sharp points beneath each letter.

Elisa, squatting on the ground, watched to see the crazy, loose-jointed wagon pass by. But it didn't pass. It turned into the farm road in front of her house, crooked old wheels skirling and squeaking. The rangy dog darted from between the wheels and ran ahead. Instantly the two ranch shepherds flew out at him. Then all three stopped, and with stiff and quivering tails, with taut straight legs, with ambassadorial dignity, they slowly circled, sniffing daintily. The caravan pulled up to Elisa's wire fence and stopped. Now the newcomer dog, feeling out-numbered, lowered his tail and retired under the wagon with raised hackles and bared teeth.

The man on the wagon seat called out: "That's a bad dog in a fight when he gets started."

Elisa laughed. "I see he is. How soon does he generally get started?"

The man caught up her laughter and echoed it heartily. "Sometimes not for weeks and weeks," he said. He climbed stiffly down, over the wheel. The horse and the donkey drooped like unwatered flowers.

Elisa saw that he was a very big man. Although his hair and beard were greying, he did not look old. His worn black suit was wrinkled and spotted with grease. The laughter had disappeared from his face and eyes the moment his laughing voice ceased. His eyes were dark, and they were full of the brooding that gets in the eyes of teamsters and of sailors. The calloused hands he rested on the wire fence were cracked, and every crack was a black line. He took off his battered hat.

"I'm off my general road, ma'am," he said. "Does this dirt road cut over across the river to the Los Angeles highway?"

Elisa stood up and shoved the thick scissors in her apron pocket. "Well, yes, it does, but it winds around and then fords the river. I don't think your team could pull through the sand."

He replied with some asperity: "It might surprise you what them beasts can pull through."

"When they get started?" she asked.

He smiled for a second. "Yes. When they get started."

"Well," said Elisa, "I think you'll save time if you go back to the Salinas road and pick up the highway there."

He drew a big finger down the chicken wire and made it sing. "I ain't in any hurry, ma'am. I go from Seattle to San Diego and back every year. Takes all my time. About six months each way. I aim to follow nice weather."

Elisa took off her gloves and stuffed them in the apron pocket with the scissors. She touched the under edge of her man's hat, searching for fugitive hairs. "That sounds like a nice kind of way to live," she said.

He leaned confidentially over the fence. "Maybe you noticed the writing on my wagon. I mend pots and sharpen knives and scissors. You got any of them things to do?"

"Oh, no," she said quickly. "Nothing like that." Her eyes hardened with resistance.

"Scissors is the worst thing," he explained. "Most people just ruin scissors trying to sharpen 'em, but I know how. I got a special tool. It's a little bobbit kind of thing, and patented. But it sure does the trick."

"No. My scissors are all sharp."

"All right, then. Take a pot," he continued earnestly, "a bent pot, or a pot with a hole. I can make it like new so you don't have to buy no new ones. That's a saving for you."

"No," she said shortly. "I tell you I have nothing like that for you to do."

His face fell to an exaggerated sadness. His voice took on a whining undertone. "I ain't had a thing to do today. Maybe I won't have no supper tonight. You see I'm off my regular road. I know folks on the highway clear from Seattle to San Diego. They save their things for me to sharpen up because they know I do it so good and save them money."

"I'm sorry," Elisa said irritably. "I haven't anything for you to do."

His eyes left her face and fell to searching the ground. They roamed about until they came to the chrysanthemum bed where she had been working. "What's them plants, ma'am?"

The irritation and resistance melted from Elisa's face. "Oh, those are chrysanthemums, giant whites and yellows. I raise them every year, bigger than anybody around here."

"Kind of a long-stemmed flower? Looks like a quick puff of colored smoke?" he asked.

"That's it. What a nice way to describe them."

"They smell kind of nasty till you get used to them," he said.

"It's a good bitter smell," she retorted, "not nasty at all."

He changed his tone quickly. "I like the smell myself."

"I had ten-inch blooms this year," she said.

The man leaned farther over the fence. "Look. I know a lady down the road a piece, has got the nicest garden you ever seen. Got nearly every kind of flower but no chrysanthemums. Last time I was mending a copper-bottom washtub for her (that's a hard job but I do it good), she said to me: 'If you ever run acrost some nice chrysanthemums I wish you'd try to get me a few seeds.' That's what she told me."

Elisa's eyes grew alert and eager. "She couldn't have known much about chrysanthemums. You *can* raise them from seed, but it's much easier to root the little sprouts you see here."

"Oh," he said. "I s'pose I can't take none to her, then."

"Why yes you can," Elisa cried. "I can put some in damp sand, and you can carry them right along with you. They'll take root in the pot if you keep them damp. And then she can transplant them."

"She'd sure like to have some, ma'am. You say they're nice ones?"

"Beautiful," she said. "Oh, beautiful." Her eyes shone. She tore off the battered hat and shook out her dark pretty hair. "I'll put them in a flowerpot, and you can take them right with you. Come into the yard."

While the man came through the picket gate Elisa ran excitedly along the geranium-bordered path to the back of the house. And she returned carrying a big red flower-pot. The gloves were forgotten now. She kneeled on the ground by the starting bed and dug up the sandy soil with her fingers and scooped it into the bright new flower-pot. Then she picked up the little pile of shoots she had prepared. With her strong fingers she pressed them into the sand and tamped around them with her knuckles. The man stood over her. "I'll tell you what to do," she said. "You remember so you can tell the lady."

"Yes, I'll try to remember."

"Well, look. These will take root in about a month. Then she must set them out, about a foot apart in good rich earth like this, see?" She lifted a handful of dark soil for him to look at. "They'll grow fast and tall. Now remember this: In July tell her to cut them down, about eight inches from the ground."

"Before they bloom?" he asked.

"Yes, before they bloom." Her face was tight with eagerness. "They'll grow right up again. About the last of September the buds will start."

She stopped and seemed perplexed. "It's the budding that takes the most care," she said hesitantly. "I don't know how to tell you." She looked deep into his eyes, searchingly. Her mouth opened a little, and she seemed to be listening. "I'll try to tell you," she said. "Did you ever hear of planting hands?"

"Can't say I have, ma'am."

"Well, I can only tell you what it feels like. It's when you're picking off the buds you don't want. Everything goes right down into your fingertips. You watch your fingers work. They do it themselves. You can feel how it is. They pick and pick the buds. They never make a mistake. They're with the plant. Do you see?

Your fingers and the plant. You can feel that, right up your arm. They know. They never make a mistake. You can feel it. When you're like that you can't do anything wrong. Do you see that? Can you understand that?"

She was kneeling on the ground looking up at him. Her breast swelled passionately.

The man's eyes narrowed. He looked away self-consciously.

"Maybe I know," he said. "Sometimes in the night in the wagon there——"

Elisa's voice grew husky. She broke in on him: "I've never lived as you do, but I know what you mean. When the night is dark—why, the stars are sharp-pointed, and there's quiet. Why, you rise up and up! Every pointed star gets driven into your body. It's like that. Hot and sharp and—lovely."

Kneeling there, her hand went out toward his legs in the greasy black trousers. Her hesitant fingers almost touched the cloth. Then her hand dropped to the ground. She crouched low like a fawning dog.

He said: "It's nice, just like you say. Only when you don't have no dinner, it ain't."

She stood up then, very straight, and her face was ashamed. She held the flower-pot out to him and placed it gently in his arms. "Here. Put it in your wagon, on the seat, where you can watch it. Maybe I can find something for you to do."

At the back of the house she dug in the can pile and found two old and battered aluminum saucepans. She carried them back and gave them to him. "Here, maybe you can fix these."

His manner changed. He became professional. "Good as new I can fix them." At the back of his wagon he set a little anvil, and out of an oily tool-box dug a small machine hammer. Elisa came through the gate to watch him while he pounded out the dents in the kettles. His mouth grew sure and knowing. At a difficult part of the work he sucked his underlip.

"You sleep right in the wagon?" Elisa asked.

"Right in the wagon, ma'am. Rain or shine I'm dry as a cow in there."

"It must be nice," she said. "It must be very nice. I wish women could do such things."

"It ain't the right kind of a life for a woman."

Her upper lip raised a little, showing her teeth. "How do you know? How can you tell?" she said.

"I don't know, ma'am," he protested. "Of course I don't know. Now here's your kettles, done. You don't have to buy no new ones."

"How much?"

"Oh, fifty cents'll do. I keep my prices down and my work good. That's why I have all them satisfied customers up and down the highway."

Elisa brought him a fifty-cent piece from the house and dropped it in his hand. "You might be surprised to have a rival some time. I can sharpen scissors, too. And I can beat the dents out of little pots. I could show you what a woman might do."

He put his hammer back in the oily box and shoved the little anvil out of sight. "It would be a lonely life for a woman, ma'am, and a scarey life, too, with animals creeping under the wagon all night." He climbed over the single-tree, steadying himself with a hand on the burro's white rump. He settled himself in the seat, picked up the lines. "Thank you kindly ma'am," he said. "I'll do like you told me; I'll go back and catch the Salinas road."

"Mind," she called, "if you're long in getting there, keep the sand damp."

"Sand, ma'am?. . . Sand? Oh, sure. You mean around the chrysanthemums. Sure I will." He clucked his tongue. The beasts leaned luxuriously into their collars. The mongrel dog took his place between the back wheels. The wagon turned and crawled out the entrance road and back the way it had come, along the river.

Elisa stood in front of her wire fence watching the slow progress of the caravan. Her shoulders were straight, her head thrown back, her eyes half-closed, so that the scene came vaguely into them. Her lips moved silently, forming the words "Good-bye—good-bye." Then she whispered: "That's a bright direction. There's a glowing there." The sound of her whisper startled her. She shook herself free and looked about to see whether anyone had been listening. Only the dogs had heard. They lifted their heads toward her from their sleeping in the dust, and then stretched out their chins and settled asleep again. Elisa turned and ran hurriedly into the house.

In the kitchen she reached behind the stove and felt the water tank. It was full of hot water from the noonday cooking. In the bathroom she tore off her soiled clothes and flung them into the corner. And then she scrubbed herself with a little block of pumice, legs and thighs, loins and chest and arms, until her skin was scratched and red. When she had dried herself she stood in front of a mirror in her bedroom and looked at her body. She tightened her stomach and threw out her chest. She turned and looked over her shoulders at her back.

After a while she began to dress, slowly. She put on her newest underclothing and her nicest stockings and the dress which was the symbol of her prettiness. She worked carefully on her hair, pencilled her eyebrows and rouged her lips.

Before she was finished she heard the little thunder of hoofs and the shouts of Henry and his helper as they drove the red steers into the corral. She heard the gate bang shut and set herself for Henry's arrival.

His step sounded on the porch. He entered the house calling: "Elisa, where are you?"

"In my room, dressing. I'm not ready. There's hot water for your bath. Hurry up. It's getting late."

When she heard him splashing in the tub, Elisa laid his dark suit on the bed, and shirt and socks and tie beside it. She stood his polished shoes on the floor beside the bed. Then she went to the porch and sat primly and stiffly down. She looked toward the river road where the willow-line was still yellow with frosted leaves so that under the high grey fog they seemed a thin band of sunshine. This was the only color in the grey afternoon. She sat unmoving for a long time. Her eyes blinked rarely.

Henry came banging out of the door, shoving his tie inside his vest as he came. Elisa stiffened and her face grew tight. Henry stopped short and looked at her. "Why—why, Elisa. You look so nice!"

"Nice? You think I look nice? What do you mean by 'nice'?"

Henry blundered on. "I don't know. I mean you look different, strong and happy."

"I am strong? Yes, strong. What do you mean 'strong'?"

He looked bewildered. "You're playing some kind of a game," he said helplessly. "It's a kind of a play. You look strong enough to break a calf over your knee, happy enough to eat it like a watermelon."

For a second she lost her rigidity. "Henry! Don't talk like that. You didn't know what you said." She grew complete again. "I'm strong," she boasted. "I never knew before how strong."

Henry looked down toward the tractor-shed, and when he brought his eyes back to her, they were his own again. "I'll get out the car. You can put on your coat while I'm starting."

Elisa went into the house. She heard him drive to the gate and idle down his motor, and then she took a long time to put on her hat. She pulled it here and pressed it there. When Henry turned the motor off she slipped into her coat and went out.

The little roadster bounced along on the dirt road by the river, raising the birds and driving the rabbits into the brush. Two cranes flapped heavily over the willow-line and dropped into the river-bed.

Far ahead on the road Elisa saw a dark speck. She knew.

She tried not to look as they passed it, but her eyes would not obey. She whispered to herself sadly: "He might have thrown them off the road. That wouldn't have been much trouble, not very much. But he kept the pot," she explained. "He had to keep the pot. That's why he couldn't get them off the road."

The roadster turned a bend and she saw the caravan ahead. She swung full around toward her husband so she could not see the little covered wagon and the mis-matched team as the car passed them.

In a moment it was over. The thing was done. She did not look back.

She said loudly, to be heard above the motor: "It will be good, tonight, a good dinner."

"Now you've changed again," Henry complained. He took one hand from the wheel and patted her knee. "I ought to take you in to dinner oftener. It would be good for both of us. We get so heavy out on the ranch."

"Henry," she asked, "could we have wine at dinner?"

"Sure we could. Say! That will be fine."

She was silent for a while; then she said: "Henry, at those prize-fights, do the men hurt each other very much?"

"Sometimes a little, not often. Why?"

"Well, I've read how they break noses, and blood runs down their chests. I've read how the fighting gloves get heavy and soggy with blood."

He looked around at her. "What's the matter, Elisa? I didn't know you read things like that." He brought the car to a stop, then turned to the right over the Salinas River bridge.

"Do any women ever go to the fights?" she asked.

"Oh, sure, some. What's the matter, Elisa? Do you want to go? I don't think you'd like it, but I'll take you if you really want to go."

She relaxed limply in the seat. "Oh, no. No. I don't want to go. I'm sure I don't." Her face was turned away from him. "It will be enough if we can have wine. It will be plenty." She turned up her coat collar so he could not see that she was crying weakly—like an old woman.

# Amy Tan

*Tan (1952– ) was born in Oakland, California, and educated at San Jose State University and the University of California at Berkeley. She has worked on programs for disabled children and as a reporter. Material for her fiction comes from the lives of Chinese-American women and the cultural ambivalence of their circumstances in the United States. Her easy and good-natured style has made her work popular with a wide public. Her novels are* The Joy Luck Club *(1989),* The Kitchen God's Wife *(1991), and* The Hundred Secret Senses *(1995). She has also published a book for children,* The Moon Lady *(1992).*

## Rules of the Game

I was six when my mother taught me the art of invisible strength. It was a strategy for winning arguments, respect from others, and eventually, though neither of us knew it at the time, chess games.

"Bite back your tongue," scolded my mother when I cried loudly, yanking her hand toward the store that sold bags of salted plums. At home, she said, "Wise guy, he not go against wind. In Chinese we say, Come from South, blow with wind—poom!—North will follow. Strongest wind cannot be seen."

The next week I bit back my tongue as we entered the store with the forbidden candies. When my mother finished her shopping, she quietly plucked a small bag of plums from the rack and put it on the counter with the rest of the items.

My mother imparted her daily truths so she could help my older brothers and me rise above our circumstances. We lived in San Francisco's Chinatown. Like most of the other Chinese children who played in the back alleys of restaurants and curio shops, I didn't think we were poor. My bowl was always full, three five-course meals every day, beginning with a soup of mysterious things I didn't want to know the names of.

We lived on Waverly Place, in a warm, clean, two-bedroom flat that sat above a small Chinese bakery specializing in steamed pastries and dim sum. In the early morning, when the alley was still quiet, I could smell fragrant red beans as they were cooked down to a pasty sweetness. By daybreak, our flat was heavy with the odor of fried sesame balls and sweet curried chicken crescents. From my bed, I would listen as my father got ready for work, then locked the door behind him, one-two-three clicks.

At the end of our two-block alley was a small sandlot playground with swings and slides well-shined down the middle with use. The play area was bordered by wood-slat benches where old-country people sat cracking roasted watermelon seeds with their golden teeth and scattering the husks to an impatient gathering of gurgling pigeons. The best playground, however, was the dark alley itself. It was crammed with daily mysteries and adventures. My brothers and I would peer into the medicinal herb shop, watching old Li dole out onto a stiff sheet of white paper the right amount of insect shells, saffron-colored seeds, and pungent leaves for his ailing customers. It was said that he once cured a woman dying of an ancestral curse that had eluded the best of American doctors. Next to the pharmacy was a printer who specialized in gold-embossed wedding invitations and festive red banners.

Farther down the street was Ping Yuen Fish Market. The front window displayed a tank crowded with doomed fish and turtles struggling to gain footing on the slimy green-tiled sides. A hand-written sign informed tourists, "Within this store, is all for food, not for pet." Inside, the butchers with their bloodstained white smocks deftly gutted the fish while customers cried out their orders and shouted, "Give me your freshest," to which the butchers always protested, "All are freshest." On less crowded market days, we would inspect the crates of live frogs and crabs which we were warned not to poke, boxes of dried cuttlefish, and row upon row of iced prawns, squid, and slippery fish. The sanddabs made me shiver each time; their eyes lay on one flattened side and reminded me of my mother's story of a careless girl who ran into a crowded street and was crushed by a cab. "Was smash flat," reported my mother.

At the corner of the alley was Hong Sing's, a four-table café with a recessed stairwell in front that led to a door marked "Tradesmen." My brothers and I believed the bad people emerged from this door at night. Tourists never went to Hong Sing's, since the menu was printed only in Chinese. A Caucasian man with a big camera once posed me and my playmates in front of the restaurant. He had us move to the side of the picture window so the photo would capture the roasted duck with its head dangling from a juice-covered rope. After he took the picture, I told him he should go into Hong Sing's and eat dinner. When he smiled and asked me what they served, I shouted, "Guts and duck's feet and octopus gizzards!" Then I ran off with my friends, shrieking with laughter as we scampered across the alley and hid in the entryway grotto of the China Gem Company, my heart pounding with hope that he would chase us.

My mother named me after the street that we lived on: Waverly Place Jong, my official name for important American documents. But my family called me Meimei, "Little Sister." I was the youngest, the only daughter. Each morning before school, my mother would twist and yank on my thick black hair until she had formed two tightly wound pigtails. One day, as she struggled to weave a hard-toothed comb through my disobedient hair, I had a sly thought.

I asked her, "Ma, what is Chinese torture?" My mother shook her head. A bobby pin was wedged between her lips. She wetted her palm and smoothed the hair above my ear, then pushed the pin in so that it nicked sharply against my scalp.

"Who say this word?" she asked without a trace of knowing how wicked I was being. I shrugged my shoulders and said, "Some boy in my class said Chinese people do Chinese torture."

"Chinese people do many things," she said simply. "Chinese people do business, do medicine, do painting. Not lazy like American people. We do torture. Best torture."

My older brother Vincent was the one who actually got the chess set. We had gone to the annual Christmas party held at the First Chinese Baptist Church at the end of the alley. The missionary ladies had put together a Santa bag of gifts donated by members of another church. None of the gifts had names on them. There were separate sacks for boys and girls of different ages.

One of the Chinese parishioners had donned a Santa Claus costume and a stiff paper beard with cotton balls glued to it. I think the only children who thought he was the real thing were too young to know that Santa Claus was not Chinese. When my turn came up, the Santa man asked me how old I was. I thought it was a trick question; I was seven according to the American formula and eight by the Chinese calendar. I said I was born on March 17, 1951. That seemed to satisfy him. He then solemnly asked if I had been a very, very good girl this year and did I believe in Jesus Christ and obey my parents. I knew the only answer to that. I nodded back with equal solemnity.

Having watched the older children opening their gifts, I already knew that the big gifts were not necessarily the nicest ones. One girl my age got a large coloring book of biblical characters, while a less greedy girl who selected a smaller box received a glass vial of lavender toilet water. The sound of the box was also important. A ten-year-old boy had chosen a box that jangled when he shook it. It was a tin globe of the world with a slit for inserting money. He must have thought it was full of dimes and nickels, because when he saw that it had just ten pennies, his face fell with such undisguised disappointment that his mother slapped the side of his head and led him out of the church hall, apologizing to the crowd for her son who had such bad manners he couldn't appreciate such a fine gift.

As I peered into the sack, I quickly fingered the remaining presents, testing their weight, imagining what they contained. I chose a heavy, compact one that was wrapped in shiny silver foil and a red satin ribbon. It was a twelve-pack of Life Savers and I spent the rest of the party arranging and rearranging the candy tubes in the order of my favorites. My bother Winston chose wisely as well. His present turned out to be a box of intricate plastic parts; the instructions on the box proclaimed that when they were properly assembled he would have an authentic miniature replica of a World War II submarine.

Vincent got the chess set, which would have been a very decent present to get at a church Christmas party, except it was obviously used and, as we discovered later, it was missing a black pawn and a white knight. My mother graciously thanked the unknown benefactor, saying, "Too good. Cost too much." At which point, an old lady with fine white, wispy hair nodded toward our family and said with a whistling whisper, "Merry, merry Christmas."

When we got home, my mother told Vincent to throw the chess set away. "She not want it. We not want it." she said, tossing her head stiffly to the side with a tight, proud smile. My brothers had deaf ears. They were already lining up the chess pieces and reading from the dog-eared instruction book.

I watched Vincent and Winston play during Christmas week. The chessboard seemed to hold elaborate secrets waiting to be untangled. The chessmen were more powerful than old Li's magic herbs that cured ancestral curses. And my brothers wore such serious faces that I was sure something was at stake that was greater than avoiding the tradesmen's door to Hong Sing's.

"Let me! Let me!" I begged between games when one brother or the other would sit back with a deep sigh of relief and victory, the other annoyed, unable to let go of the outcome. Vincent at first refused to let me play, but when I offered my Life Savers as replacements for the buttons that filled in for the missing pieces, he relented. He chose the flavors: wild cherry for the black pawn and peppermint for the white knight. Winner could eat both.

As our mother sprinkled flour and rolled out small doughy circles for the steamed dumplings that would be our dinner that night, Vincent explained the rules, pointing to each piece. "You have sixteen pieces and so do I. One king and queen, two bishops, two knights, two castles, and eight pawns. The pawns can only move forward one step, except on the first move. Then they can move two. But they can only take men by moving crossways like this, except in the beginning, when you can move ahead and take another pawn."

"Why?" I asked as I moved my pawn. "Why can't they move more steps?"

"Because they're pawns," he said.

"But why do they go crossways to take other men? Why aren't there any women and children?"

"Why is the sky blue? Why must you always ask stupid questions?" asked Vincent. "This is a game. These are the rules. I didn't make them up. See. Here in the book." He jabbed a page with a pawn in his hand. "Pawn. P-A-W-N. Pawn. Read it yourself."

My mother patted the flour off her hands. "Let me see book," she said quietly. She scanned the pages quickly, not reading the foreign English symbols, seeming to search deliberately for nothing in particular.

"This American rules," she concluded at last. "Every time people come out from foreign country, must know rules. You not know, judge say, Too bad, go back. They not telling you why so you can use their way go forward. They say, Don't know why, you find out yourself. But they knowing all the time. Better you take it, find out why yourself." She tossed her head back with a satisfied smile.

I found out about all the whys later. I read the rules and looked up all the big words in a dictionary. I borrowed books from the Chinatown library. I studied each chess piece, trying to absorb the power each contained.

I learned about opening moves and why it's important to control the center early on; the shortest distance between two points is straight down the middle. I learned about the middle game and why tactics between two adversaries are like clashing ideas; the one who plays better has the clearest plans for both attacking and getting out of traps. I learned why it is essential in the endgame to have foresight, a mathematical understanding of all possible moves, and patience; all weaknesses and advantages become evident to a strong adversary and are obscured to a tiring opponent. I discovered that for the whole game one must gather invisible strengths and see the endgame before the game begins.

I also found out why I should never reveal "why" to others. A little knowledge withheld is a great advantage one should store for future use. That is the power of chess. It is a game of secrets in which one must show and never tell.

I loved the secrets I found within the sixty-four black and white squares. I carefully drew a handmade chessboard and pinned it to the wall next to my bed, where I would stare for hours at imaginary battles. Soon I no longer lost any games or Life Savers, but I lost my adversaries. Winston and Vincent decided they were more interested in roaming the streets after school in their Hopalong Cassidy cowboy hats.

On a cold spring afternoon, while walking home from school, I detoured through the playground at the end of our alley. I saw a group of old men, two seated across a folding table playing a game of chess, others smoking pipes, eating peanuts, and watching. I ran home and grabbed Vincent's chess set, which was bound in a cardboard box with rubber bands. I also carefully selected two prized rolls of Life Savers. I came back to the park and approached a man who was observing the game.

"Want to play?" I asked him. His face widened with surprise and he grinned as he looked at the box under my arm.

"Little sister, been a long time since I play with dolls," he said, smiling benevolently. I quickly put the box down next to him on the bench and displayed my retort.

Lau Po, as he allowed me to call him, turned out to be a much better player than my brothers. I lost many games and many Life Savers. But over the weeks, with each diminishing roll of candies, I added new secrets. Lau Po gave me the names. The Double Attack from the East and West Shores. Throwing Stones on the Drowning Man. The Sudden Meeting of the Clan. The Surprise from the Sleeping Guard. The Humble Servant Who Kills the King. Sand in the Eyes of Advancing Forces. A Double Killing Without Blood.

There were also the fine points of chess etiquette. Keep captured men in neat rows, as well-tended prisoners. Never announce "Check" with vanity, lest someone with an unseen sword slit your throat. Never hurl pieces into the sandbox after you have lost a game, because then you must find them again, by yourself, after apologizing to all around you. By the end of the summer, Lau Po had taught me all he knew, and I had become a better chess player.

A small weekend crowd of Chinese people and tourists would gather as I played and defeated my opponents one by one. My mother would join the crowds during these outdoor exhibition games. She sat proudly on the bench, telling my admirers with proper Chinese humility, "Is luck."

A man who watched me play in the park suggested that my mother allow me to play in local chess tournaments. My mother smiled graciously, an answer that meant nothing. I desperately wanted to go, but I bit back my tongue. I knew she would not let me play among strangers. So as we walked home I said in a small voice that I didn't want to play in the local tournament. They would have American rules. If I lost, I would bring shame on my family.

"Is shame you fall down nobody push you," said my mother.

During my first tournament, my mother sat with me in the front row as I waited for my turn. I frequently bounced my legs to unstick them from the cold metal seat of the folding chair. When my name was called, I leapt up. My mother unwrapped something in her lap. It was her *chang,* a small tablet of red jade which held the sun's fire. "Is luck," she whispered, and tucked it into my dress pocket. I turned to my opponent, a fifteen-year-old boy from Oakland. He looked at me, wrinkling his nose.

As I began to play, the boy disappeared, the color ran out of the room, and I saw only my white pieces and his black ones waiting on the other side. A light wind began blowing past my ears. It whispered secrets only I could hear.

"Blow from the South," it murmured. "The wind leaves no trail." I saw a clear path, the traps to avoid. The crowd rustled. "Shhh! Shhh!" said the corners of the room. The wind blew stronger. "Throw sand from the East to distract him." The knight came forward ready for the sacrifice. The wind hissed, louder and louder. "Blow, blow, blow. He cannot see. He is blind now. Make him lean away from the wind so he is easier to knock down."

"Check," I said, as the wind roared with laughter. The wind died down to little puffs, my own breath.

My mother placed my first trophy next to a new plastic chess set that the neighborhood Tao society had given to me. As she wiped each piece with a soft cloth, she said, "Next time win more, lose less."

"Ma, it's not how many pieces you lose," I said. "Sometimes you need to lose pieces to get ahead."

"Better to lose less, see if you really need."

At the next tournament, I won again, but it was my mother who wore the triumphant grin.

"Lost eight piece this time. Last time was eleven. What I tell you? Better off lose less!" I was annoyed, but I couldn't say anything.

I attended more tournaments, each one farther away from home. I won all games, in all divisions. The Chinese bakery downstairs from our flat displayed my growing collection of trophies in its window, amidst the dust-covered cakes that were never picked up. The day after I won an important regional tournament, the window encased a fresh sheet cake with whipped-cream frosting and red script saying "Congratulations, Waverly Jong, Chinatown Chess Champion." Soon after that, a flower shop, headstone engraver, and funeral parlor offered to sponsor me in national tournaments. That's when my mother decided I no longer had to do the dishes. Winston and Vincent had to do my chores.

"Why does she get to play and we do all the work," complained Vincent.

"Is new American rules," said my mother. "Meimei play, squeeze all her brains out for win chess. You play, worth squeeze towel."

By my ninth birthday, I was a national chess champion. I was still some 429 points away from grand-master status, but I was touted as the Great American Hope, a child prodigy and a girl to boot. They ran a photo of me in *Life* magazine next to a quote in which Bobby Fischer said, "There will never be a woman grand master." "Your move, Bobby," said the caption.

The day they took the magazine picture I wore neatly plaited braids clipped with plastic barrettes trimmed with rhinestones. I was playing in a large high school auditorium that echoed with phlegmy coughs and the squeaky rubber knobs of chair legs sliding across freshly waxed wooden floors. Seated across from me was an American man, about the same age as Lau Po, maybe fifty. I remember that his sweaty brow seemed to weep at my every move. He wore a dark, malodorous suit. One of his pockets was stuffed with a great white kerchief on which he wiped his palm before sweeping his hand over the chosen chess piece with great flourish.

In my crisp pink-and-white dress with scratchy lace at the neck, one of two my mother had sewn for these special occasions, I would clasp my hands under my chin, the delicate points of my elbows poised lightly on the table in the manner my mother had shown me for posing for the press. I would swing my patent leather shoes back and forth like an impatient child riding on a school bus. Then I would pause, suck in my lips, twirl my chosen piece in midair as if undecided, and then firmly plant it in its new threatening place, with a triumphant smile thrown back at my opponent for good measure.

I no longer played in the alley of Waverly Place. I never visited the playground where the pigeons and old men gathered. I went to school, then directly home to learn new chess secrets, cleverly concealed advantages, more escape routes.

But I found it difficult to concentrate at home. My mother had a habit of standing over me while I plotted out my games. I think she thought of herself as my protective ally. Her lips would be sealed tight, and after each move I made, a soft "Hmmmmph" would escape from her nose.

"Ma, I can't practice when you stand there like that," I said one day. She retreated to the kitchen and made loud noises with the pots and pans. When the crashing stopped, I could see out of the corner of my eye that she was standing in the doorway. "Hmmmmph!" Only this one came out of her tight throat.

My parents made many concessions to allow me to practice. One time I complained that the bedroom I shared was so noisy that I couldn't think. Thereafter, my brothers slept in a bed in the living room facing the street. I said I couldn't finish my rice; my head didn't work right when my stomach was too full. I left the table with half-finished bowls and nobody complained. But there was one duty I couldn't avoid. I had to accompany my mother on Saturday market days when I had no tournament to play. My mother would proudly walk with me, visiting many shops, buying very little. "This my daughter Wave-ly Jong," she said to whoever looked her way.

One day after we left a shop I said under my breath, "I wish you wouldn't do that, telling everybody I'm your daughter." My mother stopped walking.

Crowds of people with heavy bags pushed past us on the sidewalk, bumping into first one shoulder, than another.

"Aiii-ya. So shame be with mother?" She grasped my hand even tighter as she glared at me.

I looked down. "It's not that, it's just so obvious. It's just so embarrassing."

"Embarrass you be my daughter?" Her voice was cracking with anger.

"That's not what I meant. That's not what I said."

"What you say?"

I knew it was a mistake to say anything more, but I heard my voice speaking, "Why do you have to use me to show off? If you want to show off, then why don't you learn to play chess?"

My mother's eyes turned into dangerous black slits. She had no words for me, just sharp silence.

I felt the wind rushing around my hot ears. I jerked my hand out of my mother's tight grasp and spun around, knocking into an old woman. Her bag of groceries spilled to the ground.

"Aii-ya! Stupid girl!" my mother and the woman cried. Oranges and tin cans careened down the sidewalk. As my mother stooped to help the old woman pick up the escaping food, I took off.

I raced down the street, dashing between people, not looking back as my mother screamed shrilly, "Meimei! Meimei!" I fled down an alley, past dark, curtained shops and merchants washing the grime off their windows. I sped into the sunlight, into a large street crowded with tourists examining trinkets and souvenirs. I ducked into another dark alley, down another street, up another alley. I ran until it hurt and I realized I had nowhere to go, that I was not running from anything. The alleys contained no escape routes.

My breath came out like angry smoke. It was cold. I sat down on an upturned plastic pail next to a stack of empty boxes, cupping my chin with my hands, thinking hard. I imagined my mother, first walking briskly down one street or another looking for me, then giving up and returning home to await my arrival. After two hours, I stood up on creaking legs and slowly walked home.

The alley was quiet and I could see the yellow lights shining from our flat like two tiger's eyes in the night. I climbed the sixteen steps to the door, advancing quietly up each so as not to make any warning sounds. I turned the knob; the door was locked. I heard a chair moving, quick steps, the locks turning—click! click! click!—and then the door opened.

"About time you got home," said Vincent. "Boy, are you in trouble."

He slid back to the dinner table. On a platter were the remains of a large fish, its fleshy head still connected to bones swimming upstream in vain escape. Standing there waiting for my punishment, I heard my mother speak in a dry voice.

"We not concerning this girl. This girl not have concerning for us."

Nobody looked at me. Bone chopsticks clinked against the inside of bowls being emptied into hungry mouths.

I walked into my room, closed the door, and lay down on my bed. The room was dark, the ceiling filled with shadows from the dinnertime lights of neighboring flats.

In my head, I saw a chessboard with sixty-four black and white squares. Opposite me was my opponent, two angry black slits. She wore a triumphant smile. "Strongest wind cannot be seen," she said.

Her black men advanced across the plane, slowly marching to each successive level as a single unit. My white pieces screamed as they scurried and fell off the board one by one. As her men drew closer to my edge, I felt myself growing light. I rose up into the air and flew out the window. Higher and higher, above the alley, over the tops of tiled roofs, where I was gathered up by the wind and pushed up toward the night sky until everything below me disappeared and I was alone.

I closed my eyes and pondered my next move.

# Peter Taylor

*Taylor (1917–1994) was born in Trenton, Tennessee. He was educated at Vanderbilt University and Kenyon College, where he became a lifelong friend of the poet Robert Lowell. Throughout most of his adult life he taught writing at a number of American colleges and universities. His last post was at the University of Virginia. Unlike many southern writers of his period, he wrote, in elegantly unobtrusive style, of the bewilderments and aspirations of genteel, resourceful people, who weave the strands of tradition into the tensions of new times with grace and persistent responsibility. His novel* A Woman of Means *was published in 1950. His collection* The Old Forest *(1995) won the PEN/Faulkner Award and is in the Modern Library series. His novel* A Summons to Memphis *won the Pulitzer Prize in 1986. His books of stories include* A Long Fourth *(1945),* Miss Leonora When Last Seen *(1963),* Collected Stories *(1969), and* In the Tennessee Country *(1994).*

## A Spinster's Tale

My brother would often get drunk when I was a little girl, but that put a different sort of fear into me from what Mr. Speed did. With Brother it was a spiritual thing. And though it was frightening to know that he would have to burn for all that giggling and bouncing around on the stair at night, the truth was that he only seemed jollier to me when I would stick my head out of the hall door. It made him seem almost my age for him to act so silly, putting his white forefinger all over his flushed face and finally over his lips to say, "Sh-sh-sh-sh!" But the really frightening thing about seeing Brother drunk was what I always heard when I had slid back into bed. I could always recall my mother's words to him when he was sixteen, the year before she died, spoken in her greatest sincerity, in her most religious tone: "Son, I'd rather see you in your grave."

Yet those nights put a scaredness into me that was clearly distinguishable from the terror that Mr. Speed instilled by stumbling past our house two or three afternoons a week. The most that I knew about Mr. Speed was his name. And this I considered that I had somewhat fabricated—by allowing him the "Mr."—in my effort to humanize and soften the monster that was forever passing our house on Church Street. My father would point him out through the wide parlor window in soberness and severity to my brother with: "There goes Old Speed, again." Or on Saturdays when Brother was with the Benton boys and my two uncles were over having toddies with Father in the parlor, Father would refer to Mr. Speed's passing with a similar speech, but in a blustering tone of merry tolerance: "There goes Old Speed, again. The rascal!" These designations were equally awful, both spoken in tones that were foreign to my father's manner of addressing me; and not unconsciously I prepared the euphemism, Mister Speed, against the inevitable day when I should have to speak of him to someone.

I was named Elizabeth, for my mother. My mother had died in the spring before Mr. Speed first came to my notice on that late afternoon in October. I had bathed at four with the aid of Lucy, who had been my nurse and who was now the upstairs maid; and Lucy was upstairs turning back the covers of the beds in the rooms with their color schemes of blue and green and rose. I wandered into the shadowy parlor and sat first on one chair, then on another. I tried lying down on the settee that went with the parlor set, but my legs had got too long this summer to stretch out straight on the settee. And my feet looked long in their pumps against the wicker arm. I looked at the pictures around the room blankly and at the stained-glass windows on either side of the fireplace; and the winter light coming through them was hardly bright enough to show the colors. I struck a match on the mosaic hearth and lit the gas logs.

Kneeling on the hearth I watched the flames till my face felt hot. I stood up then and turned directly to one of the full-length mirror panels that were on each side of the front window. This one was just to the right of the broad window and my reflection in it stood out strangely from the rest of the room in the dull light that did not penetrate beyond my figure. I leaned closer to the mirror trying to discover a resemblance between myself and the wondrous Alice who walked through a looking glass. But that resemblance I was seeking I could not find in my sharp features, or in my heavy, dark curls hanging like fragments of hosepipe to my shoulders.

I propped my hands on the borders of the narrow mirror and put my face close to watch my lips say, "Away." I would hardly open them for the "a"; and then I would contort my face by the great opening I made for the "way." I whispered, "Away, away." I whispered it over and over, faster and faster, watching myself in the mirror: "A-way—a-way—away-away-awayaway." Suddenly I burst into tears and turned from the gloomy mirror to the daylight at the wide parlor window. Gazing tearfully through the expanse of plate glass there, I beheld Mr. Speed walking like a cripple with one foot on the curb and one in the street. And faintly I could hear him cursing the trees as he passed them, giving each a lick with his heavy walking cane.

Presently I was dry-eyed in my fright. My breath came short, and I clasped the black bow at the neck of my middy blouse.

When he had passed from view, I stumbled back from the window. I hadn't heard the houseboy enter the parlor, and he must not have noticed me there, I made no move of recognition as he drew the draperies across the wide front window for the night. I stood cold and silent before the gas logs with a sudden inexplicable memory of my mother's cheek and a vision of her in her bedroom on a spring day.

That April day when spring had seemed to crowd itself through the windows into the bright upstairs rooms, the old-fashioned mahogany sick-chair had been brought down from the attic to my mother's room. Three days before, a quiet service had been held there for the stillborn baby, and I had accompanied my father and brother to our lot in the gray cemetery to see the box (large for so tiny a parcel) lowered and covered with mud. But in the parlor now by the gas logs I remembered the day that my mother had sent for the sick-chair and for me.

The practical nurse, sitting in a straight chair busy at her needlework, looked over her glasses to give me some little instruction in the arrangement of my mother's pillows in the chair. A few minutes before, this practical nurse had lifted my sick mother bodily from the bed, and I had the privilege of rolling my mother to the big bay window that looked out ideally over the new foliage of small trees in our side yard.

I stood self-consciously straight, close by my mother, a maturing little girl awkward in my curls and long-waisted dress. My pale mother, in her silk bed jacket, with a smile leaned her cheek against the cheek of her daughter. Outside it was spring. The furnishings of the great blue room seemed to partake for that one moment of nature's life. And my mother's cheek was warm on mine. This I remembered when I sat before the gas logs trying to put Mr. Speed out of my mind; but that a few moments later my mother beckoned to the practical nurse and sent me suddenly from the room, my memory did not dwell upon. I remembered only the warmth of the cheek and the comfort of that other moment.

I sat near the blue burning logs and waited for my father and my brother to come in. When they came saying the same things about office and school that they said every day, turning on lights beside chairs that they liked to flop into, I realized not that I was ready or unready for them but that there had been, within me, an attempt at a preparation for such readiness.

They sat so customarily in their chairs at first and the talk ran so easily that I thought that Mr. Speed could be forgotten as quickly and painlessly as a doubting of Jesus or a fear of death from the measles. But the conversation took insinuating and malicious twists this afternoon. My father talked about the possibilities of a general war and recalled opinions that people had had just before the Spanish-American. He talked about the hundreds of men in the Union Depot. Thinking of all those men there, that close together, was something like meeting Mr. Speed in the front hall. I asked my father not to talk about war, which seemed to him a natural enough request for a young lady to make.

"How is your school, my dear?" he asked me. "How are Miss Hood and Miss Herron? Have they found who's stealing the boarders' things, my dear?"

All of those little girls safely in Belmont School being called for by gentle ladies or warm-breasted Negro women were a pitiable sight beside the beastly vision of Mr. Speed which even they somehow conjured.

At dinner, with Lucy serving and sometimes helping my plate (because she had done so for so many years), Brother teased me first one way and then another. My father joined in on each point until I began to take the teasing very seriously, and then he told Brother that he was forever carrying things too far.

Once at dinner I was convinced that my preposterous fears that Brother knew what had happened to me by the window in the afternoon were not at all preposterous. He had been talking quietly. It was something about the meeting that he and the Benton boys were going to attend after dinner. But quickly, without reason, he turned his eyes on me across the table and fairly shouted in his new deep voice: "I saw three horses running away out on Harding Road today! They were just like the mules we saw at the mines in the mountains! They were running to beat hell and with little girls riding them!"

The first week after I had the glimpse of Mr. Speed through the parlor window, I spent the afternoons dusting the bureau and mantel and bedside table in my room, arranging on the chaise longue the dolls which at this age I never played with and rarely even talked to; or I would absent-mindedly assist Lucy in turning down the beds and maybe watch the houseboy set the dinner table. I went to the parlor only when Father came or when Brother came earlier and called me in to show me a shin bruise or a box of cigarettes which a girl had given him.

Finally, I put my hand on the parlor doorknob just at four one afternoon and entered the parlor, walking stiffly as I might have done with my hands in a muff going into church. The big room with its heavy furniture and pictures showed no change since the last afternoon that I had spent there, unless possibly there were fresh antimacassars on the chairs. I confidently pushed an odd chair over to the window and took my seat and sat erect and waited.

My heart would beat hard when, from the corner of my eye, I caught sight of some figure moving up Church Street. And as it drew nearer, showing the form of some Negro or neighbor or drummer, I would sigh from relief and from regret. I was ready for Mr. Speed. And I knew that he would come again and again, that he had been passing our house for inconceivable numbers of years. I knew that if he did not appear today, he would pass tomorrow. Not because I had had accidental, unavoidable glimpses of him from upstairs windows during the past week, nor because there were indistinct memories of such a figure, hardly noticed, seen on afternoons that preceded that day when I had seen him stumbling like a cripple along the curb and beating and cursing the trees did I know that Mr. Speed was a permanent and formidable figure in my life which I would be called upon to deal with; my knowledge, I was certain, was purely intuitive.

I was ready now not to face him with his drunken rage directed at me, but to look at him far off in the street and to appraise him. He didn't come that afternoon, but he came the next. I sat prim and straight before the window. I turned my head neither to the right to anticipate the sight of him nor to the left to follow his figure when it had passed. But when he was passing before my window, I put my eyes full on him and looked though my teeth chattered in my head. And now I saw his face heavy, red, fierce like his body. He walked with an awkward, stomping sort of stagger, carrying his gray topcoat over one arm; and with his other hand he kept poking his walnut cane into the soft sod along the sidewalk. When he was gone, I recalled my mother's cheek again, but the recollection this time, though more deliberate, was dwelt less upon; and I could only think of watching Mr. Speed again and again.

There was snow on the ground the third time that I watched Mr. Speed pass our house. Mr. Speed spat on the snow, and with his cane he aimed at the brown spot that his tobacco made there. And I could see that he missed his aim. The fourth time that I sat watching for him from the window, snow was actually falling outside; and I felt a sort of anixety to know what would ever drive him into my own house. For a moment I doubted that he would really come to my door; but I prodded myself with the thought of his coming and finding me unprepared. And I continued to keep my secret watch for him two or three times a week during the rest of the winter.

Meanwhile my life with my father and brother and the servants in the shadowy house went on from day to day. On week nights the evening meal usually ended with petulant arguing between the two men, the atlas or the encyclopedia usually drawing them from the table to read out the statistics. Often Brother was accused of having looked-them-up-previously and of maneuvering the conversation toward the particular subject, for topics were very easily introduced and dismissed by the two. Once I, sent to the library to fetch a cigar, returned to find the discourse shifted in two minutes' time from the Kentucky Derby winners to the languages in which the Bible was first written. Once I actually heard the conversation slip, in the course of a small dessert, from the comparative advantages of urban and agrarian life for boys between the ages of fifteen and twenty to the probable origin and age of the Icelandic parliament and then to the doctrines of the Campbellite Church.

That night I followed them to the library and beheld them fingering the pages of the flimsy old atlas in the light from the beaded lampshade. They paid no attention to me and little to one another, each trying to turn the pages of the book and mumbling references to newspaper articles and to statements of persons of responsibility. I slipped from the library to the front parlor across the hall where I could hear the contentious hum. And I lit the gas logs, trying to warm my long legs before them as I examined my own response to the unguided and remorseless bickering of the masculine voices.

It was, I thought, their indifferent shifting from topic to topic that most disturbed me. Then I decided that it was the tremendous gaps that there seemed to be between the subjects that was bewildering to me. Still again, I thought that it was the equal interest which they displayed for each subject that was dismaying. All things in the world were equally at home in their arguments. They exhibited equal indifference to the horrors that each topic might suggest; and I wondered whether or not their imperturbability was a thing that they had achieved.

I knew that I had got myself so accustomed to the sight of Mr. Speed's peregrinations, persistent yet, withal, seemingly without destination, that I could view his passing with perfect equanimity. And from this I knew that I must extend my preparation for the day when I should have to view him at closer range. When the day would come, I knew that it must involve my father and my brother and that his existence therefore must not remain an unmentionable thing, the secrecy of which to explode at the moment of crisis, only adding to its confusion.

Now, the door to my room was the first at the top of the long red-carpeted stairway. A wall light beside it was left burning on nights when Brother was out, and, when he came in, he turned it off. The light shining through my transom was a comforting sight when I had gone to bed in the big room; and in the summertime I could see the reflection of light bugs on it, and often one would plop against it. Sometimes I would wake up in the night with a start and would be frightened in the dark, not knowing what had awakened me until I realized that Brother had just turned out the light. On other nights, however, I would hear him close the front door and hear him bouncing up the steps. When I then stuck my head out the door, usually he would toss me a piece of candy and he always signaled to me to be quiet.

I had never intentionally stayed awake till he came in until one night toward the end of February of that year, and I hadn't been certain then that I should be able to do it. Indeed, when finally the front door closed, I had dozed several times sitting up in the dark bed. But I was standing with my door half open before he had come a third of the way up the stair. When he saw me, he stopped still on the stairway resting his hand on the banister. I realized that purposefulness must be showing on my face, and so I smiled at him and beckoned. His red face broke into a fine grin, and he took the next few steps two at a time. But he stumbled on the carpeted steps. He was on his knees, yet with his hand still on the banister. He was motionless there for a moment with his head cocked to one side, listening. The house was quiet and still. He smiled again, sheepishly this time, and kept putting his white forefinger to his red face as he ascended on tiptoe the last third of the flight of steps.

At the head of the stair he paused, breathing hard. He reached his hand into his coat pocket and smiled confidently as he shook his head at me. I stepped backward into my room.

"Oh," he whispered. "Your candy."

I stood straight in my white nightgown with my black hair hanging over my shoulders, knowing that he could see me only indistinctly. I beckoned to him again. He looked suspiciously about the hall, then stepped into the room and closed the door behind him.

"What's the matter, Betsy?" he said.

I turned and ran and climbed between the covers of my bed.

"What's the matter, Betsy?" he said. He crossed to my bed and sat down beside me on it.

I told him that I didn't know what was the matter.

"Have you been reading something you shouldn't, Betsy?" he asked.

I was silent.

"Are you lonely, Betsy?" he said. "Are you a lonely little girl?"

I sat up on the bed and threw my arms about his neck. And as I sobbed on his shoulder I smelled for the first time the fierce odor of his cheap whiskey.

"Yes, I'm always lonely," I said with directness, and I was then silent with my eyes open and my cheek on the shoulder of his overcoat which was yet cold from the February night air.

He kept his face turned away from me and finally spoke, out of the other corner of his mouth, I thought, "I'll come home earlier some afternoons and we'll talk and play."

"Tomorrow."

When I had said this distinctly, I fell away from him back on the bed. He stood up and looked at me curiously, as though in some way repelled by my settling so comfortably in the covers. And I could see his eighteen-year-old head cocked to one side as though trying to see my face in the dark. He leaned over me, and I smelled his whiskey breath. It was not repugnant to me. It was blended with the odor that he always had. I thought that he was going to strike me. He didn't, however, and in a moment was opening the door to the lighted hall. Before he went out, again I said: "Tomorrow."

The hall light dark and the sound of Brother's footsteps gone, I naturally repeated the whole scene in my mind and upon examination found strange elements present. One was something like a longing for my brother to strike me when he was leaning over me. Another was his bewilderment at my procedure. On the whole I was amazed at the way I had carried the thing off. It was the first incident that I had ever actively carried off. Now I only wished that in the darkness when he was leaning over me I had said languidly, "Oh, Brother," had said it in a tone indicating that we had in common some unmentionable trouble. Then I should have been certain of his presence next day. As it was, though, I had little doubt of his coming home early.

I would not let myself reflect further on my feelings for my brother—my desire for him to strike me and my delight in his natural odor. I had got myself in the habit of postponing such elucidations until after I had completely settled with Mr. Speed. But, as after all such meetings with my brother, I reflected upon the posthumous punishments in store for him for his carousing and drinking, and remembered my mother's saying that she had rather see him in his grave.

The next afternoon at four I had the chessboard on the tea table before the front parlor window. I waited for my brother, knowing pretty well that he would come and feeling certain that Mr. Speed would pass. (For this was a Thursday afternoon; and during the winter months I had found that there were two days of the week on which Mr. Speed never failed to pass our house. These were Thursday and Saturday.) I led my brother into that dismal parlor chattering about the places where I had found the chessmen long in disuse. When I paused a minute, slipping into my seat by the chessboard, he picked up with talk of the senior class play and his chances for being chosen valedictorian. Apparently I no longer seemed an enigma to him. I thought that he must have concluded that I was just a lonely little girl named Betsy. But I doubted that his nature was so different from my own that he could sustain objective sympathy for another child, particularly a younger sister, from one day to another.

And since I saw no favors that he could ask from me at this time, my conclusion was that he believed that he had never exhibited his drunkenness to me with all his bouncing about on the stair at night; but that he was not certain that talking from the other corner of his mouth had been precaution enough against his whiskey breath.

We faced each other over the chessboard and set the men in order. There were only a few days before it would be March, and the light through the window was first bright and then dull. During my brother's moves, I stared out the window at the clouds that passed before the sun and watched pieces of newspaper that blew about the yard. I was calm beyond my own credulity. I found myself responding to my brother's little jokes and showing real interest in the game. I tried to terrorize myself by imagining Mr. Speed's coming up to the very window this day. I even had him shaking his cane and his derby hat at us. But the frenzy which I expected at this step of my preparation did not come. And some part of Mr. Speed's formidability seemed to have vanished. I realized that by not hiding my face in my mother's bosom and by looking at him so regularly for so many months, I had come to accept his existence as a natural part of my life on Church Street, though something to be guarded against, or, as I had put it before, to be thoroughly prepared for when it came to my door.

The problem then, in relation to my brother, had suddenly resolved itself in something much simpler than the conquest of my fear of looking upon Mr. Speed alone had been. This would be only a matter of how I should act and of what words I should use. And from the incident of the night before, I had some notion that I'd find a suitable way of procedure in our household.

Mr. Speed appeared in the street without his overcoat but with one hand holding the turned-up lapels and collar of his gray suit coat. He followed his cane, stomping like an enraged blind man with his head bowed against the March wind. I squeezed from between my chair and the table and stood right at the great plate glass window, looking out. From the corner of my eye I saw that Brother was intent upon his play. Presently, in the wind, Mr. Speed's derby went back on his head, and his hand grabbed at it, pulled it back in place, then returned to hold his lapels. I took a sharp breath, and Brother looked up. And just as he looked out the window, Mr. Speed's derby did blow off and across the sidewalk, over the lawn. Mr. Speed turned, holding his lapels with his tremendous hand, shouting oaths that I could hear ever so faintly, and tried to stumble after his hat.

Then I realized that my brother was gone from the room; and he was outside the window with Mr. Speed chasing Mr. Speed's hat in the wind.

I sat back in my chair, breathless; one elbow went down on the chessboard disordering the black and white pawns and kings and castles. And through the window I watched Brother handing Mr. Speed his derby. I saw his apparent indifference to the drunk man's oaths and curses. I saw him coming back to the house while the old man yet stood railing at him. I pushed the table aside and ran to the front door lest Brother be locked outside. He met me in the hall smiling blandly.

I said, "That's Mr. Speed."

He sat down on the bottom step of the stairway, leaning backward and looking at me inquisitively.

"He's drunk, Brother," I said. "Always."

My brother looked frankly into the eyes of this half-grown sister of his but said nothing for a while.

I pushed myself up on the console table and sat swinging my legs and looking seriously about the walls of the cavernous hallway at the expanse of oak paneling, at the inset canvas of the sixteenth-century Frenchman making love to his lady, at the hat rack, and at the grandfather's clock in the darkest corner. I waited for Brother to speak.

"You don't like people who get drunk?" he said.

I saw that he was taking the whole thing as a thrust at his own behavior.

"I just think Mr. Speed is very ugly, Brother."

From the detached expression of his eyes I knew that he was not convinced.

"I wouldn't mind him less if he were sober," I said. "Mr. Speed's like—a loose horse."

This analogy convinced him. He knew then what I meant.

"You mustn't waste your time being afraid of such things," he said in great earnestness. "In two or three years there'll be things that you'll have to be afraid of. Things you really can't avoid."

"What did he say to you?" I asked.

"He cussed and threatened to hit me with that stick."

"For no reason?"

"Old Mr. Speed's burned out his reason with whiskey."

"Tell me about him." I was almost imploring him.

"Everybody knows about him. He just wanders around town, drunk. Sometimes downtown they take him off in the Black Maria."

I pictured him on the main streets that I knew downtown and in the big department stores. I could see him in that formal neighborhood where my grandmother used to live. In the neighborhood of Miss Hood and Miss Herron's school. Around the little houses out where my father's secretary lived. Even in nigger town.

"You'll get used to him, for all his ugliness," Brother said. Then we sat there till my father came in, talking almost gaily about things that were particularly ugly in Mr. Speed's clothes and face and in his way of walking.

Since the day that I watched myself say "away" in the mirror, I had spent painful hours trying to know once more that experience which I now regarded as something like mystical. But the stringent course that I, motherless and lonely in our big house, had brought myself to follow while only thirteen had given me certain mature habits of thought. Idle and unrestrained daydreaming I eliminated almost entirely from my experience, though I delighted myself with fantasies that I quite consciously worked out and which, when concluded, I usually considered carefully, trying to fix them with some sort of childish symbolism.

Even idleness in my nightly dreams disturbed me. And sometimes as I tossed half awake in my big bed I would try to piece together my dreams into at least a form of logic. Sometimes I would complete an unfinished dream and wouldn't know in the morning what part I had dreamed and what part pieced out. I would often smile over the ends that I had plotted in half-wakeful moments but found pride in dreams that were complete in themselves and easy to fix with allegory, which I called "meaning." I found that a dream could start for no discoverable reason, with the sight of a printed page on which the first line was, "Once upon a time"; and soon could have me a character in a strange story. Once upon a time there was a little girl whose hands began to get very large. Grown men came for miles around to look at the giant hands and to shake them, but the little girl was ashamed of them and hid them under her skirt. It seemed that the little girl lived in the stable behind my grandmother's old house, and I watched her from the top of the loft ladder. Whenever there was the sound of footsteps, she trembled and wept; so I would beat on the floor above her and laugh uproariously at her fear. But presently I was the little girl listening to the noise. At first I trembled and called out for my father, but then I recollected that it was I who had made the noises and I felt that I had made a very considerable discovery for myself.

I awoke one Saturday morning in early March at the sound of my father's voice in the downstairs hall. He was talking to the servants, ordering the carriage I think. I believe that I awoke at the sound of the carriage horses' names. I went to my door and called "Goodbye" to him. He was twisting his mustache before the hall mirror, and he looked up the stairway at me and smiled. He was always abashed to be caught before a looking glass, and he called out self-consciously and affectionately that he would be home at noon.

I closed my door and went to the little dressing table that he had had put in my room on my birthday. The card with his handwriting on it was still stuck in the corner of the mirror: "For my young lady daughter." I was so thoroughly aware of the gentleness in his nature this morning that any childish timidity before him would, I thought, seem an injustice, and I determined that I should sit with him and my uncles in the parlor that afternoon and perhaps tell them all of my fear of the habitually drunken Mr. Speed and with them watch him pass before the parlor window. That morning I sat before the mirror of my dressing table and put up my hair in a knot on the back of my head for the first time.

Before Father came home at noon, however, I had taken my hair down, and I was not now certain that he would be unoffended by my mention of the neighborhood drunkard. But I was resolute in my purpose, and when my two uncles came after lunch, and the three men shut themselves up in the parlor for the afternoon, I took my seat across the hall in the little library, or den, as my mother had called it, and spent the first of the afternoon skimming over the familiar pages of *Tales of Ol' Virginny*, by Thomas Nelson Page.

My father had seemed tired at lunch. He talked very little and drank only half his cup of coffee. He asked Brother matter-of-fact questions about his plans for college in the fall and told me once to try cutting my meat instead of pulling it to pieces. And as I sat in the library afterward, I wondered if he had been thinking of my mother. Indeed, I wondered whether or not he ever thought of her. He never mentioned her to us; and in a year I had forgotten exactly how he treated her when she had been alive.

It was not only the fate of my brother's soul that I had given thought to since my mother's death. Father had always had his toddy on Saturday afternoon with his two bachelor brothers. But there was more than one round of toddies served in the parlor on Saturday now. Throughout the early part of this afternoon I could hear the tinkle of the bell in the kitchen, and presently the houseboy would appear at the door of the parlor with a tray of ice-filled glasses.

As he entered the parlor each time, I would catch a glimpse over my book of the three men. One was usually standing, whichever one was leading the conversation. Once they were laughing heartily; and as the Negro boy came out with the tray of empty glasses, there was a smile on his face.

As their voices grew louder and merrier, my courage slackened. It was then I first put into words the thought that in my brother and father I saw something of Mr. Speed. And I knew that it was more than a taste for whiskey they had in common.

At four o'clock I heard Brother's voice mixed with those of the Benton boys outside the front door. They came into the hall, and their voices were high and excited. First one, then another would demand to be heard with:"No, listen now; let me tell you what." In a moment I heard Brother on the stairs. Then two of the Benton brothers appeared in the doorway of the library. Even the youngest, who was not a year older than I and whose name was Henry, wore long pants, and each carried a cap in hand and a linen duster over his arm. I stood up and smiled at them, and with my right forefinger I pushed the black locks which hung loosely about my shoulders behind my ears.

"We're going motoring in the Carltons' machine," Henry said.

I stammered my surprise and asked if Brother were going to ride in it. One of them said that he was upstairs getting his hunting cap, since he had no motoring cap. The older brother, Gary Benton, went back into the hall. I walked toward Henry, who was standing in the doorway.

"But does Father know you're going?" I asked.

As I tried to go through the doorway, Henry stretched his arm across it and looked at me with a critical frown on his face.

"Why don't you put up your hair?" he said.

I looked at him seriously, and I felt the heat of the blush that came over my face. I felt it on the back of my neck. I stooped with what I thought considerable grace and slid under his arm and passed into the hall. There were the other two Benton boys listening to the voices of my uncles and my father through the parlor door. I stepped between them and threw open the door. Just as I did so, Henry Benton commanded, "Elizabeth, don't do that!" And I, swinging the door open, turned and smiled at him.

I stood for a moment looking blandly at my father and my uncles. I was considering what had made me burst in upon them in this manner. It was not merely that I had perceived the opportunity of creating this little disturbance and slipping in under its noise, though I was not unaware of the advantage. I was frightened by the boys' impending adventure in the horseless carriage but surely not so much as I normally should have been at breaking into the parlor at this forbidden hour. The immediate cause could only be the attention which Henry Benton had shown me. His insinuation had been that I remained too much a little girl, and I had shown him that at any rate I was a bold, or at least a naughty, little girl.

My father was on his feet. He put his glass on the mantelpiece. And it seemed to me that from the three men came in rapid succession all possible arrangements of the words, Boys-come-in. Come-in-boys. Well-boys-come in. Come-on-in. Boys-come-in-the-parlor. The boys went in, rather showing off their breeding and poise, I thought. The three men moved and talked clumsily before them, as the three Benton brothers went each to each of the men carefully distinguishing between my uncles' titles: doctor and colonel. I thought how awkward all of the members of my own family appeared on occasions that called for grace. Brother strode into the room with his hunting cap sideways on his head, and he announced their plans, which the tactful Bentons, uncertain of our family's prejudices regarding machines, had not mentioned. Father and my uncles had a great deal to say about who was going-to-do-the-driving, and Henry Benton without giving an answer gave a polite invitation to the men to join them. To my chagrin, both my uncles accepted with-the-greatest-of-pleasure what really had not been an invitation at all. And they persisted in accepting it even after Brother in his rudeness raised the question of room in the five-passenger vehicle.

Father said, "Sure. The more, the merrier." But he declined to go himself and declined for me Henry's invitation.

The plan was, then, as finally outlined by the oldest of the Benton brothers, that the boys should proceed to the Carltons' and that Brother should return with the driver to take our uncles out to the Carltons' house which was one of the new residences across from Centennial Park, where the excursions in the machine were to be made.

The four slender youths took their leave from the heavy men with the gold watch chains across their stomachs, and I had to shake hands with each of the Benton brothers. To each I expressed my regret that Father would not let me ride with them, emulating their poise with all my art. Henry Benton was the last, and he smiled as though he knew what I was up to. In answer to his smile I said, "Games are *so* much fun."

I stood by the window watching the four boys in the street until they were out of sight. My father and his brothers had taken their seats in silence, and I was aware of just how unwelcome I was in the room. Finally, my uncle, who had been a colonel in the Spanish War and who wore bushy blond sideburns, whistled under his breath and said, "Well, there's no doubt about it, no doubt about it."

He winked at my father, and my father looked at me and then at my uncle. Then quickly in a ridiculously overserious tone he asked, "What, sir? No doubt about what, sir?"

"Why, there's no doubt that this daughter of yours was flirting with the youngest of the Messrs. Benton."

My father looked at me and twisted his mustache and said with the same pomp that he didn't know what he'd do with me if I started that sort of thing.

My two uncles threw back their heads, each giving a short laugh. My uncle the doctor took off his pince-nez and shook them at me and spoke in the same mock-serious tone of his brothers: "Young lady, if you spend your time in such pursuits you'll only bring upon yourself and upon the young men about Nashville the greatest unhappiness. I, as a bachelor, must plead the cause of the young Bentons!"

I turned to my father in indignation that approached rage.

"Father," I shouted, "there's Mr. Speed out there!"

Father sprang from his chair and quickly stepped up beside me at the window. Then, seeing the old man staggering harmlessly along the sidewalk, he said in, I thought, affected easiness: "Yes. Yes, dear."

"He's drunk," I said. My lips quivered, and I think I must have blushed at this first mention of the unmentionable to my father.

"Poor Old Speed," he said. I looked at my uncles, and they were shaking their heads, echoing my father's tone.

"What ever did happen to Speed's old-maid sister?" my uncle the doctor said.

"She's still with him," Father said.

Mr. Speed appeared soberer today than I had ever seen him. He carried no overcoat to drag on the ground, and his stagger was barely noticeable. The movement of his lips and an occasional gesture were the only evidence of intoxication. I was enraged by the irony that his good behavior on this of all days presented. Had I been a little younger I might have suspected conspiracy on the part of all men against me, but I was old enough to suspect no person's being even interested enough in me to plot against my understanding, unless it be some vague personification of life itself.

The course which I took, I thought afterward, was the proper one. I do not think that it was because I was then really conscious that when one is determined to follow some course rigidly and is blockaded one must fire furiously, if blindly, into the blockade, but rather because I was frightened and in my fear forgot all logic of attack. At any rate, I fired furiously at the three immutable creatures.

"I'm afraid of him," I broke out tearfully. I shouted at them, "He's always drunk! He's always going by our house drunk!"

My father put his arms about me, but I continued talking as I wept on his shirt front. I heard the barking sound of the machine horn out in front, and I felt my father move one hand from my back to motion my uncles to go. And as they shut the parlor door after them, I felt that I had let them escape me.

I heard the sound of the motor fading out up Church Street, and Father led me to the settee. We sat there together for a long while, and neither of us spoke until my tears had dried.

I was eager to tell him just exactly how fearful I was of Mr. Speed's coming into our house. But he only allowed me to tell him that I *was* afraid; for when I had barely suggested that much, he said that I had no business watching Mr. Speed, that I must shut my eyes to some things. "After all," he said, nonsensically I thought, "you're a young lady now." And in several curiously twisted sentences he told me that I mustn't seek things to fear in this world. He said that it was most unlikely, besides, that Speed would ever have business at our house. He punched at his left side several times, gave a prolonged belch, settled a pillow behind his head, and soon was sprawled beside me on the settee, snoring.

But Mr. Speed did come to our house, and it was in less than two months after this dreary twilight. And he came as I had feared he might come, in his most extreme state of drunkenness and at a time when I was alone in the house with the maid Lucy. But I had done everything that a little girl, now fourteen, could do in preparation for such an eventuality. And the sort of preparation that I had been able to make, the clearance of all restraints and inhibitions regarding Mr. Speed in my own mind and in my relationship with my world, had necessarily, I think, given me a maturer view of my own limited experiences; though, too, my very age must be held to account for a natural step toward maturity.

In the two months following the day that I first faced Mr. Speed's existence with my father, I came to look at every phase of our household life with a more direct and more discerning eye. As I wandered about that shadowy and somehow brutally elegant house, sometimes now with a knot of hair on the back of my head, events and customs there that had repelled or frightened me I gave the closest scrutiny. In the daytime I ventured into such forbidden spots as the servants' and the men's bathrooms. The filth of the former became a matter of interest in the study of the servants' natures, instead of the object of ineffable disgust. The other became a fascinating place of wet shaving brushes and leather straps and red rubber bags.

There was an anonymous little Negro boy that I had seen many mornings hurrying away from our back door with a pail. I discovered that he was toting buttermilk from our icebox with the permission of our cook. And I sprang at him from behind a corner of the house one morning and scared him so that he spilled the buttermilk and never returned for more.

Another morning I heard the cook threatening to slash the houseboy with her butcher knife, and I made myself burst in upon them; and before Lucy and the houseboy I told her that if she didn't leave our house that day, I'd call my father and, hardly knowing what I was saying, I added, "And the police." She was gone, and Lucy had got a new cook before dinnertime. In this way, from day to day, I began to take my place as mistress in our motherless household.

I could no longer be frightened by my brother with a mention of runaway horses. And instead of terrorized I felt only depressed by his long and curious arguments with my father. I was depressed by the number of the subjects to and from which they oscillated. The world as a whole still seemed unconscionably larger than anything I could comprehend. But I had learned not to concern myself with so general and so unreal a problem until I had cleared up more particular and real ones.

It was during these two months that I noticed the difference between the manner in which my father spoke before my uncles of Mr. Speed when he passed and that in which he spoke of him before my brother. To my brother it was the condemning, "There goes Old Speed, again." But to my uncles it was,

"There goes Old Speed," with the sympathetic addition, "the rascal." Though my father and his brothers obviously found me more agreeable because a pleasant spirit had replaced my old timidity, they yet considered me a child; and my father little dreamed that I discerned such traits in his character, or that I understood, if I even listened to, their anecdotes and their long funny stories, and it was an interest in the peculiar choice of subject and in the way that the men told their stories.

When Mr. Speed came, I was accustomed to thinking that there was something in my brother's and in my father's natures that was fully in sympathy with the very brutality of his drunkenness. And I knew that they would not consider my hatred for him and for that part of him which I saw in them. For that alone I was glad that it was on a Thursday afternoon, when I was in the house alone with Lucy, that one of the heavy sort of rains that come toward the end of May drove Mr. Speed onto our porch for shelter.

Otherwise I wished for nothing more than the sound of my father's strong voice when I stood trembling before the parlor window and watched Mr. Speed stumbling across our lawn in the flaying rain. I only knew to keep at the window and make sure that he was actually coming into our house. I believe that he was drunker than I had ever before seen him, and his usual ire seemed to be doubled by the raging weather.

Despite the aid of his cane, Mr. Speed fell to his knees once in the muddy sod. He remained kneeling there for a time with his face cast in resignation. Then once more he struggled to his feet in the rain. Though I was ever conscious that I was entering into young womanhood at that age, I can only think of myself as a child at that moment; for it was the helpless fear of a child that I felt as I watched Mr. Speed approaching our door. Perhaps it was the last time I ever experienced the inconsolable desperation of childhood.

Next, I could hear his cane beating on the boarding of the little porch before our door. I knew that he must be walking up and down in that little shelter. Then I heard Lucy's exasperated voice as she came down the steps. I knew immediately, what she confirmed afterward, that she thought it Brother, eager to get into the house, beating on the door.

I, aghast, opened the parlor door just as she pulled open the great front door. Her black skin ashened as she beheld Mr. Speed—his face crimson, his eyes bleary, and his gray clothes dripping water. He shuffled through the doorway and threw his stick on the hall floor. Between his oaths and profanities he shouted over and over in his broken, old man's voice, "Nigger, nigger." I could understand little of his rapid and slurred speech, but I knew his rage went round and round a man in the rain and the shelter of a neighbor's house.

Lucy fled up the long flight of steps and was on her knees at the head of the stair, in the dark upstairs hall, begging me to come up to her. I only stared, as though paralyzed and dumb, at him and then up the steps at her. The front door was still open; the hall was half in light; and I could hear the rain on the roof of the porch and the wind blowing the trees which were in full green foliage.

At last I moved. I acted. I slid along the wall past the hat rack and the console table, my eyes on the drunken old man who was swearing up the steps at Lucy. I reached for the telephone; and when I had rung for central, I called for the police station. I knew what they did with Mr. Speed downtown, and I knew with what I had threatened the cook. There was a part of me that was crouching on the top step with Lucy, vaguely longing to hide my face from this in my own mother's bosom. But there was another part which was making me deal with Mr. Speed, however wrongly, myself. Innocently I asked the voice to send "the Black Maria" to our house number on Church Street.

Mr. Speed had heard me make the call. He was still and silent for just one moment. Then he broke into tears, and he seemed to be chanting his words. He repeated the word "child" so many times that I felt I had acted wrongly, with courage but without wisdom. I saw myself as a little beast adding to the injury that what was bestial in man had already done him. He picked up his cane and didn't seem to be talking either to Lucy or to me, but to the cane. He started out the doorway, and I heard Lucy come running down the stairs. She fairly glided around the newel post and past me to the telephone. She wasn't certain that I had made the call. She asked if I had called my father. I simply told her that I had not.

As she rang the telephone, I watched Mr. Speed cross the porch. He turned to us at the edge of the porch and shouted one more oath. But his foot touched the wet porch step, and he slid and fell unconscious on the steps.

He lay there with the rain beating upon him and with Lucy and myself watching him, motionless from our place by the telephone. I was frightened by the thought of the cruelty which I found I was capable of, a cruelty which seemed inextricably mixed with what I had called courage. I looked at him lying out there in the rain and despised and pitied him at the same time, and I was afraid to go minister to the helpless old Mr. Speed.

Lucy had her arms about me and kept them there until two gray horses pulling their black coach had galloped up in front of the house and two policemen had carried the limp body through the rain to the dreadful vehicle.

Just as the policemen closed the doors in the back of the coach, my father rode up in a closed cab. He jumped out and stood in the rain for several minutes arguing with the policemen. Lucy and I went to the door and waited for him to come in. When he came, he looked at neither of us. He walked past us saying only, "I regret that the bluecoats were called." And he went into the parlor and closed the door.

I never discussed the events of that day with my father, and I never saw Mr. Speed again. But, despite the surge of pity I felt for the old man on our porch that afternoon, my hatred and fear of what he had stood for in my eyes has never left me. And since the day that I watched myself say "away" in the mirror, not a week has passed but that he has been brought to my mind by one thing or another. It was only the other night that I dreamed I was a little girl on Church Street again and that there was a drunk horse in our yard.

## ANN BEATTIE on *A Spinster's Tale*

Peter Taylor's narrators are wise people—or, at least, people in the process of becoming wise. Their explanations of their behavior are not always to be trusted—in fact, once you know you cannot entirely trust a narrator, you are on your way, yourself, to becoming wise. What might seem to be an expression that reflects the tenor of the time—by this, I mean what first strikes our ear as slightly arch, or even archaic—is often a disguise behind which the character hides: this world and these characters, in their time, are no different than we are: manners obfuscate unpleasant truths we intuit between the lines; extreme propriety can mask passive aggression.

Betsy, left motherless by her mother's untimely death, begins to intuit life's dangers and conveniently decides that they reside in and are represented by an alcoholic named Mr. Speed, who stumbles about not-so-comically outside the family house (she adds the "Mr." for propriety's sake; we see it as another attempt at distancing). When, in narration, she explains a remark she seemingly casually makes to her father, the reader will surely register some degree of surprise. She says: "My father talked about the possibilities of a general war and recalled opinions that people had had just before the Spanish-American. He talked about the hundreds of men in the Union Depot. Thinking of all those men there, that close together, was something like meeting Mr. Speed in the front hall. I asked my father not to talk about war, which seemed to him a natural enough request for a young lady to make."

Perhaps it did seem natural enough, but the reader understands that he knows that not commenting on certain things is not likely to make them any less real. He is an adult. Social form can be invoked by a young lady, and his daughter knows that—she tries, many times during the story, rather desperately to depend on that—yet what goes unsaid looms larger, and the division between propriety and passion will never be as easily circumvented as young Betsy hopes. Hers (and ours) is a world where fate deals cruel blows: the early death of a mother (like children, the adults are complicitous in not talking about her once she dies, as if silence could ensure the keeping of the status quo); terrible wars that are past and that are still to come; people trying to subjugate their feelings through alcohol. In a particularly eloquent moment, Betsy observes: "Had I been a little younger I might have suspected conspiracy on the part of all men against me, but I was old enough to suspect no person's being even interested enough in me to plot against my understanding, unless it be some vague personification of life itself."

Wow. There it is: in understated eloquence, mentioned mid-story instead of at the end, where it would have stood as the epiphany in a lesser writer's story, mentioned almost as an afterthought, in a sentence that gains momentum as it shifts into the high gear of serious meaning, Betsy lets us know—and admits that she knows—what is at stake in the world as Peter Taylor understands it, powerfully, in this brilliant and troubling story.

# JAMES THURBER

*Thurber (1894–1961) was born in Columbus, Ohio. The loss of an eye in boyhood kept him from military service in World War I, but he served in Europe as a code clerk and after some time as a reporter for the Columbus* Dispatch. *He returned to Paris in 1924 to sample the world of the expatriate. He was back in New York by 1926, submitting his humorous pieces to* The New Yorker *in its early days, working briefly as its managing editor, and then contributing regularly to its "Talk of the Town" department. Thurber had drawn before he began to write, and* The New Yorker *printed several series of his cartoons as well as fables, essays, comment, and short stories through the many years of his association with the magazine. With his friend Elliott Nugent he wrote a successful play,* The Male Animal *(1940). His zany humor—with its occasional bite of terror and dismay—follows no formula. His carefully wrought style faithfully embodies the richness of the American vernacular. Most of his books contain mixed offerings of stories, essays, fables, and cartoons. Among them are* Fables for Our Time *(1940),* My World—and Welcome to It *(1942),* The Thurber Carnival *(1945), and* Thurber Country *(1953).*

## The Secret Life of Walter Mitty

We're going through!" The Commander's voice was like thin ice breaking. He wore his full-dress uniform, with the heavily braided white cap pulled down rakishly over one cold gray eye. "We can't make it, sir. It's spoiling for a hurricane, if you ask me." "I'm not asking you, Lieutenant Berg," said the Commander. "Throw on the power lights! Rev her up to 8,500! We're going through!" The pounding of the cylinders increased: ta-pocketa-pocketa-pocketa-*pocketapocketa.* The Commander stared at the ice forming on the pilot window. He walked over and twisted a row of complicated dials. "Switch on No. 8 auxiliary!" he shouted. "Switch on No. 8 auxiliary!" repeated Lieutenant Berg. "Full strength in No. 3 turret!" shouted the Commander. "Full strength in No. 3 turret!" The crew, bending to their various tasks in the huge, hurtling eight-engined Navy hydroplane, looked at each other and grinned. "The Old Man'll get us through," they said to one another. "The Old Man ain't afraid of Hell!" . . .

"Not so fast! You're driving too fast!" said Mrs. Mitty. "What are you driving so fast for?"

"Hmm?" said Walter Mitty. He looked at his wife, in the seat beside him, with shocked astonishment. She seemed grossly unfamiliar, like a strange woman who had yelled at him in a crowd. "You were up to fifty-five," she said. "You know I don't like to go more than forty. You were up to fifty-five." Walter Mitty drove on toward Waterbury in silence, the roaring of the SN202 through the worst storm in twenty years of Navy flying fading in the remote, intimate airways of his mind. "You're tensed up again," said Mrs. Mitty. "It's one of your days. I wish you'd let Dr. Renshaw look you over."

Walter Mitty stopped the car in front of the building where his wife went to have her hair done. "Remember to get those overshoes while I'm having my hair done," she said. "I don't need overshoes," said Mitty. She put her mirror back into her bag. "We've been all through that," she said, getting out of the car. "You're not a young man any longer." He raced the engine a little. "Why don't you wear your gloves? Have you lost your gloves?" Walter Mitty reached in a pocket and brought out the gloves. He put them on, but after she had turned and gone into the building and he had driven on to a red light, he took them off again. "Pick it up, brother!" snapped a cop as the light changed, and Mitty hastily pulled on his gloves and lurched ahead. He drove around the streets aimlessly for a time, and then he drove past the hospital on his way to the parking lot.

. . . "It's the millionaire banker, Wellington McMillan," said the pretty nurse. "Yes?" said Walter Mitty, removing his gloves slowly. "Who has the case?" "Dr. Renshaw and Dr. Benbow, but there are two specialists here, Dr. Remington from New York and Mr. Pritchard-Mitford from London. He flew over." A door opened down a long, cool corridor and Dr. Renshaw came out. He looked distraught and haggard. "Hello, Mitty," he said. "We're having the devil's own time with McMillan, the millionaire banker and close personal friend of Roosevelt. Obstreosis of the ductal tract. Tertiary.[1] Wish you'd take a look at him." "Glad to," said Mitty.

In the operating room there were whispered introductions: "Dr. Remington, Dr. Mitty. Mr. Pritchard-Mitford, Dr. Mitty." "I've read your book on streptothricosis," said Pritchard-Mitford, shaking hands. "A brilliant performance, sir." "Thank you," said Walter Mitty. "Didn't know you were in the States, Mitty," grumbled Remington. "Coals to Newcastle, bringing Mitford and me up here for a tertiary." "You are very kind," said Mitty. A huge, complicated machine, connected to the operating table, with many tubes and wires, began at this moment to go pocketa-pocketa-pocketa. "The new anesthetizer is giving way!" shouted an interne. "There is no one in the East who knows how to fix it!" "Quiet, man!" said Mitty, in a low, cool voice. He sprang to the machine, which was now going pocketa-pocketa-queep-pocketa-queep. He began fingering delicately a row of glistening dials: "Give me a fountain pen!" he snapped. Someone handed him a fountain pen. He pulled a faulty piston out of the machine and inserted the pen in its place. "That will hold for ten minutes," he said. "Get on with the operation." A nurse hurried over and whispered to Renshaw, and Mitty saw the man turn pale. "Coreopsis[2] has set in," said Renshaw nervously. "If you would take over, Mitty?" Mitty looked at him

1. I.e., at the third—advanced—stage of the disease. "Obstreosis" and "streptothricosis" (below) are nonsense words for imaginary diseases. 2. A genus of herb, not a medical condition.

and at the craven figure of Benbow, who drank, and at the grave uncertain faces of the two great specialists. "If you wish," he said. They slipped a white gown on him; he adjusted a mask and drew on thin gloves; nurses handed him shining . . .

"Back it up, Mac! Look out for that Buick!" Walter Mitty jammed on the brakes. "Wrong lane, Mac," said the parking-lot attendant, looking at Mitty closely. "Gee. Yeh," muttered Mitty. He began cautiously to back out of the lane marked "Exit Only." "Leave her sit there," said the attendant: "I'll put her away." Mitty got out of the car. "Hey, better leave the key." "Oh," said Mitty, handing the man the ignition key. The attendant vaulted into the car, backed it up with insolent skill, and put it where it belonged.

They're so damn cocky, thought Walter Mitty, walking along Main Street; they think they know everything. Once he had tried to take his chains off, outside New Milford, and he had got them wound around the axles. A man had had to come out in a wrecking car and unwind them, a young, grinning garage-man. Since then Mrs. Mitty always made him drive to a garage to have the chains taken off. The next time, he thought, I'll wear my right arm in a sling; they won't grin at me then. I'll have my right arm in a sling and they'll see I couldn't possibly take the chains off myself. He kicked at the slush on the sidewalk. "Overshoes," he said to himself, and he began looking for a shoe store.

When he came out into the street again, with the overshoes in a box under his arm, Walter Mitty began to wonder what the other thing was his wife had told him to get. She had told him, twice, before they set out from their house for Waterbury. In a way he hated these weekly trips to town—he was always getting something wrong. Kleenex, he thought, Squibb's, razor blades? No. Toothpaste, toothbrush, bicarbonate, carborundum, initiative and referendum? He gave it up. But she would remember it. "Where's the what's-its-name?" she would ask. "Don't tell me you forgot the what's-its-name." A newsboy went by shouting something about the Waterbury trial.

. . . "Perhaps this will refresh your memory." The District Attorney suddenly thrust a heavy automatic at the quiet figure on the witness stand. "Have you ever seen this before?" Walter Mitty took the gun and examined it expertly. "This is my Webley-Vickers 50.80," he said calmly. An excited buzz ran around the courtroom. The Judge rapped for order. "You are a crack shot with any sort of firearms, I believe?" said the District Attorney, insinuatingly. "Objection!" shouted Mitty's attorney. "We have shown that the defendant could not have fired the shot. We have shown that he wore his right arm in a sling on the night of the fourteenth of July." Walter Mitty raised his hand briefly and the bickering attorneys were stilled. "With any known make of gun," he said evenly, "I could have killed Gregory Fitzhurst at three hundred feet *with my left hand.*" Pandemonium broke loose in the courtroom. A woman's scream rose above the bedlam and suddenly a lovely, dark-haired girl was in Walter Mitty's arms. The District Attorney struck at her savagely. Without rising from his chair, Mitty let the man have it on the point of the chin. "You miserable cur!" . . .

"Puppy biscuit," said Walter Mitty. He stopped walking and the buildings of Waterbury rose up out of the misty courtroom and surrounded him again.

A woman who was passing laughed. "He said 'Puppy biscuit,' " she said to her companion. "That man said 'Puppy biscuit' to himself." Walter Mitty hurried on. He went into an A & P, not the first one he came to but a smaller one farther up the street. "I want some biscuit for small, young dogs," he said to the clerk. "Any special brand, sir?" The greatest pistol shot in the world thought a moment. "It says 'Puppies Bark for It' on the box," said Walter Mitty.

His wife would be through at the hairdresser's in fifteen minutes, Mitty saw in looking at his watch, unless they had trouble drying it; sometimes they had trouble drying it. She didn't like to get to the hotel first; she would want him to be there waiting for her as usual. He found a big leather chair in the lobby, facing a window, and he put the overshoes and the puppy biscuit on the floor beside it. He picked up an old copy of *Liberty*[3] and sank down into the chair. "Can Germany Conquer the World Through the Air?" Walter Mitty looked at the pictures of bombing planes and of ruined streets.

. . . "The cannonading has got the wind up in young Raleigh, sir," said the sergeant. Captain Mitty looked up at him through tousled hair. "Get him to bed," he said wearily. "With the others. I'll fly alone." "But you can't sir," said the sergeant anxiously. "It takes two men to handle that bomber and the Archies[4] are pounding hell out of the air. Von Richtman's circus[5] is between here and Saulier." "Somebody's got to get that ammunition dump," said Mitty. "I'm going over. Spot of brandy?" He poured a drink for the sergeant and one for himself. War thundered and whined around the dugout[6] and battered at the door. There was a rending of wood and splinters flew through the room. "A bit of a near thing," said Captain Mitty carelessly. "The box barrage[7] is closing in," said the sergeant. "We only live once, Sergeant," said Mitty, with his faint, fleeting smile. "Or do we?" He poured another brandy and tossed it off. "I never see a man could hold his brandy like you, sir," said the sergeant. "Begging your pardon, sir." Captain Mitty stood up and strapped on his huge Webley-Vickers automatic. "It's forty kilometers through hell, sir," said the sergeant. Mitty finished one last brandy. "After all," he said softly, "what isn't?" The pounding of the cannon increased; there was the rat-tat-tatting of machine guns, and from somewhere came the menacing pocketa-pocketa-pocketa of the new flame-throwers. Walter Mitty walked to the door of the dugout humming "Auprès de Ma Blonde."[8] He turned and waved to the sergeant. "Cheerio!" he said. . . .

Something struck his shoulder. "I've been looking all over this hotel for you," said Mrs. Mitty. "Why do you have to hide in this old chair? How did you expect me to find you?" "Things close in," said Walter Mitty vaguely. "What?" Mrs. Mitty said. "Did you get the what's-its-name? The puppy biscuit? What's in that box?" "Overshoes," said Mitty. "Couldn't you have put them on in the

3. Popular weekly magazine (1924–1951). 4. Slang for antiaircraft guns. 5. In World War I the battle groups of fighter squadrons were known as "flying circuses"; the group commanded by Baron Manfred von Richthofen (1892–1918) was the most deadly German flying circus. 6. Sheltered area dug out of the side of a trench. 7. An artillery barrage from all four sides. 8. *Close to My Blonde,* French song popular during World War I.

store?" "I was thinking," said Walter Mitty. "Does it ever occur to you that I am sometimes thinking?" She looked at him. "I'm going to take your temperature when I get you home," she said.

They went out through the revolving doors that made a faintly derisive whistling sound when you pushed them. It was two blocks to the parking lot. At the drugstore on the corner she said, "Wait here for me. I forgot something. I won't be a minute." She was more than a minute. Walter Mitty lighted a cigarette. It began to rain, rain with sleet in it. He stood up against the wall of the drugstore, smoking. . . . He put his shoulders back and his heels together. "To hell with the handkerchief," said Walter Mitty scornfully. He took one last drag on his cigarette and snapped it away. Then, with that faint, fleeting smile playing about his lips, he faced the firing squad; erect and motionless, proud and disdainful, Walter Mitty the Undefeated, inscrutable to the last.

# Leo Tolstoy

*Tolstoy (1828–1910)—generally considered the greatest of nineteenth-century novelists—was born at Yasnaya Polyana, Russia, into the Russian nobility. His youth was restless and without direction. He was vain, dissolute, and immoderate, a poor student and a reckless gambler. It was only after he entered military service that he became interested in writing—autobiographical stories first, then sketches of military life as he knew it during the Crimean War. Leaving the army in 1857, he traveled in western Europe, but his disdain for the vanities of cultured life was merely deepened by what he saw in Paris. On his return to Russia he started an experimental school for children, structuring it on generally anarchic principles. At the same time he was making the major effort that produced* War and Peace *(1869) and* Anna Karenina *(1877), the novels that assure him his place in world literature. The former is an account of Russia in the years of Napoleon's conquests and his attempt to consolidate his empire by the conquest of Russia. The second is the story of a woman caught in the immemorial conflict of personal, biological, and social demands, whirled down to destruction by her inability to reconcile them. In spite of his triumph with these novels, Tolstoy, as he grew older, was painfully dissatisfied with them and considered them flawed by the earthly preoccupations he was trying to escape. He tried to appease his self-doubt by adopting a primitive version of Christianity that often put him at odds with the established church. For nearly twenty years he wrote chiefly on moral and spiritual matters, and these later moralistic writings, including the novel* The Resurrection *(1899), gave him enormous influence throughout the world as a guide to conscience. His home at Yasnaya Polyana became a mecca for pilgrims who sought his advice on the right way to live. Inside Russia his followers were persecuted by the government, though he himself remained immune from outward pressure. But he never found the inner peace for which he struggled; the turbulence of his mental conflicts moved him several times to leave his home and his wife, and on one of these tormented flights he died in a railway station.*

## The Death of Ivan Ilych[1]

### I

During an interval in the Melvinski trial in the large building of the Law Courts, the members and public prosecutor met in Ivan Egorovich Shebek's private room, where the conversation turned on the celebrated Krasovski case. Fëdor Vasilievich warmly maintained that it was not subject to their jurisdiction, Ivan Egorovich maintained the contrary, while Peter Ivanovich, not having

1. Translated by Louise and Aylmer Maude.

entered into the discussion at the start, took no part in it but looked through the *Gazette* which had just been handed in.

"Gentlemen," he said, "Ivan Ilych has died!"

"You don't say so!"

"Here, read it yourself," replied Peter Ivanovich, handing Fëdor Vasilievich the paper still damp from the press. Surrounded by a black border were the words: "Praskovya Fëdorovna Golovina, with profound sorrow, informs relatives and friends of the demise of her beloved husband Ivan Ilych Golovin, Member of the Court of Justice, which occurred on February the 4th of this year 1882. The funeral will take place on Friday at one o'clock in the afternoon."

Ivan Ilych had been a colleague of the gentlemen present and was liked by them all. He had been ill for some weeks with an illness said to be incurable. His post had been kept open for him, but there had been conjectures that in case of his death Alexeev might receive his appointment, and that either Vinnikov or Shtabel would succeed Alexeev. So on receiving the news of Ivan Ilych's death the first thought of each of the gentlemen in that private room was of the changes and promotions it might occasion among themselves or their acquaintances.

"I shall be sure to get Shtabel's place or Vinnikov's," thought Fëdor Vasilievich. "I was promised that long ago, and the promotion means an extra eight hundred rubles a year for me besides the allowance."

"Now I must apply for my brother-in-law's transfer from Kaluga," thought Peter Ivanovich. "My wife will be very glad, and then she won't be able to say that I never do anything for her relations."

"I thought he would never leave his bed again," said Peter Ivanovich aloud. "It's very sad."

"But what really was the matter with him?"

"The doctors couldn't say—at least they could, but each of them said something different. When last I saw him I thought he was getting better."

"And I haven't been to see him since the holidays. I always meant to go."

"Had he any property?"

"I think his wife had a little—but something quite trifling."

"We shall have to go to see her, but they live so terribly far away."

"Far away from you, you mean. Everything's far away from your place."

"You see, he never can forgive my living on the other side of the river," said Peter Ivanovich, smiling at Shebek. Then, still talking of the distances between different parts of the city, they returned to the Court.

Besides considerations as to the possible transfers and promotions likely to result from Ivan Ilych's death, the mere fact of the death of a near acquaintance aroused, as usual, in all who heard of it the complacent feeling that, "it is he who is dead and not I."

Each one thought or felt, "Well, he's dead but I'm alive!" But the more intimate of Ivan Ilych's acquaintances, his so-called friends, could not help thinking also that they would now have to fulfil the very tiresome demands of propriety by attending the funeral service and paying a visit of condolence to the window.

Fëdor Vasilievich and Peter Ivanovich had been his nearest acquaintances.

Peter Ivanovich had studied law with Ivan Ilych and had considered himself to be under obligations to him.

Having told his wife at dinner-time of Ivan Ilych's death and of his conjecture that it might be possible to get her brother transferred to their circuit,[2] Peter Ivanovich sacrificed his usual nap, put on his evening clothes, and drove to Ivan Ilych's house.

At the entrance stood a carriage and two cabs. Leaning against the wall in the hall downstairs near the cloak-stand was a coffin-lid covered with cloth of gold, ornamented with gold cord and tassels, that had been polished up with metal powder. Two ladies in black were taking off their fur cloaks. Peter Ivanovich recognized one of them as Ivan Ilych's sister, but the other was a stranger to him. His colleague Schwartz was just coming downstairs, but on seeing Peter Ivanovich enter he stopped and winked at him, as if to say: "Ivan Ilych has made a mess of things—not like you and me."

Schwartz's face with his Piccadilly whiskers and his slim figure in evening dress, had as usual an air of elegant solemnity which contrasted with the playfulness of his character and had a special piquancy here, or so it seemed to Peter Ivanovich.

Peter Ivanovich allowed the ladies to precede him and slowly followed them upstairs. Schwartz did not come down but remained where he was, and Peter Ivanovich understood that he wanted to arrange where they should play bridge that evening. The ladies went upstairs to the widow's room, and Schwartz with seriously compressed lips but a playful look in his eyes, indicated by a twist of his eyebrows the room to the right where the body lay.

Peter Ivanovich, like everyone else on such occasions, entered feeling uncertain what he would have to do. All he knew was that at such times it is always safe to cross oneself. But he was not quite sure whether one should make obeisances while doing so. He therefore adopted a middle course. On entering the room he began crossing himself and made a slight movement resembling a bow. At the same time, as far as the motion of his head and arm allowed, he surveyed the room. Two young men—apparently nephews, one of whom was a high-school pupil—were leaving the room, crossing themselves as they did so. An old woman was standing motionless, and a lady with strangely arched eyebrows was saying something to her in a whisper. A vigorous, resolute Church Reader, in a frock-coat, was reading something in a loud voice with an expression that precluded any contradiction. The butler's assistant, Gerasim, stepping lightly in front of Peter Ivanovich, was strewing something on the floor. Noticing this, Peter Ivanovich was immediately aware of a faint odour of a decomposing body.

The last time he had called on Ivan Ilych, Peter Ivanovich had seen Gerasim in the study. Ivan Ilych had been particularly fond of him and he was performing the duty of a sick nurse.

Peter Ivanovich continued to make the sign of the cross slightly inclining his head in an intermediate direction between the coffin, the Reader, and the icons on the table in a corner of the room. Afterwards, when it seemed to him

2. District to which a judge is assigned.

that this movement of his arm in crossing himself had gone on too long, he stopped and began to look at the corpse.

The dead man lay, as dead men always lie, in a specially heavy way, his rigid limbs sunk in the soft cushions of the coffin, with the head forever bowed on the pillow. His yellow waxen brow with bald patches over his sunken temples was thrust up in the way peculiar to the dead, the protruding nose seeming to press on the upper lip. He was much changed and had grown even thinner since Peter Ivanovich had last seen him, but, as is always the case with the dead, his face was handsomer and above all more dignified than when he was alive. The expression on the face said that what was necessary had been accomplished, and accomplished rightly. Besides this there was in that expression a reproach and a warning to the living. This warning seemed to Peter Ivanovich out of place, or at least not applicable to him. He felt a certain discomfort and so he hurriedly crossed himself once more and turned and went out the door—too hurriedly and too regardless of propriety, as he himself was aware.

Schwartz was waiting for him in the adjoining room with legs spread wide apart and both hands toying with his top-hat behind his back. The mere sight of that playful, well-groomed, and elegant figure refreshed Peter Ivanovich. He felt that Schwartz was above all these happenings and would not surrender to any depressing influences. His very look said that this incident of a church service for Ivan Ilych could not be a sufficient reason for infringing the order of the session—in other words, that it would certainly not prevent his unwrapping a new pack of cards and shuffling them that evening while a footman placed four fresh candles on the table: in fact, that there was no reason for supposing that this incident would hinder their spending the evening agreeably. Indeed he said this in a whisper as Peter Ivanovich passed him, proposing that they should meet for a game at Fëdor Vasilievich's. But apparently Peter Ivanovich was not destined to play bridge that evening. Praskovya Fëdorovna (a short, fat woman who despite all efforts to the contrary had continued to broaden steadily from her shoulders downwards and who had the same extraordinarily arched eyebrows as the lady who had been standing by the coffin), dressed all in black, her head covered with lace, came out of her own room with some other ladies, conducted them to the room where the dead body lay, and said: "The service will begin immediately. Please go in."

Schwartz, making an indefinite bow, stood still, evidently neither accepting nor declining this invitation. Praskovya Fëdorovna, recognizing Peter Ivanovich, sighed, went close up to him, took his hand, and said: "I know you were a true friend to Ivan Ilych . . ." and looked at him awaiting some suitable response. And Peter Ivanovich knew that, just as it had been the right thing to cross himself in that room, so what he had to do here was to press her hand, sigh, and say, "Believe me. . . ." So he did all this and as he did it felt that the desired result had been achieved: that both he and she were touched.

"Come with me. I want to speak to you before it begins," said the widow. "Give me your arm."

Peter Ivanovich gave her his arm and they went to the inner rooms, passing Schwartz, who winked at Peter Ivanovich compassionately.

"That does for our bridge! Don't object if we find another player. Perhaps you can cut in when you do escape," said his playful look.

Peter Ivanovich sighed still more deeply and despondently, and Praskovya Fëdorovna pressed his arm gratefully. When they reached the drawing-room, upholstered in pink cretonne and lighted by a dim lamp, they sat down at the table—she on a sofa and Peter Ivanovich on a low pouffe, the springs of which yielded spasmodically under his weight. Praskovya Fëdorovna had been on the point of warning him to take another seat, but felt that such a warning was out of keeping with her present condition and so changed her mind. As he sat down on the pouffe Peter Ivanovich recalled how Ivan Ilych had arranged this room and had consulted him regarding the pink cretonne with green leaves. The whole room was full of furniture and knick-knacks, and on her way to the sofa the lace of the widow's black shawl caught on the carved edge of the table. Peter Ivanovich rose to detach it, and the springs of the pouffe, relieved of his weight, rose also and gave him a push. The widow began detaching her shawl herself, and Peter Ivanovich again sat down, suppressing the rebellious springs of the pouffe under him. But the widow had not quite freed herself and Peter Ivanovich got up again, and again the pouffe rebelled and even creaked. When this was all over she took out a clean cambric handkerchief and began to weep. The episode with the shawl and the struggle with the pouffe had cooled Peter Ivanovich's emotions and he sat there with a sullen look on his face. This awkward situation was interrupted by Sokolov, Ivan Ilych's butler, who came to report that the plot in the cemetery that Praskovya Fëdorovna had chosen would cost two hundred rubles. She stopped weeping and, looking at Peter Ivanovich with the air of a victim, remarked in French that it was very hard for her. Peter Ivanovich made a silent gesture signifying his full conviction that it must indeed be so.

"Please smoke," she said in a magnanimous yet crushed voice, and turned to discuss with Sokolov the price of the plot for the grave.

Peter Ivanovich while lighting his cigarette heard her inquiring very circumstantially into the prices of different plots in the cemetery and finally decided which she would take. When that was done she gave instructions about engaging the choir. Sokolov then left the room.

"I look after everything myself," she told Peter Ivanovich, shifting the albums that lay on the table; and noticing that the table was endangered by his cigarette-ash, she immediately passed him an ashtray, saying as she did so: "I consider it an affectation to say that my grief prevents my attending to practical affairs. On the contrary, if anything can—I won't say console me, but—distract me, it is seeing to everything concerning him." She again took out her handkerchief as if preparing to cry, but suddenly, as if mastering her feeling, she shook herself and began to speak calmly. "But there is something I want to talk to you about."

Peter Ivanovich bowed, keeping control of the springs of the pouffe, which immediately began quivering under him.

"He suffered terribly the last few days."

"Did he?" said Peter Ivanovich.

"Oh, terribly! He screamed unceasingly, not for minutes but for hours. For the last three days he screamed incessantly. It was unendurable. I cannot understand how I bore it; you could hear him three rooms off. Oh, what I have suffered!"

"Is it possible that he was conscious all that time?" asked Peter Ivanovich.

"Yes," she whispered. "To the last moment. He took leave of us a quarter of an hour before he died, and asked us to take Vasya[3] away."

The thought of the sufferings of this man he had known so intimately, first as a merry little boy, then as a school-mate, and later as a grown-up colleague, suddenly struck Peter Ivanovich with horror, despite an unpleasant consciousness of his own and this woman's dissimulation. He again saw that brow, and that nose pressing down on the lip, and felt afraid for himself.

"Three days of frightful suffering and then death! Why, that might suddenly, at any time, happen to me," he thought, and for a moment felt terrified. But—he did not himself know how—the customary reflection at once occurred to him that this had happened to Ivan Ilych and not to him, and that it should not and could not happen to him, and that to think that it could would be yielding to depression which he ought not to do, as Schwartz's expression plainly showed. After which reflection Peter Ivanovich felt reassured, and began to ask with interest about the details of Ivan Ilych's death, as though death was an accident natural to Ivan Ilych but certainly not to himself.

After many details of the really dreadful physical sufferings Ivan Ilych had endured (which details he learnt only from the effect those sufferings had produced on Praskovya Fëdorovna's nerves) the widow apparently found it necessary to get to business.

"Oh, Peter Ivanovich, how hard as it! How terribly, terribly hard!" and she again began to weep.

Peter Ivanovich sighed and waited for her to finish blowing her nose. When she had done so he said, "Believe me . . ." and she again began talking and brought out what was evidently her chief concern with him—namely, to question him as to how she could obtain a grant of money from the government on the occasion of her husband's death. She made it appear that she was asking Peter Ivanovich's advice about her pension, but he soon saw that she already knew about that to the minutest detail, more even than he did himself. She knew how much could be got out of the government in consequence of her husband's death, but wanted to find out whether she could not possibly extract something more. Peter Ivanovich tried to think of some means of doing so, but after reflecting for a while and, out of propriety, condemning the government for its niggardliness, he said he thought that nothing more could be got. Then she sighed and evidently began to devise means of getting rid of her visitor. Noticing this, he put out his cigarette, rose, pressed her hand, and went out into the anteroom.

In the dining-room where the clock stood that Ivan Ilych had liked so much and had bought at an antique shop, Peter Ivanovich met a priest and a few acquaintances who had come to attend the service, and he recognized Ivan Ilych's daughter, a handsome young woman. She was in black and her slim figure appeared slimmer than ever. She had a gloomy, determined, almost angry

3. Diminutive of Vasily, Ivan Ilych's son.

expression, and bowed to Peter Ivanovich as though he were in some way to blame. Behind her, with the same offended look, stood a wealthy young man, an examining magistrate, whom Peter Ivanovich also knew and who was her fiancé, as he had heard. He bowed mournfully to them and was about to pass into the death-chamber, when from under the stairs appeared the figure of Ivan Ilych's schoolboy son, who was extremely like his father. He seemed a little Ivan Ilych, such as Peter Ivanovich remembered when they studied law together. His tear-stained eyes had in them the look that is seen in the eyes of boys of thirteen or fourteen who are not pure-minded. When he saw Peter Ivanovich he scowled morosely and shamefacedly. Peter Ivanovich nodded to him and entered the death-chamber. The service began: candles, groans, incense, tears, and sobs. Peter Ivanovich stood looking gloomily down at his feet. He did not look once at the dead man, did not yield to any depressing influence, and was one of the first to leave the room. There was no one in the anteroom, but Gerasim darted out of the dead man's room, rummaged with his strong hands among the fur coats to find Peter Ivanovich's and helped him on with it.

"Well, friend Gerasim," said Peter Ivanovich, so as to say something. "It's a sad affair, isn't it?"

"It's God's will. We shall all come to it some day," said Gerasim, displaying his teeth—the even, white teeth of a healthy peasant—and, like a man in the thick of urgent work, he briskly opened the front door, called the coachman, helped Peter Ivanovich into the sledge, and sprang back to the porch as if in readiness for what he had to do next.

Peter Ivanovich found the fresh air particularly pleasant after the smell of incense, the dead body, and carbolic acid.

"Where to, sir?" asked the coachman.

"It's not too late even now. . . . I'll call round on Fëdor Vasilievich."

He accordingly drove there and found them just finishing the first rubber,[4] so that it was quite convenient for him to cut in.

## II

Ivan Ilych's life had been most simple and most ordinary and therefore most terrible.

He had been a member of the Court of Justice, and died at the age of forty-five. His father had been an official who after serving in various ministries and departments in Petersburg had made the sort of career which brings men to positions from which by reason of their long service they cannot be dismissed, though they were obviously unfit to hold any responsible position, and for whom therefore posts are specially created, which though fictitious carry salaries of from six to ten thousand rubles that are not fictitious, and in receipt of which they live on to a great age.

Such was the Privy Councillor and superfluous member of various superfluous institutions, Ilya Epimovich Golovin.

4. Round of hands in bridge.

He had three sons, of whom Ivan Ilych was the second. The eldest son was following in his father's footsteps only in another department, and was already approaching that stage in the service at which a similar sinecure would be reached. The third son was a failure. He had ruined his prospects in a number of positions and was now serving in the railway department. His father and brothers, and still more their wives, not merely disliked meeting him, but avoided remembering his existence unless compelled to do so. His sister had married Baron Greff, a Petersburg official of her father's type. Ivan Ilych was *le phénix de la famille*[5] as people said. He was neither as cold and formal as his elder brother nor as wild as the younger, but was a happy mean between them—an intelligent, polished, lively and agreeable man. He had studied with his younger brother at the School of Law, but the latter had failed to complete the course and was expelled when he was in the fifth class. Ivan Ilych finished the course well. Even when he was at the School of Law he was just what he remained for the rest of his life: a capable, cheerful, good-natured, and sociable man, though strict in the fulfillment of what he considered to be his duty: and he considered his duty to be what was so considered by those in authority. Neither as a boy nor as a man was he a toady, but from early youth was by nature attracted to people of high station as a fly is drawn to the light, assimilating their ways and view of life and establishing friendly relations with them. All the enthusiasms of childhood and youth passed without leaving much trace on him; he succumbed to sensuality, to vanity, and latterly among the highest classes to liberalism, but always within limits which his instinct unfailingly indicated to him as correct.

At school he had done things which had formerly seemed to him very horrid and made him feel disgusted with himself when he did them; but when later on he saw that such actions were done by people of good position and that they did not regard them as wrong, he was able not exactly to regard them as right, but to forget about them entirely or not be at all troubled at remembering them.

Having graduated from the School of Law and qualified for the tenth rank of the civil service, and having received money from his father for his equipment, Ivan Ilych ordered himself clothes at Scharmer's, the fashionable tailor, hung a medallion inscribed *respice finem*[6] on his watch-chain, took leave of his professor and the prince who was patron of the school, had a farewell dinner with his comrades at Donon's first-class restaurant, and with his new and fashionable portmanteau, linen, clothes, shaving and other toilet appliances, and a traveling rug, all purchased at the best shops, he set off for one of the provinces where, through his father's influence, he had been attached to the Governor as an official for special service.

In the province Ivan Ilych soon arranged as easy and agreeable a position for himself as he had had at the School of Law. He performed his official tasks, made his career, and at the same time amused himself pleasantly and decorously. Occasionally he paid official visits to country districts, where he behaved with dignity both to his superiors and inferiors, and performed the duties

5. The paragon of the family (French). 6. I.e., look before you leap (Latin).

entrusted to him, which related chiefly to the sectarians,[7] with an exactness and incorruptible honesty of which he could not but feel proud.

In official matters, despite his youth and taste for frivolous gaiety, he was exceedingly reserved, punctilious, and even severe; but in society he was often amusing and witty, and always good-natured, correct in his manner, and *bon enfant*,[8] as the governor and his wife—with whom he was like one of the family—used to say of him.

In the province he had an affair with a lady who made advances to the elegant young lawyer, and there was also a milliner; and there were carousals with aides-de-camp who visited the district, and after-supper visits to a certain outlying street of doubtful reputation; and there was too some obsequiousness to his chief and even to his chief's wife, but all this was done with such a tone of good breeding that no hard names could be applied to it. It all came under the heading of the French saying: "*Il faut que jeunesse se passe.*"[9] It was all done with clean hands, in clean linen, with French phrases, and above all among people of the best society and consequently with the approval of people of rank.

So Ivan Ilych served for five years and then came a change in his official life. The new and reformed judicial institutions were introduced, and new men were needed. Ivan Ilych became such a new man. He was offered the post of examining magistrate, and he accepted it though the post was in another province and obliged him to give up the connexions he had formed and to make new ones. His friends met to give him a send-off; they had a group-photograph taken and presented him with a silver cigarette-case, and he set off to his new post.

As examining magistrate Ivan Ilych was just as *comme il faut*[1] and decorous a man, inspiring general respect and capable of separating his official duties from his private life, as he had been when acting as an official on special service. His duties now as examining magistrate were far more interesting and attractive than before. In his former position it had been pleasant to wear an undress uniform made by Scharmer, and to pass through the crowd of petitioners and officials who were timorously awaiting an audience with the governor, and who envied him as with free and easy gait he went straight into his chief's private room to have a cup of tea and a cigarette with him. But not many people had then been directly dependent on him—only police officials and the sectarians when he went on special missions—and he liked to treat them politely, almost as comrades, as if he were letting them feel that he who had the power to crush them was treating them in this simple, friendly way. There were then but few such people. But now, as an examining magistrate, Ivan Ilych felt that everyone without exception, even the most important and self-satisfied, was in his power, and that he need only write a few words on a sheet of paper with a certain heading, and this or that important, self-satisfied person would be brought before him in the role of an accused person or a witness, and if he did not choose to allow him to sit down, would have to stand before him and answer

7. The Old Believers (so called because they rejected various church reforms) had broken with the Orthodox Church in the 1600s; they were subject to many legal restrictions. 8. Good old boy (French). 9. Youth must have its fling (French). 1. In good taste (French).

his questions. Ivan Ilych never abused his power; he tried on the contrary to soften its expression, but the consciousness of it and of the possibility of softening its effect, supplied the chief interest and attraction of his office. In his work itself, especially in his examinations, he very soon acquired a method of eliminating all considerations irrelevant to the legal aspect of the case, and reducing even the most complicated case to a form in which it would be presented on paper only in its externals, completely excluding his personal opinion of the matter, while above all observing every prescribed formality. The work was new and Ivan Ilych was one of the first men to apply the new Code of 1864.[2]

On taking up the post of examining magistrate in a new town, he made new acquaintances and connexions, placed himself on a new footing, and assumed a somewhat different tone. He took up an attitude of rather dignified aloofness towards the provincial authorities, but picked out the best circle of legal gentlemen and wealthy gentry living in the town and assumed a tone of slight dissatisfaction with the government, of moderate liberalism, and of enlightened citizenship. At the same time, without at all altering the elegance of his toilet, he ceased shaving his chin and allowed his beard to grow as it pleased.

Ivan Ilych settled down very pleasantly in this new town. The society there, which inclined towards opposition to the Governor, was friendly, his salary was larger, and he began to play *vint,*[3] which he found added not a little to the pleasure of life, for he had a capacity for cards, played good-humouredly, and calculated rapidly and astutely, so that he usually won.

After living there for two years he met his future wife, Praskovya Fëdorovna Mikhel, who was the most attractive, clever, and brilliant girl of the set in which he moved, and among other amusements and relaxations from his labours as examining magistrate, Ivan Ilych established light and playful relations with her.

While he had been an official on special service he had been accustomed to dance, but now as an examining magistrate it was exceptional for him to do so. If he danced now, he did it as if to show that though he served under the reformed order of things, and had reached the fifth official rank, yet when it came to dancing he could do it better than most people. So at the end of an evening he sometimes danced with Praskovya Fëdorovna, and it was chiefly during these dances that he captivated her. She fell in love with him. Ivan Ilych had at first no definite intention of marrying, but when the girl fell in love with him he said to himself: "Really, why shouldn't I marry?"

Praskovya Fëdorovna came of a good family, was not bad looking, and had some little property. Ivan Ilych might have aspired to a more brilliant match, but even this was good. He had his salary, and she, he hoped, would have an equal income. She was well connected, and was a sweet, pretty, and thoroughly correct young woman. To say that Ivan Ilych married because he fell in love with Praskovya Fëdorovna and found that she sympathized with his views of life would be as incorrect as to say that he married because his social circle

2. A thorough reform of judicial proceedings in Russia, which followed the freeing of the serfs in 1861. 3. A form of bridge.

approved of the match. He was swayed by both these considerations: the marriage gave him personal satisfaction, and at the same time it was considered the right thing by the most highly placed of his associates.

So Ivan Ilych got married.

The preparations for marriage and the beginning of married life, with its conjugal caresses, the new furniture, new crockery, and new linen, were very pleasant until his wife became pregnant—so that Ivan Ilych had begun to think that marriage would not impair the easy, agreeable, gay and always decorous character of his life, approved of by society and regarded by himself as natural, but would even improve it. But from the first months of his wife's pregnancy, something new, unpleasant, depressing, and unseemly, and from which there was no way of escape, unexpectedly showed itself.

His wife, without any reason—*de gaieté de coeur*[4] as Ivan Ilych expressed it to himself—began to disturb the pleasure and propriety of their life. She began to be jealous without any cause, expected him to devote his whole attention to her, found fault with everything, and made coarse and ill-mannered scenes.

At first Ivan Ilych hoped to escape from the unpleasantness of this state of affairs by the same easy and decorous relation to life that had served him heretofore: he tried to ignore his wife's disagreeable moods, continued to live in his usual easy and pleasant way, invited friends to his house for a game of cards, and also tried going out to his club or spending his evenings with friends. But one day his wife began upbraiding him so vigorously, using such coarse words, and continued to abuse him every time he did not fulfil her demands, so resolutely and with such evident determination not to give way till he submitted—that is, till he stayed at home and was bored just as she was—that he became alarmed. He now realized that matrimony—at any rate with Praskovya Fëdorovna—was not always conducive to the pleasures and amenities of life, but on the contrary often infringed both comfort and propriety, and that he must therefore entrench himself against such infringement. And Ivan Ilych began to seek for means of doing so. His official duties were the one thing that imposed upon Praskovya Fëdorovna, and by means of his official work and the duties attached to it he began struggling with his wife to secure his own independence.

With the birth of their child, the attempts to feed it and the various failures in doing so, and with the real and imaginary illnesses of mother and child, in which Ivan Ilych's sympathy was demanded but about which he understood nothing, the need of securing for himself an existence outside his family life became still more imperative.

As his wife grew more irritable and exacting and Ivan Ilych transferred the centre of gravity of his life more and more to his official work, so did he grow to like his work better and became more ambitious than before.

Very soon, within a year of his wedding, Ivan Ilych had realized that marriage, though it may add some comforts to life, is in fact a very intricate and difficult affair towards which in order to perform one's duty, that is, to lead a

4. From sheer impulsiveness (French).

decorous life approved of by society, one must adopt a definite attitude just as towards one's official duties.

And Ivan Ilych evolved such an attitude towards married life. He only required of it those conveniences—dinner at home, housewife, and bed—which it could give him, and above all that propriety of external forms required by public opinion. For the rest he looked for light-hearted pleasure and propriety, and was very thankful when he found them, but if he met with antagonism and querulousness he at once retired into his separate fenced-off world of official duties, where he found satisfaction.

Ivan Ilych was esteemed a good official, and after three years was made Assistant Public Prosecutor. His new duties, their importance, the possibility of indicting and imprisoning anyone he chose, the publicity his speeches received, and the success he had in all these things, made his work still more attractive.

More children came. His wife became more and more querulous and ill-tempered, but the attitude Ivan Ilych had adopted towards his home life rendered him almost impervious to her grumbling.

After seven years' service in that town he was transferred to another province as Public Prosecutor. They moved, but were short of money and his wife did not like the place they moved to. Though the salary was higher the cost of living was greater, besides which two of their children died and family life became still more unpleasant for him.

Praskovya Fëdorovna blamed her husband for every inconvenience they encountered in their new home. Most of the conversations between husband and wife, especially as to the children's education, led to topics which recalled former disputes, and those disputes were apt to flare up again at any moment. There remained only those rare periods of amorousness which still came to them at times but did not last long. These were islets at which they anchored for a while and then again set out upon that ocean of veiled hostility which showed itself in their aloofness from one another. This aloofness might have grieved Ivan Ilych had he considered that it ought not to exist, but he now regarded the position as normal, and even made it the goal at which he aimed in family life. His aim was to free himself more and more from those unpleasantnesses and to give them a semblance of harmlessness and propriety. He attained this by spending less and less time with his family, and when obliged to be at home he tried to safeguard his position by the presence of outsiders. The chief thing however was that he had his official duties. The whole interest of his life now centred in the official world and that interest absorbed him. The consciousness of his power, being able to ruin anybody he wished to ruin, the importance, even the external dignity of his entry into court, or meetings with his subordinates, his success with superiors and inferiors, and above all his masterly handling of cases, of which he was conscious—all this gave him pleasure and filled his life, together with chats with his colleagues, dinners, and bridge. So that on the whole Ivan Ilych's life continued to flow as he considered it should do—pleasantly and properly.

So things continued for another seven years. His eldest daughter was already sixteen, another child had died, and only one son was left, a schoolboy and a subject of dissension. Ivan Ilych wanted to put him in the School of Law, but to spite him Praskovya Fëdorovna entered him at the High School.[5] The daughter had been educated at home and had turned out well: the boy did not learn badly either.

## III

So Ivan Ilych lived for seventeen years after his marriage. He was already a Public Prosecutor of long standing, and had declined several proposed transfers while awaiting a more desirable post, when an unanticipated and unpleasant occurrence quite upset the peaceful course of his life. He was expecting to be offered the post of presiding judge in a University town, but Happe somehow came to the front and obtained the appointment instead. Ivan Ilych became irritable, reproached Happe, and quarreled both with him and with his immediate superiors—who became colder to him and again passed him over when other appointments were made.

This was in 1880, the hardest year of Ivan Ilych's life. It was then that it became evident on the one hand that his salary was insufficient for them to live on, and on the other that he had been forgotten, and not only this, but that what was for him the greatest and most cruel injustice appeared to others a quite ordinary occurrence. Even his father did not consider it his duty to help him. Ivan Ilych felt himself abandoned by everyone, and that they regarded his position with a salary of 3,500 rubles as quite normal and even fortunate. He alone knew that with the consciousness of the injustices done him, with his wife's incessant nagging, and with the debts he had contracted by living beyond his means, his position was far from normal.

In order to save money that summer he obtained leave of absence and went with his wife to live in the country at her brother's place.

In the country, without his work, he experienced *ennui* for the first time in his life, and not only *ennui* but intolerable depression, and he decided that it was impossible to go on living like that, and that it was necessary to take energetic measures.

Having passed a sleepless night pacing up and down the veranda, he decided to go to Petersburg and bestir himself, in order to punish those who had failed to appreciate him and to get transferred to another ministry.

Next day, despite many protests from his wife and her brother, he started for Petersburg with the sole object of obtaining a post with a salary of five thousand rubles a year. He was no longer bent on any particular department, or tendency, or kind of activity. All he now wanted was an appointment to another post with a salary of five thousand rubles, either in the administration, in the banks, with the railways, in one of the Empress Marya's Institutions,[6] or even in the customs—but it had to carry with it a salary of five thousand rubles and be in a ministry other than that in which they had failed to appreciate him.

And this quest of Ivan Ilych's was crowned with remarkable and unex-

5. Schools of equal level in this period. 6. Charitable organizations founded by the wife of Tsar Paul I (1754–1801).

pected success. At Kursk an acquaintance of his, F. I. Ilyin, got into the first-class carriage, sat down beside Ivan Ilych, and told him of a telegram just received by the Governor of Kursk announcing that a change was about to take place in the ministry: Peter Ivanovich was to be superseded by Ivan Semënovich.

The proposed change, apart from its significance for Russia, had a special significance for Ivan Ilych, because by bringing forward a new man, Peter Petrovich, and consequently his friend Zachar Ivanovich, it was highly favourable for Ivan Ilych, since Zachar Ivanovich was a friend and colleague of his.

In Moscow this news was confirmed, and on reaching Petersburg Ivan Ilych found Zachar Ivanovich and received a definite promise of an appointment in his former department of Justice.

A week later he telegraphed to his wife: "Zachar in Miller's place. I shall receive appointment on presentation of report."

Thanks to this change of personnel, Ivan Ilych had unexpectedly obtained an appointment in his former ministry which placed him two stages above his former colleagues besides giving him five thousand rubles salary and three thousand five hundred rubles for expenses connected with his removal. All his ill humour towards his former enemies and the whole department vanished, and Ivan Ilych was completely happy.

He returned to the country more cheerful and contented than he had been for a long time. Praskovya Fëdorovna also cheered up and a truce was arranged between them. Ivan Ilych told of how he had been fêted by everybody in Petersburg, how all those who had been his enemies were put to shame and now fawned on him, how envious they were of his appointment, and how much everybody in Petersburg had liked him.

Praskovya Fëdorovna listened to all this and appeared to believe it. She did not contradict anything, but only made plans for their life in the town to which they were going. Ivan Ilych saw with delight that these plans were his plans, that he and his wife agreed, and that, after a stumble, his life was regaining its due and natural character of pleasant lightheartedness and decorum.

Ivan Ilych had come back for a short time only, for he had to take up his new duties on the 10th of September. Moreover, he needed time to settle into the new place, to move all his belongings from the province, and to buy and order many additional things: in a word, to make such arrangements as he had resolved on, which were almost exactly what Praskovya Fëdorovna too had decided on.

Now that everything had happened so fortunately, and that he and his wife were at one in their aims and moreover saw so little of one another, they got on together better than they had done since the first years of marriage. Ivan Ilych had thought of taking his family away with him at once, but the insistence of his wife's brother and her sister-in-law, who had suddenly become particularly amiable and friendly to him and his family, induced him to depart alone.

So he departed, and the cheerful state of mind induced by his success and by the harmony between his wife and himself, the one intensifying the other, did not leave him. He found a delightful house, just the thing both he and his wife had dreamt of. Spacious, lofty reception rooms in the old style, a convenient and dignified study, rooms for his wife and daughter, a study for his son—it might have been specially built for them. Ivan Ilych himself superintended the arrangements, chose the wallpapers, supplemented the furniture (preferably with antiques which he considered particularly *comme il faut*), and supervised the upholstering. Everything progressed and progressed and approached the ideal he had set himself: even when things were only half completed they exceeded his expectations. He saw what a refined and elegant character, free from vulgarity, it would all have when it was ready. On falling asleep he pictured to himself how the reception-room would look. Looking at the yet unfinished drawing-room he could see the fireplace, the screen, the what-not, the little chairs dotted here and there, the dishes and plates on the walls, and the bronzes, as they would be when everything was in place. He was pleased by the thought of how his wife and daughter, who shared his taste in this matter, would be impressed by it. They were certainly not expecting as much. He had been particularly successful in finding, and buying cheaply, antiques which gave a particularly aristocratic character to the whole place. But in his letters he intentionally understated everything in order to be able to surprise them. All this so absorbed him that his new duties—though he liked his official work—interested him less than he had expected. Sometimes he even had moments of absent-mindedness during the Court Sessions, and would consider whether he should have straight or curved cornices for his curtains. He was so interested in it all that he often did things himself, rearranging the furniture, or rehanging the curtains. Once when mounting a step-ladder to show the upholsterer, who did not understand, how he wanted the hangings draped, he made a false step and slipped, but being a strong and agile man he clung on and only knocked his side against the knob of the window frame. The bruised place was painful but the pain soon passed, and he felt particularly bright and well just then. He wrote: "I feel fifteen years younger." He thought he would have everything ready by September, but it dragged on till mid-October. But the result was charming not only in his eyes but to everyone who saw it.

In reality it was just what is usually seen in the houses of people of moderate means who want to appear rich, and therefore succeed only in resembling others like themselves: there were damasks, dark wood, plants, rugs, and dull and polished bronzes—all the things people of a certain class have in order to resemble other people of that class. His house was so like the others that it would never have been noticed, but to him it all seemed to be quite exceptional. He was very happy when he met his family at the station and brought them to the newly furnished house all lit up, where a footman in a white tie opened the door into the hall decorated with plants, and when they went on into the drawing-room and the study uttering exclamations of delight. He conducted them everywhere, drank in their praises eagerly, and beamed with pleasure. At tea that evening, when Praskovya Fëdorovna among other things asked him about his fall, he laughed and showed them how he had gone flying and had frightened the upholsterer.

"It's a good thing I'm a bit of an athlete. Another man might have been killed, but I merely knocked myself, just here; it hurts when it's touched, but it's passing off already—it's only a bruise."

So they began living in their new home—in which, as always happens, when they got thoroughly settled in they found they were just one room short—and with the increased income, which as always was just a little (some five hundred rubles) too little, but it was all very nice.

Things went particularly well at first, before everything was finally arranged and while something had still to be done: this thing bought, that thing ordered, another thing moved, and something else adjusted. Though there were some disputes between husband and wife, they were both so well satisfied and had so much to do that it all passed off without any serious quarrels. When nothing was left to arrange it became rather dull and something seemed to be lacking, but they were then making acquaintances, forming habits, and life was growing fuller.

Ivan Ilych spent his mornings at the law court and came home to dinner, and at first he was generally in a good humour, though he occasionally became irritable just on account of his house. (Every spot on the tablecloth or the upholstery, and every broken window-blind string, irritated him. He had devoted so much trouble to arranging it all that every disturbance of it distressed him.) But on the whole his life ran its course as he believed life should do: easily, pleasantly, and decorously.

He got up at nine, drank his coffee, read the paper, and then put on his undress uniform and went to the law courts. There the harness in which he worked had already been stretched to fit him and he donned it without a hitch: petitioners, inquiries at the chancery, the chancery itself, and the sittings public and administrative. In all this the thing was to exclude everything fresh and vital, which always disturbs the regular course of official business, and to admit only official relations with people, and then only on official grounds. A man would come, for instance, wanting some information. Ivan Ilych, as one in whose sphere the matter did not lie, would have nothing to do with him: but if the man had some business with him in his official capacity, something that could be expressed on officially stamped paper, he would do everything, positively everything he could within the limits of such relations, and in doing so would maintain the semblance of friendly human relations, that is, would observe the courtesies of life. As soon as the official relations ended, so did everything else. Ivan Ilych possessed this capacity to separate his real life from the official side of affairs and not mix the two, in the highest degree, and by long practice and natural aptitude had brought it to such a pitch that sometimes, in the manner of a virtuoso, he would even allow himself to let the human and official relations mingle. He let himself do this just because he felt that he could at any time he chose resume the strictly official attitude again and drop the human relation. And he did it all easily, pleasantly, correctly, and even artistically. In the intervals between the sessions he smoked, drank tea, chatted a little about politics, a little about general topics, a little about cards, but most of all about official appointments. Tired, but with the feelings of a virtuoso—one of the first violins who has played his part in an orchestra with precision—he would return home to find that his wife and daughter had been out paying calls, or had a visitor, and that his son had been to school, had done his homework with his tutor, and was duly learning what is taught at High Schools. Everything was as it should be. After dinner, if they had no visitors, Ivan Ilych sometimes read a book that was being much discussed at the time, and in the evening settled down to work, that is, read official papers, compared the depositions of witnesses, and noted paragraphs of the Code applying to them. This was neither dull nor amusing. It was dull when he might have been playing bridge, but if no bridge was available it was at any rate better than doing nothing or sitting with his wife. Ivan Ilych's chief pleasure was giving little dinners to which he invited men and women of good social position, and just as his drawing-room resembled all other drawing-rooms so did his enjoyable little parties resemble all other such parties.

Once they even gave a dance. Ivan Ilych enjoyed it and everything went off well, except that it led to a violent quarrel with his wife about the cakes and sweets. Praskovya Fëdorovna had made her own plans, but Ivan Ilych insisted on getting everything from an expensive confectioner and ordered too many cakes, and the quarrel occurred because some of those cakes were left over and the confectioner's bill came to forty-five rubles. It was a great and disagreeable quarrel. Praskovya Fëdorovna called him "a fool and an imbecile," and he clutched at his head and made angry allusions to divorce.

But the dance itself had been enjoyable. The best people were there, and Ivan Ilych had danced with Princess Trufonova, a sister of the distinguished founder of the Society "Bear My Burden."

The pleasures connected with his work were pleasures of ambition; his social pleasures were those of vanity; but Ivan Ilych's greatest pleasure was playing bridge. He acknowledged that whatever disagreeable incident happened in his life, the pleasure that beamed like a ray of light above everything else was to sit down to bridge with good players, not noisy partners, and of course to four-handed bridge (with five players it was annoying to have to stand out, though one pretended not to mind), to play a clever and serious game (when the cards allowed it) and then to have supper and drink a glass of wine. After a game of bridge, especially if he had won a little (to win a large sum was unpleasant), Ivan Ilych went to bed in specially good humour.

So they lived. They formed a circle of acquaintances among the best people and were visited by people of importance and by young folk. In their views as to their acquaintances, husband, wife and daughter were entirely agreed, and tacitly and unanimously kept at arm's length and shook off the various shabby friends and relations who, with much show of affection, gushed into the drawing-room with its Japanese plates on the walls. Soon these shabby friends ceased to obtrude themselves and only the best people remained in the Golovins' set.

Young men made up to Lisa, and Petrishchev, an examining magistrate and Dmitri Ivanovich Petrishchev's son and sole heir, began to be so attentive to her that Ivan Ilych had already spoken to Praskovya Fëdorovna about it, and considered whether they should not arrange a party for them, or get up some private theatricals.

So they lived, and all went well, without change, and life flowed pleasantly.

## IV

They were all in good health. It could not be called ill health if Ivan Ilych sometimes said that he had a queer taste in his mouth and felt some discomfort in his left side.

But this discomfort increased and, though not exactly painful, grew into a sense of pressure in his side accompanied by ill humour. And his irritability became worse and worse and began to mar the agreeable, easy, and correct life that had established itself in the Golovin family. Quarrels between husband and wife became more and more frequent, and soon the ease and amenity disappeared and even the decorum was barely maintained. Scenes again became frequent, and very few of those islets remained on which husband and wife could meet without an explosion. Praskovya Fëdorovna now had good reason to say that her husband's temper was trying. With characteristic exaggeration she said he had always had a dreadful temper, and that it had needed all her good nature to put up with it for twenty years. It was true that now the quarrels were started by him. His bursts of temper always came just before dinner, often just as he began to eat his soup. Sometimes he noticed that a plate or dish was chipped, or the food was not right, or his son put his elbow on the table, or his daughter's hair was not done as he liked it, and for all this he blamed Praskovya Fëdorovna. At first she retorted and said disagreeable things to him, but once or twice he fell into such a rage at the beginning of dinner that she realized it was due to some physical derangement brought on by taking food, and so she restrained herself and did not answer, but only hurried to get the dinner over. She regarded this self-restraint as highly praiseworthy. Having come to the conclusion that her husband had a dreadful temper and made her life miserable, she began to feel sorry for herself, and the more she pitied herself the more she hated her husband. She began to wish he would die; yet she did not want him to die because then his salary would cease. And this irritated her against him still more. She considered herself dreadfully unhappy just because not even his death could save her, and though she concealed her exasperation, that hidden exasperation of hers increased his irritation also.

After one scene in which Ivan Ilych had been particularly unfair and after which he had said in explanation that he certainly was irritable but that it was due to his not being well, she said that if he was ill it should be attended to, and insisted on his going to see a celebrated doctor.

He went. Everything took place as he had expected and as it always does. There was the usual waiting and the important air assumed by the doctor, with which he was so familiar (resembling that which he himself assumed in court), and the surrounding and listening, and the questions which called for answers that were foregone conclusions and were evidently unnecessary, and the look of importance which implied that "if only you put yourself in our hands we will arrange everything—we know indubitably how it has to be done, always in the same way for everybody alike." It was all just as it was in the law courts. The doctor put on just the same air towards him as he himself put on towards an accused person.

The doctor said that so-and-so indicated that there was so-and-so inside the patient, but if the investigation of so-and-so did not confirm this, then he must assume that and that. If he assumed that and that, then . . . and so on. To Ivan Ilych only one question was important: was his case serious or not? But the doctor ignored that inappropriate question. From his point of view it was not the one under consideration, the real question was to decide between a floating kidney, chronic catarrh, or appendicitis. It was not a question of Ivan Ilych's life or death, but one between a floating kidney and appendicitis. And that question the doctor solved brilliantly, as it seemed to Ivan Ilych, in favour of the appendix, with the reservation that should an examination of the urine give fresh indications the matter would be reconsidered. All this was just what Ivan Ilych had himself brilliantly accomplished a thousand times in dealing with men on trial. The doctor summed up just as brilliantly, looking over his spectacles triumphantly and even gaily at the accused. From the doctor's summing up Ivan Ilych concluded that things were bad, but that for the doctor, and perhaps for everybody else, it was a matter of indifference, though for him it was bad. And this conclusion struck him painfully, arousing in him a great feeling of pity for himself and of bitterness towards the doctor's indifference to a matter of such importance.

He said nothing of this, but rose, placed the doctor's fee on the table, and remarked with a sigh: "We sick people probably often put inappropriate questions. But tell me, in general, is this complaint dangerous, or not? . . ."

The doctor looked at him sternly over his spectacles with one eye, as if to say: "Prisoner, if you will not keep to the questions put to you, I shall be obliged to have you removed from the court."

"I have already told you what I consider necessary and proper. The analysis may show something more." And the doctor bowed.

Ivan Ilych went out slowly, seated himself disconsolately in his sledge, and drove home. All the way home he was going over what the doctor had said, trying to translate those complicated, obscure, scientific phrases into plain language and find in them an answer to the question: "Is my condition bad? Is it very bad? Or is there as yet nothing much wrong?" And it seemed to him that the meaning of what the doctor had said was that it was very bad. Everything in the streets seemed depressing. The cabmen, the houses, the passers-by, and the shops, were dismal. His ache, this dull gnawing ache that never ceased for a moment, seemed to have acquired a new and more serious significance from the doctor's dubious remarks. Ivan Ilych now watched it with a new and oppressive feeling.

He reached home and began to tell his wife about it. She listened, but in the middle of his account his daughter came in with her hat on, ready to go out with her mother. She sat down reluctantly to listen to this tedious story, but could not stand it long, and her mother too did not hear him to the end.

"Well, I am very glad," she said. "Mind now to take your medicine regularly. Give me the prescription and I'll send Gerasim to the chemist's." And she went to get ready to go out.

While she was in the room Ivan Ilych had hardly taken time to breathe, but he sighed deeply when she left it.

"Well," he thought, "perhaps it isn't so bad after all."

He began taking his medicine and following the doctor's directions, which had been altered after the examination of the urine. But then it happened that there was a contradiction between the indications drawn from the examination of the urine and the symptoms that showed themselves. It turned out that what was happening differed from what the doctor had told him, and that he had either forgotten, or blundered, or hidden something from him. He could not, however, be blamed for that, and Ivan Ilych still obeyed his orders implicitly and at first derived some comfort from doing so.

From the time of his visit to the doctor, Ivan Ilych's chief occupation was the exact fulfilment of the doctor's instructions regarding hygiene and the taking of medicine, and the observation of his pain and his excretions. His chief interests came to be people's ailments and people's health. When sickness, deaths, or recoveries were mentioned in his presence, especially when the illness resembled his own, he listened with agitation which he tried to hide, asked questions, and applied what he heard to his own case.

The pain did not grow less, but Ivan Ilych made efforts to force himself to think that he was better. And he could do this so long as nothing agitated him. But as soon as he had any unpleasantness with his wife, any lack of success in his official work, or held bad cards at bridge, he was at once acutely sensible of his disease. He had formerly borne such mischances, hoping soon to adjust what was wrong, to master it and attain success, or make a grand slam. But now every mischance upset him and plunged him into despair. He would say to himself: "There now, just as I was beginning to get better and the medicine had begun to take effect, comes this accursed misfortune, or unpleasantness. . . . " And he was furious with the mishap, or with the people who were causing the unpleasantness and killing him, for he felt that this fury was killing him but could not restrain it. One would have thought that it should have been clear to him that this exasperation with circumstances and people aggravated his illness, and that he ought therefore to ignore unpleasant occurrences. But he drew the very opposite conclusion: he said that he needed peace, and he watched for everything that might disturb it and became irritable at the slightest infringement of it. His condition was rendered worse by the fact that he read medical books and consulted doctors. The progress of his disease was so gradual that he could deceive himself when comparing one day with another—the difference was so slight. But when he consulted the doctors it seemed to him that he was getting worse, and even very rapidly. Yet despite this he was continually consulting them.

That month he went to see another celebrity, who told him almost the same as the first had done but put his questions rather differently, and the interview with this celebrity only increased Ivan Ilych's doubts and fears. A friend of a friend of his, a very good doctor, diagnosed his illness again quite differently from the others, and though he predicted recovery, his questions and suppositions bewildered Ivan Ilych still more and increased his doubts. A homeopathist diagnosed the disease in yet another way, and prescribed medicine which Ivan Ilych took secretly for a week. But after a week, not feeling any improvement and having lost confidence both in the former doctor's treatment and in this one's, he became still more despondent. One day a lady acquaintance mentioned a cure effected by a wonder-working icon. Ivan Ilych caught himself listening attentively and beginning to believe that it had occurred. This incident alarmed him. "Has my mind really weakened to such an extent?" he asked himself. "Nonsense! It's all rubbish. I mustn't give way to nervous fears but having chosen a doctor must keep strictly to his treatment. That is what I will do. Now it's all settled. I won't think about it, but will follow the treatment seriously till summer, and then we shall see. From now there must be no more of this wavering!" This was easy to say but impossible to carry out. The pain in his side oppressed him and seemed to grow worse and more incessant, while the taste in his mouth grew stranger and stranger. It seemed to him that his breath had a disgusting smell, and he was conscious of a loss of appetite and strength. There was no deceiving himself: something terrible, new, and more important than anything before in his life, was taking place within him of which he alone was aware. Those about him did not understand or would not understand it, but thought everything in the world was going on as usual. That tormented Ivan Ilych more than anything. He saw that his household, especially his wife and daughter who were in a perfect whirl of visiting, did not understand anything of it and were annoyed that he was so depressed and so exacting, as if he were to blame for it. Though they tried to disguise it he saw that he was an obstacle in their path, and that his wife had adopted a definite line in regard to his illness and kept to it regardless of anything he said or did. Her attitude was this: "You know," she would say to her friends, "Ivan Ilych can't do as other people do, and keep to the treatment prescribed for him. One day he'll take his drops and keep strictly to his diet and go to bed in good time, but the next day unless I watch him he'll suddenly forget his medicine, eat sturgeon—which is forbidden—and sit up playing cards till one o'clock in the morning."

"Oh, come, when was that?" Ivan Ilych would ask in vexation. "Only once at Peter Ivanovich's."

"And yesterday with Shebek."

"Well, even if I hadn't stayed up, the pain would have kept me awake."

"Be that as it may you'll never get well like that, but will always make us wretched."

Praskovya Fëdorovna's attitude to Ivan Ilych's illness, as she expressed it both to others and to him, was that it was his own fault and was another of the annoyances he caused her. Ivan Ilych felt that this opinion escaped her involuntarily—but that did not make it easier for him.

At the law courts too, Ivan Ilych noticed, or thought he noticed, a strange attitude towards himself. It sometimes seemed to him that people were watching him inquisitively as a man whose place might soon be vacant. Then again, his friends would suddenly begin to chaff him in a friendly way about his low spirits, as if the awful, horrible, and unheard-of thing that was going on within him, incessantly gnawing at him and irresistibly drawing him away, was a very agreeable subject for jests. Schwartz in particular irritated him by his jocularity, vivacity, and *savoir-faire*,[7] which reminded him of what he himself had been ten years ago.

Friends came to make up a set and they sat down to cards. They dealt,

7. Tact, knowing the proper action (French).

bending the new cards to soften them, and he sorted the diamonds in his hand and found he had seven. His partner said "No trumps" and supported him with two diamonds. What more could be wished for? It ought to be jolly and lively. They would make a grand slam. But suddenly Ivan Ilych was conscious of that gnawing pain, that taste in his mouth, and it seemed ridiculous that in such circumstances he should be pleased to make a grand slam.

He looked at his partner Mikhail Mikhaylovich, who rapped the table with his strong hand and instead of snatching up the tricks pushed the cards courteously and indulgently towards Ivan Ilych that he might have the pleasure of gathering them up without the trouble of stretching out his hand for them. "Does he think I am too weak to stretch out my arm?" thought Ivan Ilych, and forgetting what he was doing he over-trumped his partner, missing the grand slam by three tricks. And what was most awful of all was that he saw how upset Mikhail Mikhaylovich was about it but did not himself care. And it was dreadful to realize why he did not care.

They all saw that he was suffering, and said: "We can stop if you are tired. Take a rest." Lie down? No, he was not at all tired, and he finished the rubber. All were gloomy and silent. Ivan Ilych felt that he had diffused this gloom over them and could not dispel it. They had supper and went away, and Ivan Ilych was left alone with the consciousness that his life was poisoned and was poisoning the lives of others, and that this poison did not weaken but penetrated more and more deeply into his whole being.

With this consciousness, and with physical pain besides the terror, he must go to bed, often to lie awake the greater part of the night. Next morning he had to get up again, dress, go to the law courts, speak, and write; or if he did not go out, spend at home those twenty-four hours a day each of which was a torture. And he had to live thus all alone on the brink of an abyss, with no one who understood or pitied him.

## V

So one month passed and then another. Just before the New Year his brother-in-law came to town and stayed at their house. Ivan Ilych was at the law courts and Praskovya Fëdorovna had gone shopping. When Ivan Ilych came home and entered his study he found his brother-in-law there—a healthy, florid man—unpacking his portmanteau himself. He raised his head on hearing Ivan Ilych's footsteps and looked up at him for a moment without a word. That stare told Ivan Ilych everything. His brother-in-law opened his mouth to utter an exclamation of surprise but checked himself, and that action confirmed it all.

"I have changed, eh?"

"Yes, there is a change."

And after that, try as he would to get his brother-in-law to return to the subject of his looks, the latter would say nothing about it. Praskovya Fëdorovna came home and her brother went out to her. Ivan Ilych locked the door and began to examine himself in the glass, first full face, then in profile. He took up a portrait of himself taken with his wife, and compared it with what he saw in the glass. The change in him was immense. Then he bared his arms to the elbow, looked at them, drew the sleeves down again, sat down on an ottoman, and grew blacker than night.

"No, no, this won't do!" he said to himself, and jumped up, went to the table, took up some law papers and began to read them, but could not continue. He unlocked the door and went into the reception-room. The door leading to the drawing-room was shut. He approached it on tiptoe and listened.

"No, you are exaggerating!" Praskovya Fëdorovna was saying.

"Exaggerating! Don't you see it? Why, he's a dead man! Look at his eyes—there's no light in them. But what is it that is wrong with him?"

"No one knows. Nikolaevich [that was another doctor] said something, but I don't know what. And Leshchetitsky [this was the celebrated specialist] said quite the contrary . . ."

Ivan Ilych walked away, went to his own room, lay down, and began musing: "The kidney, a floating kidney." He recalled all the doctors had told him of how it detached itself and swayed about. And by an effort of imagination he tried to catch that kidney and arrest it and support it. So little was needed for this, it seemed to him. "No, I'll go to see Peter Ivanovich again." [That was the friend whose friend was a doctor.] He rang, ordered the carriage, and got ready to go.

"Where are you going, Jean?"[8] asked his wife, with a specially sad and exceptionally kind look.

This exceptionally kind look irritated him. He looked morosely at her.

"I must go to see Peter Ivanovich."

He went to see Peter Ivanovich, and together they went to see his friend, the doctor. He was in, and Ivan Ilych had a long talk with him.

Reviewing the anatomical and physiological details of what in the doctor's opinion was going on inside him, he understood it all.

There was something, a small thing, in the vermiform appendix. It might all come right. Only stimulate the energy of one organ and check the activity of another, then absorption would take place and everything would come right. He got home rather late for dinner, ate his dinner, and conversed cheerfully, but could not for a long time bring himself to go back to work in his room. At last, however, he went to his study and did what was necessary, but the consciousness that he had put something aside—an important, intimate matter which he would revert to when his work was done—never left him. When he had finished his work he remembered that this intimate matter was the thought of his vermiform appendix. But he did not give himself up to it, and went to the drawing-room for tea. There were callers there, including the examining magistrate who was a desirable match for his daughter, and they were conversing, playing the piano, and singing. Ivan Ilych, as Praskovya Fëdorovna remarked, spent that evening more cheerfully than usual, but he never for a moment forgot that he had postponed the important matter of the appendix. At eleven o'clock he said good-night and went to his bedroom. Since his illness he had slept alone in a small room next to his study. He undressed and took

8. The French equivalent for Ivan. Russians of the upper classes frequently spoke French to each other in the nineteenth century.

up a novel by Zola,[9] but instead of reading it he fell into thought, and in his imagination that desired improvement in the vermiform appendix occurred. There was the absorption and evacuation and the re-establishment of normal activity. "Yes, that's it!" he said to himself. "One need only assist nature, that's all." He remembered his medicine, rose, took it, and lay down on his back watching for the beneficient action of the medicine and for it to lessen the pain. "I need only take it regularly and avoid all injurious influences. I am already feeling better, much better." He began touching his side: it was not painful to the touch. "There, I really don't feel it. It's much better already." He put out the light and turned on his side. . . . "The appendix is getting better, absorption is occurring." Suddenly he felt the old, familiar, dull, gnawing pain, stubborn and serious. There was the same familiar loathsome taste in his mouth. His heart sank and he felt dazed. "My God! My God!" he muttered. "Again, again! and it will never cease." And suddenly the matter presented itself in a quite different aspect. "Vermiform appendix! Kidney!" he said to himself. "It's not a question of appendix or kidney, but of life and . . . death. Yes, life was there and now it is going, going and I cannot stop it. Yes. Why deceive myself? Isn't it obvious to everyone but me that I'm dying, and that it's only a question of weeks, days . . . it may happen this moment. There was light and now there is darkness. I was here and now I'm going there! Where?" A chill came over him, his breathing ceased, and he felt only the throbbing of his heart.

"When I am not, what will there be? There will be nothing. Then where shall I be when I am no more? Can this be dying? No, I don't want to!" He jumped up and tried to light the candle, felt for it with trembling hands, dropped candle and candlestick on the floor, and fell back on his pillow.

"What's the use? It makes no difference," he said to himself, staring with wide-open eyes into the darkness. "Death. Yes, death. And none of them know or wish to know it, and they have no pity for me. Now they are playing." (He heard through the door the distant sound of a song and its accompaniment.) "It's all the same to them, but they will die too! Fools! I first, and they later, but it will be the same for them. And now they are merry . . . the beasts!"

Anger choked him and he was agonizingly, unbearably miserable. "It is impossible that all men have been doomed to suffer this awful horror!" He raised himself.

"Something must be wrong. I must calm myself—must think it all over from the beginning." And he again began thinking. "Yes, the beginning of my illness: I knocked my side, but I was still quite well that day and the next. It hurt a little, then rather more. I saw the doctors, then followed despondency and anguish, more doctors, and I drew nearer to the abyss. My strength grew less and I kept coming nearer and nearer, and now I have wasted away and there is no light in my eyes. I think of the appendix—but this is death! I think of mending the appendix, and all the while here is death! Can it really be death?" Again terror seized him and he gasped for breath. He leant down and began feeling for the matches, pressing with his elbow on the stand beside the bed. It was in his way and hurt him, he grew furious with it, pressed on it still

9. Émile Zola (1840–1902), French novelist.

harder, and upset it. Breathless and in despair he fell on his back, expecting death to come immediately.

Meanwhile the visitors were leaving. Praskovya Fëdorovna was seeing them off. She heard something fall and came in.

"What has happened?"

"Nothing. I knocked it over accidentally."

She went out and returned with a candle. He lay there panting heavily, like a man who has run a thousand yards, and stared upwards at her with a fixed look.

"What is it, Jean?"

"No . . . no . . . thing. I upset it." ("Why speak of it? She won't understand," he thought.)

And in truth she did not understand. She picked up the stand, lit his candle, and hurried away to see another visitor off. When she came back he still lay on his back, looking upwards.

"What is it? Do you feel worse?"

"Yes."

She shook her head and sat down.

"Do you know, Jean, I think we must ask Leshchetitsky to come and see you here."

This meant calling in the famous specialist, regardless of expense. He smiled malignantly and said "No." She remained a little longer and then went up to him and kissed his forehead.

While she was kissing him he hated her from the bottom of his soul and with difficulty refrained from pushing her away.

"Good-night. Please God you'll sleep."

"Yes."

## VI

Ivan Ilych saw that he was dying, and he was in continual despair.

In the depth of his heart he knew he was dying, but not only was he not accustomed to the thought, he simply did not and could not grasp it.

The syllogism he had learnt from Kiezewetter's Logic:[1] "Caius is a man, men are mortal, therefore Caius is mortal," had always seemed to him correct as applied to Caius, but certainly not as applied to himself. That Caius—man in the abstract—was mortal, was perfectly correct, but he was not Caius, not an abstract man, but a creature quite, quite separate from all others. He had been little Vanya, with a mamma and a papa, with Mitya and Volodya, with the toys, a coachman and a nurse, afterwards with Katenka and with all the joys, griefs, and delights of childhood, boyhood, and youth. What did Caius know of the smell of that striped leather ball Vanya had been so fond of? Had Caius kissed his mother's hand like that, and did the silk of her dress rustle so for Caius? Had he rioted like that at school when the pastry was bad? Had Caius

1. The *Outline of Logic According to Kantian Principles* by Klaus Kiezewetter (1766–1819) was widely used as a Russian textbook.

been in love like that? Could Caius preside at a session as he did? "Caius really was mortal, and it was right for him to die; but for me, little Vanya, Ivan Ilych, with all my thoughts and emotions, it's altogether a different matter. It cannot be that I ought to die. That would be too terrible."

Such was his feeling.

"If I had to die like Caius I should have known it was so. An inner voice would have told me so, but there was nothing of the sort in me and I and all my friends felt that our case was quite different from that of Caius. And now here it is!" he said to himself. "It can't be. It's impossible! But here it is. How is this? How is one to understand it?"

He could not understand it, and tried to drive this false, incorrect, morbid thought away and to replace it by other proper and healthy thoughts. But that thought, and not the thought only but the reality itself, seemed to come and confront him.

And to replace that thought he called up a succession of others, hoping to find in them some support. He tried to get back into the former current of thoughts that had once screened the thought of death from him. But strange to say, all that had formerly shut off, hidden, and destroyed, his consciousness of death, no longer had that effect. Ivan Ilych now spent most of his time in attempting to re-establish that old current. He would say to himself: "I will take up my duties again—after all I used to live by them." And banishing all doubts he would go to the law courts, enter into conversation with his colleagues, and sit carelessly as was his wont, scanning the crowd with a thoughtful look and leaning both his emaciated arms on the arms of his oak chair; bending over as usual to a colleague and drawing his papers nearer he would interchange whispers with him, and then suddenly raising his eyes and sitting erect would pronounce certain words and open the proceedings. But suddenly in the midst of those proceedings the pain in his side, regardless of the stage the proceedings had reached, would begin its own gnawing work. Ivan Ilych would turn his attention to it and try to drive the thought of it away, but without success. *It* would come and stand before him and look at him, and he would be petrified and the light would die out of his eyes, and he would again begin asking himself whether *It* alone was true. And his colleagues and subordinates would see with surprise and distress that he, the brilliant and subtle judge, was becoming confused and making mistakes. He would shake himself, try to pull himself together, manage somehow to bring the sitting to a close, and return home with the sorrowful consciousness that his judicial labours could not as formerly hide from him what he wanted them to hide, and could not deliver him from *It*. And what was worst of all was that *It* drew his attention to itself not in order to make him take some action but only that he should look at *It*, look it straight in the face: look at it and without doing anything, suffer inexpressibly.

And to save himself from this condition Ivan Ilych looked for consolations—new screens—and new screens were found and for a while seemed to save him, but then they immediately fell to pieces or rather became transparent, as if *It* penetrated them and nothing could veil *It*.

In these latter days he would go into the drawing-room he had arranged—that drawing-room where he had fallen and for the sake of which (how bitterly ridiculous it seemed) he had sacrificed his life—for he knew that his illness originated with that knock. He would enter and see that something had scratched the polished table. He would look for the cause of this and find that it was the bronze ornamentation of an album, that had got bent. He would take up the expensive album which he had lovingly arranged, and feel vexed with his daughter and her friends for their untidiness—for the album was torn here and there and some of the photographs turned upside down. He would put it carefully in order and bend the ornamentation back into position. Then it would occur to him to place all those things in another corner of the room, near the plants. He could call the footman, but his daughter or wife would come to help him. They would not agree, and his wife would contradict him, and he would dispute and grow angry. But that was all right, for then he did not think about *It*. *It* was invisible.

But then, when he was moving something himself, his wife would say: "Let the servants do it. You will hurt yourself again." And suddenly *It* would flash through the screen and he would see it. It was just a flash, and he hoped it would disappear, but he would involuntarily pay attention to his side. "It sits there as before, gnawing just the same!" And he could no longer forget *It,* but could distinctly see it looking at him from behind the flowers. "What is it all for?"

"It really is so! I lost my life over that curtain as I might have done when storming a fort. Is that possible? How terrible and how stupid. It can't be true! It can't, but it is."

He would go to his study, lie down, and again be alone with *It*: face to face with *It*. And nothing could be done with *It* except to look at it and shudder.

## VII

How it happened it is impossible to say because it came about step by step, unnoticed, but in the third month of Ivan Ilych's illness, his wife, his daughter, his son, his acquaintances, the doctors, the servants, and above all he himself, were aware that the whole interest he had for other people was whether he would soon vacate his place, and at last release the living from the discomfort caused by his presence and be himself released from his sufferings.

He slept less and less. He was given opium and hypodermic injections of morphine, but this did not relieve him. The dull depression he experienced in a somnolent condition at first gave him a little relief, but only as something new, afterwards it became as distressing as the pain itself or even more so.

Special foods were prepared for him by the doctors' orders, but all those foods became increasingly distasteful and disgusting to him.

For his excretions also special arrangements had to be made, and this was a torment to him every time—a torment from the uncleanliness, the unseemliness, and the smell, and from knowing that another person had to take part in it.

But just through this most unpleasant matter, Ivan Ilych obtained comfort. Gerasim, the butler's young assistant, always came in to carry the things out. Gerasim was a clean, fresh peasant lad, grown stout on town food and always cheerful and bright. At first the sight of him, in his clean Russian peasant costume, engaged on that disgusting task embarrassed Ivan Ilych.

Once when he got up from the commode too weak to draw up his trousers, he dropped into a soft armchair and looked with horror at his bare, enfeebled thighs with the muscles so sharply marked on them.

Gerasim with a firm light tread, his heavy boots emitting a pleasant smell of tar and fresh winter air, came in wearing a clean Hessian apron, the sleeves of his print shirt tucked up over his strong bare young arms; and refraining from looking at his sick master out of consideration for his feelings, and restraining the joy of life that beamed from his face, he went up to the commode.

"Gerasim!" said Ivan Ilych in a weak voice.

Gerasim started, evidently afraid he might have committed some blunder, and with a rapid movement turned his fresh, kind, simple young face which just showed the first downy signs of a beard.

"Yes, sir?"

"That must be very unpleasant for you. You must forgive me. I am helpless."

"Oh, why, sir," and Gerasim's eyes beamed and he showed his glistening white teeth, "what's a little trouble? It's a case of illness with you, sir."

And his deft strong hands did their accustomed task, and he went out of the room stepping lightly. Five minutes later he as lightly returned.

Ivan Ilych was still sitting in the same position in the armchair.

"Gerasim," he said when the latter had replaced the freshly-washed utensil. "Please come here and help me." Gerasim went up to him. "Lift me up. It is hard for me to get up, and I have sent Dmitri away."

Gerasim went up to him, grasped his master with his strong arms deftly but gently, in the same way that he stepped—lifted him, supported him with one hand, and with the other drew up his trousers and would have set him down again, but Ivan Ilych asked to be led to the sofa. Gerasim, without an effort and without apparent pressure, led him, almost lifting him, to the sofa and placed him on it.

"Thank you. How easily and well you do it all!"

Gerasim smiled again and turned to leave the room. But Ivan Ilych felt his presence such a comfort that he did not want to let him go.

"One thing more, please move up that chair. No, the other one—under my feet. It is easier for me when my feet are raised."

Gerasim brought the chair, set it down gently in place, and raised Ivan Ilych's legs on to it. It seemed to Ivan Ilych that he felt better while Gerasim was holding up his legs.

"It's better when my legs are higher," he said. "Place that cushion under them."

Gerasim did so. He again lifted the legs and placed them, and again Ivan Ilych felt better while Gerasim held his legs. When he set them down Ivan Ilych fancied he felt worse.

"Gerasim," he said. "Are you busy now?"

"Not at all, sir," said Gerasim, who had learnt from the townsfolk how to speak to gentlefolk.

"What have you still to do?"

"What have I to do? I've done everything except chopping the logs for tomorrow."

"Then hold my legs up a bit higher, can you?"

"Of course I can. Why not?" And Gerasim raised his master's legs higher and Ivan Ilych thought that in that position he did not feel any pain at all.

"And how about the logs?"

"Don't trouble about that, sir. There's plenty of time."

Ivan Ilych told Gerasim to sit down and hold his legs, and began to talk to him. And strange to say it seemed to him that he felt better while Gerasim held his legs up.

After that Ivan Ilych would sometimes call Gerasim and get him to hold his legs on his shoulders, and he liked talking to him. Gerasim did it all easily, willingly, simply, and with a good nature that touched Ivan Ilych. Health, strength, and vitality in other people were offensive to him, but Gerasim's strength and vitality did not mortify but soothed him.

What tormented Ivan Ilych most was the deception, the lie, which for some reason they all accepted, that he was not dying but was simply ill, and that he only need keep quiet and undergo a treatment and then something very good would result. He however knew that do what they would nothing would come of it, only still more agonizing suffering and death. This deception tortured him—their not wishing to admit what they all knew and what he knew, but wanting to lie to him concerning his terrible condition, and wishing and forcing him to participate in that lie. Those lies—lies enacted over him on the eve of his death and destined to degrade this awful, solemn act to the level of their visitings, their curtains, their sturgeon for dinner—were a terrible agony for Ivan Ilych. And strangely enough, many times when they were going through their antics over him he had been within a hairbreadth of calling out to them: "Stop lying! You know and I know that I am dying. Then at least stop lying about it!" But he had never had the spirit to do it. The awful, terrible act of his dying was, he could see, reduced by those about him to the level of a casual, unpleasant, and almost indecorous incident (as if someone entered a drawing-room diffusing an unpleasant odour) and this was done by that very decorum which he had served all his life long. He saw that no one felt for him, because no one even wished to grasp his position. Only Gerasim recognized it and pitied him. And so Ivan Ilych felt at ease only with him. He felt comforted when Gerasim supported his legs (sometimes all night long) and refused to go to bed, saying: "Don't you worry, Ivan Ilych. I'll get sleep enough later on," or when he suddenly became familiar and exclaimed: "If you weren't sick it would be another matter, but as it is, why should I grudge a little trouble?" Gerasim alone did not lie; everything showed that he alone understood the facts of the case and did not consider it necessary to disguise them, but simply felt sorry for his emaciated and enfeebled master. Once when Ivan Ilych was sending him away he even said straight out: "We shall all of us die, so why should I grudge a little trouble?"—expressing the fact that he did not think his work burdensome, because he was doing it for a dying man and hoped someone would do the same for him when his time came.

Apart from this lying, or because of it, what most tormented Ivan Ilych was that no one pitied him as he wished to be pitied. At certain moments after prolonged suffering he wished most of all (though he would have been ashamed to confess it) for someone to pity him as a sick child is pitied. He longed to be petted and comforted. He knew he was an important functionary, that he had a beard turning grey, and that therefore what he longed for was impossible, but still he longed for it. And in Gerasim's attitude towards him there was something akin to what he wished for, and so that attitude comforted him. Ivan Ilych wanted to weep, wanted to be petted and cried over, and then his colleague Shebek would come, and instead of weeping and being petted, Ivan Ilych would assume a serious, severe, and profound air, and by force of habit would express his opinion on a decision of the Court of Cessation[2] and would stubbornly insist on that view. This falsity around him and within him did more than anything else to poison his last days.

## VIII

It was morning. He knew it was morning because Gerasim had gone, and Peter the footman had come and put out the candles, drawn back one of the curtains, and begun quietly to tidy up. Whether it was morning or evening, Friday or Sunday, made no difference, it was all just the same: the gnawing, unmitigated, agonizing pain, never ceasing for an instant, the consciousness of life inexorably waning but not yet extinguished, the approach of that ever dreaded and hateful Death which was the only reality, and always the same falsity. What were days, weeks, hours, in such a case?

"Will you have some tea, sir?"

"He wants things to be regular, and wishes the gentlefolk to drink tea in the morning," thought Ivan Ilych, and only said "No."

"Wouldn't you like to move onto the sofa, sir?"

"He wants to tidy up the room, and I'm in the way. I am uncleanliness and disorder," he thought, and said only:

"No, leave me alone."

The man went on bustling about. Ivan Ilych stretched out his hand. Peter came up, ready to help.

"What is it, sir?"

"My watch."

Peter took the watch which was close at hand and gave it to his master.

"Half-past eight. Are they up?"

"No, sir, except Vasily Ivanich" (the son) "who has gone to school. Praskovya Fëdorovna ordered me to wake her if you asked for her. Shall I do so?"

"No, there's no need to." "Perhaps I'd better have some tea," he thought, and added aloud: "Yes, bring me some tea."

Peter went to the door, but Ivan Ilych dreaded being left alone. "How can I keep him here? Oh yes, my medicine." "Peter, give me my medicine." "Why not? Perhaps it may still do me some good." He took a spoonful and swallowed

2. The highest court of appeal constituted by the council of state.

it. "No, it won't help. It's all tomfoolery, all deception," he decided as soon as he became aware of the familiar, sickly, hopeless taste. "No, I can't believe in it any longer. But the pain, why this pain? If it would only cease just for a moment!" And he moaned. Peter turned towards him. "It's all right. Go and fetch me some tea."

Peter went out. Left alone Ivan Ilych groaned not so much with pain, terrible though that was, as from mental anguish. Always and for ever the same, always these endless days and nights. If only it would come quicker! If only *what* would come quicker? Death, darkness?. . . No, no! Anything rather than death!

When Peter returned with the tea on a tray, Ivan Ilych stared at him for a time in perplexity, not realizing who and what he was. Peter was disconcerted by that look and his embarrassment brought Ivan Ilych to himself.

"Oh, tea! All right, put it down. Only help me to wash and put on a clean shirt."

And Ivan Ilych began to wash. With pauses for rest, he washed his hands and then his face, cleaned his teeth, brushed his hair, and looked in the glass. He was terrified by what he saw, especially by the limp way in which his hair clung to his pallid forehead.

While his shirt was being changed he knew that he would be still more frightened at the sight of his body, so he avoided looking at it. Finally he was ready. He drew on a dressing-gown, wrapped himself in a plaid, and sat down in the armchair to take his tea. For a moment he felt refreshed, but as soon as he began to drink the tea he was again aware of the same taste, and the pain also returned. He finished it with an effort, and then lay down stretching out his legs, and dismissed Peter.

Always the same. Now a spark of hope flashes up, then a sea of despair rages, and always pain; always pain, always despair, and always the same. When alone he had a dreadful and distressing desire to call someone, but he knew beforehand that with others present it would be still worse. "Another dose of morphine—to lose consciousness. I will tell him, the doctor, that he must think of something else. It's impossible, impossible, to go on like this."

An hour and another pass like that. But now there is a ring at the door bell. Perhaps it's the doctor? It is. He comes in fresh, hearty, plump, and cheerful, with that look on his face that seems to say: "There now, you're in a panic about something, but we'll arrange it all for you directly!" The doctor knows this expression is out of place here, but he has put it on once for all and can't take it off—like a man who has put on a frock-coat in the morning to pay a round of calls.

The doctor rubs his hands vigorously and reassuringly.

"Brr! How cold it is! There's such a sharp frost; just let me warm myself!" he says, as if it were only a matter of waiting till he was warm, and then he would put everything right.

"Well now, how are you?"

Ivan Ilych feels that the doctor would like to say: "Well, how are our affairs?" but that even he feels that this would not do, and says instead: "What sort of a night have you had?"

Ivan Ilych looks at him as much as to say: "Are you really never ashamed of lying?" But the doctor does not wish to understand this question, and Ivan Ilych says: "Just as terrible as ever. The pain never leaves me and never subsides. If only something . . ."

"Yes, you sick people are always like that. . . . There, now I think I am warm enough. Even Praskovya Fëdorovna, who is so particular, could find no fault with my temperature. Well, now I can say good-morning," and the doctor presses his patient's hand.

Then, dropping his former playfulness, he begins with a most serious face to examine the patient, feeling his pulse and taking his temperature, and then begins the sounding and auscultation.

Ivan Ilych knows quite well and definitely that all this is nonsense and pure deception, but when the doctor, getting down on his knee, leans over him, putting his ear first higher then lower, and performs various gymnastic movements over him with a significant expression on his face, Ivan Ilych submits to it all as he used to submit to the speeches of the lawyers, though he knew very well that they were all lying and why they were lying.

The doctor, kneeling on the sofa, is still sounding him when Praskovya Fëdorovna's silk dress rustles at the door and she is heard scolding Peter for not having let her know of the doctor's arrival.

She comes in, kisses her husband, and at once proceeds to prove that she has been up a long time already, and only owing to a misunderstanding failed to be there when the doctor arrived.

Ivan Ilych looks at her, scans her all over, sets against her the whiteness and plumpness and cleanness of her hands and neck, the gloss of her hair, and the sparkle of her vivacious eyes. He hates her with his whole soul. And the thrill of hatred he feels for her makes him suffer from her touch.

Her attitude towards him and his disease is still the same. Just as the doctor had adopted a certain relation to his patient which he could not abandon, so had she formed one towards him—that he was not doing something he ought to do and was himself to blame, and that she reproached him lovingly for this—and she could not now change that attitude.

"You see he doesn't listen to me and doesn't take his medicine at the proper time. And above all he lies in a position that is no doubt bad for him—with his legs up."

She described how he made Gerasim hold his legs up.

The doctor smiled with a contemptuous affability that said: "What's to be done? These sick people do have foolish fancies of that kind, but we must forgive them."

When the examination was over the doctor looked at his watch, and then Praskovya Fëdorovna announced to Ivan Ilych that it was of course as he pleased, but she had sent today for a celebrated specialist who would examine him and have a consultation with Michael Danilovich (their regular doctor).

"Please don't raise any objections. I am doing this for my own sake," she said ironically, letting it be felt that she was doing it all for his sake and only said this to leave him no right to refuse. He remained silent, knitting his brows.

He felt that he was so surrounded and involved in a mesh of falsity that it was hard to unravel anything.

Everything she did for him was entirely for her own sake, and she told him she was doing for herself what she actually was doing for herself, as if that was so incredible that he must understand the opposite.

At half-past eleven the celebrated specialist arrived. Again the sounding began and the significant conversations in his presence and in another room, about the kidneys and the appendix, and the questions and answers, with such an air of importance that again, instead of the real question of life and death which now alone confronted him, the question arose of the kidney and appendix which were not behaving as they ought to and would now be attacked by Michael Danilovich and the specialist and forced to amend their ways.

The celebrated specialist took leave of him with a serious though not hopeless look, and in reply to the timid question Ivan Ilych, with eyes glistening with fear and hope, put to him as to whether there was a chance of recovery, said that he could not vouch for it but there was a possibility. The look of hope with which Ivan Ilych watched the doctor out was so pathetic that Praskovya Fëdorovna, seeing it, even wept as she left the room to hand the doctor his fee.

The gleam of hope kindled by the doctor's encouragement did not last long. The same room, the same pictures, curtains, wall-paper, medicine bottles, were all there, and the same aching suffering body, and Ivan Ilych began to moan. They gave him a subcutaneous injection and he sank into oblivion.

It was twilight when he came to. They brought him his dinner and he swallowed some beef tea with difficulty, and then everything was the same again and night was coming on.

After dinner, at seven o'clock, Praskovya Fëdorovna came into the room in evening dress, her full bosom pushed by her corset, and with traces of powder on her face. She had reminded him in the morning that they were going to the theatre. Sarah Bernhardt[3] was visiting the town and they had a box, which he had insisted on their taking. Now he had forgotten about it and her toilet offended him, but he concealed his vexation when he remembered that he had himself insisted on their securing a box and going because it would be an instructive and aesthetic pleasure for the children.

Praskovya Fëdorovna came in, self-satisfied but yet with a rather guilty air. She sat down and asked how he was, but, as he saw, only for the sake of asking and not in order to learn about it, knowing that there was nothing to learn—and then went on to what she really wanted to say: that she would not on any account have gone but that the box had been taken and Helen and their daughter were going, as well as Petrishchev (the examining magistrate, their daughter's fiancé) and that it was out of the question to let them go alone; but that she would have much preferred to sit with him for a while; and he must be sure to follow the doctor's orders while she was away.

"Oh, and Fëdor Petrovich" (the fiancé) "would like to come in. May he? And Lisa?"

3. French actress (1844–1923), who had a great popular following.

"All right."

Their daughter came in in full evening dress, her fresh young flesh exposed (making a show of that very flesh which in his own case caused so much suffering), strong, healthy, evidently in love, and impatient with illness, suffering, and death, because they interfered with her happiness.

Fëdor Petrovich came in too, in evening dress, his hair curled *à la Capoul*,[4] a tight stiff collar round his long sinewy neck, an enormous white shirt-front and narrow black trousers tightly stretched over his strong thighs. He had one white glove tightly drawn on, and was holding his opera hat in his hand.

Following him the schoolboy crept in unnoticed, in a new uniform, poor little fellow, and wearing gloves. Terribly dark shadows showed under his eyes, the meaning of which Ivan Ilych knew well.

His son had always seemed pathetic to him, and now it was dreadful to see the boy's frightened look of pity. It seemed to Ivan Ilych that Vasya was the only one besides Gerasim who understood and pitied him.

They all sat down and again asked how he was. A silence followed. Lisa asked her mother about the opera-glasses, and there was an altercation between mother and daughter as to who had taken them and where they had been put. This occasioned some unpleasantness.

Fëdor Petrovich inquired of Ivan Ilych whether he had ever seen Sarah Bernhardt. Ivan Ilych did not at first catch the question, but then replied: "No, have you seen her before?"

"Yes, in *Adrienne Lecouvreur*."[5]

Praskovya Fëdorovna mentioned some rôles in which Sarah Bernhardt was particularly good. Her daughter disagreed. Conversation sprang up as to the elegance and realism of her acting—the sort of conversation that is always repeated and is always the same.

In the midst of the conversation Fëdor Petrovich glanced at Ivan Ilych and became silent. The others also looked at him and grew silent. Ivan Ilych was staring with glittering eyes straight before him, evidently indignant with them. This had to be rectified, but it was impossible to do so. The silence had to be broken, but for a time no one dared to break it and they all became afraid that the conventional deception would suddenly become obvious and the truth become plain to all. Lisa was the first to pluck up courage and break that silence, but by trying to hide what everybody was feeling, she betrayed it.

"Well, if we are going it's time to start," she said, looking at her watch, a present from her father, and with a faint and significant smile at Fëdor Petrovich relating to something known only to them. She got up with a rustle of her dress.

They all rose, said good-night, and went away.

When they had gone it seemed to Ivan Ilych that he felt better; the falsity had gone with them. But the pain remained—that same pain and that same fear that made everything monotonously alike, nothing harder and nothing easier. Everything was worse.

4. An ornate and elaborate form of man's hairstyle (French).

5. A comedy by Eugène Scribe (1791–1861) and Ernest Legouvé (1807–1903), written in 1849.

Again minute followed minute and hour followed hour. Everything remained the same and there was no cessation. And the inevitable end of it all became more and more terrible.

"Yes, send Gerasim here," he replied to a question Peter asked.

## IX

His wife returned late at night. She came in on tiptoe, but he heard her, opened his eyes, and made haste to close them again. She wished to send Gerasim away and to sit with him herself, but he opened his eyes and said: "No, go away."

"Are you in great pain?"

"Always the same."

"Take some opium."

He agreed and took some. She went away.

Till about three in the morning he was in a state of stupefied misery. It seemed to him that he and his pain were being thrust into a narrow, deep black sack, but though they were pushed further and further in they could not be pushed to the bottom. And this, terrible enough in itself, was accompanied by suffering. He was frightened yet wanted to fall through the sack, he struggled but yet co-operated. And suddenly he broke through, fell, and regained consciousness. Gerasim was sitting at the foot of the bed dozing quietly and patiently, while he himself lay with his emaciated stockinged legs resting on Gerasim's shoulders; the same shaded candle was there and the same unceasing pain.

"Go away, Gerasim," he whispered.

"It's all right, sir. I'll stay a while."

"No. Go away."

He removed his legs from Gerasim's shoulders, turned sideways onto his arm, and felt sorry for himself. He only waited till Gerasim had gone into the next room and then restrained himself no longer but wept like a child. He wept on account of his helplessness, his terrible loneliness, the cruelty of man, the cruelty of God, and the absence of God.

"Why hast Thou done all this? Why hast Thou brought me here? Why, why dost Thou torment me so terribly?"

He did not expect an answer and yet wept because there was no answer and could be none. The pain again grew more acute, but he did not stir and did not call. He said to himself: "Go on! Strike me! But what is it for? What have I done to Thee? What is it for?"

Then he grew quiet and not only ceased weeping but even held his breath and became all attention. It was as though he were listening not to an audible voice but to the voice of his soul, to the current of thoughts arising within him.

"What is it you want?" was the first clear conception capable of expression in words, that he heard.

"What do you want? What do you want?" he repeated to himself.

"What do I want? To live and not to suffer," he answered.

And again he listened with such concentrated attention that even his pain did not distract him.

"To live? How?" asked his inner voice.

"Why, to live as I used to—well and pleasantly."

"As you lived before, well and pleasantly?" the voice repeated.

And in imagination he began to recall the best moments of his pleasant life. But strange to say none of those best moments of his pleasant life now seemed at all what they had then seemed—none of them except the first recollections of childhood. There, in childhood, there had been something really pleasant with which it would be possible to live if it could return. But the child who had experienced that happiness existed no longer, it was like a reminiscence of somebody else.

As soon as the period began which had produced the present Ivan Ilych, all that had then seemed joys now melted before his sight and turned into something trivial and often nasty.

And the further he departed from childhood and the nearer he came to the present the more worthless and doubtful were the joys. This began with the School of Law. A little that was really good was still found there—there was light-heartedness, friendship, and hope. But in the upper classes there had already been fewer of such good moments. Then during the first years of his official career, when he was in the service of the Governor, some pleasant moments again occurred: they were the memories of love for a woman. Then all became confused and there was still less of what was good; later on again there was still less that was good, and the further he went the less there was. His marriage, a mere accident, then the disenchantment that followed it, his wife's bad breath and the sensuality and hypocrisy: then the deadly official life and those preoccupations about money, a year of it, and two, and ten, and twenty, and always the same thing. And the longer it lasted the more deadly it became. "It is as if I had been going downhill while I imagined I was going up. And that is really what it was. I was going up in public opinion, but to the same extent life was ebbing away from me. And now it is all done and there is only death."

"Then what does it mean? Why? It can't be that life is so senseless and horrible. But if it really has been so horrible and senseless, why must I die and die in agony? There is something wrong!"

"Maybe I did not live as I ought to have done," it suddenly occurred to him. "But how could that be, when I did everything properly?" he replied, and immediately dismissed from his mind this, the sole solution of all the riddles of life and death, as something quite impossible.

"Then what do you want now? To live? Live how? Live as you lived in the law courts when the usher proclaimed 'The judge is coming!' The judge is coming, the judge!" he repeated to himself. "Here he is, the judge. But I am not guilty!" he exclaimed angrily. "What is it for?" And he ceased crying, but turning his face to the wall continued to ponder on the same question: Why, and for what purpose, is there all this horror? But however much he pondered he found no answer. And whenever the thought occurred to him, as it often did, that it all resulted from his not having lived as he ought to have done, he at once recalled the correctness of his whole life and dismissed so strange an idea.

## X

Another fortnight passed. Ivan Ilych now no longer left his sofa. He would not lie in bed but lay on the sofa, facing the wall nearly all the time. He suffered ever the same unceasing agonies and in his loneliness pondered always on the same insoluble question: "What is this? Can it be that it is Death?" And the inner voice answered: "Yes, it is Death."

"Why these sufferings?" And the voice answered, "For no reason—they just are so." Beyond and besides this there was nothing.

From the very beginning of his illness, ever since he had first been to see the doctor, Ivan Ilych's life had been divided between two contrary and alternating moods: now it was despair and the expectation of this uncomprehended and terrible death, and now hope and an intently interested observation of the functioning of his organs. Now before his eyes there was only a kidney or an intestine that temporarily evaded its duty, and now only that incomprehensible and dreadful death from which it was impossible to escape.

These two states of mind had alternated from the very beginning of his illness, but the further it progressed the more doubtful and fantastic became the conception of the kidney, and the more real the sense of impending death.

He had but to call to mind what he had been three months before and what he was now, to call to mind with what regularity he had been going downhill, for every possibility of hope to be shattered.

Latterly during that loneliness in which he found himself as he lay facing the back of the sofa, a loneliness in the midst of a populous town and surrounded by numerous acquaintances and relations but that yet could not have been more complete anywhere—either at the bottom of the sea or under the earth—during that terrible loneliness Ivan Ilych had lived only in memories of the past. Pictures of his past rose before him one after another. They always began with what was nearest in time and then went back to what was most remote—to his childhood—and rested there. If he thought of the stewed prunes that had been offered him that day, his mind went back to the raw shrivelled French plums of his childhood, their peculiar flavour and the flow of saliva when he sucked their stones, and along with the memory of that taste came a whole series of memories of those days: his nurse, his brother, and their toys. "No, I mustn't think of that. . . . It is too painful," Ivan Ilych said to himself, and brought himself back to the present—to the button on the back of the sofa and the creases in its morocco. "Morocco is expensive, but it does not wear well: there had been a quarrel about it. It was a different kind of quarrel and a different kind of morocco that time when we tore father's portfolio and were punished, and mama brought us some tarts. . . ." And again his thoughts dwelt on his childhood, and again it was painful and he tried to banish them and fix his mind on something else.

Then again together with that chain of memories another series passed through his mind—of how his illness had progressed and grown worse. There also the further back he looked the more life there had been. There had been more of what was good in life and more of life itself. The two merged together. "Just as the pain went on getting worse and worse, so my life grew worse and worse," he thought. "There is one bright spot there at the back, at the beginning of life, and afterwards all becomes blacker and blacker and proceeds more and more rapidly—in inverse ratio to the square of the distance from death," thought Ivan Ilych. And the example of a stone falling downwards with increasing velocity entered his mind. Life, a series of increasing sufferings, flies further and further towards its end—the most terrible suffering. "I am flying. . . ." He shuddered, shifted himself, and tried to resist, but was already aware that resistance was impossible, and again with eyes weary of gazing but unable to cease seeing what was before them, he stared at the back of the sofa and waited—awaiting that dreadful fall and shock and destruction.

"Resistance is impossible!" he said to himself. "If I could only understand what it is all for! But that too is impossible. An explanation would be possible if it could be said that I have not lived as I ought to. But it is impossible to say that," and he remembered all the legality, correctitude, and propriety of his life. "That at any rate can certainly not be admitted," he thought, and his lips smiled ironically as if someone could see that smile and be taken in by it. "There is no explanation! Agony, death . . . What for?"

## XI

Another two weeks went by in this way and during that fortnight an event occurred that Ivan Ilych and his wife had desired. Petrishchev formally proposed. It happened in the evening. The next day Praskovya Fëdorovna came into her husband's room considering how best to inform him of it, but that very night there had been a fresh change for the worse in his condition. She found him still lying on the sofa but in a different position. He lay on his back, groaning and staring fixedly straight in front of him.

She began to remind him of his medicines, but he turned his eyes towards her with such a look that she did not finish what she was saying; so great an animosity, to her in particular, did that look express.

"For Christ's sake let me die in peace!" he said.

She would have gone away, but just then their daughter came in and went up to say good morning. He looked at her as he had done at his wife, and in reply to her inquiry about his health said dryly that he would soon free them all of himself. They were both silent and after sitting with him for a while went away.

"Is it our fault?" Lisa said to her mother. "It's as if we were to blame! I am sorry for papa, but why should we be tortured?"

The doctor came at his usual time. Ivan Ilych answered "Yes" and "No," never taking his angry eyes from him, and at last said: "You know you can do nothing for me, so leave me alone."

"We can ease your sufferings."

"You can't even do that. Let me be."

The doctor went into the drawing-room and told Praskovya Fëdorovna that the case was very serious and that the only resource left was opium to allay her husband's sufferings, which must be terrible.

It was true, as the doctor said, that Ivan Ilych's physical sufferings were terrible, but worse than the physical sufferings were his mental sufferings, which were his chief torture.

His mental sufferings were due to the fact that that night, as he looked at Gerasim's sleepy, good-natured face with its prominent cheek-bones, the question suddenly occurred to him: "What if my whole life has really been wrong?"

It occurred to him that what had appeared perfectly impossible before, namely that he had not spent his life as he should have done, might after all be true. It occurred to him that his scarcely perceptible attempts to struggle against what was considered good by the most highly placed people, those scarcely noticeable impulses which he had immediately suppressed, might have been the real thing, and all the rest false. And his professional duties and the whole arrangement of his life and of his family, and all his social and official interests, might all have been false. He tried to defend all those things to himself and suddenly felt the weakness of what he was defending. There was nothing to defend.

"But if that is so," he said to himself, "and I am leaving this life with the consciousness that I have lost all that was given me and it is impossible to rectify it—what then?"

He lay on his back and began to pass his life in review in quite a new way. In the morning when he saw first his footman, then his wife, then his daughter, and then the doctor, their every word and movement confirmed to him the awful truth that had been revealed to him during the night. In them he saw himself—all that for which he had lived—and saw clearly that it was not real at all, but a terrible and huge deception which had hidden both life and death. This consciousness intensified his physical suffering tenfold. He groaned and tossed about, and pulled at his clothing which choked and stifled him. And he hated them on that account.

He was given a large dose of opium and became unconscious, but at noon his sufferings began again. He drove everybody away and tossed from side to side.

His wife came to him and said:

"Jean, my dear, do this for me. It can't do any harm and often helps. Healthy people often do it."

He opened his eyes wide.

"What? Take communion? Why? It's unnecessary! However . . ."

She began to cry.

"Yes, do, my dear. I'll send for our priest. He is such a nice man."

"All right. Very well," he muttered.

When the priest came and heard his confession, Ivan Ilych was softened and seemed to feel a relief from his doubts and consequently from his sufferings, and for a moment there came a ray of hope. He again began to think of the vermiform appendix and the possibility of correcting it. He received the sacrament with tears in his eyes.

When they laid him down again afterwards he felt a moment's ease, and the hope that he might live awoke in him again. He began to think of the operation that had been suggested to him. "To live! I want to live!" he said to himself.

His wife came in to congratulate him after his communion, and when uttering the usual conventional words she added:

"You feel better, don't you?"

Without looking at her he said "Yes."

Her dress, her figure, the expression of her face, the tone of her voice, all revealed the same thing. "This is wrong, it is not as it should be. All you have lived for and still live for is falsehood and deception, hiding life and death from you." And as soon as he admitted that thought, his hatred and his agonizing physical suffering again sprang up, and with that suffering a consciousness of the unavoidable, approaching end. And to this was added a new sensation of grinding shooting pain and a feeling of suffocation.

The expression of his face when he uttered that "yes" was dreadful. Having uttered it, he looked her straight in the eyes, turned on his face with a rapidity extraordinary in his weak state and shouted:

"Go away! Go away and leave me alone!"

## XII

From that moment the screaming began that continued for three days, and was so terrible that one could not hear it through two closed doors without horror. At the moment he answered his wife he realized that he was lost, that there was no return, that the end had come, the very end, and his doubts were still unsolved and remained doubts.

"Oh! Oh! Oh!" he cried in various intonations. He had begun by screaming "I won't!" and continued screaming on the letter O.

For three whole days, during which time did not exist for him, he struggled in that black sack into which he was being thrust by an invisible, resistless force. He struggled as a man condemned to death struggles in the hands of the executioner, knowing that he cannot save himself. And every moment he felt that despite all his efforts he was drawing nearer and nearer to what terrified him. He felt that his agony was due to his being thrust into that black hole and still more to his not being able to get right into it. He was hindered from getting into it by his conviction that his life had been a good one. That very justification of his life held him fast and prevented his moving forward, and it caused him most torment of all.

Suddenly some force struck him in the chest and side, making it still harder to breathe, and he fell through the hole and there at the bottom was a light. What had happened to him was like the sensation one sometimes experiences in a railway carriage when one thinks one is going backwards while one is really going forwards and suddenly becomes aware of the real direction.

"Yes, it was all not the right thing," he said to himself, "but that's no matter. It can be done. But what *is* the right thing?" he asked himself, and suddenly grew quiet.

This occurred at the end of the third day, two hours before his death. Just then his schoolboy son had crept softly in and gone up to the bedside. The dying man was still screaming desperately and waving his arms. His hand fell on the boy's head, and the boy caught it, pressed it to his lips, and began to cry.

At that very moment Ivan Ilych fell through and caught sight of the light, and it was revealed to him that though his life had not been what it should have been, this could still be rectified. He asked himself, "What *is* the right thing?" and grew still, listening. Then he felt that someone was kissing his hand. He opened his eyes, looked at his son, and felt sorry for him. His wife came up to him and he glanced at her. She was gazing at him open-mouthed, with undried tears on her nose and cheek and a despairing look on her face. He felt sorry for her too.

"Yes, I am making them wretched," he thought. "They are sorry, but it will be better for them when I die." He wished to say this but had not the strength to utter it. "Besides, why speak? I must act," he thought. With a look at his wife he indicated his son and said: "Take him away . . . sorry for him . . . sorry for you too. . . ." He tried to add, "forgive me," but said "forgo" and waved his hand, knowing that He whose understanding mattered would understand.

And suddenly it grew clear to him that what had been oppressing him and would not leave him was all dropping away at once from two sides, from ten sides, and from all sides. He was sorry for them, he must act so as not to hurt them: release them and free himself from these sufferings. "How good and how simple!" he thought. "And the pain?" he asked himself. "What has become of it? Where are you, pain?"

He turned his attention to it.

"Yes, here it is. Well, what of it? Let the pain be."

"And death . . . where is it?"

He sought his former accustomed fear of death and did not find it. "Where is it? What death?" There was no fear because there was no death.

In place of death there was light.

"So that's what it is!" he suddenly exclaimed aloud. "What joy!"

To him all this happened in a single instant, and the meaning of that instant did not change. For those present his agony continued for another two hours. Something rattled in his throat, his emaciated body twitched, then the gasping and rattle became less and less frequent.

"It is finished!" said someone near him.

He heard these words and repeated them in his soul.

"Death is finished," he said to himself. "It is no more!"

He drew in a breath, stopped in the midst of a sigh, stretched out, and died.

# John Updike

*Updike (1932–    ) was born in Shillington, Pennsylvania, an only child. His mother—a writer—gave him the idea that being a painter or writer would lead him to a happy life, so he launched himself as a cartoonist for the Harvard* Lampoon *during his college years, and for a year after graduation studied drawing in England. Soon after this he joined the staff of* The New Yorker *and served the magazine in a number of capacities until 1957; he continues to contribute verse, reviews, and fiction to its pages. His fiction is often topical—people trapped in American fads and prejudices figure often in his most characteristic writing. His stories have been collected in* Pigeon Feathers and Other Stories *(1962),* The Music School *(1966),* Bech: A Book *(1970),* Museums and Women and Other Stories *(1972),* Problems and Other Stories *(1979),* The Afterlife and Other Stories *(1994), and* Short Stories *(1997). His novels include* Rabbit, Run *(1960),* Couples *(1968),* Rabbit Redux *(1971),* Rabbit Is Rich *(1982),* The Witches of Eastwick *(1984),* Roger's Version *(1986),* Trust Me *(1987),* S *(1988),* Rabbit at Rest *(1990),* Memories of the Ford Administration *(1992),* In the Beauty of the Lilies *(1996),* Toward the End of Time *(1997), and* Bech at Bay *(1998). His novels have won the Pulitzer Prize and the National Book Award, among other honors.*

## A & P

In walks these three girls in nothing but bathing suits. I'm in the third checkout slot, with my back to the door, so I don't see them until they're over by the bread. The one that caught my eye first was the one in the plaid green two-piece. She was a chunky kid, with a good tan and a sweet broad soft-looking can with those two crescents of white just under it, where the sun never seems to hit, at the top of the backs of her legs. I stood there with my hand on a box of HiHo crackers trying to remember if I rang it up or not. I ring it up again and the customer starts giving me hell. She's one of these cash-register-watchers, a witch about fifty with rouge on her cheekbones and no eyebrows, and I know it made her day to trip me up. She'd been watching cash registers for fifty years and probably never seen a mistake before.

By the time I got her feathers smoothed and her goodies into a bag—she gives me a little snort in passing, if she'd been born at the right time they would have burned her over in Salem[1]—by the time I get her on her way the girls

1. A seaport in Massachusetts, famous for the execution of "witches" in 1692.

had circled around the bread and were coming back, without a pushcart, back my way along the counters, in the aisle between the checkouts and the Special bins. They didn't even have shoes on. There was this chunky one, with the two-piece—it was bright green and the seams on the bra were still sharp and her belly was still pretty pale so I guessed she just got it (the suit)—there was this one, with one of those chubby berry-faces, the lips all bunched together under her nose, this one, and a tall one, with black hair that hadn't quite frizzed right, and one of these sunburns right across under the eyes, and a chin that was too long—you know, the kind of girl other girls think is very "striking" and "attractive" but never quite makes it, as they very well know, which is why they like her so much—and then the third one, that wasn't quite so tall. She was the queen. She kind of led them, the other two peeking around and making their shoulders round. She didn't look around, not this queen, she just walked straight on slowly, on these long white primadonna legs. She came down a little hard on her heels, as if she didn't walk in bare feet that much, putting down her heels and then letting the weight move along to her toes as if she was testing the floor with every step, putting a little deliberate extra action into it. You never know for sure how girls' minds work (do you really think it's a mind in there or just a little buzz like a bee in a glass jar?) but you got the idea she had talked the other two into coming here with her, and now she was showing them how to do it, walk slow and hold yourself straight.

She had on a kind of dirty-pink—beige maybe, I don't know—bathing suit with a little nubble all over it and, what got me, the straps were down. They were off her shoulders looped loose around the cool tops of her arms, and I guess as a result the suit had slipped a little on her, so all around the top of the cloth there was this shining rim. If it hadn't been there you wouldn't have known there could have been anything whiter than those shoulders. With the straps pushed off, there was nothing between the top of the suit and the top of her head except just *her*, this clean bare plane of the top of her chest down from the shoulder bones like a dented sheet of metal tilted in the light. I mean, it was more than pretty.

She had a sort of oaky hair that the sun and salt had bleached, done up in a bun that was unravelling, and a kind of prim face. Walking into the A & P with your straps down, I suppose it's the only kind of face you *can* have. She held her head so high her neck, coming up out of those white shoulders, looked kind of stretched, but I didn't mind. The longer her neck was, the more of her there was.

She must have felt in the corner of her eye me and over my shoulder Stokesie in the second slot watching, but she didn't tip. Not this queen. She kept her eyes moving across the racks, and stopped, and turned so slow it made my stomach rub the inside of my apron, and buzzed to the other two, who kind of huddled against her for relief, and then they all three of them went up the cat-and-dog-food-breakfast-cereal-macaroni-rice-raisins-seasonings-spreads-spaghetti-soft-drinks-crackers-and-cookies aisle. From the third slot I look straight up this aisle to the meat counter, and I watched them all the way. The fat one with the tan sort of fumbled with the cookies, but on second thought she put the package back. The sheep pushing their carts down the aisle—the girls were walking against the usual traffic (not that we have one-way signs or anything)—were pretty hilarious. You could see them, when Queenie's white shoulders dawned on them, kind of jerk, or hop, or hiccup, but their eyes snapped back to their own baskets and on they pushed. I bet you could set off dynamite in an A & P and the people would by and large keep reaching and checking oatmeal off their lists and muttering "Let me see, there was a third thing, began with A, asparagus, no, ah, yes, applesauce!" or whatever it is they do mutter. But there was no doubt, this jiggled them. A few houseslaves in pin curlers even looked around after pushing their carts past to make sure what they had seen was correct.

You know, it's one thing to have a girl in a bathing suit down on the beach, where what with the glare nobody can look at each other much anyway, and another thing in the cool of the A & P, under the fluorescent lights, against all those stacked packages, with her feet paddling along naked over our checkerboard green-and-cream rubber-tile floor.

"Oh Daddy," Stokesie said beside me. "I feel so faint."

"Darling," I said. "Hold me tight." Stokesie's married, with two babies chalked up on his fuselage already, but as far as I can tell that's the only difference. He's twenty-two, and I was nineteen this April.

"Is it done?" he asks, the responsible married man finding his voice. I forgot to say he thinks he's going to be manager some sunny day, maybe in 1990 when it's called the Great Alexandrov and Petrooshki Tea Company or something.

What he meant was, our town is five miles from a beach, with a big summer colony out on the Point, but we're right in the middle of town, and the women generally put on a shirt or shorts or something before they get out of the car into the street. And anyway these are usually women with six children and varicose veins mapping their legs and nobody, including them, could care less. As I say, we're right in the middle of town, and if you stand at our front doors you can see two banks and the Congregational church and the newspaper store and three real-estate offices and about twenty-seven old freeloaders tearing up Central Street because the sewer broke again. It's not as if we're on the Cape;[2] we're north of Boston and there's people in this town haven't seen the ocean for twenty years.

The girls had reached the meat counter and were asking McMahon something. He pointed, they pointed, and they shuffled out of sight behind a pyramid of Diet Delight peaches. All that was left for us to see was old McMahon patting his mouth and looking after them sizing up their joints. Poor kids, I began to feel sorry for them, they couldn't help it.

Now here comes the sad part of the story, at least my family says it's sad, but I don't think it's so sad myself. The store's pretty empty, it being Thursday afternoon, so there was nothing much to do except lean on the register and wait for the girls to show up again. The whole store was like a pinball machine and I didn't know which tunnel they'd come out of. After a while they come around out of the far aisle, around the light bulbs, records at discount of the

2. Cape Cod, Massachusetts, a resort area where fashions of dress are usually informal.

Caribbean Six or Tony Martin Sings or some such gunk you wonder they waste the wax on, six-packs of candy bars, and plastic toys done up in cellophane that fall apart when a kid looks at them anyway. Around they come, Queenie still leading the way, and holding a little gray jar in her hand. Slots Three through Seven are unmanned and I could see her wondering between Stokes and me, but Stokesie with his usual luck draws an old party in baggy gray pants who stumbles up with four giant cans of pineapple juice (what do these bums *do* with all that pineapple juice? I've often asked myself) so the girls come to me. Queenie puts down the jar and I take it into my fingers icy cold. Kingfish Fancy Herring Snacks in Pure Sour Cream: 49¢. Now her hands are empty, not a ring or a bracelet, bare as God made them, and I wonder where the money's coming from. Still with that prim look she lifts a folded dollar bill out of the hollow at the center of her nubbled pink top. The jar went heavy in my hand. Really, I thought that was so cute.

Then everybody's luck begins to run out. Lengel comes in from haggling with a truck full of cabbages on the lot and is about to scuttle into that door marked MANAGER behind which he hides all day when the girls touch his eye. Lengel's pretty dreary, teaches Sunday school and the rest, but he doesn't miss that much. He comes over and says, "Girls, this isn't the beach."

Queenie blushes, though maybe it's just a brush of sunburn I was noticing for the first time, now that she was so close. "My mother asked me to pick up a jar of herring snacks." Her voice kind of startled me, the way voices do when you see the people first, coming out so flat and dumb yet kind of tony, too, the way it ticked over "pick up" and "snacks." All of a sudden I slid right down her voice into her living room. Her father and the other men were standing around in ice-cream coats and bow ties and the women were in sandals picking up herring snacks on toothpicks off a big glass plate and they were all holding drinks the color of water with olives and sprigs of mint in them. When my parents have somebody over they get lemonade and if it's a real racy affair Schlitz in tall glasses with "They'll Do It Every Time" cartoons stencilled on.

"That's all right," Lengel said. "But this isn't the beach." His repeating this struck me as funny, as if it had just occurred to him, and he had been thinking all these years the A & P was a great big dune and he was the head lifeguard. He didn't like my smiling—as I say he doesn't miss much—but he concentrates on giving the girls that sad Sunday-school-superintendent stare.

Queenie's blush is no sunburn now, and the plump one in plaid, that I liked better from the back—a really sweet can—pipes up, "We weren't doing any shopping. We just came in for the one thing."

"That makes no difference," Lengel tells her, and I could see from the way his eyes went that he hadn't noticed she was wearing a two-piece before. "We want you decently dressed when you come in here."

"We *are* decent," Queenie says suddenly, her lower lip pushing, getting sore now that she remembers her place, a place from which the crowd that runs the A & P must look pretty crummy. Fancy Herring Snacks flashed in her very blue eyes.

"Girls, I don't want to argue with you. After this come in here with your shoulders covered. It's our policy." He turns his back. That's policy for you.

Policy is what the kingpins want. What the others want is juvenile delinquency.

All this while, the customers had been showing up with their carts but, you know, sheep, seeing a scene, they had all bunched up on Stokesie, who shook open a paper bag as gently as peeling a peach, not wanting to miss a word. I could feel in the silence everybody getting nervous, most of all Lengel, who asks me, "Sammy, have you rung up their purchase?"

I thought and said "No" but it wasn't about that I was thinking. I go through the punches, 4, 9, GROC, TOT—it's more complicated than you think, and after you do it often enough, it begins to make a little song, that you hear words to, in my case "Hello (*bing*) there, you (*gung*) hap-py *pee*-pul (*splat*)!"—the *splat* being the drawer flying out. I uncrease the bill, tenderly as you may imagine, it just having come from between the two smoothest scoops of vanilla I had ever known there were, and pass a half and a penny into her narrow pink palm, and nestle the herrings in a bag and twist its neck and hand it over, all the time thinking.

The girls, and who'd blame them, are in a hurry to get out, so I say "I quit" to Lengel quick enough for them to hear, hoping they'll stop and watch me, their unsuspected hero. They keep right on going, into the electric eye; the door flies open and they flicker across the lot to their car, Queenie and Plaid and Big Tall Goony-Goony (not that as raw material she was so bad), leaving me with Lengel and a kink in his eyebrow.

"Did you say something, Sammy?"

"I said I quit."

"I thought you did."

"You didn't have to embarrass them."

"It was they who were embarrassing us."

I started to say something that came out "Fiddle-de-do." It's a saying of my grandmother's, and I know she would have been pleased.

"I don't think you know what you're saying," Lengel said.

"I know you don't," I said. "But I do." I pull the bow at the back of my apron and start shrugging it off my shoulders. A couple of customers that had been heading for my slot begin to knock against each other, liked scared pigs in a chute.

Lengel sighs and begins to look very patient and old and gray. He's been a friend of my parents for years. "Sammy, you don't want to do this to your Mom and Dad," he tells me. It's true, I don't. But it seems to me that once you begin a gesture it's fatal not to go through with it. I fold the apron, "Sammy" stitched in red on the pocket, and put it on the counter, and drop the bow tie on top of it. The bow tie is theirs, if you've ever wondered. "You'll feel this for the rest of your life," Lengel says, and I know that's true, too, but remembering how he made that pretty girl blush makes me so scrunchy inside I punch the No Sale tab and the machine whirs "pee-pul" and the drawer splats out. One advantage to this scene taking place in summer, I can follow this up with a clean exit, there's no fumbling around getting your coat and galoshes, I just saunter into the electric eye in my white shirt that my mother ironed the night before, and the door heaves itself open, and outside the sunshine is skating around on the asphalt.

I look around for my girls, but they're gone, of course. There wasn't anybody but some young married screaming with her children about some candy they didn't get by the door of a powder-blue Falcon station wagon. Looking back in the big windows, over the bags of peat moss and aluminum lawn furniture stacked on the pavement, I could see Lengel in my place in the slot, checking the sheep through. His face was dark gray and his back stiff, as if he's just had an injection of iron, and my stomach kind of fell as I felt how hard the world was going to be to me hereafter.

# Helena María Viramontes

*Viramontes (1954– ) was born in East Los Angeles. She attended Immaculate Heart College. It was in college that she began writing, first poetry and then fiction. Her stories were soon published and recognized. In 1979 she was awarded the Fiction Prize for the short story "Birthday" by the University of California at Irvine in the Chicano Literary Contest. Her books include* The Moths and Other Stories *(1985); another collection of stories,* Paris Rats in E.L.A. *(1993);* Under the Feet of Jesus *(1995); and* Their Dogs Came with Them *(1996). A professor at Cornell University, she has received the Dos Passos Award for Literature and an NEA Fellowship.*

## The Moths

I was fourteen years old when Abuelita requested my help. And it seemed only fair. Abuelita had pulled me through the rages of scarlet fever by placing, removing and replacing potato slices on the temples of my forehead; she had seen me through several whippings, an arm broken by a dare-jump off Tío Enrique's toolshed, puberty, and my first lie. Really, I told Amá, it was only fair.

Not that I was her favorite granddaughter or anything special. I wasn't even pretty or nice like my older sisters and I just couldn't do the girl things they could do. My hands were too big to handle the fineries of crocheting or embroidery and I always pricked my fingers or knotted my colored threads time and time again while my sisters laughed and called me bull hands with their cute waterlike voices. So I began keeping a piece of jagged brick in my sock to bash my sisters or anyone who called me bull hands. Once, while we all sat in the bedroom, I hit Teresa on the forehead, right above her eyebrow, and she ran to Amá with her mouth open, her hand over her eye while blood seeped between her fingers. I was used to the whippings by then.

I wasn't respectful either. I even went so far as to doubt the power of Abuelita's slices, the slices she said absorbed my fever. "You're still alive, aren't you?" Abuelita snapped back, her pasty gray eye beaming at me and burning holes in my suspicions. Regretful that I had let secret questions drop out of my mouth, I couldn't look into her eyes. My hands began to fan out, grow like a liar's nose until they hung by my side like low weights. Abuelita made a balm out of dried moth wings and Vicks and rubbed my hands, shaping them back to size. It was the strangest feeling. Like bones melting. Like sun shining through the darkness of your eyelids. I didn't mind helping Abuelita after that, so Amá would always send me over to her.

In the early afternoon Amá would push her hair back, hand me my sweater and shoes, and tell me to go to Mama Luna's. This was to avoid another fight and another whipping, I knew. I would deliver one last direct shot on Marisela's arm and jump out of our house, the slam of the screen door burying her cries of anger, and I'd gladly go help Abuelita plant her wild lilies or jasmine or heliotrope or cilantro or hierbabuena in red Hills Brothers coffee cans. Abuelita would wait for me at the top step of her porch holding a hammer and nail and empty coffee cans. And although we hardly spoke, hardly looked at each other as we worked over root transplants, I always felt her gray eye on me. It made me feel, in a strange sort of way, safe and guarded and not alone. Like God was supposed to make you feel.

On Abuelita's porch, I would puncture holes in the bottom of the coffee cans with a nail and a precise hit of a hammer. This completed, my job was to fill them with red clay mud from beneath her rose bushes, packing it softly, then making a perfect hole, four fingers round, to nest a sprouting avocado pit, or the spidery sweet potatoes that Abuelita rooted in mayonnaise jars with toothpicks and daily water, or prickly chayotes that produced vines that twisted and wound all over her porch pillars, crawling to the roof, up and over the roof, and down the other side, making her small brick house look like it was cradled within the vines that grew pear-shaped squashes ready for the pick, ready to be steamed with onions and cheese and butter. The roots would burst out of the rusted coffee cans and search for a place to connect. I would then feed the seedlings with water.

But this was a different kind of help, Amá said, because Abuelita was dying. Looking into her gray eye, then into her brown one, the doctor said it was just a matter of days. And so it seemed only fair that these hands she had melted and formed found use in rubbing her caving body with alcohol and marihuana, rubbing her arms and legs, turning her face to the window so that she could watch the Bird of Paradise blooming or smell the scent of clove in the air. I toweled her face frequently and held her hand for hours. Her gray wiry hair hung over the mattress. Since I could remember, she'd kept her long hair in braids. Her mouth was vacant and when she slept, her eyelids never closed all the way. Up close, you could see her gray eye beaming out the window, staring hard as if to remember everything. I never kissed her. I left the window open when I went to the market.

Across the street from Jay's Market there was a chapel. I never knew its denomination, but I went in just the same to search for candles. I sat down on one of the pews because there were none. After I cleaned my fingernails, I looked up at the high ceiling. I had forgotten the vastness of these places, the coolness of the marble pillars and the frozen statues with blank eyes. I was alone. I knew why I had never returned.

That was one of Apá's biggest complaints. He would pound his hands on the table, rocking the sugar dish or spilling a cup of coffee and scream that if I didn't go to Mass every Sunday to save my goddamn sinning soul, then I had no reason to go out of the house, period. Punto[1] final. He would grab my arm and dig his nails into me to make sure I understood the importance of catechism. Did he make himself clear? Then he strategically directed his anger at Amá for her lousy ways of bringing up daughters, being disrespectful and unbelieving, and my older sisters would pull me aside and tell me if I didn't get to Mass right this minute, they were all going to kick the holy shit out of me. Why am I so selfish? Can't you see what it's doing to Amá, you idiot? So I would wash my feet and stuff them in my black Easter shoes that shone with Vaseline, grab a missal and veil, and wave good-bye to Amá.

I would walk slowly down Lorena to First to Evergreen, counting the cracks on the cement. On Evergreen I would turn left and walk to Abuelita's. I liked her porch because it was shielded by the vines of the chayotes[2] and I could get a good look at the people and car traffic on Evergreen without them knowing. I would jump up the porch steps, knock on the screen door as I wiped my feet and call Abuelita, mi Abuelita? As I opened the door and stuck my head in, I would catch the gagging scent of toasting chile on the placa. When I entered the sala[3] she would greet me from the kitchen, wringing her hands in her apron. I'd sit at the corner of the table to keep from being in her way. The chiles made my eyes water. Am I crying? No, Mama Luna, I'm sure not crying. I don't like going to mass, but my eyes watered anyway, the tears dropping on the tablecloth like candle wax. Abuelita lifted the burnt chiles from the fire and sprinkled water on them until the skins began to separate. Placing them in front of me, she turned to check the menudo.[4] I peeled the skins off and put the flimsy, limp-looking green and yellow chiles in the molcajete[5] and began to crush and crush and twist and crush the heart out of the tomato, the clove of garlic, the stupid chiles that made me cry, crushed them until they turned into liquid under my bull hand. With a wooden spoon, I scraped hard to destroy the guilt, and my tears were gone. I put the bowl of chile next to a vase filled with freshly cut roses. Abuelita touched my hand and pointed to the bowl of menudo that steamed in front of me. I spooned some chile into the menudo and rolled a corn tortilla thin with the palms of my hands. As I ate, a fine Sunday breeze entered the kitchen and a rose petal calmly feathered down to the table.

I left the chapel without blessing myself and walked to Jay's. Most of the time Jay didn't have much of anything. The tomatoes were always soft and the cans of Campbell soups had rusted spots on them. There was dust on the tops of cereal boxes. I picked up what I needed: rubbing alcohol, five cans of chicken broth, a big bottle of Pine Sol. At first Jay got mad because I thought I had forgotten the money. But it was there all the time, in my back pocket.

When I returned from the market, I heard Amá crying in Abuelita's kitchen. She looked up at me with puffy eyes. I placed the bags of groceries on the table and began putting the cans of soup away. Amá sobbed quietly. I never kissed her. After a while, I patted her on the back for comfort. Finally:

1. Period (Spanish); the end, case closed. 2. A small vegetable in the pepper family that has just one seed. 3. Living room (Spanish). 4. Tripe soup (Spanish). 5. Mortar (Mexican).

"¿Y mi Amá?"[6] she asked in a whisper, then choked again and cried into her apron.

Abuelita fell off the bed twice yesterday, I said, knowing that I shouldn't have said it and wondering why I wanted to say it because it only made Amá cry harder. I guess I became angry and just so tired of the quarrels and beatings and unanswered prayers and my hands just there hanging helplessly by my side. Amá looked at me again, confused, angry, and her eyes were filled with sorrow. I went outside and sat on the porch swing and watched the people pass. I sat there until she left. I dozed off repeating the words to myself like rosary prayers: when do you stop giving when do you start giving when do you . . . and when my hands fell from my lap, I awoke to catch them. The sun was setting, an orange glow, and I knew Abuelita was hungry.

There comes a time when the sun is defiant. Just about the time when moods change, inevitable seasons of a day, transitions from one color to another, that hour or minute or second when the sun is finally defeated, finally sinks into the realization that it cannot with all its power to heal or burn, exist forever, there comes an illumination where the sun and earth meet, a final burst of burning red orange fury reminding us that although endings are inevitable, they are necessary for rebirths, and when that time came, just when I switched on the light in the kitchen to open Abuelita's can of soup, it was probably then that she died.

The room smelled of Pine Sol and vomit, and Abuelita had defecated the remains of her cancerous stomach. She had turned to the window and tried to speak, but her mouth remained open and speechless. I heard you, Abuelita, I said, stroking her cheek, I heard you. I opened the windows of the house and let the soup simmer and overboil on the stove. I turned the stove off and poured the soup down the sink. From the cabinet I got a tin basin, filled it with lukewarm water and carried it carefully to the room. I went to the linen closet and took out some modest bleached white towels. With the sacredness of a priest preparing his vestments, I unfolded the towels one by one on my shoulders. I removed the sheets and blankets from her bed and peeled off her thick flannel night-gown. I toweled her puzzled face, stretching out the wrinkles, removing the coils of her neck, toweled her shoulders and breasts. Then I changed the water. I returned to towel the creases of her stretch-marked stomach, her sporadic vaginal hairs, and her sagging thighs. I removed the lint from between her toes and noticed a mapped birthmark on the fold of her buttock. The scars on her back, which were as thin as the life lines on the palms of her hands, made me realize how little I really knew of Abuelita. I covered her with a thin blanket and went into the bathroom. I washed my hands, turned on the tub faucets and watched the water pour into the tub with vitality and steam. When it was full, I turned off the water and undressed. Then I went to get Abuelita.

She was not as heavy as I thought and when I carried her in my arms, her body fell into a V. And yet my legs were tired, shaky, and I felt as if the distance between the bedroom and bathroom was miles and years away. Amá, where are you?

6. And my Mama? (Spanish).

I stepped into the bathtub one leg first, then the other. I bent my knees slowly to descend into the water slowly so I wouldn't scald her skin. There, there, Abuelita, I said, cradling her, smoothing her as we descended, I heard you. Her hair fell back and spread across the water like eagles' wings. The water in the tub overflowed and poured onto the tile of the floor. Then the moths came. Small gray ones that came from her soul and out through her mouth fluttering to light, circling the single dull light bulb of the bathroom. Dying is lonely and I wanted to go to where the moths were, stay with her and plant chayotes whose vines would crawl up her fingers and into the clouds; I wanted to rest my head on her chest with her stroking my hair, telling me about the moths that lay within the soul and slowly eat the spirit up; I wanted to return to the waters of the womb with her so that we would never be alone again. I wanted. I wanted my Amá. I removed a few strands of hair from Abuelita's face and held her small light head within the hollow of my neck. The bathroom was filled with moths, and for the first time in a long time I cried, rocking us, crying for her, for me, for Amá, the sobs emerging from the depths of anguish, the misery of feeling half-born, sobbing until finally the sobs rippled into circles and circles of sadness and relief. There, there, I said to Abuelita, rocking us gently, there, there.

# Alice Walker

*Walker (1944– ) was born in Eatonton, Georgia, and graduated from Sarah Lawrence College. After experience in the civil rights movement and as a caseworker for the New York City welfare department, she became a teacher of creative writing and black literature at Jackson State College, Tougaloo College, Wellesley, and Yale. Her short stories are collected in* In Love and Trouble: Stories of Black Women *(1973) and* You Can't Keep a Good Woman Down *(1982). Her novels include* The Third Life of Grange Copeland *(1970);* Meridian *(1976);* The Color Purple *(1982), for which she won the Pulitzer Prize;* The Temple of My Familiar *(1989); and* Possessing the Secret of Joy *(1992). She has recently published a memoir,* The Same River Twice: Honoring the Difficult *(1996), and* By the Light of My Father's Smile *(1998). Her book of essays on political social issues,* Anything We Love Can Be Saved, *was published in 1997.*

## Everyday Use

*for your grandmamma*

I will wait for her in the yard that Maggie and I made so clean and wavy yesterday afternoon. A yard like this is more comfortable than most people know. It is not just a yard. It is like an extended living room. When the hard clay is swept clean as a floor and the fine sand around the edges lined with tiny, irregular grooves, anyone can come and sit and look up into the elm tree and wait for the breezes that never come inside the house.

Maggie will be nervous until after her sister goes: she will stand hopelessly in corners, homely and ashamed of the burn scars down her arms and legs, eying her sister with a mixture of envy and awe. She thinks her sister has held life always in the palm of one hand, that "no" is a word the world never learned to say to her.

You've no doubt seen those TV shows where the child who has "made it" is confronted, as a surprise, by her own mother and father, tottering in weakly from backstage. (A pleasant surprise, of course: What would they do if parent and child came on the show only to curse out and insult each other?) On TV mother and child embrace and smile into each other's faces. Sometimes the mother and father weep, the child wraps them in her arms and leans across the table to tell how she would not have made it without their help. I have seen these programs.

Sometimes I dream a dream in which Dee and I are suddenly brought together on a TV program of this sort. Out of a dark and soft-seated limousine I am ushered into a bright room filled with many people. There I meet a smiling, gray, sporty man like Johnny Carson who shakes my hand and tells me what a fine girl I have. Then we are on the stage and Dee is embracing me with tears in her eyes. She pins on my dress a large orchid, even though she has told me once that she thinks orchids are tacky flowers.

In real life I am a large, big-boned woman with rough, man-working hands. In the winter I wear flannel nightgowns to bed and overalls during the day. I can kill and clean a hog as mercilessly as a man. My fat keeps me hot in zero weather. I can work outside all day, breaking ice to get water for washing; I can eat pork liver cooked over the open fire minutes after it comes steaming from the hog. One winter I knocked a bull calf straight in the brain between the eyes with a sledge hammer and had the meat hung up to chill before nightfall. But of course all this does not show on television. I am the way my daughter would want me to be: a hundred pounds lighter, my skin like an uncooked barley pancake. My hair glistens in the hot bright lights. Johnny Carson has much to do to keep up with my quick and witty tongue.

But that is a mistake. I know even before I wake up. Who ever knew a Johnson with a quick tongue? Who can even imagine me looking a strange white man in the eye? It seems to me I have talked to them always with one foot raised in flight, with my head turned in whichever way is farthest from them. Dee, though. She would always look anyone in the eye. Hesitation was no part of her nature.

"How do I look, Mama?" Maggie says, showing just enough of her thin body enveloped in pink skirt and red blouse for me to know she's there, almost hidden by the door.

"Come out into the yard," I say.

Have you ever seen a lame animal, perhaps a dog run over by some careless person rich enough to own a car, sidle up to someone who is ignorant enough to be kind to them? That is the way my Maggie walks. She has been like this, chin on chest, eyes on ground, feet in shuffle, ever since the fire that burned the other house to the ground.

Dee is lighter than Maggie, with nicer hair and a fuller figure. She's a woman now, though sometimes I forget. How long ago was it that the other house burned? Ten, twelve years? Sometimes I can still hear the flames and feel Maggie's arms sticking to me, her hair smoking and her dress falling off her in little black papery flakes. Her eyes seemed stretched open, blazed open by the flames reflected in them. And Dee. I see her standing off under the sweet gum tree she used to dig gum out of; a look of concentration on her face as she watched the last dingy gray board of the house fall in toward the red-hot brick chimney. Why don't you do a dance around the ashes? I'd wanted to ask her. She had hated the house that much.

I used to think she hated Maggie, too. But that was before we raised the money, the church and me, to send her to Augusta to school. She used to read to us without pity; forcing words, lies, other folks' habits, whole lives upon us two, sitting trapped and ignorant underneath her voice. She washed us in a river of make-believe, burned us with a lot of knowledge we didn't necessarily need to know. Pressed us to her with the serious way she read, to shove us away at just the moment, like dimwits, we seemed about to understand.

Dee wanted nice things. A yellow organdy dress to wear to her graduation from high school; black pumps to match a green suit she'd made from an old suit somebody gave me. She was determined to stare down any disaster in her efforts. Her eyelids would not flicker for minutes at a time. Often I fought off the temptation to shake her. At sixteen she had a style of her own: and knew what style was.

I never had an education myself. After second grade the school was closed down. Don't ask me why: in 1927 colored asked fewer questions than they do now. Sometimes Maggie reads to me. She stumbles along good naturedly but can't see well. She knows she is not bright. Like good looks and money, quickness passed her by. She will marry John Thomas (who has mossy teeth in an earnest face) and then I'll be free to sit here and I guess just sing church songs to myself. Although I never was a good singer. Never could carry a tune. I was always better at a man's job. I used to love to milk till I was hooked[1] in the side in '49. Cows are soothing and slow and don't bother you, unless you try to milk them the wrong way.

I have deliberately turned my back on the house. It is three rooms, just like the one that burned, except the roof is tin; they don't make shingle roofs any more. There are no real windows, just some holes cut in the sides, like the portholes in a ship, but not round and not square, with rawhide holding the shutters up on the outside. This house is in a pasture, too, like the other one. No doubt when Dee sees it she will want to tear it down. She wrote me once that no matter where we "choose" to live, she will manage to come see us. But she will never bring her friends. Maggie and I thought about this and Maggie asked me, "Mama, when did Dee ever *have* any friends?"

She had a few. Furtive boys in pink shirts hanging about on washday after school. Nervous girls who never laughed. Impressed with her they worshiped the well-turned phrase, the cute shape, the scalding humor that erupted like bubbles in lye. She read to them.

When she was courting Jimmy T she didn't have much time to pay to us, but turned all her faultfinding power on him. He *flew* to marry a cheap city girl from a family of ignorant flashy people. She hardly had time to recompose herself.

When she comes I will meet—but there they are!

Maggie attempts to make a dash for the house, in her shuffling way, but I stay her with my hand. "Come back here," I say. And she stops and tries to dig a well in the sand with her toe.

It is hard to see them clearly through the strong sun. But even the first glimpse of leg out of the car tells me it is Dee. Her feet were always neat-

1. I.e., by the horn of the cow being milked.

looking, as if God himself had shaped them with a certain style. From the other side of the car comes a short, stocky man. Hair is all over his head a foot long and hanging from his chin like a kinky mule tail. I hear Maggie suck in her breath. "Uhnnnh," is what it sounds like. Like when you see the wriggling end of a snake just in front of your foot on the road. "Uhnnnh."

Dee next. A dress down to the ground, in this hot weather. A dress so loud it hurts my eyes. There are yellows and oranges enough to throw back the light of the sun. I feel my whole face warming from the heat waves it throws out. Earrings gold, too, and hanging down to her shoulders. Bracelets dangling and making noises when she moves her arm up to shake the folds of the dress out of her armpits. The dress is loose and flows, and as she walks closer, I like it. I hear Maggie go "Uhnnnh" again. It is her sister's hair. It stands straight up like the wool on a sheep. It is black as night and around the edges are two long pigtails that rope about like small lizards disappearing behind her ears.

"Wa-su-zo-Tean-o!" she says, coming on in that gliding way the dress makes her move. The short stocky fellow with the hair to his navel is all grinning and he follows up with "Asalamalakim,[2] my mother and sister!" He moves to hug Maggie but she falls back, right up against the back of my chair. I feel her trembling there and when I look up I see the perspiration falling off her chin.

"Don't get up," says Dee. Since I am stout it takes something of a push. You can see me trying to move a second or two before I make it. She turns, showing white heels through her sandals, and goes back to the car. Out she peeks next with a Polaroid. She stoops down quickly and lines up picture after picture of me sitting there in front of the house with Maggie cowering behind me. She never takes a shot without making sure the house is included. When a cow comes nibbling around the edge of the yard she snaps it and me and Maggie *and* the house. Then she puts the Polaroid in the back seat of the car, and comes up and kisses me on the forehead.

Meanwhile Asalamalakim is going through motions with Maggie's hand. Maggie's hand is as limp as a fish, and probably as cold, despite the sweat, and she keeps trying to pull it back. It looks like Asalamalakim wants to shake hands but wants to do it fancy. Or maybe he don't know how people shake hands. Anyhow, he soon gives up on Maggie.

"Well," I say. "Dee."

"No, Mama," she says. "Not 'Dee,' Wangero Leewanika Kemanjo!"

"What happened to 'Dee'?" I wanted to know.

"She's dead," Wangero said. "I couldn't bear it any longer, being named after the people who oppress me."

"You know as well as me you was named after your aunt Dicie," I said. Dicie is my sister. She named Dee. We called her "Big Dee" after Dee was born.

"But who was *she* named after?" asked Wangero.

"I guess after Grandma Dee," I said.

"And who was she named after?" asked Wangero.

2. Phonetic rendering of a Muslim greeting. "Wa-su-zo-Tean-o" is a similar rendering of an African dialect salutation.

"Her mother," I said, and saw Wangero was getting tired. "That's about as far back as I can trace it," I said. Though, in fact, I probably could have carried it back beyond the Civil War through the branches.

"Well," said Asalamalakim, "there you are."

"Uhnnnh," I heard Maggie say.

"There I was not," I said, "before 'Dicie' cropped up in our family, so why should I try to trace it that far back?"

He just stood there grinning, looking down on me like somebody inspecting a Model A car. Every once in a while he and Wangero sent eye signals over my head.

"How do you pronounce this name?" I asked.

"You don't have to call me by it if you don't want to," said Wangero.

"Why shouldn't I?" I asked. "If that's what you want us to call you, we'll call you."

"I know it might sound awkward at first," said Wangero.

"I'll get used to it," I said. "Ream it out again."

Well, soon we got the name out of the way. Asalamalakim had a name twice as long and three times as hard. After I tripped over it two or three times he told me to just call him Hakim-a-barber. I wanted to ask him was he a barber, but I didn't really think he was, so I didn't ask.

"You must belong to those beef-cattle peoples down the road," I said. They said "Asalamalakim" when they met you, too, but they didn't shake hands. Always too busy: feeding the cattle, fixing the fences, putting up salt-lick shelters, throwing down hay. When the white folks poisoned some of the herd the men stayed up all night with rifles in their hands. I walked a mile and a half just to see the sight.

Hakim-a-barber said, "I accept some of their doctrines, but farming and raising cattle is not my style." (They didn't tell me, and I didn't ask, whether Wangero (Dee) had really gone and married him.)

We sat down to eat and right away he said he didn't eat collards and pork was unclean. Wangero, though, went on through the chitlins and corn bread, the greens and everything else. She talked a blue streak over the sweet potatoes. Everything delighted her. Even the fact that we still used the benches her daddy made for the table when we couldn't afford to buy chairs.

"Oh, Mama!" she cried. Then turned to Hakim-a-barber. "I never knew how lovely these benches are. You can feel the rump prints," she said, running her hands underneath her and along the bench. Then she gave a sigh and her hand closed over Grandma Dee's butter dish. "That's it!" she said. "I knew there was something I wanted to ask you if I could have." She jumped up from the table and went over in the corner where the churn stood, the milk in it clabber by now. She looked at the churn and looked at it.

"This churn top is what I need," she said. "Didn't Uncle Buddy whittle it out of a tree you all used to have?"

"Yes," I said.

"Uh huh," she said happily. "And I want the dasher, too."

"Uncle Buddy whittle that, too?" asked the barber.

Dee (Wangero) looked up at me.

"Aunt Dee's first husband whittled the dash," said Maggie so low you almost couldn't hear her. "His name was Henry, but they called him Stash."

"Maggie's brain is like an elephant's," Wangero said, laughing. "I can use the churn top as a centerpiece for the alcove table," she said, sliding a plate over the churn, "and I'll think of something artistic to do with the dasher."

When she finished wrapping the dasher the handle stuck out. I took it for a moment in my hands. You didn't even have to look close to see where hands pushing the dasher up and down to make butter had left a kind of sink in the wood. In fact, there were a lot of small sinks; you could see where thumbs and fingers had sunk into the wood. It was beautiful light yellow wood, from a tree that grew in the yard where Big Dee and Stash had lived.

After dinner Dee (Wangero) went to the trunk at the foot of my bed and started rifling through it. Maggie hung back in the kitchen over the dishpan. Out came Wangero with two quilts. They had been pieced by Grandma Dee and then Big Dee and me had hung them on the quilt frames on the front porch and quilted them. One was in the Lone Star pattern. The other was Walk Around the Mountain. In both of them were scraps of dresses Grandma Dee had worn fifty and more years ago. Bits and pieces of Grandpa Jarrell's Paisley shirts. And one teeny faded blue piece, about the size of a penny matchbox, that was from Great Grandpa Ezra's uniform that he wore in the Civil War.

"Mama," Wangero said sweet as a bird. "Can I have these old quilts?"

I heard something fall in the kitchen, and a minute later the kitchen door slammed.

"Why don't you take one or two of the others?" I asked. "These old things was just done by me and Big Dee from some tops your grandma pieced before she died."

"No," said Wangero. "I don't want those. They are stitched around the borders by machine."

"That'll make them last better," I said.

"That's not the point," said Wangero. "These are all pieces of dresses Grandma used to wear. She did all this stitching by hand. Imagine!" She held the quilts securely in her arms, stroking them.

"Some of the pieces, like those lavender ones, come from old clothes her mother handed down to her," I said, moving up to touch the quilts. Dee (Wangero) moved back just enough so that I couldn't reach the quilts. They already belonged to her.

"Imagine!" she breathed again, clutching them closely to her bosom.

"The truth is," I said, "I promised to give them quilts to Maggie, for when she marries John Thomas."

She gasped like a bee had stung her.

"Maggie can't appreciate these quilts!" she said. "She'd probably be backward enough to put them to everyday use."

"I reckon she would," I said. "God knows I been saving 'em for long enough with nobody using 'em. I hope she will!" I didn't want to bring up how I had offered Dee (Wangero) a quilt when she went away to college. Then she had told me they were old-fashioned, out of style.

"But they're *priceless*!" she was saying now, furiously; for she has a temper.

"Maggie would put them on the bed and in five years they'd be in rags. Less than that!"

"She can always make some more," I said. "Maggie knows how to quilt."

Dee (Wangero) looked at me with hatred. "You just will not understand. The point is these quilts, *these* quilts!"

"Well," I said, stumped. "What would *you* do with them?"

"Hang them," she said. As if that was the only thing you *could* do with quilts.

Maggie by now was standing in the door. I could almost hear the sound her feet made as they scraped over each other.

"She can have them, Mama," she said, like somebody used to never winning anything, or having anything reserved for her. "I can 'member Grandma Dee without the quilts."

I looked at her hard. She had filled her bottom lip with checkerberry snuff and it gave her a face a kind of dopey, hangdog look. It was Grandma Dee and Big Dee who taught her how to quilt herself. She stood there with her scarred hands hidden in the folds of her skirt. She looked at her sister with something like fear but she wasn't mad at her. This was Maggie's portion. This was the way she knew God to work.

When I looked at her like that something hit me in the top of my head and ran down to the soles of my feet. Just like when I'm in church and the spirit of God touches me and I get happy and shout. I did something I never had done before: hugged Maggie to me, then dragged her on into the room, snatched the quilts out of Miss Wangero's hands and dumped them into Maggie's lap. Maggie just sat there on my bed with her mouth open.

"Take one or two of the others," I said to Dee.

But she turned without a word and went out to Hakim-a-barber.

"You just don't understand," she said, as Maggie and I came out to the car.

"What don't I understand?" I wanted to know.

"Your heritage," she said. And then she turned to Maggie, kissed her, and said, "You ought to try to make something of yourself, too, Maggie. It's really a new day for us. But from the way you and Mama still live you'd never know it."

She put on some sunglasses that hid everything above the tip of her nose and her chin.

Maggie smiled; maybe at the sunglasses. But a real smile, not scared. After we watched the car dust settle I asked Maggie to bring me a dip of snuff. And then the two of us sat there just enjoying, until it was time to go in the house and go to bed.

# Robert Penn Warren

*Warren (1905–1989) was born in Guthrie, Kentucky. He was educated at Vanderbilt University, Yale, and Oxford. One of the original Fugitive Poets, his many publications include* Understanding Fiction *(1943); a novel,* All the King's Men *(1946); a collection of stories,* The Circus in the Attic *(1949);* World Enough and Time *(1950); and* New and Selected Poems 1923–1985 *(1985). He won the Pulitzer Prize three times and was the first poet laureate of the United States.*

## Blackberry Winter

*To Joseph Warren and Dagmar Beach*

It was getting into June and past eight o'clock in the morning, but there was a fire—even if it wasn't a big fire, just a fire of chunks—on the hearth of the big stone fireplace in the living room. I was standing on the hearth, almost into the chimney, hunched over the fire, working my bare toes slowly on the warm stone. I relished the heat which made the skin of my bare legs warp and creep and tingle, even as I called to my mother, who was somewhere back in the dining room or kitchen, and said: "But it's June, I don't have to put them on!"

"You put them on if you are going out," she called.

I tried to assess the degree of authority and conviction in the tone, but at that distance it was hard to decide. I tried to analyze the tone, and then I thought what a fool I had been to start out the back door and let her see that I was barefoot. If I had gone out the front door or the side door, she would never have known, not till dinner time anyway, and by then the day would have been half gone and I would have been all over the farm to see what the storm had done and down to the creek to see the flood. But it had never crossed my mind that they would try to stop you from going barefoot in June, no matter if there had been a gully-washer and a cold spell.

Nobody had ever tried to stop me in June as long as I could remember, and when you are nine years old, what you remember seems forever; for you remember everything and everything is important and stands big and full and fills up Time and is so solid that you can walk around and around it like a tree and look at it. You are aware that time passes, that there is a movement in time, but that is not what Time is. Time is not a movement, a flowing, a wind then, but is, rather, a kind of climate in which things are, and when a thing happens it begins to live and keeps on living and stands solid in Time like the tree that you can walk around. And if there is a movement, the movement is not Time itself, any more than a breeze is climate, and all the breeze does is to shake a little the leaves on the tree which is alive and solid. When you are nine, you know that there are things that you don't know, but you know that when you know something you know it. You know how a thing has been and you know that you can go barefoot in June. You do not understand that voice from back in the kitchen which says that you cannot go barefoot outdoors and run to see what has happened and rub your feet over the wet shivery grass and make the perfect mark of your foot in the smooth, creamy, red mud and then muse upon it as though you had suddenly come upon that single mark on the glistening auroral beach of the world.[1] You have never seen a beach, but you have read the book and how the footprint was there.

The voice had said what it had said, and I looked savagely at the black stockings and the strong, scuffed brown shoes which I had brought from my closet as far as the hearth rug. I called once more, "But it's June," and waited.

"It's June," the voice replied from far away, "but it's blackberry winter."

I had lifted my head to reply to that, to make one more test of what was in that tone, when I happened to see the man.

The fireplace in the living room was at the end; for the stone chimney was built, as in so many of the farmhouses in Tennessee, at the end of a gable, and there was a window on each side of the chimney. Out of the window on the north side of the fireplace I could see the man. When I saw the man I did not call out what I had intended, but, engrossed by the strangeness of the sight, watched him, still far off, come along the path by the edge of the woods.

What was strange was that there should be a man there at all. That path went along the yard fence, between the fence and the woods which came right down to the yard, and then on back past the chicken runs and on by the woods until it was lost to sight where the woods bulged out and cut off the back field. There the path disappeared into the woods. It led on back, I knew, through the woods and to the swamp, skirted the swamp where the big trees gave way to sycamores and water oaks and willows and tangled cane, and then led on to the river. Nobody ever went back there except people who wanted to gig frogs in the swamp or to fish in the river or to hunt in the woods, and those people, if they didn't have a standing permission from my father, always stopped to ask permission to cross the farm. But the man whom I now saw wasn't, I could tell even at that distance, a sportsman. And what would a sportsman have been doing down there after a storm? Besides, he was coming from the river, and nobody had gone down there that morning. I knew that for a fact, because if anybody had passed, certainly if a stranger had passed, the dogs would have made a racket and would have been out on him. But this man was coming up from the river and had come up through the woods. I suddenly had a vision of him moving up the grassy path in the woods, in the green twilight under the

1. An allusion to Daniel Defoe's *Robinson Crusoe.*

big trees, not making any sound on the path, while now and then, like drops off the eaves, a big drop of water would fall from a leaf or bough and strike a stiff oak leaf lower down with a small, hollow sound like a drop of water hitting tin. That sound, in the silence of the woods, would be very significant.

When you are a boy and stand in the stillness of woods, which can be so still that your heart almost stops beating and makes you want to stand there in the green twilight until you feel your very feet sinking into and clutching the earth like roots and your body breathing slow through its pores like the leaves—when you stand there and wait for the next drop to drop with its small, flat sound to a lower leaf, that sound seems to measure out something, to put an end to something, to begin something, and you cannot wait for it to happen and are afraid it will not happen, and then when it has happened, you are waiting again, almost afraid.

But the man whom I saw coming through the woods in my mind's eye did not pause and wait, growing into the ground and breathing with the enormous, soundless breathing of the leaves. Instead, I saw him moving in the green twilight inside my head as he was moving at that very moment along the path by the edge of the woods, coming toward the house. He was moving steadily, but not fast, with his shoulders hunched a little and his head thrust forward, like a man who has come a long way and has a long way to go. I shut my eyes for a couple of seconds, thinking that when I opened them he would not be there at all. There was no place for him to have come from, and there was no reason for him to come where he was coming, toward our house. But I opened my eyes, and there he was, and he was coming steadily along the side of the woods. He was not yet even with the back chicken yard.

"Mama," I called.

"You put them on," the voice said.

"There's a man coming," I called, "out back."

She did not reply to that, and I guessed that she had gone to the kitchen window to look. She would be looking at the man and wondering who he was and what he wanted, the way you always do in the country, and if I went back there now, she would not notice right off whether or not I was barefoot. So I went back to the kitchen.

She was standing by the window. "I don't recognize him," she said, not looking around at me.

"Where could he be coming from?" I asked.

"I don't know," she said.

"What would he be doing down at the river? At night? In the storm?"

She studied the figure out the window, then said, "Oh, I reckon maybe he cut across from the Dunbar place."

That was, I realized, a perfectly rational explanation. He had not been down at the river in the storm, at night. He had come over this morning. You could cut across from the Dunbar place if you didn't mind breaking through a lot of elder and sassafras and blackberry bushes which had about taken over the old cross path, which nobody ever used any more. That satisfied me for a moment, but only for a moment. "Mama," I asked, "what would he be doing over at the Dunbar place last night?"

Then she looked at me, and I knew I had made a mistake, for she was looking at my bare feet. "You haven't got your shoes on," she said.

But I was saved by the dogs. That instant there was a bark which I recognized as Sam, the collie, and then a heavier, churning kind of bark which was Bully, and I saw a streak of white as Bully tore round the corner of the back porch and headed out for the man. Bully was a big bone-white bulldog, the kind of dog that they used to call a farm bulldog but that you don't see any more, heavy-chested and heavy-headed, but with pretty long legs. He could take a fence as light as a hound. He had just cleared the white paling fence toward the woods when my mother ran out to the back porch and began calling, "Here you, Bully! Here you!"

Bully stopped in the path, waiting for the man, but he gave a few more of those deep, gargling, savage barks that reminded you of something down a stone-lined well. The red-clay mud, I saw, was splashed up over his white chest and looked exciting, like blood.

The man, however, had not stopped walking even when Bully took the fence and started at him. He had kept right on coming. All he had done was to switch a little paper parcel which he carried from the right hand to the left, and then reach into his pants pocket to get something. Then I saw the glitter and knew that he had a knife in his hand, probably the kind of mean knife just made for devilment and nothing else, with a blade as long as the blade of a frog-sticker, which will snap out ready when you press a button in the handle. That knife must have had a button in the handle, or else how could he have had the blade out glittering so quick and with just one hand?

Pulling his knife against the dogs was a funny thing to do, for Bully was a big, powerful brute and fast, and Sam was all right. If those dogs had meant business, they might have knocked him down and ripped him before he got a stroke in. He ought to have picked up a heavy stick, something to take a swipe at them with and something which they could see and respect when they came at him. But he apparently did not know much about dogs. He just held the knife blade close against the right leg, low down, and kept on moving down the path.

Then my mother had called, and Bully had stopped. So the man let the blade of the knife snap back into the handle, and dropped it into his pocket, and kept on coming. Many women would have been afraid with the strange man who they knew had that knife in his pocket. That is, if they were alone in the house with nobody but a nine-year-old boy. And my mother was alone, for my father had gone off, and Dellie, the cook, was down at her cabin because she wasn't feeling well. But my mother wasn't afraid. She wasn't a big woman, but she was clear and brisk about everything she did and looked everybody and everything right in the eye from her own blue eyes in her tanned face. She had been the first woman in the country to ride a horse astride (that was back when she was a girl and long before I was born), and I have seen her snatch up a pump gun and go out and knock a chicken hawk out of the air like a busted skeet when he came over her chicken yard. She was a steady and self-reliant woman, and when I think of her now after all the years she has been dead, I think of her brown hands, not big, but somewhat square for a woman's hands, with square-cut nails. They looked, as a matter of fact, more like a young boy's hands than a grown woman's. But back then it never crossed my mind that she would ever be dead.

She stood on the back porch and watched the man enter the back gate, where the dogs (Bully had leaped back into the yard) were dancing and muttering and giving sidelong glances back to my mother to see if she meant what she had said. The man walked right by the dogs, almost brushing them, and didn't pay them any attention. I could see now that he wore old khaki pants, and a dark wool coat with stripes in it, and a gray felt hat. He had on a gray shirt with blue stripes in it, and no tie. But I could see a tie, blue and reddish, sticking in his side coat-pocket. Everything was wrong about what he wore. He ought to have been wearing blue jeans or overalls, and a straw hat or an old black felt hat, and the coat, granting that he might have been wearing a wool coat and not a jumper, ought not to have had those stripes. Those clothes, despite the fact that they were old enough and dirty enough for any tramp, didn't belong there in our back yard, coming down the path, in Middle Tennessee, miles away from any big town, and even a mile off the pike.

When he got almost to the steps, without having said anything, my mother, very matter-of-factly, said, "Good morning."

"Good morning," he said, and stopped and looked her over. He did not take off his hat, and under the brim you could see the perfectly unmemorable face, which wasn't old and wasn't young, or thick or thin. It was grayish and covered with about three days of stubble. The eyes were a kind of nondescript, muddy hazel, or something like that, rather bloodshot. His teeth, when he opened his mouth, showed yellow and uneven. A couple of them had been knocked out. You knew that they had been knocked out, because there was a scar, not very old, there on the lower lip just beneath the gap.

"Are you hunting work?" my mother asked him.

"Yes," he said—not "yes, mam"—and still did not take off his hat.

"I don't know about my husband, for he isn't here," she said, and didn't mind a bit telling the tramp, or whoever he was, with the mean knife in his pocket, that no man was around, "but I can give you a few things to do. The storm has drowned a lot of my chicks. Three coops of them. You can gather them up and bury them. Bury them deep so the dogs won't get at them. In the woods. And fix the coops the wind blew over. And down yonder beyond that pen by the edge of the woods are some drowned poults. They got out and I couldn't get them in. Even after it started to rain hard. Poults haven't got any sense."

"What are them things—poults?" he demanded, and spat on the brick walk. He rubbed his foot over the spot, and I saw that he wore a black pointed-toe low shoe, all cracked and broken. It was a crazy kind of shoe to be wearing in the country.

"Oh, they're young turkeys," my mother was saying. "And they haven't got any sense. I oughtn't to try to raise them around here with so many chickens, anyway. They don't thrive near chickens, even in separate pens. And I won't give up my chickens." Then she stopped herself and resumed briskly on the note of business. "When you finish that, you can fix my flower beds. A lot of trash and mud and gravel has washed down. Maybe you can save some of my flowers if you are careful."

"Flowers," the man said, in a low, impersonal voice which seemed to have a wealth of meaning, but a meaning which I could not fathom. As I think back on it, it probably was not pure contempt. Rather, it was a kind of impersonal and distant marveling that he should be on the verge of grubbing in a flower bed. He said the word, and then looked off across the yard.

"Yes, flowers," my mother replied with some asperity, as though she would have nothing said or implied against flowers. "And they were very fine this year." Then she stopped and looked at the man. "Are you hungry?" she demanded.

"Yeah," he said.

"I'll fix you something," she said, "before you get started." She turned to me. "Show him where he can wash up," she commanded, and went into the house.

I took the man to the end of the porch where a pump was and where a couple of wash pans sat on a low shelf for people to use before they went into the house. I stood there while he laid down his little parcel wrapped in newspaper and took off his hat and looked around for a nail to hang it on. He poured the water and plunged his hands into it. They were big hands, and strong-looking, but they did not have the creases and the earth-color of the hands of men who work outdoors. But they were dirty, with black dirt ground into the skin and under the nails. After he had washed his hands, he poured another basin of water and washed his face. He dried his face, and with the towel still dangling in his grasp, stepped over to the mirror on the house wall. He rubbed one hand over the stubble on his face. Then he carefully inspected his face, turning first one side and then the other, and stepped back and settled his striped coat down on his shoulders. He had the movements of a man who has just dressed up to go to church or a party—the way he settled his coat and smoothed it and scanned himself in the mirror.

Then he caught my glance on him. He glared at me for an instant out of the bloodshot eyes, then demanded in a low, harsh voice, "What you looking at?"

"Nothing," I managed to say, and stepped back a step from him.

He flung the towel down, crumpled, on the shelf, and went toward the kitchen door and entered without knocking.

My mother said something to him which I could not catch. I started to go in again, then thought about my bare feet, and decided to go back of the chicken yard, where the man would have to come to pick up the dead chicks. I hung around behind the chicken house until he came out.

He moved across the chicken yard with a fastidious, not quite finicking motion, looking down at the curdled mud flecked with bits of chicken-droppings. The mud curled up over the soles of his black shoes. I stood back from him some six feet and watched him pick up the first of the drowned chicks. He held it up by one foot and inspected it.

There is nothing deader-looking than a drowned chick. The feet curl in that feeble, empty way which back when I was a boy, even if I was a country boy who did not mind hog-killing or frog-gigging, made me feel hollow in the stomach. Instead of looking plump and fluffy, the body is stringy and limp with the fluff plastered to it, and the neck is long and loose like a little string of rag. And the eyes have that bluish membrane over them which makes you think of a very old man who is sick about to die.

The man stood there and inspected the chick. Then he looked all around as though he didn't know what to do with it.

"There's a great big old basket in the shed," I said, and pointed to the shed attached to the chicken house.

He inspected me as though he had just discovered my presence, and moved toward the shed.

"There's a spade there, too," I added.

He got the basket and began to pick up the other chicks, picking each one up slowly by a foot and then flinging it into the basket with a nasty, snapping motion. Now and then he would look at me out of the bloodshot eyes. Every time he seemed on the verge of saying something, but he did not. Perhaps he was building up to say something to me, but I did not wait that long. His way of looking at me made me so uncomfortable that I left the chicken yard.

Besides, I had just remembered that the creek was in flood, over the bridge, and that people were down there watching it. So I cut across the farm toward the creek. When I got to the big tobacco field I saw that it had not suffered much. The land lay right and not many tobacco plants had washed out of the ground. But I knew that a lot of tobacco round the country had been washed right out. My father had said so at breakfast.

My father was down at the bridge. When I came out of the gap in the osage hedge into the road, I saw him sitting on his mare over the heads of the other men who were standing around, admiring the flood. The creek was big here, even in low water; for only a couple of miles away it ran into the river, and when a real flood came, the red water got over the pike where it dipped down to the bridge, which was an iron bridge, and high over the floor and even the side railings of the bridge. Only the upper iron work would show, with the water boiling and frothing red and white around it. That creek rose so fast and so heavy because a few miles back it came down out of the hills, where the gorges filled up with water in no time when a rain came. The creek ran in a deep bed with limestone bluffs along both sides until it got within three quarters of a mile of the bridge, and when it came out from between those bluffs in flood it was boiling and hissing and steaming like water from a fire hose.

Whenever there was a flood, people from half the county would come down to see the sight. After a gully-washer there would not be any work to do anyway. If it didn't ruin your crop, you couldn't plow and you felt like taking a holiday to celebrate. If it did ruin your crop, there wasn't anything to do except to try to take your mind off the mortgage, if you were rich enough to have a mortgage, and if you couldn't afford a mortgage, you needed something to take your mind off how hungry you would be by Christmas. So people would come down to the bridge and look at the flood. It made something different from the run of days.

There would not be much talking after the first few minutes of trying to guess how high the water was this time. The men and kids just stood around, or sat their horses or mules, as the case might be, or stood up in the wagon beds. They looked at the strangeness of the flood for an hour or two, and then somebody would say that he had better be getting on home to dinner and would start walking down the gray, puddled limestone pike, or would touch heel to his mount and start off. Everybody always knew what it would be like when he got down to the bridge, but people always came. It was like church or a funeral. They always came, that is, if it was summer and the flood unexpected. Nobody ever came down in winter to see high water.

When I came out of the gap in the bodock hedge, I saw the crowd, perhaps fifteen or twenty men and a lot of kids, and saw my father sitting his mare, Nellie Gray. He was a tall, limber man and carried himself well. I was always proud to see him sit a horse, he was so quiet and straight, and when I stepped through the gap of the hedge that morning, the first thing that happened was, I remember, the warm feeling I always had when I saw him up on a horse, just sitting. I did not go toward him, but skirted the crowd on the far side, to get a look at the creek. For one thing, I was not sure what he would say about the fact that I was barefoot. But the first thing I knew, I heard his voice calling, "Seth!"

I went toward him, moving apologetically past the men, who bent their large, red or thin, sallow faces above me. I knew some of the men, and knew their names, but because those I knew were there in a crowd, mixed with the strange faces, they seemed foreign to me, and not friendly. I did not look up at my father until I was almost within touching distance of his heel. Then I looked up and tried to read his face, to see if he was angry about my being barefoot. Before I could decide anything from that impassive, high-boned face, he had leaned over and reached a hand to me. "Grab on," he commanded.

I grabbed on and gave a little jump, and he said, "Up-see-daisy!" and whisked me, light as a feather, up to the pommel of his McClellan saddle.

"You can see better up here," he said, slid back on the cantle a little to make me more comfortable, and then, looking over my head at the swollen, tumbling water, seemed to forget all about me. But his right hand was laid on my side, just above my thigh, to steady me.

I was sitting there as quiet as I could, feeling the faint stir of my father's chest against my shoulders as it rose and fell with his breath, when I saw the cow. At first, looking up the creek, I thought it was just another big piece of driftwood steaming down the creek in the ruck of water, but all at once a pretty good-size boy who had climbed part way up a telephone pole by the pike so that he could see better yelled out, "Golly-damn, look at that-air cow!"

Everybody looked. It was a cow all right, but it might just as well have been driftwood; for it was dead as a chunk, rolling and roiling down the creek, appearing and disappearing, feet up or head up, it didn't matter which.

The cow started up the talk again. Somebody wondered whether it would hit one of the clear places under the top girder of the bridge and get through or whether it would get tangled in the drift and trash that had piled against the upright girders and braces. Somebody remembered how about ten years before, so much driftwood had piled up on the bridge that it was knocked off its foundations. Then the cow hit. It hit the edge of the drift against one of the girders, and hung there. For a few seconds it seemed as though it might tear loose, but then we saw that it was really caught. It bobbed and heaved on its side there in a slow, grinding, uneasy fashion. It had a yoke around its neck, the kind made out of a forked limb to keep a jumper behind fence.

"She shore jumped one fence," one of the men said.

And another: "Well, she done jumped her last one, fer a fack."

Then they began to wonder about whose cow it might be. They decided it must belong to Milt Alley. They said that he had a cow that was a jumper, and kept her in a fenced-in piece of ground up the creek. I had never seen Milt Alley, but I knew who he was. He was a squatter and lived up the hills a way, on a shirt-tail patch of set-on-edge land, in a cabin. He was pore white trash. He had lots of children. I had seen the children at school, when they came. They were thin-faced, with straight, sticky-looking, dough-colored hair, and they smelled something like old sour buttermilk, not because they drank so much buttermilk but because that is the sort of smell which children out of those cabins tend to have. The big Alley boy drew dirty pictures and showed them to the little boys at school.

That was Milt Alley's cow. It looked like the kind of cow he would have, a scrawny, old, sway-backed cow, with a yoke around her neck. I wondered if Milt Alley had another cow.

"Poppa," I said, "do you think Milt Alley has got another cow?"

"You say 'Mr. Alley,'" my father said quietly.

"Do you think he has?"

"No telling," my father said.

Then a big gangly boy, about fifteen, who was sitting on a scraggly little old mule with a piece of croker sack thrown across the sawtooth spine, and who had been staring at the cow, suddenly said to nobody in particular, "Reckin anybody ever et drownt cow?"

He was the kind of boy who might just as well as not have been the son of Milt Alley, with his faded and patched overalls ragged at the bottom of the pants and the mud-stiff brogans hanging off his skinny, bare ankles at the level of the mule's belly. He had said what he did, and then looked embarrassed and sullen when all the eyes swung at him. He hadn't meant to say it, I am pretty sure now. He would have been too proud to say it, just as Milt Alley would have been too proud. He had just been thinking out loud, and the words had popped out.

There was an old man standing there on the pike, an old man with a white beard. "Son," he said to the embarrassed and sullen boy on the mule, "you live long enough and you'll find a man will eat anything when the time comes."

"Time gonna come fer some folks this year," another man said.

"Son," the old man said, "in my time I et things a man don't like to think on. I was a sojer and I rode with Gin'l Forrest, and them things we et when the time come. I tell you. I et meat what got up and run when you taken out yore knife to cut a slice to put on the fire. You had to knock it down with a carbeen butt, it was so active. That-air meat would jump like a bullfrog, it was so full of skippers."

But nobody was listening to the old man. The boy on the mule turned his sullen sharp face from him, dug a heel into the side of the mule, and went off up the pike with a motion which made you think that any second you would hear mule bones clashing inside that lank and scrofulous hide.

"Cy Dundee's boy," a man said, and nodded toward the figure going up the pike on the mule.

"Reckin Cy Dundee's young-uns seen times they'd settle fer drownt cow," another man said.

The old man with the beard peered at them both from his weak, slow eyes, first at one and then at the other. "Live long enough," he said, "and a man will settle fer what he kin git."

Then there was silence again, with the people looking at the red, foam-flecked water.

My father lifted the bridle rein in his left hand, and the mare turned and walked around the group and up the pike. We rode on up to our big gate, where my father dismounted to open it and let me myself ride Nellie Gray through. When he got to the lane that led off from the drive about two hundred yards from our house, my father said, "Grab on." I grabbed on, and he let me down to the ground. "I'm going to ride down and look at my corn," he said. "You go on." He took the lane, and I stood there on the drive and watched him ride off. He was wearing cowhide boots and an old hunting coat, and I thought that that made him look very military, like a picture. That and the way he rode.

I did not go to the house. Instead, I went by the vegetable garden and crossed behind the stables, and headed down for Dellie's cabin. I wanted to go down and play with Jebb, who was Dellie's little boy about two years older than I was. Besides, I was cold. I shivered as I walked, and I had gooseflesh. The mud which crawled up between my toes with every step I took was like ice. Dellie would have a fire, but she wouldn't make me put on shoes and stockings.

Dellie's cabin was of logs, with one side, because it was on a slope, set on limestone chunks, with a little porch attached to it, and had a little whitewashed fence around it and a gate with plow-points on a wire to clink when somebody came in, and had two big white oaks in the yard and some flowers and a nice privy in the back with some honeysuckle growing over it. Dellie and Old Jebb, who was Jebb's father and who lived with Dellie and had lived with her for twenty-five years even if they never had got married, were careful to keep everything nice around their cabin. They had the name all over the community for being clean and clever Negroes. Dellie and Jebb were what they used to call "white-folks' niggers." There was a big difference between their cabin and the other two cabins farther down where the other tenants lived. My father kept the other cabins weatherproof, but he couldn't undertake to go down and pick up after the litter they strewed. They didn't take the trouble to have a vegetable patch like Dellie and Jebb or to make preserves from wild plum, and jelly from crab apple the way Dellie did. They were shiftless, and my father was always threatening to get shed of them. But he never did. When they finally left, they just up and left on their own, for no reason, to go and be shiftless somewhere else. Then some more came. But meanwhile they lived down there, Matt Rawson and his family, and Sid Turner and his, and I played with their children all over the farm when they weren't working. But when I wasn't around they were mean sometimes to Little Jebb. That was because the other tenants down there were jealous of Dellie and Jebb.

I was so cold that I ran the last fifty yards to Dellie's gate. As soon as I had entered the yard, I saw that the storm had been hard on Dellie's flowers. The yard was, as I have said, on a slight slope, and the water running across had gutted the flower beds and washed out all the good black woods-earth which Dellie had brought in. What little grass there was in the yard was plastered sparsely down on the ground, the way the drainage water had left it. It reminded me of the way the fluff was plastered down on the skin of the drowned chicks that the strange man had been picking up, up in my mother's chicken yard.

I took a few steps up the path to the cabin, and then I saw that the drainage water had washed a lot of trash and filth out from under Dellie's house. Up toward the porch, the ground was not clean any more. Old pieces of rag, two or three rusted cans, pieces of rotten rope, some hunks of old dog dung, broken glass, old paper, and all sorts of things like that had washed out from under Dellie's house to foul her clean yard. It looked just as bad as the yards of the other cabins, or worse. It was worse, as a matter of fact, because it was a surprise. I had never thought of all that filth being under Dellie's house. It was not anything against Dellie that the stuff had been under the cabin. Trash will get under any house. But I did not think of that when I saw the foulness which had washed out on the ground which Dellie sometimes used to sweep with a twig broom to make nice and clean.

I picked my way past the filth, being careful not to get my bare feet on it, and mounted to Dellie's door. When I knocked, I heard her voice telling me to come in.

It was dark inside the cabin, after the daylight, but I could make out Dellie piled up in bed under a quilt, and Little Jebb crouched by the hearth, where a low fire simmered. "Howdy," I said to Dellie, "how you feeling?"

Her big eyes, the whites surprising and glaring in the black face, fixed on me as I stood there, but she did not reply. It did not look like Dellie, or act like Dellie, who would grumble and bustle around our kitchen, talking to herself, scolding me or Little Jebb, clanking pans, making all sorts of unnecessary noises and mutterings like an old-fashioned black steam thrasher engine when it has got up an extra head of steam and keeps popping the governor and rumbling and shaking on its wheels. But now Dellie just lay up there on the bed, under the patchwork quilt, and turned the black face, which I scarcely recognized, and the glaring white eyes to me.

"How you feeling?" I repeated.

"I'se sick," the voice said croakingly out of the strange black face which was not attached to Dellie's big, squat body, but stuck out from under a pile of tangled bedclothes. Then the voice added: "Mighty sick."

"I'm sorry," I managed to say.

The eyes remained fixed on me for a moment, then they left me and the head rolled back on the pillow. "Sorry," the voice said, in a flat way which wasn't question or statement of anything. It was just the empty word put into the air with no meaning or expression, to float off like a feather or a puff of smoke, while the big eyes, with the whites like the peeled white of hard-boiled eggs, stared at the ceiling.

"Dellie," I said after a minute, "there's a tramp up at the house. He's got a knife."

She was not listening. She closed her eyes.

I tiptoed over to the hearth where Jebb was and crouched beside him. We began to talk in low voices. I was asking him to get out his train and play train. Old Jebb had put spool wheels on three cigar boxes and put wire links between the boxes to make a train for Jebb. The box that was the locomotive had the top closed and a length of broom stick for a smoke stack. Jebb didn't want to get the train out, but I told him I would go home if he didn't. So he got out the train, and the colored rocks, and fossils of crinoid stems, and other junk he used for the load, and we began to push it around, talking the way we thought trainmen talked, making a chuck-chucking sound under the breath for the noise of the locomotive and now and then uttering low, cautious toots for the whistle. We got so interested in playing train that the toots got louder. Then, before he thought, Jebb gave a good, loud *toot-toot,* blowing for a crossing.

"Come here," the voice said from the bed.

Jebb got up slow from his hands and knees, giving me a sudden, naked, inimical look.

"Come here!" the voice said.

Jebb went to the bed. Dellie propped herself weakly up on one arm, muttering, "Come closer."

Jebb stood closer.

"Last thing I do, I'm gonna do it," Dellie said. "Done tole you to be quiet."

Then she slapped him. It was an awful slap, more awful for the kind of weakness which it came from and brought to focus. I had seen her slap Jebb before, but the slapping had always been the kind of easy slap you would expect from a good-natured, grumbling Negro woman like Dellie. But this was different. It was awful. It was so awful that Jebb didn't make a sound. The tears just popped out and ran down his face, and his breath came sharp, like gasps.

Dellie fell back. "Cain't even be sick," she said to the ceiling. "Git sick and they won't even let you lay. They tromp all over you. Cain't even be sick." Then she closed her eyes.

I went out of the room. I almost ran getting to the door, and I did run across the porch and down the steps and across the yard, not caring whether or not I stepped on the filth which had washed out from under the cabin. I ran almost all the way home. Then I thought about my mother catching me with the bare feet. So I went down to the stables.

I heard a noise in the crib, and opened the door. There was Big Jebb, sitting on an old nail keg, shelling corn into a bushel basket. I went in, pulling the door shut behind me, and crouched on the floor near him. I crouched there for a couple of minutes before either of us spoke, and watched him shelling the corn.

He had very big hands, knotted and grayish at the joints, with calloused palms which seemed to be streaked with rust, with the rust coming up between the fingers to show from the back. His hands were so strong and tough that he could take a big ear of corn and rip the grains right off the cob with the palm of his hand, all in one motion, like a machine. "Work long as me," he would say, "and the good Lawd'll give you a hand lak cass-ion won't nuthin' hurt." And his hands did look like cast iron, old cast iron streaked with rust.

He was an old man, up in his seventies, thirty years or more older than Dellie, but he was strong as a bull. He was a squat sort of man, heavy in the shoulders, with remarkably long arms, the kind of build they say the river natives have on the Congo from paddling so much in their boats. He had a round bullet-head, set on powerful shoulders. His skin was very black, and the thin hair on his head was now grizzled like tufts of old cotton batting. He had small eyes and a flat nose, not big, and the kindest and wisest old face in the world, the blunt, sad, wise face of an old animal peering tolerantly out on the goings-on of the merely human creatures before him. He was a good man, and I loved him next to my mother and father. I crouched there on the floor of the crib and watched him shell corn with the rusty cast-iron hands, while he looked down at me out of the little eyes set in the blunt face.

"Dellie says she's mighty sick," I said.

"Yeah," he said.

"What's she sick from?"

"Woman-mizry," he said.

"What's woman-mizry?"

"Hit comes on 'em," he said. "Hit jest comes on 'em when the time comes."

"What is it?"

"Hit is the change," he said. "Hit is the change of life and time."

"What changes?"

"You too young to know."

"Tell me."

"Time come and you find out everthing."

I knew that there was no use in asking him any more. When I asked him things and he said that, I always knew that he would not tell me. So I continued to crouch there and watch him. Now that I had sat there a little while, I was cold again.

"What you shiver fer?" he asked me.

"I'm cold. I'm cold because it's blackberry winter," I said.

"Maybe 'tis and maybe 'tain't," he said.

"My mother says it is."

"Ain't sayen Miss Sallie doan know and ain't sayen she do. But folks doan know everthing."

"Why isn't it blackberry winter?"

"Too late fer blackberry winter. Blackberries done bloomed."

"She said it was."

"Blackberry winter jest a leetle cold spell. Hit come and then hit go away, and hit is growed summer of a sudden lak a gunshot. Ain't no tellen hit will go way this time."

"It's June," I said.

"June," he replied with great contempt. "That what folks say. What June mean? Maybe hit is come cold to stay."

"Why?"

" 'Cause this-here old yearth is tahrd. Hit is tahrd and ain't gonna perduce. Lawd let hit come rain one time forty days and forty nights, 'cause He was tahrd of sinful folks. Maybe this-here old yearth say to the Lawd, Lawd, I done plum tahrd, Lawd, lemme rest. And Lawd say, Yearth, you done yore best, you give 'em cawn and you give 'em taters, and all they think on is they gut, and, Yearth, you kin take a rest."

"What will happen?"

"Folks will eat up everthing. The yearth won't perduce no more. Folks cut down all the trees and burn 'em 'cause they cold, and the yearth won't grow no more. I been tellen 'em. I been tellen folks. Sayen, maybe this year, hit is the time. But they doan listen to me, how the yearth is tahrd. Maybe this year they find out."

"Will everything die?"

"Everthing and everbody, hit will be so."

"This year?"

"Ain't no tellen. Maybe this year."

"My mother said it is blackberry winter," I said confidently, and got up.

"Ain't sayen nuthin' agin Miss Sallie," he said.

I went to the door of the crib. I was really cold now. Running, I had got up a sweat and now I was worse.

I hung on the door, looking at Jebb, who was shelling corn again.

"There's a tramp came to the house," I said. I had almost forgotten the tramp.

"Yeah."

"He came by the back way. What was he doing down there in the storm?"

"They comes and they goes," he said, "and ain't no teller."

"He had a mean knife."

"The good ones and the bad ones, they comes and they goes. Storm or sun, light or dark. They is folks and they comes and they goes lak folks."

I hung on the door, shivering.

He studied me a moment, then said, "You git on to the house. You ketch yore death. Then what yore mammy say?"

I hesitated.

"You git," he said.

When I came to the back yard, I saw that my father was standing by the back porch and the tramp was walking toward him. They began talking before I reached them, but I got there just as my father was saying, "I'm sorry, but I haven't got any work. I got all the hands on the place I need now. I won't need any extra until wheat thrashing."

The stranger made no reply, just looked at my father.

My father took out his leather coin purse, and got out a half-dollar. He held it toward the man. "This is for half a day," he said.

The man looked at the coin, and then at my father, making no motion to take the money. But that was the right amount. A dollar a day was what you paid them back in 1910. And the man hadn't even worked half a day.

Then the man reached out and took the coin. He dropped it into the right side pocket of his coat. Then he said, very slowly and without feeling, "I didn't want to work on your——farm."

He used the word which they would have frailed me to death for using.

I looked at my father's face and it was streaked white under the sunburn. Then he said, "Get off this place. Get off this place or I won't be responsible."

The man dropped his right hand into his pants pocket. It was the pocket where he kept the knife. I was just about to yell to my father about the knife when the hand came back out with nothing in it. The man gave a kind of twisted grin, showing where the teeth had been knocked out above the new scar. I thought that instant how maybe he had tried before to pull a knife on somebody else and had got his teeth knocked out.

So now he just gave that twisted, sickish grin out of the unmemorable, grayish face, and then spat on the brick path. The glob landed just about six inches from the toe of my father's right boot. My father looked down at it, and so did I. I thought that if the glob had hit my father's boot, something would have happened. I looked down and saw the bright glob, and on one side of it my father's strong cowhide boots, with the brass eyelets and the leather thongs, heavy boots splashed with good red mud and set solid on the bricks, and on the other side the pointed-toe, broken, black shoes, on which the mud looked so sad and out of place. Then I saw one of the black shoes move a little, just a twitch first, then a real step backward.

The man moved in a quarter circle to the end of the porch, with my father's steady gaze upon him all the while. At the end of the porch, the man reached up to the shelf where the wash pans were to get his little newspaper-wrapped parcel. Then he disappeared around the corner of the house and my father mounted the porch and went into the kitchen without a word.

I followed around the house to see what the man would do. I wasn't afraid of him now, no matter if he did have the knife. When I got around in front, I saw him going out the yard gate and starting up the drive toward the pike. So I ran to catch up with him. He was sixty yards or so up the drive before I caught up.

I did not walk right up even with him at first, but trailed him, the way a kid will, about seven or eight feet behind, now and then running two or three steps in order to hold my place against his longer stride. When I first came up behind him, he turned to give me a look, just a meaningless look, and then fixed his eyes up the drive and kept on walking.

When we had got around the bend in the drive which cut the house from sight, and were going along by the edge of the woods, I decided to come up even with him. I ran a few steps, and was by his side, or almost, but some feet off to the right. I walked along in this position for a while, and he never noticed me. I walked along until we got within sight of the big gate that let on the pike.

Then I said, "Where did you come from?"

He looked at me then with a look which seemed almost surprised that I was there. Then he said, "It ain't none of yore business."

We went on another fifty feet.

Then I said, "Where are you going?"

He stopped, studied me dispassionately for a moment, then suddenly took a step toward me and leaned his face down at me. The lips jerked back, but not in any grin, to show where the teeth were knocked out and to make the scar on the lower lip come white with the tension.

He said, "Stop following me. You don't stop following me and I cut yore throat, you little son-of-a-bitch."

Then he went on to the gate, and up the pike.

That was thirty-five years ago. Since that time my father and mother have died. I was still a boy, but a big boy, when my father got cut on the blade of a mowing machine and died of lockjaw. My mother sold the place and went to town to live with her sister. But she never took hold after my father's death, and she died within three years, right in middle life. My aunt always said, "Sallie just died of a broken heart, she was so devoted." Dellie is dead, too, but she died, I heard, quite a long time after we sold the farm.

As for Little Jebb, he grew up to be a mean and ficey Negro. He killed another Negro in a fight and got sent to the penitentiary, where he is yet, the last I heard tell. He probably grew up to be mean and ficey from just being picked on so much by the children of the other tenants, who were jealous of Jebb and Dellie for being thrifty and clever and being white-folks' niggers.

Old Jebb lived forever. I saw him ten years ago and he was about a hundred then, and not looking much different. He was living in town then, on relief—that was back in the Depression—when I went to see him. He said to me: "Too strong to die. When I was a young feller just comen on and seen how things wuz, I prayed the Lawd. I said, Oh, Lawd, gimme strength and meke me strong fer to do and to in-dure. The Lawd hearkened to my prayer. He give me strength. I was in-duren proud fer being strong and me much man. The Lawd give me my prayer and my strength. But now He done gone off and fergot me and left me alone with my strength. A man doan know what to pray fer, and him mortal."

Jebb is probably living yet, as far as I know.

That is what has happened since the morning when the tramp leaned his face down at me and showed his teeth and said: "Stop following me. You don't stop following me and I cut yore throat, you little son-of-a-bitch." That was what he said, for me not to follow him. But I did follow him, all the years.

# Eudora Welty

*Welty (1909–    ) was born in Jackson, Mississippi, where she has lived for most of her productive life. She received her formal education at the Mississippi State College for Women and the University of Wisconsin, studying advertising at Columbia University for a brief period. Her early ambitions to be a painter were subordinated by the success of her first book of stories,* A Curtain of Green and Other Stories *(1941). Readers recognized in this and following works a writer who gives full value to the quality and spectacle of her home region and the people she knows best while at the same time she displays a cosmopolitan awareness and technical sophistication. Other books of short stories are* The Wide Net and Other Stories *(1943),* The Golden Apples *(1949),* The Bride of the Innisfallen and Other Stories *(1955),* Thirteen Stories *(1965), and the* Collected Stories of Eudora Welty *(1980). Her novels include* Delta Wedding *(1946),* The Ponder Heart *(1954), and* The Optimist's Daughter *(1972).* One Writer's Beginnings *(1984), based on three lectures Welty delivered at Harvard, is autobiographical.*

## Why I Live at the P.O.

I was getting along fine with Mama, Papa-Daddy, and Uncle Rondo until my sister Stella-Rondo just separated from her husband and came back home again. Mr. Whitaker! Of course I went with Mr. Whitaker first, when he first appeared here in China Grove, taking "Pose Yourself" photos, and Stella-Rondo broke us up. Told him I was one-sided. Bigger on one side than the other, which is a deliberate, calculated falsehood: I'm the same. Stella-Rondo is exactly twelve months to the day younger than I am and for that reason she's spoiled.

She's always had anything in the world she wanted and then she'd throw it away. Papa-Daddy give her this gorgeous Add-a-Pearl necklace when she was eight years old and she threw it away playing baseball when she was nine, with only two pearls.

So as soon as she got married and moved away from home the first thing she did was separate! From Mr. Whitaker! This photographer with the popeyes she said she trusted. Came home from one of those towns up in Illinois and to our complete surprise brought this child of two.

Mama said she like to make her drop dead for a second. "Here you had this marvelous blonde child and never so much as wrote your mother a word about it," says Mama. "I'm thoroughly ashamed of you." But of course she wasn't.

Stella-Rondo just calmly takes off this *hat*, I wish you could see it. She says, "Why, Mama, Shirley-T.'s adopted, I can prove it."

"How?" says Mama, but all I says was, "H'm!" There I was over the hot stove, trying to stretch two chickens over five people and a completely unexpected child into the bargain without one moment's notice.

"What do you mean—'H'm'?" says Stella-Rondo, and Mama says, "I heard that, Sister."

I said that oh, I didn't mean a thing, only that whoever Shirley-T. was, she was the spit-image of Papa-Daddy if he'd cut off his beard, which of course he'd never do in the world. Papa-Daddy's Mama's papa and sulks.

Stella-Rondo got furious! She said, "Sister, I don't need to tell you you got a lot of nerve and always did have and I'll thank you to make no future reference to my adopted child whatsoever."

"Very well," I said. "Very well, very well. Of course I noticed at once she looks like Mr. Whitaker's side too. That frown. She looks like a cross between Mr. Whitaker and Papa-Daddy."

"Well, all I can say is she isn't."

"She looks exactly like Shirley Temple to me," says Mama, but Shirley-T. just ran away from her.

So the first thing Stella-Rondo did at the table was turn Papa-Daddy against me.

"Papa-Daddy," she says. He was trying to cut up his meat. "Papa-Daddy!" I was taken completely by surprise. Papa-Daddy is about a million years old and's got this long-long beard. "Papa-Daddy, Sister says she fails to understand why you don't cut off your beard."

So Papa-Daddy l-a-y-s down his knife and fork! He's real rich. Mama says he is, she says he isn't. So he says, "Have I heard correctly? You don't understand why I don't cut off my beard?"

"Why," I says, "Papa-Daddy, of course I understand, I did not say any such a thing, the idea!"

He says, "Hussy!"

I says, "Papa-Daddy, you know I wouldn't any more want you to cut off your beard than the man in the moon. It was the farthest thing from my mind! Stella-Rondo sat there and made that up while she was eating breast of chicken."

But he says, "So the postmistress fails to understand why I don't cut off my beard. Which job I got you through my influence with the government. 'Bird's nest'—is that what you call it?"

Not that it isn't the next to smallest P.O. in the entire state of Mississippi.

I says, "Oh, Papa-Daddy," I says, "I didn't say any such a thing, I never dreamed it was a bird's nest, I have always been grateful though this is the next to smallest P.O in the state of Mississippi, and I do not enjoy being referred to as a hussy by my own grandfather."

But Stella-Rondo says, "Yes, you did say it too. Anybody in the world could of heard you, that had ears."

"Stop right there," says Mama, looking at *me*.

So I pulled my napkin straight back through the napkin ring and left the table.

As soon as I was out of the room Mama says, "Call her back, or she'll starve to death," but Papa-Daddy says, "This is the beard I started growing on the Coast when I was fifteen years old." He would of gone on till nightfall if Shirley-T. hadn't lost the Milky Way she ate in Cairo.

So Papa-Daddy says, "I am going out and lie in the hammock, and you can all sit here and remember my words: I'll never cut off my beard as long as I live, even one inch, and I don't appreciate it in you at all." Passed right by me in the hall and went straight out and got in the hammock.

It would be a holiday. It wasn't five minutes before Uncle Rondo suddenly appeared in the hall in one of Stella-Rondo's flesh-colored kimonos, all cut on the bias, like something Mr. Whitaker probably thought was gorgeous.

"Uncle Rondo!" I says. "I didn't know who that was! Where are you going?"

"Sister," he says, "get out of my way, I'm poisoned."

"If you're poisoned stay away from Papa-Daddy," I says. "Keep out of the hammock. Papa-Daddy will certainly beat you on the head if you come within forty miles of him. He thinks I deliberately said he ought to cut off his beard after he got me the P.O., and I've told him and told him and told him, and he acts like he just don't hear me. Papa-Daddy must of gone stone deaf."

"He picked a fine day to do it then," says Uncle Rondo, and before you could say "Jack Robinson" flew out in the yard.

What he'd really done, he'd drunk another bottle of that prescription. He does it every single Fourth of July as sure as shooting, and it's horribly expensive. Then he falls over in the hammock and snores. So he insisted on zigzagging right on out to the hammock, looking like a half-wit.

Papa-Daddy woke with this horrible yell and right there without moving an inch he tried to turn Uncle Rondo against me. I heard every word he said. Oh, he told Uncle Rondo I didn't learn to read till I was eight years old and he didn't see how in the world I ever got the mail put up at the P.O., much less read it all, and he said if Uncle Rondo could only fathom the lengths he had gone to get me that job! And he said on the other hand he thought Stella-Rondo had a brilliant mind and deserved credit for getting out of town. All the time he was just lying there swinging as pretty as you please and looping out his beard, and poor Uncle Rondo was *pleading* with him to slow down the hammock, it was making him as dizzy as a witch to watch it. But that's what Papa-Daddy likes about a hammock. So Uncle Rondo was too dizzy to get turned against me for the time being. He's Mama's only brother and is a good case of a one-track mind. Ask anybody. A certified pharmacist.

Just then I heard Stella-Rondo raising the upstairs window. While she was married she got this peculiar idea that it's cooler with the windows shut and locked. So she has to raise the window before she can make a soul hear her outdoors.

So she raises the window and says, "*Oh!*" You would have thought she was mortally wounded.

Uncle Rondo and Papa-Daddy didn't even look up, but kept right on with what they were doing. I had to laugh.

I flew up the stairs and threw the door open! I says, "What in the wide world's the matter, Stella-Rondo? You mortally wounded?"

"No," she says, "I am not mortally wounded but I wish you would do me the favor of looking out that window there and telling me what you see."

So I shade my eyes and look out the window.

"I see the front yard," I says.

"Don't you see any human beings?"

"I see Uncle Rondo trying to run Papa-Daddy out of the hammock," I says. "Nothing more. Naturally, it's so suffocating-hot in the house, with all the windows shut and locked, everybody who cares to stay in their right mind will have to go out and get in the hammock before the Fourth of July is over."

"Don't you notice anything different about Uncle Rondo?" asks Stella-Rondo.

"Why, no, except he's got on some terrible-looking flesh-colored contraption I wouldn't be found dead in, is all I can see," I says.

"Never mind, you won't be found dead in it, because it happens to be part of my trousseau, and Mr. Whitaker took several dozen photographs of me in it," says Stella-Rondo. "What on earth could uncle Rondo *mean* by wearing part of my trousseau out in the broad open daylight without saying so much as 'Kiss my foot,' *knowing* I only got home this morning after my separation and hung my negligee up on the bathroom door, just as nervous as I could be?"

"I'm sure I don't know, and what do you expect me to do about it?" I says. "Jump out the window?"

"No, I expect nothing of the kind. I simply declare that Uncle Rondo looks like a fool in it, that's all," she says. "It makes me sick to my stomach."

"Well, he looks as good as he can," I says. "As good as anybody in reason could." I stood up for Uncle Rondo, please remember. And I said to Stella-Rondo, "I think I would do well not to criticize so freely if I were you and came home with a two-year-old child I had never said a word about, and no explanation whatever about my separation."

"I asked you the instant I entered this house not to refer one more time to my adopted child, and you gave me your word of honor you would not," was all Stella-Rondo would say, and started pulling out every one of her eyebrows with some cheap Kress[1] tweezers.

So I merely slammed the door behind me and went down and made some green-tomato pickle. Somebody had to do it. Of course Mama had turned both the niggers loose; she always said no earthly power could hold one anyway on the Fourth of July, so she wouldn't even try. It turned out that Jaypan fell in the lake and came within a very narrow limit of drowning.

So Mama trots in. Lifts up the lid and says, "H'm! Not very good for your Uncle Rondo in his precarious condition, I must say. Or poor little adopted Shirley-T. Shame on you!"

That made me tired. I says, "Well, Stella-Rondo had better thank her lucky stars it was her instead of me came trotting in with that very peculiar-looking child. Now if it had been me that trotted in from Illinois and brought a peculiar-

1. A chain of variety stores.

looking child or two, I shudder to think of the reception I'd of got, much less controlled the diet of an entire family."

"But you must remember, Sister, that you were never married to Mr. Whitaker in the first place and didn't go up to Illinois to live," says Mama, shaking a spoon in my face. "If you had I would of been just as overjoyed to see you and your little adopted girl as I was to see Stella-Rondo, when you wound up with your separation and came on back home."

"You would not," I says.

"Don't contradict me, I would," says Mama.

But I said she couldn't convince me though she talked till she was blue in the face. Then I said, "Besides, you know as well as I do that that child is not adopted."

"She most certainly is adopted," says Mama, stiff as a poker.

I says, "Why, Mama, Stella-Rondo had her just as sure as anything in this world, and just too stuck up to admit it."

"Why, Sister," said Mama. "Here I thought we were going to have a pleasant Fourth of July, and you start right out not believing a word your own baby sister tells you!"

"Just like Cousin Annie Flo. Went to her grave denying the facts of life," I reminded Mama.

"I told you if you ever mentioned Annie Flo's name I'd slap your face," says Mama, and slaps my face.

"All right, you wait and see," I says.

"I," says Mama, "*I* prefer to take my children's word for anything when it's humanly possible." You ought to see Mama, she weighs two hundred pounds and has real tiny feet.

Just then something perfectly horrible occurred to me.

"Mama," I says, "can that child talk?" I simply had to whisper! "Mama, I wonder if that child can be—you know—in any way? Do you realize?" I says, "that she hasn't spoke one single, solitary word to a human being up to this minute? This is the way she looks," I says, and I looked like this.

Well, Mama and I just stood there and stared at each other. It was horrible!

"I remember well that Joe Whitaker frequently drank like a fish," says Mama. "I believed to my soul he drank *chemicals.*" And without another word she marches to the foot of the stairs and calls Stella-Rondo.

"Stella-Rondo? O-o-o-o-o! Stella-Rondo!"

"What?" says Stella-Rondo from upstairs. Not even the grace to get up off the bed.

"Can that child of yours talk?" asks Mama.

Stella-Rondo says, "Can she what?"

"Talk! Talk!" says Mama. "Burdyburdyburdyburdy!"

So Stella-Rondo yells back, "Who says she can't talk?"

"Sister says so," says Mama.

"You didn't have to tell me, I know whose word of honor don't mean a thing in this house," says Stella-Rondo.

And in a minute the loudest Yankee voice I ever heard in my life yells out, "OE'm Pop-OE the Sailor-r-r-r Ma-a-an!" and then somebody jumps up and down in the upstairs hall. In another second the house would of fallen down.

"Not only talks, she can tap-dance!" calls Stella-Rondo. "Which is more than some people I won't name can do."

"Why, the little precious darling thing!" Mama says, so surprised. "Just as smart as she can be!" Starts talking baby talk right there. Then she turns on me. "Sister, you ought to be thoroughly ashamed! Run upstairs this instant and apologize to Stella-Rondo and Shirley-T."

"Apologize for what?" I says. "I merely wondered if the child was normal, that's all. Now that she's proved she is, why, I have nothing further to say."

But Mama just turned on her heel and flew out, furious. She ran right upstairs and hugged the baby. She believed it was adopted. Stella-Rondo hadn't done a thing but turn her against me from upstairs while I stood there helpless over the hot stove. So that made Mama, Papa-Daddy, and the baby all on Stella-Rondo's side.

Next, Uncle Rondo.

I must say that Uncle Rondo has been marvelous to me at various times in the past and I was completely unprepared to be made to jump out of my skin, the way it turned out. Once Stella-Rondo did something perfectly horrible to him—broke a chain letter from Flanders Field[2]—and he took the radio back he had given her and gave it to me. Stella-Rondo was furious! For six months we all had to call her Stella instead of Stella-Rondo, or she wouldn't answer. I always thought Uncle Rondo had all the brains of the entire family. Another time he sent me to Mammoth Cave[3] with all expenses paid.

But this would be the day he was drinking that prescription, the Fourth of July.

So at supper Stella-Rondo speaks up and says she thinks Uncle Rondo ought to try to eat a little something. So finally Uncle Rondo said he would try a little cold biscuits and ketchup, but that was all. So *she* brought it to him.

"Do you think it wise to disport with ketchup in Stella-Rondo's flesh-colored kimono?" I says. Trying to be considerate! If Stella-Rondo couldn't watch out for her trousseau, somebody had to.

"Any objections?" asks Uncle Rondo, just about to pour out all of the ketchup.

"Don't mind what she says, Uncle Rondo," says Stella-Rondo. "Sister has been devoting this solid afternoon to sneering out my bedroom window at the way you look."

"What's that?" says Uncle Rondo. Uncle Rondo has got the most terrible temper in the world. Anything is liable to make him tear the house down if it comes at the wrong time.

So Stella-Rondo says, "Sister says, 'Uncle Rondo certainly does look like a fool in that pink kimono!' "

Do you remember who it was really said that?

Uncle Rondo spills out all the ketchup and jumps out of his chair and tears off the kimono and throws it down on the dirty floor and puts his foot on it. It

2. American military cemetery in Belgium, established after World War I. 3. Popular tourist attraction in Kentucky.

had to be sent all the way to Jackson to the cleaners and repleated.

"So that's your opinion of your Uncle Rondo, is it?" he says. "I look like a fool, do I? Well, that's the last straw. A whole day in this house with nothing to do, and then to hear you come out with a remark like that behind my back!"

"I didn't say any such thing, Uncle Rondo," I says, "and I'm not saying who did, either. Why, I think you look all right. Just try to take care of yourself and not talk and eat at the same time," I says. "I think you better go lie down."

"Lie down my foot," says Uncle Rondo. I ought to of known by that he was fixing to do something perfectly horrible.

So he didn't do anything that night in the precarious state he was in—just played Casino with Mama and Stella-Rondo and Shirley-T. and gave Shirley-T. a nickel with a head on both sides. It tickled her nearly to death, and she called him "Papa." But at 6:30 A.M. the next morning, he threw a whole five-cent package of some unsold one-inch firecrackers from the store as hard as he could into my bedroom and they every one went off. Not one bad one in the string. Anybody else, there'd be one that wouldn't go off.

Well, I'm just terrible susceptible to noise of any kind, the doctor has always told me I was the most sensitive person he had ever seen in his whole life, and I was simply prostrated. I couldn't eat! People tell me they heard it as far as the cemetery, and old Aunt Jep Patterson, that had been holding her own so good, thought it was Judgment Day and she was going to meet her whole family. It's usually so quiet here.

And I'll tell you it didn't take me any longer than a minute to make up my mind what to do. There I was with the whole entire house on Stella-Rondo's side and turned against me. If I have anything at all I have pride.

So I just decided I'd go straight down to the P.O. There's plenty of room there in the back, I says to myself.

Well! I made no bones about letting the family catch on to what I was up to. I didn't try to conceal it.

The first thing they knew, I marched in where they were all playing Old Maid and pulled the electric oscillating fan out by the plug, and everything got real hot. Next I snatched the pillow I'd done the needlepoint on right off the davenport from behind Papa-Daddy. He went "Ugh!" I beat Stella-Rondo up the stairs and finally found my charm bracelet in her bureau drawer under a picture of Nelson Eddy.[4]

"So that's the way the land lies," says Uncle Rondo. There he was, piecing on the ham. "Well, Sister, I'll be glad to donate my army cot if you got any place to set it up, providing you'll leave right this minute and let me get some peace." Uncle Rondo was in France.

"Thank you kindly for the cot and 'peace' is hardly the word I would select if I had to resort to firecrackers at 6:30 A.M. in a young girl's bedroom," I says to him. "And as to where I intend to go, you seem to forget my position as postmistress of China Grove, Mississippi," I says. "I've always got the P.O."

Well, that made them all sit up and take notice.

4. Star of many Hollywood musicals (1901–1967).

I went out front and started digging up some four-o'clocks to plant around the P.O.

"Ah-ah-ah!" says Mama, raising the window. "Those happen to be my four-o'clocks. Everything planted in that star is mine. I've never known you to make anything grow in your life."

"Very well," I says. "But I take the fern. Even you, Mama, can't stand there and deny that I'm the one watered that fern. And I happen to know where I can send in a box top and get a packet of one thousand mixed seeds, no two the same kind, free."

"Oh, where?" Mama wants to know.

But I says, "Too late. You 'tend to your house, and I'll 'tend to mine. You hear things like that all the time if you know how to listen to the radio. Perfectly marvelous offers. Get anything you want free."

So I hope to tell you I marched in and got that radio, and they could of all bit a nail in two, especially Stella-Rondo, that it used to belong to, and she well knew she couldn't get it back, I'd sue for it like a shot. And I very politely took the sewing-machine motor I helped pay the most on to give Mama for Christmas back in 1929, and a good big calendar, with the first-aid remedies on it. The thermometer and the Hawaiian ukulele certainly were rightfully mine, and I stood on the step-ladder and got all my watermelon-rind preserves and every fruit and vegetable I'd put up, every jar. Then I began to pull the tacks out of the bluebird wall vases on the archway to the dining room.

"Who told you you could have those, Miss Priss?" says Mama, fanning as hard as she could.

"I bought 'em and I'll keep track of 'em," I says. "I'll tack 'em up one on each side of the post-office window, and you can see 'em when you come to ask me for your mail, if you're so dead to see 'em."

"Not I! I'll never darken the door to that post office again if I live to be a hundred," Mama says. "Ungrateful child! After all the money we spent on you at the Normal."

"Me either," says Stella-Rondo. "You can just let my mail lie there and *rot*, for all I care. I'll never come and relieve you of a single, solitary piece."

"I should worry," I says. "And who you think's going to sit down and write you all those big fat letters and postcards, by the way? Mr. Whitaker? Just because he was the only man ever dropped down in China Grove and you got him—unfairly—is he going to sit down and write you a lengthy correspondence after you come home giving no rhyme nor reason whatsoever for your separation and no explanation for the presence of that child? I may not have your brilliant mind, but I fail to see it."

So Mama says, "Sister, I've told you a thousand times that Stella-Rondo simply got homesick, and this child is far too big to be hers," and she says, "Now, why don't you just sit down and play Casino?"

Then Shirley-T. sticks out her tongue at me in this perfectly horrible way. She has no more manners than the man in the moon. I told her she was going to cross her eyes like that some day and they'd stick.

"It's too late to stop me now," I says. "You should have tried that yesterday.

I'm going to the P.O. and the only way you can possibly see me is to visit me there."

So Papa-Daddy says, "You'll never catch me setting foot in that post office, even if I should take a notion into my head to write a letter some place." He says, "I won't have you reachin' out of that little old window with a pair of shears and cuttin' off any beard of mine. I'm too smart for you!"

"We all are," says Stella-Rondo.

But I said, "If you're so smart, where's Mr. Whitaker?"

So then Uncle Rondo says, "I'll thank you from now on to stop reading all the orders I get on postcards and telling everybody in China Grove what you think is the matter with them," but I says, "I draw my own conclusions and will continue in the future to draw them." I says,"If people want to write their innermost secrets on penny postcards, there's nothing in the wide world you can do about it, Uncle Rondo."

"And if you think we'll ever *write* another postcard you're sadly mistaken," says Mama.

"Cutting off your nose to spite your face then," I says. "But if you're all determined to have no more to do with the U.S. mail, think of this: What will Stella-Rondo do now, if she wants to tell Mr. Whitaker to come after her?"

"Wah!" says Stella-Rondo. I knew she'd cry. She had a conniption fit right there in the kitchen.

"It will be interesting to see how long she holds out," I says. "And now—I am leaving."

"Good-bye," says Uncle Rondo.

"Oh, I declare," says Mama, "to think that a family of mine should quarrel on the Fourth of July, or the day after, over Stella-Rondo leaving old Mr. Whitaker and having the sweetest little adopted child! It looks like we'd all be glad!"

"Wah!" says Stella-Rondo, and has a fresh conniption fit.

"He left *her*—you mark my words," I says. "That's Mr. Whitaker. I know Mr. Whitaker. After all, I knew him first. I said from the beginning he'd up and leave her. I foretold every single thing that's happened."

"Where did he go?" asks Mama.

"Probably to the North Pole, if he knows what's good for him," I says.

But Stella-Rondo just bawled and wouldn't say another word. She flew to her room and slammed the door.

"Now look what you've gone and done, Sister," says Mama. "You go apologize."

"I haven't the time, I'm leaving," I says.

"Well, what are you waiting around for?" asks Uncle Rondo.

So I just picked up the kitchen clock and marched off, without saying, "Kiss my foot," or anything, and never did tell Stella-Rondo good-bye.

There was a nigger girl going along on a little wagon right in front.

"Nigger girl," I says, "come help me haul these things down the hill, I'm going to live in the post office."

Took her nine trips in her express wagon. Uncle Rondo came out on the porch and threw her a nickel.

And that's the last I've laid eyes on any of my family or my family laid eyes on me for five solid days and nights. Stella-Rondo may be telling the most horrible tales in the world about Mr. Whitaker, but I haven't heard them. As I tell everybody, I draw my own conclusions.

But oh, I like it here. It's ideal, as I've been saying. You see, I've got everything cater-cornered, the way I like it. Hear the radio? All the war news. Radio, sewing machine, book ends, ironing board and that great big piano lamp—peace, that's what I like. Butter-bean vines planted all along the front where the strings are.

Of course, there's not much mail. My family are naturally the main people in China Grove, and if they prefer to vanish from the face of the earth, for all the mail they get or the mail they write, why, I'm not going to open my mouth. Some of the folks here in town are taking up for me and some turned against me. I know which is which. There are always people who will quit buying stamps just to get on the right side of Papa-Daddy.

But here I am, and here I'll stay. I want the world to know I'm happy.

And if Stella-Rondo should come to me this minute, on bended knees, and attempt to explain the incidents of her life with Mr. Whitaker, I'd simply put my fingers in both my ears and refuse to listen.

# A Worn Path

It was December—a bright frozen day in the early morning. Far out in the country there was an old Negro woman with her head tied in a red rag, coming along a path through the pinewoods. Her name was Phoenix Jackson. She was very old and small and she walked slowly in the dark pine shadows, moving a little from side to side in her steps, with the balanced heaviness and lightness of a pendulum in a grandfather clock. She carried a thin, small cane made from an umbrella, and with this she kept tapping the frozen earth in front of her. This made a grave and persistent noise in the still air, that seemed meditative like the chirping of a solitary little bird.

She wore a dark striped dress reaching down to her shoe tops, and an equally long apron of bleached sugar sacks, with a full pocket: all neat and tidy, but every time she took a step she might have fallen over her shoelaces, which dragged from her unlaced shoes. She looked straight ahead. Her eyes were blue with age. Her skin had a pattern all its own of numberless branching wrinkles and as though a whole little tree stood in the middle of her forehead, but a golden color ran underneath, and the two knobs of her cheeks were illumined by a yellow burning under the dark. Under the red rag her hair came down on her neck in the frailest of ringlets, still black, and with an odor like copper.

Now and then there was a quivering in the thicket. Old Phoenix said, "Out of my way, all you foxes, owls, beetles, jack rabbits, coons and wild animals! . . . Keep out from under these feet, little bob-whites. . . . Keep the big wild hogs out of my path. Don't let none of those come running my direction. I got a long way." Under her small black-freckled hand her cane, limber as a buggy whip, would switch at the brush as if to rouse up any hiding things.

On she went. The woods were deep and still. The sun made the pine needles almost too bright to look at, up where the wind rocked. The cones dropped as light as feathers. Down in the hollow was the mourning dove—it was not too late for him.

The path ran up a hill. "Seem like there is chains about my feet, time I get this far," she said, in the voice of argument old people keep to use with themselves. "Something always take a hold of me on this hill—pleads I should stay."

After she got to the top she turned and gave a full, severe look behind her where she had come. "Up through pines," she said at length. "Now down through oaks."

Her eyes opened their widest, and she started down gently. But before she got to the bottom of the hill a bush caught her dress.

Her fingers were busy and intent, but her skirts were full and long, so that before she could pull them free in one place they were caught in another. It was not possible to allow the dress to tear. "I in the thorny bush," she said. "Thorns, you doing your appointed work. Never want to let folks pass, no sir. Old eyes thought you was a pretty little *green* bush."

Finally, trembling all over, she stood free, and after a moment dared to stoop for her cane.

"Sun so high!" she cried, leaning back and looking, while the thick tears went over her eyes. "The time getting all gone here."

At the foot of this hill was a place where a log was laid across the creek.

"Now comes the trial," said Phoenix.

Putting her right foot out, she mounted the log and shut her eyes. Lifting her skirt, leveling her cane fiercely before her, like a festival figure in some parade, she began to march across. Then she opened her eyes and she was safe on the other side.

"I wasn't as old as I thought," she said.

But she sat down to rest. She spread her skirts on the bank around her and folded her hands over her knees. Up above her was a tree in a pearly cloud of mistletoe. She did not dare to close her eyes, and when a little boy brought her a plate with a slice of marble-cake on it she spoke to him. "That would be acceptable," she said. But when she went to take it there was just her own hand in the air.

So she left that tree, and had to go through a barbed-wire fence. There she had to creep and crawl, spreading her knees and stretching her fingers like a baby trying to climb the steps. But she talked loudly to herself: she could not let her dress be torn now, so late in the day, and she could not pay for having her arm or her leg sawed off if she got caught fast where she was.

At last she was safe through the fence and risen up out in the clearing. Big dead trees, like black men with one arm, were standing in the purple stalks of the withered cotton field. There sat a buzzard.

"Who you watching?"

In the furrow she made her way along.

"Glad this not the season for bulls," she said, looking sideways, "and the good Lord made his snakes to curl up and sleep in the winter. A pleasure I don't see no two-headed snake coming around that tree, where it come once. It took a while to get by him, back in the summer."

She passed through the old cotton and went into a field of dead corn. It whispered and shook and was taller than her head. "Through the maze now," she said, for there was no path.

Then there was something tall, black, and skinny there, moving before her.

At first she took it for a man. It could have been a man dancing in the field. But she stood still and listened, and it did not make a sound. It was as silent as a ghost.

"Ghost," she said sharply, "who be you the ghost of? For I have heard of nary death close by."

But there was no answer—only the ragged dancing in the wind.

She shut her eyes, reached out her hand, and touched a sleeve. She found a coat and inside that an emptiness, cold as ice.

"You scarecrow," she said. Her face lighted. "I ought to be shut up for good," she said with laughter. "My senses is gone. I too old. I the oldest people I ever know. Dance, old scarecrow," she said, "while I dancing with you."

She kicked her foot over the furrow, and with mouth drawn down, shook her head once or twice in a little strutting way. Some husks blew down and whirled in streamers about her skirts.

Then she went on, parting her way from side to side with the cane, through the whispering field. At last she came to the end, to a wagon track where the silver grass blew between the red ruts. The quail were walking around like pullets, seeming all dainty and unseen.

"Walk pretty," she said. "This the easy place. This the easy going."

She followed the track, swaying through the quiet bare fields, through the little strings of trees silver in their dead leaves, past cabins silver from weather, with the doors and windows boarded shut, all like old women under a spell sitting there. "I walking in their sleep," she said, nodding her head vigorously.

In a ravine she went where a spring was silently flowing through a hollow log. Old Phoenix bent and drank. "Sweet-gum makes the water sweet," she said, and drank more. "Nobody know who made this well, for it was here when I was born."

The track crossed a swampy part where the moss hung as white as lace from every limb. "Sleep on, alligators, and blow your bubbles." Then the track went into the road.

Deep, deep the road went down between the high green-colored banks. Overhead the live-oaks met, and it was as dark as a cave.

A black dog with a lolling tongue came up out of the weeds by the ditch. She was meditating, and not ready, and when he came at her she only hit him a little with her cane. Over she went in the ditch, like a little puff of milkweed.

Down there, her senses drifted away. A dream visited her, and she reached her hand up, but nothing reached down and gave her a pull. So she lay there and presently went to talking. "Old woman," she said to herself, "that black dog come up out of the weeds to stall you off, and now there he sitting on his fine tail, smiling at you."

A white man finally came along and found her—a hunter, a young man, with his dog on a chain.

"Well, Granny!" he laughed. "What are you doing there?"

"Lying on my back like a June-bug waiting to be turned over, mister," she said, reaching up her hand.

He lifted her up, gave her a swing in the air, and set her down. "Anything broken, Granny?"

"No sir, them old dead weeds is springy enough," said Phoenix, when she had got her breath. "I thank you for your trouble."

"Where do you live, Granny?" he asked, while the two dogs were growling at each other.

"Away back yonder, sir, behind the ridge. You can't even see it from here."

"On your way home?"

"No sir, I going to town."

"Why, that's too far! That's as far as I walk when I come out myself, and I get something for my trouble." He patted the stuffed bag he carried, and there hung down a little closed claw. It was one of the bob-whites, with its beak hooked bitterly to show it was dead. "Now you go on home, Granny!"

"I bound to go to town, mister," said Phoenix. "The time come around."

He gave another laugh, filling the whole landscape. "I know you old colored people! Wouldn't miss going to town to see Santa Claus!"

But something held old Phoenix very still. The deep lines in her face went into a fierce and different radiation. Without warning, she had seen with her own eyes a flashing nickel fall out of the man's pocket onto the ground.

"How old are you, Granny?" he was saying.

"There's no telling, mister," she said, "no telling."

Then she gave a little cry and clapped her hands and said, "Git on away from here, dog! Look! Look at that dog!" She laughed as if in admiration. "He ain't scared of nobody. He a big black dog." She whispered, "Sic him!"

"Watch me get rid of that cur," said the man. "Sic him, Pete! Sic him!"

Phoenix heard the dogs fighting, and heard the man running and throwing sticks. She even heard a gunshot. But she was slowly bending forward by that time, further and further forward, the lid stretched down over her eyes, as if she were doing this in her sleep. Her chin was lowered almost to her knees. The yellow palm of her hand came out from the fold of her apron. Her fingers slid down and along the ground under the piece of money with the grace and care they would have in lifting an egg from under a setting hen. Then she slowly straightened up, she stood erect, and the nickel was in her apron pocket. A bird flew by. Her lips moved. "God watching me the whole time. I come to stealing."

The man came back, and his own dog panted about them. "Well, I scared him off that time," he said, and then he laughed and lifted his gun and pointed it at Phoenix.

She stood straight and faced him.

"Doesn't the gun scare you?" he said, still pointing it.

"No, sir, I seen plenty go off closer by, in my day, and for less than what I done," she said, holding utterly still.

He smiled, and shouldered the gun. "Well, Granny," he said, "you must be a hundred years old, and scared of nothing. I'd give you a dime if I had any money with me. But you take my advice and stay home, and nothing will happen to you."

"I bound to go on my way, mister," said Phoenix. She inclined her head in the red rag. Then they went in different directions, but she could hear the gun shooting again and again over the hill.

She walked on. The shadows hung from the oak trees to the road like curtains. Then she smelled wood-smoke, and smelled the river, and she saw a steeple and the cabins on their steep steps. Dozens of little black children whirled around her. There ahead was Natchez shining. Bells were ringing. She walked on.

In the paved city it was Christmas time. There were red and green electric lights strung and crisscrossed everywhere, and all turned on in the daytime. Old Phoenix would have been lost if she had not distrusted her eyesight and depended on her feet to know where to take her.

She paused quietly on the sidewalk where people were passing by. A lady came along in the crowd, carrying an armful of red-, green- and silver-wrapped presents; she gave off perfume like the red roses in hot summer, and Phoenix stopped her.

"Please, missy, will you lace up my shoe?" She held up her foot.

"What do you want, Grandma?"

"See my shoe," said Phoenix. "Do all right for out in the country, but wouldn't look right to go in a big building."

"Stand still then, Grandma," said the lady. She put her packages down on the sidewalk beside her and laced and tied both shoes tightly.

"Can't lace 'em with a cane," said Phoenix. "Thank you, missy. I doesn't mind asking a nice lady to tie up my shoe, when I gets out on the street."

Moving slowly and from side to side, she went into the big building, and into the tower of steps, where she walked up and around and around until her feet knew to stop.

She entered a door, and there she saw nailed up on the wall the document that had been stamped with the gold seal and framed in the gold frame, which matched the dream that was hung up in her head.

"Here I be," she said. There was a fixed and ceremonial stiffness over her body.

"A charity case, I suppose," said an attendant who sat at the desk before her.

But Phoenix only looked above her head. There was sweat on her face, the wrinkles in her skin shone like a bright net.

"Speak up, Grandma," the woman said. "What's your name? We must have your history, you know. Have you been here before? What seems to be the trouble with you?"

Old Phoenix only gave a twitch to her face as if a fly were bothering her.

"Are you deaf?" cried the attendant.

But then the nurse came in.

"Oh, that's just old Aunt Phoenix," she said. "She doesn't come for herself—she has a little grandson. She makes these trips just as regular as clockwork. She lives away back off the Old Natchez Trace." She bent down. "Well, Aunt Phoenix, why don't you just take a seat? We won't keep you standing after your long trip." She pointed.

The old woman sat down, bolt upright in the chair.

"Now, how is the boy?" asked the nurse.

Old Phoenix did not speak.

"I said, how is the boy?"

But Phoenix only waited and stared straight ahead, her face very solemn and withdrawn into rigidity.

"Is his throat any better?" asked the nurse. "Aunt Phoenix, don't you hear me? Is your grandson's throat any better since the last time you came for the medicine?"

With her hands on her knees, the old woman waited, silent, erect and motionless, just as if she were in armor.

"You mustn't take up our time this way, Aunt Phoenix," the nurse said. "Tell us quickly about your grandson, and get it over. He isn't dead, is he?"

At last there came a flicker and then a flame of comprehension across her face, and she spoke.

"My grandson. It was my memory had left me. There I sat and forgot why I made my long trip."

"Forgot?" The nurse frowned. "After you came so far?"

Then Phoenix was like an old woman begging a dignified forgiveness for waking up frightened in the night. "I never did go to school, I was too old at the Surrender,"[1] she said in a soft voice. "I'm an old woman without an education. It was my memory fail me. My little grandson, he is just the same, and I forgot it in the coming."

"Throat never heals, does it?" said the nurse, speaking in a loud, sure voice to old Phoenix. By now she had a card with something written on it, a little list. "Yes. Swallowed lye. When was it?—January—two-three years ago—"

Phoenix spoke unmasked now. "No, missy, he not dead, he just the same. Every little while his throat begin to close up again, and he not able to swallow. He not get his breath. He not able to help himself. So the time come around, and I go on another trip for the soothing medicine."

"All right. The doctor said as long as you came to get it, you could have it," said the nurse. "But it's an obstinate case."

"My little grandson, he sit up there in the house all wrapped up, waiting by himself," Phoenix went on. "We is the only two left in the world. He suffer and it don't seem to put him back at all. He got a sweet look. He going to last. He wear a little patch quilt and peep out holding his mouth open like a little bird. I remembers so plain now. I not going to forget him again, no, the whole enduring time. I could tell him from all the others in creation."

1. The surrender of General Robert E. Lee (1807–1870) of the Confederacy on April 9, 1865, to General Ulysses S. Grant (1822–1885) of the Union, thus ending the Civil War.

"All right." The nurse was trying to hush her now. She brought her a bottle of medicine. "Charity," she said, making a check mark in a book.

Old Phoenix held the bottle close to her eyes, and then carefully put it into her pocket.

"I thank you," she said.

"It's Christmas time, Grandma," said the attendant. "Could I give you a few pennies out of my purse?"

"Five pennies is a nickel," said Phoenix stiffly.

"Here's a nickel," said the attendant.

Phoenix rose carefully and held out her hand. She received the nickel and then fished the other nickel out of her pocket and laid it beside the new one. She stared at her palm closely, with her head on one side.

Then she gave a tap with her cane on the floor.

"This is what come to me to do," she said. "I going to the store and buy my child a little windmill they sells, made out of paper. He going to find it hard to believe there such a thing in the world. I'll march myself back where he waiting, holding it straight up in this hand."

She lifted her free hand, gave a little nod, turned around, and walked out of the doctor's office. Then her slow step began on the stairs, going down.

## SUSAN DODD on *A Worn Path*

*But who is she when she's at home?* an Irish friend asks when I identify someone by name and occupation. Miss Eudora, no just-the-facts-ma'am kind of writer, has made it her serious lifelong business to let us in on just who her characters are when they're at home. Has she ever done so more clearly, more beautifully, more *deeply* than with Phoenix Jackson?

"A Worn Path" is, on the face of it, a simple, straightforward story. If it were a picture hanging in a museum, the canvas would be of modest dimension, would stand for no ornate gilt frame making a spectacle of it. No call for a viewer's eye to dart about, sorting out the picture's "busyness." No, "A Worn Path" would simply pull you inside it, keep you there, and when you came back out you'd sense you'd been long gone and far.

Miss Eudora doesn't *tell* us, of course, who Phoenix Jackson is when she's at home. Instead, she sends us packing on a rough and gloried hike in the company of a woman at home in her own skin. Alone though she is, Phoenix goes utterly *accompanied:* the sounds and smells and sights, the very air, are her sidekicks. This old woman and her surroundings fit together in a natural and familiar embrace. We take measure of Phoenix Jackson not by how the world receives her (though that comes eventually), but by the very span of her as she throws herself open to the world. Her gaze is dead ahead, her risky traverse of the creek a parade march. Every obstacle comes in for back talk. Not even hallucination can scramble her sense of direction.

To read "A Worn Path" is to have the seams of one's soul let out. The story's compassion enlarges our own; that is its greatness. Its *writing* is what brings that about, though, word by single word. Words are what paint Phoenix alive for the eye: the red head rag and striped dress and the cane fashioned from an umbrella. Dwell on the plain and perfect accuracy of the verbs (she *switches at* the brush to *rouse up* any hiding things . . . something in the hill *pleads* she should stay). Study the scrupulous choice of adjectives: the *grave* and *persistent* noise of her cane tapping the frozen earth . . . and oh, those *frailest* ringlets of her still-black hair. Listen to the perfect pitch of the dialogue, how the sounds of the words linger, ever deepening, after the simple saying: *Now comes the trial*. And: *The time come around*. And: *This is what come to me to do*.

And sometime, maybe some morning when you can't think how to begin, trace the canny route of similes running through "A Worn Path." No sore thumbs sticking out here, only the ordinary landscape of a woman's life. But tucked in among the domestic details (shadows hanging like curtains, babies and clocks and laying hens) and the expected particulars of the natural world (birds and milkweed and mistletoe) come glimpses of a life lived on intimate terms with the whip's lash, the chain's drag, imagination's (or is it memory's?) all-too-ready reference to black bodies dismembered and maimed.

Long before we learn of the singular sorrow that awaits her at home, by such suggestive images are we given to know who Phoenix Jackson is there, to know *precisely*.

# W. D. Wetherell

*Wetherell (1948– ) was born in New York City. His books include* The Man Who Loved Levittown *(1985);* Chekhov's Sister *(1990); and his most recent collection of stories,* Wherever That Great Heart May Be *(1996). He has received the Drue Heinz Literature Prize and the National Magazine Award for Fiction and currently holds the Strauss Living Award from the American Academy of Arts and Letters.*

## The Man Who Loved Levittown

You realize what I had to do to get this place? It was thirty-odd years ago come July. I'm just out of the Army. Two kids, twins on their way, a wife who's younger than I am, just as naive, just as crazy hopeful. We're living in the old neighborhood with my folks four to a room. All along I've got this idea. Airplanes. P-40s, these great big 20s. We're slogging through Saipan, they're flying over it. DiMaria, I tell myself, this war is going to end, when it does that's where you want to be, up there in the blue not down here in the brown. Ever since I'm a kid I'm good with machines, what I do is figure I'll get a job making them. Grumman. Republic. Airborne. They're all out there on Long Island. I tell Kathy to watch the kids, I'll be back tonight, wish me luck. I borrow the old man's Ford, out I go. Brooklyn Bridge, Jamaica Avenue, Southern State, and I'm there.

Potato fields. Nothing but. French-fried heaven, not another car in sight. I stop at a diner for coffee. Farmers inside look me over like I'm the tax man come to collect. Bitter. Talking about how they were being run off their places by these new housing developments you saw advertised in the paper, which made me mad because here I am a young guy just trying to get started, what were we supposed to do . . . live on East Thirteenth Street the rest of our lives? The being run off part was pure phooey anyhow, because they were making plenty on it, they never had it so good. But hearing them talk made me curious enough to drive around a little exploring.

Sure enough, here's this farmhouse all boarded up. Out in front is an ancient Chevy piled to the gunwales with old spring beds, pots and pans. Dust Bowl, Okies, *Grapes of Wrath* . . . just like that. I drive up to ask directions half expecting Marjorie Main. Instead there's this old man climbing up to the top of the pile. He's having a hell of a time getting up there. Once he does he stands with his hand shielding his eyes looking around the horizon like someone saying good-bye.

Maybe I'm just imagining it now but it seems to me it was so flat and smooth those days even from where I stood on the ground I could see just as far as he could . . . see the entire Island, right across the entire thing. Out to Montauk with waves breaking atop the rocks so green and bright they made me squint. Back this way over acres of pine trees, maybe one, maybe two lonely railroad tracks, nothing else except lots of ospreys which were still around those days. Then he turns, I turn, we look over to where the Jones Beach water tower is jutting up like the Leaning Tower of Pisa. Just this side of it the Great South Bay is wall-to-wall scallops and clams. You look left up the other way toward the North Shore there's these old ivy-covered mansions being torn down, pieces of confetti, broken champagne bottles all over the lawn. I have to squint a little now . . . I can just make out the shore of the Sound with all these sandy beaches that had "No Trespassing" signs on them, only a man in a yellow vest is walking along now ripping them down . . . not two seconds later the beach is crowded with little kids splashing in the waves. Then after that we both look the other way back toward New York . . . the old man tottering up there in the breeze . . . over these abandoned hangars at Roosevelt Field where everybody took off to Europe alone from back in the twenties, then out toward where the skyscrapers are in the distance. I see the Empire State Building . . . for some crazy reason I wave. Then in a little closer over one or two small villages, acres of potato fields, and no matter which way you look . . . Sound side, Bay side, South Shore North Shore . . . there's the sound of hammers, the smell of sawdust, little houses going up in clusters, carpenters working bare-chested in the sun. The old man is looking all this over, then looks right at me, you know what he says? "I hope it poisons you!" With that he fell off the bundle, his son had to prop him back up, they drove away in a cloud of dust.

Fine. I drive down the road a little farther, here are these new houses up close. Small ones. Lots of mud. Old potatoes sticking out of it like dried-up turds. Broken blocks off two-by-fours. Nails, bits of shingle. In front of each house or half house or quarter house is a little lawn. Fuzzy green grass. Baby grass. At every corner is an empty post waiting for a street name to be fitted in the slot on top. A man comes along in a jeep, shuffles through the signs, scratches his head, sticks in one says LINDBERGH, drives off. Down the street is a Quonset hut with a long line of men waiting out in front, half of them still in uniform. Waiting for jobs I figure, like in the Depression . . . here we go again. But here's what happens. A truck comes along, stops in front of the house, half a dozen men pile out . . . in fifteen minutes they've put in a bathroom. Pop! Off they go to the next house, just in time, too, because here comes another truck with the kitchen. Pop! In goes the kitchen. They move on one house, here comes the electricians. Pop! Pop! Pop! the house goes up.

There's no one around except this guy in overalls planting sticks in the little brown patches stamped out of the grass. "My name's DiMaria," I tell him. "What's yours?" "Bill Levitt," he says. "And what's the name of this place anyhow?" "Levittown." And then it finally dawns on me. What these men are lined up for isn't work, it's homes!

"How much does one of these babies cost?" I ask him casually. He picks at his nose, leans his shovel against the tree. "Seven thousand," he says, looking right at me. "One hundred dollars down." "Oh yeah?" I say, still casual. But I kind of half turn, take out my wallet, take a peek inside. "I only have eighty-three." He looks me over. "You a veteran?" "You bet. Four years' worth, I don't miss it at all either." He calls over to a man helping with the sinks. "Hey, Johnson!" he yells. "Take this guy's money and let him pick out whichever one he wants. Mr. DiMaria," he says, shaking my hand. "You've just bought yourself a house."

I will never until the day I die forget the expression on Kathy's face when I got back that night. Not only have I bought a house but that same afternoon Grumman hires me at three bucks an hour plus overtime. "Honey," I said, "get your things together, let's go, hubba, hubba, we're on our way home!"

I'm not saying it wasn't tough those first years. It was plenty tough. I worked to six most nights, sometimes seven. When I got home I fixed hamburgers for the kids since Kathy was out working herself. Minute she gets home, out I go pumping gas on the turnpike for mortgage money. Ten years we did that. But what made it seem easier was that everyone else on Lindbergh was more or less in the same boat. Young GIs from old parts of the city somewhere working at the big plants farther out. There were some pretty good men on that block. Scotty. Mike. Hank Zimmer. There wasn't anything we couldn't build or fix between us. I once figured out just among the guys on Lindbergh, let alone Hillcrest, we had enough talent to make ourselves an F-14. You know how complicated an F-14 is? Cabin cruisers, porches, garages . . . you name it, we built it. That's why this little boxes stuff was pure phooey. Sure they were little boxes when we first started. But what did we do? The minute we got our mitts on them we started remodeling them, adding stuff, changing them around.

There wasn't anything we wouldn't do for each other. Babysit, drive someone somewhere, maybe help out with a mortgage payment someone couldn't meet. You talk about Little League. Me and Mike are the ones *invented* it. We got the field for it, organized teams, umpired, managed, coached. Both my boys played; we once had a team to the national finals, we would have won if O'Brien's kid hadn't booted a grounder. But it was nice on summer nights to see dads knocking out flies to their kids, hearing the ball plop into gloves, see the wives sitting there on the lawns talking, maybe watering the lawn. The swimming pool up the block, the shops, the schools. It was nice all those things. People take them for granted nowadays, they had to start somewhere, right?

I'll never forget those years. The fifties. The early sixties. We were all going the same direction . . . thanks to Big Bill Levitt we all had a chance. You talk about dreams. Hell, we had ours. We had ours like nobody before or since ever had theirs. SEVEN THOUSAND BUCKS! ONE HUNDRED DOLLARS DOWN! We were cowboys out there. We were the pioneers.

I'll be damned if I know where the end came from. It was a little after the time I finished putting the sun roof over the porch. Kathy was in the living room yelling, trying to get my attention. "Tommy, come over here quick! Look out the window on Scotty's front lawn!" There planted right smack in the middle is a sign. FOR SALE! You know what my first reaction was? I was scared. Honest to God. I can't tell you why, but seeing that sign scared me. It scared me so much I ran into the bathroom, felt like being sick. Steady, DiMaria, I said. It's a joke like the time he put flounders under the hubcaps. Ginger needed a walk anyway, I snap a collar on her, out we go.

"So, Scotty, you kidding or what?" I say. Scotty just smiles. "We're pulling up, moving to Florida." "You mean you're taking a vacation down there? Whereabouts, Vero Beach?" He shakes his head. "Nope, Tommy. For good. I'm retiring. Twenty-five years of this is enough for anyone. The kids are on their own now. The house is too big for just the two of us. Carol and I are heading south. Thirty-nine thousand we're asking. Thirty-nine thousand! Whoever thought when we bought these shacks they would someday go for that?"

The twenty-five years part stunned me because it was like we'd all started yesterday as far as I was concerned. But the Florida part, that really killed me. Florida was someplace you got oranges from, where the Yanks spent March. But to actually move there?

"Come on, Scotty," I laugh. "You're kidding me, right?" "Nope. This guy is coming to look at the house this afternoon."

A guy named Mapes bought Scotty's place. A young kid worked for the county. I went over and introduced myself. "I've been here twenty-nine years," I said. "I knew Bill Levitt personally." "Who?" he asks. "Big Bill Levitt, the guy this town is named after." "Oh," he says, looking stupid. "I always thought that was an Indian name."

I should have known right there. But being the idiot I am, I take him out behind the house, show him the electricity meter. "Tell you a little secret," I whisper. "Got a screwdriver?"

I'd been helping myself to some surplus voltage ever since I got out there. Everyone on Lindbergh did. We were all practically engineers; when we moved in we couldn't believe it, all this electricity up there, all those phone lines going to waste. It was the land of milk and honey as far as we were concerned; all we had to do was plug in and help ourselves. I'm telling Mapes this but he's standing there looking dubious. "Uh, you sure this is okay?" "You kidding? There's plenty more where that came from. They'll never miss it. Twist that, jig this, weld that there, you're in business." "Oh yeah," he says, but you can tell he doesn't get it because when I hand him the screwdriver he drops it. "Oops!" he giggles. Meantime his bride comes along. Beads. Sandals. No, repeat, NO bra. "Jennifer," he says, "this is Mr. DiMaria from next door." "Call me Tommy, how are you?" The first words out of her mouth, you know what they are? "How many live in your house?" "Uh, two. My wife, myself." She looks me over, puffs on something I don't swear was a Winston. "That's not many for a whole house. If you ever decide to sell my kid sister's getting married. They need a place bad. Let me know next week, will yah?"

That was Mapes. Silver, the sheepherder took over O'Brien's, was even worse. "Hello, welcome to the neighborhood," I said walking across his lawn, my hand out. "That your dog?" he asks, pointing toward Ginger rolling in the pachysandra. "Yeah. Come here, Ginger. Shake the man's hand." "Dogs are supposed to be leashed, mister. If you don't get him off my property in five minutes, I'm calling the pound and having the animal destroyed." With that he walks away.

Welcome to Lindbergh Street.

I'm not saying it was because of that but right about then a lot of old-timers put their houses on the market. It was sad because before, guys like Scotty could at least say they wanted to go to Florida, actually look forward to it. But now? Now the ones who ran out ran out because they were forced to. Taxes up, cost of living, heating oil, you name it. Here we'd had these homes for thirty years, broke our backs paying the mortgages off, you'd think it'd become easier for us now. Forget it. It was *harder*. It was harder keeping them than getting them.

What made it worse was the price everyone was getting. Forty thousand. Fifty thousand. The ones who stayed couldn't handle it anymore thinking they'd only paid seven. The real estate bastards dazzled them into selling even though they didn't want to. That was the sad part of it, seeing them try to convince themselves Florida would be nice. "We're getting a condominium," they'd say, the same somebody told you they were getting a valve bypass or a hysterectomy. "Well, I kind of like fishing," Mike said when he broke the news to me. "Don't they have good fishing down there?" "Sure they have good fishing, Mike," I told him. "Good fishing if you don't mind having your finger sucked by a water moccasin."

You think I'm exaggerating? You expect me to maybe say something good about the place? What if all your friends were taken away from you by coronaries, you wouldn't be too fond of heart disease, right? That's exactly the way I look at Florida. Guys like Buzz and Scotty think they're going to find Paradise down there, they're going to find mosquitoes, snakes, walking catfish, old people, that's it. This guy I know in the plant had his vacation down there. He thought it would be nice, no crime, no muggers. The first night there a Cuban breaks into his trailer, ties him up, rapes his wife, takes everything they had. Florida? You guys can have it. If Ponce de Leon were alive today he'd be living in Levittown.

But anyhow, nature hates a vacuum, the sheepherders moved in, started taking things over. You have to wonder about them to begin with. Here they are starting off where we finished, everything took us so long to get they have right away. They're sad more than anything . . . sadder than the old-timers moving south. You know what these kids who stayed on Long Island know? Shopping centers, that's it. If it's not in a mall they don't know nothing. And talk about dreams, they don't have any. A new stereo? A new Datsun? Call those dreams? Those aren't dreams, those are pacifiers. Popsicles. That's exactly what I feel like telling them. You find your own dream, pal, you're walking on mine. My generation survived the Depression, won the war, got Armstrong to the moon and back. And when I say *we* I'm talking about guys I know, not guys I read about. You think Grumman only makes F-14s? I *worked* on the landing module my last two years. Me, Tommy DiMaria. Nobody knows this but Scotty and me carved our initials on the facing under a transistor panel inside of the cabin. T.DM.S.S.H. right straight to the goddamn moon. But that's the kind of thing *we* did. What will the sheepherders be able to say they did when they get to be our age? . . . Evaded the draft. Bought a Cougar. Jogged.

It's like I told each of my kids when they were teenagers. "This town is where you grow up," I told them, "not where you *end* up." And they didn't either. They're scattered all over the place. I'm proud of them all. The only problem is like when Kathy got sick the last time it was a hell of a job getting everyone together. When I think about Kathy dying you know what I remember? Kennedy Airport. The TWA terminal. Going there to meet each of the kids, trying to figure out plane schedules, time zones, who I'm seeing off, who I'm meeting. The older I get the more I think what the real problem is in this country isn't *what* or *how* or *why* but *where*. *Where*'s the question, the country's so goddamn big. Where in hell do you put yourself in it? Where?

Each of the kids wanted me to move in with them after Kathy died. Candy's a psychologist, she told me I was crazy to live by myself in the suburbs. If it was one thing people in suburbs couldn't stand it was to see someone living alone. It threatened them, they'd do anything to get rid of that reminder the world wasn't created in minimum denominations of two . . . that's the way she talks. But I told her no because the very last thing Kathy said was, Tommy, whatever you do don't give up the house. She was holding my hand, it was late, I was there all by myself not even a nurse. "Tommy, don't give up the house!" "Shh, Kathy," I whispered. "Rest now. I won't ever give it up." She squeezed my hand. I looked around to see if the nurse had come in, but it wasn't her, it was the lady in the next bed mumbling something in her sleep. "I'll never give it up, Kathy," I promised. I bent over. I kissed her. She smiled . . . she closed her eyes and it was like she had gone to sleep.

"Goodbye, Kathy," I said. "Sweet dreams, princess."

It was harder without her. I remember I'm in the back yard fixing up the garden for spring just like I would if she was still there, watching Ginger out of the corner of my eye, when Mapes's wife comes up the driveway. She stands there chewing gum. "I'm sorry about your wife, Mr. DiMaria," she says. "I guess you're going to sell your house now, huh?" When I told her no she acted mad. "We'll see about that!" she says.

Her little boy Ringo runs over to help me like he sometimes did. She pulls him away, stands there clutching him tight to her body like she's protecting him. "Never play with that dirty old man again!" she screams. "You old people think you can keep putting us down all the time! You think you can ask anything for a house we'll pay it on account of we're desperate! What's Janey supposed to do, live in Queens the rest of her life?" She's screaming, getting all worked up. Mapes comes over, looks embarrassed, tries to quiet her down . . . away they go.

A few days later I'm out there again, this time planting beans, when I hear voices coming from the porch. I'm just about to go inside to investigate when this guy in a suit comes around back with a young couple holding hands. "This is the yard!" he says, pointing. "It's a nice yard, good place for kids. Hello doggy, what's your name?" He walks around me like I'm not there, squeezes a tomato, leads them back around front. Ten minutes later they come out of the house. "You'll like it here, it's a good investment. Oh, hello," he says, "you must be the owner. I'm Mr. Charles from Stroud Realty, here's my card, these are the Canadays, they love your house." "Scram!" All three of them jump. "Go on, you heard me! Clear the hell out before I call the cops!" "But I'm showing the property!" the little guy squeaks. I had a hell of a time chasing them off of there.

The pressure really started after that. It was little ways at first. Kids that had been friendly before staying away because their mothers told them to. Finding my garbage can spilled across the lawn. Mail stolen, things like that. One morning there's a knock on the door, this pimple face is standing there holding a briefcase. "Mr. DiMaria?" "That's right, who are you?" "I'm from the county. We've come to assess your home." "It was assessed." He looks at his chart. "Yes, but twenty years ago. I'm sure it still can't be worth just four thousand now can it? Excuse me." He butts his way in, starts feeling the upholstery. He's there five minutes, he comes back to the door. "Nice place you got here, Mr. DiMaria. I can see you put a lot of work into it since we were last here. Let's say forty thousand dollars' worth, shall we? Your taxes will be adjusted accordingly."

"You're crazy!" I yell. I'm about to lose my temper but then I remember something. "Hey, you know D'Amato down at the county executive's office? Him and me grew up together." "Never heard of him," pimple face says, shaking his head. "Well, how about Gus Louis in the sheriff's office?" "Oh, we don't have much to do with them these days I'm afraid." He starts to leave. "Well, you're probably going next door now, right?" "Oh, no," he says. "This is the only house on the block we're checking." "Wait a second!" I yell. "That's bullshit. You're going to Mapes, then Silver or I'm calling my congressman. Discrimination's a crime, pal!" His eyes finally light up. "You mean Mr. Silver? Hell of a nice guy. His brother is my boss. Goodbye, Mr. DiMaria. Have a nice day."

I don't want to give the impression I didn't fight back. I did, because if there's one thing I know about Levittown it's this. People are scared about blacks moving in, only nowadays it isn't blacks, it's drug treatment centers. It terrifies everyone. It terrifies them because all they think about when they're not shopping is property values. So what does DiMaria do? I wait until the next time these sweet Seventh Day whatever ladies come around selling their little pamphlets. I always give them a dime, no one else on the street ever gives them a penny . . . they think the world of me. They're always very polite, a bit crazy. What I did when they rang the doorbell was invite them into the house for some coffee. That was probably enough to give most of the sheepherders a good scare. It's Saturday, they're all out waxing their Camaros, here's two black ladies inside DiMaria's talking about God knows what, maybe thinking to buy it. But what I do is take them outside around back saying I wanted to show them my peach tree. These ladies are so sweet and polite, they're a bit deaf, besides they'll do anything I want.

I point to the side of the house. "This is where we'll put the rehabilitation room!" I say really loud. "Over here we'll have the methadone clinic!" The ladies are nodding, smiling, handing me new pamphlets, I'm slipping them fresh dimes. "AND OVER HERE'S THE ABORTION WING!" I see Mapes and Silver staring at us all upset; if they had a gun they would have shot me.

What really kept me going, though, was Hank Zimmer. He was the last cowboy left besides me. Every once in a while I'd get discouraged, he'd cheer me up, then he'd get discouraged, I'd cheer him up . . . we'd both get discouraged, we'd take it out working on my new den, maybe his. What we used to talk about was how there were no hedges on Lindbergh in the old days, no fences, no locked doors. Everyone's home was your home; we all walked back and forth like it was one big yard.

That was long since done with now. You think the sheepherders would have anything to do with the other sheepherders? It was like the hedges we'd planted, the bushes and trees, had grown up so high they'd cut people off from each other. The only thing they wanted anymore was to pretend their neighbors weren't there.

I remember the last time he came over because it was just after I finished wallpapering the den. Ginger was whining to go out so I let her . . . that crap about leashes didn't bother me at all. Hank's telling me about school taxes going up again, how he didn't think he could pay his on social security, nothing else. "What we should do," he says, "is find other people in our position to organize a senior citizens' group to see if something can't be done." "Hank," I tell him, "no offense or anything, but all of that what you just said is pure phooey. You join one of those senior citizens' groups, women's groups, queer groups, right away you put yourself in a minority, you're stuck there. All these people running around wanting to be in a minority just so they can feel all nice and persecuted. Forget it! We're humans, that puts us in the *majority!* We're humans, we should demand to be treated like it."

Hank runs his hands up and down the wallpaper, admires the job. "Yeah, you're probably right," he says. Humans. He never thought of it that way before. We go into the kitchen for some coffee. "Now what my idea is, we find out where Big Bill Levitt is these days, we get a petition together telling him how things have gone wrong here, all these young people moving in, taxes going up, forcing us out. He'll find some way to make things right for us. I'd stake my life on it."

Hank nods, reaches for the cream. "By the way," he says. "You hear about Johnny Holmes over on Hillcrest? The guy who once broke his chin on the high board at the pool?" "What about him?" "He's moving to Fort Lauderdale, him and his wife. They bought this old house there. They're going to fix it up nice. Have a garden and all. He made it sound very appealing." "Oh, yeah?" I say. Then I remember myself. "Appealing, my ass. It'll collapse on him, he'll be back in a month. If you don't mind my saying so, Hank, change the subject before I throw up."

All of a sudden we hear this godawful roar from out front like a car accelerating at a drag strip, then brakes squealing, only I knew right away it wasn't brakes. "Ginger!" I jump up, knock the coffee over, run outside . . . There's this car fishtailing away up the street. In the middle of the pavement in a circle from the streetlight is poor Ginger. I run over, put her head in my lap, pet her, but it's too late, she's crying, kicking her legs up and down. Behind her head's nothing but blood. Hank's next to me nearly screaming himself . . . There's nothing to do but put her out of her pain with my bare hands because there's no other way. Then Hank's got his arm around me, I'm shivering, crying, cursing, all at the same time. He takes me back to the house, his wife comes over, they have me swallow something . . . the next thing I know it's morning, Hank's buried Ginger in the back near the birch tree she always liked to curl up against in the sun.

It was a while before I found out who did it. I kept on taking my walk around the block same as before, except I didn't have Ginger with me anymore. Maybe a month later I'm walking along past Silver's house, I see him out in his driveway with Mapes, a few other sheepherders. Silver is giggling. Mapes is standing to one side acting half-ashamed, but smirking, too. "Hey, DiMaria!" Silver yells. "How's your dog?"

I didn't do anything right away. We had a tradition in the old days, you had a score to settle you took your time. I waited for the first stormy night, went over there with two buckets of the cheapest red paint money could buy.

It was pretty late. I shined a flashlight at the lamppost which if you ever want to try it is enough to put one of those mercury vapor jobs out of commission for a while. Then I propped my ladder against the side of his house facing Mapes, went to work. The first cross stroke on the left was pretty easy, the upper right-hand one was tougher because I had to paint across a bay window O'Brien had put in years before. I was being careful not to drip any on the bushes. No matter what I thought of Silver I had a certain amount of respect for his shrubbery which had been planted by Big Bill Levitt back in the forties. It must have taken me two hours all told. I'm painting away humming to myself like it was something I did every night. When it was morning I woke up early, took my usual stroll past Silver's house, there on the side looking wet and shiny in the sun is the biggest, ugliest, coarsest swastika you ever saw, painted right across the side of his house big as life, the only thing bothered me was the upper right stroke was a bit crooked after all.

There were pictures of it in the paper, editorials saying Levittown had gone to hell which was true but for the wrong reasons. The entire Island's gone sour if you ask me. The Sound's gone sour, the ocean's gone sour, the dirt's gone sour. We used to grow enough tomatoes to last the winter, these great big red ones, now you're lucky if you get enough to feed the worms. Great South Bay? Sick clams, dead scallops, that's it. I remember it wasn't that long ago we used to catch stripers bigger than a man's arm, me and Scotty, right off Fire Island a twenty-minute drive away. I remember going there before dawn, cooking ourselves breakfast over a fire we made from driftwood, not seeing another soul on the beach . . . just Scotty, me, the sun, the stripers. Nowadays? Nowadays you can't even fish without getting your reel gummed up in oil; you're lucky to take one crap-choked blowfish let alone stripers.

Looking back what I think happened was that guys like Scotty, Buzz, Mike, and me had the right dream in the wrong place. Long Island's gone sour. Sometimes I remember the first day I came out here, a know-nothing kid, watching that farmer, that last old farmer up there on that overloaded Chevy looking around saying good-bye at the same time cursing it once for all. Other times I walk around the house looking for something to do. What I usually end up doing is put the record player on. Mitch Miller doing "Exodus." I put it on real loud. When they sing, "This land is mine, God gave this land to me," I start singing, too. Listening to it makes me feel stronger, so I keep turning it up, playing it again. After that I fix lunch for myself. Tuna fish, a cup of soup. After lunch I end up staring out the front window trying to figure out who lived where in the old days. Know something? It gets harder every year. O'Brien's and Scotty's are easy, but sometimes I get confused on the others.

It's like this morning I'm looking out across the street trying to remember if Buzz or Rich Ammons lived where this sheepherder name of Diaz lives now, when who do I see over on Zimmer's lawn but the same real estate bastard I chased off my place, Mr. Charles, with two young kids showing them around. This time I was really mad. I ran outside without even a coat, started screaming at them, telling them I'd call the cops, break every bone in his miserable little body if he didn't clear out and leave poor Hank alone. But what happened next was that Hank was outside, too. He was pleading with me to stop, but by then it was too late. Real estate man and kids are running into their car, locking the doors, racing away.

"Tommy!" Hank yelled, shaking his head. "They were going to pay me fifty-five thousand, Tommy!" "What are you talking about?" But now he looked away like he was ashamed. He took me inside the sun porch, sat me down on a lawn chair he unhooked from the wall.

"Tommy, we're moving south," he said. "Bullshit you are!" But he doesn't do anything, he just sits there. "We can't take it here anymore, Tommy," he whispered. "The cold gets to Marge. The taxes are too much for me. All those kids, what do we have in common with them? We're going to Florida. Saint Pete. We bought a trailer."

It was probably the next to worse moment I ever had. "You can't do that, Hank," I said, just as quiet as him. "Not after what we've been through all these years. I was going to help you out with your den. Think of all the things we could do yet. There's another porch we could add on, we could add on a pool." But he was shaking his head again. "Let's face it," he said. "You've got nothing left to work on, Tommy. The house is finished. You hear me? Finished! There's nothing left." He took out his wallet, showed me some pictures. "My grandkids. Terri and Shawn. They live down there now. We want to be close to them. That's the main reason, Tommy. We want to be close to them the years we have left."

By now I was getting mad. "Grandkids my ass!" I yelled. "You think your grandkids give a damn about you? Maybe at Christmastime, that's it. To them you're an old smelly man they don't give a damn about they never will. Take it from me, I know." But then I looked at him . . . seeing him blink, cover his face with his hands, I got feeling ashamed of myself. "Hank," I said, "don't leave me alone like this. Please, Hank. Just hold on a little while more."

"Fifty-five thousand, Tommy. I can't turn it down."

"Listen, Hank. We'll call Big Bill Levitt up. I'll say, Mr. Levitt, my name is Tommy DiMaria, I live on Lindbergh Street, you probably don't remember but you once let me have a house for eighty-three dollars down instead of a hundred. Remember that, Mr. Levitt? Remember those days? Well, a lot of us old-timers are having trouble hanging on to our places you built for us. We wondered if maybe you could help us out. We'll call him up, Hank. We'll call him up just like that."

"You and your Levitt! I'm sick of hearing about him! What has Levitt ever done? He built these places and never looked back. He made his pile, then didn't want to know nothing. Levitt? You're so crazy about Levitt, let me ask you something. Where is Levitt now? Tell me that. Where is he now? Where is Levitt now?"

Like a dope, like the idiot I am, I shake my head, whisper, "I don't know, Hank. Where?"

"Florida!"

"Hank," I said, "I hope you fry."

When I got back to my place there was a panel truck in front, two men standing on the sidewalk watching me cross the street. At the same time Mapes's wife is on her lawn pointing at me, yelling "That's him, officer! That's your man!" One of the men came up to me the moment I reached the curb. "You Thomas A. DiMaria?" he said. "Beat it!" "You live at 155 Lindbergh?" "Beat it! You're trespassing on private property, pal!" "We're from the electric company. This is for you."

I'm feeling so tired by then I took the envelope, opened it up. Inside is a bill for $11,456.55. "You owe us for thirty-two years' worth," the man said. "If we want we can put you in jail. Stealing electricity is a crime." I looked back toward Mapes's house, sure enough there he is with that same half-ashamed smirk hiding behind his Cougar pretending he's polishing the roof.

"I'm not paying," I said. "Leave me alone." With that the other man, the one who hadn't said anything before, comes right up to me, waves a paper in my face. "You better pay, DiMaria!" he said with a sneer. "You don't, we take the house!"

I didn't waste any time after that. I went out to the tool shed, took a five-gallon can of gasoline, went back inside . . . took off the cap, taped a piece of cheesecloth over the spout, went into the den.

Sprinkle, sprinkle. Right over the desk. Sprinkle. Right over the wallpaper. Then after that I went into the bathroom. I remembered those men putting it in. I remembered redoing it with a bigger tub, new tiles, new cabinets. Sprinkle, sprinkle. Right over the cabinets. Right over the rugs. Next I went up the stairs I'd built with Scotty from lumber we helped ourselves to at a construction project on the turnpike . . . up to the dormer I'd added on for the kids. Their stuff was still there, all the kids' stuff, because they didn't want it, Kathy would never let me throw it away. There's a blue teddy bear called Navy, a brown one called Army. I took the can, poured some over their fur, propped them up in the corner, poured some over the bunk beds. I remembered the time Candy cried because she had the bottom one, she wanted the top. Thinking about that, thinking about the times I sat around the old DuMont watching Mickey Mouse Club with them waiting for Kathy to get home, almost made me stop right there.

I went downstairs, the can getting lighter, leaving a little trail behind me . . . into the twins' room where I sprinkled some on the curtains Kathy sewed, sprinkled some on the Davy Crockett hat Chris used to wear every time she came out of the bathtub. Then after that I went into the kitchen. The kitchen cabinets. The linoleum. Sprinkle, sprinkle. Out to the porch where we used to eat in summer, right over the bar I made from leftover knotty pine. I stood there for a while. I stood there remembering the party we had when we ripped the mortgage up, how Scotty got drunk and we had to carry him home only we carried him, dropped him in the pool instead. Sprinkle, sprinkle. Like watering plants. Like baptizing someone. Like starting a barbecue with lighter fluid, all the neighborhood there in my back yard. Into our bedroom, over the floor, the floor where the first night I brought Kathy home we had no bed yet so we lay there on the floor of what we still couldn't believe was our house, making love all night because we were so happy we didn't think we could stand it. Sprinkle. The fumes getting pretty bad now. Sprinkle. Outside to the carport, over the beams, over the tools, over everything. Sprinkle, sprinkle. Splash.

And that's where I am right now. The carport. The bill they handed me in one hand, a match in the other. I'm going to wait until Silver gets home first. I want to make sure everyone on the block gets to see what fifty-five thousand dollars, thirty-two years, looks like going up in smoke. A second more and it'll be like kids, neighbors, house, never happened, as if it all passed in a twinkling of an eye like they say. One half of me I feel ready to start all over again. I feel like I'm ready to find a new dream, raise a new family, the works. Nothing that's happened has made me change my mind. I'm ready to start again, just say the word. I feel stronger, more hopeful than ever . . . how many guys my age can say that? That's all I want, one more chance. For the time being I'm moving back to the old neighborhood to my sister's. After that, I don't know. Maybe I'll head down south where it's warmer, but not, I repeat NOT to Florida, maybe as far as Virginia, I'm not sure.

# William Carlos Williams

*Williams (1883–1963) was born in Rutherford, New Jersey. He took a medical degree at the University of Pennsylvania and practiced as a pediatrician through the long years of his literary career. Defining himself as utterly American in taste and spirit, he became the friend, supporter, and colleague of several of the leaders of the avant-garde in American literature. His work as a poet culminated in the massive chronicle* Paterson *(1946–58), and the imagination that shaped his verse informed his speculations on our history and its character in his book of essays* In the American Grain *(1925). In his fiction as in his several plays he achieves an illuminated mirror image of the flat banality of ordinary lives. His novels include* White Mule *(1937) and* In the Money *(1940). His short stories are collected in* The Knife of the Times *(1932),* Make Light of It *(1950), and* The Doctor Stories *(1984).*

## The Use of Force

They were new patients to me, all I had was the name, Olson. Please come down as soon as you can, my daughter is very sick. When I arrived I was met by the mother, a big startled looking woman, very clean and apologetic who merely said, Is this the doctor? and let me in. In the back, she added. You must excuse us, doctor, we have her in the kitchen where it is warm. It is very damp here sometimes.

The child was fully dressed and sitting on her father's lap near the kitchen table. He tried to get up, but I motioned for him not to bother, took off my overcoat and started to look things over. I could see that they were all very nervous, eyeing me up and down distrustfully. As often, in such cases, they weren't telling me more than they had to, it was up to me to tell them; that's why they were spending three dollars on me.

The child was fairly eating me up with her cold, steady eyes, and no expression to her face whatever. She did not move and seemed, inwardly, quiet; an unusually attractive little thing, and as strong as a heifer in appearance. But her face was flushed, she was breathing rapidly, and I realized that she had a high fever. She had magnificent blonde hair, in profusion. One of those picture children often reproduced in advertising leaflets and the photogravure sections of the Sunday papers.

She's had a fever for three days, began the father and we don't know what it comes from. My wife has given her things, you know, like people do, but it don't do no good. And there's been a lot of sickness around. So we tho't you'd better look her over and tell us what is the matter.

As doctors often do I took a trial shot at it as a point of departure. Has she had a sore throat?

Both parents answered me together, No . . . No, she says her throat don't hurt her.

Does your throat hurt you? added the mother to the child. But the little girl's expression didn't change nor did she move her eyes from my face.

Have you looked?

I tried to, said the mother, but I couldn't see.

As it happens we had been having a number of cases of diphtheria in the school to which this child went during that month and we were all, quite apparently, thinking of that, though no one had as yet spoken of the thing.

Well, I said, suppose we take a look at the throat first. I smiled in my best professional manner and asking for the child's first name I said, come on, Mathilda, open your mouth and let's take a look at your throat.

Nothing doing.

Aw, come on, I coaxed, just open your mouth wide and let me take a look. Look, I said opening both hands wide, I haven't anything in my hands. Just open up and let me see.

Such a nice man, put in the mother. Look how kind he is to you. Come on, do what he tells you to. He won't hurt you.

At that I ground my teeth in disgust. If only they wouldn't use the word "hurt" I might be able to get somewhere. But I did not allow myself to be hurried or disturbed but speaking quietly and slowly I approached the child again.

As I moved my chair a little nearer suddenly with one catlike movement both her hands clawed instinctively for my eyes and she almost reached them too. In fact she knocked my glasses flying and they fell, though unbroken, several feet away from me on the kitchen floor.

Both the mother and father almost turned themselves inside out in embarrassment and apology. You bad girl, said the mother, taking her and shaking her by one arm. Look what you've done. The nice man . . .

For heaven's sake, I broke in. Don't call me a nice man to her. I'm here to look at her throat on the chance that she might have diphtheria and possibly die of it. But that's nothing to her. Look here, I said to the child, we're going to look at your throat. You're old enough to understand what I'm saying. Will you open it now by yourself or shall we have to open it for you?

Not a move. Even her expression hadn't changed. Her breaths however were coming faster and faster. Then the battle began. I had to do it. I had to have a throat culture for her own protection. But first I told the parents that it was entirely up to them. I explained the danger but said that I would not insist on a throat examination so long as they would take the responsibility.

If you don't do what the doctor says you'll have to go to the hospital, the mother admonished her severely.

Oh yeah? I had to smile to myself. After all, I had already fallen in love with the savage brat, the parents were contemptible to me. In the ensuing struggle they grew more and more abject, crushed, exhausted while she surely rose to magnificent heights of insane fury of effort bred of her terror of me.

The father tried his best, and he was a big man but the fact that she was his daughter, his shame at her behavior and his dread of hurting her made him release her just at the critical times when I had almost achieved success, till I wanted to kill him. But his dread also that she might have diphtheria made him tell me to go on, go on though he himself was almost fainting, while the mother moved back and forth behind us raising and lowering her hands in an agony of apprehension.

Put her in front of you on your lap, I ordered, and hold both her wrists.

But as soon as he did the child let out a scream. Don't, you're hurting me. Let go of my hands. Let them go I tell you. Then she shrieked terrifyingly, hysterically. Stop it! Stop it! You're killing me!

Do you think she can stand it, doctor! said the mother.

You get out, said the husband to his wife. Do you want her to die of diphtheria?

Come on now, hold her, I said.

Then I grasped the child's head with my left hand and tried to get the wooden tongue depressor between her teeth. She fought, with clenched teeth, desperately! But now I also had grown furious—at a child. I tried to hold myself down but I couldn't. I know how to expose a throat for inspection. And I did my best. When finally I got the wooden spatula behind the last teeth and just the point of it into the mouth cavity, she opened up for an instant but before I could see anything she came down again and gripped the wooden blade between her molars she reduced it to splinters before I could get it out again.

Aren't you ashamed, the mother yelled at her. Aren't you ashamed to act like that in front of the doctor?

Get me a smooth-handled spoon of some sort, I told the mother. We're going through with this. The child's mouth was already bleeding. Her tongue was cut and she was screaming in wild hysterical shrieks. Perhaps I should have desisted and come back in an hour or more. No doubt it would have been better. But I have seen at least two children lying dead in bed of neglect in such cases, and feeling that I must get a diagnosis now or never I went at it again. But the worst of it was that I too had got beyond reason. I could have torn the child apart in my own fury and enjoyed it. It was a pleasure to attack her. My face was burning with it.

The damned little brat must be protected against her own idiocy, one says to one's self at such times. Others must be protected against her. It is a social necessity. And all these things are true. But a blind fury, a feeling of adult shame, bred of a longing for muscular release are the operatives. One goes on to the end.

In the final unreasoning assault I overpowered the child's neck and jaws. I forced the heavy silver spoon back of her teeth and down her throat till she gagged. And there it was—both tonsils covered with membrane. She had fought valiantly to keep me from knowing her secret. She had been hiding that sore throat for three days at least and lying to her parents in order to escape just such an outcome as this.

Now truly she was furious. She had been on the defensive before but now she attacked. Tried to get off her father's lap and fly at me while tears of defeat blinded her eyes.

# TOBIAS WOLFF

*Wolff (1945– ) was born in Alabama and grew up in Washington State. Since his education at Oxford and Stanford Universities he has taught at Syracuse University and Indiana University. Many of his stories are collected in* In the Garden of the North American Martyrs *(1981). His books include* Ugly Rumours: A Novel *(1975); the short novel* The Barracks Thief *(1984);* Back in the World *(1985); his memoir,* This Boy's Life *(1989); and* The Night in Question *(1996). He has also edited several anthologies, among them* The Vintage Book of Contemporary American Short Stories *(1993) and* Best American Short Stories *(1994). He has received the PEN/Faulkner Award. He currently teaches at Stanford University.*

## In the Garden of the North American Martyrs

When she was young, Mary saw a brilliant and original man lose his job because he had expressed ideas that were offensive to the trustees of the college where they both taught. She shared his views, but did not sign the protest petition. She was, after all, on trial herself—as a teacher, as a woman, as an interpreter of history.

Mary watched herself. Before giving a lecture she wrote it out in full, using the arguments and often the words of other, approved writers, so that she would not by chance say something scandalous. Her own thoughts she kept to herself, and the words for them grew faint as time went on; without quite disappearing they shrank to remote, nervous points, like birds flying away.

When the department turned into a hive of cliques, Mary went about her business and pretended not to know that people hated each other. To avoid seeming bland she let herself become eccentric in harmless ways. She took up bowling, which she learned to love, and founded the Brandon College chapter of a society dedicated to restoring the good name of Richard III.[1] She memorized comedy routines from records and jokes from books; people groaned when she rattled them off, but she did not let that stop her, and after a time the groans became the point of the jokes. They were a kind of tribute to Mary's willingness to expose herself.

1. English king (1452–1485) generally regarded as ruthless and brutal.

In fact no one at the college was safer than Mary, for she was making herself into something institutional, like a custom, or a mascot—part of the college's idea of itself.

Now and then she wondered whether she had been too careful. The things she said and wrote seemed flat to her, pulpy, as though someone else had squeezed the juice out of them. And once, while talking with a senior professor, Mary saw herself reflected in a window: she was leaning toward him and had her head turned so that her ear was right in front of his moving mouth. The sight disgusted her. Years later, when she had to get a hearing aid, Mary suspected that her deafness was a result of always trying to catch everything everyone said.

In the second half of Mary's fifteenth year at Brandon the provost called a meeting of all faculty and students to announce that the college was bankrupt and would not open its gates again. He was every bit as much surprised as they; the report from the trustees had reached his desk only that morning. It seemed that Brandon's financial manager had speculated in some kind of futures and lost everything. The provost wanted to deliver the news in person before it reached the papers. He wept openly and so did the students and teachers, with only a few exceptions—some cynical upperclassmen who claimed to despise the education they had received.

Mary could not rid her mind of the word "speculate." It meant to guess, in terms of money to gamble. How could a man gamble a college? Why would he want to do that, and how could it be that no one stopped him? To Mary, it seemed to belong to another time; she thought of a drunken plantation owner gaming away his slaves.

She applied for jobs and got an offer from a new experimental college in Oregon. It was her only offer so she took it.

The college was in one building. Bells rang all the time, lockers lined the hallways, and at every corner stood a buzzing water fountain. The student newspaper came out twice a month on mimeograph paper which felt wet. The library, which was next to the band room, had no librarian and no books.

The countryside was beautiful, though, and Mary might have enjoyed it if the rain had not caused her so much trouble. There was something wrong with her lungs that the doctors couldn't agree on, and couldn't cure; whatever it was, the dampness made it worse. On rainy days condensation formed in Mary's hearing aid and shorted it out. She began to dread talking with people, never knowing when she would have to take out her control box and slap it against her leg.

It rained nearly every day. When it was not raining it was getting ready to rain, or clearing. The ground glinted under the grass, and the light had a yellow undertone that flared up during storms.

There was water in Mary's basement. Her walls sweated, and she had found toadstools growing behind the refrigerator. She felt as though she were rusting out, like one of those old cars people thereabouts kept in their front yards, on pieces of wood. Mary knew that everyone was dying, but it did seem to her that she was dying faster than most.

She continued to look for another job, without success. Then, in the fall of her third year in Oregon, she got a letter from a woman named Louise who'd once taught in Brandon. Louise had scored a great success with a book on Benedict Arnold[2] and was now on the faculty of a famous college in upstate New York. She said that one of her colleagues would be retiring at the end of the year and asked whether Mary would be interested in the position.

The letter surprised Mary. Louise thought of herself as a great historian and of almost everyone else as useless; Mary had not known that she felt differently about her. Moreover, enthusiasm for other people's causes did not come easily to Louise, who had a way of sucking in her breath when familiar names were mentioned, as though she knew things that friendship kept her from disclosing.

Mary expected nothing, but sent a résumé and copies of her two books. Shortly after that Louise called to say that the search committee, of which she was chairwoman, had decided to grant Mary an interview in early November. "Now don't get your hopes too high," Louise said.

"Oh, no," Mary said, but thought: Why shouldn't I hope? They would not go to the bother and expense of bringing her to the college if they weren't serious. And she was certain that the interview would go well. She would make them like her, or at least give them no cause to dislike her.

She read about the area with a strange sense of familiarity, as if the land and its history were already known to her. And when her plane left Portland and climbed easily into the clouds, Mary felt like she was going home. The feeling stayed with her, growing stronger when they landed. She tried to describe it to Louise as they left the airport at Syracuse and drove toward the college, an hour or so away. "It's like *déjà vu,*" she said.

"*Déjà vu* is a hoax," Louise said. "It's just a chemical imbalance of some kind."

"Maybe so," Mary said, "but I still have this sensation."

"Don't get serious on me," Louise said. "That's not your long suit. Just be your funny, wisecracking old self. Tell me now—honestly—how do I look?"

It was night, too dark to see Louise's face well, but in the airport she had seemed gaunt and pale and intense. She reminded Mary of a description in the book she'd been reading, of how Iroquois[3] warriors gave themselves visions by fasting. She had that kind of look about her. But she wouldn't want to hear that. "You look wonderful," Mary said.

"There's a reason," Louise said. "I've taken a lover. My concentration has improved, my energy level is up, and I've lost ten pounds. I'm also getting some color in my cheeks, though that could be the weather. I recommend the experience highly. But you probably disapprove."

Mary didn't know what to say. She said that she was sure Louise knew best, but that didn't seem to be enough. "Marriage is a great institution," she added, "but who wants to live in an institution?"

Louise groaned. "I know you," she said, "and I know that right now you're thinking 'But what about Ted? What about the children?' The fact is, Mary,

2. U.S. general in the Revolutionary War, who became a traitor (1741–1801). 3. A tribe native to the lower Great Lakes region, war-loving by reputation.

they aren't taking it well at all. Ted has become a nag." She handed Mary her purse. "Be a good girl and light me a cigarette, will you? I know I told you I quit, but this whole thing has been very hard on me, very hard, and I'm afraid I've started again."

They were in the hills now, heading north on a narrow road. Tall trees arched above them. As they topped a rise Mary saw the forest all around, deep black under the plum-colored sky. There were a few lights and these made the darkness seem even greater.

"Ted has succeeded in completely alienating the children from me," Louise was saying. "There is no reasoning with any of them. In fact, they refuse to discuss the matter at all, which is very ironical because over the years I have tried to instill in them a willingness to see things from the other person's point of view. If they could just *meet* Jonathan I know they would feel differently. But they won't hear of it. Jonathan," she said, "is my lover."

"I see," Mary said, and nodded.

Coming around a curve they caught two deer in the headlights. Their eyes lit up and their hindquarters tensed; Mary could see them trembling as the car went by. "Deer," she said.

"I don't know," Louise said, "I just don't know. I do my best and it never seems to be enough. But that's enough about me—let's talk about you. What did you think of my latest book?" She squawked and beat her palms on the steering wheel. "God, I love that joke," she said. "Seriously, though, what about you? It must have been a real shockeroo when good old Brandon folded."

"It was hard. Things haven't been good but they'll be a lot better if I get this job."

"At least you have work," Louise said. "You should look at it from the bright side."

"I try."

"You seem so gloomy. I hope you're not worrying about the interview, or the class. Worrying won't do you a bit of good. Be happy."

"Class? What class?"

"The class you're supposed to give tomorrow, after the interview. Didn't I tell you? *Mea culpa,* hon, *mea maxima culpa.* I've been uncharacteristically forgetful lately."

"But what will I do?"

"Relax," Louise said. "Just pick a subject and wing it."

"Wing it?"

"You know, open your mouth and see what comes out. Extemporize."

"But I always work from a prepared lecture."

Louise sighed. "All right. I'll tell you what. Last year I wrote an article on the Marshall Plan[4] that I got bored with and never published. You can read that."

Parroting what Louise had written seemed wrong to Mary, at first; then it occurred to her that she had been doing the same kind of things for many

4. Plan for rehabilitating European economies devastated by World War II, formulated by George Catlett Marshall (1880–1959), U.S. chief of staff.

years, and that this was not the time to get scruples. "Thanks," she said. "I appreciate it."

"Here we are," Louise said, and pulled into a circular drive with several cabins grouped around it. In two of the cabins lights were on; smoke drifted straight up from the chimneys. "This is the visitors' center. The college is another two miles thataway." Louise pointed down the road. "I'd invite you to stay at my house, but I'm spending the night with Jonathan and Ted is not good company these days. You would hardly recognize him."

She took Mary's bags from the trunk and carried them up the steps of a darkened cabin. "Look," she said, "they've laid a fire for you. All you have to do is light it." She stood in the middle of the room with her arms crossed and watched as Mary held a match under the kindling. "There," she said. "You'll be snugaroo in no time. I'd love to stay and chew the fat but I can't. You just get a good night's sleep and I'll see you in the morning."

Mary stood in the doorway and waved as Louise pulled out of the drive, spraying gravel. She filled her lungs, to taste the air: it was tart and clear. She could see the stars in their figurations, and the vague streams of light that ran among the stars.

She still felt uneasy about reading Louise's work as her own. It would be her first complete act of plagiarism. It would change her. It would make her less—how much less, she did not know. But what else could she do? She certainly wouldn't "wing it." Words might fail her, and then what? Mary had a dread of silence. When she thought of silence she thought of drowning, as if it were a kind of water she could not swim in.

"I want this job," she said, and settled deep into her coat. It was cashmere and Mary had not worn it since moving to Oregon, because people there thought you were pretentious if you had on anything but a Pendleton shirt or, of course, raingear. She rubbed her cheek against the upturned collar and thought of a silver moon shining through bare black branches, a white house with green shutters, red leaves falling in a hard blue sky.

Louise woke her a few hours later. She was sitting on the edge of the bed, pushing at Mary's shoulder and snuffling loudly. When Mary asked her what was wrong she said, "I want your opinion on something. It's very important. Do you think I'm womanly?"

Mary sat up. "Louise, can this wait?"

"No."

"Womanly?"

Louise nodded.

"You are very beautiful," Mary said, "and you know how to present yourself."

Louise stood and paced the room. "That son of a bitch," she said. She came back and stood over Mary. "Let's suppose someone said I have no sense of humor. Would you agree or disagree?"

"In some things you do. I mean, yes, you have a good sense of humor."

"What do you mean, 'in some things?' What kind of things?"

"Well, if you heard that someone had been killed in an unusual way, like by an exploding cigar, you would think that was funny."

Louise laughed.

"That's what I mean," Mary said.

Louise went on laughing. "Oh, Lordy," she said. "Now it's my turn to say something about you." She sat down beside Mary.

"Please," Mary said.

"Just one thing," Louise said.

Mary waited.

"You're trembling," Louise said. "I was just going to say—oh, forget it. Listen, do you mind if I sleep on the couch? I'm all in."

"Go ahead."

"Sure it's okay? You've got a big day tomorrow." She fell back on the sofa and kicked off her shoes. "I was just going to say, you should use some liner on those eyebrows of yours. They sort of disappear and the effect is disconcerting."

Neither of them slept. Louise chain-smoked cigarettes and Mary watched the coals burn down. When it was light enough that they could see each other Louise got up. "I'll send a student for you," she said. "Good luck."

The college looked the way colleges are supposed to look. Roger, the student assigned to show Mary around, explained that it was an exact copy of a college in England, right down to the gargoyles and stained-glass windows. It looked so much like a college that moviemakers sometimes used it as a set. *Andy Hardy Goes to College*[5] had been filmed there, and every fall they had an Andy Hardy Goes to College Day, with raccoon coats and goldfish-swallowing contests.

Above the door of the Founder's Building was a Latin motto which, roughly translated, meant "God helps those who help themselves." As Roger recited the names of illustrious graduates Mary was struck by the extent to which they had taken this precept to heart. They had helped themselves to railroads, mines, armies, states; to empires of finance with outposts all over the world.

Roger took Mary to the chapel and showed her a plaque bearing the names of alumni who had been killed in various wars, all the way back to the Civil War. There were not many names. Here too, apparently, the graduates had helped themselves. "Oh yes," Roger said as they were leaving, "I forgot to tell you. The communion rail comes from some church in Europe where Charlemagne[6] used to go."

They went to the gymnasium, and the three hockey rinks, and the library, where Mary inspected the card catalogue, as though she would turn down the job if they didn't have the right books. "We have a little more time," Roger said as they went outside. "Would you like to see the power plant?"

Mary wanted to keep busy until the last minute, so she agreed.

Roger led her into the depths of the service building, explaining things

5. Before and during World War II the series of Hardy Family films was extremely popular in the United States. Andy Hardy was played by film star Mickey Rooney. 6. King of the Franks (742–814) and emperor of the Holy Roman Empire.

about the machine, which was the most advanced in the country. "People think the college is really old-fashioned," he said, "but it isn't. They let girls come here now, and some of the teachers are women. In fact, there's a statute that says they have to interview at least one woman for each opening. There it is."

They were standing on an iron catwalk above the biggest machine Mary had ever beheld. Roger, who was majoring in Earth Sciences, said that it had been built from a design pioneered by a professor in his department. Where before he had been gabby Roger now became reverent. It was clear that for him this machine was the soul of the college, that the purpose of the college was to provide outlets for the machine. Together they leaned against the railing and watched it hum.

Mary arrived at the committee room exactly on time for her interview, but the room was empty. Her two books were on the table, along with a water pitcher and some glasses. She sat down and picked up one of the books. The binding cracked as she opened it. The pages were smooth, clean, unread. Mary turned to the first chapter, which began, "It is generally believed that . . ." How dull, she thought.

Nearly twenty minutes later Louise came in with several men. "Sorry we're late," she said. "We don't have much time so we'd better get started." She introduced Mary to the men, but with one exception the names and faces did not stay together. The exception was Dr. Howells, the department chairman, who had a porous blue nose and terrible teeth.

A shiny-faced man to Dr. Howells's right spoke first. "So," he said, "I understand you once taught at Brandon College."

"It was a shame that Brandon had to close," said a young man with a pipe in his mouth. "There is a place for schools like Brandon." As he talked the pipe wagged up and down.

"Now you're in Oregon," Dr. Howells said. "I've never been there. How do you like it?"

"Not very much," Mary said.

"Is that right?" Dr. Howells leaned toward her. "I thought everyone liked Oregon. I heard it's very green."

"That's true," Mary said.

"I suppose it rains a lot," he said.

"Nearly every day."

"I wouldn't like that," he said, shaking his head. "I like it dry. Of course it snows here, and you have your rain now and then, but it's a *dry* rain. Have you ever been to Utah? There's a state for you. Bryce Canyon. The Mormon Tabernacle Choir."

"Dr. Howells was brought up in Utah," said the young man with the pipe.

"It was a different place altogether in those days," Dr. Howells said. "Mrs. Howells and I have always talked about going back when I retire, but now I'm not so sure."

"We're a little short on time," Louise said.

"And here I've been going on and on," Dr. Howells said. "Before we wind things up, is there anything you want to tell us?"

"Yes. I think you should give me the job." Mary laughed when she said this, but no one laughed back, or even looked at her. They all looked away. Mary understood then that they were not really considering her for the position. She had been brought here to satisfy a rule. She had no hope.

The men gathered their papers and shook hands with Mary and told her how much they were looking forward to her class. "I can't get enough of the Marshall Plan," Dr. Howells said.

"Sorry about that," Louise said when they were alone. "I didn't think it would be so bad. That was a real bitcheroo."

"Tell me something," Mary said. "You already know who you're going to hire, don't you?"

Louise nodded.

"Then why did you bring me here?"

Louise began to explain about the statute and Mary interrupted. "I know all that. But why me? Why did you pick *me*?"

Louise walked to the window. She spoke with her back to Mary. "Things haven't been going very well for old Louise," she said. "I've been unhappy and I thought you might cheer me up. You used to be so funny, and I was sure you would enjoy the trip—it didn't cost you anything, and it's pretty this time of year with the leaves and everything. Mary, you don't know the things my parents did to me. And Ted is no barrel of laughs either. Or Jonathan, the son of a bitch. I deserve some love and friendship but I don't get any." She turned and looked at her watch. "It's almost time for your class. We'd better go."

"I would rather not give it. After all, there's not much point, is there?"

"But you *have* to give it. That's part of the interview." Louise handed Mary a folder. "All you have to do is read this. It isn't much, considering all the money we've laid out to get you here."

Mary followed Louise down the hall to the lecture room. The professors were sitting in the front row with their legs crossed. They smiled and nodded at Mary. Behind them the room was full of students, some of whom had spilled over into the aisles. One of the professors adjusted the microphone to Mary's height, crouching down as he went to the podium and back as though he would prefer not to be seen.

Louise called the room to order. She introduced Mary and gave the subject of the lecture. But Mary had decided to wing it after all. Mary came to the podium unsure of what she would say; sure only that she would rather die than read Louise's article. The sun poured through the stained glass onto the people around her, painting their faces. Thick streams of smoke from the young professor's pipe drifted through a circle of red light at Mary's feet, turning crimson and twisting like flames.

"I wonder how many of you know," she began, "that we are in the Long House,[7] the ancient domain of the Five Nations of the Iroquois."

Two professors looked at each other.

"The Iroquois were without pity," Mary said. "They hunted people down with clubs and arrows and spears and nets, and blowguns made from elder

7. Communal American Indian dwelling, in actuality a wooden frame covered with bark.

stalks. They tortured their captives, sparing no one, not even the little children. They took scalps and practiced cannibalism and slavery. Because they had no pity they became powerful, so powerful that no other tribe dared to oppose them. They made the other tribes pay tribute, and when they had nothing more to pay the Iroquois attacked them."

Several of the professors began to whisper. Dr. Howells was saying something to Louise, and Louise was shaking her head.

"In one of their raids," Mary said, "they captured two Jesuit priests, Jean de Brébeuf and Gabriel Lalement.[8] They covered Lalement with pitch and set him on fire in front of Brébeuf. When Brébeuf rebuked them they cut off his lips and put a burning iron down his throat. They hung a collar of red-hot hatchets around his neck, and poured boiling water over his head. When he continued to preach to them they cut strips of flesh from his body and ate them before his eyes. While he was still alive, they scalped him and cut open his breast and drank his blood. Later, their chief tore out Brébeuf's heart and ate it, but just before he did this Brébeuf spoke to them one last time. He said—"

"That's enough!" yelled Dr. Howells, jumping to his feet.

Louise stopped shaking her head. Her eyes were perfectly round.

Mary had come to the end of her facts. She did not know what Brébeuf had said. Silence rose up around her; just when she thought she would go under and be lost in it she heard someone whistling in the hallway outside, trilling the notes like a bird, like many birds.

"Mend your lives," she said. "You have deceived yourselves in the pride of your hearts, and the strength of your arms. Though you soar aloft like the eagle, though your nest is set among the stars, thence I will bring you down, says the Lord.[9] Turn from power to love. Be kind. Do justice. Walk humbly."

Louise was waving her arms. "Mary!" she shouted.

But Mary had more to say, much more; she waved back at Louise, then turned off her hearing aid so that she would not be distracted again.

8. The two most famous martyrs among the Jesuit missionaries in North America. Tortured and killed by the Iroquois in 1649. 9. Obadiah 1.4.

# Virginia Woolf

*Woolf (1882–1941) was born in London, the daughter of a distinguished man of letters, Sir Leslie Stephen. At her father's death in 1904 she moved with her sister and two brothers to Bloomsbury, a fashionably bohemian section of London, and when she began to publish she was firmly associated with the "Bloomsbury Group" of writers and intellectuals. In 1912 she married the journalist and political philosopher Leonard Woolf and with him established the Hogarth Press, which published so many of her works. By the example of her first novels and in essays she made a case against the heavy objective realism of such then popular practitioners as Arnold Bennett. Her preference was for lyric adaptations of the stream of consciousness, best exemplified by* To the Lighthouse *(1927) and* The Waves *(1931). In her popular* Mrs. Dalloway *(1925) she had shown the possibilities of her methods in developing the nondramatic, contrapuntal presentation of a sensitive, deranged war veteran and an unfulfilled woman committed to the maintenance of her social position—perhaps a fictional transformation of two major aspects of Woolf's own personality. In 1916 she suffered a terrifying mental breakdown; she killed herself in 1941 in fear of its recurrence.* A Room of One's Own *(1929) is a feminist tract of enduring influence, and the essays on literature collected in the two volumes of* The Common Reader *(1925–32) did much to shape modern taste with their easy, keen suggestiveness. Her stories were collected in* A Haunted House and Other Stories *(1943).*

## Kew Gardens[1]

From the oval-shaped flower-bed there rose perhaps a hundred stalks spreading into heart-shaped or tongue-shaped leaves half-way up and unfurling at the tip red or blue or yellow petals marked with spots of colour raised upon the surface; and from the red, blue or yellow gloom of the throat emerged a straight bar, rough with gold dust and slightly clubbed at the end. The petals were voluminous enough to be stirred by the summer breeze, and when they moved, the red, blue and yellow lights passed one over the other, staining an inch of the brown earth beneath with a spot of the most intricate colour. The light fell either upon the smooth, grey back of a pebble, or the shell of a snail with its brown, circular veins, or falling into a raindrop, it expanded with such intensity of red, blue and yellow the thin walls of water that one expected them to burst and disappear. Instead, the drop was left in a second silver grey once more,

1. Established as a state institution in 1841, Kew Gardens is the home of the Royal Botanic Gardens; it is in the London suburb of Kew, Surrey.

and the light now settled upon the flesh of a leaf, revealing the branching thread of fibre beneath the surface, and again it moved on and spread its illumination in the vast green spaces beneath the dome of the heart-shaped and tongue-shaped leaves. Then the breeze stirred rather more briskly overhead and the colour was flashed into the air above, into the eyes of the men and women who walk in Kew Gardens in July.

The figures of these men and women straggled past the flower-bed with a curiously irregular movement not unlike that of the white and blue butterflies who crossed the turf in zig-zag flights from bed to bed. The man was about six inches in front of the woman, strolling carelessly, while she bore on with greater purpose, only turning her head now and then to see that the children were not too far behind. The man kept this distance in front of the woman purposely, though perhaps unconsciously, for he wished to go on with his thoughts.

"Fifteen years ago I came here with Lily," he thought. "We sat somewhere over there by a lake and I begged her to marry me all through the hot afternoon. How the dragonfly kept circling round us: how clearly I see the dragonfly and her shoe with the square silver buckle at the toe. All the time I spoke I saw her shoe and when it moved impatiently I knew without looking up what she was going to say: the whole of her seemed to be in her shoe. And my love, my desire, were in the dragonfly; for some reason I thought that if it settled there, on that leaf, the broad one with the red flower in the middle of it, if the dragonfly settled on the leaf she would say 'Yes' at once. But the dragonfly went round and round: it never settled anywhere—of course not, happily not, or I shouldn't be walking here with Eleanor and the children. Tell me, Eleanor. D'you ever think of the past?"

"Why do you ask, Simon?"

"Because I've been thinking of the past. I've been thinking of Lily, the woman I might have married. . . . Well, why are you silent? Do you mind my thinking of the past?"

"Why should I mind, Simon? Doesn't one always think of the past, in a garden with men and women lying under the trees. Aren't they one's past, all that remains of it, those men and women, those ghosts lying under the trees, . . . one's happiness, one's reality?"

"For me, a square silver shoe buckle and a dragonfly—"

"For me, a kiss. Imagine six little girls sitting before their easels twenty years ago, down by the side of a lake, painting the water-lilies, the first red water-lilies I'd ever seen. And suddenly a kiss, there on the back of my neck. And my hand shook all the afternoon so that I couldn't paint. I took out my watch and marked the hour when I would allow myself to think of the kiss for five minutes only—it was so precious—the kiss of an old grey-haired woman with a wart on her nose, the mother of all my kisses all my life. Come, Caroline, come, Hubert."

They walked on past the flower-bed, now walking four abreast, and soon diminished in size among the trees and looked half transparent as the sunlight and shade swam over their backs in large trembling irregular patches.

In the oval flower-bed the snail, whose shell had been stained red, blue and yellow for the space of two minutes or so, now appeared to be moving very slightly in its shell, and next began to labour over the crumbs of loose earth which broke away and rolled down as it passed over them. It appeared to have a definite goal in front of it, differing in this respect from the singular high stepping angular green insect who attempted to cross in front of it, and waited for a second with its antennae trembling as if in deliberation, and then stepped off as rapidly and strangely in the opposite direction. Brown cliffs with deep green lakes in the hollows, flat, blade-like trees that waved from root to tip, round boulders of grey stone, vast crumpled surfaces of a thin crackling texture—all these objects lay across the snail's progress between one stalk and another to his goal. Before he had decided whether to circumvent the arched tent of a dead leaf or to breast it there came past the bed the feet of other human beings.

This time they were both men. The younger of the two wore an expression of perhaps unnatural calm; he raised his eyes and fixed them very steadily in front of him while his companion spoke, and directly his companion had done speaking he looked on the ground again and sometimes opened his lips only after a long pause and sometimes did not open them at all. The elder man had a curiously uneven and shaky method of walking, jerking his hand forward and throwing up his head abruptly, rather in the manner of an impatient carriage horse tired of waiting outside a house; but in the man these gestures were irresolute and pointless. He talked almost incessantly; he smiled to himself and again began to talk, as if the smile had been an answer. He was talking about spirits—the spirits of the dead, who, according to him, were even now telling him all sorts of odd things about their experiences in Heaven.

"Heaven was known to the ancients as Thessaly, William, and now, with this war, the spirit matter[2] is rolling between the hills like thunder." He paused, seemed to listen, smiled, jerked his head and continued:

"You have a small electric battery and a piece of rubber to insulate the wire—isolate?—insulate?—well, we'll skip the details, no good going into details that wouldn't be understood—and in short the little machine stands in any convenient position by the head of the bed, we will say, on a neat mahogany stand. All arrangements being properly fixed by workmen under my direction, the widow applies her ear and summons the spirit by sign as agreed. Women! Widows! Women in black—"

Here he seemed to have caught sight of a woman's dress in the distance, which in the shade looked a purple black. He took off his hat, placed his hand upon his heart, and hurried towards her muttering and gesticulating feverishly. But William caught him by the sleeve and touched a flower with the tip of his walking-stick in order to divert the old man's attention. After looking at it for a moment in some confusion the old man bent his ear to it and seemed to answer a voice speaking from it, for he began talking about the forests of Uruguay which he had visited hundreds of years ago in company with the most beautiful young woman in Europe. He could be heard murmuring about forests of Uruguay blanketed with the wax petals of tropical roses, nightingales, sea beaches, mermaids, and women drowned at sea, as he suffered himself to be

2. I.e., spiritualism. Thessaly: a region in Greece. "This war": World War I.

moved on by William, upon whose face the look of stoical patience grew slowly deeper and deeper.

Following his steps so closely as to be slightly puzzled by his gestures came two elderly women of the lower middle class, one stout and ponderous, the other rosy cheeked and nimble. Like most people of their station they were frankly fascinated by other signs of eccentricity betokening a disordered brain, especially in the well-to-do; but they were too far off to be certain whether the gestures were merely eccentric or genuinely mad. After they had scrutinized the old man's back in silence for a moment and given each other a queer, sly look, they went on energetically piecing together their very complicated dialogue:

"Nell, Bert, Lot, Cess, Phil, Pa, he says, I says, she says, I says, I says—"

"My Bert, Sis, Bill, Grandad, the old man, sugar,

Sugar, flour, kippers, greens,
Sugar, sugar, sugar."

The ponderous woman looked through the pattern of falling words at the flowers standing cool, firm, and upright in the earth, with a curious expression. She saw them as a sleeper waking from a heavy sleep sees a brass candlestick reflecting the light in an unfamiliar way, and closes his eyes and opens them, and seeing the brass candlestick again, finally starts broad awake and stares at the candlestick with all his powers. So the heavy woman came to a standstill opposite the oval-shaped flower-bed, and ceased even to pretend to listen to what the other woman was saying. She stood there letting the words fall over her, swaying the top part of her body slowly backwards and forwards, looking at the flowers. Then she suggested that they should find a seat and have their tea.

The snail had now considered every possible method of reaching his goal without going round the dead leaf or climbing over it. Let alone the effort needed for climbing a leaf, he was doubtful whether the thin texture which vibrated with such an alarming crackle when touched even by the tips of his horns would bear his weight; and this determined him finally to creep beneath it, for there was a point where the leaf curved high enough from the ground to admit him. He had just inserted his head in the opening and was taking stock of the high brown roof and was getting used to the cool brown light when two other people came past outside on the turf. This time they were both young, a young man and a young woman. They were both in the prime of youth, the season before the smooth pink folds of the flower have burst their gummy case, when the wings of the butterfly, though fully grown, are motionless in the sun.

"Lucky it isn't Friday," he observed.

"Why? D'you believe in luck?"

"They make you pay sixpence on Friday."

"What's a sixpence anyway? Isn't it worth sixpence?"

"What's 'it'—what do you mean by 'it'?"

"O, anything—I mean—you know what I mean."

Long pauses came between each of these remarks; they were uttered in toneless and monotonous voices. The couple stood still on the edge of the flower-bed, and together pressed the end of her parasol deep down into the soft earth. The action and the fact that his hand rested on the top of hers expressed their feelings in a strange way, as these short insignificant words also expressed something, words with short wings for their heavy body of meaning, inadequate to carry them far and thus alighting awkwardly upon the very common objects that surrounded them, and were to their inexperienced touch so massive; but who knows (so they thought as they pressed the parasol into the earth) what precipices aren't concealed in them, or what slopes of ice don't shine in the sun on the other side? Who knows? Who has ever seen this before? Even when she wondered what sort of tea they gave you at Kew, he felt that something loomed up behind her words, and stood vast and solid behind them; and the mist very slowly rose and uncovered—O, Heavens, what were those shapes?—little white tables, and waitresses who looked first at her and then at him; and there was a bill that he would pay with a real two-shilling piece, and it was real, all real, he assured himself, fingering the coin in his pocket, real to everyone except to him and to her; even to him it began to seem real; and then—but it was too exciting to stand and think any longer, and he pulled the parasol out of the earth with a jerk and was impatient to find the place where one had tea with other people, like other people.

"Come along, Trissie; it's time we had our tea."

"Wherever *does* one have one's tea?" she asked with the oddest thrill of excitement in her voice, looking vaguely round and letting herself be drawn down the grass path, trailing her parasol; turning her head this way and that way forgetting her tea, wishing to go down there and then down there, remembering orchids and cranes among wild flowers, a Chinese pagoda and a crimson crested bird; but he bore her on.

Thus one couple after another with much the same irregular and aimless movement passed the flower-bed and were enveloped in layer after layer of green-blue vapour, in which at first their bodies had substance and a dash of colour, but later both substance and colour dissolved in the green-blue atmosphere. How hot it was! So hot that even the thrush chose to hop, like a mechanical bird, in the shadow of the flowers, with long pauses between one movement and the next; instead of rambling vaguely the white butterflies dance one above another, making with their white shifting flakes the outline of a shattered, marble column above the tallest flowers; the glass roofs of the palm house shone as if a whole market full of shiny green umbrellas had opened in the sun; and in the drone of the aeroplane the voice of the summer sky murmured its fierce soul. Yellow and black, pink and snow white, shapes of all these colours, men, women, and children were spotted for a second upon the horizon, and then, seeing the breadth of yellow that lay upon the grass, they wavered and sought shade beneath the trees, dissolving like drops of water in the yellow and green atmosphere, staining it faintly with red and blue. It seemed as if all gross and heavy bodies had sunk down in the heat motionless and lay huddled upon the ground, but their voices went wavering from them as if they were flames lolling from the thick waxen bodies of candles. Voices. Yes, voices. Wordless voices, breaking the silence suddenly with such depth of contentment, such passion of desire, or, in the voices of children, such freshness of surprise; breaking the silence? But there was no silence; all the time the motor omnibuses were turning their wheels and changing their gear; like a vast nest of Chinese boxes all of wrought steel turning ceaselessly one within another the city murmured; on the top of which the voices cried aloud and the petals of myriads of flowers flashed their colours into the air.

# RICHARD WRIGHT

*Wright (1908–1960) was born on a plantation near Natchez, Mississippi, the son of a mill worker and a schoolteacher. Deserted by his father at an early age, he lived intermittently in orphan asylums or wandered with his mother from city to city in an erratic pattern that continued for him after her death. In 1927 he turned up in Chicago, where he joined the Communist Party and began to write. A growing reputation as a short-story writer was solidified with the publication in 1940 of his first novel,* Native Son, *a pathetic and gory narrative of a young black man hurled blindly into crime.* Black Boy, *a vivid personal narrative, was published in 1945, followed in 1953 by the novel* The Outsider *and in 1954 by* Black Power, *an extensive report on the Africa Gold Coast countries. Several of his stories are collected in* Uncle Tom's Children *(1938) and* Eight Men *(1961).*

## The Man Who Was Almost a Man

Dave struck out across the fields, looking homeward through paling light. Whuts the usa talkin wid em niggers in the field? Anyhow, his mother was putting supper on the table. Them niggers can't understand *nothing.* One of these days he was going to get a gun and practice shooting, then they can't talk to him as though he were a little boy. He slowed, looking at the ground. Shucks, Ah ain scareda them even ef they are biggern me! Aw, Ah know whut Ahma do. . . . Ahm going by ol Joe's sto n git that Sears Roebuck catlog n look at them guns. Mabbe Ma will lemme buy one when she gits mah pay from ol man Hawkins. Ahma beg her t gimme some money. Ahm ol ernough to hava gun. Ahm seventeen. Almos a man. He strode, feeling his long, loose-jointed limbs. Shucks, a man oughta hava little gun aftah he done worked hard all day. . . .

He came in sight of Joe's store. A yellow lantern glowed on the front porch. He mounted steps and went through the screen door, hearing it bang behind him. There was a strong smell of coal oil and mackerel fish. He felt very confident until he saw fat Joe walk in through the rear door, then his courage began to ooze.

"Howdy, Dave! Whutcha want?"

"How yuh, Mistah Joe? Aw, Ah don wanna buy nothing. Ah jus wanted t see ef yuhd lemme look at tha ol catlog erwhile."

"Sure! You wanna see it here?"

"Nawsuh. Ah wans t take it home wid me. Ahll bring it back termorrow when Ah come in from the fiels."

"You plannin on buying something?"

"Yessuh."

"Your ma lettin you have your own money now?"

"Shucks. Mistah Joe, Ahm gittin t be a man like anybody else!"

Joe laughed and wiped his greasy white face with a red bandanna.

"Whut you plannin on buyin?"

Dave looked at the floor, scratched his head, scratched his thigh, and smiled. Then he looked up shyly.

"Ahll tell yuh, Mistah Joe, ef yuh promise yuh won't tell."

"I promise."

"Waal, Ahma buy a gun."

"A gun? Whut you want with a gun?"

"Ah wanna keep it."

"You ain't nothing but a boy. You don't need a gun."

"Aw, lemme have the catlog, Mistah Joe. Ahll bring it back."

Joe walked through the rear door. Dave was elated. He looked around at barrels of sugar and flour. He heard Joe coming back. He craned his neck to see if he were bringing the book. Yeah, he's got it. Gawddog, he's got it!

"Here, but be sure you bring it back. It's the only one I got."

"Sho, Mistah Joe."

"Say, if you wanna buy a gun, why don't you buy one from me? I gotta gun to sell."

"Will it shoot?"

"Sure it'll shoot."

"Whut kind is it?"

"Oh, it's kinda old. . . . A left-hand Wheeler. A pistol. A big one."

"Is it got bullets in it?"

"It's loaded."

"Kin Ah see it?"

"Where's your money?"

"Whu yuh wan fer it?"

"I'll let you have it for two dollars."

"Just two dollahs? Shucks, Ah could buy tha when Ah git mah pay."

"I'll have it here when you want it."

"Awright, suh. Ah be in fer it."

He went through the door, hearing it slam again behind him. Ahma git some money from Ma n buy me a gun! Only two dollahs! He tucked the thick catalogue under his arm and hurried.

"Where yuh been, boy?" His mother held a steaming dish of black-eyed peas.

"Aw, Ma, Ah jus stopped down the road t talk wid th boys."

"Yuh know bettah than t keep suppah waitin."

He sat down, resting the catalogue on the edge of the table.

"Yuh git up from there and git to the well n wash yosef! Ah ain feedin no hogs in mah house!"

She grabbed his shoulder and pushed him. He stumbled out of the room, then came back to get the catalogue.

"Whut this?"

"Aw, Ma, it's jusa catlog."

"Who yuh git it from?"

"From Joe, down at the sto."

"Waal, thas good. We kin use it around the house."

"Naw, Ma." He grabbed for it. "Gimme mah catlog, Ma."

She held onto it and glared at him.

"Quit hollerin at me! Whut's wrong wid yuh? Yuh crazy?"

"But Ma, please. It ain mine! It's Joe's! He tol me t bring it back t im termorrow."

She gave up the book. He stumbled down the back steps, hugging the thick book under his arm. When he had splashed water on his face and hands, he groped back to the kitchen and fumbled in a corner for the towel. He bumped into a chair; it clattered to the floor. The catalogue sprawled at his feet. When he had dried his eyes he snatched up the book and held it again under his arm. His mother stood watching him.

"Now, ef yuh gonna acka fool over that ol book, Ahll take it n burn it up."

"Naw, Ma, please."

"Waal, set down n be still!"

He sat and drew the oil lamp close. He thumbed page after page, unaware of the food his mother set on the table. His father came in. Then his small brother.

"Whutcha got there, Dave?" his father asked.

"Jusa catlog," he answered, not looking up.

"Yeah, here they is!" His eyes glowed at blue-and-black revolvers. He glanced up, feeling sudden guilt. His father was watching him. He eased the book under the table and rested it on his knees. After the blessing was asked, he ate. He scooped up peas and swallowed fat meat without chewing. Buttermilk helped to wash it down. He did not want to mention money before his father. He would do much better by cornering his mother when she was alone. He looked at his father uneasily out of the edge of his eye.

"Boy, how come yuh don quit foolin wid tha book n eat yo suppah?"

"Yessuh."

"How yuh n ol man Hawkins gittin erlong?"

"Suh?"

"Can't yuh hear? Why don yuh lissen? Ah ast yu how wuz yuh n ol man Hawkins gittin erlong?"

"Oh, swell, Pa. Ah plows mo lan than anybody over there."

"Waal, yuh oughta keep yo min on whut yuh doin."

"Yessuh."

He poured his plate full of molasses and sopped at it slowly with a chunk of cornbread. When his father and brother had left the kitchen, he still sat and looked again at the guns in the catalogue, longing to muster courage enough to present his case to his mother. Lawd, ef Ah only had the pretty one! He could almost feel the slickness of the weapon with his fingers. If he had a gun like that he would polish it and keep it shining so it would never rust. N Ah'd keep it loaded, by Gawd!

"Ma?" His voice was hesitant.

"Hunh?"

"Ol man Hawkins give yuh mah money yit?"

"Yeah, but ain no usa yuh thinkin bout thowin nona it erway. Ahm keepin tha money sos yuh kin have cloes t go to school this winter."

He rose and went to her side with the open catalogue in his palms. She was washing dishes, her head bent low over a pan. Shyly he raised the book. When he spoke, his voice was husky, faint.

"Ma, Gawd knows Ah wans one of these."

"One of whut?" she asked, not raising her eyes.

"One of these," he said again, not daring even to point. She glanced up at the page, then at him with wide eyes.

"Nigger, is yuh gone plum crazy?"

"Aw, Ma——"

"Git outta here! Don yuh talk t me bout no gun! Yuh a fool!"

"Ma, Ah kin buy one fer *two* dollahs."

"Not ef Ah knows it yuh ain!"

"But yuh promised me one——"

"Ah don care whut Ah promised! Yuh ain nothing but a boy yit!"

"Ma, ef yuh lemme buy one Ahll *never* ast yuh fer nothing no mo."

"Ah tol yuh t git outta here! Yuh ain gonna toucha penny of tha money fer no gun! Thas how come Ah has Mistah Hawkins t pay yo wages to me, cause Ah knows yuh ain got no sense."

"But Ma, we needa gun. Pa ain got no gun. We needa gun in the house. Yuh kin never tell whut might happen."

"Now don yuh try to maka fool outta me, boy! Ef we did hava gun yuh wouldn't have it!"

He laid the catalogue down and slipped his arm around her waist.

"Aw, Ma, Ah done worked hard alla summer n ain ast yuh fer nothin, is Ah, now?"

"Thas whut yuh spose to do!"

"But Ma, Ah wans a gun. Yuh kin lemme have two dollahs outta mah money. Please, Ma. I kin give it to Pa . . . Please, Ma! Ah loves yuh, Ma."

When she spoke her voice came soft and low.

"Whut yuh wan wida gun, Dave? Yuh don need no gun. Yuhll git in trouble. N ef yo Pa jus *thought* Ah let yuh have money t buy a gun he'd hava fit."

"Ahll hide it, Ma, it ain but two dollahs."

"Lawd, chil, whuts wrong wid yuh?"

"Ain nothing wrong, Ma. Ahm almos a man now. Ah wants a gun."

"Who gonna sell yuh a gun?"

"Ol Joe at the sto."

"N it don cos but two dollahs?"

"Thas all, Ma. Just two dollahs. Please, Ma."

She was stacking the plates away; her hands moved slowly, reflectively. Dave kept an anxious silence. Finally, she turned to him.

"Ahll let yuh git tha gun ef yuh promise me one thing."

"Whuts tha, Ma?"

"Yuh bring it straight back t *me,* yuh hear? It be fer Pa."

"Yessum! Lemme go now, Ma."

She stooped, turned slightly to one side, raised the hem of her dress, rolled down the top of her stocking, and came up with a slender wad of bills.

"Here," she said, "Lawd knows yuh don need no gun. But yer Pa does. Yuh bring it right back to *me,* yuh hear? Ahma put it up. Now ef yuh don, Ahma have yuh Pa lick yuh so hard yuh won ferget it."

"Yessum."

He took the money, ran down the steps, and across the yard.

"Dave! Yuuuuuh Daaaaave!"

He heard, but he was not going to stop now. "Naw, Lawd!"

The first movement he made the following morning was to reach under his pillow for the gun. In the gray light of dawn he held it loosely, feeling a sense of power. Could kill a man with a gun like this. Kill anybody, black or white. And if he were holding his gun in his hand, nobody could run over him; they would have to respect him. It was a big gun, with a long barrel and a heavy handle. He raised and lowered it in his hand, marveling at its weight.

He had not come straight home with it as his mother had asked; instead he had stayed out in the fields, holding the weapon in his hand, aiming it now and then at some imaginary foe. But he had not fired it; he had been afraid that his father might hear. Also he was not sure he knew how to fire it.

To avoid surrendering the pistol he had not come into the house until he knew that all were asleep. When his mother had tiptoed to his bedside late that night and demanded the gun, he had first played 'possum; then he had told her that the gun was hidden outdoors, that he would bring it to her in the morning. Now he lay turning it slowly in his hands. He broke it, took out the cartridges, felt them, and then put them back.

He slid out of bed, got a long strip of old flannel from a trunk, wrapped the gun in it, and tied it to his naked thigh while it was still loaded. He did not go in to breakfast. Even though it was not yet daylight, he started for Jim Hawkins' plantation. Just as the sun was rising he reached the barns where the mules and plows were kept.

"Hey! That you, Dave?"

He turned. Jim Hawkins stood eying him suspiciously.

"What're yuh doing here so early?"

"Ah didn't know Ah wuz gittin up so early, Mistah Hawkins. Ah wuz fixin t hitch up ol Jenny n take her t the fiels."

"Good. Since you're so early, how about plowing that stretch down by the woods?"

"Suits me, Mistah Hawkins."

"O.K. Go to it!"

He hitched Jenny to a plow and started across the fields. Hot dog! This was just what he wanted. If he could get down by the woods, he could shoot his gun and nobody would hear. He walked behind the plow, hearing the traces creaking, feeling the gun tied tight to his thigh.

When he reached the woods, he plowed two whole rows before he decided to take out the gun. Finally, he stopped, looked in all directions, then untied the gun and held it in his hand. He turned to the mule and smiled.

"Know whut this is, Jenny? Naw, yuh wouldn't know! Yuhs jusa ol mule! Anyhow, this is a gun, n it kin shoot, by Gawd!"

He held the gun at arm's length. Whut t hell, Ahma shoot this thing! He looked at Jenny again.

"Lissen here, Jenny! When Ah pull this ol trigger Ah don wan yuh t run n acka fool now."

Jenny stood with head down, her short ears pricked straight. Dave walked off about twenty feet, held the gun far out from him, at arm's length, and turned his head. Hell, he told himself, Ah ain afraid. The gun felt loose in his fingers; he waved it wildly for a moment. Then he shut his eyes and tightened his forefinger. *Blooom!* A report half-deafened him and he thought his right hand was torn from his arm. He heard Jenny whinnying and galloping over the field, and he found himself on his knees, squeezing his fingers hard between his legs. His hand was numb; he jammed it into his mouth, trying to warm it, trying to stop the pain. The gun lay at his feet. He did not quite know what had happened. He stood up and stared at the gun as though it were a live thing. He gritted his teeth and kicked the gun. Yuh almos broke mah arm! He turned to look for Jenny; she was far over the fields, tossing her head and kicking wildly.

"Hol on ther, ol mule!"

When he caught up with her she stood trembling, walling her big white eyes at him. The plow was far away; the traces had broken. Then Dave stopped short, looking, not believing. Jenny was bleeding. Her left side was red and wet with blood. He went closer. Lawd have mercy! Wondah did Ah shoot this mule? He grabbed for Jenny's mane. She flinched, snorted, whirled, tossing her head.

"Hol on now! Hol on."

Then he saw the hole in Jenny's side, right between the ribs. It was round, wet, red. A crimson stream streaked down the front leg, flowing fast. Good Gawd! Ah wuznt shootin at tha mule. He felt panic. He knew he had to stop that blood, or Jenny would bleed to death. He had never seen so much blood in all his life. He ran the mule for half a mile, trying to catch her. Finally, she stopped, breathing hard, stumpy tail half arched. He caught her mane and led her back to where the plow and gun lay. Then he stopped and grabbed handfuls of damp black earth and tried to plug the bullet hole. Jenny shuddered, whinnied, and broke from him.

"Hol on! Hol on now!"

He tried to plug it again, but blood came anyhow. His fingers were hot and sticky. He rubbed dirt hard into his palms, trying to dry them. Then again he attempted to plug the bullet hole, but Jenny shied away, kicking her heels high. He stood helpless. He had to do something. He ran at Jenny; she dodged him. He watched a red stream of blood flow down Jenny's leg and form a bright pool at her feet.

"Jenny . . . Jenny," he called weakly.

His lips trembled. She's bleeding t death! He looked in the direction of home, wanting to go back, wanting to get help. But he saw the pistol lying in the damp black clay. He had a queer feeling that if he only did something, this would not be; Jenny would not be there bleeding to death.

When he went to her this time, she did not move. She stood with sleepy, dreamy eyes; and when he touched her she gave a low-pitched whinny and knelt to the ground, her front knees slopping in blood.

"Jenny . . . Jenny . . ." he whispered.

For a long time she held her neck erect; then her head sank, slowly. Her ribs swelled with a mighty heave and she went over.

Dave's stomach felt empty, very empty. He picked up the gun and held it gingerly between his thumb and forefinger. He buried it at the foot of a tree. He took a stick and tried to cover the pool of blood with dirt—but what was the use? There was Jenny lying with her mouth open and her eyes walled and glassy. He could not tell Jim Hawkins he had shot his mule. But he had to tell something. Yeah, Ah'll tell em Jenny started gittin wil n fell on the joint of the plow. . . . But that would hardly happen to a mule. He walked across the field slowly, head down.

It was sunset. Two of Jim Hawkins' men were over near the edge of the woods digging a hole in which to bury Jenny. Dave was surrounded by a knot of people, all of whom were looking down at the dead mule.

"I don't see how in the world it happened," said Jim Hawkins for the tenth time.

The crowd parted and Dave's mother, father, and small brother pushed into the center.

"Where Dave?" his mother called.

"There he is," said Jim Hawkins.

His mother grabbed him.

"Whut happened, Dave? Whut yuh done?"

"Nothing."

"C'mon, boy, talk," his father said.

Dave took a deep breath and told the story he knew nobody believed.

"Waal," he drawled. "Ah brung ol Jenny down here sos Ah could do mah plowin. Ah plowed bout two rows, just like yuh see." He stopped and pointed at the long rows of upturned earth. "Then something musta been wrong wid ol Jenny. She wouldn't ack right a-tall. She started snortin n kickin her heels. Ah tried to hol her, but she pulled erway, rearin n goin on. Then when the point of the plow was stickin up in the air, she swung erroun n twisted hersef back on it. . . . She stuck hersef n started t bleed. N fo Ah could do anything, she wuz dead."

"Did you ever hear of anything like that in all your life?" asked Jim Hawkins.

There were white and black standing in the crowd. They murmured. Dave's mother came close to him and looked hard into his face. "Tell the truth, Dave," she said.

"Looks like a bullet hole ter me," said one man.

"Dave, whut yuh do wid the gun?" his mother asked.

The crowd surged in, looking at him. He jammed his hands into his pockets, shook his head slowly from left to right, and backed away. His eyes were wide and painful.

"Did he hava gun?" asked Jim Hawkins.

"By Gawd, Ah tol yuh tha wuz a *gun* wound," said a man, slapping his thigh.

His father caught his shoulders and shook him till his teeth rattled.

"Tell whut happened, yuh rascal! Tell whut . . ."

Dave looked at Jenny's stiff legs and began to cry.

"Whut yuh do wid tha gun?" his mother asked.

"Whut wuz he doin wida gun?" his father asked.

"Come on and tell the truth," said Hawkins. "Ain't nobody going to hurt you . . ."

His mother crowded close to him.

"Did yuh shoot that mule, Dave?"

Dave cried, seeing blurred white and black faces.

"Ahh ddinn gggo tt sshooooot hher . . . Ah ssswear ffo Gawd Ahh ddin. . . . Ah wuz a-tryin t sssee ef the ol gggun would sshoot——"

"Where yuh git the gun from?" his father asked.

"Ah got it from Joe, at the sto."

"Where yuh git the money?"

"Ma give it t me."

"He kept worryin me, Bob. Ah had t. Ah tol im t bring the gun right back t me . . . It was fer yuh, the gun."

"But how yuh happen to shoot that mule?" asked Jim Hawkins.

"Ah wuzn shootin at the mule, Mistah Hawkins. The gun jumped when Ah pulled the trigger . . . N fo Ah knowed anything Jenny wuz there a-bleedin."

Somebody in the crowd laughed. Jim Hawkins walked close to Dave and looked into his face.

"Well, looks like you have bought you a mule, Dave."

"Ah swear fo Gawd, Ah didn't go t kill the mule, Mistah Hawkins!"

"But you killed her!"

All the crowd was laughing now. They stood on tiptoe and poked heads over one another's shoulders.

"Well, boy, looks like yuh done bought a dead mule! Hahaha!"

"Ain tha ershame."

"Hohohohoho."

Dave stood, head down, twisting his feet in the dirt.

"Well, you needn't worry about it, Bob," said Jim Hawkins to Dave's father. "Just let the boy keep on working and pay me two dollars a month."

"Whut yuh wan fer yo mule, Mistah Hawkins?"

Jim Hawkins screwed up his eyes.

"Fifty dollars."

"Whut yuh do wid tha gun?" Dave's father demanded.

Dave said nothing.

"Yuh wan me t take a tree lim n beat yuh till yuh talk!"

"Nawsuh!"

"Whut yuh do wid it?"

"Ah thowed it erway."

"Where?"

"Ah . . . Ah thowed it in the creek."

"Waal, c mon home. N firs thing in the mawnin git to tha creek n fin tha gun."

"Yessuh."

"Whut yuh pay fer it?"

"Two dollahs."

"Take tha gun n git yo money back n carry it t Mistah Hawkins, yuh hear? N don fergit Ahma lam yo black bottom good fer this! Now march yosef on home, suh!"

Dave turned and walked slowly. He heard people laughing. Dave glared, his eyes welling with tears. Hot anger bubbled in him. Then he swallowed and stumbled on.

That night Dave did not sleep. He was glad that he had gotten out of killing the mule so easily, but he was hurt. Something hot seemed to turn over inside him each time he remembered how they had laughed. He tossed on his bed, feeling his hard pillow. N Pa says he's gonna beat me. . . . He remembered other beatings, and his back quivered. Naw, naw, Ah sho don wan im t beat me tha way no mo. Dam em all! Nobody ever gave him anything. All he did was work. They treat me lika mule, n then they beat me. He gritted his teeth. N Ma had t tell on me.

Well, if he had to, he would take old man Hawkins that two dollars. But that meant selling the gun. And he wanted to keep that gun. Fifty dollars for a dead mule.

He turned over, thinking of how he had fired the gun. He had an itch to fire it again. Ef other men kin shoota gun, by Gawd, Ah kin! He was still, listening. Mebbe they all sleepin now. . . . The house was still. He heard the soft breathing of his brother. Yes, now! He would go down and get that gun and see if he could fire it! He eased out of bed and slipped into overalls.

The moon was bright. He ran almost all the way to the edge of the woods. He stumbled over the ground, looking for the spot where he had buried the gun. Yeah, here it is. Like a hungry dog scratching for a bone, he pawed it up. He puffed his black cheeks and blew dirt from the trigger and barrel. He broke it and found four cartridges unshot. He looked around; the fields were filled with silence and moonlight. He clutched the gun stiff and hard in his fingers. But, as soon as he wanted to pull the trigger, he shut his eyes and turned his head. Naw, Ah can't shoot wid mah eyes closed n mah head turned. With effort he held his eyes open; then he squeezed. *Blooooom!* He was stiff, not breathing. The gun was still in his hands. Dammit, he'd done it! He fired again. *Blooom!* He smiled. *Blooom! Blooom! Click, click.* There! It was empty. If anybody could shoot a gun, he could. He put the gun into his hip pocket and started across the fields.

When he reached the top of a ridge he stood straight and proud in the moonlight, looking at Jim Hawkins' big white house, feeling the gun sagging in his pocket. Lawd, ef Ah had just one mo bullet Ah'd taka shot at tha house.

Ah'd like t scare ol man Hawkins jusa little. . . . Jusa enough t let im know Dave Sanders is a man.

To his left the road curved, running to the tracks of the Illinois Central. He jerked his head, listening. From far off came a faint *hoooof-hoooof; hoooof-hoooof; hoooof-hoooof* . . . Tha's number eight. He took a swift look at Jim Hawkins' white house; he thought of pa, of ma, of his little brother, and the boys. He thought of the dead mule and heard *hoooof-hoooof; hoooof-hoooof; hoooof-hoooof* . . . He stood rigid. Two dollahs a mont. Les see now. . . . Tha means itll take bout two years. Shucks! Ahll be dam!

He started down the road, toward the tracks. Yeah, here she comes! He stood beside the track and held himself stiffly. Here she comes, erroun the ben. . . . C mon, yuh slow poke! C mon! He had his hand on his gun; something quivered in his stomach. Then the train thundered past, the gray and brown box cars rumbling and clinking. He gripped the gun tightly; then he jerked his hand out of his pocket. Ah betcha Bill wouldn't do it! Ah betcha. . . . The cars slid past, steel grinding upon steel. Ahm riding yuh ternight so hep me Gawd! He was hot all over. He hesitated just a moment; then he grabbed, pulled atop of a car, and lay flat. He felt his pocket; the gun was still there. Ahead the long rails were glinting in the moonlight, stretching away, away to somewhere, somewhere where he could be a man. . . .

# Writing Papers about Fiction

*Richard Bausch*

The American poet and translator John Ciardi used to be fond of telling a story about going around to schools speaking to groups of students as part of a poets-in-the-schools program. The idea was and is a good one: to expose young people to writers, the actual practitioners of the craft or art themselves. One morning, as Ciardi would tell it, he was scheduled to visit an elementary school, so he brought along a poem he had written for children called "The Stranger Inside the Pumpkin." The poem begins like this:

> The stranger inside the pumpkin said,
> "It's only dark inside your head."

After he had read the poem aloud to a crowded room of fifth graders, he asked, "Who's speaking in this poem?" Every hand in the room went up, and he chose a girl in front who, without the slightest hesitation, said, "Jack O'Lantern." Ciardi then asked, "What is Jack O'Lantern telling us?" Again, there was a clamor to get his attention, hands waving, little voices saying, "Me, me." Ciardi chose a boy this time. "Jack O'Lantern thinks we don't have any light inside us because there's no candle showing out our eyes," the boy said. And after this, the whole class began to talk about the truth, or lack of it, in that idea. There was even some talk about the quality of light, ordinary candlelight as opposed to the light of imagination.

At the end of the session, as Ciardi and his escort were leaving the school, the escort said, "There's a high school nearby, we have some extra time, would you mind visiting with a class there?"

Ciardi felt slightly ill-prepared, because all he had with him was this children's poem, "The Stranger Inside the Pumpkin." But he agreed to visit the high school, deciding that he would simply read the same poem, and talk about writing children's poems. To a large group of twelfth graders, young men and women, really, he read those same lines:

> The stranger inside the pumpkin said,
> "It's only dark inside your head."

When he finished reading, he asked the same question he had asked the fifth grade children. "Who's speaking in this poem?"

Silence.

He waited, intending—as he put it, telling the story—to keep waiting until the sun went down if it took that long, for someone, anyone, to gather the courage to speak. Finally one brave young man in the back of the room raised his hand. "Yes?" Ciardi said.

"Is that, symbolism?"

Ciardi would go on to say that it had taken a mere seven years of schooling to reduce this young reader to that level of stupidity about the written word.

Now, of course, this is a story, and John Ciardi used it with delight, and to great effect, as an illustration of how students learning to think critically about what they read often learn to look past the words of a piece of writing and, in so doing, miss what is obvious and quite simple. What follows here are a few general principles to help you in the task of writing papers about the fiction you'll be reading, to alleviate some of your anxiety about the undertaking, and to suggest some ways of approaching the problem of how to write a critical paper about fiction.

The following sections of this book offer some thoughts on the various approaches available to us in responding to fiction we read; the section titled "Personal Engagement" especially treats the critical response, which is what will most likely be expected of you as a student in a literature class. The matters discussed in this section are meant to suggest some ways to formulate a critical response and express it in a paper. These are not part of a list or catalog and cannot be set down like a set of commandments or rules, but they do apply to what most students face when the first paper comes due.

And perhaps the thing to be emphasized here is that how much and how well you are able to express yourself about the fiction you are studying depends to a large extent on your own attitude toward the task.

The first thing to remember when you begin to write a paper about fiction is that you must allow for what is direct and *literal* in the words on the page. A work of fiction, in spite of what you may already have internalized about it, is not a code, not something that needs deciphering, particularly, or translation into some other form of expression. One misleading question about fiction, and one of the easiest and, therefore, most often asked questions about it, is "What is the writer *trying* to say?" If the story is any good at all, the writer is in fact *saying* it, whatever it is, and the story itself makes up the terms of that saying. The writer of a good story is almost never trying to be obscure or even difficult; the experience the writer is exploring may be filled with difficulty and ambiguity, but the writer is always striving for *clarity*, trying to be *perfectly* clear.

Therefore, to read a story intelligently, you need bring only your own experience to it and strive to be *open* to what transpires literally on the page. The story will either interest you or it won't. If the story doesn't interest you, the fault may lie with you, in that you are not yet emotionally or intellectually ready for it; it is also possible that the particular story will *never* interest you, and that is one of the reasons why conversations and commentary and friendly arguments about fiction have been going on for as long as fiction has existed. But if the story does *not* interest you, if it does nothing to you, if you feel nothing reading it, I do not recommend that you choose it to write about. When you *do* find a story that interests you—and it is hard to imagine that in an anthology of this variety and size you would not find at least *one* that did so—your first order of business is to read it again. Read it several times, in fact, and you will find with each reading that you notice more about it, that its architecture becomes a bit more readily visible to you, its nature more clear.

But let me go back for a moment.

The difficulty for any new student of fiction is that while you are *reading* stories you are asked to *write* criticism. That is like entering a room full of strangers among whom an animated and widely various conversation has been going on for centuries and being asked to add something to the conversation. You read a story that you think you might be able to say something about; you even like the story. Yet even though you could sense it breaking down into its component parts as you were reading it and rereading it, when you actually come to thinking about it as a subject for a paper, your mind goes blank. There the story is, like a painting or a piece of sculpture. It is made out of words, but it is just as mute as a statue, just as much a silent, existing, created thing, insisting on its own wholeness, resisting all your efforts to take it apart.

You must understand this is not an unusual feeling for *any* reader of a truly good story. You are not being confronted with some deficiency in your own ability to *understand* or *get* it; you are simply experiencing the territory, and if you allow yourself a little confusion and uncertainty, you might find that the exploration of the inner workings of the story is fun, that it enhances your enjoyment of it. And though we live in a highly politicized time, we must never lose sight of the fact that one of the most important functions of fictive art is *pleasure*. And so the first rule of thumb for anyone assigned to write a paper about fiction is to *find something that truly does engage you*, something about which you can express yourself in terms other than the artificial, forced, exhausting phrases of false interest—that awful feeling of trying to plumb what you believe your professor wants to hear, of trying to say something as if you had the slightest interest in it, when in fact the whole enterprise seems only a little less painful than a dental procedure involving a drill.

Having found a story that does engage you—and by this I mean it has caused some reaction in you, even if that reaction is at first negative—and having read the story again and decided that you will write about it, the next order of business is to locate some aspect of it that especially interests you: its use of language, the presence in it—or lack of presence in it—of one element or another, the nature of its characters, some element of conflict or treatment of theme, the way any of its internal aspects contrasts or compares to some other story or stories, or how it reflects the values of its time and place or may be applied to the values of our own time and place or even how it may seem *not* to reflect such values, distant or near. You may discover an element of the story that speaks to you on some deeper level about yourself, about something you are afraid of, or ache for, or love. Any element of a story is worth writing about if you can have some stake in it, some actual connection to it. Writing about it is how you explore this connection.

It has been said that the best preparation for the reading of any story is to have read all other stories. That is to say that the more you read, the better able you are to respond. But even having read dozens of stories, you may feel at a loss when the time comes to write about one. So let us take the logic of the thought a step further and say that the best preparation for the writing of a piece of criticism is having read all other criticism.

Obviously, you can do no such thing in either case: no one *ever* gets to all there is that is worth reading and remembering. Geoffrey Chaucer was one of the most learned men of his time, and his library contained ninety books. I am a practicing writer of prose fiction, I read both for the love of it and as a profession, and my personal library—a modest one by modern standards—contains more than seventy-five hundred volumes. The remark about preparation is simply to suggest a truth, though; and writing your paper you will have to address the problem of what we can call "The Customs of Critical Speech." How do you begin to express yourself in the language of criticism if you have not been reading criticism? If you have had no real taste of how it is done? It is no accident that people who write poetry *read* a great deal of poetry, that people who write fiction read thousands of stories and novels (poets also read novels, of course; and novelists, most of them anyway, also read poetry); but the fact is that one reads a great deal in the form in which one primarily works. That is how we all learn to write; indeed, it is usually the thing that *leads* us to writing. Yet new students of literature are regularly asked to write criticism without having ever really been exposed to any critical writing.

To extend the metaphor of the conversation, then: you have entered this room, people have been discussing a story. The simplest, first strategy, is to familiarize yourself as quickly as possible with the manner and nature of the conversation. You do this by listening in, as it were. By reading some criticism of stories, or of any work of literary art that you already know, have already read. When I teach sophomore literature, before I give any other assignments, I ask my students to do an annotated bibliography about *Hamlet*. They must find ten critical essays about the play, read them, and then summarize them for me, merely to show that they have indeed read the essays. This is less to teach them about *Hamlet* than to expose them to the ways and means of critical speech about that great play and, by extension, about any other work of literature.

What you will find, reading in criticism, is that the work being discussed is rarely considered in its entire form or shape; that the critical writer, in nearly every case, has chosen—or discovered—some vital or crucial but always quite specific aspect of the work and is concentrating on that, tracing its use, and the ramifications of its use through the story (or its similarity or difference to some aspect of another story from the same writer, or a contemporary, or even someone far away in time or place). Notice, too, how the critical writer *uses the words of the story itself* to support what he has to say about it. The use of plot summary is always to underscore or illustrate the point, and that quotations from the story follow from assertions about it, as *demonstrations* of the truth of those assertions.

Too often, student papers about fiction end up merely summarizing the story's plot and recounting the names of its characters. For teachers of literature, there is nothing so dull as having to read twenty-seven versions of the same plot summary in a single afternoon. And falling into mere plot summary is the most common mistake students make writing papers, mostly because they do not feel confident talking about the story in any other way, they have seldom if ever experienced stories being talked about in any other way. (Much of this goes back, no doubt, to the old high school "book report," in which students are asked to recount book plots more or less as proof that they have done the assigned reading.)

Mere plot summary is likely to be a habit you will have to work some to break. And one rather simple way to break it, though at first you may find it difficult to do, is to keep in mind the fact that the audience for your paper about a given story is made up of people who are *familiar* with it.

Here, for instance, is one facet of a story you probably already know; it is a play rather than a work of short fiction, but it will serve to illustrate my point. To audiences in ancient Greece who went to see Sophocles' great *Oedipus Rex*, the story of Oedipus was at least as familiar as the story of Christ is to us (there is a reference to the Oedipus story in Homer, who predates Sophocles by hundreds of years, and the tone of that reference is that it was an *old* story, even then); hence, one of the most interesting elements of that play is the irony in which it is soaked—this mystery story in which the detective searching for a murderer finds that the murderer is himself actually contained no mystery at all to the audiences of its time; instead, there was the excruciating spectacle of Oedipus, moving ever closer to the discovery of the truth everyone in the theater already knew. To write a paper about that, you would use those lines Oedipus speaks that, given the nature of the audience's knowledge, contain the most irony. You might explore how that irony carries the play forward and informs the action; you might show how it extends to other characters in the play and how it shapes the emotions created by the spectacle of the tragedy.

The same kind of approach works when you write criticism about fiction. Your audience is made up of participants in the appreciation of some *part* of a thing with which everyone is acquainted.

So, you choose something *inside* the story, some specific element of its workings that you have noticed, and you present that to your audience, all of whom know the plot of the story, and you move through your discussion of this thing you have noticed, following your assertions about it with proof out of the material of the story, using the words of the story itself to support what you say.

But suppose you cannot find anything in the story that seems worth writing about? Suppose that, even having found a story with which you feel a connection, you are still unable to settle on some specific element of it? At the beginning of this anthology is a list of general questions (p. xxxiv), where you will find ample material from which to choose for exploring the details of any good story. You need only look over the list and then turn to your story and think through some of these questions in relation to the story. If that fails to spark something, try looking at what some of the contemporary writers in this book have had to say about stories by other writers, living and dead. You might even find one that you wish to add to, or take issue with. But as you read, see how often these contemporary writers *use the words of the stories themselves* to make their observations about those stories. Pay close attention to the ways in which they move from assertion to quotations, from the exploration of something *about* the story to the use of details *from* the story to support their claims.

To write a paper about a work of fiction is simply to take part in a civilized and polite conversation about it, with others who have read the same story, to say something meaningful about a matter of importance to you. If the story has moved you in some way, then you will be saying something meaningful as it applies to your own life, your own experience, your own interests. And in the act of expressing this, of working through the story, you become a sharper reader, you develop a more sophisticated sense of language as it is used by artists, and you become less likely to be fooled by empty rhetoric and cant, by the flood of falsity and hype all around you, by the ways in which society names and places you and makes assumptions about you and tries to control you—for whatever purpose, even if it is as simple as the ambition to sell you something you don't need. By reading good short fiction, and thinking critically about it, you not only gain the deeper pleasures there are in the contemplation of this superior art form but become more free. No less than that.

Finally, remember that fiction is about *experience,* that its truths are not necessarily—they are not even very often—merely philosophical truths, but contain the truths of *felt life;* that good stories break down the barriers between peoples and times and cultures; that fiction speaks to us across boundaries as distant as the centuries and as unbridgeable as death itself. The editors of this anthology hope you will find something that engages you, something about which you can speak passionately, in terms of the pleasure that reading good stories provides. As fiction writers—as practicing short-story writers—we take issue with the idea that the study of literature is a science; literature is far too disruptive and unruly and filled with human contradiction to be any such thing, and writers have never been in the business of engineering better human beings. Thus we encourage you to think about the stories in this book as works of art that relate to life most consistently as an *enhancement* of being—and perhaps only a momentary one at that—and that they resemble more closely all the other good stories that you may happen to be reading, or have read, than they resemble the life we actually lead, even though, in that momentary shapeliness that always obtains when a story is told, they somehow make us feel life more vividly. We hope you will make *connections,* not theories or ideology. We hope you will consider the poetry you read and hear in these prose pieces as elements of the lovely songs that exist in them, concentrating on the art of the expression rather than what you may have already been taught to search out in terms of social constructs or political "stances."

Politics is politics, and everything else is everything else.

The study of fiction is mostly the study of everything else, and politics is no more nor less important to storytelling than botany or history or psychology or religion. Most good writers are steeped in all of these things and more, without being in thrall to any of them. And by the phrase *everything else,* we mean what it is like to be alive on the planet earth at widely various points in the human journey. What it feels like being new, being crowded or alone, being in love or out of it, worrying, trying, failing; succeeding, growing old, or wishing one were older; missing lost friends, lost loved ones, or being reunited with them; fearing for one's children; living with regret, with the hope of revenge, or with an obsession; being weak or timid or confused, or consumed with fury; hating something or dreading it; wanting something and not being able to have it; grieving or gathering strength; bearing the remorseless facts of existence with some kind of dignity and with some kind of grace; facing damnation or achieving redemption. Absurdity, foolishness. Folly and heroism. What it means being alive, engaged in the struggle to be decent, and prosperous, too. In other words, the nature of the human family in all its complexity, its age-old refusal to conform to any reductive idea about itself.

# When You Write about Fiction

## *R. V. Cassill*

Writing papers about stories you have read in this book will often be a part of your class work. Writing such papers gives you the chance to organize your thoughts and comment on the emotions you have experienced in reading and verbal discussion. Properly approached, it will lead you to understand that such writing is an organic offshoot of reading, an extension of the same imaginative experience.

The general questions on page xxxiv were designed with some intent of suggesting topics and approaches you might take in dealing with one or with several of the stories that have appealed to you more than the others. To be sure, you may find that more than one question is to be engaged with any given story. The following notes will supplement and expand the questions.

For convenience in making a start on your paper, note that most of your options will fall in one of three general categories. First, you might want to assume that you are introducing a story to someone who has not yet read it. This can be thought of as the approach of a book reviewer who must give a brief but comprehensive overview of the work under consideration while enumerating some of the components that give it flavor and significance.

A second mode of approach is to suppose you are writing for someone who is quite familiar with the story but who may not have fully weighed some aspects of it that seem to you worth reconsideration. For simplicity's sake we can categorize this as the tactic of the critic who never concedes that the last word has been said on his or her subject—who, in fact, often debates prior interpretations as a means of focusing attention on points that may have been slighted.

Broadest and most open of all is the category of personal response in which your experience in reading; your values; your surprise, dismay, or delight; and your image of yourself are made a mirror for whatever a story has to offer. Here the virtues of detachment and objectivity; are deliberately set aside or postponed in favor of concentrating on your adventure as an impassioned, impressionable partner in a dialogue with the author.

None of these approaches is inherently better than the others. The sky is the limit for each. Failure and muddle lurk as possibilities—less likely, of course, for the student whose imagination and understanding have been heated in advance of the commitment to writing. Surely reading well is half the battle of writing good papers. Just as certainly, writing well about fiction stabilizes and extends your skill as a reader.

### PERSONAL ENGAGEMENT

Great critics long ago taught us that unless both the head and the heart are involved, understanding will be lopsided. Perceptions, even of the physical world, will be distorted unless we "attend and value" as Coleridge put it. While we need not argue the relevance of this in scientific studies, it is overwhelmingly important in literary education. Detachment and cool objectivity are great virtues—in their proper place. But surely the experience of reading fiction would be barren if it were not colored by passion, sympathy, and the engagement of irrational (and sometimes precious) prejudices. By the same token, writing about fiction can be a shallow exercise when it is stripped of the force of sympathy, outrage, disappointment, fear, and delight that began in reading a story.

You want—as you should—to write responsibly and truly. But from fear of falsifying we can be trapped in falsification. A perfectly legitimate distrust of sentimentality—reinforced often enough by what you have been taught in many classrooms—can choke up the emotional recognition of truths conveyed in imaginative literature. A hard heart is not a mental asset, nor is an artificial posture of impersonality a persuasive ingredient in your writing. Some of the best illuminations of literature can come from candid exposure of how, in fact, one story or another worked on the imagination of the person you know yourself to be.

Were you to note—with the greatest conceivable objectivity—that the last paragraph of "Flowering Judas" is more highly charged with dread than any that have preceded it and that this transition into undiluted terror is important evidence of Laura's character, you would still fall short of expressing what you know about the nature of such terror—and, therefore, fall short of expressing what you know intuitively of the person in the story. The external threats around her are in no way magnified at the story's end. Perhaps they are even ebbing when Braggioni relents in his courtship. At last she is terrified of what she is, of what she has become, and each one of us knows the magnitude of such dread, for we have all felt it at moments—though not in circumstances that match Laura's. It is by the recognition of our personal memory that we identify with her and recognize her story as part of our own confessional.

I risk the word *confession* with some trepidation, because I don't want to encourage a notion that writing about fiction should be an excuse for flights into autobiography merely triggered by something mentioned in a story. What is important is to find how the pattern of the story extends and clarifies the dilemmas in which we have groped as the characters do.

The right starting point is the admission that we laugh, grow anxious, indignant, or appalled, we grieve, scorn, and clutch after comfort among platitudes until we are swept by convictions generated by our reading. Then your paper must explain why the fictive evidence worked as it did on you, of all people.

Why were you amused and perhaps distressed as you read "Royal Beatings"? Here is a story about the politics of family life. Probably the setting and the members of the family are quite different from those you grew up with. Yet here is a prototype of the twists and turns by which members of every family play the others off against each other in a kind of blind ritual without reasonable objectives. However painful her beatings, Rose seems to invite them compulsively; and however shabby or distressed her memories of the family may be, in the end they are transfigured into a bond she cannot reject, does not wish to deny. By relating this prototypical formation of family bonds to what you have seen in your own family—exploring with honesty and candor—you simultaneously bring the story to life and find in life a pattern in the chaos of stressful relationships.

Falling in love, trying to manage love with its pitfalls, its vulnerability and alterations is a prototypical human experience of another sort. Stories like "The Horse Dealer's Daughter" offer variations of the bafflement nearly everyone must go through. You need not learn the sting of bereavement or the temptation to deny it or to add insights of your own. You need not have rescued a girl from a pond in the dead of winter to know that a rescued person has some profound claim on the rescuer—or to write a paper drawing on your own experience, which would touch some complications Lawrence left out of his tale.

For all its marvelous variety, the greater part of fiction draws on the major prototypes of love, war, sex, death, families, religion, and politics. And at the level of the prototype you will find in both your reading and writing the links between your own time and place and things that happened long ago and far away. The relation of children and parents is the subject of multitudinous stories—for the very good reason that though certain typical patterns occur generation after generation there are novelties we can always find to make individual experience seem painfully unique. Parents seem always to be an embarrassment to their children, by virtue of their traits, ideas, appearance, or whatever. In "Everything That Rises Must Converge" a young man named Julian hopes to reform his mother by pushing her into humiliation. That is, he tries to reeducate her without any clear idea, or much concern, about the cost to either of them if he gets his wish. Surely any but the most nonchalant reading of this story will call up the problems you have with your own parents. And just as your life situation has conditioned the way you interpret the story on a first reading, the story will influence your assessment of the situation in real life when you try to connect reality and fiction by writing a personal response. It would be vainglorious to expect either the story itself or your paper to *solve* what you feel as a personal problem. Literature is not therapy or social engineering. Yet something has been saved from the darkness when you write full tilt about the way a story has played on your judgments and attitudes toward people close to you.

"Everything That Rises Must Converge" surely engages your opinions about race and class, as well as those about families. What will you make of the moral ambiguity at the story's end? Julian's "good," "tolerant," and "unbiased" attitudes have certainly not triumphed in the test of action. Their inadequacy is exposed; they have been redefined as prejudices no better than those his mother clung to. Now, if Julian's positions happen to be those you cherish, how will you respond when you find them downgraded by the resolution of the story conflict? Will you evade the challenge by dismissing the story as "mere fiction"? Or will you risk the comfort of your convictions by setting them among contrary claims of the sort the story sets forth as part of the whole moral equation?

It is far from my purpose to suggest what response you should make—only to underline the fact that literature offers something like test cases, fictive situations in which you can make choices about where you would hope to stand.

What you write may, if it is seriously done, force you to a readjustment of values—or perhaps to an altered view of who you are and how you came to hold the opinions you do.

Emerson advises: "Put more range in your scale." Stories that go beyond the moral boundaries of your life thus far can provide that range. In writing a personal response to a difficult story, you can make choices life has not yet given you the chance to make. At the simplest level such response may be only, "I would (or wouldn't) have done (or judged) as the character did." You can create something considerably more sophisticated and satisfying if you take into account the conditioning motives the author built into the story and your own susceptibility to such motives. By playing the game according to the full set of rules required by sympathetic reading, you can keep your paper from straying into personal manifesto or autobiography.

For this kind of paper turn to those general questions that bear on the meaning and nature of human affairs, rather than those having to do with technique. For example, in Joyce's story "The Dead" you might ask about Gabriel's "generosity." It is not conceivable that the term should mean exactly the same for all of us. Furthermore, for most of us, our idea of generosity fluctuates a good deal. When we come to write about Gabriel's generosity, we can't help noting that it has variable significances in Joyce's treatment. Yes, it is genuine, but of small worth to Gabriel in grappling with the demands life puts on him. By expounding on this qualification, you should not aim at making yourself either more or less generous, but rather at refining a key term in your vocabulary of personal values.

While in most papers intended as a personal response to a story, theme and author's attitude will take precedence over a consideration of technique, it is well never to forget that all the ingredients woven into fiction condition the thematic statements emerging from it. So it follows that in this approach to writing about fiction you must not leave any of them out of account.

We find some stories that begin with quiet objectivity move to an emotional crescendo at which feeling and intuition take over. Think of these stories as good models for the paper you are writing. Borrow their devices. Imitate the tension they are built from. Wax hot, wax cold. Be lyrical, be matter-of-fact. Make a pattern of lights and shadows, risks and certainties, as fiction writers do, even though you are not writing fiction at this point. Don't neglect the tone of your paper. It is one resource for shaping what it means.

Finally, acceptance or challenge of an author's thematic statement will make you realize that in the human realm there is no such thing as a "value-free" occurrence. Stephen Crane in "The Open Boat" seems to postulate a purely indifferent universe confronting the shipwrecked men. But yet, from the magic of his art we perceive that the impassioned men are part of that universe; their concerns for their plight, their lives, and their souls transform the environing indifference. The concern you generate in a written response to Crane's work extends the passionate conflict and its circles of implication. This is how literature moves in concentric waves through the substance of life—continuous far beyond the point at which an author sends the finished manuscript to be published. The prime requirement for you is to keep it moving by an exercise of candor and intelligence worthy of what you believe literature to be.

## CRITICAL CONCENTRATION

Probing into a piece of fiction already known to your readers usually requires narrowing your subject matter in some ways, deepening and reinforcing attention paid to some aspect of it. When this is your intent, it is probably wasteful to recap the story line or central conflict—though, to be sure, there may be a need to refer to these. It may be necessary to reach out for comparisons to the work of other writers. Your progress in understanding has been consolidated by comparisons. Comparisons incorporated in your paper can weight the evidence you need to substantiate the interpretation you are arguing for. The trick is to subordinate everything irrelevant to the point you want to make.

Here again you might get valuable prompting from the general questions, for most of them are designed to focus one or another critical approach, emphasizing some singular aspect of a story. Suppose you want to hone an interpretation of Katherine Anne Porter's "Flowering Judas." Your paper will show that it is more than the account of the hardships of an American girl in Mexico in revolutionary times. Your imagination has been snagged by the title of the story and by the insistent reference to the Judas tree in the text of the story and in Laura's terror-blasted dream at the end. You note the connotations of betrayal in the word (name) of Judas and ask: Where is the betrayal in the story? Who is betrayed and by whom? You may jot in your notes that Braggioni is trying to betray his followers, his wife, and Laura. As far as Laura is concerned, you see, he is not a rapist, but he keeps in play many coercions for seducing her. The whole milieu in which she lives now is full of treacherous possibilities from which she has to guard herself to preserve her chastity and the remnants of the idealism that brought her to the chaos of the place and the times.

Having compiled the mass of outward evidence, you are ready to ask the overwhelming question. Has Laura not betrayed herself? She has said no to life in its tawdriness and no to death with its threat of oblivion. If there is nothing else, has she not chosen self-eradication? (This is not an obligatory conclusion but an illustrative one. It will suggest that a pattern of evidence must be gathered to support a thesis.)

As you see, many of the questions have to do with one part or another of the technique the author has employed. For a critical paper, an option much to be recommended is for you to examine a single aspect of technique as this is exemplified in a number of stories. You could begin with the choice of a single item from the "Glossary of Critical Terms" (p. 1722).

Were you to start, say, with "point of view," you would need to select a group of stories illustrating the range of possibilities in stories told in the third person. (In first-person narration, the point of view is more narrowly restricted to that of the narrator.) In "Babylon Revisited" you will see that the point of view is closely limited to the thoughts and experience of the central character. Also there is such a close connection between the language of this character and that used by the author you should categorize these as examples of an "effaced narrator" (see "Glossary"). In "The Road from Colonnus," on the other hand, not only does the point of view shift from one character to another, one is constantly aware of a clear distinction between the voice telling the story and that of any of the characters it includes. The point of view in "Hills Like White Elephants" is completely detached and impersonal, as if it were that of a disinterested third person present on the scene, eavesdropping as he watches a pair of strangers. The detachment of the early part of "Flowering Judas" is by no means as impersonal or unemotional, and it is shifted in the last passages to a very intense identification with Laura's interior monologue.

In these cases—or in others you might choose—you should acknowledge that the material and focus of interest (see "Glossary") have influenced the handling of the point of view. To indicate the probable reasons for the author's choice in each case will help you display your working knowledge of the critical term you are illustrating. Matters of tone, use of flashback and imagery, pace, immediacy, omniscience or objectivity—in fact, all or any of the aspects of fiction—can best be treated by assembling a number of examples from different story sources.

Analysis of character and motivation is not precisely a consideration of an author's technique. It draws, as well, on your knowledge of human nature and behavior and on the way one is revealed by the other. Yet it is a prime mistake ever to write about a character or action as if these existed in the actual world rather than in your reading. After all, what we may know of a fictional character is what the author has developed by means of his or her choosing and by a selection of evidence or by some form of special pleading to engage the reader's sympathies. Because, in matters of literature, we are concerned with life as it is exposed by arrangements of written words, a truly critical approach obliges us to examine the means used to represent actuality. If you choose to limit your examination of "The Chrysanthemums" to the character and motivations of Elisa Allen, probably you would show how Steinbeck set up a sequence of revelations that altogether add up to what we can know of her. There is, first of all, her appearance as she works among her flowers. We are told her age and that her attire seems to masculinize her. Her husband's comment about her "gift" adds another touch to the picture. Her speech and behavior in the scene with the vagabond tinker shows us the turbulence of her suppressed yearnings. In the aftermath of his visit we see evidence of its effect in her husband's exclamation, "You look so nice!" Then, after she has been hurt by the rejection of the gift, she flares up to wish she could see men bloody each other. Her quickly suppressed resentment rounds out our sympathy with her predicament. The art of arranging such evidence in the meaningful sequence of a story line is what you ought to account for in writing about character. If you can *show* how meaning has been developed by the writer, you have gone an important step beyond a mere statement of that meaning.

While it remains very much worth critical scrutiny, "The Chrysanthemums" is one of the most conventional and straightforward stories in this collection.

As such it could be used as a norm against which you could measure the peculiarities of some that are deliberately unconventional—"experimental" as we say. "A Hunger Artist" and "How I Contemplated the World from the Detroit House of Correction and Began My Life Over Again" are striking examples of unconventional subject matter and unconventional presentation. They offer special challenges and opportunities to the writer of a critical paper.

The subheads of Oates's story indicate that within the unconventional sequence the fundamental elements of fiction are somehow given their due: "Characters," "Events" (for action and plot), and "Sioux Drive" (for setting). But where Steinbeck wove these elements into a continuous narrative following a simple chronology, Oates segregates them in categories to imitate notes made in preparation for writing a coherent account. Reading about the adolescent girl and her adventures among some desperate characters in the seamy side of Detroit may seem very much like solving a jigsaw puzzle. We find a few bits and pieces that fit together. Once they are assembled in our mind the patterns revealed indicate whether other details have to fit in. When we reflect on the story after reading it all, we can remember that there is a chronological sequence of events no more at odds with our common experience of time than that of Steinbeck's straightforward presentation.

It should occur to us that if we were really reading notes compiled by a disturbed girl, the chances are very great that we could not retrieve such a chronology or be nearly as certain of when, where, and how the details spewed forth could be fitted in. In a word, the author has taken pains to select details that can be linked together by normal association, and then to plant clues of time and place that assist the reader in following the patterns of sequence. Your detective work in writing analytically would involve locating, sorting out, and illustrating the types of clues used to make this, in fact, a polished story rather than the jumble of notes it pretends to be. For example, you would note that "weeks later" is a perfectly conventional indication of the time involved between the theft of the gloves and the girl's running away from home. "In the end I think he turned me in" marks her move from Simon's room to the House of Correction. The newspaper account of Raymond Forrest's death and the "new haircut" noticed by the psychiatrist also serve as time markers, as do numerous other physical details correlated with phases of the girl's flight and return. For purposes of a critical paper, you might think it enough to show how the author has achieved unity and coherence under the pretense of incoherence. Or you could go beyond this to speculate about what may have been gained or lost by the indirections of the imitative form. What you learn from your writing evidently depends on how far you want to push it. And on how much effort and insight you will pay to get what you want.

## THE REVIEWER'S APPROACH

A good review will not simply aim at reducing the story to capsule form or be content to point out the interest of the subject matter. True, enough of the story line should be sketched to show the essential conflict the author has exploited. But beyond this, the reviewer wants to illustrate the flavor of the work, its dependence on the language of perceptive narration and of dialogue. Even the briefest review can be enhanced by quotes from the work being introduced. It is with a preliminary selection of usable quotations that you might well begin your preparation for writing.

So you must develop the habit of seeking out such key words, phrases, or lines as will serve to lure your readers into sharing your reading experience. If the option of using direct quotations doesn't suit your intent, then some salient detail of character or action can be chosen to serve in much the same way for topic sentences or leads.

*For example:* At the end of "The Open Boat" one of the four shipwrecked men is dead.

*Or:* Success in competition may mask a deeper failure. ("Rules of the Game")

*Or:* A doctor's professional motives are sometimes at glaring odds with his emotional impulses. ("The Use of Force")

*Or:* Following one's preference in this world is a quick way to exit from it. ("Bartleby, the Scrivener")

Each of these declarations raises a series of questions. Answering those questions and linking the answers is the way to compose a paper that fits the requirements of a review.

If such samplings of your author's language will be useful in showing the flavor of his work, you would do well to make sure they can be handily retrieved when the time comes to put them in your paper. A simple way of doing this is to underline them while reading, mark them with a highlighting pen, or jot them in a notebook. The point is that composition is a growth process. The first steps of writing are taken while you are still reading.

By the use of quotations you give a dramatic and vivid quality to the page you are creating, just as the author being reviewed created the world that you mean to open. Your review should partake of the thing reviewed.

In reviewing, you mean to give a broad and general view of your subject, not neglecting the lively particulars. You mean to indicate what sort of story it is, starting perhaps with general qualities and moving toward the particular. For example, In John Cheever's "The Enormous Radio" it will be important to note that the main protagonists, the Westcotts, are living the generalized conformist American Dream in an apartment in New York City. They are by no means rich, but they are prosperous enough to acquire luxuries like the giant radio, comparable to the material goods their neighbors in the apartment complex acquire. It is from this general specification that the ultimately ghastly action begins to develop. The outsize radio is an ultimate prize for consumers in a consumer society. When it first begins to display its uncanny powers for rendering the lives of the neighbors all too transparent, the Wescotts are at first amazed, then amused, presently disgusted, and finally horrified to realize that their lives are just as tacky as any in the building. This progress of attitudes is clearly important in presenting the theme of the story, so it should be given prominence in the review—certainly as much prominence as the comic device of the radio itself. If you have traced the meaning of the downward progress to humiliation and shame, you will not need to spell out the moral (though this story certainly has a moral, it is not delivered by the outcome of the plot).

When the plot is the main vehicle for expounding the meaning or the moral of a story, it may well serve as the backbone for your review. Some stories have very little plot, and that should be noted if you have discovered what besides plot is the author's chief means of expression. Alice Walker's "Everyday Use" has a simple, strong plot: Virginia Woolf's "Kew Gardens" has no discernible plot. That should not lead us to say that one of these stories is better than the other. In fact, you should seldom or never express an outright judgment of merit when writing about a piece of fiction.

It is almost always unnecessary and usually ill-advised to tell your readers flatly whether you liked the story, or how much. The tone of your paper, if it be honestly and thoroughly done, will sufficiently indicate the value you give the story. Salting quotes will give clues to your readers about what particularly engaged your sympathies. If you find something really good, the way you write of it should convey the value you place on it. Leave it at that.

Let me recommend, again—without overstressing—the advantage of borrowing quotations to liven the prose of your writing about fiction. Some of the best student papers I have graded have been distinguished by the integration of well chosen quotations with the student's expository passages. Others have done without. Yet even in the latter cases, I inferred that somewhere, at some stage of preparation, the writer had gathered them as notes or underlinings, still using them as guidance in reconstructing the spirit of the original.

# Writing Fiction

One of the very good ways to learn more about the art of fiction is to practice it—to take the plunge and write stories of your own. It is also a very natural outgrowth of the emotional and intellectual excitement that reading the top-flight work collected here has generated. Whether or not you have written any fiction before, like most people you have been *telling* stories for most of your life. The next step is to make the more complex effort of giving them a written form of the sort your story has taught you to respect. Often teachers offer the option of writing a story as an alternative to preparing at least one of the papers required in a course where the main emphasis is on improving skills in reading. The relation between reading and writing is so important—and so intimate—that more than one form of written work can help you read with keener enthusiasm and a constantly expanded understanding of what can be communicated in fiction.

Courses specifically devoted to fiction writing are enhanced by the guidance offered in masterful variety by the authors whose finest efforts are assembled in this text. In years to come great work will be done by some of you in writing classes who are now beginning a serious apprenticeship, learning your craft by a devoted scrutiny of what has been accomplished by remote and recent generations of fiction writers.

Thus whatever the nature of the class—and whatever your long- or short-range expectations may be when you set out to write your first, or fifth, or twentieth short story—it must be obvious as a general principle that models of short fiction can discipline and accelerate your progress. To be sure, everything will depend eventually on the quality of your personal and unique imagination, your judgment, your dexterity with language fit for your subject, and the excellence of your observation of life. The happy truth is that drawing on models will not impede your personal talents—it will release them by sparing you the waste and frustration of striking blind.

Surely the writer you hope to become must be an observer and a listener, sharp-eyed and attentive to experience, and with the ability to retain or recall things seen and heard: the shape of a child's mouth when his birthday balloon pops in his hands; the words your sister used to describe a new boyfriend to your parents; the atmosphere in a forest clearing on a summer day. And if you are already very good at such observation, the chances are that your reading of stories has been an essential part of your preparation as an observer.

The genius of fiction is to train readers in what it is *important* to take note of among the incredible profusion of details and events crowding everyday existence—to train us to select what counts, what signifies, what fits with other details of observation to give a sum of meaning to patterns emerging from the superficial chaos of life. In a word, readers of fiction are continuously modeling their habits of observation on that of writers who, in their turn, no doubt, modeled theirs on a continuous narrative tradition still evolving.

But when we have conceded the inevitable role of models in the formation of skill and craft in writing fiction, we may still became bogged down in a widespread prejudice that, I will guess, is stirring in your mind as you read this. You may have a vaguely reasoned, but stubborn, resistance to the very idea of following models. To do so smacks of imitation, and the cardinal motive for creative writing is to be *original,* is it not? You want to write stories to free yourself from the formulas and limitations that inhibit your other kinds of writing.

Seriously, I know you want to—and should—turn out something original when you are ready to do so. Seriously, I believe you haven't a very good chance of doing so until you have learned more ways of observing and shaping your material as the masters of the art have done. When students in creative-writing classes don't or won't accept good models for their development, all too often they begin half-consciously to model their stories on each other's. The blind follow the blind, and standards are much lower than they should be for all the investment of labor and good intention.

Having gone thus far in trying to persuade you to use what is freely offered by excellent models of fiction in our text, I had better come down to specifics about the ways you can effectively go about it. Actually using these stories as models, in all the ways they can be used, requires more than devout appreciation. It requires putting words on paper, whether as exercises, as notes, or as part of a story of your own.

## IMITATION AND COMPARISON

To begin with a bedrock, basic form of exercise, let me note that some writers have found it useful to copy passages word for word from an admired example. Such "slavish" copying (let's face the term at once and have done with it) may have the merit of training you in habits of syntax and verbal rhythm that worked well for writers from whom you intend to learn. Word for word copying might be good for a daily—or occasional—warm-up exercise to get the juices of your imagination flowing. As an icebreaker it can coordinate the sheer mechanics of writing with word processor or typewriter or pen or pencil with a flow of idea and emotion into words on paper. (Though I won't take time to go into this now, please believe that a writer should never, never, never consider the physical means of composition to be a matter of indifference.)

Better than this, a bit of literal copying may be a specially rigorous way of *reading,* which forces you to pay some attention to each word without skimming. And if you have the devotion to make it so, it may be the occasion for pondering the function of each word and each syntactical element as these build into sentences and paragraphs.

Please don't just nod over my suggestion and pass on. Far better to grab your portable and type out the first paragraph of Frank O'Connor's "Guests of the Nation." Had you noticed before how this first person narration is identified as such by the three pronouns *me, we,* and *our?* How the time of day (dusk) is made more concrete by the lighting of the lamp? How the crucial word *chum* (a synonym for "friend") is emphasized by repetition and set in opposition to the word *divil* (a synonym for "enemy" or "hated adversary")? Yes, of course you can understand the meaning of the paragraph without dwelling on such trivial indicators of the situation and the conflict to come. But *by* dwelling on them—as you are privileged and perhaps enticed to do in the exercise of copying—you may learn something almighty precious about a potent and economical way of getting a story started. Your task will be slavish only if you let it be so. And as much can be said for any other assignment, even if self-assigned.

Yet, your verbal imagination will no doubt be more constructively engaged if you base another sort of exercise on O'Connor's paragraph (or a passage from some other story you admire). It is this: following his sentence pattern closely, substitute language and subject matter of your own. Your subject might be the relation of two antagonistic groups in your school or community. As you know, the narrator need not be yourself, but can be an imagined character. Whichever way your imagination veers, the result might be something like this:

> At lunchtime the pockmarked Nicaraguan boy Manuel would jingle his change and ask, "Amigos, you up for it today?" and Scott would say, "Why not, amigo?" (since we pretended we also spoke Spanish) and the smaller Nicaraguan Greniero would brush off a table and roll out his own set of dice. As often as not Martin Stark would join us to watch and get angry at Greniero's style, which was pretty gaudy, and read him out the way he did us "Come on you clown, why are you wobbling the table?"

As you see, we have made a transition from outright copying to parody. And though this example of parody (or the one you will now write) may be only a warmup for truly original composition, pause to reflect that parody *can* be pushed to the level of the highest art, as readers of Joyce's *Ulysses* know so well.

Most of the time when we are developing our own material with the guidance of models, we aren't so committed to a single text or author as in the case of parodistic exercises. Although we continue to learn by a sort of imitation and constant comparison, our comparisons usually range freely over three distinct items: (1) our own manuscript, in whatever state of development it may have reached; (2) the segment of reality we mean to represent; and (3) the story telling tactics and styles of several writers who have dealt similarly with similar subjects.

Particularly in matters of diction and dialogue we continue this simultaneous three-layered scrutiny as a natural part of the writing process. We go on observing and listening to tangible things around us—in fact observation is now intensified because we have given it focus by beginning to write about some segment of observable behavior, and we listen more intently to test whether people like our fictional characters really do speak as we are saying in our story that they do. We want to add more beads to the string, so we listen for characterizing utterances we have not been able to imagine or remember. And—while we are verifying our writing in progress by what might be called fieldwork—we are turning back to the text of this book to see how Mansfield or

Woolf, Hemingway or Faulkner, Oates or Munro have handled confrontations like those we are writing about. We reassess Hemingway's exploitation of understatement, Faulkner's probing with highly charged rhetoric—and are encouraged to remember that either tactic is available to us if we can fit it to the material we are now developing. We turn to the pages of our predecessors for promptings, and when we are lucky we bring away something which sharpens what we have begun.

What we are searching for in such repeated comparative surveys is probably not something we can directly parody, but a principle or an approach suitable to many fine stories. Thus if we turn to Williams's "The Use of Force" while we are at work on a story in which the voice of the first-person narrator is a necessary component, it is not at all with the aim of imitating the particular voice Williams has created, but to see as sharply as we can how small modifications of flat and rather impersonal language can further individualize the character beginning to emerge on our own pages. And to see how this author has fused the idiosyncrasies of speech with the flavor of the situation being recounted. It is very important to remember that Williams's effects are not and could not be achieved merely by inventive manipulation on his part. Clearly he has listened—in actuality and over and over again in memory—to a voice that is finally remorseful. One of the most valuable things you can learn from choosing his story as a model is that you must go into the corners of your world and back in to the dark labyrinth of your own memory listening for the timbre of such a voice.

Dialogue passages in such stories as "Hills Like White Elephants," "Great Falls," and the climactic last scene from "The Dead" can teach you, first of all, what to listen for in actual conversation and, second, how to structure the patterns of ordinary speech into revealing and dramatic sequences. As you become a keener listener, you will note that dialogue is not usually a matter of question and answer or direct responses to purely rational propositions.

The man in Hemingway's story says: " ' . . . But you've got to realize—.' " Without waiting for him to finish the sentence the young woman responds, " 'I realize. Can't we maybe stop talking?' " Her impatient breaking in reveals better than any explanation that could be provided by the author how weary she is of the persistent argument. Yet, just a moment later her despair of reaching agreement is modulated when she catches at something he says and echoes it back. " ' . . . if it means anything to you,' " he says, and she answers, " 'Doesn't it mean anything to you? We could get along.' " Even in despair she is still fighting to make him really hear something besides his own voice, his own wish. If you read such a passage aloud—instead of copying it on your computer—you will see how skillfully the author has implied the tones of voice of the two speakers. In some comparable scene in one of your own stories you can use the same effect.

In "The Dead" Gabriel Conroy asks his wife, " 'And what did he die of so young, Gretta? Consumption, was it?' 'I think he died for me,' she answered." At first glance this may appear to be a direct response on the wife's part. But look again at the context of the question and answer. The powerful shock in her reply comes from the fact that the two are speaking in quite distinct levels of discourse—his mundane, hers mystic and profound. It is from this revelation of incompatible modes of adjusting to reality that the resolution of the story emerges.

These examples illustrate the principle that what we call dialogue is often, in truth, two or more monologues rather loosely fitted together by the circumstances of the scene.

Even when you are not intentionally searching for model fragments of written dialogue, you will come across one sort or another of striking examples that you will want to collect for later reference. It is a fairly simple matter to photocopy such passages and keep them handy in a notebook or file—a very good practice for the writer commencing a serious career.

## STORY-GENERATING MODELS

As the Canterbury pilgrims went on their way, a story told by one of them prompted a story from another. So it goes with all of us. When we hear or read a story, we are reminded of something we have to tell. Like the spreading wake of a boat, waves of memory veer out, stirring flotsam that has lain dormant on the beach, activating inert material we have not yet quite imagined might be the stuff for a story of our own. It will be like—and yet fascinatingly different from—the example that stirred the waves of imagination.

Consider Sherwood Anderson's "I Want to Know Why," which deals with a boy's disillusionment following a moment of triumph. Surely very many of its readers will be reminded of similar shocks in their own lives. It would not be surprising if a lot of them toyed with the possibility of writing about how such a common disappointment seemed very particular and very personal to them—or that most of them felt balked by uncertainty about how to come at their material, which is plentiful enough but unmanageably formless in the rag bag of memory.

Well, a story not only stimulates a reader's memory, its form gives bold hints about the way you might shape up what you are moved to write about. Anderson opens his story with the *arrival* of the narrator and some other boys, at Saratoga, where the climactic race will be run. Then, in an apparently rambling fashion, the boy's feelings about horses and racing are spilled out. In fact these clumsy declarations are put forth as a preparation before the horse Sunstreak is named—before they are all summed up and focused on the actual drama of the race and the disillusioning aftermath when Jerry Tillford brags in the company of prostitutes.

A decision to follow Anderson's example would, first of all, oblige you to concentrate on the end, the dramatic resolution of your fictional situation, and then to measure out the necessary preparation of material, feelings, and circumstances required to give full force to this resolution. In a word, the model shows you how to construct your story backward, starting to work from the end and adding the material required for the opening. What feelings and what qualities will your central character have? I haven't the faintest notion. But you have more than a faint notion—the more you review your material and cull the possibilities, something approaching certainty will be established, for memory works that way once we guide it by fictional craft. Of course in your reminiscence you will be directed by the need to choose a character who has the potential for jolting the protagonist as Jerry Tillford jolts the narrator. That is, you may have to invent, or change, the personages when those you remember do not quite fit the requirements of the story.

Almost as universal as Anderson's basic story of the loss of innocence is the situation in Walker's "Everyday Use." Much of the tension in the American experience generally is the conflict between those who have clung to the places where they have their roots and those who have "gone to the city"—migrated in search of a broader or more fulfilling life. Most students returning home during their college years find themselves caught in a cross fire between old values and new ones. Walker built her story around a number of physical details of setting—the grassless yard, the churn, and the quilts—which have different values and potentials for the stay-at-homes and for the daughter who has briefly returned.

In preparing to write a story about the return of an offspring to the original home you might well begin by (1) listing a number of such specific things in the setting you know or imagine, (2) by noting after each one of the potentially different values they might have for those with conflicting lifestyles, and (3) imagining or simply remembering the characters who would be most likely to clash in their perception of the cardinal values in such possessions.

Making lists of the sort here called for is not at all the cut-and-dried matter you might suppose before you try it. Selection of sights and sounds, names and voices, thunderstorms and carnivals, the furniture in church basements, things stored in attics or garages—picking over such things, mentally following streams of association, and then building complete sentences around the things named in your list is creative work of the richest kind. It is a preliminary shaping of the substance that will give life to your finished story. There is no rule for choosing which of the concrete details you assemble will function most effectively in the development of plot, characterization, or theme. But, rather than trying to select details to fit some predetermined idea or outline, you ought to be always eager to follow the significance suggested by the details themselves. Thus an imitation of Walker's approach can be transformed into something uniquely and unpredictably original.

Many of the same suggestions can be made if Joyce's "Araby" is chosen as a model. Again the basic experience is close to being universal—humiliation in an encounter between romantic expectation and banal actuality. (None of you could convince me you haven't pushed some childish desire until it burst in a shattering embarrassment, that you haven't found yourself "driven and derided by vanity." Conversely, I am sure that the meaning and circumstances of what happened to you were different enough from those in Joyce's story that they are worth telling. So this model will serve, as it probably has already served, for hundreds of excellent new efforts.)

We note that "Araby," like "I Want to Know Why" and "Everyday Use," is told in the first person. We may concede there were ample reasons why this mode was chosen by the three authors. Yet, just because you may be modeling your work on theirs, this does not mean your story will or should be told in the first person, however close to your actual experience it may be. The decision whether to use first- or third-person narration ought to be based on some trials and some sketch work in both methods. You might learn something useful by recasting the final scene of "Araby" as a third person account with a somewhat altered point of view (probably one more detached from the consciousness of the main character). You will find that much more is required than a simple change of pronouns from first to third person if either the emotion of the story or the significance of its resolution is to be retained.

Suppose you were to rewrite "Everyday Use" from the point of view of the daughter Dee, in either first or third person. What modifications would have to be made to reveal the same significance in the circumstances? Some useful answers to such a question will occur to you from purely passive analysis. Better answers—and ones much more useful to you as a committed student of the craft of fiction—can come only from your putting on paper at least a partial rewrite of your model. However much you respect that model in its published form, you must realize it came to that form through a series of authorial choices of the kind you are forced to make in your reconstruction.

Probably most of the stories in this text could be used as pathfinding models as you develop conceptions of your own. But, as a matter of practical fact, no one has time to follow so many leads systematically. You will be served best by choosing those that are written in a more or less contemporary idiom. Great as they may be, Poe, Hawthorne, and Melville wrote in an epoch when both diction and conceptions of man in society were different from those you have grown up with. Some of the practices of earlier masters could be downright misleading to you in this latter part of the twentieth century.

Yet, even as I put down this commonsense warning, I am teased with a hankering to see someone write a totally up-to-date "Bartleby." Wouldn't it be worthwhile to take something marvelous, old, and outmoded and make it new?

## MODELS FOR REVISION

Today there is a good deal of talk about the use of word processors taking the curse off revision—the implication being that revision is always unpleasant, though necessary, and that use of a labor-saving device is the best way to have done with it.

My own experience has always been that revision is simply a continuation of the imaginative act of writing, and for me it has been the most pleasant part. It is in revision that the nice touches can be laid on, the tones and colors harmonized, and clarifications made to show the precise meaning of what was often cloudy or indistinct in some phases of the compositional process.

To go even further, let us admit that revision is not merely the final phase of the process. It has been going on since the concept first began to take shape. Very few of us write as much as a sentence on paper without some juggling and readjustment of an idea and the words that seem fit to express it. We change the nouns and verbs that first entered our minds; we add or drop some adjectives or move them around in the process of inscribing a sentence on a page. As the sentences follow each other, we keep shifting our thoughts by reviewing what has already been put down and what is now required to keep the story flowing and to prepare for what is still to come. At the end of a page or the end of a draft of the whole story, our minds are still teeming with reasons for the choice of wording we have made and the possibilities that have been rejected. Or, if this still-bubbling mental activity *isn't* continuing, then no word processor is going to be of any help.

The only absolute requirement for revision is that there must be something to revise. This means that in your initial surge you have got something on paper. Something that won't shift and fade and drift away as a purely mental construct often does. Something that can be examined and reconsidered on the morning after, marked for change, or cut apart and repasted. A writer is not a day-dreamer, but is a worker with paper, and the joy of the craft can only be experienced by the trials and revisions made on paper. You have finished a story only when nothing remains to be done to improve it.

This is worth repeating for emphasis: Just because you have written a story through from beginning to end, this does not mean you have finished it. If it is good in the form you have first given it—even if it is published or publishable—it may be bettered by revisions. It may be brought closer to what you have to say; it may be modified to fit the editorial requirements of one publication or another. This text contains a major work by William Faulkner, "The Bear," which can be found in two other published versions, both very interesting as examples of revision—particularly interesting in their relation to what has come to be regarded as the definitive version included here. In 1925 Faulkner published "Lion: A Story," which contains not only episodes leading to the death of the great dog and mythic bear but a great deal of the language you will find on the pages of this text. Yet (among other significant differences and omissions) "Uncle Ike" McCaslin is only a peripheral character in that first version, narrated by a boy far less personally involved with or conditioned by the bear's fate than Ike will be in the definitive text. Though the other magazine version (published almost simultaneously with the appearance of the present text in book form) is narrated in the third person, the character of the boy is held to about the same dimensions as in "Lion: A Story." In this intermediary version, the climactic episode is the attack the little fyce dog makes on the bear, with the lessons about courage to be learned from that. But the revision that shows the great range of Faulkner's maturing conception moves Ike McCaslin to the center of the action in the forest and focuses in his life the major themes and conceptual conflicts.

You need not be already a successfully published author to take to heart the example of Faulkner as he coaxed greater and wider significance into his material by his revisions. When you have a "finished" draft of a story in hand, you have come to a point where it is natural to pause, take a long hard look, and weigh the possibilities still to be wrung from material you have successfully coaxed this far along. Such points offer a natural occasion for comparing what you have done with examples from the text that may prod your imagination with suggestions for improvement.

Suppose that, for reasons that seemed sufficient, you began your story with a striking line of dialogue and moved directly into a scene beginning the central action. Now you will reflect that the risk of such a brisk leap into the action is that the characters are more shallowly drawn than they must be to bring out the significance of what they are doing or saying to each other. While it is certainly not necessary to explain characters before you let them move, background information, histories, and individual idiosyncrasies must be incorporated somewhere and somehow without impeding the movements of events.

When your work is fresh and hot—and unfinished—on the desk in front of you, the time is favorable for comparing your opening presentation with those of Joyce in "A Little Cloud," of Lawrence in "The Horse Dealer's Daughter," and Hemingway's "Hills Like White Elephants." Joyce begins with a generalized, fairly extended summary view of his character before he moves him into the scene with his friend Gallaher. Lawrence begins with dialogue that is part of an ongoing present scene (though this is stretched to permit the author to weave in some of the background of the family now in a moment of crisis). Hemingway begins with a scene that is almost purely objective and pictorial. He strikingly avoids giving any information about the characters or where they have come from. Before the story is done we will know what is essential to be known about them, but this emerges entirely from their dialogue.

A careful study of just these three stories in comparison with your own material may suggest to you what you can cut and what you might need to build up in terms of background information for the reader. The value of analytic comparison can be enhanced by actually cutting up photocopies of your own work and pasting them together to make them conform to your models. It should go without saying that you cannot move paragraphs and scenes around this way without some rewriting to make the pieces fit together in a coherent whole.

Before undertaking a second draft of your story, it is worth reconsidering and making comparisons of all the elements of fiction you have learned by reading and discussion to identify. Consult examples of descriptive passages, narrative passages in which long stretches of time are compressed, and scenes. Note that the lush and detailed description that opens "Kew Gardens" functions in a certain way to serve the peculiar demands of that story, while the descriptions of Parisian street scenes accomplish something distinctly different in "Babylon Revisited." In "The Open Boat" an insistent series of sensory descriptions of the ocean and the shoreline runs as an accompaniment to the adventure of the shipwrecked men, vivifying their experience and contributing much to the reader's inferences about what it all means. "The horizon narrowed and widened, and dipped and rose, and at all times its edge was jagged with waves that seemed thrust up in points like rocks." "The color of the sea changed from slate to emerald green streaked with amber lights, and the foam was like tumbling snow." "On the distant dunes were set many little black cottages, and a tall white windmill reared above them. No man, nor dog, nor bicycle appeared on the beach." Surely such a series of pictorial renditions is worth imitating if your story requires its characters to be immersed in conflict with their environment—just as surely it would be inappropriate if the conflict were more confined to personal oppositions.

In "The Veldt" Bradbury plays a very nifty trick in his description of the images projected on the nursery walls. That is, instead of describing them as if they were, indeed, *pictures,* he slants the descriptions forcibly to make them seem as if he were talking about direct encounters with the dangerous African habitat itself—as in the twist of his fantasy, they turn out to be. Descriptions of the barbecue stand in "A Good Man Is Hard to Find" intensify the atmosphere of grotesque contemporary reality. The coming of dawn at the end of "Barn Burning" serves as an indirect revelation of the emotional state of the boy who has—for good reasons—betrayed his own father. You can and should continue your list of examples, make a collection for convenient reference, *and* remember that no one descriptive device is suitable for all kinds of story objectives.

How long a period of time is covered by the action of your story? If it is several years, months, days, or even hours, the chances are that you will need to account for the longer stretches with what I am here calling *narrative passages*—those in which the language is specifically adapted to show persisting as distinct from immediate action. Time is compressed by statements on the order of "during July he exercised daily in the college gym." There is a tendency for such passages to become thin, flat, and lacking in concrete detail. In the example just given, no picture is drawn of the person at his exercise, the weather or the mood of the summer, or the sounds, sights, and smells of a gym during this season. In a fully finished story this will not be the case—as you can see by taking the example of, say, de Maupassant in "Boule de Suif."

Part of "Everyday Use" compresses time just as effectively—without losing richness of concrete detail—in the reminiscence of the narrator. "I used to think she hated Maggie, too. But that was before we raised the money, the church and me, to send her to Augusta to school. She used to read to us without pity. . . . She washed us in a river of make-believe, burned us with a lot of knowledge we didn't necessarily need to know. . . . Often I fought off the temptation to shake her. At sixteen she had a style of her own; and knew what style was."

These are brief examples, and you will want to collect more. As you accumulate them from other stories that reach over too much time to be presented in continuous scenes, pay particular attention to the time modifiers that indicate the action is an extended one—"she would often," "by the time he graduated he had," etc. These mechanical connectives can, and should, be given the function of keeping your story vivid and convincing, just as the detail and dialogue of a scene will do.

Perhaps for the beginning writer scenes are the easiest part of writing fiction. At least, the most fun. In such writing you are more likely to have ready-made models from life as you observe it. A conversation begins, and the exchange back and forth between characters builds naturally, because the response of the second speaker is roughly governed by what the first one has said. You follow the example of movies, in which essentially everything is revealed by a succession of related scenes, requiring no authorial account of what has ripened or changed in the interim between them. But the more demanding a craftsman you become—coming up hard against the difficulties of fitting one item with another to make a fictional pattern—the more you'll perceive the need for specific models.

A number of stories in this text consist of a single scene, and we turn naturally to something like Updike's "A & P" for a precise examination of the way in which the characters are brought into the reader's view, how their encounter is progressively complicated, and how the concluding action gives point and meaning to the dramatized spectacle. The mere presence of the three girls in the store and the narrator's appraisal of them would have made a fictional scene, in the bare technical meaning of the word, but it is the intervention of the store manager in the midst of the scene that makes it, all by itself, a story in which no follow-up material is needed to round it out.

Compare "A & P" with "Everyday Use"—another story that contains only a single scene. In the latter the design is significantly different. The author sets up her characters and their traits with an extended expository passage before the main action starts. What is then required of the scene is that it dramatize the traits already enumerated and show what they amount to when brought to the test. The correspondence between the mother's analysis and what Dee (Wangero) reveals by her spoken lines should be closely analyzed as a model for what can be intensified in a scene you have written that may have been perfect in its verisimilitude but lacking in point.

With material requiring a number of scenes for its full development not only does one need the aptitude for getting the most out of each scene but there must be a suitable design for the sequence in which the scenes will be laid out, and a series of connectives to move economically from one scene to another. There is also an ever-present question of proportion—which of the scenes can be treated summarily and briefly, which must be given some amplitude. Fitzgerald's example in "Babylon Revisited" can be useful for a start in learning such management. Mark the beginnings and ends of all the scenes in this story, and then ask of each one: What is accomplished to advance the story by this scene? How have we been brought into it from the preceding one?

The first, between Charlie and Alix in the bar, is what may be called an "establishing" scene. It presents the main character on his return to a once-familiar environment and ticks off some changes in him, in the places he is taking another look at, and in his judgment and perception.

The next full scene takes place in the home of Charlie's in-laws. But how has he come there from scene one? He has taxied across Paris (a bit of drab and routine transportation that *should* have been omitted—except that the author uses it to give another glimpse of the Parisian setting and to record Charlie's regret at having "spoiled" this good place for himself). The second scene serves to demonstrate the bond of affection between father and daughter—and to signal the potential for opposition, hostility, and dislike between Charlie and the woman who will be his chief antagonist in the principal conflict of the story.

The third scene gives us Charlie alone in the city that once proved an irresistible temptation for his dissipations. It is a test intended to demonstrate (to the reader as well as to the character himself) how far he has recovered from the previous crackup. It climaxes in his rejection of the woman who encourages him to plunge into vice once more. He has not failed the test. As the section ends, his hopes are bright for showing that he is now fit to reclaim his daughter.

What occurs in the first scene of section II is crucial preparation for the outcome of the story. Not only does Charlie have a pleasant, promising lunch with Honoria, he seems to have once again side-stepped formerly destructive temptations by his coolness to Duncan and Lorraine. But what the author has, in fact, accomplished here is to plant a superficially successful evasion as the time bomb that will presently blast Charlie's prospects and hopes.

I will not take space here to complete the map of scenes that round out the design of this story. Having indicated how you *can* block out the elements of design in a story with several scenes, I'll only say, *Do it,* and do it conscientiously with the intent of making use of what you learn from it in revising the design of whatever similar project you are engaged in. If the scene pattern in "Babylon Revisited" only partially resolves your problem, take another story, or several, and bear down until you get what you need.

Though I cut short my analysis of this story—and of others herein mentioned—I would like you to believe that in a long career as a writer and teacher I have knuckled down on repeated occasions in which I trained myself with exercises and analyses of examples of craft. I tried early and late to take over as much as I could from admired writers who went ahead of me. Much earlier in my comments you may have been jolted by the suspicion that what I was actually recommending could not be finished within the limits of any given semester or year of work.

Quite so. I did not truly intend to lay out a program limited by the duration of a class, but to offer an approach to getting good use from your reading of fiction, taking it as a guide to a craft that none of us will ever completely master. We are on an endless quest. Semester by semester and year by year we do our best with such native abilities as we have and with the skills we are acquiring for the sake of what can be done next year. The better you work along lines I have indicated here, the better you will work along lines I have not mentioned or maybe haven't imagined yet.

With that hopeful qualification, I turn you back to your own reading and writing and to other teachers—those who meet with you regularly in the classroom and those you will only know through their published works.

# Writers on Writing

Any writer, I suppose, feels that the world into which he was born is nothing less than a conspiracy against the cultivation of his talent—which attitude certainly has a great deal to support it. On the other hand, it is only because the world looks on his talent with such a frightening indifference that the artist is compelled to make his talent important.

*James Baldwin*

Most of the basic material a writer works with is acquired before the age of fifteen.

*Willa Cather*

I start with a tingle, a kind of feeling of the story I will write. Then come the characters, and they take over, they make the story.

*Isak Dinesen*

Read, read, read. Read everything—trash, classics, good and bad, and see how they do it. Just like a carpenter who works as an apprentice and studies the master. Read! You'll absorb it. Then write. If it is good, you'll find out. If it's not, throw it out the window.

*William Faulkner*

A book ought to be an icepick to break up the frozen sea within us.

*Franz Kafka*

Looking back, I imagine I was always writing. Twaddle it was, too. But better far write twaddle or anything, anything, than nothing at all.

*Katherine Mansfield*

There is only one school of literature—that of talent.

*Vladimir Nabokov*

Beginning a book is unpleasant. I'm entirely uncertain about the character and the predicament, and a character in his predicament is what I have to begin with. Worse than not knowing your subject is not knowing how to treat it, because that's finally everything. I type out beginnings and they're awful, more of an unconscious parody of my previous book than the breakaway from it that I want. I need something driving down the center of a book, a magnet to draw everything to it—that's what I look for during the first months of writing something new.

*Philip Roth*

We work in our own darkness a great deal with little real knowledge of what we are doing.

*John Steinbeck*

Writing doesn't require drive. It's like saying a chicken has to have drive to lay an egg.

*John Updike*

## *Margaret Atwood*

## Why Do You Write?[1]

You learn to write by reading and writing, writing and reading. As a craft it's acquired through the apprentice system, but you choose your own teachers. Sometimes they're alive, sometimes dead.

As a vocation, it involves the laying on of hands. You receive your vocation and in your turn you must pass it on. Perhaps you will do this only through your work, perhaps in other ways. Either way, you're part of a community, the community of writers, the community of storytellers that stretches back through time to the beginning of human society.

As for the particular human society to which you yourself belong—sometimes you'll feel you're speaking for it, sometimes—when it's taken an unjust form—against it, or for that other community, the community of the oppressed, the exploited, the voiceless. Either way, the pressures on you will be intense; in other countries, perhaps fatal. But even here—speak "for women," or for any other group which is feeling the boot, and there will be many at hand, both for and against, to tell you to shut up, or to say what they want you to say, or to say it a different way. Or to save them. The billboard awaits you, but if you succumb to its temptations you'll end up two-dimensional.

Tell what is yours to tell. Let others tell what is theirs.

## *Toni Cade Bambara*

## What Is It I Think I'm Doing Anyhow?[2]

When I replay the tapes on file in my head, tapes of speeches I've given at writing conferences over the years, I invariably hear myself saying—"A writer, like any other cultural worker, like any other member of the community, ought to try to put her/his skills in the service of the community." Some years ago when I returned south, my picture in the paper prompted several neighbors to come visit. "You a writer? What all you write?" Before I could begin the catalogue, one old gent interrupted with—"Ya know Miz Mary down the block? She need a writer to help her send off a letter to her grandson overseas." So I began a career as the neighborhood scribe—letters to relatives, snarling letters to the traffic chief about the promised stop sign, nasty letters to the utilities, angry letters to the principal about that confederate flag hanging in front of the school, contracts to transfer a truck from seller to buyer etc. While my efforts have been graciously appreciated in the form of sweet potato dumplings, herb teas, hair braiding, and the like, there is still much room for improvement—"For a writer, honey, you've got a mighty bad hand. Didn't they teach penmanship at that college?" Another example, I guess, of words setting things in motion. What goes around, comes around, as the elders say.

1. From *The Writer on Her Work*, Vol. II, ed. by Janet Sternburg (1991). 2. From *The Writer on Her Work*, Vol. I, ed. by Janet Sternburg (1980).

It will be a pleasure to get back to the shorts; they allow me to share. I much prefer to haul around story collections to prisons, schools, senior citizen centers, and rallies and then select from the "menu" something that suits the moment and is all of a piece. But the novel's pull is powerful. And since the breakthrough achieved in the sixties by the Neo-Black Arts Movement, the possibilities are stunning. Characters that have been waiting in the wings for generations, characters that did not fit into the roster of stereotypes, can now be brought down center stage. Now that I/we have located our audience, we are free to explore the limits of language. Now that American history, American literature, the American experience is being redefined by so many communities, the genre too will undergo changes. So I came to the novel with a sense that everything is possible. And I'm attempting to blueprint for myself the merger of these two camps: the political and the spiritual. The possibilities of healing that split are exciting. The implications of actually yoking those energies and of fusing that power quite take my breath away.

## *Raymond Carver*

## On Writing[3]

Back in the mid-1960s, I found I was having trouble concentrating my attention on long narrative fiction. For a time I experienced difficulty in trying to read it as well as in attempting to write it. My attention span had gone out on me; I no longer had the patience to try to write novels. It's an involved story, too tedious to talk about here. But I know it has much to do now with why I write poems and short stories. Get in, get out. Don't linger. Go on. It could be that I lost any great ambitions at about the same time, in my late twenties. If I did, I think it was good it happened. Ambition and a little luck are good things for a writer to have going for him. Too much ambition and bad luck, or no luck at all, can be killing. There has to be talent.

Some writers have a bunch of talent; I don't know any writers who are without it. But a unique and exact way of looking at things, and finding the right context for expressing that way of looking, that's something else. *The World According to Garp* is, of course, the marvelous world according to John Irving. There is another world according to Flannery O'Connor, and others according to William Faulkner and Ernest Hemingway. There are worlds according to Cheever, Updike, Singer, Stanley Elkin, Ann Beattie, Cynthia Ozick, Donald Barthelme, Mary Robison, William Kittredge, Barry Hannah, Ursula K. LeGuin. Every great or even every very good writer makes the world over according to his own specifications.

It's akin to style, what I'm talking about, but it isn't style alone. It is the writer's particular and unmistakable signature on everything he writes. It is his world and no other. This is one of the things that distinguishes one writer from another. Not talent. There's plenty of that around. But a writer who has some

3. From *Fires* (1968).

special way of looking at things and who gives artistic expression to that way of looking: that writer may be around for a time.

Isak Dinesen said that she wrote a little every day, without hope and without despair. Someday I'll put that on a three-by-five card and tape it to the wall beside my desk. I have some three-by-five cards on the wall now. "Fundamental accuracy of statement is the ONE sole morality of writing." Ezra Pound. It is not everything by ANY means, but if a writer has "fundamental accuracy of statement" going for him, he's at least on the right track.

I have a three-by-five up there with this fragment of a sentence from a story by Chekov: ". . . and suddenly everything became clear to him." I find these words filled with wonder and possibility. I love their simple clarity, and the hint of revelation that's implied. There is mystery, too. What has been unclear before? Why is it just now becoming clear? What's happened? Most of all—what now? There are consequences as a result of such sudden awakenings. I feel a sharp sense of relief—and anticipation.

I overheard the writer Geoffrey Wolff say "No cheap tricks" to a group of writing students. That should go on a three-by-five card. I'd amend it a little to "No tricks." Period. I hate tricks. At the first sign of a trick or a gimmick in a piece of fiction, a cheap trick or even an elaborate trick, I tend to look for cover. Tricks are ultimately boring, and I get bored easily, which may go along with my not having much of an attention span. But extremely clever chi-chi writing, or just plain tomfoolery writing, puts me to sleep. Writers don't need tricks or gimmicks or even necessarily need to be the smartest fellows on the block. At the risk of appearing foolish, a writer sometimes needs to be able to just stand and gape at this or that thing—a sunset or an old shoe—in absolute and simple amazement.

Some months back, in the *New York Times Book Review*, John Barth said that ten years ago most of the students in his fiction writing seminar were interested in "formal innovation," and this no longer seems to be the case. He's a little worried that writers are going to start writing mom and pop novels in the 1980s. He worries that experimentation may be on the way out, along with liberalism. I get a little nervous if I find myself within earshot of somber discussions about "formal innovation" in fiction writing. Too often "experimentation" is a license to be careless, silly or imitative in the writing. Even worse, a license to try to brutalize or alienate the reader. Too often such writing gives us no news of the world, or else describes a desert landscape and that's all—a few dunes and lizards here and there, but no people; a place uninhabited by anything recognizably human, a place of interest only to a few scientific specialists.

It should be noted that real experiment in fiction is original, hard-earned and cause for rejoicing. But someone else's way of looking at things—Barthelme's, for instance—should not be chased after by other writers. It won't work. There is only one Barthelme, and for another writer to try to appropriate Barthelme's peculiar sensibility or *mise en scène* under the rubric of innovation is for that writer to mess around with chaos and disaster and, worse, self-deception. The real experimenters have to Make It New, as Pound urged, and in the process have to find things out for themselves. But if writers haven't taken leave of their senses, they also want to stay in touch with us, they want to carry news from their world to ours.

It's possible, in a poem or a short story, to write about commonplace things and objects using commonplace but precise language, and to endow those things—a chair, a window curtain, a fork, a stone, a woman's earring—with immense, even startling power. It is possible to write a line of seemingly innocuous dialogue and have it send a chill along the reader's spine—the source of artistic delight, as Nabokov would have it. That's the kind of writing that most interests me. I hate sloppy or haphazard writing whether it flies under the banner of experimentation or else is just clumsily rendered realism. In Isaac Babel's wonderful short story, "Guy de Maupassant," the narrator has this to say about the writing of fiction: "No iron can pierce the heart with such force as a period put just at the right place." This too ought to go on a three-by-five.

Evan Connell said once that he knew he was finished with a short story when he found himself going through it and taking out commas and then going through the story again and putting commas back in the same places. I like that way of working on something. I respect that kind of care for what is being done. That's all we have, finally, the words, and they had better be the right ones, with the punctuation in the right places so that they can best say what they are meant to say. If the words are heavy with the writer's own unbridled emotions, or if they are imprecise and inaccurate for some other reason—if the words are in any way blurred—the reader's eyes will slide right over them and nothing will be achieved. The reader's own artistic sense will simply not be engaged. Henry James called this sort of hapless writing "weak specification."

I have friends who've told me they had to hurry a book because they needed the money, their editor or their wife was leaning on them or leaving them—something, some apology for the writing not being very good. "It would have been better if I'd taken the time." I was dumbfounded when I heard a novelist friend say this. I still am, if I think about it, which I don't. It's none of my business. But if the writing can't be made as good as it is within us to make it, then why do it? In the end, the satisfaction of having done our best, and the proof of that labor is the one thing we can take into the grave. I wanted to say to my friend, for heaven's sake go do something else. There have to be easier and maybe more honest ways to try and earn a living. Or else just do it to the best of your abilities, your talents, and then don't justify or make excuses. Don't complain, don't explain.

In an essay called, simply enough, "Writing Short Stories," Flannery O'Connor talks about writing as an act of discovery. O'Connor says she most often did not know where she was going when she sat down to work on a short story. She says she doubts that many writers know where they are going when they begin something. She uses "Good Country People" as an example of how she put together a short story whose ending she could not even guess at until she was nearly there:

> When I started writing that story, I didn't know there was going to be a Ph.D. with a wooden leg in it. I merely found myself one morning writing a description of two women I knew something about, and before I realized it, I had equipped

> one of them with a daughter with a wooden leg. I brought in the Bible salesman, but I had no idea what I was going to do with him. I didn't know he was going to steal that wooden leg until ten or twelve lines before he did it, but when I found out that this was what was going to happen, I realized it was inevitable.

When I read this some years ago it came as a shock that she, or anyone for that matter, wrote stories in this fashion. I thought this was my uncomfortable secret, and I was a little uneasy with it. For sure I thought this way of working on a short story somehow revealed my own shortcomings. I remember being tremendously heartened by reading what she had to say on the subject.

I once sat down to write what turned out to be a pretty good story, though only the first sentence of the story had offered itself to me when I began it. For several days I'd been going around with this sentence in my head: "He was running the vacuum cleaner when the telephone rang." I knew a story was there and that it wanted telling. I felt it in my bones, that a story belonged with that beginning, if I could just have the time to write it. I found the time, an entire day—twelve, fifteen hours even—if I wanted to make use of it. I did, and I sat down in the morning and wrote the first sentence, and other sentences promptly began to attach themselves. I made the story just as I'd make a poem; one line and then the next, and the next. Pretty soon I could see a story, and I knew it was my story, the one I'd been wanting to write.

I like it when there is some feeling of threat or sense of menace in short stories. I think a little menace is fine to have in a story. For one thing, it's good for the circulation. There has to be tension, a sense that something is imminent, that certain things are in relentless motion, or else, most often, there simply won't be a story. What creates tension in a piece of fiction is partly the way the concrete words are linked together to make up the visible action of the story. But it's also the things that are left out, that are implied, the landscape just under the smooth (but sometimes broken and unsettled) surface of things.

V.S. Pritchett's definition of a short story is "something glimpsed from the corner of the eye, in passing." Notice the "glimpse" part of this. First the glimpse. Then the glimpse given life, turned into something that illuminates the moment and may, if we're lucky—that word again—have even further-ranging consequences and meaning. The short story writer's task is to invest the glimpse with all that is in his power. He'll bring his intelligence and literary skill to bear (his talent), his sense of proportion and sense of the fitness of things: of how things out there really are and how he sees those things—like no one else sees them. And this is done through the use of clear and specific language, language used so as to bring to life the details that will light up the story for the reader. For the details to be concrete and convey meaning, the language must be accurate and precisely given. The words can be so precise they may even sound flat, but they can still carry; if used right, they can hit all the notes.

## *John Cheever*

## What Happened[4]

A few years ago I stayed with my family in a rented house on Martha's Vineyard until the second week in October. The Indian Summer was brilliant and still. We went unwillingly when the time came to go. We took the mid-morning boat to Wood's Hole and drove from a brilliant day at the sea into humid and overcast weather. South of Hartford it began to rain. We reached the apartment house in the east Fifties where we then lived just before dark. The city in the rain seemed particularly cavernous and noisy and the summer was definitely ended. Early the next morning I went to the room where I work. Before leaving the Vineyard I had begun a story, based on some notes made a year or two earlier in New Hampshire. The story described a family in a summer house who spent their evenings playing backgammon. It probably would have been called "The Backgammon Game." I meant to use the checkers, the board and the forfeits of a game to show that the relationships within a family can be extortionate. I was not sure of the story's conclusion but at the back of my mind was the idea that someone would lose his life over the board. I saw a canoe accident on a mountain lake. Reading the story over that morning I saw that, like some kinds of wine, it had not traveled. It was bad.

I come from a Puritanical family and I had been taught as a child that a moral lies beneath all human conduct and that the moral is always detrimental to man. I count among my relations people who feel that there is some inexpugnable nastiness at the heart of life and that love, friendship, Bourbon whisky, lights of all kinds—are merely the crudest deceptions. My aim as a writer has been to record a moderation of these attitudes—an escape from them if this seemed necessary—and in the backgammon story I had plainly failed. It was in essence precisely the kind of idle pessimism that I had hoped to enlighten. It was in the vein of one of my elderly uncles who never put a worm on a fish hook without stating that sooner or later we will all be corruption.

In order to occupy myself more cheerfully I looked over the notes I had made during the summer. I first came on a long description of trainsheds and ferry-boat landings—a song to the engines of love and death—but the substance of this was that these journeys were of no import—they were a kind of deception. A few pages after this I came on the description of a friend who, having lost the charms of youth and unable to find any new lights to go by, had begun to dwell on his football triumphs. This was connected to a scathing description of the house in the Vineyard where we had spent a pleasant summer. The house had not been old, but it had been sheathed with old shingles and the new wood of the doors had been scored and stained. The rooms were lighted with electric candles and I linked this crude sense of the past to my friend's failure to mature. The failure, my notes said, was national. We had failed to mature as a people and had turned back to dwell on old football triumphs, raftered ceilings, candlelight and open fires. There were some tearful

4. From *Fiction and Human Experience* (1959).

notes on the sea, washing away the embers of our picnic fires, on the east wind—the dark wind—on the promiscuity of a beautiful young woman I know, on the hardships of island farming, on the jet planes that bombed an island off Gay Head, and a morose description of a walk on South Beach. The only cheerful notes in all this were two sentences about the pleasure I had taken one afternoon in watching my wife and another young lady walk out of the sea without any clothes on.

It is brief, but most journeys leave with us at least an illusion of improved perspective and there was a distance that morning between myself and my notes. I had spent the summer in excellent company and in a landscape that I love, but there was no hint of this in the journal I had kept. The conflict in my feelings and my indignation at this division formed quickly in my mind the image of a despicable brother and I wrote: "Goodbye, My Brother." The story moved quickly. Lawrence arrived on the island on a voyage of no import. I made the narrator fatuous since there was some ambiguity in my indignation. Laud's Head had the accommodating power of an imaginary landscape where you can pick and choose from a wide range of memory, putting in the smell of roses from a very different place and the ringing of a tennis-court roller that you heard years ago. The plan of the house was clear to me at once, although it was unlike any house that I had even seen. The terrace, the living-room, the staircase all appeared in order and when I pushed open the door from the pantry into the kitchen I seemed to find there a cook who had worked for my mother-in-law the year before the year before last. I had brought Lawrence home and taken him through his first night at Laud's Head before it was time for me to walk home for supper.

In the morning I unloaded onto Lawrence's shoulders my observations about backgammon. The story was moving then towards the boat club dance. Ten years ago at a costume ball in Minneapolis a man had worn a football uniform and his wife a wedding dress and this recollection fitted easily into place. The story was finished by Friday and I was happy for I know almost no pleasure greater than having a piece of fiction draw together incidents as disparate as a dance in Minneapolis and a backgammon game in the mountains so that they relate to one another and confirm that feeling that life itself is creative process, that one thing is put purposefully upon another, that what is lost in one encounter is replenished in the next and that we possess some power to make sense of what takes place.

On Saturday I took a train to Philadelphia with a friend to see a football game. The story was still on my mind but when I thought back over what I had written, looking for weakness or crudeness, I felt assured. The football game was dull. It got cold. I began to feel uneasy at the half. We left in the middle of the fourth quarter. I had not worn a top-coat and I was shivering. Waiting in the cold for the train back to New York I saw the true worthlessness of my story, the scope of my self-deceptions, the flights and crash-landings of an unstable disposition and when the train came into the station I thought vaguely of throwing myself onto the tracks; but I went instead to the club car and drank some whisky. I have read the story since, and while I see that Lawrence lacks dimension and that the ambiguity will estrange some readers, it remains a reasonably exact account of my feelings after returning to Manhattan after a long summer on Martha's Vineyard.

## *Anton Chekhov*

## Selected Letters[5]

### *To D. V. Grigorovich,[6] March 28, 1886*

. . . If I do have a gift that should be respected, I confess before your pure heart that up to now I haven't respected it. I felt that I had it, but got used to considering it insignificant. There are plenty of purely external reasons to make an individual unfair, extremely suspicious, and distrustful of himself, and I reflect now that there have been plenty of such reasons in my case. All my friends and relatives were always condescending toward my writing and constantly advised me in a friendly way not to give up real work for scribbling. I have hundreds of friends in Moscow, a score of whom write, and I cannot recall a single one who read my work or considered me an artist. There is a so-called "literary circle" in Moscow: talents and mediocrities of all shapes and sizes gather once a week in a restaurant and exercise their tongues. If I were to go there and read them a mere snippet of your letter, they would laugh in my face. During the five years I have been roaming around editorial offices I managed to succumb to the general view of my literary insignificance, quickly got used to looking at my work condescendingly, and—kept plugging away! That's the first reason. The second is that I am a doctor and am up to my ears in medical work, so that the proverb about chasing two hares has cost me more sleep than anyone else.

I write all this merely to justify myself to you in the smallest way for my deep sin. Up to now I have treated my literary work extremely lightly, carelessly, haphazardly. I do not remember working more than a day on *any single* story of mine, and I wrote *The Huntsman,* which you liked, when I went swimming! I wrote my stories as reporters write their news about fires: mechanically, half-consciously, without worrying about either the reader or themselves. I wrote and constantly tried not to waste images and scenes which I valued on these stories, and I tried to save them and carefully hide them, God only knows why.

Suvorin's[7] very friendly and, so far as I can see, sincere letter, was the first thing to impel me to look at my work critically. I began to get ready to write something significant, but I still have no faith in my own literary significance. Then suddenly, completely unexpectedly, your letter came. Forgive the comparison, but it acted on me like an order "to leave town within twenty-four hours!" that is, I suddenly felt an absolute necessity to hurry, to get out of the place I was stuck in as quickly as possible. . . .

I will liberate myself from deadlines, but not at once. There is no possibility

5. From *Anton Chekhov's Short Stories: A Norton Critical Edition,* edited by Ralph E. Matlaw (1979). 6. An important writer in the 1840s and the later part of the century (1882–1899), who had written to Chekhov on March 25, 1886, praising his outstanding talent and urging him to write more seriously. 7. A. S. Suvorin (1833–1911), influential publisher of the conservative paper *New Times,* became Chekhov's closest friend.

of getting out of the rut into which I have fallen. I don't mind starving as I have already done, but there are others involved too. I give my leisure to writing, two or three hours a day and a little bit of the night, that is, time that is suitable only for trifling work. This summer, when I will have more leisure and will have to earn less, I will undertake something serious. . . .

*To A. S. Suvorin, October 27, 1888*

. . . I sometimes preach heresy, but I have never yet gone so far as to deny a place in art to topical questions altogether. In conversations with the writing fraternity I always insist that the artist's function is not to solve narrowly specialized questions. It is bad for the artist to undertake something he doesn't understand. We have specialists for specialized questions; it is their function to discuss the peasant commune, the fate of capitalism, the evil of drink, shoes, women's diseases. The artist, however, must treat only what he understands; his sphere is as limited as that of any other specialist's, I repeat that and always insist on it. Only somebody who has never written or had anything to do with images could say that there are no questions in his realm, that there is nothing but answers. The artist observes, chooses, guesses, compounds—these actions in themselves already presuppose a question at the origin; if the artist did not pose a question to himself at the beginning then there was nothing to guess or to choose. To be as brief as possible, I'll end with psychiatry: if you deny questions and intentions in creative work you must acknowledge that the artist creates unintentionally, without purpose, under the influence of a temporary aberration; therefore, if an author were to brag to me that he wrote a tale purely by inspiration, without previously having pondered his intentions, I would call him insane.

You are right in demanding that an artist approach his work consciously, but you are confusing two concepts: *the solution of a problem and the correct formulation of a problem.* Only the second is required of the artist. Not a single problem is resolved in *Anna Karenina* or *Onegin,* but they satisfy you completely only because all the problems in them are formulated correctly. The judge is required to formulate the questions correctly, but the decision is left to the jurors, each according to his own taste. . . .

You write that the main character of my *Name-Day Party* is a figure who should be developed. Good God, I am not a brute without feelings, I understand that. I understand that I cut up my characters and ruin them, that I ruin good material for nothing. Honestly speaking, I would gladly have spent half a year on the *Name-Day Party.* I like leisure and find no attraction in hasty publication. I would gladly, with pleasure, with feeling, and in detail have described *all* of my main character, his soul while his wife was in labor, his trial, his nasty feeling after the acquittal, I would have described how the midwife and the doctor drink tea at night, I would have described the rain. That would only have given me pleasure, because I like to delve into things and putter around. But what can I do? I begin a story September 10th with the knowledge that I must finish it by October 5th at the latest. If I delay it I break my promise and I remain without money. I start the beginning calmly, I don't restrain myself, but toward the middle I become uneasy and begin to fear that my story will turn out too long: I have to remember that the *Northern Herald* has little money and that I am one of their expensive collaborators. Therefore my openings always promise a great deal, as if I had started a novel; the middle is crumpled up and timid; and the ending is like fireworks, as though in a short story. When you fashion a story you necessarily concern yourself with its limits: out of a slew of main and secondary characters you choose only one—the wife or the husband—place him against the background and describe him alone and therefore also emphasize him, while you scatter the others in the background like small change, and you get something like the night sky: a single large moon and a slew of very small stars. But the moon doesn't turn out right because you can see it only when the other stars are visible too, but the stars aren't set off. So I turn out a sort of patchwork quilt rather than literature. What can I do? I simply don't know. I will simply depend on all-healing time. . . .

## *Joseph Conrad*

### A Familiar Preface[8]

It is very difficult to be wholly joyous or wholly sad on this earth. The comic, when it is human, soon takes upon itself a face of pain; and some of our griefs (some only, not all, for it is the capacity for suffering which makes man august in the eyes of men) have their source in weaknesses which must be recognized with smiling compassion as the common inheritance of us all. Joy and sorrow in this world pass into each other, mingling their forms and their murmurs in the twilight of life as mysterious as an overshadowed ocean, while the dazzling brightness of supreme hopes lies far off, fascinating and still, on the distant edge of the horizon.

Yes! I, too, would like to hold the magic wand giving that command over laughter and tears which is declared to be the highest achievement of imaginative literature. Only, to be a great magician one must surrender oneself to occult and irresponsible powers, either outside or within one's breast. We have all heard of simple men selling their souls for love or power to some grotesque devil. The most ordinary intelligence can perceive without much reflection that anything of the sort is bound to be a fool's bargain. I don't lay claim to particular wisdom because of my dislike and distrust of such transactions. It may be my sea training acting upon a natural disposition to keep good hold on the one thing really mine, but the fact is that I have a positive horror of losing even for one moving moment that full possession of myself which is the first condition of good service. And I have carried my notion of good service from my earlier into my later existence. I, who have never sought in the written word anything else but a form of the Beautiful—I have carried over that article of creed from the decks of ships to the more circumscribed space of my desk, and by that act, I suppose, I have become permanently imperfect in the eyes of the ineffable company of pure esthetes.

As in political so in literary action a man wins friends for himself mostly by

8. From *A Personal Record* (1988).

the passion of his prejudices and by the consistent narrowness of his outlook. But I have never been able to love what was not lovable or hate what was not hateful out of deference for some general principle. Whether there be any courage in making this admission I know not. After the middle turn of life's way we consider dangers and joys with a tranquil mind. So I proceed in peace to declare that I have always suspected in the effort to bring into play the extremities of emotions the debasing touch of insincerity. In order to move others deeply we must deliberately allow ourselves to be carried away beyond the bounds of our normal sensibility—innocently enough, perhaps, and of necessity, like an actor who raises his voice on the stage above the pitch of natural conversation—but still we have to do that. And surely this is no great sin. But the danger lies in the writer becoming the victim of his own exaggeration, losing the exact notion of sincerity, and in the end coming to despise truth itself as something too cold, too blunt for his purpose—as, in fact, not good enough for his insistent emotion. From laughter and tears the descent is easy to snivelling and giggles.

These may seem selfish considerations; but you can't, in sound morals, condemn a man for taking care of his own integrity. It is his clear duty. And least of all can you condemn an artist pursuing, however humbly and imperfectly, a creative aim. In that interior world where his thought and his emotions go seeking for the experience of imagined adventures, there are no policemen, no law, no pressure of circumstance or dread of opinion to keep him within bounds. Who then is going to say Nay to his temptations if not his conscience?

And besides—this, remember, is the place and the moment of perfectly open talk—I think that all ambitions are lawful except those which climb upward on the miseries or credulities of mankind. All intellectual and artistic ambitions are permissible, up to and even beyond the limit of prudent sanity. They can hurt no one. If they are mad, then so much the worse for the artist. Indeed, as virtue is said to be, such ambitions are their own reward. Is it such a very mad presumption to believe in the sovereign power of one's art, to try for other means, for other ways of affirming this belief in the deeper appeal of one's work? To try to go deeper is not to be insensible. An historian of hearts is not an historian of emotions, yet he penetrates further, restrained as he may be, since his aim is to reach the very fount of laughter and tears. The sight of human affairs deserves admiration and pity. They are worthy of respect, too. And he is not insensible who pays them the undemonstrative tribute of a sigh which is not a sob, and of a smile which is not a grin. Resignation, not mystic, not detached, but resignation open-eyed, conscious, and informed by love, is the only one of our feelings for which it is impossible to become a sham.

Not that I think resignation the last word of wisdom. I am too much the creature of my time for that. But I think that the proper wisdom is to will what the gods will without, perhaps, being certain what their will is—or even if they have a will of their own. And in this matter of life and art it is not the Why that matters so much to our happiness as the How. As the Frenchman said, *"Il y a toujours la manière."* Very true. Yes. There is the manner. The manner in laughter, in tears, in irony, in indignations and enthusiasms, in judgments—and even in love. The manner in which, as in the features and character of a human face, the inner truth is foreshadowed for those who know how to look at their kind.

Those who read me know my conviction that the world, the temporal world, rests on a few very simple ideas; so simple that they must be as old as the hills. It rests notably, among others, on the idea of Fidelity. At a time when nothing which is not revolutionary in some way or other can expect to attract much attention I have not been revolutionary in my writings. The revolutionary spirit is mighty convenient in this, that it frees one from all scruples as regards ideas. Its hard, absolute optimism is repulsive to my mind by the menace of fanaticism and intolerance it contains. No doubt one should smile at these things; but, imperfect Esthete, I am no better Philosopher. All claim to special righteousness awakens in me that scorn and anger from which a philosophical mind should be free. . . .

I fear that trying to be conversational I have only managed to be unduly discursive. I have never been very well acquainted with the art of conversation—that art which, I understand, is supposed to be lost now. My young days, the days when one's habits and character are formed, have been rather familiar with long silences. Such voices as broke into them were anything but conversational. No. I haven't got the habit. Yet this discursiveness is not so irrelevant to the handful of pages which follow. They, too, have been charged with discursiveness, with disregard of chronological order (which is in itself a crime) with unconventionality of form (which is an impropriety). I was told severely that the public would view with displeasure the informal character of my recollections. "Alas!" I protested, mildly. "Could I begin with the sacramental words, 'I was born on such a date in such a place?' The remoteness of the locality would have robbed the statement of all interest. I haven't lived through wonderful adventures to be related *seriatim.* I haven't known distinguished men on whom I could pass fatuous remarks. I haven't been mixed up with great or scandalous affairs. This is but a bit of psychological document, and even so, I haven't written it with a view to put forward any conclusion of my own."

But my objector was not placated. These were good reasons for not writing at all—not a defence of what stood written already, he said.

I admit that almost anything, anything in the world, would serve as a good reason for not writing at all. But since I have written them, all I want to say in their defence is that these memories put down without any regard for established conventions have not been thrown off without system and purpose. They have their hope and their aim. The hope that from the reading of these pages there may emerge at last the vision of a personality; the man behind the books so fundamentally dissimilar as, for instance, "Almayer's Folly" and "The Secret Agent," and yet a coherent, justifiable personality both in its origin and in its action. This is the hope. The immediate aim, closely associated with the hope, is to give the record of personal memories by presenting faithfully the feelings and sensations connected with the writing of my first book and with my first contact with the sea.

In the purposely mingled resonance of this double strain a friend here and there will perhaps detect a subtle accord.

## *Ralph Ellison*

### An Interview[9]

ELLISON: Let me say right now that my book is not an autobiographical work.

INTERVIEWERS: You weren't thrown out of school like the boy in your novel?

ELLISON: No. Though, like him, I went from one job to another.

INTERVIEWERS: Why did you give up music and begin writing?

ELLISON: I didn't give up music but I became interested in writing through incessant reading. In 1935 I discovered Eliot's *The Waste Land* which moved and intrigued me but defied my powers of analysis—such as they were—and I wondered why I had never read anything of equal intensity and sensibility by an American Negro writer. Later on, in New York, I read a poem by Richard Wright, who, as luck would have it, came to town the next week. He was editing a magazine called *New Challenge* and asked me to try a book review of E. Waters Turpin's *These Low Grounds.* On the basis of this review Wright suggested that I try a short story, which I did. I tried to use my knowledge of riding freight trains. He liked the story well enough to accept it and it got as far as the galley proofs when it was bumped from the issue because there was too much material. Just after that the magazine failed.

INTERVIEWERS: But you went on writing—

ELLISON: With difficulty, because this was the Recession of 1937. I went to Dayton, Ohio, where my brother and I hunted and sold game to earn a living. At night I practiced writing and studied Joyce, Dostoevski, Stein, and Hemingway. Especially Hemingway; I read him to learn his sentence structure and how to organize a story. I guess many young writers were doing this, but I also used his description of hunting when I went into the fields the next day. I had been hunting since I was eleven, but no one had broken down the process of wing-shooting for me, and it was from reading Hemingway that I learned to lead a bird. When he describes something in print, believe him; believe him even when he describes the process of art in terms of baseball or boxing; he's been there.

INTERVIEWERS: Were you affected by the social realism of the period?

ELLISON: I was seeking to learn and social realism was a highly regarded theory, though I didn't think too much of the so-called proletarian fiction even when I was most impressed by Marxism. I was intrigued by Malraux, who at that time was being claimed by the Communists. I noticed, however, that whenever the heroes of *Man's Fate* regarded their condition during moments of heightened self-consciousness, their thinking was something other than Marxist. Actually they were more profoundly intellectual than their real-life counterparts. Of course, Malraux was more of a humanist than most of the Marxist writers of that period—and also much more of an artist. He was the artist-revolutionary rather than a politician when he wrote *Man's Fate,* and the book lives not because of a political position embraced at the time but because of its larger concern with the tragic struggle of humanity. Most of the social realists

9. From *Writers at Work,* The Paris Review *Interviews,* Vol. 2, ed. George Plimpton (1963).

of the period were concerned less with tragedy than with injustice. I wasn't and am not, *primarily* concerned with injustice, but with art.

INTERVIEWERS: Then you consider your novel a purely literary work as opposed to one in the tradition of social protest.

ELLISON: Now, mind, I recognize no dichotomy between art and protest. Dostoevski's *Notes from Underground* is, among other things, a protest against the limitations of nineteenth-century rationalism; *Don Quixote, Man's Fate, Oedipus Rex, The Trial*—all these embody protest, even against the limitation of human life itself. If social protest is antithetical to art, what then shall we make of Goya, Dickens, and Twain? One hears a lot of complaints about the so-called "protest novel," especially when written by Negroes; but it seems to me that the critics could more accurately complain about the lack of craftsmanship and the provincialism which is typical of such works.

INTERVIEWERS: But isn't it going to be difficult for the Negro writer to escape provincialism when his literature is concerned with a minority?

ELLISON: All novels are about certain minorities: the individual is a minority. The universal in the novel—and isn't that what we're all clamoring for these days?—is reached only through the depiction of the specific man in a specific circumstance.

INTERVIEWERS: But still, how is the Negro writer, in terms of what is expected of him by critics and readers, going to escape his particular need for social protest and reach the "universal" you speak of?

ELLISON: If the Negro, or any other writer, is going to do what is expected of him, he's lost the battle before he takes the field. I suspect that all the agony that goes into writing is borne precisely because the writer longs for acceptance—but it must be acceptance on his own terms. Perhaps, though, this thing cuts both ways: the Negro novelist draws his blackness too tightly around him when he sits down to write—that's what the anti-protest critics believe—but perhaps the white reader draws his whiteness around himself when he sits down to read. He doesn't want to identify himself with Negro characters in terms of our immediate racial and social situation, though on the deeper human level identification can become compelling when the situation is revealed artistically. The white reader doesn't want to get too close, not even in an imaginary recreation of society. Negro writers have felt this, and it has led to much of our failure.

Too many books by Negro writers are addressed to a white audience. By doing this the authors run the risk of limiting themselves to the audience's presumptions of what a Negro is or should be; the tendency is to become involved in polemics, to plead the Negro's humanity. You know, many white people question that humanity, but I don't think that Negroes can afford to indulge in such a false issue. For us the question should be, what are the specific *forms* of that humanity, and what in our background is worth preserving or abandoning. The clue to this can be found in folklore, which offers the first drawings of any group's character. It preserves mainly those situations which have repeated themselves again and again in the history of any given group. It describes those rites, manners, customs, and so forth, which insure the good life, or destroy it; and it describes those boundaries of feeling, thought, and action which that particular group has found to be the limitation of the human condition. It projects this wisdom in symbols which express the group's will to survive; it embodies those values by which the group lives and dies. These drawings may be crude but they are nonetheless profound in that they represent the group's attempt to humanize the world. It's no accident that great literature, the product of individual artists, is erected upon this humble base. The hero of Dostoevski's *Notes from Underground* and the hero of Gogol's "The Overcoat" appear in their rudimentary forms far back in Russian folklore. French literature has never ceased exploring the nature of the Frenchman.

## *Gail Godwin*

## Becoming a Writer[1]

On weekend mornings my mother sat at the typewriter in a sunny breakfast nook and wrote stories about women, young women like herself, who, after some difficulty necessary to the plot, got their men. In the adjoining kitchen, my grandmother washed the breakfast dishes and kept asking, "What do you two think you could eat for lunch?" My mother and I would groan in unison. Who could imagine lunch when we'd just finished breakfast? Besides, there were more important things to do than eat.

Already, at five, I had allied myself with the typewriter rather than the stove. The person at the stove usually had the thankless task of fueling. Whereas, if you were faithful to your vision at the typewriter, by lunchtime you could make two more characters happy—even if you weren't so happy yourself. What is more, if you retyped your story neatly in the afternoon and sent it off in a manila envelope to New York, you'd get a check back for $100 within two or three weeks (300 words to the page, 16–17 pages, 2¢ a word: in 1942, $100 went a long way). Meanwhile, she at the stove ran our mundane life. Still new to the outrageous vulnerability of widowhood, she was glad to play Martha to my mother's Mary. In our manless little family, she also played mother and could be counted on to cook, sew on buttons, polish the piano, and give encouragement to creative endeavors. She was my mother's first reader, while the stories were still in their morning draft; "It moves a little slowly here," she'd say, or "I didn't understand why the girl did this." And the tempo would be stepped up, the heroine's ambiguous action sharpened in the afternoon draft; for if my grandmother didn't follow tempo and motive, how would all those other women who would buy the magazines?

To my grandmother's mother, my mother played father; she was the provider, who took her skills off to the next town on the weekday bus and returned home at night, rumpled and exhausted and as in need of being waited on as any man. Lucky for her, most of the men were overseas at war, and the *Asheville Citizen-Times* needed reporters. Out she went daily; at the new Army hospital, she interviewed wounded soldiers who had flown back home; she followed

1. From *The Writer on Her Work*, Vol. 1, ed. Janet Sternburg (1980).

Eleanor Roosevelt all over town one day and bore the brunt of the restaurant owner's ire when Mrs. R. insisted upon bringing her black friend to lunch; she interviewed Béla Bartók in her college French; whenever Mrs. Wolfe called up the paper to announce, "I have just remembered something else about Tom," my mother was sent off immediately to the dead novelist's home on Spruce Street. It was not uncommon, during blackouts, for my mother to arrive home via police escort; they at the *Citizen* did not think it proper that a young woman should be alone in all that darkness; but the other side of this special treatment was that, after the war, she was told her skills would not be needed anymore. "The men need their jobs back, you see."

My preschool occupation consisted of being the adored Child on whose behalf this family had been created. For if I had not existed, these two might have worked out different plots for themselves. My elegant, feminine grandmother, doted on by men who wanted to protect her, would not have remained long on her own. My mother was still young, pretty as any of the girls who stepped off trains or entered fateful rooms in her stories; she had a master's degree in English ("The Stage of Inigo Jones": her thesis); an only child, she had been brought up in comfort, riding around the country on passes—her father was with Southern Railways—shopping almost daily for clothes from the moment she could walk with her mother (I can open her college diary today and read about the rose silk pajamas they bought, or the yellow taffeta tea gown, and what movie they saw afterward) and I know (also from the diary) that in the years just before me her main problem had been choosing between men. At Chapel Hill, she often had five dates in one day—and the energy of the true candle-burner-at-both-ends; she thought nothing of staying up during what was left of the night, typing nineteen-page term papers, or writing her own plays. But at home one weekend, she was playing bridge with her girlfriends on the porch when a man limped by. It was Mose Winston Godwin, the handsome local bachelor, who had snapped his ankle playing tennis. My mother's little dog, incensed by something in the man's gait, rushed down the stairs and bit his good leg.

And that was that. Sealed. My mother's fate. And mine.

GIRL MEETS MAN. MUTUAL ATTRACTION. THINGS DEVELOP. A PROBLEM ARISES. CONFLICT AND DOUBT. RESOLUTION OF CONFLICT. FINAL EMBRACE. The formula was unvarying. All the stories that bought my clothes, my storybook dolls, my subscriptions to children's magazines, were contained by, were imprisoned in that plot. Did my young divorced mother, while typing in that sun-filled breakfast nook, ever have moments of bitter irony when she was tempted to rip out the "happily ever after" lie she was perpetrating, and roll a fresh sheet into the carriage and tell her own story? It would have been much more interesting. But who would have bought it? Not *Love Short Stories,* nor any of the other pulps—nor any of the "slicks" for women, either. When you write for the market, you lock yourself willingly into the prison of your times: a lesson I learned early. Now I sit in my dentist's office and leaf through women's magazines whose fictional terrains support, quite matter-of-factly, divorced mothers, unmarried mothers, even well-to-do suburban wives who may or may not "keep" that unplanned-for last child. And I think of the writers of these stories, safely within the ideologies of their *zeitgeist*, and I wonder what parts of their own stories they still feel obliged to suppress, what dark blossomings of their imaginations still lie outside the realm of the current "market"? Yes, even in these "liberated" times.

It is this realm that I fight; it is the dark blossomings, the suppressed (or veiled) truths that I court. Not always successfully. Like my mother, I, too, am the child of my times.

Here is a story that my mother did not write: a woman, coming home late from her creative writing class, walks past the Casa Loma nightclub, on the way to her bus stop. She sees a man go in, a handsome, laughing, well-dressed man with his arm around a platinum blonde. Upstairs in the nightclub, the band is in the throes of "Stardust." The woman downstairs in the night, alone, has been up since six that morning, teaching at two schools, teaching, among other things, Romantic Literature. She has been unable to collect a single child-support payment from the handsome man because he has moved to another state. But now he has sneaked back into this town, unable to resist his old haunts. He has not seen the woman in the rumpled tweed suit, downstairs in the night. An irresistible impulse rises in her. She goes to the nearest phone and calls the police and identifies herself. They remember her, from her wartime job at the paper; many of them have taken turns driving her home during the old blackouts. She has my father locked up. She misses her bus but boards the next one and rides through the starry night, a weird joy throbbing through her veins and making her feel lightheaded. When she arrives home, she gives in to another irresistible impulse and wakes her little girl. "It's almost midnight," cries the grandmother, "are you crazy?" "No," she says, smiling. She hugs them both. She will keep her secret for tonight, as it will just upset her mother, who fears scandal as much as disease. "I want Gail to see the stars," she says. "They have never seemed quite so close."

But if the next day was Saturday, her "free day," she probably sat down and fabricated yet another fortuitous beginning. Girl would meet man, at work, at a party, on a trip. (A biting dog would create the wrong tone.) And once set on her romantic treadmill, she has only to stand in place—or even sit—and let her author make it happen for her: the mutual attraction, the developing passion, the necessary conflict, the happy ending. The final embrace is a blind one, containing no foreknowledge of difficulties, no intimation of separation or sorrow—and certainly not the sort of retributive prank against one's former beloved that would send a weird joy pumping through one's veins.

My mother's specialty was the representative heroine, not the singular, the "passing strange." For practical reasons, she must keep editing the most interesting parts of herself out of the heroines she sent to New York. To explore all those oddities and promptings that rustled like wings in her soul at night, while she—who longed to write a love scene as it really was—lay beside her small daughter? Ah, better not, better not. For practical reasons, for reasons of sanity as well.

"Your mother always did have a sense of humor. Not that I felt much like laughing that night they came and hauled me out of the Casa Loma. But, do you know, you can get the best view of Asheville from its jail? All those ranges and ranges of blue mountains cradling the town. Especially when it's lit up at night. By the time your Uncle William came to bail me out, I had organized the other prisoners into a clean-up squad. They were nice fellows, just a little beleaguered, that was all. We were going to wash down the walls and then whitewash them over." My father laughed, thirteen years after the fact, a few months before his own suicide. "I was sort of sorry to have to leave. It was an interesting experience, being in jail."

Fact and fiction: fiction and fact. Which stops where, and how much to put in of each? At what point does regurgitated autobiography graduate into memory shaped by art? How do you know when to stop telling it as it is, or was, and make it into what it ought to be—or what would make a better story?

Choices, choices.

The child of two women, I sat down to write my first story at age nine. What was the story about? A henpecked husband named Ollie McGonnigle, who insults a man one morning only to come home that evening and discover that his wife has invited that same man to dinner. And, moreover, that man is—THE MAYOR OF THE TOWN!

My mother remarried. One of her ex-GI students from her Romantic Literature class. She wrote a novel about a college teacher, courted by several veterans, each of whom had a story to tell about his life and about the war. The teacher marries one of the veterans. This novel, called, *And Not to Yield*, contained, to my memory, some of the most erotic love scenes I have ever read. Amazing, when you think of it: the sheltered little girl and her grandmother, sitting down each evening to read the next installment of *And Not To Yield*. It was fiction, of course. My grandmother had not approved of the new groom, but this book was interesting. Hmmm. "Your mother certainly knows how to keep a reader's interest," my grandmother said, moistening her thumb to turn the page. "Kathleen Cole writes like an angel," wrote the publisher to my mother's agent, "at times. At other times, she is much too facile . . . and sentimental."

I went to a private school run by a French order of nuns. I was the poorest girl in the class, the only one who could not fork up the twenty-five dollars for the eighth grade trip to Washington. What story did I write in those days? One about a little rich boy, who lived all day behind elegant iron gates and had everything he wanted—except a friend he could confide in.

My mother miscarried her first son. Her husband got a job as a management trainee at Kress, for forty-five dollars a week. A courtly older man in town, the renowned local portrait painter (also the teacher of my mother's former creative writing class), painted my mother's portrait in oils. In the portrait she wore a jade green silk blouse and a gold Chinese pin. She also wore an enigmatic smile. She started a new novel about a famous woman writer, with two men after her. One, her ex-husband, was now her literary agent, who always leveled with her about her work. The other was a celebrated portrait painter. She also had a daughter, "pretty but selfish." The daughter got to marry the boy she loved: the son of the painter. The portrait painter, who has been looking for the "perfect woman" to paint, chooses another woman in town, a less beautiful but selfless woman who has been a wonderful mother. At the end of the novel, the successful writer-heroine is told by her ex-husband that her writing has become too facile and shallow. Having lost both the portrait painter and her writing, she turns to religion. When she has chastened herself sufficiently, she remarries her ex-husband. This novel was called *The Everlasting Door*. It went the round of the publishers. Take out the religion, some publishers said. Take out the sex, said others, and maybe a religious house would be interested.

Begin again.

My mother had a baby girl. I was fifteen and fell in love with an athlete nobody approved of but me. But we were going to move from that town soon, to Norfolk. Kress moved my stepfather often, and what I wanted to do more than anything was "stay out all night" with Larry. So I lied, and did. We didn't "do" anything, of course: it was 1953, and it had been drummed into me often enough what my most valuable commodity was. But the girl I was supposed to be spending the night with "told," and I was disgraced. I lost all my friends the same week I moved from that little South Carolina town. In Norfolk, we knew not one soul. There was a whole summer ahead of me in which to smolder over the injustice of society. I borrowed my mother's typewriter in the hours she wasn't using it and wrote a short novel called *I Broke the Code*. I have this piece of work before me now. An interesting artifact. Part truth, part lie, part gauche attempt at craft ("True, some will believe the worst, but I like to think that every small town has a forgiving streak that crosses right down its center like the railroad tracks.") and part cliché ("A wave of shame rushed through me."). Pretty disgusted with the results, I condescended and sent it to *True Confessions,* who returned it with the reader's note clipped to the top: "Some good writing but overdone. Also *much* too long. Also nothing much happens."

My mother had another miscarriage in Norfolk. Like me, she had no friends yet. So she organized a local Toastmistress Club, her civic specialty, begun back in Asheville when, after hearing a Red Cross volunteer open her speech with, "Ladies, our deficit is astounding," my mother decided it indeed was, and that women should do better than this. Now Norfolk women flocked to learn how to organize their thoughts and project their voices before crowds. My mother was gratified; her spunk returned. "Oh, what the hell," she said. "I am going to sit down and write a dirty novel that will really sell." *The Otherwise Virgins* was set on a college campus in the South. It had three heroines: Debby, a poised and beautiful redhead, president of her sorority, who unbeknownst to her friends was formerly a callgirl in New York until a southern senator decided to adopt her and give her a new start; Lisa, a dark-haired freshman, also beautiful, but spoiled and determined to win the love of Mark, an ex-GI just returned to campus; and Jane, a minister's daughter, a shy and scholarly girl, who joins Debby's sorority and rooms with Lisa. Complications arise when Mark discovers Debby on campus. He remembers her from her other life. They had a night together before he shipped out with his regiment for France. Further complications arise when Jane discovers she is a lesbian and deeply loves her roommate, Lisa.

I loved that novel. What excitement, during those dreary summer days in Norfolk when we knew nobody, to read each new page as it came out of the typewriter. My mother sometimes wrote twenty pages a day; a compulsion came over her during novels, it drove her to the end. Unlike me today, she always wrote with the completion taken for granted. It never occurred to her that she might get stuck, might not finish. She had always finished her stories for the old wartime pulps—unfinished stories didn't sell. A photographer from the Norfolk paper came and took my mother's picture at the typewriter, flanked by her sixteen-year-old daughter and her seven-month-old daughter. "Mrs. Cole writes novels and starts toastmistress clubs in her spare time," the captions read.

"*The Otherwise Virgins* has come heartbreakingly close," wrote the agent, many months and submissions later. "What the publishers seem to feel is that this novel is neither fish nor fowl. The campus life is realistic, but the situation is implausible. Also the World War II background is dated. Perhaps if you made it the Korean War and took out the part about the Southern senator . . ."

But if she took out the southern senator, she must take out Debby's past life, and if she took that out, there went the plot. And the Korean War had only ended the year before. Besides, we were moving again, across the river to Portsmouth. My mother consoled herself by starting another Toastmistress Club.

The writing bug did not bite again until a year later. We had been talking about my father and whether I should invite him to my high school graduation. She sat down and wrote a story about a selfish playboy father who suddenly takes an interest in his seventeen-year-old daughter, whom he has not seen for years. He invites her to come and live with him in his sumptuous house. ("Keep it," his rich second wife had said. "I never had a happy moment in it.") The girl goes, but ends up being more of an opportunist than he. She abandons him after two months when the rich ex-wife offers to send her to art school. "Nothing is going to stop me from reaching my goal," the daughter writes in her farewell note which she leaves with his housekeeper. "Maybe you're thinking I am ungrateful. But really, these two months have been so little in comparison with all you could have given me in seventeen years." She has even taken the curtains and bedspreads from her room.

"I'm not that bad, am I?" I asked.

"Of course not, darling. You're ambitious, like she is, but you would never have taken the curtains. I've brought you up better. But I needed her to be as ruthless as she is because I wanted this story to have that fated circular shape, like Greek drama."

Twenty years later, my mother, my sister, and I sat in my sister's girlhood bedroom, talking about a novel I had written. "I don't care," Franchelle was saying. "She'd better never put me in a novel again. I don't like being frozen in print for the rest of my life, forever wearing those silly panties and short skirts; and I'm *not* big like that, she's made me into some sort of amazon-freak."

"Darling," our mother said, "the sister in *The Odd Woman* wasn't you. Gail just took parts of you, the parts she needed. Writers work that way."

"Well, I wouldn't know. I'm a lawyer and they don't work that way. Besides, it *hurts*."

Tears filled her eyes and she ran from the room.

"It's unfair," I said. "She's being unfair by not trying to understand."

"It's difficult when you haven't written," agreed my mother. "Now I understood why you had to make Kitty a more passive mother than I am, also a little stupid; that was necessary to your overall plan . . ."

"Passive! Stupid! Kitty? Kitty was a beautiful character. I worked hard on Kitty."

"She was a lovely character," my mother said. "I thought she was awfully well done. But what I mean is, I knew she wasn't supposed to be me."

"But she was!"

"Well, there was something left out, then."

The magazines rejected my mother's story about the father and daughter. "Well-written, but there are no sympathetic characters," wrote one editor.

My father floored everyone by showing up for my high school graduation. He had to introduce himself, as I had no idea who he was. I flung myself, weeping, into his arms and he invited me to come and live with him.

"It was a little scary," my mother told me a long time afterward. "I felt I had somehow made it happen by writing that story."

The house of the real father was not sumptuous, and his second wife (not rich) still lived in it with him. It was he, not she, who sent the ambitious daughter off to college. He could only afford the first year: his playboy days were over; he sold cars for his wife's brother-in-law. In real life, it was he, not the daughter, who left first. For some reason, he took off his watch and placed it on the bedside table. His wife returned from the grocery store and found him lying on the floor, but with his head off the rug to spare her the necessity of dry cleaning it. He needn't have worried; it was a neat job. The coroner found that the first shot had misfired. So he had made his decision twice. There was no explanation, no farewell note to anyone. The daughter was in her third year of college, on a scholarship now. She was rewriting *The Otherwise Virgins*, updating the Chapel Hill campus her mother remembered from too long ago. Mark became a Korean War veteran, as it was now 1958 and there was plenty of information to look up on that war. "I give it to you," said her mother, now the mother of a little boy, too, and soon to be the mother of a second. "If you can do anything with it, you're welcome. I've somehow lost the urge." In her fourth year of college, the daughter would try and fail to complete a story about the father's death from the daughter's point of view. Many years later than that, she would finish an unsuccessful draft of a novel called *The Possibilitarian*, about a man of lost possibilities. Later again, her fourth published novel would contain a southern playboy uncle, Ambrose Clay, who shoots himself neatly in the head at the age of forty-nine because he has not kept his promises to himself. We know this is his reason because he leaves his niece, a young painter who will be warned by his failure and pursue her promises because of it, a loving note. Like the real father, Ambrose at one point is a car salesman, but I made him sell Mercedes. Unlike the real father, Ambrose had wanted to be a good novelist—as the real mother had wanted.

Fact and fiction, fiction and fact. Shapeshifting into one another. Sometimes fact cries out for fiction; sometimes fiction cries out for yet another fiction. Sometimes fiction redeems fact. And sometimes it doesn't.

Miss Gail Godwin
*The Miami Herald*
Fort Lauderdale, Fla.

November ___, 1959

Dear Miss Godwin:

Haven't I seen this novel before? You say you have just finished it, but I'm sure I recall the kindly southern senator and I'm sorry to say the plot is still as implausible as ever. Regretfully, I am shipping back *The Otherwise Virgins* to you under separate cover.

Sincerely yours,
Lurton Blassingame

Oh, Jesus, how could I have been so stupid? I thought my mother's agent was Ann Elmo. But obviously, at some point, she must have switched. Why can't I pay attention? What a stupid, self-defeating thing to do!

Failures often come in clumps. The next was the letter from my bureau chief.

August ___, 1960

. . . I have spent more time working and worrying over your future than I have spent on the entire rest of the staff I combined. I must confess I've been a failure. I apologize for my mistakes. But the fact remains that I cannot see any further benefit from my efforts or yours and I am convinced it would be to your benefit to find someplace to "start over." This has been harsher than I intended it to be. I really feel badly that I have failed to make a good reporter out of obviously promising material. I hope you can use this experience somewhere but I'm afraid you won't do it successfully until you look facts in the face and at the same time quit expecting to get to the moon in one day.

Failed! A failed writer, a failed journalist, at twenty-three. I don't know what to do. I'd rather die than tell my mother I was . . . fired. I'm afraid to kill myself, though. I don't have his nerve. I'll get married.

Divorced and twenty-four, I used the slow hours at my job at the U.S. embassy in London to work on my novel, *Gull Key,* about a young wife left alone all day on a Florida island while her husband slogs away at his job on the mainland. (He is a newspaper photographer.) Her discontent swells like a tidal wave . . . neighbors bicker and age and are held back by their children, making her wonder if marriage and motherhood are for her . . . a tryst with a sensitive man met in the art section of the public library provides the denouement, in which the husband "finds out" and his fist comes crashing through the glass door which she has locked against him and she bandages it up and they decide to separate. The final scene shows the heroine, chastened but re-energized, driving north on AIA, a modern Nora fleeing her doll's house in her own compact car. After a dozen English publishers turned it down, I sent it off to an agency I'd seen advertised in a magazine.

WANTED: UNPUBLISHED NOVELS IN WHICH WOMEN'S PROBLEMS AND LOVE INTERESTS ARE PREDOMINANT. ATTRACTIVE TERMS.

Many months went by and no response. I called directory assistance. The agency had no phone. I went around to the address. It was an empty building. I had made only one copy of *Gull Key*.

The City Literary Institute was located in a cavernous old building in north London. Somebody said it had been a prison in Dickens's time. But once I discovered it, I attended it every Tuesday evening with the desperate faith of an afflicted person attending a religious shrine. I was badly in need of a miracle. I was twenty-seven years old and had not yet become what I had wanted to be since the age of five: a writer. True, I wrote every evening, long, exhaustive entries in my journal to compensate for my boring days. I had stayed for three years in my cushy government job—helping the British plan their holidays in the U.S.—when I had only intended to stay one year. I had begun countless stories and novels, but there was something "off" about all of them. Either they had the ring of self-consciousness about them, or else they started too slowly and petered out before I ever got to the interesting material that had inspired me in the first place, or else they were so close to the current problems of my own life that I couldn't gain the proper distance and perspective. I have the 1964 journal before me now. Following a long quote from John Updike, which begins, "Her face, released from the terrible tension of hope, had grown smooth. . . ." I have begun a story of my own:

> The knock on the bedroom door turned out to be, that Sunday morning, the knock of Richard's mother, instead of Richard.

This gets nowhere, after a page, and I begin again:

> She had not slept well the night before. Things had come to a premature crisis with her and Richard, and though he took her home with him every weekend she had begun to feel in the position of a rejected lover . . .

At this point, I become disgusted with fiction and impatient to record, for my eyes only, what the real situation was. I was trying to get a rugby player to propose to me. He cared for me, but his mother cared infinitely more.

> Andy's mother rushed into the room, sat down on the bed and hugged me. She smelled of violet water. She said, "I just can't lose you. I love you like a daughter. If you go back to America, I'll have to go, too. I just can't understand it. It's sheer *stupidity* on his part. He'll lose you and then when rugby season is over he'll go crazy. He wrote to me this week, it was a lovely letter, he added up all your qualities, almost like 25% for this, 60% for that. Then he left a small reservation! As if you weren't a superwoman already! He said he'd never been so near the brink before, but that he needed time to see. I know he's going to fall for some faery doll of twenty. Or marry one of these English society types. If he can't rise to *this*! . . ."

Easy, in retrospect, to see the problems with the first two fictional openings. As well as the possibilities of the "real" opening. But in 1964, I could see neither and was in despair.

Our teacher at the City Literary Institute was an appealing woman who looked as though she had stepped out of another century. She wore her dark hair like Charlotte Brontë; her skirts were much too long for fashion. She had a rich, dramatically paced voice with which she read to us from the great writers. (When I reread Chekov's "Anyuta" recently, it seemed flat without Miss S——'s enthusiastic intonations and pregnant pauses.) But however she looked, our teacher was a thoroughly modern woman and somewhat of a heroine. She worked daytimes as an editor in a prominent publishing house, did interviews for the BBC on weekends, and taught these classes to support herself and her small illegitimate son. Miss S—— not only knew what good fiction was, she could tell you why it was good; she at once zeroed in on me, and, with a modicum of English tact, told me why my fiction wasn't working. That she was *able* to tell me, moreover to prescribe exercises to correct my faults, was my good fortune. What if I hadn't found my good angel, Miss S——? Later, when I was back in the U.S., and had become the writer I wanted to be, I tried to track her down through my English publishers, but to no avail. She seems to have vanished into thin air, she and her beautiful little boy, who would be almost a man by now. When I teach writing classes today I try to emulate her, try to match her standards.

The first exercise she gave me was: write a story of 200 words. Two hundred words is less than a typewritten page. Therefore it is necessary to get to the heart of the matter at once. What I had achieved accidentally in my journal entry about Andy's mother, I must learn to do on purpose.

Write a story of 300 words. Write a story of 450 words, beginning with this sentence: *"Run away," he muttered to himself, sitting up and biting his nails.*

When that must be your first sentence, it sort of excludes a story about a woman in her late twenties, adrift among the options of wifehood, career, vocation, a story that I had begun too many times already—both in fiction and reality—and could not resolve. My teacher wisely understood Gide's maxim for himself as writer: "The best means of learning to know oneself is seeking to understand others."

One of the exercises I like to give in writing courses is: imagine a person as much unlike yourself as possible; then write a scene, from that person's point of view, in which he/she is getting ready for bed.

At last the evening came when I was invited by Miss S—— to read my latest story aloud to the class. I was up to 4,500 words by then. The story was about an English vicar who has seen God, who writes a small book about his experience, and becomes famous. He gets caught up in the international lecture-tour circuit. My story shows him winding up his exhausting American tour at a small Episcopal college for women in the South. He is at his lowest point, having parroted back his own written words until he has lost touch with their meaning. He fears that, given the present pace and pressure of his public life, he will never again approach that private, meditative state of mind that brought God into focus in the first place.

Many drafts and two years later, this story, first titled "The Illumined Moment—and Consequences," later "An Intermediate Stop," would get me accepted into the Iowa Writer's Workshop. "She has some affectations, but we'll prune them," wrote the member of the reading committee on the bottom of my application.

A decade later than that, I was winding up my own exhausting reading tour in a fluorescent-lit classroom in Kansas City. It was an adult education course in Creative Writing. As I watched the members file in, many looking more exhausted than I felt, I wondered how I could manage to keep them awake for an hour. Beginning to panic, I leafed through the handsome leatherbound volume of my story collection, a Christmas gift from my publisher. All the stories I usually read—my "tour de force" stories—seemed much too long. Moreover, I had read some of them aloud so often that they were beginning to sound as if they had been written by somebody else. I suddenly lit on the vicar story, buried humbly among its flashier sisters, and it was like greeting an old friend who has known you "back when." I had never read this story aloud since its London debut, many a draft ago, in Miss S——'s class.

To fill in the time—for this group certainly deserved their hour's worth—I began by telling my audience the genesis of the story they were going to hear. Once I, too, had attended an evening class, like this one, after working all day at a job . . .

As I began to read them the story, my tiredness diminished; I could see them perk up, as well, for they were "in on" things. They were no longer "Gail Godwin the Visiting Writer's Audience," they were people like me, on the same quest. With a wonderful jolt of recognition, I realized that my life was imitating the action of my vicar story, written all those years ago. For his resurgence came when, facing his last audience before the journey home, he turns his notecards, worn from too many previous lectures, face down on the rostrum. And standing before them, "a man like any other, no vision standing between them," he takes them into his confidence, gives them a guided tour of his English landscape, that private long-ago place where he had been granted his vision.

After I had read my story to Miss S——'s class, its most interesting member came up to me and pronounced himself pleased. Though he never turned in stories himself, he could be depended upon to deliver penetrating judgments upon the work of his classmates. His name was Dr. Marshall, and even the astute Miss S—— was a little in awe of him. He was a tall, dark, scowling man with a slight limp who came to class with a motorcycle helmet under his arm, often accompanied by a horsey-looking woman carrying a motorcycle helmet under her arm. Tonight, however, his companion had not come, and after we had discussed certain religious images in my story, he told me he was a psychotherapist. We discovered we lived on the same street in Chelsea, and he rode me home that evening on the back of his Vespa. Within two months we were married and I had time, as did my character Dane Empson, the American girl in *The Perfectionists*, to meditate amply upon the consequences of our impulsiveness. It had been, on both our parts, a "nervous attachment, rather than a sexual love," as D. H. Lawrence described the marriage of the couple in *St. Mawr*, a work I had the misfortune to discover *after* I became Mrs. Marshall. For one year, we did our best to drive each other crazy—and both almost succeeded. Our union finally dissolved a year later in a nightmarish vacation in Majorca; the figurative truths of that year, if not the literal ones, were to become my first published novel. But to give credit where it is due, this man who was impossible as my mate was the person who may well have made it possible for me to start being the writer I knew I had it in me to be. And I don't mean the obvious, that our marriage was to become the material for my novel.

As I have mentioned, he was a psychotherapist, and during our year together I saw him do wonders for several people. Some doctors are extraordinarily gifted as diagnosticians, and he was one of them; also, he was willing to try the most unorthodox of cures. This bothered me at the time; more conventional than I am now, I wanted him to declare himself a Jungian, a Freudian. Meanwhile, off he went to a scientology lecture, to see what useful ideas he could derive from that controversial organization. My own "cure," ironically, was derived from a method he had picked up from the scientologists. It consisted in asking the patient the same question over and over again until the patient comes up with an answer that sets off a feeling of "release" in him, a relieving certainty that he has at last *really* answered the question.

Shortly after our fiasco-vacation in Majorca, and just before I was to depart for the United States for a visit from which I suspect both of us unconsciously knew I would not return, we sat under a very old mulberry tree, which was staked and wired together to preserve it as long as possible. It was known locally as Sir Thomas More's mulberry, though that would have made it more than four hundred years old. The building where we lived was on the land that had once been his.

"I am going to die if I can't be a writer," I said.

"Why can't you be a writer?" he asked.

"Because . . . I don't know . . . something keeps getting in the way."

"I see. But why can't you be a writer?"

"Because! I told you, something never quite . . . jells."

"Hmm. But . . . why can't you be a writer?"

"Oh, I don't know. Look at my mother. She wrote and wrote and wrote. And nobody ever published her novels. Heartbreaking."

"Yes. But why can't *you* be a writer?"

"When I write in my journals, it's fine. You know it is, you bastard, you've read them yourself, without my permission. They flow, they're real. Whereas, the minute I put on my writing hat and sit down to 'write a story,' I bore myself to death. I kill it, I kill the whole thing."

"I see. Why can't you be a writer, then?"

"Because . . . because . . . OH, GOD! Because I'm afraid I might fail!"

The sun was weakening, cold for June, but I felt very warm, as if I'd been given an injection of some warm energy. "Good God," I said, "That's it! That's it, you know. What a spineless, lily-livered fraidy-cat I have been!"

"Yes, that's it," he said, in his cool professional voice. But I saw the blood come into his face: the blush of exhaltation: he knew he had freed me. Even if it meant freeing me from him.

In Iris Murdoch's novel *The Black Prince*, a writer says, "I live, I *live*, with an absolutely continuous sense of failure. I am always defeated, always. Every book is the wreck of a perfect idea. The years pass and one has only one life. If one has a thing at all one must do it and keep on and on and on trying to do it better."

I love that statement. Its stark pessimism is comforting. That statement expresses my feelings about my own work.

I work continuously within the shadow of failure. For every novel that makes it to my publisher's desk, there are at least five or six that died on the way. And even with the ones I do finish, I think of all the ways they might have been better. Rodin was right when he said that even an achieved work is never perfect; it is always susceptible to a modification that can make it better. But I believe that with enough practice and skill and good faith, you can learn to recognize when the work is achieved. There is such a thing as fussing too much; it can deaden the work. There is also such a thing as stopping too soon; this gives the work a kind of incompleteness that is more annoying than it is mysterious. Learning when "enough is enough" is the discipline of a lifetime. Perfection, however that ideal is measured, may not grace the work, but it should be sought during the process of the work.

I think the most serious danger to my writing is my predilection for shapeliness. How I love "that nice circular Greek shape" my mother spoke of; or a nice, neat conclusion, with all the edges tucked under. And this sometimes leads me to "wrap up" things, to force dramatic revelations at the expense of allowing the truth to reveal itself in slow, shy, and often problematical glimpses.

But my serious danger is also my strength. And so I must fight its temptations and preserve its rights at the same time. For it is the part of my talent that *selects* from what Henry James called "the rattle and the rumble" of ordinary existence, and fashions these literal happenings into another kind of truth called a story.

An example. That "story my mother didn't write." True, she attended a creative writing class in the evening; and she held down several teaching jobs during the day. (Or was the creative writing class during that earlier time, when she still worked on the newspaper?) True, one evening, she spied my father, delinquent in his child-support payments, slipping up to the Casa Loma club. And true she had him locked up. And once, when I was still small enough to be picked up, she carried me outside in her arms to show me the stars. All the rest, including the weird joy she felt, is my interpretation. And the events that did happen did not all happen on the same night. That was my timing. What did I hope to gain by telling the story this way? Well, the night becomes the backdrop on which I glue five isolated events that add up to a certain truth about my mother's situation at that time.

But what about the *other* truths you lost by telling it that way? you ask.

Ah, my friend, that is my question, too. The choice is always a killing one. One option must die so that another may live. I do little murders in my workroom every day. I must commit some now, in order to bring this piece to a close.

This account of my own unfolding as a writer has been the truth. But it is also full of lies, many of which I'm not aware of. But in one sense, perhaps the most important, it is all true: it could have been written by nobody but me.

What I have chosen to tell, how I have chosen to tell it, and what I have chosen not to tell, express me and the kind of writer I am.

I am my mother's child, weaned on shapely plots; the child of the woman who knew more about herself than she dared to put into her heroines.

I am the daughter of a man who, when locked up in prison, discovered it afforded the best view in town; who would whitewash the walls of the prison if he was forced to stay there; who would look back on prison after he was out of it and reflect on the interesting nature of the experience.

I am—thanks to the efforts of those who have loved me (and to some who have not) and thanks to the examples of people who did their work well, and thanks to the efforts of myself—my own woman.

I am haunted at this moment by what I may write next. The good thing about becoming older is that you gain time from that much more experience and can see where the real stories are. So many landscapes impose themselves upon the one I look out on as I write this. So many people present themselves before my inner eye, turning themselves this way and that, reminding me of their myriad aspects. I'm a novelist and a teller of tales, in a room alone, looking out on rain-washed grass, garden, trees, yet seeing as well a French chateau, a path in white rock in New Mexico, a dormitory room, a marriage bed. I'm watching a roomful of personalities parading their traits before me, giving me a fashion show, enticing me to buy. "I'm unique," says one. "So am I," says another. "I, too," says another. "Me, me!" cries a fourth. And all of them are right. Each of them is unique. And the more I write fiction, the more I want all of them. The more I understand: I am in all of them; all of them live in me.

I am also haunted by "the story I might not write." How I long to sneak into the future and snatch away the retrospect of one who could say: *"Oh yes, she wrote about this and this and this, while all the time, as close to her as her own skin, lay her real story, her true story, the whole story, the best story of all."*

What is that story?

Oh, you know-it-all daughterly ghost of myself, I am going to shake you within an inch of your life, I am going to wrestle with you all the rest of my days, I am going to employ all my tact and strength and wiles to force you to give up your secret!

## *Ernest Hemingway*

## An Interview[2]

INTERVIEWER: Do the titles come to you while you're in the process of doing the story?

HEMINGWAY: No. I make a list of titles *after* I've finished the story or the book—sometimes as many as a hundred. Then I start eliminating them, sometimes all of them.

2. From *Writers at Work,* The Paris Review *Interviews,* Vol. 2, ed. George Plimpton (1963).

INTERVIEWER: And you do this even with a story whose title is supplied from the text—"Hills Like White Elephants," for example?

HEMINGWAY: Yes. The title comes afterwards. I met a girl in Prunier where I'd gone to eat oysters before lunch. I knew she'd had an abortion. I went over and we talked, not about that, but on the way home I thought of the story, skipped lunch, and spent that afternoon writing it.

INTERVIEWER: So when you're not writing, you remain constantly the observer, looking for something which can be of use.

HEMINGWAY: Surely. If a writer stops observing he is finished. But he does not have to observe consciously nor think how it will be useful. Perhaps that would be true at the beginning. But later everything he sees goes into the great reserve of things he knows or has seen. If it is any use to know it, I always try to write on the principle of the iceberg. There is seven-eighths of it underwater for every part that shows. Anything you know you can eliminate and it only strengthens your iceberg. It is the part that doesn't show. If a writer omits something because he does not know it then there is a hole in the story.

*The Old Man and the Sea* could have been over a thousand pages long and had every character in the village in it and all the processes of how they made their living, were born, educated, bore children, etc. That is done excellently and well by other writers. In writing you are limited by what has already been done satisfactorily. So I have tried to learn to do something else. First I have tried to eliminate everything unnecessary to conveying experience to the reader so that after he or she has read something it will become a part of his or her experience and seem actually to have happened. This is very hard to do and I've worked at it very hard.

Anyway, to skip how it is done, I had unbelievable luck this time and could convey the experience completely and have it be one that no one had ever conveyed. The luck was that I had a good man and a good boy and lately writers have forgotten there still are such things. Then the ocean is worth writing about just as man is. So I was lucky there. I've seen the marlin mate and know about that. So I leave that out. I've seen a school (or pod) of more than fifty sperm whales in that same stretch of water and once harpooned one nearly sixty feet in length and lost him. So I left that out. All the stories I know from the fishing village I leave out. But the knowledge is what makes the underwater part of the iceberg.

INTERVIEWER: Archibald MacLeish has spoken of a method of conveying experience to a reader which he said you developed while covering baseball games back in those *Kansas City Star* days. It was simply that experience is communicated by small details, intimately preserved, which have the effect of indicating the whole by making the reader conscious of what he had been aware of only subconsciously. . . .

HEMINGWAY: The anecdote is apocryphal. I never wrote baseball for the *Star*. What Archie was trying to remember was how I was trying to learn in Chicago in around 1920 and was searching for the unnoticed things that made emotions, such as the way an outfielder tossed his glove without looking back to where it fell, the squeak of resin on canvas under a fighter's flat-soled gym shoes, the gray color of Jack Blackburn's skin when he had just come out of stir, and other things I noted as a painter sketches. You saw Blackburn's strange color and the old razor cuts and the way he spun a man before you knew his history. These were the things which moved you before you knew the story.

INTERVIEWER: Have you ever described any type of situation of which you had no personal knowledge?

HEMINGWAY: That is a strange question. By personal knowledge do you mean carnal knowledge? In that case the answer is positive. A writer, if he is any good, does not describe. He invents or *makes* out of knowledge personal and impersonal and sometimes he seems to have unexplained knowledge which could come from forgotten racial or family experience. Who teaches the homing pigeon to fly as he does; where does a fighting bull get his bravery, or a hunting dog his nose? This is an elaboration or a condensation of that stuff we were talking about in Madrid that time when my head was not to be trusted.

INTERVIEWER: How detached must you be from an experience before you can write about it in fictional terms? The African air crashes you were involved in, for instance?

HEMINGWAY: It depends on the experience. One part of you sees it with complete detachment from the start. Another part is very involved. I think there is no rule about how soon one should write about it. It would depend on how well adjusted the individual was and on his or her recuperative powers. Certainly it is valuable to a trained writer to crash in an aircraft which burns. He learns several important things very quickly. Whether they will be of use to him is conditioned by survival. Survival, with honor, that outmoded and all-important word, is as difficult as ever and as all-important to a writer. Those who do not last are always more beloved since no one has to see them in their long, dull, unrelenting, no-quarter-given-no-quarter-received, fights that they make to do something as they believe it should be done before they die. Those who die or quit early and easy and with every good reason are preferred because they are understandable and human. Failure and well-disguised cowardice are more human and more beloved.

INTERVIEWER: Could I ask you to what extent you think the writer should concern himself with the socio-political problems of his times?

HEMINGWAY: Everyone has his own conscience, and there should be no rules about how a conscience should function. All you can be sure about in a political-minded writer is that if his work should last you will have to skip the politics when you read it. Many of the so-called politically enlisted writers change their politics frequently. This is very exciting to them and to their political-literary reviews. Sometimes they even have to rewrite their viewpoints . . . and in a hurry. Perhaps it can be respected as a form of the pursuit of happiness.

INTERVIEWER: Would you say, ever, that there is any didactic intention in your work?

HEMINGWAY: Didactic is a word that has been misused and has spoiled. *Death in the Afternoon* is an instructive book.

INTERVIEWER: It has been said that a writer only deals with one or two ideas throughout his work. Would you say your work reflects one or two ideas?

HEMINGWAY: Who said that? It sounds much too simple. The man who said it possibly *had* only one or two ideas.

INTERVIEWER: Well, perhaps it would be better put this way: Graham Greene said that a ruling passion gives to a shelf of novels the unity of a system. You yourself have said, I believe, that great writing comes out of a sense of injustice. Do you consider it important that a novelist be dominated in this way—by some such compelling sense?

HEMINGWAY: Mr. Greene has a facility for making statements that I do not possess. It would be impossible for me to make generalizations about a shelf of novels or a wisp of snipe or a gaggle of geese. I'll try a generalization though. A writer without a sense of justice and of injustice would be better off editing the Year Book of a school for exceptional children than writing novels. Another generalization. You see; they are not so difficult when they are sufficiently obvious. The most essential gift for a good writer is a built-in, shock-proof, shit detector. This is the writer's radar and all great writers have had it.

INTERVIEWER: Finally, a fundamental question: namely, as a creative writer what do you think is the function of your art? Why a representation of fact, rather than fact itself?

HEMINGWAY: Why be puzzled by that? From things that have happened and from things as they exist and from all things that you know and all those you cannot know, you make something through your invention that is not a representation but a whole new thing truer than anything true and alive, and you make it alive, and if you make it well enough, you give it immortality. That is why you write and for no other reason that you know of. But what about all the reasons that no one knows?

## *Henry James*

## The Art of Fiction[3]

It goes without saying that you will not write a good novel unless you possess the sense of reality; but it will be difficult to give you a recipe for calling that sense into being. Humanity is immense, and reality has a myriad forms; the most one can affirm is that some of the flowers of fiction have the odour of it, and others have not; as for telling you in advance how your nosegay should be composed, that is another affair. It is equally excellent and inconclusive to say that one must write from experience; to our supposititious aspirant such a declaration might savour of mockery. What kind of experience is intended, and where does it begin and end? Experience is never limited, and it is never complete; it is an immense sensibility, a kind of huge spider-web of the finest silken threads suspended in the chamber of consciousness, and catching every airborne particle in its tissue. It is the very atmosphere of the mind; and when the mind is imaginative—much more when it happens to be that of a man of genius—it takes to itself the faintest hints of life, it converts the very pulses of the air into revelations. The young lady living in a village has only to be a damsel upon whom nothing is lost to make it quite unfair (as it seems to me) to declare to her that she shall have nothing to say about the military. Greater miracles

3. From *Partial Portraits* (1905).

have been seen than that, imagination assisting, she should speak the truth about some of these gentlemen. I remember an English novelist, a woman of genius, telling me that she was much commended for the impression she had managed to give in one of her tales of the nature and way of life of the French Protestant youth. She had been asked where she learned so much about this recondite being, she had been congratulated on her peculiar opportunities. These opportunities consisted in her having once, in Paris, as she ascended a staircase, passed an open door where, in the household of a *pasteur*,[4] some of the young Protestants were seated at table round a finished meal. The glimpse made a picture; it lasted only a moment, but that moment was experience. She had got her direct personal impression, and she turned out her type. She knew what youth was, and what Protestantism; she also had the advantage of having seen what it was to be French, so that she converted these ideas into a concrete image and produced a reality. Above all, however, she was blessed with the faculty which when you give it an inch takes an ell, and which for the artist is a much greater source of strength then any accident of residence or of place in the social scale. The power to guess the unseen from the seen, to trace the implication of things, to judge the whole piece by the pattern, the condition of feeling life in general so completely that you are well on your way to knowing any particular corner of it—this cluster of gifts may almost be said to constitute experience, and they occur in country and in town, and in the most differing stages of education. If experience consists of impressions, it may be said that impressions *are* experience, just as (have we not seen it?) they are the very air we breathe. Therefore, if I should certainly say to a novice, "Write from experience and experience only," I should feel that this was rather a tantalising monition if I were not careful immediately to add, "Try to be one of the people on whom nothing is lost!"

• • •

There are bad novels and good novels, as there are bad pictures and good pictures; but that is the only distinction in which I see any meaning, and I can as little imagine speaking of a novel of character as I can imagine speaking of a picture of character. When one says picture one says of character, when one says novel one says of incident, and the terms may be transposed at will. What is character but the determination of incident? What is incident but the illustration of character? What is either a picture or a novel that is *not* of character? What else do we seek in it and find in it? It is an incident for a woman to stand up with her hand resting on a table and look out at you in a certain way; or if it be not an incident I think it will be hard to say what it is. At the same time it is an expression of character. If you say you don't see it (character in *that*—*allons donc!*),[5] this is exactly what the artist who has reasons of his own for thinking he *does* see it undertakes to show you. When a young man makes up his mind that he has not faith enough after all to enter the church as he intended, that is an incident, though you may not hurry to the end of the chapter to see whether perhaps he doesn't change once more. I do not say that these

4. Clergyman (French). 5. Come on now! Surely not! (French).

are extraordinary or startling incidents. I do not pretend to estimate the degree of interest proceeding from them, for this will depend upon the skill of the painter. It sounds almost puerile to say that some incidents are intrinsically much more important than others, and I need not take this precaution after having professed my sympathy for the major ones in remarking that the only classification of the novel that I can understand is into that which has life and that which has it not.

• • •

Nothing, of course, will ever take the place of the good old fashion of "liking" a work of art or not liking it: the most improved criticism will not abolish that primitive, that ultimate test. I mention this to guard myself from the accusation of intimating that the idea, the subject, of a novel or a picture, does not matter. It matters, to my sense, in the highest degree, and if I might put up a prayer it would be that artists should select none but the richest. Some, as I have already hastened to admit, are much more remunerative than others, and it would be a world happily arranged in which persons intending to treat them should be exempt from confusions and mistakes. This fortunate condition will arrive only, I fear, on the same day that critics become purged from error. Meanwhile, I repeat, we do not judge the artist with fairness unless we say to him, "Oh, I grant you your starting-point, because if I did not I should seem to prescribe to you, and heaven forbid I should take that responsibility. If I pretend to tell you what you must not take, you will call upon me to tell you then what you must take; in which case I shall be prettily caught. Moreover, it isn't till I have accepted your data that I can begin to measure you. I have the standard, the pitch; I have no right to tamper with your flute and then criticise your music. Of course I may not care for your idea at all; I may think it silly, or stale, or unclean; in which case I wash my hands of you altogether. I may content myself with believing that you will not have succeeded in being interesting, but I shall, of course, not attempt to demonstrate it, and you will be as indifferent to me as I am to you. I needn't remind you that there are all sorts of tastes: who can know it better? Some people, for excellent reasons, don't like to read about carpenters; others, for reasons even better, don't like to read about courtesans. Many object to Americans. Others (I believe they are mainly editors and publishers) won't look at Italians. Some readers don't like quiet subjects; others don't like bustling ones. Some enjoy a complete illusion, others the consciousness of large concessions. They choose their novels accordingly, and if they don't care about your idea they won't, *a fortiori*,[6] care about your treatment.

• • •

If you must indulge in conclusions, let them have the taste of a wide knowledge. Remember that your first duty is to be as complete as possible—to make as perfect a work. Be generous and delicate and pursue the prize.

6. Even more certainly (Latin).

## *D. H. Lawrence*

## Why the Novel Matters[7]

Me, man alive, I am a very curious assembly of incongruous parts. My yea! of to-day is oddly different from my yea! of yesterday. My tears of to-morrow will have nothing to do with my tears of a year ago. If the one I love remains unchanged and unchanging, I shall cease to love her. It is only because she changes and startles me into change and defies my inertia, and is herself staggered in her inertia by my changing, that I can continue to love her. If she stayed put, I might as well love the pepper-pot.

In all this change, I maintain a certain integrity. But woe betide me if I try to put my finger on it. If I say of myself, I am this, I am that!—then, if I stick to it, I turn into a stupid fixed thing like a lamp-post. I shall never know wherein lies my integrity, my individuality, my me. I *can* never know it. It is useless to talk about my ego. That only means that I have made up an *idea* of myself, and that I am trying to cut myself out to pattern. Which is no good. You can cut your cloth to fit your coat, but you can't clip bits off your living body, to trim it down to your idea. True, you can put yourself into ideal corsets. But even in ideal corsets, fashions change.

Let us learn from the novel. In the novel, the characters can do nothing but *live.* If they keep on being good, according to pattern, or bad, according to pattern, or even volatile, according to pattern, they cease to live, and the novel falls dead. A character in a novel has got to live, or it is nothing.

We, likewise, in life have got to live, or we are nothing.

What we mean by living is, of course, just as indescribable as what we mean by *being.* Men get ideas into their heads, of what they mean by Life, and they proceed to cut life out to pattern. Sometimes they go into the desert to seek God, sometimes they go into the desert to seek cash, sometimes it is wine, woman, and song, and again it is water, political reform, and votes. You never know what it will be next: from killing your neighbour with hideous bombs and gas that tears the lungs, to supporting a Foundlings' Home and preaching infinite Love, and being co-respondent in a divorce.

In all this wild welter, we need some sort of guide. It's no good inventing Thou Shalt Nots!

What then? Turn truly, honourably to the novel, and see wherein you are man alive, and wherein you are dead man in life. You may love a woman as man alive, and you may be making love to a woman as sheer dead man in life. You may eat your dinner as man alive, or as a mere masticating corpse. As man alive you may have a shot at your enemy. But as a ghastly simulacrum of life you may be firing bombs into men who are neither your enemies nor your friends, but just things you are dead to. Which is criminal, when the things happen to be alive.

To be alive, to be man alive, to be whole man alive: that is the point. And

7. From *Phoenix I: The Posthumous Papers of D. H. Lawrence,* ed. Edward O. McDonald (1936).

at its best, the novel, and the novel supremely, can help you. It can help you not to be dead man in life. So much of a man walks about dead and a carcass in the street and house, to-day: so much of women is merely dead. Like a pianoforte with half the notes mute.

But in the novel you can see, plainly, when the man goes dead, the woman goes inert. You can develop an instinct for life, if you will, instead of a theory of right and wrong, good and bad.

In life, there is right and wrong, good and bad, all the time. But what is right in one case is wrong in another. And in the novel you see one man becoming a corpse, because of his so-called goodness, another going dead because of his so-called wickedness. Right and wrong is an instinct: but an instinct of the whole consciousness in a man, bodily, mental, spiritual at once. And only in the novel are *all* things given full play, or at least, they may be given full play, when we realise that life itself, and not inert safety, is the reason for living. For out of the full play of all things emerges the only thing that is anything, the wholeness of a man, the wholeness of a woman, man alive, and live woman.

## *Doris Lessing*

## An Interview[8]

LESSING: I think I've always been a writer by temperament. I wrote some bad novels in my teens. I always knew I would be a writer, but not until I was quite old—twenty-six or -seven—did I realize that I'd better stop saying I was *going* to be one and get down to business. I was working in a lawyer's office at the time, and I remember walking in and saying to my boss, "I'm giving up my job because I'm going to write a novel." He very properly laughed, and I indignantly walked home and wrote *The Grass Is Singing.* I'm oversimplifying; I didn't write it as simply as that because I was clumsy at writing and it was much too long, but I did learn by writing it. It focused upon white people in Southern Rhodesia, but it could have been about white people anywhere south of the Zambezi, white people who were not up to what is expected of them in a society where there is very heavy competition from the black people coming up.

Then I wrote short stories set in the district I was brought up in, where very isolated white farmers lived immense distances from each other. You see, in this background, people can spread themselves out. People who might be extremely ordinary in a society like England's, where people are pressed into conformity, can become wild eccentrics in all kinds of ways they wouldn't dare try elsewhere. This is one of the things I miss, of course, by living in England. I don't think my memory deceives me, but I think there were more colorful people back in Southern Rhodesia because of the space they had to move in. I gather, from reading American literature, that this is the kind of space you have in America in the Midwest and West.

I left Rhodesia and my second marriage to come to England, bringing a son with me. I had very little money, but I've made my living as a professional

8. From *The Doris Lessing Reader* (1988).

writer ever since, which is really very hard to do. I had rather hard going, to begin with, which is not a complaint; I gather from my American writer-friends that it is easier to be a writer in England than in America because there is much less pressure put on us. We are not expected to be successful, and it is no sin to be poor.

INTERVIEWER: I don't know how we can compare incomes, but in England it seems that writers make more from reviewing and from broadcasts than they can in the United States.

LESSING: I don't know. When I meet American writers, the successful ones, they seem to make more on royalties, but then they also seem to spend much more.

I know a writer isn't supposed to talk about money, but it is very important. It is vital for a writer to know how much he can write to please himself, and how much, or little he must write to earn money. In England you don't have to "go commercial" if you don't mind being poor. It so happens that I'm not poor any more, thank goodness, because it's not good for anyone to be. Yet there are disadvantages to living in England. It's not an exciting place to live, it is not one of the hubs of the world, like America, or Russia, or China. England is a backwater, and it doesn't make much difference what happens here, or what decisions are made here. But from the point of view of writing, England is a paradise for me.

You see, I was brought up in a country where there is very heavy pressure put on people. In Southern Rhodesia it is not possible to detach yourself from what is going on. This means that you spend all your time in a torment of conscientiousness. In England—I'm not saying it's a perfect society, far from it—you can get on with your work in peace and quiet when you choose to withdraw. For this I'm very grateful—I imagine there are few countries left in the world where you have this right of privacy.

INTERVIEWER: This is what you're supposed to find in Paris.

LESSING: Paris is too exciting. I find it impossible to work there. I proceed to have a wonderful time and don't write a damn thing.

INTERVIEWER: To work from *A Man and Two Women* for a bit. The almost surgical job you do in dissecting people, not bodily, but emotionally, has made me wonder if you choose your characters from real life, form composites or projections, or if they are so involved you can't really trace their origins.

LESSING: I don't know. Some people I write about come out of my life. Some, well I don't know where they come from. They just spring from my own consciousness, perhaps the subconscious, and I'm surprised as they emerge.

This is one of the excitements about writing. Someone says something, drops a phrase, and later you find that phrase turning into a character in a story, or a single, isolated, insignificant incident becomes the germ of a plot.

INTERVIEWER: If you were going to give advice to the young writer, what would that advice be?

LESSING: You should write, first of all, to please yourself. You shouldn't care a damn about anybody else at all. But writing can't be a way of life; the important part of writing is living. You have to live in such a way that your writing emerges from it. This is hard to describe.

INTERVIEWER: What about reading as a background?

LESSING: I've known very good writers who've never read anything. Of course, this is rare.

INTERVIEWER: What about your own reading background?

LESSING: Well, because I had this isolated childhood, I read a great deal. There was no one to talk to, so I read. What did I read? The best—the classics of European and American literature. One of the advantages of not being educated was that I didn't have to waste time on the second-best. Slowly, I read these classics. It was my education, and I think it was a very good one.

I could have been educated, formally, that is, but I felt some neurotic rebellion against my parents who wanted me to be brilliant academically. I simply contracted out of the whole thing and educated myself. Of course, there are huge gaps in my education, but I'm nonetheless grateful that it went as it did. One bit of advice I might give the young writer is to get rid of the fear of being thought of as a perfectionist, or to be regarded as pompous. They should strike out for the best, to be the best. God knows we all fall short of our potential, but if we aim very high we're likely to be so much better.

## *Guy de Maupassant*

## The Novel[9]

The man who seeks only to amuse the public by already known methods writes with confidence, in the candor of his mediocrity, for the ignorant, the idle. But those on whom all the ages of past literature weigh heavily; those whom nothing satisfies, whom everything disgusts because it does not come up to their dreams; those to whom every flower seems to have been plucked, to whom their work always gives the impression of a useless and common labor—arrive at the opinion that literary art is an intangible, mysterious thing, only partially revealed to us in some of the pages of the greatest masters.

Twenty verses, twenty phrases, may suddenly thrill us to the heart as a surprising revelation; but the following verses resemble all verses, and the prose that follows resembles all other prose.

Men of genius, doubtless, do not experience this anguish and torture, because they have in themselves a resistless creative power. They do not sit in judgment on themselves. The rest of us, who are simply conscientious and persistent workers, can only by continued effort fight against overwhelming discouragement.

Two men by their simple and lucid teachings gave me this power of persistent effort—Louis Bouilhet and Gustave Flaubert.

If I speak of them and of myself in this place it is because their advice, summed up in a few lines, may be useful, perhaps, to some young writers with less self-esteem than is usually found in literary débutants.

Bouilhet, with whom I formed a rather intimate acquaintance about two years before I gained the friendship of Flaubert, by dint of repeating to me

9. From *The Novel* (1887).

that a hundred verses, or even less, insured the reputation of an artist, provided they were faultless and embodied the essence of the talent and originality of a man, even of second-rate talent, made me understand that.

I also learned that the best-known writers have seldom left more than one volume; and that the first essential is to have the luck to find and discern, amid the multiplicity of subjects that present themselves, that subjects that will absorb all our faculties, all our ability, all our artistic power.

Later on Flaubert, whom I sometimes saw, conceived a liking for me. I ventured to submit to him some of my attempts. He kindly read them, and replied: "I do not know if you have talent; what you have shown me proves that you possess a certain degree of intelligence. But do not forget this, young man, that talent—to quote the saying of Buffon—is merely 'long patience.' Keep on working."

I did so, and often revisited him, as I perceived that he liked me, for he laughingly called me his disciple.

For seven years I wrote verses, I wrote stories, I wrote novels, I even wrote a detestable play. Of these nothing survives. The master read them all, and on the following Sunday at luncheon he would give me his criticism, and inculcate little by little two or three principles that sum up his long and patient lessons. "If one has any originality, the first thing requisite is to bring it out; if one has none, the first thing to be done is to acquire it."

Talent is long patience. Everything which one desires to express must be considered with sufficient attention, and during a sufficiently long time, to discover in it some aspect which no one has as yet seen or described. In everything there is still some spot unexplored, because we are accustomed to look at things only with the recollection of what others before us have thought of the subject we are contemplating. The smallest object contains something unknown. Let us find it. In order to describe a fire that flames, and a tree on the plain, we must keep looking at that flame and that tree, until to our eyes they no longer resemble any other tree, any other fire.

This is the way to become original.

Having, besides, laid down this truth that there are not in the whole world two grains of sand, two specks, two hands, or two noses exactly alike, he compelled me to describe, in a few phrases, a being or an object in such a manner as to clearly particularize it and distinguish it from all the other beings, or all the other objects of the same race or the same species.

"When you pass," he would say, "a grocer seated at his shop door, a janitor smoking his pipe, a stand of hackney coaches, show me that grocer and that janitor, their attitude, their whole physical appearance, including also by a skillful description their whole moral nature, so that I cannot confound them with any other grocer or any other janitor; make me see, in one word, that a certain cab horse does not resemble the fifty others that follow or precede it."

I have stated elsewhere his ideas on style. They are closely related to the theory of observation which I have just explained.

Whatever be the thing one wishes to say, there is only one noun to express it, only one verb to give it life, only one adjective to qualify it. We must search, then, till that noun, that verb, that adjective, are discovered; never be content with an approximation, never resort to tricks, however happy, or to buffooneries of language, to avoid a difficulty.

We can interpret and describe the most subtle things if we bear in mind the verse of Boileau:

*"D'un mot mis en sa place enseigna le pouvoir."*

"He taught the force of a word in the right place."

There is no need of the eccentric, complicated, multifarious sort of Chinese vocabulary, which is inflicted on us at the present day under the name of artistic writing, to enable us to describe every shade of thought; but it is necessary to discern, with the utmost lucidity, all the modifications of the value of a word according to the position it occupies. Let us have fewer nouns, verbs and adjectives with almost incomprehensible meanings, and more varied phrases, differently constructed, ingeniously turned, sonorous and full of skillful rhythms. Let us endeavor to be excellent stylists, rather than collectors of rare terms.

It is, in fact, more difficult to turn a phrase to suit one's self, to make it say everything (even that which it does not express), to fill it with hidden meanings, and with secret suggestions which are not formulated, than to invent new expressions, or to seek in the depths of old forgotten books all those that are obsolete and have lost their significance, and for us are only dead words.

## *Bharati Mukherjee*

## A Four-Hundred-Year-Old Woman[1]

It took me ten painful years, from the early seventies to the early eighties, to overthrow the smothering tyranny of nostalgia. The remaining struggle for me is to make the American readership, meaning the editorial and publishing industries as well, acknowledge the same fact. (As the reception of such films as *Gandhi* and *A Passage to India* as well as *The Far Pavillions* and *The Jewel in the Crown* shows, nostalgia is a two-way street. Americans can feel nostalgic for a world they never knew.) The foreign-born, the exotically raised Third World immigrant with non-Western religions and non-European languages and appearance, can be as American as any steerage passenger from Ireland, Italy, or the Russian Pale. As I have written in another context (a review article in *The Nation* on books by Studs Terkel and Al Santoli), we are probably only a few years away from a Korean *What Makes Choon-li Run?* or a Hmong *Call It Sleep.* In other words, my literary agenda begins by acknowledging that America has transformed *me.* It does not end until I show how I (and the hundreds of thousands like me) have transformed America.

The agenda is simply stated, but in the long run revolutionary. Make the familiar exotic; the exotic familiar.

I have had to create an audience. I cannot rely on shorthand references to my community, my religion, my class, my region, or my old school tie. I've had to sensitize editors as well as readers to the richness of the lives I'm writing about. The most moving form of praise I receive from readers can be summed

1. From *The Writer on Her Work,* Vol. II, ed. Janet Sternberg (1991).

up in three words: *I never knew.* Meaning, I see these people (call them Indians, Filipinos, Koreans, Chinese) around me all the time and I never knew they had an inner life. I never knew they schemed and cheated, suffered, felt so strongly, cared so passionately. When even the forms of praise are so rudimentary, the writer knows she has an inexhaustible fictional population to enumerate. Perhaps even a mission, to appropriate a good colonial word.

I have been blessed with an enormity of material. I can be Chekhovian and Tolstoyan—with melancholy and philosophical perspectives on the breaking of hearts as well as the fall of civilizations—and I can be a brash and raucous homesteader, Huck Finn and Woman Warrior, on the unclaimed plains of American literature. My material, reduced to jacket-flap copy, is the rapid and dramatic transformation of the United States since the early 1970s. Within that perceived perimeter, however, I hope to wring surprises.

Yet (I am a writer much given to "yet") my imaginative home is also in the tales told by my mother and grandmother, the world of the Hindu epics. For all the hope and energy I have placed in the process of immigration and accommodation—I'm a person who couldn't ride a public bus when she first arrived, and now I'm someone who watches tractor pulls on obscure cable channels—there are parts of me that remain Indian, parts that slide against the masks of newer selves. The form that my stories and novels take inevitably reflects the resources of Indian mythology—shape-changing, miracles, godly perspectives. My characters can, I hope, transcend the straitjacket of simple psychologizing. The people I write about are culturally and politically several hundred years old: consider the history they have witnessed (colonialism, technology, education, liberation, civil war, uprooting). They have shed old identities, taken on new ones, and learned to hide the scars. They may sell you newspapers, or clean your offices at night.

Writers (especially American writers, weaned on the luxury of affluence and freedom) often disavow the notion of a "literary duty" or "political consciousness," citing the all-too-frequent examples of writers ruined by their shrill commitments. Glibness abounds on both sides of the argument, but finally I have to side with my "Third World" compatriots: I do have a duty, beyond telling a good story or drawing a convincing character. My duty is to give voice to continents, but also to redefine the nature of *American* and what makes an American. In the process, work like mine and dozens like it will open up the canon of American literature.

• • •

My theme is the making of new Americans. Wherever I travel in the (very) Old World, I find "Americans" in the making, whether or not they ever make it to these shores. I see them as dreamers and conquerors, not afraid of transforming themselves, not afraid of abandoning some of their principles along the way. In *Jasmine*, my "American" is born in a Punjabi village, marries at fourteen, and is widowed at sixteen. Nevertheless, she is an American and will enter the book as an Iowa banker's wife.

Ancestral habits of mind can be constricting; they also confer one's individuality. I know I can appropriate the American language, but I can never be a minimalist. I have too many stories to tell. I am aware of myself as a four-hundred-year-old woman, born in the captivity of a colonial, pre-industrial oral culture and living now as a contemporary New Yorker.

My image of artistic structure and artistic excellence is the Moghul miniature painting with its crazy foreshortening of vanishing point, its insistence that everything happens simultaneously, bound only by shape and color. In the miniature paintings of India, there are a dozen separate foci, the most complicated stories can be rendered on a grain of rice, the corners are as elaborated as the centers. There is a sense of the interpenetration of all things. In the Moghul miniature of my life, there would be women investigating their bodies with mirrors, but they would be doing it on a distant balcony under fans wielded by bored serving girls; there would be a small girl listening to a bent old woman; there would be a white man eating popcorn and watching a baseball game; there would be cocktail parties and cornfields and a village set among rice paddies and skyscrapers. In a sense, I wrote that story, "Courtly Vision," at the end of *Darkness.* And in a dozen other ways I'm writing it today, and I will be writing, in the Moghul style, till I get it right.

## *Alice Munro*

## What Is Real?[2]

Whenever people get an opportunity to ask me questions about my writing, I can be sure that some of the questions asked will be these:

"Do you write about real people?"

"Did those things really happen?"

"When you write about a small town are you really writing about Wingham?" (Wingham is the small town in Ontario where I was born and grew up, and it has often been assumed, by people who should know better, that I have simply "fictionalized" this place in my work. Indeed, the local newspaper has taken me to task for making it the "butt of a soured and cruel introspection.")

The usual thing, for writers, is to regard these either as very naïve questions, asked by people who really don't understand the difference between autobiography and fiction, who can't recognize the device of the first-person narrator, or else as catch-you-out questions posed by journalists who hope to stir up exactly the sort of dreary (and to outsiders, slightly comic) indignation voiced by my home-town paper. Writers answer such questions patiently or crossly according to temperament and the mood they're in. They say, no, you must understand, my characters are composites; no, those things didn't happen the way I wrote about them; no, of course not, that isn't Wingham (or whatever other place it may be that has had the queer unsought-after distinction of hatching a writer). Or the writer may, riskily, ask the questioners what is real, anyway? None of this seems to be very satisfactory. People go on asking these same

2. From *Making It New: Contemporary Canadian Stories,* ed. John Metcalf (1982).

questions because the subject really does interest and bewilder them. It would seem to be quite true that they don't actually know what fiction is.

And how could they know, when what it is, is changing all the time, and we differ among ourselves, and we don't really try to explain because it is too difficult?

What I would like to do here is what I can't do in two or three sentences at the end of a reading. I won't try to explain what fiction is, and what short stories are (assuming, which we can't, that there is any fixed thing that it is and they are), but what short stories are to me, and how I write them, and how I use things that are "real." I will start by explaining how I read stories written by other people. For one thing, I can start reading them anywhere; from beginning to end, from end to beginning, from any point in between in either direction. So obviously I don't take up a story and follow it as if it were a road, taking me somewhere, with views and neat diversions along the way. I go into it, and move back and forth and settle here and there, and stay in it for a while. It's more like a house. Everybody knows what a house does, how it encloses space and makes connections between one enclosed space and another and presents what is outside in a new way. This is the nearest I can come to explaining what a story does for me, and what I want my stories to do for other people.

So when I write a story I want to make a certain kind of structure, and I know the feeling I want to get from being inside that structure. This is the hard part of the explanation, where I have to use a word like "feeling," which is not very precise, because if I attempt to be more intellectually respectable I will have to be dishonest. "Feeling" will have to do.

There is no blueprint for the structure. It's not a question of, "I'll make this kind of house because if I do it right it will have this effect." I've got to make, I've got to build up, a house, a story, to fit around the indescribable "feeling" that is like the soul of the story, and which I must insist upon in a dogged, embarrassed way, as being no more definable than that. And I don't know where it comes from. It seems to be already there, and some unlikely clue, such as a shop window or a bit of conversation, makes me aware of it. Then I start accumulating the material and putting it together. Some of the material I may have lying around already, in memories and observations, and some I invent, and some I have to go diligently looking for (factual details), while some is dumped in my lap (anecdotes, bits of speech). I see how this material might go together to make the shape I need, and I try it. I keep trying and seeing where I went wrong and trying again.

I suppose this is the place where I should talk about technical problems and how I solve them. The main reason I can't is that I'm never sure I do solve anything. Even when I say that I see where I went wrong, I'm being misleading. I never figure out how I'm going to change things, I never say to myself, "That page is heavy going, that paragraph's clumsy, I need some dialogue and shorter sentences." I feel a part that's wrong, like a soggy weight; then I pay attention to the story, as if it were really happening somewhere, not just in my head, and in its own way, not mine. As a result, the sentences may indeed get shorter, there may be more dialogue, and so on. But though I've tried to pay attention to the story, I may not have got it right; those shorter sentences may be an evasion, a mistake. Every final draft, every published story, is still only an attempt, an approach, to the story.

I did promise to talk about using reality. "Why, if Jubilee isn't Wingham, has it got Shuter Street in it?" people want to know. Why have I described somebody's real ceramic elephant sitting on the mantelpiece? I could say I get momentum from doing things like this. The fictional room, town, world, needs a bit of starter dough from the real world. It's a device to help the writer—at least it helps me—but it arouses a certain baulked fury in the people who really do live on Shuter Street and the lady who owns the ceramic elephant. "Why do you put in something true and then go and tell lies?" they say, and anybody who has been on the receiving end of this kind of thing knows how they feel.

"I do it for the sake of my art and to make this structure that encloses the soul of my story, which I've been telling you about," says the writer. "That is more important than anything."

Not to everybody, it isn't.

So I can see there might be a case, once you've written the story and got the momentum, for going back and changing the elephant to a camel (though there's always a chance the lady might complain that you made a nasty camel out of a beautiful elephant), and changing Shuter Street to Blank Street. But what about the big chunks of reality, without which your story can't exist? In the story "Royal Beatings," I use a big chunk of reality: the story of the butcher, and of the young men who may have been egged on to "get" him. This is a story out of an old newspaper; it really did happen in a town I know. There is no legal difficulty about using it because it has been printed in a newspaper, and besides, the people who figure in it are all long dead. But there is a difficulty about offending people in that town who would feel that use of this story is a deliberate exposure, taunt, and insult. Other people who have no connection with the real happening would say, "Why write about anything so hideous?" And lest you think that such an objection could only be raised by simple folk who read nothing but Harlequin Romances, let me tell you that one of the questions most frequently asked at universities is, "Why do you write about things that are so depressing?" People can accept almost any amount of ugliness if it is contained in a familiar formula, as it is on television, but when they come closer to their own place, their own lives, they are much offended by a lack of editing.

There are ways I can defend myself against such objections. I can say, "I do it in the interests of historical reality. That is what the old days were really like." Or, "I do it to show the dark side of human nature, the beast let loose, the evil we can run up against in communities and families." In certain countries I could say, "I do it to show how bad things were under the old system when there were prosperous butchers and young fellows hanging around livery stables and nobody thought about building a new society." But the fact is, the minute I say *to show* I am telling a lie. I don't do it to show anything. I put this story at the heart of my story because I need it there and it belongs there. It is the black room at the centre of the house with all other rooms leading to and away from it. That is all. A strange defence. Who told me to write this story? Who feels any need of it before it is written? I do. I do, so that I might grab off this piece of horrid reality and install it where I see fit, even if Hat Nettleton and his friends were still around to make me sorry.

The answer seems to be as confusing as ever. Lots of true answers are. Yes and no. Yes, I use bits of what is real, in the sense of being really there and really happening, in the world, as most people see it, and I transform it into something that is really there and really happening, in my story. No, I am not concerned with using what is real to make any sort of record or prove any sort of point, and I am not concerned with any methods of selection but my own, which I can't fully explain. This is quite presumptuous, and if writers are not allowed to be so—and quite often, in many places, they are not—I see no point in the writing of fiction.

## *Flannery O'Connor*

## The Nature and Aim of Fiction[3]

If you go to a school where there are classes in writing, these classes should not be to teach you how to write, but to teach you the limits and possibilities of words and the respect due them. One thing that is always with the writer—no matter how long he has written or how good he is—is the continuing process of learning how to write. As soon as the writer "learns to write," as soon as he knows what he is going to find, and discovers a way to say what he knew all along, or worse still, a way to say nothing, he is finished. If a writer is any good, what he makes will have its source in a realm much larger than that which his conscious mind can encompass and will always be a greater surprise to him than it can ever be to his reader.

I don't know which is worse—to have a bad teacher or no teacher at all. In any case, I believe the teacher's work should be largely negative. He can't put the gift into you, but if he finds it there, he can try to keep it from going in an obviously wrong direction. We can learn how not to write, but this is a discipline that does not simply concern writing itself but concerns the whole intellectual life. A mind cleared of false emotion and false sentiment and egocentricity is going to have at least those roadblocks removed from its path. If you don't think cheaply, then there at least won't be the quality of cheapness in your writing, even though you may not be able to write well. The teacher can try to weed out what is positively bad, and this should be the aim of the whole college. Any discipline can help your writing: logic, mathematics, theology, and of course and particularly drawing. Anything that helps you to see, anything that makes you look. The writer should never be ashamed of staring. There is nothing that doesn't require his attention.

We hear a great deal of lamentation these days about writers having all taken themselves to the colleges and universities where they live decorously instead of going out and getting firsthand information about life. The fact is that anybody who has survived his childhood has enough information about life

3. From *Mystery and Manners: Occasional Prose,* ed. Robert and Sally Fitzgerald (1969).

to last him the rest of his days. If you can't make something out of a little experience, you probably won't be able to make it out of a lot. The writer's business is to contemplate experience, not to be merged in it.

Everywhere I go I'm asked if I think the universities stifle writers. My opinion is that they don't stifle enough of them. There's many a best-seller that could have been prevented by a good teacher. The idea of being a writer attracts a good many shiftless people, those who are merely burdened with poetic feelings or afflicted with sensibility. Granville Hicks, in a recent review of James Jones' novel, quoted Jones as saying, "I was stationed at Hickham Field in Hawaii when I stumbled upon the works of Thomas Wolfe, and his home life seemed so similar to my own, his feelings about himself so similar to mine about myself, that I realized I had been a writer all my life without knowing it or having written." Mr. Hicks goes on to say that Wolfe did a great deal of damage of this sort but that Jones is a particularly appalling example.

Now in every writing class you find people who care nothing about writing, because they think they are already writers by virtue of some experience they've had. It is a fact that if, either by nature or training, these people can learn to write badly enough, they can make a great deal of money, and in a way it seems a shame to deny them this opportunity; but then, unless the college is a trade school, it still has its responsibility to truth, and I believe myself that these people should be stifled with all deliberate speed.

Presuming that the people left have some degree of talent, the question is what can be done for them in a writing class. I believe the teacher's work is largely negative, that it is largely a matter of saying "This doesn't work because . . ." or "This does work because . . ." The *because* is very important. The teacher can help you understand the nature of your medium, and he can guide you in your reading. I don't believe in classes where students criticize each other's manuscripts. Such criticism is generally composed in equal parts of ignorance, flattery, and spite. It's the blind leading the blind, and it can be dangerous. A teacher who tries to impose a way of writing on you can be dangerous too. Fortunately, most teachers I've known were too lazy to do this. In any case, you should beware of those who appear overenergetic.

In the last twenty years the colleges have been emphasizing creative writing to such an extent that you almost feel that any idiot with a nickel's worth of talent can emerge from a writing class able to write a competent story. In fact, so many people can now write competent stories that the short story as a medium is in danger of dying of competence. We want competence, but competence by itself is deadly. What is needed is the vision to go with it, and you do not get this from a writing class.

## *Edgar Allan Poe*

## Review of Hawthorne's *Twice Told Tales*[4]

Were we called upon however to designate that class of composition which, next to a poem [of moderate length], should best fulfil the demands of high

4. Originally appeared in *Graham's Magazine* 20 (May 1842).

genius—should offer it the most advantageous field of exertion—we should unhesitatingly speak of the prose tale, as Mr. Hawthorne has here exemplified it. We allude to the short prose narrative, requiring from a half-hour to one or two hours in its perusal. The ordinary novel is objectionable, from its length, for reasons already stated in substance. As it cannot be read at one sitting, it deprives itself, of course, of the immense force derivable from *totality*. Worldly interests intervening during the pauses of perusal, modify, annul, or counteract, in a greater or less degree, the impressions of the book. But simple cessation in reading would, of itself, be sufficient to destroy the true unity. In the brief tale, however, the author is enabled to carry out the fulness of his intention, be it what it may. During the hour of perusal the soul of the reader is at the writer's control. There are no external or extrinsic influences—resulting from weariness or interruption.

A skilful literary artist has constructed a tale. If wise, he has not fashioned his thoughts to accommodate his incidents; but having conceived, with deliberate care, a certain unique or single *effect* to be wrought out, he then invents such incidents—he then combines such events as may best aid him in establishing this preconceived effect. If his very initial sentence tend not to be outbringing of this effect, then he has failed in his first step. In the whole composition there should be no word written, of which the tendency, direct or indirect, is not to the one pre-established design. And by such means, with such care and skill, a picture is at length painted which leaves the mind of him who contemplates it with a kindred art, a sense of the fullest satisfaction. The idea of the tale has been presented unblemished, because undisturbed; and this is an end unattainable by the novel. Undue brevity is just as exceptionable here as in the poem; but undue length is yet more to be avoided.

We have said that the tale has a point of superiority even over the poem. In fact, while the *rhythm* of this latter is an essential aid in the development of the poem's highest idea—the idea of the Beautiful—the artificialities of this rhythm are an inseparable bar to the development of all points of thought or expression which have their basis in *Truth*. But Truth is often, and in very great degree, the aim of the tale. Some of the finest tales are tales of ratiocination. Thus the field of this species of composition, if not in so elevated a region on the mountain of Mind, is a table-land of far vaster extent than the domain of the mere poem. Its products are never so rich, but infinitely more numerous, and more appreciable by the mass of mankind. The writer of the prose tale, in short, may bring to his theme a vast variety of modes or inflections of thought and expression—(the ratiocinative, for example, the sarcastic or the humorous) which are not only antagonistical to the nature of the poem, but absolutely forbidden by one of its most peculiar and indispensable adjuncts; we allude of course, to rhythm. It may be added, here, *par parenthèse,* that the author who aims at the purely beautiful in a prose tale is laboring at great disadvantage. For Beauty can be better treated in the poem. Not so with terror, or passion, or horror, or a multitude of such other points. And here it will be seen how full of prejudice are the usual animadversions against those *tales of effect* many fine examples of which were found in the earlier numbers of Blackwood. The impressions produced were wrought in a legitimate sphere of action, and constituted a legitimate although sometimes an exaggerated interest. They were relished by every man of genius: although there were found many men of genius who condemned them without just ground. The true critic will but demand that the design intended be accomplished, to the fullest extent, by the means most advantageously applicable.

We have very few American tales of real merit—we may say, indeed, none with the exception of "The Tales of a Traveller" of Washington Irving, and these "Twice-Told Tales" of Mr. Hawthorne. Some of the pieces of Mr. John Neal abound in vigor and originality; but in general, his compositions of this class are excessively diffuse, extravagant, and indicative of an imperfect sentiment of Art. Articles at random are, now and then, met with in our periodicals which might be advantageously compared with the best effusions of the British Magazines; but, upon the whole, we are far behind our progenitors in this department of literature.

Of Mr. Hawthorne's Tales we would say, emphatically, that they belong to the highest region of Art—an Art subservient to genius of a very lofty order. We had supposed, with good reason for so supposing, that he had been thrust into his present position by one of the impudent *cliques* which beset our literature, and whose pretensions it is our full purpose to expose at the earliest opportunity; but we have been most agreeably mistaken. We know of few compositions which the critic can more honestly commend [than] these "Twice-Told Tales." As Americans, we feel proud of the book.

Mr. Hawthorne's distinctive trait is invention, creation, imagination, originality—a trait which, in the literature of fiction, is positively worth all the rest. But the nature of originality, so far as regards its manifestation in letters, is but imperfectly understood. The inventive or original mind as frequently displays itself in novelty of *tone* as in novelty of matter. Mr. Hawthorne is original at *all* points.

In the way of objection we have scarcely a word to say of these tales. There is, perhaps, a somewhat too general or prevalent *tone*—a tone of melancholy and mysticism. The subjects are insufficiently varied. There is not so much of *versatility* evinced as we might well be warranted in expecting from the high powers of Mr. Hawthorne. But beyond these trivial exceptions we have really none to make. The style is purity itself. Force abounds. High imagination gleams from every page. Mr. Hawthorne is a man of the truest genius. We only regret that the limits of our Magazine will not permit us to pay him that full tribute of commendation, which, under other circumstances, we should be so eager to pay.

## *Katherine Anne Porter*

## An Interview[5]

INTERVIEWER: You once said that every story begins with an ending, that until the end is known there is no story.

5. From *Writers at Work,* The Paris Review *Interviews,* Vol. 2, ed. George Plimpton (1963).

PORTER: That is where the artist begins to work: With the consequences of acts, not the acts themselves. Or the events. The event is important only as it affects your life and the lives of those around you. The reverberations, you might say, the overtones: that is where the artist works. In that sense it has sometimes taken me ten years to understand even a little of some important event that had happened to me. Oh, I could have given a perfectly factual account of what had happened, but I didn't know what it meant until I knew the consequences. If I didn't know the ending of a story, I wouldn't begin. I always write my last lines, my last paragraph, my last page first, and then I go back and work towards it. I know where I'm going. I know what my goal is. And how I get there is God's grace.

INTERVIEWER: That's a very classical view of the work of art—that it must end in resolution.

PORTER: Any true work of art has got to give you the feeling of reconciliation—what the Greeks would call catharsis, the purification of your mind and imagination—through an ending that is endurable because it is right and true. Oh, not in any pawky individual idea of morality or some parochial idea of right and wrong. Sometimes the end is very tragic, because it needs to be. One of the most perfect and marvelous endings in literature—it raises my hair now—is the little boy at the end of *Wuthering Heights*, crying that he's afraid to go across the moor because there's a man and woman walking there.

And there are three novels that I reread with pleasure and delight—three almost perfect novels, if we're talking about form, you know. One is *A High Wind in Jamaica* by Richard Hughes, one is *A Passage to India* by E. M. Forster, and the other is *To the Lighthouse* by Virginia Woolf. Every one of them begins with an apparently insoluble problem, and every one of them works out of confusion into order. The material is all used so that you are going toward a goal. And that goal is the clearing up of disorder and confusion and wrong, to a logical and human end. I don't mean a happy ending, because after all at the end of *A High Wind in Jamaica* the pirates are all hanged and the children are all marked for life by their experience, but it comes out to an orderly end. The threads are all drawn up. I have had people object to Mr. Thompson's suicide at the end of *Noon Wine*, and I'd say, "All right, where was he going? Given what he was, his own situation, what else could he do?" Every once in a while when I see a character of mine just going towards perdition, I think, "Stop, stop, you can always stop and choose, you know." But no, being what he was, he already *has* chosen, and he can't go back on it now. I suppose the first idea that man had was the idea of fate, of the servile will, of a deity who destroyed as he would, without regard for the creature. But I think the idea of free will was the second idea.

INTERVIEWER: Has a story never surprised you in the writing? A character suddenly taken a different turn?

PORTER: Well, in the vision of death at the end of "Flowering Judas" I knew the real ending—that she was not going to be able to face her life, what she'd done. And I knew that the vengeful spirit was going to come in a dream to tow her away into death, but I didn't know until I'd written it that she was going to wake up saying, "No!" and be afraid to go to sleep again.

INTERVIEWER: That was, in a fairly literal sense, a "true" story, wasn't it?

PORTER: The truth is, I have never written a story in my life that didn't have a very firm foundation in actual human experience—somebody else's experience quite often, but an experience that became my own by hearing the story, by witnessing the thing, by hearing just a word perhaps. It doesn't matter, it just takes a little—a tiny seed. Then it takes root, and it grows. It's an organic thing. That story had been on my mind for years, growing out of this one little thing that happened in Mexico. It was forming and forming in my mind, until one night I was quite desperate. People are always so sociable, and I'm sociable too, and if I live around friends. . . . Well, they were insisting that I come and play bridge. But I was very firm, because I knew the time had come to write that story, and I had to write it.

INTERVIEWER: What was that "little thing" from which the story grew?

PORTER: Something I saw as I passed a window one evening. A girl I knew had asked me to come and sit with her, because a man was coming to see her, and she was afraid of him. And as I went through the courtyard, past the flowering judas tree, I glanced in the window and there she was sitting with an open book on her lap, and there was this great big fat man sitting beside her. Now Mary and I were friends, both American girls living in this revolutionary situation. She was teaching at an Indian school, and I was teaching dancing at a girls' technical school in Mexico City. And we were having a very strange time of it. I was more skeptical, and so I had already begun to look with a skeptical eye on a great many of the revolutionary leaders. Oh, the idea was all right, but a lot of men were misapplying it.

And when I looked through that window that evening, I saw something in Mary's face, something in her pose, something in the whole situation, that set up a commotion in my mind. Because until that moment I hadn't really understood that she was not able to take care of herself, because she was not able to face her own nature and was afraid of everything. I don't know why I saw it. I don't believe in intuition. When you get sudden flashes of perception, it is just the brain working faster than usual. But you've been getting ready to know it for a long time, and when it comes, you feel you've known it always.

INTERVIEWER: You speak of a story "forming" in your mind. Does it begin as a visual impression, growing to a narrative? Or how?

PORTER: All my senses were very keen; things came to me through my eyes, through all my pores. Everything hit me at once, you know. That makes it very difficult to describe just exactly what is happening. And then, I think the mind works in such a variety of ways. Sometimes an idea starts completely inarticulately. You're not thinking in images or words or—well, it's exactly like a dark cloud moving in your head. You keep wondering what will come out of this, and then it will dissolve itself into a set of—well, not images exactly, but really thoughts. You begin to think directly in words. Abstractly. Then the words transform themselves into images. By the time I write the story my people are up and alive and walking around and taking things into their own hands. They exist as independently inside my head as you do before me now. I have been criticized for not enough detail in describing my characters, and not enough furniture in the house. And the odd thing is that I see it all so clearly.

Interviewer: What about the technical problems a story presents—its formal structure? How deliberate are you in matters of technique? For example, the use of the historical present in "Flowering Judas"?

Porter: The first time someone said to me, "Why did you write 'Flowering Judas' in the historical present?" I thought for a moment and said, "Did I?" I'd never noticed it. Because I didn't *plan* to write it any way. A story forms in my mind and forms and forms, and when it's ready to go, I strike it down—it takes just the time I sit at the typewriter. I never think about form at all. In fact, I would say that I've never been interested in anything about writing after having learned, I hope, to write. That is, I mastered my craft as well as I could. There is a technique, there is a craft, and you have to learn it. Well, I did as well as I could with that, but now all in the world I am interested in is telling a story. I have something to tell you that I, for some reason, think is worth telling, and so I want to tell it as clearly and purely and simply as I can. But I had spent fifteen years at least learning to write. I practiced writing in every possible way that I could. I wrote a pastiche of other people, imitating Dr. Johnson and Laurence Sterne, and Petrarch and Shakespeare's sonnets, and then I tried writing my own way. I spent fifteen years learning to trust myself: that's what it comes to. Just as a pianist runs his scales for ten years before he gives his concert: because when he gives that concert, he can't be thinking of his fingering or of his hands; he has to be thinking of his interpretation, of the music he's playing. He's thinking of what he's trying to communicate. And if he hasn't got his technique perfected by then, he needn't give the concert at all.

• • •

Interviewer: You are frequently spoken of as a stylist. Do you think a style can be cultivated, or at least refined?

Porter: I've been called a stylist until I really could tear my hair out. And I simply don't believe in style. The style is you. Oh, you can cultivate a style, I suppose, if you like. But I should say it remains a cultivated style. It remains artificial and imposed, and I don't think it deceives anyone. A cultivated style would be like a mask. Everybody knows it's a mask, and sooner or later you must show yourself—or at least, you show yourself as someone who could not afford to show himself, and so created something to hide behind. Style is the man. Aristotle said it first, as far as I know, and everybody has said it since, because it is one of those unarguable truths. You do not create a style. You work, and develop yourself; your style is an emanation from your own being. Symbolism is the same way. I never consciously took or adopted a symbol in my life. I certainly did not say, "This blooming tree upon which Judas is supposed to have hanged himself is going to be the center of my story." I named "Flowering Judas" after it was written, because when reading back over it I suddenly saw the whole symbolic plan and pattern of which I was totally unconscious while I was writing. There's a pox of symbolist theory going the rounds these days in American colleges in the writing courses. Miss Mary McCarthy, who is one of the wittiest and most acute and in some ways the worst-tempered woman in American letters, tells about a little girl who came to her with a story. Now Miss McCarthy is an extremely good critic, and she found this to be a good story, and she told the girl that it was—that she considered it a finished work, and that she could with a clear conscience go on to something else. And the little girl said, "But Miss McCarthy, my writing teacher said, 'Yes, it's a good piece of work, but now we must go back and put in the symbols!' " I think that's an amusing story, and it makes my blood run cold.

## *James Thurber*

## An Interview[6]

INTERVIEWERS: Is the act of writing easy for you?

THURBER: For me it's mostly a question of rewriting. It's part of a constant attempt on my part to make the finished version smooth, to make it seem effortless. A story I've been working on—"The Train on Track Six," it's called—was rewritten fifteen complete times. There must have been close to 240,000 words in all the manuscripts put together, and I must have spent two thousand hours working at it. Yet the finished version can't be more than twenty thousand words.

INTERVIEWERS: Then it's rare that your work comes out right the first time?

THURBER: Well, my wife took a look at the first version of something I was doing not long ago and said, "Goddamn it, Thurber, that's high-school stuff." I have to tell her to wait until the seventh draft, it'll work out all right. I don't know why that should be so, that the first or second draft of everything I write reads as if it was turned out by a charwoman. I've only written one piece quickly. I wrote a thing called "File and Forget" in one afternoon—but only because it was a series of letters just as one would ordinarily dictate. And I'd have to admit that the last letter of the series, after doing all the others that one afternoon, took me a week. It was the end of the piece and I had to fuss over it.

INTERVIEWERS: Does the fact that you're dealing with humor slow down the production?

THURBER: It's possible. With humor you have to look out for traps. You're likely to be very gleeful with what you've first put down, and you think it's fine, very funny. One reason you go over and over it is to make the piece sound less as if you were having a lot of fun with it yourself. You try to play it down. In fact, if there's such a thing as a *New Yorker* style, that would be it—playing it down.

INTERVIEWERS: Do you envy those who write at high speed, as against your method of constant revision?

THURBER: Oh, no, I don't, though I do admire their luck. Hervey Allen, you know, the author of the big best-seller *Anthony Adverse,* seriously told a friend of mine who was working on a biographical piece on Allen that he could close his eyes, lie down on a bed, and hear the voices of his ancestors. Furthermore there was some sort of angel-like creature that danced along his pen while he was writing. He wasn't balmy by any means. He just felt he was in communication with some sort of metaphysical recorder. So you see the novelists have

6. From *Writers at Work,* the Paris Review *Interviews,* Vol. 1, ed. Malcolm Cowley (1977).

all the luck. I never knew a humorist who got any help from his ancestors. Still, the act of writing is either something the writer dreads or actually likes, and I actually like it. Even rewriting's fun. You're getting somewhere, whether it seems to move or not. I remember Elliot Paul and I used to argue about rewriting back in 1925 when we both worked for the *Chicago Tribune* in Paris. It was his conviction you should leave the story as it came out of the typewriter, no changes. Naturally, he worked fast. Three novels he could turn out, each written in three weeks' time. I remember once he came into the office and said that a sixty-thousand-word manuscript had been stolen. No carbons existed, no notes. We were all horrified. But it didn't bother him at all. He'd just get back to the typewriter and bat away again. But for me—writing as fast as that would seem too facile. Like my drawings, which I do very quickly, sometimes so quickly that the result is an accident, something I hadn't intended at all. People in the arts I've run into in France are constantly indignant when I say I'm a writer and not an artist. They tell me I mustn't run down my drawings. I try to explain that I do them for relaxation, and that I do them too fast for them to be called art.

## *Leo Tolstoy*

## What Is Art?[7]

*The art of the future not the possession of a select minority but a means towards perfection and unity.*

People talk of the art of the future, meaning by art of the future some especially refined new art which they imagine will be developed out of that exclusive art of one class which is now considered the highest art. But no such new art of the future can or will be found. Our exclusive art, that of the upper classes of Christendom, has found its way into a blind alley. The direction in which it has been going leads nowhere. Having once lost hold of that which is most essential to art (namely, the guidance given by religious perception), this art has become ever more and more exclusive and therefore ever more and more perverted, until finally it has come to nothing. The art of the future, that which is really coming, will not be a development of present-day art, but will arise on quite other and new foundations having nothing in common with those by which our present art of the upper classes is guided.

Art of the future, that is to say, such part of art as will be chosen from among all the art diffused among mankind, will consist not in transmitting feelings accessible only to members of the rich classes, as is the case to-day, but in transmitting feelings embodying the highest religious perception of our times. Only those productions will be esteemed art which transmit feelings drawing men together in brotherly union, or such universal feelings as can unite all men. Only such art will be chosen, tolerated, approved, and diffused. But art transmitting feelings flowing from antiquated, outworn, religious teaching;

7. From *What Is Art? And Essays on Art* (1959).

ecclesiastical art, patriotic art, voluptuous art; transmitting feelings of superstitious fear, of pride, of vanity, of ecstatic admiration of national heroes; art exciting exclusive love of one's own people, or sensuality, will be considered bad, harmful art, and will be censured and despised by public opinion. All the rest of art, transmitting feelings accessible only to a section of people, will be considered unimportant, and will be neither blamed nor praised. And the appraisement of art in general will devolve not as is now the case on a separate class of rich people, but on the whole people; so that for a work to be thought good and to be approved and diffused, it will have to satisfy the demands not of a few people living under similar and often unnatural conditions, but of all those great masses of people who undergo the natural conditions of laborious life.

Nor will the artists producing the art be as now merely a few people selected from a small section of the nation, members of the upper classes or their hangers-on, but they will consist of all those gifted members of the whole people who prove capable of, and have an inclination towards, artistic activity.

Artistic activity will then be accessible to all men. It will become accessible to the whole people because (in the first place) in the art of the future not only will that complex technique which deforms the productions of the art of to-day, and requires so great an effort and expenditure of time, not be demanded, but on the contrary the demand will be for clearness, simplicity, and brevity—conditions brought about not by mechanical methods but through the education of taste. And secondly, artistic activity will become accessible to all men of the people because, instead of the present professional schools which only some can enter, all will learn music and graphic art (singing and drawing) equally with letters, in the elementary schools, in such a way that every man, having received the first principles of drawing and music and feeling a capacity for and a call to one or other of the arts, will be able to perfect himself in it.

People think that if there are no special art-schools the technique of art will deteriorate. Undoubtedly it will deteriorate if by technique we understand those *complexities* of art which are now considered an excellence; but if by technique is understood clearness, beauty, simplicity, and compression, in works of art, then even if the elements of drawing and music were not to be taught in the national schools, not only will the technique not deteriorate but, as shown by all peasant art, it will be a hundred times better. It will be improved because all the artists of genius now hidden among the masses will become producers of art and supply models of excellence which (as has always been the case) will be the best schools of technique for their successors. For even now every true artist chiefly learns his technique not in the schools but in life, from the examples of the great masters, and then—when art is produced by the best artists of the whole nation and there are more such examples and they are more accessible—such part of school training as the future artist may lose will be a hundredfold compensated for by the training he will receive from the numerous examples of good art diffused in society.

Such will be one difference between present and future art. Another difference will be that art will not be produced by professional artists receiving payment for their work and engaged on nothing else besides their art. The art of the future will be produced by all the members of the community who feel need of such activity, but they will occupy themselves with art only when they feel such need.

In our society people think that an artist will work better and produce more if he has a secured maintenance; and this opinion once more would prove quite clearly, were such proof still needed, that what among us is considered to be art is not art but only a counterfeit. It is quite true that for the production of boots or loaves division of labour is very advantageous, and that the bootmaker or baker who need not prepare his own dinner or fetch his own fuel will make more boots or loaves than if he had to busy himself with those matters. But art is not a handicraft, it is the transmission of feeling the artist has experienced. And sound feeling can only be engendered in a man when he is living a life in all respects natural and proper to man. Therefore security of maintenance is a condition most harmful to an artist's true productiveness, since it removes him from the condition natural to all men—that of struggle with nature for the maintenance both of his own life and the lives of others—and thus deprives him of the opportunity and possibility of experiencing the most important and most natural feelings of man. There is no position more injurious to an artist's productiveness than the position of complete security and luxury in which in our society artists usually live.

The artist of the future will live the common life of man, earning his subsistence by some kind of labour. The fruits of the highest spiritual strength that passes through him he will try to share with the greatest possible number of people, for in such transmission to others of the feelings that have arisen in him he will find his happiness and reward. The artist of the future will be unable to understand how an artist, whose chief delight is in the wide diffusion of his works, could give them only in exchange for a certain payment.

Until the dealers are driven out, the temple of art will not be a temple. But the art of the future will drive them out.

## *Eudora Welty*

## An Interview[8]

INTERVIEWER: Your interest is in psychology also, so that a story such as "Why I Live at the P.O." is a comedy of hysteria. The humor comes out of a pathological behavior.

WELTY: No, I tell you I don't think of them at all as being pathological stories. I know Katherine Anne Porter refers to the girl as a case of dementia praecox in the introduction [of *A Curtain of Green*]. She believed I thought so, but it's far from what I was doing in that story. I was trying to show how, in these tiny little places such as where they come from, the only entertainment people have is dramatizing the family situation, which they do fully knowing what they are doing. They're having a good time. They're not caught up, it's not pathological. There is certainly the undertone, you're right, which is one of wishing things

8. From *Conversations with American Authors,* ed. Carl Ruas.

would change. Even though Sister goes and lives in the post office, she'll probably be home by the weekend, and it could happen all over again. They just go through it. I've heard people talk, and they just dramatize everything—"I'll never speak to you again!" It's a Southern kind of exaggeration. There is something underlying it, needless to say. That's what gives it its reason for being.

INTERVIEWER: But the current beneath the humor is despair, isn't it?

WELTY: I know in those early stories I have a number of characters where something visibly is wrong, they're deaf and dumb. Although I didn't think about it, it was a beginning writer's effort to show how alone some of these people felt. I made it a visible reason which is, of course, inside everybody. I must have chosen that as a direct, perhaps oversimplified way. I was not aware at the time that that was what I was doing—for instance, the story about the feeble-minded girl, Lily Daw. Nearly every little town had somebody like that in that part of the world, and the whole town made it their business to take care of her. They wouldn't usually send her away to the Institute for the Feeble-Minded unless they really reached an emergency, which they felt this was. Everybody takes care of everybody to the point where it's not taking care at all. You could see the futility of what they were doing. It was something I observed, just as I observed how people talk in exaggeration. All these things are rooted in a reality which I can use for the story, but I didn't invent it.

INTERVIEWER: "The Wide Net" is a comedy of misunderstanding between newlyweds. The young wife threatens to kill herself, and the husband calls the community together to drag the river for her body. Your description of the forest in autumn is elegiac, knowing that all things must come to an end, and yet inevitably return.

WELTY: That's exactly how I felt when I was writing. They were going on an excursion. Old Doc says, "The excursion is the same when you go looking for your sorrow as when you go looking for your joy." Young love is a mysterious thing, and anything might have happened. Things could have been very terrible. William Wallace, who was so inarticulate, could fish and dive down to the bottom of this water. That's part of it, because they wanted the presence of mystery and the possibility to be there. That's about the season of the year, the fall and the changing times.

INTERVIEWER: Young lovers acting out the drama in the fall reminded me of Chekhov, and I wondered if he influenced your concept of the short story.

WELTY: He certainly was my ideal. I didn't consciously try to base things, although that is an acknowledged method of teaching yourself. I guess I never thought I could base anything on a master like that.

INTERVIEWER: Did your reading determine your direction?

WELTY: I'm sure it must have done it indirectly, but not directly. I feel that when I'm really working on something, I'm not aware of anything but the story. I'm not thinking of myself, or of another writer. I'm just trying to get the story the way I want it. Those things can certainly help and bear down on me, but it's done at other times. Then they are worked out in the story without my conscious knowledge.

INTERVIEWER: When you began writing, did you identify with the Southern tradition?

Welty: I'm self-taught, so I really didn't. I just wrote stories. I was befriended by Robert Penn Warren and Cleanth Brooks, who published me in *The Southern Review;* I met Katherine Anne Porter fairly early; and they were already long-established writers, but we had no group. We're all such individuals, I hardly see how we could. I'm thinking of Walker Percy and Peter Taylor and many more. We all met in the course of things without seeking one another out, just meeting as life opened and enjoyed each other.

Interviewer: Katherine Anne Porter was a lifelong friend, and I wondered if she was involved with the direction of your writing.

Welty: I don't know that I would have known how to take any kind of direction. What she did for me that was so great was to believe in my work. This was like a bolt of lightning from the sky, that people whose work I loved thought well of mine. It made me feel that I was really in the world, that I had understanding and some readers. That's the greatest thing you can do for somebody.

Interviewer: You have this independence in your work. Does it carry over also to publishers, because they are at such a geographical distance?

Welty: I don't think about that end of it when I write. All I want to do is write that story, and I had such a long wait before stories appeared. I began writing six years before a story appeared in *The Atlantic Monthly,* which was my first national magazine, but from the beginning they were welcomed by university and college magazines. I was published, which gave me a sense of reaching somebody. I don't know what would have happened to me if I'd waited to be published to write the next story. One blessing about living at home—although I imagine I would do it anywhere—is that I write just the way I want to, and when I want to, until I get it nearly as I can to what I want. Then its fate is up to the other end. I've always been blessed with wonderful editors and agents. I didn't even realize how extremely lucky I was.

# Glossary of Critical Terms

**Action** Most simply, what happens to, or what is done by, the characters in a story. A somewhat more technical usage—in which "action" is nearly synonymous with **plot**[1] —makes the term signify a unified sequence of events with a beginning, middle, and end.

**Allegory** A literary work in which the characters and their situations clearly represent general qualities and types—as, in an animal fable, each animal may represent a type of human personality. Often the characters of allegory represent abstract vices or virtues such as avarice, charity, innocence, or prudery. See **symbol**.

**Ambiguity** Any story or element in a story that can be interpreted in different ways is said to be ambiguous. Ambiguity can be a fault that obstructs clear communication, but it can also provide enrichment by clustering associated and complementary meanings. See **irony** and **paradox**.

**Atmosphere** The enveloping spirit or mood of a story. Used in the same sense as in actual life, it might describe the feeling that prevails at a family reunion, a funeral, or the beginning of a vacation. See also **mood** and **tone**.

**Author intrusion** Explanations or statements that go beyond a rendering of the situation to make an interpretive comment about it. The author seems to address the reader directly, abandoning the illusion of his or her tale to deliver an opinion.

**Character** 1. One of the people who has a part in the story. 2. The quality or the sum of the qualities of such a person. In most stories we can easily distinguish between central characters—on whom most of the author's attention is focused—and the minor characters—who play some part in the development of the situation. *Round characters* are those presented as having the complex or contradictory qualities that we note in most human beings. *Flat characters* are those who display only a small fraction of normal human complexity. Most good stories will show examples of both flat and round characters according to the requirements of the **focus of interest**.

**Chronology** The clock or calendar of events presented in a story. Chronology may be straightforward—with the narrative beginning at the earliest and running uninterruptedly to the latest point in time—or complicated—with the narrative opening somewhere in the middle and leapfrogging backward or forward. Faulkner's "The Bear" provides an excellent example for study of complicated chronology. See **flashback**.

**Climax** The outcome of the main **action** of a story. That point at which the reader can see what the complications were leading to. Often the climax is a decisive encounter between characters who have been in **conflict**.

1. Words in boldface type are defined in this glossary.

**Coherence** The consistency of various parts of a story. We expect a character's speech and actions to be consistent with his nature. We expect certain consequences to follow from a particular act, certain feelings to rise from disappointments or rewards. Certain kinds of language will be in keeping with the material described. See **unity** and **style**.

**Complication** The emergence of a problem out of the interaction between characters and the situation that prevails as the story begins. See **exposition** and **resolution**.

**Concreteness** Joseph Conrad wrote: "All art . . . appeals primarily to the senses. . . . My task . . . is, by the power of the written word, to make you hear, to make you feel—it is, before all, to make you *see*." Fiction renders those concrete details of sensuous experience from which moral and emotional interpretations can be made. Fiction *shows* an action in progress. See **credibility**, **illusion**, **setting**.

**Conflict** The active opposition of characters, ideas, ways of life. A dynamic test of the capacities of one thing or person to overcome whatever competes with or frustrates it or him. Conflict is often considered the soul of fiction, because it gives rise to suspense, drama, and the emotional tension that sharpens our intuitions about characters and the values they are contending for.

**Convention** Any aspect of the literary art that has been established by earlier and repeated usage as part of the way in which language represents experience. Punctuation, syntax, and the alphabet itself are conventions. So are such things as the use of a narrator, the freedom of the author to substitute his or her language for that of the characters, the use of paragraphs in dialogue passages.

**Conventional** This term frequently has a pejorative meaning—though it derives directly from **convention**, without which no communication would be possible. When used disparagingly, *conventional* means that the writer has tried to find approval by clinging to familiar narrative types and procedures, and noncontroversial values.

**Credibility** Is the author telling you something that is unbelievable because it is impossible? If it is possible, is it probable? There are degrees of credibility in all reports of human events, and we measure what we read in fiction much as we measure history or the daily news. Just because a report is credible it need not be interesting, emotionally convincing, or intuitively comprehensible. See **concreteness** and **illusion**.

**Denouement** A synonym for **resolution**.

**Description** Those passages devoted to a presentation of the appearance of characters or the setting. Descriptions may appear in passages of dialogue, but they are usually provided by the author or narrator.

**Dialogue** The actual speech of characters in a story, usually punctuated with quotation marks. See **illusion** and **immediacy**.

**Diction** The choice and arrangement of words. By disciplining their vocabulary to a degree of conformity with the passions and actions of the story, writers enhance their power to convince. See **illusion** and **unity.**

**Didactic** A story is said to be didactic if it deliberately teaches some lesson about the way people should behave. The use of fiction for such teaching was one of its traditional justifications. Most modern fiction tends to show humanity as it is rather than as it should be, but even such stories point to general values and distinguish between admirable and contemptible behavior. See **moral** and **parable**.

**Distance** Like many other valuable terms that are now conventionally used to discuss fiction, this one is both metaphorical and ambiguous. It may mean the distinction authors preserve between themselves and their central characters (also called **objectivity**). It may refer to a use of language that separates the adventure described from the experience of the reader. It may mean a lack of **immediacy**. The author may choose to let crucial events take place offstage. In such a case they seem to be taking place at a greater distance than events presented directly to our eyes.

**Dramatic** This term is most useful in fictional criticism when it is taken to mean "like something presented on the stage of a theater." The modern writer of fiction tries, most of the time, to *show* us an action rather than simply to *tell* us about it. The writer sets a stage and peoples it. However, the term *dramatic* is also quite properly used in a different sense as a synonym for *exciting* or *suspenseful.* See **concreteness** and **objectivity**.

**Effaced narrator** In third-person narration we frequently find that part of the description and narrative is given in a language attributable to the character whose point of view has been assumed by the author, while other parts are in a language that must be attributed to the author's own understanding and observations. This latter is said to come from the effaced narrator, the speaker standing hidden behind his or her character.

**Episode** A single part of the continuing action of a story.

**Episodic** Usually signifies a loosely constructed or incoherent series of actions. See **coherence**.

**Exposition** That part of a story—frequently at the beginning or near it—which gives information about the characters and their situation before the action begins to change them.

**First- and third-person narration** In first-person narration the story is told by a character who habitually refers to himself or herself with the pronoun *I*. In third-person all characters are referred to by third-person pronouns and the story is told directly by the author.

**Flashback** A break in the chronological sequence of a story made to deal with earlier events. See **chronology**.

**Focus of interest** Whatever the author tries to make most prominent in his or her narration. May be **plot**, **setting**, **characters**, situation, a social problem, or a moral enigma.

**Foreshadowing** Hints of things to come. A foolish, impulsive judgment on a small matter hints that a character may be similarly susceptible in the great crises of life. Sometimes foreshadowing is accomplished by a prophetic episode, sometimes by author's language or by the dialogue.

**Form** A term so broad that it sums up all the others in this glossary. The totality of conventions exploited and modified by an author in his or her creative act. See **convention**.

**Illusion** No story provides optical illusions. Sensory experiences can only be evoked by language; they cannot be duplicated. Nevertheless, in varying degrees, stories can provide the sense that one is morally and emotionally involved in a situation shared with fictional characters. *They* smell the roses and feel the pain of a stab wound, but the reader envies the former experience and sympathizes with the latter, much as he or she would if the experiences were real. See **credibility**.

**Imagery** 1. Figures of speech. Similes. Metaphors. 2. More generally, all descriptions that prompt the reader to visualize characters in their setting. These visualizations, in turn, set off imaginative analogies that extend the implications of the story beyond its literal limits.

**Immediacy** The effect or illusion of sharing the experience that the characters in a story are undergoing. An author may gear all the devices of language, including dialogue and a use of the present tense, to promote this effect. It may be enhanced by a deliberate choice of subject matter that will play on the reader's enthusiasms or apprehensions. See **illusion**.

**Interior monologue** Sometimes—more popularly—called **stream of consciousness**.

**Irony** A discrepancy between what is expected and what is revealed. It may be found either in language usage or in the working out of the action of a story. Surprise endings always depend on some sort of irony, often crude. Irony may appear in the difference between a character's understanding of his or her situation and the reader's estimate of it. See **paradox**.

**Milieu** The political, social cultural, economic, and intellectual aspects of the **setting**. Milieu is to setting as Greek culture is to Greek geography. See **setting**.

**Mood** The prevailing feeling of a story, generated by language, **setting**, and the quality of the action. The term is naturally analogous to the moods of our experience—grim, gay, solemn, remorseful, angry, ecstatic, melancholy, anxious, etc. See **atmosphere**.

**Moral** The instructive point of a story. (See **didactic**.) The lesson drawn or to be drawn from the outcome of the action. While modern taste inclines away from the pat and clear morals that once adorned a lot of stories, a shrewd and important moral in fiction will have the same worth as a shrewd and important axiom delivered without fictional illustration. Handsome is as handsome does.

**Motivation** The internal and external forces that compel a **character** to take **action**. Sometimes these forces may be chiefly psychological, sometimes sociological, and sometimes a matter of hostility or opportunity in the physical environment. For **credibility**, motivation should be consistent with **character**.

**Narration** 1. A synonym for story-telling, whether the story is told by literary means, by the cinema, or in pantomime. 2. In fiction, narrative passages are to be distinguished from *descriptions* and *scenes.* In narrative passages the **chronology** is condensed so that relatively few words will encompass the events of an extended period of time. Most writers of short stories use narrative passages to fill in the links between events given a scenic treatment.

**Narrator** In **first-person narration**, the character who tells the story in his or her own words. It is not uncommon in third-person narration for one of the characters to tell an extended story. In such a case it is quite proper to refer to him or her as a narrator.

**Novella** (or sometimes **Novelette**) Term of flexible usage, referring basically to the length of the piece of fiction so described, somewhere between a short story (up to about twelve thousand words) and a novel (thirty thousand words or more). Because some complexities and developments beyond mere length are involved, it is probably best to think of this class of fiction as being defined by notable examples—as in this text "Heart of Darkness," "The Bear," "The Death of Ivan Ilych," and "Death in Venice" represent this intermediate category.

**Objectivity** Telling a story without bias; telling a story without the interpretive comment to be expected from a partisan or sympathetic observer.

**Omniscience** A **convention** in which the author speaks directly to the reader about events that will come in the future and other matters beyond the knowledge of the central character or of all the characters. This contrasts with the discipline of adhering to the **point of view** of a single character and is little used in modern practice.

**Pace** The speed at which writers develop any given part of a story. Usually they will hasten over unimportant things, slow to give a detailed view of what is essential.

**Parable** A story told to point a **moral** or teach a lesson.

**Paradox** A statement that appears to be contradictory or inconsistent with common sense—though it may be quite true.

**Parody** Mimicry of a work or a style of expression. Sometimes the mimicry is undertaken to make fun of what is parodied; sometimes it is done in a sincere effort to gain the understanding that comes from painstaking imitation. Parody is akin to paraphrase, the translation of a work into your own language to make sure you have grasped it.

**Pathos** The pity roused by the situation or the misfortunes of the characters in a story.

**Pattern** Another metaphorical and ambiguous term. It is generally taken to refer to changes in the relative position of the characters—as if they were pieces on a game board, shifted, developed, and sometimes sacrificed by the progress of the action. Thus if Character A is happy and prosperous in the beginning and becomes poor and wretched while Character B moves out of poverty and achieves happiness, there is said to be a "crossing pattern." The term may also refer to the way the author lays out blocks of material. If the author provides a number of small episodes not linked with transitional passages, he or she has made a "mosaic pattern."

**Plot** Consists of the phases of action in a story that are linked together by a chain of causal relationships. Event A causes or provides motivation for event B. B causes C, etc. Where this chain of causality is not apparent, the story is said to be **episodic**. A well-made plot leads from the potentialities revealed in the **exposition** directly to the situation left in the wake of the **resolution**. Plot may be subordinated to some other **focus of interest** in many stories, but it is one of the most important aspects of fiction, for we understand things best when we are shown what caused them to be as they are.

**Point of view** The events of a story may be told as they appear to one or more participants or observers. In **first-person narration** the point of view is automatically that of the **narrator**. More variation is possible in third-person narration, by which the author may choose to limit his or her report to what could have been observed or known by one of the characters at any given point in the action—or may choose to report the observations and thoughts of several characters. The author might also choose to intrude his or her own point of view. See **omniscience**.

**Protagonist** Chief **character**.

**Realism** An interest in and emphasis on life as it is. In literature this does not mean that writers copy what they see and hear. (Perhaps that is impossible, anyhow.) It means that they will select from their observations the material suitable for constructing a story that faithfully represents what they have understood.

**Resolution** The point in a story at which the **conflict** is decided one way or another and the struggle concluded. The expectations of the reader and of the characters have, at this point, been confirmed or refuted.

**Satire** The satirist aims to correct, by an exposure to ridicule, deviations from normal conduct or reasonable opinion. The chief tool of satire is to exaggerate deformities to the point at which their absurdity is unmistakably apparent.

**Sentimentality** An author's attempt to produce an emotional response greater than is warranted by what he or she has to tell. While the student should not be fooled by sentimentality, it is well to remember that the symmetrical and equal fault is hard-heartedness, a cold insensitivity to the trouble and joys of the human condition.

**Setting** The physical and cultural environment within which an action takes place. The stage that serves to demonstrate the qualities of a **protagonist**. An arena suitable for the **conflict**. Weather, urban uproar, the majesty and menace of the ocean can signal moods of human characters. See **concreteness** and **milieu**.

**Short Short Story** (also called for convenience simply a "short short") In recent years there has been a growing interest in stories of a length less than that typical of short stories in general. Writers, critics, and readers at all levels have become more sharply aware of the effects obtained in pieces of minimal length, and they are more and more frequently published in collections. Fables, moral **parables**, epiphanies, prose poems, and thin slices of life may be usefully considered as examples of this general type.

**Stream of consciousness** A fictional device or **convention** in which the author undertakes an imitation of a mind responding to exterior experiences. Frequently it involves a free association of ideas in which normal syntax and logical coherence are suspended. It is usually intended to shortcut the processes of reflection and reconsideration that stand between raw experience and logical statement. See **convention**, **immediacy**, **interior monologue**.

**Style** A writer's habitual way of expressing himself or herself is his or her style. Examination of it requires consideration of vocabulary, sentence patterns, and other compositional elements. More generally, the appreciation of an author's style comes with a recognition of the way his or her mind plays with experience and literary form.

**Symbol** An act, a person, a thing, or a spectacle that stands for something else, usually something less palpable than the named symbol. The relationship between the symbol and its referent is not often one of simple equivalence. Allegorical symbols usually express a neater equivalence with what they stand for than the symbols found in modern realistic fiction. See **allegory**.

**Tension** The emotional and intellectual force generated by disparate potentials within a literary work. In every **ambiguity** there is a tension between the primary meaning and the secondary meanings of a word, phrase, or larger unit of expression. There may be tension between a comic tone and pathetic subject matter. See **ambiguity** and **tone**.

**Theme** The unifying point or meaning of a story. Often the theme is implicit in the outcome of the action. It is rarely directly stated, though often it is closely paraphrased by an author's observation or by a statement made by one of the characters.

**Tone** A wide-ranging, metaphorical term that usually invites analogy to the tone of voice in which a speaker relates an episode. The speaker might be trying to make light of something that frightened him or her. If we conclude he or she is doing so, the fear will seem magnified by the attempt to disguise it. Tone reveals a storyteller's attitude toward the material.

**Understatement** The technique of playing down or underemphasizing a statement. It is a rhetorical trick intended to bring the imagination of the reader into play with a resulting magnification of emotional response. The style of Ernest Hemingway offers some of the best modern examples of this device.

**Unity** The shape and consistency of a story. When all the elements and devices of storytelling have been harmonized and nothing extraneous has been included in the text, we speak of it as unified. See **action**, **coherence**, **diction**, **point of view**.

**Voice** May be the characteristic mode of expression of a first-person narrator. (See **diction**.) Sometimes the term refers to the total, individualistic effect of all the devices a writer habitually employs, the combination of tactics that distinguishes his or her work from other fiction.

## Permissions Acknowledgments

**Margaret Atwood:** "Death by Landscape" from *Wilderness Tips* by Margaret Atwood. Copyright © 1991 by O. W. Toad Limited. Used by permission of Doubleday, a division of Bantam Doubleday Dell Publishing Group, Inc., and McClelland and Stewart, Inc., The Canadian Publishers. "Why Do You Write" from *Nine Beginnings* by Margaret Atwood. Originally published in *The Writer on Her Work,* Vol. II, 1991, edited by Janet Sternburg. Used by permission of Phoebe Larmore Literary Agency.
**James Baldwin:** "Sonny's Blues" was originally published in *The Partisan Review.* Copyright © 1957 by James Baldwin. Copyright renewed. Collected in *Going to Meet the Man*, published by Vintage Books. Reprinted by arrangement with the James Baldwin Estate.
**Toni Cade Bambara:** "Gorilla, My Love" from *Gorilla, My Love* by Toni Cade Bambara. Copyright © 1971 by Toni Cade Bambara. Reprinted by permission of Random House, Inc. "What Is It I Think I'm Doing Here Anyhow?" by Toni Cade Bambara from *The Writer on Her Work*, Vol. I, edited by Janet Sternburg. Copyright © 1980 by Janet Sternburg, reprinted by permission of W. W. Norton & Company, Inc.
**Andrea Barrett:** "The Littoral Zone" from *Ship Fever and Other Stories* by Andrea Barrett. Copyright © 1996 by Andrea Barrett. Reprinted by permission of W. W. Norton & Company, Inc.
**Donald Barthelme:** "Me and Miss Mandible" from *Sixty Stories* by Donald Barthelme. Copyright © 1981, 1982 by Donald Barthelme, reprinted with the permission of Wylie, Aitken & Stone, Inc.
**Charles Baxter:** "The Disappeared" from *A Relative Stranger* by Charles Baxter. Copyright © 1990 by Charles Baxter. Reprinted by permission of W. W. Norton & Company, Inc.
**Ann Beattie:** "Snow" from *Where You'll Find Me*. Reprinted by permission of International Creative Management, Inc. Copyright © 1991 by Ann Beattie.
**Madison Smartt Bell:** "Witness" from *Barking Man and Other Stories* by Madison Smartt Bell. Copyright © 1990 by Madison Smartt Bell. Reprinted by permission of Houghton Mifflin/Ticknor & Fields. All rights reserved.
**Gina Berriault:** "Who Is It Can Tell Me Who I Am?" from *Women in Their Beds: New and Selected Stories* by Gina Berriault. Copyright © 1996. Published by Counterpoint. Reprinted by permission.
**Amy Bloom:** "Silver Water" from *Come to Me* by Amy Bloom. Copyright © 1993 by Amy Bloom. Reprinted by permission of HarperCollins Publishers, Inc.
**Jorge Luis Borges:** "Pierre Menard, Author of the *Quixote*," from *Ficciones* by Jorge Luis Borges. Copyright © 1962 by Grove Press, Inc., translated from the Spanish copyright 1956 by Emece Editores, S.A., Buenos Aires. Used by permission of Grove/Atlantic, Inc.
**Ray Bradbury:** "The Veldt" by Ray Bradbury. Originally published in *The Saturday Evening Post,* 1950. Reprinted by permission of Don Congdon Associates, Inc. Copyright © 1950 by the Curtis Publishing Co., renewed 1977 by Ray Bradbury.
**Kate Braverman:** "Pagan Night" from ZYZZYVA. Copyright © by Kate Braverman. Reprinted by permission of the author.
**Ivan Bunin:** "The Gentleman from San Francisco" from *Stories and Poems of Ivan Bunin*, translated by Olga Shartse.
**Frederick Busch:** "Bread" from *The Children in the Woods: New and Selected Stories* by Frederick Busch. Copyright © 1994 by Frederick Busch. Reprinted by permission of Houghton Mifflin Company/Ticknor & Fields. All rights reserved.
**Raymond Carver:** "Cathedral" from *Cathedral* by Raymond Carver. Copyright © 1981 by Raymond Carver. Reprinted by permission of Alfred A. Knopf. "On Writing" from *Fires* by Raymond Carver. Copyright © by Raymond Carver. Reprinted by permission of International Creative Management, Inc.
**R. V. Cassill:** "The Rationing of Love" from *Patrimonies.* Reprinted by permission of the author.
**John Cheever:** "The Enormous Radio" from *The Stories of John Cheever* by John Cheever. Copyright © 1947 by John Cheever. Reprinted by permission of Alfred A. Knopf, Inc. "What Happened" from *Fiction and Human Experience*. Copyright © 1959 by John Cheever. Reprinted by permission.

**Anton Chekhov:** "The Lady with the Dog" from A. P. Chekhov, *Short Stories and Novels.* Translated by Ivy Litvinov. Reprinted by permission of the Ivy Litvinov Estate. "Gusev" from *The Portable Chekhov,* by Anton Chekhov, edited by Avrahm Yarmolinsky. Copyright © 1947, 1968 by Viking Penguin, Inc. Renewed © 1975 by Avrahm Yarmolinsky. Used by permission of Viking Penguin, a division of Penguin Putnam Inc. "Selections from Anton Chekhov's Letters" from *Anton Chekhov's Short Stories: A Norton Critical Edition* by Ralph E. Matlaw, editor. Copyright © 1979 by W. W. Norton & Company, Inc. Reprinted by permission of W. W. Norton & Company, Inc.
**Robert Coover:** "The Babysitter" from *Pricksongs and Descants* (New York: E. P. Dutton & Co., Inc.). Copyright © 1969 by Robert Coover. Reprinted by permission of Georges Borchardt, Inc., for the author.
**Julio Cortázar:** "A Continuity of Parks" from *The End of the Game & Other Stories* by Julio Cortázar, translated by Paul Blackburn. Copyright © 1967 by Random House, Inc. Reprinted by permission of Pantheon Books, a division of Random House, Inc.
**Malcolm Cowley:** "James Thurber" by Malcolm Cowley, editor, from *Writers at Work, First Series* by Malcolm Cowley, editor. Copyright © 1957, 1958 by The Paris Review, renewed © 1985 by Malcolm Cowley, © 1986 by The Paris Review. Used by permission of Viking Penguin, a division of Penguin Putnam Inc.
**H. L. Davis:** "Open Winter" from *Team Bells Woke* by H. L. Davis. Copyright © 1939 by the Curtis Publishing Co. Renewed 1953, 1981 by H. L. Davis. By permission of William Morrow & Company, Inc.
**Isak Dinesen:** "Sorrow-Acre" from *Winter's Tales* by Isak Dinesen. Copyright © 1961 by Rungstedlundfonden. Reprinted by permission of Random House, Inc.
**Susan Dodd:** "Public Appearances" from *Old Wives' Tales* by Susan Dodd. By permission of the University of Iowa Press. Copyright © 1984 by Susan Dodd.
**Andre Dubus:** "The Intruder" from *Dancing After Hours* by Andre Dubus. Copyright © 1996 by Andre Dubus. Reprinted by permission of Alfred A. Knopf, Inc.
**Stuart Dybek:** "We Didn't" from *Antaeus* #70 (Spring 1993). Reprinted by permission of International Creative Management. Copyright © 1993 by Stuart Dybek.
**Ralph Ellison:** "King of the Bingo Game" from *Flying Home and Other Stories* by Ralph Ellison. Copyright © 1996 by Fanny Ellison. Reprinted by permission of Random House, Inc.
**Louise Erdrich:** "Machimanito" from *Tracks* by Louise Erdrich. Copyright © 1988. Reprinted by permission of the author. First appeared in *The Atlantic Monthly.*
**William Faulkner:** "Barn Burning" copyright © 1939 by William Faulkner. Copyright renewed 1967 by Estelle Faulkner and Jill Faulkner Summers. Reprinted from *The Collected Stories of William Faulkner* by permission. "The Bear" copyright © 1942 by William Faulkner and renewed 1969 by Estelle Faulkner and Jill Faulkner Summers. Reprinted from *The Uncollected Stories of William Faulkner* by permission.
**Timothy Findley:** "Dreams" from *Stones* by Timothy Findley. Copyright © 1988, 1990 by Pebble Productions Inc. Reprinted by permission of Delacorte Press, a division of Bantam Doubleday Dell Publishing Group, Inc., and Penguin Books Canada Ltd.
**F. Scott Fitzgerald:** "Babylon Revisited." Reprinted with permission of Scribner, a Division of Simon & Schuster, from *The Short Stories of F. Scott Fitzgerald*, edited by Matthew J. Bruccoli. Copyright © 1931 by The Curtis Publishing Company. Copyright renewed © 1959 by Frances Fitzgerald Lanahan.
**Richard Ford:** "Great Falls" from *Rock Springs* by Richard Ford. Copyright © 1987 by Richard Ford. Used by permission of Grove/Atlantic, Inc.
**E. M. Forster:** "The Road from Colonus" from *The Collected Tales of E. M. Forster* by E. M. Forster. Copyright © 1947 by E. M. Forster. Reprinted by permission of The Provost and Scholars of King's College, Cambridge, and The Society of Authors as the literary representatives of the E. M. Forster Estate.
**Mavis Gallant:** "Bernadette" from *My Heart Is Broken* (New York: Random House, 1964) by Mavis Gallant. Copyright © 1957, 1960, 1962, 1963, 1964 by Mavis Gallant. Reprinted by permission of Georges Borchardt, Inc., for the author.
**Gabriel García Márquez:** "The Handsomest Drowned Man in the World" from *Leaf Storm and*

*Other Stories* by Gabriel García Márquez and translated by Gregory Rabassa. Copyright © 1971 by Gabriel García Márquez. Reprinted by permission of HarperCollins Publishers, Inc.
**George Garrett:** "Wounded Soldier" from *An Evening Performance* by George Garrett. Copyright © 1985 by George Garrett. Used by permission of Doubleday, a division of Bantam Doubleday Dell Publishing Group, Inc.
**Gail Godwin:** "Becoming a Writer" from *The Writer on Her Work*, Vol. I, edited by Janet Sternburg. Reprinted by permission of Gail Godwin.
**Nadine Gordimer:** "A Soldier's Embrace" copyright © 1975 Nadine Gordimer, from *A Soldier's Embrace* by Nadine Gordimer. Used by permission of Viking Penguin, a division of Penguin Putnam Inc.
**William Goyen:** "Ghost and Flesh, Water and Dirt" from *The Collected Stories of William Goyen* by William Goyen. Copyright © 1952 William Goyen. Reprinted courtesy of the Doris Roberts and Charles William Goyen Literary Trust c/o Wieser & Wieser, Inc., New York, NY.
**Allan Gurganus:** "Nativity, Caucasian" from *White People: Stories and Novellas* by Allan Gurganus. Copyright © 1991 by Allan Gurganus. Reprinted by permission of Alfred A. Knopf, Inc.
**Barry Hannah:** "Testimony of Pilot" from *Airships* by Barry Hannah. Copyright © 1978 by Barry Hannah. Reprinted by permission of Alfred A. Knopf, Inc.
**Tom Hawkins:** "Wedding Night" by Tom Hawkins. Copyright by Tom Hawkins. Reprinted by permission of the author.
**Ernest Hemingway:** "Hills Like White Elephants." Reprinted with permission of Scribner, a Division of Simon & Schuster, from *Men Without Women* by Ernest Hemingway. Copyright © 1927 Charles Scribner's Sons. Copyright renewed 1955 by Ernest Hemingway.
**Amy Hempel:** "In the Cemetery Where Al Jolson Is Buried" from *Reasons to Live* by Amy Hempel. Copyright © 1985 by Amy Hempel. Reprinted by permission of Alfred A. Knopf, Inc.
**Zora Neale Hurston:** "The Conscience of the Court" by Zoral Neale Hurston. Reprinted from *The Saturday Evening Post* © 1950 by permission.
**Shirley Jackson:** "The Lottery" from *The Lottery* by Shirley Jackson. Copyright © 1948, 1949 by Shirley Jackson, and copyright renewed 1976, 1977 by Laurence Hyman, Barry Hyman, Ms. Sarah Webster, and Mrs. Joanne Schnurer. Reprinted by permission of Farrar, Straus & Giroux, Inc.
**Ruth Prawer Jhabvala:** "Passion" from *A Stronger Climate*. Used by permission of the Harriet Wasserman Literary Agency, Inc.
**Charles Johnson:** "Moving Pictures." Reprinted with the permission of Scribner, a Division of Simon & Schuster, from *The Sorcerer's Apprentice* by Charles Johnson. Copyright © 1985, 1986 by Charles Johnson.
**Edward P. Jones:** "A New Man," pp. 207–221 of *Lost in the City* by Edward P. Jones. Copyright © 1992 by Edward P. Jones. Reprinted by permission of William Morrow & Company, Inc.
**Thom Jones:** "The Pugilist at Rest" from *The Pugilist at Rest* by Thom Jones. Copyright © 1993 by Thom Jones. By permission of Little, Brown and Company.
**James Joyce:** "A Little Cloud," "Araby," "The Dead," from *Dubliners* by James Joyce. Copyright © 1916 by B. W. Heubsch. Definitive text copyright © 1967 by the Estate of James Joyce. Used by permission of Viking Penguin, a division of Penguin Putnam Inc.
**Franz Kafka:** "The Metamorphosis" and "A Hunger Artist" from *Franz Kafka: The Complete Stories* by Franz Kafka, translated by N. N. Glatzer. Copyright © 1946, 1947, 1948, 1954, 1958, 1971 by Schocken Books Inc. Reprinted by permission of Schocken Books, published by Pantheon Books, a Division of Random House Inc.
**Jamaica Kincaid:** "Girl" from *At the Bottom of the River* by Jamaica Kincaid. Copyright © 1983 by Jamaica Kincaid. Reprinted by permission of Farrar, Straus & Giroux, Inc.
**William Kotzwinkle:** "Jewel of the Moon" from *Jewel of the Moon*. Copyright © 1985 by William Kotzwinkle. Reprinted by permission.
**Patricia Landers:** "My Life as a Mollusk" from *Farmer's Market* (Vol. 12, No. 1), 1995. Reprinted by permission of the author.
**D. H. Lawrence:** "Why the Novel Matters" from *Phoenix: The Posthumous Papers of D. H. Lawrence* by D. H. Lawrence and edited by Edward McDonald. Copyright © 1936 by Freida

Lawrence, renewed © 1964 by the Estate of the late Freida Lawrence Ravagli. Used by permission of Viking Penguin, a division of Penguin Putnam Inc.

**Sharyn Layfield:** "The Coggios" from *The Ploughshares Reader*. Reprinted by permission of the author.

**David Leavitt:** "Gravity" from *A Place I've Never Been* by David Leavitt. Copyright © 1990 by David Leavitt. Used by permission of Viking Penguin, a division of Penguin Putnam Inc.

**Ursula K. Le Guin:** "The Ones Who Walk Away from Omelas." Copyright © 1973 by Ursula K. Le Guin; first appeared in *New Dimensions 3* from *The Wind's Twelve Quarters;* reprinted by permission of the author and the author's agent, the Virginia Kidd Agency, Inc.

**Doris Lessing:** "An Interview With" from *The Writer on Her Work*. Copyright © 1988 Doris Lessing. Reprinted by kind permission of Jonathan Clowes Ltd., London, on behalf of Doris Lessing. "To Room Nineteen" from *The Doris Lessing Reader* by Doris Lessing. Copyright © 1985 by Doris Lessing. Reprinted by permission of Alfred A. Knopf, Inc.

**John L'Heureux:** "Brief Lives in California" from *Desires.* Copyright © John L'Heureux. First published in *Comedians*, Viking Press, 1990. Reprinted by permission.

**Sandra Tsing Loh:** "My Father's Chinese Wives." Copyright © 1994 by Sandra Tsing Loh. First appeared in *Quarterly West*. Reprinted by permission.

**Robie Macauley:** "The Chevigny Man" from *The End of Pity and Other Stories*. Copyright © 1951 by Robie Macauley. Reprinted by permission.

**Bernard Malamud:** "Angel Levine" from *The Magic Barrel* by Bernard Malamud. Copyright © 1950, 1958 and copyright renewed 1977, 1986 by Bernard Malamud. Reprinted by permission of Farrar, Straus & Giroux, Inc.

**Thomas Mann:** "Death in Venice" from *Death in Venice: A Norton Critical Edition* by Thomas Mann, translated by Clayton Koelb. Translation © 1994 by W. W. Norton & Company, Inc. Reprinted by permission of W. W. Norton & Company, Inc.

**Bobbie Ann Mason:** "Shiloh" from *Shiloh and Other Stories* by Bobbie Ann Mason. Copyright © by Bobbie Ann Mason. Reprinted by permission of International Creative Management, Inc.

**William Maxwell:** "The Thistles in Sweden" from *All the Days and Nights: The Collected Stories of William Maxwell* by William Maxwell. Copyright © 1995 by William Maxwell. Reprinted by permission of Alfred A. Knopf, Inc.

**Bharati Mukherjee:** excerpt from "A Four-Hundred-Year-Old Woman." Copyright © 1991 by Bharati Mukherjee. Originally published in *The Writer and Her Work*, Vol. II. Reprinted with permission of the author. "The Management of Grief" from *The Middleman and Other Stories* by Bharati Mukherjee. Copyright © 1988 by Bharati Mukherjee. Used by permission of Grove/Atlantic, Inc.

**Alice Munro:** "Royal Beatings" from *The Beggar Maid* by Alice Munro. Copyright © 1977, 1978 by Alice Munro, and from *Who Do You Think You Are* by Alice Munro. Copyright © 1978 by Alice Munro. Reprinted by permission of Alfred A. Knopf, Inc., and Macmillan Canada. "Prue" from *The Moons of Jupiter and Other Stories* by Alice Munro. Copyright © 1982 by Alice Munro. Reprinted by permission of Alfred A. Knopf, Inc., and Macmillan Canada. "What Is Real?" from *Making It New: Contemporary Canadian Stories.* Reprinted by permission of the Virginia Barber Literary Agency, Inc. All rights reserved.

**Vladimir Nabokov:** "Signs and Symbols" from *The Stories of Vladimir Nabokov* by Vladimir Nabokov. Copyright © 1995 by Dimitri Nabokov. Reprinted by permission of Alfred A. Knopf, Inc.

**Hua-ling Nieh:** "The Several Blessings of Wang Ta-Men" from *Writing from the World.* Reprinted by permission of the author.

**Joyce Carol Oates:** "How I Contemplated the World from the Detroit House of Correction and Began My Life Over Again" from *The Wheel of Love and Other Stories* (Vanguard, 1970). Copyright © 1970 by Joyce Carol Oates. Reprinted by permission of John Hawkins & Associates.

**Tim O'Brien:** "The Things They Carried" by Tim O'Brien. Copyright © 1986 by Tim O'Brien. Originally published in *Esquire*. Reprinted by permission of the author.

**Flannery O'Connor:** "A Good Man Is Hard to Find" from *A Good Man Is Hard to Find and*

*Other Stories*, copyright © 1953 by Flannery O'Connor and renewed 1981 by Regina O'Connor, reprinted by permission of Harcourt Brace & Company. "Everything That Rises Must Converge" from *Everything That Rises Must Converge* by Flannery O'Connor. Copyright © 1962, 1965 by the Estate of Mary Flannery O'Connor and copyright renewed 1993 by Regina O'Connor. Reprinted by permission of Farrar, Straus & Giroux, Inc. "The Nature and Aim of Fiction" from *Mystery and Manners* by Flannery O'Connor. Copyright © 1969 by the Estate of Mary Flannery O'Connor. Reprinted by permission of Farrar, Straus & Giroux, Inc.

**Frank O'Connor:** "Guests of the Nation" from *Collected Stories* by Frank O'Connor. Copyright © 1981 by Harriet O'Donovan Sheehy, Executrix of the Estate of Frank O'Connor. Reprinted by arrangement with Harriet O'Donovan Sheehy, c/o Joan Daves Agency as agent for the proprietor and by permission of Alfred A. Knopf, Inc.

**Tillie Olsen:** "Tell Me a Riddle" from *Tell Me a Riddle* by Tillie Olsen. Introduction by John Leonard. Copyright © 1956, 1957, 1960, 1961 by Tillie Olsen. Introduction 1994 by Dell Publishing. Used by permission of Delacorte Press/Seymour Lawrence, a division of Bantam Doubleday Dell Publishing Group, Inc.

**Luigi Pirandello:** "War." Reprinted by permission of the Pirandello Estate and Toby Cole, Agent. Copyright © 1932, 1967, by E. P. Dutton, N.Y.

**George A. Plimpton:** "Ralph Ellison" by Alfred Chester and Vilma Howard, edited by George Plimpton; "Ernest Hemingway" edited by George Plimpton; and "Katherine Anne Porter" by Barbara Thompson, edited by George Plimpton from *Writers at Work, Second Series* by George A. Plimpton, editor. Copyright © 1963 by The Paris Review. Used by permission of Viking Penguin, a division of Penguin Putnam, Inc.

**Katherine Anne Porter:** "Flowering Judas" from *Flowering Judas and Other Stories*, copyright © 1930 and renewed 1958 by Katherine Anne Porter, reprinted by permission of Harcourt Brace & Company.

**V. S. Pritchett:** "The Fall" from *Selected Stories* by V.S. Pritchett. Copyright © 1978 by V. S. Pritchett. Reprinted by permission of Random House, Inc., and Sterling Lord Literistic, Inc.

**Philip Roth:** "The Conversion of the Jews" from *Goodbye, Columbus*. Copyright © 1959, renewed 1987 by Philip Roth. Reprinted by permission of Houghton Mifflin Co. All rights reserved.

**Charles Ruas:** "An Interview with Eudora Welty" from *Conversations with American Writers* by Charles Ruas. Copyright © 1984 by Charles Ruas. Reprinted by permission of Alfred A. Knopf, Inc.

**Jo Sapp:** "Nadine at 35: A Synopsis" by Jo Sapp from *Flash Fiction* (Norton, 1992). Reprinted by permission of the author.

**Irving Shaw:** "The Eighty-Yard Run." Reprinted with permission. Copyright © Irving Shaw. Originally published in *Short Stories of Five Decades*, Delacorte Press.

**Isaac Bashevis Singer:** "Gimpel the Fool" by Issac Bashevis Singer, translated by Saul Bellow, copyright © 1953, 1954 by The Viking Press Inc., renewed 1981, 1982 by Viking Penguin Inc., from *A Treasury of Yiddish Stories* by Irving Howe and Eliezer Greenberg. Used by permission of Viking Penguin, a division of Penguin Putnam Inc.

**Lee Smith:** "Intensive Care" from *Me and My Baby View the Eclipse* by Lee Smith. Copyright © 1988, 1990 by Lee Smith. Used by permission of G. P. Putnam's Sons, a division of Penguin Putnam Inc.

**Jean Stafford:** "In the Zoo" from *Bad Characters* by Jean Stafford. Copyright © 1964 by Jean Stafford. Copyright renewed 1992 by Nora Cosgrove. Reprinted by permission of Farrar, Straus & Giroux, Inc.

**John Steinbeck:** "The Chrysanthemums," copyright © 1937, renewed 1965 by John Steinbeck from *The Long Valley* by John Steinbeck. Used by permission of Viking Penguin, a division of Penguin Putnam Inc.

**Amy Tan:** "Rules of the Game" from *The Joy Luck Club* by Amy Tan. Copyright © 1989 by Amy Tan. Used by permission of Putnam Berkley, a division of Penguin Putnam Inc.

**Peter Taylor:** "The Spinster's Tale" from *The Collected Stories* by Peter Taylor. Copyright © 1969 by Peter Taylor. Reprinted by permission of Farrar, Straus & Giroux, Inc.

**James Thurber:** "The Secret Life of Walter Mitty" from *My World—and Welcome to It.* Copyright © 1942 James Thurber. Copyright © 1970 Helen Thurber and Rosemary A. Thurber. Reprinted by arrangement with Rosemary A. Thurber and the Barbara Hogeson Agency.
**Leo Tolstoy:** "What Is Art?" from *What Is Art: Tolstoy* by Maude, © 1960. Reprinted by permission of Prentice-Hall, Inc., Upper Saddle River, NJ.
**John Updike:** "A & P" from *Pigeon Feathers and Other Stories* by John Updike. Copyright © 1962 by John Updike. Reprinted by permission of Alfred A. Knopf, Inc.
**Helena María Viramontes:** "The Moths" is reprinted with permission from the publisher of *The Moths and Other Stories* (Houston: Arte Publico Press—University of Houston, 1985).
**Alice Walker:** "Everyday Use" from *In Love & Trouble: Stories of Black Women*, copyright © 1973 by Alice Walker, reprinted by permission of Harcourt Brace & Company.
**Robert Penn Warren:** "Blackberry Winter." Copyright © 1987 by Robert Penn Warren. All rights reserved. Reprinted by permission of William Morris Agency, Inc., on behalf of the Author.
**Eudora Welty:** "A Worn Path" from *A Curtain of Green and Other Stories*, copyright © 1941 and renewed 1969 by Eudora Welty, reprinted by permission of Harcourt Brace & Company. "Why I Live at the P.O." from *A Curtain of Green and Other Stories*, copyright 1941 and renewed 1969 by Eudora Welty, reprinted by permission of Harcourt Brace & Company.
**W. D. Wetherell:** "The Man Who Loved Levittown" from *The Man Who Loved Levittown*, copyright © 1985 by W. D. Wetherell. Reprinted by permission of the University of Pittsburgh Press.
**William Carlos Williams:** "The Use of Force" by William Carlos Williams, from *The Collected Stories of William Carlos Williams*. Copyright © 1938 by William Carlos Williams. Reprinted by permission of New Directions Publishing Corp.
**Tobias Wolff:** "In the Garden of the North American Martyrs" from *In the Garden of the North American Martyrs*, by Tobias Wolff. Copyright © 1976, 1978, 1980, 1981 by Tobias Wolff. Reprinted by permission of the Ecco Press.
**Virginia Woolf:** "Kew Gardens" from *A Haunted House and Other Short Stories* by Virginia Woolf, copyright © 1944 and renewed 1972 by Harcourt Brace & Company, reprinted by permission of the publisher and The Society of Authors as the literary representatives of the Estate of Virginia Woolf.
**Richard Wright:** "The Man Who Was Almost a Man" from *Eight Men* by Richard Wright. Copyright © 1940, 1961 by Richard Wright. Copyright renewed 1989 by Ellen Wright. Reprinted by permission of HarperCollins Publishers, Inc.

Every effort has been made to contact the copyright holders of each of these selections. Rights holders of any selections not credited should contact W. W. Norton & Company, Inc., 500 Fifth Avenue, New York, NY 10110, in order for a correction to be made in the next reprinting of our work.

# *Index of Titles*